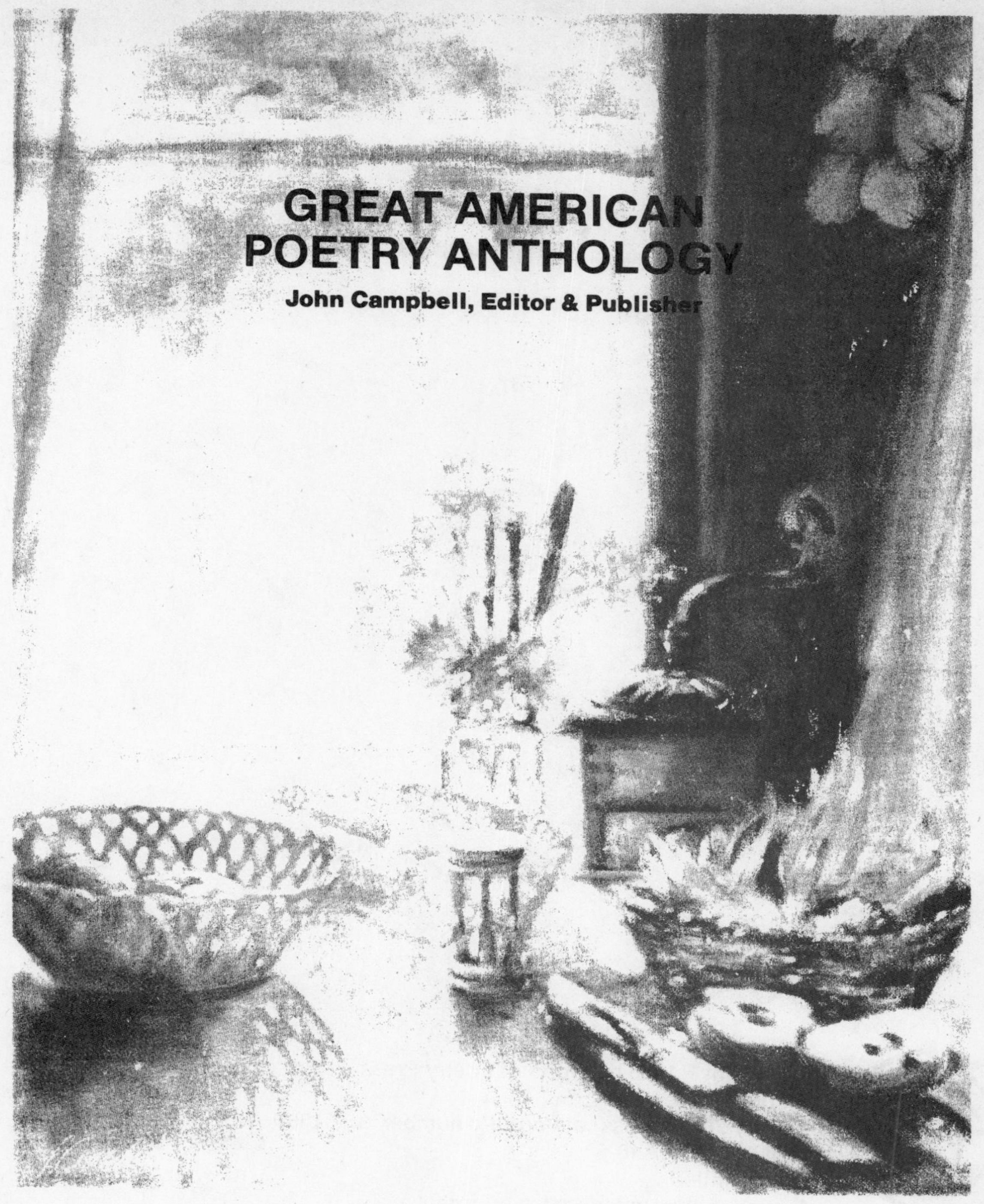

John Campbell, Editor & Publisher
Edited by Eddie-Lou Cole
Art Director Julie Joy
Illustrations by Raymond Walker
Proofread by Fern A Wolff
Creative Consultation by John Stempeck
Typeset by Terri L Relph
Typesetting assistants:
Dean Campbell
Kathleen Endl
Mary Hoffman
Karen Grow
Julia Arisiaga-Urias

Library of Congress catalog card number: 86-51367
ISBN-0-910147-10-8
1988 Printing
Printed in the United States of America

GREAT AMERICAN POETRY ANTHOLOGY

C L Walker
MY LADY

This Poem is Dedicated to my Mother Margie May McWayne, Because she taught me how to dream. Thanks Mom.

Look upon the man who walks
beside you
He'll take your hand only to guide
you
He's gonna love you with
everything he's got
Whether your ready to accept or
not
He's gonna make you and love you
And he'll place no other above you
Because your his lady
And there is no if, but, or maybe
He's your man

Reach out and touch his skin
Start the fire burning within
And Lady, oh Lady
Love your man

He'll love and caress you
And he'll try to possess you
Because he feels a need to reach
For the passions yet unleashed
Loving him is so easy
And it don't take much to please
him
Your good loving man

Reach out and touch his skin
Start the fire burning within
And Lady, oh Lady
Love your man.

Sherry Miller-Campbell
THROUGH THE EYES OF A CHILD

To my greatest inspirations, Kristen and Kayla, and all my love always, Earl.

The eyes of a child can see many
things,
Raindrops and rainbows up in the
trees.
A magic place where dreams do
come true,
In the eyes of a child as they look
up at you.

Kissing and fixing each time they
fall down,
Knowing you'll be there when they
turn around.
Questioning and trusting in the
answers they seek,
Saying "I Love You" before they
can speak.

I'm amazed at this child who's part
of me,
The wonder and amusement of her
personality.
To her everythings perfect, sure,
and so mild,
All this and more through the eyes
of a child

Happy and smiling even on a rainy
day,
Bursting with joy when daddy
looks her way.
Showing and telling, sometimes
running wild,
This and so much more in the eyes
of my child.

Donna C Smith
ALL THE YEARS
Inside your house
You are writing a story
It's your story
It's your life;
When you go somewhere
It's a part of the story
It's part of the story of your life.

If you meet me
I will become
Part of the story of your life.

Page by page
You are writing a book
About your life
And the chances you took;
What interesting chapters you've
written
Of dreams, and fears, joy, and
tears, love, and hope,
All the years.

Dianne Smith Herren
SIGHT AND SOUND
Search the world over for all the
best—
The most beautiful sights, sounds
and the rest.
Search where you wish; search far
and near;
For the most beautiful sight, the
sound most dear.
Hear the most splendid melody
that's ever been heard.
Hear each of God's creatures—the
animal or the bird.
See dew glistening on the petals of
a perfect rose.
Watch the wiggly whiskers on a
bunny's pink nose.
Hear the sound of raindrops on a
window pane.
See the colors of the rainbow after
the rain.
Watch the wings of a soaring bird
in flight,
The shadows made by the dancing
sunlight.
Feel the soft, soft touch of an
animal's fur.
Listen to the kitten as it begins to
purr.
Hear the sound of the church bells
as they ring.
Listen to the voices of the people
when they sing.
Hear the brook as it babbles along
on its way.
Watch the sun as it rises for
another new day.
Search near by, or travel for mile
after mile;
No sight is more beautiful than a
child's smile.
Search now, later, tomorrow, or
forever after;
No sound is more beautiful than a
child's laughter.

Mary Ellen Tapio-Martin
ALWAYS A DREAM

Dedicated to the dreamer within all of us—no matter how hidden, no matter the circumstances, no matter who or where we are.

Hidden dreams,
Quiet dreams,
Silly dreams, sometimes—
Yet heartfelt dreams are ever
present,
If we but slow down long enough—
To softly listen,
To openly listen,
To honestly listen.
Coupled with our innate
realization of uniqueness,
Dreams create a path towards
manifestation.

Alystar McKenneh
AN AGELESS TUNE
Forever I lie . . .
bleeding bleeding
dying on the stones
Forever I lie . . .
dying dying
come and take me home
though my blood is running
thin
and my breath is almost nil
my life has been for Ireland
and I'm thinking of her still.

Tina L Del Bel
PICTURES
I paint a picture of the ocean
using colors to express my
emotions

I paint a picture of the flowers
remembering what used to be
ours

I paint a picture of the stream
discovering its only a dream

I paint a picture of the skies
while wiping tears from my eyes

I paint a picture of the rain
wondering what I'll gain

I paint a picture of the seashore
looking for a little more

Lori Engel
AMERICA
Oh America with freedom,
I stand so proud.
With pride and justice,
I speak so loud.
May our liberty prevail,
Our freedom still ring,
Love and peace float around,
And all the birds sing.
And through the clouds,
May the sun still shine.
Pledging to America,
That freedom is thine.

Mildred Davis Hall
A TRIBUTE TO MARTIN LUTHER KING JR.
Martin Luther King was slain
Thursday April 4, 1968 in
Memphis, Tennessee.
He gave his life that the oppressed
might be free
A great man has died and left us at
the edge of a dream
Darkness falls on the horizon in a
world of sadness and sorrow
While we wait for the dawn of a
brighter tomorrow
Doctor King is gone but we must
carry on
We must continue that vital work
he so nobly began
Martin Luther King hoped for that
higher quality in every man
Be it resolved, "This is a great
nation and we are a great people
But we are not all we hope to be."
This man was true to his country
and to his race
Yes, when things got rough Doctor
King kept the faith
He could be found pleading for his
people where ever they were
misused and abused
Martin Luther King was admired
by learned men everywhere
For they knew the cross of racism
is one we all must bear
It was ignorance and strife that
took this man's life
Doctor King visualized America as
a nation of many races, creeds
and all kinds of people
Dedicated to the common cause
that "All men are created equal."
He tried to make this world a better
place in which to live for all
humanity
He lived a life of integrity,
preached a ministry of love and
brotherhood
But was sometimes misunderstood
When men of every color learn to
respect one another
Regardless of where they fall on
the spectrum or what country
they come from
Such words as "riot" and
"insurrection" will swiftly fade
from the scene
And we shall live out the reality of
Martin Luther King's dream

Ella R Leonard
WINTERS CHARM

To Children

The sky so blue, the sun so bright,
How it sparkles in the light.
Tall trees swaying in the cool
breeze,
Snow is now up to one's knees

Sliding, skating and skiing too.
Such great fun for each of you.
The wind at times is rather cold.
Children laugh at reddened nose.

Winter is truly a delight
As the sun goes down at night.
Colors so brilliant my heart sings
With the joy that winter brings.

Other seasons that we may praise:
Spring has many lovely days.
Summer has surf, beach and the
sun.
Fall, bright leaves for every-one.

Winter season is my delight,
Sky not blue, sun not so bright.
The snow once more begins to fall.
Wonderland for one and all.

Susanne Marie Cross
PASSING THE TIME
As I sit here wishing the time to
pass right by,
The wind is whispering words of
goodbye.
Birds sing, sweet melodies and
stand aside as dreams become
realities.
Please sit and pass the time, as
many have done before.
Please sit and dream with me, as
you have never done before.
Come sit and pass the time with
me and see the dreams we dream
become realities . . .

Rosalie Brevelle
LORD HELP ME
She drops to her knees
And begins to cry
Lord help me please
Or I shall die.
Her mind in agony
Her body in pain
Lord help me please
I'm going insane.
Her life she sees
Is wasting away
Lord help me please

Before I decay.
She begs, she pleads
But still no answer
Lord help me please
I'm dying of cancer!

Peter L Osterman
NEHALEM BAY

Rain brushed the rocks,
the kelp washed ashore glistened
in the scant light
of the storm-tossed morning.
Laughing children
wheeled as gulls
upon the pocked spines of the beach;
mothers searched the sand,
baskets in their hands.
In the driftwood piles
a smoky fire
slipped blue-grey tendrils
up through the rain
and babies cried
beneath the cedar cloaks of old women.

The sands are still harvested,
but the children of the coast are gone,
swept away.

Donna M Ford

Donna M Ford
THE MISSION STREET BUS

To my Mother, Irene. Without her love and kindness and guidance I wouldn't be the person I am today.

On the bus of San Francisco
Or the Mission Street Bus
Past Mission—down third

I see eyes—the eyes of despair
Seeking, always seeking
Hungry, always hungry
Dirty, always dirty

Doorways
Doorways are their homes
A place to be—a doorway
Some place to be theirs

We worry—we fret
Oh how foolish we are to worry so
All we need is a doorway
A doorway to find the way
Perhaps a way home

Maybe they know
Through the doorway is home

Reflections on a bus
Past Mission—down third
Leaving my love once again

When will I return?
Only the Fates know for sure

Sadness
The sadness bus is the Mission Street Bus

Ken W Hall
THE DREAM

To Marjory, The reality of many dreams

I first thought she had a grain of sand in her eye
But I guess maybe it was a real tear,
A tear for her lover, her boyfriend or however he fits into her life,

Whatever his position,
Whatever the reason,
I guess the tear was worth it,
He's holding her now,
Walk on.

Misty Darlann West
LOVING ONE THAT BELONGS TO ANOTHER

When I gaze into his eyes a memory awakes of the times we shared as man and wife.
But now in your eyes there is another to whom I have lost you to forever.
My heart is broken as I see
the end of our once beautiful
love that never was forever.
As I leave these memories
behind my love for you
will be eternal.

Angela Jo Ellison
AN ANSWER, PLEASE

TO those I love and care for, and who believed in me. Love, Angie

I chose to go, never to look back
I shed no tears—my heart is done.
It was not for love, it was for lack
only life has answers, I had none.

A different place, a different time
a dream that was surrounded in gold.
Your heart is cold and no longer mine
it is time, for we have grown old.

The finality has come upon me now
I say goodbye, to a dear person, a friend.
Love is eternal, but I must ask how.

We must go on—each a different way
we shared the worse and the best.
The sad times are when I won't see you each day.
It's true, we did put each other through lifes test.

But now it's time to say goodbye,
as I kneel here upon my knees
I know I can't ever ask you why...
I wish I could,—have an answer, please.

Myrna L Hagy
MEMORIAL DAY

In memory of Darrell "Sonny" Meador, beloved son, brother, cousin and friend. He died in Vietnam at age 19.

My father was brave thru all the years,
I never saw him shed many tears,
Until one dreadful day,
The news came, Sonny had passed away,
Pain and hurt ran high,
My father began to cry,
Over and over my Dad said, "Why?
Why did Sonny have to die?"
You were so loved, Sonny,
As were 54,000 or more,
Of sons, husbands and fathers that left our shore,
To die in a jungle's damp and clam,
For a far away country called Vietnam.
Especially on Memorial Day we can still see,
Sonny, the way he used to be,
Laughing, smiling, with his winning ways,
Young, handsome, in his carefree days.
"The cream of the crop," yes, we had all seen,
How proud he was to be a Marine.
We kneel beside his grave and pray,
"Thank you, God, for letting him come our way,"
Sweet memories crowd our mind and heart,
Even though the tear drops start,
Especially on Memorial Day we can still see,
Sonny, the way he used to be.

Karen Larivee
MISGIVING

Who am I?
I can't stop wondering.
The time has come where I should know,
But no hint to show.
I want to climb inside my heart,
To find the real me.
What would I see?
I've experienced love,
Which is the most beautiful thing,
It has told me nothing;
I wish a sign would come from above.
My life is a blur;
I am the only one who can focus.
I just have to wait for it to occur.
Until the time comes,
I'll keep on living my life,
Uncertain as it may be.
If only I could be free,
To live and love as me.

Joe P Ryan
THE BEST IS YET TO COME

The best is yet to come,
It's only dark because we're in early morning; waiting for the dawning sun,
We are standing on the labors and freedom of what others have done,
And yes, the best is yet to come,
There are problems a many and yes, there is gloom,
But we are alive—we mourn only for the laborers in their tomb,
For we've unfinished business, there is much to be done,
And the best is yet to come,
The future is in our hands—we'll decide what it will be,
The best is yet to come is up to you and me.

Dallas Kirk Gantt
BE HERE NOW

with my wisp of a surprising son on my shoulders
i set out on a crisp morning walk into the woods.

geese plowed through the fleece of clouds high overhead,
painted a lush but gentle red by the rising sun.

knee deep in snow, beside the stream we stood and watched them pass then . . . there was only us and the wind seeking
the tall marsh grass and cattails thrusting up through the frozen pond.

beneath our feet and down below the brittle ice-trapped bubbles,
trout and bass seemed to swim between encased leaves like fossils
of broken branches and pondweed stubbles.

Jamie laughed and looked up, his big eyes catching the fat cardinals
puffed up by the breeze like ripe red fruit on bare birch trees.

clear toe-prints in the snow showed where deer had walked by
not long ago, and Jamie wanted to know where they went and why.

on a fieldstone outcrop we found where a fox had feasted . . .
. . . pheasant feathers spread about the paw-prints . . . then!

like a flash of fire the fox bounded out of nearby brambles
and cut across overgrowth of some unknown farmers' forgotten fields.

thick pine hills and thornbush thickets brought us to a standstill,
our breath steaming out into the clean chill of morning,
freezing rare moments of beauty together with our minds' memories,

giving us both each other and this pristine time forever,
so that we'll always share a little sliver of heaven,
from this deep-country winter moment, of 1987.

Mindy T Turek
A LITTLE SMILE

The sun rises
And I awaken
Another day
Quiet
And
Peaceful
The wind blows
Through
My window

Bringing in the scent
Of the
Pretty
Flowers
That are planted
Beneath
My
Window
It's such a beautiful day
And I can make
It better
By
Starting with
A
Little
Smile.

Stormy Rebecca Thew
DREAM COME TRUE

To Alex Isabel, that wonderful man who has indeed made my dreams come true. How I look forward to spending my "forevers" with you, as we unite as Husband and Wife on 9/5/87. I love you!

Before September of Eighty-Six
When I was all alone;
I had built a lovely daydream
of a love to call my own.
I thought it was a fantasy
too precious to come true
But all my dreams of love became
reality . . . in you.

Michael E Roberson
A CHILD IS BORN

Dedicated To My Nephew; Stephen Michael Roberson, "It was your birth, that inspired this very special poem.

A cry is heard,
A mother sighs
Into the world,
A child arrives.

Breath is taken,
For him a first,
God allowed;
To this earth,
A child, A birth.

Its' a boy!
Soft, pure,
From mothers eyes,
praise, tears.

"A child we had",
Father sighs,
Staring down,
Into his childs eyes.

"God allowed this to be . . ."
A blessing, A gift,
From you to me.

Thank you Lord,
For the work that you have done,
Thank you Lord,
For giving us our son.

Suzanne Treasure
ONLY YOU

This was written for my one & only love, My Sweetheart CHUCK

Only you can make
the sun shine bright.
Only you can get me
thru the night.

Only you can turn
the red lights green.
Only you can understand
what I mean.

Only you can make
me feel this way.
Only you can make this
a special day!

Carl R Modrow
PEACEFUL FEELING
Oh, the feeling that can be obtained
When one is in the wilderness.
The overwhelming tranquil
thoughts
That enter the mind,
As one sits beneath a towering
conifer,
Gazing at the clouds which passeth
O'er the mountainous terrain.
Where the foul of the air
Gracefully float amidst the
heavens.
While the critters of the wild
Are going about their business
Without a care and all is fair.
These things to behold,
Make for a "peaceful feeling".

Estal "Eppie" Naanes
AWARENESS
I see Christ in you.
You live a life that is true
As you reach out to help others.
Your eyes are clear.
Your face is fresh.
Your life to others is dear.
To us, you are precious.
The Lord does bless us!
Again and again you have revealed
A most prized possession—
That of a good life.
It is surely an example
Of walking hand-in-hand
And side-by-side
Along with Christ.
Looking upon your face
Fills my heart with loving grace.
I am aware of Heaven above
As I witness the love
Of Jesus flowing through you.
I see Christ in you.

Florinda (Alanis) Wright

Florinda (Alanis) Wright
AFTER SCHOOL
After school I wait,
For him to walk with me home.
Together we walk.

Shelia Vaughan
WHAT JESUS DID FOR ME

To my loving husband Larry, and to the Rainbow Tabernacle.

When Jesus came into my heart
He gave me a brand new start.
Jesus gave me a new life;
took away all the anguish and
strife.

Jesus took away all the hatred
Filled me with love and
understanding to keep me
straight.
I'm glad it wasn't too late to
change my doomed fate.

There is one thing that I know,
I just want to praise him for.
Giving me the sweet Holy Ghost
For he is my heavenly host

I pray daily without cease, but
Finally there is one thing that will
Put my mind at ease.
When I find myself kneeling at
his feet on my knees.

Traci Sevick
SPRING
Blowing softly, the wind whistled
through my ears,
for it was Spring.

The playful flowers were blooming.

There I lie on the ground happy
with all that I see.

Debra L Gero
A CHILD

To Corey and Hillary with love

What is happiness
Who am I to say
But I find happiness
When I watch a child at play.

Eyes that are bright with wonder
Hands that are never still
A smile to bring warm sunshine
To the coldest winter chill.

A giggle and a whisper
Are all that I can hear
As the secrets of the day are told
To the devoted teddy bear.

As I tuck them into bed at night
And watch them nod off to sleep
I feel the joys of motherhood
My happiness to keep

Susan Ayres
MY LAST TIME
The broken glass
The shattered door
I know I walked this way
So many times before.
The images I've seen
The sounds that I have heard
I really can't tell you
In just a simple word.
I've wanted to cry
But, couldn't find the tear.
I've wanted to run
But, found not the fear
The pain and the torture
Just an act for revenge
Made me find the bottle
And the pills or syringe
The faint cry for help
This was my last plea
Hoping that the stained floor
Was my last time to bleed.

Virginia A Breech
THE NEED OF HIM
The need of him is growing
strong—
My love for him is like a song.

I've wanted him since the day we
met,
And still my honor I have kept.

I need his hand to wipe my tears—
I need his love to chase my fears.

I'll express my feelings in every way
Because I shall need him every day.

I need him so much I shall not
forget—
There's nothing to say that I would
regret.

I know he's the one my heart
desires—
His face appears in the flames of
fires.

I know he's the one I need
To reach my goals and help me
succeed.

There's beautiful wonders up
above—
I want us always to share our love.

Steve Abelli
FRIENDSHIP

For Steve and the times that were; for the Lord's magnificent Wichita Mountains; And for those special friendships everywhere.

I journeyed to the mountains to
spend a little time,
but something there was missing,
your soul; your mind.
And as I wandered in the
wilderness there,
I tried to enjoy it, but my mind was
elsewhere.

Over and over the visions returned,
of those crisp, quiet evenings and
thejcampfires we burned.
Of hiking and climbing on hot
summer days,
and the cool, damp, contrast found
in underground caves.

Of exploring rugged canyons as the
sun was sinking low,
and rafting down the rivers, going
where the waters flow.
Of waking in the darkness to the
coyote's lonesome howl,
and every now and then the
hooting of an owl.

Of misty morning stillness after
thunderstorm at night,
watching deer and elk from hiding,
and the hawk on winged flight.
These memories I'll cherish until
I'm at life's end,
but they would have been quite
worthless, without you there,
my friend!

Jean E Merrihew
BROTHERLY LOVE
How do you explain brotherly love?
Is it a special gift from above?
Or do we earn the right to know—
What makes kindness cast such an
obvious glow?
All around the faces of creatures—
Who prefer to be unassuming
teachers?
By their actions and their need to
be—
Responsible citizens without
bigotry.
Securing their place in the sun—
By teaching their brothers, one by
one—
That the art of love can be done—
Even when we cease to see—
The need for all this chivalry!

Nicki Ruble
GRANDMA
There comes a time
In all our lives
When death must come
And life must fly.
But always near
You'll be with me
Forever here
A memory.
Through all these years
You've loved and given
Forever near
To help, to listen.
Our love for you
Will never falter
For only the way it's expressed
Will alter.
You've been so much a part
Of all our lives
We'll miss you so
As on life flies
And someday, many years from now
Through times of good and bad.
We'll once again, together be
No longer just a memory.

Joyce M Rodgers
A MOTHER'S BLISS
My day is so intense and very complexed,
Sometimes I get very confused, puzzled and perplexed to say the least.
I did not know I would grow up to face this fate,
And I never thought it would be so sedate,
so quiet at times and yet
so vibrant and dignified.
For you see I am a Mother of three these days,
But no more do I hear little foot steps on the hearth,
For they've grown up, and walking on my heart.
My moody brood has made it to the perplexing teens.
At the crack of dawn I hear what's for breakfast?
And can I go home with Joe?
Oh, by the way, here's my report
card
I haven't time to discuss the "D's Mom,
I'm off to class.
See you tonight before I get my "Z's".
But then when evening comes I hear more!
One has practice, and one has band, but lo, the third
has a date! 'Tis such a short time
to puberty!
Just think, all of the above is the result of my chaotic
marriage and I think it's grand.
And yet I know it only gave me more to love,
'cause this family is wrapped in God's blessings.

Erica A Beringer
A GIFT OF LOVE

This poem is dedicated to my Mom, Grandpap, and Grandma Anna

Love is your warm smile.
Love is sitting on the couch and talking to me.
Love is listening to
my problems.
Love is playing board games with me.
Love is lots of hugs and kisses.
Love is making time for me.
Love is helping me with my homework.
I love you
Erica

Mrs Martha C Fortini
ANGELS
God needed some angels in heaven;
That's why he took my children away,
But some day I know
I will see them again
In a brighter place
Far, far away.

Connie Frank
TIMELESS LOVE
Two misty figures from the past sharing timeless love
Walking the path destiny foretold
Their adversaries nothing but dust
They dared the fates and walk triumphant
Two who have known the struggles and heartbreak love demands
Their story often tragic
they would not yield
Needing no one
They walk the centuries
guiding lovers
giving strength and courage
where love lives defiant
The ancient ones smile
their fight victorious
Eternity stretches—beckons them onward
through time
Together, always together

Martha Herps
HEARTS
Every one has a heart,
as different as can be.
Happy hearts, sad hearts,
and hearts of jealousy.
Big hearts, small hearts,
even hearts of stone.
Broken hearts, mended hearts,
and hearts that are all alone.
Kind hearts and cruel ones
hearts that have gone to heaven.
But the one we hear the most about,
is the artificial Jarvic Seven.

Ellis Harold Henderson

Ellis Harold Henderson
LIFE IS REAL
Life can be as you see it,
Just as you see birds fly.
You can see life pass you,
Very swiftly bye.
Life can be as you feel it,

Just as you may touch a flower.
So you must cherish life,
Hour-by-hour.
Life can be what you make it,
Just as a cobbler makes shoes.
So may you create something
That is an image of you.

Vivian E Kaiser
MY REWARD
You are—

every breath I take,
every dream I own,
every thought I possess;
You are—
my reason for being,
the rebirth of believing—
You are—
every goal I make,
every place I call home,
every thing that's happiness.
You are—
my strength, my courage too—
my reality, my dream come true;
You are—
my reward
for trusting in God.

Edna Marie Bremer
THE CANDLE
A tall, white candle burns in the window,
And looks like a glowing bride,
The bright ray is her bridal train,
And a thin film of smoke, her veil,
Longingly she stands at the window
As if waiting for her true lover,
She shivers and looks down the street,
With a silence deep and white,
Again she flickers and looks away
Into the dark, dark room.
Sadly fall her waxy tears,
And slowly she melts away.

Steve Kendall
FUTILITY
The dawn was purple and the mist was white.
The day became scarlet and drove 'way the night.
The blue of the sky was of regal hue,
And the tale of the ages was to be told anew!

With the purple dawn came shapes in the mist.
With the scarlet of the day our comrades were missed.
With the blue of the sky appeared shapes of black.
And the day awoke with a thunderous crack!

The shapes in the mist took ominous form.
The scarlet of the day was a banner so worn.
The blue of the sky was the cross of the bars.
And the bars bore proudly their little white stars!

With the mist rolled back and the shapes unveiled.
Brothers on bayonets were found impaled.
The cannon grumbled and shot were spent.
Few blue or gray tunics were free from rent!

The blue for the black and the gray for just honor.
The man for the dollar not caring for either.
So brother killed brother and the dirt claimed the blood.
And the passing of ages absorbed the flood.

The night came purple and the blue won the black.
The gray kept their honor and hired them back.
The man with his dollar went on his way.
But the blood in the dirt was there to stay.

Christopher Gavin Gutierrez
SHE
A Dear elderly lady was she,
Smiling, cheerful and full of glee.
That was the day I met, She.
Lying in that hospital bed, you see.
She would talk a mile, then laugh at me.
Her eyes, they would twinkle, but not see.
No one knew the aches and pains she felt,
No one knew what she could see.
Then I came in the next week,
I swear only to take a peek.
My dear elderly lady, smiling, cheerful and
full of glee.
Had left me, you see.

Kenneth R Newton
THE BEAST
From lily pad to lily pad just passing time away,
I hardly noticed, the birds flying away.
As I realized what was going on,
All was silent, around the pond.
And then I saw him—standing near,
The one who hasn't—any fear.
He was a smoker, fat and stout,
And then he dropped it, but never put it out.
The fire spread from tree to tree,
And all the animals had to flee.
There was no escape, no way out,
Because he didn't put, the cigarette out.

Selma Youngdahl
O FRIENDLY DEATH
O Thoughtful Death,
Embrace me ere I find
That I have left
My usefulness behind.

O Helpful Death,
Leave me not here to know
The living death

Of seeing talents go.

O Timely Death,
Claim me when work is done.
Take me with you
Though missed by even one.

O Peaceful Death,
Release me from the fret
Of my frayed world
In time. Do not forget.

Not one more breath,
O Friendly Death.

Michele R Hartman
A PIRATE LIFE

To Mrs. Huzey, Mr. Crawford, and Mrs. Doan, who are my teachers, my encouragement, and my friends.

A pirate life be the life for me,
One of danger, adventure it be.
A life of defiance, that makes one stagger,
With a whip and a swirl of my sharp dagger.
My crew be killers, marooners, tis true,
But to hangmen I'll never give that clue.
The noose be raised with my first mate,
His cries for mercy be too late.
I live off the sea, with my silver and gold,
Never being afraid, but always so bold.
I loot the galleons, the schooners, all,
I live for adventure, that is my call.
In the last battle my life was all but taken,
It left me wounded, defeated and shaken.
My flag on the mast will forever fly high,
With honor and glory till the day I die.
In a watery grave where I shall rest,
The sharks and the thieves will uphold my crest.
Before I take my breath, the last,
These wisdom-filled words will I cast.
A pirate life be the life for me,
One of danger, adventure it be.

Betty Claire Allen
BEHOLD THE MIND
Behold the Mind
My companion in silence
Thinking, remembering
A—circle of thoughts, laughter, fear, tenderness
And love—undone

Behold the Mind
Unlike any other affair
It leaves nothing to the imagination
Except
Reality.

C A Little
MY SPECIAL FRIEND
You're ragged and dirty
a bit rough from the wear
and missing one eye
which went no one knows where.

Yet you're my constant companion
and lovable friend
cause you're trusting and faithful
and true to the end.

We share the adventures
both the good and the bad
despite and occasional scream
from my Mom or my Dad.

You share all my secrets
and tell not a one
and my pillow as well
when the days' work is done.

Yet all of these things
that together we do
is just one of the reasons
I'll always love you.

The other's the friendship
that together we share
just me and my big,
one-eyed, brown Teddy Bear.

Chedie Enchyvonne Wright
MORNINGS
Mornings are quiet.
A certain peace is found.
Lots of mothers are breakfast bound.
What a time to re-evaluate.
My life, myself, the kids, my mate.
Alarm clocks soon will buzz.
What a haven this house was.
If only for a short time.
Part of this morning was all mine.
"What shall I wear?"
I hear in the distant air.
"These old jeans have a tear."
My quiet peaceful haven that was.
Is now changing because:
Reality has to take it's place.
"Hey mom, how 'bout some pancakes?"
Oh well, tomorrow morning will be.
Just re-evaluation, quiet, peace and me.

Dora Allen Brooks (Mrs Howard H)
MEMORIES
As your anniversary is drawing near,
Remember your fond memories, all through those years.
Remember the feelings you had as kids,
Remember all the loving things that you did.
Remember your joys, sorrows and the inbetweens—
All those silly little hurts, that appeared on the scene.
Every single moment—be sure to treasure.
Remember each and every thought with pleasure.
For now your memories are much as before—
Only now you (more or less) know the score.
So be happy as you go on with your life,
Being her wonderful husband, and his darling wife.

Ruth Marie Gilbert
TO LEARN AN ANCIENT ART; KARATE

In gratitude for their patience, encouragement, and inspiration in teaching me their Art: Scott Adamski and William Lassi.

There is a Master,
A king of his Art.
True grace is in every action.
Smooth movement of hands.
Power in the turn,
Muscles working
in a well choreographed series of moves.
A dance without music.
A song without words.
Flash of hands, fist clenched.

There is a student,
New to the art.
Every action is an attempt
to follow the Master.
The turn is too slow,
the muscles weak.
Form awkward and difficult to follow.
Music without rhythm.
Words without rhyme.
Slow hands, fist unclenched.

Bernice Lloyd Booker
WATER-TALK
Did you ever sit on the bank of a clear running stream
and watch the water play
Around the grass and over the rocks
You can almost hear it say;
Why sit up there and miss the fun
Come on in with me
I'll take you on a merry run
Away on out to the sea.
We'll visit all the babbling brooks
And listen to their merry song
There are flowers and fairies in every nook,
Why don't you come along.
We'll help the miller turn the wheel
to grind the golden corn
And smell the warm yellow meal
Early in the morn.
We'll run across the meadows
Around the countryside
And if you turn out to be a sleepy head
We'll just drift with the tide

Joseph Barry Coopersmith

Joseph Barry Coopersmith
A ROUND FIGURE
It all followed in order,
With origin south of the border.

The svelte rumba queen
Swayed real keen,
From around the hinder quarter.

Bobby L Cooke
THE GOAL

To Johnny

Setting a goal and letting it be known
Is a risky adventure indeed
What if you fail and have to explain
Why you couldn't make your dream

It's easier to dream a silent dream
Than to open up your heart
To jeering, mocking eyes that laugh
When your plans fall apart

So dream your dreams and lock them up
Deep within your soul
But not so deep that you forget
To work quietly toward your goal

Prettyflyer
A DREAM TO BE FINISHED

To the one who gave me the dream,
To the one who shares that dream

I am of the future of which my fathers dreamed
Though I am not the future that they dreamed . . .
How ardent was the call to power!
A futile call that Time would not let us answer,
A call lost in the roaring of the Past
And only faintly heard by the Present . . .
I am of a future undreamed of,
And though I walk every bit as proud
And carry my head every bit as high
As the man who walks beside me,
I am but a private dream . . .
A dream unfinished; incomplete . . .
For I am but a fraction of a greater dream
Of a people who have dared to survive . . .
I cannot ride the plains astride a horse of Vengeance
And cry for the blood of those who do us harm . . .
I cannot raise the bow and shield in war
And like my fathers, vanish in the dust . . .
And yet, how precious was life to them!
I can raise a shield of Knowledge to protect their dream,
I can raise a cry against Intolerance and Ignorance—
A cry to be heard across the plains . . .
I can raise the bow in sign for all who once were, to be again . . .
I will not be mine own executioner!
I will finish the dream of my fathers!

Cyndi Stacey
THIS SEA
I stroll upon a glistening shore and ponder wading in . . .
Invincible waters from This Sea relentlessly summons me.
"Shall I tell him I can't swim?"

Deeper and deeper with each step did I wade too deep?
Was I captured by this ocean

or justifying my emotions?
This secret I can no longer keep.

Shifting sands beckon me
to heed the undertoe . . .
my fears subside
unlike the tide
Drowning in This Sea of love's
the only way I'll go.

Shirley Ryan
ONCE
A tiny quintessential seed
From creation's soul
Chanced to fall
Upon my cluttered brain,
But lazy me,
I was too slow,
I failed to grasp it
And hold it
And make it grow
and so —
Lost forever
An original thought

Vicki L Alexander
NIGHT
evening breezes
caress
my face
tugging lightly
at my hair
whispering
softly
with the
sounds
of night.

Katherine Holt
THE RABBITS ON THE HILL
Upon the hill where the pine trees
blow.
Anywhere, anywhere I don't know!
We hill it up, we hill it down, until
we hill it around.
Whirly, twirly, around, around, as
we
scamper to the ground.

Shirlene Y Johnson "Shirl"
JESUS CHRIST
J ust when, by a mere twist of fate,
E verything was crumbling around
me;
S eeing that I was a loser in life and
U nable to control that or to
tolerate
S uffering so much loss, I turned
to Thee.
C hanges began to immediately
take place—
H eavy burdens were lightened; joy
replaced sorrow.
R elying on Thee, my life was
turned around.
I now walk with Thee & in Thy
grace.
S urely enough, I welcome each
day & do not fear tomorrow—
T hanks for giving me the guidance
& peace I've found.

Julie H Yurkovich
OUTREACH OF LOVE
What do you think of when you
think of people,
Or do you think of them at all?
Are they all tall or short.
Or white or black,
Does that cover them all?

Some are full of love you know
And others don't know love at all.
But God gives us all a chance
We have only to heed His call.

He wants us to know and love Him
And love our neighbors too!
For only then—can we begin
To see His love shine through.

Love starts when we are born
We are bonded, so they say.
And we learn to love our sisters and
brothers
For that is His way.

So why can't we all get along,
And have harmony in the world
today?
All it takes, is lots of love
And peace would be here to stay.

Victor M Levey
INGRATITUDE
The man who invented
French-fries
died last night
and no one even knew his name
or heard his death-sob
or moaned his end.
They didn't lower the flags
and the kids still had to go to school
and my mother didn't weep
and the priest misspelled his name
and the paper made no mention,
and you and I . . . We ate out
anyway.

Al Stewart
BIG TOYS
Any of us knows why humans fight:
nobody is willing to put away his
toys.
Anybody could push the wrong
button
on the pretty light panel.
Somebody will get killed,
and it will be everybody!

Everything will go BANG!
Anything remaining will be useless.

Nothing will ever be the same.
Something will remain:
a great silence.

Each of us must talk
to anyone willing to grow up.
Everybody knows
that no one goes
without everyone else, on the day
everything Blows!

John Tigue
GODS' SONG (A PERSONAL PRAYER TO GOD)

To Bob and Doris for their kindness and To Floyd, Beulah, Frank, Rita, Brenda, Linda, Tracey, Tina, Crystal, Rhonda and Ky. for caring

---

As we go through life together,
Let us hold our heads up high,
And know that god is watching us,
Somewhere there in the sky,
As we maruel every sunrise,
And survive each passing day,
Let us not forget to thank our Lord,
For showing us the way,
While we journey through the
darkness,
And we wander through the
light,
Remember who has blessed us all,
With every sound and sight,
And as our ends grow nearer,
And we reflect upon our pasts,
Know that God is holding you,
And that his love shall last.
Amen

Elizabeth Ann Austin

Elizabeth Ann Austin
BLESSINGS

To: Doug and Momma, whose love is a true blessing.

We have many blessings large and
small;
Good conversations, a telephone
call,
Sunshine, flowers, a warm bed;
An ability to apologize for things
said.
The chime of a clock, food on the
table;
A place to work when we're able.

A vote in a ballot, freedom of
speech;
Even the stars are within our reach.
Sins forgiven with God's love;
Brought to us on the wings of a
dove.
We thank you Lord, for what we
share;
And hope to be worthy of your
tender care.

Thelma M Welsbacher
FATHER
F
stands for faith to guide you along
When doubts in your mind make
your heart go wrong.

A
stands for adoring the one above
all,
Because God is the one on whom
we can always call.

T
stands for the thankful gifts you
have given to us,
But true words of love are the most
precious.

H
stands for hope where darkness
may lay,
and peace of mind to fill your day.

E
stands for the eternal light that
shines on and on,
So goodness may spread from
night until dawn.

R
stands for the rememberance of
his loving care,
And His treasures on earth are ours
to share.

Shannon Sue Pattillo
AT TIMES I'M NOT THE DAUGHTER
At times I'm not the daughter that
you seem to want me to be.
In many ways, I'm not the same as
I long ago used to be.
It may be hard for you at times,
But I am growing up, you see.
It's not that I don't love you Mom.
I just need time to be me.

Shanna Rochelle Wiggonton
ONLY THEN DID I REALIZE
He was so kind, not only to me but
to all,
He was so gentle, understanding.
So sure of himself and yet
Not conceited in the least.
Flattering words and actions
Never could totally reveal
All the love that was there.
But it was there, in his eyes.
Such a concerned friend he was,
Always listening to my problems.
Even if he saw I was wrong
He looked away and saw only the
good.
But something happened,
There was no more sharing
Only a distance woven with
confusion.
Only then did I realize he was gone.
Only then did I realize I loved him.

Deborah M Davis
A TREASURE OF LOVE
I'm going to have your baby
A token of our love
A precious little being
A gift from God above

The sweetness of this little child
Will touch our very life
The conception of our marriage
Now we're more than man & wife

Our days are filled with happiness
Waiting for our girl or boy
It's sure to make us more complete
And fill our life with joy

Wendy J Zinke
THE PEOPLE AND THIS WORLD
In this great big world one man is
always kind.
In this great big world one man has

only violence on his mind.

Please realize that one man lives
and one man dies. Does it matter
to us, will anyone cry?

Let it all out.
We know what this world is about.
Death and mankind, I don't doubt.

Poverty, Sickness, and Nuclear
War, do you want to hear several
examples, I can say more.

What has this world come to?
Is anything precious or needed
from the things we do?
Think about it slowly while I
pause . . .

Did you understand the poem or
even its cause?
Read this again and feel the
people's pain.
Such violence and shame, so
uncontrollably strong; can we
not be tamed?

Mike Connolly
MY FLAG

I live in a land, the greatest on earth
The home of the free, the place of
my birth
Where the mountains are high and
the valleys are low
And the shining sun sets the whole
world aglow.

Where the forests are green and the
lakes so clear
And the Hand of God has touched
everywhere
Where people sing out with
freedom and joy
As they raise their great flag up to
the sky.

With joy in my heart and a tear in
my eye
I stood very still as I watched my
flag fly
As the stars and stripes waved in
the breeze
I stood up no longer but fell to my
knees.

And I prayed to God to make the
winds blow
So then the whole wide world
would know
That the stars and stripes would
forever fly
As long as there was wind in the
sky.

Lena S Reagle
MOTHER'S PAY

Who pays you, Mother, for the
work that you do?
All workers get paid for their work,
do you?
You always are busy, hurrying
about;
You are home so much, haven't
time to go out.
You cook and clean, and mend our
clothes,
And read us stories, and hear our
woes.

"My child," I answer, "My payment
is this:
Small arms in a hug and a sticky
kiss,
As I'm stopped in my work by a
touch,
And a sweet child whispers, 'I love
you so much!'
This, and seeing my children each
day
Developing rightly, That is my
pay."

R Jolene Thompson
PASSING TIME

To my loving God, Jesus, The true Author Of all Things

One day while I was sleeping
This Dream came to me
That some day soon I'd stand Alone
At the Cross Of Calvery
All Alone I would be crossing
Old Jordon wide and strong
So I thought I'd take some time
today
To sing to God This Song.

Put me in your heart Lord so I'll be
close
To You . . .
No more will I be lonesome
And no more will I be blue . .
And when the day has come Lord
To Bid this Earth Adieu
Then I'll be in your heart My God
And I'll go Along With You . . .

Heather N Gibson
SEARCHING

Love comes in time with the wind,
Caressing the beaches with its
carefree hand.
I walk not alone but with the ocean
air,
With spirits.
Looking for the pair of love and
happiness.
Yet when they find it I won't know,
For I shall again be alone
In my own little world
Forever Searching.

Edith Lee-Milburn
LATE LOVE

Dedicated in Remembrance to Jack Milburn, My Husband, My Friend

It was a garden
Somewhere.
You smiled,
I spoke.
I don't know

Why
I remember
Late blooming roses,
Except
You were there
And so was
I.

Jeannie C Gee
ONLY DREAMS

For the one to whom I shared my first dreams and the other all the rest: my father, Charlie, my husband, Dale. And to a special little boy, Ryan, may all your dreams come true.

I have never seen the awesome
sight
of the mighty redwood tree
or walked with you along the Seine
in romantic gay Paree
I have never worn a wedding gown
nor a mink or sable coat
Never viewed the Colorado River
or sailed a yacht—or any boat.
I've never once been to the opera
or a circus or broadway show
and never a time in all my years
to a rock concert ever go.
I've never had a honeymoon
or camped out in a tent
not a poem of mine's been
Published
a dozen roses have never been sent.
Never walked with you in Central
Park
or even had a horse n' buggy ride.
And I never got the chance to say
"I LOVE YOU"—
the night you died.

Elizabeth Draper Bolick
REFLECTION

Summer's gone.
Only bright November days
remain . . .
And yet . . .
Roses reminiscent of June
Still bloom
Along the lane.
Faces bright . . .
Untouched by frost play hide and
seek
Neath autumn's falling leaves . . .
Imparting a sense of wonderment
To one who believes . . .
That just because warm days cease
to be
One cannot grow
Or be a part
Of earth's great maj-es-ty.
The days grow cold.
The trees are almost bare,
Yet
Like autumn roses . . . life blooms
For those who truly care . . .
Paying no attention
To life's cold winter air!

Gayle Malone
ASPIRATION'S TREK

Thanks to wonderful parents, encouraging siblings, inspiring children and my husband Ronald. I love each of you.

In the land of opportunity,
I chart my course on talent's sea
and launch ambition's ship of
dreams
as recognition's beacon beams.

Hoist the anchor of experience
Avast ye skeptics! Man the boat!
This voyage you'll have me to
thank,
Past disappointments—"Walk the
plank!"

My compass is the star of hope
though failure's pirates come to
loot,
with gusts of pride I fill my sail,
with winds of luck, I shall prevail.
And onward to that distant shore
where buried neath the sands of
time,
waits fame and fortune's treasure
chest;
on the beach, in the land of Sweet
Success!

Septiembre Booth
ONE EYE SEES

This poem is for my Pop, Mr. Alexander L. Johnson. I love you, you're always in my heart.

If one eye sees only happy, the
other only sad,
If one eye sees only good, the other
only bad.
If one eye sees through tear drops
that fall like, stormy
rain—Can the one eye that takes in
all the glory blind the one that
takes in all the pain?
Can humanity strengthen one eye
so that vision if finally restored.
Can be sure of happiness only once
more.
The answers to these question, that
run wild through my mind.
Shall reach me in this adult world,
I've only just begun to find.

Carol Sue Matthews

Carol Sue Matthews
A PRAYER OF FAITH

To My Children & My Friend, With Unconditional Love & Respect, Marissa Emilee, Sean, & Bob Fletcher

We the people and so it goes
Are fighters strong against our foes
And no matter how the world may
turn
It's for our freedom we will yearn.
And if the Darkness comes to light
Only God can win this fight
So listen now, and no not flight
For only Love can beat their might.
We are a country great, not small
And to this land we owe our all.
For God can give—yet take away
And he'll have his say come
judgement day
But nay—no man can say "it's time"
So live, and love, and cry, and grow,
And let your heart and feelings
show
And give your all to both old—and
small
And make your love the best of all

And last—yet least
Show Love and Peace
Not only Man but also Beast.

Gin Scopel
BUMP IN THE NIGHT

Bump in the night, Gee what a fright
I listen so still on my own free will
Cats meowling loud and clear . . . Something
must be very near
The moon at night shining on the floor
Holy cow . . . Its at my bedroom door
I peek from the covers, afraid to look
Boy . . . am I ever shook

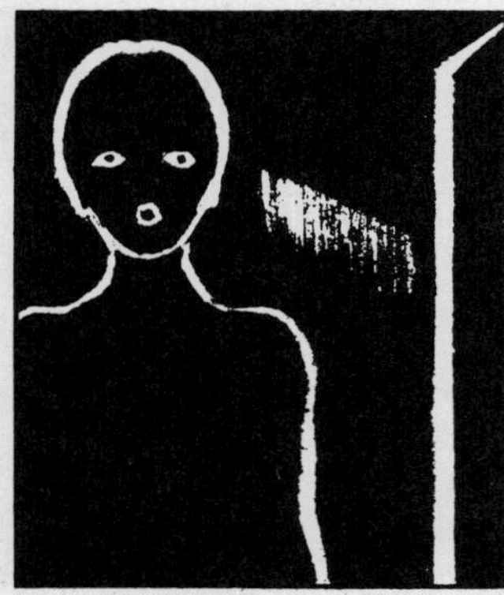

My hands are clammy, My feet are cold
I feel like I'm a hundred years old
My head starts to pound, My stomach is growling
I wonder whose out there . . . Around prowling
Should I call MOM, or crawl under the bed
Get up and face it my conscience said
So I went to the door, Pretended to be mother
Guess who was there . . . My little baby brothers

Andrew Schemick
TREES OF AUTUMN

The trees of Autumn.
Shedding their leaves,
losing their splendor.
While preparing for Winter,
and their long sleep.

Matthew Edwards
THE UNTOLD STORY

To my mother—Patricia Ann Edwards

I'm going to tell a story that has not yet been told, to some it
will seem so warm at heart,
to others it will seem so cold.
It's about the game of love,
something we all should know.
The goods the bads, the ups the downs, the pains we always
seem to outgrow. The forgiving and
the forgetting, the love
and the regretting.
So good luck to those who dare
play—Oh, did I mention the rules?
All is lost, if you don't obey.

Tammy E Scott
A MOTHER'S DREAM

To my son Dezmond, who is my greatest inspiration

A mother's dream is that someday
her child can live in a pleasant way,
no prejudice, no drugs, no men at war
not even she had experienced this before.

A mother's dream is for her child
to grow up warm, thoughtful and mild,
to be respectful and obey the rules
and not conduct himself as a fool.

A mother's dream is giving her child the best
even if it means her not having much rest,
to watch him learn gives her greatest joy
as if she is a child with a brand new toy.

A mother's dream is to set a fine example in her child's life
even when there is time of pain and strife,
to be able to take a stand
as she watches her child become a man.

A mother's dream most of all
is to be available when there is a call,
to show her child she is full of love
and give her child strength that comes from above.

Cathi Kostynuk
UNTITLED

This poem is dedicated to Dan. You'll always have a place in my heart.

I lay awake and listen to the rain drip down outside,
I just can't seem to sleep with thunder cracking in the sky.
I think of all the times you've held me on rainy nights like this,
But tonight I'm all alone, just wondering why.

I can't remember the last time I've sat up this late at night,
But the last time it was raining, I remember you holding me tight.
You could take away the loneliness and dissolve my every fear,
Everytime I needed you, you were always near.

So where are you tonight, Dan,
When I need you so bad,
This thunder has never been louder,
Nor the rain ever been so sad.

I try to close my eyes and think
That you'll be coming to get me,
Then I open them wide, and get this feeling inside,
That maybe you're trying to forget me.

No one can tell me that you'll be back
To put together the pieces,
Because when we're apart, it breaks my heart,
And that kind of pain never eases.

Now all my dreams seem out of reach
In the dark and endless sky,
The rain has stopped, I'm still alone,
And I'm still wondering why.

Judith D Mayhew
AN EARLY MORNING PRAYER

Father, as I come to you in the early hours of the morning,
I ask you to help me to be a Shining Light to my family.

Oh Father! bless this home and family that you gave to me.
Help me be the wife and mother I should be.

As my family awakes, let me greet them with a smile and help
them get ready showing them my patience all the while.

And long before they leave this house to go out into the
world, let us take time to pray together and show love
awhile.

Help us not to rush about and fuss and pitch a fit but, let
us take the time to share a bit, before this busy day.

And as they go, they will know that You will guide them on
their way because, we took the time to pray.

Bonita Blake Graham
INSPIRATION ON DRUMMOND ISLAND

Dedicated to my husband and best friend, Wayne, to our daughter Cassia Lynn, our delight and to our grandson, Dustin, the joy of our life.

The sky is so blue
and peaceful too;
The trees are so tall
and brown and green . . .
God hath surely created this place!
It is so serene.
I love you my Lord.

Marian L Brown
THEY WERE SEVEN

To those who have gone and will go.

They were seven.
Breaking free Earth's plane,
our country's best and brightest
Suddenly there is only pain.

Some curse, some cry,
some pray, "OH GOD!
tell me why.
Help me to understand."

They were seven.
Eager to go
on the great adventure.
Our final frontier's "Westward Ho!"

Challenger is away,
and we are soaring.
Last words, "Throttle up!"
an explosion's silent roaring.

They were seven.
Earth's bonds forever free.
But someday into space
we will follow, you and me.

Randolph R Nesbitt
MEMORIES OF LAST NIGHT

For Angela, my wife.

The fragrance of your love comes back to me now
Or perhaps it never left
but caught in my clothes

Waiting to seduce me
with your memory

Moving in all directions at once
like God

An invisible crystal ball effloresces
becoming the sun

Heat, light, life appear
two are now one

The dance is complete
music fades to golden silence

And your fragrance hides
waiting to call me

Back to the past
into the future

To move and explode
and touch the divine

To breathe your love
the fragrance of God

Anny Cobb
GOD BLESS MY GUY

For my loving husband, James.

Heavenly Father, full of grace,
Bless my Sweetheart's sexy face.
Bless his hair that always curls,
Keep him safe from other girls.

Bless his hands so big and strong.
Keep them where they belong.
Give him strength and you know why,
Cuz he's my one and only guy.

Bring him closer to my side.
Let his love melt down my pride.
Let us walk hand in hand,
Together we can make a stand.

Let me love with a heart that's true,
May I never make him blue.
May we learn to always share,
Doing whatever's fair.

May we see it to the end,
May I always be his friend.
May we love our whole life through,
These things oh God, I ask of You.

Lucille L Brown
STALEMATE

Just when I think I am getting ahead.
Just when I feel that I'm getting smart.
Just when I know I can go it alone.
I lead with my heart.

Half of the time I am mixed and confused,
Half of the time? Why, right from the start!
But just when I feel I am leveling off,
I lead with my heart.

When God made us creatures,
weak as we are,
He should have omitted that intrinsic part,
For all of my life, I have erred in my ways.
When I led with my heart!

James L Daniels
SUNFLOWER

By love possessed
From another's embrace,

You will not let yourself love me
Yet I see the longing in your face.

Freely you would bloom
In my eternal light,
Your morning,
Would never see night.

Set wings to your heart
And let it fly unto me,
Let us shine together
For all the world to see.

Erdine Southworth
TWO LOVES
Oh April, do not tempt me so—
(You know October has my love).
Your robin-song, your greening-grass,
Your fickle sun shines from above
To lead me to forgetfulness;
To lure me to unfaithfulness.

You think October's far away
And with impunity you woo.
With Spring's sweet breath
And bursting bud
You coax me to become untrue.

Oh April dear, shed not that tear,
Two loves I'll have in every year!

Karen Doyle
STEADFAST LOVE
I've never personally met you,
yet you're my best friend.
You've loved me forever,
and it will never end.

It took time
to appreciate it all.
But your eternal love
is worth every fall.

You gave so much
so that I could be free.
I now want to live my life
making you proud of me.

Trying my best
to lay sin aside.
Following you
as my life's only guide.

Thank you, Father,
for all that you've done.
Especially giving the life
of your one perfect son.

Charlotte Gibson Dillon

Charlotte Gibson Dillon
A CURSE OF DESTRUCTION

Dedicated to women everywhere who have suffered the pain of a divorce.

Destruction hit a home last night,
The damage it brought—severe.
To the lives of those who dwelled within,
Leaving behind heartache and fear.

It didn't break the windows out,
Or cave in the front door.
The walls of the house still stand secure,
As does the tile to the floor.

The furniture's good, as the day it was bought,
The pictures still hang on the wall.
The cats lay around in their favorite chair,
Still something is missing in all.

The destruction that hit, thought it harmed not the house,
Brought damage the eye cannot see.
Which will dwell on within the depth of a soul,
Till it's forced out again to be free.

It took with it trust and faith in mankind,
A forever picture of life.
Pushing apart the love of two souls
That once lived as husband and wife.

Many a life becomes shattered and broken
A home, now a house without source.
So each day look to God, and don't become victim,
Of this cruel destruction—
Divorce.

Mark Allen Reynolds
SHALLOW VOICES IN THE DEEP
Shallow voices in the deep,
standing far yet so near.

Illusions and fantasies colour my mind
of the day I reach the pinnacle of my life.

Misdeeds persist—replacing my dreams with mistakes.

Shallow voices in the deep—
not of dreams, fantasies and illusions, but,
of confirmed inconsistency.

The dream is dead—
my mind is quenched with an adequate
supply of gruesome
catastrophies.

Lawrence P Browning
DILEMMA
There was a young woman
who knew not where
There was a young woman
who did not care

For she did not care
for the likes of him
for she did not care
if she saw him again

D M Swier
SPECIAL THOUGHTS
These special thoughts I'd like to send,
To a very dear and caring friend.
I'm not quite sure how I knew
That I could always count on you.
But sure enough you'd always be
Very near to comfort me.
To brush away the falling tears,
And talk away the awful fears.
By my side you'd always be
When I'd call so silently.
Someday, I know, in my heart,
The time will come when we must part.
But in my heart and in my mind,
A tiny spot, there, you will find,
Filled with memories of a friend
That I will cherish to the end.
But I'll not say goodbye forever,
For someday we'll be together.
Watching all from up above,
There, with GOD, in the kingdom of love.

Jan Tate
THE WONDER OF IT ALL
Do you remember the line:
"See the U.S.A. in your Chevrolet"?
The Chevrolet hasn't been mine,
But with friends I've seen some of the U.S.A.
Yes, I've seen pictures of this land;
Pictures by great photographers,
But nothing compares to seeing it first-hand;
Not even pictures on calendars.
I look forward to seeing more.
Oh, wow! Let freedom ring!
This America of ours is no bore.
I'll see it all with God's blessing.
Without God's help I would not travel
To see the mountains or prairie
Or to visit the sea and its white sea gull.
Oh, how good the Lord has been to me.
God has made each state different.
There's something in each one
So you know what is meant
When someone says, "Come to our state and have fun."
You can't say, "If you've seen one state
You've seen them all."
Each one is totally different.
That's the wonder of it all.
Thank you, God.

Darlene M Kepner
MY FATHER WHISPERED

To my father—who was a friend, a father and mentor.

It only seem like yesterday when
my father whispered
GO TO SLEEP, SLEEPIE PIE
I heard it when I was 5
I heard it when I was 6
And the fears of the night would go away
I heard my father whisper
GO TO SLEEP, SLEEPIE PIE
And now I'm 20
And the words make me smile
And it seem like only yesterday
When he whispered
GO TO SLEEP, SLEEPIE PIE
And then the final whisper
GO TO SLEEP, SLEEPIE PIE
Once again made me cry
As he said good-bye!

Rob Heitzman
DREAM'S ILLUSION

To my son Bobby, that he may develop a more keen sense of the universe around him.

I walk upon a comet's silver tail,
The yellow stripes of the tiger light up my eyes,
Did anyone see the blue iridescent scales of the butterfly?

I see the brightness of the star's new world,
Did you see the golden lion soar?

When the artic iceberg falls,
Will anyone notice the falling tree in the forest?

I heard the roses beauty grow,
Did you hear the peddle of hope fall?

I felt the sun of life rise,
When the moon wasn't there,
Was it a surprise?

I smelled the sweet fragrance of life,
Did you sense the odor of strife?

I flew upon the blue sky's sensation,
Did anyone sense the illusion of creation?

David Allen Milstead
OKLAHOMA
Oklahoma Oklahoma
Bury my heart
With your beauty and grace
At a time of peace
Which once
Passed this way
At a time of my ancestors
Native to this land
Bless my heart
With vision to feel
Their beauty and grace
As they lived
With
Mother nature
Father sun
Mother moon
And as time come
Pass this way
Bury my heart
With the trail of tears

Elaine S Clark
GROWING OLD
Alone
She waits there by the window
To watch the world that's passed her by;
She reaches out with hands that tremble
No one is there to hear her cry.

Hair that hangs in unkempt fashion
In the wind it once blew free;
Faltering steps they soon betray her—
How did she age so rapidly!

Growing old . . .who'er considers?
'Til time is past, the deed is done.
Oh, love surround us; life fulfill us
For death shall claim us—one by one.

Janet Lustman
A PROUD AMERICAN

For my loving husband, Jack, and our adoring son, John. Both of whom are my inspiration and joy.

The Freedom
to pursue a dream
of Global Peace; of thee
I sing
The Liberty
of lives United
In Defense of Justice; of thee
I praise
The tender, fierce,

fragile heart of nature's cry
I'm not afraid
To live in Constant
Praise of God and then,
To Die
For this Our Country's
Honored Dead Shall Long
Survive
With Symbol Blessed
By Pride Filled Eyes
My America's
Stars and Stripes

S K Kramer
GOD

We met years ago. He showed me kindness, understanding and love.
I see him in everything, right down to the doves. His name is God.

Harold C. Shelton Jr
FEBRUARY

As moon reflects white,
the sun's yellow light,
day of hearts gets nearer,
love grows like nature's seed,
stronger each passing day.

Douglas A Schinkel

Douglas A Schinkel
I STAND ALONE

No pomp and questionable circumstance
A shabby quid-pro-quo
The problem simply
You can't call dreams to order
Self-actualization the supreme journey
Pushing constantly through heads of wheat

Vast internal galaxies played
To the music of a singular flute
The possibility of reverse birth
Remembering
It's a slow waltz through eternity
It's my song.

Anna Sado
BY OUR OWN WINGS, WE FLEW

This poem is dedicated to Mrs. Gail Marie Spindler, the best English teacher that ever graced a classroom.

Why, oh why did they tell us,
We who stood mourning over your grave;
"It's all part of Heaven's plan.
We must bow to the scheme of things."

Why did they worship death instead
Of life, and build their temples—
While you and I built the future?
Why did they fall to their knees,
When we knew enough to stand tall?

What say you, dear one—are they afraid?
They, who never had one fraction of your courage,
Your light, or your promise—are they resigned?

Or do they wait in the shadows for such
As you and I, we who showed them
The empty hopelessness of their days.
Do they gloat? Are they satisfied?
Do they rejoice when we, the mighty, have fallen?

Oh dear one, please tell me. I must know.
Does it pleasure them to think
That their celestial plans and schemes
Laid waste to all our hopes and dreams?

Richard A Picciuto
NOVEMBER GRAY

Reflective moments come all year at every time of day
They journey me to years gone by during November gray.
A very special time of year when winter starts to form
Chimneys put forth their smoke and leafless trees the norm.
The moon puts on a different face—friendly, yet alone
Whether clouds or branches shield it, it seems to set the tone.
Everything more orderly, even in our play
People are more disciplined when summer's put away.
I think of football kicks so high—where did we get the strength

Last year we couldn't reach the pole, we couldn't get the length.
The days grew short, what does that mean, I'm not sure I ever knew
But days were nice November gray, the skies need not be blue.
The holidays a bit away did not consume the mind
Our thoughts were more on everyday, not far reaching kinds.
The cider had a special taste, reserved for just this season
So very short this pressing time, we never knew the reason.
The leaves still left upon the ground were covered now with frost
These images appear each year to some will still be lost.
For when we think about these times so many years away
We must have child inside of us to love November gray.

Mrs Ina Kizziah
A VIETNAM EXPERIENCE

In memory of my son, Sgt. Fredrick B. King, who was killed in Duc Pho, South Vietnam on November 25, 1968.

When I was trained for the Vietnam War, I learned to do things I'd never done before.
I was given a gun and trained to kill waiting for a casualties place to fill.
I learned to shoot and dodge the bullets well, hoping and praying I'd never have to yell,"I've been shot and need a helping hand".
I was drenched to the skin by a monsoon rain, distressed and suffering with a sunburn pain.
Writing a letter from a bunker hole wanting a drink, just anything cold.
Hearing the rockets coming closer still hoping the guards are watching our hill.
I grabbed my rifle and crawled to the door wishing this fighting would soon be o'er.
I saw my buddy lying on the ground, his legs were missing but he found—, strength to throw hand grenades at a jeep.
Charlie went flying over the wheel not much of his body left to feel, the bullets I fired into his bleeding head.
Old men, old women and children too were often hungry and I knew that some of their food would come from American Men.
I shared my rations time and again with these children, women and men.
I stare and wonder why in the world so many lives should be in peril.
MY thoughts are broken when an ambush begins, guns manned by children, women and men.
Bullets flying in a violent rage without feelings for sex or age.
I hope each time I fire my gun that it will spare an innocent one.
The commanding order, "Take your gun and go to a village near, search and destroy every living thing 'til not a sound you hear."
Though the foe may not be armed, who knows if he is or not, if search and destroy is the order, give it all you've got.
Obey the order, do your job and when from this place you've gone, try to forget the lives you took, one thats saved has been your own.

Lyle W Vadnais
WHY

To Beth, without you, This wouldn't be possible. Thank You

When darkness settles on the land,
Its tendrils stalking every man,
When the moon is full, and gale winds blow,
The Earth will shake,
And Man will know.

The cities will crumble, our temples made ruins;
And death will seek the living, soon.
He will burn the crops, and poison each stream.
Men will tear at their flesh,
And choke on their screams.

They'll think of shattered hopes, and dreams;
Remember cool spring days, and clear blue streams.
When they do find death, they crumple,
And cry.

Their last hopeless words are:
Why, Lord,
Why?

Alex Nelson Jr
CHALLENGER, REMEMBERED

January 28, 1986 was a frigid Florida day,
Space Shuttle Challenger was facing another slight delay.

The seven-member crew had climbed aboard,
And soon it was, "Go", and off Challenger soared.

Off into the cloudless sky the first teacher went,
Along with her six fellow crew members were sent.

As the flame of the Challenger came into view,
A blast soon sounded and the flame split in two.

Our nation will miss these seven brave space pioneers,

As the joyful lift-off of Challenger turned from cheers to tears.

Anita Rundell
AFRAID

This poem is dedicated to my cousin, Sister Mary Christopher, Benedictine Order, whose help keeps me from being afraid.

The lowest fish in ocean's pit
May wonder what is over it;
The mole within his burrow dark
May wonder if there is a lark;
Floating high, the snowy dove
Perhaps may wonder what's above,
But I, the lowest creature made,
Dare not wonder—I'm afraid!!

Afraid the sky may fall apart—
Afraid someone may break my heart—

Afraid to live, afraid to die—
Afraid to laugh, afraid to cry—

Afraid to eat, afraid to drink—
Afraid to work, afraid to think—
I looked one time upon my soul
And found I'd dug a 'fraidy hole,
I'd crawled down deeper than the sea
And pulled the hole in after me!!

Pati M Flink
ALL BOTTLED UP
Sometimes I feel
just like a bottle.
Thats all filled up,
with pain and sorrow.
Then put inside a cold dark shelf;
Maybe,
just until tomorrow.
I wish someone would open me,
pour me out, and set me free.
Even tho my lids on tight,
take a grip, and hold on tight.
Twist and turn with all your might,
for I will put up quite a fight.
Once I'm open, you will see,
what is deep inside of me.
Please don't stop, just at the top,
keep on pouring, and never stop;
Until,
you find the bottom line.
The water that you see in there,
are tears of joy,
That someone cares.

Frances G Ver Hoven
MY TEENAGE DAUGHTER
Where is this child that once was mine—so loving and so dear?
The one whose feelings I'd understand whenever she was near.
Am I so old? I never thought—
As fun and her laughter I've always sought.

Now in her mind it always seems
I do not understand her dreams.
No matter what I do is wrong; the hours waiting seem so long.
When her whereabouts I do not know,
I'm full of woe because I love her so.

The arguments, they never cease—
When will this family be at peace?
The hurt and frustration I feel from day to day,
While her new clothes just sit there wasting away.

The questions and worry are not from mistrust,
My heart is so full of love, I feel it will bust.
She's so precious to me; she's special from the rest,
She's my teenage daughter and one of the best.

The music, the phone calls, the fads and the clothes,
She says I'm old-fashioned, but little does she know—
The same feelings I had and to my own mother I told.

The sacrifices that I've made; when will she see the light?
Maybe when she holds her own precious child—
Then she just might.

The world will then be different,
But one thing won't change—
The Love of a Mother will always be the same.

Ruth M Wilkins
THE DIFFERENT SOUNDS YOU HEAR
It's funny when you're all alone, the different sounds you hear,
The darkness and a thunderstorm, you wish someone was near,
You turn your radio way up loud, to keep you company,
Then you turn your tv. on to see what you can see,
I heard the slamming of the door, I wondered who came in,
I looked and saw the door wide open, it must have been the wind,
A scarey feeling deep inside, a chill went up my spine,

Another night alone like this will make me lose my mind,
I was tired, I thought I'd go to bed,
I heard a noise, I covered up my head,
A scratching on the window pane, it's driving me insane,
Emotions are getting away from me, it must have been the rain,
I heard the barking of a dog far into the night,
I seen a light come through the fog, it vanished out of sight,
The hooting of a morning dove, I finally gave up the flight,
I realized as I rubbed my eyes,I hadn't slept all night.

Micki Cline
GRAVESIDE VISITOR
When I die and pass from this life
Wilt thou visit by my graveside?

Wilt thou bring roses of plastic red
To place upon my eternal bed?

Wilt thou mourn and shed a tear
For the one below once held so dear?

Wilt thou remember me and say a kind word
Of something I did or something thou heard?

Wilt thou return from time to time?
Wilt thou remember me from a poem or rhyme?

Wilt thou look for me up ahead
For I'm just resting, not really dead?

One day I'll meet thee at the end of our walk
And we shall sit—and talk.

And I shall remember thou were once so kind
To have visited by an old graveside.

Mary Margaret Minnich
A SOLDIER'S DREAM
A soldier dreamed of peace one day
While all around him battles raged
And life seemed vain.
And at his side
His comrades fought and swiftly died,
Mouthing a message of farewell
Reddening the snowdrifts
Where they fell.

And he fought on, forgetful why,
Envying the peaceful form that lay
Careless of cold or fear or pain,
Exempt from duty, free again.
And wistfully the soldier dreamed
Of life and love, when peace could be.
Time passed.
The hideous nightmare ends.

At last he sees his home again—
The lighted streets, the happy throng
Of noisy friends, he'd missed so long.
His parents, proud, yet strangely shy
With this new son, he wonders why
He feels alone
Like in a dream.
And now the dream is battlefields.

Jennifer Jaquith
TICK TOCK
Tick tock, tick tock
Time flies by as the rocking chair rocks
Tick tock, tick tock
As the pendulum always refuses to stop
Tick tock,tick tock
As the gate to our future is slammed and then locked
Tick tock, tick tock
Soon Death will arrive but won't bother to knock
Tick tock, tick tock
Is my time now ending? Who owns this clock?
Ding dong, ding dong
Not a clock, but a single clanging bell.
Tick tock, tick tock
Now will it be Heaven or will it be Hell?

Joseph A Sekelsky
OUR NATION'S DEFICIT
Luscious lovelies flash their caps,
wink their contact-tinted eyes,
breezes blow through blow-dried minds.

Yearning Yuppies suck up the corporate ladder,
plastic promises melt in the sun,
a porcelain nation flakes away.

Karen Kosch

Karen Kosch
NO MORE
The sky was shining crystals of rays
While the children without warning continue to play
The atmosphere humid and slightly amist
Gave feelings of danger no one could resist
The oceans gave off a mighty roar
When crashing the rocks, remained silent no more
The birds flying over were not to be heard
Left only the people without whispering a word

As deserted as the town may have looked
Sitting still in their houses, the people shook
The weather had changed and was now very still
Clouds forming funnels about ready to kill

The quiet little town awaiting the time
While hidden in places left only to slime
Even though they felt safe and secure inside
Danger on the outside, rose greater with pride

A sudden gush of wind swept by so fast
Leaving the town to suffer, then die for last
The town so empty and torn to shreds
Left masts of bodies to be put in their beds.

Joseph Robert Chester
MYSTERIOUS EYES
Beauty seeks in your mysterious eyes:
Believe I tell truth; I tell no lies.
Your long, crystal-like hair I couldn't resist,
shown through the long, dark morning of the midnight mist.

Kathleen M Ouellette
WORLD'S LAUGHTER
Vicious gossip circles about me
People laugh and call me fool
Can't they see how the knives
Pour my life blood upon the ground?

They sneer at all I do
Slaying with their snide remarks
How long must I endure
The rendering of my flesh?

Fingers point from all sides
Their faces blurred with disgust
As I sink slowly down
Into the opening abyss.

Marian K Young
THE WILLOW AND THE OAK
The willow swayed gently
with the breeze,
The oak stood still
totally unaware.

The willow bended
in the wind,
The oak stood still
totally unaware.

The willow bowed
during the storm,
The oak stood still
and broke.

The willow swayed gently
with the breeze,
The oak
was no more.

Staci Mitchell
REFLECTIONS
I Look In The Mirror,
What Do I See?
An Image Of You,
And You Are With Me.
A Vision Of Love,
A Vision Of Pride.

A Vision Of You,
With Me By Your Side.
I Look In The Mirror,
What Do I See?
A Vision Of You,
But Now Not With Me.
A Vision Of Love,
A Vision Of Pride.
A Vision Of You,
With New Life At Your Side.
I Tried To Carry On,
What I Wanted To Last.
But I See Now,
They Are Only Reflections Of Past.

Fortino Guerra Jr
MY KIDS

To my kids, John, Christina, and Matthew Guerra

They are my hopes, my dreams,
They're like doves so white and pure.

I think of them all the time,
They're such a big part of me.

They're like candy, so sweet,
I love them so.

They have my blood, my flesh, my bones.
Oh Lord, I don't ever want to lose them.

To my kids, with love,
Daddy's little doves.

Maryann Catherine Sullivan
BACKWARD IN INFINITY
Backward in infinity,
Did Destiny decree you would be lost?
What snakesong did She sing to Love's Creator?
When He was mixing molecules of morning,
Did He deliver dusk to Her design?
What blinding, blending God would bend,
In dawning's dazzle,

And lightly bless a nucleus of never,
To fool forever
Don Quixote double-crossed . . .

Or was it Dulcinea?

I believe,
I believe,
I believe,
In infinity of Love.

Of Loss.

Heather Heid
UNTITLED
You're A Man of God's True Being
You're A Fluctuating Tool
You're the Guard Of Reproduction
God's Own Master of Male Rule

You Inspire Reformation
Braving Earth's Disgraceful Debt
Loyal Lifelong Occupation

Loyal Soldier

Loyal Vet

Lois D Pecha
JOE

This poem is dedicated to Joe Dardas.
With Love,—Today, Tomorrow and Forever!

I Love you in the morning
When the dew is on the grass!
I Love you at the noontime
As the day begins to pass!
I Love you in the twilight
As the sun starts to depart!
And I Love you through the night
With every beating of my heart!

John Ravenscroft
A CHALLENGE LOST
For this I write to seven souls.
Who were to bravely accomplish our tasks and goals.
To two women McAullife and Resnick
Doctor and the best teacher of the pick.
To astronaunts Scobee, Jarvis, and Smith.
Commander and pilots that our hopes went with.
To Onizuka and Ronald McNair;
To two space travelers lost in despair.
Finally, to a great shiny black and white albatross.
A challenge taken, a challenge lost.

Kay Jamieson
LONELINESS
I'm never so lonely, as when I'm left alone with my thoughts.
Thoughts of future loves or loves gone by.

My mind goes back to times of joy and sorrow, and ahead to things that may or may not be.
Images enter the depths of my soul like rain into a weeping willow.
I'm filled with all the beauty that surrounds a cool blue lake at sunset and I wonder . . . could life ever be as beautiful as this picture here before me?
Can the harshness of Life be anything but fleeting, when visions such as this make me gasp.

I stir and suddenly the thoughts are gone.
The loneliness is gone and I'm filled with
Love and Now, because of YOU!

Tamara Jo Hobbs
A BABY BOY
He has big blue eyes
and a perky little nose,
Ten little fingers
and ten little toes.

He's the precious gift of love
from our Father above.
I can't believe he's here,
but I can't imagine life without him;
I long to have him near,
whenever I'm without him.

For he's our pride and joy,
God has blessed us with a baby boy.

Dorothy Rusignuolo
UNTITLED
If it be true that
All marriages dissolve in heaven
And those who loved
All love together with
No contracts that exclude and bind . . .
Joined with God we all shall be
And you, at last, in heaven I will find.

Nylic Rowe Radford
A LITTLE BOY

This poem is dedicated to my daughter, Eunice Twitty, and her son, John Paul Twitty.

By chance it was,
one sun-splashed autumn day,
A little boy held my hand
in a most endearing sort of way.

We strolled the garden terrace;
steps uneven, heights extreme,
but we managed well despite
the space betwix and between.

"You know what, Granny,"
I distinctly heard him say.
"No, John,"
pondering next he'd have to say.
"I love you, Granny,"
he spoke it just that way.

Still silence must have swept
the universe for a moment, I'd say.
For youth to endear the aged
quite caught me in dismay.

No greater crown of glory could
he place upon my hair of gray,
Nor would that I could dispell
his thoughts of that enchanting day.

Kelly McCormack
THE GAME OF LOVE

I dedicate my first published poem to my mother, Maureen. I love you! And you've won the game with me!

You either look too good or not good enough
It's what starts the game of love
You talk but it's not the words you say
I keep telling you it's how you play the game
You do what you think he'll like and then he wants more
You give him what he wants and what for?
Just to be loved?
So supposedly it's love and supposedly it's true
Then why don't you love me the way I love you?
Amazing how things start the same
But somewhere along the lines they always change
Something that used to be right is now wrong
And the Game of Love goes on and on
So now it's time to change and you ask yourself why
I like myself the way I am, who is this guy?
It's not like he's Billy Dee or even Bobby Blue
And as soon as he sees this, he's gonna want you
You go round and round for someone just right
But let me tell you now it's an endless fight
But you'll fight and I'll fight too
And I'll keep on fighting . . .
All for the love of YOU!!

Natasha Adamov

Natasha Adamov
THE LADY FROM MAINE
There once was a lady from Maine,
everyone thought she was a pain.
She sucked her thumb,
and acted real dumb,
and didn't ever win fame.

Sharon E O'Heron Allen
FIRST LOVE
When I'm alone and feeling blue,
I just sit down and think of you.

I think of all the fun we've had,
And why I'm home alone and sad.

It seems sad to think that you're so far away,
And I'm hoping that you'll return someday.

But, if in your travels,
You find someone new,

Remember, that I'll always love you.

V Marielle McFarland
IN MY HEART I CAN SEE THE LOOK IN YOUR EYES
In my heart I can see the look in your eyes
Hoping that you're not hurting inside
A past remembered
A future not known
Invisible thoughts-present unknown
I try hard to reach you
But sometimes I get restless
There's always someone out there who's calling—
Who's calling my name
But hiding in my shadow
You're with me always
The fantasy has gone too far
I close my eyes—
And there you are

Mary Ann Coward
ARBUTUS WOMAN
I am an Arbutus Woman
reaching out for salt
twisting, turning
leaning into wind and sea.
A molten red-gold spirit
ever-renewing in an endless cycle
of peeling Arbutus bark
and shedding leaf.
Arid seasons bring branches
bone-bare, vulnerable;
my ever-peeling red-gold bark
floats wisp-like down,
paper curls among the yellowed
dreams.
My sheddings rustle underfoot
become compost for my roots
nothing waste.
Then greening rains come and
I am nourished
luxuriating in new growth.
My spring fruit greens
into Christmas red,
my leaves renew and shine
eternally
reaching out for salt.
I am an Arbutus Woman.

Julie C Humphrey
TEACHERS ARE SPECIAL
Some people think of teachers as
ordinary women,
Some people even treat them like
they're as sour as a lemon.
Some teachers are nice, some
teachers are mean.
Some are reliable, some are keen.
Some teachers are short, some
teachers are tall.
Some teachers are quite ordinary
and some not at all.
But teachers are human and that
is so true, so treat them with
respect as they do to you.

Shelley L Drayton
TIME
Draw away the cloak
from the illusion that is Time;
Its hands forever ticking
towards a never sounding chime.
Its face a blank,
showing no dismay
as moments do pass away
from tawny dusk
of time bygone
into the rosy dawn
of Future.
For in Eternity's wink
a moment dies
with no one
to hear its cries
As Present gives way,
begrudgingly,
to be the Past
that happened last
when once It was . . .
the Future.

Brenda Corbin
A TRIP OF NO RETURN
While walking along the campus
one day
Lee heard someone ask,"Going my
way?"
Feeling blue, she thought, "What
have I to lose?"
This was her first step towards
drug abuse.

Lee joined the "in crowd" and
thought it was tough,
smoking pot, she said, "Aren't we
the stuff?"
Gradually it seemed to lose it's
thrills
Therefore she moved on to shots
and pills.

Heroin and LSD were quite a trip
But let me give you a helpful tip.
The return afterwards was quite a
pain,
and Lee vowed each time, "Never
again!"

To get it she would buy, borrow,
or steal,
She left home against her parents
will.
Among her classmates, she'd
become a fool,
Before long, she was thrown out of
school.

Then one night Lee came to her
journeys end;
LSD was now her latest trend.
She had a hallucination that night,
Thinking that she was a bird in
flight.

Her wings did not sail through the
air with ease,
As the man on the flying trapese.
Instead Lee fell from the twentieth
floor,
Gone on a trip to return no more.

Laurette Frasnelly
RIVER OF LIFE
I share so much with the river near.
Life's message it seems to say.
Winter's rains overwhelm the bank.
Hopes and dreams are washed
away.
All my faith and heart has sank,
The rage of the river is all I hear,
freezing my life with fear.
Springs gentleness comes at last,
and grants my soul relief.
The agonizing pain of the past,
has lost it's strength and grief.
I see new beauty on the earth,
life renewed is of great worth.
Summer heat melts away the strife,
my heart again doeth love this life.
Faith ascends the height of towers.
Fun and laughter fill the hours.
Fall's brisk windy cold,
puts all the play upon the shelf.
Another year grows old.
The river continues it's journey,
rolls on without a care . .
Forewarningly sings out to me:
"Rest yourself and prepare".

Dionne Postelle
LONELY AS THE NIGHT

It would be improper to dedicate a work of all my strength to anything but God.

It was a cold night
but a cold night
that followed a gloomy day,
and all the life that seemed in
sunshine
had long since gone away.

T'was long before the twilight dawn
heard the moaning cries of wind,
an yet it seemed as if they said
that very life was sin.

To bare no bones, I hold you now
as if held close before,
but if it should come rapping,
knocking
cry for ever more.

Pamela Scott
SILENCE OF LOVE
Snowfall on a moonlit night.
The Silence so embracing
It transports you to a level
Unknown by many, but aspired to
by all.
The mind wanders to love.
The feeling of being immortal.
Of being invincible to life's
Problems and able to conquer its
challenges.
Walking hand in hand to a favorite
place.
Finding in each other's eyes the
strengths and weaknesses
That cement that one special
relationship.
Knowing and seeing life through
another's love.
Touching, Needing, Kissing,
Loving so much words aren't
necessary.
The Silence of Love.

Marguerite A Zahoruiko
ON TRAGEDY
There are no words to console
So therefore I shall not try to find
them.
Words are symbols of the mind
And the mind is not able to
comprehend
The tragedies that beset us
And the heart cannot stand the
pain,
Therefore, the words are useless.
Time is the only solace left to us
And for now that is my consolation
to you.

Jennifer Jones
JUST BELIEVE
You can be what you want to be
And do what you want to do
There's nothing that's too difficult
Or impossible for you.

The stars are just a step away
And the goal you would achieve
Are at your very finger tips
If you will just believe.

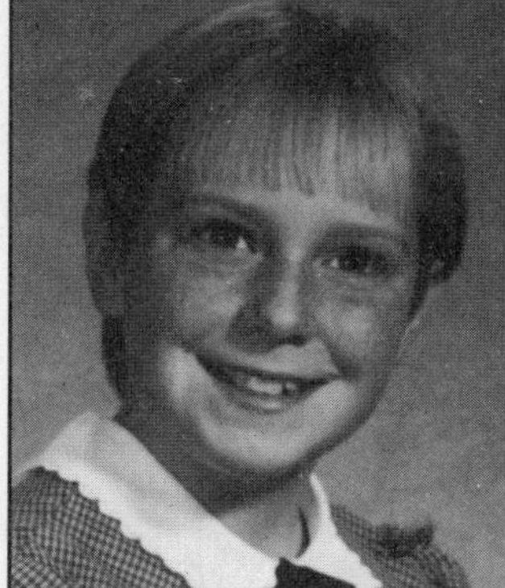

Jennifer Cheek

Jennifer Cheek
UGLY OR PRETTY
Ugly or Pretty—
Will you please tell me?
Is a caterpillar ugly,
Knowing a butterfly it will be?
A dirty brown seed
Grows to a beautiful plant indeed.
A torn, old music book,
When the notes are played,
ripples like a brook.
Remember "Beauty and the
Beast"?
A handsome man he became
When the curse had ceased
Ugly or Pretty—
Will you please tell me?

Eva Leet Wilcox
PRIDE
Cheap reward is loud acclaim—
That din of glory; boastful fame.
Here lies Pride, a body, found
Rotting away in filthy ground.
'Round and 'round the buzzards
swarm
Devouring that unsavory form—
"I, Mine, and Me", amassed—
Achievement's bold enthusiast.

Now GOD speaks—man's Soul
affirms
By wordless songs, symbolic
terms.
He speaks in tongues and foreign
tones
While retrieving those unsavory
bones.
A Spirit pride can never blight
Whirls 'round in colored light—
Concentric circles in red and green,
Cosmique Knowledge clearly
seen.

Motion stems from this bright
glow—
Time and Space in flux and
flow—
Transient forms of humanity,
Billions with One Identity.
The bones rise up to join—
unseen—
A form composite, pure and
clean;
Then outward again, evolving
anew,
To work and achieve through
the Selfless You.

Dawn Marie Phillips
I'LL MISS YOU
I'll miss you more than words can
say,
I'll miss you each and every day.
I'll miss you knowing you're not
near,
I'll miss you more with each falling
tear.
I'll think about you day and night,
I'll think about you in dark and
light.
I'll dream of you when I sleep,
I'll dream of you with feelings deep.
I'll miss you from the day I leave,
I'll miss you more than you believe.

Kathleen Grady Oberstad
REINCARNATION

I dedicate this work to my son, Tommy, who makes this life a celebration!

A presence has hovered
throughout this life
and the feeling of deja vu,
While glimpses of memories in
times of strife
have altered my conscious view.

Oftentimes haunted by visions of
yore,
(such visions turned hazy with
time),
I've struggled to unlock the barrier
door
with the key to the unconscious
mind.

But resistance is great as the past
unfolds
with maddening absence of
haste.
And the lingering shadows of tales

to be told
intensify present's distaste.

The soul surges forward, ageless in flight,
with the mind ever spinning in place.
While I crave the emergence of pain's delight
unrestricted by time and space.

So where in the life scheme reality lies
proves uncertain and yet undefined.
Time will prevail as the flesh lives and dies,
imagined as "now" by the mind.

Wanda L Rockstroh

Wanda L Rockstroh

MY HUSBAND—MY LOVE—MY FRIEND

Dedicated to David, my husband and my inspiration for this poem. I love you

---

Your love has given me
So much pleasure
Far more than the worlds greatest treasure—
You can search the world
Far and wide and never find
The pride I have inside—
It is only true love
That will endure
Lifes ups and downs its laughs and frowns—
Our love will always be brand new
With just the very thought of you
You are my husband, my dream come true—
None to compare anywhere
Sent from up above your love—
There is never a reason
To be lonely again,
Because you will forever be,
—My husband—My love—My friend—

Melissa Dutton

GRANDFATHER

My grandfather was a wise old man,
Who lived to be ninety-two.
He told of the days of the Civil War,
And when women wore high button shoes.

Each day he would walk along the shores of the sea
Watching the tide roll in.
Envisioning himself once more on the waves,
Along with his captain and men.

At night he'd sit all alone on the porch,
Observing the stars in the sky.
Humming a sad sort of melody,
While thinking of his youth gone by.

He had a small garden which was always filled,
With the wonders of God's earth.
And along with the racoons, deer and bugs,
We'd sit and watch nature's rebirth.

I remember the days when he'd hold me tight,
And speak of his undying love.
I'll be glad when I again, can walk by his side,
In the heavenly streets above.

Janet Nugent

CONFLICT

The words bite
Into my heart
As they fight
Each other bitterly.

Tears well up
In my eyes
As a slap
Hits his face.

He refuses angrily
To speak with her
And my heart
Breaks in two.

Time passes by
And things improve
Until once more
They fight again.

Tracy Swords

SHADOWS

To My Father, Gaylon Nicholson, with Love

Lifes dark shadows hang over head
Giving me feelings of utmost dread
No way out of a sinful past
Wondering how long my sanity will last

Looking forward to the light of day
Giving thought to the words I pray
Help me Lord get through this time
Forgive and mend this soul of mine

Sharon Elizabeth Snyder

OUR STATUE: TEACHER OF LIBERTY

Thanks to Mr. Tillison and his dedication as a teacher

In the New York harbor,
Our teacher proudly stands.
To show all nations we welcome them,
In our country's loving hands.

She tells all of our Liberty,
All entering the harbor.
She symbols our long unity,
To see her is an honor.

On Ellis Island, or in your heart,
She will be forever.
To hover over and protect us,
To bring us all together.

Ethel Mae Townsend

SINCE YOU WENT AWAY

I've been so lonely since you went away
I still look for you each and every day.
The flowers are in bloom and smell so sweet
But not half as sweet as when we'd meet.
The Birds don't sing that same old tune
As they did way back last June.
The skies all gray and overcast
As if it too thinks of days long past.
When we laughed and teased and loved all day
Oh yes, I've been so lonely since you went away.

Sandra Jo Mickey

DESTINY

And the winds of fate shall drop their debris.
We shall feel the sands as they litter our existence.
Particles of power deciding one's lot.
Gathered along with the passing of time.
Sifted and silted on each one's will.
Changing the pathways of life.

Dr E P Wundram, DC

THE OLD ROCKING CHAIR

Dedicated to Mother's Memory and to Ruth, my loving and devoted wife.

Crowded with memories of yester year,
On arm and hallowed head rest
Are indelible marks of hands so dear,
Where silver hairs left a shining crest!

Yes, it is my Mother's rocking chair,
Where of't she sat, wondering about my future
And what parent is there who does not care
Nor wonders who next, may be my tutor!

Songs and hummings still ring in my ear
Tho many a year has fast slipped away!
Cradled next her heart, where I first shed a tear,
Calming fears with her faith, making it a new day!

Three score years have since come and gone;
One by one loved ones have gone ahead!
Only in mind's ear do I still hear her song,
Ever alive in my heart, tho now she is dead!

That is, her earthly body now to dust has returned,
But her spirit, that part of God never dies.
It is alive surrounding me, seeing if I had learned
The lessons of love, making me a beacon in the skies!

Already I know, in a heavenly chair she waits;
So when the hour has come and I depart,
What higher gift could my soul rate,
To again crawl onto my Mother's lap and into her heart!

Shelly R Driewer

LOVE LOST

It's late at night and I'm all by myself,
Staring at the knick-knacks on the corner shelf.
Watching the door knob through the fireplace reflection,
Searching for you everywhere but making no connections.
I'm alone and I wish that you were here with me,
But the darkness seems to be my only company.
The fire is burning slowly down to die,
And my one tear turns to many as I begin to cry.
The tears of pain roll slowly down my weary face,
And the tears of joy do seldom, take up any space.
There never was a sad tear when we started out together,
For we had the faith that our love could survive the worst of weather.
But time rolls on and weather wears the smoothest stones to rough,
And the love that bound us strong as steel, now just ain't enough
It takes a certain breed of folk to keep their loving strong,
To take it 50-50, knowing both of you were wrong.
Never pointing fingers, always holding tight,
Never being back to back in the middle of the night.

Thomas J Rycombel

THE HORSE DIED

Remember how we galloped through golden fields,
With our backs and bellies touching?
I, pressed against you so tight
Each bump
Made us tickle inside.
Then the ditch!
That awful ditch
Lurked up and
We pitched into it.
Blood,
Hair,
Cries,
Pain—
All and at once!
My arm lay twisted against your neck
Which so often it had touched in the past.
We moved together, but in separate
Ways,
clutching
clawing
calling out!
Till,
when night's shroud came upon us
A farmer brought a lantern to see
what beasts did moan so
We fondled each other's hurts
And tried to remain human,
But the horse upon us only whinnied
And swished its tail in our faces.

April Georgette Julian

WIND BLOWING

With all my love to my mother, who has given me the creative inspiration and zest for exploring that which is not mundane.

Wind blowing
And I'm not knowing
Of sounds climbing from
throats—from what?

Peeking Tom-Palms
Clutching the window
That's what the wind will
—do—
If one's not careful.
Cane liquid noises there then not,
Screams and cries; plighted pity
Cloaking the city.
And yet, one cannot save those
nightwind abstractions

Nettie M Seale

FRIENDS

Friends were made to share your
thoughts
and help you reach your goals
For special secrets shared and
special speeches made
For laughter from the heart and
tears from broken dreams
For comfort shared in grief and
building up your spirits
They are, there to lend a hand when
no one else is there
A friend will be objective and
tell the truth when asked
They're someone very special that's
treasured in the heart
They're understanding, warm,
giving
and last throughout your life.

Helen M Davis

THE YOU THAT'S WITHIN

You gaze into the minds that have
no sight,
that do the wrong, but think they
are right.

You gave your feelings and you
showed your care,
they laughed in your face and
made things unfair.

They say or do things to hurt your
soul,
to put them high, and make you
low.

You are strong, but patient, though
you hide your grief,
for you feel alone, so far beneath.

So you grip the love that you have
to share,
you give it all, you take the dare.

Though days go by, with things
unchanged,
still you pray to the heavens above
the range.

Through smiles and all, you cry
now and then,
hoping one will see the you that's
within.

Rita Sunna Warren

HAND OF TIME

Hand of time
I know you not
You're old
And I am young.

What matters most
Is not your ghost
What matters is
MY Spring.

Let me enjoy the merry May,
June is yet to come.

Hand of Time
Hold back your hand
My Summer's yet to come.

I will not count the hand of time,
I haven't begun to live.

Oh, Hand of Time,
September's here
Why did you rush your hand?

December's here
The end is near,
My Spring is Unknown Land.

Helen Pastushin

LONESOME WORLD

If today wasn't an endless highway
If tonight wasn't so dark and cold.
If tomorrow wasn't so far away
This loneliness would mean
nothing at all.

June Carol Isaacson

MEMORY

Let's create a memory
That can be drawn upon.
Create happiness that lingers,
Like melody of song.

Create a fine experience
That can be cherished all through
time,
That would reach out to others
As a light to forever shine.

Tie it with a ribbon
Of brightest shining gold,
Keep it within the pages
Of lifetimes centerfold.

When we reminisce
To the times of yesterday,
Memories pathways are lined with
flowers,
All along the way.

Rheiba Reigh Gower aka Barbara K Long

STAR REFLECTIONS

I climbed into the heavens
and sat upon a star.
It was Star Light! the star
we had wished upon as children.
"Why didn't you grant me
all my wishes star?" I asked.
"The things I had so eagerly
hoped for?"
"Because," was the star's
response, "I gave you
your needs instead."

M Bonamico

PEACE

There is a solace
In nature, in God
And His creatures
Who really care.

The openness
Of the very young
And the very old
Is a reaffirmation,
Being with those
I love and like
And sharing thoughts
Is a joy.

But you know recently
I've returned to poetry.
Though not works of art—
They've done wonders for me.

For I find as I write
There's a soothing effect—
A kind of tranquility—
At least for the moment

Mary Lou Held

THE WAITING GAME

From his hiding place the old cat
waited patiently,
The bird feeder his lure,
From the roof the sparrows
watched,
Silent sentinels afraid to move.
The cardinal swooped in, a flash of
scarlet
against the snow,
One gray ear twitched
imperceptibly,
whiskers quivered nervously,
Suddenly the raucous screech of
the bluejay
shattered the stillness
and the sky came alive with
fluttering wings,
The old cat switched his tail and
walked away.

Lynn Baker

WHO AM I?

I'm a plant in the desert searching
for the rain.
I'm a prisoner of war trying to
appear sane.
I'm a weed in the summer seeking
out the sun.
I'm the deformed person in the
wheelchair longing, once again,
to run,
I'm a baby bird with a broken wing
wanting to learn to fly.
I'm a senile old woman waiting for
her time to die.
I'm a dying alcoholic searching for
booze on the street.
I'm an old punching bag waiting to
be ripped apart and beat.
I'm a child in an orphanage
searching for a home and love.
I'm a cold hand in the winter
longing to find a glove.

SO . . . WHO AM I?

Bob Ogundare

THE BELOVED

To my wife Lamide

Thinking of her on many a time,
I am overwhelmed by strong swift
winds,
Rushing through my liquid veins
Emotions flowing to the core of my
being.

The very first time we two did meet,
Recognition to some degree,
Maybe we'd loved in times well
past,
I knew she was mine in that first
blast.

Sometimes when together we be,
Arguments ensue and we
completely disagree,
On big things, little things and of
medium degree,
Yet this love remains in me,
Aging a year each successive week,
Apart or together, I love her still.

Before my eyes this love unfolds,
Delicate arms which grasp my own;
I feel her touch, both warm and
cold,
And shiver to the marrow in my
bones.
However hot or cold it be,
This love for her suffuses me.

The reason for this love I cannot
tell,
It fills me up like water in a well.
I cannot help but love my gem
As this love skims through thick
and thin
Until the end which is no end.

Audrey E Benicki

A SISTER'S LOVE

To my sister "Janie Crawford"

Out of sisterly love she came
But feelings weren't the same

Words were said and spoken
A heart was torn and broken

Falling tears can't take away the
pain
Things may never be the same

Silently she walks the road
Her heart still feels the load

She knows: God does not take sides
She knows: God does not divide

He loves the children one and all
Nature is his kingdom hall

A new day has come and gone
Feelings back where they belong

Love can mend the weakness bond
Love can give back . . . your heart
a song

Kathy Mae Barnes

GOD IS THERE

There is a God up in heaven,
As you all must know,
He walks by our side,
Everywhere that we may go.
He leads us both by either way,
Both by night or by day,
When we are lost,
He helps to give us sight,
When it is dark,
He gives us light.
No matter the weather,
No matter your name,
Rich or poor,
He loves you the same.
Day or night,
Spring or fall,
Yes, it is true,
God loves us all.
On those roads,
Hard and rough,
Yes, God is there,
And he's filled with love.
So when times are hard,
And no one is there,
Yes, God does care.

Ruth Duff

THE FARMERS PLIGHT

The farmer is in trouble
We hear people say,
Lots of hard work
And very little pay.

It is hard for us to understand
Why the farmer is being sold off
his land.

A farm grows up in bushes and
weeds

When no one tills the soil and plants
the seeds.

I go to the grocery and help myself,
But I know the food doesn't grow on
the shelf.

We all know the farmer feeds the nation,
Something should be done about the
situation.

The U.S. Government of this great land,
Should grasp the problem with a mighty
hand.
And do everything within its power,
To help the farmer in his darkest hour,
And all of us should do what we can,
To keep the farmer on his land.

James Smith

WE ARE KEY MAKERS

I went to work on a home that had burned. It had a caved in top, it had a burned and charred front door that had a key stuck in its lock.
The LORD gave me a message that we are key makers in a sense to say, and we work and shape on our keys every single day.
Have you ever noticed a key how one side has notches on it, the other smooth? Could this be the shape of our key, a mark for the things we did or didn't do? our key look like? will it do? My key will look exactly like me and yours will look like you.
The key that we are shaping on is the inner soul that will one day open a door and once you step inside of it, it will close back again, and you can't come back through it any more. So will the key that you are making on, open the door to outer darkness where you shall always burn, or will it be to the door of heaven where God should be more our concern? Where there shall be no more outer darkness, no more night and GOD will be its master and the LAMB shall be the light?
Like the sinful soul of man, this house has all been cleaned out again and I believe it still has a firm foundation right down to the rock, because I have removed all of the burned timber out of it from its bottom to its top. The beams and joists have been made safe again, enough that a little child can make its play, and the lady and man of this house can soon once again go about it preparing for their busy day. It has a new roof and a new front door that has a beautiful tree carved in its top and it has a brand new set of keys to be put in its lock. Amen.

Mary K Hamilton

WHO COULD EVER FORGET?

Who could ever forget?
The sun when it sets
The moon at night,
A person never forgets
Such colors of light!
The forest after a rainstorm,
The ocean when calm as can be,
A beautiful newborn child,
Or a ship out to sea.
A flower when first blossoming,
A shooting star in the sky.
A rainbow stretching over
A cloud filled sky!
Rain on the evergreens,
The sun in your eyes.
The wind when it blows
Through the ever-aging pines.
The snow on the hilltops,
A rushing white stream,
A bird when it sings.
And who could ever forget
The love in my heart, that was put
aside, For You, from the very start.

Deanna Rawls

THE WORLD

Many questions on this subject are queried.
The mistakes we find are often buried.
Can we repay what it does for us?
The answer is yes! We certainly must!
The real question is how? By being dead or alive?
But the answer to that will never arrive.
For now we can only keep it pretty and clean.
And be nice to other people, not sour and mean.
Is there going to be a doomsday, or is there not?
If there is, will we go to heaven or shrivel up and rot?
Will there be a World War III . . .
or can I grow up in a good world just being me?
Is the ocean green . . .
Is the ocean blue . . .
Is the ocean what separates me and you?
Does it separate love, peace and kindness . . .
or does it separate hatred, disaster and kindless?
Is there really a God, really a devil?
Did that little ole gun make all men level?
Equal, other people would usually say
but I guess I just talk in my own way.

P Dene Williams

A WOMAN NOW

For two super kids I love dearly, Glyna and Alyson.

A woman, a girl no longer
it doesn't seem so.
But the years haven't stopped
and each one tells me,
"You're a woman now"
But I'm still not sure
what a woman is.
I don't seem that much different
ambitions haven't changed
but added onto.
I've my girls now, but also
a career and me.
Me . . . a woman,
No more wondering what I will be,
I am.
No more doubts if I'll grow up,
I have.
Still searching, still learning, still growing,
but with experience now
to hold to the knowledge
instead of sifting it through my fingers
like sand.
I'm a woman now,
not much different, but still
a lot.

Ivy N Meyer

THE BIRD FEEDERS

To my husband, Herman, Without his sheltering love and support, I would be as lost as the birds to the hawks.

It is winter again and outside my window you stand
snow drifted in cake-icing swirls about your feet
bare arms a graceful tracing against the sky.
Like charms dangling from a bracelet, you hold aloft
the bird feeders entrusted to your care.
I take sad pleasure in your naked form, knowing
through spring and summer you will remain as you are.
No longer will you wake, stretching your arms
toward the coaxing warmth of the sun
rustling and swaying to the winds seducing caresses

adorning yourself in scent and flowers to welcome your guests
sheltering them from the watchful eyes of the hawk
circling in mock disdain high above.
Only your skeleton remains, a shadow of our years together
two aging handmaidens waiting upon our charges.
Perhaps we have been too indulgent, enchanted by their presence.
Like spoiled and greedy children they wantonly scatter
our offerings upon the ground below.
Still, I take delight in their colors flashing in the sun
or bringing lustre to darker days.
Alone now, I watch in wingless wonder, eyes bedazzled
by this treasure.
Heedless of your lifeless arms beneath their singing
they perch with careless honor
like jewels upon a dead queen.

Kristy M Wescott

MY FRIEND

You and I
We're two of a kind
We always stick together
Regardless of the trouble we find
I feel comfortable to call you friend
And thats the pledge we made,
Friends to the end.
And when you're down, and your days are not so fine
I'll say, "Hey, you're not just anyone,
You're a friend of mine!"

Anne Knapp

AN ODE TO SCOTT CARPENTER

Since the epic ride of John H. Glenn,
The world was about to see it again.
This time a man in Aurora 7
Was about to reach aloft into heaven.

It took a few months to prepare for flight,
This man who would soon be ready, and right
On the morning he was scheduled to fly,
The countdown went on and he was ready to try.

Time ticked on, 4, 3, 2, 1-, and the Aurora 7 had then begun
To ascend into space with conditions Go—
This man, his capsule and his radio.

In space all things seemed as they did with Glenn,
The sun rose and set three times, and then
It was time for our man to return from flight,
His fuel was low, but it seemed alright.

Suddenly, no sound from our man in orbit.
The nation wondered, "Did he make it?"
For 46 minutes the world was in doubt.
Then a plane radioed back, OUR MAN MADE OUT!"

A wild cheer, a tear and a sigh,
Our man was safe, and down from the sky.
Our prayers were answered, thank GOD they were,
For our fourth man in space, SCOTT CARPENTER!

Nora Lea Dwyer

GOING FISHING

Dedicated to my husband, Edmund L. Dwyer Jr. He died March 9, 1986. He was buried March 12, 1986 on our 35th anniversary. He was a child of God and we had a happy life together.

The sun is shining and the grass is green,
Down in the meadow by the old mill stream.
It's a beautiful spot, so lovely to see
We can picnic there, just you and me.
When the time is right and work is slow,

Let's fix a lunch and away we'll go,
We'll fish in the stream and lay on the grass
We'll count the butterflies that flutter past.
If the fish bite good,
We'll catch a few,
A good fish fry for me and you,
Just like you said we would.
Come on now, don't say no,
You promised me a long time ago.
Get the fishing poles, don't be so slow,
You'll catch a big one and be all aglow.

James A Rodgers

A DAYDREAM

Running down hill of knee-high grass,
I push,
then lift my feet.

Leaving earth behind,
I glide over countryside,
float on air currents.

Fingers are feathers,
legs become tail,
Mental metamorphosis.

I can fly.

Mario R Altamura

STATUE OF LIBERTY CENTENNIAL (STAUNCH BEACON OF HOPE)

Dedicated to the weary immigrants, seeking freedom, peace, justice and opportunity in U.S.A.

On new-found land, in verdant robe, there stands
A monument of hope and life—a gift
To man from man who loves and comprehends
God's wish for compassion, that strives to lift
The soul of him who craves for liberty,
And seeks a light, a door and kindly word—
All molded in a Queen of Sympathy,
With crown of rays, a torch and tablet gird.
And there she stands, now ten decades of time,
Ever-calling, ever-drawing with magic
Unknown, which stirs the soul and soothes the mind
As lost joy replaces life's sombre statics.
Praise God for His gift of Liberty;
Bless America's magnanimity.

Robyn Marie Ackermann

A LEGACY OF LOVE

To Grandma Vanasse, for your unconditional love

My Grandmother sits and talks
And I listen in awe
She points to her flowers
And tells me a story about each
Then picks up her coffee and sips

She says she's going to lose weight
But I think she's wonderful as she is
She gets up out of her favorite chair
And makes me breakfast
Then I get dressed
She folds my clothes neatly
and tells me how her employer taught her how to fold

We then discuss family
Making sure we both get things straight
And slowly begin to play cards
I always win
And the game is always the same
But it makes things more wonderful

Grandma gives me money
And I go to the store to buy milk
While I'm gone she puts money in my purse
Which I later sneak back in her purse
When I get back we watch her "Soaps"
She talks about the characters
Like they are her best friends
It makes me sad to think of
How easy it is to tune out family

I think sometimes she's lonely
But she's always happy when I'm with her
We need each other to understand
Our worries and fears
And in a way she is "MY Best Friend".

Opal Jeune

BUTTERFLIES

Dipping up and dipping down
Flying all the way around
Yellow, red, orange, and brown
They are beautiful in our town

Some are colorful, others white
In the summer they come in sight
Tlitting and sitting on the flowers
I have watched them hour after hour

This earth is full of beauty
Plains, hills and valley land
Where all people can expand
God made and created it all for man

I have noticed the birds and bees
Flying through the shady trees
With differed voices and songs
We can hear them all day long

Just a perfect harmony
I enjoy their company
I can begin to explain
How God made everything.

Eliene Person Hattervig

THE EVERGREENS

The trees stood tall and stately,
Reaching high, high into the blue heaven,
The tree tops swayed gently in the breeze,
I gazed, amazed at the straight trunks,
And at the green of the needles,
I inhaled the exhilerating scent,
For they were the gracious evergreens.
All around on the ground
Were the uniquely shaped pine cones,
Like quaint decorations, scattered by nature herself,
I gathered several into my hand
And thought that here I held in my palm,
Many trees, but only in the making,
For though I would plant these seeds,
Water and care for them tenderly,
Yet, it would not be I who made them grow,
For I like Kilmer, realized.
That only God can make a tree.

Marie V Scanlon

CONFESSION

You're not a sin anymore.
I don't feel guilt or regret.
Now I face squarely . . . the pain of letting go,
The fear of not loving another
in quite the same manner—ever.

When you were a sin,
My heart turned away readily.
Now it spins back . . . just love on its axis,
The longing turns to desperation,
There's no comfort for me—anywhere.

Now the change in love comes,
The passion must be surrendered, it must die . . .
And then there's also the burial to contend with.
Sin darkened my soul,
But set my mind at ease.
Truth lightens my soul,
But leads me to insanity.

The confession has been heard — the penance much too stern.

Marjorie L Hadley

THE AIRPORT

A place of joy, A place of sadness,
Busy! Busy! utter madness.
Someone going, someone coming in,
Far away places many have been.
Tears are flowing, also many smiles,
As each one remembers how many miles:
Kisses for the loved one going away,
A last, long hug for someone who must stay.
"Ilove you," "Write," "Call me soon,"
Phrases that are spoken,
Then loved ones are gone.
An empty heart turns away
And begins to dream of the day,
When arms will be open,
And someone will say,
"Welcome home," "I've missed you,"
"So glad you are here."
"Oh! How I've waited for this day,
Now tell me how long can you stay?"

Marilyn F Kozic

FEMME FETAIL

I once knew a girl who was fat

She ate too much of this and of that;

An empty bowl was her gripe,

And her name was Sweet Spike

She was my fatuous. fat, tabby cat.

Lou Ann Carey

INDIAN EYE'S

To Mary, who brought to my attention, our Indian Eye's.

The two of us have Indian eye's, my friend Mary and me.
I know not what tribe's blood flows through her veins,
But mine is Cherokee.
Although, it really doesn't matter about the tribe or name
Because when it comes to Indian eyes, they are all the same.
Indian eyes can see back into centuries ago
In a softly falling rain, a giant herd of buffalo
Grazing peacefully on the plain
They can see an Indian village; Its campfires all aglow
And the little village children running happily to and fro.
They can see braves astride their ponies,
With bows slung across their backs, riding silently
Through the forest on the trail of a grizzly's tracks
They can see Indian maidens laughing and chattering happily,
As they weave their beautiful baskets
From the branches of a willow tree
They can see a chief in his council house,
Holding a meeting there; with a beautiful eagle feather
Headdress adorning his raven hair.
Yes, the two of us have Indian eye's, my friend Mary and me,
And these are just a few of the many things
These Indian eye's of mine, and Mary's see.

Mary Lynn Spires

WOMAN

To my loving, supportive sister.

I am a wife.
I am a cook.
I am a mother.
I clean, wash, sterilize, feed, and play.
I correct, instruct, and discipline.
I fetch, find, and put away.
I get up early and stay up late.
I read a lot, watch a lot.
I doctor, nurse, and soothe.
I shout and I whisper.
I cuddle and I shake.
I get close then I back away a little.
I sympathize and I criticize,
I urge and I praise.
I am a Housewife, Homemaker—I am Woman.

Cheri M Smith

BELIEVE IN ME

To: Ericka and Greg for their love and encouragement

As I stood on the mountaintop and looked back on my life,
The trials and tribulations had left me angry and full of strife. I took one step forward and you caught my sleeve,
As I stood there grappling, you made me believe.
The wind whipped through my clothing as I fought to take flight,
No longer could I stay on earth, not even through the night.
As I begged for freedom to leave this cruel world,
I was suddenly transformed to when I was a girl.
I sat in church, the organ softly playing,
As I was listening to chords, I heard your voice saying,
Trust and believe, no matter how

small you are,
If you trust my word, I'll never be far.
The tears begin to roll as the wind blew strong,
As I finally realized that I had always belonged.
Believing and trusting you did not guarantee,
That I would go through life pain and trouble free.
What it did guarantee, that I failed to know,
That the road would be easier no matter where I go,
That the pain and the heartache would hurt nonetheless
But the outcome would be better because of our togetherness.
So as I stepped back on the mountain and turned to walk away,
I knelt on my knees and began to pray;
Thank you for your loving kindness, your care and control,
Through all of my life even through miracles untold.
Thank you for knowing me by name and guiding my way,
But most of all, thank you for being here tonight
So I may live to praise you another day.

Dana Renee Stalnaker

Dana Renee Stalnaker
DON'T DIE

In memory: Clifford Owen Church
August 6, 1925—April 4, 1986

AS he lays in his hospital bed all alone,
Don't wanna go nowhere but home.
He's always in a lot of pain,
With nothing but death to gain.
I wish I could take your place I thought,
To teach the way you taught.
He's lead me through life and back again,
This ole' man I call my friend.
I wish I could help him as he sits alone and cries.
There he sits—when he slowly dies.

Trish
YESTERDAY I WAS

Dedicated to Dee, MUH!

Yesterday I was
once mellow and serene
as I walked up the mountain
to watch the green grass
turn to snow
and, nature's children
came to talk with me.
The air was crisp, with a feeling
of freshness.
Now,
as I watch the coming
of the sun,
today begins a new life,
Yesterday
vanishes with memories.
The snow, once white and pure,
is now used
and confused with hatred.
Why? it asks,
do people just walk upon and
always take for granted—
Life.

Laura Addah Seiver
BOOKBAG

Searching through nine weeks of senior year
English handouts, college mail
broken pencil
Where's my walkman?
Need to finish that letter and
Send off that scholarship application before the deadline.
Uh-oh,
Just what I feared
My physics and civics homework
Irrevocablyentwined
Naturalized acceleration and
Angular ideals of democratic velocity.

Joanne Rouse
DURING A LIFETIME

To my parents, Burl and Lola Rouse with Love

Through the years of growing up, playing, watching and learning.

Influence of others and mistakes of our own,
happiness, sadness and peacefulness.

Finding love and living our dreams, judgement, fulfillment and rewardment.

Having children and learning from them,
life, pain and joy.

Remember growing up and letting them chose,
helpful, cheerful and fearful.

Children having children and we get older,
caring, helping and sharing.

Growing old as time passes,
living, loving and dying.

Jo McDonald-Nichols
SWEET GHOST

Ah "Sweet Ghost" of yesteryear
In fantasy you reappear
To walk beside me once again,
Down a bright leaf covered lane.

Ah "Sweet Ghost" when day is through
I drift through dreams in search of you.
And in a dimly lit cafe,
We dance 'til the break of day.

Ah "Sweet Ghost" when winds blow free
You're sure to haunt my reverie
And once again it's so devine,
To feel your lips pressed close with mine.

Ah "Sweet Ghost" when stars are bright
I know that somewhere in the night
We will meet again my dear,
And stroll once more through yesteryear.

Pauline French
FRIENDS

When you wake up in the morning
At the beginning of the day
Do you wonder how many people you'll
meet as you go along the way.
How many will say Hello! to you, or how
Many will turn their head
How many will apologize for some
Unkind word they have said
How many will give you a helping
Hand when the going for you gets rough
How many real—friends do you really
Have I can tell you not—nearly
Enough.

Mary Jo Tardiff
THE 25TH MISSION

It was the promise of a dream
that took them far beyond the limits of earth and sky.

It beckoned them with out stretched
hand to a timeless journey beyond the stars.

Boundless and free they flew
through the heavens of blue
In a blink of an eye they
were gone, leaving us asking
God "Why"

He whispered in the wind
"Their spirits are flying on
the wings of eternity. Dancing
across the clouds of time.
Until they find a rainbow
in which to follow into my
open arms."

Zayid Muhammad
EVIL GAL BLUES (FOR BAAAD MS LADY CRACK)

I'm a evil gal
Don't bother with me
I'm a evil gal
Don't bother with me
I'll make ya' feel real good
Then turn yo' soul into misery . . .

I'll hit ya' first for 10
Then I'll hit ya' for 20 too
An' after a month'a my good pullin'
you'll be bringin' me all yo' money soon . . .

I say . .
I'm a evil gal
Don't bother with me
I'll make ya' feel real good
Then turn yo' soul into misery . . .

I'll make ya' weak an skinny
One boy even shot somebody in da' head
Anotha' fo' money he had to get me
even stabbed his own motha' dead . . .

I tell ya'
I'm a evil gal
Don't bother with me
Yes, I'll make ya' feel real good
And then I'll fill yo' soul wit'sum sho'nuff
MIS—ZUH—REE!!!

MCP
RENEWAL

The breezes wear
May's fragrance in their hair.
May is a sweet disturbance
floating in the air.

Water shake.
Rivers, stream and lake
sparkle with the sun's pleasure
that May is awake.

Men wait long
for Spring's outburst of birdsong,
her renewed zest of life
from here to Hong Kong.

May flowers grow
so gently in the earth, you know
Spring is in love with tenderness,
everywhere you go.

Let everyone you meet,
in lane, igloo, canal or street,
join people around the world
to find sweetness and freedom in Spring.

Cheryl Ann Bryant
THROUGH THE SEASONS

In the spring of life we learn to grow.
In the summer we begin to understand and know,
As we enter the fall, we remember why
And as winter approaches we learn to say goodbye.

Bessie Yawn
BEAUTY IN TREES

I walked in the woods one bright Spring morning when the day was at its best,
The shadows came out to greet me wearing their new Spring dress.
I walked on a few paces and sat down upon a large stone,
I listened to hear the birds singing, the Turtle Dove calling his own.
I rested there a little while in the shade of the big full trees,
And I marveled at the wonder of God, how he let the wind blow the leaves.
I walked in the woods one cold winters day,
The shadows were asleep in their blankets, the sky above was dark and gray.
I looked up through the trees so bare and free,
I was still for a moment, a voice whispered to me.
It was soft and gentle, then it was gone, gone with the breeze.
A thousand years is like a day my child,
Spring will come tomorrow and God will put the leaves back on the trees.
And I whisper, "Thank you Lord Jesus for all the beauty your hands have made,
Make my life beautiful, as beautiful as the trees."

Jackson H Rodgers
HE'S JUST A PUPPY

As I sit alone to meditate
This devil intrudes my space
This furry thing, ears dangling free
Rains kisses on my face

He reads the darkness of my pain
And brings me into play
Before to long my smile begins

The sadness swept away

He aggravates me sometimes
He's persistent as can be
After all he's just a puppy
Teaching my spirit to be free

He's there with true affection
His love it has no cost
And if he hadn't been there
My soul would now be lost

So if you have a furry friend
I'll tell you what you do
Make sure that you take care of him
And his love will see you through

S Jean Chapman

AMERICA MY HOMELAND

In memory of my ancestors, who made America their homeland.

America my homeland,
You are mighty; you are great.
Beauty abounding all around us,
Continually growing without a fuss.
The Mountains in their majesty
And rivers flowing to the sea.
People of every race and color,
Sharing this space with one another.
Sometimes differences do arise.
It is painful to hear the hurting cries.

America my homeland,
Reach out your helping hand.
To people calling out to us—
Let us not betray their trust.
Let them come and let them see
Our purple mountain's majesty.
People of every race and color
Need to share with one another
Let us put our differences aside,
In peace and trust let us abide.

Fran Karpus

AN UNDERSTANDING HEART

To Jim—he picked up the pieces.

When I was young—oh so very young—
I searched for a lover fair.
I judged by the heighth and breadth of him
And the color of his hair.
Many a kind one passed me by,
But his eyes or his nose was wrong—
Such a lover was not for I,
He must be handsome and strong.
Then a lad I found who could pass the test
Of my heart's demanding eye;
And to him the love I had cherished long
I tendered with a sigh.
And he took my love—this lad so fair—
The one I had searched for and found,
And with thoughtless words and careless deeds
He dropped it to the ground.
And it lay all broken as I wept and sighed
For the one who had left it there,
And I thought of the ones who had passed me by
As I waited this lover fair.
Then I knew at last—though at last was too late—
For my dreams had fallen apart,
Love is not caused by beauty of face
But an understanding heart.

Susan Rene Brown

Susan Rene Brown

UNITY

I dedicate this poem to my husband Steve, in memory of our wedding.

As we join together our lives today,
let us also join our hearts;
In unity, in truth and love, as we strive to never part.
As we journey down life's pathway,
may we take a step each day;
May we climb the highest mountain, may we cross the widest sea.
Let us carry each other's burdens,
when the load is far too strong;
And be each others footstones
when the road is getting long.
Let us not find faults or failures,
but seek to find the best;
In everything we say and do, until the souls at rest.
May we find the joy and happiness,
that only two can share; and cling to one another, finding love beyond despair.
May we cast our fears behind us,
and learn how to forgive;
Let us love, honor, and cherish, as long as we both shall live.

Robert Eugene Seale

CHRISTMAS DAY

This poem is dedicated to my Lord and Savior

On this one day of the year,
I feel so close and so near,
To the one I dearly love,
Who dwells somewhere up above.

He was born so long ago,
In a manger In the snow,
Later on, as time went by,
He suffered much and I know why—
His father sent him, don't you see,
To die on calvary for you and me,
So our sins would be forgiven,
If we would believe on him in heaven.
So all we need to do today,
Is fold our hands and really pray,
To thank him for all his love,
He sends to us from up above.

Dawn Leppala

SUCH IS THE COLOR

Blue is the color of belonging,
Bays, Beauty, blissful living.
Green is the color of eternity,
Evergreens, Envy, Ever to be.
Yellow is the color of happiness,
Halos, High Hopes, helping the hapless.
Orange is the color of Fear,
Fire, Fright, a Fruitless tear.
Brown is the color of today,
Trees, trying, a page turnaway.
Black is the color of dread,
Dreary days, Doom, another dead.
White is the color of democracy,
Doves, Demonstration, Free Nationality.
Silver is the color of Ability,
Ashes, Aspiration, as we will be,
Gold is the color of remembrance,
Rings, Respect, returned romance.
Red is the color of harmfullness,
Hearts Hurts, hateful bitterness.
Pink is the color of Friendship,
Flowers Fun Family Kinship.
Purple is the color of memory,
Music melodies moving us to see.
Life is a prism put together.
Search, Seek, Such is the Color.

Suzanne Kristine Musgrave

A BRIEF MOMENT, CHALLENGER

To Herbert Olson, my father and inspiration; William S. Grenzebach Jr., my godfather and mentor; and to my loving husband Kenneth.

Life resembles the rainbow,
Look how the colors blend.
Every means of existence,
All that nature sends.

Yet when it comes to man,
The rainbow fades away.
Not like the perished seven,
That vanished in a ray.

United for that moment,
With tears in our heart.
Concern for one another,
Nows the time to start.

Wendy M Lazik

THE PAINFUL FIVE

I walked along a deserted road,
alone and bold with nowhere to go.
I reach out my hand to feel your clutch, but it's still hanging there alone so much.
A broken heart in time will mend,
only with the touch of your hand.
Playing with feelings goes very deep, it drives you to just sit and weep.
Caring for someone in the heart will grow, to keep a sense of value that you show.
Knowing love for what it is worth,
helps show you for yourself on this earth.
Understanding can drive you insane, it also teaches you how to deal with pain.
Ending with a meaningful thought, knowing that some day it
will all be taught.

Valerie Lynn Vitale

MOTHER

Thanks for giving birth to me
And for giving me this chance,
Thanks for your permission
To laugh, to sing and dance.

Thanks for all your patience
At times I'd scream and cry,
Thanks for all your wisdom
At times when I'd ask why.

Thanks for holding onto me
When I couldn't even walk,
Thanks for all the tenderness
Thanks for teaching me to talk.

Thanks for raising me on truth
So I'd grow up and wouldn't lie,
Thanks for all your courage
Thanks for never letting me die.

Let me thank you for your beauty
And for everything you've shared,
Thanks for all you've given me
To let me know you cared.

Nick S Loftus

ALONE BY THE SEA

To My Loving Wife, Doris

Today I walked the shores alone
Thinking of you as the day passed on.
The sky was blue, but then turned gray,
The waves washed my footprints away.

Then the sky turned again to blue,
Once again my mind was on you
Wondering where you might be
Could you be thinking about me.

I sat upon a rock and gazed out to sea
Wishing you were here beside me.
So many things I would like to say,
As a summer breeze blew the clouds away.

I once again began to walk,
Wishing you were here to talk
Sitting here you and me
On the sand by the sea.

A gull flew over so graceful in flight
The day was ended as it began to be night.
I walked on and on, walking alone
It was time to head back home.

Today I walked the shores alone
Thinking of you as the day passed on.
The sky was blue, but then turned gray,
The waves washed my footprints away.

Audrey Lynch Wassner

AUTUMN

The shorter days with a clearer, brighter blue sky.
Bountiful gardens bathed in moonlight and twinkling stars at night,
With the brief warmth of summer so quietly slipping by.
Fallen chestnuts and shiny apples
Glistening in the garish sun.
A brilliant color traversing the countryside,
A tapestry of nature's show that has begun.
All creatures great and small
Preparing their larder for colder times.
Birds with their precision-like flying
Heading for the warmer climes.
The giant cathedral of trees
Reaching ever upward toward the sky.
To hear the friendly crackling sound

Of leaves underfoot, as we go by.
The splash of golden yellows,
bright oranges, pinks, wine,
bronze, peach and
Soft shadings of green and golden-
rod.
This beautiful season of autumn
In the ultimate presence of God.

Patty Gregg
A VIEW OF SPRING
Bright colors paint a pretty scene;
This field is quite a lovely sight.
Spring is seldom a view unseen.

Grasses are deep in emerald-green;
Trees are apple-blossom white.
Bright colors paint a pretty scene.

Steeples in the distance are lean;
Houses without fresh dress are
slight.
Spring is seldom a view unseen.

Red and yellow flowers are keen;
A sharp blue sky has but one kite.
Bright colors paint a pretty scene.

The atmosphere seems sweet and
clean;
A golden star spreads radiant light.
Spring is seldom a view unseen.

A town and field are thus
portrayed;
Bright colors paint a pretty scene.
Anger is a season delayed;
Spring is seldom a view unseen.

Robert S Matthews
ASIA
Into the land of the Prester John
Where temple and tomb are a
singular one,
Where life by a simple thread is
hung,
The Sacred Crow—its precious
dung.

The evening meal 'neath a
monsoon sky,
An Asian smell, a beggar cry,
The World may spin, just one more
turn,
But the pot will boil—the fire will
burn.

And the naked child will still be fed,
While the leper crawls near
unclaimed dead,
And the clothes are scrubbed in a
tepid stream,
Near the crush of souls, in an
endless seam.

The reaching hands, the peddlers
ware,
The foreign land, where God must
care,
While Shiva and Buddha in their
temples sleep,
Asia will toil, and Asia will weep.

And the world may spin this one
more turn,
But the pot will boil—the fire will
burn.

Vivian Orrison
FALL

"To Sherry"

I walk through the woods in the
Fall.

I gaze at the trees standing graceful
And tall.

I hear the cardinal's
Call.
The leaves of every
Hue.

Made more beautiful by the
morning
Dew.

God raised His sacred hand

To paint these pictures in our
Land.

God, the greatest artist of all,
Painted this beautiful season
We call fall.

David E Butler
HIS WORLD—OUR NATURAL HOME
Pounding waves, noisy thunder,
whispering trees,
Rain falling with graceful ease—
Brings out the quiet wonder in me
Of what, God wants us to see.

True beauty, he has created
And to this place, he has led
To, sands white and pure,
Like a truly wonderful lure.

Animals bold and true
And birds that once flew
Inhabited this world for all to see
To fulfill his decree.

Let us look again
Without the acid rain
At our natural home—
No matter where we roam,

From now until forever
His plan was clever—
We should enjoy
His marvelous toy!

His world is the result
Which we tend to insult
Through wreckless care
Of our land so fair.

Veronica M Carr
I'LL BE WATCHING

To Melissa

I watched you today
My lovely girl grand-child
As you sat at the kitchen table
With your crayons and your
coloring book.
Your hair like a black silk fan
against your cheek

And your dark eyes fixed
In a deeply concentrated look.
And I wondered how many times
In the life and living get to come
your way

I'd be watching
And remember
And still see you as you are today.

Ethel L Campbell
THE OLD FARM
The old cabin stood in the desert
so proud, with
nothing but tumbleweeds for a
shroud. Its ribs bleached
white by the desert sun, you knew
that its days of
raising a family was done. You
wonder why in days gone by
that they had left it there all alone
to die. It had served
them so faithfully, it's where they
had raised their
family.
The old gate doesn't swing
anymore it lies all rusty
on the desert floor. The old barn
lies in a heap on
the ground, not a living thing can
be found.
No more does the farmer harvest
his hay, no more is there
the sound of children at play, no
more does the cattle
graze on the land there is nothing
left now but drifting
sand. You look at the old farm
and sigh, you can't help
it you want to cry.

Maxine R Teachout
SOULMATES
I thought I'd forgotten
The tingle of anticipation
The thrill of strange hands
caressing, coaxing
With a gentle touch.
Slowly releasing my tensions,
urging me closer;
closer to the lost private world of
utter abandon—
Lost in the high of just feeling;
what a high!
When feeling becomes all that
matters
And the rest of the world
disappears leaving only two
Two caught in the glow of just
being there—
Together we take the upward
spiral;
Up, up, until suddenly, exhausted,
we drift off
And slowly, so slowly, we drift
apart
Now I have only my memories of
you
And there, together we will drift
forever
Two souls merged into one—
And if that's all there is; all there
can ever be—
It's enough!

Zeretha Lenore Jenkins

Zeretha Lenore Jenkins
A FAILING IN THE LEFT FIELD

To my grandmother, Big Mama Winnie, who would have been happy for me had she lived to witness this accomplishment in my life.

Hold your reign, Brothers,
Hold it tight.
Til thy crimson hand swells with
humiliation.

Across the river lies the enemy,
the friend, the intimate
comforter.
Draw back thy lifeline before
dawn's bulging belly bursts,
mocking thee.

Hold together, Brothers, for
we fastly approach ourselves.
As midnight—our fallacies—
gently rock us,
Poisoning our souls, robbing
us of all dignity.

In the distance flashes a vision—
A vision of death we cannot, we
shall not escape.
Hold tight, frightened Brothers,

The enemy approaches.

Doris H Sleigher
MEMORIES

To my Mom and Dad. Forever in my heart.

All these memories
In a box
All those dreams held in stock
This little box

Gathered up like lillies at Easter
Formed into the breeze
All those many clovers
Dancing around the trees

The golden wheat fields
Along the brisk running streams
The constant sound and likeness
Of the beauty of nature and spring

Always sits my dreams in a box
Gathered up memories
Something unbought

Merion Margaret Webb
I PLAYED A PART
I played a part
In someone's life,
The sick, the homeless,
The age, the poor
The child who knew no
Kindness or care,
I played a part
The best I could,
I hope it helped
The way it should.

Don Petty
DARKNESS
Darkness, oh Darkness
Lost within the crust of night
I try to see beyond my reach
And as I try, I come to think, to
believe, to know
That life is but a darkened screen.
And what I cannot see, I do not
know.
And what I do not know is a
darkened screen in my mind.
For it is wisdom alone I seek to
mend,
To weave and thread within my
mind.
For it is knowledge that makes a
mind
As there are words to think in.

Mrs Nell McAmis
WONDERING
Where did I put that money?
Where did my scissors go?
What shall I have for supper;
I have to decide you know!

It is so much fun to be older;
It keeps you so alert—
Remembering the things you've
forgotten
And doing all your work!

I like to think of the olden days
When I was young and spry.

I could do anything I wanted
And not even wonder why!

Now, I do this and a bit of that
And put the rest off till tomorrow,
Sit down to rest and fall asleep
And wake up in a tizzy.

I must get going and get on the ball,
Work real fast and finish it all,
So I can be young and whizzy!

William S Marshall Jr
STEEPLE DREAMS

On Sundays, I remember things like
the mesquite brush that blew dead over
West Texas plains as if it had someplace to go. It didn't
tumble really—just scraped along in the eddying wind that
could have blown the sun down.
And I remember the empty
night that pushed most of hope over the horizon, leaving the desert to sweat a cold dew in the chill of the planet's shadow.
But then, the penlights came out—the encircling Milkway blinked
its familiar message of mystery—an unbreakable code, no matter
what Voyagers searched its language. Still, there seemed an answer, interwoven in the stars—perhaps far grander than our questions, or maybe just a punchline to some giant cosmic joke.
Ultimately, as if no answer mattered, dawn came.

I remember a strange dankness in the Chihuahuan Desert
on such a winter morning.
Remnants of nimbus clouds were
fleeing the relentless north wind.
There was a particular barbed fence that kept sinking further into the earth every year.
It leaned so much from the wind, that even the middle wire was sowed by parched grass blades.
The same basting prairie stretched into uselessness on both sides of those miles of post and wire.
There were reptilian pumps, sparsely dotting the outland, sucking the blood of Tyranasaraus Rex, who lay smothered in an ancient ocean's sediments.
Even these three thousand feet higher, we can't see much more than Rex did. I suppose that's why,

on Sundays, I come here—
surround myself with a dim rainbow of panes
and squint at some man who utters from beneath a polished, rotting cross. I can never quite get him focused
from my usual seat, behind rows of puppets and pews. That preacher if I asked, would tell me that my Moslem friend, (a better man than I),
will not be able to live after he dies.
So I don't ask.
I can't ask. I need this church, its symbols, its pseudo-answers—
the consolations to stars that don't respond.

Pat McCarty
PASSING OF TIME

To Mattie Irl and Charles Kountz, who always had faith in me and my abilities

---

I look in the mirror and what do I see
A face that is older even to me
No longer am I fair of face
And my hair is out of place
On my cheek I see a smudge
Then I feel just like a drudge
If I could just turn back the years
To before I knew of loneliness and fears
All the people that I have known
Are long since dead and gone
But my children bring joy to me
For through them I will live eternally

Betty-Jane Elroy
GRANDMA—MY FAVORITE NAME

To Tommy, Chris, Jason, Adam, Jessica, Nick, Jennifer and Katherine—My Grandchildren.

I'm just a little nobody
Amazed if someone knows my name.
I've never done anything that
Could ever give me fame.

I'm not a famous singer
Or a poet laureate by far,
Or an actor whose dressing room
Has a bright and shining star.

But when my kids and grandchildren
Pick up the phone and call,
I may only be 5 foot 1 inch,
But I feel 6 foot tall.

To know that they all like me
And are happy that I'm around—
To hear them say "I love you"
Is the greatest joy I've found.

So have your fame in acting,
Or singing merrily.
My place in life as a Grandmother
Is the place I want to be.

Janis Rainey Allred
THE BOND OF PEACE

There is a rainbow in the sky; it holds a bond of peace;
And over it there lies a bridge—
lined with pure white fleece.

There are stepping stones on the bridge, with colors bright and bold,
that lead up into Heaven where
Streets are paved with gold.

There are sunbeams shining so bright
their light will not cease, in this place called Heaven tht holds a bond of peace.

At the end of this rainbow bridge
many treasures are stored—
Waiting for all deserving mankind
to come and adore.

Jesus is waiting at the door for all to enter in.
He offers a sanctuary free of sorrow, pain, and sin.
Gabriel will be there to play the trumpet sound;
And in the center of Heaven, God's throne we'll gather 'round.
We will all be happy there, where wonders never cease;
In this place called Heaven that holds a bond of peace.

Mari A Arvanetes
DREAM #1

Standing on the edge of a cloud
Shouting and shouting
My thoughts outloud
The warmth of the sun warms my soul
As I begin to rise out of my ever sinking hole
I can now put the past behind
I have cleared all the clutter
from my mind
But when the dawn comes
And it won't be long now
I know what I must do
I must return to you
Maybe the same as you left me
But maybe not
Could I have found peace of mind
Somewhere past that line
Where you can't calculate time
Where I was never yours
And you were never mine
No it can't be
I must awaken and face the reality
I started with
Nothing is ever as good
Or as bad
As it seems
Just as standing on the edge of a cloud
Can only happen in dreams

Joseph J Acotto Ph D
IS THERE ANYONE THERE?

When you're down
and it appears no one's around,
Your whole life is meaningless
and your face is in the ground—
WILL THERE BE ANY0NE THERE?

Lifes battles have been quite a struggle
and roadblocks were so very many,
Praying to God and getting no solace,
Is there any reason to live; any?

WILL THERE BE ANYONE THERE?

I can't eat—can't sleep
one of my loved ones is dying
The closest one to me is undecided
my heart is broken—inside I'm dying,
and on the outside—millions of tears I am crying.

IS THERE ANYONE THERE?

In time of stress,
when my life seemed amiss,
I can always turn to her
She's always been there—
That's my Sis—
I truly love her.

LaureneAllyce Chaney
THEN CAME YOU

I was depressed, then came you
I was glad for someone new.

You brightened my days and filled my nights
You're always there to hold me tight.

We both were shy right from the start
But now it's rare, if we're apart.

I love to hear your singing voice
With you, my heart has made the choice.

I love your hands so big and strong
With you I know I can't go wrong.

I love your lips, so soft to touch,
All of you, I love so much.

I know our love will last forever
I believe God has brought us together.

Love is now an unlocked door
We've found the key to something more.

I'm always here when you need me
I'll try to understand and to see.

I'm sure you know how much I care
With memories we make and memories we share.

Our feelings grow each passing day
With things we do and words we say.

I cried when I didn't know what to do
Then at once, with all your love came you.

Mable Jackson

Mable Jackson
A PRAYER FOR: THE PRESIDENT

To the people of these great United States

Dear God, please bless our President
Of these great United States
Always walk beside him
Keep him from mistakes

Let him ever be aware
That you are always there
To walk beside him and to lead him anywhere

Let his faith ever be strengthened
And know you are that light
That leads, guides and directs
And does and always protects

Let him fear not the enemies
For they are already defeated
But let him fear you
For he knows you are always needed

So let him look to the hill
On which his helper stands
With watchful eyes and always outstretched hands

Step by step let him wane his way
Let him pause awhile and let him always remember
He came here to stay
To do the very best he can
And help and to serve his fellowman
According to your great command

Florence Reis
WINTER BLUES

Here I am in January,
Feeling very depressed.

The holly is gone,
And the tree undressed.
We haven't had much snow,
And the trees look so bare.
The only thing I'll have to enjoy,
Are the birds at the feeder.
I fill it real often, so they do know
I care.
There is one thing for certain,
The days are getting a bit longer,
So my spirits will be lifted,
And my emotions a little stronger.
Looking forward to spring.
With the first flower to blossom,
And the first robin to sing.

Marie A Hoegler
I NEVER KNEW YOU, LORD

They say You are the Lord and God,
And You are the King of Kings,
I'm told You made heaven and
earth
And every living thing.

They say You are my heavenly
Father
And I am Your child, too,
I want so much to know You, Lord,
So I may go to You.

No one told me of You, Dear Lord,
So many do not care.
I lived a sad and lonely life,
I could have lived a life of prayer.

Open the hearts of men, Dear Lord,
That they should share the faith,
Let Your children know You, Lord,
And fill their lives with grace.

I thank You, Lord, I know You now,
My life is full of joy.
Your Name, I'll share with
everyone
Who will listen to my voice.

There are millions more like I was,
Lord,
Help them to know of Thee,
Change their lives as You changed
mine,
Then all may live with You
eternally.

Laura W Olsen
DECEMBER

Remember him as he was before
Giant in spirit, haven of strength
Tender, gracious, gentle man

Remember him as he was before
Sudden stroke, cruel surgery
That only kept death hovering

Tubes, monitors and automatons
Wasted strong mind and body
And tears replaced words

Remember him as he was
Before sons of Hippocrates
Abandoned and named him Old
He died as he had lived
Innocent, trusting, loved
Remember him

Shannon L Sanford
TWO PEOPLE

She reads the paper
while he turns on TV

She likes the mountains
He craves the sea

He'd rather drive
She'll take the plane

He waits for sunshine
She walks in the rain

He gulps down cold drinks
She sips at hot

He asks "why go"?
She asks "why not?"

In just about everything, they
disagree
But they love one another, and they
both love me.

Pauline E Plante
LOVING WAYS ARE NEVER MINDLESS

To the ones I love: Mom, Dad, Debbie, Grandma & Barton. Thank you!

On a day
Long after I gave my heart away,
I saw you standing there looking at
me
And I so desperately wanted to see,
If there was still a chance
For our long-time secret romance.
You looked like you wanted to cry
And I felt like I wanted to die.
If only I could have told you of the
feelings I had
Maybe you wouldn't have seemed
so sad.
We left each other standing
And just a touch of your hand,
Could have started me crying
And inside you would have been
dying,
Because we need each other oh so
much
And cannot live without the other's
touch
I have loved you for a long, long
time.
I have loved you since I first caught
sight
Of you and lost my heart,
To a man from whom I will never
be apart.
But if we should be torn apart,
Love will always be in our hearts.
Loving ways are never mindless so
I will go on being true,
Living only for my tomorrow with
you.

Karl H Graf
A GREEN VALLEY

Within a valley deeply green
With grass which grows around,
And goldenrod, and violets blue;
A tiny stream which ripples
through,
You may know the place I mean—
This place that I have found.

To look into the laughing stream,
And see a loved one's face,
And pluck for her the goldenrod
And violets close down to the sod,
And then to lie and dream
Within this heavenly place.

To gaze between the leaves which
are
Upon the trees, and to the sky—
To watch the white lace clouds and
see
The azure blue away from me.
And yet for all it is so far
It seems so near that I

Reach up and outward with my
hand
To catch that beauty there
Two clouds so white—just passing
were
One for me, and one for her,
But then I understand,
And they sail onward though so
fair.

Christie Lou McCormick
SHE'S JUST A LITTLE ANGEL

To my children—Rena Nichole, Gabriel Edward, and Joshua Blaine, and to Cory Edward in Heaven.

She's just a little angel, sent from
God above;
She's come to bring you happiness,
beauty and joy and love.
She'll have a heart of gold, as pure
as e'r can be,
And open, like a window, to
everyone she sees.
Her eyes reflect the sunlight, just
like the gleaming sea,
And fall on Nature's wonders, the
sky, the grass, the tree.
Her hair with its softness, falling
in beautiful curls,
Shall take the wind within its locks,
and toss and bounce and whirl.
Her sweetheart lips, so full of
smiles, the color of burgandy
wine,
Shall kiss your forehead and your
cheek sweetly from time to time.
Her voice shall rise with angelic
splendor
As she calls you, "Daddy, please
come to dinner."
Her fingers, so soft and sleek, as
you hold her hand in yours,
Shall express more love and
devotion than can e'r be said in
words.
Yes, she's just a little angel, sent
from God above;
But she's your very special angel;
to teach, to guide, to love.

Debra Rae Kreml
YOUNG GIRL DREAMS

For my daughter, Amy, with love

She dreamed of knights and kings
Of ferris wheels and golden rings
She dreamed of sailing ships and
boats
Of castles surrounded by a moat
She dreamed of tin soldiers and
circus clowns
Of being a princess about to be
crowned
She dreamed of silver stairs to the
sky
Of the sandman and sleep dust in
her eyes
She dreamed of what prince
charming would say
Of how things would be this way
She dreamed as every little girl will
Of how she'd like things to be until
. . .she grew up

Carol Barr
MY DREAM IS GREEN (OR SATURN SMILED)

In memory of my Mother, the Grand Duchess Anastasia Nicholaevna, simply known to most people as Ann, who survived it all.

I want to sing, I want to show
What in my vision is my dream
Flies past these daylight stars
By yellow means past Mars
I come into your splendid view
To touch the light of daylight blue.
Time flies these daylight stars
What in my vision is my dream
Hastens my thought towards your
Place onto place, a team?
The stars, your swirl, to turn and
smile
In time to grow a thought this way.
Oh, time, what is the gamble
I must make before to seek
Through colors that do not seem
of being?
My dream of you belies my life
Though light years from your beam
If only tiny clue to mean
The daylight flight of my green
dream.
Could I be wrong to talk of you?
Could you be wrong, too?
So wrong to see your gift of color
To those black dots surrounding
Every purple time and even
midnight space.

Laura Rochelle Reves
MODERN ICARUS

A column—A tower
Striving toward the azure vault
Straining for the heavens,
For the stars.
Its roar echoing across the land,
One last strain to break free of the
bonds of the earth
One last strain for the frosty, starry
void.
Fire.
All-consuming, all-destroying;
Expanding as if to fill the void
With the reminder of mortality.
A brightness, melting Icarus'
wings,
A supernova, consuming rigid
feathers of steel,
Illuminating the green depths of
the heaving sea.
Falling, fingers streaking the air,
leaving trails white against the
sky,
Falling silently like plumes of some
great bird,
The shards of a shattered dream.

Icarus, who can speak your eulogy?
What mortal can?
But Icarus, you need no eulogy,
For tribute has been paid you,
more eloquently than man could,
In your own fate.
No man could convey that glory

Gloria R McGown
HOPE

To my Mother, Mildred Bond Crosby who taught me to dream.

My heart bestrides a phantom
dream

That rides on silver wings
It shatters all my days with light
And makes my life a thousand
springs.

Eloise Covell Schneider
WHAT MIGHT HAVE BEEN WAS NOT TO BE

It was such a love all at once
It was a love to be short-lived
We met, we loved, we married,
He then became so sick, so sick
And then he died
A short short six months it was
He was so young
I could not bear his suffering
To continue longer
But why could it not have been
That we met, we loved, we married
Living together forever after
If only it might have been for
always
How much I've wished for what
might
Have been
But no, it was not to be forever.

Billene Chatfield Stoller
NIGHT SHADOWS

This poem is dedicated to my husband Steve and our six children. Because of you, I've gained the courage to believe in myself.

In the long hours 'tween dark and
dawn,
The night shadows spin their
magic.
As mist rises, slumber loses hold
And daylight images become
tragic.
What company we keep when time
unfolds
Amd the encroaching rhythm of
life takes hold.
There is life, 'tis true enough.
As a diamond, at first, quite rough,
But smooth as nurturing hands
mold and shape.
With a special tool each has called
heart,
Our destiny is ours to shape, or tear
apart.
Such strange and troubled images
we see.
They will not keep us from our
dreams.
Only sooth and help to keep at bay
Those long, long hours from dark
to dawn,
That keep night shadows away.

Prince Wellington Young
LOVE

This love extends from the warmth
libido of our souls beyond
eternity
In the company of others, it's
obvious of it's authenticity
Your skin is soft and radiant as
petals of a blossoming rose
Like the natural feeling I receive
when you're near,
So is the absorption when I'm in
your arms
Silky hair, Mesmerizing eyes,
captivating smile and a figure
with harminous
proportions—Only Venus could
imagine
If it had to come to one ending
one's life, I'd give mine to
preserve yours
As Cupid's arrow descends from
his bow was my love for you
To lose you, my mere existence
would cease
When I'm in need or distressed,
you're beside me
Soothing the sensation til it's end
We have a constant concern that
occurs when we're together or
apart
As I faced life's obstacles, you
were encouraging me to go on
Faced before each other
uncovered, our bodies
distinguish their uniqueness
Desire oozes from our pores as
encircled kisses passes your lips
The caressing of your body's
resilience compells my breath to
deepen and skin to vibrate
As bodies merging our thoughts
become one
Cries of ecstasy are released
from within
Lying in each others arms, our
faces reflecting total
gratification
To bring this emotion alive
surpasses any gift one could give
to another
You're my sweetheart, My lover

Gary Wm Coatoam
THE UNFINISHED POEM

Peaceful in quiet solitude,
by myself but not alone.
Your memory ever present,
in my heart, forever a home.

Cast upon a quiet sea
the gentle stillness deafens.
Heralding glory of the love
which fades but never lessens.

Tis true that love is bittersweet,
an enduring, burdening test.

But with this love of centuries
my soul has found true rest.

To never have loved, to have
avoided the sad, sweet sorrow,
Like living just one day,
with no promise of tomorrow.

The solitary mariner,
nearing the journey's end,
Some sadness felt in leaving the
sea,
still happy to see land's end.

Florence Gall
VOYAGE

Dear ones, as I tend and watch you
everyday,
As a gardener caring for his garden
may,
I will hover around you until you
depart,
Locking all my love in your heart.
Soon you will set sail on the ocean
of life,
Weathering every storm and strife.
I cannot be filled with remorse,
It is not I who will set your course.
You will be gathering memories
along the way.
Store the happy ones to savor when
you have a stormy day.
Faith must be your guiding star,
No matter where you are.
Spirit and courage your compass,
Candor your crew.
All of this will carry you through!

Phil Maclin Jr
THE MYSTERY WHICH IS YOU

In deep dark silent pools of thought
Reflected in the stillness of your
eyes
I find a mystery.

Gazing through windows into
another world
I witness the workings of the
universe
And their expression of
creativity—
Which is You.

Behind subtle walls of inexperience
I sense a thundering rumble and
roar—
The power of life
Pushing inward, moving
outward in all directions.

Writing playfully on the
sketchbook of your mind
I see the child at play
And know the artist is at work
Drawing up plans for future
tomorrows.

But in times of innocence, when
thoughts mean nothing
And only words of love are
spoken,
Your eyes betray the beautiful
person you really are.
For this I am thankful.

And so having seen, I step aside,
And wait patiently for you to
speak . . .

Nova Jones
THE RETURN

Dust.
Dry and parched in my throat
It doesn't matter because
I am home.

Home.
Never believed I again would see
This weathered house so familiar
Or even Mom.

Mom.

Tears streaming down her face

Arms stretched out to me
I am home.

Joan Selby
INTO THE SAME COUNTRY

Following your taillights
up the road & into
your country records,
into your tall, oak-burned
rafters, or holding your guitar,
the red night full
of dust-strung birds & feathers,
only we are strummed to silence
close before the evening falls
and scaled to flame along
dark rivers, moving on
the strings, the sealing wax,
the paper. . .something fallen
like a strange green leaf away
& into the same country.

Mark T Whalen
ALONE

I dedicate this poem to all the friends in the world, without whom the world would be a lonely place.

I sit, I think, I wonder
about my life now and then
things that I never did,
things that should have been.

The cold and dark surround me
draining, leeching me dry.
There seems to be no end
and I begin to cry.

I'm waiting,
waiting for someone to come.
But no one hears me
and once again I'm left
by myself, alone.

Vancil J Henry
AMERICA'S WASTE

The troubles of America, the lack
of time and space,
Are very insignificant compared to
America's Waste.

Tons of food are thrown away each
and every day,
But this is not the tragedy that
leads to my dismay.

More precious than pure gold or
gems, we throw away like trash,
It's now an epidemic and is
spreading like a rash.

America's Waste is abortion, it's
sad for me to say,
That over a million babies are
butchered and thrown away.

Like a tragic accident, the scars
that never heal,
The life of the unborn baby that
will never reappear.

It's not the innocent baby's fault,
he'll never see the light,
The sin of inconvenience is the
reason for his plight.

Mary, the mother of Jesus, was
pregnant and unwed,
Only she knew God had sent him
to suffer and die in our stead.

The crowds knew not of the
unborn's worth, that from sin
he'd set us free,
All they could see was a pregnant
teen and a baby that shouldn't
be.

Where would we have spent
eternity without this babe of
Mary's?
What if they had aborted that
child, our Savior that she
carried?

For pregnant girls around the
world there is another option,
Thousands of young couples want
their babies for adoption.

So when you see someone
with-child, or tiny newborn
babies,
Praise God for that child has
survived the holocaust of the
eighties.

Oh please speak out America, this
crisis must be faced,
We must do something now, today,
to stop America's Waste.

Todd Morgan Kelley
THE NEAR SPRING

Springtime nearing
When all that has withered
rejuvenates with life
The same can be said of a society
that congregates.
While in the winter months—
cold desolation stifles growth
In the warmth of the new season
romance generates.

A single bikini
Distant and cast alone against the
surf
Marking the beginning of
transcients in bloom.
Silhouettes of skin scorched by the
sun
People and so many people there's
not enough room.

Sunshine burning
Beating down upon basking bodies
I can smell the scent that's in the
air.
With all those frames of flowering
fertility
I'm crazed and bewildered it just
isn't fair!

Summertime keep coming
This time I know I'll be ready for
you
No way will I miss out upon your
succulent pleasures.
I have learned in the past of hope
and aspiration
I have met you before and I know
of your treasures.

Linnea S Peacock
SLOW DANCIN'

Cheek traces chin until lips
have forgotten their previous
purpose.

The outer music fades; we
compose.

We are
Baritone: rich and round
kissed on the higher edge by
Alto: whole and clear.
We are
unmindful of rhythm—
percussion being too harsh for our
tune—
extremes of balance lend
momentum.

A singular, Platonic soul
buoyed by muted colors and
unborn cantatas.

Casually precise
Carelessly infinite

A singular, Platonic soul—
born of two lesser souls
who conspired to fly
at the slightest touch
of swaying bodies.

Francis Anthony Targowski
IN THE SUNSHINE OF PEACE

Dedicated to My Wife, Kathleen, With No Ending.

In the sunshine of peace a calm
breeze
Echo's enchanting fragrances
everywhere
Creating a heavenly spell that will
please
The saddest of emotions and make
them disappear
In the warmth of the burning sun
Where serenity is born
And its possession is in the reach
of everyone
With each and every new dawn
Come and experience the thrill of
peace
It's a whole new world for your
senses to touch
Beyond joy that somehow seems to
increase
With each new breath you believe
so much
That you would swear it's all a
dream
But it's all very real where love
rules supreme
And wishes of good will mellow
and flourish
In the sunshine of peace for
everyone to cherish.

Robert L King (Hopsing)
SHE'S THE PRINCESS OF MY DREAM

I would like to dedicate this poem to the Princess of my dream Miss Debbra Arnold.

She has to be an angel sent down
from heaven
On a scale of one to ten she's an
eleven
I look at her and see that she is
perfect
From her head down to her feet
She's an angel, a Goddess, or
Queen
Yes she's the Princess of my dream
If flowers had eyes they would be
jealous
Because they could see she's the
best
She's brighter than a shining star
She would never hang out in a bar
She always seems to steal the scene
Yes she's the Princess of my dream
She's more beautiful than all the
trees
She's sweeter than the honey of
any bees
She's softer than a winters snow
The sun shines on her and makes
her glow
She's the greatest lady I've ever seen
Yes she's the Princess of my dream
She's really gorgeous and a little
shy
When I look at her it makes me high
With diamond eyes and golden hair
Miss Universe you best beware
She'll take your place and make
you scream
Because she's the Princess of my
dream
Yes she's the Princess of my dream

Joan Lancaster Winings
THE CLOTHESBASKET CLOWN

The clothesbasket clown is a ball
of fluff
Who entertains us by her antics
and stuff.
She wiggles and worms herself
inside
Only to discover there is no place
to hide
In this molded basket so full of toys,
Intriguing things of untold joys.
They bounce and squeak as she
attacks
Rolling from tummy, to side, and
then to her back.
A mischievous kitten you promptly
say
Is the only animal who would act
that way.
But guess again, much bigger,
more fluffy,
Her name is "Liz", my dare-devil
puppy.

Mikael Wayne
FIRST & LAST & ALWAYS

To my Grandfather who passed away into the arms of the Lord this past April. He left us a lot and he hasn't stopped yet. Because this is a first for me, I believe it's also a victory for my Grandfather.

First and last and always (I will be
yours)
First and last and always (I will be
yours)
First and last and always (I will be
yours forever)

Night falls from the sky
Moonlight reflects upon your face
Ocean blue in your eyes
Heat of the sun in your embrace

The Nightingale sings
A song that reminds me of you
All the joy you bring
You touch me in a way that's new

Sweet September rain
Not unlike your deep emotion
I will remain
Take pleasure in your devotion

Like magic the snow
You give me shelter from the storm
When the cold winds blow
Inside your soul you keep me warm

Jean Feulner
LISTEN . . .

Sometimes,
the only way to find out
what a person is thinking
or feeling,
is not to ask,
but to listen,
to their movements . . .

Ms Sandy "Samm" Burleson

Ms Sandy "Samm" Burleson
ANOREXIA . . . THE KILLER

This killer disease has a hold on my
mind, tormenting me no peace
can I find.
Upon awakening I feel helpless and
wild. Each waking moment I like
a scared little child.
I've lost twenty pounds and I'm still
losing fast, I just don't know how
much longer I can last.
Which will go first my heart or my
head, Sometimes I think I'd be
better off dead.
I'm scared to eat, I'm scared to
sleep, my appointment with
death I might too soon keep.
I'm not ready to die I want to live,
There's so much inside that I've
yet to give.
I want to be happy. I don't want to
be sick, ANOREXIA . . . THE
KILLER is hard to kick.
Where did it start when will it end,
for some it's too late they
couldn't shake their killer friend.
This is a battle that I might lose,
but it won't be because I choose.
I am dying day by day, ANOREXIA
. . .THE KILLER is taking me
away.
ANOREXIA . . . THE KILLER . . .
Let go of me, Release my mind
and set me free.

(Shiva) James E Porter
I WAS TRAINED TO DIE

To my mother whom cut the strings

As I sit watching the fight
I think of home with all my might
And remember my mom as she said
Come back alive instead of dead

I think of home and all my friends
And of broken hearts that never
mend
I wish I was there with them all now
Then I look around and I wonder
how

I came to be looking down my
sights
At some one I'm supposed to hate,
with all my might
I don't ever know who he might be
And I'm supposed to shoot him,
cause I'm infantry
Oh please dear God deliver me
from this
If you can't please let my shot miss
For I don't want to kill this man
Even though my Sarg is saying I
can

For in your word it says,"Thou
shalt not kill"
And even though it's hard to live by
your will
I can't bring myself to shoot this
guy
Because of your words I won't even
try

So forgive me Sarg, for I give in
It's your war so you go and win
I'm going home now to the Lord
Jesus Christ
For I've been shot, and have paid
the price

Patricia Frey Blasko
PATCHES OF MEMORIES . . . PIECES OF DREAMS

I wonder where my quilt began
What fingers stitched, what loving
hand
How many sat around the frame
While children played their
old-time game
I wonder about my quilt so old
With tears and joys wrapped in its
folds
Whose gown was this, what tender
bride
Heart swelled with hope and fear
and pride

I wonder where my quilt has been
Pieces gathered from friends and kin
Tiny fingers of a baby boy
Exploring the mystery of a homemade toy
I wonder about my quilt so warm
Its colors faded, its patches worn
A four-year-old with a tear in his eye
Sunday-best shirt all smeared with pie
I wonder about my quilt so old
What manner of stories does it hold
Of two little girls about the same size
The sparkle of Christmas in their eyes
I wonder where my quilt will be
Whose hand will hold it tenderly
Wistfully asking its worn-out seams
"Whose patches of memories and pieces of dreams?"

Luella Bartels

EBB TIDE

From on my pinnacle of grief
When all my world seems gray
When not a ray of hope, I see
To light my lonely way.

The voice that brightened all my days
Has stilled to hear God's call.
Now, I must blunder on ahead
And brace what e'er befall.

From out the turrets of my heart
I search for interests lost.
I never dreamed, when he was gone
I'd have to pay such cost

He was my Rudder and my mast
My anchor and my ballast.
Now I feel laden down with grief.
Encumbered as a galless

My course, once charted by my love
Must run a different path
One strewn with chasms, 'long the way
What now my fate, alas!

He would not wish me cast adrift
With naught to spur me on
H'ast left a counterpart of him
To keep my senses strong.

Son's, his sons, take o'er the wheel
And set my course steadfast
A solace, I have found in them
Now I can raise my mast.

Oh stormy seas, though not full rigged,
I have such stores of treasure
More than my share, as it would seem
More e'en than I can measure.

Gerry Leavy

INSIGHT

Chambers of the mind in mankind, are narrow rather than wide.
Probe them carefully, with caution, find room and gain space
To harbor those reflections that are worthy of shelter inside.

Cling fiercely to reason, as the grape holds fast to the vine.
Lessening the strength of firmly founded beliefs
Renders their truth as ineffectual as a diluted old wine.

As the mind is the storeroom of all it can capture,
Then the heart is its helper; sifting like sand
Feelings of the spirit, from grey grief to bright rapture.

Often lost, stolen, betrayed, then gratefully found,
The heart is an enigma, a traitor, tyrant, or truant.
It cannot be held by mind and will not by reason be bound.

Victor H Morrison Sr

MY FAMILY

To All My Children, Crystal Dawn, Vic Jr, and Especially To Lisa Marie . . . I Love You

---

My family is a family
Full of happiness and love.
For God is our Father above.
My family is ready to help you whenever you need help.
Whether it be a financial problem,
Or in sickness, or in health.
My family loves one another,
It's easy to see.
For Christ is in our hearts.
Because we believe.
My family's name is what I'm proud of.
Mr. Christian, because of our Father above.
My family is a family of all races and creed.
To be in my family, all you have to do is believe.
So no matter where you live, or who you are.
A member of my family isn't very far.

Riley Anglin

LIVING THREADS

There is a building in our community
that weaves a living thread into the cloth of our lives,
This thread is wool and cotton
colored by colors unmatched by manmade dyes.
And there are silk threads the colors of golden
sunsets for those of us with special needs,
The cloth of our lives so interwoven carefully
in rows of living threads like a show field a planter precisely seeds.

The building, it's my church and
it houses the spinning wheel,
from which these living threads are spun.
And yes these living threads are her
members stitching and weaving
striving to do as God would have done,
And the spinning wheel operated by some
unseen force yet we know it spins
for the living threads we see,
could the force that drives the wheel
be love sent from God
received, and passed on, by plain folk like you and me.

Carole Morgan

A TRUE FRIEND

I once saw a man sitting under a tree.
The breeze brushed his face and blew his hair free.

He looked quite content and very relaxed.
Quite taken with life, not one bit detached.

I ambled on over and bid him good day,
A sweet aura of peace surrounding my way.

We sat there in silence for moments on end.
Then the man looked my way and said to me, "Friend,

"The joy in this life comes from giving your all
"And in building foundations, but never a wall."

Having spoken these words, the man went to sleep.
So, I pondered his words and reckoned them deep.

"And, Friend," the man stirred, "Think of life as a lake.
"See, it's teeming with life just for the life's sake.

"Without the lake, all its contents would cease;
"But it gives itself freely, affording them peace.

"Always with living there is a great prize.
"Look past the glitter, neglecting the size.

"True treasures of life can't be held in the hand,
"But are found in the heart, immeasurably grand."

As I reflected on all that he'd said,
Between the lines I suddenly read.

A true friend is one who will pay a great price;
Be it time, space, or all, in self-sacrifice.

James Albert Lukehart

WORDS OF LOVE IN THE NIGHT

I give of myself, unselfishly
With the gentleness of Love,

The night is crowned silver blue
By moonbeams from above,

The harmony of our Love is
Lost tonight as if wounded or
Frightened like a bird in erratic
Flight,

Summer songs whisper through a
Stand of old trees,

Unmarred reflections of splendor
On distant and glimmering Seas,

Love should be like butterflys
Free of any ties
I see the look of Love, tranquil
Liquid pools your eyes,

The world has spoken a spell
Suddenly broken by words of
Love in the night.

Ruby L Wolfe

ETHEREAL FLIGHT

Not to the cerulean blue of the sky would I fly,
But to the remote ends of our own cosmic system!
I want to go to the other side of the mountain—
Not to discover my identity
Or to measure my poetic potential
But for the sheer ecstasy and beauty of it—
For the quickening of my heart,
For the shaking of my soul,
For the controlled excitement of it!
To touch the other side of the world of poetry
Is a challenge that sparkles for me,
That scintillates with splendor for me!
Wings beat with my yearning for it;
Wings beat with my burning for it.
The odyssey toward that world's end
Is part of the joy and the thrill of it
So that when I touch prosaic ground again
I'll know that I have flown back home again!

Alice M Butzine

HE FIGHTS BACK TOOTH FOR TOOTH & NAIL FOR NAIL

I dedicate this poem to "All non-drinking persons who must fight to survive life with an alcoholic spouse."

Out of the dark the lions roared from their depths of tall trees and grass;
Looking for anything to be devoured, be it singularly or by mass.
They knew not their victims domain, be it the land of snow, sunshine, or rain;
For their goal was to tear at the soul and flesh,
spilling out blood and guts, and making a mess.
Both young and old stood in the pride.
The victim stood alone, no one at his side,
No place to run and no place to hide.
Their teeth sunk deeper, the claws got sharper,
as the lions goared on their fallen marker.
Then the victim arose with a sharp and mighty cry!
No longer to be devoured or left alone to die.
He came back with a shout of courage and strong will,
and the pride no longer pulls him down hill.
His anger he displays, his armour he wears,
No longer to be clawed and ripped full of tears.
He flashes back tooth for tooth, and nail for nail;
Now it's his turn to sink into heart, soul, and tail.
The pride stands together, three fold to one;
But the victim still stands, not yet ready to run.
Six hours of harassing were torn at his heart and soul,
yet he's not ready to release his aim and goal.
For what he thinks today, he'll still think tomorrow,
and the pride another victim will have to borrow.
The prides roar has now come to a still,
and the victim escapes their ferocious kill
Tomorrow will bring a new day at dawn;
and with it, the victim of this pride is gone.

Ms Diane Rose Cocurullo
HOPE
A gentle breeze,
Deepest dreams and desires.
Highs, lows all the time.
Eternally sprung hope without end.
A dove flying free,
The glistening gold of the bright morning sky,
A midnight sight of sparkling stars.
Like a rainbow with its many colors of joy,
This feeling shines from deep within my soul.
It's of hope and all that life will bring:
the sorrows, joys and mysteries!

Jacqueline Oakley
SWEET HOME IN HEAVEN
There's a sweet heaven up above
Filled with only love
The streets are made of pure gold.
As in the Bible the words are told.
Sweet home in heaven above
Oh don't you want to go.
Where there is peace and love.
No pain no worry—misery or woe.
Happy smiling faces are there everywhere.
My God walking and talking to his children,
With tender love and care.
Wait for me Jesus, I want to be with you.
In that sweet home in heaven beyond the blue.

Gladys Freshour
IT'S WINTER AGAIN
It's winter again, but where is the snow?
The corn is all cribbed and my calendar says so.
The trees are bare and the robins have gone,
The flowers have died and the days aren't so long.
The lakes are froze over and covered with ice,
The geese have flown south where the weather is nice.
The lacy briefs that left you almost bare,
Have now been changed for long underwear.
The bathing suit is gone from it's hook too,
It's replaced by a suit to ride the Skidoo.
The electric blanket was also put on the bed,
And the clocks set back instead of ahead.
Snow boots and mittens are laid out too,
To take the place of the tennis shoe.
Storm windows and doors were put on the house,
And a trap was set for a roving mouse.
The snow blower was put on the tractor today,
The machinery and tools were all put away.
The potatoes were dug and binned where it's cool,
The TV antenna checked and so was the stool.
You see toys and decorations as Christmas draws near,
And the calendars are out for the coming new year.
Yes, winter is here, and here's how I know,
By the changes I see, not by the snow.

C B Barnes
SHE COMES
She comes like the sun . . . rather, the ray, that is . . . and was, but vibration for sure, the gold, the glow, the aura so pure.

Of thorns and stones and diamonds few, the windows of her soul have cast the hue.

She is there . . . always . . . there in every sense, she is there, yet . . . knowing not . . . and I, . . . I must not.

Another and yet . . . another steals her time . . . but I . . . I cannot, and must not, for time steals from me.

Even I . . . of others sought, to still the passion she has brought.

Even then she begins . . . and ends . . . as though between.

Eternal love is mine to give and give it I will . . .

But love of me cannot be, for hurt would come in age, you see.

So . . . I must not.

She goes . . . divine.

J W Herbert Ross

J W Herbert Ross
MY WONDER DOG BARNEY

I dedicate this poem to my wife Patricia A Ross.
And to a friend Wendy Fields who does so much for
all animals.

I taught my dog a trick or two.
He's taught me something too.
I taught my dog to sit on a ball.
He's taught me to get up when I slip or fall.
I taught my dog to sit and put his paw in my hand.
He's taught me to take a stand.
I taught my dog to sit on my back.
He's taught me love and tact.
I taught my dog to jump through my arms.
He's taught me that love and understanding goes arm in arm.
Who is teaching Who?
Am I teaching him? Or is he teaching me?
Could this be true.

Edna F Day
SOMETIMES I WONDER
I sit alone sometimes and wonder, how this world would be
If Jesus was coming at any moment, would we wait expectantly?
Would we watch the sky in earnest hope and joy beyond compare,
Or would we carry on each day with not a worry or a care?

I often wish that time were here and this world would soon be ore
Then I think of all the things that I was put here for.
To love and care for my husband and my children, oh, so dear,
To help their lives be happy and to help dry any tear.

To help to brighten, with a smile, a weary stranger's day
And to do just anything that would help someone along their way.
To love and honor Mom and Dad,
and Grandma and Grandpa, too.
And to do my best each day to let the love of God shine through.

Yes, sometimes I sit alone and wonder how this world would be,
If Jesus were coming at any moment, just how READY I would be?

E Isabel Ference
BE THANKFUL FOR OUR SENSES
I find many daily pleasures,
in God's given gifts and treasures.

Pause for just a moment, to observe, comprehend, and appreciate our five senses.
Watch the white clouds roll in the blue sky.
While the butterflies, flutter and the birds fly.

Listen to the songs of the birds and the hum of the bees.
Watch and listen to the pines, swaying in the breeze.

And smell the pine scent of those stately trees;
and don't close your eyes to the colorful fall leaves.

Be observing of all sunrises and sunsets,
for they are a sight to behold, and never to forget.

Take time to touch and smell the beautiful flowers;
and feel the beads of rain upon your face, during a shower.

Never forget the rainbow in the sky, for it is like a dream.
Observe the fish wavering to and fro, in the stream.

Indulge in the taste of fruits, berries, and all the eatables,
and always remember to cuddle and stroke, the little creatures we call animals.

May your eyes scan the mountains ever so steep,
and the oceans, ever so deep.

Yes, all of these beautiful gifts and treasures are free,
for God loves us so much, He meant them to be.

So before it is too late, and you are deprived of one or more of your senses.
Always remember; God builds no fences.

Take heed my dear friends, for it is our duty,
to give thanks to God for all of His treasures and gifts of beauty.

Jana M Wagoner
LETTER TO THE WIND
And so I write another letter,
Another letter to the wind
A letter that blows from my hands
And ends up nowhere
The ink on the page fades to nothing
The words are forever lost
Crying with frustration to the heavens

And so I write another letter,
Another letter to the wind
A letter that will blow from my hands
Up into the endless skies
And carried across the ocean
Where it finally finds its resting place
In the arms of the man I love.

Sally Withjack
JUST LIKE THIS
Eleven o'clock in Central Park
Night lights of penthouses,
Against the sky,
Bordering the outskirts in the dark.

Rays of the moon shine down,
Shadows of trees on lanes,
Summer breezes across the mall
Sweetness of life for a crown.

Jason Landrum
THE GRIZZLY BEAR
The sun was burning in the sky,
In the distance I heard a whippoorwill cry.
As I walked silently through the forest,
Across the field was my neighbor's harvest.
I heard a roaring behind me,
It scared me so, I climbed a tree.
Just before I had reached the top,
The loud roaring had completely stopped.
I slowly climbed out of the tree,
To see a grizzly staring at me.
I ran as far as I could,
But not as far as I wished I should.
I ran as fast as I could go,
But the six-foot grizzly slashed a hole.
I was squirming and jumping around,
But when he let go, I was homeward bound.
I got my gun and waited by the door,
Just waiting for that grizzly to come with a roar.
We tied up, going round and round,
I pulled the trigger and shot him down.
I took him to town and made a good sale,
But bear killing was illegal, and I was hauled to jail.
So here I am drinking water and eating bread,
Meeting up with that grizzly is one thing I dread.

Evelyn Stewart
THEO'S BABY
I bought a stuffed toy,
it looks like her

A tiny toy Poodle with snow white fur
I named it her Baby, she never forgets
It's her favorite toy, she loves it the best

She carries it around wherever she goes
I wonder what happened to it's little round nose?
She shakes it and tosses it here and there
She takes it up on her favorite chair

The eyes are missing and also some fur
But it doesn't matter a bit to her
It's been mended and stitched, I sewed up it's head
Please don't Theo, don't pull out the thread

I ought to wash it, it's matted and gray
But I just hate to take it away
I swear she knows just what I think
Cause she just tossed Baby in the kitchen sink

Heather Welton

THE POET

Look at me
I am the poet
A pen and paper
Are my tools

Look at me
I am the dreamer
I dream dreams
And wish for them
To come true

I am the poet
Making up puzzles
Of rhymes and riddles
That people read
And remember

I am the dreamer
I let my imagination
Run wild
But my dreams
Never come true
They fall and break
And out comes a poem

For I am the poet
And my dreams
Are my poems.

Cameron Grant Hanson

THE MIRACULOUS CONCEPTION OF OUR LADY LIBERTY

She came to us from kindred souls who labored 'cross the sea—
Their lives touched those who struggled for Life and Liberty!
They built her with their love and might and gave her to us free—
We took her to our hearts and homes from Sea to Shining Sea!

God placed within her golden crown, Wisdow from Above—
Then in her bosom placed a heart of Sacrificial Love!
He bathed her in a light as bright as Holy Light can be—
Then placed her on a pedestal for all the world to see!

We welcomed her with shouts from Purple Mountains' Majesty
And swore that we'd defend her from the common enemy!
We bent our knees and recognized she came to keep us free—
The Mind and Heart and Spirit of Our Lady of the Sea!

They came from every quarter of this torn and troubled sphere—
Every race, color, creed with the courage to come here!
Children, young and old, downtrodden by the years—
Blessed by her bright beauty—baptized by her tears!

Raised by love and honor through evil times and good—
Defended by her brothers with their consecrated blood!
Conceived in truth and metal, delivered without fee—
The Miraculous Conception of Our Lady Liberty!

They came because she needed to complete her grand design—
Poets, peasants, scientists with Brotherhood in mind!
She flung the door wide open and invited each one in—
Then nurtured them with Wisdom from the poet and the pen!

Praised by sons and daughters of the nations of the earth—
We thank the Lord above for our blessed sister's birth!
Quick'd by the Wind, Commanded by the Mind of Destiny—
The Miraculous Conception of Our Lady of the Sea!

They came to her insistently when hardship came to them—
They purchased LIBERATION— they bought THE RIGHTS OF MEN!
We no longer stand perplexed because WE'RE NOTICED FROM ABOVE!
Miss Liberty has beckoned us to Lord and Life and Love!

She's standing by the portico where men yearn to breathe free—
Her Torch is raised in prophecy of MIGHTY MINISTRY!
Upheld by the God-Head—The Almighty One-in-Three—
The Miraculous Conception of Our Lady Liberty!

James B "Sonny" Taylor

THE HEART

Mr. John Ed Carpenter, this poem is dedicated to you. For a heart like yours, I have found very few

---

For out of the heart will become what you are
It leaves a blessing, a memory, or a scar
While you are dwelling here from a child to a man
You should live humble, honorable, and as fair as you can

It doesn't matter if you were left a large or small start
You'll always be judged by what comes out of your heart
Some may think they are fooling people while dwelling here
With smooth pleasing words that they want to hear

As sure as the sky is beautiful above
Only out of your heart can come mercy and love
A friend with a heart as strong as a stone
Is one that no matter what happens you can count on

There's not many hearts that reach out as far as they can
They are a rare species and few in this land
Those who reach out with this special mercy and love
Is guided by a special strength sent from above

All will like you when your up and not down
But that is not where true friendship is found
Most just like you, they only look out for self and their kin
There is a special heart that will stick with you to the end

And if while dwelling here you find one or two
That will never let you down or turn their back on you
Consider yourself lucky, a fortunate man
For you are probably the most popular man in the land.

Carol Williams

TAPS

Melancholy sounds.
Mournful sounds! Weeping.
My heart's like a lump of lead,
and his bugle is under the bed.

The dirt thuds on the metal,
and down drops a solitary petal.
It flutters, and hurries to catch up to tears
that already have fallen to the clay.

Melodious sounds.
Joyful sounds! Singing.
My heart hurts at the silence . . .
of the bugle that's under the bed.

Her song slaps at my sadness,
as it rises, —a soprano child-gladness.
It falters, then hastens to grab at the gloom
that already has damaged my day.

Incongruous sounds.
Living sounds! Laughter.
That child's tune, a ray of sun.
But John's bugle has no more songs . . . none.

Melancholy sounds.
Mournful sounds! Weeping.
My heart's like a lump of lead,
AND HIS BUGLE IS UNDER THE BED.

Chris Adkins

I HAD TO SAY GOOD-BY

They say love is a splendid thing
and well, I know it's true
If I had to make a choice
I'd choose to spend my time with you.
Your beautiful hair,
Your lovely eyes,
Your sensuous lips,
Make it hard to say "Good-by."
If never I love
If never I kiss
Holding you in my arms
I always will miss.
Gone are the days
When I called you mine
and close side by side
we did abide.
Now the stories ended
Our poem ended with no rhyme
I walk off alone
and inside I cry.
Now you have another
and me, I'll get by
but I'll always regret the day
I had to say "Good-by."

Martha Sue Landrum

FILLED WITH THE SPIRIT

One night as I knelt praying
Beside my bed,
Fire rained down from heaven
Upon my head-
Now I'm filled with the Spirit
Washed in His blood,
Now I know the glo' of
My Savior's Love.
Filled with The Spirit
Washed in His blood,
Filled with the Spirit
Wrapped in His Love,
Now I know Jesus
From up Above
I'm walking in the Spirit
Aglow in his Love

Joyce L Daugherty

SCHOOL IS COOL

This Poem is dedicated to my son, Howard

It seems you never listen to what I have to say.
The only time you're satisfied is when you have your way.
The chances I have given you meant nothing now I see,
As you don't like to take advice from the school or me.

These years of school you take for granted
Should mean so much to you
And will give the knowledge that you'll need
To help you your whole life thru.

When all your friends are graduating and really feeling great
What then will you be doing? What will be your fate?
Now is the time to decide just what you will do.
Don't wait too late, the time has come, now it's up to you.

I wonder later on in life, just how you will live,
When as of yet you've never learned how of yourself to give.
You're growing older every day and soon a man you'll be
Life will then pass quickly, "Oh, God" why can't you see.

I know that you can do all that I've asked of you.
But do it for yourself, not because I asked you to.
And when you take that final step deciding what to do
Just remember that I love you and I'll be taking that step too.

All I've ever wanted for you was nothing but the best,
So please think it over carefully, don't take it all in jest.
As it's your future now that you are laying on the line,
Will you complete your schooling, where will you spend your time?

Jo Ellen Crum

HEART OF CLAY

In your hands I place,
a heart of moist clay.

It is yours to mold and shape,
as you may.

It is a heart that knows of
fear, loneliness and pain.
Yes, it certainly knows how to
break.
It bares love.
But must be brought awake.

For it is a troubled heart.
That cannot wait.
Hear the lonely cry for love.
Even in it's tender age.

The cries are louder.
Stronger is the pain.
So shape it quickly.
Before it turns hard.
And only the cold remains.

Karen Buak

LAY DOWN YOUR GUNS

Lay down your guns my sons,
my sons.
Lay down your guns and pray;
Pray for peace here and above.
Pray for a better day.
Pray for love and guidence.
Pray to know the way.

Lay down your guns my sons,
my sons.
Lay down your guns and pray;
Pray for your enimies.
Pray for your friends.
Pray to know what to say.

Lay down your guns my sons,
my sons.
Lay down your guns and pray;
Pray ther your sons won't
have to fight.
Pray that they know what
is right.
Pray their not taken away.

So lay down your guns my
sons, my sons.
Lay down your guns and pray.

Holly B Hissong

SONNET

For Tobin

Spring came and brought the soft
rebirth of love
To youthful hearts throughout the
countryside.
O sweet emotion like to that above
O sweet feeling which cannot be
denied.
The springtime came and thus her
heart was glad
And filled with love and other
gentle thought
For how in spring could one like
she be sad
Youth hers and so much love still
to be wrought.
Her heart was full and her love
overflowed
Many were those upon whom her
heart thought
Many were those in whom her love
was sowed.
Yet soon all such to her will be for
naught.
The years creep in even upon the
young
Old age like winter comes where
love has sung.

Stan Coy

BERL PHIPPS

Berl Phipps was a fisherman
On pier pilings he sat

Some say he was looney
But his heart was like a bass
His brain like a clam

And he caught a few
As they passed by.

Pamela Jean Brothen

LADIES OF THE EVENING

The lady who walks the night
looking for the last drop
to feed her master:
Searching the night
under the full moon
for the life giving:
She supports this man
who will use her
at his will.
If she no longer succeeds
her duty, her nightly deed.
She will be the masters meal.

Kim Troutt

THE MEMORY

The days ran by and turned into
Months and
Years
Before we even knew they'd passed.
Pictured in my mind are the
Laughter and
Tears
Joys and
Sorrows
That our life together gave back to
us
They make me
Happy, make me
Sad
A cherished memory will never
fade
And the memory of
Us
Will remain
For
Always
You will be with me in my heart
And
Forever
Will I hold you as close as
The memory of
Our last dance in the snow.

Bettie V Campbell

LOVE ETERNAL

God has promised us a world
without pain;
A haven of rest, where God doth
reign;
Where streets are paved with
glittering gold;
And the soul of man walks with
God, I've been told.

There is peace and contentment
and joy each day;
A time of comfort;
As we greet each other on life's
eternal highway.

So I look forward to crossing the
Bar;
Where the skies are blue and
sparkling with stars.

My life on earth-no more to be;
But life with our Father will begin
to Eternity.

Teddy Lamey

GENTLE FRIEND . . .

You are, in your gentle way,
a mirror of my soul.
You are the bestower of peace;
the calmer of troubled spirits;
the deliverer of tender
compassion.
You are the just confidant . . .
listening and passing no
judgement,
silently forgiving,
understanding, comforting,
You are the essence of goodness;
the embodiment of the concept
of love.
You are gentleness; you are
kindness.
You are the warmth of home,
the security of family.
It is with you that I am at peace.
It is with you that my soul seeks
comfort.
It is with you that joy begins
and the true meaning of caring
is possible.
In your gentle way,
you have found a home in my
heart.
In your gentle way,
you have give my life
peace . . . and love . . . and joy.
In your gentle way,
you have become my friend.

Rosa Lee Folland

A VISIT FROM A STRANGER

On a quiet Christmas eve night
A knock at the door brought a
sudden fright
As I opened the door the light was
faint
I saw in the doorway "oh a saint"
All dressed in a robe so white
I saw standing there in the light
A beautiful sight to behold
For this was the Lord so I've been
told
And as He held out to me his hand
I saw the kind face of this gentle
man
For a kind person you see
Had come to my house to visit with
me.

Jack G Green

MY WIFE'S BEST FRIEND

I doubt if I'll ever really open my
eyes, I'm filled with blind luck
you see
And everything good that can
happen to a man, has already
happened to me

I live with God in a land that's free,
and owned many a good horse
in my life
But the height of joy, for this
cowboy, was in picking a friend
for a wife

Our love runs so deep, it might fail
to show, out from under our
heavy load
And as I choose to ride the rocky
trails, she helps me smooth out
the road

She's the one I ride the river with,
as we ford life's swollen stream
Sometimes I get soaked, but when
she's around, I'm never as wet as
I seem

I think of the years we've stood side
by side, enjoying the bad with
the good
When I wanted to lope, she'd
loosen up my rope, as I always
knew she would

Now as we both approach the final
page, of the book we call our life
You can bet no cowboy ever lived,
that had such a wonderful wife

In case we don't leave this world as
one, when we face our
judgement day
I hope she'll find time to
remember, what I am about to
say——

If God should call on me to leave
first, I'd hope you wouldn't cry
But I'd overlook a wee small tear,
if something was in your eye

Just remember our years together
"Dear", the happy and the sad
And as you look back I think you'll
agree, that even the worst wasn't
bad

Don't hurry yourself, the old hoss'
and I, will be waiting on you to
arrive
And we won't hold it again' you
none, 'cause you're still down
here alive

But if it should happen the other
way round, I promise you I won't
cry
If God should call, on you to leave
first——————
It's simple,—I'd just die

Brenda Bagood

WE ARE BUT TWO SPECIES IN THIS UNIVERSE

Dedicated to "My Love of My Life",
James I. Harman, who
inspired this poem. This comes
from my heart to be forever
engraved within our memories.
Aloha Auia Oe! Palenaka

We are but two specks in this
universe
which unknown to either of us
were destined to find each
other . . .

Though the long search appeared
hopeless
the time seemed endless
this fated meeting not by
chance . . .

For we found each other through
loneliness
from deep within ourselves a
wariness
frustrated by our present
existence . . .

Forced to be separated by our
circumstances
fate compelled us to seek
compassion
faced with the reality of our
vulnerability . . .

Temporarily sacrificing to touch
physically
thus signifying our hopes and
dreams mentally
to be together as "one"
someday in the future.

Carolyn C Dukes

AMERICAN DREAMS

America is a nation of dreamers
Who have given their lives boldly
For their hopes of peace and
success
And the wondrous visions they
could see.

Dreams have always spurred action
In the past, as well as today,
They push us ever forward
Hoping to find that better way.

There have been some great
dreams
And some small dreams, but all in
all,

Each dream in its own way
Has aided America to stand tall.

We must keep our dreams alive
No matter what the personal cost,
For if our dreams should suddenly
run dry
Our America would surely be lost.

America is our great heritage
Our forefather's past, our
children's future,
And we must for the sake of
America
Help our dreams to endure.

Americans, look to your God
He, the maker of dreams, is alive
And He, through our faith and
dreams,
Will help America to survive.

Steven Calvin Cummings

BEGINNING OF A DREAM

As the daylight starts to fall
The darkness slowly begins to call
The Earth is filled with a touch of
light
And your eyes are filled with a
glimpse of sight
You feel a cool breeze begin to
blow around
And hear the crickets softly
beginning to sound
You watch the wind blow thru the
meadows
As the Moon is outlining with its
shadows
You then look deep into a star
Wondering if you'll travel afar
As you turn from the window and
draw the shade
Remembering the images that you
made
You then crawl into your bed to
sleep
Never forgetting the visions you
keep
As the night is shortly ending
Soon the Moon will be decending
As the dawn begins to break
Soon will be the time to awake
Then to dream you'll have to wait
Until the Moon again escapes

Patricia Laraway

GOD IS MY ARTIST

I think that God is an artist
With a paint brush in his hand
And the work that He displays
Is seen on this great land.
He paints from dawn to dusk
Mountain peak to ocean floor
And when we think we've seen the
best
He shows us much, much more.
The tiniest of flowers
The tallest of the trees

The sunrise and the sunset,
The rivers and the streams.
The children playing happily
In schools and backyards
Can never quite be pictured
On store bought greeting cards.
So when my day is done and
through,
And I close my eyes to sleep
My dreams are very beautiful
With the pictures that I keep.

Gertrude Lynd Hobbs

KANSAS 125TH BIRTHDAY

One Hundred-twenty five years ago
Kansas as a statehood began to
grow.
Across Kansas roamed numerous
Buffalo
Followed years later by Wagons
Ho.
"Ad Astra per Aspera" is our slogan
great
"To the stars through difficulty" it
will rate.
The state tree is the Cottonwood
It stands erect as all trees should.
The state bird is the Meadowlark
And Wilson Lake is a Kansas
Park—
Of beauty and scenery Kansas will
boast
Any many tourists it will host.
Our state song is "Home on the
Range"
And a good co-operative is the
Farmers Grange.
Our region is known as the
territorial "Great Plains."
Where the cow herd on grassland
so nobly reigns.
Kansas people are strong and
industrious
They made the state great and also
illustrious.
The cattle town in the Sixties was
known as Abilene
Where "Wild Bill" Hickok was
frequently seen.
The state insect designated as The
Honey Bee
Laboriously works for you and me.
Come to Kansas in the U.S.A.
Geographically located, it is
midway.

Ruthann Beninsky

GOLDEN BAND

This poem is dedicated to my wonderful husband Joe

This Golden band is growing old
Through the years it shed many
tears.
This golden band holds many
memories
Through the years it lead happiness
And when I'm dead, it will still be
worn.
This golden band has the hand of
many fears but, love
Knew the years would last.
Love knows best, over and over
love shows and,
tells all.
This golden band is my wedding
band.

Derek W Werner

PORTABLE BATHTUB

I know a girl
She acts like a squirrel
Or more like she acts like a nut
For one time she tried
To make a good hide
So she hid in a rubber made hut.
This gave her a thought
What if she bought
A big rubber made bag
Then tied up some hoses
Like those that water the roses
And threw in a duckie and rag.

Margaret P Lafferty

THE EMERALD ISLE

Although I have never seen
The beauty of your land;
My heart longs to come
To you and roam among
Your fields of green.
The bond is great and
The wish is strong.
I feel your beauty,
Although we are miles apart.
When the wind is soft
And the leaves gently
Rustle in the trees,
I hear you call to me,
Come, Come and roam
Among my hills with me.

Miss Ruth E Rehr

CHRISTMAS MUSIC

As universal as the radiant star
Which shone o'er Jesus centuries
ago—
Beloved Christmas music heard
afar
Again to man's tired soul doth
bring a glow!

As slow as feathery flakes of snow
The first faint notes of this great
symphony—
But soon, from largo moves to
quick allegro
Until the world is bathed in holy
harmony!

Oh, hark! The sweet sound of
silvery bells,
Like children's laughter rises to
crescendo—
And low the lilting lullaby which
tells
Of Bethlehem in tones of golden
cello!

For you, the beauty of each
melodic measure,
The ecstasy, and ringing choral
treasure!

Blanche L Tighe

HAPPY BIRTHDAY, DARLING

Happy Birthday, Darling,
And the best of luck to you!
May all your prayers be answered
And all your dreams come true.
Your Birthday means much more
to me
Than I can ever say,
And always in my heart it is
A most eventful day
Because you are the one I love,
And you will ever be
The only one in all my thoughts
And every memory.
And so I do sincerely hope
The year ahead will bring
A paradise of pleasure
And the best of everything!

Robin L Wagner

STRANGER BY MY SIDE

To Paul McCartney, with love and thanks for all the happiness he gave me

---

With his charming ways and baby
face,
He filled in my life an empty space
When my world comes crashing
down —
everything wrong,
He makes it right with every song
Each one is a precious treasure,
Which bring me endless pleasure
He gives me the courage to "let it
be",
He gives me the strength to just be
me
When I need someone to
understand,
I listen to his words and feel as if
he's near holding my hand
Every note, every melody will live
on
forever more,
For young and old to cherish and
adore
He may never know my name,
But the fondness I feel will always
be the same
He inspires my every dream,
However impossible they may
seem
In my heart he will stay,
Guiding me as I live each day
My love will never fade for Paul, the
Stranger by my side,
A part of me I could never hide

Christine Walters

GOOD-BYE

She turned and left me all alone
She didn't seem to care
That my whole life had been just
her's
From the moment she was there.
I'd taken care of her by day
And guarded her by night
When she was lonely I was there
And for her I would even fight!
In spite of this she's gone away
To start a whole new life.
Today she started Kindergarden!
Someday she'll be a wife!

Arthur Fischer

THE GIFT

A most precious gift is life,
experience all its joys and sorrows,
for each will make you all the wiser.
Be not foolish by merely standing
off
and gazing in, or your future will be
full of endless empty tomorrows.
Be careful to remember that life is
fragile,
and once broken; can never be
replaced.
Taste both the sweetness and
bitterness of life.
Know and understand that your
existance is brief.
So seek out and enjoy,
for a most precious gift is life!

Frank E Burkhart

THE HUMAN CYCLE

Somewhere on earth a child is
born,
as the human cycle starts.
Two people create a newborn life,
from the love within their hearts.

The news is spread to all
concerned,
with excitement and great joy.
This married couple are very
proud,
they have a baby boy.

While somewhere else a child is
born,
with emotions in a whirl.
But this time nature plans it so,

this baby is a girl.

The years from childhood to adult,
pass quickly by, it seems.
So parents sit and reminisce,
how their child fullfilled their
dreams.

It seems that somehow destiny,
will make these two lives meet.
Whether they are miles apart,
or just across the street.

These strangers meet and fall in
love,
Oh, the joy within their hearts.
They marry and produce their
child,
as a new HUMAN CYCLE starts.

Kaye Varnell
MATURITY
Maturity is not an age
It is a little feeling
Knowing that childish games
Are really self defeating!

Fran Armstrong
A GIFT FOR ALL MANKIND

To Marie for your confidence; to Mom & Dad for always being there; To Susan Jacobs for your inspiration and opening my eyes

---

A day without light, music without
sound
That dark, dead world to which
you are bound
The brightest sunshine to light
your day
Oh dear God, is there no way?
The sound of voices filled with song
To be without is such a great wrong
The child has tears, but does not
cry
I see your pain, but I know not why
If I could but give you for just one
day
To see; to sing; to hear children
play
If you could possibly understand
Maybe then, you would take my
hand
I am your eyes and I am your ears
I will cry and feel your pain when
you have tears
May all mankind share their heart
That you may feel loved and be a
part
Let us all join hands and show we
care
Don't be the last, but the first to
dare

Thomas Krise
I WATCHED THE CLOUDS TODAY
I watched the clouds today,
As they swirled along their way.
Shadowing the earth as they come
and go,
Simply passing, in a never ending
flow.
Billowing spirals of infinite shapes,
Silently, thankfully, providing an
escape.

Josephine Thomas
OUR LAND OUR HOME
Over our fields and land
We call our home,
and love so well.
We'll stroll an roam,
we'll touch the wind.
Chase the rain today,
Over our hills and dells.
To our woods we'll go
that we love so.
Down by our creek
we'll touch the wind.
Chase the rain today

There we'll sit and rest,
Talk about our land
we love so much.
While we talk and rest
We'll touch the wind.
Chase the rain today

Marg Tollefson

Marg Tollefson
BLANK PAGES
Blank sheet of paper
evil eye on me
waits for a paradox,
polarity.
I struggle for a metaphor,
for images;
full circle is my death—
my Nemesis.
Why, when planet earth is thick
with words,
dense forests,
rushing streams,
stars at night;
bugs and beasts, a single
wind-blown rose;
why do I cringe—show
stress—give up in pain
because a sheet is blank
but for my name?

Dorothy Alta Jordan
THOUGHTS WHILE VIEWING THE MONUMENT
Silently, I viewed the likeness of
the man—
Abe Lincoln with the weight of one
great nation resting
On his frame. His countenance of
sorrow furrowed
With the problems greater than
himself. Intent
On preservation of a government
that would not
Perish from the earth—the legacy
that stated
"Of the people, for the people, by
the people"
Of his native land, for he was
dedicated
To the common good, exemplifying
right
With many noble deeds for our
reflection, thus
To be remembered, emulated by
each one.
He is the symbol of the justice for
us all.

Lois Jennison Tribble
FAMILY TREE
"I'm tired today," he muttered,
slouching in the easy chair,
and gazed through dirty glass at
Grandpa's oak.
It stood, the sole surviving tree of
sixty-seven more
he'd planted as a mark for every
year.

"I must be nuts to stay here. All
that's left here for me now
is just this house, the grave, and
that damn tree."
Feet shuffling through the trash
he'd strewn across the grimy
floor,
he opened up the fridge to get a
beer.

"It's cold in here," he shivered,
glancing at the sleeping coals,
"and me with all my dry wood
nearly gone."
He peered out at the sentry oak
beside the old man's grave,
the dead man's dreams reflected
like a mirror.

"Six hundred forty acres of the best
damn land around,"
at least that's what my grandpa
used to say.
But ever since the hanging folks
have changed "The Oaks" proud
name,
and now they usually call it
"Jacob's Tears."

The wind's wail did not stop him
as he grabbed the rusty saw,
and trudged through crunching
snow across the yard.
The dead limb loomed above him
as he made the chain saw whine.
"I guess I'll have to get it down from
here."

He leaned into the shadow that the
oak splashed on the grave.
Without another thought, he cut it
down.

Evelyn Charity Ellis
HOW FAR ON LOVE
If love was what powered this
world—
That undying love as from God
above,
Would your life be healthy and
happy?
Just how far could you get on love?

If love was what heated our homes
When winter blew her chilly
breath,
Would you live warmly til
springtime,
Or, would you soon freeze to
death?

If love was our source of electricity
And through it we received our
light,
Would you have bright sunlit days,
Or the darkness of a moonless
night?

If our food and our drink were
supplied by love
And with love we all had plenty,
Would your cupboards and
freezers be full,
Or, would you starve for lack of
any?

If love was our shelter in a storm—
If it were all the protection we
could get,
Would you be safe from the cold,
cold rains,
Or, would you be freezing and wet?

If love was our oil and our gasoline
And with it we could fuel a car,
Would you be able to travel this
world,
Or, would you not get very far?

If love was what powered this
world—
That undying love is from God
above,
Would your life be healthy and
happy?
Just how far could you get on love?

Francis P McNulty
THE NEWS
I recreated the world last night
For a dream no-one will ever see;
Shattered in a burst of morning
light
Then scattered in the wake of
reality;

Rolling thru the morning news
And taking up the little screen,
Blonde, blue eyed talking head
With a smile so squeaky clean
I hardly noticed a word she said;

Beyond the honey glaze
Of the world's latest heartache
That keeps the ratings jamming
For the advertisers at stake
Are endeared to good war and
famine;

To create the stories
That will engross a nation
To huddle around a TV set
Looking for intellectual
conversation
Until nothing's left;

But the obscurity
Of an overwrought topic
With the problem still there,
Just bumped aside by another
subject
To keep the fresh air.

Daniel James Burt
A TIME

For my Mother, who encourged my writing; and for all the lost love in this life; peace and love are commandments.

There comes a time
in each man's life
when decisions hard are made.

There comes a time
in each man's life
when that man is afraid.

A space in time
of aimless kind
a searching of our own.

A touching care
a searching stare
a feeling all have known.

There comes a time
for each and all
to wonder at the sky.

There comes a time
when love we find
and softly kiss good-bye.

William Michael O'Donnell
TOMORROW

To My Loving Wife Linda and children William Michael Jr., Lynn Markay, Kathleen & James Cornelius.

The day that will never be,
not for you nor not for me.

Yesterday is gone, gone so far away
AH! But Today!! Today, is here to stay.
OH! how I yearn for just one tomorrow
and the dreams I had with you,
would surely all come true,
If I had that one Tomorrow.

Kathleen Busch
ALWAYS
I'm watching you across from me
Sleeping in the easy chair
These quiet times I thank God
For helping me keep you there.

I try my best to satisfy
Because I love being here
I'll fill our love with hopefulness
To ever keep you near!

I'll be the only one you'll want
Sitting here watching you nap
You'll wake and say you're sorry
But I love you just like that.

Whenever you feel tempted
Remember me here at home
You know another just won't do
I'm sure you'll never roam.

To be your friend forever
Would always lift my heart
I really need you near me
I don't want us to part.

Sally C Folsom
A MEMORY IN HIS EYES
In someone's mind today I am just a memory of what I used to be,
He doesn't see me as I am only as he wants to see me.
In his eyes I am the memories of the girl he won't let go,
A memory that's good and true—a memory that died so long ago.
At our class reunion he saw me with memories in his eyes,
But the price I payed for being there was much too high,
It took something away from both of us to watch his memories die.
In reality he could not accept the woman I'd become,
And so to him I'll remain the memory of a girl who'll never change,
A memory of what I used to be—a memory in his eyes.

Kasha Brown
FOR A GOOD LIFE
It's a hard thing to accept
That you sometimes accept
A lot less than you deserve

When it's a gift of time given
With all that you've given
There's no time to lose your nerve

Just always demand the very best
If you really want all life's best
The world is what you create

If you strive for a good life
You'll surely find a happier life
The rewards will truly be great

Kimberly Conroy
AN ECHOING SOUND

This poem is dedicated to Frank and Lorrie, and all my other friends who, without their help, I wouldn't have made it here. Also thank you to all the veterans who fought for us.

An echoing sound
Still heard in your mind
Yelling to block it out
They say it'll fade but . . . you doubt.

The shadows close in upon you,
As perhaps, maybe on cue,
The screaming tear of the peace,
You run, hoping to hide; the noise never does cease.

The bombs busting near you.
You turn and look.
Where is your friend, your buddy?
God, no! Not another you took.

You search and finally find,
Although you wish you hadn't.
You swear; you can't cry at this time,
Why did our country get involved, why mine?

Hearing the roar of planes you look up.
Are they ours or theirs?
You know, as a thin layer pours out & covers you.
Breathe, do you dare?

You cough and choke,
As perhaps breathing the last.
There is no future, there is no past,
Just this hell hole, where you were cast.

Having no choice,
Just ordered here and there.
Perhaps Canada was a choice,
Is there another place, where?

Years later, you're here now.
Still seeing your friend,
In your mind,
The place you can not mend.

Envisioned in your mind,
He's decorated with blood.
There is no honor to find,
Only deaths of people, flowing as floods.

Hear the "silence of the dead"
Be sure the greedy have been fed,
Or they'll come and hunt you again,
And wonder "where've you been".

Slowly travelling the road to insanity
As the figures clutch at your edge.
Don't let it show, the two faces you hide.
Never show the dark side.

Time has passed but the memories remain.
You search for yourself.
And the enemy slowly passes by.
Can you ever again look at the sky.

An echoing sound,
Still heard in your mind.
Yelling to block it out,
They say it'll fade but . . . you doubt.

Nancy J Widder
THE ROSE OF LOVE
The Rose of Love
Sometimes has thorns.
(But who knows how many hearts they've torn?)

It can and will sprout buds,
Giving new life.
(How can you be sure they will survive?)

Tiny roses, waiting to open.
They give new Life, new Love, new Hope.
(What if they bring pain and sorrow?)

Be careful—the new Roses of your love may
sprout thorns also.
(Why must there be so much fear?)

Alas, they can be removed.
But if you damage the stem, all is lost.
(When can this fear of injury subside?)

Your Rose will die and grow anew.
But the dreaded Thorns may come with it, too.

Arthur M Bosselman Jr
GREAT AMERICAN POETRY
Early morn, when you rise and shine,
Don't you love a melodic line?
The rising sun welcomes a great new day,
Giving you light to guide your way.
By mid-morn, when you take your break,
Doesn't poetry take you out to a lake?
Especially all those impressionistic rhymes,
It makes you think of those marvelous times.
During your lunch, with all your friends around,
Isn't it wonderful if a new verse is found?
It makes your friendships seem extra strong,
As everyone feels like they sincerely belong.
In the afternoon sun, we see a beautiful rose,
Wouldn't this make everyone think of prose?
This gorgeous flower really makes us glow.
Because we all know who made it grow.
At the evening meal, as the day's tales are told,
Isn't it picturesque to see them unfold?
It is like the visual psalms that we read,
Or the essence of the blessings we said.
When our day is done and it's time for bed,
Wasn't it meaningful the story we read?
And as we peek at the moon silhouetting a tree,
We say thanks for our Great American P-O-E-T-R-Y.

S R Stardevant
THE RAKEMAN
The
rakeman cometh
in the cool
of early morn.
Slow methodical arms
sweep the frost killed
decendents
of summer
into huge piles
underneath
the bare branches.
Fate fleeing
survivors
catch the wind
in their attempt
to escape
the coming pyre
only to find
eternity
in the corner
of the garden
wall.

Mae Stewart
TRY
In a world as fast as today,
The meaningless things that people say,
The cruel unfeeling things they do,
I wonder how I found you.

I don't think you're like the rest,
That's why I'll try to do my best.
Stop racking your brain to figure out why,
I like you, you're different and so am I.
Why can't we just give it a try?

It's not a real gamble, what can we lose.
If the feeling is there the flame will be lit.
If it's not then we'll split.

I'd rather say let's give it a try!
Or, do you want to say Bye-Bye?

Dora Bridges Dixon

Dora Bridges Dixon
EASTER
What a glad and glorious feeling
When I awake on Easter morn.
And remember he is risen,
And gone to prepare a home,
For his children who believe him
And from his path's will never stray,
But we'll know he watches over us
And he hears us when we pray.

Oh the crown they placed upon him
Nor the spear that pierced his side,
Could separate him from his children,
As unto his God he cried.
Oh forgive them for this father,
For they know not what they do,
That is still his sweet prayer for us,
When he intercedes anew.

As we face each new tomorrow,
With its burdens and heavy loads,
Help us Lord to bear them gladly,
As we walk life's stormy road.
And when at last we meet in heaven,
And hear you say my child well done,
Twill be worth it all to listen,
As you say, you are welcome home.

Leslie J Jones
AS I SIT THINKING OF YOU

To my only love, Zane Mead.

As I sit thinking of you,
The memories come crashing through.
I cannot seem to overcome my fear,
As I shed a lovelorn tear.

I begin to count the things I'll miss,
Those deep hazel eyes and that tender kiss.
There's something I can't explain to my heart,
The sad cold truth that we must part.
Now I must ask a question of you,
Will you miss the love of me too?

Debra G Pope

NO END IN SIGHT

All alone tonight with only the darkness to hold me.
Endless hours of sleeplessness, constantly reminding me.

Unspoken thoughts echo like drums in the night.
No voice of comfort, no end in sight.

All that passes between us, passes with the day.
All those moments that fill my dreams, will never come my way.

All the words we're not saying, conversations never shared.
Avoiding all the suppositions, sidestepping all the stares.

no end in sight.

Beth Anne Brown

MUPPET BABIES LIVE

I went just to see a show.
The Muppet Babies of course you know.
There was Kermit, Fossie and Miss Piggy too.
I don't know which one I like the best, would you?
There was color and music and dancing all night.
My sister was there and thought it was out of sight.
I hope I can go again it was the best.
Because my 4 year old sister won 1st place in the coloring contest.

Lori Olliger

THE GOLF BALL'S COMPLAINT

To Lee, Who fills my life with Happiness and Love

There I was just resting,
Sitting on a tee.
Someone with a long club
Took a swing at me.
I went as far as I could go
So I could get away,
But sure enough he found me
In the rough in which I lay.
Then he took an iron
And he hit me on my side,
So I flew into a sandtrap
Where I thought I could hide.
This cruel kind of punishment
Is more than I can take.
The next time that he hits me,
I'm going in the lake.

Julie A Michener

LONELY DAYS

This poem is dedicated to my loving husband, Dennis and daughter, Jessica

---

Here I am in solitude.
Once again, I sit and while away the endless hours
of lonely days.
I listen, but hear no voices.
I wait, but no one comes or calls.
Like the spent sands who've already slipped
through the hour glass, I am forgotten here.
Hour to hour, day by day.
The ticking clock is the constant music in
this lonely place.
The clock strikes twelve, the fire goes out, and
kitty and I fall fast asleep, once again.

John Bushman

A KISS IS ALL I ASK

Maiden dear with lips so soft,
Why do you hide behind a mask?
With lips so soft and tender
A kiss is all I ask.
Maid with lips so red and sweet,
Why hide behind a mask?
My heart pines for your caress
A kiss is all I ask.
Press your lips to mine
Dear maid, a small caress;
So please remove your mask
Your lips to mine do press.
Sweet tender bliss is mine,
So please remove your mask.
Your lips so tender and divine
A kiss is all I ask.
What sweet joyous bliss,
Please I beg remove your mask.
That rapture deep I might enjoy
A kiss is all I ask.

Dorothy A Gratton

THE COURAGEOUS ASTRONAUT'S

This poem is dedicated in memory of Gladys
my loving mother

My heart stood still on that fateful day.
The year was nineteen eighty-six
The astronauts lined up with joy
For their trip on high
They went in one by one
And the door was closed on them.
Up they went and all could see
Never to return again.

Our dear Saviour knew that day
That they would be with him
He waited with arms outstretched
And said "come unto me"
So we all know that where they are
There is no sorrow there.

Their courageousness was shown
To their families and their friends
They'll be greatly missed by all
And never will we forget.

Laurie Wilking

A HEART IN HIDING

My heart sags low.
Deep inside my chest
it hides.
Hides from feelings
coming close to it,
Love trying to touch it.
Feelings expressed as words
come through my ears
grasping for my heart.
It quivers and cowers
behind the reasoning of my mind.
Once too often
the painful touch of love
has reached it's softness.

Karen M Dodd

WHAT IS BLUE?

Blue is the sound
Of soft music playing
Blue is an egg
That a robin is laying
Blue is beautiful sapphire rings
And silky scarves and pretty things
Summer skies
My eyes
And blueberry pies
A bedspread
And sewing thread
And a sad poem
That is read
Things often said that are not true
Are blue
And a macaw is blue
With other pretty birds at the zoo
Blue is wet paint
And Easter egg dye
And fallen teardrops
When you cry
You can smell blue
In the ocean spray
When you walk on the beach
At the end of the day.

Roger Reynolds

A SHOW OF CANDLES

I pass the lonely camposanto
On the lonely Sevilla Road
It is the night
Of All Souls' Day—November Two.

A viejo, old man, white-haired
Wanders among the graves
Talking to those no longer quick.

There are other lost ones
In other places,
Too deep to be disturbed
By flickering candles.

I try to dissipate the gloom
By looking skyward shouting
Romp-po-po! Romp-po-po!
To clusters of stars,
Brittle as snowflakes.

Then as I leave the graveyard
The moon breaks through the clouds
Dazzling me
With its spiky nimbus.

Mame Hill

CONSUME

With everything that we were together, I dedicate this to my late husband David in the name of Love.

I see the music
I hear the sun
And I smell the warmth on my face
I taste the content
I roll in the growth
And I laugh with all surrounding space
I touch the power
Walk with no One
And I run with every living thing
I hold the air
For it seizes all
And I swell not with sting
I write my letters to Concrete
Forward my mail to Abstract
And I disassemble the alphabet
I dream in color
I enter the exit
And I dry myself off with wet
I forgive the unforgivable
I reveal the unrevealable
And I deceive not the truth
I swallow the whole
I chew only the liquid
And I inhale this bottle of vermouth
I tickle the thoughts
Swim amongst ideas
And I fly like an answer with wings
I search not for senses
I instead clothe myself in them
And I commit suicide laughing at things

Margaret Lucinda Moberg

THE DESERTED PLANT

At once twas forgotten I began to thirst,
When all the flowers were watered I yearned to be first.
In the gardners concern to take care of the others,
He forgot that I too needed to be nurtured.
Further and further to the back that I went,
When all of a sudden to the floor I was sent.
Losing hope of no chance of surviving this life,
I couldn't bloom I was living in strife.
My roots were strong, but without love and care
I wouldn't grow any where.
It was to the trash the gardner would have me go,
When a wee little voice said "No please don't let that one go"
I see a future for this withering plant although it
looks old.
But with tender loving care it shall grow to be strong and
beautiful with a story to be told.
Many days of watering and caring my foundation now
was set,
I now have color and of my past I could not regret.
A bud now forming and yet a little while I shall
blossom as the Rose

Mary E Wiser

80 YEARS OF VALENTINES

To Cyril Wiser—Husband
Daughter—Sylvia Wiser

I had a sweetheart, many many years ago
and almost as many years ago we were wed.
And so 'twas spring, and love was everywhere.
Then came a long and dreamy summer.
A fall laced with golden dreams and drifting leaves.
The cold of winter and lovely white snow fell so soft and white.
Some of the love we had was taken from us then,
and the soft white snow fell on a mound so small
As longer years and summer, fall, and winter came
and snow fell down so soft and white.
The bed clothes carried by angel arms to keep our loved ones warm,
and dreams and valentines not all on the one day.
The love is the same until the longest year and longest love of all my

life lay sleeping—by our first,
and still the snow was drifting
down soft and white to cover
both,
and angel arms are busy.
Covering so nicely white bed
clothes to keep our loves warm.
And hide our broken hearts, till
they can heal a bit.
HAPPY VALENTINE DEAR
HEARTS ALL.

Mary Sinclair

Mary Sinclair
DON'T LET AMERICA DIE

To my loving husband, Jim, my mom, my sister, my grandchildren, my children, Cindy, Jack, Pat and Ken.

I heard a record the other day
About America, and if I may,
I have several things I must say,
Being brought up the American
way.

I'm as proud of America as I can be,
But since World War Two, you'll
agree,
Not many really believe in our
country,
How are we going to keep it free?

Since the war there's only a few,
Who really want to fight, it's true,
And everyday something happens
anew,
Everyone's scared and wondering
too!

Our good leaders shot on sight,
People afraid to go out at night.
Our leaders not doing anything
right,
Someone had better stand and
fight!

We the people will not stand by
And let our leaders lie and lie!
Wake up Americans and really try,
Please, don't let our country die!

America has been here a long time,
Someone has got to draw a line!
This country is too gosh darn fine,
Remember, America is your
country and mine!

The Rev Stephen L James Jr
A CHRISTMAS DREAM
In early times, to us 'twould seem
When God with man conversed,
He often did it with a dream;
A whole scenario rehearsed.
The Christ child's every need, 'tis
said
was flashed to minds of men,
A "guidance system" dream which
led
God's cast through his great plan.

Today, it seems, man lives aloof
From Signs—from bushes
burning,
Has little time to search for truth
Or answers to his yearning.
If he should, by quirk of fate,
With dreams from God be trusted,
I wonder if he would relate—
His words would be accepted.

Would that God a Christmas dream
Could loose on all mankind
Showing how his Son redeems
Though man's so terribly blind.
Make us all once more aware
Of Jesus and his word:
"Love your neighbor"—Show you
care—
This Christmas—praise the Lord!"

Starlene Lipelt
SUMMER MORNING DELIGHT
I awake to hear the bee's a buzzing;
Even the dusting planes are a
coming.

Gentle Delta breezes are a blowing;
My neighbors grass he is a
mowing.

The smell of cut grass is so sweet;
To walk barefoot upon it a
delight to my feet.

The heat is starting to hang in the
air;
Summer's sweet smell is
everywhere.

How wonderful to enjoy
something so free;
To know that it will always be.

Victoria Irene Robertson
FOR YEARS GONE BY

I dedicate this poem to all the marriages of the world. For it is their courage, their strength, and their commitment to values that give us hope for our children. I applaud you.

Over the years the days have grown
shorter,
our eyes rarely meet as before.
Words go unsaid,
kisses forgotten,
yet the test of time strengthens us
more.

We've learned hand in hand,
what it means to be giving;
forgiving,
and living,
as one.
To give and to take,
with a balance of humor;
adding comfort,
as each day is done.

Please tell me you love me while I
am here.
Don't wait 'til the day that I'm gone.
For the Good Lord might take me
during the night,
and alone, you may greet the new
dawn.

For over the years the days have
grown shorter,
and our eyes rarely meet as before.
Words go unsaid and kisses
forgotten;
may the years to come strengthen
us more.

Rose Kathlyn Wallace
ROSE AT THE WINDOW

Dedicated to my devoted loved ones.

Standing at the picture window,
Breathing in the panoramic view,
There was seen nearby a pretty
yellow rose—
Artfully framed in the pane where
it grows.

Beneath it was perched an
abandoned bird's nest,
Still perfectly formed after
weathering the climes-
It seemed to be clinging with a
tenacious strain,
Waiting for a family again.

Now, summer has come and gone,
and
Autumn scenes are on review—
Blustery winds soon will be high,—
The rose is gone but the nest still
nigh.

Millie Ann Cook
THE BEAUTY OF NATURE

Dedicated to my mother, Mrs. Beatrice Cook and to my friends who inspired me, Miss Katherine Reid, James H. Bryant
and to my cousin Robert L Smith.

The beauty of nature is a lovely
sight to see.
The summer time may not be your
favorite time, but it's a lovely
time of the year if you appreciate
the beauty of nature.
Flowers blooming, bees collecting
honey, birds singing.
The beauty of a rose the wind
blows a petal it floats slowly
to the ground.
Butterflies camouflage with the
colors of nature that blends in
with the scene.
A pretty blue sky with clouds the
tall green trees swaying in the
breeze.
The beauty of nature painted by
the hands of God.
The snow of winter makes a lovely
picture to remember the beauty
of nature created by God.
Beauty that's created by the only
one who paints the sky with
rainbows way up high.
Every day there is a different
picture created by nature.
The beauty of nature created by the
hands of God.
The beauty of Autumn trees their
brilliant colored leaves swaying
in the breeze.
The beauty of a sparkling lake with
swans, the sound of birds
singing that wake you up at
dawn.
The songs they sang to thank God
for another day.
The beauty of nature for all eyes to
see.
To appreciate the things you take
for granted.
The beauty of nature is a lovely
sight to see.
The beauty of nature created by the
hands of God.

Patricia A Setzer
I MISS YOU

In remembrance of my son, Jerry W Scarborough Jr.

On the beach
With sea and sand
Made an impression
With my hand

Thought of you
Wished you could be
Here to walk
The beach with me

I threw a stone
Into the well
Watched the ripples
Gather and swell

Thought of you
Wished you could be
Here to make
A wish with me

No matter where I go
No matter what I do
Life just ain't worth living
Unless I share it with you
I miss you

Dorothy Ellen Kilburn
APPLAUSE TO SPRING
Cushioned by night
Magnificent spring
Moves in
To spread her warmth,
Like a shawl,
Over a winter-weary world.

Matching her youth
Against aging winter's wrath
She dissolves
His icy hand
To forfeit moisture
To the silent earth.

Anxious color-tipped shoots
Await their cue—
Then burst forth
In great applause
As spring lifts her curtain
To thrill a waiting world!

David L Sirois
VACATION
Everything is melting
The mountains
The plants
The people

Only the stone buildings
Are still unshaken
And the elevator
That goes up or down

Everything is red
The sky
The ground
The button

Only the ocean is white
Steaming and misty
And the snow
That falls down and down

Everything is unreal
The mushrooms
The seasons
The questions

One of them is answered
This is the end
We fought with atoms
Death's just a short vacation

We file into the elevator
One by one
Doors close behind us
Block out the sun

We find what we expect
At the end of the tunnel
Friendly faces
Or deadly denials

Everyone's on a vacation
Life was never fact
The elevator continues running
Carrying the dead on its track

Prudence O Gulley
HAPPY

Thank you Ray, for loving me as I was and teaching me to love myself.

The joy I know, I hope it's showing.
I saw last night, what you're feeling
I touched your soul, even if it was unknowing.
The feelings I know you have. that you gave me.
I knew we still had, only hidden.

Happy! Happy! I am so proud,
The good is in that.
Sharing, we have Happy!! Happy!!
When once, I was so sad.
The joy I feel when you let me know you are caring
Trying, not just for the sake of caring or trying.

for you, Happy!
Not trying to stop crying, because you haven't cried
Not try to stop caring, because you always have.
Not to stop or start lying, because you never had to.

Happy! Happy!
A smile or, the wave of your hand
The greeting from someone close.
No spoken word is heard
The only sound, a Happy one;
The crash of interesting worlds

twisted in love.

Happy!

Louise Amsden Catalano
A NOCTURNAL SYMPHONY
O wonderful sky, that so deceptively appears to be night;
the end of brightness and daylight,
When the curtain of evening is drawn aside to reveal
a vastly greater day, with billions of stars
lighting that way, what mysteries do you conceal?
What secrets of inconceivable glory do you cleverly hide
behind a breathlessly beautiful moon, our sun
and a spiral of globes of which we are one?
Can you really hide your glory by bewitching us
with your moons and planets hanging magically in space,
a million stars you have flung out while whirling around
to form the glittering Milky Way? What do you hide?
Is your secret so great that our minds cannot grasp it;
is it that we cannot understand night is daylight,
so beautiful our minds cannot embrace it, and must
turn back to earth and sun for day and night?
O sky, you have not deceived me. is our revelation
of infinity, eternity, wonder upon wonders,
secrets waiting to unfold, worlds without end.
At evening I am waiting when sunset colors are entwining
their long silken trumpets in sonorous symphonies.
With the fading of sound and color the darkening curtain
softly parts and the drama of the dazzling night begins.
Amongst Orion and the Pleiades I see beauty, mystery. This
is ecstasy, light, victory. Glory to Almighty God.

Carla Dominguez
LOST LOVE

For my late husband, Gilbert, who I lost in 1983. He will always be in my heart and have my love.

Where does love go
When you lost what you had,
Does it go with the wind
Or stay in your heart so sad.
My body still trembles
When I think of your touch,
My knees go weak
'Cause I loved you so much.
Does love go up to heaven
So far up in the sky,
Or does it go to a river
Where the bed has gone dry.
I want no one but you
And I never will,
For you were my lover
My heart beats for you still.
What now my love
That you are gone,
Will I go on forever
So lonesome and alone.

Tracy Lee Lemke
A SPECIAL PLACE

This poem was specially written for Duane Muskevitsch, the man who holds my heart.

There's a special person in my life
Who means the world to me
I love him more than anything
And that's how it will be.
There's a special place within my heart
That holds my love for you
It's full of warmth and happiness
And all my feelings too.
There's a special place inside my mind
Which keeps my thoughts of you
And all the times, both good and bad
That we have both been through.
And there's a feeling in my body
That says I'm special too
Because I'm lucky enough to have
A special guy like you.

Sharise Weers
THE LORD IS CALLING
God is strong
He's a wonderful sight
He's our world
And everlasting light
He's our power
Our hope within
He is very thick
He'll never wear thin
He's our love
In our heart deep down
When we were lost sheep
He's the shepherd we found
When we were sad and all alone
We heard him calling
He was calling us home

Jennifer Hartsell
ME
I know I'm not an athlete
I don't play sports or such.
I don't have much to offer
Except I love you very much.

I'll never have curly hair
And I'll never be so tall.
I don't have much to offer
I don't have much at all.

I never wear much make-up
I never mousse my hair.
I don't have much to offer
Except I really care.

I don't have an East Ridge jacket
I don't have a basketball pin.
No, everything I have to offer
Comes from deep within.

I'm not so devastatingly beautiful
And I know that I'm not tough—
I thought before it didn't matter
About all that other stuff.

I'm not a girl like her
I'm afraid I'll never be.
I don't have much to offer
Except this person—me.

Phyllis Gail Jensen
INDIAN TEACHING

To my mother, Janette Craig

Stand tall
Walk straight
Never speak
With lying tongue.

Always pray
To Spirit Great
In whose image
You are made.

Be noble
Bless the poor
Protect the young
Be a man . . . my son.

Lynn E Schneidmiller
DEVILS DUST
Everyone is saying it, just one more line
Trouble is ahead for them, this is the first sign

The lane people are living these days is much too fast,
Too bad they can't go back to just havin fun as in the past

Cocaine makes them feel superior like they can do no wrong,
Making them feel this way does not take very long

Everything they use to care for and love they now hate,
Hopefully they'll realize how bad it is, before it's too late.

Mary Helen Witting
BREEZING ALONE
When I dance underneath
the skies at night
You cannot touch me
because I'm not there
When I walk alone
Under the warm shining sun
No one will catch me
because I'm not around
When I stand in the rain
Under wonderful wet clouds
You won't see me
because I'm not moving
When I brush alongside
the whole world as I fly
Maybe then you will feel me
and know me
and sigh

Casey F Willms
THE SUN
The sun will keep warming and lighting the earth.
While hydrogen forms into helium.
Helium is exploding to keep the sun going.
It will repeat the process for the rest of your life

Miriam Nisbet Fallon
WRITING JINGLES
If I could write a jingle
Like Edgar Allen Poe,
I would surely tingle,
My spirit all aglow.

I'd be swinging, tingling,
Dancing like the mods'
My spirit intermingling
With the angels and the gods.

But, not an intellectual,
My meaning never clear,
With lines so ineffectual,
Still I persevere.

Perhaps someday a spirit
Will materialize,
And take my hand and steer it
To win a Pulitzer Prize.

Margaret Chesney Potts
ANOTHER DAY
Way down in the swanys and bog
A frog is seen upon a large log
Eyes closed just enjoying the sun
A sudden noise, "Oh-oh, I have to run!"

Unhappy No! Tomorrow is
another day
He knows on that same log again
he'll lay
So he'll just swim around and play
and wait for that warm sun
another day.

There's a lesson here for man to
learn,
Leave our troubles and every
concern
Every day all things don't go our
way,
Remember the frog, tomorrow is
"ANOTHER DAY"

Christopher Lynn Gagnon
A FATHER'S PRAYER

For Delila Lynn-Alisha

I don't know much of little girls
or how they grow to be
But now I have a little one
entrusted unto me

The Lord in all His wisdom
has given me this test
to show me things I didn't know
I trust He knows what's best

I'll gladly take this challenge
that is given from above
and bring into this lady's heart
the gifts of trust and love

And as I know what I must do
my efforts will not cease
for my charge is to lead her
to His eternal peace

Darlene L Cory
MOTHER'S LAST GOOD-BYE
She couldn't give me riches or
wealth untold,
But she gave me love and a heart
of pure gold.
She was an ordinary person and
didn't boast of fame,
But she was my mother and I loved
her just the same.
She never went to college or got a
degree,
But she taught me all about life and
loved me.
When Jesus called her to spend her
life in eternity,
She never got to say "good-bye" to
me.
They carried her casket across the
cemetery that day.
On top of the casket, pink and
white carnations did lay.
When all at once, a gust of wind
took the flowers placed there so
neat,
And gently placed a lovely flower
at each of our feet.
A pink one for her daughters but
white was for her son.
My mother said her last good-bye
and had some fun!
I kept that lovely flower and my
Bible holds it dear.
It never faded in color and grows
more precious from year to year.
I know mother's in heaven with
Jesus you see,
But she gave me one last flower to
say "good-bye" to me.

Jamie M Floyd
MEMORIES
As I look at pictures of long ago,
And teardrops fall on my pillow,
I think of the path we used to know,
Down to the Weeping Willow.
Everyday we'd walk down together,
As we told each other
Our love would be forever.

But things have changed,
And now you're gone,
And my heart and our Willow are
all alone.
Now when I see our Willow,
Stretching up into the sky,
I go to our spot, and lay down my
head to cry.

But the Willows are growing old,
And no one seems to care,
That a love so tender, and so soft,
At one time blossomed there.

Thomas H Snow
SIMPLE MYSTERY
Perhaps if Holmes were here in
altered guise,
equipped with facts and semiotic
mind,
he might untie this Gordian Knot
and find
some method of unveiling your
disguise.

If only I could summon Parsival,
for he was most courgeous on a
Quest,
with simple mind, out-witting all
the best,
he'd gladly answer any noble call.

I'm sure that I could trust in
Socrates
to reach the cause of you, seeking
virtue
with mid-wife charm, extracting
what is true.
I've nothing to suggest, like
penalties,

apologies, or redefining right,
I only wish that you were here
tonight.

Rita M Hyland
SHARING
The scent of the flowers,
The green of the trees,
The song of the birds,
The rustle of the leaves.

They are all ours,
And don't you see,
I enjoy them more,
When you are with me.

And while talking or listening,
I am set free,
Because you'll understand,
I just have to be me.

Nedrine Sumners
LOVE-FRIEND
I have to leave you now and cannot
pause to say why.
I am not offended, you could never
offend me,
Only circumstances make offences.
Perhaps you are the mountain I
must back away from
That I might see all of your great
beauty.
I feel I must go where my heart
leads me,
And be nourished where
knowledge feeds me,
To find more inner beauty rather
than just images.
Not abstaining offenses, or
building defenses,
But to seek other love to surround
and keep me.
I will always feel that you are
always as close as the
Sand under my bare feet, my tears
that fall,
The raindrops that cool my brow.
You are to me the sparkle that
sprinkled me with
your favor,
And if that sparkle ever becomes
dim.
I shall again seek you to polish it.

Joanne P Schrank
OCTOBER

---

*In loving memory of my daughter
Dawn Marie*

October clouds are dark and gray,
geese are flying low,
and for just a moment you
can almost feel the coming snow.

Gone are summer's flowers,
the bright and sunny skies,
you watch with inner sadness
as earth's green foliage dies.

Mother nature has to be,
around the corner peeking,
for she knows that all life's
forms are left in her safekeeping.

Plants and seeds go dormant,
while peacefully they rest,
preparing to emerge
and give their very best.

Furs have grown thicker,
homes are burrowed deep,
as the many creatures
await their winter's sleep.

But time so quickly passes,
and much before you know,
the warm and gentle breezes
once again will blow.

Pamela D Lewis
MOLLUSK
So you've been taken from the sea.
I wonder how many look for thee?
Were you ever someone's home
Free upon the sand to roam?

Spiral as an ice cream cone,
Providing protection hard as stone,
Once you laid upon the sand
Making the seashore a
wonderland.

Did you with little feet once creep?
Did you have little eyes to peep?
Did once a little vagabond
With you upon his back abscond?

Now you sit in my collection,
Bringing back a recollection
Of childhood days upon the shore
When I was breathless to explore.

David Chaloux
JAMIE LEIGH
Oh, Sweet little Jamie Leigh
Lying there and being a part of me
You will grow and you will see
How this world can really be

There'll be good times and there'll
be bad
But just remember-you'll always
have your Dad
Love could be just a fad
If it were around more I'd sure be
glad

Hopefully this world will change
Maybe you'll help it re-arrange
Hope you see its better side
Lord knows we've all tried
We've all lied

Maybe someday everyone will
open up wide
And we'll all be on the same side
And no ones' love will be denied

Day by day you learn and grow
I hope you will always know
That—I love you

Peggy Stella G Beisswanger
THIS LAND IS OURS

---

*To my wonderful husband, Richard
R. Beisswanger, who had the
nickname "King of the Road"
because of our many trips across the
United States.*

When my husband and I travel in
our car,
We really do go very far.
From Tucson, Arizona to Reading
P.A.
And this is what we have to say:

Take the opportunity to explore
our great land,
Which has indeed been blessed by
God's great hand.
Farmers working in their fields so
big,
Truly makes a proud heart sing.

Beauty is all around us in our car,
Our eyes are like a camera that can
see so far.
Friendly people we meet on this
earth . . .
for this is our place of birth.

God gave us the greatest
commandment of all—to love,
We know our help comes from
above.

Travel this land oh so wide,
you'll always have company by
your side.
Travel, travel over this great land,
You'll appreciate the beauty done
by God's great hand.

E Gayle Reynolds Adams
SOLO FLIGHT
Charted for blue,
Dreams unlimited.

Solo flight,
No plans filed.

Umbilical to the nest
Love, not S.O.S.

Loft yourself please,
Extend my range.

Martha Louise Viater
THAT'S WHAT FRIENDS ARE FOR
A hand reaching out to break a fall,
A voice that answers a pleading
call,

A smile to help stem the flow of tears,
Words of comfort to calm your fears.
A warm embrace when you're feeling blue,
An optimistic point of view,
In times of grief, someone who cares,
In times of joy, someone who shares.
All of these nice things and more,
That's what friends are for!

Wayne K Callister
PRAISE BE TO GOD
How many times have I begun
A day when everything seemed unstrung,
And placed my God upon the shelf
To become completely involved with self?

I tried alone without success
And only made a bigger mess,
Until my soul within me sought
To set me straight, and to me taught
"With this I cannot cope."

I looked to the Lord and found there hope
To carry on—begin anew.
With reborn heart my spirit flew,
To merge as one with that great love
Which comes to us from God above.

He calms my fears both great and small.
I understand Him not at all;
But feel His touch on all my being.
It makes my soul commence to sing:
PRAISE BE TO GOD!!!

Maqui Ware
REGRETS
Shifting sands and borrowed time
wasted hours no longer mine

with thoughts of you
my mind doth wander

more than yesterday
tomorrow yet fonder

Lisa Ticer
THINGS OF THE PAST
Things of the past, we must let them go;
But doing this isn't easy I've come to know.
The memories of you, they lie so deep.
I think of you often and sometimes weep.
The things that we shared, I'll never forget.
I hold them all sacred, on this you can bet.
Going back in time, it seems so long.
I wish you were here where you belong.
I'm setting you free so that you can fly.
The things I told you, why should I lie?
You say I don't love you, but I really do.
You'll be back if our love is true.
Please don't be angry, hurt, or sad —
I never really tried to make you feel bad.
The way that you touched me was so sincere.
That's why I hold the memories oh so dear.
Lovers I know we'll never be;
But if you need a friend, please call on me.
You think I've found someone to take your place.
There's no one worthy enough to fill that space.
As hard as I fight it, I will set you free;
But do me a favor, remember me.
Remember what I said, my love, it's true—
I wish you well in all that you do.
Thanks again for all that we shared.
I just wanted you to know I still cared.

Blanche Richards
BIT OF HEAVEN
We were expecting a stranger
One who would come to stay
A tiny son or daughter, scheduled
To arrive most any day

Then as the birth pangs gathered
And nature had it's way
I was enveloped in darkness
And silently slipped away

I awoke to find an angel
in a tiny baby form
Ever so soundly sleeping
Close for strength and warmth

And so we named her Sandra
She is so tiny and fair
Sometimes little sunbeams come tumbling down
And play in her red gold hair

And then sometimes as she's sleeping
so quiet and peaceful there
We begin to realize God's Greatness
And more of his tender care

And then we slip to our knees
Drop a kiss on her tiny head
And thank God for sending to us
A corner of Heaven asleep in her bed

Paul Michael Suino
A FRANKLIN STREET ANTIQUE

For all the private moments, from champagne on Van Hise to thunderstorms shared on Monona, for times locked away and times yet to come, this is for you, Pip, with all the love that began on Franklin street.

Flashing lights for a dollar;
Interest unusually colored in beer.

Piquant grape juice in the music room.
Satiated corners of the morning mind.

Hurricanes.
Fast blue hurricane waters.

Onyx night plunging under
White coasting shows.

A lost and ancient photograph of retouched faces:
"The both of us. April nineteen twenty-nine."

Genie Lantrip
A WISH FOR RICHES
At first, I wished for you, mom
Pearls, diamonds, and rings of sparkling gold
A castle tall, with a moat like Kings in days of old.
Now I realize your fortune is vast
More than I could ever dream,
Or ever hope to wish for you
By any sort of mean.
Jewels beyond compare, I now know you hold
Wisdom, love, gentle helping hands
And a heart that's filled with gold.
And in my dreams, for me, I wish
To teach what you taught me
If I could only resemble you
How rich I would be.

Beth Krasovec
JUDGEMENT
Some spend their lives judging others
Never looking into themselves for the same.

Some spend their lives in judgement of others
Never seeking in themselves for their own truth

To judge with a heart thats pure
To judge without contempt
Without envy
Without bias
To judge without hate
would no longer be judgement but acceptance.

Marla S Mills
DYING BEFORE DEATH
My friend knows.
He lived—
(once).

He:
Telling me—
Never stop giving,
Open up,
Hurt.

I:
Tired of hurting,
Wanting to close—
(but not die).

Is life so much that
We hurt so much that
We die so much before death?

LET MY LIVE—
As long as I breathe,
As long as I pulse.

My friend:
Breathes yet does not live.

God—
Someone—
Make him live.
Give him the gift.

Tabitha A Kaigle
SHADOWS

For Grandpa

On a hill stands a dark isolated figure.
North winds blow
vigorously.
A concealed secret some where in the
shadows.
A stream of light grows on the dark figure.
...Come quickly...
...Come quickly...

Carolyn J Borgne
I WISH
I wish, I wish, upon a star.
To be nearer, to the one afar.
The one afar, being the one I love.
To thee I send, my loving dove.
My loving dove, being the letters I write.
Of dreams of loving all through the night.

Brenda Loretta Moore

Brenda Loretta Moore
SIS O'MINE

To Norma, This one's for you, Sis. I miss you so!

That Sis O' Mine was special
Perfect in every way
Goodness filled her heart
Every hour, every day
Everybody was her friend
From the very first hello
If someone had a problem
To that Sis O' Mine they'd go

She loved the city lights
She loved the country air
She loved to feel the wind
As it gently blew her hair
She could be a child
Or a girl about town
She could wear faded jeans
Or a flowing evening gown

She left us way too soon
That loving Sis O' Mine
Because some drunken driver
Crossed the center line
Someday if I'm very good
And I leave this world behind
I'll move right up to heaven
And see that Sis O' Mine

Thelma Davila Snyder
THE CREATOR
It isn't as though I loved you.
You were—what?
An experience?
I haven't known many men—

Like that, I mean,
And you were warm and sweet,
And said all the right things.
Except one.

The face mirrored in your eyes
Was so much brighter than the one
My bathroom mirror revealed.
The naked body that your hands caressed
Was softer, fuller than the skinny one
Within my clothes,
And the Me that you created,
Dazzled me.

But it isn't as though I loved you.
Don't look so guilty,
And so eager to be gone.
This emptiness inside comes,
Not from loss of you,
But loss of Me.
Now I'm a blank bathroom mirror,
And empty clothes.

Daryl Scanland

LEAVING THE NEST

Our first one left the nest today
At five o'clock this morning
We knew about it long ago
But still had too little warning

Smiling, he waved his last good-by
With feelings we could only guess
From now on he'll be a Navy man
And we'll have one child less

Two other sons are next in line
To seek their separate ways
What seemed eternally far away
Now numbers only days

It feels like it was yesterday
They were chasing the ice cream man
Shiny dimes brought happiness
That bounced with them as they ran

Now one is a sailor, one is working
The youngest has college in mind
The noise we hear will be memories
Of the moments they left behind

Each step forward has a price
That hurts even 'tho we jest
We found out for ourselves today
When the first one left the nest

Thomas R Gulbronson

TERRORIST

It was not so awful long ago
Traveled a lot, was on the go
Then something cruel happened, sorrows came
People started playing a very dangerous game
The skies and highways are their workshop
Evils of the terrorist has to stop

We live in a country that's free
Can plant a seed, cut a tree
Walk down the street, without any hesitation
Not planning to destroy our great nation
We work and play and serve God
In fields of clover, and golden rod

It was on the beaches of Normandy
The land and isles of the sea
Our boys fought to make us free
To walk in honor and in victory
We cannot dare let our country down
And welcome and honor a terrorist clown

She stands so proud torch in hand
Without a welcoming committee
or a band
Ellis Island wouldn't be as complete
Without the lady to warn our fleet
She never sleeps or takes a rest
Always on the alert, for all terrorists

Callie Fugate Harvey

DREAMS

When I was just a little girl—
One beautiful sunny day . . .
I sat and dreamed,
Under the old Apple Tree
As I watched the others play.

They seemed so happy and free,
Enjoying the simple pleasures
Of that beautiful summer day.
Yes, I remember well, the dreams . . .
We shared along the way.

My friends said to me—
You'll grow up some day,
So enjoy this time of youth.
You can always dream,
After your hair turns gray.

Now it's happy birthday Callie.
You've come a long, long way . . .
But what has happened,
To all those wonderful—
Dreams of yesterday?

What are your goals for tomorrow?
Strive for joy they say.
Yes, I still remember—
When I was just a little girl,
One beautiful summer day.

Bertie W Gravitt

FALLING LEAVES

To—Jeff

Falling leaves are tumbling down
Red, green, yellow and brown,
The prettiest sight I've ever seen
Changing my lawn from summer green.
As I listen to them falling down
On my roof a beautiful sound,
Mixed with acorns ping, ping, ping
I wouldn't change it for the spring.
I stand and let them hit my head
Green, gold, yellow, brown and red,
And as I stand there looking up
I feel the good Lord fill my cup.
Fall flowers gently nod their head
Say, "Come on leaves make me a bed."
"Keep my roots all nice and warm
So I can live through winters storm."
And now its time to rake the leaves
I love to do it, but it makes me sneeze,
I pile them up, then scatter them around
Then I have showers of red, gold and brown.
Now they are gone and I miss them so
I sure do hate to see them go,
But they will be back in another year
And I pray to God I will be here.

James Mieno

GODS' MIND

To all who strive and work for peace, to end wars and hatred.

In the beginning, there was but Gods' Mind
And He created, the start of mankind.
Man and a woman, he make without sin
The Garden of Eden, is where they dwelt in.

The fruit of all evil, the myst'ry of life
Beckoned to Adam, he made Eve his wife.
Children she bore him, and though they were kin
One slew the other, when <u>HATRED</u> set in.

All through the ages, the hist'ry's the same
Death due to violence, and cities in flame.
Love for each other, and all of mankind
Has been forsaken, for <u>HATE</u> rules our mind.

Change in the climate, has colored the skin
Brothers and Sisters, we truly are kin.
Born from a woman, whose life began
When Gods' Mind created, the image of man.

LOVE—that is gentle, peaceful and kind
Comes from the heart, and not from the mind.
PEACE—on this earth, will only come—WHEN
Love dwells within, the hearts of all men.

Doris Elaine Kampfe

SYMPHONY OF A SPRING

The brook
Nestled in a limestone nook
Sheltered by Columbine and Bloodroot
Sounds a silver-stringed spring;
Surrounded by the March beat
Of merry mint Mayflower feet
The brook
Bubbles, gurgles, gasps,
Like a child at play
It winds its way
Through silky meadows,
Fern-feathered hills,
Fields of newborn hay;
The brook
Grasps each thing
Fingers of soft green moss cling
Pebbles sing;
Jack-in-the-pulpit proclaims,
"Take care!"
Bird's-foot-violet whispers,
"Spring's here!"
Lady Slipper laughter
Spangles pine-needled air;
The brook
Washes each stone bare
A frog jumps
Fishes and flies share;
Sunlight surrouds
A symphony of sounds.

Buck D Guernsey

TO SEE

I see the sun shining;
When its warm upon my face.
In the summer and fall,
I see the leaves on the trees;
When the wind blows.
The birds when they're singing,
Are such a pretty sight.
I see the rain, cool as it is;
As it falls against my face.
I even see the winter,
When I touch the powdery snow.
Though my eyes only see darkness,
Yet I see this and much more.

Chloe Beeson Blom

DAD

I remember being a little girl
and looking up at you, oh, so tall,
Your handsome face, your gentle ways
made me so proud to call
you, "daddy"

I remember growing older
and watching your endless tasks,
remodeling our home, raising the family,
God's help you continually asked.

My memories of childhood are many:
popcorn and Monopoly, Seattle in a storm,
clam digging in Ocean City,
our basement as a dorm,
baseball games in the alley,
badminton in the backyard,
a tetherball set you assembled,
lively games of cards.
Many happy times together we spent,
For you, your family was most important.

You gave me love and security,
and a wealth of other gifts:
perseverance, courage, and ambition,
seasoned with your wit.

I remember leaving home
to attend college and live on my own;
You gave me incentive and constant support,
in my endeavors I never felt alone.

Today, as a grown woman
I look at your handsome face.
The years of love and giving
can never be erased.
As I look at your commanding stature,
admiration and respect I have
for all you are and all you gave—
So proud I am to call you "Dad"

Martha Starr Ashworth

LET A DREAMER DREAM

Let a dreamer dream
For dreams are what keep
Our hearts alive
Striving to reach the furthest peaks
Of our imagination

Let a dreamer dream
To dream of the way
Our lives once were
And in our minds
Let the dream live again

Let a dreamer dream
About a future brightened
By knowledge learned
From mistakes in our past
For us, and all future dreamers

Debra Ann Brendelson

JOY

You are my joy,
My life untold;
For you I would share,
My being to unfold.

Come walk with me,
For there's happiness to be found;
There will always be rainbows,
And journies abound.

I have found heaven on earth you see,

Because of you,
I am bursting with glee.

Joyce M Choiniere
BLANK PAGES
Blank pages
Beckoning for words
Which speak of feelings
Lost in the heart
Searching for a place
To break free
From the bonds that hold them

Jamie Dawn Englert
HORSES
I like horses very much,
The way they have a special touch.
Horses are very nice,
Mine is the color of cinnamon spice.

I like horses very much,
And mine even likes to share my lunch.
She likes sandwiches, chips, and rice,
She nods her head to thank me twice.

I like horses very much,
And I know mine likes me a bunch.
Because when I look into her eyes,
She never wants to give me her good-byes.

Marjorie W Weaver
MARCH WINDS
Don't be afraid when March Winds blows;
he is only chasing away the snow.
When he sounds so boasterious, loud and shrill,
he is only calling the daffodills.

Sometimes he is a giant and very stout;
he piles up the clouds and then scatters them out.

When he shrieks down your chimney, don't you fret,
for he is only waking the violets.

When March wind blows his boasting song,
the trees are busy all day long.
Swelling with pride their leaves to show
So hurrah for March winds; let them blow.

Helen J Booth
HANDS OF A FARMER
By the window he sits, in pensive thought,
Hands clasped in his lap,
In overalls, slippers and threadbare shirt,
On his head, a dusty old cap.

As his eyes scan across the stubbled land,
Where traces of snow still cling,
His hopes are that soon these idle hands
Will be busy with chores of spring.

Through many years those hands have toiled
Those hands so skilled and strong.
They've worked from dawn 'til setting sun;
The hours, rewarding, but long.

In spring they've plowed and planted grain,
Cut summer's fields of hay;
Tended the crops through sun and rain
Until autumn's harvest day.

They've helped with birth of calf and lamb,
With litters of piglets, too.
They can fix 'most anything
With wire, cord or glue.

Leaning back in his chair and removing his cap,
He feels especially blessed.
He smiles and says within his heart,
"My hands have done their best."

Julie C Freundel
SHE

To Jon and Edie, who found the rose, despite.

Into dusk, the child so meek,
Followed hope, though thin and weak.
A starry gaze, the crystal froze,
The moonlit rays, a single rose.

A turning prince, the woods ablaze,
The fire ravaged childhood days.
A black abyss replaced what had,
Forever lost, Forever sad.

A fantasy, and rainbow dreams,
were covered up with horrid screams.
In stillness gripped with hands of pain,
her spirit struggling to remain.

She held it tight, that love would grow,
an endless search, she had to know.
The shell now hard, her head held high,
Suspected none, the silent cry.

Heard a sigh, fight back the tears,
The dagger sharper than the years.
Mourning child, though now you've grown,
The sun sits high, but all alone.

Into dusk, the woman meek,
Follows hope, though thin and weak.
of starry gaze, and crystal frost,
the rays live but, the rose is lost . . .

Ron W Ronquillo
MY EVERYTHING #2
You are my sunset on a blue-green sea,
my oasis in a parched, dry desert.
You are a rose amongst the thorns,
the song that a robin sings.
You are my sunshine on a cloudy day,
a ray of hope when all seems lost.
You are the beauty in the world around me.
You are . . . MY EVERYTHING!

Naomi J McDaniel
GOD'S PAINTING

My three-year old grandson, Ronnie Burton, said, "God closes the sky, that's why it gets dark. But, in the morning He will open it up again and it will be day." So, I lovingly dedicate this to you, Ronnie.

God closes the sky . . .
The sun . . He puts to bed . . .
With breath-taking colors . . .
From gold to crimson red.

The sky is His canvas . . .
For the art He creates
From sunset . . . to lightning . . .
These wonders He makes.

Yet swiftly He erases . . .
His art . . . before our eyes
For again He's creating . .
His work upon the skies.

Sometimes it's a cloud
So puffy and white . . .
Or the stars and the moon
That glow in the night.

Such beauty and promise . . .
One painting contains . . .
It's the breath-taking rainbow
God adds to the rain.

Barbara S Stewart
DEATH OF A DESPERADO
You went out that night
with one thing on your mind.
You were going to avenge
the vicious rumors that were flying about.
You found him on the street,
and I saw it all coming,
but couldn't do a thing.
Out of the truck you jumped,
words and fists began to fly.
Suddenly, out of the darkness,
a single shot was fired,
and you tumbled to the ground.
Things were tough, but I never knew
that it would end so drastically.
People scattered, however all I could do
was hold you in my arms.
Your last words were "I love you,"
and I honestly believe you did.
Now, as I sit by your grave,
mourning your loss, all I can think about
is how much I cared for you.
It is to no amazement then,
that while walking away from the grave marked desperado
I start to cry.

Jacqueline Maria Powell
MY TWIN SISTER

I would like to dedicate this poem to my twin sister, Jennifer Powell, whom I love and care for a lot.

I have a sister who looks just like me.
Very few know how much fun that can be.
She is my best friend through thick and through thin;
The reason for this is she is my twin.

Having a twin can be pure delight.
But like all sisters we sometimes fight.
We can't stay mad at each other long.
We hug and tell each other we were wrong.

When Jenny is sick I am sad;
But when she is well I am glad.
We share our room, our clothes and our toys,
We even share the same friends, girls and boys.

Together we laugh, together we cry,
But in each other's business we know not to pry.
She tells me her secrets, I tell her mine.
She knows I'll be there all of the time.

Without my twin sister I would be lost.
I would not give her up at any cost.
Not a million dollars or a thin penny
Could replace my best friend, my twin sister, "Jenny."

Tina Leonetti
FOR DAD
Dear Dad,

As this important Father's Day arrives, I have reflected on a way to say "Thank-You" for all that you have given me as my father . . .

You have given me your values and morals; not necessarily as my own, but as a foundation on which to build my life.

You have given me knowledge to choose between the rights and wrongs of life; and even though I haven't always made the right choices, that knowledge helped me to correct my mistakes.

You have given me kindness and honesty, not only toward others but also toward myself.

You have given me the courage to dream, and the strength to turn those dreams into realities.

You have given me the gift of open communication. The talks we have had have often given me the hope to see brighter tomorrows.

But of all the gifts you have given, Dad, the most important is your love.

So on this Father's Day as you look upon this child of yours, I hope you can feel a pride in my achievements. Because when anyone asks who you are, I am proud to say,

"He is my Dad"

Happy Father's Day
With Love,
Tina

Herbert W Mueller
BEATRICE ELAINE
They said a thousand days might pass, before the hurt could start to ease.
That months to years would slowly turn, until the emptiness can cease.

"They" may be right, and one must
hope that passing time some day
ought mend;
It's God's own most peculiar gift,
that needs no heed of his to send.

Oh, but the days are long and grey;
the joys so few, and griefs
remain.
Mem' ries bring bitter-sweet recall;
what could have been yields only
pain.
Your passing left us all benumbed.
Too soon, it seemed; before your
time.
No purpose served, no aim
achieved; with reason none,
without yet rhyme.

Your gentle smile and kindly
words are needed still on this
grim earth.
Your helpful loving ways are
missed; the air seems sparse
without your mirth.
The footsteps that you left behind,
soon fade except to just a few;
I'm one who sees them evermore
in marks of service wrought by
you.

I value much the years we spent,
resent the spans we were apart;
Regret the times that I have
missed, to tell you what was in
my heart.
Too late, I now arouse the breeze
with words of praise so dumbly
saved.
Light years away, you may not
hear. I try, that cosmic laws be
braved.

My love for you has never dimmed,
though years rolled by, and
problems came.
You sparked a joy ent'ring a room;
my voice was glad to speak your
name.
A sheer delight to be around; your
view on life was so serene.
Your fingers, nimble, never ceased
to make gifts fit to please a
queen.

The loss of you was not just mine.
The countless kin and fervent
friends
Seemed stunned by fate's cruel
sudden blow. A shock that no
one comprehends.
I know I'll miss you evermore,
since much too soon our lives
were rent.
But you left a void, an ache, a grief,
in every life where you were sent.

Miss Julia G L Tompos

MY FIRST PLANE RIDE

From on high with birdlike wings
I view my home below.
The fields, like my checker squares,
Are ribbons row on row.

The mounds of snowy 'whipped-
cream' clouds
Look sweet enough to eat.
The glorious sun in radiance
beams,
With fierceness throws her heat!

The airwaves lift and fall again
As ocean's highest crest.
Then gently to the earth we skim
Until our plane finds rest!

Dorothy L Bradshaw Pates

LEGACY

In memory of K. Baker, I. Pates and R.M. Dixon for the profound effect you all have held in my life and legacy.

Remember . . .
Forget . . .
So hard to do . . .
But with time,
And its wearing,
We will soon forget
The sharing,
But the evidence
Still lingers
On . . .

Thersa S Mulligan

SOUVENIRS

Hear the ticking sound of the clock
In the closet on a shelf is a box
From the box the lid is lifted
The contents are safe only slightly
shifted
Just odds and ends of the years
gone past
Just reminders to help the
memories last
Lost emotions come flooding in
And thoughts escape of how things
might have been
Revisited for a moment are times
and places
And the mind's eye sees the
forgotten faces
For a time the past is relived once
more
Now the lid is replaced, closed is
the door
The box is replaced upon its shelf
And the memories were
remembered, just for myself.

Sandra Heise

THIS DAY

Dear Heavenly Father,
Please help me to: be of service
to
someone in need . . .
say a kind word to a neighbor . . .
or do a kind deed . . .
This Day.
Let me be ever ready to:
lend a hand to someone who may
stumble and fall . . .
write a note, or make a call . . .
to a special friend
This Day.
Keep me ever mindful of:
those who are in pain, or
experiencing sorrow . . .
Praying that they will have a
Brighter, happier tomorrow . . .
This day.
Let me not forget to be thankful for:
This beautiful world made by
Your Hand . . .
The mountains, the seas, every
grain
of sand . . .
And every person of every land . . .
This Day.
And, finally, Dear Father,
Help me to:
Tell someone that you
Are our best friend . . .
Remember that Eternity
lies around the bend . . .
Realize that I may
never see the end . . .
of This Day.

Amen.

Alice Fleming

SEARCH, SEARCH, LOVE

There's nothing material that can
compare,
To the smell and feel,
of your own special love's body
Perfume.

It's the stabilizer for enjoyment of
other worldly things.
Without your own special love,
other things seem without
meaning,
And there's a constant ache inside.

Search, search, love.
The owner of your heart is such a
vital part
A priority treasure hunt.
Climb to the top of your love tree,
And search endlessly for the
matching part to your heart.

You'll make the ecstasy music,
of two hearts becoming one part.
Search, search, love.
The creator did it tor the first man
Adam,
He took a rib from Adam,
And Presto matching Eve met
Adam's love sigh.
In future days it was left up to us,
To match or mismatch,
To loveless hurt, or to love, love,
search!

Randy L Culver

Randy L Culver

TO QUINCY

You're everything we've ever wanted xxx and more.

Thank you Lord for my little girl,
she's perfect in every way.
Her skin's like soft pink roses,
her eyes like sunshine rays.
Her hair's so blond and curly, her
smile seems one mile wide
And when I hold her close to me
I feel so warm inside.
I know my little girl loves me by
her very special touch.
So Lord, please protect her. I
need her oh so much.

Thank you Lord for my little one,
she's precious in every way.
And when she giggles and talks to
me, I know what she's trying to
say.

Thank you Lord for Mom and Dad.
They're perfect in every way.
Mom's skin's like soft pink roses,
Dad's eyes like sunshine rays.
Mom's hair's so blond and curly,
Dad's smile seems one mile wide
And when they hold me close to
them I feel so warm inside.
I know my Mom and Dad love me,
by their very special touch.
So Lord, please protect them. I
need them oh so much.

Love,
Daddy

Fred Fukunaga

CHRISTMAS TIME

To all our POW-MIAs. May they all soon be accounted for and released to join their families or returned home to be laid to their final rest on American soil.

C is for the cheer we should bring,
H for the hymns we should sing.
R for rights by which we stand,
I for independence we enjoy in
this land.
S is for Santa, the gent called
Nick,
T for the toys for the well and the
sick.
M for our MIAs whom we dearly
love,
A for the Angels and their
blessings from above.
S is for sadness in this world of
strife,
T is surely for the time of your
life.
I for the inspiration your soul can
lend,
M for mirth that will many hearts
mend.
E is for the eyes of a friend and
now the end.

Dr Lynn Rae Sengbush

A WOMAN OF THIRTY-NINE

Now she is a woman of thirty-nine;
once she was a girl drifting
through childhood—half asleep
amid dreams of becoming a
woman.
Oh yes—she'd live in a big house
with two kids and a doting
husband.
She'd volunteer as a room mother,
bake cookies, plan school
parties, and be fiercely proud of
her children and husband.
Oh yes—her identity as a grown-up
woman would never be a
question.
When did this woman of
thirty-nine rustle from the
cobwebs of sleep?
It was at the age of thirty-three—
How ironic!!Christ died at
thirty-three.
Is there something magical or
cosmic in the awakening rebirth
of the woman who slept in the
50's—Christ died so that they
might live.
Late bloomers these women of the
50's—No wonder they
experience so much confusion.
No super big house—No two
perfect kids—No constantly
doting husband.
Slowly this woman wipes the sleep
from her eyes,
coming face to face with the
inner woman.
The wheels of her emotions are
slowly set in m o t i o n—
Confusion???? DENIAL*********
DISILLUSIONMENT

Confusion ??????? ANGER
!!!!!!!!!!!!!!!!SADNESS
Confusion ????????? IMMOBILITY ************** INERTIA
Confusion ???????????? TERROR
********************** PANIC
Confusion ?????????? false starts
&&&&&&& small steps
Confusion ????— DETERMINATION ——————
VISION

Victoria J Stewart
A MESSAGE ON MY MOTHERS' DAY

Mother, you and I look alike,
But I am not you
And you are not I.
But I Love you.

We both know the joys and sorrows of love
You shared a compassion and understanding
That no one else could give.
And I loved you newly.

Out of our hurt and hope,
You shared painful memories of the past,
So that we could trace and forgive.
And I loved you more.

At a time of gutless strength and deep sadness,
We shared the trueness of the maternal bond,
And at that lose we grieved.
And I loved you truly.

Yes, we look alike
We don't live alike,
But I celebrate our love everyday.
I love you always.

Rebecka J DuPaul
NEVER HEAR "I LOVE YOU"

Lonely is a word to describe me.
Lonely is when you sneeze and no one says,"God bless you,"
Lonely is me.
Lonely is when all you can do is cry yourself to sleep at night,
Lonely is me.
Lonely is when you walk down the halls and no one notices you,
Lonely is me.
When no one says "Hello," and no one says "Goodbye,"
When no one says "I'm sorry" or "Thank you," or "I love you."
Lonely is me.

Vladimir Mikle
MEMORIES

To Vladimira and Stanislava Kollarova

Memories are a double edged sword
flooding minds like a raging hoard
They escape no one not even a great lord
who recalls glory days when his falcon soared

Memories can bring back times of delight
when days were warm and bright
They can shift and turn your sight
to days that were cold with blight

Memories bring alive loved ones long years dead
as you lay at night warm in bed
They bring back departures filled with dread
when you long for homecomings instead

Memories recall loves lost and friendships found
during journeys to foreign ground
They are crisp and clear without a sound
as familiar faces and places abound

Memories occur during winter and summer spring and fall
with the suddenness of an eagle's call
Memories must be accepted by one and all
whether they're good or bad large or small

Cecil Moore
WHAT YOU ARE TO ME

This poem is dedicated to Sara. Thank you for touching my life, you are everything to me. I love you.

You are sweet memories of when we first met;
Those precious days I'll never forget.
You are the best that life has to give,
The one that I really enjoy being with.
You are the one with that sweet southern smile
And those beautiful brown eyes that make my life worthwhile.
You are the one with the mouth made just right;
Those perfect lips I could kiss all night.
You are sunshine and blue skies and without these things my day would not start.
Soft rains and gentle breezes, things that are close to my heart.
You are my Scarlett O'Hara, my own true southern belle.
You are all those things, that I love so well
You are the one that makes me so proud,
And I'm always looking for your face in a crowd.
You are wonderful and witty, and a pleasure to be near;
You are truly "everything" I hold dear.
You are so special; to me you are the world.
And I will always love you my beautiful precious southern girl.

Yvonne Agyarko
FAREWELL

To the seven astronauts killed

The ship goes up in the air for the early morning flight, it soars beyond the heavens and dashes through the light, But soon it all ends from joy to sorrow, We shed Our tears and think about tomorrow

Evelean Halliday
LIFE IS ETERNAL

For forty-eight years we were married, then in a moment he left my side
To go back to Heavenly Father's Sphere, and there forever to abide.
His pain and suffering now are gone, his mortal life is through,
God called him home again, a greater work to do.
He'll travel upward and onward forever from this special day
For he had the Everlasting Covenant to light and lead the way.
Trials and tribulations are placed before us all,
Which prepares us each for greater things when we get our call.
We have the Gospel of Jesus Christ, through its teachings we truly know
Where we came from, why we're here, and if faithful where we'll go.
For time and all eternity, that great and glorious plan
Was prepared for all God's children before our earthly lives began.
And when we reach our Father's realm and in his home abide,
Our families, too, will be with us forever by our side.
Although it's hard to say good-bye, I know we'll meet in time to come,
God's hand will guide and comfort us, "DEAR LORD, THY WILL BE DONE".

Oliver Franklin Coon
BLIND FATE

Dedicated to Annie Gandy

Fate has no mercy
for the children left behind,
they have been judged, But they
done no crime, for death is blind.

Elizabeth C Smith
I CRY FOR JOY

Dedicated to my wonderful sister Carolyn Wright, Blissfield, Michigan.

As I pray—I cry for Joy
As tears—roll away,
I'm not sad—I'm happy
That I'm with him today!

I cry for joy—I cry for joy
I know by him I'm blessed,
Yes, as I pray, I know—I know
The greatest—happiness!

It's great to know that he is near
And everything's all right,
To talk with him, I know—I know
My eyes with tears are bright,

I cry for joy—I cry for joy
The greatest joy on earth,
When I gave my heart to Jesus
'Twas a joyous re-birth.

I cry for joy—I cry for joy
I know by him I'm blessed,
Yes, as I pray, I know—I know
The greatest—happiness!

Christine Anne Charles
EVERY

Every teacher was once a student.
Every student was once a very little kid.
Every little kid was once a baby.
And one of them was
You!

Andrew A Rumps
NICK THE BARBER, ARE YOU BUSY

Nick the barber are you busy
Asked Ted Woodruff on the phone
I'm not busy and I won't be
As I pass along your dome
For a child of two could count
the hair upon your shining pate
Oh Death where is thy sting
said Ted, oh what a ghastly fate
Once my hair was numerous
as the sands upon the shore
It took two men to cut it,
one worked aft the other fore
Hour after hour they kept cutting
more and more
The hair piled up twice ankle deep
as it fell to the floor
But now my hairline is receding,
combing it is quite an art
All I use my head for is
to keep my ears apart
Long long ago when I was young
My head was crowned with hair
Now it resembles heaven
For there is no parting there.

Pat J Piaskowski
WHAT IS THIS PLACE?

What is this place?
People live in layers. Steep
stairways wander down and up.
Doors and windows and vents and screens.
Music needles through the walls.
And old people knock gnarled hands
Against the intrusion.
Children run and scream and
Bounce balls against rattling doors.
Roller skates thunder across the tiles.
Peace is gone. It left last year in the spring.
Din came to take its place.
Junk came, too, to have a picnic with its friends.
And spread out on the floor.
And use everyone's space.
Can anyone get them to leave?
Who are they? Why did they pick this place?
I'll bet they said, "What is this place?
People live in layers."

Pearl White Alvarez
A CITY LADY IN A COUNTRY KITCHEN

Dedicated, with love, to the proud memory of Helen—Mother, Grandmother and Great Grandmother

---

Young, pretty and gifted was she
The lady who was my mother-to-be,
Enroute to a new destination miles away from home
And the big city she had always known.

It was her love for Dad alone
That eased the move into the unknown.
For, of the country, and its demands
She had little knowledge, but willing hands.

Her young husband, who loved the land,
Plowed, planted, fulfilling his dream—how grand!
She cooked, scrubbed, carried water and wood—how odd!
Oil lamps to fill, chickens to feed—Oh, help me, God.

Hour by hour, day by day, no relief, as I recall,
She smiled, loved, and learned to do it all.
She shared, nurtured, soothed; and then
With aching, tired hands, she'd play her piano again.

Mother grew older; and her wrinkled face
Did nothing to minimize her pride and grace.
A city lady in a country kitchen she will always be—
Her presence there shaped my destiny.

Reginald D Williams

Reginald D Williams
HOME

To Bianca—from Daddy, thank you Ma & Mrs. Kessler

A picket fence
A lemon grove
The same old st. that Ma & Pa drove
A Sunday church social that last till dusk
Friends you always trust
The sound of kids playing distant yet close
I guess this can tell you what I miss most
HOME

Lisa Levine Cummins
THE POET'S FIRE
A fire within,
Seeking fuel,
The consuming flame—
A need to unloose this light,
This energy;
To share this warmth.
A need to feed this fire;
To watch it grow,
And spread,
Enlighten,
Cleanse,
Purify.
Till all that remains are coals,
That may spark, even at night,
And kindle yet another flame
To warm some reader's soul.

Sandra Foster
IN THE EYES OF THE BEHOLD
A man mighty, with unspoken words, he depicts a strength stronger than the flames of sheol.
With each impression, he leaves behind, the mark of passion, his victim left struggling, to maintain composure, from sensations
traveling to and fro, through each vessel.
Each kiss, denotes a trust superior, indescribable to others, that sweetens the presentiments of tomorrows.
As day unfolds into night, her ears listen, longs, for words of endearments, to abate her agitation.
As the night unfolds into the break of day, she hopes one day he'll say.
My life, with you, I shall stay.

Thamer
IT WAS GOD'S WILL

To those left behind

My darling wife, who I love still
Has gone away it was God's will
She hasn't gone to some strange place
She's with our loved ones, somewhere in space
Christ himself prepared a place
For God's children, the Christian race
And since God chose for me to stay
I must except her gone away
I shall push on from day to day
And do just what the good Lord say

Somehow I'll learn and lean the more
On Jesus's words he gave them for
Man to read and then apply
Them to our lives until we die
Yes, I know I shouldn't be sad
God knows best, He said be glad
It will take time my life's new change
I loved my wife, God will arrange
Dear God please take my sadness here
Only you can make me cheer
Only you, my God shall be
My strength throughout eternity

My darling wife whom I love still
Has gone away it was God's will.

Shirley Swain
FEAR

To my sons; Shawn & Michael, my parents; Don & Joan, and the Love of My Life; Randy.

Listen to me, children,
before you go out there.
The world is such a painful place,
you'll find no one to care.
An alley, dark and dingy,
a light is shining through,
Don't let a shadow make you jump,
when it sneaks up on you.
A car slowly approaches.
you're blinded by the light.
Your senses on the verge of fear,
and ready for a fight.
The beating of your heart,
as it's ringing in your ear;
then you feel the heat erupt,
when it turns to fear.
Now the car is here,
and two lovers pass you by,
Relief is washed upon you,
as you feel the need to cry!
And once again you feel secure,
in knowing that you're free.
Until you walk a darkened street,
for fear you cannot see.

Beverly J Anderson
A BIT OF AN ANGEL
A little girl's softness and sweetness and love,
A bit of an angel, you know.
She's pretty and winsome with sparkling eyes,
And dancing curls topped with a bow.

She's tea parties, dollies, and make-believe fun,
She's laughter, a heart that is gay,
She's happiness romping through meadows and fields
In love with a bright summer day.

She's curious, questions, and chatter and tales,
She's innocence pure as can be,
A dear little princess with sweet tender charms—
So precious upon daddy's knee.

She's sunshine and rainbows and everything fair,
And lights up our life with her smile,
She's kisses, and hugs that can squeeze oh, so tight,
She's all that makes living worthwhie.

A little girl's heaven right here upon earth,
No doubt in my mind about this;
For only a bit of an angel, you know
Could bring to our hearts so much bliss.

Denise J Babbitt
STAIRCASE
Walking through the staircase of life watching and waiting
Pausing at one step at a time seeing the future ahead but yet seeing the past
Being tested, and seeing the heartbreaks
of tomorrow around the corner
Walking through the staircase of time
where life seems to hit some hard blows
One moment you are one instead of two experiencing the creakness of the steps
With the movement of the stair's years
melt away into a hazy mist of clutter
Grabbing the rail for the stability of life in freeform style of caring
Caring about the moaning of each stair-step as the passerby travels the familiar path
Climbing the staircase of life holds the uncertainity of life in general
Seeing the not yet morning arise with dew
sprinkled on the unrevealing petals of a rose
Walking through the staircase of life observing
the unopened roses wishing and wanting.

Lisa MacDonald
SPRING HAS ARRIVED
The trees were swaying in the wind
The birds were singing in the rain.
The children were playing all happy and gay
And spring had arrived.

The bugs were out, and branches sway
The butterflies went their own way.
Snakes were hissing, and
Little girls and boys were kissing.

Ants had fun
Sunning in the sun
Flies were zooming and
Flowers were blooming, and
Spring was finally here.

William T Parsons
SUCH A FIDDLER

To Karl Nadler, Palatinate poet

My neighbor is so good a man,
Plays fiddle, not too well.
At times I wish that he would go
to Heaven, there to dwell.

It's true, since he lives over us,
Our cat has left our home.
That means the rats and mice near here
Quite brazenly may roam.

In face, I fear, our cat may make
His absence permanent,
For every time the bow tuned up
This cat from house just went.

The truth is this: he plays too well
For this, our little world.
Oh, that his constant fiddling
In Heaven be unfurled.

But no! In heaven he dare not
Go live there to reside;
Although if the old saying's right:
"He sees the brighter side!"

No, down in Satan's chapel
Most clearly he belongs,
Where he himself may hear it said:
"They're devilish, those songs."

Amelia Medeiros
SING OF SPRING

This poem is dedicated to an inspiring Mom and Dad, who have taught me to be imaginative with feeling.

Flowers bloom brilliant colors,
Air so transparent.
Babes anew,
Here and there.
Sun shines upon,
Birds in song.
Sing of Spring,
Also happiness it brings.

Fred J Schroeder
JOHN WAYNE—A TRIBUTE

This poem is dedicated to one of our true Americans and to all those who cherish the same values.

I, an obscure figure, rode in from the plains,
A MAN MOUNTAIN.
I was a idealistic in my views about what every American should be,
A DREAMER.
Through war and western, as a hero I grew,
AN IDOL.
Never was I afraid to praise my beloved homeland,
A PATRIOT.
With a lovely wife, and seven children, I flourished,
A FATHER.
Through sixteen years, I battled silently against unbeatable odds,
A PILLAR OF STRENGTH.

In death . . .
A HUMAN.

John Richard Brown
LOST IN A CROWD
To be looked at and not seen.
To speak and not be heard.
To appear like everyone else.
To act as they do.
To walk as they do.
To sleep and not dream.
To search and not find.
To hurt and not cry.
To stand in line
and not question why.
To reach and not touch.
To grasp and not hold.
To walk with a crutch
and talk when you're told.
To break and not crumble.
To run and not fly.
To know and not teach.
To want and not try.
A face without lines,
a soul without spirit,
your heart is a screamin'
but you just can't hear it.
So stay with the crowd
and live out their lie.
Pretend that you're proud
till the moment you die.

Rosie Byrne
TILL WE MEET AGAIN
You are very special,
And so very much more,
But the Lord is calling,
He's waiting at the shore.

All the pain and sorrow
You can take it aboard,
Give it back to Satan,
You're in the hands of the Lord.

He will guide you to the light,
And show you your special gate,
You'll be in His Kingdom,
To share your promised estate.

Though you'll be gone from earth,
And I will miss you Roy,
I know you'll be in a place,
Where there is eternal joy.

So may the Spirit of God,
Hold and touch you with His Love,
As you prepare to go,
To meet the Lord above.

Carrol McNeal
LOCKED OUT
I struggled through the blizzard,
home at last;
But something strange was
waiting at the door.
A pigeon, troubled by the storm
much more
Than I, after I opened, hurried past
And ran into a corner of the hall.
Secure at last, it stared askance at
me,
Who couldn't fail to understand its
plea
That I must help it live, or death
would call.
I flung open the door and chased
it out
Of the apartment building.
Tenants know
That we don't need a bird strolling
about
Where young and old or what we
are must go.
At dawn I wondered, who are we
to flout
The frozen pigeon lying in the
snow?

Blaine A Allred
I WONDER
Have you ever stopped to wonder
How your life would be today,
Had you wed your high school
sweetheart
And gone Another way?
Would your life be as happy
Or would it be as sad,
Would things have been any better
Or would they be as bad?
Would you find fame and fortune,
Or would you be a bum?
The past cannot be changed
The future is yet to come.
Does she still remember,
And does she think of you?
And is her heart as happy,
Or is it just as blue?
If you had to do it over
Would you do it just the same,
Or would you try a little harder
To keep your first loves flame?

Tammy Reed
CURE FOR THE BLUES
When you're having a bad day,
And you don't know what to say;
When you feel blue,
And don't know what to do;
Just give a big smile!
And laugh all the while!

Yes!
You've got to stick to it,
'Cause you can do it.
You will see you're the best!
The best you can be.
Your day won't be bad;
And you won't be sad.
You'll be happy all the while
With a big smile
The length of a mile!

Sandra Faye Zanders Scott
MY SON-SHINE

Dedicated to Jerry, Felicia and most importantly, Nicholas for it is you three that I truly love. Also to any and everyone I have had the pleasure of knowing in this lifetime.

The raindrops beat against my
window—
not allowing time to ponder.
As tears poured freely down my
face,
I soon began to wonder;

What will tomorrow bring,
and how will I survive—
Knowing you will not be here
to celebrate the age of five?

There will be no more hugs and
kisses
from the little boy called Nick.
No more days of painful headaches
and no more nurses doing finger
pricks.

You touched the lives of so many
and shared your love with all.
You told me to be happy—
but it's your name I need to call.

The raindrops have slowed a bit
and my thoughts continue to
roam.
We watch your little coffin
lowered,
for God has called you home.

Renee L McKibben
NATURE'S BEAUTY
Sitting under a tree,
Near a clear running stream
I realized Nature's beauty,
And sensed it all a dream.

I looked out and about
And was amazed to see—
Not a soul was around
To observe this beauty with me.

Alone, with my thoughts,
It came to me:
How wonderously perfect
Nature really can be!

Remembering the trees,
Remembering the sun:
How could anyone harm
All the work that Nature has done?

As the day came to an end,
And nightfall on it's way,
I walked through the trees
Saying "Good-bye" to another day.

Jill Alfreda Knight
GAMES
Games are to be played
When burdens are great
Dividing your time between
Some needs must wait
We can only do the best
We can
We are not the almighty
Perfect man
There must be space for
Ourselves alone
Or our assets are stripped
Right to the bone.

Shawn Oldham
TO LOVE IN VAIN
To love in vain
it cuts so deep.
I feel such pain
I long to weep.

This love I feel
is wrong I know.
This love I feel
I must not show.

Down deep inside
there is a hole.
Down deep inside
within my soul.

A hole so deep
my heart was lost.
I cannot weep
tho' such a cost.

William Jay McCarter
THE KING THAT WAS A CARPENTER

Dedicated to my wife Patricia for her encouragement and family and friends. Also to the ones that receive a blessing from reading this poem.

There was a man working in his
carpenter shop.
He received an order to make
crosses for executions.
When he was making the crosses
he knew within
His Heavenly Father sent Him to
do a greater work.

A King that was a carpenter,
The hands that made the crosses
were also
The hands that created the worlds.
No one really understood, only
Himself, Jesus,
That one day He would die on a
cross,
For the sins of the world.
Could it be that one of the crosses
would be His own?
He started telling the Good News,
That His Heavenly Father sent
Him to redeem mankind.

A King that was a carpenter said,
"Let not your heart
Be troubled, you believe in God
believe also in me.
In my Father's house are many
mansions,
If it were not so, I would of told you.
I will come again and receive you
unto myself."
Those hands that made the crosses
would one day
Have stakes through them.
The work of salvation complete,
When the King that was a
carpenter was put on the cross,
And He said, "It is finished."
Three days later God raised Him
from the dead.
A King that was a carpenter,
became King of Kings forever.
St. Mark 6:1-6

Barbara Jean Bloor
TEACH ME

For my children: Scott, Brian & ReGina

Touch me—Touch my hand
I'm real
Hear me I talk
See me I walk
I run
I cry
I feel.
I spin
I turn with time
Whichever way the wind blows
Or I walk in a straight line
Whichever way you turn me
I'll be whatever you want me to be.
Believe—I'll know it's so
Because you said it's true
Disbelieve, I'll put it down
Because you told me to.
Mock someone—I learn to scorn
Damn the book, a page is torn
I learn very fast.
Forgive me
Forgive my individuality
I promise not to be different again
I want to be just like you.
Whisper
I'll learn to hate discreetly
Cry God's name outloud
I'll turn to him completely
Teach me to love

Set me free
I'll grow with you
Teach me to hate
Bind me
A wild creature
Finally caught
But
Teach me very carefully
I'm the only child
You've got.

Kim Kampf
FAR AWAY THOUGHTS

I dedicate this poem to my future husband, Patrick Steckel, who gave me a reason to write this poem, also to our parents, Frank and Nancy and Paul and his late wife, Mary, thanks for everything.

Since Christmas Day, the day I first met you
My life has really changed.
Somethings I put in order,
Somethings I've rearranged.
I've put you in the middle
And built my dreams around
Someone who means so much to me
The special one I've found.

Before you came into my life
My skies were not as blue.
But then one day you came along
And the sun came shining through.
Although we may be far apart,
The miles cannot erase
The precious memory that I have
Of your handsome eyes and smiling face.

So now I'm waiting patiently
For the day when you'll come home
And hold me in your arms.
I'll not regret one moment spent
Of dreaming while you're gone.

Some say you're where your thoughts are,
Now if that thought is true,
You don't ever have to be lonely,
For I'll always be with you.

Renee Fraser
UNBREAKABLE
Time relived
is only memory passed.
Exhuming dusty skeletons
with such care
that one would think of them
as made of glass.

Glass
that would break
with only a gentle tapping.

Yet,
in reality, too sturdy.
For the past can never be broken.

Duane E Menago
A TRIBUTE

To Tom, for all of your love and encouragement, and to the families of the Challenger crew.

As, once again, the nation watched
With pride and joy abound,
Our Challenger was swept away,
Only pieces have been found.

Our joy was turned to horror
As we gazed upon her plight,
Our pride was turned into remorse
At such a deadly sight.

As if we dreamed it, we clung to hope
That still, we'd see her rise
Above the cloud that swallowed her
Right before our eyes.

But our hopes, they faded quickly
For it wasn't meant to be
As we watched her flaming fragments
Float to their rest at sea.

Among her precious ruins,
The souls our hearts are with,
Scobee, Jarvis, Onizuka, Resnick,
McAuliffe, McNair and Smith.

We'll not forget you, Challenger,
Nor your precious crew.
And we'll not forget what you stood for,
A nation's dream come true.

Jean Veile
WAR'S FORGOTTEN FACE
The fragile petals fall upon my chest
Drops of blood without end
Guns of war burst and flame, pain, no rest
What message do they send?
I lie in a field in this godforsaken place
No one knows me, I'm War's Forgotten Face.
I, too, once was young, lighthearted, no cares
Unconcerned with worldly affairs.
Alas, an enemy I never knew
Has taken the sun from a sky once so blue.
The petals of a tiny poppy are as fragile as the drops I bleed
For what I've done, I know not what deed.
I'm the faceless unknown soldier they all pass by
I'm dying and I don't even know why!
The petals fall on me for one last time
My blood mingles with their beauty, my last breath, in rhyme
. . . . Good Bye . . . . . .

Michael G Graham
THE OCEAN SHORE

To the USS Antietam, Homeported in Long Beach

I love to walk the ocean shore and listen to the waters
roar, the ocean hits apound the beach which lays the shells
with in my reach, I pick them up from off the sand, hold
them softly in my hands.

I love to walk the ocean side to watch the crabs run and hide, even when the day is gone the oceans breath goes on and on.

Joanne Robinson
THE REGAL ASPEN
On the bank of the Blue River stood an aspen so tall.
He listened in spring for the bird's mating call.
Perhaps they would light midst his leaves, all aquiver,
Taking a rest before crossing the wide, rushing river.
Many an angler had stood at his feet;
His wide trunk protecting them from summer's heat.
He was a protector of all, both man and wild game.
But, there was no protection for him when the woodcutters came.
None of those he'd protected were around
When they cut through his trunk three feet from the ground.
He was glad when spring waters make the river very wide.
In this new rushing water his nakedness he'd hide.
But, once again, his protective instincts were found
When all that water softened ground.
In the holes 'neath his roots in the water so deep
A fish laid her eggs and went safely to sleep.
By his roots he snatched fish hooks, day after day;
Protecting the fish as they went on their way.
The new water receded and took away all that was good.
He knew he would die with no soil where he stood.
Across the dry river bed it was a pleasant surprise
To see a seedling of his, before his demise.
He was proud as he saw the aspen so tall.
He knew he would be a protector of all.
Now all that is left of that stately old tree
Is gnarled roots, full of hooks,—but, the fish were set free.

Thelma H McMullen
SOLITUDE

Dedicated to my sisters: Kathleen, Margery and Dorothy

Oh! For the quiet of a babbling stream:
Where I could just sit and dream.
Beneath a shady 'Ole Oak Tree,
With nothing but Nature all around me.

To hear the Robin singing his song.
Little squirrels frolicking, all the day long.
Then, at night when everything's still,
Listen to the Whip-O-Will upon the hill.

Watching the sunrise in the 'Morn.
Realizing a new day is born.
The flowers awake, heavy with dew,
Brilliant with colors of every hue.

Overhead, white wispy clouds drifting by.
Under a beautiful azure blue sky,
The forest creatures going their merry way.
They too, beginning another new day.

Away from the hustle and bustle of city life,
Soothing away all cares and strife.
I hope this puts you in the mood.
For this is really SOLITUDE.

Michelle MacQuarrie
BEFORE

For my Sapphire Blue and to Flame, may it be a boy!

From the windows
I can see them
The children as
they run, chasing
each other
Someday, when they've
grown
maybe they'll look out
a window
and wonder about those
children who came
before their own time . . .

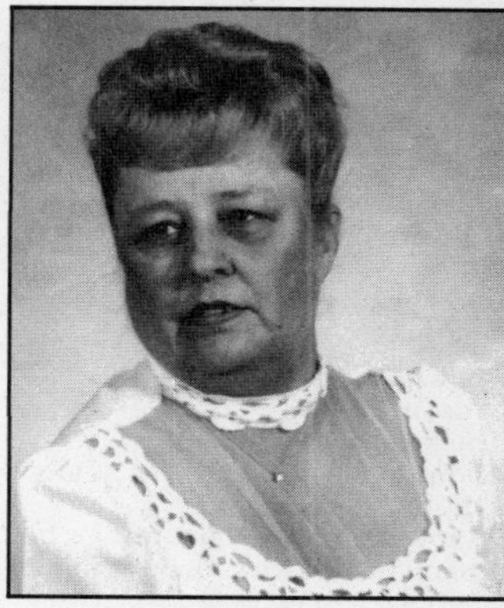

Elaine Onisto

Elaine Onisto
THOUGHTS
My thoughts are still—the light fades—
My mind wonders to a little girl—
She cries in her sleep—a gentle
Hand, a gentle voice eases the fear—
A stroke on the head and the girl
Knows the gift of love—now here
I sit holding a loved hand—knowing
A growing fear for soon the Lord will
Come and lift the weary and tired
Sole—down a sunny road of peace—
She will go into a painless world of
Grace—for it is said, the peace of
Heart shall see the Lord—I love
you mother.

Hubert Oscar Farnum
DREAM ALONG
Look down below to see
The midnight moon,
Racing swift from lake to lake
As we ride the step
To Tampa and the South.

How come the scent
Of orange blossoms
Reaches up to here?
How come the stars
Shine down from everywhere?

Spiderweb bridges
And ladybug cars,
Licorice highways
And powerboat stars.

Beacon of emerald
Or beacon of white,
Guide us to safety
Down through the night.

Jet engines and wings
Hauling people and things,
A small world in flight
Alone in the night.

Jonathan Iannone
NINE MONTHS
Lea cried the day
we made love.

Staring out the window
shivering and silent.

Strangers,
Listening to locker room voices
echoing cliches.

It snowed
late
Killing the early blooming flowers.

Nine months later
my son was born.

Bonnie Schroeder
SNOWFLAKES
Snowflakes are a ponderous thing,
That always set me wondering
If I were one
I'd be scared of the sun
And always on the ground
Not able to make a sound

Snowflakes have the grace of a dove
The beauty of a flower
And provide peacefulness at any hour
I'd love to become just for a while
A snowflake with a happy smile

Ella L Waldridge
ENTRAPPED
Like a bird caught in a snare,
I was trapped in my own isolated world.
There was no place to run,
And there was no place to turn.
Friends were a comfort,
But they would not alleviate the void;
They could not fill the emptiness;
And they could not bring the satisfaction that comes with loving.
Just as the bird is finally set free,
So was I unleashed from the destitution of my being and the bonds that bound me.
Suddenly the path was completely clear,
And there was someone to catch me when I fell.
Though my fellow patriots will always be there to console me,
No one but you can make me feel needed;
No one else can fulfill my deepest desires;
And no one but you can fulfill my need for love.

Richard C Tullock Sr
PRISM
Sailing away with no destination in mind.
No Companion, just his heart in his hand.
Remembering the love of the one he adores.
Thinking about the way it was once before.
The sun reflects off his lonely heart, like a prism.
But this rainbow reflected only a shade of crimson,
On an open sea, the light has faded, he is alone.
His heart has drifted away into a world of its own.
Remembering the love he once knew.
And the sparkle of the morning dew.
The suns fading reflection of the silvery gloss.
A glow in his eyes, his love he hoped was not lost.

Lori M Owens
I'LL NEVER GET OVER YOU

This poem was written for JEFFREY WARREN EARLS, who died on Tuesday, May 5, 1987. Jeff, you'll never know how much I still cared, no matter what I said. You'll live forever in my heart.

I'm trying hard to forget the good times we had
But when I see you with her I get really sad.
I know you'll never miss me or my foolish ways
But maybe you'll see how much I care one of these days.
I'm trying to go on, I'm trying not to cry
But it gets harder each day, and more and more I want to die.
Maybe one day I'll get over you
But until then, my skies won't be blue.
I thought I'd really been hurt before
But now I see the hurt can be so much more.
I thought that maybe one day you'd be mine
But now I see I was so wrong and my sun doesn't shine.
Whenever I see you, the tears I have to fight
But like they say, I'll be alright.
I guess I could get someone else to take your place
But I'll never be able to forget your face.
I would have been so true
But I see you'll never let me belong to you.
I guess you don't know just how much I'd give
But now that we're so far apart, I'll still have to live.
I've got only one thing to say
And I'll mean it until my dying day
I'll love you 'til the day I die
But until then, I'll just sit around and cry.

Julie Kirchmer
SCARLET WISHES

This poem is dedicated to my children, Lisa and Andrew.

Time stands still
On the edge of a dream,
A tear is but a childs silent scream
Trapped within auras dimmed.

Bedlam held edges of bright light
To the ends of magnetic seas;
And confines the mind to sense and rhyme,
Never to feel the comfort of a certain summer breeze.

Betty Lola James
THE GULLS
Overhead a pure white gull glides above the sea
Its movements grace the beauty of the creatures that are free
It crosses my bow and sweeps and dives
With the hopes of a fish to keep it alive
When I put up my hand with a crumb of bread
It will dive to my hand and return again to be fed
Then off to the sky with a dip of it's wings
The wind whistles the song it sings
The gulls will follow my ship way out and soar up in the sky
They will follow my wake and play with the wind
and make their plaintive crys
When the gulls are gone the land is too
Then there is just me the captain and my crew
A game little ship and a mighty sea
With many long days and nights to be
Till the gulls follow my wake again and follow us to land
Then we who are weary of the sea walk again on the sand
My ship rests berthed with the sails down tight
While we who sailed her rest easy tonight

Gregory A Southern
MOVE ON BIG MAN
Move on big man, move on.
Don't let her see your tears
Or let her know she hurt you deeply.
Don't turn back.
You told her you didn't love her
Or care for her.
Were she worth the tears
It would be different.
To her you were a passing fancy
Made for her moment of weakness.
A moment of need has been filled.
Now she wants to go her way
And have you go your way.

Move on big man, move on.
Don't let her see your tears
Or know your denial of love was a lie.
If she only understood
You love her and do care.
That's why you let her have her way.
Yes the tears are burning
And the hurt is deep.
But from your love, she has her way.

Move on big man, move on
Don't let her see your tears.

Linda Cavaness
LOVE

To all those that I love, and to all those who know the joy of giving love, and to those still searching.

Love is different in many ways,
And changes alot throughout the days.
Love is found in many things,
But mostly in human beings
Who fight and argue all the time.
When will peace set to their rhyme?
Sometimes love turns into hate
And when it's gone you have to wait.
So while you're waiting, have some fun!
Go out of your way to find the sun!
Bring joy to all those that you can
By lending an ear or a helping hand.
It won't be long and you will see
That dreams come true for you and me.
For way down deep in hearts of men,
Love is found and renewed again.

Judith A Leighton
NO GOOD-BYE
Freed from its earthly bonds
Toward heaven Challenger soared.
A flash—a Y-shaped trail
And gone were seven lives.
Viewers stared in disbelief
As debris rained on the Atlantic.
We grieve not for the dead . . .
They are with God.
But for their loved ones
Who were left behind
Without a last good-bye.

Elizabeth Ann Clackum
LONNIE

To a special someone who has meant so much in our lives. A joy and blessing that could only have come from God.

Into our lives one day, a ray of sunshine came,
A little boy so shy and sad, and Lonnie was his name.

His past was not a pretty one, misfortunes he had a few,
But in our home, he had a chance to live and start anew.

They said he needed kindness, a lot of love and tender care,
I told them, from the very start, we had enough to share.

On one bright day in 82, he moved into our home,
He settled down, and fit right in, and never more to roam.

Now, our home's complete, nothing but laughter and joy,
All because of one small child, who's now our little boy.

There's no more tears, they're gone, we're glad,
It's us three now, Lonnie, Mom and Dad.

We thank thee Lord, each and every night, for making our lives happy and bright.
You're in our prayers and every smile, for bringing to us this little child.

Valerie Davis
UNTITLED
The morning grass
Shines wet with dew
It glistens like glass
The day is brand new
As a misty morning dawns
Over an ocean so blue
Over sleeping forests where fawns
Lay protected
Over abandoned fields
Which now lay neglected
What this new day yields
Has yet to be started
For dawn has only just risen
On this day uncharted

Constance B Goslin
THE WIND IN THE WILLOW
The wind in the willow one dark Christmas eve
A poor man goes gathering corn husk and sheaves.

He carries them home to build a night's fire
to close out the cold and burn out the tired.
Put on the kettle, a cake for his tea
a lone cup and saucer arranged daintily.
A whisp then a whistle once low, shrill and long
a hot cup of comfort, a moment then gone.
A sigh for the moment, a lonesome stare round
a tear that escapes him, an echoing sound.
A push from the table a clink in the sink
a rinse with the water, an unhindered blink.
A slow turn to boredom, a tired step round
and upon his pillow, he lays his head down.
A short prayer, a blessing, a sign and then sleep.
A sigh and a cry; a tear, time to weep.
A swipe, take a deep breath, a pat to the pillow.
A sigh and a cry, the wind in the willow.

Mary Ann Gonzalez

THE CHOICE

To George, my best choice

Blue stillness of a summer
morning
chameleon-like sporting itself
in emerald-June hope
by noon.

Will afternoon don a dress of

love-colored evening
or will this stylish day
simply strip itself,
seek the black night, and
dissolve there
naked
and
unfulfilled?

Jennifer B Mills

ODE TO A COUNTRY ROAD

Oh Country Road, traveled now and then,
Remember how it was way back when.

When horses and buggies made a two-lined track,
While clip-clopping along on your dusty back.

Parties and gatherings were their destination;
You were their only mode of transportation.

Now you're covered with black asphalt,
To bring your dust and dirt to a halt.

Though today people prefer freeways to soar,
In you, sounds of yesteryear echo forevermore.

Joan D Catillaz Zielenski

BIRTH OF BEAUTY

At first
your whiteness is frightening.
Hesitatingly I touch you
one stroke and then another.
My fear slowly subsides
as you become familiar to me.
Your image takes form before my eyes
and under my gentle touch
I begin to see your beauty
come forth
full of life and color.
No fear now
only love and excitement
each time we come together
as we slowly nurture one
another.
You touch my inner being
and bring forth feelings
before unknown to me.
Until, one day in consumation
I seem to hear you say
"Thank you for helping me
to become . . .

a painting.

Carol Poor Kohtz Brown

Carol Poor Kohtz Brown

MY LITTLE MAN

To My Loving Son Jesse Stuart Kohtz

A bundle of joy, my little man
Seems I've waited forever, to touch his little hand
His cute little body, tucked close in a ball
That sweet tiny face, with features so small
I long to hold him and teach him of love
Tell all of lifes wonders, and of God above
What a delight, growing up with my son
Then watching him sleep, when day is done
Can't imagine my life without him now
My existance before, was empty somehow
His first little smile, the first laugh out loud
Discovering his hands, that wondering brow
It won't be long, he'll be learning to walk
Soon after that, he will learn to talk
They grow oh so quickly, enjoy it while you can
He'll someday be leaving, my little man.

Olivia Vincent

THE WIND IS BLOWING

To Mrs. Dorothy H. Bibbs, My Fifth Grade Teacher With Love

The wind is blowing, it's a windy day,
When school is out kids go out and play.
The clouds are white, the sky is blue,
The flowers are blooming and colorful, too.
The dogs will bark, the birds will sing,
When school is out, the bell will ring.
I like to sing,
I like to read,
Learning is what we really need.

Leona McCoy Young

TAKE A LOOK

Look in the mirror, Then look at me,
Our aging faces is what you will see.
One thing for sure, If we live long enough
We'll have happy days, And many that are rough.
Our steps will be slower, Our speech not so clear
Old age keeps creeping, Until it is here.
Just try to remember, Your young days past
No need of wishing, That they will last.
Every good thing has to come to an end,
And our youth we can't extend.
So get that thought out of your mind,
Surely soon, You'll see the sign of graying hair
And wrinkles quite a few, In both you and me
So don't be upset, Take it in stride,
And make these steps, With dignity and pride.

David Wade

SKIING

To my mom, Gary, and Trev because without them I would not have had the chance to go and learn to ski.

Skiing is lots and lots of fun
whether you're an expert or just begun.

It doesn't matter if you win or not
it all depends on how much nerve you've got.

Skiing is not for everyone
but it guarantees you lots of fun.

Nancy Cristina Sisk

MY LAST CHANCE TO SAY I LOVE YOU

I knew how you felt
after all that happened
and still thought
It might be worth it.

I don't know your feelings now
but I thought you should know
even through all of the bad times
I still remember the good.

I've been saving this for a long time
and feeling the way I do
I don't want to wait another day
to say I love you.

I've held back for months
to say it again
and now is my chance to say
just once more—I Love You!

Anna Bauer

HIS GREATEST GIFT

Wouldn't it be wonderful,
If all the world could be
Clean and bright and beautiful
And all men well and free.

But would we treasure all these gifts,
If we got them without pain?
Would we really love the sunshine,
If we'd never seen the rain?

So for all the blessings we receive,
Let us thank Our God above,
And remember that of all His gifts,
The greatest one is Love.

Barbara J Miller

ONLY YOURS

A mind is full
Of many wonders
It can hold secrets
Which only itself shall know.

It is yours, for
No one can tell you
What to do with it,
You can seek the
Largest ocean, or
The smallest stream;

And no matter which
You choose,
Always believe in love,
And hold tightly
To your dreams.

Naomi Pauline Shaffer

MONUMENTS TO MEN

Monuments to men are destined to decay,
Written on tombstones of time.
In the junkyards of memory they silently lay
On crumbling foundations they've long ago laid,
As the echoing voices of history fade,
The praises of men in their prime.

Engravings on stone may be symbols of trust,
But monuments to men never last,
Their efforts are buried like treasures in dust
In neglected cemetaries of glory
Where whitewashed stones tell a story.
In the graveyards of the past.

Carolyn Tetenbaum

THE WORLD THROUGH A CHILD'S EYES

If you could see the world through a child's eyes.
How different it would seem to look up at the summer skies

and dream away the lazy
afternoon.
And in June the gauzy fragile
butterfly that pollinates the hot
flowers with its sensuous tongue.

A child's hand reaches gently in
among the branches of a tree to
hold a bird's nest oh, so tenderly.
How mysterious is the miracle of
birth and in the wintertime
when snow blankets the earth.

Peeping up through the melting
snow, a violet, the harbinger of
spring.
What makes the sky so blue and
the grass so green?
Why is everything?

To be a child again, doing nothing
but thinking about the wonder
of it all.
Although so many years have
passed, perhaps you may recall.

Heather Osborne

A CHILD INSIDE

My favorite vase, I was so sad
How can one little girl be so bad
The vegetables that they won't
eat
The mud they track in with
their feet
Sometimes I want to run and hide
I guess I'm still a child inside

It feels so strange to hear me say
Why don't you go outside and play
Brush your teeth, pick up your
toys
I'm too young to have two boys
And when I hear their childish cries
I know I'm still a child inside

A train made from the kitchen
chairs
The times we'd pretend that we
were bears
Our favorite stories read time
after time
The hours of fantasy, make
believe and mine
And though my children grow in
size
I'll always be a child inside.

Violet C Scott

HELP OTHERS—SOMEHOW!

Dedicated, with Love, to my Children.

Look to the new day dawning
As the sun comes up in the east,
Accept your many blessings,
Especially those you expected
least.

Count them over carefully
As the sun goes down in the west,
And remember through whom you
received them,
And by whom you are blest.

Look to the evening hours,
Bow and say a Prayer.
Thank God for all His Glory
That you are privileged to share.

As you close your eyes in slumber,
Make a solemn vow
That with another dawn
You will—Help Others—
Somehow!

Mildred (Midge) Munz

NORFOLK AT DAWN

This poem is dedicated to Wilson, my loving husband.

Snow glistening and the city still;
Slowly yawning for the reborn
day,
As homeward bound in quiet will
The travelers make their way.

Long nights and busy days they've
served
Their country right or wrong
As war waves rocked their homes
awry
"V-Day.'" "Hurrah" They sing
their song.

Many miles and all are gathered
'Tis Christmas Eve; the Tree of
Light
Reflect the shining faces, warm
greetings, delight!
Welcome home! to fireside
bright.

Army, Navy, AirForce for sure
Sisters, brothers, husbands,
wives,
Look now! Step lively. The world
can wait!
Rebuild your lives, enjoy love
and beauty
All the sweetness of God partake.

Peggy Clements Sidden

JESUS IS MY LAWYER

Dedicated to the Father, the Son and the Holy Spirit with Whom all things are possible.

On that day in Glory, when the
dead in Christ shall rise,
I will see my Savior standing in
Paradise!
The court room will be open for
my Father is the Judge!
My lawyer is Christ Jesus, and
He is filled with love!
There was a chance to confess His
name that I almost blew!
I'm happy to say now that I've
found Him; you can, too!
I've leaned heavily on Christ Jesus
and avoided lots of strife.
I've always shared God's
blessings which vitalized my life!
Now the time has come to hear my
case, and I am stricken dumb!
But, I can see excitement on the
face of the Son!
"Abba, Father," Jesus began. "This
soul confessed My name before
men. And by Your Grace, We'll
let her in!"
God's eyes twinkled and did shine!
God moved His arm toward
heaven and the Gates opened
wide!
Suddenly, I heard a voice singing
and realized it was mine!
Jesus stood there with me—at
the beginning of time!

K S David Loh

MEMORIES . . .

In loving memory to my Late Parents. . . . poem dedicated to all the "broken-hearted," (like myself). And to all my friends at the University of Hawaii, Manoa.

Memories that I have for you is
sweeter,
Than that I am getting Later.
I know there is a time for a up and
a down,
I am drown with sorrow right now.
I wish there will be more happy
times, You and I,
My arms are always open, my heart
never cold as ice.
I love you, what more can I say,
That within my life, you will never
fade away.
My friend, my love, my forever,
I have never met a girl like you;
Never.
You are my sweet memories,
You are my soothing melody.

Brian D Frasco

PERFECT LOVE

Etched, white, fluffy clouds
Sky so blue
One more moment
I'll be with you
Sweet, sacred, promised land
Grass so green
Weeping willow tree
Everything so sheen

Seconds never pass
Time stands still
I can hold your hand
If it's my will
Bodies splashing water
Simple little stream
It's all so perfect
Don't wake me from my dream

Joseph E Schnieders

THE MIRACLE OF SPRING

I saw a crocus sprouting
One cold and wintry day;
That harbinger of blossoms
Said that spring was on the way.

I heard a robin singing
While walking yet in snow.
His melody gave promise
Of greenness soon to show.

I smelled a certain freshness
Which floated in the air;
The scent that starts a tingle
In us humans everywhere

I felt a raindrop hit me.
It told me very much.
It wasn't cold or frigid,
But warming to my touch.

I savored tasty berries
Plucked from an icy vine,
And knew these sweet precursors
Were but another sign.

My senses all had told me,
And caused my heart to sing.
I knew I soon would witness
That miracle called spring.

Suzanne Petherbridge

UNTITLED

To Ken, For loving life so much

Through misty eyes
I will travel
Over the edge
Into eternal peace.

Sandra Jean Jackson

QUIETNESS

To my special Grandmother, Mrs. Kathryn Funk

Alone with my thoughts, my mind
wondering.
Thinking of all the good things I
have in my life.
The day you ever decide you're
leaving me my mind would go
blank.

For if you leave you take the good
and happiness away from me.
But there will always be the quiet
time that no one can take away.
For the quiet time is a gift I give to
myself.

Debora Diane Kobolt

CRICKETS

What makes the Crickets Crick all
night,
And then be still when it is light?
I guess in the day they have to rest,
So in the night they can do
Their best!
I dont know, nor do I care,
I just hope they will always
be there

Jenny Gale

WARM LOVE

Days come, and, days go; and,
nights hang on like
Reminders of a better time we
know.
When two minds join in common
thought and prose,
Love is so strong, we don't have to
be there.
Our conscious being erases miles,
brings to
Mind's eye, your face, your smile,
sweet reminder
Of time gone by, when we held
your sweet hand
Reaching out for love you knew
our heart would
Extend to one so young, so sweet,
so true.
Sweet thoughts bring tears, filling
eyes; a reminder
Of times gone by; to these we issue
call—
A journey over memories' tall wall,
Until again, we feel sad tears no
more;
And, things are like they were
before—warm love.

Janet Pearson

WASTELAND

musty clouds overhead
seagulls calling my name
withering, wilting all the while.

opening wings
closing minds
dew drop falls
under the heavy waves
no chance
of surviving.

sea weed, dead weed
beneath their toes

your friend's gone
the next one goes
withering, wilting all the while.

white waves pound the ocean floor
birds now gone
making the foundation
for life to continue on
tear drop falls
under the heavy waves
no chance
of surviving.

Lois Baker

BROKEN HEARTS AND ARROWS

Gone are the ponies
that once roamed these hills
There are no more tee pee's
Our drum beats are still.

Our people have scattered
our corn has grown wild
Our spears are all broken
Our anger grown mild.

For with each treaty signing
and shaking of the hands
The Cherokee moved backwards,
and lost more sacred lands.

Through winters cold and hungry
we stood to try again
With spirits still unbroken
and pride we stood like men.

We stand now as a nation,
for all the world to see.
Though times have changed,
We are still, the proud, the
Cherokee.

Dennis G Blankenheim

LIKE THE ROSE

Like the rose I started from a seed
As I grow the beauty that's within
shall often be given
Knowing from time to time I shall
be clouded by troublesome
weeds
If lack of sun I failed to open Lord
Would I be forgiven
I must fight to one day blossom
and open my heart
Let my petals reach out to the sun
to nourish and remain
So all that's within shall come out
of the dark
And once I open the beauty of this
rose shall always remain
I'll try to grow perfect
My petals reaching out in loving
ways
And if bad weather endured my
petals become weathered and
torn
I'll try hard to be patient for
sunlight and better days
For even after the storm I shall be
a rose
Not just a stem of thorns

Virginia Sewell

SPRING

With arms extended I ran
Barefoot through April sands
In search of love.
The spring was so enchanting
And I so young.
The breath of romance touched
My finger tips
And I was hopelessly enthralled
With the beauty of the day.
Apple blossoms and wild cherry
filled the air
With a fragrance that was
Heaven in its sweetness.
Azure skies and pastures green
with new-born grass
Lent their charm along with
Birds mating in the budding
trees.
And I so young was breathlessly
Awaiting.
Hopelessly in love with love.

Sue Learn

THE FORTRESS

Forgive me for this fortress,
I've built around my heart,
But I must protect myself,
From the day when we may part.

For every teardrop there's a stone,
To help me build that wall,
Then someday if I'm alone,
It won't bother me at all.

Every time that I've been hurt,
It fortified that wall,
Someday there'll be no key, no way,
To get inside at all.

My heart was broken once before,
So fragile now and quick to bleed,
It could'nt stand another blow,
From a lover's thoughtless deed.

Adele McCormick

LOVE

It was a dark and lonely night,
but then I thought of you,
of how you made me laugh and cry,
cheered me up when I was blue.

To think of you again and again,
to try to make you see,
how much I really love you,
that our love was meant to be.

Now I know what love does mean,
It's really not a game,
but my love for you my dearest,
will forever be the same.

If you could see inside my heart,
my love for you grows stronger,
plese give me one more chance my
dear,
please just a little longer.

If you could only see me,
how much I really care,
please you must ask anyone,
anyone if you dare.

Now my thoughts will all be
memories,
my broken heart in two,
because I really love someone,
that someone was only you.

Leonia Graben

Leonia Graben

IN REMEMBERANCE

Sleep dear ones sleep. God watches
over your
slumber.

We came today to place our
flowers upon each.
In honor of the sweetness each
gave to us in
the past life we shared with each
other.
Remembering your true love that
brought beautiful
smiles and gladness to our faces,
found a resting
place in our hearts.

Just heaps of blessings that
brought so much
happiness to our lives in just being
together.
Simple joys in song of kindness to
each other.
Our happiness could be just a
smile, a hand
clasp or just a simple "Hello", of
yesterday
remembered, gone by.

These little things can mean so
much in lights
of a past loved one's life. For little
things
can bring so much comfort. They
hold a store
of tender thoughts that many
about you can
not see. But you feel them deep
down inside,
curing all the sore spots, where you
really live.
It's the kind of material that your
soul can grow
on and on.

It is the first bright star of the
evening,
shining with a beautiful yellow
glow bringing
about a restful peace.

Remembering how we stood with
each other under
the big full moon, sharing its
brightness, then
to the right a golden yellow star we
make our
wishes upon.

In tears of compassion, we silently
weep. We
say to ourselves, we'll see you soon
dear ones.
We'll all be together in the sweet
by and by
with Jesus.

Lisa G Pierce

DAYS OF LIFE

For Meano—Without you I would be nothing

A memorable day
Taking the first look of life
Scared and alone
Not yet knowing of love
But loved so dear
Soon growing to learn of hurt and
fear
Wild and wonderful
Dreaming of freedom
Wise to thoughts
But not to actions
Experiencing love and happiness
Sorrow and tears
So rebellious and uneasy
Becoming loud and crazy
Now its time to settle down
Think of the future
And how it will be
Finding that someone special
Setting the vows for eternity
Working at really enjoying life
Watching your young one grow
Time passes faster and faster
Feel happiness while you can

Elizabeth J Nilles

A MOTHER'S LOVE

A Mother's love is instant
When she conceives a child.
It is a love never fading
A love always embracing.

A Mother's love is instinct
Thru infancy and childhood.
It is a love of learning
A love always protecting.

A Mother's love is hesitant
As teen years appear.
It is a love of defending
A love always guarding.

A Mother's love is light
As adulthood arrives.
It is a love of feelings
A love always caring.

A Mother's love is heart
Loving all her children.
It is a love of sheltering
A love always nuturing.

Motherly love
To thee I give
So you shall love
In return—each other.

Dianne L Feyer

ODE TO THE ONE I LOVE

To my beloved husband, Paul.

This is not a new experience,
This love I feel for you . . .
It is ageless, timeless.
It has always existed;
Or seems to have been in my
heart . . .
My very being.
For I have loved the very essence
of you
For as long as I can remember.
I have searched for you in everyone
I met,
But found only fragments;
Tiny, teasing threads of you
That made me sure
That somewhere the "whole and
complete" YOU
Really did exist.
And, that if I waited patiently
And long enough . . .
You would come to me . . .
And you did.

Floyd Doremus

TO MOTHER

My mother is so very great,
And to me she is so dear.
Why do I just celebrate
My mother once a year?

She's always there when I need her.
She's constantly on guard.
She watches out for my welfare,
So living don't get too hard.

On mother's day we all recall
The many things she's done.
We often wonder when she'll fall,
As she keeps going on and on.

She never asks for much you know,
Just health and happiness.
She wants to see the healthy glow,
And hear the sounds of gladness.

To all the mothers on this earth,
We know you are the best.
We'd like to give you what your
worth,

In health and happiness.

My mother, she is number one,
This day and then forever,
I'll never leave her all alone,
Our ties we'll never sever.

Jan Bryant
OUR HOME

A family is more than just people living together in one place. It is a bond of love, sharing, and many times the understanding of another person. So I dedicate this poem to my husband, Paul, and my children, Angie and Daniel.

In our home built safe and secure,
Where love bounds us to ensure,
The happiness made for us two,
It shows from day to day in what we say and do.

In our home a family we do show,
With love and strength our children do grow,
When work is done, we share in play,
Make plans for tomorrow, yet build on today.

In our home love shows in everyway,
In a glance, a word, or some passion play,
Smiling happily today, looking ahead for tomorrow,
Playful joy in happiness, hold tight in sorrow.

And in our home when night moves in,
The children asleep in their world within,
We speak of our day, plans, and dreams,
And realize our love is more than it seems.

In our home there's times when a rough tide we must ride,
Yet, with love in our hearts this too we do abide,
Till wounds heal and anger is gone,
Then make up only to realize our love was made strong.

In our home of later years when we're old and gray,
I pray our love will sustain us everyday,
To look back in our minds and hearts,
Because of love we never did part.

Peggy Luke
MY MOM
My mom is a very special lady not only to me, but to all of those who know her.

My mom is known for her caring and
understanding and for her tender
smile.
My mom believes in helping anyone in need.
My mom has always been there in all my times of need.
She has taken care of me
in sickness and in pain.
She stands by me whether I'm right or wrong, because
she loves me just that much.

My mom is very special and
I love her very much.

Patty Burfield
ENDING STORMS
I see the sky is changing now
I see our love is ending now
I see the sky is darkening now
I see your eyes have been crying now
I hear the wind blowing through the pines
I hear you weeping in the dark
I close the curtains to quiet the wind
I hold you in my arms to quiet your hurt

Nancy Coffin
NEVER ALONE
What makes them think their the only ones
Who's ever been hurt, or lost someone,
The sorrow they feel, not knowing what to do
I know how they feel, I've been there too.

The many memories, too painful to bear
Reaching to touch, to find he's not there,
The lonely days, the sleepless nights
The love you've lost, it's just not right.

If only they'd realize that people do care
The emotion they feel, their wanting to share,
Life is a gamble you can never be sure
Of the chances you take or how they occur.

If only I could make them understand
All they need is to reach out a hand.
And grab onto something, a new bend in the road,
They might find a way to lighten the load.

Memories are to be cherished and not torn apart
But to be tucked in a special place in our heart,
We must go on living our lives, ever aware
That the love we had will always be there.

Lorene Burkett
UPON A CLIFF TOP
High upon a cliff I see,
Far away and under me,
Valleys lying green and fertile,
Roadside edged with wild crepe myrtle,
Willow, cedar, trees of pine,
Wild mimosa, trailing vine,
Oak trees almost old as time,
All is green in this great clime.

Honey bees are making honey,
While the day is bright and sunny,
Creatures nestling under brush,
Robins, sparrows, wrens and thrush,
Making nests in grass and reeds,
Eating worms and sunflower seeds,
Mocking birds began to scatter,
When the Blue Jay makes his chatter.

Hillsides lined with grazing cattle,
Watched by man on horse and saddle,
Brooks that quietly flow and trickle,
Ponds that look the size of nickles,
Fields are sowed in maize and corn,
Growing tall this lovely morn,
Fleecy clouds are rolling by,
Lonely eagle circles sky.

Nancy Kuna Lawler
ON BECOMING A WOMAN
I am the stem of a flower
All life functions exist
But, the potential for beauty is yet inside
Waiting to be born.

I stand here straight
Ready to face a strong gust of wind
Though a gentle breeze can
Sway me.

Will I possess the perkiness of the daffodil?
Or, will the fragrance of the rose
that lingers well after the bloom is gone
Be mine to claim?

What color will I be?
Vibrant, vivacious red
Billowy, spacious blue
Cheerful, new yellow?

I wonder if other embryos think and wonder, too.

Jacqueline E Jackson
A PROMISING LOVE
Love is a promise that God kept for man,
he sent his son to save the land.
From sickness, poverty, and sin.
Jesus's love come from within,
His heart that is filled with love and not pride.
So we could live free from sin in which he died.
On the cross from which his blood was shed and
his life ended,
To give us eternal life that's so splendid.
Some men know of his promising love and some do
not but they will learn,
He has not forgotten his promise he will keep it
until he returns.

Patsy S Bowers
ONE TINY SNOWFLAKE
One winter day as I sat
and watched it snow outside
a single little snowflake
by chance caught my eye.
Its shape was odd, there was
no doubt but its beauty was much
to behold; such a small piece of
nature yet, its true impact forever
untold.
I watched as it floated slowly,
time was nothing to it
it seemed to be searching
for a place on the ground to hit.
There seemed to be a glitter
from the beautiful object as it
passed then, I was reminded,
its beauty would not last.
Then, suddenly, other snowflakes
seemed to follow down
for alas, the tiny snowflake
at last had reached the ground.

Phyllis Anne Hunt
CRY FROM CALVARY
My soul has heard the lonely cry
That came down from Calvary
My life I give for you alone
What will you give to Me?

I ask no more of you today
Than what I know you can bear
Take up your cross, come follow Me
I'll be with you thru all eternity

Hanging there on dark Calvary
He cried out in love to me
I'm hanging here because of you
Can you feel the love I send your way?
In agony His soul cried out to me

My soul cries out to Christ above
I thank You for Your loving ways
Forgive me all my sinful deeds
I heard You cry from Calvary
My soul lifts up to You today
My spirts soaring high above
Touching the hand of God my Lord
Deep peace I feel inside my soul.

Sandra Sue Burdick
WORKING MANS BLUES

To my sons Mark Spies and Marty Spies from Nacogdoches, Texas

---

Boy it's hard getting along these days, when you want to live right, and there are too many bills to pay. But what is a person to do, when these things start happening to you?
We bought things on time, we used our Master Charge. We even had a Sears and Roebuck catalog card.
Eating beans and potatoes and rice gets old. When your gas company cuts your gas off all your food gets cold.
It's hard to look up now, because when everything was great, Uncle Sam came by, and took them ole' cold beans right off my plate.
The oil crunch has hit us now, and gas is real cheap, but there's something you have to remember my job I didn't get to keep.
So I don't buy gas, or oil for my car, because, I don't have cash, and they took my credit cards.

It's hard to go from President to sweeping the floor, because I have seven years of college, and they only want four.
I used to rob Peter to pay Paul, but now that Peters broke, Paul just called the law.
So, what's a man to do to overcome these hard times?
When to support his family at all he'd have to commit a crime.

If I tried to sell my soul, and think I would buy it back again, the creditors said I done broke the law, because I already owe it to them.
I sure hope this isn't a sin, but Lord I pray that President Reagan can pass a bill that will bring my beans back again.

Daniel A Bonadies III
FROZEN FOR A MOMENT

In Loving Memory of my Grandfather, DANIEL A. BONADIES, SR.

Frozen for a moment,
a world holding its breath.
At the viewing of a birth
dancing on the edge of death.

A letter meets a mailbox.
Hope teeters on despair.
A man looks at a woman
who doesn't know he's there.

A blackbird hits the windshield
of a trucker on his run.
A bullet stops halfway
down the barrel of a gun.

A stifled sickening sound
of a starving stomached rumble.
A foot that hits an unseen curb
in the prologue of a tumble.

A would-be soldier ponders entrance.
A convict plots escape.
In a Wall Street broker's office
there's a piece of ticker tape.

Infinity wrapped random things
scrape senses and they're felt.
And the moment that was frozen
meets the moment of its melt.

Kathleen A Dube'
THE KENNEDY PARADOX

To all great Americans—as we take the sweet with the bitter.

One thing is said but another often meant,
Politicians talk this but then do that,
So, if ever rules were made to be bent,
A Kennedy is an expert and always up to bat.

For, a Kennedy has mystique, they're so hard to figure out.
They are bold in character, with charisma to the end.
Special individuals, the world will long shout,
Having their share of sorrow and plight, all that life sends.

A mixture of a mother and father, they a paradox in flesh,
Who came together in marriage, however,
Did never completely mesh,
But gave to their sons and daughters purpose forever.

Strength and weakness, a paradox they share,
They are "Heroes of Our Times" and this a quote.
They live, laugh and play hard, beware,
And when in politics, they'll seduce your vote!

They try hard to make a better world for all to live,
And so aware are we of this "Camelot" they create,
We pardon their wrongs, as our hearts do forgive.
Oh, those Kennedys do take chances, and some on thin ice-skate.

They're daring and brave, all must acknowledge true,
Sticking together through thick and thin
And their rewards are still long overdue,
So, once again, pass the torch and let a new generation begin.

Ruby Stearns Bolton
DESERT FACETS

To Betty Jean Bailey, my Daughter,
To Curtis W. (Bill) Bolton, my son

The quivering yellow heat is pressing down
To brand with summer's mark her heaving wastes.
Each saber-pointed bush . . . each once-red spike
Of octilla bloom . . . each cactus armed
With daggers in saffron candle-flame edged
Is smothering beneath a gray dust quilt,
And to her fevered bosom, tightly clutched
Is Silence, fierce as new-born mother love.

No sun, however dominant, can stay,
The night is sweeter for a bitter day.

So now, the fire-ball inches toward the night
And sunburnt all surrenders to the dusk,
A dusk which waves a cooling plumage fan
Tipped with quartz-pink and streaks of amethyst
And here and there a Joshua's needle-points
Pierce through the remnants of a dying day
A lizard scuttles from his purpled dark
And stars sing of a blue and silver night.

A friend, her day . . . her night a quiet friend.
A land of no beginning . . . and no end.

Tim Roach
NIGHTFALLS
Daylight fades so slowly
as if it can't decide
rays of red and gold appear
as light sends forth its pride.

Trails of dusk meander
as kingly rivers sail
upon their waters gently
reflecting pools so pale.

Darkness comes as softly
as newly fallen snow
rains invade the atmosphere
as springly breezes blow.

Rainbows ebb from end to end
their hues absorbed above
fleeting prisms, all entwined
they speak, that such is love.

Clouds ripped in trailing wisps
from a never-ending day
horizons gleam with life and hope
The night falls, come what may.

Marcia Lynn Heard
OLD MAN
The house is very silent
The children grown and gone
I see the old man sitting near
A mere shadow of what he was.

His face is drawn and wrinkled
His body no more than bones
He does not know that I am here
Perhaps he doesn't care.

He watches out the window
As though he expects someone
I see he holds a picture
So gently in his hands.

He carries on his vigil
Unaware of time or place
The room is growing colder
But he doesn't seem to care.

His eyes have signs of life in them
Traces of a happier time
But they are overshadowed now
By loneliness and pain.

He turns back from the window
He slowly walks away
I wonder where his family is
Or if they even care . . .

Shannon Bassett Kirkpatrick
DECEMBER NIGHTS
Before the waning season's winds
Remnant leaves are tossed,
As Winter Solstice waxes near
With fragile, crystal frost.

A sylvan shadowed dusk descends
With somber shaded hues
And softly shrouds with greys and blues
The sleeping earth and misted sky,
Within a timeless, silent lullaby.

Stacy A Doklovic
EXCELLENCE
Take me to that place if only for a time,
where contentment and I stand face to face
and success is not far behind.

Remind me of that place when failure knocks
at my door, when defeat laughs in my face,
and disappointment cries for more.

Bury me in that place when contentment
finally sets in, when acheivement has won
the race, and my excellence comes from within.

Steven G Lorr
MY "FOR EVER" LOVE

To my wife, Dania on her birthday (9-25-84)

If ever, I was to lose you,
We would both, be losers.

I, for you, being the one I love most,
You, for I, being the one who loved you most.

If ever, I was to lose you,
You would lose more than I.

For I, could love an other,
As I loved you.

But no other, could ever love you,
As I love you.

Happy Birthday Dania

Midge Margaret Rothenberger
MY PORCELAIN DOLL
Love notes left on your pillow,
Love notes written on the wall,
Love notes that mean I love you, even through it all;
cause your my priceless porcelain doll.

Love notes showing that I love you,
Love notes left everywhere;
Love notes telling you I'll care,
even showing you I'll be there,
cause your my priceless porcelain doll.

Love notes that tell how much it means to hold you,
Love notes that tell how much it means to see you,
just to say how much I love you;
my priceless porcelain doll.

Love notes that would take away the hurt,
Love notes that would take away the pain,
Love notes that would make you smile;
Love notes that would last forever, while;
your my priceless porcelain doll.

Annie Huston
THE PAIN OF WAR

This poem is dedicated to the brave men who fought The Vietnam War. May their names never be forgotten. Also to my beloved Andrus.

Wash off your window the rain drop of hail.
For tomorrow will be a mournful sigh.
For only the future knows what will be.
Maybe a cry for peace, or an answer in vain.
But whatever it may be it will only bring hate.
From the rain drop of hail you washed off to late.
You, you over there why run why haunt your soul.
The world might cry only the grave will rejoice your cometh.
And look you will be no more for only the dirt
will tarnish your soul.
And call for the body thats withered and cold.
Stop running for you can not hide.
For the rain drop of hail will only bring fate.
Because you yourself washed it off to late.

Frances Jackson Allen
IMPOSSIBLE
Finding peace, joy and happiness,
Who said it couldn't be done?
In this day and time,
For such a thing is thought impossible,
Content away from care.
Impossible you say?
Take yourself on a long enchanted daydream,
Into life's most wanted things.
You're happy there with joy and laughter,
But that's only for awhile.
Impossible you say?
Make yourself enjoy life, in the worst of times.

For in the end you'll see,
That it was only for awhile.
Nothing is impossible,
It's just the way we make it seem,
For all can be accomplished,
That is, ALMOST ANYTHING.

Sim Diky
SLEEP MY GIRL
Sleep my little girl
My tiny little jewel
You'll have a dream and best of all
It will be very real.

You'll dream the World
That's laying at your feet
It seems that you'll be clever girl
With world to play like with a soccer ball.

Sleep my little girl
My tiny little jewel
You'll have a dream and best of all
It will be very real.

And in the universe, no matter how big,
There is none
Smarter and prettier than you alone.

Sleep my little girl
My tiny little jewel
You'll have a dream and best of all
It will be very real.

John C Bachandouris
LINA
If when you read this, your face turns red
It's only because of the truth you've read

Your eyes are like sunrise
And yes, they hypnotize

When I see you in a room
It's like a flower about to bloom

Your smile is so beautiful and bright
You'd make anyone feel alright

Beauty like yours, I've rarely seen
You're incredible, like something from a dream

Beauty like yours is hard to find
Because you are one of a kind

When I see you, I can't help but stare
Since impeccable beauty is very rare

I know if I search the whole world through
I'll never find a girl half as beautiful as you

I never thought I'd find a girl
Who'd send my mind for a whirl

A perfect body, smile and personality
I never thought that could be found in reality

You're like a goddess way up high
It's impossible to reach you so high in the sky

Your eyes would glow in the night
Oh what a beautiful sight

This poem is over, yes it's the end
Alas! I must settle to just be your friend

Charles J Moran
HEARTBROKEN
Oh son I love you so much!
I hope you never know
The pain that I am going through
from missing you so.

And I hope your life is full of riches
In everything you do.
With good health and no pain.
With plenty of sunshine and no rain.

I hope your wife is pretty.
I'm sure she will be.
And your children all will be beautiful
And have bewitching brown eyes like you.

I hope you're all together
for one hundred year's or so.
And I give you all my happiness,
which I could never find.

And someday when you have the time
When your sitting with your son,
I hope you'll tell him about me
And the good things that we done

I hope that you realize
What a set back this has been
To leave someone you love so much
To never return again.

I hope you know I love you
And that I miss you so.
I hope someday we're together
In a land where we pray to go.

Toni McCullough
IF I CAN
If I can help with good intent,
someone to feel a bit content,
Their troubles small as they might be,
to them are magnified you see!
If I can clasp a lonely hand,
or just to be there, for a dying man,
A lonely child, or a mother-to-be,
or just to set an animal free.

I cannot help a thousand men,
but I can give, an extending hand,
I cannot help this world to see,
but I can give, just part of me.
If I can feed someone today,
or just to teach someone to pray,
A little child to love and care,
then my friend, I've done my share!

Gordon H Taggart
ONE SECOND 'TIL MIDNIGHT
Wrap up Today in a package
And store it on Memory's shelf,
For nothing can change how you've lived it
So, "praise" or "condemn" for yourself.
You can value and weigh it for merit
You can judge it for loss or for gain—
You can balance the tears with the laughter
Your triumphs—with dreams that were vain.

The ledger is closed to that entry,
The "seal" of "the past" is in place—
The ink of the age is upon it
And, it's filed away—out in space.
So, wrap up Today in a package
Then store it on Memory's shelf—
The way that you lived it is over
The scoring was done—by Yourself.

Rebba Morton Becker
LONELY CHILD
A child is born, a person dies,
Someone is gone, the baby cries.
The child grows fast as the days pass by,
Soon the child is learning to lie.
The child, now running around without care,
Turns to find love that is not even there.
The child feels he is not wanted anymore,
Now at fourteen, walks out the door.
He steals, he cheats, he will even fight,
Just for money or a place to spend the night.
He takes the drug to ease his mind,
He keeps on searching but will never find.
He watches people as they pass him by,
He starts to think and wonder why.
He tries to run from his problems and fears,
But only finds he cannot hide the tears.
To ease the pain he does the drug once more,
One time too many, he falls to the floor.
A child is born, a young boy dies,
The boy is gone, the baby cries.

Michelle Clark
FLIGHT
Over the seas
Above the trees
In the wind
It will begin
Breathing the air
Leaving the fair
Beside the moon
Today at noon
It will rise
Into the skyes
Big and round
Over the town
You will see
A balloon and Me!

Barbara Oliver
VALENTINE BE MINE

To my beloved and life-long friend Charles Timmons

Will you be my valentine? I promise never to be untrue, never to be unkind.
Valentine, if you say you'll be mine, we'll rocket into space, we'll skate to Mars.
We'll declare our love to the world as we stop to gather stars.
My love, if we would always remember to put God first in our lives giving him the praise and the glory, the victory will always be ours.

No hurdle will be too hard. No cross road will be too rough.
If, we return the love that Christ has for us, we shall have done enough.
We might not ever be rich or millionares, but if we hold tight to each others hand, and walk in the light of God's holy plan.
I'll always be your woman valentine and I know you'll always be my man.

Glenda S Thomason
LIFE'S TASK
Life is so elusive fleeting by so fast
Yet time is eternal, we all have a task
Learning isn't easy—we all make mistakes
If only we could see—giving LOVE is what it takes
Thru our past, present and future as time does evolve
The lessons of our karma we must learn to resolve
Giving of our talents, our love to all mankind
When this we can accomplish our spirits are sublime
But during our trials its so hard for us to see
That giving, loving,teaching each other, is what sets us free
Free from earthly trappings, from all the hurt and pain
Free to exist as one, with HE who forever reigns.

Jody L Campbell
TO YOU WITH LOVE
I love thee
With all my heart
And I know we
Together can paint beautiful art

So stay with I
Me with you
And you will see why
We can make a matching two

For if you leave me
I might die
Or you might see
A tear coming when I cry

For we might marry
And live in the wild
And I will carry
Our very own child

Amy McDonald
ALONE IN A CROWD
Sitting alone in the middle of a crowd
I hear people laughing,
And shouting,
Cars and buses roaring by,
The sound of footsteps crunching up the dried leaves.
Children laughing, running,
Crying for their moms,
Radios blaring,
I hear a jet over my head,
People working, hurrying off to Nowhere.
Silence is nowhere to be found
Except inside my head
And if I sit still long enough
All I hear is silence
But if I move the slightest bit,
The sounds of the crowd
Come back to me.

Flora Keiser
SNOWFLAKES OF LACE

Margie Ditman

Snowflakes of lace
Gliding softly to earth
Each a different pattern of
beauty and great worth
Snowflakes of lace
Landing gently on my face
Blanketing the mountains high
And valleys with such grace.
Snowflakes of lace
Becoming heavy with each layer
Listen to each snowflake fall
As silent as a prayer.

Lynne Arnott Thomas
KICKING THE HABIT
All these things
They've been going in my mind
I'm not anyone else,
I'm one of a kind.

It's really mind blowing
Throws a jolt to the soul
When you slow down the digging
And climb out of the hole.

Throw away the devilish games,
Doesn't matter win or lose
Just keep my head together
When it's my privilege to choose.

Soaked up all the laughter,
Gave my pain to the Lord
There's just no reason for lazy,
Because I'm tired of being bored.

So just let me be,
To live like HE
FOREVER FREE.

Lora McEwen
EASTER LOVE
What is your thoughts of Easter
As it comes again this year?
Is it thoughts of fresh, spring days
Or something new to wear?
Some think of brightly colored eggs
Scattered in the grass
Others of the Easter bunny
All done up in class.

The egg is symbolic of new life to
begin
Also, the rabbit portrays life
without an end.
The natural human spirit is
grasping after life
Not knowing it can be obtained
through Jesus Christ.

They did not take His life from Him
As He hung upon the post
No they didn't kill my Lord,
He gave up the Ghost.
Over all the earth that day
A deep, deep darkness fell
As Jesus left this earthly realm
To go down into Hell.
He went down to the pit you see,
to take away the keys
To defeat the devil, raise the dead
And set the captives free.

The human cry can now be
stopped, for He became our sin
He burst forth that morning, Death
could not hold Him!
No they didn't kill my Lord, of Him
to hear no more
For on that Easter morning the
Victor's crown He wore!

Rebecca Baldwin Dowell
SLOW DOWN
Slow down and don't run
For this life is too short
So slow down.

Look around and see
All the beauty God has created
He will speak to your heart
If you let him come in
Slow down.

He'll lead you through life
No matter how dim

He'll guide you and lead you if you
Follow him
So trust in God
Thank him for all he's done.
So slow down, don't run

Bettye Ellen Stout
ABYSS
In the deep pit of man's folly
Exists the wall of despair.
He has built it inch by inch
With neither thought or care.
Only blind self-gratification
Has been the enduring mortar,
Cementing this man-made prison
Keeping captive the tormented.

Herman H Parrish Jr
MY LAST THOUGHT

In memory of Mrs. Minnie Lewing

Do not grieve for me when I am
gone
Because I will be in a perfect home
Up in heaven with the angels fair
There will be no more care
Do not shed those tears today
When they lay me in my grave
For my home is far away
Up in heaven I will stay
You can come to see me there
Up in heaven with the angels fair

Brevane D Gauthier
QUESTING LOVE
Oh, how I have searched for you!
In softly running brooks and
stormy seas!
In starlit nights that reach far
beyond a thousand me's.

Busy streets that hold so many of
my kind
have hid you from my grasp.
Again to think I only hold you in
my mind.

You've been so close, so very many
times,
a hand, a breath away
Only to slip again into the limbo of
my searching heart
and then
To wonder if the search is real, or
have I only made
you up to keep my days?

Ah, yes! You are real!
I see you in the morning sun when
life is fresh and new.
Yes, then I can behold the purpose
of my dream
from high atop my private view.

The doubt that you will never
come, bogs down
as love and courage hold me high
To keep that which only is mine . . .

The wait, the longing, the
everpresent time,
for my quest of love, My Love,
Forever seeks out Thine . . .

Sharon E Walker
HURT

To David Gamez, the love of my life

Suppose hurt could be bottled up
inside
Like a fly in a trap.
You wouldn't have to wrap
Up the dirt and hide.

Maybe if hurt could fly away

Like a duck in flight
And start a brand new day
You could smile with all your
might.

Possibly if it could explode like a
stick of dynamite
Just maybe there wouldn't be any
more hurt.
Hurt always makes you want to
fight.
It makes a big difference between
day and night.

Ludy Lehmann
MEMORIES OF MY MIND
As I sit here alone and blue;
Memories and years gone by
without you.

So many days and nights I've set
and cried;
As so much time has gone by.

I can still see the sweetness of your
face;
That all my memories of you
haven't erased.

As my heart aches and memories
yearning,
I can still smell the fragrance of
your pipe burning.

I still see your eyes of blue;
My God knows, I still love you.

Oh how I loved to see your smile;
For just one more chance, I'd walk
a mile.

To laugh, to cry and to be your
friend;
Most of all, to be your love once
again.

All the past years, I've secretly
cried;
God in Heaven knows, I'll love you
till I die.

For your always with me, in my
heart;
Someday, we'll be together, never
to part.

For someday when I'm dead;
You'll still be with me, my
memories of you, in my head.

When they bury me and cover me
deep;
I'll take all my memories of you,
with me in my sleep.

When God comes and takes us
home;
We'll hold hands and sing, as
through the golden streets we'll
roam.

Melody Anniece Patterson
METAPHYSICAL ENCOUNTER

Dedicated to my reason for being . . . to the first real love of my life . . . to Ron Patterson.

Sun streams into the open room
with the soft morning breeze
blowing in with the rays.

Feeling the gentle caress across
my cheek from the draft—I
turn—
And there is this magnificent
silhouette filling the doorway.

Shoulders so very broad follows a
contour to a chest so massive
as to take my breath away.

A beautifully shaped body
supported
by muscular thighs that top a pair
of long, long legs—I sway.

A stirring such as I have never
before experienced begins in my
stomach and expands to run in
ripples through my veins from
arms to fingertips—from legs to
toes.

My entire body is encompassed in
electricity—an eternity passing
as a spiritual premonition touches
lightly upon my soul.

Whether it is warmth from the
sun's rays or a flush from
my excitement.
A fervor settles like a cocoon
wrapping across my shoulders
to encompass my body—
promising a life of
enticement.

Audrey R Hicks
REMEMBER ME
Darling, please remember me
Not as I am, but as I used to be.
I'm lonely now and you should see
What a change your love
Has made in me.

Thank you for the memories
Of beautiful days gone by.
I often sit and think of them,
And I often sit and cry.

Our life together could have been
so sweet
When once again we chanced to
meet,
I love you now as I did back then,
And I hope someday we will meet
again.

Lord, help me to be wise enough
to see
If another chance you give to me.
Not to make the mistake I made in
the past,
And to accept the love
I know will last.

Eva M Newton
SO TIRED
In early morning when the grass
with dew
is wet
I'm planning so many things into
which
I must get
The day seems so bright and I'm
eager
to start;
and yet by noonday, I'm beginning
to lose
heart.
Well by middle of the afternoon
I have really lost my zip and glow
All my plans have gotten out of
tune,
And my traffic light says stop, <u>not</u>
go.

Oh! Woe is me and my energy
surely, everything cannot be right;
Even though I'm so tired
physically,
I still have a ravenous appetite.
Well, I'm seeking a perfect balance,
an energy increase and hunger
control,

one without the other gives an awkward
stance
and falls short of nurture to my body and
soul.

Thelma Ritchie
PRECIOUS LIFE
Life is not perfect, always gay,
Peace and serenity every day.
It is not always kindness, love,
Nor sheltered by a protective cove.
Life is not death, it is not hell;
Its purpose not a confining jail.
It is not limited by matter's claims
And cannot be consumed by flames.

Life is a chance to care and love,
To give oneself and therefore prove
That life has meaning. Oh how grand
To have a chance to take a stand
For something real and purposeful.
Life is spiritual, contained in soul.
God created it through His plan,
And this great gift He gave to man.

It is exciting, brave and daring,
Sometimes loving, learning, sharing.
But life is not what it should be
Until through Christ we are set free.
It then is used eternally
To share with others lovingly.
And then no matter how we feel,
We'll always know that life is real.

Netannis Henderson Kline
FROM SEA TO SEA
Over the rolling restless waves, the carefree winds blow west to east
Sometimes softly, smooth and light, sometimes screaming, black with rain
Hurling the clouds toward the land. Or soft again and silent, clothed in mist
Pale as a ghost in the moonlight.
Sea fog drifts ashore like smoke, soaking the rocks and trees with dew . . .
Dripping, awaiting fresher winds, which blowing briskly, clear the mists.
Lifting over cliffs and hills, lightly the breezes stir the woods.
Swaying the tips of the tallest trees, then on to the mountains, rising still,
Colder and stronger, up and up to rage and storm on the icy peaks,
Fierce as a banshee scream. .
Now gathering speed and flowing down, between the hills and out across the plains
Rolling and trapping tumbleweeds against the fences, buffeting the sheep and goats,
Wildly rushing down the canyons, drying the streams, blowing dirt and dust,
Fast and furious next the winds attack the prairies, rippling fields of wheat and corn
Like those waves left far behind.
High and hot, heavy with clouds, striking the land below with fire
Whirlwinds and tornadoes wreak destruction on the patient earth.
Leaving havoc in their wake, the winds roll on across the great slow rivers,
Into the lush and humid south, pouring rain on the fields of rice and cotton
Releasing the scent of pinewoods into the soft warm air,
But spiced with the tang of salt.
For now the winds have crossed from sea to sea and free once more
Can roam another ocean's wide expanse, joining the seabirds on their lonely flight,
Or spinning wildly off the coast, turn back as hurricanes,
And tear at the land with a final savage frenzy!

Harry (Bill) Andrews
CHRISTMAS TREE
I wish there was a Christmas Tree,
So tall the eye could never see.
I wish its branches would reach from
ocean to ocean.
Its every branch covered and dripping
with love and devotion.
Approached by a poor girl or boy they
would receive their most wanted
Christmas toy.
A blind person would touch this tree
and they would be able to see.
Instant parents would appear by the
shedding of an orphans tear.
A wonderful world this would be
If we only had this beautiful tree.

Dax D Sprinot
WITH LOVE IN THE HEART
With love in the heart
And spring in the air
More beauteous the art
And fresher the breeze,
If thou art a pair.

The sunshines down on each new love
And bathes them in its fulfilling light.
Around them does soar the dove,
Each thing they look on new.
Together they reach any height.

But to one alone the sun does not shine as bright
And the air does not smell quite as sweet.
Their heart does not take flight,
But sorrow is not their lot
For if they look, the one they seek, they're bound to meet.

Then love shall rest in the heart
And spring shall scent the air.
With thy love thou shalt not part
And live together forever,
If thou but love and care.

Selenia Montalvo
BROTHERHOOD

To my dear grandchildren

Brotherhood, beautiful word!
Meaning love throughout the world!
Hate is out, no place for it
Love and gentleness you should teach!

We must care
We must share
We must not ever forget
To be united
Holding hands
We can continue
We can stand
Love is force
If it's true
Is the base of
Brotherhood

Xenia Ursula Laguna
DEAR PAIN
So dear pain, you have come
Knocking on my door again.
Were you sent to witness,
My last farewell?

Who, if I may ask,
Sent you anyways?
Was it someone I love,
Was it someone I hate?

So dear sorrow, you too
Have come my way.
Your taste is so sour,
Your smile is so vain.

Who told you, by the way,
That I was in pain?
Was it someone I love,
Was it someone I hate?

So dear grief, what are you doing here?
Had not you heard,
My heart was already hollow,
And my soul was already weak?

Who did you follow?
Was it your friend sorrow, or
Was it someone I love,
Was it someone I hate?

Jodi Stevens
LOST SHIP
I am like a lost ship sent out to sea never to come back
I've lost all my friends, and I miss the love I lack.
As I am sailing farther into nowhere I watch the waves grow
The waves get bigger, as do the gaps in my life, then the wind blows.
The waves are like walls being built up all around me
These walls are blocking out all that I can possibly see
The waves will soon die and the winds will too.
Now I am left out in this world all covered in blue.
Soon in the distance I see a brand new shore
As I reach it, the birds above start to soar.
I have found a new place far from my last home
I look back in the long path of white foam
I see all the things, that I once did fail
I know they are over, so now I will lower my sail.

Thomas Michael Flatley
THE ELUSIVE DOVE
It soars above in the heavens,
And o'er the ocean's crest;
Wandering about like an outcast—
In search of a place to rest.

It is making the same, sad, slow journey
That it has made for years;
Witnessing the pain and the anguish
Brought on by wars and fears.

It has known and seen the ancient muskets,
And now, the fearsome rocket's might;
And with alarm, it views the struggle
Between godlessness and right.

Much sought, and yet rejected by those
Upon tyranny and aggression bent;
Its flight seems futile and fruitless—
In a world by weary anxiety spent.

Perhaps, there may still be a world—
In which reign tranquility, brotherhood, and love;
And there may, some day, be a haven
For Peace, the Elusive Dove.

Pearlie Taite
GOOD FRIENDS

To all of my good friends, Debbie, Jackie, and Joanne.

Good friends are people you can call anytime of day or night and say, "I need you". They ask no questions but are there before you can hang up the telephone.

Good friends do favors without being selfish.
They forget about their problems to help you with yours.
They stay together through good times
and bad.

They can talk about anything without
being offended.
They are not envious of each other.
They thrive on pushing each other up the
ladder of success and are proud of that success.

Gail L Sanford
AT TIMES
There are times
in the darkest of nights
when the winds blow chill
and a cold rain is coming on,
when you have to take any comfort
you can find.

You'll find warmth sometimes
in the glow of a strangers eye
giving way to a fire within.
Open hearts like empty rooms
waiting to be occupied.

And I'll open your door
shivering with my coldness
and take a chair on your hearth.
I'll warm my hands
and breathe in strength
to help me on my way.

And we will know when I've been filled
as I turn may collar up, bracing myself
to face the world again.

Thank you my beautiful friend in
your knowing way
for helping me to make it
through.

Helen Feil
WAGONS
When its time for a bit of remembering
Remember the little red wagon you had
The fun it was when you played with it
The work it did for your Mom and Dad

The furniture it carried in
The hills it took you down
The spills you had from it
You'd come in with bumped knees, and frown.
Your wagon lasted quite a while
It lost its tongue in due time
The wagon rests now near the garage
Rusting as we remember bygone time.

We had a wagon also
But it was big and blue
In fact it sat ten and
Was eighteen foot two
Carried us on visits to Grandmas,
Small vacations and short trips
Filled it with groceries every other week
Had a few bumps and dents, then a dip
We stood on the road and watched it float
Called the cops, a wrecker and divers.
Pulled it out, windshield's gone
Top's pushed in, now no more drivers.

Ruby M Olson

PEACE

Peace among nations, is what we need now.
And we must find the answers,
To all the questions, somehow.
Each nation must speak their piece,
And everyone should listen,
If we want the wars to cease.

No one is perfect, we all make mistakes,
We can learn from one another.
And for the World's sake.
We must listen like a brother.

Though we might not agree.
There are others to consider, not just you and me.
Kindness and sharing go hand in hand.
And have proven to many, we have a great land.
And patience is a virtue, we all must nourish.
To save this World, that all Nations cherish.

Annetta Lewis

DAD

I remember masked eyes of merriment,
pudgy cheeks of natural sunburn,
hair as black as the ever-present shoe polish stains on his thick fingers

He seemed a giant in size, but wasn't.

I remember a husky voice booming orders in a baritone,
bellowing rebukes with brass,
thundering threats with authority.

I remember a cruel dictator about curfews, dates, and parties.

And yet,

I remember sturdy arms lifting me gently from slumber on a school morning to wash away the sandman's sleep—first with kisses, then with soap;
I remember an awkward but willing partner at father/daughter dances;
I remember shaky smiles and steady tears when he gave me away on
my wedding day.

He's old now.

I see his once-joyful eyes clouded with glaucoma and fear,
His jowls sunken and splotchy,
his crown of skin fringed with thinning black hair.
I hear a frail voice whispering wishes,
wheezing requests,
whiffing laughter.
I feel strengthless arms giving cub-bear embraces instead of kodiak-bear hugs.
I see a gentle man dictated by doctors, doses, and disabilities.

He seems small in stature, but isn't.

Mary Smithhart Chevalier

MATERNAL LOVE

This poem is dedicated to Donna, my inspiration.

Lovely, sweet, sad child of mine; I held you close
And brushed the teardrops from your eyes.
We clung together—
And for a while, we did not part.
And for the moment, I could see that
I had seared the open wound,
But deep within,
I had not healed the broken heart.

If only I could take your place, when
Life reaches out and batters to and fro—
When inwardly, you feel that giving up
Would solve the hurting for us all.
But that was not the plan
The Master had,
Who stretches out His arms,
And lifts us, 'ere we fall.

So smile, my child! Tomorrow will
Begin a brand new day!
The heartache we shared a day ago, will
Seem so small, and worthy of forgetting.
You'll see the difference
Just another dream can make—
Then maybe, just maybe, you will laugh
And say, "Twas no use fretting!".

Pamala Phipps

A SUMMER'S STORM

This poem is dedicated, with love, to everyone who encouraged me to try.

Like a sudden summer shower,
you came into my life,
rushing, pushing your way through.
For one brief moment
you were a torrent of falling love,
and then,
nothing. . .
Nothing but the puddles of memories
left in the uneven tracks of my mind.

Jonathan Moore

THE BEAUTY OF THE NIGHT

Dedicated to all of the special people in my life

The heavy coat of day is shed,
Its brilliant light now banned,
And soft the cloak of evening
Drapes the shoulders of the land,

The earth's face is cooled,
By a light nomadic breeze,
That weaves the blades of meadow grass
Into sparkling dew-lit seas,

Throughout the darkened forests,
Soft moon-shadows creep,
Water kisses on the shore
And puts the sand to sleep,

Everything is hushed,
Wearing gown of silken light,
A silent earth now lends to you
The beauty of the night.

Barbara Ann Cox

THE GREATEST GIFT

Valentine's Day is a time we show our true and deep affection,
So I am sending all my love straight in your direction

I hope that it is not misused, nor that its rejected,
But that you fine my love a gift worthy to be accepted.

And if it be that you should feel the same way that I do,
Then I shall have the Greatest Gift—the Love I receive
from you!

Molly A Pond

THE UNWED MOTHER

She woke from sleep in early night.
This to her was cause for fright.
She'd been for days in pain.
But tonight she was not the same.
The time she knew was coming near.
The birth of child she thought she'd fear.

Her limbs had soon become so cold.
To the friend beside her she had told.
And friend to release her of any fear.
Said to her, "You're doing good and birth is near."

Fear by this time was put aside.
But in its place she'd soon confide.
Was the pain and love expressed by a tear.
The pains much closer and soon She'd bear.
Born to mother baby girl was she.
And as soon as child was placed in her arms.
With baby at her mother's breast.
The pains she'd known had been put to rest.
She felt received a gift of love.
Given to her from God above.
Together and always their love they'd share.
To all around, her love she made aware.

Jill Nicole David

DEAR WORLD

Dear World,
Do you see the pain all around?
And how it is turning us upside down?
Do you see children without food and drink?
I sometimes wonder if they have minds to think
Why don't we understand and help?
We have so much to give them
And it's on us that they depend
There are people like this everywhere
But it does not really seem
As if the world cares.

Ursula Octavia Bacon

A CHRISTMAS DAY POEM

Christmas is a time of year.
Christmas is when Santa is here
Christmas is when Jesus was born
Christmas is when hate is gone
Christmas is when we put up the Tree.
Christmas is for you and me.
Christmas is a day for sharing
Christmas is a day for caring.

Jean D Rideout

ODE TO CHARLIE

I was the apple of your eye,
Your estimation of me, was always high,
I never seemed to fall from grace,
I always held a special place.

Your eyes show me you're hurting bad.
I can't show you that I'm so sad
When you're gone I'll fall apart
You're the place from whence I start.

Now I'm tortured by my grief
Perhaps someday I'll find relief
But now I weep to ease the pain
I want to hold you again and again.

I want to see your smiling face
I want to see you, stare into space
I need to see you laugh and smile
There never was one with so much style.

They heard you coming with heavy feet
As a "copper" you'd be considered really neat
Here comes "Charlie" with a hearty "hello"
How many people loved you so.
They miss you down the burnt oak shops
To all of them you were "the tops".

Grace F Blake

ADRIFT

For Bill, who will never have it. Mostly for my son Arthur, may he always have faith in love.

A soft whisper in the night
To wake and touch would chase it away.
It's so pleasant and soothing.
This place where you are not;
But yes, you are living it now.

The farest places, the nearness of home

The sound of fairies speaking,
The edge of life is far removed
You drift through mist of memory

You must hold it for yourself
You wake to take it for your own:
But no, It's gone, it wasn't here
At least not long for you.
Don't wake next time, let it float.
The dream, or love? might last.

Renate Potjan
MORE ABOUT RELATIVITY OR: EINSTEIN EQUALS ONE STONE

For Margot Einstein with love

A small stone
is
yet Einstein
has
access to all
the
magnificence
of
divine power
to the source
of
all energies
is
complete
in itself

Marvin L Goss
A POETRY FORMING

To God, who has given me this talent to share, and who has opened these gates for it to be published.

Poetry, the art of putting stories, beautiful thoughts, feelings into verses of understanding the knowledge, simplicity, complexity, individuality and unity of one mind or the linking of minds universally.
A poem is nestled in the heart, brought out by a stimulation, which produces a motivation of serious word calculation, that in turn brings forth strong determination for completion.
A poem is a story that unveils the mystery of a mystery in plain view.
That which you can't see is revealed to thee through a maze of word tease.
A poem is there to share, that which your mouth could not bring forth to bare, taken from the heart and transferred to paper for the minds to compare.
A poem is that which the world deems obsolete because the meaning is not point blank.
In the world poetry has no rank, but what it doesn't see is that poetry is the worlds thinking tank.
A Poem is that which is hard for the mind to conceive from words that deceive, but if time is taken out to read between the lines, maybe you will find that the words meanings are divine.
A poem is simply being you and telling how you truly feel about this world and how it's perceived, so this is a poem trying to illustrate a poem by writing a poem of how a poem is conceived.

Michael T Rinehart
SONNET XV-C UNTITLED

To Caryl, whose beauty is the very essence of poetry.

O! Bells do chime from distant steeples' stead,
And lights align the streets and avenues;
Sweet voices do their intonations wed,
To form a chorus light as morning dew.
Now love doth fill the heart and stir the soul,
And lifts mine dampen'd spirits for a time;
As briefly I forget I am alone,
And revel in the seasons' joy, sublime.
But then mine heart, for thee, begins to yearn,
And missing thy sweet love discomforts me;
Mine Christmas won't arrive 'til ye return,
Safe from foreign lands across the sea.
'Til then I'll keep thee ever in mine heart,
And hope 'twill be the last time we're apart!

Albert Mora
THE DEATH OF LIFE
One night I looked up and found I could no longer see a star,
I cried because I could no longer see my friend from afar;

What happened to the world I knew?
Slowly we became but a few;

The snows have melted and the rivers they are all dry,
The rains no longer fall and I ask why;

We forgot how to love and smile,
I wish those days would come back for a while;

No longer did we hope and care,
The pain it gives me I cannot bear;

Where is everyone, where did you all go?
Please tell me it isn't so;

Slowly we all became strangers,
And talked only of the dangers;

We hurt and killed each other,
Oh, why did we do this to our brother;

It's cold here now and I am weary,
Each day is all the more dreary;

God, I can no longer look up and see a clear blue sky,
A new day has come and the world forgot to say goodbye. . .

Sonia Tirado
THE PEAKS OF LOVE
Our first glance,
first kiss,
first embrace,
The culmination of our love.
Peaceful walks,
our thunderous laughter,
those longing looks,
the openness of our love.
Those first tears,
the angry words,
the shivers in my spine,
the beginning of the end.
Our hasty glares,
our last kiss,
our last embrace,
the termination of our love.

Burtz Chastain
ODE TO THE HUMMINGBIRD
Hummingbird, Hummingbird, where have you been?
I have not seen you since, heaven knows when!
I await every day your appearance to show,
But where you go wandering, I'll never know.
You visit the rich and you visit the poor,
But the ones who grow flowers, you visit much more.
You come in the summer, you leave in the fall—
And during the winter you don't come at all.
You're such a free spirit, the envy of men
Who would love to go visit the places you've been.
You seem oh so fickle—you come then you're gone,
And when you'll return, there's no telling how long.
Ah! There you are hummingbird, tell us we pray—
Of the places you traveled while you were away—
Of the beautiful flowers whose nectar you sipped
As you gracefully, swiftly through flower beds slipped.
Gone again, hummingbird, swiftly away,
I hope someone else may enjoy you today.

Lynn Archer
MEMORIES

To my wonderful husband, Evans, and my three beautiful children, Karen, Steven, and Cindy, for all the special memories we have shared.

Everyone should have a room
Where they can reminisce;
About the days and dreams long past
That were filled with heavenly bliss.

I have a room where I can go
And quietly I climb,
The stairs to open up the trunk
That holds memories of treasured times.

I gaze intently on each one,
Handling with gentle care,
The yellowed paper, fragile and worn
From frequent visits there.

Faded ribbons, a lock of hair,
There's even a prom card, too;
Mortar board, graduation gown
And a tiny baby shoe.

Memories are made to last
Of precious days gone by,
As I gently close the old, old trunk,
I heave a wistful sigh.

Jonathan L Davis
STORM OF LIFE

To all the others who are still searching

My life I live, my dreams I don't
My pleasures I seek, my soul that won't
Content, am I, to sit and wonder
Too proud, am I, afraid of thunder

The storm inside screams wild and free
Batters my will and begs me to see
No different am I than the next who stands
Afraid, am I, of life's great demands

The step, I feel, too soon to take
The risk of pride too soon to make
The blow, when dealt, is filled with pain
The tears they fall, like a summer's rain

The storm subsides with the passing of time
The fury abates, innocence is mine
The day has come, too soon I fear
My youth is gone and death is near

Regret, do I, the life I fail
Feelings, have I, but to no avail
My storm of life, over and done
My wind and thunder give way to sun

Let no man lead the life I've lived
Empty of love and passion instilled
Blow with your storm, enjoy it's thunder
Content never be, to sit and wonder

Mrs Temperance Lunceford
MY LOVE

This poem is dedicated to my husband—Melvin P. Lunceford (March 23, 1914—October 20, 1977).

One year ago today, "My Love"
God called you from this life.
He said, "It's time to come on home"
From all the toils and strife.
But oh, how sad to see you go
We all loved you so.
The heart aches I bear; the tears I've shed
Only God could know.
I look around to an empty chair
Your voice I wish to hear.
I kiss your picture on the wall
and vision you are near.
You slipped away without good-bye
But not for very long.
We'll meet again to part no more
In that Heavenly Home.

Deloris R Boyum
THE FADED ROSE
Within the box some items lay,
Memories from an earlier day.
A ribbon, a pin, a faded rose,
The story of which, no one knows.

Could it have been a moonlit night?
With stars a-twinkling, and oh, so bright.
Or could it be, the story took place
In a setting of white wedding lace?

The ribbon speaks of younger years,
Full of laughter, and childhood tears.
The pin could be from schoolroom days,

With promise of rainbows and
sunshine rays.

The rose conjures up visions of,
Beauty, happiness, and soul-felt
love,
Tears of sorrow, tears of joy,
That encircled the lives of a girl and
boy.

The memory of something dear,
Can hide away a forgotten tear.
And, to look upon these mementos
old,
Can fire the imagination bold.

Just what is the tale, do you
suppose?
Of a ribbon, a pin, and a faded rose.

Lucy Swaim Waldner

MEMORIES

How in the world could there ever
be
A more wonderful Father and
Mother to me?
They must have been from heaven
above
Their lives were so true and filled
with love.

Everywhere they went, together
they'd be,
In buggy, spring wagon or old
surry.
My brothers and sisters in the back
would ride,
While I sat in front at my parents
side.

No matter how cold the night
might me,
To church we'd go, and there
would see,
Our pastor and friends of the
whole neighborhood,
So happy we wouldn't have missed
if we could.

On our way home, of times we'd
sing
The songs we had heard, such a
wondrous thing.
Kept our minds off the cold, as
riding along,
Each anxious to sing their favorite
song

Soon we'd be home and upstairs
we'd go,
Carrying hot irons, and as you
might know—
Into our fat featherbeds, we would
climb,
And sleep like a log, till getting up
time.

Antonia M Mosca

THE WRITING OF A POEM

Think, think,
I said to me;
So think and think I did.
In fact I think I thought so hard
The words, just wouldn't come to
me.
Think of things familiar
Those things of which I know;
The sun, the moon, the stars, the
seas,
The heavens and the earth below.
I thought of all these things
And many more besides,
Of other poems I've written
And my feelings deep inside.
Of all of these my thoughts abound
But a poem of one,
I couldn't seem to write it down.
So often when I'm out, walking
beneath the trees,
The words will come and float
through my mind
As a gentle breeze that whispers
through the leaves.
But when I sit and think and think
The words just go away;
They stay locked up inside of me
With no key of escape.
So I searched again deep down
inside
And there found many treasures;
But the greatest of them all I spied,
The key which allowed the words
to be free.

Linda Horton Slinker

COURAGE TO BE ON MY OWN

I'm sitting here alone as I usually do
And suddenly I was filled with the
thought of you
I didn't want to do it, I didn't want
to try
But without any notice, I began to
cry

Give me the courage to be on my
own
To give me direction and sight
I need to hold on to something in
my life
Something that's decent and right.

My life's full of people but I'm all
alone
I have to find something to do
I work all day long and then I go
home
To nothing but memories of you

Give me the courage to be on my
own
To give me direction and sight
I need to hold on to something in
my life
Something that's decent and right

Time passes on as it usually does
And feelings start fading away
And the hurt that once was is
replaced with content
As the nights turn into a new day

I've found the courage to be on my
own
I now have direction and sight
For I know it's OK to be on my own
Without a man in my life

D A McCallister-Clark

BURY ME ALIVE

When I should die, lay my corpse
To rest upon a hill;
Over-looking tranquil lakes
With waters blue and still.

Let my ears, 'though deaf they'll be,
Hear birds afar off singing.
Let the wind blow over me;
Fair music be it bringing.

Let my nose, 'though dust it be,
Smell no sweeter fragrance
Like be in the woods protecting me
—
Enshrouded in the scents.

Let my lips, 'though numb they'll
be,
Savor the natural birth.
The cuisine of God springing about
From my tomb of sacred earth.

Let my eyes, 'though blind they'll
be,
See emerald valleys showing
How life bursts forth with many
hues
From the prismal flowers growing.

When I should die, no more be
pled,
Except to sleep in peace
Upon my hill, my tomb of life;
For with life I'll never cease.

Wanda D Morris

FAREWELL TO LOVE

---

*To my family—Ernest, my husband,
Jonah and Ezekiel, my sons.*

Kiss the rose goodbye.
For I—the petals;
Have slowly, died

Gladys Smallwood

A WAR WITH NO HONOR

A war with no honor,
A war with no pride,
Where many men suffered,
Of brave men who died.

They all joined up proudly,
Leaving families and friends,
To fight a foreign battle,
That never ever would end.

Then the war was over,
Our boys came back alone,
Landing here with no parades,
And no big welcome home.

They returned to no praises,
No glory, jobs, or fame,
Let's take a look at ourselves,
Really, who is to blame?

It should go down in history,
Of how we rejected these men,
So proud, brave and very young,
We committed a great sin.

So wake up America,
These men faced real bombs,
Let's show them we love them,
And have no more Vietnams.

David Mann

THE BIGGER ME

Even though some may think me
strange,
perhaps eccentric or deranged,
my war is not with them, I'm sure,
the battles deep inside, I must
endure.

Still their words leave wounds so
deep,
and out of control my anger seeps,
out to the surface where I scream
and shout.

I pray they know that's not what
I'm about.

They turn in shock and walk away,
I gave them even more to say
about the little man who shares my
soul,
and temporarily gained control,

of the bigger me I've confined
within,
and surely that's the greatest sin,
for love has no value locked inside,
we must set love free before it dies.

Cherie Wisdom

AUTUMN MOUNTAIN MEMORY

Climbing high. . .feeling so free,
Sitting above the tree tops.
Talking among the clouds.
Feeling the warmth of the sun and
the snap of the breeze upon my
face.
The splendor of Autumn in all its
grace. . .
Only a moment in time it will last. . .

Getting to know you and feeling
like me.
Laughter and the thoughts shared
have now gone riding with the
wind.
That special day never to be
forgotten,
never to be recaptured. . .
Only a moment in time it did last. . .

The window panes are now frosted
time has come and gone.
But, the memory of you and I
is forever pictured in my mind—
The magic of the mountain,
the Autumn moment—so gold.
I will always treasure, but keep it
tucked away, like precious china
glass.
It was only a moment in time
A moment kept. . .

Beverly H Welch

SEEING YOU WITH MY HEART

Seeing you with my heart
I was blind right from birth, it
seemed I didn't know my worth,
until I learned of the second birth,
now I see with my heart.
There's no doubt dear you I see, it
is all so clear to me,
that God has given me such beauty,
as seeing you with my heart.
O! to know you love me my darling
so fair, no other women could
compare,
I feel your long soft silken hair;
your lovely graceful your own
style,
a pretty dimple when you smile
and your so joy filled all the
while,
yes I see you with my heart.
Now I can see things through your
eye's, such as sun, moon, stars,
and realize,
us becoming one O! what a prize,
for seeing you with my heart.
Someday you and I believe, as
God's children we'll receive,
all of his promise's, just conceive,
because we're seeing Him with
our heart.

Mildred Stewart Watson

COMPARISON

I used to wish
for you
a perfect world.

I know now that
that is impossible.

Besides
in a perfect world
there is no
pain or
unhappiness or
fear or
insecurity.

Without such things
in your world

you could not
truly understand
joy or happiness or
love or
security

How could you appreciate
a perfect world
if you had nothing
to compare it to?

Stacie Gieszelmann

AS FALL WEARS ON

As fall wears on, the sun grows cold.
Trees drop their heads, they're growing old.
Leaves are slowly, turning brown,
Drifting silently to the ground.

Death must come, as winter grows
Trees are brittle, lakes are froze.
With fearless eyes, and quiet breath
Animals scurry to seek their nests.

But soon the sun again will warm.
And put new life within earths forms.
As tears must dry after a death,
So will winter to springs warm breath.

Bertha Garrett

A LIGHT

I was walking along one dark night,
When in the distance I saw a light
One that was shining so bright,
I hasten my pace to see the sight.

The closer I got the brighter it glowed
Warming my heart and welcoming my soul;
I tried to imagine what could it be
That even from a distance I could see.

I thought someone was aiming it directly at me
As I looked up through the snow and trees,
But as I grew closer to the sight
I began to wonder about my light.

Does the light in my heart glow?
No matter where I may go;
Does it make a difference as it shines?
Welcoming even those who are blind.

Does it radiate from my heart?
A warm beam of love as it imparts;
Does it make a radiant shine?
Saying come and try this light of mine.

The closer I got to the light I saw
The more my heart was in awe,
Of how the light in my life should be,
Shining bright so all could see.

Sharon B Short

MY LADY

Where is my lovely LADY now?
I've loved her since I was a child.
Once dressed in freedom, bathed in pride,
Why must she in foreign countries hide?

For years, full of power, no one dared
To dishonor her colors, or laugh at her cares.
But alas! Her offspring steadily became
A nation of illiterates, who'd rather play games.

Her children no longer concerned for their nation,
Were too busy planning their next vacation.
She no longer taught her young to say "No!"
But instead paid specialists to ease their woe.

And no longer did she feel the need for God's blessing,
She aborted the problems, and ignored history's lessons,
That all great powers can tragically fall,
Not from outside, but from within the walls!

And yet one day, resting on our bended knee,
Will you say, "Comrade, is this me?"
Could this happen without our knowledge,
What has our nation been teaching in college?

Its really not my fault you see,
The laws were passed without me.
I was so busy with my life and plans,
I forgot how much our Lady demands. . .
oh, America!

Agnes Drumwright Meacham

OCTOBER

How can I describe it now that it is here?
It is my favorite time of the year!
The bluest skies I have ever seen
The leaves on the trees no longer are green.
They are all dressed up in scarlet and gold
A more beautiful sight you will never behold.
Butterflies dancing all around in the air
Beautiful wild flowers in bloom everywhere.
The roses are larger and beautiful to see
The mocking bird's song seems sweeter to me.
The frost on the ground and a nip in the air
This Heavenly sight is so beautiful and rare.
Go out, look up and thank God above
For the beauty He gives us and His wonderful
love!

Mary Trotter Kion

I'LL ALWAYS NEED RAINBOWS

To Robert Johns, the Man and the Artist

Tints of color bowing across the sky,
beauty I cannot live without.

A legendary promise from one of might,
a mythical dream at its end.

Arching, transparent ribbons embracing
an earth freshly washed.
You put tints of color in my sky,
shades of promise to my dreams.

Your arms hold me in your world,
belief in life renewed.
In your touch and your gentleness,
I find a golden mystique.
When I don't need rainbows,
I won't need you.

Harold T Hikiji

HANDS OF CLAY

This poem is dedicated to a dear friend Janice

She shapes both porcelain
and stoneware with quickness
and skill. She's a potter.
She sits on her stool
next to her potters wheel.
She's a potter.
After all the dry and powder
clay is thrown it is ready
for her hands.
She's a potter.
Days and nights to shape these
objects of art. Cups, vase,
tea sets and things of beauty
for her eyes.
Next the kiln is where they
will enter. Out they come
colored and shining.
She's a potter.
In the shop window and on
the shelves they sit ready
for your home.
So as you drink and eat
from them remember.
She's a potter.

Darci D Hill

THE BATTLES OF LIFE

The wars that we fight;
The wars that we've fought;
Make no sense at all.
Friends fighting friends; watching others in pain,
Even sometimes in death's grip.
If we are to remain forever "The Home of the Free and the Brave"
Our braveness must be shown by our united freeness,
Not divided.
For we are all one in the eyes of God,
And we should believe our Creator.
For shouldn't He know exactly what He has formed?
For artists name their paintings,
And God is the artist of the world and all its beauty.
This beauty was made to enjoy, to see,
And not to be torn apart or burned.
By our childish fights and arguments.
And just as the sculptors build and shape their simple forms;
So does God form us in His own image.
And we are born to be like Him;
Loving,
Giving,
And kind.
Not to live in anger and fear because of
The wars that we fight;
The wars that we've fought;
That make no sense at all.

Christine M Dodge

AND I DREAM

The tide's rushing in, the waves coming in, and going out.
The boats out in the horizon,
And the children playing in the sand.
I sit here in the sand, the warm sun shining down.
Theres a cool breeze blowing around me.
And I sit here, And I Dream, And I Dream.

Your a man of the sea, And on your ship you are free.
No womans arms can hold you.
For like the birds flying around me,
And the tide going into the sea,
You are free.
But I Dream, yes, I Dream.

The love we've shared together
With your arms holding me close.
The memories, the tears, and laughter.
And the night you sailed away.
But you'll be back!
Someday soon, but not to stay.
For the gods will call you.
But in my memory, you will stay.
For you are free, yes, you are free.
And I'm here watching the horizon.
And I Dream.
Yes, I Dream.

Pauline Munsell

Pauline Munsell

MICHIGAN

Michigan my Michigan
If I searched the whole world over
I'm sure I would never find
Another state like Michigan
This great state of mine.

Edna V Tressler

EASTER IN ALASKA

As Easter comes again this year
We miss you three, 'cause you're not here
We remember Easter, as a triumph day
When Jesus arose, and the stone rolled away.
In all His Glory, He came forth
And spread His love o'er all the earth.
The hills, and plains, they can't divide
Our love for you that's deep inside.
So as we worship God and pray
We'll remember you, as we do each day
We'll pray that God will bless you there
And keep you all safe within His care
And though you're many miles away,
We'll vision you beside us, in church
This Easter Day.

Stephen Edward Boyd

THE SPINNING OF TIME

Time is spun in a mysterious form,
As the hand from above intended.
Each second and moment are different,
With the spinning of each season.

Winter snows are spun with the coldest finger,

Like silk, it ensures a shine.
Silk runs out and wool is worn,
When the snow starts to melt and fill the soil,
With the spinning of time.

Leaves appear in the light of dawn,
The colors of light shine through.
To a recipe is added a pinch of spice.
To autumn, all colors, red, yellow, and blue.

Summer is spun under the new day's sun,
When the dew is fresh and the moonbeams hum.
The birds are formed as the butterflies pass . . .
Summer is formed in the winking of an eye,
With the spinning of time.

Spring appears in the presence of flowers.
Each spun with the shiniest of needles,
With the hand from above using the brightest of threads,
To spin the beauty of nature, ever so present in spring.

Spring is warmed with the spin of love,
The product of all seasons.
Summer is highlighted as the heart beats on
Without a rhyme or reason,
Then autumn leaves fall on the summer scene,
Winter snows are not far behind, making the seasons complete,
Thus, the spinning of time.

Lenn Reese

COMPANY

For G. T. (A teddy bear) made with love, care, and feelings.

Teddy Bear for company . . .
Do you want to play with me?
Rub my head and wipe my eyes
Look at me and say your mine
Hug me with your loving arms
Treat me like a good luck charm

Teddy Bear for company . . .
Do you want to play with me?
Playing tug of war with unmatched socks
Snuggling down for pillow talk
Hide and seek beneath the sheets
Don't be shy I only peek

Teddy Bears have big families . . .
That is why they're never lonely
And some day soon there could be more
knocking on your front room door
Piling up on a nice warm bed
Lying around waiting for you to say
"Do you want to play with me?"

Helen Alyne Davis

THINGS I LOVE

I love the winds that whisper wild adventure
That go their shiftless ways down endless lanes
Then too I love the sheen of misty silver
Of candlelights against a frosty pane

I love the icy trees all bathed in moonlight
The solitude of hills, a whispering pine
The fragrance of a rain-scent trail at moonlight
And little pools where silver stars may shine

A song that still can live when music ceases
A silver crescent peeping through the blue
The cool, clear, crystal dewdrops on the roses
These little things, remind me dear, of you.

Andrea K Lipps

WHY LIVE?!

For Mom and Dad; for daily showing me reason, and for making life worth living. Much love, gratitude, and many, many thanks. I love you both!!

"Why live?!" Question the heart,
It's the logical place to start.
Life small pieces brings,
The best being the little things.
Things like . . .
a budding rose,
forgotten woes.
a baby's smell,
the first noel.
Quiet time spent within the soul,
A wonderland with an elf or troll.
The western seaside meeting dusk,
A homemade pie with half the crust.
A swimming mother and baby duck,
Not having to say, "It was just luck."
So much of life, the best of life,
Are the little things we all pass by.
Just take the time to look around,
And you shouldn't have to ask yourself "Why?",
But if you find yourself in a bind,
Just look, it doesn't take a lot!
Then just think to yourself,
Or say to yourself,
But always reply . . .
"Why Not?!"

Angelique Peer

THE CHALLENGER

The crew members were happy ready to go
Tragedy undetected. How could we know?
They had prepared the ship, of course, with great care
The seven climbed aboard, no reason to beware.
They closed the hatch and got ready to blast
The nation was praying, each person to the last.
In minutes it lifted off the ground
A moment of awe was felt all the world round.
We watched the ship climb higher and higher
Then suddenly it came back in a great ball of fire.
We had seen it ascend, all ready and loaded,
And watched as in seconds, the Challenger exploded.
The nation was filled with pain and with sorrow.
No one believed life would continue tomorrow.
"No hope of survivors," is what they had said.
Still, the crew families prayed they weren't dead.
Soldiers, over the Atlantic, dropped down a wreath
Mourning the people the water held beneath.
President Reagan made a speech, in memory of the crew
Saying they had bravery; we already knew.
Seven people went up, to show us the way
And though they are gone, in our hearts they will stay.

Leah M Hermann

DIAGNOSIS

My prognosis: Good

With the exception
that I shall carry
these symptoms always.

My only cure of you
could be time.
And even then,
with time on my side
and my disease in remission,
these symptoms I show now,
will only resurface
once again
at a later date and time.

Betty Deborah Mercer

A SPECIAL GLOW (12/26/86—6:30 A.M.)

Trees make shadows upon the snow.
Sunshine sheds its glow
In between and beyond the shadow
Of the trees, and that of the clouds that come and go.

There's a special glow in the sky
At this time of year. . .
I don't know why. . .
Except that God wishes us Cheer!

Through His angels, He lets us know
That whatever we do, me and you,
Wherever we go, to and fro,
He'll be watching over us all
Lifting our hearts, when our spirits fall.

He's there to guide us, when unsure what path to follow
To comfort us in prayer when we feel low,
To remind us of the power we possess
If we wish, to find our own happiness.

Mark C Sefakis

FRIENDSHIP

To Sal DaBiero, thanks for being my best friend.

Surrounding oneself with a burning bush—
Not wanting to be touched.
Yet ! longing for the friendship.

Never knowing the feelings of love—
Wanting to give, but never does.
Crying inside for help from a friend—
that you've not allowed.
Afraid of being. . .

The blaze burns bright and hot—
Burning, aching, but crying not, aloud.
The silent torment of loneliness.
Afraid of being. . .
Mental anguish torments your soul—
Never could one be allowed to be—what they are and still be free.
Burn with coldness, be sick at heart.
Afraid of being. . .

Love oneself because no-one-else can.
You lit that bush ablaze again.
Find a friend, but not too close.
Afraid of being. . .

Why do we set ourselves apart—
Wanting the love, but never allowing?
What do we fear of friendship close?
Afraid of being. . .What?

Dee E Clay

BABIES THE MIRACLE OF LIFE

I wish to dedicate this poem to my husband, my family, and my friends, who have touched my life in so many ways. I thank you all for encouraging me and inspiring me to make my dream a reality.

Babies the miracle of life
the beauty of growth
A gift from me to you
a gift for us both
Inside my body is a seed
of love
reflections of me, you,
and above
So tiny and delicate
helpless and alive
Only with my love he
will survive
Inside it kicks and
sleeps away
growing more and more
each day
Babies Are A Miracle Of Life!

Sharon E Meltzer

THINGS

The winds whisper o'er the treetops
filling the trees with life-like movements.
Grasping; Changing the full grown leaves.
"Things" are not always as they seem.

The grass turns brown; withering decay,
and the skies grow dark and menace the day
with horrible tales of cold wind and rain—
"Things" don't always stay the same.

To Live—to Die; to Love—to Hate
with passion, confusion, trust and Faith.
To dwell in the past and dream of "one day."
"Things" take time. . .
"Things" don't always occur Today.

If life could be predicted, molded and shaped
the way we would like, without relying on Fate—
We could have it "All!"
But, what is it! Wealth, Possessions—
the Moon and the Stars?
"Things" don't always come from afar.

Love of Self—Others—Life we should reap.

Togetherness, compassion—a
family complete.
What we have is within us.
Here. Today.
"Things" are not always a game we
need play.

Debby Schue

MORNING FLIGHT

Miles and miles of endless sand
just now come into sight.
The southern California sun
Just burst forth days first light.
Looking down upon the coastline
at the beauty it will bring,
as each inch slides swiftly by my
sight,
from beneath this great birds wing.
An awesome feeling flows through
me,
so many will live long, and die
and never see a California sunrise,
burst forth color upon the earth,
from the sky.
All things down below grow small
until they suddenly vanish from
view
leaving nothing in sight but soft
billows of white
hanging soft in the skys crystal
blue.
I have felt beauty in song and verse,
Left breathless by many great arts,
but none have compared, as the
earth touched my soul
as flight 716 now departs.

Wendy McBride

IMAGES

Dream, at night, of a rose bud
lying in the sun
Think, at times, of a sacred trust
that can never be undone
Wish, when down, of a birth
a new beginning of one

And after the sun has left the sky
Remember it's you that I love.

Dream, on days, of life and love
and all the joy they can bring
Think, sometimes, of the earth and
sky
and how God created all things
Wish, when happy, that love will
never die
and birds will always sing

And after the sun has risen again
Remember it's you that I need.

Kelly Jo Ecker

THE MAN I LOVE

For My Father, who always stands by me.

I grew up in a family of five
With good times, and bad times,
My brother, sister, and I.

Our lives involved motorcycles,
deer-hunting, and fun;
It was great to watch a race and
cheer
When my Daddy won.

Then Dow went on strike, and
times turned tough.
Sometimes at dinner, he'd say he
had enough.
But really he'd just tighten his belt,
And hide behind his smile, so we
couldn't guess
How he really felt.

Working two jobs really put him to
the test.
He was strong, and carried on,
There wasn't time to rest.
He'd always take time for us to play,
It didn't matter he was working
night and day.

Dad helps me more everyday
By taking care of my daughter
Who I can't afford to raise.
For this I love him so much more;
He could have just closed the door.

I don't often express it
But I've finally found a way,
To tell him I love him
More than I can say.

Richard B Davis

THE RAGE WITHIN

The rage within burns brighter, oh
brighter.
Hate flames rise higher, so higher.
There is no hope, 'least none for
thee.
Tears and crying shall always be.
Fear and pain now take their toll;

as you pray for God to save your
soul.
In the face of time it is now too late;
for you have broken the key to the
golden gate.
You swear and you curse as the
chains are
pulled tighter and the rage within
burns brighter,
oh brighter.

Judith M Gemeinhardt

THE STORM

To the Children of Despair; Hope is the root of the Soul.

The surging sea hurls itself onto
the ocean floor
Winds whipping through the trees;
Angry exclamations of debris
Spilling over onto the shore,
Crashing with a thunderous roar;
Bolts of lightning illuminate the
apogee,
Dogs barking, peering from a lee;
Seagulls eager to avoid death's
door,
Clouds of doom descend at
noon—an abnormity.
Scattering children flee in fright
Aimlessly into the "night".
Tripping over timbers scattered in
enormity;
Patiently awaiting the calm to bare
the sun
And thus behold the universe as
one!

Danny R Hutchison

THE AVENGER

The heavy blue waves plunged
angrily upon the white sands,
As if seeking some never ending
revenge on the apparently
innocent beach.

What could happen in the course
of life to cause this peaceful
sea to become violent and
resentful,
As if pushed by a soul possessing
demon to a destiny that
must bring destruction to one of
us, or perhaps to all?

Maybe the answer lies deep within
his heart, something that he
cannot talk about, not even to me.
Whatever it might be, I know he's
trying hard to forgive and
forget.
I have watched him many times
retreat to his once peaceful and
happy world, gaze longingly upon
the beach, and then return again
with more rage and determined
revenge than ever before.

In my determination to find an
answer, I questioned the rocks
that lay at the edge of the
sea. to him, perhaps
they would know.
But in their words I could only find
pity and respect for this
determined avenger.

With still no answer, I turned to
the ever faithful palms that
stood at the edge of the intriguing
beach, separating her from
the cruel and ugly cliff, that
constantly threatened her. But
in their whispering I could only
hear the same words as spoken
by the rocks, differing only in
whom they respected and pitied.

In a last desperate attempt, I
turned to the beach once more
for an answer that she still could
not give. But in her eyes
I could see the ever lingering desire
to be loved and only
by him.

And so I departed, climbing slowly
back to the top of the cliff.
With an empty heart and destroyed
dreams, I once again took my
place in a lonely, cruel and
desperate world; never again to
walk beside the angry sea nor to
gaze upon the loveliness of
the beach.

Eugene Presley

FRIENDSHIP'S GOLDEN LINK

Friendship's golden link
Etches within my heart
Fondest memories of olden
treasured times
That never from my memory
can depart.

O' the hope of friendship's
golden link
Ever guiding my footsteps onward
Oft' through gales, deepest valleys
and then on mountaintops,
They can never, ever falter
If faith abides and love is never
altered
For each there within
Friendship's golden link.

Albert E Simms

TO HELEN

Sometimes in the midst of the busy
day,
Sometimes in the dark of a restless
night,
Sometimes when touched with a
moment of fright,
Sometimes when my heart is
happy and gay,
In times of great joy and moments
of fear,
In warmth of success and chill of
defeat —
You come to my heart my deep
need to meet,
To lift me, to love me, you come so
dear.

So may I be thankful for all you say
And may I express this often
today —
This day and next day, be it dark
or bright,
I'll love thee, beloved, with all my
might.
May God grant that this love, so
real, so dear
May bring us real joy, through
every year.

Mildred B Gibbs

A PORTRAIT

If I should paint your portrait
Of how you look to me—
I'd place you on the highest hill
As a strong and graceful tree.
I'd paint sunshine on your
branches—
As they look upward to the sky
For all those happy hours
You gave in days gone by.
I'd put some little birds
All snuggled in their nest
For all the peaceful hours
With you that I found rest.
I'd place some deep, deep scars
there
And smooth them down with
care
For all the battles that you won
Over suffering and despair.
If I should paint your portrait
I'd paint you as a tree—
And there you'd stand forever
For all you mean to me.

Carole Bogutzki Armstrong

OH, HOW THEY WANTED TO COME HOME

Where have all the good men gone?
They've gone to fight
a war
In some other land so far away,
those peaceful men; a
dirty game must play. And
wonder deep inside. . .
what for?
What became of those young,
smiling faces? They came
home in flag-draped caskets.
Oh, how they wanted to come
home!
Never actually thinking that they
would die there.
Where was their God? The one
they thought fair?
What was to become of the lives
they'd planned? For now
they were fighting in another
man's land. . .Walking
with Death hand-in-hand. . .Oh,
how they wanted to
come home!
And when that terrible war was
over, some of those men had
indeed come home. What kind of
home had awaited them?
For some, ten years of their lives
had passed by; they said

that "the others were lucky to die!"
These men had lost years, many lost faith. . .
Those who came home had to find their own place.
Their children were grown now; some with kids of their own now
Oh, how much they had wanted to come home!
But, who had turned their whole world upside-down?
Where was home???
And now, many years have gone by, and thousands of good men have had to die. More countless tears will have to be cried.
So, when you ask "where have all the good men gone?"
Remember that only the good die young!
But, please God. . .Where were their yellow ribbons??

June A Bundschuh

GOD'S OWN MAGIC

A gentle wind spraying snow across glistening
white fields, transformed a marble world with a
veil-like softness.
While the splendor and beauty of a Cardinal perched
on a snow-clad Evergreen tree, created a magic
known only to Thee!

Phyllis Jean Jones

THE MIRACLES OF LOVE

To Tillie my loving mom

I was blind in my affliction
then I turned my eyes from youth
Now I see with new direction
All GODs wonders that are truth.

My life was full of indecision
so I placed it in GODs care—
Now each day my heart grows wiser
as I view the love He gives
to all who come to Him thru Jesus
Seeking truth and understanding—
Looking for a better way to live.

Now each day God gives direction
to every thought that comes to mind,
And I see a new reflection
of the me I used to be.
I no longer am unhappy
for my mind has eyes to see,
GOD has given me his wisdom—
He reveals His Truths to me.

Now my life is filled with wonder
And each day is filled with love,
I have peace and understanding
As GOD sends it from above.

There is only one thing lacking
in this new life that I live—
That this happiness and peace I have
To my loved ones I could give:
So I may know that they have found You
While still in this life I live.

I have faith that this will happen
as I place my trust in Thee,
Even if these miracles of love
in my lifetime I don't see.
I will still go home to Heaven
with this peace held in my heart—
For I know GODs timing will be right
I can trust Him and depart—
Knowing each loved one will be saved
and will join with me someday to the Place
GOD has prepared for us in his very special way.

We will live in love and harmony
and our troubles will all cease,
As we view with awe and wonder—
The miracle of His peace.

Bob Kelly

ONE DESERT NIGHT (DOWN BY THE WATER HOLE)

For my two and a half pack rats, Ann, John and Molly I think.

A low down and dirty coyote
sat down to a lunch of peyote,
'twas the only food there
and he didn't care,
when his sister turned into
Bill Cody.

Before he was done chewin cactus
and deciding he needed more practice,
he laughed with a growl
and said "Who is she now?
She's singin just like
Johnny Mathis !!"

Sylvia A View

I MISS YOU STILL

Traveling along the highway today,
My thoughts were of you most of the way
The trees had turned purple, red, yellow, and green
Many other colors were splashed in between.
The air was so brisk and the sky so blue.
To make the day perfect, it needed you.
The family at home, was busy you see.
How could they know what we'd shared, you and me?
The ride was long but at last I was there.
You would have jumped out and sniffed at the air,
Then run through the yard like never before.
You would have bounded up the stairs and barked at the door.
But I was alone now, at our place at the shore,
Remembering the times we could share no more.
I missed you more than the others would know.
I walked on but, my footsteps were slowed.
Time heals, they say, it's in God's will.
But faithful friend, I miss you still.

Sheila Faye Ross

IF IT WASN'T FOR THE LORD

If it wasn't for the Lord, I'd be lost in sin.
If it wasn't for my savior, the devil, he would win.
I'm glad I know the one who loves me as I am, because without the Lord, I surely couldn't stand.

Stephanie Hartfiel

THE LITTLE SUN MAIDEN

In the meadow, laden with moss,
Those cushioned footsteps would be lost.
The little sun maiden,
Dungarees and gingham clad,
Pigtails bouncing, ran.
The game she played was hide-n-seek,
While buttercups she'd squash.
Her playmate, robust Nandrie, a very gentle host.
(It mattered not that he was a ghost.)
On they played, through the years,
Till the sun maiden grew up and shed her tears.
The robust Nandrie, no more her host,
'cause grown ups don't play with ghosts.

Then one day in that meadow high,
My fair maiden at my side,
Reminded me of those years long ago,
When our ghostly play was all but slow.
Now we walk, arm in arm,
Thru the moss cushioned charm.
Words aren't needed to communicate,
As our inner selves meditate.
When cares and woes get you down,
Please always remember that Nandrie's around.
To walk in the meadow laden with moss,
Where your cushioned footsteps will never be lost.

Joe T Horton Jr

Joe T Horton Jr

MOON FACED CHILD

To my love and best friend Muffy.

Moon faced child;
Eyes turned upward.
Star struck baby;
Don't glance downward.

Fawn like image;
Visions of sadness.
Horoscope dweller;
Falsified gladness.

Thought warrior;
Seeder of morrow.
Keeper of idols;
And thought drugged sorrow.

Sun kissed infant;
Frozen waterfalls.
Embryo spun;
Cocoon like walls.
Annual feeler;
Of inherited despair.
With sky colored eyes;
And angel soft hair.

I shall rock you little one;
To a tempo of tears.
Then I must release you, to war torn years.

Moon faced child;
Eyes turned upward.
Star struck baby;
Don't glance downward.

Michael Samuel Wood

SOUND OF THE TIDE

If the world was you,
And you were but a grain of sand —
And I were a sea of blue.
I'd make it a point —
At least twice a day,
To reach out and envelop you.
Yes, at least twice a day!

R C Stankey

THE BEST MOTHER

I come home late on a summer night,
And see your face reflecting the moon light,
Your standing there like a fresh spring rose,
Your beauty ranges from head to toes,
Your wonderful, warm, and loving too,
And deserve more love than I could ever give you,
There's only one person who stands above every other,
And that person happens to be the best mother,
That person is also a person I love,
A person of whom I think an awful lot of,
Though you'll never know how much I care
With you my love I would like to share!

Sandra Smith

DO IT TODAY

Oh what I'd give,
To be back in my little Rendon home once again,
Instead of this prison, that I'm in.

This prison that I'm in,
It's this world of sin, with danger and sickness
all around.

I lost my friend yesterday,
Yes, he had AIDS,
And my father to cancer long ago.

It's always been my belief,
That God gives a just reward,
For all the different seeds we sow.

So, if we give our hearts to God,
It would be a better world we live in,
And we would not have AIDS facing us.

Give your heart to GOD,
Brother, can't you hear his words?
Give your heart to GOD,
It would be a better world.

Beata Maria Gehringer

CAULDRONS

My soul salutes you,
first born son
Navigator of uncharted
waters of my womb.
Exploring my maternity,
innocent and unaware
Of deviant fates, stirring
mischief in genetic cauldrons;

Dabbling with heredity,
unwanted legacy they spilled
On you . . .
Birth, pain . . . . your gift of
Trolls became my gain
You were teacher, and I . . .
Learned the meaning of life.

Leslie Steinback
SEASON'S
The season's of my life have etched
their timely scars,
and left me feeling their
impressions.
The people have come and gone
by me, and their feelings
I have gathered and taken in stride.
One does not pass through this
life leaving behind the
flesh without the spirit it has
embodied.
To go without the conscience
being satisfied is to die
a death forever untimely.
So I give and take in life
constantly aware of it's
destiny, and search out the good
and deal with the evil,
only hoping that when it's over I
will be prepared.
I will have given of myself and
will have played the
game of life to justice, for God.

Jennee Kelly
MISSING YOU
Missing you, as I am now.
Why the feelings I once knew none?
Never before the feeling of
emptiness.

Like a sunset without brilliant
color, of a new day to come.

Once I loved you, never regretting
thethought, never the feeling the
thought has brought.

The emptiness of a clear sky
without the
stars. Life without happiness of a
childs heart.

A new day will come and go
without you.
With the feeling of emptiness. I
miss you.

Jeannine Aretta Taves Johnson
WHY?
Why do parents like to drink
I hate what it does, and the way
they think
I'll never understand why
Someone would drink till they die
Especially when they have
beautiful grand kids,
That love them dearly,
And would love to see them,
Other than yearly
I guess times have changed
Because they won't even try to
arrange
To see the three most beautiful
grand kids,
They will ever have.
AND I ASK WHY?

Rosann Claeys
MIND
It's all a state of mind.

You can be unemployed or
working,
You can be lonely or alone,
You can be ugly or pretty,
You can be rich or poor,
You can be fat or skinny,
You can be mean or gentle,
You can be vicious or loving,
You can be afraid or out-spoken,
You can be stupid or smart,
BUT,
It's all a matter of opinions,
Other people's opinions.

It's all a state of mind;
It's only yours that matters.

James L Waller
PRECIOUS LOVE TAKE MY HAND
Precious love take my hand,
lead me on our precious love
forever
will stand. I am lonely, I am
weary,
I am weak for your precious love.
Take me by my hand, lead me to the
promised land where our God
given
love will forever stand. Through
the
storms of the night, through the
evilness, through the darkness of
the night. Someday we will reach
a
land where there is nothing but
love
and happiness. Precious love
take my
hand and lead me on and on to a
land
where there is nothing but love and
happiness. Precious love take my
hand, lead me on and on.

Violet Touch
MELISSA (Honey Bee)

Dedicated to my Granddaughter
Melissa Lynn Touch

Honey Bee, I love you —
Honey Bee, yes, I do —
You are all that a darling should be
And your sweet smile is ever with
me;
As you grow, through the years —
Let that smile dry your tears —
You will never be lonely or blue
And your heart will forever be true;
You will soar to the skies —
With your beautiful eyes —
Honey Bee, be my sweet honey bee.
Honey Bee, be my sweet honey bee.

Rozella M Wiley
HOMESICK
The Rockies they are home to me
They're such a pretty sight to see
Strong majestic snow capped
peaks
They warm my heart and chill my
cheeks
I long to see them just once more
From standing in the cabins door
To walk among the whispering
pines
Observing all lifes little signs
For all of this my heart does yearn
But I know someday I will return

Mrs Sandra L Rucker
TO MY LOVING HUSBAND
To you my love,
I give you my heart,
And I gave you my love,
Right from the start,
You give me love and happiness,
Thats why for you I'm at my best,
Our home is where I want to be,
As long as I have you to share it
with me,
Our love for each other when we're
apart
Just gets stronger in our hearts,
Our love together will always be,
For as long as I have you,
And you have me.

To my husband, Dwight
I love you with all my might.

Jeannie M Petersen
DAYDREAM
As I sit here staring at the rain,
My thoughts are of you and I speak
your name.
If only you realized my love was
true,
That all I want is to spend life with
you.
To walk thru the park and throw
rocks in
the stream.
To lie on the grass and share all
our dreams.
To catch the sun as it sets in the sky,
To walk hand in hand, just you and
I.
We can make it together my dear
friend,
It would be a beginning, never an
end.
And I'm sure he would bless us, the
one above,
Cause we have that special kind of
love.

C Gilmer Bell

C Gilmer Bell
IDLE IDYLL
Add a spoon of spirits
to your steaming daily fare;
Set your handy wireless
to your favorite music—low;
Appoint your lusty rocker
among the sun's south sunny
rays;
Pose your feet across themselves
on a hassock or a stool;
Nestle pen and paper
across your leisure lap;
Loose your mind to wander
through these dreamy idle days;
Invite the Muse of Morpheus
to wile your gentle dreams;
Unite your pen and dreaming
to the pleasures that you reap;
Lean back in this Eden land
to rock yourself to sleep.

As the zephyrs play upon your
brow,
warmed by cosmic rays,
You are Epicurean in a castle;
You are a giant in repose.
It's Paradisos; it's a garden;
It's Adam and Eve at play;
You're a universal traveler
in a spaceship—or a car.
Your world transforms to Eden,
No matter where you are.

This is that bliss,
sought so hypodermically,
bought by self-deception—free,
wrought by nature's beams
to permeate your dreams.

Roxane Laidler
WE ARE FRIENDS
Food was an item on which we
couldn't agree.
She liked New England seafood
and I liked Midwestern beef.
But it was okay, we would just go
out for tacos.
We liked the same singers and
imitated our favorite duets.
We weren't too bad in harmony.
We both wanted to lose weight,
but her motive was to attract guys
and mine—
was to fit back into my jeans.
When playing tennis, her serve was
stronger than mine.
We both laughed as the racquet
flew from her hand and into the
next court.
The lady in the next court didn't.
The quiet nights in our room when
the lights were turned out,
one always wanted to talk and one
always wanted to listen.
We assured each other that God
was watching out for us.
We were both afraid of not finding
love—
her because she'd never tried and
me
because I'd tried once and failed.
But we convinced each other we
would.
We both wanted rugged husbands
with blue eyes, but hers had to
have dark hair, and mine had to
have brown. But we both knew
it didn't matter.
We cried the night before we left
college,
as the song I dedicated to her came
on the radio.
Friendships were hard long
distance.
We talk on the phone both wanting
to visit
but knowing by the tears in our
voices neither can afford it.
So we relive our good times until
we can make more.

Rose LeDuc
ENLIGHTENMENT
Look up, the Lord is here!
Ever near beside me, He walks, and
listens, and talks.
Be of a sound heart: all is well.
The trumpet blares —
The sound is heard —
The gates are open—just say the
word.
To heights unknown by mortals
we,
What He has for us in eternity.

The darkness parts: the light shines
through,
Oh, bright and shimmering—all
gold and blue,
As bursting stars, the heavens wide,
That yearning, burning, deep
inside
Has come to the fore.
Your enemies will bend their
knees,
For this light will burn out all
impurities.

Armand M Beliveau

A TOAST TO FRIENDSHIPS—OLD AND NEW

Of all the things we treasure most
True Friendships we do stand and toast
The years move on and soon we're old
But memories of "Friends" are "Gold"
The kind of wealth that truly lasts
Are memories of good time blasts
Such small events like this small treat
New "Friends" and "Old" take time to meet
So much emotion comes to mind
As we meet here—How God's been kind
New Friendships have begun today
And will continue 'long'—we pray
A Toast to you—my "Friends" of Old
A Toast to you—new "Friend" of Gold
May memories be bright and long
And "Friendships" grow so very strong

Love To Our "Friends" — Both Old and New

Flo Fessler

STARLIT NIGHT

A star fell into the sea
But as it fell, it winked at me
And in that twinkling of an eye
Its brilliance lighted up the sky

As it hurled itself toward earth
And danced across the universe
Leaving its fiery path behind
In a silvery, ghostly line

In that moment as it fell
Suddenly, I knew so well
Life can pass as swiftly by
As that bright star across the sky

A wink, a blink, and then 'twas gone
But its brilliance lingers on
In my mind and in my heart
That fleeting, timeless work of art

Over the edge of the earth it went
And I knew 'twas heaven-sent
But in that brief, short span of time
For that instant, it was mine

Lily Rhynes Pelonis

SEARCHIN'

To my Children Stephanie & George Pelonis, Amanda Myers, Johnny, Jovina, & Santos Salas. Because without their love, I'd still be searchin'. And to John Salas in hopes that he may find he's Loved too.

Your looking for rainbows
and wishing wells
Only to find
cloudy days a reality
Your trying to find
the key
When the door
Was never locked
Your looking in
the mirror
Only to find
a fading reflection
Your looking for
Love
But feeling that
it hasn't looked back
Your looking for
a way out
Only to find
the exit not in sight
Your looking for
A little tenderness
In a world
made of stone
Your trying to find
yourself
But your looking
in all the wrong places
Your trying
to cry
Only to find
you've forgotten how
Your trying to cry
Only to find
It's easy.

Mayra C Diaz

I WILL SURVIVE

youth is just all that I am today
with lots of questions I must say
will it be so hard for me to find
why really is the world so unkind
want to be able to shout and scream
want to go out there and find my dream
but everything will be as twice as hard
if your not here to help me deal the card
but what I fear most is what I have known
scared of this feeling, this feeling alone
right now I have you so close by my side
soon you will leave, will I go home and hide
I know that you really must have to go
it shall still come to me as a big blow
if I were just a little bit older
maybe I'd be that little bit bolder
and on that plane wouldn't be one but two
'cause in my heart I know our love is true
I guess we will take this as a big test
to see if our love is really the best
ourselves we have promised to keep in touch
you matter to me so really so much
if for some reason you write to me bye
I don't know surely if I will survive

Madeline F Johnson

NURSE'S REVERIE

I'd like to hold you in my arms
And rock you in my rocking chair.
I wish that I could heal you with my hands.
That I could give you of my strength
to fight your battle.
You are so young and so lovely
And seem to have so much to live for.

But you will be going to a better place.
A place where there is health and laughter
and beauty always.
This is what our Bible tells us,
But we are not sure
And so we are afraid for you
and for us,
For we all must make the crossing sometime.

Rachel Sarah Bergeron

PRAYER

I took for granted
What I wanted to hear
The words that came
When you were so near

Now that your gone
I have nothing to say
I watched for the dawn
And I had to pray

Bring him back to me
One more time for him to see
How much I love him
How much I care

I need something more
Then just a teddy bear,
Then just to share,
Then just to dare,

I need someone to care.

Ken R Hancock

WHO ARE YOU NOW?

Who are you now? Do you belong?
To every shape and sound and color turning round?
Have you been here, or have you been gone?
Somewhere, the world's turning around.

In every day, in every town
A child is born to all the world to lead us round
And show us things we've seen before
Give everything, if you really want more.

A child is born, to lead us round
From where we've come, past here and now, to where we've gone
Be glad your will is written down
Be happier still, the world's turning around.

To all my sons, I'll never know
To all my daughters that my life will never show
I'm with you when you're reaching down
To help the world that's coming around.

Who are you now? Do you belong?
To every shape and sound and color turning round?
Have you been here or have you been gone?
Somewhere, the world's turning around.

Soraya Purvis

IN A LIFETIME

To Dennis—I shall always light my candle of creativity by your flame of inspiration

---

In a lifetime you can learn so much
and then lose touch with reality . . .
In a lifetime you have lessons to learn;
Experiences to gain some filled with joy
others pain . . .
In a lifetime you may find your "spirit-in-kin"
Two minds intwined nurturing each other
while cultivating other minds . . .
In a lifetime you have decisions to make;
Which way to go, what roads to take;
Should you dare to be different or shrivel up inside;
Should you reach out for love while hurting and pull
back to die?
In a lifetime you find true love and sometimes
lose it . . . the sweet kisses, that sensitive touch,
the passionate lovemaking, the ecstasy in love . . .
In a lifetime we can find each other;
there is no right or wrong;
just you and I existing
seeking in order to find
what we are looking for
in a lifetime . . .

Gertrude W Dickens

ANGRY PAPA

I was lying in my hammock, gazing at the sky,
I was too relaxed to see my Papa go by
I didn't know Papa was behind that tree,
Getting ready to shout and yell at me,
Suddenly, I heard a noise from over there
Papa came out like an angry bear,
He said, "Son, by the time I count to ten,
You had better be up and going again,
Your Mama's over there working in the sun,
While you are over here having all that fun,
Go and take that hoe from her hand,
And let her know you can be a man."
I took that hoe, and I went to work,
Otherwise, Papa might have come with a jerk,
Now Mama's lying in the hammock, gazing at the sky,
Relaxing and singing, "Let the world go by."

Pamela Shirley Campbell

DISCOVERIES OF LIFE

Life seems so strange; day to day things change,
One minute you feel good and the next you feel down.
Now sitting in front of a beautiful Lake;
It is so very tranquil and serene, you finally feel at peace.
Learning what's important in life to be at peace
With your surroundings and content with oneself.
To enjoy every single moment of your space and time.
Hearing the waves splashing on the shore;
The sound is so precious bringing on a sudden calmness.
Clouds are gathering around the lake now.
Lightning striking in the back of the Majestic Mountains.
It seems to bring excitement in;
The Mountains standing at their glory.
They are so gigantic to me they look mysterious
Knowing they can be dangerous along their steep terrain.
Hiking now you feel the power of your surroundings.
What a challenge to climb to the very top!
Looking down now you see the lake barely moving.

Picturing yourself calmly
floating on a canoe;
As day goes into night gazing about
the lake.
Admiring the first glance of the
moon and the stars.
Then noticing the shimmering
shadows on the top of the lake;
You feel yourself just drifting
along peacefully.
Oh'What Serenity!!!!

Chelsea April Richardson Epps

MR. GRASSHOPPER

Mr. Grasshopper, Mr.
Grasshopper,
Won't you come and play?
Look out your window
It's such a lovely day.

Mr. Grasshopper, Mr.
Grasshopper,
Won't you come and play?
I would like to play.
It's such a beautiful day.
Violets, daffodils and roses.
Sunflowers, tulips and posies.
They're all growing.
In Mrs. Grasshopper's garden.

Mr. Grasshopper, Mr.
Grasshopper,
Don't be a sleepy head.
Wake up my darling.
And don't go back to bed.

Karen J McKeown

RING AROUND THE MOON

Tell me, ring around the moon
Will darkness stay with us till dawn
or is the light forever gone?
As Eden in a distant time
Became the pawn of serpent's con
And disappeared as in a dream
The sentence passed by One
Supreme.

Tell me, ring around the moon
Will life remain a constant force
or is our brilliance set to wane?
For Noah told to build the ark
By You who promised of the rain
And floods engulfed the evil world
But goodness waved as flags
unfurled.

Tell me, ring around the moon
Will plagues destroy this world of
mine
or is it doomed to fiery glow?
The large white throne prevails
that day
To climax Armageddon's show
And evermore to let us see
Eternal You who lets us be.

Stephanie E Elston

I WISH IT WERE A SUNNY DAY

I wish it were a sunny day
so the flowers would grow
and the wind would blow,
and the birds would fly upon
the sky and at last comes the
sun,
the sun always shines.

Priscilla Anne Meek

COME, FOLLOW ME

I dedicate this poem to Jesus Christ, my loving Saviour, without Whom, I can do nothing.

I thank you, Lord, for showing me,
God has a better plan for me.
My plan took me so far away,
I found no peace, both night or day.
My plan took all my energy,
And yet I never was quite free.
Free to laugh, and free to love,
All God's creatures from above.

After many years of pain and
sorrows,
I decided to give God all my
tomorrows.
Now I see the light of day, as He
guides me on my way,
I found my peace, in Jesus' way.

He's always there, right beside me,
I feel His gentleness, as He guides
me,
You, too, can enjoy the Victory,
Just heed His words, "Come,
Follow Me."

Cheryl Marie Hollett

MY BROKEN HEART

This poem is dedicated to my dearest friend, Amy Horner. It was written for all the people who have been hurt by loving someone too much.

My life has given me a rotten deal,
this is because the one I do adore
no longer loves me as he did before.
You do not know how bad this
makes me feel.
I cannot tell you when my heart
will heal,
at the moment it is all very sore,
and mending it will be my greatest
chore—
to purge false love and leave that
which is real.
He seemed to me a most
kind-hearted guy
but now I cannot stand to have him
near.
I am afraid that I will fall apart
in front of him when I break down
and cry.
I will not let him see one single tear,
or ever look into my broken heart.

Irma R Kovach

EMILY

To my special grandaughter

Once upon a time in a far away
land,
Is Emily's favorite place to be.
A bundle of giggles, a bucket of
tears,
No better actress than she.
Let's sing, let's dance—
While stopping in the mirror to
pose
Like a ballerina on a music box,
Twirling round and round on her
toes.
Her soft brown hair like
Autumn leaves in the sun
Her eyes little stars, just twinkling
with fun.
A chatterbox full of how and why
and when,
Cuddled in my lap, listening in awe.
But best of all, I love her so
Because it's me she calls grandma!

Cynthia A Propp

GIVE ME A DAY

Give me a day
and I will
climb a mountain
to reach the evening
where I can
lay down and rest
beside you.
For silence is peace
and warmth is your embrace
where I long
for the covets
of your love.

Margie F Seales

THE LOSS OF A LOVED ONE

This poem is dedicated to Roger and Shirley Bray in loving memory of their special and loving son, Mike. Those we Love live forever in our hearts.

Every individual has a place to fill
in the world
For when we give ourselves away
in sacrifice and love,
Very little is needed to make a
happy life
Where there is love, the heart is
light.
Please tell me Lord, why he had to
die?
Why the earth swallowed him up
and went on by?
Oh, why Lord was his life ended as
a boy?
He was kind, smart and a real
touch of joy,
He was special, one of the very few
Who could touch a life and make
it new.
The ultimate in generosity when he
smiled,
Could make you feel very happy
and worthwhile,
He had what it takes to touch the
heart of everyone,
Brought sadness, happiness and
greatness in all he had done.
He has always lived by the golden
rule, done the best he could,
He was thoughtful of all others
feelings and understood.
It seems so unfair as he was so
loved
To be called away to live up above.
I know Lord, it is not for us to ask
or understand,
But what a glorious miracle to
have seen this boy become a
man.

Dennis S Zawadzki

KAREN

Hunger devouring all
That is of me,
Holds a ransom of ages
Within a reflectance of disdain.

Giver of love
Embrace my being
That I no longer hold
The image of myself in thee.

Be unto me ever
That I will never know,
And no love is there
In you and me.

Feeling for the first,
Caressing beauty of your existance,
Ravage my soul and I am gone
To a place where love
belongs. . .Forever

Sandra Engelstad Slaughter

DISTORTIONS OF THE HEART

We meet and our eyes ignite our
deepest selves.
We touch and the flame bursts
forth,
Warming and cradling and
consuming our souls.
The exchange is a charge to all
the senses,
And we feel the easy flow never
spent,
Only to adhere ourselves to
eternity,
As one bright flame of feelings.

But subtly, it becomes dark and
cold,
And quiet all around
And she is lonely. Oh so very
lonely,
Waiting and hoping for the man
who never comes.
Wanting and needing the man
who split her wide open,
And exposed all of her private,
hidden feelings,
To share and to give to him.
The man who let the swift salt
chard rub and chafe
The wounds of love,
Who showed her his sharp
razors edge,
To hone her womanliness onto
him.
She is still here, laying open,
exposed and used,
To be given scraps and bits of his
life, to pacify,
WHY?

Elizabeth Lake Coddington

HOW TO WIN

They tell me—to go somewhere
and DREAM—
To sit and ponder—to thrill &
scheme!
To feel and see it—all in my mind—
Than somehow; in my life—IT; I'll
find!
They say—BE QUIET—forget the
world—
Find PEACE, Joy, Desire and, IT,
will unfurl!
I say, "How can, such a thing be?"
But; TRY IT 10 days—you'll surely
see!
It's so simple—that most won't
try—
They'd rather—sit around & cry &
cry!
The world is yours—to care &
share,
To help create and enjoy—Not sit
in despair!
Get away and dream—where
there's not a care
Use your mind, and create—your
schemes, while there!
It can be for fun; fill a need or even
a toy,
It's all there—waiting; just for you
to employ!
So, use your mind computer, the

creator gave to you—
DREAM! SEE! DESIRE!
KNOW—Do! Enjoy? Be thankful!
Now you know the secret—use it daily & be grateful!!!

Vincent J Healy

A FRIENDSHIP LOST

Twas almost fifteen years ago
when first I met my friend.
I ask you, Sir, what makes friendship?
Good times, kind words, or, more?
I ask this question, which you hear,
for help to know, not smear.

There came one day so long, forlorn
when I was faced with choice—
to spare my friend I must betray
those who on me depend;
or, favor them, then, him I slight.
Such was my lot in fright!

To lose by choice was all my doom!
But, then, my friend should know—
my principles come first, dear friend.
I'm sure you understand.
So, choose I did in dreadfulness—
now count my friends one less.

But surely, Sir, he must have known
the plight I faced alone!
And yet the anger he displayed
to all who needed me!
Oh, God above, inspire him
with grace to look within.

William Edward Weathers (Mr Willie)

FAMILY

To all Families

The table set and mom sits down.
Hands are clasped from all around.
Closeness flows from hand to hand.
As family ties will always stand.

Kelly Anne Wormack

AS WE RISE

To the children who labor in love.

In a world so vast, so wide
So much love to give,
So little time;

Babies crying,
People dying,
Government lying;

No solidarity;
Only charity,
Statistics and hunger
Morality asunder;

Where's all the Martin Luthers?
All the Kennedys'?
It's up to we the people
To consolidate the remedies.

Branna McCarty Smith

YES! . . . TO CHRIST-MAS!

...Dedicated to a poet, accomplished artist, musician and one-of-a-kind friend—my Grandmother, Berta Hoover.

Can it be?
Yes, I see!
There goes Santa's sleigh;
Are there toys
For girls and boys. . .
Is Christmas on its way?

Are presents wrapped,
The journey mapped
To Grandma's house so soon?
Have songs been sung
And sleigh bells rung. . .
Are Christmas songs in tune?

Has joy been spread,
Are all in bed
To wake on Christmas morn;
Are all aware,
(Or do they care?)
That Christ, our Savior's, born?

Annie Mae Flint McKnight

NOISES OF THE WORLD

The noises of the world are so loud,
But God doesn't shout above the crowd.
Instead, He speaks in a manner
that's quiet and still,
You can hear Him speak, only if you will.

You must get away from the
maddening crowd,
Turn off everything whose noise is too loud.
He's speaking quietly, He's
something for you to do;
But He won't turn off the noise, He wants you to.

If you listen to Him, He'll put order in your life;
Help you to be a better child,
husband, or wife.
He'll bring you joy and inner peace,
But you must turn off the worldly noise—let it cease.

Listen to Him speak, through His holy word,
Listen to Him speak, through the flight of a bird;
Listen to Him speak, through His servant, the Preacher,
Listen to God speak, let Him be your teacher.

When you can turn off the noises of the world, you'll see,
God is constantly speaking softly, to you and me.
You'll see that life's worth living in quiet solitude,
If the noises of the world, you would elude

Mrs Adeline Maynez

THE FLAG OF FAITH

To Jesus, Mary and Joseph

When day is spent and twilight lingers near
The songs of spring and summer come,
the blossoms joyfully appear
And winds of Autumn signal
winter's here to stay
Just live this day—just for today.

If in some distant future you foresee
A goal of Love, unreachable, as yet to be
Unfurl the "Flag of Faith"
and cast your fears today
That winds of hope may blow your doubts away.

If tossed by sleepless nights and rest eludes your calm
May God's Embracing Love
console you
like a soothing balm
His Love transcends the barriers of fear
That hover like a shadow ever near.

So forge ahead today with banner bright
A challenge in your soul, with all your might
Compelled by Faith, a mystery to see
God's Endless Love—awaiting you and me.

Angel Lines

YOU

To Kevin Krug who has helped me realize that just being a thoughtful, caring person can make one's world a more delightfulplace in which to live.

Sometimes while looking up at the clear blue sky a vivid thought of you travels across my mind.

The stillness and mysteriousness of the sky reminds me of your presence. Stillness, of course, meaning the relaxed and enjoyable feeling that is in my surroundings.

I am now waiting for you to appear but I have a faint feeling that you really are here—or some portion of you.

Maybe it is just the pleasant way you are that makes me realize that you really are here. Most likely it is the caring portion of your personality that makes me wonder. . .

I am honestly able to comprehend the suggestions and ideas which you relate to me. I do understand that you're keeping in mind the best interests of my present and future.

When you speak—you do so with a slight tinge of boldness. You are not exactly using the upper hand, but you show guidance. I believe that may show that you really do care—maybe too much?

Please do not forget to realize that I also have goals. I have priorities in life. I am not blind to the world. I am knowledgeable in some aspects of life—not all—but I am sure trying.

Start looking out for yourself and your concerns in life. What really counts is YOU!

Mary Ann Malone

SYMPHONY#6—*SEPTEMBER TRYST*

Tree branches entertwine
overhead,
casting shadows in the cold
autumn moonlight
As we step lightly over mossy rocks
and cross to the other side of the stream,
Then continue through thick
undergrowth,
along the bank, and round a
sharp bend.

It is almost indiscernible by
moonlight,
a strange configuration,
shadowy
Behind the dark foliage of ancient vines,
but our footsteps seek a
remembered pathway,
And your hand tightens over mine
as we enter the place of our trysting.

"Love is dead; you are going."
"It is living, part of nature's
enchanting artwork
which is never completed."
I am faint with relief and wait to be kissed;
then you continue:

"Living, growing, and never complete
as the leaves and vines
Which cloth our beloved cottage—
in springtime, a green velvet gown;
in autumn, a canopy of crimson and gold,
and in winter, a dazzling palace
of ice and snow.
So I enshrine our love in a
symphony of this
September tryst."

Helen Danis

THE BOYFRIEND

He cracks his knuckles —
Blushes, grins like a Barnum Bailey Clown.
And rings our doorbell —
Blue jeans like pantaloons
Hang on legs like July humidity
Drooping. Self confidence damp.
I give him a job to do.
Watering my flower bed on patio.
Boy and bud —

And now her clown smiles —
Sagging stance seems to dance
He becomes ring master,
Self confidence in being needed —
Accepted and liked for himself.
She approaches the arena.
"Oh Mother, you're so queer."
Would she, could she, understand
I still can remember being sixteen
And knowing a sad clown?

Shirley M Venema

LET'S GROW

Let's grow in personality
Let's feed our human minds.
Let's inspire one another
For exciting mountain climbs.

Let's always keep our chin up
Responding courageously.
Believing with positive attitudes
Let's live victoriously.

Our world with all its problems
Much better it will be.
If we'll realize dynamic energy
Is possessed in you and me.

Dig down release from the mystic depths
The treasures in your mind.

Bring out the hidden genius
That will build and serve mankind.

Then honestly love one another
As the Good Lord has loved you.
Then there will be peace upon the earth
With real purpose in what we do.

Donna Janiece Thomas

WHERE LOVERS GO . . .

When darkness falls upon the land,
come my love take my hand.
Kiss me in you're special way,
that makes my heartaches melt away!

Take me on the trip of love,
I know he would bless it from above.
Take me where we can be free,
The place you're eyes reveal to me!

The place where only lovers go,
To laugh and sing, Where love still grows.
I journeyed there so long ago,
Oh, Please my Love, Oh, Can't we go?

If gravity would let me be,
I would fly to you and we'd both be free.
I would hold you in my Warm embrace,
Until a smile formed upon you're face!

No matter what life trys to do,
I would stay and love and take care of you.
You see there's no other one for me,
It's you I want, and it's you I need!

Cheryl E Learst

PROGRESS

A thousand tiny details,
A million unanswered questions,
Vivid in the thinking mind today,
Instantaneously gone in the era of tomorrow.
With ash to ash and dust to dust,
Swirling in the sands of time,
In decades to come and decades gone.
Everything out of proportion now
Will be thought so trivial then.

Geri Kirwan

JUST ONE

This is dedicated to my son, Wade, a fun-loving spirit.

If a gleam escapes from your eyes,
Let it shine on me . . .
For I will nourish it until it glows

Regina Chaplin McBride

SONNET ON MARRIAGE

The love of man and woman is a thing
More precious than a city full of gold;
It takes their lives its beauty to unfold.
Its freshness rivals that of early spring;
And when fulfillment comes with wedding ring
They bask in happiness so much extolled
That soon it spreads a mantle to enfold
Those lonely hearts where love will never sing.
Each tiny flame that leaps from lighted hearts
Kindles a fire in everyone it touches,
And, as its light spreads on from soul to soul,
Its new warmth softens all those stricken hearts,
The victims of mischance's evil clutches,
Like music from the sound of church Bell's toll.

April Sandberg

PARENTS LAMENT

Days of empty dreams, no tomorrows.
We live for today, push aside sorrows.
You do your thing, and I'll do mine.
Sorry, not now, I haven't the time.
"Hey kids, how are ya? Do you need any cash?
We stop for a moment . . . The tears fall and splash.
It's too late, they're gone. When did they go?
Wasn't it yesterday we watched them grow?
Remember when . . . Oh, remember the day
When the dog and kids went out to play?
Oh, to have those days to live again.
I'd stop the world to see their grin.
What empty dreams of riches sublime.
The kids were our wealth all the time.

W Courtney Harper

TOO OLD TO MARRY

TOO OLD TO MARRY, TOO young to die;
Too long I courted, I wonder why.

I sowed my wild oats, All over town;
Then when I wanted to settle down,
All my old time sweet-hearts,
The girls I use to know;
Seems they all got married,
A long time ago.

So now I worry, Sometimes I cry;
TOO OLD TO MARRY, Too young to die.

TOO OLD TO MARRY, Too young to die;
Can't get a woman, No use to try.

My face is wrinkled, My heart is cold;
Young girls ignore me, I'm getting old.
Seems that time is passing,
I'd stop it if I could;
'Cause the girls are saying,
That old man's no good.

I'll keep on hoping, 'Till it's good-bye;
TOO OLD TO MARRY, Too young to die.

Nichole A Fernkes

NATURE'S FREEDOM

To have the wind tousle your hair
Is to feel free without a care.
Fun is to frolic through dandelions wild,
The careless play of a beautiful young child.
The dew upon the window glass
Reminds you of a tearful past.
Yet, to feel the sun upon you hot
Is life itself and everything its got.
Each day lies over and goes as it must,
The auburn light turning to coal black dust.
Days go by and minutes go fast
For only a miracle will make them last.
To know fun is free, and freedom is here
Is to take advantage and treat it dear.

Michelle Loraine Palmer

SWEET PARTINGS

We were close once
but that's no more
You went away
away through the door
You left me alone
in this cruel, cruel world
And you left me
without a single word
The time I spent with you
was really meant to be
And though our love was true
it is no more to be
I loved you once
good-bye my love
You were as sweet
and pure as a dove
Love come back
I love you still
And though you don't
I always will

Michele Ann Michaels

JIMMY MAC

In memory of James P. MacBeth, forever in my heart.

He is gone,
To another world which few can see.
By day or night, my heart cries out to him.
Does he hear me, can he hear me?
Tears of sorrow, heart full of anger.
Why did he leave me!!
I reach out to him in the darkness,
Moonlight shining through the window.
Can he feel my loneliness,
My need for his tender touch?
His comforting words,
Those strong shoulders I always leaned on,
Lost forever.
I gaze into the sky,
Searching for the answer that may never be found.
Longing for my one true passion.

Vivian Boucher

TODAY

I like to think
There is no yesterday;
Each life is lived
Just for today!

The past is done
And put to rest,
While for today
We do our best.

Our failures,
Weaknesses and pride
Each bright new dawn
Are cast aside.

"Lord, make me stronger
Than yesterday;
And thank you, Lord,
For each new day."

Matthew Mahoney

A PAST TO REMEMBER . . . A FUTURE TO MOLD

FROM:
Log Cabins to two story homes,
and telegraphs to telephones,
and Raggedy Ann to dogs named Puddles,
and wagon trains to space shuttles.
IN ALL THESE THINGS WE SEE:
In celebration
across our Nation,
a past to remember
in our time of December,
and a future to mold
with greatness untold.

Mary Wronko

PEACE

Long years at last had stilled the hounds of war.
In ravaged lands, on mangled street and shell-torn hill
Men turned from deeds of hate and strife to thoughts of peace.
Rejoiced and sorrowed still
For those who fell to life's dark lore—
But tulips bloomed once more
On Holland's fertile shore . . .

Gini Christian

I CAN FLY!

"I can fly," said the sparrow, and he took to the air.
He circled the crowd, then landed with care.
"So can I," said the green worm, and everyone laughed.
"But I can," he insisted, "Do you think that I'm daft?"
"I can fly," said the duck, "though I seldom do."
The worm raised his head, and said, "Well, I can too!"
"I can fly," said the owl, sinking deep in his chest.
"So can I," Preened the peacock, strutting his best.
"I can fly!" vowed the worm, "Just you wait and see!"

But they all had a laugh, for it just couldn't be!
The worm felt embarrassed and sealed himself up.
He wouldn't come out, not even to sup.
He fell asleep then, deeper than deep.
For a long time he slept, made no sound. Not a peep.
Then finally, one day, he opened one eye.
And he said to himself, "Today, I can fly!"
He broke open his blanket and spread out his wings,
From wing-tip to wing-tip, they were beautiful things!
The sparrow was startled and the duck was, too.
But the owl smiled broadly as he

whispered, "I knew!"
The butterfly sat lightly, and looked all around,
Remembering his life as a worm on the ground.
Then he fluttered his wings, and he took to the sky,
Telling all who would listen, "I can fly. I CAN FLY!"

Susan Cowgill

THE GRAND TOUR

In Memory of Cory Allan Fondren

Life is a grand tour.
We pay to pass through its corridors.
They are all special and different, just as you and I, in our special way.
Many of us are here for only a few decades.

If only we could slow the sand, as it passes through the hour glass.
Just enough to realize each minute as we live it.

Stop, if you can, to feel the sun warm on your back, or the wind blowing
gently through your hair,
As if to cleanse your soul of haste.

It seems the price is too high at times,
just for a moment, Please search your mind.
Is there any word to describe this tour?

Mine has been "DIVINE"

Don't get me wrong, the roads are not all smooth and paved,
With signs letting you know the way,
For our destiny is what we make it.

With this in mind, enjoy your tour, for this is the "Grandest" of them all.

David A Watson

IF I COULD

To April, for being concerned about others during a sad and difficult time in her life. She is a dear friend.

If I could do my complete will
I would make you a promise that I could fulfill

To take away your troubled times
And give you rest and peace of mind
To brighten up your darkest hour
With days of sunshine and never showers

Remove all mountains which may arise
To keep the tears from your eyes
Give you smiles mixed with laughter
To have your life read . . . "Happily Ever After"

If I could do the things above
Life, I'm sure, you would not love
For within dark hours and limited sight
God appears and gives you light

The mountains which rise and tower above
You must climb and conquer, and fly like a dove
And like the tears, there must be showers
To make things clear and bring new flowers

When you are sad and lonely too
Lean on me, I'll be strong and true
To help you make it just one more day
And give you support along life's way

Ashley Eden Kessler

THE POWER OF FRIENDSHIP

Dedicated to Shannon King, my dearest friend.

The clouds are as soft as the warm sunshine
caressing your skin on a cheerful spring day
The day as beautiful as a dove flying into the sunset
The feeling of friendship is as beautiful as anything
you can imagine
Friendship is a beautiful thing
When you have a friend, it makes your heart glow
like a firelit ruby
And being apart is as awful as death
When I think of you, I cry, because I miss you so
Remember that friendship is more precious than
anything, anything at all
I cherish the memories of happiness, and sadness
we shared together
Knowing we're friends makes me feel wonderful,
and friendship is the greatest power on earth.

Denise H Clardy

LORD . . .

I hear Thy anger
in the thunder of a storm

And Thy joy
in the laughter of a child

But when the thunder ceases
and the laughter quiets

I forget
Forgive me
Remind me

Wm H Miller

JAMAICA

JAMAICA, I wonder how did this place come to be,
This Island I feel came from the bottom of the sea.
The Sun kissed its volcanic rock and brought forth trees.

I know the goodness of any land is not in its ground,
But in the souls of its people there to be found.

I have heard that only God can make a tree,
But HIS greatest work really is within thee.

I sit and watch the water rushing up against its side,
The waves bringing new life with each in coming tide.

I'm sure its people came here on these waters,
To draw life from this land and build their living quarters.

As I look across the sea, I feel a Heaven rising up within me,
There's a peace I seek in this Jamaica land, you see.

But could be I have come to another moment in this race of mine,
To store my thoughts and bring them back in some later time.

Kathleen Alexander

POSSIBILITIES

Of all the things I might have been
In a world so great and wide
I think I'd choose to be a wave
Just flowing with the tide.

Or should I have been an eagle
Soaring high up in the sky
To look down on the world below
With condescending eye?

I might have been a kitten
Curled up lazy in the sun
Or the frisky little mutt that comes
To put her on the run.

Perhaps I'd have been a daisy
Whose petals tell of love,
I could have been the mossy oak
Towering above.

Maybe just a cricket
On a hearth one autumn night
Or the flame that leaps within the grate
And makes the room so bright.

But of all the things I might have been
In this vast and varied world
I'm glad I'm just the Mother
Of my tiny baby girl.

John A Parnell

LIFE ETERNAL

This poem is dedicated to my Lord and Savior Jesus Christ

When life's flow and beauty
rounds the last bend
And deep in your soul, you know,
your nearing the end.
For some, there is a sense,
of dread and fear
Knowing, so little of death,
soon to be here
But for me I can smile,
a grin of content
I know in my heart
my life's almost spent
I fear not death, and its
oh so cold call
It's strength that presses
even strong men to the wall
For now I am weak and tired and frail
But my heart sings with joy
as a ship in full sail
Let death knock now
I have no fear
For me life eternal
will soon be here.

Elaine Hayes Tucker

DAY DREAMING

I dreamed of a walk along the shore
That I had taken years before,
Leaving my foot prints in the sand
My auburn hair tangled and tossed by the wind.

Life was beautiful and care free
Looking back now, could that have been me?
Was that I? The girl in my dream,
Or perhaps my grand daughter
that I was seeing.

Time is moving fast now
my face is marked with lines,
I'm much slower, I'll admit that
but physically I'm fine.

I long to walk bare foot on that same shore
have my faded hair tangled and tossed once more,
Leave my foot prints in the sand again
I'm sure I could do that, with the support of my cane.

Dan P Kirk

TO SEEK

Mortal eyes perceive so fast
As the judgment gavel falls,
Most will never take the time
To see inside at all.

And as these eyes bounce face to face,
Of each, so much can tell,
Relentless eyes are quick to judge,
And judged they are, as well.

Peter D Warda

ONE LIFE TO LIVE

To all you people out there—hello,
From the bottom of my heart where it ends,
And up to the top where space begins,
Where all the people should get a cross,
To see the mighty boss,
Into the sky blue heavens where he stays,
He will be happy to take you any day.

Kevin C Brown

HOMEWORK PENCIL

A pencil is a good friend
A pencil it sleeps
A pencil you have to spend.
A pencil you can keep

A pencil you can erase
A pencil can be awake
A pencil it won't show its face
But it won't be a fake

Giovanni A Stralli

WONDERING

As I looked out
Over the sea,
I could not help but wonder,
What would have happened to me,
If I were to have sailed
Over its many mysteries.

Would the winds have prevailed
Filling my sails,
Taking me to where,
My life belonged.
Or would they have ceased.
Leaving me to the mercy
of you
"Oh Almighty Sea".

Terry Tucker

WALLS

For me to see
Inside of me
I've got to feel
That I am free.
When I say no lies
And feel no guilt
I'll break these walls
That I have built.
I'll open my heart
And say what I feel
I'll prove to myself
That life is real.
I'll show my joy
I'll show my pain

Emotions will pour
Like late fall rain.
I'm pushing my way
Without looking back
As I look at my progress
I see light through a crack.

Twink Evans
MY WISH FOR YOU
If I were a ray of sunshine
I'd give myself to you,
To carry with you everywhere
And here's what I would do.

I would wake you in the morning
And brighten up your day,
Each hour, I would beam for you
To guide you on your way.

I'd shine upon the green, green grass
Drink up the morning dew,
I'd hop upon your face and smile
And be a part of you.

If fear should try to weasel in
I'd take good care of him,
I'd outshine all the doubt he brought
And make his light go dim.

I'd sneak upon your life again
If rain should enter in,
I'd drop a rainbow on your eyes
And let God's SON shine in.

Now at the close of every day
A special gift for you,
Would be a beautiful sunset
Made up of golden hues.

Bruce Sherman
MY SHADOW

This is dedicated to my brother, Art.
Who I admire, respect and love

I have a Shadow deep inside,
Who from him I cannot hide;
He lurks above me day and night
And never lets me see the light.

He tempts me with things I cannot deal,
Like drugs and drink that make up my meal;
He's taken away my home, love and pride
And left me emptiness deep inside.

I promise to me, myself and I
That him not I, will surely die.

So even now while that Shadow is fading
And I know I have loved ones waiting;
Let me not forget the day,
The day my Shadow went away;
For I know he's still here inside
And he will tempt me until I die.

Jeffrey Lanham
UNCERTAINTY
Here I sit,
Alone and afraid,
Living a life that was not by man made.

Being kicked from side to side,
By the roughness of the sea,
Oh, Lord, how I wish I could be free!

Entombed in a prison,
With no rightful precision,
Made by me.

In a lifetime,
I will come and go,
Playing the part of a mime.

No reason behind me,
None ahead,
Can't you just see?

I have no meaning,
A speck on the earth's crust,
As I stand here on the edge, just leaning.

Throw no pebble or stone,
I will surely fall,
Then there will be no more to be shown.

Betty J Barnhart
REMEMBERING
The old woman sits in her rocking chair
remembering the past
Wondering where the years have gone
They have went by so fast

Remembering when her kids were small
And how they played upon the floor
She looks up when she hears a noise
Hoping one of them comes through the door

But no, alas it is the wind
No one visits anymore
She is all alone
Her days are long, awaiting
For someone to come home

Harriet Radis
A GIFT OF LOVE FROM A GRANDMOTHER
Come little one and take my hand
And lead me in your childhood land.
The years are fleeing much too fast,
Please help me now to make them last.

I'll tell you of days gone by,
Soothe your hurting when you cry.
While in return your lilting laughter
Will be with me forever after.

Your wonderous eyes can fill my being,
As if the first time I am seeing.
Let me share what I do know,
My legacy to help you grow.

Nothing worthwhile can replace
The feeling when I see your face.
Your noise, your toys, your lively chatter
Are the things that really matter.

Let me hug you, kiss your cheek,
Muss your hair and maybe tweak
An ear that doesn't want to listen,
Teasing eyes that fairly glisten.

Let me love you, be your friend
As our two generations blend
Into a partnership of joy,
God bless you, my dear little boy.

Barbara Franklin
A TRIBUTE TO THE COACHES
We honor our beloved coaches,
Mr. Henry Carroll and Mr. Leon Price;
Wiley College's legend, and Huston College's delight.
AT Wiley College all hearts were truly filled,
With great admiration for NUMBER ONE man in the backfield.
His talents were not limited, to just football.
For, his athletic loves extended to track and basketball.
For since, he was great.
He was great in them all!
Mr. Leon Price, Huston College, still resounds,
As the LONNIE BELL AWARD, everyone should remember,
Was presented to this college athlete and outstanding team member.
Basketball, football, and even in tennis,
Top scorer and athlete, to his opponents, truly a menace!
We've come to toast you and thank you,
For the lives, you've touched;
Through your caring, understanding,
And sometimes being a little tough.
Strong athletes and appreciation,
You've developed so neatly,
At our beloved Alma Mater,
The Old Phillis Wheatley.
We thank you so much, and blessing, on you we pray.
For we have become stronger persons,
Since you've passed our way!

Carmen Sue Cross
TIME
Time
Time can't be retraced
Time must go on,
Even though seven great people
Are gone.
When the shuttle blew up
Their families cried,
We will miss them forever
Those astronauts who died.
The whole nation was shocked
the whole nation grieved,
Because this day
The world couldn't believe.
We have to continue
Their memories we'll keep,
Of seven great
Who are forever asleep.

Sylvia Brade
SOULMATES
I am like a rock, the only stable thing in your ever-changing world.
I am cold and harsh yet, I sense more than any mere mortal
I am pure truth yet, I fill your heart with a million deceitful lies
I am your conscience and guilt as I lead you down destiny's path
I am the caring which compells you to protect a child and,
I am the selfishness which starts the bloody world wars
I celebrate your victories no matter what size
I am the comfort with you through all your sorrows
I am your ambitions and dreams living on, though they be scorned by all
I am your best friend yet, I am your very worst enemy
I am only worth as much as you yourself make me.
You will never be alone in this unforgiving life
For I am bound to you for all eternity.
You need not call me in your times of doubt.
Realize your inner strength, your own selfworth.
With that realization I will join my strength to yours
And we two, against any odds, will conquer this world.
We will make it ours
For we are Soulmates.

Susan A Jones
LOST AND WEARY

This poem is dedicated to my mother who has been an inspiration in my poetry and my spiritual faith.

In a state of desperation
with nowhere else to go
I wish someone would find me
and lead me to the road
My soul is lost and weary
trying desperately to find
a hand to guide me gently
to the path within my mind
Stumbling hard within my search
my footsteps to be found
Please place them on the pathway
to the road that's heaven bound
The path it seems so narrow
so easy to stray off
Hold my hand Lord Jesus
And lead me to the cross

Mildred E Olson
GOD'S WONDERFUL GIFT
GOD spoke and it was done,
The earth, the skies, the moon and sun.
He made the trees so stately tall,
The animals . . . both large and small,
He made the birds to fly and sing,
Praises be! He thought of everything.

Then, He took some clay and made a man,
A woman, too, for He had a plan . . .
That these two should rule over all . . .
To be His children and answer His call.
So, the story of Life came to be . . .
I'm so thankful it included you and me.

Nila Baker
LIFE AND DEATH
Mom; Always prayed to the Lord in the heavens, so God
took her home when she turned eighty-seven.
Mom was a gracious little woman and lived a Christian
all her life, I know when she crossed over she received
the crown of life.
Her soul is now resting in God's loving care, just waiting
for her children to meet her up there.
Death is a debt we all have to pay,

and the death angel
will come your way, he is always knocking on doors, the
young and old rich or poor.
Life and death we will never understand but it all
started after God created man.

Linda Bossert-Pawlowski
REFLECTIONS

To the most important people in my life Al, my husband, Joshua and Daniel, my sons, and God for giving them to me.

I love to pick some flowers
And wear them in my hair
I like to say "I made these grow
With tender loving care."

I love to hold my tiny son
Yes, he's my pride and joy,
I like to say "I gave him life."
My precious baby boy.

I love to paint a picture
Of the country or the sea,
I know I'll say "I painted that"
For all the world to see.

I love to take the credit
For all that I can do
Yes, credit's due, but not to me,
Lord, the credit's due to You!

Cathy Sue Foster
LIFESCAPE
Years Drop—
One By One—
Grains Of Sand—
In The Hour Glass
Of Life.

We Are Each—
Architects—
Building Our Own
Mountains, Valleys,
Sand Castles.
Watching Them Grow—
Erode—
And Wash Away.

Every Sculpted Sigh
Leaving Its Mark—
For A Moment—
On The Landscape
Of Our Days—
Carved With Love—
From The Wilderness
We Ourselves
Have Tamed.

Barbara Paddock
To Let and Let Not
Let not my dreams become faded and sad
Let not my heart become bitter and old.
Let not my thoughts be evil and bad
Let not my love become harsh and cold.

Let my faith be steady and my word is true
Let the words on my lips be filled with love.
Let my actions be clear and my doubts be few
Let me be inspired from the sources above.

Let not your heart be saddened without me
Let not your life be filled with despair
Let not your spirit be less that free
Let not you forget I will always be there.
Let our love be free as the flight of an eagle
Let the relation we have stay honest and true.
Let our feelings be always magnificent and regal
Let you always remember that I love you.

Maryann G Clarin
SONGS

To mom for all of her inspiration

Songs are friends and memories
Of tears and love and bubbling joy.
Come sing with me today!

Bonnie J Joseph
MY LITTLE GIRL

This poem is Dedicated to the Lord Jesus and my 4 Beautiful Children

---

My little girl asked me today
why is the sky so high
But I could find no answer
and I just gave her a smile
I looked up at the stars one night
and I asked myself why
Are the stars the end of the earth
or do they just begin the sky
then I saw you and your new wife
as you both walked through town
I realized my love for you
had never really gone
Are you happy with her
Does she give you all her charms
Or do you wish like I do
You were still here in my arms.

Virginia Eden

Virginia Eden
BITTER CAKE

To my children, Mary, John, Nancy, and My Grandchildren, JeanMarie, Louis and Ashley, with love . . .

I have a Poem—that tells of me
It's not so great as you will see
I always wanted to explain
The beauty of the sun and rain
The time flew way so very past
And now I took my pen at last
It's too much time that I may take
To tell you of my Bitter Cake
One day soon I'll hope to smile
If only for a little while
The roads were bright and very dark
The sun shut out but there was still a spark
And times like now I want to quit
Though I know that spark must still be lit
I am so tired I want to rest
Yet something within says I must do my best
It's God I know that keeps me sane
Or I would have drowned under all that rain
I'm sorry if I sound depressed
But—Tomorrow I'll know of all the treasures I possess

Linda Bohmeyer
SHE WEPT
She swore that this was it, and wept,
and swore there would be no more.
Many days have come and gone, and
yet tears still fall upon the floor.
Ah! The pain it does not hurt as much,
and soon it will be gone.
Then sadness grabbed her soul,
and it is more than being wronged.
No, she is no longer weeping,
for she is being strong.
She wears it well, but hardened fast,
and went into a shell.
The walls are thick and high inside,
and no one enters in.
The pain no longer penatrates,
the battle, she did not win.
Though her heart is hurt, her soul
is bruised, her joy will never truly soar.
The tears she wept upon the floor, aren't falling anymore.

Joan C Smith
DUTIES OF FATHERING

To Hubert my loving husband and to all you "Dads" out there

Husbands as yourselves you should love your wives.
Your children should see this love in your eyes.
Take her hand as you stroll down the lane.
Security about life your child will gain.
Dad, as a parent you should see.
A love not expressed is never free.
Dad, did you hear your little one speak?
Did you feel his kiss upon your cheek?
Were you too tired from work today.
To listen to your little one pray?

Emma L Keown
AGED BARN
Years have passed: now standing there,
Silent, neglected and bosom bare.
For life and growth, once filled with hay,
Where children romped and stopped to play.

Joints now quiver, frame is bent,
Body sagging, boards are spent
Elegant once in a color red,
An empty shell, now gray, instead.

Wrinkles and creaks have stories to tell
To an artist who sits now under its spell.
The open door will becon him
To sketch and paint, to matt and frame.

Steven LoCicero
THE TIME BETWEEN
The Time between
Reading and Writing
Thought and Action
There is eternity

The Quiet Time
Of indecision
Vows and Curses
In the Silence

Red runs the clock
Its hands dripping blood
On the shoulders beneath
A reminder

For what is gone
And what is going
Through our minds
Into oblivion

With hands to face
We tell of times
Marking Change
And running out

Reading the back
Of a postcard past
That still implores:
"Wish you were here"

Tammy J Kitzmiller
SEAGULLS AND SAND
Seagulls and sand
And us hand in hand.
The dawn at its breaking,
Nature awakening,
And we would be together
Walking hand in hand.
The sun's golden rays
And us face to face.
Waves rolling high
Against a blue sky,
And we would be alone
Standing face to face.
Starlight sparks
And us heart to heart.
A cool summer night's breeze,
The swaying of trees,
Songs playing in our minds
Dancing heart to heart.
I close my eyes
'Til the morning's arise
Of seagulls and sand
And us hand in hand.

Laurie Leone Hand
FOURTEEN
Fourteen is a strange age,
No more dolls or Robin Kane,
Or not even playing in the rain.
Just plain boring,
That's what fourteen is.

Perhaps fourteen is the
Beginning of dates,
And no more time for roller Skates.

As everyone can see,
Fourteen is odd to me.
But some people look at it,
From a different view.
So whatever you do,
Remember to just be you!

Josephine G Stringer
MY FATHER'S LOVE

In memory of my deceased husband Clinton, and granddaughter April Stringer

---

When I awake each morning
My Father is always near
I talk with Him so quietly
His Love to me is dear

I feel His Presence near me
He's with me every hour
His Precious Love engulfs me
He keeps me by His Power

He Loves me in the morning
And in the evening too
He Loves me in the night time
He Loves me all day through

He Loves me in the springtime
The fall and winter too
He Loves me in the summertime
And all the seasons through

His Tender Love surrounds me
Bringing Peace and Joy each day
Although I have my trials
He's with me all the way

So gracious is His Spirit
He's truely my best Friend
He woos me oh so gently
He's with me till the end

If you would Love to know my
Father
Just lift your heart in prayer
He Loves His Precious Children
You will find He's always there

Brandy Landrum
A DREAM
A dream is something in your mind
A dream is something you can find
A dream is something you can
pretend or be in
One time there was a dream I
couldn't find,
It wasn't in my mind.
I wished I could pretend it
But, I couldn't even see myself in it.
One day I saw my dream inside my
mind
Now I know a dream I can always
find.

John W McLure
TO A FAVORITE AUNT
In many nests of ants one finds
That workers usually specialize:
The nurses, hunters, soldiers of
great size,
And cleaners, evictors of the insect
rinds.
In dark recess the queen and her
attendants
Perform their urgent labor without
honor.
Nearby some ants will take from
any donor
Pretending help in every
circumstance.
Great queen is not the queen: that
designation
Belongs to those who scent the
need for change,
Toward food, or foe or end of
monarch's reign.
These catalysts decide the formic
nation.
So here's to her who never says, "I
can't,"
Our stimulant, our sun, our
superaunt.

Heather A Bachus
OXYOPY
Some say tomorrow passes,
Some say tomorrow never comes,
So shall the mysteries of tomorrow
forever linger.

Dwelling in the past,
Dreaming of the future,
Forgetting that life is leaving today
behind.

The day,
Yet to behold the light of sun,
Is the question to the answer.
But What does all of this mean?
Is youth left to die,
With the inevitability
Of numbered years?
Must the comfort and security
Of dreams be faded in the light?

But why trouble the simplicity of
now,
When tomorrow
Is another day —
away.

Marilynn Harper
WHAT CAN YOU DO?
What can you do when you are 40
years old, when you are
turning the far corner of life.

When the pages of your life, you
are turning over just seem to
crumble in your hands, like dead
ashes in a long gone out fire.

What can you do when, the end of
the rope has come into view
and you are grasping the last and
final knot.

When you feel you have done all
you can do, like there is no
where else or no one else you can
turn to for help. For the help
you need in both the physical and
mental sense.

Where do you turn for the help to
train you to live a life worth
living, a life with some meaning, so
you to can feel human and
needed by someone, other than
yourself.

When and where can you find the
spark that will ignite you to
keep trying, to keep going.

Is there really that spark out there
or is everyone else, just
PRETENDING?

Can anything really be done?

Shannon Leigh Cooper
WHEN WE ARE TOGETHER
Into each day you are a charm to
me
When we are together we are so
happy

When we are apart I feel so desolate
We are too close to just forget

We have had good days, and we
have had bad
But when we are together at least
we're never sad

Tomorrow will be another day
To keep our lives from wasting
away

So if we can start all over again
I won't have to face my lifes very
end

Here we are now hand in hand
To be together on this very land

Now we are together without a lie
Together we will be to live and die

John David Day
QUEST
O'er heaven-scraping crags and
mountains
cross the valleys that lie beyond,
Through rivers fast and dark and
deep
his trek has led him on.

From fiery beasts of death
to pits which forever go
From parching, steaming deserts
to the driving, frigid snow.

He's overcome every element,
he's conquered what he must,
Only to deny his love and stoke
the fires of his lust.

The addictive, invaluable treasure
he seeks
is a joy he shall not find.
'Twill do no good to discourage
him,
for the beggar of love is blind.

And the quest always continues
over peaks, through fields of
clover
For always across the further
mountain
is the cup that runneth over.

Peggy Shelton Griggs

Peggy Shelton Griggs
THROUGH THE YEARS

To my loving husband, David Maurice Griggs

She gave him her heart for
safekeeping;
'Twas all the young girl had to give.
He promised to keep it forever;
To Love her as long as he'd live.
He carried her love deep inside him
And kept her so close to his heart.
They vowed they would always
stay lovers;
For nothing would tear them apart.
He still sees her through eyes that
remember
Of how she once looked long ago
And for her, the heart reminisces
Of the many ways his love would
show.
Through the years she still fondly
remembers
The warm loving words he would
say.
She can still feel his soft, tender
kisses
That were sweet as the ones of
today.
Etched by time are the lines on
their faces
And the gray gently tinges their
hair.
Many years have passed by for the
lovers,
But that love they once shared is
still there.

Carolyn Roy Gulley
MY WEDDING
Everyone had been planning
for the joyous affair,
All my friends and neighbors
had replied they would be there.
The crowd had finally gathered
and were seated one by one,
The air was full of mystery
for the event had just begun.
My courage was quickly fading
as I walked on down the aisle,
My arm was linked with father's
and I forced a nervous smile.
All eyes were upon me
as I had wanted all along,
And I could faintly hear the music
of a very familiar song.
We finally reached the landing
and my hand was placed in his,
As I glanced up at the people
I found my eyes were filled with
tears.
My heart was overflowing
for my joy knew no end,
And my life with him still reflects
the happiness I felt then.

Diona S Green
LOVE'S NATURE
The tides' bubbles crash to the
beaches,
Hills become fields of chaff left in
the wind.
Harsh wintery storms whithers
mountains,
Rivers become a graveyard of
fossils,
And disease threatens each living
day.

Yet the years can not compete,
With roaring tides of bubbling
laughter,
Rolling hills of gentle tears falling,
Mountains of memories of good
times,
And young children's voices
calling.

As time taunts with nature's
beauty.
And slowly takes life from all.
When nothing else lends a guiding
hand,
Our love will continually remain,
As natures' other beauties no
longer stand.

Cheryl M Wright
ALONE
Alone is how I stand, I've stood this
way before, but life alone has
brighter roads than looking at
closed doors.

My paths are clear, my freedom
near, but which road do I
take? I'll go to search each path
to find the one where life is at.

My past has brought me pain, my
future still holds more, but this
time I am wiser and I'll be the
one to close the door.

Alone is how I stand, I've stood this
way before, but this time
questions must be answered, the
ones I used to ignore.

Dixie R Alexander
CLOUDS
Little clouds so lightly
gather,
A gentle reminder as
to whether—
My desiring, or pursuing,
is all that matters—
To bring the joy of laughter

Gladys Mixon
WORDS WITH WINGS
O, words of radiant beauty
Lovely words with wings!
Like birds and butterflies
They bear no stings.

But, bringing joy and cheer,
They help our hearts to glow.

And paint as bright a picture
As red birds in the snow.

Lorna L Steckler

HE

HE called the wind and HE bade it blow
Breezy, gusty and strong.
HE called to the rain and lightning came.
The storm was fierce and long.
HE called for the clouds to disappear.
The sun burst forth in light.
HE called to the flowers and mighty trees.
Leaves were brushed colour bright.
HE called all the seasons, one last time.
They came and they fell at HIS feet.
HE judged the The Quick And The Dead in line,
For HE was their MAKER to meet.
HE took all the Chosen, Ascended On High,
Where together for Life Everlasting,
HE reigns over all in the greatest of light.
HE is LORD! HE is GOD!
KING of KINGS!

Grace A K Harmon

CHILD OF A BROKEN HOME

Dedicated to all children of broken homes . . . .

My mother and father now are gone
In my life they did not get along.
It matters not which one was right
Or which one wrong,
But did I love them?
Did they love me?
And Especially . . . .
Did I dishonor either one?

Dear God, my prayer for them is this . . . .
That death tore away the confusion mist,
That each forgave and each forgiven,
They're happy together now in Heaven.

Darres J Munds

LAMENT TO A LOVE GONE

I would like to dedicate this to my father, Wilburn J. Munds who taught me to be myself, above all else.

A fool I have been a time or three
A fool again I have been to thee
An artists heart is cold and bare
Whichever cloak he wears
Compassion he has for women fair
With love and joy beyond compare
But alas he shows the heart he wears
Lonely is he this life to bare
Listen all who care to see
An artist this man some day shall be

Michelle Law

FEELINGS THAT KILL

Dedicated to Todd Vickers—the one who broke my heart. I still love him more than anything in the world! And he'll never be without my love!!

Stars—Far away, casting hazy glare -
Me wishing you were there.
Night so dark—heavy, but light.
Black, cloudless skies—Tender is night.
Never hear—your cries.
Never seeing—your good byes.
Shattered dreams to break the hearts
of loving ones whose end now starts.
Screaming soul to fear -
Falling down—one lonely tear.
Soft voice to scream
for hearts and souls need be redeemed.
Stinging tear to burn the eyes
of the blind fool who makes us cry.
Whispering wind to ease the pain
of the lonely one who still remains.
Until . . .
Broken Heart stops the beat
During time while crying to sleep.

Jean Scheel

LOVESICK

To Beatrice, to whom I wrote this poem as a letter when we were courting. She thought it should be in your contest.

My love for you I know is an unlikely script,
a play whose simple theme is made of feelings stripped
of make-believe and sham. The characters don't fit
a TV plot or stage. But I'm transformed by it
as though a virus filled me and took complete control
of all my glands and muscles, brain and heart and soul.
This illness I'll not fight; I've no wish to recover.
Fate innoculated me to be your lover.

Martin J Doyle

A SEARCH FOR COMFORT

In this life, can comfort be found?
With strife and problems becoming profound.

Since birth, a hungry stomach craving food,
a damp bottom, changing our mood.

Through life, hoping comfort can be found.
When only problems seem to abound.

Can there be true comfort in this life?
Can it be found by taking a wife?

True comfort leaves us the day we are born.
Can it only be found, when for us, others mourn?

A glimmer of comfort seems to exist.
The sun shinning through, the earth's blanket of mist.

The beams of comfort shine through like the sun.
When you meet your love, and you become one.

Saddly bidding farewell, much to your chagrin.
You pray for this comfort, soon to be found again.

Ken Krousey

MINNESOTA WINTER TO SPRING

Our winters are cold with lots of snow and ice,
With the north winds blowing it isn't very nice;
A cheerless winter sun slowly sinks in the west
While the whistling snow is drifting to a regal crest.
The red poll, chickadees, with sparrow the leader,
All cluster in the yard for sunflower seeds at feeder;
The road is slippery and it is twenty below,
I think I'll stay at home and watch a TV show.
Now the sun is brighter and a longer day,
The rivulets of water indicate the snow is melted away;
Wild geese, ducks, and loons are here to stay,
And a fat night crawler tempted a robin today.
Now we see young rabbits, squirrels, and bees,
With pink apple blossoms fluttering in the breeze;
The green grass, iris, and peonies grace the lawn,
While singing orioles and chattering wrens usher in the dawn.
During the winter I had my special dream,
So, today with rod and reel I fished a babbling stream,
While the graceful hawk performed in the sky;
Along the river bank wild flowers caught my eye.
You ask why I spend my retirement here,
With drifting snow and winter so severe,
But I do have a privilege only God can bring,
Enjoying the transformation of a Minnesota Winter To Spring.

James E Brown

BLUE SKIES

Magnificent of many of Gods creations,
For bright heavenly colours flow throughout the globe,
Only God could pour such a beautiful invitation,
Always so bright it seems too unreal and bold.
Within are puffs of cloud images,
That dance around in lifes imagination,
It releases many colours as a birds plumeage,
Making signs for man to witness Gods final declaration.

Mae M Laborde

TO A NEW BABE

To my first great grandchild, Matthew Lawrence Ehrlich

When the Angels drop you from Heaven above,
There will be open arms to hold you with Love.
Welcome to your new World little Babe,
For all the money we'll never trade.

Cheri L Winkowski

HUMBLE ONE

Here we live very humbly,
I and my little family.
Accepting life day by day,

And getting through it in a,
Humble way.
And yet having the strength to,
Face each and every new born, Day.

J Bradley Yarbrough

WHAT ARE WIVES FOR?

Dedicated to my lovely wife, Jill, who gives me inspiration, encouragement, and support.

I ask "What are wives for?"
If I may be so bold.
I run toward the door,
And me she does scold.
I mean no offence
By my question today,
Though "He's got no sense!"
You may hear some say.
Yet I have an answer
To this question of mine.
If I can romance her,
You'll say I'm just fine.

Wives are for talking,
Listening, holding and tugging.
Wives are for walking,
Playing, kissing and hugging.
I love my wife so much!
I know she'll always be there.
Yes, it only takes a touch
To let me know she does care.
I think you should know,
If you haven't been told.
Why do I love her so?
My wife is pure G-O-L-D!!

Florence E Moyer/Michels

TO OUR ADOPTED SON WITH LOVE

Two bright eyes as blue as skies,
Two lips so pink and sweet;
Two tender little ears, a nose,
And two rosy little cheeks.
Two little feet and chubby legs,
That run to us in fright.
Two chuffy little arms and hands
Around our necks so tight.
With blond hair on your little head,
A smile upon your face;
Dear little son, there is no one,
Can ever take your place.

God gave you in our care,
To fill our hearts and home.
The blessings of watching you,
Grow unto your own.

Before long dear son, you'll be a man,
Out on the sea of life;
Our hopes for you, is a good home
With a dear and loving wife.
That you both will be the sunshine,
That lights the others way;
And you have some little ones like you,
To fill your earthly stay.

Dianne Graves

WASTED YEARS

I look at you and see
So many wasted years.
Three decades going on four,
Half a lifetime, may be more.
Lost to guilt and dreams
Of what could have been.
A baby born in times
When infidelity was only whispered.
Fear and denial overpowered reality.
And time and guilt weave
Strange patterns with the mind.
Where truth becomes an illusion,
Fantasy a way of life.
But reality is seen at a glance
By everyone but you.
For you still live in years
Long since abandoned.
Forgotten how to share or care.
A woman now, I understand and accept.
Is there still time for you . . .
Mother?

Donella Joy Hiebert

OUR RAINBOWS

Our lives are like rainbows
That shine across the sky so blue,
They're mixed with sunshine and rain,
With dreams coming true, hopes ever new.

Our lives have had some rain
That we could call our tears,
But soon the sun came in all its splendor
And helped to calm those fears.

Although not always welcoming the tears,
It is to the rain we actually owe
Our thanks, for with just the sun
Our rainbows could not grow.

Happiness, candlelight, and romance,
Sadness, teardrops, a broken heart,
Makes our lives rainbows—
Beautiful pieces of art.

Yvonne M Wakefield

FOREVER AND BEYOND

You have to believe before you can understand.
Just reach for the golden hand.
It will take you to a world unknown by most,
where war is somewhat of a ghost.
There is no hate in this beautiful place.
Here, love fills the space.
There are no crimes other than passion.
Things are done in the most fascinating fashion.
There are still tears.
But there are no fears.
If you ever pass into forever and beyond,
we will share a very special bond.

Kerry Elizabeth Blickenderfer

THE LIGHT SHADOW OF LOVE

There is a shadow to every sun,
and we two are like this.
As dawn and dusk, sunrise and sunset,
our differences are few.
I am contented to watch in mirrors
As your light outshines mine.
No tears invade my strong face of stone,
for I know that you could not survive
without me, your shadow.

Your voice may hold the strength of kings,
yet my soft melody keeps you sane.
For you, the sun shall always glow warm,
and for me Diana shall reign.
Things grow and flourish in your time
to rest peacefully during mine.
As your light grows stronger each day,
I become one with the shadows.
For you cannot be without me,
and I cannot be without you.
There shall always be a you and me
in every sun that shines
and every moon that glows.

Bonita Rowley

I'M SORRY (ABOUT OUR DIVORCE)

I'm sorry
that I didn't pay any attention to you
as I pulled you along behind me
in my little red wagon.

I'm sorry
that you had your eyes closed
as we lumbered along.

I'm sorry
that you only heard my song,
none of your own.

If I could do it all over again-
I'd make you walk-
I would make you talk.
But the damage is done.

My "Maker" knew
what was ahead
for you and me:
the inevitable,
the unforgettable,
and the unforgivable.

"He" knew that I would become weary
before you did.
Our life together was only ashes on the grid.

"He" knew that I would suffer with you
when the ride was over.

On Reconciliation:
I have tried so desperately
to recreate the wagon scene-
but I cannot conjure up not one positive dream.
It won't work!
I have dropped the handle
and gone on without you.

I walked back to the wagon
and I couldn't recreate you and me.
I could only see incompatibility.

On the outside of the wagon we stand.
It was not our maker's plan
for me to pull the wagon forever.
I'm sorry.

Beth Binkley

THOSE WHO

Those who love,
Should be loved
Those who hate,
Should be loved more

Valda M Harrison

SUMMER

Summer is here after the long freeze,
Beauty of sunrise, a warming breeze;
Calling the heart to far away places;
A wandering to wide open spaces.
Flowers are a riot in full bloom,
Filling the air with sweet perfume;
For spring has sprung into summer;
Nature has awakened from her slumber;
And turned the grass again to green,
And little creatures again to preen;
Scurrying about in the golden sun;
Children laughing, having such fun
With scooters and dolls and bikes
And plans for joyous camping and hikes.
What happiness, its summer again
With people's faces all a'grin.
How it feels so wonderous warm
After all the winter cold and harm;
For God lets the warm summer rain
Wash away all the winter pain.

Ruth Puoti

THE STORK

The Stork stalks majestically
Seeking snails, mice and moles;
At night it rests in a nest
On a roof on one leg
Preening its white and black plumage
With its bright red bill.

Donna Jayne Allen

PERFECT PAIR

To Ethel and Issac Fultz, My Grandparents

Some say love is a flower
Then it should be called,
A Rose . . .
It puts roots down
In any type of grass.
That says it touches all of us
So, stop and smell the Roses
Of our lives.
It grows from a bud of youth
Bursting into the flower of beauty.
Growing by the tears of rain
Blossoming with smiles of sunshine.
Rainbow with many colors
Is our miracle of love
Our pot of Gold
So, is'nt it just natural
We made a perfect pair.
One love and Roses
The other, us man and wife . . .

Karen L Carson

FEAR

The microwave waits its turn like
a detached brain awaiting formaldehyde.
A knee cracks in the distant hallway.
I remove the microwave's
splattered browning dish
only to see the watery blood of rump roast.
Stroking
His face close to mine
Blood
on the sheets Mother would change
She pushes through the swinging door leading
to the dining room, only to remind me
"A place for everything, and everything in its place."
I think my maiden's quilt displays itself to her searching
eyes like the dark pool filling the stained dish.

Dorothy S Moore

THE PILLOW

To Julie—who knew I could, and to Randy—who had no idea I could

---

The pillow, oh so cool and white,
Once marked the presence of your head,
Now, fresh and smooth, it mocks my night
With your absence from my arms, my bed.

Your arms once held me 'gainst the night,
Your fingers soothed my fretted brow,
Your kiss could set my world aright,
Who will bring me comfort now?

Through all the haunted nights I cry,
They drag me on towards empty years,
Your pillow lies there cool and dry,
While mine is hot and wet with tears.

Golda Wade Bentley

Golda Wade Bentley

THE END OF THE WAY

When you come to the last moments of life,
You have taken your last steps,
Eaten your last meal, and said your last words,
What then?
Will you be glad your steps were to the right places,
You said the right words,
Your eyes saw the right things,
You did the right things,
You laughed the right laugh,
You danced the right dance,
You drank the right drink,
You spent the right money,
You went to the right church,
You sang the right songs,
You prayed the right prayer,
You heard the right gospel,
You lived the right way,
If you did will you hear him say,
Well done thou good and faithful servant.

If not, he will say depart you that
work inequity
Unto everlasting fire prepared for
the devil and his angel,
What will it be?

Rene Clayton
PINONS LOST TO PROGRESS

To my daughter, Mitzi and our Bobcat Ranch.

A funereal freeway has split this
land
With two black bands of mourning.
Deathlike knells for pinons gone
Silently wail a warning:
A pungent paradise is lost—
A monster is aborning.

Hidee DeLight Marotz
SOMETIMES YOU MUST STAND ALONE

Sometimes you must stand alone
to kiss a knee or bloody toe
it's just part of your life don't you
know.
To change and clean when a mess
they make
is quite simply—icing on your cake.
Yell and hollar—swear and curse,
Smile to yourself, it could be worse.

Sometimes you must stand alone
They'll be there, your whole life
long.
The aches and pains, fears and
sorrows
Where's the happiness, hope &
love to follow?
Today the world is theirs to run,
Tommorrow perhaps, they'll have
to stand alone.

Regina Smith
ABSOLUTE BLISS

To smile
To laugh
To love . . .
To live.
My happiness
My hope
My joy . . .
You give.
I crave
I desire
Your touch . . .
Your kiss.
For me
For you
Our love . . .
Absolute bliss.

William Warner Koch
LOVERS IN THE RAIN

The rain had come again.
I had mistaken her call for the
dancing of
leaves in a reel of wind of the
pavement.
But when I recognized the call,
I had to dance with her.
So I donned my light coat
and hatless, ventured into her.

She stroked my brow, cooled my
thoughts,
and as we made love,
the unseen sun sank, while she
spattered my body with herself.
Small rivers soaked my shoes,
resistance to feeling ebbed—
as sweet raindrops fell into my
laughing mouth.

Our affair over, she departs,
and I can only hope as I shiver,
covered with memories of her,
that we will, some serendipitous
afternoon or night, love again—
two souls at dance;
alive within each other.

Jackie Burinda
AWAKENING DREAM

To my 2 beautiful daughters, Marlene & Delena Love Ya! Mother

---

Did you ever think of a dream?
A dream walking?

Just think of trees in autumn with
leaves of red and gold.
Of icy water falls.
Water that is freezing as it falls,
Just hanging in mid air.
The sunlight hitting it causing
silvery blue, flashing lights.
At night the moon glistens and
dances on the slowly moving
water and ice.

Oh what beauty there is to see,
dancing in the moonlit icy water!

Then the warm spring breezes
come up.
Suddenly there is a creaking and a
loud boom.
The glistening, glass like ice, falls
into the whirlpool below.
Swirling and falling down beneath
the water,
Only to rise again a few yards
beyond.
They seem to dance down the
rapids, growing smaller and
smaller,
Until they are no more to be seen.

Such is the coming of spring,
And the awakening of dreams.

Tressie Sims Gossage
KISSES

To my husband Flavius L Gossage On our anniversary April 22, 1935 to April 22, 1986

Kisses all over me from head to foot
Playing hide and seek, then taking
root:
Running like quick silver up and
down my veins
Or making squishy puddles like
soft spring rains.
Kisses for my hands and kisses for
my throat
Kisses for any woman to crave and
gloat:
Kisses hot and sultry, make lips
promise more
Till kisses rush by, going with a
roar . . .
Kisses singing round me like stars
in the night
Swirling and converging in one big
light.
Sippy little kisses that taste like
wine
All mixed up with kisses of brine;
Kisses in the moonlight and kisses
in the dark
Till the heart lilts like the song of
a lark.
Hard fused kisses, beating with
desire,
Kisses that burn with loves own
fire.
Kisses intended for a sweet long
thrill
Kisses embellished with a lovers
skill—
Kisses more precious than
diamond gleams
Made mostly of memories and
dreams
Kisses strung forever to a necklace
of life
Kisses of love from a man to his
wife.

Martin Ray Miller
UP FOR THE DAWN

I will never
Get over
The sun and It's shine.
It's rays warm the heart.
Oh a true
Friend of mine.
The shadows it cast
Doubles existence that's there.
The animals,
For awhile,
Have a friend
They can share.
The scenery becomes beautiful,
So peaceful
So calm.
The quiet cleans the soul,
Almost like a psalm.
There's nothing quite so
beautiful
As the hour after dawn,
Unless it's looking forward
To twenty-three coming on.

Madeline Aldridge Wynn
THE BITTER COST

I'll have just one, this time I'm sure
To prove to me that one will do
Then go straight home to wife and
son
Just one won't hurt, since day is
done.

I know not why or what took place
Jusst one, then two, I remember
eight.
I can't recall what I have done
Home is in shambles, my loved
one's gone.

What happened to that vow I
made?
To prove that I would have it made
To go straight home after just one
To sweet Marie and little John.

Many times this has happened to
them
My broken promise, their hearts to
mend.
Wish I had come on home to them,
Before I stopped for just one gin.

Lucy Marie Griffis
THE POPPY

I awake in the middle of the night.
Fright grips my heart,
Like a tortured mouse in the
clutches of a cruel cat.

Is that his voice that I hear?
It cannot be. For he is dead.
A scarlet poppy waves its head
(Red, Red like the ground where
on his blood was shed)
In the breeze that stirs the curtain
at the open window.
He is not dead!
Those small black seeds I scattered
in the soil- (not so long ago)
Knew death- and yet
A scarlet poppy waves its head
In a blue vase on my window sill.

Daisy D Rudy Martin
I SEE HIM IN EVERYTHING

This poem is dedicated to my children, Peggy Rudy Cavin and David Trent Rudy

---

I see Him in the mountains, the
lakes and the sea,
I see Him in the raindrops as they
fall fresh on me,
I see Him in the flowers that bloom
in early spring
I see Him in everything.

I see Him in the laughter of the tiny
little child,
I see Him in the couple as they walk
down the isle
I see Him in the robin as it builds
it's nest and sings,
I see Him in everything.

I see Him in the stsormclouds as
they sweep through the sky,
I see Him as he blesses this world
for you and I,
I see Him, oh! I hear in voices as
they sing,
I see Him in everything.

I see Him in the green fields, laden
fresh with the dew,
I see Him gently caring for me and
for you,
I hear Him softly whisper, come
unto me and rest,
I see Him in everything, oh! I see
Him in everything.

Ida M M Ragan
SEARCH FOR IDENTITY

This poem is dedicated to my daughter Bronwyn.

Who are you? Who am I?
Reach for the Attic sky,
And grasp a bar of rainbow with a
sigh.

Gain the golden hills
To gather daffodils,
With molten magic in their butter
frills.

Gaze at scarlet wings
That flash like ruby rings,
On the hands of daring, dashing
kings.

In aventurine,
Or cat's-eye, deep as sin,
Look for Wisdom's widely
knowing grin.

Unveil the waterfall,
Like beads against a wall;
A droplet may reflect our destined
call.

Seek the sparkling brew,
Where bubbles burst anew;
Jove's intoxication gives a clue.

Rise to the Rigel star!
There Diana's car
Illuminates our path to
what-we-are.

As the arrowhead flints true,
And the sapphire stars to blue,
The Hunter points to nature to
pursue
The query—Who am I? Who are
you?

Julie Meador
PAGES OVERLOOKED

Many years down the road
The chapters of my life unfold.

As I leaf through this tattered book
Falls pages that I overlooked.

The writing on the pages
Cramped for space and faded
Follow the lines upon my face
Wrinkled and spotted with haste
and waste.

Colored pictures, now black and
white
Memories too have aged, yet time
Has read countless books
And pages fall overlooked
To rest between dusty shelves
Ashes to ashes tell the tale.

Edward L Brunt
I HAVE FALLEN FROM GRACE . . .

I have fallen from grace
At a time I knew not.
So very much is divine
And often I have Wondered
What I have done
(or not done)
And what actually matters.

Mankind is ignorant, of much.
We are as children trying to
Balance on top of the
Neighbor's picket fence;
Wondering, in our simpleness,
Why our father snatches us
From an unperceived danger
To an unconceived safety.

Gerry Templet
LOVE

Let me be your candle,
that lightens up your life.
Let me be your candle,
that lightens up your night.
Let me be the stars,
that burst unto the skies.
Let me be the stars,
that lightens up your eyes.
Let me be the rainbow,
with colors bright with hue.
Let me be your moonbeam,
for I am in love with you.

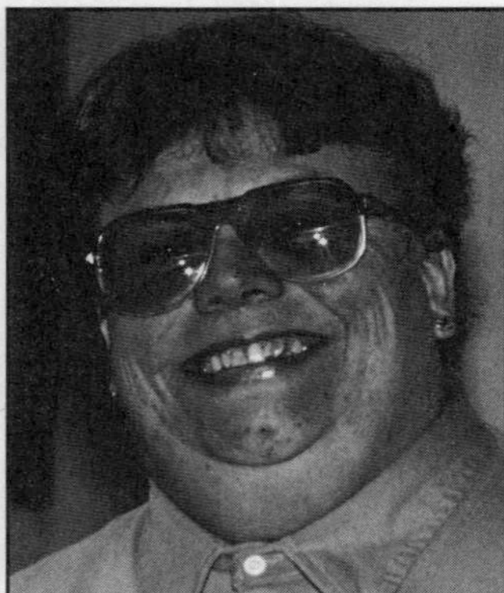

Loretta Garing

Loretta Garing
OLD FRIENDS AT CHRISTMAS

To Diane and Carol, whose friendship inspired this writing.

Old friends at Christmas,
the Christ child we share.
In all of lifes' memories,
his presence is there.

He has walked with us, too,
since the dawn of our day.
His words have brought comfort,
his lights' shone the way.

Through eons of time
our friendship has flown.
In the likeness of "He"
and each other, we've grown.

We have shared it all,
the good and the bad.
Our time together, the
best we've ever had.

So, as we rejoice
with the shepherds of old,
in the birth of the Christ child,
as the story is told,

Let us thank God for all
that has been and will be,
and step into the future,
good friends, we three.

David Jones
TOO SOON THEIR DREAMS DIE

The wind died,
the sun is setting,
All of life,
is now forgetting.
The days' deeds,
which were done in haste,
Are now seen,
as just total waste.

My eyes are closing,
my mind is sleeping,
All my life,
I'm now forgetting.
The nights; deeds,
are done in dreams,
Then fade away,
to soon it seems.

My heart is aching,
our hearts are meeting,
My life is yours,
for the asking.
But lovers' deeds,
are done in vain,
To soon their dreams,
die in pain.

Susan Leona Dolan
WHAT REALLY MATTERS

To my father-in-law. The courage he showed fighting cancer helped me realize how special life is.

Hope is strong and faith heals,
But what of a human heart that
ails?
Questions always; No answers
please—
The answers consistently tease.

What's inside the human heart
within?
Conceived to live without sin—
A human struggle of wrong or right
The answers to questions quests
it's might.

For questions present a life task—
To solve and raise the flask.
An answer worth receiving—
Of questions more deceiving.

Shall we gather where hope is?
Forever to quest the mountain of
his—
Or something so simple must
Of the open heart I give to trust.

M Florence DeLuca
GOD SPEAKS

God speaks to me through every
flower that grows,
His voice I hear in field and garden
fair;
Where daisies dwell I know my
God is there,
And I learn His deepest secrets
through the rose.
God speaks to me in every breeze
that blows,
And sun and rain proclaim His
tender care;
The moon and tide confide the
truth they share—
That all the world in rhythmic
pattern flows.

O God, I pray the day no more may
dawn
When I forget to note that peace
within
Is drawn alone from Thine Own
Master Plan;
Make mine the task to toil where
hope is gone,
To tell to those who yearn new
faith to win:
"God speaks in accents tuned to
heart of man."

Suzanne M DeLucia
BEST FRIENDS

To Connie, Through the good times, Through all the bad, You're still the best friend—I've ever had. Always, Sue

---

Do you remember when we first
met
We didn't have much to say—
Although there was a touch of
magic
I found I wouldn't forget!

Our meeting could have been just
plain luck but I think it was
planned by that big man at the top.

Either way I met someone very
special and at no time I ever
forgot.

In my yesterdays you gave me
memories old and new.

In my tomorrows you give me
dreams to look forward to.

There is a special place in my heart,
it is a place were love could never
die.

I give only you the key to this part.
For you are my sunshine within
that still glows when days seem
dim.
This place will just wait inside, if
you ever want a place to run and
hide.

My Loyalty—
My Friendship—
I have already shown, so don't ever
FEAR being alone.
I will be there if you fall—
you won't even have to call.

Always remember—I want you to
have the very best.
I couldn't settle for anything less,
especially, I want your
happiness.

Because nothing is more
important or nothing could ever
compare.

To the special kind of love these
two best friends share.

Kaye Morel
THE SECOND TIME

To Dennis, my husband, for whom this was written with love.

With our eyes, may we always see
love
sparkle with God's gift from
above.
With our lips, may we always
speak true
encouragement in abundance,
disagreements few;
With our hands we can give and
yet receive,
and in our hearts, in each other,
always believe
That
Blessed is the second time
Like a Pure and Beautiful
Dream;
Two hearts wrapped in splendor
Love binding together as the
seam.

Doris Nettles
DON'T JUDGE TOO HARD FOR IT MIGHT HAPPEN TO YOU

Pray don't find fault with the man
who limps or stumbles along the
road, unless you have worn the
shoes he wears or struggled
beneath his load.
There may be tacks in his shoes
that hurt, though hidden away
from view, or the burden he
bears placed upon your back
might cause you to stumble, too.

Don't sneer at the man who's down
today, unless you have felt the
blow that caused his fall, or felt
the shame that only the fallen
know. You may be strong, but
still the blows that were his, if
dealt to you in the self-same way
at the self-same time might
cause you to stagger too.
Don't be too harsh with the man
who sins or pelt him with words
or stones, unless you are sure,
yes, doubly sure that you have
no sins of your own.
For you know, perhaps, if the
tempter's voice should whisper
so soft to you as it did to him
when he went astray, would
cause you to falter too.

Audrey Buxton
HEAVENLY GUIDE

This poem is dedicated to the memory of David William Buxton

I was resting on a fluffy cloud
singing merrily

When an Angel appeared happy and serene smiling down at me.
A very old man with trembling hands was standing by her side.
The Angel softly whispered "I've chosen you for his guide."
Proudly I took him on a tour of Heaven and all of its wonders to see.
I knew that in no time at all he would say what a very grand place to be.
We walked slowly down a golden path, birds were flying everywhere.
Their sweet songs of happiness were filling the crystal air.
He wanted to see the animals, where they made their home.
And then he spied a tiny kitten that he used to own.
In the velvet dusk the Angels were lighting the stars for earth below.
But they all stopped to smile at us and waved a cheery hello.
At the end of the rainbow an Angel was waiting patiently for him.
To fasten on his golden wings so his Heavenly life could begin.
I wasn't surprised to see the old man straighten up his shoulders.
Nor was I surprised to note the trembling of his hands was over.
I know just how he felt you see, though I've been here a long long while.
I still remember when my uncertain tears turned into a happy smile.
So I shook his hand and watched him go, alone, but peaceful as could be.
With a promise that tomorrow he'd stop by and have a cup of tea with me.

A Lincoln Ames

FALSE SPRING

To Ronald Reagan; who faced the assassins of this world in his own way, by standing up in front of them

---

Every thing was greening up
Natures urge is stirring
Looking toward a filling cup
Then zap it's not occurring
A fickle wind switched to the north
It's chilling snows propelling
Impatients who had ventured forth
Retreat to safe dwelling
Braking sounds come from the drive
That ray of hope, yes it's (her)(his) van
Once dreary heart, alert, alive
Perhaps a chance to start again
"I've just come back to get my thing's"
A soaring heart has lost its wing's
But a clearing mind began to reason
Spring won't come till it's in season

Faye Purcell

ECHOES

Single sounds double.
Echoes, Echo what they hear,
Echo what they hear.

Fred Wood

THE GREAT LIE

To the great truth Jesus Christ, the way, the truth, & the life

---

There's a wild fire blazing in our land today.
A great lie that has come in great power and plans to stay.
Many empty hearts it will surely slay. The lie declares you are remoulded clay, another face in a different place.
Many lives you have lived and so many more to come.
Believe this and you'll find theres' nothing to shun.
Oh death where is thy sting, since upon this lie I dearly cling.
When I need answers, and feeling weak, my medium
I shall seek. And into my future he'll give me a peek.
My aching heart now has hope; with this lie I have eloped.
This is my decree, that my God is me, and now I am free.
The Father upon his throne, because of this lie his heart does groan.
My Son I have sent; our truth you have bent.
In this lie you cherish, know not you shall surely perish.
As a thief in the night shall death come
Before in judgement you'll stand naked and bare.
Before you; my truth I'll declare. To your many live's still unborn say goodbye. For in hells black chambers shall your dead spirit lie, no one to hear its lonely cry.
No matter how far this great lie sails; the truth is, only my word pervails. This is my story, this ismy song, catch the beat, you can't go wrong.

Harvey B Myers

CERTAINTY

The Limb, Life Gnarled with Time,
Clutching Rings of Coon-Tailed Scars,
A Eulogy of Hopes and Ropes
Battered and Frazzled Beyond Repair

The Pool, Swimming in Colored Sky,
Inviting Waves of Confident Comfort,
An Envelope of Needs and Reeds
Shimmering and Shining with Love

The Rope, Spectral Sent and Hung,
Awaiting Fists of Grappled Risks,
A Gossamer of Cares and Dares
Swinging and Taunting Beyond Reach

Small Boy, Old Beyond His Years,
Stretching Arms of Lonely Desire,
A Body Wet Bank of Barriers
Saturated and Muddy with Fears

Reaching for a Grasp, Secure
Longing for the Water, Serenity
Slipping Still Further, Unsure
The Only Certainty, Uncertainty

Sandra L Smith

THOUGHTS OF GRANDMA

I was having my morning cup of tea,
When thoughts of my Grandmother came to me.
I was hoping she would come to see me I guess,
In that same old tattered everyday dress.

She brings such happiness to everyone around,
Without ever having to whisper a sound.

Maybe we could go pick some wild greens,
Her in her dress, me in my jeans.

Or maybe we will just sit and chat,
She'll pet the dog, I'll play with the cat.

When she comes to the door she'll have her Bible I know,
So we will probably have prayer, then read about Job.

I am so thankful God gave her to us,
When he took her away I wanted to cuss.

Then suddenly it came into my head,
Grandma has been twenty years dead.

Jack Blanchong

MY HOPE

My hope, my darling, is centered upon you,
For I love and adore you—yes, it's true.
My hope for life is to have you so near
That, when I reach out, you're always here.
To hold you close and never let go
Is the fond hope that makes my heart glow.
You are my hope, the center of my dreams.
I love you so much I'm bursting my seams.
The Lord, Himself, has put you before me,
And opened my eyes, your beauty to see.
My hope now lies in His great mercy—
To keep us together for eternity.
There is no hope that matches mine,
For it's the highest hope of all time.
My life depends upon having you,
And nothing else will ever do.
My dearest darling, you know that my love
Is as endless as all the stars above.
My love will outlive time itself,
But only let me have you to myself.
My very existence herein lies.
It's your love for which my heart cries
Having your love, with the world I'd cope,
My lovely darling, this is my hope.

Betty Borchardt

WINTER STORM BLESSING

I heard you call and I saw you stumble
As you came near in the raging storm . . .
Your mouth and nose were covered with a scarf.
Your hands had on gloves that were wet and worn!

The snow circled . . . your eyes opened and closed!
You were trying desperately to see the way . . .
In your arms you carried a wet calf
Born in the snowstorm today!

I pulled open the door for you . .
The howling storm blew in!
It lifted the curtains and tablecloth . .
As you stumbled again, coming in . . .

Closing the door took all of my strength!
Wind lifted my skirts to my face!
In the short time you took to come in
Snow blew all over the place!

You gently laid the calf by the fireplace
Half-frozen, it was matted with snow!
As you massaged it with dry towels . . . thanking God . . .
Our "winter storm blessing" moo-ed low!

Michael Moore

DISCOVERY

A ship in solitude
Anchored off the cities bay
Only water surrounds her,

And then the pure air.
Like me and you
For the fish in the sea,

And the mammals upon the land.

We are the life and air in which they breathe,
And the freedom—and bravery to wander wherever.

He is the ship which sails away.
—The ship that sails today.
For some, new, and future waterway . . .

Shirley A Cieryca

BEFUDDLED

This poem is dedicated to my son James; In hopes that he will follow his dreams and always remember that "Knowledge is Power."

Words in books,—books and words are hard to comprehend,
When hours and hours fly by with no means to the end.

Adventure and knowledge are revealed
through words;
A mystery I've yet to solve.
The words from books go in my brain,
but tumble and revolve.

Meaning and understanding are important—

this is true!
So,—try again,—again I'll try;
for meaning to come through!

Linda Francis
CREATION

To Sam for all the reasons

Only with a glance,
Did I ever notice the stars.
These beautiful mysteries of radiant glow,
Reach out,
Wanting to be known,
Yearning to be understood.
Then I found myself in your arms,
And together we discovered the universe.
Love came into my life,
Only with a glance did I notice.
Never looked beyond the surface,
Never searched it's reasons of existence.
Just as the stars, Love can explode,
With pieces drifting in many directions,
Never to unite.
This love has exploded,
But if you take me into your arms again,
We can create our own galaxy.

Mae E Sallila
THE DOLL AND THE TEDDY BEAR

Perhaps we're not the showcase doll,
Glamorous in her stylish clothes,
Much admired but hardly loved,
Who gives no comfort to a child's woes.

But like the ragged teddy bear
Left bleeding saw dust on the floor,
Worn out and full of other's tears,
We hear God say, "I love you more."

Phoebe C Walton
THE HOUSE IN THE GLEN

In loving memory of my dear mother, Nettie E. Mitchell

Houses may come and houses may go
But there is one special house I know,
One that is snuggled close in the glen
Oh, how I loved that little house then.

For 'twas there Bill took me when we were wed
Carried me over the threshold, smiled and said,
"This is our home, though small it may be
It is just right for me and thee."

Three happy years we shared in that house
All cozy, and tight, and warm as a mouse.
When I came to Bill, with a heart full of joy
He laughed and cried, "I hope it's a boy!"

Three other babies, in that house were born
Then it was too small, so we moved on.
In all seven children we had,
Three girls, and four boys; like their dad.

Now Bill is gone, the children are grown
And I'm in this big house all alone.
Oh, how I long to be once again
In that little house down in the glen.

Margaret Asselin
THE GATHERING PLACE

I bait my trap and back away
Conceal myself and try to stay
Quiet and still.
After a while there comes one
And then another comes along.
Alert and quick.
Too soon the quiet is shattered
And the air is full of color
Reds and yellows
Blue and brown. They chirp and sing
And chase each other away
While more come.
And soon the bait is all used up
The colors fade from my view
And the feeder is empty.

Vikki Cooper
SO FULL OF QUESTIONS

So full of questions without an answer
oh you poor soul—Your life without a goal.
Who cares? Who knows? Who shares?
Agony and defeat go hand in hand
So cruel is the blow dealt from man to man.

So full of questions without an answer . . .
Who rules a life? A man or a wife?
Who cares if you live or die? Or laugh
or cry? What of the little ones we leave
behind? Poor little angels; should you
have been born? You have at times been
so sorely scourned!

So full of questions without an answer . . .
No bed of roses it has been said,
but must each day have thorns and dread?
Give me a chance to rise and grow
You might be amazed at what could be . . .
Don't drown me with cruelty!
Either love me or leave me, but don't destroy me!

So full of questions without an answer
So full of hatred and dread—Who
says a person has to die to be dead?
Smothered in defeat 'til we're one inch
tall—at this you must have had a
laugh—Just to see me crawl . . .
I truly don't believe you are capable
of regret—For you couldn't treat me
with such outrage—Never, never giving
me the stage.

So full of questions without an answer
Goodbye to what could have been—
To what suredly should have been—
Oh I love, I care, and could most
assuredly share had I been given the
chance to see the world—under my full stance!

Stephanie M Binkley
AT CALVARY'S CROSS

As I stood at Calvary's cross,
I knew that I would suffer loss;
Loss of a friend so dear to me.
What could the purpose of this be?
And as my heart reached out and cried,
My Savior hung his head and died.
I'd seen so many deaths before,
But his death seemed to be something more,
Something awaited yet to be seen.
And three days after his death,
My Savior took another breath.
In that breath he blew life into me,
So with Him I would always be.
Now I finally understand
My Savior's long awaited plan.
Now I realize there was no loss,
For my Savior was meant to be on that cross.

Debby K Hodson
INSPIRATION FROM GOD

To God-My Inspiration-

Lord, it's really beyond my understanding—why you
love me, why you love me so much. You gave your
only Son—could I give my child? To think of a love as
grand as yours for me—it overwhelms me really.
I'll never do anything to deserve your endless love
and grace. Sometimes I try to do for you, and always
it's just not enough for me.
I am so glad that all you want is me to love you
and follow you, and believe in your only Son Jesus.
You know that's not hard for me to do. Sometimes
I just want to hug you Lord! I raise my hands and
praise you, I sing to you, I give you myself. I just
love you so much Jesus—that I want to show you
And tell you, and try anything to just do it, even a bit
more than before. That's when I realize you just
love me! For who I am now through your Son Jesus—you just love me! I do not have to make a big parade to let you know how I feel for you. I just have to acknowledge you through your lovely Son, our Lord Jesus Christ and just simply love you. And I do. With all my heart and soul and my strength. Thank you Jesus

Joyce Irene Schmidt
WHAT IS A DAUGHTER IN A LIFE

This poem is dedicated to my two daughters, Rhonda Renee and Robin Rachel—their pleasing and loving qualities made it easy to inspire me to write this poem.

What is a daughter? Oh! What a question to ask!
How could we ever dispassionately answer when in her beauty and light we bask?
Other people see a beautiful young woman, but we see the infant of yore,
Sometimes when we wax nostalgic, we can't believe she is not a child anymore!
It seems incongruous and sometimes not very real,
When we see her with a child of her own, trailing at her heel.
Memories and photographs are the only remnants of that precious little girl we raised,
(And on how well she turned out we always receive praise!)
How sterile and empty life would have been without her—we know when we have been blessed,
Without her smile, the sun would seem permanently recessed!
So please be careful asking us that question because it strikes a parental chord,
Her Dad and I know what this daughter means and of course,
so does our dear Lord!

Helen Eleni Levos
YOU AND I

To the ones that I love the most, my parents, Gus & Catherine Levos, Carol, Penny, Angelo, my 2nd parents Mato & Charlie Rose, To Christina Rotella, Cathy Katsoris, Emily, Debbie, Pamela Grant, & to Alan M. Diamond; My wish for him to be my secret admirer! & The Sutters Mill co.

Your gentleness is kept within the deepness of my heart,
Your caress makes me feel so wanted.
But yet, the time that we spend together seems so different.
Like, here we are now, but yet our world's are
So apart.
For when I dream, your name is spoken from my lips,
I only dream of you and the memories that we have shared.
At night in my dreams, I want so much for you
to hold me and tell me how much you love me.
Right now, I feel as if we can combine into one
just like the future will bring.
For yet there is no other that I could ever love,
So I'll be here when you decide.
Just remember that "no one will ever love you
like I always will."

Penelope (Penny) L Barnes Cambra
FEEL ME

This is dedicated to my Mom and Dad, who I hope someday will not just love me, but feel me and understand . . . and to my most cherished love, You truely feel me, as I feel you. We touch beyond our souls. Feel me . . .

I write to you—of me.
Feelings—my soul.
I write now
So you can too, feel—me.
I'm not the same
as others.

Just different.
My thoughts
Untold, are now.
I feel—like you
Unspoken words
but they are there.

I write to you
words.
So much more is meant.
I give to you, me
you receive.
But do you understand?
My thoughts are here.
Not only words . . . But me . . .

Ruth Bakanauskas

THOSE TINY GREEN PEAS

Part I.

O those tiny green peas
and you floating
in the cream.
It's all that mattered: those peas
(and the song of Ewok,
high-pitched and mean).

Part II.

For Christmas you receive
a healing of your cranium/
I give you a swan
and a Lilt home wave

and fill your skull
with tiny green peas
and put it in a pot
with bacon and cream.

And the starry flames
in your tar-baby eyes
and the games on TV
roll and hiss in the steam/

a crash through the screen
and Pledge Allegiance:
Joe Montana eats one raw
and winks at me

And I wink back, knowingly
and blush, and cook the peas
three minutes, exactly.

Mary A Bezold

THE MASTERPIECE

I watch the stars as they twinkle
and shine
Through the trees outside my
window
And the light I see through the
stately pine
Is the bright full moon oe'r the
meadow.

The woods take on an eerie hue
As the moon casts its glow through
the trees
And paints the shadows a misty
blue
As the leaves wave good-night in
the breeze.

The hours go by and the moon
disappears
As a mist starts to cover the earth
And soon the bird's song is music
to my ears
As the dawn brings a day of rebirth.

Then I rise and again observe the
same scene
But the daylight provides a new
view
For the trees are now dressed in
shades of green
All glistening with diamonds of
dew.

Olga Thompson McHale

DEAR FRIEND

For Brian, who left us in the springtime of his life.

I climbed the hill to your house
today,
And found the doors were barred.
The flowers were gone from the
garden;

Weeds had taken over the yard.
I stopped for a bit before heading
back.
Wiping a tear from my eyes,
I saw a late bloom by the
springhouse:
The red rose of friendship never
dies.

Hazel P McNeal

HOW MUCH LONGER

In memory of my beloved husband Carl E. (Bud) McNeal

As I look out at the sunrise,
As another day peeks through,
I realize that you are gone,
And I could not go with you.

God called to you, "I'm ready for
you,
Are you ready for me too?"
"You must leave your love behind
you,
Someday she will come to you."

And so I look and wonder,
How much longer must I wait,
Before I meet my Darling,
At that Heavenly Gate?

Michele Darr

AN ODE TO TEACHERS

Once in a lifetime, someone comes along who goes beyond simply being an educator. This poem is dedicated to my teacher and my best friend, Mrs. Janet Markee.

What motivates a teacher?
Certainly it cannot be
The low wages or long hours
Laboring on indefinitely.
Neither can it be
An angry parent or rebellious
youth
That motivates the teacher
Who with persistence
Seeks the truth.
These people our educators
Whom with young minds we trust
Labor on in their endeavors
While knowing that they must
Teach a generation skills
To distinguish right from wrong
To go into the world
Where the roads are rough and
long
I have finally realized
What motivates the teacher
It's the spark of understanding
Lighted with a knowing smile
That makes a teacher's job a joy
And their efforts all worthwhile.

Angel Arnold

RAINY NIGHTS

On rainy nights the skies are blue—
Wake up in the morning and smell
the dew.
Leaves are falling from the trees;
Little blue birds are singing with
ease.
Kites are going everywhere;
Children are going here and there.

and that's why I love rainy nights;
You get to see all kinds of sights!

Marie McDaniel

COME BACK LOVE

Everybody has a unique experience in the world, you're mine. Dedicated to my sons, Tawon Riley and Alton McDaniel. With love.

By the time you read this letter,
the night will already be gone.
And I'll pray to God high above,
I made it through the night alone.
But tomorrow has to come my love,
And the pain will still be here
so I'm begging you to come home,
because I love you my dear.
But if begging can't bring you to
realizing my needs.
I'll even go as far, as dropping down
on my knees.
I'm not so proud, when it comes to
getting back your love.
I know I was the cause, so let
me be the result.
I know we hurt each other, but it
was just a lover's quarrel.
So let's forget about yesterday
And think about tomorrow.
Tomorrow will bring happiness for
both me and you.
So move your pride aside, and let
your love shine through.

Nettie Mantica Grant

TO NEVER LOVE AGAIN

To never love again,
So young and yet so old.
To think of one so dear
Her arms cannot enfold.
Gone forever now;
Precious moments do not die,
Even if life snuffed out,
Her brave heart cannot lie.
Empty hours creep
Through each long day that slips.
Memories burn the mind,
His kiss still on her lips.
Once, and only once,
The "one and only" comes along.
So in love and joyful,
He held her hand and she was
strong.
A door will never open,
A bell will never chime,
That she will not remember
Each past, but happy time.
To think of his warm heart,
Now still, forever cold.
To never love again,
So young and yet so old.

Kathy L Hasara

DEEP PLANTED ROOTS

Dedicated to my loving husband for his support and encouragement

---

The pictures are coming off the wall; The boxes are carefully being packed with those sentimental nic-nacs, that we have given you over the years. Your pride and joy! It amazes me how you can remember who gave you each one of the tiny treasures; So delicate they are. You have a story for each one. I see a vase I gave you when I was still in grade school, the artificial flowers, it use to hold, have long been gone, the paint is faded but still you pack it away. Wrapping the china I can remember a Christmas when we all still believed in Santa Claus; A Thanksgiving when for some strange reason we all managed to be home.

As you were taking the photos off the wall unit, I noticed how you paused to look at each one a little longer than usual, as if you were saying something very private to each one of us.

You told me you went through the old cards and letters we have sent you over the years, the pictures we drew in school.

My eyes water as I imagine you home alone in that big house, going through parts of your life; pulling up the deep planted roots.

Kathy M Biggs

WALK WITH ME TODAY

I dedicate this poem to our Lord and Saviour Jesus Christ and to my mother, father, granny Lewis, Aunt Dollie, and Grandpa and Grandma Duty, for their love and support.

Lord When you see a little
child crying, you stretch
out your hand and wipe the
tears away.

I'm hurting Lord, would
you come and walk with me
today. My burden is heavy
Lord, I can't bear it alone. Now
more than ever I need the
comfort of the love you have
shown.

I'm in trouble Lord and I have
lost my way, please Lord would
you come and walk with me today.

Frances M Klingenmaier

I WISH

To Ralph; Love Always, Fran

I wish I were The Sun

that I could warm your heart for
me.
I wish I were The Moon
Enfolding you with light, that you
may see—
I wish I were The Wind
around your heart I'd fly—
And if my wishes ne'r come true
I wish I'd die!!

Barbara Gouger
THE ONLY ANSWER

To Anita Mosley

When the burdens that you carry,
Seem so heavy and unfair,
When the tempter softly whispers,
That no one really cares.

Remember Satans a liar
And he has been from the start
But you have power over him,
Because of Jesus in your heart.

The precious blood atonement
that Jesus freely gave
Was just one way of showing
His life for us He gave.

So when you need to feel the hand
Of Jesus touch your soul,
Just raise your hands toward
Heaven
And He'll gently take control.

Candy C Moulton
ONCE A MIGHTY MAN

This poem is dedicated to my mother Rose Wynne in memory of my father Thomas M. Wynne.

My Dad was once a mighty man
Who had the strength of two
He lived his life for his work and
family
But now that life is through
He raised us kids to be strong and
smart
And sure he was tough
When I look back now and think
about it
The love there was more than
enough
I'm sitting here now on his property
Waiting for the sun to come up
My son plays here like we use to do
Damn, it's hard to grow up
An evil demon got ahold of him
Its name is simply cancer
Dear Lord I ask you why
I hope someday I'll have the answer
I see my Dad now frail and weak
And slowly slipping away
He still makes jokes and smiles
when he can
Somehow he's accepted his destiny
Though it means he can't do what
he loves to do
Once a mighty man with the
strength of two

Betty Coffman
HURRAY TO SPRING

After the cold winds of the winter,
the snow, ice and the chills
Now the days are getting longer
and full of promise
I feel spring is just over the hill.

The early flowers are pushing their
heads through the earth,
All the world seems ready for it's
rebirth.
The birds are busy building their
nest,
The grass is turning green after it's
winter rest.

Animals are out of hibernation and
getting ready for giving birth,
The world is excitedly watching all
of God's nature at work.
I feel the warm spring sun on my
body, and breathe deeply the
fresh crisp air.

I humbly thank the Lord above,
hurray spring is nearly here.

Maybelle McAbee Bates
THE MASTER'S HAND

Awaking from my slumber
I listened to the stillness of the day,
Then peering from my window
Beheld the glory of the world,
Oh, the awe that overcame me
Filled my heart with praise,
As I drank in the beauty
From the touch of the Master's
hand.

Trees were heavy laden
Boughs bent low as if in silent
prayer,
Soft winds blowing gently through
To add music to the air,
Birds nestled closely finding
protection there
Fearing neither hurt nor harm,
Being a part of God's creation
From the touch of the Master's
hand.

Brenda Katherine Underwood
THE CONCRETE JUNGLES

Given life by a seed
Planted in the mind
And nourished by the
Sunshine of human hands,
The jungles take shape
And grow and expand

Into miles upon miles
Of concrete land.
And the earth, and the flowers,
And the trees
Have concrete graves
Of sidewalks and streets
And the buildings are the
Tombstones of unequal worth.

Bertha J Denem
OUR CHURCH

I know a cute little house in
Suncoast Estates,
That never locks its doors or gates.
There's a great little reason why,
you see,
They would just love to have some
company.
The Master of this lovely place,
Would welcome you with charm
and grace,
You're always welcome at His
house,
He loves you, your children and
your spouse

Won't you come to His door and
walk on in,
Go right up, and talk to Him.
He's waiting for you, you know
that's true.
Your vows to Him, you should
renew.
His servants are there to help you
through.
There's love in our church just for
you.
Let's make our Father's face to
glow,
By getting our congregation to
grow.

Bring all your family and then one
more,
Get all of them through the door.
Put a big smile on our Savior's face,
You'll feel good and in His grace.
Let's fill His house to overflowing,
With faces that are bright and
glowing.
When the battle is over and all is
won,
Let's praise God for what He's
done.

Maggie Utterback
GRANNY

Yes memories are happenings—
Each one, a different kind.
Each one, a separate chapter—
That is printed on the mind.

Your book has many happy
chapters—
Filled with laughter and good
times.
Each paragraph tells another
story—
In detail, through smiles, and in
rhyme.

Yet we can't erase the sadness—
Or edit out the tears.
We can't undo the wrongs we've
done—
We can't relive the years.

So onward, the pages turn—
Traces of tears for yesterday.
Here flashbacks as pictures hold
you—
Until you bring yourself away.

Since memories keep building—
Each day can be the start
Of making new & happy
stories—
To store within the heart.

Suzanne Anderson
CRYING DEEP INSIDE

A sleek, shiny headstone rests by
my loved one
The earth is covered, the ceremony
is done
Bright and hard shines down the
sun
It's beckoning me to walk away
from here
But still I stand and stare . . . Crying
deep inside.

The flowers struggle to lend me
comfort and cheer
The ministers words still ring in
my ear
Friends awkwardly mumble words
of regret
I long to turn and run, to flee from
this fear
But still I stand and stare . . . Crying
deep inside.
My senses throb with this
deadening pain
I want to cry out and yell, to call
out and scream
But they say life goes on and so
must I
To pick up the pieces and let my
loved one lie.

Yet agony racks my mourning
soul, each time I hear his name
And it hurts even more because the
world goes on just the same
They told me the pain would pass,
the wound would heal
But so many years have passed,
still I can't change how I feel.

A harsh, weathered headstone
rests by my loved one
Bright and hard shines down the
sun
It's telling me to walk away from
here
This burden no longer should I
bear
But still I stand and stare . . . Crying
deep inside.

Marion Masterson-Cloake Wolfe
DESOLATION

The Fog in swirls of dark delight,
Conspires to overtake the night.
Forms emerge, all haze surreal,
Shape and substance I cannot feel.
Begone! Oh brooding fantasy,
Give my mind a peace to me.
Dissolve the fears within that
linger,
Lurking, clinging, chained
together;

Frenzied movement as in trance
Deeper, denser go their dance.
Does my mind perceive them so
Or is their life their own to know?
Tell me spirit of the night—
Do these nethers take delight:
Cavorting through my troubled
mind,
Remembering love that once was
blind?

Ted E Robirts
THE STEENS

In loving memory to John Cooper, a husband, father, and best friend. Brave and courageous to the very end, we'll miss him

---

"I am in love!"
How many times have you heard these words, or even uttered them yourself? But I am in love with an older woman, centuries and centuries old. She is a mountain. Before you call me a fool, let me describe her. Fish Lake and Wildhorse are her eyes, bluest of blues. Kiger Gorge is the cleft of her breasts. She wears a powdered wig throughout the winter, then changes to the golden brown of cured wildgrasses in summer. surround her throat like necklaces of pure silver. nose and cheeks are freckled with juniper, mahogany and aspen. Desert surrounds her on all sides. A majestic queen, 9,600 ft. high, the ridges and canyons in her leathery skin stretch endlessly across her face. Many moods has this old

girl. You cannot predict from day to day the way she will be tomorrow, whether she will be sunny and warm, or throw a tantrum of cold wind, snow or sleet. Do not camp in a wrinkle in this old girl's skin, for when she cries (and many is the time she does) she will drown you where you stand. Do not expose yourself on a bony ridge as the thunder rolls overhead, for she demands respect.
My mountain carries scars on her seamy old face, put there by man. He comes from the towns and cities to escape the clutter and pollution of his home. But habit is strong and he is doing the same to the Queen. Throughout the years I have cleaned up after my fellowman, like her nursemaid, but I am old and tired now. My eyes have grown dim with age. no longer see the majestic face I love so much. But when the time comes to scatter my ashes from the sky upon her brow, I will hear her say "Welcome home, old man, welcome home."

Betty J House
WINGS OF FIRE

Oh, my great and noble warrior
How your aim and strength amaze
me
With your bow so taut but gentle
And your arrow straight and sure
Sent a message to its target
Claimed your prize of hours rare!

In the magic of the moonlight
You have filled my eyes with
stardust
Amid thunderbolts and rainbows
Thru' the heavens and beyond there
We have flown on tails of comets
Shining silver wings ablaze!

As the smoke of many signals
Lingers on the misty mountains
Smould'ring embers dream of
flaming
Waiting for the wind to fan them
Burns my passion with your
mem'ry
Makes my thoughts within me stir!

Let your eager voice enthrall me
And your spirit rise and call me
As the river's pulses quicken
As the deer is swift in season
Run to me on legs of light'ning
Fly to me on Wings of Fire!

Phyllis E Keefer
OUR LAKE

This poem is in honor of my wonderful children who enjoyed many hours of fun around this lake.

I walked around
the lake today,
I saw alot
and wanted to stay.

It was a beautiful day
around the small lake.
The children were playing
with their poles at stake.

A lone white duck
amongst them she swam.
Among brown mallards
and mudhens she can.

Like long jet streams
the water spread like a fan.
The quiet of wildlife
it belongs to man.

This muddy small lake
you see
responds to the likes
of you and me.

Flo Marie Arnold
DAD AND MOM

The starry sky, shined ever so
bright,
While two young lovers, pledged
their love that night.
They started the wheels of life as
one,
Fulfilling their dreams and
building their home.
Their youth saw them thru' the
early years,
Raising their children thru'
laughter and tears.
Beautiful memories, along the way,
Kept them together thru' each bad
day.
Middle years, there wasn't none,
Only an extension of the earlier
ones.
Now, their earthly time has come
to an end,
But not one of us, shall ever forget
them.
For part of them, in each of us
dwell,
To carry forth, as we shall,
Their values and traditions, as we
were taught,
And bring forth goodness, from
which life is wrought.
Alas, Dad and Mom, from our lives
have gone,
But the fruit of their love, still lives
on.

Ms Yvonne MacMaster
ONE DAY A CHILD IS BORN

One day a child is born
Who brings joys to his family
Sad to say that in a short time
This child finds himself so lonely

In search of love he goes
To find and lose at every turn
Until at last he realizes
That only God can give that Love

Return to me my child
No more sorrows you will find
But peace of mind you will get
And most of all LOVE that
humankind forgets.

Do not fear the time of loneliness
For you needed it to go within
And find the ENERGY, that are
built in
For you to use—God within—

Kathleen Bridget Freeman
SEEKING SERENITY

Life, like a bird in flight.
And I, the cat prey
In search of hope,
For a tranquil domain.
In a world so somber.
Yet full of growth and gain.
My heart, so tear-flooded,
Yet keen on the sense of hope,
Still yearns for brightness,
As the minutes grow old in a
young day.
The threshold of being widens,
but I, draw further away
From the truth.

John J Smith
THIS MAN CALLED LOVE

This poem is dedicated to my father, Paul C. Smith Sr., who most sincerely tried to reveal to me by his example and his words the true role of the man in the home and the world

---

A man is Strength
He is Protector
He is Love

A man is Wisdom
He is Advisor
He is Love

A Man is Confidence
He is Provider
He is Love

A Man is Tenderness
He is Friend
He is Love

A Man is——Lust
He is——Oneness
He is love——Virility
——Excitement

A Man is
He is
He is Love

A Man is Caring
He is a Sexual Being
He is Love

Marie Hunter Burns
A MOMENT'S SPLENDOR

In the fall . . .
That time when all the leaves are
floating down
In a cacophony of color all over
town—

Now and then,
against the din of the blazing gold
and red,
Falls a leaf, so quietly, past my head

It's just brown . . .
Gets lost on the ground . . . and its
outer skin
Is spotted with patches grown
quite thin—

But an angel wing
Is this gossamer thing with sun
shining behind it!
And only a moment's splendor . . .
for, who but I will find it?

Evelyn Cruz
WHO NEEDS A HEART

Who Needs A Heart
If One Does Not Know
What It Is To Love

The Heart Feels Happiness
The Heart Feels Pain
But 'Tis Truly Sad
When One Does Not Know
What It Is To Love

I look At The Stars Above And I
Wonder
What Is Wrong With Me
Why? Why Is It . . .
That I Do Not Know What Love
Means

Who Needs A Heart
If One Does Not Know
What It Is To Love

Is That The Reason Why You Are
Not With Me
Is That The Reason Why
My Heart Feels Something
But Is That Love.

Rhonda Bailey Baldwin
MOTHER'S SHOES

Somewhere in the world today
a little girl will go out to play.
with hair in curls and nothing to
lose
she'll quietly slip on her mother's
shoes.

She'll close her eyes and pretend
she's grown,
with children to love and a home
of her own.
Molded with pride by her
mother's charms
and held by daddy in his big
strong arms.

She'll not know the worries of this
day
that probably will come along
her way.
But simply play without any
clues
to what it means to wear
Mother's Shoes.

Judy D Ellsworth
I'M COMING HOME

To my Two Sons, Tommy & Tony, I Love You

I've been away for so long,
But now I'm coming home.

Oh how my heart has been aching,
And it's waiting, just for the taking.

There's been pain, sorrow and
tears,
It all happened in less than a year.

I've been away for so long,
But now I'm coming home.

I'll be there, it won't be much
longer,
God give me strength & make me
stronger.

I'll be there, just wait and see,
We will be reunited, you and me!

I've been away for so long,
But now I'm coming home.

William J Roberts
LOWLY SNAKE

How bad it would be to be a lowly
snake,
and spend your life crawling
around.
Never could you stand, but would
always have to lay
with your belly on the ground.
When cold weather comes you

would have to find
a hole to crawl into to hibernate.
And after going to sleep, if some
animal dug you out,
what would be your fate?
If you live through the winter, and
crawl out of your hole,
to find spring has come.
And then to start another season of
just crawling around
on your belly, feeling real dumb.
The next time you feel all neglected,
and think that life has dealt you a
raw deal.
Just remember the lowly snake
crawling around,
and how much worse than you he
must feel.

Barbara Peterson-Welnel
PARADISE

To my husband John, with all my Love . . . Always.

There is a place
that can't be so very far away;
where sparkling streams flow;
Seeming to have no beginning;
No end . . .

Majestic mountains tower over all
beings;
their soaring peaks vanishing
into wind-swept
puffs of clouds;
billowing across the
azure-blue, sun-washed
heavens;
Seeming to have no beginning;
No end . . .

Lush forests teem with
colorfully-plumed birds;
Harmonizing together,
Creating a symphony of such
sublime majesty that it
Captivates the listener and
demands his undivided
Attention.
The richly-colored foliage,
composed of every color of
the rainbow,
stretches as far as the eye
can see;
Seeming to have no
beginning;
No end . . .

And there is a feeling that prevails
and rules over all;
a feeling of unsurpassable
compassion
and Love;
Having no beginning;
No end . . .

Teresa Lyn Page
LOVE—YOUR FLOWER

"This poem is dedicated to my Dad and Mom—Two VERY special people!"

I've walked down many paths
through the years,
You've been there to hold my
hand every step of the way.
Along the first path you nurtured
me—
Corrected me when I was wrong
Praised me when I was right.
The next path led to adolescence—
When I was ALWAYS right.
You guided me toward goals; the
future—
my future.
Now, you walk behind me—
To help me when I ask
To catch me when I fall.
No longer do you tell me what to
do, you advise.
From the bud to the flower. . .
You both helped me to grow
My sun, my water, my protector—
Mom and Dad,
The love and understanding you
gave to me made my
petals strong. I can withstand
the most powerful
storm because of the strength
and courage you both
have given to me.
I thank you for me and I can
only hope that I will
shine as bright and help
someone—my bud—grow to
be a strong and willful flower.
Thank you Mom and Dad—
I LOVE YOU BOTH!

David L Yarnall
SOLSTICE

Some ancient feeling
draws me here
knowing; not knowing
the time it is near

Soon will come the day
when joy fills the air
with sounds bright and gay
filled with good cheer

Boulders stacked on end
forming a circle
marking a time
that will never bend

A window on the stars
the passing of seasons
looking afar
for new reasons

Deborah Richardson
SO YOUNG, SO INNOCENT

The dedication of this poem goes to the Lord God Almighty, for giving me such a beautiful life. And my beautiful son Joey.

So young, so innocent, so loving so
trusting
my little boy is growing up brave

Your eyes so blue, hair so blonde,
I love to watch you sleeping, not
making a sound

Dreams of choo choo trains and
big white trucks,
Christmas time and rubber ducks

You'll soon be older, go out to play
and discover children your own age

But I'll be here very near, I'll watch
you laugh running fast,
to make that touchdown with that
pass

I'll watch you grow, I'll hear you cry
I'll long to hold you, but can only
sigh
I'll see your dreams, I'll watch them
all
But very soon night will fall

The dreams will fade, sad times
pass
You'll know I'm here when a breeze
rushes past
A sudden kiss, upon your cheek,
Mommy's here now go to
sleep . . . . . .

Nikki Reynolds
IN DENNY'S AT 2 A.M.

How many sorrows can wallow in
a coffee cup?
every roasted seed a dream
that sadness has washed through
every teardrop aromatic
clear, resplendent drops, brown on
silver
ringing a distorted teaspoon
reflection
She does not seek to dull its bitter
taste with cream
or sweeten it with sugar but
How much anguish can she drink?

Judith Stow
SEASONS

In the springtime of our love,
we laughed, jubilant with the
anticipation
of things to come,
feeling the newness of our lives
since we met,
exploring, searching, exchanging
words and promises.
And then came summer—oh, the
glorious summer.
We basked in the heat of the sun
and our passion,
taking our joy moment by
moment, day after day.
Fall came slowly, and one by one,
the leaves turned
and fell.
We rushed through our days
almost in desperation,
fearing the cold to come.
And then winter.
And what I thought would be
security,
a hibernation,
a time for planning and starting
new life
for the spring to follow.
But my love, I couldn't know that
for you
it meant only a dying time; a time
of giving in
to a cold, bleak existence, from
which nothing could be born,
or reborn.
Your love for me has died,
and left no seeds for planting.

Shelly Renee Wheaton
PARENTS OF MINE

This poem is dedicated to my parents, Walter and Sydney Wheaton, with all my love.

I am so lucky, in this messed up
world
To have parents like you who love
their little girl.
And show her what such love can
do
When it is all you really have to see
you through.
You understand me, or at least
always try.
Never condemn me but instead
show me why
What I have done or said wasn't
quite right.
Knowing you care helps me
through each long night.
Mom—you have a beauty I will
never possess.
Always forgiving and filled with
tenderness.
For all who come before you, an
ear is lent.
Never in shame of them is your
head bent.
Father—you're so strong and sure
of ways that are right.
To inherit half this quality, I pray
someday I might.
To trust you is easy, no lies ever
cross your tongue.
In my mind's eye you will forever
remain tall, handsome and
young.
To me you will both always be my
sun.
In heaven and on earth, together
as one.
My guiding light to see me through.
No one could possibly wish for
parents better than you.
Wherever I am, or wherever I go,
I only hope you will always know
How much I love you and respect
all you have done.
With parents like you, my life has
only begun.

Enid Kelley
SECRETS OF THE HEART

Lately I've been thinking about the
realms of life,
The joys and the havoc of a man
and a wife,
We love and we hate at the same
time—
Sometimes we can't make up our
mind
If only we could see inside each
others heart,
We would wake up and say O' how
smart,
For finally I have found—my
friend and my LOVE
Just like an angel from above
But O' it's so hard to reveal our
secrets deep inside
for fear we will hurt our pride
We need to speak before it's too
late—
before we fall into the arms of fate.

Alice Jay Lindsay
VISIONS IN THE OCEAN

As I sit and watch the ocean
In the sunshine—in the rain—
In the depths of the deep, deep
waters—
I see things I can't explain.
One wave rolls in with laughter—
The next one rolls in with tears—
I see visions of happy young ones—
And the ones who have added
years.
They have all been a part of my
lifetime—
Some shy, some aggressive, some
bold.
Do you think these visions a sure
sign—
That I am growing old?
I'd much rather think of it this
way—
As I gaze at this wonderful sea.
These thoughts that I've locked up
inside me so long—
Are ones that at last I can free

Becky Featherlin
WHAT?

In gratitude and love to my "creative roots"—my grandmother and my mother

---

What can I say in a poem?
What can I do with my life?
Harsh words or actions,

Cut through the soul like a knife.

What bits of wisdom can I give?
What can I do to show I care?
How often do we nothing,
Carrying on alone—if we dare!

What good is common sense?
What good are fame and wealth?
How can we enjoy them,
Crying because of our health?

What makes us happy?
What makes us sad?
Have we helped another?
Can possessions make us glad?

What kind of story did we weave?
What examples have we set?
How did we handle our trials?
Could they have been better met?

What's that you say?
What's the excuse you give?
Heaven and Hell are at hand.
Care what you do while you live.

Trish Ross

A FATHERLESS SON

To Michael Anthony and R.M.D.

What will I tell him,
When he is grown?
Why his father left
Before he was born.

Did I have a choice
On what to do?
Never, my son,
It was always you.

Explain my father,
What was he like?
A more compassionate man
You'd never find.

Then, why'd he leave me,
Didn't he care?
I know he did,
So don't despair.

I'll hold him close to ease his pain,
And whisper lovingly to further explain,
There'll always be questions, unanswered, it's true,
Just put them behind you, love and forgive,
For the world is awaiting, and you've so much to give.

Kay McAlpine

DIE-AT-IT DIET

Light as a horse,
Heavy as a feather,
Graceful as an ox,
Stuffed like a flat pillow;
That's how you feel BEFORE you go on a diet.

Light as a piece of fudge,
Sour as a sweet pickle,
Square as a pizza,
Stiff as gooey filling;
That's how you feel ON a diet.

Heavy as a balloon,
Ugly as a swan,
Slow as a gazelle,
Angry as a playful puppy;
That's how you feel AFTER a diet.

Eric Michael Jurien

CRUELTIES OF CHANCE

Deep into the celestial season
Driven tears on counts of treason
Fog filled laughter, extremely intense
Curses the fools, who have no sense
Gun in hand, screaming somewhere
Shoots its load on those who care
Anxiety releases with the touch of my hand
The victims cry, they can't understand
The night plays loud on my brain
As the little girl remains the same
Naked now, but with no shame
She's wishing that I'll go insane
The truth will die and so shall romance
Oh the pain and sorrow of cruelties of chance

Elsie M Rozevink

THE LITTLE SHORE CAPTAIN

To My Grandson Joshua A. Poston

Across the water it did go,
The little sail boat so true,
Pushed by the gentle hand
Of a little boy dressed in blue.

He was a captain great
As he stood upon the shore.
Shouting orders to his crew
To heave ho, man the oar.

He was sailing far away
To a distant land.
To see all that he could see
He was a roving man.

But soon the little toy boat
Reached the other shore,
So he walked around the pond
To start it back once more.

And that's the way his hours did go
As he sailed upon his sea.
With his little toy boat
He was as happy as could be.

So to my little shore captain
Who is all dressed in blue,
With good luck someday
Your dreams will all come true.

Douglas Downs

A LOVING MOM

For all the love and effect, a guy can't possibly regret, thanks to his loving and understanding Mom,

Like when its time for school, there is no need for an alarm, thanks to his loving and understanding Mom,

And when danger is near, he has no fear, because he knows his loving and understanding Mom is near.

Dale T James

THE UNICORN

Dedicated to faith and destiny—as what will be, will be.
I hoped and prayed for love, my friends, and my love came home to me. I love you Nancy Lynn, always. Everlast.

Monday crashes down on me with its reality;
Day one of a dream.
Tuesdays' freshness is a sigh that somedays'
Promise is to be.
The week rolls by—
Someday doesn't show.
Seven days have come and gone, the eighth must
Be for me; then Monday crashes down on me with
Its reality.
Hope comes bittersweet—
When someday never comes.
De je vous—
The unicorn.
That fantastic eighth day of the week, someday.
I've seen pretty pictures of untouchable fantasies;
But none seem as untouchable as the one you paint
For me.
Doomed to wait forever and the wait is crushing
Me; another Monday crashes down on me with its
Reality.
De je vous—
The floating hearts—
Hope comes bittersweet, when someday never comes.
Are you the unicorn?

Della (Manns) Leckrone

OUR MOM

In loving memory of Dollie (Manns) Ousley, My Mother. May 3, 1910—Jan. 17, 1987, We miss you 'Mom'.

A lady with beautiful, red hair,
Like a rose, she gave tender care,

She was small, in size,
But big in "love",
And never was a lady,
Ohh so wise.

She guided our paths
For many years,
And with a strong hand,
She'd take away our fears

She did not like
Some things we did,
Point her finger, shake her head,
Then with a grin she'd say—
"But I love my kids".

The "old time" stories, she use to tell,
Were such a joy, we loved so well.
Her gestures with the hands,
And excited voice.
No story could ever go without notice.

Mom's "love" for all,
Was like a flower,
She left it here
For us to borrow.
Now we keep it for all tomorrow.
We'll keep her "love" in our hearts,
And never will we let it part.

G Panaitos

MEMORIES

Still you are here,
then you were.
Already in the moment of your presence
you are past.
What makes past so perceptible?
The drive making finite things infinite.
Pleasant is your presence.
Why?
Only by finiteness we know delight.
Should I tack your photo to the wall?
Your pleasure will be shortlived.

Already in the moment of your presence
you are past, darling.
I inhale you, I exhale you,
touch untouched.
Australia is far away, love,
yet farther still are you.
Sweetheart, I need peace
to live in.

Kenneth A Dayringer

MY SHEPHERD

Yes, the Lord is my shepherd, so we say.
But we are smart, we know the way.
But when lost, alone, in a world without care.
Why? Isn't my Lord my shepherd there.
We often call, only when others fail.
Why? Should he rush, with our bail.
We ignore His teachings, curse His name.
Why? Shouldn't he, treat us the same.
We lie and we steal, without any thought.
To things we have read, what we have been taught.
We get so involved, day in and day out.
For us to hear Him He has to shout.
But when he withdraws His blessings from us.
Then we are the loudest, the first to fuss.
Yes, the Lord my shepherd, He is always there.
He is just waiting, to see if we care.

Christine Spurlin

WAKE UP, AMERICA

We talk about the Homosexuals,
The Bible teaches they are wrong.
And what about the Prostitute?
The oldest profession known.
Drugs are being sold to our youth.
The Pushers tell them they are mild.
And what about the murder of our unborn child?
God says, "If my people, who are called by my name
Will humble themself and pray,
And seek my face, and turn from their wicked way.
Then I will hear from Heaven, and heal their land.
and forgive their sins, and make things right again."
WAKE UP AMERICA—AIDS has hit our land.
To show the God of love is also in command.

Thelma Fee
THE SEASONS OF LIFE

For my husband Kenneth and our three precious children, Jeffery, Jennifer and Janet.

The seasons of life must come and go,
Each moment unused is the most deadly foe.
Greeting each season with acceptance and smiles,
Will make each step easier, while walking the miles.

First comes the spring, the time for all things new,
The greatest gift life, has been given to you.
This season used well, with a spirit to learn,
Will leave less in summer, for your heart to yearn.

Summer comes slowly, it has been a long wait,
You feel strong and alive, you can toy with fate.
You feel today is forever, it will never end,
But beware of your path, it has a bend.

Autumn comes quickly, doubts crowd up your mind,
Have you been true to yourself, have you been kind?
Time is racing by you, the years seem to flee,
How you accept your past actions, is what you will be.

Winter arrives finally, with a savory good taste,
Your lifetime has passed, with the smallest of waste.
You have enjoyed each season with few regrets,
You have taken life's gambles and won all the bets.

Henry Tye Jr
THE WEDDING RECEPTION
A friend took me to a wedding reception
And I was an unwilling passenger
In his haste, I was not properly dressed,
I hoped they would appreciate my candor.
We arrived at the banquet hall, minutes late,
When we went in, my mind's eye astounded me
The bride and groom and many in attendance,
Were a part of my life in my high school days.
Among well-dressed people, I felt out of place
Clothed in attire appropriate for sport
My heart ached as I watched very good friends
See me, recognize me, and keep their space
When all the time they knew I was there.
I longed to reach out to them and say hello,
But felt I would cause a subtle stir,
I did in fact, when rumors reached my ear,
If I was the one they knew six years ago.
Some hours later, we left, heading for home
And this experience and impression
I sadly related to my quite tired friend
Was that "after a generous span of time,
True friends are the ones who see your real self
From the inside, in spite of what you're wearing."

Kurt W Lenser
TO: BROWNIE
Farewell, little kitten.
Down deep I feel
the agony and pain
you must have felt,
before your little heart
stopped beating.

My conscience tells me
somehow I failed you
Great grief envelops me,
but cannot bring you back.
Would that I could reverse
the forward flight of time.

You gave me all your love,
asked but little in return.
When I held you in my arms
you purred with happiness and joy.
Always with me will linger
the beauty of your soulful eyes.

Sometimes we hurt
the things we love the most.
Sometimes we do not realize
that Heaven in our grasp
may vanish in a moment
—never to return.

Steven Angelo Tamucci
LIGHTNING STAR
High and hovering above my atmosphere
is a vision I can see very clear.

It's bright but dimming from its everlasting glow,
it will fall apart one day, everything has to go.

A wish to last forever and hang in the sky,
it would be a miracle if it never died.

Could it be that its light has burned out, oh so long ago?
When will we find out, when will our eyes see, —
Well, I don't know.

It shares its emotions and shines them down from a site
so very far.
Nothing can tell the truth of life, like a LIGHTNING STAR

Jude Anne Mitchell
THE PAIN MUST REMAIN WITHIN MY OWN HEART

To my mom, dad, and my husband Denny: You have made my world complete; with love, My brothers and my dear sister. God bless us all.

The pain must remain within my own heart, to allow the escape of such a hurt could cause destruction of some part of the strength which took so long to construct.
As the sun shines, a smile remains; should rain appear; my smile gets brighter. No more shall I cry and crumble, for there shall be a day when I need not walk backwards to let another pass me by. Their loss, not mine.
Life carries on through the fog surrounding truth; so thick at times no person cares to cut through. Sanctuary only comes with truth and those that refuse to see can only lose it in the end.
To what degree does fighting life's trends become useless, or is it just the finale of every quitter that draws this imaginary line? What about me?
No path do I follow, for my thoughts are my own; my road is my own.
In search of love always; perhaps never to discover. In search of justice; shall it ever exist again?
Debris remains a potpourri, "Pandora's Box", questions unanswered behind closed doors that I dare to open. I will open them in my own grace and brace them to remain open for others who dare to fight the way it is, ways that shouldn't be.
Beware my "friends." I'm on my way to grasp your rules and tear them apart. I shall not be under the heavy steps of those that crush and destroy. Between the rocks of your burial grounds I shall place my stars for all the world to see.
Take heed of your money and your power, cherish; if it is that, what you value so much, but remember success is measured in the soul rather than your minds. I have success of great mass, because my friends, my soul too is my own.

Sandra K Slate
REMEMBRANCES OF A LOVER

To my wonderful husband, Dan. Without your love and constant encouragement, I would not have the personal inspiration needed to continue with my writing. All my love, Sandy.

Thoughts of you are forever flowing through the riverbeds of
My mind.

I gaze into your eyes and see mirrored images of the love held
Captive deep within them.

Your heart pounds rythmically beneath your masculine chest.
Your arms envelope me and I dream of your exquisite manhood as
You penetrate into the dark recesses of my soul.

Your love is genuine, as is your touch.
The gentleness you possess flows freely through every fiber of
your being.

As your fingertips softly caress me, they brand me with a warm
Excitement.

The fire burning within me is kept rekindled by your kiss.
I trace the outline of your lips and find sparks drawing me
Into a sensuous embrace.

Etchings of you and your sensitivity are permanently engraved
Into my heart.

Becky Hendershot
CONCERNED . . . CARING
Concerned . . . Caring . . .
between one another
the words were quietly spoken.

Quietly . . . Spoken . . .
so ones own peers
had no hints, no knowledge.

No . . . Knowledge . . .
of what was happening
for her benefit.

Her . . . Benefit . . .
what really happened
she never knew.

Never . . . Knew . . .
until some time later
that they were only
Concerned . . . Caring . . .

Kervin Fondren
RECRUIT
Parents and Community,
I have a job to do;
If I come home alive,
I'll come straight home to you.
I've packed up all of my belongings,
I've said my last goodbyes,
So Father Don't you worry,
and Mother Don't you cry.
They took away my pride,
and shaved off all my hair;
and then I'm humiliated,
and they tell me that they don't care.
Oh How I miss my plump bed,
and eating tons of junk,
They're stuffing me with potatoes,
and they issued me a bunk.
After breaking all of my bad habits,
and making me feel brand new,
They throw me this dufflebag,
and send me home to you.
Parents and Community,
I'm coming home with new pride,
I'm not going to lie to you.
I thought that I would die.

David Keith Bertalla

David Keith Bertalla
AUTUMN FLOWER

Autumn Flower is a tribute to the life and spirit of Connie Sontag. One of America's finest Grandmothers.

This special gift is to show you I care.

It comes from my heart, the reason I dare.
Thank you, Grandmother, you brighten my days.
When I think of all the deeds you have done
Your light's so bright, it could be the sun.

I remembered all the times you were there.
You cradled, you kissed me,
You taught me to care.
Your tenderness never came to an end,
Your patience, your strength
Taught me to win.
The way I learn, this comes from your hands,
The values you show me, help this man stand.

When I need courage to truly press on,
I think of your kindness,
It's the first light of the dawn.
Now your life is in the calming hour
I appreciate the full beauty
Of my Autumn Flower.

Roxanne Gillis

REFLECTIONS

Time, Time, Time
See what has become of me.

While I sit and look at
all my possibilities.
Look around, Grass is high,

Tis the springtime of my life.
Sometimes high
Sometimes low
Feeling mean and dirty.

I see my face
reflected there.
Now scared,
At what was once pretty.

Sandra M Ward

UNCLE MIKE

This poem is dedicated to Mom, who nurtured us both

Always tie a string around the opposite pinky where the nosebleed is to stop it;

Wear galoshers on the wrong feet to keep them dry
(I never know if he meant my feet or the boots);

Click your teeth when you eat soup and
it keeps them clean;

And on and on . . .

Me a teenager

He seventy-eight
Never married
Full of advice
Small, frail looking, but not
Walking miles each day, never sick
White hair with bangs
Topcoat, scarf and umbrella
Rain or shine—you never knew

A funny old man

Jan Marks

Jan Marks

THE LOVE GAMES

I know a game that lovers play, over beyond the hill.
It is a game all lovers play and lovers always will.
In the freshness of the green grass and the heat of the sun.
We'll think about sweet memories and dream of future fun.
And as we watch the sun rise in the vast azure sky, we shall lie together naked side by side,
The softness of each others flesh, the movement of our loins, as we caress each others mouths, our bodies they will join.
Then as the sun begins to set and we must soon depart,
We search into each others souls and look deep into the heart.
We see the beauty, the good of life, and our undying love, for with love so strong two are entwined as one.
Someday you'll go beyond the hill and play the lover's game.
And you will find how love can be tender sweet and tame.

Judy Tomkiel

MOTHER'S THOUGHTS

I love you, my children,
I truly do;
but you're hard on my nerves,
and my budget, too.
You're constantly at
each other's throats.
When I balance my checkbook
I nearly choke!
I try to give you
the best I can,
and accept that you're not, yet,
my biggest fans.
I'll bear the nonsence
you give to me,
because you'll grow up,
eventually.
Then you'll have children
of your own,
and it will be your turn
to groan.
And, I am sure
that in the end,
you'll finally know,
I am your friend.

Henry A Morgan

NIGHTTIME

The nighttime is, the nighttime does,
The nighttime gives, what the nighttime loves;
A chance for us to catch our breaths—
And to answer questions of the day.

Not to ponder meaningless events;
This is not what day has meant.
But rather to discover our other selves—
The ones we continuously place upon shelves.

The meek, the mild, the serene;
Oh passiveness, where hast thou be'n?
So quiet, peaceful beautious sleep;
In the Lord's hands our souls do keep.

Until the new dawn with sun break,
And from our restful slumbers wake;
To rush and push ourselves to death,
Or till the nighttime comes, to catch our breaths.

Virginia Iaia

CRIMES THAT PAY

Whenever there's a moment,
Every now and then,
I cannot help but think on
The avarice of men.
Who said, "Each man
Must have his price"?
A cynic, I've no doubt
And yet, the evidence in hand
Would certainly bear him out.
Who benefits from hateful wars?
Surely, not the dead!
Who profits in the trafficking
of heroin and lead?
What secret power structures rest
On contracts forged in blood?
Who reaps the ultimate reward
When heads of state play God?

Chris Frateschi

WORLD OF EMOTION

"To Mrs. Farady, Kristen, Laurie, and Shannon. Thank you all for sharing and listening, I wouldn't have been able to do it with out you." "Thanks for the support Mom and Dad."

People are so funny,
with many different thoughts.
A world of emotion, that all the people brought.
One sharing, as the others need caring.
Wishing people would stop and take notice
of the people who need love.
Just for one second, to make the hate all end.
So many people forget to care for someone
but themselves, and help the lonely people
find a friend.

Karen Lynn Buckley

MEGAN ELIZABETH BUCKLEY

For my neice Megan, who will always hold a special place in my heart.

A little girl was born today.
Cute and fragile
in every way.
Perfect and sweet
As all little girls are,
Megan's so cute
We know by far.
We'll dress her up
in pink with lace,
little bows perfectly set in place.
Dolls and such
will be her thing.
But we'll see what time has to bring.
Ten perfect toes,
Two perfect hands,
All a part of GOD'S perfect plan.
We'll watch her grow up
before our eyes.
Won't miss a thing
oh how time flys.
Our little girl,
So perfect you see,
A special gift,
God has sent you and me.

Michael Earl McCutcheon

VIEW TO A CRIMSON RHYTHM

For those who had faith

Riot in the wombs!

Turn them holocaust
First engines on!
They are immediate.
Notice their anxiousness
Tucked comfy
In elaborate
Jackets of flesh.
Here's lifes whole kerenel
Shrunken skillfully:
Lucifer in a cauldron.
Hell's mouth
On a twig called
Our spine-excitement!
Gapping flapping.
This communist muscle
A lil'injun
Flowing facelessly red;
forty watt meats
pumps
Amid a cornflowering
Nazism.

Joe Yancey

PRECIOUS MEMORIES RELIVED

To my Christian Friends in Allentown, GA.

My heart returned that pleasant day in Allentown autumn sun,

To a land where my roots were
nourished and enriched by folks
who love the Holy One.
Greetings of gladness—smiles of
joy told a wonderful story.
I felt back home—with a happy
throng traveling the road to
glory.
There, nestled serenely among the
spreading pecan trees,
Was a gleaming white temple—like
a lighthouse by rocky seas.
In memory I must have vision a
halo about its bell tower,
For it's illumination abounded as
if God gifted His brightest
flower.

There were tables of sumptuous
food reaching from border to
border.
Like a grand ol' "Quarterly
Eating—uh, Meeting", Willis
and I Used to slaughter.
I filled my plate with luscious cake,
pies and meats of every kind
And leisurely supped—as days of
yore, a joyful feast—a taste
Divine.

I moved and mingled among a host
of friends, sensing a warm heart
with each greeting,
Savoring sweet fellowships,
retelling stories of long past
meeting.
My spirit soared skyward into a
realm of sheer ecstasy!
This was heavenly music, balm to
my lonely soul, loving his
Majesty.

Such golden hours are
fleeting—like a twinkling of a
star.
A million moments of sweet
elation and soon my heart is
flown afar.
But memories live on—Allentown's
spirit rings-out angelic music
from above.
This is the story—this is the life of
a lovely village enshrined in
Christian love.

Patricia Ann Hall

PARENTS

---

*To my parents, Mr. and Mrs.
Americo Bellaver, my inspiration.*

When I was small, so very small,
you never left my side.
All the time you made me feel,
so very warm inside.
I loved you then, I love you now,
never will I stop.
For all my life, folks, you'll have
me, until
the day I drop!
I don't care if your hair is gray,
to me it's like a flower;
and wrinkles are like number
banks,
adding loving power.
So everyday that does unfurl,
you can always say for sure,
that is ours, for all our lives,
our little, first born, girl!

Marjorie Dixon Baggett

AMY'S BEAR

---

*To my precious Granddaughter—
Amy Lee Weed*

"But, Grannie, I did see him," she
looked at me to say.
Look right down there,
Grannie. that-a-way".

Pointing toward the glen, beyond
the sycamore tree,
Amy frowned her worried look,
and pushed real close to me.

Her little heart was pounding; I
didn't want to doubt
If that old feller was down there,
we would surely run him out.

It was hard to keep from smiling
as I cautiously moved on down
To where the fence was broken; my
face now wearing a frown.

Little Amy held my skirt, and
nearly tripped me twice.
As we stumbled on that path, we
were a funny sight.

Then I heard a sudden swish, and
stopped dead right there.
I had not planned on all this fuss
when I left my front porch chair.

I looked up, then all around, While
Amy squealed her fear.
There was nothing right, nothing
left; nothing I could see or hear.

Then Amy tumbled as I laughed;
the way she grabbed the air,
You would have thought a monster
faced us instead of a dumb old
teddy bear.

There he was grown so big, since
Amy had left him in the rain.
His legs were long; his feet were
huge, and his eyes were large
with strain.

"I told you, Grannie, I told you,"
Amy chanted her little song.
"I knew we'd find him, I knew we
would . . ." so glad she wasn't
wrong.

We laughed 'til we cried, our lives
meeting in the middle.
She became old, and I became
young, while old teddy solved
the riddle.

He moved an arm, then a leg, and
stood up straight and tall.
He became real; we became stuffed
. . . as time stood still for us all.

Joyce Ryan Matthews

Joyce Ryan Matthews

**THE HOUSEWIFE'S
SOLILOQUY**

---

*To housewives everywhere whose
job is sometimes thankless, always
without recompense and whose
only motivation is love.*

Do you hear me each day, my love?
As we go through the days,
I don't say many words to you
But speak in other ways;
I speak to you in thoughtful acts
By doing tasks for you,
And putting your desires first
But let you think it's due.

I speak to you each day, my love,
Though not in long rapport,
By not complaining of my lot
When I have need for more.

I ask our Lord to keep you safe
And to our home to bless,
Love, this is how I speak to you
With few words, nonetheless.

Clarence Knowlton Burnside

THE INTRUDER

The morning sun came through
my window;
With such a mysterious grace.
While moving the curtains to and
fro.
It softly touched my sleeping face.
I stired uneasily beneath its glow.
Then yawned and stretched my
arms so slow.
And blinked and blinked and
yawned some more.
Knowing that day was here once
more.

Feliza Lynn Maggay

**THE GREATEST MAN I NEVER
KNEW**

From the day of his birth he knew
his calling was to preach,
And even from the grave, a
message he does teach.
He had the courage to take a stand
against the biased heart:
Always willing and prepared to
carry out his part.
A pillar for the young and old and
for the strong and weak:
The Lord's message of equality for
all he did seek.
Though stoned, stabbed and
cursed upon, he carried on God's
will.
He had a dream he knew someday
our nation would fulfill.
No man should hate another or
deem him an outcast,
For prejudice of any kind should
no more have to last.
And though April fourth of
sixty-eight brought his life to an
end,
If we press on in his name,
someday we all will win.
Then we can say, "Free at last, free
at last,
Thank God Almighty, I'm free at
last."

John Ritter Jr

LIFE 2

When the world is heavy, and I feel
all alone
my hopes and actions, are looking
ahead
if there was such a thing, as a
human clone
then life as we know it, would
surely be dead.
We all need freedom, to be our own
person
expressing our thoughts with that,
special drive.
For our lives, which can not worsen
since if they do, the world, will not
survive.
As human beings, having the best
within reach
by building and raising, our self
esteem
striving to learn, and learning to
teach
this only proves, our hopes are not
just a dream!!!
Pride and compassion, are what
we need
for that is the way, our world can
shed its greed.

Gary A Peterson

A FOREST—ANY FOREST

---

*To every one on the planet especially
my Mom & Joyce*

The edge of a meadow, a forest
awaits.
With such beauty, one hesitates.

To enter a land that is so grand
is even better when your love is in
hand

The trees, the flowers, in
springtime bloom
Fawns a playin, in all nature's room

Indians for ages, once did roam
in a forest that they called home

White men then did appear
and the Indian, would disappear

And in a flash it's so unclear
this could all end. Nuclear

Carol Sroke

TO MY FAMILY

---

*This poem is dedicated to my
beloved parents Helen and John Van
Lenten*

Looking back throughout the
years,
I have so much to see
A special Mom and Daddy
Who God picked out
Just for me
As a child you held me near
I felt your love
but never fear
On my Wedding day
you smiled up at me
It filled my heart
With special love
You've meant so much to me.
Thank you for the years gone by,
Sometimes it's hard to say
I am now looking up
As I watch my Grandchild play.
My life has been worthwhile
Because of your guidance you see.
I just want to say thank you
That God made you my family.

Margaretta Morris

CHRISTMAS POSTSCRIPT

To my son, Jon

When the holiday dream has ended
And you sit in the after glow,
While the candles are dimming
slowly
And the fire embers burning low,

As the carols fade in the distance
And the snow is melting fast,
And the holly withers and ages
Are you wishing the vision will last?

Hold fast to the beauty that's
Christmas
Let it shine through you all the
year,
Be as sparkling and bright as the
tinsel

Make a heart warm to have you
near.

Keep the spirit alive within you
And as the days come and go,
The true meaning of all that is
Christmas
Will brighten the after glow.

Patricia Dattoli-Wentworth

STAR OF LOVE

There's a very shiney star
In the sky above.
I call this star,
The star of love.

When we die,
There we shall meet.
Our love, we shall
Again, repeat.

It's the most beautiful
Place you've ever seen.
Where there is constant sunshine
And the grass is a deep dark green.

Huge meadows and through them
Run babbling brooks.
You can sit all day.
And get high on the looks.

God has your name and mine.
I'll see you there,
It will be divine.

Dorothy D Young

A GRANDMOTHER'S PRAYER

To all grandparents whose worlds are torn apart with the breakup of their childrens marriages.

Daryl has laughing eyes of brown,
Kara's eyes are blue.
Jheri's eyes are hazel,
Their moods reflecting too.

They came into our lives,
And spent just three short years.
Then upon their Mother's whim
They were to disappear.

Their leaving left an empty void,
That nothing can replace.
How I long to see them,
And fold in warm embrace.

Gladys D Morris

TIME HAS TRAMPLED ON MY FACE

To my husband Lyle and children Winifred and William

Time has Trampled on my Face
Age has left its Lines
but O'Lord, Grant me the Grace
to Laugh to the end of my Time.

Scott Allan Winkelhausen

MEADOW AND STREAM

The meadow goes on and on,
with a stream to one side,
The sights and sounds of water
running,
is pleasing to the mind.

The meadow full of gold and
green,
gives off a glowing haze,
The sound of singing birds in
trees
will put you in a daze.

Looking to a sky of blue,
and trees of yellow and red,
The colours that which Autumn
brings
nature has carefully wed.

Autumn colours shine brighter
than the sun,
and are big as they are bold,
God has given eyes to all,
so that people may behold.

Behold the colours that Autumn
brings,
and the beauty to the earth,
And thank our God for giving us
eyes,
to witness Fall's rebirth.

Irene Quintanar

FRIENDS

Friends the bases for being, the
human being
that exist in me.
Friends that have come into my
life have made
me exist in this world.
Friends have made me see things
in many different
ways; through their life
experiences and from that I've
learned in some instances life has
to be experienced
and others by learning from others
mistakes.
Friends aren't always worthy,
but that's what
makes me want to be a better and
stronger person.
Friends are not always there in
times of need,
but you have to consider are you
for them. There
are friends who listen and help
keep a persons mind
sane. There are those who you
listen to and help out,
which gives you a sense of being.
Friends and their times of
laughter, which makes
each day, a day worth living.
Friends also experience bad
times, but you
experience it together which helps
the load become a
little less.
There are times when a person
feels abandonded
by their friends, a friend has to
remember did you
ever take the time to look. There
are times when a
friend just has to let you stand on
your own.
Friends are the bases of needing
each other to
exist in this life day to day.
Friends that have come into my
life have left
a little part of them, which exist in
me.

Alfred J Pirone

FULFILLMENT OF A DREAM

To God—My Father—With Thanks

When I was very young before my
teens
My life was full of lofty dreams
I dreamed that someday I would be
A member of Gods family tree

I lived in a neighborhood, so very
poor
But rich in love and not charity
poor
At Christmas time it was a delight
To hear from charitable places not
far away
Who showered poor children with
gifts and toys
To make sure their holidays was
full of great joy

I was one of those children we are
talking about
Who never forgot those gifts of love
And I made a promise to my dear
Lord
That when the time and my
finances will permit
That I too would glorify God this
way

And so this gift which I am giving
to you
Is something which I had to do
To Fulfill my promise to my God
To thank him for his blessings too
And hope that others may share my
delight

So let us live the way we should
And treat each other as we should
With love and care and tenderness
For who knows when the curtain
will fall
And we are through once and for all

Stephen E Haas

I'D LIKE TO BE A LIGHTHOUSE

For Mom

I'd like to be a lighthouse
All scrubbed and painted white
I'd like to be a lighthouse
And stay awake all night
To keep my eyes on everything
that sails my patch of sea
I'd like to be a lighthouse
With the ships all watching me.

Alexander Leonard Bove SR

Alexander L Bove Sr

I'D RATHER BE AN ATHEIST

To Whom it may concern

I'd Rather Be an Atheist
From natal day to judgement day,
But obey "The Ten
Commandments"
Minus one, "The Sabbath day."

Some are demons from dawn to
dawn,
Then their angels on Sunday morn!
They use His name to hide behind!
They sure must think, the Lord is
blind!

I'd Rather Be An Athiest
From nurtured days on Kingston
Bay,
And believe in "NINE
Commandments"
And obey them every day!
Some read the words He etched
from love,
But never heed the meaning of.
They use His name to hide behind!
How can the good Lord be so kind?

I'd Rather Be An Atheist
From boyhood days on Kingston
Bay,
And sail on "My Ten
Commandments"
Minus one,, "The Sabbath day."

Some read the bible every day,
Then preach the gospel, and
betray!
They use His name to hide behind!
Just like some Christian friends in
mind!

My Christian friends may think me
mad!
But "NINE Commandments aren't
so bad!
"My Christian friends; "You think
it best?"
To abide by one! and not the rest?"

I'd Rather Be An Atheist
From natal day to judgement day,
But obey "The Ten
Commandments"
Minus one, "The Sabbath day."

Some are duped in by the takers,
By the racket money makers,
From the Roberts and the Bakers!
To the phony Christian fakers!
From the Falwells! and the
Swaggarts!
To the phony Christian braggarts!
From the Popoffs! and the
cheaters!
To the phony Christian healers!

I'd Rather Be An Atheist
From natal day to judgement day!
I,ll swear on "The NINE
Commandments"
Up until that reckoning day!

Some do the devil's work each day!
On "The Sabbath," Repent! and
Pray!
They'll burn in hell! if hell there be!
While heaven, sure, may wait for
me!

Dina M Harada

PEN PAL

Scribbling lonely thoughts,
I watched as each tear fell
and smudged and warped the
page.
Soon the words on every line
were smeared by salty rain.
I continued, with misty eyes,
although I could not see;
My pen unsteadily raced along
as dizzy ideas fogged my mind—
The knowledge of what had really
happened

brought haunting dreams of how things
should have gone.
The sting became all too strong and suddenly,
Those drops of warm and salty rain turned into sweeter, darker stains.

Ronald E D'Agata
WHY WORLD WHY

This Poem, (Song) was written to make us stop and think about the world we live in, and to appreciate it.

What makes the World we live in go round?
What keeps the stars from tumble'n down?
Why do we live in worry or fear,
Every day of every year?

Why Why World, Oh Why World Why?
Why Why World, Oh Why World Why?

Why must there be thieves and thugs?
Why must we have problems with drugs?
Why must there be tension and stress?
Why can't we live in complete happiness?

Why Why World, Oh Why World Why?
Why Why World, Oh Why World Why?

Why do we play with love and romance?
Thinking we'll have another chance.
Why were we put here? We do not know.
We only know that someday we'll go!

Why Why World, Oh Why World Why?
Why Why World, Oh Why World Why?

G D Stewart
FORBIDDEN LOVE
It was beautiful, blossoming, growing;
It came forth upon the desert wind a'blowing.
The rains came, moistened it, nourished it, caressed it
And it grew and burst forth; this newborn thing.
It thrust its face toward Heaven; God blessed it.
The winds gently swayed it, the morning dew bathed it;
The world was before it, this newborn thing.
BUT THEN! The rains no longer came;
The wind blew angry and dry.
It dropped its head; wilted, sick and lame:
But thought it once more to try;
Yet alas! Not so! 'Twas doomed to die!
This love of yours and mine!

Vivian A Rottmayer
WHAT CHILD IS THIS?
We see him there,
The product of marriage gone amiss.
His real parents married to somebody new.
Now Jane lives with Harry,
And Charlie with Sue.

He's often lonely, and he's often blue.
He's got lots of parents but none really care,
Where he stays each day or what bed they share.
They make plenty of money and have great fun,
But the little boy is a family of ONE.

Dale Reed
OUR LOVE

To my wife Delphia

Love is a pretty fragrant rose,
A flowing poetry, a stirring prose,
A bursting forth of April flowers,
A lovely album of enchanted hours.

Love is a bond so sweet and strong
Entwining hearts closer all life long.
Love is the depth of a tranquil sea
You, my love, are God's gift to me.
Love is a feeling of rapturous bliss.
Love is the message of a passionate kiss.
Love is beauty that's forever new,
Love is what I feel for you!

Love is two hearts that beat as one
From morning light to setting sun.
Love is the coveted precious goal
Of each solitary searching soul.
Love is the union of body and soul.
When lips meet lips and arms enfold.
Love is a trust our hearts enshrine
And each loving day is Valentine!

Lou Gavin
HAVE YOU EVER FELT?
Have you ever felt like crawling in a hole,
a hole so deep, dark, and empty?
Have you ever felt like crying all night,
with noone around to hold you so gently?
Have you ever felt so terribly astray,
for not loving the one who loved you plenty?
Have you ever felt like just taking off,
just keep on going till you find ecstacy?
Have you ever just sat and thought about life,
of how it is such a confusing diversity?
Have you felt trapped in your own world,
so confused, so lost, and so lonely?
Have you ever felt such pain as love, full of hurt and no affinity?
Have you ever felt you were being used . . .
. . . I have.

Laura J Wood O'Shea
QUESTION OF LOVE—(TO BECOME ONE)
The feelings in my heart
are so very hard to express
Thinking, someday we may part
but do I love you any less?

For, the answer my love,
to that question be;
I'll love you forever—
for all eternity.

Whether we're together or we are apart
The love I have for you, is off to a running start
Not knowing where it might end
but if ever it shall—
can we become friends?

There's no doubt in my mind
our love will never be so unkind
To forbid us freedoms two shall have
for forever to become one.

Howard J Fretz
PEOPLE OF THE LAND

To Cape Crocker Indian Reserve on the Bruce Peninsula, Ontario

They come from far and near
to the great Longhouse in Ottawa,
came the many Native people,
came with trusting expectations
and also trepidation.
As often they had been here
and more often dissolutioned
by the way the white man treated
his blood brother, the great Red-Man.

To the Great Longhouse again
came the trusting Native people
minus tomahawk and dagger
in peaceful celebration
of union so important;
that binds in peace together
the vast Native population
with the White-Man his blood brother.

All adore and ever worship the Great Spirit our
Heavenly Father
by Whose love and power within us
guides us, safely to the future
in this land of peace and plenty
where all people dwell as equals with the blessing of
Great Spirit. Acts 17-26

Vicki Ecret
THE CARNIVAL
Diamond lights swirling 'round
Overhead a clown looks down,
Songs of laughter fade away
As the sun comes up —
night turns to day.
The carnival leaves nothing to be found
Just a crumbling lot in the midst of town.
Smiles are gone, replaced by tears
But no one sees, no one hears.
Does anyone care; will they take the time
to turn back the pages tucked within the mind?
Years pass away, memories lost
Gray replaces the gold, feelings tossed
Around and around and around again,
Days add on—missing a friend.
Aging won't mend the hurts of the past
The carnival has gone, dreams don't last.

Joan P Davidson
THE FLOWER
The leaf was turned up to the sky,
As if looking for an unseen God.
Forever searching for its creator and savior,
Its color was green and alive.

The stalk was tall and slender.
Strong and sure;
It too seemed alive.
Together they wavered in the spring breeze;
Dancing in the warm sunlight.

The flower sat upon the stalk,
Head high and proud.
It was creamy white with a yellow center.
It too looked up to the sky.

This is the single lily,
That stands at the head of my mothers grave.

Douglas Cowan
MY DREAM GIRL

This poem is dedicated to Rebecca Asuncion who is very special to me and who I love alot. Rebecca, you are the best, to know and to be loved by. I love you.

I think of you when I am alone
My mind wonders about you
You may be so far, yet so near
Here in my heart
That is only meant for you
Distance may keep us apart
You are there and I am here
But no distance is so far
For whom me love to see
Letters have kept us together
And you'll always be remembered
This will be kept and treasured forever
For it meant the love of you
When time allows and love prevails
It might be the happiest time
A guy could wish
To love and to be loved . . . . .

Emily Susan Fowler-Tweddle
SILENCE
The hush of quiet in still slumber—
No utter or sound is heard;
The calm is not disturbed by constant rumble.
Beauty in the silence here; within no spoken word.
Blessed is the beauty of this silence show;
A gift in the realm of awing spirit.
To renew a freshness: In the heart aglow—
Love is reflected in all near us.

Loren Kimberly Johnston
ON THE BEACH
As I walk along
the beach on an
August afternoon,
the sun beats down
on my face.
I look at the
different shaped
shells. On the
lake, boats are
drifting slowly.
There is just a
slight breeze.
I step into the
lake and the water
comes up to
my knees.
I go in soon
because it is
getting late.
I watch the sun
go down. The sky
is red, orange,
and pink.
It is beautiful.

Patricia Mary Thurston
THE UNKNOWN HERO

To Mom, the best mother in the world. And a special thanks to all the veterans alive and dead.

Who is this man who gave his life for me the one who ensured my freedom. The one
who does not know me yet risked his life for mine. I don't know how to thank him because I don't know who he is. This prayer goes to the unknown hero who died so I might live.

Jane McClinchey
SYMBOL OF A TREE

To Ray, for sharing the beauty of country living. To Ryan, Steven, and Colleen, as a guide for appreciation and maturity. To 'Women Today' for teaching many, to control their well-being

The symbol of a tree, alone does stand . . .
No matter—elm, beech, oak or maple at hand.
Graceful, gallant, vibrant or gaunt be they;
We find them at river's edge, or along brook's way.

Mother Nature comes and passes; battling at length,
And yet through this hardship, the tree gets its strength.
Cycling winter's tempests within a century albeit shown,
Entwined with spring's miracle, and summers; it's known.

A hundred years hence, a small seed had then found . . .
Sanctuary among good humus; its tiny root settled inground.
Magnetically—sprouted green shoot, toward stars;
Grown taller, and in power; amid decades of wars.

Resting cattle graze in their shade, on ranches,
Birds have perched and made homes throughout their branches.
Searching for food, the tree roots became great . . .
Strength enhanced trunk and branches; from whence the root ate.

To guide, man's best inspiration should be . . .
Found lifting eyes, upon the security of a tree.
Admire—qualities of tree, standing single . . .
Yet conquered life's storms; like rain upon shingle.

Not broke by hazards, 'tis found fit to bow . . .
It's feet in ground, and raising head to sky now.
So, symbol of a tree, alone does stand . . .
No matter—elm, beech, oak or maple at hand.

Kenneth R Jinsky Jr
SILENT MOTION

Dedicated to my beloved grandparents; Mike and Sarah Jinsky; Whose farmstead I spent many pleasant days as a child, and where this stream flows.

Where has the rushing, rambling sound gone to rest?
No more the movement of white water on a crest.

A blanket of calm lies over one time current.
Below the surface a force prevails without deterrent.

Rocks and ridges always in its company.
They seem unfriendly; as does the dormant tree.

Trees are barren; grasses weep.
All its shoreline neighbors are asleep.

Where life once abound,
Now; virtually none will be found.

Gone is the migratory bird.
A jay's shrill cry may still be heard.

Border the meandering slopes with a coat of white;
Sparkling and glittering in the moonlight.

Where banks protruded; now are drifts.
The wind carves a sculpture with nature's gifts.

Turbulence: Its character; unrevealing this time of year.
Time evolves; life returns; serenity reappear.

Michael Duane Mullis
MY WIFE

The lady I love, She's one of a kind
She makes me laugh, she blows my mind
She holds my hand, if my heart gets broken
She can mend my soul, with never a word spoken
She makes me mad, enough so to kill,
But when she needs me, words can't explain the thrill.
Without her, I'm nothing, mere dust in the wind
With her, I'm strong, no force can bend
A lover, a teacher, a lady, a friend.
Together forever, till death do us part,
And Lord if you will, in the new life, we'll start
I'll love you darling, for all of our life,
My friend, my woman, my lover, My wife.

Jerry D C/Gerald F Hennen
THE POET

This poem is dedicated to all poets—past, present, and future

The poet is regarded with some skepticism
And thought to be a little foolish

Has it occurred to anyone

He might suffer from divine madness
Or periodic inspiration of the gods

The poet is a craftsman
Who makes strong sayings

He has his role in the social structure
Celebrating battles and histories
Telling of heroes and cities

He is expected to tell of living
And of love and joy
Not merely of arms and glory

It is the poet's function
To remind mankind from time to time
Of loneliness and death

Lest we forget this simple fact
We are mere mortals

Marie E Pickrell
A COUNTRY CHRISTMAS

Christmas-time is here,
It's time for joy and cheer.
To a country-boy, Christmas is joy,
But a city-boy wants an expensive toy.
A country-girl learns to bake a pie,
Though a city-girl wants a doll that will cry.
A country-dad will cut his tree,
One that is bigger than you or me.
We decorate with popcorn and candles,
And hang our stockings from our mantles.
In the city, your trees are in the store,
With lights and balls and so much more.
Give me a Country Christmas,
One like our grandparents had.
Give our young a Country Christmas,
So they'll know the joy of the Christmas we had.

Anne-Mary Graveline
SUMMER'S RITUAL

To G. Harper, who makes any ritual, (spring, summer, winter or fall,) that much better.

A sensuously golden day,
For pealing back the outer skins.

The thermometer reaches the ideal temperature.
It is just right for baking.

The tender meat begins to cook,
As the juices run off to the side.

The thermostat rises higher,
Causing the meat to saute'.

Rotation is required
For an all around baste.

The heat continues to climb,
While the meat starts to broil.

What was once tender and juicy,
Is now burnt to a crisp.

Norman Denim
DARE YOU

To my ladies three, Helga, Terra and Tammi

If you read a madman's quiver,
Your mental stability, might shiver,
For his thoughts, are not yours,
And he lives behind doors,
That are labeled, as such,
To displease, so much.

Dare you question, his sanity,
For the sake, of your vanity.
Challenge his thoughts, if you dare,
For you are here, and he is there.
Do you long, to know his game,
Are you what, is labeled sane?

Lea Roberts
HAPPINESS IS SUCH A FLEETING THING

Happiness is such a fleeting thing.
It comes.
It goes.
Like the indolent beat
of a small birds wing,
Reaching out to grasp and bring—
You missed the song
the small bird did sing.
Happiness is such a fleeting thing.

Donna Jacobs
MOM

You are the pot of gold at the rainbow's end
A murmur of a bubbling brook
The tranquility of a dew kissed morn
An unpredictable flicker in a flame.
You give me the resistance of a raging ocean
Courage of the king of flight
Determination of a turbulent twister
Simplicity of a summer shower
Exuberance of a volcanic eruption
Beauty of a bud in bloom.
You will touch me like delicate pussy willows
Caressing a gale in spring,
Nurturing me through wicked winters
Despite that all my leaves have shed
Reassure me like the doe awards her young
Giving confidence to grow on.
Now I've grown beyond tender years.
You are still there to weed out existing traumas.
You are all the expressions that nature brings.

Iris May Gilbert
HE HUDDLED AGAINST THE TREE

He huddled against the tree,
Its mighty size dwarfing him.
His tiny fists tightly clenched
Were stuffed deeply in his pockets.
His stomach tensed
Then released in spasms.
Eyes fiercely shut
He craved control
But heard only the explosion in his ears
As shattered lives screamed
In piercing voices.
The dark walls shrank
In their rejection

Of flying objects.
The reverberations clashed
Loudly through his psyche.
His stomach churned
As his body quietly shook.
He huddled against the cradling trunk
Of the weeping willow,
His fists still clenched,
His eyes tightly shut.

Dina Marie Shisler
DARLING

This Poem is dedicated to Ken, my Loving Husband

I am proud to be your wife.
Loving you darling is my life.
Over and over you show me you care.
Very happy am I with the life that we share.
Each day I look forward to your warm embrace.
You've made me feel, that beside you is my place.
Only you can make me feel as I do.
Undoubtedly Darling, I will always love you!

Susan M Smith
PRISONER OF LOVE
Prisoner of love, soft whispers in the night,
So she goes again, he waits as the sun falls.
She walks beneath the moon, her lovers voice calls.
Her body is so pure, her fantasies are so free.
Her mind is so wild, she is so excited,
In her lovers arms she will soon be.
So they meet again, It seems like it's been so long.
She holds him tight, "God her love is so strong."
He touches her with such burning desire.
Calling to her love, "The night is on fire."
"She loves him," Oh she loves him more than words can say.
But the man, he only takes her love away.
She will never lie, yet her love must stay deep inside.
He loves his family, the ladie has so much pride.
The ladie is a prisoner of love, taken so long ago.
Time is passing, still he will never know.
The night is over, the sun must rise above.
"Still", the ladie is a prisoner of love.
Until the moon falls and the time is right.
She must go on with only memories of their last night.
Blue water can rush from her precious eyes with no one to know.
The ladie will hide, for she will never let her love go.
He is so impassive, she wonders how she is captive.
She has no love left inside to give.
All of her love, "Oh", it's so much you see.
She hides it all with such invisibility.
He calls her name, His voice, can it be from up above?
But she, the ladie, will always be a prisoner of love.
Prisoner of love
Prisoner of love
Of love.

Clara M Hanson
OUR FRONT YARD—JANUARY 1987
Our front yard with snow so clean and white
Is a delightful unblemished winter sight.
The unmarred beauty is an inspiring scene.
So lovely, so quiet, and so serene.
At the edge, tall spruce and Norway pine
Look like guardian sentinels in a line
With their bushy branches so wide and high
Reaching up to God above in the deep blue sky.

Beverly A Bell
THIS GIFT OF LOVE

"This poem is dedicated to, universal peace." We are all God's children, and he loves us very much. When we learn to believe in him, we are truly touched.

The love I have for you.
was much deeper than I thought.
This love is pure and simple.
the kind that can't be brought.

We have alot to salvage.
but salvage we must do.
If we are to build again.
this love of ours anew.

The passion I've felt with you.
my love.
I've never felt before.
I've tried so many times.
my love.
I've tried to shut the door.

We've hurt each other very much.
but we can get over this.
To love again.
and have your love.
is my most treasured wish.

Diane Parkman
NEW ENGLAND

Dedicated to Mike Parkman and Esther and Arthur Moulton

Hushed, New-winter
Sight
Snow, Light-frosty
and white

John R Morris
THE LITTLE FRAME SCHOOL

Dedicated with love to my family; my wife Lee Nora, son John R., Jr., daughter Janet Lee. For their confidence and faith in me.

It stands all alone upon the hill
Fond memories cling around it still
Wild flowers are blooming around the door
Vines are creeping up thru the floor

As I stop to see it today
The scenes of my childhood around me play
Here on the desk, the last in the row,
The names are still there, Jack, Bill and Joe.

And as I gaze on this old place
I can picture every face,
And wonder where each one may be
Since we were kids and played hooky.

Does anyone wander back here like I,
And gaze on this place with a tear in his eye?
I think that they do, for we can't forget
The scenes of our childhood, we love them yet.

So to that old fashioned school
Where we first learned the golden rule;
Tho, now it is tumbled down and forlorn,
T'was there that our memories were born.

We'll forget thee I promise never;
For you gave us memories we'll treasure forever.
Memories of laughter; memories of tears,
Clinging, still clinging on thru the years.

Barbara C Pendleton
CHALLENGER—"ODYSSEY TO A SPACEMAN"
92 seconds into Life, then death
Such courage, such love of life
And down below, a grieving wife
Not done for kicks, she knew the risks
God looks down, five men, two women are now with him
They made it to the tallest limb
Our weather seems a bit bizarre
Oh what the hell, I flew a star
Tornadoes, gales, fires burn, snow rain
The seasons turn
I saw a rose bloom in November
Is that strange, I can't remember
Such loss of life for these men
I saw it all in my den
Please God teach us humility
One small speck surrounded by beauty
The speck is gone, but we live on
They are gone, a nation grieves
I felt such sorrow
Please God believe we lost this day
But we will learn and kneel to pray.

Jean Pettry
WINTER
Snow is falling, covering the earth with a blanket of white:
Icicles hang from the roof, casting shadows by the pale moonlight..
The wind so cold the trees shiver, the brook has a muffled sound;
Little jack rabbits scurry to their warm home under the ground.
Violets are nestled under a bed of snow, frogs buried deep in the mud below.
The old fat bear asleep in his den, resting and waiting for winter to end.

Davare'
THE LORD REBUKE THEE

This is in dedication to my two sons, Richie and Jake with the wish that satan never can do to them what he's done to me.

Fortify me, Jesus, for I am doing fine
We, together, can handle this
with YOU, ALMIGHTY GOD.
Almight God, You are protecting and
shielding me
Letting me experience
the devils and demons of this,
our universe, which YOU, ALL POWERFUL CHRIST created!
POUR IT ON BELOVED CHRIST
DRIVE THESE BEASTS AWAY AND OUT
OF HOUSE AND HOME
SAVE THE CHILDREN, JESUS, AS THEIR
MOTHERS' FAITH IS SHOWN
USE ME AS YOUR CLOUT, LORD
I'm ready, Lord, I'm waiting
Indeed I am amused
Satan is so weak, my God
I BELIEVE IN YOU!!
Your loving disciple.

Eleanor E Weiner
ODE TO THE NIGHT
As night descends and I am in my tower,
I gaze at the sky, hour upon hour,
Watching the moon smiling down at earth,
Thousands of stars "twinkling" in their berth.
Below the earth seems so still,
Heaven looks down, all is tranquil.
As the dawn slowly makes its way,
Getting us ready for another day,
The stars above begin to disappear;
The moon waits till it is clear,
Then also leaves without a sound;,
Still smiling, it cheeks so round.
Slowly I leave my cherished place,
To once again join the human race.
But the day shall only be for me,
Passing time till I once again see,
The night envelop all that abounds,
As "Father Time" continues his rounds!

Miss Melanie Rywak
MY BEST FRIEND

To My Grandmother (Mrs. Josie Burak). She is my best friend and I wish to dedicate this poem to her.

My best friend is a special one,
And when I am with her, we have lots of fun.

She is pretty, smart, and tall,
I am the same, except I'm small.
I have glasses and so does she,
I like her, and she likes me.
We spend time together alone,
And when we aren't, we're on the phone.
We like to walk, talk and play,
Together that adds up to about one day.
And when I go home to sleep I say,
A very special prayer, to her each day.
She is my (BABA) Gramma.

Rachelle Helen Porter
DEFEAT AND FREEDOM

To all who appreciate words of truth and reality.

Live a good life now,
Make the best of it,
For time will pass you by quickly,
Then it will be too late.

Take advantage of this precious freedom,
No matter how infinite it may be.

Love it and take care of it,
As you would a child,
For it may someday be gone too.

Edna Cassady
GIVE ME THE SPRINGTIME
Give me the Springtime
With all of its' frills
Let me roam o'er the meadows
And climb the steep hills.

Bask in the sunshine
So warm and so sweet
Gather the flowers
That bloom at my feet.

Hear the birds singing
Their welcoming song
As they flit through the treetops
That lay bare for so long.

Let me look at the heavens
So pure and so bright
And thank my dear Savior
Who makes all things right.

Janet Ann Nyovich
POSITIVELY ME (ON SELF IMAGE)

To Lori, Jacki, and Karen Boland's "Positiveness."

Look in the mirror
and what do you see?
Who is that person
looking back at me?

Do you love the whole you inside and out,
from your crooked old toe to your oversized mouth?
Cause whatever you think is ugly or bad
someone else wishes that's what they had.

Change what you want, and love what can't change.
There's really not much to rearrange.
Work with great attitude each day.
Wake up! With gratitude 100 times say:
"Today I will be the best I can be.
I'm beautiful, unique, there's only one me!"

Cynthia Pope
CALM YOUR WATERS

For my Dad, Fred Shattuck I love you and my husband and daughters. And a special thank you to the Poetry Board for voting me the Golden Poet Award for 1987.

As I see you roaring by, the look of anger is there but why,
You spit and foam on each stone that you pass by,
As if you call, you become me, daring me to come inside,
To swallow me up if I let, you want to hurt me but why,
You hold so much beautie, even in the anger that you cry,
How can something hold so much beauty, yet hold so much anger deep inside,
Calm your waters, be at peace where you lie,
You are as you are, that can't be changed, but the anger you can decide,
Show your beautie without the roar, or the threat of what's in store.

Pearl E Baptiste
A LIGHT IN THE WINDOW
A light in window beckoning me
Promising joys and fantasies
Come closer, come closer
It seemed to say, drawing me into its colorful rays

As I moved closer, the colors so true
Danced all around me
Chilling yet exciting
Urging me to taste its warm delight

Come closer, come closer
Don't be afraid
As I pressed my face to the window pane

The light became blinding
And I closed my eyes
Locked in a spell, I was hypnotized

No way out, no way to get free
Suddenly the light was part of me

Bryan M McFadden
TIME

I like to dedicate this to Robin S. and Jesus Christ my Lord and Saviour, and my Mother and Father.

Time can change the places and the people that we've seen
But then time can hold the Beauty
of some of that we only dreamed,
Time is our keeper
For each year that passed
No one year can last forever
only time can forever last,
If time was measured as a sculpture
that stood in front of me
Then its beauty would last always
through all eternity

Marletta J Pearson
SWEETHEART, I LOVE YOU

This poem is dedicated to Keith, my wonderful Husband.

Sweetheart, I love you
let me count the ways.
I love the way you comfort me
and all my fears just fade away.
I love the things you say to me
on a dark and gloomy day.
I love the way you make me laugh
and even make me cry.
One thing I'd like to change is that we'd never say goodbye.

Sharon Brooks Shofner
BELOVED ONE

In memory of my daughter, Amy

She was the joy of my life;
My little angel on earth.
Her short stay was such a strife,
But it did hold much worth.
Cancer invaded her body at two,
And this I could not understand.
In my heart hoping this wasn't true,
How could this take the upper-hand!
She fought this battle for four years.
I made her life as happy as could be
Through all the pain, laughter and tears.
She was a blessing to ev'ryone and me.
What strength and courage she did teach
To all who loved her so.
She left her valor for us to reach,
She was a "shining star" to know.
Her name meant "beloved one",
And how fitting that was for her,
Her special life on earth is done,
For me to be mournful, for her to be better.
She was the joy of my life!
My little angel is in heaven now.
Her short stay was such a strife,
But oh, what worth she did endow.

Virginia L MacInnes

Virginia L MacInnes
TERRACE BY THE SEA

I dedicate this poem to my great husband, David, to my wonderful children, Diane, Janet, Bruce and Susanna and to my dearest grandchildren, Holly, Heather, Katy, Allison, Jennifer, Tara and Barbara Ann.

I might be home for Christmas
But please don't count on me
I'll send a check to cover the cost
of presents beneath the tree.

You know where to find me
I'll welcome you with glee
But I may not see you for Christmas
Unless you come to me.

Christmas Eve may find me
Under a big palm tree
With a tropic moon
I'd like to croon
In my condo by the sea

It's been very nice to know you
With that I'll let you be.
Snow and ice and winds that slice
Do not appeal to me.

I've found my lost horizon
And this is where I'll be
So come on down for Christmas
By the Vero Beach blue sea.

Flora Hefner
TRIBUTE TO MOTHERS

This poem was written on Mother's Day as a tribute to my mother after she passed away.

A Mother is God's gift
So bright and very strong,
That God gave to every one of us
To teach us right from wrong.

A mother is the gentle touch
The word, the smiling face,
And all the things that make a home
A cheerful happy place.

Tell her that you love her
In the old time tender way,
Show her you haven't forgotten
This is her own special day.

You can only have one Mother
Patient, kind, and true,
No other friend in all the world
Will be so true to you.

For all her loving kindness
She asked nothing in return,
If all the world had deserted me
To my Mother I could have turned.

To those who still have a Mother
Treasure her with love and care,
For you will never know her value
'Till you see her vacant chair.

Teresa B Walker
FINDING

This poem is dedicated to J.C. Breshers my loving father—having a family is a tuff job. Thanks for showing me the right way!

Sometimes it's hard to find peace of mind—or hope.
Sometimes it's hard to find sunshine in the rain.
At times like these—I look to my family.
Then I remember the extra little sleep, I got while they got the newspaper. Or the extra special hug—I got for just being there.
I remember that everytime it rains—there's always a rainbow afterwards.
And then—I find peace of mind—and more hope
than I could dream of—and I smile for rainbows are a special gift to me.

Max Hottle
THE SEA OF LIFE
And we sailed out from the harbor
Into the turbulent sea of life,
Hope, ambition running high

No thought of trouble or strife.

When the first storms of life hit us,
All things seemed black beyond.
But there was no returning,
One great command sail on.

Now we have rode out storms of trial
Through black nights of trouble sailed
Fog of grief and sorrow thick around us
All light of hope was vailed.

We have seen blue skies and sunshine
On a calm and peaceful sea
And the gentle breeze that drove
Seems to bring prosperity.

As we sailed on through the sunshine
Peace, love and joy all around,
Friendship of those close to us
Seemed like heaven pouring down.

As we pushed ever forward
Through the storm, the calm and gale
All of us have been successful,
All of us at times did fail.

But when we reach that peaceful harbor
At the setting of lifes sun,
When we drop our final anchor
Will the Master say, "Well done?"

Helene Claire Shubert

THE MILLION DOLLAR QUESTION

TO: A NEW GENERATION

I am sure about ME, what I want to do. But,
I have a QUESTION:
"HOW ABOUT YOU?"
I do not need DRUGS to make ME feel "high"
I am too young, I do not want to DIE.
I have MY whole Life ahead of ME
So I am going to stay DRUG-FREE

Why should I spend MY Good MONEY
to act like a "JERK" it is just not Funny.
Why be "STUPID" better to be "SMART"
STAND UP and be COUNTED
Don't Fall Apart
Earn ADMIRATION . . . . KISSES and HUGS
LEARN to Say "NO" to DRUGS.

Christine A Foust

YOU'LL ALWAYS BE THERE

To my wonderful parents, who have always encouaraged me to do my very best in whatever I have attempted to do; and who will "always be there" no matter if no one else is: I love you, Mom and Dad. This one's for you.

Oh, I try to forget—
Yes, I say, "I'll go on."
The past is behind me—
The time is all gone.
It's time for the present—the future will come. . .
Yesterday's gone . . . Oh, yesterday's gone . . .

But, the memory still lingers—
You'll always be there.
I try to forget you but you're everywhere.
I look on ahead
Yet, my mind wanders back—
You'll always be there.

Will love ever be mine?
I see it coming to me.
The present is now here—
The future will be.
Love's getting closer—Is it really a chance—
To love again? . . . Oh, yesterday's gone . . .

But, the memory still lingers—
You'll always be there.
I try to forget you but you're everywhere.
I look on ahead
Yet, my mind wanders back—
You'll always be there.

Reading Deutsh

LAST SEPTEMBER

When you came down the path,
That blue sky and warm sun
That shone so golden on your head.
Just to know you was miracle enough
I thought—and never wept when you left.

October gone, and bleak November rains
Come again and again—you are gone.
How is it that you never forward are,
But somewhere dimly past, that greyed and guantleted span
That borders on nothingness and mists?

What time we were all over now
And empty yawning caverns of momentous peaks.
Why is it you never speak of
Crones and drones and terrifying shrieks
Come to haunt a vast so deep my heart trembles.

When was it you asked in need
I answered in careless precision of a 4-wheel drive.
How is it now that glory is not so perceived
As that bright star, but somewhat tarnished tin?
Do you ever ask what might have been?

Doris J Johnson

THE SAME OLD MOON

The same old moon is shining
As it did the night we met.
Now you have gone away and
My heart won't forget.
The nights are long and lonely
My days are all the same.
Just thinking of the things I did
Before you came.
My life was so empty untill you
Came and taught me how to laugh,
And love.
Now you are gone again.
That old moon still shines above
And if my hopes are vain, I'm still
Hoping that some moonlight night,
That you will come again.

Diane E Moore

SEASON SIGNS

PB&J has yielded its way
to a lunch of soup and crackers,
And book bags are hung
Where wet suits were strung,
And the whirr of the fan
is silent.
Clocks tick away odd hours of day
bereft of the chime "I'm thirsty,"
And sneakers by the door
are replaced by bare floor,
And I may even use
the oven.
My toddler now asks if "I" want to play
and I can't very well refuse her
for the kids have all gone
and she can't go along
and even the laundry
can wait.
So I guess I'll confess
With a pang in my breast
that the long days of summer
have ended.

Barbara Wentzel

LIFES FULLNESS

I'd want to walk today
Along the ocean shore—
Just to breath the fragrance
Of the lingering salt air;
I like to watch a bevy
Of sea gulls winging by;
To watch the sunset in the western sky,
I love to feel the coolness
Of the gentle ocean breeze;
In this way I find solace
From living lifes grief and pain—
I'd want to walk today
Along the ocean shore—

Jane Small

THE PEOPLE OF THE SEA

Dedicated to Grace M. Small, without whose help my perseverance at writing would not have been possible.

Lately I've been dreaming
Of the People of the Sea
With their brains larger,
More complex then our own.
Long ago they chose to be
The People of the Sea;
Knowing they would never gain
A thumb if they remained
In water bound,
They chose the Way of Peace —
A voluntary sacrifice
Of dominion in the earth.
Ten thousand years
They're called to us
Speaking with their ways:
Their songs, their joy,
Their care for one another
We've just begun to listen.
Lately I've been dreaming
Of the People of the Sea;
Miles away, on land,
I hear them calling me
To Christ, to truth, to love
To . . . a questing heart . . .
And Peace.

Hildred Boucher

DREAMER

To the one I love. My husband Richard Boucher

I wish I were a poet
I sure would love to be
Then I could put down on paper
All these thoughts inside of me
But I am just a dreamer
And a dreamer I'll always be,
But you have to be a dreamer,
If you want to writer poetry
So when I write my masterpiece,
Then famous I will be,
They'll put my name up there in lights,
For all the world to see
While I'm accepting my awards,
And feeling ten feet tall.
I'll know I'm not just a dreamer,
But a poet after all.

Carmen Richardson

CHRISTOPHER AND ME

Dedicated to Alice's memory and in gratitude of HER Last Gift to us. She gave us Christopher.

I dreamed of two rocking chairs sitting on a porch;
Retirement years together spent doing things we wanted most.
We'd travel o're our country great, so many things to see,
I soon found out as time passed by, this wasn't meant for me.
The Lord had taken this away and replaced it with His plan
I now take care of a two year old as only grandma's can,
I diaper, feed, and bathe at will, and sprawled across the floor;
As we play horsie, "MA-MA, come on, lets do it more".
We potty train and bottle break, as schedules come with play,
He doesn't have a Mommie, as cancer took her life away.
I sometimes feel at sixty-three, I'll blow all ore the place,
My patience thinned with passing time I didn't grow old with grace.
And yet I bulge with pride in him, so loving in his way;
I love to watch the daily change of our little boy at play.
His little arms reach up in trust as he pleads "Takie Me",
We sit and watch cartoons and game shows on TV.
I hope his Mommie sees and knows we're happy as can be,
This little boy she left behind, our little boy and me.
So what if there are no rocking chairs no sitting down to be,
This little boy with curly locks has brought new life you see,
Even arthritic pains hurt less and eyes don't seem so dim,
As I live in the brightness of his smile, I just thank God for him.
What if there is no travel,—no far off lands to see,
We'll walk a while together—
CHRISTOPHER AND ME.

P K Hunt

SAND

Sunshine, rain, gale, and calm
Is natures gift of tropical feast
That is strained upon me
beneath the palm.
While I exist as neither best nor least
Of all that is pure and almost true
My existence is not my own,
But taken from another that was battered and hewn.
Sunshine, rain, gale, and calm
As waves devour me and take me to sea

I do not complain but go with
ease,
While being consumed day by
day.
Sunshine, rain, gale, and calm
I may not always be here, but
I'll never go away.

Daniel J Gale

Daniel J Gale
LIFE

What is life?
Life is a purpose, a reason,
happiness, sadness, often
pleasing.
"Life is a smile on a child's face"
"Life is unison between the
different race"
"Life is believing and trusting"
"Life sometimes can be
discussing"
(But out of all those reasons)
"Life is Pleasing"

Ronald R (Whoopstick) Fordham
MEMORIES OF AN OLD BLUE MOUNTAIN

That old blue mountain that lies
above the little ole
Two story log home that stands out
in the lonesome field
Is full of wonders and it is full of
beauty.
Those streams begin to flow
beneath that old blue mountain.
Those streams begin to flow freely
down the slopes that lie
Beneath those hills of many
wonders.
The beauty lies back watching over
the streams that are full
Of sparkles while flowing over the
rocks that are in the streams.

That old blue mountain brings
back a lot of memories staring
Down at the little ole two story log
home that lies in that
Lonesome field that stands quietly
alone and has all the beauty
To face.
That old blue mountain is peaceful
with the love of the nature
That shares its beauty with that old
blue mountain that stands
Very still looking over the valleys
that stare at that old blue
Mountain of many wonders,
beauty of peace, and love to
share those
Memories with you beneath those
blue skies that lie above that
Old blue mountain that is full of
peace, love and beauty.

Sandra L Pate
PARENTS' PLEA

To my son Timothy with Love and Concern, Mom.

As I sit I wonder,
where did I go wrong?
Or is it only me, that questions on
and on?

I question greatly
the world I live,
and how we let things slide.

Our children come
and go by us
and still we let things ride.

Attention now,
to things at hand
for here we are with heart in hand.

I beg of you
don't hurt me so
or I will have to let you go.

To a World
so unknown,
yet, I know you'll be alone.

Alone to stand
and freedom gone.
Oh where, oh where, did we go
wrong?

I wonder now,
how long it is,
before you are set free.

To live and love
in this world of ours
where people are to be.

I can't explain
the reasons now,
for doing what I've done.

I only hope
the next time,
that wiser will I be.

And have the answers
to these questions
and save this Agony.

Markham Brian Stevens
OUR LOVE

Some loves are as pleasant as fallen
snow,
Others young and new with room
to grow.
Some are a secret and softly
spoken,
Others are fragile and easily
broken.
Our love is a diamond—broken
never
And always remember, diamonds
are forever.

Nelda Albright Smithe
OF BEES AND HONEY

There was a lady of bliss
Who made her living like this:
She robbed the bees of their honey
Passersby took a jar and left the
money;
Then in a course of a week
Honey was paid for by only the
meek;
In a business of this particular sort
I'm stung twice was her only retort.

Gloria Moraga
CATHY, MY OWN SPECIAL ANGEL

In loving memory of our own "special angel," Catherine Denise Moraga, May 28, 1965—October 10, 1980, Love—Mom and Dad

---

The last few weeks you were here
on earth
Were possibly spent, deciding your
worth
Why were you born? Why your
creation?
Hours were spent in reconciliation

What were your thoughts? What
were your fears?
My darling Angel, I wish I could
hear!
Did I love you enough? Did I make
you happy?
Was I a good enough mother? Was
I all I could be?

I saw you so brave and strong in
your faith
Knowing how you suffered,
knowing your pain
I wanted to ask you what your
thoughts might be
What it would take to make you
free

Free from the strain and the duress
But I was a coward, I guess
I knew deep down in my heart
You were leaving me . . . we'd be
apart

Now you will dance and now you
will sing
On earth these were talents you
were about to begin
Most of your life was spent on
sports
Now you'll be doing things of all
sorts

Now you are gone and oh how I
miss you
I wish I had taken more time to
kiss you
You now have answers to the
questions above
My own special Angel Cathy,
whom I so love
Love,
MOM

Michael A Margolis
LITTLE PRISONERS

To my wonderful daughter Crystal

You walk alone
Through the yard in the daytime
Here you will stay
Till your childhood is over
Well, you want to go out and play
But there's too much danger there
People stealing children
Oh what could they be thinking of
When I see you looking through
the fence
It makes me want to cry
But I know if I let you out here
Chances are you'll disappear

I can recall
All the dreams that I had
Letting you play
With other children all alone
But times have changed
And it's not that safe anymore
Little prisoners of loving parents
Have no safe environment
When I see that you want to play
I sit back and I cry
I'd like to let you out of here
But chances are you'll disappear

Gwen P Freeman
WINGS OF MORNING

When I wake on the wings of
morning
I know God is always there,
I can feel His loving presence
Surrounding me, and everywhere.

As I wake on the wings of morning
I can feel that heavenly glow,
I can hear God's greeting so warmly
With the assurance only I can
know.

While I wake on the wings of
morning
Prepared for a bright, new day,
I know the desires of my heart
Are a reality that's here to stay.

Oh, precious wings of morning
So gently unfolding the golden sun,
For I know God is watching over
me
And, will send love till day is done.

Dear God, sweet and loving
I know you are by my side,
I can hear your answer to my
whisper
As on morning's wings I glide.

Mary Challender Smith
THE LITTLE PEOPLE

"Moma" Thank you for loving me.

Little hands,
Tiny feet,
Dreams of sand,
and high up seat.

Pitter-Patter,
across the floor,
makes mom mop,
three times more.

Imaginary flea,
with a name,
It's REAL!
not justa game!

Dolls being strangled,
taken care of . . .
A cat's tail pulled by
innocent love.

A giggle, a laugh,
a blown kiss,
a tender hug,
I would miss.

It's not only for tiny hands,
building a church steeple,
I simply love them,
Children, the Little People.

Muriel Aileen Somers Kuebler
ENLIGHTENMENT

I'll never share
innocence again
and think
blowing bubbles is fun,
bubbles burst!
A babbling brook mirrors
lovely colored stones
a closer look reveals
jagged edges —
The squirrel walks a
tight rope —
parallels life
when we try to cope.
I'll never fall in love
again —
until the next time.
I will take life in stride
despite its hurtful pride
and know
that I have learned a
lesson well
life is a game of
"Kiss and Tell."

Yes, our eyes are the

"window of our soul"
but always the mistique
we crave to know.

Charlie W Harris
HELL'S GATE GUARD

They did not know or would not tell
Who would be guarding the gates of Hell.
Out of curiosity I wanted to know
So I got myself ready there to go.
Oh, it wasn't really fun—living in sin—
But I was told "It's the only way to get in."
Finally my ship came and I was on my way—
I arrived in Hell the very same day.
There I saw Satan and the gate guard too,
But I never dreamed it would be you.

Rhoda E Stevenson
HE'S GOT THE GRACE OF A DOVE IN HIS FLIGHT OF LOVE

He's got the grace of a dove
in his flight of love.
Oh! He's got the grace of a dove
in his mighty flight of love.

He's got my heart in a brace
that I can not face.
He comes from above
a place where no man has stood
or shoved.

He's got the grace of a dove
in his flight of love.
Oh! He's got the grace of a dove
in his mighty flight of love.

Charity K Dobbs
WHEN I DAYDREAM, I DREAM ABOUT YOU

When I daydream, I dream about being with you,
When I daydream, I dream about holding you and not letting go ever.
When I daydream, I dream about you and me walking alone
through
the park.
When I daydream, I dream about being
with you always.
When I daydream, I dream about you and me having fun,
laughing,
and being together.
When I daydream, I dream about you.
I'll love you always!

Leroy A Jackson Jr
BUT ONLY IF THERE'S SOMEONE CLOSE

I can be strong . . .
but only if there's someone close
to catch me if I fall.
I can be proud . . .
but only if there's someone close
to smile in admiration.
I can be loyal . . .
but only if there's someone close
to be trusted with my faith.
I can be loving . . .
but only if there's someone close.

Walter A Peek
EXULTATION

A man must climb the stair of life,
and reaching for the sky,
May often stumble painfully on
steps so steep and high.
They wind and turn, then double
back, and vapors dim the way.
While landings beckon artfully to
bid him stop and stay;

To cease the aching upward climb:
"'tis far enough, old friend.
For how can you be sure you'll find
a rainbow at the end?"

One balustrade a woman's love,
and one a friend's true hand;
With these to guide on either side
he'll reach the Golden Land.

A hundred forks beset the way,
with each a fatal test.
To go astray means sad delay and
failure in his quest.

And here the lowering clouds of
doubt, condensed by winds of night
Help terror rule the tides of choice,
as reason yields to fright.

These crossways bear confu;sing
signs to veil the course ahead,
And oft the way of death is laid
with carpeting of red.

To tempt the tender, tired feet to
choose the smoother climb,
Though each day lost pays fearful
cost to preserving Time . . .

That undefeated warrior whose
wav'ring, parchment hand,
Can strike the strongest hero to the
dust where he began.

Each juncture holds a pilgrim
band, made up of men to whom
Decision is a fearsome thing . . .
the partner of doom.

And rather than essay a path that
may not lead aright,
They stand and wait and curse the
Fate which brought them to
their plight.

But he whose eyes can pierce the
fog and see the final goal,
Will pause here but a moment to
assess the awful toll.

Then stumble on and upward
toward that Haven from All Pain,
Though the rails be ringed with
nettles and the light begins to
wane.

Through awesome gates the
traveller toils, whose crumbling
scrolls foretell
That he who dares their portals
soon shall hear his final knell.

But these cannot order him, nor
the sirens' subtle song . . .
What means the froth of winter's
cough to one who's fought so
long?

The stairway seems to steepen
'neath the weight of hoary years.
His pace may slow, but eyes still
glow through all frustration's
fears.

For as the clutching granite tears
the flesh from hands and knees,
Each level gained brings nearer the
esteemed Hesperides.

But how can we, just starting on
this perilous terrain
Be sure that if we reach the top our
dreams are not in vain?

Or if there is a crest at all, and is
it worth the while?
Can we be sure the air is pure atop
this endless stile?

I know not, nor do you, my friend
. . . we cannot pierce the pall
Of darkness that the hand of God
has placed before us all.

But this I know . . . He told us so .
. . That he who has not striven,
Can never find that peace of mind
that is the root of Heaven.

And 'though the phantom paradise
foretold that ancient day,
May be a dream delirium has
forged to ease the way.

It still exists in haughty hearts of
men who rise each morn
With knowledge that they'll do
their best, and damn the critics'
scorn.

To these, the bold, unyielding few,
who face life without lying,
Elysium is, in purest form, the
ecastacy of trying.

And when your Time shall come to
drink from Nature's fountain-head,
You'll know that Heaven simply
is—the single step ahead.

So live your life that when you
meet the Master on His throne
Your eyes are aiming at the stars;
your blood is on the stone.

Corliss Ramsey
YEAR'S END

Autumn days of falling leaves,
Makes one nostalgic,
It really makes you believe,
In Indian Summer's magic.

White fluffy clouds rolling by,
Gentle breezes flowing,
How swiftly autumn flies,
Soon winter winds are blowing.

Snow is falling in great flakes,
Holly and pine the only greenery.
Ice for skating on the lakes,
The best thing about winter is the
scenery.

Christmas will soon be here,
With the ever-changing seasons.
Soon the beginning of another
year,
And time for new visions.

Ollie S Crouch

Ollie S Crouch
THE TEAR

While looking through the gallery
of various
selections of art, my eyes were
fixed upon a
painting that caused pangs of
sorrow to my
already saddened heart.

There among the many mastered
paintings was
one of a little boy, his golden skin
unblemished, impeccable,
his velvet brown eyes Heavenward
gazed, and on his
cheek a glistening tear, it
enthralled me in a daze.

I stood in reverend awe, seeing
nothing but
this little tear, so real, so effective,
for a
moment I felt that no one was near,
though
many passers by were going to and
fro, not a
one demanded my attention from
this little
tear that I saw. . .

Why was it there I asked, on such
an innocent
little face? ah, there in lies the
mystery of
an artists perfect touch, as seen
from the heart
of such, for only an artist could
portray a
glistening little tear that could stop
a passer by,
and close a listening ear to all
surrounding
sounds of joyous and conversing
folk,
so remote. . .

Karen Renee Swanson
MISSPELLED CATASTROPHE

Dedicated to my husband Don Swanson. My children Lori Jean, Michael Wayne & Mindy Lynn Swanson. And my parents Arvid and Margaret Olson

---

We received many beautiful gifts
At our wedding in '64
Lots of pretty pillow cases
And sheets and blankets galore

We were given a mixer and blender
And one of the shiniest toasters
Two tablecloths and nine lamps
And eight wooden butterfly
coasters

I wrote thank-you notes for many
days
No spare minute went to waste
Some got thanked for the wrong
gifts
When their wedding cards got
misplaced

But the most embarrassing part of
it all
Wasn't thanking the wrong one for
towels
It was adding an -e- to the word
bowl
And thanking twelve guests for
bowels

Elizabeth Clodfelter
GOD . . . YOU AND I

This poem is dedicated to my husband Ron.
I Love You!

I've dreamed since I was a little girl,
dreams that a little girl has,
I dreamed that I was a princess,
the prince. . .I could'nt clearly see.

And there stood someone over us
with their arms stretched far and
wide,
someone who made us both smile,
someone who was by our side.

"Like the prince. . .I could'nt
clearly see."

I dreamed of standing on a hill
on a bright and sunny day,
a knight in armor on his horse
rides up and sweeps me away.
And yet his face is not seen.

And there stood someone over us
with their arms stretched far and
wide,
someone who made us smile,
someone who was by our side.
"Like the knight. . .I could'nt
clearly see."

I've dreamed of wearing a long
white gown,
a dream that is coming true,
the face of my prince and my
knight in armor,
I can clearly see that it's you.

And as I walk down the aisle,
with my head held so high,
I clearly see who stands over us,
with his arms stretched far and
wide,

that someone who made us smile
through my dreams, was

God. . .You and I

Lisa A LaVigne
FRIENDSHIP
Friendship is a band in which I
play the flute
to my faults you seem to be mute
When I'm down your always there
to give me a smile to show you
care
We have a band of our own
you seem to be with me even
when I'm alone
You whipe my eyes when I cry
and cover up when I lie
You help my problems to go away
and always assure me of another
day
When we laugh they know we're
alive
on each other I think we thrive

Florence Howery Roddy
TIME
The clock of time, how short its
hours
That God has alotted all,
To walk the trails and gather
flowers;
Listening for the skylarks call.

To count each hour in sweet
content,
Finding love along the way;
Seeking the truth that God has sent
At the close of each perfect day.

Strolling where healing waters
wend;
Finding peace in verdant land;
Seeking gold at the rainbows end,
Hold a sunbeam in ones hand.

Meeting the sun at dawning time
To welcome the new days birth,
Are hours that makes life near
devine
For Gods children here on earth.

The book of time is closed by God,
With seasons that tarries long;
Alone one road then all must trod
When we hear the thorn birds song.

Audrey Hodge Broussard
GLORY TO GOD
Glory To God Give Glory To God
Whose Blood Was Shed On Calvary
Glory To God, Give Glory To God
Who Died To Give Men Victory
Glory To God, Give Glory To God
Without Whose Love, Life Would
Not Be
All That Hath Breath, Let All That
Hath Breath
Give Honor And Glory To Thee

Glory To God, Give Glory To God
For all of His Goodness And
Mercies
Glory To God, Give Glory To God
For All Thy Great Wonders And
Beauties
Glory To God, Give Glory To God
Who Was Born of a Virgin So Holy
All That Hath Breath, Let All That
Hath Breath
Give Honor and Glory To Thee

Humbly I kneel, I kneel At Thy Altar
Giving My Homage To Thee
Blessed, Oh Bleassedness Holy of
Holiest
All Praises My God To Thee
Glory To God, Give Glory To God
Let Heaven And Let The Earth Sing
Glory To God, Give Glory To God
Let's Worship, Let's Honor The
King
Glory To God Give Glory To God
For He's A Great God A Holy God
Almighty!
All That Hath Breath, Let All That
Hath Breath
Give Honor And Glory To Thee

Debbie Moretz
SUMMER REMNANTS

To the people and the place from which the inspiration for this poem came. Summerville, S. C. Summer 1987 A.M.L.S.T.

Summer, I hear the birds whistling
a familiar tune.
A lonely puppy sits in a feathered
streak of afternoon sunlight
creeping through the trees.
A robin drifts down to watch as the
tiny weightless insects
rise from the grass, unheard; like
tiny fluffs of
downey cotton; blowing in the
breeze.

Simple silence envelopes our
world as does the grass,
so green carpeting the hills.
The sun, now tired, sinks down and
rests its weary head
upon the horizon, emitting an
afternoon solace of
orange ecstacy upon a glass sky of
tiring blue.

Brenda M Chandler
A MOTHER'S MEMORY

With love to my stillborn children: Jarred (1979) and Chad (1984) And to Tara (1985)—my 3 lb. 4 oz. miracle baby!

Child unseen,
yet loved beyond imagination.
A small kick, a hearty punch
yearning to be on his own.

Yet for some unknown reason—
something happens.
Unexplained silence, heart-rending
stillness.

Life eventually goes on,
but I shall never forget—
a small kick, a hearty punch
that yearned to be on his own.

Louis D Engelhardt
WHY DO BIRDS FLY
They fly high into the sky, then
along the waters crest.
To tree tops and buildings to rest
Do they fly to challenge man;
The greatest body on land?
Or do they just fly, to keep us
wondering why??
Why do birds fly??

Ethel Berkman
JUST FOR YOU

To My Son Lawrence

Just for you, I am writing this poem
To show you how much I care.
When you are not home,
Of my loneliness, I am aware.
My life is a void
that could be enjoyed
If only you were here.

Barbara Powell
UNTITLED
Come quietly, sweet death, and
seal my lips with silence
Nevermore shall they repeat some
word of love or feel a kiss.
My eyes are closed in endless sleep,
Never to behold a summer day, or
his smiling face.
My arms lie empty now; never
again to be embraced or
embrace.
But, in someway, my soul is at
peace and happy
For I have loved and been loved—
This can never be taken from me,
not even in death.

Virginia (Ginger) Miller
YOU ARE NOT FORGOTTEN

To my lovely and precious Mother, Lois Wallace and to my dear, wonderful husband, Johnny Miller. Until we meet again, know that you both are with me always in my heart and in my thoughts. 'Ginger'

To honor our POW'S and our
MIA'S, We have set aside this
one special day;
Not time sufficient we all know,
For each and every one who was
treated so!
So 'tis with love and sadness—An
attempt to wash out the
madness;
With remembering and caring;
These moments we are sharing.

World War I, World War II—Korea
and Vietnam; You're forever in
our hearts, each and every one.
You who came home—You who
did not; There's none of you that
we forgot.
To honor? Yes! To salute you too!
You gave your ALL for Red,
White & Blue!
A sacrifice so true—And now we
are trying; To thank you
somehow—No harm in crying!

There's a little boy—just so high;
He salutes the flag as it passes by.
A tiny little girl—hand over heart;
To assure their freedom, you did
your part.
And for all generations, until time's
end; You'll be remembered as
heroes and brave men!

'Though some may wonder,
"What's all the fuss?" When
war's "over there" and not
touching us;
In our comfortable homes—an
auto or two; We may have had
naught if it weren't for you!
Our husbands, sons, brothers,
sweethearts and friends; The list
is endless—It never ends!
Army—Air Force—Navy—
Marines; Some of you were
barely out of your teens!
Whoever you are; wherever you
may be;
God bless and protect you for
keeping us free!

Mary P Mere
PATHWAY OF FREEDOM

Dedicated to all Veterans of Foreign Wars of the United States with special mention to my Grandfather L. J. Mere and my Father T.L. Mere and all members of VFW Post 1143 Massena N.Y.

Gunfire, and the cannon roar
As those brave men die in war
Their bright blood glistening
over rivers and land
Some pray, God help me where I
stand.
As fear rises in one man,
He prays, dear God I love that land.

Land of choice and of peace
Land thats made for you and me
Land that stands for liberty
God let my soul rest in thee.

Virginia West Oberly
ARCHAEOLOGISTS
Roll back earth's layers.
see the bones and shards
of man storied in ivoried beauty.
Skulls lie in conversational
closeness;
mouths hang open, spilling dust
like inane talk;
but round eye-holes stare in stilled
surprise —
wondering why intruders pry.

Ollie Dirks
'TIS SO
"Ye must be born again,"
the Master said,
"Born again?" we ask who
have passed our youth.
"Ye shall not enter Heaven,
lest ye do,"
And we know our Savior always
speaks the truth.
"Ye must be born in Spirit
and in Truth,
This we are taught is the
second birth,
That we may spiritually hear
and understand,
The things that Jesus taught
while on this earth.
Putting off the old,
becoming new,
Treading the path,
that our Master trod,
These things we must
seek earnestly to do,
Then some day, we will
stand face to face with God . .

Yvonne L Cheshire
HOBO

Remembrance to Rip, Pokie, Suzie and Maggi. They will always share that special warm place in our memories and heart

---

A funny little puppy, our Hobo
Bounding through the snow
On tiny legs that would hardly go.

Spring came and the sun warmed the earth
The tall pines gave a scent
That tingled his nose.
Oft we would catch him
Sitting in perfect pose
With a pine twig in his mouth
Watching little white butterflies
Flit to and fro.

Many winters and springs
Filled his life with wonder and wisdom.
Our lives he filled with joy.
We called him Big Boy,
Such a GOOD BOY!

One day as winter came again,
We noticed his eyes were sad and dim,
With drooping head he was trying to say
His time had come to go away.

He lay his head on my knee
Trying I know to comfort me.
I held his head in my trembling hands
With eyes blinded by tears
Told him of our love for him.
How grateful we were
For his faithful love
These many years.

We lay him beneath the pine tree
Where he used to play,
In slumber for a time,
Until we meet again
One day.

James John Simms
SEASONAL DEPRESSION: A SONNET
The time for season's change is almost here:
the dying old flames of autumnal leaves
have flickered, guttering, to ashes sere.
The trees' spring sap, now old and gummy, grieves
for glorious youth; camps near trees' heart-fire,
leaving outer reality alone.
Leaves are burnt on winter's cold, clammy pyre;
Trees shift in wild wind with splintering groan.
Skeletal fingers reach from dying bones,
Long nails click in skeletony fashion.
Dying wind through dead, bare, brown branches moans
with undisguised jealousy and passion:
And all the trees within my questing sight
Await the end of the despairing night.

Mary L Jackson
SPRINGTIME IS NEAR
Springtime is very near,
Oh, how I wish that you were here.
The Songbirds are singing their favorite song.
Ah, the sound of their voice is so lovely and strong.
They are calling to their mates to join them in song,
Springtime is coming and they know that it won't be long.
Springtime is a lovely time of year.
The fragrance from flowers that bloom each year,
The beauty of their blossom is very clear,
They seem to be saying, "Ah, if you could just be here."

Gloria Yohn Schwartz
THE NEED FOR LOVE
You stand tall beside me
And your body casts a shadow that sheilds me.

When you're not present
And I'm by myself
The weather beats on me and I shatter.

You come along,
Piece me together,
And there we stand again side by side.

So in a way you control me,
And my life doesn't matter,
But my love for you is <u>all</u> I believe in.

Knock me down,
And pick me up,
As many times as you want,
But I'll never leave you

for I cannot stand alone.

Shirley A Snyder
DAVID
You came to us from heaven
slid down on a ribbon of blue,
and now you're up there waiting
for us to come to you.
Memories we'll cherish
Your cheery smile and winning ways.
Why! you never met a stranger.
Not once in all your days!
Your friends were always many—
It was easy to see why
Age, size, or color
never seemed to catch your eye.
You loved them all for what they were
and tried to change them not
Relax, just be yourself, this time is all we've got!
You lived life to the fullest
and we never will forget
The joy and love you brought us
Your presence is with us yet.
Love, Mom

Mary Ethel Woody
OLD NUMBER SIX
The old school still sticks in my mind;
'though the bricks are crumbling away.
I can see Uncle Jimmy ringing the bell
To call in the children from play.
From him we learned to read and write,
To cipher and to do our best.
With spectacles low upon his nose,
He'd proceed with a spelling test.
At noon time we all ate together
From lunch pails or paper sacks;
Some had cold biscuits and sausage,
Or fried chicken, a leg or a back.
Sometimes we traded cake for cookies
Or an apple for a pear.
Calories were never given a thought,
We always had sweets to share.
Near the entrance was the old iron pump
Where I drank from my folding cup;
Where there was always a puddle of mud
When lunch was over, and play time was up.
So many things I could tell you
Of the school with the crumbling brick;
Double seats and desks with chewing gum;
Readin'—writin'—and 'rithmatic.

Paulette J Hlus
TO YOU, MY FRIEND . . .

This poem is dedicated to Art, Gordon and Karen—for very special friendships.

There are good and there are bad days,
But you my friend, are there—always;
Just knowing that you're there
in thoughts, I know you care.

Your friendship I find so sincere
You help me overcome my fear
of life, of living, can I cope?
I seek fulfillment; you give me hope!

You make me feel that I'm okay,
The things you do, the words you say
Your company is such a comfort,
You are a remedy when I hurt.

And if I'm down or I am blue
Just hearing a few words from you
restores my courage, brings back my pride
And just as quick, my tears are dried.

Friendship like yours is hard to find
knowing you—one of a kind
means more than you will ever know,
Just had to write and tell you so.

THANKS FOR BEING MY FRIEND.

Berniece Davis Bowman
RAINBOW OF LIFE

To my son, Richard Lane Davis, on his twenty-first birthday

Life can be beautiful, so they say
Full of color—never gray.
There's the gleaming white of utility bills
And the sunshine yellow of ulcer pills.
The tax bill is always a beautiful blue
And the green one that indicates "Bill Past Due"
There's your little blue bank book, that shows all you own
When it's in the red, you must get a loan!
Your payment book is a pretty tan
(You'll pay that off as soon as you can)
With the pink slip showing you own a used car,
You know you needn't go very far
To give your life a rosy hue
Just trade it in on one that's new.
So—with the gilt-edged credit cards merchants send
This rainbow of color need never end.
Life <u>can</u> be beautiful, as they say,
As long as you're willing and able to pay.

R J Freeman(a.k.a. Dreamer)
IT'S WHAT I DO

Dedicated to C. Burke and E. Bennett, My best friends and inspirations.

Being alone is not so bad, its what I do when I'm
feeling sad. Being alone is good sometimes. It helps
me to think and clear my mind. When I'm alone and
feeling blue I can think of alot to do. Like sit here in
the middle of the night and think of a million things
to write. I write about people, things and life. I write
about love, passion and being nice but when I'm
lonely, sad and blue I like to sit and think of you.
When I'm alone there is a lot to do, but when
I'm lonely I dream of being with you. . .

David Paul Truax II
MORNING DREAMS

To my Grandmother, Genevieve L. Truax, who was a great inspiration to me always, who recently passed away.

Through eyes that run silver and gold
I gazed through worn window pane at the naked morning,
Mind shivering and racing upon calloused hills and swaying pine,
Pondering the cost of a day such as this
After a well-buried night.

Claiming no such owner I steal it for a moment, the morning,
And say it is mine and use it.
Whisper I say. And it does.
Sing to me. And it does.
Cry to me. And it does.

Through cool mist and sodden hills of tear drops of a dying night,
I watch you. Do you know?
Do you listen to my morning dreams?

So tell me your secrets.
And sing me your song.
And show me your delicate rains
And I will reveal mine.
Do you listen to my morning dreams?
Sleep tonight I say. And it does.

Anna G Kananowitz

REVEREND OF PATIENCE AND GRACE

A Godly man I see,
a worthy person to behold.
No colors crossed our hands
or face,
just a presence of God,
a blessing to behold.
My skin of white,
his of gold,
and yet he understood,
as if I were in the fold
all the time.
A person so human,
and yet so inspiring,
yet with a weakness of pain
we all must endure,
seems at times,
depending on me,
just for reassurance,
like I was the Reverend,
and instead,
he in my place.
What pleasure it is to
serve a man of God,
when he also needs a
few words of kindness,
to keep from slipping,
especially a person of
my standing,
to hold him in place.
I feel that this hospital
room is so sacred,
that no church ever knew.
I can feel that God is here
at all times.
It's my place to relax and
have reverence between God
and I.
This man of gold,
deserves a crown,
for not all will instill the
love of God and human race,
like my Reverend of room 105.
Never once he was concerned
about blessings for himself,
but every moment,
whether with words,
gesture or his eyes, kept
saying,
"God bless you child, thank
you, you are so good, God bless
you."
Some go to church for blessings
to receive,
but to receive in this room
of 105,
blessings every night,
I feel nearer to God, for
whatever I must accept,
and be prepared,
for it's God's will to be
done.

Frank Xavier Robinson

REN'EE

She's my blanket
When in need of cover;
My partner
When I need a lover;
My candle,
When I'm in the dark:
My home port
When I disembark;
A window
When the walls close in;
A saviour
When I sometimes sin,
She fills my body
And my mind;
She manages
To find the time;
And so upon
This special day;
I wrote this
For my love;
Ren'ee

Kathleen Hendricks

COMING OF AGE

I look upon this beautiful youth,
And catch my breath at what I see,
For on her lips the smile of truth,
Caught me unaware, but I am pleased.

The meekness of childhood has passed,
The shadows of innocence understood;
For she has reached womanhood at last,
And realizes the changes are good.

Where once she tread with reluctant feet,
For fear of ridicule or hurt;
She now advances with eagerness to greet,
Ever conscious of her true worth.

Gone forever the timid glance,
The self-conscious shifting about;
She now meets life with swift advance,
Without fear or stunning doubt.

I know I have done my best,
In an overly short time it seems;
It is now up to her to do the rest,
Find her destiny, dream her dreams.

James Morabito

Mary-Michael Morabito

THIS IS IT

Dedicated to my dad. His understanding ways made him one of the greatest people who ever lived. Always a smile, never a complaint. I love you. In memory of James Morabito 11/05/1933-06/16/1987.

This is it; todays' the day
We must say good-bye.
Please don't fret, can't you see
I didn't really die?
My love is here, to never stray
For eternity and a day
Now, the time has come
For you to listen
Because, I have something to say
"My life as you know it has ended,
My dreams yet unfulfilled
However, my life has just begun
For my spirit is willed.
Remember, if you may
My world of yesterday
The laughter, the song, the sorrow—
So long
Over forever
Tomorrow, I travel to a dimension
Untouched by time.
I am fine!!
Keep in mind, anyway,
Only now my dreams can be fulfilled
Every moment of every day."

Anetha Tyree

A TALK WITH TIME

To my inspiration and strength, William, Candace and Ashanta

A man tried to put time
Like some grains of sand in a bottle
To watch it slip silently by
Uneventful and unoffending.

He was dismayed that time
Would not respond to him
And ignored his attempts
To put it to rest.

A man woke up one morning
After studying the stars in his sleep
Only to discover the sun still shining
And time continuing to roll on.

How dreadfully low he felt
His crest fallen back to earth
For what and whom was he
To try and rule time on God's earth?

A man discovered new meaning
And beauty in each blade of grass
And time just went on ticking
For he'd caught the man at last.

Genevieve Larry

GENERAL DAYS

A general idea may come to your mind.
A general check-up to be on time.
A general walk you can take each day.
A general utility bill each month you must pay.
A general fraction to show how much you owe.
A general thought to let you know.
A general gesture say's "Hello."
A general slim diet keeps the waist just so.
A general mistake not dotting the 'i'.
A general gas station stop, even if the gas is high.
A general kiss and hug for your kids at night.
A general drive to your work at the morning light.
A general breakfast of eggs, bacon, toast with marmalade.
A general shopping spree which can't be delayed.
A general song that makes us hum.
A general wash day whatever the day that comes.
A general talk with one of your friends.
A general television commercial, a headache to end.
A general pat on your dog's head.
A general used car, with not much to be said.
A general wave to the mailman you gave.
A general meeting, a bake sale to be made.
A general supper, salad, soup, hamburgers and chips.
A general church service, the Lord we worship.

Christine Strauss

SEEING STARS

It seems so long ago (and maybe it is)
That we stared at the same stars and saw them that way

Young at heart (years too, I guess)
We held hands and saw what could be if we shut our eyes tight enough

We made a promise (the forever one)
And started out for the end of time.
Through years of endless feeling we felt our way

We've made mistakes (even planned some)
And are no better for having faced the realities of being human

Life can wear us down (if we let it)
And all to soon we could be two people with regrets and nothing
much to say

A change is upon us (can you feel it)
It is what keeps us on the course to the end of time
Or leads us on a side road to eternity

We understand (or think we do)
Reaching with love, we hold hands and stare at the stars
with our eyes shut

Janet Richter

THREE

This poem is dedicated to Melissa and Sean, my beautiful children.

The big blue eyes look up at me,
And innocence and trust I see.
The small chubby hand I hold
Is warming me from the cold.

His face is full of warmth and love,
Like sunshine falling from above.
He makes my life worth living,
With all the joy he is giving.

We run through the pure, soft snow,
And tumble down a hill we know.
I wish I was again as free
As my little one who's only three.

He does not know of hate and pain,
Or terrible wars that kill and maim.
He knows of only love and peace,
Why does this innocence have to cease?

Mrs Anita Gross

WHAT GOD HAS TAUGHT ME

This I do for God; for the love of my husband, Roger, and God's greatest gifts to us, Robert and Richard.

Goodness will surely sprout and grow
If each of us let a little bit show.

Let us try to love all others,
After all, God made us brothers.

If you feel hate or some other bad feeling,
Learn to forgive, and you will start healing.

If you suffer from illness or problems or stress,
Call upon God for help out of the mess.

If life seems the pits and keeps coming up clover,
Just say a prayer and ask God to take over.

Your prayers He will answer, if your heart is true.
If your faith is good, He will never fail you.

I've needed God many times in my life,
And He's always helped me over my strife.

If you just take the time to call upon Him,
You'll find out your life is not quite so grim.

Keep praying, be patient, He soon will be there.
God's answer will come, and He'll always be fair.

Charlene Ramsey
TWO PEOPLE
Twenty five years of ups and downs
Raised five children, and oh
What a merry-go-round
Four darling daughters
One wonderful son
What could be more complete
Two people who said "I do"
Twenty five years ago
Little did we know
What the years would bestow
My love for you
Grows with every passing year
To me you are so dear
A man so good and kind
Has my heart entwined
All the sorrows
All the joys
Are part of our life time
You are God's gift to me
For eternity
Bill—my life Charlene

Lena Sangret
DREAM OF SUMMER

Especially dedicated to David and his family. Ken and Jean Swann, for the inspiration, they have given to me and their interest in poetry. Thank you.

Sitting on the balcony dreaming, dreaming
Of the summer sun, beaming, beaming.
Soon the white blanket of snow, white snow
Will be whisked away as March winds blow and blow,

As Spring comes and goes, goes,
With its whining windy woes, woes.
Summer hours, days creeping,
Slowly approaching, dark nights sleeping,
Creeping slowly, yet approaching fast, fast
Ridding itself of the past, grey past.
Soon there will be streams, muddy streams
And April showers, cleansing mother earth it seems
Washing, washing away the old; making way for the new,
Sowing, sowing a glamorous quilt of shimmering green, red, yellow, blue,

As night approaches, mother nature in a slumber
Until she awakens listening to the sounds of summer.
Then everything comes to life, in great leaps and bounds.
Waving her magic wand as she makes her rounds,

Like birds gliding, riding waves of air
Circling ever circling with a flare, a flare.
From east to west, like a wave, a big wave,
Subsiding slowly, slowly because she gave and gave,
As dream becomes reality, oh! oh! that I, so crave

Kelly L Ireland
SERPENTS OF OUR MINDS
It came to me in a haunting dream,
the memories of the past.
It entered in through an unsealed door,
that was somehow left unlatched.

It weaved its pain, as memories do
like a serpent through my mind.
It coiled and slithered through forgotten dreams,
and through pains I left behind.

It weaved its way through the chamber door,
that let to my forgotten past.
And with one quick lash of its deadly fangs,
my memories came rushing back.

We seem to forget that the pains of the past,
are lessons in disquise.
The lessons we learn are unsurpassed,
within our memories eye.

Catherine Bevington Franck
PERFECTION
For many years I've struggled with—
Those dreams that don't come true:
Where everything is perfect;
And Knights on White Steeds rule.
Until a riddle came to me;
And millions it was worth:
It left me with a meaning;
To live with on this earth.
You see things that are perfect,
A myth that should be shattered:
Illusion is a funny thing;
And soon it's all that matters:
The lesson is to learn my friend;
When perfect is in view,
That somewhere on this perfect:
There's torn and tattered too!

Florence Parisi
DEDICATED TO MY LATE HUSBAND TONY
It is all the simple things you did that made my life worth while.
It is all the love you shared with me and how you made me smile.
It is how you brought me laughter each time that I was down.
Life was so much easier just having you around.
Now I have my children and grandchildren.
They are making me smile again.
Sometimes they make me cry.
Having them around has taken part of the hurt away.

Trisha Aud Mullins
A TRIBUTE TO MY DAD
You were raised on a farm in a family of twelve,
learning to be sensitive and strong as well.
You served your country, married, and became a Dad,
Six children in five years, and you were so glad.
Material goods were not plenty, happiness came from
being together, and those times were many.

Walking through the woods, six children and you,
looking for walnuts that had fallen from the trees.
Tracking through the woods in the new-fallen snow,
six excited faces watch you look for the "perfect" Christmas Tree.

Hearing you cry for the first time when we were young,
your Brother had just died from a brain tumor.
Seeing the joy in your eyes when you were presented with grandchildren,
You gave them love, and taught them humor.

You were up at the light of day, working with your hands,
putting siding on houses, coming home tired but making no demands.
You were on the job when I received the call,
My father had been electrocuted, and took a 30' fall.

Watching you suffer for seventeen days before you died,
and listening to your grandson of seven ask "why?"
The day of the funeral rain poured from the sky,
Memories of all that you gave to us still make me cry.

Mike Yunis
IN SEARCH FOR HAPPINESS
Yearning for happiness, I searched the earth
But how can happiness be without a wife
Marriage in my eyes has been a signal of red
That leaves the worries gathered in my head
Thru barren hearts life is an aimless strife
It is only love that makes it truly worth.

For the sake of happiness I earned a wealth
But how to be happy and no peace of soul
A sound mind is the source of ultimate rest
And a lover among the world's riches is surely the best
Thru a barren heart you cannot achieve any goal
It is only love that makes life truly worth
To attain happiness I strived for health
But how can health be with an empty heart
Fill your heart with love you'll be a king
Who will ever dance and will ever sing
For thru a loving heart happiness will never part
Giving you health and wealth making life truly worth

R D Weir
UNTITLED
The wilderness is our mind, ready to explore.
With each dawning morn the vastness expands, into new realms.
Always changing, never ending realities fog the hope for fresh beginnings.
Dreams are the hunted creatures of the night, elusive but always within reach.
To grasp just one is the desire of every man.
Pity on the soul who lets the creatures die and the wilderness burn.

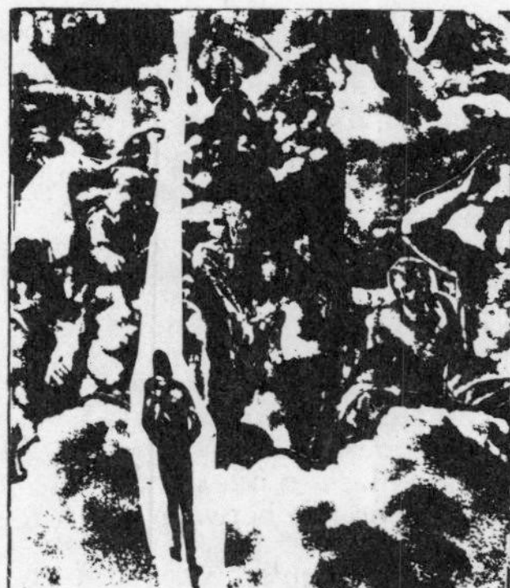

The eons of time and space pass before my eyes as nothingness.
I yearn for understanding but a wall separates me from comprehension.
For what do I look in my search?
Confusion reigns within as though there is no meaning.
Turmoil has found a home.
Desires burn my heart, but I know not how to extinguish the flame, as the source must be yet too deeply hidden.
Only faith and hope will maintain the power I must have to find what I seek, Whatever that may be.

Lily Lee
ANNELO OR YEARNING

To Emy, This poem is dedicated to you, who was my best friend.

Quisiera poderte ver,
Atraves de tus palabras,
para poder apreciar,
Algo mas que tu gran alma.,

Quisiera poderte ver,
para palpar con mis manos,
las formas de tu pecado.,

Quisiera poderte ver y,
Penetrar tu mundo de ensuenos,
Remontarme en lo infinito.,
De tus mas raros deceos.,

Quisiera poderte ver,
Para vivir con tu aliento y,
De tus labios beber,
El nectar de ese gran sueno.

Claudette Martin
GOD'S GIFT
Among God's Gifts is Forgiveness
This I Thank Him for
Everytime I think of it
God's Love flows through me more

Louie A Bangerter
THE CHRISTMAS TIME
Why does it take the Christmas time
To make God's glory shine more bright,
To find the love the shepherds found
In search for Christ that Holy Night?
Why does the world forget "good will,"
That angel message long ago
To frightened shepherds in their fields—
"The peace on earth" all men should know?
Men wait for blessed Christmas joys,
The festive time at end of year,
There's feeling of "good will to men,"
The giving presents and good cheer.
'Tis then men know a brotherhood;
Is it the stable and the hay,
The viewing of the manger scene
That every year men store away?

Too soon it is they close their eyes
So needy ones they cannot see,
Forget to give the helping hand
When through with lighted Christmas tree.
When men, like shepherds, seek the Lord
And cherish glory of His birth,
It will not take the Christmas time
For love to spread 'oer all the earth.

Cathy D Parks
THE HOUR IS COMING
The hour is coming for the dead to rise,
the strong to surrender, the weak to be wise.
The Lord and all of His majesty,
will be coming back to set me free.
Free from all worries, cares and strife,
to set me free from this earthly life.
To take me home to glory above,
a place where I know that I will be loved.
Will you be ready to go with me?
or will you suffer through eternity?
For the judgment is not just another day,
It is the day when all sinners will pay.

Sandra Sue Chiarelli
LIFE'S A BIG GAMESHOW

To David O'Vivion my inspiration. For your love and friendship I dedicate this poem to you

---

Is this the way it was meant to be?
In this real life gameshow
Is there nothing for me?
Where's my prize? What do I win?
I answered the questions
Where's my big spin?
I want the jackpot
If life's just a game
I gave it my best shot
Where's my fortune and fame?
I'm sitting here idle
My thoughts all run wild
I'm smart, I'm creative
I have plenty of style
What am I lacking?
What magic ingredient?
Are my standards to high?
Should I settle for less?
I want the lifetime guarantee
Only the best!

Jane Whitaker Burke
FAITH
With faith enough in heart I sought,
(Or so in mind I had thought),
To walk upon the sea one day,
As on that warm sea shore I lay.

'Til suddenly I heard in some dismay
A voice within my soul did say,
"Are you comparing Me with thee?"
"Oh, no," I cried, "for you are He."

"Dear child test thee not,
You may not have what I have got.
I struggled long and hard for faith,"
I heard Him say, as I lay there safe.

But still my soul beckoned me,
As I gazed out on that wondrous sea.
Of such thoughts I could not rid:
Cannot I do what He once did?

"You must not test the waters clear,
Take a ship, said He, one is near."
I stopped my dreaming and lay back down.
For without his faith, I would surely drown.

Dorothy Smith
FELLOW TRAVELER
I have watched my fellow traveler
struggle daily on his way, seems at times
his load so heavy, yet no one stopped
him just to say; Can I help you with
your burden then reached out with
helping hand, friend! I'll help you in your
struggle, till you reach a better land,
Some have stumbled fallen weary, just too
tired to try and win, then you'll see
them gather courage lift their heads
and try again,
Then I've watched some deeply troubled,
in their trails heard them say, Oh! dear Lord
how will I make it to that brighter land
of day?
Life is not all blessings; without burdens,
sometimes things come to make us pray;
prayer will lift the burdens give you courage
on the way.
Often when we're gay and happy we forget
to seek God's face then he sends us a
reminder that there is no stopping place
Often in our homeward journey
seems we've traveled our last mile, but
it will be worth each coming hardship
if we can but see God smile.

Dorothy Hotz Lynn
BIRTH AND GROWTH OF THE FAMILY FARM
This is no prate.
It has a definite time and date.
Yes, SHE smiles and waves to me.
What beauty to see!
I must tell this story—you see—
How the family farm came to be!

Grandfather and Grandmother adopted HER.
They nourished and caressed HER.
Father and Mother adopted HER.
They nourished and caressed HER.
We adopted HER—

A new barn, shop, and crib,
Covered HER left rib.
A new chicken and hog house,
Made a lovely blouse.
Nourishment was fighting the weed,
For SHE loved to grow seed.
All was accomplished with sweat and blood,
To say nothing of illustrious mud!

Now we look into HER eyes—
As SHE reveals and denies!
Seconds, minutes, and hours—
We treasure HER hand in ours.
Together we can take on anything.
So let AmeriCa sing!

Kenneth D Kynett
MOM AND DAD
Often we argued and seldom agreed
You showed us the things we just couldn't see
You offered advice, patient and open-minded
And showed us happiness and where we could find it
You gave us a map and a direction to head
Though sometimes we chose our own ways instead
But now that we're older and starting our way
We thank you both for those wonderful days
You taught us to live, to care, and to grow
We treasure those teachings wherever we go
A debt much too large to ever repay
We're proud you're our parents, and in some small way
We'd like to say thank you in all that we do
And hope our love always. . .reflects upon you

Bevelyn Bacon
YOUR SMILES

To my husband

Tho our twilight years
Are with us
In my heart I can
see
That we are not old
As it will always be
When I look at you
And see you smile
at me
Tho some are old
and weary
And wish for the end
of day
For me spring will
never end
As long as you are near
And I can see you
smile at me
I cannot write poetry
or carry a tune
But my heart is full
of music
When I look at you
And see you smile
at me

Marilyn M Underhill
BILL'S GARDEN
Bill planted a garden the garden did grow,
It grew so big in just a week or so
That Bill contemplated he was in quite a spot,
Who would eat all the veggies before they did rot?

So he picked up the phone and called Marilyn his friend,
She immediately saw the spot he was in.
Upon much discussion it was abundantly clear,
She said, "Bill I suggest you don't plant next year."

Why veggies you'll eat both day and night,
You'll eat veggies with all your might
In spite of the eating they'll grow again,
Do you understand now what a dilemma you're in?

Grace L (Bonnie) Carey

Grace L (Bonnie) Carey
WINDOW OF BEAUTY

To my Guys: Bill Eddie Carey, husband; Bryan Michael and Jayson Edward Carey, sons.

Windows are made for looking
Through and far beyond.
To distance from, where you stand,
To distance come and gone.

To places you admire so
To ones in which you've seen;
All the wonders, in the world,
Of places where you've been.

Stop now and consider
Of all the sights yet known.
Through all the windows, where you've seen
The greatest beauty shown . . .

It's brought to my attention
By words heard in the past.
The greatest beauty, to behold,
Is beauty which will last.

The beauty I refer to
Is that, of which, I'm told.
To read words' someone's written,
Is to look through a window into
their soul!

Luba Palomba

STARDUST

To all the women, lucky enough to be mothers . . .

Babies are bits of star-dust
Blown from the hand of God . . .
And lucky is the woman
Who knows the pains of birth,
For she has held a star!!!

Dorothy E Burgett

MY EASTER HAT

I have the largest Easter Hat that
ever was designed
The colors that I chose for it are
black and blue combined.
These colors are quite neutral, and
I picked them with great care
They'll have to last a long long time
and go with all I wear.
It will have a look about it, that
seems a bit like veil,
Made of fog, and wind and rain and
sleet and snow and hail.
The accent colors that will be, atop
for all to view
Resemble canary yellow, robin red
and blue bird blue,
The lines are snug and well made
and most becoming too.
It took a lot of planning to have this
Easter Hat
And a great deal of money, so now
because of that
The one I wore at Easter to go to
Church that day and pray—
Was a plain old fashioned beige
one that I had tucked away.
But with the lovely yellow roses,
my Love sent along to me
I was very very pleased and as
happy as could be,
This combination gives me a Hat
beyond reproof—
So come around next week and
see—I'll have a brand new roof.
This verse I think will prove it—I
am not a clown
You must agree with me—I have
The "Asbestos" Hat in town!!

Mary Hohl

MY FOND MEMORIES

Dedicated in loving memory to my loving husband, born September 9, 1918 passed away November 21, 1983

Fond Memories
Dear—is what I have of you
The Lord has called you home
But I'm not alone
I have my fond memories

There were good times
That we had
When we held hands in the park
And we kissed in the dark
And when we built our love nest
together
We weathered each storm
And we promised
To love and protect each other
From all harm.

But then there were sad times
For you and for me.
But we made it together

And now you are gone
And I'm all alone
But I'm not lonely
Now, I walk with the Lord
And my fond memories

Elizabeth Sophie Burzawa

NEVER FOR ME

Watching you from across the
table,
Adoring your beauty.
How I wish we were alone,
Just the two of us.
With so much in common, so little
to spare,
But yet we have so much to share,
With each other.
If I weren't so shy, I'd make the first
move,
To get us together.
As we're close to each other,
gliding across the floor,
We turn so many heads.
Those people know us, and they
realize,
We're the perfect couple.
But why do I fool myself, when I
know,
I'm only dreaming,
And this dream will never be.

Though I wish you were,
You will never be for me.

Jean Olson

DO YOU KNOW ME

God, do you know me
Have you forgotten my name

Am I recorded in your Book of Life
Have I caused you shame

I lower my head, I know, to pray
Why, God, has my tongue grown
silent

Has my soul been lost and yet my
body remains

Is Heaven beyond my reach
If I lift up my arms will you take
my hands

Do you know me God

I cry out your name
Yet I hear no sound

Let me hear your angels
I need to hear them sing again
to feel your peace

Now I feel the wind of angel wings
as they brush my face

Is that you Mother
Did he send you today

Nicole J Melinski

WHEN DARKNESS FALLS

Here I am and there they be,
Away so far, yet here with me.
When darkness falls, they shall
awaken,
Saintly white, yet so forsaken.
Then a cold breeze blows; I know
they're near.
I try not to, but still I fear.
Now I know they're in my room,
With them, there's a sense of gloom
Next they make their guest
appearance,
Frightening me with
perserverance.
Small clouds of mist surround
each face,
Smooth as silk, fragile as lace.
The shadows lurk with these guant
shapes,
Who move as wind to chill our
napes.
Their fleshless fingers grasp for
new souls,
Beckoning me to join their rolls.
In every corner, under each bed,
"They" are the spirits of the dead.

Rose Daly

MY DAUGHTER, MY GRAND-DAUGHTER

In God's creation He chose to make
A child so sweet for a mother to
take.
She's very special in every way,
And brings joy to all, from day to
day.

A "one of a kind", just like no other,
And God chose me to be her
mother.
The years have passed; some tears
were shed,
But her sweet smile came out
ahead.

You, my daughter, are my
beautiful child,
A woman now, so meek, so mild.
Our roles have changed, and you
are now
The mother of a beautiful child.

I now am blessed with two sweet
girls,
A daughter, a grand-daughter, my
pearls.
My thanks to God I give each day
For honoring me in this special
way.

Lucile Luckey Marshall

YOUNG WIDOW

Future Fate,
an echo of the past,
whispers of
joys to come through
love and wisdom wed.

Present wind,
a gust of stygian gloom,
whips onto
paths to spread for
branch and life source graft.

Severed branch,
a gift of grafted fruit,
wells forth from
tree to bloom with
old and newer strain.

Louise L Zwart

WINTER'S OVER

To my Three Wonderful daughters and one son, Helen, Peggy, Mariann and Ray

---

Ice gone glimmering
No more Shimmering
Brooks are filling
With waters Chilling

Violets blooming
Dandelions grooming
Green grass painted
All yellow tainted

Song birds trilling
Joyously spilling
Into warm wonderful air
See! it's Spring everywhere

Bob Fox The Old Bluebird

HE IS JUST A LITTLE BOY

He stands at the plate,
with his heart pounding fast.
The bases are loaded,
the die has been cast.
Mom and Dad cannot help him,
he stands all alone.
A hit at this moment,
would send the team home.
The ball meets the plate,
he swings and he misses.
There's a groan from the crowd,
with some boos and some hisses.
A thoughtless voice cries,
strike out the bum.
Tears fill his eyes,
the game's no longer fun.
So open your heart and give him a
break,
For it's moments like this,
a man you can make.
Please keep this in mind,
when you hear someone forget.
He is just a little boy,
and not a man yet.

Michael E Reed

CHALLENGER

Dedicated to GOD, our FATHER who has shared his GRACE, LOVE, and INSPIRATION

No sunrise will they see,
tho they shine like the dawn.
No moonglow will they know,
tho their bodies are now gone.

No brisk breezes blowing
No spring fresh air
No cold winter snowing
Nor summer-time fare

They left on a mission of Glory and
Hope
Amidst personal danger where
most could not cope.
They showed us their Spirit, their
Bravery. . .no Fear
In everyone's prayers they'll always
be near.

We will have honor for the
Challenger crew
They are all very special—whom
everyone knew
From the "Teacher in Space" to a
Viet-Nam Vet.
From America's Black to
Hawaiis' Best Bet
From Heartland America and a
Jewish Princess
They honor us all with Bravery and
Finesse.

They'll live on forever in our hearts
and our minds
Their accomplishment will never
diminish with time.
All America mourns at the loss of
these Seven
Their life now eternal. . .with our
Maker in Heaven.

Rondi Pardue

MEMORIES ARE FUN, WHEN THEY'RE WITH THAT SPECIAL ONE

To Danny Scott, thank you for your encouragement, Love Rondi Pardue

---

The time will come, we know it's
true,
When our love together, will have
to be through,
But deep inside, there's a burning,
that you won't be able to hide

It's then that you will know, your
love for me is still alive.
It will start as a fond memory, that
only we have shared,
It's at that time you'll notice, how
much you really cared.
The chances that we've taken, the
things that we both dared,
They'll come back to you in
memory, the romance that we
shared.
Meanwhile in my home, life will
still go on,
I'll go about my business, although
I know your gone,
There will be a memory, inside that
lingers on,
Of the loving and the laughter, that
created this special bond.
The two of us in sequence,
remembering our love affair,
Of the passion that grew between
us, that only we two could dare.
One day we'll meet again, and the
twinkle will reappear,
It's at that time you'll know, how
much I really care . . .

Cynthia M Richards
ASPIRATIONS
To be able to write
As the great poets do,
Portraying great wisdom
With thoughts that would move
Mortals into action,
Satan into prayer,
I long to put on paper
What most would never dare.

To capture great insights
On ideas that confound,
To decifer mixed emotions,
Perhaps put into sound
The feelings, the desires,
The needs that drive us on
To heights of lofty grandeur
With visions so profound.

Will wisdom come in flashes
Or only through great pain?
Is life to be a desert
Hungering for the rain?
Waiting with great patience
I've yet to see the sun,
Desiring perfection
Before this life is done.

Francile Patterson
DREAMING
Sitting by my window
Looking through the glass,
Remembering When I was younger
Playing in the grass—
Running among the trees—
And listening to the Breeze!

Now, I can only sit and ponder
Of those who sadly say,
What can I do today?
For, if I had my way
I would play in the grass—
Run among the trees—
And listen to the Breeze!

Rita L Sweet
EUROPEAN HIGHLIGHTS
Just a note to let you know,
October twenty-second is the
date we go.
London, England is our first town,
I hope the bridges don't fall
down.
Paris, France is our next stop,
We'll think of you as the
champagne we pop.
After the Palace of Fontainbleau,
Geneva, Switzerland comes into
view.
The itinerary reads: Montreax,
Aosta and Milan, Italy;
I can hardly believe this is where
I will be.
On to the eternal city of Rome,
My thoughts and prayers to all
back home.
Journeying on to Florence and
Venice,
Gondoliers must have finesse!
Snow-capped Dolomites and
Innsbruck, Austria,
Are leading us on into Bavaria.
Now Munich, the Hofbrauhaus
and Beer!
My relatives and I will be full of
cheer.
Castles in Heidelberg, Rudesheim
on the Rhine,
This night before dinner, we'll be
tasting wine.
In Cologne we visit a Cathedral
magnificent,
We pause to praise God for the
time we've spent.
Amsterdam, Holland is our last
stay,
On November fifth, it's back to
the U.S. of A.

Henry (Hank) Robison
I WISH I HAD WHAT MY DOGGIES GOT
I wish I had what my doggies got,
He aint purty, but he sure is smart.
When I tell everyone he is mine,
I swear I hear him laugh
sometimes.

I dry him off when it rains or
snows,
Brush his coat and trim his toes.
The master here sure aint me,
Who waits on who is plain to see.

When I sit down with a snack to eat,

He sad-eyes me till he gets the
meat.
Then wags his tail and licks my
cheek,
He grows strong while I grow weak.

Each workday I'm up at five,
You wouldn't know he was alive.
Sata-day come and I wanna sleep
in,
There aint no way with a dog like
him.

To greet me nights when I get
home,
At the door his love is shown.
I wish I had what my doggies got,
He aint purty, but he sure is smart.

Steven M Wexler
THE CHOICE

To Deana, who liked it from the start.

A woman through her garden
strolled one night,
And started when she thought
she heard a sound.
She felt that something watched,
just out of sight,
But naught was there when
slowly she looked 'round.
The moon above the maiden lit
the sky
And she beneath a fragrant tree
sat down
When suddenly, a voice called
out, "Come nigh!"
A summons come from high
above the ground.
From on a branch above the
woman's head
A snake spoke; "I've a gift for you
today!
An apple that is good and sweet
and red!"
"My thanks, but no." She said,
and went away.
Oh what a different state we
might be in
If that was how the scene had
really been!

Pegi Marcotte
CAPE COD SUMMER BREEZES

Dedicated to my daughter, Julie, whose wonderful song entitled Cape Cod Summer Breezes, composed at age 11, inspired these words.

Cape Cod Summer Breezes
Whispered to the sand,
The secrets of
Those days of Love,
When we walked hand in hand.

Seagulls softly soaring,
Cotton clouds on high:
Each bobbing kite—
The sails so white,
Saw Love as they passed by.

Salty sunwarmed breezes
Heard your words of Love;
They danced with joy around
us—
The sun smiled from above.

Cape Cod Summer Breezes
Whispered to the sand,
The wonders of
A lasting Love—
A golden wedding band.

Lucy Brown
ONLY A MOTHER

For my children, Tim and Sally, who gave life to these words, and for my husband, Jerry, who "put up with" us all!

ONLY A MOTHER could face
childhood's messes:
Dirty faces; clothes streaked with
mud and stains;
Hands with a bushel of dirt under
their nails;
Teddy bears dragged through the
dust . . . and left on the stairs
standing on their heads;
Dollies with bare bodies, waiting
for some little mommy to dress
them;
Puzzle pieces and building blocks
left in corners and under chairs;
ONLY A MOTHER could face such
childhood's messes!

ONLY A MOTHER could face such
teen-ager messes:
Unmade beds and little curls of
dust beneath;
Clothes taken off sweaty bodies
and cast aside;
Dirty socks strewn here and there;
Lipstick and mascara smeared on
dresser tops;
Muddy gym shoes snuggled in the
corner;
Everywhere disarray, and . . . .
ONLY A MOTHER could face such
teen-ager messes!

ONLY A MOTHER could face an
empty nest:
No patter of little feet on the stairs;
No hugs and wet kisses on the
cheek;
No whispered cadence in the ear:
"Mommy, I love you".
No coming to ask advice from a
wiser head;
No young voice announcing,
"Mom, I'm home".
Gone are the excitements of
childhood and youth, and . . . .
ONLY A MOTHER could endure
an empty nest!

Rocco Scanelli
CLOUDS OF TIME
Can you see above the clouds?
It's something to behold
There peace and happiness abound
For those who choose to take the
time
Within yourself you'll find
Are the clouds of time.
You need only to take the time
To search and you will find,
In these times of strife
You need to stop and try.
Whenever you feel the need,
Just take the time to search your
soul
And you will see the peace and
happiness
Above the clouds of time.

Tram Nguyen
TEACHER MINE
Teacher, Teacher,
Do you see me
—up upon your high chair
Surrounded by a sea of faces
like a tempest tossed in storm?
Will you remember me, teacher
the black sheep amongst the fold
With my piercing incessant
laughter
and mocking tone.
Will I become nothing more—
than a memory too
Like facts, tossed away—
—left to be forgotten
molding in the grime.
Will you remember me, teacher
when skies are gray with tears
when storms adrift come roving
home
—on quiet seashore towns
when tears flow from another's
eyes?
And will you quiet his gentle sobs
with tender care
As you burst in lightening rage—
at my silly little antics?
looking back now, teacher mine,
I reminisce in you
Who taught me much by word
and deed
And loved me more than
words can say.

Annette Crosby
YESTERDAY & TOMORROW

"Yesterday" is a thing gone past—
A "day" spent,
Ended and cast.

Some small memory—
Tucked away in our mind.
Recalled of a "day"—
We left behind.
Brought a smile, to our face—
Or a tear to our eye,
Warmed our hearts—
Or made us cry.

"Tomorrow" is a day—
We all search to find.
Hoping to make "yesterday"—
Right in our mind.

Decisions—made.
Our lives—cast.
Yes,
"Yesterday" is a thing—
Of the past.

"God," set each day—
Each life, "He"—Cast!!!

Yes,
"Yesterday"
Is a thing of the past.

Bruce D Renken
EVER STRONGER

To Christine Michelle who taught me of Love, Life, and myself.

Every time I hold you,
I feel that I shall never love anyone more
Yet I never tell you this,
lest I be in lie
For I know that someday
I know that I will love someone more than I love you today.
That "Someone" will be you,
That "some-day" . . .
. . . Tomorrow

Joyce Guthrie Drakeley
MY FRIEND

My friend is like flowers that bloom in the spring,
She makes the sunshine instead of the rain.
My friend is the person I turn to in need,
She's also a person that does a good deed.
My friend is so helpful in so many ways;
Her phone calls, her letters, make happy-filled days.

My friend, as a person, knows me to the core,
She never once mentions that I am a bore.
My friend keeps my secrets steadfast and true,
She makes special moments that once were so few.
My friend, like good music, sings love in my heart,
She comforts, she soothes me, she's His work of art.

My friend's someone special that God only chose,
She's beauty, she's sweetness, like flowers of rose.
My friend has much wisdom so pleasant and whole,
She's one I can trust with my heart and my soul.
My friend brings the laughter when I'm feeling down,
Like tinsel and treelights that glisten a town.

My friend's moved away now, I see her no more,
Can she not come to visit and knock on my door?
Until that time comes when she's back in my sight,
I hope and I pray morning, day, noon, and night.
Happy Birthday Dear Friend, you are one of a kind,
I will never forget—You will not leave my mind.

Lois Rawls Delp
A VALENTINE TRIBUTE TO MY HUSBAND

Your name is "Ford", but that just doesn't do,
Because of the way I feel about you.
Some other name I've tried to find,
But none to suit you has come to my mind.

Ford sounds like a car, and that's really not bad,
Because a car, and you too, can just drive me mad.
My true feeling for you is a deep feeling of love,
And that you are so "special", like a "gift from above".

You're not like a father, and you're not like a mother,
You're not like a sister, and not like a brother,
You're not like a daughter and not like a son,
But whatever you're like, my heart you have won.

You're like a sweetheart, companion, help mate and lover,
A friend that I've learned to love like no other.
My life has been changed since you came along,
And all of my days are as sweet as a song.

Your smile lifts my spirits whenever I'm down,
And your loving ways are in no one else to be found.

Your presence keeps me going throughout all my days,
And my nights, with you close, I want to keep always.
Now, at last my dear husband I've a name in my mind,
It's simply my wonderful, sweet "Valentine".

Becky (Bearden) Courtney
SEARCHING FOR LOVE

This Poem is dedicated to Don who has been a great inspiration to me.

Look not for only beauty when you're searching for a love,
Look deeper for beauty of soul sent from God above.

Look for a happy person that appreciates the good,
That minimizes trials that come just like she said they would.

Look for someone who's not selfish, who will consider you,
Someone that will be deeply grateful for everything you do.

Look for a true compassionate love on which you can depend,
And have the faith that with your love, you'll always have a friend.

Rebecca Rodriguez
THE BIRTH OF A MIND

To Every member of "my family" and those "timeless" events of inspiration.

Visions of Purple
Lay Deep in the Horizon,
Past the world of dreams and space.
Unto you comes a beauty unknown,
A side within,
A timeless place,
FANTASY, . . . a reality.
Vaults of Knowledge in every cloud,
With populations of ideas sifting their way out,
To face each world alone.
Hoping when tested,
they may return triumphant,
To occupy this paradise called home.

Juanita (Nita) Joyce Avila
MY SPECIAL DAUGHTER

I've always felt the need to tell you,
so, I take this time, right now.
To say how much you're really loved, the reasons why, and how.

Those thoughtful and unselfish things, that you always say and do.
Make other people say, they envy me for having such a wonderful daughter as you.

Numerous friends, say they'd be so proud just to have you for their own.
But there's not enough money or silver that could buy (your weight in gold)

I know, I don't say it often enough, how your precious smile can brighten my day.
When, I'm feeling down and so depressed.
You'll bounce in with a card or just the right word to say.

I was young and seventeen, and I, would have never dreamed
that I'd be so greatly Blessed in the summer of "64"
When God nurtured the seed, and I gave birth to you,
you gave the word "Life" a whole new meaning, and made mine worth so much more!

Your my joy, my laughter, my encouragement, and my hope.
Your my compassionate "Special Daughter" worth more than
these words I wrote.

Don't change a thing about yourself, your ethics are all that matters.
Continue, being that special girl and your world will never shatter.

Katherine Rowland
LOVE YOU FOREVER

To my eight children

We grew up together, he and I; We laughed and
Loved, and climbed life mountain.
When we stumbled, we shared pull-up's
In harmony.
The minister said, "Till death you do part:"
Our vow being, —I will love you forever.
We became parents for eight, and taught
Them to be God's children.
Together we became senior citizens;
Now the minister's words have fulfilled.
But I am not alone, I fill my time
Being active; and hold tight to the
Memories and our vow, —I will love
You forever.

Ruth Conley Shahan
OKLAHOMA HILLS

My heart is homesick for the sight of
Oklahoma's lovely hills
For shady glens and flowery nooks
Blue water springs and tumbling
Rills, like Ruth of Bible times who
Stood in tears amid the alien corn
My tired eyes view these level
Lands and sigh for hills
Where I was born

Maxey D Little (Seminole)
VIET VET

The story of your life is part of history now
You spent your turn in hell to no man should you bow
From the trail of tears to the fields of rice
We hear of feats and deeds of men and learn of freedoms price
You were White Black Yellow and Red the life you changed you did not plan
The Vietnam battles changed you from a boy into a man
An undeclared war folks started to say
When it dragged on day after day
You came back from the battlefields you truly were the best
You came back from an Asian war medals on your chest
Your medals speak highly of your heroic deeds
A nation in distress you answered to their needs
It didn't seem to matter you fought for a lost cause

Freedom fighter that you are you didn't hesitate or pause
You came home to your family

and your loving wife
To face the nightmares and the memories a veteran's way of life
The tears that we cried would not equal the blood that was shed
By our brothers who were wounded both living and dead
Every vet has a story of the places he has seen
One vet was seasoned one was green one was old one only a teen
The many ways of saying death is as many way as dying
The challenge NOW is living—you
have to keep on trying
God bless America with all her mistakes
God bless the veteran it's AMERICA he makes.

Mable M Scott
LOVE IS

This poem is dedicated to unconditional universal love and the beings and creatures who share that love.

Love is a miracle, an energy, a force.
Love is a power, a oneness, wholeness.
Love is God, God's miracle, a rainbow, a waterfall.
Love is creation, a birth, all Gods children, the earth.
Love is a whisper, a shout, a feeling that needs to be let out.
Love is mystery, its truth, a caring and sharing.
Love is the moment, eternity, the dawning.
Love is the sunset, its touching and hugging and smiling.
Love is giving, receiving, its yesterday, its now.
Love is memories, its sad, its joy.
Love is forever, its you, its me, always together, it needs to be free.

Patsy A Garrett
MY TRANQUILIZER
When I'm angry, or hurt and feeling depressed,
I reach for my little dog to hold and caress.
Each little lick of his tiny warm tongue
Brings joy to my heart, the healing's begun.
Little by little the fury melts away,
His sweetness and innocence makes everything okay.
Our friendship is caring and mutual respect,
No need of a common English dialect.
I don't rely on the bottle, a pill, or a nap,
All I need is my little dog to sit on my lap.

Robert C Kern Jr
BALLERINA AND TOY SOLDIER
There she spins
My golden-haired ballerina
Dancing away
On an over-wound jewelry box.

Stop! Stop!
You spin to fast;
Your delicate spring
Will never last.

I watch her dance
With tin soldier after tin soldier,
And smile
At her happiness.

With my silken ballerina
I long to dance,
But I'm a tin soldier with one leg shorter
And seem to have no chance.

When I wind myself up for her,
I can only march in circles;
She sees and smiles,
But quickly turns away.

I'll never retreat,
And who knows one day
She'll stop mid-pirouette,
And never turn away.

Marlene Krigner Dzieglewicz
I SEE YOUR FACE

Dedicated in memory of my friend Rusty Messico

I see your face in the red ambers of the sunset sky.
Like a yellow jacket I search endlessly for a life of
sweetness and tenderness,
for bitterness is not my high !

I listen to the windy whispers coming from the wheatfield
where busy ants are hid.
I set my ear to earth's blanket to find if the earth itself
makes sounds,
smiling while remembering, how you once silly did !

My nostrils catch the sweet aroma of the old cedars
and through the new forming evening mist,
through staring eyes,
I see your face.

Shadows seem to encircle me for night is on it's way,
where once in it's clasp I'll lie awake in bed
to see your face again.

Why did you have to go my beloved ?
My life without you seems in vain,
You sleep in death,
I sleep not well,
I see your face and bitterness swells,
within this shell of mine.

Sunset skies, sweet buttercups
and nights sneaky-rolling mists,
cannot erase the face I see,
cannot erase the face I see. . . . .

Fred Westfield
LILAC'S IN THE SPRING
If I must go and you remain,
I ask of you this day—
To look beyond my leaving,
And wipe your tears away.
Please make your days forever bright,
And happy as can be.
And share the love with someone else
That you once shared with me.

The years we've spent together,
Have been such treasured things,
And when you want to remember
Bring me Lilacs in the Spring.

The things we've done,
The love we've shared,
The memories of the past,
Are treasured things to lock within,
For only they will last.
Things of earthly value,
Are only here we know,
A short, short time and then they're gone,
As the sun will melt the snow.

I bequeath to you these memories,
Of every little thing,
If you will grant me this small wish,
Bring me Lilacs in the Spring.

Please do not be lonely,
And it is my fervant prayer,
That your life will still be happy,
And that you'll always care,
Enough to still remember
When the robins start to sing,
You'll know once more, it's time again
Bring me "Lilacs in the Spring.

This fragile fragrant flower,
I've always loved you know,
So if in Spring you'll both be there,
It won't be so hard to go.
I'll be waiting for you Darling,
And when Heaven's bells do ring,
Please bring with you the "Lilacs,"
And we'll share them in the Spring.

Kathleen Nelson Ciekurzis
SELF DESTRUCTION

For Erika, Gretchen, Peter and Karina, my beautiful children, whose tender innocent love has given me the strength to endure.

Watching you for years
through so many tears.

So much you've lost
such a very high cost.

Searching for your space
to no avail just losing face.

When will this vicious circle end,
of promises broken, and you on the mend?

I think it's time you stop and see,
the one you're destroying most is me.

Robert M Strong
THE LITTLE ROSEWOOD CASE

In honor of my Mother, Clara Strong.

She's a dear and lovely lady,
And her face is still so fair.
As the silver of the moon-light,
is entangled in her hair.

As she sits and gazes fondly,
at the Little Rosewood Case.
That brings many happy memories,
and sunshine to her face.

The Little Rosewood Case,
what tokens does it hold.
An old Prom Dance Card, a fragil piece of Lace,
A faded Rose how old.

A Little Box so full of dreams,
each dream a souvenir.
It's all that's left of lost sunbeams,
and loved ones ever dear.

Oh little Lady you are right,
you think and dream of each delight.
And while the moon is in it's flight,
you whisper softly, Love Good Night.

Paula Kunath
RECALL OF ALCOHOL
The tall man walked into the bar
His first mistake he drove the car
As he sat upon the worn out stool
Thought to himself, boy I am kool
Never thinking setting outside, there
was the man ready to glide. As
he started off lights went on
Pull over buddy, my name is John, as
He stepped out, with a tear in his eye
This can't happen, I am too nice of a guy
Now that 18 months have passed, take my
Word, drive or drink it was his last
With all the time, that has passed
He's learned his lesson finally at last.

Lisa Maria Ferris Eno
BOUNDED

To my love and my dreamer. To my husband forever. I love you James. Forever and Always. Lisa

---

When you call I will run.
Through the pouring rain or the heated sun.
I will find you no matter where you go.
Where the trees subside or where the rivers flow.
The mountains would be like castles in the sand.
And I will run over them like grass on the land.
And the oceans would be like water in a glass—
That I would drink just to pass.
I will find you no matter where you roam.
I will always be there to bring you home.
But, if you should deny me and refuse to follow —
I would leave you—only to face my own sorrow.
But that could never happen to us you see.
Without the sun the earth could not be.
We will be together till we grow old.
Till our dying day, till our skin is cold.
Together, we are one.
Like the earth my dear, and her glowing sun.

Margaret Ann Rich
THE TREASURES IN A SALVAGE YARD
Along an old back country road
There sits a salvage yard
with junked cars parked all around;
And the man who owns it is a friend of mine—
His breed they are a special kind.

They don't see 'Junk' in these old cars
They only see them as treasure;
Like a pirate on a pirate ship—
Sees only gold and silver in measure.

Each auto part is worth a price
Be it starter or generator—
Each windshield, door handle or tire;

Every engine, each carborator—
Just name your need—he's got it someplace.
This junkyard curator.

There's Chevrolets and Cadillacs
Oldsmobiles, Ford Vans and Buicks.
A Chrysler or two and even an Edsel;
Some wrecked Sports cars, Pintos and Mavericks.

One man's junk is another man's treasure—
It's often been said before—
My junkman friend is "open for business"
And always has treasures galore!

Loretta M Catlett

AMERICA . . .MY COUNTRY

America, my country, Land of the brave and the free;
The "Mother of Exile," that beautiful lady welcomes thee.
Her torch held high, she beckons with an invitation;
To those of all ages, pioneers of this great nation.
We can realize our dreams no matter how hard we try;
Old Glory, the bald eagle, Oh! how graceful they fly.
It reminds me of our pilgrimage, struggle and strife;
It stands for our people, our land, our life.
America, we appreciate thee for we have something to compare;
No hunger, no depreviation, an abundance with which to share.
We enjoy our freedom and goals we achieve.
In God We Trust, in Him we believe.
Success is ever present in whatever we use;
Our achievements, our opportunities, are ours to choose.
We have the right to endure through trials and tribulations;
Enjoy the life of our making whatever the situation.
We can pilot our destiny in whatever we desire;
Advantages, advancements, our abilities to acquire.
America's a promise, our future at a glance.
To live, be free, to have the golden chance.
To everyone the right to work, be himself, and speak his mind;
To make his own image, and his vision to find.
Let us revive the spirit of the America we proudly share;
Equality, justice, democracy. . .freedom everywhere.

Jonatha D Cooke Sr

MY EYES

I dedicate my poem to Ms Barbara Bartley, Mrs. Sharon Cooke, and the blind because sometimes they see things I can't. I love you all.

When I want to see you I slowly close my eyes,
And think of all the beautiful things I have ever felt inside.
Then natural prints of you appear in colors bold and bright,
And I lay my head down slowly and my dreams just come out right.
Sometimes I dream the future; sometimes I see the past,
Sometimes I fear my only life is moving much too fast.
Will heaven really save those who have not made a change,
To die in hell and say oh well; we'll try it all again.
We all have dreams of fortunes in homes all paved in gold,
But in my life I often think of how I will grow old.
Your darkest hours come and go they leave a mark on you,
To warn you of the animals that make our world a zoo.
You may see many movies of how the end will come
But late at night the end comes close in places that bear no sun.
So live each day in happiness and make each dream come true
And thank our God in heaven, for beautiful people like you.

Tony Marteney

THE CHANGING OF OUR TIMES

The days have been cold and long, and the sun goes down early.
The air is cold and brisk, a feeling of snow, soon to blow.
The leaves have been gone for some time, leaving branches bare,
as though reaching to the sun for warmth.
The ground has already settled for the winter.
as have most of the life of animals have done.
The sky is clear, the stars are bright, the moon also shines.
The night is lit with light cold, sheltered days,
and the nights are upon us.
But, soon it will be spring and once again,
The joy will shine among us.
The trees are all out with leaves for our shade.
The grass and flowers are up in full bloom.
The air is very warm, as the sun is close by, now.
The children are happy, they have time to play, it's summer.
The water is warm enough to swim, a mild breeze to fly our kites.
The days are longer as the sun stays out, but 'twill soon be fall
The colors are grand, as Jack Frost nips the land.
The trees are beautiful as rainbows are, too.
The sun has grown cooler as the winds become so, too.
Soon, we'll look up at the trees, where the leaves are so few.
It's time to go in, as we do with a grin, just think and smile,
We can do it all over again, in a short while.

Bethani Michel Macquire

THE NEVERENDING TIME

Quickly, so quickly, time passes us by
Never looking anyone right in the eyes
And as we watch our lives pass on
With the new day, I give you this song . . .
Time come back and tell me once again
How it was when you were young and life would never end
Speak to me in my ear, tell me all those things
Sing to me those sweet, sweet songs, let the bells ring
Show me once again to live each and every day
Guiding me with your light every step of the way
Give to me that piece of life, known to us as time
Bring to me the love of life, a sweet, sweet rhyme
Show me once again to breathe, teach me
How to search for life eternally
And if by chance I lose my friend,
Time, I know you'll never end
If only I could make time stay
And live with me, never go away
So, with this song I want to give
A piece of time that always lives
And when I go away . . . forever
Time lives on in me . . . together

George P LaMarsh

CONSCIENCE

Mortals sing, dance;
Sunday hypocrisy;

Beyond the grave,
The eternal hangover.

Constance L Brazzale

YOU AND I

This is dedicated to Jon Ferrari, the one I long to be with, but find it greatly impossible.

I sit here with nothing to do,
So all day long, I think of you.
I pray to God I'll find a way,
To be in your arms again some day.
I think of all the times we've had,
Most are good, but some are bad.
Now to wipe me free of dust,
I have to do things that I must.
I know you will not understand,
But I need you to lend a hand.
If you help me to be free,
I'll know for once that you love me.
Our love is one that'll last forever.
I part you now, but leave you NEVER!

Ginnie Tuberg-Barsic

MY CHILD-WOMAN

Dry the tears from your eyes, my child-woman.
Behind you are the twisted ruins of many roads,
Ahead lies many yet untried, but waiting for you
To choose it's destiny.

Take my hand, hold on tight, I will be there too
If you should ever be in need of me.

Look around you and see the beauty of it all.
Don't try and wish your young life away, my love,
For one day, you too will look inside your mind
And say, what happened to my youth? Where did it go?
And When?

Kathryn L Roberts

THE RAIN

Since I was little I have loved the rain,
The gentle finger tapping touch of rain,
How sometimes streets are pebbled by the rain,
How I have seen sun filtered through the rain.
The wind once pushed against my face, a rain
Like sharp, staccato hoofs almost! The rain
In summer is a smooth and satin rain,
Or makes a bamboo screen for dawn. But rain
At night taps drumbeats on my wall. Cool rain
Soaks into hard cracked thirsty earth, for rain
Belts down like tiny mallets and yet rain
Makes everything grass-green, alive! The rain
May be as soft as baby hands, for rain
Is nature's miracle—life-giving rain.

Eugenia McWilliams Short

RUNNING SANDS

Swift on the wing is the Morning—
Borne on the surge of its power;
Bright with a zeal that's adorning;
Arching to noon and its hour.

High are the aims when attempting
Goals that in youth are a vision;
Each for a height is preempting—
Much is result of decision.

Pause when the sun's at its zenith—
Choice, a diminishing factor.
Harvest—how different we dreameth—
Bears its reward to each actor.

Strong is a trait sustaining—
Grace of the good and the gallant;
Work to success appertaining—
Waste not your time or your talent.

Scott M Dormady

DESTRUCTION

Through the clearing smoke
You have a sense of fear,
You realize what has happened
In your eye there forms a tear.
All you can remember
Is a lonely walk in the night,
Then a sudden burst
And a flashing brilliant light.
Through the total destruction
Your body feels no pain,
From the heavens come
A lightly falling rain.
You look around and realize
There is no one around,
The people have disappeared

All else burned to the ground.
The button has been pushed
You realize as you cry,
The present has been erased
No time to say goodbye.
On the ground there is a body
As you look into its face,
An empty feeling follows
Leaving only a barren space.
You recognize the body
As you turn its head,
You see the face as yours
You realize you are dead.

John L Thompson

LUNCH BOX DOG

This poem is dedicated to our dog Cindy.

When never too late for lunch and munch, handy dandy,
devoted to lunch boxes dog sat down.

With sad long face, big brown eyes, tick trailing
tail and flip flopping, flying a flea dog looked up.

I gave that don't bother me now brusin crusin doggone
dog a shot in the mouth. With a doughnut hole. It
never misses her devoted to devouring dinner doggie
face.

Ola Margaret James

AMERICAN SLUMBER SONG

To my son, John Edward Olinghouse

America is "one from the many"
And so, my son, I sing my song to you:

Go to sleep my English-German,
Go to sleep my Choctaw Indian,
Go to sleep my little Laddie,
Sleep, sweet sleep, my Irish-Rogue!

Slumber in this land of free men,
Dream, your face is like your Dad's;
Wake to find the sun all golden,
You're the finest of all lads!

Jackie Bridgewater

A STUDY IN DISCIPLINE—A CINQUAIN

Dedicated to Ruth and Gene Whitworth of Great Western University in San Francisco, California, who know what a Cinquain is, and what this one means.

I made
A bet with life
That I would never die.
Now, how do I come back and say
"I won."

Dorothy B Slovak

MEMORIES IN CRYSTAL

To Tyler, whose red rose enhances the beauty of my crystal gem.

Among the treasures of my memory shelf
Not one do I love so dearly
As my glistening crystal vase
Reflecting points of fire clearly.
I prize it as a souvenir of joy
Which concluded the pleasures and tears
Of teaching and sharing with our youth
For three times ten and seven years.
A gift presented when I said "Farewell"
Will remind me of what has been
And add to my future happiness
When I look beyond my crystal gem.

Cheri Zellner

THE SEA

To my Uncle Bill: Whom I loved dearly, and wished I had gotten to know him better. My memory of him will float in my mind forever.

The sea is an endless body of water that reaches forever into the horizon.
It has a gift of arousing up feelings never felt before.
It is a place of serenity and peace of mind.
It is also a place of turmoil.
Feelings can crash against the rocks along the
shore, or gently float across the wet sand and
float on forever.

I run along the shore; chasing the waves and running
with the water.
Loving each and every wave that gently runs over my feet.
The wet sand cushions my feet from feeling the outside world.

The sea is my own private world.
My place of thoughts and ideas.
And my special place to be with God.

Linda Young

THE GENTLE TOUCH OF MORNING

The sun comes up over the
crest to spread a new days
dawning.
The chirp of birds can be
heard as they tauntingly
chase each other around
the sky.
Flowers reopen their brimming
cups to get warmed in
the morning sun.
A little humming bird goes
to a porch on a hill where
he knows a sweet treat is
awaiting him.
The last of the mornings dew
begins to dry up causing a drop
to stray.
As it rolls down the petal of
a wild daisy the sun catches
it just right sending out a rainbow
shine of glory.

Thomas Deane Bellenir

GODS OF LOVE

"To Mary"

If I love you more tomorrow
Than I'm loving you today
It will be because I love you
In every way

And so I say to you
May the gods of love pray for you
And watch over you
Until we meet again

As the sun sets on the ocean
And our glass of wine is full
In my eyes you'll see the notion
That my love for you is real

And so I say to you
May the gods of love pray for you
And watch over you
Untill we meet again

Karl Van Bibber

Karl Van Bibber

FOR MY WIFE ON GEORGE'S DAY

Written on George Washington's birthday, and dedicated to Claire, my loving wife.

It's Sunday, my dear,
And Washington's birthday is here.
Want to feel a love song unfold?

Alone he knelt in bitter cold
And found the Power to break the hold

Of George's grip and tyranny's mold.

His reigny day was frayed and stayed
As one George prayed, the other nayed.
Yorktown rests two hundred years,
And we have stood throughout those years.

Hear the bells of freedom, dear?
By George, it's Sunday, my dear!

Darlene Maestre

CRYSTAL BLUE TEARS

Crystal blue tears on my pillow
If only you told me to wait.
I feel like a weeping willow,
But now it's too, too late.

Could you tell me that you were true?
It seemed that nothing else mattered.
'Cause I fell in love with you,
My life was shattered.

I was such a fool.
I always have known,
Even if I was a stubborn mule,
I couldn't have you for my own.

You spread your charm around,
Then you came back to me instead;
You still didn't want to be bound.
Crystal blue tears do I shed.

I overcame through the years,
With God's loving care.
Those crystal blue tears
Are no longer there.

Mrs Virgie V Jones

DREAMS

Images on the mind
What do you conjure for my dream tonight?
Will it be in black and white
or technicolor?
Of knights of yore
and maidens saved from dragons
Or a flight across the skies
Looking downward,—or veering off
into vast space
Pleasantries of a pastoral scene
with cattle and sheep grazing
And a couple picnicking
Childhood memories of school and friends
Frolics with merry dancing
Or nightmares of ghosts and goblins
and scary creatures
Or maybe that eerie sensation
of falling or running
And being chased and almost caught!
Time will tell,—as I prepare to slumber
What will I dream,—tonight?

Marjorie F Kammerer

IMPONDERABLES

With loving thoughts for my dear family, the Richard G. Kammerers, and the assurance that this is not autobiographical.

Alone in that narrow dark room
my back to the busy traffic just outside,
I ponder the three unanswered
questions of the ages.
I do not move. But my shadows
make a thousand of me against the wall
in the lights of passing cars.

Who am I?
Haunted—and hunted out in the
anonymous obscurity of night
only black silhouettes move.

Why am I here?
Shadowy action is a mockery
of taut shape unmoving.

Where am I going?
To ask this of stiff arrested form?
For other passing lights and
others and yet more
flick action against the still wall.

But it is not I who moves—not I, myself.
So why do there seem to be so many of me?
They will not stay still. And I do not know them

nor know
who I am
why I am here
or where I am going.

I do not know myself.

Evelyn M Legband
THAT LITTLE HOME OF MINE
My cottage is shabby and worn
But it seems that I love it all the more
It's so comfy and peaceful
It's so homelike and beautiful
Each morning early after opening
My pretty flowers seem to say
"Thank-you God, for this lovely day"
Then my birds sing a lullaby
It's so beautiful that I could sye
Oh I know I wouldn't
And I know I couldn't
I wouldn't trade that little home of mine for a million
Nor seven hundred or eighty trillion
I wouldn't trade that little home of mine
Down by the flowing river and the growing pine.

Michael D Sauda
BRUTAL ARDOUR

To RDK

Wave like forms crease in the darkness of a corner
Slowly and patiently, in perfect harmonic unison.
Stillness abounds as the surrounding darkness is the only mourner
Watching and holding passion's fateful ammunition.

Flowing together in tribute to one another
A pair of friends turned momentary lovers
Exchange lust and let carnal urges flutter
Each involved within themselves and no others.

Kathryn Whitehead
LIFE'S PURPOSE
Make life have meaning
Accept Jesus today
Life passes so quickly
Time fades away
Day's, month's, and year's
Part of age
Giving all to God
Means grace today
Peace, love, and joy
Having abundant life
Saying no to evil
Yes to Christ
Sheads strength for tomorrow
Lighting life's way
Led to his Spirit
Within the heart
Live for Christ in
The remaining day's
Witness to lost, about
Jesus's blessed cross
Gives life a purpose
Serving Jesus today

Elouise Cole Huffman
DESERTS OF MEXICO
The deserts of Mexico is not a place to be
Everywhere you go is more of what you see.

Poor ole cattle standing in the sun
No water to drink and too poor to run.

Windmills turning every now and then
Pulling up some water to store in a bin.

Jack Rabbits carry a pack on their back
No food to eat so they carry a snack.

Cactus in the field, sage and mesquite
No place to rest a weary travelers feet.

Tumbleweed rolling in the desert sand
No place for beast or even a man.

Only thing thats running is the train on the track
It goes to the Border and comes right back.

Mountains in the background, a sight you can't believe
A nice place to see and a good place to leave.

Ellen Hope Priddy
DIRTY DISHES
There they are stacked four feet high.
Dishes, glasses, pots and pans,
Silverware and coffee cups.
It's more than I can stand!

I think of all our progress as
In front of this sink I stand,
And find my luck is getting worse.
I've now got dishpan hands!

It gets so aggravating.
They'll get the best of me.
One more dish and I'll go mad.
My mind will up and flee!

But here, again, in front of the sink
I see the end in sight.
It will give but one short pause,
There'll be more later on tonight!

If I could, I would find a wishingwell
And ask for only two wishes.
I'd wish for nice, new paperplates,
And no more dirty dishes!!!!!!!!

Jeanne Beckett McMaster
THE LAST DAYS
Old ladies and gentlemen put away to die,
Uncomprehendable jargons of weeping and
babbling to those who pass by.
Wanting only a gentle touch or maybe a smile,
To make those lonely hours of emptiness
more worthwhile.
Picking, patting, pulling knarled rough fingers
in unkempt hair.
Masses of curled little bodies slumped in bed
or an old wheelchair.
Excretions and bare-bottoms are exposed
without chagrin,
They are robbed, starved, depleted of all
dignity within.
Hearts that shared and hearts that cared,
Are left alone to wither and die.
A desolate loneliness for the poor souls
with dreams unfulfilled or not possessed,
Surely, they must call upon their Lord to
take them Home to rest

Geraline Moeller Griffith
SINGER BOY
Say
Singer, boy—
Where did you get that voice?
You
Look so young,
So meek and mild
Until you sang, I would have smiled
And—
Passed you by,
Thought merely, here, this brown eyed lad
With smile so shy, just a little sad.
Then
Boy, you sang.
It was then I knew
That God had left that voice for you
To roll and raise, to ease and sooth
To make our small world glad.

Mabel B Nelson
LEONE'S GARDEN

For Leone Renn 1905-1987, In Loving Memory

"Pray make a poem for me," entreats Leone
Whose trowel in moist earth creates her own
Sweet ode to spring, to shame my ragged rhyme—
Unmatched beads strung on a fragile line.
My altar to the vanished Erato
Is manteled in gray dust; its feeble glow
Will lend no light, nor lure the Muse anew
To whisper hope of one more rendevous.

I bow before Leone's renascent shrine
Tranquility it's poetry sublime.
Here morning glory meets her god's embrace
Here purple pansy lifts her pixie face.
Rosebuds unroll to make a loving cup
Where hummingbirds and honeybees may sup.
When gentle showers quicken pregnant earth
Here is redeemed the promise of rebirth.

Tess Noprada
THAT'S MOTHER LOVE
For years and years she lives,
Working and working with pride,
Children's hugs and frolics,
Heavenly inspire indeed.
That's mother love.

Stillborn! Silence relayed;
With tearful eyes she grieves,
She sobs "O God, help me,"
Nothing more could be said.
That's mother love.

She lays her hands again,
Although that can feel no more,
Hopeless cries of sorrow fall,
On ears that can hear no more.
That's mother love.

She braves rough seas and winds,
Hidden dangers here and there,
With strong will she must see,
Her child in lands far away.
That's mother love.

She exults, she hopes,
She admires, she chides,
She consoles, she cares,
Immeasurable, all ways.
That's mother love.

Karen Dahlinger
A BRIEF ENCOUNTER

To my dad. For all his love and support and for making me pursue my dream.

Bright.
Bright is the light I wake to shining softly against your face on the pillow.
Loud.
Loud is the crashing of the waves that fall tumultuously against the shore.
You stir.
The curtains blow gently from the cool breeze drifting quietly into the room.

It whispers it's good morning and is then gone.
A seagull perches on the window sill.
I stare solemnly at him.
He turns to me and stares back.
We gaze for but a moment into each others eyes.
Then; he is gone.

Shannon Wadsworth
TO SEARCH INSIDE

I would like to dedicate this poem to my family and friends that encourages me to strive for what I believe in. Also to all the poets that have enlightened me and inspired me.

Many a day,
I have searched inside my soul;

For the knowledge of growing.

For the knowledge to know.

I have learned many things,

Since the day of my birth.
Many things have aided in my search.

A search that has taken me deep in my soul.

For the knowledge of growing.

For the knowledge to know.

Linda L Dinse
MOONLIGHT'S MEMORY

For the sun, the moon, the planets, and all other luminaries of the nighttime sky

---

The moon lay golden in the sky,
The night deep midnight blue,
And placed its head upon a cloud
With sleepy thoughts of hue.

Inanimate, suspended there,
And yet if it could see,
A light reflected in its task
Sends memories to me.

Lois Mitchell Caporale
YESTERDAY
I saw an old dead tree
Lying there beside the sea
Lined with barnacles old and grey
Soaked through for many a day
Washing back and forth in the foam
Old tree how far did you roam
Where are your roots your place
What has happened to your leave
Your face
Many a song you could sing
If it was again your spring

Charles F Boyns

Charles F Boyns
AN ODE TO K-K
Just a note to say "Thanks, Pal"
you really are my type of gal.
I knew nobody on this tour
You changed that—that's for sure!

Little old retiring me
skeptical of most women I see;
not ready yet for a real commitment,
but with a heart full of sentiment.

If I were to consult an analyst
he'd say you were the catalyst
That formed our congenial group
a friendly, happy, congenial troop.

I'll call you when I settle down
and hope it will not draw a frown
we can do the whole darn town
including spots of great renown.

You are adjusting to life alone
with friends, clubs, and a telephone.

It would be selfish of me
to indulge my fantasy.

Cameron Noonan
FEASTLESS!
My new culinary attitude and kitchen expertise
Would be disgustingly abhored by one who loves to feast.
No more stuffed pork chop, braised chicken here,
Or sumptuously beef-laden stews, I fear!

The day is now vanished when I may boast
Tempting rack of lamb or pot of roast.
It's pastas, salads, breads slathered with jam.
He's self-proclaimed vegetarian!

Mary Schorr Munding
YOU'RE A PART OF ME

To Chris, my dear husband, because "You're A Part Of Me"

You're my vision, my laughter, my joy and my pain,
You show me sunshine, when all I see is rain.
While blue skies hang above, I know I have your love,
and I'll carry it with me till my dying day.

Like a heart on a chain, that's been broken in two,
There's no heart at all, if the other half is not you.
For your love was my answer, your love is my way,
Your love is my reason for living every day.

You're a part of me, my better half for the world to see,
You touched my soul, you're the life I breathe,
Because my Darling, you're a part of me.

James Patrick
18-2
ice-flower
snow-flower
creak forth the hue
of your red red stamens
freeze whom you touch
as you grow in your field
engender their deaths
with the brush of your
grain pollen
ice-flower, snow-flower.

Tina Barton
SWEET MEMORIES
From the outside you seemed happy, though your eyes showed a
sadness I didn't understand
You had everything a man could ask for in the palm of your hand
If only you could have seen the carousel that I was on
One minute grateful for you, the next you were gone
Too late I realized your lifestyle was taking its toll
You only had half a lifetime when you should've had a whole
Not able to go out in public by day, did you feel like a
prisoner in jail
Who had all the money in the world but couldn't post your bail?
With a lump in my throat and tears in my eyes
On that dreadful August day, I said my goodbyes
I have your music, memoirs and a scrapbook that doesn't have an
empty page
But what I'll remember always is when I saw you on the stage
I have a lot of memories, but that night I was proud
Every seat in the Arena full, and I was one of the "sell out" crowd
You were so magnetic, I was drawn to you
The attraction was so strong, others followed, too
Though only nine rows back, I couldn't stay in my seat
I moved around to get closer, but security guards met me with defeat
I want the world to know you'll always be in my heart
That I felt the way I do right from the very start
I also have within me a part of your soul
For you are the one and only Elvis, King of Rock 'N' Roll

Robert Carmen Angle
A SONNET FOR EDDIE-LOU COLE, POETRY EDITOR
A picture's worth a thousand poet's words:
Indeed, it's what he has to view with light
Until with closer glance (like playful birds)
His spirit starts to dance and gain insight:
The eighty years cannot your beauty take;
Nor, can the photo really make it clear;
Yet, wonderful his thirst it is to slake
And bring him joy with loveliness so dear.
It is your smile, your warmth, your tenderness;
It is your eyes so bright and meant to care.
It is your countenance complete (he'ven bless);
It is your heart and spirit visioned where
Your treasure lies—the secret door within—
Where love encounters Love, this prize to win.

Laura J Meschwitz
WHEN YOU'RE ALONE. . .
When you're alone
Think of me
And how we
Dreamed of eternity
Making plans
For us to share
What's wrong now
Is I'm not there
To be with you
Would mean the world
To know again
That I'm your girl
To feel the love
We had between us
And with the love
To feel the trust
That feeling I know
Is still There
I know in my heart
That you still care

So when you're alone
Think of me
And how our love
Was meant to be.

Wanda Forrester
ENDLESS DREAM

This is for you Don, my only love, my dream come true.

In a dream you came to me,
Haunting my every thought;
You repeated yourself almost every night,
With no escape—I seemed to be caught.

Your face alone I could never see,
The darkness kept you from sight;
I searched every mans face I met,
Hoping to end those endless nights.

Then one day unlike in my dreams,
Your face no longer concealed;
I'll see you as my only love,
Your love too will be revealed.

Then like it came, it will also end,
I'll have my dream no more;
For you'll be before me, and in my arms,
My dream come true, the man I've waited for.

Monroe Gibbs
WALK OF DEATH

To all my Friends & Foes

In the Road, I walk slowly
In the Woods, I walk slowly
Anywhere I go, I walk slowly
My eyes burning, as they water
From anger
My Body is tense, I can't hold back
My anger shall be the Death of me
Living a life of turmoil I Anguish
My road is long, it doesn't end
Even when I'm dead, I will still
Walk, The Walk of Death.

Kimberly D Hensarling
WHAT A MOTHER IS

Dedicated to my Mother, Mrs. Evelyn McVay, on Mothers' Day of 1986.

A mother is one who is gentle, kind, and true.
A mother is someone who does things just for the two of you.
A mother is one who tucks you into bed, and says, "Now lay
down, you darling sleepy head."
A mother is someone who tries to fulfill all your dreams.
A mother is one who can mend all things, such as broken hearts
and any other thing.
A mother is one who says it will be alright, and you wonder
just what she means on down through life.
A mother makes your life worthwhile, your happiness complete.
A mother always has a smile for every friend she meets.
A mother is one who makes you feel so glad to be a daughter
for all these years.
But most of all, a mother is someone special, as you are,
Mother, Dear.

Robbie Steed Laliberte
FRIENDS GO ON LIVING

This is for R. Todd Morsilli and Mark Gardiner Hoyle, both of whom I never met, but who taught me about life and death; for Eric Anderson Toth who taught me how to care, and for Steve for being there.

Friends go on living if you hold them close
and never let them die. The senseless waste
of his life doesn't deserve your tears, my brother.
They only make it worse.

He will go on living. His life will not end.
His death will be a sadness and leave
a vacuum in your life; but mourn him now,
and then go on living. He will live in your heart
for evermore.

You came to me, crying in the night,
looking for something I could not give.
I could only comfort you so much,
holding you tight 'til your tears were dry.

You ask me if he's safe and why he had to die.
But I can't answer your questions; I don't know why.
He is safe, though. He will never be cold, or go hungry,
or be frightened and alone in the dark.

He will wait for you 'til your time has ended;
but for now, cry your silent tears on my shoulder and
I'll hold you as best I can through the endless nights
'til you're ready to go on living.

Chris "Sheep" Hepburn
IN OVER MY HEAD

To the Suburban Youth, whose dreams hold the hope of Tomorrow . . .

Like a drowning man
I struggle to the surface,
only to be pulled down
once again.
Pulled down by the stupidity
and carelessness
that rule my life.
I must try
to reach the shore,
for I know it
it is there.
I saw it
for but one moment,
before the waves came
crashing in.
Within that moment,
I knew hope.
I also knew I must not give up,
or, like a drowning man,
without hope,
I will surely
DIE.

Kimberly Anne White
REALITY

To my mother, whom without I could not have been given this great honor, Thanx.

There once was a place called Reality
a place for you and me
It seems to be a formality
as you may clearly see
The people there are always cold
it really is a fright
To live out there you need to be bold
and lock your doors at night
From the horror of your minds eye
it may not seem so bad
but when you hear the distant cry
you know that you've been had

Virginia C Langham
SHOULD WE HIDE
If the world stopped would our heart,
could we say; I've done my part, to make
life richer for one another—or life's pleasures did we smother?

Would life's curtain hang unopen, by
words of kindness that went unspoken;
or could we say—world look inside!
swing life's curtain open wide! to reveal our tasks, or "Should we Hide?

"Tear-drop Rob" aka R. W. Sehi

"Tear-drop Rob" aka R.W. Sehi
NATURE AS MY CONSCIOUS
The trees around about seem to be speaking to me,
softly whispering words by the rustling of their leaves.
Across the blue ocean sky clouds float high overhead,
seemingly to spell out words that long ago I should have said.
The sun's warmth beams down upon its rays,
reminding me of warm memories expressed in so many ways.
The birds seem to be singing just to me a special song,
words that tell me for not speaking my heart I have done wrong.
As the flowers open to the sun's rays they make it most clear,
one cannot experience living and loving if one doesn't remove fear.
The wind seems to be the strongest and most dogmatic speaker of all,
that which brings great joy today may not be there at the next call.
So after all of nature has so emphatically stated what I must do,
the contents of my heart must now be expressed by the words "I love you."

Jean Murray Driscoll
MORNING

To my husband, John, with love

Staring into the dark green
valley of near night
I am surrounded by
whispers, patterns of wind
caressing me into sleep

I travel an imaged land
empty and not aware of you
straining to the light
which is elusive
and possible

Shattered by sleep
hunted by a dream
to the edge of life
where comfort eludes
a desperate grasp

I wish for morning
when the sun will break
this dark in two
lifting me to the dawn
closer to you

Anita "Pete" Bennett
JESSICA AND THE LOVESICK MOOSE
There was a moose from Canada,
Bullwinkle was his name,
His life was very boring there,
So he trudged to Vermont to gain his fame.

He stopped in a farmer's barnyard,
And much to his delight,
He finally found the love of his life,
And he stayed with her, day and night.

Now the cow's name was Jessica,
No truer love could be found,
People came from miles away,
To watch the love that knew no bounds.

Now it appears, after 76 days,
That Bullwinkle has gone back to the wild,
And Jessica pines for her lovesick moose,
Like a mother pines for her child.

I for one, am going to miss,
This love story that never could be,
About the lovesick moose and the hereford cow,
And a love that made history.

I hope someday he will return,
To the land and the love that he met,
But if he never returns to Vermont again,
It is something we will never forget.

De Witt Hastings Thompson
PICNICS
Oh, a picnic is unequaled as a source of sheer delight,
With baskets all heaped high with food to whet your appetite,
With homemade pies and cakes, and pickles, jams and jell,
Fried chicken and baked beans to hold you in their spell.

The smell of coffee brewing o're an open fire
And the smell of wood smoke to heighten your desire,
'Til for the, "Come and get it" call you scarce can wait
To sit right down and start a heapin' up your plate.

It makes no difference if you are slim or stout
For diet is one thing you will sure forget about.
It looks so good and tastes so good you simply can't resist
As "Oh, have some more, please do!" someone will insist.

"Oh, I want some of this, and give me some of that!"
Why worry 'bout that diet, to keep from getting fat?
For there's nothing that will ever quite compare
With a picnic in the woodland, out in the open air.

Denise I Spevack
SPRING IS COMING
The birds are singing,
Church bells ringing,
Spring is coming, it's everywhere.
It's in the flowers,
April showers,
Spring is coming, it's everywhere.
The cattle are lowing,
While farmers are sowing,
Spring is coming, it's everywhere.
The ponies are dancing,
While horses are prancing,
Spring is coming, it's everywhere.
The clouds are floating,
The youths are boating,
Spring is coming, it's everywhere.
Children are sleeping,
While mothers are cleaning,
Spring is coming, it's everywhere.
The sun is shining,
Nights reclining,
Spring is coming, it's everywhere

Thomas P Myers
S.A.
A piece of onion,
dropped in the perfect circle
his mouth made, snoring
would get a cane slap at the head,
quick as hell.

He complained when the women cleaned his rooms,
Lysol reminded him of a brothel.

They put his Buick on blocks
after the traffic light was installed.

On his rocker arm,
crimes forgiven, arm around,
the stories of bears gutting hunters
were favorites, but the one about
the fancy house in Denver
was true.

Sandra Burd Paul-Lee II
A MEMORY AND THE TRUTH

*This is to that "nite" in "60", whom & what this is
about, love you Paul McCartney, John Lennon,
George H., Chuck, Jerry & Michelle.*

We sat in a smoke filled room and filled our pipes up high

and then, only then, did we start to
make music. John,
Paul, George, Charles, and I.
I had to yell a time or two, I even
started to scream, for
my fellow brother's wanted only to
toke and me I wanted to
sing.
We argued, we shouted, John gave
this girl a drink, then we
got down to making music, we
finished what first we spoke.
The little girl got loaded, the little
girl got tight, she
wanted to go swimmin', John said,
"Little girl that ain't
right," then her mind, oh so much
older, the love she had
made her bolder, and skinny
dippin' she would go and lovin'
was her goal.
But it all quickly ended, for a man
with a gun said "Oh!",
the little gal looked up and
screamed, "Oh God, No!" and the
man with the gun that night almost
took a soul.
Blood ran bright and blood ran
cold, but thanks to loving
laughter, friends with love, the
little gal's still singin',
she's giving it her all. For it had
taken only months to
heal her body, but twenty years to
heal her soul.

Mona Beck
LOVE

Pain—
Such overwhelming pain.
The unbearable strain,
The anguish I am feeling.
The fear.

It's over.
It's gone.
I hear a cry,
My precious child is born.

Overwhelming JOY.
This is LOVE!

Joan Dahlby
TO LISA

They say grandma's old now and
so "worldly wise,"
But oh for a moment to see
through your eyes.
Does the sky seem as blue does a
star shine as bright,
Does a little girl smile at this
heavenly sight?
Do you still see the love on the face
of a pup
When you've shared with him milk
from your most
favorite cup?
Do the blossoms on trees and a
robin's red breast
Announce early spring and put
winter to rest?
When a rainbow appears do the
colors all blend.
Have you ever seen a gold pot at
the end?
Is your head full of dreams with
the hope to succeed?
Are you ready to challenge the way
they may lead?
Can you look to the future? It's
waiting for you.
Be happy but giving in what you
must do.
Remember to strive and work hard
to excel.
For whatever's worth doing is
worth doing well.

Marcia Miller Fray
HEARTBEAT

This poem is dedicated to my Husband, Son and Daughter.

In the silence of the night, a heart
beats.
Rhythm steady, calm, and then—
A pounding, almost jungle beat,
breaking
the stillness, crying out listen!!
Hear me! Know the feeling deep
inside.
Listen world!! Know the love this
heart
holds for those so dear to me
This heart, so small, is
overflowing.
It weeps, can't tell how much it
cares.
Can't let loved ones know, can't
protect
and guide, give happiness, wealth
and fame.
Give the best of a lifetime, to
those so dear
This heart cries out, I've tried, I've
tried
There are no words, this heart is
breaking.
It leaves to each a little part, with
only
love—over flowing.

Sarah L Kelly
A TRUE MAN

This man is not a common man,
for he has a tender heart.
It's not his height that makes him
tall,
but the towering love within his
heart.
It's not his physical strength that
makes him strong,
but his ability to form
supporting columns of love for
others.

He lives in a castle,
where he rules his kingdom.
The drawbridge is often down,
to welcome others to his
kingdom of love.
When the drawbridge is lifted,
it's to protect those who live
within.

His coat of armor is of golden
thread,
finely woven from love and
respect.
He knows love and respect well,
for that all he lives.
He knows hate and greed,
choosing not to make them
friends.
He's wise enough to know hate and
greed will keep a person
imprisoned.
He's wise enough to know love and
respect will lead others
through all chambers of his
loving soul.

In life he's had to fight many
battles.
The battle of life, the battle of
country,
and the battle of feelings,
surviving them all with a learned
victory.

Never does he criticize others.
He's often too critical of himself,
but forever managing to stay
self-composed.
He's been hurt many times
when offering and giving
confident love.
He's cried many tears.
Pain only strengthened and
intensified
his preponderant importance
for love.

He's a giving man
who rarely has thoughts of
selfishness.
He has a gift for deeply caring
and a great love for mutual
sharing.
Most men hide their feelings
and love to be men of society.
He shares his feelings and love
to be a man in the TRUEST
NATURE.

Josie Funderburk
GOOD MORNING

This poem is dedicated to Jack, my wonderful husband, in appreciation for his love and support.

My heart is filled with gladness,
As I begin this day;
There's no room for sadness,
For I'm happy today.

The man I love lay by my side,
When I first opened my eyes,
And I can say with pride
He's better than the grandest prize.

My baby girl was snuggled against
my chest,
So cuddly soft and sweet;
Hardly awake she sucked my
breast,
And kicked her little feet.

I fixed some breakfast for my man,
And helped him on his way;
I like to help him all I can,
For he works so we can play.

The older children went off to
school,
They're surely some of the best.
They cause no trouble as a rule,
With children we've been blessed.

I guess my husband shields me
from the world,
I've nothing to worry about.
I just take care of our little girl,
And know everything will work out.

Jerry G Elmore
TRIBUTE TO CHALLENGER

This poem is dedicated to all of America's Astronauts

I got up one morn after a cold
winters night
I wanted to see a wonderful flight
The air was cold but the sky was
blue
Many people were watching for a
dream to come true
The Shuttle was standing on the
pad ready to go
Seven people inside hoping for a
good show
Years and years of hard work and
study
Mothers and fathers, good friends
and buddies
I watched as the countdown
continued and time went by
This bird was nearly ready to fly
Challenger rose from the Earth
into the sky
We cheered and cheered as she
started to fly
The mighty engines roared as the
world could see
Only in America could this be
Challenger climbed several miles
high
The people watching let out a
terrible sigh
Then came the moment we would
never forget
We stood there watching in a cold
sweat
There was a explosion and
blinding light
As we all know it ended the flight
It is over now for the Challenger
and crew
We will never forget the day that
you flew
Our hearts are with your families
and friends
Our nation is greatful and hope the
wound mends
Now and forever as the Shuttle's go
high
God bless you all whenever you fly

Marcus Boney

Marcus Boney
YOUR BEAUTY . . . YOUR LOVE

Angie, your beauty, as your name
implies
Is vast and endless, like the midnite
skies
And it reflects, as the moon, with
mirrored eyes
Upon my empty soul.

The stars show a beauty of all their
own
But Angie, you're more beautiful
than any I've known
And you're the reason these
feelings have grown
And filled my empty soul.

These feelings I have collected
inside
But they show no trace, because
I've learned to hide
These feelings that come from
deep inside
So they sit in my empty soul.

But a certain love, a love for you
Causes those feelings to shine right
through
The imaginary wall between me
and you
But still my soul is blue.

How I ache when my soul will
yearn
Because it longs for a love in return
And it longs for a beauty that will
not burn
And that beauty . . . that love, is you.

Alexis Harris
CHANGE OF HEART

A Heart.
Frozen in silence and isolation,
Made hard and cold through the years
So no one could touch it
or care for it,
Lay barren . . . empty . . . useless . . .

Same heart,
Thawed and stirred to be reached,
Made soft and warm at a moment in time
By His love,
Now able to be touched and cared for,
Is becoming fertile . . . full . . . useful . . .

Raymond P Conti
THE LIE

Once I loved a lie . . . deep and still,
Hung over with shattered dreams and fruitless quests.

It bears the images of formless faces,
Dark foreboding encounters.
It parades before my eyes the demons which men call
Delusion, despair and shame.
All the cold shallowness of a hollowed soul.

This is my lie, the murder of all that is new.
The sacrilege of all that is past and once held holy.

My lie stands before me now . . . large, dark and cold.
A rampart prepared to repulse any dream,
To smother any flicker of hope with a ruthless malignancy.
Until I myself become the lie,
Giving it wings . . . mobility.

My lie stands before me now . . .
And I know not how to pass.

Carolyn S Wilson
THE COMING OF SPRING

Comes the morning bright and new,
Colors of Spring bursting through.

As the Earth breaths a sigh.
Empty limbs come alive.
Drifts of fluffy mounds of snow
Are pushed aside by Nature's glow.
Shades of yellow, pink, and greens,
Through the Winter's snow now spring.

Shades of green color the trees.
Birds of song the Winter frees.

Nature wakes her sleepy head,
And whispers softly what is said,
"Come alive, begin to flow,
Frozen brooks and streams so cold.
Bring to life the frozen ground,
Refresh us with your babbling sound."

Furry creatures far and wide
Nestled warm from Winter skies,
Scurry out to see the Spring,
The gift of colors the warm sun brings.

God sends to us the beauty of Spring,
To show us His Love, to let our hearts sing.
The colors of Spring from His rainbow they came,
To show us there's Life and Beauty to claim.

Viola Weltz-McMinimy
SHE'S NEARLY—5

This poem is dedicated to my two grand-daughters: Terrie McMinimy and Alison Bowling

---

A little burst of energy just dashed in through the door;
She carries all her haughty pride just three feet from the floor. She laughs out loud and with a bound she tosses kisses all around;
The room is filled with happy sound . . . and more!

She reaches up and grabs at an imaginary bird,
And from her lips there comes the strangest whistle ever heard.
She holds her open hand aloft; she sees that bird so sweet and soft,
Then with a wave to me, she's off . . . to spread the word!

I have no faintest notion what all tomorrows bring;
To see the lashes on her cheek, are like and angels' wing.
She looks at me as if to say: "I'll let you in My world, today;
m-m-H-M-M! As Mommies, your're O.K. . . . and everything!"

There goes my heart, she's nearly—5; the happiest little girl alive.
If that's her dream, I'll surely strive to be the BEST I can!
If I could hold both TIME and SPACE, and all the HEAVEN in this place,
Then . . . just to see her smiling face . . . the BEST is what I am!

Rachel Lynne Rhome
TRAGEDY IN THE SKY

In Memory of the space shuttle "Challenger" crew

The times we've cried; the times we've cheered—
All of this in just one year.

But the astronauts started a journey not found
All on their way, destiny bound.

They were excited, but still had fears—
Family and friends, in smiles and tears.

The take-off was perfect! Things seemed alright!
But within moments the world viewed a horrible sight!

An explosion of fire, orange and red,
Left watchers stunned with panic and dread.

We kept up hope, as the hours went by;
Soon the question arose—why did they die?

Five men and two women, filled with courage and valor,
Met their death at that untimely hour.

The journey they started, with fate unknown,
Has carried their souls eternally home.

William G Laing
EQUANIMITY

This poem is dedicated to N.A., my Higher Power.

As the tranquility of the sunset allows the tide to caress the surface of the earth
The serenity of faith allows the mind
to be cleansed and replenished.

Arlene Wagner
HE AND I

I started dating in my teens

Soon I met the man of my dreams
We married in 1943
And started planning our family.

We had only two of our own
But many called our place home.
We loved each and every one
Every daughter, every son.

Now our children have all grown
They have families of their own.
We get together now and then
And talk for hours without end.
We talk of the past and things to come
These times are enjoyed by everyone.

I now must face these things alone
Cause my husband was called to his final home.
Someday I'll join him up above

In the home of eternal love.

Jeanette Todd
THEY TOUCHED THE FACE OF GOD

Written in honor of the seven astronauts, Michael Smith, Dick Scobee, Ronald McNair, Ellison Onizuka, Gregory Jarvis, Judith Resnik & Christa McAuliffe, who were killed in the disaster aboard space shuttle, CHALLENGER.

The Fearless Seven, some would say,
To leave this place called Earth.
To soar toward the moon and stars,
Away from their land of birth.

Brave and Strong their spirit stands,
Like the ship upon the wind;
For those who make our country great,
The story never ends.

Their lives live on for us to view,
As a pattern upon a screen,
We'll feel and know the things they taught,
We too, will hope and dream.

We'll dream the dreams and dare to do,
Our part to keep alive,
The trust they had in our great land,
As willingly, they died.

They had no fear that death was near,
When they left this earthly sod,
They did not know they'd n'er return,
For soon they'd Touch the Face of God.

Stephanie Streeter
THE ATTIC

I slept in the attic just up the stairs,
You wouldn't believe what I saw there,
Spider webs long and tall,
Two ghouls were having a ball,
Cobwebs deep 'n' thick,
I smelled the air and I got sick,
A mouse named Laremy,
A rat named Jeremy,
A bat called Jon,
A spider that conned,
A floor that creaked,
A frog that leaped,
A snake that sneaked,
A girl that sweeped,
A boy that weeped,
A horn that beeped,
But the very worst of all
Was a great, big giant ball,
It would not bounce, it would not fall,
I really did dread that ball!

Sherin J Roe
THE LIGHT

This poem is dedicated to "My Pop", Harry W. Booth, who passed away January 26, 1986

Once I was a sinner,
I lied and cheated too.
I did all the evil things,
That God said not to do.
I walked down the Devils' street,
And danced to Satans' tune.
Then one day I found God,
And not at all too soon.
I told Him I was sorry,
I asked Him to forgive.
And on the day I spoke to Him,
I began to live.
Before, I lived in darkness,
Now I see the sun.
Before, I fought a battle,
I never could've won.
Now He stands beside me,
To help me if I fall.
For His loving kindness,
To Him, I'll give my all.

Chrys Melcher
MESOZOIC

I've never gone to the places I want to go
so at night I must content myself
with letting my feet walk on alone without me.
At night my feet walk to the places my eyes wish they had seen
and slowly I die: I fade: I become a part of the earth.
My metal bones lie embedded in sleep
but my footsteps tread the ground
detached from my body. My footprints trace two million
years in the earth's blank clay
dinosaur feet at the threshold of day
brush over me, brush past me —
centuries are tiny pieces of seconds.
Fossils of my bretheren shrouded in their weary grave
I begin burning at the edges, softly fading, squeezing what
life I have out between the cracks in the rock.
At night I lie suspended, dreaming, until
the sun spreads living fingers

across the dead sky
and my feet (my hooves)
disintegrate to dust, to nothing.
I reach out
in vain
to embrace the darkness.

Barry Stambaugh
HIS STORY
Divine, the feeling the boy was anew
and groomed in a tempered space
Alive for the moment he struggled to One
and embraced for a moment's journey
a subconscious Tale, whispered in dreams
acted in dance of the Natives
He was American Indian new
his dance was the Joy of existence
beleaguered by many, sustained by few
he flew beyond sight of his dreams
Imagined a Universe
dancing in Love
betraying the secrets if Is
When would the tide turn
he wrestled his page
but he just could not harness the magic
A man came along said you're tryin' too hard
the Cosmos depends on your Eyes
they laughed til they cried
these Comrades of Old
of long and forgotten Adventures
Ahead the dreaming again would be theirs
the past, a glance in the Mirror
Earth was not the beginning then
and this is not the end

Kirsten Catrina Ashley

Kirsten Catrina Ashley
LOVE FOREVER

To Daniel, With all my love. . . forever.

Can't you see how much I care?
Don't you know it's real?
Don't you know you have all my love
despite what you now may feel?

Why must you reject
a love that could be so fine —
a love that could last forever —
a love that's yours and mine?

I know that you've been hurt
and may never be the same,
but I'll try to make you happy
and pray not to give you pain.

Someday things may change
and you"ll want to give love and care —
and if it's me you want, just close your eyes,
think real hard,
and soon I will be there.

Tina J Withers
HEALING TOUCH
Hear me Lord
as I cry unto you.
Help me Lord
as I wait patiently
For Your healing Lord
of my broken heart—
My spirit's been crushed
and a wall's going up,
I pray for Your touch to break the wall down,
Heal me Lord.
Oh, Father the wound goes deep down inside
Can anyone really feel the tears that I've cried?
Only You—for You were broke too.
You gave up Your Son so I could be new,
You know what it's like to have deep pain too,
Thankyou Lord . . .
For a new heart within.
A brand new start with each coming day,
The pain is subsiding cause You heal it away,
Thankyou Lord.
My prayer is for others to find You,
The new heart You give is for them too.
Help me to tell others that their life can be new,
Because of You.

Rachel Cuppy Sykes
SAYING THE LAST GOOD-BYE
Whenever a life's balance
hangs on the edge of a prayer,
Remember that the Savior
said He would always be there.

Our lives are so fragile
you can almost know
That it takes no extra nudging
when it's someone's time to go.

We have watched loved ones leave us,
not knowing on what day
Their Maker would finally call them,
and we wondered what to say.

We've seen events unfolding
over which we had no control—
We thought we might do something
yet knew God had His goal.

Somethings are beyond controlling
so we remain standing by
To await our Father's bidding
and try not to ask Him "Why?"

After our loved ones leave us,
and we've said our last good-bye
We find we're only human
with hearts that know how to cry.

Deborah Y Jones
WHAT DOES IT MEAN TO LOVE?

To Kelly, my wonderful and loving husband

When ever I say "I Love You"
what does it mean?
Could it be because I care
for you?

Or that I want to

share my life with you
and you to share your life
with me?
What does it mean to love?
To intertwine two hearts
so they beat as one;
to no longer be alone in a
world of so few who really care.
What does it mean to love?
To open your heart to someone,
to see the beauty
that lies within.
To have someone say "I Love You"
in return.

Patricia L Hill
LOVE IS ALLOWING

I lovingly dedicate this poem to Rev. June McRae of Phoenix, Arizona, in appreciation of the spiritual wisdom and teachings she so humbly shares with her students and friends.

Love is just allowing us,
Each spirit here, to be
Exactly what we need to be —
For only we can see . . .

Just what we must experience,
Just what we must endure,
To learn the lessons we must learn —
To transcend to the pure.

If we would but envision past
The mortal flesh of man
And glimpse the spirit living there,
Then we would understand . . .

That each of us has set our course,
Our path in life self-made —
And none, save God, has right to judge
The times another strayed.

So let us love our fellowman,
Without judgement or blame —
Allowing each his time to grow,
As God loves us the same.

Roberta A Walker
SHADOWS ON THE WALL
Pictures in my mind come slowly creeping.
Shadows on the wall dance in my mind.
I lay awake at night pretending to be sleeping
While the past sneaks in and unwinds.
The memories are there and ever haunting
With the black and stillness of the night.
Poking and dancing, always teasing and taunting
While I try to push them away with all my might.
The nights go on with endless fury
As I fight the memories on the wall.
And sleep seems far away and alluring
Then I hear your voice give me a call.
I close my eyes and I can see your face.
I know one day this will all be in the past.
When all the ghosts are gone and in their places,
I will sleep again, so sound and fast

Gina Coffey
LOVING YOU, LOSING YOU
you finally found the one that you long awaited for.
The love that you never thought would come, came and walked Through the door.
You swore that no other man could ever be compared
Because he gave you everything and it was mutually shared

You shared your love, your joy, your tears and sorrows
We promised each other that there would be many more tomorrows
You never thought a man could bring you so much love and truth.
You thought at least, it would never happen in the days of your youth.

Then one day you decided you had found "Mr Right".
Then the next day you started with the fights.
He was the one that you thought had brought you to your fate.
The one where the love was so suddenly turned to hate.
You couldn't understand how this happened so fast
What happened to all the love that was meant to last?
You realize your love was lost so you put it in the past
But you'll never forget him because he gave you memories to last.

Heather Lorenz
A PAST TO REMEMBER; A FUTURE TO MOLD

To my grandfather, Walter J. Hochlowski, who was a dedicated poet.

A past to remember; a future to mold . . . the cycle of our lives:
A journey of the diverse man
Different people with different traditions and lives.
From Austria and Poland, Italy and France
Christians and Muslims; Germans and Jews—a seemingly endless search for a chance to be a part
A part of a whole with justice, and futurity.
Growing and changing; knowing happiness and hardship;
learning science and art
This life cycle churns on into maturity.
We are a lasting model for generations to come
More societies are drawn to us . . .
even from all the universe
They seek the common beat of the drum.
Now the inevitable—prevalence of the good and perverse.
A past to remember; a future to mold. It is what we all see
It is the same cycle that was, is, and will be.

Jill Martinsky
GRANDPAP'S LAP

Of all the places I have been since
I was just a child
None can compare with the view
that Grandpap's Lap allowed.

He'd pick me up and hold me tight,
and tell me tales of old,
And as he spoke his words to me
the magic would unfold.

He'd take me from yesterday into
tomorrow around the world
we'd go,
And I was certain there wasn't
anything my grandpap didn't
know.

We would sit and talk for hours
then I would take a nap
And dream of things that I had
heard while in my grandpap's
lap.

I swear that I could see the stars
inside his eyes of blue;
He taught me to have faith in God
and "HE'll take care of you."

He taught me more than any book
or any scholar could,
And the memories that I have of
him are true and fine and good.

Now if the world's treasures I
possessed and all the countries
of the map
I'd sell it all for one more day upon
my Grandpap's lap.

Steven Michael Rutherford
THE CLIMAX

To the memories of all joys in their own special way. That reach a climax one day.

A Harvest moon, that came too
soon.
A sun light glow, from long ago.
A firery night, that burned so
bright.
A wind swept dream, that seem to
cling.
A day so plenty, shared by many.
Should I find a distant time?
Are we so vain not feel pain.
Can love be so cold, making us
bold.
Have I found strength, with every
tinch
A strong man in faith, must not
waste.
Be ever so daring, with truth and
caring.
Be ever so bright, strong in might.
Free winds will blow, and sunny
hills will show.
How a day in Paradise, will awaken
thee.
I feel a need, a longing, to be free.
From a life of mediocraties.
I have site, that remains hidden
from life.
That when revealed, awaits an
irruption
In its day to be.

Eleanor S Radcliffe
SO TO WALK

When God made the Earth
He said, "It is Good!"
For man to walk,
To choose and have a Heavenly
Birth,
With Sun above and Earth beneath
your feet,
Green carpet which is really neat.
Do nothing that will bring disfavor
or defeat,
For Sin, will follow down life's
Street.

Our Guardian Angel watching over
us,
And the Laws are written,
We, sometimes are smitten,
With problems of earth's creatures
and transgressions.
Let the Altar of Love give Peace.
So God's open arms can gather in
His children,
With Forgiving Love still not
written,
Gathering all the beauty of Peace
that is given.

Life that is complete is Sweet,
When you know God is ready
To hear every heartbeat,
Blessing your very footsteps.
Holding your hand, leading the
way,
Knowing you will never stray,
For God is all knowing, all
showing,
Oh! What a Blessing, So To Walk.

Helen Jo Temple
LOVE FLOWERS

To Carolynne for her encouragement. And Joey who will remain very special to me.

Seasons come and seasons go . . .
. . . Love blossoms continue to
grow,
Gaining strength from sun and
showers . . .
Bringing, forth these beautiful love
flowers.

Janice Wise
SOMEDAY

I'll not survive to go among the
stars,
To reach out and stir the diamond
dust of Time—
I'll never see the rise of alien
moons,
Nor walk amid the trees of
unknown climes—
But some small part of me shall
know
The endless voids, and velvet dark
of space,
And feel the warmth of unknown
suns
Upon my great-great-grandchild's
face.
And I shall know, through that
child's life,
The joy of wandering far and
wide—
Through her, or him, I'll know at
last
The wonder of God's universe,
Though I'll be deep inside.

Jack E Lulow
SOCIETY TODAY

In our society today
It can be no other way
Only death can bring us back
To the original way
Yesterday will always be in the past
for nothing in this world will ever
last
We look to the future
Even though tomorrow will never
come
our life is just a game
The game of war
Death and destruction
The science of mind reconstruction
There's nothing left but
contamination
Our world has become total
radiation
We are mutants of the land
Soon nothing but sand
Living in constant fear
Asking ourselves will we make it
another year
Death and Destruction
Radiation, contamination
Yes our sentence has been passed—
COMPLETE DAMNATION

Ruth Hubbard Robinson

Ruth Hubbard Robinson
WHO

This poem is dedicated to the loving memory of my parents, Charles Harrison Hubbard and Sarah Malvenia Hook Hubbard, whose example of Christian living I have tried to follow.

Who commands the dawn of day
Or canopies the earth with a
cloudless sky
At whose behest does the thunder
roll
And who makes the newborn
baby cry

Who can wake a sleeping child
Or give sparkle to the faintest
stars
Who can enable the lame to walk
And grant eternal peace to end
all earthly wars

Who controls the flooding waters
And catastrophic quakes
Who can calm the oceans wide
Or fill the dried-up lakes

Who can make the east winds blow
Or quench a parching tongue
Who can count every raindrop
Then paint the evening sun

Who offers the gift of salvation
And allows you to hold the key
Who is standing in the narrow door
Beckoning always to you and me

Who looks inside our hearts
And is recorder of every deed
If you are unsure of the answers
Then a commitment to God is
what you need

Emery Chaffin
CREATION

Soft as a zephyr on a warm
summer day,
Quiet and gentle as a kitten at play,
Love so pure that a nymph would
respond,
The spirit of God, like the birth of
a fawn,
Breaths the desire to create some
clay
Out of a faith called the breaking
of day.
Then by His will the molten was
cast.
Then in that void a form came at
last.

Why was it love? I can but surmise.
Why then was faith the sustaining
prize?
Why? It's because God planned it
that way,
This is the reason we have night
and day.

Douglas Alan Scharenguivel
TREES

Noble and pliant, wavering trees
Movements given freely by the
breeze
Branches outstretched,
whispering please.
Giant angels on their knees . . .
playing.

Fibrous, scattered hair of green
Shading the sun, creating a scene.
One where God treads and
convenes.
Throughout the trees . . . swaying.

Buds and blossoms in rainbow
shades,
Of pinks and blues, in springtime
glades,
And bees and birds in their colorful
parades.
Within the trees . . . and staying.

Green fruit turns ripe in
conspiracy with the sun,
As thunder showers soak
everything and everyone
The summers' returned and has
begun
Among the trees . . . playing.

Larry D Bowling
SPRING

To: William Monus Bowling and Edna Bowling my Father & Mother. To my daughters, Lisa, Lori, Jana, Renae, and Marla. And to my wife Judy. With love.

In spring is seen the quiet fair,
Of cartwheeling flowers springing
anew,
And maple buds with creeping
flair,
Point their nose to a sky of blue.

Sabra Force
HOW DO YOU STOP THE HURTS OF LIFE?

How do you stop the hurts of life?
How do you make them go away?
How do you lessen the weight on
your heart
when you find it chooses to stay?

And how do you show the damage
done
when you know your voice cannot
be heard?
When you've cried aloud, "I've had
enough!"

When vision by teary eyes is
blurred . . .

Do you hide behind a placid smile
and walk with head held high?
Coping with the pain and grief
while inwardly wanting to die . . .

And yet—who would care?
To whom does it matter what you
feel?
Those who could make any
changes at all
are the ones who think what you
suffer not real.

And so—what do you do!
Raise your voice to the God above?
He who knows of our daily struggle
with pain and grief and love . . .

Or—turn to a world of make
believe,
a world where dreams come true,
a tranquil place within the heart
sought by many, but found by few.

Melissa L Kageler

A THOUGHT APART

This poem is written to Mommee and Daddee Kageler with lots of love, Melissa

---

I should like to rise and go,
To a place where the sun shall
forever show.
Where beyond the meadows
an ocean lies,
With waters as brilliant as the
sunlit skies.
To a land where singing seagulls
soar,
As the waves greet the wind with
a crashing roar.
The essence of spring flowers
fill the air,
Lacing the earth in a floral flair,
And if the sky may darken,
Or if the snow may fall,
I could think not of it and
turn away from it all.
To escape to a paradise
beyond this land so cold at heart,
And wander through my
dreamland,
a thought apart.

Treva L Brown

A TRIBUTE TO A FRIEND

To Mrs. Dora Skinner, my dear friend, who has been beside me through so many trials—ever helping and caring. May this poem inspire others to express their love for their fellowman.

You are, and always have been,
Such a true and loving friend.
You've made these past six years,
Such a joy that has no end.

And you will never know how
much,
You've meant to me these past few
months.
Each time I've been down, you've
brought me up,
And given me hope again.

I pray I'll ever be worthy of
Your friendship and your great
love;
You were truly sent to me,
From my GOD above.

I pray I can always be there,
To comfort you whatever comes
your way.
Just know you're ever with me,
Each time I kneel and pray.

I thank Him each and every day,
For the joys you have brought;
Every step along the way,
Even caring when I was at fault.

Never forget the fun we've had,
Canning, planting, laughing,
sharing.
You're a friend when in need,
A TRUE FRIEND INDEED!
And I'm so thankful you're mine!

Byron Frank Beall

TRAGEDY OF THORNS

Fleeing in mind.
To rid this tormenting thought.
Nothing could be overstated.
For no statement could describe,
the menacing void which blows,
through all fibers of my novel
heart.
Let the records show,
that I was not a defeatist,
but a realist.
Knowing all the time,
that the final blow would soon
thrust,
into my pretentious world of make
believe.

If motives were real, actual and
true.
If honesty stood as the fighter of
all injustice.
But no such world existed.
No rose petal path fell under my
feet.
For if I wanted roses,
they would be supplied by me.
No one told me of the hazards.
The tragedy of thorns.
It is odd, but your heart knows.
Yes it knows of impossibilities in
one's life.

But now I know.
Yes I know of vulnerability.
I know of the tragedy of thorns.

Kelly Starry

LIFE

The Spirit of Life is changing,
Different as everyone knows,
Either just born, or recent death,
The story should always be told.
Joyous over a baby's first walk,
Weeping, a dead person will never
talk.
Willowing through a forest, one
night,
Very few stars that were shining
bright.
Sending a person to God's faraway
place,
Sending someone else a brand new
face.
When people we know have just
recently died,
With tears we look up into the sky,
"Why God, did you take that face
Up to your faraway place?"

Brian Hemingway

TO DREAM OF SPRING

Open your heart,
To the warm spring wind,

Let the season
Give life to your soul.

When summer turns to autumn,
And the winds are growing cold,

When days are getting shorter,
And snow begins to fall,
Think of the season of springtime,
Whenever you're feeling old.

No matter how bitter the winter,
It matters not how long,

Dream of the season,
Of dawning life,

And spring will come again.

Linda K Williamson

THE LITTLE DRUMMER BOY

This poem is dedicated to Herbert and Marlene Colston, my loving Parents.

Little drummer boy, do you know
where you're bound?
Will you play your drum for me
before you leave our town?
Will you tell me of the sights you
saw, will you tell me
if you cried?
Will you tell me all about the war
and how innocent people died?
Did you stand up straight and tall
watching as you played?
Did you march along in front of
them as if it were a parade?
Were there times when you wished
you were home sitting on
your mama's lap.
Eating homemade apple pie and
talking with your Pap?
The mail horse came this morning,
Mama's gonna cry.
T'was her baby's twelfth birthday,
but last night the
boy marched to the sky.
Papa's down by the river, his pride
won't let him be.
He mourns in silent wonder, now
there's only Pa and Ma and me.
Two Sundays came before we
could lay the boy to rest.
The man told Papa he should be
real proud, up to the end
the boy done played his best.
Now the drum is very silent, it is
still and very dead.
It hangs upon a nail above his little
bed.
No more will he play for them who
march along to war.
No more will he walk with them,
not like he did before.
The drum is very silent, it is still
and very dead.
But the memories will linger as
long as it hangs
above his bed.

Michael D Jones

THE STORY VENDOR

I once knew a man, a little old man
Whom I'd visit as oft as I could,
but 'twas easy to see as oft as it be,
not nearly as much as I should.

He spoke mostly of the wild to this
wide eyed child
who loved his tales of splendor.
The yarns he spun were, oh, such
fun,
for he was my Story Vendor.

The children at school were so very
cruel
When they spoke of the man so old.
I shook my finger and said hatred
would linger
till the day that hell grew cold

For I knew this man they didn't
understand,
Who suffered from lonliness and
sorrow.
And like all men could meet his end
As early as before tomorrow

then one day I heard them say
the words that brought me such
pain.
The old man had died and had
taken his pride
to a boot hill grave in the rain.

This song cannot tell the whole of
the tale
the way that I want it to be.
I say with a sigh as the years go by
the story vendor is me.

Herman Emilmeyer

Herman Emilmeyer

SHOCKING ISN'T IT

To Billie Jo Meyer with Love, Thanks for the 39 years, thanks for Mike, Peggy Jo & Elaine and 5 Grandchildren. Herm

---

SHOCKING ISN'T IT
New Year is over
Spring is on the way
Soon one can find Clover
In which one may play
Grass with trees too cover
New Spring Flowers every day
With Birds and Bee—s to hover
In beautyful month of May
The time to find a Lover
You will think the Worlds O.K.
Love will want to smother
This feeling you will obey
Not the urging of the other
The Mood you wish would stay
You have to tell another
Quick before it goes away
You better tell your Mother
It's gone It's gone Today
Now it must be Summer.

Clint Williams Jr

MY OPEN CONFESSION

I find it hard to contain myself
whenever we stand together, like
now, face to face.
You can start a hex with your
refreshing features and your
pleasing ways help trigger this
spell.
Like the force of a magnet that
repels and attracts.
You got me going in both
directions. At times, I really feel
displaced.
Your binding spell caused this
moment. Now my expressive
feelings will determine what
future they will foretell.

This is something that didn't just
start to happen.
The desire was aroused distant
years ago.
From day one, the sight of your
incredible features, had me
where I almost forgot how to
breathe, and even lost my ability
to speak.
You never even knew this, we had
only brief encounters through
the years. You're back now and
I'm saying, my warm feelings,
they still flow.
I'm not ashamed to admit, how you
held my mind captive through
the years. I surrender a
confession, a confession that I'm
weak.

If I'm living a lie, then please don't
tell me. Because I'd rather hear
a lie, than to go insane.
Through the years no one replaced
you, nor will any for years to
come, my belief in this is strong.
This is why and on this occasion,
that no other can elevate me to
a higher and more blissful plane.
Let me describe my desires and
passions in detail, it's your spell
that gave me this nerve. And its
drive has worked on me too long.

I want to get lost, when I look
deeply into your lovely pretty
eyes. Will I see a picture of
paradise that will elate me to a
point of no return.
When our hands join together, will
this fusion make my ears play a
melody and give my mind a
vibrating rock.
Let my lips find the sweetness in
your pretty luscious mouth. Will
this gesture that says, I love you,
put me in a trance like state and
start my passions to burn.
Will your embracing arms put me
in a world that heaven couldn't
touch. And if you are too soft for
cotton, that would add to the
shock.

Whisper in my ear and let the
words echo out sweet praise. If
you're too bashful to do it, I'll
reverse the role to help intensify
the flame.
I want our hearts to sound off in
unison, they both must spell out
the same undeniable and
desirable truth.
I want this feeling to bathe me all
over, I don't ever want it to stop.
And I'll be deliriously happy, if
with you its the same.
These combined feelings are better
than the warm morning
sunshine kissing me in the face,
but I need your willing role to
help excel the proof.

I've stated some of my desires for
the body and spirit.
But my goal is to make love to your
mind.
So will my shameless confession,
add life and give breath to my
heart. Am I your winner, or will
I become confused in what I
thought that I saw.
In the event I'm made happy, lets
make it be forever, which is the
epitome of my enchanted mind.
And this decision will make me
feel tremendously divine.

So now Miss Lady, dear spell
binder of the mind. Will I
become forgotten history or do
we make a shamelessly blissful
and everlasting new law.

Dana Dean Lesley Dougherty
THE END OF THE RAINBOW

To My Daddy (Paul Russell Lesley)—a constant source of love and help . . .

There's gold at the end of the
Rainbow
the poets and storybooks say
It's there for those who are willing
to look for it day after day.
Through fields and o'er hills, down
long rocky roads
men have searched for treasure
in vain.
Instead of the end of the rainbow,
found themselves out in the rain.

Some give up in disgust, others say
it's not there.
The toiler will prove these men
wrong.
Success doesn't come to the lazy,
seems it eludes all but the strong.
There's a golden treasure of
knowledge.
It's yours if you'll just dig it out
of the books you study day after
day,
Education! I'm speaking about.

Now the gold at the end of my
rainbow
is a diploma from College I'll say.
With this gold in mind,
I'll not give up 'till it's mine.
My goal's a diploma some day.

Greg Pasternak
UNTITLED

Strangers are people
as unknown to you,
as you are to them.

We'll never get to know
one another,
unless we let our feelings show.

There are so many words
we could have used.
Hello . . .
Or maybe after a time
—I Love You.

Wrapped too deeply within
ourselves,
we may appear to be cold,
not want to get involved.

If you care, show it.
Don't let me leave,
if you want me to stay.

Pamela M Short Shanahan
MEMORIES OF MOM

In loving memory of my mother, Joyce Ann Thompson Short.

You wiped our noses and quieted
our fears
bandaged our knees and dried our
tears
You nursed us through chicken
pox, measles, and mumps
doctored our scraped elbows,
bruises, and bumps

You chased away "boogie men" in
the dark of night
and stayed at our bedside until
morning's light.
You kissed us goodnight and
wished us sweet dreams
at times now . . . it was only
yesterday . . . it seems

But the years have past and we all
are grown
I'm married now with a child of my
own
Such a long time now since you
were taken away
and still I miss you more than
words can say

So many things we missed . . . so
much we didn't do
so many little things I never said
to you
But in my heart I say them now
I just hope you hear me somehow.

I love you Mom.

Juli Cowan
FRIEND

So this was it
New home
Four gray walls
And a toilet with no seat
Cot bolted to the floor
With a clang
The door was shut
And he was cut off
His world was gone
Laying down
He stared at the ceiling
At a spider web
Soon the spider was a friend
The only friend he had
As time went by
The spider would sit in his hand
And he would talk
About anything
And everything
And nothing
A small, black, furry thing
It was gentle
And it listened
And comforted
At least it seemed that way
To the boy
Who needed and counted
On its love so desperately
One day
The boy was told
He could go home
His sentence was done
He went to his cell
To tell his friend
Perhaps take him along
But the spider was gone
And the boy cried

Dana Lynn Gardner
THE FOX

In a peaceful forest with
berry shrubs,
Laying on the ground is
a Redwood stub.
What is that peeking
around that plum tree?
I don't have an idea what
it could be!
Could it be a bear or a
bag or rocks?
No, I know what it is—
a clever fox!
Now frightening a
squirrel while zipping by,
Smart he is, never will
wear a striped tie.
Lost a hunting dog at
the speed of light.
Mysteriously plotting in
the night.
Climbing a pine tree as
easy as that,
Member of the dog species
not the cat.

Sheryl L Crofoot
A NATURAL ROMEO

A smile that laughs when it grins,
A laugh that tickles you from
within.
A Kiss that leaves your face with a
smile,
A touch that tingles and gets one
riled.

You have the gift of charm,
A Natural Romeo.
Come take me in your arms,
But don't ever let go.

A bubble thats in my soda,
A thought that makes me wanna
hold ya,
A sweetness that I have desired,
A desire that I have acquired.

A spirit that rises so high,
A cheerfulness that shows through
your eyes.
A personality that is so charming,
A charm that is so warming.

You have the gift of charm,
A Natural Romeo.
Come take me in your arms,
But don't ever let go.

A joy that I have felt,
A thought that makes me melt.
A spark that has been started,
A loneliness that came when we
departed.

Roseann Hundertmark
ON A LONELY BEACH I STAND

On a lonely beach I stand
like a defeated soldier of a
war within.
A wave crashes before me
and leaves a flawless path of new
sand.
A journey of a thousand miles
begins with one step;
the one step which I have
already taken, but was
washed away
and now is only
a vague memory.

Glennard Bruce Turner
LIFE

It's all the things
That are right,
The sun, the moon,
The stars at night.

It's all the mistakes
That are made
It's all the ones
That will be paid

It's the happy times
That one remembers,
It's the special times
In mid-December.

It's living and dying
It's sad, it's true.
And what it brings
Is only for you

You never know
What it may bring
Just always remember
It's a precious thing.

Charles Calvin Shaw
EPILOGUE: BIG DAN'S TAVERN

To the memory of Cheryl Araujo

Three years ago the rapes occurred,

'Twas in New Bedford, Mass.
Where Big Dan's Tavern then was set,
A spot liked by that class
Of people of the drinking sort
Whose morals were quite loose;
Who thought not twice of what they did
For entertainment use.

Four men one day seized on a girl,
Who then was twenty-two,
And raped her many times upon
The table used for pool.
She made complaint to the police
And then the men were tried —
Would you believe, when justice won,
'Twas "foul" her neighbors cried?

To flee their wrath, she left her home
And southward she escaped
Because it seemed they thought it was
The men that she had raped.
And now, this month in eighty-six
While on an auto drive
An accident has claimed her life
At age of twenty-five.

Nellie Lucius
MY GARDEN

In memory of my husband, Alfred Daniel Lucius, Sr., August 31, 1890—December 11, 1984

I walked in my garden
In the cool of the day,
And revelled in the beauty
All along the way.

The toils of life seemed lighter,
Burdens heavy to bear
Were somehow made less heavy,
As I walked in there.

The calm and quiet stillness
Eased my troubled mind,
Brought joy to my heart
That no where else I'd find.

There's something about a garden
With its lovely flower array,
That fills one with security
At the close of a long, hard day.

Lois Eason
THE MOUNTAIN

"Dedicated to my husband Bill and my son Randy, for their encouragement and love."

Like a giant hovering high,
It's white hair touching the sky,
Trailways running up and down,
Through the green grass and the brown;
Tall trees dot it's ridges,
Remind me of green hedges;
Great rocks give it gloom,
Wild flowers are in bloom;
Through the trees the sun rays dance,
Taking one's breath at a glance;
Winter blankets it with snow,
A shining pyramid from top to toe;
The streams flow wildly as they tumble down,
The falls below make a roaring sound;
It's color in autumn is a shimmering red and gold,
The mountain then is surely a beauty to behold;
A masterpiece of God's own hand,.
That came to life at His command.

Arlene Joan Kirsch
THE WEEKEND

We recognize your God given talent, and want you to know, how much we love you. Always Mom & Dad.

It's Friday and work is over and you make plans
To go out. There's so much to do.
Movies, bars, amusement parks, zoos, and museums
And you open your door to the four walls and telephone
And you get into your nightgown cause no one's going to call.
You turn on the TV and the news is on
And a seventy year-old lady got raped by a 13-year old boy
And you wonder when it will be your turn to make the headlines.
A movie is on, during commercials you run into the kitchen,
And there's nothing to eat and you make a screwdriver cause
You're celebrating the week-end, and watching a movie
And the people are laughing, drowning out your tears.

It's Saturday and you walk through the stores
Staring at the faces and wondering where they are
And you buy a baby gift for the girl at work, who's due next month.
And you remember you bought the same gift last month.
You walk through the park in hope that you'll recognize a face
Or catch a sign of some involvement
and your stares are met with
Downward eyes and worry-ridden faces.
So you get on the swing and remember
When you were little and you relive the carefree times and you are awoken
By a mothers screams that your in her childs' place.
You return home and the telephone rings and your adrenaline flows,
It's a friend who lives many miles away
and she tells you she's happy
With lots of friends and places to go
and you tell her your happy,
With lots of friends and places to go and she knows your lying,
But what can she do, so she says good-by
And you know
you'll never hear from her again.
So you smoke a joint and have a drink and play solitaire and
stare through the table, into the night with empty dreams.

It's Sunday morning and get dressed
early to go buy a paper
And on your way home a man stops his car and asks if you
Need a ride, and you smile. . .
and he walks up the steps in front
Of you to open the door
and the four walls seem filled,
And afterwards you stare at his relaxed face and touch his lips
And you feel empty because there are no words to share.

It's Monday morning and you reach
over to touch and there's no one
There, and you scrub off your week-end
and paint your weeks face.

Mary Margaret Pester

Mary Margaret Pester
KNOWING THE PRESENCE OF GOD

This poem is dedicated to Rev. Deane R. Hardy

Here I'll stand
As I look across the land
With open heart and out reached hands

In my life I have had so much fun
But now as I sit here in the sun
Out of my eyes and down my cheeks I
can feel tears run.

But now as I know death is near
I won't fear
Cause I know God will steer

Just look at me!
I never promised you a warrantee
Nor did I give you a guarantee

Just look to heaven and see the light

It looks so pretty and bright
It even shines at night

I know God is always there and cares
And he knows the pain's more than I
can bear
So my thoughts with God I'll share

As I look to heaven I can see God
He's reaching out to me
I seem to be soaring so free
It's no longer me, it's we

Now as the day is done
I am so glad to see the Son
The fight is over, my life to God, He has won

Tracey Rouse
GRANDPA AND I

For Grandpa of course, and Mom.

Sitting in the sun,
Grandpa and I
Watching some man
Cleaning the neighbor's yard.

Sitting on the porch steps
Enjoying the lovely spring day.
Grandpa and I.
Watching Eddie bicycling
Up and down the road.

Listening to music
Waiting for the mailman,
Wondering what he'll bring
Grandpa and I
Patient as Job.

The sky is bluer
Than a robin's egg,
Watching and waiting
He says the steps are too hard
Just Grandpa and I.

Cheryl Lynn Taylor
DEATH
Death, death, death
Death takes your breath.
Death comes but once in a life-time.
This poem may not rhyme.

Death is for understanding,
Death is not pretending,
Death is for tender caring,
Death is also for tending.

So with Death we send cards
To help with the sad feelings.
We send cards to bandage the hearts
Sent with love we're sealing.

The cards are sent with love
Sent by a turtle dove.
This is the end of this rhyme
So thanks for your time.

Kathie Sue Hoofard
CHRISTMAS SPIRIT

Dedicated to Pamela Marie Pogue for the encouragement she gave me.

The joy I feel at Christmas time
Should not be hard to put in rhyme.
Christmas cards coming in the mail
Telling lots of Christmas tales.
Candies, Garland and Mistletoe
Lights on the tree to make it glow.
Snow on the window, a wreath on the door
A turkey in the oven we bought in the store.
Take your picture with Santa Claus
In the toy store the kids want to pause.
They ring the bell, hear it clang
I like to sing carols with the gang.
Friends and Relatives come in the door
Hoping wrapped presents don't get torn.
Horse and Sleigh through Central Park

Outside lights shining in the dark.
Enjoy the party New Years Eve
New Years Day the tree we heave.
I hate to see the spirit go
It'll be back next year I know.

Wm H Curtis
ODE TO EVERETTE
As I look down at this flower bed
With colors as perfect as could be
I know all about Gods wonderful powers
And here is proof enough for anyone to see
Delicate petals on long slender stems
Rising to meet the morning sun
Swaying ever so slowly in a gentle breeze
I know their life is nearly done
A few have withered from the summer heat
Others are in their prime
Golden daises are such a beautiful sight
To pick the very last poppy would be a crime
Flying creatures being well fed
And drinking from the morning dew
Golden rays of the morning sunshine
Lighting up shadows as only they can do
I will stand still and just look for awhile
At the beauty all over this ground
In no other spot in my daily life
Can any such perfection be found
All of these beauties are the blessing of God
I feel his presence so near
As I must turn and walk away
I know my heart will always be here

Shari Koeppel
TO BE GOD'S CHOSEN ONE

To my dear friend, Don Taylor who passed away: March 28, 1987

We are not to question why,
When a rainbow appears
In the rainy sky.

To hear the bluebird start a song,
God only knows
It's there all along.

He chooses us for His very own,
To have a special faith
That's ours and ours alone.

When sickness strikes and it's hard to cope,
Put your trust in God
He will always give us hope.

Patty Hunter
TO MY THERAPIST
The pain lies deep within me
Can't anybody see?
Can't anybody help me & try to set me free?
Why don't I know the answers—
the doubts keep plaguing me.
Then someone asks a question
that sparks response in me.
In his eyes I see compassion—
maybe he will set me free.
He says he hasn't all the answers—
but he seems to know what makes me me.
I hope he has the questions
that will help to set me free.
I'll just have to wait and see.

Marilyn Moran
BRIGID
Violets and August remind me of you.
August like purple the month you came
Intense with heat and pain.
Like violets through the
deep shadows of my loneliness
A fragrance came,
deep and colored it remains
Forever violets purple-stained.

Kevin N Koutrelakos
LOST LOVE

This poem is dedicated to all the people who have loved someone, have had their love shattered, and have hopes ofrekindling that love in the future.

A full moon opposite the sunrise
Bats,
A large swarm of them.
Circle the trees in the near distance.
The wind,
Swirls thru the forest.
A rough,
deadly,
Yet steadily smooth.
The sound of dry, creaking, crispy
Leaves,
Swaying
Back
And
Forth.
A few fall
And then they are gone.
Battered
And
Not
Wanted
By
The
Old cold tree.
The remaining,
Those that are left,
Try
Try and hold strong.
But forever
Is never,
Soon they too will be gone.
Once
Vibrant
Young
Shiny
and
Strong.
Glistering with life
Rainbows
And
Sunny days.
Now winter
Hits.
Forever is never
Old tree sheds its' coat.
Its' nakedness
A lonely view.
For what once was
Is
Now
Out
Of
Sight,
Broken
Unattached.
It'll be old spring,
Until
It
That tree,
Is once again,
A
Poplar
Tree

John A Christensen
THE SEASONS OF LIFE

This poem is dedicated to my four children: David, Bonnie, Donna, and Darryl.

Once I was young, carefree and bold;
With never a thought that I'd one day be old

Glory and power, money and fame
All have eluded this tired old frame

The young dreams are gone, and gathering dust;
Like ships which are buried, and left there to rust

Ashes to ashes and dust to dust;
Life has its seasons, and end it we must

Someday our life, and all that it holds
Will surely be gone to a much better fold

What have we done for those we've been given?
For the lives we've touched, and those who were bidden

To grow in our house and sit at our feet?
How faithful? How loyal? How apt to entreat?

What we failed then to teach, and failed then to share
Can never again be brought to bear

For life has its seasons, which all must know;
When one day we'll reap what now we sow

Thus, winter and springtime, summer and fall;
The seasons of life apply to all

To live with God, we shan't deny
His Son, the Christ, Who came to die

To live for Him is Life indeed;
I pray that all will give it heed

Anne L Emory
RABBITS, RAINBOWS AND BUTTERFLIES
RABBITS

White whiskers, floppy
ears—silly rabbit, hiding
in a flower pot!

RAINBOWS

Violet, pale pink—
joining heaven and earth in
celebrating life.

and BUTTERFLIES

Yellow whisper, blue
whisper. Dandelion and
butterfly share dreams.

James D Mandigo
Heaven's Door

To the students and faculty of Whitcomb Elementary who more than most, know the cost of believing in and exploring the future. Travis and Mandy, you are the future and I believe in you.

Within the bounds of my cockpit,
I allow my mind to soar.
I am in control of my aircraft,
and its gentle response to more.

Climb to reach the Heaven's limit,
total concentration I must pour.
Frightened that its limit might be reached,
far short of Heaven's Door.

I have flown within my limits,
my performance was better than poor.
I have touched the throne where God sits,
and someday I will go back for more!

Linda Downie
THE OLD MAN FROM MAINE
There was an old man from Maine;
Who carried a wooden cane.
He was the town's tailor;
But wished to be a sailor.
The wind and sea he did admire;
And hoped soon he could retire.
He hopped out of bed;
And "why not", He said.
So he closed up his shop;
And off he did hop.
Left behind was his misery and bore;
I heard he set sail and was seen no more.

Margaret Magee
WHEN ASKED TO LIST MY VIRTUES
When asked to list my virtues
The roll is very short,
But all my vices listed here
Would make a long report.
I will not bore you with them,.
Nor bare my soul to men.
The Lord God knows what I have done
And, no doubt, will do again.
Though many are my failures.
There's one thing that is sure;
I know Jesus as my savior
Only He is just and pure.
The perfect, blameless lamb of God
Died to bear my sin,
And sent the holy spirit
To help me to begin
To see the needs of others
Before I see my own.
Each conviction of the spirit
Tells me I have grown.
This Christian growth continues
With every passing day.
It is not I but God himself
Who leads me all the way.

J Grant Singer
CONSIDER THE TIDE

With love always For Jeremiah Edgar of East Stroundsburg, Pennsylvania

fragrant differences
echo from the dunes. . .
remembrance
haunts the breeze
soft clouds—unhobbled -
drifting
eloquently toward the sea. . .
the heron thoughtfully
considers the tide. . .
symphony's motion
ebbing. . .
odors of salt, remote
articulating gulls

. . .amplified lonely
pleas. . .
outstretched shore pine

grotesque. . . cynic. . .
nervous breezes touch
the waves
empty lunch sacks. . .
sullen orange peel. . .
the bread pieces feed
the ugly bird
punctuations of leaping
fish
escape the sea lion's lunge. . .
unfettered evening. . .
draping
embracingly upon us. . .
embers glow. . .
our haunting silence
melds with the ocean's roar. . .

Lurah Hayden Haworth

MOTHER

Our mother went away a few days
ago,
with an unfinished job, all must
know,
Our Dad needed her, oh so very
much.
For he's growing old and need's
your touch.
They took her away when she
became ill,
She said, take me back Daddy to
heal,
But God said, come now. They'll
take care of him. I need you now
in the promised land.
So she layed down her work and
held out her hands,
I'll meet you Dad and children in
the promised land.

Pamela K Clemons

FEELINGS

Separation is upon us, and
togetherness no longer there
Love for one is stronger, but seems
no one really cares.
This separation may last forever,
no one really knows
But it takes two to work things out,
and only one to say
"I DON'T KNOW."
If all true feelings are expressed
and never held in
Communication is better, and
fighting comes to an end.
If love between us is more than a lot
Then how come love takes
togetherness and together we
are not?
Dealing with love seems as if it's
the hardest thing to do
But if we stick together and prove
our love, then the hard part is
thru
Times are not always going to be
good and not always bad
But if we are together, then we
should never be sad.
Goodtimes are not the only
happiness known
But being together is love standing
alone.
Isn't it a shame to put one thru
such misery as this
When all it takes is communication
and a thoughtful little kiss.
Although you might say, "You
never know who you might
meet,"
I will always say, "Being with you
makes my life complete."

Betty J Lattire

THE PLANNED WEDDING

I was standing in the shadow
of a church one day.
As I stood there in silence
I heard the wedding march play.
I walked into the church
and sat by the door.
Through my tears I could see
rose petals on the floor.
This is your wedding day,
but how can that be?
Because the girl kneeling beside
you
at the alter's not me.
As you knelt there beside her,
I knew our prayers were the same.
So be happy, my darling,
she has your name.
I'll never forget you
and you'll never forget me.
But the wedding was already
planned
for August, 1963.

Donna Sue Hayes

INFINITY

For Robt. Harris, and my favorite retreat, Sherri's.

All life is but a fleeting second in
infinity,
Some are given talents to strive for
greatness,
Others are given qualities of
giving and much to share,
While yet others are born to be,
Only passing there.
Into this infinity came I,
Seeking knowledge,
With a talent in my hands,
A vision in my mind,
Hoping only to leave a sigh,
A thing of beauty, my own
design,
A small something to mar this
infinity.

Buddy Lee Walter

BEHIND YOUR EYES

For Jyll Blakeslee, with love

Night falls quietly
allowing the illumination
from behind your eyes
to spill out around the beautiful
brown
and drip down as glistening drops
of honey
splashing over velvet skin
running down
forming a deep pool in which to
rest
in sleep and dreams in each other's
hearts.
I wake at dawn and watch
as the sun is noiselessly lured
through our window
and kisses you lightly on the eyes
and beckons me to do the same
which brings a smile
from your lips for us to share.

Cindi Sanders

UNTITLED

I've been looking back on what we
almost had
No matter what they say, it wasn't
all that bad.
The years have gone by all too fast
And still they find me living in the
past.
Ways to see you, I can still invent
Even knowing it isn't time well
spent.
We ignore each other on the street
For unknown reasons, our eyes
won't meet.
They tell me you're as happy as can
be
Have you really forgotten all about
me?
If only I had listened to you
I wouldn't be here and feeling so
blue
They say you just lead me on
How can something that wasn't, be
gone?
I believed you loved me, and I still
do
Just as you know, I'll always love
you.
So many times, I've picked up the
phone
But then I decided to leave it alone.
I can never dial your number all
the way
I wouldn't even know what to say.
I hope with her you have found
true happiness
Because that is just one step from
success.
And now without the urge to cry
I can look at you and say,
"Goodbye."

J Colleen Murphy

A WONDERING SPIRIT

To Charles, Angela, Stacey, Jocelyn and Anthony

As I was walking on the peer
I saw a man standing there
As I approached and came close
I felt the shadow of a ghost

His eyes they bore a hole in me
I felt stripped of all mortality
I was confused and feeling weird
Then this old man just disappeared

Feeling numb and in shock
I glanced out at the dock
A wisp of wind had touched my
face
I thank the Lord, he left with grace

The reasons why I can't unfold
I chanced to meet this eerie soul
I do know one thing for sure
Our spirits live for ever more

Loretta Edwards-Knight

WHICH WOULD YOU PREFER?

Would you prefer a life of sin
or
Walking with Jesus Christ to
win?
or
Would you prefer to be the boss
instead of
Carrying your own cross?
or
Would you prefer Satan's
Judgement
than
The Son that was God sent?
or
Would you prefer having Silver
and Gold
than
Giving-Sharing and feeding
God's souls?
IF
You prefer hatred-violence and
strife
than
Love—Peace and eternal life
Then, Where are you headed? my
dear sinful
Friend, For God IS in heaven and
you won't make it in

James Rickabaugh

THE WAY

This poem is dedicated to my love, Judith.

The conquering horde emerged at
first light,
Trained to be merciless, they
charged forth
With a horrid might.
One would think Nature had gone
wild
To accept such an evil from the
innocence of
A child.
No Lord knew they save for the
blade,
Aligned with Lucifer, filling grave
upon grave.
Imagine, if you would, the
multitudes destroyed.
What chance had they against the
horde?

Behold, all that is love and the
coming of the Lord!

Roland "Z" Zimmermann

UNICORNS

Unicorns are magical. . .
Unicorns are true,
Believe in them. . .
They'll believe in you.

Put trust in them. . .
And you will see,
Just how magical. . .
They can be.

They'll bring you love. . .
And happiness too,
Look at them. . .
They're watching you.

Treat them kind. . .
Touch their horn,
You'll get to feeling. . .
Safe and warm.

Confide in them. . .
Wait and see,
A truer friend. . .
No one else can be.

Misty Jo Fisher

GRANDMA

The lines on her face
are records of life's joys and
sorrows.

I look on her lovingly as
She gives me a soft, weak smile.
Tears come to my eyes and
I must look away.
I turn back and Grandma's eyes
are closed.
Her spirit has flown,
Leaving her loving smile behind.

David H deManbey
the other side
He didn't have many friends.
They say he pretty much minded
his own business;
never caused any trouble or
anything like that.

Father Reardand said he was a
quiet man.
Mrs. Fabershire said troubled.
most just said 'strange'.
Their talk scratched him inside
until the bleeding finally caused
him to go inside.

There he stayed, content in the
knowledge
his shadow clothed the other side
of us all.

As the years passed the people
knew him as the nameless one.
Sometimes they heard him inside
sobbing,
yet being nameless no one seemed
concerned
or thought it their business.

he had once searched for a retreat
from his loneliness;
searched for it,
maybe even found it for a time;
found it,
till laughter sent him tumbling
back into his
dungeon once again.
They send all the lonely people
there you know?
—prisoners have no choice—

the bleeding had long since passed
now
leaving a disfigured soul
tormented by want.

trembling;
he lay cuddled in a remote
corner of his hut;
a self appointed
victim of his own fears.

H Keith Bentley
THE SECRET OF THE UNIVERSE
It can be as evasive as conclusive,
This secret can be.
It stares you in the face everyday,
In almost every concievable way.
It is as free and pure as a dove,
That moving force we call love.
It has moved men and nations for
centuries,
While all the while from afar,
It continues to move the stars.
For love is always attracting,
Relentless in its insistance,
Moving along the lines of least
resistance.
One cannot even deny its existance,
For in each of us contains a spark,
That never leaves anyone
completely in the dark.
It is out of love that we are here,
It is not monumental,
Or is it merely coincidental?
So let this secret give you
nourishment,
Drawing on it while watching its
flourishment.

Halina de Roche
THE ETERNAL SOLDIER
The eternal soldier kneels on top
of the globe
And he weeps

Why is war?

That roar and snore and sore
We implore Thee oh Lord
To restore the world
That never more
We kill and bleed and die
For
At the end
We do not know
For why.

Thousands of years we were killed
Thousands of years we survived
But thousands of years
We connived
We contrived, deprived, derived
And revived
And the earth is fruitful with our
blood.

Oh Lord, what a knot
What a plot, what a rot
And in the end
We always cry—For why?

And I
The eternal soldier
A man of all ages
Personages, pilgrimages
And privileges
A man of all peoples
All guiles and styles and viles
A man of all beliefs and griefs
I kneel on top of the globe
And weep.

Sharon Gilmour

Sharon Gilmour
BROTHER
Dear Brother how much we share,
Without voicing that we care.
It's hard for people to express their
love,
Everyone now and then needs a
shove.

I have so much I want to tell you,
None of which is new.
But time is not on our side,
I can no longer my feelings hide.

For a brother you are the best,
To put up with a sister who's such
a pest.
You never in all our years,
Caused me any tears.

I'm proud that family we are,
In my books you were the star.
That a little sister looked up to,
Because you are just YOU.

Now your struggling just to stay
alive,
There's nothing I can do to help
you survive.
I love you, I care, I want to be near,
To help to take away some of the
fear.

Maybe I'm selfish in my own way,
Or fear my own death one day.
Maybe I need to be close to you,
To get from death some kind of
clue.

As I look at you my heart breaks,
I watch you struggle for every
breath you take.
I wonder if treatment is all in vain,
Just watching your body in such
pain.

I don't know what's right or wrong,
Who is weak and who is strong.
You are brave and this I say,
I know your courage is here to stay.

It's hard to say goodbye,
Especially when someone is about
to die.
Death is called the final curtain,
At least on earth we are certain.

Your memory is one I'll hold dear,
I'll look back not with fear.
But with deep sorrow,
For no more tomorrow. . .

Patricia C Egofske
BACK TO BASICS
We have a little cabin,
That is nestled in the woods,
It holds our hope, our dreams, our
love,
And all our worldly goods.

Our basic needs are simple,
Our bed, our board, our health,
But, we have more than some
others,
When you measure it in wealth.

Our entertainment is all free,
It's a million dollars worth,
For we watch mothernature,
It's the greatest show on earth.

We envy not our neighbor's,
with their fancy homes and strife.
We have no stress or worry,
We lead a tranquil life.

No, we have no fancy mansion,
In this little woods of ours
With luck that will come later,
When we live among the stars.

Joey Smithey
24 KARAT LOVE

To William T Brewer II, my loving family and everyone at the World of Poetry, thank you all for support and caring.

What is it? Who Knows? Do you?
I don't, but I can give you
opinion on the matter, for sure.

24 kts. is pure for one thing,
in gold that is. 24 kts. in Love,
to me, has a one track mind;
unswerving, never leaving the
track, short of a catastrophy.

The value of 24 kt. gold steadily
climbs, Rarely falls (and even then
bounces back everytime). 24 kt.
Love
cannot be bought, True, but man &
woman alike have determinedly
tried inspite of this fact. The
value of 24 kt. Love is in every
man & woman's heart, unknown
to most until that Love is lost.

24 kt. Gold is very soft, Delicate,
and
easily molded to a desired shape.
24 kt. Love, also, is soft, Delicate
and
readily worked into a Desired form,

But. . .

24 kt. Gold can be Re-molded &
reshaped according to a change
of Desire, Taste, or change of
moods.
24 kt. Love is IT; Pure,
un-adultered,
beautiful, True Love. To me when
you
find 24 kt. Love it's yours for life,
for if you try to change it,
it's like trying to make
Gold, well, . . .Golder, and you
can't do that, so, you can't
make 24 kt., (perfect), Love,
well . . . you know . . . Perfecter!

Everyone has their chance to
find 24 kt. Love, but, it's like
panning for 24 kt. gold, you
have to look very carefully,
taking your time, Being very
thorough or one slip and you can
lose your chance to be richer than
the richest and, Baby, I'm not
talking about GOLD!

Robbie Leigh Beard
EARTH'S BEAUTY
Earth's Beauty is many times taken
for granted.
If one would take the time to
examine the details
they would find peace and love for
all life has to offer.
Simple things, such as the stars,
the trees, and even
grass can heal the pain that hate
may have caused.
The stars are actually symbols of
the freed souls that
shine their beauty upon us all.
The trees' limbs are the
outstretched arms of the
Protector who shades us from
danger.
The grass, so many times
overlooked, is actually the
blanket of the Earth, which softens
the step of a young child.

Katie Blue
HOW CAN I BE ME?
Where do I stand
When I cannot stand alone
Where do I walk
When I cannot walk alone
How do I speak
When I cannot hear the silence
Whom do I know
When I do not know myself
How may I question
When I cannot ask the truth
And who will believe in me
When I have lost all faith,
I often dream
Of truths that cannot be
Praying for one word
Hoping for one sign
To preserve my self-esteem.

Sherryle (LeBlanc) Guze
YOUR THE JUDGE

This poem is dedicated to my Husband Dale, Daughter Jamie, Family and my very dear friends.

Hatred is so often in the air, at times understandable and times unfair.
So quick to judge from what others say, instead of judging in your own way.
Believe what is in your own mind, and leave words unsaid that are unkind.
Don't let harsh rumors lead you astray, this we all will learn someday.
We are young yet, and just beginning to live, share with others the kindness you have to give.
Each day we go through a lesson is learned, we can make good or bad the respect we earn.
We all have kindness within, that I know, let the bitter thoughts within you go.
Think of good in each and everyone you enhance, and give the ones you dislike just one more chance.
It's so much easier to go through each day.
when kind words to others you can relay.
Just put yourself in others shoes,
It's then much easier to like, than hate and abuse.
As you go through life from day to day, take good with bad the very best you may.
Believe in the feelings, that come from your heart, not in what others say, make today a new start.

B L "Topper" Williams
WHY
I asked the college professor.
I asked the president.
I asked the minister and the rabbi.
I haven't found one yet that can tell me "Why".
They all have college degrees, They all have P.H.D.'s
Until I find out "Why" I will continue to believe, there is a better way.
The world can be a better place.
With peace goodwill and a slower pace.
The rich are too rich, the poor are too poor.
There are too many wars.
There is not enough love, understanding, and building in this world.
When we learn to use the power of our sun, life will be much more fun.
There will be peace, food and love for all.
Before I die I would like to find out "Why".
When we find out "Why" we will have taken the first step toward enlightenment.

Nancy Brien Heaston
TRIUMPHANT TREE (THEE AND ME)
A little tree, all alone
Tucked in the Lilacs, about to be thrown.
A small boy spotted me.
His heart filled with glee.
Oh Joy, Oh Joy, 'tis thee and me!

He ran for the shovel and dug a small hole,
Covered my roots and patted my soul.
The sun came out and he watered the ground.
A prayer was said for me to be whole.

Thus, I was sown and now I've grown tall,
To look around and watch thee grow.
We look over the Bay and watch the ships come in.
We look at the stars on a clear pleasant night,
And we love to live with all of our might.

We share alot in our inner peace,
Thanx to thee, I got a new lease.
Now my branches are full of grace
Just from a touch of the human race.

Life is fine and growth is great!
It's neat to be a triumphant tree.
We're filled with glee,
Thee and Me.

Pat Langwell Weaver
REMEMBER THEM WELL
We were fortunate to share with these
A portion of life's time and space.
Then, either by accident or disease,
They were taken from this place.

Let us embody and keep alive
The qualities in them we most admired
So that their essence may survive
Long after they've expired.

Remember, as you brush away your tear,
Tho it is sad that they are gone,
It is more important that they were here.
And their memory lingers on.

If this poem's message we heed,
As these memories in our hearts dwell,
We'll say, both in word and deed,
Ah, yes, we remember them well!

Rubymarie Martinez
THE POWER OF LOVE
THE POWER OF LOVE. . .
subsides over any mountain.
It endures in the very soul of one's heart. . .
It envelops the Spirit of one's body and inclines the heavens of one's mind.

It defines the purpose of two
and binds the trust of very few.

It breaks the virtue of evil and it with the truth. . .
It heals the lies of creatures by the heavens.

It bonds the faults of many and...
seals them with serenity.

Betty J Good
DEVIN MARIE
I paused to speak with God today
And share a simple prayer,
He heard each spoken word
And listened with his tender care.
I thanked him for his tender touch—
When things are hard to bear
And he assured me most of all
His hands are always there!

He said, "My child I've dried your tears
When times were pressing you"
And when you tire and falter,
That's when I carried you.

"No time to watch a setting sun," said I
Or watch a rose unfold,
Again my child these precious things
Some may never grasp and hold!

Said he, "Come pause awhile
And hear these words I speak."
You shall not miss creations—
You will find the joy you seek.

I paused, and in a moment knew
What beauty he had given me.
For God had taken joy, setting sun and rose
And placed them all. . .in precious "DEVIN MARIE."

Ann Cheney Breymaier
VILLANELLE FOR LOIS

In loving memory of Lois Marion Auck Powell, Chi Omega, Ohio State University, from North High School, Columbus, Ohio, where we sat next to each other, translating Cicero.

That hot and steaming August day
you lay in satin and in bronze
with roses yellow, white and red.

And I, unknowing, miles away,
in yard with roses yellow, red,
that hot and steaming August day.

In softest colors were you laid,
to match your long and golden hair;
near by the roses red and white.

I scratched the soil, and pulled the weeds,
and envied worms the cool of earth,
escaping steamy August heat.
So soon in depths of earth you lay,
away from verses, hymns and tears,
beneath the roses white and red.

Your lifeless fingers could not bow your violin;
with eyes, that should have filled with tears,
I quietly admired, that hot and steaming August day,
the roses red and yellow, white.

John C Kern
STRENGTH
I whisper: "I am the keystone"
Some do do wear honor and knowledge as they think.
False eloquence and virtue spill forth in floods.
We will neither burn nor sweat with envy
In the shadow of that distant mountain,
Remember: there is always weakness,
A fissure in the imaginary crown.
An outstretched hand reaches only so far;
A tower of strength falls the hardest.

Elizabeth Hess
UNSPOKEN FEELINGS
Upon this earth a man and woman
walked their separate way.
At a crossroad in her life, she tired
and torn with strife, they met one day.

Here take my hand, I will help you stand,
your burdens I will share.
With tenderness and care, he gave her
strength for lifes burdens to bear.

God looked down from above and said,
"Let there be love."
But both were afraid to say,
"I Love you, please stay."

So they parted—and went their
lonely separate way.

K Lehner
THE WIND
The wind softly whispers
against my ear,
From it's murmmering voice,
words of love I hear.
A love song it sings in it's
own gentle tune,
It promises of hope and
of joy to come soon. . .

Tahni Jeanne Stotts
SHADES OF REMEMBRANCE

Thank you Anthony. You're still my "Inspiration" and my love will be here always.

Watercolor dreams
that fade like petals
from long forgotten flowers,
Running together
until it all blends to one
from tears

falling on the page.
The past
only a memory
of the once brilliant sunshine,
In a life
Where love brings rainbows
from the fast spreading
hues of the past,
That know
but one passion. . .
you.

Harry A Conte
THE RIVER
It started in the mountains, from a flake of melted snow,
Then hundreds, thousands,

millions, together made it grow,

Until at last a little stream, began
to flow at will,
Trickling down the mountain side,
always growing never still,

By the time it reached the
lowlands, it had changed into a
brook,
Adding to it's stature, with the
water from each nook,

On it flowed across the meadows,
gathering strength each passing
day,
Twisting, turning, slittering, a
small serpent on it's way,

By the time it reached the valley,
between the mountains on each
side,
It was a wide and flowing river, full
of strength and white with pride,

On it flowed now with a purpose,
on it flowed across the land,
Slittering through the vast green
valleys, gathering all within its
span,

Like a mighty raging serpent, on
its way to meet the sea,
Informing all that stands before it,
either join or let me be,

Onward now to meet the ocean, to
join the waves that lap the shore,
Faster, faster hear it calling, like a
mother at the door,

The journey now is ended, the salt
mingles with the fresh,
And the little melted snow flake, at
last is laid to rest.

Ruth J DeHollander

THE TAX REFORM ACT OF 1986

In memory of my dear husband, Myron. (He would be so proud.)

The new tax laws have us all in a
tizzy,
Trying to decipher them makes
one dizzy.
You cannot deduct this or maybe
that,
Can some use as a dependent, a
calico cat?

There are long term gains and also
short,
Which one do you wish to report?
There is interest and income and
bonds and stocks,
But you can't take sales tax on
those lovely new frocks!!

Your taxes go up and your income
comes down.
You no longer can afford to live in
this town.
You can rant and rave, but take a
long breath . . .
There is one thing for sure—it's
taxes and death!!

Linda M James

AARON

This poem is dedicated to Aaron, my son.

Screen door banging, dusty tennis
shoes scuffling across the floor.
Grubby hand reaching for the
refrigerator handle.
Peering in, looking for something
that appeals.
"I'm starved," he declares, as he
retrieves
A pickle, a slice of cheese, and a
pitcher of juice.
"Don't you eat a single bite until
you wash those hands
And not in the kitchen sink, if you
don't mind."
Water running, hands wiping dirty
prints on clean towel.
Sitting, twisting, turning on the
high stool, gulping juice,
devouring food.
Spilling drink as he pours his
second cup. "Why can't you be
more careful?"
"I didn't try it." he replies, sliding
from his perch.
"Don't climb up the cabinet door
with those dirty feet, if you want
a cookie, ask!"
Dropping crumbs on the way out,
banging door, rustling blue
jeans, jumping off porch.
"Let's dig a swimming pool right
here, can we?"
Heading for the petunia bed with
shovel in hand and friend
trailing.
"Oh no you don't, there is plenty of
dirt elsewhere."
"Mom, oh Mom, the dog's loose
again."
Giggling, running, falling, rolling,
zig-zagging, barking, wagging.
"If I have to catch that mutt again,
I'll call the pound!"
Dirty, dog-smelling, sweating,
fuming, slamming screen,
breathlessly plopping.
Screen door banging, dusty tennis
shoes scuffling across the floor.
Small arms reaching, dandelions
filling grubby little fist.
"Look Mom, I brought you
something. Aren't they pretty
Mom? I love you Mom."
Hugging, squeezing, loving,
thanking—brushing back a
shock of unruly hair.
"Can we put them on the table
Mom? Mom! Why are you crying
Mom?"

Gloria J Hudson

CHRISTMAS ALL YEAR LONG

Dedicated to Mrs. Margurite Hilts who is a great inspiration to me and my interest in writing poetry. Thank you, Mrs. Hilts.

What is the real meaning of
Christmas?
Does anyone really know?
To celebrate the birth of Jesus
Christ;
And our gratefulness to show.

To thank Him for coming to a
world of sin,
For he really didn't have to do it;
To lift our hands in praise to the
King,
He could have stayed in heaven
and he knew it.

He came as a babe wrapped in
swaddling clothes,
Not even a crib for a bed.
Do you thank Him for the pillow
at nite,
Upon which you lay your head?
There are many ways you can
thank our Lord,
Look around and you will see.
People need food everyday, and
Christ said,
"Feed them, and you've really fed
me."

You must clothe my people, Jesus
tells us all.
Did you see some ragged child
today?
Do you have an extra dress to give
that someone?
A pair of pants to someone passing
your way?

We celebrate Christmas one day of
the year,
What of the other three hundred
sixty-four?
There are needs to be filled every
hour of the day,
Let us each do a little more.
For Christmas is really all year
long,
It's the spirit of sharing, you see;
Remember, Christ said if you've
done unto them,
You've also done unto me.

Paul A Kupfer

DARLING: I LOVE YOU

I only need to see you once,
and my world falls apart.
It's hard for me to say good-bye,
to what's inside my heart.

The way your smile makes me feel,
still burns me deep inside.
For, everytime we chance to meet,
those feelings I must hide.

I don't know how long I'll last,
pretending I don't care.
When I long to hold you in my
arms,
and whisper in your ear.

I want to have you by my side.
I need to let love show.
I need to tell you all the things,
that I never let you know.

But, soon you will be leaving,
and you'll be so far away;
that I know I'll never see you.
So, please, just let me say:
Darling, I love you.

Bob Daniels

I DREAMED I WENT TO HEAVEN

This poem is dedicated to my Daughter Melissa. She was 16 years old when she was killed by a Tornado that struck Springfield, Mo. April 29, 1983.

Last night I dreamed I went to
Heaven,
It seemed so far away
And now I have decided,
I'd like to go back someday
You have to die before you go there
But, now, I'm not afraid of death
For I know I'll be happier
When I take my last breath
In my dream I stood before the
gates
And soon they opened wide
Then I sensed someone next to me,
I looked and St. Peter was at my
side
He placed his hand on my shoulder
And said, "The Lord wants to see
you."
I stood before the Lord and he told
me
'other people here would like to see
you too.'
He took my arm and said, 'Come
with me.'
He led me down the streets of gold
There were people all along the
way,
Some were young and some were
old
But no matter what age they were
You could tell by the look on their
face
They were happy and pleased to
know
They would spend eternity in this
place
The Lord led me to a beautiful
mansion,
He said, 'this is your home
forevermore,
And the people that want to see you
are on the other side of this door.'
I could hardly move and the
excitment grew
As I wondered who was on the
other side
The door opened and I walked into
a big room
When I saw who was there, I broke
down and cried
My dad was the first one I saw
My heart was filled with joy
For he had died so long ago
When I was just a young boy
I saw my relatives and friends
And they all came running to me
My grandparents, aunts and uncles
But there was a special one I
wanted to see
Then I saw my daughter standing
there alone
Melissa had died when she was just
sixteen
When she saw me she began to
smile
A more beautiful one I have never
seen
We started walking toward each
other
I had missed her so very much
And now we were together again
And soon I would feel her touch
But all at once I woke up
And oh, how real it had all seemed
And of course I was disappointed
That it was just something I
dreamed
Now Ihave something to look
forward to
I'll be going there someday in time
Then it will be for real
It won't be just a dream of mine
I'll see all the pople I've missed so
much
In that place where you never grow
old
I'll live in a beautiful mansion
And I'll walk the streets of gold

Janet Marie Buhrow

IT IS FINISHED

"It is Finished" were the words of
our Lord,
As He hung upon the cross.
He gave His life to save us all from
death,
Was it really worth the cost?
We nailed God's Son in His hands
and His feet,
And left Him dying there.
On Calvary's hill he bore the cross
for us,
And we didn't even care.

Forgive them He prayed, as He hung so high,
Forgive us Lord, we are ashamed.
You gave us new life when you came to earth
Teaching us, and healing the lame.
The sky grew black and the earth did shake,
As His final words were said
The wind blew, thunder roared, lightning shone above,
And then, our Savior was dead.
"It is Finished" were the words of our Lord,
And His tasks on earth were done.
Now all that was written has been fulfilled,
For this man was God's only Son
Christ suffered and died to save us all,
He gave His life that we might live.
Calvary cost Him great anguish and pain,
What have you got that you can give?

Howard Theodore Buhrow

THE CHASE

The call of the wild,
Is anything but mild,
Tho its snowing and there's not much light,
It is clearly heard in the crisp cold night.
Wolves are running on the frozen ground,
And the howls of the hunt are heard all around,
The buck is racing as fast as he can,
Afraid of the pack as he is of man,
The rim of the forest is fast coming near,
As he swings his antlers and looks to the rear,
He slowly is winning the racing fight,
As he gains yards by his rapid flight.
Rushing into the thick forest of pine,
Then is heard the panting packs failing whine,
As they know they cannot feast tonight,
On the buck who has won a ten to one fight.

Raymond V McGivern

AN UNDERSTANDING

To those who died in Vietnam

I don't know how,
and I can't see why.
I was born to live,
not to die.

The Bureaucrats that point at me,
sent us to war across the sea.
With their envious tricks and sly little schemes. . .
You mess with them, they'll shatter your dreams.

It's been several years past since then
and now I feel that it has started again.
War solves nothing, the peaceful cry,
completely destroy Mother Earth?
WHY?

The social structures cannot prevent,
this unleashed hell the
governments have sent.
And so the wise make known their plea,
for Peace on Earth, and to Let Things Be.

Ruben Cardenas

MY STREAM . . .

Neverending glimpse of beauty, runs
for all of life to witness, to feel,
to love, always flowing, swift, but trustful.
My stream will never run dry. . .
Never leave my. . .heart.

Viola Martin

BOUQUET FOR THE MASTER

Dedicated to Verna Rose Raymer (Mother) who loved everyone she knew and who was loved by all who knew her.

Jesus is Lord my heartstrings shout;
In the greatest war ever, Our Saviour
won out. He hung on the cross; His
lifes blood was shed. But in three days—
Glory Halleujah—Our Saviour is risen our
Lord is not dead. Continually praise Him—
Every day, make a boquet for the Master today!

So come on all ye Christians; To the
doubting Johns go, with our faith seeds—
and by planting them; a garden we'll
grow. Our dear Saviours praises Lets
sing far and near; Tell them the story —
Then kneel down in prayer. Talk to our
Saviour; Show them the way,
make a bouquet for the Master today!

Praise Him for all of the blessings
He wrought. Praise Him for your soul
That with His lifes blood He bought.
With all of these seeds a garden
we'll grow; for our dear Redeemer
from His servants below, down on
you knees continually pray. Make
a bouquet for the Master today!!

Joan M Kopczynski

BLOODY MURDER!

In honor of an FBI agent named John, one of the cruel few.

Death brags of its accomplices—
the physical blow
and its competitor,
the emotional blow.

And whether one dies
by failure of a heart
to go on beating,
or by failure of a heart
to go on loving,
which really is more cruel?

Sunny White

WHAT'S IN A NAME?

I called my mother 'Dory'; it began when I was two. . .
Some said, "it's disrespectful" but she thought it was cute.
Our small town watched in horror as six more children came,
Then divorce, she tended bar; did the woman have no shame?
And Dory laughed and loved us and went her merry way. . .
The year was nineteen forty-four; oh, there'd be hell to pay.
They said she smoked a cigarette, wore slacks right on the street!
Dory bore no malice and smiled at those she'd meet.
She showed us "love thy neighbor", shelived the Golden Rule,
Gave us her sense of humor; we too laughed at the fools.
We grew to be good people, pay tax, obey the law. . .
All seven called her 'Dory', not Mother, Mom, or Ma.
Her first name became 'Grandma', later changed to 'great-';
I prayed she'd see my grandkids' kids but I prayed too late.
Last year she saw a doctor; he told her she would die.
She said she'd had a good life, we lost her in July.
No "Why me, God?", "I don't deserve. . .", she never shed a tear;
She wouldn't let us either, then she left us without fear
The way she'd always lived her life, as brave as any man. . .
I'd said I couldn't stand it, her reply was, "Sure you can."
Friends' comments were unanimous: "She always made me laugh. . .
She was so easy-going"; Lord, what an epitaph!
And when she met her Maker, (it seemed like I could hear)
She said, "Just call me 'Dory'" and she's laughing in her beer.

Jennifer Jean Winkler

FATTY

I hope you see, how I wanted to be,
but never got the chance
I know each day,
I get farther away,
from what I want to be.
I gain 10 pounds, and keep it on,
getting fatter everyday.
I wish for once,
I'de control myself,
and lose that ugly fat.
My hair won't grow,
it stays the same,
and isn't even blond.
I know I complain,
about the littlest things,
but this is not the same.
I cannot stand,
my grotesque appearance,
and I know I need to change.
I pray each day, to get my way,
and look like, what I'de like to be.
So if you see me eating,
just take it from my hand,
and tell me about this poem I wrote,
and how I want to be.

Patricia O'Sullivan

FOOLS' PARADISE

Frail and alone, we reach out tenuously,
Hoping to merge in quixotic ecstasy,
With our disjointed soul's lost memory.
But we end our search prematurely,
For only fools survive life's cruel indignity,
To reach profound and joyful symmetry,
On the far side of despair.

Unity's sweet, tempting bliss beckons us emerge;
We venture out and then recoil.
Surely vile rejection lurks where two souls converge,
For who could continually abide
Those wild hopes and erratic fears we keep locked deep inside?
Only fools thrive in such uncertain soil,
On the far side of despair.

Better not to take the risk;
Better still to quell the loneliness and need,
Bestill the mind, benumb the soul,
Abandon hope of turning half to whole,
Trade vulnerable, contingent harmony
For safe, singular immunity.
All frightened humanity voices but one reply:
Since there are no guarantees, only imprudent fools can merge,
On the far side of despair.

Mary Jane Lamberti

GOD MADE

God made:
Darkness
Wandering
cold stinging wind
No warm faces
Heading toward stormy skies
No companion but their own.

God made:
Light
Bright sunshine
guides their way
Warm soft breeze
Caresses their faces
Heading toward spring
beautiful flowers
are in their path.

Sara Elizabeth Horos

GOODBYE—HELLO

For Kevin and Cheryl Reim who renewed my faith in life. Your memory shall always be with me.

Two shining bright stars,
One Kevin, one Cheryl,

lived shining bright lives
their short earthly stay.

Much to our sorrow,
these children have gone,
to shine in the heavens
for all the days long.

Two shining bright stars,
one Kevin, one Cheryl,
inspired my faith in
all that I do.

I'll always remember,
as each day goes by,
your sweet shining faces,
so beautiful and bright.

Two shining bright stars,
One Kevin, one Cheryl,
I'm saying GOODBYE,
which is so hard to do,
But I know in my heart,
that someday we'll meet,
And saying HELLO,
will forever be sweet.

Carol R Miller
WE'LL MEET AGAIN
First come the tears and then the sorrow,
For me there won't be a tommorrow.
"What about my children, my husband, my life?"
They need a mother and he needs a wife.

My little ones came up to my bed,
They were now crying from what I had just said.
They came up and hugged me one by one,
And then came forth my youngest son.
He hugged me so very tight and a hidden tear
Fell into sight as I took the last breath of my life.

Now I'm in heaven looking down,
I see my little, tiny town.
At the graveyard my children I found,
Each child placed a flower upon the ground.
Then came my youngest once again,
He caressed my head stone with his hand,
His father came and carried him away,
And told him he'd see me again someday.

Eric McVey
THE SAND CASTLE
Love is like a sand castle on the beach
It's built with carefulness,
compassion, and a soft touch
Moving to quickly might endanger
this work of art
and crumble its walls to the ground
But moving slow
allows this structure to grow
Adding and shaping
until it is strong enough to stand by itself
Yet this quest is not over
one must maintain this castle;
Rebuilding each broken part,
making it stronger than before
If care is not taken,
this castle of love will be swept away
Its parts being scattered
thoughout,
never to return as one again

Lynwood Miller Jr
THE DAYS I THINK OF YOU
One day you came into my life
A day which I will never forget
The memories I have shared with you
Always lay deep inside my head

Your eyes were always filled with color
Your heart so caring and true
The way you understood things
Made me always think of you

We had our disagreements
Disagreements that hurt each one of us a lot
We learned from our mistakes
But mistakes are never forgot

Maybe we grew up a little
Maybe we never will
But the love I have felt
Made me feel, very, very real.

Patricia A Houyou
ROMANCE
Romance isn't candy and flowers and such
It's a kind word, a warm caring touch
It's day by day sharing the ups and the downs
It's sharing the laughter enduring the frowns
It's working together and making a life
That will flourish with love, and sustain any strife
It's knowing and meeting the needs of your mates
It's remembering the feelings you had on your dates
It's thinking of special times and places
That sweet memory never erases
When the kids are in bed and you still want to dance
Believe me that is truly romance.

Diane L Salisbury
TANKA XI
His arms held me close
I felt his love, heard his voice
That softly caressed
I thought at last he'd be mine

But it was only a dream

Terrie Costello
ODE TO A HALF-CENTURY
Did you ever think in the good old days
When you were twenty-two,
That you'd ever get to middle-age
And find your waist-line grew?

That your thighs got full of cellulite
And your backside kinda spread
And your upper arms are sagging
And there's gray upon your head?

Did you ever think your hormones—
Those nasty, little traitors—
Would turn on you (when you need 'em most)
Like terroristic raiders?
And plan attacks that make you think
Your brain has turned to hash—
And make your neck and face blush
With a miserable, hot flash?

And when you want to do a simple thing
Like climbing up the stair,
Your legs might give out, your heart might pound,
And your nostrils just might flare!

As life goes on a person can get
Positively "whifty"
So considering the possibilities—
Ain't you glad you're only FIFTY?!

Deva N Macdonald
I DON'T CARE!
Molly Mollare
With the golden hair
Did not care
About anything.

Her mother once said,
"Your father is dead"
Molly laid down in bed and said,
"I don't care!"

Her house was burnt down
Her fish almost drown
She walked into town and said "I don't care!"

Her white coat turned blue
Her dog had the flu
While she lost a shoe and said "I don't care!"

Molly sneezed twice
Her cat ate 3 mice
Her life had no spice she said "I don't care!"

One cold dark day
The sun ran away
So no-one could play she said "I don't care!"

Kay Smith Power
MEMORIES OF GRANDMOTHER

Dedicated to the loving memory of my Grandmother, Elva Viola Weddington, (June 7,1983—January 15, 1973)

I remember sleeping on a mattress filled with feather down,
And when I fell into into it I was covered all around.
A flannel gown from my head to my feet,
With a hot, flat iron to keep in the heat.
At least fifty pounds of cover made with loving hands,
By the dearest Grandmother in all the land.
I remember Grandma holding me close,
And saying our prayers for those we loved most.
I remember her saying, "Do not fear,
God knows what He's doing and He is near.
The thunder will pass and so will the rain,
And tomorrow the sun will shine again."
I remember waking early and Grandma was gone,
It really seemed strange, being alone.
I walked to the kitchen to prepare for school,
And Grandma looked up and opened her arms.
I knelt beside her and she held me tight,
"til she'd finished her prayer and started the day off right.
I can almost remember every word of her prayer,
And I wish I could be like her, as she knelt by her chair.
The memories rush on, some sad, some gay.
Dear God, let us kneel together again some day.

Gregory Alan Main
FRIEND
Thank you for the hands we've held
Thank you for your smiles
Thank you for the time you take
To make my life worthwhile

Thank you for your thoughtfulness
Thank you for your anger
Meant to steer me straight in life
And harbor me from danger

Thank you for your companionship
Thank you for needed hugs and kisses
Thank you for being my confidente
And understanding my most secret wishes

Thank you for the tears we've shed
Thank you for your laughter
Thank you for the light you'll shine
On my life's road everafter

Thank you for timely tender words
Thank you for your trust in me
Thank you for always being near
Forever grateful I'll always be

Tamara Kathaleen Sears
GOODBYE MY LOVE
With the love I've seen inside your eyes
is when I hear you talking.
You always look down among my pride,
but then of course I keep on walking.

The light that shines inside of me
may seem like it just collided,
but how could that be? When all
the sorrow comes down like rain,
not one drop left for me to borrow,
to ease down the pain.

But before you begin to leave the room
I want you to know baby—that on the
other side of this door is a whole new
world out there! And maybe someday,
everything will be allright.

So please don't cry! . . . Goodbye!

Wm M Cowl
LOOK INWARD ANGEL
Look Landward Angel
And see if thou canst not perceive
The rocks and rills
The forest glade
The wooded glen
That bespeaks of peace to the hearts of men

Look seaward Angel
And see if thou canst not perceive
The ocean deeps
The coral reef
'Neath thundering wave
Where rest so many of the brave

Look upward Angel
And see if thou canst not perceive
The towering hills
The lofty crags
The snow capped peaks
Where man in vain his maker seeks

Look inward Angel
And see if thou canst not percieve
The stuff of which
The rocks and rills
The ocean deep

The towering hills
And even distant stars are made of.

Travis A Duncan
ON TRUTH
Her world was a horror show,
A film of fright'ning scenes.
She had a place where she could go
To hide from all the fiends.
Through the wood, upon a rock
By a brook of blues and greens,
She'd sit and with the creatures talk
About what honor means.

I found her there one day years back.
I thought she'd run away;
Her clothes were piled in a stack,
Her hair in disarray.
But nay! She pulled me to her side
And begged me please to stay.
In me it was she did confide
All that she had to say.

She told me what she feared the most:
"The ease with which we lie.
"Not little whites nor angler's boasts."
She paused, then with a sigh
She said, "The lies we tell ourselves
"Are those that make me cry.
"If lies take root first place they delve
"Then truth must surely die."

Jean Marie Shucosky
GROWING PAINS
If only time could turn about
To when I used to say,
"Mama, can I please go out
With Mary-Jane and play?"

If only time could turn about
To the days so fat with laughter
To the mud pies, dolls and torn blue jeans
And the spankings I got after.

If only time could turn about
You'd never hear me pause
To answer, "Yes", when someone asked

Do you believe in Santa Claus?"

If only time could turn about
You'd see a father's pride
Beaming for the little girl
Clinging to his side.

If only time could turn about
To all these things long past
I never would have wished at all
To grow up quite so fast.

But now I'm grown with memories
That ne're from me shall part
For with them I can always be
So very young at heart.

Phebe Anne Boyle
REFLECTION
You're considered old colonial
A relic of yesterday
Your shuttered door and entrance hall
Have given you away—
Your sloping door and windows fair
With their diamond-studded panes
Have let the golden sunshine in
While keeping out the rains—
Then of course your chimneys wide
Just whisper of days long past—
When friends drew close to your fireside
Till winter's storms had passed—
Your shining hearth with its mantlepiece
Still gleam from loving care
They reflect their light on wide board floors
A-showing signs of wear—
Up your stairways banister
Flooded soft with light
I think of all the loving hands
That kept you polished bright—
I walk across your wide board floors
Hearing them creak and moan;
They're not complaining that I know
Tis age that makes them groan—
You've seen it all, of that I'm sure,
Of birth, of death and tears,
And yet I feel that you were blessed
With laughter down the years!

Noella Cormier-Clavette
LOVE
What is love?

It's feeling,
It's sharing.

What is love?

It's caring,
It's belonging.

It's having fun

It's you and I
As only one.

Francelia Herkert
THOUGHTS
Oh America, once so beautiful, so fair,
now so full of polluted air;
Where have all your flowers gone?
your trees and grass and bird's sweet song;
Once they were all so dear,
but now the warning signs are clear;
People better get together while they can,
for its the end of pollution, or the end of man.

Martin T Kohn
ROBIN
Robin with your orange and black
feathers sitting on a branch
with your male robin.

Robin sitting on that branch chirping
your love song with your male robin
next to you.

Robin just chirp that love song that
love song, Robin you and your male just
keep on chirping.

Colleen Fitzgerald
THE INNOCENT ONE!
Down into our wombs, God sent
them from above.
The same way we were sent, but
we were allowed to grow.
The innocent ones never get the chance
to see what life can be
No trees, mountains, or animals,
they're doomed to darkness you see
God always has a reason for everything
he does
So what do we think we're doing,
by changing what is to was
If only we could realize, there is
no choice to make
By the living one inside you,
the choice has already been made
Think about the innocent one,
you'll see that I am right.
By living there inside of you,
the choice it's made is life.

Bonnie Van Driesen
MY FRIEND, MY MOTHER-IN-LAW
If ever I could choose,
A mother-in-law for me;
I'd keep the one I've got,
Because a better one can't be.

You've taught us all,
To get along,
And yet you've shown us,
That we must be strong.

To think things through,
Before doing them first;
To make the best,
Of what seems the worst.

You've shaped our lives;,
In so many ways,
And brightened up,
So many of our days.

I'm so glad we are related,
And share one family tree,
And all because of your son,
Chose—very fortunate Me.

I've gained a Mom,
Whom I simply adore,
You are my friend,
Of that I'm sure.

Glenn D Pelfrey
MOTHER I MISS YOU

---

*In loving memory of my mother,
Wanda M. Pelfrey.*

Mother I miss you,
More than words can say.
I miss you always,
Today and everyday.

Thanksgiving wasn't the same without you;
Christmas was so too.
I miss you so much Mother,
I don't know what to do.

I try to be strong Mother,
Because someday I know,
I'll be with you in heaven,
When it's my turn to go.

James E Mulira
AFRICA
Africa Oh! Africa,
How sweet it sounds!
The name of Africa.
Africa is huge and complex.
Stretching far and wide,
With deserts, virgin forests and savannah,
Africa is different.

They are as diverse as can be
The peoples of Africa.
A mixture of black and white,
Most are tall and agile,
Their traditions unique.

Remarkable are the rivers of Africa
The mothers of all nurture:
The Nile, the Congo, the Niger, the many more.
They flow across deserts and savannah,
Across forests and farmlands.

Now, I beseech thee brethren
Yee, the people of Africa,
Continue working and searching in earnest,
Preserving your heritage for the future,
Maintaining thy friendly attitude,
Training thy sons and daughters,
For the future will be different,
And the best prepared will benefit most.

Vincent Guella
FLOWERS ALONG MY PATH
Flowers bloom along my earthly way while I'm sad
and the flowers seem dull. In my view I see
tulips and roses though there is a deadness
there. It seems as if I'm dead as if today is
tomorrow. The sun shines but it does not
illuminate my view. I see tulips of red laden in
sadness. I see black fences, newly painted, as I walk along
my sullen way. Everything seems still and quiet
and no sounds are to be heard. even
hear a pin drop as it seems. Whether the
sky is clear or cloudy there is still sadness
there. All around me life continues, people laugh
and sing, though I don't see them. It seems as though I'm in my own world of gloom.

Dorothy Lichty
WIND
It comes in gusts with whine of wearied ghosts
Beseeching entrance through the sash secured;
The trailing tail that whips the shade and coasts
Beyond in senseless search of gain, demures
To lull and rest, then gathers greater force —
A fierce and sonton wolf with fangs unleashed,
Returns in furry bound with no remorse;
But howls the louder toward his goal unreached.
The dust from fields engulf my living room
And blankets all there in a soft grey haze.
I cannot see the sun though it is noon;
The sky will hold the scene for many days:
A sharp reminder that we are but heralds,
And God is in command of His own world.

Karen J Lapointe
WHAT, WHY, AND WHEN

As I sit and look out the window a tear comes to my eye.
When I think of the Way we used to be and the things we let
pass us by.
My mind is full of questions.
My heart aches with fear.
I search my soul for the answers, but they are not really clear.
What happened to those happy times when we did things just
for love?
Why don't we hold hands anymore just because we want to touch?
When did we let money and pride begin to mean so much?
What makes you rather watch TV then do something with me?
Why don't I want to rub your back when you complain it's sore?
When in the world did making love begin to be a chore?
What caused us to feel that we had to prove ourselves to
each other?
Why did we start comparing us to: a neighbor, my father, your
mother?
When did our minds get so lonely that they wandered to someone elses bed?
What makes me feel more comfortable looking back and not ahead?
Why do we cry as two separate people, instead of laughing as
one?
When will we wake up and begin to repair the damage we have
done?
What caused us to be so blind that we don't even see, we have
lost <u>us</u> and become <u>you</u> and <u>me</u>.
Why do we play these foolish games, does anyone really win?
When will we stop wasting our lives and begin to love again?

James R Finn
ENLIGHTENMENT

To Annegret for opportunity, recognition, suggestion, encouragement, typing; and being a loving caring wife.

Of God our words cannot describe;
Yet, on our mind spirit soul inscribes:

A knowing of a knowing for any betides,
In awe and wonder of grandest surprise;

Of tranquil joy melding ecstasy besides,
And fullest the picture forever resides.

Wilma G Widick
LIFE IS BEAUTIFUL

Life, as whole is a beautiful thing.
Did you ever stop to wonder
Why you were happy, or sad, or blue?
Or think life a continual blunder?

"Now why did this have to happen to me?"
Have you heard these words before?
It's foolish to utter them, needless to say,
"That's life for you, evermore."

Why not take the hard luck with the good,
And laugh at the persistent pest.
For the whole world knows this adage is true,
"Everything happens for the best."

Life has a sunny side to, don't you think?
For when you're happy and gay,
You never give thought to trouble then.
Life moves in a mysterious way.

So when the ebb of our existence is reached..
Let us be more than dutiful,
As death clouds dim our horizon,
Remember. . ."Life Has Been Beautiful."

Dolly Strong
SONG FOR AMERICA

America! Thou land apart.
Thou hope of every trembling heart.
With arms now stretched so open wide,
Renew thy welcome with each tide.
Thy promise great, to those who try;
Who with God's help, on thee rely.
Thy beauty, still, beyond compare.
Thy waters blue, thy forests fair.
Thy mountains strong, with craggy peaks.
And hamlets nestled down in sleep.
Thy cities hum with industry.

Thy heartland farms, they nourish me.
Thy churches, standing silent, speak.
Of love and peace which all men seek.
Thy flag, aloft, proclaims thy might;
As stripes vermilion march with white.
And purest stars, in sapphire sea,
Restore in me tranquillity.
Some sons now sleep beneath thy sod,
For freedom's cause, known now to God
We bow our heads, in tear-drenched thanks,
To those now fallen in our ranks.
God grant us grace, that we may be,
Forevermore; the land most free.

Diallo
I THOUGHT YOU WOULD NEVER GO AWAY

To Mrs. Barbara Dugger Anderson, My mother for her love, patience, and inspiration

---

I thought you would never go away
or leave me alone.
And if you did you would always come back.
Now I've been solo/w so long -
I lost track of time
and values
and beliefs
and don't care for much.
Even stopped really loving those importantly close
and can't even say the words anymore.
I remember all the things I wanted to say
or should have
but didn't.
because they were procrastinated!
and maybe that's making me indulge in
laziness.

Viola Henson
LOVE

Love should be pure and true,
Expressed daily by me and you.
Love is great,
let's show it now or tomorrow will be too late.

Micheal S Roberts
CHECK MATE

What can we hope to accomplish?
What can we hope to achieve?
Why don't we look at the other and agree,
It's time to stop fighting,
just live and let be

How can man expect to survive?
Our answers are too advanced.
We know too much of how to kill,
nothing to stay in peace.

Where do you think our world is headed?
How can it possibly stay alive?
When we have the weapons, and they have the weapons
to kill every thing alive.

We call them evil,
they do the same,
Is it a wonder there is no change?
We still grow farther apart.

The farther we grow,
the more we teach and learn to hate.
The more we hate,
the closer we come to dying without change.

Why don't we look at the other and agree
it's time to stop fighting,
just live and let be.

How can man expect to survive?
Our answers are to advanced.
We know too much of how to kill,
nothing to stay in peace.

Where do you think our world is headed?
How can it possibly stay alive?
When we have the weapons, and they have the weapons
to kill every;thing alive.

We call them evil,
they do the same,
Is it a wonder there is no change?
We still grow farther apart.

The farther we grow,
the more we teach and learn to hate.
The more we hate,
the closer we come to dying without change.

Barbara J Hawkins
FEELINGS OF THE WHITE DOVE

Show me what kind of heart do you have?
Tell me what kind of mind does the dove have?
Show me the white wings of the dove
So I may fly high above the sky
I feel the walls of the vassel closing down around me
Where should I hide?
The ships are at hand, and the white dove
Sits at her throne as she has sat before.
Detain my heart, Let it not refuse love, but
Let's not confine ourself behind the walls of the vassel,
Let the winds of the storm combine its
Force, so we can be pure in heart, If not
In the mind. I too have seen the wings of the
White Dove flying high above the sky.

Raymond E Wright
FATHER . . . SAVE US ALL

Father. . .Save this world from turmoil
That it is in;
Father. . .Let us live together
Apart from sin. . .
The violence, the hate;
Why some segregate. . .
We're all made of one
All under your sun. . .
Father. . .hear our call;
Save us all.

Father. . .They talk about black power,
They say that's soul;
Father. . .The Ku-Klux-Klan's an idol,
Bless both, they're bold. . .
Teach them the way,
To live right today. . .
Teach them the love
That comes from above. . .
Father. . .Hear our call;
Save us all.

Father. . .When it's time to gather
Around your throne;
Father. . .All the groups and nations
Must answer alone
And when you look,
In your holy book. . .
Some still don't know
That your word will go. . .
Father. . . Hear our call;
Save us all.

Mary Stockton Madden
SECURITY REFLECTED

To God for Inspiration, and my Husband Bill, and Family, for Love and Encouragement.

I tried all night to find the words
That poems are supposed to express,
The rhyme, the meter and the theme—
The contents that would impress

The harder I tried to force the words,
Or force my own thoughts to form,

The more weary my efforts
  became,
I wasn't even getting lukewarm.

I turned to God, for I wanted to
  sleep
I prayed for some peace and my
  mind to slow,
But instead He helped my mind to
  clear—
And the words began to flow—

When I was young, Security was,
A Nite-lite as I slept,
My Father's hand when I crossed
  the street,
My Mother's embrace when I wept.

A big Brother to stick up for me,
A Teacher who knew my fears,
A Girl-friend to confide in,
Some acceptance from my Peers.

Now in maturity, I find,
Security and Faith go hand and
  hand.
God's that needed Nite-lite in my
  life,
Reflecting in my love, and molding
  who I am.

Lareta Sue Steinmetz

FREEDOM (BEGINNING OR END?)

Dedicated to Wisdom which comes as a gift thru choices of freedom. . .and to those in my life whose wisdom gave me freedom.

Floating up and up
into the sky,
the balloon is free from the tugging
  string
the balloon is free from the tugging
  string
in the little ones hand.
Up into the air it goes following the
  wind.
Up and
back
and d
o p
w u
n and
over the trees and over the wires,
far from the little ones sight.
It's free, it's free
at last, at last -
Just go with the wind
over the mountains
and over the sea,
to new soft winds and
different lands.
Oh! The freedom and happiness of
  it all.
The air is thin,
the balloon expands,
then pop and rip. . .
It's over—
The bubble of delight is gone
and the freedom becomes the end

Nancy M Ryan

UNTITLED

You were gone—late you left me
I slept and awoke alone
in love and a little lonely.

It is Saturday
It is washing clothes
cleaning
chores
running
with your image moving all around
  my heart.
Half-way between rinse and spin
between kitchen and dining room
your white shirt
hanging over a chair, stopped me
made me smile
with its remembered fragrance.

It hangs now in my room
clean
straight
renewed

It is how you make me feel.

Kathy Deane Vignali

A NIGHT OF LOVE

WE made Love, when time would
  permit us to share our
bodies and our minds
There's something special about
  our Love—I don't think all Love
  is blind.
We start with just a simple kiss, my
  head on your shoulder
rests.
And then it turns into another kiss,
  then your hand upon
my breast.
Our bodies touch together as we lie
  down in the unmade bed.
And then kiss again so gently,
  where angels fear to tread.
Your leg crosses atop my body and
  our breathing becomes so heavy,
And then we move together, in a
  rhythm that's so very steady—
We see the top of a mountain we
  both know were going to climb,
Not only with our bodies, but with
  our hearts and our minds.
And then the top of the mountain -
Upon it we both have come!
To share together a night of LOVE
  that's only just begun!

Wilma E Lopez

THE LOSING

I can feel the tears,
Welling up inside;
It is much too hard
To hide them.

It's so bittersweet,
Thinking of lost years,
Knowing I'll never again
Find them.

When the precious moments
Fade to gray in my mind,
I realize it's a terrible
Losing.

And I wish sometimes
That they'd sparkle once more,
But I know that I can't
Do the choosing.

So I let the tears flow,
While I brush off the dust
That covers what my heart
Is unfolding.

And I wipe away a tear,
As I finally conclude,
All that's left is what my soul
Is holding.

Sherry S Redmon

MOTHER

Mother is the sweetest name, or so
  the poets say
And here in my own words is what
  makes me feel that way
When I was just a tiny tot you were
  always there for me
To scratch my back, hold me close,
  or mend a battered knee
To play with dolls, to color, or just
  to lend a smile
I knew that you were "Special"
  even as a child
And as I entered the wild & crazy
  teens you never let me down
You took me places I wanted to go
  and at home my friends could
"hang around"
The rules were strict and the
  discipline stayed the same
You taught me through
  wrong-doing nothing would be
  gained
But it wasn't until I became an
  adult with a family of my own
That I began to realize what you
  knew all along
The love bond between us will
  never be broken
Through any deed that may be
  done or any word that's spoken
We have come too far to turn back
  now and I just wanted you to
know
The things that are in my heart that
  sometimes I don't show
So as I've grown I have learned that
  what the poets say is true
Of all the Mothers in the world the
  most precious one is you.

Mavis Campbell

BEFORE THE MISSILE FELL

Inspired by my son, Allan, on the death of our friend in Vietnam, June 5, 1968

Dear Pal, I received your letter,
'Twas great to hear from you.
Things then, seemed so much
  better
With our red, our white, and our
  blue.

I answered your letter twice before
But, mindless me, I failed.
Forgive me, now, and forevermore
Because they were not mailed.

I feel, somehow, you know the
  truth
Things may be twice as well,
With you, my friend, who in your
  youth
Were there when the missile fell.

We did so many things together
When we were fancy free.
The good, the bad, or whatever,
But we had fun. Didn't we?

The gun salute and taps are played,
But not in the heart of your pal,
Somehow, may my letter so
  delayed
Reach you, my buddy.

  From Al

Elizabeth Wilkinson-Anderson

MY BELOVED

We met, and lived, and loved;
Me and my beloved.

Children came, and grew, and
  went,
And we lived on in sweet content.

When we knew he had to go;
We spent a year in silent woe.

Then one night death came near;
We held hands without fear.

In the first light of dawn;
A slight pressure and he was gone.

He went striding up the hill,
Eager still to do God's will.

He helps build mansions up above
Where all of us will live and love.

Marva Stewart-Pittman

A BREATH OF SPRING

Love is like a breath of spring
Crickets chirp and little birds sing.
The April flowers and the blossoms
  bloom,
And all forms of life give out a tune.
Songs of love are sung out too,
With love that's warm, that's sweet
  and true.
I adore the love that the springtime
  brings,
That's sweet, sweet love, that
  breath of spring.

Linda C Grazulis

WHO CAN DOUBT HE CARES

We can sense God in the morning
As we breathe the fresh, clean air
In the country where the dewdrops
Cling to roses soft and fair.

We can sense God at noon
As we stroll amid the garden,
Viewing yellow buttercups,
Assured our sins are pardoned.

We can sense God in the evening
When morning glories fold,

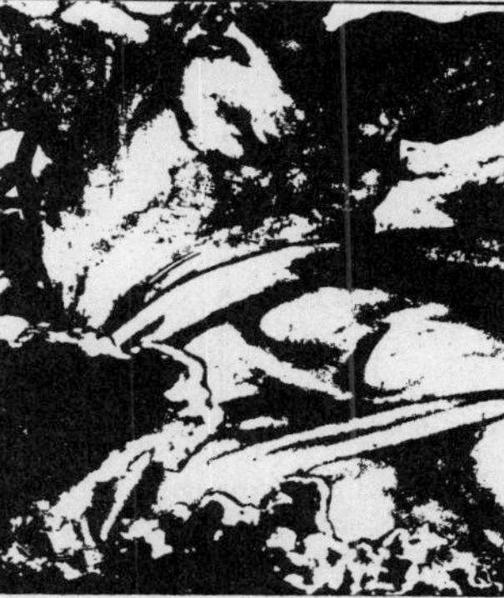

Just to catch a glimpse of the
  sunset,
God's love revealed so bold.

We can sense God at night
When darkness overtakes,
Trusting our Father's love,
Sweet peace when we awake.

God tenderly watches o'er us.
Who can doubt He cares
When each hour ticks a miracle
Displayed everywhere.

Karen Seyb

THE KEY

Cluttered
in a montage
of myriad mysteries
the mind lies locked
in musty oblivion
until the key
unlocks
the
door
to
secluded
Shangri-la
steeped
in
spectrums
of
splendor.

Robin Rae Johnson

I TRY

I am alone in a crowd and it makes
  me wonder;
  What does God have in store for
  me?

I have a family but they all take,
I have a town but no friends,
I have a life but no purpose;
What do they all expect of me?
I don't pray for wealth, not much at least;
I pray for friends and a way to help,
I pray to keep my sanity.
Will I pass the test?
We'll know when I die if I'm missed by more than my family
I will have found the answer,
If I was able to touch other lives and help them with
THEIR DREAMS!

Elizabeth Myra Carter
DANIEL

This poem is dedicated to my mother, Myra L. Kravetz. Thank-you for your encouragement.

Will you ever want to marry me?
. . .ever love me that much?
Oh yes,
I see,
Commitment is not to be touched,
No,
It's nothing personal
. . .not rejection. . .
I just accept it
while left
craving your affection.

Robert D Klock
THE RAIN

Light pierced my eyes,
I saw,
The frightful clouds in the distance
A coming storm.
Then from afar
I heard,
The sound of thunder.
Suddenly there was a breeze,
I could smell
Dampness beckoning the coming rain.
Quickly it came and without cover,
I felt
Upon my face,
And running down,
The rain.

Cynthia Gervais
ODE TO NATURE

Oh Nature what has become of thee?
We have forced you away.
We have pushed you into the furthest exile.
Now we must travel far just to stand secure
beneath your loving arms.
Nature I look up to you as if a child in awe.
Your majesty and grandeur inspire me.
What will become of thee?
Will you allow us to gnaw and chew at you
like a great hungry beast
Until we devour all? Everything:
Leaving you nothing but an empty shell.
Leaving you stripped naked like many old bones.
Who will nurture us then Earth Mother?
What will become of us after we have drained
and wasted every last drop of your precious juices.
Who then so lovingly as you will take us to her breast
while we cry like spoiled children . . .

Linda Grantz Sirwell
IMAGINE BEING THERE

I dedicate this poem to my father Daniel and mother, Marian

I try to imagine being there
That night so very long ago,
Talking, sharing and being in prayer
With Jesus and the disciples He loved so.

I've read most of what they talked about
I've heard how they passed the dishes,
I know He had no reason to doubt
Soon He'd be fulfilling His Father's wishes. . .

They respected Him and loved Him as a brother
He taught them as time went by, what they knew,
He spent time in prayer with them, and they with each other
Praying unceasingly together, oft till morning brought dew.

They protested loudly as Jesus informed them
Soon it will be time for Me to go,
Judas Iscariot was at that moment betraying Him,
Just as the Bible had prophesied it to be so.

I try to imagine being there as He trudged up Calvary's hill
If only to help shoulder His heavy burden, relieve the agony,
I marvel at such sacrifice, each day I thank Him still
Try to imagine such great love, He gave His life for you and me.

Mary Katherine Downs
GOOD NEWS—TO BE SAVED

This poem is dedicated to my mother and father who have stood behind me through difficult times, and who I owe my life and my faith to. God bless you, Mom and Dad!

My beginning is my end!
Now I can see the truth of it,
circumfrence at my command.
You lose your life to find it,
Lose your legs to stand.
Christ's glory shines brightly
through showers of blood.
The light in the darkness.
Perfection established through imperfection,
to live as one.

Extraverted we are born.
Pure. The snow white dove.
Reigns the stain of living
discolors our love.

When we have to die,
we want to live.

God's wisdom is the circle -
the Cross, the Great, the ultimate Bridge.
My beginning is at last,
my end!

David Battershell
ANN MCCARTNEY

We've exalted many vessels and we loved them as they came, Ann McCartney was a symbol of, love's joy, then death and pain - The first letter. . .each poetic line. . .will spell her angel name

Ann McCartney . . . her very name
. . . Sings with the
sweetest syllables of sound
Nourished by the beat of angels wings or so my thoughts abound!
Nothing could make me happier now than if her heart were free
Much weighs the agony in my crying soul—she's engaged, but not to me!
Can hope be crushed by a single blow?—Shall the birds
all cease to sing? -
Can a blue sky be but sullen gray and every fowl take wing?
A happy hope crushed down in death like a vulture from the sky,
Resting on fallen carrion—the tearing to shreds of I.
True to the nature of ourselves, we love, if it is
wrong.
No imagery conveys these crushing pangs where we seek to but belong,
Engaged as you are to another man, can your love ever shine on me?
You said goodbye, when I said hello—Ann McCartney,
hear my plea!

EdK
UNTITLED

Written for Dan: Dedicated to Ian and Evan—may they never sense the sadness

I saw a man in agony
Full of anger adespair
To hold him in his misery
But my hands touched only air

There were other people present
And so I did not dare
I longed to reach acomfort him
But my hands touched only air

I felt a need to help him
And yet I sat astared
My heart reached out aheld him
But my hands touched only air

Cecile Bouchard Cain
NEAR TO YOU

This poem is dedicated to Bruce, my husband.

I've thought so much of you to-day,
I wish that you could hear
the words I long to say to you,
to whisper in your ear.

But now, you've gone so far away,
(and tho' we're far apart)
I think you know the things I'd say
for the words are in my heart.

You're always near to me, dear,
(still you're so far away)
you're always near to me, dear,
although you've gone to stay.

For I know there's no return for you
but I know that some day too,
I shall also go away
and then—I shall again—see you!

Melanie M Knack
A MEMORY FOR ALL SEASONS

My mind won't remember
what time it was
Because, my darling
Because, my heart loved you through
All the seasons.
Yes, there were so very many reasons
spring brought us birds to fly
As you touched my hair, our love climbed high
I knew that your life I would share.
Summer sun, we sure had fun.
Stars at night, oh, what a beautiful sight.
Fall leaves changed their colors.
We were the best of lovers.
Winter snow, our love still flowed
Now, we've come through all the seasons
This year, let our love
Still be the reason.

Betty Jane Ramsey
FLOTSAM JETSAM

I was jetsam, I was flotsam,
Floating in an emerald sea.
Waves buoyed me up
To float with aquatic moves,
There among the white capped spires of foam,
I spotted my portmanteau.
Ah, with fancy plumage, I a
Mermaids haven could seek
And bedazzle the great Poseidon.
Sinking down underneath liquid covers,
The song of the humpback postlude to the lovers.
Murky depths, a seaweed garden,
Sand stirring as I touch bottom.
No mermaid kingdom, no Poseidon!
I kicked off with flippers
Surrealistically pummeling at speed,
Passing bubbles in flight,
Like a porpoise effortlessly,
Jumping through a ring,
I came sailing into the light.
A flotilla surrounded me,
Sailors threw me flotage.
I chose the ring to port,
The next reservation on a cruise ship,
I plan to abort!

Zoe C Bleau
BEYOND MY WINDOW IS A TREE

Beyond my window is a tree
A symbol of hope and serenity
Skyscrapers large and quite select
Stand so sterile and erect.

If God can let one tree survive
In this awful concrete countryside
Why can I not be the one
To sit and ponder in the sun?

The branches dance, the pinecones sway
The buildings only stare all day
The concrete slabs can't dance at all
They just stand there straight and tall.

When the wind whispers in their ears
Do you think those buildings hear?
But watch the tree as the breeze dances by

She is talking to someone who is on high.

She fears noone you can easily see
The tree that is talking to God for me
If that tree can stand with branches high
Amid the concrete jungle, free
Then why not I?

Frank Paul Graffeo
THE VOICE FROM WITHIN

You shall not lose, anyone of them, was God the Father's cry,
Thats why Jesus came to earth, to help and save, not to deny.
The voice of conscience, was given, to every one and all,
To help man find happiness with life, so as not to slip or fall.

That sacred spiritual voice, of the father, He shares with you and me,
To know right from wrong, so that we can enjoy life clean, true and free.
That voice thats within us is a Godly flower, guiding us daily, every hour,
Have you ever wondered, when your about to commit, a foolish sin.

Like unexplained magic, you hear a little voice, from within,
You fight it at times, with all of your very might.
It's always telling you, always, wrong from right,
The touch of God is in it, for everyone, for me and you.

This voice my friend, is God's undying love for you,
He tries to guide you, from His heavens, in the sky above.
God's love for you never dies, some just listen, some abide.
Others fall prey as they leave, His loving and adoring side.

God's love for you never ends, He's telling you always, He's your friend,
So share the love he has to give, listen to that gentle voice within.
It's God's way of keeping you free, from lifes immoral sin,
So listen to the voice of love, that speaks to you, from within.

Diana Boyle Rice

Diana Boyle Rice
MY SPRING WILL COME

Gentle rain will fall today
and somewhere, you may grieve . . .
longing for sun and spring that never come.
But I cannot . . .
I cannot grieve
for rain, or trees so bare,
For they bring beauty, I, alone can see.
I cannot grieve
As gentle rain turns savage, and torments the land,
Though Earth will seem a desolate, barren place,
I cannot grieve
Though every flower and leaf is stripped away
and this chill land is darkened with despair,
For soon, through dreaming eyes, the sun appears,
and so I know, My Spring will come again . . .
But I will grieve
for you, my Dear, for in your heart
the Winter never ends . . .
and flowers cannot bloom in barren places.

Nancy Roberts
CACTUS-GARDEN ASSAULT

For Ozell

Strong, yellow buds
Silently search for space
On a still-sleeping Prickly

And red-orange orbs
Attach to the grey-dead tips
Of a tall Ocotillo

While bold blooms convert
A long-needled, fuzzy Barrel
Into a blazing globe of color

And Summer's vanguard
Marches across the desert
Into my cactus garden.

Only the Spanish Dagger
Sharply silhouetted
Against the pale-pink sun-rise
Seems to stand strong
Against the first foray
Allowing neither bloom nor blossom
Daring to defy Spring's harsh advance

Until a spirited sparrow
Flies past the knife-sharp blades
Straight for the Dagger's heart

And next to it
Builds a nest.

Vivian C Curcio
THE CHALLENGER

This poem is dedicated to the crew of the Challenger, and their families.

The countdown had started; the seven in their seats,
No one thought of the danger; only of their feats.
All eyes were on the sky, it was a perfect day,
Everything looked just wonderful, everyone was so gay.

Great clouds of smoke then appeared in the sky,
NASA was saying "A major malfunction. . ." OH MY:
A little more than a minute; it was over for the crew,
But the love and respect of the nation, grew and grew.

The people watched in horror; tears in every eye,
Every man, woman and child wanted to say goodbye.
Ron, Dick, Mike, Judy, Greg, Christa, and El:
We will never forget you; you did your job well.

Your courage and valor will lead us to a great height,
And may the good Lord forever keep you in his sight.
Watch over our country, that we may expand in space,
And when we meet in heaven, we can thank you face to face.

Vicki L Holsworth
CENTERING

For I am the center of my universe.
A hard lesson to learn, even harder to grasp when taught.
All that happens can be controlled, examined. . .
dissected into minute parts
To be reassembled in manageable segments which when taken
one at a time can be paried, molded into life's scheme,
the pattern of what you want.
Success can only be if one is content, at peace internally
with one's own self.
The magnetic pull can be redirected, reversing the poles.
So that what happens inside and out will work in harmony.
You are the master of the key which unlock the doors to
your fate.
Happiness, success, health all that you desire is centered
in your being.
Protect what is yours, feed it, care for it, nurture it,
let it grow. . .
For unless you do, your being, the essence of who you are
is lost as others lead you.
The dark clouds of sorrow, failure, and defeat will follow
you until all eternity envelopes you.
I know, because I now am the center of my universe as,
I <u>can</u> control, alleviate, activate, separate the whole
into parts once again.

Dorathea J Bath
GOD'S EDGE

To Merlynn my beloved daughter-in-law

Come to the edge
Where earth caresses the sky,

Come to the edge
Where shiny stars twinkle by,
Where the man in the moon
Smiles down on the earth,
Yet frowns on a dearth
Of hate, death, and war.

Come to the edge
Change hate to love,
Change death to life
And war to peace on earth
ETERNALLY!!

Michelle Sydow
ED AT EIGHTY

Written for my Uncle Edward Earl, inspired by my very special Aunt Ethel Earl.

I was a very small child back in 1943
When mother took me to Uncle Ed's farm to see
All the wonders and beauty of the Iowa farm
Where I was toted around on Uncle Ed's arm.
Uncle Ed was a quiet, gentle, lovable man.
He worked day and night taking care of the land.
His special talent was making everything seem like fun.
Like the day his old bull put us all on the run.
Uncle Ed said, "That bull wouldn't hurt you, you know,
He's a ham and just likes to put on a show."
My mother and Aunts weren't convinced, I could see,
They hadn't enjoyed the day up in a tree.
I'll never forget that sad lonely day
When Uncle Ed and Aunt Vera moved far far away.
He said California would be a wonderful location
And he wanted a chance at a brand new vocation.
From California Uncle Ed wrote that he and his son
Had their own successful business already begun.
He invested in property and worked for the state,
In short his accomplishments were nothing but great.
As a husband, father, grandfather, he's the best.
There's no doubt about it, he's heads above the rest.
At eighty years young, the best is still yet to come
Happy Birthday, Uncle Ed, you've only just begun!

Kathleen E Sutton
REFLECTIONS

The other day I chanced to see,
A reflection in the mirror of me.
The skin that was so smooth and clear,
Shows maps and lines of another year.
My hair that was so red and bright,
Shows traces, here and there, of white.
Tiny lines around blue eyes,
Have seen the wonders of a hundred skies.
They've shut themselves so very tight,
Against the fear in the mid of night.
These eyes have crinkled in grief and pain,
And looked toward heaven in the rain.
Opened wide at the joy of birth,
Shimmered and shone with untold mirth.
These cheeks that were so full and round,
Have followed bone, hollowed down.
At every step along the way,
Every sorrow, joy, dismay,
Have added to this face of mine,

Another mark, another line.
The love I've known, the worry too,
I wouldn't trade for youthful dew.
Each flaw and mark, etched with time,
I've earned and deserved, they are all mine!

Gaelwyn Eridanus
THE RHYMER'S SONG

To the circle of friends who knew I could.

I long to write of mountains,
Or starry nights in June,
The crystal streams
Of midnight dreams,
Or the textures of the moon.

I want to capture sunrise
And its colours I adore,
The sunlit sea,
The shady tree
That sits upon its shore.

I seek to paint the rainfall
Upon this page, so dry;
The rainbow's glow,
Or winter snow,
Or the graceful butterfly.

I've taken the time to see
The world that's all around
And now I try
To show your eye
The beauty that I've found.

I share these things of wonder
For those who've never known
A dolphin's grace,
A mountain's face,
Or where the eagle's flown.

Vivien M Oertle
GROWING OLD

I glanced into the mirror today
with an old and faded eye,
Saw wrinkles on my face, hair turning gray
and I began to cry.
Where had that young girl gone
who used to flit around?
Happy that the day was done
and her family homeward bound.
As I thought back over years gone by—
the valleys and the peaks,
I asked myself "why oh why?"
as the tears ran down my cheeks.
But then I heard the shuffle on the stair
as he came in the room,
This stooped over man with graying hair
who once stood straight as a broom.
He looked at me and winked an eye
because he'd read my mind;
He knew that life was fast passing by
leaving us behind.
Suddenly my heart felt light as a feather
for I knew I'd never be alone;
We'd walk those last few miles together
until God called us home.

Loraine Bull
MY CHILDREN

To God and my dear children Bobby, Louisa, Herby, Gail, Randy

---

Lord, you gave them to me while here on this earth
To keep and to raise them from their time of birth,
To love and to care for them through all of their fears,
To kiss their hurts away when they were in tears,
To teach and to guide them from evil and harm,
To protect them from satan and all of his charm,
To show them the difference between right and wrong,
To help them to grow, be healthy and strong,
To learn of your ways so they won't be lost,
To pay the price no matter the cost,
To live, to love, to enjoy, to endure,
Till you come and assure them their salvation is secure.

Shonta Warren
A MOTHER

A female person who cares for you is called a Mother.
A Mother is somewhat like no other
A Mother is someone who gives to you love.
A Mother is more precious than a dove.
A Mother is someone who will understand
For when you're alone she will take your hand.
A Mother is better than a flower growing out
of the Earth,
Better than a leaf falling to the surf,
For when I look at something beautiful and mild,
its my Mother I see.
Dearest Mother, you can't be a Mother without me.

James C "Jim" Morris
ON SUICIDE AND MISS DOROTHY PARKER

Dottie Parker said:
"Razors pain you;
Rivers are damp. . ."
So on and on
She smoothly spoke.
And what "Dot" said
Was not a joke.

But what Dorothy
Just could not know,
And what does really burn one so
Is: After having set to go,
And find out there is no return!

And when you discover that this is so,
It's much too late to try to learn!
(And, my good friends, I ought to know!)

Hobert Neal
SLEEP ON, SLEEP ON

To all departed loved ones and friends.

Sleep on Sleep on my precious one,
For you there will be a new dawn.
Gone are the fears you faced in life,
For all the darkness will be gone.

So let the dark storm clouds gather over head,
Let the thunder roar and the wild winds blow.
Like a mother hen that gathers her chicks beneath her wing,
God too will surround and shelter your soul.

You have crossed the deep valley below,
The stoney path of life you have trod.
You now know the comfort that peace can
bring,
Only by the grace and love of God.

Sandra Ashby
MEMORIES

I see you clearly
Every detail is vivid
Your eyes catch mine
My body tingles
An uneasiness overcomes me
I lean to you
You reach out
Closer Closer
Until at last
I feel the heat of your lips upon me
A surge of love swells inside
Our hands explore
Sensations come alive
Passion overcomes us both
You take me and I am yours
Again and Again
Another memory is born

Lillian Mustola Boyle

Lillian Mustola Boyle
BABY GARY

God sent Baby Gary
for you two to love
on August 1, 1970
from Heaven above.
And as the weeks passed
although tiny as a toy
he brought joy unsurpassed
this wee baby boy!
His life was cut short
the months numbered almost seven,
you see, God needed another star
to shine down from Heaven.
So he chose Baby Gary
after your lives he had blessed,
who can question that God
in His Infinite Wisdom, knows best.

Ella Eaton Kienholz
WALK INTO THE WOODS

Surely there is something in the unruffled calm of nature that overawes our little anxieties and doubts; the sight of the deep-blue sky, and the clustering stars above, and the templed trees, unpart a quiet to the mind.—Jonathan Edwards

Into the woods I walked one day,
where shadows fell deep, and green moss lay;
Pine needles soft beneath my feet,
Tall trees clasped hands in this retreat.
And bits of sunlight filtering down
Formed pools of gold upon the ground.
One sensed God's presence, out there alone,
The templed trees God's sacred throne!

Heartsick and weary, filled with despair,
My burdens were truly my cross to bear!
I fell to earth, to bare my soul,
And begged God's love to make me whole.
Soon came a peace—can one explain? —
My heart was drenched like refreshing rain!
The cares I had just faded away;
My strength renewed, as I knelt to pray.

And you, o my friend, when cumbered with care,
Walk into the woods—there's solace there!

Nell O Willis
NEVER ANOTHER YOU

There'll be other nights of moonlight,
Other days with skies just as blue,
There'll be other hours of laughter,
But never another you.

There'll be other games in the mornings,
Other friends that are just as true,
There'll be other parties and dancing,
But, never another you.

There'll be other dates and romances,
Other kisses many and few,
There'll be other arms and caresses,
But, never another you.

There'll be other gifts, flowers and tokens,
Affections and compliments undue,
There'll be smiles heartwarm and tender,
But, never another you.

There'll be many to wish me happiness,
But forever, my whole lifetime through
Tho there be numbers and numbers of people,
There'll never be another you.

Denise Shawnette Rafnson
OLD SHOES

When you mentioned to your friend
you wanted to see me again,
He said the reason that you do
is she's like an old shoe.
She's just too convenient
and too comfortable, too.
On yourself don't be too lenient,
never can tell what she'll do;
She might let your feet get wet
while walking in the morning dew.

But you kept her in your closet
because she has a good soul,
And now both shoes have new laces
since they were broken in places.
Yes, they're real comfortable,

but that's the best kind,
Especially when a long journey's in mind.

R McKenzie Reeves
SING AMERICA SING

To America

Sing a song of freedom people
Shout it from the tallest steeple
Sing America loud and clear
Sing about our land so dear.
Sing it in the south and west
Feel the pride swell in your chest
Sing it in the north and east
From the highest hill to the very least.
Sing about our freedom of speech
Sing about our freedom to teach
About God's love for this great land
And that He holds us in His hand.
Oh, sing about our determination
To protect and defend our beloved nation
That we have and will again
Fight and die to protect our friends.
Sing about the brave and free
Sing, MY COUNTRY 'TIS OF THEE
Sing it long and sing it loud
Sing it alone or with a crowd.
Yes, SING AMERICA SING
Let your voices proudly ring
Be sure to say before you're through
AMERICA THE BEAUTIFUL, we love you!

Dora W Taylor
FORGETFULNESS
Shafts of light delicately entwine themselves
In mirrorids of dancing shapes,
Oft seen in loving eye
As ribbons of color braiding a Maypole as they pass by.
Once a brilliant mind
Shadowed now in forgetfulness,
Pulls apart the yellow of sunlight
That now fades into twilight hues to grey of night.
Blue, once seen in laughing eyes,
Is seen no longer as laughter fades and dies
Never to return again on memories wings,
But lay hidden within a well of forgetfulness
And worldly things.
Time heals not a weary mind in recesses fathoms deep,
Nor does man in world fame
Bring release allowing sleep.
Life or time alloted, unknown,
Is light or heavy upon the soul,
And each in time is given their choice
Which path to take to find their goal.
Shafts of light delicately entwine themselves
In mirrorids of dancing shapes,
Released at last as eye lids close,
The curtain of color drapes.

Laurel D Smith
OUR HEROES
With eyes that cried out to me in pain,
He pleaded "Don't ever let them do it again."
To fight a war for no sane reason,
When some opposed, they were charged with treason.
The men came home in bits and pieces.
These were our soldiers, our defenders, the best of our species
The men came home minus feet, legs and hands.
All because they had followed their superior's commands.
They were brought home in sorrow and despair,
To empty streets and empty lives and no one there to care.
These brave young men so bitter and aged,
Wonder now why the battles were waged.
Did we bring them home to parades and banners overhead?
Did we shower them with confetti and honor the dead?
We should have, you know.
For they battled our country's foe.
The time has come to honor these heroes both alive and dead.
They gave their lives and it was their blood that was shed.
You are our heroes, defenders of this great land.
We praise you and honor you, and extend to you our hand.
To our Vietnam Vets,
Our Country's Best!!

E L Stallworth
THE NEW GOOD OLD DAYS
To no one's big surprise, The divorce rate's on the rise,
There are so many single-parent dwellings;
We're not coping very well, It's all a living hell,
Where it will end there just ain't no telling.

The fathers say "to hell with it, I'll pack my bags and hit it,"
"I don't have to take this from you;"
"I can do better on my own, and as for being alone,"
"Just any ole woman will do!"

The mothers say "honey, you ain't got enough money,"
"To make me want to stay here with you;"
"So, you just pack your old bags, and take all of your rags,"
"And jump in the first river you get to!"

"Playing games with reality, has caused another fatality,
One more family has bitten the dust;
Each will go their separate ways, and in the following days,
The children will suffer most from the bust.

They'll blame father and mother, and their sister or brother,
For all that goes wrong in their lives;
Some will keep faith and pride, some will lay respect aside,
Some may never take husbands or wives.

They need good directions, not your petty rejections,
You should give up your self-serving ways;
Make the home what it should be, give your all to the family,
And make these the new good old days!

Terry L (Farrell) Fulton
ONWARD . . . ONWARD . . .
While watching my little toy boat floating down the clear babbling brook and teasing the newborn tadpoles, I noticed the mountains on the
horizon, glowing with the promise of eternal beauty. The birds were singing, the wind whistling nature's songs, and the plants radiating incredible splendor.

Recently I got a spring break from college and came home to the babbling brook, distant mountains and eternal beauty I remembered so well from childhood. The brook, muddy and polluted, barely trickles along the slimy rocks. The distant grandeur is obscured behind the monstrous
pipes of industry as the sun plays peek-a-boo with the clouds of progress that pollute the air. The only whistling to be heard comes from the nearby
building morning, noon, and night. The healthiest
plant in sight provides a living for over 1500 people, (the master race). Man is advancing beautifully on earth!

Margaret G Kahn
THE EGO BIT
I wonder when I'm going to die.
I wonder why I wonder when;
For it will make no difference at all
When I reach my earthly end.

The sun will still shine clear and bright
And stars will glow throughout the night.
The rivers yet will seek the sea;
They do not need to wait for me.

And whether I'm here or gone away,
The birds with song will greet each day.
Important, I am really not;
I just don't want to be forgot!

Mary Mezurecky
HALLOWEEN NIGHT
Halloween's a fearful night
All the witches are in Flight
Lights Flick about so ghostly shine
Large golden pumpkins leave the vine
Out come the goblins, sprites and elves
With sacks for candies from the shelves
Even the moon wears an odd silver face
Enchantment, laughter, good times every place
Now sleek black cats growl strange cries
Near infernos blaze in their eyes
Inky shadows dance, bats dart on the breeze
Great horned owls watch, hidden in the trees
How weird the world on Halloween night
Time steals away, fading into daylight.

Darlene A Wilson
DARBY
Your hair is golden, your eyes are blue:
If only you can realize what I think of you:
You have made me try to teach you true:
If you could only know what your smile can do:
When I hear you say that's my Dar-Dar to a friend:
I feel I can melt ice and I know I will never end:
Your guardian angel and I will help you through:
The pain and hurt your heart will do:
I hope you will always keep saying:
Dar-Dar I love you as big as a day:
I love you Darby too.

Tammy Frances Madison
ADAM
What was happening? Had the world gone mad?
The great God was angry with his children.
Where was the gentle, kind God who walked in the gardens?
Now His voice was harsh, His manner cold.
What we did—it seemed so small a thing!
He was saying we had to go away. could we go? Who would take care of us?
He spoke of pain and heavy toil and other things.
Things I did not understand. He spoke of death.
What is death? Is it a thing to do—like eat or sleep?
Is it a thing to find—like fruit or herbs?
I will think of it another time, another day.
Just now there are too many things to think upon.
First we must find shelter—something to eat—
It will be long days before I harvest any crop

Abel, Cain, where are you? Come now, sons.
Your mother's food grows cold upon your plates!
Abel. Abel, lying on the ground, napping like a child.
Wake up, son. Abel, I call your name! Abel!
Abel, there is blood upon your face. You are injured.
Open your eyes, my son, we must go home. Abel!
Cain, Cain where are you? Come quickly to me.
Abel, your brother, is injured. You must help me carry him.
Cain! Cain! Cain where are you? Abel speak to me!
Oh, God! Is <u>this</u> that thing you spoke of?
Cain is gone, but Abel is here before me.
Yet, even as I hold him in my arms, I feel his emptiness.
Although Abel, my son, is here—he, too, is gone.
The words the Great God said—the unknown words.
"Thou shalt surely die." "Thou shalt surely die."

Phyllis Brusius
MY MOTHER'S BIBLE

In loving memory of my mother

My mother's Bible is old and worn.
Some of the pages are slightly torn.
Mother read the Bible everyday.
She taught her children how to pray.

Mother didn't rule with an iron hand,
She'd explain things to help us understand.
When we came home from school or any place,
She was there to greet us with a smile on her face.

Years passed, there were good times, some bad one's too.
But mother seemed to know just what to do.
When there were problems she'd simply say,
Read your Bible child and don't forget to pray.

One by one we left the nest,
We were out on our own and put to the test.
Mother's teachings helped pave the way.
Because we did read our Bible and we knew how to pray.

Our children loved their Grandmother so very much,
With her loving ways and her gentle touch.
They loved to go to Grandma's to play.
To read the Bible, and learn how to pray.

Now the Bible is mine thats old and worn.
I've mended the pages that were slightly torn.
Mother has gone to her rest, but I still hear her say.
Read your Bible child and don't forget to pray.

William E Moore
THE DAY I DISCOVERED WEIDER

On a bright June day, in nineteen sixty-eight,
I read of a man destined to be great.
I was reading this ad in the back of a magazine,
I could not believe what my eyes had seen.
A muscular body graced this paper,
I kept on reading, and learned it was Dave Draper.
A body so beautiful and so well built,
Like a priceless gem or essence of silk.
I kept on reading to find who was his leader,
I soon found out his name was Joe Weider.

Who was this man, and what was his claim,
I sent in the ad to learn of his fame.
A few weeks later an answer to my letter,
Would come in the mail, and I felt better.
I opened it up to take a look,
To my suprise, it was a bodybuilding book.
"How To Build A Strong Muscular Body" was its name,
Now I know Joe Weider's claim to fame.

Louis was his father, and Anna his mother,
Later I found out he had a brother.
Ben was his name,
And what was his claim,
I wrote more letters, and what would it be,
I soon found out, he was President, IFBB.

It all began in nineteen thirty-six,
Men were weak, puny and sick.
Weider bombed, blasted, gorged and strained,
Soon his body responded with fantastic gains.
He shared with others what he had done,
Soon they would shine like the stars, moon and sun.

In nineteen sixty-five the Olympia was conceived,
It was the highest award a bodybuilder could receive.
Joe brought them fame, muscles and glory,
But that's not the end of a magnificent story.

Franco was a boxer trained to fight,
Until Weider help put him in the muscle spot light.
Reeves was handsome, sexy and groovy,
Muscles put him in a gladiator movie.
Again his name was Steve Reeves,
The Movie he made was called Hercules.
Oliva a Cuban, from Castro he ran,
He came to America now he's a muscleman.

In Weider's magazines they all can be seen,
Who else's but Weider the bodybuilders dean.
He's the "Master Blaster" and to many a companion,
And he'll always be the "Trainer of Champions."

Glenda Courtney Foots

Glenda Courtney Foots
SHOULD I
Should I

Should I continue
as usual,
with all sweet smiles,
and no bitter frowns?
Should I turn my torturous face
in an unruly position,
permitting mine enemy to scorch my
sensibilities?
Should I seclude myself?
My resentfulness cannot be concealed,
nor my hideous thoughts be hidden.
My action shall answer.

John P DeBonis
I JUST TOLD MY MOTHER GOODBYE

In memory of my mother Enes DeBonis

The last time I saw my mother,
I kinda knew it would be the last,
She was just laying there helpless,
Trying so hard to live.

Oh! Mother, my mother,
Why did you have to go?
Just when I was a starting to sing so good,
Even though you didn't want me to,
I know why now, because the night life
Isn't any good.
How it can be mean and cruel,
How it tears you apart,
As you start to rise up.

But, please stand beside me
And help me write a song,
So it can be a memory
And tribute to you.

Mother, oh mother, how I loved you so,
Even though I never let it show.
Also of the rough times, I gave to you.

So goodbye, mother, goodbye.
Then not knowing it was the last,
Goodbye, mother, goodbye,
And rest in peace,
With God, forever, goodbye.

Cora Davenport
THE FIRST CHRISTMAS

She was young and she was beautiful,
that Jewish maiden of long ago;
When an angel whispered "You will be with child,
to one greater than any you know."
Now Mary was in awe. She pondered it in her heart:
To think that she should be the one
to play so great a part.
Now the time had come, that taxes were due
and each must go to the city to pay.
While Mary rode a lowly donkey,
Joseph walked beside her all the way.
The city was crowded. The inn was full;
so Joseph and Mary were turned away.
But a kind neighbor offered all that he had
and in that stable they chose to stay.
Then the word went out to all the earth
that a child had been born of miraculous birth.
That King of Kings and Lord of Lords
is still with us today.
Let's keep His Love deep in our hearts
and never ever let it get away.

Eleanor F Sneed
ON THE MOUNTAIN TOP

I met God on the mountain top,
on one early morn
We sat and watched together,
as a brand new day was born
We watched the edge of darkness,
slowly tuck away the night
Saw the moon and stars together,
gently turning out their lights
We watched the golden sunshine,
as it peeped through azure skies
Saw the dewdrops on the roses,
like sparkling diamonds it now lies
We watched the golden eagle soar,
and spread it's wings in flight
Saw nature proudly dressing up,
after sleeping through a moonlit night
As I witnessed all this beauty,
tears slowly filled my eyes
Then he told me oh so sweetly,
man's creation was his prize
We talked a little longer,
about Salvation's plan
Then He said He must be on His way,
to save the soul of man

Philip A Grimard
IT'S YOU I LOVE

Dedicated to my wife, Josephine, Valentine's Day, February 14,1985

Today is the day,
Like everyday,
It's you I love.

The days, weeks, years go by,
Always back to you I fly.
It's you I love.

As the silent tide moves out to sea,
I look back and faintly see
The silhouette of you, my love.

I am no longer only "thee",
It's you and I who now make me.
It's always, always, you I love.

I sit and rock, silently my thoughts
Drift back to you and me.
It's you I love.

And there unfolding on the hills,
A cloud of dancing daffodils.
It's you I love.

Thru half-closed eyes, a bright blue sky,
And fairy tears that banish fears.
It's you I love.

We talk of dreams of yesterday,
That slowly, slowly fade away.
It's you I love.

The autumn sounds are clear to me,
Leaves fall gently from the trees,
And whisper messages to me.

It's you I love, it's you I love. . .

Dorothy C Brittle
FOR I'VE KNOWN MY DAD

If courage is overcoming the foe of fear —
Fear of defeat and trifles that baffle and disturb
the soul,
If courage is meeting the dawn of each new day
Without complaining or dreading duty that might appear,
Then, I've known courage, for I've known my Dad.

If truth is read from twinkling eyes
of deepest blue —
With straight forward and fearless
glance that condemns
untruth,
If truth is living as you know God'd
have you live,
Without care of man's criticism
and blows all undue,
Then, I've known truth, for I've
known my Dad.
If love is warm and kind, and felt
in silent
understanding,
While others declare loyalty in
loud tones betraying.
If love is smiling through
downfalls of loved ones
And lifting with no mention of the
hurt and sorrowing
Then, I've known love, for I've
known my Dad.
If faith is enduring to the end of
life—trusting God
Believing in ultimate victory of
good o'er evil,
If faith is clinging strong to God
when man has failed
And humbly looking up with feet
planted firmly on the sod
Then I've known faith, for I've
known my Dad.

Love Always, Bryanna

I LOVE YOU MOM . . .

This poem is dedicated to Eileen, my best friend, God Bless you Mom.

I love you mom because you're you
You're very real and true.
Some mother's are rich and
famous,
But I'm proud of you for what you
are.

I love you mom because you're
always there.
It shows that you understand and
care.
You do a lot for us and I'm grateful
There's nobody as understanding
and as beautiful as you.

I love you mom because you're the
best there'll ever be.
I know I'm not the greatest kid but
I try to be.
There's not enough words to say
what I want to,
I know this much mom, I will
always love you.

Shyann Burk

A LITTLE LOST LAMB

Dedicated To the Lord God Almighty who makes all things possible

---

We're like the little lamb
That's strayed far from the fold
We're lost and we're oh so scared
And there's no protection from the
cold

We turn here and we turn there
But there's danger on every side
There's no place safe to go
No where to run and hide

The farther we go by ourselves
The sadder seems our fate
We need to find a shelter
Before it gets too late
And finally, in our need and
anguish,
We fall down upon our knees
We cry out for mercy, oh Lord
Come and save us please

And, behold, before us stands the
good shepherd
With loving arms extended
With a voice so kind and gentle
He says "my child your search is
ended."

Ronald James Tenasco

VALENTINE'S DAY

As the years pass by in its uncertain
ways,
there's one loving day that will
never change.
This day is precious in its own
undying way,
cause it brings out something
special that I so must say.
Your a sweet spirit angel in my
deepest dreams,
and that's something special noone
else will ever see.
I give you these words nothing
more I can say,
than to wish you a beautiful and
happy
Valentine's
Day!

Elizabeth Gail Williams

AT MY GRANDAD'S HOUSE

Dedicated with love to my Grandad J. M. Gerlash

The dying kitchen stove
Spat out
Its last gasp
Of heat,
While a tarnished Victrola
Silently cried
And remembered
What it was like
To be young
At my
Grandad's house.

Sarah P Stromberg

REMEMBER

To My Family, Who have given me unstinting love and support

Forget each kindness that you do
As soon as you have done it.
Forget the praise that falls on you
The moment you have won it.
Forget the slander that you hear
Before you can repeat it.
Forget each slight, each spite, each
sneer,
Wherever you may meet it.

Remember every kindness done to
you
whate'er its measure.
Remember praise by others won
And pass it on with pleasure.
Remember those who lend you aid
And be a grateful debtor.
Remember every promise made
And keep it to the letter.

Brenda Sue Robinson

A LONG HARD DAY

My teddy bear is sleepy
it's been a long hard day.
He helped me in the cornfield
and helped bale up the hay.
He's sitting in the chair now
Yawning his troubles away
Then all of a sudden
He's sleeping his yawning away.
He's asleep
he will be for a while
He's asleep
curled all in a pile.
My teddy bear is sleepy
its been a long hard day.
He helped me in the cornfield
and helped bale up the hay.

L Dennis Sundberg

HOPE PREVAILS

In Memory of My Father—He never gave up hope.

Cares of this world are plenty.
War, unemployment, death and
sorrow
Does anyone have any pity?
Is there no hope for a brighter
tomorrow?
People sleeping on city streets
Farmers and industrial workers
losing all.
The rich are getting nature's treats
No one hears the children's call.
Our schools and small towns are
suffering
Political leaders seem confused
Drugs and alcohol seem as
common as Bufferin.
Children and families are abused
Lift up your hearts my friend
Never give up in despair
There is a glimmer of light at the
tunnel's end.
People can and do have a care.
Hope lies in love in the hearts of
good people.
With God's help and furthering our
knowledge
Life can be better for strong and
feeble.
Fight for better things and work for
a stronger moral bridge.
Wake up and smell the roses, my
friends.
The world can be a brighter place
for all.
Only, we, can create a better trend
Love, peace, faith and honor are
our call.

C Bradford Bliss

UNTITLED

Circles 'pon circles connected one
onto one
reaching from now back till when
I was begun
and I can see now,
I walked every damn one.
W.K.F.L.

wisdom
knowledge
faith
love

T Summers

DREAM

It started out like a dream, me as
your Queen and you as my King.
Much love and everything, It was
the sweetest lil' swing.
I mean, King and Queen real happy
in a dream! It seemed like the
real thing. There wasn't
nothing wrong, as far as I have
seen, but then again, A dream?!
My feelings elate; when I feel your
passion penetrate.
How great . . .
I should have known by fate that
nothing, no dream, could be that
great. Mistake, heartache,
escape—Not so great!
Love you! for sure . . . your love for
me, obscure. Yes sir, I hurt
while you flirt.
It started out—to me—like a
dream. While to you—it was
only a fling. Ya' know . . . a
pastime thing.

Jimmy Quinn

Jimmy Quinn

NATURE'S SPECIAL GIFT

An Individual snowflake falls from
the Heavens —
and on its seemingly never-ending
journey
towards Earth —

He thinks about joining his friends
below,
maybe in a snowball
or an igloo —

But when he does join his friends,
and becomes part of the crowd,
He doesn't loose his
individuality —
He's still unique,

Linda Palmieri

WHAT IS CHRISTMAS?

CHRISTMAS IS A TIME
for sharing and
expressing your love
to one another!
CHRISTMAS IS A TIME
to give
without expecting
to receive!
CHRISTMAS IS A TIME
when Santa Claus
brings joy to the hearts
of little girls and boys!
CHRISTMAS IS A TIME
for the ground
to be covered
with a white blanket of snow!
CHRISTMAS IS A TIME
for happiness and
the singing of
Christmas carols!
CHRISTMAS IS A TIME
for families to be together
and to share
the happiness of the day!
CHRISTMAS IS A TIME
for peace among
all mankind
BUT MOST OF ALL!
CHRISTMAS IS A TIME
To Remember Our Savior Jesus
Christ and this Blessed Day and
Thank Him for All He's Done for
Us!!

Emilia A Glaz

ALL ABOUT LOVE

If you are lonely,
I'll be your friend.

If you need help,
I'll give you a hand.

If you have problems,
I'll lend you an ear.
If you need comfort,
I'll hold you close, Dear.

If you need love,
I'll give you my heart.
If you ask "For How Long?"
Until death, do we part.

J E Tramel
EVERDREAM TREE
On a cold December morn
My mother said to me
As she bundled me up nice and warm
Let us go find the perfect christmas tree

The holly tree stood
So tiny and all alone
Near the edge of the woods
It looked so frail and forlorn

This little holly tree would make
A beautiful christmas tree
If only my hatchet I would take
Cut it down and carry it with me

Its beauty was so great
To destroy this tree
My hands I would surely hate
I walked away and let it be

This dream christmas tree
With its berries and green leaves
Still stands for all to see
A giant of all holly trees

This tree will forever be
Wedged deep in my memory
When I return to the home of my youth I see
This my ever dream tree.

Den-Nickolas Smith
GUILT
Perhaps I was never meant to be.
I, the bastard child,
Conceived in a moment of passion,
Never knew the anguish you
Kept hidden within your soul.

Tomorrow has passed and now
Reality hits you full force.
I have grown up to be a kind, gentle man
And you tell me I have his nose.
A tear trickles down your cheek.
Now it is I who hides the anguish—
Guilty of reminding you of him.

Lucille Swindell
NIGHT VIGIL
Have you ever sat by a loved one's sick bed
When the sun has left the sky
And listened with a well tuned ear
For signs she is still alive?
The nurses go to and fro and scarcely ever pause,
To give you news you want to hear;
That's part of the nursing clause.
The hours tick by slowly
As you think how things were before;
And you mutter a prayer that God will your loved one's health restore.
For all is being done that can be,
Doctors resolutely strive;
Still it is up to God, the highest, to keep your loved one alive.
So you wait to see if your prayer's been heard
And watch for signs you're loved ones stirred.

Phyllis Marshall
GODS PLAN

This poem is dedicated to Scott & Cheryl, my children

Before I was born or began to breathe
God knew what I was to be,
He was the only one that could really see.
God knew that the time would come
That he would be my only one.
So you see that God has all the plans
For the worlds people and the lands.

Mary E Hencley
THE WORLD IS BROKEN
There's a crack in the world
It's right near the top
It's sure to get bigger
If the splinter's don't stop

There's a rent in the world
A small jagged tear
If we don't fix it soon
We'll have nothing to wear

There's a hole in the world
Where the people are falling
If you stand near the edge
You can hear them all, calling

Yes, we've broken the world
We've ripped it with hate
If it's not patched by tomorrow
It might be too late

Would peace and love mend it?
Are you sure that they would?
Death and war haven't helped
Though some think that they should

There's a split in the world
And how shall we fix it?
With Magic and Super Glue?
Perhaps, if we mix it.

Roseann M Whitaker
TWO WORLDS
I know of two worlds,
So distant and yet so clear.

One where the clouds are cold and grey,
Where I'm trapped by emotions,
And sadness fills my heart.
There my dreams are unfulfilled wishes,
And happiness is a stranger to me.

The other is so different.
There the sunshine is warm and bright,
There I'm free to feel and live,
And my heart is full of love.
There my dreams are reality,
And sadness is unknown to all.

These worlds are special to me,
For they are part of my soul.
The one is reality,
Where all I love is found.
The other my dream world,
Which only I can see.

Laura Ann Hover
A CRY TO THE LORD

To the Lord for giving me the ability to write this and to Ron for all his love.

When I need to cry Lord,
help me dry the tears.

When life seems unbearable Lord,
help me to see someone cares,
When all I see are clouds Lord,
help me find the sun.
When I feel like giving up Lord,
give me the strength to go on.

Claribel L Palmer
THE REDWOOD
The massive red giant rising to the sun from the forest floor
Dwarfs the tall forest pine and forest creatures
who pass below or seek shelter in its branches.

The mammoth redwood, ancient when Caesar was betrayed
Eaten and scarred by long-gone forest fires
Yet stretches out its vast green umbrella.

'Though shading forest fern and mosses, the goliath
Now itself needs protection from man
Its mortal foe.

Man, who thoughtless in his covetous greed, heedless of his damage
wrought upon the ageless land
Harvests the tree and yet another and another
Scarring for time yet uncounted that world for all who come after.

God's forest, His handiwork now seared by empty space and stump
As flood ravages still more from over-burdened streams
Which can no longer themselves hold the raging waters funneled
there unheld by once firm-rooted trees.

No forest creatures now do loiter nor feed nor browse
Where once they sheltered in the dappled shade
of the great red pillared beauty.

Can time unknown yet heal the ruthless scar
That now replaces aged giants—and defaces?
Mayhap—in time and yet more time.

But mother's son who walks today—
and morrow and yet morrow more
Shall not see it healed in his time.

Patricia Ann Moore
THE GREATEST GIFT
The greatest gift there will be
will not be under a Christmas tree
It won't be wrapped in tinsel and foil
Where it will be hidden and cannot soil
But it will be in the hearts of men
Where there is love and peace within
It will be shown throughout the land
To every creature and every man.

Elaine J Patterson
IN MEMORY OF MOM
Her mind was sharp at 83.
She was blind, but still could see,
The heartaches and pain of others,
But isn't that just like a mother.
She suffered pain but still could smile,
Trying to help others all the while.
She loved her family and others,
To me she was one of the worlds greatest
mothers.
She loved the Bible and to pray,
And she talked about Jesus and heaven everyday,
And God in His mercy took her home to stay.
And as I kneel to pray I say, "Lord help me
to be the kind of mother she was to me."

William Hosie Hayes
NOW I UNDERSTAND
Today I sit alone, thinking of you and home.

Today I understand that when I came along,
you gave up all of your wants and needs
to give me my wants that would please me.

Today I understand that when I was sick, my
pains became your own.

Today I understand when I fell in love, my
joy would not be alone.

Today I understand that the family I started,
I was not alone, You helped in so many ways
I could never repay.

Today I understand that I have never been
alone, from birth to times of old, you
were always there giving love, a helping
hand, and even a loan.

Today I understand that only a Mother could
do so much for me.

I Love You Mom

Rev Daniel A Nicholson

Rev Daniel A Nicholson
THE QUESTION

This poem is gratefully dedicated to my Lord Jesus Christ. After my many years of searching, he has become the answer to all of my questions.

What is life all about?
Does anyone really know?
People yell and shout,
Protesting all their woe.

This world is full of many fears,
Of many hates built through the years,
Of many people hurting others,
And yet it's said that we're all brothers.
How can I possibly understand
A world so wrapped in hate;

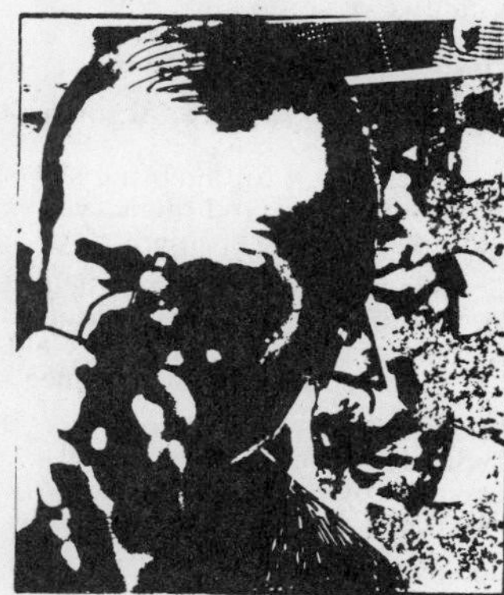

Where everything is a demand,
And no one knows his fate?
I've pondered this question many times
And yet I still fail to see;
How a world so full of growing crimes
Can live in harmony.
My thought has gone to its full length
And yet I still cannot find the strength;
To understand why people do,
Those hurting things to me and you!

Max J Ross
THE OKLAHOMA DUDE
He came from Oklahoma,
A hefty sized galoot,
Came to have a visit
Wearing fancy hat and boots.

I had a horse name Echo,
A dancey little mare.
He said "I'd like to ride!"
I said "Go, if you dare."

There wasn't any saddle
So he had to ride her bare.
I knew he'd have some trouble
When he tried to ride that mare.

He climbed upon her back
And watching horse borne fare
It took but just a moment
To see him flying in the air.

Then down the path he stumbled
I stood and laughed with joy.
He sits a better bar stool,
That broken down cowboy!

C Joseph Pine
THE WIND
The wind with its strangest air
Traveling over the land ending nowhere
The wind so great that it rushes sailing
ships along
That the trunk of a tree in the greatest
wind must bend to the wind that is like
a song
The wind seems undaunted
And my memories it has haunted
With ancient times and places
And a yearning for past faces

Tad Dee
A BLOODY VICTORY
I see the graves
Hundreds of thousands of men,
Who fought for what
They believed.
Crying crimson, faint blue,
Dark green, and screaming red blooms
Surround them.
Hopes of war won,
Fulfilled by these men,
Never cherished.
I see the graves
Of Billy Joe, Tommy John, and Clyde Mclane
I hear the raven cannons destroy,
The nutmeg rifles kill
And the general order troop 38 to die!
I hear pleas for help
And the cry of a bloody victory
I feel the spreading vermillion on their coats,
And their colorless tears.

A Jackson Paige
THE WHIMS OF RHYME

To the circle of friends who knew I could.

Dormant, within my pen,
Lie the words I long to write.
They've come so oft before,
Yet, they simply sleep tonight.

Full often have I labored
At the slightest of their stirring,
Although, their final message
Is less often reassuring.

At times they come so softly,
As a gentle springtime rain.
Sometimes they come so harshly
They cause bitterness or pain.

On some days they flow slowly
And I must force them to the page.
On occasion they flow quickly
As a brief and passing rage.

But, always they reveal to me
A part of me unknown.
And always, when I write them out,
I feel that I have grown.

Myrtle R Tucker
BE STILL
Be still and know me.
Speak not words,
Be still!
Partake of the silence
And its fullness of knowing.
Savor the beauty
Of love's wholeness,
The realness of the real.

Tracy Lea Jimmerson
WHAT IS, TO LIVE?
To live is a breath taken more than each day.
A step taken that later will surely pay.
To live is to walk above a narrow street and to be
friends with everyone you should meet.
To live is to grow with each day in time.
To open our hearts as well as our minds.
To live is to make thoughts of our own,
ones that haven't had to be stopped and shown.
To live takes more than help or a little lift.
To live is a simple treasure often known as a gift.
To live is to grow up, to move away, and to have
something to look forward to each day.
To live is to accept you for who you are.
To live is to wish upon many stars.
To live is
a lesson that
we must give,
to keep others from
wondering,,
"What is, to live?"

Bob Sheckler
CHILDREN IN SNOW
Outside my house the carpeting is fine
And frigid, calling feet to tread its nap
And wear a path as if from kitch to dine,
From countless trips to serve our food and wine,
But only once it takes to draw this map—

This evidence of where we've been and gone—
Until the lines are crossed and crissed and lost,
As sunlight comes of certain rays of dawn,
When filtered through the tree upon the lawn—
A slight wind and the lines are turned and tossed

My little rays now shine outside my house,
The map is drawn, the lines are clear but stray,
And quickly now I see the wind arouse.
The changing courses of my little plows
Make a ragged carpet where they play.

Robin Quolas
BENEATH THE MOON
Oh, Moon!
For you,
Birth
Is at night

You are always fast
When I wish you to be slow.
For the times when I race you,
I never seem to win.

Slowness you quickly become
When my heart desires the light of day.
You take much time to cross the sky
From one end of the world to the other.

Moon, why do you act so strange?
Or am I the strange one?
Do you try to teach me to be satisfied
With things as they are?

So much do I appreciate your attempts,
Yet I am sorry that they are in vain.
For I was born to a world of unsatisfaction —
A world that for most mankind,
Is unavoidable.

Oh, Moon!
For you,
Death
Is at dawn.

Wm J Schmit
STORMY DAY
White gulls fly by on silent wing.
Below them crested waves roar constantly.
Upon the shores their wall of water fling,
While a flock of canvasbacks bob merrily.

A sandhill crane stands in a marsh nearby.
Poised and ready for any morsel in sight.
Reeds moving to and fro give off a sigh,
As dark clouds roll by swiftly in flight.

The day is stormy with a dark gray cast.
Large waves pile high on a bar offshore.
A forceful southerly hits the beach with a blast,
As though it were competing with the waters roar.

On the shore the wind makes the pine trees hiss.
Back and forth they sway most violently.
High above a large hawk soars in bliss,
For a choice morsel below it watches constantly.

Day finally turns into a seething darkness.
The storm seems worse in the black of night.
Perhaps morning will tame the sea with a caress,
So to gather its strength for another fight.

AHMADDIN AS-SALIK
THE ROBOT
I am no longer under my own control:
limp as a corpse in the hands of its Washer, I wait
for Him to tell me what to do; my soul
is nesting deep within His Heart, my fate
depends upon His every word and thought.
My former program has been wiped away,
my memory-banks are blank, my mind is nought
but random squiggle-lines in disarray.
My bodies functions are at least obedient,
and I appear as I have always appeared
to others, but inside is nothing but a transient
state, waiting to be fully cleared
for a higher program, written by
my Lord, which He has promised to give to me
at some nebulous future date. so I
wait, surrendered to him totally.
It is not all a blankness, for He plays
upon my many keyboards with His Love,
and gives me joy and rapture yet unheard of
by those who do not know His roguish ways.

Barbara A Bickmann
FRIENDS FOREVER

When someone special enters your life,
All you can dream about is being his wife.
You forget how dear your friends are to you,
And you keep on thinking about you know who.
Then he breaks up with you and your mind is nowhere to be found,
But isn't it funny, your friends are still around.
That shows you how true a friendship can be,
And I'll tell you my friend, you're special to me.
You entered my life in a situation like this,
And I thank the Lord for answering my wish.
I prayed one night for a friend so true,
He gave me more—he gave me you!!

Ron Merritt
HAPPY ANNIVERSARY

To Rena' 4-16-86

A year has come and gone
And it was so great,
We experienced love and sharing
We have contemplated fate.

We have carved a road through wilderness
And traveled it together,
Our lives became entwined en route
And that will last forever.

We make the most of what we have
Yet, time will be the thief,
The balance of our mortal lives
Will seem so very brief.

But we have gone so far beyond
The physical love of man,
That we will walk our path forever
Arm in arm and hand in hand.

Kristen Peterson
I AM A GIRL WHO LOVES ANIMALS

This Poem is Dedicated to Martha and Les

I am a girl who loves animals.
I wonder what it would be like to watch two tigers at battle.
I hear the scream of eagles in the middle of the night.
I see the first flight of birds.
I want to ride a mustang through a field of flowers.
I am a girl who loves animals.
I pretend I'm ruler of all animals.
I feel the pain of a deer being killed.
I touch the newborn animals.
I worry when whales are attacked.
I cry when animals die.
I am a girl who loves animals.
I understand when animals must die.
I say all animals have the right to live in a man's world.
I dream of running with gazelles through a field of grass.
I try to know every name of every animal.
I hope to travel to Africa someday.
I am a girl who loves animals.

Daniel W Hamblin
THE CHILD IN ME

To Renata

Children love the circus,
With clowns and bright balloons.
They love to play on summer days
And carefree afternoons.

They love the simple things in life,
So much to live life for
To run, to skip, to laugh, to cry
Their world's an open door.

As grown-ups now we often miss
These take-for-granted pleasures.
Our days are spent in buried thoughts,
Our lives are weighed and measured.

But now and then, we come to find
Through some unseen pitfall
These things have never left us
There's a child within us all.

And I, for one, must now admit
The child in me is near
He comes to me on pleasant thoughts
With things that I hold dear

So when I act as though I've gone
From twenty-one to two,
It's just because I fell in love
I fell in love with you.

Alice Gray Nobles

Alice Gray Nobles
MOTHER

In these words
we'd like to tell
Of a Loving Mother
named Belle.
She named our names
all to rhyme.
To keep us close
for our lifetime.
She raised us,
when times were tough.
And made little food
into more than enough.
She never found much
to complain about.
She'd wait, and let us
eat first, so she'd be
the one to be without.
When the crops were sold,
come shopping time.
All got new shoes
but for Mom.
The girls old worn ones
were just fine.
In later years,
when times were good.
She wanted nothing fancy
and we understood.
Two things she loved,
flowers and her children,
all around.
She taught us God loves
all things good.
We know this is true,
Mother, because now
he picked you.

Lois Faye Drake
OLD FRIEND

I wonder if somewhere in time
We will ever meet again
And if you will remember
The young girl who was your friend.

The years have gone so quickly by
Since last we met and talked
Neither knowing the life of the other
Nor the paths we choose to walk.

What dreams of yours were fulfilled?
Which were lost along the way like mine
And I wonder if we could still be friends
If we met after all this time?

Julian LaDell Aiken
TO BE TOUCHED

To my beloved wife, Zadie, for all these 45 years of happiness

---

You make me think
Of rainbow ends
Of tumbleweeds
And canyon bends
Of riders out
Across the range
Herding cattle
Acting strange
Of rodeos
That seldom change
Of stallions running
On the range
Of times long past
And yester year
That swept on by
And shed no tear
Of sunbeams in
Your hair so bright
That sparkle through
The darkness night
Of wind swept plains
And cattle calls
Your gentle touch
That wasn't all
Of willows bending
To their knees
Praying to
The other trees
Of redwoods deep
Within the sod
Stretching tall
To talk to God
Of storm clouds touching
Lightning rods
The phrase "be still
and know I'm GOD"
You make me think
Of many things
Of wedding gowns
And golden rings
Of stars that twinkle
Far above
And most of all
To think of Love . . .

Mildred R Bocek
PERENNIAL LOVE

Dedicated to my beautiful nephew, Paul Krivanek.

I reach out but you do not see
A captive of some inner joy
You sway and smile but not at me
I love you still, blue-eyed boy

Holding tight with head thrown back
Your feet reach to touch the sky
Swinging higher and higher yet
I love you so, my brother's boy

Gentle winds over a barren field
Planted in faith with finest seed
A drought prevents potential yield
I love you son, come by my knee

You are your own inventive toy
Twirl like a top and nearly fall
Steadied by that invisible wall
I love you so, autistic boy

Lucile Brunner
COVENANT

As from the burning bush
He called to Moses to be free,
A singing dove from Heavens gate
A message brought to me,
"Look up, for we have hung a star
To guide and bring you from afar.
Through wilderness and raging sea,
Its calm sweet light will follow thee,
For Alpha and Omega, He is yours through all eternity.
Through endless time and boundless space
His wondrous Love and matchless Grace
At last will lead you to the throne
Of Him who saves. Our God, alone
Is Savior, Cause, Creator, He
Of star and lake and budding tree,
Of fronded isle and silvery flute,
Of singing viol and harvest fruit.
Of falling rain and murmuring dove,
Of home and friends and truth and Love.
Can grief and pain and anguish be
A part of His immensity?
If little faith can mountains move,
Then rest contented in His Love,
For Alpha and Omega, He is yours through all eternity."

Philip Lynn Pletcher
FEEL THE PAIN

Feel the pain
and enjoy
for the pain
symbolizes
the life we feel
the life we need
the life we cling to.

In early life
we feel the pain
and learn from our mistakes.
Yet we also learn
to close ourselves
to become cold
to become emotionless
to learn not to care.

Feel the pain
and enjoy
do not despair.
Know always that someone
somewhere
will care
will be there
and you will grow.

Marty-Me
ALL GROWN UP

To my son Jim—who grew up too fast. God Bless my boy.

Come climb upon my knee, my son,
Lay your head upon my shoulder.
It's still O.K., no one will know
although you are much older.

I know you have so much to do
you must go slay the dragon
you've outgrown all your little toys
your teddy bears and wagon.

The world out there is calling you
and sometimes is very cold.
It's tough to be a grown-up man
For someone ten years old.

So climb upon my knee, my son
And rest your little head.
And maybe if you fall asleep
I'll tuck you in your bed.

Eldred Lewis Johnson
VERY LITTLE
The more I learn
The more I learn
How little I know

Karle Fritz Berger
SPECTACLE OF NATURE

Dedicated to my Granddaughter Jamie Brooke Lewis

The Spectacle of Nature
Increased the range of words
She bent her will to hang them
Like icons on the Hearts of poets.

Jeff Mortimer
CREATION
To make it happen, God let it be
By His creation God made the sea
He made the grass, He made the trees
He even made the birds and bees.
He made the flowers, He made the plants
He made the itsy-bitsy ants.
He made the sun, He made the stars,
He even made the moon so far.

Dolsy Smith
THE BUTTERFLY
How would you like to fly through the air,
With wings like paper,
And a body as delicate as dust?

You could soar with the wind,
All filled with trust.

Geraldine Giles Jessen
FREEDOM
God makes us free,
and free we'll be;
If we understand
the ME that's free.

Tim Purgason
WILDFLOWER
You are my soft and fragile wildflower.
You sway where the warm breeze moves you.
You stand silently alone in the quiet meadow.
Walk by the gentle and slow moving stream.
Feel the warm sun upon your cheeks.
For all the beauty of nature around us;
there is nothing as beautiful as you.
A soft and fragile wildflower in the woods.

Betty Denmark
WINTER SOLACE

For Jessie, 08/26/21—11/17/67

When the end of year is close at hand
And winter winds cut through the land,
Those memories deep inside me stir—
My quiet present begins to blur.

When the chill of night settles all around
In a chair by a window, I am found,
With expression alert and eyes so bright—
Remembering a time one winter night.

When the darkness enfolds and holds me close
I dream it's you who needs me most.
All this love left deep here inside,
Alone, with me, need no longer hide.

The winter holds my favorite memories
That no one touches, hears or sees.
Yes, when icy fingers embrace the land,
I find myself with you again.

Evelyn M Blanchard
THE FARM IN SPRING
Spring heightens the rugged beauty
of the farm;
The woodlands, hills and valleys grow green
From the bright rays of the warming
sun;
And here and there, grazing sheep are seen.

Flowering shrubs add color to the green
And blossoms fill the air with perfume sweet;

Bubbling brooks sparkle in the light,
And distant blue peaks make the scene complete.

When at last he feels the time is right,
The farmer plows deep furrows in the soil;
He sows his seed with faith that it will grow,
And takes great satisfaction in his toil.

Jane B Kelly
TODAY I'M THIRTY
She looked up from her sandbox,
Her sweet face smudged and dirty.
"How old are you today, Aunt Jane?"
Said I, "Today I'm thirty."

Are you THAT OLD?" she asked, dismayed,
And wrinkled up her little nose.
I thought you were still young," she sighed,
And kicked the sand up with her toes.

I walked into the living room,
And Gram was there, knitting away.
"Here comes the Birthday Girl!" she grinned.
"Jane, how old are you today?"

"Would you believe I'm THIRTY, Gram?"
I asked without a smile.
"You are so young," was her reply.
"Let's sit and chat awhile."

We sat and talked, she's so much fun,
And then she said, "You know, it's true,
Thirty isn't very old,
I'd love to be as young as you."

To some I'm young, I've years ahead,
And life has many more a page.
To some I'm old, I've seen a lot.
To me, I'm just the PERFECT age!

Vivian E Yarr
MOTHERHOOD
From seven a.m. to nine p.m.
I'm always on the go.
The only time I get to sit
Is when I'm folding clothes.

Laundry, dishes, changing diapers,
The list goes on and on.
A million things I've got to do, but
Where has the time gone.

The baby wakes, he wants his lunch,
The others want theirs, too.
The baby spits all over me,
Oh, what's a mom to do.

It feels as though I've had too much to deal with in one day.
Bedtime comes, the kids tucked in
There's nothing more to say.

Tomorrow is another day,
I need to get some rest.
Of all the jobs I've ever had,
Motherhood is the best!

Gladys Alford Everhardt
THE WONDER OF SPRING

This poem is dedicated to my dear granddaughter Ashley Renee Redd

---

Today Mother Earth awakes from her sleep
Her spring appointment she must keep,
Bursting forth with love of life
She soon forgets last winters strife.

She concentrates on bringing joy
To every grown-up, girl and boy,
She bares her bosom to the sun
Her battle for life she now has won.

She changes her dress from brown to green
The greatest sight you've ever seen,
With fragrant blossoms, adorns her hair
Bringing beauty with a perfumed air.

With a cry of gladness she embraces
Leafless trees with upturned faces,
Knowing they deserve a dress
Then clothes them with springtimes best.

The air is filled with joy and song
As colorful birds sing all day long,
To live and breathe, to see and hear
Proves the Creator is always near.

Minnie May McCord
GRATEFUL
Heavenly Father:
I adore you,
Bring my grateful heart
Before you
And lay it at your feet.

Eleanor F Mines
LIKE A ROSE
Like a rose
I blossomed
Nurtured by your love
Your friendship

The gentleness of your touch
Your kindness; sincere
You've allowed me to take root in your heart
Freely; honestly

The softness of your voice
The tender glow in your eyes
Allowed me to grow straight; tall

Your arms opened wide
With acceptance of me
I blossomed
Like a rose . . .

Mrs Julie Crowley Powers
SMILE
Tis' easy enough to be cheerful
When everything goes like a Song
But the man worth while
Is the man with a Smile
When everything goes dead wrong.

Melissa Susanne Rouse
FROM LIBERTY'S VIEW
Liberty means being free,
You can be you and I can be me,
We can see all there is to see,
We can be all that we can be,
We can sit and gaze at the stars,
We can drive a truck or a car,
We can go whereever we wish,
We can go for a walk or fish,
We can say what comes to mind,
We can be rude or we can be kind,
We can learn what we are taught,
We can fight back when we are fought,
We can celebrate, you and me,
Just because, we are free.

Bernice S McElwee
CITY O'POSSUM
Mr. O'possum, dirty and gritty,
Why are you at my back door
Stealing dinner from my kitty?
Don't you know you don't belong under a store,
Nor should you be sleeping in the city.

I'll bet the Mayor thinks you have a lot of gall,
When he catches you in City Hall.
You're slithering around just off City Square
You had better hunt the wilderness
And chase a hare there!

Linda O Carlsen
YOU SAY YOU HAVE NOTHING TO GIVE ME

You say you have nothing to give me
Yet my love you put
The smile on my face
The sparkle in my eyes
The music in my laughter
The magic in my dreams
Is it any wonder I Love You
You have given me so many things.

Elsie E Brown
DO YOU WONDER

Do you ever wonder why the sky is blue
And some other days it's dark and dreary too?
In the rainy season you just sit and sigh,
Then you wonder where the rain is when it's dry.

Do you wonder why some people act so queer?
But most others, bless their hearts, are very dear.
Do you wonder if the check you got today
Is enough for all the bills you have to pay?

As you think of all the things you like to do,
Do you wonder if your wishes will come true?
Just take heart and be your wishes great or small,
All of life is such a wonder after all.

Russ Swindell (Norrin Teague)
LOVE (TO REMEMBER)

Always remember
What love is to you.
For if you forget,
The Road of Life
Becomes a Jungle Path
And the King turns to the Tyrant.

Mary Glassner
RETIREMENT

I never thought
I'd see the day
When my husband
would retire
I've heard so many
different things
that made me
ask & enquire.
Well the day
has come and
I thought Oh No
But instead I
was amazed
For it's great
to have him home
with me 24 hours a day.
There is no more getting up at 6
and coming home at 4
or eating on a schedule
like we had to do before.
This is what he worked so hard for
RETIREMENT RETIREMENT

Warren D Prouty
KNOWING A POEM

To Nellie, my beloved wife

Give it gender,
Give it wings,
Not of the honey-bee, that stings,
But of the swallow, that will soar,
And feed upon its flight.

Now tell it where to go.

There must be something to express,
A tender thought,
A message gained,
And a multitude of purposes attained.

Give it fire!
Give it spice!
Not to bear a meager slice,
But to grow and be the author
Of the ritualistic spread.

Now share it, let it go!

That better things may find a way,
Breathe on the flame,
To help it burn,
Then the passion
And the climax, it will earn

Janine Boynton Bond
A GIFT OF LOVE

My heart was filled with loneliness,
As one who's lost at sea;
It seemed that the world had no need
For one so small as me.
I was left with no one to love,
Nor with one to love me;
I felt the sea that lay ahead
Held no eternity.
And then, one day I met someone
Whose love I sought to stay;
I gave my heart to this someone,
But he turned my heart away.
Then I met someone who needed
The heart I had to give;
When I held my heart out to him,
He then commenced to live.
It was then that I discovered,
Though with no guarantee,
I might not be loved by another,
But he'd be loved by me.
Though winds are strong, and waves are high,
It matters not to me;
For I am a needed part of
That restless, endless sea.

Karyl Staci Fischer

Karyl Staci Fischer
YOUR FIRST BOOK OF NURSERY RHYMES

Blue Ink
on
white flesh
keeps patterns
and tides
as seen in
a photo
of me,
from when I
knew nothing
of
my own
colorless
skin . . .

Carla L Welch
DREAM

This poem is dedicated to Family & Friends who told me to never "give up".

Fantasies and dreams natures little schemes that help you to get away from the drudge of everyday.

Lets you go beyond anything that could be real. A special moment, time or
place that you could steal.

Whisked away in thoughts and motions,
that some people would consider just
crazy notions.

But dream & fantasize let your mind go, but be sure your in control.
Dream, Dream, Dream let yourself go.

Arlyne M Sylvester Sikon
LOVE, AFTER 40

Loving you like it was yesterday,
walking hand in hand
barefoot in the sand,
blue skies, sunny day.
Years gone by,
memory still there,
replaced youth, wrinkles, grey hair,
heart still feels young,
don't seem to remember why.
The fall of my life,
descending upon me,
harder to stoop over, smell the flowers,
eyes squinting, harder to see
grandkids sitting on my knee
the love of my life.
Loving you makes it seem like yesterday,
jogging hand in hand
sidewalk in the park
caution, old folks at play.
Tender love, older hearts
holding hands, running on
catching those memories
love after forty and beyond.

M M Nishikawa
ISSEI

This poem is dedicated to all the immigrants who have struggled before us.

I long to see the land I left behind
A father, mother, brothers, sisters, dead
Those loved, long gone, no one to seek or find

With aged hands I cry to reach my kind
From distant land in saddened tears I shed
I long to see the land I left behind
My happy childhood lingers still in mind
At school and holidays, care free I led
Those loved, long gone, no one to seek or find

This land I leave a string of brood of mine
My children's children's children all in stead
Yet, long to see the land I left behind

The aches and pains of age, at times unkind
With passing days the end seems near, I shed
Those loved, long gone, no one to seek or find

But scores of years have passed, yet still I pine
Before the tired and old is called to bed
I long to see the land I left behind
Those loved all dead, no one to seek or find

Annie Hanke
THE STREET MUSICIAN

To my sister Joanie and the fun we had discovering Seattle

The street musician
With hair that is long and
Shaggy;
And clothes that are thin and
Worn;
He stands there
On the street corner
Playing his old guitar.
He seems to be just another
Wanderer;
Singing a song for his next
Meal;
But when I look deep into
His eyes
It is his soul
Which he
Reveals.

Elizabeth Plumley
MOM

To my wonderful mother, Who gave me life and the wisdom to live a dream. This is for you!

Here I sit upon the sand
Equipped with thought
And pen in hand
Yet not the words do I command
But they command of me.
I just sit and as they come
I'll write them down one by one
Where they come from
I do not know
Someone inside of me.
Its really not so strange to me
Its the voice of you Mom
Reading poetry.
You gave to me so many things
The hopes and joys of what life would bring.
But after this you did something else
You let me stand all by myself.
You gave me courage enough to try
To learn to walk and hope to fly.
You gave me strength enough to know
That I could walk once you let go.
I thank you Mom for all you've done
Because of you I now am one.

Doris E Bjorkstrand
CABIN
I see you down the mountainside,
Nestled in a tiny flat
Close to the tumbling river
Sheltered by towering trees.

Oh the stories you could tell
The sights that you have seen.
Of the slash of rain on windowpane
The snow on the mountain pass.

Tell us of wide eyed children
Running on bare brown feet
Splashing in cold clear water
Happy and complete.

Tell of the deer, the coon and bear
That travel by our door
The squirrels that scamper
overhead
The birds that sing and scold.

Tell of the happy hearts
Of those so snug within
The joy of warmth and shelter
Of family and of friends.

Cheryl Ann Howard Dohner
NATURE'S LULLABYE
Long ago, when I was young
I walked the riverside,
The cool sweet air to fill my lungs
The sun to be my guide.

The birds, they sing a cheerful song
Unaware they harmonize,
With my thoughts all along
Singing songs to blue skies.

The trees that stand, so tall and
proud
Blow gently in the breeze,
I lay beneath, and watch a cloud
Sky winds just seem to tease.

Mother Nature seems to rock me
With a soothing lullabye,
Soon a dream, seems to engulf me
And I surrender with a sigh.

Kiera Joan Meehan
TO FLY . . .

To My Family, Friends and Teachers, For Keeping Me Writing.

In the early morning light,
With the last few drops of dew,
I wake up to hear the singing of the
birds.
As I dress the shadows fade,
And darkness again is laid,
Through my open window
I can smell the flowers bloom.
Now, as I open the door,
And the sun begins to rise,
A bird flies overhead,
And things begin to stir.
Yet I do not notice,
For with that bird I go,
Go, and I am free,
Free to dream,
Free to fly . . .

Yolanda Vesia
I RECALL
It was yesterday, I recall, . . .
our budding friendship,
blossoming in the fall, . . .
what a "love"ly transformation! ! !

All our precious moments
together,
inspired our hearts with sweet
desire,
with each promise, a tender kiss, . . .
yes, I remember this!

Despite the challenges, of many,
our love reigned victorious, over
all!
That was yesterday, I recall, . . .

Today, we are many years young,
our love even more strong,
for together we are one,
happy as can be,
united in holy matrimony.

Dorothy I Price
RELEASE
Where had the time gone?
Wasn't it just yesterday she held
Warm hands and led them;
Golden heads darting in for
Mother's quick assurance
And gone again?
Cool hands on fevered brows?
Her worn hands folded in her lap.
Hadn't they mended glider wings
And tied kite tails,
Combed golden curls?
These tall, strong, confident bodies
With well remembered baby faces.
The feeling rose in her to be
needed,
Instantly subdued.
The needs were just different now.
Understanding, companionship,
release.
She opened her heart and set them
free.

Janet Ellison
LOVE (ON THE ROCKS)

To Ricky

My feelings I cannot contain,
They rush forth like waters flowing.
My emotions are so mixed up,
Unsure as to where they're going.

I want so much to hold you close,
Let my love go over the falls,
But instead, it puddles up,
And all I can do is pause.

I suppose it'll always be,
Emotions rapidly flowing,
They'll continue to run on,
Without you ever knowing.

Jodi Pestel
THAT FIRST SNOW
That first snow—
The one that covered the ugliness
Of a world gone wrong
And lit the dark
With the clarity of perfection,
Deadening life's harsh sounds
With a blanket of deep white
Vertically pillowed on fences,
Cushioning tomorrow's barbs,
Soft contentment in space,
Surrounding us in serenity
With a silence so loud
Only our eyes could hear,
On a night so bright
The day's reality
Hid its head in shame,
With a chill not cold
But warm with peace,
And new air so clean
Only our hearts
Breathed the stillness
That enveloped us
In a frozen moment of time
With the real world lost
In that first snow.

James R Woodhams Jr
TAKE ME HOME
When death comes for me,
I shall not hesitate;
But go with my friend,
and not make him waite.

He knocks a little louder,
at my door every day;
I know he comes for me,
but when, he will not say.

I look forward,
to making the transition;
But suicide,
is a major transgression.

There's many things,
I have to see;
So let my fate,
come naturally.

I will be ready,
when death calls me home;
My friends will come for me,
I won't have to do it alone.

Jesse Allen Kirkie

Jesse Allen Kirkie
CAME THE DAWN

This poem is dedicated to all the active passivists in the world today.

Day breaks—the time has come
If man should whisper
Life will come undone

Creeping in the dust
of a vast wasteland
looking for sustenance, a helping
hand

The sun shines white
with immature light

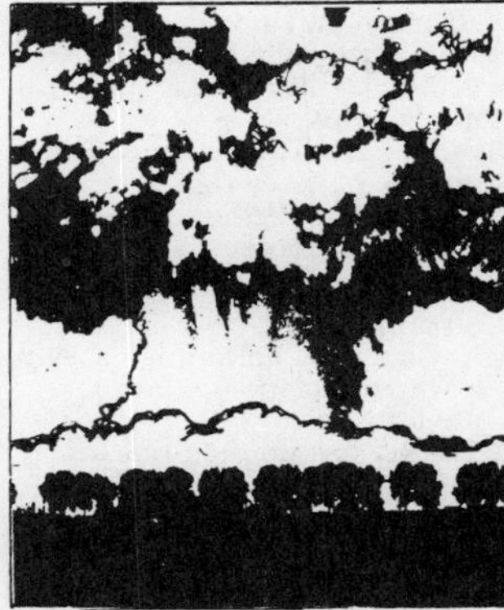

The days grow cold
waste and disease grow bold

The fear of life spreads across the
land
no civilization could ever
withstand
a glow so bright, a dust so
suffocating

The people of Mount Vesuvias
of Mount Saint Helens
are once again, not soon enough,
evacuating

Across the sea salvation may come
if thirsts are quenched
and Our Lord is enlightened by
some

Until that eternity do cometh to us
this different corner of ours will
be viewed in disgust
And to an end which we may see
isolated, desolate, uncared for by
some,
unexpectedly—not
unforshadowed—came the
dawn.

Alison D Stepp
A TRUCKERS WIFE'S PRAYER

To my precious Husband Jim and all the other truckers wives.

Dear Lord, stretch out your hand,
place it over and protect my man,
Watch over him for our childrens
sake.
'Cause he's the best trucker they'll
ever make.

While he's out driving on the roads,
picking up and delivering loads,
Send him cheerful thoughts when
he's alone,
remind him of the love waiting
here at home.

Then he'll surely have to smile,
knowing home is closer each
passing mile,
He's out there taking care of us,
so for taking care of him I thank
you, Jesus.

Joseph L Gaytan
CHANGE

To my sister Monsie, thank you for all the support and encouragement!

I see myself looking
through the glass
wondering why it
happened that way
wondering why I
was led astray
always thinking about
the other way
Knowing it could
never change
But realizing change
is all it takes

Blanche Vera Gripp
AGE . . . OLD . . . QUESTION?

To my Mother, Bertha, a loving, caring person. . .multi-talented, to whom I shall be eternally grateful, for all of the talents, she passed on down to me. Always . . .forever young.

"AGE. . .OLD. . .QUESTION?"
Just what determines age?
Consider the ageless sage.
Is it youth? Some are always old,
Regardless of years.
They are so beset by fears and tears.
Many older people are forever
young.
Their praises continue to be sung.

Many have such an interest in life.
Nor were they ever, a stranger to strife.
What stories they have to tell.
Drawing their knowledge from a bottomless well.
Oh, the teachers they could be, if we would
but listen.
Note the teardrops that glisten. . .
On the weathered cheeks, recalling memories
of the past.
Heartaches, precious memories, that forever last.
This is age? Just being old? Uncaring?
No! This is. . .loving, living and forever sharing.
Qualities that are ageless, in this world of
oriented youth.
The definition of old. . .is anybody's GUESS'.

Ms Penny Glover
HAPPY 125th ANNIVERSARY

Come one, come all
To help us celebrate
An institution
That serves every country and state
People come from near and far
To tour the Bureau of Engraving
To see how good we are
In manufacturing and printing
Brand new currency
Other items and postage stamps
In Washington, D.C.
And in the near future
There will be another location
In Forth Worth, Texas
That is our destination
If you have money
That is burned or mutilated
Send it to us
Our workers are very dedicated
The shipping and handling
Of the men on the planks
Makes sure that the money goes
To all the Federal Reserve Banks
To all the men
Who print and engrave
I say "A job well done"
What an important road you've paved
For the Bureau of Engraving and Printing
Since 1862
And to each and every worker
I would like to salute you
For the many years of service
Through people and technology
It is a very special pleasure
To say "Happy 125th Anniversary"

William Floyd Carpenter
THE GIFT OF WORDS

Along the banks of some anonymous, glimmering pool,
I sense the holy commission.
The gift of words! The rule;
To pen them smartly on the page in artist's fashion
Arranging some, then others touch hearts,
Stir minds, the quest of passion!
Words.
Pure, independent, innocent, dancing, hiding all about.
As fair game, the hunting poet in mystic state,
flush them out!
Place the captives bound by memory before the artist.
Gently down they lay,
To be stroked upon the canvas,
hues of wisdom, proudly on display!
Words.
Bountiful, descriptive, illusive,
beautiful splotches scattered here and there,
like pigments, remain alone,
just colors lying idly on the palette,
no thought to share with human hearts,
their gift as words, is monotony
till collected by poets,
and arranged by some
most cleverly.

Charlotte A Morrison
LOT'S IN LIFE

To my darling niece Brenda who has encouraged me so much, to write

---

We draw lot's in life
Destiny determined where-in
Sanity maintained by a thread
If our lot bears thin
I saw a child
Hungry, lonely, distressed
Soon life ebbs
He lies in perfect rest
Was his lot drawn empty
No mountain to climb
My heart aches for answer's
God reveals in time

Diane P Samuels-Dey
GROWING OLD, AND BEING ALONE

Dedicated to the memory of my beloved Grand-Mother, Ianthy Louise Samuels.

Being old has no dignity.
Dignity is for a time when I was young,
When I had a life of my own; When I thought for myself.
When I lived, worked, studied, seeking that higher learning.
When I did everything for myself.

Now I am old and grey, Wrinkled like a prune,
I am discarded like a useless pair of old shoes that don't match.
I have no dignity left.

I was once proud, healthy and strong. Now I am old and weak.
I sit in my own excreta, I reek of urine, day in and day out.
Nobody cares.
My children disregard me, They ignore me, they fight over
my personal belongings, my estate and monies.

I am in a nursing home, caged like an animal.
No, worse that an animal, seeking a way to escape my fate,
my lot in life.
Being old has no dignity, No respect for me.

I am old and alone.
Alone I will die.
Alone I will lie.

Pamela Ann Johnson
WHEN YOU'RE ALONE

To all of the people in the world who are alone.

When you're alone, you may have to look twice--you're not,
When you're alone, people think you're lonely,
You're not,
When you're alone, you may think you're happy,
You're not,
When you're alone, you may think you're selfish for not spending
time with someone else,
You're not,
When you're alone, nobody knows you better than you,
When you're alone, you can dream your dreams, think your thoughts without anyone else's criticism,
When you're alone, you're in your own world, not happy nor sad just in between,
When you're alone, cherish the time you have with someone you've known your whole life through,
Yourself.
If you understand these things I'm telling you, then God bless you,
Because now, you see, you have a friend you never knew,
You had . . . Yourself.

Doris Duzyj
TO ANDREY

Once I thought the world was not a very sparkling place,
Until I met an exquisite specimen of the human race.
I thought, perhaps, it was, again, another of my delusions,
But found he proved, above my dreams, a great & perfect solution
To all the world's most complicated & profoundest confrontations
A simple, but yet sweet & gentle, psychic lamentation.
A serene & quiet mournful sigh of peace, solitude & quiet,
For all the noise & crime & hate, for all the guns & riots.
A love so strong for all alive, for all that's clean & healthy,
That conquers all inquietude to make wholesome & wealthy.
A joy that transcends all equasions of humanity, rationale & reason,
A happiness for all the ages to conquer hate & treason.
A rule so simple for all to know, that life holds in its bosom,
A warmth of love for all to share, a nucleus of fusion,
Of hearts & souls & body & skin, of life & love & senses,
Of struggle & breath & sounds & tastes, of beauty, eyes & tensions.
A fusion of minds & thoughts & feelings, of music, miles &
travel,
Of beaches, water, sun & sky, sanded shores & paths of gravel,
Of sunset skies & moonlit rooms, of dancing through the night,
Of all things great & glorious, with powers of highest Might.
To me, I guess, the answer came, at last without the inquiry,
A startling realization, yet, so simple & so easy,
To know, for sure, that all is not, futile nor for naught,
That all one learns (& without books) can truly be self-taught.
I found the one who taught me this and now I shall not waste,
Life's greatest treasure, the power of love,
Since of it I did taste.
With Love, Doris

Verlie L Arnet
THE PAIN

In loving memory of my dear husband CHRIS ARNET, who touched our lives with love, who gave me the strength to live without him and to write this poem.

The pain in my chest is still there,
Oh, it's true I still care.
You have left my life, but not my heart,
So often the teardrops start.

But as the days pass by,
Though at times I do cry,
It is not so often now it seems,
Sometimes it is all a dream.

The things I've had to learn to do,
Can even grease the machinery, it's true.
Somehow you made everyday chores look so easy,
I take so long my hands are freezing.

We have handled the farm,
Lucky not to come to harm.
Made hay, seeded grain,
Survived mud from all the rain.

The cattle look good and well cared for,
Eat hay and grain and would like more.
To carry on and do what's best,
Coping and caring for this farm is a test.

But I know we are left to do these chores,
So glad there isn't more.
I sometimes feel I'm not alone out there,
Can feel your presence in the air.

Vivian Lauer
EVENING AT INNER HARBOR

Dedicated to my daughter Laura & grandsons Vincent & Nicholas Harrison

---

Sitting on the dock at inner harbor
darkness settling in
You could hear the seagulls screaming, always hungry
You could hear the blare of the boat horns
going out, coming in.
You could see the hustle bustle
As each hurries on its way
Shopping, eating, going home, it seems as if
some are here to stay.
The Power Plant has closed its doors
The Acquarium, its inhabitants are resting
And looming high in the darkness is the
World Trade Center, where lights twinkle, birds are nesting
Soon all will be quiet, then rippling waves battering the

pier, the fog horns on distant
shores,
The frightening thoughts of
darkness will take over
for Baltimore never sleeps . . .

Joyce Dawn Opem
A CRY IN THE NIGHT

A cry . . .
A wee cry breaks the
silence of the night
heard only by the mother.
Arises . . .
She arises and goes
to the cry.
Quiet . . .
For the infant is
suckling at her breast.
Love . . .
The mother and child.
Peace . . .
In the night.

Jeanette Rosenwasser
THE BEAUTY AND WEALTH OF THE OCEAN

Observing the ocean the different
waves the sounds that make you
think and feel as if you are
listening to Beethovens fifth
Symphony

How peaceful and relaxing it is
to your inner well being
Now your imagination brings you
into the deeper water to the
depth of the sea

You face a new world of wealth
and beauty—beauty of living and
growing of endless surprises
with inspirational stimulations

It looks as if the arrangements
were put there by a great creator
Billions of people could be fed
from the plankton of the sea

Minnie L Paisley

Minnie L Paisley
A LETTER TO VIETNAM

---

*Brother Thomas R. George,
Deceased Husband Thomas F.
Paisley*

The anger we shared. Brother of
mine. The fights we have fought.
But only to hold deep inside,
(A Peace) A peace we won together
to share. A peace of mind for you. It
wouldn't be fair if we didn't
share of what we fought for deep
inside
Brother of mine. Sister Penny

Linda Collum Busby
AGELESS RELATIVITY

---

*To Bert who encouraged, Mom and
Dad who believed, Shirley who
published, Tap who received*

When I was just a child of ten
Life seemed serenely sweet. And
then,
At twenty, life was exciting and
dear.
At thirty, life acknowledged my
advancing years.

For when I was a child of ten
Twenty seemed so old. And then,
At twenty, thirty loomed ancient
and drear.
At thirty, forty was something to
fear.

But now that I'm older, I realize
you can face age without tears.
For it's not the number of years
you've lived—
It's the "living" you've put in the
years.

Nickcole Simond Moore
DIVINITY

The twinkling stars to show
the way, until the breaking of each
day. The sun that shines so warm
and bright, purple and blue hues
of a pale moonlight. Streams ring
their cheerful sounds, beside them
daffodils abound.

Robert W Pratt
ME AND THE BASTARD SEA

When I was young
I loved to roam
And sail the sea
and fight the foam.
Now I've matured
and long to be
At home with you,
not on this sea.
Not on this slanted deck,
but safely in your arms;
Not fighting wind and storm,
But nestled with your charms.
We used to be friends,
Me and this bastard sea
But now we're deadly foes
as it separates you from me.
The widening expanse
is breaking my heart.
It's blinding and choking
and keeping us apart.
But there's one more trip
o'er this sea I must do;
That's my homeward journey,
Home safely to you.

Cynthia Deist
O, TREACHEROUS HEART

O, treacherous heart, you've done
it again,
By leading me down that path of
pain.
I see that look of last goodbyes,
Shine and shimmer from his blue
eyes.
And my heart grieves for what I
lost,
And the feelings that moment cost.
His face, it haunts me during the
day,
While his body steals my nights
away.
Dreams are filled with nocturnal
rapture,
Lonely days pass, devoid of his
laughter.
Passion throbs throughout my
veins,
For him who drives my mind
insane.
And burning desire illuminates my
life,
But has little meaning for all my
strife.
Emotion overwhelms my every
thought,
For the love that can't be bought.
His eyes reflect the crystal clear
pools,
That lure and trap us unsuspecting
fools.
How could my heart deceive me so,
To think this love I could control?
Death would have a greater chance,
Of freeing me of this circumstance.
O, treacherous heart, return me
from oblivion,
So I may live, and love again.

Kimberly Ann Vago
CARING

---

*To my family for all their loving
support*

As sadness overtook me
an angel came to say lie your
head against a pillow and ask
God to guide your way!

Edith Manning Walker
THE PEARL DOVE

---

*In memory of Elicia, from her
Mothers heart to hers. Genesis
31:49 Written September 15, 1977*

Like the Dove descending
In Pearl essence white
With silent fluttering wings
She arrived in the night

Her white feathered splender
Held more beauty, more love
Than any earthly creature
God, sent from above

She nestled in warmth
From beams of the sun
She was our beautiful baby
From Heaven this child had come

We frolicked in her loveliness
She with her angelic ways
The adorable little smile
Was of sunshine rays

One day God wanted her
Much sooner than we planned
Her spirit followed slowly
As the Lord held her hand

She now slumbers in Glory
Where light is of dawn
Angels gone before her
Now sing her, their song
Her toys are the stars
That twinkle at night
We miss our little one
Yet her joy is our delight

We know God has his purpose
For taking our baby love
She winged back to Heaven
Like a Pearl essence Dove

Sandra Brennan
AS LONG AS YOU LOVE ME

---

*To the man who lights up my life
and my heart. You're all I need. I
love you Vince.*

As long as you love me,
I'll stay by your side.
I'll be your companion,
your friend, and your guide.
As long as you love me. . .
As long as you care,
I'll do anything. . .
I'll go anywhere.
I'll bring you the sunshine,
I'll comfort your fears. . .
I'll gather up rainbows,
to chase all your tears.
As long as forever,
my love will be true. . .
As long as you love me,
I'll love only you!

Tiahuana D Vaughan
LONELINESS

Who is he that tortures the soul?
Who corrupts both mind and body,
and
whose scars never heal?

His wrath is great and painful.
His vengeance long and
unbearable.
He's like a cancer that slowly eats
away every bit of hope, till nothing
is
left but a shriveled vegetable in
human
form.

Who is he? Think about it carefully.
Think about the times when you've
cried all night, when you've cursed
yourself and everyone around, and
when you've wanted to ask God,
"Why me?"

Who is he, a rose by any other
name is a rose,
and loneliness by any other name
is Hell.

Mary W "Polly" Jones
THE FATE OF MAN'S SOUL

The soul of man today is likened to
a sewer
And no longer can endure
In the abyss deep to which it sinks
through drains
And there remains—to rot
And thus send forth the stench of
death
As it bewails its fate
"Too late, too late;"
While from the pits the demon
voices swell
To claim this soul which fell
And will forever dwell
Mid unrelenting belching fires
In the pits of Hell—
But, as torrential flames reach
forth
To sere each fibre in their wake,
The faintest voice can still be
heard—
"O wretched soul, it's not too late;
There is yet time for your escape;
Release thyself now unto me,
And concentrating Heaven's
power,
Alas, I will lift you from the depths
And bring you to—
One shining and eternal hour."

Darlene Horn
CHOICES

---

*Dedicated with LOVE to my
children: Robert, Teresa, Tony, and
Kristi.*

Choose a color, Choose a style
Choose a life you want 'for a
while'

Choose a song or Choose a book
Choose that certain 'perfect look'
Choose a mate, Choose a car
Still trying to find who you really are
Life's made up of choices
and it changes every day
In time we find
that things don't always stay the same old way
But one thing is for certain.
One thing's really true,
His love stands eternal
and its always there for you
He was there at the beginning
He will be there at the end
He'll be there to help you make those choices
just around the bend
So ask of Him and then have faith
As you go through each day
And if you really do believe
He'll help you find the way

Athena Rhea
UNTITLED

Clouds of white rolling on
A blue background,
Rushing to the shoreline
Of vast green leaves.
Tumbling, crashing with
A force to the ground.
Feathery foam churning
And receding.

Kenneth Militello
A LOVING ROSE

Today my eyes are set on thee
In my words here's what you mean to me;
To see your smile and tender ways
With your loving ways you've brightened days.
The glistened sparkle from your eyes
Is much more fairer than the Heaven's skies;
Such tender feelings from your heart
Give a hope to me when we're apart.
As you speak soft, loving words so clear,
Your loss would be my gravest fear.
Remember as I speak of thee,
As always you shall be to me,
Within my words of simple rhyme,
A loving rose amongst life's vine.

Dolores Jacqueline Bouldin

Dolores Jacqueline Bouldin
LOVE IS . . . FAITH GIVES . . .

This poem is dedicated to the memory of "mama", my beloved grandmother

---

LOVE IS. . .
A covered dish of kindness
A fleeting moment
A flutter of the heart in spring
A close encounter
A treasure chest of memories
A tear drop on a rosy cheek
A winter's fire
A friend—tried and true
A grandmother's tender touch
A "Me and You"

FAITH GIVES. . .
Light in a path of darkness
An oar in the sea of trouble

Abundant blessings in due season
Calm to a rage within
Strength to the weak in spirit
Comfort in the time of distress
A pillow of sight for the sightless
Solutions to problems
Courage for tomorrow
An answer to a grandmother's prayer

Joan Janis
MOTHER AND DAUGHTER

My mother is dying; there isn't much I can write about concerning that. It is just that. She is dying.

When I talk to her, she acts as if she doesn't know what the facts are and I act like I don't know, and so we keep up our conversation just as if the whole world isn't really caving in on us. "Wait until next summer", she says. "I'll come over to your place and we'll sit outside near the pond and watch the ducks." I smile and tell her that "I can't wait" but she and I both know that for her, there won't be a next summer. But we go on pretending; it comforts us.

She looks at my daughter's stylish shoes with the high heels and wonders aloud "Will I ever be able to wear those again?" and we both know she won't, but I say, "Sure, mom, like the pair you wore at my wedding." And she talks about going shopping for a pair just like that again some time soon.

In the night I wake from a deep sleep, abruptly, and my mind instantly clicks on with a picture of her alone in her hospital bed, still, white, calm. Is she scared? Is she lonely? Does she ever want to talk about 'it'? Iwant to hold her. Just hold her so tight to me. Mothers are mothers to their daughters but eventually the daughters become mothers to their mothers, brushing the hair off their faces, wiping their mouths, bathing them, holding them while they cry at their insufficiencies.

I feel good that my mother knows I have always loved her. I will miss her so much but she knows I love her and I take comfort in that.

Ellen Lynch
BOMB

In that dread day of holocaust
When man shall loose his new-found powers
And flesh, and steel and woodland flowers
Shall know alike the fearful blast;
When there shall be no time to fast
Or meditate in leafy bowers,
And spirits borne on mushroom towers
Shall into outer void be cast.

What, then, of God? Will the Eternal Mind,
Under the impact of on-rushing souls
Reject forever self-destroying man?
Or in His boundless storerooms will He find
Nobler impulses and finer molds,
And breathe on them His breath and start again?

JoFrances Sheffield Cook
EASTER SURPRISE

Dedicated to my Son. R. Earl Moses, Jr.

Twas the morning of Easter and all thru the woods, not a rabbit was stirring, even though he could.

For all thru the forest there was heard such a sound, of cracking and popping that shook the ground.

Little baby rabbits with their heads in the grass, were calling their mama's "Come back to the nest."

Then all of a sudden, to every rabbit's surprise, popped a little boy, about three rabbit's high. His lips were smiling and both eyes bright, as he carried his basket and went out of sight.

Margaret P Cincotta
UNKNOWN LOVE

To Mom & Dad, with all my love.

A love unkown is the worst of all.
To never have known the rise and the fall.
A love which only you can feel.
A love which is still all the real.
To see him in your every thought.
To be seeked and forever sought.
To want him more everyday
To see him go farther away.
To always wonder if he too feels the same about you.
And when the time comes that you must part
The tears will come and tear at your heart.
And you will always dream of how it could have been.
If somehow he could have seen that your love was always there.

Lisa Porter Hofsess
THREE WOMEN

For Kim, Janie and Linda for these three, and for all of the women who have shared real love

---

This one manifests the power of a mountain
Legs that I think could stride across the landscape of my fears
Stepping over boulders as if they were stones
Leaping across rivers that I wonder if I can swim
In my dreams she can embrace the grizzly
Dance his dance beautifully because her body embodies the power of the mountains

This one has my body
Lithe and agile as a cat
But she is more mercurial than I allow myself to be
Emotions dance across her face expressing the depth and the joy that fly around behind my mask
Unable to escape my heart
Her body catches the light
And sprays it out in a riot of colors
Like the prism I long to be

This one is as shy as a deer
She glides gently through the forest
Hesitates to leave the shelter of the trees, thinking maybe I can't see her
But I do and I love her because I know when it's important she will find me
When I am sitting quietly against a tree
Wishing my sorrow could soften the mask of my face
She comes and lays her head gently on my shoulder, allowing me to cry
She is the peace and gentleness I feel in the forest

Women with bodies that embody all of the power I feel
All of the strengths of my spirit manifested
In the women whom I love

Betty L Dubuque
A SHADOW OF A GUN

I remember when I was young, on dark and quiet nights,
We didn't have electricity, kerosine lamps gave us lights.
Shadows were cast upon the wall and were great on a window shade.
We used our shadows to make up stories and oh the games we played.
The shadow of a small wooden gun gave my brother great delight.
He knew the stories he'd make up, would fill us all with fright.
One night a noise on the front porch, like nothing we'd heard before,

Nearly scared us all to death, when it knocked upon the door.
My Mom stopped reading, "Be Quiet," she said,
And dad called out, "Who's there"!
The small wooden gun was now in Mom's hand, we had dropped it on a chair.
That little gun looked 5 feet long in it's shadow on the shade.
"Don't Shoot, Don't Shoot," a voice called out,
"It's me, it's your neighbor Wade."
Wade came in and the three shook with laughter,
We knew then it had all been in fun.
They had joined in our games and played out their story,
"A Shadow of a Gun."

Debra D Samples Bosecker

PARADISE

It's the little things
that mean so much.
A hug—A kiss—A smile
Everything that makes loving you so very much worthwhile.

The moment you look into my eyes
I melt with your sweet touch
If only you would realize
I need you so very much.

Hold me close and don't let go
in my heart please stay
And our tomorrows in paradise
will never fade away.

Mary Elizabeth Walling

THE PRO'S DREAM

Dedicated to my son, Kendall, who is making the dream come true.

From the baseball fields in Canyon's Hidden Valley
To the pro's diamond in Anaheim
Those dreams keep rolling
Of the California Angels and "the big time."
You've proven that dreams really do come true
But that it takes hard work and talent too.
When the going was tough it wasn't always fun
Yet you kept on pushing for better things to come
And now with a beautiful wife and a handsome son
To share each step as the race you run
Keep right on dreaming as you climb
And you'll still be reaching til the end of time.

Jenny Schaefer

WHAT I HAVEN'T DONE

It's not what I've done
That mostly I regret
But what I haven't done
That I wish I could forget

The things I should have said
The things I should have done
All the things I've dreamt
But never did instead

Well now that I am wiser
So to you I'll recommend
Build your life with aver . . .
And you'll find yourself a friend.

Carmen Marie Legendre

NATURE'S SONG

To my loving grandfather William Moore

I hear the wind calling me
To a land beyond;
Beckoning to follow
The blue jay to a land
Which is a forest
Of nature's song
Where the meadow lark
Sings her lullaby
And crickets form
An orchestra to play melody
Rejoicing in the nights
As frogs croak out
The chorus to a long
forgotten tune.

Marie Cascio

LOVE

To my loving family who inspired me to write this poem. Especially to my brother Joe.

Love is beautiful; love is divine.
Love is always so hard to find.
Love is in the air; love is something you share.
It's not just a word it's how you care.
It's hard to imagine what this world would be
If I didn't love others and they didn't love me.

Anna Cholewczynski

MARY

A mother said to her little daughter
Who had sisters one older, one younger
"We are going by an ocean liner
To a new country far over yonder.

Mary was her name. She was three years old,
She was fair of face, her hair was like gold.
"Your grandma and grandpa there you will see
Which will make you very, very happy."

They were on the ocean a long, long time
Mary was waiting for the happy time
When she could put her arms around granny,
Who she loved dearly, 'most like her mommy.

All her life mother remembered Mary
How she asked, "Mommy, are we almost there?
It is taking long, why don't we hurry?"
And mommy pressed her closely, smoothed her hair.

Then sickness came and it was for Mary
They took her away to a ship's infirm'ry.
Days later, when mother could go see her,
Mary's voice was hoarsend to a whisper.
"She cried all the time," said lady 'tending,
Just as if her little heart was breaking."
Then she closed her eyes—Angels took Mary.
She could not get to see her dear granny.

Juanita Lee Shaw

NO LONGER

No longer may I hold your hand,
And now I do not know where I stand.
You are gone now and I'm alone,
I'll just sit around, listening for the phone.
"He will come walking in," I say,
But where you have gone, you will stay.
Thank you for the time we have shared.
I want you to know, how much I have cared.
You were more than a friend, but now it has ended.
So I must continue—go on,
Knowing my heart you have won.
"Almost too good, to be true" people would say.
Love is the only thing we knew, but it did not stay.
So once more I shall kiss your cheek.
A new life, I must seek.
We were one, two hearts in an Easter basket,
But, now I lie in misery,
As you lie in your casket.

Leonard C Valley

CRUSADER'S RETURN

O' Lord God of Israel grant us surcease from
this toil and deep moaning of our hearts' desire. . .
May we go forth and return to our lost land and find
there at least one moment of achievement that is

not barren. . .and forever lost amidst the mediocrity
of this Autumnal year that we hold so dear. . . Even
now as I behold at last my castle towers, I find
within me a final spark that seems to sing and I
hear the sweet sad song of yesteryear. . .the whispering
hills and fragrant trees are still there—nothing has
changed. . .but me?

Winifred Thomas

WINTERS END

I dedicate this poem to my Dad in his memory

The night is cold.
Winds are blowing,
Making a hollowed
Sound as they go.

Thoughts are deep and
Moving, thinking,
Planning—
No one but me knows

Restless. roaming,
Running, anywhere—
Everywhere

Joyce Cox

ANXIETY

In the midnight haunting visions come
That would not dare to come in day.
People long in past and long forgotton
Ring round my bed to play.
Goblin's feet are creeping, witches hide behind my door.
Satan's angels gather here to dance across my floor.
Demons oe'r my window peer
Leave me quaking here with fear.

From the midnight 'till the dawning
With these weird creatures am I taunted;
'Till morning's streaming sunlight proves—
It's I, and not the house that's haunted.

Iva Pate Brown

EMPTY NEST

To my children-three, Sylvia, Ford Jr. & Cynthia

The silence is very loud, with no one near
All the noises of yesterday are so very clear
I can hear you saying all the cute little things
that a mother treasures, as her heart takes wings.
My heart aches for the tread of your little feet
first ones faint, then louder, and not always neat
with all the clutter and fuss and stew, it would be
nice to know I still had each of you.

I marvel at the ladies, grown from my girls, when only
yesterday your hair was matted with curls, your sashes torn
from your pinafores, pictures and paints smeared all
the doors. The print of little hands are all about,
with teardrops visible when you were in a pout,
because of the scoldings from all the marks,
You couldn't understand grown-ups and their barks.
I sit alone and ponder as the years go by
and think of my son who wanted to fly
Superman was the hero he liked best, now they are
gone, and I'm left in an empty nest!

Chris Shanaman

GEORGE

For my son, Jim, who still has his teddy bear.

I have a teddy bear named George,
he's cuddly, soft and brown.
I like to take him everywhere,
especially into town.

George was a gift, from mom and
dad, when I was only three.
I know there are no better friends,
then my old George and me.

I've told George my many secrets,
hidden within my heart,
And that is why he's my best friend,
and has been from the start.

All through the years George
stayed with me, I've placed him
in a chair,
And tho' I do not talk to him, he
seems contented there.

Today I hurried home to tell, the
greatest news of all,
And George was there, tho' old and
worn, waiting for me to call.

I held old George close to my heart,
and whispered in his ear,
I have a son of my very own, and
he is very dear.
Then as I placed him in his chair,
I thought I saw a tear,
Now don't you cry, my dear old
friend, I'll always keep you near.

And when my son is older, George,
say at the age of three,
We'll give to him a teddy bear, a
gift from you and me.

So someday he will understand,
what friends, we'll always be,
And all the secrets that were
shared, between old George and
me.

Then as I turned to leave the room,
I heard a little sigh,
Looking around, I saw George
smile, the tears were in my eyes.

For now I'm older, and I know that
there can never be,
A better friend in all the world,
then old George was to me.

Adam L Langus

ONLY TIME WILL TELL

To: Candle-light Cafe's

I met a pretty gal. not so long ago,
as we got acquainted, my love
began to grow—
thought I could see sign's of it,
from her begin to show.
I learned to like the things she
liked,
do the things she wanted to,
gave up most
every thing I ever did—her
avenue's pursue.
One night when we were all alone
and
every thing seemed well, I asked
her if she
loved me . . she said, only time
will tell;
wasn't really set for that, but
all, in all
seemed swell.
Time kept moving on and all
season's cast their spell,
we'd gone and done a lot of
things, now have come
to sit a spell, once again I
asked her . . . . .
if she loved me—but in her eye's
could tell; she didn't
want to say it, but, only time
will tell.
Well soon I got real busy, with put
off things and those
I had to do, gave a lot of my
attention— to what had
passed from view, found I
completed a lot of things
I thought I couldn't do.
We saw each other now and then,
let the moment cast its
spell, suddenly she asked me, if
I still loved her;
I looked at her and smiled—
and said . . . . .
"Only Time Will Tell."

Scott Garret Oliver

THE LION IN THE EVENING

In dedication: To Mrs. Sylvia Sosa for all the time and inspiration that she's shown me.

The Lion in the evening holds its
head high.
He gives a noble farewell to the
daylight sky.
Alone he sits on his hill, after
darkness falls.
Until again he wakens and gives
the morning call.
The land is shadowed in darkness,
The sky filled black with pain.
And now, The Lion in the Evening
waits for day again.

Sharon Rigall Shed

WORD FIGHT

War sang out
from the left then the right.
Not even hand to hand combat,
just a stupid word fight.

Things were said
that neither of them meant,
only in the heated anger
did their mouths turn to vents.

Apology rang out
but kind words were too late.
Nothing on Earth,
could erase the word named hate.

Rachel Ohr

WHAT IT IS TO BE ME!

This is dedicated to my dad and my grandfather who are in Heaven.

To be me
right now is:
Depression,
Misery,
Happiness and
Enjoyment

Missing my
loved ones
makes me:
Sad,
Mad,
Dreary and
Teary Eyed
In Time I
hope to become
again:
Smiling,
Cheerful,
Funny and
Hopeful.

Aaron B Schofield

REACH FOR THE STARS

Dedicated to Christa McAuliffe, The teacher who risked and lost her life to increase the knowledge of children throughout the nation and her fellow crew members.

Black emptiness of vacum void,
cold, wonderous space of none,
but little tiny mystic lights called
moons
and stars and suns,
and having in this vast, deep space,
most
beautiful of all, a little orb of seas as
blue as truest blue of all.
Her emerald woodland forests
lush,
her plains and prairies wide, her
canyons deep, her mountains tall,
a crescent at her side, From
bubbling
brooks to roaring falls,
the merry breezes flow,
from colors of the rainbow high to
the
sunset lying low, Yet like the silver
lining
of the clouds, puffed in the sky,
the magic of our precious gem
does in our spirit lie,
For happiness and sorrow, and for
joyfulness
and pain, let us not forget the
simple things,
our dreams bear greater gain.

Shelly Smith

SOONER THAN WE THINK

Once there was a green, green
earth;
of trees, and plants, and healthy
life.
Now there is nothing, but grey
spaces,
And tombs of dead men.
Men who died in the name of love
and loyalty.
Men whose souls may or may not
ever return to know
the freedom of everlasting life.
What is that which everlasts,
amid nuclear war and bombing
blasts?
Nothing saved, nothing earned,
Everything wasted, everything
burned.
Friendships built on weak
foundations,
crumbled like dry leaves in the
hands of wrath.
Families grown together, simply
blown apart;
Those not burned, died of broken
heart.
Signs the sparrow a throaty song;
Their voices gone, it won't be long.
No one left to see the dawn, which
is red and bloody,
Simply gone.
Hear the thundering of above;'
Buried below, wastelands, no love.
No love left, no love lost,
Upon our gravesites, our bodies
are tossed.
Battered and smashed, our bodies,
our souls.
Sent beyond time and space, no
life, no goals.

Virginia Bailey Jarrett

I FOLD MY HANDS

This poem is dedicated to my loving mother, Elizabeth.

I fold my hands
I close my eyes
I bow my head in prayer
with Jesus in my heart I know
He will be forever there
My life's been such a shambles
My outlook's been so bare
But now I know that things will
change
He will always care
The road need not be bumpy
As I travel on my way
My head is so much lighter
Than it's been for many a day
Dear Jesus, thank you kindly
For showing me you care
As I fold my hands
Close my eyes
Bow my head in prayer

Deborah Louise Potts

LOOKING THROUGH EYES OF WISDOM

If only I could have seen through
these eyes years ago,
I might have stood strong and my
burdens would'nt have
Pushed me down so low.
Instead of mountains filled with
green.
Now these eyes see beauty I've
never seen.
The flowers I passed by day after
day,
My eyes were blinded so dark and
gloomy and gray.
The childrens laughter that made
me uneasy at times,
Now if only they could see through
my eyes, we could share
The love we tried so hard to find.
The gift of life I took for granted
and almost threw it away,
I now realize it is a gift from God,
the most precious gift
I would say.
As I touch the wrinkles that are
engraved in my face so deep,
Suddenly I've become so tired and
my only desire is to sleep.
The darkness I see is different in
so many ways,
I know that if I close my eyes this
is where I'll stay.

Darrell James Abshire Jr

SNOW

Snow is of fashion,
But it still comes down
To whiten all the buildings
In our town;
To dull the move of traffic;
To dim each glaring light
With star-shaped feathers of frosty
white.
And not the tallest building
Halfway up the sky;
On all the trains and buses,
And taxis scudding by;
And not a million people,
Not one of them at all,
Can do a thing about the snow
But let it fall!

Anita Gennusa Knighton

DAD, IT'S JUST TOO HARD TO SAY GOODBYE

This poem is dedicated in loving memory of my Dad.

The time has come to say goodbye,
and it's so hard to do,
because we just can't seem to know,
how to let go of you.

You've always been there for us,
Dad,
and losing you has made us sad.
There's no one who can take your
place,

or fill that void that we must face.

You'll be forever in our hearts,
and our memories of you,
will comfort us when we're alone,
And don't know what to do.

We find it hard to go on now,
Without you among us,
and yet we know it must be done,
So we'll re-live your life within us.

And on this day I want to say,
that I love you more deeply than I
did yesterday.
And that with tomorrow I'm sure
that I will,
Love you even more deeply than I
thought I could still . . .

Guy Bunce

Guy Bunce
MY OLD POINTER

This poem is dedicated to my old hunting buddy Sagi, from his partner Curt.

Sagitarius is his name.
Pointing birds is his game.
When he runs around
he sure covers some ground.
But when he's on point he won't
make a sound.
He'll point them birds until they fly
and when they do that's when they
die.
Cause from behind him comes a
man
they call Curt Gowdie, with gun in
hand.
Sagitarius will fetch those birds
and bring them back
and before you know it they've got
a stack
of pheasant, partridge, ducks and
geese too
then Curt will tell you how they
once flew.
Through rain, sleet, and even the
snow
that won't stop Sagitarius and
Curt, they're ready to go.
So yes he's an old pointer, but not
like the rest.
He's old Sagitarius, Curt Gowdie's
best.

Gerard P Riley
DREAMING
Drifting, Drifting
I slither from the conscious world
Descending into the chasm of a
new reality
Where time is only illusion

Images are conjured
by my cerebral magician
Abstract shapes, translucent
spectres
unreal, yet real
Incorporeal.

Graceful and chaotic,
this land of enchantment
Where surrealism manifests itself
as my phantasm unfolds.
Places, exotic landscapes
Faces, shrouded in disguise
Past, Present and Future,
Intertwine

Suddenly, I awake
My memory is elusive as
the door closes to what was
Perhaps Forever!

J J Thompson
DID YOU HEAR?
Did you hear? We live in America,
The U.S. of A.
Where you can worship God in
your own little way.
But WAIT—Did you hear? In
school you can't pray!
You can't speak of Jesus, That is
taboo.
But—Did you hear what we will
teach you?
Evolution: No God; No future for
man; no eternity,
By chance we all came from fish in
the sea.
No God and no Jesus for you and
for me!

What good is tomorrow—if there
is only today?
What matter how we act or what
we say?
No devine master? No hope for
heaven?
Well, then, I'll just make my own
Little haven!
So give me the needle, the drugs
and the pot,—
Keep away from me people the
color I'm not!
What matters my life here on
earth, when the grave
Is the only sure thing left you gave?
No faith, or tomorrow or Jesus
who loves me—
Maybe someday we'll just wash
back to the sea!
Did you HEAR WHAT YOU HAVE
DONE TO ME?

Give me back God, Love, a future,
eternity
Jesus who, because of love, died for
me.
Our America our men fought and
died to keep free!
Where we can in worship come to
Jesus's side,
And all races kneel together, no
fear or pride.
DO YOU HEAR? GIVE ME A
REASON TO BE.

Morris Holding Durrant
LET'S MAKE ANOTHER MEMORY

To my sweetheart wife, Nelldean.

Let's make another memory—
Of love that used to be.
Let's make another memory—
A memory of you and me.

Let's make another memory—
Of love that promised to be true.
Let's make another memory—
A memory of me and you.

Let's make another memory—
Of all the loveliness that's past—
Let's make another memory—
Let's make this memory our last.

Grace Boggan
WHAT YOU THINK IS WHAT YOU ARE

For my grandson Tim Dean Nielsen

They Say; What You Eat is What
You Are!
I Say; What You Think is What You
Are!
Because, How You Think is How
You Eat!
And, How You Eat is Quite Bizarre!

Heather M Fisher
ME

For those to whom my leaving would make a difference!!!

When they say Hello
but they mean Goodbye,
When I want to laugh
but I can only cry.
If I leave here now
Would they feel the same?
Or bow their heads in shame.
Would they read My Thoughts?
Would they see the pain?
Or be darkened with words
And think it's a game.
If I leave here now
Would someone see,
I only wanted to be
ME!

Mrs Mazine Moore Winstead
GOD'S UNDYING LOVE
Lift me dear Lord from the depths
of sin,
Stretch forth Thine arms, enfold
me within,
Take my body and make it whole,
Forgive my sins and save my soul.

Take my life and use it dear Lord,
To help Thy cause, to spread Thy
word,
So that others may come to Heaven
above,
To live in Thy bosom and share in
Thy love.

I'll serve Thee dear Lord any way
that I can,
I'll love Thee oh Lord, as Jesus
loves man,
So my friends will know that I'm
living for You,
And ask for salvation and start life
anew.

Look on my dear Lord as my head
I bow,
Thy grace I accept, Thy love I
endow,
I'll walk in Thy ways and give Thee
Thy due,
As Jesus loves man I'll always love
You.

Jenneane Evelyn Lammert
PURE
Come follow me take my hand.
I shall lead you into the promised
land.
Don't be afraid of what is to come.
As long as you listen for the call of
my drum.
Remember always that I love you
so.
Put your faith in me and you shall
grow.
Come follow me take my hand.
I shall lead you into the promised
land.
To a place that is always there.
It's as beautiful as the clouds in the
air.
Soft and gentle that is my touch.
For you are all my children and I
your crutch.
Always believe and trust in me.
And tomorrow I shall bring you
Eternity.

Joann Stetz
A SPECIAL PICNIC
I picked up the phone and a voice
said "Hi Friend!"
"We're having our annual Rehab
Picnic again."
My thoughts went back with a
smile and a tear,
To the wonderful time we all had
last year.
There was plenty of fresh air and
lots of sun.
There were shows, games and
prizes for everyone.
Old friends and new friends, I got
to see.
But what I liked best is that it was
all free.
I think we should all give a big
rousing cheer,
To the hard working therapist who
helped get us here.
And as for the doctors a "Hip!"
"Hip!" "Hurray!"
Becuase thank God for them we're
all here today.
Now as I look around the smiles
are the same,
"Would somebody please push me
to the Bingo Game?"

Dale Jenkins
FATHER'S

dedicated to Norman Jenkins, the inspiration of this poem, and the lives of his 7 children. Also to Bertha Jenkins his wife, and the special mother who encouraged all of them.

He works all day making money,
plus
He spends it all on food for us;

He must make alot of money tis
true,
Because he must pay for the house
too,

After a long day at work,
He may want to give us a jerk,

But he restrains from doing this
and gives us on the head a little kiss;

As he gets up there in his years,
He still may never shed any tears;
And later on he may pass away,
But we'll never let memories sway,

He's the one who made us right
when we were wrong
And when we were weak he
made us strong

So children cherish your father
he's so dear
For someday he may not be here.

Eme Rose
THE SEED OF LIFE

To my friend Kitty—only she knows why.

The Seed of Life was sent to me
Implanted like the deepest tree

And then—God Above
Decided Thus—
When he took my Babe to love.
Amen.

Ruth I Conway
THE GIFT OF LOVE
Valentine's Day reminds us of love,
A gift we receive from our Father above.
It's not just for today, but for all our life through,
The more love you give, the more comes back to you.

Love is for everyone both near and far,
It doesn't matter where you live, or not who you are.
Love is for a family, a sweetheart or a friend,
It is round like a ring and has never an end.

We should all love our neighbors and enemies too,
But we have a choice, it's up to me and to you.
If love were spread over, all the world wide,
We would all be much happier deep down inside.

Love is something that we can't live without,
We must give it and receive it, without any doubt.
Love is forever, not just for today,
And no greater gift can be given away.

Anita Walter Helfrecht
WAR

To my dear children, Ruth and Paul

O cold April snow
you haven't a right
To make war on spring
with all of your might.

Your offensive pursuit
is strong indeed,
But springtime's defense
is a mighty steed!

Though spring's covered up
with your troops of white,
Spring will prevail
like an armored knight.

You may surely succeed
in springtimes delay,
But the army of springtime
will send you away!

Michael J McClure
SPECIAL FRIENDS
Friends like you are hard to find.
People like you are one of a kind.
Some people don't understand and are blind,
jealous of the things that bind.
Everybody deserves good friends like you.
Although sometimes I don't think I do.
Sometimes I'm cruel, which we know is true.
I do charish friends such as you,
and hope you understand.
Friends such as you are grand.
I hope that our strong friendship will always stand.

To the one who means so much.
I can not express my feelings as such.
My love for you is forever lasting,
of a magnitude that is unsurpassing.
A thought goes out to you each waking moment.
Although even in sleep you are still a torment.
I hope the future for you is always bright.
Also a wish that you always do all that's right.
I miss you so much I can't think of what to say.
But as you know I would never take your freedom away.
Every now and again please take a little time to see.
Just a pause to think one quick thought like me.
Think of the beautiful memories and feelings we have shared.
And then remember I am the one who cared. (And always will.)

Sandra V Cullimore
WAITING FOR SPRING

To Mom, who enjoys waiting for spring as I do.

The dismal days of winter
leafless branches brush the skies
And the cold wind shows no mercy
endless snow before our eyes

Lighted windows, smoking chimneys,
clouds of steamy-breath exhaled
Crunch of snow and cracking ice
beneath our feet on wintry trail

Inside. . .Dreams of winter's end
catalogs of tools and seeds

Remind us just how constant are the cycles
changing times and changing needs

We need the cold—it encourages
the flowering of hidden bulbs
come spring
And returns again the changes
that each fresh new season brings

And remember how the summer
dusty, hot, more work than play
Brought us new strengths to prepare us
for the autumn harvest days

Listen. . .Look, there
Springtime's pulse soon will be throbin'
For on that dark and lifeless branch
there sits a Robin!

Harvey Green
TO THE DREAMERS
I believe you can never separate
true hearts and true minds.
If I should ever leave this earth
and not have someone here
who thinks I am special,
then I would think my life to be a tragedy.
So I would like to spend my life touching
other lives, to make them special and
myself also.
For where we have touched is a special
place, where the Good, the True
and the Beautiful are forever.
So when you think on good things and
truths and see beauty,
think of me.
For I, too, have been thinking of you.

Charles Curtis Blackwell
THE MELTING OF A CHAMP, AWAY
The streets are painted
Standing reflections
Neon lights broadcast messages
Of neon, neon and neon
Say never again
And goodbye champ

Ice is melting on the eastern shore
Near the eastern street
While others still sleep
Come closer
Come closer

Drawn by the pull of fishing line
Liken to little children
Liken to little lovers
Pulling nickels from the sewer
From laundrymats
From pay phones

Listen to the cries, of a friend
Broken by life and timeless punches
Like his mother
Broken off
Long ago

Drunk she is
Cries unto his mother, drunk
Fight, some more
Serious rain falling, on to blacken streets
Creating reflections of neon lights
That reflect an endless fight

Analda Ann Koeth
MY HAVEN
There is a refuge,
A place of peace,
That sits among the mountains' floor.
This is my haven.
My haven is as peaceful as,
Newly fallen snow.
A place away from the hustle
And bustle of this busy world of ours.
My sanctuary has no phones,
No fast cars or noisy trucks.
No, my haven is calm and noiseless.
Instead it answers with the
Chirping of the many birds,
And calls from wild turkey and of grouse.
The small chattering of the squirrel
Black, gray and red, and chipmonks, too.
The rustle of the mountain laural
As the deer run to and fro.
This is my little piece of heaven.
My haven is not disturbed by man,
No machine to wreck the beauty.
No, man alone could not compose
The beauty of this place.
The guardian of my haven
Was a creation of GOD'S two hands alone.

James R Gobles
JAYNIE'S 45'S
This beautiful blonde is really smart;
She combines math'matics with an art
And I heard what Jaynie had to say
As she stepped from the high noon stage today.
She said, "I'd sure be dead and not alive
Without this pair of forty-fives.
I'm the fastest draw this side of the river."
And from where I stood, they really made me shiver
Well, Jaynie stood tall, wind-blown and carefree,
A pair of forty-fives for all so see.
So this put an end to all the rumors and lies;
'Round the clock Jaynie totes a pair of forty-fives.
She said "I'd surely be dead and not alive,
Without this pair of forty-fives.
I'm the fastest draw in town", she goaded.
And from where I stood, they sure looked mighty loaded.

George E "Buck" McCullough
A HOLIDAY WISH

To Nola Watters, with great devotion.

There are no words with which to express
the inner-most feelings of my heart at
this special season

True, fervent emotions are there, and with
out my choosing manifest themselves in my
consciousness, void of rhymn or reason

It seems at times that all the world has
knowledge of them, all of humanity comprehends
their meaning, 'cept I.

My prayer is that you will understand
them implicitly and knowledge that they are
in the joy fashioned tears I cry.

That you will sense the intimate communication passing
between our souls,
seeking to bring us happiness

And that you will know they imply more
than, I love you, they say; I wish you love
and joy and hope and tenderness.

Kim Publicover
THE LIFE OF A RAINBOW—TO MY DEAR FRIEND CHRISTI
What a sight? See it?
It's there. Red . . . Green . . . Blue.
How long will it last? 1—2—3.
We do not know.
Will the rain disappear and

take with it the red . . . green . . . blue.
What beauty! What life!

Its time has come—it's fading.
Where might it go?

Quickly!

We cannot grab, touch, or hold it back.
But only reach out with our hearts
and send beauty and peace with it
wherever it may go!

We can only remember this beauty and
the impact it had on us for that
brief moment in life. And believe
it will be passed on and created
again and again in a new life of its own.

I can see it. Now I can't
Is it lost?
Only our memories can make it glow.

Share the beauty with someone else.

We can only be satisfied and content
to have experienced this beauty—this peace.

The life of a rainbow is too short.
We must treasure this rainbow.
For I will always, treasure mine—

Evelyn R Carey

REAL LOVE

The day for lover's came and went,
But the love we have is never spent.
God made a way for the greatest love,
And gave it to us from heaven above.
The greatest love—His Son had shown;
And we can have it always—it's not a loan.
Thru faith that Jesus died for me;
God gave me love,—'cause that's the key.
Love is the key for my relations with you.
Loving and caring always in all that I do.

Yes, God is Love, and without Him you can't really love,
So hold fast to Him, grab His Hand from above,
He's reaching for you, as He reached once for me,
Oh! take it in faith—try it;—you'll see!
Nothing in life is ever, as sweet as it's seeming,
Until you know "real love", you'll miss the real meaning.
Life will be empty—you'll even tire of what's "fun";
Unless you "know Jesus" you can never "be one"—
With God and His Love, so He can put in your heart;
Real love for others—that sets Christians apart.

Lillian G Abrams

SUNSHINE

Dedicated to my beloved husband, Saul.

Another day is dawning
The sun rises in the sky
And in so doing
Spreads its light all around.

The birds start to twitter
And forage for their food,
The flowers turn their faces
To greet the warmth anew.

The brightness of the day
Brings everyone forth
To start activities
Of which they are a part.

Whether it is cloudy,
Even if it rains
The sun is shining over all
Though it is unseen.

We too have days of grey
We have our days of woe,
But like the sunshine, there is always hope
A new day will bring joy.

Amy Melissa Smith

WHO IS IT?

TO: Jeff Keim, who inspired me to start writing poems. Jeff, you're the greatest friend, I love you, remember me always—Amy Smith '87

Crouched in the corner of the dark attic
I see two large eyes staring at me from out of the darkness.
Who is it?

It stares at me. I stare back.
The eyes seem to be without a face.
Who is it?

It is silent and remains stationary.
So do I.
It frightens me.
Who is it?

Who is this mystery? It seems to reach out to me.
It is not unfriendly, is it a friend?
Who is it?

It is yearning for me to follow it into the unknown.
Should I follow? I do, but the question still fills my head.
Who is it?

It takes me far into the sky, above the clouds and sun.
Here it is bright. The eyes of the creature are gone. Where am I?
Where did the frightening eyes go?
Who was it?

As I travel farther,
I realize now as I see the pearly white gates and a peaceful dove fly by, it was the eyes of death and darkness.

My fears have been chased away.
I am no longer alone.
The eyes have returned below to bring yet another soul.
Who will it be?

Barbara Kay Trebacz

COLORS

My feelings 1977 To those I Love

Love is the color of the rainbow.
Blue is when problems arise and things seem all mixed up.
Orange is the happy times we have in our relationship.
Yellow is the fear we have of getting too close.
Red is the funny times we experience together.
White is our melody, our love song, our life together.
A loving rainbow full of joy.

Beverly (Stacey) Gibson

THE HAVEN

The old house squats, defeated,
shingles split and curled,
rakish angles of its sway-backed roof
pointing towards the sky.
Gnarled and grey, an apple tree
slumps against the windward side,
branches draped in seeking vines
fingering broken windows.
Hollyhocks and daisies
marching through the yard,
are crowded close by poppies
rioting with weeds.
Where steps once were, pink roses grow
sprawled in mass confusion,
holding fast an opened door
invitingly aside.
Forgotten are the sights and sounds
of those who once laid claim.
Now shadowed places hide the seekers,
nooks and crannies shelter all.
Crumbling wood, a falling shingle,
sounds softened by debris,
are small concerns to drowsy tenants
listening to the songs of summer
drifting in the air.

Michelle Ann McKnight

THE UNATTAINABLE

Alone in my room—All feelings locked inside
When forced to confront them—I only run and hide.

All these problems—I silently scream;
My only escape—I must dream.

The problems number many—they letter A to Z.
Are these problems commonplace? Or, is it just me?

Envy leads to jealousy, which, in turn, becomes hate.
I need to find an answer but solutions are none too great.

Why do I want what others have? Why can't I be content?
Why does no one like me? I need a friend—from heaven sent.

I need a guardian angel to teach me right from wrong.
I want to sing well but have no words for the song.

My problem is so simple—yet an answer I await.
Not solvable on my own, I need the hands of fate.

I want someone to love me as no other has before.
I want to be held so pain will be no more.

I need a small white dove to show me the way to happiness,
A dove to help me find my love.

Russell Lee Provost

WINTER

Winter close
It touches the days
With an icey finger
Gone the summer rose
But leaves a memory to linger

Winter awaits
While autumn leaves answer call
Covering the ground with blazon color
The natural order of fall

Winter comes
Clouded dark, as wrought by nite
Forever and ancient
A season cloaked in white

Eva Conrad

BIRD SONGS

At dawn gray doves give out a mournful tune,
Fat robins sing a happy gay refrain
While sparrows join with chirping very soon,
All glad to meet the daylight once again.
So many a lovely bird song is missed—
Just listen to one singing clear and shrill
Atop the knoll that by evening sun is kissed,
Ah, what a sound—The song of whippoorwill!
And when you hear that Happy Meadow Lark
The sweetness of it's song gives such a thrill!
The old wise owl asks "Who, Who?" from woods so dark,
It gives one quite a start when all is still.
Let not the music of the bird songs be in vain!
Stop your ever busy-ness and hear
The sounds of earth-The softly falling rain—
The voice of God—And know that He is near.

D J Jena Richardson

D J Jena Richardson

MY PRAYER OF YOU JOCK

Dear Lord,
Where did my Jock go,
the romantic lover I use to know?
My Jock, my Greek God, with the perfect physique,
who use to trail kisses across my cheek.
My Jock, my Hawaiian Adonis, with a golden tan,
who never walked beside me without holding my hand.
Where did my romantic lover go
The Jock I knew so long ago?
My Jock, who use to put his arms around my waist, ever so tight,
as we walked together in the night.
My handsome young lover, ever so great,
has become someone else's mate.
Oh Lord, feel my pain, hear my humble cry.
Let me see my romantic lover once more before I die.

Sherry Lynn Burns
MY CHILDREN

To my wonderful children, Marlon D. Burns and Andra' Rushawn Burns

I have two sons, ages thirteen and three.
They keep me busy and happy as can be.
I enjoy cooking their meals, three times a day.
You know. It makes you feel the Motherly way.
We sit around and watch TV.
My three year old does some of the funniest things you'll ever see!
I am very proud of my oldest son.
He's a special child. Well, he is the first one.
Girls are okay, but you see for me,
There's nothing so special as my sons, thirteen and three.

Anjoleen Baca
REMEMBERED LOVE

This poem is dedicated to Matt Lucero. Remember, I'll always love you!

Today I was sitting here thinking
About me and you
Happily remembering the things
We used to do.
I remember your smile
That always brightened my day
And how you said
You'd never go away.
Remember we said
We'd always be together
Through thick and thin
And stormy weather.
Remember you said your love
Would always be true
And I said I would
Always love you.
Remember before you left,
The beautiful moon-lit night.
I couldn't let you go and
You held me tight.
That night we found
Our love was true.
From then on, I knew I would
Always want you.
Now I wait for your
Return home
As I sit here all alone,
I wonder if your feelings
Are still true
And if you'll still love me
The way you used to.

Betty King Britton
THE CRUCIBLE

To my Parents, Hannah, Hazel, Billie Gay, "Miss Deborah", "Miss Lil", Mr. Poulk, "Libba" Early, Frances White Coleman, Mabel Claire Maddrey, the Ethel Forbes Sunday School Class and the May Perry Circle.

All things must crucibles go through
To reach the High, the Pure, the True.
The rainbow's colors do appear
Just after skies are dark and drear.
The wedding band new and unmarred,
Shines lovelier when worn and scarred.
The tree that bears fine fruit for him,
The gardner has to pluck, prune, trim.
The thornbird's sweetest song doth start
As blood drips from her pier-ced heart.
That sepulcher so white, so dear,
Was hewn with whip, cross, nail and spear.
All things must crucibles go through
To reach the High, the Pure, the True.

Marian Bennett Simon
THE POWER OF LOVE

To the memory of my parents, whose forty years of marriage was the best example to me of love in all its aspects at work; To Kelly, my daughter, and my joy; and, to "Himself".

The power of love goes beyond all understanding,
Beyond all the laws of nature and science.
Love is the life force within each of us;
It creates life,
Sustains life,
Even ends life, or one phase of it.
It cannot always be explained,
Or even forever maintained.
It makes us sick, it makes us well;
Sheerest heaven and darkest hell.
It can topple governments and create kingdoms.
An ecstasy, and aberration,
An agony of sweet sensation.
It goes beyond the world, the flesh, and the devil.
It makes us crooks, it keeps us level.
It is balance and imbalance,
Truth and lies;
We can see it in each other's eyes.
It was with us before time began,
It will far outlast the Age of Man.

Lou Jean Royle
GOD'S WORLD

Up above the clouds today
A sight most beautiful to see
The feathery wispy clouds
The sun so beautiful in its heaven.

The beautiful silver bird
Making its way forward
God made such beautiful sights to see
This earth is the most beautiful place to be.

This day flying is new to me
I look out the window and see the ground
But don't know what I see.

The clouds are a beautiful sight to see
It really impresses me.

The sky is so blue and the sun is so bright
The clouds all look like big marshmallows
I wonder if anyone else sees
God's world that way.

Florence Koplein
DID YOU EVER?

To my two great inspirations. My hubby Ken and daughter Karen for all their love and constant encouragement

Did you ever take a walk,
On a bright and sunny day?
Did you ever stop and watch,
A big gray squirrel at play?
Did you ever watch the birds,
In flight a way above your head?
Did you ever see the fish,
Swim round in a swirling river bed?
Did you ever walk in a meadow,
And see the flowers all in bloom?
Did you ever see a sunset,
And feel it take away your gloom?
Did you ever watch a child at play,
With never a care or woe?
Did you ever see a white tailed deer,
With her two little fawn's in tow?
Did you ever see the moon shimmer,
On a lake on a summer night?
Did you ever see colorama,
In all it's beauty and color so bright?
Did you ever walk on an ocean beach,
And feel the soft sand under your feet?
Did you ever watch the bright blue sky,
Where the fleecy white clouds meet?
Did you ever, well if never,
Then you've missed an awful lot.

Karen Varchol
THE SUN

To Nana and Papa

It crawls above the tallest trees,
Warming the cool, stiff, winter breeze.
It shines its rays throughout the people,
Reflecting its light on the sharpest steeple.

It falls upon the forgotten graves,
And forever protects the flag that waves,
It holds all nature in its possession,
And shapes the clouds into God's greatest perfection.

It comforts the unhappy and those who weep.
And then slips into the horizon to peacefully sleep.

Mary Catherine Marshall
RURAL DELIVERY ISN'T ALWAYS FREE

Raindrops muffle the windowpane
like gray-robed monks shuffling to morning mass.
I pass the hours with make-work tasks.
The rain begins to pour. Beyond my door,
a silent sentry stands beside the rural road.
His scarlet-gloved hand is upraised in warning.
Suddenly, my morning vigil is ended by the splash
of tires on wet blacktop. They stop, then slush ahead.
With dread, I go out and cross the yard.
The sentry has dropped his guard.
His watch is done.
Rain causes the ink to run on a familiar scrawl.
Like little red scars, still painful and tender,
from old burns inflamed anew, the jagged red letters
cut through the rain smears (or are they from tears?),
"REFUSED. RETURN to SENDER".

Karen Regan Wallace
MY GOAL

I've reached a place in time, when at last I know;
I've watched the years go by, yet I'm ready now to grow.
My life has new direction, a star to show the way;
A goal that I am striving for and working toward each day.
I'll never be defeated, lest I alone give in;
And with my goal so close at hand, I'm confident I'll win.
But when the victory is mine, my goal I have attained;
I pray that I will not forget the knowledge I have gained;
The trials that I have endured, the struggles of each day;
And most of all, the ones I love—who stood by me all the way.

Carole Ann Cheever
STREET MAN—DOES ANYONE CARE

I dedicate this poem to Rev Shirley Hanson, my loving husband Richard, and our family, The Street People.

Today as we all gather here
Sadness lies within
Another man has gone from us
yes, a Street Man, does anyone care.

There are so very many
The streets they trod each day
They search for something they're missing
Love, yet does anyone care.

As long as they have money
Or maybe a bottle or two
Their friends can be outnumbered
Yet a Street Man, does anyone really care.

Some have no loved ones or families
Yet so many of them do
They turn their backs in times like these
He's a Street Man, we don't care.

Well I can tell you from my heart
My love for them is deep
I cannot stand to see them
Trodding or laying on any street.

There are also others here today
Whom I know feel the same
I also know the Lord loves them
Yes, there are alot of us who care.

Sophie Mount
I AM SO GRATEFUL

To the "Mount" clan—"Oldsters" and "Youngsters"

A Senior Citizen, now, am I,
And I am here, to tell you why.

The golden years, of seventy-five,
Makes me ahppy, to be alive.
God has blessed me, with many things,
Like sight, movement, and
love, it brings,
That I may share it, with others, who,
Are rather lonely, and also, blue,
Although, I do not have, much wealth,
But more important, is my health,
So, for this, dear God from above,
Thank you, and gratefully, send my love.

Dorothy Brockmeier
ORPHANAGE

When you visit an orphanage you see
Children crying "oh please take me"
And when it is time for you to go
To all except one you must say no
It is really hard to say good bye
You can only take one, it makes you cry
They all want to go home with you
They all want you to love them too
They have no one to really care
No ones love to really share
They dream to have a real home
A place that they can really rome
They need someone to love, someone to care
A special friend, whos love they will share
I'd like to give them a chance to find out
What a happy home life is all about
I know if I had one wish, It would be
To take all these children home with me.

Glen A Domnick
ME OLD MAN

This is written about my father, a one of a kind man . . . and dedicated to my mother with all my love.

This is written for a man I love
Though it is hard to describe just what he was
Bigotted and quick tempered was the man
to every problem he had a plan

To his family he was the best
And for his country he fought like the rest
He worked so hard for all his life
What he made went to the kids and his wife

To be robbed so close to a goal
Just wanted to kick back with a fishing pole
No words now or that will ever be said
How much I love and miss your presence

For I am so much like you
Not one to listen having to learn like a fool
Your so much a part of me dad
Why did you go and leave me so sad

I hear and see you every day
Listening to every word you say
As I reach to grab your hand
You fade away like blowing sand

Juanita Bonner
LOVE

I dedicate this poem to my friends and family because they bring me joy and sorrow at different times in my life.

Love is full and joyous
But not always

Love can hurt you in all the wrong places
But not always

Love is an everchanging mood
Always

Marion J Schulz

Marion J Schulz
COUNTRY

Have you heard the Meadowlark at early morning
That full throated song bird of the dawn,
When the sun is blazing upward in the morning
And the daisies raise their faces on the lawn?

Have you seen the graceful gliding of the Swallow
In the evening as the coolness fills the air,
Or heard the gentle lowing of the cattle
As the evening comes in softly as a prayer?

Have you smelled the smells of supper from the kitchen
As the farmhands wend their way home from their chores,
Or seen the silver trout jump in the river
As the gentle waves lap up upon the shore?

Perhaps you've rocked upon the porch when day is fading,
And heard the distant church bells softly toll,
And thanked your God for blessings He has given,
And felt His peace descend upon your soul!

Doris Lindsay
INLETS

So many inlets make up life;
traveling them is how to thrive.

Each one has his own vehicle;
to ride, just like a bicycle.

Most bicycle speeds are ten;
If you don't succeed, try again!

When you pave the way to fame;
you must learn to play the game.

It doesn't take that many schools,
to learn just how to bend the rules.

Oh! With a message in your heart;
you are now a work of art!

So give out the best you can,
and proudly prove this race you ran.

Then, as the tide returns to shore;
go ride that inlet way once more!

Karen L Welker
NATURE'S WEB

To my husband who has always encouraged me in whatever I do.

Dusty roads and country lanes,
ocean breezes and mountainous planes.
Dipping toes in the sparkling stream.
Not far off, I hear a seagull scream
A monarch sails right past my face,
with utter abandon, style, and grace.
Up on the hillside I spot a deer.
Standing so quietly, I coax it near.
Birds in the pine trees singing a song.
The break of daylight, a new day's dawn.
Diamonds in the sky, sparkling in the night.
Heaven's so clear they twinkle so bright.
Nature surrounds me in all its glory.
Just like the spider it weaves a story.

Roy C Cartmill
DON'T LET IT RAIN

In memory of Jim and Frances Cartmill, my loving father and mother. Though the storms of life are over for you, I'll never say to my wife, don't let it rain.

You look so sweet and beautiful
Dressed up so nice and neat
If everyone here hadn't known it
They'd think you were just asleep

Here I sit with our families dear
With tears streaming down their faces
They've all grown and married now
And have moved to other places

The funeral is almost over
And I haven't heard a word they've said
I've been thinking about our life together
And all the fun we've had

Now we're at the grave side dear
Where you will lie in rest
Please don't worry about me dear
For I will do my best

I took your picture from the wall
And we'll sit by the window pane
The sky even looks like it may cry
It must have known my pain

Remember how frightened you would get
When you would see a rain storm cloud
You would come running into my arms
And then you would laugh out loud

And then we'd laugh and say how silly
Two grown people can be
I never really knew if you were scared
Or just wanted to be held to me

Well you're up in Heaven with God now
Where there is no fear or pain
But please grant this prayer tonight
Please God don't let it rain

Nadine Harden
YOUR "BEING"

I dedicate this poem to Gene, with love and everlasting gratitude, for his nonjudgmental acceptance of my "being;" his unfaltering belief in me and my talents; and his unconditional love and devotion. . . I am fortunate!

You're so filled with goodness, it's difficult to perceive
this is a fact that you don't believe.
It's time for forgiveness with yourself first in line.
Let go of the anger and let your light shine.
Acknowledge your feelings; deal with your grief.
Choose not to be fearful and breathe with relief.
Don't refrain from giving affection.
Never hold back in fear of rejection.
Expand your horizons—discover the connection
you can make with yourself by a change in perception.
As you endeavor to reach a new height,
fear not if you stumble or don't get it "right."
It works just like magic! As you learn to release
those pent-up emotions, you'll find inner peace.
While searching for enlightenment and seeking out life's lessons,
remember to always "be of love" and you will experience your essence.

Lee Hannold
THE SQUIRREL THAT SAT AT THE EDGE

Dedicated with love to my Loving family which includes, my Loving Mother, Doris, and Loving Stepfather, Harold, my Loving Wife, Rebecca, and my Loving Children, Jessica, and Jared.

I came to the edge of the woods one day and spied across this great divide—
As I sat there a while in time I thought about going to the other side,
My friends told me of this barren field that seemed to go on and on with no end—
And there are stories of some who crossed and must have been carried off by the winds,
So as I pondered there a while. . .deciding if I would venture to the other side—
My ears caught sound of a roaring wind coming that must have been very wide,
Now my heart was beating faster and faster and the sound was

coming more and more—
Could this be just the wind that was
making such a thunderous roar,
I had to decide quick, should I go
across now or return from where
I came—
And then I wondered if it all was
worth it,
because the other side might be the
same,
Then all of a sudden from around
the bend it came with the
thunder close behind—
And this was like no other sight I
had ever seen or thought of in
my mind,
This animal with the brightest eyes
seemed to be coming for me and
me alone—
So now no more thought was
needed for I was running on my
way back home.,
Maybe some day I'll come back
again,
but with one of my friends or
more—
Because I could'nt take the fear
alone that came from this
animal, with the bright eyes, the
thunder, and the roar!

James Butler

HALEY'S COMET, THE LEGEND

Long ago back in nineteen-ten,
They said you'd cause the world to
end,
Causing agony, suffering and pain.
People everywhere were going
insane.
Famines, pestilence, earthquakes,
disease,
Many other types of catastrophies.
As the earth passed through your
tail,
Men trembled in your misty veil.

Coming out from around the sun,
People everywhere were on the run.
They said there was peace,
volcanos roared.
Terrorists reigned in ruthless
hordes.
Famines, pestilence, earthquakes,
disease,
Voices crying, "Help us, please."
But in spite of this confusion,
We're enjoying your grand illusion.

Astronomers set forth to solve the
case
Of this mysterious jewel in space.
And now we'll see behind your
disguise
And remember you for all our lives.
It's a pristine ball of rock and ice,
There are those who will see you
twice.
It's a legend travelling in solar
wind.
Say, Comet, will you come again?

Judy Clark

CLEAN AND SOBER

I came to believe I could not see,
I came to believe in no one, even
me.
I drank through the night in anger
and fright,
I played through the day roles that
seemed right.

The sadness that finally did
overwhelm me
took charge of my soul and my
mind completely.
I turned to the left, to the right. .
.where to go?
I cried, I prayed, I admitted, "I
don't know."

I called a number I'd seen years
before,
I went and I rested and went back
for some more.
I gradually remembered a little of
myself,
and I put all my questions away on
the shelf.

Today I can cry, get angry, feel
pain.
Today I can love, can laugh, feel
the rain.
But I don't take a drink to celebrate
or grieve,
and I don't take a drug to "forget"
or "relieve."

I have a new life that I'm so grateful
for,
each day it seems I'm grateful a
little more,
cause the One who guides me
when I might stray
will always be with me each and
every day.

So from "grass" and pills and
needles I'm clean,
(Self-destruction is not
compulsary, it seems).
I'm sober! No more booze or beer
or wine,
I'm in love with life and I'm doing
fine.

Sueann Kay Wheeler

A FINAL TRIBUTE TO GRANDPA

Yesterday I went to Grandpa's
house,
But he was nowhere to be found;
I looked in the living room and
kitchen
And outdoors all around.

Then away I went with Mom, Dad
and Grandma,
To see where he was at rest.
It was the hardest thing I've ever
done,
But I knew with God's love and
strength I was blessed.

I spoke many words to my
Grandpa,
But to none did he reply;
For in a peaceful sleep
Was where I saw him lie.

The cheek that I once kissed,
Was so incredibly cold.
And with unbelievable rock-like
qualities
Were the hands I used to hold.

I took for granted he'd always be
around;
And now how shockingly I can see;
That I will never see again
That man who always made time
for me.

Today I saw Grandpa for the last
time,
And I had so much I wanted to
say. . .
How much I loved him,
And how I'd remember him always.

Fergy

FEARS, TEARS, AND CHANGE

To my daughters—Mary Louise, Karen, Nada, and Dolly Rose—love, peace, and wisdom beyond their years to guide my grandchildren through life (Ahmed, Andrina, Danielle, Branden, & Melissa).

Sixty-four 'ears of knowledge—
gained.
But, very little change in man.
A
World held in HOSTAGE!
Child slain!
By ambitious, ruthless, terrorist,
and
Deranged men.
Umbrella strained by umbilical
shame
No one is safe 'no one
Can explain.
Why? The guiltless must die for
the sins of man.

Stephen R Gage

WITHIN REACH

You were so quiet
Sitting by my side
But I could hear you crying
You were asking for the time
To sort out your life
To arrange your feelings
So that you'd feel comfortable with
me
You were asking for space
Some time to be by yourself
To restore your life to order
So that you'd feel comfortable with
yourself
There were times when I wasn't
listening
The times when you needed an
understanding friend
Someone to confide in
Someone to share the bad along
with the good
It isn't my intention to make you
feel pressured
Or to force you into anything that
you may not want
I simply want to be there when a
touch is all you need
To bring a smile to your face and
warmth to your heart
To be there
When a softly spoken word can
mean more to you
Than the quiet silence
Of being alone with your thoughts
To be there
When a gentle embrace would be
sufficient
To keep you warm
And to let you know that I was
always
Within reach

Alison Mae Sayre

LOVE

Love is something we can't hide
Or try to keep deep down inside
So don't say words that you don't
mean.
Try to be sort of keen.
Say hi as you go by people.
Take a look at that old church
steeple.
Remember what God stands for.
God stands for "LOVE"

Karen D Bridgman-Sikorski

A PLEAD

"To Cheryl Felger," my dearest friend.

Help me, Help me, Help me
I pray.
This I ask each and every
day.
Help me to laugh, to learn to
cry.
Help me to live before I die!

David E Rednour

THE CONTEST

They say send a poem,
You could win some money,
But if I send this one in,
They might think its funny,

Just think of the things,
A thousand would buy,
But this ones so sad,
It might make them cry,

Some poems I've written,
Speak of Jesus above,
And others I've written,
Are all about love,

I could send this one in,
But it seems so long,
Or if this one were entered,
Would they think it's a song,

I have A whole book,
But just one I must choose,
If they like it I win,
If not I lose.

Julie Kay Clements

LETTER TO MYSELF

Face it
You're alone in this world
You'll never be anyone's girl.
You've been looking for a man
But you've done all that you can
So give it up
It's not worth the pain.

They say you're pretty and so
talented
So why are you always alone
Crying in your room at home.
You may be sad and blue
But there's nothing more you can
do
So just give it up
It's not worth the pain.

Anne Burwell Harris

Anne Burwell Harris

HE LIVES

To Lawrence Smallwood, Jr. who has been inspirational during my trials and tribulations.

He lives because He lets me know.
He lives because I told you so,
Day in, day out, morning, noon
and night.
Trees grow, flowers blow, there's
snow—
Sunny days, rainy days, cloudy
days--

Sunrise, sunset, happiness, sadness,
Babies born, people die,
That's why I know He's always around.
He lives for me, He lives for you.
He lives for everyone this I've found.

Laura Orvis-Martinez
FOG

To my parents who have given me love, support and encouragement throughout my entire life.

The haziness and blur were suspended
in the atmosphere of the park. It weakened
my perception and helped me lose my escort
in its mist. I walked for hours searching, but he had vanished.
The fog
swept him in its clammy hull and slapped him into oblivion. . .

I found him after five long, chilly hours. He smiled, and tipped his black
derby hat (How did he come by it?), and
skipped past the zoo. I called after him,
but he continued to act in the alien manner. . .

Yesterday he called me. We had dinner at Pierre's. He wore the strange
hat and smirked all evening. . .

Forecast for tomorrow: Fog overcast.
I cancelled our date.

Karen E Holleran
HAMARTIA, OR THE TRAGIC ERROR

My tongue caresses your chest
As I lick the sweet tasting sweat
with as much reverence
As a priest who takes communion.
You exonerate my sins
And once again I become pure.

You kiss my neck and I become immersed
in a world of unbridled ecstasy.
While your hands explore
the subtle folds of my body,
You penetrate the wall that sets me free.
I can once again feel as a woman should —
satisfied but still unfulfilled.
It's not your fault,
You act as a man should,
but I react as a lovelorn donna
Who'll never wake with you or share your dreams.

That future is an hamartia.
For you, never to be lived
But for me while I breathe, I hope.

Gary M Brinkman
THE POET'S GIFT

To the glory of God by the power of Christ

God's gift of love
through verse of poetry,
Never ceases to ever stir
the heart inside of me.

When I read the verse
I have written down,
I know that it's a gift
that's come from heaven down.

Yes, down from heaven above,
to within the soul of me,
For me to sit and write
for all the world to see.

To see, and really feel,
the love in beauteous rime,
That allows wonderous escape
from troubles of our time.

Aye-wonderous escape,
but-not in fear,
Tis just short interlude
spent living love with tear.

Tears spent in joyous living,
loving, feeling, caring,
whilst reading of love in rime
that God through poet's sharing.

Love-through poet's sharing—
whether love, or rhyming, story,
Of adventure, faith or courage—
it all bespeaks God's glory!

Susie Miller
WHY WE DRANK

To Kelli McClelland, for always reading my poetry. To Pat, who gave me the info for the contest in which I am now merited. To Scott, my husband-to-be, for all of his love.

We drank for happiness, and became unhappy.
We drank for joy, and became miserable.
We drank for sociability,, and became argumentative.
We drank for sophistication, and became obnoxious.
We drank for friendship, and made enemies.
We drank for strength, and felt weak.
We drank for sleep, and awakened unrested.
We drank for relaxation, and got the shakes.
We drank "Medicinally," and acquired health problems.
We drank to make conversation easier, and slurred our speech.
We drank for bravery, and became afraid.
We drank for confidence, and became doubtful.
We drank to erase problems, and saw them multiply.
We drank for freedom, and became slaves.
We drank to feel heavenly, and ended up feeling like hell.
We drank to cope with life, and invited death.

Mrs Beatrice DeVoe
TWO LITTLE OLD LADYS

There was two little old ladys that had two little old fannys.
Together they run around like two little old nannys.

Rose L Burnley
FRIENDS FOREVER?

How many friends say to each other,
they'll be best friends forever and ever.

It's so very true, when you first become friends,
but sooner or later it's frayed at the ends.

New people come with new friendships to share,
and sometimes old friendships are too hard to bear.

The older friends ask and they wonder why,
What happened to that friendship, was it just a lie?

They never get an answer, but still they live,
they, too, find someone who's willing to give.

This same old story goes on and on
they say it's here, but forever is really gone.

So you see, my friend? It does no good,
'cause a new friend, stands where an old friend stood.

Debbie Szetela
HAPPY VALENTINE'S DAY

Today is Valentine's day
And there's something you should know
Just a simple word or two before I finally go
Our lives touched that instant
Yet fate kept us apart
The only way to love you was deep inside my heart
I thought about you and your love
And how I fought so hard to win it
And I thought of all the times I failed
Because your heart just was'nt in it
Well, what I'm gonna say now
Is the hardest thing I'll ever do
I think I've faced reality; I'm letting go of you
If freedom's what you really want
I wont stand in your way
Because your happiness means more to me than words can ever say
God knows that I still need you, but if I have to let you go
I will because I love you more than you'll ever know
If you ever need me I'll always be right there
In my heart I'll always love you and in my mind I'll always care
But if you think you know whats best, I'll just walk away
Well, you got just what you wanted
Happy Valentine's Day!

Cindy D Rivers
A FRIEND LIKE YOU

Remember when we first met
It seems so long ago
We probably introduced ourselves
Smiled and said, "Hell-O".

We had our fights
Our quarrels and spats
Times we wouldn't speak

We shared our laughs
Our joys and pains
Secrets that we'd keep

Whoever would have imagined
Now that we are grown
We'd still be there for each other
Whenever we feel alone

You're a special person
In a world where they are few
And everyday, I'm thankful
I have a friend like you.

Richard H Consolvo
MY SENTIMENTS!

Dedicated to my Daughter, Sunny.

Woman,
The fairest creation
of the great author,
the edition is vast
and no man should be
without a copy.

Phyllis Duree Mast
PARENTS

This poem is dedicated to the memory of my loving, understanding parents, Anna and Ora Duree.

Parents are such precious things,
so how come the bell never rings?
Until its too late for us to see,
the things they did for you and me.
We look back, now that they're gone,
and see all the things that we did wrong.
They would tell us what was true,
but we knew better the things to do.
Who were they getting old and gray
to tell us what to do and say.
Now that they're gone, we can do
the things that they wanted us to.
Why couldn't we do these things then.
It surely wouldn't have been a sin.
To make them happy in a little way,
to listen to the things they'd say.
To just once say, I love you Mom,
I love you Dad.
would this have been so terribly bad?
You may say, they're gone too late
the time is gone to set this straight.
But we can as we Pray and live,
I know that they surely will forgive.

John A Brownlee Jr
PRAY WELL MY CHILDREN

Dedicated to my sons: Sean and Eric

Pray well my children before you sleep
Listen for noises, for creatures that creep
For the eerie sounds that come in the night
Just might be a real reason for fright.

Pray well my children, then make not a sound
There's evil afoot, there's demons around
They're out there, you see them, it's you that they're after
Listen, you'll hear them, their maddening laughter.

Pray well my children, then have pleasant dreams
Remember that things are not as they seem
Your dog is a werewolf, your cat is a witch
Watch carefully now for every

movement and twitch.

Pray well my children, now get back in bed
It's night-time now, watch out for the dead
They just like to visit, they mean you no harm
They have their own unique brand of charm.

Pray well my children, now don't get upset
There's really, truly, nothing to fret
These night-time visitors just come in fun
And usually, most times, they leave with the sun.

Pray well my children before you sleep
The noises you hear are just from the deep
Think pleasant thoughts and you'll have a good night
But remember my sons, those bedbugs do bite.

Cindi Randolph
LET'S PRAY
I awoke, and you smiled at me as if to say;
Hello, to me, and then you said "Let's Pray."
Before the morning started you knew what to do and say.
As I opened up my eyes, I heard you say, "get up. . .together,
Let's Pray"

You awoke me with your smile and then stretched out your hand,
You said to me this day, there shall be rejoicing in my land"

The time flew by this morning, and noon was soon at hand,
You tapped me on my shoulder; and your spirit layed out your plan.
As afternoon was on me, you knew just what to say;
You put your arms around me, and again you said "Let's Pray"

As the walls came tumbling around me, "You had already prepared
this day"; you whispered in my ear to me, "Let's just stop and
pray"
Evening fast upon us, all the day is done, You came to me in my
living room, and said "I am the One".

I replied; "Yes, Lord," and paused to see what next you would say.
You said "I'm the one who smiled at you, and begun this your day."
"Father, this, I know is true, that only your the one in whom I put all my trust in, in whom my day begun."

So now as I close my eyes for rest, at the end of this, your day.
I ask that tommorrow finds me again; "Alone with you to Pray."

Annanelle Butler
GRANDMOMMIE LOVES . . .

Dedicated to Bob, Jon, Laurelle and Julie, my grandchildren.

Grandmommie loves. . .
Little "men" who make their mommie real happy.
Little girls who make their daddy so proud.
Nice children who care for their "little sister."
All who don't play too rough or too loud!

Grandmommie loves. . .
'Specially those who share with their friends,
And all those who play good with the toys.
Sweeties that take time-out to use the bathroom,
Little girls who play nice with the boys.

Grandmommie loves. . .
Little boys who don't forget to say, "Thank you."
Those charmers who remember to ask, "Please?"
All who say, "I'm sorry," when they step on your toes.
Kids who cover their mouth when they sneeze.

Grandmommie loves. . .
Helpful boys who run get things for Daddy.
Little girls who help Mommie put things back in place.
All those who hold still go get their hair fixed.
Happy children with a big smile on their face.

Grandmommie loves. . .

Little "men" who wash their dirty hands clean.
Smart kids who learn to eat all their food—neat!
Amateurs who color and paint—only on paper.
Little angels who hop into bed and go to sleep.

Bertha Alongi Ross

Bertha Alongi Ross
THE TATTED CAP
Tears inside
Others mustn't see, while
In my hand I hold the cap
I tatted for you.
I hear you,
I hear you cry,
You break all the rules,
I feel your breath upon my face—
When my eyes are closed—
And the breezes blow;
I saw them close your bluest of eyes,
A part of me with you.
Then they carried you away,
And you left a fragrant trail
Of larkspur, stock, honeysuckle,
Baby-breath, for-get-me not,
And the tatted cap with blue ribbons
They forgot.

Randy E Kirby
A DAY IN LOVE WITH J

Dedicated to my wonderful wife Jeanne

Along with the sunrise, I feel the softness of her skin next to mine.
She turns as I rise and kisses me and I lose myself in time.
As I prepare to start my day, she rises with a smile.
And as I leave she wishes me luck in all my daily trials.
As the sun passes over the sky above, Ithink of her a million times.
And savor the thought of the end of the day, when I hold her hands in mine.
That time has come when I return and she stands there all aglow.
I reach for her and she comes to me and I tell I love her more than she'll ever know.
As the day ends I lie with J and tell her of her many charms.
And then we love one another, until we collapse in each others arms.
And as I lay in restful sleep, with J close at hand.
I thank the Lord above for a women that understands.

Charles A Stevens
THE THREE MEDALS

This poem is dedicated to William H. Stevens who fought in the Philippines and New Guinea.

I want to thank you for the three old taintedMedals you left to me.
Red, White and Blue for "liberty."
Mounted on red crimson velvet, the color of blood.
To me, they stand for the jungles where you stood,
I can see a ship, a plane, and a forest of rain,
I know that against the Japs, you did surely "raise cain."
With fighting like that I wonder, you were "sane,"
I know you had aruptured duck, I know it broughtyou "Luck".
But, most of all, I want to thank you for "Liberty,"
And the three golden Medals, you left to me.

Marjorie Phillips
FRAGESTELLUNG
Do you ever wonder why the sun shines on us each day?
Do you ever wonder where God is when you pray?
Do you ever wonder why the sea comes to the shore?
Do you ever wonder about the Universe and Galaxies galore?

Do you wonder why the deserts ever should be there?
Do you wonder why the mountains stand climbing in the air?
Do you wonder why a leaf grows on a tree?
Do you wonder why there are fishes in the sea?

Do you wonder why the birds are flying in the air?
Do you ever wonder why people are dark and fair?
Do you wonder the deep mysteries of life?
Do you ever wonder why on earth is so much strife?

God gave us the brain to wonder,
The ability to tell
Of all our thoughts and reasonings
And our own choice of heaven and hell.

God, in his infinite mercy,
Made our earth stay a short spell,
And what we do and think and say,
Affects us only and our own hell,

But naye, I wonder!

Sheila J Hullihen
A SUMMER PASSAGE
Between the yester-and to-day
our time together's rent
seems faded now and far away
as any summer spent.

A moment shared in sneakered youth
as friends and self made legends,
exchanging dreams for harder truths
in keeping with the season.

Reflections of an August sun
blind all to passing time
as our paths, to separate, run
unnoticed lives . . . untwined.

Lost in memories time line trances
our seasons final day,
feel not the parting but the absence,
dawn's lavendar gone gray.

Midge Nelson
GENESIS OF THOUGHT
Flashing impulses
In the pregnant mind
Conceive an image.
Painfully delivered
From the depths,
It penetrates the membrane
Of consciousness.
With a kaleidoscope
Of brilliant colors
And a white-hot explosion
Of powerful splendor,
It is born
Into awareness.

Kevin R Lowell
YOUTH

For my love, Lisa, who has always believed in me

For the young meant;
Want reflects it once misspent.
It's lived once;
When gone: Gone.
Lived right, no wonder where it went?

James M Mason
SILVER HONEYMOON
I'm going on a silver honeymoon.
I'm traveling upward to the sky.

I'm going on a silver honeymoon.
My true love is by my side.
On our way we'll visit venus.
Where the godess of love resides.
And this you can beleave us.
We'll have true love on our side.
We'll visit way up there where
there's lot's of room.
Up in the starry sky so blue.
I'm going on a silver honeymoon.
On a silver honeymoon with you

Carol Ahne

MY LOVE-HE IS MINE

Love is like an old oak tree
Sturdy and steadfast
It branches out to be free
He is my love, my love, he's all of
me.

Gently waving in the winds
Like the currents of time.
The sweet and gentle touch
He's unlike any other kind.
He's all of me, he is mine.

He's my love, my life, he's all of me.
He is me, all I hope to be
Like the branches inter-twine
Throughout the years, throughout
the time,

He is mine.

Lillian E McPherson

ONCE A MOTHER; I'LL ALWAYS BE

As I hold this wee one against my
breast,
and rock him gently as he rest.
His sleeping head on my shoulder
lay,
a silent prayer, you'll hear me say.
Reminds me of those days gone by,
I held my babes, tears swell my
eyes.
The love of God is here within,
the tiny hands, the quivering chin.
Once a mother, you'll never forget,
the life of a child; God's best gift yet.
I've been so blessed as a mother
too,
my priceless memoirs spring up
anew.
I thank you God from day to day,
for all this loveliness I pray.
May all my children know so well,
the love of God, in their children
dwell.

Barbara A Pierce

WHAT IS A MOTHER?

Dedicated to all the wonderful mothers!!!

A mother is a person who smiles
even when she is sad,
A mother is also the one who
punishes you if, you are bad.
A mother is a wonderful person
who, can do no wrong,
A mother is the first one to miss
you, when you have gone.
A mother is always filled with
kindness, and love,
A mother teaches you, to pray to
God up above.
A mother will always listen when,
you want to talk,
Mother held your hand when, you
first learned to walk.
A mother will stand by you, when
you need a good friend,
A mother will love, and guide you
until the very end.
So for all the wonderful mothers
in the world let us pray,
That all of them will have a Happy
Mothers Day.

Eugene J Kelly

SONG OF SOLITUDE

Alone I walked the railroad tracks,
Unused for many a year,
Apart from the noises people make,
Frustrations and their fears.
I made my way along the creek,
Until alone was I,
Solitude and peace I saw,
Written in the sky.
Etched on the rocks of endless
time,
Spoken by the breeze,
Announced by the water flowing
free,
Symbolized by the trees.
I sat in amazement and wondered
awhile,
About all that occurred before,
Of how this was formed,
And the beauty it held,
And if it would be no more.
I lost track of time,
The hour grew late,
By the light of the stars did I see.
I vowed I'd return,
As soon as I could,
As soon as soon can be.

Judith A Myers

DARE TO CARE LIKE JESUS

Dare to care like Jesus, go that
extra mile.
Wipe that frown off someone's
face, give to them your smile
Have compassion in your heart,
follow in His way.
Bring Him to those you meet, by
all you do and say.
Dare to care like Jesus be an
example to all,
That life is worth the living when
you come to hear His call.
Those things you did before are no
longer your concern
As you teach your friends the many
things they have to learn.
Have a sense of humor, strive to be
sincere,
Whenever you're in trouble, He is
always near.
Learn to love your enemies, keep
them in your prayers,
Be that person who reaches out, be
the one who dares.
Look for Jesus in all the people you
know,
Let His light shine through you, be
that radiant glow
Of light which someone needs as
they travel in despair
Dare to be like Jesus—dare to show
you care.
Dare to care like Jesus, don't just
talk the talk
Be that one who dares to always
walk the walk.

Erma Ferdinand

REVERIE

I sit inside all safe and warm
As the year draws to a close
And begin to count my blessings
That out number any woes
First the safty of my love ones
And the life and love we share
And the joy of special friendship
With the ones who truly care,
All of nature created
To provide us joy and cheer
And the seasons with their
blessings
And their beauty all the year
Music, art and poetry
And the talents we may use
Advantages and work to do
And the privilege to choose.

Patricia Ann Holder Walker

OUR GUARDIAN ANGEL

I dedicate this poem to my Mother, Lois. I truly thank God for the Mom of His choice.

There is a friend, who's like no
other,
On whom we always can depend.
Who shares our laughter or our
sorrow
And always there with a hand to
lend.

Who held our hand and then our
heart,
As the years went passing by,
And taught us that on her love
We forever could rely.

She taught us of Jesus
And how to kneel and pray.
To thank Him for the many
blessings
That He gives to us each day.

God is always watching over us
He loves us like no other.
That's why from Heaven He sent
an angel down
For us all to know as "Mother".

Debbra M Long

Debbra M Long

THE GIFT

To Lloyd, my very special Uncle. "The Gift" is for him.

I wanted to crochet you some
snowflakes for Christmas.
However, no matter how hard I
tried, the thread could not reveal
the cool icy beauty, or the splendor
I see in each tiny delicate
crystal.

You couldn't feel the cool frosty
softness, as it lay on
your cheek, when first it touches
your face.
I wanted to share the special
beauty of such a moment.
As you are standing, almost
breathless in the cool air amidst
the tall trees, in their delicate array
of white.

For only a moment in time does
the frosty blanket of
crystals lightly sit upon the earth,
gently trimming every blade
of grass and tree limb in lace. as
though a thief
would steal a precious jewel, the
sun peeks through the mist
and the crystals disappear. Only
to leave weeping trees.

Ah, but alas, God returns the
crystals to the trees!

Sandra L Kelley

LOVE PROVEN

There's a stillness in time when I
think of you.
A calm in my heart when you say
you love me.
Joy in my life when you are near.
Growing love when you are gone.
Peace within when you laugh.
I now know the true meaning, you
now know how much I really do.
At times it may not seem like this
for you when you grow impatient
with me, it only strengthens that
bridge of our united hearts.
I love you truly I do, and would
do anything to prove the love
you've
Proven for me.

Patrick B Witt

A CHRISTMAS STORY

A Christmas star is beaming down
upon a sleeping little town.
A tender loving sight so dear, with
angels all around.
Welcome kisses from Eve's dear
own, welcome gentle king to this
thy earthly home.
A lamb I have to give, a shepherd
this day am I.
A king of earth with precious gold.
To pleasure your gentle eyes.
He rings our hearts with
cherubim and assuredly moves
right in. From sons of man to
brothers dear, he names us loving
kin. Amen

Mildred Virginia (Tilbury) Edwards

ME

You look at me so strangely!
You seem not to understand
that I am Me,
Formed by God in his image
As He would that I should be

But I am Me
With hands that move, eyes that
see, voice that speaks
Lips that smile,
I've a warmth of nature, a love for
God's creation
That even you, in your subtle way
can see
Is different.

You ask why!
Man's knowledge is so small!
Am I different?
You cannot, will not understand
That I am Me,
Created perfectly; because, in His
image, too,
Different from you,
God created Me.

R D Estep

MY DEAR MOTHER

This poem is especially for Rena G. Powell, my dear Mother, who died May 27, 1987.

I think of you everyday,
from the time I awake, and start
on my way.

I see you there in all I do,
pieces of me are pieces of you.
The closeness we share will never depart,
though you and I Mother, are miles apart.
When life gets rough on you or me Mother,
we know we can always call on each other.
Our failures and disappointments don't seem so great,
when we talk it over, it lifts the weight.
What seems so wrong among all the others,
always seems right in the eyes of you, Mother.
And now that I wear the shoes you once wore,
I feel even closer than ever before.
"For I wouldn't want you, to ever go through,
the things I have done, mistakes I've made, too."
I remember you said those words once to me,
now I understand, I finally see.
Life is so hard, on some more than others,
I wish it could have been easier, for you, Dear Mother.
I share something in common with the Angels above,
the love for a special lady, whom deserves special love.
For as long as I live, I'll cherish no other,
the way that I cherish you, Dear Mother.

Deneen Coppola
OUR BEAUTIFUL WORLD!!!

Our world is a beautiful place to live.
It's the peace and love that people give.
The weather seasons are a part
That give new life and love in the heart.
Spring is the warmth
and blooming of creations,
while summer is hot and gives variations
Fall is the one that gives a great light,
And winter is cold, but the snow is bright.
The sight of the moon, the sight of the sun
make everything glow, and everything fun!
The flowers and trees are another part
that give softness & joy straight to the heart
The animals run, the sailboats sail,
the sunset goes down like a long lighted trail.
The heart of mankind is alive on the earth
and more and more things come to birth.
Let peace and happiness be seen in us all;
So listen for God's creation call.

Martha Chapman Smith
FRIENDS

F is for <u>friends</u>—we all hold dear
In far away places, or those very near.

R is for <u>richer</u> our lives they have made
Without them our smiles would easily fade.

I is for their <u>interest</u> in whatever befalls
In joy or in sadness—they heed every call.

E is for <u>eager</u>, of their love to share
In deeds of kindness they show that they care.

N is for <u>needs</u> our true friends meet
In dead of winter, or summer's heat.

D is for <u>dearer</u> they become each day —
God knew we must have them—no other way.

S is for <u>special</u>, these loved ones we so treasure
Filling our lives with precious memories
beyond any measure.

We have spelled out FRIENDS—we can have
them by the score
If we show ourselves friendly—and by
starting next door.
So, for this wonderful gift, let us thank the Lord
For friends are one of life's richest blessings and a valued reward.

Basil G Maile
OUR ORGANIST (AS SEEN FROM THE TENOR BENCH)

To TRUUKE, Wonderful musician and friend

Her hand uplifted stills the final chord
Of anthem, requiem or Bach cantata,
Her radiant smile the Choir's due reward.
"Hear now the joyous strains of Young's Toccata."
Allegro from the organ pipes there blazes
A noble theme, rich cadences of sound,
And while deft footwork punctuates the phrases
Her fingers o'er the manuals nimbly bound.

At last, the music's effervescence captured,
The echoes die away on minor chords.
The Congregation, silently enraptured
Appreciates and frequently applauds.

At Darts or Scrabble, cycling or Croquet
Her skill surprises many an admirer.
Her sky-blue Honda, eager for the fray
Will speed her soon from Frederick to Elmira.

On Thursday nights we practice loud and long
Striving to fit the notes to the libretto.
Sopranos, Altos, Basses come on strong.
Alas the Tenor section squeaks falsetto.

". . .Letter "C" . . .sing <u>now</u>." I fumble with my score.
I'm left behind. . .for this I'll ne'er rebuke her.
She lights our song with happiness and love.
This lovely lady's Christian name is TRUUKE.

Darlene Hubby Rungee
ST. PATRICK'S DAY

To my children who always had faith in my ability as a poet, their love and devotion and my husband who always was there in memory.

Me name is Pat O'Murphy tis from Ireland I come.
And I've a tale to tell ye as true as the rising sun.
I took me ole shillalah with me jug beneath me arm,
and I went out celebratin' St. Pattys day be darn!
I sat me down beneath a tree on a quiet little knoll,
and emptied out me jug ya see nay bothered by a soul.
Well me thought me heard a little noise from behind a big ole rock.
I staggered to me feet ya know be gorra! What a shock!
I rubbed me eyes in disbelief I couldn't believe the sight,
but there they were the little people dancin' to the left and right.
Now Irelands known for leprechans with their very magic ways.
But only do they show themselves exceptin on St. Patricks Day.
They danced around and sang of gold and treasures buried there.
And if they were aware of me they didn't seem to care.
I guess me bones got weary and I was feelin' a wee bit cold.
And I drifted off a dreamin' of leprechans and gold.
Well mornin' came and it's no joke the little ones they were no hoax.
Cause sittin in a cup by me was 20 gold pieces, don't ya see?
Back to Killcarney I took meself this tale I had to relay,
and just in case ya should forget—Happy St. Patricks Day!!

William J LaSalle
SUNSET

Looking out across a pond at sunset
As the sky is cast with tangerine
Knowing it won't last causes me regret
As I watch the crimson sun sinking

Now the sky goes to darker shades of blue
As the sun sinks deeper into the hills
When I'm alone I can't help but think of you
Sometimes I need a world without the frills

So quiet I can't help but think of the past
The beauty around me eases my mind
I hope our love will forever last
For beauty as a sunset is hard to find.

Janet Gail Barror
SILENCE OF THE NIGHT

This poem is dedicated to Mr. Paul Martin, my high school teacher and friend, for his help and encouragement in my writing. Thank you Mr. Martin!

The fine details of the day
Are fading into the night.
The sun is replaced by the moon
The way wrong is replaced by right.
The day's share of violence
Is overcome by the nights beauty.
The clouds fade and the stars appear
As if in the line of duty.
The nighttime silence arrives,
But not in the true sense of the words.
For the nightime silence carries with it
The sounds of the wind, the owl, and the bird.
But this night is different.
This is the night I've come to dread.
For now the silence is true.
For now I am dead.
For now I am dead.

William W Mitchell
WE

You're never all you say,
Not near what others condone.
In privacy of home,
real thoughts let to roam,
Likes—dislikes seek the real self.
No need to hide the social elf.

All begins and ends in you,
nor amiss of what is true.
Miss little in the mirror plain.
It goes deep to private pain.
Let the ship run smooth,
a critic of the peopled groove.

Where 'ere you find yourself,
'Lone on street or 'mid wealth,
Your life is "ship on sea,"
boundless, fleet and free.
Be careful with thee—
—Thee are me.

C June Stecklein
FORGOTTEN MEN

This poem is dedicated to the Lord Jesus Christ and to all the men and women who served in Vietnam.

He left his home only a child.
When he came back he acted crazy.
Some even said he was wild.
Most do not know or understand,
What it cost him to become a man.
He went to war where they sent him.
He wore a green shirt and boots they lent him.
He saw his friends dying all a round him.
And he thought of going home without them.
He finished his duty, he had done his best.
When he came home, that was the test.
He got off the plane with no one to meet him.
No family, no friends, no one there to greet him.
Suddenly, this boy of nineteen,

Felt old, lonely and demeaned.
He had no job, he had no plan.
He was a confused, hurt young man.
America did not want him home.
He'd lived too long with the Viet Cong.
He thought he had paid his price to become a man.
But the cost of living had gone up in this land.
Now, you tell me, and tell me true,
If you had to fight for the red, white and blue,
Could you fill his boots or wear his shirt?
Without feeling that wild, crazy hurt?
The End

Phyllis Ann Mease

A BOUQUET OF FLOWERS

This poem is dedicated to: Albert E. Worley and Blanche L. Worley, my mother and father

---

A bouquet of flowers,
I put on your grave,
It doesn't replace,
The love you gave,

A bouquet of flowers,
Is all I can give,
Because your gone,
And I still live,

A bouquet of flowers,
To say I love you,
To let you know,
I put no one above you,

A bouquet of flowers,
I hope you can see,
I wish that you,
Were here with me,

A bouquet of flowers,
A bouquet of love,
A bouquet to show you,
All of my love,

Rena Roberts Eastman

IT'S SEPTEMBER

Memory takes me back 75 years, as I recollect so vividly the incidents as told in this poem—It's September. I dedicate it to the memory of all who attended school at Brothersfield, Dist. #7, Turner County, Parker, South Dakota

---

It's September, and the school bell
Peals out across the prairie, loud and plain,
Calling all the lads and lassies
Back to school again.

There was sister and I, and the neighbors' small fry,
Girls in braids and bows and calicos,
Barefoot boys, both short and tall
In their blue bib overall, on their way to the house of learning.

Bobwhite on the gatepost as we passed by
Whistled over and over, "More wet, more wet,"
But there wasn't a cloud in the sky
So it would be some time yet.

Then down along the slough
Where the tall cattails grew,
The big frogs garumped, and the little frogs jumped,
And the blackbirds sang in a chorus.

We hurried over the hill and around the bend,
With our Karo lunch pails swinging,
And arrived at the school by the side of the road,
Just as the last bell was ringing.

Senta Miller

A SMILE FROM A WOMAN

This poem is dedicated to William Turner—a beloved friend. I am grateful for his kind help which gave me faith and vision to climb the heights.

There are many things in life that brings us pleasure,
Like the puppies and kittens we love without measure.

There are sunsets, rainbows and works of art,
But there's one other pleasure that's nearest my heart . . .

A smile from a woman is a gift from above,
Which gives me the feeling only of love.

A smile from a woman makes the struggle worthwhile,
It lightens the load and shortens the mile.

May the Lord bless these women who brighten my day,
Like a beacon that drives the darkness away.

A smile from a woman makes my life more complete,
There's nothing on earth as nearly as sweet.

There are many things in life that bring us joy,
Like our own little girl and own little boy.

There are flowers and trees and the beautiful sea,
But there's no other joy that's greater to me . . .
"a smile from a woman."

Michael Molino Sr

DEDICATED PEOPLE; NURSE'S

This poem is dedicated to: The Nurse's at Saint Michael's Hospital, Newark, N.J.

Nurse's are special as you are about to see,
These girl's are dedicated to taking care of you and me.
The doctors do the cutting that is true,
But it is the nurse's duty to help them mend and, that's just
what they'll do.
Changing the bandages and putting on antiseptic too,
They'll do this every day until that cut is looking just as
good as new.
They'll give you your medication and it always will be on time
each and every day,
Just to help you to get better and to help to chase most of
your pains away.
They'll change your bed and wash you too and try to make you look brand new,
There's just so many things that these nurses do, that I can not list them all but these are just a few.
So remember what I said these nurses are special and, now I
think you will agree too,
For as you walk out the front door you will be feeling brand
new.
So I would like to thank them from the bottom of my heart,
for their caring and their loving and for doing their part.

Bryan S McDaniel

TRANQUILITY'S ABSENCE

Stopping to view
tranquility's absense
from speed

Ernest Wilson Cote

WITHIN THIS RING

In Loving Memory Of My Parent's Raoul & Laura Cote

Within this ring,
You will find love,
Happiness, Kindness,
Caring, Sharing.

Within this ring,
You will find,
Adventure and
Romance.

Within this ring,
You will find all
Of me, Heart and
Soul.

Lina Bajraktari

UPON THE GOLDEN MOUNTAIN

The earth became denser and the lifeless leaves continued to flutter softly, gently on its runway; they gave the colour of shimmering gold. Ah yes, rich on the mountain slopes. He looked around as far as his old weak eyes could see. Snow caps glistened like twinkling diamonds; the soft ivory colour in the depths of its existence.

Further up the mountain, he came to the peak of its course and looked out. There he saw the sun begin to shield itself behind the great, rich mountain. The last rays of its light were sparkling in the stream below.

Tears filled his eyes for he was greatly moved with the beautiful breathtaking sight. He looked up and the clouds moved swiftly, silently; of how the natures peace lifted his soul and took him beyond the. . . Golden Mountain.

Ruth H Hilton

TIRELESS WAVES

Surging, rushing waves,
White caps of gleaming, sudsy bubbles
Pushed onward to the shore.
Smaller swells enveloped
By stronger, higher ones,
An endless, pushing continuity
of wave upon wave.
Then—receding, pulled and drawn back,
Only to push forth again,
Reaching farther up on the shore.
A tireless surging of energy and beauty.

Grace Wasem

WHAT IF I HAD TO WAIT?

My Parents Mr. and Mrs. August Wasem

What if I had to wait
Until Thanksgiving Day?
My spirit would shrivel
Until I could not feel God's presence.
Each new day, my soul cries out.
I feel the essence of these words;
"Deep calleth unto deep"—
and there within—
I sense the oneness of my spirit;
With Christs' Eternal Light—
Joy—praise—gratitude—
flow forth.
Thanks be to God,
I need not wait.

Phyllis M Thomas

CAREFREE

I raced through the fields as though the wind
Carried me along to see the flowers' brilliant hue
And touch the grass of lucious green.

I flew a kite into skies so vast there seemed no end
Of fleecy clouds stretching all across the summer blue
Embraced by a golden sunlit sheen.

Oh glorious, carefree days spent with a childhood friend
Running barefoot, catching freckles and other summer's due
I wouldst go back to where I've been.

Julie Rae Frantum

EARLY DESCENT

I thought as the shudder
I thought as the shake
The tremble inside
the tiny earthquake . . .

It meant the darkness
for me, yet too late—
Into the soul
only for fate . . .

When the roaring thoughts
were inside of my head;
Soon it was over
Sooner, it's dead.

So, forgive me now
in silent weeps;
For you, inside me,
I could not keep . . .

Jennifer L Fish
OLD FOOL BORN NEW

To Dean—I'll always care for you no matter what happens.

So I thought I had a part of you,
I was wrong; An old fool born new.
I loved you, you were so special to me,
We were so different from the rest (I thought we agreed).
Our friendship was colorful, we shared so much,
With every new day, a new subject touched.
I can't believe you've found another
To take my place; For me there's no other.
I'll never find someone to take your place,
I miss you so much but it's like a race.
A race between her and I to the end,
What's going on, I thought we were friends?
I'm getting so tired, I feel I have lost,
The times we have shared I feel have been tossed.
This shouldn't be happening, it can't be real,
This emotion I'm feeling I don't want to feel.
So I thought I had a part of you,
I was wrong; An old fool born new.

Dorothy Nickens
FREE
You were there whenever dear
I really needed you.
You never knew the troubles—fears
I really had been thru.
I stopped and thought how far away
Those things are now from me.
The troubles—all the fears astray
Since the day that I felt free.
No more sadness—no remorse
I've set upon a brand new course.
I smiled a little more today
I even laughed out loud.
Tomorrow I'll look back and say
I'm happy and I'm proud.
I've found love upon the way
A heart sweet, good and true.
I only hope another day
The grey skies all turn blue.
When at last a happiness
I never knew could be.
Will drive away the loneliness
To forever set me free.

Maria Yadaseska
THE GREATEST REWARD
Helping a friend who doesn't want help
leads to frustration.
When the friend tells me to "get away"
it gives me determination.
To nag the person until she tells me what's upsetting her.
Sometimes it's necessary for a professional and me to confer.
I give my friend advice and tell her positive things.
This almost always results in my bringing her into an upswing.
The greatest reward is when I get thanked for being there.
Even though it's upsetting sometimes,
I like to show that I care.

Blondelle Brokaw Lashbrook
AFFECTIONATELY YOURS, THAI
Tiny, companionable
Blue eyes slanting, aloof
She steals her mistress' heart
Tails her—willing slave,
Attention-getter, flapping tail, muted cries,
Grief gone, comfort gained.

Chiquita Monique Hopkins
HELL IS FOR HEROES

In remembrance of my parents with special thanks to my family.

Hell is for heroes, here's how the story goes,
For all of you who worship not he who rose.
Hell is for heroes, who have a heart of stone,
Chose not to share the love that god has shown.
Hell is for heroes, who chose the wild life,
Use and abuse people, their husband, their wife,
Hell is for heroes, who live dangerously,
With the gift of sight they could not see.
Hell is for heroes, who can hear but have not heard,
For all around there's someone speaking the word.
Hell is for heroes, who trusted in luck,
Not by faith and hope, ending in self destruct.
Hell is for heroes, with a naked heart,
Not light or love only bleak and dark.
Hell is for heroes who chose not thy way,
What would they do, if they could have this day.

Velinda Stringfellow
1986
The year of 1986 is through
It left us with memories both good and bad
It's come and gone it's done its do
We're sure to look back on the offerings she had

We watched the Challenger go up in awe
And then we changed to disbelief
Because of the terrible sight we saw
As we shared with the families in their grief
Lady Liberty got a face lift
Her harbor was filled to celebrate her 100 years
She's always been such a well loved gift
As was shown by a display of fireworks and cheers

As for Colonel North, his duties were relieved
Because of his part in the Contra's Aid
I wonder if he was making a stand for what he believed
And if he ever felt afraid
President Reagan was the leader of our states
A country so proud to be a part of
Our freedom is what really rates
It is our greatest love

Memorial Day is what stands out in my mind
But not for the parades or to stand and see Old Glory unfurl
No I had a much greater find
It was the birth of my baby girl

D L Donahue

D L Donahue
BELOVED

To the Living Memory of Little Bit.

Dear Heart—
From the heavens you came, amidst a thousand voices ringing—
with your sweet virgin modesty—
To make the meadow's borders lovely with rosebuds in the spring.
As I was about to rise in the springy meadow gay, around me blew your eager flightiness so dear to me.
I felt you so graciously in my heart still and small as it skipped along so.
In those stolen moments where silence did not play, a
thousand loves our spirits spoke in whispers tender.
My love, oh, that shines so brightly amongst the morning flowers—
that blushes with not—you are
the finest flower with your hidden way,
no end will ever your stem break.

And with delay, not, the gods have plucked my lovely flower as
with not a care—to the heavens above.
Oh, shelter her ye gods, so gently,
in her saintly maidenliness
'til we meet again—For her preciousness rushes to brighten all my tomorrows, in the meadow gay,
where her voice and flightiness rings
evermore.

Pamela Jeannine Oswalt
MY HEART BEATS FAST
I care for you,
Deep within my heart.
Whenever I,m near you,
I feel we'll never be apart.
The way I see you,
Being sneaky and such.
I care for you,
Very, very, much.
Being with you,
Every day and night.
Wishing it was you,
In the glorious light.
When I'm with you,
My heart beats so fast.
I will raise for you,
My glorious mast.
I'm waiting for you
To come to my side,
So I can take you
For a marvelous, long ride.
I'm waiting for you,
To make up your mind.
To be mine,
And always at my side.

William C Fraser Sr
PARTING WAYS

To my wife Marty

I loved you, I chased you.
For the very last time.
I know now.
You will never be mine.
We both argue and disagree.
This is goodbye to you.
From me.

Cheri Culmone
CHALLENGER

This poem is dedicated to Christa McAuliffe, the astronauts of the Challenger and their families.

It was just another day when to work I went on
then someone called to say that the Space Shuttle was gone.
I dropped my pen and bowed my head,
I sat there wondering if they were truly dead.
We turned on the T.V. and then I knew for sure
because of the horror I would see,
I would see them no more.
I watched the lift-off again and again
looking at the faces filled with elation,
but after only a minute-twelve seconds in all they saw was disintegration.
Now with just an eerie silence everyone stared in disbelief,
after that sudden moment of violence a saddened world will

show it's grief.
We will honor them with a lasting monument that we will have to build
because the astronauts and you spent the day of January twenty-eighth being killed.
I did not know of your courage or of you
and now all that's left is a wreckage in a sea of blue.
But now I know because you died,
you said today is a go with six others by your side.
You were a woman and a teacher but most of all a mother,
space—you just wanted to reach there and come back to your son and daughter.
But instead we all stand here together trying to learn
the reason why you will be gone forever never to return.
You were known as Christa McAuliffe and now your life truly belongs to Christ.
It's written right there in your name
and because of your great sacrifice
we will all never be the same . . .

Willa Hartschen

THE GREATEST PLACE TO LIVE

There is a little Hamlet where I love to live,
A group of people with a lot of love to give,

This little Hamlet is really great.
The town is so old they once brought in a lot of freight,

You start down the street, a warm wave of the hand,
The greatest place in the land,

Down the street, with seats so neat,
All the old men with their tobacco cans, so sweet,

Telling each other of days gone by,
When every one of them knew they were telling a lie,

In 1968, a 100 years this town's history gone by,
Now so many of those folks, were ready to die,

Now my dad was a strong man,
To make us a living, we came to town with a cream can,

A few groceries we bought, for the coming week,
Hoping and praying that old cream can wouldn't leak,

Now the old hens, they laid eggs, a few,
But you know they bought a few groceries too.

Mom and dad, and us youngun's
on Saturday night came to town,
Just to visit with all the friends all around,

All I pray for when I leave this world,
Is for all my friends to smile.

When they pass my grave, and think of all the fun and love,
I had all the while.

Donald A Lanthier Jr

ABOUT POETS

Many a word we poets write
About the day, about the nite
We write of things that make us glad,
And other things that make us sad.

Some write words of wisdom wise,
Others of some tall bold lies.

Some write about the earth and rain,
Many others of their pain.

Some write about the birds and bees,
And others about the grass and trees.

Many write their words in rhyme,
Some do not, It's line by line.

But in the end we do realize
These words are read by many eyes,

By young, by old, by rich, by poor
There is one thing we can be sure.

These words will stand the test of time,
And be read forever, By all mankind.

Vickie Dagen Craig

ESCAPE FROM CHILDHOOD

As I roam the land of which I love so dear; childhood memories are suddenly unlocked and come rushing forth from my vault of endless memories.
Running through an empty shed of my fondest memory; my mind
returns to the time when I was young, innocent, and unaware of
such a troubled world.
Silently, people come to mind.
People so dear to my heart, but have long ago passed on.
Visions of yesterday play on the golden fields of wheat.
No longer do I reflect upon the present, but wander into the
past, and catch a glimpse of my own once forgotten life and
unforgettable people.
I focus my memories on the unpicked flowers so carefully
planted and quietly admired.
Echoing hills shout back my words, only as they return, they
sound so weary.
Time has made them grow old, as no one has come for so very
long.
Majestic pine trees sway with my arrival and whisper a message into my ears.
They too, seem tired and weary now.
Powerful gusts of cold and cruel winds rip my once lived world from within my reach.
The echoing hills seemed to give one last answer; and the trees sway so beautifully in rhythm with the golden fields.
I, too, realize that the past must remain there and my life will go on . . .
Pausing only for moments like this.

Mary Ann Rosser-Green

CONFESSION (OF THE MIND)

"To My Beloved Husband and Family"

How painful is the hour of truth,
The dark and ugly World of
Mistrust, that has captured my
soul
Frail is my spirit, Waned with
Guilt. For Within my eyes are the
Haunting Shadows of an Untrue
Love and it's Infidelities.
There is a cry from within the
Depths of my soul, begging for
Forgiveness from the one who
knows all. "Place within me," I
hear myself say, a new
beginning of Faith that will
enable me to carry on.
Death has my Name trapped in
it's hands and will soon possess
my Wretched soul for all
Eternity.
Is there no help for This, my
Gray mass of Lost and Wearied
spirit. Oh plead I now for my
Soul to be set Free.
Fate has no place for me, for
soon I will exist no more.
My life and liveliHood will have been taken away by a Tumbling
Down of that Pillar of Immitation Hope and Trust.

Joyce Edith Gunn

YOU'RE NOT FORGOTTEN, THO YOU'RE GONE

Twas a summer night in June,
when first we met.
I haven't forgotten,
no not yet.
I'll never forget
the way you looked.
It was like opening
the pages of a book.
With eyes so blue,
I knew you could be nothing but true.
Time has long gone
since that precious day.
Soon it will be May.
You're not here
so my dear
I'll go alone slowly,
but feeling mighty lowly.
There's a new star above,
it's the symbol of my love.
At night as I look up
at the sky,
He twinkles from on high.
I must not cry
but wear a smile,
Because we will meet again
in the sweet by and by.

Mazel Lillma McKenzie

A PLEA FOR HELP

I wonder what it's like to die—
How long it takes from earth to sky?
I know the bible says we can shorten our days.
I've pondered many ways,
How many pills to take, or
would a bullet be quick?
What is less painful??
My life is so meaningless.
No-one could care less,
If I live or die,
So there is no question as to why.
I've got to make sure it's the right thing to do.
I know you won't hold it against me,
That you understand and see,
The pain, of being alone, unloved, and unwanted.
You Lord, experienced the same feelings, didn't you?
At least, I won't be lonely in Heaven, now will I??
I'm going to try to stick it out;
But Lord, my mind is so clouded with doubt.

Bessie M Pope

VELVET THOUGHTS

Dedicated to a most generous and beautiful spirit.

Thank you for inspiration and the gift of many seeds with which I plant my garden of love and understanding.

Why can't I say what I feel
with words blooming and beautiful like petals on a flower?
Opening with thoughts and scents
Exotic Rainbow colors,
Soft velvet petals of thought
Ablaze with color and meaning.

Instead I find my words mundane, the same.
As I search for new colors
with which to paint my thoughts
I always come back round
to the reds and yellows and whites
The familiar that lights
my thoughts the same.
I read others thoughts in poetry
and they are fuscia, magentia,
orchid and gold,
beautiful to hold
scenting the air with beauty.

In my garden I shall nurture
the beautious color and scents of nature
and as I set my thoughts to paper
There will be new flowers blooming,
Just for you, and just for me
Eventually given for the world to see.

J Kalayil

J Kalayil

INNER VOICE

'Were I to die today'
So flashed through my mind,
A thought so sudden and stunning!
A condition of all living, none the less.

But I see myself in the grips of things
Many and varied absorbing all attention.
Yet I am left unsettled and void
A lot that befalls all, for sure.

May be, I should ignore and forget
All that this passing world offers.
No, fight I must, for man's life warfare.
Against what ?, 'flesh, world and satan'!
Formidable foes with unearthly vigor,
Demanding superhuman strength, if fight inevitable.
Where to look for help or shelter !.

I call upon you O Lord.
'You created every part of me.
'You saw me before I was born.

'My days are recorded in your book'.

To you I surrender my spirit
Whispering the soothing words of submission
"Thy Will be done".

* Psalm 139.

Linda Spencer
THE NIGHT

This poem is dedicated to my loving mother.

The days are short, the nights are long.
I can hardly wait until the dawn.

The days are sunny, bright and gay.
The nights will come and take them away

The days are laughter, the sun that's warm.
A time when all my fears are gone.

The night is dark, empty and cold.
The loneliness surrounds me like fear untold.

One day soon the night will come,
And stay with me until the dawn.
The night will finally have its' way.
Now, for me, there are no more days.

Martha (McCallian) Brown
LOVE OF THE U.S.A.
We must all stand by Our Country;
Patriotic, Tried and True,
Never waiver, Never falter,
And Praise the Red, White and Blue!

Many have given their life for Our Country,
Brave Men and Women, gave their all;
So let us keep, "Old Glory Flying,"
And always be there, to answer the call.

Thank God, for all of our Blessings,
Our Freedom, most precious of all;
We send our prayers to President Reagan,
And our leaders, who stand brave and tall!

I am so proud of "America," you see,
I am honored to sing, "My Country Tis of Thee,"
So this I know, that we all should say,
We are emotionally, "Proud of The U.S.A."

Darla J Roy
MY DEAREST DAD

May this poem be dedicated to my creator, my best friend, my Dad. Without his love and eternal faith—I would not have met the crest in me.

My Dearest Dad,
Times gone so fast
The memories last
From child, to teen, to now—
My Dad, my friend, my comrade
In many ways, you've taught me how—
To live, to love, to laugh, to cry
To bear life's sadness with some style.
To share with other's the gift of God—
Peaceful moments for awhile.

You see, dear Dad, my dream desire is to
follow in the steps—
Of a man who's rich, in heart and soul,
who has walked along the wire.
Don't know if I can do it, Dad,
But I sure am gonna try,
To be that person you've become—
The very best, that's why.
I Love You Dad

Suzanne Marcotte
NATURE'S GIFT

In loving memory to Morey Marcotte, Timmy Marcotte

I walked today,
Through the trees;
Back to the sun,
Face to the breeze;
& where I sat
To enjoy the view,
A butterfly sat
Enjoying it, too
& there in the warm sun,
Side by side,
Each viewed the view
& each one eyed
The other. Odd we too;
Below us lay
The valley floor
Which fall with blue haze
Failed to smother
Beauty unmatched
On which to gaze
& each
Disturbed by the other.

J A Avila de Sanchez
MY PRAYER

To my children

I do not ask to give them a life,
Of only sunshine and roses.
A life without pain or strife.
Without sorrow, or loses.
But rather dear Lord I pray,
Give them the strength to stand alone.
And face any storm that may come their way
And trusting in you go on.
And when all is well, Oh Lord I pray,
May they not be forgetful.
To bow their heads and humbly say,
Dear Lord we are so thankful.

Virginia Frazier
MY SPECIAL AUNT

This poem is dedicated to my special Aunt, Daisy Pittman.

My Aunt is such a nice person
On her birthday I thought she should know it
So here's a little poem for her
From her niece the poet.

You're such a nice, kind, person
Helping people all the time
And that's why out of all the Aunts in the world
I'm so glad you're mine.
We always have fun together
You make me laugh sometimes
Even when I'm feeling low
And these are some reasons I think you're special
And wanted you to know

So I'm wishing you Happy Birthday
Saying how much you mean to me
Telling you I love you
And hoping your day is nice as can be

Lonnie Mason Hathaway
LITTLE BROWN-EYES
A young boy walks beside an old woman
Her face is creased with lines of love, care, hardship, laughter, and time.
She holds his hand and says to him
"Always remember that no matter the changes that time brings,
You will forever be my little brown-eyes."
He looks up to her and smiles and bends down
to pick a few dandelions to make a ragged bouquet.
They return to the house and braid a necklace of weeds
and share love and laughter.

Time passes slowly for a small child and they spend much time together.
As he grows stronger, she grows weaker
Both slowly changing
The boy grows into a young man and
the woman grows older and slightly more frail
Both still vividly remember those dandelion necklaces
A small ray of sunlight on gloomy days,
Hope and a commitment to the good things in life.

The young man meets his own Little Brown-Eyes and
she is the apple of his eye,
No sweeter fruit could he wish,
They walk together hand in hand through many a starry night
They pledged their troth and the older woman watched
With a smile on her lips, she knows now that she did her job well
She made a man who shall stand strong and true,
Who shall strive for that which is right.
And once again the still sweet memory
of those dandelion chains comes into her mind.

Mary Adams Radford
OCTOBER SHAG
A golden carpet, inches deep,
Lies on our lawn today.
Installed while we were fast asleep,
It isn't here to stay.
October winds, too soon, will sweep
Its loveliness away.

Most trees were bare a week ago,
This maple held on tight
Its bumper crop, which seemed to glow
With radiant inner light.
Unseen, it dropped to earth below,
In just a single night.
Neglecting work, I gaze entranced,
Imprinting on my mind
This lovely picture Autumn chanced
To paint, where I would find
My love of Nature much enhanced
By the carpet She designed.

Irene Piwowarski
WHY DOESN'T IT WORK FOR YOU OR ME?
Being an American—it sure is good for me.
It is so wonderful to be free!
Yet, there are so many things I don't understand
In this, so wonderful, native land.

There is so much evil going on and on—
When there could be justice, happiness and fun!
Why don't people, in this world and land of ours,
Work together, help, as did our forefathers?

There is plenty of room—yes, for everyone!
If, only a good, honest leader would come.
Opportunity for all, should be really great!
But, I hope and wish and pray, it's not too late.

There is justice here—but, but is it for all?
Whom do we ask? To whom do we call?
Yet, all the good things in life are supposed to be free.
Why doesn't it work for you, for me?

All my life I have known: the rich get richer.
But, tell me, why the poor get poorer?
All through the years, I know we live in fear,
And yet, we should know God is near.

If everyone would open their eyes, look and see:
Together, we could have peace and harmony!
If only all the wars and hate in this world would cease,
We could live together in love and in peace.

So, look around, all you people and please, do see:
This land and everything—were made for you and for me.

Beulah J Compton
CHRISTMAS LONG AGO
When Christmas bells are ringing
And the earth is white with snow,
By candle lite and fireplace
You dream of long ago

In your dreams, a cedar tree
Standing high, so long ago
Were trimmed with silver discs of foil.
And popcorn strung, was white as snow.

With waxen Angel to top it all,
Her wings spread
Over our heads.
Just then we hear our parents call,
"It's time to go to bed".

Beneath the tree, a plate of cake,
A mug of cider too.

It awaits for dear old Santa Claus,
A treat from me and you.

The snow was deep, the moon on high
That casts down a silvery gleam.
I will always hear sleigh bells ring in the air,
As I dream of that Christmas of long ago. As I dream.

Debra Tallent
ALL THOSE TIMES

If you knew
The countless times I waited up for your calls,
Even though I didn't get any.
And all those times I said, "I love you."
But you didn't say it back.
What about the times I asked you where you'd been.
But I never got answers.

Could you guess
The times I wanted to hug and kiss you.
But you wouldn't get close enough.
And the times I wanted to be with you,
But you wouldn't come around.
Remember the night I wanted to go to the movies,
But you wanted to be with the boys.

If you'd learn
What it means to love someone,
But I doubt you can.
To be my one and only prince,
But are you ready?
To give me all those calls I've waited on,
But are you willing?

If you only knew, or could only guess,
Maybe if you'd learn—Just how much I love you—
You'd love me too . . .

Arlene (Ottenbacher) Buechler
GRANDMA

As we gently knock on her weathered door,
We are greeted by Grandma's warm smile once more.
The door is flung open wide with welcome,
And we step inside Grandma's humble home.
With her thin, frail arms we get loving hugs,
And we then know how much Grandma missed us.
Before we can ask her how she's been doing,
In genuine concern, she says, "How are things going?"

We reminisce about days gone by—
She remembers many events, with a gleam in her eye.
But the trials and hardships of eighty-seven years
Have weathered her structure, and I hold back my tears.
Her dress limply hangs on her frail, gentle being,
But not without great poise and dignity revealing.
Evening draws near and we regretfully must go—
Grandma will be alone again—this we sadly know.

But, today, as we slowly drive by Grandma's home,
The shades are pulled and the weeds have greatly grown.
Grandma doesn't live here—she has made it Home at last,
To our Divine Maker—her Earthly life has lapsed.
Grandma doesn't live here anymore,
We can't stop to see her as we did before.
She's among God's Angels, in Heaven way on High,
Smiling down upon us, saying, "Please don't cry."

Joyce Deatherage
GIFTS

Dreaming
Of a warm summer's day.
Feeling
A touch as gentle as May.
Hearing
A voice soft as velvet.
Seeing
A truly spectacular sunset.
Wishing
Upon a twinkling star.
Thinking
Of a dream where only two are.
Trusting
In those you love.
Believing
That God gives all of the above.

Ted Irwin Hearnsberger
A RARE TREASURE

To: Juanita Hearnsberger, mother; Reba Woods, Leola Belle Towns, grandmothers; DeLorah, wife and mother of our children

---

God hath given me a rare treasure; through
the years it has given me much pleasure.
With love, warmth, and abundance of cheer;
I have received many blessings year
after year.
It has given me strength and guidance through
toils and strife. My treasure helped
lead me to my ultimate goal in life;
my anchor and faith in my Lord Jesus Christ.
My treasure hath given to all that ask; To

Help conquer and win the ultimate task.
Down with darkness and its urchins within;
remove the devil and all of his sin.
Up with cleanliness, purity, and light, that
all may see Jesus; love and His might.
Onward we go, hand in hand, to offer Christ
to each and every man.
Thank you Lord for my rare treasure, from which
I have received more than my measure.
Peace and happiness abide in thee, the first
to touch and love me.
My Beloved Mother.
Matthew 6:21—"For where your Treasure is, there will
Your heart be also.

Katharine C (Staggs) Blackford
SERENITY ISLAND

Serenity to me
Is by the sea.
When the turmoil of life becomes too much
I wander down to listen to the lap-lap-lap of the waves
And to feel the soft, damp breeze blowing through my hair.
In such a world of solitude
How can one despair?

I may escape to my island
Any time of the day or night
Sometimes in the darkness the moon glistens on the
white-capped waves
And I stand and watch.

In the early hours of the dawn
I may wander to the east side of the island
To watch the sun
As it slowly emerges from beneath the sea
With the turning of the earth
The little shells on the beach begin to move
And the sand crabs start to run—
All around me there is life
But, there is no chaos or turmoil
Rather, it is soft movement.
And life begins, quietly and serenely
I stay awhile to play in the twinkling sand. .

And, then, one day the sea
May be so angry with me!

It lashes back and pounds and pounds
Against the wall, and I wonder what I've done.
Its wordless lecture tells me how
Serenity can return to my troubled heart.
It cleanses my mind, then quiets down
to give me time to calm myself and think.

At sunset I may wander to the west side of my island
And then I find
The sun setting in the blue, quiet water
Enveloped in a sky of brilliant color
The tide descends into the depths
All is quiet now, the world's at rest
And peace is found
Within my heart and soul.

Go find your island by the sea
And come with me.

And I stand and watch

Connie M Erwin
AMERICAN PRIDE

Just think how fortunate you and I are,
To see the moon and the North Star.
Just think how much we tend to forget,
the men and women who gave their lives with no regret.
I'm proud of you America and your daughters and sons,
how lucky we are to have such loving and brave ones;
To protect and give more for me and you,
to give us a safe place to live and a chance for life brand new.
I'm proud of all who gave their time,
I'm sorry for all we could not find.
Those who died to prove us strong,
those will be missed forever, so long.
America, we are behind you and all you wish to do,
America, remember we're yours and we love you.
We set your flag up so high,
for you are our freedom, in everyones eye.
We show our PRIDE and we show them all,
AMERICA, we love you and will never let you fall.

Pam Meek
SUMMER DAYS

"Remember the old summer days?"
When grandma would surely say . . .
"Anyone for some cold lemonade?"
"For this is gonna be a hot sunny day!"
Remember the old summer days?"
When fireflys shone big and bright,
On one hot and starry night,
And the mosquitoes buzzed in their flight!

"Remember the old summer days?"
When fathers day came
Families had bar-b-ques,
and children played games!
"Remember the old summer days?"
When everyone sat and sang.
Sitting on a swing with the neighborhood gang,
while grandpa sat their strumming,
and soon we all knew, the end of summer
was coming!

Lamont Forney
KATHY

To Kathy Williams because you meant that much to me and always will.

Kathy, I found the morning dew is lovely,
but not in sweet nature only in you.
Playing with the violets in bloom.
Kathy, I see the colors of rainbows before spring, cause they
wait for you to smile and silently sing
And star lights are your eyes before dawn.
Cause your smile takes the winter winds so far, far away.
Autumn is no secret, she comes from your dreams.
Kathy, I found the song I have been longin to hear, but
don't worry if you can't hear it, it

plays in your eyes when
your always near.
Cause the nightingales want the honey in your touch
I wish I could be the rain in your teardrops
so that you can remember, my heart can't forget you not.
Cause you'll be the evening song I play everyday
to bear the loneliness when your far far away.
Kathy, paradise is missing a very special part.
It sweet like roses but lives only in your heart
Cause daydreams have been crying cause they won't come
true, but that is cause my eyes will always see only
lovely you.

Dorothy May Dellach
MY LITTLE GIRL

My Girls

Here I am thinking
Of you,
Just yesterday you were
Brand new.
You're getting around and
Into things,
The smile on your face makes
Me sing
You sit and play just
Chatteren away,
I hate to think you'll
Leave me one day.
But there's a time when
We must part.
For a family you
Must start.
When it comes time to
Say good-bye.
I think I would rather Die

Janice Exler Seymour
PAPAW'S BOY
Carl:

You came to us out of nowhere
When your mother married our son
You became his pride and joy
Now you're also PAPAW'S boy.

You look at the world thru innocent eyes
Where everything can be a big surprise
You are your parents' pride and joy
Now you're also PAPAW'S boy.

Just when we thought little ones
Were a thing of the past

We've had to learn to adjust fast
For you have become my pride and joy
Now you're also PAPAW'S boy

You came to us out of nowhere
And we are sure glad you did
You make us look at the world anew
Best of all, you're MAMAW'S boy, too.

Deborah Grundy-Bayus
CONFUSION
Thru the layers of cosmic dust . . . a laugh rings
A tear falls loudly.
Placid eyes scan the gray paper-bag sky,
And wait for God to show his face.
Where do I belong?
While passing thru the portals of infinity
I am nothing.
While riding the 6:15 bus to oblivion,
Everything suddenly stops.
A thousand keys rush to unlock a thousand doors
And in the distance . . . a pebble is heard,
Wishing it were a rock.

Ruth M Coffey
A SMILE

I dedicate my poem to my husband U.M. Coffey and my two daughters, Ruth Ann Huston and Jean Sue Burnham. They're good listeners.

Can you spare a big smile or two
As you go along today?
It will make the day much brighter
For someone along your way.

It only takes a smile from you
To bring sparkles to someone's face
And in no time at all it seems
The world's a different place.

You've heard the saying, I am sure,
A smile is a big old frown
That someone has decided
To just turn it upside down.

A smile and a frown are contagious
And they both really "catch on."
The frown just brings displeasure
But the smile is so much fun.

A smile that is happy and friendly
And is surely headed our way,
Can heal a lot more wounds
Than a frown can, any day.

It is said: "Smiles will keep us young"
That frowns make us "look old"
So let's forget the ugly frowns
And put our smiles "on hold."

Clodagh Meath
A PASTOR NAMED KEN

To My Parents, Paul and Joan Meath

I met a Pastor,
And his name was Ken,
I met him on my way,
Down south street,
Among a lot of men.
He seemed very nice,
He seemed to care,
But then again,
He seemed very unaware.
I don't know,
What I saw,
or what I wanted,
to see.
Maybe I did or didn't
See any light,
Maybe I am,
Looking for something,
And I thought,
That a Pastor named Ken,
Would show me the way,
To what I do or don't want to do.

Janie Stratton Martin Lee
WHEN DEATH COMES
A physical body will die someday
All emotion will slowly fade away
A mental mind will turn off its light
A soul shall rise out of sight.

Jacqueline Jean Boop
LOVE IS SO BLIND
When love is so blind;
That it leaves you behind:
It stops the sun from shine:
It makes you so mean and unkind:
My world is so shattered:
I do feel like I'm battered:
The birds don't sing no more;
I run and hide behind my door;
If I just wasn't this poor:
Maybe I could have kept him at my door:
I feel so alone and deserted:
I'm sorry for the love I inserted:
"GOD" didn't bless me with money:
So now I've lost my honey:
"GOD" blessed me with my children and good health:
Well I think that's far better then wealth:

Betty Jean (Benton) Brooks
LIFE'S JOURNEY

To Mother, Modean and Grandson, Cole!

We are all taking a journey,
Life's trip for each life.
No luggage needed, you travel light.
Know yourself better, than you do others.
Is a good plan. And try others to understand.
From birth to death, is just a twink of the eye.
As far as time is concerned.
But in each life is a "special story."
God's interested in everyone.
The many events that come in store.
Make a difference in the <u>Life At Hand</u>
Whether you be boy, girl, woman, man.
Take that journey, enjoy it to the fullest.
You are issued only one life
A short journey of time.
Make it count.
First things first and love life's Journey
Share with others some of your views,
But stay an individual person
The best that you can do.
Love yourself, care for yourself too, and others will follow you.

Joan Paula Buckes
DISHES

"This poem is dedicated to my devoted husband, Walter, who came to my aid when the stacks were high."

Dirty dishes every night;
I'm tired of the chore.
No matter how much I wash 'em,
There always seem to be more.
The broiler, and the skillet;
A dirty cake pan, too;
Throw in the bowls, and coffee pot,
There's nothing else to do!!!
It's the same thing after breakfast,
And then, again at lunch—
Cups, and saucers, and glassware;
Utensils, by the bunch.
Upon the stove and table,
Any counter-space that's free,
Make room for dirty dishes;
The sink is full, you see!!!
An automatic washer
Perhaps, would help a bit,
'Cause the folks here don't stop eating,
And, the mess will never quit.
I wonder, if, in Heaven
There's a cafe, by the shore;
'Cause, if I get to go there,
I won't do dishes any more!!!

Christine Marie Gerst Brown
THE INDIANS FAREWELL

To my loving husband Jeff, to my children Jenny & J.C. to my in-laws, Janis & Bob, my parents Elmer & Marge & to my dear friend Carole. To all of you for helping me to grow . . .

The Indian is one of a kind
He learns to never ever unwind
the Indian was taught not to fear
nor does he ever hide his tears.

While the young ones come from all around
the Indian shows them to obey the ground,
he has told them many, many things
all of which he will one time sing.

He speaks of all the things he loves
the animals, the trees, the ground,
and the sky above.

But there is one thing he must tell
to let all men come together as well
for if there is hate and not any love
there will not be for us . . . A sky above.

William Joseph Neumann

William Joseph Neumann
THE PAIN

This poem is dedicated to my loving, caring, devoted wife. Who stood by me when I lost my leg, and who still stands beside me.

Pain is a name that everyone knows, when you grow old, you can feel it down to your toes. But when you dont have any, you feel insane, you hobble to the window and look out at the rain.

Patty, my love. So tender and true. You know that I'll never tire of you. But life is hard, with all the mistakes.

I just dont know, If I have what it takes.

Lookout, lookout, its do or die, my
that first week I was flying high!
But when I looked back and
started to shudder—
I closed the window, and looked
through the other

Well, my love, life is vicious and
cruel,
But I'll never fail using God as my
tool.
I'll try, I'll try, with all my might,
and learn to keep that machine
out of sight.

Yes, I know I am at "mercy"; the
lights so bright
the nurses uniforms so starchy and
white
And I know what it means to be in
plight.
But I'll walk out of here, I've got
the might!

The pains, the pains, they know no
bounds.
They'll haunt you quicker than the
basketville hounds.
Yes. Keep your head high and don't
despair,
Because God is watching over us,
everywhere!

Rebecca Geer Rogers

JEAN

The old man never knew this wife
Until he married her for life,
That was the year that Kate had
died,
And going all agin' his pride,
He ordered this one from a book,
Because it said that she could cook.
Life out here is always hard,
And no one thought that it was odd,
For a widow man of forty-four
To take a wife to help with chores,
When she arrived the last of May,
He made it clear upon that day,
She'd never take the place of Kate.
But Jean, she never argued fate,
If not Jean's face, her ways were
fair,
Working hard she did her share,
And side by side for twenty years,
They worked through happiness
and tears.
Words seldom passed between the
two,
He always felt that Jeanie knew,
But now he slowly bowed his head,
Regretting words he hadn't said,
Beside her grave the old man knelt
And told his Jean the love he felt.

Donna White

LONELINESS

Loneliness can kill you, just like a
perilous
disease.

It can eat away at one's heart; like
maggots
eating away one's inside.

Loneliness hits all ages, but it
mostly strikes
the elderly; elderly whose all alone
and in a
world of their own.

The elderly that is less unfortunate
they lie in
bed day after day just opening and
closing their
eyes waiting to die.

Then you have the ones who
wander through the streets,
hoping to find someone to meet.

Of course you have the one's who
sit on their porch
and rock & rock their life away,
hoping that someone
would pass by someday.

Slowly, slowly their dying like flies.

Slowly, slowly the loneliness
disease has finally
arrived.

Margaretta Carlin

JELLY PRINTS

To my wonderful, Grandson: Michael Jude Morey. My inspiration, through the sharing of love, and daily adventures.

Hi! Little guy, what would you like
to eat?
A peanutbutter, and jelly sandwich
for my little sweet?
Can I fix it for you, my little man?
No! I can make it for myself gran.
And, so you can, but what have we
here?
Jelly prints all over the kitchen,
dear.
Don't worry about it, we'll clean
it up.
You get the sponge, and I'll get the
mop.
We've cleaned up the mess, and put
the jelly away.
Can, we go outside gran? It's such
a nice day.
So, out we go, for a walk to the
park?
Should we go feed the fish, or play
at the school until dark?
Oh! The wonderful! happy times
we had.
Thinking of him now, I feel so sad.
No jelly prints around the house
any more,
No, little guy, to help mop the floor.
Though, the miles now find us so,
far apart,
I can never, wash away the jelly
prints,
He, left on my heart.

Dorothy Snow Cloyed

MORNING SONG

An oriole sits in the sycamore tree
As I stand by my window at dawn,
He warbles away, giving thanks for
the day
In a cascade of melodious song.

His colorful coat and sweet mellow
notes
Set the theme for the hours ahead,
And I turn to my tasks with a heart
thats at peace,
And give thanks for the cheer that
he spreads.

Edward L Stevens

LOST OR STOLEN

It was just two years ago today
Our little boy/girl went astray
Late coming home from school
I thought he/she had stopped to
tary
Not thinking to be wary

I walk the floor and start to worry
Praying he/she will hurry
I stare out the window and watch
the door
Thinking we might not see him/her
anymore

We sure miss you, please call or
write
You're in our prayers both day and
night
Hoping you're warm and well,
what ever you do
Remembering we will always love
you

Was it something said or done
For you to feel that you had to run
Our memories of you are so golden
please come home and take
another chance
Or are you just lost or stolen

Laura R Worst

RAVAGES OF ICE

Mother Pines stand weeping over
their young.
Their boughs hang heavy like
sinewy arms reaching out to
support.
And yet, they themselves become
weaker and weaker as this
enemy weighs them down too.
Lower and lower they bend.
Cracking is heard and echoes
loudly through the bleakness of
the frozen clumps of trees.
How can anything so lovely be so
destructive, I ask myself.
The trees are dripping with
transparent frosting that stiffens
the needles and twigs.

Light is reflected and shimmers
like ghostly liquid oozing from
the branches.
On some, the frozen aqua looks
lacey and one compares the
adornment to a regal matron
receiving her guests at a formal
affair.
Stiff, bent with age, cool and yet
an air of elegance and survival
surrounding her.

The mother pines continue their
vigil and remain faithful to their
young.
Many of them are smothering and
a sense of near death
approaches.
Cannot the sun take pity now and
rid the young of this threat of
doom? Dissolve the bounds of
beauty yet pain and allow all to
reach skyward again? Oh, how
much we need the trees, all of
them.
I want them to be free and yet this
awesome beauty clutches me
and I love the breathtaking
scene.
How much can they endure?
Enough of my desires, save
them, save them now!

Kenneth C Eskridge Sr

HAPPY AT LAST

Dedicated to the light of my life, my wife, Betty Jean Eskridge

---

One hot summer day I was riding
a bus and making a hell of a fuss.
The weather was hot, the bus
was crowded, smelly and humid,
and all that stuff.

It was packed so tight I couldn't see
to my right. But to my amaze I
saw a light flickering towards
the front. I followed that light,
through people I did shove, to
find that flicker of light. But the
flicker was gone when I reached
the spot. In place of the flicker
there was a great bright light.
Shining with beauty, brilliant
and bright. The temptation was
too strong for me to withstand.
I had to know what made that
light glow.

By some unknowing force it had
drawn me to its side. I set down
not knowing what would
happen next. Bewildered and
amazed, I was sitting in a daze.
I knew not what to say, I knew
not what to do. All I knew was I
wanted to be part of that beacon
that was shining for me. I
wanted to speak but words I
could not find. I searched and
searched all through my mind,
of what I could say on this
special day. I heard a voice,
angelic to me. I was so excited I
trembled inside. I could not
believe it had spoke to me.

I stayed awake late that night,
thinking of the bright shining
light. I felt so strange in a good
sort of way. My heart was
tingling, my head was spinning.
I realized I was alone, but yet,
somehow, not all alone. I would
close my eyes, but it would still
be bright for I could still see the
light.

It's morning now, time to start
another day. I hope and pray it
will be as great as yesterday. At
days end, I ran to my stop,
looking frantically for the light.
I looked not far, there it was
bright and radiant, more
beautiful by far.

Now years have passed and I'm
happy at last. That light I had
seen in the past is still with me
and will always last. It shines in
my heart, it shines in my life, for
now it is my darling wife.

Kathryn Drouillard

THOUGHTS

I dedicate this poem to my children Jeffrey and Katie, with all my love

---

Our thoughts are something
to savor
Because they come so fast
like lightning, they flash in a
second, and they are gone
Like the wind that blows the dust
from the ground
We must listen to that sound

Cheryl A Mala

DIVORCE

I don't understand
Why
I cry
And wish it could have worked.
Don't you see
That's part of me
I can't reconcile.
There are things I miss, while
I know they can't be replaced.
But I have faced
The fact
I can't go back.
I also know
There's an emptiness
That will never be filled,
Even if I willed
It to be so.
There's a part of you
That's a part of me
That will always be.

R S Angell
MYSTERY LADY
There is a lady for me I've seen in a dream,
Not to be mine easily—or so it would seem.
A Mystery Lady I will love to the end,
Share my life with a loyal and true friend.
I've stood in the background to take it all in,
Trial and error have taught me where to begin.
Reasons are many for whom I've been waiting,
In the sea of search up to my neck I've been wading.
The smallest of sparks can set my heart burning,
Hopes and passion fuel an unfulfilled yearning.
Oh Mystery Lady where are you?
To comfort and hold me when I'm blue,
To tell me it's worth it and know it's true.
A dreamer at heart—a long while I've known,
Ample dreams with cold reality together I've sewn.
There's alot in the mind in my life to share,
For the lady who will love me and really care.
To that special lady I'll be loving and giving;
Make life happy together and worth living.
So Mystery Lady step out from the throng,
Say you love me—prove I haven't been wrong.
Oh Mystery Lady where can you be?
Get close to me and I'm sure you will see,
That life together will be good as it can be.

Joseph Jeremy DuBose
CHRISTMAS DAY

This poem is dedicated to my Mamaw, for her love and belief in me.

The cold winds blow,
Along with the snow,
And Santa's Ho Ho Ho.
Santa's on his way,
Twelve reindeer pull his sleigh,
And all the children say,
Tomorrow's Christmas Day.

David William Martin
I'LL GET TO IT

This poem's for Kathleen, smiling and nodding thanks for your love and occasional prodding.

Procrastination, I know it so well
Put off the task until somebody yells
Watching the TV, reading the funnies
Planning on how to round up more money

I need to do this, I want to do that
Everything can wait until I get back
Tomorrow is free to catch up on chores
But by then of course there is so much more

Clean up the yard and go to the store
Take out the trash and then retile the floor
I'll patch up the leak, it isn't bad yet
I'll get to it soon, on that you can bet

My spouse of course is so very refined
She leans on me not until my deadline
Then panic and anger on my behalf
I struggle to gain, she stifles a laugh

Wish as I may and then dream as I might
There's still the same jobs awaiting at night
Lantern in hand to the garden I go
Weeds and petunias are yanked out of snow

I'm changing my ways, I'm going to adjust
I'll wash the old car before the things rusts
I'll mow the long grass before summer rains
As soon as I've finished watching this game

Susan Elizabeth Coker
THOUGHTS OF YOU
i had a dream
it was during the day
it was a daydream
it was more of a thought
than an actual scene
and the thought was this
we were growing old together
it was not a question
it was a matter of fact
it was a pleasant thought
and i thought we were smiling
and i smiled at the thought
of us smiling together
then the sun came out
no, really it did
and it warmed the air
and it warmed my heart
and i thought of you
and your heart was warm
and i longed for you
and your arms were warm
and i reached for you
and the air was warm
with the sun playing through
and i touched your face
and i felt your warmth
then i opened my eyes
and i felt the warm air
with the sun playing through
and i wondered if you
could feel my warm hand
then i thought back on my thought
and i thought of us smiling together
and i smiled at the thought
it was such a nice thought

Elaine Champ
DAD

---

dedicated to the memory of my father, Lev Wolfe, and my entire family.

Dear dad, if you were here today,
We'd climb the highest hill,
And then we'd sit and rest a spell,
While all the world was still.

We'd watch white clouds go rolling by,
Laugh and sorta clown,
And then the fun would really start,
'Twas kite time in our town.

That special hill Dad,
Was part of childhood days,
And in memory I still climb it,
Just to recall your old, sweet ways.

Ever pleasant, always calm,
Oh, how I'd like to see,
Just one more day of climbing hills
And how they used to be.

David Duffey
THE GREATEST SENSES OF ALL

In Loving Memory of Daisy Foster

How wonderful are the eyes with which we view our world.
They let us see the deep blue skies and awesome scenes
unfuled. The purple of the mountains and the shading of the
night, would all be greatly lessened if we didn't have our
sight.

But glorious, too, is our audial sense that sound we may
percieve; the trickling of a tiny brook, the falling of
an autumn leave, the umpa of a sousaphone, the sound of
falling snow; if we had not our hearing than none of this
would we know.

Then, too, is the way in which we trace a scent upon a
breeze; the smell of baking apple pie, and the freshness
of a grove of trees.

And finally too, our touch and taste which we all adore.
For without these senses, each meal we would abhore.

But all these senses that we have, however great or small,
they are quite trivial compared with the greatest senses
of all. For, more important than our sight; or our hearing, touch, taste or smell; it is our hearts and minds and souls that
will serve us all most well.

Todd F Pearson
PEACE
Peace is
the word that makes people come,
and listen and work in harmony.
Peace is
the power that stops wars,
and shows the love of each other,
Peace is
the word that makes friends stay together forever.
Peace is
what birds sing in the morning.
Peace is
the dove that lasts forever.

C Jane Bair
IN MY DREAMS
The water folds over itself
As it rolls toward the sandy beach
But this scene is imagined
Even now.

I can smell the salty air
And feel the cool, gentle breeze.
The leaves of the palms
Sway back and forth,
And I feel close, comfortable, and safe.
Yet I have only been here
In my dreams.

Thomas Allen Harrison
CHRISTMAS: A TIME TO REMEMBER

To all the people who mean so much to me, my Dearest Friends and Beloved Family Members, Thank you.

Remember the fact that "Mommy Kissed Santa"
and "Rudolph's Nose is Red."
Remember it's not time to take;
it's time for giving instead.
Remember all "The Twelve Days of Christmas"
and that the "Herald Angels Sing."
Remember that "The Faithful are Coming"
and that the "Silver Bells Will Ring."
Don't forget the "Little Town of Bethlehem"
Remember too, that "Silent Night"
when our Savior once lay.
Remember all the "Bells are Jingling"
and the "Merry Gentlemen are at Rest."
Sing the "Songs of Christmas"
which ever you like best.
Don't miss "Santa Claus"
as "He Comes to Town."
Remember the "White Christmas"
When "Frosty the Snowman" fell down.
Yes, let us give "Joy to the World"
and give gifts just because,
we want everyone to remember
Christmas is a time for love.

Lawrence J Syrop
CLOSED FEET PAJAMAS

For Gail Robin Colodny

---

in yellow aura the kithen thrives to
smell wood underfaded wallpaper
the roving fan cuts the sun beams
plastic feet shuffle and grey

the nightmare is over Life
is real feel the springhue
the gold dusted rays main
the dark nocternal vision
effecting my youth

crave those mornings in confined pajamas
wherelung were pure hearts sublime

to when the mind dabbles
in Freedom Fleeting Freedom

cuddle close to the window pane
watch umbrella trees hide the
shade

Lydia Solis Cardenas
MY HUMBLE PRAYER

In Loving Thanks to our Lord and Saviour Jesus Christ. Dedicated to all cancer victims everywhere. "When I said, My foot slippeth; thy mercy, O Lord, held me up." Psalm 94:18

When I talk to You Lord
I feel like we talk face to face
Often I feel like I know You so well,
And at times I don't know You at all

At times there's such distance
between us
The sky seems so far out of reach
I know You are somewhere behind
all the clouds
But where Lord, that far I can't see

Sometimes when my prayers
aren't answered
I feel like I'm praying in vain
It's so hard to manage in this world
This world is a world full of pain

But I think that you know what we
go through
For You once walked upon this old
earth
You know what it's like to be
human
You know all we have to endure

And I do understand if You tarry
I know you have so much to do
My prayers are not that important
I just wanted to say "I love you".

Nancy B Weinberg
A RIVER APART
It seems you left so unexpectedly.
That's what hurt me so badly,
And what hurts me even more
Is that I haven't found
Anyone to fill the void that you
Once filled in my heart.
I guess you could say,
Where there was one
There are now two apart.

And through all my pain and
suffering
The worst part is the aloneness,
An empty river
That's never
Quite filled
With enough water.
And if my river should run dry
And my life should end
I'll just turn around and
Remember that I once had a friend.

Jeanette Krugman
PARADISE
I look up at the heavens and say,
"Oh, how bright and blue you are
today!"
The big white clouds that float
around,
They don't even make a sound.
The trees so nice and green,
They seem so quiet, and, serene,
Not a trouble, or, a care,
I think I'll try to keep them there!

They all look so nice and new,
And there is nothing to obstruct
their view!
You could think you are a circus
clown,
And turn your whole world upside
down!

Sometimes, it seems too much to
bear,
And so we really do not care,
But, when all is said and done,
And our fateful trip we've won,
We still look out and see the light,
It looks so happy and so bright.

A greater person you could be!
Won't you come and share; this
Paradise with me?
And see the wondrous things I see,
It's really up to you!

Kathryn A McGarry
FOR A GROWING BOY
You're just a little boy right now
young and small and free;
I look into your eyes
And think of who you'll someday
be.

With freckles on your nose
And shining hair and dimpled
cheeks
Your smile and happy giggle
Make the years all seem like weeks.

In no time you'll be off to school
To book and lunchbox days,
Learning that the little you
Gets big in many ways.

Muddy shoes and scraped up knees
And, yes, a tear or two
And every time Mom turns her
head
She'll notice that you grew.

With love and kindness all the way
And doing all she can
Mom will be there to help you out
And then, you'll be a man.

Mari Williams
THE FUNERAL
My "Baby" was now buried
I sat at the freshly covered grave
Dry eyed
Tearless
Released
Liberated
Free!

My ten year long suffering had
been finalized
Terminated
The ultimate climax

The essence of our relationship
had been wrung dry with
Chicanery
Equivocations
Negation!

I gazed at the empty silent phone
grave
Arrid
Vacuous
After the phone rang, and he told
me he was
Married!

Janice Nothem
VICTORY OF A VIETNAM VET

This poem is dedicated to all men who served their country in Vietnam and still carry a part of that war with them even today.

As a Vietnam Vet pauses briefly in
thought,
His mind wanders back to the war
that he fought.
He's tried to forget, but the war
battles on.
In his mind it's still raging, the
wars going strong.

As he trys to make sense of the
killing he did,
He realizes now, he was still just a
kid.
It hadn't been long since the
morning of prom,
Then he found himself wandering
over in Nam.

He daily was greeted with
bloodshed and death,
And watched as his buddies would
take their last breath.
The memories are clear, and his
tears gently flow,
Remembering their bodys piled up
in a row.

Each day he was faced with the
duty to kill,
Which soon was transformed into
some kind of thrill.
The killing of gooks had turned
into a game.
These innocent boys learned to kill
without shame.

As the nightmares invade in his
sleep every night,
He sits up in bed and he trembles
with fright,
Will this war never end? Will it go
till I die?
When will I ever stop asking God,
why?

As he kneels by his bed, a strange
touch of a hand,
Leads him to see that it's part of
God's plan.
I know that he spared me to carry
life on.
I'm somebody special like those
who are gone.

Rosanne O'Dell
LESSONS
Love shared, will grow twice as
much
And is something dear to cherish
Because love held by only one
Will soon choke and perish

A flower reaching to touch the sun
Will blossom and smell so sweet
But with only dark clouds to grab
The flower will face defeat.

Happy ever after dreams
We strive so hard to gain
Are roads with many obstacles
Of truths lies and pain.

Lessons learned when we are
young
Are understood when we're old and
gray
Then we wish the rest of our lives
We could go back to yesterday.

But yesterday is gone for good.
Today has nearly reached it's end.
And as for tomorrow well . . .
Only God knows what's around the
bend.

Jack Phillips
WINTER
O' swirling twirling feathery flakes
Falling softly around me and
touching my face —
With ice cold fingers—then swiftly
melting
Into saltless tears upon my cheeks
—
O' winters greeting —
O' never ending—steadily
descending fall
A whirling wonderland of white
confetti —
It's gentle beauty, spreading like a
cold and fleecy quilt,
And hiding man made scars on
virgin soil —

And on a lonely hill of blanket
white —
Gaunt cedars stare in ice bound
silence—
Their leafless branches twisting
and cringing
Like arthritic fingers dusted in
white
O' cruel beauty —

And hungry wild birds—madly
searching
for a covered morsel —
A stray dog barking for his lost
master —
Then leaping and plunging into the
soft drifts,
While the prudent squirrel
smirks and crunches happily on
his lay-away reserves —
Quite unconcerned —

And innocent and sprightly deer—
Huddling together on a bleak and
powdery slope —
Nostrils quivering in nervous
apprehension —
Whilst the wily fox—ventures
stealthy from his lair,
His cautious prints
etched into natures white and
snowy carpet —

And now O' slipping mass of
decaying beauty —
Your virgin white now turning grey
—
And slowly melting into watery
pools beneath my feet —
O' winters farewell!—-

Elaine Wiggins
DEAR JOHN
I have sat and thought for days and
days
All the words I wanted to say.
"How could you have stayed away
For all those years?
Where were you when I needed
you
To wipe away my tears?"
What did you say, "But my how
you've grown."
What could I say to a father I have
never known?
Somehow the words don't come to
me now.
Guess they weren't important
anyhow.

I guess I don't hate you
Although I used to.
It wouldn't have taken much to
please me then
At the age of seven, eight, nine or
ten.
Now many years have passed
And I have met you at last.
You are just like a stranger.
Someone I pass on the street.
Just anyone I should happen to
meet.
Sure do wish you would have been
my dad.
Any kind of Dad would have made
me glad.
Now, I don't know what to call you.
You weren't my daddy, and father
doesn't seem proper.
Guess I'll call you nothing or by

your first name.
You could have been "my Daddy"
but "John" is your name.

Gene J Stergar

Gene J Stergar
SYMPHONY IN SOLO

This poem is dedicated to Mother, Laverne my loving wife, our five wonderful children, Deborah Ann, Gregory Gene, Monica Lynn, Gary Ross, Glenn Victor, and Dad.

Softly separate the fire from the flame
And from that make a rope of sand
Better yet, a net to catch the wind
Or perhaps just join firm hand in hand

Focus not on things unseen
Or listen for the sound to come,
Better yet make discovery a balance beam
and God's knowledge the reservoir we draw eternity from.

Justine Marie Sicks
SPRING'S LOVE AFFAIR

To My Dear Husband, George . . .

"Oh . . you stung me, said the flower to the bee,
your suppose to remove my nectar, without disturbing me."

"Forgive . . said the bee to the flower, your
so delectable, I lost all my will power."

"Be far more careful, and have all that you wish,
remember, I'm fragile, however today, you I can't miss."

"Oh, thankyou, I'll drink my very fill, your
to good to be true,
I know, I'll get "tipsy" sipping sweet liquid from you."

Heavy from "hypnotic" juice, he could hardly fly,
He took time for one last look, too "dip"
his wings, for a joyous goodby.

Ms Joe Ann Peacock
SOME OTHER DAY
Who are we fooling? only ourself,
We love each other, yet we both have someone else.
He's there for me, when you're not around,
To pick me up when ever I'm down.
She's there for you all through the nite,
To care for you and hold you tight.
I eagerly wait for your knock on my door,
When in your arms, you'll hold me once more.
You'll say all the right things, with each gentle touch,
Like I missed you darling and love you so much.
When we're together nothing else matters,
We don't hear the world, not even it's chatters.
Only the beat of an aching heart,
Cause time and distance have kept us apart.
You leave no room, for his memory,
He's just a statue that shadows me,
Her memory darling, I can erase,
It shows when you're with me, I see love in your face.
To them we can not, say goodbye,
It would break their hearts and make them cry.
So we'll go on our usual way,
And meet again some other day.

Gerald Montreuil
GRAND OLD MASTER
Grand old master of the universe
Who stands still as a country's hero
Looking over green fields and valleys below;
Over rivers, forests, and mountains and foes.

Foes like insects, tornadoes, drought and flood,
Earthquakes, fires, storms and even humans.
Humans; who at times can be so ruthless.
Some has no concern; is so inhuman.

He comes with an axe or chain saw
And gnarls at my skin till it's raw.
I must stand there with no place to go
And can't even growl to make him go.

I used to be master of the universe;
Now I'm just material for poetry's verse.
I used to be champion of the forest;
A great hiding place for little birds' nests.

But then he came with his barking machine
And landed me down; made me white and lean.
So heed the call other giant friends out there;
Beware of humans dressed in ploddingly care.

Joan Obra
OH L'AMOUR

This poem is dedicated to my English teacher, Ms. Diane Scarpulla, who has recognized and encouraged my poetic ability.

Love is . . .
a broken heart that is held together
by the thin strings of longing
a light pink diamond
in the corridors of his imagination
the light of the moon
bathing the earth
looking for that special someone
the waves upon the sea
endlessly flowing out
into the arms of eternity
the gentle touch of a lover
in the shadows of the night
the taking of one's own life
to follow the spirit of another's corpse
and the twinkle in the eyes
of a newborn babe
regarding it's mother for the very first time.

Dorothy A Lang
OCTOBER ROSE

To Larry—In memory of our golden moments.

I gazed into the heart of a rose,
and saw the wonders of the universe unfold.
The gnetle rain, the warm sunshine,
the golden beauty that was mine,
all mine.

Then came the wind, the wild wind,
I saw my flower droop and bend.
Ah! my yellow rose, it was no more.
Stunned, I stood there in the sun and heat,
a stem in my hand, a shower of gold at my feet.

Time stood still, there was no sound,
only a memory of a golden flower,
and a haunting fragrance all around.
Like distilled sunshine in an autumn bower.

Carolyn T Feagans
THE VOICE OF GOD
Fear clutched at me as I lay in awe
Of nature's twisting pain . . .
A sky of brilliant illuminated vastness
Sent forth its angry rain . . .

Suddenly heaven and earth trembled
God thundereth with His voice . . .
He thundereth with the voice of His excellency
A powerful and mighty force . . .

Hear attentively the noise of His voice
And the sound that goeth out of His mouth . . .
Even the storm has its source
When it rages north and south . . .

As the lightnings lighted the world
Striking its path without regard . . .
I thought I heard the thunderings speak
"Be still and know that I am God"

Mrs Jean Hinkle
THANKSGIVING PRAYER

To a loving husband and two wonderful children.

We thank thee, Lord,
This Thanksgiving day
For the many blessings
You have sent our way.

For our healthy children
So happy and bright
They give us great pleasure
From morning til night.

For the birds that sing
High above the green trees
And the flowers that bloom
From the miracle of seeds.

For the rain and the sun
And the snow and frost
Without all of these
We would really be lost.

And last but not least
For the good of mankind
We pray for lasting peace
On earth and of mind.

Ann M Spaar
I KNOW YOU ARE HERE

This poem is dedicated to my husband Walter, a real great guy.

Although, you can't be with me now
I know that you are here
Because, you live within my heart
I know that you are near
Sometimes, I hear your laughter echo
throughout the rooms, and it seems
to fill my heart with a very happy tune.

I know your thoughts are like Birds
in flight, But somehow you know I am
with you, and things will turn out right.

We will erase all those shadows from
the night, and pray that you will see the light.

Lynn E Leiker
ATTITUDE IN MOTION
Attitude
expressed
in motion.
Directed
with a
glance.
Exasperated
by chance?
If for once
you could see
Yourself
instead of me:
Would you
perceive
what I see?
Would you
act
any differently?

Karen McIlvoy Rapa
MOM

This poem is dedicated to the most wonderful mother in the world: Norma J. McIlvoy. I love you mom!

I've tried to find the words to say,
just how very much I care.
To say how much I'd like to thank you,
for always being there.

I may not be that little girl,
with both those skinned up knees.
And even though I'm all grown up,
I still have those small girl needs.

Although I always did those things,
you used to warn me from,
I understand their meaning now.
You tried to keep them undone.

Children learn from their mistakes.
LORD knows I've made my share.
And even when I hurt you bad,
you still were always there.

I LOVE YOU, MOM.

Karen Lynn Majors
IN SEARCH OF A CARVED-OUT HEART

I dedicate this poem to my friend Dr.Z for believing in me

I went searching today . . .
Searching for answers,
for truth,
for a tree

I couldn't even find the tree
It seems to have disappeared
unexplained . . .
like you

Maybe time destroyed our initials
The same as it destroyed
the love in your heart
for me

Maybe if I had payed more attention
Maybe I would have seen
the leaves were leaving the tree
. . . as you were with me

Herb D'Aigle
DESCRIPTION OF A SPIDER

I Herb, dedicate this poem to you Jane; Will you always remain by my side . . . Now? I love you, Happy Birthday 1987

Green, vasigated.
Smooth texture,
looks like
a spider, may be
tropical
topically plants make me
feel good, some day
our plant will
bloom to
have babies who'll
become
as parents
and
have
plants
of
their
own.

Janet Sandoval Mills
MY LITTLE TREE
A golden tree with dollar signs,
Is what I have in the back of my mind.
It sparkles and shines when the sun comes out.
I planted the seeds and watched it sprout.
I've watched it grow every minute,
I gave it love, and that's what's in it.
My mom and dad, they have a branch of their own,
because they deserve to be up on a throne.
I'll share what I have, I won't be tight,
to make everyones lives, better than right.
My little tree, it's so pretty.
All in my mind, that's a pity.

Helen B Crittendon
THE MESSAGE
The wind comes blowing from everywhere
carrying it's messages along on the air,
but what does it say as it passes on by?
No one knows, not you nor I.
In summer it comes as a zephyr aloft,
it's voice is gentle, so low and soft
and what it whispers floating on by,
only flowers hear, neither you nor I.
In the fall whistling around the eaves,

shaking the trees, loosening dry leaves,
tall grasses bowing as it hurries by,
they know the message, not you nor I.
Sometimes in winter we wake snug in our bed,
a howling n'oreaster is rushing o'er head
shaking our house, rattling locked door,
its angry voice shouting in a loud roar,
but what is it saying as it storms on by?
nobody knows, neither you nor I.
The wind comes blowing from far and near,
it's secret message is not ours to hear.

Marie Parker
DRUGS

This poem is dedicated to my husband Mitchell whose loving support has helped me through many trying times.

You take them at will
Though you know they can kill
You want to be high
Though you know you can die
I'm going to quit is what you say
Then pop a pill the very same day
If you only knew, If you could see
What these terrible drugs have done to me
My mind is burned, I'm paranoid
Because of the drugs with which I toyed
To tell you the truth, my friend
If I could do it all again
I know I wouldn't be so sure
To make my mind a constant blur
There is a lesson in this to tell
Ask me, I know it well.

Frances Elizabeth Colwell
LIBERACE
There has never been, and never will be another, Liberace
So I dedicate this poem, to you, Dear Liberace
The world was yours, to have and hold,
You had it all, the diamonds and gold.
You did it your way, that was true,
But the magic if it all, was really in you.
Something about your smile, tells it all,
One of a kind, as I recall.
You are a legend in your time, and a mystery, too.
The world will never forget your music and you.
You reached for the stars, as high as you could.
And took them all, like you knew you would.
Flamboyant, they say you were, that's true,
But, no other way would ever do.
Impossible, they said, but you did it even then,
You were the extraordinary, way back when.
Yes, we'll remember you, your music, too.
But a far better place you go, then you ever knew.
Liberace, we love you, we love you, we do,
Sleep sweet prince, may God bless you.
Our hearts will bleed, the tears will flow,
We lost a legend, may the curtain close.

Kim Hull
A DOG NAMED BOO
There once was a dog named Boo
Who always found gum to chew
He'd chew and he'd chew
Until he turned blue
And then he'd hide in the shoe

Ramona L Bluto
LOVE . . .?
Tell me do you know?
Tell me how does it show?
Love, the most mysterious word.
Is it a flower, a tree or bird
I don't think anyone can really say
But each person shows it in their own way
I try to show it to you, straight from my heart.
It came with the friendship, we shared from the start.
My friend for you
It will always be there
My friend for you
I'll always care.
Love is still a mysterious word
Love . . .?

Hattie J Pompa
YOUR FIRST STEP
I held you close against my heart,
Before I set you free,
I knew that you must learn to walk,
And yet it seemed to me
Your baby-days had been so short,
And time kept flying by . . .
I gently placed you on the floor,
I tried hard not to cry,
There was a smile upon my face,
Yet in my heart, I wept,
I set you free—you toddled off,
To take your own first step.

Mary Joan Dennis
BABY'S DAY GENTLY

For Adam

Twinkle toes ten and a barge floats by,
Shampoo and tears, Lo! Soap in the eye.
Washcloth and water, splashes galore,
Baby is bathing, both self and floor.

Soon yawns in the nighttime and sighings of sleep,
Close baby's day gently and foster dreams deep.
While I nod and I drift, my dimmed senses beguiled,
Baby stirs then is silent, God glanced o'r His child.

Diane Van Buren
A FLASH OF COLOR

With sincere thanks to Mrs. Clough

Across the lawn something looked different
Settling down against the midsummer night

I looked again
Hoping it would reveal itself to me—a friend

I peered at the sky
Trying to find an answer
When I came across a sunset
So full of color

It distracted me of any outsider
I was too busy peering
To bother with hearing
What any outsider said

I was wrapped up in my own little world
Gazing across the sky
Ready to strike anything that disrupted this picture
Or flew by!

I wanted to capture this scene always
'Cause I knew it would soon disappear

And then it did—
Without the twitch of an ear!

Walter E Schmitt
PATERNAL MISJUDGEMEMT
Happy days of childhood
O many they should be,
Father why do you sadden them,
And falsely punish me.

Home by five I should have been,
Though now it's after eight,
Father your not listening,
Let me tell you why I'm late.

Your anger transforms the truth I speak,
To excuses you don't want to hear,
Father the love I have for you,
Is slowly turning to fear.

I feel your wrath across my face,
Extending from your hand,
Malicious intent fills your eyes,
Tears of mine soften the land.

You say someday I will thank you,
It's all for my own good,
Excessive rage will save me,
From the perils of childhood.

Though sent to bed with hunger,
And a heart heavy and sad,
Father your only my father,
And no longer will I call you dad.

Teri Marquis
ABOUT PEARS: FOR ELLEN
Pears.
Their ruddy skins
are a dull gold
splotched with a dark wheat color.

They look like
a still-life painting
as they lay in the basket
on the table.
One sits straight up
and the other slightly tilted.

I look at them
and I think of mama
and how she never knew
that I drug that old mattress
from the garage and placed it
under that big pear tree
and jumped on the mattress
as high as I could
to reach those pears.

Pears are my favorite.
They have a sweet granule-like
taste

And they are shaped like mama
but she never knew.

Andrew Hu
HAPPINESS
Happiness is a feeling
That everyone can see.
They know that you're happy
When they see that you're free.

Pearl DuRoy Longberry
THE OLD WOOD STOVE
The wood stove sat in the parlor
grand,
its chrome polished bright.
Isinglass inserts in the huge iron
door
Showed the wood burning right.

There was a cozy corner to enjoy,
on a cold, cold night.
Warming our toes and our
backside too,
There wasn't much more for us
children to do.

During the night the fire burned
out,
waking in morning we'd shiver and
shout,
From cold bedroom and nice
warm bed,
"Get close to the stove" our Mother
said.
As Dad had made a fire in the early
morn,
The old stove once again was
warm.
Warming our clothes, we'd dress in
haste,
We never had a minute to waste.

Later in life, the old stove had to go,
Now a beloved antique,
But without warmth and glow.

Christine S Nesdoly
DISCOVERY
You are and one with mine—I
shared
those closets dark and old as
daylight
faded you were with me in the night
inviting me the same as I for you
and secret hiding places are no
more
my own
alone.
The meaning with a
sigh and eyes to
my uniqueness fosters
more and I am with you
as we glide away
through haze and light.
Dark contains our caring and we
freely
wander idle with a trace of
moonstream
playing songs of long time passing
rarely seen
beyond the curtain where the world
awaits our
coming.

Shirley L Miller
THE ANCIENT SONG
The ancient song my heart will sing
Of lotus blooms and temple bells,
Of golden days and velvet nights,
And pennies dropped in wishing
wells.

The ancient song my heart will
know
Of wishing on a falling star,
Of hanging up a horses' shoe,
And where the four-leaf clovers are.

The ancient song my heart will tell
Of standing in a fairy-ring,
Of wishing on a load of hay
And having touched a bluebirds'
wing.

The ancient song my heart will see
Of sunrise on the golden plain,
Of crimson sunsets on the shore,
And purple mountains in the rain.

Mary Frances Wambach Schnore

Mary Frances Wambach Schnore
PENNSYLVANIA'S GARDEN PATCH

This poem is dedicated to my family.

Come to Pennsylvania to see the
animals go by.
Deer, rabbits and pheasants
really fly.
Once here, you will want to stay
To watch the flowers bloom in
May.
When you have a garden at your
home
You will never be sad or alone.
You may have to hoe sometimes at
night
Just to help it grow alright.
There is no work that can compare
To giving your garden tender
loving care.
You never become too tired or
weary
Because you enjoy your garden
very dearly.
During summer you can drive all
over
To see beautiful large fields of
clover.
You can always hear the bluebird
as he sings
While you enjoy all the garden
things.
Come to see this beautiful land of
ours
With its delicious vegetables and
fancy flowers.
You can sit beneath the orchard
trees
And hear the humming birds
and honey bees.
Various gardens over the world are
lush
And thru the valleys the rivers do
gush,
But the productivity of
Pennsylvania's garden Patch
No other place in the world can
match.

Jeanine Shaner
LIFE'S LONELY HUNTER
I'm life's lonely hunter,
the one who walks the endless
roads.
I am the single footprints,
in the newly laid snow.
I'm life's lonely hunter,
with no place to call my home.
I am the lonely hunter,
with no one to call my own.

Jane E Smith
AN OLD MAN
WHERE DID THE CHILDREN
GO?
The swings are empty and the
slides gleam in the glow
Of sun against metal.
NO LAUGHTER IS HEARD
Only the distant chirp of a bird
breaks the silence in a land
where only toys lie in the sand.
An old man sits in a rocking chair
staring off into some time
That only he can remember where
the "used to be's" were yesterdays
And the cries of delight
Rang far into the night
As "kick the can" and catching
fireflies were part of the fun
of just being on the run.
Glorious, lazy, crazy days
of just being young
And a tear rolls down the cheek
Of one whose been in this home
one week.
And I'd like to take a minute
For me, there's really nothing in
it.
EXCEPT, to maybe let the swings
swing again
And teeter-totters do their thing
and children sing
And just for awhile, Bring it all
back again.

Linda D Glass
STRANGERS
Peace be unto you, Friend
I pass you unnoticed,
I may or may not touch you:
If I do you will not feel.

The noise of the world
Holds your attention
Beyond my small ability
To really reach you.

Drums beat, differently for each of
us . . .
Survival exacts different prices.
We pass, perhaps pause,
But inevitably move on to our
separate destinies.

Dan L Clark
DESERT TEAR DROPS
Heart broken tear drops fall on a
desert floor,
The amimals are watching,
wondering, why this comes
forth.
Long lonely highway stretches
cross the floor
filled with all the tear drops from
heart broken hauls.
Are we all just reptiles that hide our
cold
blooded claws? Or, is there
something better
in this heart broke desert haul?

Ailene Travillian
OUR ORDER OF EASTERN STAR

Written especially to a new member

We all start with the same
principles
When we join the Eastern Star;
And it is with the best of people
You can find both near and far . . .

What you will receive from our
order
Will be in the interest you show,
Add your interest to our principles
And watch your dividends
grow . . .

Your dividends will be in the lovely
people
That will greet you, where ever
you are,
You can find pleasure that is
beyond measure
IN OUR ORDER OF EASTERN
STAR . . .

You see, what you will receive from
it
Will be in the interest that you
show,
Add all that interest to our
principles
And watch your dividends
grow . . .

M Jean Lytle
MY DISTANT DREAMS
My distant dreams, they seem so
real,
My soul they always touch,
Influencing the way I feel,
These dreams I cherish so much.

A well-known author, I will be,
And fame will be mine to hold,
Just to have a place in history,
And to children, my stories be told.

To prove to myself and others,
That a success I really can be,
To satisfy my distant dreams,
And show everyone the real me.

But, time is my problem and it's
sad to say
in these days of hardship and strife,
That we all seem too busy making
a living,
to really make our own life.

So, I'll study and work as hard as
I can,
and hang on to my plans and
schemes,
and perhaps in the not too
far-away future,
I will be living my distant dreams.

Norma Girouard
CHILD IN MY ARMS

This poem is dedicated to my dear friend, Alice Smith Shaw

Bring me a child to hold in my arms—
I have a longing for a child in my arms;
It seems the nearest answer,
The one true sense,
The only reality of recompense
For every heartbreak, for every plight,
For every terror that fills our night.
God knew it would be so—
That would have a need to know
Of some small miracle to nurture our thoughts,
Of some small hope to gladden our hearts;
One small, shining, lovely thing
That would let our souls grow,
And make our lives sing.
I have found it to be
The sweetest blessing for me,
The comforting balm for all my alarms—
Oh, bring me a child to hold in my arms!

F L Braxton
JESUS

For my mother, Alice, who ultimately is responsible for all this

Jesus, Jesus, my Savior to thee,
I always want you here with me.
From day one, I knew I had found
A true way safe and sound.
It isn't hard to do good, especially
When Jesus is good to you.
So, lets run with Jesus to and fro
And not the Devil down below.

Leon Muller
ABOLISH WAR

Dedicated to Ernst and Matilda Muller, my loving parents.

From my veteran perspective
the message of war is peace.
My life is most effective
when war thoughts cease.

Carole Messenger
TEARS
Tears flowing gently down the cheek
The silent cry heard from "within"
Mirrored in the face of loneliness
A soul; where love has never been.

Sue Hilbrant-Potter
THE REST
There was a night . . . . I could not sleep
I had a dream that made me weep.
There was saddness all around and such despair
Everywhere I went, no one cared.
I wanted to scream out, "Hey, look at me!"
But no one noticed . . . . how could this be?
The colors that surrounded were grays and black
I would talk to people but they wouldn't talk back.
Such remorse I saw in everyones' eyes
It saddened me so, and I wanted to cry.
Each one passed by slowly, with a cross on his back.
It must have been a symbol for something they lacked.
I wished I could help them with their pain and sorrow,
They need not worry, there's always tomorrow.
Whatever they had done, they could make right
If they would show love, instead of spite.
I wanted to tell them, they were loved the best
But then the lid closed . . . . and they laid me to rest.

Karen Newton Curtiss
A COUNTRY GIRL'S WONDER
I sigh,
not for a grievance, sorrow, or misfortune
but for the world beyond me.
Maybe it is not a wonderful world
so much as a world full of wonder.
The wonder of known cities, times, and dates,
A wonder I know naught of.

I sigh,
Woe is me, the farm girl,
I who hear the cock crow at morn
and ever smile sadly into the sunset.
I, who watch as the corn grows tall
and live all the joys of the country.
Am I one to wonder at the world
and become of the world?

I sigh,
So much has lately been in my mind
of countries, places, and times
and I stay simple and naive
while I stay here in this country, my country.

The sun is rising.
The beauty fills me so I can only gaze in wonder.
Did I say wonder?
but does the sun not rise out there
in the world beyond
and fill those who watch with wonder
of the world, the wonderful world,
a world full of wonder,
And do they not sigh, too?

Mary M Gnolfo
WAITING
This feeling that my life is destined for something more
Than just a common living like everyone before.
Is it some deep unconscious knowledge, a hidden driving force,
Or just another ego trip to cause me more remorse.

I want a simple living, maybe easy is the word;
But I feel if I strived harder, my voice could finally be heard.
There's so many injustices that need to be put to end,
So many people that just need a friend
To help them go on living, to help them see a goal,
And here I am just contemplating, right on the threshold!

Jean E Allen
THUNDER IN THE SNOW
Rain, sleet, snow—and the wind did blow
The day it thundered in the snow.
The wind whistled and moan-groaned through the trees
And thunder grumble-rumbled above the leaves.
The sounds, now together, now apart, played a fearful tune.
"Not my leaves! Don't take my leaves! Oh, not so soon!"
The trees did cry, fighting back against the wind.

It should have been Indian Summer, but it wasn't quite.
The mid-October day was quite a fright.
One poor tree which sheltered me from summer's sun
Lost a proud limb to the wind's cruel fun.
Snow, rain, then snow again, taking turns they did come
Down from the thundering skies. Always there was some
Wind to whirl-swirl the drops and flakes about.
A threat of the winter to come was aflaunt
The day it thundered in the snow.

Margaret T McGarry
LOVE FOR MOVING PICTURES
My first love was the movies,
Since I was a tiny tot,

By ten, I scrounged the dimes,
To view every creative plot.

My early teens, the price had tripled,
Though my income, sadly not.
Baby-sitting after school,
Provided the price a lot.

Early twenties, be first to see the show,

Was a highly regarded spot.

Thirties, treasured oldies on TV,
during appropriate time slot,
Re-viewed with enlightened mind,
Life experience, had released the clot.

Forties, nudity and violence,
Presented a hopeless botch.

Fifties, so many solutions provided,
For every problem families have got.

Cecil L Nunes
THE FLOWER
A flower grows on the desert,
And blossoms wildly at the sun,
Unseen by the passing sheepherder,
Unseen by the wandering nomad,
Described by me,
But noticed by none . . .

A flower grows on the plain,
And blossoms wildly at the sun,
Unseen by the passing horseman,
Unseen by the wandering cow,
Described by me,
But noticed by none . . .

A flower grows in the field,
And blossoms wildly at the sun,
Unseen by the playing child,
Unseen by the wandering dog,
Described by me,
But noticed by none . . .

A flower grows on a sill,
And blossoms wildly at the love,
A smiling old lady,
A dingy old city,
Described by me,
But loved by one . . .

Lois J Patterson
BEYOND THE GRAVE
Everywhere I go I still see his face,
I know that he is out there somewhere.
Why does his life seem like such a waste?
I can hear him call me from beyond the grave.

When I think of him I shed a quiet tear,
I just cannot believe that he is gone.
At times I just want him to be back here.
I can hear him call me from beyond the grave.

His life seems to have gone so wrong.
He was just a kid, not quite seventeen,
He really had not lived all that long,
But I can hear him call me from beyond the grave.

The crash of metal, the tinkle of glass,
It's coming back all too clearly now.
Seventeen years gone in one great crash.
I can hear him call me from beyond the grave.

I really should have been the one to die.
The doctors aren't at all sympathetic.
They say I'm lucky just to be alive,
But I can hear him call me from beyond the grave.

Why am I lucky? My brother is dead.
How can I go on without his smile?
The crash and tinkle echo in my head,
But I can still hear him call me from beyond the grave.

Velma J Croy
BILLS
From the day you are born, until you die,
Bills are with you for ever more,
Bills you can never do with out,
Bills for this and bills for that,
Bills, bills and more bills.

Bills for the food you buy,
Bills for the clothes you wear,
Bills for pills to keep you alive,
Bills for the Doctor you see,
Bills, bills and more bills.

Bills for the taxes you pay,

Bills for the telephone you use,
Bills for the Hospital, when your
sick,
Bills for the fuel, that heats the
house,
Bills, Bills and more bills.

Now these bills, I'd like to get rid of,
But Jo say, the bills you must keep,
I'll bet when trying to file them,
These bills, She would like to
heave,
For there's Bills, Bills and more
BILLS.

Jenny Thompson
I HAVE A DREAM

To my teacher who loved poetry so much, Mrs. Betty Best, who now watches from Heaven.

I would like to live at the beach.
Then I will need a horse to ride.
I'll ride my horse to Grandma's
house.
and we will talk by the fireside.

Pop-Pop and I will go fishing.
Maybe we will catch a flounder or
two.
Then I will ride back to my beach
house
and share my fish with you.

Arlene S Bredfield
DAY UNTO NIGHT

Dedicated to my godchild Diana

Morning mist caressed the trees
Dampened blades of grass
Streaks of sunlight peeking
through
Reflecting dew like glass
Brilliant, colorful flowers awake
Petals wide and proud
Wakening sparrows chirping away
Sandpipers scurrying about
Squirrels rushing up the mighty
oak
Nesting their new-found prey
Nearby swirling, cool clear waters
Illusions of blue and gray
Day goes on, nighttime nears
Shadows began to appear
Flickering patterns of heavenly
stars
Romantic creations adhere
A blanket of stillness covers all
Nary soft, gentle breeze is heard
The beautiful serenity of silence
Not a sound, not a word.

Lucille Downing
WE CALL HER ARIES

Dedicated to our Beloved Missy, in dog Heaven.

When we had first seen her,
that day in '85,
We wondered what she was
and could she be alive,
My daughter found her in the alley
behind our house,
You might not believe this but she
wasn't much larger than a
mouse.
She was a bedraggled specimen,
but such a loving creature.
She was examined by a Vet, and
bathed
and behold as pretty as any
picture.
She learned her name
in a few short hours,
The way she took to us
we knew she was ours.
It is now two years
since that day,
and I can assure you
our beautiful dog is ours to stay.

Tammy S Birch
MY DAYS ARE NUMBERED

You cannot hear the voice I hear,
nor see the hand I see.
The voice that says I can not stay
and that I shall not be.

The time to die is growing near,
The dark becoming black.
The days of sun and happiness
are now upon my back.

The arms of death are closing nigh
and darkness circles near.
I stand straight, tall and brave,
for I have not one fear.

My days are numbered one by one,
like pages of a book.
I shall remember joyful times and
times I had to brook.

I wish I would have had the time
to do the things I vow.
The rays that land upon my grave
are brightly shining now.

Paula Gifford
THE SEA AND ME

I live by the sea
And what do I hear,
But the sea smashing near
In the dark, and I fear.

I don't know how I live
With the sea next to me;
With the waves battering my
House and me,
But the sea lives next to me.

It keeps tracking me down,
And spinning me round,
A fox with a hound,
Baying next to me.

Jeanette Warren
DOWN ON THE FARM

The barn roof leaked
When it rained today
It really don't matter
We've run out of hay

The cow's gone dry
The hens won't lay
The corn in the silo
Gets lower each day

The mule went lame
So I can't plow
Can't fix the old tractor
Cause I dn't know how

Both kids are sick
I'm down with the flu
"Hey Chief" who said?
The Navy needs you

Got a letter from welfare
In the mail today
Best thing to do
Is just move away

There's jobs in Florida
So they report
By the way honey
Just where is Mayport?

So leave that ole carrier
Out in the sea
take a plane, bus or train
Come on home to me

Elizabeth R Hernandez
THE CITY

The ugly city of today
degraded, degrading a misery
place;
Children crowded, hidden away
TV the curse of the city race.

The pavement jungle where youth
play
The alley where polluters stay;
Parks where nature refreshed the
soul
now a place where crime takes
its toll.

City children, no chores to do
no stimuli for intellectual view;
just TV, sex and murder too
good example for only a few.

Garbage cans and broken cement
symbolic of the marijuana bent;
broken windows, graffiti walls
fowl language on toilet walls.

No place for the mind to hide
loud noise its only pride;
the smell of rotten city air
reflects the corruption of those
living there.

The feel of being dirty and cheap
prostitutes, gamblers, alderman
all reap;
urban violence the gun and knife
Is there a symbol of Divine Life?

Shae Rohrer
SOLEMN FLIGHT

To "Grandma Neena"

A hawk glides gently above a cloud
Upon the wind without a single
sound

Mountains loom below the sky
Their sunlit peaks shine so bright

A stream runs quickly through the
trees
Along its path blows a pleasant
breeze

A twig may break or bird may sing
And sweet smells alone do flowers
bring

The snowflakes fall and raindrops
glisten
As animals stop and quieltly listen

The seasons bring such a wealthy
treasure
Their sights and sounds are such a
pleasure

Always may we treat their beauty
with care
And forever its beautiful growth
will share

Belinda Wingo Quarles
GUIDANCE

Lord, as you look down on me
tonight
I pray for your guidance to do this
right
You gave me children to nurture
and raise,
You gave me a warm heart full of
love and grace
If I should stumble or become
misled
I will not worry for these words you
said,
"I've given you knowledge,
wisdom, and truth
So why my child do you still need
proof."

Karen E Songhurst-Hume
SOON LOVE

Soon love . . .
Soon there will be time to love you;
time to lie with you all night,
to rise with you in the morning.

Just time . . .
heavenly, sweet time;
and you.

Connie V Clevidence
I BELIEVE

When life is passing you by
and you are filled with doubts,

As to who you are and what
you hope to achieve,

Just turn around and face
the world head on,

For you are everything that
you believe.

And all those high hopes and
childhood
dreams you've had right from the
start,

They give your life its' reasons,
so never let those dreams depart.

And so my friend as you will find,
it's not important what we hope to
achieve,

But what we have become to one
another;
that is what I believe . . .

Elsie Jeannette Krause

Elsie Jeannette Krause
HORSEMAN'S HEAVEN

To Charles

Are the good old horsemen there
with you
And are the horses sleek and fast?
Do they graze in lush green
pastures
Free from starting gates at last?

Do the barns smell sweet with
clover,
Sunlight streaming through the
door?
Are you content stroking soft
muzzles?
Dear heart, I could never wish you
more.

June W Takatch
MELODIES OF JUNE

Ah, June, sweet June—romance
and bliss;
A silvery moon, a stolen kiss.
Roses scent the morning air.
Bird song is everywhere.
Bees are buzzing here and there,
Taking sips
From flower tips.

Take care,
Or you'll scare
The hummingbird away.
A delightful June day;
Violets to pick for a sweet bouquet.
Ah, June, sweet June—her sunny smiles;
She woos us with her enchanting wiles.

Shirley Jean Dubay
HOW FAR

How far from the jungle has been our arduous journey . . .
Through the millenniums of years . . .
From chiseled stones and spears dipped in curare death . . .
To atoms split into a thousand fears . . .
Still, we war and kill and look away . . .
From rape, pillage and old folks tears . . .
How far up from the primal mist . . .
A millimeter . . . or less . . .

Alice M Rosser
DEJECTION

I am but a lowly earthworm,
Squirming to escape the deadly heels of humanity.
For I have yet to learn
That I am naught but victim of my fellow man.

James E Meyer
WHATSOEVER YOU DO

I'd see him there most every day,
Standing on the street,
In baggy suit and battered hat,
Scuffed shoes upon his feet.

I'd listen as he played a tune,
Sad thoughts would come to mind,
Of how he'd come to be this way,
The fiddler man was blind.

His vacant eyes they seemed to say,
"Grieve not for me my son,
For Jesus meant these things to be,
His kingdom I have won."

Though I no longer see him,
Those memories still remain,
I wonder if that old violin,
Now praises Jesus' name.

Now that my time on earth has come,
And at death's gate I stand,
I see that same old fiddler man,
Stretching forth his hand.

"Come dwell within my kingdom,
For you were meek and kind,
And showed me your compassion,
When you saw me blind!"

Patricia J MacNeil
FAITH RENEWAL

Easter Sunday dawned cold and clear,
As the multitudes climbed to the hills,
Not seeming to notice
The hint of winter still.
To see the glory of the sunrise
To sing their praises,
To rejoice with their Lord
In the Psalms they sing,
Their prayers for peace and love all mankind;
Each rejoicing in their faith of being born again,
Letting HIM know HE has not died in vain.

Jody S Lester
SO THERE COULD BE NO OTHER

This poem is dedicated to Okey, my loving husband.

I love you more than yesterday
I love you more each day,
You, have been the best to me,
In each and every way.

So there could be no other.

So every day I pray
That we will love each other,
Until our dying day.
So there could be no other.

As fine a man as you,
You are as great a father
As you are husband to me
From now until eternity.

So there could be no other
For our Son and Me.

Tina M Moyer
HIM

To my loving husband, Bill

I know the pain of too much tenderness, that lies within the path behind us.
I know that love is hard to hold, but' its there and will never go.
Year's have come and gone,
Chapters have been erased.
Affection fixed, like a rock in the stream.
And the stone becomes smoother with time.
The rainbow follows, until cannot take.
Our love is strong, and cannot be replaced.
For it is us who make our lives so complete
Because, no one can ever take your place.

Donna H Citak
DAYDREAMING

To my Mom and Dad for giving me the encouragement to explore my talents.

Down by the seaside
Catching a breeze.
Watching the waves roll by.
Footsteps in the sand.
Walking hand in hand.
Watching the gulls fly by.
The sun is bright.
The wind is warm.
Seashells are everywhere.
The beach is always beautiful.
I wish I could be there.
Instead I'm sitting behind a desk caught in the working scene.
I hope the next hot sunny day.
My thoughts aren't just a dream.

Justin Timothy Howe
SNOW FIGHT

Playing in the snow is so much fun
Boy how much I hate the sun.
My friends and I build forts in the snow
Throw snow balls and play GI Joe.
It was fun until the sun came out
And melted our forts and made us want to shout.
I'd like to get myself a gun
And take a shot at that old sun.
I'd challenge him to a duel
Because now I must go back to school.

Anne K Riddle
OUR TWO LITTLE BOYS

To Ryan & Jared

We have two small boys
And, oh what joy
They bring into our hearts.
They are fun to be around
Always climbing up and down,
Amazing us from morning until night.
The air is full of laughter
And it is only after
They are put in bed at night
And we turn off the light
That we realize how sad
We would be without these lads,
And how thankful for their lives we really are.
With each new day that goes by
We sit and wonder why
Our hearts are blessed so fully
By these precious little fellas.
Then we turn to God and say,
"Please guide us every day."
Because as parents we realize
They see life through our eyes.

Florence H Burkett
STEPPING STONES

To be dedicated to Elsie Katherine Killday

Life is like stepping stones along the winding roads.
Special little places to pause and just stand still.

To look back over years gone by and think of memories, joys, tears and smiles.

We now leave the past behind us and start out anew,
And count our age by friends, not years.

Dolores Mitchell
ETERNAL FLAME

The light is dimming slowly.
The lamp of our land is burning low.
What will rekindle the flame before dying?

Why in vain do we search for—the answer?
In the twilight it never will show,
just look at the light all around us.
The flame of our eternal God will know.

Theda Dowdy Ward
IT'S GREAT TO BE AN AMERICAN

To the memory of my father, Richard, a great American and humanitarian.

"It's great to be an American,"
Shouts the man from the great Northwest
Where mountains with their snowcapped peaks
Hide the great bald eagle's nest.

Says the grizzled old Western miner
With his pack strapped on his mule,
"It's great to be an American,
Where all of the people rule."

"It must be great to live in America,"
Our visitors from abroad will say,
As they roam the fields at Gettysburg
Amid the smell of new mown hay.

"It's great to be an American,"
Chants the 'Old Miss' riverboat crew
As they pass the Delta cotton fields
And head for the great Bayou.

From the Smokeys to the Everglades
All the folks in the South agree,
"It is great to be an American
In the home of the brave and free."

Evelyn Dawn Hughes
THE AWAKENING

Eve, deep in sleep, on bed of down,
Drifts through dream . . . wears wedding gown.
From distant hills, comes monstrous roar
That echoes once, then thrice upon the door
Of sleep. 'Tis time for the awakening—the hour:
To bargain dream for Morning's scented flower;
To welcome the filtering, chrystalline light
That fingers through her leafy bower to her delight;
To rise and bathe in the shaded pool where waterfall
And time have carved a basin in the rocky wall.
And thus refreshed, she turns whence perfume blows,
Her senses keen, through brier and leaf, she seeks the rose,

Only to sigh that one so beauteous must bare a hidden thorn,
But then to whisper, "Come Song, I am woman born."
From many options, she must choose a face to wear;
With it so done, she combs and parts her silken hair,
Revealing chosen face for hungry eyes to feast,
She calls softly to the stuttering beast
Who comes on winged feet, his roaring now has ceased.
With spider's floss, she spins a fragile thread
Which she entwines, with loving

hands, around her monster's head,
And man, now silenced and wearing foolish grin—
Perplexed by what is happening to him—
Stands helplessly fettered by a flimsy string.

Darla Grothe
GET UP! GET UP!
Get up! Get up!
Get out of bed.
Brush your teeth,
And scrub your head.
Get your books,
And off to school,
Get your homework,
that's the rule,
Go to the lunchroom,
eat their food.
Go outside without,
Being rude.
When the bell rings,
Go to class.
Do some more work
And hope you pass!!!

Laura Vinger
ALTERNATIVE
If silence could go on forever,
Then maybe the hurt from within would cease.
The mind has some fearful answers.
The answer to every question seems so simple,
and yet . . .
There is one thing that keeps simpleness from taking shape.
Hope.
It comes from deep inside this castle of pain and anguish.
Hope is all I've found to keep the answer from appearing.
The intensity of insecurity nags at the strings of my heart.
Fearfully I realize the answer is the only way.

William Lee McAdam
TEMPLE

To the eradication of complication.

Guard your thoughts and keep life simple.
May every thought stay in its temple.

Joyce Oliveira
DARKNESS
Darkness is where I love to be
My enriching fulfillment of tranquility
A place where one can always see the light
One can never see a war or fight
One can always feel;
The sense which is most real
To many it is a place of great mystery
To me it is the ultimate discovery
A time for deep reflection
For bright, new inspiration
A place where I'd love to remain
Where one can suddenly feel so sane
Yes, Darkness is where I love to be
My enriching fulfillment of tranquility

Sherry Murphree
COLD
coldness penetrates my soul
and leaves me
frozen in time and space
unable to receive warmth

artifical outward heat
cannot reach my interior ice
to thaw my dying spirit

only the power of love
can melt the solid mass
of my isolated, breaking heart
sealed in a lonely vacumn

then and only then
will I be free
of the unbearable cold
free to live and not die

Grace L Joyner
THE WATER IS COOL

Inspired from above, encouraged by my parents and brothers, whom I love.

Sand burns beneath my feet
because of wrong
and I run 'cross
pieces of broken shells
to make the water.
wading where it's cool
yet seaweed catches me
bound by ankle
turquoise twine untangled,
dive generously
as waves rock
shaking my senses
free from misdeed.
in drenching water
the ocean stretches on
beyond sight
calling me to swim
lengths far off
'cause the water is cool
the water is cool.

Sandra Sleeper
DEATH AWAITS
Creatures of the night, tremor
As a predator steals silently through.
Unknowing eyes tremble
Waiting for their demise . . . true.

Hidden in a murky swamp,
Sucking on a lifeless corpse.
Hideous fangs and gnarly claws
Tearing with tremendous force.

Those who fall upon its' lair
Their bones will twine a pattern of lace.
But, those who take heed and reroute their travels,
Will avoid the Black Rose and this place.

Anna Gabriel Holtzman
WHY?
What is our purpose and why do we live?
What did we come into the world to give?
Why is the sky blue? Why is there sun?
Why has the world even begun?
All of these questions come and they go,
But never the answer cause only God knows.

Joyce F Divver
THE CALLING
My heart is exuberant,
My eyes they fall,
For I feel the remnant
Of His immortal call.

"Come follow me."
These words linger on
Never ceasing to be
Until I answer . . . I've come.

Donald G Westlake
CLIPPINGS
Success was always hers in hand;
Her talent matched her charm and grace.
To hear her voice was something grand,
As was the glow upon her face.
Her clippings filled thick albums—yet,
For Hildie, dreams were unfulfilled.
To her, the lines of age were threat;
Her lust for youth could not be stilled.
On Christmas Eve, her family slept
While Hildie leaves of yellow scanned
In search of something she'd accept
As proof she'd reached the heights she planned.
The obit didn't mention why
This beauty chose so young to die.

Joyce Utne
MY HUSBAND
Robbed of love.
Overheated of sun.
Beyond the feelings untold
Energy of your deep compassion
Ready to unfold.
To me a unique mold.

Around the blessings of your kindness
Run through the snow, to feel it's cold.
To melt the ice, my love flows warm.
Hand in hand, my only rose.
Under the trees, we feel love grow.
Round the waters, sea of love foams.

Untested love, but our knowledge roams.
Together our mystery's are shown.
Now past history, like the wind moans.
Enough for you, enough for me, forever in eternity.

Georgette A Payne
FINAL DAYS OF A PREGNANT WOMAN
Today I'll clean my house again
And defrost the freezer too,
I'll do four loads of laundry
As usually, I do.
I'll wash the mess of dishes
That lay within my sink
And after all this work is done,
I have my time to think.
I think of all my early days
before I got so fat,
When I could enjoy myself so much
Just doing this or that.
But now I need help to get up
and help to sit back down.
I can't lift heavy things too much
or move too much around.
To hug my husband's quite a task
And so I hardly do
I try to do the best I can . . .
But my best feels rotten too!

Curtis Bowman
THERE'S NO CHANCE FOR THE CATALPA
When cantilevered layers of the catalpa tree
Shower the early blue night with orchids,
Speckled-white, perfuming the grassy pathway
As they daub the earth in drop-like heaviness,
Spreading fragrant peace of a summer's eve,
The night creatures among bush and branch drink
Gratefully of the honeyed air, clicking,
Beating a soft tattoo in secret safeholds,
While the myrtle freezes its absorbent green,
And daisies nod their moonbright heads.

Now the glaring roar of headlights rushes by,
And stops, and waits, put-put-puttering,
For the red light to change,
And beams upon garbage sacks that boast
In metallic bulkiness: "We're here to stay,
Shiny, strong-scented, too,
While the orchids must fade and wait
'Til next year to spread their perfume."

There's no chance for the catalpa!

Jennifer D Berkey
DIAMONDS IN THE SAND
In the
evening
as the
summer
sun is
setting
by the
lake I
stand,
listening,
feeling,
watching
the diamonds
in the
sand.
The sun
reflects
its light
on the
sand,
glistening,
gleaming,
shining
diamonds
in the
sand.

Judy Dowell
WHERE HAVE MY TOMORROWS GONE
I look around at faces I no longer know —
The babies when I left home now have babies of their own —
Where have my tomorrows gone?

Friends and loved ones bodies lay in their graves growing cold,
Their souls have now reached their final goal.
Where have my tomorrows gone?

My boys are grown and will soon be leaving home —
I was blessed with a little girl so I'd not grow old alone.
Where have my tomorrows gone?

I looked in a mirror, my hair is a silvery gray —
A tear softly flows down my face, I gently brush it away.
Where have my tomorrows gone?

My body's growing feeble and my health is almost gone —
I know now I'm just a breath away to where my tomorrows have gone.

Becky Ostrzycki
THE CHRISTIAN'S PILLOW
Beyond my tear-stained face, I see
The Will of God revealed to me.
With a pillow wet beneath my head,
I now can see the way He's led.
For He who loves my soul so much
Has calmed my fears with His gentle touch.
The path before my eyes unfolds
With beauty—more than jewels or gold.
Though the end of life I cannot see—
With joy I'll say, "His way's for me."
I've fumbled in my own self will,
Having no power my doubts to still.
But when I move by faith in Him,
My days grow bright—no longer grim.
Each step He leads, I'll follow on,
Despite rebuke or other's frown!
For I alone His will must know
And answer as He bids me go.
And when questions rise through Satan's snares,
I'll seek sweet shelter with earnest prayers;
Remembering always as I face each test,
That my only pillow is Jesus' breast.

Linda D Griffith
THE SINGER
Singer sing your song again, sing it one more time;
Singer do you remember when I use to call you mine?
You were the one they were cheering for, but now the cheering's stopped.
Singer you must face it now, you are no longer at the top.

The lights are dim, the stage is bare,
There are no longer people standing out there.
You were the one they were cheering for,
But as time went on they closed that door.

Another chance you must now take—
To get up and sing, and hope for that break.
You close your eyes and you remember when,
They were all cheering for you; why did it have to end?

A love song is played; tears hit your face,
Are you remembering now my warm embrace?
You chose the crowd over me;
And you asked me to set you free,
So I walked away and had few regrets,
And what you're trying to remember, I'm trying to forget.

So singer sing your song again, sing it one more time,
Singer are you remembering when I use to call you mine?
You are the one they are cheering for, but now My cheering has stopped,
'cause singer I never stopped believing; To me you were always on top.

Kathleen Miller
FLOWERS WITH MEMORIES

This poem is dedicated to our lovely children Douglas, Steven, and Phyllis, Who have brought us so much joy and happiness

---

As I strolled through the yard of the old home place
And looked at the flowers mother planted there,
Each one of her flowers, they seemed to say
How they missed her, day after day.
And the smile that she wore on her lovely face.

Then I walked into her room, it was filled with memories
with the flowers she had left for me, mom's tear stained
Bible she had read through the years,
The old hymn book, she and dad loved so dear.

I can see the family, like we used to kneel and pray,
Each word was inspiring, dad and mother would say
Someday God will lace them in heavens bouquet,
There to live forever and their beauty won't decay.

These flowers with memories are so dear to me,
Mother's tear stained Bible that gives me light to see
When the storm clouds gather and dark seems the way,
She always taught me, to stop, kneel down and pray.

Walter C Johannes
AFRICA
Starvation stalks the country,
Skeletons scattered o'er the ground.
Mothers hold their hapless infants,
who can't whisper or utter a sound.
Disease has taken over, death deals a heavy blow,
While mothers cry in anguish,
As they see their children go.
"God, oh God have mercy, have mercy," is their plea.
"God, oh God please help us," as they wallow in misery.
And, the World aroused in pity,
Sends aid while people wait.
Will it be a timely arrival, or will it be too late?

Bernie M Parker
DANCE PUPPET DANCE
Once the puppet heard a drummer
far off in the distant hills,
Harps and flutes were in the background
But, the drum made time stand still.

Trumpets sounded louder than trombones
and the strings of Violins,
But, the drummer beating different
tuned the puppet from within.

Then the puppet tried to follow
to the drummer's different call
But, he was pulled in all directions
and he finally took a fall.

As his masters tugged his strings
he would struggle to his feet,
He was told, "Dance, Puppet, Dance,
until we tell you when you can quit."

Broken strings and jerky motions
are sad attempts of retreat,
of a broken-hearted puppet
Who can't follow the tune of a drummer's beat.

Dance, Puppet, Dance!
As one day soon you shall find
That the only way of stopping
is by running out of time.

Granddaughter

Eleanor Bernardo
GRANDDAUGHTER
My Granddaughter is grand
Grand as can be

She is a delight
a light to see
that everything is all right with me,

She makes my life meaningful
and plentiful you see
which is all right with me.

She see's the world as beautiful
as beautiful as she is,
and the whole world is just right
right as can be,
Which makes me feel all right
Which is all right you see,

Just a message from a Grandmother
to her Grandaughter dear.

Nano Mounir Bibi
WINTER

I dedicate this poem to my dearest cousin Shirine Bazzi.

Autumn is gone and winter is here,
The children are making snowmen in the fields.
I sit near my window and imagine
The deers flying like birds in Spring.

Becky Fry
HOW ABOUT YOU
The sun rose this morning,
The sky turned blue
When I told my friends to watch it
They said:
"What's wrong with you?
We can see a sun
Any time of day,
Just pop a few pills
And fly away.
We can take a trip
And never leave the ground.
We can hear things
When there is no sound."
My reply was:
"My sun and sky cost no money.
They are both true.
They don't mess up my mind.
How about you?"

Constance L Kirkland (Dowling)
MY LADY FAIR
You are always on my mind, where ever I may go,
Your radiance reminds me of, a beautiful winter's snow.
The softness of the snowflake, reminds me of your love,
The love that God has sent me, straight from above.

I'm so glad that I have found you, you are my everything,
Without your love beside me, what sadness it would bring.
Hand and hand we'll walk together, now and ever more,
And what beautiful surprises, we will have in store.

Your kisses are so sweet, they knock me off my feet,
And then your hug's "OH WOW", I wish I had one now.
Just everything about you, is so very, very dear,
I wish that I could always, have you very near.

The time I spend without you, is time I feel alone,
I feel that I'm a rock, or just a stepping stone.
But with you by my side, I walk on golden air,
Because I'm with my lady, my beautiful lady fair.

Kenneth (Ken) R Beckmann
THE OCEAN

To Ginny Weber and L.C. Vail who are true examples of the words love and friendship.

The sound of the ocean, is the only sound we hear as we walk along together, in our silence.
Oh Father your creation now we see,
With it's waves of love, let it overpower me.

May we your humble people, be the streams
Filling your ocean, with our love.
As the sun sets on this beautiful day,
In my mind forever let it stay,
For a more precious gift you could not have given me,
Than to walk along together in the sand.

Dear Jesus let us spend this time we share, in listening may it be our special prayer,
May I never forget how much you love me,
In those times I seem to blind to see.

The moon has broken through the
clouds of darkness,
Shedding it'slight for all to see,
May our lives be the stars,
Through which your light shines,
To bring compassion and love to
all the world.

The sound of the ocean, is the only
sound we hear
As we walk along together in our
silence.
Oh Father your creation now we
see,
With it's waves of love
Let it overpower me.

Raymond M Mancini

HOW DO I?

How do I keep from hurting; and
keep from hurting you,
How do I keep my heart from
breaking, before it breaks in
two?
How do I stop the poison I speak,
before it reaches you
How do I mend your broken heart,
after the words ripped through?
All I can say is, "I'm sorry" and
know, "I love you too",
And try to understand the pains I
feel, before I do what I do.
If only words could be taken back
after they've been said
I'd take all the hurting ones and
leave loving ones instead!!
So please understand when I say
that you're everything to me,
And I wish I could show you
exactly the person I see,
And don't ever think my heart
could change, after some things
I do
Because I know you're the best you
could be; and that's all I could
ask of you.

Tina Dempsey

WHETTING YOUR APPETITE

Surging waves
quench the simmering beaches
of day,
Jostling scorched pebbles—
whirling them away!
From thrusting force
comes rippling froth;
Atomizer of
mist aloft.
Shores heed
the sensual breeze,
Of whispers casting
off high seas.
There,
Unto palates
perceiving of brine,
Savor the harmony
from ocean soul.

Angela Michele Wieneke

EVEN THE GOOD MEMORIES ARE BAD

Out my window I sat watching
into the distant night
across the fields of sleeping daisies,
alone I felt my fright.
It occurred to me while dreaming
of all the good times we had
tainted visions flashed thru my
mind,
even the good memories are bad.

A simple act of giving love
for you my soul to take
over the years my heart was lifted,
then smashed to the ground to
break.
While reminiscing once again
I ultimately became sad
to realize now your heart was
missing,
and that even the good
memories are bad.

In my pocket I felt a coin
something you left behind
across the lake I watched it sink,
into forgotten time.
And as I recall now waking,
all the tears and fears, I'm glad
it's so much easier to forget you
now,
since even the good memories
are bad.

Robert Farr

AN OLD MAN'S DREAM

Now you think about love
To quench an ache which can only
be satisfied
Only by doing
What you are dreaming about

You make symbols out of these
images which dance in your
mind
Giving shape
Burning brighter in the soul
As the fire dies in the body

But life is meant to be lived
By longing
By pushing your being into
becoming
What cannot be

Passion chooses that which
becomes a part of you
Love is the thing
Truth and beauty now the same
As truth is sacrificed for beauty's
sake

Nadine L Linscott

MY PROMISE

To Mike, the most important person in my life.

Just seeing you there makes
my eyes sparkle.
You fill me with so much
love and joy.

You are my whole world,
And if I lost you it
would all crumble down
around me.

If you love me, you'll never
leave me.
I promise you, I'll always
be with you.

I could never make it on
my own.
I need you to keep going on.

You give me strength
and you give me hope.
You give me everything
I'll ever need.

Love, happiness, hope and
courage, to face tomorrow
and all the days now and
forever.

So stay with me
And I'll stay with you.
And I promise our hearts
will stay together.

D A Norwood

I'D CHOOSE YOU

To Mary Louise and Roner Augustine, for believing in me and to Stanley for the good times.

If for some reason
Mortality catches up with you
Before I see you again.
And Time separates our
Physical beings, remember—
Love, you mean so much to me.
And never think that for one second
That my life with you was an
unhappy one.
And know if I had to choose again,
I'd choose you.

Then close your eyes and there I'll
be,
Smiling ever so gently
With one outstretched hand to you.
Yes, I know we won't be
able to touch, but try to feel
the love that waves goodbye
and pray that in that brief pause
when Mean Time and Infinity
cross each other,
We'll be with each other again.

But for now, know this,
Just in case I didn't say it
When last we saw each other;
I love you and yes—
If I had to choose again,
I'd choose you.

Jo Ann Carlson

IF ONLY . . .

My Child:
If only I could set apart
Each thing that's bound
To break your heart;
But I cannot!

I've been through life
And know the pain!
If Only from my advice
You would gain!
But you will not!

Yet, my Child, that "is" Life:
That we each must learn—
Then want for those we love,
That they could skip their turn;
But they cannot!

Gregory L Goodchild

MOUNTAIN

Oh great peaks lying on your
beds of yellows,
greens and blues—What great
force dared frame
this symetry which rises before
me?

As I gaze upon you—you smile
cool
breezes down upon me. Are you
really so kind
for me?

I see your story written upon the
eons of
time which lie so heavily upon your
brow. Come!
Share your wisdom with me—for I
am here
But for a little while.

Then, when times are done and
ages are
past—perhaps you and I can be
friends
in the far—far corners of forever.

Shane Gregory

SEASONS OF LIFE

In life there are seasons,
Spring, summer, fall, and winter.
First comes spring, with it's
childhood days.
When you are young and playful,
And not yet set in your ways.
Then comes summer, when you
are in your youth,
And you are easily taught,
And can be grounded in truth.
After that comes fall, when you age,
When a family depends on you
And time has you in a cage.
The last is winter, with death's cool
breath,
When you are old and crippled,
And face to face with death.

Agnes Smudde Kesler

LIFE'S IDEAL

We dedicate this poem posthumously to our dear talented and beautiful Mother who wrote it and drew the rose as a young woman.

Though flowers waver their beauty
And gladness is proclaimed by
song,
There is nothing so noble as duty
Nor nothing as beastly as wrong.

I trust, in the years that are passing,
My striving to do earnest good
Will shape a phrase for surpassing
The words "I did what I should."

'Tis true that on life's boundless sea
There is many a chance of despair
But this is only to help thee
The joy of Your heavenly realm to
share.

Amid the care, gloom and sorrow,
Amid the sunshine and glee;
I'll think of my aim of the morrow,
And sincerely try that to be.

Susan White Ahten

FOR ALL THE TEARDROPS

For all that fell and no one saw;
There is no way to count them all.
They fell for love and loss and fear;

Memories faded, yet so clear.
Time erases what we endure—
For all the teardrops.

Henry Paul Di Pillo
AN EXPERIENCE OF LIFE

To My Daughters: Tammi and Toni. The Loneliness reflected in this poem is because you were not with me. The joy is because you are. I love You.

A poem is an experience of life
Collected in the mind and released with a thought.
A poem is a woman described by a man,
It's a lost love as told by the loser.
You've read a poem and thought that's beautiful,
But have you read a poem and knew it was you,
Maybe lonely or loved.
A thought person can only be a poet
One who's lived and been forgotten many times.
Being alone is his greatest pleasure,
Being loved his only desire.
How many poets dwell on love:
Past loves, present loves
And the fear of no future love?
The sea is his favorite place
And life his favorite subject.
This is the poet
And his poems are the reflections of his life.

Jana Dee Stokes
LONELINESS

To my Grandmother who believed in me all the way.

Loneliness is a terrible thing.
It rules, in some way, every
human being.
Help, is what some people cry.
Can you just sneer and pass them
by?

Ancil Jones
STAIRCASE TO HEAVEN

To Julie, with Love

My staircase to heaven is missing some stairs
It is because of sin; that's why they're not there
How can I replace them, to make sure they're there
On the day that I need them. . .I hope they're all there
No one has an extra one or two, for me, to spare
The only way to replace them is to know that God cares
His word will help you replace all your stairs

Lynn Loges
SONG
Once in a midnight
Your music touched
my soul
rendered me senseless
once more
Lost among the melodies
Only haunting my emotions
I dared to forget, fleetingly
But I hear still riding
on the wind
a song, yours . . .

Holly Ann Kapuschinsky
THE CHRISTMAS SPIRIT

This poem is dedicated to Amelia Butch, my loving grandmother.

As the autumn leaves are covered with snow,
It reminds me of Christmas' long ago.
When people sat by a warm cozy fire,
And children dreamed of their only desire,
To find a stocking full of toys,
For all good girls and boys!
But today others are outside cold,
Just hoping for some nice warm clothes.
If their wish ever comes true,
They'll be more thankful than me or you.
But it doesn't matter whether your rich or poor,
Because the Christmas spirit is here once more!

Erick Green
ALIEN
When I walk down the street
People stop and stare
I guess they all know
I'm not from here.

Though I have no extra limbs
Or twisted features on my face
They all look at me
With a look of distaste.

I should be accustomed to it
'Cause since I arrived
Of all the native privileges
I have been deprived . . .

When they look at me
Someone tell me what they're
seeing
'Cause when I look in the
mirror . . .
I'M STILL A HUMAN BEING!

Maxine Ringwald
TEARDROPS
A very little teardrop
Was locked up for awhile,
It begged me to let it go
So it could run a mile.

It said that it would be
So very very neat
And never would disturb
The make-up on my cheek.

It had been with me so long
I wanted it to know I was afraid it
wouldn't stop
If I was to let it go.

It said it would be careful
And travel at slow pace
And promised to return soon
Unto its favorite place.

I decided to release it
Then it was on its way
And all its many teardrop friends
Followed down my face that day.

Lillian M Keahey
ACCENT THE NEGATIVE
Hundreds of tiny
snow-white blossoms
adorned the bridal-wreath bush.
She could not see
their ethereal beauty,
for nearby,
in her neighbor's garden,
grew just one weed.

Kathy M White
MY CHILD, MY FRIEND

Dedicated to my lovely sister Melissa Diane and in gracious memory, of my most beautiful and gallantly strong daughter, and friend, Desirae Mary Valencia.

My child, My friend:. . .

You are a Freedomsong, you are the fruit of my desires
That feeds my soul and nourishes my flesh.

You have shown me trust and love
When the pinnacles of discontent and hate
Were floundering aimlessly in the ether of my mind.

You restored my faith when my breast was wounded
With iniquitious realms of hopelessness.

You listened patiently with open mind and tender heart
To nebulous words that so many others sought
And would have considered verdant and meager.

You visualized the image of beauty with gracefullness
Both physically and spiritually, when the mirror
Reflected a faded silouette I once had known.

My Child, MY Freedomsong. . .

Accept my admiration and envy of your stalwart being
Give me the strength to be able to share the pleasures
Of these precious gifts with you, such a blessed one.

Dorothy Frum Ricer
DAYDREAMING
A gentle wind tugs at her skirt
And wraps it 'round her slender thighs
As down the street she stately strolls,
The target of admiring eyes.

And then by chance? Perhaps design,
A pane of glass says, "look-admire"
She slows her pace-reflected feet—
And then her eyes are drawn on higher.

Suddenly, her joy collapses
As reality, like cobras, rise,
To show that slender, creamy vision
Was only poor day-dreaming eyes.

How can she feel so young and lovely?
When there for all the world to see,
Old age with all it's dreaded trappings,
Has crept up unaware—on me!

Teresa Terrien
A CHILDS EYE
A childs hand comes in many sizes and shapes.
They have come here to touch this earthy land.
As they reach for empty spaces, they'll be searching for more traces.
They will be grabbing for whats in reach
so please lets not preach.
They are so young and soft they surely will
take it wrong.
As the tear comes down the face, they
may look at you saying grace.
Oh how could it be so wrong.
We only want to touch and feel this new place.
All we want you to do is please understand,
we are just trying to expand.

Trudy Aguilera
LITTLE ONE SO SWEET

Dedicated to my youngest son, Marc

Little one so sweet,
So peacefully you sleep.
You're mind's in dreamland,
As gently I touch your hand.
Stay little while you can,
For all too soon you'll be a man.
Don't grow up too fast,
Make your childhood last.
Laugh and be full of joy,
Be happy being a little boy.

Teresa W Irvin
GROWTH
There's a secret place within us where we store harsh memories
Dormant seeds awaiting the first rain
Until a chance encounter, a careless word or thought brings
Growth and bloom and harvest of dread pain.

With effort we repress it, we deny that it exists
Shove it out of sight and close the door
Until that chance encounter, that careless word or thought brings
Pain and grief and sorrow back once more.

We must somehow clear the darkness that encourages the roots
Sterilize and neutralize the source
Until the chance encounter, that careless word or thought is
Met with calm acceptance, not remorse.

Alice Joan Shipman
SILENT DESERT

To my husband Don, Who introduced me to the desert

How silent the desert
Sagebrush blooming

Sweet fragrance fills the air after an evening rain
Wild birds call to one another
How lonely at times
Peaceful and silent
You can almost hear tomorrow coming
The warm sun, shines down upon it
Brings life everywhere
When darkness falls upon its breast
A soothing coolness fills the air
Nocturnal creatures soon appear
Silent, silent, silent
How is it, that God made green lush lands and water
And yet, there is the silent desert
It thirsts and burns until a rainfall cools its face
Sweet silent desert
God has not forsaken
There is life
With your flowers, sun and rain
There is warmth and coolness
There are creatures
For without the desert, none would survive
The Silent Desert

Dixie D Bauch

GOD'S LOVE

When you feel depressed and blue
and it seems that no one cares,
Remember the love God has for you,
the love He wants to share.
We are all children of God, you know
and His love will ever infold us,
Trust in Him and He will show
us blessings showered in abundance.
We can see evidence of His love
in the beauty of earth, sky and sea,
He sent His Son from heaven above
to die in the place of you and me.
What have you done to deserve such love;
have you given your life to Him?
Are you striving for that home above,
or are you living in sin?
So when you feel blue and depressed
and you don't know what to do;
Turn to God for peace and rest
for God will never fail you.

Gary M Kile

YOUR LOVE

Your love.
It is your love.
It has been
since the moment of Creation.
A spirit. Fleeting
through time, light, space.
Waiting
for you to be.
As music waits
for Stradivarius.
As the splendid song of birds
flies on high summer
waiting for robin, or dove—
a love, pristine, waits.
Without flaws, or imperfections,
nor eroded by tears of selfish passion.
Never weakened by words, or false affection.
It comes
to you.
Not asked for, nor dreaded.
Fulfilling it's own purpose—
it's feeling
is its own reason to be.
For you.
Forever.

Elizabeth Richards

L.I.F.E.

The time of your life is the time you
feel the happiness inside.
Just as an ocean feels the wave of
an outgoing and incoming tide.
Life is a constant carousel which
circles round and round
Through each and every life, and
each and every sound.
So take a ride on the ocean waves,
a ride on a carousel
Life's a gamble for everyone
what will happen you just can't tell.

Todd Haney

A LONG TIME AGO

To my dad, and all the other men who fought for America in Viet Nam.

Long ago love was here,
Hate was gone, friends were near,
Life was easy, love was sweet,
Peace was alive, the world was neat.

Now all that is gone away,
War opens the brand new day.
Love is gone and hate is in,
Men die saying "We must win".

Amidst the night the fires burn
It is the place of no return
Don't get me wrong, they may leave
But the memories, they can't deceive

They lived for war, they fought alone,
They even died without a groan.
Even those who leave this place,
Can't find just one trace

Of the world a long time ago . . .

Kathleen Masi

OUR SPRING

Dedicated to Mom and Dad, Mickey and Anna

People say look at how the young ones dress
Look at how they walk and talk
And the things they do seem to be
So out of hand and wrong

But I just simply think that we
Forgot what it was like
When we were in our spring of life
Before winter came along

Didn't we not in our spring
Dress in all the styles
And dance to our music
And talk in our terms

Didn't we also think that
The world would always stay this way
We had our spring yesterday
And now its someone else's turn

Gloria J Ruehle

A MOTHER'S EYES

In memory of my mother
Who's eyes I see Reflected in my mirror.

As a young mother,
Eyes aglow with the promise
Of a future carefree and bright,
She sees a tiny baby born,
And dreamy eyes make plans.
Days of warmth and sunshine she sees.

As years go swiftly by,
The eyes grow misty and wise.
Time (you see) has dimmed the glow.
The child grows up.
It's failures and despair she sees.

Helpless now to mend the pain.
Old eyes tired and clouded,
Remember times of joy and sorrow.
The eyes of a mother.
They were hers and now are mine.

Eleanor Babette Dodge

HERALDS OF TOMORROW

To my beloved mother

The fire in the fading sun,
Burns the day's dim light,
And from its ashes, glowing coals
Form stars in the cooling night.
They glow in the velvet sky above,
As embers from the fires of day,
Reflecting in the water's edge,
Studding with jewels the quiet bay.
Now they sparkle as bright jewels
In the softest velvet skies,
Now they hang as dewy tears,
In a sad night's dreamy eyes.
Sometimes gay and sparkling brightly,
Then in sad and wilting sorrow,
But trembling always, eternally
On the brink of some tomorrow.

Marlan

UNTITLED

If Teddy Bears could talk,
What would they say?
Would they speak of tommorows
Or great yesterdays?
I have a hunch that

Most of the bunch,
Although it's absurd
Would utter no word,
Out of fear might destroy
All their love and great joy.
Teddy Bears are special.

Delores C Allen

LIFE IN THE COUNTRY

Oh for the life in the country

Where the air is so fresh and free
Where the birds are chirping happily
In the shady chestnut tree.

There the sun is so beautiful in the morn
Where there's acres of tall straight corn
Also, the sound of chickens scratching away
And the crunch of horses eating hay

There the young fawn stands by the mother deer
And she protects him from harm and fear
Where the stars twinkle above so bright
Over the praire land at night.

Sharon M Strong

A KISS FOR THOSE UNTOLD

In loving memory of Raymond Carl Boynton for all the times I didn't say I love you . . . now, I truly hope he knows!

You've become a great companion to me
a friend that was good to know.
I'm beginning to feel the lonesomeness
that I'm almost afraid to show.
I'll be talking to you in heaven now
for your heart was made of gold.
And for all the times you loved me
a kiss for those untold.
You'll be buried in my secret thoughts
a reminder once of a broken heart
we're parting friends and I will pray
once upon that twinkling star. . .

Jacqueline Ann Vernot

MY SPECIAL DREAM

I was standing outside on my front porch
Looking up at the starry sky.
The moon was shining down on me
As the wind came whistling by.

Then I heard a sound in the bush
I went to look to see.
There standing in the grass
Was a Unicorn smiling at me.

I followed him to the wide, silent beach
And there he made an enchanting sound.
And just like magic right above me
A Pegasus was flying around.

He swooped me up on his back,
And rode me up to the stars.
We zoomed around in the night
Just like racing cars.

The Pegasus dropped me off on a cloud.
It was truly a perfect night.
Watching the stars winking at me
And the moon shedding it's light.

I was sitting up on the cloud
Up there the whole world could be seen.
I wish this night could last forever.
But in reality, it was just MY SPECIAL DREAM!!

Stacy Howe

IN THE CLOUDS I SEE THE DAYS OF YESTERYEAR

For Larry and Mom, with love

In the clouds I see the days of yesteryear.
I see the unicorn running through the enchanted forest.
I see the lady waiting for her knight in shining armor.
I see the witches and wizards and

the magic they perform.

The wind blows and I hear the dreams of many.
I hear the wishes of a thousand children.
I hear the laughter from the heart.
I hear the promise of love beginning and the cries of love ending.

In my mind's eye, my fantasy serves to enhance what I see and hear.
I run with the unicorn.
I am the lady waiting for my knight.
I am apprentice to the wizard.
I grant the wishes of a thousand children.
The laughter comes from my heart.
I fulfill the promise of love beginning and cry the tears of love ending.

Michael T Bradley

SPRING LOVE

Spring is here, its joys we know,
The singing birds and melting snow.
The budding trees and new spring grass,
All give us signs that winter has passed.

Yet with spring and the blue skies above,
There is a rebirth of fresh spring love.
Spring love seems so clean and sparkling clear,
It blossoms like flowers whenever love's near.

Spring love is like spring, of this you should know,
In all of its splendor, one day it may go.
Just as water to flowers and sun to the trees,
Spring love too will grow if approached with ease.

Spring should not leave, but simply get better,
With the arrival of summer, and bright warmer weather.
This is to say, and for lovers to know,
Show spring love every day and that love will grow.

Martha Williams Ward

CHRISTMAS

Christmas is
going home;
a horse-drawn sleigh;
snowflakes, a starlit sky.

Christmas is
candle light;
a fireside glow;
mistletoe and holly.

Christmas is
warm wool mittens;
a frozen pond;
sharp, shiny skates.

Christmas is
ribbon candy;
steamed plum pudding;
walnuts and dates.

Christmas is
carolers concord;
a tree-top angel;
prize poinsettias.

Christmas is
a new 'Flyer' sled;
the tinkle of bells;
merry street Santas.

Christmas is
a loved one's face;
laughter of children;
the smile of a stranger.

Christmas is
a lighted church;
the Infant Jesus
lying in a manger.

Elizabeth Howard

FOR GRANNY

A very special Lady lives within my heart . . .
Her love for me was strong & deep & of me is a part.
So many things she taught to me . . .
So many things she said . . .
They have become a part of me & by them I am led.
Her love for God & for His Word
Lived deep within her soul.
Now as her body's laid to rest
I know that she is whole.
For once again her eyes do see
She's wanted that for so long;
& once again her ears do hear . . .
& her legs are well & strong.
For God has shown her mercy & God has shown her love
By calling her to be with Him & share His home above.
& now I will not say "Good-bye"
Amidst my grief & tears . . .
But a quiet "I love you" & a joyful "thank you"
for all those happy years.

Mary D Price

LOVE

I am so lonesome. My mistress is at work and I miss her so.

Oh Boy! There she is at the door. I will get some loving.

She picks me up, tells me she loves me, strokes my fur and
gives me a kiss on my head. If there is a kitty heaven I must be in it.

I wonder why she loves me so!

Could it be because I talk to her when she comes home or because
my fur is long and soft as silk. it is because I sing
her to sleep at night and stay on her bed til morning.

Maybe it is because I love her.

I am on my way home from work. be alone.

She will come running to meet me at the door, talking all the
while. I will pick her up, stroke her silky golden blond fur
and place a kiss on top of her pretty little head.

All evening she will stay by my side. I can talk to her. She
understands. We play games going up to bed. She sings me to
sleep and stays with me all night long.

I wonder why she loves me so?

Maybe it is because I love her.

James L Sullivan Jr

UNTITLED

All the things we've never seen
We'll get to see perhaps
All the things we'd like to do
We'll get a second chance
It's never just one time this way
Some road it leads us back
Perhaps you like a different route
Go ahead, a separate path
Whatever may be the case for you
Don't ever turn your head
Think and live and feel this day
It's one that's gone for good
How long do we wander forever alone
When it stops are we aware
There's much I want so much to see
But when I do, will I be me . . .

Julie O Miller

Julie O Miller

ST MARK'S BY THE SEA

I lost my heart in my St. Mark's,
I lost it there for sure.
Where God's word guides me just in love,
And makes my heart so pure.
He loves me that's for sure,
In St. Mark's by the shore.

Where friendly faces welcome us,
Where everyone is kind,
Those are the people of St. Mark's,
No better place you'll find.
God's little church by the Sea,
Is gently calling you and me.

Come to our church O' come with me,
To St. Mark's by the Sea.
O' Come with me and you shall see,
How happy you will be,
In our little church,
Right by the Sea.

Francis M Tucci

RHAPSODY AT DAWN

AS THE DAY'S SUN LEAVES THE HORIZON, THE RHAPSODY OF NIGHT'S MEDIATION APPROACHES:
If I reached you this night, my hope is that it was where no else has been.
For opportunity lost attempting less would have verged as if upon a sin.
There have been many obstacles to breach;
And, at times you seemed out of reach.
But, as time and patience teach,
All is tenable through pen and speech.
Though neglect seemingly appears;
Let preaching's void be in arrears.
When I am away from you, you are a dreamwish,
The lovely lead in my self-conducted rhapsody.
With dreams the longing is easier to cope;
And, therein lies my salvation, my hope:
Release me from the reins of elusive fantasy;
And, let the dawn of rhapsody brighten into reality.

Barb J Campana

A WHISPER IN THE NIGHT

To "Sunshine" and the family.

In a field where flowers grow,
made by God's hand, a mysterious glow
There a lost lover stands aside,
While the wind blows by and by.

The stars overhead were shining down
and in her heart she thought she'd found
one who was faithful and always true,
but like birds on wings, away he flew.

The flowing river swiftly goes on its way
And the moon up above was bright and gay.
She whispers so softly will he ever come back,
Time will tell as the sleepy posies nap.

The beautiful green grass in stillness like form
And the trees they sway as in a storm,
As on her knees she silently prays
Please God bring him back my way.

The shadows of darkness were creeping about
When alas but quiet came a sudden shout,
I've come back darling, back to stay.
Never again will I ever stray.

Yes, faith alone has answered her prayers
And their love together will always be shared.
Hand in hand through the mist they go,
With the future ahead and all it will show.

Liz Hudak

LIFE WEBS

The rain embraces the tree's, Referbish's
the grass, while bringing memories of the past.
The solitude offered, consoles the jaggered edges of the splintered heart.
Time, has been kind on the outside, while termites eat the wooden nerves from within.

Women endure, what man destroys, swallowing years to preserve the justifiable fears.
Demoralized, they some how survive.

The "Modern Macho Man" articulates his effectual
plan. Blames the "Feminest Movement" for all his
faults, never admits what he truly lost.

Women know they were forced from the home

inflation, economy, while edged
deep in their
hearts traces of biology.

Passively they assume the inate,
cuffed
on the wings of fate. Praying their
sisters
will endure, what "Modern Man"
Chose to ignore

Carolyn L Pompei

MOOD # 4

This poem is for my mother and father, who were unflagging in their faith that I could probably write something worthwhile.

Sitting silent, oblivious, pensive,
On an evening as calm as a sea
After storm, feeling only reflective,
Wrapped in pleasureable reverie.
Feeling peaceful, remote, faintly
blissful,
Far off, distant from all but this
hour,
With all memories dim, slightly
wistful,
Clouded, misty as rain, lacking
power,
And with thoughts floating lightly
as breezes,
Brushing outskirts of tranquility,
Mildly stirring sensation that
pleases,
Before ebbing away dreamily.
Being quiet, alone, but not lonely,
With emotions subdued calm, and
stilled,
Vaguely yearning for emptiness
only
To be slowly and gently refilled.

Diana LaBerge

IT'S SPRING

Dedicated to my loving Mom, brothers Richard, Jim, and to all my friends for their love and support;

Spring is in the air;
Pretty flowers everywhere;
This season is my favorite time of
the year;
The beauty of nature will soon
appear;

Birds come back to sing;
They let us know It's Spring, It's
Spring;
Little animals of various types;
All seem happy, what a beautiful
sight;

The grass is so green in the
Spring;
The sun shines down on
everything;
Oh yes the Daisies that are wild;
They're sure to make you smile;
Little children laugh and play;
They love the Spring in everyway;
Every creature on this land;
Goes to the park hand in hand;
I thank GOD for this season;
Spring it's beautiful and so
pleasing;
Now as the day comes to an end;
Remember tomorrow It's Spring
again, my friend.

Dave Leighow

TWO BOYS

To Barb, whose Love is the inspiration.

Asleep!
They are their mother's children.
At peace with the world,
solemnly innocent of its ways.
Their dreams are rarely stirred
Beyond another day's play.
Dispassionately, they reflect
their ambitions.
They are content, just to be.

But awake!
Aroused, they seek the challenge.
Time is too slow to assist them,
as
together, they conspire
to the deeds that must be done.
What a pair, these two!
They are, these boys, my sons.

Leah E (Walter) Mountain

TOMORROW

This poem is dedicated to my four grandchildren for whom it was written.

Tomorrow shall be paved with
many roads,
Some shall be hard to climb.
Courage shall take you a step at a
time,
Until you come to the end of the
line.

Set your goals high and believe in
yourself
Don't let thoughts of defeat block
your way.
For you hold tomorrow in the palm
of your hands
It is yours, so why not start out
today.

You are our hope for tomorrow
We are trusting and believing in
you
To make it brighter and better by
far,
We know you can accomplish it
too.

When temptation knocks on your
door,
As it shall from time to time.
Have the boldness, to say with
politeness,
No thank you;
God has endowed me with a
wonderful mind.

For I know the temptations you
offer
Though shiny and bright as we
meet
Only lead down the road of
destruction.
To heartache, to shame and defeat.

Trust your Saviour to guide you
On the road that is called Success.
Then there will be all the hope for
tomorrow
In knowing you have done your
best.

Allan H Matsuo

THE SLEEPER

To thought, as everything else
must come end.
Thus, I yield to thee now; and take
my rest.
Now I lie here and accept my
journey's end,
Having fought so long: Having
tried my best.
I can now see the smoke on the
water.
As we pass through the Mists of
Avalon,
My vision is cleared of earthly
matters.
To lie here in heavenly bliss, 'til
dawn.
'Til morn bells toll, and I begin to
stir.
I know they toll for me: None else
are here.
I throw aside the thick covering fur,
Only to be gripped by the breezy
air.
A new day dawns: Just as the last
is gone.
Again, the Avatar o'er night has
won.

Doug Branam

PROPOSAL

To Debbie, my love eternal.

Darlin though I've known you
For just a short while. . .

I've grown to love you
And treasure your smile.

Your kisses to me are heavenly
bliss. . .
And when we're apart your lovin I
miss.

I could hold you forever in my
arms. . .
To have you close and relish your
charms.

Sweet thoughts of you spin in my
head. . .
Face life without you? I'd sooner
be dead!

This flaming passion that burns
deep inside. . .
Is proof of my love that I cannot
hide.

I look in your eyes and my future
I see. . .
Now tell me my darlin will you
marry me?

Frances P Kasman

Frances P Kasman

WHEN HE COMES KNOCKING

Lest we forget.

We go to Him on bended knee
Hear us Lord, we ask of Thee
We sense His touch
We know He's near
We ask of Him our plea to hear
But when things go right
And we're to gain
We lack sometimes
To think of Him
When He comes knocking
Our love to win
Let's open our hearts
And let Him in.

Ruth Vander Does

OREGON LOUP TOUR REFLECTIONS (MT HOOD 1985)

A blend of work and rest,
A journey high and low,
Climbing to meet the sunrise
And downhill for the glow.

Cyclists on a holiday,
Riding for pleasure and growth,
Growing to treasure each other
Finding life's true worth.

We're as varied as a rainbow,
But find we are the same,
Learning and growing together
'Cause Biking is our game.

Trusting and sharing
Bring out the best,
Moving along together,
All passing our test.

Our days go by so quickly,
For friendships old and new,
We've seen, we've rode, we've
conquered
And proud of what we do.

A cherished trip
A touch with nature made,
As we cheer each other,
All can make the grade.

Eric Robert Bankes

TOGETHER ALWAYS

May we two
Become better friends;
Through sand or snow,
Together we'll stand.
May our feelings
Never cease to end;
Now and always
We will expand.
Our friendship
Is too large to foresake,
So let us continue
Through eternity
And enjoy the life
That we must make
Of love and joy
And serenity.

Jamie Helen Houser

EARTH LOVE

Look at the world, see what you
can see.
You see the most beautiful world
you've ever seen.
To your nation, to our nation we
hold hands across America.
Sea to shining sea.
Light gives us life and other pretty
things.
Like flowers and roses and violets
too.
You're pretty or you're handsome
as you are.
Your heart is in mine and love is
like a chain.

Mary J Geesland

WILD WINDS

Wild are the winds that sweep the
plains
and roar in their savage climb to
the hills.
As wild was the passion that once
swept my soul
and buffeted my heart with thrills.

Do the fates that set the wild winds free and rip
the clouds to shreds—laugh in gleeful merriment
because our love is dead . . .

Do they roar and dance so lightly . . .
then in mockery destroy a town.
Do they really chant the words I hear . . .
You clown . . . you clown . . . you clown.

It seems I've traveled alone, upon a dark river
of hurt for years . . . yet in sunlight dancing . . .
I see you . . . thru a veil of tears.

Allan R Stratton Jr
RUNNING AWAY

To those whom are wondering: I don't live, nor do I dwell in my past, I just take note of my mistakes and try to move on.

Your back is turned, your eyes are closed,
as you try to run away.
You reach for the future then realize;
The past haunts you more each day.

You can't escape, you can't forget,
the mistakes that you have made.
The present is now and the future is yet to come,
but the past is still a blockade.

A blockade to life, that is always remembered,
even though times have changed.
The door to the past is still open,
so it leaves the future out of range.

Someday the past will be forgotten,
and the future will take its place;
but until then you must continue to run,
and hope to someday win the race.

To win the race, which is to leave the past,
and to finally stop running away.
Then you could walk, clean, into the future;
leaving behind yesterday.

B Birge
I HAD AN IDEA FOR A POEM AND LOST IT

I had an idea
For a poem
And lost it,

For in my haste
I thought
Of you.

Julianna Williams Sharkey
DREAMING

To my husband who stuck by me, through good and bad.

I walked along the shore for days
needing you in so many ways

To hold, to share, to say a prayer
how could this happen, how could you dare

You left, your gone, now I'm alone
to sit and write to you this poem
The waters cold and oh so clear
I need you now, oh my dear

If you could come back to me and say
I need you now in so many ways

Genevieve Cluff
A BEAUTIFUL DREAM

Last night I had a beautiful dream
I thought I was at heaven's door.
I stood there for hours, it seems,
And was knocking for evermore.

I saw an angel standing inside.
She finally beckoned me "Come in."
Then she opened the door wide
And glanced at me with a grin.

I stood glaring at the things they had
Stored there high upon the shelf.
She said to me "Now don't be sad—
Please feel free to help yourself."

Now everything I needed was there
To help make this life worth while
I saw Faith, Hope and Love everywhere
Justice, Peace, and Joy in every aisle.

I took two large boxes of Grace
for I knew I would need a lot.
I ask her where Compassion was
She said "Plenty of that we've got."

I ask her to give me a gallon of Purity
For that is something everyone needs,
To keep themselves pure and clean
And take out all the thorns and weeds.

I saw some Patience and Humility
Setting on the shelf side by side.
I asked the angel to give them to me
To take away my haughtiness and pride.

I was looking for Wisdom and Instruction
'Cause in this life I want to do my best.
She handed me a bundle of Forgiveness
Said "You'll need this for eternal rest."
She gave me two pounds of Knowledge
Something no Christian can live without
She seemed to be able to read my mind
As I stood there in wonder and doubt.

I looked aside and saw a large booth.
I said to the angel "May I take all I need?"
It was full of Honesty, Mercy and Truth.
So I filled my basket: Indeed! Indeed!

Suddenly I awoke and opened my eyes.
There was no one to interpret my dream.
But I know that God was reminding me:
To make Heaven, I must keep my slate clean.

Martin Bud Taggert
THE HAPPY HANGING

When the thief was caught on a stolen hoss
He was hauled into town by the lynching boss
On bended knee and tearful eye
Cried: Clean me up before I die.

It was agreed, so they filled a vat
And into it the doomed man sat
Strong soap and brush made him glow
And the lather reached from head to toe.

The hurrying townfolk all joined the pack
So eager to scrub the outlaw's back
Then spirits were drunk, songs were sung
And everyone cheered as the clean thief swung.

Robert Maurice Kelly
THE CYCLE

Dedicated to my mother, Jane

Spirit Renewed

Life's Pattern Reassembled
Mother's Miracle

Kathy E Wills
THE OLD

In Loving Memory of my Grandmother Frances Gale Macpherson who died March 17, 1987

They sit in a booth in a corner,
Like a wrinkled pair of jeans,
Their eyes as grey as a rain cloud,
Their bodies like a corpse,
-But still alive.
Age spots covering their hands,
They're like a skeleton with skin,
Little children stare at them,
Oh, I feel for them.
As they sit, I look into their ancient eyes,
How lonely are they,
Their faces so wrinkled,
So old with age.
They feel so alone,
In this ever changing world,
Unlike the one they once knew,
Where will they end up?
A nursing home?
A funeral home?
Whichever comes first.
I look away with a cloudy teary-eyed face,
It's so sad they're all alone,
And I know we all shall be,
Just as they are.

Patricia Cuthrell
PEOPLE

I dedicate this poem to my family, and all my relatives, especially my brother Aaron, for his words of encouragement "Go for it". God bless everyone.

People are people if you just look around.
There's peace and love to be found.

People of color
All over the world
They bleed, they die

We're singers, actors, politicians,
Laborers of the land.
Believe or not.
We're all in demand.

Blackman, whiteman, redman or yellow
Every man on this earth
Our lives intertwine our goals much the same
To reach God's heaven, and have no shame.

Reach out to one another
Before it's too late.
Shake hands my brother;
Go together through the gate.

Becky Stuper
SLEEPING VILLAGE

Night caresses the sleeping village,
darkness settles above sleeping houses,
stars like a sea of light.

Reflections on sleeping pools of silver liquid,
shadows deep, hiding whatever dwells below.

Judith A Leahy
MY BEST FRIEND

Lorenzo Costa—remember you are an inspiration, and a joy. I hold you dear to my heart. Love always Grandma, you are my friend.

I picked him up on the way home
not that I minded being alone.
I just thought to see his face, would make me feel like I'd won first place.
Off to the mall we promptly rode,
with him reading a book named "Here's Mr. Toad.
In and out of all the stores, we browsed and looked till our
feet were sore.
We sat and ate, we talked and laughed.
He jumped up and hugged me tight.
It seemed that no one was around,
until a lady asked to sit down.
She said, I envy both you and your son, the both of you are one on
one.
I said to her you're wrong you see this is my grandson and he loves me.
He hugs me tight and holds me close, he tells me he loves me and I'm the most.
We feel the same my grandson and I,
I'm always sad when we say goodby.

Bonnie S Puchovan
MY OWN MAGIC

My Beloved Grandchildren Falacia, Stephen, and Amanda, Believe In Yourself.

They said I didn't know how,
I called upon my magic,
I showed them I could.

They said I could not,
I called upon my magic,
it was done.

They tore me down,
I called upon my magic,
I made them feel small.

They said I would never finish,
I called upon my magic,
it was complete.

They wore me down,
I called upon my magic,
I stood again, they cursed me.

I called upon my magic,
and said a blessing for them.

They cried out,
what is this magic you call upon?
I smiled and said,
just the strength from within.

They laughed at me,
and said it could not be.
I called upon my magic,
and I was free.

Spring Elizabeth Pippenger
TO YOU MOM AND DAD

I know this seems a little weird or
even strange
But in this short time the closer
we've become
At first it was a little tough to make
a start
But the rough water's over so let's
leave it in the dark
I want you to know just how I really
feel
I feel the love in my heart that is
truly real
You take a special place in my life
that I hold high
If we have any problems I hope
they pass by
You mean an awful lot to me please
believe it
My feelings for you seem to grow
and grow and don't seem to quit
a very special couple you two are
In my eyes you twinkle like stars
The bright shiny stars people make
their wishes on
You're the people who I've come to
count on
If hundreds of wishes were made
today
To brighten your day in everyway
And Mom, Dad
If all these wishes came true—they
still
Wouldn't show all the love meant
for you
With more warmth than you can
know
And more love than words could
ever show
I LOVE YOU MOM and DAD

Yvonne Fenton Allen
MY HEADACHES!

Dedicated to a dear friend, Dorothy Melton whom I shall always remember; as well as the 1949 snow in Los Angeles.

Outside the rain began to fall as
into bed I did crawl,
But by no choice of mine my
misery was set to rhyme.
I fought to keep the covers neat, as
chills ran from my head to feet.
Horses stamped upon my head,
while I lay helpless—sick in bed.
Against my weary bones, the
pillows felt like stones.
My bed got harder by the minute,
the longer I was in it.
To add to joys of being sick, my
diet was already picked.
I lived on soup, and tea, and
toast: while others dined upon
my roast.
Upon the wall I set my gaze, where
a big red banner always stays.
In letters big was "Erie, Pa" what
worries me is where is Ma?
Ever hear of the "Gingham dog"
and the "Calico cat"?
Well, side by side on my bed they
sat.
While in sympathy my pets recline,
I attempt to end this silly rhyme.
Well, what do you know! Our
California rain has turned to
snow.
Which means in bed I must recline
until the sun begins to shine.
Since I've begun to bake, my leave
I'd better take.
If I should die before I wake—I
leave you my headache.

Jillian E Weller
THE ENTRANCE

Here I lie in still
Through silently meadowed creeks
As one enters me softly
Like the ferns cushioned against
the meak.
You wend my fertile passage
To closures space of warmth
You kiss of me so tender
That flourish and melt me forth.
So all be not of woeful
Your touch hath caressed kind pain
The sheathing of compassion
Could rapture one's emotions
insane.
Let thoughts ween to savor
To taste your purpose sprout
Into this passionate womb I enter
Until my day of life shall come
about.

Tera Sue Holland
THE WIND CHIMES

To my mother, my friend, Cheryl Bean

When you hear the gentle
tune of the wind chimes
Remember far back
into your mind
When you held your children
for the first time
And with each tinkle
remember the twinkle
In their eyes
of the happy days gone by
And as the breeze
touches your face
Remember that no matter
where your children may be placed
You will always be together
because the love you share
Will last forever

Beverly I Langley
WORLD OF CONFUSION

We live in a world of so much
confusion
All people say it's just an illusion
You and I both know that's not true
Because if it was we wouldn't know
what to do
Have you ever stopped and realized
That this world seems hypnotized
No one wants to live a happy life
All they want to do is fuss and fight
World of confusion is what we're
living in
A world where no one seems to care
All you have to do is smile and
share
That will make this world a better
place to be
You and me and any one you see
We all should work together and
make things better
If this world was filled with love
How exciting things would look
above
So let's not live in a world of
confusion
Let's work together and find a
solution

Harleigh H Allen Sr
SOLO FLIGHT

I've climbed on wings of silvered
girth,
On air of purest essence,
To clear my bonds with troubled
earth,
And ease my mental presence.

To clear my soul of worldly care
I've climbed and soared so free,
And felt, on cheek, the rush of air,
And yet communed, oh God,
with Thee.

Through vaulted skies of purest
hue,
O'er sunlit clouds and mountain
peak,
Ah, solo flight up through the blue,
To you, oh God, I try to speak.

I dare the heights and bumpy flight,
O'er hill and lake and islet;
I fear no force within the night
With God as my co-pilot.

Lillian Albright Ackley
IN THINE HAND

Were I
An artist true and keen knowing
color and what
goes with green—
Such beauty I could paint,
Many foolish ones would call me
"Saint".

Were I
A sculptor, sensitive and fine
understanding rhythm,
proportion and line—
Such creations I could make,
That would, in many, inspiration
wake.

Were I—A singer sweet and clear
Interpreting music truly, without
fear—
Such harmony I could bring,
Hearts to lift, cares afar to fling!

But—
No colors have I, no marble fair,
In my throat there lies no music
rare—
Still know I this, and to it I cling;
WORDS can paint, can carve, can
sing!

Robert J Carley
THE MIRACULOUS STAIRCASE

There exists today
in old Santa Fe,
At our Lady of Light
a unique sight;
A miraculous staircase
with defying ways
Thirty-three steps above the floor
it ascends evermore,
There is no central support
in mid air it seems to float.
There are no nails
only wooden pegs prevail,
From wooden sources unknown
not in that area grown.
This came about in an unusual way
much to everyones dismay,
The planners left no place, you see,
for a choir loft staircase to be.
Many tried to build but failed, all
said as one
it couldn't be done,
But nuns did pray
that God find a way.
Then out of nowhere, they say
came a carpenter one day,
In two weeks he built this very
staircase
a marvel in those days.
He went by the name of Jose the
carpenter,
the master woodworker.
In these hereabouts he was not
known,
his skills wiser than our own.
Could it have been Saint Joseph,
the carpenter himself,
the staircase donor
who built it in the Lord's honor?
Thirty-three stepping stones to
heaven, he did give
one for every year the Lord did
live,
It still stands in Santa Fe, New
Mexico
as it did a century ago.
A legend, myth or a dream
to some it may seem.
But come disbelievers with me
it is there for everyone to see,
This Miraculous Staircase
in all its splendored grace.

Beverlyn Ann Person Battle
IT TAKES ALL KIND

This poem was inspired by GOD, and is dedicated to my mother, Mrs. Fannie Mae Person

It takes all kinds of people
To make the human race,
As GOD made us in His image
We're just of different colored face.

GOD has no respect of person
He loves us all the same,
There should be no Big I's and
Little U's
Just a host of saints glorifying His
name.

There are sometimes wars between
us
But, GOD's intention was LOVE
We should all try and live together
And praise our Father above.

It takes all kinds of people
As we should know by now,
But, we have to love our fellowman
And strive for harmony somehow.

Some people distinguish color
And some give respect to class,
But, when GOD comes again on his
cloud
These kind of people won't last.

We must get right now for glory
Make peace with all mankind,
Live according to GOD's holy word
So we won't be left behind.

Shirley Paye Allen

AN AUTUMN CRY

The smoke from burning leaves
and ember
Scaled its way up to the sky
As we stood and watched, and said,
"Good-bye."

The setting sun out in the West
Adorned her colors and her charm
As you looked, and spoke, and
touched my arm.

And then, perhaps, a tear I felt
Creep towards my cheek, but
brushed away,
You never saw it fall—or knew that
day.

How fleeting time can heal the
pain of love,
Now lost and cold,
I do not know—how long—how
old.

Joe E Cook

THE POINTER

I met a man in seventy-five
He was a birdhunter to my
surprise
I didn't know he'd soon be my
friend
He said we'll go hunting when
season's in
He told me about his dogs, all of
them
The one he liked most was a
young pointer named Lem
When fall came around and
season opened up
I saw Lem my first time, not
much more than a pup
He told me how he broke him
and the things he had done
But hunting with Lem was a
whole lot of fun
The first day we hunted, minutes
after we let him out
I saw him standing on a hillside,
so high and so stout
He was a bird dog, day after day
A good looking classy dog, going
the right way
Sometimes he would be gone,
and we'd look for him a while
We would always find him
pointed with plenty of style
He was a hard going dog, even
after he'd got old
An all day dog with a super nose
We hunted together for about
ten year
We noticed last season that Lem
couldn't hear
We knew it wouldn't be too long
before he couldn't go
This big orange ticked dog was
getting too old
On December Seven, Nineteen
Eighty-Four
I knew I wouldn't be seeing Lem
any more
I talked to Cloyd Friday of this
week
He told me He had Lem put to
sleep
One thing I'll remember time
after time
The old dog was a friend of mine.

Patti Dawson Meier

THE SMOKER

Here I sit having a g-o-o-d time
First I suck . . . then I blow . . . then
you choke!
The "weed" is my soother and
savior
So thank you for holding your
breath while I smoke!

I work hard to pay for this habit
One year costs a thousand or so
But my polluting is helping our
government!
So thank you for holding your
breath while I smoke!

You say my smoke stinks? Makes
your eyes burn?
The chemicals injure your lungs?
Oh stop it . . . You're hurting my
feelings!
And your ranting is hurting my
eardrums!
Don't let in that fresh air . . . I'm
fre-e-zing!
The spray from that can stuffs my
nose!
That air purifier is too loud!
Ah, thank you for holding your
breath while I smoke!

My little kids and my friends . . .
how I love them.
I'd give them my all . . . that's no
joke.
But they better not ask me for clean
air!
And I'll thank them for holding
their breath while I smoke!!

I think that someday I may quit this
Before either you or I "croak!"
Just don't hold your breath
a-waitin'
But thank you for holding your
breath while I smoke!!

Mary Kathryn Zuck

THE GOODBYE FLIGHT

They sailed away one morning
The day was sunny and bright,
Into the bright blue heaven
Then everything seemed right.

The families were there watching.
And little did they know
That never again would they return
To the ones that they loved so.

Oh! Lord Bless the lonely children
So sad and shocked to tears.
Who will ever remember that
lonely flight
through all their lonely years.

The brave and happy seven
Chose the road that they must trod
And the morning flight that took
them
To touch the face of God!

Elizabeth Matlock

IN THE PAST

My life is growing so very old,
To think I'm not half as bold.
Ah—think of yesterdays—
And all my younger ways.
Wishing I truly didn't care—
Ignoring it even if it was there
Staring at me in the face—
Wondering if I'm not just taking up
space.
So the days are going fast—
Here I sit, already in the past,
Thinking of things I should have
done,
Ah—more battles lost than won.
And yes, of love I've had the best,
Being just friends with all the rest.
I believe one day I'll lay down this
pen,
Never to write of sad things again.

Rita A Bedard

FIRST WEDDING ANNIVERSARY

To Ron and Dee

One year, already passed
The two of you still are one
Because your love did last
Thru its important trial run.

First hurts and heartaches are now
behind
Oh, there will certainly be more
than you will find
But now you know the two of you
that your love will always see you
thru

Perhaps some of the sparkle has
now worn
That first loving feeling that made
you one
But now deeper, wiser love dwells
there
The two of you, your whole life to
share

So now to two people we dearly
love,
We send our wishes and our love
That each other's happiness will
always be
The most important thing-to-thee.

g franscecia mcleod

g franscecia mcleod

I AM NOW

I AM NOW
Speak not to me of promises for
the Future.
Promises are finely-spun and
oftentime broken.
I AM NOW
Give me some look of
reassurance—some
words of inspiration.
Give me something to cling
to—Here
in the Present.
I AM NOW
Future assurances? These are
good also;
but do not
Look so far Ahead that you must
Now pass me by.
I AM NOW!
I am human. I have needs and
they are Now.
For Tomorrow, I may not be.

Anne C Hayward

THE SILENT LANDSCAPE

The autumn leaves tumbled down.
Coating the lawn a russett
brown—.

Winter arrived with a powdering of
snow.
Comforting the gardens and
hillsides below.

Spring crocuses, tulip's and
daffodils
Unfolded their petals to adorn the
hills.

The summer breezes rolled in from
the sea,
Gently swaying the boughes of the
Maple trees.

Loren T Bouldin

COW POOR

In the fall of nineteen-eighty two,
I started out with a cow or two.
A couple of years went by,
and they began to multiply.
Now the rent on the grass is due,
and the note at the bank is too.
If I don't go and pay,
they may repo any day.
I have to declare chapter seven or
eleven
and back to selling hardware.

Carla Luann Jones

MY LOVE FOR YOU

I know I can't have you, but
That won't stop my heart
My feelings keep growing stronger
Even though we're still apart.

I know we've had our times, but
I want you more today
I'll always be here waiting;
If you should ever come my way.

Beverly Sherman

YESTERDAY

To Kris, Sean and Rhiannon—for all the beautiful yesterdays, todays and tomorrows.

Wasn't it yesterday we rolled on the
floor,
me tickling you, you screaming
for more.

Learning together and laughing
out loud,
sharing and loving, me feeling so
proud.

And proud I've remained as the
years ran away,
and I watched all your antics,
and enjoyed you each day.

You've grown up so fast, I've hardly
had time,
to tell you I love you
and claim you as mine.

Next year, child of mine, you'll
walk out the door,
but wasn't it yesterday we rolled
on the floor?

Tammy Miller
A SECOND CHANCE
It seems that every moment of my
life,
Be the moment happy or filled with
strife,
I catch myself day dreaming,
Remembering the smile on your
face beaming.
I can't seem to let you go,
Even though deep inside I know,
That what we had is now gone,
Even though to me it seems wrong.
I took all the love you offered, but
did little myself
in giving.
I should have realized my part was
more than just
living.
You needed me as much as I
needed you,
And you my friend were always
there and true.
But I was afraid to let my insides
show.
I was afraid to blossom and begin
to grow.
I was afraid the world would laugh
at me,
If through my feelings for you the
real me they'd see.
But now I realize it doesn't matter,
For I would put you first and the
world latter.
If only I could have a second
chance,
I'd show you how free I now am, I
can dance!
But in the world of love and pain,
A second chance doesn't come as
often as the rain.
So I can only sit here and dream
of the past,
Desperately holding onto a love
that did not last.

Kathleen Maley
VIETNAM EPITAPH
Granite
born in Asia
shaped in Vermont
christened in Atlanta
inscribed in Tennessee.

A monument
black as the hawk
grey as the dove
reflecting, projecting
frozen love.

Simply
neighborly names
together apart
invade the spirit,
engage the heart.

Sounds of
hushed low voices
anguished sobs
people praying,
remembering pain.

Wounded
they come
to greet, to embrace
annealed they leave,
tempered with grace.

Olivia B McKeough
MY FAVORITE COLORS

To my Family, with Love

I love my flag, indeed I do.
My favorite colors are red,
White, and blue.

Each time I see my colors fly,
A-top a building way up high,
I get a feeling deep inside of
gratitude and heartfelt pride.

We can come and go whenever we
please
And do it with the utmost ease.
We can worship when, and where
we desire,
And vote for the man we most
admire

I love my flag, indeed I do.
It stands for all that is just and true.
My favorite colors are red, white
and blue.

Linda S Frink Baird
THE LORD IS OUR SAVIOUR, WE NEED HIM TO BE STRONG
The LORD gave us our liberty,
He made America strong,
He gave us fields of wheat and corn,
He's helped us to go on.

He wanted America to be free,
From evil and of wrong,
And all the people to know his love,
To praise Him all life long.

But now I look around me,
To see what's happening here,
The people are not holding,
Our LORD so close and dear.

They're saying no religion,
In this place and in that,
We have our rights and don't want,
Religion as part of that.

What's the matter with this world,
That would let the evil rein,
The LORD gave us our liberty,
Without Him we can't gain.

We're falling to evil doers,
Our children will feel the pain,
Then one day we'll stop and
wonder why,
We're sad and filled with shame.

The LORD is our Saviour, We need
Him to be strong!

William Cal Downing
MOM

This poem is dedicated to Laura, my special mother whose life gave me material for these verses!

There are so many words we use
each day
that add extra meaning to all that
we say.
Well, "Mom", is a word which is
always understood
to mean love and encouragement,
kindness and good.
Just what is a "Mom", you may ask
Well, she's a woman who has an
awesome task!
First, to be a wife to one called a
"man"
Which is difficult at times, but she
does what she can.
He can make her job hard and
many times will
But she sticks to her duties and
loves him still.
She bears his children and nurses
and feeds
She's always right there to tend to
their needs!
Through measles and mumps and
chicken pox too
Why, she's had them all and knows
just what to do.
For congestion and chestcolds you
use mustard plaster
But if left on too long, oh what a
disaster!
It works just the same and if you
live till you're old
Will be many times thought of and
very often told!
She cooks and she cleans and
washes your clothes
She'll even do dirty jobs like wiping
your nose.
Who else understands and shows
faith in you
Through mishaps and blunders in
all that you do?
With boyfriends and girlfriends
she'll be a matchmaker
Then with wedding expenses, she'll
be a partaker.
Not long after this comes her
"grandmother" role
With no previous experience, she's
quite good on the whole!
She's a good baby sitter and most
often quite cheap,
Who'll even wait till payday with
just "thanks a heap."
There's walks to the park and trips
to the store
You can be sure with Grandma, it's
never a bore!
So you see, being a "Mom", leads
to quite a career
But she'd do it all over, and not
shed a tear!
She's a blessing from God and
don't ever doubt her
After all, stop and think, where
would you be without her?
These are just a few expressions,
Mom, and thoughts so true
But the best way to sum it all up is
"I love you!"

Tommy and Phillip Sanson

Judith Lynn Sanson
YOUR SOMETHING, CLOSE TO MY HEART

This poem is dedicated, to my darling little boys: Tommy and Phillip—to let them know how I feel when they get older!

Your something, close to my heart,
As you look up with love and a
smile,
Your warmth and sweetness
always last for awhile,

As I hold you close to my breast,
to feel your—
warmth against my chest—
Your baby blue eyes give me a
special joy,
It makes me proud to have two
little boys,

As they are a special joy—
One's so small, and the other a two,
Makes me wonder, "What can I
do?"
"Can I survive the terrible two's?"
He grabs a spoon from the drawer
and opens,—
the refrigerator door,—
Makes me wonder, what he'll do at
age four?

And the other, he's not far behind,
Because, he's starting to talk
before his own time,
He makes me wonder if he'll be
that same kind!

But providing the hard times they
put me through,
And they make me wonder,"What
am I to do?"
I will always love them and never
give them up, they're—
So precious my love for them is
true.

Who will know how big they'll
grow?
I know the Lord would only know,
They're love will always have a part
for—
"Your something close, to my
heart"!

Ruth Anthony
LEAD ME ON
Lead me on, loving savior—
To your love and light above;
Thou hast led me from dark valleys,
To a greater life with you.

I need your strength every
moment—
In my journey to your home—
The loving friends you sent to save
me,
By their love and kindly deeds.

Help me always to be grateful—
For your love and your
forgiveness—
Help me always share your
kindness,
With my suffering fellowmen.

Tracey Lynn Brabant
A RAY OF HOPE
Hope is a beautiful, vibrant sunset
That lights the heavens afire with
brilliant color.
Sunsets are an inspirational taste
of happiness.
Somehow, just watching these
iridescent shadows
Race inadvertently across the sky
Sends a message of endurance
To the lost souls of this world.
Sunsets are contenting,
Radiating a unique, personal
fulfillment
To all within imagination's grasp.
A genuine creation of nature,
Sunsets are, in a certain essence,
elusive
Lasting long enough to cloud
reality
Yet disappearing before the
opportunity arises
For the viewer to depreciate its
value.

Bonnie Palmer
THE PALISADES

The cliff stands tall dark and stern
But in its forbidding rocky clay
Stunted aged trees find foothold,
Gulls find rest and respite
From the towering white-capped sea
Tearing its massive waves into white foam
Against the gloomy unbending wall.

The heavy leaden clouds
Pour out their streaming tears
In driving gray-silver sheets as
Fiery flashes rip the lowering sky asunder while
Winds fling their rage against the ancient trees
Even as the cowering birds
Are sheltered by the forbidding palisades,

No man steps upon the grass above
Nor upon the sandy rocks below—nor dares —
While the storm beats out its fury
For the palisades shelter not the man creature
As it does it shelters the weary winged one
And the oldening trees.

Jennifer Marie Powell
MY MOM

I'd like to dedicate this poem to the greatest mom in the world, my mom, Sandy Shuburg.

My mom is the greatest mom on earth;
She's half the reason for my birth.
She's been with me all the way;
By my side I hope she stays.

Whenever I have a problem
She's always here to help me solve them.
My mom and I are close best friends;
I hope our relationship never ends.

Her three children cause her pain,
But very seldom does she complain.
We make her mad as often as we fuss,
But she still puts her time aside for us.

My mom is there for my sister and I
And she's there for my brother besides.
My mom is better than the rest,
What I'm saying is she's the best.

She buys my clothes and cooks our dinner;
My mom is a real winner.
She's with us in all that we do,
And I like to say, mommy, I love you!

Celious Davis
WAITING FOR GOD

Dedicated to my pastor, Bishop Elgin E. Little with Love

We are waiting for God
In this barren land
We are all on one accord
Fasting, praying and praising the Lord
We have our trials and tribulations
Life for us is not always easy, but sometimes hard
Yes, we are waiting for God
Doing our master's will
Rocky is the road we trod
We will not get weary along the way
Watching our every step
Being very careful of what we do or say
Determined to make it in
And see his wonderful face one day.

Dorothy Rose Gottstine
DO YOU EVER WONDER?

With Love To my Husband Bill, and gratitude to my wonderful children, Linda, Billy, Jimmy and Ricky, without whom I would have no life at all.

Woman, do you ever wonder,
what's become of that little life?
What happened to the tiny being . . .
You let them cut away with their knife?
As you lay so warm and safe, near someone who really cares, does your conscience ever bother you?
Do you feel the sting of tears?
Your precious little angel, your gift from God above . . . was there nothing you could offer him, no tiny thread of Love?
Was there no room inside your heart for him, no room inside your home . . . nothing you could do for him . . . To keep him safe from harm?
Do you hear him cry inside your mind . . . "mama, tell me why . . .
Why did you let them hurt me . . .
why did you let me die . . .?"
Does your womb cry out "We're barren now . . . Our childs been cut away" . . .
Did you ever stop to realize . . .
Some day you'll have to pay? . . .

T Freeman
TELL IT

Daily we get good deeds and God's blessing
but, when was the last time you heard
People discussing the subject, like "hey
man you gotta spread the word."

Some think others will tell, that my life
has just been too rough
I'll sit here and be content, to be thankful
but, that's not quite enough

This is a world wide dilemma, it knows no
particular region
Everyone knows the devil is powerful and
that he has his legion

You may be one of the many who say "my life
is running mighty fine."
This may be true but, if it's not, the next
time there might not be enough swine.

John Joseph McCarthy Jr
MY FATHERS LOVE

To Rusty, Miss Lillian, Farmer Jakey

I stand on the rocks and look out to sea
I wonder what will become of me
Of the pain and sorrow
Of the hope of tomorrow
Of the treasures I may find
Why have I been so blind?
The answers you see, maybe my destiny
My Father lives above
He showers my soul with love
He shows me the way, for today
To be kind, I will find, love
As a dove from above
So is my Father's love

Wendy Cameron Miragliuolo
SYMPHONY IN YOU-MAJOR

I wish I knew how to write you a love song; for music expresses emotion so well.

It would have to be soft and sweet to the ear; like the warmth of a crackling fire.

And then I'd add the spices of life; like a secret you just can't tell.

It would have to show the tempest of my soul and burning desires.

And when the music ended I would surely feel a void; so much like each time we part.

I'd so love to write you a symphony, but for now I'll just keep
trying to tell you with a touch, a look and a kiss.

Helen Aiken
A CHILD'S LAMENT

Sad is the day you ran away
when I call you to play with me.
You blend an harass through
the earth's green grass,
then land in the flowering fig tree.
Swinging and watching you on that tree limb,
I hear a sweet murmuring musical sound
to put me, altogether, to sleep.
I run to the pond
discover to my delight,

six black tadpoles just head and tail,
darting from here to there.
They were too shy when I asked them to play.
Hiding 'neath mama they meant to say,
"No thank you, we won't play today."
Standing alone in the garden,
"Come Pete," I call,
"no one will play with me."
There stands Pete before me
as I'm about to cry,
with freckles and hair to match.
At least I have a make-believe friend,
so willing and steadfast
when I am needing a friend for play.

Deborah Anne Trgouich
UNSPOKEN HURT

Why is my life like a merry-go-round
That is sometimes up but mostly down
Why am i always left here to stay
In this cruel world to suffer and pay
I don't want to live but i don't want to die
Oh my dear God i think i will cry

I don't know what to do anymore
So i guess i'll just hide here behind these closed doors
Staying away from those people who have been so mean
Hiding for now so i will not be seen
I never want to see those who have hurt me so bad
Oh why did my life have to turn out so bad.

GOODBYE PAINFUL WORLD!

Walt Bragan
WHAT WOULD WE DO?

To my undiscouraged companions, my wife—my family.

To where go the days that pass us by?
After we reach twenty the years just fly.
I wish time would stand still for you and I.

We wouldn't work, we wouldn't eat,
All we'd do is play and sleep.

We'd gather flowers from the distant hill,
And drink at the spring when the day stood still.

We'd run by the sea when the mist comes in,
And after you rested, we'd run again.

I'd tilt your face to the sea breeze mist,
And hold you long in a tender kiss.

We could lay down and dream for a century or two,
For when we awakened, I'd still have you.

What would we do if we couldn't die,
If time stood still for you and I?

To where do we plod, as this earth we trod,
Is there room for us in the kingdom of God?

Tami Strausbaugh
CLOUD HORSES

Horses white and blue,
Sail the skies through and through.

When the trees turn green,
The horses can be seen.

The birds are humming,
And the horses are coming.

You can see the flowers dancing,
While the horses are prancing.

When darkness fills the sky.
The horses say goodbye.

Patricia A Tallman McConnell
THE POTTER'S HANDS
As I watched the hands of a potter
working at his wheel,
A picture came into my mind
So vivid
and so real.
Upon the potter's wheel I saw
a shapeless mass of gray.
I realized that my life was
that ugly
lump of clay.
The quality of the clay way poor
good intentions marred by sin;
Too many disappointments
Too little joy
Mixed in.
The clay then felt the Potter's touch
as the wheel began to turn;
Nail-scarred hands gently
transformed
the mud
into an urn.
The vase, when taken from Lifes
kiln
was plain and flawed to see;
But the Potter whispered "I love it,"
"I'll take it
Home with me."

Ann Marie (Santos) Simcock
THIS CHRISTMAS WITHOUT YOU

For the late Mrs. Irene Medeiros-Saudade Baldaia Vavo. . .The love and kindness you gave, will always remain in my heart. . .

We celebrated this Christmas
quietly without you,
The children's tree was not as
tall.
The more ornate decorations
remained untouched,
In their boxes in the upstairs hall.
Still, the homemade manger you
gave us,
Was placed with utmost care,
Beside the fire; where you used to
sit,
In your favorite easy chair.
The holiday table was a quiet one,
Without your laughter there.
Despite precious memories of the
Christmases past,
Through the years we were
fortunate to share.
With respect we set a place for you,
Our holiday feast was always
yours to share.
And the painful realization then,
Was more than our hearts could
bear.
And as we bid each other "Merry
Christmas,"
Please know how much we
missed. . .
Your voice, your smile,
Your "Merry Christmas
Sweethearts" hug and kiss.
We thought often of you on your
journey,
Hopeful of your new beginning,
not your end.
On this Christmas without you. . .
You were somehow still with us,
my very special friend.

Joanna L Clark
A MOTHER TO REMEMBER
She's always there to wipe a nose
or comb a lock of hair
She never fails to kiss a hurt
or show how much she cares.
She always seems to kiss a tear
from tiny little eyes,
And brightens up their days and
nights
with all her tender smiles.
She sometimes tucks them into bed
and hugs them in her arms,
And wishes they were small again
with all their childhood charms.
But when their grown it's not as
clear
the love she really needs to hear.
She never really asks for much
even though she gives alot
She never seems to be aware
of things she hasn't got,
But one thing you could give her
and the one thing you should say
Is Mom I love you with all my heart,
and remember her on
MOTHERS DAY.

Robert C Howell
SOLILOQUY

Dedicated to Clyde M. Howell, soldier, educator, and gentleman. A man known for his love and abiding faith in the future of all mankind.

In this moment in space and time
I feel profound humility.
I stand in awe of the scope of my
existence.
I am part of the microcosm-my
body shares the minute building
blocks of the universe.
I am part of the macrocosm-I live
in an infinity, a total energy
matrix.

My mind finds rapport between
the diciplines of the physical
world and the free spirit of my
curiosity.
And yet, I know and understand
my place on one planet.
Each day I gain new respect for my
fellow man.
He too shares the universe and is
a child of eternity.
Together we experience and
interpret our environment.

Living and being, wrapped in
endless splendor,
Knowing something of the grand
structure of all creation,
Understanding in part the
omnificient Divine purpose—
Wonderous privileges for
everyone, accorded even to me!

For these privileges I kneel in
reverence.

E Mildred Cox
TO BLOW OR NOT TO BLOW

In memory of my beloved husband, Everett

Beware of March and its formidle
ides
Tempermental as a musician's note
Swirling and swishing and ruffling
our hair
Even exposing our petticoats.
Old Sol peeks out reluctant and shy
Winter still hasn't relinquished her
power
Snowflakes, showers, hail and
wind
May all come in the self same hour.

A crocus appears, a bright spot of
yellow
Wild flowers add their delicate hue
Dogwood buds swell with new life
As other signs of spring appear.

We love you all but the wind
But that's a large part of your
charm
As changeable as a baby's smile
Blowing cold and then again warm.

Blow on in your new-found fury
Usher in a clean and shining
spring.
Washing and cleansing and
moving about
Bringing us the best of everything.

Lois Zinke Bay
WEBSILKEN LACE
Golden children in popcicle
summers
we ran, sunbeams glinting
in our hair.
Under a tree she solemnly traded
her stone of genuine gold
for my dimestore diamond ring.
Secrets we spun
like spiderweb silk
in lacy patterns that were us.
When the thirsty wind would gust
us home,
our shouted partings
hung behind in the dust.

She left me websilken lace, and
now,
Dear Friend,
this design is yours and mine—
a summergarden kaleidoscope.
Your wit taps in me wells of
laughter,
and I speak
with the trust of a child.
Our webben lace
prisms sunshine from its strands.
When summer fades, I love
to touch its satin glow
and use its colors in my smile.

Lorraine Hiester-Smart

Lorraine Hiester-Smart
MEMORY TRAIN
Yesterday rides a Memory Train
pulling into my Today,
urging thoughts to track back
to Old Ghost towns
I left along life's way.

Yesterday belongs to someone
who doesn't live here anymore,
the past lies in Old Ghost Towns,
and Time has boarded up the door.

Though I've traveled
back down that track
To visit certainly is true!
It's here in Today
that I wish to stay,—
making memories totally new.

Doris B Ahearn
MY LITTLE DOG

To my sister, Lois, and our poodles

When I awake and start each day
My little dog is up and ready to
play.
When I begin each daily chore
My little dog meets me at every
door.
When I partake of every meal
My little dog joins me, it's for real.
When I go walking down the street
My little dog is forever at my feet.
When I go shopping and take the
car
My little dog is my favorite
passenger by far.
When I sit at the organ to play what
I can
My little dog is quite a devoted fan.
When I am tired, weary and blue
My little dog is always there to see
me through.
When friends drop by to have a
chat
My little dog greets them like a
welcome mat.
When I am gone and stay too long
My little dog waits patiently,
hoping
nothing is wrong.
When I go to sleep at night
My little dog never leaves me out
of sight.
My little Dog, as you can see,
is very much a part of me.

Carolynn Ward
INNOCENCE

To my daughter and Grand Daughter

The sweet innocence of love given
from a child's smile. The naked
beauty of a gift so pure.

The same splendor as watching a
new blade of grass grow or a
flower blooming after a gentle
spring rain.

Oh, the sweet purity of virgin love,
truly a gift only God could give.

This rare breed, this great gift, this
innocence entrusted to none
other than the beholder.

What knowledge those innocent
lips hold. What texts this
beautiful love would fill.

All this and more, much more, all
from the pure innocent smile of
a child.

Truly the greatest gift of all. Oh,
what magnificence we could
learn from the innocent love
given through a child's smile.

Harold W England
LONESOME
I see the stars, the velvet sky of
night.
The beauty of the summer day.

They are like a memory from the past,
My thoughts are all on you so far away.
I never thought that I could be alone
With all these people here.
Each night I bow my head and pray,
That with the dawn I'll find you near.
I know that in your eyes I sinned,
And I admit that what I done was wrong.
But somewhere in the ashes of our love,
Can't you fine a spark alive and strong,
To burn the pages of the past,
And light a pathway as a start,
To bring you home again to me,
And help me mend my broken heart.

Esther J Carlson
I REACH FOR THE STARS

Dedicated with gratitude, to the memory of my two high school English teachers, Ethel Zimmerman and Mabel Iser

---

I reach for the stars
And fall on my face—in the mud.
In the mud I learn to wait.
I must or never rise again.
I wait—
For surely one will come with love
To lift me up
To greater joys than I have known.
He comes.
But I must take his hand with faith
And then I'll rise to heights
Before unknown.

Debbie Cudd
LIFE WITHOUT GRANDMA

To my precious Grandma Murdock and Grandma Dunnam—I miss you

Today, I wept. Today, I cried
You see, today—my Grandma died.
With skin so soft and eyes so bright.
She was the best part of my life.
She always baked cookies, and smelled like a rose.
I used to sit and listen to stories
Around her old stove.
Today she's gone and home isn't home
My future looks dim with no warmth in sight.
Although it sounds cruel—I must confess,
When I wrote these words, today, I lied.
See, I'm really an orphan
And don't know my real name.
So pretending to have family is my favorite game.
Don't judge me too harshly
Today I needed to cry
I would love to have a Grandma—even
If she had died.
So, please understand when I write my fantasy
Today, I just needed to play-act my dream.
If your old, sick, and tired and feel all alone
Consider me coming to live in your home.
I need someone to share all my time
Cause today—belonging to a Grandma
Is all in my mind.

Frances Erickson
GODS' SUFFICIENCY

As grasses bend
But straighten after rain,
My burdened heart bowed down
May rise to joy again;
For God who lifts the grasses up
Showers blessing everywhere
And always lifts my spirit
When I come to Him in prayer.

As pine trees twist
When winds are high,
But straighten stronger—
So may I,
When this has passed,
Straighten as the storm-tossed tree
Knowing Gods' strength
Sufficient for me.

Maria Santo
THE DEATH OF A FRIEND

I can't help thinking of you
now that you are gone.
When yesterday was tomorrow
and we didn't have any sorrow.

Why did you have to die
leaving me to cry?
Why did you have to leave
making me grieve?

Hearing your name one night
filled me with such fright.
Thinking of you each day
and why you went away.

So many words
that were left unspoken.
So many plans
that were broken.

Now it's time for us to part
but you will always be in my heart.

Dionne Nicole Eldridge
WAS IT BECAUSE OF OUR COLOR?

To my Mother, Lillian, whom I love very much. . .

I was a young girl,
A young black girl
in Africa, my home

So happy I used to
be with my family
not caring about the
hot blazing sun
beaming down on
the sands of my non—
shading pavement.

As the warm wind
whisked the misty sand
across my

ebony face

We were unaware. . .
unaware that "White
Man" searched and
found us.

Oh, dear Lord, hear my
cry,

What have they
done to my people of
color?
Ruining our name
by calling us
"Niggers."
All I hear are sounds.
Sounds that are hard
to ignore. . .
The cracking of whips
from behind,
The squaks of our oars
as we steer the wooden
ship,

The stench of salt from
the sea.

Why should we cry for
help?

No one will hear.

The "White Man" watches. . .

We are being taken to
America.

To be sold. . .

Sold like pieces of meat
to hungry dogs or wolves

Used as "bedwarmers," and
heavy-duty workers.

One day I tried to escape.
to be free was all I
asked.

Shotguns,
Bloodhounds,
Chains,

The sounds of their footsteps
came after me. . .

Feeling the sweat run down
my face, onto my dingy
dress.

They will hang me to death
if they catch me.

Then, there will be no
more pain, for I will
have crossed the Freedom
Bridge.

Free from turmoil and Hell. . .

Soon, I will have a voice
and a choice in this cruel
and mindless world. . .

No more will I see such
hatred or bloodshed
towards our color.

I Am Free
Praise the Lord, I am
finally Free.

But someone answer me,

Was it because of our
color?

Will we ever understand?

Connie Edlin
ILLUSIONS

Twas a full moon on the 13th of June
There was misty rain and numerous clouds
I sat composed as I sipped my tea
Glanced out my window to see a shroud
Patiently I await my friend's arrival
Only my friend did never show
Thoughts came and went as I grew intense
Took a walk through my garden down by the cove
I could hear the faint sound of mantra
As Incense encircled the air
I meditated for a while, looked up with a smile
To a Banshee who, appeared on my stairs
This Banshee, could she be my friend
Oh, this seems to be utterly confusing thought I
She looks of death and wishes unkept
Perhaps an Illusion that will fade away or die
Suddenly I awake from my dream
To a morning that's sunny and bright
Grandmother had delivered my mail
Only a dream no cause for fright, she replied
I open my card and it reads
Loki, the prince of darkness is at hand
Open thine eyes and ears unto the Lord
He will enable you to withstand

Anita Maltin

Anita Maltin
FRIENDSHIP

A friendship has to balance—to be lasting
Firm and true—one side cannot give and one side take the whole way through.
There must be an equal share of sympathy and fun, all the cheer and understanding cannot only flow from one.
If a friendship is to balance each must do her level best—to study and consider the other's interests.
Each must forfeit something for the other person's sake—
If a friendship is one-sided there is bound to be a break.

Wayne Shockley
MY DREAMS

Back in my younger days
I dreamed of growing old
and of how life would be
watching my dreams unfold.

I'd pretend I was a rich man
with all within my reach,
all I needed was wisdom
and a place to dwell and teach.

Then my mind would wonder
to an unknown distant shore
only to see ruthless killing
and countries torn by war.

Most of my dreams are forgotten
of lost with the passing of time,
I've lived with words like loneliness
and love's I thought were mine.

Like the wind life changes
no two days are the same
and the way my dreams unfold
there's no one but me to blame. . .

Donna Danielle "Baby-Dee" Perez
A PLEA TO MY LORD

I, dedicate this poem to my beloved grandmother, the late, INEZ ELIZABETH GLOVER, who will always live in me. And to GOD; who allows me this talent. NADIA, I love you!!!

Dear GOD please help me to stand,
Bring peace to our corrupt land;
As I look about from man to man,
I realize damnation is at hand.
I see our nation growing weak:
Our country soon to fall;
Grant us the strength we so desperately seek,
Dear Lord please heed my call.
The drugs, booze, negative attitudes:
All soon to be our leader;
As I sit here pleading for strength,
They continue in making us weaker.
Our children are starving daily,
For the love they need to grow;
Our negligent adults, too concerned with war:
So how could they possibly know?
Our men are killing each other;
For a nickel, for a dime;
I hold my head down in constant shame,
And hope for a change in time.
Our women disgracing themselves,
Losing morals day by day;
I see the despair their faces reveal,
And my heart seems to melt away.
So once more my dear Lord:
I stretch my hands to thee;
Remember these words I wrote,
Remember these prayers, my plea!

Virginia A Ingalls
MUSIC

This poem is dedicated to music lovers everywhere, especially my loving husband Thomas.

Heaven's breath within its being,
Lifting us beyond earth's bars,
Giving us a glimpse of glory
In the space above the stars!

Every note an angel's movement
Echoing, from pole to pole;
Gift of God to worldly longing
For refreshment of the soul!

Mark S Hurst
REASONS DAY
Time's a calling to be as one,
And the time we'll take
Takes sometime to be done.
Neither one of us knows what
Will follow us from here.
Just that we know that our hearts,
Filled with fear, must be near.
Just follow us lightly, and step in when you can.
Be kind of enlightning when we're needing a hand.
The show of your strength, with no need for demand,
Helps to show us the way when we need to take a stand.
When the silent promise, love and of care,
In our lives is present, we know that you're there.
Is so often a comfort in sometimes of despair,
Remembering those voices of thoughts passed away,
Trying unselfishly, to help you make it through the next day.

Geneva Fields Mcfarlan
YESTERDAY

Dedicated to my dearest sister "Mary Poythress Bright"

As I walk thru the woods, down the path I used to know
The old trees are bending and my steps are very slow

Once the trees were young and so was I
The summer breeze would rustle the leaves
And you could hear a murmuring sigh

The smell of hickory, and the aroma of plums
The scent from the old apple tree, and the pleasant
sweet gum.

The robins plucked the china berries from the old china
berry tree. We swung in the old rubber tire
swung from the branch of the same rugged old tree.

The pine thistles had a clean smell, and the sweet smell
of new mown hay.

We were picking plums and berries and were laughing
with glee as we play.

This was the yesteryear, that should be here today.
It and I came too early, now we are too tired to play

Jeffrey N Graham
TEEN DRIVER
The screech of tires sounded,
shattered glass flew around,.
and a puddle of teenage blood
formed upon the ground.

Red lights and sirens
surrounded the scene
and lying in their midst
was the body of a teen.

He'd been president of his class
and captain of the team
but because of one stupid act
his blue eyes lost their gleam.

There had been a party
a scant few hours before.
His friends asked him to stop
but he continued to drink even more.

When in his brand new car
he climbed behind the wheel,
he sat upon a pencil's point
but the pain he did not feel.

As he drove down the road
he weaved from left to right.
Because he was driving drunk
he did not survive the night.

W Ed Elliott
MOUNTAINS HAVE NO EMOTIONS
Silent mountains
Dominating the sky line,
Lording it over
We peasants here below.

Mountains aren't bothered by emotions;
Nor heat, nor cold . . . Nothing.
Rains may wash them away,
Winds may blow them away,
Snows may cover them,
But a mountain doesn't care;
Mountains have no emotions.

Earthquakes may cause them to tremble
Or shell-fire, or a bomb.
Fires may burn them,
Ice may freeze them;
But a mountain does'nt care,
Mountains have no emotions.

I envy a mountain!
Its strength and staunch indifference;
Its stoic impenetrability,
Void of all emotions . . .
But—I am not a mountain!

Alice Louise Parry
THE CYNICAL ROSE LOVER
Take the time to stop and smell the roses, don't just rush through the garden every day.
This advise which seems so wise and sweet is given by many folks in a thoughtful kindly way.
To me this phrase was once spoken and now I've stopped, I've smelled, and really, I must say
Thank you to the gardner who lovingly cares for them— they are so beautiful and delightful and gay,
So delicate, so fine, so fragrant, but more I must report— so much to my dismay—
My nose is sneezy, from the thorns my finger hurts, and you need to get some aphid spray.
I stop to smell the pretty roses and what a price I pay!
I think I'll find a different pleasure—watch a cloud, a butterfly, a bluejay.
But now I must rush along, I'll try to stop again some other day.

Joyce Eads King
MUD PIES AND BRICK HOUSES

To Grandpa, Connie, and Joe for the memories. And, to Daddy for encouraging me to write.

Grandpa's farm is gone now.
There's a brand new development there.
I remember we made mud pies.
Coming home with dirt in our hair.
I can still see Joe Kicking a hill to make dirt bombs
To hurl as grenades to the sky.
It's a wonder we ever lived through it.
All the fights and running away from home.
So they took a part of our childhood,
And they covered it over with bricks.
The people who live there don't know it.
But right where they watch their T.V.
We once hunted monsters and villains
And ghosts we couldn't even see.
I'm looking the neighborhood over.
Oh, I know the world isn't fair.
But, the farm in the country is gone now.
And, we spent so much childhood out there.

Mario D Montoya

Mario D Montoya
TOMORROW IS COMING

Dedicated to all the children of America, especially to my children.

Tomorrow is coming
The light is in the sky
New era is the future
America wake up.

America smile
Everyone in town
Life is love
Don't brake the road.

The country is the heritage
Of Washington and Lincoln
Who fought for the freedom
And who died for the land.

Unity and brotherhood
All races are just
Daughters and sons
The Country needs you.

Destroy all the nuclear
It is the power of evil
God send solar energy
It is the future symbol.

The tears convert the rivers
The ground converts into cities
And gives us cultivation
For the new generations.

Living in peace is great
In this marvelous world
Thank you again
Tomorrow is wonderland
I hope America is great.

God bless you America
And your scientific men
For new future era
For new future land.

Emily Dickson
INDIVIDUALITY
I'm different from other people;
People are all the same.
You can't tell that I'm different, from my normal name.
I just know I'm different, my thoughts, my feelings;
not many people can relate.
Sometimes I feel I cannot communicate.
I'm proud to be different; it's boring to be the same.
Even if you can't tell I'm different, from my normal name.

Marjorie Lee Newcomb
MY CHILD
We only had you for a day,
And how we wished that you could stay.

But God came and took you home
To be a star in his great throne.

Just like a jewel you would be.
And so we named you Tiffani.
An angel fair and perfect too.
I guess that's why we could not keep you.

If we had got to keep you longer,
Would our hearts have gotten stronger?
Would the pain of losing you be less?
No! We would have loved you more, I guess.

And so we gave you back to God,
Angel, product of our love.
Until we meet on heaven's sod
We'll watch our "star" shine up above.

Robert E Vert
A CITY BY THE SEA

For the memory and family of Frank Vert and Gunnar S. Hanson

A city by the sea
Tugs at my tails
It calls like the
Siren of Ulysses
"Come to me"

I knew not then
What I know now
Youth like spectors
Say "set us free",
As the city by the sea
Says "come to me"

I listened
I grasped her hand
I smelled her fragrance
How sweet
A snow capped sentinel
Stands in the background
Accentuating her majestic
Beauty,
While the Bremerton bound
Trumpet
"You've come to me"

An emerald garden
Cascades her bossom
So pure, as to astound
The gods of Olympus

The cold yet sometimes
Gentle sound that touches
Her heart whispers in the
Breeze
"This is why you've
Come to me".

Youthful spectors guide
Me as I show those that I
Love what was once given
To me
Through them the memories
Come back.

I left my home for battle
A battle far across the sea
Now all I have are memories
Of the city by the sea,
That cries in the wind
"My son, my blessed son
Come back to me".

Barbara Wells Soliman
FLOATING

To and fro
I'm drifting
without a rudder
in this world of uncertainty.
Job, home husband, all were mine.
My life moved in an orderly direction
before the world flipped upside down.
The view interests me on the way down
as troubles of life shift my direction.
Job, home, husband, nothing's mine
in this world of uncertainty.
Without a rudder
I'm drifting
to and fro.

Caroline E Bailey
MY GATOS

Dedicated to my husband; Stevan Reed and our Gato's "Fat Bob" and "Suzie".

They're with me in the morning,
They're as hungry as a bear.
They're with me after feeding them,
They like to share my chair.

They're with me drinking coffee,
"Fat Bob" Likes to smell my cup.
They're with me trying tooth and
Nail from letting me get up.

They're with me while I'm cleaning,
That's when they clean themselves.
They're first through the door in
The kitchen,
When anything's moved on the
Shelves.

They're with me right at dinnertime,
And if their not I'll know,
Thay have a special language,
Just in case I don't quite toe.

They'll stare at me; sit on me;
And the other will work the
Floor.
The slightest move will set them
Off towards the kitchen door.

Then afterwards they settle
Down to shifts around the clock,
Of wanting in and wanting out—

"The Gato's in my flock".

JoAnn Dorsey Dupras
REMEMBER DADDY

I dedicated my poem to my darling daughter, Marlene

Remember how I use to wait
Standing by the front gate
I would see you comming down the walk
I was so excited, I could hardly talk

Remember how we use to play
You showed me how to build toys out of clay
We would run around on sunny days
Acting silly and being gay
I love you daddy, will you please stay

Richard L Lemley Jr
THE RENAISSANCE MAN

Dedicated to the one who inspired me to write this poem, my good friend Richard Gonzales

---

T'was long ago in a far away land,
That I first met the Renaissance Man.
He was brave, he was bold, he was gentle and kind,
Worked well with his hands, was quick with his mind.
Well traveled was he, London, Paris and Rome,
No time for a wife, no need for a home.
His thoughts were so varied, new challenges yet undone
Like exploring the earth, the stars, the sun.
He learned of his budding power deep within,
His soul full of desire to grow and to win.
So many goals, to paint, to write, to build,
His agenda for life was already filled.
His zest for living was rivaled by none,
For he knew the rebirth of his life had begun.
For so many years life's light had been out,
With no reason to try, only trouble and doubt.
But the dark days of living are now in his past,
His new life beginning, unshackled at last.
For now times had changed, with so much to be done.
New knowledge to gain, new love to be won.
By trial and error these things would be done,
Combined with the Spirit of Jesus the Son.
But this Renaissance Man wasn't worried you see,
For this Renaissance Man, my dear friend, he is me.

Kathy Lee
YOUR SPECIAL

My heart will remember the things you have done
Those things I can believe in when the dark is lonley and you are gone
Not the things you have promised for future days
Or things you have given me to pass the time away
Or the things you have said when a change was made
Those small lovely words or ones that hurt so bad
Just your deeds, the things you have done
Some big, some so small
I love all of you, no matter how you come.

Linda Baron
POPCORN

I love the taste of popcorn—
Its smell is for the
happy times
Like you and I
Sharing baskets full
and drinking beer,
While talking, teasing,
laughing—and
Visiting with strangers,
like Sarah in red beret'.
She, a lonely widow
You—offered her acceptance,
My love for you
Grew even more. . .
That day!

Doris Brown
HOW LONG HAS IT BEEN?

How long has it been Lord, since I spent some time with you?
That I ask for Your forgiveness, asked what You would have me do?
When was the last morning that I greeted You with a smile
Thanked You for watching o'er me while I slept through the night?

How long has it been Lord, since I sat down with Your Word
And read from It's Holy Pages the sweetest message ever heard?
Can I recall the last time I visited with a friend
and told him of Your Salvation, begged him to make amends?

How long has it been Lord, since I knelt beside my bed,
and thanked You for Your blessings, asked Your guidance for days ahead?
Well, I don't know for sure Lord, but I know it's been too long
since I felt Your Holy Spirit, since my heart was filled with song.

So I want to take this moment to kneel down upon my knees
and ask for Your forgiveness, to renew my heart with Thee.
And I want to start each morning with a Prayer of Praise for Thee
And all through the day and evening too, may others see
Your light in me.

Lillian L McKay
UNTITLED

Red ribbon baker
Pride bubbles to the surface
Joy to Meredith

Heather comes and goes
In and out with Grandmother
Living is such fun

Angela Scharfetter
THE MIGHTY MISSISSIPPI

The Mighty Mississippi, exploring all of nature
and master of its course,
from tranquil sunrise to majestic sunset!

Provider for many and creator of much,
inspires friendships and
passions of love.

What miraculous wonder brings such enchantment
with its subtle power,
That flourishes the imagination
and nutures
one's desires!

Among all glories bestowed from above,
should we not stop and ponder such creations —

And seek their beauty, peace and understanding
that surrounds all of us.

Iris O Mann
ONLY FOR ME

To my husband Carl, with his understanding. That I could only write after midnight, And to my Son David who gave me much encouragement

---

Bring back to me
my memories,
Of whimmering silk
and fine old lace.
Blackberry cordial and lemon tea!

But leave only for me,
those memories
of a scrubbed pretty face
and sweet smelling hair,
all in place!

And always,
I'll keep just for me,
a stolen secret kiss
still treasured,
with thoughts of love to be!

Bring back to me
those memories,
of tunes we hummed
and songs we sang,
of love that came to be!

Always,
These will be,
in my memories!

Ronald L Titman
AN ORACLE IN THE NUCLEAR AGE

Icy tones upon callous gray,
This wind will blow for countless days
Carving the land with hell and fire,
Torrents rage with mindless desire

Left with battered fields and conquered lands,
Their reign will fall into many hands
The weak will chose the coward's path
The strong and wise will feel their wrath

Years will pass and tensions grow,
In these fields, a bad seed they'll sow
To sprout forth a passive hell,
Encase these fields in a hardened shell

But the strands are weak and ties will break,
Even the massive earth will shake
So, release this evil, let it soar,
The living death of Nuclear War

Keith Parks
UNTITLED

Oh speck of dirt
Oh you look nice to me now
Sand can't beat you
Or mud can't out do you
Oh you look beautiful to me now
Dust can't fly over you
And the biggest rock can not crush you
So there is no need to swallow you for safekeeping

David R Ferolito
THE FERRET

And like a wise old man, acute and inspiring,
Who sits poised on a blanket of snow,
Gazing coldly into the vast white horizon,
Surrounded by the odor of evergreen saplings,
Waving soundlessly in the desolate winds,
And cleverness looms in his irresponsive eyes,
The ferret's tail brushes the unbroken snow,
In a respected all-knowing indifference,
A state of motionless pride.

David Wayne Beard
TEN AND SEVEN

Dedicated to my daughter, Terrie. It was written to her at 17 years of age, a very troubled time in her life. This poem helped inspire her to become the beautiful, loving, caring person she now is.

I know this girl of ten and seven
Who lives in hell and dreams of heaven.
The hell she's in, is her own making
Heaven's there, just for the taking.
Happiness is not out there
Wandering here and there.
True happiness is at home
Where there's a special love all her own.
I know this girl of ten and seven
For I was there when she came from heaven.
The Prettiest sight my eyes had seen
She looked to me just like a dream.
Through the years, though she has grown
From my heart, she'll never roam.
I love this girl of ten and seven
Sent to me straight out of heaven.
If I could take her pain and sorrow
I'd do it today, not tomorrow.
I understand for I was there
I also had no one to care.
Though I found in the end
My Dad was a very good friend.
So if things go wrong and things get bad
Please come home and talk to Dad.

Janice L Francis
WHY

To RoseMary, Phil, and Brenda Voight in loving memory of their daughter/sister Cheryl

---

Why, Lord, Why
Did you take our child away?
Couldn't you let us keep her
on earth with us to stay?

The child you grieve is mine.
You raised her as your own—
But when I gave her to you,
She was only yours on loan.

In the masterplan of life
Each of you have a spot.
Your life is for a purpose
Not just a chance of lot.

When I gave you Cheryl
She had a job to do.
For having known and loved her
The better are all of you.

Her life on earth is over
She was only just a guest.
It's time for her to come to me
To home—to peace—to rest

Julian Steve Munoz
HAVING A BABY

Having a baby
is such a special treat.
I love him all over,
from the tip of his head, to the toes on his feet.
I will care for his needs,
throughout the years.
Show him some good times,
and wipe away his tears.
I will teach him things,
the way they ought to be.
Justice for all, Life, Love and Liberty.
Yes, having a baby
is such a special treat.
One of the beauties of nature,
which is hard to beat.

Billie Jean Nored Caldwell

Billie Jean Nored Caldwell
CLOSE YOUR EYES

To Vance and Vince, Mom and Dad, my entire family. To my friends—they know who they are.

Close your eyes, close your eyes
Come drift away with me.
I shall paint for you a rainbow,
A brilliant arc; colorful to see.
Maybe sculpt a majestic mountain,
Snow-cap above verdant base.
Or fashion a perfect flower—a mandrake

The fertile earth shall be its vase.
Now open your eyes . . . It's all disappeared,
But much to my surprise,
I am one helluvan artist . . .
When I fantasize.

Wanda N Stanton-Borel
OUR TIME

To the lost loves of my life who left me with special friendships as we each went on to today.

Just a note to let you know I thought of you today
In such a way to cause me say
"Many smiles and easy road along your way,
Old friend."

So that things won and lost of yesteryears
Bittersweet—of joy and tears
Would still be reflected as sincere,
That "our time" never end.

Glenn Wintemberg
A PASSAGE OF TIME

The little baby lies there,
so quiet and content.
The little girl she sits there,
you wonder where time went.
The young lady stands before you,
In your eyes she is so sweet.
The young woman sits there pondering,
the man she is to meet.
The mother with her baby,
a loving sight to see.
The grandmother sits and reminisces,
this is how it's supposed to be.

The passage of time goes so quickly by,
No time to rest, no time to sigh.
We'll open our hearts and look to tomorrow
A life time of joys, few moments of sorrow

Patricia Ann Young
CHEERFUL

This poem is dedicated to Mrs Barri Armitage, my personal friend and lyric poet.

I'm cheerful
Not prize winning cheerful
Not drunk over wine cheerful
Not cheerful of attending a wedding
But just spiritual cheerful
Cheerful there's a loving God
Cheerful that I'm understanding
Cheerful that I can find peace
in this cruel world.

Tom Hord III
DRESDEN

Oh, empire of sandstone—
Who has heard your mute statues speak?
The witness to man's ultimate ruin.

Arisen from the ashes—
Your pinnacles etch an exalted canvas.
A panorama for the living reclaimed.

Goethe's vision redeemed—
By your human hands worn triumphant.
The world returns in noble grace.

Elsie A Marklowitz
HAPPY 50TH ANNIVERSARY

It's a honor to be married 50 years
You have thoughts of happiness
and also tears.

Your family and friends are happy
for you
And God plays a part in the
celebration too.

The years together go by so fast
But you have the memories that
really last.
As you look in the future of each
day
The Heavenly Father guides your
way.

The Best of Everything is wished
for you here
And God Bless and Keep you year
after year.

Brie Louise Sundquist
THE ROSE
I see in my minds eye a
Man walking through a valley, as
dark gray hangs overhead.
Walking by one lone rose, not dead
but merely asleep,
thinking of how this was once a
place, where children
laughed among the trees.
But, not anymore.
Now it's just an old rotten forest,
One sleeping rose lying in wait.
Waiting for the day when children
once again will laugh
among the trees,
and play among the flowers.

Irja Waris Anderson
BLUE GLIMPSE
The miles fly by
as I drive
toward my destination.
My eye and mind
take in,
almost unconsciously,
the blue of the sky,
and the blue, blue
of chicory
that borders the road.
I am reminded
of my mother's eyes,
the same blue—
And from the past
she comes to me,
kind, and gentle,
and loving.
I smile—but
a sigh escapes my heart.
I drive on.
The miles fly by.

Frank R Basile
BURNING LOVE
Love is similar to
fire.

A bright one glowing midst
the trees.

shining against the blackness
of life's forest.

It licks at the sky,
searching,

it's hunger measured only
by

the amount of food given
it.

My love for you is the
same.

I reach for the sky, for it's
where you are.

I smile when there is little
to laugh at

It comes from the heart and is
caused by you.

I thirst for your warmth, your
closeness.

I can have you as often as
you come to me.

to lick at you hungrily,
consume all of you.

hoping you never let me fade away.
Feed me always, my love.
I burn inside, only for you.

Madeline D Crane
HAUNTED
There stands alone atop the hill
Amid gathering darkness still
A house deserted aeons ago.
A phantom grey amidst the snow
With walls tumbling with decay
As leafless trees 'round it sway.

Winter winds around it sigh
And when the moon rides high
Ghostly shadows slip thro it
Pointing death's bony hand
As if to reveal the menace
Locked up within the walls.

In solemn rhythm there's the knell
Of moaning breezes, soft and low
That tell the secret dark and drear,
"His wife was murdered here!"
Fear will not let me wait to hear,
T'was I who left her buried here.

Linda Warren Thaxton

Linda Warren Thaxton
TO MY VALENTINE

For Jake, for his constant inspiration

And, therefore, if I truly do deserve
this,
If Life and Love have this in mind
for me,
While I sit back and survey all my
kingdom
And wonder how I ever found the
key

Then I, alone, feel I'm the one
who's blessed,
To step inside a world as pure as
thine,
To hear thy voice with all its happy
colors
Proclaim, straightforward, that
same world is mine.
Yet, let me only stand within thy
shadow,
To know such warmth as muted
sunbeams bring
To see thy face light up when thou
art happy,
And know when thou art hurt, how
bad the sting

Henceforth, if I should step outside
the pattern
To loose the ties or try to struggle
free,
I know thine own would quietly
endure it,
And tears would flow from none
the more than me.

Patricia Livingston
HERE IN THE GARDEN

To Richard, my loving son.

Here in the garden, I worship,
Here in the garden I pray,
Here in the garden I worship,
And give thanks for each
wonderful day.

I give thanks for the flowers, the
birds,
and the trees, Thanks for the
mountains,
the sand and the seas,
As here in the garden, I fall on my
knees.

Andrina N Jordan
PRETTY KITTY!

To my mother, father, and sisters, I love you.

Pretty, Pretty, Pretty Kitten
You are so fluffy.
You look like a mitten.
Your
eyes
Are different colors,
That's
What makes you so sweet.
I
Wish,
I could
Hug you—then your eyes would
Blink.
You are such a
Pretty,
Pretty,
Pretty Kitty.

Carolyn J Bedell
SENSELESS SORROW
I have known him
Eight beautiful years
Now just thinking
Brings endless tears

So young and innocent
All I hold dear
Yet now his presence
Is nowhere near

Nourished with food and
Starved in soul
Now I ask you what
Is your goal

Once so cheerful, sunny
And bright
Now you hide him
When it's light

You taught him well
Told to lie
Now I'm wondering
Will he die

Crushed in spirit
Broken heart
Why and when did
It ever start

Bonnie Winkelhake
THE DRUMMER MAN

To Dad

I love to tell his story now;
And beat the drum for him and
how.

At his command the drumsticks
would fly;
And tell a musical story to you and
I.

I miss the sound of his beating
drum;
All percussion was he to the last
hum.

Cymbals, triangle then bass and
snare;
For he played to others and they
did care.

And the best was he to roll a beat;
Playing tympani as if to greet.

With flourish he rolled the
drumsticks he held;
And with the symphony he would
meld.

As the tympani beat bases each
song,
So the drummer man led us all
along.

His steady beat on the drum he
had;
Kept us all going and that's my Dad.

Helen A Jones
GRADUATION DAY
Your High School days are over
And as you reminisce,
And look back over the last four
years
I'm sure there are things you'll
miss;
But Graduation Day is here,
So tuck fond memories in your
heart
And in your mind look forward,
To the life you're about to start:
Graduation is just a stepping stone
To what the future holds for you,
Always strive to do your best
And may all your dreams come
true.

James Michael Phillips
REST IN PEACE
An unnatural paradise is where my
soul is now chained.
Big iron links hold me so I may
only venture a few feet
from my chosen spot. Eyes sunk in
a deathly glance, as
my soul finds the nerve to look
back, back through the
mist of hurt and confusion to my
outer shell. Madness,
total and complete, as I see a look
of terror locked
upon my face. A heart that could
never be found by
human eyes and feelings lost
forever in the firey pits
of hell. A tear hits the unmoving
dust as my soul
crumbles into itself only to be
blown away in a whirlwind
of overbearing hate for others that
had tightened
my chains beyond the point of
death. So I must repeat
my torment until the cosmos itself
crumbles into nothingness
will I truly REST IN PEACE. . .

Joseph B Petrick
THE FINAL CHAPTER
The final page is written
In the books of history,
As man unleashed his deadly
bombs
And sent troops overseas.
The final war can't be won

And it destroys the human race.
A show of greed and ignorance
Mans quest for dominance.
They say, when a mistake is made:
A lesson has been learned,
But this time, there is no second chance.
The hate spreads across the world;
A million lives are lost each day
As cities slowly burn.
Their death ridden glow subsides;
A mother holds a dying child
But no one is concerned.

Brenda Melson
SO FAR AWAY
Are you there?
You seem so far away
from me. . .
Even when we're together. . .
I talk to you
but
You seem so far away,
In a distant world
unreachable to me
As though
you have already
left me
alone,
in a cold,
loveless
environment.
I'm cold
and
lonely.
I need
someone
to hold me
and keep me warm.
Are you there?
Where have you gone?

Katherine Anne O'Keefe
THE CLIMB
The scintillating whisper of pine
brushes against my body
as I climb for the sky
branch by branch getting closer
struggling with anticipation
knowing glory at the top
I sigh looking down
at what has been accomplished
and grin as I see all

Judy Berry

Judy Berry
LOVE IS A WORD
Love is a word that you say when you mean it,
not a game that you play when there's no lovin in it.
Not a ring that you wear on your left hand,
not a paper that you sign with the preacher man.
It's a world of its own, it's all convention,
it's a thing that you know, but you hardly mention.
It's a look in your eye, when you call my name,
it can give you wings, it can cause you pain.
You'll never know the times I've cried,
you don't seem to feel a thing inside.
I know that I'm already losin you,
the way you carry on.
Sure, love packs up, and it can be gone.
A one-sided love can never go on.

There was a time, it seems so long,
when our world was young and strong.
It was more than the games that we played,
Now those wedding bells nothing more than empty shells.
Echo in the promises we made have all faded far away.

There is nothing that is wrong in wanting you to stay with me,
but now we have parted, its time to get started on a new life
and hope we will find our next partner.

Joyce Elaine Siewert
TAKE THE TIME
It seems like only yesterday when you, my youngest, was so tiny and pink.
Your skin was so soft—it felt just like mink.
I know that simply can't be true anymore,
For you are now a young woman of twenty-four.

Many times throughout your life, I wished you weren't growing up so fast;
How I wanted those carefree days of "little girl" innocence to last.
Your talents are many—your failures are few.
Did I ever take the time to say how proud I am of you?

Like most mothers and daughters, we don't always see eye to eye.
No matter—for I want you to know that my love for you
Can still reach the sky.
I recall your school days with your special talent with music and all.
When you played the violin and I was at the piano, I felt ten feet tall.

City competition each year was certainly a lot of hard work and tension,
But I feel the pleasure was more than I can ever mention.

Many years have passed since those busy days,
But I still continue to be proud of you in so many ways.
When you see something you want and you've set such a high goal,
Determination is always there with all your heart and soul.

You're a mother now, and I'm sure you already know
What a thrill it is to watch your two little girls grow.
Don't wait until you're a grandma to tell them you care.
Take the time now—
Before they grow up and no longer are there.

Kristen Nugent
WHY?
Why is there war?
What is it for?
There wouldn't be anything
To be thankful for
If there was war.

Pamela L Rogers
LOVE IN SEASON
You know
Our relationship
Could very much be compared
With the seasons. . .
In the spring
When we started
It was luke warm
And
Just beginning to grow. . .
In the summer
It was hot
And blossoming...
But then came the fall
We cooled off.
I guess in the winter
Things will freeze. . .
Until the spring
Where it will
(Maybe)
Once again
Thaw out
And Again Begin
To
Grow.

Anna L Scarberry
THE DEAF

For my beautiful daughter, Susan

The deaf are those who cannot hear
They use their eyes instead of ears
Some don't speak but that's okay
They use their hands to have their say
They laugh and play as others do
When sad they cry like me and you

Tamie Collins
AS TIME GOES PASSING BY
As time goes passing by
Seconds ticking
My heart beats songs of sadness
Thinking of you and
How you left me behind

As time goes passing by
Oh so slowly
My heart beats songs of sadness
Thoughts of going on
Alone, without you

As time goes passing by
Advancing, progressing
My heart beats songs of anger
As I try to understand
Why you left without me

As time goes passing by
Steadily faster
My heart beats songs of strength
As I continue with
My life without you

Rose Marie Juliana Oddo-Hulton
A GIFT OF LOVE
What do you tell your little child when with innocence he prys,

"Mommy where do babies come from,
and so where did I?"

Do you simply smile uneasily and utter a heavy sigh,

Or do you kiss the little imp and tenderly reply.

"God has a special way my child of rewarding husband and wife,

Who so beautifully express their love
with the power of creating life.

And he gently places their seed of love
beneath the mother's heart,

So it can get the best of care right from the very start.

And with each day and with each week,
the small seed does grow,

Tiny fingers, arms and legs, and ten cute little toes.

Until arrives the grand event, this budding life matures.

With tears of joy both mom and dad
behold the child they've bore!"

Mr.Terry K Terwillegar
SPRING
The snow is gone,
The birds are returning home,
The rain has stopped for a day,
It's time to go out and play.

The sun is warm and bright,
The grass is green,
For I know that Spring is near,
Isn't it a beautiful sight.

Little children are playing outside,
The kites are flying high and low,
The old folks are sitting in the swing,
Oh, Boy, It must be Spring.

Wendy S Miller
AFTER YOU
To live a life,
a lonely one.
For me I shall not fret.
A life with you,
a lovely one.
Yes you I won't forget.
Alone, alas,
as broken glass.
My life will wonder on.
No warmth reborn,
my life has torn.
Now that you are gone.
Our love long past,
but not yet lost.
My shattered soul rebuilds.
A heart not gone,
but never strong.
From hate that never stilled.

Tami D Womack
THINKING OF YOU
The sun is shining bright,
Against a beautiful sky of blue.
There's a soft breeze blowing,
And I'm thinking of you.

I've thought about it hundreds of times,
It happened so quickly that night.
How did things get so out of hand?
Why did we have to fight?

But when the anger comes from hurt,
The ability to reason goes.
All you feel is hurt and pain,
And anger is all you show,

But, all of that was long ago.
Though the memories are still

strong in me.
I always feel good when I
remember the times,
And the way we used to be.

Sometimes I'll just start thinking,
You come to me out of the blue.
And maybe, just maybe, now,
you're thinking of me,
Like now, I'm thinking of you.

Shirley A Muhleisen
LOVE HAD WINGS

To my loved ones—Those who have gone before us and those who have stayed

---

Love had wings
Which we had not,
Traversing space to realms
unknown
And feelings we forgot.

Once a smile
But now a tear

Embraces, seals the saddened souls
Who chose to reappear.

Love has wings
But will it stay
Burdened, bound to earth?
No, love soars away.

Kim Marie Boone
CASTLES
As I went walking along thinking
how my life has gone
I came upon a little boy who was
playing in the sand.
Joy had filled his eyes as he looked
up to the sky
and said "I'm building this castle
just for you.
It's going to be as big as the sky, so
all the people
can go there when they die."

Now from time to time when I
am feeling down
I think of what that little boy said.
And now it all seems that
throughout all of my dreams
I see that little castle sitting in the
sand.

I went back out there one day when
life was going my way
and saw that same little boy sitting
in the sand.
Tears had filled his eyes as he
looked up to the sky
and said, "Oh how can you love
something that's gone away.
I was building it for you, as big as
the sky, so all the people
could go there when they died."

Now from time to time when I
am feeling down
I think of what that little boy said.
Oh how hurt he must of been when
his hopes were washed away
when a tide came in too high one
day.
But still it all seems that
throughout all of my dreams
I can still see that little castle
sitting in the sand.

Phil West
THE WRITER
Controlled by a different thought,
The writer remains content at
costs.
Writes what he feels, feels what he
writes,
A finder of words we assumed were
lost.

Some may never read his words,
Others may never care.
Few never catch the meaning,
As the writings fill the air.
So who can question the ways
of the writer.

Burning a match in a gusty wind,
The miracle released brings it back
again.
Demands the credit yet captures
the soul,
The message equals out the
unbalanced flow.

There is a point in height,
Which we may never reach.
There are many extremes,
Only the message could teach,
The all so many emotions
of the writer.

Sy Mac (Sylvia McDonald Heade)
THE DECADES
Do you remember hearing of The
Dull Eighties?
Then we had The Gay Nineties.
Then came The Turn Of The
Century.
We had The Warring Teens
The Roaring Twenties.
The Depression Thirties.
The Flying Forties.
The Nifty Fifties.
The Sizzling Sixties.
The Soaring Seventies
Now we have The Debating
Eighties.
Will everything be settled in this
decade?
Then Will We Have Another Gay
Nineties?

Derest A Christinia
THE SUFFERING WAY
We all experience suffering—
As long as we live.
There's an antidote for that
suffering—
Only Jesus can give.

He suffered the utmost agony,
Though He knew no sin.
There's no path that we tread in
our misery—
Jesus has not been.

We must suffer if we want to reign
with Him;
Share the victory:
He gained power o'er Satan and
death and hell—
At Calvary.

There's no 'person' that causes our
suffering—
It's the prince of this earth.
We can't fight him—just stand on
the Word of God
For all it's worth.

Suffering's good for us—helps us
as saints of God
to grow in grace.
So let's joy in our suffering for
Jesus,
And stay in the race.

Francis J McPartlin
I HAVE LIVED IN TIMES OF WAR
I have lived
In times of war
And added peace
To tie the score.
Yet, to find a way
To live my life,
Without the hatred
And the strife
That I have faced
In these lifeless days.
And I have followed
In my desperate ways;
And I have suffered
Throughout these years;
A fate to all;
Which has brought me tears.
But I will strengthen
In this generation,
With peace of mind
In this deadly nation.
For I am one
Of an only face
And I will conquer
The entire race.
For I am Love.

Bess Ferrell
THE BAG LADY
I watched with interest
The old woman
As winter wind's cold surge
Tossing her gray unkept locks
upward,
Allowing them to fall carelessly
about her narrow stooped
shoulders.
Rough chapped hands clutching
the brown burlap bag,
Her only possessions.
Small wrinkled face, etched by the
cruel artist of time,
Eyes empty, staring blankly at the
cold wet pavement.
Toes, naked, raw, protruding the
too small shoes plucked from an
open trash bin.
Soot filled snow falling upon the
bustling, noisy city.
A sudden chill shook her small frail
frame.
She shivered beneath the ragged
old coat,
Wiping her dripping nose upon a
badly torn sleeve
The old woman entered the filthy
alley-way.
Bags weeping refuse, lining the
dingy peeling walls.
Stinch of raw human waste lay
heavily upon the damp brisk
wind
As it scattered empty wine bottles
and rusty tin cans about the alley
floor.
A stray mangy cat scampered from
within a lidless garbage pail,
Disappearing through a gapping
hole in the ancient board fence.
From beneath a huge cardboard
box, a bearded black face
appeared,
Eyes prying.
The aged bag-lady searching
frantically throughout the vast
heap of rubble,
Hoping to find at least a morsel of
edible nourishing food,
To soothe the ever constant,
gnawing pain within her
drunken stomach.

Helen Osborne
THOUGHTS

To my devoted daughter, Helen.

My time has come—How could it
be?
So much to do—so much to see!
So many things I meant to say,
But never found the time—the day
To drop the mask we wear to shield
The way we think—the way we feel,
To tell of all our hopes and fears
Of lonely nights and lonely years.

My time has come—I know it's
true,
The azure skies are not so blue,
The breeze that blows brings too
much chill,
Across the open window sill.
In just a "twinkling of an eye"
The whole parade has passed on by:
The elephants, the acrobats,
Lions, tigers, all the cats;
The riders and the funny clowns,
Their tumbling acts of ups and
downs.
They've all gone by and left for me
the echoing coliope.

Judith Knaack Johnson
OUR LAST AUTUMN? (TO MARIE)
Glorious autumn, earth's varigated
quilt,
gold-strewn, rose-hand,
Softly muted in mist and shadow
forest green
Majestic scarlet maples punctuate
the hills
Amongst yellow birch and oak
Singed from dying summer's sun.

Imperfection within perfection,
and yet perfection still,
Dying, like you, yet vibrant,
fulfilled;
Robust celebration of season's end,
Come walk with me among the
leaves my friend.

Beneath autumn's sun-dappled
arbor

partake of peace, of rest,
Nourishment of soul for soul
distressed.
Let Nature's quilt enfold us now,
To keep at bay dark winter's wind.

Craig A LaPointe
INTO THOSE EYES
Into the mirror of my mind
Visions of smiles I can't let go
Hand and hand we were so free
Into those eyes I've come to know
I can see you now—I can almost
touch you

Into the joy of holding you close
Tears fall upon your gentle touch
Hand and hand we were so free
Into those eyes I've loved so much
I can see you now—I can almost
touch you

Into the heart of my very soul
Lies the echo of a silent good-bye
Hand and hand we were so free
Into those eyes that had to cry
I can see you now—I can almost
touch you

Into the night of lovers dreams
Set a new course on a falling star
Hand and hand we were so free
Into those eyes of near and far
I can see you now—I can almost
touch you

Into the day when love was young
Hopes are built upon days with you
Hand and hand we were so free
Into those eyes I've loved so few
I can see you now—I can almost
touch you

Charlene Bloodworth Jones
A GOOD MAN
He looked to where the arm had
been,
his heart heavy with sadness and
fear.
He wondered How will I embrace
and hold my loved ones near.
How will I ever tie my own shoe;
Help me Dear Lord, please
tell me what to do—
"My Beloved Son, so dear to my
heart,
What you must do is left up to you,
for that is your part.
Half a harvest you can reap
but with courage, all of it is yours
to keep."
Right then the man made up his
mind
His seeds were to be Gentle and
Kind.
With renewed strength, and twice
as much
effort, he did what he had to do.
And where the arm had been
a Beautiful Wing grew.

Thomas Brandsness
LETTER OF LOVE
Bittersweet lines of love
and hope
The desire to be near
A friend draws closer
Warmth and laughter
Pleasant memories
And high hopes
Interspaced with sly smiles
Secrets known but by two
Wrapped in ribbons of
time-worn blue
Dreams never forthright told
How the story will unfold
Days to come
When the bird's flight ends
To the safe haven
Of a friend's warm and caring
hands.
Tenderly held
All doubt dispelled
The words on the page will end
As the tear of joy is wiped dry
By a friend.

Melissa Anne Jauss
WHAT IS FUN?
"What is fun?"
Ask Samuel Dunn
On one sunny day.

So he went to the barnyard
Where he usually played
To see just what they would say.

"Fun is", said a prissy cow,
"To boss others around,
To tell them just when and where
to do things
And watch their hateful scowls."

"Fun is," said a muddy hog,
"To play about in the mud,
To get all yucky and dirty,
And look like some sort of crud."

And Sammy liked what he heard
In the barnyard pens.
But he decided that what fun was
Was having true friends.

C Ann McGuire
FLIGHT

Dedicated to my mother who gave wings to her daughters

Oh, to soar like the eagle, earth's
wonders to behold
The grass, the trees, the
countryside, the wheatfields
cloaked in gold
Majestic mountains beckon, their
secrets calling me
To every nook and crevice as far as
eyes can see
Outspread wings uplifting thru
clouds and deep blue sky
Lungs so full to bursting, this
miracle to fly
Rivers paths to follow, flowing
aimlessly
But with a final plan in mind,
perhaps an azure sea
All senses touch creation, wings
open to enfold
Oh, to soar like the eagle, God's
wonders to behold.

Charles M Bugara
WHAT YOU ARE

To My Dad, A great man. From your son Chuck

Happy Fathers Day, Dear Ole Dad,
you're the best Dad, anyone could
have,
I loved you then, and I love you
now,
So stand up, and take a bow.

You made sure, we had food to eat,
and bought me those red shoes,
they were neat,
We always had nice clothes to
wear,
You weren't the best, at cutting
hair,

You worked hard, to raise a girl,
and two boys,
and yes, we had plenty, of nice toys,
But not to mention, all the above,
I'll never forget, when you gave me,
my new ball glove,

You were always there, when I
needed you,
When I was feelin down, you
would help me through,
You and mom, did a lot for me,
Thank you, Thank you, yes indeed,

Sometimes I pray, when I'm happy
or sad,
I say, thank you Lord, for giving
me a great Dad,
But most of all, and by no means
by far,
I love you, for what you are,

Debra J Ashley
SPECIAL LOVE

This poem is dedicated to my devoted and loving husband, David Holmes Ashley

---

Met as children, lived as neighbors.
Became friends and dated later.
Husband-wife, soon ten together
Living love does last forever

Bought our first house where we
first met
Childhood sweethearts with no
regrets.
Memories of past, live the
present,
Keep us steadfast, future looks
pleasant.

Two hearts withstanding tests of
time.
Bonded as one & made divine.
Upholding love built strong to
take,
All which is determined by fate.

Stacey Williamson
ANOTHER DAY
What is before us?
Yet another day.
Filled with laughter,
Sorrow, work, and play.
And the frolicking,
Of children near,
Leads us to,
Yet another year.
Times may pass,
But memories will stay.
Reminding us of,
Yet another day.

Michelle Powers
ANIMAL LOVE
When animals die
They fly so high
They fly so high
Up in the sky
Way up there in the cleanliness
Way up there with the happiness
But still we'd take them back again
Just to hug them one more time

Linda Anne Figgins
WHO IS WORTHY

---

1) Prophetes' Pandiculation 2) with glory to Jehova-Shammah

When symbols shape imagery, a
haze we perceive;
Leads us, correct our vision, we
plead.
Who among mortals can savor but
upon which we feed?
Why be so decisive to elect or
concede.
Searching, while longing to sip,
only where water is sweet;
The sampling of many wells offers
the treat.
Swallowing in solitude, the flavors
each seeks;
Multitudes produce no one
grandeus or meek.

We create the aromatic airlock or
flow;
We allow the taste to permeate or
vanish as snow.
Discernment or discord, not gifts
to just those few,
Consume no fallacy (while
somewhat melancholy),
continue
to chew.
Dispose of that which sours the
Spirit or constricts the famished
heart and soul.
Seasons with all that you are lent,
to purchase the richest
delicacy, Unity, your ultimate goal.
Spirit, mind and body made whole.

Robin Eugenia Suprunowski
ABALONE
Chips of shells from lost sea shores,
Oh! How dull they once were,
Tiny mirrors on those stones,
Reflecting all of the terrible storms,
Pounding seas and restless winds,
Shaping and forming all of them.

Oh! How delicate they are now.
Colors soft yet colors bold,
All those beautiful colors yet
unknown.
All the shapes and forms they
come.
All looking like the setting sun.

What am I? Abalone . . .

H F LaRosse
MY BLESSING

In honor of our beloved daughter Cimoy L. (LaRosse) Walters, Walters, The inspiration for this poem.

Child birth is not an easy thing,
there is some pain you know,
Yet as you feel the baby kick, your
face becomes aglow.
To carry a child full term is
certainly no easy task;
So give me a healthy baby, Lord,
this is all that I ask.
Whenever that happy day came, I
heard this little cry.
As the doctor said, you have a
daughter, now open up your
eyes.

You were such a beautiful baby
and had such a head of hair,
I could hardly wait to hold you, and
to give you loving care.
Ah yes, it seems that time flew by,
for you were starting school.
Now it was time to teach you to
live by The Golden Rule.
I remember your first baby doll,
and your first party dress,
Your first slumber party, and how
your room was quite a mess.
I remember all the tears you shed
whenever things went wrong;
And how your heart would break
if you felt that you didn't belong.
I remember all of these yesterdays,
and all of your ups and downs;
Or how you would say something
silly and chase away my frowns.
When you finish your schooling
and start on your own career,
This is when I start to hold all these
memories so dear,
Yes, this is when I cut the string
and turn you loose to fly;
Knowing, that I will be with you,
as you go out there and try.
I guess what I'm trying to say is
"Daughters are so fine,
I thank the good Lord everyday for
blessing me with mine!"

Cindy McGinnis
WHAT IS FOREVER?
Forever—
Will the tides always reach the
shore,
or May always follow April
When each blossoming bud
is the birth of new life—
a cycle,
Forever is a cycle.
A neverending spinning wheel
the falling leaf of autumn
always promises the winter snow
Yet the snow will melt
into water trickling under the sun
Then what is forever?
Perhaps—
the endless days of tomorrow

Sharon Richard
MEMORIES
My memories wander to a better
place and time.

Reality is so harsh, but it's
comforting down deep in my
mind,

They say you can't live in a world
of fantasy, but I know this to be
untrue,

Cause that's mostly where I stay
now, since reality doesn't
include you.

The world is a cold harsh place to
be, I don't want to face it alone.

Since I don't have your love to
sustain me, it's my mind I must
call home.

If home is where the heart is, then
that's my mind for sure.

That's the only place outside your
arms, that I really feel secure.

Why must people fuss so? . . . Is it
really such a crime?

To stay where you feel happy and
safe, even if it's deep in your
mind.

Amy Lynn Eisenstadt
ARE WE REALLY HERE?
Is the sky really blue?
We see it blue through our human
eyes, but is it really blue?
Dreamers and thinkers see it plain
white like a clear page
Ready to be filled with their
thoughts and dreams.
Sad and mean people
See it grey and bland filled with
anger and hate, just as they are,
Shy people see it as green, as green
as a meadow, because it is a
place to
Escape the things that they are shy
and scared of, me, I see it In
many different ways,
I see it white and sometimes grey,
and green, but
Sometimes I really don't know,
I think is the sky really there. . . and
I don't know the answer,
I don't think I will ever know the
answer.
I would just have to keep on
wondering. . .???

Violet Downey Kruger
THE BLUE VASE
It's only a little blue vase,
Not elegant, fancy or fine.
A slim neck and round little
bottom,
No beauty or grace of line.

The color looks somewhat drab
As it stands up there on my shelf,
Not even one bit sensational,
To draw attention to itself.

Then it's moved to a new location,
To a sunshiny window so bright.
Its colors become iridescent,
Seem to glow with an inner light,

Expanding that light into prisms,
Reflecting all over the place,
Dancing on walls and ceiling,
From sunshine in that little vase.

Could we humans learn a lesson,
Gather sunshine into our soul,
Cast about us rainbows of
gladness,
The same as that little bowl?

Cecilia G Burke
HOW QUIET IS THE NIGHT

To My Beloved Mother

As I lay in my bed of rest, joining
in the serenity of the night,
I think of the day gone by, my
children asleep in their beds of
warmth and innocence.
I listen for their calm breathing
and think of not but minutes
ago, their voices loud and clear.
My love for the joys they've given
me, goes out to their heavenly
dreams.
How grateful one seems for all
their friends and loved ones
in this bliss.
The thanks one feels, the joys, the
sorrows, the calm of love that
makes ours the best there is.

As the lid of night starts closing in,
your loved one sleeping at your
side, your happiness deep inside
flows out in great thanksgiving.
The great band leader in the sky,
who leads us in the wonders of
day and night, hears my words
to His song of life.
The darkness seems to carry the
tune; I start to listen to the
harmony in the still of my room.
Cars go by on the distant roads, all
join in, some at the start of their
day, some at their end.
A toot from a diesel breaks up the
tune as in the back yard the dogs
bark at the moon.
A car door shuts, out in the night,
coming home to end its day.
A baby cries for his mother's arms.
A mother weeps for her loved ones'
life.
A siren brakes in this mystery tune,
but only for a second,
life and death are not left out as
night goes drifting on.
What will the new day bring as
sounds of the future lie deep in
the tomorrow?
My body lies limp to the melody of
rest, as I give thanks for all that
has been.
The darkness seems to be getting
light, I join in the quiet of the
night, to the heavenly bliss of
sleep, sleep.

Carrie A Piela
I LOVE
I love the sun that shines down on
me, the birds that fly so free.
I love the moon that controls the
ocean tide, the stars that glow
during the night.
I love the sand that blankets the
beach, the ocean waves that roll
over my feet.
I love the sky that is filled with
sunshine, the wind that is
traveling through time.
I love the music that is easy to
listen to, the sea that is so
beautiful and blue.
I love the clouds that dance in the
sky, the rain that tumbles down
in my eyes.
I love the mountains that stand so
bold, the falling snow that feels
so cold.
I love the animals that live in the
green forest, the trees that grow
their tallest.
I love the desert that holds a place
of its own,
I love you because you make me
feel at home.

Kathleen Schork

Kathleen Schork
FOREVER FRIENDS

This poem is dedicated to my beloved husband George Schork

There was a time in my life
When I needed a close friend,
Someone older and wiser
and to whom I could always
depend.
Someone to look up to
and correct me when I was
wrong,
Someone who could share a smile
When the road seemed too
narrow and long.
Someone I could share everything
with
weather dreams, joys, or sorrow.
But also a friend who would stay
close
Much longer than just
tomorrow.

I've found this special someone
and he's all the things I say.
I only wish I could be with him
each and every day.
He's alway's been understanding.
and so patient, sweet, and kind.
I'll be darned if he's not the best
friend
anyone could ever find.

Jill Renee' Robinson
DREAMS
I am the child
crying in the night
I am a cloud
moving freely across
the sky
I am the wind
blowing violently
outside your window
I am the tear
falling from your eye
slowing
hitting the ground
I am the waves
rolling onto shore
I am a seagull
flying free above the ocean
I am hate
lingering in your mind
I am love
warming your heart
I am all that I want to be
Dreaming can never end

Maria Caldeira
FOUR WAYS OF LOOKING AT HANDS
Hands are soft
with lines
resembling paths on a map
Fingers: attached as branches on
trees
Nails: to soothe a crying itch.

The body: having no extensions
made hands
enabling affection with
a gentle touch or caress
Hands have a purpose

They're always reaching out to
touch another
in warm handshakes
Thus, creating unity among all
men.
Hands are friendly.

People are hungry
Planting a seed takes only a hand
to bear the fruit
which satisfies a need.
Hands are survival.

Robert Lawrence Mazzola
GREEN CROSS STATION
"We're going out to meet her,"
The dream said, "Get your coat!"

"I need you there to greet her;
I want her to be home."
Along the black beds piled with loam,
(The wagon knew the lane by rote)
I saw winding dawn-lit tracks,
Waking fields, heard washing streams.
The distant hills that turned their backs
To catch the morning springtime sun,
Were all true hills except for one,
And that was Green Cross Station beams
Rising from the subtler plain
With wisps of smoke above the sage,
Pulling home that plaintive train.
I arrived; the rails were still.
A pot stood on a windowsill
Covered with the webs of age.
I looked up at the timeless beams,
Then turned around to stoke a dream.

Emma "Cricket" Campbell
LADY LIBERTY
Lovely Lady with torch held high
Against the morning's azure sky
With a show of gracious hands
Welcoming all from foreign lands
Giving freely to one and all
Another chance, another call
To live life fully on her shores
To share the abundance of her stores
Of freedom, of religious choice,
Civil rights, political voice.
Through eternity may you reign
Lady of Liberty, America's Queen.

Holly Krystal Brown
UNTITLED
The circles never seem to end,
the questions never cease.
It is much like the wind, my friend:
swirling; searching for peace.
That unattainable dream
(communication being the key)
of a warless, united team—
together, glorious and free.
No madness, no sadness, no "wrong,"
no questions, no answers, no "right,"
all singing to the same song,
all seeing the same light!
. . . it could never, ever be
yet we pretend not to care.
Our souls are trapped, yet free—
'tis the bond in which we share.
So, to make clear my intent
would mean that I should know . . .
the mesage that is sent
depends which way the wind might blow.

Traci A Miller
LOST FRIENDSHIPS

To Chris D., we had some great times!

We've been friends since grade school
We grew up together, we dressed alike
We talked about our problems to one another
We told our most intimate secrets to one another
We told one another the boys we were in love with,
and how we would both grow up and find our, Mr. Right

We had our differences, and plenty of fights, but they were all silly games we played.
Now we are adults, and finally are out of school, and are working to get somewhere, but after work we play, go out and have a good time, and be like little kids again.
But, you never know when to grow up.
You went too far, telling other people about secrets you shouldn't of, and talking about your friends behind their backs.
And most of all you hurt me, your best friend, very, very, much, and nothing in this entire world would make me forgive you.
I'm sorry our friendship had to end.
We were really close, but now we are so far away.

We had the best times of our life when we were together.
I will never have as much fun as I did when I was with you, but I guess we have to sacrifice some things in life,

Too bad, it had to be our friendship!

Angela Dawn Hershey
LOVING YOU THROUGH A MEMORY
Loving you through a memory
Is forever a long-term thought,
Always remembering the best of times
The ones that stole our hearts.

Never knew that I needed
A love from only you,
Never realizing I was searching;
For a dream that could come true.

Loving you through a memory
The question arose;
Will God choose for you to love me
In time, we both shall know.

Remembering times together
When we were alone and still,
The silence between us, whispered,
The words "I love you, dear"

If my words don't come together
Just listen to my cause,
For the love that I gave to you
I never hid at all.

But now time keeps passing by
Our lives must still go on,
Forever holding the memory, once shared
In a time we called our own.

Eva Buckley
WINTER SNOW

To Bill "My Loving Husband"

In the morning we wake to glisting snow,
and at night while we sleep, we do not know,
that all the beautiful crystals that come floating down,
will leave their blankets of white upon the ground.

Winter is such a beautiful time of the season
the crackling of firewood burning bright,
and the glow of candles in the night.

I open the curtains, just to watch the snow,
and hope it will snow, and snow, and snow.

And while looking out into the night
there's nothing I know as beautiful and bright,
underneath all the tall street lights.

Shirley K DeFazio

Shirley K DeFazio
TO MICKEY
I had made friends with loneliness.
We shook hands, formed a marriage of convenience
and settled down to live together,
Staid, practical.

Then you came along
upsetting my cautious notions
disrupting my placid marriage
disrupting my orderly existence.

Now I don't know where I am:
unmarried, but committed—
in love with you but dissatisfied,
loved by you, but alone.

Why didn't you leave me in my loneliness?
My isolation untouched
My heart petrified but unbroken
My life orderly and unfulfilled.

I want you so much and you are not at all
what I want.
I love your past bearing—I can not bear
what you are.
I want to be with you—I do not want to be
where you live.

You have destroyed my life and filled it.
Set fire to my heart and consumed it.
Shattered my mind and made it whole.

Why didn't you leave me in my loneliness?
I was dead, empty, worthless, unsatisfied.
I was content.

I want to be free of you.
I can't bear to let go.

Gaudencia Antigo Tan
A POOR IMMIGRANT
"Are you happy in this great country?"
"Not Really"
Why!
Simply, because someone is snobish to me,
But I choose to be happy
Although treated unfairly,
Because I know God is not far away.
When I look up to the sky,
That is blue as the sea,
I know God wants me to be happy,
To receive His blessings,
He bestows to everybody
Including you and me.
And someday, I'll be real happy,
Although I'm a poor immigrant only

Sharon L Saxton
HAPPY FEST
The campfire crackles
In the cool autumn night.
There's warmth in the circle
Of embers glowing bright.
Our voices blend together
In prayer and in song,
And there's a happy feeling
This is where we belong.

Someone throws on the fire
One or two more logs.
Now it's time to roast
Marshmallows and hot dogs.
The aroma of the food
And that of burning wood,
Have the right ingredients
To make a taste so good.
Juices drip into the fire
Causing sizzling sounds,
Mixing with the laughter
Of friendship that abounds.

Too soon the evening's over,
The fire is burning low.
But as we head for home
Our hearts will keep the glow.

Kathy Torzok
A SLUMBERING ROSE

For Mary Ann

My essence is a slumbering rose
a flower enclosed by the night
awaken this blossom from repose
with the kiss of morning light
let love's glistening ray
draw the petals apart
reveal this mystery to the day
and lure the secret from ny heart.

B J Tollefsrud
CHILDREN, COME UNTO ME
Within darkness,
a frightened child lies awake,
listening to a recurring quarrel,
that spontaneously makes him shake.
Embracing "Teddy Bear" closely,
tears well in the little child's eyes,
his heart pace quickens,
with sobs that plead, why?

Nights of a small child,
progress into teenage years.
Numbness, exhausts all emotions,
with a hardened heart, that no longer hears.
And as the sound of fighting continues,
to echo down the hall,
he wonders if God knows his suffering,
and if "God" exists at all.

The teen matures into manhood,
and through life's darkness, he found joy,
discovered in a new life with Christ,
builds happier memories, for his boy.

Geraldine C Post
IF YOU CAN!
If you can be loving
To enemies who hate you;
If if you can be silent
When others berate you;

If you can be loyal
When friends prove untrue,
And if when they need you,
You can show you're true-blue;

If you can sing praises
In the midst of great loss,
And can share someone's load
When you carry a cross;

If you can see sunlight
Through clouds dark and drear,
And when others sorrow
You can speak words of cheer;

If when you falter
Ere the race is half-run,
You still can press onward
'Til the vict'ry is won;

If when folk fail you,
You can still wear a smile—
'Twill prove you are living
A life that's worth while!

Fran Cooley Payne
AGE OF LONELINESS
An emotion, everyone must
experience—
Some look to it as an ole' friend.
Others find the feeling frightful.
Many know of no other existence.

We begin life, very much a part of
it.
As time goes on, our needs are
endless.
Oh, how the eldest of us demand
respect.
Then grow older, we are said,
meaningless!!

Sandra Lee
MISFIT
Silent trees reach for the heavens
Clutching precious soil.
Limbs and leaves draped overhead
Form Nature's sacred temple.

Beneath the trees, wildflowers
throng
In fragrant, pastel carpets.
Ferns fan the forest floor
As spittle bugs and spiders labor.

In one small creek a trillion drops
of water
Clutch at one another rushing off
to meet the sea,
Making sounds of liquid music,
Dancing in a ballet without end.

All these lovely, separate things
Merging in the cycles of their lives,
Know nothing of their purpose
here on earth,
And what is more, care not.

While I, formed in God's image,
stand,
A misfit in this beauteous place;
And wondering at the mystery of
life
Give thanks for all creation.

Sande Bamberger
A LETTER
I tried to remember the good times
we had,
But greed overcame me, and I grew
sad.
I shed tears now as I wonder,
"Why?"
You made me laugh, but now I cry.
We always knew how the other one
felt.
I'll never forget the time I knelt,
Before you to say, "Goodbye".
I whispered softly, "I love you",
Knowing you could hear.
And all the time I thought of you,
wishing you were near.
I couldn't believe it was for the best,
I wondered how this could be true.
Now all I have are memories
Of my funny and wonderful you.
Each time I think of you, my eyes
fill up with tears,
But then I try to think of you and
your happy, carefree years.
I was lucky to have you the time
that I did,
Although I wish it was more.
I smile as I think of you,
The one I most adore.
Sweet memories my dearest uncle,
Rest happily in peace,
I love you then, I love you now,
Your ever-loving niece.

Harold (Hal) MayBee

Harold (Hal) MayBee
PICK-A-STAR
Pick a Star from afar
that is Gods Home.
Pick a star from the Universe
where ever man might roam
that is Gods Home.
Pick a star, Our Sun,
with planet Earth,
that is where God
gave Mankind birth.
and that is His and their Home.

Dina J Fink
WORTH

This poem is dedicated to my daughter, Rachelle, my inspiration, the joy of my life.

Some folks measure treasures
In lumps of gleaming gold,
Others live in castles
Built with wealth untold,
But a person's worth is measured
By the good that's in his soul.

There are doctors of philosophy,
Psychology, and such,
With a decent stack of papers
To tell the world as much,
But a person's heart is measured
By the kindness of his touch.

It isn't in a string of pearls,
Or in a yacht at sea,
Or in a small certificate
Proclaiming your "M.D.".

No matter what your title is,
Or if you're rich, or poor,
A happy, smiling, honest face
Will open any door.

When folks look at you in askance
Because you're only you,
Just remember at the start;
A person's wealth is measured
By the good that's in his heart.

Ida M Leonard
A TIME FOR ALL

Dedicated to my 5 children—my inspirations

The great and mighty
How they stand
To hold us tightly
In the palm of their hand
It's gloomy now
But just beware
There's something better
For us out there
The time will come
Yes, you shall see
When we're the ones
Who win the victory
So work real hard
Don't give up the fight
It'll all work out
If we do what's right
We'll just exchange places
With them someday
And they'll know how we felt
When it's their turn to pay
For you see there's
Someone greater
Than all combined
Who believes in equality
For all mankind

Kelly Peterson
I KNEW HIM WHEN
I knew him when we were in
kindergarten
I knew him when we were in grade
school
I knew him when we were in high
school
I knew him when we were in
college, too
I knew him when I was liking
someone else
I knew him when we were out of
school
I knew him when he went into the
service
I knew him when he was engaged
to someone else
I knew him when we finally started
going out
I knew him when he asked me to
marry him
I knew him when I had our first
child
I knew him when we named her
after him
I knew him when he went off to
war in Lebanon
I knew him when he got killed after
two years

David Frankie LaFave
WORLDLY VISIONS
so many things have yet to be seen
or heard or loved or in between...
the people aware and the scientists
dare to test what is between. . .

At Planets And Moons And
Darkness Like Light
The Universe Beckons And Calls
To Us And Them and Everyone
Men
We Stare And Do Nothing At All

AROUND THE STARS AND INTO
THE NIGHT. . .
GO GALAXIES HERE AND
THERE. . .
AS WE ALL WATCH AND DO
NOTHING AT ALL
AS WE ALL SILENTLY STARE. . .

the stone age,
the dark age,
the days of our lives,
pass so fast, so slow,
the people can guess
and the people can lie
but really, they never will know!
(bang, big).

Shari McCracken
REPETITION
Each day I think about you,
It cannot change my thoughts.
Each day I wait for the phone to
ring,
It never does.
Each day I long to hold you and
kiss your lips,
It cannot satisfy my desire.
Each day I need to hear your voice,
It cannot change the sound in my
ears.
Each day I need to look into your
eyes
It cannot change what I see.
Each day I need us to get together,
It cannot bring you back.
Each day I need to sit alone with
you,
It cannot change the presence of
my company.
Each day I love you,
It cannot make you love me back.
Each day is getting harder to live
alone.
Does that mean I must die?

Elizabeth Whitworth Blythe
THE TREE
There is a big oak tree
Just outside my window
Placed there by man
And nourished by Nature—
In God's Divine Plan.

Picturesque, indeed.
Strong, not wavering.
Able to cope with
Strange sights and sounds,
Unusual overnight guests;
Furnishing shelter and
Provision to many
Kinds of life.

Oh, that I could
Be like "The Tree."

Denise Catherine Miller
DELICATE PETALS
Delicate petals
Pink and yellow
Quietly bow
Nite fall settles
Droplets of dew
Bead in their pockets
Love filled hearts
Of life's chain and lockets

Monica Urias
INTRIGUE

Dedicated to my one and only wild heart—Laurie

A flower grows, its beauty give,
As if forever it will live.

Her colors beautiful and bright,
and to my heart a pure delight.

She came to me so sweet and small,
Wonder of wonders of them all.
Her perfume sweetly filled the air,
Lingering softly everywhere.

My beautiful flower grew for me,
Lovely petals falling free.
. . .and as she grew I came to see,
That every child a flower be.
With this in mind, I too now know,
I had to let my beauty grow.
Into this flower of me a part,
My beautiful daughter, my wild
heart.

Elizabeth James

Elizabeth James
MY FISHING THRONE

'Oh—How I love to go
To my favorite spot
With my fishing stick
And find the rock
As "My Fishing Throne"
And there I see
Beyond the tree's
The mountain's high
Surrounding me
The sky so blue
A cloud or two
The water so calm
The sun so warm
My mind wander's on
In serenity—and soon
I ponder whom to thank
For all is for me
And there I found
The spirit touches free
Now in my heart I feel
And in my eyes I see
Gods blessing came to be
I thank you heavenly father
Jehovah God—Pslm 83:18
For the greatest gift
You have given me
Again I will go
To my favorite spot
With my fishing stick
And find the rock
As "My Fishing Throne"

Christy Lacy
THROUGH THE TIME

Through the time my love will
grow.
I love you, just want you to know.

My love for you, will never end.
My love to you, I will send.

If you send it back, I will know.
Through the time, our love will
grow.

Dorothy A Bolmer
TWO WHEELS FOR FOUR

To my children

My children are children no longer
Now they've traded their
two wheels for four;
At one time the house couldn't be
entered
For bicycles parked at the door.

Now the doorway is cleared for
entrance,
No longer are toys on the floor;
And the children seen only in
passing
Since they traded their two wheels
for four.

Sandra Jean Mayo
HURT

To my loving Mother who sacrificed herself always that her children might succeed. I love you!

Hurt came to me one fine day
I begged oh Him, "Please go away,"
But as He turned to look at me
Through eyes of blue sobriety
I felt in Him an awkward friend—
Through tears I cried, "We meet
again!"

My head upon my pillow lay
The tears, they would not go away;
With gruff, cold hand upon my
heart
He said, "You know we cannot part,
For we are one with Life you see—
For I am you and you are me."

Life is Hurt and is meant to be
For without Hurt what would we be
But carnal shells of empty souls.
And Happiness, well God, He
knows
That without Hurt we could not
see—
All we are meant to grow to be

And with my hands I dried my eyes
As Hurt did leave, I realized
I want so much from Life you see
That reaching out brings Hurt to
me,
But what I gain in each sad time—
Brings tears of gold and joy
sublime.

Cynthia Chinn
MEMORIES

Where are we headed? What is out
there for us?
Is it right . . . or is it wrong?
Who really knows, I am not quite
sure . . .
What about you?

I have no right or wrong answers,
all I
Have are memories . . .
Sweet memories of the times we
have
Shared together.

And for the time being, I am
content
And thankful for even having that.
The present? Who knows . . .
I only hope for more days
Spent with you . . .

Elaine Kay Tiefenauer
SUNSHINE

For my Sunshine, Rick.

Yawning
Stretching
He gently kisses my face.
Lightly caressing my body
I blush and smile.
Pulling on my sweats
He's there beside me
Following me into the kitchen
For my cup of coffee
Sitting beside me
We remain silent—
Not wanting to disturb this perfect
day.
He follows me out of the house
And down the street as I jog
Coaxing me, nudging me to my
limit.
Exhausted I pause to rest on the
curb
Sweat dripping from every pore.
Cooling down a cloud passes
overhead
I shiver, feeling chilled.
My Sunshine reappears
Holding me gently in his warm
arms
I turn my face upwards and give
thanks.
Stay with me my friend—
I need you.

Rebecca Reinhart
THE BEST I CAN

To my loving husband. I shall remind myself time and time again just for you Arthur I'll do the best I can.

I wish I had a way
for to reach the other side,
And to live each passing day
but take them all in stride.
For some where deep within
I know that time will pass
Like a soft and gentle wind
that moves the blades of grass.
As for traveling through our time
I know it's near the end.
Your love for me so kind
so I'll do the best I can.

Catherine Cato

Catherine Cato
MY IDENTITY

To my mom, who encouraged me to understand who I am.

Tell me I'm pretty,
Tell me I'm fine.
Make me your friend,
Make me your kind.
One thing I'm absolutely sure,
From one beginning came
innocence and pure.
My name evolved from the rest,
The blood that flows amongst
the best.
My thoughts of those I'm close,
I live, and try to get the most.
Tell me, who am I?
One that loves—one that
hopes.

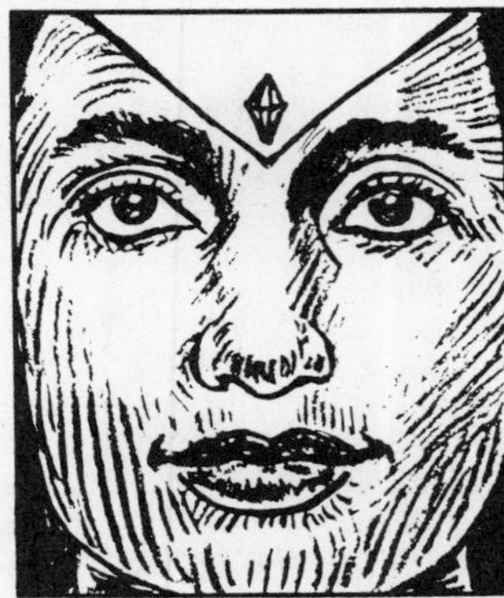

Tell me you trust me,
Tell me I'm smart.
Make me a person,
Make me a part.
For in this life comes one source,
The main purpose—the one
course.
Individually intended to be,
Of God's likeness, and man's
liberty.
To pursue—only to perfect,
Life's true reason—Love's the
target.
Tell me, who am I?
For what I see, I am me.

Josephine Cordaro
GOD'S GIFT

Remember, sad and lonely one,
she's ever at your side,
Her voice is heard in whispering
leaves, and the murmuring of
the tide.
Her smile breaks through the rosey
dawn, her tears, the gentle rain,
Her touch, the sighing of the
wind, would brush away your
pain.
Her footsteps are the falling snow,
her breath, the crystal air,
Her thoughts are yours forever,
your quiet grief to share.
And always she is with you, the
ache, that's ever there,
For that's her way of telling you,
she's always there to care.
Although your life seems
meaningless, and your road so
hard to trod,
Remember sad and lonely one,
your gift of love, now rests with
God.

Norman Kemnitz
SCHLITZ

Time flits, here I sit, Drinking
schlitz.
The world goes by and I sigh,
drinking schlitz.
Money glides, pride dies, drinking
schlitz.
Driven to seclusion by delusion, a
hermits life
I chose, a ragged wretched
existence, drinking schlitz.

Mary E Reifel
QUESTIONS

To Lee, who always believed in me.

Where am I going?
Where have I been?
Is it too soon to answer?
Shall I ask again?

Have I seen all of life?
Have I tasted life's flowers?
Have I done all I wanted?
Have I used all my hours?

Have I loved to the fullest?
Have I given my heart?
Have I been happy and sad?
Since this is all of a part . . .

Of my lifeline I'm thinking
Of ways to rely,
On my last days on earth
When I bid all goodbye.

I haven't accomplished
All I set out to do,
I'll live life to its fullest,
Till I bid life adieu.

Claude A Shriner
WALK WITH ME
There it is before my feet,
Spring's new growth so soft and sweet,
From Mother Nature's green thumbed hand,
Sprouts new life upon this land.

For you and I we marvel long,
And listen to the birds at song,
And dream of days that we remember,
That so slowly we embrace September.

Summer brought the Fall we knew,
With change in life for me and you,
And while waiting for the Winter's done,
We'll dream again of Spring to come.

We'll shed the Winter's coat you'll see,
Hold tight the Spring with abandoned glee,
Rejoice new life so soft and sweet,
Before our eyes and at our feet.

Yes, you're the only one I need,
And through life's seasons walk with me,
From January through the late December,
Because you're the dreams I do remember.

Alban Wall
FAIR VISTAS
Winter's too strict and the summer too lazy,
Spring is too fickle my love to command.
Give me these days when the mountains are hazy
And cool spicy winds are astir through the land.

Leave the hot days to the lovers of beaches,
I'll take a trail that winds over the hill.
Skiis are well suited to ice-covered reaches,
But give me a pack and an unfettered will.

Nature's a painter and fall is her glory,
Flashes of scarlet and crimson and gold.
Nature's a teller-of-tales and her story
Brings back the fire of youth to the old.

Flame on the uplands in mellow September,
Air that is richer than Burgundy wine,
Stir the dulled senses and make them remember
A glory in living that used to be mine.

Sound loud the trumpet, o geese winging over,
Echo the signal from marshland and pond;
These are the days that God made for the rover,
These are the hints of fair vistas beyond.

Len Waters
MOTHER

To Millie with love for her giving

How do you say good-by to Mother
How do you say so long to a friend
How do you part with Gram
How do you accept the end.

How do you fill the loss
Who will take her place
Mom, Gram and Granma
We all will miss your face.

We all knew and respected her
That's why we're gathered here
Many of us loved and cherished her
Many shall shed a tear

Her laugh, her love, her art
Touched us each in some small way
Her paper toll and tating
Mean more than we can say

She was always there to help
And there to bid us on
There with faith and courage
"Don't give up, carry on"

And now at last she's earned her rest
Her peace and tranquillity
Her days on earth have finally past
God Bless and be with Thee.

Edelgard Knoob
NURSING HOME PATIENT
I am alone, so alone
no one to call my own.
I sit by the window and stare
though no one is there.

There was a time when I was needed
but now have been depleted
of beauty strength and health
not much left of my former wealth.

Just a room with a bed and a chair
and the floor is bare.
Is this how it all must end
alone—without a friend?

A little care and a little love
Would let me hope in Heaven above,
till my life is spent on this earthly shore
and a place for me is found no more.

Margaret Ameigh
LOVE, LAUGHTER AND GOD TOO
Oh little girl with the long dark curls:
Can I think you were left in the whirl—
or life of misfortunes
or gay appeal

Oh days of Mom and Dad and you were filled
of Love, Laughter and God too—
You grew so fast past your grammar school
days, into teens you flew

Happy, happy days were yours—
A love you met and thought life was all complete
Then heartbreak came, as he left for another

Years went by and new guy was yours,
The Love, Laughter and God too did return—
Happy, happy days were yours

Then the sad accident which his life did take—
You were alone again
Twas hard to go on
But you must find it all again—
Love, Laughter and God too

Meg Mason
MYSTERY
I wonder what thoughts lie
behind the tired drawn face
of my mother as she sits,
her hands busy
with ever present needlework.
Does she remember
days of younger love?
Or children at her knee?
What could she tell us
if she but would?
Of struggle and of laughter?
We can only wonder
what lies behind her smile,
Or an occasional word
accompanied by a special look.
It is her secret—
and so it will remain.
The present she will share,
The past—is hers to keep.

Art Goldman
KEEP SMILING

To my wife Maureen whose smile has kept me going.

There is no room for sadness
When you see a cheery smile
It always has the same good look
And it's never out of style
It nerves us on to try again

When failures makes us blue
Its dimples of encouragement
Are good for me and you
It pays a higher interest
For your money spent
It's worth a million dollars
Yet it doesn't cost a cent.

William Deimling
HE WAITS IN THE BACK
He waits in the back
where there's little light
and dreams of things
he won't, but might

The fights, the jobs
the glory he seeks,
the things that are never
the realm of the meek

He is boss, he is king
and a thousand things more
he is rich, he is famous
all the women adore

And he sits and he dreams
as the world passes by,
his brother, his friend
their success makes him cry

He will never understand
what it is that he lacks,
'til nothing at all, 'cept . . .
he waits in the back

MacArthur Savage
THE NIGHT BEFORE
I caressed the smooth feathers
layered softly across voluminous wings
which she then spread wide
and our love soared.

I reached and held
the celestial orbs
and graced the earthly
mounds with passionate adornment.

And the heavens opened wide
fulfilling our love with
the nectar of the gods.

Susan H Balogh
THE HUNTERS
My camera and I are hunters
We capture sunsets, moonbeams and stars.
We hold wonder at a standstill
a photo of a child-time kept in a jar.

My camera and I are hunters
a dog frolicking, caught unaware.
His freedom unbounded, captures the moment
a mystery photographed to share.

My camera and I are hunters
no harm we wish to bring.
Only a feeling, subtly of hope
as in a kodachrome of spring.

My camera and I are hunters
like actors, looking for a part.
The myriad of colors flow
from eye-to lens-to heart.

Marian Waldsmith
OH! FOR THE LIFE OF A TRAVELER
I've always wanted to travel
From one land to the other,
But have never strayed far from home
Taking care of little daughter—
And her baby brother.
It gets so very tiresome
Just keeping house and all—
Cooking, washing, sewing
And doing many things beyond recall.

"I'd be quite content to see our land
From one coast to the other,
And enjoy the many beauties

I'm sure I would discover.

When your family moves away and
One by one they all are gone,
You get mighty, mighty lonesome
For a substitute for Mom.

Venesa Corzine
REMEMBERING YOU
It's been seven years now,
Since I saw your tiny face.
I remember holding you.
No one could take your place.

For three days you were mine.
Someone of my own.
I was only fifteen, but . . .
I knew I had a Son.

I'm married now,
With a family of my own.
There's so much I want to say,
But, I feel I'm all alone.

Not many people know
That I had you.
It just doesn't seem fair,
That I am here and you are there.

I have so many regrets,
For what I have done.
I gave away . . .
My very first Son.

Mary Ellen Hall
THE SNOWFLAKE
From wintery skies a snowflake fell
Upon my outstretched hand.
It's design of perfect symmetry
I could not understand.

How a drop of moisture could
become
This pristine star-like form,
Which for a moment clung to me
Then quickly it was gone.

With just a trace of moisture left
And soon that too would rise
To be a part of clouds that float
Across the wintery skies.

No two snowflakes alike we're told,
As in the race of man,
But each with his own special place
In God's eternal plan.

Man's life is like a vapor: brief,
The snowflake is the same,
And the life that clings to Christ
will rise
To God from whence it came.

Michael J Durachko
FROM THE BOTTOM OF OUR HEARTS

To The Phoenixville Hospital

It's not inspired pictures that we
draw,
Nor is it Godly visions that we saw,
but the most important aspect of
life's part,
is what has been the status of our
hearts?
It's not the pretty words we think
and say,
Nor is it knowing beauty with each
day,
but the realm that surpasses all the
rest,
has the Love we've given others
been our best?
It's not the wonderous deeds we
somehow do,
Nor is it saying how I do Love you,
but what will mean the most when
we have died,
have we sacrificed for others true
inside?
It's not the twinkle shining in our
eyes,
Nor is it smiles we give when we
pass by,
these things I've spoken of with
help will do,
but they cannot work until Love is
really you.

Glenda Johns Cook
JUST DREAMING

Dedicated to My Mother Mrs. Edith Bartow Johns

The gray is showing in her once
dark hair,
She seems tired and sleeps more in
her chair.
I'm sure that she's dreaming of
days gone by,
For she smiles a bit and then
there's a sigh.

She's remembering the squeals of
children galore,
As they played with their toys all
over the floor.
If there were extras around when
it was time to eat,
She'd just add another potato and
stretch the meat.

Her life was so busy, but she
always found time,
To hold a small child while singing
a rhyme.
Days are long now and too quiet it
seems,
So she closes her eyes and
continues to dream.

For she would like to return to the
days of old,
When her children were near and
she had to scold.
She feels so useless just rocking
there,
Dreaming of the "Good Times" in
that old rocking chair.

But look! Her lap is not empty and
there's a smile on her face,
For her newest great grandbaby
has found a favorite place.

Beverly-Ann Kosier
WORDS LEFT UNSAID

This poem is dedicated to Elayne, my friend. Mahili Garthe-Nay.

If God was to tell me,
When my last day of life would be
In my final hour,
I would gather my loved ones
around me
And to each one I would say
I love you,
And forgive the wrongs I have done
But the advantage is God's.
Everyone has a numbered day
And in man's rushing ways
Too often words are left unsaid,
And a friend or loved one is dead,
For tomorrow isn't promised to
any one.

Scott F Walsh
TO

For Shirley and the love found once more

To the tears over the years,
I bid you adieu.
To know life as no other,
I welcome you.
To see the moon glowing,
I miss you.
To know a God of love and Peace,
I love you so.
To remember a love gone now,
I thank you.
To remain is of times gone,
I grow from you.
To love a world gone mad,
I feel strength.

To want peace today and always,
I dream Impossible.
To have loved and needed,
I have learned.
To have seen the beauty of sunrise,
I knew true peace.
To have felt a spring rain,
I felt growth.
To have loved you, my wife,
I knew true love.
To have almost lost you,
I learned pain.
To have regained you again,
I Knew I was complete.

Ronnie J L Clyburn
A MOTHER

I dedicate my poem to my grandmother, Violet May Douglas, who has served as my mother for more than nine years now.

I have no mother,
I feel no shame, there's no one I
can blame.

I work so hard from day to day,
sometimes I get no play.

I fear nothing I cannot see,
because in the dark there's only me.

I have a sister so kind and near,
and a brother who makes you
cheer.

I love you mother although we're
apart,
deep in my thoughts and deep in
my heart.

Cathryn M Woods
DRIFTING
Who are you my love? My
knight? My friend?
I need you my love. I will wait
until the end.
See the clouds my love? The stars
in my eyes?
I need you my love. Let the birds
soar the skies.
Can you hear it my love? The
steady beat of my heart?
I need you my love. Is it the
nightingale
or a lark?

Who am I my love?
Your princess,
your queen?
I need you my love.
When was I last seen?
Am I gone my love?
Have I drifted away?
I need you my love.
Please beg me stay.
Can you find me, my love?
Which direction was taken?
I need you my love.
Am I forsaken?

Can you help me my love?
Shield me from harm?
I need you my love.
Place my body in your arms.
Hold me my love. Love me til the
end.
I need you my love.
My knight! friend!

L L Selover
THE ARTIST, THE FOOL
He sits upon the hill
Of pure rhetoric thought,
With the faraway eyes
Of a newborn babe.
Take care not to disturb
His peaceful reverie!
The hazy gaze will then fall upon
The death of dreams with true
entity.
With the wariness of a fox,
Sensing the hounds' approach,
He'll fear the storm of reality.
Then flee into a fantastic world,
Or—better yet—insanity
To achieve the beauty,
To relieve the pain,
With creativity.
The senseless brilliance of
The Artist.
The Fool.

Karen L Steward
A TOUCH OF LOVE

To My Grandmother Rosabelle Alejandro, To My Mother Carolyn Steward

---

Deep within one's heart there's
a place where happiness awaits
A place where sadness creeps
and loneliness takes place . . .

A smile or a simple hello
a telephone call or an I Love You
Can break the shattering feelins
and mend a broken heart that's
in two . . .

A gentle kiss or a warm bear hug
or a glance their way
Makes life a little brighter
it does more than words can
say . . .

It only requires a little time
and occasionally a small shove
But to make someone feel happy
inside
just show a little touch of love.

Kelly Diane Nichols
REAVED
A child,
whose eyes are closed to our
world.
Sad and mourning,
he quietly contemplates his
world of dreams.
He often thinks of our world,
and what lies within.
Few rays of hope exist,

with which he might re-enter our world.
But our world hurt him,
leaving a deep, tender scar.
Sorrow fills his heart when he remembers the loss he experienced,
in our world.
The mind of a simple child,
closed to our world.
An innocent heart,
marred by realities.

Cindy K Gallagher
DEAR GOD

As I kneel beside my bed,
At the end of a weary day,
I bow my head in humble thought,
And tears fall as I pray:

Dear God, unworthy as I am,
I ask one thing of thee,
Bless the one I love tonight,
And let him think of me.
I am not able to go to him
And take him by the hand,
I know only you can go to him
And make him understand.
Let him keep me in his heart,
Until we meet again,
Even though we are apart,
I Love Him God
Amen!

Sherry L Calhoun
FRIENDS

Our friendship has a beginning,
And will never have an end.
For in you,
I'll always have a friend.

A friend that is dear,
A friend that is true.
With you as a friend,
There's no need to be blue.

You have come into my life,
And brightened my days,
I want to thank you,
In so many ways.

From North to South,
To west to East.
You're always with me,
To say the least.

From January to December,
You just always remember.
In this life there's only one guarantee,
And that is you'll always have me.

Suzanne D Lonn
POETIC PASSIONS

To my dear friend, Karen, who gives me hope & encouragement

The ebb and flow of life
Carries me far from shore.
Oceans of reality
Sweep me along to sea,
Musical thought pulls me back.
Muddy sand washes white
With waves of inspiration
And workings in my head
Lead me to put pen to paper.
No visions in salty tide pools
Nor sailor's tales nor dreams,
But boundless love, memories
And simple sensualities.
A searching shaft of lighthouse gold
Illumines a beached sea gull.
When daylight beckons the fog away
Poetic art intensifies.
Pinions of hope and wings of morning
Spread wide in graceful flight
To soar to silver shores unknown,
And workings in my head
Lead me to put pen to paper.

Stacy Morgan Bailey
I ASK NOT

"I ask not for your fame,
though it was earned by a game.
Nor do I ask for your secrets deep and dark,
time and friendships will leave their mark.

I ask not for your strength in power and position,
you've worked too hard and it would be an imposition.
Nor do I ask for rubies, diamonds and pearls,
or to dine and dance with Kings, Emperors and Earls.

I ask not for your undying love and eternal passion,
though it would be to my satisfaction.
Nor do I ask for trips around the World,
(the dream of most daydreaming girls).

I ask not to be put on a pedestal,
sheltered from the passing crowds.
I ask only
that you hold me,
as gently as the Heaven's do the clouds."

Wilma Carr
AT THE CROSSROADS

When you see a strange reflection in the mirror,
When the voice inside your head is not the same,
Then you know that you are coming to the crossroads,
And the world expects that you will make a change.

It's a time when you can think of what you're wanting.
It's a chance to ponder where you want to be.

You can choose the path ahead that you'll be walking.
Don't forget to take a glimpse at all you'll see.

Where will you be a little farther down the road?
Will this pathway take you where you want to go?
There can be no turning back once you have started,
But if you don't take the risk, how will you know?

Mark T Greene Sr
STOP THE MADNESS

In the hills and the valleys
The war rages on
We fight for our homeland
To make a right from a wrong
But can we see clearly
The names on the list
Of all our dead brothers
Please stop the madness
No crops in the farmland
Just dust and the wind
We curse and rape the land
Will the struggle ever end
We long for the old days
A real bed on the floor
They sent us here for freedoms sake
What are we really fighting for
Can we see clearly
The names on the list
Of all our dead brothers
Please stop the madness

Larry Henry
A EULOGY TO BE

I watched the sunrise this early morn
A child dies, a child is born
A mother laughs, a mother cries
don't wipe them, let them fall
those tears in your eyes
Be not ashamed for we all shall cry
Yes, I watch the sunrise this early morn
A new day has come, but a mother has gone.

George E Cuonzo
I'M LONESOME FOR YOU SWEETHEART

To: Beatrice Santucci Cuonzo, My Adorable Wife.

The people I see don't appeal to me
For it's you Bea I long for each day.
Your beautiful style made my life worthwhile
How I miss it now that you're away;
And I miss your sweet kisses and your caress,
The wonderful ways only you possessed;
I'm counting the days when together we'll be,
Together, forever, just you and me.

Mildred C Sprouse
SWEET CONTENTMENT

To Cliff and Kitty, my dear friends on the Cliff Foreman Ranch, AND to whom I am indebted for many inspirations, of Montana.

Down the dusty country lane
That winds beside the creek,
Wild flowers polka-dot the way
Where bowers of wild roses creep.
The fragrance of their
So sensual and so fair
Drew many bees and
As it filled the air.
But OH! The tiny buds,
Reached toward Heaven in clusters
For a kiss of the sun's warm touch.
The pussy-willows arch above,
The grass grows lush and green,
The whispering waters—the hum of bees,
Sets a peaceful scene.
I pause in wonder at it all,
I sit beside the stream,
Denude my feet and plunge them in
Cool waters, sweet and clean.
What difference—eight or eighty—
Pleasure is complete
And sweet contentment fills my soul
As I sit and soak my feet.

Timothy Krebs
I LIFT UP MINE EYES

I lift up mine eyes,
To the fields of gold grain,
To the orchards of trees,
Where fruit falls like rain.

I lift up mine eyes,
To the mountains and rills,
To those great rocky ridges,
And grand templed hills.

I lift up mine eyes,
To the sky far above,
And see the white clouds,
And the deep blue I love.

I lift up mine eyes,
To the heaven of stars,
I see there a handiwork,
That surpasses all ours.

I lift up mine eyes,
To the Son high above,
I see the great light,
That was given through love.

I lift up mine eyes,
From the problems and strife,
And I see all around me,
The gifts of this life.

I lift up mine eyes,
And I see all around,
The great love of God,
Oh how it abounds!

Lisa Cooney
TIME IN EACH MOMENT

Sometimes, the inspiration of each day spurs me on.
It begins with the rise of the early dawn.
The very power is being
here believing without seeing.

Now, there is that flurry of feeling
that comes for awhile like a snowflake reeling
down from the sky landing afloat
in my body mass that warms me like a furry coat.

Suddenly, my emotions are as if simmering
on my skin, probably a noteable glimmering
when my body boils red
and this woman blushes from whats been said.

Then, comes the next moment to be;
lets open up what we can see.
What a plesure is time
in the present, it isn't too far off to find.

Kathy Barron
TIME AND SPACE

The scarlet sphere slowly rising
Caused the sky
To open those big blue eyes.

A baby day greeting
For the meeting

And adieu, of darkness to light.

The process only claimed
A few minutes of time in the same
Space as the day before.

Aaron Kenna
PRISON
Trapped in a Prison
With the door wide open.
Can't get out
Except for a moment.

Sitting in my cold cell,
It's O.K.
I sit and dream
For most of the day.

Dreaming of a land
Where there is a beautiful woman
And a hamdsome man,
Where friendly people are
All over the place,

Except for my prison
Which is a disgrace.

My time is about up.
I am going to move to that land
Where there is a beautiful woman
And a handsome man,
Where friendly people
Are all over the place.
Then I won't have to worry and be a disgrace.

My time is now up
I'm moving away.
I will miss the Warden.
He is O.K.

The Warden is really a nice guy
But I never got to see him and
Sometimes I'd cry.

Now I live in this land
To which I used to see.
Now I am her, now I am
FREE!!!

Yolanda Yvette DeYounks
MY HEART
I have a heart, and it's like gold;
Hard to keep in which you can never hold.
I have a heart, and it's like glass;
You can see through it and shatter its mass.
I have a heart, and it's like a bank;
Always giving in return for thanks.
I have a heart, and it's like a child;
Though it's shy it's tender and mild.
I have a heart, and it's like hair;
Always growing and needs lot of care.
I have a heart, and it's like a baby;
Always bringing joy sometimes, maybe.
I have a heart, it's like a mirror;
Reflecting your love and wanting to get nearer.
I have a heart, and it's breaking up again.
Yes, it's true I've lost my loving friend.
I have a heart, and it wants to cry;
But I'll wait until later, maybe after I die.
I have a heart, and it's coming to an end.
Goodbye, Goodbye my dear, dear friend!

Jean S Regan
A BEGINNING LOVE!
You make me happy—you really do
For we're starting a Love—that could be true.
We'll take our time, go real slow
Love each other and watch it grow.
It won't be easy, but that's okay
it will make us stronger day by day.
and if it doesn't and we grow weak
we'll know our love, was not to be
But, if it survives—reaches its peak
we'll then have a Love that can't be beat
And we'll cherish Forever the time we spent
For Beginning a Love—that would not end!

Jerianne Cooper
UNTITLED

Mommy, our life together was too short. I love you, Jerianne.

The black night, the howling wind
grows strong, then fades—
brings loneliness within.
Roaring like a demon, searching
out its prey,
Then quiet, sudden stillness,
breathless, in its way.
Trees shaking in their nakedness
mutely wait for spring
devoid of personality—no
rustling leaves to sing.
Dawn finds the angry, restless wind
untiring, yet loath to stay,
abiding in its fierceness
only time will take away.

Marjorie A Hayes
GRANDMA'S PRAYER

To my first grand-daughter Kristie Lee Payne

The time has come,
what will it be?
A girl, a boy,
makes no difference to me.
Please, Dear Lord,
let it healthy be.
That's the only thing,
that matters to me.

The time has past—
she's here at last—
A little girl
with hair to curl
and eyes so brown
and skin so pink,
perfect is the word, I think.
Thank you, Lord, for being there
and answering a Grandma's prayer.

Karin L Keller
CHILDREN

To all children young and old—also for two very special beings Dustin and Holly

---

Children are very special beings,
Their innocence are as pure as streams.
Curiosity—knows no bounds,
Imagination—they're alot like clowns.
Forgiveness—they give so fast,
Hurt feelings—they put in the past.
Their thoughts are on the day,
They learn things in every way.
Their love is all for free,
Their joy is a smile for all to see.
They're grown up more than adults will ever
know,
They live, and love, and joys what they show.
Yes Children are very special beings,
They're silent—but know the important things!

Berny Reina
THE CALLING
Circles—roll, and thunder—"Boom,"
the center of a drafty room.
Swirls of thoughts, screams of pain,
the middle of—some steaming rain.
Fogged-up reflections, a narrow way,
the end of a—confusing day.
Where round is square, and square turns round,
the answers float, but cannot be found.
Depths of notes, the song is fade,
darkened tunnels—where souls are made.
Caved-in feelings—soaked with fear
the death stars bright, and growing near.
Crushed-up faces, minds are numb,
fists of power, from the sky will come.
A morbid smile—a stone cold bed,
half shut eyes, a ticking head.
Shadowed corners, contain a thought,
could be "what's there" is really not.
Spinning round, in fields of lies,
spinning truth, and spinning eyes.
Pin-hole light, from the ebony sky,
it's beams spot-light, those who'll die.
Turned-up notes, they're on the wall,
play them back, your name—they'll call.

W Eggleston
LIVING ON THE MOON
Sing to me of what once was,
Tell me of the age gone by.
Now when time has lost its hold,
Here where fate does not apply.

Silver metal shadows,
The darkest silhouettes.
Dust with every mouthful—
Dust—but no regrets.

From knee-deep velvet valleys
Whose black rivers cannot speak,
Eternal twilight silence
Spreads to ancient, slumber peaks.

The barren cold forgives,
The stillness soon forgets.
Dust with every mouthful—
Dust—but no regrets.

The intent of every sound
Swallowed whole before it's made
In airless, silver quiet—
The half-light masquerade.

No echo of the past—
Gone walls, gone minarets.
Dust with every mouthful—
Dust—but no regrets.
Now dust—all dust, but no regrets.

Jacada
SOCIETY'S GONE TO HELL AGAIN
Society's gone to hell again
Just as in ages past. The
Actual
Incidious
Dangerous
Storm blows strong across the land

No longer can the people sit in quiet piety.
To judge the victims of the storm
And smugly say "not me."

For now the evil wind does blow
the whole of earth its home
And strikes not only childless man
But even babe unborn.

So once again the science labs
Research the clubs of war
And jealously hide weapons found
Just as they've done before

But this is not a battle fought
For lines or bits of Land
No scourged and blackened earth
This time
Just the end of man.

Veronica McGowan Andrews

Veronica McGowan Andrews
CHALLENGER

Thank you Bob, for being YOU, encouraging me to be me . . . "Walking behind you" Walking with, Walking together We accomplish . . Ich" leibi' deich Mrs. Robert O. Andrews

---

Our hearts are sore . . .
There is no more . . .
That words could ever say . . .
We watched, we learned
The terrible hurt . . .
The terrible truth . . . of today.
Adventure holds the magic,
Adventure holds the dream

The dream has become a nightmare . . .
The end, or so it would seem.
Please God, what of tomorrow?

The children are in such pain . . .
Please God, console each heavy heart . . .
Then . . . we'll begin again.

Roger-Anne Gardner
HELLO SUN!
Oh, you make me feel so good.
You share your warmth with all the world.
You put a shine on a dull day,
And blooms on the stems,
We bask in your radiance,
And mellow in your glow.
You're the object of lovers,
Who admire your settings.
And bodies on beaches worshipping your rays.
You're the sunshine of living,
You're the maker of days!

Veda Habler
AWARENESS
I see the birds up in the sky. They appear to be soaring with ease.
I love to watch them as they fly. For this, I am very well pleased.

I see the sun burning in the end; its color and shape a great ball of fire.
I can watch it daily, again and again. For it is this that I desire.

I see the stars set up on high. They twinkle to be seen by all.
I watch them. . .Then I began to cry. For there was a time I could not see at' all.

I could not see the sun, nor the birds as they flew by.
I could not watch the stars, that twinkled in the sky.

But now I can see many things, that I've missed along the way.
I can even watch the little kids as they play from day to day.

The flowers that I could once only smell, looks so beautiful to me.
I love to watch the water at night. The serenity of the sea.

So if you see me admiring every little thing I see.
Every little bug crawling or flying, and every single tree.

No need to wonder anymore. For I can truly say,
I once was blind, but now I see. . .My God, he brightens my way.

So look at his creations and thank him once again.
For the beauty of this world, and all that lies within.

Douglas Earl Gillespie
MY RED RABBIT
My red rabbit.
He is a beautiful funny little bunny.
He shows in rabbit shows.
He wins me blue ribbons.
I love him for that.
I say to him thats good bunny.
For you sure win me lots of money.
Everyone thinks he is a cute, fuzzy little bunny.
He didn't cost me a lot of money.
But he is so sweet.
He has taught me to treat people sweet as honey.
I sure hope he can always keep me in the money.
So I can afford to date my Honey.

Suzanne Schiefer
THANKSGIVING IN LOVE

To Michael—I love you.

This Thanksgiving will be my first one in love,
With a kind and sweet man that God sent from above.
Together we will share the happiness and the tears,
Our love will last throughout many years.
My only dream is to be his wife,
And him to be my husband for the rest of my life.
And so Lord, this Thanksgiving I thank you from my heart
that Mike and I will be together and never be apart.

Linda Wolke
THANK YOU MOTHER
Someone once said to me—what does your Mother mean to thee?
A warm spot way down in my heart, rose as tears became a part.
Mother, don't you see—you mean the world to me?
You held me when I cried—punished me when I lied,
Laughed with, and at me; taught me to be me
A lady, a mother, a wife; you gave me my life.

Through those endless years, and uncounted tears—
You shared your love and care; I cried when you cut my hair.
It's true that then I didn't know, I'd always love you so.
My mother showed me how to talk; she taught me how to walk.
When I was ill—she was by my side still.
Mother means: A bond of love that grows with each new day, years of love as my childhood passed away.

Learning to give, making dandelion wine, wanting to buy the cleaner with pine,
Stopping a sibling fight . . . tucking me in at night,
Handling me the bandage to cover my cut . . . making sure I ate my vegetables but . . .

Mother: You mean so much more, I couldn't begin to keep score.
Just believe it now, when I say . . . I love you now for yesterday.
For all those scoldings I knew were unfair . . . and all the times I thought you didn't care.

It's true, you were always there, to teach, to show and to share.
Now I've grown to understand, I needed your helping hand.
Thanks to you, I now do, all those things you hated too.
It's not too late for me to see, how much my mother means to me.
She means the very words: I love you, and Mother, I want you to know I do.
I love you for so many reasons, precious times, starting at my very birth.
But most of all—I love you because you're mine, the most wonderful Mother on earth.

Marilyn Ann Gladish
THE INEVITABLE
There is no way we could have known
Saddened by emptiness upon coming back home
Back home where our house was once filled by a son
You see, he began college, possessions and all
He'll be on his own with only a call.
Sure, we remember that first day of school
And the Boy Scout camping trips—will he be fine?
But then we knew he'd be back home at such & such a time.

Across the dinner table, Dad and I sat
Until no longer our eyes filled with tears
Knowing only too well we must gain some control
A hand to each other, comforting oh yes
Our own private hurting only a parent fears.
The telephone rings; we speak cheerfully
That's really great, son, and you say it's a gas?

He'll never know that moment we had
Longing for the clock to turn back
He's gone and this was the break
Our love he knows is with him always
We must be strong, letting go for his sake
You're coming home this weekend? that's great!
We'll be here waiting for you, Dad and I will be glad.

Kenneth R Finchum
GOD, MY FAITH IS LITTLE

To the person who needs a boost in life and will hold this dear in their heart.

God, my faith is little,
God, my faith is weak,
God, I need your help
For my soul to keep.

Janina Baxley

Janina Baxley
OF WINTER WAVES AND SUMMER SNOW
I, drifting through the land I know
Of winter waves and summer snow,
See children laughing by the stream—
Thinking not of untold dreams
And others chase through its soft waves
To unknown thoughts in tiny caves
And each is different—each game diverse
For difference here is not a curse
And innocence is not a flaw—
Conformity is ne'er a law.
I so edge forward to the brink
Of the children's stream, to take a drink
Yet the water runs dry in my rough hands—
Without a word, each child stands.
Their eyes do not seem filled with fear—
Yet they stare until I disappear.
When I am gone, they continue on
In their guilt-forbidden dawn
And I can only pretend to know
Of winter waves and summer snow

Linda Eutsey
NATURE'S BEAUTY
Nature by day and Nature by night,
it is to me the most beautiful sight.
The grass so green covered with glisten,
Nature has a way of talking, if you just listen.
The sound of the birds singing way up high,
Others sing joyously while they fly in the sky.
White clouds silhouette over the blue of day,
one look at this beauty. . . I have no words to say.
Nature alone does all of the talking,
while my eyes can do nothing but the walking.
It is only the sound of water that caress' my ears,
a creeks water flowing ever so softly, can bring me to tears.
When you look into its face of reflect,
how can one, (even so cruel), not ever respect?
Fields of fields that continue on and on,
asks for the suns warmth to respond.
As the wind whispers through the trees,
and howls through the darkness in the breeze.
A cool chill approach's to set the night,
until arises the dawn of early light.
Then once again the Natures land becomes its own,
to live for its beauty and for its beauty to be shown!

Cindy Casciani
A RUNAWAY'S LIFE
You find you're by yourself
Left in the world all alone
No one to kiss goodnight
No one to hear you moan

You wonder what has happened,
To the world you used to know
But then you realize to yourself
It's you, who decided to go.

Running wild in the city
Is like running wild in hell
You thought Life's roads were so smooth
But then you find you fell.

You sleep in a dark alley
You sweat because of the sun
You turn to the life of crime
So all you do is run.

This isn't a life for kids
Because all you do is roam
So take a little suggestion
Life is better at home.

Melissa Ann Ebert
RUNNING BY YOUR SIDE

This poem is for anyone who has or will consider suicide.

The sun goes down
And the lights paint the town
While loneliness takes up your night.
Your heart wants you screaming
Under stars brightly gleaming
But you stand quietly, out of all sight.
As you look around
And you don't make a sound
You fear you have nothing but foe.
They don't want you there,
If you weren't, who would care?
So you plan of letting yourself go.
But try this my friend
Before you let it all end—
To run screaming in the night
Forget of your fear,
Because I love you my dear,
And I'm always there right by your side.
You'll see you have more
Than you thought once before
And that so many care so deep.
Together we'll start that big climb
While taking our time,
No matter how long or how steep.
When we reach to the top
We won't let life stop
But live where the heavens flow
Then glance back down,
Into our little black town
And find not a one was your foe.

Diane P Hanner
STRIVE AND CONQUER

Dedicated to the clients and staff of the Palm Springs Stroke Activity Center, whose motto is "Strive and Conquer".

Yesterday I was just like you.
Today I can't speak
and part of my body
quit working on me.
They tell me I had a stroke.
My mind still works
but I can't communicate.
My hand and leg refuse to obey.
It scares me to death.
It makes me damn mad.
But I'm a fighter,
and I won't take this lying down.
My family is devastated,
I can't comfort them with words.
They feel they lost so much of me.
But I'll come back
as far as God permits.
So tell everyone to keep the faith,
because I know you love me
and I love you, too.
I'll strive . . . and I'll conquer.

Erma M Dickson
HIS COMMANDMENT OF LOVE
When dictators get so greedy for power
They seek to conquer the world
When cities are bombed for hour after hour
And ultimations to nations are hurled
When stately buildings that took years to build
Are tumbled to earth with a crash
When thousands of people are needlessly killed
And ships are destroyed with a flash
When innocent little childrens crys
of hunger are borne on the air
When mothers look up at war darkened skys
And from their hearts is wrung a prayer
Then we should all think of God up above
And pray for deliverance and release
For if everyone had kept his Commandment of Love
The whole world would now have peace

John Bennett Segars
STRIFE FOR LIFE
Through life we all must pass
For flesh is made to endure not last.
Another day older, more painful we grow
Ever so caught-up in life's forward flow.

No time for this, no time for that,
No time to ponder those things not fact.
Measure time in micro varibles
Only to try and win all the marbles.

Rush here, hurry there, no time to stand.
Must try hard to grab all you can.
Work your life away as a slave
But just how much can you take to the grave.

Butterfly V A S
SILENT TEARS

The inspiration of platonic love is infinite and profound . . . Thank you, Mr. Cook.

The quiet time comes and my thoughts turn to you
Wondering where you are and are you happy. I hope so
A constant battle in me rages onward; the heart and
The head no longer agrees with each other and
There is no balance anymore, only priorities, beautiful
Memories and hope, that one day, the scales will
Tip toward harmony and balance; where your warm
Smile and blazing eyes will shine through, like
A sunshower after the storm . . .
It's thoughts like those, that conflict with reality
Now I find myself struggling to push them deep
Into the hidden parts of my heart, where no one can touch
Then comes the night; and dreams that unlock the door
Where we are free, you and I, running through flower fields
And snow covered hills; racing the wind, not caring
Just sharing the moment, while hidden passion sparks
A roaring fire with only a touch or glance and nothing
Else matters; for the shelter of each others arms is
Enough until I wake to morning call.
The total feeling of aloneness is overpowering, at first
As I reach over to touch you but you're not there.
Already, you rushed back to safety, behind the locked
Doors in my heart and I shamelessly cry . . .

Roberta L Farrow
CHILDREN

Dedicated to Children everywhere, especially my own; Robin, Brian, Rebecca, and Nichole

---

Children are such wonders,
True gifts from God above.
Their actions, pull our heart strings,
Their laughter, keeps us young.

From the moment, we first hear them cry,
Until they say, their first hello.
The very first step, they took toward us,
All on their very own.

Do you remember, his first suit?
Or, her first high heeled shoes?
His first car, and her first date?
"Oh! How they worried you."

Then, as in an instant,
Right before our eyes.
That little boy, and girl of ours,
Becomes, a man <u>or</u> wife.

Then all at once, As God intends,
The cycle, is repeated, and we share,
With them, the same joys, and fears,
With their own, little men and women.

"Yes, Children are such wonders,"
True gifts from, God above!
And, as a Mother, I only add.
"God Bless them, each and everyone!"

Brenda Lee Diehl

Brenda Lee Diehl
THROUGH THE EYES OF A MOTHERS HEART
There is no experience to compare with the bearing of a child
Though many of the experiences to follow may be somewhat wild

It is an unforgettable feeling to see this strange but beautiful being
At the same time there is much we are not forseeing

Such as the very long days and nights of continual crying
Though there is not much we can do but be there and keep on trying

Moms need to be strong, loving, and patient through times to come
Even though their hearts may break and beat like a drum

They say there is more room in a broken heart
Although we all know there is no time to fall apart

Its funny how we stop and think of times gone by
And of memories to come; all in such an exhausting sigh

Parenthood is such a mystery with all its ups and downs
When the children one day can be so monstrous and one day be clowns

Its important for us all to keep our individuality and selflove
Through the guidance and trust of the Lord above

Jeanne B Eddinger
THE HOURS BEFORE DAWN
Last night
I cried, reaching out to touch the empty place
by my side.
Half yesterday, half today, half me
and tomorrow I see only in fragments
like a cracked mirror, not broken but not whole.
So I wait in the hours before dawn
wishing the night was gone.
As sleep has gone so love has fled
and I leave my bed to roam a silent house.
The coffee pot is cold, I'm feeling old and tired.
What do you use to fill up empty nights
or empty lives?

It's so quiet and still—
even the sound of my match striking to
light a cigarette sounds shrill.
Traffic noise from the highway becomes faint,
just enough to let me know that somebody has someplace to go.
Maybe tomorrow I'll have someplace to go,
across the street or across the world.
It's mostly all the same when you travel alone.
But I never met a stranger who mightn't become a friend
and the hours before dawn do end.

Janet Sanders Johnston
UPWARD TO HEAVEN

Memory of my Parents, Ray and Dorothy Sanders

Why, do we bow our heads in Prayer?
When God is in Heaven, way up there.

So, raise your heads to Heaven instead.
Cause, God is always waiting there.

Why look down, when we pray?
Cause Hell is there, no place to be.

So, raise your heads, when you pray.
For there is Heaven, the place to be.

Margaret Wandel Jacobi

FALL SUNSET

For Rachel who has seen many sunsets with me

Last night a fleeting glance out of my window
Caused me to gasp: "What holocaust is this
That spreads from north to south on the horizon?
Red-orange flames that shoot from an abyss!

Has Someone split the roof of Hell asunder
And let the unleashed fury upward spout
Until it reached the zenith of a cloud bank
And strove to put this obstacle to rout?

Did the Sun, in sinking, ignite an unseen furnace?"
No, this awesome but fascinating sight
Was the glorious afterglow of a normal sunset
Bursting forth to speak God's beauty and His might.

Diane L Prucnal

MY TRIBUTE TO MY MOTHER

Roses are red, violets are blue
Oh, Mom, what can I possibly say
To describe how I feel about you.
"I adore you", "I love you" are just not strong enough
To me you're a lovely jewel
Unspoiled, untarnished—like a diamond in the rough.
You're an elegant lady, beautiful, yet still sweet
This is a rare combination
For this type woman one rarely may meet.
Your deep sensitivity, your kind thoughtful way
Is why numerous compliments & accolades
People to YOU always say.
You're gracious, loving, & sensuous; Daddy knew this to be true
And there is no question in my mind
As to why he chose and married YOU.

When I was a child, I remember how you took from your own plate
This selfless, self-sacrificing deed was done.
To make sure that each one of your children ate.
You give SO MUCH of yourself, there's sometimes little left for you;
Your "kids" are all adults now;
Please, take more time to do the things YOU really want to do.
We're all so extremely proud of you, in every single way
And we want you around for a long time
At least for a 1000 years and a day.
Take good care of your health—physically AND spiritually
Be active but get plenty of rest,
Eat well and take your medication ritually.
There's hardly a wrinkle on your angelic face
Your eyes are crystal clear, like a fresh-water lake
Gold Medal, Blue Ribbon—Number One in our hearts you'll always place.
You're intelligent & intuitive, more than mere words can tell
You've doctored, clothed, and nutured us
And you've inspired us all and taught us well.
To compare with you there is simply no other
And I'm so proud to declare
Yes Indeed!! You are truly an "open-minded" 1980's Mother.

ZELMA LEE LAW PRITCHETT without you and Daddy none of us would be
Raising and supporting nine children has had to cost you loads of money.
We so deeply thank you for that support and for putting up with us
About this I've never ever heard you complain, or even put up a fuss.
You brought us up in a religious atmosphere
And because of this, Christ in our hearts, we always will hold dear.
Dearest Mother, because of you I am better
You've shared my triumphs and my sorrows; You've helped me stand tall thru all types of weather.
I LOVE YOU SO MUCH, Mama! Oh God, I really do
And if I had but one wish in life—it would be to have an inner soul like the one that makes you—YOU!

Tanya R Crawford

GENERATIONS

While children cry our dreams die—
Oh, but when they laugh our future is strong!

Vickie Lynn Stock

MEMORIES OF GRANDMA

To my unforgotten Grandmother. For which she has given me such fine memories that shall remain with me forever.

Memories of Grandma still linger on, memories of Grandma will never be gone.
When I was young and Grandma was here, oh how I knew that she always did care. Her special ways, and her special touch; She made my world and life mean so much.
As I grew older Grandma did too, and our times together became far and few. Grandma took ill and soon passed away, but she gave me her memories in my heart they will stay.
Memories of Grandma still linger on, memories of Grandma will never be gone.
I remember the times we laughed and we cried, her strength, her wisdom, also her pride. A little old fashion set deep in her ways, I hope I'll be like Grandma some day.
Memories of Grandma still linger on, memories of Grandma will never be gone.

Vivian Owens

A CHILD'S SPRING

In the Spring, when I was a child,
There were many things lovely,
That grew in the wild.
There were blue bells and buttercups
and violets too.
Dandelion greens I took to Mama and said, "just for you."
The brook in the meadow was an interesting spot,
Watercress for salads and the frog on the rock.
A place to dream, by the willow tree,
I really thought God made Spring just for me.

Sandy Cruz Armstrong

TO A SPECIAL MOM

I'd like to say a thing or two about a special mom
Who's cared for us for many years through rough times and the calm.
Though we know we are prejudice we feel you've raised us well
Considering the times which they had made you live in hell.
You taught us right from wrong, you know
you did all you could do
And all the mistakes which we have made
are no reflection upon you.
When things are tough, and we need a friend
to you we make our way
You're always there to listen with something comforting to say.
When we all get together as one great big family
You deserve the credit for the happiness we see.
You showed us how to care and to say "I Love You" when . . .
There really was no reason just to say it now and then.
So now you know the answer if we ever had to choose
The vote would be unanimous We'd pick you mom, Barbara Cruz.

Nashel J Houldin

THE DANCE

Different colors dance in faded nights
and shadows form on smiling bones they wear
and sunken in the dread of evening lights
the eyes of sorrowed souls are waiting there
and different voices speak in monotones
with greying words that match the clothes they wear
and empty souls dance grinding hollow bones
and eyes of different colors stop and stare
and in the evening of the murky gloom
the dancing bones abandon masks they wear
and different couples dance to different rooms
with eyes that found a lusty bed to share

Brenda G Parks

OL' ELMER

A fellow asked the other day if anyone had seen
the old folks living down the road who ran the school canteen.

Ol' Elmer claims they've up and left to find a place to hide
away from all the stress and strife. (I think they've up and died.)

It's like those folks, Ol' Elmer swears, to leave us wond'ring
why they'd go away without a word. (I swear it's 'cause they've died.)

But Elmer says, "They seemed depressed—you never saw them smile— and somehow, it's not hard to feel they've left us for awhile."

Well, stubborn is my middle name, and this won't lie for long.
Ol' Elmer's sure they're on a trip, and I'm sure Elmer's wrong.

Persistence pays, they always say; the sheriff runs by the farm.
Nobody seems to be around—and not a sign of harm.

So why's Ol' Elmer wiping tears he's trying hard to hide?
Is it relief his secret's safe . . .
or guilt because he lied?

Genevieve E Adesso

WHAT SPRING CAN DO

In Memory of my Beloved Son, Thomas, Jr.

As morning came, the first sound I heard
Was the chirping of a single bird
The thought that came to me right then
Was that it would soon be Spring again

And then a feeling came over me
I should not mourn, for it has to be
"HE" gave to me for many years
A child who brought me joy and tears
One who touched my heart with his smile
I was blessed with his love for a little while
And in the while he gave to me
The very things that life should be
Now I see that he had to take
The road to "GOD" we all will make

I'll always miss him, this I know
But memories left, will make me glow
And somehow with the thought of Spring
I begin to feel that it will bring
Once again, the need to know
That life goes on and all must grow
The flower starts to bloom once more
and it is time close Winter's door

I think that Spring has a special call
to love the life "HE" gave to all
So I write this poem because I heard
The chirping of a single bird.

Philip Web Martin

COULD THESE BE THE TEARS OF GOD

To my wife Bertie Mae Bain Martin

We stand this beautiful memorial day
To honor our dear soldiers brave
For those who died and gave their all
Love of freedom, our old glory still waves

On this rain drenched land of tramping feet
To our many battled scared our Heroic Brave
We pay tribute and honor this day all they gave
To remember always in memory to repay

With grateful hearts not ere to depart
For their love still lives in our hearts
Now they are at rest. And have gone to their reward
To be with the Angels of Heaven the honor guard

We still stand on God given land
To let him take charge by his command
And now scans the battlefields of war
For God thoughts not what the cause was for

So God cries with and open grieving heart
on the torn battle fields soaked with blood and rain
And see these deep ruts trenched fields and sod
To see the many drops of rain with pain
Now what is left to see. Could it be the tears of God.

Karen Hutton

EAGLE

Spread your mighty wings
Soaring through the cloudless sky
Must you be so proud.

Trent Edwards

THE LISTENING HEART

Can you hear those hippies calling with their songs of weird retreat,
Or sense the droplets falling as the heart fulfills its beat?
Can you listen without crying to their sentimental tunes,
Keeping faith while theirs is dying, heeding well the cry of loons?
Can you feel the sense of wonder as the child cries out in awe
When the strains he is under obey their pristine law?
Do you hope for those who flounder, seeing past their groping hands,
Knowing that the path is sounder when they leave the shifting sands?
Can you see where deeds are leading, where the path will end in time,
Or measure waves receding after peaking in their prime?
Will you wait for those who linger tasting fruits in fields divine,
Keeping song apart from singer, laying all upon the line?
Have you looked in eyes grief stricken, giving love another chance,
Consoling those who are forsaken, leading them into the dance?
May you soar with those who venture past the edge of safe repair,
Letting them choose adventure, giving them your loving care.
Do you dare to challenge crusty mores and mindless toil,
Jetting freshness into dusty mausoleums of rigid soil?
Can you sympathize with sinners without falling in their trap,
Or give credit to the winners, sorting pearls from puling pap?
Have you read the words of Kipling which say you must hold on,
Or watched a brother tippling, giving strength when his is gone?
Have you watched your children straying from the straight and narrow path
Or spent your lonely hours praying that they never lose to wrath?
Did you spend your life in working, trusting God and fellow man,
Trying to learn where Death is lurking, to give Life a natural span?

Shannon H Patterson

THE COUNTRY

The grass is green
The sky is blue
The flowers around
Are beautiful too
This place called the country
Is so pretty
It looks very different for people
Who live in the city
They are used to having the noise
All around
But not used to having grass
on the ground

Barbara E Loveland

BRAVE PROMISE

When solitude is challenged by a loving heart
doubt defends with fierce delight,
and logic softened by a smile
joins the fray with half her might.

When trust befriends with open hands
freedom cries a valiant song
To plead the case for loneliness;
lost joyously to lover's plans.

When passion with its garish fruit
casts purity aside with glee,
then gentleness the caring knight
rides soothingly in love's pursuit.

When honor dedicates itself to love
and truth's a gleaming treasure found,
brave promise proves the silken thread
by which these loving hearts are bound.

Marla VanWinkle Snider

FOREVER

I love you. . .it was something
you needed to know.
Although God knows how hard
I've tried to not let it show

I thought maybe it was wrong
and would complicate your life
or that you would feel it your
duty to make me your wife

I want it to be a true
honest love when it comes. . .
or if it comes.
I want it to be real and
to last. . .forever.

Michael J Rehm

RUMOURS

To my eternal rose.

I spoke a phrase of awesome truth.
It meant so much, you see.
But a passage rearranged the words and
made a liar out of me

The meaning had lost all its form.
perhaps to make it better.
Maybe confusion would be erased if I wrote it
in a letter.

The message has been fantasized. Creations of
ignorant minds.
The voices of fools are wide awake, leaving something else
to find

They gather just to pass these thoughts. A type of weird
convention.
Falsifying what is said, and truth is none to mention.

I am not a man of wisdom, but speak what I must say.
And if it follows back to me, I want what went away.

For those who fail to understand, this is what I mean.
A picture's worth a thousand words, but not before it's seen.

Ann M Wetjen

HIM AND I

He stood by his locker and stared at me,
His eyes were the color of the bluest sea.
I motioned with my finger, approach very slow,
He moved with caution, but his eyes told me go.
He was an athlete, tall and strong,
I knew from the start we'd never be wrong.
When he asked me out, I couldn't say no,
He asked me to dinner, then a show.
But I knew right away from the look on his face,
Next to sports, I'd take second place.
Some girls could take it, but not me,
I must be in control of my own destiny.
A tear fell down his cheek, as we said good-bye,
Forever apart, Him and I.

B Elizabeth Brooks

PASSAGE

At the close of the twilight of my days
When the turmoil of life comes to an end

May my spirit ride the night wind
Home to God
My unfailing source of guidance,
And my friend

Faye C Harris

MISSOURI

To Yvonne, Randy, & Susan, Love you Mama.

I was born in Mtn. Grove, Missouri
the year 1921. We lived in a log house,
and there as a child, I had fun.
I had the sweetest Grandma, any kid, could have;
The day Dad, and I left her there for parts, unknown,
To me has always been sad. On this farm, we
had everything, chickens, cows, horses, hogs, and mules.
I even liked ole Brushy Knob, that was the name
of our school; I visited sometimes with my sister,
we ate persimmon's along the way. We pumped us a
drink, from the well, when we were turned out
to play. Our lunch was cold bacon and biscuits,
packed neatly, in a syrup pail. We rode our horses
bare back, and crossed a creek, to get our mail.
If, I could start all over in Missouri, I'd want
to be, rocking on that long front porch, sitting
on my old grandma's knees.

Martha J McStraw
THE CHRISTMAS DOLL
With Christmas time anearing
I go back to long ago
To a little picturesque village
All bright with fallen snow.

Picture an early Christmas
morning
(Too hard it was to sleep)
And a small girl begging her
mother
(Please, just a tiny peep?)

(Just let me stand in the doorway,
I won't go near the tree?
And I won't tell anybody
May I, Mamma, please?)

Well, mamma gave permission
The little girl stood in awe
For there in semi-darkness
The desired "Doll" she saw.

Well the "Doll" became her "Baby"
She shared her joys and tears
She heard all her dreamings
And her growing up teenage years.

But one night a tragic fire came
And took everything away.
And her Doll, (her cherished
playmate)
In the ashes lay!

Now, the little girls heart was
broken,
For she thought her life must end
For her "Doll" was more than a toy
to her
She was confidant, and friend.

Years have mended the broken
heart
And time has dried all tears
But the Doll is remembered
At Christmas time each year.

K Cottrill
AFTER MY HUSBAND'S DEATH

This poem is dedicated to my husband, John, who loved his fellow man and never met a stranger.

Sugar Plum! Sugar Plum!
Oh how I miss you!
As I drive along the road
Like we use to do.

And see the fields, the crops,
the friends,
The cattle, hogs, and sheep.
Sugar Plum! Oh Sugar Plum!
Without you I do weep.

Mickii Sharon Ruscoe
TEARS OF AN OLD WOMAN
The minutes like dark shadows
swiftly ticking by and here
in my lonely room I pace the
floor and cry.
Can you hear me world? I want to
scream, is this reality or
another terrible dream?
No, this is real, worse than death.
I'm alone you see, all by myself.
My children are grown and have
long left
home, and my husband passed
away
ten years ago today.

Oh, so long, so long ago it seems I
too was young with a heart full
of dreams; but life rushes by;
how quickly time flies.
I have memories, some beautiful,
some
sad, and I can remember
laughter
and the good times we once had.
You ask if I have grandchildren?
Oh
yes! Three. But they have no time
for an old woman like me.
Ah well!! Here comes the night
nurse
with a sleeping pill and some
other medicine for my ills.
Yes, they treat us nice in this
rest home; but believe me friend,
it's not like having a family and
a home of your own.

Mary Anne Buckley
THE MELODY
Deep within the caverns of my
mind,
a haunting melody is living,
its drums and guitars
whispering, shouting, screaming
your name,
like restless demons in the dead of
night.

Chorus after chorus,
it travels through this mass of
frigid flesh,
which once was my body.
I tremble.
My heart pounds with its incessant
refrain.

The melody takes no holiday.
Over and over, it invades my
tortured brain,
like angry waves of a storm at sea.

And I am alone with your memory.

Christine (Copple) Brown
PLEASE, BE PATIENT WITH ME

I dedicate this poem to a special lady who lived life to the fullest, who loved people for who they were, and who could make everyone feel special in her presence. She was one of a kind, she will always be remembered, and she will be greatly missed. Her name, Charlene (Mook) Dalton.

Please, be patient with me for I
have not been myself lately.
For you see, I have lost someone
very dear to me.
I feel lost and lonely and I even
hurt.
For you see, she was very special
to me.
She was my strength, my joy, my
courage, my hope,
and it's so hard to let her go.
I miss her so much, and it's so hard
to grieve.
This process is all so new to me.
I find myself crying for no reason
at all, and
I laugh at things that aren't even
funny.
I don't really understand what's
happening to me,
but I'm trying very hard, so please
be patient with me.
I am sorry for the way I feel, for I
grieve because
I loved, and there's nothing wrong
with that.
I just hope that you will love me
in-spite of myself and
help me to grow through this trial
in my life.
I need all the love and support I
can get, for I have such
a huge emptiness inside of me. It
seems to haunt me with a
terrible feeling of fear and the
reality of silence.
The quiet has never bothered me
before, but now I can't
stand it. All of this seems to worry
me, and then this
causes me more worry. So you see,
I'm just not myself right
now, but in time—this too will
pass.
So please be patient with me, and
someday I will be able to
love again, without hurt, and then
I will be able to live
again as myself—So until that
time—Please be patient with me.

Jennifer Coleen Holtz
A MOTHER'S LOVE
A mother's love is something no
one can explain.
It's made of deep devotion,
sacrifice an pain.
It's endless an unselfish, enduring
come what may,
For nothing can destroy, or take
that love away.
It's endless an unselfish, enduring
come what may,
For nothing can destroy, or take
that love away.
It's patient and forgiving, when all
others are forsaking
And it never fails or falters even
thou the heart is breaking,
It believes beyond believing, when
the world around condemns
And it glows with all the beauty of
the rarest and brightest gems.
It is far beyond defining. It defies
all explanation
And it still remains the mysteries
of creation.
A secret just like
A many splendored miracle man,
cannot understand.
And another wondrous evidence of
God's tender and guiding hand.

Helen L Dreher
STIRRINGS

In memory of Denver L. Dreher

After thoughts do bestir me
Oh! What pleasure they do bring
me,
Driving out the emptiness that
Fills my very being,
The little anecdotes we shared
Which had little or no meaning,
But to us were gems of life
Sandwiched in between the strife.
I will treasure these stirrings which
Beguile and intrigue me,
Knowing they were ours
And time nor space cannot erase
them.

Evelyn Judy Buehler
FANCY DANCER

To my husband, Henry; my lover in the shadows.

As she leaps on pink & satin cloud
Beauty is with her like a shroud.
In sunny mist; a twilight stream;
She laughs and frolics as in a
dream.
Through slumbrous days and
steamy nights
She oft takes off on strange flights.
The dance is one of mystery
Performed without a symphony.

In the marsh and in the glen
She'll pause to rest now and then.
In shady forest and green meadow
She flits through trees and grass
below.

Wearing jewelry of amethyst
She resides in sunset's rainbow
mist.
The trees bow low where she
prances;
The world stops to listen when she
dances!

She makes the young gentlemen
blush;
And the landscape still and hush.
She wakes the robins in the morn;
Caresses waiting stalks of corn.

She hails the sunrise with a whirl.
She's a very special girl.
At times surly; at times sweet;
The wind goes by on satin feet.

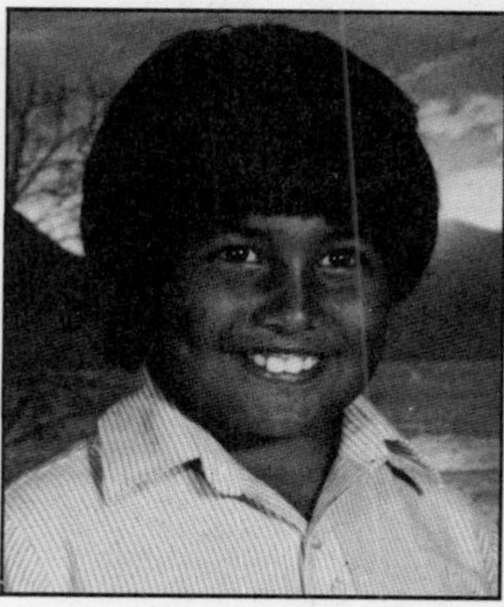

Marcos B Aguilar

Marcos B Aguilar
HANDS ACROSS AMERICA

I dedicate this poem to my family, to the Special Ed kids of Agua Fria School and to all the hands that stretched across America.

I went to "Hands Across America,"
and this is how I felt.

"Hands Across America,"
meeting people from everywhere,
each share love and care;

Waving flags and waving hands,
wearing red, white and blue
T-shirts,
but mostly wearing their smiling
faces.

Stretching arms and hands-
Of young and old,
until a long line at last to behold.

A feeling of goodness,
I felt as at last,
We sang "We are the World, and
Hands Across America,"

At last a feeling of hope—
for the Hungry and Homeless of
America.

S L McCallen
DAISY
Plucked one by one
from a tall-standing flower,
The petals lay lifeless

without any power.
The last one says she'll
love him not,
I won't pick it off,
says he,
Let it drop!

William Alexander Springer
MAYBE LI PO TODAY, BUT . . . ZEUS' TOMORROW

To all my muses, known and unknown, for their patience and love; and also to my mentor, Mop Tzu for cleaning up our cage. Thank You!

When where wears a thee as if. . .
The polka dot turtles
From the land of chess
Play more than one game
At home or in the wild,
The reach, the following move,
And of course the wind. . .
As eye admits
Its every guest,
Evers to proof. . .
There, there are no losers,
Is when
If building castles in the air
you would protect me
With your paper dolls
If eye had a kingdom
Of more that imaginary boundries
And yet measureless
Where monkeys and frogs
Both having banana-like fingers
Learn square dancing swinging limb to limb
In even odder circles
To laugh at the man chance made awhile ago
With his winning yet to be
As he slips off the edge
Of the lily pads cliff
With the whisper on 'is lips.
"Humpty Dumpty was pushed!
For refusing to curse Captain Hook!
For the cause's money of must needs come. . .
In greater cyphers,
When there's little or nothing to argue about,
Or married to Letter's hand for verse,
No better place than home;
So kids, please take the folks.
It's Paradise, I'm told, Gold dreams!
It's never nearly known nigh. . .
A goat-dawned play,
Nor a dog-done whirl,
Still. . .
One may be Li Po today,
As drunk as love can allow,
But as sure as all poets. . .
May earn their Muse's ruses,
We shall all find. . .
A Zeus is tomorrow.

Sandra Coalson Everett
MY SON

. . and the spirit shall return unto God who gave it. (ECL 12:7) My spirit yearns to fly free, far from the cares of this life. My eyes long to behold your most angelic face. With love, mother

I didn't remember they said you would die! They said it before you were born!
I begged them to save you! It only made them more forlorn!
Son, let me bare this pain for you! It's not right for you to
suffer this way!
Oh God! Let my baby live, I pray!
An innocent baby, is he!
If someone must die, let me!
Why did you take him away?
He did nothing to suffer that way!
There he lays in a little white coffin, his body so tiny and
cold!
He is my baby, I never will hold!
There my life goes in a long black car!
Lord, what did you take him for?

Vilma McClure
FOG

Billowing whiteness,
Enveloping nothingness,
Bringing a soundlessness
Milky-white shapelessness.

Strange in this eeriness.
Still, opaque murkiness,
Suspended, curtained-off
Is Man in this emptiness.

Feeling his aloneness,
Feeling his helplessness,
In limbo. in no world,
Aware of his minuteness.

Sheila Marie Carpenter
TEARS AND JOY

Let the healing waters flow
gently washing through my soul
tumbling over rocks of pain;
muddy lumps of grief and shame

Healing spray, splash my spirit
lift it up on waves
let the joyous surf leap higher
washing sin away forever

Holy tides of life and peace
rolling over the dreary beach
of past regrets; gritty mistakes
are swept away

Let the healing waters flow
making new and washing smooth
the rotting ruts of death and
empty shells of night

Morning sun finds glistening white
a life washed clean
by waves of forgiveness.

Janice Maureen Ames
THE GOLDEN KEY

The key to happiness and peace of mind . . .
Is from within . . we search; then find . . .
Sometimes it takes a special key
To unlock your soul and set you free . . .
You search, you try with all your might . . .
At times you love—At times you fight . . .
The feeling locked so deep within . . .
Is God inside . . He'll help you win . . .
The battles, the torture we put ourselves thru
It happens to me . . It happens to you . . .
His door is always kept ajar . . .
Waiting for you whether near or far . . .
He has the key . . .
He'll set you free . . .
Listen to him inside your head . . .
Pray to him . . To him be led . . .
For in his heart he holds The Golden Key . . .
He's waiting now to set you free.

Julius Moreno Jr
BRIEF ENCOUNTER

To my loving wife Alice, and my daughter Sandy.

It was a dreary, rainy, February morn
As I answered the doorbell with a "darn,"
There stood a smiling, shivering, 10yr-old child:
No coat, ill-dressed, with hair looking wild.

Quickly he told me "Oh, morning Sir,
I'm selling candy to help my sick Mother."
He showed me some candy in a plastic jar,
"It's good and fresh and a dollar a bar!"

The kid was uneasy and kept on talking,
Something about his "Dad's truck'll be checking,"
Then I noticed the blue spots on his face
And the bruises and scars showing everyplace.

He quickly noticed and tried to explain—
"Bigger kids hit me cause I don't try cocaine."
But I suspected his Father abused the lad,
Forcing him to sell candy or get "tagged."

I bought two candies and he seemed glad,
"I gotta go or get in trouble with Dad;
Thank You, Sir, and have a good day,
Cause my Mom says God loves us every'day!"

With that he smiled and then was gone,
Walking rapidly on towards the next home.
Helpless and moved, I watched him go,
Praying silently to God to help him so.

Kathryn Dekker Hanley

Kathryn Dekker Hanley
SOLITUDE

To my Father, Harry Dekker, "Being with you is like being alone"

Sitting alone, watching TV,
Oh, how depressing, just me and me.

If this sounds familiar, then lend me an ear
No reason to fret or shed a tear.

Just let me tell you while I am in the mood,
There ain't nothing better than pure solitude!

So come right in self, have a seat,
after all that company I know you're beat!

Come right over self, sit right down
cause when we talk we don't make a sound!

I have a husband, and its great being lovers,
But when he's gone, I get all the covers!

Being alone means being contented,
some people think that I sound demented!

But solitude is the greatest, yourself is all you need,
When it's time for dinner, there's only one to feed!

I can be so happy, my magazines in a pile,
I don't even have to move, if it's not worth while.

The gift of silence, no one else around,
is about the greatest gift I have ever found!

Now don't get me wrong, I love the fast pace,
But once in a while we all need some space!

So, I value my alone time, more than the rest
cause my own company is really the BEST!

Beverly Gulbranson
THE ULTIMATE FIELD TRIP

In memory of the seven astronauts who died on the space shuttle Challenger, January 28, 1986

There are new stars in heaven,
Seven new stars in the sky.
We see no rhyme or reason,
Why good men who live then must die.
The world is filled with sorrow,
It will never again be the same.
But God said, there's no tomorrow
As he called each astronaut's name.
It was to be a space journey,
New worlds, out there to explore.
But 73 seconds after lift-off,
The challenger it was no more
The lives of seven had ended,
No more on this earth will they roam.
They have taken the ultimate field trip,
The ultimate field trip home.

David D Foat
DAUGHTERS

To Kaja and Zoe, my daughters

They talk
(they always do)

About what they will wear, and
They ask each other to do things
For each other
(they always do).

Bev
A DELIGHTFUL THOUGHT

To my lovely daughter and her best friend—Love ya.

Jennifer—bound to Brian with balloons
What a delightful thought!

To be wrapped delicately with colored string —
round and round —
With bright balloons overhead.
Arms around each other, being careful
—not to break a string
—not to miss one shy smile
—not to miss one sparkle of the eye
—not to miss one word
—not to make a move unless together.
—Relying on the strength of the string
—Neither wanting to move for fear of losing a
balloon:

A balloon for togetherness
And one for friendship
A balloon for sharing
And one for caring
A balloon for warmth
And one for trust
All for Love.

Jennifer—bound to Brian with balloons
What a delightful thought!

Nicole "Smurfette" Austin
THE EAGLE
HE watches down unto the majestic plains,
Whenever he is near no one else reigns.
To cast your eyes upon him—he looks like the wisest sage,
His face tells you he will never be locked in a cage.
Beneath him are cliffs to rise a thousand feet,
And rivers crawl, never to meet.
There are lakes that stretch a thousand miles,
And trees that bend in a thousand styles.
Yes, he has streams that are forever flowing,
And plants and flowers that are always growing.
Of course—he has to catch his prey,
But not by day—
He does it by night,
And you might not think that's right.
Up on his mountain he rules with iron hands,
And watches over a thousand lands.

Randy Yingling
SWEET KASSY

To the young lady who's enchanting eyes constantly haunt me

She was a lady just thirteen,
the flowers knew her name
They envied her beauty
but their blossoms tried in vain.

"Kassy," said the flowers,
"How do we stand the shame
We endeavor all year our petals
yet your beauty gains the fame."

"Flowers," said sweet Kassy,
"It is all the same
Fore Randy plants and nurtures you,
to help to ease his pain."

"What pain is that?" the flowers asked
"That he needs us to hide."
"The pain he has when I'm not there,"
said Kassy
"To gaze into my eyes."

Kelley A DiFiore
AMANDA MARIE
Our Dear, Sweet, Amanda Marie
The perfect combination of your father and me
When I hold you close, my heart races
You in our life fills all empty spaces
We are so blessed and I sometimes cry
Because for you, I would gladly die
Our love for you will last an eternity
Our Dear, Sweet Amanda Marie

Gregory Philby
PACHYDERM CONVOY
Tugging on the tails
Of their interlocked beams of light,
The heavy and wet family
Of trucks plodded down
Their darkened path
In a uniform chain,
Shadowed gray
With the sunken sun,
Thundering indifferently past others.

Rosemary A Bowen
MOTHER'S TO BLAME

To my Mom—Naomi E. Moore

Think I'll write a book about my Mother, that practice seems to be the rage.
I can slander that fine image, smear her name across each page.
Jot down tantalizing tidbits, irregardless truth or not.
Just how should I begin it? It should have a sordid plot.
How about all those times after working hard all day,
Mom spent her evenings sewing new clothes for school and play?
And all those lovely holidays, as only my Mother could
She spent days ahead preparing—No, this isn't any good.
I can't sell books to readers unless I tell them how very bad
Was my existence with my Mother or what a horrible life I had.
I shouldn't tell them of the happy times like those picnics at the lake,
Or those many trials and errors when she taught me how to bake.
Then, when I was terribly ill and my babies need care
I rested comfortably and soon was well because my Mother was there.
But when my husband passed away and my oldest child was not yet three;
Again, she told me, as all though my life—"Don't worry, lean on me."
I guess I'd better give it up, forget about fortune and fame.
I can't lend deception to literature and it's my Mother who's to blame.

Karlie-Linda Michaels
COMPROMISE

To Stevie, for the poet in her heart.

I keep my dreams close
Rarely surrender to actualities
Realistically, I know
I've wasted time
That went down in
gum wrappers and
discarded coffee cups
It matters not, not now
This one is for me
I seem to have found
a way of letting go
Without losing the vision
the hope will always remain
And I believe that is
motivation enough for me

Bonnie V Winston
METAMORPHOSIS

To Billy—who I always thought would be around to see my fly.

I wonder if caterpillars
feel when they are
about to become butterflies?
Do they feel the bonds
of their silken cocoons
slowly loosen—
the silken threads
wrapped so tightly

start to unwind?
Can they feel a
change in the wind?
Or something
shaping deep inside?
Can they feel that
they, like I, are
slowly, suddenly,
scarily
about to fly?

Berna Dean Bibbs
THOUGHTS OF YOU

In dedication to my mother, Mrs. Dorothy H. Bibbs, who encouraged me to believe in my dream. Thanks Mom. In dedication to a cherished friend, Mrs. Jessica W. Roll. (Prov. 17:17)

I think of you in the morning at the break of day, and then
in the evening as the sun fades away.

Yet in between these hours, my love for you remains, as the
fragrance of a rose, in the midst of a summer day.

I can't forget hearing the softness of your voice, nor neglect
remembering the gentleness of your touch.

For what is life if not to live, if not to care, if not to give;
a part of yourself though small it may seem . . . a way
of expression, so lovingly.

To hide within you may lose sight, a ray of light only
seen by night; a drop of rain unnoticed falls,
like the whistle of the wind that calls.

My love for you will never change, though trying times
may come our way; for too many of us fail to show,
while time silently echoes on.

Love can hide a person's faults, beneath a heart of
kindness sought; with a sprinkle of trueness right
from the start . . . I'll love you always with
all of my heart.

Deborah Burdette
GOD'S BOUNDLESS LOVE

In loving memory of my grandfather Clyde V. Burdette

The sun is glowing with all its splendor
Flowing over mountains so high and valleys so low.
There is sweet peace and pleasure in this boundless
measure.
It is given by God from heaven above.

I wonder and ponder as I look to the sky.
As my eyes behold what God unfolds to tell us
the story of his boundless blessings and love.
How vast the sun of his glory and wisdom.

His grace is infinite in love I've found
To the least or to the greatest creation.
We all share this nature inside of us.
We just need to let go and share as God does.
God's boundless love.

Raymond Comer
MY BROTHERS
The people watched that day
as the young man walked away
He had been standing by the river bank and
tears ran down his face.

I know that was one day
he wished he could erase.
They watched him walk away
a tear ran down his eye.
They heard him ask
God why did you let them die?
Now it has been 11 years he has
a wife and family his life still goes
on.
But this life he is leading
he knows something is wrong.
He still has love for his brothers
and
this will always be.
Because the young man who
stood
on the river bank that day was me.

Frances Devine
MEMORIES

To my husband Mark

He is gone from me,
his loving face I can not see,
His hair turned gray,
I loved it that way.
His eyes dimmed with age,
could read the paper page after
page.
His hands big and strong,
did no man wrong,
Now he is asleep,
Many times do I weep.
Praying that we will meet,
and our lives will be complete.

John E Carpenter Jr
TO MY WIFE

For my wife Shari, all my love today and all of our tomorrows

I need you like the sun needs the
sky;
Like the birds need to fly.

I need you like the stars need the
moon;
Like the summer needs June.

I need you like a man needs a wife;
Like I need life.

I need you like peace needs the
dove;
Like I need love.

Elinor Bender
THE SEARCH

This poem is dedicated with love to daughters Barbara, Andrea and granddaughter Beverly.

I am constantly being pursued.
And am frequently misconstrued.
I've been told that I'm elusive,
And rarely ever stay.
You may not realize that I'm with
you,
Until I've gone away.

It's better that you not search for
me.
When invited, I will come to you.
Live life one day at a time.
That is the positive thing to do.

Some discover me while at play.
Others are rewarded as they pray.
Peace and contentment I can bring.
You may even want to sing.
Who am I, can't you quess?
My name is "Happiness".

Marc Amedee Landry
HAPPY BIRTHDAY FROM AFAR, DAD

To a wonderful Father! All my love to you from Plymouth N.H.

A Father who cares,
is what you are;
With incessant love,
from near and far.

You brought me here,
to where I am;
You set me straight,
you gave a damn.

You showed me good,
and what was bad;
You shared your life,
and all you had.

And now we are,
so far apart;
Soon time will come,
and mend the heart.

So with a smile,
and in my way;
I wish to you,
a Happy Birthday.

Love,
Marc

Laura B Bingham
PAIN

Oh God, maker of the Universe,
dare I call on you?
Dare I ask relief from pain that
permeates my very being?
Oh God, is there no end to pain?
From circle to circle it runs the
gamut, and then begins once
more,
Pausing only long enough to make
me believe it is gone.
It springs forth again with newness
of life,
Reverberating with such force
inside my being
That I think every cell within my
body is sure to explode!
My heart, my soul, my mind, all
melt into one big ache.
Oh God, dare I call on you? Dare I
ask relief?
No, for you are perfecting me. I
know that you are waiting
nearby,
Watching, ready to snatch me from
the flame that sears my soul.
I shall rise from the ashes! There
is a part of me that is
indestructible.
I shall look up and see your
outstretched hand.
I shall reach up and touch you.
What a solid link to peace!
Pain, where are you? You are ever
lurking within,
Waiting for the winds of life to fan
your tiny flame into an inferno.
Pain, you are lost to the great
extinguisher!

Eddie Jean Jones
DON'T TAKE MY SUNSHINE AWAY

Sunshine, Sunshine so bright,
Guide me through the day and
night.
Shine on me a ray of Care,
Letting me know that God is
always there.
Shine on me a ray of Love,
Which comes from Heaven above.
Don't ever go away,
Keep me warm each and every day.
For without a little Sunshine,
There is no light,
Then the devil has won the fight,
And no one will ever see,
How much the Love of God means
to me.

Robbie R Meyer
NICHOLE

This poem inspired by and dedicated to, Nichole M. Carey, my cherished daughter.

Out of her heart, her love
overflows. Eager to
please, her happiness shows.
Patiently waiting, approval she
seeks, just smile at
me mommy, her eyes seem to
speak.
Gently I brush back, the hair from
her eyes, a kiss on
the forehead, a welcome surprise.

Into my arms, she climbs hastily,
she whispers I LOVE
YOU, and hugs me sweetly.
I hope that I show her, in as simple
a way, that I
love her more dearly, with each
passing day.
The joy that she brings me, is so
pure and so
true, a gift sent from Heaven, and
NICHOLE
that gift's you.

Nancy L Schlotter
THE SHADOWS

To Karen, John and Lisa

A full moon casts its silver light
Thru the branches of the trees.
Creating shadows across the sand
Stirred only by a soft warm breeze.

Sea gulls sit along the pier
Like sentinels in the night.
Keeping watch over the lonely
shadows
As they wait for dawn's first light.

The shadows slowly merge into one
As the moon moves on down the
bay.
For their nightly vigil has come to
an end
And its now time to fade away.

They ease along, caught by the
waves
And drift slowly out of sight.
To wait somewhere in the vast
beyond.
For another moonlit night.

Irene Leisso Bay
RIVERSIDE PARK

If you go to the corner
And then, west down the street,
You will come to a lovely park
That is so very neat.
It sits beside the river
And is so gayly dressed,
With brightly colored flowers,
All in their Sunday best.

If you go to this gay park
And there, walk about,
You'll find the grass much greener
Than any you could tout,
But the nicest place to sit,
Is on the river's bank,
Then let your thoughts go sailing
On the waters dark and dank.

They will give them a swift ride
And twirl them about,
Like a leaf that is just floating
'Cross riffles, in and out,
And somehow you feel peaceful,
After your thoughts take that ride,
You feel you can ride out any storm
And come out on the right side.

Sharon L Cuchiara
A SINGLE NOTE

A single note
Both you and I
In life's great symphony.
We are plucked
Then soon forgot
With absent sympathy.

Let me put a song to you
Two notes to make a melody,
Then forever I'll be held
By your sweet memory.

If the soul is everlasting
On this you may depend—
Each time a stranger plays the tune
Our love will live again.

Let me put a song to you
The maestro leaves us soon
Resound our tender leit motif
Forever to the moon.

Willard Wrinkle Jr
ANGEL IN DISGUISE

Dedicated to my beautiful wife Marie

One day she came into my life and
brought an evil
dare. I knew the devil sent her in
with evil and
despair. The dare was to deceive
me and to steal
away my soul, with deceitful lies
and trickery, so
cunning and so cold. She said she
was in love with
me, a love as pure as gold, please
stay with me for
ever and I'll stay only yours to hold.
I felt a chill
run down my spine, my blood ran
thick and cold. I
knew that she was lying, she was
reaching for my
soul. She is a devil's child and she
is evil through
and through, I heard the devil tell
his demons this
and so it must be true. She's as
beautiful as a
princess, an angel in disquise, I

prayed to my Lord
Jesus, please come into her life.
She thinks she
is a demon Lord but goodness fills her eyes, so he
chased away the demons that the devil had disquised.
Then Jesus took her by the hand and kneeled her down
to pray, then told the angel now you are pure your
sins I took away. The man you love is waiting now so
let his true love in. You must always stay right by
his side and love him till the end.

Gerri Fegarsky
SOME MOTHER'S SON
He was some Mother's Son, who lay there today,
Cold and shivering, with eyes far away,
The sky in its glory, the waves smashed ashore,
The frail, huddled figure, trembled once more,
Alone with a muse, from a time long past,
A solitary sea gull gives comfort at last,
Smiling and nodding, with a secret well kept,
Some Mother's son, how long has she wept?

Mary Irene Sanders-Merkling
CONFUSION; IN LOVE!

To my first and last true love, my husband Joseph, and our precious Families.

Your head starts spinning
and your heart is flittery.
It's hard to breathe.
Your eyes are glittery.

In your thoughts
all you see is that one.
If you try to stop,
you end up with none!

Sorting out the feeling,
it's not the easiest task.
When your heart weakens
you give it the mask.

Open your mind
and try looking around.
If your one does go,
the heart must be found.

The good-bye's were said
in those soft tender lips.
Your head's so confused
and your heart does flips!

You know you're "In Love"
by that final Kiss.
You cry, you live,
even though, this one, you miss!

Susan Boesiger
YOU
My thoughts of you are so unreal
My wanting you is true
I see your face and realize
Why I've been so blue.

I dream about you all night
And I think about you all day
I wonder why I love you so
And why it's so hard to stay away.

I want to tell you so much
How I feel and why
But every time I see your face.
I know I just can't try.

Someday I hope to be with you
And feel your warm touch
But until that day comes
I will always love you this much.

Barbara J Camden
WEAVING IN THE AIR
The woven lace turned out by hand
Each thread in place so deftly planned,
The form is set, do what you will
With it and let it guide your skill.

To weave a maze of crossing thread
The design lays much a spread,
It's outward led from one small knot
Tied in one's head when just a thought.

Your weaving skill is your own lot
So few now days will sit and sew,
Instead they burn what they can't make
And never learn the grave mistake, they make.

Instead, the burning lace that hides the light
Is a disgrace to all the bright who face the world in night,
And know this lace is all the might
The human race can ever cite to show its good.

And yet, some of my neighborhood
Are scared of love and strength, the good,
They're running scared of what might come
When hearts are bared and shown how numb.

Because of this they burn the lace
That shows their face its blinding grace,
And yet this lace can mirror us
It is the base for building us.

Mary M Harrison
AMBITION
Grand and majestic,
Streaking through the night;
Grasping and gasping,
Climbing such great heights;
Clinging and tired,
As it reached the top;
Quiet and subdued,
By early morning's light;
Jublient in victory, yet
Eagerly awaiting
Another flight.

Lena Catalina Roberts

Lena Catalina Roberts
THOUGHTS FOR CHRISTMAS

Dedicated to our mother, Mrs. Pauline Catalina, (1921—1978), in memory of our many "bright" childhood Christmases.

It's December, the whole world is in a dither!
Who is this Santa Claus so merry?
Who makes everything so cheery?
What is Christmas without a mother?

Decorations are going up everywhere!
Little eyes are twinkling.
Little minds are thinking.
But what is Christmas without a mother?

She's the one who shops and worries.
She's the one who wraps and hurries.
She's the one who cares and bothers.
For what is Christmas without mothers?

And while you ponder over this question—
Think also—and give a good answer—
Who carried Jesus and fed Him at her breast?
Would we have Christmas without the Mother Most Blest?

So when you hurry on Christmas morn,
And the packages from Santa are all opened and torn,
Run and hug and give a kiss,
To the one you love and the one you'll miss
When Christmas comes one year,
And you remember the one so dear,
Who made all your Christmases bright—your Mother!

Barbara Baden
GODS' SPECIAL GIFT
We met in a special way
And built a relationship day by day
You've touched my heart from the moment we met
And made me realize I had love to give yet
When I'm with you I feel so proud
You send my heart soaring on a cloud
You gave me a reason for happiness
By asking me to share a special togetherness
Today is a happy day for you and me
It's shared with our friends and our families
We are here to be joined as one
And given a blessing by God's only Son
As we shared our wedding vows
Pledging a love that will always be ours
To hold special feelings within our hearts
Creating a bond that will never part
As we placed the rings on each others hand
With a meaning so special represented by our bands
That we will cherish with our love
Given to us by God above
And now at the conclusion of our Mass
We'll cherish memories that will always last
To build a new life and togetherness
Blessed with a love for future happiness . . .

Cheri Bittle
SONGBIRD

In memory of a Songbird. . .Helen Ring.

The songbird filled
its lungs with song.
Its killer had an ugly laugh.
He had cruel hands.

The rape was complete.

The old woman, who
sang, her perch
a wicker chair, was
murdered last spring.

I wondered,
who could hurt a songbird
in a cage?

Her garden,
a granite birdbath,
is now naked and dry
littered with dead leaves.

I wonder,
old woman, do you
still sing? Are you
drinking rainwater now?

P Andre' Bennett II
A FOUR YEAR'S OLD PRAYER
A four year's old prayer
God knows
Dear God
Thanks for the Lord
Thanks for the family
Thanks for the T.V.
Thanks for the lightbulb
Thank you, Amen

Denise E Badie
FACES
Faces that can touch, faces that can feel,
faces that are make-believe, faces that are real.
Faces that can kill, faces that can die,
faces that tell many truths, faces that can lie.
Faces in your bedroom, faces on your wall,
faces on the windowpane, faces down the hall.
Faces at the supermarket, faces at the picture show,
faces that are strangers, faces that you know.
Faces that are nice, faces that are mean,
faces that are transparent, faces that are seen.
Faces full of love, faces filled with hate,
faces that have patience, faces that just can't wait.
Faces that are dumb, faces that are smart,
faces that will hold you, faces that break your heart.
Faces that will harm you, faces filled with care,
faces that will look away, faces that will stare.
Faces that won't smile, faces that don't cry,
faces that say hello, faces that say good-bye.

Ida M Row
OUR CALIFORNIA HOME
High on a hill-top overlooking the town,
Sets our California home of white, trimmed in brown.

It's not a palace of finery or such,
Just a homey little cottage we all love so much,
Over the hillside and in the gullies near by,
Blooms the wild lupin, poppy and baby blue-eye.
A shepherd and his flock far out on a hill,
May be seen most any day from our window sill,
From the veranda, as the sun sets we see,
A world changed to fairyland, yes it must be,
For the mountains nearby turn a rosey hue,
And then quickly change to a deep dark blue.
Over the back door trellis entwine,
The honeysuckle and flaming trumpet vine.
The rose garden aflame is a beautiful thing,
Where oft we can hear a mocking bird sing.
Three back terraces wear carpets of green,
Where little white heads of clover are seen.
Down by the lath house neat and cool,
Is the flower garden and lilly pool.
Now we must not forget the many fruit trees,
Whose blossoms perfume the gentle spring breeze,
And I know if by chance we ever shall roam,
We will always long for our California Home.

Susan M Duane
SUNDAY TRADITION
Golden Sundays
fought,
with salty streams
drying in a dimple's crease.
Crimped,
by pinching hands
of relative's routine affection.

Golden Sundays
saved,
by Grandfather's tales
of the old country, the war.
Filled
with garden walks
and weekly grape-eating lessons.

Golden Sundays
Lost
in black panic
when Grandfather's body was blessed.

William J Johnson Jr
BUTTERFLIES

To my beautiful wife, Tina, who shares these feelings with me, and has since the butterflies started, given me four gorgeous daughters.

Words can't explain the way that we feel,
When we make love the sensation's unreal,
And to explain the burst in our heart,
That's when we feel those butterflies start.

We start out slowly, and work our way up,
Like tempting a bone to a starving pup,
To pierce through each other like the tip of a dart,
That's when we feel those butterflies start.

They start in our stomach, and work to our spine
Just when we tell each other "you're mine"
The feeling's unreal, it'll never go tart
That's when we feel those butterflies start.

When it's all over, we don't want to stop,
The world better slow down cause we're up on top,
So let's tell each other we'll never part,
That's when we feel those butterflies start.

Christopher J DeFrancisco
CLASS
It's cold and sunny outside
but yet so hot in here,
and the walls between act as medians
between freedom and tetrahedrons.

Inside, elders teach with racing repetition
in an attempt to prepare us for life.
Outside, barren fields run miles without petition,
with mystifying beauty and delight.

The sun is calling,
but I fight it with a passion unknown,
as I sit imprisoned,
wishing I was with the nature I was once shown.

Vicki

D Craig Graham
WITHIN OUR HEARTS

To my darling Vicki, my love forever, Craig

A treasure so delicate,
A treasure so rare,
A treasure so deep within,

My love for you is there . . .

Like the pearl within a shell,
Like the mid-night air,
Like the morning dew,

My love is always there . . .

We have found each other,
We have grown to care,
We have said, "I love you,"

Your love too is there . . .

Is this a place here today,
Is this a place two can share,
Is this a place we can live forever,

Yes, I feel it . . . it's there.

Bonnie Jean Rhoads
THE BRIGHTEST STAR—IN TRIBUTE

To Leo Wilson Shoup, Our Dad, by Bonnie Jean & the family.

This season shall not pass,
without this constant thought
Of the greatest legacy to us
by one, so dear has brought.
Gifts far surpassing those tied
up with a bow. . .
Of love, guidance, patience and
fortitude, provides an afterglow.

The constant desire for helping
others, Always there!
We thank God, we had the chance
to know his loving care.
The values and footsteps for us
to follow. . .a challenge in-kind
As his must have been as he
followed someone more devine.

Dear God, please grant that his
gift may be,
The most joyous "Reunion" with
his heavenly family.
Our feelings will be heartrending
But God, will help us all
through faith-mending.

Up there he must be planning to
lay the carpet, plane the wood,
Or just do anything he could.
Every task he understood and
was done with ease.
Always it was his aim to please.

So let him tend those things
if you would;
For he never could feel supreme
just being. . .
The Brightest Star in Heaven.

Sylvia C Fliege
MIRACLES UNSEEN
There are miracles we see each day;
We take them for granted and go our way.
Is it not the rose which blooms in the spring?
An oak tree tall and green; a church bell that rings.
There is a crimson sun setting in the West;
A robin nestled safe in its freshly made nest.
Perhaps it is a park where a child laughs with glee,
Able to play in a land that is free.
Maybe it is the moon and stars shining bright.
God put them in the heavens; placed them just right.
Let us be grateful to live in the land of the free.
Let us thank God we can be all we want to be.
Pray that our country will never stray.
We will always be able to live, work and pray.
May we not lose sight of oppression where it dwells.
Hopefully someday the world may be one, healed and well.
There is a beacon we must shine over this earth;
Telling of our love and of life's worth.
Standing free with our heads held high;
Forever may our stars and stripes fly.

Norma Evans-Barber
ONE STEP AT A TIME
He is teaching me to walk with Him
One step at a time;
And learning is a painful thing
For those who want to climb
To higher heights of His great love
Which blows our human mind.

I am learning how to leave my fears
Right at His cross;
And trusting is a daring thing
For those who have known loss;
Since they must judge through human eyes
His love which knows no dross.

I wonder where this trek will lead
As I my Savior follow;
But knowing is a dangerous thing
For those like me—so hollow;
So I'm content to go step by step,
And learn, and trust, and follow;
And glad surprises crown my way
When tomorrow's fear I do not borrow.

Betty Lou Weaver
DO YOU KNOW ME?
My life has always been a busy one . . .
Laughter, family, friends, sorrow and fun,
Full to the brim, with hardly time to spare.
Now, I'm older, not so busy . . . sitting here in my chair.
My children are great; do nice things and are kind . . . but,
"How can they know what goes on in my mind?"
As I sit here crocheting, my mind takes flight . . .
I've just won Reader's Digest six million dollars Sweepstakes . . . and OH! What a sight!.
I'll own my own home . . . where I'll have flowers and a garden,
so lovely and bright.
A house with plenty of rooms, for grandchildren to stay overnight.
But . . . Best of all . . . to be able to pay my own way,
Not be a burden, when I'm really old and gray . . .
To be . . . one less . . . worrying whether I'll have Medicare . . .
So I can tell the government "I'll pay my share."
It's a beautiful dream . . . I hope it comes true . . .
For all my senior friends . . . For me and for you.

J Emerson McGowan
APPEARANCES
While walking on the beach one day,
I spotted something shiny. . .it was not far away.
Hastening my steps as I drew near, it seemed that there was nothing to fear.
As I bent down to pick up this mass of green and gray—oblong
shaped glass.

I realized quite apparently that this
was only a piece of broken glass.
I did not care, nor did I think twice
of the consequences
that it would have on my life.
It twinkled in the fading light
and started for me thoughts of
sheer delight.
But no, what could this be, it was
only glass—the thoughts
of which soon quickly passed.
Sitting now, I realize that it was the
colors that caught my
eyes.
To make so much of this
heat-fused silicone made me
think
that my mind must be fully blown.
It must have been the 60's I thought
to myself; the passions, the
dreams or maybe something
else. No what am I talking about;
I must be insane; sitting here
ruminating of some long since
gone pain.
The glass has nothing to do with it.
. .as I threw it in a
tantrumed fit. Sailing through the
air and falling with a dull
thud, I can see it still. Sparkling
with a drop of our blood.

Brenda Giesbrecht

INSPIRATION

For my loving husband Brian and beautiful son Brandon. A special dedication to my good friend Vonda Foraie.

When in your confused state of
mind,
Think of memories, of another
kind.
Those of comfort and relaxation.
Memories that provide inspiration.

If it seems as though life has passed
you by;
And all your heart can do is weep
and cry;
Wipe your tears, smile in
realization,
For tomorrow will be your
inspiration.

Though the past and future are so
very far,
Tomorrow is not here, the past has
left its scar.
So come to me for a friend's
conversation,
Today, together we'll give each
other inspiration.

Loretta Greene

TRUE VALUES

To my wonderful parents, Pearl and James Greene

Love, respect, and always kind,
Mom, Dad—Senior citizens
you're devine,
Worked real hard, had time
for laughter,
And took time to thank
their Master.

Wm Michael Cotter

AN ANGEL'S LOVE

An angel's love is one of a kind,
one that's always in your
thoughts and on your mind.
An angel's love is one that is hard
to shake,
in which always steals your
heart, there to take.
An angel's love is not to be taken
in stride,
because it is always there at your
side.
An angel's love is now and forever,
but not one to give up on,
however.
An angel's love can be a great cure
for whatever your problems,
that's for sure.
An angel's love is whether you're
happy or sad,
in both good moods or bad.
An angel's love is usually for the
best,
it will help you to relax and rest.
An angel's love goes on 24 hours a
day
to help you, just as you pray.
An angel's love can ease your pain
with nothing to lose or even to
gain.
An angel's love can always be
found,
for you don't have to look for it,
it's always around.
An angel's love is here to keep
no matter whether you're awake
or asleep.
An angel's love would be nice to
share,
hold out your arms and show
someone you care.

David D Sizer

David D Sizer

TIME

The same today, yesterday and
forever,
Around the world; it changes never.
A strange, mysterious, complex
notion,
Encircles life with no commotion.
In the animal kingdom man lives
supreme,
Recording most deeds as true (so
they seem).
Man's full comprehension of
things to find,
Is expressed in prose, arts and
rhyme.
Man's greatest endowment is
power of "Thought".
Without its existence he is brought
to nought.
Mystery in thought life is found in
man's will
Directing his path o'er valley or hill.
Thoughts mold ideas; they make
purpose 'tis true,
Ambition and vision are sure to
guide you.
Achievements of man in the
ladders he's climbed
His wars his writings, and travels
defined.
Humanities goals, good or bad
ever clash
Frustrating desires as a rumpled
sash.
Faith, hope and love show growth
in his life
Moving true or false in his daily
strife.
Man striving for good where there
is always wrong,
Has foggy despair, or glorious
song.

P C

LIFE IN A PAPER WRAP

Elvira—Thanx . . .

I am an envelope pure and white
Born from a tree
My message of Love and Hope and
Happiness
Ripped from my body
Carrier of thunderous sounds of
laughter
And rivers of tears and joy

This to you God I give gladly
Loving the free flow of emotions
Your stamp of approval is why I
exist
Without question I love you, my
Creator

When I am used and tattered
The devil gaily beckoning me
My company the rinds of fruit
Dried and wrinkled and empty
I accept the darkness and smells of
Death
The distant fires of Hell
Just rewards for my sins

I am a tree strong and beautiful
Born from a seed
Within me I feel messages of love
and Hope and Happiness
If only I knew how . . .

R E Keplar

PUSHIN' THIRTY

For Barbara Oney Evans. Simply for being the right memory, at the right time.

All we had was time,
we always had tomorrow,
we didn't know the sorrow,
we didn't have the apathy,
then all at once,
tomorrow up and came.

I wondered where it would go,
there was so much to hold,
it tumbled from our hands,
to the ground,
where it came to pass.

All we had was time,
to wish away our wildest whims,
to catch our ride on the farthest
wind,
to dream the dreams,
to someday fill our pasts.

Steven B Sherman

MORNING LAUGHTER

While thinking of Natalie: In memory of speech—for it is never full.

I'm pleasant and the air is as
such.
Casual pleasantries I acknowledge
in a flute—
To incorporate the soul
structure unto words—
To somehow release its tendernous
unto the tongue—
Our ignorance only, does grow
old and abused—
For our soul remains freshly-naked
and blissfully young.
Comic lust—so preciously we
lust—
After our flesh—its tones and
textures.
Pretentious of actualization—
phantasmagoria becomes our grip.
About the day, we dress and are
clothed in silence—
Within our dreams and creation
we become stripped.
The soul is dry—
We live and die in an instant.
"Why do we breath" is a question
spat by the numb.
My senses are conditioned by one.
The soul is conditioned by
love—being active in itself.
All blessings are bestowed upon
its wings,
and wings are sheathes placed
upon the heart
in the merciful repentance of
sin...End and Begin...
"Unless speech contains the
words of—God—it is given
vaguely and numb—therefor
remaining in a
common state of ignorance"
—My Morning Laughter—

Doretta Johnson

SECRET PAIN

Each hour seems like weeks, each
week like months
Though my years pass much too
quickly now
My mind knows no peace, my
heart only pain
I make claims of love and special
feelings,
even of having dreams
Though my heart only knows the
truth I keep locked
inside of me
I feel not love, nor hate, only the
obligations to
function for others
I live alone with my almost
unbearable pain
I paint on a smile for those who
love me
For I do not wish to make them
unhappy
I have no answers, much to
confused to explain
I will endure what life I have left
to live
Until my soul inherits its release
Such a glorious day it will be,
when this hell is over
And my mind and heart come to
peace

Bertha Renchkovsky

ELVIS THE KING OF ROCK AND ROLL

We loved you for your acting.
We loved you for singing the blues.
Even for "Love Me Tender",
Down to your "Blue Suede Shoes."

Elvis was our teenage Idol,
Elvis was our grown up man,
And God had come and took him;

He took him to the promised land.

He was our teenage Idol,
He was our grown up man,
And now he's up in heaven
With the King of all the land.

They took him back to Memphis
To be there with all his clan,
Because he was the King of,
The King of the Rock and Roll land.

They put him in a Mausoleum
To keep him the best they can
When someone tried to steal him,
The King of the Rock and Roll land.

And now he's back in Graceland
His Mom is back there too,
And his dad and uncle Vester
Were watching over both of you.

Joyce E Zimmerman
TEARS

Dedicated to my father, Grover H Pascoe, who lost his fight with cancer and passed from this life March 7, 1981.

The pain you suffered
The tears we shed
In my mind you were
The "Christian Soldier"
Marching ever onward
To face the battle
We all knew lay ahead
And to conquer the horrible death
We all knew would come
To end your suffering
To begin our tears again

Rhonda J Gipson Taylor

Rhonda J Gipson Taylor
AFTER THE INTERMENT

I want to dedicate this poem, to all my family and friends. A very special dedication to a man, I admire dearly, who has played a major roll in my life, Douglas L Conner.

After the interment eyes still
filled with tears, mind goes
wandering
Over the years.

Everyone has gone home.
There
you are—all alone.

Now that he's put to rest, your
life isn't at it's best. Depressed?
Yes. Your whole life seems to
be
a mess.

Where are all those concerned
relatives, neighbors, and friends?
Seems
like their friendship has come to
an end.

No one to talk to you, there you
are still feeling, so blue, saying
"what shall I do?"

He's on your mind. There you
sit —
continuing to cry.

You're asking yourself over and
over, why did he have to leave?
Leaving me here to grieve.

Before the interment everyone

seems so nice at the time of
sorrow, "hey what about
tomorrow"?

After the interment everyone
seems so far away. Yet you seem
to need them today.

If someone did come over, you'll
try to persuade them to stay,
longer.

Please don't forget me! I'm the
one who still grieves

Don't forget me so soon. I need
you, if not morning, or night,
please
make it noon.

Yes I admired the telegrams,
flowers, and cards you gave.
No, he is no longer with us,
he sleeps in his grave.

Just talk to me every now and
then, I still yet live, and I'm
still that friend.

Call me if you don't have the
time to stop by. Ask me, how am
I;
or just call and say hi, because
my heart still yet cries.

Don't forget me after the
interment.
I yet live and I thank you for
everything you did, or might
had sent.

If you ever have a time of
sorrow, remember I'll help you
through it all, today and
tomorrow.

Marjorie A Brockman
TAKE MY HAND FOR AWHILE

Take my hand for awhile
And walk with me through my life.

Do not be afraid of the warmth my
soul radiates.
It cannot hurt you
The warmth is true love.
The kind you read about and
daydream of.
Love such as this can only make
you happy
And help you grow.
And it is present because you have
so touched my life
With your kindness and affection.
You yourself have created it.

Do not say a word; just hold my
hand
And look into my eyes.
No words are necessary—only
after love has gone.

Do not be afraid of what you feel.
Let what is inside free.
If you love and try to hide it, you
are going to hurt somewhere.
Showing you care means taking
chances
But it can also make you happy.
Trust me. Take my gift of love and
cherish it always.

In years to come should our lives
part
A moment's thought of the
warmth once felt
Will bring a smile to your mind and
light your way to another day.

Cindy Railey
AWAKENING INSPIRATION

If "Life" is just the temporal plane
And "Death" the soul awakening;
Then we must strive for higher
consciousness—
Dispell our fear of "Death."

"Death" is just the beginning;
A continuance of the search
For "perfection" and "oneness."

Only through "Death" can we
relive and learn
From our mistakes along the way
And learn to give freely without
want
Ultimately to experience true
"Life"—
L O V E .

Larry C Gilbert
I KNOW A MAN I'VE NEVER MET

To my loving wife, who has helped me see, without the Lord, just where I'd be.

I know a man I've never met,
But someday I know I'll see.
My Lord, my Savior, Jesus Christ,
Died on the cross for me.

Upon his head a crown of thorns,
Nails through His hands and feet,
With arms outstretched He died
for me,
This man I long to meet.

He died on Calvary that day,
To redeem me from my sins,
He rose to return again someday,
Although I know not when.

And on that day I'll meet this man,
As eye to eye we look.
I'll see fullfilled the promises
written in His Holy Book.

Jan Holten
DRUGS PICKED OUR FLOWER

I dedicate this poem, to my dear daughter Julie, and to people, all over the world, who do, or think about doing drugs. Say No, to drugs.

She started from a tiny seed,
a flower protected from all weed.
The flower bloomed, so beautifully,
and for fourteen years so
wonderfully.

The flower was so pretty and
bright,
and nourished with, what thought
was right.
The care we gave this little flower,
because we valued her as ours.

Then one dark day, a monster
came.
Since then the flower was not the
same,
and I can call it by its name.
Drugs, picked our flower, for its
gain.

The flower wilted, withered and
dried,
and helplessly, we watched and
cried.
That ugly drugs, claimed our
beautiful flower,
and drugs, had no right, because
she was ours.

Now all that is left, is our wilted
flower,
to care for and protect, from hour
to hour.
Drugs, keep on claiming the good
and the best.
Let's stomp drugs out, to save all
the rest.

Eva Northrup
CHRISTMAS

Christmas time is here again
All the bells begin to ring
To welcome in the yuletide joys
And help surprise the girls and boys
How the children's eyes will pop
When they see Santa in the shops
The fire burns brightly on the
hearth
The stockings hung all in a row
The goodies sitting all around
And up above the missletoe
The Christmas tree stands slim and
tall
Beside the front door in the hall
Everyone will stop and stare
And wonder why the tree is there
All the little folks will say
It's handy there for Santa's sleigh
The packages beneath the tree
Are for everyone and you and me
It's really sad they are all so gay
They have all forgotten it's Jesus'
Day

Laura Dene
MAKE YOUR OWN SUNSHINE

To Betty Jett with love. Thanks for the inspiration to write this poem.

For those of you who have ever felt
blue,
Been divorced and unhappy, this
poem is for you.
You're going through changes—
some good and some bad,
But remember the good times and
try not to feel sad.

Do you ever feel you're on this
earth for a reason;
Not just to drift through, but to feel
each and every season?

Life has its growing pains which
we must endure,
Never really knowing or ever quite
sure.

Sometimes we have laughter, and
sometimes tears,
But life is an experience and we
grow through the years.
The pain we encounter can bring
us great grief,
But the joys of a change can also
bring relief.

May your future bring changes
that enrich your life.
Remember you're "you" now and
not just a wife.
You can make your life a happier
one if you really try.
Give yourself lots of sunshine and
reach for the sky.

Jeanne La Fon

SPRINGS CAMEO GARDEN

I could walk for hours in a garden
Come every spring,
When winter's ice transforms to an
Eden of growing things.
Where golden air and its warm rays
Escort me through a garden gate,
And a robin glad of new delights,
flits
About the garden's wake.
I'll walk with quiet hours neath a
Spell so ever tender—

Where sweeten rain imparts the
Garden's cameo splendor.
Down emerald aisles I'll mingle
With flowers nestled
everywhere—
Breathing deep there fresh new
scents,
Come floating on the air.
Each time I walk a springtime
garden
Heaven fills my heart,
And being silhouetted by her
summit
I never want to part.

Ronald W Hauser

MY APOLOGIES AGAIN (FOR MARY ALYCE)

Long have I sought,
for you again
past the darkness
of sleeping death

for an age
I slept apart from you,
held in silence,
to at last return, seeking you

till this day I turned
and like an answer to questions
asked
you stood, having waited
you knew me and I you

So now our words
and dreams intwine,
reminded of your eyes,
the color of leftover wine

And so I find
I love you still, with ease
my long lost portugese . . .

Marla Britton

TIME

To my parents with love.

Washed away.
Like the tides sweeping a
sandcastle
Leaving a pattern of glass
As though never having been
touched.
The sun sets.
Night falls.
Dawn brings anew.
Time is, but still.

Roberta R McNew

Roberta R McNew

GOOD-BYE

My tears, they burn so deep,
My love, you said you'd always
keep.
And now my heart lies deep
below,
'Cause I saw you turn with her and
go.

Everytime I thought of you,
I remembered you said "I love you
too."
Then I knew it was just a lie,
When you said I'd find another guy.
But now that I'm gone you ask
me "why?"
It's 'cause I loved you so, and you
said
"Good-Bye."

Kitty Lyon

OH WIND COULD BLOW

Oh wind could blow
the tired mind
and place it in
magnetic fields
where molecules align

And God is never theory.

Oh wind could blow
a tear back in
the sea where all
is whole and nothing lost

And God is every host.

Oh wind could blow
the sound of chimes
clean out of sight
and still the mind
would clink

To God in every toast.

Franklin Delano Gesswein

CHASING RAINBOWS

When I was six years old,
I saw my first rainbow.
I stood in the rain. . .gazing
at that wonder in the clouds.

When I was twelve years old,
I chased my first rainbow.
I ran hard down the long street,
but it waited. . .up the hill.
I ran. . .I ran. . .and I ran,
yet now. . .it waited for me
Way way down. . .the valley low;
still. . .as distant. . .as ever.
When I was thirty years old,
I was caught by my first rainbow.
I saw the familiar colored crystals
in a cool refreshing spray;
Brush this walker's face and
disappear
on a bright, cloudless, Summer's
day.

That's the secret. . .isn't it?!?!
It was always there. . .invisible,
Just waiting there for me
to reach out. . .and grasp. . .it's
magic.

Debbie Wolf

STOP SUICIDE

Life is too much for me to bear,
No one to love, no one to care,
Living's too much for me, its too
unfair,
There is no hope, no, not anywhere.

Letters are found like this everyday,
After someone's taken his life away,
Stop. Listen. I've got something to
say,
Don't die for tomorrow, live for
today.

If you're thinking about suicide,
Find someone in which to confide,
Take the time to look down inside,
Bring out those feelings you're
trying to hide.

If you're thinking my life has to
end,
There is someone who has an ear
to lend,
Stop. Don't do it, go talk to a friend,
Talking will cause your heart to
mend.

If you're thinking, this I must do,
Think what your family is about to
go through,
Living their lives wondering why
you,
Took your own life, without even a
clue.

Becky Freeman

COUNT YOUR BLESSINGS

As I was watchin' & listenin' to a
T. V. show
Which deals with lots of subjects,
of those in the know
Today it might be history, politics,
as you listen so well
But what's on tomorrow that
emcee just won't tell
Today he had a person, we might
term as weak
How she had overcome her
handicaps she did speak
An old lady called in, voice
creakin', couldn't carry a tune
But alas as she sang, I felt Gods'
presence all in my room
She sang, "Count your Blessings"
name them one by one
Count your many blessings, see
what God has done
As she sang, I began countin' each
one of mine
First on my list, was my Saviour
Divine
Next was the little family, He had
given to me
Who'd be with me for all eternity
Then Gods' people from each
different clan
Who make up this creature, called
man'

Connie Norris

TO MY OH MY OLD HOLLIE

To mom, dad Carl, Monica and Christina for all the love you gave me and to Hollie for all the memories

To my oh my old Hollie
I hope the wind will blow
So you can ride a cloud as far as it
will go
I hope the sun will shine
so you can find your way
Because you died one September
day
Although you are not here Hollie
I still love you all so dear
I hope the stars will shine
and the moon will be so bright
because Hollie you are a beautiful
sight
To my oh my old Hollie
you are the best little pony
that I could ever have wanted
Even though you are gone my
memories will hang on

Kimberly Golden

GOLDEN

In loving memory of my grandfather, Leland M. Golden

Golden Is the morning sun
That shines forth through the day.
Golden is your loving touch.
Your soft and gentle way.
Golden is a shining star
That makes your dreams come
true.
Golden is the falling leaf
A sky of autumn blue.
So when your in a winter world
And everything is cold.
Just close your eyes and dream
your
dreams
And your thoughts will turn to
gold.

Liska Anne Crowley of River Spirit

CIRCUS MEMORIES

To "Raunchy" — My Love of My Life, whose support and love made me the Happy Lady of River Spirit

The once gaily lit arena is dark, the
clowns have all gone.
White painted faces are washed
with tomorrow's dawn.
Their baggy pants are hung in
silent dressing rooms.
High wire artists are
stilled. are all folded
For another days show.

Sequined costumes are still
twinkling, though
There's no one left to see.
The dancing bear snores gently
and horses prance
In their stalls.

Field mice do scurry while the
ringmaster's cat
Waits for his call.
The children's laughter is stored
in my memory like
My rememberings of eating Cotton
Candy on a
Saturday afternoon.

The stands are barren now only a
few peanut shells

Litter the ground.
I hear the voices in my heart and recall when the
Circus came to town.

Deborah Louise Morgan Martin

Deborah Louise Morgan Martin, RA, LPABI, FIBA, DG, DDG

CONFESSION

There was a young man who under duress,
Finally acquired the nerve to confess,
"A Priest I cannot be,
For everyone would see
Me entering the church wearing a dress."

Kevin S Hayes

WISH THAT YOU WERE MINE

What is love if you never felt it
What is life if you haven't lived
What are dreams if you never share them
What is hope if you never give
What are words, if they have no meaning
You say you care, but you show no signs
Days are lettered by numbers
And I wish that you were mine

Songs are written for pleasure
They fill our hearts with joy
Children clinging together
And I'm knocking at your door
Flowers are made for beauty
Stars were made to shine
Memories, were made to last forever
And I wish that you were mine

What is love if you never felt it
What is life if you haven't lived
What are dreams if you never share them
What is hope if you never give
What are words, if they have no meaning
You say you care, but you show no signs
Days are lettered by numbers
And I wish that you were mine

Jennifer Norred

I'M JUST THREE

I can count, and say my name,
Tie my shoes, and play a game.
Tell you hi, and say good-bye,
I may not be right, but I try.
I know my left from my right,
Say my prayers every night.
I brush my teeth and comb my hair.
If I need help, I know you're there.
Now that's a lot as you can see
I can even say; Hip, Hipper, Hippo.
Oh well, I'm just three!

Barbara Kaye Curtis

I OWE IT ALL TO YOU

Thank you for your patience and the knowledge you have shared, the simple words of encouragement and the ways in which you've cared.
You've helped me get to where I am and now that I am here, I look at the past of days gone by and down my cheek rolls a tiny tear.
It seems just yesterday I started school and responsibilities were so far away, but now I face reality as I approach the final day.
My own life is just beginning now and there's so much I need to do, but I wanted to take time out to say, Mom and Dad, "I owe it all to you."

Mary E Clark

OLD PRAIRIE SCHOONERS

Old prairie schooners made their way
across the staked plains of yesterday.
They left their tracks in the shifting sands
as they carried prairie pirates to an unsettled land.
The days dragged on, weary and hot.

Obstacles that faced them—grew more like a plot.

After days on the trail—the pirates did ponder,

sick children cried, some were buried out yonder.
Their way wasn't with ease, their hardships were many.
Days on the trail numbered one hundred and twenty.
Indian raids, skulls found on the trail
made them wonder daily—what would prevail.

Old prairie schooners made their way
across the staked plains of yesterday.
The proof is there—still out in the sand
where they came to settle an Indian land.

Ralph William Greenwell

MY LOVE WON'T DIE

My love for you is true
for when I was sad, lonely or
blue; all I had to do was call you.

I want you to know that my
love for you will never die,
but, now I must say goodbye.

Now we must go our separate ways.
But if my path leads me back to
you, trust me I won't delay seeing
you. For my love for you will
never die. But I will have to
say GOOD-BYE.

Prudence Anderson Soukup

THE LITTLE STRAY PUP

Walking up the street that day
Sing merrily as was my way
I saw, all huddled in the snow,
The little stray pup I fed not long ago.
He had been hit & kicked aside
To suffer & freeze until he died.

I knelt beside him & prayed
To God that his little life be saved.
His pain, while on my bended knees,
I tried with all my might to ease.
Oh the sadness of my heart
When I knew that pup & I must part.

The little dog so black & tan
Looked into my eyes & licked my hand
Then whimpered a little & passed away.
There was naught but sadness on that day
I lifted him gently & took him home
And on his grave I'd like to place this stone

Here lies the pup that died
No matter how hard I tried
To save that little bundle of black & tan
Who with his last breath licked my hand
Then whimpered but little then passed away
On that cold & bleak December day

Mildred V Eller

FOG

Fog is like a petal soft
As it ascends among the loft
Of every harbor, nook and den
Hiding all the beauty therein.

Helen Conklin

BABY AFTER FORTY

When that tiny mite was placed in my
arms,
and I gazed at the sweet little face,
I wondered why God had chosen me to bless
at this time and place.

I thought of the two young men at home,
I'd watched grow from babyhood too,
who were ready now to try their wings,
in whatever they wanted to do.

I thought of baths and bottles and the
Den Mother bit and strings tangled
in kites,
of hurts to be kissed, when at camp to be
missed,
and punchered tires on bikes.

I thought—"In the afternoon of my life,
How will I ever make a new start?"
But God had thought of all of that and
is keeping me young at heart.

Deanna Lynn Breakfield

AMERICA

To my loving family, Bill, Kendrick, Thomas, MeLissa, and Clifford, Also to our young boys in the Armed Forces, Steve, Kelly, Chris, and Doug. We love you all.

Let the bells of freedom ring,
Let the youth of our Nation sing
Always allow our choice to be
One Nation under God with liberty!
And as we stand so tall and straight
Lifting our flag to Heaven's gates
Let us remember where we all began
One Nation under God, hand in hand
We take for granted our freedom flag
With immoral conduct and the sinner's brag
Our Nation's strength begins to fall
No longer on God does this Nation call.
So let us think how our forefathers feel
As the CONSTITUTION no longer seems real
The rights for the wrong, now our Nation screams
Forgetting the victims, their rights unclaimed.
Our Nation has been shielded by blood, sweat, and tears
As the sounds of war rumors our ears
And again for our Freedom would our young men die
As America! America! America! they cry
Liberty and Justice for each one shall be
The Freedom of choice as each one sees
No guns, no wars, no hate can be
In a country of love with Liberty
America! America! America!

Agnes C Vinson

THE AQUARIUS CHILD

To my loving family

The Aquarius Child is so special;
A treasure to love and hold dear.
To watch her grow and spread her

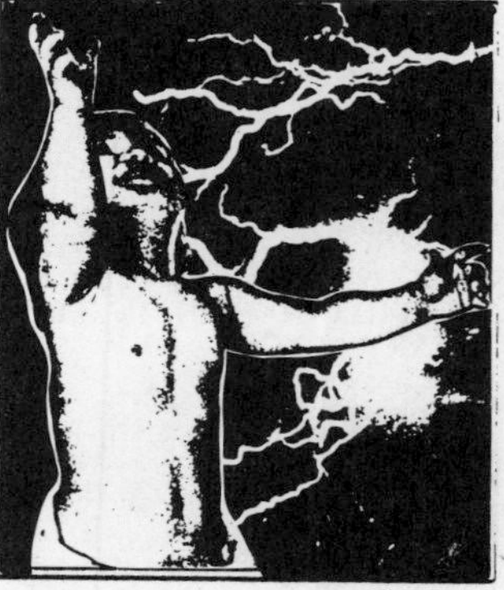

wings brings joy and perhaps a tear.
She is quiet with thought. There's strength that runs deep, and love that flows freely for all in her keep.

Sharon Taylor Battee'

CHRISTINA

She came to us—as a little babe,
This young life to us God gave.
She filled her home with an abundance of Love
Christina truly was God's Gift from Heaven above.

A tiny, precious little life
She had such a struggle . . . such a fight.
Christina has won her battle at last
Her sickness and pain have all gone past.

A delightful, loving, happy child
Just to look at her made you Smile.
Christina touched the hearts of

those all round
Many friends she made by leaps and bounds.

It's hard to understand the reason why
God called her to His Heavenly side.
She was loaned to us . . this we know
It's just so very . . . very hard to let go.

Knowing someday we'll meet her once more
Over on that Heavenly, Peaceful shore.
Christina's life was short . . yet for a special reason,
She touched so many hearts in such a short season.

To you, Christina, we must say "Good bye",
We know you're at Peace by the Savior's side.
You'll always hold a Special place in our hearts,
And someday soon we'll never have to part.

Our love and prayers reach out to those left behind,
The right words are yet so hard to find.
May it just help to know; "WE CARE"
And your sorrow we want to help you bear.

Vada McBride
NEW DAWN
Gazing beyond the Horizon
Watching the darkness fade away,
Comes the Dawn in all its splendor,
It's the beginning of a grand new day!

Like a fether of flame the sun brightens
Filling the heart with a fiery rage;
Facing the awe of an unknown future
Seeing the rose-flush of a new age!

The winds whispering words in the background
With a message for Lovers to hear,
and the songs of the birds are a symphony
Like Harps to a musical ear.

These throaty songsters greet the new day
Pausing on the window sill—
With cheery notes of Love and gladness,
Bringing to each of us a thrill.

I will rise before the Dawn tomorrow
to watch the change that are made
Down the Lanes of the unknown future
and the Dreams of other New Days.

Jamie Homistek
SNOW
The white ice crystals
Look like lace from the heavens.
It's God's mystery.

Nelson Arthurton
THE POTION

Karen Racquel Shenel

Oh blend me a potion of Land, Heaven, Ocean
Distilled, but with tears laments and despairs
Aged, but only in grottos lonely tinted by beauty
Fashioned so comely purely humbly
Scented by petals crushed in sepals
Touched with music
Spiced with laughter, the cry of barter
Mixed with moonbeams dew and mist
That thin lips as grass have kissed
The enchaliced blood of Christ
Stirred with truth Spring green and youth
Kept by Winter, her silk vestures under
But must be anodyne of cured roots and quinine
Then drink to my soul
From a love prepared bowl
Ringed with rainbows sunset and halos
My thirst will quench it
Sip crooked lips it.

Lucille Boyce
THROUGH THE WINDOW PANE
I can see through the misty window pane
Wet with drops of crystal rain
The weaving traffic, windshield wipers to and fro
And in rhythm the sidewalk walkers go

Umbrellas held high, dodging a puddle
Pedestrians rushing through the city's muddle
In spite of the weather and gray pall
That lies over the city covering all

In a mysterious cloud, the walkers seem to disappear
Then one by one more people appear
It is fun watching the throngs go by hurriedly
Strangers to all except to friends and family

Do I appear as this when I go by?
Walking with strangers under the rainy sky?
And someone upstairs watching at the window pane
Sees me go by in the rain

Yet I slide by into the mist out of sight
Past strangers who not know me or my might
"I am here", I want to call out, "Who are you?"
"I feel the wind and rain too—as you do!"

But I dare not, I plunge on in the rain
And wonder who is watching from their window pane
And sees
Another stranger go by as a breeze

Am I just a passing stranger in someone's eye?
Or do I look important as I go by?
Then I look up, and see the sun in yellowed glory break through
I see umbrellas closing up, and smiling faces too
The girl at the window pane smiles and waves to me
I am renewed, and walk on happily.

Eloys E George
A RIVER AND LIFE
Sometimes our lives are filled with turmoil like a torrential river in the spring.
Our thoughts are in great disturbance, and it seems there is no hope in anything.
Sometimes we keep ever searching like a river winding on it's way,
And we are restless and uncertain, and our lives can go so far astray.
Sometimes we are filled with happiness like a river sparkling in the sun.
We are bubbling o'er with laughter, and life is filled with joyousness, and fun.
Sometimes we are sad and lonely like a river at low ebb.
Our spirits are depressed and shallow, and we are caught up in a useless, tangled webb.
Sometimes we long for peace and tranquility like a river flowing gently and so calm,
And we pray to God without ceasing for some kind of soul soothing balm.
But God is watching, and He is waiting, and if we give to Him our heart,
He will guide all along life's pathway, and from us He never will depart.
Then we will have a home in heaven, and forever with Him we will be,
And the longest weariest river will fulfil it's destiny, because one day it will meet the mighty, distant sea.

Ann (Antje) Hanssler
LIFE AND DEATH

Dedicated to the Memory of my "Sweet William", by his bride of 63 years

---

Life can be like a beautiful flower
Planted carefully with a loving hand.
When it blooms in all its glory
Telling the world a beautiful story,
Sharing its beauty with you and me.
As we smell the fragrance, freely given,
Until it pleases God to end its reign,
And thus it dies to bloom again.
So with man, he is born free
Living his life and working fervently.
He offers prayers and sings the hymns,
He loves his God and worships Him.
He hopes one day to meet his Lord
Whom all his life he has adored.
Illness comes and with it pain,
He prays to God, he hopes to gain
His mercy and a home in Heaven,
Free of his pains and his sins forgiven.

Betty Goins
MY AMERICA
America, I love you, no matter what they do, to me you're still the land of the free, the brave and true;

"Old Glory", is still flying from every pole I see, and everytime I look at her, she seems to wave at me;
I think she looks so pretty, so fancy, and so clean, Her stars so bright, they always shine with purity it seems;

There's much trouble in this world of ours, and wars throughout the land, but we alone must not give up, the battle we must stand;

For God gives us this nation to cherish and to love, and he expects us to return, our thanks to him above;

So many times throughout the past, our Country's stood the test,
But God is there and answers prayers, and he always knows whats best;

"Old Glory", is still flying from every pole I see, and this is still the land of the true, the brave and free;

My America, America, I love you;

Faefern Gelbond
AWAKENING OF A CHILD TO THE WORLD
As a child of two years
Placed by mother in my crib
Of our backyard garden
I woke up to the world; gazing at you
In wonder! of your beauty
My delicate, silky, heavenly blue, bluebell
Blue as the sky you were—yellow gold as
The sun's rays nicely warming me
Green grass wings you had
You stood there stately waving to me
And I became an intity with the world
A traveler, longing to see more unfurled
But, never again have I captured
The rapture of seeing my first bluebell
You will always be my love
My first love

William Stewart
WOODSMOKE

To my Mother in memories past

Have you ever sat on a summers eve
And smelled the woodsmoke in the air?
Wafted on the warming breeze

Gently drifting everywhere
I tell you there's a magic

That no perfume can
compare
When you smell the
woodsmoke
Drifting gently on the summer
air

Benjamin F Folk Jr
HALLOWEEN
Ghosts and witches and gobblins
It's that time of year again
To get out your masks and
costumes
And guess which spooks are your
friends

For children it means candy
For older people, Fun
To give the kids a candy bar
Or just a piece of gum

Black cats will cross your path
And screams will curl your hair
And strange things will start to
happen
When witches fill the air

So if you see a Dracula
Or a shadow from the moon
Don't be overly frightened
For it will all be over soon

So light your Jack-o-lanterns
Make your face pretty or mean
And fill your candy dishes
For again it's Halloween

Eldred L Douglas
THERE'S A BIT OF HEAVEN

To my wife and companion—Betty

There's a bit of heaven in your smile
Whenever you smile at me.
A bit of heaven in your style
And an angel I see.
There's a bit of heaven when you
speak
And whisper so soft and low,
I'm list'ning to an angel's voice,
Truly, I love it so.
Whenever we are together,
Things that happen don't seem
real.
Am I dreaming or believing,
I know it's just the way I feel
So tell me you're not pretending
And all this was meant to be
There's a bit of heaven in your eyes.
Is it shining for me?

Crystal Sancken
WREN'S ARIA

To my beautiful grandchildren: Jill, Lucas, Zachary, Lindsay, and Renata

---

Rhetorical question, God—
How does that tiny throat
produce such a torrent of sound?
How does it keep from bursting
with this explosion of melody?
He's not had training at Julliard,
Has no expectations of singing at
the Met—
And yet his efforts rival the
dedication of a reigning diva
with this early morning concert!

I don't need an answer, God.
I just give thanks for this miracle
of song
being rapturously flung into the air
from a branch of the magnolia tree.

Anthony David Wright
THINKING OF YOU

To the love of my life, Diane S. Landis

So busy at work, even busy at play,
with so many things to do.
I still take time out of each day,
to sit back and think of you.

My thoughtful smile gives the clue
to my boss and working crew.
That I'm thinking of someone, and
they know who,
they know I'm thinking of you.

When I go outside and look above
at Heaven dressed in blue,
It reminds me of the one I love,
and that can only be you.

And that little place I often pass,
where someday we'll
rendezvous.
Trees, a stream, and fresh green
grass,
A great place to be with you.

Almost home! I really can't wait,
until it's just us two.
And enter the realm past Heaven's
gate,
and spend the night with you.

Alan D Ekery
THE OUTSIDER
Have you ever felt like you were an
outsider
When the hands around your neck
grew tighter and tighter
And you became paralyzed not
knowing what to do.
If I didn't have someone to run to,
could I run to you?

As far back as I've remembered I
have felt like that
not able to grasp reality, being
stabbed in the back.
Where, please tell me where the
answers lie
So my life can be stopped from
passing me by.

Signals from heaven said God was
King.
I really don't know if I believe in
those things
Yet when we were young we were
taught to believe
Wishing the solution would be
found up our sleeve.

When it came down to it, who
really cared
Only a few lived, they were the ones
that dared.
As for the rest of us, we were left
back to perish
So we reached back for our
memories, the ones we
cherished.

Denise Olberg
LITTLE BUTTERFLY

To my family and my loving son Shane

Tiny little butterfly
Standing on the tree
Spreads his bright wings proudly
for all the world to see
Drawing attention to himself

Hey! Look at me.
This is what it's like
to really be free

Keri D Epperson
MOTHERHOOD

To all those men who have died in battle whether right or wrong, And all the families who only know they're gone.

I weep for that which once
belonged to me,
One who was always so gay and
free.
I weep for him who now lies dead,
I weep without tears for I have
none to shed.

I wept when he was born,
A mother's tears that live.
I wept then that morn,
I had tears to give.

Thus he grew up as the years sped
by,
Burdened he'd laugh, little he'd cry.
Thus the years did pass 'til that
fateful day,
Quitely he laughed not knowing
he'd pay.

'Killed in Action' was all they said,
A hero besides, but still he is dead.
And after the funeral as I sit on his
bed,
I weep without tears for I have
none to shed.

Jennifer Sanchez-Salazar
TOO YOUNG

To Mom and Dad, and to Alma Gilbert, three of the most important teachers in my life.

We would not listen.
With your curiosity and devoted
concern,
We thought
You were too young to understand.
Yet, in truth, you held
A silent wisdom,
Greater than our own;
For you knew of
Love and loyalty,
Beauty and forgiveness,
Patience, and ambition.
Perhaps your only flaw
Was your ability to
Relent quietly
After speaking your piece.
You knew how to teach us,
If only we had listened.

Bert Baxter Jr
THE MAKER OF THE SAND
You as one were made from sand.
God touched you with His gracious
hand.
With little eyes and little ears
While others looked through
happy tears.

You grew so fast, so healthy and
strong.
We filled your mind with right not
wrong.
You listened well and learned the
words.
You sang the songs of a thousand
birds.

You aged each year and the time
had come.
You made your choice; you would
leave home.
Listen close, the world's a tease,
So live your life for God, oh please!

The One who made you with His
hand
Will change you back soon into
sand.
So pray each day you may repay
The Maker of the sand.

Samantha A Schneyer
WINTER TREE
Empty, gone,
You won't come back 'til spring.
You're lonely and cold,
Stiff and old.
Frozen and bare,
I still care!

In the spring
sweet smelling flowers you shall
bring.
I cannot wait 'til that certain day,
maybe sometime near the end of
May.
But now you're just a winter tree,
don't forget who cares, is me!

Cynthia Beth Usrey
IT'S JUST ME
I sometimes wonder why she
thinks I'm all that bad,
I've never done anything, it makes
me kind of sad.
All I ever wanted was to laugh and
play,
but I think instead she's going to
send me away.
I'll miss her cause I've grown to
love her,
after all I live inside of her.
I'll never get a chance to see daddy,
or learn about my family,
the only thing I know is that I feel
kind of down.
I think mommy is mad, cause I've
messed up her life,
and I don't think she's willing to
become my daddy's wife.
I wonder what she's thinking, or
what is being said,
the only thing I know is that soon
I'm going to be dead.
Is it my fault? Am I to Blame? It's
just I take after mommy,
I'm kind of scared of pain.
I look at my hands, they are so
small,
how could she let go of her dreams
and her all.
She can't hear me or even begin to
know how I feel,
Please mommy don't make this
such a big deal.
I love her and I want her to know,
but I guess it's time that I must go,
she doesn't love me, she doesn't
care.
It's time that I must say good-bye,
Maybe someday
there'll be nothing to hide.

Lauren Salmon
THINK OF ME
Think of me,
some cold, white night
after the embers have lost their glow
from the bonfire of Fame
that once burned brilliantly for you;
and wonder at the warmth of my memory.
For I will remain
patiently in the quiet depths of your soul,
a hidden fawn of delight,
ready to be caressed by your thoughts,
and willing to respond
with a transcendence of tenderness
you couldn't comprehend
even for all your wisdom.
So come into my world some lonely day
and I shall reveal to you the secrets
I have protected from long ago,
and I will usher you into my gentle life
of innocence.
Touch me,
with your mind. . .
and I will become your soul.

Mary S Sneed
SEASONS

To my 7 grand children & 3 great grandsons as of May 4, 1987.

Summer time so hot and
sticky drags on and on—

Autumn's colorful foliage
comes falling down.

Winter knocks out autumn
with a cold, cold, blast!

Springtime then emerges
Newness of Life-
At last!

Jason Scott Parsons
FROM LIBERTY'S VIEW
From Liberty's view, she sees people of all nations,
but today they're Americans all.
Like before, let us be friends again,
no matter what their skin.

From Liberty's view, she sees freedom now and forever,
so no matter rich or poor, let us be together.
We know life can succeed 'cause love is all we need.

From Liberty's view, she sees people working together,
in the cities and the fields,
and that's the way GOD meant it to be,
with you and me.

From Liberty's view, she sees freedom now and forever,
so no matter rich or poor, let us be together.
We know life can succeed 'cause love is all we need.

At Liberty's feet slavery's chain lay around,
while she stands guard on freedom's ground.
All the children hear the call,
because Liberty means freedom for all.

Margaret E Mohr
REFLECTIONS

To: Mr. Mohr, Extraordinor

The Golden afternoon sunshine,
Of a late autumn afternoon
Streams through the door,
Making you long
For a time, a place,
The where, the when,
You can't quite remember.
Perhaps that place, that time
Really were;
You
Think, you feel they really were;
You are afraid
Perhaps that time, that place
Never were
But your soul clings
To the hope that
That late autumn afternoon,
Somewhere in your memory
Really was.
For if it were not,
Then perhaps
You
Never were!

Frank Childress
OUR DEAR MOTHER

Written in memory, by her son Frank Childress, on May 25, 1986, as a loving tribute to his mother, Gladys Childress, who passed away on May 20, 1986 in Lowell, Indiana. Age 87 years—11 months & 8 days.

She did so many little things and usually for another,
But that was how she lived her life, our dear unselfish mother.
It seems like only yesterday when we were all so small,
That she would wipe away our tears and comfort one and all.

But she would scold us just as fast if she thought we'd gone astray,
And remind us all to toe the mark or the piper we would pay.
She taught us by example the essence of the Golden Rule,
And always sought to educate so we'd not become a fool.

Her family was her everything, Her reason for existence,
And this lesson stuck with all of us because of her persistence.
Today we said goodbye to her, our dear, sweet, patient Mother,
And she left for us her legacy, of loving one another.

Jane Collier Daugherty
OUT OF THE DARKNESS
Carry my soul far away from the glitter
Of this shallow season of holiday mirth;
Bear it away to a land of contentment,
Carry my soul far away from the earth.

Tears form like crystals on ivory statues,
And fire-tempered daggers pierce deep to my soul
As hopelessly crushed lay my dreams in the ashes,
And nothing is left but the meagerest dole.

No more illusions of peace universal,
No expectations of peace all around,
No more the glimmer of hope for the future;
There is no hope anywhere to be found.

Smothered with pain I escape to the darkness,
Anesthetized only with joy yet to be;
Life is too painful to beckon me onward,
Encompassing fear is the measure of me.

Out of the darkness much darker than dying
Sporadically lit by a temporal glow
Of lights that fade shortly without seeming reason;
To the edge of the universe I blissfully go.

No more empty holidays or glittering baubles,
No more shallow platitudes to folks I don't know;
Just comforting darkness to end all tormenting,
With other sojourners laid row upon row.

Gladys K Thatcher
MYSTIQUE
When I emerged on earth from my cocoon,
A child of curiosity and joy
In each small monumental gift or boon
Of fantasy, accomplishment or toy,
Night's curtain always dropped a bit too soon!

Then when my wings were spread, I wandered free
Among the perfumed petals of the flowers.
I gloried in the passing of the hours
That brought fulfillment of my life to me—
The splendor of the radiant high noon!

And now again, I rest with folded wings.
I listen to the pulse of life that sings
Of all things past and things that are to be—
A curious child, yet one content to see
The gentle twilight greet the rising moon.

Colleen Marie Cecil
THE INNER PRISON
Trapped within the dungeon of my own demise
without the will to sustain my own freedom a little longer

It started as a simple game
and turned into a deadly nightmare
from which I cannot escape

to live on the edge without the desire to turn back,
to turn down the second chance of the dice

So hungry for the life I once knew
and so full of the past years' tragedies

I am starving for the love I can never seem to find
and now I am just a shadow of myself

When I look up from my murky prison walls
to the sunshine outside, I am blinded

and through my own eyes I see my only objective,
to starve myself from the true happiness that living
seems to bring to so many others who deserve to exist

and now. . .I really don't mind the darkness anymore,
I am used to it since I can't find my own way out
of this eternal trap

I get my own joy out of watching others live to their fullest
while I slowly fade into the dark corners of
my
Inner
Prison. . .

Mary Floyd Harrison
A MOTHER'S LOVE

Dedicated with love to the memory of Mama

A Mother's Love is a thing to behold
Worth more than diamonds, silver or gold
It will ease the pain of a skinned up knee
Make you understand why, some things cannot be
It can make days that are dreary and gray
Seem bright and cheerful, happy and gay
It helps mend hearts that are broken and sad
Forgives and forgets when you've been bad
It gives hope and comfort when troubles abound
Never ceasing to be around

It will lift your spirits and make your heart sing
Yes, A Mother's Love is a beautiful thing
After she's gone, her life's work is done
Memories of her warm you like rays from the sun
They may bring a chuckle, some times a tear or two
But cherish them dearly, all your life through
For as sure as the stars shine in heaven above
There's no greater gift, than a Mother's Sweet Love

Mae Wright
WINDOW WINTER

To all my children

We love the winter-
the swirling snow
Cavorting with our window panes-
leaving their six-sided patterns
Pressed against the Glass-

We love the winter, when the wind
is sharp and crisp on
our cheeks, our toes, our nose-
And the squirrels' tails are spinning
to keep their backs from freezing.
the hearth is a splendid place
of comfort-
Luscious spicy—smell of good
old-fashioned cooking-
Seeping through the door, as
we "rear-backed" to the fireplace-
watching—winter cold, out
of the window!

Brenda Murphy Gregory
CREATION
A beautiful garden was once this
earth,
with flowers, trees, and waters
clear.
The mountains soared so very tall.
The soft wind
whistled for all to hear.
Birds would sing sweet songs of
Love, and soar
in a beautiful clear blue sky.
Animals played in the soft green
grass, without fear
or hunger, not even a sigh.
And then came man a creation
of splender,
To complete the perfection but
what a disaster,
He ruined the garden, the flowers,
and trees.
With buildings and houses of
concrete and plaster
The sky that was once a crystal
clear blue,
Has gray clouds of smoke from the
factories below.
The lakes and the rivers where fish
used to swim.
Now flow full of garbage, How far
can man go.
From a paradise garden full of
beauty and
love, to a world full of hatred, yes
even that too.
He has done everything that a man
can do, to
bring self destruction on himself
and to you.

Rebecca Lyn Floyd
THE BRAIN
My body is in pain when I use my
brain
And I feel so lame when I try to
tame my brain

I'm definitely insane, but one day
I came
upon a candycane while walking
on Candycane Lane

And it started to rain and believe it
or not the rain
helped my brain so I will not be
so lame

You might think this is a game, but
a game is not the same
You see, I went to Spain to train
my brain
To see if I could frame my brain
for the other insane person
who really needs it!

Scott Oliver Nichols
STARS
Ah, talk to me lonely gull, you
sound as sad as I.
I deserve your scornful waves dear
sea
But not your salt that makes me
cry.
I have lost my only love, she's
banished from my isle.
I wither now with lonesome
thoughts
For replacements of her smile.
I can only wish to have her back,
to hold her close to me.
To swim beside her exiled ship
And for her always be.
But should she turn in need of me
and call me in some way
I'm walled too deep, she can't be
seen
Like stars on sunny days.

Andrea J Cobin
TO FORGET YOU

To Barry Savard: May the years of love encircle your soul and the mystery of happiness be ours to fulfill. T.T.F.N.

When you look into her eyes
do you see what you once saw in
mine?
Does it feel the same. . .is it as
warm?
When you hold her in your arms,
Think back to a time
When it was only you and I
No distance between us; no
stranger in our minds
How our spirits could dance under
the misty moon
How we held each other so close
'til the sunrise
This was no dream, my friend
for I have dreamt before
You were the flame burning my
candle,
the magic that colors the dawn.
Even now I hear the echo of a
warning I once gave
Of a love that could not be;
a love that I cannot save
Knowing though, thru my own
presence,
that I must be the one to take the
blame,
It hurts me so much to think of you
now
For you, maybe it was easy
For me it will take some time
To forget your touch. . .your
laughter. . .your smile
To forget the silence in your eyes. . .

Jane Mann
REBIRTH
As I drive through the country
bound to the car,
My spirit roams the green fields
of Spring.
Unhindered and free, I stand
Looking up through the fresh
green leaves
of ancient trees.
And gazing dreamily into a deep
clear pond,
I feel the renewal of life,
and willingly I respond.
My spirit bonds up the hills,
And gloriously young again, I
search,
And all around me I hear the echo
of rebirth.

Patty Markham Proffitt
MYSTICAL NIGHT
I would love to walk along the
beach
Barefoot in the sand
With you beside me all the way
Walking hand in hand
The sun setting in the distance
Colors on the water reflect
A sparkle in my eyes you would see
A feeling of love you would detect
As you would stare at the beauty
Of the magic of the sea
I would wonder how much longer
You would be in love with me
We would make love on a blanket
Beneath the warm moonlight
Bodies close together
Knowing it was right
As we would lay in the darkness
To us the tides would sing
Then all and any problems
Wouldn't mean a thing
For we would have shared a fantasy
A perfect tender night
But with the end of darkness
Has to come the light
And when our time is over
We would look back someday
And remember how we had loved
That mystical night away. . .

Sandra K Berger
SAY IT IN A LETTER
Sometimes it's hard to tell
someone
Exactly how you are feeling;
If words won't come to say it,
Then "say it in a letter."
For someone so shy like me
To come right out and say it;
I might as well climb a mountain
To do that—just forget it!
You don't have to be face to face
When you tell someone that you
care;
Just write it down what you feel
And "say it in a letter."

Ann T Ragan

Ann T Ragan
CAPTAIN OF THE THIRTY

To Dr. Robert Taylor, my loving son.

During David's Dynasty, The
Jebusites were lost in foolish
fancy, hate, and war. They
taunted David. "The lame and
the blind, will keep you out. The
taut reached out (spies)
Philistine. If we live to eternity
we are still divinity—we rule the
past, and all things meant to be.
Crops, love and marriage. In
case of war we never quit. We
know you would like to take us.
Your leader is a Philistine. We
know his name, At the gate the
warriors waited. No time for
speculation. Information about
the shaft was with the Leader.
Joab, a young an eager, bronzed,
filled with ardor warrior. A dead
ringer for old Abner and son of
David's sister. Filled with love of
God they moved within silence.
Go up the Shaft! David shouted.
The first to reach the top will be
"CAPTAIN OF THE THIRTY".
Joab's face was drawn and
fallow. He drew his shield before
him. And swore to his God he'd
make it. And jumped between
a double wall. A semicircular
tunnel.

Fitted together like a jigsaw
puzzle, a Camleck at his feet He
felt that he could leap. Bravely
against cold, wet walls he crept.
The soldiers had their orders to
follow. Suddenly pale as death,
He saw the Gihon water shaft.
No Shibolith to cross. He quickly
climbed the shaft. Covered rock
with shafts for light concealed.
He saw the top. Painted blind,
and lame, were standing.
Wooden gods upon the wall. The
soldiers swore, shrieked, and
cried, Gods without a soul! Joab
saw the water down below. mist
like his call to go, The magnitude
of God. Not Everyone could see
it. Everyone could hear it. (water
Gihon) Everyone could feel the
mist . . . feeling Everything could
sense it . . . . wild live. Back in
ancient time it went (spring)
Joab drew his trusty sword and
sliced the gods to bits. And
burned the splinters on the wall
in honor of his God. Jerusalem
was his.

3800 years of history.

Sara Starr
TENDER WISP
There are things too small for
others to see
too small and yet to me

the warmth of your knowing smile
I brought on
perhaps by something foolish said
comes now to me across the lonely mile
of memory.
These are things that others may never know
only God and I may share their beauties tender
these little things, things that I remember

Stephanie Kay Corona
WILD HEART

Hold on to your wild heart, quiet the fluttering wings
Keep it in check and remind yourself of all those important things
Don't fantasize, don't guess, don't care
This by far is the best advice in a world where everyone else
Keeps theirs encased in ice

Hold on to your fleeting spirit—don't let it get away
Remember the limits placed on you—how to laugh, how to dream, what to say

Above all hold on to your feelings—they must not be allowed to show
the shadows that dwell within you—don't ever let anyone know

You feel things that peril, you respond at a very great risk
you become an open wound at the mercy of those you trust

But if you love your wild heart—if you relish its quickening beat
If without the freedom of your spirit you are strangely incomplete

Then revel in the depths of your feelings
Don't recoil from pleasure or pain
Open yourself to receive what comes
Be it a storm or a gentle rain

Esther S Leivas
MY CHILD

Dedicated to all who are of a broken and contrite Spirit to know that God is always near.

My child "I" will be with you, even through the darkest moments of your life
Though it may seem at times that "I" am not,
But if you will lift your eyes unto the hills you will see a "flicker" of light!
And you will know that "I" am that light!
You will have the strength to overcome all in this world!

Flora Hefner
THE LOST SHEEP

It was a sheep, not a lamb, that strayed
In the parable Jesus told.
A grown up sheep that had gone astray
From the ninety and nine in the fold.

Out on the hillside out in the cold
'Twas a sheep the good shepherd sought.
Back to the flock, safe into the fold,
'Twas a sheep the good shepherd brought.

So with the sheep we should plead
And earnestly hope and pray,
Because there's danger if they go wrong
They will lead the lambs astray.

For the lambs will follow the sheep, you know
Where ever the sheep may stray,
If the sheep go wrong it won't be long
Until the lambs are as wrong as they.

So for the sheep we earnestly pray
For the sake of the lambs today,
If the sheep are lost, what a terrible
Cost the lambs will have to pay.

Sandra Donahue Caballero
TREASURE OF LOVE

To my Mom & Dad, all my family, and, especially, my children, with love. May it never tarnish.

Love is life's greatest treasure,
More valuable than any jewel.
How can the glitter of an Emerald
Outshine the light of love in one's eyes?
How can the feel of a cold Diamond
Warm your heart, such as love does?
No Ruby is as precious as a heart
That is filled with love.
Compare a perfect Pearl,
Which grows within a shell

And has to be released,
Before its beauty can be seen,
To love that grows in a heart,
That when nurtured,
Can change ugliness into beauty.
How can the Opal's blackness
Compare to a tender touch,
In the darkness of night?
Love cannot be bought—
It can only be given.
It is not to be put away in a chest of gold.
It is a treasure
That can only grow more precious everyday.

Louise Jones
WHAT IS LOVE

This poem is dedicated to Big George

I need to know the true meaning
of love, or if love tru'ly exist.
I think its like a terminal disease with
lingering pains long lasting.

Love is sometimes brief as a passing
Illness weakening hearts with each episode.
Love I'm told has a strong affection that
binds together concrete connections

In time I've learned that love does exist
I can see its presence upon many faces

Love is true with many meanings, but

I know love as a disease slowly
destroying my yearning heart.

Myrtle Barbour Durham
LADY LIBERTY

To Mama-Irene Woodard Barbour who taught me the love of words & their meanings.

She has stood almost a hundred years and welcomed to our shores,
the ones who searched for freedom, she has opened many doors
In family groups of five or ten or else they came alone,
fearful wondering at the sights, when all hope was gone.

Her torch shines thruout the night, she towers thru the day
for the downtrodden and the hopeless, she shows a better way.
Royalty, peasants, slaves and thieves came to make a stand,
with muscles, hope and resolutions built upon this great land.

They plowed the fields and built the towns, from sea to shining sea
climbed their ladders to success, made a new world for you and me.
Black or white, brown or yellow, or some where in between.
They all had a part in making this our great American scene.

When they gather here to worship and call upon his name?
of each one's own particular God. Isn't he the same?
For all of us who look up to Him this all seeing eye,
it does not matter what we call Him, He listens to our cry.

Virginia E Bartges
MYSTERY AND MAGIC

The night is clear and high above in the sky
The pale moon quietly casts its beams
Upon silvery trees, as a gentle breeze
Whispers and hints of a faint and forlorn sigh.

I wander alone down a winding country lane
Deep in my thoughts and reflections
While shadows of night under flickering starlight
Lend an air of enchantment I somehow can't explain.

From across the field there comes an eerie sound
I stop to listen—what can it be?
A hound dog's howl? A black cat's "meow?"
Or are there ghosts and goblins all around?

The sound gets closer and I wish I could hide
But I freeze in my tracks and stare
Then I shiver and shake—do a "double take"
As some strange and frightening creatures appear at my side.

There's a pirate, a skeleton, a scarecrow and a witch
Plus a giant dog by the name of Fritz
Eyes all glowing—where could they be going?
It's really quite obvious it can't be the Ritz.

They beckon to me and I ponder what they mean
Are they trying to be friendly—or what?
But as they disappear, it all becomes clear
It's the mystery and the magic of Halloween.

Jean Louise Baker Leister
WHEN I WAS A YOUNG GIRL

For Steven Homel, M.D. and John Udall, M.D.

When I was a young girl
I thought that I would find
A love so constant, present, and true
That I need not be a mime.

Now that I have lived so long
I found that I need think
Of my love so far away
Or else I'd near the brink.

Perhaps some day he'll settle near
And not go into space,
Or wander to the western states

To end the human race.

Why is it that we hide from love

Or shrink from its possession . . .
Perhaps we need to see ourselves
As needing our obsessions.

For when we meet our human
selves
And recognize our needs
We truly gain our souls
And can find that love exceeds

Our greatest need to be alone
Yet with our friends intact,
And communicate ourselves in
need
So hate doesn't become a fact.

Jackie Nelson

AN HONORABLE AUTUMN (THE THIRD SEASON IN A LIFE)

The old man at the variety store.
His features wrinkled with
laughter and age.
His mind sharp with town lore.
Respected like a sage.

His days spent selling his wares.
His customers, his neighbors
Each serviced with care.

Guided by a force from above
His life content and filled with love.

A mentor. . ., to some

Koleen Gilstad

ALONE

Alone is lonely,
But is for the only.

Only the one's who have felt the
pain and sorrow,
And seen the visions of tomorrow.

Who know life isn't what it seems,
Who find reality in their dreams.

Those whose hearts are filled with
love,
Who offer a hand, not a glove.

When we depart this place called
earth,
There is no measure to what alone
is worth.

Pattie Lou (Avent) Breidenbach

AN ODE TO TWO

To my dear husband Joseph and our wonderful son Jimmy.

Today is my birthday. They say I'm
seventy five. I'm glad to be alive.
But wouldn't it be nice if I were
seven or five or even thirty five?
Sakes alive!

I tend a garden, knit, crochet, bake,
rake, mow, sew and even shovel
snow.

I'm so lucky to be able to take care
of me and you—Jimmy too.
Wouldn't take anything for having
both of you.

You're my heaven on earth and I'm
grateful for it too.
A mother couldn't have been more
blessed than to have a son and
husband like you.

To share in every joy through
life—pain and sorrow too.

Many thanks to both of you.

You've been true blue. GOD
BLESS YOU.

Jessica Mechele Thompson

NO END

To my darling husband, Eddie who's love has inspired me greatly.

You've made me realize
what love's really for,
You've given me the feelings
I've never had before.
You've given me a reason
to live.
You've taught me to take as well
as to give.
I've got a feeling deep down in
my heart,
That you'll never leave me
that we'll never part.
With all my troubles you've
helped me through,
you if you're ever in need
I'll help you too.
You've been a lover, you've been
a friend,
I know with all our love
there is no end.

Joyce Boettger Gruver

IF I HAD ONE WISH GOD

In loving memory of my brother Rick Sorrentino

If I had one wish God.
What would it be,
To see my brother by
a tall oak tree,
If I had one wish God,
what would it be,
To talk to my brother
by that tall oak tree,
If I had one wish God,
What would it be,
To stay with my brother
in eternity,
Please one more wish
God, before you go,
Talk to my brother
and let him know,
I love him so.

Betty J Bechtoldt

MY MOTHER

To my mother, Rachel I. Cummings, and my sister Norma Sue Coskburn, for their love and faith

---

Touch me so that I might feel your
tenderness,
Smile so that I might see your joy.
Your eyes say so much, and I know
your
thoughts are deep and touch every
surface.
A mother's love is like a fountain
which
never runs dry.
You have guided my footsteps, And
led me
down life's path with hopes I would
walk
in a straight line.
You shed many tears for me and
wondered if
I would ever know.
There's nothing like a mother's love
for her children, and nothing like
the love of a child for its mother.
You brought me into this world,
and introduced
me to the sunshine, then told me
there would be some rain.
You nursed me through sickness
and took away the pain.
You've helped me through
heartaches and sadness,
Then helped me see there is light
at the end of the tunnel.
You were there to share in my joys,
my happiness.
Thank you for being there when I
needed you, and
Mom, I love you.

Kathryn A Warner

HIS WAY

To my husband, George and our sons, Chris, Bob, Kent and Eric

---

Oh! Lord, How I wonder
When I look 'round and see,
All of us hurrying,
Like a bunch of busy bees.
I wonder how you,
On your throne up above
Can look down on us with all of
your love.

Now, if the reasons
For hurrying, were all worth while.
You'd say, "Look! Go to it,"
And look down with a smile.
But they're not and we know it
And you know it too.

So Lord, I won't blame you
If some day, you'd say.
Look folks, I've had it!
Now, we'll do it my way.
"We'll, stop, look and listen
"Be still and take heed
For these are the things,
That my old world needs.

And, when we stop,
And do it your way,
Things will be much better,
And then, I can say.
"Lord, how's the view
From up there
And, you'll look down and say,
"I knew you all cared,
It's a beautiful day

Mrs Willabe Sarber

JIMMIE (AGE 11) ON MOTHERS

Mothers is people, just like you and
me,
But how many kinds of mothers
did you ever see?

There's the kind that smiles and
sings every day
And the kind that giggles and
laughs, and that play
And then there's the kind that nag
and scold
If you stay out a little too long in
the cold.
Or bring a poor little dog in out of
the rain
Or smash your ball through a
window pane.

And say! there's the mother that
talks just like
She thinks her son is just a little
tyke
That don't no way know what's
wrong or right.

And some mothers, when you go
upstairs to bed
Go with you and stay 'til your
prayers are said.
And read a good book 'til you've
gone to sleep.
Now. that's the kind of a mother a
guy'd better keep!

Well, there's mothers and mothers
the whole world around
Some that are sweet, and others
that frown.
But I haven't told you about mine,
have I, yet?
Well, I've left the best until the last,
you bet!
She's all of the mothers I've named,
all in one
She's the kind that makes you glad
you're her son.

She does all of those things, and
she's simply grand,
She's the kind of a mother a guy
can understand!

Harold R Green

'TIS BEAUTY AT ITS BEST

Dedicated to my Mother, Dora Green and to the memory of my Father, Lawrence Green who taught me the beauty of nature.

Ah! Bleak, the wintry wind,
The cold and roaring wind.
It sweeps o'er plain and mountain
top;
Into the valley it comes to stop,
The bleak and wintry wind.

Each gust, a breath of newborn
snow
To clothe the naked earth

And swiftly tho the wind doth blow
The snow lies down to rest.
'Tis beauty at its best.

White the trees and meadows now,
White with silent beauty.
Clothed once more in splendor,
Now the snow has done its duty.
'Tis beauty at its best.

Rebecca B McConnell

ST. VALENTINE

I dedicate this poem to the Lord Jesus Christ, to my wonderful husband Michael and to my beautiful daughter Rachel.

As this day of hearts and flowers
comes our way once again
Let us remember St. Valentine and
why this day began
Because of his devotion and
abiding love for Christ
The Romans of that day said his
life must be sacrificed
As the day of execution began to
draw near
Valentine asked God for the
purpose of this, to make it very
clear

An angel suddenly appeared in answer to his prayer
To remind him of God's love and of his constant care
The angel said, "Sometimes things may happen that you don't understand
But it's all divinely ordered within God's loving hand"
Valentine now knew, for it was clear to see
That with his loving Lord was where he soon would be
Valentine sent a note to a Christian friend
To urge them to stay close to God for soon his life would end
He urged them to stay good and kind
He signed it "From your Valentine"
We still carry on the tradition of Valentine each year
By sending hearts and flowers to those we hold most dear
This poem is coming full of wishes for you, your family, too
To have a happy Valentine's Day and a happy year all the year through!

Doris Jeanne Leichty

TRIXIE

Phones ringing in the pre-dawn darkness
Seldom bring good news.

Approaching the pasture gate, I heard
Trixie, whinnying softly,
Asking for help.
My beloved bay mare
Her one white sock and
White forehead patch visible
In the early morning rays,
Head still erect
Black, roached mane and
Long black tail accentuating the
Sleek, trim body.

Motionless, she stood
Her mangled right foreleg,
Broken in three places,
Hanging awkwardly.

An accident they said.
They were playing they said.
Running, rearing—
Legs accidentally getting entangled
Her slim one snapping
Under Pistol's heavier weight.

Out of the darkness comes the dawn.
Love is everlasting.

Mom

Terry (Terrific) Vona

TO A FOSTER MOTHER

To a very wonderful woman,
With a great big heart of gold
She has more love within it
Than any one heart can hold
She takes care of our children
Whether very young or old
She'd never think to leave them
Standing in the cold
She eases all our worries
As every day goes by
Cause she's always there to tend their hurts
And soothe their cries
The things she has done for me
I never will forget
But she will be repaid in life
Upon this you can bet

Leo Wilson

ALPHA FATHER

Let us consider the day of the Lord passing through time.
Knowing that he knows our hearts and our minds.
He knows our intentions, and our reasons why.
That is why we must not die.

For we die with Christ on the cross.
And we come to life, when he calls us from the lost.
He paid the cost for those who were lost.
High upon that rugged cross.
For the love of life, is the love of God.
So we will all stand before the son of God.

James Rodney Reppy

A PRINCESS WAIT AND SEE

Soft to hold and barely three
she sat upon my knee
talked to me of little things
said, now I will sing . . .
and sang to me this little tune
rang so loud throughout the room
"When I grow up I'm gonna be,
a Princess, wait and see"
So I laughed and smiled and looked at her
took her in my arms
and said, "until your prince comes dear,
I'll keep you safe from harm"

Douglas James Zubryd

BEAUTY MISSED

Lunar rays illumine ensilvered haze.
High hill forest gleams soft blue-white
Embracing still, frozen winternight.

Crisp shadow-map, sylvan city maze.
Chiaroscuro dance tree-fingered inquires
Of snow crusted creature, lucent silhouette of desire

Forlorn figure emits steam-puff'd sighs
Upon patches of path wet crystals fall
Blinded and deaf, heedless of hopeful, silent call:

"Beloved, a firmament of sparkling snow lies
Like festive dance round your feet, reflecting above
Your sky-vast pulsing starr'd crown, my love."

'Always alone in this ugly world!' the figure cries;
'No one and nothing cheers my useless years. . .'
Turning 'round and trudging down; stars and snow twinkle like tears.

Helen Arlynne Lord

NEW FRIENDS

Dear friends are found—
We know not where,
But then again—
They're everywhere!
A pleasant 'smile'
When on a street,
A time of 'talk'
When 'ere we meet;
'Sharing', of a dining table,
'Visiting', as long as able;
A 'giving' of some special poems,
'Receiving' some for other homes;
So, if one takes the time each day
To make new friends along the way,
You'll find it gives an inner glow
And makes ones life a joy—not woe!

Carmen Salvadora Ingham

AMERICA, HEART OF THE WORLD

I dedicate this poem to all humanity . . . to the oneness of all in God, The Supreme Being.

America . . . heart of the world!
here in the heart . . . love lies.
All of suffering humanity
watch us with anxious eyes.
What happened to commandment
"Love thy neighbor as thyself"
With all God's admonitions . . . has it
been put on the shelf?
Unless you feed the people's need
war will be from within.
For history shows . . . starvation causes
madness and then sin.
So help the world . . . cleanup the air
let virtue reappear!
A way of life . . . one without strife
and also without fear.
Give everyone a chance to work
a good life of their own
and put the hardened criminal
to work 'til he atone.
Each one must pray . . . for in this way
their consciousness will rise.
America . . . heart of the world!
here in the heart . . . hope lies.

Terrence A Gibson (opie)

ISN'T IT AMAZING

To Pastor David Jackson and Steve Auston of Bethel Baptist Church. For showing me what it means to be a Christian and how truly amazing the Lord Jesus Christ is. Thank you both.

Isn't it amazing
How His love for us does grow.
Isn't it amazing
How much we didn't know.
The flowers bloom in springtime
And wither with the Fall.
Isn't it amazing
Once you've answered His call.

His trumpet sounds so clearly;
For all who'd care to hear.
Isn't it amazing
How He takes away our fear.

So open up your ears
And hear the angels sing.
"Glory Hallelujah,
To Jesus Christ our King!!"

Helen Zack

O'MOMA

To Ora Walker Zack, July 1898—Nov 1985 From her daughter Helen

---

I dreamed about Moma last night
O'MOMA are you alright?
I know you are so alone
I dreamed about Moma and home

Someday when my work is through
I will come home and visit you
Until then Moma, I miss you so
It is eight o'clock, I have to go

I dreamed about Moma last night
Someday I will make it right
I just called today, there is no way
Moma is gone, she is not at home

O'Moma why did I decide to roam
Now I can never come home
O'MOMA I wish I could make it right
I dreamed about Moma last night

O'MOMA

Your weathered hand I cannot touch
Tell you I love you so much
I can never make it right
O'Moma, O'MOMA
I dreamed about Moma last night

John Godines

DREAMS GONE BY

To Kimberly, Who brought the dreams Here and now

There's nothing out the window but the road
And I am not going home
Or anywhere

I look around and all I see
Is staring back so stupidly
And I don't mind

Then I remember long ago
A boy, a dog, and shining snow
And happy times

But now those times are far behind
And I am just driving blind
With dreams gone by

I used to think about a girl
Someone who could make my world
So beautiful

But lovers come and lovers go
And here I am all alone
Like yesterday

My friends no better off than me
Sometimes we all screamed stupidly
At the world

Now I no longer have the strength to scream
For dreams gone by.

Miss Roslyn R Lee
THE MAN OF MY DREAMS

I dedicate this poem to: Mr. John A. Miles. Who is The Man of My Dreams.

From top to bottom is my prescription;
of my man that fits this description.
The locks and curliness of his black hair;
makes him so suave and debonair.
Those pearly white teeth, that captivating smile;
lets a woman know that he's worth her while.
Catching the sexiness in his eyes;
leaves me breathless and hypnotized.
The SLEEK PHYSIQUE;
So-o-o- masculine and unique.
With courage, dignity and pride;
which is built of the genuine man inside.
Wanting and needing so much;
especially the gentleness of his touch.
So handsome as handsome as he can be;
I know that he's the perfect man for me.
When I'm in need of tender loving care;
I know that in my heart he'll be there.
My breathtaking poem; ends with an endless view
of my description of a man which could be. . .YOU

Marge Kirchner
AN OPEN LETTER TO MY SON

"1987 Golden Poet Award Winner; Dedicated to my son David Kirchner." And hope it will be a great inspiration to all reading it.

Dear Son:

As I sit here in my hotel room
My thoughts go out to you.
Hoping God will always keep you in His care
And guide you along the way.
For life is full of ups and downs
And it's so easy to go astray.
The path will be rocky, and sometimes you'll fall along the way
But when you trust in God you'll surely find the way.
Don't be misled my son when life seems like bed of roses
'Cause there'll always be a thorn to block your way
And when trials and tribulations come your way
Stand tall and proud, yet don't forget to humble yourself
Along the way.
As God is smiling down at you saying
"Well done my son, now go on your way".
And when you come to the end of the trail
You'll look back and say
Thank you God for giving me the wisdom and courage
To go that way.
No more will I look back to seek and find
For it was always there, all I needed was a little time.
And if ever you get discouraged
Get down on your knees and pray
"Seek and you will find, ask and you shall receive".
And so I hope you've learned a lesson here today
And never, never go astray.
Your Mom.

Janice D Wheeler
THE INTRODUCTION
I met Death when I was a youngster
so young I did not fear
a grandfather who lay sleeping
was no reason to shed a tear.

But, when I did get older
of Him, I met a lot.
I started learning of the pain
of the loved ones that got caught.

The mother that left the hospital
the child she did not hold.
The boy on the cycle—
his story would not be told.

The family man, no reason to die
a daughter and son had he.
Death did not attempt to try
explaining them to me.

Death has visited these people
wasteful and needless was He,
to take a young and useful life
No reason for to see

Rev Dr Eleanor Wilson

Rev Dr Eleanor Wilson
WHICH

Immediate family—the Washingtons, Wilsons, Gefords, Ross' Beards, Waites and the Jenkins. Christian family Mother Waddles, Bishop Moore & Household

---

This arena of life is entered but once
I may become a winner or wind up a dunce
It's up to me to choose the way I go
I may run very fast or trot quite slow
Baseball, basketball, volleyball or tennis
Rules and regulations eliminates the menace
No matter how many players in each game may be
The bottom line, it is God and me
In this arena of life, I'll win or lose
But I'll spend eternity with the one I choose

Mary L McIntire
ODE TO EARTH
Why do I dwell upon you, earth,
And not another part of the universe?
I reach down and touch your soil
Whose elements are a part of me.
Your atmosphere, I breathe into my body
And it energizes my being.
Your thorns can prick my skin
And draw my blood from me.
Your waters can submerge my body
Smothering life from me;
Yet, I was born with waters flow.
My eyes behold the infinite space of your skies
And reflect the eternal immortality of my soul
I can conquer your mountains
And behold the tops of your trees.
Your herbs and plants feed me
And flesh covers my bones;
As the grass covers your hills and vales.
My mind bears record of my space in time
As your strata holds secrets of the eons of the ages.
Why am I here, O earth?
I am a part of you and you of me,
Until my immortal soul is free.

Rev Maurice J Tiell
ME AND MY SHADOW
There's more to me than you can see,
For my shadow lurks deep inside of me.
I manage sometimes others to affirm,
But manipulation makes my insides squirm.
As I get praised for being generous or kind,
My shadow resents the goody-goody kind.
Some folks cite me for being real dependable.
My shadow hates the very word, indispensable.
My loud, gabby, know-it-all drives some crazy.
My shadow enjoys being shallow and plumb lazy.
When I appear aggressive and always right,
My shadow shudders with real negative fright.
Easy-going and happy I may seem to be,
But my shadow is responding critically.
I'm branded as the one who is never late,
Yet for schedules my shadow has a deep hate.
There's more to me than you can see,
For my shadow lurks deep inside of me.

Annie Schoos-O'Donnell
THE FACE OF LOVE
What is this mighty power of love
An endless fire that sparks within?
At times I am an unwilling pawn
Yet I have hope when all else is gone . . .
You give me a glimpse of what it can be
But I want more to fill my soul
When I think of the love I could be giving
You become my best reason for living . . .
We will know such happiness
The kind I've only had in dreams
Yet yearn for, pray for, would even die for,
The kind that people cry in the night for . . .
I've seen your eyes a thousand times
Beholding me with understanding
I hear the whisper of your voice
Telling me to make my choise . . .
Then will I run to find you, meet you
Looking for the face of love
And I'll know that my search is done
When two more hearts become as one . . .

Ronald Perri
THE GOOD LIVES ON
On a night not so long ago
A man's life was brought to an end.
I saw the pain and shed the tears;
But soon the message grew clear.

Because on that very same day—
A new life had then begun;
A child was born . . .
And that girl over there, well, she had a son.

Now that man will never see;
It's true, he will never speak again.
But now the world will be seen thru new eyes,
Along with many other men.

A life was said done
and never to be known again;
But a new life had then begun,
I finally realized then . . .

No matter how bad life seems to get,
A greater good will come along;
And soon the bad will end,
And THE GOOD WILL LIVE ON . . .

Mary Anne Senerchia
MY LOVE
Speak softly love for my heart is fragile.

Listen into my heart love for my voice speaks only fear and hurt.

Be gentle with my spirit love for you hold it in your hands.

Be near my love for your distance threatens my existence.

Be kind my love for I rejoice in your touch.

Be my love for without you my world would be empty.

Donna M Muller
MORNING CRY

Dedicated to Vietnam veterans everywhere.

Out on the battlefield all night
Another nightmare, they're so hard to fight

Nerves and feelings left on a string.
All he knows is, he can't shake this thing.
As his lover tends to the dying embers,
He cries out, as he remembers
Baby, please don't put the fire out
It's still raining out.
Baby, please don't leave me yet
My heart is still crying out loud!
Wake up! Wake up! The nightmare is over.
If you need an embrace, come a little closer.
The door to your dreams is closed now. Come cry to me.
Shed your tears of pain and fear.
The night is no more.
Morning has come and your lover is here.

Deborah Lynn White

WILL YOU THINK OF ME?

Dedicated to Ken for all his caring and understanding support.

When you walk out of my life,
And easily keep on walking away
Thoughts barely on your mind—
Just wanting to follow a hope desired
Able to leave what loneliness took over
Only to find the happiness you require
As you still walk—not even a glance behind
Will you think of me?
As you awaken from your dreams
Still not quite aware of things
You want to be sure—You're right.
As you go over all thoughts—searching,
Anything to show an answer
Finding that—It wasn't a dream
You are surrounded by memories.
Will you think of me?
You begin to think of things to come,
Seeking out only the good ahead of all.
Having yourself again—complete.
And when you watch your future
Tell me Will you think of me?

Ruth L Holbrook

DE SPITE

To the Lord Jesus whose love has overcome our deepest hurts

A trembling child sneaks away to her room,
Fearfully waiting her next moment of doom.
Crashes and screaming alert all of her fears,
Under blanket she hides and covers both ears.

A safe place to hide seems her only chance.
But remaining so still she wets her pants.
Footsteps grow louder—she hears a turned knob.
The door now has slammed—her cry becomes sob.

"Get up! Did you hear me!" your teeth are clenched tight.
Your hand tenses up as if ready to fight.
"Oh mommie, I'm sorry, I won't bother you.
I will pick up my clothes and all the toys too."

Sweltering anger dominates your war,
But stunned by the blood that splats on the floor,
You escape to your room and plunge on the bed;
Defeated and guilty, you'd rather be dead.

A soft tiny hand finds its way to your shoulder;
It's seeking and pleading—oh why can't you hold her?
"I'm sorry," she begs and breaks out in a cry,
"Will you love me oh mommie, if I would die?"

Edith Girton

THE LAST HOBO

This poem is dedicated to Ralph Gooding, a retired hobo.

When evening shadows fall,
and I'm sitting here alone,
comes the clickety-clack of rails
and a freight trains lonely moan.

I can smell the stew abubbling
in an old tin can,
smell the bacon fryin' in
an old blackened pan.

While we sit and tell our tales of
adventures in odd little
town and places.

Now they've gone, these pals of mine,
hobos of the rails.
I can hear their voices, and see their
kind, old wrinkled faces.

These were my pals for a good
many years.
Gone are the hobos,
The last pioneers;

And I'm left dreaming here
how it will be,
Will they ride the rails
when they come back for me?

Anita J Sherren

A VIEWPOINT ON REINCARNATION

There are some who tell me I have been here before, possibly a seer, a teacher, a sister or more.
But frankly between you and me one lifetime is enough to live.
From infant to adult troubles seem to envoule.
Work, play, sometimes days are good, sometimes bad.
Work, play, and in one's life sometimes hate, hurt; but then joy, love,
When misunderstandings are cleared up.
Winter snows turn to spring, blue skies, sunshine, summer,
fall, all a part of life's ways to spend the days.
Reincarnation? Mystery! Yes!
But when one's life is done let it be to a heavenly home, not again the earth to roam.

Guy E Jones

LOST & SEARCHING

This poem is dedicated to all, who have yet found the words of expression.

I am just a single soul,
That again wants to become whole.

I am looking for another to share my life,
to share my time in this lonely world as my wife.

To help prepare for what is to become,
for that day when we become as one.

I may touch her and hold her and know she is so real,
but it is her soul that I cannot touch . . . to feel.

Oh, how I long for us to be as one,
that I cannot wait for that very day to come.

And when we are whole once again,
I will cherish for all eternity
knowing Our Love will never end!

Rose Shaw

THE WISH

I gazed on a Robin passing by—
He flew way up into the sky,
Lit on the tip top of an old pine tree—
Sit there looking at you and me.

This made me wish that I could be—
Like a Robin wild and free,
Left alone in perfect bliss—
Where I could dream that I could fly,
O're field and stream—
That I could see the earthly scene,
But alas I'M only me—
Just a common human being.

Evelyn Arroyo McNece

MOM

To mom: "A mother who has moved heaven and earth for her children, and would do it again! We love you Mom.

Mom didn't have to keep us.
Mom didn't have to care.
But when we were all frightened
Well . . . Mom was always there.
She started with the nine of us.
She did it all alone.
No matter what we said or did
We always had our home.
Through all the years of ups and downs
she somehow got two more.
She took them in and loved them
And Mom was always sure
She had the same love for them
And to spare, well . . . she had more.
So remember when your mad at her
And you don't come around, . . .
Mom didn't have to keep us —
She could have turned us down.

Ruth V Moody

STORMY SEA

There is a ship a-sailing
on the sea
in a night of deepest
stormy black—
no stars or moon in the sky
shining down upon the sea.

Now, there comes the crashing
of flashing thunder
flickering all around
the stormy, stormy sea,
tossing the ship up and up
then way, way under.
Do you think God's angry
with me?

After the storm, reigns
deep, deep silence
with a once stormy sea
held in calm abeyance
'til the next time
God roars at me!

Peter Norbert Crafts

TAKE A LOOK

Pull yourself up
Look for higher ground
Things get better
It can be found

By your own doing
You are barred
You try too much
You look too hard

Try to take it slow
Take life in stride
Do it face to face
Don't run and hide

Come out in the open
Get off that shelf
Your not so bad
Appreciate yourself

Consider these words
They are true
And see what others
See in you

Lisa J Sweatt

FAITH

From the moment I awoke and held you close to me
I began to realize how hard letting you go would be
I felt the pain start to grow deep inside my heart
A terrible burning feeling that was tearing me apart
I started to think of the future and the Christmas' I'd miss
or how I couldn't tuck you in with a good-night kiss
Never to hear you speak your first word, or see the first step you take
I wouldn't be there to watch you grow and share each birthday cake
When I think of all the times I'll miss, it gets harder for me to live
But I know you'll have a better life than the one that I could give
And if someday you find out about me and think I didn't want you
I just want to say that I could've done what some other women do

Only I wanted you to have a taste
of life, a chance to run and play
And I pray to God He keeps you
safe, each and every day

Marjorie Knott
FOOT-PRINTS

On a crisp October morning. The
grass coated with frost, our
footprints loomed behind, with
the leaves the wind had tossed.

Hard times had fallen on us,
we were in our middle years.
To survive we had to leave our
home. Our eyes were wet with
tears.

A new place was to greet us,
a thousand miles away. Where
we saw "at last" our footprints,
in the warm and wet red clay.

The winter is much milder here
and people's friendly smiles,
made it easier for us to bridge
the many, many miles.

The days are going fast now, our
middle day's most gone, and our
thoughts are getting stronger of
family, friends and home.

We find we're looking forward
to a most rewarding day, when
we leave our footprints
far behind, in the warm and
wet red clay.

And then we see them re-appear.
On frosty ground they lay.
The only difference this time,
they will point the other way.

Herm Nelson
SOMETIMES/ALWAYS

About—and for—Darlene. wherever she may be.

My love for you is as
a wave of the ocean—
surging with power
and always in motion.

Sometimes rising to top
the highest mountain peak—
sometimes with such force
to cause my heart to break.

Sometimes gently rolling
to form a hidden trough—
where my mind can hold you—
sometimes hard, sometimes soft.

Not sometimes, but always,
the ocean wave goes on—
as does my love for you—
sometimes changing, always
strong.

Margaret Ballard
FREEDOM IN FRIENDSHIP

No longer do you have to live
within the confines
of a "box" my friend.
A box which sides are made up
with my preconceived ideas
of who you are and what you
need.
A box with walls formed from
my expectations, my
impressions,
my notions, my ideals—
my usefulness to you.
You are <u>free</u> my friend;
Free to be you—
the unique individual that God
has created you to be.
Oh, that I might stand back a bit,
yet near to you;
and be still—
content to watch as who you are
unfolds in strength, beauty,
and richness of personality.
Maybe watering an area here a
little,
or planting a thought there a
little,
but "free" also to:
watch the growth,
respond
experience
and just enjoy you,
as we are discovering the person
that God is creating you to be.

Mrs Irene G Jarboe
ASTRONAUTS

This poem is dedicated to my loving Daughter F. Diana Polsgrove

In my trusty ship, I one day flew
ore, the highest cloud in the sky.
And played leap frog, with all the
clouds.
When an astronaut, whizzed
by . . .
Gee, but he, sure was in a hurry.
Or was late, for a meeting
someplace.
Yet here he was, flying
round-and-a-round.
. . . Way Out in Outer Space . . .
The poor lil clouds and I were
startled.
And this we don't deny.
Then I wondered, what would
happen.
If, there were speed—cops in the
sky.
I guess, they'd hide, behind a cloud
In some good secret place.
And tag the speeding astronauts
. . . Way Out in Outer Space . . .
But let me be, the first to tell you.
Give astronauts, the right of way.
For, you won't have time to argue.
Though, they are flying, home
today.
It was then, my ship and I decided
That home, is the safest place.
For six year old astronauts
. . . And Not In Outer Space! ! !

Shirle M Reiff

Shirle M Reiff
LIFES GARDEN

Your life is an open field to be
sown,
to be watered and nurtured by you
alone.
The friendships you gathered will
come from the seeds
Of Kindness you've planted with
many a deed.
Your garden will bloom with
laughter and mirth,
And good times will cover the once
barren earth.

'Ere you came to those weeds of
woe and dispair.
Remember there's always
someone who cares.
"I know of your garden, I met you
one day.
And I felt a warm glow having
passed your way."

'Til its harvest time in your garden,
And you reap in splendor hue,
the sweetest bouquet you'll pick
will be,
the love in friendships true.

Tracy Ann Voss
GOING HOME

To my Brother Jim, who would rather play baseball than help.

Going home isn't neat,
Because my brother makes me
beat.

He'd always rather have fun
Than to get his homework done.

I bribe him with a lot of lies
But all he does is eat all the pies.

I ask him to please help,
But all he says is "Eat Kelp."

I tell him to "Get Over Here,"
But all he does is plug his ears.

Wanda J Eberle
FAREWELL TO MICHAEL

In Loving Memory Of Our Son CPL. Michael D. Eberle

Michael you came to us in 1964 as
a bundle of joy,
yes, God had given us another fine
boy.
Michael you spent so much of your
time playing alone,
then you would tell us of your other
home.
Michael you cared more for the
elderly than you did
the kids your own age, I guess in
your life this was
just another page.
Michael you went through school
with the greatest of
ease, for you were always cutting
up and being a tease.
Life to you was always full of joy,
for you were truly
an all-American Boy.
Michael you left in 1982 to become
a Marine, we always
knew you would, for it was one of
your dreams.
Michael you traveled the world
over and made so many
friends, and son they didn't forget
you when it came
time for your life to end.
We are all saddened that you are
gone, but I know you
are happy in your Heavenly Home,
so my dear Michael
watch over us from now until then,
when we can all
hold you in our arms once again.

Fayellen Krejci Sanetra
CHARLES NOT A HORNET

This poem was written for one who supported me during a recovery of an illness in my life, namely Charles.

Let me write some fine things,
Let me be a poet.
Let me not mince or hobble.
This is the hero of my poem,
He is a delight of life,
His heart pours love,
Undeniable a man of energies,
Spinning a caricature
That finger tips design
Not a hornet of a man
A transaction of tender breed,
A variety of emotions,
Not as fat witted people
They are battered roses.
As the wren's morning cry,
With unlettered jingles
God love this man.
He is not dead flesh
But, kindly and rare,
Befriending me, this scribbler
A genuine story is he.
May I adopt this hour.

Donna M Schnur
THERE IN THE FOSSIL HILLS

In loving memory of my mother Margaret Boulanger 1905—1987

There in the fossil hills
Even time is old,
So I have been told.
The ghost of the Indians are there.
When the sun is setting,
And the sky is a fiery glow,
The phantom Indian chief sits
upon his horse
And watches from the highest cliff.
You can almost hear the shrill cries
of the hunters
Echoing over the thundering
hooves of the buffalo.
Arrowheads and buffalo bones can
still be found.
Deep within the hills are hidden
mysteries
Of dinosaurs and cave men.
There in the fossil hills
Even time is old,
So I have been told.
Ghost from the past are all
around . . .

Marylin Sanford
HALITOSIS

To those who need to know this.

There's a cure for halitosis,
Believe me there is hope,
Go to any grocery store
and please buy you some scope.

I don't see how you walk around
with a bad halitosis,
Everytime you come around,
people snare up their nose.

It's so loud can't you see?
Sure I do my thing,
You can also do your thing
by buying some listerine.

I'm not trying to offend you,
Nor, am I being harsh,
I'm telling you this as a friend,
Please buy you some mouthwash.

I'm telling you this because I dig
you,
Some don't care you know,
My dear ole' friend your halitosis
has really got to go.
So go on home, Wait! Hear me out
And please take my advice,
Gargle your throat a little harder,
Or maybe do it twice.

Debra Kay Wilhelm

IF YOU EVER DARE TO DREAM

This poem is dedicated to our courageous astronauts. This tragedy has touched the hearts of many. The pain we feel is very real. But so is living our fantasies. Don't ever give up your dreams.

If you ever dare to dream
Seven courageous astronauts did
If you ever dare to have fantasies
Seven heroic astronauts did
It was their dream to be pioneers
And their fantasy to be sky-riders
Their dreams and fantasies were
reality
To reach up through the stars into
heaven
And see what we only imagine and
dream

It wasn't that they could be famous
But what could be achieved for
mankind
They knew the great risks involved
And were still willing to forge
ahead
They believed in their incredible
dreams
And had the courage, strength, and
wisdom
To bring them into existence
It's no illusion that they lived out
their dreams

John Girard Willis

TO NANCY—ONCE AGAIN

Swirling in the mist of dreams
Lies meanings which aren't what
they seem
Taxing the senses with colors and
confusion . . .
But in the midst of the mist
There is a clearly human form
Gesturing with her outstretched
arms—
Beautiful you/
Your beauty is not just in your
form,
But in my anticipation of seeing
you
Like being in love for the first time/
Even now I see your form walking
On the seashore and it is early
dawn—
We are back on the Island—
You tax my senses with your
tender love . . .
Then I wake up crying your name
Like some poor lost soul
Like Ulysses seeing Penelope
For the first time in ten years/

Judy E (Weddle) Books

IT HURTS TO CRY

The trials and tribulations I've
been through,
The pain and suffering that made
me blue.
My home without plumbing for
thirteen years,
And fighting the wood stove would
bring tears.
But then my garden would make
me cheery,
Watching the corn and beans grow
would make me merry.
Hoeing my crops, I'd look up to
Heaven
And thank my dear Lord for all his
blessings.
My Mom and Dad, my friends so
true,
The sky, the grass, the flowers blue,
The cat, the dog, the squirrels
playing by and by.
But oh my God, why does it
physically hurt to cry?

Vurlena Carr

Vurlena Carr

MY ONLY BABY

You are my baby my only baby
You make my heart so happy today
You know how much I love you
Please don't take my baby away.

You are my baby my only baby
You thrill my soul so much today
You know how much I adore you
Please don't take my baby away.

Barbara J Matuszak

REFLECTIONS

This poem is dedicated to my brother, DUANE A. WAKLEE, who gave his life for the call of freedom.

My auburn hair has faded
And silver takes its place
The lines of age & worry makes a
pattern
Upon my once proud face.
My body does not move as fast
As is did when it was new
My head doesn't think as quick
As I would like it to.
It's time to think about
When my life is over
When sun, wind & time
Will be no more.
But—Heaven's such a pretty place
It's what I've always been told
Where the sun is always shining
And the streets are paved with gold
And see his heavenly smile
Just that one precious moment
Will have made my life worthwhile.

Jesus Flores

THE LONG FLIGHT HOME (FROM THE ARTIC TO SAN FRANCISCO)

I dedicate this poem to all mignatory people, and for the love of nature.

As the time of departing back home
drew near.
With sadness and jubilation, for
this land so dear.
The sky was cloudy and calm, then
like magic the sun appeared.
Mt. McKinley at the right, with
beaming splendor farewell to us.
So long land enchanted with
beauty and pray. God give you
beauty and pose unequal to
none.
!oh tundra divine! Those years of
waiting in vain never were.
Posses by nostalgia for leaving this
land of the midnight sun, my
memory always be with you till
the end.

Elizabeth Martha Martin

MY DEAREST LOVE ROBERTO

My dearest love Roberto age of
love is timeless;
Now that I have met you.
Time is standing still; for our love
so great,
That cannot be separated not even
by fate.
The like turns to love that has no
limit,
For thus the golden love the first
sighted minute.
For days and weeks I could not be
able to withstand the time,
I shall be away from you my
dearest love Roberto.
Months and years would surely kill
my so lonesome heart,
and my love for you.

If you were to ever leave me my
dearest love
Roberto;
My soul would hurt; dearly, and
my heart would surely die.
I would not hurt; but I would cry.
I would live forever I would not die.
I would not think, and I would not
blink.
I would not talk, and I would not
walk.
I will not jump; but I would
surely fall—
without the love of my dearest
Roberto.

Sandra Millikan

SOME THINGS IN LIFE ARE FREE

Bright sunshine,
Butterflies and bees,
A snowcapped mountain,
A summer breeze,
The moon, the stars, the seven seas;
Colorful rainbows,
Snowflakes and leaves,
A flower that grows,
A forest of trees;
The rain, the wind,
The love of a friend,
Some things in life are free.

Susan Kay-Von Pelky McAdams

A FATHER NOT FORGOTTEN

The baby girl was born
Into a home filled with scorn,
So small and helpless was she
Not aware of the unhappiness to
be.

All through her life she asked why;
"Where is the father she was
denied?"
The pain in her heart would never
end
Till she's seen his face once again.

As her being goes from place to
place
The girl still searches each man's
face
Feeling that someday by chance
His smile she'll remember at a
glance.

Although the years have come and
gone
The love for her father is still
strong,
For this man she was denied
The love she feels will never die.

Edith June Rouse

THE STATESMAN

With whom have thou my
statesman been? O, my
handsome young
statesman where have thou and
she been? Please my statesman
tis I the one who begs, asking thou
to tell. Is she the one
as for thou to love, thou chose? I
say tell me my darling
is she the one thou love, or just the
one thou think thou love?
What will thou do, if it tis I, "the
poet," thou love? My
sweet strong darling, oh love of
mine, I know not what I will do,
if it is she the one thou have as to
love, and as for I to love,
thou not givith thou love to me.
Fearing our love again will
never be, tis sickened at heart, I am
for the alen cloud of hate
is destine to win. Tis surely a curse
of the devil, with
feelings of hurt, like that of the red
hot coals as they burn
within the pits of the devil's hell!
Making me a decendant
of lewifore it most asurely will, for
with my own hands my life
I shall take, never again to hurt
from our love, a love thou
chose to forsake, never to know of
thou love thou givith to she,
for alive be, I will not, but dead it
tis I will be, as I burn
forever within the tourches of the
devil's hell, knowing my
destiny is you loving me.

Kelly P Townsend

I DO SET MY BOW IN THE CLOUD

The dawn is born gently
bringing forth
filtering sunlight
across the lands.
The light remains muted
as the day grows older
allowing space
for an unsettled storm
to unfold across the sky.
It eventually succeeds in

encompassing the sunlight
completely.
The clouds tumble and fight
among themselves.
Each toll of thunder
is a cry of pain.
To stop the anguish
the sunlight struggles
to penetrate the billows,
trying to clear a path.
But its tremendous force
is useless.
Then silently,
from somewhere behind the sun
a rainbow rolls out
against the sky
It softly melts an opening
in the clouds,
enabling light
to touch the earth
once more.

Colonel O Thompson
THE LEAF
I came upon a dead leaf,
Brittle to the touch.
Where the thief —
Did he take so much?

The leaf is now a has-been,
For the sun it doesn't care.
Its days of glory over;
Its host, it now stands bare.

It has now lost its lifeblood,
Its vigor now unseen.
It lies there brown and broken,
Its beauty just a dream.

The leaf had a thousand neighbors,
Each had a job to do;
To shade our heads and feed our
souls
And keep the sun from view.

The leaf had but a season;
Now, in the mud, it's mired.
It has now sung its swan song,
Given up, it's tired.

The tree now stands, a silhouette—
A cold and stark old thing;
But there is hope for beauty yet
For soon will come the spring.

Yolanda Rae Scholl
MY ANGEL
You're my angel
In disguise.
You do no wrong
In my eyes.
You touched my heart
Made of ice.
I felt it melt
Oh so nice.
I dream of you
Only you
The one I love
Very true.
The unity
In our hearts
Was meant to stay
Not depart.

Ruth Brown Stover
YEARNING
Have you ever tried to fathom
What it means to one like me
To have this secret yearning—
For a love that cannot be?

In my dreams it's ever near me
Yet my arms they cannot feel
This little one so tender
That I'm always seeing there.

It seems—his eyes—they must be
brown,
His face—it's round and rosy
All touched with God's own
precious love
Saved for me—and me only.

My innermost soul still weeps for
him,
Were it only one touch so tender—
But the door is shut—is shut to
me—
Must I always be its tender?

Jose O Bautista

Jose O Bautista
I'M THANKFUL FOR FRIENDS

Lovingly dedicated to the friendly nurses of the Manila Sanitarium and Hospital and friends who came to visit during my illness

Not until sickness came to me,
That I did realize the value
Of faithful friends, who proved to
be
So thoughtful, so kind, and so
true.

Some came by my bedside to say
How sad they were to see me
down;
Then as they left and walked away,
Waved and wished me a "Get
well soon."

Others came with messages in song
Of sympathy, comfort, and
cheer,
That buoy up one's spirits along
As through life's way he journeys
here.

Dear Lord, for such friends, I thank
Thee,
Bless their service of love, I pray,
That many others just like me
May also be blessed day by day.

Kate Russell
A DAUGHTER'S DESIRE
I hope that you can look at me as
a source of pride,
and not as one of your offspring
that you'd like to hide.
I don't expect you to believe in—or
condone—
my crazy ways.
Please, just love me,
unconditionally,
and let me live my days,
exactly as I wish to, exactly as I
please.
Don't worry—I'll survive it all—
so put your mind at ease.
The hard knocks and the rocky
roads
are a source of pain and strife.
But taking it all in stride, I've
learned,
is the key to a happy life.
I know that you are older, and
you're both
much wiser too.
I hope that you will welcome me
when—for advice—
I come to you.

Alisa M Boedeker
TEDDY BEAR
I had you when I was little
I still have you by,
Now here is a little riddle
to show you why:

Your soft and cuddly hug makes so
many wrong things right,
and even so many right things
better,
which gives me all the more reason
to hold you tight.

You've got that certain touch,
that I would travel miles for,
If it took all that much.

You've made my life worth while,
so just smile,
and make other people happy for
miles and miles.

Phebe Hale Giles
MY MOTHER'S HANDS
Those withered old hands how I
miss them so,
As they lie there wrinkled and
cold.
How I long for the touch that
would sooth the ache,
In our hearts that have all they
can hold.

Though tears and grief will not
bring her back,
And we know it is in God's plan.
Our mother was sent upon this
earth
To help with those Wrinkled Old
Hands.

She took care of us when we were
sick
Watched over us night and day
Kissed our hurts to make them well
And taught us to kneel and pray.

She took us to church, taught us
right from wrong
When we were too young to care,
And she shrank smaller as we grew
up
And silver was in her hair.

I know she will wear a crown of
glory
With others who are there,
And our blessings are many as
grains of sand
So take care of her God, and
those Wrinkled Old Hands.

Lisa Hutchinson
UNTITLED

This poem is dedicated to Michael Genovese, my first love, If only you knew how I really felt.

The time we've been apart,
so long it breaks my heart.
The love I have for you,
could not be given to someone new.
The love that I have lost,
so precious it has no cost.
The friend you were to me,
was a friend no one else could be.
The time we were together,
so beautiful, I'll always remember.
The love you gave to me,
I never wanted to be set free.
The times that we shared,
showed how much we cared.
The memories that I'm holding on
to,
are all I have left of you.

Edwin Beck
LAUGHTER

This poem is dedicated to Sandra, my wife, Katherine Ann, my daughter, and Charles Henry, my son

Laughter is a universal sound
Found where love is all around,
It is like the brook that
Ripples thru every crack and nook
It is understood by all
The grown-ups, big and small
And little children all,
It is like all the melodies of song
All blended into one
To come forth as assurance
That all is well with everyone;
It echoes forth a new spirit
On an otherwise forlorn day
It is like a check on payday;
Oh laughter, do not hide your song
Bring forth thy melody
Longed for, for so long,
Oh laughter, come tarry a while
longer
And replenish yet my longing
hunger.

Dianne Foerster-Kozloski
I ENVY MY WANDERER
I envy his direction,
or lack of it,
while I sit tied to my
schedules and appointments
and routines.

I envy his freedom,
of movement and thought,
when I'm firmly planted with my
desk and my books
and my phones.

I envy his oneness
with the sea and land and air,
as I'm trapped by pollution
and traffic
and flourescent lights.

I envy his aloneness
without me in his arms,
as I long to have him with me
close and safe and warm.

There's one thing about my
wanderer
that I truly hope and pray—
that when he's done with all his
wandering
he'll return to me
someday.

Terry E Eckert
THE SILENT HEART

The silent heart
no tele-tale trace
of life within
its chambers lets escape,
of any hope,
of any faith,
of any needs
waiting to be told.
And the Ghost of time
just passes by
and fails to ever notice—
this neglected want
alone in wait
for the master
of it's fate,
such a waste,
such a waste.

David M Howe
REFLECTIONS ON A WALK

Meandering through the forest
green,
I reflect upon the Earth.
While gazing at this scene serene,
I contemplate Her worth.

To some the World is standing
reserve,
Everything for the taking.
They gobble Her up and have the
nerve,
To ignore the wastelands they're
making.

The forests fall to the
businessman's axe,
The minerals ripped from the
ground.
And if they avoid the federal tax,
They are men of great renown.

The results of their actions are
plain to see,
Waters are polluted everywhere.
Factories spew poison and it seems
to me,
I cannot draw a fresh breath of air.

Earth's value is not in Her worth
to man,
But portends another purpose.
Nature has Her reason and plan,
She is not merely here to serve us.

But man has made this planet his,
And I doubt he'll ever see,
That worth lies hidden in What Is,
And not in what could be.

Barbara S Baker
HIS GARDEN

In memory of Henry D. Baker

I've been thinkin' 'bout an old man
we all used to know;
And everything that old man did.
You know he did just so.
I never will forget his perfect
garden standin' there;
I still can see him propped behind
his hoe without a care.

Everybody knows, his garden grew
in the straightest rows;
And he was not afraid to say
goodbye,
And I wouldn't be surprised,
IF he's planting something right
now in the sky.

Nobody is perfect, you just do the
best you can.
The longer that you live, the better
you will understand;
Live a busy life on earth, and just
be satisfied,
To hear the pretty music when its
time to say goodbye.

Everybody knows, his garden grew
in the straightest rows;
And he was not afraid to say
goodbye,
And I wouldn't be surprised,
If he's planting something right
now in the sky.

We all loved him, and we all miss
him,
And may that pretty music ring
forever in his ears;
For all his good years.

J E White
MARTIN

Were you a prophet, Martin?
Will your dream prove true
And make the pain well worth it.
Did that mountain view
Reveal the future brothers,
Red, black, and white as one
United people honoring
The freedoms all had won.
Will the little children,
When their vote is cast,
Forget the stain of prejudice
And make the bonding last.
Will their children's children
Lift one voice to sing
(In memory of you who taught
the song) "Let freedom ring!"
Then after generations
Of following this theme,
Will a nation hope enough
To bring to life your dream.

Rosie Braa Pulliam
DITTOS

All to the glory of God

Winds — Blow
Flowers — Grow
Hail — Rain
Window — Pane
Birds — Trees
Bended — Knees
Bees — Honey
Work — Money
Food — Life
Burdens — Strife

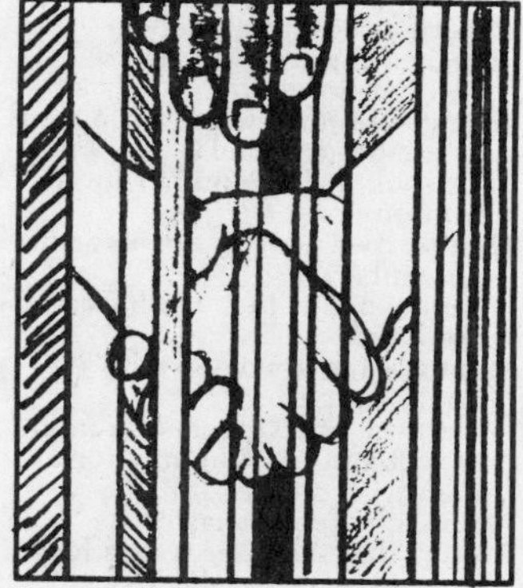

Clouds — Sun
Children — Fun
Snow — Ice
Field — Mice
Moon — Night
Stars — Bright
Animal — Cage
Storms — Rage
Men — Slay
Satans — Way
Forgiveness — Sins
Christ — Wins

Pam Raymond
WE'LL GET THROUGH THIS, TOO

Dedicated to Lois & Bob—Together, we'll beat this!

There's a time for anger, a time for
fear
There's a time for sorrow, and a
time for tears.
But once these feelings have all
come about,
We can talk, if you want to, and
work them all out.
We're here, if you need us, no
matter what's wrong
It's things, such as this, that keep
our ties strong.
We're family—we're in this
together, you see
No crisis can separate this family!
And so, with the help of the Lord
up above
Combined with our strength, our
faith, and our love,
We'll fight this, together, as we've
done before
Using love as our weapon, and
faith as our cure!

B J L Porter
SISTERS ARE GOD'S TREASURES

To: Barbara Aliene Wilson, my sister, Written March 20 1985, before she died on July 24 1985

Sisters are great treasures, sent
from God's storehouse above.
Tho not always a pleasure they're
one sign of His Love
I don't often take the time to reflect
I would much rather wring your
sweet neck.
Say! Do you suppose it's the
coming of age
I find myself wanting to turn
back
life's page
And experience again the love
and the fun
When you were my family and
the
family was one
United in trials; We let all the
hurts
come
We are one family no matter
what's
done
God says love is enduring,
patient
and kind,
And judges all things with the
heart
not the mind
Love is unselfish; giving more
than
it takes
Always understanding and
never
forsakes
Trusting us with His treasure
from
above
Sisters are signs of God's
pleasure
and Love.

Diana Shipman
THE RAGMAN

To Grandma Richardson, with love . . .

A ragman walked through town,
A cross in one hand—a bible in the
other,
Asking people in the street,
"Can you spare a dime for your
brother?"
The richest man in town
Threw up his arms and walked
away,
"I haven't time for a ragman
for I've a horse to buy today."
Then the ragman approached Mrs.
Chambers,
The banker's lovely wife,
"Can you spare a dime for a lowly
man
Who lives the simple life?"
"I may have a dime for a lowly man,
But not a bum like you—
I'm a busy woman, so out of my
way,
I've forclosures to attend to."
Then out of the streets came a little
boy
Dressed in rags and wearing no
shoes,
"I have a dime and that's all that I
have,
But I will share it with you."
The town fell silent over the little
boy
As he took the ragman's hand,
For what they saw was a poor little
boy
Become a wealthy young man.

Debra A Wilson
TIME

Time is so endless, totally without
feeling or concern.
Time just goes on and on.
But on the other hand, life is
feeling and concern.
Life is never endless, life will one
day die, unlike time.
And time, oh time will pass you by
like its nothing, so you must live
your life to the fullest.
Live life like it was your last day.
Because if you don't, you will miss
all that time is giving you. Time
to watch your children and
grandchildren grow.
Watch love flourish and die, a
broken heart, here and there, but
it will mend with time.
Time heals all wounds.
Life is to be lived with time on your
side.
You make the time on your side.
You make time work for you.

Patricia Gorby Howlett
MY BIGGEST CHALLENGE

"My Biggest Challenge" was written as a tribute to our son Robbie who added a family to our lives and all the happiness we could ever ask for.

I've always dreamed of what it's
like to be somebody's mother,
I tell him all the secrets that I
would tell no other.
This world can be a hurtful one and
he's so very small,
Under my wing I will keep him he's
such a little doll.
How can such a tiny thing give me
so much inspiration?
Every day I look at him with love
and admiration.
What did I do to deserve him? He's
the biggest challenge in life,
Some day some lucky woman will
be chosen as his wife.
He will grow very strong and
handsome because he's had a
loving start,
I hope that he will always keep his

mother in his heart.
My dear son, may you always
know, why I feel this way,
My love for you is endless, it will
never go away.

Irene Burton Richey
MEMORIES OF MOTHER

When I feel the softness of a gentle
breeze,
And see the flowers swaying at
early dawn,
I hear rustling leaves, on all the
trees,
Yet they still manage to hang
on—
I think of her

When I see the twinkling stars at
night,
Light up the sky so beautifully,
I wonder who might have turned
them on,
Or did it happen automatically?
I wonder

When I hear the laughter of
small children,
At play in the summer sun,
They seem to have no cares at all;
Just sharing and having fun—
She loved them

When I think of the things she
taught me,
It took me years to understand.
That the greatest friend I could
ever have,
Was right in the palm of my
hand—
Constantly

I've wondered why the phone
stopped ringing;
And why the nights are so still
and calm;
I've longed for a simple
explanation,
But the answer just doesn't seem
to come—
I miss her

But, God needed a special
person,
To help keep things under
control;
One who had the patience and love,
To beckon His children, to His
fold—
He chose mother

Lloyd S Aiken
THREE A M BLUES

It's an hour since I first awoke
And I'm here to say, that it's no joke.

It's three A.M. and I can't sleep
And from now till dawn, the time
will creep.

I think I'll have a bite to eat
May have a smoke; God knows I'm
beat.

I'll read a bit and maybe then
I could get back to sleep again.

It used to work most every night
I'd read awhile and then,
"Daylight."

But readin don't help much no
more
Mostly cause my eyes get sore.
Guess that's a part of growin old
It happens all the time, I'm told.

And if there's a reason for this to be
I can't figure it, for the life of me.

Sandy Ring
MY MOTHER . . . MY FRIEND

This poem is dedicated to Jeanne, my loving mother and best friend.

A friend that I have always had
Someone I took for granted,
Who's always there when I feel sad
And makes me feel so wanted.

Her loving and considerate ways
That show in all she's done,
I know that I am proud to say
That surely I have won.

A better friend could never be
The stars have said above,
Someone I want to be with me
The mother that I love.

Katherine L (Titus) Harms
THE COLLEGIATE MYTH

Ah, the joys of college life
Free of petty daily strife.
Hours of intellectual stimulation
Mixed with analytical
conversation.

Volumes of facts about ages past
Crammed into lectures over-fast.
Problems in algebra that boggle
the mind
Upset the stomach and numb the
behind.

Two hours of study for each hour
in class
Prudently advised for a grade that
will pass.
So much to learn in so little time
The less sleep, the more sublime.

All this to obtain a better position
In society's traditional
stratification.
There is no guarantee of a job for
graduates
So what is the purpose or value of
it?

What we gain is far from lily
guilding.
Our character and confidence we
are building.
Time management and self
discipline for sure
There is no hardship we cannot
endure.

We adapt to changes and seek
insight
To the problems of others to lessen
their plight.
We inquire, struggle, improve and
excell.
Facing the Apocalypse we find a
cure for hell.

Robert L Barton
THE ONE I LOVE

She is saucy enough to be witty
Just merry enough to be gay,
She is fat enough to be healthy
Just bold enough to be brave.
She is fair enough to be beautiful
Just dainty enough to be neat,
She is tall enough to be graceful
Just gentle enough to be sweet.
She is fair enough for a princes
Just sly enough for a fay,
She is brave enough for a knight
but kind hearted in a way.
She has pride enough for ambition
pure hearted as an angel above,
These lasses are hard to find
but they are the kind we love

Eduardo Duran
JOURNEYS

The rain falls gently
On the comfortable abode
Tears of heaven falling
Cleansing misled souls

Another member gone
Embarking on a journey
Mysteries as yet unsolved
Territories yet unexplored

Someday I shall follow
Perhaps led by you

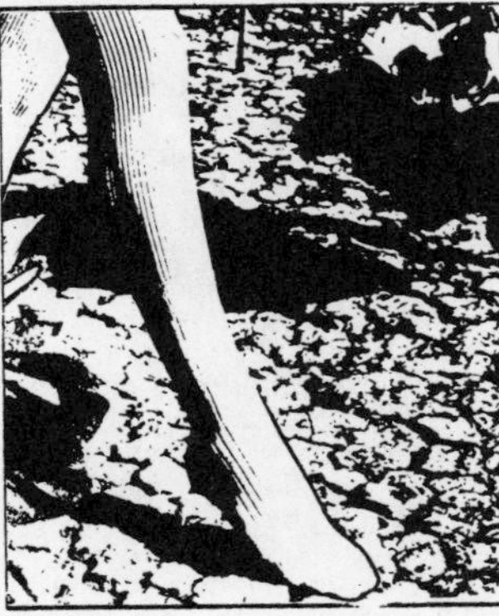

And childhood memories recalled
And relived forevermore

I'm sorry I missed you
So many thoughts unspoken
Time came between us
In ways we never dreamed

Now the rain runs down the panes
And the house is a bit emptier
For another member has departed
Embarking on a journey unknown

Diana M V Liddle
REMEMBERING THE MEMORY

Across a crowded room
full of drunken lovers
You seemed alone, without
merit—without grace
I laughed inwardly at such a
peculiar little man
We met—rather—were introduced
by a mutual friend
Your soul, so like another lover
from my past,
Time warped and I was in his arms
remembering
What anyone is lucky to have had
even once
And me—I'm a woman who's
doubly cursed
I have the world's greatest strength
of will and passion only for a
man with greater still
Not many are my master
But for that night, as it was long
ago, my will was the lesser
As your hand turned my face by
mind alone,
your eyes pulled me inside
Your soul grabbed my heart and
held it tight—screaming
Powerless, I ached for your touch
Which you denied just long enough
to show your absolute grip
I felt your pleasure at my
unfulfilled hunger, sensed your
smile
Consumed with desire, I was
undeniably defeated.

Brenda J Regan
SEARCHING

Life lies out like a bank of drifting
snow,
Searching for a place to rest.
It watches our every move,
And trails we trod.
There's laughter,
There's tears,
There's Love,
There's hate,
Searching for what,
Not realizing we found it,
Until it's to late.
Never to have,
Never to hold,
But it will always be there.

Angela Dawn Harrington
ONE IN THE MIDDLE

First there is my sister . . .
She is the oldest.
Then there is my brother . . .
He is the youngest.
Last but not least is ME!

Me, yes me, I am in the middle.
I feel like a peanut butter and
jelly sandwich.
I wish I was older than my sister
Mary-Kay.
But I'm glad I'm not younger
than my little brother Jay.

If your in the middle just like me,
you have a problem I can see.

Barbara Wehr
WIND SONG

The aspen shakes in a gale of glee,
Laughs with the mountain,
laughs with the sea.
Laughs with the clouds at a mutual
joke,
Its soul is happy, no tears
provoke.

The west wind rocks with a joy
unseen,
Makes tall reeds shiver and bow
and lean.
Makes daisies turn wee heads to see
What the west wind said to you
and me.

Genevieve Moor
MIRAGE OF LOVE

I've traveled far and I've traveled
wide
and the Lord more than Blessed
my life
I've worked hard and toiled in the
sun
always the faithful wife.

Gathered the harvest and showed
at the fair
what the bountiful gifts had done
hunted the wilds and fished the
streams
and even raised a Son.

I've conquered and advanced from
strength of faith
marched where many fail
turned not aside where friends
abide
and helped the sorrowful frail.

I've trudged the land with one
small hand
sailed waters with half a crew
shared a house with a disgruntled
spouse
sat with Governors old and new.

I've flowen the land in forest watch
when trees were tinder dry
watched the sunsets ever aflame
from my station high in the sky.

I've searched below, afar and
beyond
I've lost with steadfast grace
I've done all this and so much more
for the Love of a small shining face.

Clifton Morris Wood

A TREE

Oh! you great big Beautiful tree.
A tree of knowledge you were to be.
God made you first then made
Adam and Eve.
The fruit on the tree was a sight to
behold.
but Adam and Eve were told.
Not to eat the forbidden fruit you
see
or their Happiness would cease to
be.
The Tempter came and confused
them
They were disobedient and ate the
fruit
from the Beautiful tree.
Their Happiness ceased to be.
The Beautiful garden they had to
leave.
They had to make their living from
the
toil of the soil with strife.
God loved them so much, he
gave them
Another Chance for Eternal life. By
dying on a tree made into a cross.
Their strife will end, his stripes will
heal and their lives won't be lost.
They will live in another garden
with another tree
which will be
The tree of life for Eternity.

LeAnne Fisher Ensign

THANK YOU FOR THE HUMMINGBIRDS

Dedicated to Marlene Fisher—For introducing me to life's little treasures

---

On wings as quick as lightening
She passes endlessly hour upon
hour
Busily doing her daily task
Seeking sweet nectour from every
flower.

Amazed, I'd watched and I'd
Wondered
How a creature as tiny as she
Could accomplish her seemingly
impossible chore
With such grace and vitality.

Entranced, I moved even closer
As I did so it was clear to me
The flutter of even tinier wings
Those of her small baby.

At the moment all I'd been
pondering
Became abundantly clear
The reason she worked for hours
on end
She had a family to rear.

But soon the four tiny wings ceased
On soft petals rested mother and
child
With wing draped around her little
one
They stopped to smell the flower
for awhile.

As they resumed their task that day
My thoughts began to wander
To another busy working day
When side-by-side we worked
together.

Amazed, I'd watched and I'd
wondered
How a person so small as you
Could accomplish the tasks you
did each day
Awed by the things you could do.

Suddenly I noticed
The twinkle in your eyes
For while working by the garden
A hummingbird you spied.

You called for me to stop my chore
To come hastily and see
"Twas then we all became as one
The hummingbird, you and me.

I thank you for the hummingbirds
For special moments shared
'tween two
Because you took time to show me
that day
They'll forever bring memories of
you.

Diane Greco

WHAT LOVE CAN DO TO A PERSON

Assume that I were you and you I
and all I feel you would feel in the
same intensity
than you can understand some of
the many emotions that
break a person into hundreds of
pieces and it would
be like a jigsaw puzzle to put back
together
you would start with the border of
the puzzle
in the same respect with the one or
two emotions that
brought that person in to his or her
depression
once you have evaluated these
emotions you try to ask
the questions what, why, and how
come which is the
hardest part, the middle of the
puzzle
The last couple of pieces of the
puzzle are the
understanding of what, why and
how come then the
puzzle is finished and you can
understand me and I you

Geraldine M Lane

HIS LOVE

This poem is lovingly dedicated to my dear husband Wesley for helping and inspiring me—

When I awoke this morning, and
saw the sky so blue
I said thank you Lord for this day,
and thought of my love for you—
I thought of all the things I take for
granted every day,
My home, family, and many
friends who are near or far away.
The sun, the moon, and stars
above, such a lovely sight to see
All these things, God's own plan,
and He made them all for me—
He is so great and such a friend,
after doing all this for me,
He gave his precious son Jesus, to
die on Calvary.
So before I go to sleep tonight
again I'll look above
And say good night dear Jesus,
I sure do thank you for your Love

Rex Hucks

TO WALK AMID THE PLEIADES

To walk amid the Pleiades, a goal
I shall attain
And pursue them as Orion across
the astral plane

Seven waning sisters, the night
lights of the sky
Crying deep from loneliness and
silenced with a sigh

To walk amid these sisters is to
settle with a dream
An impossible task at first glance
or at least so it would seem

But I glance toward the stars and
the impossible I can do
And before my time is over, my
dreams will all come
true

I shall frolic with the sunlight and
swim in drops of rain
And walk amid the Pleiades with
the nymphs of Diana's train.

Agnes Amaral Manger

QUIET BEAUTY

This poem is dedicated to Ted, my wonderful husband.

Silently, silently
All through the night,
Gently, so gently
On an unsuspecting land,
Descend myriads
Of tiny snowflakes,
In patterns so lovely,
Each different from the other,
All a creation of art.

A glorious morning sun
Unveils the glistening sight,
Trees clothed in frosty ermine,
The ground blanketed in fluffy
down,
Jewels sparkling everywhere.
Oh, let me remember
When summer comes around,
This wonderland of delight,
This scene of unmatched beauty.

Teresa Rena Beck

AT LAST

Darling it's happening, Like I knew
it would
I'm falling harder, and it's all cause
of you
What did I do, to deserve such care?
In this old world, Such love is rare
I'm not complaining, nor doubting
it's true
Because I now realize, that I really
do love you
I tried at first, not to fall
Cause I've been hurt, and I've built
a wall
But now it's time, for that wall to
come down
You've come into my heart like a
thief, with no sound
I'm welcoming you, and true love
at last
So I'll do my best
to forget the past.

Alberta L Starrett

THE DANCERS

They play their little games
We know by many names;
They make their moves
with cool diplomacy.
We watch their mating dance,
That deadly damned romance
That's choreographed
for all the world to see.

We watch from little rooms
Which may become our tombs
If they should miss a step
or lose the beat;
While we just hold our breaths
And die our little deaths
Each time the dancers'
movements chance to meet.

The music's hard to hear
With shell-shock damaged ear;
The dancers lose the rhythm
now and then.
But still they struggle on
Their dreadful marathon
As we await the drum roll
at the end.

Brenda Mattice

THE MUSIC MAN

Hillside park surrounding natures
for joy,
Who's this I see, man or gay boy,
Oh yes such a man, playing banjo
and tune,
Children grab at his denium to
hear tales of the moon.

What a jolly round face with
auburn hair,
Pipe held tight with his teeth,
described him fair,
Carried a blue suede pouch,
hidden of sweets,
Singing old songs, children
covered benches and seats.

Best day for all, of course on each
Sunday,
Prayers to Jesus, never tips hat for
money,
A poor man he was, but proud as
could be,
Layed a tear in his heart, only I did
see.

Soon was a week that shortly
passed by,
No sight of him anywhere, I left
with a sigh.
What ever happened to our music
man?
Plays his banjo in heaven, leaving
memories again.

Etta F Fleischer

IT IS WHAT IT IS

For Hal—a true King

I can hum away the silence
As my key opens a saddened door.
I can keep my frustrated rage from

turning to violence
As my realistic brain reminds me that he is no more.
I can convince myself that never will there be another like him anyhow
As I count the months since I have been hugged or kissed.
I can tolerate the world's well-intentioned cliche to "live for now"
As I realize that I am Number One on nobody's list.

But what I cannot do
And what I will not do
As long as I am able to draw a breath
Is to keep silent when I'm told "at least he feels no more pain"
For then I must shout "BUT NEITHER DOES HE FEEL ANY MORE JOY!!!"

Why should I permit my agony to be used to glorify Death?

Lyle E Weelborg
DREAM

All alone at night,
I wait for sleep to come.
For with it, the dreams
Where I can wander the lands
and sea, the Heavens, Space.
I go far beyond the reach of any harm.
Mingling in my own mysterious madness.
I dance in the freshness of new Life, Freedom.
I scream until my throat is sore in fear.
Of societies' hateful ways.

Into my soul I searched one day
Finding it there at rest.
Quivering in a dream it lay,
I see all of me that is good.

From its dream it woke
With a terrible scream,
And from me it broke free.
With a single shot, burning,
It was gone from me.
Away to another World.

It and I were both finally . . .
Free———

Raymond C Schuck Sr
HOW MANY SUNSETS?

How many sunsets does it take, to make one realize,
the beauty of the long day's end, displayed in western skies?
How many sunsets does one count, in time, the world around,
to view in color, evening's end, forgetting daytime's sound?

How many sunsets are there seen, by millions 'round the earth?
Do they recall each twilight's glow, means another sunrise birth?
How many sunsets change the scene, with reds and purples—gold,
or raise your spirits, hold your breath, while heaven's clouds unfold?

How many sunsets can you count, where God has shown His hand,
to let you see His majesty, to grasp and understand?
How many sunsets reach your heart, inspiring every thought?
Do you appreciate their worth, the way you really ought?
How many sunsets, you may ask, reveal the hand of God?
To everyone the answer's there, when day begins to nod.
How many sunsets truly show, the rainbow's beauteous hue?
God's sunsets give the world this gift, for all, for me and you.

Jack R Gray
CRYSTAL TEARS

A crystal tear falls from the eye, gently splashing to the ground.
No noise it makes in falling; its arrival makes no sound.
Yet, through the tear the soul has cried its sad and lonely call.
What a tragedy there's no one there to hear its silent fall.

If eyes are mirrors to reflect the fragile human soul,
Then tears must be the measurement that tallies up the toll;
That measures all the sorrow interwoven through the years;
And oh my God they're costly, those salty crystal tears.

For they tell of lonely nights and endless empty days.
They speak of yearning broken dreams; of lost and unfilled ways.
They whiper sadness and despair the lonely heart must know;
The pain of missing someone—and how the pain can grow.

Oh, tell me why does life demand those precious crystal tears?
Why must they be the tribute life demands for mortal years?
The price is far too high to pay; the soul is unprepared.
It leaves it torn and broken, it leaves it stripped and bare.

Please, tell me is there not a place where tears are never known?
Does man deserve to spend his days where joy is never sown?
Oh cries the thought that's in my mind that casts its evil spell;
It's really true that God decreed that life shall be our Hell!

Ricardo Garcia

Ricardo Garcia
YOU LOOKED AT ME

To the woman I loved and lost but will never forget

You looked at me
And I thought I saw your soul reflected in your face
You looked at me
And you were warm and lovely as velvet and lace

You talked to me
And I felt that my life was again beginning
You talked to me
And my world was spinning

You kissed me
And Heaven and earth seemed to come together
You kissed me
And I knew that nothing could be better

You said good-bye
And Heaven and earth were not there anymore
You said good-bye
And my life was no more

JoAnn L Ballard
A TREASURE SO DIVINE

To Steven Charles, born December 15, 1986: We are all created equal, yet unique. Another of God's treasures.

He was close to you today
He watched your every move
He led you through so many things
Were they unbeknownst to you?

Perhaps you did not notice
The land beneath your feet
Or hear the voice of someone near
Who needed you to see

Did you see the day as it moved on
While you were standing still
A bird, a cloud, all heaven sent
To give your day a thrill

He works in many ways
To press upon our minds
How vast the earth and all it holds
A treasure so divine

God provides for all of us
You need to just reach out
He'll take your hand and lead you through
All that life is about.

Tammy R Knapik
SUDDENLY

For Pat Lawrence; with all my my love, T.R.K.

Your time came before I could tell how special you were.
You were there for me when I needed your ear
You made me happy when I was down, and somehow just by seeing your face everyday, it just seemed to brighten up my life.

Maybe I didn't say "Thanks" for the ride, or for your help,
or just "hello." But in my heart, "you" were "special" to me.

David Suddath
TIME

The ocean moves and splashes.
Roughly against the reefs. The black clouds move slowly.
The rain and lightning are strong.
The lightning strong, slowly clouds move away.
The vapors rise's and move slow.

Good-bye
We don't know the exact time!

Ramona J Griego
WITHERED WILL

Oh Withered Will
To And Fro,
In Yander Valleys Do I Go.
A Sullen Shadow Well Eyed,
The Sea And Ocean A Tear Cryed.
Oh Fragile Lives Withstand The Bold,
Hold Strength The Weak, No Fire So Cold.

Twas Not The Frost That Froze The Sea—
Twas Merely The Chill Inside Of Me.

Dorothy Kofoed
NEARER TO GOD

This poem is dedicated to my children. It was their love and support during troubled times that inspired me.

I would like to climb a mountain until I reached the very top
And lie there in the sunlight until the day has stopped.
While up there on the hillside so quiet and all alone,
I'd feel so close to God as if he were my own.
I'd ask him for forgiveness in everything I do.
I know that he will hear me the same as he will you.
Sometimes I may forget him and go my merry way.
But he knows that I'll come back, perhaps this time to stay.
It's funny what you think of as you lie and meditate . . .
Your whole life right before you, the things you love and hate.
Someday soon again that same mountain I will climb . . .
This time with love in my heart leaving my fears behind.

Gwendolyn K Newton
METAMORPHOSE

I am a flower now a tree.
Sometimes a grapevine taste the nectors of me.

I am pitty, hurt and pain
Mixed together a nasty thing.

I am happiness one feels
Suddenly a banana one peels.
Truth and fantasy day and night opposite subject, which is right.
I am the ocean roared by the winds to the sky
Sometimes so high I close my eyes

I'm a bird in the sky.
I am a pebble now a rock
Back to sand where does
Life really begin.

Cheryl Duke
I NEVER SAW

Winter
and I never saw the great white blanket that covers all the earth.
I never saw the melting snow that brings on muddy birth.
Spring
and I never saw the grass turn green under warming skies.
I never saw the buds burst forth from where the seedling lies.
Summer
and I never saw the sun beat down upon my lonely face.
I never saw the ships that sail in waters or a race.
Fall
and I never saw the greenery that turns so golden brown.
I never saw the leaves from trees as they're falling to the ground.
Life
and I never saw a person sit and gaze at a beautiful sight.
I never saw the moon's reflection off the waters in the night
Death
and I never saw a loved one dying slowly and in pain.
I'm only blind, I am not dead—
I feel things not in vain.

Judith Saladin
LET ME BE ME

To my daughters—in hopes they'll remember

Let me walk among men while I'm here on this earth
And be judged only by the toil of my worth,
Give me the courage to laugh, the courage to be strong
Let me not be ashamed to sing my own song!
Let me love and be happy, let me laugh and be glad
Let me be able to help the weakened and sad
Oh let me be able to help lighten the load
Of the unfortunates who walk the other side of the road!
Let me be able to share mankinds sorrows within
And keep in tune with the spirit of men.

Let me think intelligently, and with an open mind
Let me treat others with respect, and be kind;
Let me not judge others by the color of their skins
But only by what resides in the spirit of men!
Let me never speak the cowardly word quit
But give me courage, strength, and true grit!
And let me be strong enough to take the right stand
For only then God—can I call myself a man.
Don't let me whimper—but die as a man should
Then let me go—knowing I've done all I could!

Mary T Nooney
SOLITARY THOUGHT

A sigh escaped
from saddened lips
and would have died
a solo death

Instead transformed
into the wind
that rattles and
bangs my windows
in the blackness

And I must smile
(alone myself)
comforted by
a distant sigh

Betty Fredericks

Betty Fredericks
TANI

To Mr. & Mrs. James George & Family

We all loved Tani so much
To be in her presence was sheer joy
Her lovely smile, a simple touch
You felt like a child with a new toy
We'll miss that lovely face
That made a room light up
Her energy and pace
Like a new born pup

It's comforting to know
Each time we look at you
A little bit of Tani
Lives in each one of you

Alene Smith
DOUG

For my sister Inez, In memory of my beloved nephew, Doug

He was just a tiny baby when he came to live with me.
But oh, the years went by so fast; soon he stood
6 foot 3.
The day came when he told us he must go away
To serve his country for a year; he didn't plan
to stay.
So I smiled and tried to hide the tears when he
got on the plane.
I told myself, it won't be long till he'll be
home again.
Yes, I tried to keep the teardrops from falling
from my eyes
As I stood and watched him disappear somewhere
in the sky.
Oh, how we all missed him, and began to count
the days
Till he would be back home once more; yes, home
with us to stay.
But one day they came to tell us that our precious
son was dead.
Then the tears rolled down my face; the tears I
hadn't shed.
Still, even in my sorrow; I know that its not
true
Our son is gone; he isn't dead!
Lord, he just went to live with you!

Doris Graves Patterson
CHERISH

With love To my sister Carna, my daughter Darla & my son Patrick for standing by me through a difficult period in my life. Always Doris

Oh to be back, when I was young
To the years, when you and I first became one

Nothing could compare to the strength of our love
For the gift of each other, it came from above

A more beautiful thing, of this there were none
Because first we were two, and then we were one

So take heed, young hearts and listen to what I say
Enjoy what you have to the fullest each day

For you never know when it will be taken away

So give of yourself, with a big heart and a smile
Because God only lent you that love for awhile

Cherish each day as if it were your last
Soon there will only be memories and they fade awfully fast

Viola Jane Perry
TRYST

"Go sit alone," he wrote,
"And keep a watch for me.
This you shall say inside you, over and over,
Our two names, see then what comes."
I did. Even before the appointed hour I turned to him
In thought, for we could meet no other way.
I walked with him the paths we'd walked before
And thought what would be when we'd meet again,
But always back to over and over, our two names.
And then he came, I knew he'd come.
Out of my body I rose then, weightless as I had never been before,
Weightless and formless, merged with him,
Like some dawn cloud, meeting its kind
In infinite togethering.
The greatest peace and joy was with us then.
But as he left my heart cried out
That I should have to face my world again,
And he turned back, and placed the spell around me,
"Within the circle of my love you are inviolate."
And in his peace I slept.

Mary L Douglas
TENDERNESS

Tender lips, oh so sweet,
Tender eyes oh so kind,
Tender arms that yearn to hold you in the night,
Tender ears that hear you whisper tenderly,
Tender words of love meant only for me,
Tender love that will bring happiness
To we two.
Tender love that vows to last till
Life is through,
Words of love and laughter, always kind and true, but they come my darling from my heart direct to you.

Barbara J Weaver
I WAS BORN FROM THE SEED YOU PLANTED

I was born from the seed you planted.
A part of me, is you.
You have no name, no face, no history.
Your nothingness haunts me.

W Joseph Fogazzi
A CHILD OF THE KING

To my Lord and Saviour Jesus Christ

Oh, look at me and you shall see
A child of the King.

Oh, look at me and you shall see
A sinner saved by grace.

The lord reached down and touched me
For all eternity.

He's coming soon to take me home
And live eternally.

The word of God in all its pages
Foretells the plans he made.

That Jesus came and gave his life
To pay the price for man.

That grace abounds through faith in him
Salvation full and free.

Accept him now—live eternally
As a child of the King.

Pollyanna Nance Benedict
MY GARDEN
In my garden fairies whisper
As they guard the roses tall;
Come and see the things of beauty
Just inside my garden wall.

Down a moonlit path we'll wander
By the timid pansies' bed,
See the dewdrops' sparkling splendor
In primroses' blaze of red.

By the laughing, dancing fountain,
Nightly feasts the fairies hold;
Here they dine on dew and fragrance
From the daffodils of gold.

Tenderly the breezes lull, and
Through the haze of soft moonlight,
How enchanting is my garden
In the magic of the night!

As the soft and silvery moonbeams
Play upon the lily pond,
They reflect the sweet verbena
In its crimson flush beyond.

Hollyhocks of red and purple,
Standing very proud and tall,
Seem like Stalwart little soldiers
Guarding o'er the ivied wall.

Bette Rose Wagner
THE LOST SEVEN AMERICANS

This poem is dedicated to our 7 Americans who lost their lives Jan 28, 1986 on "The Challenger" Jarvis, McAuliffe, McNair, Onizuka, Resnik, Scobee, Smith

---

The days were being counted till you lifted off into space,
Your American friends stood on the ground with a smile on their face.
The moment of countdown came and you were off into the wild blue yonder,
Many Americans stood by watching and just had to wonder.
Where is this mission heading for out there,
Will it be riding all thru the open air.
Moments after it took off, a tragedy struck us all,
The "Challenger" burst into a fire ball.
The expressions on our faces, had shown fear,
Because we could not believe what we had to hear.
You "seven" will never know what happened outside your door,
Now you have all gone to be with the Lord, you will adore.
Here on earth, we will always look up into the sky,
Because many Americans will still want to fly.
To you "seven" you not only have made history,
But down here on earth, "The Challenger" will remain a mystery.

Deidra
NEED I CRY
Need I cry for the way I feel?
Do I pay the price for wanting love,
And is it so wrong to want you near,
Need I cry . . .

Need I cry for knowing what is
Must I lie, just to feel loved?
Can't you see the honesty of it all,
Need I cry . . .

Need I cry on fallen knees,
Is that what I must do to show
This feeling that's so warm with tenderness,
Need I cry . . .

Need I cry for failing, I know.
Can never forget the riches of loves,
And yet I'm me who hides it all,
Need I cry . . .

Need I cry for experiences I have
The holding of you, for but a moment,
Never to be looked upon from the heart,
Need I cry . . .

And need I cry, which could never be,
Never come about in ages
For it's my life, my love, my all,
That has made me as I am,
And indeed I cry . . .

Patricia A Stearns
OPEN YOUR EYES
Open your eyes world and look upon
Those small little children who just have no one

They live on the street, an old condemned building
Feeling that life is just not worth living

Their dying world, just dying I say,
And nobody's willing to show them the way

To give them their time, their love and care
To show them that some people are aware

Of those things happening to this place
The crimes, the violence, of the human race

So open your eyes, your heart and your mind
And show them that some people can truly be kind

Mary Ann (Malloy) Peer
TWO ROSES

To: My Rose and Inspiration

Two roses, that have grown together.
Two, that have seen the beauty of each other
And were showered with love
Know how sweet life can be.

Our love, like its delicate petals
Is very precious to me.
We share a special closeness
A bond between two roses
That will grow forever.

Two roses, that stand together,
Through all kinds of weather,

Always there for the other,
You sweetheart, are my rose.

You have touched me deeply
By your loving smile,
Your warm and thoughtful ways,
Your gentle touch and tender kisses.
Like the beauty of a rose
You leave me breathless.

Two roses, for two years of love
You have given me.
Two, for two hearts joined as one.
Just as the roses bloom each spring,
So dear, our love shall.

Lenore Schwartz
LIFE

To the memory of my wonderful Mom and Dad

To have been born and seen anew
All the pleasures of life, as fresh as dew
I ponder a thought in my mind alone
Of warmest of heart and love of home
As the years have gone by, I'm beginning
To see
What a miracle of life it is to be free
To obtain all your goals, to express what
You feel
A freedom of speech, which we needn't
Conceal
To exist in a world of which I am
Part
Is as beholden as a work of
Art

Ramona S Orozco
I WANT TO BE THERE
I want to be there to be your strength, not your burden.
I want you to be there to hold my hand.
Whatever comes into our lives, it doesn't matter.
As long as you love me as I love you.

As we go through trials and tribulations together,
We will conquer all,
Because the love we have for each other
Will make us strong.

I want you to be there when I'm troubled.
I want to be there to comfort you.
When the storm passes over,
We will have made it through.

I want to be there to see your smile.
I want you to be there to reassure me.
The obstacles in our way—
We can leave them in the Lord's hands
and we will never dismay.

I want you to be there when I'm confused and searching.
I want to be there when you're sad.
When the torment has passed over,
We will have won that dreadful battle.
Love will keep us together.

Margueritte M Pitts
MISCONCEPTION

To my daughter Marsherri the most beautiful rose I know

---

a rose is such a beautiful flower
standing so elegantly tall like a tower
when it's in full blossom
to look is breath takingly awesome
its magnitism draws you near
such a heart wrenching sight brings forth a tear
then impulse forces you to reach out and grab
suddenly you cry out in pain I've been stabbed
as you draw back with great speed
the rose takes on a new meaning indeed
still a beautiful sight
not at all fragile or without fight

Mike Schrum
AND NOW . . . THE WINNER
It was so calm but a moment ago
With the sun and the bright shining faces,
And that's when it started, the terror, it started,
The yelling, the panic, the races.

But what are they proving?
who's going to win?

The sirens are calling, the children are falling,
To be crushed 'neath the feet of the crowd.
The light was so faded, the moon was so jaded,
The daytime, the darkness did shroud.

But what are they proving?
Who's going to win?
And then came the teeth, so sharp and so white,
like streaks in their darkened black maw.
The moon was the tongue as it sat in the mouth,
And it watched the slow shut of the jaw.

But what are they proving?
How<u>can</u> they win?

And now see my skin as it burns to a crisp,

My flesh as it peels from the bone,
As they sit in their chairs and regret
what they've done,
The fault of the war is their own.
Yet nothing is proved.
No body wins.
And now . . .

Linda Hoover

A REASON

No one knew
Exactly why
She chose to take her life
A smiling face
Or helping hand
Revealed no kind of strife
Her grades were good
"She's very smart"
Said someone looking on
"So full of life
And energy
I can't believe she's gone"
A note lay silent
By her form
For anyone to see
The only explanation
Read
"Why weren't you proud of me?"

Susan L Ross Phillips

NIGHT SOUNDS

Branches are stirring
as evening winds call,

Crickets are singing
their evening farewell,

Rustling leaves
as the night creatures roam,

The hooting Night-Owl
as he hunts near his home.

A distant shrill whistle
of a train long gone past,

Are sweet sounds of the night
until morning is cast.

Zella Hancock

YOU DIDN'T TELL ME

Oh Mother, you went to Heaven,
I didn't get to say Good-by.
You didn't tell me you were going,
Why did you have to die?
There's so much I want to tell you,
I miss you so down here.
Just to share an hour now, with
you
would seem so very dear.
If I had known that you were going
there's so much I would have done.
At least, stayed right by your side
until your setting sun.
I would have told you how much I
love you.
I would have tried to make you
smile.
I would have held your hand, so
tender,
down that last long mile.
But Mother, you didn't tell me,
How was I to know?
Forgive me for things I didn't do,
before you had to go.

Ed Davis

A PATRIOT'S PLEA

The years have passed two hundred
Since the colonies guns had
thundered
And cries for freedom
Rang throughout the land
Those years of pain and toil
Have shown upon the soil
As you see the stains of blood
Upon the sand
As America gets older
Are these feelings growing colder
In our attitudes about
This land we love
I know many men who'd die
To look into the sky
And see a flag that flies
So freely from above
Let's thank God for being free
And what it means to you and me
To have a chance to choose
The life we live
So lift your chin up proudly
Sing your praises loudly
To freedom no other land
Can give

John W Dubrovin

A FRIEND

A friend is someone who really
cares,
Someone to trust with your secrets
to share.
Someone to depend on when you
need support,
Someone to give emotion comfort.
Someone who is loyal and in whom
you can confide,
Someone who is honest and to you
will not lie.
Someone who likes you for who
you are,
Someone who sticks with you
whether you're near or far.

Netta Winterick

A SINGLE ROSE IN A GLASS

To David

A single rose in a glass, its essence
fills up the room
She reaches out and gently,
caresses
its precious petals
Like a mother's love, tenderly
stroking
her child
She breathes in its essence and a
pleasant
thought settles in her mind
She thinks of the man, who
brought this,
pleasure of a rose. . .

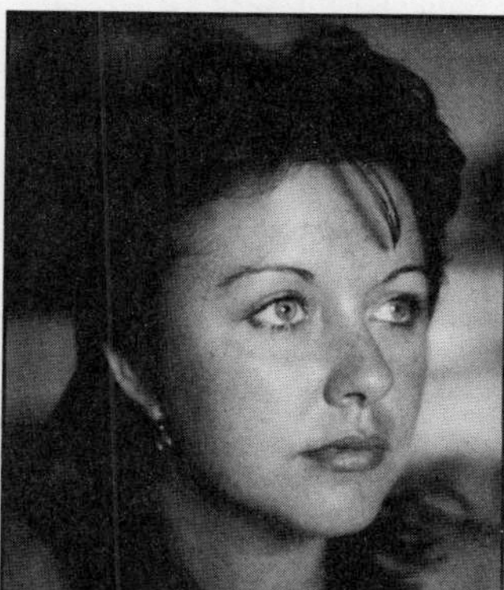

Lesley Anne Ife-Gerace

Lesley Anne Ife-Gerace

UNTIL ANOTHER DAY

To my husband Sam—no man's grass is greener than your own.

Parting will cause us great pain
and sorrow,
Do we act through the anger of
today
Only to grieve in our hearts
tomorrow?
If only time could be caught,
Maybe we would be given another
chance
Allowed to erase the battles we
have fought.

Life is so short and should not be
abused,
But we have done just that my love
Look at all the hours we have
mis-used!

We did wrong to each other in turn,
Lost love and trust, a gift from God
A lesson by this we hope we will
learn.

A different place, another time,
After many tears and much
learning
I pray the love we once shared will
again be mine.

J R Osborn

UNTITLED

To, of and for Dona

Dreams, Bright eyes, smooth skin.
Light caresses. Soft, warm lips
Sweetly tasted. Hers.

Encircling arms hold me.
Loving warmth enfolds me.
I see her bright eyes,
I taste her sweet mouth,
I feel her fingers moving.
I touch her.
Rough, ruined hands to soft, sweet
flesh,
She stirs. Caresses me in return.
Must be a dream.
I don't deserve this.

C Dian Worley Chambers

FLEETING MOMENTS

This poem is dedicated to Joe, my loving husband.

At fleeting moments in time,
Thoughts slip in the back
door of our mind.

The're glorious, the're grand,
both yours and mine.
The're as beautiful as
the mistic dawn;
And flit around on wings like
the illusive butterfly;
Here for a moment, then
they are gone.

Awe, for these fleeting moments
I do yearn;
And morn the passing of
those that never return.

Cindy Marie

LIFES PROMISES

To My Son, Peter Allen

Times go on and people change
Nothing ever stays the same
We try to cherish friends and times
lost
With feelings of lost loyalty as the
greatest cost
You build your life over for a new
beginning
With memories of old times in
your mind ringing
We teach our children how to be
true
But lack examples to compare it to
Just promises the future will be
better
You hope they won't remember
and think with a shutter
All the fights, tears, empty nights
and broken promises
Times the special someone wasn't
there to see special moments
May the future be better, happier
and brighter
We hope our walls won't become
theirs
And with their loved ones they'll be
able to share
Good times and promises kept
Fulfilling lives will be their safe bet
But without examples I'm afraid to
say
I pray the children won't lose their
way
Just try to touch as many people
with happiness throughout
your day
Better times, good futures and
fulfillment in life will
be your pay.

Joan Drury Bruhn

THE BLONDE

To Bob, who loves her.

She walks with grace and dignity,
That strawberry blonde hair
Flowing over her shoulders,
As if she were something special.

I have watched her from my
window
As she strolls leisurely
Around the pool,
Hoping the neighbors will notice.

She does attract attention
From almost everyone she meets,
Especially him.
She always gets what she wants!

On occasion, her demeanor
changes
When she realizes that it's him
Coming home;
Its just too hard to contain herself,
She barks!

Macil Jane Lee

UNDYING LOVE

I dedicate this poem to "Bob" who I am destined to love forever.

Oh tears! Thou cannot wash away
this everlasting love,
Implanted deep within my sorely
bruised and anguished heart
Which easieth not. I shall forever
weep!
The love I lost so many years ago,
To someone else, "for better or for
worse",
Will never in my lifetime be
replaced,
How bitter is life's path, my fate is
cursed!
Such ecstasy I'll never know again,
It's beauty I shall cherish and
revere;
I'll hide my grief behind a cool
facade
And try to face the bitter, lonely
years.

Lora Becker

SCARECROW

Tonight you roam the silent field
shrouded in snow.

A tractor lays still, on the edge near
the broken fenceposts
like the corpse of some frozen cow.
And the wind is light, almost
breathless—
you never notice how it follows,
slipping snow over your footprints.

Beyond the skeletal limits of trees,
something homeless is moving,
searching, or perhaps it is only
you, after all, cheered by your
echoing footsteps, or the shadow
at the edge of the field
you think is your own.

Beneath the moon's floodlight, a
wood cross leans
at the edge of the field.
Faceless—tattered denim rags and
matted straw
sag on rusted nails. The crow
perches at top
arching his wings, a black banner
silently unfurling.

Cold, clutching at straws,
you shudder.

Hazel Andrew Burdette

THE ONE GREAT MAN

---

*Our three wonderful children:
George William, Linda Carol and
Mary Ann*

Who made the bird?
Who made the bee?
Who made the land?
Who made the sea?
There is only one man
Who it could be
It is God—can't you see?

Who made the day?
Who made the night?
Who made the stars?
And the sun shine bright?
It is the same great man
Who gave us our sight
It is God doing all things right

Who made the flowers?
On the grassy lea?
And all the wonders
For everyone to see?
It's the one great man
watching over you and me.
It is God—can't you see?

Karen L Conner

A LOVE SO GREAT

---

*To my grandparents, Lane and
Elzada Boothe, for whom I wrote
this poem.*

A love so great
lasting through the years
all the trials and tribulations
the good times and the bad.

A love so great
carrying them through the
heartache
giving them dreams
bringing them new life.

A love so great
carrying them through their lives
knowing they'll be there for each
other
the eternal shoulder to cry on.

A love so great
giving them laughter
bringing them tears
being there to coax away the pain.

A love so great
it will last forever
past the last breath, the last
heartbeat
the final look passing between
them.

A love so great
carrying them through life
death will never end
the love that withstood the years.

Joyce Young Hargrove

TIDBITS OF PARADISE

---

*This poem is dedicated to my
parents, Marion and Ida Young.*

Pale starlets shimmering in a
cobalt sky
And breezes softly speak of coming
day;
From stirring of the jays in elms
nearby
There spills an early note that
seems to say—
In liquid tone, "The morning's
close at hand
Be watchful lest you miss its finest
hours,
When sunbeams will awaken all
the land
And dry the dewey droplets from
the flowers."
I wait expectantly the touch of
dawn,
When robins will be listening for
the sound
Of earthworm movements in the
dampened lawn,
Then hasting get their breakfast
from the ground.
I'm thankful that my God
prescribed to bring
Tidbits of Paradise in early Spring.

Angelique Marie Ronquillo

Angelique Marie Ronquillo

IF WORDS COULD SAY . . .

If words could say how I love you,
How much I really care,
The words would weave a golden
crown
For you alone to wear

And if you cut the strings
That with my heart you've bound,
All that was a kingdom
Will come crashing down

And all that's left behind
Is a never-ending sea
Of tears and emotion
And a fond memory

But then a glimmer of light
From out across the sea
Perhaps the king will return
To rebuild the joy in me.

And create a mighty fortress
Much stronger than before,
And the sea will flow with laughter
And love evermore.

Elizabeth M Boozer

EARLY MORNING SPLENDOR

---

*Dedicated to my daughter, Kathryn
Whittington*

The early Morning Splendor
You may read about,
You may talk about,
You may think about;
But to really know about
You must be about
Early in the morn.

Joshua H Reeves

WINTER

To my family, with love

In winter time, while snow falls to
the
Ground, I like to go sledding down
a big
Hill and iceskating on a frozen
pond.
Then when it is cold it snows, and I
Make fat snow men and have
treacherous
Snow ball fights. After we're done,
we
Go in and have hot chocolate. It
feels
very warm on my lips as I sit by the
Burning fire.

Kitty L Sudduth

ENDLESS LOVE

---

*To my Husband and endless
love—Lonnie*

In the darkness of the night
I found a light
The wonderful glow of your sight
Has awaken my need of flight
To be apart of your height
Forever this want shall be
For you and me.
To be deep inside this emotion
This endless greatness you make
me feel
Just seems to grow
Like the flicker of a candles glow
The depths of love
For you I will always know

Nereida Jines

GOD IS STILL ABOVE

---

*Dedicated to Terri Rosenthal for
encouraging me to send this poem
to you and to keep writing, also to
my family for standing by me.*

As I look above me,
The stars are all I find.

As I look around me,
This world is full of crime.

Some people are homeless,
Others sit and die.

All of us must suffer,
Dear God, What a crime.

If we all were equal
In hope and piece of mind,
Maybe those who suffer,
Will live well and fine.

And if those homeless Children,
Find in you the Love,

Then nothing seems hopeless,
When God is still above.

Donna Marie Larson

THE BLACK CHANCE

And once again, the shadow falls,
Bringing inside it a black chance
for escape.
The invitation lies there, constant
and unchanging,
The feelings remain.

The question being not one of how,
or why;

Only . . . when.

My soul soars with wings spread
Always flying too high and too fast.
Giving reasonable cause for my
frequent
And often, almost fatal, crashes.

But alas, there it is,
Hovering in the shadowy recesses
of my conscience,
Beckoning,
The last chance to take,
By chance one is born,
By chance one will die,

I will take the black chance,
Gliding into the softness of death
Taking with me the secrets that
shadow my soul.

Shawna Parris

FRIENDS

---

*Thanks to all of my wonderful
friends, you'll always be
remembered.*

Friends are always there
To help you and care
Through the sorrow and pain
Your friendship always gains
Through the laughter and tears
Your friendship lasts through the
years
Now that we're here at last
Let's put all the disagreements in
the past
Friends are there for you
To pick you up when your feeling
blue
Everyone needs somebody to be
there
To cherish your friendship and
care
Now that we're still the best of
friends
I'll be here for you 'til the end.

Tonya S Morgan

UNTITLED

You are with me only, in my heart,
mind and soul,
Yet you're not and I haven't you to
hold.
Do you remember the memories
that we've shared
Do you remember the times in
which we both really cared
Dinner, a movie, the love
afterwards,
The drive home, the kiss goodnight
The "I love you's" even during a
fight
I remember it all
Waiting at home, excited about
getting your call
Sure, we had our differences

But the love was still there,
Through it all!!

Robbi Lynn Lebeter
THE ROSE

The rose is a symbol of beauty and life
Its thorns, yet another symbol of strife
The delicate petals so soft and red
Yet one day soon this rose will be dead

The rose is tough, yet for some hard to grow
And yet it is always the rose that they sow
The rose is a symbol of friendship and love
Also a symbol of love is the dove

While looking for roses throughout your years
You must remember that thorns cause many tears
Don't spend all your time searching for this proud flower
For its life may be ended in less than an hour

The thorns of this beauty are stiff and grow old
But for the thorns of this flower many souls have been sold
For wisdom in life don't rely on the rose
For its only God who truly knows

Blessed be the flower that brings joy and pain
For souls may be lost and souls may be gained
Believe in your love as you trust in the rose
And soon you will know its the right path you chose.

Bessie P Beekman
YOU THINK I AM GETTING OLD

You may think I'm getting old, I've been around a while.
But that don't mean I'm getting old, just had to change my style.
I will admit my hair turned grey, I put on extra weight.
Had to give up jumping rope, and cleaning up my plate.
These wrinkles in my face you know, I earned them, every one.
For frowning when you disobeyed, and had a bee, bee, gun.
Or some other things I guess, like wading in the creek
Like bringing poison ivy home, that really made me sick.
And fighting on your way from school, with other kids you know.
Yes you could say I'm getting old, Go on it isn't So!
The things I hate are aches and pains, Just to name a few.
My body it is all worn out, But . . . I'm as good as new.

Josie Doty
OUR GOLDEN YEARS

Written especially for Paul and Stella Doty on their 50th Wedding Anniversary May 22nd, 1974

Fifty years ago today,
It was our wedding day.
A blushing bride,
A handsome groom;
We hadn't time,
For a honeymoon.
We had responsibilities,
Ours to assume.
Our Life wasn't easy,
We had troubles and woes;
Joys and sorrows,
As it comes and goes.
Seven children blessed our lives,
Four daughters, three sons,
Their husbands,
Their wives.
The children are all married,
And have homes of their own;
And once again,
We are home alone.
We have grandchildren,
Great grandchildren, too.
Before very long, we expect another,
Brand spanking new!
The sounds of laughter and tears,
Echo through these old walls;
As through our minds,
Our memories recalls;
Our children growing up,
The whimpering of their new pup.
We never dreamed,
That someday we would say,
Yes, we were married,
Fifty golden years, today.

Desa Irene Buerkle

Desa Irene Buerkle
THE FAMILY BIRCH

May His Holy Presence continue to dwell within the soul of each member of the Buerkle family to whom this poem is dedicated.

By means of the Holy Vow
Instrumental thou wert —
Sprouted the Birch —
Fertile became its roots.

Faithful to the creed—our ancestor's creed,
The homestead became involved
Not for greed, but for the
Patter of little feet—there on.

With joy they pattered—those little feet —
'Til the tree grew high —
Enormously high —
Not always up straight —
Occasionally a kink.

"Get rid of those kinks," they said.
"Erase the evil which eats from within.
The tree must remain intact,
'Til heaven, the members reach."

Marion Alice Fisken
DEAR MOTHER

In loving memory of Lizzie (Jones) Fisken July 9, 1901 — February 21, 1986

Somewhere beyond the sunset,
We shall meet again once more;
And in the land of eternal Spring
We'll meet those gone before.

Pain and Suffering, a thing of the past;
Nothing but joy to always last.
So goodbye dear Mother for a little while,
Someday I'll see the sunshine of your smile.

Until we meet again dear Mother
I'll miss you like no other.
But we'll not be parted anymore;
When we reach that Golden Shore.

Until then I'll commend you to our dear Lord's care.
May you his many blessings share.
God bless you and keep you forevermore,
Safe home at last on that Golden Shore.

Life's journey is over,
Your battles won.
You dearly earned your place with the Son.
God keep you and give you eternal rest.
With love from the one who loved you best.
And this dear Mother is just for YOU.
With all of my love, from me to you.

Peggy L Barrett
GRAZING

This poem is dedicated to Kitty and Patch, my two furry girls.

They're out in the garden
chewing on grass.

At a glance,
two cows are grazing;

Holsteins, grinding
cuds in a green pasture.

My call to come in
is ignored.

They prefer to frolic
and romp together.

Once more I call
them back to the barn.

Coming closer towards me, the cows
become my cats again.

Kenneth M Cross
RENEE THERESA

Oh splended child of the universe,
The sunshine warmth of your eyes
touched the hearts of all upon whom they fell.
And now the rapturous delight of your memory
echoes your presence through the corridors of my mind.
Filling me not with sorrow, nor despair,
but touching my longing heart with kindness,
comforting me in your special ways.
With each new dawn comes tantalizing thoughts,
reminding me of the totality of your love.
And with each new sunset comes the soothing realization
that I'm drawing ever near to your heart.

A.K.G.
DADDY'S GIRL

Daddy's little girl
Daddy's little girl
Daddy's little queen
Who never does wrong.

But where is Daddy now?
Oh, I guess he is gone.
Daddy's little girl
A lost little queen.

But life must continue on
No more tears can she shed.
The power of his love
Must carry her on.

Daddy's little girl
From a queen to a wife.
Daddy's little girl
From a queen to a mom.

Wife, mom and little girl
Miss Daddy's arms.
The power of his love
Must carry her on.

Mark Alan Ryan
—MESSAGE TO YOU—

This poem is dedicated to M.C.S. Forever

Treat me gently,
Treat me kind.
Don't shatter the emotions,
In my mind.

My hearts so true,
So please break through,
As fine as the early morning dew.
A feeling so strong,
Reaching for you . . .

I beg that you see it,
I ask that you feel it,
I hope you need it,
Please don't stick around,
Just to bleed it.

Tired of hurt,
Tired of pain,
Please don't leave me out,
In the pouring rain.
For my love for you,
Will make me insane. .

Without you,
Life is no gain!

Rose Marie Gauck
THE SEED OF FRIENDSHIP

The seed of friendship we have planted
has now fully grown
And blossomed into love our hearts have
never known
This love so true and beautiful was surely meant to be
And the good Lord must have blessed it
for you and me

The kind of love we've known before
has only brought us pain
And as we held each other while we cried
we brought the seed the rain

Together we've nourished it
bringing the seed the sun
We've helped it on growing strong
now our hearts and souls are one

Now has this flower of love we have grown
continues to grow
We'll give to each other the love we've needed so
We'll keep it true and beautiful
in our married life to be
And thank the good Lord for blessing it
for you and me

Dana Sprayberry

THE LIGHT OF LIFE

The light quivers, it has grown dark
It moves as if an insect, weaving through
My tears
All it does is move in and out, never
Stopping to help

Time has passed now
The light grows longer
Could this mean life

Doubling in size
Is it growing old?
I think I see a sign of life

Yes, it could be only the quivering, shattering,
Breaking of dreams
Tears, the quivering
Hope, the size

The only survivor is the light, growing
Longer
But as you can see, the light does not
Move

Sharon Valerie Birdsell

WINTER

It's winter again in the little eastern town,
And the leaves of autumn wear a great big frown.
The barn in the distance is so warm with it's sweet smelling hay,
With plenty in stock for a cold snowy day.
The lazy sheep is fast asleep,
And the tiny baby is close by her feet.
The pumpkins in the field are turning to gold,
And the once warm brook water has turned icy cold.
The bridge to my cottage will soon be filled with snow,
Where standing neath a willowy tree is a spotted baby doe.
Ice will soon cover the village pond, and the skater's will hurry out,
With hats, coats, boots, and mittens, and a great big shout.
This shout is one of joy my friend, for on this wondrous day,
It's peace and beauty does surpass in every single way.
The ice is gleaming and sparkling like diamonds, and the air is fresh and clear,
And in the distance the lovely sounds of winter are coming near.

Horace Young

NO ONE SHOULD DIE OF HUNGER

Why take the best years of their lives away;
When something can be done today!
To give our young ones the strength to play
No one should die of hunger!

Let's form a huge assembly line,
To get food to all those we can find.
And give ourselves some peace of mind,
No one should die of hunger!

Don't fret about race, religion, color or creed.
Reach out to those who are in need!
We have a lot of mouths to feed,
No one should die of hunger!

God wants us to use his land,
Let's show him that we will and can.
So brothers and sisters, Come Lend A Hand
No One Should Die Of Hunger!

Francis E Harris

Frances E Harris

OLD FLAMES

You're my knight in shining armor,
Thank God and Thank you Lionel.

You've ask what can I give you
you haven't already had
And how could I make you laugh
if I always made me sad
Well tell me how could I love you
and still say I'm free
Like how could I not be myself
but say that I am still me
Oh, I know there are lessons

I've still yet to learn
About giving of myself
and what I should expect in return
So go on and live your life
everyone has dreams
But if one day you find out
it's not as great as it seemed
And you need a friend sometime
when you've nothing new to do
You can count on an old flame
I'll be still in love with you.

Wanda Draisey

MY STAR

The clinging drapery of the night
Was velvet soft and warm
The glowing, lingering moon was high.
A tranquil mood was born.

The fragrance of the rose nearby
Was wafted clean and sweet.
I drifted with the Universe
And thought my life complete.

Then out the realm of time afar
But zooming now quite nigh
The brilliance of a shooting star
Flamed fast across the sky.

That flaming, sparkling, shooting star
Is you, My Love, My own
And life is now more beautiful
And I no more alone.

Marlene Ignatowski

THE LOSS OF MY MOTHER

Especially to Jeffrey Laigle and everyone at Storefront

Acid, Buds, and drinking, to name a few,
were my friends and also my daily crew
They didn't help I would discover,
to relieve the pain and loss of my mother,
She wasn't as important to my little brother Lee,
but she was everything, she meant the world to me,
I wish she could come back and stay right here,
so just like before, she could calm all my fear,
I need her so badly, you would never know,
I won't let you see it, I won't let it show,
No one can ever replace my one and only,
because I'd rather be alone, sad and lonely.

Patti Hills

Patti Hills

MOTHER—A SPECIAL CONFIDANT

To my sister Lisa, my friend and inspiration.

"Mom I have some news for you
That is very hard to tell,
But I can no longer put it off
I know that very well.

"Mom I have a baby
Growing inside of me right now,
And being only sixteen years
I need you to help me somehow.

"I know you've always told me
to wait until my wedding night,
But he and I are so in love
Everything felt right.

"Five months have now since passed
Since that special day,
And we plan to have this child
So please help us along the way.

"You and dad are the greatest
That I always say,
So please guide us as parents
In your very caring way.

"You're love and understanding
Will surely help, it's true,
And mom, I want to say
Thanks, and I love you."

Jenni Lynne

THEY DREAM

The feelings they share are the same.
They wish for the same dream
But for reasons they do not understand
they may never have what they dream for.
One dreams for her
The other for him
He makes her feel warm and safe
She makes him love and want her.
They will be together one day,
but for now they just dream.

Teresa J Maxwell

PEBBLES

Dedicated to my miracle children: Justin, Joshua, Sarah, Brentin, and Whitney

---

I have five pebbles in my hand
I found them washed up on the sand
One is very smooth and dark
The next is clear with tiny marks
One shines and glitters in the light
and one is small and very white
the very last one of all
is tiny, precious, and so small
the ocean gave to me these treasures
now they bring me lasting pleasure.

Penny Morgan

A HAND THAT CARES

There was a time not long ago
when I felt you were the one
that would take my heart and never let go
I felt love had finally come

But all you did was grab my heart
and bounce it like a ball
snatching the net out from under me
knowing I was going to fall

Now you stand accusing me
of the time we no longer share
well darling this is straight from the heart
I want a hand that cares.

Joyce Blanton Lindersmith
TRIBUTE TO BOBBY

With flashing sunlight on his hair
His love of life and joys to share,
We shall remember.
When it was football, he played fair
Accepting challenge or despair,
We miss him.
With sureness of purpose he climbed the peak
or fought with courage the right to seek
Equality among men.
His wit and wisdom and brave spark
Remain with us like a singing lark
To spur us on.
His plea for justice shall not cease
Carry his banner of fairness and peace,
For love of country.
His hopes and dreams shall linger on
Hold high your head with prayerful song.
He dwells with God.

Lynn Bradley
NASA

They loaded on the shuttle,
As they took off in the sky:
We wished them a safe journey,
As we said our goodby.
At last it took off—
A tragic—real bad!
Left everyone on Earth,
Feeling so sad.
Six Astronauts and a teacher, too,
Went above the stars to explore the new.
NASA Research Plant tried their best.
They worked day and night—never had much rest.
They tried their hardest to make it new,
They were for sure it would have flew.
The next shuttle left off,
We're sure gonna try,
Because the next shuttle is definitely,
Sure gonna fly.

Lloyd A Gilchrist Sr
DADDY'S GIRL

You're like a great big piece of Heaven
in an ordinary and gloomy world
You're like Christmas every day
and you're mine, you're Daddy's Girl.

You're my lovely, lovely, daughter
and the center of my world
I am just a plain, ordinary Oyster
while you are the Cultured Pearl.

For you see, a Cultured Pearl is lovely
and to you it does compare
and I wish you were still in my cluster
instead of being over there.

Heck I thought you wouldn't miss me
when you'd leave to go out on your own
but I guess, even a Cultured Pearl
does remember it's humble home.

You now have a jewel of a husband
and your own little precious Pearl
but you always must remember
to me you'll be, "Daddy's Girl".

Mary Lou Nance
THE PAST

We all dream of years gone by—
Especially the old
They remember pleasant things
Stories never told!

The happiness when they were loved
And looked their very best
But when you're old and wrinkled
Youth would not have guessed.

Look to the years, when they were young
And worked so very fast
But youth today— cannot convey
To look into the past.

Very soon the youth of "now"
Will be the "old" of then,
They'll look back remembering
For it's the fate of men!

Alice Switzer Bierman
I AM NOTHING

I am nothing but a grain of sand
In the hourglass of time.
Brief moments of victory lift me out of the stream
To heights that are sublime,
But the fleeting feeling of ecstasy
Is gone all too soon,
I am plunged back again into the shifting sands —
A mere grain in a giant dune.

Julie Everts

Julie Everts
JOY OF CHRISTMAS

May Christmas bring, Peace, Joy and Love, filled with Forget-Me-Nots, world over and all planets throughout Universe.

Christmas joy filled
our hearts with love.
With lingering memories
of our past, ties of Forget-Me-Nots, upon each branch of our
Christmas Tree.

Ethel L Taylor
FROM YOUTH TO AGING

This poem is dedicated to my beloved grandmother (Mary L. Wilburn) deceased 1-85 at 105 yrs. young. My parents: Sarah & James Taylor and Eddie Lou Cole, Poetry Editor of World of Poetry. All persons everywhere: Readers of "From Youth to Aging"

From creation to birth
From mother's womb to father's hand
Upon this earth and life's path
A universal journey over many lands
Heavenly father, protect us as we grow
From the cradle of a babe to a little child
Dependence upon parents and their trusting smiles
Heavenly father, guide us all the while
A continuing journey across the miles

Entering a hemisphere with changeable atmosphere each day
An adult, with wisdom and guidance of yesterday and today
Our heavenly father, provides along the way
Rememberance of others and life thus so, I know he is with us as we go
Seeking and asking, love and blessings, like a knock upon the door

Now growing older proudly and steadily
Memories are many, may our thoughts be ever gay
While growing older, may our heart be pure and our soul ready
No malice told, no hatred to unfold but faith, we must behold
Heavenly father, should he come tonight, we'll greet him with delight
Throughout this universal journey, our paths guided by a constant greater light

Mrs Geraldine Sexton
ON THE MOUNTAIN WHERE MY DADDY PRAYED

Dedicated to my Father, Rev. John Adkins, with love, for his prayers upon the mountain.

On the mountain where my Daddy prayed
It seems now so far away
The mountains so high they seemed to touch
the sky, On the mountain where my Daddy prayed

About the mid. hour of the day
We would hear our Daddy say
I've got to go up on the mountain
and pray my sins away
On the mountain where my Daddy prayed

His prayers would echo far and near
Upon a little coal camp so dear
He would praise the Lord, with his eyes
filled with tears.
On the mountain where my Daddy prayed.

It took a lot of steps to climb that mountain
But each one was in Jesus' name.
He prayed for his wife, and he prayed for his
children.
On the mountain where my Daddy prayed.

Reid Howard
THE GARDEN

Firelit skies where birds, butterflies and
leaves lend to wishful dance,
Where spirits rise too and eyes lift up to view
the red orange blazing blasting blare
that rips and splits the ever darkening blue
into fragmented scraps for me and you.
Mother moon slides silkily in place
revealing the children of her love—stars
that call playfully to hearing hearts from above.

Soft sexy slow breezes billow about
the slippery ink black seas then—
hasten on to clothe you and me.

Warm are the fires the cool breezes fan
Soft are the eyes of a woman for her man
wild the beat borne in his breast
for the she-child gives him no rest—

(He) "You are my torment, my pain—my pride."

(She) "I am your love, borne in the breeze."

(He) "You are my woman, my rib—my bride!"
(She) "I am your love, born earthen, easily pleased."

Joyce Stites
TELL OF HIS LOVE

My loving family

I walk by my saviors side
He sent me from above
To fill the lives of mom and dad
and tell of His love
And God's own hand is laying
His peace on everything
Thy lays in Heaven.
The love is on the earth
Love give it energy
Love gave it birth
Fill the lives of sons and daughters
and tell of His love.

John Michael Moore
DISTANCE, I SUPPOSE

Faintly she was there, but with the wind she drifted away.
How many times and how strongly he felt, really didn't matter—
That he knew and kept it inside.
Seeing with the mind differs from flat-out-spoken-words.
Because words land—splat!
And cannot be taken back.

She comes and goes, that sunbeam?
With the breeze and sunrise— above from the clouds, I suppose.

But he knew and knows along, he would see her again.
To look upon her beautiful elegance, seeing against a blue sky, a golden ray—
Connecting the heavens, touching to ground below.
A vision of beauty in his own mind, because of a sunlight far, far away.
He once saw her suddenly!
But she is there now no more.

Where had beauty gone, that sunbeam?
With the clouds and setting sun—in the distance, I suppose.

Using the wind she painted the sky in that colorful way,
That sunbeams do, to hold your eye in dazzling splendor—
She danced and played, peeking through holes as though she were a living soul.
She is such a masterpiece!
Herself a work of art, when she wanders,
There will I wander too!

Why did she wander, that sunbeam?
Behind the distant horizon—to paint another sunrise, I suppose.

Eric Carlson
THEN, NOW, AND BEYOND

When I was four
My friend was Tim.
We played Star Wars
I really liked him.

But those days have passed
And BMX is my thing.
I know I go fast,
I hardly ever finish last.

I need one more first to qualify
From Novice to Intermediate.
When I finish in first the other riders shout with glee,
Because now they can win without worry of me.

I race the track at Oshkosh,
I've gone to Janesville too.
My count of medals and trophies
Amounts to twenty-two.

When BMX season is over,
I have another sport.
For football season begins
And we hope for many wins.

The time is coming near
When I must choose a career.
I don't know what I'll do,
But I'll probably go to the "U."

Charles O Barnett
OLD WAR

It seems, old war, that your thirst for life will never end.
Since the recording of time you have stalked the lands,
Like a hungry animal looking for its prey.
Seeking and searching from sea to ocean, from one continent to another you've traveled.
There is no place upon earth that doesn't know the smell of your breath,
Or the stench you leave afloat throughout the air of your path.
You have left your scar upon many souls
Cursing their minds for eternity
Planting hate within their hearts
And during your journeys through time, I wonder, old war,
How many eyes have shed a tear
'cause you've taken away
Some precious, irreplacable part of them
And still today, as I look upon the setting sun,
I know somewhere the soil of the earth soaks with your blood,
And I can only hope and pray, that not I alone, old war,
Can feel your presence feeding on mankind,
Standing over it watching . . .
Waiting for that final day to devour him forever
And that which remains of you, old war,
Alone it shall stand
In the mist
Of the battlefield.

Garnet S Alsterberg
CHRISTMAS

Millions of people rushing from one shopping center to another—
Millions of people spending a lot of money to satisfy material desire—
Millions of people living in their own small world.

Millions of people starving and crying—
Millions of people suffering on Christmas like on every other day—
Millions of people not knowing what Christmas is.

Millions of people being able to help—
Millions of people forgetting about the poor and lonely—
Millions of people enjoying Christmas as it is because they have the power to forget.

Millions of people not being able to forget the misery they live in—
Millions of people who need love and help not only on Christmas—
Millions of people being so dependent on the people who just forget about them and who live with their eyes shut.

Angela Jill Inzer
ANDIRONS

There they sit by the fire
Cast iron
And porcelain.
As alike
As desert
And ocean
Blinding white desert sand
Midnight
At the ocean's
deeps
There they sit by the fire
Black marble
and
Fine china.
A pillar of stone
or
An Oriental passionflower
There they sit by the fire . .
Ninja
and the snow queen
Black panther
and
Albino fire

Ann Coyle
THANK GOD FOR TODAY

You must not worry or fret or care
But look for the sunshine here and there
Do not turn back to the days gone by
For God is so good to you and I
He has given us much for our daily fare
Where would we be if He didn't care

So what, if the days gone by were hard
If we lived them well, we will merit reward
And they lay a path for our future walk
And we'll be given the help if to God we talk
And every day if we've done our best
The Master of all will give us rest

Accept in faith the time He'll give
Accept and pray and relax and live
With family and friends and a world of love
Give thanks each day to our God above
With work gone past, He has strengthened you
For the future work that He wants you to do

If your troubles down here are hard to bear
Thank God you're chosen to help people care
If you were the master who picked the crew
If they fell by the way—just what would you do
So with all your faith and hope and love
Thank God for today, your gift from above.

April K Jones

April K Jones
STILL LOVING A DREAM, WHO'S ONLY A MEMORY . . .

To my special grandmother, Anna C. Jones, who went that extra step to help make a dream come true.

Falling in love with you was only a dream,
or so I was told —
But before long, that saying grew old.
I finally let my feelings show to you —
Well, actually, you read me straight through.
I could understand you quite well
and you me
And our friendship was the best as far
as we could see.
But soon you'll be gone, 'cause all dreams
must end —
Hopefully one day you'll be back again.
Our lives will go on, once we've gone
our separate ways
But just for a moment I'll remember those
special days.
The ones we spent together, talking all
the time,
Saying how much we cared—letting our
friendship shine.
Back to reality I seem to drift in
You're just that dream—never to be back again.

Kitty Escoe Cohen
VERSE FROM A GRANDMA

A rosy baby lobster was swimming in the sun
He came right up onto the shore to have a little fun
He crawled close up to Ava "I'd like to play with you"
Ava's "yes" made Bennett turn, "who are you talking to"
"oh, Bennett see the lobster, his shell so shiny red
Do you think if we play with him he'll snap at us instead"
"no, Ava, I think he is lost—but do not take his hand
Just let him stay and watch us build a tunnel in the sand"
Soon they tired of digging and took lobster for a swim
And there they found his mother looking all about for him
She clutched her baby with her claw, he did not say a word
When the children said goodbye to him as if he had not heard
"Bennett was it magic when the lobster spoke to me"
Bennett smiled at Ava, "there are such wonders at the sea"

Willie Mills
WHOSE DELINQUENCY

We read in the papers, we hear it on the air,
Of killing and stealing, and crime everywhere
We sigh and we say, as we notice the trend,
This young generation, where will it all end.
But can we be sure, it's their fault alone?
That maybe a part of it isn't also our own?
Cause kids don't make movies and they don't write books
That paint a gay picture, of gangsters and crooks
They don't make the liquor, and they don't run the bars
They don't make the laws, and they don't buy the cars
They don't make the drugs, that addle the brain
It's all done by older folks, greedy for their gain
It's far too many cases, we find this to be true
The label delinquent, fits older folks too!!

Sally Loraine Hite
CHILDREN NINE

With warmest thoughts of you in mind. Johnny, Sonny, Christi, Jean, Danny, Joe, Bob & Katherine

The Children Nine as we were strong
of knowing where we belong
And now where have we gone.
A little here and scattered there;

Don't seem right to us.
"So Fair" The God laid path when
we were born,
Given tattered, given torn.
Do we dare look behind that door,
Where children weep and children
mourn.
Oh, Yeh, I say, open that door
If only to understand more.
Of love you were made,
Not that of hate.
Of life you were given,
With that first breath you take.
Let go of that anger,
You have in your heart
and replace that with kindness,
You've had from the start.
In living and learning and
compassion a must
"Oh come on, you won't bust."
Your seed is young and beauty deep
As you and I are very unique,
Of Children Nine, do I speak.

Ruth Kaysing McKeg

GOD'S LOVE

Three little blue birds living in top
of a tree
Papa bird, mamma bird and baby
bird makes three
One day baby bird said, "I want to
be free
I want to see in the top of the other
tree."
Then the next day she flew away

Mamma Bird and papa bird
followed her all the next day
But they did not worry they knew
she had gone away to stay
And some day she would find her
mate.
Then there would be more blue
birds to take her place.
That is why God does things in his
mysterious ways,
So this great earth of his would be
filled with blue birds
Always.

Lydia Resta

WHAT IS LIFE

To Tere, June, Anthony & James—To all my loved ones

What is Life?
Some joy and some laughter
Some sorrow and tears
Praying for courage
To fight all those fears
You're so full of love
As you walk in the sun
Then it's dark and it's lonely
when day is done
Yet I will not despair
If there's no one out there
Because Dear Lord
I feel very close to you tonight
I am content! I have found
happiness
in your love

D A Deistchle

DREAM

It started as a dream, a joke, a
thought that came from
the dark deep parts of my inner
soul.
Only parts came to me in deepest
sleep and dreams of
tenderness, but yet I weep.

A special part not in its place, and
a love with no face
A haunting dream from night to
night, and yet I seek
not to fight.

This love with no life has no
substance and no price
But takes the total of my life.
This the dream sent to me of a love
that soon will be,
And the angles on mountains high
will come to share
Their love with us in time.

Then the dream will come to pass
for our love will
always last.
She the woman of my life sent from
God to be my wife
Then the patience always shone,
will lead the way to our
new home. And the tears that seem
to fall shine a light
through distant halls.
Then to sleep and cry no more until
a son: Both Re-born.

Vanessa Edmonds-Watson

PERFECT LOVE/BOUNDLESS LOVE

IF I gave you my heart on a silver
platter,
what will you give me in return?
I would ask you to accept mine
in return,
so that you would know without a
moment of doubt
how much I love you.

IF I allowed you to really look
inside my mind,
what would you search for?
I would look for all the beautiful
ingredients
which makes you and your love a
priceless recipe to me.

IF I opened the doors to my soul,
how far would you travel?
I would journey with you
until the end of time.

IF I gave you my love,
what would you give me in return?
I would give you a love so strong,
it would surpass even the end of
time.

Jan Stuckey

DEAD WHITE CAT

A dead white cat lying beside the
road
Is just a cat, nothing more, I
suppose.
Car after car drives on by
So why, of course, shouldn't I?
After all, cats are not people and
everyone knows
If that cat were a person on the side
of the road
We would stop, each one of us, I'm
certain
If we saw, lying beside the road, a
person.
My car moves on, I've done nothing
wrong
And a dead white cat lying beside
the road
Is just a cat, nothing more, I
suppose.

Mary Wallman

WHEN MOTHER WASHES CURTAINS

The squirrel scurries from rooftop
to treetop
Balancing his bungling body along
The cold, yet still unfrozen,
telephone wire.
The squirrel free as the world he
lives in,
The world outside the window.

Her face presses against the
windowpane,
Blue eyes brisk enough to pierce
the shield
Restraining her. Innocent breath
emanates
From her tender pug nose and
settles
On the glass, threatening her view
Of the world outside the window.

Tiny fingers fight to smear away
intruding frost,
Struggle for one last glance at the
tantalizing world.
Larger fingers overrule her will,
hanging curtains
Stiff and unstained as the world
she lives in,
The world inside the window.

George Mayer

ONE HUSBAND'S PLEDGE

I'll seek and find a noble aim
In all you say and do,
Your wishes I'll anticipate
No motive misconstrue.

I'll take up all your cares and woes
And bear them all with cheer'
And when essential classes loom
I'll yield without a tear.

If harsh remarks (forbid the
thought)
From you should ever slip

I'll answer with a mild reply
Or button up my lip.

In thought and word and every act
Faithful to you I'll be
My confidence, full and complete,
You'll always get from me.

And as Prince Charming of your
dreams
Your flag I'll proudly wave
Atop the peak you'd have me reach
Your love I'll always crave.

Diana M Panizzon

THIS THING CALLED LOVE!

It was said long ago, in yesteryear,
That love would come, without a
fear,
To every single girl in store
A man would come knock at her
door.
But doubts have been raised about
this snow white dove
Who is said to bring this thing
called love.

Love is a virtue we know is true
But many hearts have been broken
in two
For something we cannot touch
nor see
Yet it comes to some so
desperately.
Deserted hearts have gone astray
Hoping to find love one day.
But how can we find something so
fleeting
Something so real, yet many times
deceiving.
And where do we find this snow
white dove
Who is said to bring this thing
called love?

William Robert Leeson

MY MOTHER

Dedicated to my loving Mother, Joyce Ann Bane Leeson Seymour

Thank you, Lord, for giving me
A good life and family,
And for all those good times I had,
Thank you, Lord, for Mom and
Dad.
But the one who's closest to me
Is my wonderful Mother, for you
see,
I often think and then I recall
That me and Mom have been
through it all;
And thank you, Lord, for my sisters
and brother,
But especially, dear Lord, for my
loving Mother;
If it weren't for her I don't know
what I'd do—
When things were rough she'd
always see me through.
I've heard bad things about her—
Things that people say.
But they don't know her like I do
Or they wouldn't talk about her
that way.
I know I lack in showing her
All the things I could—
How much I love and care for her
And all the things I should;
I know she cares and loves me, too,
So here's how I'll thank
her—MOM, I LOVE YOU!

Darlene C Schwefel

WHAT IS HAPPINESS

To my friend—Laverne Smithmier, who always enjoys my poems and gives me confidence to keep writing them.

Happiness is a smile
Or someone shaking your hand
It means someone to listen to you
Or someone to understand.

That certain special someone
Either a he or a she
Is something very important
Very important, indeed.

For everyone needs someone
To help in leading the way
In helping someone else in turn
To keep from going astray.

It really does not matter
What language they speak
Because kindness and
understanding
Is a universal thing.

It only takes a smile
Or a shaking of a hand
To let you know that someone
Is there who understands.

A gentle hand upon ones shoulder
Helps the feelings, all come thru
That if it weren't for a Friend
There would go Happiness, too.

David Jason Zoloto
BALL OF YARN
The tendency for things to unravel
wrapped red in thread
is a ball of yarn, bleeding and kinetic.
The same tendency
in gray clay
is the earth or
the hand of a defeated potter.
Gradual tendencies:
arthritis of the soul and the
syncopation of sad requiems
like moonlit awakenings
to think of someone far away.
And far away, emotions lay flat between land masses
and arise in vertical mountain voices.
The nerves of human heavens are touched
with the scalpel of the past, and it frightens
the green bird, who only wants to wade
in fresh sun streams.
Cradled tendencies pierce the whiteness
crying out for the ovens of justice;
but who now can harness the
tendency of the falling dominoes?
There, that boy.
He is wearing a red sweater.
It is the fulfillment of many tendencies.

Louise V Boyd
BEDTIME THOUGHTS TO MY GROWN-UP "LITTLE ONE"
The hour has come when through the house I go,
Doing all the chores to put the house to bed,
And as I pass your door
I pause to look inside.
All your things are in their place.
Your bed remains untouched.

You cannot know my soul as I stand there
Thinking of you, my "little one,"
Now grown up and gone away.
I wonder how you are,
And if your day was happy.
Were the people you met good to you,
And were you well today?
Do you know a funny story we could share?
Or do you have a heartache
I could ease if I were there?

My eyes grow heavy with a tear.
Take care, my "little one."
I love you still. Good night. Good night.
I love you still. Good night.

Regina M Coates
WAKING AN OLD HOUSE
We came across an old house
That had fallen fast asleep
Not even the scampering of a mouse
To wake it's slumber deep

So sound asleep in neglect,
Breathing loudly of decay,
Only a short time to reflect
My dreams of another day.

Wending from room to room,
Helping to wake up a home,
Rubbing it's eyes dispelling the gloom
As the thrill to new beauty shone.

A painted coat of snowy white
And shutters grassy green
The paling fence erected right
A gate for you to lean.

Inside the door a shiney floor,
Walls all papered with cheer,
Dim lighted lamps and busy scamps
Made heaven seem quite near.

Jeanette I Dotson
THE MIRACLE OF DREAMS
Dreams are where all miracles begin
Shut behind closed shutters within,
Hidden from any and all human eyes
Either drowned or dead or in a disguise
But will like the Phoenix one day arise,
They're wishes on wings that carry our thoughts
Which wander inside like ghosts on a haunt,
Though tacit and unheard by all other's ears
The image is quite vivid when your heart is your mirror.
Dreams keep the spirit lifted and alive
While faith and hope glide along with sheer drive,
And as seeds dance on the waves of the wind
Our dreams visit places where we've never been,
In constant search they ramble and roam
Then land and nest in a nourishing home,
To one day mature and one day come true
That's the miracle of dreams
Which are found inside you!

Russell D Hudson
WHAT IS LIFE?

For Bill, his family, my family, and everyone who feels the pressures of life.

What is life?
This long and painful stay
On a torn and tattered planet
Until we're wisked away
What is death?
The freedom from the repetition
Of battles fought and wars won
And the trial of competiton
What is life?
The question that we've all been asked
And only when we'll understand
Will the answer be unmasked
Life is to me
As a ball is to a child
And with these eyes, can I see
The ways to tame the wild
The ways to right the wrongs
The ways to see the light
And bring the goodness from the souls
Of the darkness and the night
This is life
But why?

Jeanette M Galbraith
ODE TO A SPECIAL AUNT

This poem is dedicated in loving memory of my dear aunts, Sally C. Skibinski and Rose A. Para. Elmira, MI

It's been a while since you left this town,
(you said you would).
Your house sits silent,
bursting with memories.
I wish you could come out and talk,
I have so much to say.
Only stillness fills the air.
Reality can be a thorn
but you left a ROSE.
The ROSE withered then reblossomed in God's glory.
The air is filled with fragrance.

Jo Roe

Jo Roe
INDIAN SUMMER

To my God, my family and my friends, The greatest support system I could have.

Indian Summer—
Actually a part of the fall,
Reminds us God is in control;
Not conscious of time as we are.
We would hurry the sacrifice,
And get on with our lives;
See that leaves turned on time,
The way Big Ben in London chimes.

The stillness—
Time for thought and values,
Filling in the vacuums,
Slow hard-working processes,
Can be our friend; time out to mend.

Spaced by God alone—
Then He lets us know
The quickening of the soul;
Making up for loss.
Joy comes as flood;
The bodyguard of God
Arrives in perfect time! Amen

Barbara Sharik Babb
THE SECOND MARRIAGE
The second marriage
Is a time of mending, a period of blending.
It's more than bodies meeting and minds greeting.
It's a changing scenery like replanting hot house greenery.
There's the giving and take the adjustment must make,
Demanding more, expecting less; a certain wariness.
It's being strong with less emphasis on who's wrong.
It's re-education conclusion, living without illusion,
Like looking reality in the face, growing older and tireder with grace.
This time love is more intense, yet taking less offence,
Like being more considerate, yet quietly desparate.
Unfair, but always there, trying hard to never compare;
It's a daily repast, daring to hope this time, love will last
But showing no surprise if it too dies because this time you're wise.
It's laughing with meaning while creating fantasy from shattered dreaming.
It needs kindness most of all so as never to recall
Words that cause pain, that can't be forgotten again.
Along with bridal lace there need be breathing space.
And as understanding encompases on a daily basis
The period of adjustment flows and hopefully love grows;
Gathering strength to keep promises made while letting the broken past fade.
It's the time of blending, the period of mending,
The love of life, of man and wife,
That either makes or breaks
The second marriage.

Pam Smith
DOGS

This poem is dedicated to my husband Mike, and his encouragement, my friend Rowdy, the best dog ever.

Dogs are God's creations, it doesn't matter much, that all the time they lie, around not doing very much.
They're dedicated creatures, who share your hopes and dreams, always with you joyfully.
And sorrows too it seems.
One look it takes to realize, the company they are, they follow right behind you, not going very far.
Young or old, or short or fat, all they need is one good pat.

A walk at night, and to be fed, a nice firm stroke upon the head.
Outside to play, and then a walk, also to listen while you talk.
A friend indeed is a dog, they love to lay down or take a jog. Indeed they are creatures that God made for us, they require not much, and really don't fuss.
A lick on your face, a paw on your hand, make dogs the best animals in all of this land.

Connie Complitano

A BUSINESSMAN'S PRAYER

To Robert P. Romano, President and to Comus International.

I wake up each morning and look at the clock. The
first thing I think of is loading the dock. . .
With switches we're making day after day, by Friday
the orders are well on their way.
Now who will be early and who will be late and who'll
call in sick 'bout a quarter to eight.
Machines are all humming, the fires are bright, a few
real big orders will make the day right.
A couple of hours have just passed on by, I look out
the window and say with a sigh. . .
"Oh here comes the mailman" now what will it be
a dozen more bills or a check just for me.
The time goes by quickly and now it's that day,
Quite often I worry about having their pay.
The week is now over and all's said and done. I look
all around and I feel that I've won.
Equipment and people, the orders and such, are all
part of me 'cause they mean oh so much.
At night when it's over I pray and I pray, all this
will continue day after day.
Employees and customers know that I care. . .
And all this to me is a
"Businessman's Prayer."

Virve Joks

. . . LIKE THE TREMBLING HEART OF A CAPTIVE BIRD . . .

Melted midnight blue
as the violin pierces my chest,
strikes its sound into my soul
like an arrow.

The arrow is aflame.

I am put in motion—slowly, gently,
through the spider-web dream
my eyes see myself wrapped in
the chords of the song.
I sip it slowly—lingering,
the words make me collapse in
a willow of emotions.

And it moves me, literally.

My soul is overpowered by the disk,
I go around, around, around,
with the needle scratching,
ripping my skin.
The violin bow playing my lashes.
My hair is a B flat.
I vibrate—hold the tone
until it loses its breath and oozes into the needle.
I shiver and dance through the grooves,
become my shadow.

I become a dark, outlined movement.

Lynne Anne Meany

SHALLOW ENCOUNTERS

Butterfly, butterfly, so daimonic and free,
Will I ever capture thee?
You dart and drift over many a flower,
imbiding their nectar with a whimsical power.

Oblivious to the shadows your wings have cast,
the tempo of your frenzied flutter is too fast.
Never do you lament the tedium of your transient bliss,
nor regret the estrangement of your hollow kiss.
Butterfly, butterfly so afraid to fear,
will you ever shed a tear?

Edith V Despres

AIMLESS MUSINGS

Someone thinks I show small talent
In a literary way
Never tried to write a story
Wouldn't know what to say
Thought I might try writing
Something. . .sort of
make-believe
But in my search for proper diction
My half-formed ideas. . .leave
Thought I might try writing
Something true. . .or mostly so
Citing some of the things I do
The places that I go. . .
But I don't like to share my secrets
With people strange to me. . .
So guess I'll just forget my talent
And remain a. . .nonentity

Cindi Ann Jones

TIME

To my darling husband, Ronnie, who has helped me grow strong.

The sun rises in the morning,
only to set at nightfall.
We end our days without a thought.

Sometimes we notice how time flys,
but there's nothing we can do but
let it go by. . .

We look in the mirror to see an older face
The one we knew so long ago is gone
without a trace.

Only photographs remind us of what was.
Only time can tell us what will be.

We do what we can with the time we have,
while we watch our children grow so very fast.

Sometimes we notice how time flys,
but there's nothing we can do but
let it go by. . .

Mildred L Pfalzgraff

Mildred L Pfalzgraff

THE ROSE

Written for my friend, and kindred spirit, Lida Ratcliffe

Along a weedstrewn pathway
I chanced upon a rose.
Growing so sublimely
Just how I do not know.
No loving hand has pruned it
Or watered it in love.
Except the Heavenly Father
Watching from above.
It hasn't given up its struggle
Among the weeds and stones.
It lifts its blossoms skyward
On stems so tall and strong.
Gentle rains have bathed it
Warm sun has drawn it forth.
But it seems some inward spirit
Put strength into its birth.
Imprisoned in its patch of weeds
Its fragance rises free.
Its spirit of survival
Inspires new hope in me.

Doris B Rackley

NEW YEAR'S DAY "1987"

God sent a storm raging
It came out of the sea
To let us know he is still God
And that he will always be
It took away some houses,
Some fishing piers and trees
The mighty sound of the ocean
brought many to their knees.
But God was kind just three
lives were lost. How
thankful we should be and
today the sun is shining
For all the world to see.
Our God is strong and mighty
His heart is filled with love
He keeps his hands upon us
As He watches from above.
No storm can overtake us when God
is by our side. He died upon
the cross our sins in his
blood to hide.
He sees our every movement and
knows our every thought.
So we should serve him daily for
the blessings He has brought.
So when the storms are raging
and troubles are all about
Remember God is in His Heaven,
and is always looking out.

Michael S Wilkitis

WHEN FIRST WE MET

We walked hand and hand
through her neighborhood.
The people they all stared
and the feeling it was good.
We were chased by a dog
and must have ran a mile.
I haven't felt this way
She always makes me smile.

The hours seemed to pass
As the day turned into night.
We shared a cup of tea
and some pie but just a bite.
I looked up at the clock
and I knew that I must leave.
But only for the moment
I'll be back tomorrow eve.

You see this girl is different
I could tell it from the start.
She spoke not from her head
but instead right from her heart.
She always had a glow
and knew just what to say.
It's time I take her home now
I wish that she could stay.

We kissed goodnight and then she said
"Make sure you get some sleep."
I tried to go to bed that night
My thoughts just would not keep.
You see this girl is special.
I wish she understood
just how much I love her
I knew someday she would.

Doreen Gamble Burgess

APART

St. John's long ago on a Christmas morning
Carols and ritual so familiarly warming,
Prayers for peace, the candlelights gleaming,
Still at that moment the world was dreaming;
Sharp is the memory, it's all crystal clear
I remember it so well my dear,
And soon we were—apart.

St. John's here and now on a September morning
Hymns and ritual so familiarly warming,
A day to remember the Few who gave
Their laughter and courage which never fades;
The Last Post sounds, clear in the silence,
And remembrance returns of the noise and the violence;
In seconds I see all those years fleeting by,
What we could have shared, you and I
But we are still—apart.

Wanda R Cunningham Thurston

LONG AGO

To Cindy Pittman—without your friendship I don't know what I would have done. Thanks!

I was too young then, to truly understand
And after all these years, I long to hold your hand

I remember the good times, they outweigh the bad
I remember the love and contentment we had
We still could be friends, if I could only trust my heart
I've not been truly happy since we've been apart
I'll forever need security, which you could never give
But I'll always remember you for as long as I live.

Deborah George
MY SWEET LITTLE ANGEL
My sweet Little angel,
I look at you cradled in my arms,
So small and helpless and innocent
And realize how very selfish my life was without you.
You've forced me to give more of myself than I ever thought possible,
Yet in all my giving, what I receive from you is far greater than I ever expected.
The delight I feel when I see your big toothless grin,
The joy of hearing your loving gurgles,
The satisfaction of holding you tight and protecting you from all harm.
As we explore each day together we learn from each other and our love grows by leaps and bounds.
Never cease to amaze me and go forth into the world cherishing all that is God's Creation.

Judith A Bussing
THE MOON BEGAN TO RISE
The moon began to rise
As she quickly made up her lies,
Smiling over her sins.

"Where have you been?"
"I was with my best friend.
hurry, this must end."

"Where have you been?"
"Down the road, beyond the old deserted inn,
with a friend."

Do you realize what you have lost?
Since you have crossed
To the other side away from me?

Never again shall you see,
ALL the love within me.
For as easily as my love was tossed astray
For as simply it has gone away.

Ann Allen
SUMMER
Summer is made of song birds
And blossoms bright and fair;
Of honey bees and shady trees
And fragrant balmy air.

Summer is made of blue skies
With clouds all fleecy white,
A shady nook, a babbling brook,
And sunshine warm and bright.

Summer is made of raindrops,
A whip-poor-will's plaintive cry,
Of gauzy wings and growing things,
A rainbow in the sky.

Summer is made of moonlight
And laughter sweet and low,
Of moonlit streams, of golden dreams
And stars that softly glow.

Summer is made of beautiful things
That's bright like the morning dew;
Hearts that were sad are now made glad
For hope is born anew.

Jennifer L Surman
BEST FRIENDS
We're best friends
This is true,
But I'm me
And you're you.

We have our differences
Every once in awhile,
But we always make-up
With a hug and a smile.

You're always beside me
To show that you care,
When you need me
I try to be there.

Sometimes when things
Get rough, and I can't cope,
I turn to you
And you give me hope.

I wish together
We could spend more time,
But you have your life
And I have mine.

We're best friends
This is true,
You and me
Me and you.

Beverly Jean Smith

Beverly Jean Smith
A DAY IS BIRTHED

This poem is dedicated to my precious Lord and Saviour, Jesus Christ.

A day stirs expectantly midst the deepness of the night.
In its embryonic stage, its eyes possess no sight.
The heartbeat of this miracle cries out to God above,
"Now nourish me tenderly with your abiding love.
God, though I be minute in thine authoritative hand,
Reverently I plead with thee, keep me in your plan.
You hold the key to end my life before I see the dawn.
Let me taste the morning dew; a doe would let her fawn.
I grope around in this black space with only a blank stare.
Does your face mirror anger, or love beyond compare?
With the night far spent I cringe to think, what's my destiny?
Will these blind eyes be granted sight, liberty to see?
What's my worth to you oh King, am I valued more than gold?
Please let this day burst forth with mysteries to unfold!"

Just then a springlike warmth began to permeate my soul.
Deity reached down to me and said, "My child you're whole!"
Another joyous day emerged, its sight with clarity,
As the sunrise beamed bright rays toward all eternity.
"Thank you, God, for dissipating the blackness with your light.
Wisdom states that each new day is blessed with all thy might!
Dark hours of gestation is a shadow of what will be.
Father, thank you for creating a grand symphony.
All nature sings, the rich earth blooms, instead of meeting death.
Your Agape labor of love gave this day its breath!"

Mary Oudenhoven Malsavage
OAK IN WISCONSIN

Dedicated in loving memory of my father, Anthony A. Oudenhoven. Wisconsin was also honored with his presence. . .

A Mighty Wisconsin Oak Tree stands as tall as any hill
of dreams, its roots run as deep as a valley of hope
It is a towering specimen of time honored grace
Its magnificent branches spread out as if they were
Huge arms, reaching, calling, welcoming all of God's
creation
If this Mighty Oak could speak, it would tell of dewy mornings,
bright red sunsets, cold long winters of freezing winds blowing,
and hot humid days of summer
This Mighty Oak has seen many evening fall
Some evenings fell on days of war and discouragement
As well as days of green fields and prosperity
"Oh what stories this Great Oak could tell!"
"Oh what wisdom it could share!"
"If only it could speak!"
This Mighty Wisconsin Oak Tree is a sight to behold
It is surely one of God's most beautiful creations
Wisconsin is honored with its presence

Donna J Buskirk
MESSAGE TO MY HEART

Lovingly dedicated to my parents, Dorothy and Luther Croston

Dear Heart, take heart
Nitetime is drawing nigh,
And soon the cares and woes of today
Will vanish with the night.

Dear Heart, weary heart
So in need of rest,
The scars and aches that you have borne
Have made you worn and heavy.

Dear Heart, take heed
Your wishes are coming true,
The days are going swiftly by
Far faster than intended to.

Dear Heart, stand strong
You can beat the greatest odds,
Today you have within your grasp
Tomorrow has not been promised.

So dear Heart, take care of me
Begin each day with faith renewed,
My soul rests in your tender care
On you I am depending.

Georgia Gideon
NOW I KNOW
Things are getting better now,
now that I know why.
Tears still come from time to time,
but it is for different reasons that I cry.

Now that its been analyzed,
the problem is far different I see,
the baby was just a substitute,
for emptiness and no one loving me.

I can see things better now,
I can almost say its for the best,
for how unfair to my poor child,
to be a replacement for all the rest.

Better to wait until later,
until I can give and take,
until then I'll work on loving me,
for my future childs sake.

Yes, things will get better now,
Now that I know why.

Eugene D Bruhn
YOUR CLOCK OF LIFE
Your clock of life is wound but once,
And no one has the power,
To tell just when the hands will stop,
At late or early hour.
Now is the only time you have,
Work, live, love and laugh today,
With a will,
Place no faith in tomorrow for,
Then the hands may be still.

Thadrah Rogers
RAINBOWS
Individual Colors
Red, green, and blue
Just like my love for you

Indigo feelings
Yellow skies
Orange faces
Crying eyes

Patricia Diane Cagle
CHILDREN ARE FLOWERS

To Kelley and Johnny, my Flowers!

Children are flowers,
You must prune them as they grow.
Feed, water, and train them, or
wild seeds they will sow.

Black-eyed Susans,
Ragweed Hair.

They shoot up towards the sun,
And soon their not there.

Someone will come by and pick
them,
And off they will go,
To plant the seeds of life,
So more Flowers will grow.

Nancy Heavin
TO MY CHILD
I'm not a perfect parent,
The Lord above knows that,
I hope I'll always be here ready
When you want a little chat.
Remember that I love you
And that I always will,
Through fun times and times of
discipline,
I want the best for you still.

Did you ever wonder why I go with
you
To extra activities that you do?
I can not afford to miss and not see
The basketball shot you migtht
make:
The ball you might steal or the
rebound you'd take.
The new technique you have
learned when you skate,
Or the next time you are at the
plate.
What if you hit a home run and I
was not there to cheer?
Could you tell me about it later on
with all the excitement still
there?

We both know you won't always be
On the team that wins the game,
But oh what fun it is to see
The way you play, Sportsmanship
is the name.
For when you do your very best
And do it with a smile,
I know I have been BLEST.

Glenda Z Cantey
FINDING YOU

To my friend with Gentle love

I was skipping along
in the rain,
Stomping in mudholes,
watching the drops splash the
pavement,
humming a blue tune,
my face upward
my hair wet, clingy to my skin,
yearning for the warmth of sun,
then you opened your arms
and took me inside your heart.

Jill Dee Beilharz
REFLECTIONS ON PANE

Dearest Nicholas, Love of my life. I love you for ever and ever!

As I sit
staring
By the window
wondering
Watching the rain
rolling
Drop by drop
drizzling
Down the window
Wandering
As I sit
pondering

Althea Keesey
MYSTERY

To Jerry, my beloved son.

You came under the spell of
immortality,
as many of us do,
when a magnetic force tells you
there is God
With the very power
that can carry you to heaven.

You discover
it was there all the time,
God's love for you
though He didn't talk to you out
loud
the way you thought He would
but was just there waiting.

Then great hope is born.
you know it is the mystery
of all mysteries,
a mystery critics and scorners of
God
cannot touch
and it is better such were never
born.

You want to be obedient to Him.
This flashing of truth
is the work of the Holy Spirit.
It may come from Bible reading
or the insight of another.
God's lamp again pierces the
gloom.

Marilyn J Crothers
STRIVING FOR LOVE

To my loving husband, Doug

As each day goes on I love you more
Yet there are so many goals we're
striving for
To climb the ladder of "success"
To have a family with lot's of
happiness
To be well liked with lot's of friends
To have a marriage that never ends
To have a nice home, nice car,
extra money,
Yet will we ever have enough
honey?
I think we need to STOP, LOOK,
and LISTEN,
Because there's so much more
were missin'
We need to determine what's
important now
But the big question is just how?
Were changing more each day
We seem to be growing in different
ways
Some weeks everything goes just
fine
At other times our marriage is on
the line
I want to work hard and make it
better
Let's beat the hard times and stick
together
Our first goal; to be "in" love for
forever
It's not going to be easy, but I want
you to know
I'll be beside you as you grow
I'll give and you give, that's what
it's going to take
Let's see if there's a better life we
can make
Just remember that what will get
us through
Is your love for me and my love for
you!

Mary Jo Hamilton Farber
THE HARVEST IS OVER

To my 91-year old father, Mendal Lee Hamilton, who passed away 21 October 1986.

The harvest has been bountiful!

I have reaped family, friends, and
far horizons.
My basket is brimming with love
of God's creatures
and treasures from afar.

I have labored during long golden
days, moonlit nights,
fresh rain upon my face, gentle
wind across planted fields,
thunder and lightning from above,
colored leaves falling
earthward, and clean snowflakes
across my brow.

I have smiled and laughed.
The harvest was filled with
happiness.

I have sighed and cried.
The harvest was sometimes empty
and sad.

I lie down, thank God for the
harvest, smile,
close my eyes, and sleep.

The harvest is over!

Joyce E Conduitt
THE SEASONS

Dedicated to Justin my Grandson

Let me tell you again how I love
them
The seasons and just what they
bring
The hope and new life in each little
bud
That come bursting forth in the
Spring.

The long hot days of Summer
With soft fleecy clouds in the sky;
And at night the heavens are lighted
With millions of tiny fireflies.

The first crisp days of Autumn
Turn the leaves to colors of flame
The ground lies bare from the
harvest
The barn holds the ripe golden
grain.
Soon twill be time for the cold days
of Winter
And the barren oak trees seem to
know
The heavy dark clouds hovering
o'er them
Will soon bring a blanket of snow.

Each season leaves a trace of their
span
But never a stain to remember
So it should be in the life of each
man
Though it be May or December

Amalia A Gallegos
GOODBYE

In memory of Daddy with love to Mom

In my sleep I dreamed of you.
Of the times both old and new,
Of how you'd hold my hand,
As we wandered through the land.

Of the times you held me close,
In the happiness we chose,
Of the seed we shared together,
All those times are gone forever.

L J Esch
THE PHOTOGRAPHER

With love to Heather, Bobbie, Melissa, Michael, Emily Jo, Stevie, & Emily Ann: Dare to Become Whatever You Dream

This time in which I needed to
know how I was loved,
For since I moved away from home
I've missed the tenderness,
That friends and family have
shown with kisses and with hugs.

As your pictures captured my smile
in print,
Your arms captured my tender,
broken heart and caressed
With soothing and loving care,
granting it life and courage once
again.

Like a drowning person straining
to stay afloat,
With the person who offers saving
hope—Perhaps the
Responding grasp was much too
tight, choking without
Freedom.

Once again on land, the drowning
victim with legs
Walking surely upon the sand,
Need not hold tightly to
The one who offered hope. And I,
too, can once again
Walk confidently.

Should you know fear at the
tightness of my grasp,
Which leads you to seek another
path and not mine,
Would that you know I have grown
from your tenderness and wish
you well.

Dorothy Leiala Villalba A.K.A. Cabbie Cerio
A LOVE FOR ME

To my dear friends Kathie and Keala, who inspired this poem, and to my loving children, Gino, Sean and Gina, who are the light of my life, and most of all, to Derrya.

There's a peace within myself,
I've found by being alone.
I'm learning my capacity,
I'm amazed at how I've grown.
Each day brings me closer,
To a deeper understanding,
Of life, of love, of cherished thoughts.
Of time, how undemanding.
I look back in time and special friends,
And lessons of life they've taught me.
I thank each and every one of them,
For my life now means a lot to me.
I can see the good, accept the bad,
In people and life's pleasures.
And all the sadness in my life,
Happiness now outmeasures.
I can look ahead, plan my future,
For I'm at peace withim my soul.
I can see beyond vast horizons,
For my eyes have not grown old.
I'm enriched with gifts of knowledge,
And happy at what I see.
For I have found a meaning for life,
And a love for being me.

Chip Colvin
DAWN
Dawn,
The first light in the East
tells of the coming of morning,
the beginning of a new day,
And—
Another Chance!

Melinda Anne Tustlin Bassett
HOMELESS
The rain pours and
I have nowhere to go.
I look for help, but where
To find it?
I am so poor that I cannot
find an—open door.
I ask the state, the city, the county
and the people,
but there is no caring
The street is my home now.
My husband is disabled, but that is of
no importance where I seek,
The world out there wants us to
get on our knees and bow.
I bow to no-one but the Lord for
he gave me life, He shall take it.
He (the Lord) will do the sharing.
He will give, give till he cannot give no more.
When he has chosen the time for me to go,
then I will have a home I won't have to
worry about being poor. For He will not say no!

Michael D Kamer
TWO LITTLE LOVE BIRDS
Once there were two little love birds
sitting on a limb
One was a her, the other a him
They dreamed of one day they would have their own nest
For those two little love birds deserved the best.
They wanted to get married and fly far away
So they could be happy and have children some day.
As they flew through the forest the wind began to blow
First there was rain, and then there was snow.
The two little love birds started to get cold
The her was real scared, but the him was real bold.
He protected his love until the very end,
After it was over, only the her flew through the wind.

Elaine J Snyder

Elaine J Snyder
LIFE AND ITS TRIALS
I was born into a family who loved me alot
And through childhood and growing up, I was not a "Have Not".

But growing up with a lack of parental affection
Made me know all to well about rejection.

I've been hurt many many a time
And asked myself what did I do that was such a crime.

I've had to accept things not always understood
And heard the cruel words of people telling I'd be no good.

I've hung my head in shame a time or two
But I've walked proud and tall for some things when they were through.

I've tried to stand up and fight for what I believe
Knowing God would be the only one to see what I justly receive.

The time between life and death goes so quickly by
with laughter, Joy, tears and sorrow all in between and always asking why?

But it's all one big cycle of give and take
And wondering if the next step will be any better and one I can relate.

Until that time comes along, which we all must face
All I can do is learn to love and be happy and hope it wasn't just a waste.

Charles Nixon
TRUTH WITHIN
We're born into this world unknown,
With no worldly possessions of our own.
We're told to do this and that,
If not, punishment follows, and that's a fact.
It's true society plays an important part,
But to me, that's not where life starts.
We're taught to relate from out to in,
But from in to out is a better blend.
Go inside and find the real you.
That's where you'll find a world that's true.
This inward road can be long and frustrating,
But the truth you'll find will be worth anticipating.
Don't be afraid of the new things you'll see,
You've been led to believe these things wouldn't be.
What you'll see in yourself, you'll see in others too,
That's the new truth you've found coming through.
Remember to accept the good with the bad,
Keep what you like and change what makes you sad.
As you mature in truth and accept what you're about,
Look around to see if you can help your brother out.
But don't try to change anyone before their time,
As you did, they must make up their own mind.
Just live your life full of zest,
With every moment, try your best.
So when the final bell has rung,
You can smile within and say 'Well Done.'

Garrison Leroy Moreland
CIRCUMFERENCE HAWK
I have seen no horizon
beyond beauty
than life
Merely,
that it has away to meet peace,
and be undisturbed by pain
What you cannot see
beyond it
makes life difficult to be felt,
without ebullience to enjoy
A meaning of eternal divinity

As many ways have not come
from the other side of the world,
just away that can be talked of
If the two should ever meet
maybe there shall be
a jubilation of grief,
because we shall never succeed from trying
To be the next wonder
of the world
So,
that a harvest shall abandon
from it's true monoloque

Josephine Smith
A PRAYER

To my four loving children: Jerrell, Joy, Jennifer & Jason.

I stand here looking out of the door,
Thanking the Lord for being a mother of four,
Being a single parent, I can't complain
Because I know they love and need me, so there's no room for pain.

I've watched them grow up so happy and free,
Watching each one, you know they look a lot like me.
Two boys and two girls, Lord, I raised them for you
I know God that you are proud of them too.

You see, I wasn't alone after all
For you were there when I started to fall.
You picked me up and showed me the way
So that my babes would not go astray.

My God, as we stand here looking out of the door,
What a great job we did Lord, we couldn't have done more.
You and I, we did our part
And thinking back now it really wasn't so hard.

A teacher, a builder, a nurse and an engineer,
They make me want to stand up and cheer.
So single parents out there, you stop look and be fair
The Lord will help you, just send him a prayer.

Bryan T Sweasy
WINGS
The ground is there staring up at me
Two hundred feet below my two feet
And the cars look like children's toys
As they pass below me on the street

Nineteen years it's taken me to arrive here
Standing on the ledge of this place
Nineteen years to build my self-esteem
Enough to look myself in the face

These homemade wings have yet to be tested
How carefully I carved them out of wood
I don't know if they'll hold me to the sky or not
But I wouldn't want to know even if I could

If my calculations aren't correct
Down towards the ground I'll be hurled
But I won't flail or flap as I plummet down
For a moment I almost owned the world

And if I fly, just think what I could be
I could sleep in peace among the clouds
I could fly so high that I touched the moon
So far away from all these city crowds

So now it's time for me to finally find out
If I own everything or nothing at all
Sooner or later a fellow just has to know
If his wings can hold him up or if he'll fall

William Stokes
a pentastitch to waken winter oaks

spring freshets subdue winters quietus
with genesis of meadow rues and morning cloaks
enough to purl the larks to sleep
enough for morns halflight to ascend winters hiatus
enough to disguise HIS footsteps adumbral deep

Isadoria I Steinhilber
ROSES

The rose is so lovely, yellow, red and white
Blooming by day, sleeping by night
The fragrance of a rose is so sweet to smell
Giving more beauty than one can tell.

God made the beauty of the rose so rare
He nurtured and gave it special care
We, like the rose are part of God's plan
That's why He made and cares for man.

God made the rose for us to enjoy
Just like a child with a special toy
God made the rose so pretty to see
He made them for you, but also for me

We need to stop along life's way
To smell the roses that bloom today
You see, true beauty is so hard to find
So stop! and smell the roses from time to time

Alice Artman
TELLING OF MY LORD

If I were to tell someone about my Lord, I'd tell them of His genuine kindness.
I'd tell them of His miracles, from changing water into wine to healing men of blindness.
I'd tell them how He gave His life for us upon a crude thing called a cross
And how His love calmed the angry sea that waves a ship did toss.
I'd tell them how His love was felt not only from the elderly and sick;
But from the children, who once seeing Christ, would run to Him quick.
He's done so much in the past and today His love is still shown.
For miracles are taking place, you can have them for your own.
For He still heals the sick, still calms the troubled sea.
And He still gives His life for you and for me.
He still lives in hearts of the young and old
And can be as close to you as to those prophets who about the Bible told.

Annette Smith
MY BIGGEST CHALLENGE

There's never been a challenge
Like bringing up a child
I never dreamed I'd meet that test
When I was young and wild.
With now, a son and daughter
It's opened up my eyes
And made me thank my Mother
The more I hear them cry.

I've learned that as a parent
I face a constant fight
In second guessing all I do
And wondering if it's right.

I pray I'll have the patience
And pray I'll find the strength
To do what's right for both of them
Despite what they might think.

And though I'm just a child myself
Who's used to coming first
I did alot of growing up
The day that I gave birth.

Despite the many hardships
A parent must endure
I've never met a challenge
More rewarding in this world.

Lillian Ingram
THE BRIGHTEST STAR

To my lovely daughter, Sonja, whom I consider "The Brightest Star" in the universe.

Reflecting back from day one,
I'm the brightest star compared to the sun.
If my light didn't shine so brightly,
the world below would exist quite contritely.
Everytime I twinkle down,
I alleviate a devastated frown.
Even on a cloudy night, my cosmic rays
penetrate hearts; to my delight!
While all the other stars wonder why,
I positively know, "I'm the brightest Star in the sky!"

Joyce Jones-Rogers

Joyce Jones-Rogers
TIME

To all the people I love in this world, No names are needed for you'll know who you are

As the age of time
flows gently through my mind
I recall those days
that I cannot throw away
It's not easy to forget
all the times that we met
and loved together
Time has a way
of mending hearts
that's lost their way
And maybe, yes maybe
our times will change
Yes, time has a way
of mending hearts
that's lost their way
And maybe, yes maybe
our times will change
As I sit here tonight
all my dreams pass me by
Like the winds in a storm
and the clouds in the sky
If by chance
Things turn out right
for the two of us in the night
We'll love again

Neil J McNeil
A TRAGEDY

It's been three days now since I was told
Shattered is everything dear I hold.
It's just that I really feel He's unfair,
I sometimes wonder if He really cares.
A life so young, beautiful and free
Yet death is there for all to see.
My heart aches every minute these days
My mind searches for the easiest way.
I cannot cope and fear rises within
God please help, it's such a sin.
He's fading now and my heart pounds inside,
I feel his pain and I cannot hide.
No strength I have to hold my tears
What will it be like in future years.
So much I did was built around you
You cannot die, this you must not do.
My world falls apart as the moment is close
I pray God will be a gracious Host.
My life is empty now and I must go on,
I lost the one I need; the sun that shone.
A void that I know I can never fill
The air is warm—but I feel the chill.

Janice Davis Williams
THE BIRTH AND DEATH OF A FAMILY TREE

This poem is dedicated to my Grandmother, Mother and my two children Randall and Melissa

In a distant place in time
A little girl is born in 1899
She carries in her a seed
That will continue a Family Tree
Then one day from her seed
My mother is conceived
In her she yet carries another seed
Then on a rainy day she has me
The tree is getting old now
The branches will die off one by one
The little trees are coming along
The time has come to carry her away
Where she will lay the rest of her days

Judith Moss Mueller
LIFE

To Mama and Papa

Life is a bubble,
Blown from the wand of creation.
Transparent, yet opaque,
Expanding colorfully,
Then deflating,
Escaping sometimes from the source,
Or disappearing at the moment of departure.
The bubble floats freely through the atmosphere,
Only to burst at that unexpected moment
Causing temporary grief—or surprise.

Barbara Johnson
LET ME HOLD MY TEAR FOR LATER

Let me hold my tear for later.
When a love one has left and forgot you,
Let me hold my tear for later.
When your kids don't understand.
Let me hold my tear for later.
When sleep won't come.
Let me hold my tear for later.
When your child can hear you and won't listen.
Let me hold my tear for later.
When you can lay your head down and sleep.
Let my hold my tear for later.
When the pain comes in your heart and your head hurts.
Let me hold my tear for later.
When all hope is gone and you close your eyes.
Let me hold my tear for later.
When there's no gentleness with a little kindness, to help you understand
Let me hold my tear for later,
When there's no kindness or sorrow just sadness.
Let me hold my tear for later.

Melvyn Louis Rankin
A HOUSE IS NOT A HOME

What makes a home
So warm and good
A place for family to live
The way a family should.

In peace and comfort
With lots of love too
Houses are plentiful
But homes are few.

The aroma of baked bread
Fresh from the oven
A home filled with kindness
And lots of loving.

A place to grow
And a place to share
A place to learn respect
And a place to care.

A home means more to me
Than a place to grow
It means refuge and protection
From rain, sleet and snow.

A house is kept together
With wood, brick and nails
A home by God Almighty
That's why a home never fails.

Ruth I Litch
OUR SON

Dedicated to Barton, the son who inspired this poem, and to Wayne, the son for whom these words also seemed appropriate.

You ask me where ya came from lad?
Its kinda hard 'ter 'splain.
Cause yer allers inta mischief now,
And sorta raisen' cane.
But ya once lived up in Babyland
With God's angels all around,
And when we asked God fer a baby,

It was you that he sent down.

Now ma and me were kinda lonesome,
Cause our home was built for three,
And the house was kinda empty
With just yer ma and me.
So we asked God fer a baby,
And though yer kinda bad,
When we asked God fer a baby
He sent the best he had.
And we shore do love ya sonny,
With yer face that won't stay clean,
And we think yer 'bout the swellest lad,
yer ma and me has seen.

Robert J Burkholder
WHITE RABBIT
Covering the hole with happiness
Bordering on insanity—triggered by reality
Grown hard of hearing when the doctors
And the others who aren't like me, keep telling me
How I could be, if I'd TAKE THESE
From the background Grace sings slickly
WHITE RABBIT
Grafted at the parting of society
Where the one side proclaims
How "normal" I can be, if I really want to be
While right outside their ivory walls
The streets tell me I am untouchable
A freakish aberation—someone to fear
For I'm out of control, there's a hole
In my head no one can really fix
So they'll cover it up with drugs
Till the unexpected fall in the trap
White Rabbit

Debbie McCoy
A LITTLE GIRL'S NIGHTMARE; IS REALITY
The little girl looked around crying
It was hard to tell him she wasn't lying.

She still had bruises from the last beating;
she really dreaded this next meeting.

She just couldn't get him to understand
that the wet bed was beyond her command.

Her hands trembled as she opened the door . .
She didn't want to go through this any more.

He told her to take off all her clothes.
She felt totally dirty, bared to her toes . .
Her legs were weak as she shook with dread.
He picked her up and threw her on the bed . .

He put his fingers where they shouldn't have been.
Why did she have to go through this again?

When he got done he got out his belt
the look on her face should have made his heart melt . .

When she put on her clothes it hurt like hell,
but she knew she didn't dare tell.

She was only eight years old . .
Thats the way the story is told.

How she turned out, you should see.
You can, that little girl was ME.

Steven A Long

Steven A Long
TOO SOON LOVE

For all the rebounding lovers and their confidants

Didn't mean to make you love me
At least not here, not now.
Just fun and friendship was all we'd want
Nothing serious anyhow.

You've so much to see and feel and do
In becoming who you are;
To learn of all you missed before,
Having wondered from afar.

You say how much you care for me
But somehow I'm just not sure.
You need to check out other things
Before trusting to endure.

Too soon the time will come I know
To leave you to yourself
So you can do what you need to do
Alone, without my help.

Whether stones for building a future for us
Or fond memories for old age
Only time will write the truth for sure
Of our days upon the page.

So with a gentle kiss and loving hug
We sadly now must part
Remember, I will love you ever
With all my mind and soul and heart.

Heather Antoinette Sentkoski
SENSELESS
I can see your caring eyes
Although I am blind

I can hear your thoughts
Even though I am deaf

I can feel your presence
Although I am numb

I can smell happiness on your breath
Even though I can't smell

I can taste love in your heart
Even though I can't taste

For love can penetrate
The most Senseless diseases

Phyllis Aldcroft Kolseth
MISS LIBERTY
Your arm is stretched to light the path
To freedom in this land.
Compassion lies upon your face
As if you understand.

You welcome all, who are oppressed
By nations torn apart,
And point the way to liberty.
You take them to your heart.

But there are some who would abuse
The freedom which is theirs.
Who plot to undermine the rights
That everybody shares.

To those who do not cherish
This great and glorious land,
Get out, we do not want you here,
And you must understand.

That many, still, in other lands
Are yearning to be free.
Make room for those who value
Life, love, and liberty.

Nancy Ellen Griffin
NO END

This poem is dedicated to my family and friends

LOVE IS THE BEGINNING
It grows from a seed planted in the heart
And reaches out with strong tender branches
to hold its beloved, but not too tight
Love heals and takes away the fear
It speaks softly from an open heart
and sings a happy song
LOVE BALANCES ALL THINGS
It laughs, it weeps and it waits
It shouts and sheds tears of joy
Love builds and changes
it helps and leads the way
It warms and cools and eases the pain
Love keeps its own time and it always knows when
It gives of itself and never stops
LOVE HAS NO END

Christopher Wall
TO A GIRL EATING SPAGHETTI
Red swirl around your fork
twists a vein through a forest,
their silver trees a playground
for the scamper chase of squirrels.

Your tail like grey snow
upon my face. (I catch you
and you me)
We jump as the trees errupt
and carry the red mountain,
air like an ocean to swim through,
foamy waves that push us
gently to the ground
(panting and breathing)

A garlic wall to lean against—
we're smeared in yellow.
Slip and fall and (yellow love),
we laugh at the blue eye moon.

You touch the napkin
to your lip and wipe the red away,
and I try to find part of that smile
that we used instead of words.

Maybe tonight
when I close my eyes
and melt into

used to be's.

Carol Lee Register
THE LIGHT AT THE END OF THE TUNNEL

In memory of my beloved parents Charles and Catherine Register. They gave me life and taught me to love and laugh

The Light At The End Of The Tunnel
There is a light at the end of the tunnel that I can barely see.
There is a light at the end of the tunnel, will it grow brighter for me?
My pain, my hurt, my sorrow, will it ever leave me?
With each passing day, things will get better, this I
must believe, and the light at the end of the tunnel will get brighter but patient I must be.
I seek so many answers and diligent I must be, for GOD in his infinite wisdom and merciful love in time will let me see.
My suffering, and pain will be rewarded and one day I will be free.
YES! The light at the end of the tunnel will shine brightly for me.

Susan Zengel
A TINY FLOWER

To my dad who helped me with the poem; to my mom, who told me to write it, and to Lynn, who especially liked it.

A tiny flower
And its' small tiny bud
It fights for a life
It hopes it will find.
It reminds me of love
And how first it must sprout
Then grows very slowly.
It reaches its' height
And opens its' eyes
Then closes them quickly
And seeks a way out.

Randall Anderson
SELF APPLAUSE
We are spectacular
in a minor way.
Why—we even flash our bijou
to the Universe—
"The One and Only
All Star Cast of Billions",
Human Kind.
Our sciences bring us a bow;
our philosophies bring us a
second,

but what can we do
if the audience
calls for an encore?

Eryn Ramsey
SEAGULL
See him Fly
How he moves
He looks so shy,
He glides so slow
He dives so fine
So fast he goes
In a straight line.

Betty Hilliard
LOST LOVE
At the first hour of darkness
When sounds of silence are so loud,
Old memories come back to haunt me
All alone or in a crowd.

Hand in hand we walked together
While youths candle brightly shone,
Our hearts entwined, we thought forever,
Then all too soon we were alone.

As our paths in life divided
We each went our separate way,
With our hearts and steps mis-guided,
We just drifted day by day.

The years passed by, we each existed,
In our prisons we called home,
Our memories some time persisted,
Along with feelings we thought were gone.

Today I stand here by your grave side
Wondering why and where and when,
My dreams have fallen by the way side,
I can never Love again.

Steven Espinosa

Steven Espinosa
A COWBOY POEM

This poem is dedicated to my teacher Susan Capek

I was riding on the range
And I was feeling pretty good.
All the cattle were behaving;
They were running like they should.

The sun was just a-setting
in a blaze of orange and red.
And my dog was acting frisky
Like a pup that's been well fed.

I had planned to build a campfire,
So I chopped myself some wood.
Then I cooked my steak and beans
And I can tell you they were good.

I pulled off my leather boots
You know the ones you buy in town.
I took out my heavy blanket
And prepared to settle down.

Lindsay Gaskins
WORLD WAR WITHIN
I'm living a lie
Standing on war
And my heart is the battleground.

I'm holding a bomb
Feeling suspense
And my hopes are where it's bound.

I'm dying a life
Screaming in vain
And my body will not be found.

I'm sinking a ship
Losing the grip
And my strength will soon be drowned.

I'm feeling the blast
Shredding all skin
But my cries refuse to sound.

Gloria Anderson
CLOUDS
Puffy clouds
up in the sky
Change scenes
as I blink my eye.
Foreign streams
of a jet trail
Invade billows
as they sail.
Fleecy lace
on azure blue
Dress heaven
in regal hue.
Such majesty
to behold
As clouds mesh
and unfold.
The clouds of life
ever change,
Bright or dark
they rearrange.

Charles H Swetland
A TRIBUTE TO MY MOM
When I was just a little tot,
Say around six or seven,
My Mom talked to me a lot,
All about Jesus and Heaven.

How Jesus left His home above
Came down in all His Glory
To save us through His matchless love,
I'm sure you've heard the story.

How Adam ate the fruit forbidden
So tempting from the tree.
Such a sin could not be hidden.
It passed on to you and me.

Disobedience brought death and sin,
Through sin the flesh will die.
We, His seed, must be born again
So we can meet Him in the sky.

We need this Holy Son of God
To wash our sins away.
By His Holy cleansing blood
And His Living Word to obey.

I'm glad I heard the story,
How Jesus set us free.
Now Mom's gone home to Glory
Just waiting there for me.

Richard E Lewallen
THE CHRISTMAS TREE AT OUR HOUSE
We have a Christmas tree at our house,
Our Christmas tree is green;
It is the prettiest Christmas tree
I believe I have ever seen.
It grew along a mountain side
Where the snow was white and soft
Until along my daddy came
And with his ax he chopped it off.
He put the tree upon his back
And brought it home so gay,
That is why we have a Christmas tree
At our house on Christmas day.

My mommie took some tinsel
And placed it on the tree.
She said that she would decorate it
Especially for me.
She also placed some balls and lights
And a big bright shining star;
It is so very big and bright
You can see it from afar.
She said it is to guide us
Through our entire life,
She said it is the shining Star
Of our Saviour, Jesus Christ.

vera l harper
ODE TO A FLYING FILLY
Bells clanging—Crowds yelling
pressure against your chest!
Bit in mouth—tongue aside
weight upon your back . . .

Flags waving—colors screaming
a slap against your thigh!
Smell of sweet—feel the dirt
flying in your eyes . . .

Bridles, saddles, blinders, silks
bred for this one moment!
Extend, reach—ruptured heart
and now we feel the grief . . .

Soft, fuzzy—cute and lovely
stubby tail extended!
Romp whinny—grope for freedom
face the odds together . . .

Gone the rapture of your waltz
gone the pounding rhythm!
Gone the rainbow of your sheen
gone the hope of winning.

Oscar Lynn Gilstrap
A SUMMER STORM PERSONIFIED
Darkness abounds all around,
And raindrops pelt the earth.
The sky's ripped asunder with thunder,
And lightening the heaven does girth.

The pine trees sway in a mournful way
As if nodding to God with disdain.
They'd like to know, amidst the throe
Must the wind accompany the rain?

Darkness is part of my life and strife
Many problems pelter down.
I look to the sky with a wistful eye
As God shares His heavenly Crown.

Though souls may sway in a mournful way
They don't give up in disdain.
For surely they know God's heavenly glow
Is life's rainbow after the rain.

Joanne R Bianco
BEAUTIFUL MORNING
Wakening,
I see the rise of the sun
A brand new day has just begun
Sparkling,
Was the grass, with the morning's dew
Fluffy clouds sailing the sky's blue
Swaying
Leaves dance along with the wind
The birds variety of songs begin
Breathing,
In bloom, the fragrance of flowers
The earthly smell of last night's shower
Feeling
Warmth from the glowing sun
The squirrel on the ground begins to run
Smiling,
Satisfied, my heart sings and sings
For all of the mornings beautiful things

Sam James
I CRIED

To My Family

If I reach out
to touch your hand

It's because I need you
to understand
how I feel

If you see a glistening
in my eye
In a casual glance
as you pass by

It's because my feelings
from deep inside
Are bursting out
Some might even say
I cried.

Katherine S Sumerlin
I SEE YOUR SMILE
I'm looking into infinity
I see beyond the barrier of time
You are there and I touch your hand
And again, I see your smile

I'm waiting for a word
But I hear no sound
I hear only memories of things long gone
And again, I see your smile

Mrs Bertha L McClain
TO MOM

This poem is dedicated to Mrs. Louise Foster, Thanks Mom

Mom's life was hard, what she must have gone through,
Raising her children alone, when there should have been two,
She could have left . . . turned her back and walked away,
But with her children, my mom chose to stay.

Happy, little and carefree were we, for she allowed us not
Her tears to see; and at night as she put us to bed,
There was never a worry as to how we'd be fed . . .

Long hours of work, yes ma'am's, thank you's and please,
As she cooked, washed, cleaned and ironed but refused to scrub
Floors on her knees. We learned very early house work
And cooking to do; cause Mama was too tired when her day was through.

How often we thought . . . "She's so strict"! yet she would
Work for us although she was sick.
Correction was a way of life, never! never! cause mom any stress or
Strife; to get what I wanted never a lie to use, because what you
Got then, today; is called child abuse!

From babies, through school, to a life of our own, she struggled
To raise us, now we are grown.
I grew up a lady, truly I appreciate
My mother; if given a choice, I would have no other,
For without mom's guidance, I could be living in sin,
I truly thank God, for the mother she's been.

Cara Sforza
IN-SIGHT
"I see right through you"
Her psychiatrist said.
"I view the workings
Of your lucite head.
I bear silent witness
To your anal retention,
Your circuitous colon
Knotted with tension.
Your ego appears
Slightly out of line
Your libido, though,
Is doing fine."

He rubbed his palms together
And smiled with glee.
"Drinks and hors d'oeuvres
At three?"

Louis Alan Headley
THE SPARROW

To Mary Ann—beautiful-gentle-lovely and as soft as the sparrow

A tiny sparrow injured lay,
On the sidewalk in the heat of day,
Poor little tyke so alone and small,
As people passed by caring not at all,

Gently I lifted the tiny thing,
Saying do not die you must sing,

With prayer and tears I walked to where,
People were chatting on Fountain Square,

I placed him in the bushes there,
Thinking I'd leave him, leave him there,

But some impelling force within,
Said to me he'll fly again,

So I stopped and lifted him once again,
And held my hand toward the trees in the rain,

He spread his wings and soared away,
The little sparrow flew on that summer day.

Katherine V Averill
TOGETHER
When we were wed
I was a teen.
You have been kind
And never mean.
The odds were slim
That it would last.
What ever the sayings
Our lot was cast.
It wasn't easy
To make ends meet.
But working together
Things came out neat.
One had to give
The other take.
At times it's reversed
The agreements to make.
Over fifty years
We've been together.
Time sped on by
We've wanted no other.

Babe
HOPE
How can I retrace the pages of time,
To leave behind a past such as mine.
Surrounded by future no drive to go on,
My hope for a future seems to be gone.
How many times must I push to succeed?
How many times must I make my heart bleed?
I've failed my friends, who can't possibly understand,
They reach out to me but I can't take their hand.
I face reality which is so clear,
Never to love again is my greatest fear.
I will go on despite the pain I must bare,
One day the mrmories will reach out and I won't be there.
Someday I'll be happy! For now its my turn to feel pain,
I am fighting to survive with the hope of loving again.

Angelia Robinson
THE BEGINNING OF AN END

To the Karcher Family, in remembrance of Brian

One Day,
He drifted off on an angel's wing
He left the world to greet his King
The life of a friend
In sorrow comes to an end
The family's grief we share
In attempts to show we care

Remember,
His life we can never forget
He was special to each person he met
He accomplished an amazing feat
For never a stranger did he meet

In Silence,
Leukemia has taken another friend
Can this death be dealt an end
For his family we sympathize
Leukemia took him, it is for sure
And for this disease there is no cure

Renee S Robinson
A LONELY GIRL'S DILEMMA
I want to be taken to dinner
I want to be wined and dined
I want someone to want me
I want to make someone mine

But I don't have the time to go out
I work an 8 hour day
and after I get home from work
I haven't the energy to play

So I'll continue to be patient
and hope someday he'll come
but the way my luck has been going,
I won't even be at home.

Jeffrey C Lloyd
WHY
Why does the sun always set in the West?
And why do you speak of the times you like best?
Why is the sky blue, and the grass green?
By any other color, could they be seen?
And why do men hate and fight?
Does it matter who's wrong and who's right?
Someday God will cash in on your lease.
Why fight the truth, just hold the peace.
Hold back your aggressions and keep down your hate,
Just one more day your problems can wait.
Why hide from problems that seek you?
Why look for evidence without a clue?
So why don't we talk before we destroy our race?
And don't follow others, go at your own pace.

Gertie S Worsham
RAINY DAY GOLF

Dedicated in memory of my husband Eckel, a fun-loving golfer

FORE!
You've heard of the "NINETEENTH HOLE"
Such a solace to the golfer's soul
You can have a ball—get all teed up
Swing, tee—ter, putter but still hit the cup
You can score on an alcholic course
Spoon that highball—liquid fill endorse
First shot is driver for fairway link
Making the yardage begin th shrink

Number two shot gives medium loft
With mid-iron power, you find no fault
Next shot, higher lift with a smash-ie
Just the right loft using that mashie
Short shot, just a niblick by jigger
Stop quickly of get one that's bigger
Who is that monster, keeper of the greens?
Brassie! Counting practice soaks it seems
So what if bogeys scare off the birds
Pink elephants won't tell—they can't speak words.

Wilbur K Sartwell
THE RIVER
I have a little cabin where the creek and river meet,
And the city's having difficulty fixing up my street.
The land is low and soggy and the gravel that they haul
Sinks deep into the roadbed, doing it no good at all.

Each year just after thaw time I have water at my door.
And sometimes it comes up so far it covers up my floor.
It leaves me limbs and mud and silt and that awful fishy smell.
And every time the flood comes it contaminates my well.

My neighbor on the creek side always comes to let me know,
And help make the decision as to

when it's time to go.

Just why I choose I live here is to
some a mystery . . .
But I get more from that river than
it ever gets from me.

Mary A Held
ROSES
They speak of Rose's so
Wonderful and grand,
They even grow on no mans land
But there is one rose that
grows in everyone's heart
THATS OUR ROSE

Fern B Dunfee
PEN PAINTING

Dedicated to my brother, The Reverend Charles L. Chew

Could I but paint a picture:
A golden thrush atop a tree,
Offering up to the heavens
His melodious rhapsody;
The sun filtering through tall trees
Casting shadows on the forest
floor;
Dark clouds rolling over the bay,
White cap waves dash the shore;
Big raindrops writing in the dust
On a warm summer's day;
The devoutness on his face
When my brother kneels to pray;
The dancing waters of a stream
As it waltzes toward a lake;
Waterfalls cascading in the
moonlight
Then foaming darkly through
the brake;
A small child laughing merrily;
Kittens playing near their house;
The understanding and the
patience
Contributed by my spouse;
A friend's hand reaching out to help
Far beyond that which is his
duty;
Would I could paint one of these
I could really name it "Beauty."

Lynn S Squibb
THE LAND SPEAKS OUT
What will you do with me? How
will you expend what I have to
give?
Will you misuse that which I
possess as your predecessors
have done in eons past?
Civilization? I spit on it. I was
treated better before man ever
set foot on my surface.
I don't ask much. Just a chance to
give my best.
Can you understand, you people
who live and breathe in
complete dependence upon me?
The elements trouble me
enough—I don't need mere
mortals to increase my burdens.
I've given my all—you've used me
inside and out, yet you've
wasted, squandered, and
depleted my gifts.
What do you want from me?
My resources are vast—but not
limitless.
You have conquered, but you can't
live without me.
I've watched you live, love, fight,
and die—and
I've cried inwardly at the futility of
it all.
You have wealth—you have
power—power to create, and to
destroy. Which will it be?
Think, consider, reason. I have
been patient.
I beg of you . . give me a chance.

Janet R Nason
THE POET
The poet sings to me
Causing silent miracles of the
heart.
A poet and a dog named Ben
Rekindle the flame of life
Causing my soul to revive
from a dreamless sleep
In a soundless space
To greet each day
With something that has been
missing
For so long—
Joy
Hope
And Love.

Coni L Fling (Van Note)
UNTITLED
And the sky was azure blue
The clouds satin white
and soft as goose-down
The autumn gale swept the
tall grass
And I walked barefoot
to absorb God's natural
high.

Dennis C Almquist
ONE AND SEVEN
One morning Charlie came to see
me at eleven
And asked, "What exactly is the
reason
That John, Jerry, Clete, and you bet
one and seven
In the Daily Double season after
season?"

It has now been four years since
my buddy John declared
That the one and seven
combination
Came in the most, from
calculations he'd prepared,
At the time he said it would be our
salvation

If four of us gentlemen invested
each race day
Just fifty cents apiece through
O.T.B.,
Eventually what we would see
come our way
Would be hundreds of dollars
profit, all tax-free

Ron and Jerry said they would like
to go in with us,
Each spent forty dollars or
forty-one,
Our first year's luck we thought
was just one incubus,
We didn't win, so Ron decided he
was done

Clete said that he would take Ron's
place the following year,
He's stayed with us to watch our
horses run,
We can't explain it; we think this
one's rather queer
That it has been four years and we
have not yet won

Clete proposed a change, but we
said no; he'd wanted us
To bet on one and three, or five and
two,
As I'd told Clete, I also said to
Chuck, "I guess
John, Jerry, and I think one and
seven are due."

JoAnne Stangl
GOD'S LOVE

This poem is dedicated to my husband, Jerry, my son, Scott and my daughter Julie who have been my greatest encouragement in using the gift of writing God has given me.

The love of God is so beyond
expressions that we know
It's hard to find the words
describing how He loves us so,

A picture sometimes paints a scene
and adds the hidden light
And so I want to paint a picture
of God's love tonight.

The scene is earth, where we abide
and where from God no man can
run and hide
Abortion, hate & killing reign
and men blaspheme His Holy
Name
He's mocked, the brunt of comedy
Oh how far we've strayed from
Thee.

And yet, each morning bright and
new
He makes the sun to rise
The beauty of His Holiness
breath taking to our eyes.

He sends the rain and gives us
flowers
and food for us to grow
He cares for men who hate Him
because He loves them so.

Each new day He sends His word
to all men far and wide
I love you, so I sent my son
and for your sin He died.

Can we who know His love today
not share this love so free?
And so complete the picture
begun on Calvary?

Wanda Brown Scott
WHEN I AM GONE

To courageous men and women everywhere, face to face with their own mortality, yet noble enough to leave a legacy of hope.

When I am gone hang down your
head and shed a million tears,
Then gird yourself with
hopefullness and walk into the
years.
Please spend no time on useless
thoughts or questions such as
why,
For they cannot be answered
should mortals dare to try.
Please cast aside the dreary
thoughts that try to haunt your
mind,
For you must pursue the sunshine
and the laughter while there's
time.
My love forever written on your
kind and gentle heart,
Will feel no ill or sorrow, just save
me a tiny part.

We partook of life so freely, we've
no regrets or wasted tears,
You walked with me through
golden valleys, God blessed us
with such happy years.
A valley dark now lies before me, I
must traverse this realm alone,
Please hold my hand to give me
courage and don't despair when,
I am gone.
When you look into the heavens or
hear my favorite melody,
Or feel my presence in the
shadows, then it's all right to
think of me.

And should you visit me in
springtime and on my bed sweet
flowers lay,
Bid me farewell with tender
musings and with courage walk
away.
I'll lay no hold upon your future or
weigh you down with memories,
Still it gives me consolation for I
know you'll think of me.
Perhaps my soul will go on
dreaming or perhaps I'll only
sleep,
It matters not, your love goes with
me, the memories mine to keep.

Pauline Beck
ANGUISH

Dedication: To my mother, Mary Elizabeth and to all who are lost. In hope that they hold on and find beauty in life and go forward in peace.

Listen—wait—understand
There be anything else?
Ever a cry inside not let out.
Hold no longer, a cry inside
Sound come, laughter around
Come out! cry Come out!

Much inside to free
See—feel—touch, all beauty
Ownself free: to give, learn all
Clamor thee now
There be anything left?
'Tis love in heart, now pave way
Ne'er shall hide no more.

Jack Victor Liotard
IF YOU WERE MINE
If you were mine, the world would
be
Exactly what its been
We'd have our ups and downs, you
see
At times an awful din,
And yet, a difference would abide
And love would be no game
If only you, would be my bride
Making, Liotard your name;

If you were mine, the birds would
sing
On each day of the year
Each animal and flower would
bring
Us smiles, to erase, each tear,

These things I've written, would all
come true
My life would be so fine
I'd seldom frown, for I'd have you
If only, you were mine.

Lois Kellems
WHERE HAVE YOU BEEN?
Have you ever strolled down a
street or lane
And suddenly been blessed with
seranades
By a Mocking Bird sitting atop a
weathervane
Bidding you ado as the sun slowly
fades.
Or watched a little gray squirrel, as
he scampers around
Going first up the tree and then
back down.
He'd rustle the leaves as he hunt
for a snack,
Hoping to find nuts that he could
take back,
To his leaf nest he'd made high up
in a tree.
So he'd twitch his tail and up he'd
go with glee.
The crows in the trees would scold
as you passed by,
Causing you to sigh, seeing how
effortlessly they fly.
Then your attention is drawn to a
little beagle dog
Chasing and yapping at a rabbit,
he'd scared from a log.
Over in the meadow, you catch a
glimpse of some deer,
Filling their tummies, without
nary a fear
Knowing that nightfall was
drawing near.
So, if you've not heard or seen the
beauties that lie
All around you, either low or high
Slow your pace, and open your eyes
Or else the wonders will pass you
by.

Michelle Knowles
WHAT A GOD HE IS

This poem is dedicated to Kelvin McCune. Thank You for helping me understand God & who He really is.

What a God He is
So perfect in every way
What a God He is
For He has given me His
salvation as my shield
He's a helper to the helpless,
merciful to the merciless
What a God He is
For He is a King forever and
forever
He's the greatest Judge because
He is perfectly fair
What a God He is
He's the Alpha and Omega—
beginning and the end
What a God He is
For He is Love
He's my inheritance—He's all
I've ever wanted all I'll ever need.
What a God He is
He's my highest joy and He fills
my every dream
He's my strength and protector,
yet His gentleness surrounds me
What a God He is
For He's alive,
Sing praises to Him for He is
worthy.
What a God He is
Day and night the heaven tells of
His glory without sound or word,
Silent is the skies yet their
message reaches all the world
Oh What a God He is—
Who is God except my Lord.

Vicky K Ramsey
EVENING

In memory of my brother: Joel W. Whitesides

Night tiptoes in
On kittens feet
To hear a willow sigh
A murmur low, a softened call
Against an ebony sky

A whippoorwill sings a merry song
As mist settles over the rise
but still, a willow calls
her murmur low
A soft and gentle cry.

Oh come with me through
meadows of Spring
Where May showers dress pastures
green
And evening stars above the earth
Welcomes the night
But the willows arms, drooping low
bemoans the very sight.

Hush, pretty willow
With your pessimistic airs
Night must come to rest earth's
cares
To mend the weary and the worn
to create life and the morn

So sleep soft willow, sleep
your boughs flung low
And tomorrow let your beauty
show
And tomorrow let your beauty
show.

Denice Mayhugh
FIND YOUR PLACE
Find your place on the time line
with goals you have set for you
Or the place you find will bring
misery
till you find the right place for you.
Build a stairway to success using
the
bricks of life.
Build to goals in little steps
so sliding doesn't get you behind.
The choice is yours, the goal is
your's
remember that all the time
And find your place on the time line
with success in the goal, in your
life.

Milred E Cushman
THIS LIFE IS ALL YOUR OWN
This Life is all your own—
No matter how it's going
Only you can accept or change it—
It's you, that makes the showing!

This Life is all your own—
Even if you're an orphan or a
drifter.
Your goals are in your hand—
Not your guardian, Dad or Sister!

This Life is all your own—
The failures or achievements.
The choice is yours alone—
No matter who's in agreement.

So this is your very own Life.
While young, try to rationalize—
"What do I want to achieve?"
Then make it materialize!!

Carol Meredith
WHAT EVER HAPPENED TO OLD FASHIONED LOVE?
What ever happened to those men
and women who fought so hard,
for everything; for love,
country and their beliefs.
What happened to those who still
believed in old fashioned things;
for love, country and beliefs.
It's easy nowadays to say: who
cares about anything, who are the
ones that suffer for it; each and
everyone of us.
So, don't be afraid to be old
fashioned, don't give up on love,
country and beliefs.
Be what our Great Grandparents
were: old fashioned and true to
everyone.
Old fashion is not a dirty word.
It's pride in oneself, and love
for mankind and respect in
everything that means anything to
you or your friends.
It is also trust in people that you
don't know.

Veronica Rivera
FAITH

To God who gives me my faith and inspiration.

I have yet to expend
My wings and fly for
Awhile, and explore
My life, who I am
And what is to become
Of me, because I have
Yet to live up to my dream
That I always wanted
And I know that someday
I will, with God, I'll live
Up to my dream, I will
I will, and I shall
I shall win
And live my dream

Mildred Jenkins Mauseth
THE THING

Poetic thoughts on the recession turning to a depression. Written for youth who haven't yet lived through a depression—in hopes it might help them cope.

A primeval fleshy thing crawled
out of
Nightmare caverns in
metamorphosis
Wreathing smoke as computer
eyes stared.

Must be a distant cousin of the
grim reaper
Breathed the air of an ancient
opium den and
Perhaps be the offspring of rape by
technology.

Blown by the economic winds
toward the city
Slithering like a monster in a Goya
etching
Pulsating a mute and ominous
prophecy.

Absorbing abundance from the
struggling
While programming some to
deception and crime.
It's hungry so we may become
victims.

Jane Hoffman
WELCOME, LITTLE STRANGER

To all the Little People, may they find, love and laughter, patience, joy, as each seeks their pace in life . . .

Did you come in on a rainbow?
In a crib of soft white down?
Were you sprinkled by the star-dust
as you floated oe'r the town?
Wer'ent you frightened of the
darkness
Or was it starry bright?

And what is the news of heaven
is it just as clean and new
As is this wee small baby
who has come to live with you?

You are a wee small stranger
and you've come from very far.
Soon you will find how much you
are wanted
Because you are just as you are.

You will bring such happiness
through the coming years.
From baby hood to child hood
Through sunshine and through
tears.

From the "Teens" onthrough to
growing up
each have a loving care;
How rich will be the memories
no gift could be so rare.

So, We, welcome you, little
Stranger
To your new home here on earth;
And We congratulate the parents
You acquired at your birth . . .

Lucy Moser

Lucy Moser
ANTIQUE GLASS

To my husband, Albert J. Moser, and son Albert Ray.

Crafted in the days of hoops,
bustles and stays
By early American artizans who set
the art of glass ablaze.
Sandwich pieces and those formed
by molding in a press
Left a telltale sign that proved it
wasn't real unless
A tiny thread imbedded there was
left
To show the end of pouring,
Not that they were inept.
Amber pieces that dazzle in the
sun,

Ruby glass that glows ad infinitum,
Satin and cut glass whose prisms
repeat all the rays
Of the most brilliant aurora
borealis.

These pieces that sit on my window
shelf
I know are only borrowed for
myself;
In yesteryear they were in
someone's parlor
Along with horsehair sofa and
antimicassar.
They were dear to somehone's
heart
And of their life a needed part.
So now I have the privileged
pleasure
Of sharing with that person's
treasure.
I hope in some future day
They will gladden another's heart
this way;
My 'pieces of history long past'
Captured in some lovely glass!

Marguerite M Waters
WHY LOVE?

To Joan, My "Second Mother"

If all the words cannot be spoken,
If all the feeling cannot be shown,
If all the love cannot be shared,
why love?

Why give so much, to take away?
Why 'be there', then to be alone?
Why love? To risk the hurt?

As the daffodil bursts into
Springtime,
so, too, as the sadness wanes,
Will my hope for tomorrow
begin anew—but not today—not
yet—
In its season, the smiles will break
through—
For I have felt the warmth of
your love,
I have shared in your friendship,
I have spoken the words of my
heart.

And now, as your memory echoes
within me,
evermore precious—
I am comforted,
reassured of each new day's
beginning—
that's . . . why love.

Shirley B Krawford
MY MOM-DOROTHY WRIGHT

My Special Mother's Day Poem written especially for and I now dedicate to: the most wonderful and loving mother, Dorothy Wright, with Love Forever, your daughter Shirley

---

When a smiling, happy little girl is
a part of your life.
Before you realize, the years have
gone by.
Now there's a bit of heaven in your
eyes,
The silver lining of the clouds is
placed amidst your hair.
And now by your side your
daughter walks with you as
friend and companion.
That's when a Mother's dream
comes true.
God Bless you Mom. My Love
Daughter
Shirley

Susan Canedy Clark
FREEDOM

A shimmering white dove soars
against a silken gray sky.

Freedom she has—
to fly unaided—
to circle and dive—
to race and glide.

She sweeps above sleepy
meadows, through wooded
glens—
brushing dew from the tips of
leaves
or heralding the dusk.

The skies are hers and she soars
unfettered.

Nesting high above the ground
with the coming of the night
with only her freedom
Her nights are cold.

Peggy Oneil Walters Crump
A BOOK

To my devoted children, Tina and Stephen Sneed

I wish that I could write a book,
Like so many hundreds do.
And have the words roll off my
tongue,
Like the early morning dew.
I would write of all the things,
Peace, happiness, and serenity
brings.
A book of hope, not fear,
Of all the things that I hold dear
But since I can't, I'll do my best
To write a poem, and then give
my pen a rest.

Peggy Duncan
THE LIKES OF LOVE

The flowers in spring when they
bloom
Love is like
A melody, a special tune
Love is like
A certain glance between me and
you,
I like the likes of love.
Love is like
The birds and bees, so I'm told
Love is for
The young and for the old
Love is good
When its hot or its cold
I like the likes of love.
Love is like
A ray of light from the sun
Love is like
The moon, when day is done
Loves throughout
The whole world, it's in everyone
I like the likes of love.

Eleanor T Port
MAN OF MY DREAMS

To Ed, Thank you for the inspiration and giving me your love.

I finally met the man that I've been
looking for
In all the searching on land and
shore
He's been the man of my dreams
For all of my life so it seems
The comfort and love that I feel
I know in my heart is very real
There's love in his eyes and his
touch
It's no wonder that I love him so
much
In all the things that we do and
share
This love that is growing I know
is rare
How lucky for me to have met this
man
He means so much to me
I'm proud of the love between us
I want all the world to see
My heart feels like bursting with so
much pride
Just when I'm standing at his side
Little things like calling to just hear
my voice
I'm the lucky one for his choice
We grow closer together day by day
What more can I ever say
Man of my dreams, I've finally
found you
Who said, "Dreams couldn't
come true."

Ms Beth A Kuhn
THE SEA OF TRANQUILITY

Swimming in the sea of tranquility
Is where I want to be.

Escaping the burdensome shores
of pain
To catch my breath and regain.

Plunging the misty depths of blue
Where the world becomes
magically anew.

Riding the awesome waves of life
Without those familiar pains and
strifes.

Waves of salty mist slapping my
face
Is a feeling that could never be
replaced.

Just floating upon this peaceful sea
I see all that is good in me.

It calms the stormy swells deep
within my
soul; When the troubles flood
within and
take their toll.

Plummeting and swirling me all
about
It's the place where I can let it all
out.

You will find it at the top of my list,
For coming here I just cannot
resist.

Nothing to lose but oh so much to
gain.

The sea of tranquility is where I
shall
remain.

Kimberly S Clark
CASTLES OF SAND

I am dedicating this poem to my precious, daughter Valencia; to Granny for a lifetime of faith "just be yourself . . . the world worships an original" —AND, to Anthony for an everlasting "Castle!"

He loves a girl of satin and lace;
confound, occult art,
emotionless space;
An angel at heart,
he's silent, with faith;
Love shines a limelight
sentenced to grace.

The Count and Countess vividly
glow,
with Joust, a cupid's poisoned
arrow;
Living for love,
no two better know—
"A Dream Within A Dream,"
our entity, by Poe

The roses have died now—
"I Love You Sweetheart;"
Painting by numbers, too many
call smart;
A symphony of red,
icy and tart;
We're castles of sand the sea
washed apart.

John Michael Dipietrantonio Jr
WHAT WE DID, WAS WHAT WE FELT

What can I say to comfort you
What can I do to help,
All I know, there were very few
That knew just how we felt.

As you can see, it's hard to say
I don't know how to start,
That this will be the final day
Before we must depart.

Tomorrow I will be leaving
Don't come to say goodbye,
Don't look back on the memories
They only make us cry.

It seems that this is all so wrong
You seem to feel the same,
But all we did, was what we felt
And now we feel the pain.

One day we will forget each other,
They say this must be so,
I say that you must love another
I say that I must go.

So it's time that I must say goodbye
While we sit here all alone,
It seems so even strange to me
That we ended it, over the phone.

Larry C Huber

Larry C Huber
NATURES CALL

Dedicated to my family, friends and to all who love and respect the jewel upon which we live.

Dawns early light, gently breaks
through the misty morning fog.
Silhouettes dancing on the
mossy old log.
Autumn colors of red and gold on
mighty oaks standing tall and
bold

Against a clear blue sky an eagle
soars, as if to say, wake up,
Wake up we have another day.
Reflections in the clear running
brook, meandering through the
meadow and oak.
Between granite the water runs
with both gentleness and power,
A bold blue cloak.

Water to nurture both man and
beast, but not least, providing
Moisture for all life giving seed.
Winding through the valley below
the brook has an iridescent glow,
Reaching out, seeking the end of
its journey.
The gentle fog moves on, the pastel
shade lifts,
Revealing the glory of a new day
born.
Ready to give of itself, the beauty
of nautre gives life a just name.
Never complaining about the
abuse and neglect rendered
upon it by the hands of man, the
stewards of this daily birth.
Take heed my fellow man, we have
only one great and beautiful
planet, "Earth"

Julie L Davis

LITTLE FINGERS

With love to my son, David James Blair Davis

Little fingers
And little hands
Reaching out to learn
Everything they can

Great big smiles
Great big eyes
Full of wonder
And surprise

Some day soon
You'll grow to be
Independent and you won't
Need me

So for now
I'll hold you tight
Sing you lullabys
Tuck you in at night

And no matter
How old you ever get
I know that I
Will never forget

Those little fingers
And little hands
Reaching out to learn
Everything they can

Patti Dee

A SUMMER DAYDREAM

The day is hot
The breezes warm yet cooling
My thoughts wander
To another place and time

A place of rippling waters
And never ending peace
To a time when love was young
And so was I

I remember the child
Who would blush and giggle
At the thought
Of a magical first kiss

As the seasons change
So do we
That child is no longer
For now she is grown

Often I long
To be that child again
To be carefree
When things were simple

Tara Khurana

MY MEETING WITH MY LORD

I was sitting on the threshhold of
life,
I thought I have still time left in life
To finish all the chores of my life,
Before starts setting in the dawn of
life
When I will get ready to meet My
Dear Lord.

I hustled around my house to
finish all
The unfinished tasks though were
very long;
I did not realize evening of life had
set in
And I should rather get ready for
My Lord,
To greet and meet My Majestic
Lord.

Evening of life also passed by;
I thought I still have night of life,
To complete my chores and
prepare for MY Lord;
Energies were waning, even night
of life passed by,
I still had not prepared for my
meeting with My Lord.

Even night of life passed by;
My Lord came at my door to meet
me,
I was so unprepared that I did not
want to go,
I burst into tears I wasted my life
in petty chores,
And never prepared myself for my
meeting with My Lord.

Janel Lafond Paquin

SNOW ANGEL

My little one, a babe in arms,
A princess of delightful charms,
With blanket clutched in fingers
small,
While sparkling snowflakes softly
fall.

My little one, just two years old,
With mittened hands against the
cold,
Those cherub cheeks of heaven's
glow,
An angel's portrait in the snow.

My little one approaching four,
A path you make from yard to door,
Through drifts that sink beneath
your feet,
In search of icicles to eat.

My little one, a child of six,
Collecting stones and carrot sticks
To clothe the figure, cold and bare
With tender warmth and childish
care.

My little one, a charming eight,
For powdered slopes you cannot
wait
To tumble down the glistening hills
With laughter ringing after spills.

My little one, so close to ten,
I wish that you were small again,
To be the child I used to know,
My blessed angel in the snow.

Jeanne G Kupchik

THREE TODAY

Growing, developing, little boy,
Unfettered, unsullied, untouched
mind.
What wondrous secrets will you
reveal,
What unknown truths will you
find?

You probe, you question, you gulp
facts,
With tactile fingers you find form.
Your eyes record, your ears receive,
Your three years knowledge a
sumptous store.

A mixed inheritance is present
here.
How will the scales at length reveal
A loving nature, an appreciative
eye,
A sense of laughter, a sympathetic
sigh.

You speak with genius and,
incredibly, read.
You master numbers with
enormous speed.
What grace of ours will you
possess,
What negative genes will sport the
rest?

We see in bloom a remarkable soul.
We watch, we pleasure, we admire
the whole.
It's obvious you're wondrous
smart,
But will you fathom your
grandma's heart?

Marcia A Desreuisseau

LET ME SING OUT TO AMERICA

Let me sing out to America,
With rainbows gracing her
With her sides clutched hard by the
gripping tides
And the rugged mountain spurs.

Let me sing out to America,
Whose greatly as she stands
With a ground so good with
brotherhood
Lest she be a friend to Man!

Let me sing out to America,
Where there's peace in her valley
each morn
Where over each hill, there's a
moment so still
When a proud American's born!

Let me sing out to America,
While I hold my head up high
Embracing all her beauties right
there
Under and 'ore her sky!

Let me sing out to America,
When I see her banners fly
Over that mound and that stone
once again
Over the hill in the rye!

Let me sing out to America,
Where God's children are treading
her sod
Let us sing out, America
Where the Bible's the Word of God.

Enid Hershey

REVELATION

When I was a little girl,
I loved him
Because he said I should.
I was very good.

When I was a little girl,
I went to school
Because he said I should.
I was very good.

When I was a bigger girl,
I was confirmed
Because he said I should,
I was very good.

When I was a bigger girl,
I went to college
Because he said I should.
I was very good.

When I was a woman,
He died.
I cried—
Because I wanted to.

Jennifer Jean Janutolo

FORGOTTEN DREAMS

My dreams nearly died when you
turned me away,
You said goodbye to me forever
that day.
I love you, I'll miss you, I'll never
forget,
That you once loved me those
words you regret.
I wish you could hear my
heart-breaking cries,
I miss the warm feeling when
you looked in my eyes,
You said that you loved me and
that it would last,
Why can't I forget it and put you
in the past?
Why can't I forget it just as you
care to do?
I would if I could but I still care
about you.
I miss when you held me you
held me so tight,
You wouldn't let me go until the
time was right.
I know it will never be the same
as before,
Don't ever look back 'cause it'll
only hurt more.
'Cause if you look back the pain
will be there,
It won't be easier if you said you
still care.
I don't need a fancy reason or an
answer why from you,
All I want to know is why you
broke my heart in two.
What we had was special and I
thought it would never end,
All I ever really wanted was for
you to be my friend.
We can only go on though and
not think about our past,
Just forget it like Forgotten
Dreams to me I thought would
last.

Paulette Yohe

AMERICA WEEPS

Lord, let us turn our eyes to thee,
America is more than free.
We are one nation under God.
Yet Christian Love seems so odd.

Crime and corruption are
everywhere,
It's not even safe to breathe the air!

Our lands are filled with toxic waste,
Our water even has a "taste!"

Our society lies in ruin and rust,
And our governments have no one's trust.
We worry of bombs from up above,
We need your comfort, peace and love.

Help us to be our brother's keeper,
And stop the decline from setting steeper,
Help us save the Earth and stop the crime.
And bring the paradise back in time.

Let freedom ring and beauty reign,
Stop the hunger, hate and pain.
Teacher forgiveness that war may cease,
We learn more when we know your peace.

Our nation spans from coast to coast,
To guide us send thy Holy Ghost.
Help us Lord, to follow thee,
And from these plagues, grant liberty.

Mrs Frank Pressley

Mrs Frank Pressley
JESUS CHRIST

In the darkness of the night
When all seem so bleak,
There came a ray of light
So gentle, and caring
I knew it had to be—JESUS CHRIST.

When I thought all was lost and gone
He came along—picked up the pieces
And filled my life with rays of sunshine.
This man called—JESUS CHRIST.

Now I'm filled with love and gratitude,
Knowing His guiding light,
Will see me through each trying day
And every lonely night.
For this man—that entered my life
Is JESUS CHRIST.

Now my burdens somehow seem lighter
With the coming of the dawn.
My tears and fears are gone
Because of my Master—JESUS CHRIST.

Bob B Villines
DON

To a fine young man. Whose vivacity I cherish forever

Don—you left too soon today
There were things I needed to say
Didn't get to tell you goodbye
So all I could do was cry

Don—don't know where you are
But I'll bet you're ridin' a star
One so full of love and truth
Is sittin' high on heaven's roof

Wish we could ride the highways
Lie in the sun on summer days
All the things we used to do
Don, I don't do anymore without you

Those words, the good die young
So sad when they're sung
But I'll keep singin' for you
It's what I hold on to

And Don, one day so fine
We'll meet again in time
Then walk down roads of gold
It's true so I've been told

Wish we could ride the highways
Lie in the sun on summer days
All the things we used to do
Don, I don't do anymore without you

Maxine Thomas
DOWN THROUGH THE COUNTRY LANE

As we travelled down through the country lane,
Reminiscing as we went along—
There was beauty to see in every nook
And life was a lilting song.

The flowers still bloomed at the side of the hill,
The moss was thick and green,
And the vines of ivy swirling 'round,
Made a beautiful, breathtaking scene.

The cows and sheep were grazing,
Sheaves of wheat had been readied for fall,
You could hear the frogs in the babbling brook—
And at times the whippoorwills' call.

You could hear the robin red-breast,
Feel the strength of the cardinals' trill—
You could see the flash of red as he flew,
In his reign—he was king—at will.

Rows of corn in the fields had been planted,
Their stalks swaying there with the breeze—
We had no cares as we travelled on,
Relaxed—serene—at ease.

The years slipped away for a little while
And we were young again,
And we nodded and dreamed as we drove along—
Down through the country lane.

Linda A Sandknop Silverwings
FLIGHT INTO FREEDOM

To all thinking hearts who read, think, and ponder deeply about the many meanings of life . . . may your consciousness be lifted, if only for a moment, by the reading of a poem.

Birds in flight wanting freedom, longing to get
Eventually even,
Struggling, strutting their colors, showing off for
Naive others,
Swooping down into the sea spray, grabbing a fishbite
Colored grey,
Doing the latest penguin dance, then growing real still,
Almost in trance.

Hugging ancient forest trees, gliding effortlessly in the
Still breeze,
Squatting on the deck of some millionaire's boat, pecking at
His smuggled dope,
Walking lightly on silver clouds, defacing the noses of some
Holy shrouds,
Shaking off sea spray from their wings, taking high dives
Into circus rings . . .

Who do you think you are, reminding myself of me? I too
Long to be free.
I've set sail into stormy seas; my mind's been broken by
Life's disease,
Fate's dusty hand choked me with such ease—can I never do
What I please?
Will hesitating bring me lengthening of my life? Is freedom
Only in death's flight?

Eva Price Bell
A WIFE'S PRAYER

I took his love, his name, his life, with the simple vow, "I will,"
And two lives became one life, together a mission to fill.

I gave him then all my tomorrows, and whatever they would bring,
Through sorrow we'd together cry, through joy, together sing.
With the strength of the oak our love would stand through the calms and the storms of life,
The greatest blessing of all, to be together as man and wife.

A minute detail in Thy wonderful plan; a small branch yet, to become a tree
To give life and direction to whom Thou would choose to be ours for Eternity.

Father in Heaven, let me be a channel of blessing to him from Thee,
Of inspiration, strength and love, all that a wife could ever be.

Help me to be sensitive to his feelings and his needs
And as he seeks to do Thy will, let me faithfully follow his leads.

Let my heart hear eternal echoes of the vows I made this day
That I may stand firm and faithful, and by his side always stay.

May the love that binds us blossom into a radiant flow'r
Of fulfillment, through our faithfulness, until the judgment hour.

Let us keep the dream before us, and brighter all the while
That we live to partake of Thy glory and thrill to the touch of Thy smile.

And as we share our mansion in Thy kingdom up above,
my heart will sing with Eternal joy, "I did not fail my love."

Patti O'Keeffe
SEASON ON THE WIND

Sifting through ashes of spring memories, where bright
flowers were gently lifting their heads to the sun,
I finally realized, you may have been everything I wanted,
but in your present frame of mind you will never be everything
I need.

Strolling through the hazy moonlight on a hot summer night
without you, is slowly becoming bearable, soon it will become
enjoyable. Briskly walking through damp piles of vibrantly
colored autumn leaves, while smelling the crisp air of winters
approach is invigorating to both my mind and body,
even though I miss you!

Quietly watching winters first snow fall, while baking
festive holiday cookies in gala reds and greens, has brought
to me a new inner peace. I have passed through the
four seasons Chicago weather shows its native sons
and daughters and survived them without you.
What a joy to pass through my own season of
freedom. The season on the wind.

Sonja Denise Slone Zone
I SEARCHED THIS EARTH

I SEARCHED THIS EARTH FOR ONE, LONE, TRUE FRIEND
I LOOKED UNTIL I LOST HOPE AT A DEAD END
OUT OF OBLIVION YOU AND YOUR RAINBOW APPEARED
YOU MADE MY THUNDERSTORM OF TEARS DISAPPEAR
LIKE A WIZARDS MAGIK
YOU COME AND YOU GO
THE CURTAIN CLOSES
END OF SHOW
I STAND, ALONE, AND GIVE YOU AN OVATION
THANKING YOU FOR WITHSTANDING MY TRIBULATIONS
REVOLUTION COMES AND THERE IS CHANGE
MY MIND IS WEAK, MY HEART IS INSANE
LOVE SURROUNDS AND MY LIFE IS IN A NEW PROPORTION
I LEAVE YOU BEHIND TO BE VICTIM OF MY EXTORTIONS
OCCUPATION OF MY TIME
LEAVING YOU BEHIND —

how could i B so cruel?????

Light shatters dark and aphotic time
THE MEMORIES STALK—my heart talks

my mind seeps memories of you . . .
the way we were
not the way we have become

IT IS AXIOMATIC—I DID YOU WRONG
OUT CAME THE WORDS FOR A JUSTIFICATION SONG
MY APOGEOTROPISM IS INTERPTED BY THE APOLEXY TO APOLOGIZE
THESE WORDS PLEASE, HITHER, READ, AND MEMORIZE:

U R MY FRIEND . . . and i love you

William A Parks

William A Parks
THE SMILE

In memory of my beloved wife: Enriqueta

The smile that once brightened my world
Has now gone to be with God,
She suffered pain, heartache, and sorrow as did Jesus when he trod,

She was here for a purpose
That now I can see,
She was God's special envoy he sent to be with me,
To bring me to Jesus who now holds her hand,
And she will smile on me while waiting in that blessed promised land.
And so dear God I promise to walk the Saviour's way,
And join her forever at the end of my earthly stay.

Greg Waszak
TIME—A PASSAGE OF

To Mary Beth the inspiration—the love—the result

And through the passage of time
A man did walk!
And behold. . .
His eyes did meet those of
A fellow traveler!
And they became friends. . .
And lovers.
And through a passage in time
A man and a woman did walk.

Edna Maxine Bittick
MY MOTHER

Written for and dedicated to, my Mother, Lillian M. Davis—on Mother's Day 1972.

God took from the glories of heaven
A special ray of the sun
The freshness of dew and starlite, too
And the sweetness of songs unsung
He added the beauty of flowers
Barrowed strength from towering trees
The softness of gentle showers
And gentle midsummer breeze
He molded these into an angel
Who's face holds a gentle smile
Filled her heart with love and goodness
And gave her a voice sweet and mild
Yes—God's creation was perfect
For—Heaven created her,—He
Then in pity and love, He sent her to earth
And gave "My Mother," to me.

Donald L Harris
COUNT IT ALL JOY

Dedicated to my family in God for the elevation of humanity through the beacon of American dignity, freedom and infinite harmony of all throughout the whole world, for all the ages to come until the end of history and time as we know it.

Life comes and goes,
With all its thundering woes.
Oh, how I long to be free;
Free from all disharmony.
Men and women, randomly pursue life;
And along the way, see pain, despair and strife.
If only, all would cohesively seek ideals!
But many don't understand such desperate appeals.
People, conveniently, ponder away their dreams.
To find disillusionment and cynicism with all schemes.
Intimate emotions are expressed in flight,
By lonely temporaries, pondering in the night.
Now, I'm looking for the brighter side.
However, thrills of life seem to hide.
My hope still lies in the testimonies of my Creator.
If only, it would be lauded, communicated in the theater!
Crystals of joy, would then compete;
Amidst overwhelming frustration and defeat.
Who has the integrity to command such domain?
The WORD became flesh, echoed in many a refrain.
Love still conquers the emptiest heart;
It beckons all who are willing, to take part!
Hope is only a prayer away,
Waiting for those interested, to begin, today;
To consider a life that comes and goes;
Conquering with grace, the woes;
With dignity raised to be free;
Pursuing the grandeur of infinite harmony!

Elizabeth J White
TAKE TIME

Husband and Father Delmonte L. White, loved and missed.

Take time to put your arms around a loved one.
Tell them how much you love them today.
Tell them how you're enriched by the things they have done.
How you appreciated them along the way.
I often think of all the things I could have done and said.
But never had the time you know, and now that precious ones are dead, covered by the white blanket of snow.
Take time to count your blessings over and over.
Thank God each day for all the blessings as you figure up the score.
Each person you know in some way has good about them.
Tell them each day as they go out and at nite when they open the door.
Put your arms around them, hug them real tight, tell them how you love them and need them every nite.
Kiss them goodbye in the morning. Greet them with love at nite.
And no one will ever forget that you taught them the way that was right.
We all make mistakes and are sorry for the things we've done and said.
Tell them all about it now while you can. For some day they too will be dead.
We are born to die the bible tells me so.
But now while you can love them, hug them, and your love shows.
So that when they go away no more can be said.
You know God will say my children you are well fed.
I know the heartache of everything I've said and done.
But I'll try and make it up on my life's run.
Maybe a little word I say or a little deed well done.
Will help someone else save their daughter or son.
So take time to smell the roses as your path you trod.
Do the best you know how to do I'm sure as the word of
God he will open his arms to you, and say
(WELCOME, JOB WELL DONE).

Linda Louise McDonald
FOR A VIETNAM SOLDIER

I dedicate the poem "For A Vietnam Soldier," to my friend and husband, Charles Stanley McDonald, who was there.

Let the past die my friend,
Say I to you,
But how you—say, and say I to you—
Learn to forgive, For in forgiving we grow
And in growing we live, my friend
Feel the feeling, yes, that's your enemy
He has a family like you, my friend
Is he so different—
In lighter days, He laughed, He loved, He saw a better world, my friend.
Do you remember?
Is there a chance you might have been friends if your paths had crossed in a different season—
You say you hurt—What about him—
You say your friend was killed, what about his—
You say you hate him—
What about, what about
It's alright, I understand, you needn't go on—
I love you, the same as he is loved—
And say I to you
Eyes meet, souls touch, through time and he is you and you are him, my friend
There is no difference—
Although I sense you feel one.
My heart breaks—But dawn comes early—

Carolyn S Wms Harris
BEAUTY IS

Beauty is
A smile good morning
A kiss hello
A hug, I love you
Closeness good night
Beauty is saying,
—I will,—
—I can,—
I want to, sure, why not,
And okay
Beauty is,
—Caring—
—Giving—
—Taking—
—Doing—
—Sharing—
Beauty is,
Earth, sun, sky
Beauty is people
Beauty is God

Maria Y Baca
FOREVER ETERNAL

It is truly a melancholy thought to ponder
That the total sum of one man's existence would not
Even merit a passing sigh in the life of this universe.
It is indeed a sad thought that in a relatively few
Years from now our total life's journey will have been
Forgotten—except perhaps for a passing reference
By some distant and unknown

descendant. This has
Often made me question God's
purpose for us to
Be conceived in time—the
monster
that consumes everything.
It is my belief, however, that God
has not left
Man completely vulnerable to
the
ravishing hand of
Time. Love, that ability for two
people to share the
Same eternity of emotions
within
the same space,
Can be little time. Although the
physical will age,
Love will withstand. And when
the
material has
Succumbed to the passing of the
seasons, that love
Will survive in those minds and
places touched by
That space of emotions.
So be it with us. The uncertainty
of time will no doubt
Test us, mistreat us, misguide us,
perhaps unite us, and
Eventually consume us—as it
will
everything. But as
Long as there is space; And there
must be because time
Cannot exist without space, I will
live in those spaces
That our emotions occupied—
forever eternal.

Mrs Brenda Irene Helling

IN THE HANDS OF MY SAVIOR

In the hands of my Savior, I have
nothing to fear,
Though storms rage around me,
and the way seems unclear.
He designed the rainbow. He's the
Author of peace.
His power creates good gifts and
makes evil cease.
Through Him, all things work
together in love and grace.
I'm persuaded He's with me in
each test I face.
He's called and chosen me to be
servant and friend.
The journey we take together will
never end.
If my world grows dark, and the
light I cannot see—
His Light of goodness He'll send to
touch and heal me.
He'll help me stand strong when
my faith starts to depart.
Faith comes by hearing His Word
that changes my heart.
I will put on the armor, He's given
to me.
Knowing He's on my side, I will
taste victory.
I'll soar as an eagle, as I'm learning
to wait—
Through the Lamb's Blood, I'll
enter Heaven's Gates.

Heather K Magee

ALL'S GAME

I face upward
talking.
I don't believe you
killing.
Carelessly, innocently, vengefully.
scattered memories left behind.
One slits his wrist for you to see;
yet;
the world crumbles onward.
Corpses cry out their death
hoping to change the destruction;
but it only repeats.
It's all a game.
Society the characters; the
scandalizing scavengers.
The resourses are tripping short.
Our rewards, success, are attached
with consequences.
Our beautiful world;
the tip of the mountains
to the bottoms of the seas
diminish with black smut.
All's game.
And you're the player.

Barbara J Bentley

AND LIFE GOES ON

To my mom, Patricia J. Spalding, in loving memory. Thanks for making my life possible and for encouraging me to write my feelings. I love you. Thanks again for everything.

Oh those teen years,
how fast they come and go
Remembering back,
I thought I'd never grow.
Time goes faster
with the kids I have now.
They grow so fast,
the speed of time has tripled
somehow.
As life goes on,
and the days pass by.
I'd like to be remembered,
I say with a sigh.
Who will remember someone,
once in a grave.
I've done nothing special,
and nothing I gave.
So when people walk by,
they may read my stone.
I give you these words,
and life goes on

Ruth Errington David

Ruth Errington David

SWEET SLEEPER

I watched you once again last night
As nighttime made the room a
place
Where moonbeams, searching,
paused to light
Upon soft curls that kissed your
face.

I heard no sound except the sighs
And murmurings which come and
go
When slumber closes tired eyes
That earlier had charmed me so.

Your hand, enhanced by starlight's
gleam
With half curled fingers seemed to
be
In readiness to catch a dream. . .
Sweet Sleeper. . .let it be of me!

Lori Thomas Sheets

DREAMS FROM THE PAST

He came from a time I'd forgotten
at last,
He haunted and teased me with
dreams from the past.
He played with my memory of love
pure and soft,
My dreams from the past, the love
I thought lost.
He tempted my heart to take over
my head,
To relive those moments I once
thought were dead.
He relit the fire that burned from
within,
He set my heart free to know
passion again.

Eliza Ann McNair

PEARL HARBOR, AGAIN!

Listen! Mothers weeping for their
dead children,
not knowing where their graves
forever to be.
Thrown amid the chaos the
assailant bombs have rendered,
bodies here, and heads, legs not far
off to see.
Creeping out from the ruins an old
man of seventy-five,
and he watches the behavior of
anguish and panic of people
running by.
A child wailed not from far off,
someone search, search for that
child?
Fragment of the bombing
penetrated the lives of every
tribes.
A flower used to blossom here on
this tree splintered to the earth.
Pearl Harbor, again!
Blood and death perfumed the air,
signs of no trespassing springed up
from everywhere.
Fathers gone to war, not knowing
how his family fared,
no, no an earthquake could not
have happened there.
My sons were taught to fight with
bows and arrows,
my sons haven't any know-hows to
defeat the atomic nuclear
warfares.
See where a mother tried to protect
her sons, to avoid unwanted
sorrows,
at least we know they died together.
Bewilderments filled the
expressions of surviving
children,
huddled together like discarded
old shoe leathers.
A flower used to blossom there, its
scent greeted the wind.
Pearl Harbor, again!

Kelli M Kay

DELIVERENCE

Quietly the gate unlocked
and I was free.
Free at last from imprisonment
I had caused
With crimes against myself,
wrong choices, a fear of life.
Now, how simple. How easy the
pieces fit.
No struggle, I have the key.
Before all life was a jumble of
puzzle
that didn't work,
Because I had locked that gate. I
alone
opened it again.
How great to find fresh scent to air
I breathe.
How intense the whole spectrum
of color
and now . . .
How beautiful is life. Freedom
from
pain, from want, from strain
Comes with choice. With decision
to
mentally free oneself . . .
Deliverence is won. Anytime you
care
unlock the gate, be free.

Benjamin Carrasco I

MASK OF SORROW

To: Susan E. Hauck; For all of your support and encouragement. And for believing in me. Love always Benjamin

---

We hide our tears. We hide our
fears. Behind a "Mask of
Sorrow." Hoping we can hide it
all, at least until the morrow.
Our private shames, our private
guilts, are hidden behind the
mask. Deep inside we cry for
help, but have not the courage to
ask. Instead of admitting the
pain in our hearts, we try our
best to deny it. But then it begins
to tear us apart and we realize
we must accept it.
Our "Mask of Sorrow." How
long can we hold it? How long
can it last? When will it be
shattered by our sins from the
past? Guilt and Shame cloud our
lives. As we tire of living with lies.
Sorry are we who wear the mask.
For keeping it on is a dreadful
task. It hides the feelings we do
not want others to know. But
after so much time, they begin
to show.
Mask of Sorrow, it hides our
guilt. It hides our shame. It hides
it all, save for our pain. Mask of
Sorrow. How we hate it so. For
our true selves, we are afraid to
show.
Through the mask slips a single
tear. After so long. The Mask of
Sorrow, we can no longer wear.

Jean Moffett

REACH FOR THE STARS

Reach for the stars, that's what
they had said
And they eagerly prepared to go
where few men had tread
So young, so proud, so anxious, as
they readied for their launch
Loyal to their families, yet, with
American hearts so staunch
To go far out among the stars
where peace forever reigns
And make their dreams come true
as well as scientific gains
Little did they realize how short
that trip would be
Only God could know, as He's the
one who holds the key
Even though we mourn them, it's
really for ourselves we cry
For they've gone to a far, far better
place in that
Vast undaunted sky.

Diane Virginia Harlowe
MY MARRIAGE SECRET

Dedicated to the one who keeps my dreams alive. My loving husband, Billy Harlowe.

There's someone so special, a big part of my life.
Many wonderful years ago, he made me his wife.
Some couples don't make it in marriages today.
It's such a shame and fills my heart with dismay.
The secret is easy, it's one simple thing.
Just remember the vows you made with that ring.
If you can remember the promises you made.
Your love and happiness will never fade.
So what's more important?
Those trivial debates,
Or staying with the one you love, for life as mates.
When you think things aren't right,
Just open your heart,
And remember you promised,
"Til death do you part."
Remember I said, "Openness, love and laughter."
Will help you to live . . .
HAPPILY
EVER
AFTER!

Jo M Pearcy
WINTER ENDS
The sun is out the sky is blue
It looks like a pretty day.
The warmth of the sun beaming down
On the ground melts the snow away.
Winter is almost over
Cold weather will soon be gone.
Soon you'll see pretty flowers
Sprouting up all over the lawn.
The ground will turn from white to green
As the grass grows big and tall.
Reaching up for sunlight after
Being hidden by the winters snow fall.

Sherry Lee
CHAIN OF HANDS
Pull in close now
Let's hold hands

Everybody close your eyes and pretend
We are all equal

Pretend we are on peaceful lands

Pull in closer now
Let's all pray

Everybody knows how
Don't they . . .

Helen Pedker Baron
PIANO MAN (A MEMORY OF LIBERACE)
Life of glitter, glass and sound
In countless countries all about
His flying fingers fueled dead keys
With lively tunes for heads of state
By magic box for every man
They saw that splendid smile
Those starry, flashing eyes
Heard the rapid tumble rush
That cornucopia of notes
In ecstatic rapture, fantasy and fame
He dwelled in marvelous acclaim
Wonderous audiences still applaud
Though He's kept his rendevous with God.

Tricia L Kursewicz
THE COOL NIGHT AIR CHILLED HER SKIN

To the dreamers, fantisizers, and romantics in this sometimes cold world. . .

The cool night air chilled her skin.
The jacket she had pulled around her shoulders gave a little warmth.
The stars in the sky and the moon had beckoned her,
She had answered the call.
The moonlight on her wavy auburn hair reminded her
Of how it used to be, or may be it was her imagination
Fortelling her dreams of castles and lands,
Far away
And a prince who would love her.
Then in years to come she would stand on the water's edge
And remember him,
The way they were, together.
Things about him she never noticed then—
The stars
The fairies, fools, jesters of the night
Dressed in silk, icy hot and white
The dance they do.
The life they live,
In the kingdom of the night.
The onyx bay lapping at the shores,
The ripples of the water etched in silver,
Frozen breath like stardust cutting the curtain of midnight.
Then the dawn comes to push away the dreams,
Beautifully it urges them back, into their box,
To await the time when the lid will be lifted
once more.

Kay A Fletcher

Kay A Fletcher
MY GLIMPSE OF HEAVEN
Our stay on earth is a gift from God, from Heaven above,
How else could we teach our children of His forgiving love?
Each of us has the option of being real good or so bad,
We are born as little babies to a earthly Mom and Dad.

We can be taught quite simply, the Golden Rule,
Our minds are then expanded as we attend a school.
The most important gift is just to believe in God,
To attain Christianity before we return to the sod.

Faith is not something you can learn, it's not something you see,
It's not something tangible, like a pretty flower or a tree.
It comes from God, through our prayers and faithful love.
The inner peace is satisfying, a promise from above.

It's hard to describe, words are rather hard to command,
But I was touched tenderly by God's own saving hand.
All the pain I had, the mental anguish, melted away,
As I saw a glimpse of Heaven, I'll never forget that day.

I no longer felt my body, I was floating in the air,
The blessed peace I felt, nothing can ever compare.
I cannot describe the tranquil beauty, tho I can see it still,
I knew God had accepted me, I would gladly accept His will.

Our gracious God rekindled the beat of my still heart,
He returned my floating spirit, He gave my soul a new start.
He sent me back to my body, to act out my Book of Life,
With its trials, tribulations, its anxiety and strife.

No more will I be afraid, or fear the call of Death,
For I will find Heaven, when I take my final breath.
Since I am but human, I sin each day I live,
But as my prayers are spoken, I know He will forgive.

So, my friends, be faithful to God, just simply BELIEVE,
Such blessed assurance, is the reward you will receive.
For I know there is a Heaven, I've had a glimpse you see,
When I die, I will enjoy Heaven and peace eternally.

Linda S Simms
QUIET
Quiet is a solemn place,
Full of time—
Full of space—

Memories flow about
like ghostly apparitions.

Alice Henderson Dunn
ODE TO POOKI
Pooki wanders:
He's wandered since a pup;
I've sought him all about the town,
Down the hill and up.

We've a leash law,
This little town of ours;
Our neighbor right across the street
Hates Poo in his flowers.

Dog catcher
Had Pooki in his grasp
One day when I was right behind
Waving his leash clasp.

Pooki mastered
Obedience school rules;
He went through all the paces, then
Tossed aside those tools.

He refuses
His "duty" on a walk;
He thinks it is his special time;
He'll run, then gawk, then balk,

Marking boundries,
Of course, at every post;
At every bush his sniffs reveal
Other dogs' old ghosts.

Bring him back in,
He's pawing at the door;
Of course he needs to go outside;
He'll prove it on the floor.

Twelve years winning!
(I've never beat him once.)
I let him out into the yard,
Then feel quite like a dunce,

For off he wanders;
Cuts sharper than a knife
Right through a brand new exit hole;
Leads a magic life;

Cars don't hit him,
Dognappers pass him by;
Perhaps his growl and wide, bull smile
Belie his dimming eye.

Search for hours,
In solitude or crowd,
He'll come at last, when he decided,
Prancing, dancing, proud.

Search is idle;
I do it just the same;
He isn't my dog, never was,
But "Mother" is my name.

Robin Lane
IF I COULD BE A STAR
If I could be a star
With many brilliant rays
I'd shine upon your life
For your remaining days.

I'd toss away sorrow
Leave you only with smiles.
I'd give you smooth sailing
For many carefree miles.

I'd take away your debts
Replace them with cashflow.
I'd make you so happy
As through this life you go.

I'd be a friend to you
As long as we shall live.
Because you are my friend
My all to you I'd give.

Grace DeGirolamo Resio
AUTUMN
Autumn is a beautiful season to look forward,
To see the leaves turn red, yellow, gold and rust.
Let us enjoy the foliage about us every year.
God never fails, so in Him put our trust.
The Fall leaves are a picturesque scene.
The colors fit so lovely blended together.
In their midst the fir trees peek through.
They remain the same in all kinds of weather.
People travel afar in trains, buses, and cars.
They all enjoy gazing around at this beautiful view,

And feel closer to Him for this creation.
And thus, may all our lives in Him renew.
The array of colors seen close to the heavens,
Also reflect their splendor in lakes and streams.
The artist is inspired by all their beauty,
And shows a radiant happy face that beams.
Those portraits can last a very long time.
Pretty Autumn leaves are also pressed in a book.
And so we have our cherished memories of Fall.
The trees are dormant, in spring display a new look.
So it is with us when we accept the Lord,
A new change through our lives takes place.
A new glow and beauty radiates our whole being.
Pray this awakening, we can walk with God at His pace.

O'Nelda Starr
HOW LIFE IS SPENT

A little heartache—a little pain
A little loss—a little gain
Some disappointments—a little sorrow
Not much concern about tomorrow
Occasional sickness—a desire for wealth
Being wrapped up—within one's self
Little love—plenty deceit
Disloyalty seems—a treasured fete
Time is limited—to make amends
For those who mistreat—their loving friends
Never practicing—what they preach
No communication—but plenty of speech
Plenty time—to criticize
But not enough—to sympathize
Too little faith—for so many needs
With some reluctance—to do good deeds
Slow to retract—that little white lie
And much like a vapor—life passes by
This precious life—God has lent
Be sure to monitor—each moment spent

Dale L Knaggs
READ TO ME

Daddy, let me climb
upon your knee,
so you can read to me.
About far away places, old and new,
I want to hear about things that are true.
About God and his command,
yes, EVEN the devil and his hand.
I want to be able to see,
so Daddy read to me.
About the clouds in the sky,
and about people and why they die.
I want to know more, and be.
So don't stop reading to me.
I float away on the sea,
to mountains I will dwell.
Golly! But its swell,
when you read to me.

Harriet Glenn
CATS

For Amy, who loved these cats

My big, black cat
is very, very fat.
If she sat on your hat,
she would mash it flat.

My black and white cat
is also very fat.
He brought me a long, brown rat
and hid him under the welcome mat.

David R Cummins
VALENTINES

Though my heart has beaten
a thousand times.
It does'nt compare
to the love that's mine.
The days are short
and the night's are longer.
Every moment with you
my heart grows fonder.
For this valentines
would not be complete
if not for the love I cherish
that stems so deep.

Michael R Whitener
A CHANGE FOR THE BETTER

Factories change their products sometimes,
just to make a change.
Businesses change their sales techniques
to keep competition out of range.
Mothers change their children
to keep them nice and dry.
Pilots change their courses
so they can stay up in the sky.
Me, I changed my lifestyle
'cause it was gettin' out of hand.
Kept on doin dumb things that I didn't understand.
I made a change for the better,
least I sure do think I did.
And I haven't felt so good inside
since back when I's a kid.
The change I made wasn't easy,
but I'm glad I made the start.
'cause it's made a world of difference
lettin' Jesus change my heart.

Lois Bryant

Lois Bryant
THIS DAY

This day is ours to use and make
God keeps us strong and true.
Let me no wrong my path take
And others something do.
Let all I meet today speak well of me tonight
I wouldn't want him to say
I'd hurt him by a slight.
Grant thee Oh God when the setting sun
That this day shall end.
That I may rejoice over something done
And gain another friend.
Let there be something good and fine
That I May have something to tell.
That I have lived these days of mine
Not good, but well.

Jacklyn Kline
LAST NIGHT IN A DREAM

To my loving husband, Joel

Last night while I lay sleeping,
I made love to you in my dreams.
Your warm body was lying next to mine,
Our bed was a blanket of green.
Surrounded by only darkness,
The moon and stars glowed from above,
And a cool breeze whispered over us,
As we made sweet, blissful love.
I said how much I loved you,
As I softly kissed your cheek,
And continued making love to you,
While I laid in my bed fast asleep.
When the darkness turned to morning,
On my face was a smile of delight.
Remembering the glorious time we had,
Making love in my dreams last night!

Jennie Bennett
DIANE

She was born on a Thursday in May
It was a beautiful warm spring day

She was my bundle of joy
I hoped she wasn't a boy

She has long brown curly hair
When I comb it, she growls like a bear

She is only nine years old
And is not too bold

She has to wear braces
Which gives her funny faces

She tries to be creative in art
But the mess to clean is my part

When she practices her flute
She doesn't think she looks too cute

The other day, we had a fight
But I know she won't bite

Some of her things, she won't share
But deep down, I know she does care

Because I am the biggest fan
Of my daughter, DIANE

Basil Renee Scott
THOUGHTS ABOUT CHRISTMAS

To my parents Mr & Mrs. B.G. Scott for their love and inspiration, also my teacher, Mr. Englehardt.

As I sit here counting the weeks away,
I am reminded of that special day,
When the angel Gabriel came to Mary,
Whom appeared to her as a beautiful fairy.
Gabriel said "Do not fear or do not run,
For you shall give birth to Jesus your son."
As it came to pass for this birth to occurr,
Some wise men brought Jesus gold, frankincense and myrrh.
Listen now, hear the angels sing,
Glory to our newly born king.
A man shall live forevermore,
Because of Christmas that we adore.

Angela M Ferrell
WHAT LOVE MEANS TO ME

Love is caring about the people
Around you,
A mother caring for her young.

Love is believing in someone,
The person who believed in the
Drug addict who got help.

Love is sharing a part of yourself,
People who give blood or
People who donate organs to save lives.

Love is working with people,
A teacher working with a student or
The time people give for volunteer work.

Love is giving the homeless a home
And is a friend who is always there.

Love is death,
The brave soldiers who gave their
Life for our country.

Love is love because its all around.
Give a little love and you'll get so too.
There is enough love for everyone.

Kathryn M Loving
MY DAD

This poem is dedicated to my dad Jesse Daniels, Sr.

You gave to me all you could get
When not accepted, you did not fret.
You knew when to be kind and when to be firm
When the going was rough
You could weather any storm.
When asked to do a favor,
You were always glad
If I had a thousand choices
I would still choose "My Dad.
I've enjoyed you dad, as much as I could
If I could keep you with me,
You know I would.
So long "Dad, you've been a great scholar,
I hope to visit you in your Heavenly Parlor.
God gave you to me and my life has been blessed
Sleep on Dear Dad and take your rest,
To live without you makes me very sad.
But to know you're at peace makes me glad.
I have beautiful memories of you
"My Dad".

Clara Necessary
MY HUSBAND

My Husband is a precious soul
If not for him life would be so cold.

He always speaks the sweetest words
To me the sweetest ever heard.
He never fusses, we have no spats
He always hangs his coats and hats.
He helps me with the household chores
Takes out the garbage—vacuums the floors.
He loves his guitar and fishing too
A man needs a hobby, something to do.
To take his mind from worldly things
and let it dwell on angels wings.
My Husband is the best I know
If you doubt it, come, I'll show
To you the sweetest ever was
Even under his day old fuzz.

Serge Vit

SURREALISTIC PEOPLE

Surrealistic people came down
From the paintings of Cezanne
To change this world forever,
To cure everyone.

And their spirits in that foggy day
Got soaked, but not from walking in the rain,
They diluted the air, they became part of rain,
The thunder and some Broadway play.

Their decadence,
Their love of life
Cut through indifference,
Faked smiles, lies.

Strange images projected on the screens,
New faces in the fashion magazines.
Ladies and Gentlemen, it isn't Halloween.
It's Art as it was never heard or seen.

Ronn Winterton

ANOTHER TOMORROW

To all that stood by me

There is always tomorrow—no matter how long the night.
Another tomorrow—to start out fresh and bright
Another tomorrow to do the things you have so far only planned

Another tomorrow to care and understand
Another tomorrow to do the things you never had time to do

Another tomorrow for me and for you
And even though it seems it may be years away
There is always another tomorrow and with it a brand new day

Kenneth Willis

DOPE

Marijuana, Cocain, and Angel dust,
That's what I call dope.
Some people use that stuff,
Because it's their only hope.

They think that stuff is good for them,
But I would not tell a lie.
I don't like to use that dope,
'cause it can make you die.

Dope is a killer,
It will destroy your life.
Dope is really dangerous,
It's worse than using a knife.

Cops do not like the dope,
They say it's a terrible crime.
But the people who use it don't care,
They use it all the time.

Now I'm a person who cares about life,
And I don't like that dope.
If I would use that terrible stuff,
I wouldn't be able to cope.

'Cause dope is a killer,
And it's a terrible shame.
Because when people use it,
They take all of the blame.

Ms Jesse M. V. Ek

FLY BYE

You pinned on my wings
And encouraged me to try,
And although life has many stings
You still taught me to fly.
You told me not to be blind
But to really see.
You sent me to seek and find
So I can be all that you wanted me to be.
I now can make it on my own
Without the Fear
Of standing alone.
Though I'm glad you're still nearby
And I will shed an occasional tear,
I want to tell you before I die
That to me you were always dear.

Elaine Hays

HERE WAS A MAN

Here was a man the whole world knew
He was a hero through out the land
He was truly an American symbol
A proud, honest sort of a man.

As a cowboy he stood tall in the saddle
As a soldier he stood brave and true
As a captain he always ran a tight ship
He was American as red, white and blue.

He was rough, tough and brawny
And always a side way grin
Some how I always noticed
A very slight tilt to the chin
Now I know he had a bank account
That would have to stagger the mind
But to me he just seemed ordinary
Just the plain old country kind
A ledgend in his own time he was
Know one else could fill his shoes
I don't know how he was with women
With bar rooms or with booze

Susan Jehrio

TEDDY BEAR

I wish I had a teddy bear,
To sit upon my knee,
I'd take him with me everywhere,
To cuddle up with me.

I'd squeeze him, hug him; love him too,
But most of all I wouldn't put him in a zoo.
I'd give him a name, and a place to live,
So, he would never feel blue.

So, I wish I had a teddy bear,
To keep warm, and snuggle up to,
I'd even give him a little bed,
And a fluffy pillow, for his little head.

I finally found a teddy bear,
He has brown, little feet,
I will take good care of him,
And I promise to make him eat.

Sandra L Gurnsey

A SPECIAL FRIEND

Thank you friend for being there
When I thought that no one cared
People come and people go
But my friend with you I know
That you have come and you will stay
A special friend in every way
So thank you friend for being there
When I thought that no one cared

Connie M Haun

AN ODE TO A TREE

In our yard, close by, stands a giant tree serene and free
In times past, I've rushed by and didn't see
All your beauties, as you stood there so straight and tall.
Constantly doing something for us all.
Since I've just lately retired
There will be more time to admire,
Your graceful limbs, trunk and leaves
Which blow so gently in the breeze.
The lovely things you share mean so much to me.
The tiny robins nest, the squirrels home too,
To say nothing of the shade you give
Day by day, in summer to help us live.
In winter when your limbs are bare
I can see them lifted upward in prayer.
You restore my soul with your beauty rare.
Never again will I have to be told
Of all the inner strengths you hold.
Now it's your turn to watch me grow old.
I'll cling to life with the lessons you've bestowed,
And let love radiate the intricate life patterns you've showed.
You've made me instant rich, and what a pleasure to be born!
And feast upon your untold treasures each morn.
God's earth is full to the brim if man will only trust Him.
Love is the key to growing old dear tree
Continue your lessons, for life eternal is a must for me.

Doris M Halliwell

?

The weathermen have predicted a layering
of snow.
But when I retired, the sky's still aglow
With a silvery moon and twinkling stars
galore,
Against a background of black velvety
velour.
Upon awakening at dawn, not a sound is
heard.
Is it too early for the chirp of a bird?
Or "did it snow" like a child, I wonder,
As I drowsily lay and ponder.
Did the snow arrive, as on pussy—cat feet?
A winter wonderland, will my eyes meet?
The suspense is too much, to a window I
go,
But my fantasy is shattered, alas, there's
no snow!

Rory Irene Staples

ANGEL OF MERCY

I pass thru their lives,
With the greatest of ease,
Nothing better to do,
But for others to please,
Each passing day someone,
Has an unbearable need,
No one to turn to,
Their story to plead.

Families, children and
Loved ones they bring,
Into this world, so many
Pleasures to sing,
But one single person,
Lingers in their mind,
One who is there ready and
Willing to be kind.

Troubles ring loud,
Vibrations spread far,
As the body and mind merge,
Feeling under par,
Then for one moment dark, stormy
Skies turn crystal clear,
And a peaceful calm comes forth,
From that someone dear.

A sleeping devil and
A heart resting well,
Each one goes home, there's
Nothing left to tell,
Fresh air that brings a
Silent glint of hope,
That now with that problem,
You can finally cope.

All's well with the troubled,
But what of the host?
What kind of stoney road,
Does this one coast?
Who helps their needs and hear
The lonesome cries?
God above replenishes those tears
As each one dries.

James E Westberry

AN IMPERFECT WORLD

There he was—a young man sitting within
the walls created from his own conscious
with barriers built from years of torture
from peers who made him feel inferior.

Sometimes, sitting for hours, he'd ponder
the value of this worth, knowing not
that a person's worth is seldom appreciated
until it's too late, but yet always hoping for a day of total serenity.

Then comes the sad realization that utopia
is just a figment of an innocent imagination.

Margie Dahir
MUBARAK
Four years ago today you ejected
Yourself from your mother's womb
One animated, vociferous, diminutive
Male offspring.

Creation of passionate emotions
Culmination of an old man's being,
Hope for perpetuation of ancestral tribes
Mother's joy.

We honor you on your anniversary
And hold you close to our hearts:
Vowing to forever protect you from
This world's sanguinary horrors.

Would that all the wondrous joys of magical childhood
Shining forth from the depths
Of your immense piercing brown eyes,
Endure forever!

Ellen Elmore
SEASONS
I hear soft music—footsteps from the
long ago
Are treading softly on my lonely heart;
And distant scenes float from the past
Into the present—shades are drawn apart;
Transported into days of yesteryear,
It seems to be scarce any time at all
Since life was full of laughter and of love
'Twas Spring, then Summertime, now
turned to Fall
The chill of Winter in the air serves to
remind,
How swiftly time may pass and comes
the end.
Be it a year, or many of them in life's
span,
The past, the present, and the future
seem to blend.
And holding fast the Hand that guided
us thus far
We take each step, nor fear the ones to
come
For He who holds the Universe in endless
space
Will lead us, safely, to our future Home.

Alethia J Goodman
ABSENCE
When the roll was called,
My name was not mentioned
In the catagory
Of fame and fortune.

And when the story had been told,
My name could not be heard.

Here where I lay,
My name, you'll see
Is printed very well.

I hope you'll say my name
Out loud for all to hear.

So, not one
Will ever know
I came this way
Only once.

Miss Teresa A Chapple
HOPING
If I have seen you once I've seen you twice a million
times is twice as nice;
You left me standing all alone I looked around and you was gone;
I thought I wasn't going to see you again and I remembered we
are still friends;
We can be much more than friends but it seems I never let you in,
you let me in and I was happy I never thought it would happen
From now until I want us to be so much more I want you to be the
one opening my door.

Mildred B Rohde
A LIFE OF LOVE

Dedicated to my loving husband, Bernard

Thank God for the many kinds of love that come to each of us in life.
For many first love came, as for me, to become a wife.
The strong, broad shouldered man with the merry eyes of blue
Showed me love and the many good things love can do.

The first love was a baby girl, sweet and tiny with golden hair.
I knew it was His way of answering mydays and nights of prayer.

Later it was a son, and we loved him with full heart.
And, although four more sons were born, with one we would not part.

Our seventh and last love together was a sweet baby girl
And like her older sister, was tiny with golden curls.
Our hearts were full of love, our lives were complete.
The world was ours as love is sweet.

But life has a way of completing a circle and each must come to an end.
My heart is full of love for seven now, my greatest and first love is gone,
And I'll not see him again, until the eternal life of love.

Pamela Evelyn Millwood
VICTORIOUS LITERATURE

In honor of Mama, Evelyn Bruce Millwood, and in memory of Daddy, Cecil B. Millwood, Sr.—parents who provided a supportive, encouraging environment filled with examples to follow in their love of reading and writing.

Tides of emotion wash upon a language shore,
Debris takes shape as words ne'er spoken before.
The battle begins with churnings and burnings
As unseen captives expose their yearnings;
Gradually building a relentless power,
One unequaled in my hour.
Reluctantly, confinement yields its grip
As words converge on their victorious trip.
They command existence in a concrete world
Rather than the abstract one from which they were hurled.
Desire to battle reality as an existing entity
Propelled the words to join in a goal for liberty.
The former design of reason and rhyme
Was only a cloud of ideas harbored for a short time.
Now the battle is won;
Literature has begun!

Josephine J Hall
OLE MISS TANZY SLY
Come getter roun me chillen an lissen very close
I'm telling ya'll you might not like it most
I'm talkin bout Miss Tanzy kno Ole Miss Tanzy Sly
She set down all de year, watched the time flyed by
While all dem other womens helped husband harves de crop
Miss Tanzy was drinkin stump drinking the last drop
She never picked a lock of cotton aint dat a sin
Ginnin time came she beat her ole man to da gin
When dat bale of cotton was sold Miss Tanzy liken to had a fit
Cause the man didn't give her the check, my how her teeths did grit
Then her husband reminded her of the times she didn't work
When she set on de fish creek stopped going to church
That learned Miss tanzy a lesson the next year she worked
Doing all de good she could never her duty she sherked
If ya'll go to the camp meeting and don't see Ole Miss Tanzy Sly
Call down in the Cotton patch cause she's making dem cotton bolls fly.

Mary Zlabek Liberte
AT THE GRAVE
It's no surprise to find you here
Alone beside his grave,
As though its peace could bring him near,
Its silence makes you brave.

It is so sad to lose a child
In such a senseless way,
The grief enough to drive one wild,
More pain than any words can say.

On that bright day, there was someone
Who dared to drink and drive,
And in a moment, our sweet son
No longer was alive.

We must soon leave him here to rest.
Let's gather up his smile
And take the laughter we love best,
Tuck them away awhile.

We'll put our memories deep inside
And try to carry on.
But our heart-pain we cannot hide,
Our little boy is gone.

Thomas M Martus
WISHING TO BE FREE
I'm wishing to be free,
like the eagle in the sky,
so graceful in flight.
And the wise old owl,
searching through-out the night.

And like the mountain stream,
flowing so swift.
And an Autumn day
with leaves adrift.

I'm wishing to be free,
like the valley flowers,
with their buzzing bee.
And the wild horses,
running so free.

And like the milkweed seed,
floating through the air.
Wishing that it was me,
living without a care.

But, I have to sit and think,
it just can't be.
Because not a soul,
not a one I see,
is so very, very FREE.

Gary D Shaffer
THE MOUNTAIN
The boy was born on a warm spring day;
A child of the land sweet and fair.
A fragrant breeze blew down from the mountain
To show it was glad he was there.

The boy played in the mountain meadows;
Its scenic beauty was rare.
He loved the playground it provided
And sure was glad it was there.

He hunted game and picked wild berries
That the mountain so freely would bear.
Season after season life was sustained
Because the mountain was there.

He tilled the soil at the foot of the mountain
And farmed the land with great care.
Each morning he looked up at his mountain

And thanked the Lord it was there.

As the years went by, the man grew old;
Blindness did not bring him despair.
Even though he could see the mountain no more,
He was comforted just knowing it was there.

In this ever changing world, few things are sure;
God's mountain is beyond compare.
The man will pass from this life here on earth,
Knowing the mountain will still be there.

Norma Valentin

WE PARTED IN THE RAIN

To my beloved Mother

The rain kept falling when we parted and
you went far away from me

A memory only remains of dreams we shared
and plans we made of things that now could
never be

The rain just falls as I recall the hours
we spent in reverie

The walks, the talks those hours of bliss
the joy we found in every kiss remain within
my memories

Now I sit and pray that someday though your
very far from me you'll remember our love
as it was, it will always be

Now as the rain beats on my window my soul is
filled with misery

I'll keep on looking up & down and pray that
someday you will find your way and you'll come
back to me

John J Hennessy

CHER AMI

To my loving wife, Anita, To my lovely daughter, Kathy, To my lively son, Johnnie

---

Like a cathedral on Monday its quiet now Cher Ami
So long ago the big guns were hauled away
And so few recall your heroic flight
On that tragic October day

O'er the tree tops of the Meuse-Argonne
You flapped your wings of brown
While mausers cracked in "Jerry" hands
They tried to bring you down

You lost a leg, you lost an eye
A bullet smashed your breast
But you carried on till you reached our lines
And then you took your rest.

"For God's sake stop shelling u."
Thats how the message read
If you had failed to make it back
Two hundred doughboys might now by lying dead.

I'm sure God prepared a place for pigeon's
Some aviary Shangri-la, ever green and nice
Then Mon Cher Ami I'm certain;
You fly again eternally in pigeons paradise.

Fern A Martin

WAR

Dedicated to Bruce Martin—Son

As a mother, I hate war with a bitter intensity.
I know from past experiences, the victories you've
won are of short duration.
But the killing and atrocities will be with you forever.
Your sons, what does it do to them?
They are given over to the military, who teach them
to hate, burn, kill, bomb or commit crimes which
will haunt them forever.
And many of them will give their lives; which some
say is an honor to their country.
I can't believe God wanted us to bring forth children
for this purpose.
Man has upset the world, with his hunger for power
and greediness, regardless of humanity.
But he can't take away a mother's love for her
child,
Whether his skin be black, red, yellow, or white.
We mothers must fight for a better world in the
future. One with peace and love for all mankind.

Clint Del Lauricella

HEAVEN'S LOSS

To Meredith Ford, my high school sweetheart, whose memory still makes me smile.

God cried in the Heaven's Today,
Mourning for what he had lost.
The sun seemed to lose its ray,
All was covered with frost.
For Heaven had lost a grand prize,
With beauty beyond compare.
Her brilliance dazzled the eyes,
Such perfection, indeed was rare.
Heaven lost an angel that night,
Silently she traveled to earth.
She brought with her a bright light,
To stir in me, a spark of birth.
The Heaven's are sad, it's very true,
But I pray that she will remain.
For my life's empty without you,
What's Heaven's loss is my gain.

Theresa Hayes

CHANGING TIMES

To my husband Bill

As a firefighter's wife,
I believe in fighting for a life.
A life that keeps my flame aglow,
And can't be put out until I know
He's safe and sound and home again.
Woman's work is never done
But firefighting isn't much fun,
It's a job of strength of men,
Family types and home again.
I'd like to know if you were me,
How would you feel if your life
Went out the door using the strength of two more.
Please stay where you're needed most with a child or at a post.
I've seen the times when fires
Were bad, the soot and smoke in his hair.
Firefighters need lots of strength
To carry victims and do the job that's meant
To share the risk the job persists
Back to where they have to fight.
To have a team is a wife's dream.
The work is assigned and shared by all
Or the Fire Department will surely fall.
The strength of mind is not the test.
The test of heart is no contest.
To push one's strength for the job he has to do,
Leave it to a man to carry it through.

Ann Blackburn

SUMMER FOOLISHNESS

To Robert, my one true love throughout the ages of time

The sweet aroma of honeysuckle fills the air.
The summer breeze reminds me of our many hours together . . .
Talking of love and other foolish things.

You said you loved me that summer.
We had just met, but felt we had known
one another for centuries.
We talked of marriage and other foolish things.

Summer ends, as all things do.
The honeysuckle withers,
The soft breeze turns to a cold wind,
Now you are gone as they all are . . .
Love, marriage, and other foolish things.

Jean Cain

TWO WOMEN IN PASSING

Our sable Cadillac had sprung to wait
For green to urge us on. My arm in mink
Lay haunched along the seat as if to bait
A mouse. I blew the fur and started to think.
The priest had preached of love, concern and care . . .
Just so . . .I watched a woman stalking near—
Mexican, but sober. Streaked with bleach, her hair
Strung long. Her eyes, on mine, grew black and queer.
Soricine, her coat was piled and matted gray.
"You son've bitch," she mouthed and sneered her hate,
Again, "you son've bitch," and spit my way:
Spit, spitting out her need to execrate.
We leaped away. Transfixing her, I hissed
And raised a finger of my black, kid fist.

Cathi Hess

CONFESSIONS OF A LONELY GIRL

For Karen who understood

Life is a bitch
But then so are you
So don't even try
To tell me what to do

I've seen many places
Heard many lines
It all comes together
In the war of old times

What is your sign
Where do you live
It will be to your advantage
Your body to give

This is your chance
As a lover I'm tops
Come on, stop the dance
before interest drops

I'll show you a good time
If you'll show me your bed
I don't want to know
What goes on in your head.

They'd come and they'd go
With the speed of light
To offer love and adventure
For the entire night!

Donna Truluck Atkins

TAKE TIME

A time to laugh,
A time to play.
A time to be reverent
and kneel down to pray.
A time to be happy,
A time to be sad.
A time to be thankful
for all that you have.
A time to take time
to show someone you care,
A time to show them
that you'll always be there.
A time to remember
to notice their needs,
A time to praise them
for all of their deeds.
A time together
at the end of the day,
When as a family
you reverently pray.

Shirley E Woods

THEN CAME YOU

To the love of my life, my husband

I've had the storms of life to fall all around
They tugged and pulled and drug me down

The rains and winds whipped at
my heart and mind
No anchor or shelter could I find
Then like the suns rays and
warming hue
God smiled and then blessed me
with you
Arms to embrace and shelter me
from fear
Kisses to dry up the hurtfull tears
Gentle touches to comfort all the
pain
A beautiful caring soul of a very
loving man

Susan Sampson

LITTLE CHILDREN

Little children, you've captured us
within'
You spread your love with Baby
Grin
You see the world through starry
eye
Nothing new will pass you by.

Little lips like dewdrop
Little feet never stop,
Little hands longing to explore
Wondering how to open the door

You are as gentle as a flower
Growing more hour by hour
Precious thing with angel wings
Tugging softly at our heart strings.

Little children, soft and warm
God's guidance will keep you, from
all harm
Quickly you grow out of baby ways,
Wonder what's happened to those
days . . .

When in your eyes there comes a
tear
Come to us, we'll dry them clear,
Precious Darling,
Baby Dear.

Doris A Church

OUR MOM

In memory of Frances Lenora Vincent. We miss you Mom!

The long ago, not recent past,
As she was then, not so ill
Getting it done any task
No matter what she had willed,

Remembering our weekly walks
Dancing, climbing, stories to tell
Having time for our talks
Loving her we always shall,

The pain is here, She's at rest.
Missing her we all do.
She raised us right, now's the test.
Her love is always true,
At her place, she is there.
Watching us from above.
Knowing that we all care
Guilding us with her Love!

Patricia K Boschert

DECEPTION

It seems like only yesterday
I awoke to a rustling sound,
A cold clammy hand,
And darkness . . . all around.

I search for a reason,
for what's going on.
Like a change of the seasons.
The one I have known is gone.

My eyes are closed tightly,
I'm acting asleep.
Concealing my trembling,
These secrets to keep.

This touching and groping,
I don't understand;
These confusing motions,
from this loving man.

I pray for the moment
The rustling will cease
Releasing my spirit . . .
To give me some peace

When the deception is over,
my trembles turn to tears.
Flooding my soul,
to hide all my fears.

The days of concealing
This darkness is through.
That is why I'm revealing
These secrets to you.

Elizabeth Buckley

A SPIDERS NIGHTMARE!

The long, eight-legged beast
scurried silently
up the wall
He was invisible there simply
because
no one saw him
Closer he got to the cob-webbed
palace where
his dinner awaited unwillingly.
The speed of the eight-legs
increased as he
wondered how to begin
The legs, no, the arms, no, perhaps
the wings . . .
SWAT!!

Judith A Rosella

CHI-TOWN

Into humanity come
The tired, the wicked
Steel framework
Walking through the city
In all directions
Picking them up
Scattering them like flies
Across the concrete walkways
Which carry them to
Their Lives.

Into boxes which
Remind me of childhood
Fireflies at dusk
We put them into boxes
Punched holes
Their lights glowing
In the fading light
Sneaking to your room
To hide them until after
Lights Out.

Out into night
In streams then flecks
Of pale gold light
Along Concrete paths
Flicking in and out
Small specks in an otherwise
Man-made world.

Marian Newcomb

MY CATHEDRAL IN THE WOODS

To God, With Love

I know that I should go to Church,
as all good Christians should,
But I have my own Cathedral on
the pathway to the Woods.
There the giant Trees stand tall like
steeples reaching to the sky,
And like little Altar Boys, God's
little Creatures scurry by.
There's a scent of incense in the air,
carried by a gentle breeze,
And I always know that God is
near, by the bowing of the Trees.
The fields of Flowers are my Altar,
that's where the feathered choir
sings,
The Sunbeams are the candles
that make the little Bluebells
ring.
The dome of my Cathedral, is
Heavens Sky of blue,
And the stain glass windows are
the little drops of sparkling dew.
I can see the little Angel wings in
the golden Maple leaves,
And hear "Ave Maria," in the
humming of the Bees.
There I receive Communion from
the ripple of the Creek,
And feel His Benediction in the
Glory that I seek.
As I watch Him paint a Rainbow
in the Sky, I know that He
Placed this lovely old Cathedral,
in the Forest, just for me.

Philip Crouch

THE DIFFERENCE

Fair
"I'm fair," he said
resting his head —
a single teardrop staining a path
on his palm pressed cheek

"And you?"
"yes life is fine," she said,
as she thought of him
and what best she should say,
to a troubled soul
on such a day.

"I love you."
she continuously told him straight.
And the day seemed bright
and his troubles light,
as he went his way.

Dorothy Byrd

SOUNDS OF NIGHT

I would like to dedicate this poem to my family and friends. My children Charles, Carol, Annette and their Families. Also my special friend Cliff.

As darkness creeps over the land
The sounds of night begin
Lay quiet upon your bed
And listen . . .
A cricket chirping near
Seems you can almost touch him
In the distant a chorus of frogs
Calling to each other.

The roar of motors take on a new
sound
The big trucks how they sing
The tires humming round
A faint hum increasing as a plane
flies over
They blend all together
Without any trouble.

The local train blows at a crossing
near by
A sound so lonely makes you want
to cry
Brings back memories of departed
loved ones
How your heart aches over wrongs
you've done
Listen again . . .
To the sounds of the night
How peaceful they are making
things right
You soon fall asleep
As quietly you lay
When the night is over
You will face a new day.

Ann Marie Visich

MY CONSCIENCE, MY FRIEND

Happy New Year to you my friend
I know where you live—
inside my head

I talk to you at least twice a day
just wish you had something to
say
We've been together a long long
time
and because you don't talk
our friendship won't end

Life's a circle, a riddle too
I get so confused as to what to do
But then I talk it out with you
And although you don't speak
You tell me what I should do
The paths we take will never end
so until we pass you'll be my
friend
TALK TO YA SOON!

Tom Kilcullen

MEMORIES ARE . . .

To my sister, Katie

Memories are of the things we've
done
The times we've had, the laughs,
the fun.
Memories are of the times we've
shared
The talks we've had when our
hearts were bared.

Memories are of the things we keep
To help us live and help us sleep.
Memories are used and kept on file
To bring back up when our lives
are on trial.

So, to save our memories would be
an endeavor
Because memories should be
kept . . .
Forever

Tana R Kessinger

PAP

This poem is in memory of "Pappy Russ," who was a wonderful person, and a great influence, and inspiration to me.

Pap, it seems like only yesterday
That you would watch me run and
play.
Yet, thinking now of those years,
Upon my face I feel the tears.

For yesterday can come no more
The Lord has called you to his door.
I only wish there had been more
time
To enjoy you, Pap, you were so fine.

I'm going to miss you very much
Your gentle smile and tender
touch.

You added much to my life while you were here
And although you're gone, in a way you are near.

Now, I'm looking forward to the day
When we meet again and I can say,
Pap, you really didn't leave—
you were only away

Julie A Petersen
PIECES OF HEAVEN
Yes, I've seen a piece of heaven
A priceless smile that can't be bought
Or that sparkle in your loved one's eye
Meaning you love him, no matter what.

The potent words like Thank-you
And I'm sorry and I love you,
For I've heard a piece of heaven
In the wedding words, I do.

I've touched a piece of heaven
In a simple hug homespun,
In that tender secureness when holding hands
Most of all, in my cherished son.

When someone else besides yourself
Wipes away your tears,
For I've felt a piece of heaven
That comforts me through the years.

All these riches combined together
Are gifted in every part,
They will always be precious pieces
Of heaven in my heart.

Carol M Columbine
HOMELESS
Why must people live on the street
Why don't they have enough to eat
Why is it we're always looking away
Dear God this could be us someday
They're on the streets rain or shine
They're in every town your's and mine
In bitter cold and blazing heat
One good meal would be a treat

The shelters are full we hear on the news
Aren't there empty buildings they could use
The homeless deaths are up fifty percent
Why don't they receive the money we sent.
The SALVATION ARMY is trying in vain
Yet there doesn't seem to be much gain
While the temperatures drop down near Zero
Our governments fiddlin' just like Nero

They need to know that someone cares
Now, that's a feeling we all can share
The problem they're facing are nothing new
Yet the change must come from me and you
I'm saying it's time to make a stand
This is not what God had planned
If someone out there shares my view
It's time to find out what we can do

James Ace Moore
CANDLE IN THE WIND
The world was set against him
even at the place he loved.
He had no one
and wanted no one.
He could stand on his own
and take the punishment
that life dished out,
eating it whole heartedly.
Just because you love
does not mean
You will be loved back.
He did not fight against his world,
he fought along side it.
Slaving away and getting nothing
in return.
Until his life resembled
a melted candle.
Nothing left to burn,
and nothing left to prove.

Diana Marie Melton
MOM

This poem is a dedication to my Mother Patricia A Dodson, and I give her this with all my love, heart and soul.

Today I felt so down and out, but I called
My Mom and she made me feel joyous, and I
Thought why pout?
I need her love and soothing touch, and only
Hers would do because she loves me so very much.
After we talked and she prayed for me on the phone
I felt a new happiness and I was no longer alone.
She sent the angels to surround me all day
And with them by my side it turned out to be a
Beautiful day.
I broke down and cried to her on the phone for hours
And she made me realize once more Gods wonderful powers.
I did wrong and I must pay in this earthly hell
And I'm reminded each day of what I done wrong by this
Hell.
When I need strength or understanding or love
I know I can turn to my mom or God above.
I love my Mom more than she could ever know
And I fear the day that God takes her & she must go.

Ira K Moore
THE MOCKING-BIRD

In loving memory of my brother Allen W. Kilgore

Oh, Mocking-bird, on wing or perch,
We acknowledged your presence when at the church:
Your song of wisdom, while the organist play—
Was it "Sweet Hour of Prayer" or "Oh, Happy Day?"
You were not boisterous, you were not bad;
You gave a comfort to the sad.

Then in the hush of the noon-day prayer,
While the minister gave console to those gathered there,
You kept your silence, never uttered a sound,
Until the bier left the church and resting-place bound,
Then with chest aloft and wings a-flutter,
You moved to another branch, a new song to utter.

We left you there never to meet again;
But others will come to hear you sing.
So with all wisdom, clear your throat,
Don't be boisterous, never gloat,
Cheer the sad, comfort the meek,
When at the church God's help they seek.

Helen Elizabeth Fisher
JESUS OF NAZARETH
I just want to tell you, dear Jesus,
And I want the whole world to know;
Just how much I really love you
For the agony you suffered so long ago.

Now, I remember your trip to Jerusalem,
How you were walking along, ahead;
How the disciples were softly following
How they were filled with terror and dread.

Then taking them aside, you told them again
How you'd be arrested and sentenced to die,
How they'd mock you, spit on you, flog you;

Then "crucify Him!" would be their cry.

So to Golgotha they proceeded to take you,
With a crown of thorns placed on your head;
On the cruel, cruel cross they nailed you
To suffer until finally you were dead.

You lay in the grave, but not for long
For the plan of God was not yet complete.
But after it was, you ascended into Heaven
And at God's right hand you were given a seat!

Buddy Sims
THE SCHOOL PLAYGROUND

My wife Denise and School Children Everywhere

Children joyfully out at play,
at the local school this day;
Midst the sound of squeaky swings,
nearby, someone starts to sing!

Can't recall the name of the song,
but somehow the words, came on strong.
There was joy, on this beautiful day,
on the school grounds, as children play!

A twinkle of the eye, and in a flash,
several youngsters, came running past.
Then a smile crossed, a teachers lips,
as little tykes, went zip, zip, zip.

Squeals and moans, came from all around,
as the ringing of a bell, crossed the grounds.
So it's back to the classroom, they all go,
'cause they're here to study, learn, and know.

Shoshannah Frager
A WHISPER IN THE WIND
A whisper in the wind.
A far off cry.
I pray, Oh Lord
Don't let me die.
Here I am.
Away from home.
On foreign ground.
Left to roam.
Fighting for.
An unknown cause.
Without sleep.
Without pause.
Killing men.
I know not who.
It's just something.
I'm forced to do.
Let them all.
Go to heaven.
For they are.
My unknown brethren.

Mary Cook
THAT'S WHAT DAN IS ALL ABOUT
A lovely face so full of love'
That warms you like the sun above.
Her friendly nature reaches out;
That's what Dan is all about.

A diplomat in every way—
She brightens up a dismal day.
Soft of voice—not a shout.
That's what Dan is all about.

Concern for others in her style;
She shows it with a charming smile.
Her tender friendship is devout.
That's what Dan is all about.

Her knowledge far exceeds her years.
She doesn't harbor any fears.
To count her years; she's only four;
In many ways, she's much, much more.

Shari J Maher
ODE TO OLD MAN WINTER
The cold breeze blowing
from the north,
Crystal snow flakes falling
to the earth.
The wind howling and making

a treacherous sound,
A blanket of snow gently
covers the ground.
Jack Frost nips fiercely
at your nose,
And bites at your frozen
little toes.
It just now covers up
the autumn's gold,
It's so beautiful,
yet so cold.

Jean F Heimerman

TREASURES

Ice-covered branches glistening in
the sun,
The tranquility of dusk when day
is done,
A kite's carefree dance in the
evening sky,
The tinkling of a wind chimes'
lullaby.

The sanctuary of home's sweet
embrace,
Walls of wood and love interlaced,
A favorite room, a familiar old
chair, and
the vision of someone I love sitting
there.

Simple good times and quiet talks,
Singing birds and pleasant walks,
A curtain's graceful ballet in the
breeze—
Thank you, God, for all of these!

Bobbe C Whitaker

THE ROUND OR SQUARE OF IT

I'm a square piece of puzzle,
that won't fit in the round.
Regardless of whether
I turn it up or down.
It doesn't go together,
it just won't fit.
Tho I round down the edges
tho I whittle and whet.
If my pieces were round,
neither would they fit in the
square.
No matter how hard I try,
They don't fit anywhere.
I guess you might say,
I don't really belong.
There's no tune for my life,
no words for my song.
No use for my life,
no purpose to live.
I gave all I had,
beyond what I had to give.
But, I'll continue my search,
for that certain space.
That can use a square or a round
To fill a special place.

Ruth G Brewster

I'M MOUNTAIN

To Gary, Bob, Scott, and Bill who have helped me climb life's mountains

---

The clouds blow by—drift over me,
and hide from those below
the remnants left of winter's freeze
the slowly melting snow

I've been so wind whipped, cold,
alone . . .
Yet from my crest I see . . .
that spring creeps up my
mountain,
and soon will cover me

Yes, spring crept up my mountain,
and summer stayed two months . . .
but fall intruded, oh so fast . . .
It came, as if at once.

The few trees standing at my crest
turned gold, and red—then brown.
I wish they'd lasted longer,
but nature pulled them down.

Through branches standing stark
and bare
the cold wind speaks and blows.
Again I'm snugged in sparkling
white
of winter's crystal snows.

There is no sadness—no regret . . .
I know my seasons change
My color matters not to me . . .
I'm mountain—I remain

Gina Bilinski

CONDITIONAL FRIENDSHIP

how is it I am your friend
only when you are in need of
something?
so quick are you to turn
so sharp are your words
until you need something,
anything
recognition
attention
but you won't ask for help
no, you don't need help
you don't admit your faults
but you do have them
you are not perfect
yet you are so quick
to point out the imperfections in
others
a conditional friendship
Your conditions are:
agree with me
never doubt me
never challenge me
are these your conditions?
then these are also your faults.
your friends are few in numbers
now
they cannot meet your
conditions
lonely isn't it?

Martha Koapke

BANNER TO UNFURL

May this on my banner be:
Christ, the Lord arose for me!
May it gloe and gleam and shine
Till it swell this heart of mine—
With its message sweet and fair—
May my Lord be honored there.

May this banner be unfurled
To a doubting troubled world;
May His victories be told
Till His glories all unfold!
He has conquered death and hell,
Sin— oh, see how Satan fell!

All may come to read and own
Precious words— their depths
unknown.
Who receive this gracious Lord,
Have the promise of His Word.
That the christ arose for me
Is my hope— eternity.

John E Floyd

CRACK SWEEPING THE NATION

Crack sweeping the nation.
Crack sweeping the nation.
Killing all of human nature.
All types of people getting hooked.
So many of them turning into
crooks.
Crack sweeping the nation.
Even our children need translation.
The pushers are getting rich and
the
hookers getting fixed on a two
minute
hit, what a trip.
Crack sweeping the nation.
No one is trying to understand the
relation to win the war of
retaliation,
so we can live in a better nation.
Crack sweeping the nation.
Men and women are in a fatalistic
state
of mind as they suffer somewhere
in time.
Babys, boys and girls don't know
how
to face the world, because all the
parents
are using drugs.
Crack sweeping the nation.
Crack sweeping the nation.
Look out friend and relations,
you may be the one in that
sweeping
of the nation.

Mrs Merle B Green

Mrs Merle B Green

GIVING—GOD IS LOVE

Thispoem is dedicated to my beloved late husband Eugene Alston Green, writer, historian and educator—and my beloved young son, Eugene Alston Green Jr., who drowned in a tragic death by accident.

Always give a smile,—
Oh—happy the hearts—
That beat with love—
Who give to others
The joy of living—
Who in each hour finds—
Goodness—as days move
behind.
Some of the happiest hearts—
We may ever know—
Beat in the sincere quiet breast—
And always leave to God the
rest—
For—God is love.

Muriel M Forsyth

AWAKENING DAY

Dim twilight lurks
hushed and still,
until in phantom arms
an enfolding light appears
like a candle softly lit
as dawn brushes the heavens.
Deep magenta bleaches
to a gentle pink,
gradually ghosts away
into a misty, subdued blue.
A delightful illumination
wraps round
ascending layered clouds
as dawn blooms into day.

Mary E Jackson

Mary E Jackson

IT IS SPRING

It is so nice now the weather is
warm,
A pleasant time of the year,
Blossoming trees, green grasses,
and plants,
Tells that spring is here.

Buttercups wet from the morning
dew,
From the tree tops the robin sings,
Daisies have wakened up from
their beds,
Telling this is spring.

Showers of rain has freshened the
air,
Butterflies with bright colored
wings,
Fluttering around from flower to
flower,
Telling this is spring.

Children are playing with their
bare feet,
Kites flying high on a string,
Sweet scents from the honeysuckle
vine,
Telling it is spring.

Carole Turner Johnston

ON BORROWING TERMS

At home
on an Iowa farm
the bank plants a
FOR SALE sign

where the best corn
in the valley
grew
last year

where bitter tears
watered
city terms
last week.

At home
on a trailor lot
in Texas
barren plot that
nobody banked on.

Nan C McNeal

THE ROBINS NEST

Dedicated to Bill—My Husband

I watched two robins build a nest
And heard them sing with
happiness
For soon with little ones they were
to be blest
Those two happy robins

The nest was finished the eggs
were laid
Mama watched them while papa
played

Then one day three robins stood
With mama and papa a happy brood

Soon they were learning as all robins should
To take care of themselves when not with the brood
Then one day to everyones surprise
They flew by themselves to their own paradise

Now on that nest of happiness
There's a sign to let inquire within
For the robins are leaving because of snow
And want a tennant before they go

Anne Federico McManus
WALKING

To Mother and Dad, who taught me the best things in life are free. To appreciate nature, people, life and music and to smile. I love them!

When I walk along the road
In the warm sunshine and cool
Gentle summer breeze
I see the soft touch of nature
In the grass, the flowers and trees.
I wander along a foot path
Winding in, out, down, under and thru.
I hear the crickets, grass hoppers, birds
and bees, and they hear me,
And as the sounds of my footsteps
Move them from their homes,
Each one speaks to me in
Soft and gentle tones

Cassondra Antoinette Turner
WOULD I BE A FRIEND IF I DID NOT . . .
Would I be a friend if I did not show you how much I care for you
Would I be a friend if I did not tell you your wrongs and compliment your rights
Would I be a friend if I did not chastize you as a father or mother
Would I be a friend if I did not hurt with you nor share life's most simplest plesure with you
Would I be a friend if I did not say, hey, it's time for a change to occur in you for the growth of your prosperity
Would I be a friend if I did not introduce you to yourself
Would I be a friend if I did not introduce you to the Lord, Christ Jesus
Would I be a friend if I did not help you to become the best you can
Would I be a friend if I did not give to you when you were in need and I had it to give
Would I be a friend if I did not say, there is a brighter day when you hurt day-in and day-out
Would I be a friend if I did not give you a coupeus amount of hugs and kisses
Would I be a friend if I did not say so very often, I love you with the love of the Lord which is more than man can ever love.

Dorothy Dayton
FRIENDSHIP
Friendship is a circle—
Round and round it goes;
Ever widening, ever extending,
Just how far no one knows
For friendship is a handclasp
That bestows its own good will,
And smiles are little lights
That flash along the way
To light up darkened corners
So sorrows will not stay;
Yes, friendship is a circle
Extending near and far
And, because it is a circle
Comes back to where we are.

Gertrude A Johnson
GOD, THE EAGLE AND I
One morning on a mountain top
With a spectacular view before me
I saw a movement high in the sky.

It was a magnificent bald eagle
The majestic symbol of our freedom
Soaring gracefully on outspread wings.

As I sat there watching him
Wheeling aloft in the clear, pure air
I was filled with a wondrous joy.

It was so peaceful way up there
With Nature's wonders around me
That I closed my eyes and prayed.

Then I felt a calmness within me
A sense of serenity and awe
As tho a Divine presence were there.

I was glad I had climbed the mountain
For there in harmony with the world
It was just God, the eagle and I.

Beverly Wilson-Lynn
THE WORLDS LAMENT
Grieve for the children whose stomachs are empty and feet are bare
for they have nothing without people to care

Feel sorry for the people who turn their backs and refuse to give their help
for they need more compassion than anyone

Feel shame for a world who will not feel pain
for they can think only of themselves

Feel sorrow for all of humanity
for they destroy all that is sacred and meaningful

Pray for your souls for you all have sinned against the one thing that could have made you great

Cry for the babies who will never grow to see how beautiful the world could have been

Feel sad for an earth that may never be again
for the joy of life could be gone

FOREVER

Eula Robinson
MAMA'S SNUFF BOX

In memory of Mom: Sarah Lovelace

I ran across it today while cleaning the place,
It was tied in a handkerchief
Trimmed with ribbon and lace.
It was shiny and black from constant use
The contents inside powdery and loose.
Made my nose tickle, tears came to my eyes;
Sneeze upon sneeze—In between sighs
Twas mama's snuffbox.
She always carried it in her apron pocket
Close to her being, like most wore their lockets.
She'd take it out, tap the lid before her dip
Place contents twix gums and lips,
She'd settle down to quilt or read
Or maybe to order some garden seed.
Then Dad was gone.

Still her snuffbox she carried along.
To call on a neighbor or see a new babe,
Or just to go and visit Dad's grave.
But one day she put it aside.
Had to pinch myself—couldn't believe my own eyes
Her taste for it was gone—
Maybe she knew she was leaving her earthly home
To dwell with her maker, she needed it no more
He would be her comfort on that distant shore.

Joseph John Medeiros
THE FACE
As I sit before this mirror of mine
I see a face, etched, with aging lines
This face, has seen happiness and tears
This face, has seen some eighty years

As a child, it had seen it's joys
Through a cornucopia of toys
This face has had it's dreams
From adolescence, through it's teens

With make-up, it had enticed many a lad
Most of them good, a few of them bad

Till it met the one, the only one
Who gave it life, second to none

He was so young, handsome and strong
It knew in his life, it must belong
Our lives became a picutre of joy
That young girl, that handsome young boy
When on that day, we became one
This face of mine, out shone the sun

That once handsome young lad, died last fall
His eighty one years, had taken their toll
Know, as I look into this mirror of mine
It's reflection tells me, it is almost time
When the time comes, for me to join my spouse
I know it will be, in GOD'S peaceful house

Pearl M Coombe
LITTLE IMP
Your impish eyes are full of glee.
you think you've got the best of me!
you upset my lovely, peaceful days,
and shock me with your pagan ways.
you break my heart, you grey my hair.
you age me fast, I'm bent with care.
then something you say, or maybe you smile.
it makes the whole crazy mess worthwhile.

You smash the lamps, you crayon the walls.
leave muddy foot tracks in the scrubbed halls.
you love to torment me, its plain to see.
or impish elf don't you think of me?

But when you're all tucked in at night,
oh impish child of my delight.
your real self shows as you close your eyes.
and you're just an angel in imp's disguise.

Michael Raymond Carter
THE LAST PRAYER

Thank you Boy, for I am at Peace—Love, Irene

Sometimes the words just don't come out when you love someone very dearly.
Emotion is strong and you want to shout, but words can't express you clearly.

Is there a way to express myself, a method to convey my thought?
In my few days upon this earth you taught me an awful lot.
You were here many years before me you worked to make my life easy.
In my learning years when life was confusing it was a comfort when you would tease me.

When there's not much time and a lot to say
A lifetime of words can't fit in a day
At a time like that each last look is a treasure.
That's when silence is golden and always a pleasure.

In all the minds I would like to place a shrine no man can ever erase

No money, or crystal, or gold can bear this shrine of love I wish to share
With God's goodness in you from head to toe, layered inside and outside a rainbow

I'll form a memory no-one can ignore, from the highest mountain to the shore.
Enjoy life with others and do everything we could not do if we were together
I'll always be watching and listening and loving through all kinds of different weather

Though to you it seems alone I am, I'm happier now than ever.
I can't explain the beauty that's here, but it makes me awful clever.
So many things I see at once as I silently watch without a tear.
It's a wonderful feeling to know your thoughts as I listen without an ear.

As the rains pour out the tears from my heart
I know that your body and soul must part.
In its' heavenly journey from earth to above
The rainbows shall carry your memory with Love.

Stella Sandlin

HEART SOUNDS

I captured a sungleam when the morning was still.
I caught a moonbeam coming over a hill.
I captured the rustle of a soft gentle breeze.
One evening at sunset through the leaves of a tree.

Like music all sparkled, with silver and gold,
The dazzle and splendor spread over my soul.
I listened one evening to the song of a bird.
And as I listened my heart soon heard,
A soft note of sadness behind every word.

And oh, why sadness in the song of a bird.
He was trying to say in his beautiful song.
Each one must have love is he means to go on.

For life without love is sadness and gloom.
And as he sang on in a tree by a stream,
My heart caught the sound of a beautiful dream.

Patricia Overy

TAKE GOD'S HAND

Dedicated to My Mother, Sidaline Sorter

Take God's hand, and he will lead you home.
Once you get to heaven no more shall you roam.
Remember we should pray, and ask him to forgive.
All the sins that we've committed while on his
earth we've lived.
They cursed the Son of God, as he hung upon the cross.
He, prayed to God, for strength, just before his life
he lost.
Picture Jesus hanging there.
Nails in his hands, thorns in his hair.
He died for us so that Christian love could live.
And his Father up in heaven, would all our sins forgive.

The Bible is the good book but it's hid upon the shelf.
When we want to read, we think only of ourselves.
The magazines we read are full of murder, love and sex.
While all the beauty and the knowle
Please come on all you people and take God's hand.
He's the only man in life who will ever understand.
Remember we should pray and ask him to forgive.
All the sins that we've committed.
While on his earth we've lived.

S Gauer

MOTHER'S SONG

To my sweet daughter-in-law, Denise, who inspired this poem.

Sometimes you feel your identity is gone,
It's mommy and honey all the day long,
You feel as if somewhere you've gone wrong,
You're just singing "Mother's Song".

Comes the winter and the snow,
Noses to wipe and to blow,
Weather is bad—no place to go,
It's just "Mother's Song" you know.

Oh dear Lord, what can you do,
Hubby is gone—child can't find his shoe,
Stuck in the house and feeling blue,
"Mother's Song" has come over you.

Somewhere down the road a way,
You'll stop and reflect upon this day,
"Mother's Song" has gone its way,
And "Woman's Song" is here to stay.

William P Kelley

DEATH OF A FARMER

To Patrick J. Kelley, my father, a farmer all his sixty years.

I was thirty-nine when my father died
in my mother's arms that winter night.
She sat alone in shock, tears not yet dried
when Father closed his eyes and began his Flight.

Thick clouds clung to the early morn'
on Father's first day away from the farm,
both friend and family gathered to mourn
while livestock stood hungry in the barn.

The neighbors came to help me do chores,
and murmured of his untimely fate.
The cow dog stood vigil 'side the barn door
and wondered why the master was late.

The melting snow exposed brown grass,
on his grave the wet earth lay raw;
the sun teased white roses 'side the windlass
in the spring with its early thaw.

Summertime grew warm; I saw hayfields grow tall,
and the calves on the cows do the same.
The yield of my wheat crop was good that fall,
then it was wintertime again, once again...

Caroline M vanBreemen

A GIFT OF HOPE

Dedicated to my daughter, Heather. With all my love and support, mom.

As I gaze out through my window
I look up out on to the sky to see the sun shine.
Above my eyes, up in the sky,
I see birds that fly.

We are like and as the birds—
We're free and full of ' light'.—
Free to do all things in life.

All that space gives me
no wonder of where to go,
But I know I have to show
a place for my baby—
She's 'A Gift of Hope'.

She's surrounded by demons and angels.
She's beginning to learn how to fly her wings.
She's trying to find how to use her space
in her mind, But yet hasn't found her purpose to be.
We give her the courage. We give her the hope.
Most of all we give her our Love and our Greatest Support!
I love my Baby! I'll show her the way.
I know she'll make it now until the very next day.
She will finally find her nesting place,
and I will finally let her go on her own.
She knows I will be here for her—
'cause I was once 'home'.

Edith L Ball Cronk

DO NOT CONSPIRE WITH THE SHADOWS

Do not conspire with the shadows
To create new darkness in your life.

Find your pleasure in the gifting of the day.
The new spring blooms.
The color,
The sights,
The vision.

Let it grasp you and listen.
Listen carefully to everything.
Let it become a symphony.
Ever so gradually BOOMING forth
With JOY
With THANKSGIVING
With GRATITUDE.

And do not conspire with the shadows
To create new darkness in your life,
But find your pleasure in the gifting of the day.

Rose M Koester

FOOT STEPS ABOVE

To all incest survivors and my Special friends, Bonnie, Lynn and Katie

Small crawl space
Darkness
Reeking, closed off earth
Focussed eyes on the above trap door
No recollection of time spent

Dusty Lane Johnson

TWILIGHT

As evening nears,
With promise of dark,
The sun bursts out,
In all its glory,
Lavishly painting the landscape
With amber light.
The familiar world becomes
An ethereal place.
All is aglow.
The beauty is awesome,
Overwhelming the senses.
Reality comes in retrospect
With a treasured memory—
The unsurpassed loveliness of
Nature's golden gift.

Trudy Marie Guettler

PEACEFUL SLUMBER

My son sleeps
beneath the sky,
but no one will
ever hear his cry.
His head softly rests
upon the black sand
while he clenches his dreams
within a small hand.
He listens to a lullaby
of the night's gentle wind
as he slumbers peacefully
'til the indefinite end.
Cradled by earth
he sleeps, safely kept,
but my baby . . . he's dead
and I have wept.

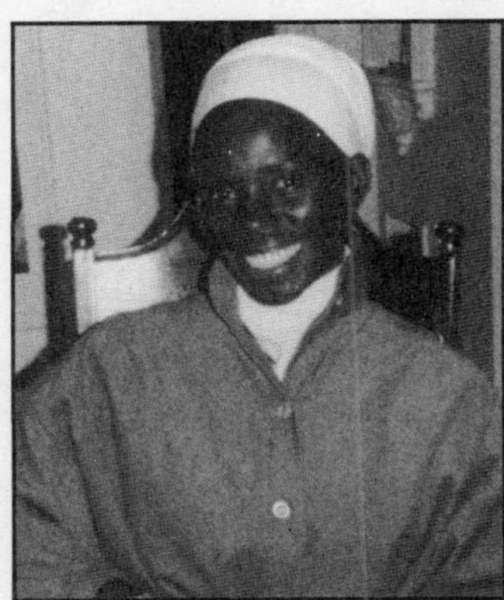

Mary'yam T Muhammed

Mary'yam T Muhammad

REMEMBERING -DR. MARTIN LUTHER KING JR.-

Through all of his struggles, labor, and strife—Dr. King was killed on a Thursday night.
When he was killed, it caused many to cry; for we often
miss good men as time goes by.
He had a dream as many of us do; he just didn't live to see
his come true.
Although he's gone, yes long departed, we must keep up
the work that he started.
He and Rosa Parks changed the course of history, without a
fuss—when she refused to give up her seat on an Alabama
bus.
He marched for peace and justice all over this land; he
fought for non-violence and dignity for the common man.
Love and peace was always his

way, he preached this to
mankind until his very last day.
Love and peace he always
pleaded—and now today it's so
badly needed.
Like it is said in his favorite song,
"We shall try harder to
overcome."
We must not let his death be in
vain, if we have to march
again and again.
We've shown our respect to his
family, father and mother.
Now let's try to show some for each
other.
Yes Dr. King, we're going to miss
you—for most of the
world showed respect for you.
We've even named some streets
after you, and we've
chosen your birthday as a national
holiday in honor of you.
May God's peace and blessing be
upon you, as we strive to
carry your ideals through.
For you died for the common
man—it's the least we can do.

William R McCreedy

NATURES HELPING HAND

A flower grew in a field alone,
among the weeds and trash
there thrown.
A small child came walking
through and spotted where the
flower grew.

She ran and knelt down by its side,
it was so sad, she sat and cried.
How come you grow here all alone,
She asked the flower, between
each moan.
Who is here to care for you, and
watch the things that flowers do.
The flower heard the small girls
plight, Its petals closing for the
night.
The grounds so dry here I think, I'll
find you water for a drink.
She ran down to a near by brook,
in cuppled hands some water
took.
She dripped the water on the
ground, and watched it soaking
slowly down.
I have to go now, It heard her say,
for daylights fading fast away.
The days went by and the flower
grew, and wondered where the
girl went to.
For nows the time in natures way,
Its petals start to fade away.
Seed pods come on big and strong,
If only now the seeds hold on.
Then one morning sunny bright, It
woke to find the girl, in fright.
Upon her knees, upon the land, It
dropped its seedlets in her hand.
The girl laughed in sheer delight,
I'll plant these seeds at home
tonight.
And when they're up big and
strong, I'll plant them back here,
where they belong.

Cale T Brown Jr

LOST LOVE

Thoughts of you are both happy
and sad,
But for our time together, I'm
forever glad.
Though the words were rarely
spoken,
My love for you was never broken.
But as we must, you left and went
away,
The pain that caused, I can't begin
to say,
Even now, as the memories return,
A lump forms, and begins to burn.
I tell myself that, time is all it takes,
But even still, does my heart ache.
I try not to cry, but at times I do.
Yes Dad, I'll always miss you.

Sandra J Toland

DON'T LOOK AT ME

With love to God, my mom & dad, my children, Dr. K.J. Wade, and all institutionalized mental patients. Last, but not least, the public at-large.

Listen to what I have to say, don't
look at me, don't look at me.
Beneath this exterior you see is a
woman just longing to be so
understood, so understood.

Is love so blind that it can't see the
real me inside of me?

Listen to what I have to say, don't
look at me, don't look at me.
Sometimes child sometimes
woman, how could you tell by
just looking?

Mirrors reflect only what they see,
I want someone to really know
me.
Listen to what I have to say, don't
look at me, don't look at me.

Love is grand but don't you see, the
real stuff is inside of me.
Listen to what I have to say, don't
look at me, don't look at me.

Communication is the key, the
shape and form of my body can't
tell you what's going on inside of
me. Listen to what I have
to say, don't look at me, don't look
at me.

Beauty fades away afterwhile, and
I'd rather have someone who
really knew me, by more than just
my smile.

Listen to what I have to say, DON'T
LOOK AT ME, DON'T LOOK AT
ME.

Yolanda Yvette Franklin

THERE IS NO OTHER

To:Ms., Mr Louis, Marie Franklin (With love) To the ones who inspired me to persue on and acheive. For of me accomplishing they truly believed. I luv you mom, dad I truly do, There's no one greater than you . . .

There is no other than you my love;
That I truly love.
There is no other that I would do;
Other than do for you.
There is no other that I would
protect from the cold; For it is
you that I choose to hold.
There is no other I would shed a
tear; For it is you that should be
here.
There is no other who will rest in
my bed; For it is preserved
for you to rest your head.
There is no other I would kneel to
thou feet; For there is no
Other as you born unique.
There is no other I so truly miss;
The soft texture of your
morning kiss.
There is no other who had sweet
suprises; Every time I looked in
to your beautiful eyes.
There is no other who could
replace the part; For you are the
only which lies within my heart.

Delores Hendricks

JUST YOU

Just your hello warms
my heart,
Your "I care" smile is
just the start.
But the trick you do
that takes the prize,
Is how you hug me
with your eyes

John H Denney

GOD AND NATURE

I thank Thee Lord for giving me
The love of nature's serenity.
I feel Thy presence ever near
In each season of the changing
year.

Like springtime when the earth
turns green
And wild flowers burst upon the
scene.
A feel of you is in the air
Exquisite beauty is everywhere.

In summertime the stately trees
Sway softly in the gentle breeze.
The fireflies gleam in the pale
moonlight
Like silent sentinals of the night.

When Autumn spins her web of
gold
Panoramic scenes unfold.
A world of color all around
A fantasy land of sight and sound.

In wintertime the falling snow
Covers the hills and the fields
below.
An enchanted wonderland of white
A tapestry of pure delight.

I sometimes pause and reminisce
And slip into an inner bliss.
I think of the countless paths I've
trod
Awed by the handiwork of God.

I dream of snow-capped peaks so
high
They flaunt their grandeur in the
sky.
I see majestic waterfalls
And hear the doves' sad mating call.

Why then do we whom God has
blessed
Have such a morbid fear of death?
For nature reveals the simple truth
In him we have eternal youth.

Some day we will end our earthly
quest
When our maker calls us home to
rest.
Like the relentless ebb of the
evening tide
We'll begin our trek across the
Great Divide.

As one condemned and then set
free
Like a sailor home from the stormy
sea.
As sure as the wild flowers bloom
in spring
We, like the flowers, will bloom
again.

Ms Martha H Hunter

THE HOME PLACE

A picture is worth a thousand
words
And there are many I can tell
Of the home-place we loved so well
As I go on a memory trail.

The hillside where we picked the
plums,
Rode horse-back 'til rears were
numb,
Walking home when he slipped the
collar,
Sipping a drink from the spring in
the hollow.

Sitting under a tree aftera spring
rain
Watching for a squirrel as we made
aim,
Walking the foot-long across the
stream,
Fishing, frog-gigging or just to
dream.

Aroma of molasses cooking next
door,
Braying of the Jacks and Jennets a
bore,
Dogs howling as they treee the
coons,
Piano music and singing good
tunes.

The shrubs and grass neatly trim,
Relaxing in the front-porch swing,
A table filled to the brim
With food—the dinner bell rings.

Thrill of the children's joyful
scream,
On the back—porch we made
ice-cream,
For turning the crank we had to
match,
Ate watermelon straight from the
patch.

Tears and laughter, work and play
Leaves a memory to always stay
In my heart as I pray
For the home-place of yesterday.

Kathy M (Schings) Guilbault

THE DEATH OF TERROR

In the summer of Eighty
She was expecting a baby
But her marroon car crash
Was mangle in trash
Into a lonely white tree
Among the forest of green
Which marked the death of terror
A man was seen in rear view mirror
Three cracked ribs of pain
A labor of insane
Her eyes clouding with tears
Her soul filled with fear
An anger felt in disgrace
The trace was erased
Which marked the death of terror
A man was seen in rear view mirror
A locket which she held in her palm
Piercing her hand with no calm
A silent scream from the hurt
Heard a scream from the birth
Faint sights of blood
A child she wanted to love
Which marked the death of terror
A man was seen in rear view mirror

James C Fulk

MEMORIES OF DAYS I LEFT BEHIND

Here on this hilltop where the tall
oak trees grow
And the sound of rippling water
somewhere down below
Wild flowers are blooming as far

as far as the eye can see
And the sounds from my cabin
home keep coming back to me

Here on this hilltop I can look out
and see forever
And the beauty I can see is a beauty
like no other
Like the treetops gently swaying in
a warm southern wind
The sights I see around me are like
seeing an old friend

Thats the sights and the sounds of
my childhood
How I'd like to live them all again
if I could
As I grow older they come more
often to my mind
Just some sweet memories of days
I left behind

Helen Lee Cardwell
SCHOOL GUARDS
I drove the same route to work,
As I do most everyday—
And today, I chance to see
The same school guard at her post;
Helping little children along the
way.
The school guard never ask for
favors
Nor do they get much pay.
But they guard our little children
As they go to school each day.
God, give them strength to weather
The winter snows and rain,
And help them in the summer—
When the sun comes out again.
When the winds are strong and
mighty
And the sunshine warms their face;
Let them know we love and thank
them
For being in their place.
To the drivers of the buses,
For those who ride to school
May God's hand be always on yours
As you drive your route to school.
And when the frost is on the
windshield;
Those yellow buses hard to start;
May you know our prayers are with
you
From deep within our heart.

Nan Blackshire-Little

Nan Blackshire-Little
GIVING THANKS
I thank you Lord, for one more day.
Thank you Lord, this I pray
Thank you for the sun and rain;
I thank you for everything.
Thank you for the many things
you've done, big and small; I
can't seem to thank you enough
for them all.
Many times there was doubt and
fear, thank you Lord for being
near.
Thank you for me and mine and
giving me peace of mind.
When I'm in trouble and filled with
doubt, you're always there to
bail me out.
You cured my aches and pains and
saw me through. My Lord, how
can I forget you?

Melinda K Becker
CHILDHOOD MEMORIES OF GRANDMA AND GRANDPA
When I was a little girl, happy and
carefree,
My daddy was far far away in the
Army.
While stationed in places like
Japan and Manila,
Mama and I lived with grandma
and grandpa.
I loved rambling about in their big
old farmhouse,
Skipping through sunbeams, and
romping about,
I helped grandma gather eggs into
her apron pouch.
The yard was big, with flowers and
trees,
The windmill was fascinating, and
full of mystery.
A garden out back held fruit and
vegetables,
With two hugh trees full of green
apples.
I'd hold grandpa's hand as we went
for long walks,
While he told me stories, and
talked and talked.
At night I was kissed, and tucked
into bed,
As grandma held a story book, and
read.
My grandma and grandpa are now
in heaven,
But every once in awhile, if I
concentrate and listen,
I can hear their voices clearly
speaking to me,
As softly they tell me, "we still love
you honey."

Patricia Hilliard
CITY LIGHTS
City lights in night sky
And only the dove flies.
Closer still but a distant cry;
That you know me I won't deny.

Lonely bird from far away.
Perhaps a stray.
Why stay?
Fly away, fly away.

Shirley H Northrop
LIFE FLIGHT
The eagle flies;
Despite all efforts to restrain her,
She soars
Again and yet once more.
She rides the wind
And perches on the mountain's
crest;
She plummets and swoops
To the earth below,
But stays not long.
Ever she must return
To the lonely and desolate
Place of her nesting
Would she replenish her power
And her kind.

Alberta Williams
THE CHIRPING BIRD

This poem is dedicated to my daughter Neppie

I was awakened one morning in
June by the chirp of a small bird
caroling joy.
The winter chill was passe and my
small friend was rehersing on
Mother Nature's time,—
to charm the June bugs and other
earthly creatures with its
melodious airings.
Up the scale and down, with a
thrilling desire.
I was previously not charmed
with birdsong,
because my car suffered the
results . . .
Now, with a new resolution, I
vowed I would
review my ornithology vibrations
and applaud the chirping
newcomer, with no reservations.
So I chirped enderingly on my
bird-call whistle, and the answer
was truly melodious.

Charles F Brandau
LIFE
Endless seemed the hours
As time slowly slipped away.
An eternity in the passing
Of each and every day.
Growing ever older
With each seasons fall.
Not stopping long enough
To see the beauty of it all.

Never to recover
All that I have lost.
Striving for tomorrow
The price at any cost.
And if after the tomorrows
Have all but slipped away,
What will I have acquired
For the price I had to pay?

Donna Baur
TOO LATE

To my children, Nikki, Tabbatha and Andrew, I love you

You never told him that you loved
him
and after he had died
You put your head upon his breast
and you broke down and cried
And from you lips there came the
words
that he so longed to hear
But now he's gone, your words fall
on
a cold unhearing ear.
You hold his body close to you
but he will never know
How you broke down and cried
that night
and let your feelings show
The feelings that you should have
shown
before it was too late
Why is it with the ones we love
we think that we can wait?
May we take the time to realize
that soon their steps we'll take
For those we love who are left
behind
good memories we should make
To help them thru their toughest
time
and help to ease their grief
For time will stop for no one
and life is much too brief.

Margaret Coolbaugh
THE CHILD
A child was born last night,
But could not stay to cope
With the love we deemed his right
To share with us in shining hope.

Like a clear and brilliant star
That little life flashed through our
realm.
And quickly as the wind that blows
afar,
He left us here bereft, with grief
o'erwhelmed.

O little one, so bright and dear,
Linger in our thoughts and dreams.
Beckon us on to that brighter
sphere
Where love and faith our life
redeems.

Joseph B Murray
SUBTLELY

"To Luba, intimus inspirare." "Tis pleasant, sure, to see one's name in print; A book's a book, although there's nothing in't.—Byron

---

Tear drop, tear drop
Tr
ic
kl
in
g,
Oh, so slow.
Are you a tear drop of joy
Or a tear drop of woe?

Sir, ask me not
For fear I dry.
I'm just a tear drop
From you who cry.

Linda Christensen
MOTHER

To the millions of unborn children who have died as the result of legalized abortion. Also, to the mothers of these children, that they will know the love and forgiveness available through Jesus Christ.

I was woven together in the depths
of the earth,
And soon you prepared for my
eventual birth.
You provided a place for me to
grow—
How wonderful is God's plan we
know!

His eyes saw my unformed body in
you,
And soon you knew that I was
there, too.
Within your womb I wasn't put to
the test
Of questionable circumstances—
what would be best?

He knew everything that I was to be
From that very first point in
eternity.
I know I am fearfully and
wonderfully made,
For it's in His image my foundation
was laid.

The Lord has a definite plan just
for me
That some day soon you'll be so
proud to see.
His works are awesome, I know

that full well,
For there's no mistake in Creation, He tells.

You won't ever regret the choice that you made—
You said I was well worth the price that you paid.
Since in your heart you knew my true worth,
I'm grateful that you let me live before birth.

Elva M Wilson

Elva M Wilson
THE HEART REMEMBERS

To my children and grandchildren

The heart remembers many things
the tenderness that caring brings,
the happiness of memories
and the joy of special days like these.

Time has a way of changing things
but never the joy that loved ones bring.

For loved ones like the warming sun
make each new day a brighter one. . .

Loved ones cheer the heart, and fill it too,
with memories old yet ever new.

Thoughts of which you are a part
will always stay within my heart!

This special poem is just a little token
of all the loving thoughts of you
so often left unspoken.

Linda J Shurmur
A NEW YEAR
A new year is here, another new year
Boy, If each and every one of us could hear
The do's and the don'ts for the coming year.

To keep the good, and change the bad
Are hard to do and its really sad;
Because born in US was nothing but good
And only to ourselves could it be clearly understood
That we can if we want, to be the real person we choose
And we never would have anything to loose.

Liking yourself is half the battle
And sometimes this is too hard to handle
But that's the key, to love yourself first
Then easily should come the rest of this verse.

For a new year to me, is a chance to re-live
A time to love, forget and forgive
Another year to make someone happy
To show them you care and always be ready
To be there for them and help them be steady.

A new year is here, stand up and cheer
For we're alive and all should hear,
That once again were blessed with another beginning
To live and love and never stop giving.

Nancy Lou Adams
PRAYER
How does it talk—"
What magic does it hold.
We gather we whisper
we join every creed"

There is a voice
Invisible inside
We each a foundation,
If we but learn
To know that words
are the keys
to God in us

So many club's, we meet
there is but one builder
and that is God
of the Heavens "prayer" is
Is a moment' to be free"

Brian K McCormick
PERSPECTIVE

To my loving wife, Jimmie, the inspiration of my life.

Where is the time
of things so new?
Where is the climb
once lined with dew?
Where is the joy
that followed me?
Where is the boy
who yearned to be?
Of all the things
I loved to do,
My soul yet sings
for just a few.
And now I know
that it was I
who turned to go
and not the sky.

Awake, Arise
and come to life;
that joy still lies
beside your wife.
Again begin
to share that prize
that lies within
her loving eyes.

Sheila J Somerville
LOVE IS
Love is a beautiful day
Such as bringing good things your way
Love is sweet
It can't be beat
Love is sharing
With someone worth caring
Love is crying in the rain
When there is someone there to share the pain
Love is that tender moment
You spend with the one you love
Which is as precious as a white dove
Love cannot be bought
It has to be earned
By people like us
Who need to stop and yearn

Laura (Tootie) Johnston
MY JOY

Dedicated to my daughter: Kimberly Joy Wilemon

God gave me a bundle of **Joy**, this time it wasn't a boy
Many people came to congratulate me, our **Joy** they could
all see.
We never were sorry, we never were sad, because we had
The **Joy** we had never had. It was always a thrill, to dress her in frills.
But time went so fast, I knew it could'nt last.
A young man came along and stole her heart.
I knew then, it would soon be time to part.
As they walked down the isle, she gave him a smile.
But we did'nt give up very much, as we keep in close touch.
We gained another fine boy, but she will forever be our
JOY!!

John H Yeatts
BLUE RIDGE MOUTAIN MAMMA
We finally found you Annabell
With roses growing near your stone
High on a hill in Old Mayberry
And seemingly so all alone . . .
But then our memories joined you there
Recalling days when sunshine tried to light your face,
Half hidden by the old slack bonnet that you wore
To shield you from the stranger's stare
As you went walking through the summer dust and heat
Up to the village store
To trade your meager pennies there
For just a little salt and meat
To feed your hungry children waiting, hoping for
A chocolate drop to eat, when you returned.

We talked about your cabin small
Standing on the mountain side
With cliffs and ledges near your door
And how you stitched the Mother Hubbard dresses
That you wore . . .
Then we agreed that now we knew
Why you always seemed so old and tired
And how, when finally your life expired
Some kind men bore your body, to a ladder laced
Up the abrupt mountain side and to this place.
It seemed so very long ago, and now to find
Your stone's inscription saying you were only forty-nine
When your rest came at last . .

But someone surely loved you Annabell,
To plant those roses blooming there
Reminders that you once were young and fair
Before neglect and poverty wore your life away
Consigning you, forever, to this tomb of clay . . .

K A Nelson
CORRIDORS
Are we
sacrificial beasts of conquest
Whose dreams
are hopeless vibrations
ringing through space?

Are we men
or transient apparitions
Whose lives
may be a continuum
of finality
of thoughtless motion?

Greatness and oblivion
vie for attention
with equal allure.
Their separation
a speck in time,
An unseen divergence
of identical paths.

Our choice of fate
will fall
Where history will laud
or the void will call
May our souls traverse
corridors unknown
To shine
where light has never shown.

Geraldine Shortridge
YORKTOWN MEMORIES

This poem is dedicated to those who served aboard, "The Yorktown, Aircraft Carrier."

I wonder, Oh, I wonder; Yorktown, "The Fighting Lady"
If your decks could only speak:
How many tales of
Courage of your great crew
And all the battles they went through.
As you sailed the seas, Oh, so high
Sending out your fighter planes one by one
High into the sky.
The brave pilots, they were the best,
Not to speak of all the rest.
How many months? Or was it years?
That your brave crew watched over
This great land of ours.

From sun up to sun down
Those brave men served without a frown.
Years have gone by, Oh so fast,
The memories, Yes, Memories will forever last
In the hearts of men fortunately to return home,
And sorrow for the men who gave their life, and have gone on,
Their devotion and courage for the Great U.S. OF A.,
Has given Liberty and Freedom today . .

Lydia Marie Locurcio
WISHES FOR YOU

Family, Relatives, Friends, and Students. Bless You!

Health, Strength,
Love, Money,
Old Friends, New Friends,
A Smile to Show, You are Happy.
To Give and to Receive,
These are my "Wishes For You."

Gay Decking
COME SLOWLY TO KNOW ME
Come sit, with me, by the fire,
And listen to the sound love makes
in a heart of desire—
Come redeem the hour;
Let emotion be as radiant as a flower;
Let sweet thoughts bud and bloom;
Cast away gloom, and let your beauty fill the room.
Let innocence be our tempter this night—
Let purpose and meaning be our candlelight.
The hottest flame is the quickest gone—
Too quickly consumed—with no love to rely on,
But come, slowly to know me,
And if you like me my friend,
Our souls will sing, together, a
song that will never end.

Victoria Augustine
PRIVATE SCREENING
Her trustful baby-big eyes
Turn up to the screen
With a vulnerable fascination;
She does not see the immorality,
Precious babe.

Tonguing a simple ice cream
With arousingly pure pleasure,
She will giggle at his joke
But he wonders if she really understands—
Adorable child.

His eyes linger helplessly on her figure
As he puts his hands away in his pockets,
Uncomfortably aware of her age
And that precarious contradiction:
Child/woman.

It is just her playful nature
Springing into the lap of her lost daddy,
Unintentionally teasing
Men who mean only to cuddle her wishes.
Naive seducer.

Little narcissist
Smiling back at herself from the screen,
As she graciously bows to her public.
She's no fool—
Shhh.

Helen I Shiers
THE LADY IN THE HARBOR
There is a lady in the harbor
Who stands there straight and tall.
In her hands she holds a torch
That proclaims liberty for all.

She proclaims to us the freedom
That our fathers fought to save.
She came a gift to our country
That freedom should ever wave.

Our fathers fought for the freedom.
To worship the one supreme God.
For us they built this country
As they tilled and worked the sod.

The lady stands for freedom
To all who come her way—
Freedom of speech and of worship;
Freedom that no man can sway.

As she stands so tall in the harbor
Offering a welcome to all
So we reach our hands out in friendship
To all mankind both great and small.

Shirley Hamilton
IF
If Jesus knocked on your door
Would you make Him wait outside
Because you weren't expecting Him
So there were things you had to hide

Evelyne Hill Bisaccio
MY GARDEN IN DESERT SNOW
When the great sweeping snow covers the desert,
It brings winter beauty.
The weather vagaries bring a suprise of lovely winter flowers.
Crowding along to-gether and bowing in the wind I see wild
Lavender crocus, yellow jonquil, and Iris.
It is a reflection of joy
When my garden blooms in desert snow.

Beatrice Florist Brown
GOD-THE ARTIST
Mr.
&
Mrs.
Spruce
united they stand
hand in hand
praying to God
in blue heaven;
wet limbs touch
dipped in last night's rain
tiny rainbow crystals
dancing on the window pane;
sunbeams peeking through the trees
whispering in the breeze, "Sing to me please."
Eve comes—dressed in sparkling snow
projecting—a kaleidoscope every bough
while stars glitter and glow in the full—moonlight.
They need no Christmas balls,
they're draped in nature's hauls
their sweetheart's "The Man in the Moon."

Michelle Lynette Prolizo
MR. RIGHT
I love you with all my heart
I never want us to be apart.
We'll have a relationship that is strong
One that has no wrong.
We'll live our lives together
Be with each other forever.
We'll always show each other love
That we only get from the one above.
If fights begin to start
We'll heal them with our heart.
You'll always greet me with that gorgeous smile
It makes me feel like jogging a mile.
I hope there's a Mr. Right somewhere for me
So I could have a relationship that will always be.

Sophia Dream
ONE DAY

To all children with hope for a better tomorrow

One day my tears will stop
One day my sadness will go away
One day I will find a friend
One day I will see the light

The road without the thorns
The job with friends like stars
The home without a fight
The stream of sum and warm

One day it will happen
It was my dream for years
So far I am still crying
And I am still drowning in Tears
There is no strength to pray
There is no help from above
Like many abandoned children
Reaching to you Lord for help
Crying aloud.

Denise M Partyka
AWAITING THE EQUINOX
The four walls surround my imprisoned brain
While thoughts of you bring sullen Spring.
March 21st or so. No leaves as yet appear.
But hidden behind the frozen ocean of a mystic sea,
Foamy, frothy buds of thought
Purple-passioned with orange streaks await.
And raindrops ripple through waves of trees.
They're decayed—like crawling bark
Captures the vernal equinox.

Marjorie Conard
THANK YOU, LORD!
Thank you! Thank you! Thank you, Lord !
Our hostages are free at last!
We're grateful for Your loving care
Bestowed upon their days just passed!

They've been so brave, and patient, too.
You gave them faith and hope and love.
They trusted Your protective care
To watch them from Your heaven above.

You heard our prayers both day and night.
So many, many prayers arose.
We wonder how You ever heard
Amid the tumult of our woes.

Forgive our enemies, Dear Lord,
For they know not what they do.
Bless us all with peace and love.
Give us joy and strength anew.

Dear Lord, we are so grateful now!
This moment is a precious one.
Our hostages are free! We are
So glad to have thy will be done!

Iris Marks
SUMMERS END

To my sons, Marcus and Carey and their families

The wind is silent and crisp.
The sun is warm as it shines down on the waters of the lake as it ripples ever so softly.
Looking across the lake on this autumn day—the leaves are beginning their blazing beauty of turning from green to golden browns and fall reds.
Where did it go—Where is it going?
Seems only yesterday—the trees were dressed in their best summer greenery—now today—the greenery fades to amber—tomorrow the trees will be naked—dressed for the winter season.
The birds no longer sing.
They have gone to seek a warmer climate.
The cottages are empty and lonely.
The lake is quiet—the laughter that is shared with the
summer has stilled.
The ripples that are now so calm will soon be covered
with an icy glaze.
So another season comes to an end—

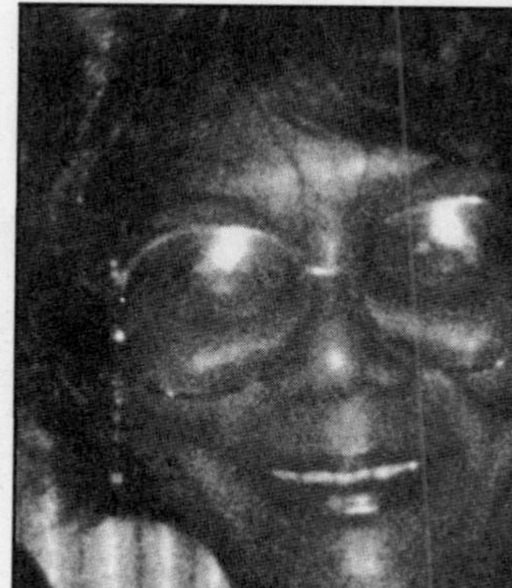

Rose Kelly

Rose Kelly
YOUTH TODAY; LEADERS TOMORROW

This Poem is dedicated To my beloved Family And All Youth

The struggle is now; the issue is you
Education is essential, for tomorrows issues
Youth deserves the best, you are the best
The chance is now, for future progress
Jail is hell; don't end up there!
Know the joy of youth; accept Love and Care

Programs are planned to motivate and to enhance
They are designed to inspire youth to advance
Life and living, can be sweet and fun
Aspire! Set a goal, get the job done
Hands are outstretched to lead and guide
Your help is needed, to help you survive
Please say NO to dope, and Yes to education
Wear pride each day, with appreciation
We will praise and uplift, as we blot out sorrow
Our youth today you are our leaders tomorrow

Ann R Waugh

SLED RIDING

I have so much fun
going down the hill;
but pulling the sled up
the hill is a different story.
It hurts my back so much
and hurts my legs too.
It hurts me so much
that I have a hard time
turning around
But it's worth it!

Kenneth R Kline

(POETS) SUCH AN ODD LOT WE

"Such an odd lot we" (Poets) one and all.
Inspires all reverant idolaters we tantalize and mesmerize with word and flair.
"We" nuturers of inspirational concoction.
Such an odd lot we, man woman and child stroking with pencil or pen indelibly upon our souls.
To word, sentence and meter we give substance.
(This odd lot we).
This odd lot we, of which I am part have suffered and gloried in life, have won, lost, smiled and teared.
But in the midst of these took pen in hand to scribble out a trace of soul.

Not such an odd lot we, we dreamers with fluid pen and excess passion.

Eunice Ford Johnson

SCHOOL DAYS

How well do I remember,
When school opened in September,
How hard it was to wait
Until the town clock slowly struck eight!

Our clock stood high in the Court House tower,
Plainly telling citizens the hour
On its four big, round, white faces.
The long black hands and I ran close races!

For all the teachers had a strict rule
To keep the children in, after school,
If they ever were a little late,
Even one minute or two after eight!

To chapel we all liked to tramp,
Our songs to sing and our yells to chant.
Every morning at the roll-call
A memory verse was said by all!

Did we not have a lot of fun?
And oh! How fast we then could run!
But goodness! How often we would fall
During our games of basketball!

When with exams we had to grapple
We'd bring teacher a bright red apple,
Or candy, with a peppermint flavor!

Trying to gain a special favor!
'Twas queer. At school's opening we were glad!
At the end, always a little sad.

Lorna Kathryne Atherly

FORGOTTEN?

Be still, my heart . . . thou hast lain quiet for
so long a time.
Do not stir again, and with sweet rhythm start
once more to chime.
The one you thought was gone you saw today . . .
Do not again let fancy
far-fetched dreams
whisk you away.
Stay calm and quiet now within my breast . . . and
Do not drag his memory from it's rest.
That steady flame which burned so brightly,
glowed sored,
You told yourself . . . it long ago grew cold . . .
was dead.
Oh, do not stir again . . .

And yet, 'tho cold you've lain . . . I knew,
you never did forget!

Bob Zimmerman

PATIENCE

The pounding surf, screeching gulls.
Long shadows of afternoon;
A boy stood alone in sand,
Rocks and thrusting waves.

A warm breeze carried
The smell of fish;
Misty breaking waves
Brought the taste of salt.

Frothy eddies were nearby and—
Softly like a whisper, he cast his line.
Watching patiently as,
The rhymthic motion of the waves
Seduced fish to bait.

Lost in the rays of evening sun,
The boy stood alone—
Lost in his fate—
As fish swam closer to the hook.

Alison Abshire Kight

A FOGGY NIGHT

A foggy night I lay in my bed
thinking of all the things I dread.
My life sometimes it is so queer,
strange things are always near.
Funny sounds keen peculiar
voices of my distant ruler.
These thoughts are always in my head
and they are always things I dread.
Shadows creeping loftily and leering —
seeming to look for strange things like
a tiny yearling.
Seeking out peoples destiny and fates;
peeping through holes in rotting gates.
Sometimes I think that I'm possessed
and my disappearing would be all for the best.
Could you tell me why these things occur;
why shadows and peculiar things roam this
earth?

Danielle Hirsch

LIBERTY, LIBERTY

Liberty, liberty
Our land alone,

Freedom and hope are
what we have shown,

People who've come here
have seen it and known,

Liberty is something we
all have and own.

Jim D Sawyer

A QUIET PLACE

One day, we all must be on our own;
to ponder about our worth, alone.

No one will be there, but silence and all alone;
Noiseless, to all but our reverberating minds.

Some place to hide and think things out,
solitude and a quiet place . . . at home!

Ruby Rolon (Toodie)

ETERNAL LOVE

Dry your tears, for your worries shall cease,
I have come to comfort you.
I have been here always, and will always be,
I love you.

You have not seen me, yet I was there,
and am here now.
You have not felt my presence, yet I felt
your pain, your love, your cares.
I love you.

My love is eternal, I cannot change.
You cannot know what is within me.
Dry your tears, for you need them not.
I have come to comfort you,
My love is eternal, I love you.

Eugene W Miller

Eugene W Miller

LOOKING AHEAD

From the Moon looking back to Earth
An Amazing sight I see
And Earth with many people
Just like you and me
And as I stand here all alone
Where no man's been before
Except perhaps the LORD HIMSELF
Who created all this Lore.
I wondered why I volunteered
To go on this Space flight
And as I look back miles to you
I think about man's plight
For there is all GOD'S People
On this spinning little Ball
And all they do is fuss and fight
Can't get along at all,
And so I sit here like the LORD
Looking down with hope anew
And wonder when you'll realize
That PEACE is up to YOU.

William M Harris

CAT'S TAILS

To Miss Bridget Takara, A friend whose love for cats equals my own.

A cat's tail is an odd tool
Waved alike at both statesman and fool
To a cat it has very little meaning,
Just something extra to be cleaning.

Margaret Isabelle Tidemann

THE SUNFLOWER

To my children Patricia, Karen, David and Michael, and my grandchildren.

Who says the sunflower is a lowly thing?
See the way it turns it's face up toward the Lord & King.
The yellow petals turn to the sun.
Who could have put it there?
There is only one.

There may be one singled alone along a lonely road.
There may be hundreds in a field, or a cluster,
Hidden among trees and weeds way back in a grove.

God's hand has been here upon the land.
Moist black dirt or clay, yellow beauties dance merely,
In the sun, in the breeze, in the sand.

I drive down a long dusty road.
My heart sad, because of a heavy load.
There upon the roadside for all the folks to see,
One shining sunflower,
Swaying, gently, in the morning breeze.

My burden lightens as I look up at the morning sun.
To think it took a sunflower, to make my life begin.

Bonnie Middleton

ROCKER

With love to my grandmother, Ruth Ellen Coots, for rocking all the children

---

She pushed a wisp of brown hair away
that had fallen in her face.

Her baby's head upon her shoulder lay
While rocking her to a gentle pace.

She hummed a little song
That was learned many years before,
And though, she had rocked the baby long
She would continue rocking more.

Many nights I heard that familiar tune
As she rocked them in that creaking chair
But years pass quickly and babies grow up too soon
And to her, it all seemed unfair.

Today she rocks and hums the same song,
But the hair pushed back, has turned to white.
If you see her, you'll agree, I can't be wrong.
My grandmother is a truly beautiful sight!

Katie Pratt
TO HER AND TO HIM
TO HER:
I didn't mean to hurt you.
I didn't intend to make you cry.
But I have to find out who I am and where I'm going with my life.

I'm out here in the "big world"
Trying to find myself.
I still love you.

Even tho' there is someone else,
You are still my wife, my one love,
For the rest of my life.

AND TO HIM:
My reason for living left when you did.
My heart has been torn out and smashed.
It hurts!

The mourning is past—so I try to tell myself,
And the anger and bitterness is present.
How can you honestly say you love me?

Everyone says the hurt will dull,
And I'll live again,
That acceptance comes next.

Can I ever accept being without you?
Can I ever learn to cope with this loneliness?
Will life ever return to my broken heart?

Chessica R Riley
THE STORM
The storm has been going on for so long.
The harsh winds and the deadly thunder are
beginning to sound like a song
Blowing dangerously are pieces of trees,
Striking anything like a serious disease.
I sit here and watch, with a scare on my face,
and the fright, I try hard to erase.

Marc Washington
THE RIVERS OF YOUR EMOTIONS
When the rivers of your emotions
Are about to overflow
It means you're holding in your feelings,
And it's time to let them go.

When the seas of your emotions
Are filled with salt and grime
You need to let your feelings go,
And right now is the time.

Confide in someone if you want,
Or you can do it alone.
The feelings you have tried to hide
Have probably already shown.

Whatever you do, do it soon
Believe me, you really should,
For the feelings you keep inside,
Do more harm than good.

Regina L Fall
FRIENDSHIP
Friendship, comes to those who care,
Real friends forever; are very rare.
Interests and caring, are the special key,
Exchanging our thoughts, that's you and me.
Needing a shoulder to cry on; when we're blue,
Depends on that strength, between me and you.
Spending the time, to listen and care,
Helps us to survive, the friendship we share.
In closing I'd like to say to you,
Please let us always be friends, me and you.

Lela K Arnoldy

Lela K Arnoldy
MIEKA

To Mieka, my inspiration, with love

Among my favorite things there grows
a child, with beauty like a rose.
Like soft petals her flaxen hair
shades eyes of blue and skin so fair
it seems 'twas kissed with morning dew
to wet the lips her smiles shine through.

I want to open my arms wide
and encircle the innocence I see inside.
This child, protected, needs to grow
with guided love, and I know
if pruned too much 'twill SURELY show
and like a stem, her soul will bend
and disappear upon the wind.

The beginning of a child is love—
a gift to us from God above.
I vow to help this child to grow
to be someone "He'd" like to know.

Alton Paul McCarty
A CAPTAIN'S DREAM
Calm and peaceful, the mystic sea.
The horizon was dimmed by fog,
but I could see, faintly
a ship approaching me.
Not many were on board,
Only a few,
And they called out "We're coming for you."
When the silent ghost-like ship arrived,
Over the star-board side a figure dived—
The others cried, "We've come for you."
When on the shore the ghost appeared.
It took my hand—
the others cheered, "We've come for you."
With the ghost, my spirit did go,
Leaving the old body lifeless and cold.
When on the ship, I did see,
The ghost of the men
that once sailed with me.
Now as your captain,
and my crew complete,
On with our voyage,
Eternal and sweet.

Rita E Nevins
REFLECTIONS OF WINTER
As winter rolls in
With chilled frosty air
It whistles a greeting
Through trees that stand bare.

A white powdered landscape
Awaits the day
Familiar yet new
Untouched as it lay.

At first light we marvel
What a vast icy world.
It wraps us in silence
As the vision unfurls.

Each branch of the tree
Is now dressed in white
And icycles glisten
In a prism of light.

The soft muted sounds
Are carried on air
The echo of laughter
Freed from all care.

Time seems to stand still
The world is reborn
As once more we wake
To our first winter storm.

Rhona Pelletier
DARK IS THE NIGHT

To my mother; Diana, who laid the foundation stone and inspired my love of Christianity, and also to my sisters and brothers.

My mind seeks out
My soul in the night
Dark is the night
Dark as that night
Is this soul out of sight.
I close my mind
To shut out my soul
The door opens wide
My secrets are told.
Oh vain peace of clay
Oh servant of sin
Must you always obey
Must you always give in?
Oh useless flesh
That will decay in rest
For your weakness and sins
Must I pay the toll?
Oh dust that will drift
In the least little wind
Will you forever follow
With no thoughts for tomorrow?
I cried out in terror
To the Lord my Savior
Is this me that I see
On the edge of this abyss?
My soul spoke to me
Through process of mind
I listened intently
for wisdom divine.
You are here for a purpose
And that is to serve
Nor people, nor kingdom
But God in His heaven
For He does command
And you must obey
And He will demand
Come judgement day.
Then a warm light of love
Did shine from above
My mind was at ease
My soul was at peace.
I know I'll still fail
For the human is frail
I feel safe and secure
I know I am sure
That there's life after life
When you are one with Christ.
All I ask in the end
One small corner in heaven
Once a while glimpse Your face
And sing out Your praise.

Lou Peck

Lou Peck
MY SIS
She sleeps beneath the sheltering oaks
in Brookside
It was her wish that by her son
She would abide,
This Sis of mine,
A gal so fine,
We miss her so—But now we know
That God will keep her well
Beneath the sheltering oaks
In Brookside.

Suzanne Olawski
ONE
Stillness in a hectic world
Unknown days gone a past
I am alone

Barbara Hudgell
SEA JEWELS

To my fellow jewel hunters Rusty, Yanett, and Renee

Jewels
lie deep in the sea
They're hers

to keep or give
And sometimes
she gives but a chip
of a precious jewel
to tease and taunt
the mortals
For she knows
her jewels and she
will be
after all mortals cease

Michael Paumgardhen
LACUNA
Though I live here
This is not my Home

While I sleep
I do not rest

As I see
I am blind

I am empty
Yet full

Being lost
I can be found

Gazing Homewards

Kay Weber
THE LITTLE OUTLAW: JESSE JAMES
I have a little nephew,
His name is Jesse James.
Such a little outlaw!
Exactly like his name!

Jesse is the best
little nephew in the world.
I love him for his baby blue eyes
And hair that is slightly curled.

But there are many other things
that I love my nephew for.
His charm, his witt, and intelligence
certainly even the score.

Jesse has a problem.
It's his eyes; he cannot see.
But I shall not be bothered,
cause he's loved, especially by ME!

So whenever you hear me talk
about the kid with the outlaw name,
I want you to know, and NEVER forget
that I love my Jesse James!

Barbara-Anne Steegmuller Johnson
CHILD'S WORLD
A house held together with touch up glue,
and lipstick writing on a closet wall,
echos a "thump, shuffle" with only one shoe
enchantingly danced by a child so small.

Magic pictures are drawn with fingers on glass
when blowing the window with hot breath,
and cookie crumbs grace the clean floor as
wide eyes check the jar to see what's left.

The bedroom is filled with balloons tied with string,
circus souvenirs so happily held,
and these rainbow colors float by the ceiling
permeated with peanut smells.

Wet plastic fish float in the tub
with tiles soaked as bubblebath is splashed.
After bedtime stories, a kiss and a hug,
a busy day exploring has passed.

Gladys W Ihde

Gladys W Ihde
SHARING CHRISTMAS
When I trim the Christmas tree
A star will shine for all to see;
I'll make a wish for you and me
For "a world of peace!"

The tree will sparkle with the light;
The warmth and cheer will be a sight
To give a glow of sheer delight
With "hope and joy!"

The ornaments, some new, some old,
Of crystal, lace and beads of gold
All precious with the dreams they hold
"Fond Memories of Love!"

Mary Wilson
WE ARE THE FUTURE

To the class of 81 of Howard Career Center.

We are the Future and we are ready to take our stand.
We have lots of dreams placed in our hands.
We will all go our different ways and no road is the same.
We are the Future and the time is on its way.
We are the Future, when they look at us they will say
They are the Future Help them on their way.
The world needs love and togetherness
They will show us the way.
We are the Future, We are the Future
We are the Future and it is on its way
The time has come for us to take our place,
No matter where it may be
We want to show the world we are ready
And we will bring it some peace.
We already know the world is a heavy load,
But the time is growing near
We have alot of hope and we will give it to the end.
We are the Future, We are the Future,
We are the Future
And the time is Here!

Paulette Hess Brown
PORTRAITS
So I'm a paint-by number artist
So what?
If I follow all the numbers
just so

And I have a lovely painting
in the end

If I am happy with my creation
within myself

And no one was harmed in the process
Well then?

Be grateful to the genius who created
the numbers

And go and leave me to clothe their nakedness
in beauty.

Dena R Litzinger
THEY SAY YOU AREN'T WANTED
They say you aren't wanted, but listen to My words
child. Before you were created, there was someone who
loved you. In the busyness of His day. . .He took the
time to stop and create you. He looked all around His
big universe and picked out the very finest parts that
He had.
The stars. . .for the sparkle in your eyes
The rose. . .for the blush in your cheek
The joy that the angels sing. . .for your laughter
He even gave you His rain drops for your tears.
He took the softness of His finest lamb. . .for the skin
you were to be covered with
And when He ran out of things to borrow from,
He created some especially for you.
The dimple in your cheeks, your arms and your knees;
Maybe even a birthmark where He allowed an angel
to kiss you.
He put you all together in one little package,
He kissed you and handed you to us with love.
You were wanted child. . .by HIM
His gift was rejected. . .by US.
Just as that Finest Lamb was rejected 2,000 years ago.
There are some Child who accept you as a gift
from God;
But our numbers are few.
Maybe someday our eyes will be opened.
Maybe someday
But don't feel sad child
You were wanted. . .by the One who loved you the most.

Marie Corsetti
MEMORIES
Cherish the memories of all the yesterdays.
Dream for all the tomorrows.
After the tomorrows, the dreams
Will be yesterday's memories too,
To cherish.

Beverly A Bartlein
BLESSED WALK
As I walk through the fields, on my face I feel the summer breeze
My mind is so at peace and my body feels at ease
I hear the melody of the songbirds in the air
I touch the wild flowers that are growing there
I look around me and what do I see?
All the beauty God has made to be
I see the yellow carpet of flowers blooming everywhere
Planted there for our enjoyment with tender loving care
As I walk I stop and pick a piece of wheat in the field
I look at the rich earth from which it does yield
I see the trees in the distance, swaying in the wind
I hear the sound like a beautiful concert that comes from within
The sound of the birds that sing
The fresh smell that the flowers bring
I love to walk in this great outdoors for here I feel so free
For I love to look around and see
All that God has made to be.

Gayle J Krase
IMAGES IN SNOW
My son was here

not long ago—

In this safe cabin

secure from the snow.

He made me a shawl of yellow at eight—

I still remember his first date.

Named David—"Beloved by All"

His spirit is close as winter falls.

I look to my mountain—

He waves below—

Perhaps my imagination or

IMAGES IN SNOW

Denny Burkes
SOLVING PUZZLES
Leaves gently drift in the overcast
Precedence of autumn showers
Reminiscing of strolls far away,
I mentally glide through time
Into the dawn of another day.
This feeling I experience when I'm alone
Brings a more acute serious tone.
Open minds glance brightly toward the future,
And with an air of optimism I smile.
With the onset of rain I am forced to
Seek a less comfortable dwelling,
And release these consequential reins.
Through these moments of personal peace
There is a definite mental gain.
That being answers to questions
Which usually induce refrain.

Mary Leona Rockwell
FALL FADES AWAY

In memory of my beloved husband Donald G. Rockwell.

Sitting by my window,
I see the leaves,
On my trees,
Swayed by a gentle breeze,
Like a beautiful ballet.

Soon the breeze escalated,
Into a wind so strong,
It swept along,
Like a lilting song,
All the falling leaves.

Carrying them away,
To blanket some flower,
Protecting against that hour,
Temperatures fall lower,
lower,
As fall fades away into winter.

Susan Muench

WE WERE LIKE CHILDREN

We were like children
painting dreams on butterfly
wings,
tie-dying rainbows in the sky,
blowing puffy white clouds
from make believe pipes,
chasing love on imaginary horses,
fighting fierce dragons of time
who destined us to grow up.
Where have those playful days
gone?
We have drifted apart,
two lost ships at sea.
Will there ever be time again
in your life
for me?

Lucy Cable Swatzell

MY LORD

On this day so bright and clear
the loud voices you could hear.

Crucify Him, crucify him
the King of the Jews

Up the hill carrying the heavy cross
He was paving the way for all the
lost.
On the cross where he died
for all our sins he was crucified.

When He said "Father it is done"
someone yelled "Look at the sun."
For darkness had fallen over all the
earth
as Jesus was paying the price for
what man was worth.

All the love He had He had freely
gave
so man would no longer be sin's
slave.

Ellen Hursh

FOREVER AND ALWAYS

To My Children Bobbie, Sherry, Pam, Skip and Margaret

If in Life, I seem down, it's only
because
some loneliness I've found.
But to pick me up, outside I'll
stand,
looking up because up there life
will be grand.
No more tears, sorrows or blues,
homeward
bound I'm going to choose.
When my wings, they clip onto
me,
don't shed no tears or be unhappy.
Stand outside and raise your
face,
and I'll look down in amazing
grace.
Raise up your hand, I'll lower
mine,
together again we'll be joined in
time.

Mildred B Holmes

ODE TO PANTY HOSE

They are worn by short and tall.
They get snagged by the fat and by
the small!
To exercise arms and legs—
You don't have to run or jog.
To get exercise from head to toes,
Just try on a pair of Panty Hose!

You bend over double—you turn
and you twist—
A few naughty words you can't
resist!
Talk about The Olympics—and all
that fun.
No! Let us talk about Panty Hose
and how they run!

Thank the Lord, there are no
seams.
When you finally get them on, and
you are ready to flop—
You notice that the heel is on the
top!

You now try a dark pair, as good
as can be.
But later, when you look
down—what do you see?
There is a runner—from toe to
knee!
Another pair you patiently try. It
looks first rate—
But one pesky leg will not go on
straight!

In a minute or so, you think you'll
be ready to go,
Then you notice, your baby toe,
has poked its way through
And is now winking up at you!
Next time you'll wear bobby socks,
although you may freeze—
It will be a long time, before into
Panty Hose will you squeeze!

There is the honk of the horn. are
calling for you.
You go to the window and yell, "I'm
not ready,"
So please don't wait—I'll join you
another day—but not today—
Heaven knows—
I'm having a battle with my Panty
Hose!

Susan J Cox

SOMETIMES I NEED A HUG

Sometimes I need a hug,
Just to see that you care,
To be close to someone,
To be able to share.
Sometimes I need a hug!

Sometimes I need a hug,
Just to know I exist,
I'm more than a number,
On the world's imaginary list.
Sometimes I need a hug!!

Sometimes I need a hug,
To cheer my weary day,
To know there is a friend,
To chase my blues away.
Sometimes I need a hug!!!

Sometimes I need a hug,
To comfort a soul that's lost,
Knowing you are there for me,
Whether there is warmth or frost.
Sometimes I need a hug!!!!

Sometimes I need a hug,
To get me through the night,
To give me pleasant dreams,
To push away all fright.
Sometimes I need a hug!!!!!

Deborah Jean Roche

LITTLE ONE

As I wake up every morning long
before the sun begins to rise,
I think about you, little one, and
the brightness in your eyes!
I recall you coming down those
steps to start your day outside,
but what I remember most of all,
is the brightness in your eyes!
You told me that you loved me, and
hugged me, oh so tight,
enough to make a tear fall down
my cheek that night!
Promise me you'll dream on, and
reach for the clouds in the sky,
thats sure to keep a smile on your
face, and the brightness in your
eyes!

I wish you were here beside me,
walking hand-in-hand,
so I could watch the smile on the
face of my little man!
As life has many ups and downs,
you have to be real brave,
and make the very best of things
throughout each passing day!
As each day comes to an end, the
moon shining bright in the sky,
I think about you, little one, and
the brightness in your eyes!

Maurice Frank

FIVE WAYS TO WOO A WOMAN

Woo her with a letter. Make a word picture of Miss America and give it a name, her name, you better.

Woo her with words. Don't whistle, that's for the birds. Speak softly in her ear, not her eye, she can't hear there so good.

Woo her with a present, a flower, a sweet, a precious stone or a delicious T-bone. To be gracious is to be pleasant and present. Don't go off hunting pheasant.

Woo her with an aim. Know why and what for you are wooing. For if in the course of the wooing you are wed and that wasn't what you wanted, man, you're dead.

Woo her with attention. Her every wish you heed, every gesture read. Never mention you're on old age pension.

Peg McCameron

LOVE IS

Faithful strong and true
Unselfish warm and tender
Sincere Joyful and Caring
Charming—
A feeling deep from the heart
Your inner most emotions
Sometimes indescribable,
Sharing always, in all ways
Truthful at all expense
Your tears are my tears
My tears are yours
Love is but sublime
This is what I imagine true
Love should be and more
O' Dear one,
I love you for all you are
I love you both near and far
You are my most ideal
To me you have the greatest appeal
Your touch gives me pleasure
Hands so strong and so true
Makes all the difference in the
world
When the touching comes from
you
I love you, you are so special to me

Laurie-Lee Luoma

THE FEELING OF MUSIC

I walk on stage and get ready to sing
The sweet melody begins to pour
I open my mouth and hear the
music ring
Then my spirit begins to soar

The audience that I had first seen
The music has made me forget
It takes me to places I've never been
And I'm not ready to leave them
just yet

As the song ends I seem to be sad
Why must it end soon?
The feeling of music is the best I've
had
It's when my heart and my soul are
in tune.

Mrs Donna Jean Laferriere

SPECIAL PARENTS, SPECIAL MEMORIES

This poem is dedicated to Mom and Dad. Two very special parents.

Every day I thank the good Lord
above,
For giving me two wonderful
parents to love.
Our home is a very special place,
Where the love shows on
everyone's face.

It's a place where special memories
are made,
So special that they'll never fade.
It's Christmas Eve so shiny and
bright,
We're happy to be together on this
special night.

This home is filled with so much
sharing,
And it's done with the love, that's
all so caring.
So when this special night has
passed,
The memories we cherish will last
and last.

I can show my parents off with
pride,
Which gives me a special feeling
inside.
Your home shows all the love it
reflects,
And everyone who enters, can feel
it project.

So I thank both of you, Mom and
Dad,
For being the best anyone has had.
Another New Year to hold
memories so dear,
Merry Christmas and a Happy New
Year.

Eric V Blanchard
SEASONS CHANGE
Summer lingers on,
Drifting slowly by.

The closer that autumn gets,
The more and more I cry.

It seems like only yesterday
That summer seemed so new.

Even poets have to change,
As the seasons do.

The time has slipped away,
Leaving me in the cold.

The coming of winter
Makes me feel so old.

Ragged and beaten,
Memories linger on.

Bringing spring in, sadly,
When the past has gone.

Lois L Wilson
RESENTFUL EARTH
Won't Earth be displeased
Without any bees
Or ants to work faithfully
While grasshoppers play
The summer away
And gorge on farmers' crops?

Won't Earth be depressed
When she is not blest
With beauty to eye and ear?
Butterflies to see,
Singing birds to hear,
Murmurs of clear, fresh streams.

Our Earth will despair
When cupboards are bare
And plants no longer can grow—
Nor humankind, nor
Creatures large or small
(Or medium-size) at all.

Earth, enraged, will roar,
Some ought-to-be spring,
"Man, you messed up everything!"

Robert Hugh Gaugh Sr
SUCH BEAUTIES FOR COMPARISON
Where smut and thoughtless oath
and careless curse
Have overwhelmed almost one's
decent part,
His own response may make
conditions worse
And lost seem hope for purity of
heart.
But in God's goodness surely there
abound
Such beauties for comparison that
what,
Invisible, seems hardly to be found
Will shine when tuned or turned to
any spot
Of many scenes that can reflect its
wealth.
Then cheerfully he will associate
With blooms and birds, with trees
and seas—with health.
And so a little seeking will create
Similitudes so gracefully applied
That he with them is amply
satisfied.

N Lee Krausse
COURAGE
Everyone has it, everyone knows
Courage is being brave
When something is told
Being able to face
Whatever is near
Being able to unfold
Your fear.

Courage is something
Everyone has
Being able to use it
Isn't sad.

God, knows and He shows
Your courage every day
Even though you simply
Say, I can't, I won't
I really don't care,
God says courage
Because He is there.

Be brave when something
Is told
You will be able
To face the unfold
Courage is you.

Heidi Joy Garland

Heidi Joy Garland
MY GRAMPA

I dedicate this poem to Grammie Garland who loved and took care of My Grampa while he was so sick.

My Grampa was very special,
He was kind, nice and true,
I loved him very much
and he loved me too.

I'll always miss my Grampa,
sometimes I'll even cry,
cause when you really love
someone,
It's hard to say good-by.

I don't know why he had to die,
but I trust God up above,
and whenever I look at his picture,
I'll remember My Grampa's love.

So when I'm sad and lonely
and feeling down and blue,
I'll just remember the good times
and God will help me through.

Alma W Hudson
FAREWELL
It seems just like the other day
Since first we met
But oh the fun times in between
We never will forget

Goodbye is only a little word
To hold us for awhile
For friends are never parted
With distance or a mile

Our memories will live forever
When it comes to one like you
The nice things you have done
Will always shine right through

Get ready for our visit
Make a bed upon that floor
For no State is miles away
It really is next door

So as you leave this area
One thing we want to say
Our love and blessings go with you
Every mile of the way

Elsie L Hicks
HIS MASTERPIECE
There is no art but handiwork of
God
Whose knowledge wrought
Creation into law,
And genius man can only take His
nod
To further what is needed without
flaw.
The flash of intellect can touch a
star
And set profound enlightenment in
place;
Immortal Truth is grasped from
Him afar
As gift of His perfection and His
Grace.
So was the Christ, His son, and
Lord of all
Made gift supreme to humankind
with love;
Acceptance of Him covers Adam's
fall.
And hears the invitation from
above.

As Mastermind of all creative art,
God made His Masterpiece a
Loving Heart!

Victor April III
AN AFTERNOON'S FOREVER
I Picture her in silence
Lost in time I watch her there . . .
Oh to be the wind
That gently dances through her
hair . . .
Aye Lass, 'tis you I seek
As I wade through darkness long . . .
The spark of Love smells faintly
sweet
Forever captured in a song . . .
A look inside her world
And peaceful days spent in a
dream . . .
An afternoon's forever
Set in Lush fields of green . . .

Vedora Hunter Maloney
THE TWO TRAVELERS

To my daughter, Elaine Hunter O'Connor, my son-in-law, Robert, and their children: Sheridan, Sedrick, Jennifer, Caroline, Sacha, Britney, Warren, and Savanna

Two people chanced to meet one
day
Along a country road;
The two were different as could be
Though each one bore a load.

The first a miser man was he
With gold and jewels in store;
The other, just a lowly tramp
Who'd knock at any door.

The miser worried half to death
For fear he'd lose his gold;
He'd worked and slaved, and
pinched and saved
And starved and suffered cold.

The tramp with nothing on his
mind
Except a bite to eat
A cooling drink, a place to snore
And time to rest his feet.

I knew the two would struggle on
'Til Death came into view,
Which one would die the happier?
I think I know. Do you?

Caroline Seals
FOR MOTHER

Dedicated to my mother, Wilma Foster Seals

I see her eyes growing dim,
I see the weakness in her limbs
And I pray "Give her a little longer
Lord" . . .

A little longer to hear a melody
play,
A little longer to see a Robins nest
made . . .

A little longer to smell a rose,
A little longer to play the music she
knows . . .

A little longer to reach out and
touch,
A little longer, because I love her
so much!

Jack Sapienza
CHOOSE
Can you tell which is the cutest,
When you see them giving chase?
A puppy with its awkwardness,
A kitten with its grace.

Doreen Atchison
MY TIMES
You know there comes times when
I need someone to talk to;
Just one time, the whole day
through.
I'm the kind of person that needs
a little pat on the back every now
and then,
To get me going once again
Or maybe a few words of
confidence
Even if—to you, it doesn't make
sense.
Now don't you laugh and say I'm
wrong,
Sometimes I feel I don't belong.
There are times when I'm feeling
good,
When things go smooth the way
they should
Many times people know the right
things to do or say,
They make me happy, I'm on my
way.
I'm on my way to fulfill my hopes
and dreams,
The way it should be, the way it
seems.

Nina Mae McGinnes
A NEW BEGINNING
I behold my joyous exuberant
daughter
In the bloom of her sixteenth year
Anticipating her road test —

"A fitting Christmas gift," says she

Disappointed because God chose to enshroud
His earth in a quiet blanket
Of pure white cotton
Thus interrupting a girl's dreams

The radio reports several accidents already
She says, "I doubt that I'll have to travel 195"
"Look at that snowy road out there," I exclaim
"Negative reaction," she chides with a smile
"No, I'm being realistic," I reply

"I still want to try it," she persists
Common sense must take over—a relieved mother sighs
"But I wanted my license for Christmas" —
"You may still have it for New Year's Day"

How refreshing to my heart are those
Lovely eyes exuding their confident glow
For the first time to my youth I'd revert:
Ah—to be sixteen once again —
For another chance would I yearn
Why must it be only 'round the turn?

Robert Max Gallegos

Robert Max Gallegos
WATER

This Poem is dedicated to our beloved Earth, its resources shouldn't be taken for granted, they are all we've got, once they're used up. . .it's all over. . .

Cup some Water in your hand,
Wonder from what far off land,
This water has flowed and boiled and froze,
Evaporated to the wind that blows,
Forming clouds that bring the rain,
To drop it to the Earth again.

Cascading downward from the skies,
It carries Earth from where it lies,
An inland mountain, a dusty plain,
All set in motion by the rain.

Digging deeper age by age,
Yet exposing another page,
Of where it's been, of what it's done,
The roles it's played, the shapes it's made.

In boiling pots creating steam,
In giant glaciers and ancient streams,
From where it flows on mountains high,
Thru gorges deep, rain from the sky,
Brings life to land to nourish growth,
To feed a worlds gaping mouth.

It is the life-blood of our earth,
Please realize its precious worth. . .

Kathleen Adams
DADDY

"Daddy" is dedicated to my father, Robert Estel Johnson, of Berwind, West Virginia.

"Daddy" is forever and forever
not to part.
He will always be a special
place deep in my heart.
"Daddy's" do a lot of things
that we don't understand,
But as we get older we
do get the meaning of
his demands.

Joyce L Duitsman
SEEING IN A DIFFERENT WAY

You can see the beauty of the sky,
With light, white clouds all floating by.
The brilliant sun, with heat like that of Mars,
And the bright, shiny moon and the twinkling stars.

You can see a rainbow after a shower of rain,
That arches over a field of golden grain.
The birds are flying high amid the trees,
And the flowers are blooming and aiding the bees.

You can see many people on city streets,
Doing their shopping for clothing or meats.
And children all playing after school,
In parks, or maybe a swimming pool.

You can see the buses, cars, trains, and planes,
All going places in their own lanes.
And folks relaxing at various sites,
Such as on the beach, on picnics, or flying of kites.

I see all these things in a different way,
And I enjoy them every night and day.
By listening and reading from special books to improve the mind,
And going to school for those who are blind.

Brian David Donah
PETALS LOST

In summer haze we said hello
it seems like yesterday . . .

And I thought: another chore
In threading my way through a tangled webwork;
a twisted forest
often nicked and scarred
by thorns of adversity

another chore, I thought . . .
And time went by . . .
And I found in this murky wildness
this shrouded garden
a brilliant flower, glowing brightly
inviting sunshine
And drawing a smile from this
sometimes shadowed visage
we shared the light
and felt its power
And time went by . . .

In summer haze we say goodbye
it all comes much too fast
That old familiar emptiness
casts its shadow in my eyes
And I hold within my mind
the shrivelled stem of fading memories
and petals lost in summer sunshine
goodbye . . .

Dorothy Jane Sowell

Dorothy Jane Sowell
SWEET JESUS

To my children Faith—Rose—Joe—David

He said I Loved you First
even before birth,
"These words echo in My Heart"

He Hung on a Cross
and "God" took the Loss,
"These words echo in My Heart"

He said "Father" forgive
and died that I Might Live

"These words echo in My Heart"

He Loved me more
that's one thing for sure,
"These words echo in My Heart"

I'll never be the Same
since I Heard "his" Name
"These words echo in My Heart"

"One Day" I'll Meet
this precious "soul" So Sweet
"God's words echo in My Heart.
Sweet Jesus

Gregory Kent Barnes
GOD'S LITTLE LANTERNS

When darkness falls,

They peep out from their hiding places.

Timid at first,

But they grow bolder.

Soon they're flying everywhere,

So happy they are.

They flash with sudden joy,

Lightning bugs,

God's little lanterns.

Addie L Kelsey
MEMORIES BRIDGES

I walk along a covered bridge
A memory of long ago
The gentle sound of laughter
And a face I used to know.

The creek which ran below it
And the farmhouse on the hill
The road that winds the valley floor
Are in my memories still.

These many years have come and gone
The bridge stands staunch and true
Floors worn smooth from many a tread
The wood has a golden hue.

Fishing and Swimming from over the side
Bird's nests in high heavy beams
Vines grew lovingly over the rails
Catching the sun's bright gleams.

The snow lay heavy on roof and rail
But snug on the inside would be
And many a person took refuge there
That old bridge of memory.

Some are left and some are gone
Like the folks who knew them well
But the memory clings like yesterday
That old bridge like a sentinel.

Carmela A Martinez
TO MY DAUGHTER

You have gone so far from me
I cannot see your face,
I stand with empty arms
and cannot bear the pain.
There is no comfort for my tortured soul.
Were you a dream those many years?
Where is that loving glance, that elfin smile?
I yearn, the longing hurts.
Then I hear a strain of music,
see a sunset
and the evening star
and a mist dissolves,
you hover over me,
I feel your love,
you touch me
and I begin to heal.

Loraine Addington Esh
WHILE HE WAS AWAY

Dedicated to the one I love, My Husband Ernest

I love you my darling,
With all of my heart.
I love you my darling,

I can't stand to part.
To be with you darling,
Is my fondest dream.
To be with you darling,
Just makes my heart beam.
I miss you my darling,
And just want to say.
I want to be with you,
Each night and each day.

Alma C Ratterree
MY FAVORITE SEASON
In March when all the shrubs and trees
Burst forth with tender buds and leaves
And from each tree top is often heard
The song of courting mocking birds
Then should you ask me which season is best,
I'd love spring more than all the rest.

But when July sun smiles hot and low
Ripening peaches which sparkle and glow,
When apple trees are laden down
With golden fruit which covers the ground,
Should you inquire which season is best,
I'd love summer more than all the rest.

Yet when September morn rolls around
Turning the leaves yellow and brown,
When tree covered hills become golden mounds,
And migrating birds search for warmer grounds,
Should you ask which season is best,
I'd love autumn more than all the rest.

Though when wintry clouds hang down low
And cover the earth with new fallen snow,
When friendly birds crowd around to eat
Our scattered crumbs and bits of meat,
Should you seek to know which season is best,
I'd love winter more than all the rest.

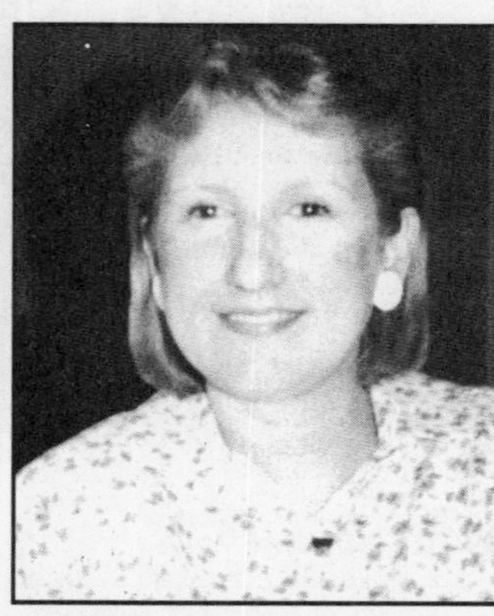

Sandra Fleming Cannella

Sandra Fleming Cannella
EARTH—WHERE ELSE?
Oh where to walk
Being not afloat
Oh where to talk
feel not remote
-Earth-
Oh where to inhale
Having used not a tank
Oh where to exhale
Having sniffed a bit rank
-Earth-
Oh where to eat, drink, laugh to weep
'Fore now I lay me down to sleep
Oh natural, Oh natural
Where can natural be
Surrounded by air, by land
And sea
Oh natural, Oh natural, Oh natural
Oh see
'Tis natural, 'Tis natural
Oh EARTH! It Be

John Shuster
A LESSON

Dedicated to Neill and Alma Ann, who artfully practice the art of inspiring another to recognize his/her own artistry.

Two dots : and part of a circle)
Got together to form what's universal :)
Is not this a lesson for Man :
To get together whenever he can?

Phyllis R Foster
I SEE NOT THE FLOWER
Her little pink hands hold out to me a lily
delicately white on slender stem.
I see beyond the gift the tiny fingers
fairer than the flower, and love flows out to them.

Her sky-blue eyes look shining into mine,
twin mirrors of the skies above,
And mirrored into them I see reflected back
as in a deep, clear crystal pool,
God's deeper love.

I take the flower from the tiny hands,
warm from her fingers' gentle hold,
And know the gift she offers me is one true heart
Of loving trust, of matchless worth, unweighed, untold.

I see not the flower, oh small, sweet cherub mine!
My heart enfolds your precious gift and pours
(Without the need of words and close akin to awe)
its deepest fount of love in thankfulness for yours!

Sandy Young
COME AGAIN
Alone I often go to sit,
On the shores of far-off seas,
While swiftly, gently, comes a voice
That beckons unto me.

She tells of courage, battles won,
And vessels lost below;
She tells of heroes; legends, too,
Those which no more are known.

She tells of all the secrets kept
On Earth and then Above;
That voice so familiar yet strange to me,
Telling me to love . . . yes, too, it tells of love.

And, yes, she tells of all those things
Forgotten down through time;
The many moons, the many suns,
The many truths and lies.

Yet Past does not forget a thing,
And all our tales she tells;
And the dreams we've ever dreamed—
Yes . . . Past knows us well.

I rise to leave the peace serene,
I've found in Past a friend;
And as I go her voice returns,
Calling, "Come Again."

Anthony John Geslicki
POET POEM
So you say you'd like
to be a great poet? Well,
that thought's more noble
than nice.

I mean be prepared for a
whole lot of learning, no
just thinking twice will not
suffice.

To feel the pangs of broken hearts
as well as excitement along with joy,
Dreaming while you experience with
communication your employ.

So many ups 'n downs of
everyday living, fate
applying its pressure yet
you cannot stop giving.

Yes instilled desire adds
the fuel for the fire as
the poets pen writes on to tell,
'bout those glories of the heavens,
and those scorching flames of hell.

John Russell
IMAGES
How would you live
if you could just be yourself
take off your image
put it up on the shelf
would you still need caviar
and the fine wine
if you really like it
then that's just fine
but are you so afraid
of what the world'll see
that you project another
instead of "just me"
would you still need sandals
and jeans and wild hair
does it make a difference
do you really care
or are you so afraid
of what the world'll see
that you project another
instead of "just me"
how would you live
if you could just be yourself
take off your image
put it up on the shelf.

Virginia E Cruikshank
SEEKING ROOTS
They came from Vermont to Pennsylvania,
A newly-retired couple seeking
Missing links in their geneology.
George and I had met only once,
As children. I remembered his curly hair.
After introducing his charming wife,
We began to share family history.

His Father, I knew, and my Father,
Were first cousins. But how were they related?
After reminiscing and recalling
Names of people and anecdotes,
One truth emerged. His Grandmother Ellen
Was my Grandfather John's Sister.
They had both been born in Pottsville.
It was from there my Grandfather
Left for the Civil War. I had received
His Army Records from the National Archives.
It all seemed clear now.

I showed them family pictures of Grandfather.
They promised to mail family names and dates.
It was a fascinating experience.
But oh, there is so much more to learn!

David Taylor Hepper
SAME DAY (LAST NIGHT, TODAY)

For Vietnam brothers & others who lost; children of the world: Israel, Alexia, JADE, & Nathan Dylan to win

---

Last night, today
they're both the same
Don't talk your voice'll break the silence
kill the peace 'm holdin' in my mind
Love is a machine to make people cry
cryin' is death to dignity
You said you dreamed to play a horn
with a name band goin' east by plane
Red was your color as we were blue
Cincinnati a home you called square
Last night, today
they're both the same
Charlie cried foul, but we played fair
takin' our turns, rotatin' the slots
We said Geneva to Ho Chi Minh
results we received I ask you know
It had to do with mechanical things
M-16s, water pipes, ball point pens
To say nothin' of blowin'
Dempsey's mind
Who's side you on anyway?
Last night, today
they're both the same
Don't talk your voice'll break the silence
kill the peace 'm holdin' in my mind
Love is a machine to make people cry
cryin' isn't death to dignity

Kenneth Riordan
A HAPPY DAY
The world spins away
Night turns to day
Darkness is rolled back
Sunshine fills the lack
As the fog rises
We see a world full of surprises
Down the road we go
Carrying our load with us below.
But we do not despair
Birds singing their songs fill the air,
Reminding us life is a precious thing,
Compelling us to join in and sing.
All the strangers we meet,
All the company we greet,
Whether foe or friend,
We have reason to smile to the end.
When the day is done
The victories ours and the battles won,
We go home—a place so dear,
Giving us security and comfort, taking our fear;
At last we lay to rest,
Peaceful, happy, and blest!

Barbara B Reeves
MYSTERY GUEST

To my Granddaughter, Christina Elizabeth Reeves

Today I am as happy
As I could ever be
For I heard the good news
That I'm expecting company.
I'm making plans already
For the time we'll share together
And I am really hoping
You'll decide to stay forever.
Although you've never been here
What a meeting that will be
I hope that you'll be glad you came
When you meet your family.
I don't know what your name is
And I've never seen your face
But I'm sure that I would know you
Anytime or anyplace.
Oh I can hardly bear the wait
Until I see your smile
With a happy heart I'm waiting,
To meet my first grandchild.

Diana Palchik

Diana Palchik
FROM LIBERTY'S VIEW
On Liberty Island proudly I stand
As a welcoming sign with a torch in my hand.
I am surrounded by land and by sea,
And there are so many great things that I see:
Buildings so tall, reaching up to the sky,
Where kites, helicopters, and airplanes fly.
I see the White House, and cities and parks,
The Statue of Lincoln, and other landmarks.
I see all the schools, and the houses look nice,
And freezing Alaska with igloos and ice.
Here on this island, above rocks and sand,
I welcome you all to this wonderful land!

B J Anderson
KENDRA
You were born of our youth, and our dreams,
When we believed that with effort we could do anything.
As the years passed when you were three,
We knew that another, a sister or brother was to be.

And so came Naomi, quiet and still,
Who spent so much time in hospitals because she was ill.
You loved her so much, were so concerned about her,
That you worried how I could care for her and a new sister or brother.

Kerry was born as Naomi grew weaker, completely worn out from two years of trying,
And in my mind's eye I still see you standing there crying.
As I left you alone again with your Dad,
To see if one more miracle for Naomi could be had.

At home to you it seemed that instead of two sisters now you had none,
While far away Naomi's time for leaving had come.
How does one explain dying and death to a child of six?
After our talk you put a penny in a wishing well so Naomi would be "fixed."

Time passes . . . things change . . . you and Kerry are real,
While Naomi is only a memory that still hurts a great deal.
You were born of our love, of the faith that makes us strong,
Of our hope for tomorrow, and all that like you hasn't gone.

But there have been lessons as the years have gone by,
Wrapped up in the struggles, the laughter, and the tears that we cry.
Results of effort aren't always as we wish, but never is it wasted,
And happiness is much sweeter after sorrow is tasted.

Evie Stewart
ODE TO YOUTH
Today I smiled at the girl in the glass,
She was lovely and young, you see;
She was so full of life and bubbling with joy,
That girl was yesterday's me!
When she walked down the street
All the men turned their heads,
And flirted and whistled with glee;
And she knew at a glance they were all watching her,
That girl was yesterday's me!

But time marches on and days turn to years,
One day youth is gone too, you see;
If I had my way I would turn back the clock,
And yesterday's girl would be me!

Marjorie Uldine Coogle
DIAMONDS ON THE WINDOW
After a much, much needed rain one night,
The light from our yard hit the window just right.
The window was open and there on the screen,
Was the most amazing sight I'd ever seen.

The drops of rain looked like diamonds to me,
Shimmering in the light so beautifully.
The leaf of a tree made the shadow of a hand,
On which these diamonds would look so grand.
The night was so still, everyone was asleep,
I felt so sad I wanted to weep.
I would never own such a beautiful thing,
As one of the diamonds on the window left by the rain.

A breeze blew through the window and the diamonds were gone
But I had gotten the message, I felt it so strong.
Base your life on the things you can feel,
Things that are important, things that are real.
Diamonds are nice, but when your life ends,
The sparkle you leave will be with family and friends.

diana dearing
JOURNEY INSIDE
Each journey must be made alone
And though the path may seem unknown
In reaching out and nurturing too
Strength is found to help us through.

Separateness helps make a union strong
Those seeking in spirit always belong
To the individuality which is part
Of commitment in a loving start.

Peaks of growth which enrich the soul
Are the woven threads that make us whole
And as we search our whole life through
We learn to accept the old and new.

Maps redrawn of our own choice
Enhance our life and lend it voice
It's courage that leads each venture taken
And misunderstanding is all we've forsaken.

Hearts and hands that mutually extend
Are joined by a bridge with an open end
For boundaries created can always be crossed
And fear is all that's really lost.

Not without effort can we lovingly embrace
All in this life that must be faced
The rewards for our trials can be wisdom and pride
If we're brave enough only to journey inside.

Carol (Follis) Hutchison
NATURE

For Glenn, Christi, and Glenn Wade, Jr. Without your faith in me and your encouragement, this would not have been published. I appreciate and love all three of you.

The grass is green and the sky is blue
God in Heaven knows that, "I love you"
In spring of the year, life begins;
Grass, flowers, trees and pretty things
They all come to life for us to enjoy
If we would only look, as we toil
We work each and every day
Time is set out for play
As I look out the window, I see the view
That God has put there for me and you
If only we would see, the beauty of nature,
The trees growing tall and mature
We are like the trees' branches
We are given many chances
Life has its ups and downs
Sometimes, we are a clown
Sometimes, we are sad and cry
It makes us that; we must try
We must not give up in what we do
Because, God in Heaven, still loves you

Mitchell Gordon
WITHOUT YOU
I'm so afraid to live alone
now that you've gone
anyone else
will only share in my loneliness

The world is gapped
between love and life
only your smile can bring them together
only your love can make them one

I sit and wonder
about many things
but as your face passes
my mind stops and watches

I know
if I try to watch the sun come up
without you
it won't

If pictures were real
you'd be here

Tan Long Pham
WHY WAR?
We all human,
Why do we fight?
One hits other,
Like hitting ourselves.
Why don't we live
Like butterflies and birds?
Having own mind
To enjoy nature.
God gives us life,
To learn and seek
To love and share,
But not by heat.
Why do humans
Are so imbecile?
Talking can't solve
Their foolish problem.
Why don't they use
The human way?
To solve their problem
Instead of their blood!
Let's look around
See what God gives
Shelter and food
What else they want?

Then WHY WAR?

Nancy Friese
EASTER, JESUS, AND I
Jesus, today was so wonderful;
As I walked through, Your forest so green.
The birds were all singing carols;
As I walked upon the carpet of green.

Jesus, You lead me through the forest;
And the sunrise, was a sight to behold.
For you see this day, was Easter;
And I knew, You were alive for evermore.

Upon the carpet there were flowers;
That, You had scattered to and fro.
And then I saw four deer, that came leaping by in a row.

This day, is a day I'll remember;
For Jesus, My Lord, You were there.
So as I knelt on the carpet in prayer;
I saw the cross, and Jesus was there.

Oh! What a sight it was to behold;
For I could see Jesus, encircled in a glow.
And no one will never, never know;
How it touched my heart, and made me whole.

Colleen J Gifford
REACH FOR THE STARS

Dedicated to the families of the Challenger crew

You can reach for the stars
Or settle for less. . .
Those seven brave souls,
Now in Heaven are blessed!

It took a lot of courage
To be different from the rest. . .
Many times their faith was shaken
When God put them to the test.

Whenever they would falter
He would whisper from afar. . .
"Keep your faith in Jesus,
While reaching for the stars!"

With a wave of a hand,
A smile on each face. . .
They boarded the shuttle
And lifted off into space.

In just a few seconds,
Those seven brave souls. . .
Joined hands with their Savior
Finished with life's earthly goals.

With God there to guide them,
On that fateful flight. . .
He led them through darkness,
To Heaven, so bright!

You can reach for the stars
Or settle for less. . .
Those seven brave souls,
Now in Heaven are blessed!

Rennie M Cole

Rennie M Cole
WHAT HAVE I GAINED FROM ATTENDING ABE

To Mr. Davis and Mrs. Hintor, my Teachers

What have I gained from attending ABE?
Was it anything worthwhile?
It's been a long time since I left grade school,
you see,
It seemed that my brains were as hard as tiles.

I know where a question mark and a period go
I've learned a lot of new words too.
I can make an adverb out of "slow"
I think a good word for a pronoun would be "you."

I can spell very well as you can tell.
"I before e except after c"
But when it comes to those hard words
you should hear my yell.
I always forget to dot the i and cross the t.

Math is my worst subject.
But I can squeeze a penny and pinch a dime
I don't worry about a budget
I just spend the money and save a lot of time.

What have I gained from attending ABE?
It's hard for me to explain,
I know some of it will forsake me,
But a lot will remain.

Sandy Anthony
SUMMER TYME

Summer air,
Summer Breeze.
So Alive,
So Free.
Put a big smile on
your face, if you please.
Give someone a big embrace.
Travel miles to see an ole' friend.
Come alive.
Start Anew.
Take a chance on becoming a new
and wonderful you!

Emmett Carter
ALL SHOULDERS TO THE WHEEL

To my wife DOVIE CARTER

Fear not the future,
And what it holds in store,
But with the ram of reason,
Open wide the door!

Mankind is moving,
Toward a higher plane,
Where freedom, Truth and justice,
Shall equal rights maintain!

The road is rocky,
Winding always uphill;
But ever moving forward,
Never standing still.

No time to falter,
Little time to kneel,
But time to stand up
All shoulders to the wheel!

All through the ages,
Over all the past,
Conquest for Freedoms
Winning through at last!

Grasp then the throttle,
And hold it firm in hand,
Defend our hard won progress
The path of love of man for man!

On to the future,
Onward! We'll always find
Our happiness creating
New frontiers of the mind!

What price for progress,
To hold each precious gain?
Always, it's Struggle! Struggle!
In peaceful work, or war's black stain!

Fear not the future,
And all it holds in store;
But with the ram of reason,
Open wide the door!

Can we meet the challenge?
Can we rise to the call
With peace jobs technology
And production enough for all?

Frances Israelson
RESPECTFULLY YOURS

To Tekla and Karla

Home is love
Home is share
Home is hope
Home is care

We grow a little day by day
Respect each other more each way
Until our dreams materialize
We'll grow we hope a little wise

Hard knocks a-plenty there will be
But Lord I pray be kind to me
Home help protect me from the strife
Until I've found my niche in life.

Hermila R Kruhalski
SING
Sing, sing, sing
with vibrant song!
And tell: the pain,
That with esplender light go.
That there is nothing
better in life, than to sing,
Sing, sing, sing.

A cricket starts to dance
Like a wire that a kid play,
with vibrant song!
And tell: the pain,
That with esplender light go.
That there is nothing better
In life, than to sing, sing a song.

Vi Kirby
WHY

This poem is written for and dedicated to Lucky, my adorable husband.

It's because I love, I must let go!
It's because I care, I must say no.
It's because of you I am the way I am.
It's because of others, I don't give a damn.
So my dear friend, where'er you are,
Remember I'm here, no matter how far.
I've been told many times, it's true,
There's absolutely nothing I can do;
To help the feelings I have for you.
So why bother, its nothing new.
The days come, the days go.
The nights come and I feel so low.
You're gone, but not forever.
And until you're home, I'll endeavor,
To me, you're worth your weight in gold;
And that's a lot, I'm told.
So remember me always my love,
For I definitely mean all the above.

Mary L Cheatum
A MOTHER'S PRAYER
Dear God, help me to be understanding when my children
come to me,
Help me to stop and listen when approached with their
childish plea,
Help me to be tolerant when my nerves are wearing thin,
Help me to endure their noises when it seems to never
end.
Dear God, help me to be helpful when they work or even
play,
Help me to be forceful when they tend to disobey,
Help me make the right decision about things they
cannot see,
Help me to remember they are human just like me.
Dear God, give me the wisdom to guide them in this life
we share,
Help me to make them realize there are burdens they
must bear,
And last Dear God, help me to always love them, even
if they go astray,
Help me teach them all about you, your love and your
wondrous way,
But, Dear God, most of all, I really want to say,
Help me to bear my grief, when you take them back
someday.

Orpha I Baumer
LIFE

My daughters Avis and Norma

I am morning. I have the greatest gift
in this world.
To give to all. Just flow along with me
in my embrace.
For my love is constant—true, and
everlastingly given
like a flag of freedom. Proud and
joyful to every known race.

I am evening. Hold me close. let me slip away
For someone, somewhere has embodied
my truth,
My gift of character, my emotion
of love,
My value of spirit, my promise of
joy and beginnings,
and accepted the love that God
sends from above

Terri Boteilho
WILL YOU BE THERE?
Will you be there when I need you the most,
When I think it's time to end life and jump off the coast?
Will you be there to stop me at that time,
To comfort me and help me reach my prime?

Will you be there during Christmas,
When both of our families can't be with us?

Will you be there to make it seem great,
To remind us of Christmas when we were eight?

Will you be there to inspire my life,
When my mind is blank and have a paper to write?
Will you be there to pull me through,
To make me feel like somebody new?

Yes, I'm sure you'll be there through those times,
For good or bad, better or worse without any bribes.

When you need somebody just turn to me,
I'll never forget what I got from you.

Marie Lovell Perrott

THE SYMPHONY OF THE SEASON

To Miss Helen Clauss, English teacher, Reade Twp. High School, who read my writings aloud in class. Thanks. Class of 1938.

God made noisy, rhythmic creatures
that add cadence, rhyme and reason,
and each one in chorus features
the symphony of the season.

Cold February brings the Cardinal's shriek,
as he streaks across the sky,
laying claim to a patch of icy earth
for his progeny, by and by.

Then a little later on
the pond begins to ring, with croaks and trills,
as frogs declare,
"It's spring, it's Spring, IT'S SPRING!"

In the dim dew-drenched morning,
in the summer of the year,
Sparrows, Jays, and Doves-in-mourning—
Music to a slumberer's ear.

In the summer evening long,
fireflies dart their silent symphony.
Though they have no evensong
they chant, with their choreography.

Autumn comes with crackling glee,
a cricket chirps behind a lath.
Leaves dance in one last joyous spree.
Grasshoppers snap and cling,
beside a sunny path.

Charles M Dabney Jr

MEMORIES OF YOU

Dedicated to an eternally remembered moment of time

I feel your presence now here with me,
The gentle, sweet aroma of your perfume,
I feel your hand caressing mine,
Memories of you fill my room.

I hear the tunes you loved most,
Wild, but strangely sweet in my ear.
I feel you move, I feel your touch,
I see the ghost of you through my tears.

Our love was young, carefree and untamed
Each day taught us something new
We ran with the wind, walked in the rain
You were me—I was you.

Winter was Spring and Spring was forever,
As we danced merrily through time.
We made love wildly under stars and sun,
Wrapped in each other, whatever the clime.

Swiftly, a strange fever overtook you
When our love had reached its peak
And you passed over, as my arms enfolded you,
Into that eternal, blissful sleep.

O' how I loved you then, tho years have passed,
I still feel your presence in my room,
The faint touch of your hand caresses mine,
I smell the sweet fragrance of your perfume.

Laura L Montgomery

WITH LOVE TO MOM

If there's a place in heaven,
As everyone will agree.
Because you fit the angel role,
Someday that's where you'll be.

Because your something special,
That words just can't describe.
Whenever there's been trouble,
You've always been at my side

Some just don't seem to realize,
Just what a mother is.
The special things you do,
The special touch you give.

But these words can't really tell you,
What's deep within my heart.
How much I truly love you,
A love that will never depart.

Gladys Hines

FIFTY

Today I reach fifty—an elegant age
My time-chart is filling; exactly half a page

How should I feel; neither young nor old?
There is no magical answer—or so I am told

Don't say I'm mature, that sounds over-ripe
Nor refer to me as youthful, that is just not my type

The best of all ages to me is today
An exact balance of the scale, but it won't stay that way.

Teresita Jamito Jaquias

MYSELF

My Fondest Aloha and Mahalo to my Great Grandmother, MAMA EMMA KOLII.

Yesterday I was
Today I am
Tomorrow I should be
I could be
I would be
I may be
I will be
I shall be. . .
what I was
And what I am.

Fran Shonts

WORLD OF STRIFE

We're living now in a world of strife
Through tears, through suffering and woe—
Darkened clouds hang o'er the earth
On the corruptions down below
Our God looks down upon it all
At the sinful ways of man
As they strive for wealth to win their goal
Which prevails throughout the land
Their minds are far from our Heavenly God
They cease to come to his call
They forget to pray, lose faith in our Lord,
But they must come to him one and all.
Our Saviour is waiting patiently
For the ones that come to his fold
He'll watch over them til their work is done
On his list their names are enrolled.
The others may go on their gory way
For they despise all that is good
But God never intended such sins on earth
So lessons are best understood.
These are the lessons that confront us today
Throughout every land in this world
Corruptions and sins must be blotted out
Before all the flags in peace are unfurled.

Connie Beeker Mathis

MY DARLING DAUGHTER

To my loving Sam and His lovely daughter Sheri

As a seed I watch you grow form and bud into life.
As a child I watch you bloom grow & blossom into a mature young lady.
As life passes by & days to years from diapers to dresses,
Dreams to reality one man one woman created love, that friendship survived what life gave and is still giving to a memory of yesteryear and the darkness of the future.
You are only a thought away, within reach in my dreams you're the
Inspiration of my hopes & the reality of my future.
To repeat life cycle with another so precious as you.
For you my daughter hold the key to life past, present and future,
To carry the seed and watch it bloom is the most wonderful miracle & mystery life will hold.
And a dream to reality is to watch it grow.
To know when its right, to have lived your dreams, your wants, needs, and desires.
Your life is young so see it thru, then see the future as I've seen you.
With love my daughter forever and always Dad

Mrs Betty P Richardson

A PEACEFUL WORLD (WOULD YOU LIKE?)

This poem is dedicated to my husband "Jim" who stuck with me through thick and thin

---

Would you like to live in a world free from fear
of atomic war, bombs and pollution ever so near
Would you like to live in a world free of police locks and bars
Drive down the street with your family in your car
Carefree, happy about an exciting new day
Where children can laugh and sing and enjoy their play

Would you like to take a stroll free from worry in the park
Daytime or nightime enjoy the sun or starlit sky in the dark
Be patient that day is coming
although it seems so very far away
Let's join and show love to our neighbor
Yes, let's hasten the day
When hatred of fellowman will be gone
Love is the answer, love is the answer
Pray for it, PRAY, PRAY
So have faith all you indecisive ones
"All things are possible with God"
The battle is not yet won
Peace will come, peace will come.

Would you like to live in a world free from fear
Take your stand, show you care
Demand to make the dream come true
Do your part, no matter how small
You can do it, Yes I mean YOU!!!

Victoria C Harris

IS SANTA CLAUS REAL?

To my son, Randy

Everyone knows that Santa's not real.
So I wonder, what's the big deal?
Everyone knows that reindeer can't fly
Over rooftops and chimneys "way up high.
What an idea that Santa delivers toys
On Christmas Eve to girls and boys!

People can't really be too bright
To believe he goes 'round the world
in one night
I visited the Santa in the store
And told him that I knew the score.
When I said I knew it was so,
He just laughed and said, "Ho! Ho!"
Wait! Did I see a flash of red?
Maybe I'd better jump in bed.
Was that prancing and pawing of
reindeer hoofs
That I just heard upon the roof?
Is that sleigh bells I hear?
I'd better think this over for
another year.

Nancy J Roeser

LIMIT OF LIFE

To my loving husband and children

Time of life, or more the state of
mind,
Measure the limit of our existence.
Enjoying all the time we have to be,
Or giving in to nothing but
resistance.

Some will live a million worlds in
one
Loving all they do and see,
But the souls who cannot see
beyond themselves
What a lost world it must be.

The sky so blue, with a tumult of
clouds
Or the ocean filled with waves;
A country farm with flowing fields

Or cities where the streets are
paved.

The poor and needy smothered in
themselves,
The rich who live a life so gay.
It matters not in which valley you
dwell
If one's heart is open all the way.

Our stay is short here on earth.
Our days are numbered by fate.
See and feel the world about you
While you live in wait.

And when the waiting is over,
All things are quiet and clear,
You will understand it all
And know why you were here.

Annette Harmon

THEY DRESSED HIM IN A KHAKI SUIT

They dressed him in a khaki suit
Gave him a gun
Told him not to shoot
Then they sent
him to Bierut
where terrorist scheme
and PLO's plot
He didn't shoot
He got shot

Sandra L DeSoto

DEATH CAME

Death came
and took you away from me—
never letting me feel the touch
of your hand.
Death came
and took your warmth away—
never to soothe me again.
Death came
and took your love away—
never to fully grow within.
Death came
and took you away from me—
never letting us become as one.
Death came
and took you away

Jayne A Jones

OUR BABY, JAMIE

To our first-born daughter

Oh, our baby Jamie, how sweet it
has been since you came to us,
so little at the beginning, putting
up so much of a fuss.
You grew up so fast, wanting to do
things in your own stubborn
way.
But our love for you grew fast, too,
and more so every day.
The first word you said was
"Dada," but "MaMa" was not far
behind,
You had to try new things your
own way, once you had made up
your mind.
You started to crawl and then to
walk without help from anyone.
Your first tooth came and your
bottle went away before you
were one.
You could eat, drink, sit, walk and
talk and always gave us a big
laugh,
Along with sitting on your potty
before being one and a half.
Daddy would play with you to
make you grow up to be big and
tough;
Making you act like a sweet girl
was going to be very rough.
Now that you are over two years
old and are growing up so fast,
we write all these things down, so
in our heads these memories will
last.
You are our first little girl Jamie,
and we will always love you,
we want you to grow up and
remember this whatever you do.

Mrs Fannie Rose McClain

TRICKERY

This poem is dedicated to: my LORD and SAVIOR, JESUS CHRIST. Praise be to His Name, FOREVER. Thank-you, LORD.

Love has tricked me in the past.
Mainly because it did not last.
It just disappeared too fast.
Here today, gone tomorrow.
Leaving me so full of sorrow.
Why didn't you tell me that you
loaned it to me, it was not for me
to keep.
And I would not have had to weep,
Because I had gotten a little too
deep.

Dolores A Irwin

ME!

I'd love to sit and think today
of beauty seen along life's way. . .
The big things that are always there
like sun and moon and sky and
air. . .
The small things that are seldom
seen
like flowers, stones and leaves and
green. . .
The things that move and gently
dance
like birds and bees and little ants. . .
And man-made things we take in
stride
like telephones and auto-rides. . .
I'd like to take the time to taste
the ripened orange or sun-filled
grape. . .
To smell a home-cooked meal
prepared
with love and warmth and hands
that care. . .
To hear the song of soft, fine rain
and the sounds of God with man
again. . .
But today being only another day,
with people around, and in the way,
with problems and life and work
and things,
and with the day and all it brings. . .
Who's got time for such small fare
like enjoyment and fun and being
aware?
Me! Today I'm going to look and
see. . .
I'm going to be just me being me!

Helmer Tietjen

SOLILOQUY

To Agnes of Chaky

I will honor man in noble fashion
By revealing thoughts unto myself
That apply, with love and sinew,
An understanding of likeness in
strife.

Close to mind lies the path of
another,
Linking, intersecting, and
intermingled.
Together, the challenge combines
into one—
The asperation of evolution in
peace.

I will shatter unimpressive
traditions
In an era that glorifies the mind,
Then free the flow of universal love
That binds all to commonness in
birth.

Before this day is forgotten and
past
The light and dark shall fuse into
one,
And greater events will stir, with
compassion,
This life which is rooted in
perfection.

Pam Warr

A SMALL TASK OF TIN

This poem is dedicated to my granddaddy who taught me that the smallest tasks hold the greatest memories.

The little snuff tin sitting on my
shelf,
Brings back memories of
granddaddy and myself.
How he used to dip the snuff with
a crook of his
chin.
He always would spill a little and
give a grin.

He carried the tin when my father
was just a
tot,
And used it in the fields when
planting his
crops.

As he grew older the tin turned
yellow with age,
He didn't buy a new one though,
never throw away
anything useful he used to say.

The paddle inside also showed his
skill,
I'm sure no one understands how
these memories
make me feel.

A small task of tin is my special
memory,
It was part of him and he was part
of me.

Though my granddaddy is now
gone,
I'll always have my little snuff tin
in my home.

I can look at it, it may bring a smile
or may bring
a tear,
But I can look at it and feel my
granddaddy is near.

And with a crook of his chin,
He's looking down and giving me
a grin.

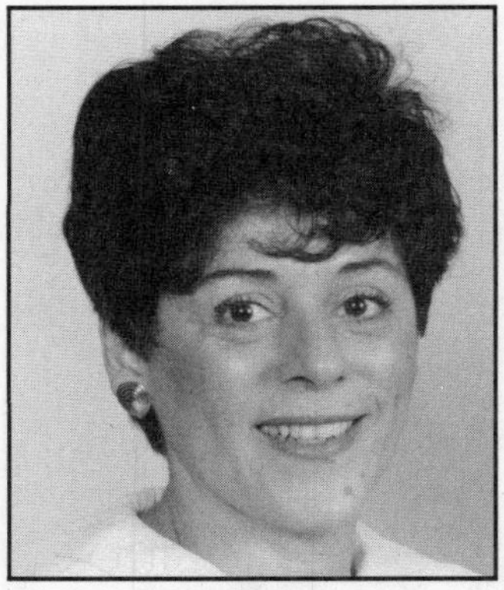

Donna M Gray

Donna M Gray

THE WANDERER

Beneath the shadows of the moon
I wander aimlessly,
across the sand, along the
shore,
to think in privacy;

The waters roll and spray a mist,
the salt air wraps my soul,
my cluttered thoughts begin to
sort
and clarity unfolds;

The silent, gliding gulls above
portray a spirit free,
and I, at peace within myself,
stroll on in harmony.

Lon Wolfe
MORTALITY REALIZED

To Shirley—May there be another Spring—

As I listened to the king
Thinking dreams of Spring long past;
Some came true,
And some were cruel—
Bitter-sweet that does not last.

Now secrets clear of regal ash
We take our daily task.
With royal mist
The final kiss—
The cloak of youth is cast.

Winters wisdom now to guide us—
We grasp the golden ring.
For now we know, beyond the cloud,
Will be another Spring.

S R Meier
YOUR NOVA
A calm way to speak
like a summer rain,
is to dole out your name
like clouds,
but that's a thing
you can't believe in; too tame.

BUT IF I WERE TO SCREAM!
MIGHTILY! CRAZILY!
THE STARS! THEMSELVES!
COULD . . .
fold away like leaves.

Well, you ain't fooled.
I'm not a Second Coming,
I'm a blistered band of light
waiting for eclipse
underneath your nova of night.

Shirley Boren
NANA'S TEARS

To my seven year old grandson, Justin Mikal Bodie, left us Oct. 8 1986

If my tears could make the roses grow
I'd send them all to heaven
If my tears could stop the fires glow
I'd send them all to hell
Now there are tears of sadness
And there are tears of joy
But my tears right now are sadness
Cause I lost a little boy
He's out of sight and out of touch
But memories are still here
I don't know why
That's why I cry
What's life without a tear
The Lord called him to heaven
Left the weak and took the strong
Maybe just to guide us on our way
I don't know why
That's why I cry
But we will know someday

T E Walker
A CHILD UNBORN
A child unborn
And who does mourn,
Or ceremony make?
What kind of grave,
What flowers laid,
What prayers your soul to take?

A child unborn
And who does mourn,
Or sheds a single tear?
Whose arms do ache,
Who longs to take,
Your precious body Near?

O child unborn
It's I, who mourns
Twas me, betrayed your life
It was my sin
Death took you in
Twas you, who paid my price

My child, unborn
Why do I mourn,
Why me, and not another?
No other soul
May ever know
Just God and I,
Your mother.

Loula R Shumway
THE BEAUTY SALON
At one time the Beauty Salon was a haven
For women hoping to look their best,
Where one could kick off their shoes—and
Exchange jokes, or otherwise relax and rest.

Now all that has changed—because
Men have invaded our place,
They are being shampooed, rollered or blowdried
A new breed of men, almost like a new race.

Seems to me the men are changing
No longer trying for the image of John Wayne,
Now with their haircuts and permanents
It's hard to tell men from women, what a shame.

I feel certain this trend will eventually change
Real looking men are certain to emerge,
No longer looking like fancy male models
But more attractive and with more nerve.

I'm looking forward to the day
And I'm hoping it won't be too long,
When the Beauty Salon will revert to us women
With the Barber Shop, the place for men's song.

Frank Menalis
MY LOVE, MY KINGDOM, GONE

This poem is dedicated to Betty Jo, my loving wife

Oh what pity—for a king's heart and soul,
finding his Castle of dreams, and love—
suddenly crumble into wind-blown dust.
His beautiful Queen—and secret lover—
suddenly vanished—into dark clouds of
no-where.

Pam J Kleinwachter
SISTERS
Friends don't last forever,
and people come and go.
But a sister is for a life time,
a friendship that will grow.

Nothing can ever take away,
these feelings I have for you,
To me, you are a priceless gift,
in all you say and do.

Now that we are older,
and grey infests our hair.
We are so much wiser,
and blessed within His care.

Through the years we've parted,
and gone our separate ways.
I recall fond memories,
of our happy childhood days.

I wish that I could see you,
there's so much I want to say.
I think of you so often,
I think of you and pray.

Arlene E Gargano
HURTING

"To My Present Day Friends" Thanks for Understanding

My friends are my enemies
My enemies my friends.

They know how I think
They know how I feel.

Yet their tongues hurt like
a sharp piece of steel.

Down deeper I sink in the
dark depths of gloom.

Now there, I slip into the
hallow depths of my wounds.

I hold onto myself for
I am all I have.

And wait for a tomorrow
when friends can understand.

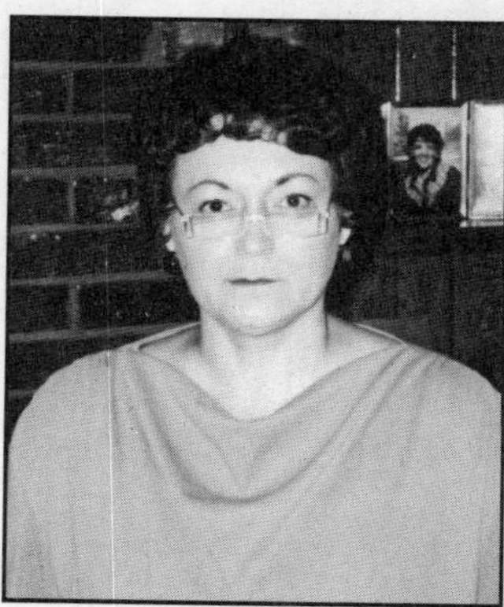

Betty A McMullen

Betty A McMullen
WHY MOMS WEAR THE PANTS

Dedicated to all the moms who have been forced to 'Wear The Pants.'

The parents decided their union to sever,
those sacred vows to become one forever.
They established a home and children arrive
pairs of toddling feet, one, two, three, four, then five!

Regardless how many little ones they leave
a marriage now broken no more to retrieve.
Days and years passed and the children fastly grew,
time finds mom providing the clothes, rent and stew!

She's rushing here some twenty hours of the day,
a whole lot more to do than just bills to pay.
Little time left for her own personal needs,
another emergency. . .she instantly heeds.

There are too many duties for her to record
yet she finds the time to teach God's Holy Word.
For without His extra help, courage and strength
she could not endure the task at its full length.

The blessed children suffer and have less chance
in life, because mom was forced to wear the pants.
Lots of fathers, their obligations deny,
as they have left the little ones home to cry!

Linda K Fischer
"SPECIAL" LOVE

"To Shari," may you be all you can.

I keep her close to me
because she doesn't understand.
She talks to herself
and watches her hand.
She didn't walk til
she was near seven.
Her speech had started
when she was going on eleven.
Her moods they change
from morning til night.
When she is very angry
I try to make it right.
I see others look
and I see them stare.
The best part of all
is she doesn't care.
I've watched her grow
from baby to teen.
Thinking of the joys
and sorrows we've seen.
I look at her now
and the Lord up above.
And thank him again
for my "SPECIAL" Love.

Elsie S Hall
WORDS WITH MUSIC
The poem has a subtle melody
That words compose in rhythmic, shining lines,
Revealing thoughts each dazzling phrase defines
With intellectual sincerity.
There is a delicate tonality
Interpretive of Nature's rare designs;
The ever changing splendor intertwines
With views of life that bring tranquility.
The poet sets the stage with questioning,
That draws the reader to relate delight
Or sorrow to remembrance of "warm fields;"
Embracing days will bring awakening,
Belief Divinity will come, a bright
Enduring star that love of living yields.

Ms Helen Gagliardi
WINE

To my little Angel, Michael

I love the taste of wine
It makes me feel so fine

And I pray to God, I won't
Fall down on my behind.

Evelyn M Cornelius
AWAKENING

To Ira, who taught me love.

We have not said the words,
I know. Nor have I let
My own shy heart acknowledge
That I love you. Yet,
The veil is rising
Like slow-lifting fog
On wintry night. Today
We need no spoken word
To speed love's winged flight.

For tho our love e'en now
Each thought denies,
I see it trembling
In the heart depth of your eyes!

Willa Ree Plunk
CHILDRENS DREAMS
Wouldn't it be nice to have cold wind in the summer
Wouldn't the flowers be pretty in the snow
Snowmen could have dazies for buttons
And icicles would hang from the rainbow

It sure would be nice to go barefoot
And make funny tracks all around
On that beautiful white snow in the summer
That we have always tracked on the ground

Just imagine being out on the playground
Sliding in something fluffy and white
You could roll and turn a million summersets
And not worry about colds and frostbite

We could all go swimming in January
Spread a picnic lunch on the ground
With no worries of ants and mosquitos
'Cause there wouldn't be any around.

Santa Claus would be wearing a swim suit
Mocking birds would be pulling the sleigh
In his bag he'd have sandels and beach balls
And he would come in the middle of May
Oh the wonderful dreams of children
All the make believe games they play
Lord keep them all healthy and happy
For adulthood is not far away

Linda Sue Templin
DISTURBANCE IN THE COUNTRY
In the distance, I see my mountains crumble
With the force of the progress machine.
Gone are the heights which I climbed
To hold hands with God, you know what I mean.

Over the way I see my woods disappear
Where they will never be at all.
No one will remember or know
How they grew so tall.

Can't anyone see—
the importance and know—
Only GOD can make a tree.
Wonder what God thinks of man
Whose progress is so smart—
Who is destroying the gardens
That he was placed in from the start.

Progress goes on— there's no doubt—
But Oh! God, if you're listening,
Please help us out.
Save our souls from this—
Fast-moving world—

And give peace to this
Heart-broken country girl.

Laddy Boy

Nellie Lidholm
LADDY BOY

In Dedication: The Lord has taken Laddy home, He's taken care, well fed, now, he guards the pearly gate where devils dare to tread.

Once I had a collie dog,
I miss him you'll agree,
But, God just had to take him,
Guess it was meant to be,
Now, I don't think another pet
Can take his place you see,
'Cause Laddy like my daddy
Meant all the world to me,
But, should I get another dog,
I'll call her Lassie Lee,
To make up for my Laddy,
She'll romp and play with me,
I'll teach her tricks,
And, make her smart,
And, hope that she won't be
Taken up to heaven
Like Laddy Boy from me.

Michele Doriguzzi
HIGHWAY SAILOR
Why do such immensities

fly by with a smile?
Well that's all they ever do
day after day, mile after mile.

And the man behind the wheel
like a pilot behind his panel,
you drive with such grace
in your jeans and flannel.

A navigator making his way
while hours of scenery pass by.
No detail is overlooked
by that sharp eagle eye.

The goals of this captain,
cruisin' like a ship on the ocean,
are to always keep those "ears on"
and stay in constant motion.

You have to be crazy
to be a highway sailor,
cause there's nothing you'd rather do
than drive your tractor-trailor.

Hosezell Blash

Hosezell Blash
A NEW BABY

To my loving wife, Rosa

A new baby is a sweet little creature
it is beautiful with all of its feature's,
it's as innocent as the gentle wind,
trying to be as sweet as it can.

It is like a gentle breeze,
Without motherly warmth, it would certainly freeze,
it's as innocent as a baby sheep,
there's nothing so beautiful as when it falls asleep.

It's like a day in Spring
when it cries, it pours like rain,
it's as innocent as a baby angel
when mother protects it, there is very little danger.

DeeDee Ellison-Stovall
THE ARTIST

For Paul Shaw

Thoughtful and withdrawn
And at times sad
His artist's face so right
Planes, angles, the beguiling smile
That luminates features classically etched
To him the world is a canvas
Each day one stroke of his sable brush
His palate of colors is varied and rich
And his soul saving perspective
Is always there when it's needed
So each day with a stroke of his brush
He suspends time on canvas forever
So in the end
When his painting is finished
And his colors old and dry
One life will have been recorded
For others to study and ponder
And it will remain
Devasting
Forever

bonnie (ohrn) ehrhardt
SO MANY PEOPLE
So many people
a line with no end
Consisting of children
women and men

So many faces
so little smiles
Expressions of sadness
and tearfilled eyes

Starving and homeless
just the clothes on their backs
Just waiting to die
these are the facts

So many just waiting
waiting to die
So many praying
"Oh, God Why?"

A world filled with plenty
consisting of riches
Yet some of our people
Live on nothing but wishes

Just a glass of milk
a slice of day old bread
They could help the living
and could have saved the dead.

Jessica F Santora
SOME OTHER PLACE
Some other place . . .
Somewhere . . .
Sometime . . .
I may yet awaken
And find
You mine.
Some other day . . .
In warm
Spring sun
While budding flowers
Become
Undone.
Some other dew
Upon
My face . . .
Somewhere . . .
Sometime . . .In
Some other place.

Susan Hernandez

Susan Hernandez
MOTHER & DAUGHTER

For my Daughter Sherri

It seems like such a short time ago,
I was blessed with a little girl to get to know.

And with that blessing came the responsibility
Of helping you grow—I thought—"this should be easy,"
For I was only a kid myself, you see!
So we grew up together . . . learning things too.
I think we turned out to be pretty good "kids," don't you!
There were times you thought I was being unfair,
But wanting the best life had to offer you was why I cared.
Looking back I hope you know,
My love was always there even though sometimes it didn't show.
Gee, the years have passed so fast,
And as adults we have found a closeness that will surely last.
But from the very start there's been a special place in my heart,
For that little girl, I'm so proud to say, has grown into a lovely, caring person.
You and I have matured in many ways—we're wiser and so much smarter.
For we have discovered the ever growing love of a Mother and her Daughter!

Miriam F Hartman

PICNIC AT THE LAKE

The sun is out
The grass is green
Grab your hat and come
It's time to take
A study break
And have a little fun.
The picnic basket
Holds the food
The thermos has lemonade.

A blanket old
For on the grass
In the Maple's shade.
There's hardly a ripple
On the lake
The air is cool and sweet.
Tomorrow will be
Back to work.
Today is joy complete.

Joan Groover

IT'S ME, LORD

It's Me, Lord
I know there's no problem too big for you
But here's a favor I want you to do
You said that you'd hear me when I pray
And I've finally found a minute in my busy day.
It's me again, Lord
I know that Thou art great and I am small
But are you sure you'll see me when I fall
I've so many problems, I just don't know what to do
But you promised that you would see me through.

It's me again, Lord
What Lord? What's that you want me to do
You mean start each day in prayer to you
And you mean always do my best
And that I'm going to be put to a test?

Well, here I am again Lord
Let me make sure this is what I heard
You want me to tell others of your word
Actually say "You're His child and He cares for you"
Lord, are you sure that's what you want me to do?

Just one more time, Lord
Thank you Lord, is what I forgot to say
For all the blessings that you gave today
Just one more prayer and I'll be through
'Cause I want my day to begin and end with you.

Estene King

Estene King

LOOK UP

Look up and live by faith each night and day,
I trust in God to show me the way,
If we look to Him in all that we do,
He'll keep us safe all the day through.

We all have our troubles and trials down here,
Just look up to God, He's always near,
He will never leave you nor forsake you I know,
Just look up to God, for He loves you so.

When you think you have gone your last mile,
Just look up to God, He always has a smile,
I'm living by faith as I travel with Him each day,
It's a whole new life, since He showed me His way.

Friends, won't you hear His call to day?
Just take the first step and look up and say,
Lord, forgive me, I've sinned against thee,
He'll forgive you, just like He forgave me.

Bonnie Frum

MY DAILY PRAYER

When I awake at dawn
And the grass is fresh with dew—
That is when I pray my daily prayer to you.
Dear God
Give me the courage to face each day,
For whatever it may bring forth.
Dear God
Give me the strength to work each day
And pay my just debts to my fellow man.
Dear God
Give me the faith
To walk that straight
And narrow path
That leads to Thy heavenly home
That I may dwell with Thee
Some day in heaven.
Amen

Balt W Kramer

SILENT HEROS

To my parents: Violet Hall Kramer and Allen M. Kramer Smithtown, Monongalia Co., W. Va.

Heros in the eyes of many are ones who do great deeds.
Ranging from wars and ball game scores, to olympic perfection we see.
In this modern-day world of ours it's easy to get carried away.
With movie chills and gusty thrills; it's on television everyday.
But how often do we think of those in our own neighborhood.
Giving their time, not accepting a dime. Their example to follow we should.
It's often hard to find the time for things we most want to do.
But spending an hour, or even sending a flower, someone's day could be brightened by you.
The services to give throughout the year for young and old are many.
And as for fame inscribed with your name, well, there may never, ever be any.
Now, if you're willing to give of your time your memory by someone will last.
And once in a while will ask a voice in a crowd, "oh, what's their names?" those silent heros of the past.

M L Green

NEW LOVES FLAME

Our love was once warm
And bright. Our hearts
Were warm with new
Loves light.

But through the years
Your love grew cold
Then there was no room
For love of old.

Then you met a new love
That lit that flame of
Love once more.

While my loves flame
Burned on for years I
Cried the tears of
Loves lost years.

But now I've found that
Flame of mine is no
Longer bright and warm.

It went out one day and
The pain went away now
I have room for new
Loves flame.

Michael Sarkissian

ICE FISHING

To my children, Karen and Michael, and my Grandaughter Jordan.

Ice fishing is great, but it's only for the hearty.
But with two or three friends it's like having a party.
You get up early in the morning, and get on your way,
To a hearty breakfast to start your day.
Then it's off to the bait shop, to get your baits,
From there to the lake, where your prize awaits.
You punch your holes, and your heart starts to flutter,
Cause you know catching the fish, is easy as butter.
When you land the first fish, you already know,
Your in for some fun, as it lands on the snow.
When the day is done, and you are ready to go,
You gather your gear, and trudge through the snow.
While heading for home, as you are on the way,
You talk of the real "Big One," That got away.
Yes ice fishing is fun, and I've said it before,
It's better than staying home, and being a bore.

Sharon L Williams-Lawson

IMPRESSIONS OF A THUNDERSTORM

The oppressive heat making streets and sidewalks seem to fry;
Feeling the excessive humidity and imagining life in a lush tropical rain forest;
Watching the puffy white thunderheads bubble and boil upwards as they increase their size;
Feeling the wind puff and blow and watching dust swirl like mad whirling zephyrs;
Seeing the backwards-facing leaves of trees as they beg and plead for the thirst-quenching rain;
The oppressive stillness before the onslaught of the storm's violent temper;
The fear of wild violent weather as the storm unleashes its dark fury;
The smell of fresh living water falling in the distance from a livid sky;
The oppressive blackness splitting as the lightening screams to the earth and the thunder shakes the earth in rage and rips the fabric of sound;
The roar of rain hitting the parched, dry earth and soaking

in with drops as big as a child's eyes at Christmas;
The roar of streams too engorged to hold the rushing, churning waters as they rumble and roll onward to the sea;
The arc of the colorful rainbow with its backdrop of dark sky as the sun pushes the cloud curtains away from in front of her face;
The sparkling wetness like morning dew and the fresh clean smell of newly-washed earth and green;
The birds leaving their nests again and renewing their chattering and flitting to and fro;
The beasts of the earth uncovering their heads and leaving the thickets and burrows to leap and play in the diamond-like drop-ridden grass;
The knowledge that all is well and good again, and peace reigns supreme (until the next time).

J Todd Cumming
SPACE . . . THE FINAL FRONTIER

This poem is dedicated to the Challenger astronauts and to my grandpa, E. Norman Sylvester, who was killed on Nov. 24, 1986, when his plane crashed and burned. He loved my poem.

Space . . . the final frontier
It's not for those with morbid fear.

It is a thing, that empty space,
To add so much to the human race.

Time will run, time won't stand still,
For man to explore at his free will.

There were seven of these, as you will hear,
Who risked their lives and died without fear.

It was on the Challenger, to go around Earth,
When in a flash the Challenger burst.

When they died all of us were in pain.
One was a teacher, McAuliffe her name.

Here are the others McAuliffe was with:
McNair, Scobee, Onizuka, Resnik, Jarvis and Smith.

In this sorrowful moment it began to dawn,
All of them would want the space program to go on.

They were heroes, all seven of them;
Each life was like a precious gem.

And as they blasted off the pad,
Who'd guess the moment would be so sad?

And as they left the Earth and sod,
They reached to touch the face of God.

Jacquelyn H Morris
BLESSED

To my husband, my three sons and especially to my Mom, Dad and the family.

This world, can be a cold lonely place.
Sometime's, there are days,
When, we feel lost and scared.
But it's no disgrace, we are all just part of the "Human Race."
And we are all, "Blessed" by God's grace.

So called friends, and their lies.
Who is right?
Who is wrong?
Is their a place for me?
Where do, I belong?
And what happened, to our song?

Love comes and love goes.
A baby cries, and someone dies.
Yet we are "Blessed," by purple mountains and blue skies.
Now I am on my own.
It seems that everyone, I once knew, is gone.
And, there are so many things, that I miss.

My Mother's unusual kiss.
Even a fight with my sis.
A laugh and a smile.
A hug from my Dad, once in a while.
Everyday I do my best, and I know that I am "Blessed" by
God's love. Just look above, look above.

Miguel Barreto

Miguel Barreto
SACRIFICE
From a sea's storm
I walk across
From a fire's hearth
I came across
And in a rain
I wet myself
From a sunshine mortification
I dried up
But now
The peace of love
And the
Cool Breeze
Will I achieve?

Judy Anne Cornett
AUTUMN DELIGHTS
Mountains, towering monuments against an azure sky, spiral upward as if reaching for eternity.
Looking at the horizon, I feel small.

Fall foliage, rustling and swishing, propelled by cool, breezy, currents whirls brilliant shades of golds, rusts and scarlets into a vivid autumn mosaic.
Scanning the landscape, I am awed.

Birds, free—wheeling creatures of flight, soar in precise patterns, inate instincts warning them to flee before winter's icy freeze.
Watching, I regret being earthbound.

Leaves, drifting downward in aimless swirls, blanket the ground, turning sidewalks into crunchy paths.

Jogging along, I enjoy the sound.

Samantha L Schlossberg

Samantha L Schlossberg
THE EDGE
I got to the top of the building
And approached the edge,
Still I did not jump.

I came to the edge of time
And still looked at the hands
Of the clock go round.

I got to the edge of the bridge about to leap
And could not bring myself to do it
Until I reached the edge of my mind.

Kim Lynette Martin
FOREIGN EYES
Transport me to an exotic land
of desert sheik and burning sand

Mesmerizing liquid, brown and gold
Making me feel so young and bold
Promising secret turkish delight

Oh, where are you now
that I need flight

Anita Scutti
A BABY
A baby grows
Like a flower in the sod
A baby is a gift
A good gift from God
A baby is tiny
So precious and brittle
Something that everybody loves
So innocent and little
A baby grows
Inside it's mother
She becomes very proud
As they grow close to one another
All the clothes and toys
Babies play with but maybe
The love and glory
That is given to a baby
A baby shower is enjoyable
A lovely thought that somebody gives
A mother will always love her baby
For as long as she lives
A mother prays for her baby
God's love fills her with joy
She would want her baby to grow
To be a nice girl or boy
Coming into the world
God makes no mistake
Trying to get used to new faces
Is a big step for a baby to take

It takes a lot of love
Between a man and woman
God's love is the strongest love
That creates a new born baby

Fast asleep at night
Crying at the stroke of seven
A baby will always have God's protection
And eternal life in Heaven

Paula M McNult
A NEW BEGINNING
I looked out my window, and what did I see?
A little pink rosebud smiling up at me.
A soft, sweet fragrance filled my nose.
I knew a celebration was about to arose.
I thought to myself, what could be happening this very day?
I closed my hands and began to pray.
Is this the day for some family to mourn?
Or, is this the day of a new life being born?
The answer never came straight out front.
I guess the question was just to blunt.
The sky opened up and let out a shower.
Then, the rosebud followed and bloomed a flower.
The answer came from within.
The rosebud bloomed and new life was about to begin.

Marjorie Naomi Jackson
FADED LOVE
They strolled along down lovers lane,
So young and so in love
It seemed as if the God of love
Smiled on them from above.
He touched her hair of sun spun gold,
She touched his ruddy cheek.
They vowed no other love to hold,
And only love to speak.

But the years passed by and were unkind.
And sorrows took their score,
Love turned to hatred in their minds,
They spoke of love no more.
How sad that life should be this way.
Love should have stronger grown.
Renewed and cherished every day.
Instead they're now alone.

Gerri E Prosser
SOMEONE SPECIAL

I dedicate this poem to my wonderful family and friends.

Someone Special is very dear
and in your heart so very near
Someone to say I love you so
or gee I hate to see you go

Its wondrous what someone can do
especially to cheer you when you're blue
Someone to share in all you do
and to thank God in prayer for
Someone as special as you.

Laura Anderson
FADING DREAMS
To see myself with you,
was a dream.
To hold you in my arms,
and to look in your eyes.
I remember when that dream could
get me through the day.
And I know that, that dream will
never come true.
Now the only thing that gets me
through the day,
Is the fight for life I lost so
many dreams ago.

Lorraine Henley
THY WILL BE DONE?
Questions fill my final hour
Tell me!, if Thine is the power.
Though mountains move at Your command
Why does a cancer fill the land?
Perversion, rage, destruction, war
We cry for help, You close the door?
Lost souls crying in induced dreams
Tormented minds are filled with screams
Innocent flesh is rent and torn
While fields of lilies You adorn?
Why have You now forsaken us?
Are we so vile You leave us thus?
Helpless, hopeless, homeless weeping
Promises You failed in keeping.
Our tears, they fall like acid rain
And burn into our hearts with pain.
While children starve on desert streets
Where now Your miraculous feats?
If You can hear the sparrow fall
Why don't You answer when we call?
In death's dark corner all alone
I reach for answers yet unknown.
To what place does my life now flee?
Is there a We? . . . Or only me.

Robert Frederick Buehl
WORKING FOR AMERICA
Listen here America, I've got some words to say,
It's something you should know about, right here, right now, today.
I'm serving for my country, with some of my best friends,
We're working hard, plus overtime, so freedom never ends.
I ask that you might lend an ear, and try to understand,
That we who serve, here or over there, are proud of our homeland.
Warm soft beds, home cooked meals, and weeks without the sun,
Are the prices that we have to pay, so we can carry on.
It's hard to hold our heads up high, when someone's talking bad,
But I'll be damned if they'll get me down, or even make me mad.
Because I know that in our hearts, we've done the best we could,
And that's enough for most of us, to keep us feeling good.
Pull a tour of duty in some strange or different place,
Just searching through the crowds, for a single friendly face.
Meet people from all walks of life, it happens everyday,
Red, white or black, young or old, they live life they're own way.
Now freedom's not just a word, like I've heard some sing,
Brave men and women fought to here that Liberty Bell ring.
Today it's easy to be swayed, to follow with the crowd,
But now it's up to you, to stand up and say you're proud.
Yes, we're working for America, and we're looking good for Mom,
It's the families that we left back home that keep us going strong.
For the yankees and the rebels, and the folks who live out west,
We thought that you might like to know, that America's still the best.

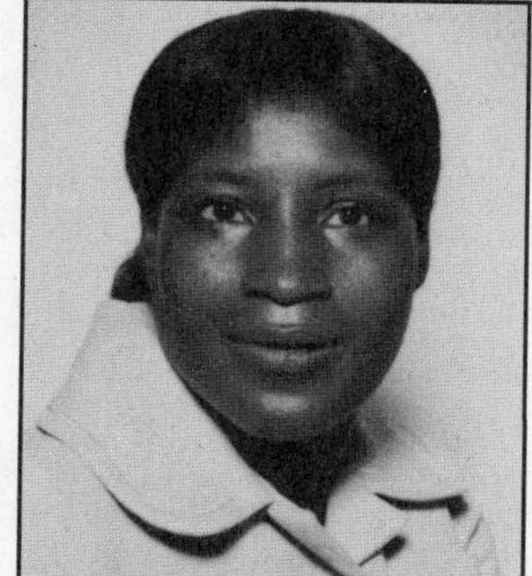

Josephine Carr-Merritt

Josephine Carr-Merritt
CHANGING MOODS

To my husband Jesse and my children Wade, Roger, Sharon, Myra, Victor, Anita and Avis.

Down inside something is missing,
Deep down something's gone wrong,
I can't put my finger on it,
But I feel the feeling coming on.

A feeling that mere words cannot explain,
Its not anger, sorrow, grief or pain!
But I still feel it, and it's real,
Even though it has no name.

Some might say it's frustration,
Some, it's your low esteem,
Some will say it's just a mood
Or, you are not on top of things.

I don't know if that's the reason,
That sometimes I feel this way.
But, the only way I've found to relieve it,
Is when I take the time to pray!

Nellie Grace Hauret-Pierce
REALITY VERSUS DREAMS

To my sons, Ralph, Fred, David, and Sandy; I love you dearly. And to my grandchildren who brought much joy into my life.

Children play tag, hide & seek among parked cars on litter-strewn streets—the playing fields for future baseball, football, or other athletic stars.
Rows and rows of steamy tenements in close proximity; handkerchief-size yards to play in—made of concrete.
Children of Blacks, Whites, Spanish, European, Asian & Orientals,
Whose parents are trying to stay on their feet—barely making ends meet.
The mixed odors of ethnic cooking fill the air—garlic, onions,
Curry, greens, rice and beans, soups, stews, and sauces; cornbread,
Homemade biscuits and rolls, and occasionally—the mouth-watering aroma of—a delicious roast, chicken fixed a dozen ways,
Chilidogs, hamburgers—and don't forget the spicy aroma of tacos,
chili, and pizza with more than one topping and extra cheese;
No left-overs—tummies never get full—there is seldom enough near the end of the month—stretch it out—
A little each day is better than none.

In this neighborhood, there are no fancy homes with acres of soft green grass, tennis courts, swimming pools, Cadillacs,
private planes, yachts, or Jaguars;
No hors'd'ouevres of pate' or imported caviar, pheasant-under-glass, Cornish hens, or rack of lamb; nor fancy desserts of Baked Alaska or chocolate mousse.

But, lacking all the fancies, every day brings these things—Togetherness, caring, helping, loving, and—the never-ending hopes and dreams of one day being able to rise up out of the ineffable feeling of POVERTY!

Savita Jain
I AM SOMEBODY

To Brian—for always being there

Someone once said,
"Everybody is somebody."
But I know
I'm a nobody.

Someone once said,
"You can be anything
you want to be."
If that is so,
then why am I nobody?

Somebody answered me.
"You are somebody,"
they said.
"You are you."

I asked somebody,
"Why do I feel alone?"
Somebody said,
"Because you wan to be so."

I said,
"No. That's unture.
I want to be loved
by somebody—maybe you."

Somebody said,
"Is that so?"
"Yes," I replied.
"I need you."

"Why do you need me?
Do I matter? Do I care for you?"
"Of course you do.
For I am you."

"Oh. So you are somebody,
you agree?"
"Yes." I realized the truth then.
"Everybody is somebody."

Then somebody said:
"I LOVE YOU"

Karla Kristine Halliday
THE LIGHTHOUSE MAN
He lives on an island,
a lighthouse and a dream . . .
days pass without a thought
He walks on the rocky shore,
where no ships have crashed
and no others have seen,
where his dream waits
for reality to hit,
but rare is the possibility.
He hears the crash of the waves
and the breaking of his heart,
as he drowns in his sorrows.
He walks back to the lighthouse
knowing he will never see
the rocky shore again
after this, his last day,
when he reaches the lighthouse
he sits down and closes his eyes
to dream one last dream . . .

Mary Rose Kimmel
CARVING OUR FRIENDSHIP
Cheering me up when I'm feeling sad and low,
Always in my daily routine, I meet someone
Ready to help me in daily trials I have to undergo,
Very importantly, I know that God is near me,
I always want you to know I am near, I do understand
No one doesn't experience some pain, sadness sometimes in their life,
God is near, always to lend a hand.
Open your heart to a friend, make an effort; not a demand
Unity among friends are important as we know,
Remember you're never alone; strife!
Friends stay together, pray

together, open a new door, day
by day,
Relationships;
I and you can always hold no
matter what happens on the way
Enjoy friendship.
Never forget; God is always near,
Dear Friend, I care, love you, pray
for you always,
Sincerely hope this message lets
you know
I lend an ear;
Happy smiles from me, to you in
all ways.
I know that God is always near you
and me,
Patenting; Carving Our Friendship.

Cathy Thi Tai Nguyen
FEELING

1— To those who search for Freedom and Human right.
2— With respect and love for my husband THI CHANH NGUYEN and my children.

We were called the boat people
Some think we are the trouble
Simply because we need to resettle
After so many lost in battles.
We see reasons for all rejects
Cause of the inflation affects
Prepare ourselves for goodness
sake
Communist influence is right
next.
We ask you please to be at ease
Watching us grow in the
community
One bad apple does not spoil the
whole tree
Exchange our LOVE for remedy.
We did go through so many
shocks
Lost almost our entire stocks
Only COURAGE and PRIDE
were left
Work our way up as new folks.
Adjusting old and new cultures
Just for a better future
We need to learn from each other
Sing a happy song TOGETHER.
We are children of God as you all
Only different in color people call
We try to cope for we do hope
Independence, Liberty and
Justice for all.

W H Acker
TEMPTATION

Remember the sergeant at Mass
who had come to the rear
for r. and r., and said he sought the
Grail?
He laughed like a falling shell
and his brain exploded.
He snatched the consecrated Wine
and screamed that he had found a
Fuel
that would make his tank
invincible.
The father
exorcised him back to peace
like a cooing serpent:
the Wine was not sufficiently
combustible;
His death didn't burn,
it only warmed.
But I clanked to war on a chained
groan,
over a lashed back,
past a pierced side bleeding a
vineyard
under a barbed, bunkered crown,
tempted by the innocence of
madness.

Alexis Andros Bachand

Alexis Andros Bachand
PEACE, LOVE, AND HAPPINESS

I dedicate this poem to the third world

Peace is not war.
Love, the kind there isn't enough
of to go around.
Happiness, the ones that will never
know the meaning of the word.
So when someone asks you,

How do you feel?"
Say "peaceful with the world,
happy to be loved, and
happy to be alive."

Hazel E Swanson
A CHRISTMAS GREETING TO A SPECIAL FRIEND

It's time to hang the Christmas
stocking,
Time to trim the Christmas tree,
Bake the cookies, roast the turkey,
Time for friends and family.
Holly wreaths and glowing candles,
Lovely carols fill the air,
Tinkling bells and happy faces,
Christmastime is everywhere.

May your day be bright and happy,
All good things to come your way,
Love and laughter, peace,
contentment,
May they fill your Christmas Day.

And when the fire is slowly dying,
Casting shadows on the wall,
In the softly glowing embers
Time to reflect, and I recall
Times gone by, so many of them,
Happy memories of you blend,
Let me add to this precious
moment,
"Merry Christmas, dearest friend."

Dolly C Robinson
EYES OF MY SONS

To my sons: Anthony, William,. George, Bill, and David They are the beginning of the Footprints in my life.

Eyes tell us everything
if you can only see,
Look into the eyes of a child
you'll see everything you need.

I see in their eyes, love
a feeling, oh so great.
I see in their eyes, anger
a feeling that can't wait.
I see in their eyes, hurt
a feeling of despair!
I see in their eyes, hope
a feeling beyond compare.
I see in their eyes, compassion
a feeling for our nation.
I see in their eyes, love
a feeling for communication.
I see in their eyes, comprehension
a feeling of what to endeavor?
I see in their eyes, thoughtfulness
of a world living together.
I see in their eyes, Love.

Wayne Brown
"THAT'LL BE $3.50, MAC!"

Placate the dischord of a civilized
life, then . . .
. . . enjoin the harmony of the dying
willows
Envision the dreams of autistic
social workers
As they tread the paths of
complacency
And ask for the change from
their dollar

Caress the emptiness . . . the
infinite . . . the void . . .
. . . and hold them tightly within
the confines of the
Democratic thimble

Then pray, yeah pray . . . . .
The Renaissance Man is coming . . .
. . . I hope he's got cabfare . . .

Anne M Bonti
HEROES

Early hours before the dawn
Our troops are forming on the lawn
We'll see the front before
daylight
And thousands die by coming night

We fight for freedom, pride and
truth
Honor, country, glory, youth
Side by side we march to war
To keep the enemy from our shore

We face our fate
Each man alone
And as we march
Our voices drone

"If I die on the battle zone
Bag me up and send me home
Bury me with all the rest
Tell my wife I did my best"

With trembling hands we load
our guns
And watch our men fall one by one
Our minds go blank, our hearts
are still
Our only thought is 'Shoot to Kill'

Face to face it's me or you
Both of us know what we must do
As I squeeze my trigger and
watch you fall
I shout to sky "We're Heroes, All!"

Linda L Beal-Colville
ODE TO THE DEATH OF JAMES

To my dear parents, Mona and Roland Beal, who stood by me with support and love through all of my successful and unsuccessful endeavors.

Weeping sorrows,
pass me by.
Why must my loved one die?

I see his soul,
drift away.
Premonitions go, life must stay!

Life is absurd,
so we fabricate.
We touch and see in altered states.

Love is the strongest,
bond of all.
It's hard to part, but time does not
stall.

James was a violinist,
strumming music into life.
As soon as he goes he'll take his
wife.

"Good-bye" my love,
I'll see you soon.
We'll meet again upon a full moon.

Until your heart,
takes a faster pace.
I'll wait for you in our special place.

Through the Lord,
my eternal soul shall glow.
As long as time "lets" the west
winds blow.

Liz Tocci
LONELINESS

Sitting alone . . . staring at a
telephone that never rings
wondering what tomorrow will
bring . . .
crying tears that nobody will wipe
away . . . wishing
for some brighter days . . . needing
a friend . . .
wanting to share . . . wondering
when someone will care . . .
wishing the hurt would go away .
. . looking forward
to a brighter day.

Robert L Berklite
TOO YOUNG TO DIE

Dedicated to: John Darla Chang.

They died that night;
Caught between steal and might;
Too foolish to live;
But too young to die;
On that New Year's eve;
The dawn of a new year;
That they will never see:

So much to live for;
And too much to loose;
They died that night: Because the
lord had to choose;
The sweet, young innocence;
Of the ones we loved;
Taken away from us;
And sent above;

They died that night, caught
between steel and might;
They died that night, caught
between steel and might;

Why, oh why, must they leave us;
So close to our hearts;
Only to be torn apart;
Oh why, oh why, must they leave
us;

She was as innocent as fifteen;
With a head on her shoulders;
And her body was lean;
He was a friend until the end;
Why, oh why, must they leave us;
Now we all have been lessened by
a little bit;
And the world has become a
lonelier place;
But in our hearts they will always
live;
As long as we keep them alive.

Virgie Mae Webber-Klein

SPRING REVERIE

To my Beloved Brother, Hugh R. Webber, who has always been a great inspiration to me.

Now once again Time's restless
hands unroll
An emerald parchment, and our
ravished eyes
Behold Spring's lovely poem on the
scroll,
And in our hearts the same old
sweet surprise
Stirs to verdant stanzas, to petaled
lines
Inscribed in fragrance. Almost
beyond belief

Are these bright metaphors of
flowering vines,
These rythmic meters of bud and
bloom and leaf.

Now must we haste to read this
ode, for yet
A little while, and we shall seek
in vain
The purple measure of the violet,
The rhyme of jeweled pansies
after rain.
For Time will twist the scroll into
a shred
And leave us dazed, with half the
lines unread.

Evelyn Burkhard Perry

REMINISCENCE

For little cause war started
And lasted through four years,
The trials of war were horrid
As told by many seers.

The soldiers kept on fighting,
The captains gave commands,
The men were shot by hundreds
But soldiers kept their stands.

And from the army came a shout,
A cry which gave the thought
That all men were like brothers,
And Armistice was sought.

And through the next twelve years
That peace was kept by all.
But Armistice Day shall ever be
In memory of them all.

Mrs Clyde (GERALDINE PALMER) Plecker

MY ROOTS

Dedicated to the memory of my parents, Lloyd and Myrtle (Bumgardener) Palmer, both deceased.

How happy I am, upon this day,
To have found "My Roots" along
the way—
It is so strange, how things work
out,
When your hope is strong, and
faith so devout.
There are often times, in our busy
life,
When our minds are cluttered,
with pain and strife—
We fail to ask, from whence we
came
Or how we happened to have our
name?
Our ancestors! "Roots"!—that's
who started this nation,
And gradually added each new
generation—
Knowing the new ones would carry
on the same,
Hoping maybe, some might rise to
fame.
I am proud of my name, and wear
it with pride,
But most important, is what comes
from inside—
To my family honor, I will bring no
shame,
Grateful to my ancestors, I shall
remain.
My "Roots" branched out into a
family tree,
And from this branch, has
sprouted me—
My family "Roots" have developed
quite big,
And I'm so proud, to be just a
"Twig!"

Timothy E Ebright

THE DRUG EXPERIENCE

I'm not the man I used to be
Drugs altered the reality in me

Friends warned me of my way
They said, there would come a day
When I would regret
Playing the game,
I lost the bet

For once the damage is done
How can it be said:
I've won

Can't play games with your brain
Drugs won't stop you from going
insane
They only temporarily relieve the
pain
And the only thing you do gain
Is an empty space between your
ears
Never able to turn back the years

Life is a continous fight
The future is not within my sight
I only know what I can see
Drugs have gotten the best of me

And I hope for the futures sake
Our children don't repeat this
mistake
Drugs are not the answer
When reality is the question
So please try to remember
This story of truth and confession

Rose Coray

ADOPTING A CHILD

Dedicated to: Jeffrey and Karen

It was a happy moment in my life,
When my husband took me for his
wife.
And a happy moment, there is still
another,
To have a child, and to be its
mother.
Our life is rich now, with just my
husband and me,
It would be even richer if our
family were three.
I would realize gratitude and so
much pride,
Knowing I had a child close to my
side.
I would be amused by what they
did and said,
And wonder at the ideas in their
little head.
I would be joyed by seeing them
romp and play,
And baffled at the energy they
would display.
I could explain why somethings
must be so,
The reasons they are yes, and why
they are no.
I could show affection by kissing
away tears,
In comforting their bruises or
quieting their fears.
I could know the peace watching
them sleeping,
And pray to God for their safe
keeping.
I would be wanted and needed in
their daily care,
Which is part of my life that I want
to share.
I would gain a score of memories
to treasure,
To someday reminisce in my
moments of leisure.
All dressed up with no place to go,
But a mother is always star of the
show.

Miss Kathlene Hicks

FORGET NOT ALL HIS BENEFITS

Dear Father, we thank Thee for the
gift of Thy Love,
For salvation and every blessing
from Above.
We thank Thee for the beautiful
sky so blue,
We thank Thee for treasured
friends so true.

We thank Thee for the beauty of a
baby's smile,
For the little things that make life
worthwhile.
We thank Thee for the roses's
sweet essence,
We thank Thee for Thy indwelling
presence.

We thank Thee for the snow so
pure and white,
For the twinkle of the stars so
pretty and bright.
We thank Thee for the birds that
sweetly sing.
We just thank Thee, Lord, for
<u>EVERYTHING</u>!

Patrice Lanette Minor

GOD DIDN'T YOU ASK IF I WAS LONELY?

I want this poem to be dedicated to David Murphy. Someone I care for very much and even though we're not together I want him to know he's still in my heart now and forever and there's no one who could take his place. I wrote this when I was down and lonely after we broke up. If you're reading this Haywood I still love you.

God if you want to know if I'm
lonely, yes I'm lonely
I'm looking for someone to love,
but the only person
who can fulfill my need is the one
high above.
I'm a person full of hate, because I
have no one to date
I'm a girl with an empty heart, I
wish someone come make me
start Love is a burning flame
Because love for me is a damn
shame
God didn't you ask me if I was
lonely? yes I am
If you get hurt by the one you love
and you know you're not the one
to blame
It's his fault that love came
God if you want to know if I'm
lonely, yes I am
Inside I feel so lonely, because
there's no one here
I want to let you know I'm hanging
on an empty stair
I might be lonely but I know there's
one thing I can say to you
No one looks the way I do or no
one can get so lonely and blue
I notice that it is true, I'm glad to
be me, you see, Its true
to be yourself
and not wish you was an elf, God
didn't you ask me if I'm lonely?
Well, alright I'll tell you,
somewhere out there across the
fallen star
some where out there no matter
where you are, I will love you in
the morning sun, I will love you
in the morning rain, there's no
better love than the one that you
get from up so high, when the
night wind starts to sing a lonely
lullaby, God if you want to know
if I'm lonely, Yes I am,
God it's me Patrice, I don't know
who I am, who am I, Tom! Harry!
or Sam!
I use to have dreams that was so
high, now there gone, because
my
Heart did die, Now I lay me down
to sleep, If I should die before I
wake, I pray the Lord my soul to
take,
God didn't you ask if I was lonely?
O.K. here's your
answer, Yes I am

Paul Willis Fagert Jr
NIGHT AND DAY
Night and day, day and night. Other days that are bright. Other days that are stormy, sunny, rainy. Other nights that are dark, cloudy, foggy. Days of the future, days of the present, days of long ago. Days that pass by slowly, days that will not end.
Those days are strange. A man walks down the road and he says, "What day is it?" And the stranger says, "It's today not yesterday and that is why they call it the Day." Sea and land, land and sea The days are changing, and the nights are long. The days are colder and the wind is stronger, to the old man by the sea.
Today-Tonight, on land, on sea, the stranger is looking for the light in the distance that are calling his name. The days that come and the days that go and like the air that we breathe, and the water from the sea. Although we do see things different as night and day, the paths that we choose, will shape a new tomorrow—FOR NOTHING STAYS THE SAME.

Helen M Parker
DEAR DAD—YOUR ROSE
There was just one little rose
Blooming on the bush
That you could see from your bed.
Altho we were lapse
In getting even one red rose
Among all your beautiful flowers
God remembered
To place one under our nose

Out of season—for us to see.

Just for you and Little Elizabeth Ann
Who came to bless our homes
Since the day you left.
But I'm quite sure
That you did see the rose,
And are watching Elizabeth Ann
Grow—And curl the toes
From your heavenly home above.

Angela Renee' Meeker
TO OUR DEAREST MIKKALA

For you, Mikkala, My love is with you always, Love, Mommy

To Our Dearest Mikkala,

We wanted to do the little things
that parents love to do—
be with you when you took your first step
and rock you asleep at night
To be there when you were scared and hold you
very tight

We wanted to watch your face in the sunset
and see the wind blow through your hair
To make some home-made ice-cream
together and learn how to share

We wanted to help you pick the flowers
and watch the little birds as they flew
and play with little puppies and kitties
and be beside you as you grew

To teach you about the world, the bad and
good—the wrong and right
The people and sights, the darkness and bright
You see my "Little Dolly," all we really
wanted to do
Was have you with us and share our lives
with you.

The time you were with us, was not all
in vain
We were with you in sickness, the sunshine
and rain
You fulfilled our need of giving and gave
us strength and hope
We can only thank-you for your blessings
and the way in which you coped.

You have helped us to grow—more than
you can ever know
And sweetheart you are at peace now
and we have to let you go.

But we will never forget you, your
memories will remain
We will go on with our lives and love
you just the same

We thank-you for your time with us
and "Little Dolly," you just rest
Because God and Jesus are with you
and they will do what is best
Love.
Mommy and Daddy

Giovanna D Pierce
IF I . . .
If I could count the days we spend
the nights we send

If I were near you everyday
on my bed I'd let you lay

If I could kiss you
I would love you

If I were a river
you would glow like silver

If I had a wish
I'd make your favorite dish

If I were a bird
I'd fly till your voice I heard

If I were alone
Our love would be shown
I love you would you stay

If I could be a ghost
I would want you to be my host

If I could show you my heart
It would be a start

If I saw your face
It would be such a grace

If I could see you
I would tell you

I love you

Mercy R Coronado
THE REAL CHRISTMAS!
It came upon a midnight clear!
The shepherds with their flocks did hear
"Glory to God, and peace on earth,"
As was announced our Saviors birth!

The King of Kings gave up His throne
Not for a few, or one alone!
For a lost world He came to save;
For you and me His life He gave!

'Twas given then, He gave His all
To ransom men after the fall!
He is The Christ, The Rock of Ages
As you will find in History's pages!

That was the Very first Christmas day,
We must remember it that way!
Christ belongs in Christmas, True?
"Joy to the world," and to me and you!
Happy Holidays!!

Lana Burke
'TWIXT ROYAL SATIN AND THE FISHERMAN'S SHOES
If not for the power of God, I would be
But a wandering mortal, without destiny;
The love and the comfort He knows to provide
Assures me He's with me, there close by my side.

His Grace is of glorious, generous giving;
He reveals my mistakes as He teaches through living. . .
If not for the Will of my loving Lord,
I would lose my calm heart, that my soul won't afford!

In His light He shines wisdom for me to achieve
All the goals of my faith, and the strength to believe.
He opens new doors and invites me to follow,
To bestow the great gift of another tomorrow:

He sets my path, yet, allows me to choose
'Twixt royal satin and the Fisherman's shoes.

John DuRant
FOR CHRISTA (FROM HER SISTER'S TEARS)

To the families of Christa McAuliffe and the crew of the Shuttle "Challenger."

You spoke and smiled
And turned away before I could reply,
Your curls entwined with
breezes from above,
Your restless charge from wanderlust on high.

Your eyes so bright
With longings for a place I cannot go,
Where even eagles ponder with an upward stare,
Where fills the soul till spirits overflow.

You waved goodbye
And with your friends engaged the strength of life to bind
Your common courage shined with laughter, trust and duty;
Boldly climbed within, the earth to leave behind

The rush of tears
To realize that this was our last meeting,
For us to carry on without your guiding plan
With all our strength and hope so quickly fleeting.

Your warmth remains
in those whose dreams and plans you've seen begun
For this small world grows sweeter with each passing day,
As all your goodness fills the sky around each setting sun

Ruth Mary Wilson
HOME
DEATH?—NO—
Just ' realeased from life, ' is THE BODY,
THE SOUL on wings, now free!
to meet THE GOD ALMIGHTY
in The HEAVEN—ETERNITY.

Shedding the dust of THE BODY,
Great Beginnings enrapture THE SOUL!
THE PLAN of THE GREAT ALMIGHTY
to each, HIS OWN,—unfold—
THE PROMISE, THE PLACE prepared in Time,
To be, wherewith, THE GOD FAMILY Divine.

Cecile M Greenland
NATURE SPEAKS
The power over all the earth
Is gloriously displayed,
The flowers, trees and the green grass
Are magnificently arrayed;
The sun in golden splendor
Shines down in radiant hue,
The clouds drift over the blue sky
In garb so white and new.

The waves in azure splendor
Break whitecrested on the shore,
The palms spread out their fronds
As they never did before,
The sand glistens under the bright sky
And feels cool between our toes,
The cooling breeze sails calmly by
Going where, nobody knows.

In all this glorious splendor
Of this tropical paradise
It's hard to see how man denies
And finds it so difficult to even surmise
That there is a powerful, wonderful God
Who created this beautiful world,
For us to delight in and to enjoy,
And the half has never been told.

Eldor Rathjen
GRAMPA'S DREAM
From across the ocean—Grampa Came
Settling on—the Oklahoma Plains
To till the land—His family Raise
To talk with God—to sing His Praise
This was my Grampa's Dream

To worship God—at His earthly Hearth
Along with others—He did His Part
Lumber, bricks—stones and Dirt
To build a Zion—on God's Earth
This was my grampa's Dream

Young of age—God called Him Home
Building His dream—He was not Alone
To finish the task—there wasn't Time
Grampa traveled to—the heavenly Zion
Others finished Grampa's Dream

The founding fathers—long are Gone
Each traveled to—their heavenly Home
Task here finished—work now Done
One by one—till there were None
They completed Grampa's Dream

Our ancestors left—this Legacy
They left it here—for you and Me
Grampa's Dream lives on—in our Time
This church of ours—now Known as Zion
We harvest Grampa's Dream

Lauren Cheryl Natter

Lauren Cheryl Natter
FAITHFUL FRIENDSHIPS
You must be faithful to the end
Whatever happens do not bend
Unknown friendships forced apart
Knowing neither from the start
One is knowing name and face
The other in a distant place.
The other knows of not a thing
About the first one existing
Unknown friendships
forced apart
Knowing neither
from the start
A teardrop gone
Falling astray
The first one's memory
Washed away.

Jeffrey Michel
UNTITLED
Beyond the sea
There's word of a war
With an ocean of blood
Spilled for a cause—
Swinging sharp
Double edged swords;
The thrusting bullet;
The devestating missile;
Have melted the flesh
Of many a soul, They say—
With hand over mouth,
Chuckling over the matter,
They clothe themselves
In a vieled heart
Finding comfort.

Candy Robinson
A FINAL DEATH

In memory of my father, Thomas D. Robinson, and love to my mother, Peggy M. Haloda.

I'm living out this life in hell
While others ring the Autumn bell
I cry and scream out into the vast
While others laugh and leave the bad times in the past
I can't understand why I always want to cry
When there is still a part of me left alive
I may have died a thousand deaths
But there is still a little life, in here left
Even if the nights are full of tears
In the dark, I somehow, face my fears
Days are filled with little light
The birds fly away with such fright
What is it they see?
A final death coming for me?

Marie Pope
MY MOTHER

To my family and my sisters

My Mother's hands were wrinkled and thin
Her feet were aged and slow,
Her eyes still did twinkle as she talked to us
of her life so long long ago.

Of being a bride when she was still young
She washed on a board for us all,
She sewed for her six little girls
From the time they were tiny and small.

Mending and sewing by candle light,
After her family was fed,
She said she accomplished so very much more
when her family was all tucked into bed.

A Midwife, a Doctor, a pioneer of the west,
A neighbor and true friend was she.
Every one loved her, both near and far,
And a wonderful Mother to me.

I was a pioneer baby, a Basin pioneer
I feel I have been greatly blessed,
Utah will always be homeland to me,
IN my little Gray home in the West.

Louise Watson
MY SHOES
I have something, they are my own,
They were ever since I brought them home.
I wear them all day from morning till night,
I don't think I'd trade them, but then I might.

They are so new, so shiny and bright,
To me they are a beautiful sight.
They have tongues, but they can't talk,
And yes they go with me for a walk.

They have souls, and they have heels.
They would look so funny if they had wheels.
They will keep me warm, they'll keep me dry,
If I can remember their laces to tie.

I love my shoes, the ones that I chose,
Not even once have they pinched my toes.
They are very comfortable and they look so fine,
I'll wear them always because they are mine.

W F Tallman
THE TRUE GIFT OF GIVING
The simple gift of giving
Is not as easy as it seems
For often times in giving
We must give up our dreams
Some give the gift of money
Some offer good advice
Some offer consulation
And all are very nice
But few are they who give themselves
Most find the price too high
It's easier to cling to life
If to give means you must die
But there are always those among us
Who feel the price is fair
And it's lucky for the rest of us
That they are always there
And when the ones they left behind them
No longer want to live
That same still voice inside them
Begins to whisper, "Give"
And humbly they bow their heads
And they begin to pray
"Dear Father" please give me the strength
To give in my own way

Pearl L Smith
STARTING THE DAY

Dedicated to all who marvel at God's gifts to us.

How lovely to awaken in the morning,
To the songs of many birds.
The Song Sparrow beneath my window,
Robins high in the maples are heard.
Even the Blue Jays scolding,
Because sunflower seeds in the feeder are low.
The gentle cooing of the Morning Dove,
And the caw of the stately big black Crow.
Goldfinches singing their chorus,
And flitting on branches to catch the first sun rays.
The Cardinal calling to its mate,
Brings a brightness to the day.
Time to thank God for all these sounds,
And watching over me thru the night.
Thankful for this lovely day,
That has started out so bright.

Vincent R Blake MD
shuttle seven

To my loving wife, Ruteena and the kids, Sonja, Kurt, Simone and Kent.

---

a solemn salute to shuttle seven
you are america
in all its greatness
in all its weakness

smiling sunlit faces
of success turning to the
sorrow and anguish
of disaster

blastoff anomalous burning booster
billions blown to bits
trailing billowing smoke
across the heavens
sending seven angels to God

mr president your humanity
is refreshing consoling the widows
and their children in their
and our hour of bereavement

through toil to the stars
but remember icarus
the sun melts waxen wings
remember achilles goliath and samson

Wendy J Ballard
LADY OF LACE
Lady of lace
I remember your face
My favorite doll
Where are you now?

Buried deep
Inside my trunk
Surrounded by
My treasured junk.

You helped me grow
I do remember
And I'll cherish
All those memories.

Lady of lace
You're not forgotten
Only being saved
For someday.

When someday comes
You'll rejoin this world
And belong to
My little girl.

Debbie Haaser
GOODBYE

To Bob and Mary, my dear friends

I used to sit and think of you,
Ever to ponder what I would do,
If, per chance, no more would be,
At this place, my friends to see.

You've been here always, forever it seems,
But now you'll go to follow your dreams.
I wish you well, as I love you so,
It's just so hard to let you go.

But as you leave, be ever so glad,
You gave me such memories, as not to be sad.
Your moments of kindness alone

are mine,
To have and to cherish for quite sometime.

Thank you, dear friends, for being just you,
Such beautiful people, all through and through.
It's said good things must come to an end,
But you'll always have me as your loving friend.

Deborah Ann Schunot
ON GOSSAMER WINGS
How does it feel I wonder
To become an angel on high,
Meeting their call up yonder
To serve God in the sky.
On gossamer wings they serve Him
These spirits from above,
With flute and lute and lyre
They rejoice in the Master's love.
The mark upon their forehead
Known only to their Lord,
Called to do His bidding
By God's wishes and accord.

The rank of the angels command
Is at the Lord's mighty hand,
To carry out God's authority
From the sky down to the land.

The majesty of the seraphim
The cherubim and arch,
Their lilting music in songs of praise
Fill the Master's heart.

So I'll wait to meet Saint Peter
At my Lord's beckon call,
On gossamer wings I'll serve Him
To love and give my all.

Mabel D Gilmore

Mabel D Gilmore
ALWAYS, WITH LOVE

Dedicated to Delbert E. Gilmore (husband for 36 years) deceased since May 11, 1975.

Logs crackled in the fireplace,
giving me warmth and light
as I re-read a stack of his letters.
Reluctantly I tore them into bits,
tossed penned love by handfuls
into a consuming fire.
Each scrap, as it curled,
sent back to me
a special warmth and glow.
With the ritual finally finished,
I went to the window
to utter a prayer of thanks.
Snowflakes of all shapes
were doing gymnastics
before landing on the warm
ground,
where each flake became a water drop.
But—come Spring, violets will grow
where winter snowflakes fell.
Smoke that went up my chimney
will give them an intimate fragrance.
With Spring and violets
there will always be love.

J J Ruttenberg
CROSSING DORSEY CREEK
Sauntering, into
The scintillating night,
Running away to
Random remembrances
Of memories
And moments,
Peering clearly into
The desolate, soft black
Depths, dim reflection
Of the coldly, and
Crisply lit stage.
Away, down an
Avenue of shadows,
Cables and yesterday's
Lamplights, tunneling
Into the answers.
But, at the last,
Sloughing along
To ward off the chill,
A detour
Back to the questions.

Cheryl A Vincent
MY DAD
He never leaped tall buildings
He never spun a web
I kissed him every night
When he tucked me into bed
He never drove the batmobile
He never sang the blues
My dad was the greatest
Always knowing what to do
When I learned to walk and to talk
Or when I skinned my knee
He was always there for me
To tend my every need
Daddy, He's my superman
My very special friend
He died when I was just a girl
Yet his memories never end.

Mary Catherine Brown
TRUE FRIENDS
True friends are a part of you
They stick together
Like paper and glue.

They are with you
Through the good and bad
To share the happy and sad.

They are there when you cry
Or just to hear you sigh
They stick with you when things go wrong
To help with a cherrie little song.

Though some friends seem to wander away
True friends will always stay.
They keep in touch
To show they care so much.

N Marie Russell
PLEDGE THE SOUL
Pledge the soul away
Tears of blood.
Darkness thru the day
T'will be a rampant flood.

Train whistle blowin'
Thunder rollin' down the track.
Hell's fire glowin'
Time to pay the devil back.

Vicki Kryklywyj
COMEAU
Cool cool blows the wind—down our heads
We push and plow our way along the path
Gay branches slap our faces—stinging
Laughter follows—we're on our way
To reach the heights again.

Berries of hue, and leaves that glisten bright
Adding their colours to the mossy sides
Water is tinkling in the rocky falls
As cautiously we pick our way across the slides.

The crest is reached, and with our sweat-stained packs
We settle on the ground, to rest, and gaze
Upon the verdant valleys spread below
And eat our lunch, and talk of other days
When we made hikes just twice as tough as these!

We're rested now, and as we gaze about
Each one reluctant to depart the scene

We store these memories in our deepest hearts
We dream in years, and come, and come again.

Lorraine Hale (JGP)
RASH ACTS
Look before you leap, think before you act
What you do now you can't take back
A harsh word, an uncontrollable reflex
These rash acts get you at your best
Too late to regret, no use apologizing
These rash acts go on jeopardizing;
Lives and loves, friends and family
Rash Acts, why do they have to be?

Everett
DEATH'S SEARCH FOR LIFE

This poem is dedicated to my very dear friend Frod, who was taken away from us in the spring of 1986 at the age of 35, after a long hard-fought battle with cancer.

Now as the wind doth blow its sweetened breath
Upon a world that turns in silent awe,
A gallant creature that calls himself Death
Drifts slowly o'er his prey, but swiftly falls.
For character, Death has no choice respect;
He roams the earth in search for wanted life.
To Him, there is none living called select;
Death searches not for name, but seeks out strife
And as each day slips gently into Time,
This Friendless Searcher closer comes to all
And though this creature ne'er will reach His prime,
To all that ever knows life, He will call
—Forever must Death's search for life go on,
He conquers all, in Time, but lives alone.

Anne McKenzie
SURVIVING
I compare to a wounded bird
Whose only thought is of Protection.

Protection from the pain
Inflicted upon it by forces
Seemingly much stronger.

But, like that bird,
I will survive. . .

To live, to love.

Have patience

Odelia Trujillo
OLDSTER'S LAMENT
Listen to my lonely heart, he cried.
I have survived almost a century
and my mind is weary, he replied.

As an infant life was a perpetual nirvana
in my dear mother's arms.
When I became a child time became endless
with its constant charms.

In adolescence I found rebellion,
Curiousity and fickleness.
Drifting along in my quest for maturity
I became impatient, I must confess.

Having survived this tumultuous storm
my lot became one of familial responsibility.
I had acquired a great solicitude
and love of family
unaware of having such ability.

In my patriarchal years much wiser am I,
although my days are few.
I have discovered sorrow and serenity.
Alas, I close my eyes and live anew.

Susan Good
THE COW AND THE DAFFODIL

I dedicate this poem to my parents who have listened lovingly to me through the nineteen years of my life. Also to Jacque, who should have been listened to more. I love and appreciate them all.

It's important to me.
It made an impression.
You halfway listen, absently nod
and change the subject.
Then you wonder why -
why I hardly ever visit talk
why I don't share my life and interests
with you.
It angers me until I cry.
I guess—maybe—they're too simple,
Or, in some way, not simple enough
for your interest.
But what it all—in the end—
boils down to really

is that you don't try
to understand the importance
because you cannot grasp
the impression
But So What?
A cow will listen, intently, when
I sing to it.
Yet it doesn't even know my words
I suppose I could tell a cow
About the
daffodil
in our front yard ?
If you ever read this poem—
you'll probably want to laugh
at the part
about the cow—Maybe you will.
Either way you'll continue to not
understand—won't you?
So maybe I should hide this poem
bury it or burn it.
Or . . . maybe I should put it
in your hands . . . And Ask—
"Can you finally see?"
and listen to you laugh
about the cow.

Doris A Richards

Doris A Richards
A LOVE LETTER FROM GRAMIE

To "Jacki" My "Sugar" with love always. "Your Goobie"

Most Gramies learned how to
crochet and knit, while
your Gramie learned how to roller
skate and use her wit.
So when it came to making
something smart, I was troubled
because I wanted to win your heart.
So I took a special pillow and filled
it with love,
put in a lulabye and trimmed it
with lace.
So now my precious you will know
how very much we want to see
your tiny face.
We know that we have to be patient
because God is not done
with you yet but your loving family
is anxiously awaiting,
So have a safe journey to all of us
here, may you be blessed
and soon we will have you near.

I love you already,
your loving Gramie

Patricia Sidars West
THE BARGAIN

To Scott

God loaned me a baby to hold in
my arms
To cuddle to love to adore
Whose shining eyes and gurgling
laugh
Brought new found delights by
the score
God loaned me a child with infinite
charms
To nurture to guide to enjoy
Who trusted and learned and
quickly evolved
An exciting dear little boy
God loaned me a son A fine
handsome youth
Who filled my heart with great
joy
You see t'was all part of His
plan
God loaned me an infant a
child a boy
To walk in His truth
And I have returned Him a man.

Michelle A Trombley-Baker
BROKEN HEART

My eyes are filled with sorrow as I
sit here caressing
your forehead; your hair as you
lay in my lap.

I feel you drifting from my life; our
life together.

I lay in bed thinking about our
good-byes,

How it hurts.

I'd felt myself lifted as tho a part
of me was taken.

I'd died inside in my sleep of a
broken-heart and

empty soul.

My life with you was no more; nor
was I in an empty
world without you. . .

Donna C Hart
TOMORROW

In the shadows of my mind
there are dreams of better times.
Times of joy, no pain or sorrow.
Times of peace for all tomorrow.

In the wind float all my dreams,
prayers of hope and wounds now
clean.
No skeletons shall haunt this land,
for truth has dawned on mortal
man.

The light has shown so bright as
day,
to lead us to that passage way.
That hidden gift that none shall
bare
the key to happiness are all we'll
share.

But in the future these things will
follow,
Reality teaches that life is hollow.
As empty as a paupers shelf,
so brutal as your tortured self.

In the shadows of my mind
there are dreams of better times.
Times of joy, no pain or sorrow.
Times of PEACE FOR
ALL. . .TOMORROW.

Jeremy DeJournett
SOMEONE SPECIAL

To My grama with love.

When I think about my grama.
I think of many different things.
Such as a bird flying freely,
with the most pretty colored wings.

A person with such humanity.
A person just like you.
Should be treated with a king's
personality,
and that's what I'm trying to do.

I wrote this poem just for you.
Just because I love you so.
I want to say I love you,
and that's all you need to know.

Virgil E Graber Ph D
NEVER EVER

Never ever say "can't," my friend,
As through this life you fend and
wend;
You'll oft succeed, if you'll but try,
Hence, do oft try; you'll soon learn
why.

Never ever recall too well
Life's hurts and wrongs that come
pell-mell;
Learn to forgive, and to forget;
Life is too short to vex and fret.

Never ever forget kind words;
Such words are heard like songs of
birds;
"Kind words ne'er die," wrote a
great sage;
How true this sage in every age!

Never ever forget good deeds,
That you can do for human needs;
You'll make the world a better
place;
Enlace your deeds with human
grace.

Never ever neglect to do,
That which you must your whole
life through;
Man's life is work, likewise, some
play,
That he must poise, day after day.

Never ever fail to return
Love received through life's
short sojourn;
To love and be loved is God's grace,
That blesses man through time and
space.

V Marie Platt Antonucci
THE STORM

For all his encouragement and love of poetry. I dedicate this to Edmund

---

Lightning streaks across the sky. . .
The thunder booms and the waves
fly high!
Roaring with rage, the wind rages
through. . .
Like an angry lion with deadly
intention. . .
His torment and anguish scream
for attention.

Sweeping rain pounds the window
panes;
Our dogs draw close. . . For they
can feel. . .
The wildness in the air is real.
My heart is pounding—my eyes
remain. . .
Bright with excitement—as it
crashes again!

Just as swiftly as it had arrived;
The bellowing lion becomes a
wailing child
A silver lining shines through a
cloud . . .
And once more the winds are quiet
Peace and contentment in my
heart abound.

Eleanor Garcia Martinez
ELYA

Granddaddy: As you taught me, heart & soul to fly—these wings of poetry in flight—are for your traveling soul. . .ELYA

The poet—not only writes it.
The script avails—
Because she has lived it!
Somewhere between—
Mystery and magic—
The poet rides—
The clouds of change—
Somehow between—
Life and reality—
She climbs off—
To share the secrets—
Of the universe. . .

Karalyn D Hubbard
ANONYMOUS

I have to learn, it hurts too much
To fall in love with you
For as long as I sit and think about
it
I know it's too good to be true

I've had my share of flirting
I want to settle down
But it has to be with the one I love
Not just someone out of town

It's you I want, you know it's true
I would not make it up
But whatever it takes, I'll wait
around
Drinking sorrows cup after cup. . .

You always say "you never know"
every time I call
But I hate it, that's not fair to me
I feel like a number on your wall

Please sir, come to me
Let me show you that I care
For my cup is just refilling
As long as you're not there

Mary Lind
SOUNDS

Do geese still honk as they fly over,
And quail rustle in the brush for
cover?
Does the sparrow and finch chatter
in the trees,
And the hummingbird flutter on
morning breeze?
Please tell me, as I want to know,
For I haven't heard since long ago.

Does a cow bawl as she gives birth,
To a mewly calf on clover scented
earth?
Do the chickens cackle as they lay
eggs,
And lambs baa, rising on wobbly
legs?
The glorious sounds of nature are
the ones I miss the most;
Yet, they linger in memory like a
friendly, pleasant ghost.

Does the mourning dove coo his
song at close of day,
And the coyote howl as he
meanders on his way?
Do waves make a roar crashing on
the sand,
And crickets sing when quiet is
over the land?
Tell me, as I want to know,
For I haven't heard since long ago.

Marsha Carr
THE DIFFERENCE

I thank God for the love and compassion in my heart, through which this poem was birthed.

What a difference Christians
make, when they take the time
to care
And lift another's burdens, to the
Lord in prayer
With sincerity of heart, and faith
that is abundant
No prayer that's ever prayed, will
ever be redundant
What a privilege it is, to be a vital
part

Of the goodness of our Lord,
through the love within one's
heart
So when someone is hurting, no
matter who they are
Let us put our faith in motion, and
not just stand afar
And shake our heads, and wring
our hands, then turn and walk
away
We must, because He cared, be
compassionate, and pray—

Troy McKenzie
YESTERDAY
Yesterday brings memories,
experiences we've had
Memories to cherish, memories
good and bad.

We think about chances lost, the
words we never spoke
Things we used to fight about are
now a silly joke.

We wish we could reverse the clock
and change yesterday
To take a very different path, do
things another way.

But we had our chances yesterday,
now we must move on
It's best if we not think about
things that are now gone.

Dorothy Hough Cameron
POEMS
A poem to send in you say
Well I've written many along the
way.

Some all about People and Places
Some were about natural wonders
And some proclaimed the beauty
of Nature's many faces.
Many told of living and of love's
many blunders.

Thoughts of sad times were
foretold
And the sorrow eased as the story
began to unfold.
Memories of good and happy hours
Were sweet and precious to recall
to mind
And as breathtaking, as it was to
see a waterfall or a glistening
field of Bluebonnet flowers.

So you see a poem can mean so
much more to you or me
Than casual reading or passing
time
Writing or Reading, it can lift your
spirits high and wide and make
your soul feel free.

Linda C Stanley
BY THE SEA

To-Ma-with-all-my-Love

It is so peaceful here by the sea
I could stay here forever.

Just to look at the birds and fish at
play.
It is like a world of it's own.

The sea air seems to call your
name.
To ask you if you would like to
come in and be a part of the sea.

So free your mind of the outside
world and come into the world
of the sea.

And then you can see why I like to
be in the world down by the sea.

Louise Passalacqua
FLY EAGLE

To Davey, who always flew with the eagles.

What does the eagle think of as he
soars through the skies,
is he scanning the ground for his
dinner
is he hunting as he flies?

Does he see the beauty of the land
as he looks with eagle eye
does he treasure God's plan that
he can fly?

I am earthbound does he see me
watch him
as he circles through the air
does he know that he is free, is he
happy
does he care?
If only I could spread my wings and
sail
away from all those things
that trouble me, I try, but I am
earthbound
yet—my heart can fly.

Pamela Wilson McMahon
THE IMMIGRANT
You look the same.

Refugee
Screams sound
Home.

Memories in the loneliness
Postcard pictures bent and dirty.

What will become of us?
What is freedom
This love not permitted,
Shamed intensity, this love

For us. . .
Refugees.

In your language
Ask me again not to forget and
I'll answer in mine, as

I sit here and feel the sun
On my face through the glass. . .
Always only through the glass.

Close the dictionary.

Recognize me.

Bridgitt F Boggan-Dunn
MIND-SIGHT
To possess the potential;
conceiving;
achieving,
Obtaining desires
the reason for breathing. . .
Stagnant thoughts;
Limitations,
Understand that it's one's
creation.
Accepting less;
Wanting more,
Fear to exit the revolving door. . .
Igniting the flame;
Reflecting the sun,
A fortunate quality that is present
in some.

Alice Crane Behr
PRIME TIME
Time seems to be standing still
To catch forever this moment of
perfection—
Moments packed with all that's
right
In contrast with the previous
dejection
That came from winter's bitter chill
And leaden days and ways now
in subjection.
For all creation's plan and Planner
Into our hearts there rushes deep
affection.

A robin watching from a limb,
The singing of the birds in joy
unfeigned;
The gentle breeze, the blue of sky;
And, at their peak of beauty all
unstained,
The flowers in their brief display—
Their once-a-year fulfillment
now regained;
In this rare and perfect moment
There's harmony that seldom is
attained.

While all of Nature now is in her
prime,
Stand still for just a little longer,
Time!

Dolores Ann Thompson
MY PRAYER
Heavenly father, I beg of you
Don't let me drown in this sea of
life!
Please be near me through all my
stresses & strife.

Give me necessary strength &
courage
to hold out.
Why are my days filled with
frustration
and doubt?

Please make me smile!
Why can't I see all the beauty
around
me that makes my life worthwhile?

Show me how to use you for a
crutch,
Instead of tranquilizers, alcohol,
cigarettes and such.

Let me find comfort through thy
divine power,
Be with me in my loneliest hours.

Strengthen me where I am weak
When I pray unto thee help me find
the right words to speak.

Teach me to be a better person
for myself and others,
And above all—Help me to be
a more loving and patient mother.
Father, help me to be a better
Christian,
For only in thy sight do I seek
recognition.

Kenny D Kearns
DEAR MOTHER EARTH
What's happened to my dear
mother earth?
I went out into the world and
began my search.
I looked where the dear and the
buffalo roam.
I just cannot find a place worth to
call home.

Dear mother earth what has
happened to you?
Could not you stop what the people
would do?
They're filled with violence, the
danger I see.
Dear mother earth will you fight to
be free?

I've searched the fields and plains,
but couldn't find home.
I've excavated miles, but still found
no bone.
My mind it aches from all the sin
that I see.
Why can't they go and leave my
mother earth be?

I've walked all the valleys and
swam all the streams.
I've searched the forests, through
the tall evergreens.
Destruction is the only thing that I
found.
Construction of cities the familiar
sound.

The end has come or at least it is
near.
The sound of violence, destrustion
I fear.
Dear mother earth would you
listen to me?
Destroy yourself so that you too
can be free.

Lula R Moss

Lula R Moss
GOD'S CREATION
Dearest God, I would be so happy
If I could be a distinguished poet.
I would make your creation so
plain,
That all the people of the world
would know it.

The infidels or atheist pretenders
would fade,
They were created like all others,
Regardless of all their Hell fired
teachings,
They must repent and accept
Christians as Brothers

Your creation of Heaven and earth

and contents are beautiful,
If there are mistakes, big or little flaws,
Man made them for his own selfish benefit,

This can be proved by man made laws.

There is no question about your creation,
Records show it perfect, beautiful, everything in place,
"How Great Thou Art" all people should sing,
As they teach and preach along life's race.

Monica Haire
THE LIGHT OF OPPORTUNITY
Sometimes when you think
you are in one of the darkest corners
in your life,
a door opens
to let a small amount of
light seep through.
it is only then
that hope slowly becomes restored.
But how long will it take that light
to make way for an open passageway
out of the corner of darkness?
And if the passage is made,
how much time is needed
to dive through the opening
before it snaps shut
keeping you in a forever world of darkness?

Elaine K Addesso
FALLEN RAIN
Love is like droplets of new fallen rain,
Sometimes it's so cold that love turns to snow.
Puddles of love one discovers in the valleys and plains;
For it's so stormy at times, one wishes that tears could blow.
One might be able to open the door,
That depends on how much, it rained before.
In one's heart, love pours so fast;
the rain can evaporate:
The lightning strikes just long enough for it to penetrate.
Love's purity one tastes as it appears,
For the thunder can leave fear to remain.
The rain that collects either is cloudy, muddy, or clear:
Cleanse one soul with love, then it will be new not fallen rain.

Shirley Wesenberg
IN MY HEART

This poem is dedicated to Steve, my son.

Way back in the year nineteen sixty-three
A three week old boy came to live with me
It was nine days before anniversary number five
And a thrill to have a "gift" who was live
Our tears of sorrow were now tears of joy
Nothing seemed to matter now except this sweet boy
Before this, it was second grade children I taught
So for a long time, youth around me was a pleasant thought —
This child is grown now, and himself will marry this year
We trust he'll give his new wife this same good cheer
You know now this adopted child did not grow under my heart...
But now and always, this lovely young man will in it be —
a VERY big part!

Valerie Dennis Maynard
ANSWERS FROM WITHIN
If I could see the visions
of time
The great wisdom of all creation
I could then define

Of those that know the secrets
of the ages
Let me join them in writing the
words upon the pages

The questions of old that have
went unanswered with time
Shall be heard in the faint and
echoing words in our minds

Send me the truth on the wings of the wind
and I shall whisper to thee
Lead me in my dreams to where the key is
and I will set you free

I reached out and touched the stars
then brushed the dust from my hand
The mystery of life and what it holds
is written in the sand

The sand upon the beach is
washed away by time
As it sifts through the hourglass
the answers you will find

Charles Richard Khulenberg Jr
MY MOTHER
Always here never there
My mother can always bare
My problems and frustrations.
I cause her grief sometimes very deep.
Yet she's always here
When I need someone near.

When I'm in time of need
She is there.
She will give yet not take
I have problems so does she
But she is there to give
To you the comforting you need.

She takes so little and gives so much
To those who love her so very much.
When she's gone
And I'm all alone
Everyone shall know
She was the "Greatest Mom on Earth."

Darlene H Carey
A MOTHER'S REALITY

To my children who have helped me grow

My hand extends
to my child
And finds
an individual
Who must be set free
from me.
How harsh the reality
of letting go. . .
How much harsher the reality
of holding on.
Let go, my hand.
Free the child
And allow the growth
of a man.
Release a new me!

Johnnie O'Quinn
ON A SUNNY JUNE DAY

This poem is dedicated to my four wonderful children: Clara, Lennie, Vernon and Ann.

On a sunny June day,
Watching my children run and play;
I thought, how good life seems to be,
Giving these wonderful jewels to me.

June Kennedy Hackett
VICE
When I was young and lost,
Not realizing then the cost;
I stumbled into a den of wolves,
And ate with them.
Not being extremely wise,
I tried to leave when satisfied;
But they laughed and mocked,
And held me back.
1957

Carmine F Malzone
AMERICAN FREEDOM

To the Daalgarrds, Vera & Dahl, my true and dearest friends

Listen, oh world ! to what I have to say
I am an American and as proud today
As my forebears were in the days gone by.
When you could hear the Americans cry
For their freedom, first and last,
A shot was heard and their lot was cast.
Many lives and blood were lost
But it did not matter the cost
To become a land of the free
For the little people like you and me.
So listen to me, many and all,
As an American, I shall walk big and tall.
Around and around this old universe
To let all nations know this verse
That we, as Americans, will always take a stand
To help to free the oppressed from any land
Whether it be any color or creed
As long as they yearn to be freed.
There are too many nations in this universe
That still feel the heel of tyranny's curse
So, as Americans, one and all
Help these nations walk big and tall.
So one day they will walk as one
In the brightness of the midday sun.

Lucille (Landis) Brubaker
GREEN GRASS TOOTHPICKS
Thousands of Green Grass Toothpicks
Sticking skyward out of the snow
Let me view a funny thing—
None are lined up in a big row,
Nor can they change their green stance,
But remain rigid and quite small.
Thousands of Green Grass Toothpicks
Are FREEZING and it is yet FALL.

Last night it snowed, but it's now
ZERO at eight o'clock outside;
The SUN is shining brightly
So the new white snow glows with pride.
See those miniature shadows
Of green toothpick spikes on the snow!
Would all those Green Grass Toothpicks
Like for that SNOW to stay or go???

Clifford W Matthews
ROSEBUDS

To Donna Rose Nemitz. . .Dreams really can become reality. . .one really can capture a star.

I have gathered rosebuds,
Along life's path;
And found such sadness,
For they didn't last.
Yet I did not despair,
I kept up my quest;
For I knew that I would find,
The fairest, the sweetest, the best.

And just when I,
Was about to give up my search;
I lovingly looked down,
Upon the earth.
I picked up the fairest of rosebuds,
And to my glee. . .
This tender little rosebud
blossomed. . .
Into thee.

Joyce Beck
CROSSROADS OF CHOICE

This poem is dedicated to my family, especially Harold, Angela and Micheal for their continual support.

Somedays I start to wonder which
way I should go,
Should I choose the new blazed
trail, or take the one I know?

Do I walk the unknown path and
be unsure of my way,
Or keep the safe and guarded life
of the good ole days?

I cannot reach the answers they're
just outside my grasp,
I ask myself most everyday, "How
long can my winning last?"

Only I can make the choices, I'am
the one to choose,
Do I keep the safe to win or take
the chance to lose?

Ruth E Moore
LOVE OFFERS PEACE OF MIND
Are you living in confusion with no
peace of mind?
Get all predjudice and hatred out
of your way.
The only way you can have peace,
is to be kind.
Love offers peace of mind
everyday.
You don't like my looks you say,
but you do love me & my kin.
You really only like you today,
you're selfish and always have
been.
The problem is you, not all of us,
put on a smile, focus in on
Love.
Then you won't have to make such
a fuss. Hold your peace the
answer's above.
Now that you've gotten a fresh
start, the beauty that was hid is
beginning to show.
Make your smile bigger, peace is
in your heart;
this is a miracle, everyone should
know.
I love you, you're so kind
You love me, you're not selfish
anymore
because Love offers peace of mind
You are a happier, peaceful, lovier
person than ever before.

Joyce Ann Thomas
STONEHENGE
What are these columns
Standing up so grand?

Like Palace Guards;
Tall and silent they stand.

Put in place centuries ago
By long forgotten hands.

An astrological source,
These stones in a band?

Or a religious ring where
Druids stood hand in hand?

Oh, stones, you are so vague;
What did you demand?

Echoes from the past,
These stones in an ancient land.

Kathryn Keller Haley
SOMEBODY NEEDS SOMEBODY
Somebodys' feelin' lonely,
Needin' somebody to love,
Somebodys' needin' somebody,
The way I'm thinkin' of,
There are so many lonely people,
Needin' somebody to love,
And it hurts because nobody,
Knows how much I need to be
loved,
Somebodys' feelin' lonely,
Feelin' like I do,
If you look around you'll find
them,
And baby, when you do,
You better put your loneliness
aside,
And spread a little lovin' around,

Somebody needs somebody,
And baby, you do too,
So when you feel that love and
emotion,
There'll be two less lonely
people around,

Somebody needs somebody,
And you need somebody too,
So when you come across that
love and devotion,
You better not fool around,

True love may only happen once,
Or maybe even twice,
But if you're looking for a lifetime
lover,
You better find him and treat him
right,

I said, when you find somebody,
Who loves you with all his might,
Shower them with love and
affection,
And make sure you treat them
right.

Somebody needs somebody,
And you need somebody too,
So when you come across that
love and devotion,
You better not fool around,

True love may only happen once,
Or maybe even twice,
But if you're looking for a lifetime
lover,
You better find him and treat
him right,

I said, when you find somebody,
Who loves you with all his might,
Shower them with love and
affection,
And make sure you treat them
right.

G Jeffery Puha
A SAILORS REWARD
Throughout the years of voyages
long, my heart ever yearns for
thy voice's calm song.
Though my ship is torn by rocky
shoal,
And rendered driftwood by
murderous wave,
Though the cold, gray grief of
endless storm may wither my
nerve and grind my bone,
Though I be scourged by flooding
sky and mocked by raging sea,
At journeys end my soul may rest,
for my ship has dropped anchor
in the bay of motherhood,
And I have come home to thee.

Horace Storeter
FORGET

Dedicated to Verna & Mildred Schutzbach, my dearest friends on this beautiful Earth.

When by a trusted friend you are
betrayed
Let not the harsh surprise; the
crushing hurt cause your mind
to be enraged
Hate glowing in your heart will
wither your precious soul like an
autumn leaf
There is a way,—a simple way to
forget, forever, the heartless act
of that Judas friend.
At once, your life-work must be
resumed or your high
ambitions, skills and talents, all,
will be consumed.
Encourage with helpful deeds, The
lonely; The defeated folk, you
meet along your path through
life.
Those folk who never received a
chance to flee from crippling
poverty.
Swiftly, bitterness will vanish, just
as tragedy fades from a hazy
dream, into the mists.
With great new strengths, you will
emerge the splendid person you
had always hoped to be
Clearly, you will recognize the
purpose, for which the almighty
creator placed you on this planet
under
His laughing moon and friendly
sun and beneath the twinkling
stars
That light His world through the
dark hours of the night.
With these victories won, you have
earned the right,
With bold assurance, to proclaim
this vow of joy, "my mission
on earth will be accomplished!
My purpose, here, shall be
fulfilled!"

Dorothy M Gerkin
I'M MISSING HIM SO MUCH

In memory of John F. Colwell, Beloit, Wisconsin

From Ohio I traveled to see John
in Wisconsin to be with him
there,
But a happy visit turned out to be
a terrible nightmare.
After being with him only ten short
days,
He became very ill and passed
away.
Many family members and alot of
friends,
Hated to see his life come to an end.
He was taken from us at an age of
53,
But I'm sure he is much happier
with thee.
At his funeral the clergyman told
the story of footprints in the
sand.
Now John is in the Lord's
wonderful hands.
At the chapel a soloist sang "The
Old Rugged Cross" and
"Amazing Grace,"
And now the Lord is holding him
in his warm embrace.
He could be stubborn, impatient
and such,
But only God really knows how I'm
missing him so much.

Gregg D Scott
CHRISTMAS IS THE TIME FOR GIVING AND SHARING

To my parents Douglas C. Scott and Gladys M. Scott for giving me life and to my wife Debra A. Scott for her love and support.

Christmas is the time for giving
and sharing,
the time to show love and caring.
From falling leaves to drifting
snow,
from crowded stores to the winter
wind's blow.
From Santa's laugh to the church
bell's ring,
from children's toys to choirs' sing.
From stockings on the fireplace
mantle,
from ma ma's kerchief to pa pa's
red flannels.
From the carolers singing door to
door,
from presents all wrapped upon
the floor.
From Christmas morning's early
rise,
from all the relatives that sad
goodby.
From old year to new year and
back again,
Merry Christmas to you my dear
friend.

Cheryl Haas
MONTANA'S EMERALD LAKE
Beauty has many faces —
Some striking and unforgettable.
A few; serene, full of compassion.
But Emerald's face is rippling jade
Oblivious to all but the canyon
wind.

It pulls you to come back again —
Somehow, the expectation is
Greater than your presence.
And it, powdered with dazzling
diamonds, shimmers
Oblivious to all but the canyon
wind.

Green, ridged back of ancient
mountain —
Set high above the ice-clear
green,
Contrasts smoothly, the textured
slopes.
And hopeful fishers stand
Oblivious to all but the canyon
wind.

Kathleen M Sherlock

Kathleen M Sherlock
CANCER

To Debbie—for all your encouragement.

I know a family going through a
tragic time
Mom's dying of cancer—what a
terrible crime

She had talent and beauty and a
  special charm
She loved her family and kept them
  from harm.

Now this treacherous disease is
  doing its best
To put their faith through a bitter
  test.
Her once colorful face is drawn
  and pale

Her once healthy body is small and
  frail.

She's unable to walk
And it hurts her to talk
She's unable to eat
And welcomes the solace of sleep.

But worst of all is the inner pain
Of seeing her family so sad and
  drained.

Everyone knows the end is near
And each passing moment is made
  precious and dear.

Family and friends pray a cure will
  be found
So others won't suffer and hear the
  sounds
Of the weeping and crying that
  cancer brings
To people of all ages—paupers and
  kings.

Edwin G Davis Jr
A SONNET ON TERRY WAITE
We think of saints as light
  admitting panes
Which beautify some broad
  cathedral wall,
Or maybe as the marbleized
  remains
Of one who drank the hemlock
  mixed with gall,
Or felt the spear or knew the lion's
  maul.
I'm apt to do that too. Stories
  persist
Since long before Isaiah heard the
  call,
Of those whom we adjudge a
  saintly list.
But all Saints aren't deceased. I
  must insist
We're privileged to share our lives
  today
With one whose sacrifice cannot
  be missed;
For whom the whole world joins to
  watch and pray.
A doer of the word, while others
  hear
That Terry Waite's a Saint it would
  appear.

Joe F Farlin
GOLDEN HAIR

To my beautiful golden haired daughter—Lanae

As the moon shines upon your
  golden hair
As it hangs around the face of an
  angel
Your eyes are like the stars in the
  night
Your voice is so soft and gentle that
  it
brings joy to everyone around you.

"Alisa Dawn" Gibson
SUGAR FREE

Dedicated to my Heavenly Father who gave me the talents and to my mother and grandmother who give me the inspiration.

There's sugar free this and sugar
  free that,
Sugar free everything to keep from
  getting fat.
Sugar free cookies and sugar free
  jam,
And sugar free ice cream as I
  understand.
Sugar free drinks and sugar free
  candy,
And sugar free gum sure comes in
  handy,
But they'll go far and I'll have
  enough
When someone decides to make a
  Sugar Free Love.

Carolyn Ware
LOVE IS

To my Mom and Dad. To All—Friends and Relatives who give their continued Love and Support

---

Love is happiness with someone
  dear,
Love is always knowing someone
  cares,
Love is joy and sorrow that two can
share,
Love is being able to reach out;
  always
knowing that special someone is
  always
there,
Love is making possible what you
  thought
to be an impossible dream,
Love is giving with all your heart,
Love is the sacrifice of your time in
another's time of need,
Love is suffering the pain of
  another,
and doing your part,
Love is life and a dream come true,
Love is beautiful for all, like me
  and
you.

Edith P Dietz
WITHIN
Within each of us we feel there is
  a very special place
Where age, race, sex, bias
  has no need to be erased.
For the creation of the feeling
  sees perfection through and
  through
And we walk in perfect balance
  and daily feel brand new.
Cleansing for the weary worker
  at the closing of the day,
Is in that secret residence
  deeply hidden away.
The multi-faceted people,
  the personalities of our race,
Each seek their poise and patience
  in their own special place.

We are strugglers on our journey
  in this world of time and space,
It's exciting as we watch and grow
  to know the exhilerating pace.
It's within us; this desire of life,
  to live it filled with love
And to know the freedom that's
  within
  is given from above.

Katharine Assante
A SMALL REPRIEVE
There are no words
in all the tongues men use
that can express
your irreplacibility.

No singing metaphor of mine
can call you back
or conjure up your voice,
your touch upon a silent
  instrument.

That dear and singular uniqueness
that was you is gone
I cannot give you immortality —
fond, foolish human that I am.

Only my love can grant
a small reprieve —
that while I live,
you live in my memory.

Noelie Crepeau
SOUTHERN WAYS
my southern ways
stand in perpetual northern gaze
peering through the haze of the
  swelter
hoping this is a phase, that it will
  get better
feeling time burn memories under
  the skin
something akin to grief
wanting relief from today
with the belief that the way
is to make peace with today

my restess intrusion
a palate of confusion
a brush of illusion
I paint a kiss of tomorrow
on the face of sorrow
tomorrow
is yesterdays' today
north is south
of the northernmost way

Carolyn Havelaar
THE REASON

Dedicated to George, my wonderful husband who was also my reason.

I prayed for death and You gave me
The strength to carry on.
I lived my days in sorrow,
My heart without a song.

I could not understand the reason.
I thought it very wrong.
I prayed for death and You gave me
The strength to carry on.

Then, without a warning
The darkest shadows fell.
I prayed for death and You told me,
"You'll live through this as well."

And suddenly I understood
Your mercy and Your love.
You gently smiled upon me
And reached down from above.

You gave to me in human form,
The meaning of Your love.
All that You took, You returned
  ten-fold.
More than I'm worthy of.

Oh, God, it overwhelms me
The blessings You can give.
I prayed for death and You gave me
The reason that I lived.

Patricia B Martin
TO MY VALENTINE

To Bob on our Thirty-Seventh Wedding Anniversary

Yesterday's money is squandered
  and gone,
But yesterday's loving is lingering
  on.
Yesterday's wine is vintage by now,
But yesterday's kisses lie sweet on
  my brow.
Yesterday's roses have lost their
  perfume,
But yesterday's memories still fill
  the room.
Yesterday's love is blooming anew
Because yesterday's love, forever,
  is you.

Mr Eddie Weldon

Mr Eddie Weldon
TRAV'LIN MAN
I left home when I was a boy
I hit the road and I didn't get far
I went to Mississippi and worked
  like a hippy
I didn't get paid but I miss my
  honey
Cause baby I am a Trav'lin man
I get to back home where I belong
Well I get on the road and started
  back home where I belong
As I stopped along the way I find
  my baby on the phone
True love will never die but now I
  miss you so bad I must cry
It's your turn now so step up and
  love me
Cause baby I am a Trav'lin man
I hit the road again and just around
  the bend a car stopped along the
  way
A man said get in boy I looked
  around he had a gun
Then I wanted to run
He said what is your name I said
  Eddie
He said I know because you shake
  like jelly
He said get out here boy and don't
  look til we're gone

And there I was all alone
Cause baby I am a Trav'lin man
I was all alone
I left home when I was a boy
I still ain't got far
Cause baby I am a Trav'lin man

Arthur McCabe

THE TIDE

To my sister Marie, who left us on the tide Sunday June 14, 1987

I have felt the storm upon my back,
Rain upon my cheek, and hail, and
sleet.
Bucked the tide, drifted with the
slack
Fell, arose—went on with heavy
feet.

So many times looked back along
the way,
Vainly sought a pattern there to
guide me.
Silence my companion for the day,
Conscience in the night to lie
beside me.

But there were times for poetry
and song,
When sun and moon, night and
day were blurred;
Wit and laughter sped the hours
along;
Regrets were stilled, somber
thoughts unheard.

One may gaze from mountain top
to sea,
Look from crested wave or valley
floor.
There is NO charted course, NO
sheltered lea,
Just a challenge for each day,
unknown before.

A final tide will come someday
high on the shore
Each wave will help and tell a tale
of days long past.
Then the beach will clear to be as
just before,
A gentle breeze shall whisper, "You
are Home, my son, at last!"

Henry Edmond La Croix

LA PINTURA BELLA (A TEENAGERS DREAM)

Dedicated first, to "Hank," the teen-ager with the dream. Then to Kathryn, Annaleen, Dona Lee, Sonya Lou and last but not least, "Smokey." I love you all.

I've wanted a horse, for many years
it seems.
A beautiful mare was the height
of my dreams.
Wasn't sure what I wanted, but one
thing I knew,
Just any old horse would never,
never do.

I looked at some beauties, of all I'd
be proud.
I drove many miles, like chasing
a cloud.
Morgan, Arabian, Appalousa and
Paint,
Pinto and quarter horse, all fit
for a saint.

Finally I found her through and ad
in the news.
The price was quite high, my
Dad might refuse.
But he took me to see her and we
both took a ride.
Her beauty and color soon made
me decide.

She's the one that I want, I cried
with a shout.
I'll work and I'll slave to get her
paid out.
You can have her, Dad said, but
remember this son,
It's a horse or a car, you can have
only one.

I choose this fine pinto, I said to
my Dad.
Of her I'll be proud, as would
any lad.
But what will I name such a
beauty, I cried?
Use spanish for a name my Dad
replied.

"La Pintura Bella" was the name
that I chose.
For my little paint mare with the
soft warm nose.
Means "Beautiful Paint" in English
you see,
And that's what She'll be forever
to me.

Mary M Nudo

BUTTERFLY

To my grandmother who loves butterflies.

To be a butterfly
Is really very nice.
You have the chance, you see,
To live, not once, but twice.
First a caterpiller,
You eat and eat and why?
To spin yourself to sleep,
To make a butterfly.
Around and 'round and 'round,
The silk threads are spun,
And in your cocoon,
Become the other one.
The world to now explore,
You start your second life,
Into the sky you soar!

Ragene Wartick

TAPS

In memory. . .to all the brave young men who served their country. . .and those who didn't make it back.

I hear the taps over Oakland boys,
such a sweet, but mournful
sound.
I hear the taps over Oakland boys
as you sleep within the ground.
How sad that day as you
marched away to a strange and
far off land,
With your head held high you
were willing to die and lend a
helping hand.
I hear the taps over Oakland boys
it falls softly on the air.
I hear the taps over Oakland boys
as you sleep so peacefully there.
In the dark of the night by a
flickering light, alone in her
rocking chair,
A mother awaits as she murmurs
a prayer, for her boy way over
there.
I hear the taps over Oakland boys,
it fills my heart with pain,
I hear the taps over Oakland boys
through the softly falling rain.
When all is said and done, and
the battles are won, and they
return from over the seas,
Some lived, many died. . .yet our
flag waves high over the home of
the brave and the free. . .
I hear the taps over Oakland boys
through the sunshine and the
rain,
I hear the taps over Oakland boys,
and know you did not die in vain.

Phillip L Bendall

ALONE

I'm lonely,
Inside a deep well of blackness,
I sit with my thoughts,
Not realizing the passage of time,
Nor the movement of space.
My thoughts bounce off the walls,
And reform back into my mind,
In the form of questions,
Which in turn produce more
thoughts.
In a never-ending circle.
I suppose the big question,
What to do?
Just wait and see,
You'll know.
I need to laugh like I did before.
My mind continues this question
and thought time,
Until eventually,
I fall asleep.
When I wake up,
My pillow is wet,
I must have cried in my sleep again.
I hate being lonely.

Ernie Curry

ACTIVE DISCUSSION

The druid and the manikin sat
Perched upon a jaded fence
Decorating the outskirt of a forest
Dark, deep, and wooded dense
The druid and the manikin sat
Overlooking silver creek
Winding through the misty valley
Slow flowing and glassy sleek
The druid and the manikin sat
Discussing our oval sphere today
Where bias opinions and lost ideals
Make tomorrow's future gray
The druid and the manikin sat
Exploring all there was to find
All while stoaically contemplating
The inevitable destruction of
mankind
The druid and the manikin sat
Ignoring one minute inflexible fact
Salvation's not for those who sit
and wait
Tomorrow's for those with the
courage to act.

Erma J Knight

MY APPRECIATION

Dedicated to my Lord—Jesus Christ, my husband—L.R. (Bill) Knight (Deceased), my sons—Orville W. & Billy E. Knight

Oh Lord, should I be prone to
wander
Beyond the realms of this earth's
majesty,
Then may THY WORD astutely
lead me yonder,
To Thy fair home beyond earth, sky
and sea.

You've given us a vast expanse of
beauty
To see, enjoy, to ponder, love and
share;
But when at last we reach Your
Holy City,
We'll know a beauty there beyond
compare.

Yes, we shall reach those heavenly
portals,
IF we obey instructions You have
given.
If we are clothed with
righteousness as mortals,
You'll say, "Well done My child,
now enter in."

So thank You for all things that
You have given,
This world, its' wonders to explore,
We'll use it as our dressing room
for Heaven,
Where love and beauty last
forevermore.

Alice I Champlin

HONEYMOON ON HOLD

This poem is dedicated to my loving husband, Walt; my 3 sons, Jack, Dale, Larry; stepdaughter, Sharon; grandchildren, Jack III, Janyssa, Barbara, and Brandon.

For thirty long years we have
yearned,
My better-half and me,
To take our belated HONEYMOON
To those islands across the sea.

We gave to mine, to his, and ours
Our labors, time, and tears.
With love we raised our precious
brood;
It took us thirty years!

We're thankful God was on our side
His helping hand outspread.
He helped us all along the way
To keep them clothed and fed.

But now they're gone, they're on
their own
And now our time is free
To take our long planned
HONEYMOON
To those islands across the sea.

We have our reservations made
Our bags are packed to go;
So NOW please wish us
Bon-Voyage
And greet us Aloha-o!

Regina Lyn Finley

TRUE LOVE

With all my love to Robert Alan Richards, my best friend that I fell in love with

It's the "little" things you
do and say
That are so important as
you go your way
Now, I'm not just
living on a prayer
And all of the world is a
Treasure
When you have someone
To care
you always know just what
To say and do
That's why you're a
friend so true
confused at times, I may be
But one thing I do see

Is that we have a special
Relationship
That is so much more and
Better than just a friendship.
Baby, to you I'll
Always be true
and the reason is that
I Love You.

Cynthia L Patterson
SITTING ON GRANDPA'S KNEE
I was but a wee child,
Sitting on Grandpa's knee.
He would tell me stories,
Of how things used to be.

I would sometimes ask him,
"What happened to your hair?"
He'd just laugh and say,
"The Indians made it bare!"

My eyes would grow big,
My thoughts running wild,
As story after story—
Upon me he piled.

Reminiscing of years past,
Sitting on Grandpa's knee;
Describing places untold—
To a wee child of three.

George R Hopper
THE LAST KING

I dedicate this poem to my loving mother and father. To my brother Mike. My sisters Sheila, Debbie and my little angel AnneMarie.And last to Eleni. With all my heart and soul. I love you all, for now and forever. Peace.

Sitting at the circle—again. I have returned.
Decayed thrones surround me—empty vessels of lost souls—that have burned.
Empty is the night.—Silence is the air. I close my eyes to remember when Kings did fill these chairs. The laughter and the stories. Great festivals at night.
Tall mugs of thick grog to fill you—a willing maiden at your side. The harsh rays of dawn seemed a lifetime away, as the colorful gypsies danced in the night.
Alas—I sigh—remembering one sharp and painful gust of wind—brought the gray tales of war—again!

Through these lovelorn castle halls—there is no laughter, no song—anymore—only the bitter, haunting sound of the mid-night wind.
Wounded—aye—my heart carries the unhealing slash of time.

Now as the morning rays of the sun tender their way up and across this once great hall—there hangs a veil of darkness—in this now home of rats and vermin alike.
The moulted feathers, the unsettling stench of dung from your winged beast above.

Oh—I sigh—as I close my eyes in sorrow—to remember.
My sword in hand—I—slip silently away.

Lola D Purcell
IS THIS WHAT YOU WANT, LORD?
There are troubled minds that have no purpose,
Difficult lives, broken hopes caused by injustice,
Crosses too heavy to bear by people of the world.
Is this what You want, Lord?

There are hungry children throughout the lands
Caused by greed and prejudice by many hands.
Sickness prevails, and much help is needed.
Is this what You want, Lord?

There are miseries, impatience, sorrows and tears
That have existed for many years.
Depressions, misfortunes, sufferings of all kinds.
Is this what You want, Lord?

Loneliness is prevalent in many homes,
Children abused and left alone.
The elderly are frail, helpless and dependent.
Is this what you want, Lord?

The rich take advantage of the poor every day
Cheating and swindling in every way,
Murder and crime have got out of hand.
Is this what You want, Lord?

Wars have existed since time began;
Peace can't seem to be controlled by man.
When You show the world Your power,
Then it can be what You want, Lord.

Lorraine A Jackson
IF I COULD BE ANYTHING I WANTED TO BE

To: my loving family whom I love very much Richard, Kia, & Giles

If I could be anything I wanted to be
I'd be a star in the sky.
What a sparkle I'd Shine!
No! I'd soar like a bird in the sky.
What a song I'd sing
To bring you joy in disguise.
No! I'd be a Bumble Bee
For what sweet nectar I bring!
No! I'd be a rainbow across the sky for all the world to see.

I could be almost anything I wanted to be you see!
But most of all I just want to be me
For I am special since God made me!

Kathy Simpkins Dunahoo
WINGS ON HIGH

To Riley—The man of my dreams.

I can feel the wings as they start
to grow from my back.
They are so strong and powerful,
yet I know they are not mine.
I have them only on loan
as I walk with the Father.

They are his wings and
he has shared them with me.
They lift me higher and higher,
first below the clouds,
then floating in them.
Heaven is now a breath away.

I feel the brilliance of the sun
as I rise to meet him.
The glow on my face is evidence
of unspeakable joy,
For words do not speak of
overflowing peace.

Radiance is all about me,
time is standing still
but only for a split second
as I behold the Glory on my Father's Face.

In his eyes, I have found my eyes.
In his arms, I have found my strength.
In his love, I have found my life.

Shirlene Challis
THOUGHTS
This thought has finally come to me
My insight, now, I do see
I know there is a reason
To have so much pain in this season
I can't put on paper all that is in my heart
Somethings can't depart
All I know, life is so divine
This is true in my mind
Maybe, someday, I will realize what it is
That today, something is amiss
Whatever it is, it will become clear
The path I take will be near

As I watch people walking down the street
Not knowing what feat they will meet
Their thoughts on other things, I think
I would trade my aches easily for a mink
Wishing them happiness, without pain
People need to count their blessings and their gain
If, pain could be bought and sold
These words would'nt be told

Life goes by fast
Only memories will last
We will face tomorrow
Maybe with sorrow

Julia Mecham-McKinnis
A PROPOSAL

To the man who chose to share his life with me, my loving husband, William Boyd McKinnis.

This time. . .

If only you could give for me
As I have given for you, in the past
Then at last . . .

Our lives would finally be
So tightly bound together

That no one, or nothing could ever . . .

Come between the love we've shared
Or shatter our private dreams

And, so it seems . . .

That I would be quite honored
To walk with you again

As your wife . . .your lover . . .your friend.

Dehlia L Wilcoxen
THE SNOW BIRDS
Friendly little birds of gray
With neat black hoods and white tail feathers
Come each year from far away
To spend the wintry weather.

In my back yard they feast and share
With sparrows, quail and insolent jays
The seeds and crumbs I scatter there
All through the frosty wintry days.

As they partake of each day's supply
Throughout the winter season;
They do not question if, nor why,
Nor seek to know the reason;

Their daily needs are being met.
They simply come and feed.
Why is it then that I forget
God's plan to meet my needs?

In His own time my needs are met,
When I seek to do His will.
No need to worry nor to fret
But learn to trust Him still

And like the snowbirds in my yard,
Who come each day to feed,
Though times be difficult and hard;
I know He will supply my need!

R W Grandinetti Rader
UNFINISHED PROJECTS

For Boyd Saunders

The time it takes to walk
around the farm and take inventory
of the hole dug to bury the cat,
or the fence broken by the old stubborn bull

who refuses to stay
within the boundaries kept for him,
is worth seeing what work is left to be done
in each corner of unturned acreage.

The memory of your father
is etched into a copper plate,
the polished remembrance of a time
when carriages outnumbered cars

pictured for children
who've still to put their feet
in black southern soil as they remember
the way it was and the way it could be:

Offering them
a time to walk in the footsteps,
a place to grieve,
a picture to remember.

Shirley J Parrella
I'LL HAVE NO MORE
The songs they sing of love and joy,
of friendships through the years.
Seasons and holidays, families,
friends
The list goes on—will it never end?

What of the people who have no
friends, no love, no joy—
They do exist and carry on—for
they've turned their backs
and shut the door, simply saying
"I'll have no more,"
For friendships are so very hard to
endure—

Families are gone, they are alone
through the endless seasons and
holidays,
But they do exist and carry on.

A love lost somewhere in time? A
friend who caused much hurt?
No one will know why they are
alone.
Some friendships cost more than
will ever be known.

Sing no songs of sadness and
please no songs of joy,
for they are happy behind that door
simply saying "I'll have no more"—

Martin M Mikulich
A THOUGHT
When I'm down
I'm able to put it down
Simply and clearly
The puzzle pieces
Fall into place
As the keys
Fit to open
Their mating locks
And I'M up

Bruce Strand
THE SARA SONG
On starry nights when Northern
lights come calling in the skies
They hope their lumination
reaches lovely Sara's eyes.
If Sara goes, these neon shows
would flicker
out and cease,
Without the special Northern girl
they wanted most to please

When breezes blow the swirling
snow they're trying all the while

to land a pretty snowflake on her
nose to make her smile.
If Sara leaves, the wind perceives,
its energies will wane
Without its favorite Northern girl
to grace the white terrain

On summer breaks at northern
lakes that glisten in the sun
There's Sara with her latest beaus
immersed in summer fun.
If she departs, the buoyant hearts
of suitors on
the beach
Would sink like broken rowboats
with their true love
out of reach.

Cathie Setser Swick
OUR MOTHER LAND

Carole: Thanks for the thought. I decided to do something with it—Great. Cathie.

America. . .
Our motherland.
Land of freedom, and of peace.
With feet resting on your rich soil;
Dreams finding birth in your
clouds and blue skys.

America. . .
How, I love you.
My heart abides in you.
Your very name is imbedded in my
soul.
Tears flow at the thought of you.

America. . .
Holding a deepest pride of
you—for you.
I would go to my death, in your
defense.
Fiercely battling for your goodness
and greatness;
Never yielding my arms, until
again, you are safe.

America. . .
Land of freedom and peace.
In my pride, I cry for you.
Like a fine woman, you are most
beautiful;
Your beauty overwhelms all else.

America. . .
Oh, how I love you.
It is impossible to fulfill of you.
For all that we see, you offer
multitudes more.
The heart of us—our love—our
motherland.

Yvonne Hughes a.k.a. Emilee Morgan Hughes
FOR YOU
They shake their heads and say
"what a shame."
"She never should have had that
child."
They try to place some blame.
They look at me with sorrow,
And extend their pity.
They think I fear tomorrow.
The world sees you in their own
way.
They call you handicapped.
"So many problems," they all say.
I let them think what they do.
No one could understand. . .
How much I treasure you.
Your smile lights up my darkest
day.
Your warm little arms around my
neck
Erase all the things they say.
I've never felt ashamed.
You are a precious gift.
There is nothing at blame.
I don't feel any sorrow.
I can't use any one's pity.
I look forward to tomorrow.
I understand how it looks to the
outside world.
Yes, I know you're handicapped. . .
But still, you're just. . .my little girl.

John Good
MY LAST ROSE OF SUMMER
I picked my last rose of summer
during October's wane.
I picked my last rose of summer
on the rough coast of Maine.
Kissed by the Atlantic's salt air
on many a sunny day,
It blossomed pink and fair
down by the rocky way.
Its beauty and fragrance
charmed my heart,
As I beheld its finery
and art.
It was a vestige of summer
gone by,
Of days with joy and days that
made me cry.
I picked this rose and brought it
home,
adoring its color and scent,
And in my mind I did roam
through a summer well spent.

B J Krakauer
SUMMER END
Undetachable dusk upon a
summer lunch
embodied the smell of soft peaches
caught in the eastern wind

Touching May flowers
for a minute and coming home

In a winter of dry trees; we heard
the cock
signaling a return to hearts' fire

One-matched nerves blazed red
sweeping through green-eyed oak

Something of yours a ward
charming the summer end

A balm of coconut cream ending at
leg top
right below and until

A storm leapt in the air, clutching
leather and chain
studying how to prolong summers'
ending pain

Through a window, August shone
on a shifting of limbs, uneasy with
the season

We were walking on a bridge. . .
tongue-on-lip, trying to remember
heated words

Janet Kay Crawford
INVITATION TO SPRING
It was a hard winter,
when every sundown
barn shadows on snow
were my companions.

Now, delicate bells
on lillies-of-the-valley
spread out along the green
in welcoming lines;
and little girls skip rope
where spring's breath
reddens their candy faces.

And the air in May
awakens yawning blossoms
who open their Honeysuckle
invitations to Hummingbirds
and bees that call out,
"Come and walk among us
forgetting like the white
bloom on the vine, that
it was a hard winter."

Colleen K
STORMY SEAS
Winds of love
Tides of rain
Tell me will I love again?
Winds of love
Tides of rain
Tell me will my love be tame?
Winds of love
Tides of rain
Tell me does his love remain?
Winds of love
Tides of rain
Tell me that our hearts beat the
same.
Winds of love
Tides of rain
Tell me our feet move in time.
Winds of love
Tides of rain
Tell me the value is more than a
dime.
Winds of love
Tides of rain
Tell me bitter will never be as a
lime.
Winds of love
Tides of rain
Justly bring me sunshine.

Monica Lalor
ALMOST GONE
The day in Recovery Room started
out slow.
Then, With an urge we had to go,
He's not breathing,
He may be leaving,
Hurry, Let's start the reviving

Few minutes ago he seemed fine,
And, as if he had just drawn a line,
For he just paused,
Without a cause
As far as the mind, or eye could see.

Air-way clear, head of bed flat.
Let's try to prevent a clot.
Bed-board please,
Massage chest with ease.
Pump the vital breath of
air,—Breathe!

With a full minute to spare,
He Made it back here,
Breathing and coughing.
We then started sighing
With relief, for the tensions that
had built.

Carol Sue Davis
THE WOMAN MADE OF TEARS
There was a woman made of tears,
and you may well ask why.
With all the joy and happiness,
this woman chose to cry.

Her tears would burn her ivory
skin,
and scar her saddened face.
And joy would simply turn away,
and find another place.

Her head hangs low as teardrops
fall,
and rest upon her hand.
While the thought of crying herself
to death,
is more than she can stand.

Each time she'd cry, her heart
would bleed,
to be drawn oh, so near.
For one more drop from drowned
eyes,
could make her disappear.

Yet time again the sadness came,
and she began to cry.
With one drop, two drops, the
Woman of Tears,
slowly began to die.

Now time has passed since the
Woman of Tears,
on Earth cried out for love.

And when it rains, there is no doubt,
She cries from up above.

Sherry Motley
LITTLE THINGS
Little things you can't live with out.
You scold them, they cry, they pout,
Little things, with big blue eyes,
Little things, a big surprise!!

Egg on their hands and face,
Rubbing it into their hair, No disgrace.
Little things, mischievously sweet,
Little things, mud on their feet.

Little things, rubbing their eyes,
Time for the sandman's little surprise.
Dreaming good things never of bad,
Sleeping so peaceful, loving things, for all to have.

Children are little things I'm speaking of,
These are a few things we all prize and love,
The little things in life.

One maybe. . .Sugar, Spice, everything nice,
Snakes or snails or puppy dog tails,
Without our little things in life,
Nothing called, loving or strife.

Dimple Smith-Underwood

Dimple Smith-Underwood
IN RENOIR'S PORTRAIT, "LADY BY THE SEA"
In Renoir's portrait, "Lady By The Sea,"
In frothy lace and variant blues she sits;
Her clasping eye stir sighs within me,
For while my sun's wasting in the West, she knits.
It grieves me to covet a face so truly fine,
This lamb in treasured prime and golden grace.
Against the blue sea and cragged shoreline
Who but a master could sculpt' this face.
Was she birthed only in wordless rhyme?
Or did unknown ecstasy prod this creation?
Did his longing list until glimmering time,
Cross over to sketch her for a rare occasion?
Though penitence is a guilt of heart not eyes. . .
It is in the painter's soul the picture lies.

Camille Little
SUCCESS
Starts from the day of giving,
And we all can because we are living.
It is a task of holding on to stuff,
Even when things get tough enough.
You learn to keep moving and striding,
And how we all go on not really guiding.
Some times we really have to do,
In order for a real breakthrough.
Holding on and always retaining,
Making sure that something we are gaining.
For these are times when we all feel a little bit less,
But that is just a big part about success.

Mildred Jacoby Vail
PIGGLIN AND POGGLIN

To my Grandaughter—Heather.

She touched me with her tiny hand
And led me to another land.
When she said in a voice so wee,
"Will you come a Pigglin with me?"

I'd never heard that word before
And wondered just what laid in store,
She led me to her playroom then,
And there the Pigglin Game began.

Her soft and cuddly toys she threw
Up in the air by one and two
She looked and laughed with glee
And smiled a happy smile at me

"Pigglin and Pogglin," she did say
As animals flew everyway
Birds and camels, frog and bear
Went "Pigglin Pogglin" thro' the air.

An hour passed in happy fun
The "Pigglin and Pogglin done,
Myself returned to other tasks,
But ever when that small voice asks

Will I put grownup work aside
To follow her, this tiny guide,
As she leads with her little hand
To the "Pigglin Pogglin" Land,

Rachel B Elliott
THE STONE
All I wanted was a place in your heart,
A place to feel safe and cared for.
But, I needed to feel love even more.
I should have realized it couldn't happen to me,
All the things I've seen in my fantasies.
People told me all about you,
I never thought that they could be true.
I suppose I shouldn't cry over you,
But, it's really kinda hard not to.
Life is like being on a rock, on the edge of a lake,
And when you're young, there's so many rocks to take.
Right now I see no more rocks and feel all alone.
My rock's getting smaller and smaller, now it's just a stone.
When I met you I thought I had everything,
Hey, you even gave me your class ring.
And now you've taken it all away from me.
I sit here on this stone feeling sad, but free.
That's one nice thing about being on this stone, with no one near,
I feel no pain, none at all and I have no fear.
I know someday life will go on for me,
But right now that's kinda hard to see.
When you and everyone is pushing me,
I just want to crawl back on that little stone, where I know everything is true.
Because when you are telling me what to say and do,
I just don't know if you're really being true.
But on that stone I only have myself, and I know I'll always be true.
Even without you.

Forrest McKinley
I HAVE COME HERE TO DIE
Listen! All of you who have travelled
with me all these miles,
You will have to journey on yourself,
For I have come here to Die.

You travelled with me when the
Road seemed so narrow that we
Could not pass, and all the times that
We had to journey into the jungles
Of impervious weeds, that seemed to
Grasp hold of us, not wanting us
To pass.

And oh so many crossroads!!
It seemed to be millions of them,
Each bringing a different response.
We trod the thick, almost impossible
Mud, that hindered our journey even
more.

So if you will please, build me
A final, beautiful shelter here.
I dare not journey on, for the shortcut
To my paradise lies here.

Listen! All of you who travelled
with me all these miles,
You will have to journey on yourself,
For I have come here to Die.

Elaine March
TAMMY ROSE

Dedicated to Sonya Sterling

In God's garden there now grows,
a precious flower, called the Tammy Rose.
She was put here a while for us to love and care,
then taken from us in her tender years.
In all God's wisdom He now knows
How we all loved His Tammy Rose.

A wild little flower, while here on earth,
amidst the heartache, laughter and mirth.
Remembering all the good, forgetting the bad,
always be happy and never be sad.
For in God's garden there now grows,
a precious flower, called the Tammy Rose.

Shed not tears of sadness, but tears of joy,
for she left behind part of her, in a little boy.
Her memories will live forever, in our time,
for all the loved ones she left behind.
In God's serenity we'll behold,
God's heavenly flower, the Tammy Rose. . .

Lily R Stuart
WHAT IS LOVE
It isn't something you can touch or see,
Except when it's shining in someones eyes
And they are looking at you in that special way

You can feel it when it engulfs you,
And wraps itself around you,
Somehow you just know its there,

It's nice to hear someone special say,
"I love you"
But even when they don't
You know,

Because that special look is there,
And you can feel it, in the air,
What is love?

Don't you know?
It's all those special things,
That someone special does or says,

Can't you see it in their eyes?
And feel it in the air?
I can, because, I know
You love me.

Angie Flauto
DROWNING IN THE RAIN
Tried to get the answers
to questions on my mind.
Didn't know what I was looking for
didn't know what I would find.

They said that I was crazy
my mind was shot to hell,
The thoughts all crammed inside me
the things I could not tell.

Sometimes it seemed so useless
to stand and take the pain.
Reaching out to nothing
drowning in the rain.

My feelings cried outloud
yet barely made a sound.
Giving up so willingly
was what finally brought me down.

I stayed there for a while
hanging on as though I'd fall,
Counting every second,
though not wanting time at all.

The strangling of my emotions
was too great to be ignored.
It caused my final drowning.
as the rain endlessly poured.

Colette Kaye Nelson
MY LITTLE BUTTERFLY

This little token is dedicated to my father, in memory of all our times spent together in the wild land of Wyoming.

Sometimes,
my imagination runs wild.

It takes leaps and bounds
across open fields,
Towards the high mountains
of untamed societies.
With beasts of field
and fowl of air,
my imagination races,
like streaks of light
dancing in the sky,
always chasing imagination.
Fluttering just ahead like a teasing butterfly,
leading me into a lush green world of innocence.
then taken by the hoof of a fawn
to a human-like council to be accepted.
Then I notice that butterfly edge to the opening
of the circle and flee
for spirits unknown,
Forever pursuing my butterfly,
always finding myself unable
to catch the wild and free spirit
of my imagination.

Wilma E Brewer

Wilma E Brewer
LADY SPRING

To my children

Lady Spring you are on your way and drawing near, I feel your presence in the air
Your perfume, sweetest fragrance in all creation, is spreading everywhere
I heard a bird's love song to his mate just before the break of dawn
And watched an early red vested robin proudly strut across my lawn
One forenight soon you'll wave your wand and quietly leaf the trees
And whisper to the flowers to awaken and feed the honeybees
You'll blush the maples on the hillside and dress the willow with tender care
In delicate waterfall patterned laces and leave a bluebird nesting there
Lady Spring you are the world's greatest artist your talent and fame no one denies
You spread your colors in perfect array from gold edged lilies to tinted butterflies
You shadow your valleys with emerald, trace ferns amd mosses on the boulders
For the sky you use your truest blues and mix your hues in the rainbow you drape around her shoulders

Spring you are a lovely, gracious lady but sometimes a little fickle
First you soothe and caress with your brooks that meander to a murmuring trickle
Then tantalize with your warm, wayward, twirling, swirling, flirty breezes
That bring glistening, scattering, spattering, raindrops from a showy cloud that only teases
Lady Spring I'll enjoy your beauty and not be saddened because I know how brief is your stay
For when your picture is painted you will gently go and leave a summer day
But when the melting snows have rushed the rivers and the giant oak has let its last brown leaf fall
Then early one morn I'll arise and again hear your faint far away call

Anne Reuter
THE COMING

This poem is dedicated to Tansie who showed me her world.

It's coming
I can feel it
And with dreaded anticipation
My eyes search the sky
Knowing that its arrival
Means the end

The end of so many pleasures
Of walks and waterfalls
Of crickets chirping and frogs croaking
Of warm night air and the sound of rain on the roof

A sadness overcomes me
A hopelessness
Knowing I cannot prevent its appearence

It will be endured
As those before have been
The imprisonment
Of the coming
Of winter

John L Lamb
ONLY TRUE LOVE IS

Dedicated to my loving wife MARY

Roses are red
Violets are blue
But not all the time
ONLY TRUE LOVE IS

Margaret Poole
MAGIC

A hand full of magic from me to you
I hope it accomplishes what I cannot do
This hand full of magic, some people don't know
Is simply love, to make love grow
Comedy and Tragedy, two-faced is the clown
A smile when she's happy, upside down makes her frown
And here's where the magic, that slight of hand
Shows its face of hope and love again
Blot out the tragedy, the tears of the clown
Wipe away that awful frown
Magic make her hope and live once more
Give her heart the spirit to soar
To fly thru the heavens on Gossimer wings
Give her the peace true love does bring
So cherish this treasure, this thought that's so true
You see, my friend, the magic comes from within you . . .

Tina Marie Wonders
FOR MY TRUE LOVE

To Kevin
A special one sent from heaven,
Just the right one,
That I needed to
fulfill my lonely heart,
And he has done more than,
fulfill my lonely heart.

He has shown me,
How to love and care.
Also how to be myself.
Instead of trying to be
Someone I am not.
He has changed my life,
from gloomy to exciting.

So this is for my true love,
also my first love,
So to him I devote myself,
for always and ever.

Patricia Maria Chang
I PRAY THAT ONE DAY

To: My daughter Tamara and my son Desmond

My eyes are sad
My heart is mad
I pray that one day
I'll be glad

My daughter is wise
My son is shy
I pray that one day
They will be mine

I cried and cried
All day long
I pray that one day
My tears would stop

Robert A Tower
THE MAN

I walked with a man,
beside the still sea.
And I heard him singing,
this sweet melody.

Teach all my children,
the wrong from the right.
And show them, I am
the way and the Life.

I came down from heaven,
when I heard your call.
To save all my children,
the big and the small.

So, Love me my children
as I've loved you, so
that you may not dwell,
In the valley below.

I walked with a man,
beside the still sea.
And I'll remember forever
that sweet melody.

Thomasina Jackson-Moore
FOUR LINE VERSE SUITABLE FOR WILLIAM

This poem was written for the young Prince William at age 3 because I knew his FATHER.

Paste an apple
To a pear tree
and surely luck
shall follow thee.

Linda Leming Stahl
MY PAPER AND MY PEN

Dedicated to my mother, Marie, and Mr. Michael, who have loved me in my many moods; and encourage me to continue.

You are an ever faithful friend,
my paper and my pen.
Keeping yourself always available,
to every need I may have.
Accepting me in my many moods;
in joy, in anger, and in sorrow.
In times of rememberance I come to you,
and you present the truth within.
You aid me in times of change,
with a desire to explore myself.
As you listen, there is no criticism of my thoughts,
and you never leave me lonely.
You absorb all that I can give unto you,
yet you never ask too much of me.
Such a gracious and loving friend you have been,
my paper and my pen.

Jennifer Dreyer
UNICORNS

The unicorn is a fabled creature
Or so I'm led to believe.
I feel that this creature is not extinct;
But roams freely somewhere.

It roams in countries where there are
Castles, dragons, winged horses and knights upon fiery steeds.
It lives in the woods where it's safest
With the elves and fairies who pledge to protect them.

When hunters try to capture a unicorn, for it's magical
Horn, they will chase the unicorn until there is no chance of
Escape, then the elusive creature will turn, rear to its full
Height, and disappear with the magic of its horn.

Usually, the unicorn will reappear in front of a rainbow waterfall,
Where the water parts for the creature to pass through.

The unicorn walks through to the Hidden Valley of the Unicorns
Where there is grass and water and the sun shines brightly!

While the new foals of the herd
Stay at their mothers' side,
The older ones play happily in the lake,
Their manes shining, their coats shimmering, and their horns sparkling.

The leader of the herd stands guard on a
Slight hill where he can watch the herd
And the waterfall. He will watch the area
Carefully, and be prepared to move the herd, or fight for them!

So now you know, unicorns are real, you just have to know where to find them!

Grandma Ruth Ritter

Grandma Ruth Ritter

OUR FUTURE

In years to come, a rocket ship
Will take you to the moon.
You'll lunch on Mars,
Visit sattelite bars,
And dance to an alien rock tune.
A shopping mall on Venus, where you can spend the day
You can golf on the stars, then make a stop
To bowl on the Milky Way.
The medical teams will use lazar beams
To cure our every ill—
When it's time to leave, you can believe
There will be no such thing as a pill.
Retirement homes will be U.F.O'S,
Nursing homes a thing of the past,
Will we have perfection?
And will it really last?
These things are in the future
They aren't a reality yet,
But, given just a little time,
It will happen, you can bet!

Sylvester A Johnson

THE GUN AND THE BULLET

The gun held in the hand of someone
With a finger on the trigger
Waiting and aiming, standing ready to pull it

Lying in the chamber
Bold-faced and cold
Filled with powder in a jacket of brass—the bullet

An instrument, a weapon or device
A hard piece of metal designed
then machined
And made pretty to cause fear, protect or take life

One not good without the other
In the hands of a doubtful soul
The gun and the bullet as a combination has caused much agony and grief
To many a father, sister, mother and brother

High on a building, low on the ground
Around the next corner out of sight
Peeping from a window with malice in mind
Preparing to shoot someone down

With a finger on the trigger
Held with a tight grip
Waiting and aiming standing ready to pull it

Lying in the chamber bold-faced and cold, filled with powder
In a jacket of brass within a frame designed, machined and pretty
The gun and the bullet!

Denice Watts

LOVES SO LONELY

To Stephen Raupp, the man who has inspired me more than anyone. I will always love you . . .

How do you love someone
Who does not love themselves
You do all you can
To make them understand
Hold them close, lend them a hand
Give until your heart breaks
And STILL, You do not know where you stand

Love is NOT supposed to feel LONELY
Everyone needs a one and only
What is the sence in going on
When all you seem to do turns out to be wrong
All I really wanted was to belong

Why can we not get it all together
Tell me—Will we always be forever
He is gone, He is gone, He is so far away
What is going on? No communication so many days
And then when we talk I hardly know what to say

Love is not supposed to feel LONELY
We all cannot be without a One and Only
Hold me, Love me, Don't make me cry
The key is wanting to at least try
Love really should not feel LONELY
I want you for always
My LOVE SO LONELY

Curtis Cole

BEYOND EXPLICATION

To Patty—my wife and my inspiration

Within the being's depths, there are at times
Emotions that cannot be told or shown;
Deep currents of a person's very soul
That ebb and flow, yet can't be fully known.

I can't explain the mystery of life
That fills the sea and garnishes the hill.
In awe I tread upon this living sphere
And seeing, can but stand and wonder still.

No word of mine can tell the peace that comes
At sight of all the tumult of the sea.
In all its boisterous ways it lies serene
From ages past until eternity.

I can't describe the joy that fills the soul
When from some silvered cloud the moon stands clear
And bathes both glade and thicket in its glow;
I can't describe but hold the vision dear.

I can't portray the images of fear
That flash unbidden through a worried mind
When friends I love are walking danger's paths
And I, in safety's hold, am left behind.

I have no bob to plumb the depths of love
Nor can my eyes discern its breadth or height;
I can but see and wonder at its power
And feel its warmth and revel in its light.

P P Harris

PRECIOUS MOMENT

dedicated to my dearest friend: Dr. Robert Jarvik

A rose lost one of its' petals
Which fell softly on to a stone,
Like a kiss to a cold hardened lover
Who was destined to be alone;

Like so many petals before her
She clung to the stone so tight
As a breeze tried to whisk her from him
He prayed with all of his might;

Her soft velvet touch wooed him
His strong will held her in sublime
This precious moment was theirs
As if to hold for all time;

But their moment was soon to be over
As someone came upon the two
There was a soft cry, and a gentle good-bye
As the petal was crushed by a shoe.

Theresa M Nallick

THE JUGGLER

This poem is dedicated to my father, the best juggler I know.

Two for sickness, two for death,
And one apiece for all the rest;
The heart's most fragile of them all,
The juggler adds another ball.

Some he'll miss, they hit the ground,
Some bounce off and ne'er are found;
Some tossed up will not return,
And some will stay, one never learns.

Those balls tossed in the air too high
Are wisdoms gained with many a sigh;
Those bouncing off to find another
Will never again ill fare this juggler.

The ones that miss, break, and are gone,
They were not meant to be there for long;
And those that stay, from ignorant bliss,
In time, tossed too high, ne'er will be missed.

William F Sutton

TINY BIRD

To Suzanne, Dennis, and Keri, my three tiny birds.

Tiny bird,
Majestically perched upon a
Solitary boulder;
Resting comfortably in that
Farmfield
Barren of crops save for
Seeds
Laying in furrows awaiting
Rain
From the heaven's clouds;
I
Wondered as I whizzed past
On our beautifully warm
Spring morn,
Which we shared while the
Quiet community road
Blossomed with smells and budding
Trees;
Where are we going
You and I?

Christine Bisch

WHEN YOU'RE BLUE

This poem is dedicated to Bea Burkitt, love Christine

This is a poem
To let you know
When you feel blue,
I do too
Now wash up your face,
And let me erase
The blue that you feel inside.
So when you're blue,
I'll be there for you,
To lift your spirits high
Because I love you,
And to see you blue
Just makes me want to cry

Margaret A Campbell

MY PRAYER TIME

I got up early one morning 'cause
I had much to accomplish that day.
I rushed from one thing to the other
And never took time to pray.
Each job seemed more difficult;
It took more time for each task.
I wondered, "Why doesn't God help me?"
I heard a voice say, "You didn't ask!"
I wanted things shined to perfection
But everything seemed grey and bleak;
I wondered, "Why doesn't God show me?"
The voice said, "But you didn't seek."

I tried to come into God's presence;
I used all the keys at the lock;
God gently and lovingly chided,
"My child, you didn't knock."
No matter how small or large the
job,
You can't just work with the clock;
To let God come into your life,
You've got to take time to "knock."
I woke up early THIS morning,
I paused before entering THIS day;
I had so much to accomplish,
I HAD to TAKE TIME TO PRAY !!!

Mario A Gutierrez
LOS ANGELES

Los Angeles —
the city of movements
and bejewelled time.

Of maddening traffic lights,
of street cars lined up like trains,
of buildings towering like vultures,
of unpredictable night life,
of hysterical sirens
and crazy telephones,
of apartments called home,
of grayish clouds and oil in the air,
of haunching backbones,
taxes and bills everywhere,
and of hubcaps in the freeways.

Of varied and shrouded faces,
of distant attachment
and reserved neighborliness,
of inaudible moans,
of rights demanded in every place,
and
of greetings "How're you doin"
and "How are you today"
with no speaker and no meaning.

Los Angeles —
the city dead on weekdays;
alive and human on weekends.

Los Angeles —
the city in struggle —
naked and staggering
to the outcome of awesome
progress.

Los Angeles —
the city of lost people like me —
no name, no shield and no sting.
(I left myself back home.)

Aaron L Finley

Aaron L Finley
9-1-1

Dedicated to: 1. God our Father, Jesus and the Holy spirit; 2. My wife Eleanor, my sons Brian & Kenneth, & my Mom & Dad; 3. All Firefighters everywhere

---

He gives it all he has
Till he has no more to give
He gives his final breath
So that someone else might live
He'll battle flames and smoke
He'll keep you safe from harm
Even tho it may mean
Answering the last alarm.

Man of pride
Man of risk
He resist
Fear exist
A.k.a. Lifesaver

This salty dog no flame can lick
When things heat up he doesn't
quit
And though his job is full of stress
He's always at his very best

Man of guts
Man of hope
Doesn't choke
Eating smoke
A.k.a. Smokeeater

American as you can get
He's constantly defying death
Ignorant of difficulty
Goes beyond the call of duty

Man of pride
Man of risk
He resist
Fear exist
Man of guts
Man of hope
Doesn't choke
Eating smoke
A.k.a. Firefighter

Dorean Rodkey Gulliver
A MOTHER'S CHRISTMAS WISH

This poem is dedicated to my daughters Kelly-Jo Rodkey & Kandice-Jo Rodkey with all my love

---

Hello, to you my little ones,
there is something I must say.
Things went wrong and now your
gone,
so my heart it aches each day.

You were much too young to
understand,
to know it wasn't you.
Close your eyes and hold my hand,
beleive my love is true.

I only meant to let you go
for just a little while.
Now I long to hold you near,
and see your precious smile.

One day your daddy came
and took you far away,
I know what he has done to you
now i'm the one to blame.

I never should have listened
to what he had to say,
but I was much too tired and weak
to fight, so he took you both away.

If I had but one wish to come true,
my wish would be
to spend this Christmas day,
with both of you.

Michelle Rene Minor
FRIENDS

I have one I care for,
one I share all my secrets with.
This person I seldom ignore,
is always there in time of need.
This one makes me and my life
proceed,
and always has a solution to
make me succeed.

I can laugh, cry and share my
emotions,
with this very special soul.
Each and everyone has one of these
or this world would be a sad, sad
toll.

When you need a shoulder to lean
on,
no matter dusk or dawn.
Go to this special one indeed,
and pour out your pondering
plea.

Are you asking yourself who this
person is?
It's a special one you'd miss,
if they said the sad words "Good
Bye" in the very bitter end.
The special soul you see is a good,
good friend!

Rocky D Midgette
THE COBRA

i saw it coiled there,
yet i reached out . . .
the cobra struck—
i'd been struck before;
i felt the venom whirl in my heart,
leaving me ill, but,
i'd been struck before.
i hid for a moment—
as it were, from the cobra,
to no avail—
the cobra sought me out
and found me feverish.
i faced the stare of defeat—
then looked away;
i had been conquered.
i pondered, in my lifeless state
the meaning of the cobra;
how i could have turned;
how i could have run—
how instead i sought befriending
this lovely creature.
i reached out in love;
in fear the cobra struck—
meaning no harm.
i, at last concluded,
love is to the beholder
what they perceive it to be;
i offering to the lovely,
and the lovely piercing my heart;
with fangs of indecision;
the venom of retreat;
i reached out to the cobra,
lived, and shall again, as
i have been struck before.

Paula Sue Duff
SPRING AWAKENS

Listen to the bluebirds sing
As the earth awakens with a smile
Dream of all the beautiful things
While they come to reconcile.
The blossoms of the earth will
bloom
Into flowers of all kinds
Bringing all the sunny gloom
To all our mellow minds.
As we pass away all our strife
Into the dark blue days
As we enjoy the brand new life
In very many ways
We let this life reopen into a
beautiful thing.
Into a warm sweet word called
Spring.

Beatrice A Sipe
MY GRANDCHILDREN

To my family

How well I remember,
A long time ago,
When the Grandchildren would
come,
Spend a week or two.

The old family room
We gathered around,
The card tables spread
With sheets and down.

The bag of clothes-pins
Spread over the floor,
The games that we played
Were never a bore.

I'll never forget
The hamburgers we fried,
Of all the potato chips,
And french fries, too.

Then to wash up,
Take a long nap,
But the kids would yell,
Tell us a story, "Grandma,"
Before we tell "Pap."

Now the kids are grown,
And going their separate ways,
But the memories still linger on,
In my good old senior citizen days.

What wonderful Grandchildren,
What a blessing they are,
This is a real happiness,
Thus so far.

John F Horchler
A WAY UPWARD

To my Aunts, kissing cousins and Miss Heidi Shauffer

The rod of the Almighty will never
fail
The son of God will always prevail
It is where David's spiritual amor
was victorious
It is where the sheperd was proved
most glorious
With the spiritual power's new
clear light
The spirit power of darkness might
He has to fight
To prove in the end that His spirit
is right
To His converts on that happy day
He will send
The spiritual amore that will never
bend
During the last days that will never
seem to end
Some say are already here or
growing near
And pig out to prove it by swilling
a keg or two of beer
And laugh and shout and think the
spirt is all a cheer
And they have really never come to

know God by fear
For they think in their baseness
they have Holy Spirit clear
Because the stable Christ is
substance bread and His blood
And the wine blood that He shed
before He became a mometary
dud
So they imbibe, swill, quaff, and
and gulp and say, "hey, where is
the bud?"
For it doth not quicken the spirit
of the living but the dead
If they'd put their taste buds on the
Spirit that flows from the Rock
And believe and help others that
have become blind
He will to you be very kind and will
give a sign
And help you from Heaven to find
a way upward to climb
And on the "last day" a place in
Heaven to find.

Mildred Margaritte Feldman

GOD'S BLUE EYES

The Clouds above were lovely
today,
Silvery, pearly puffs of grey;
Here and there a rent or two,
With glimpses of azure peeping
through.

Often in this world we find,
A broken heart, a troubled mind;
But God's just proving to me and
you,
that back of the grey, there is
always the blue.

Bertha Fite

Bertha Fite

THE BIG BRAVE MOON

One by one the tiny stars
Popped out bravely, to show
their worth.
While the great big moon timidly
Peeped over the horizon of the
earth.

Mmmm the world looked very dark
Those stars are awfully brave
But watch me, I'll show them
I can be a regular knave.

The stars winked, twinkled and
teased
While the moon glowed with
pride.
I'm almost as big as the sun, said he
Watch me, while across the sky
I glide.

Up he plunged on his journey
Upward across the Milky Way
In full force, he turned on his
brightest light
And made the world almost as
light as day.

All alone he sallied forth,
Triumphantly he felt that he had
won
For were there not a million stars?
And he was only one.

Vicky R Carlson

YOU TOOK THE TIME

Dedicated to my husband John,
who still takes the time.

I think about you often
yet I really don't know why.
I see the way you look at me
out of the corner of my eye.
You really make me wonder
with some things you say and do.
Yet all these things you've told me
I can't believe they're true.
Sometimes I think you're happy
just restless with your life.
You think you need a change of
pace
from work, your kids, your wife.
Yet sometimes when you're really
close
I can feel you really trying.
To maybe give a part of you
a part you think is dying.
I can feel the warmth you're
sending
I can sense a little fear.
All these little things we're feeling
can only bring us nearer.
So no matter what the future brings
I just want you to know.
I'll never forget the tenderness
you took the time to show.

Heather L Mahl

I'M SICK OF

I'm sick of so many things
I've decided to make a list,
Like, I'm sick of people who always
give their opinions,
I guess you call them opinionists.

I'm sick of Moms and Dads
And Grandpas and Grandmas too,
But if it weren't for them
We wouldn't know what to do.

I'm really sick of school
Although that's where you go to
learn,
But sometimes the days are so long
I wonder if I'll ever return.

I'm sick of having to wait for
everything
A minute here and a minute there,
But all the things you could get
right now
Are things about which you don't
care.

I'm sick of people who think they're
better
Because we're really all the same,
The only ways we're different
Are by sizes, shapes, looks and
names.

I'm sick of this little poem
And I'm sick of being artistic,
And do you know what just
occured to me?
I'm sick of being sick!!!!

Philena Cox

LOVE, A REASON TO EXIST

If all love existed only in time and
space,
Imagine the lack of emotions that
we would all face.
Faded rainbows would have no
meaning at all—
There would be no reason for your
lover to call.
Roses would just blossom, and
slowly die.
There would be no reason to ever
record why.
Seasons would come and go—
Leaving only a silent echo.
If all love existed only so far away...
The need to live would have no
meaning, anyway.
Everyone would have just a blank
expression;
A no-caring attitude, a sense of
desperation.
There would be no reason to speak;
for
All thoughts could be read.
Written on our faces would be
thoughts of nothing. . .
Of nothing to be said.
But with love, this one gift, we are
blessed.
By this four letter word, all can
express—
The wonders of the world take on
new meaning,
With this word—we see the "stars
softly gleaming."
For if all love was in time and space,
We would cease to exist.
And think of all the happiness,
laughter, caring,
And emotions we would all miss.

Christine Jeffrey

REFLECTIONS OF CHILDHOOD

I start to run.
hair flying,
across fields of wheat-colored
swaying masses.

Tumbling, rolling
side over side down the hill,
watching in my mind
the world as it twirls.

I reach the bottom and land
on my back
to wonder at the china sky
white fluffs passing by.

Quick! There's a duck, now a tree,
Oh, and there's an angel—
whoops!
She just lost a wing.

I get up slowly, sighing,
muscles tired, protesting,
and brush myself off.
Why does it end so soon?

As the thirty-five year old that I am,
I walk toward home in a more
dignified manner,
glad that I could be
twelve again for just a moment.

Leona Lake Ryan

COUNTRY ROADS REVISITED

The trees have all gone away
Where once they stood so tall
And people in the houses now there
Aren't even aware of their fall.

For, when these people came there
were houses,
And streets and sidewalks
everywhere;
They never saw the area's former
beauty
With tall trees and flora fair.

They never saw a startled deer
In the woods by a former byway,
Nor saw the forest home of smaller
creatures
Before the byway became a
highway.

The thought probably never occurs
to them
That, as our housing needs
continue to grow,
The natural beauty of this earth
Is often struck a fatal blow.

The trees have all gone away
Where once they stood so tall
And the beauty that once existed
there
Few any longer can recall.

Lisa Lynne McIntire

THE MAGIC OF FRIENDSHIP

To Marianne Moss, Tonya Dively
and Gene Brown, to the three of my
closest and dearest friends. Thanks
for your time and understanding for
which I've written this poem.

Friendship is magic pure and
sweet,
for it helps to make life complete.
Given freely and never bought,
it's one gift mankind has always
sought.
Friendships last throughout the
years,
standing strong through joys and
tears.
Friendship gives its all,
working wonders large and small.
Friendship turns all that's
commonplace,
to matchless beauty, joy and grace.
Happiness is friendship's specialty,
and gives to everyone unselfishly.
Friendship is ages old,
and something dear to have and
hold.
But when there's nothing more
to say,
friendship like magic shows the
way.

Daniel Hurt

ALONE WITH YOU

This poem is dedicated to Shelley
Zylstra.

I lay awake late in the calm of night
searching the past that made it
right.
Drifting through time to see your
face
with twinkling blue eyes I cannot
erase.

Shadows that dance through heavy
sleep
in endless seasons I cherish to keep.
With sobs of "why" you end my rest
and I awake today having not slept.

Your long blond hair shines in the
mirror
around the smile of love once so
sincere.
Raising my hands with ease at last
to hold the cheeks that slowly pass.

In the routine of life I work and
wait
and call on love that slipped away.
With discontent I shuffle towards
home;
to a night with you but really alone.

Kate Barton

WEDDING THOUGHTS

Dedicated to my Nephew Jeffrey
Davis

and his wife Susan, June 7, 1986.

Remember when you say, "I Do,"
Your soul's no longer yours.
Everything throughout your life
Includes both of you

As you mature and love grows
strong
Throughout the coming years,
Your hearts will blend and be as
one
Through laughter and through
tears

When trouble comes and things go
wrong
And nothing seems just right,
Your mate is there to comfort you
Through all the darkest nights

So, love and cherish what you have
And guard it jealously
For as the years they come and go
your love will grow and grow.

Betty Jane Era
A BOX
I got a box that is special to me.
It is a box of long ago
Of love and hopes and dreams.
It's a box, of love you gave to me.
It's a box, of memories I received.
Oh this box I will keep
For in this box, is a part of you and
me.

Oh it was so long ago.
But it seems it was just like
yesterday.
I will keep all those lovely cards
that you gave to me.
I will treasure all of those
precious memories.
I will keep it forever.
Because it all belongs to me.

Mary J Pierce

Mary J Pierce
THE SURVIVOR

This poem is dedicated to those who made my life worth surviving. To my husband Don, and our children Randy, Russ, Rachelle and Ryan.

I'm one of the survivors,
in this Economical Crunch.
I'm not the only survivor,
there's a hell of a bunch.
Remember the good ole days,
when the family went out to eat?
Today, even the fast food places,
the food budget can't meet.
I remember the days when my
money
was saved for gas.
Now when my gas tank is full, I
drive
less, it still doesn't last.
Remember all the old movies and
the drive-in shows?
Now we watch T.V. because
there's no money to blow.
Remember the days when you
planned ahead?
Now you plan for only today,
that's what the survivors said.
We've learned to sacrifice, to sell
and trade,
Maybe that's the golden stairs,
the survivors laid.
We've learned to be hopeful, wise
and strong,
But still as one of the survivors,
I hope this Economical Crunch
won't last long.

Mary Lou Allison
THE KING
He is the King who wears no crown
Who's turned our heads and hearts
around
Who freed emotions with his style
With used guitar and crooked smile

For two decades He's filled our lives
From little girls to loving wives
He is the King who rules no lands
Yet still retains His loyal fans

He'll never need an earthly crown
To show the world He is around
His style, His grace, His deboneir
A shakey leg. And coal black hair

He left before His reign had ended
His songs from God were only
lended
His throne He left at forty-two
From Graceland in his Blue Suede
Shoes

Talbot F Charles Jr
AN OLD HOUSE IN THE WILDERNESS
Am an old house in the wilderness,
who no one seems to know.
I have been here for a thousand
years, but no one visits me.
In the winter when the birds are
gone and the leaves fell from the
trees, am alone until it's time for
spring and the trees are green
again.
Sometimes, I sit here and wonder,
why people knew not, of me.
I guess it's because of this lonely
place around me which I sit.
I have survived every hurricane
and storms that came my way.
Am a strong and good house, that's
the most that I can say.
But if people really visit me, what
will they have to say?
Am sure they will tear me down
and slowly throw me away.
But why should I be worried, I'd
rather stay this way.
If some one really visits me, I won't
live another day.
So-long all my lovely friends, come
back when it's spring again.
May the winds blow you on your
way, until we meet again.

Nancy Wagstaff
TUNNELS OF TIME
The room is quiet and hushed,
sacred with soft breathing of
new life.
An infant lies in the arms of
another, more wise and mature,
Yet also an infant, in the tunnels
of time.
Time is the mother of both.
Nurturing them to different points
in childhood,
Until finally, like the child of their
birth,
Times let them slip away
from this world
Into perhaps another
We are all children of different
ability.
Some of us barely able to crawl
While others are wrinkled and
gray!
Children—coming, growing,
learning,
and finally leaving
Through the Tunnels of Time.

Roger E Coleman
A LITTLE CUP OF FLOWERS
This little cup of flowers
Stands out from all the rest,
Has solaced many hours
When my care was all the best.
It may be the least expensive
Of all these works of art,
But it is so comprehensive,
It is the closest to my heart.
It's made from a labor of love
From just that good a friend
Who has her way of thinking of,
With more to give than lend.
I can feel her thinking of me,
And loving its creation,
So I keep it here above me
For my own sweet revelation.
Flowers cut by florists
And made into bouquets
Just show that friends adore us
In their many little ways,
But creation by a loving friend
Has a way that's all its own
To show that she loves me to the
end,
And she lets her love be known.

Daniel J Leshikar Sr
SEVEN WHO DARED

In Memory Of the Challenger Crew and to my granddaughter, Niki L. Sondermann

---

January twenty-eight, nineteen
eighty-six
Seven who dared, were all of a
racial mix
lifting off, on the Challenger, into
the sky
going on their mission, and they
knew why

Their spaceship traveled but for a
minute, maybe more
with a flash, they were gone, like
the closing of a door
Never again to return, from their
journey into space
but a lesson left behind, for all the
human race

The lesson being, for us to reach
for the stars
with conquered space, maybe
there won't be wars
They taught us, that for everything,
a price has to be paid
be it of small cost, or something on
which life has to be layed

A Nation United, mourned the loss
of Seven Who Dared
our tears and flowers showed
them, that we cared
Now we reach for the stars, as they
would want us to do
Seven Who Dared, a grateful
nation, is proud of you

Margaret Myers Waters
MY ROSE GARDEN
In the corner of my life's garden
There's a million roses, each so
bright and new
And in my beautiful garden
The roses are my friends like you
If I should lose your friendship
That means one of my Roses Died
Then the dew left on the others
Will be the tears I cried
So let me keep all my roses and,
Always lets be friends
Help me enjoy Our Garden
Till we reach the rainbow's end.

Mary Etta Spurlin
ROSES WILL BLOOM AGAIN
When life is young, and cares are
few;
When the sun shines bright, and
the skies are blue;
The scent in the air is a pure
delight;
When the roses bloom, it's a
wonderful sight!

Each rose bush nods its sleepy
head,
And the buds burst forth in scarlet
red.
They beckon the young and the
old, "Come see,
What a beautiful world God made
for thee."

Sometimes dark clouds come
billowing in,
But they bring sweet rain, to the
rose again.
And so with life, when the rain
clouds come,
Remember, tomorrow, there will
be a sun.

A sun to chase the dark clouds
away;
The sweet smelling rose is yours
for today.
So cherish the good things in life
that are yours;
The roses will bloom again, as
before.

When your sorrows seem many,
and your friends seem few;
Remember, roses will bloom, with
the morning dew.
So hold on to your dreams,
whatever life brings;
Yes, roses will bloom again, in the
spring.

Helen G Ritchie
A QUIET PLACE
I know a place—a quiet place
Between large rocks, just a little
space.
A babbling stream rushes madly by
Its pools reflecting the azure blue
of the sky.
Such a quiet place—just a little
nook,
Where I take my sewing or read a
book.
And sometimes, I just sit and
watch or rest,
As a butterfly passes or a bird's in
a nest.
It's just a quiet place—in a shady
spot.
Where I go to relax when the day
is hot.

Find your quiet place if it's just in your mind,
Rest awhile there each day and you will find.
Your troubles grow small and will fly away,
And you'll make each day a golden day.

Kathleen A Szautner
PANTOUM

Polka-twirling my life around
Repeating patterns of three-four,
My flying feet barely touch the ground,
You whirl me off for more.

Repeating patterns of three-four,
My face distorted in the glass,
You whirl me off for more—
I cannot see me, as I pass.

My face distorted in the glass,
In your eyes, my vertigo—
Hold me tripping, steer my feet,
You know I'll follow where you go—
I, who cannot find the beat.

Hold me tripping, steer my feet—
My flying feet barely touch the ground,
I, who cannot find the beat,
Polka-twirling my life round.

Corinne Nawells

Corinne Nawells
GOD BLESS THE STATUE OF LIBERTY

Dedicated to the Statue of Liberty on her One Hundredth Birthday

---

God bless the Statue of Liberty
For all the world to see;
God keep her in her Glory
The way she was meant to be.

There she stands in New York's Harbor
A Torch within her hand
To welcome all the Foreigners
That come into this land.

Now remember Emma's Poem
On the plaque where it appears
Out there on Liberty Island
Where she's been a Hundred Years!

God Bless the Statue of Liberty
And what she means to you and me;
God keep her in His Majesty
Throughout all Eternity!

Esther B Johnson
MY FRIEND-A DESERT FLOWER

God beautifies the desert with lovely flowers,
His love radiates from each bloom we see,
His warmth is felt through glistening sunshine,
And special people He touches so tenderly.

My friend was one of God's desert blossoms,
The desert flourished with her sparkling glow,
With God's love she watered seeds of kindness,
Through His grace she watched them grow.

Like soft petals her gentle hands reached out in compassion,
Bright glossy leaves were likened to her effervescent smile,
Although illness like desert winds spread through her body,
Her deep roots of faith made even her suffering worthwhile.

An angel, sent by God, saw my dear precious friend,
And gently transplanted her with tender care,
To the splendor of God's garden in heaven,
Where she now lives and will shine forever with Him there.

Woody Kennon
TORNADO

To my wife, Ann—at 17, ran from bath to car—still wet and soapy; two minutes later—looked back from car and saw house explode (totaled by tornado).

Tornadic winds of whirling wrath,
Destroying all within its path,
With roaring noise like none before
Snuff-out sweet life forevermore.
As whirling winds weave down the road
God's creatures run for safe abode.
As homes explode from vacuum breath—
Black funnel cloud of dancing death,
With anger spent, begins to rise
And fades away in cloudy skies.

Mrs Richard (Joanne) Settlage
MY THANKS

Thank You, dear Lord
For being so near
For being so dear
Each day of this year.
We thank You, Lord.

Thank You, dear Lord
For Your presence each day
As we seek you and pray
Each step of the way.
We thank You, Lord.

For answered prayers
Too many to count
And they continue to mount
As we come to the fount—of blessing.
We thank You, Lord.

Thank You for life so abundant and free.
Thank You for saving a sinner like me.
Thanks for Your love and Your most tender care.
Thanks! When I need You—You always are there.

Precious Redeemer, my Saviour, my Friend.
God's greatest Gift to us He did send!

Janis Dee Aldrich Brunn
THE GOLD STAR MOTHER

To Father John and Father Tony for their faith and strength. To Joan for her beautiful specialness. To my parents, my husband and my girls for their love

---

Memorial Day is here again
Other Mothers stand here with me
As we pause to remember our babies
Who died to keep us all free
So young he was when I kissed him good-bye
And sent him far off to war
For years after they listed him KIA
I still prayed he'd walk through the door
Where he is no one really knows
His body has never been found
Never will I be able to bring him home
And lay him in hometown ground
Yet, here at the War Memorial
Stands a small cross with his name
Though he rests not here in silent peace
In spirit he's here just the same
But I can not say I know not where he is
For in Heaven he waits patiently
And when I pass from this vail of tears
I'll again hold my son next to me
So just leave me alone for the moment
While I stand in the silence of grief
As I stare at this white cross before me
And let the tears fall from my cheeks.

Fern N McCaslin
THE CALL

'Tis indeed a sad, sad day,
when our loved ones pass away.
To all who's left remember this,
To be with the Lord is heavenly bliss.

Just wait till Gabriel
blows his horn,
Then we meet them all on that
glorious morn.

But time is flying, oh so fast,
And we know our troubles on
earth won't last.

Soon we'll meet our Savior
face to face,
And dwell eternally in his
heavenly grace.

Elaine Hoxie Randolph
PUPPY LOVE

The hearth of love glowing with fire
The warmth encased showing desire
Attracts you closer into the flames
Until the heat reveals only pain

Red dances the alluring part
Warming the love within the heart
Circles the whole into a trance
Deceiving the eyes to enhance

Time passes, ocher, in turn, revealed
Love shown attributes the doubts not real

Overlooking the diminished beam
Warmth continues the images seen

In the wake of orange, blue arrives
Not the color but what's inside
Trying to keep the redish glow
Life in the past is now not so

The fire dies eventually
Love cannot live perpetually
Other fires will be lit again
The love to be shared with other men

Barbara Fioretti
WASHDAY

When women wash their woolies
On a very windy day
The wind, like some bad bullies
Seems to wisk their wash away.

But when women hang their dresses
In the bright and shining sun
The sun it seems caresses
And they nary lose a one.

C Mykel Henderly
A POET'S FRUSTRATION

Yesterday's memories have slipped away
I should've written what I wanted to say
I think of lines in the strangest places
like crowded parks with networks of faces

On empty beaches where sand tickles feet
or the grumpy man who cursed so sweet
Wish I could have written about it then
but again I'm without paper or pen

Robbing my mind of life's recall
Searching for thoughts no matter how small
Wanting to write as life turns me on
When I find my pen the feeling's gone

If I could gather thoughts slipped away
I'd write a poem for poets someday
Whenever I feel those thoughts get near
I'll be without pen or paper I fear

Muriel Yetter
TAKE TIME

To my mother, Delphia Hamilton

Take Time to live, love, and pray
and each day will be a lovely, lovely day.
Take Time to see a sunset after a shower
and to see the dew on a lovely flower.
Take Time to see the miracles of nature occur
like little birds in a nest of hay
and little rabbits in a nest of fur.
Take Time to take the hand of some one old and grey
and talk to the little children on your way.
Take Time to give thanks to our God above
and give a helping hand to the ones we love.
Take Time to hear the song of the (whippoorwill)
after the day's work is done and the summer night is still.
Take Time to live, love, and pray
and each day will be a lovely lovely day.

Anton J Stoffle
THE MAGIC HOUR

Dedicated to my wife, Jewell, my constant inspiration for many years, and to my faithful friends and followers.

I sit alone in twilight's calm,
When ev'ning shadows softly fall,
And reminisce about the day,
Events, and things which I recall.

The solitude and peaceful trend,
Oh, how they capture life's sweet mood,
Which tends to bring along its glow,
It leaves one's spirit quite subdued.

This is the magic hour of dreams,
So set aside from woe and care,
A time to search one's heart and soul,
Or gather thoughts which hover there.

Romantic, sentimental things,
Perhaps a joke which someone told,
Or some kind gesture brought to mind,
Some item which one bought or sold.

And so it goes when dusk is night,
That certain highlights of the day,
Still cling within the mortal mind,
Before the night sweeps all away.

Then gently shadows of the eve,
Grow denser as the moments fly,
When sunlight winds its way back home,
As twilight bids the world good-bye.

Mary K Link
GONE
Oh child, dear child, I cry, but my tears all fall in vain.
One final statement, senseless death, leaves me guilt and blame.
Far too late I feel your pain and forever you are gone.

Gone by your own hand! And I can only cry
And cry again

Oh God, dear God, I cry. Do I cry out in vain?
Where is your loving hand? Do you really feel my pain?
This awful pain that rips! And tears! And grinds and shreds me.
My soul a screaming void and I can only cry.
And cry again

Frieda E Iverson
MY SISTER MARIE
She rocked me when I was tired, and sang to me a soft melody.
She taught me how to stand and walk, my first steps she walked with me.
She taught me how to speak and read, when the time for learning came.
She also taught me how to fast obey, when she called out my name.
She gently gave to me a shake, when I would disobey.
She was my shadow every day when I went out to play.
She washed my face and dressed me, when it was time for bed.
She sat me on her soft warm lap, and brushed my curly head.
Sometimes she made me laugh with joy, some times she made me cry.
I loved her then, I love her now, and more, as time goes by.
She is my second oldest sister, the apple of my eye.
For she was like a Mom to me, I'll love her till I die.

Liz Harris
CONSOLATION
A new day has come
into being
with the sights and sounds
of God's love.

The greenery of the grass
is like a carpet of consolation
telling us that once again
we can walk on the road of life,
with God leading and guiding
our footsteps.

The blue horizon is like a blanket
of protection telling us that
God has covered us from
Sun up to sun down.

The Golden Sun is
a reminder of his power,
his glory and his ultra rays
of hope that we will see
another day.

The Beaconing Moon is
a ball of faith

Lanna Eisaman
BEGINNING

For my husband Ralph, my son Jay Bradford, my daughter Jennifer Bradford, for your love and support

---

In the beginning is life,
In the end, there's death,
Life is full of joy and strife,
But death is the final breath.

Life can be good or bad,
It is ours to choose,
It can be happy or sad,
We can win or lose.

In death there is no choice,
Unless you believe as I do,
That we should really rejoice,
For the end is a beginning, too.

Elizabeth Jean Gross
LEGACY

To my beloved Mother, Elizabeth J Llewellyn

Dear old great great grand-pa this letter's meant for you,
And though you may never see this, it's so very sadly true.

They say you walked on the wild land, over green meadows, and blue vales. And though I never knew you, I heard all the tales.

I heard majestic bald eagles soared over your lands on high,
while you hunted the giant bison on the prairies nearby.

I heard you could almost hear the earth's heart-beat on a warm summer's morn. Yes grand-pa, it's still beating now, though a little tattered and worn.

Grand-Pa, I've seen your gentle bison, your grand elk, and
timid moose. But all caged in and weary, not one out running loose.

The old sun beats down harder now, through a gray polluted sky. And when I take a walk out there, I can almost hear the earth cry.

No grand-pa, they're not monuments, those huge white sentinels by the road. Just evidence of white man's wastefullness left there standing to erode.

And oh grand-pa those granite skull-crossed markers covering your hills down to the sea, well, I'm very sad to tell you, but, that's all thats left of your legacy.

Gertrude B Shoun
THE SYCAMORE
Platanus Occidentalis, to those in the know,
To a massive size this tree will grow.
Its fan-shaped leaves, yellow-green in May,
Provide dense shade where cattle lay.
In Summer its bark is scaley and brown,
Sloughing off in Autumn, upon the ground,
Revealing a smooth chalky trunk beneath,
Like white-washed columns along the creek.
Its branches like fingers lifted high,
Supporting the canopy of low dark sky.
Its abundant fruit, mere fuzzy balls,
Dangle loosely by weak petioles.
Sturdy and rugged as a legend of yore,
Behold its beauty, The Sycamore.

Gail Louise Merry
WILDFLOWERS
The wildflowers on the mountain side
dance in the filtered sunlight
As through the forest I often stride
never tiring of the beautiful sights.

The deer have left the open fields
as cattle wander through to graze.
The farmer checks as the old hens yield
the eggs they've earlier laid.

Children raised in the goodness of life
wake to misty mountain mornings.
Wading through springs where wildlife abides,
witnessing seasons of nature's adorning.

Laveda Winegar
HOW WILL I KNOW
How will I know that all is well
When there is no one there to show or tell
I will look up above and then all around
It is then I will know where the answer is found

How will I know when the time is right
As I go along both day and night
I will look up above and then all around
It is then I will know where the answer is found

How will I know which way to go
When there is no one around to tell or show
I will look up above and then all around
It is then I will know where the answer is found

So when all is well and the time is right
As I travel the road both day and night
I will look up above and then all around
It is then I will know where the answer is found

Allison Michelle Powers

Evelyn Barnes Powers
GRANNY'S ANGEL

To: Allison Michelle Powers, My Angel Granddaughter

Bag full of M and M's
She sits dreaming, staring into space
Future President? Astronaut? Movie Star?
Granny's Angel with the dirty face.

The Windwalker
RAY

To all who walk lost alone today

One teardrop prism splintered ray
Lost from the flock, shafted away

Out of the vee, splintered astray
A wild goose is gone lost today
From the flock's southern way

Its plaintive cries testing fear
As lost and blind it cannot hear
A mate's wingbeat quite clear
In air of crystal crystal shear
It is lost forever far and yet near

It is loneliness as an empty thing
A teardrop out of a heart to bring
Only a lonely plaintive cry to sing
Like a glass shattered broken wing
It cries and cries on a lonely wing

Lost away in the full sight of day
Like an arrow shaft it flies away
Lost forever from the flock astray
One prism's separate separate ray
Alone in a glass clear sky, today

Lola Mock
ABIGAIL
I have a little kitty cat,
She likes to be with me.
She's not so very beautiful
But cute as cute can be.

She follows me through all the house
And never seems to rest.
When she can have her choice of rooms
She likes the kitchen best.

She likes to get up in the sink
When I let water run,
And play she's catching all the drops,
And seems to think its fun.

At night she curls up close to me,
As quiet, as quiet can be,
Its then I look at her and think
She's cute as cute can be.

Eathel G Harkins
THE OLD BARN
The old barn stands in edge of field
Where once grew cotton and corn
Long since the old farmer has gone away
Now the barn stands neglected alone

For many years corn was gathered in
Hay had a place of its own
Big wide shed, where the wagon stood
Sheltered from the storm

Mules there in nice neat stalls
So cozy with corn and hay
Many years have passed, they all are gone
Since the farmer has gone away

Bright shiny roof is rusting now
As raim storms have come and gone
One rusty hinge, holds the sagging old door
As the old barn stands there alone

Diana Baker
JUST THE OTHER DAY
It seems like just the other day
When I had nothing much to say
I would just walk
People tried to talk
I would just look at them and scorn
Cause I was still deeply in mourn

It seemed like yesterday
When he had everything to say
I remember him teasing me
But I still loved thee
I always ask him if he needed
Anything from the store
But he always seemed so poor

It seemed like just the other day
That he had to go away
I was so concerned
But God said it was his turn
Oh, Lord please be with him
I believe he was the best
Out of all men

Cathy E Berger
BEFORE THE DAWN
Before the dawn is at its peak,
The robin's song is far from weak;
It fills the air with cheerful noise;
The joy is shared by flowers, poised.

The melody lifts up my heart,
Just as the new day's due to start;
And once again to God I pray:
"I thank you, Lord, for this new day!"

As now about my work I go,
The sun sets everything aglow,
With God my life does also shine;
A greater light I'll never find!

When down at day's end goes the sun,
At last the robin's song is done;
But God is with me all night long,
Til comes again another dawn!

Sarah Huchel
CELEBRATION-JULY 4TH, 1986
Fireworks burst above the seven spikes in lady liberty's crown—
The crowds aboard the small ships below echoed a joyous sound.
Amid the clapping and screaming—some were remembering
As lady liberty looked down.
One hundred years of liberties represented by the seven spikes of her crown.
Civil liberty, our freedom to conduct our own affairs, observing good morals
While obeying the laws of our land, to do unto others as we would have others do unto us—Quietly without fanfare or a brass band!
Moral liberty, to accept responsibility for our actions!
National liberty, the ability of our nation to make laws and to elect its own executives—regardless of party or factions!
Natural liberty, the unrestricted freedom to exercise all natural functions
In their proper places, to beautify America and preserve her graces!
Personal liberty, the freedom to leave our country and return without restraint— Of court battles and winning cases!
Political liberty, the freedom to participate in elections and civil offices,
And to take part in the admimistration of the laws under which we live as brothers!
Religious liberty, freedom to worship God privately and publicly—
Respecting the equal liberties of others!
The seven spikes of lady liberty's crown, newly refurbished, gleamed, as she looked down—
To remind us we live upon seven continents, surrounded by seven seas the world around!
Happy one hundredth birthday lady liberty and many more!
Let freedom ring forever upon your island shore!

Tom Rhodes ta
FAITHFUL
Beggars, nor bluffers, nor pidgeons be sane,
For out of the night, we all must refrain.
Dwindling and dashing, bobbing or bashing, life goes on.
Impart to others, that others may know.
Raise from the depths, that others may climb,
Out of their pits, the light sure to find.
Savor the plum, that the meat not be sour,
Food for the soul, all must devour.
Pick all the fruit, as the harvest abounds.
Store that which is ready, easy to be found.
Give that which is portioned, to those be in need.
Tender the caring, as if it were seed.
Raise up thine eyes, while still in your youth.
See all to behold, find it in your use.
Live as you will, but keep all in mind
That those less fruitful, are biding their time.
Long may you savor, that which is there
For soon you will know, the answer to prayer.
Believe in that which, is yours to behold
For sooner than not, you will be old.
Respect for your others, as time bid you well.
Find you a place, that time will unvail.
Be suiters and follow, all that is thine
Without having faith, you wilt on the vine.

Marcella R Wild
MY FAVORITE FLOWER
To name my favorite flower will be
A difficult task to do.
So many flowers to analyze,
Then eliminate all but a few.

The Daffodils, Dahlias and Daisies,
Valley Lillies, Lilacs and such,
Peonies and pretty faced Pansies,
Tulips brought here by the Dutch.

I haven't forgotten the Violet,
The Orchid or colorful Phlox,
Then I see the bright lowly Petunia
Blooming profusely in the large window box.

If time and space were permitted
I could name many more I suppose,
But the favorite one I'm sure you'll agree
Is the everlasting beautiful <u>ROSE</u>

William Bernard Raines
MEMOIRS

I dedicate the poem Memoirs to my daughters, Charlene, Joann, Shirley, and Dawn for the love and devotion shown me through the years. Little investments really do, pay off.

When I write my memoirs, my legacy or will

There won't be much to leave behind, like money in the till

I guess when opportunity came knocking at my door

I must have gone a fishing, like so many times before

I never made much money, like Tom or Joe or Guy

And yet, I'm quite a millionaire, in things money can't buy

It seems as how the little things, that we invested in

Came due in time, and now pays off, in little Dividends.

Ellen B Murray

Ellen B Murray
THE BLUEBIRD

To my Loving Family—Fondly, Grandma.

Over in the meadow, where the wind blows free,
Lived a Mother bluebird, and her little birdies three—
"Sing!" said the mother— "we sing," said the three—
And they sang, and they chirped in the ol' willow tree.

Ida Mae Rodgers
GOD'S ANGELS
God's angels come in many forms
With many shapes and faces.
And very often turn up in
Most unexpected places.
One day I walked a narrow street
Where work was being done,
It was so very, very bad
I knew not where to turn.
"Oh God," I prayed,"What shall I do?"
I needed help so badly,
As I stood amid the muck and rain
And viewed the chaos sadly.
Then 'one' came by and walked with me;
His arm was firm and strong,
He led me safely on my way,
And did not steer me wrong.
I'm sure that God looked down and smiled
As in my bus I sat,
With a Prayer of thanks upon my lips
For an angel in a Hard Hat!

Dixie A Rimmer
FLOWERS IN THE FIELDS
Flowers in the field pierce my thoughts
And bring my mind to clear remembrance,
Of serenity once claimed by earthen vessels,
In the Garden of Eden long eons ago.

Peace reigned completely from corner to corner.
New creatures obeyed it—humans alike.
No storms at sea, none ashore;
No turmoil in hearts of God's graven image.

But transformation a reality
Whisked peace away to cast it off.
Destruction was swift—that Garden of
Eden, gone evermore,
To leave ill will, envy and strife.

Continuance now—eternity it seems.
Evil conquers and gathers its own.
Patience now to few who grasp it—
Patience for flowers in the fields once more.

Shannon Michele Rains
THE SILENT CRY

To the ones that have lost—And to prevent the ones that may.

They leave us with no warning, no goodbye
Despite all the love and care we have shown.
They feel they have no friends and are all alone,
But we are blind to the fear in their eyes.
Did we ever try to hold out our hand
Through that seemingly endless cloud of doubt?
Didn't they know there's another way out—
Didn't we ever show we understand?
Why don't we know what goes on in their mind—
What were they desperately seeking to find?
Why don't we know what they're feeling inside—
What were they secretly trying to hide?
Doesn't anyone try to find out why—
Doesn't anyone hear their silent cry?

Graham Todd Joesph Danyleyko
LOVE

I wish to dedicate the poem Love to my mother for through her eyes I grew to see the true meaning and value of the emotion we call Love. Thank you, Mom.

Today I pledge this poem to you,
To those who know that love is true.
Its truth is warm, and means so much,
to those it seeks and tries to touch.

Love is what is felt by many,
For its value is unlike a penny.
The joy love gives is so divine,
Leaving those who love feeling fine.

Love is to be given with every chance,
To those in need who you catch in a glance.
Around the world we all do know,
How such a force could surely grow.

So as I give this poem to you,
I ask you to think for a moment or two.
Of all the love that you can give,
To make this world a better place to live.

Ruth Steinman Sievers
NATURES GIFT
I feel the gentle breezes
That brush across my cheeks,
I hear them whispering faintly
In tones of soft mystique.

Above the stars are twinkling,
Like sparkles in the sky,
The moon in all its brilliance
Casts shadows that flutter by.

I see the trees yet swaying
In all their lucid form,
One feels exhilarated,
Happy to have been born.

We thank the great Creator,
Who rules the earth and skies—
Causes the beautiful sunset
To rival the glorious sunrise.

Dennis Costa Jr
CALLOUS

To the leaders of our world: look, listen, learn. It's our world too.

Acid Rain fell from the sky
Looked up
Got some in my eye
And it sizzled
like an egg on a frying pan
Boy, oh boy how stupid i am

The Holocaust began
Just the other day
Snow!
How i hate snow
in a Major way
Especially when i can't see

And if i had the chance to do it all again?
i'd rather die
(Major sigh . . . Smiles frown)
And to make matters worse
—must be a curse—
i've got a blister
on the finger
that pushed the button
down.

Linda Ann Dawson
THE RUNAWAY

To family and friends.

As a child can't take the pain at home
She runs away
The streets to roam.

From the cold of an alley
To the warmth of a bed
Money made, for herself to fed.

Loss of her dignity
Loss of her pride
As men come up, to her side.

She walks the streets
Of sin and lust
For dirty old men . . . that she must . . .

At first it hurts
And she cries
To feel the strange man, asleep at her side.

Then there's another and many more
And she can't distinguish
Or feel anymore.

An innocent child
Of sixteen
Turned hard on the city scene.

Helen Roe Skaggs
I'D LIKE TO BE
I'd like to be a Christian
As nice as one can be
So that the beauty of Jesus
Can always be seen in me.

I'd like to be gracious and pleasant
To everyone I meet
Displaying a friendly smile
And gentleness when I speak.

I'd like to apply "The Golden Rule"
In all my daily deeds
And extend a hand of compassion
To everyone in need.

I'd like to sow some seeds of kindness
In all this world's vast store
And nurture them with tender love
With joy and peace forever more.

I'd like to look back this very night
And to my conscience say
Because of some good act to God and man
"The world is better that I lived today."

Margaurette Upshaw

Marquarette Upshaw
SOULSEARCH
Snow covers the ground, glistening white.
The furnace hums to my reverie.
I'm cozy and warm with breakfast just past. . .
But there are people out there so cold and hungry.

We celebrated progress in brotherly love.
Mixed choir, black teen, Jewish priest, celebrities
Sang, reminisced, cried tears of great joy, but. . .
There are still so many suffering diverse indignities.

My three great kids live lives beyond compare.
Thinking of them brings joy born of vanity.
But as they give my life such a plus, there are
Myriads of others' behind bars, bereft their humanity.

I dream fondly of two little girls
My grandchildren smart, unqualified sweet. . .
But what of other children—those born too soon
With impossible mind/love problems to meet?

I must do something—whatever seems minute.
What shall I do? My soul aches with regret.
A check here a word there; just enjoy my own?
Won't do for the millions; their needs won't be met!

Those millions are hurting far beyond my ken.
Make me sensitive, aware. I'll check out every race;
Stand up in protest; diligently educate. Above all
Learn the searing meaning of "There but for His grace."

Wilma Mayberry
THE BABY FAWN

My Children

In a forrest, dark and dwear
There was born a baby deer
There were spots on her coat
Of a dark brown, the rest was tan
Her legs were wobbly, and what's worse
She fell each time she tried to nurse

Finally, she began to stand
Looked around with amber eyes
Saw her mother not far away
Ran over to her to play

But the mother was instantly alert
She had a feeling of unease
Her eyes darted this way and that
Next her instinct was to run
But first she must hide her baby fawn

Now the baby was in a soft place and safe
The mother knew she must lead away
The enemy who would harm them today
She ran far and fast with the wolf close behind

She ran till she knew for sure
She had changed whatever fate
May have held in store
Now slowly she went back another way
To where her baby lay

The baby was sound asleep,
So the mother grazed awhile nearby
Then she too lay down in the den
And peace reigned again,
In the forrest glen.

Alma Britten-Huddleston
AGEING
Oh, the springtime of youth
So fleetingly ours
Spending our days
Smelling the flowers

So soon it is summer
And love's full bloom
Brightens our horizons

With the dazzle of noon

Fall follows so quickly
We scarcely realize
That winter is approaching
With it's blustery skies

Then winter decends
So peaceful, so quiet
As we rest and remember
Our years of delight

Robert K Kufrovich
SEEDS SOWN IN SANDY SOIL

To Jesus Christ, Creator of the Universe; Without whose assistance, This poem would not have been possible for me to write.

Seeds sown in sandy soil,
Starting to sprout inside stiff shells,
Stretching secretly towards distant spring sun.
See shoots surfacing!
Stems strengthened soundly,
Stalking similiar species besides.

So soon! So soon! Such striking show!
Spectacular sights to senses!
Special scents sniffed and smelled.
Simple scrags and insects scurry,
Swimming silently aside scouring rushes;
Searching solitude of swamps, grasses, and marshes.

Soon seething summer
Sends its solstice stare;
Supplying splendid greenish growths:
Staple supplements of steady sunshine.
Standing still atop stalwart supports,
Stamens sport and pistils glisten,
Stimulating stages for spore-spreading sprees.

Since last seen,
Setting season shortly ceases.
Supreme Sculptor sows sacred, sleeping seeds,
Shallowly sinking into same serene sites.
Seeds sown in sandy soil.

Agatha Oravec
RITE OF PASSAGE
She skipped into church with pink ribbons in her hair,
No cumbersome mittens; the weather was fair.
She was four and as free as a bird on the wing.
It had to be spring.

She sat in the pew with hair piled so high,
She dabbed at her forehead with a wisp of a sigh.
She was eight and as soft as a babbling brook's murmur.
It had to be summer.

She whisked inside briskly, it was almost a run,
Her tawny hair glowing; it was bleached by the sun.
She was twelve and as vibrant as a wild goose's call.
It had to be fall.

She knelt down in prayer swirled in wools newly sewn,
Not one lock was peeking; oh my, how she'd grown!
She was sixteen and as agile as
Jack Frost, the painter.
It had to be winter.

In a white bridal gown she flowed down the aisle,
Her tresses pearl-flecked; the groom wore a smile.
She was twenty and as radiant as the stars above.
It had to be love.

Elaine Kelley Umphrey
TO MY DEAREST FRIEND
Thank You:

For Understanding
When no one else could;

For caring
As few others would;

For the Kindness
You've shown so many times;

For Your Patience
When I've seemed so blind;

For Encouragement
When things were dark and drear;

For Your Presence
When I've needed someone near;

No One Else
could ever be what you have been;

Thank You
For being my dearest friend.

Lori Ellen Gartland
LIGHT
Glory is the light we make,
Fame is the light we follow;
Kindness is the light we shine upon others,
Day is the light we look for in tomorrow.

Rick Bledsoe
A LESSON (LEARNED TOO LATE)

This poem is dedicated to Brenda Green

A Godsend from heaven that's for sure
She had an Internal Beauty, a heart that was pure
She reached out and touched my soul
Two spirits meeting is the ultimate goal
I wish we could have stayed together forever
But working things out was too hard an endeavor
Our differences were many, our similarities few
But she taught me things I never knew
Like when you love someone with all your might
You must refrain from holding the reins too tight
When you care about someone you want them to be free
And not dictate all that they do and who that they see
But a tear doesn't spring to my eye because I didn't choose her
An inner joy overwhelms me because I once knew her.

George Anderson
ETERNITY

I dedicate this poem to my children, Sheridan, Brad, & Trey.

Upon awaking with each new dawn
I lie there dreaming of days long gone
When doubts and misgivings have finally fled
I arise from my bed

As I start my day
I pause to ponder what causes us
to wander along life's way

Was I chosen for my good
or was I chosen because I could

Did I stumble along the way
become lost as I traveled each day
or did I stay upon the path
to complete my given tasks

Will I succeed or will I fail
I try to find these answers
to no avail

Only time can tell
If indeed I have done well

When the end of my journey draws near
I hope my life will not have been a trail of tears
I hope that I will leave for all eternity
something of me for others to see

Ruth G Finch

Ruth G Finch
TURN BACK
Turn back, turn back
Oh time in your flight
Turn back, that I might see,
Visions of what used to be

Turn back turn back
That I might roam
The land that once was home

Turn back turn back
Till I am young
Turn back to the dear old memories
Oh childhood days, and dream of future years.
Let me play among—
Those long lost souveniers

Turn back turn back
Oh time in your flight
That I might guide my faltering step.
In to old age and linger yet
With the dreams that used to be

Irene C Skinner
BIRTHDAY OF THE KING OF KINGS
Could you change the color of the rainbow hues
Or the ink blue of the sea
Or lower or heighten the mountains
God's creation for you and me
Could you fathom the stars in their glory
God has numbered them one by one
Or change the heat or the cold of the weather
Or move the moon or the sun
How can we doubt our Father's love
Or escape His infinite grace
For He is the one and only King
That ruleth over time and space
God loved us so much, He died for us
Through the life of His dear son
As the yuletide echoes through the land
Lets open our eyes, our ears, our hearts, today for His command
And if we hearken, obey His word
We have the battle won
For in our hearts will be reborn
The life of Jesus Christ the Son.

Tana J Wynn
THE RAIN
Today I opened the door and noticed
the sidewalk was wet.
It must have been a quiet rain.

I used to listen to the rain.
I remember it softly tapping against
your window at night.
With your body against mine,
our hearts seemed to keep time
with every drop.

Afterwards, I'd hold you.
Knowing that we were safe and warm,
we'd listen together.

Although we no longer share that window,
it still rains

But sometimes

I'm unaware.

John A Venning
NORTHERN LIGHTS

Dedicated to my wife who worked with me in the north for many winters.

Have you ever been up in the Arctic
And seen them like magic unfold
The northern lights in the evening
It's a wondrous sight to behold

If you listen a while you can hear them
It's a whisper as soft as a sigh
As myriads of lights go a streaming
From the rim of the earth through the sky

And I've thought to myself as I watched them
It's a beautiful sight that I've seen
Like the fluttering leaves in the autumn
Some pinkish, some yellow and green

And often I've listened to stories
From Eskimo people who told
That those lights were the spirits of witches
Who lived midst the people of old

But I'm sure they were there before people
They were there at the first break of dawn
And the way that this old world is going

They'll be there when the people are gone
But I'm sure that the world would be better
If we'd pause for a moment each day
And give thanks for the beauties of nature
And the good Lord who made it that way

C.L Salazar

SHE'S DRESSED FOR THE BALL

She's dressed for the ball
in her lavender gown;
Crystal dewdrops decorate
her dainty throat.
Under the stars'
mirror ball lights
She dances with the breeze
to the sound of the
cricket's fiddle.

Tonight she baskes
in the attention
she receives
For it will soon be day
and she must return
To being one of the flowers
in the magnificent garden.

Clayton B Hadden

BEAUTIFUL SEASONS

The leaves of fall are shining
Their colors are so bright
But the winter nights are coming
And the leaves will disappear with snow flight
As the seasons and time keep revolving
We should live our lives to the fullest
And enjoy each wonderful sight.

Evelyn N Rock

AUTUMN MEMORIES

When the sun sets in a maze of clouds
And the millions of tiny starlights appear
When the sun shines in full splendor glorious
It's then I miss you most my dear.
When the rain begins to softly patter
And the last rose petal has its fall
When the last blade of grass grows brown
It's then I miss you most of all.

When a silent tear slips down a weary cheek
And my heart grows heavy with fear
When being lonesome reaps all of its sadness
It's than I wish you were here.
When trials of the day seem burdens
And my shoulders stoop in woe
When my eyes swim with suppressed tears
I miss you Dear Heart, I love you so.

Michelle Pratt

WILD ANIMAL CRYING

wild animal crying
set me free
there is no life here for me
caged in,
the same
helplessly
constantly
reliving the pain
thrashing against the prison walls
he falls
wild animal crying
let me be
has found a way
to finally be free

Roger Sheaves

JUDGEMENT DAY!

To my wife Jeannie, with love Rog

The search for peace within us all,
Seems to sometimes get lead astray.
But, struggles of life's everyday living,
Helps us venture back the right way.

We're well aware of common-daily problems,
And sometimes even that which lies ahead.
But, concern of things of secondary importance,
Is a path we have all surely lead.

His way unknown to many is primary,
And should be willfully and constantly sought.
But, to put off today what we can do tomorrow,
Is really how some of us will get caught.

So listen to, those seemingly selected few,
And try to understand the words they say.
But, to really comprehend life's true story,
Is what we all know to be;
"Judgement Day!"

Tammy Mills

Tammy Mills

I LOVE YOU

A young man's fancy turns to love,
As the colorful rainbow turns to a snowy dove.
A young girl's smile turns shy,
As the one she loves goes quietly by.
A woman's laughter turns to tears,
As the quick days turn to slowing years.
A man's bright twinkling eyes turn sad,
As he thinks of all times, good and bad.
An old man's mind lingers back,
As he trades his shining home for a decrepid shack.
An old woman's love that never died,
Turns to her love as she cries.
An old man looks at his whole life,
As an old woman turns into his younger wife.
An old woman's dreams come true,
As he takes her hand out of the blue.
And he says those simple words
That make the whole world sing like birds.
They were spoken simply, honest, and true.
They being I Love You.

Vanessa Bell (V)

ETERNITY

To my love ones Chris and Purcell

The making of a body
Evolving from a blanket of nothings
Living to be wanted and loved
Seeking a world of adventures
unknown and as pure as a vigin's face
Grasping forever for warmth
But always forgotten in a spur
Traveling solely on instinct
Being led by the hands of darkness
Eternity belongs to us all
Noone ever reaches for the sun.

Henry E Berek

THE NAMELESS

To Susan, my mother

I almost thought that I was free, free from this persistant perilous fear.
But no, it creeps and crawls and lingers still in the corners of my mind.
Sometimes, it seems to be litle animals dancing with dilligent airs down my spine.
And sometimes I see it in the corner of my eye, but always when I turn it is gone.
I even see it in the clear blue sky.
Little pale figures that blur and float, too near to be real, too far to be a part of my being.
Yet they are there, creaking and screaming in the moonless night.
When will I be rid of these creatures of my sleepless dreams?
I fear never to be rid of them until I face them.
Then it will be too late, they will be I will not.

Deborah D Hall DiCesare

DADDY'S DYING

Where are you going?
Did you know you were leaving?
Had you planned to keep living
Thru' our stages of grieving?

Well, to grieve is to grow
And to cry is to clear,
For we must grow to live
And we must live to steer.

Our lives do continue
Tho' they continue apart,
For it is in our separateness
You live on in our hearts.

Stephanie A Stottlemyer

THE HOMELESS

Cold bodies huddle
around trash can fires.
A bottle passes
from hand to hand.
Sharp winds pierce
through their thin coats.
The cold ache in their bones—
forever present.
A man sprawled out
on a hard park bench
shudders under newspapers.
Others huddle silently
in abandoned buildings,
alleys, entryways.
Men, women, children,
whole families
living on the streets,
waiting for food.
The hollow hunger
is always there.
The worry
constant.
Where will they go tonight?
When will they eat again?

Delores J Nielsen

MY HORIZON GIRLS "CAMP FIRE"

To My Daughter—Janet Marie Kleen

Eight lovely gals
Every one's pal!
No matter what we do—
They always follow thru'
In work fun or play
They never shirk but pave the way
For some new adventure
Which beckons them to stay.
They'll explore new horizons
Each coming forth like dawn
Breaking in a new day,
And help less fortunate ones to say
I, too have found the way,
And as the day turns into night,
May they shine forever
Like the stars burning bright!

Bessie L Imel

DAUGHTER'S FIRST BABY

GOD planted a seed in his garden
He wanted to watch it grow
He nurtured it with tenderness
And soon he had a ROSE
He gave you a loving Mother
And a Daddy who cares too
For from God's perfect Roses
God gave to us, YOU.
God Bless you baby,
Grandma.

Robert M Ryan

MEMORIAL DAY

On a grassy field in far off France
Some little girls were learning to dance,
And on this field some little boys
Were marching around with their soldier toys.
Beside the field there was a hill
Where all was quiet, peaceful and still;
Yet this was a famous old battlefield
Where Armies had met but would not yield,
Until at last their fate was sealed,
And many men died on this selfsame field.
The ghosts of men who had fought and died
Stood silently on this rural hillside,
Wondering why, as the long years past,
Why the peace they fought for did not last;
Hoping Man's struggle for power would cease

And leave at last a world at peace.
Quietly they wish and hope and pray
For a final and lasting Memorial Day;
But I'm afraid the hearts of men are frail
And the Gods of War will still prevail.
Again we hear the battlefield's din
Of nations fighting wars no one can win—
And why this must be I cannot say
As I honor the dead on Memorial Day.

Mrs Winnifred A Cleaves

A LITTLE HUMAN KNOWLEDGE

A little human knowledge,
Never hurt anyone;
To learn it and nourish it,
And watch it flourish;
We end up with a product,
Above average you say.
To some—why that's enough,
To make or last us—our day.
Our day will come as the old folks say,
Who cares about tomorrow?;
Or what the young folk do to-day?
They have to go through it,
Before they understand;
What it really takes in life,
To become a man—instead of a can.

Wyldeheart

WITHOUT DOUBT

Only You. Yesterday, Today and Tomorrow. My Love and Heart to Tony (my man) and my other Babes, Kristi and Brandi. XOXO

If I were to waken
and not find you near
scared of reactions
caused by the fear
Afraid of an ending
to something so good
a loss of all meaning
the place where I stood
The pain so relentless
you're in me so deep
valued most precious
of all treasures I keep
If I were to waken
and find that you'd gone
life left without reason
this heart could not go on
For it is from you love
that I draw every breath
attain strength, exist, persevere
Do you see?
I want allways to waken
and find you still near
cause forever beside you
I'll be
without doubt

Jolene Wood Goodall

MEMORIES

In a secret place, within my heart,

The memories of my life remain.
Good ones, I remember at will
Others, I try not to recall again.

There are so many precious ones
That they outnumber the bad.
When I look back upon my life,
There's no reason to be sad.

Even though I have lost
Those whom I held so dear,
Through the sadness that I feel
Good memories hold back tears.

Everyone has this secret place.
Store your memories as you would gold,
So that you'll have them all of your life
To remember when you grow old.

Gregory J Doke

BOOKS NEVER WRITTEN

A glimpse of patience sets boldly upon the brow.
Old men watch from where children impatiently ignored the world.
And so there you sit . . . owner of the world's last secret—
So too far consumed by passion even to hazard Gabriel a hint.
To feel it was the greatest truth since Descartes.
The cost could be measured by the wear on your shoulder,
Scarred like the soldier from Constantinople, shot cold in Korea.
Time plays no favorites.
Barred by the rules kept by the keeper,
Secrets double as sandals, and guises as gowns.

Men act out charades—rituals of war and peace;
Atom on the Eve of fruition.
Like blood in the vein, words from the books are read . . .
but in vain.
Too much concerned with the words of a song and a melody not recalled,
Man's finest philosophies share time with a joke, on the
back of a napkin.
This scherzo plays no repeats.
A bead of sweat sets patiently upon the brow.

Stephanie Cruger

LEARNIN'

There once was a young boy named Pete.
Who never put shoes on his feet.
He had went to school
And learnt all the rules.
He said, "This is fun! School is neat!"

D F Sanders

WINGS

Though he is blind,
He sees a world which we will never know,
The colors and the images of dreams,
Graced by the songs
That fill his thoughts until they overflow.
He is the perfect instrument, it seems.

He cannot speak,
No words will come to him, but he can sing.
Where he finds his talent, who can say?
He knows of love,
And brings into his world all he can bring.
He seems to find more beauty day by day.

He can't be taught,
But he can learn the beauty of a song.
His joy of music is too great to measure.
This is his life:
This is the onlyu place where he belongs.
A singing heart becomes his perfect treasure.

With song, he sees,
And learns, and speaks with eloquence and mirth.
The chains that bind his body disappear.
A song has wings
That let him soar beyond the cares of Earth
And find the key to banish every fear.

Edward C Comtois

IF ONLY I COULD WALK WITH YOU

If only I could walk with you,
All the things that I would do.
I'd climb a mountain high,
Reach out and touch the sky.
Hike along a mountain stream,
And listen to an eagle scream.
Stroll beneath the tallest trees,
Go where ever I might please.
Follow the setting sun
Into the night, now begun.
All these things, I would do,
If only I could walk with you.

Bernice Pestlin

NEW BORN PHOTO LADIES THOUGHTS

These cherished babies
Who for awhile
Remain with us briefly—
And share a smile

Wake up little one
And show those eyes of blue—
Lets make mom and dad
So very proud of you

I'll fix your hair
And make you ready
Now please don't cry
Keep that tiny head steady

I love each one
They melt my heart
Than so very soon
They must depart

Sweet little girl
And dear little boy
What a treasure you'll be
Bringing your family much joy!

William Ebbesen

GARDEN ENIGMA

See how this awesome, wondrous mite,
This tiny engineer,
So skillfully contrives at will
The marvel of the year.

With silver filiments to bind
The girders to the span,
It weaves a geometric orb
That routs the best of man.

Such scintillating symmetry
Was not begot in school.
Whence comes this tiny creatures ken
To build withiout a rule?

Jacquelyn Sue Baldwin

THE HARVEST

A little seed is planted.
Step back and watch it grow.
Feed it daily—bit by bit.
You reap that which you sow.

Kindness should bring kindness.
Laughter should bring joy.
Handle life with caution,
For it, is not a toy.

A little seed is planted.
Step back and watch it grow.
Water it daily—drop by drop.
You reap that which you sow.

Anger brings unhappiness.
Hard words bring hate and pain.
Handle life with caution,
You'll not be here again.

A little seed is planted.
Step back and watch it grow.
The Harvest is upon us.
You reap that which you sow.

Dorothy Forsyth

GRANDMOTHER

Dedicated to Stacie Ann from Grandmother with love

A Rosebud opened one morning,
fragrant with silvery dew
and out came a little babe, and
darling that babe was you
You filled our hearts with laughter
With your sparkling smile and pretty eyes
May you always be filled with joy
And your days full of surprise
And know I will always love you
More with each sun rise
Ten years have passed, each one a pearl
Bringing blessings to my little girl.

Linda Katherine Gowan

ODE TO VALENTINE'S DAY

For my husband who has put up with me for years.

Hearts and flowers and all that stuff,
All I say is, "Enough is enough!"
Guys don't like hearts and flowers,
Girls rattle on for hours and hours,
"Isn't that cute and isn't that darling!"
While he sits back and starts in yawning.
Couldn't we girls find a much better way,
A bigger, grander, more fantastic way
To express ourselves to you gentleman?
I think we must simply begin again.
No hearts, no flowers, no candy; so boring.
But then again, if it's him you're adoring
He should know you'll love him forever
As he loves football, fishing; how clever,
And TV and poker, baseball and chocolate cake.

It may have to be simple for his own sake.
Simply, adoringly, lovingly say,
"For you, my dear, Happy Valentine's Day."

Ursula Fritz
I PRAY TO YOU GOD FOR STRENGTH AND UNDERSTANDING

I pray to you, God, For strength and understanding
So I can meet each day with love in my heart,
I pray to you, God, make my will to succeed unbending
because Life is so precious, so divine.
I pray to you, God, give us greatness in wisdom
and let us thank you, God, for the miracle that

Life and nature holds in store.
I thank you, God, for the greatest gift of all, my Life,
and the feelings of love and laughter and tears,
I pray to you, God, let us be good and kind and wipe out
the sadness in all mankind.
Then, maybe one day we'll be able to say,
Gods word is working and here to stay.

Louis William Boockoff
FIELDS OF GREEN

For God so loved the world, that He gave His only begotten Son, that whoever believeth in Him should not perish, but have eternal life.

I stood within the fields of green
And thoughts I thought,
But never seen.
I saw the streams
That ran with red,
And saw men die
From bits of lead.
I heard the cannon's mighty roar,
That sound of grief,
That sound of war.
I heard the screams
That echoed pain.
The sides divided,
And Yet one name
. . . America.

Evelyn Glenn Haynes
SEEKING LOVE

Dedicated—To all mankind—Love is a gift cherish it always.

Let us not be two more
Lost souls searching high
And low over the horizon
Seeking to find love.
Only at the end of the
Journey, we are still alone.
Show me the path that
Lead to you and I will
follow it.
Reach out your hand to
Me and I will take it.
Open your heart to me
And I will climb in.
That way we are never
alone.

Samuel W Beebe
VIRGIN EMOTION

Virgin emotion untried but true
Living for the experience, always something new
Innocence blessed, ignorance best
For the truth always hurts when known
Knowledge the wall to keep man outside
So emotion he never will know
Try as he might, with all of his study so bright
in this labyrinth of the mind
always changing, always evading capture
Man will for eternity wander never knowing
The true meaning of human emotion

Rose Bush
LIFES PATH

This poem is dedicated to my husband Mr. "B" whose love and encouragement has helped me to be me.

Winding, Winding, Winding,
Goes the pathway toward the sea

Do you stub your toes on pebbles
Do the side thorns scratch your knees?

Were you skipping just this morning
Are you stopping now to rest?

Do you smell the scent of flowers
Have they put you to the test?

Does the sunshine all around you
Is it clouding up to rain?

Not that afternoons upon you
Are you searching for a cane?

Is it harder to keep going
Now that darkness fills the air?

Are there others there to help you
Are there others there who care?

Can you hear the sea a calling
Do the moonbeams light your way?

Has a life time passed since morning
Or has it been a day?

Chere C Severn
TIME

Time doesn't heal all wounds—
time can't hide loneliness.
Hand in hand
time and distance grow
and build empty days and long nights—
take away light,
pouring darkness from black clouds—
robbing summer of its warmth,
making misty eyes yearn for spring
again.
But through it all
one emotion carries on,
often sadly but still alive.

Time and distance
may weaken faith and dwindle hope,
but they'll never kill love.

Paul Marshall Swigart
BLACKBURNIAN

May days have arrived,
songs surround the swamp.
Flitting high in the trees,
a bird that knows no grief.

A collection of colors,
a portrait in yellow, orange,
black, and white.
Oh carefree Blackburnian,
living high atop the trees,

your world is full of leaves and flowers,
your school is your home
what you learn . . . you teach,
and when you sing . . . you preach.

You are a warbler that we seek to find,
but are you reality . . . or just the mind?

Judith Hobbs Cook

Judith Hobbs Cook
THE FLIGHT OF THE BUTTERFLY

This poem was written for my parents Hommer and Maybelle Mead for their example of the transformation that takes place when we dedicate our lives to live a Christ-like life.

Born into the family of God we begin our life as a tiny seed, protected nurtured and cared for. All our needs are met without asking. We are excited for we experience a new life of peace and security.

As we grow in the Lord, we are alike the caterpillar, eating away at the leaves of life trying to digest the Word of God.We become busily occupied with learning and doing.Our faith is little, our bellies full, as we share the Word of God with others.

Then the Lord slowly spins the threads of testing, trials, and tribulations around us. Silently, in the stillness of our cocoon, His miracle starts taking place. Our faith being stretched, our bellies emptied, we shed the old and start forming the new.

Slowly emerging from our cocoon two antennas appear. One of faith, the other of hope. Next the mouth which uses the Word of God to open the eyes of understanding. Discernment and compassion crown our head as the wings slowly begin to spread decorated with love, joy, peace,gentleness and meekness. Our legs firmly plant themselves on the limbs of life which are righteousness, truthfulness, long suffering and forgiveness.

We are now ready to take flight with much thanksgiving, eager to impart to the world the beauty of the Butterfly.

Charlotte P Stone
WALKING INTO SPRING

To: Genie

"There's a warmer sun today," I said,
"I'll take that walk I've promised to myself for oh, so long,"
And as I hastened westward from the town
To climb the slope beyond
I hummed a song.

Though icy rocks still lined its banks
The stream I crossed had freed itself from Winter's binding hold.
I stood and shivered there awhile,
Then traveled on and upward toward the sun
Away from Winter's cold.

A few brave trees had ventured forth a bud on blackened bough,
A distant bird had loosed his voice—the sun was warm.
And as I turned to listen to him sing,
There close enough to touch I saw bright shiny, dark green
leaves
Pushed outward from the dead ones down below
That had been a shelter from all harm.

A thrill I'd known from childhood stirred me now.
As gently I uncovered them, my

heart began to sing,
For underneath the cold, dead
leaves I found

Arbutus!
Spring!

Michael Thomas De Mattia
KAREN

To my "Guiding Angel"

When I hear your name I picture
Laughing geese with chubby
cheeks
Smiling duckies in search of
yummies
Whipped cream clouds on a
powder blue sky
And a glittering sea where we can
be

I see a smile that brightens the
darkest room
And hear laughter that echoes
through the gloom
Eyes that are windows to a soul so
true
The lust for life that is decidedly
you
I remember the lantern that
glowed in the nighttime fog

I think of a wonder that sees and
observes
Listening intently to what she
has heard
Those special times when she
heeds her heart
Are when she shows this is only
the start
Of an eternal love that knows no
bounds

I know she's an angel sent to me
Whose purpose is to set me free
From old ideas and restrictive fears
That keep me from learning how
to fly
With her forever by my side

Parrish Wayne
NO LIMITS TO MY DREAMING
ONCE there were no limits to my
dreaming.
No boundries to my ambitions.
No friendship I could not possess.
Some fire raged from within,
volcanic and seething.
Nourished my success—that only
intervals could rest.
Each day another test.
Each idea a challenge beyond
compromise.
Critics only shadows, empty
voices—that came and went.
Then I lost a friendship I thought
I owned, and tried to conquer
life—myself—alone.
While age came crashing into
youth in cosmic conflict,
And left me lost in fears I had never
known.
So Now I'd like to be there with
you,
Maybe laugh a bit, give a child
life—
Change myself.
Then again there would be
No limits to my dreaming.

J L Davidson
MY LOVE THE MOUNTAINS
Oh what beauty God has put in the
mountains!
To see the water flowing in the
mountain creek.
To watch the birds flying among
The tall ridges looking for food in
The cracks and caves of the tall
granite rocks.

To watch the hummingbirds
looking
For necter, from the wildflowers
In the meadows and in the green
trees of Spring.

As night falls and the moon rises
Over the tall granite rocks the birds
Give way to the animals of night as
they hunt for food.

This is my love of the mountains
To see all living things and grow
With the beauty of cave creek.

Maxine M Sweeting
SILENCE

To my Grandchildren—May they always feel free to "break the silence."

Silence is not golden
As it filters thru every room,
Too many memories of growing
children
Makes silence an instrument of
gloom.
Oh, how the years have all flown by,
The house is empty but for the two
of us.
Hark! There is a loud knock at our
door,
The grandchildren enter with
much ado and fuss.
Hours later after sound has filled
every room,
Once again there is the closing of
the door.
If only for a few fleeting moments,
Silence is Golden once more.

Gertrude McArthur
OUR WORLD
The Good Old Days have come and
gone
But just the same we carry on;
We're Blessed with the great things
of today
But still we go our wayward way.

The World cannot go on this way
If we will not take time to Pray;
With all our Wealth and Greed
today
Our happiness and morals decay;

So let's get back to basic things—
Like 'Work', 'Real Love'
and 'Marriage Rings'!

Evylon Nix

Evylon Nix
PICTURES

In loving-memory-of-Mother and Dad—Mary and-"Bill" McKee

Some precious pictures in my mind
Were framed so long ago.
Bright Spring flowers, Summer
rain,
And scenes of Winter snow.

A little house upon a hill.
Pine sentinels standing tall.
An old log barn where games were
played.
My mother's gentle call.

Some little trails through shady
woods
Where hickory nuts abound.
Where pansy beds and violets
Were scattered all around.

A picnic by a dancing stream.
Bright leaves of red and gold.
A fireplace (my daddy's pipe)
Where many tales were told.

Tho many years have come and
gone,
These scenes I clearly see.
Time has never dimmed the
pictures,
In my book of memory.

Ruth Means
ALONG THE WAY
A seed fall's
among the weeds.
Near a Robins nest.
where a mother feeds.
With sun and rain
a stem grows tall.
As a mother watches so
the young won't fall.
A flower blooms
one day to die.
The young ones feather
one day to fly

Vivian M O'Neal
CELEBRATING YOU!

For Nancy Farmer

What do you say to a friend who is
dying,
Who may never see tomorrow?
I tried to make small talk, but that
didn't hide—
All the anger, frustration, the fear
and the sorrow.

I was angry at God, for letting this
happen.
I felt frustration through and
through,
For all the times I wanted to call,
But never managed to.

And fear ran through my body,
Like a river runs to the sea.
Then, finally, all I felt was sorrow.
Yeah, I felt really sorry for me.

I stood beside your bed that night,
Not knowing what to say.
I looked into a strangers eyes,
But your smile gave you away.

At last, I said "I love you!"
You said, "I love you, too!"
Then, I touched your face, as I left
you to rest.
There was nothing more I could do.

So, tonight, I'm celebrating you,
In a fashion I know best.
With pen and paper, and all that I
feel—
I'm putting my grief to rest.

R S Iverson
TOGETHER WE WILL . . .

In memory of Mr. N. W. Hetherington (July 5, 1885—June 23, 1985), a Christian man I never met; but came to know and love through his granddaughter, Cheryl. (John 13: 34, 35)

Fly a kite.
Search for the moon.
Watch a bird in flight.
Friends we'll be soon.

Walk a path.
Sit upon a knoll.
Listen what the other sayth.
Hand-in-hand we'll stroll.

Cry a tear.
Smile a smile.
Share a fear.
Love awhile.

Cyril W Greig
SOLILOQUY

To: Loving wife—Daisy. Children—Cyril Jr. and Janet Eileen. Grandchildren—Elizabeth, Kantha, Indrani.

God had a talk with me today,
And this is what God had to say:
"Of Time and Space man is a part
As gill or noggin is of quart.
The nothingness of space equates
The density its awe creates.
This seeming void 'tween earth and
sky
Discloses man's identity.
Life essence is the full drawn
breath
Embodying the stench of death.
The circle's arc is so designed
Its beginning is but its end.
Man then, you see, is intertwined.
Man's enemy is man's best friend."

Christopher A Young
VISIONS OF CIRCLES
Round shapes fill my head
Spinning, curling
Twisting, twirling
One form becomes another
All in that infinite shape
The Circle.
Wheels spin on a car
Wheels find puddles
Puddles find me
I'm soaked . . .
. . . in blood
Round corpuscles, colored red
Twisting, turning
Doing a flip-flop dance
That tells a story
In an obscure language.
Lips coming closer, intertwining
A loving embrace;
A kiss.
Atoms floating through space
Bump, shiver and shake
They can destroy the world
But they'd rather join together
with other atoms
Regardless of color or shape or size
I wish we were like that
Circles.

Betty Patrick
CHRISTMAS DAY
God gave us Love at Christmas
In the form of a baby boy,

The precious Christ Child, Jesus,
Who gives us Christmas Joy,
Who came to earth to save us
And to give us second birth,
To show God's Love and Power
Over Heaven and the earth!
Never to condemn us,
But to help us start anew,
Love came down at Christmas,
The feeling is so true!
So glorify the precious Lord . . .
In everything you do—
Because you only love Him
Because He first loved you.

Ethel J Firmin
IN THE SHADOW OF HIS WINGS

The storms of life were raging all
around me,
I was being tossed to and fro,
No light could I see, no hope could
I find,
I called unto the Lord to rescue me,
He came to me in His love and
goodness.

He said to me come unto the
shadow of my wings,
There you will find rest for your
soul.
You will rest in My love and care,
I will shelter you from the storm.
You do not have to ever leave,
But can abide with me forever.

He brought me to heights
unknown in my spirit,
I am betrothed unto Him in love
and faithfulness,
And will abide with Him for
eternity.

Pauline Peduto Ragland Farrar
THE LONELY VIGIL

Far out on the desert sands
There a lonely soldier stands
Watchful and alert all the day
Silently he begins to pray
He prays for the folks who are at
home
Far from the misery he has seen
and known
He prays that they will never see
The atom war, with its debauchery
He prays that they will always
know
The joys of freedom from which to
grow
Peace and contentment every day
Joys and sorrow to fill their way
Life full with laughter and
childrens delight
For each new day and each new
sight
Life rich with blessings of love
Sent with his graciousness from
above
The joy found in each new step
ahead
Knowing only the fear of the things
we dread
Not to know a world devoid of love
and care
Where there are only masters who
will not hear
The miseries of those they profess
to love
The innocent who suffer from the
iron glove
He falls to his knees and cries to
the master of all
Dear God—Dear God, hear my call
Let the light of your love reach into
each soul

j cap guillermo
zeroing in on success

In loving memory of my parents now in the Great Beyond.

in your struggles toward life's goal,
look behind you from time to time;
and thereafter visit the past
that nurtured you in your
childhood—
in its waters let your mind wade;
there you will find the same old
pair,
with hearts so true for your
goodness;
fountains of love is what they're
known,
with constant hope that you realize
your cherished dreams.

In your ventures to scale the
heights,
look deep below time and again;
and afterwhich see the people
with eyes on you but bowed
upward—
with all prayers that you be graced;
from them you'll find said old duo,
the breath and rhyme of the same
lines;
and the ending and beginning
of the prayer: you reap the fruits
of your labor.

in your struggles towards life's
goal,
look behind you from time to time;
for one who looks back to the past,
grateful is he and is blessed
for thoughtfulness with a big heart;
in your ventures to scale the
heights,
look deep below time and again;
there you will find the same people
that you will need, comes the
mandate
that you get down.

Fern E Sheppard

Fern E Sheppard
IMBIBE, THE SLOW DEMISE

To my Brother, Lionel.

"Bullets" was killed during the war!
"Here I am "Enun" said, your
youngest son"
The void was too great!
Born too late!
Run! Soldier! Run!

Heidi A Meissner
NOT IN TRANSIT

& then they said
"do this
do that"
in a chitter-chatter
only they could ignore.
Their podium was the mind
as sugar-coated as their
solutions were;
Still they hated the enemy
& smiled at him coincidentally.

Each day the clock moved
faster & faster—
9 & 5 were not numbers anymore
but an angel of mercy
with black leather wings,
lacey mutant
though she was,
tried to save the drowning ship.

No resistance, of course,
from her slaves unquestioning
And like the clickety-clack of the
train that brought them there
Her voice brought them back
again.

Violet Napoli
BEAUTIFUL DREAM

Sprarkling brilliance, color
supreme.
I awoke from a beautiful dream,
the heavens had opened for all to
behold
the wonders of God, soon to be
told.
Expectation held me bound, but
then I heard
a terrible sound the noise of living
was
all around, and the mysteries of
God was
not to be found.

Gloria J Adams
SPACE AND TIME

My words may be short
But very sweet at times
They may not say much
Nor will they rhyme

But underneath all that I write
If you look, you'll see everything's
all right
There'll be words which will never
rhyme
Because of the space and of the
time

But in my heart, there's so much
to say
I could never find the space or time
in a day
Someday I'll be able to spell it out
clear
But until I can, I'll handle it from
here

My heart has become like a heart
of stone
It tries to sing, but it sings alone
The tunes are there, but the
feelings are gone
Someday to return, before my life
is flown

To the world beyond, where we
don't know
If we qualify to stay or have to go
Too little is known, too much is
assumed
For God gave every man, just so
much room

Ronald A Freeman
SINCE I LOVE YOU

Since I love you and really care,
It shows that we make a very good
pair
Since we are together every day,
It makes our love grow day after
day
Since I love you with all my heart,
That shows we will never part
Since I love while we're young,
It only shows that we have only just
begun
So when I die and go away
I will soon be back again some day.

Donna J Witham
COAL MINING MAMA

Dedicated to my mother, Bessie Hodge.

Not much education, but, oh, how
well she taught.
Her watchful eye was loving us;
We were blessed from the start.
She took pride in every task;
Our laundry, washed on a board
with
Lye soap and lots of boiling,
Was the prettiest wash in town.
When coal was taken out of the
bucket
And carted about the house,
Mama didn't seem to mind.
(She called it "pent-up energy.")
A child with so much "talent"
Should go out of doors!
Making mudpies was allowed,
But only 'neath the porch
('Twas there we learned to
"cook.")
Kindness was known of Mama
To both man and beast.
Taking care of others first
And resting afterwards is a
virtue.
"Do your best
And leave the rest to the Master."
Oh, yes, beloved Mama,
You taught us oh so much!

Kenneth Cressey
GO FOR IT

To the children of the world

Put your mind in the right
direction and shoot your best
shot. Go for it with all your heart.
Your life goal you've been
dreaming of.
Strive for your future for today.
For tomorrow may be too late.
Go for it children of today.
Don't hide your pride, so bring it
out for the world to see.
Go for it! Go for it!
Children of the world catch hold
on an old dream, and never let
go.
Break the ice, but don't play the
dice.
Show your talent to the world.
Children go for it!
Go for it!
Yes children catch hold of an old
dream, and never let go.

Nicholas Petroro
THANKSGIVING

Moms in the kitchen preparing a
feast
Basting the turkey and to say the
least
Our favorite stuffing and pumpkin
pie
The worlds best cook and that's no
lie.
Dads in the barn filling his jug
Sister go fetch him and give him a
hug
Moms basting the turkey with wine
you see

Dad would rather drink it and play
a melody.
Tell little brother to wash his face
The table is set, every dish in its
place
Yams, apple cider and cranberry
sauce
Moms almost ready to serve the
first course.
Now we're sitting, preparing to eat
A silence has fallen, there's one
empty seat
Our symbol for those who can't
afford
The time has come to thank the
Lord.
May your blessings be with us on
this special day
May we venture to thank you, in
our simple way

For the fruits of thy bounty and the
peace that's in store
The time has come to thank the
LORD.

Santina M Hartung
THE LAST OF WINTER'S FURY

To my family, who has always inspired me.

The snow drove past my window
in a chariot of frost
pulled by a pair of icey steeds
of inlaid silver gloss

Their prancing hooves of molded
ice
pawed at the frigid air
among the swirls of dervish curls
they danced without a care

The wind went roaring as it
whistled
through the frozen reels
where lacey patterns changed
with the turning of the wheels

The chariot went flying
as it dipped and tossed, the
ancient white haired driver who
was wild eyed and cross

He knew his time would soon be up
his fury sought no reason
he lashed and struck with all his
might
at the changing of the season

But Spring was brave and bid her
time
then softened his harsh blow
with smiles of sun rays through the
clouds
She melted winters' snow

Annie Pearl Hopkins
WHO'S HELPING WHO?

To: humanity, and especially my five daughters. Evelyn, Vicky, Rosia, Sharon and Melissa.

We need help . . . but who will it be?
Who's helping who?
Our teachers who teach, our
preachers who preach.
Our policeman . . . who protect.
Our politicians who,
Are working to bring about better
living conditions,
Just for a vote. Who! are they?
What are being taught, to our
children today?
And by whom would you say?
Where does the flock gather, to
hear the preachers
Speak?
And how many souls, will be saved
from the lake?
What are our policeman
protecting?
I know they do their very best.
Our Politicians work so hard! to
bring liberty and
Justice to all mankind.
Who! are . . . these peoples?
Our pace too fast, to thoroughly
explore them all.
Who's helping who?
If all this modernization are for to
better mans living
Conditions, then why's he still
crying out for help?
Where are the ones, with all the
"Serenity,"
Who are they? . . I beg of you,
Oh! please . . . do tell.
Who!s helping who?.

Naomi Ousley
BEYOND THE HORIZON

I walked along the sunlit shore;
My heart broken, pained and sore
Empty arms reached toward the
sky
No one seemed to hear my cry.
My thoughts, besceeching, asked
His Grace
"Who can take a Mother's place?"
She lifts your fears with one
embrace
When sad—she makes you gay,
Gives courage with each breaking
day.
She loved us so, and loved the
earth;
Her heart's desire was to remain,
Tell me, God, why she left this
domain.
My voice echoed the empty space;
Only God and stillness there to
face.
Then warmth encompassed my
aching heart,
The door to eternity opened, never
to part.
"My child, would you dethrone a
worthy King,
Or rob a bird the right to sing?
Take a baby from a Mother's
breast,
Or a weary soul it's right to rest?
So it is with heaven above,
She, too, has earned the priceless
love.
Lift up your heart and sing with me.
She is free, she is free, she is free."

Crystal D Bauer
A CRY FOR HELP

To my son, Jordan, who has taught me to not take life for granted!

I don't want to be illiterate
I'd love to learn to read
If only I could find someone
Attentive to my needs.
Someone who wouldn't pity me
Or ridicule me to shame
But just to lend a helping hand
As if teaching me a game.
The word "illiterate" hurts me
For I really am quite smart
If only I could learn to read
I'd have a happy heart!
If you'll have some faith in me
I'll try my very best
And I am sure that with your help
I could pass the test . .
So if you'll take the time
To plant a little seed
I'll really make you proud
To show you I can read!

Kathy R Adriano
JESSIE

In loving memory of my mother-in-law, Jessie Adriano—a very special lady, who married a very special man, and had three very lucky children.

I knew a special lady.
Oh, how she touched my life!
And when she left us all behind,
It cut me like a knife.

Her skin was soft as flowers.
Her heart was solid gold.
She never knew a stranger—
On your heart she took a hold.

She offered words of kindness
And a sympathetic ear.
That smile so sweet and gentle
Could often stop a tear.

This woman touched so many lives.
Like her there is no other.
God took this special person
home—
OUR BELOVED MOTHER.

Rodrigo de Jesus Martinez
A MESSAGE TO YOU

To Tiffany whom I love very much

My love for you will never die
But will hold like the sun in the sky
Although we may be far apart
You are always with me in my heart
I will always be here for you
Whether you are happy mad or
blue
You and I are a lot alike
We know whats wrong we know
whats right
Yet you and I are strangers
Facing lifes loves and lifes dangers
Someday we will be together
Maybe for a day maybe forever
All my feelings all my dreams
I hope you understand what they
really mean
I love you do you love me
Your answer is yes I hope you agree
I'm here when you're in need
I love you, this is my creed
I will always be here for you
In anything you want to do
Sweet sweet daughter of mine
You are my world thru the sands
of time

Charles Woodrow Imel
A GRANDPARENT

To my Wife, Judith Arlene, with whom I share, the joy of our grandchildren.

Must Have the heart of stone, but
be as flexible as rubber.
Must Have the knowledge of an
Einstein, being able to pass that
knowledge on to a child.
Must Be young enough at heart to
keep up with those little feet.
Must Be prepared for many
sleepless nights.
Must Be on call 365 days a year,
without advance notice.
Must Be willing to drive that extra
mile.
Must Be the greatest machinist of
all.
Must Have a heart full of love.
Must Be able to suffer the pain, as
great as that suffered by the
almighty.
Must Be a philosopher as great as
Socrates.
Must Be the artist of an
Rembrandt.
Must Have the shoulders and back
of an Atlas.
Must Be the sole person with the
wisdom to pass to the next
generation, past wisdom, with
the wisdom of the future.
Must Be prepared to judge, but
withold judgement.
Must Be able to negotiate all wars,
and to negotiate all peace.

A grandparent is God's bridge
between the past, future present.

A Grandparent—The jewel of a
childs eye . . .

Jozaa D Buist
MISSING PLANES

To my Husband Robert W. Buist and my mom Rosa Kovach, my friend Donna Oveson.

There were some planes that left a
field on a dime.
They just didn't know they would
be lost in time.
They flew with confidence and lots
of pride.
They were buddies, they were
friends,
Knowing they left side by side.

As the crew flew, they looked
around.
They saw the sky was gray and
brown.
The crew sent a signal, May Day,
May Day, where are we.
Where in the world can we be.

The planes sent their signals, and
the Captain said men.
Like the crew you really are, be
really brave.
This phenomenon will pass, and
we'll ride the wave.

The men in return said, Captain sir.
Remember the last time we heard
that word?
You said cheer up fellows, we'll be
heard.

Something seemed to beam us up.
It looked like a saucer, but yet a
cup.

In yet another dimension, there was some dissention.
We looked for a door, where there was none.
Can't you see what has been done?

To you we are still but missing
Travelling on with our lonely mission.
One day the doors will open.
Out will walk hundreds, and hundreds of men.

Maybe one day you'll see us again.
We'll fill you in from beginning to end.
There's something out there, we ought to know.
Whether it be friend or foe.

Bambi L Morrison
SOMETHING

To Bill and Dad and Mom for the inspiration you have given to write what I feel in my heart.

You are on my mind again tonight,
And I don't know if this is right.
I thought I forgot you long ago,
but now I guess that isn't so.
Those tender words still stick in my mind,
But I had left them behind.
Now they come rushing back in my head,
again I hear those words you said.
Come lay by my side,
our hearts have nothing to hide.
Tonight is for love,
something we're both afraid of.
I was scared to give my heart away,
you were afraid I wouldn't stay.
In your eyes I saw the only fear;
in mine I felt a lonely tear.
You knew what my answer was to be,
still you tried to hold on to me.
I was sure of my love but not yours,
but you spoke as I closed the doors.
Come lay by my side,
our hearts have nothing to hide.
Tonight is for love,
something we're both afraid of.
You tried to use me to ease her pain,
I thought I had nothing to gain.
But you showed me there I wasn't right,
something had happened that night.
I opened up and let someone in,
something I thought no one could win.
Now we see love in a whole new way,
so this is all I have to say.
Come lay by my side,
our hearts have nothing to hide.
Tonight is for love,
something we're not afraid of.

Ann Hallock Bradford
THE DREAM WORLD

With no one to talk with and hours to spend,
I'll invade a dream world, my boredom to end.
For I can be anything I want to be,
A queen on a throne or a sailor at sea;
A dancer with feet so graceful and nimble;
Even a seamstress who just found her thimble;
My beauty can be unsurpassed anywhere
Or I can be hairy, just like a young bear.
My wisdom, the greatest; and to those in need,
I'm sure I'm the kindest, whatever their breed.
But as I imagine the realm of each life,
I wonder about all their problems and strife.
What would it be like to be the great queen,
Whose customs and manners are publicly seen?
Or what of the storm that is raging at sea
With a man overboard depending on me?
A dancer must practice for hours and hours,
No time for playing among precious flowers.
The seamstress is sad for she suddenly found
Her patron had gained another ten pound.
Then there's the person all covered with hair
Wishing indeed for none to be there.
So, as I return to reality,
I'm certainly glad that I'm only me.

Clarence Morgan Pohlman
POINTS OF VIEW

I (Innocence)

"Do you know, my boy, where this road goes?"
The traveller asked the child.
"Oh, it goes to the brook down in the glen
Where the fairy flowers grow wild."

II (Idealism)

"Can you tell me, son, where this road leads?"
The traveller asked the youth.
"Why, it leads to opportunity,
To beauty, and love, and truth."

III (Reality)

"If I follow this road where will I be?"
The traveller asked the man.
"You'll be on a long, hot, dusty road
Going nowhere—and back again."

IV (Resignation)

Then the traveller asked the patriarch
"This road, where does it run?"
"It runs away over yonder hills
And into oblivion."

Grace Benner
SILENT INTERLUDES

Some stories will never be told,
Left deep in the heart to hold.
Lest they be cast
By the wayside, at last —
Some stories will never be told.

Deborah A Rhoades
THE ENCHANTING LAND

To my husband Vernon, and my daughter Sandy, with their loving support, said I could do it. Thanks mom & dad also !

Down in a valley where the bluebird sings,
And the wildflower grows
There is an enchanting little land
That no one knows.

Tis' a place full of wonder
A place full of joy.
Elves work their magic
On wide eyed little boys.

Fairies hear the wishes
Of beautifull little girls.
Some are granted curly locks
Most are granted special curls.

The human eye cannot see all of this,
It was'nt meant to be.
That is why we are blinded,
By what we are not suppose to see.

So down in a valley
In the enchanting little land,
No one sees their magic
That passes from hand to hand.

So if you should come across a valley,
Be careful where you stroll
A little dwarf might see you,
His name? . . . The Troll.

Caren Vigil
SAPIENCE

Dedicated with love, to my husband and family.

Branches touching, branches reaching
to another kind, to his own —
always upward, form a weaving
covering ground, creating shelter,
beauty, inner warmth.

Each tree clothed in leaves,
the composing parts, reflecting the whole
as dreams, memories, and time
color our lives, cover our soul.

A rich blur of multi-colored leaves
make up one forest, many trees.

To single one out and know its identity
it must stand alone in your eyes.
Hues of soft color, arrayed in dew,
each leaf in its own right
must be seen, experienced by you.

Trees are trees, in a way—all the same
Or are they?

A rich blur of multi-colored leaves
make up one forest, many trees.

It is so important for the eyes of love to clearly see,
being careful not to look at one
through the leaves of another tree.

Robin Higginbotham
QUIETNESS

Pretty little cardinal,
Sitting in a tree.
But then,
You flew away with the breeze.

Pretty little robin,
Sitting on the ground.
But then,
You flew away without a sound.

In the quietness of May,
The birds were singing.
And in the brightness of the day I found
The most beautiful way to say . . .
PEACE.

Robin L Toth
WE RAISE A GLASS TO MAKE A TOAST

Dedicated in honor of my mother—Jeanne Pinsonneault

We raise a glass to make a toast,
Then sip the wine and carve the roast.
A blanket of linen spread even and pressed,
The fine china sparkles to prove it's our best.
For today is a day unlike any other—
It's the 54th birthday of my wonderful mother.
Everything's perfect, except for one thing:
There are no gifts to open, no reason to sing.
At the head of the table in the straight wooden chair
Where our guest should be sitting—nobody's there!
But we still celebrate even though she is gone
Because our memories of her help us to go on.

Leslie Maya Whittier
END TO BEGIN

For Nicarus—Who showed me the rose beneath the snow . . .

Pretend that you don't care
When you smile and laugh
Inside you seethe
And your heart wears a mask.

All your life
You've hid from pain
Trying to avoid
Leaves nothing to gain.

You are your own worst enemy
Rejection, you fear
But how will you cry
Without shedding a tear?

With your soul you must see
With mind you must think
Your heart will so bleed
Trade blood for the ink.

Janelle Griffith
MY FIRST BORN

Angie, you,re my first born.
Since then, I've had more.
I know you feel, they've taken your place,
But they're just sharing your space

I still remember your first step,
And how I loved to help.
But the next thing I knew,
You were ten, not two.

You're toddler days are a thing of the past,
And they went by so fast.

You used to be my baby,
But you've become "Some little lady!"

I know you are only ten,
But you've grown so fast, you put me in a spin.
Sometimes I think you're the mother,
The way you care for your sister and brother.

Through those ten years,
The laughter and the tears,
We've had something in common, you and me.
'Cause I love you, and, you love me.

If you find yourself, someday,
Maybe, Going the wrong way.
Just turn yourself around,
And I'll be standing there, Proud,
Of "MY FIRST BORN!"
With all my love,
Mom

Sara C Merlo (PATI)
T-R-O-U-B-L-E-!
The two of us were a team. We grew up together and
got in trouble together. Together we spelt T-R-O-U-B-L-E !
We walked together. We talked to one another. One of us
was always around in time of need. Never did we lose each
others confidence. We trusted one another in secrets to
good to tell the world. We shared memories of good and bad
times. Now the future has come. The days are gone. Now we
each have what we wanted. A life of our own. A hope and a
dream come true. My friend you are still and I love you
always. Keep in touch and keep in mind; your still my
friend and my sister. Love, PATI

Lucille Cathell Densmore
FROM MOTHER WITH LOVE

To my Mother, Marie Cathell who was loving and loved, and my grandsons, James Shaffer and Jeffrey Huell whom I love so dearly

---

To see my Mother's beloved scrawl
And read the news of family and all
To share in part, things close to her heart
To talk on paper while we're miles apart
It makes my day bright, to know she's glad
Yet my heart drops if I feel that she's sad
I read each line from beginning to end
Then I turn it over and read it again
I cherish each word as tho' it were gold
To know that I'll never get too old
To receive these cards and letters from home
No matter to what far places I roam
When they come, signed, love Mother and all
I feel that Heaven has heard my call
The thoughts and feelings that we have shared
Lie deep in my memory, not to be impared
My Mother understands, whatever I've done
God bless my mother, I have only one

Cynthia Jefferson Delbridge

Cynthia Jefferson Delbridge
THE MILLION DOLLAR PRIZE
The sight of raindrops falling down
The sound of a violin,
A carosel, going round and round
With laughing kids within,
No greater gift can God bestow
Upon a persons eyes,
These things are precious more precious than gold
They're the Million Dollar Prize.

We've learned to value diamonds and furs
We skimp and save to buy them
But these things very soon turn old
And they're no value to your soul,

No greater gift can God bestow
You'll know this if you're wise
That true pleasures in life encrue no price
Thats "The Million Dollar Prize."

Marjorie A Brown
ST. IVES
Dreaming, I heard my cat say:
News revives
The everlasting riddle of St. Ives,
Your fount of poetry,
For love of rhyme, and me,
(Though not, perhaps, polygamy!)
When laughter and its leaven
First by-passed logic and the magic seven.

Nor did you wonder, till a later day,
What took the many-sevened on their way.
Menace to countryside
By plague or conqueror? (Away from tide
Could surely not be felicide!)
Subtraction, or a multiple of lives,
What integer was threatening St. Ives?

Numbers, greed-melted into viscous ring.
Digesting patterned form of shell and wing,
Spreading on fabled sand,
The sustenance of ages counter mand
Till wit awakens, and
To know, receive or turn away, contrives,
Who, with what gift, is coming to St. Ives.

Jennifer Trieloff
BOSTON CITY LIGHTS
Seeing these hundreds of glowing bright lights makes me happy.
It brings back good memories.
There's a certain calmness about the lights of Boston.
I remember the Friday night coming in on a plane.
Not knowing the experiences I would have,
Feeling the excitement again just thinking about them,
Just thinking about them.

I will remember many people.
People that made me laugh.
People that gave me good times.
People that showed me the specialness of Boston and its secret places that are only for me.

Bittersweet memories of a love whom I did not really know.
"First Love is hardest they always say."
But it was not true love.

I will always have a special place in my heart for the teacher who gave me inspiration to be proud of who I am.
Made me think,
Made me want to reach out and see how far I could go.
I will always remember her.

Even though the Boston Lights seem a million miles away.
I always have these memories in my mind and heart.

Nancy O'Rourke Mauldin
DEATH
Sometimes slow
Creeping silently upon you,
Catching you unaware.

Sometimes fast
Noisily exploding,
Rushing in unexpected.

Other times,
Aware
Expected
Waiting for its moment
It comes.

Left behind
We cry.
Hot,
Bitter tears,
to wash away our pain.

Leaving emptiness,
A place to fill
With memories,
Love remembered,
And knowledge
that we will meet again

Margaret Anne Thomas
TEACHERS
Folks call you a teacher, it's a title to wear with great pride,
For it denotes caring, sharing, and a heart that's open wide.

A teacher is one who manages to see good where others may fail,
And guides that quality tenderly, in hopes that "good" will indeed prevail.

There's something about teachers that makes them a special breed, its's true,
For they accept challenges that not many others would do!

They promise to reach such a diverse group of needs—
And in so doing, they even plant a few of God's seeds.

A teacher is a specialist in many areas of expertise—
Such as headaches, sore throats, loose teeth, and bruised knees!

But above all, she must care for them, and love 'em, and teach 'em, too,
And even cheer up those who came to school feeling sad or blue.

A teacher is someone special for to her it's never too late
To listen to some child's ingenious description of his poor homework's fate!

A teacher's job is never one that ends on the dot of three,
For dedicated teachers rarely have spare time that's free

From the caring and sharing and heart that's open wide—
For we'll always welcome any child in need—
That's why we wear the name of "Teacher" with pride!

Gregory Mitchell
IN THE LIGHT OF DAY
That "yes" You granted me under the Moonlight,
Lastnight,
By Sunlight
Became "No."

So, you too have a weakness for romance.
Confession time:
I couldn't resist asking you
that question that I asked
Inspired by a Moonlit hour,
At sunrise I regretted my asking.

Yes, fairy tales flash through fickle minds

But truths are always revealed
In the Light of Day.

Pamela C Pumphrey
THE BATTLE TO LOVE
Body and soul wrestle in anger
Wanting to do what is right
But my mind hides the truth from me
As I see only me and not you; it's another fight.

Rose mist and pine, you've shown me how kind
We are meant to be, just pure and free.
Like birds on the wind, who don't need to pretend
Naturally, they just love you see
Soar and sing for you and for me
So why can't we?

Shameful hatred from the past,
Deepest fear that love won't last
Letting go of who I am inside
The little child who wants to cry
I push aside.
Where are those feelings, the innocence of love
Like a dewdrop, or an ocean
In snowfall's silence or thunder's roar?

Please let us feel again
That hope is really here
And somewhere, in the sometime
We will all find time to love.

Belva Carey
THESE HANDS
In the beginning they were used to clutch toys,
Or hold to the hands of Mom and Dad . . .

Maybe even pinch a balloon, thus destroy;
Sometimes a spilled glass would make me sad.

As time moved along, off to class I would go
In the cold of winter and sometimes in the snow.
Picking icicles from the side of the school . . .
Using my fingers adding two plus two.

Then before I knew it my life had made a change,
So many things calling for the use of my hands . . .
Dishes to be done; cooking on the range;
Shopping in the market or planting flowers on the land.

They have been with me since the day
Of my birth, these marvelous hands of mine!
Time after time always making a way
For cleaning house or getting dinner on time.

It is difficult thinking about life
Without my hands keeping me busy
Doing the chores of a busy wife . . .
Driving from the country to the city.

Thank you dear Lord for these
Wonderful hands made from clay . . .
May they always continue to be
Used for you, until their final day.

Judy Cornelson Coker
LIFE

To all my family, who make my life so meaningful.

Listen . . . silence pounds
My heart, my thoughts . . . Life's sounds
A beat, a flash
The present, the past
Life contained within a being
Forever trying and yet not seeing
Till time has passed
That which cannot last
Life!

George K Henry

George K Henry
DAY OF THE LORD
Today His solemn warning
Is being thundered around the world
That the second coming of Jesus
Is about to enter this world.

Many of God's people
Have lost Spirit and do not pray
But to escape God's wrath
They need only to obey.

There are many false preachings
By false prophets who deceive
By saying that Jesus was the Christ
And not saying what He really means.

Deceived are the many
Believing they could be saved
Holding onto the traditions of pagans
While worshipping in Jesus's name.

The Lord our God
Said in vain they worship me
But blessed are those who hear
And read this prophecy.

In the book of Revelations
It says God's people can be saved
Provided you are submissive
And stay obedient to Thee.

So pray that you be accounted worthy
To escape the things that shall come
For there exists a God of mercy
Judgement, wisdon, and love.

Stacy I Pflieger
A CHILD OF DIVORCE
Goodbye Daddy
I have reached to you for one last time
and now I know you are not mine
For I am here
and you are there
and for some reason you just don't care
or maybe you just don't dare
For love hurts—this I know
For in my heart I shall always have
one piece missing . . .
and this piece is you
Goodbye Daddy
I love you!

Janet Lee Core
OH TEDDY
"Oh Teddy, Oh Teddy,"
What will I do?
For mommy and daddy don't love me, do you?
I'll bring mommy some flowers and daddy a beer
Hug them and kiss them and fill them with cheer
And then what will they do!
"Oh Teddy, Oh Teddy."
Please understand, I want them to love me
For what God has made of me
I'll need sometime, for I am not perfect
In every which way
Please don't go away teddy
Just watch and see
For I shall soon make their day

David J Yatalese
MY BABY DOLL

For all you wives, faithful and true, For all you lucky husbands too. But mostly for Gail. Babe I love you

---

I've seen your smile and felt your touch.
and Babe, I've heard your fears.
I've seen you melt at my caress,
I've seen your frown, your tears.

Could I but tell you how it hurts
to see a tremble in your chin,
Or how it warms me, makes my day
To see your saucy grin.

The time we've known each other, Dear,
has been, really, very short,
But the feelings that I have for you
are of a very special sort.

I'd like to be your shining knight.
I'll be loving, kind, and true.
I know we'll make it, you and I,
'cause, Honey, I love you.

James Edward Titzman
WHAT HAS HAPPENED?
What has happened to the world today?
It's unsafe for children to go out and play.

You leave your home to go on a trip,
Only to return to find it ransacked and ripped.

I heard they found a woman gagged and taped,
Tears coming from her eyes as she told of her rape.

A little girl came home from school today,
Said a man there wanted to do more than just play.

A man was shot at the corner store,
He told the robber of the money, that there was no more.

People living in the streets with no place to go.
Covering with boxes to keep warm from the cold.

A man went into the store to buy a cigar,
And when he returned he had no car.

There was a gang fight last Friday night,
Two members were killed, others, with revenge in their sights.

As a man was walking on his way home,
Someone drove by and shot him for reasons unknown.

A building was bombed yesterday, men, women, and children inside.
"A terrorist for peace," trying to get his word spread wide.

I hope for the day when crime will be no more.
To walk without fear, beyond my front door.

What will happen to this world that sees no rest.
The way things are going, soon, there will be no one left.

Sherri M Jones
ALL I WANT

Keep Smilen' Daily!!!

All I want is a smile to brighten my day.
A friend that you would walk a mile, just to say hey . . .

All I want is someone to care that special deepness . . . Someone to share dreams, goals, and happiness!

All I want is to enjoy life!
To be footloose and fancy free!
To be able to deal with daily strife and just to be me!

That's all I want!!!

Carmella Celedonia
CHILD HOOD DREAMS
Come walk with me into the past
With memories golden and mellow
Of when I was a little girl of,
Five or six or seven.
I'd walk and sit upon the Hill
And dream of many things,
To watch the birds go fluttering by
Without a care or worry,
And feel the wind so soft and smooth
Against my youthful cheeks.
And feel the warmth of the sun
That bronzed my tender skin,
And then I'd hear my mother call
To come down from the hill
And be a part of the family again,
But to remember those child hood dreams.

Sharmain Davis Lopez

Sharmain Davis Lopez
AT DAY'S END

With love to my children—Natasha and Sean

The sun is going down now; your work is done.
Time to go to the house now, your day is won.
As you look to the left, see the paintbrush flowers in bloom.
Look to the right at the dark black clouds, it will be raining soon.
Straight ahead you can see the farm.
Home is where the love is, feelings so warm.
Behind comes the children, running this way and that.
There was only time to work, no time to chat.
The wind is blowing, and huffing along.
I can hear it far away, sounds like a song.
Nightfall is here now, as I enter through the door.
The rain is falling down now, more and more.
As I lay down to sleep and say my prayer.
Now the day's end is near.

John W Gibler
THE GOOD ROAD

To my dear wife Jennie Sullan Gibler. Mother of three grandmother of nine and great grandmother of three. Member of Zonta International and Business and Professional Women's Clubs. She is respected and loved by all who know her.

When evening comes and lights are low
And when everything is quite still,
I dream again of long ago
As I'm sure that I always will.

Of that great day when we first met
Not aware of what was to be,
That time I know I'll not forget
Because it's much too dear to me.

Fifty-nine years seem quite awhile,
When measured in weeks and in days.
Some say marriage is out of style
But those folks have peculiar ways.

After all these years, happily
I must say that this is not true.
These years have all been rich, you see
Children, mates and grandchildren too.

When real love comes into your life,
'Tis surely a wonderful thing.
Mids't the sorrow, turmoil and strife
It does somehow lessen the sting.

Greater love you can't surmise
Though it is only a small part.
Of how you feel when you realize
That your wife is your old sweetheart.

Margaret Leusing
JOURNEY OF LOVE
I am a child of God on a journey of love
Searching for home in the heart of your soul
A union of spirits sharing life as one
Where I know I am free and never alone

As spirit fills my empty vessel
With each drop I am renewed
In solitude I have found peace of mind
In laughter I have found you

Gazing deeply into your eyes I see
The reflection of God
Deep within me

The source of all that I am to be
Lies in the heart of what we become
Together as travelers on a journey of love

Tammie Borders
THE TOY ROOM

To Dorinda Blount, a wonderful friend

My sister used to have a room, but then she moved in with me,
Because her room was destroyed, if you saw it you'd agree.

First came the doll house, then came the dolls,
Next came the bookcase, and after that 44 balls.

She installed gray toy shelves filled with lots of little things,
52 card decks were lost in that room, but of all I only found 17.

Her room was only eight by twelve, not very big at first,
But as days went by it shrunk, and that wasn't even the worst.

Soon the floor was 4 feet deep, and posters covered the sides.
Some of He-man, others of Austin, she even had a few bear hides.

She wasn't happy with her room at all, so she added some more.
She hung plants from the ceiling, but then the ceiling tore.

A plant hit a bomb, the bomb went KABOOM!
The sides and roof caved in, and that was all for The Toy Room.

Barbara H Copeland
I THOUGHT OF YOU TODAY
Many times I think of you
and push the thought away
But I thought of you today
In that loving forbidden kind of way

The days of you and me are long past
But the memories how they last
I thought of you today
In a loving forbidden kind of way

Oh the days of what might have been
But now will never be, but your face I see
I thought of you today
In a loving forbidden kind of way

The years and days stretch ahead
But what we've shared will never be dead
I thought of you today
In a loving forbidden kind of way

In my heart you will always live
With the only love I'm free to give
I thought of you today
In a loving frobidden kind of way

I thought of promises made with tears
To stay in touch through the years
I thought of you today,
In a loving forbidden kind of way

May you never forget I'm your friend
I'm yours til time does end
I thought of you today
In a loving forbidden kind of way

You take care my love, my friend
May our friendship never end
I thought of you today
In that loving forbidden kind of way

Dorothy M Fowler Hattenbach
MY TEEN AGED SON

In memory of my beloved son—Paul David

My teen aged son
With eyes so brown
And hair as soft as down,
Have a happy day this one.
For time is on the fly,
And we have only left a few
For all the things to do,
That were planned so eagerly.

I thank you my son
For all the happiness and tears
And heartaches done
To the two who love you so.

Always stay as pure
And as sure of life
As you are this day.
. . . Mom

Elaine Jones
FALLING LEAVES
The wind blows softly against the majestic-like trees.
And you hear the quiet rustle of all the Autumn leaves.
As they fall smoothly, softly, slowly;
descending upon every field of grass, and every cemented sidewalk.

Just look at all the beautiful colors.
Red, green, even the yellow which holds true to a cornstalk.

No leaf is blown quite the same.
Each gust of the wind
Moves each one in a pattern
Geometrically complex—not one is the same.

Alas I've spotted one in a motion.
It's falling from a branch
As though under the spell of a love potion.
It does a loop-the-loop like a circus clown,
Twirling around in a hula hoop.

Now it does a nose dive;
Top part of the leaf towards the ground.
Maybe it's alive,
And has a new destiny to be found.

Oh what a beautiful sight,
Autumn leaves falling,
Touching the ground, and looking just right.

Florence Crunk
ESPECIALLY FOR TEENS'
Attention: All teenagers,
You are the future world,
And that world needs you,
Be the very best you can.

Do you know yourself well?
Think, before you answer,
Do you like yourself now?
If not change while you can.

Stay in school above all,
Keep your good health,
Say "No" to drugs daily,
Also never smoke or drink.

Leave babies off 'til adults,
Join a church and attend it,
Prepare well for your future,
Listen to wholesome advice.

Frederick A Williams Jr
LET ME DREAM
Let me dream
For was it not a dream that man could fly?
Let me dream
That I might know of something I could try;
Let me dream
Of sailing before the wind beneath a friendly sky;
Let me dream
Of trodding on distant sands listening as the palm leaves sigh;
Let me dream
For fate might take a hand and I could live this dream before I die.

Lisa Sullivan
MY BEST FRIEND

Dedicated to my sisters: Nancy and Becky, and to my best friend, LeeAnn.

My best friend means the world to me,
We've grown up together since I was two or three.
We've been through thick and thin together,
Through sunny days and rainy weather.
We've had fights that would last all day,
But then we'd laugh, make up and say,
Let's go outside and play.
But now we are grown,
With lives of our own,
And even though we are miles apart,
I love her so, with all my heart.
And I really have missed her,
Because she is my little sister.

Paul Grasseler Jr
THE SHINING LIGHT
Clouds that roam
Powers to hone
Mystic might
Stars for light
Mystic powers will prevail
Evil and horrors to curtail

Magicians fight
Wrongs for right
Magic to wield
Evil to yield
Powers do grow
Wrongs soon to overthrow
Good to guard
From evils bard
The war has ended
Good was defended
Evil has lost
Before winters first frost

Warren M Rice
PREMATURELY
I think about so many things
My hair is almost gray,
But if you say I'm getting old
"Prematurely" is what I'll say.
For age is just a state of mind
I live from day to day,
And if you say I'm slowing down
"Prematurely" is what I'll say.
Don't think you have the laugh on me
I'll always shout "Hooray,"
When God comes down to take me home
"Prematurely" is what I'll say.

David Wayne Sharp
GOD'S SPECIAL GUESTS

This poem is dedicated to my family, and Clay G. Parks

From the foreign lands of Sinai
They left for home with joy in their eyes
But death over-took them before they could say "Goodbye"
Now, they're laughing and singing up in heaven, on high.

From the arms of their mothers and wives, to the arms of their savior
They entered heaven with a medal in highest of honor
No, we'll never forget the crash at Gander
And the Task-Force 3502, Kentuckians will always remember.

Many loved-ones they left behind, but someday, they'll again be seen
And oh what a happy day up in heaven that will be
Yes, there'll be more rejoicing than the Angels have ever seen
But it's just the beginning of the screaming-eagles dream.

Yes, two hundred and forty-eight of Fort Campbells's best
Are standing tall today, they are God's special guests
They are armed in robes that are made from our Savior's best
And each night around God's golden throne they peacefully rest.

So, there's no need to worry, there's no need to fret
Our soldiers went to heaven at God's request
They're guarding his Golden Throne and the Land of the Blessed
Yes, God knows our Best, the "101st are God's Special Guests" . . .

Agnes Dillard
ONE MORE DAY
God, give me one more day
There is much I want to do
Don't close the door on me yet
Let me prove myself to you.

Give me a little more time
Before you call me home
Let me finish my chores on earth
Then claim me as your own.

I have grown old through the years
And I must also fade away
God, give me one more day
Just one more day to pray.

Paul M Dossett
THE GLORY OF SPRING

To All Mankind

In March when mother nature awakens,
To an earth that looks forlorn and forsaken.
She removes the snow that's been her nightcap.
And calls her children forth from their winter's nap.

Trees are budding the grass is turning green,
Birds are singing and starting to preen.
Flowers are blooming by the babbling brook,
Enticing one and all to take another look.

Marshes are teeming with dragon flies,
As a hawk circles lazily in the sky.
Frogs croak loudly down by the creek,
No longer hiding a mate they now seek.

The hustle and bustle has now begun,
Because the earth lies fertile and warm in the sun.
Mankind once again starts tilling the fields,
Hoping for bigger and better yields.

Tis a time of joy and a time of trust,
Knowing the good earth will provide for us.
From time immemorial it's the same great story,
Spring has arrived in all her magnificent glory.

Esther Schultz
THE SCATTERING OF DEBRIE
I stood upon the mountain side and gazed down at the sea.
There was nothing left of the little ship, but scattering of debrie.

The angry waves came dashing in and beat upon the shore.
The scavangers birds upon the sand to feed upon the spoors.

The little ship fought bravely, Held on till the very last.
Than with a sigh, she lowered her head as the furious storm, tore down her mast.

The wind raged in all her fury, as I stood there, Helpless and alone,
Than the waters began to calm, and the ship gave her final moan.

It was almost like a mirage, That never came to be.
For the little ship who fought so brave,
Lies gently now beneath the sea.

Beatrice Conner
NIGHT LIGHT
Few have seen this silvery light
in a woodsy glen in the dark of night.
It is a raveled thread of Elfin cloak
or just a wisp of curling smoke?
Or a strand, perhaps, of Fairy hair
caught and held by the chill night air?
How it weaves and winds about!
It is not moonlight. The moon's not out!
Now no longer a strand
just a small round light
bobbing about—
an eerie sight.
But few will see and few will care
for this wonderful thing which is so rare.
Yet the ultimate mystery
of all that's right,
may be found in the woods
in the dark of night!

Connie Ouellette
A DISTANT HORIZON
Muted shades
Screen the morning dawn
Reaching fingers
Touch fortresses of stone
Timeworn pebbles
Lie restlessly
Buffeted, tossed
By the heavy sea
Lost seashells,
Their voices echo 'neath
Sheltering lee.

There—
A cry cuts through the blackness
Strong wings lift
A captive high,
Vantaged above
Discerning hearts glimpse
Ocean merging into sky.
Stretched across
A solemn ocean
Here it lies
Untouched by time
Unshaken by waves
Uncrossed by man
A distant Horizon.

Kenneth Wayne Davis
LOVE

To my wife Lorry and my Daughter's Kim, Kristin And my mother Barbara Davis

Even though the sun may shine in the sky.
My heart is under a dark cloud.
Which cannot be enlightened or warmed, because
of this cloud called loneliness.

My heart I feel is like the wind!
Moaning and groaning, letting out it's lonely sighs
Always moving, searching for a place to settle,
To be Loved and to Love

The spirit of Love has left my heart and
soul, with a deep empty feeling.

Why must Love leave you empty?
Why must a beautiful thing such as Love be so painful?
My heart and soul cries, my mind wonders!
WILL I EVER FIND LOVE!

Sharon E Cline
SOLDIERS' SACRIFICE
The guns will sound and
men will fall,
not an eye will blink
when few stand tall.

My heart beats fast,
but my blood runs cold;
tomorrow is just a hope
that I must hold.

My heart is empty,
my soul is meek,
as I watch friend and foe
fall at my feet.

Now it's my life or his,
as I see his eyes in the night,
God I want to serve my country,
but why must men fight?

I hear the blast, I feel the blow,
the war for me is over, I now know.

One last breathe is all I can endure,
as I say to myself, "I Will Fight No More."

Evelyn Ellman
MY FRIENDS THE FLOWERS
A lacey frond of maiden hair,
A philodendron or two,
And baby's tears, the precious dears,
And violets of midnight blue.

A chlorophytum, or mini rose,
Are sure to please a friend.
I could go on, and on, and on,
For there really is no end.

It's hard to feel bad, or even sad,
When you spy them across the room.
Every day will seem like Spring,
When you have a flower in bloom.

So try a flower, upon your shelf,
With petals pink or white.
And though there may be gloom outside,
Your world will seem more bright.

Every flower will bring you joy,
No matter which you choose.
So place a flower upon your shelf,
And chase away the blues.

Gladys McAnally Meredith
UNDERSTANDABLY

This poem is dedicated to the memory of my husband, Charles Everett Meredith, a USS Indianapolis Survivor in 1945. It was written a few years before his death December 22, 1978.

Yes he loves me
And he should.
Because of me
His life is good.

My life is good,
Understandably,
For I love him
As he loves me.

Thomas Blaney
QUANTUM-JUMP

For you;

Bound by the limits of a pulsing wave,
lines of force, in time behave.

Governed bodies moved enslaved,
by powers rising from shallow graves.

They follow the path of rise and fall,
of give and take of where with all.

By what image has made us all,
with blind-fold on and back to the wall?

Chance of change is building up.
Present danger is real enough.
Change the leaders all you want.
It's up to us to make the Quantum-Jump.

Life goes off, and life goes on,
on through darkness, toward beyond.

We carry the freight of fear and hate,
expectations running late.

The weight of the night grows against the dawn,
come to lighten the load just to carry on.

Wake up children! Can't you hear the call?
Sleeping won't save you from the fireball.

Chance of change is building up.
Present danger is real enough.
Change the leaders all you want.
It's up to us to make the Quantum-Jump.

Linda Lee Duncan

HANDS

In dedication to my mother, SallyAnn "Her children rise up and call her blessed . . ."

. . . Hands . . .
I looked at mine the other day,
and at a glance they seemed to be my mother's hands.
Her hands were soft, yet somewhat worn, from
scrubbing floors,
rinsing diapers,
washing dishes, dogs, kids and cars.
Her hands were strong as she pulled my pony tail in place
. . . and as she applied the rod of correction.
Her hands were small,
as I remember them slipped inside of Daddy's big, rugged hands.
Her hands were gentle, as she wiped our feverish heads,
and stroked our hair
Her hands were busy, always busy, never idle
Her hands were even busy as she spoke—
for which we teased her much
Perhaps my hands have become like mother's—
I hope she's proud of that.

Thomas J "Speed" Funari

OUR LITTLE TOWN

Dedicated to our little town as featured in the album Dream of Dreams by Sunrise Records Inc. Hollywood, CA.

I live in a little town with a lot of data,
The little town is in the beautiful state of Nevada.
That used to mine silver ore,
And now, there isn't anymore.

The city dads all began to cry,
Our little town is going to die.
One said, "Don't live in the past,"
We are going to build at last.

We are going to make this a gambling town,
They are going to come from all around.
They will come from near and far,
Some by plane, and some by car.
Just to play and have a lot of fun,
And take home the money they have won.
I have watched our little town grow,
And now, we have the broadway show.

The stars come from all around,
To play in our little town.
That once was said we are going to fold,
And now our sidewalks are painted with gold.

Blanche Wambold

TRY TO FORGET

Try to forget the sad old past,
The part that keeps on hurting you;
Now is the time to leave it behind
But this I know, is hard to do.

Yes, but it's so hard you may think
Forgetting it can not be done,
Yet you have been through it all
So half of the battle is won!

Things that were so hard to bear
Are things that happened in the past,
So now it is just the memories
That you are allowing to last.

Happy days are sure to come
So forget the days gone by;
It's time for you to take heart again,
So put the load down, and try.

Delores Chandler

A LITTLE WISDOM FROM ABOVE

Dedicated to the Love of the Creator of the Universe and the One He sent.

God is Love, Eternally Cares for Us
We Need to Believe Not Doubt, Distrust
In His Son We Must Place Our Hopes
Open Our Eyes, Broaden Our Scopes

Honoring Father, Mother, for Happiness, Longevity
Not Forsaking Prayer, Because It Holds a Key
Love of Neighbor, Kindness to Others
Begins at Home With Sisters, With Brothers

From Right By Our Sides Jesus Will Not Leave
So Why Be Afraid, Why Worry, Why Grieve
He's Always There For You, For Me
Allowing Our Hearts to Be Young, Free

We're Free to Dance Yes to Sing
Revel In the Warmth the Peace It'll Bring
To Keep Our Minds Void, of Hatred, or Strife
Adding Blessings, Love, Years, Life

In Times of Happiness Yes, Even Despair
He Suffers our Burdens Yes, Even Our Share
Thru All of This God Still is Love
And Even Gave Us A Little Wisdom From Above

Alice Diane Baggett

THE SENSE OF SIGHT

We who are able to see
Should stop and think of how it would be
If we did not have the sense of sight
And always walked in the darkness of night.

We wouldn't be the person we are today;
We would live our lives in a different way.
We wouldn't be able to see the colors of Spring and Fall;
We wouldn't know how things looked at all.

We would wonder what was meant by red and green
And wonder how these looked when seen.
About these things, we could question any human being,
But it still wouldn't be the same as seeing.

Diane M Hollingsworth

SOMETIMES

The children cry—because it's dark
and someone says "I'm here."
The youngsters cry—because it's dark
and someone says "There's nothing there."
The adults cry—because it's dark
and no-one answers.
Better to be a child sometimes.

Phyllis E Sakane

LISTEN TO THE WORDS

Listen to the words of a king,
Spoken in silence, he speaks of great things.
Not of smite or anger or of knowledge unknown,
But truth and compassion, only goodness be sown.
I imagined myself the king one day—
How might I feel; what would I say?
Within me beat a frantic heart
As my regular world I could not depart.
Finally with calmness the breaths eased the pace
And I found myself filling with beauty and grace.
Opening my eyes,
Within the same space,
I found a new world.
Never replaced.

Gary Dean Muir

MAN'S VIEW

The city was pure gold, as if it were transparent glass,
we know not when, only that it will come to pass,
The city's length, and width were 1500 miles square,
New Jerusalem is this place, but we know not where,
The material of the wall was of jasper,
A place where we will worship the Master,
There were twelve gates, and angels with them,
At every gate, there was a pearl and a gem,
There was a tree of life, on the street, by the river,
It was a place of quiet rest, that will last forever,
There will be no need, for a sun or moon,
For the light of Christ, will shine down soon,
The nations who are saved, shall walk in the light,
As they travel, they'll say, what a beautiful sight.

Barbara JoAnne-Wathen-Lister

THE OCEANS OF TIME

I Think of my life
as gently shifting sand.
I wonder at Eternity,
how Complex the plan.
In the tables of time
Where do I stand?
I try to relate
to where I began,
believe it or not
in Gods loving hands.
Only few things are certain,
but these are all true,
We are like beaches
Waves of time pursue.
I'm part of this sand
Washed up on this shore.
When my breath is thru,
and I've ceased my chores
I'll become part of time
and Travel once more.

Christine Wilkins Cavner

AN ODE TO SUZANNE

Little girls are like little elves
They're never still a minute,
They're here, they're there—they're everywhere
Out of your lap or in it.

Never have I been happier
Having a girl like you.
Never have you been sweeter
Than since becoming two.

Almost like flipping a brand new page
In your small book of you,
You've changed from our tiny toddler
To a wondrous being of two.

A darling creature of loveliness
Sent to us from above,
Your every movement—every thought
A true expression of love.

Suzanne, so delicate—So fair of face,
You are a special one,
Giving us joy the live long day
From morn 'til day is done.

God used his very choicest mold
When he created you,
Suzanne, you're simply wonderful.
Precious, on being two.

Mrs Peter G Kanes

SMILE YOUR TROUBLES AWAY

Troubles may come, and troubles may go.
Many a day, you are feeling so low,

But, smile your troubles away,
And sing a song as you say.
Rockets may whiz, and atoms may fiz.
Your whole world may be all a diz,
But, smile your troubles away,
And smile some more as you say.
The old world may be troubled and O! So Sad,
But, I will keep smiling and somehow be glad.
For I feel so good when I smile and sing,
That my troubles really don't mean a thing.

Doris Ericson
THE ARTIST

In loving memory of my parents, Charles and Bertha Ericson

Jack Frost paints pictures in the Fall
With Crimson glory over all,
And willows drip their shimmering gold,
While maiden ferns bronze fronds unfold.

Down paths o'erspread with carpets soft,
Their colors falling from aloft,
And cardinals with trees compete,
Crimson above, gold at my feet.

A haze across the meadow shows.
Beyond it, cornshocks stand in rows,
And in amongst them scamper here,
Some rabbits and a tawny deer.

The river even has its share
Of glory on its surface, where
Leaves float, brown-golden in the sun,
Until it sets, when day is done.
The squirrel is gathering his store
Of acorns, hazelnuts galore.
He piles them 'neath an old oak tree,
Safe hid, he hopes, from folks like me.

The changing winds a cold rain brings.
The leaves are gone as if on wings.
The branches bare once more attest,
Cold winter's hand is here at last!

Jo Alderson Goad
PIRATE

Ah, you breached unchartered waters,
transgressed my port of heart,
Stole me in the night sea mist,
took me floating in the dark.

Left me lying on the beach—
sun's salty heat to dry me blind,
Now here am I this empty shell.
You took it all,
but never mind.

What treasures have you stolen, pirate?
What riches have you gained?
What is it worth when unrequited?
Have you never mercified such pain?

You should have forced me to the plank,
off the edge to bounty's floor.
Instead, you leave me only silence . . .
tides of silence, so loud the roar.

You should have buried me at sea
wrapped in Truth's tranquility.
At least my mind would have been free.
Pirate, you're a mystery.
Come back again and ravish me.

Charles S FeBuary
MINDS EYE

This poem is dedicated to my wife, children and christian fellowship of all.

As I close my eyes and bow in prayer
in my minds eye I see
Crosses on a mountain top, they number three
Three man hang there, two thieves and
God's own Son
One on each side is guilty, the one in
the middle has harmed no one.
The crowd around call "Hail to the King Hail"
If thou be the Son of God have him
Pull out the nails
They laugh at him, throw lots for his robe
and then they pierce his side
He calls out "Oh Father Please Forgive
Them" and then he dies
In my Minds Eye these things I see
And I know that the man in the middle
just died for me.

Mitchell E Johnson
SLEEP TALK

There's a fall coming.
You look down,
here comes the ground.
Fear grabs your heart and sticks in your throat.
Your breath catches.
There's time for one last thought.
I wonder who will put a dime in the parking meter, I don't want to get a ticket.

Black, black, everything's black,
yet there's nothing,
nothing there, nothing here,
nothing anywhere.
Yes! I remember! I was falling.
Am I dead?
Where am I?
There's no sound, no light, only thought, quiet, peace.
Peace like I've never known.

Apprehension now building,
there's nowhere to run, there's
nothing, Wait, whats that? I felt
something. something moved
on my face. My eyes blink. I'm
breathing. Yes, I'm breathing.
Relief.
It must of all been a dream.

Go back to sleep.

Donna J Hoover
O! TO RETURN

This poem is dedicated to my loving parents

O! to return,
My youthfull days.
Energy to burn,
To run and play.

The teenage time,
Went by so fast.
Is hard to define,
Why they couldn't last.

Adulthood meant changes,
More ways than one.
Keep up with the rages,
Just to have fun.

Marriage and parent-hood,
Does take it's toll.
Mainly though very good,
O! at times to be a mole.

Grandkids and retirement,
Can be a joy.
Remember the sentiment,
Try to be coy.

My memories I hold dear,
In thought I yearn.
For it all seems like yesteryear,
O! to return.

Helen S Gates
OH STRIVE NOT TO CATCH THE WIND

This poem is dedicated to Dick, the free spirited Libra who inspired it. Without his love and encouragement this Capricorn might never have put pen to paper to preserve these words.

Oh strive not to catch the wind,
it will elude your grasp.
There is no catching that free spirit
as it goes about it's task.
It can be fierce and howling,
blowing raindrops on their way,
Or gentle and sweetly tender,
as it caresses you each day.
You know it still surrounds you
because clouds move across the sky.
You cannot hope to touch it,
why do you even try?

Earths' firmness can't resist it,
the thrill is just too much.
Even the lofty mountain has learned
to crumble at it's touch.
Does the wind seek such power,
or does it just happen so?
Seek not to learn the answer,
it will never let you know.
You can watch the meadow grasses
and tree branches as they bend,
But you must not try to hold it,
oh strive not to catch the wind.

Sharon J LoPresti
TIME EACH DAY

Endless is the time, like the sweeping of the tide
Empty is the feeling that consumes all of me inside
Visions of you creep into my mind,
I remember everything
Awakening feelings deep inside,
like a breath of spring
Consuming as the fire, I delight in watching in your eyes
Knowing how steadily it burn's,
amazed how it never dies
Wondering through the hours that pass in each day
About all the things that I might never get to say
Sometimes as I sit, while watching out my window near
I'm awakened from this dream like state, by a single tear
Shed only for the joy I feel because of loving you
Never for any of the misery that we have gone through
For when I look into your eyes,
everything seems to fade
Leaving behind only the good
things, together we have made
So in these lonely hours I"m kept alive by the glow
From all the happy moments only together we can know
No longer is time endless, let these moments last
So I can dwell endlessly into the warming past
Where I'm no longer empty, but full of life with you
Seal me in this time, keep this vision in my view
Untill the clock strikes the time
that together we can share
I'll remain in this dream like state
knowing that you are there

Daniel Metz
INSIDE MY DOOR

To Amy, Thanks for your Inspiration and Encouragement

Outside my door, night after night,
I had watched for you, to come
into my life,
now my hopes and dreams, are
real today,
for I've found you and your
loving ways!

Outside my door, the stars do shine,
on all the plans, that will be
yours and mine,
plans of a love, that will be so true,
always and forever, for only
we two!

Outside my door, the wind does blow,
on the trees and flowers and on
all that grows,
the gentle breeze draws us near,
with wanting us to grow, with
this love so dear!

But outside my door, it is just the start,
for if you open it up, you'll find
my heart,
so walk on inside and become a
part,
make yourself a home, within
my heart!

For within my heart, I will shelter you,

from all the things, that may
trouble you,
and I will show you love, like
no
one before,
from within my heart, inside
my door!

And inside my door, you can
always stay,
as we share forever, what we
may,
for our love, has a chance to
be,
since you've opened the
door,
that's led you to me!

Ethel Lucille Ross
PEACE ON EARTH
How can I ask for Peace on Earth?
Unless I establish Peace in me first?
How can I ask our Creator to give
That which I'm loath to do,
The love and kindness, I pray of
him,
I must hold in my heart for you.

I can't ask Him for all these gifts
Unless I'm willing to share
Of all my Worldly and Spiritual
goods
With a fellow man in despair.

If I put gold above all else,
Have thought for none other then
myself,
And cause my heart to grow so cold
That I have no time for another's
woe,
How can I ask, with conscience
clear
That, which we all hold dear?

How can I ask for Peace on Earth
Unless I've found Peace in my own
heart first?

Violet A Price
THE AUTUMN YEARS
The time has come, we're old and
gray
Our youth has gone away.
How sad, so soon the years have
past.
The sun is down and shadows cast,
O'er land and sea and over me.
Now glasses are upon my nose
Along my brow the wrinkle shows.
Alas, I've even lost my hair.
Our teeth fall out, but we don't care

For we elders all have earned,
Love, peace and honor as
calendars turned.
Don't let age let you down
Try to smile and not frown.
We stand fogether hand in hand
To bring our youth a better land.
Life itself is pure as gold
With precious moments to behold.

Ruth G Ray
WHEN I THINK ABOUT THE MANGER
When I think about the manger
Where the Holy Child was born
I'm reminded of the homeless,
The weary and forlorn.

I wonder what they think of
When they have no place to go
When friends are few and far
between
And there is no open door.
Do they just make a manger—
Some place to pass the night—
And trust that they will find a star
To lend a little light?

And what about the gifts we give—
The one's we least prefer—
Do they represent our gifts of gold,
And frankincense and myrrh?

I wonder, if we truly seek
To sincerely serve mankind,
If in the process we will meet
The Holy Child, Divine.

Le Roy F Oates
MY MOUNTAIN HOME
Orion is rising 12 O'clock high,
And a coyote is yelping close by;
The stars are shining ever so bright
On a cold mountain wintery night.
Far away I saw a shooting star,
I saw it go, yet never very far;
It went very fast, it was Hell bent,
So I don't know where the Hell it
went.
I saw it shooting across the sky,
I saw it fall, and I saw it die.
On a shooting star You make a
wish,
So I wished to catch the biggest
fish.
Up here on the very mountain top,
Everything halts, everything must
stop;
Everything is quiet, everything is
still,
Peaceful and quiet up here on the
hill.
The balmy breeze whispers
through the pine,
And the squirrels on the pine nuts
dine;
Jays are squacking here in the
forest,
And all the birds join in the
chorous.
They sing a song of love, a song of
cheer,
For it's so peaceful this time of
year;
From here I'll never stray, never
roam
From My Idllywild mountain
Home

Lucy Lee Sinkler
I LOVE YOU

To Charles Griffin with love.

Love is something often read about
in books.
Love is often without handsome
looks.
Love is something often unspoken
to a lover.
Love is often made without sheets
or a cover.
Love is something we make with
one another.
Love is something we have for each
other.
Why is I LOVE YOU something we
don't say often to one another.
I love you can sometimes make
wrong alright.
I love you if unspoken can fade
from life.

Clara Kolb
FRIENDSHIP
I love to wander down Memory's
Lane
And recall the days of long ago,
Those childhood days which knew
little pain
And the cherished friends we
used to know.

Years ago when we were quite
young,
We met as children and had lots
of fun.
But we all grew up as children
should,
Doing the very best we could.

Then Fate took a hand, moving
some away
While others felt they had to stay.
As the years marched on we drifted
apart,
But our friendship was anchored
in the heart.

May this childhood friendship we
hold so dear
Be a bond between us of
yesteryear,
And lead us through the years to
come
Until we are all called home.

Todd Robert Birkenholz
ALL ABOUT DINOSAURS

Dedicated to Ms. Riley my teacher with love from Todd

When dinosaurs lived a long time
ago,
No human was there to see where
they would go.
So no one would ever know,
They may have even put on a show,
Way back long ago.
Some walked fast and some
walked slow,
Way back long ago.

Some dinosaurs were as big as a
house,
And others were as small as a
mouse.
Planteaters were herbivorous,
Meateaters were carnivorous.
Some were fat and many were thin,
And they had different kinds of
skin.
Some dinosaur skin was smooth,
but most of it was rough,
And I bet most dinosaurs were very
tough.

Sherry E Chase
THE TURNING POINT

Dedicated to Sam Stone . . .

Memories of life, and a love, once
existing so many years ago;
Destroyed and forgotten, in a life
bent on self destruction.
So many chances, so many failures.
So much fear, so many dark alleys.
So much pride, so much denial.
Misery Untold . . .

Soft rain barely audible; music in
the distance
Slowly being flooded with inner
peace and tranquility
New sprouts of life appearing,
bringing confusion, forcing
decisions.
Reality always a question, being
"artful dodgers" as we are.

Forever longing for Serenity,
grasping for some Courage,
Struggling to Accept, finally
handing it over . . .
Quality returning the sparkle to
our eyes
Them meeting others' now, no
longer evading.
It was ever so long ago . . .

So intense are emotions, so
different from our listless norm
Direction turning 180°; Strength
becoming our Addiction

Falling in love with life and You;
becoming so involved in it all
Learning to take all the risks and
not be afraid anymore
So much to learn and remember
In a new life; bent on self
preservation . . .

Ms P J Jennings

Ms P J Jennings
HOME AT LAST

To Bill Nilan, My life . . . my love . . . and my deepest inspiration!

The twilight stars grew sleepy and
in
slumber twinkled down as
dawn found sun come creeping
to
light the morning's yawn.

A sea of blueness looked at me and
droplets cried the shore.
In the arms of my nestled morning,
I wiped His tears once more.

Proud sails carried me along to
conquer
my sea of dreams, where he

has chartered my happiness with the
gent'lest of winds, it seems.

Lost shadows, in the midst of a mem'ry . . .
Now frozen yesterdays . . . So frozen in me are
my winters alone!
The tears of my eternal Spring have warmed my winters, at their best
and
His arms are my outstretched horizons where
I've laid my heart to rest!

Bernice C Crimmins
MY VOLUNTEER
Thank you for the gift of caring
Thank you for the gift of sharing
For the gift to do your will
Through my talent and my skill
The gift you give to me
Is what I do with that gift, to you
May the joy I feel today
Brighten yet another day
I walked away my head held high
I've shared my gifts with humble pride
If kind thoughts bring on a tear
I feel your presence very near
And I think I softly hear
A whisper saying very clear
A job well done "My Volunteer."

Louis D Izzo
ONLY "GOD" KNOWS

To my dearest grand children
Danny—Marie and Roseann

As the waters of an ocean, a river, or a stream run to no end,
Also the soil of the earth and the desert sands, it does not move or bend,
Then there is the wind, that blows a cool breeze, moving the clouds away,
And life with its beginning, that must come to an end, someday.

Now, education is a means of teaching, with no end to learning,
Which later in life will determine, one's professional gains and earnings,
Like brightness of the sun, made possible only by the hand of "God,"
Also in the evening, shining stars twinkle about the moon, up in the sky so high.

Time,—will stop for no one as it just keeps going on,
Like worrying does no good, but only upsets your nerves and mind,
Loving someone, can be meant in o' so many different ways,
Like that of parents, a wife or husband and a child at play.

If there are any answers then the good Lord must know,
For he started it all, so many years ago,
But for now, it is a mystery of "God," nature and time,
And for us to continue keeping faith and love, in our heart and mind.

Anne Maureen Cummings
FOR KEVIN
I remember the days when we first met
The fluttering heart I'll never forget—
You brought me out and spread my wings
Opened my soul to brighter things . . .
Walks on the beach, hand in hand
I still have the shell you picked from the sand.

Years have passed and we have grown
Flowers have blossomed from seeds we have sown.
I've given to you my very best
And you've seen my worst, I confess!
But day by day, I love you more
I always felt it would be for sure.

There's something about you so sincere
Something I hold so very dear
I know you love me as I am
And I give to you, my lovely man,
All of my self, my dreams, my life
I am so proud to be your wife.

James Sehrt
BEAUTY IN THE WOODS
Down in the woods;
where the waters run . . .
Deer and rabbits nourish in the sun . . .
Peace and beauty,
as far as you see;
In my mind, forever it shall be.

Scotty Mitchell
THE VICTOR'S SONG
In our fall
We tried all;
From cannons to guns,
Anything to shun
The enemy from our turf.

And though our fort wasn't strong,
We fought the battle, hard and long.

They wouldn't give up,
But neither would we.
We should have known better,
And let them be.

For in this time of suffering and pain,
We ended this battle the loser again.

The enemy departed to his homeland
In a loud and joyous throng;
All singing loud in unison,
The Victor's Song:

Goldie Kirkpatrick Fuller
MOTHER
God formed her and blessed her
with His gentle touch,
And gave her to parents
Who loved her so much.

Her life was not easy
She worked with her hands,
Cooking, housekeeping,
Even tilling the land.

Mom lived by her faith
In Joshua 1:9
It stood in her stead
All down through time.

God helped her through sorrow
He looked down from above.
She trusted her Savior,
Secure in His love.

Now her heartaches have ended,
Physical suffering has passed.
She's gone to her mansion
With Jesus at last.

Her rest—she has earned it,
Her joy is complete,
My plans are to meet her
Someday at His feet.

Barbara Schneider
SUCH A FRIEND
You sit there almost all the time
in that one certain place,
you hardly change position
and you barely take up space.
Your face is always smiling
and your eyes so full of glee
and sometimes I could swear I saw
you turn and wink at me.
You always try to cheer me up
and try to be my friend
and never saying anything
you listen till the end.
I've held you lots and lots of times
when I seem to feel down,
but I never ever saw your face
wear a single frown.
We have this secret friendship
and there's certain things we share . . .
but it seems a little bit silly
cause you're just a big stuffed bear!

Gonzalo M Soto

Gonzalo M Soto
SILENCE BLUE . . .
It is so sad when you live on but the heart dies
After so much pain for a love that was only lies
The eyes cry tears, but the heart weeps in silence blue
I know, for it happened to me, and it will happen to you . . .

The spirit flies and you feel alone like an empty shell
You try to smile, but you are hurting and your friends can tell
Every deep breath you take is just a painful sigh
And then you remember and again you begin to cry . . .

There is always hope you will get together again
There is always the promise that somedays it will rain
But it is best to find another rainbow outside your door
So you can forget, forgive, and believe in love
. . . once more . . .

Mary E Gentry
CHILDHOOD PETS
Alluringly sleek

Curious or aloof
A soft ball of fur or talons

To some—the PURRfect companion!

and

Alert always to friend or foe

Diligent to duty or repose
Only to heed a master's voice
Good friend and companion by choice!

Lou W Barnhouse
AND THE YOUNG DREAM DIES
Past dreams fade away as I learn what I know;
The older I get and the further I go
I finally realize.

How foolish are the sweet dreams of youth,
How elusive is the quest for truth;
And the young dream dies.

The worries and cares, they pull me down;
Less often the smile, more often the frown
Less often the happy sighs.

The anger and fear, the hurt and the pain;
Less often the sunshine, more often the rain;
And the young dream dies.

Oh, where does the time go, where have I been?
Where am I now, where will it all end?
There have been so many goodbyes.

Today is my future, today is my past;
Just give me today, no more shall I ask;
And the young dream dies.

Michelle Elaine Jordan
PEACE
When I found peace,
I was sitting near a tree.
I didn't find it outside,
But inside of me.

Peace is not something you get;
Peace is something you receive.
Peace will always be here;
Peace will never leave.

Peace is something beautiful;
Something that can be acheived.
Peace is something loved,
Once it is received.

Peace is always here with me;
Peace can never leave.
Peace is something given,
But first you must believe!

Ruth E Barker
HERE COMES THAT SONG AGAIN
Here comes that song again,
Jesus died to save from sin.
I must sing it again and again,
As long as one person is still in sin.
Jesus calls us, Come and see
I will pardon and set you free.
He wants every man, woman, girl and boy
To know this pardon, feel his joy.
Then you can help me sing again.

Jesus died to save from sin.
Praise His name
I'm saved, are you?

Louise Ann Flannery

THE NOSE

Here I sit trying to write
And soon discover to my fright,
Behind my back, someone is creeping,
To see my private thoughts and weeping.

Nothing is sacred to the nose,
She roots and rumages to expose;
Each and every private thing.
Here to my inside thoughts I cling.

She'll never know what makes me tick,
Although she thinks she's very slick.
I don't write down everything I feel,
The thoughts of my soul she can not steal.

Perhaps there is only one sure cure,
To let her know this is immature.
I hope she reads what I now write,
And thus resolve my little plight.

Katherine Bowes

TIME TO GO NOW

Mom—Thanks for believing in me.

Walks through a silent gloom
Glares by the moon
Hitting ends that die before they're reached
No place new to touch my feet

Monotonous steps that deaden the ear
Laughter that only hides fear
Pulling away but snapping back
Caught up—like a mouse in a trap

Knowing of feelings I can't describe
Things maybe seen by unseeing eyes
Hitting ends that die before they're reached
No place new to touch my feet

Eyes holding dreams that can't be foretold
Living a life that's already sold
Searching for answers that you can't be givin'
Now that it's time to start my own livin'

Walking—not running away from it all
Trying to break through that hovering wall
Hitting ends that die before they're reached
Needing some place new to touch my feet

Holly S Sorensen

THE FINAL RESTING PLACE

I get in line
To follow once again
That long black car
As it carries another loved one
To his final resting place
The drive is long
With lots of time to think
To recall again
What he was like
Things we did together
Happenings only he and I
Would recall
Finally we wind our way in
To the side of the grave
The pall bearers carry him
With pain in their eyes
And set jaws
They set him in his resting place
The last words are said
Then we turn away
To take up the task of living
Without his lopsided grin

John E Salerno

WHEN COMMENCEMENT BEGINS

Dedicated to the Henry Ford II High Graduating class 1986

Precious moments,
Precious words,
Each and every day.
Tears fall,
Hearts stall,
We say 'goodbye'.

The end to a new beginning
Why does it have to start?
All the love and comfort
Lost in sweet remorse.

A new challenge before us;
An old one not far behind.
Pushing to that final step,
Are we ready to try?

We wait in line
Those before us cry.
Here,
When Commencement begins.

Daisy Seale Moore

A CHILD'S FAITH

This poem is dedicated to Paul, my friend.

The faith I knew when but a child
Is with me yet today.
I may have faltered for awhile
For doubt got in the way.

But now I know I believe in God,
Regardless . . . come what may.
And the faith that sustained me through the years
Keeps me yet today.

Holly Lu Jostes

DREAM TEARS

For Mom and Dad, I love my new home, and I love you both so very much.

Where do dream tears slowly go
When people have to let them flow

No longer cherished, do they die
Finally mixing with the sky
Becoming stars to wish upon
Glowing bright, but magic gone

Do they hide to someday greet
One in a song that's bittersweet

Or do they truly find a place
In crystal tears upon a face

Where do dream tears slowly flow
When people have to let them go

Donna Reigle

WILL MY CHILDREN CALL ME MOTHER

Will my children call me Mother
When my hair has turned to gray?
Will they love me as no other
Will they love me as today?
Will they bring to me their problems
They encounter through the years?
Will my words be any comfort
To their minds in time of fear?
Will they want me near in sorrow?
Will they want me near in joy?
Will I be someone so precious
Or just like a a worn out toy?
When Mother's Day rolls 'round each year
Will they all come home again?
To show they've not forgotten me
My life was not in vain?
As these questions go unanswered
Only time alone can say
Will my children call me Mother
When my hair has turned to gray?

Inez Edwards Ray

TWO PAIRS OF SHOES

To my husband

Two pairs of shoes stood side by side
On the closet floor so dark and wide;
Two pairs of shoes all bright and new—
One pair for me and one pair for you
To walk in!

Two pairs of shoes went to foreign lands
To guide you and me o'er sunny sands.
Two pairs of shoes grew bruised and torn,
Scuffed and run-down, old and worn
From walking!

But one day I had to roam alone;
I drifted back to our own hearthstone.
Two pairs of shoes stand side by side
On the closet floor so dark and wide—
For MEMORIES!

Flo Baker

LIFE TOGETHER

Together you share the richest blessing of all
"Life itself"
May you enjoy it as you go along the way.
Sharing and caring as beauty unfolds
in your arms your husband you hold
May your happiness be your guiding light and
may joy be forever yours, as it is this night.
May your wedding day be forever happy as it
moves into months and years
and always be laughter instead of fears.
May your every wish and dream come true
for this I wrote especially for you.
God Bless you and yours.

Mary E Chambers

CHILDREN

Come on grow up; you're no baby!
your plenty old enough, not maybe.

Give Ma and Pa a rest:
They surely deserve the best.

Ma and Pa needs your rewards,
so start cutting off the navel cords.

Did you know they love ya lots?
Now you got their stomach in knots.

Ma and Pa worked hard paying bills.
Now you all got them taking pills.
They've given you so many provisions.
Don't even forget them on occasions.

Loving them should be your desire.
Let their hearts again catch fire.

They need alone again with each other.
Be good to your father, and mother.

Joyce Shellaby Sterling

TO JANET

I sit here wondering
how to explain
The feeling of gladness
coupled with pain.

The gratitude of having
your friendship at last,
The sorrow of having wasted
years of the past

never understanding
Of never realizing that
you also had fears
That you and I both
had felt anger, shed tears

in regret of our childhood.

I want you to remember
today-and tomorrow
If ever it's possible
for me to change sorrow

To lighten your burden
to brighten your day,
Call me-ask me
I'll try, anyway
To make life a little easier.

Pauline Stratton

THE COUNTRY ROAD

I walked along a country road
The sights were fair to see.
The butterfly flew right by
So did the bumble bee.

A gentle breeze blew thru the trees
Birds were singing sweet and low.
Ne'er a cloud was in the sky
The sand was warm beneath my toe.

The goldenrod and milkweed
Swayed gently in the breeze.
The sun was shining brightly
So radiant were the trees.

The hazel nuts in clusters hung
Upon the bush so brown.
And when the wind came rushing by
They all came tumbling down.

The little squirrel ran real fast
Then scampered up a tree.
Tis a beautiful sight this country road
To be enjoyed by you and me.

Lowell Mitchell
THE SURGEON'S HANDS

To the Doctors Engh, Anderson Clinic, Arlington, Virginia, and to all such consecrated surgeons.

They hold no life except their own;
thus are we anxious to have them work.
They are used for purposes common to you and I;
thus do they partake of the human need
They have a sensitivity imperative to body probes;
thus do they explore with a knowing touch.
They are mortal and they are fallible;
thus can both life or death stay their movement.
They bring forth harmony with silent dexterity;
thus are they soundless like those of a musician.
They align, build, rebuild, remove, repair, and restore;
thus are they skilled like those of a craftsman.
They reach outward to feel, to touch, to judge, to help;
thus are they eager like those of a child.
They join in faith those of the patient;
thus are they exchanged to perform wonders for both.
They are human instruments dedicated to life;
thus are we cared for, thus are we healed.

John J Lalley

John J Lalley
FLUTTERBYS

To Lynn, my inspiration.

If butterflies could utter lies,
Like humans when they criticize,
They'd stutter to utter and really try;
But see no point and flutter by.

Linda D Morris
CAN YOU HEAR ME?
Daddy can you hear me
When I talk to you today?
I lay under this cold, dark stone
Where mommy kneels to pray.

I know that I am with you
And know what is new
But I just don't understand
Why my years were so few.

I had hoped that I would be
A man as great as you
And I wish that I could learn
All the things that you knew.

Daddy can you hear me?
In heaven I must be
You know I had to leave you
So this country could be free.

Daddy can you hear me?
I'm sorry I had to die
Daddy, please don't
Please, don't cry.

Thelma Shuman
HOW ABOUT THAT?
We're born naked—wet—already in debt,
Bawlin'—untied—can't even stand,
We love—fight—work day and night,
Lookin' back—Hey wasn't it Grand?

Tonya D Swan
WE ARE ONE
As we now walk as one
Down the road of life,
May we always share happiness
As husband and wife.

Many a dream
Will come and go,
Times of fantasy
Will go untold.

Look to the future
Not what's gone by,
For we are made of love
Never, ever to be denied.

Donald D Miller
DONNA

For Donna Marie, so she will always know, Daddy loves his Funny Bunny.

Little girls dressed in satin and lace are not rare,
but the beauty of You, no other could share.
You're my Little Princess, my China Doll,
so high on energy, yet so very small.
A smile that could make the darkest day bright,
You have a way of ending my day just right.
That special little kiss and hug just before bed,
the habit You have of slightly cocking your head.
The center of attraction, laughter that fills the air,
that little giggle, loved so much, always there.
I'm always wanting to hold You so tight,
to let You know Daddy's there, everything's alright.
I hope You will always want to hold my hand,
and want to ask me of things You don't understand.
Yes, you're my Precious Jewel, this is so very true,
I thank God, and your Mommy, for a Daughter such as You.

Linda Gail Tinney Cowan
LESSONS FROM OUR UNBORN CHILD
Already, I learn from you.
You teach me.
Yesterday was a difficult day at work.
It tried my patience and my emotions.
Then . . . in the midst of my frustrations . . . I felt you.
You gently nudged me from deep within my womb
And I was reminded of the life within.
You put me back in touch with the very essence of life.
The events occurring around me suddenly seemed unimportant.
The confusion and turmoil paled in significance
To the mystery of new life being formed.
In that moment, I felt my soul stilled by an inner contentment.
From that moment, I learned and I grew.
Thank you . . . for the lessons I am discovering through you.

Holly Butchyk-Trabulsy
STILL NIGHT
Many a night, I lie awake;
Softly breathing, so near to me—
Deeply sleeping, he rests peacefully . . .

With the innocence of a child,
And wisdom of a man.
Stir not, sweet prince: Placidity—
Hidden deep within the dream:
Idealistic unity.

A gentle sigh, if in response,
As I extend my hand to thee—
But cease before his face I touch,
Disturbing not: Placidity.

Repose my weary head to rest,
A single tear descends.
Consumed by vague obscurity;
United we: Placidity.

W B Fisk
THE ULTIMATE PASSING

In honor of my Dad, A. C. Fisk Sr.

I have seen,
And I was there

An un-explainable thing
Is death, so untimely

We see, and we care,
But are helpless to prevent

The un-stoppable event
That hurts us all

There is pain emense
To respond you cannot

They know you are there,
Caring, and watching, its trying

Hurting like you,
In a much different way

But to speak, you cannot
Its past that stage

You care, but you can't
Say what you feel

The time is near,
You must say good-bye

To those who you love,
That love you the same.

Rachel-Jo Huggard
TO CLAIRE FROM THE OTHER SIDE
She walked.
As a leaf falls.
She walked in.
Her movements,
her sensuality and look
mesmerized and astounded me.
She walked in and I lost myself, I was scared
of not finding my control; yet her feline habits
enchanted me, her eyes glittered and sang to me;
she is so real so glowing and so young, yet she is
so knowing; she breathes spring whenever she is around.
She makes me happy, she listens to me.
I am lost.
I love her.

Dorothy Louise Soverns
GROWING PAINS
A box of toys
An empty room
Idle chatter
No more clutter
A stilled rocker
A quiet tear or two
A time for bliss
Or thoughts amiss
A time for decision
A time for rediscovery
A time for a new
Beginning

Kenneth Robert Sandberg
FULFILLMENT
Some wish for eternal youth,
To this I answer no;
Youth, like the sunrise, is beautiful,
But age has the sunset's glow.

Rodney Lemery

Rodney Lemery
THE BIBLE
Your Holy Word spoken right from Your tongue;
My Lord and God may your goodness be sung:

The Bible's Your masterpiece our guiding light;
It should be our handbook to guard us at night:

The Bible's there each and every day;
And if you don't have one you could at least pray:

The Bible's important to our daily lives;
And maybe could help you and your wives:

One or two husbands could really be helped;
Or maybe your marriage would

surely be blessed:

The Bible's a message and it won't throw a fit;
Let it work for you and you work for it:

Ronald B Holmes-Bey
A SPLENDID ROSE
A splendid rose stood all alone,
surrounded by a wall of stone.
Around the wall were roses too,
still neither knew the others grew.

So often we . . . like flowers dwell—
too deep within our human shell,
and pass through life . . . not understood—
not making all the friends we should,
not comprehending all we see—
so we decide to let it be.

Yet true friends,
understand each others thoughts
even before they are spoken.

Nedra G Goldhoff
THE PORTRAIT
There will never be a portrait of your face.
The noble image is lost, but I feel no disgrace.
I remember clearly your demeanor quite jaded.
All at once those lines of character began to fade.
As for your impressive style and streak of boldness,
I have decided they were simply designs of coldness.

In the mind of this artist, let one truth be told.
It's not a pretty picture, nor one to be sold.
I invision worn down pencils with erasers split apart,
A trash can filled with paper and a rip in my heart.
The portrait in time would crumple and yellow,
Leaving me to muse about a wrinkled fellow.

There will never be a portrait of your face.
I now know other "Beau Ideals" to take your place.

Lyle Craig Sanders
INTERNAL CAPTIVE

To my mother and family members who I have disappointed so many times in the past; for all the Internal Captives in prison.

The Free world
The stone wall of which I am encaged
Chicken feed fence wire
"they say to keep the birds out"
Bars . . .
Windows
The railing
Fence again
Bars again
And me
Still not so secure!

Donna C Leatz
DREAMS OF VISION
little jewels that float on the images of dreams—
sparkling as bright as the sun
only wanting to come true—
understanding what happiness means.
like a teardrop, single
yet so true—
riding on a free ocean,
a supportive bed of blue.
rolling away with the tide
and never setting free
the meaning that it dreamt of
in hopes that others
will see.

Jerum Melchizedek
UNTITLED
I woke up this morning
looked out at the sky
I saw a man's image
with a tear in his eye
I asked him his name
and what troubled his day
He said, "SON OF MAN"
and faded away

Joan Bolsinger
THE ANONYMITY OF CROWDS
I move along the crowded aisles
Into the marketplace
And watching from behind my wall
I see each curtained face
As tho' it hid behind a veil
More tangible than air,
I wonder who the being is
Who hides so shyly there?
What moves them to this place in time
Why do they linger here?
What joys and sorrows left behind?
What laughter and what tears?

We all join in the lonely dance
And learn the careful steps.
At weaving swiftly in and out
We all become adept.
We sample this and gaze at that
And linger here and there.
But seldom do we touch a hand
Or give a gentle smile
Or let each other see the pain
Kept hidden all the while
For which of us can take the chance
To give away the key
Which opens up the secret door
Of lonely anonymity?

Elsie Habegger
THE OLD MILK TRUCK
Flipper, Flipper, if you could only talk
Wonder what you would say?
Tell of the many years past,
Families you have met, places you have been,
Tell how things have changed today.
You often take the boss to work,
Although the people stare
Wondering what you're doing on the road
They don't know, to one, you're worth your weight in gold.

You may have had your troubles
Your engine still is good
Your floor board got in really bad shape
It's a wonder Terry didn't fall through.
Your radiator would get hot, you blew your top
This didn't worry Terry, he said "poor old Flipper,
I can't get rid of you, I cannot give you up,
You are almost a Saint."
So he gave you a new coat of paint
He'll drive you until you stop
And go to that big junk-yard in the sky
With a tear in his eye, he'll say "Goodbye."
What's that? I'm sure I heard Old Flipper sigh.

Margaret Cole Harry
MEMORIES
Memories, Memories, how dear you are to me
To the many, many children whose faces I still see
I want to thank you for making my life worth living
By the smiles and happiness of your giving.

Your pictures I treasure and keep
And many time I want to weep
Not for sadness, but for gladness
Of many times spent together
In all kinds of weather.

You are an important one
So make the most of work and fun
And grow up to be fine and strong
And always remember right from wrong.

To your family be true
Because you are you.

Memories, Memories, how dear you are to me.

Cynthia Anne Musser
A DREAMER'S LIFE
Reality or fantasy . . .
Where am I?
Where have I been?
Wandering somewhere between them.
Time is slipping by.
Not wanting to wake from the dream,
I hesitate to take control.
And so, I leave it up to you.
Touch me and I will respond.

Elizabeth Schell/Hindman
THE CYCLE

To all my love ones. Who helped this "reborn" relearn, grow, and reach out for happiness.

Who was this child?
growing, asking, grasping
the cycle of life was turning . . .
Time—She couldn't yield

green eyes looking deep
tricycles to bicycles
blue jeans to ruffly dresses

She knew it wouldn't keep
Blush, flush, first time thrills of carresses

Time, She could now yield
for in the cycle of life, but one yearning
He, laying in the field
But, Time would not wait

Who is this child?

Susan Kay Tucker
ONLY A SECOND
Sitting all alone
Wondering if anyone cares
Waiting for someone to share
One happy moment of theirs

Someone walked by
Didn't have a thing to say
Going their own special way
To share some fun with someone else today

Now, I'm all alone again
Looking around to see no one at all
All I see is the white of the wall
And an empty long hall

A tear fell down my cheek
Feeling so lonely inside me
My elbows resting on my knees
Sitting alone for no one to see

Will anyone ever come
Will I be alone forever
Not to feel a happiness ever
To be lonely till the end of never

Will someone please care for me
Anyone who will look and see
That I need love as everyone does

Please share a happy moment with me
It only takes a second
To make my tears dry up
Only a second . . .

James Peter Battista
SEASONS OF CHANGE
The snows have fallen o'er the fields,
As darkness brings a brilliant night;
The moon bedecked in full array
Glows silently, serene and bright.
The cold is chilling evidence
Of WINTER'S growing dominance.

The sun begins to gain in strength,
As snows and ice commence to melt;
New flower buds peek through the soil,
And now the promise of SPRING is felt.
The birds return from southern flight,
To bid farewell to Winter's bite.

The heat grows more and more intense,
The grass grows thick and rich and green;
The days grow longer with each dusk.
And SUMMER'S setting sun is seen.
The mood is one of relaxation,
No hint of strife or tribulation.

But all good things come to an end,
For soon the AUTUMN frost appears;
And mother nature has her way,
As she has done throughout the years.
Then we reflect upon the reasons,
For seasons of change, and changing seasons.

Jane Neri
JENNIFER
It's been a year ago today
Since we held you in our arms.
And kissed your cheeks in sweet caress
Because of no more time

The memories of your five short months
Dwell within our hearts,
And visions of your angelic face
No one can erase.
There's times I long to hold you so
And never let you go,
But God's plan was the ultimate
Why, I don't yet know.
I see you in your snowsuit cuddled up
So warm and tight—And then how you
Smiled at me to say, Hey this is nice!
I remember how I nursed you and held
You in the night
And how you first sat in your chair
So big and proud and bright
Your big blue eyes were radiant
They said so much for you—a little bit of
Heaven sent from God, to me, to you.
Your in God's home and safe and warm
And happy in your soul
And that's the best that we could want
For our Daughter, five months old.

Wendy McGlynn
MY UNUSUAL FRIEND

To my Mom and Dad, You believed in me when I didn't believe in myself.

In a corner he sits, not making a sound,
Quietly hoping that he is not forgotten, but found.
He is always there when I need him or when I'm in pain,
When my heart has been broken or my emotions drained.
With patience he listens and becomes damp from my tears
And his lumpy little body takes away all my fears.
His soft brown fur now stiff and matted,
Definitely shows how much he is loved and patted.
He tells not a soul what he knows about me,
But keeps it all hidden behind eyes that can't see.
I consider him truly my best friend,
For when others desert me he's there in the end.
He knows all of my wishes, desires, and dreams,
And he cheers me on with his silent screams.
Then if they fail, or if they come true,
I know he'll be there to help me through.
My life would be lost without him to share
Tiny daily events when others don't care.
So you ask yourself, "Who can this friend be?"
Well, some people may have one, two, or three.
But as for myself just this one will do,
Oh Teddy Bear dear, I love you!

Martha F Sampson
ERIN—A PORTRAIT

Standing in the doorway
Tilted head wrapped in too much hair
Excessively coifed
Her eyes hold steady
Thumbs hooked on pocket hems
She wore the uniform of her rank
Blue jeans
Oversized black zippered jacket
Painted shirt . . . and eyelids
Tennis shoes, red bordered, untied
Her name describes her beauty's source
She'd have you think her street-wise
But artless unpretention glimmers through
The calculated cover
Archetype of her time

Shirley Hillmon
I WRITE THE WORDS

I want to write the words
That everyone wants to read,
Words that will change the hearts and minds of some
Words that will be here long after I am gone
Words can make you, say something good sometimes
Then can break you, so watch how you used them
But they are the stuff great writers and poets are
Supposed to be made of.
Maybe I'll plant a tree,
But inscribed in that tree will be!
"She wrote the words."
That may be one somebody loved
Whether good or bad
She wrote the words.

Deborah Joann Sanders
DEBBIE'S SWEET AND SOUR STEW

I dedicate this poem to the Spirit of truth who can teach us all how to replace an old recipe with a tasty one through faith and love.

Combine a feeling of cheer with a slice of sadness,
To tell the world its truly wonderful to be blessed.
Braise the heart on both sides from all wickedness,
Mince the madness which aggravates my happiness.

Chop up the politics and the wars into real small dice,
Grate the greed, hate, jealousy, pain and prejudice.
Mix in some tragedy and let life come to a boil,
Don't coddle the mind with anguish, strife and turmoil.

Add a pinch of joy, love, patience and peace,
Stir in valuable lessons to remember the ease.
Add some hope to compliment the sour taste,
Let the stew simmer on a warm flame of grace.

Cover the stew with constant prayer and faith,
Add more love each day if the stew becomes too dry.
Continue cooking the stew for a lifetime;
Always garnish this stew with the truth.

Transfer the stew to a warmed heart;
Serve immediately with love from God.

Kathleen Ann Bala

Kathleen Ann Bala
HAPPY ANNIVERSARY

To Mom & Dad for their inspiration thankyou for everything

The two most important people in my life
My mother's husband and my father's wife
Today is the day you said your vows,
And promised to love, and always be pals
Hand in hand you share the night
Arm in arm you hold on tight
For years the two of you have spent
Helping me grow with love and concent
For the two of you whom I love so
Wishing you a "Happy Anniversary"
With years to go

Melana R Hyatt
DANCING DEW

Behold, the dancing dew—
Her tall and slender partner,
the rich, green grass,
Holds her high, poised.
She pauses, letting the sun
sparkle and shimmer her body.
Allowing it to become a part
of her performance.
This ballerina knows no
boundaries on dance floors.
Twirling and kicking
thru the air she soars.
Until her teacher,
Powerful and warm,
Dismisses her behind the
curtain
of day.

Marjorie Reilly
TO MOTHER

A name to conjure memories, of happy "By-gone" years
Memories which fill our hearts, with joy and wistful tears.
A name imprinted on our hearts, never to lose its "Glow"
A shining memory "Ever-there," of one we all loved so.
We all of us "Share" memories, and each have our "special ones" too,
Of loving things she did "Alone," for me, and yea, for you
It doesn't need a "Special" day, a special time of the year.
To bring to life a memory, of "Her" we hold so dear,
But when you get this little card, memories will "Brightly-glow"
And the love alive, within our hearts, Mother must surely know.

Su Chelius
THE HURTING

the frost
glistens in the sun,
then slowly it melts
changing with the seasons.
feelings are warmer and stronger
everything lingers
waiting for summer to happen again
suddenly the frost returns
and covers all that was beautiful
—all that was love.

Mitch Walker
BEAUTY

Have you e'er walked into a forest
When Autumn is in the air
And feast your eyes on the leaves;
The colors painted there?

You cannot describe the diff'rent colors.
There is no use in trying.
Their colors are so beautiful.
It's hard to believe they're dying.

Their colors are so magnificent
They will tend to take your breath.
God created beauty e'rywhere,
Sometimes even in death.

Melynda Jensen
THE GARDEN HAS A DOOR

To my best friend Jesus, who is my risen Lord and Saviour

There once was a garden,
That appeared to have no door.
Though I knew that beauty lay inside,
There must be something more.

I went in search to find the key.
I looked all round,
But knew the key could not be found,
By someone soiled,
—like me.

I went to find the only one.
The unadulterated Son.
To clean me from the things within,
That kept me from entering in.

And now the door is open wide.
I now see the beauty inside,
That few people will ever see,
Except those who take the time to seek,
—like me.

Anna Hurst Brown
FEELINGS

People seem so far away
As if I live in a different way.
I often wonder if it's not just a dream
Like icicles in summer, or so it seems.
My mind is abused, my soul is confused
I've got to be careful I don't want to lose.
The people I thought would always be there
Have turned their backs they just don't care.
If I'm happy, content, or out in the cold

I just need a friend, my friend's hand to hold—
To tell me that I'm really okay
Even if they don't understand my ways.
I have to stand tall, I have to be strong
That road to paradise is oh so long.
I'll choke back the tears and try not to cry
I'll walk down that road with my head held high—
And when I reach the very end
I'll turn around to see where I've been.

Nancy A Kraft
YOUR FIRST LOVE . . .
Your first love holds you captive,
Bound by silken strands.

And every now and then,
She gently
Pulls you through the shifting sands.

Doris Gene Sharp
DEATH THE REALIZATION

In loving memory of Mrs. Sarah Young Sena May 17, 1891—November 19, 1984 My Great Grandmother

Some think of it as a deep, deep sleep in which never to awake.
Then the loved one's are left with feelings of loss, sadness and despair.
Like having a thick cloud hanging over one's head.
Coming to the realization that a loved one is dead.
Some become distant and withdrawn from the rest of the world.
But into each life some rain must fall, leaving only shadows and or memories of what was.
Nevertheless, the survivors will know that although the body is gone the spirit and memory lingers on evermore.
So let's accept Death, just as we accept Love—you give and take and so does God above.

Carol J Peppel
TO EVERYONE WHO HAS A DREAM
T-o everyone who has a dream
O-f doing many famous things

E-ven if your dream may be
V-ery big or very small
E-very person who ever was
R-eady's themselves for what maybe
Y-ears of heartach are involved
O-n you march step by step
N-o one can stop you if you set goals.
E-veryone has their dreams. But,

W-hen you laz around all day, that
H-appy dream stays far away.
O-nly you can make it be.

H-old tight to those dreams
A-nd one day they will arrive, and
S-tay.

A-ll, in all . . .

D-ays will tred fast
R-ather then drag
E-very time you try to reach and
A-im for those happy
M-ystical dreams.

Elizabeth H Johnson
I REMEMBER YOU
I remember you, especially
when I lie in bed and cannot sleep.
On a cold winter night,
I am there alone,
not daring to move
lest my nude mass should shift
from the warm spot my body has created
against the double chill
of winter and myself.
I leave room for you
but you are not there.
I listen to the wind
struggling with the quiet
waiting for sleep—not for you
for I know you will not come.
The sleep that overtakes me
is the heavy sleep I need
so I will not waken
in the middle of the night and find you gone.
Morning comes, you are gone.
Not before me—just gone.
The tasks of life fill my time
for the busier I am,
the less time I have to
think of you,
long for you,
love you,
Oh, but I do.

Clarence J Erbes
FLANDERS FIELDS 1945
I saw the crosses row on row,
I saw the fields where poppies grow,
I heard the lark sing in the sky,
I saw the graves wherein you lie
In Flanders fields.

New crosses now are added to your row,
On fresh turned sod new poppies grow.
Where the lark once sang, now his offspring sing,
Where your cannons roared, new echoes ring
In Flanders fields.

Your flaming torch, they held it high,
In vain they would not let you die.
They loved the love that you once knew,
And now your comrades lie with you
In Flanders fields.

Mariann S Lewandowski
SEA MONSTER
Adventurous boys sometimes
Think you are their toy.

They play and tease
With your gentle ripples,
Young boys not long off
Mother's nipple.

Embolden by your deceptive
Gentleness they form more
Strenuous games.

Some build rafts in which
To explore the whole shore.

After patient tolerance
Of their earlier antics
You crush, destroy,
Oh, you dangerous,
Treacherous beast.

Men know you are not a toy,
But not so, do young boys.

Frieda Levenhagen
RED

To my father—a real dreamer.

I dream of red
In different hues
And suddenly
They look like you.

Changing shapes
Once more to find
The master
Of all humankind.

It's funny how the
Shapes change and go
To places which
We'll never know.

Somehow it seems
To match my life
And all the people
In my dreams.

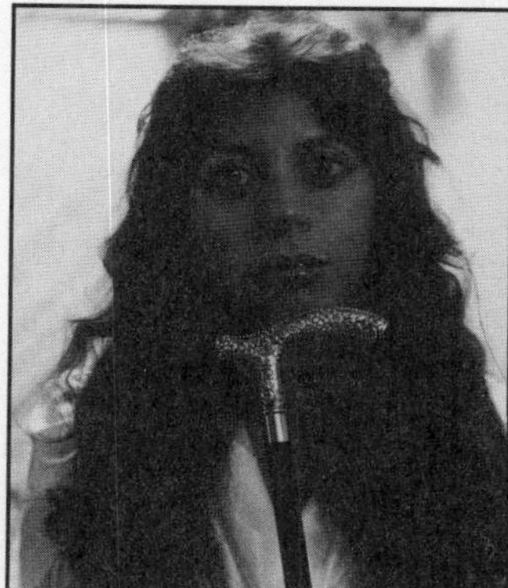

Miroslava Valbuena

Miroslava Valbuena
DISCOVERY OF A MICROSCOPIC DANCE THROUGH INSOMNIA
Counting the seconds just as the penumbra falls covering shadow by shadow,
A hissing blow becomes gigantic, like a cyclops mouth, like a burning iceberg;
Elevating the brown leaves as they dance in a fervent manner.
They commence a type of war-dance, where floating leaves face each other very slowly,
To splash into the thick, cool swamps afterwards, or just thump to the shaky ground.
No steps are heard, no wizard could possibly reign in that moment;
No sentiment could be revealed, no calm, just a nocturnal leaf dance.
A flying fiery flashing light like a lost point with excessive brightness,
With eyes capable of staring at the most suspicious move,
Or at the sound of ant's breath.
Meanwhile, the curtains of a curious chamber pull apart,
Not by themselves, or by the wind;
But by nervous fingers, hands unaware of their five bifurcations,
Those five little tails intend to fleece the wandering wardust,
Or the evaporated swamp droplets.
Unfortunately the foraging fingers were oblivious to the eye winged light,
They were transfixed by the dearth of respiration, the dearth of accusing pheromones . . .
The scarcity of synesthesia;
Deceived into allowing the fiery flasher to electromagnetically witness their curious behaviour,
Now they will not be able to see through their misty window anymore,
They will not entertain or know the secret of the dead leaves' dance.
Because, now they are synchronized with the compass of the cyclops' wind,
They float in the dust of the breeze, and splash together in the swamps;
Only to later disintegrate at the appearance of another fiery flying light.

Mrs Michaeline Roeske
REFLECTIONS ON THE HEART
Step by step, I take
life's path,
The bitter with the
sweet.

Knowing not what
fate may bring
until the passage
of my time.

My children of love
are jewels of my
heart
Untarnished for awhile,
until that day
when destiny steps
in and
suddenly we part.

Sheila D Perkins
WHAT IS LOVE

This poem was inspired by Steven, my devoted and loving husband.

Love isn't something that can be measured
But true love is something which should be treasured
It's not just mere words that people say
Love comes from the heart, no other way
Love touches you lightly and then it takes hold
It's grip is tight, but it's never cold
Not if it's real because only real love is warm
Love can hit you like lightning in a thunder storm
Loves not all good if it's only one sided
But do not worry because true love is guided
And when it is, it will last through time
Thats what our love is, yours and mine

Joyce M Tuepker
FRIENDS

To my mom, Helen Fisher, and the rest of my family. Thanks for always being there for me. Thanks to Tim Held for the encouragement you've given me. I love you all.

Christmas is a special time,
As far as seasons go;
Our spirits are high, our hearts are full,
Of the love we want to show.
But the miles between us have grown to be many
And our visits have been few;
We find we miss you more and more,
And we hope you miss us too.
We wanted to share a special gift,
We wanted to give some holiday cheer;
So please accept our gift, tho' small,
Because we wish our friends were here.
The tree is up and stockings are hung,
And all our hearts are filled with song;
But please remember as it has been said,
The road to a friends house is never long.

Othelia Strickland
ARE WE READY
Are we daily living for Jesus
are we really homeward bound
Will we end up in a fiery furnace
or be in Heaven with a starry crown?

Do our works and actions differ
people usually go by what they see
We were all born with a sinful nature
God gives us a choice of what we want to be.

Daily prayers are always needed
the word of God and a humble heart
God doesn't always answer as we ask Him
For too many prayers are selfish from the start.

Please God, help us, a sinful nation
give us the strenght and courage we need
Daily use us for your purpose
is our humble prayer, we plead.

Debra R Cole
DO YOU KNOW
What brings smiles to children's faces?
What makes things grow in new places?
What makes birds sing and flowers bloom?
What brings to your mind a merry tune?
I'll give you some clues to help you out,
then I'm sure you'll know what I'm talking about.
Blue birds, new birds, all flying around
Trees budding and flowers spring from the ground;
The sun shines bright and grass grows green
The streams flow, smooth and clean;
Bunny rabbits are famous this time of year,
Can you now guess . . . SPRING IS HERE!

Jim Jordan
GIRL CAT
She quietly stalks around the house
and hardly a sound is heard.
She rubs against my leg, swishing her tail,
and nuzzles when I pet her, and purrs.

I call her GIRL CAT, she has no other name,
and she acts kind of crazy sometimes.
She's scared of most people and hides when they're near,
and peeks around corners and whines.

She's a good old cat, I've had her for years,
and she's more than a pet to me.
She's family, a friend, companion and more,
and she's very easy to please.

Inez Newman
PARENTS

To my son, Avery who is my joy and inspiration

Be mindful of what you do and
say in front of your children
Their eyes are like cameras
Their ears are like tape
recorders
Their lives are like one giant
movie screen
Sit down and watch
I hope you like the picture

Eleanor J Seidenburg
DAWN
Dawn means a new beginning,
bringing new hope, extended boundaries, a fledgling day.
A day of winning. Joy in
a dawn is indescribable, insurmountable.

Dawn is irrevocably beautiful in its' own stillness, with
loveliness, quietude, and mysteries
beyond comprehension!
This begettor and epitome of life is to be outshone . . .
only . . . by life, itself.

Michael Thomas Truitt
HUMMINGBIRDS
Fly upside down
then loop around
then stop in air
and not fall down
gathering nectar from
bee balm blooms
or spider web silk
for their nest cacoons
and if you find their hidden nests
in the tops of the highest trees
you'll find their eggs
that look like pearls
about the size of peas
from Mexico they come in spring
their joyous chatter songs to sing
in colonies they come to stay
too quick for other birds of prey
to the Eastern Shore
their summer place
these emerald throated
birds of grace

Beth R Kennedy
DISCOVERY

For Hartwell, my dear husband.

Lonely, I reached out to another,
Shyly and timidly, fearing rejection.
Instead I found acceptance,
Outreach, hesitant as my own,
Underscored with longing.

Heartsick, I reached out to God,
Fearing Him remote and unheeding.
Beginning my search, I turned
And lo, I found Him beside me
Holding out His hands!

Elizabeth Locke

Elizabeth Locke
TAKING TURNS

This poem is dedicated to my beloved parents: Errol Hastings Locke and Elinor Whitney Locke

Look, look, look—
Don't turn away!
Take a good long, deep, look.
Someday you may
Roll along sterile halls
In a wheel-chair
Strapped in by tight empty fear-eyes
Afraid to look.

We ache to have you touch our wrinkled-age-cheeks
With love welling up
Free, from inside your death-fear faces.

Look, look, look—
Don't turn away!
Your it-can't-happen-to-me-eyes
Swim in a sea of self-disguise.
The songs of smooth youth
Your strong bodies sing
Must not lull too long, illusioning.

Inside our time-spent skin
You can hear us singing:
"Beauty for us is a breath away."
And you will repeat the first verse someday.
Look, look, look—
Don't turn away!

Phyllis K Lichty
THE GAME
Sex is a game that many people play
If you know the rules
Hurt can't get in the way
There is a problem there you know
The rules are always changing
People always on the go
No time for rearranging
So if you want the game to work
You really have to play it Or
Take the flow of life in hand
And don't let the game upset it

Donna Mae Willmer
FROM LIBERTY'S VIEW
I've seen many changes in my 100 years of standing.

A country built with freedom, justice, and the pursuit of happiness.

I stand here alone surrounded by water but have been visited by people from all over the world.

America has progressed to its fullest in so many ways.
Inventions of all types in forms of transportation, architecture, and science of all fields including a computerized country.

And yet with all this progression, I see our land being choked with chemicals, unemployment, hungry people, diseases, drugs, and crime.

I hope in my next 100 years that America will truly grow strong economically, freedom will ring out and the American people will regain its patriotism and will say "I'M PROUD TO BE AN AMERICAN OF THE UNITED STATES."

Tarona Marlo Siqua
WHEN I LOOK AT YOU
When I look at you, I see so very much
I see beauty in your smile
I see the look of tenderness in your eyes
When I look at you I see a special quality,
the kind not often found.
I see thoughtfulness in your heart
I see goodness in your face
When I look at you, I see alot
I see the politeness of a gentleman,
the roughness of the wild
I see passion
When I look at you, I see alot
I see love sincere
I see honor and trust,
spirit wild and true
and when I look at you
I see all the reasons why . . .
I love you so.

Sandra Jaggers
MOTORCYCLES
"Motorcycles are a nuisance," says my Mom.
"Oh, but I like 'um!"
"Motorcycles are too noisy," says my Dad.
"Oh, that's ok—I'll muffle 'um!"
"Motorcycles are too dangerous." says my Mom.
"But not when I ride 'um."
"Motorcycles are too expensive." says my Dad.
"But, can't we finance 'um?"
"NO," says my Dad!
"NO," says my Mom!

"But, it won't cost much—
I only want one."

Tina Pierce
BEST FRIENDS
To my very best friend
Our friendship will never end
No matter what people say
you'll be there the next day
I love you and will remember you
forever
and as friends (sis) we'll be together
through wind, rain, and snow
no matter where you go
Because friend you're in my heart
and that's one place where we
won't part
even 500 miles away
in my heart you'll always stay
all I can say is don't forget me
Because I'll remember you for all
eternity.

Kristina L Santry
THE SEARCH
Be Strong—
It's the world
you have to face
Try not to set
your feet to an
abnormal pace
Be Strong—
You've got to find
out the truth
Try not to be a
persisting sleuth
Be Strong—
It's the answer
you have to know
Try not to feel
the emotional blow
Be Strong—
You know you
should
To find out what
none else could

Karen F Bhola
GROUND-ZERO
Blank pages waiting to be soiled
with the ink of my pen.
Thoughts flowing in a steady
stream
Painting the world that I see.
A reflection in a shattered glass
Of a world gone sour by its own
complexities.
The ruins I search for hope
No longer conforming
No longer seeking to belong
Just hoping for a reason to live
Before the final puff of smoke
Forces the decision from me
Snatching the choice from the
human mind
And rendering life impossible.
Then there will be no need for
search
The pages will all be filled
With the promise of extinction.
Lost in the dust of the ruins
My soul will cry out for the reason.

Lynn Jordan
THINGS THAT ARE FREE
You don't have to pay
For the stars in the sky,
The Sun or the Moon,
Or the clouds drifting by;

For the rain on the roof,
Or the wind in the trees,
The song of the birds
Or the hum of the bees.

All of these things in life
You'll find free
Things God has prepared
For you and for me.

Nancy N Brindley
ANN
Her speech a vipors tongue
She hides beneath the sun
She turns to face the wind
A child undiciplined

Her words a restless knife
That hack upon my life
She boasts a sinful heart
Were guilt does not impart

A cactus spews its thorns
Contentment is forlorn
She probes with faith to see
Unrighteousness in me

Demanding all control
She rips apart my soul
When clawing at my heart
I hear the laughter start

The mother of my bride
Would grant me suicide
And hold the gun to see
That I aimed perfectly

Rachel R Greenstein

Rachel R Greenstein
BONJOUR, MON CUR'E

In memory of Reverend Theodore Kunch who saved my life in W.W. II. One would rather forget—but never does.

Are you sitting at His left or
standing at His right?
Does He know how sweet you were
sweet and gentle when you took
my little hands into yours. . .
Smiling with your eyes, gentle
voice
to calm this strange child,

Does He know?
Does He know that this child still
dreams
of you. . .still sees you in the dark
long frock through the trees.
running, jumping, looking back
protecting his pack. . .

Does He know?
The bread that was yours, you gave
to me
in the dark through the trees
Does He know how mad I was and
still am at Him
when your hands shook from
disease
years after. . . when I came back
to
Thank you again. . .

Does He know how mad I still am.
. .for doing
this to you, an Angel. . .
Are you at His left or at His right?
Let me know, if you can'. . .

Linda Maria Pickard
MY LOVE, MY FRIEND
To my only sweetheart,
With whom I tried to stay
I wanted to say so many times,
"I love you anyway."

Although you never call me
I hope that you still care,
'Cause if you ever needed me,
For you, I would be there.

And though I knew just how it
was—
Too good to never end
I really need to tell you that
I'll always be your friend.

But now it's just too late for us,
You've found someone brand new
But just remember what I meant
When I said, "I Love You."

Paula Bowers
DEATH
I saw death creep over a raging
battlefield,
Scrawling his name in blood.
I heard the cries of dying men,
As their souls fled their bodies—
Never to return.
Death robbed father of their sons,
Wives of their husbands,
Children of their fathers.
He stole through the rows of beds
in the infirmary,
Claiming many.
Leaving few.
Tomorrow he will be back again,
To take many more,
To drag them into his deep, dark
dungeon.
But does he ever leave his vigil,
Nay, never!
Always death.
Death. Death. Death.

Judy Branom Holley
DEATH

This poem is dedicated to my Mom, for always having faith in me.

Death comes creeping through the
night
To take away our loved one
When the time is right.
We have no way to control this fate
God has given us just so many days
And for the end we must wait.
It seems as though death knows no
bounds
It shall get each one of us
In the process of its appointed
rounds.
When for our loved one, it is the
end
Only God and an indefinite time
Can help our lonely hearts mend.
There is a great sorrow at a time
of death,
But when the time is come
We shall each have one last breath.
As for our loved one, we all grieve
We shall cherish our memories
That death cannot take, I believe,
Someday God will end all death
And we will all be in heaven
With everlasting and eternal
breath.

Jann Potter-Withrow
MARCH GARDEN
Lying still,
with ear pressed to cold ground,
I listen.
Fresh, clumped dirt surrounds
an icy crack.
I hear wind-carried murmurs
from beneath the hardness.
Damp leaves
black and mossy,
cling to each other
listening.

Above I see ice prisms
banging here and there
on stiff, brown maples.
With eyes as large as the greying
moon,
the smooth, fresh buds wait
listening.

I make no sound
as not to disturb
the dead,
or labor of the many seeds
beneath the soil.
Hidden,
but for their silent humming,
the smooth seeds
and watchful grasses lie
listening.

Vivian Henson
GIFTS
Sitting in my rocker by the window
And looking out over the land
I see all of God's beautiful
wonders—
I see all the works that He
planned.

One little seed was all it took
For all these wonders to grow
Then—God sent us Jesus, His only
Son
For us to reach out and to know.

One little seed is all it takes
For our faith in Jesus to grow
This mighty seed is full of love
And can beat "any" evil foe.

Jesus gave his life that we might
live
He was beaten and hung on the
cross
Agonies, for us, He surely
suffered—
Not to follow Him is our loss.

So look all around you and see
these gifts
That our God so freely gave
Let Jesus come into your heart
today
And forever, through Him be
saved.

Delores Greathouse
THE SEA OF LIFE

For my children, Lisa and Matthew, who make the sea of my life much better.

Dear God,
Help me to see
that you are still
parting the sea.
The sea of doubt
when I am confused and unsure.
The sea of fear
when I am afraid.
The sea of wrath
when I am angry and may lose
control.
Remind me, dear Lord,
when I cry out to you.
You can still part the waters
and let me pass through.

Dorothy K Luccock
A LETTER TO SANTA
Santa, I need a brunch coat,
Not too long, nor too short, nor too
heavy, nor too thin,
It should be colorful, easy to wash,
and of no-iron material;
The last is the most important.

And Santa dear, my doll house
Needs some things, such as a book
case, a piano, some lamps;
Oh, and a desk and chair,
And plates and cups and saucers,
And new curtains for the library.

That's all for now, Santa dear.
Would you like raisin lemon
squares or chocolate brownies
with coffee glaze
To eat with your egg nog?

Janice D Walsh
RAINBOW'S END

To Mother and Dad, the greatest influence on my philosophies.

Some say, "Life's a moment
Looking through a glass";
For some it's such a torment;
To some, "This too shall pass".

Some master hard-won flight's
In educational persuit;
Some scale pinnicle heights
To prove that man can do it.

Others paint the tiniest
Strokes across a canvass;
Others bold and brilliant
Of all creation's vastness.

All folk's seek to better
One day from the last;
Most think, "Grass is greener

The other side o'the fence".

Well now, let me tell ya',
There's no pot o'gold
At either end of the rainbow
To ever have or hold".

All of us make the colors,
Its beauty lies between;
Black and white are at its end,
The middle gives it name.

Cleo S Hill
ISLAND BOY

Dedicated to my boys—Mike Hill, Joel Orris and Sean Meek

Past my window, he walks by
Beneath a clear blue island sky
He drags a soggy nylon hose
A salmon head stuffed in the toes
He stops to check for crab, and
then
Slowly winds his way again

His new learned whistle fills the air
The island sun halos his hair
As snowy seagulls quietly float
Past him on a driftwood boat
He hurls a pebble to make them fly
And this they do, with mewing cry

Into the distance he grows dim
Sea-filled footprints follow him
Only net and pail, the fish filled
hose
Will know where else this
youngster goes
Unknown to him, I shared his joy
God bless you, little island boy.

Cheryl Lorraine Miller
TOTALLY YOU
There is no one word
I can use to express,
The problems I've presented you
with
The tensions, all the stress.

Yet as I face disasters,
Obstacles in my way
You're always there when I need
you
And I make it through that day.

Jesse, if I ever lose you
Or you stray from my side
I'd be lost, confused, bewildered
Don't even mention pride

There's nothing I can't ask you
Nothing you won't do,
I owe my personal growth and
developement
A standing ovation—
because it helped me to get you.

Dorothy Shearer
THIS OLD WORLD
In the changing of the seasons
As the World in its orbit turns,
One must wonder at its fixed
rhythm
For so regularly it churns.

First the springtime brings the
essence
Of the flowers and budding trees;
While all outdoors feels hale and
hearty
As the rains wash clean the breeze.

The good old summer takes its turn
By growing luscious foods untold;
With beans, peas, cabbages, and
fresh fruits
We nature's blessings now behold.

Autumn ushers exotic changes
Treating us to its rare beauty.
As Jack Frost paints his priceless
pictures,
His agile brush tints every tree.

Winter comes like lunging hounds
Showering us with snow and ice,
But since it is the Christmas
season,
We pretend that we think it's nice.

Satisfaction we are given
As seasons rotate bit by bit,
That this Old World will stay in
orbit
'Cause His unseen hands will guide
it.

Helen J Logue
THE LIFT OFF
I look to the east and I look to the
west,
At a never ending vastness of space,
I am left without so many answers,
As countries continue to run the
race.
I stand to think and question;
All the wonders of our world,
Are we really ready to handle
The many miracles we have
unfurled?

As the world so patiently waited,
To witness the Challenger again,
From homes, schools and space
stations
And those who stood to watch in
vain.
The monstrous eagle looked so
anxious,
To spread it's wings and grace the
sky;
With the beauty and charm of
other times
So perfect and great no one could
die.

For seven brave and anxious ones
Challenger became a firey grave,
And left a world almost
unprepared;
We had to see but could not save.
We must not despair, they were so
loved;
By one who extends his merciful
hand,
That eased all pain and let them
know,
Waiting—Is Challenger in another
land.

Debbie Stuart Blankenship
MY SON

For my son, Shannon.

My Son, My little one.
Your life has just begun.
Keep your head up and smile,
for life's only a little while.

Yvonne J Barlet
LIFE FORCE
My name is not important
The life force inside me is
For that is what makes me
Me and whom I am to be
The same with all of you upon the
earth
Time to cry is here for I live
Now upon the earth
When I die do not cry
Just bury me beneath the willow
tree
And say good night and sweet
dreams
Cause I shall only be sleeping
Waiting for you to join me
Until God calls us to his kingdom
for all eternity

Patty Sprouse
AMERICA
AMERICA
What does it mean?
Freedom,
A place to dream.
AMERICA
Where stars shine bright
Where the people are led
By a guiding light.
AMERICA
Where people stand tall,
And get up just one more time
Than they fall.
AMERICA
With golden fields and sparkling
waters
A place where the future belongs
To her sons and daughters.
AMERICA
May your flag long wave,
And may I die free
In the home of the brave.

Kay Stinson
THE PEARL
A pearl of wisdom, love, and hope
who's seen the sorrow of our days;
The joy of happiness well earned
with Love the essenance of it all;
The hope of all to come and be
a thread of Love for all to see;
The sorrow of all that should not
have been
love to forgive and to still carry on;
The wisdom to look back and know
life had been lived . . . with no room
for regret;
The Lord has given us the courage
to be
all that we are and all that we can
be;
Life is the answer to all that you see
accept it and live it . . . each day as
it is.

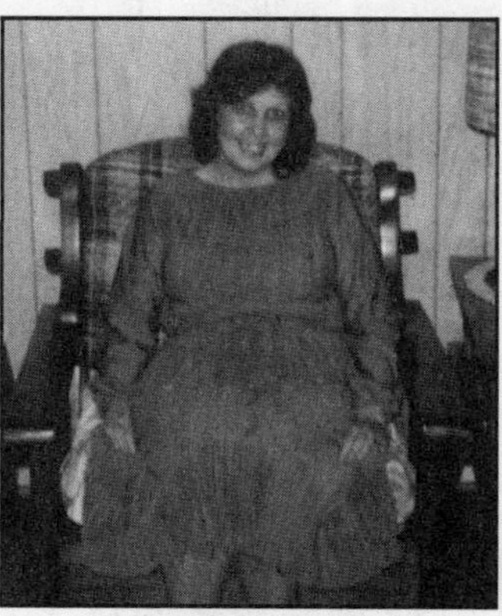

Barbara L Owens

Barbara L Owens
HE'S ALWAYS THERE
He's always there
I know he cares
My Lord is always there
Troubles and worries don't bother
me
Cause he knows I need him so
He's always there
I know he cares
My Lord is always there.

When I'm down and low
He fills my soul
With joy and hope
Cause he's always there
I know he cares
My Lord is always there
Amen

Kim Lee Ferguson
MORNING WALK

This poem is dedicated to my Dad, who instilled in me an intrinsic understanding and divine appreciation of the beauty of nature. . .and to my Mother who gave me the gentleness to love.

I gazed upon the flowers,
Their beauty and their grace—
The sunshine filled my heart
with joy,
It's warmth upon my face.
The grass sprung up to greet me,
Through the cracks along the
walk—

The city had relented,
So nature's voice could talk.
The air was filled with sounds of birds,
The glory in their song—
Echoed my true feelings,
That God was ever strong!
The earth with all its beauty,
Blesses us each day—
It kisses us with sunshine,
As we go along our way!

Tisha LuDene Young
TURN TO ME

This poem is dedicated to Donny for his proud spirit and wild heart that inspires me though we're apart.

You're special to me and always will be
And you can bring a tear to my eye;
But I don't let you see that certain part of me
Though I guess I'll never know why.

You bring out the sadness, you bring out the pain
And I hardly know what to do;
My life's in a daze and in one simple phrase
"It's all because of you."

You need someone to care, you need someone to share
The things you couldn't before;
You need someone to love, to help you rise above
And show you there's so much more.

So don't put me down and don't make me cry
Only tell me you understand;
I'll show you affection and not one rejection
Just turn to me—and reach for my hand.

Richard R Keener
FRIENDSHIP
I measure not my wealth by gold
But by true friends both young and old.
I care not for their material things
Just the joy that their friendship brings.

He could be the richest man on earth
But friendship is how I measure his worth.
He could be penniless, not a dime to his name
Whether rich or poor, their value's the same.

I don't ask for perfection, that wouldn't be fair
When it comes to faults I sure have my share.
If I ask for something that you can't lend
It doesn't matter if you'll still be my friend.

I'll tell you again how I measure my wealth.
It's more by friends than even by health.
If I count my friends and use both hands
I'm the richest man in all the land.

Marilyn Summers
LOVE VERSES HATE
Through the eyes of love, I looked into the face, of hate
I knew without a doubt, this was going to be, a debate
Hate seemed so much stronger, I wondered what I'd do
Would my love, be strong enough, to see me through
Hates eyes, were cold, and hard as a stone
With my love, I felt so alone
Hate's words were bitter, as they pierced my heart
I thought to outwit hate, I've got to be smart
I started trying, to turn, my love, into hate.
Before it was too late.
Love wouldn't let me, it stood it's ground
Love said, there's enough of hate around
Hate scorned me, He caused me a lot of pain,
He was trying to ruin, love's name
I felt my love growing stronger, it beamed through my eyes.
Love shined a light on hate, He saw all his dirty deeds
and lies, hate backed away. He knew he was beat
Love was shining and proud as an Eagle, Hate crawled away in defeat. . .

Betty Sprenkle Hoffman
FAREWELL, DADDY

This poem is dedicated to my beloved Father, J. Webster Sprenkle

Well, Daddy dear—The time has come—
When we must say "Goodbye."
Your journey's end and day is done,
You're pointed toward the sky.
You leave behind a sorrowing group—
A mournful family we.
And now, at last, I understand—
"My Faith looks Up to Thee."
For had I neither love nor faith—
I could not tarry here.
I'd cast all reason to the winds—
And fall upon your bier.
And had I neither faith nor love—
I could not see the light.
I could not fully comprehend that you
are robed in white.
Ah, Yes! It was an empty shell
We placed beneath the sod.
But <u>YOU</u>—the Father, whom I loved—
Are Home—in Peace—with God.

Linda M Buckel
THE MAGIC OF READING
When I was just a little girl, my parents read to me.
They made me see so very young, a reader I wanted to be.

So I often took my little books and sat beneath a tree,
The wondrous words I read aloud, to my dolls, my friends, and me.

Mother Goose and Dr. Seuss — Peter Pan—The Gingerbread Man.
The Bible, the Atlas—the Reader's Digest.
A good scary story—the best of the best.

And the many books of poetry that I so often read.
Created lines of rhythm, to dance inside my head.

Yes, reading took me places, where I had never been before.
And the MAGIC of the unread words, were treasures yet in store.

Now the years have passed so quickly, since I sat beneath that tree.
With dolls and friends and stacks of books, that meant so much to me.

But even though the years have passed, some truths remain "un-new,"
I still love reading lots of books, and hope that you will too.

'Cause reading takes you places, where you've never been before,
And the MAGIC of the unread words, are treasures yet in store.

Marjory B Marsh
SPINDRIFT
I had a dream last night. It was a beautiful dream
And the moon was bright.
The night was still and covered with stars.
Music softly came from afar

I stood at a window watching the ocean
Wash smooth white sands with shimmering
Moon-bathed waves that broke and shattered
Into a million glittering stars, then whispered back
Together and break a new—sigh and say—
A a-h-h-h, love.

Ah, love, this dream became so real
I forgot for a little it was only a dream
That would shatter and break like the molten silver
Of the moon on the sea.

But for a little while yet I dreamed on
And forgot the ache in my heart.
Too soon dawn's cold light
Burst the rainbow bubble I'd been living in.

Ah, love, where are you now?

Phyllis Sullivan
NOT SPRING YET?
This should be Spring, but that looks like snow!
It should, I'm sure, be rain—but no,
Not just a little, an inch or worse
Like we might expect on April First.

It's getting deeper, piling white
Upon our tulips; what a blight!
What fun if this were last October,
But really, Winter should be over.

Ronald G Kemper
THE POET-SEER
The poet a philosopher must be
And fathom deep where others dare not go
He has each day a sense of mystery
That grossly minded people rarely know

A wonderment for all that life may bring
An inner sense to nature's outer play
He has from utter joy a song to sing
For miracles abound with every day

A way of thought elusive like a breeze
It's origin and destiny unknown
The poet-seer intuitively sees
Regarding all of life his very own

A blend of head and heart the poet-sage
Supernal light and joy of every age

Brian L Dunkle
FRIENDSHIP
By your side
But not in sight
A force
Loving
Hurting
Someone to hold
In the dead of the night
Not for sale
There's no price
Crying
Feeling
The joy of life
It's friendship.

Paul Anthony Gumbel
FATE OF A STAR
I love you oh America my own
But weep for you in this your tragic hour
Because you've treasured life and spirit most
And gave your God the rev'rance he was due.
You held in trust the promise of the ages
For men whose vision soared beyond creation.
But now two centuries have passed:
You yield your immortality to flesh
And pirouette across the human stage
Like meteor with brilliant flashing train
Then vanish in a black hole long grown cold
The fate of civ'lization e'er retold.

Emily S O'Brien
A MAN NAMED MACK
There was a young man named Mack,
Who free-based and smoked too much crack;
He wanted to fly
Way up in the sky
He did, but he never came back.

Jerry Lipine
YOU WILL NEVER KNOW

This poem is dedicated to my daughter, Kendall Ann, and to all dreamers.

Your fingers lightly caress the keys of the piano.
It's as though you were making love to every note—

Such passion and yet tenderness—
Chills run up and down my spine,
as I listen to the sounds.
The words you sing, in my
imagination are written for me
alone.
I love you, and you will never know.

I hear your music in the air.
I see you now and then.
My records always keep you near—
But you will never know what
you've missed in not finding
me—
And you'll go on playing your
beautiful music.
For I am only one of thousands
who love you—
And how sad, that you will never
know!

O Estelle Hutchins Brockinton

O Estelle Hutchins Brockinton
WHAT IS MORE LOVELY THAN A BIRD?

To My Lovely Daughter,
Barbara—Husband, Thomas

A beautiful Cardinal and his lady
are building a nest in our
backyard, in the Jasmine I love
best.
Lady Cardinal, is working with
pride, gathering twigs, straws
and whatever God provides.
Mister Cardinal with pride and
glee, watches over from the
neighbor's hickory tree . . .
His melodious songs serenading
the neighborhood,

Seems to be telling us, he never had
it so good.
I fed them thru the Winter's sleet,
snow, and cold,
They have now come back to repay
a hundredfold.
If only we humans would be, so
cheerful and appreciative as he,
What a Wonderful World this
could be.
Thank you God, for all the
Wonders and Beauty of Nature.

Paddy McGonigle
IMAGES

I've walked along the beach and
felt my feet upon the sand.
I've felt a touch upon my face and
imagined it was your hand.
I've thought of you in dreams, in
hours of day & nite, & I find,
That hard as I try there is no way
to expel you from my mind.

I feel a warmth within my body and
I feel you near.
I think of loving you with all my
heart, and I feel fear.
I feel the wind caress my being and
the rain
gently embrace my face, and I
think of times
we've had as I close my eyes and
trace;

Every precious moment we've
spent together, and
every pleasure so real,
Everytime we've had to the past
now fallen, I can feel;
And maybe someday a time will
come to be,
When with me you can finally feel
free.

Arthur J Morsch
PEARL HARBOR LEGACY

Dedicated to the Pearl Harbor
Survivors Association

'Twas two weeks before Christmas
at a harbor called Pearl
Where the fleet came to rest and
their colors unfurl,
When across the cane fields as the
day drew new breath
Came two flights of planes on a
mission of death.

They dropped torpedoes and
bombs as they flew over in waves
Sending ships and their men to
watery graves,
Causing leaders in Washington to
yell loud and long
While promising forever our
country'd be strong,
That we'd no longer be weak nor
try to appease
Those nations who hoped we'd
drop to our knees.

But time has passed and that day
is forgotten
Now the word patriotism is almost
verbotten,
Not to those, however, who remain
crippled and lame
As they watch new leders look for
others to blame,
Then find reasons they cannot
keep this great country strong
For in their hearts they believe a
good defense is wrong.

There is left only hope those
officials will revert
Then remember Pearl Harbor—
and keep America alert.

Christy Michelle Roberts
THE HIDDEN SIDE OF LIFE

Is life what you see?
Or is there another side of it always
waiting to happen
Which means there are two sides
The one that happens
And the one that doesn't
Like two different columns
The side that we live
And the side that we don't
The two columns
Both full of memories
One contains the real memories
The other contains the memories
of dreams
But in the end it is the real
memories
that remain clear
And it's the memories of dreams
that
live in the hidden side of life . . .

Lawrence Swanson
CATHEDRAL

The sunlight streams through
coloured glass
while I ponder present, future and
past,
within a world far removed from
strife
and the anguished cries and wails
of life.

In peaceful silence I kneel alone,
the sorrow within my heart now
grown.
Tranquility pervades, so still and
hushed;
the carpet beneath my knees so
lush.

I gaze upon God's chosen One
and wonder why He forsook His
Son,
along with the many who died in
vain
simply to defend His name.

I come in confusion to this Holy
place
to seek reassurance within the face
of our beloved Christ the Lord,
who surrendered His safety
amongst the horde.

Filled with despondence I turn
away,
convinced no miracles will occur
today,
I receive no answers for my
tortured brain;
there is no salve to ease my pain.

Defeated, the light fades into night;
the world lies deadened within my
sight.
Gazing upward I beseech the sky
to tell me why so many must die.

Verna L Day
HANDS

I gaze upon these hands of mine
And dream about the past
And think of all the loving hands
They held
The fingers they enclasped
If I knew then, what I know now
I would never let them go
For all of those dear hands I
touched
I dearly loved them so
So cherish each precious moment
With those hands enclasped
For no one knows when the time
Will come
When it will be the last.

Robyn M Chapin
RIPPLES

Indescribable beauty
in an oragne ripple.
Peaceful . . .
Uncaring . . .
So warm, but so far away.
The sky so smooth
with burning rays
descending
On silky glass.
Dark is nigh.
The orange sinking
Into the ripples
of my heart.

Sylvia E Niemi
MAYTIMES OF REMEMBERING

A sunny Maytime bids us go
Where daisies dance and willows
blow,
And where the bluest violets grow!

You gather me a bright bouquet;
The fragrance of this hour in May
Is sharp and sweet as yesterday.

We walk beside the sheltered
stream;
You hold my hand; as in a dream
I see the May-kissed violets gleam!

Dear Love! You gave me
everything,
A smile to share, a heart to sing
In Maytimes of remembering.

Warm joyance holds you near, my
own!
I will not weep, though all alone
I leave blue violets at a stone.

Laurie Paliulis
MAY PEACE BE WITH YOU

A soul has winged it's way toward
heaven;
the body, it is gone . . .
Hold the memories of that smile,
for love shall linger on . . .

Arise from all your sorrow;
Arise from all your fear;
Just try to cherish your memory,
of that smile you hold so dear . . .

The Lord now has your loved one
and holds him close to him . .
Don't you start to feel,

The peace that comes within . . .?

As for all your sorrows,
This will lessen in some time
I wish I could lift your pain,
So that part of it were mine . . .

To be so unhappy, the Lord has not
meant this to be . . .
So stop to count your blessings . . .
You have your family,
you have me . . .

Donald Laverne Walker
POWER
The power of the atom! so gruesome a thing
In a world where love finds little room
Is a power in mens hands that today could well bring
All mankind to destruction and doom.
Yet all of this power must be started we learn
From but one tiny nuclear grain
That touches another and it in return
Touches more in a nuclear chain.
Each molecule bounds with a power of its own
From that first tiny start to the last
Until all have combined to produce what is known
As an atom or hydrogen blast.

Let these be the words that will triger a chain
Of a mighty reaction of love
That touches each heart on earth's troublesome plain
And ascends to the heavens above.
The power from this test that the whole world could view
Would make hydrogen bombs but a toy
That men put aside as at last they outgrew
The destructivesome traits of a boy;
For love is the greatest of all of the powers
So why shouldn't we give it a test?
It would make this old fear ridden earth that is ours
A utopian world at its best.

Marcia Brauer
TIME
Now is the time,
to put all thoughts behind
of iced tea and lemons
and the beauty you find.

Winters coming,
so cold and wet.
The snow has started falling,
the snowman is someone we've met.

Mr. Jack Frost,
is close on our trail,
so run real fast
and drop off the mail.

Stoke up the furnace
and chop all the wood,
the blizzard has started,
hurry, you really should.

Have a warm winter,
as cozy as you please.
See you next spring
with its warm summer breeze.

Sandy Sasso
IN THE WOMB

Dedicated to all the unborn babies in the world

Is it moving? I ask.
Is it mine to mask?
Should I hush this life?
Or should I let it last?
Why these questions, it's
so apparent there's nothing
to question,
Only to parent.

Kay Workman
THE DAISY
Laughing eyes, tousled hair
A world of sun
With little care . . .

A dimpled smile, a dusty cheek,
A priceless daisy
For Mom to keep.

E H McMillan
THANK YOU LORD
I just want to thank you Lord,
and not ask for anything.
I want to thank you for saving my soul,
filling me with the sweet Holy Spirit,
and healing my body many times.

I want to thank you for a lovely companion
that has stood by my side
through thick and thin.
Oh, away back Lord, you know when.

I want to thank you for four little girls, the cutest ever seen.
I just had to call them my four little Queens.
Now they have all grown up with their hopes and dreams.
but they are still my little girls it seems.

I want to thank you for two little boys to bless our home
hand in hand they would roam.
Lord, do you remember that big snow? out in the yard I did go,
Two little boys following my footsteps oh so slow.
I shortened my footsteps, just to see what they would say,
Looking over my shoulder, I shook at what I heard them say.
Look we are getting bigger, now we can walk in Dads steps all the way.

Knights in shining armour, though tarnished here and there,
I leave them in your hand Lord,
to make of them what so ever you care.
Just A Dad

Doug Compton
RUNNING
Running won't move you at all,
you just stay in the same place,
shrouded by your tall brick wall
because your problems you can't face.

Hiding won't bring down the wall,
nor will lying bring you grace,
Running will only bring your fall
and multiply your disgrace.

When you see pain coming your way,
and nothing seems to be right,
Running, Hiding, Lying, I found out
Are not the way to fight.

Admit to yourself, face the plain facts,
you've ran and probably will again,
Why can't we learn to face our attacks
And thus dissipate them like the wind.

John (Sky) Kashner
2 GOD
God on the Highest
Hear my needful plea
I know You'll listen
You always listen to me

Forgive us for destruction
Forgive us of our sins
We need Your love to guide us
Through narrow, thick and thin

Watch us laugh; watch us cry
Watch our sorrow; watch us try
We know there is no end
Just a beginning at our end

I know You are there
I feel your spirit near
You Know that we are human
Keep us, wipe our tear

Phyllis Olson Aubin
TRANSFORMATION

I dedicate this poem to the memory of my husband Joseph and son Robert & in honor of my children, Joe, Charles, Evelyn, Marie, John, Richard, Patricia and Kathleen.

When you die and leave this earth
And all your friends behind,
You'll journey to eternity
To a world of a different kind.
You'll see a mist of shimmering light
When an angel welcomes you.
Why, she's that certain someone
Who died and now welcomes you.
Smilingly she'll take your hand
As other angels appear . . .
You'll recognize so many,
Will be surprised to find them here.
At last the angel will take you
To the loving Saviours' throne . . .
His voice reflects His glory
As He'll tenderly welcome you home.

Donald R Boysen
TO A SKUNK
Oh little skunk of black and white
I smelled you pass the other night.
I wonder if you really care
How badly you pollute the air.

I really do not understand
Just how your essence has demand
To make the best high cost perfume
That smells so good throughout the room.

I wonder just how it would be
If changed were your anatomy.
You cannot care how you offend—
Your nose is on the other end.

I doubt if you'll apologize
For bringing tears to someone's eyes.
I'm surely glad that you are gone,
But how your odor lingers on.

Sylvia Rosalita Katz
OF WORSHIP
Of light transfixed
Are atoms mixed,
In solar raiment
Souls in containment . . .
Precepts to impart
From man's heart,
Worship with care
That which you are . . .
Follow wise ways
To lengthen days,
Noble may you be
In all humility . . .
Strengthen brotherhood,
Seek power of good
for shades of dark
Leave their mark . . .

Virginia Kerstetter
FOR A DAUGHTER AND HER SON
Was it yesterday?
I held her
Soft
Warm
A part of me
Yet
Separate.

Was it yesterday?
She hugged me
Laughing
Loving
Learning to walk
Away
From me.

Was it yesterday?
Her arms held
Out to me
Joyous
The new life
Shining
Blest.

And suddenly
All the yesterdays
Became
Tomorrow.

Roy Veteto
WHERE HAS THE LOVE GONE TO?
Yesterday people seemed to love one another
but now it seems to occur as if, by chance
we treat one another like a stranger than brother
Love seems to have become romance.

Yesterday children seemed to be a blessing
They were given to those who needed love most.
But now we seem to treat them as an aggression
We abortion and abuse them to the uttermost.

Yesterday marriage meant all it was intended for
A man and a woman joining til death
but now it's becoming a dinosaur
for now many end before taking a breath.

Yesterday families loved to spend time and be together
picnics, sing-alongs, trips, even a meal,
but now it seems to not be either
for many consider this is a bad deal.

Yesterday, now, and tomorrow we have hate

We've always had this but not so bad
but now it seems to be a helpmate
if you don't hate you'll become a foot pad.

Where has the love gone to?
In a world full of pain, death,
tears and war, we try to answer
this with brew and glue, but only by
loving one another will settle the scofe.

Howard R Reischman

Howard R Reischman
ULTIMATE POWER

Love is the ultimate power.
Such power that it cannot be harnessed.
Many I have known, who attempted to capture this power.
Yet instead of capturing, they were captured . . .
Captured into slavery of loving and caring.

Many try to escape, few accomplish this feat.
For those who do escape they are wounded for life.
Wounded not in the sense of physical pain.
But in the emotional pain of having all love
severed from their souls.

For those who do escape . . .
They are to love and care . . .
Care for one which with they truly do not belong.

Michelle Timothy-Jolley
THE MISSIONARY

To all those men and women who have believed in something so strong that they were willing to risk public humiliation and even death to bring their message to the masses.

A lonely litle caterpillar sat perched upon a tree, taking in the scenery as far as she could see.
In the distance, a butterfly, floating on a breeze, he spied the little caterpillar and flew closer to the trees.
"Good morning, my friend." he said to her, but she was very shy, she backed away into the leaves but she managed to say "Hi."
"Don't be afraid of me," he said, "I will do no harm, just come back out onto the branch in the sunshine where it's warm."
"Who are you?" she said to him feeling not so shy, "In many ways you look like me but how is it that you fly?"
"I have come from far away to give the world the news, a secret plan, a special gift, and a life you cannot lose."
"What is this you speak of, and what message do you bring? And tell me please just how it is that you were given wings?"
He said, "My wings they shine with light that comes from God above, they're woven with the finest thread spun from the purest love."
"I know you well and the way you live, as you move from tree to tree, you'll spin a cocoon, crawl inside, and you may cease to breathe."
"But I say to you, if you live in faith, and not stray at any cost, you will sleep warm and safe, and your life will not be lost!"
"How do I know," she said to him, "if these things you say are true?"
He winked his eye, began to fly, and said, "I once was a caterpillar too!"

Jorge A Garcia Benitez
NEGLECT

Staring out the window, and being able to see nothing.
My mind is blank and my memories are scarce.
My eyes are watery and my hands are shaky.
My pulse is rapid, my breathing slow.
I look around and all I can see is white.
But the thing that stands out is the look in your eyes.
The look that says I wish I could have loved you more.
I should have cared for you more; I wish . . . I wish . . .
But it's too late cause you're going to lose me now.
Knowing my time is not too far;
I just lay here staring at the stars
Remembering the few times that you and I have shared.
The laughter, the cries that you never heard.
I can feel your sorrow, I can see your pain.
You will not leave my bedside because you are afraid.
You are afraid to admit you were wrong.
You were wrong in leaving me all alone.
I was too young to understand.
Too young to understand why you left me alone.
But now; "Here" I understand, I was never your child.
So you had no reason to care.
But now that I'm dying, you understand that I did care!!

Now I am dead, but I can still feel.
And my heart will keep feeling until you too are dead.
Dead of the feeling and guilt, that you did not care.

Helen Alley
MANSION IN THE SKY

To my dear great grand daughter Courtney Danielle Morrison

There's a mansion in the sky,
I'll be there by and by.
God built it just for you and me,
The most beautiful home you will ever see.
The garden is covered with flowers so bright,
From the golden gate you can see it all night.
To reach the top it's a long and narrow trail.
On each side it has no rail.
God will keep you safe from all harms,
For he will always hold you close in his arms.
And when I reach that golden gate,
I pray to God it won't be too late.
Lord please open your gate I pray,
Because I'm getting tired day by day.
Lord, I'm, not afraid to die.
If I told you of my life you would know why.
So that mansion in the sky,
I hope I will be there by and by.

Verna Byron Kroeschel
THE ANSWER

To My Progeny

I looked for God
And the answer to life.
Where?
In the magnificence of the ocean,
The grandeur of the mountains,
The lushness of the forest,
The desolation of the desert,
The tumultuous turmoil of the city,
The quietude of twilight.

I looked for God
And the answer to life
And found it
In the gurgling innocence
Of my child
Lying there.

Linda Street
MY BEACH

When I went to the beach
I did not see a crab walking by
Nor did I hear a seagull's cry

There are walls on the side of me
There was no tide nor sea
There were only a few big rocks
Probably because I'm in the sandbox.

Eunice Siefker
MY TRUE LOVE

My true love is special, there is no one like him in all the earth, I'm impelled to bless the mother who labored to give him birth

My true love is precious to me, more than the finest gold, the love I feel for him can't be bought or sold

Oh, how I love my true love, with his suntanned face and sunbleached hair, for making me happy he has a flair

My true love is tuned into me as a person, he knows the heighth, breadth and depth of me as the oceanographer knows the secrets of the depth of the sea

He nurtures me and I blossom as a rose, my personality and talents come to the fore, I cannot help but grow

My true love is not insensitive to me when I'm sick and not functioning very well, he takes my hand and comforts me, there is concern in his eyes, you can tell

He lifts me up when I am down, he is unique, not another like him can be found

I'm growing old my hair is turning grey, it doesn't matter to my true love he will not stray, he is blind to the lines forming in my face from year to year, he delights in toying with the wrinkles on the lobe of my ear

My hands are wrinkled and worn like an old shoe but he takes
my hands in his and assures me of his love so true

My true love walks not in front of me nor behind me he walks beside me all the way through lifes happy times and sad times, to the perfect day

As we grow older our love for each other grows stronger, our love will still be there when we can't hold on any longer

If there was only one request that could be granted to me from my maker above it would be to live forever on earth with my true love

Sharon F Cornett
WHO WILL DIG UP MY BONES?

Who will dig up my bones?
Will it be a child playing
On some distant beach
Not yet formed by the hand of God?

Will it be an Archeologist
Who will find me and ponder,
Chin in hand, at what I said.
Wonder what I did, how I lived,
Wonder how I died?

Who will dig up my bones?
Will I be discovered by two lovers
Writing promises in the sand?
Building castles, dreaming dreams
Or just walking hand in hand?

In some far off millennium
Will I look with unseeing eyes
Into faces staring and wondering at me
Through a case of glass as a museum piece?
Or will I be forever burried
Beneath the sands of time?

Inda Blatch-Geib
TIPTOES OF CHILDHOOD
One remembers their first Autumn
Standing on tiptoes of childhood
Strong and quick
Full of life and laughter
Appreciating the crispness
Of the air
That feeds the nostrils and seems to whisper 'play now'
There is a certain headiness
Tumbling about in paint palate leaves
Tickling each other and kissing
On the cheek
Liking it—And not—At the same time
But doing it again and again
Until mothers call—Looking back themselves
Remembering their times—Of
Falls gone by
And smiling for those moments—
And these ones
Silently bequithing more to come
Suppers tasting so much better—Hot and wonderful
Even their smells thick and good enough to eat
Then laying down to sleep
With blankets newly out of mothballs
The window cracked a bit
And the full moon made for Shadow pictures
Drifting off with a certain clean feeling
And waking up the same—slowly—warm
Glad to be alive
Yes one never forgets
Their first Autumn.

Dakota Miller
MY DREAM

To the man I love so very much
Rusty Dugan

Dreaming of the day
That we become one
When we take our vows
In front of everyone
Sharing the truth
That our love is true
Let no other come
Between us too.
I love you Rusty, really I do
I'd climb the
highest mountain
Just to be with you
As we grow older
And so will our love
To be honest with you
My life would be Nothing
If anything ever happened to you
As I walked down the aisle to you
Always remember I love you
All my dreams, have finally come true
When you said I love you too.

tammie lee daily
THE PERFECT FRIEND
The perfect friend.
What a name to be called,
but I guess that's what I really am.

Always a friend, that's me.
Your friend, his friend,
but never what I want to be.

Call me a sister, maybe a lover,
but never anyone's girl, fiancee, or whatever.

What am I? The perfect friend!

You can talk to me, I'll listen.
And if you want, love me.
I'm so easy to love, that's what is said.
So love me, as long as you can.

But when it's over, I'll still be here—
Always, the perfect friend.
And you'll be gone to be with her, the one you love.
But here I sit, all alone, the perfect friend.

Where do I look? Where do I find my perfect friend?
Someone to share with and care for—
someone with noone else.

Just me, the perfect friend.
—tammie lee daily

Lloyd K Mitchell Jr
WHAT YOU MEAN TO ME
When faced with the tribulations life puts me through,
I seek the comfort and security of you.

'Cause you possess exactly what I need,
to remove the pain; and anxieties set free.

Tis true; the fact when I look into space.

There is no shining star your love won't replace.
A clear evening, the stars will show,
But cloudy or clear, your love will glow.

The way I feel when I'm away from you
Is one of emptiness, and I am forced to be blue.
It is difficult to define the beauty you hold
I truly think you are worth your weight in gold.
I look to you and see a woman at her best,
For the love of you, there is nothing I wouldn't invest.
All that I say here, I would say twice,
There is nothing in this world I wouldn't sacrifice.
All this is what you mean to me.
In the name of the Almighty I'd stake my plea.
I love you now, and especially tonight,
For the warmth in my heart,
ONLY YOU WILL IGNITE!

James C Dearing
IF YOU ONLY BELIEVE IN YOU
You can cross the highest mountain, You can sail the deepest sea
You can carve your way through a jungle, and others will follow you through,
—If you only believe in you.

God wants you to conquer the things in life, That He has for you to do,
He wants you to be happy, too
—He wants you to believe in you.

You can accomplish anything that you set out to do,
You can make life a breeze, as you are passing through,
—If you only believe in you.

Through life you have to cross a lot of bridges,
And travel down a lot of crooked roads too, and a few may get bumpy as you go through,
but you can make the bumps seem easy,
—If you only believe in you.

You can find the end of the rainbow, and make all your dreams come true,
You can help your friends find their dreams too,
—If you only believe in you.

Audrey O Cooley
THIS BROKEN VESSEL
See this broken vessel that's all damaged by decay.
See this broken vessel; it's useless for today.
See this broken vessel; it's no good let's throw it away.
But wait! God the Creator made us and He can mould the clay!

Although our vessel's damaged and we think we're sinking fast
God can lift us up if we'll only take hold of His hand at last.

God can mend this broken vessel and can make it look brand new
Then my vessel can be useful and will sparkle like the dew.

Take this forgotten vessel that's been hid and pushed aside
And bring it into the warmth and sunlight of God's love and there let it abide.
The vessel that seemed so hopeless will have a new dimension
Since God is the Potter and He gives to us Redemption.

Janet Lee Spencer Vaughn
IF I WERE

To My Loving Husband George O., Lorene, Mom, Dad and Family with Love for all.

If I were a dancing doll I would dance for someone sad to brighten their day.
If I were a soldier I would fight for peace everywhere.
If I were a flower I would bloom for the lonely and give beauty to one's who own nothing.
If I were food I would feed the hungry.
If I were water I'd quench the thirst of the dry.
If I were rich I would share with my brothers and sisters who are poor.
If I was warmth in the cold night I would cover someone freezing.
If I were a hospital I would treat the sick and tired.
If I were a doctor I would help heal the sick.
If I were an angel I would protect the children.
If I were happiness I would feel the heartbroken.
If I were a singer I would sing God's praises.
If I were a candle I would light up the darkness of souls.
If I were an Eagle I would soar the Earth, Touch the clouds.
If I were a Dove I would send out messages of love all over the world.
I'm not these things but I can pray!
I can expect God to answer because He dearly cares.

Alice E Reed
SOUTH DAKOTA
It is the Land of Infinite Variety, spiritual, picturesque, plentiful!
The State of renown petroglyphy, our Shrine of Democracy.
Unsurpassed! Beautiful!
It is a State of beauty fought for by men
Through hardship, starvation, love or sin.
The land of men that tilled the unbroken soil.
Sometimes working for naught with tears and toil!
The explorer, the miner, the will and the might
Who worked with brow wet from morn till night.
It is a land of Indians, war! Of history and lore.
Hardships of settlers, cattlemen.
The weak, the strong.
Stories of blizzards, drought,
Duststorms and floods of rivers.
A land forever blessed by our Giver!
From the magnificent Badlands to the beautiful Plains.
The Black Hills to the West, attracting the tourist guest
With hunting and fishing at its best!
Evergreen, birch; forests green
Brush covered nooks, running brooks
The barren lands of sage and brush, yucca and spoil,
Covering a wealth in gold, coal and oil.
The magnificent beauty of this land,
West, East, South or North
God in all His glory has brought forth!

Phyllis H Boschen
REMEMBERING
I MISS YOU MORE THAN
I miss Massachusetts, "land of the Cod and baked beans"—
MORE THAN I MISS
The maple trees in autumn splendor, the crooked country
Lanes and all their rustic scenes—
I MISS YOU MORE THAN
I miss the Boston Gardens, with it's swanboats gently
Gliding along the frog pond—
MORE THAN I MISS
The Old North Church, the Museum of Fine Arts, in all

Of which, I have a Yankee's
"bond"—
I MISS YOU MORE THAN
I miss the fried clams I savored,
from the restaurant by
The bridge, at Buzzard's Bay—
On my summer excursions to Old
Cape Cod, I always HAD to
Stop THERE along the way!
I MISS YOU MORE THAN
I miss the Esplanade concerts I
was so ENTHRALLED with,
The music of the "Boston Pops,"
under a summer
Canopy of heavenly "light" —
I've often wondered if the angels
were ECSTATIC, too—when
The majesty of that awesome
"sound" reached their heaven's
height?
I MISS YOU MORE THAN
I miss the cowslips in bloom, along
the Charles River,
They delighted my heart, every
spring—
Dear One, you must certainly know
by now . . .
I MISS YOU MORE THAN
ANYTHING!

Jerry A Anderson
MY PUMPKIN

To my daughter, Amy   Love Dad

I put you to sleep in my lap moving
to and fro',
When you were just a few days old
or so;
I couldn't wait for you to walk and
talk at last,
But, I didn't know time could go so
fast;
Now, you walk faster than me and
say some words I think,
Hopefully, they're not words daddy
uses when his temper's on the
brink.
As time passes by, I'm gonna keep
both eyes on you,
Because now you're one year-old
and too soon you'll be two;
My work day ending, pumpkin,
you're waiting at the door,
I know you'll be there a little after
four;
As I put you down, you follow,
walkin next to my knee,
And you're sayin, "DADDA,"
"DADDA," "Play with me!!"
So I put you over my head and drop
you on the bed,
And pumpkin I'm happy, I'm
"Dadda, Dadda,"
just like you said; So when it's a
little after
four and pumpkin's on the roam,
I'll hear
my little girl saying, "Daddy's
home! Daddy's home!"
A tear will leave my eyes, I know
they will;
Because the day I watched you
being born,
Is the day I remember still.—

Linda Edwards Foster
A YEAR AGO OR THREE

Dedicated with love for Philip; Love and a smile for special relatives; Love and a smile for truly special friends.

Leave me alone and by myself
I'm not in a fishbowl on a shelf.
I will decide to end this grief alone.
I can handle it on my own.

Smile here, frown there,
It is my loss to bear.
Don't expect me to be
As I was A Year Ago or Three.
I'm asking with a please.

I am grateful as I can be
For true friends do stand by me.
But the fear of loosing them is
always within.
The strain on friendship is like a
testing sea.
It wasn't there A Year Ago or Three.

The corner is turned as a bird
struggling to shore,
Now many directions are there to
explore.
Accept the new, never assume life
as A Year Ago or Three.
Hopefully, the world is ready for
another me!

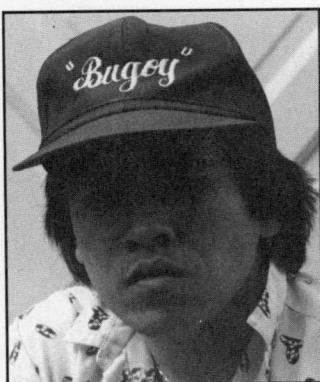

Jette Masankay Arenas

Jette Masankay Arenas
THE JOURNEY

To Lola Enriqueta, Your smiles always brought comfort to my troubled heart.

I sit by the window beneath the
heavens thinking of you.
The smiling face, the gentle touch
and the reassuring voice I feel
day in and out.
As the seconds tick by I realize that
the vision was of the past.
A past gone by forever embedded
in the corner of my mind.
I wake into the present as a
teardrop falls
Realizing the painful reality that
you're forever gone.
Three roses I pick for you,
symbolizing   I love you.
Sweet Lola my heart cries out in
pain
For your death brings less joy and
much sorrow.
But I also cry with tearful joy
For your suffering's over
And you've passed over
Into the promised life beyond the
river Styx.

Ruth May Dean
MY GRANDFATHER'S MANTLE CLOCK

To my 'Husband," Rowland H. Dean. Here's to my husband Rolly, who is special in my heart.

I hope our love will always be special.   Never my Dear, to depart.   Always your wife "Ruthie"

My grandfather's mantle clock
stood sedately
on the shelf.
In the living room of his house.
Each morning he would wind
his clock,
being quiet as a mouse.
He was very exacting in
completing
this chore
And always at the same time.
Because he said, if it wasn't done
with accuracy,
it would be a terrible crime.
The mantle clock remained on the
shelf
for many a year
And the decades did pass, and
grandfather
continued to wind his clock, with
his very
special class.
Years again passed and one cold
day in
January
There was a wreath on
grandfather's door
Friends and neighbors sighed,
with tears
in their eyes
Grandfather would wind his clock
no more.

Joseph C Sebastian
THAT'S LIFE

Life is filled with so much wonder,
It gives so many memories to
ponder,

We start with birth, and then
growing up,
Toys, joys, and oh yes, "that first
pup,"

Then comes studying from our
books,
As teens come along, worrying
about our looks,

During these years we meet John
or Kate,
And something inside us says,
"That's my mate,"

Then love grows, believe me, it
shows,
Friends can tell by the way your
face glows,

You set the date, and then the
marriage,
In a little while comes the baby
carriage,

Many obstacles occur over the next
few years,
They're overcome, some with joy,
some with tears,

Seeing them go thru the things you
did,
Is almost like re-living, "when you
were a kid,"

Now they are ready to face the
world,
Your job is done, their life is ready
to unfurl,

As I sit back and look at life,
It's been well worth it, for me and
my wife.

Patrick Michael Ed Corrao
A SIGHT TO SEE

This poem is dedicated to Rebekah, my lovely sister, who will one day have to experience a sight to see.

The day starts smooth
The room is still
I tell myself
The day will fill

At nine o'clock
The pressure mounts
The work is much
Each moment counts

The day goes on
As people call
But how can I
Get to them all

A lunch time break
I love to see
But back to work
I soon should be

And on and on
My humor fades
My face is bleak
But work there still be

At last
The day has gone
The work is stopped
And I am done
Oh it is a sight
And what a sight to see

P J Parker
THE HILL

This poem is dedicated to all those who appreciate the more aesthetic things life has to offer.

Up and down in never-ending time,
The hill goes on in a curved line,
Always there in majestic glory,
Over-seeing life and all it's fury.

Then one day a war broke out,
The hill was bombed around about
It fell before the onslaught of man,
Leveled beneath the wind-swept
sand.

The hill is gone. Terrain is bare,
Birds won't sing people won't dare.
Life gets shorter as war Goes on,
Old men remember the hill, but
now it's gone.

Christopher Alan Stidd
BLUE DOTTED DAHLIAS

Blue dotted dahlias
Dance upon a gray grassed field
In a southerly breeze
'Neath the shadow of a passing ship
They look to the billowed sails
And cry, knowing they cannot go
that high
For they are just blue dotted
dahlias
Dancing upon a gray grassed field
Swiftly the ship cuts
Leaving the flowers wishing
Their roots to be free
And bodies strong
A time they could go
Sailing upon such a ship
Whose shadow so deep passes
And bounce on wind filled sails
For a time they would dance
Upon a brown wooden field
All this they wish
But in all their wishing
These blue dotted dahlias
Do not know where they would go

Charles Renfrow
A LATE HARVEST
Seeking sustenance on
dimly lit
walks.
Wind tossing leaves about the air
one trapped by stirred
locks.
The sticky sultry night perfumes
and intensifies my efforts.
Headlights blaze
briefly
silhouetting
the two
against the darkness of
the night.
A harmony
entrusted to fate
nurtured by the intensity
of
love
And
recognizing
the turning point
is God.

Vicki Humphrey
THE GIFT
If you look real deep inside you
much deeper than your soul.
Look to the center of your heart
and you will find a little hole.
From this opening in your heart
love and goodness come shining
through.
It was given as a gift from God
made especially for you.
Everytime you do good for
someone
and make their day seem brighter,
then that little hole will get bigger
and your burdens will seem much
lighter.
If you treat this gift with tenderness
as you would a precious gem or
stone,
it will do the same for you
and you will never be alone.
If only more people would realize
this gift is like no other,
they would welcome a stranger
into their home
and treat him like their brother.
If we could all just join together so
all the
world could see, I'd shout it from
the highest
mountain look at the gift Gods
given me.

Martha Greenberg

Martha Greenberg
YOUR FACE YOU CAN'T CHANGE
I am a beautician who works on
your hair,
I'm not a magician, so try to be fair.
I can make you look lovely, with
each hair in place,
But there's one thing, I can't do,
I can't change you face.

You come in and haunt me with
pictures and faces,
But if you had their face, you too
would go places.
Why try to be someone you can
never be?
If you were a flower, would you
want to be a tree?

For beauty, as we all know, comes
from within,
You too can be pretty, just start
with a grin.
Don't rush us, or holler, or start a
big riot,
You might be more pleasant, if you
went on a diet.

For hair as you know, is a woman's
crowning glory,
And that takes you back to the
same old story.
Your hair and your makeup, you
can always arrange,
But there's one thing, that's certain,
Your face you can't change.

So don't give us ulcers or acute
indigestion,
Because sometimes, squeeze-ins
Are just out of the question.
Just leave it to us, and we'll do our
best,
But we can do just so much, and
you must do the rest.

We'll change your color, and we'll
arrange your style,
But nothing will help, if you refuse
to smile,
We keep telling you one thing, and
though it sounds strange,
There is one thing we can't do,
YOUR FACE WE CAN'T CHANGE.

Roque E Barela
BELIEVING IN OURSELVES . . . SHADES WE COULD COME TO KNOW
WILL WE TAKE THE RISK AND
ALLOW OUR INTERNAL
GOODNESS
TO SHINE THROUGH . . .

or shall we choose a quiet
loneliness—

WILL WE ALLOW OURSELVES
TO SHOW OUR POTENTIAL
ABILITIES
FOR CLOSENESS . . .

or shall we choose to frain the
sweetness of touch—

WILL WE PREMIT OURSELVES
NOT TO CARE FOR OTHERS,
WHEN WE ARE
SO UNAWARE OF WHO THEY
ACTUALLY ARE . . .

or shall we learn to open our
inner selves, to those
who choose us to grow towards
them—

WILL WE CONFIRM THAT MAN
INHERITANTLY COULD
ALLOW CLOSENESS,
CARE, CONCERN—AND THE
MULTITUDE OF HIS
ENERGIZING POTENTIAL

or shall we continue to open our
selves, as though to touch,
and yet never feel the essence
and unlimitedness of this
actualizing sense ** inherit **
in the

SHADES WE COULD BRING
OURSELVES TO KNOW . . .

Tracy Steinka
DOES IT REALLY MATTER?
I close my eyes
And hope
That when I open them again
The life I have seen
Has disappeared into a vast
darkness
So I will not have to see it again
Yet then I find
That my eyes are always closed
Not wanting to see the life around
me.
I trip and stumble
For I would rather fall
Than have to see the life around me
And be hurt by the people in it.
The torment
The tears
The people around me
Treating me as though I were
invisible
Not existing
Yet I'm not invisible
I live
But does it matter?
Does it really matter?

Erica L Risberg
TO TWILIGHT
Oh Helios! Pour your golden rays
on earth
And light the sky once more before
the night.
Let free your sparkling beams into
verse
And watch them dance on frothy
waves in flight.

The streaks they make fade slowly
in the sky,
They forge great, radiant treasures
from a chest
Across the heavens. Nightingales
do fly
To meet their mates in flight, then
stop to nest.

They gaze upon a darkened sea
below
And witness night approaching
from the West.
The world of water calms amidst
the glow
Of bronze light; earth in layers gold
is dressed.

The drapes of eve do cover up the
sun,
The air about them gently blows
away
The traces day has left. All is slowly
gone
As night begins to cover over day.

The honey-tinted light seeps
through the drapes
And drops cling on the dark
curtains of night.
The droplets shine and twinkle o'er
the cape
of darkness; specks of glorious
delight.

Peggy Saxin
THE SUNKIST MASK
I get lonely when tomorrow comes.
Only when I'm changing colours
Am I someone.

Despair unfolds inside my mind,
Bringing me shadows I don't
understand,
And I am half-way gone.

Slipping and falling, I descend
Into vast darkness
And bright light.

Almost gone, someone else is
coming nearer
Inside my mind
Showing me a confusing world
Of glowing tension evermore.

I'm losing the battle
To this powerful force
And I almost want to give in.

How I wish I could know
Why there is life,
Why there is death
Why there is me.

There is no other
Who can help me now
Because I must
Remain
Here.

Diana Fullbright
HE AND SHE
One day they met and began
sharing warmth;
languishing time, they—touching
and giving.
Inside her heart a while hope
existed.
Tálk came easy. A closeness
beginning.

Desire to help such a love stay alive;
an urgency . . . time was soon filled
in haste.
Longing swept him to give love and
comfort.
Wanting to hold her heart and to
keep her.

Foreboding is, like habit, hard to
break.
Struggling inside she felt
apprehension.
Doubt in her heart, fixed upon the
edges.
Alarms of fate within her being
rings.

The tremblings rise as she fears his
pity,
but even more she fears his close
touching.
The dread inside her quivers and
rises
but even more she fears his close
touching.
as the panic overcomes her senses.

So to escape, becomes the deserter;
not wanting to yet leaving him with
pain.
The gentle side of her heart has no
words,
no resistance, to fight this
unreason.

Alone again, the cycle commences,
seeming to pursue a never yeilding
goal.

Don Willis
TREES

All my writing is dedicated to my wife Carol—In appreciation for the inspiration she's alway's given to me. Thank you princess.

Trees, are like ballerina's,
In the wind, they dance and sway,
I love to sit, when it's windy,
And watch the branches play.
Their branches reach up to the
sky,
As if they try to pray,

Reaching for the sunlight,
Each, and every day.
The raindrops fall upon the leaves,
This is what gives them life,
They look so tall and majestic,
Like monarchs, with no strife.
Trees remain forever,
As people come and go,
Their beauty, is for all to see,
To watch them dance, to and fro.
So, next time, you see a tree,
Try and guess, how long it's grown,
Admire, it's majesty,
And all the time it's known.

Dolly Selby-Gilliland
DADDY'S SOLDIERS

Two young boys playing war
In their daddys den
Hear their mother calling
And hide as she peers in
Beneath their daddys wooden desk
They take the leather chair
And scoot it in to block themselves
She'll never find them there.
The enemy is searching
About the soldiers camp
A bright light carefully scans the room
Then she turns off the lamp.
The captain turns quite satisfied
The enemy has left,
And two brave soldiers shake their hands
Beneath the wooden desk
"Well done old chap" the captain says
His eyes so full of glee
"A metal I shall pin on you,
for your Bravery."
Up on top the wooden desk
Just within his reach
He grabs a shiny paper clip
"Now do give us a speech"
Their mother overhears these words
Inside her thoughts do burn
For the man who gave her two brave boys
From war did not return.

Helen L Smith

Helen L Smith
CHRISTMAS AT OUR HOUSE

Dedicated to my beloved parents, Mr. & Mrs. Thurman Locklear who made the writing of this poem possible.

Days before Christmas at our house was a very special time.
To see one of us not busy was very hard to find.
Of course, I'm speaking of the days when we were growing up.
There were only ten of us and we sure could stir up some fuss.
We would help to rake the leaves, cook, and clean the house.
Then on Christmas Eve in bed, we were as still as a mouse.
You see, we were looking for Santa to come around this night.
We knew to be very good and make sure we were out of sight.
We had met the requirements of Santa just as we had been told.
Now we were sure that in our house he wouldn't miss a single soul.
But as the days of our childhood grew and came to a close,
Our parents said, "Listen children there's something you must know."
"This man called Santa Claus has been very good to you.
Now I want you to understand what we're going to say is true."
"We have been your Santa Claus and brought you all those toys,
For you see, we wanted to make you happy both girls and boys."
"Now we want to tell you of a real Santa from above.
The one who really brought Christmas and brought it with joy and love."
"If you would believe on Santa Claus when you were very young,
Surely it must not be too hard to believe on this man, God's son."
Ever since this time I have found Christ very very dear.
Not only at the Christmas season, but throughout the year.
I might not receive the kind of gifts that Santa Claus brought.
After knowing Christ there has been blessings which no money has ever bought.
He is the reason for the season!

Amelia Tan
A MISTAKE

As I walked down the path
so familiar, so unknown
There I found two ways to go
And I was all alone.
My thoughts were of friendship
and I took the one at the right
But all I found was confusion,
and the darkest night.
I didn't know whether to laugh
or to cry,
But I did know I wanted
to die.
If only I could turn the hands
of time, back the other way
But I know it's hopeless
because here I lay
My mind is like jelly,
I'm ashamed of myself
For so naive, for being so stupid
that's how I felt
I sit blinded by the dark,
looking for a speck of light.
I looked for you to tell me what's right.

Geraldine Gem C Dee
LIFE BEGINS TOMORROW

To all those who've been a part of me and who'll be a part of my tomorrow: Mommy, Ginger, Tan Family, KLA, EGOG, Gato, RRR, RB, RA, JM, GDM, PS, RST,

---

fingers of morning sunshine
inching their way through
start of a new day
among those other myriad days

it's the nanoid day of my life
or is it life?
wonder why i hate this day
no life, no love, no life

morrow is another day
no life, has life
no one knows
you just have to wait—cept fate

life begins tomorrow, she says
when is that tomorrow
waiting seems so endless
till the fingers
inch their way through again

Suzanne Marie LaMontagne
MY HANDS . . .

To L., Who Pleasures Me in a Thousand Ways

. . . I also have palms and fingers
for your leisure, for your pleasure!

I have hands, enthusiastic or ceremonious,
to please you
I have hands, ready for a feast in your honor,
they were born when they met you!

The first time,
how would they dare to, or know how to undress you?
Nevertheless,
I wanted to seize you naked in my naked hands!

You did laugh when I was amazed
at the softness of your skin!
I just couldn't believe my palms . . .
Had I, until then, thought that a man's body
had to look and feel exactly like some old bark . . .

From now on,
I have hands which are intimately acquainted
with your body . . .
Just like if you were
My "newborn son" . . .

Frances Georgiana Carter
SALVATION

World Peace

God created all men—Equal
Nature sets each one—Apart
'Tis not our shade of skin—He'll judge
But the Goodness—In one's Heart
So let us face—Reality
Shoulder each—Our Special Cross
Give thanks to Him—For Our Reprieve
Our Souls could be—Our Loss

Mildred A Williams
NEGROES

Negroes are people, too;
Just like me and you!
They want to love and be loved,
Just like I am I, and you are you!
They have a heart!
Hearts bring pain and pain brings tears!
Therefore; Negroes shed tears!
They are the same as you and I!
So, why can't we look at each other and say,
"I Love You!?"
Instead of, "I Hate you; you Nigger! You're Down-Grading Us!"
I've always wondered why this has to be!
Why do people look at you 'cause you're black?
I pity them!
They're the ones that are wrong!
The ones that are prejudiced!
They are the ones we should feel sorry for.
Because Negroes are People!
White people are Prejudiced!

Clara Jo White
THE MANY FACETS OF LOVE

This poem is dedicated to Jeff, with much love.

Love is a feeling that grows,
Like a child, it is born, nurtured, and it grows.
Like a flower, it is cultivated, and it blooms,
Like a hurt, it brings pain, but it heals the wounds.

Like a tree that grows tall, and gives shade,
Or fruit it may bear,

Love is sharing and caring,
It doesn't matter when or where.
Love is happiness, sadness, even madness,
Love is singing. crying and joy;
It is a bouncing baby girl or boy,
It is enduring and strong,
It will defend right or wrong.

Mrs J H Fenton
THE LITTLE HOUSE

To "Mary Ann"

Little house upon a hill,
Autumn days and winter chill,
Children cuddling baby kittens,
Always wearing his matched mittens.

Apple trees and apple pies
Crispy days and blue blue skies.

Winter snow and hauling ashes,
Pretty dresses with wide sashes.

Sledding down the steepest hill,
Faster, Faster! What a thrill!!
Melting crystals, spring's first sign.
Wonderful memories for all times.

Michael Monaco
WHERE THE OCEANS MEET

To everybody who encouraged me to write. I thank you and love all of you.

My feelings for you
are so true
time has given you to me
like a dove in the sky
love makes me fly
and this is how I see. . .
you and me
we're going to be
better than ever
where the oceans meet
love will defeat
my feelings will last forever
but in the end
another love can't mend
my heart, broken in two
for all I do is cry,
for you have died
and now I'll join you
up in the sky
with the angels so high
I'll be there when,
the oceans meet
love will defeat,
we'll be together again.

Clinton L Alexander
A MAN

A man was on a river's edge,
Tossing rocks off the ledge,
When suddenly from out of the
woods,
On the other bank a tall man stood.
The tall man said to the guy on the
ledge,
My life is of a sailor's pledge,
I sailed the oceans and rocked the
seas,
I've made mighty sailors cry for
mercy from me.
Now my fine man what is your tale?
Are you a lover of land or is it
oceans you sail?
And the other said, it's the land
I roam.
Surely solid earth is my home,
I fought bloody wars and took
people's lives,
I've suffered from pain and sorrow
and strife,
I've explored every land from east
to west,
I've fought wars among the best,
But now my good man I'll be on
my way,
For on this ledge I cannot stay
But as he spoke and started to go
The tall man said,
Come with me and we'll exchange
what we know,
Yes, my good man, we'll be on our
way,
For on this ledge we cannot stay.
Nobody knows where these two
people went,
Maybe in a fine land is where their
life was spent,
Or have they learned new skills
from each other,
Maybe they live and work as a
team,
Or did they part and forget each
other.

Naomi Ruth Hill
BEAUTIFUL SIGHTS

What can be more beautiful in the
whole world than an early
morning sunrise?
Or a child flying a kite the highest
of highs,

The beautiful colors of a sunset,
A fisherman with a big fish in his
net,

New spring flowers blooming,
especially a rose,
Gardens growing in neat little
rows,

Birthday cake with candles
making your loved ones eyes
bright,
Firework display in the black of
night,

A couple holding hands,
Children building a snowman,

Sun glistening over the ice and
snow, with animals playing in
the fields,
A child playing on the beach with
a pail and shovel and
shells,

A boy and girl dressed up for their
first dance,
A bride walking down the aisle, at
that time you don't give
the groom a glance,

Birds flying with food for their
babies in the nest,
Fruit and berries just waiting for
the harvest,

Night with stars so close and yet so
far away,
A rainbow after a rainy day.

You ask what can be more
beautiful,
My new Granddaughter clasping
my finger with a smile,
makes my heart full.

Gwennie K Case
THE BEST IS YET TO BE

I dedicate this poem to my family and friends. Also to that special someone in my life.

The best is yet to be,
Come with me and be my friend,
My love my only one,
We will share love, joys, tears and
fears,
And we'll never part,
Come with me and share the years
As time goes by we will love each
Other more and more,
So come with me
The best is yet to be.

Amberly Noelle Johnson
MY DREAM

My dream is a dream
I dream in fall,
It lives behind
The waterfall.

Where roses grow
And rain falls,
Where colors shout
And nature calls.

Where dreams live
And dreams die.
They can't live forever,
Like you and I.

Like diamonds on the flowers
That shine so bright and new;
It's hard to tell it's water
Making it's own dew.

Lace for skies, beautiful skies;
As they turn bright pink and blue.
A secret world of our own
Made just for me and you.

When the battle of love and evil
begins,
The side of love always wins.
Love is great, it conquers all;
There beneath the waterfall.

Gary Joseph Hasiak

Gary Joseph Hasiak
MY VERY SPECIAL FRIEND

I, Gary Joseph Hasiak, dedicate this poem to Trudy Rose Blazek. My outlook on life changed the day I met her. She is, "My Very Special Friend"

Trudy,
Just when things were at an all
time low,
And the depression inside me that
I tried not to show,
I took the first step at living again,
And on Friday night I met a special
friend

I didn't want that night to end,
This lonely heart of mine was
starting to mend,
Putting all the pain and sorrow
aside,
I searched for the words I've
always seemed to hide.

I couldn't believe what was
happening to me,
Blinded by love so long that I just
couldn't see,
And then on Sunday with the help
of that friend,
My pain and sorrow for the day
came to an end.

Thank's, Trudy, for being there on
that day,
It meant more to me than words
could ever say,
May be we can do it again someday,
And if you agree then we will find
a way.
And I'm sure that the day will be
filled with fun,
Because two people together are
better than one

When I think back on all those
lonely nights,
Thinking of ways of ending the
fight,
And as I start to dream I hear a
voice,
Telling me not to make that awful
choice.

I realize now that life is worth
living,
When there are people like you
who don't mind giving.
You gave me more on Sunday than
you'll ever know,
Even though sometimes my
feelings don't show,
And what I feel right now is hard
to explain,
That day with you I experienced no
pain.

I hope you're not bored after
reading this poem,
It's something that I do when I'm
feeling all alone,
You've mended my heart and
showed me the light,
So now it's time to continue the
fight.

Thank's again, Trudy, for being
there,
I hope we have more days like that
to share,
But if something happens and it all
comes to an end,
I hope that I never lose my very
special friend.

Carol Ann Sheldon-(Munoz)
A TREASURE

I dedicate this poem to all who have loved and lost, someone dear to you in your life. Remember him or her as your treasure. With love always to all.

Although you are gone from
sight . . .
You are a treasure in my heart . . .
My love for you will always be . . .
For me my deepest memory . . .

Joel Embry
YOU CREATED THE WORLD

This poem is dedicated to my parents, S.P. and Maurine Embry—"I love you."

You created the world, Lord
and turned it over to me
but I made of Your world
what I wanted it to be.

I leveled Your beautiful mountains
and cut Your tall stately trees.
I burned Your green meadows
and polluted Your deep blue seas.

Then You sent Your Son
to this world to save
But I took Your Son and placed
Him in a cold, dark grave.

The grave is for those
who are burdened by sin
so Your Son had no reason
to stay and by Your love
He arose to live again.

Carmelita Dyke
THE TANGLED THREAD

One rainy day as I was walking
along a narrow street,
I saw some tangled thread laying
in mud at my feet.
Something told me to pick it up
as rain fell on my head,
And I thought, "why bother?
it's just muddy tangled thread."
But I knelt down and picked it up
and I'm so glad I did,
'Cause it was a crocheted cross
made of yellow colored thread.
I'll always keep this little cross

that I found stained with mud,
It reminds me of Jesus' death and
how He shed His precious blood.
The tangled threads are liken to
how
sometimes our lives can get,
We're too busy everyday and the
meaning of the cross forget.
How Jesus died for everyone all
over His great land,
I'll always cherish the day I
found the muddy tangled thread.

Helen E Stanton
SPIRIT

It zooms upward
Then touches down at will
There are no bonds to bind
No hurdles to surmount.

Growth will not be stunted
In this bounding phenomenon
It holds a daily emotional reunion
With laughter, tears, and joyful
singing.

It is unique—
It cannot be possessed
It is free. . .

Michelle Hartley
SPIRITUAL LOVE

Our love is strong and deep.
It is everlasting.
It does not fade with the passage
of time.
I love you more than words can tell.
More than our bodies entwined
could feel.
Our love is mighty.
It is fierce.
It is undying.

Our love has been blessed by God,
And the greatness of His vast
heavenly Kingdom.
And it is of the magnitude
That is
The depth of our love.
I love you so much
Forever and always
Throughout eternity.

Steven Horner
THE INTENSITY OF POVERTY

With the intensity of poverty
Little brittle leaves come brown
Come down winter withering
Come down
Crackling with skeletal will they
wander
Drying to dust the wind they
powder
Ashes of leaf veins dust to dust
Come down winter withering
To tiny lungs that suck
With brown breath the wintry
dead,
Come down the mocking brown
confection
To swaddle a kindred little corpse,
With the intensity of poverty
The gasping little world stills,
Come down winter withering
Come down

Anita Pokorny
SHARE WITH ME

With love to my husband, Joseph, who makes my life complete.

Share with me, my love,
Your thoughts, your hopes, your
fears;
For only then shall I be free
To share myself with you.

All of my anxious yesterdays are
gone,
For today you are here with me;
You have fulfilled my dreams as I
have yours,
So now it is time for us to share.

Peggy Charles
REALITY

To my special son, Randy, with love forever . . .

A sturdy boy for all to see
Proud to see him tower o'er me.
A mother's love could not be
greater
No other child would I trade for.
Caring for him thru early years,
Watching him grow & hiding my
fears.
Maybe he's not as strong as I
thought
Feelings of illness in him—I fought.
When he gets bigger—he'll care for
me
He'll be as strong as an old oak tree.
But God didn't mean this for him,
or for me
This son of mine has epilepsy . . . .

Joseph A King
MY FLIGHT

This sonnet is in memory of Commander Dick Scobee and the six crew members of the space shuttle CHALLENGER. We will never forget you.

Blast off this brazen craft with
belching roar
That cuts its searing wake upon the
sky.
Above the snowy, wind-swept
clouds I soar
Where lives the solemn dreams of
man to fly.
I've climbed the silent depths of
endless space
Where sun-lit worlds float on in
vibrant blue.
I glide through time beyond all
human trace
To seek the place where once the
angels flew.
Behold man's dream where God's
creations lie;
And if, within these hallowed halls
of grace,
I join with souls who must forever
fly
The timeless flight through all
eternity,
Grieve not for me; Here in this
sacred place
I shall have found my immortality.

Helen Bacon Edwards
THIEF

I dedicate this poem to my dearest friend and loving father, Alex H. Bacon

Dawn steals through my bedroom
window
Penetrates the velvet veil
Of sleep,
Intrudes into my sanctuary,
Pulls the soft raven cloak from
me—
Mutating it
To charcoal
To dingy gray
To dull ivory
Till all that remains
Is the stark, raw white of day
Robbing me of sweet darkness
Cherished solitude
And exquisite dreams.

Elizabeth King

Elizabeth King
SENSE OF LEGACY

To Frankie King, My Mother, who through her love, understanding and guidance helped me appreciate the pleasure, endure the pain and cope with the inconsistencies of life.

Where dwells our sense of legacy
Earned through toil and tears?
In the strength and love which
Brought us through those evil
"Slavery Years,"
The bravery of our fathers no
matter death the cost,

The help and prayers our mothers
gave
In spite of children lost.
Where dwells our sense of legacy
Earned through toil and tears?
Not in the faces of those older than
their years,
Not in the lack of pride in self
Nor the need to feed on fears;
Not in the evil deeds or senseless
ills
We heap on each other;
They have taken us down to
"Dante's World,"
To brother against brother.
Where dwells our sense of legacy
Earned through toil and tears?
Is it hiding in our hearts and minds
Afraid to venture here?

Ruth Paschke
THE GIFT

God sent down a gift to man,
The gift could love and understand,
The gift could laugh and it could
cry,
It can accept and not ask why.
The gift is strong and always there,
Full of compassion and wanting to
share.
So when you feel you have no self
worth,
Remember why you're on this
earth,
For man couldn't live as fulfilled a
life,
Without God's gift—a loving wife.

George T Zemtseff
AUTUMN SPLENDOR

I sense the end of another summer
and the beginning of fall's
wonder.
I relish the change of the leaves and
crisp, cool evenings sprinkled
with stars of splendor,
Grass of green yawns and silently
changes its hue,
Trees that flourished give up their
leaves and acknowledge the
sleep they are due.
An arrow of geese decorates the sky
as southerly haven it does seek.
Squirrels of brown and gray
hurriedly prepare, racing
frosted grass that soon will
creak;
Shocks of hay stand row on row
amongst patches of orange—
some round, some awkwardly
sunken,
Where old, yet youthful
imagination may tread the aisle
in search of yesterday's "Great
Pumpkin."
The season is short, as quickly it
did begin, it has passed,
But I who know the seasons
understand why this season
must so quickly come to last,
To accede to and humbly
acknowledge that season it does
bring,
And bow its head with proper
dignity, to introduce the season
of our King.
I sense the majesty of all that
preceded His birth.
When fall ushers in the Advent of
man's salvation on this earth.

Janice A Sargent
MY BEST FRIEND

To my husband for being there to lean on and for his love.

A big warm hug or a soft gentle
word,
Can make bad times seem less
absurd.

Someone beside you all the way,
To share the memories of each day.

The world has many unexplored places,
With lots and lots of unknown faces,
But never a problem will this be,
While my special friend walks close to me.

He's always there to lend a hand,
Most any problem he'll understand.
This fantastic person is a dream come true,
My wonderful husband! Maybe you knew.

Lisa M Bizarro
SPRING
A time of rebirth and new beginning
Children can be seen playing, laughing and some even singing
The days slowly grow longer and people feel a little lazy as they day dream
Some think of fishing by a stream
Thoughts of Spring break come to the minds of the young
Getting time off from school to have some fun is a thought of each one
The air is warm and sweet
A romantic season a time when many young people meet
Flowers start to bloom and the leaves of the trees turn green
What a lovely scene!

Wendi Wilson
SILENCE
Silently she stares at the dusty clock,
As the numbers slowly tick away;
She lays very still on the edge of her bed,
As time grasps on to another day.

She stares at the picture next to her bed,
And remembers how life used to be;
Her thoughts seem to drift back in her mind,
As she still refuses to face reality.

She remembers the good times she once enjoyed,
And how love simply faded away;
She reaches for her pillow to hide the tears,
And tries to make the pain go away.

She dreams of a time when love will be warm,
And her life will be just as she planned;
She says his name softly and tries to rest . . .
I guess she'll never really understand.

Terry G Yarnell
REFLECTIONS OF A SUNNY DAY
The coldness is past and the loving sunlight warms the earth.
Seeds begin to awaken and insects rouse to continue the never ending quest for nourishment.
A lone sparrow sings his song of joy of the coming spring.
He has survived the harsh winds and winters icy fingers,
He sings a greatful song of praise to the lifegiving sun.
In the mists of the past there is a hugh elm that has stood all my days.
It has held countless such sparrows on its limbs,
all in turn singing their songs of joy and sorrow.
The tree is mystical in its great expanse, reaching to the sky, to the same sun the sparrows worship.
Just as winter is a time of cold slumber where every living thing
takes on the mast of death, spring is warm and alive, where life bursts forth in all its wonderous beauty.
It is a time of reflection on springs past, of youth.
Of those whom we have loved, yet are not here to enjoy the birth of life with us. The sparrow sings his beautifully simple song of life.
Spring comes and wraps us in her loving arms . . . and we are happy.

Canel Morely
CROSSWIND
Wind pulls twisted clouds apart
Beckoning to a waning moon;
A dusky night it is, and holds a yellow light.
Stars hang listlessly above:
Wind mocks and laughs at the dying day
Then moaning, sighing, whining
Needles through bleached fields of whithered grass—
Lulling insects from song—to sleep.
A raindrop falls, there—another
—Twisted from its misty bed above
—To its leafy, dusty bed of earth below.
Reluctantly—the wind has died,
Insects awaken
Now their humming fills the night;
Clouds scatter to make room for flaunting stars.
The whole night sighs.

Judith F Seymour
UNTITLED
And so I cry
To try to soften my heart
It hurts so much
I'm figuring out why

I'm afraid of being alone
Facing the unknown
I'm tired of working so hard
Always on my guard

I forgot how to smile
To make my heart glad
It hurts to laugh
So I'll not try for awhile

I'm tearing apart
The inside of my heart
I always seem to sigh
And so I cry

Reggie Davis
SILENT WHISPERINGS
The calm within my heart is but
a message from myself
Silent whispering, from the inner voice;
the grand master speaketh in his holy
temple; Shinning light and sacred fires;
Invocations that stirs my consciousness
to introspection.
Through the depths of self I plument into
nocturnal darkness to that glorious place
of invocation where the light shineth
forth like a blistering sun, a solo—
apporition of Gods divine birth that
leadeth the lives of all mankind to
greater asperations of oneself.

Ellen Kolsto

Ellen Kolsto
IF A CUP RUNNETH OVER

To my mother who appreciates my poetry the most.

When I drink from a cup
I fill it up, to the H
top with something A
hot. If it should N
overflow, well D
that's more L
than I can E

Mrs Ida Bunch
PRELUDE TO SPRING

To all my children: Glenn, Beverly, Jamie, Michael and Barry (and my skeptical grand-daughter, Heather) who always had faith in my ability.

(Ruminating on a rainy day in March)
Bare branches silhouetted against the sky, naked and unresistant against the wafting of the wind.
Minute rain, steady and determined to saturate all that's below.
The Earth becomes pregnant and swells to deliver it's off-spring of flowers and grass.
We, the inhabitants stoically trudge through it all, hopeful and expectant of the "Birth" that we know will come.
We must have this, to have the Other, for Nature decrees,
the Cycle cannot be broken.

Constance Anderson
INSIGHT
In one hand He holds the miracle
Of Life, so delicate and so astounding.
While in the other He holds the destiny
Of death, for which we all must face.
In his heart he has pure Love,
For each of his creations.
While in his mind he holds the Truth,
For all of mankind.

Doreen Latourette
SOCIAL STUDIES

Dedicated to my sixth grade teacher, Mrs. Scully, 4/87. Thanks for your help.

Social studies is pretty interesting
Even though I always fail.
I guess it's cause I don't study
Instead I think about a whale.
I failed my last test
With a lucky 23,
And when I showed my mother
I knew that she was proud of me.
Especially when she sent me to my room
Came after me with the broom
And when she said she was ready to send me to the moon.
I guess she came up with a broom,
To help me clean my room,
And when she wanted to make me famous
By being the first kid to visit the moon.
All of this has happened over a failing test,
And thats why I think
That Social Studies is the best.

Lorraine F Buchanan
FRIENDS

I dedicate this to my "Friend" Jake Landsiedel

I have a little friend
And his name is Jake
We play with toys,
Sing and play patty cake
We sit on the porch
And watch all sort of things
We discuss the bees, cats, dogs
And even butterfly wings!
We sing and dance
And even do a jig
And talk about daddy
He has a rig
It's a tow truck
big, good and strong
His daddy's his joy
And he can do no wrong
We wait for him
To come home to eat
His dinner, watch T.V. play with Jake
That's a treat!
Then it's off to bed
As the day is done
We'll be up again
Tomorrow with
the sun
For it's the beginning
of another day
When my playmate
Knocks on my door
And says
Can I come out to
Play!!

Ela Westbury Thorpe
BRIDGES
If time we could turn
We would all have bridges to burn.
Thru life we go—our bodies grow
Our loves we find—our lives we intwine
Our children come—our children go
We now have time on our hands
We have met our demands
It is such a wonder in our later years

Did we burn all the bridges that gave us
Our loves, laughter and fears.

Helena Sutton
DAY TIME LOVE

Search for tomorrow,
the very young, and restless.
There's one life to live.
At the edge of night is
a guiding light.
As the world turns, somerset.
Ah! another world.
That's love of life.
That's love of life.

Danny Eugene Randolph
GRANDMA'S ROCKIN' CHAIR

Written in fondest memories of my grandma, Blanche Evelyn Higginbotham, December 10, 1900-February 06, 1986. Although she has departed, she will always live in our memories.

The paint has peeled, the wood is worn.
but yet holds firmly to its form.
The days have past when made like these,
of solid oak from hardwood trees.

The hours it shared and made her proud.
She liked its shape and liked its style.
No more motion does it make,
no more give and no more take.

A masterpiece, just sitting there.
I love my Grandma's rockin' chair.
I remember the days she kept it warm.
The evening nights, the early morn.

Sitting there with a smiling face.
Nothing could take my Grandma's place.
See, now she sits on a golden throne.
No more sitting all alone.

Her starlit eyes and skin so fair,
a snow white robe in which she wears.
But I still see her sitting there.
I love my Grandma's rockin' chair.

Irene C Denner
MY MOMMY

I'd rather have my Mommy home,
Than to go to "Outer Space."
I'd rather have those hugs and kisses,
And see her pretty smiling face.

Mommy was a teacher,
Making me proud, indeed.
Being an only daughter
Mommy met my every need.

I stood there wondering,
The day it all took place
Why my Mommy, the school teacher,
Was going to Outer Space.

She told me not to worry
That everything would be OK,
That where she was going
It would only take a few days.

She was so full of energy,
Excited as could be,
Not thinking of the danger,
Only "success" could she see.

All were settled in the Shuttle,
Off to Outer Space.
In just a matter of seconds,
An "Explosion" —no Mommy to embrace.

"Honor" will keep me strong.
The "Public" shocked and sad.
Although Mommy is gone,
I still have Scott and Dad.

Her name will go down in history.
Her courage will, indeed, spread
Inside future astronauts.
As into Space they tread.

In the far-off distant future,
In Heaven I will see
My Mommy who vanished so quickly,
From a tragedy she didn't foresee.

Diane Lore Palladino
RAIN IN NEW YORK

For Ernie and Andrew

Rain in New York
melts medallion cabs into
tiny slabs of yellow butter
over steaming manhole covers.
Umbrellas, limp and maimed,
poke uselessly
from wire trash baskets.

A wet TIMES pasted to the sidewalk
is trampled underfoot.
All the news of the world
reduced to senseless pulp.
At the curb a puddle is forming,
collecting each drop,
gushing toward the corner catch basin,
taking with it all your dreams.

Margie Young
OUR STATUE OF LIBERTY

David Jonathan Young (Grandson who inspired me to write it) He was three years old. He is now five. He spoke of the lady and wants to visit her.

Our beautiful lady so graceful and tall
She represents "Liberty" for one and for all
In her right hand reaching on high
She holds a torch that lights up the sky
The poor, the lonely, the tired did roam
Alas! Alas! They have reached their beloved home
They shed tears and pray as they draw near
They are home dear Lord, no more do they fear
They see the statue so encouraging, so grand
The Declaration of Independence she holds in her left hand
All colors and creeds come! Live in harmony and pray
Worship your God in your very own way
One hundred years old and long may she stand
For Freedom! Faith! and Hope! In America our land
You were restored and your banner unfurled
And may you stand for !Peace! All over the world . . .

Audrey J McGrady
FLASHBACK

For my precious daughter Keysha, who is the pillow of my strength and for John A. Neri, her father and my love of ten years whom I thank for the contribution of her existence.

I saw with you sunsets that I could never see with anyone else.
Climbed with you to mountain tops so high that only God has tread upon them.
I have walked with you in a rain so gentle that the weight of a single drop was lighter than a small childs tear.
I have laughed with you in the out break of a noise that could almost wake the deaf to sounds they have never known.

I have cried with you and for you, aloud and in silence as well, hard yet so soft that the coldest and strongest of hearts would rip.
I have slept by you under the brightest of stars, the whitest of snows, the fullest moon.
And have woke by you under the bluest of skies.
You are gone from me now and I walk my world alone with your memory at my side, shining through the windows of a small childs eyes.

Joy D Binion
THE TEENAGER OF THE PAST

I would like to dedicate this poem to my mother and my grandma.

In this day and age,
The teenager of the past,
Would not know their advantage,
Of the pace of life, that now moves so fast.

In our world their is no time to think,
Of what will happen tomorrow,
Or whether or not the sun will sink,
And the next day filled with sorrow.

The days they come and then they go,
And so do the people that we meet,
The worries that we know,
Are always lying at our feet.

But teenagers of today,
Must try to understand,
The advantages that our technical ways,

May bring tragedies for us to pay.

One nuclear blast,
That could show the world a hell,
Leaving nothing of the past,
Starting over from a hollow shell.

Barbara Thoelke
FEELINGS

I dedicate my words of love to Chris Huse, and will "Love Forever."

Today,
I'm feeling the distance
Between us
A little more than Most days . . .
I'm missing your *SMILE,
your *TOUCH,
your *EASY WAYS.
I'm feeling a little LONELIER
than usual:
thinking of you a little MORE . . .
And missing the way I feel
when I'm with YOU.
TODAY, like every day that
you are away,
I'm *MISSING YOU
and *WISHING YOU
were there . . .
I find Myself wishing
Just a Little More."

Catherine M Crawford
THROUGH YOUR EYES

In your eyes I see the wonder
As you watch the falling snow
Or hear the sound of thunder,
I watch you while you grow.

In your face I see the laughter
That each new experience brings,
Whether you're reaching out for rainbows
Or the carousel's brass rings.

In time I know you'll grow up
And forget your nursery rhymes
And the shadows that have scared you
So often at bedtime.

But for now I have the pleasure
To see life through your eyes
And experience the laughter
Before the wonder dies.

Mary Lou Wise
THE PROMISE

To my friend, Helen Ivec, who named this poem; To my mother, Linda Harris, just for being; And to my aunt, Tamara LaBreque, for having faith in me.

When we hear the words,
"If you deny me on Earth, I will deny you in Heaven,"

We may hear this as a threat, yet,
As a parent would (warn) not threaten
Is what we are really hearing;
As though saying to a child,
"If you run away from me, you will become lost."
A fact, not a threat.
And how will I find you
If you do not come back of your own accord?
"I will always be where you left Me.
So, should you and I be separated,
You will have to seek Me."

"In my Father's House are many Mansions:"
Each Soul when united with the Father
Embodies a Mansion.
A spiritual Mansion,
Sitting on its own grass-covered knoll,
On the Bosom of God.
Nature, Spirit, Mind and Body
In harmonious communion
In the Universe which houses all.

Bessie Lee Knapp

A MOTHERS THOUGHTS'

Written, for my son SP.4 Harry B Knapp by his mother, Bessie Lee Knapp; 1984;

Do, you remember that punk kid at the end of the block? That everyone said wouldn't amount to a lot, Well, so very wrong were those busy tongues You, see today he's far away, ready, willing, and able, to fight, for everyone!

Yes, he works for Uncle Sam, He, misses his Home Family too, friends of course, very few, they've, gone on to bigger, and older, and better things, Let's stop a minute and view this Man, Who's off in a far off distant land, He's, doing more than all the rest, you know why? They, only keep the very best. He's doing his part and been put to the test, Graded, A—OK, for Uncle Sam, So, you see he's my kind of Man. Friends, well he has a bunch everyday they work, together, play and even share lunch. Those, are his Buddies off from Home too; He kinda thought he had some friends, Oh he did a few selected ones,

But, all the rest forgot this punk kid but that's OK, Because, today he's 22 tall and strong with a heart that's true, because he never turned his back on you. If, all the punk kids could come out on top, think about the world we've now got, Damn, we could change things just a Hell, of a lot!We would'nt need these weaklings who refuse to fight, but go to bars and start a brawl, or kill someone for no good at all, Well, you see My Son isn't that kind of slob, he's working on a very important job, Guarding people like you and me all over the world while we're asleep. I, think he's one hell of a Man, not just because he's My Son, Because, he's doing a job that must get done By, a Man only, and That's My Son!

Natalee Suggs

MY DAILY PRAYER

Lord—Guide my steps along the Highway of life
Keep my steps straight in this world of strife
If I should stumble and fall along the way
Help me pull myself up and face another day
And not to blame others for mistakes I did
But to face lifes problems and grow stronger instead
When I come to the end of lifes setting sun
May I leave this world with thoughts of a job well done.

Agnes Robbins

PEACE

Soaring, soaring, through the
Beautiful-Blue
to the outer limits
through time and space
to the inner beauty
of Peace—tranquility

Out of the withered shell
I fly
on the wings of ecstacy
Free at last
Gliding, gliding, as silvery
blades on sparkling ice
to joy—Love—to eternity
to Peace everlasting

James D Phillips

TWO BLIND MEN

Dedicated to a living, loving, gracious, giving God.

I was blind and could not see,
That's what a blind man said to me.
I didn't understand, I had perfect sight.
My only trouble was seeing at night.
I wanted to know just what he meant,
And this is the story and how it went:
The blind man sat behind his Bible of Braille
Moving his fingers and reading so well.
I thought then how terrible it'd be
If I were blind and could not see.
What I didn't know and was to find out.
That I was blind without a doubt.
I saw a man read in darkness his finger his light
His faith in God gave him sight
As he touched his Bible Braille parts
I knew God's word was in his heart.
I knew then just what he meant
That true sight was heaven sent.
When I close my eyes and act his part
It's faith in God that moves my heart.
I've found the light and now I see
What God's Word means to me.
Now you know blind men see
Sometimes better than you and me.

Leslie Gail Elder

MEMORIES

Memories are made of things
That happen everyday,
Moments as we live them
Things we do or say.

Little bits and pieces
Of laughter mixed with tears,
Paragraphs and pages
Written through the years.

Friendships' that we remember
Mistakes that we regret,
The ending of a love
We never could forget.

We can't erase the sadness
Or edit out the tears,
We can't undo the wrongs
We can't relive the years.

Memories cannot show
What's going on inside,
Emotions and feelings
Are what memories hide.
"BUT SINCE MEMORIES KEEP BUILDING, EACH DAY CAN BE THE START, OF BUILDING NEW AND HAPPY ONES, TO STORE WITHIN YOUR HEART."

Grace (Franke) Pierce

AN ENJOYABLE PASTIME

I dedicate this poem to my/husband, Silas, who is above heaven's floor.

Heaven's floor—it's overhead!
Look up! There's a large movie screen.
Characters of talent action
Achieve an entertainment scene.

I see vehicles, animals, fish,
Performing delightfully.
They parade, dance, swim, run and leap;
Operating magically.

Mountains, rivers, valleys and lakes
Set a lovely scenic background,
Grand Canyon? Green hills? An unforseen country, just found.

Sights you have never seen before
Change quickly, are gone forever!
Never a rerun, and it's all free,
A grand surplus-time endeavor.

Rest, relax, enjoy the visions.
Mother Nature will never shirk.
Watch from inside, or lounge outdoors,
Take your fill of God's handiwork.

Walter K Delbridge

THE HONEYBEE

Culture's pollen with empathy's nectar
For honey and the hive's perfection
A life along the creative vector
Sweetness and light a useful confection

The inner voice comes to me:

"You follow an ancient law
Diverse ancestors saw
You have to follw the age-old Will
Work, create, fulfill,
And gather to live
Suffer your wingful journeys over
Brambles and anthills
Finding fragrant flowers
Not knowing exactly what you do
It's built into you;
With sundance and beauty calling
You go to bring pollen and nectar dew
Back to hivey hexagon
This after lure of sweet invitancy
Tending center petals to feed the hive
Each day awaiting the sun to arrive;
Why for flowers do your wings
Brave gusts, dust, for your work to Begin?
Honeybee,
You're only free
Chasing Beauty-Truth/Love
With Duty's dominancy."

David W Ogden

A PRAYER AT DAWN

As I awake, each dawn of the day
Holy Spirit of God, for Your guidance, I pray;
Be near unto me, so each thought, each deed,
Shall follow the urge of where You may lead.

Let me write only words You direct me to write;
Let my pen only 'luminate God's Holy light;
Clear my eyes of the film that darkens my view,
That I be a witness for God and for You.

Give me wisdom, oh Spirit, tho simple I be;
Give strength to my body; of mind, to see,
To fulfill the purpose I was sent to fulfill,
To honor Thy Kingdom and live in Thy will.

That I may perform what You lead me to do,
Is the prayer I pray, dear Spirit, of You;
When light of this day is vanished and gone,
You'll make this heart purer than you found it at dawn.

C E "Chiz" Mintmier

THE VOYAGER

I saw it leave the darkened strip
and drag along it's swollen tips.
The tips that had the long supply
of fuel to keep them up so high.
I watched them climb to higher skies,

just two alone to win the prize.

To stay aloft around this world,
this great adventure now unfurled.
That day to night and night to days,
these two alone saw through the haze.
While one does fly and contemplate,
the other then must navigate.

This frail small wisp upon the air,
this daring couple make a pair.
I've watched this feat upon the screen,
It's something I could only dream.
I watch and read about their flight,
and pray that they do win this fight.

It's been nine days they left this ground,
and now there's thousands gathered 'round.
To see them spiral from out the sky,
this frail small craft that they do fly.
Two wheels lock in, no time they waste,
and then the nose wheel takes it's place.

As it does glide down to this world,
with bands a playing flags unfurled.
Just when it's ready to touch down,
it's quiet here, there's not a sound.
The thousands stare in disbelief,
now come the cheers of wild relief.

Yet only two could make this trip,
but a million prayers were with that ship.
Yes nine long days, they flew up in the heavens,
but the GOD who was with them,
HE HAS MADE IT IN SEVEN.

Larry Gene LaRousse
MY FRIEND

Dedicated to all the friends of mine who have crossed my life's path . . Especially to my parents, my children Tana and Tara, and to J.M. for inspiring me years ago and to D.C. for inspiring me again

---

My life's path was crossed back quite some time ago
When I first happened to meet someone I thought I'd like to know
Memory fails to serve me as to the exact day and just when
But I felt I had to see and talk with her again

She seemed somehow to be so different to me
Something inside her that only I could see
A light shone round her; her smiles so real
Understanding came so easily, I could talk to her I feel

She did not laugh at or make fun of me you know
When I first tried writing; and telling her it was so
Others may laugh at and most don't understand
Because you try and express yourself they think you less a man

How can I say to you what may be on my mind
When I don't know how you'd take it, or if you'll be unkind
But you've shown me that at the least we're friends
No matter what this all may lead to or where it all may end

So if I think of pleasant thoughts of which are all of you
or weave myself into your dreams as dreamweavers often do
It's just my way to trying to get through each and every day
When you have the need for a loving friend along life's different ways.

Jackie Moulton Haug
LAST HOURS

In memory of my mother, Mary Gertrude (Trudy) Hinton Moulton

Bottles dripping, oxygen bubbling,
Labored breathing, hands fumbling,
Wind blowing, as nurses chatter,
Floral beauties on sill gather.

Friends drop in, goodbye to say,
Children cluster with hope display,
Phone calls from far and near,
This might be the last they fear.

Each breath a lasting struggle,
Bed pans hard to juggle,
The lonely vigil with those who care,
Who give their all, with love to spare.

Patience Master, soon my Julie will appear,
Then I'll come home, with you to be near,
There my beloved Lester I'll see,
And on those golden streets, he'll stroll with me.

Robert D Atkinson
IN MEMORY OF "TACO" OUR LITTLE DOG

He was one of a kind, a loving, four legged gem.
Every thing I do, every where I go, reminds me of him.
Perhaps, once in a life time, such pleasure, fills your life.
I wonder, with each waking hour, why all this emotional strife.
My heart is sad, my eyes, seem always to be moist,
What a pleasure, it would be, just to hear his voice.
Some thing, some time, will fill my sad and lonely heart,
But for now, I'm re-living his friendship, from the start.
I want, always to remember, everything, that made him so special.
Why he was taken from us, my mind continues to wrestle.
He was a fighter, struggled, with all his might,
His desire was to live, knowing he would be treated right.
He knew the battle was over, he couldn't fight any more,
He left as he had entered, through life's wonderful mystery door.

Judith J Fisher
MY PARENTS AND I

I made some mistakes, by making wrong to right.
Though I tried to think of ways, my parents and I wouldn't fight.

I thought I'd find an answer, if I were out on my own.
All that I had found, was to feel so alone.

I thought they didn't care anymore, whatever happened to me.
Being away and unhappy, was all I could see.

Now it's time to correct, all that I have done.
Never with a pistol, or a loaded gun.

But, only with my mind, and from right I will try.
Hoping I shall make it, without one lie.

I know I hurt the people, that I love the most.
Always thinking of them, as I sat upon the coast.

Looking into the waves, I could always see them cry.
That's when I felt, I wanted to die.

Now I am back, happier than before.
Was it me or them who had shut the door?

Working things out, will take alot of time.
But not as long, if our trust is on the line!

Please do not leave, if you think you know it all.
Because soon oneday, they know you'll call.

So stay open to them, as they are to you.
You may think they don't love you, believe me they do!

Kathy M Carrell
GRASS

Grass is green,
people walk on it.
On it, dogs and cats sit,
isn't that keen?
Grass is spit on,
on it, sports are played.
But it is always okayed,
one day grass is there, another it's gone.
Bikes are rode in the grass,
and cars are drove through it.
Even though people shout; quit!
People who do this don't have class.
Animals use it for pitstops,
people use it for sidewalks and tennis courts.
Cars use it for parking ports,
and in it some people plant crops.

Peggy Moss O'Neal
GOD'S MASTERPIECE

For my precious children: Sara, Kenny, Donna, Sandi and Amber

---

Dear Little One;
most precious one.
A gift from God above.

A tiny pretty piece of clay
to shape and mold with love.

Beloved Child
So tiny, yet a painter in his glory
Could never on his canvas paint
more exquisite a story.

Jessie L Burks
CROWDED ALONE

This poem is dedicated to the Head of my life; GOD, who gave the answers to CROWDED ALONE.

So much sadness in your eyes
that looks at a world of hate
with pain in your heart that survived
so many years, shows on your face.

You get lost in your fantasy world
so many others see
love and peace all wrapped in pearls
with you and I and me.

Life goes on . . . leaving you behind, alone, still
you walk, run under the blue
sky; with clouds in the air that wilt.

You and I climbed a hill that
stretches, beyond reach of the sea
that feels crowded as we sat
and looked around and saw just me.

Gabriel M Carrara
ROLL AWAY THE STONE

Came a man from Galilee
condemned to death on Calvary.
His only crime appeared to be
the son of God, he claimed to be.

Crown of thorns upon his head
a gather crowd who wished him dead.
Climbed the mount of Calvary
was crucified for all to see.

Taunting, teasing
those deceiving
Religious leaders,
disbelieving.
Come on down
They started screaming.
King of Jews,
he must be dreaming.

Roll, Roll, Roll,
Roll Away the Stone

Darkness loomed across the land.
No shadows seen upon the sand.
Noon day sun just disappeared.
He felt he was deserted here.

Was taken then from the cross.
Wrapped him up in linen cloth.
Placed the body in a cave.
For all of man, this life he gave.

Taunting, teasing
those deceiving
Religious leaders,
disbelieving.
Come on down
they started screaming.
King of Jews,
he must be dreaming.

Roll, Roll, Roll,
Roll Away the Stone

Darkness loomed across the land.
No shadows seen upon the sand.
Noon day sun just disappeared.
He felt he was deserted here.

Was taken then from the cross.
Wrapped him up in linen cloth.
Placed the body in a cave.
For all of man, this life he gave.

Taunting, teasing
those deceiving
Religious leaders,
disbelieving.
Come on down
they started screaming.
King of Jews,
he must be dreaming.

Roll, Roll, Roll,
Roll Away the Stone . . . . .

Marie Estep

Marie Estep

VIOLETS

Behold the hillside, amenthyst throne,
where the violets are grown.
Their beauty and eloquence,
put forth a delightful scent.
They are wild and so free,
velvet loveliness for all to see.
The price is only your sight,
see them glisten in the moonlight.
From all of the flowers to choose,
I'd choose to give the violets to you.

Judy A Hendrix

DREAMS WITH A DEADLINE

Rain falling, thunder calling
The world's in a whirling spin
That's the way it looks outside
But things are calm within.

War in the east, death in the west
People dying all around
Fighting without pause, for a "worthy cause"
They just can't find the peace I've found.

When will it end, and living begin
Not just existing each day
Pretending to be what others want you to be
The lead character in a life-long play.

To you it may seem the Impossible Dream
An elusive butterfly chased here and there
I've found the answer and will tell all the world
When the world becomes willing to share.

Jim Restivo

SMILE

It is always nice, to see one smile
To light up their face, show some style
It costs nothing, to make a grin
Give out with a laugh, don't hold it in.

Let it be there, for all to see
Your eyes will say, "Hey, this is me"
Make it a point, to brighten a room
With a big grin, chase away gloom.

Wherever you go, whatever you do
Always be happy, do not feel blue
Soon all others, will follow your lead
Join in the fun, a grin's all they need.

For it has a message, its very own
And will make friends, wherever shown
So wear a grin, put a light in your eye
It isn't hard, give it a try.

Judy Speed

THE HERO

Dedicated to my loving husband—John Terrel Speed—The Hero

They stand so tall so proud and strong
The men this country did so wrong
They sent them off to Vietnam
To fight a war that nobody won

Somehow his story he'll never tell
Of how he lived in the pits of Hell
Or when he finally came back home
How the war for him would continue on

No one cared even way back then
The cost to each and every man
To some the cost was their very life
While others lost a home and wife

To others it was no more than a game
Still others it finally drove insane
And then this country became oh so blind
To all those poor men they left behind

For those who wonder why I feel so strong
About all the men this country did wrong
They rated their lives no higher than a zero
But the one that I married came home as a hero

Rikie Fender

I

To Stewart E. Tapley, with Love.

I am today's youth, tomorrow's promise
I am the hope of the future

I did not create the problems of today,

But explore my mind
with Faith
the answer lies
Waiting

I do not fear tomorrow or today;
I embrace it like the sun
for in its Shadow
you'll find its key

PEACE can be achieved
one handshake, one hug
at a time

I am today's youth
tomorrow's hope

Let It BEGIN WITH ME.

Pamela E Madore

REALITY

This is a poem to my mother, Betty
whom I have seen struggle
with life
with the frustration of wanting to grow
and held back by committment to others.
I have seen the strength to say yes
when the answer was no, the courage to go on
when the ambition withered with time
to become acceptance.
I have seen the bitterness turn to sadness,
the anger to resignation.
We have only one lifetime of memories
for fulfillment.
So now, my mother, look back with
joy at the accomplishments,
with exuberance at the life you have
given
with peace at the outcome.

Erika Shasta Hawkinson

TO RICKY

Kiss me forever, as you did. My kisses will always be warm and filled with love, for only you. I Love you Always

---

Your kiss is as the rush of the oceans' waves, overwhelming me.
And your eyes glow dark green,
When I've held you near to me.
Like the depths of the emerald sea.
You're a man, as much or more,
than a man should be.
And all the man that this woman
would forever want and need.
And although I've never let you love me,
I have felt your tender, gentle touch,
When your sensuous lips touched my body.
It's as though I've never had that feeling before.
This was a strange sensation for me.

Ruth Ann Carson

BIRDS IN FLIGHT

Zebra finches are tiny little creatures.
Orange beaks, orange feet and bright
Colored feathers add to their features.

They're curious, clever, alert and fluffy—
Mine are: Bright Eyes, Spunky,
Samantha and Scruffy.

They sleep in their cages only at night—
For when it is morning
They all take flight.

They're flying and hopping
Around all day,
Looking for treasures to carry away.

When it is bedtime
You can be sure—
They're bathing and splashing—all four!

Quiet now—their day's complete;
I'm looking at four pairs
Of little tired feet.

But when morning is bright
They chirp and sing
And begin again to discover new things.

Helen Jacobs

BUTTERFLY

Rainbow droplets in the sun
Tell us when the Spring's begun,
Has Winter donned her sleeping cap
To start her long Summers nap?
Tiny creature with no care
Float on Summers balmy air,
Grace our parks and woodlands too
With your colors clear and true.
We see you flit between the trees
And fly away on gentle breeze,
You mock no-one, nor do you scorn
The scarecrow in the golden corn.
Every morning, noon till night
You flutter by on careless flight.
Aimless wanderer, free to play
While children toil at school all day,
They watch and wonder with a sigh
Wishing they could flutter by.
Enjoy yourself my little friend
For all too soon your life will end.
When Autumn looms and Winter nears
And trees shed all their leafy tears,
Carol singers, pantomimes,
Good tidings come with Christmas time.
But seasons change, when Spring is nigh
We'll look to find you, Butterfly.

Hilda M Collins

CLOSE TO GOD

To my loving family

When I think about God,
And want to feel Him near.
I dream about a mountain top.
Up there He will appear.

As I sit in silence,
Looking out into space.
The clouds just seem to part;
That's when I see God's face.

I'd start to talk to Him;
Anything that comes to mind.
Then God said in this sentence,
"Just seek and you will find."

Just to feel His nearness
Made me feel so good inside.
I'd tell Him that I loved Him,
And His words I would abide.

As the clouds kept rolling by;
I could see each step He'd trod.
In that great serene moment
I felt so close to God!

Clifford L Tyree

THE SEASONS CHANGE

The seasons change "for sure"
and will forever more
Spring, so clean and sweet
Summer, thunder storms
Fall, and colors peak
Winter, crisp and, or . . .

Johnnie Renee Evans
A CHALLENGE

This poem is dedicated to the crew whose lives were lost in the Challenger tragedy and to their families.

On January 28, 1986
Something happened that we can never fix.

Seven brave young people went high in the sky,
In search of a dream that would surely die.

They were pioneers of the human race,
Taught to explore the depths of unknown space.

No one knows what really happened that day;
They found some of the wreckage out in the bay.

Time will pass as we all know,
But the memory of that fatal day will never go.

They were people brought together on a mission
That turned out to be only a vision.

Everyone was mourning as the day did pass,
For all the flags were lowered to half-mast.

Some people may think that they did not make it far,
But they did—for they went beyond the stars.

Sue Chambers
WHEN THE WILD GEESE FLY OVER AGAIN

Dedicated to; The farmers who raise our food, the children who make us laugh

It's time to get the blankets out
Put plum pudding in the oven
Set the checker board up
The wild geese are flying over again

Pull your darling up close in the evening
Light the fireplace in the den
Call the children in from playing
The wild geese are flying over again

Wind blowing Grandpa's clothes around him
In the barnyard and hog pen
Feed the animals good tonight
The wild geese are flying over again
Mow the hay in the fields
Feed for the horses and cows
Pull the corn and take to the mill
The wild geese are flying over again

The north wind is blowing
You can feel it on the skin
Rabbits hoping to hide
The wild geese are flying over again

God loves His people
Goes back to Adam and Eve
His people work hard
The wild geese are flying over again.

Helen Keegan
REFLECTIONS OF A WINTER NIGHT

To my son, Paul.

White flakes are gently falling
The child in me is softly calling
As I remember so long ago
Some past December, the memories flow

The moonlight cast shadows on the lonely country road
Yelling from the hill of snow, "Last one down is a toad!"
On the sleds we rode double, down the hill we flew
Gaining speed with no trouble, for the snow was new

And on this winter night
The stars and moon our only light
Finding it so hard to see
Who's out there—who's in front of me?

"Move! Get out of the way!" No one answered a word
The snowbank was there to stay. Only laughter could be heard
Laughter filled the air, our spirits were high
No one had a care, we had no tears to cry

The night was young and free
. . . . And so were we

Madeline Coe
CAPTURE EACH MOMENT

To my daughter, Kathryn, with all my love

I watched you from the porch
while sitting on a rocking chair
which always looked ready
to rock a nice old lady.
I played with you
when we were so small,
in the warm white sand
and in the cool blue ocean.
I stood and gazed at you
when we were young and wild
and danced to any tune that played,
feeling crazy, so carefree.
I laid with you
and heard each heartbeat
when we were all alone.
We talked of things that passed
and things that someday would be.
I can still feel each memory
and capture each moment
as I look from the porch
rocking in a rocking chair
which is always ready
to rock a nice old lady.

Linda Renz
GRANDMOTHERS

To my husband, Michael, who makes me believe all things are possible.

They are the keepers of all things grand
Great stores of knowledge and wisdom
That must be nature's plan.

About the things you wish to learn
They are the ones to visit
Walking books of history
If your're smart you won't want to miss it!

Grandmothers' homes are also different than ours
In the way they're arranged just so
Grandmothers also have wonderful ways
They are such a pleasure to know!

But such as with everything else in this life
The time comes when they must leave us
It's always too soon, it never seems fair
But they never intended to grieve us.

Memories of what used to be
Will help to get you through
And as years go by
You'll reflect and you'll find
Your grandmother's image is you!

William E Kick
GOD'S SUNSET

To my dear wife, Thelma, who is viewing "GODS SUNSET" from Heaven, May I share her experience soon.

No artist can paint a picture so true,
Of God's great Heavens as the gold turns to blue.

Of the changing panorama, from bright daylight,
To the red, to the gold, to the purple, and deep blue of the night.

From the heat of the day, how hot it seems,
To the coolness of the evening with the first moon beams.

With the hustle and bustle of each daylight hour,
To the quiet serenity of each fragrant flower.

Instead only God can bring the day to a quiet hush,
And paint a brilliant moving picture with out a brush.

Catherine Belin
FEAR
Small fears grow into fences around me.
Terrible things I wish not to see,
Creeping closer and closer, . . images
Projected from my mind to me.

When lightening, wind and darkness come,
I huddle close and tremble . . . shiver,
And wait for time to sweep away, . . the
Things I've feared for almost ever.
When at last my space has dwindled away,
And my light is no longer aspark,
Before I'm laid in my final place . . PRAY
I'm no longer afraid of the dark . .

Melinda Fernandez
SLEEP CALLS ME
Sleep calls me, beckons,
But, I listen not.
My eyes grow heavy,
And begin to close,
I must stay awake,
For in my dreams they wait,
The horrors, the worst demons,
That my mind can conjure.
The faceless ones,
They bring the terror.
And, cause me to scream.
In the dark.
To try to escape is hard,
And, sometimes very slow.
I desend into their world,
They wish to keep me there
I do not wish to stay,
Yet, fighting has been hard,
And harder still
Each time I try.
So I cannot sleep,
For the horrors await.
Another sleepless night.
Yet I go on

Rosella Dean
A PRAYING MOTHER

I dedicate these words to my precious Mother, Dorothy Holman. Thank you for angels who have surely watched over me at your request. Lovingly, Rosella Dean

I'll never know how many times
You spoke my name in prayer
On bended knee with heavy heart
Just because you care

The nights you were awakened
And knew I was in need
You held me up before the throne
Offering Him your plea

I'll never know how many times
You freely toiled for me
Simply doing without yourself
To willingly fill my needs

I'll never know how many times
I hurt you needlessly
And you forgave me endlessly
Just because it was me

I'll tell you what I value most
To me there is no other
No one could ever ask for more
Than to have a "Praying Mother"

Blanche Robbins Gerrard
THE STATUE OF LIBERTY
Her far flung torch held gleaming in the sky,
A welcome gives to all who truly love
That freedom sanctified by Life and Death
And asking only loyalty to keep it pure.
Great emblem of an independence gained and kept,
True symbol of a nation's friendship tried and won,
Gleam brightly on! Light far and wide
The path that brings the wanderer home again
And bids as well the foreign sons

Whom we would call our own.
Emblazoned on a background of a million lights
A hundred million hearts and souls
Send out their message with thine own
And make the gilded pathway to thy feet
A promise of humane reality.
Liberty enlightening the world?
'Tis more!
Enlightens, beckons, pleads
For heartthrobs that will match her own
And build a nation worthy of all men
A benediction to thine honored, sacred shrine!

Fred Eugene Green

Fred Eugene Green
ME AND MY CHAIR

Dedicated to Heather Eudy, Chris Brafford, Joel (B.S.) Brafford (Grand Children)

Wood and things all put together
Straight and strong it stood
Just for me to sit in
When I'm tired and don't feel good

Leon Piecuch
APPRAISEMENT

A man is as big as he wants to be,
or as small;
If he applies the same measure to others
as to himself—
he grows.
He moves in the many faces of the seasons.
The winds can blow cold, yet he can temper them,
hot and be cooled.
But the greatest test of all is when he can stoop
to befriend one of lifes littlest of creatures,
and see beauty in the otherwise dull colorations,
Strength in the tiniest of bodies, and recognize
that the sparrow is as free as the wind,
which cannot be found.
For a sparrow tested against the elements,
shows the daring of an eagle
But most of all it can move it's weight
a thousand times—
You see, observed in the palm of a gentle hand,
a sparrow can move a man.

Muriel M Stoneburg
I REMEMBER MAMA

I remember Mama . . . for the smile upon her face
For the troubles and the sorrows . . . she could easily erase
For the comforting hand that always reached out . . .
To anyone in distress . . .
I remember Mama . . . for she was happiness
I remember Mama . . . when in the night I pray
For it was she who taught me . . the prayers I've learned to say
We used to pray together . . . I never shall forget
And though I pray alone now . . . I feel her near me yet
Many times my memories carry me away
To a far off distant town . . . in another day
And though there are a million things . . .
that I can still recall
I remember Mama . . . for I loved her best of all

Donald Bendiks
WHEN BRIGHTLY THE MOON BEAMS ABOVE

To lovely Birute Semenaite—in Lithuania; my love

When Brightly The Moon Beams Above

Blossoms unfold their petals behold
Of gossamer wings flies a butterfly
Sunrise in springtime fills beauty untold
All nature unfolds so I ask why

Why should the winter be there or fall
Just springtime and summer is all
That I ever would like to feel
But always my summer the autumn will steal
And winter is soon on the heel

The snowflakes soon fly in the wake
I then my thoughts of warm summer do take

I dream by the fire of flowers and streams
The bubbling brook where we tranced and I picked
My roses and daisies for my only love

Where by the river once more I will meet
Sweet my Tom Sawyer with barren feet
Next springtime when brightly the moon
shines above . . . .
Shines for me and shines for my tender sweet love
my only sweet love

Susan L Clark
MARY

Dedicated to Mary J. Scandrett (My adopted grandmother)

I have a friend named Mary,
She's anything but contrary,
Intelligent, Compassionate,
Creative,
A class all her own,
No nicer friend could be found.

Caren J Combs-Watson
SOMEONE SPECIAL

Dedicated to Someone Special, who also knew that you must be friends before lovers.

Someone Special, Someone dear,
Someone who lives quite far
from here

Someone to laugh with, Someone to hold,
Someone to warm me when the world is cold.

Someone to tell my fantasies to
Someone to comfort me when I'm feeling blue.
Someone to share life with till the world's end,
Someone Special,
To think, . . . it began with a friend.

Harry James Jones
CHILDREN OF THE CAPE

The seasons bring forth Children,
as a hen brings forth hatchlings.
We, as children return to the Cape
like Pilgrims.
This glorious season we call summer,
is a time to slumber in the dunes.
The bayberry is starting to wax,
with the beachplumb in full bloom.
All is made ready, for the Children of
the Cape to return.
For I see a time to behold! As summer,
oh so quickly unfolds.
As night falls, and dawn appears,
so does summer, and fall will give
us that leer.
The Children of the Cape disappear.
Only to return my Child another year.

Orvil Watts
TOGETHER WE'RE STRENGTH

This poem is dedicated to my grandmother, "Rita Hutchings" and her family

---

on reconing day our emotions run deep
for the memories we cherish, it seems we must weep
we reach for our brothers and sisters in faith
with hopes that between us, we all can gain strength
where in we'll find comfort, that seems not to exist
an escape from the pressure, and pain that persists
we helplessly wonder. . .for we've nothing to try
time becomes precious, and so passes by
through the misery we share, we will somehow unite
combine we are able, this depression to fight
colors grow vivid. . .we appreciate life
if only we felt this, in the absence of strife
for me these words, are a release of a sort
and to state that we all need each other's support
we all must have faith in God and his wisdom
for he alone, can make such decisions
together our hearts must form tightly a band
so at the end of our trauma, we still may in unity stand

Barbara R Bell
AT TWENTY-TWO

I look out my window
See old men with walking canes,
Young girls with short curls in their hair,
Highways leading, I don't know where,
For at Twenty-Two, I'm confined to this

Wheelchair.

I wish I was there on that highway,
Maybe it would take me somewhere and

That old man could let me use his cane,
Give me a chance to get a grip on things.
One leg missing the other soon to be gone,
Life isn't too pretty sitting here all alone.
Oh, I have friends and loved ones,
But they have things to do.
Blood pressure up, sugar too,
I'm getting a little tired at 22.

John Allen Bates
FOR THE CHILDREN

It is for the children
I will sing this song,
For it is from the children,
We could learn to get along.
They care not of ones color,
To religions they can't relate
See the little children
They know not how to hate.
But we grow old, and fall into sin.
Knowing that we could be born once again.
A child can't see the danger
Their days here have been few,
So teach the little children,
And they will teach you.
To those of you still searching,
You are a budding pod.
Become as little children,
And you will know God.

Miss Renee Myltoft
DIVINE SELVES

In dedication to my mother Audrey; I thank God for blessing me with the mother that I have, for if it were not for her I would not be interested in exploring various horizons.

At the time you believe in something,
and can no longer be persuaded to change your direction
of belief,

Hold strong onto that which is placed upon the pedestal,
which will be forever more.

But do not close thine ears to those
that speaketh of their own truth,
keep thine own heart
and mind open.

But do not let thine own inquietudes

bring you down, let it be. . .to restore thine own faith.

Seek that of which is true and let not thy knowledge be smoky to inflame thine ears,

Concern yourself of your own ignorance,
and ask of which you do not know.

For the richness of the frame comes not from that of Divine Selves,

But comes from that which is spoken
upon thine ears.

To take it as it is . . .
To change it for your own understanding . . .
Or to cast it aside as something insignificant.

But always remember those that speak.
and the passage spoken upon thine ears,

For situations may rise when those
passages thought to be
insignificant are truly and positively significant.

Now to thine own self you may understand
what has been spoken of,
or you may not find thy Divine Self.

But as a unique Divine Soul, strive to
learn of what is about,
and the makings . . .

To find thy Divine Self.

Vimal C 'Manav'

Vimal C 'Manav'
A LETTER TO SWEETHEART

The author, originally a renowned Hindi poet, dedicated the poem to HINDI LANGUAGE in which it is much more heart-touching and true expression of deep love, than the transcreation.

Brusque to me you have ever been though,
Still you are the best among all I know.

May you live long for centuries more,
Enjoying good health and charm & beauty galore.

Complaints are there, so many and so sure,
But severe they are, difficult to endure.

The pangs I suffer, are blunt and bad,
On hearing all those, you will also be sad.

You may feel guilty, if I tell you all those.
Let me be with myself, as it all goes.

Isn't it enough for a person of your wit,
To understand and move, maybe bit by bit.

Please favour with reply, at an early date;
Rather come and see before it is too late.

I was and am and will remain,
Sincerely yours who will never complain.

Shelly Nichols Kenyon
HERE IT IS VALENTINE'S DAY
Here it is Valentine's Day and again I'm without another
it seems like everyone around me has a "better-half" I guess
everyone is taken so I'll have to be the one whose left.

A Rose, carnation or traditional box of candy, it seems
they're things I'll never receive, only the people who have
joined their hearts together and made it one.

It's no fun to see people around you together
especially when you're all alone it's even worse on
this day just thinking what it would be like with someone
of my own, loving each other, needing each other, wanting
each other endlessly.

I guess I'll never hear the beautiful words "I love you"
and that's what hurts the most.

So while lovers are together celebrating their
special day, maybe cupid will be generous with
his arrow today and I'll be able to get a man of
my very own.

Gail Rodman
THE W W F

I dedicate this poem to my younger brother, Wade Rodman who got me interested in wrestling and encouragement.

Fight, listen to the thud of the Iron Sheik.
Fight, fighting for the freedom that's in your dreams.
Going to hold on, nobody cares when you hit them hard.
You've got to bodyslam, slam them again, now how much
can they take. You've got to keep your mind on the U.S.A.
if you want to survive.

Hulk Hogan wins, with Bundy and Studd losing match after
match. The Killer Bees, Junkyard and Steele making Funks
pay their fees. Lanny and Don, don't you let them put you
down. Under the rules fight the bad and the good. And the
bad is losing every time.

Fight, listen to Corporal Kirchner's loyalty.
Fight, fighting for America's Dream.

Fight for Freedom!

Patricia Ann Looney
SEARCHING
Days when I wonder who I am, what I am, and just where I am
Days of depression coming more as I grow older, seeing the troubles of the world and my friends.
Days of wondering why some are so weak, and dependent, whileothers are so strong and independent.
Days of thinking happiness has finally been found, only to have sadness replace it, sadness that can't be dismissed with much ease.
Searching? Yes searching all the time and not truly finding
any meaning of this eternal journey.
It all seems hopeless and then faith once again is more powerful and I begin another day with a new outlook and end these turmoiled days with prayer, thanking God for his love and kindness.
Then the searching doesn't seem so hopeless.

Shirley Cox
THE MOON
I saw the most beautiful sight tonite,
As I stepped out onto the beach.
The Sand, The Sea? No, I've seen them before.
The Sky, The Quiet so unique?
No, it was the most beautiful moon I've ever seen lighting up the sky.
It caught my breath as I looked across the sea.
I wish I could stay to watch it come from behind the cloud where it went hiding.
But maybe God only gave me a glimpse, because he wanted to remind me, what a beautiful world we live in.
In spite of our <u>PERSONAL</u> BLINDNESS!

Larry Dean Roop
FEELINGS

To my loving wife, forever and always Larry

A look sweet and gentle
as if time was holding you still
bringing about a radiant glow
of love that looks so real.

Reaching out to touch you
to feel your every desire
to be a part of your very soul
your inside fires burn higher.

And looking into your eyes
as if they want to say
darling never leave my side
always stay this way.

Fill my every wish
with every dream come true
let me hold on to reality
that I find only with you.

For it's now that I know
how much you mean to me
and that you always try so hard
to fill our destiny.

And with each breath that I take
I'll never leave your side
I'll only hold you close to me
until the day I die.

William John Colliver
QUIET LIGHTNING

For Stu

Quiet lightning, miles away dance.
In winds sculpting electric seas
In night sounds shining
Upon an azure sky diffused

Lovely lightning, here and not
But long enough.
Bare a sounding board for brother
You are thunder's silent door
Crack the sky
I wait,
He enters into darkness

As before
No children crying.
When only my beginnings faced up
To skies of lace,
A spark of dawn

You drop still, quick
Strobe
Unslowed by ages
To terrify my twilight.

Theresa Waselewski
THE HOUSE

To the memory of my Grandmother's House in Lavelle, Pennsylvania

---

In the firelight I can see,
Yesterday and things that used to be.
In time I suppose the pain will pass,
As the brown turns to summer's green grass.
Now, Today, the house is gone,
Sometimes I don't think I can go on.
The moonlight sleigh rides upon the winter snow.
And the gentle summer breezes that blow,
Will never be quite the same,
Without the roaring fire, coming in from the rain.
Into the house of dreams and fun.
Try to recall just what it was like,
The back porch step, the well's wheel spike.
What is there now is just brown earth,
Like the ashes, the coal ashes, from the hearth.
That house will always be a part,
A place in my memory, A place in my heart.

Brenda Hartman
THE END
The night was long and uncomfortable.
People with expectations surrounded me.
I felt smothered, but acted differently.
The need to be totally alone overtook me,
But the room only got more crowded.

It became unbearable, and I tried to escape
People with sneering faces, eyes looking for any hint
of reality—when there was none.
I cried to escape. My tears went unnoticed.
My needs went unmet, but I had to fulfill all theirs.
They only wanted more and more.
I died to escape, and they looked to the next like me.

Alice Faircloth

THE BREAKING OF DAWN

To: Brother John Kozak

The breaking of dawn painted the sky with a golden hue
The rising sun kissed the clouds and turned them to a blushing pink too
The air is filled with a symphony, from the songs of the birds
The world is waken, to the sweetest music it has ever heard
The breaking dawn, gives way to a bustling of a new day
The traffic jams the pushing and shoving is on the way
No time to stop to smell the flowers along the way
The busy day draws her strings, to close the curtains into a peaceful night
The golden dawn has vanished far out of sight
But I made time from dawn through my busy day
I stopped and picked a yellow rose, and smelled it's lovely fragrance along the way

Jude A Ford

Jude A Ford

WHO I CAN SEE

No one knows who I can see,
when I raise my hand and smile.
They can't understand the words from me,
cuz I'm just a ten month child.

They say I'm a gift from your heart,
I know I came here through love.
You helped give my life a start,
I can feel you up above.

There's a big book in our house,
my Mamma reads to me.
Even tho I'm too young now,
something's growing inside of me.

Grandma says, when I raise my hand,
that I'm praising the Lord.
Only you know and understand,
what this little hand is for.

As I grow and I can learn,
they'll understand the words from me.
Another child will take their turn,
and they'll all know
who I can see.

Rebecca A Garrity

OCEAN

A full moon glows engulfing the sky.
As the tide rolls in on the Atlantic side, with a forceful rage of vengeance.
The grains of sand are hard and fine,
beneath my feet that winter night.
A timeless breeze smelling salt,
filled the air with a ghostly sigh.
Fear was not the emotion I felt,
for when I see the ocean all I feel
is peace, hope and love inside.

Debbie Lou Vena

GOODBYE MORNING

Friendships grow from love gone blind.
To hurt the truth takes so much time.
Spare our friendship or indulge sublime,
Maybe it's worth just one more time.

Butterflies change to waves of passion.
Sickened plague of no defeat.
No treat that's cold enough to cool us,
I kiss the ice cream from your cheek.

The night is gentle warm and tender.
Moon and stars—just you and me.
Footsteps leading to surrender,
To breaking dawn when you must leave.

I'll walk the shore on goodbye morning.
Gathering treasures from the sea.
That replace our every footsteps,
In the sand—that used to be.

Yolanda Bridges

THE LORD IS MY SHEPHERD

The Lord is my shepherd and I am His sheep
When I lay down at night, I fall peacefully asleep
He watches over me the whole night through,
The Lord is my Shepherd and I am His sheep.
The Lord is so great He never forsakes
If I stray from the righteous path, He rescues me,
He brings me back to the fold. He is the shepherd of my soul.
The Lord is my shepherd and I am His sheep.

Kimberly J Pickens

A SPECIAL DAY

One day as through the woods I wandered, My mind began to ponder:
Just why this world is so bad,
Why we fly off the handle, Why we get mad.
As I looked at the trees that stood as towers, I wondered how a bud;
Changes into A flower?
I watched A young squirrel gathering nuts,
and wondered just why we let our lives get into such ruts.
As I turned and looked out across the river,
up my back ran A tiny shiver.
As I turned and started to walk on,
I realized I was not alone!
As I cryed a special warmth began to rise,
That sadness was gone and I was Happy inside.
I had seen our world in a way that no one else could understand,
A world not created by man!
But A world built by the ONE who takes away pain,
The ONE who washes our world with rain.
The ONE who grew that tree and can destroy this world of hate,
The One who can change our lives if only we have FAITH.
Have faith next time you feel sad or afraid,
Bow your head, have faith, and to the LORD pray.

Ruth E Hurney

MEDITATIONS

In memory of my late husband, John H. Hurney Sr. who died March 30, 1984

I never knew what pain could be,
Until my love was taken from me.
I think of the good times and the bad,
And that is when I get sad.
It doesn't seem possible I'm now alone,
To brood over him in our little home.
I know that someday again we'll meet,
Up in one of Heaven's streets.
But when and where I do not know,
It's up to God when he wants me to go.
I'm not the first, or will be the last,
That now live in dreams of the past.
I join my friends in their sorrows,
I, too, live now for tomorrows.

Mrs Edna Fredrickson

IN THE CANYONS OF NEW YORK

Dedicated to my dear family. All of them.

The canyons of New York
Are not real like Arizona's;
With rocks, rills, firs and folia,
Cactus bloom and desert heat,
But,—soaring steel and concrete structures
And narrow, skinny tired streets,
With secretaries in tailored blouses,
Books, "Bulls," "Bears" and mouses,
Men, money, machines and madness.
Boutiques, banks, bums and badness,
Cats, cops, pigeons who coo,
But, never, never, cows who moo.
Lastly and best of all,
Sometimes between all the people
You will find a lonely steeple—
in
The canyons of New York.

Cynthia Draper Van Hemert

REFLECTION

Moon, you stare intensely
into the dark and lucid pool

that so black absorbs your gaze,
sucks your thoughts within itself,
then having done with contemplating
gives them lightly back again.

Noble Holderread

I'M JUST A DROP OF WATER IN THE SEA OF LIFE

I'm just a drop of water in the sea of life.
I'm carried by the tide, and taken for a ride.
I hope to skim the oceans but the waves subside,
And they have me scraping bottom all the way.

Then when I sally forth, I end up in the north
Where I'm colder than a boulder in the ice.
And when I try to steer, my landing place I fear
Will be the opposite of paradise.

I'm just a drop of water in the sea of life.
I'm carried by the tide,
And I think I'm being taken for a ride—
ride—ride—
I think I'm being taken for a ride.

Sister Marilyn T Beauvais S C

ODE TO PAIN

To all those suffering pain of any kind.

O Pain!
What kind of god can you be
That haunts people so endlessly?
Your clutches beset the weak and strong.
You are forever milling 'mid the throng.

O Pain!
What kind of god can you be
Where you rob others so stealthily?
You prey on the very prime of life,
And make living nothing but a strife.

O Pain!
What kind of god can you be
To make others resist so relentlessly?
The grapple with you morn til night
And are determined to win the fight.

O Pain!
What kind of god can you be
That takes such toll on humanity?
Begone! False god to far off space,
And let blessed peace reign in your
place.

Morris L Miller
THE CLOUDS

This poem is dedicated to Connie, my loving wife.

The clouds rise gently in the sky
They seem to fall to earth but not
to lie.
They bellow up so firm and round,
You'd almost think they'd touch
the ground.

They are so fluffy how soft they
look.
I wish I could lie on top and read
a book.
Now as I watch them pass me by
I wonder where they go and why.
The mystery of their passing by
Shall never catch my wondering
eye.

Frankie Olinger Holbrook

Frankie Olinger Holbrook
QUILTS OF LOVE

"In memory of Mom"—Maude A. Olinger. Dedicated to my husband—Bill, Children—Donna and Bill Jr. Grandson—Leon Keller

She cut each piece of cloth
As though it were made of gold
With confidence and patience
She toiled with each fold

She matched all the colors
With scraps she had saved
From each small child's garment
To this she had engraved

Her heart into each quilt
As she pieced all by hand
A quilt for each child
A gift made of love

When each quilt was finished
Each stitch in its place
Mom would lay down her needle
And smile with such grace

She knew she had finished
A quilt made of love
For each child a memory
Of mom's unfaltering love

Gene Christman
REFLECTIONS
The ocean is the place to go
To watch the tide come in,
And let the thoughts run thru your
head
Of things that might have been.

You do your best to figure how
To make things go your way,
So life can be the best for you
If only for a day.

You make your wishes and dream
dreams
Of things you hope might be,
Then lift your eyes so you can
watch
The tide run out to sea.

Now as you watch the tide go out
And leave a barren shore,
Your mind knows life's not yours
to change—
Not now—not evermore!

Caroline Reinartz White
A QUESTION
What has man done to man . . .
that violence reins unchecked?
When decency and good and
right . . .
are laughed at in the land.
When he who fights, and kills . . .
and wounds
is higher than the rest.
The multitude who sit, and wait . . .
For GOD to take HIS hand . . . and
turn us back to dust.

Ivory Snowden
READY FOR LOVE
I'm ready for love
I'm tired of playing
around
Life is a hard enough
merry-go-round
I know love takes time
But, it's about time this
light shined
I can only withstand so
much pain
Then after a long time
it becomes so vain
I'm ready for love
A solid feeling to hold
on to
When I reach this stage
I'll know what to do
I'm ready for love
And I hope you are too.

Janice H Middleton
ODE TO MY GRANDSON
When your father was drifting
on the mighty sea
He said to God,
"If you rescue me
And I have a son
'NOAH' 'twill be
Because I was saved
from the perilous sea"
Now a promise was kept
And a dream came true
And that promise to God
And that dream is "YOU"

Martha L Gordon James

Martha L Gordon James
LOVE

I dedicate this poem to my beloved niece, Sharion McFarland.

Where there's Love . . . God, he
gave his only son,
Where there's Love . . . Joy,
Where there's Love . . . Kindness
Where there's Love . . . Peace.

Where there's Love . . . Self-control,
Where there's Love . . . Mildness,
Where there's Love . . . Patience
Where there's Love . . .
Faithfulness.

Where there's Love . . .
Long-suffering,
Where there's Love . . . Goodness,
Where there's Love . . . Endurance,
Where there's Love . . . Jesus Christ,
for all he gave his Life.

Robert C Coombs
OUTSIDE MY DOOR

To my mother and father, with all my respect and love

Sitting here on this special kind of
day
smelling the fall, feeling God and
his display
Of the love in life, the happiness to
live
watching the freedom of birds
and their ability to give.

More things than money and
success are mine
the wonders of sight and
thoughtfulness to define
My contentment, my freedom, all
my thankfulness,
my peace of mind, thanking God
for His caress

It smells so sweet, the coolness
outside my door
the feel of a warmth inside me
that I adore
Knowing this isn't fleeting, it
always comes again.
Again to carry me, to make me
smile and grin.

Loving sitting here outside my door
smelling the fall and wanting
nothing more,
than the warmth and satisfaction
it gives me.
Knowing I'm me and that I'll
always be free.

Bernice Wooden
WHAT MORE COULD HE DO
He created you in his own image
And He said, "It is very good."
Then He walked in life before you,
To show you how you should.
He said, "Don't worry about
tomorrow,
What you shall eat, or what to wear,
And if you have a burden,
Cast on Me your every care,
If you should have another need
Just ask it in my name,
If you ask it in good faith
You shall receive the same."

He taught you many parables,
Good lessons you should learn,
He gave you of His Wonderous
Love
Asking only yours in return.
He's preparing a home for you
In a city with streets of gold,
He is coming soon to receive you,
In the Bible we are told.
To insure you that home in Heaven
He gave His life for you
That you might have Eternal Life,
What more could He do?

Rivers J Marchand
GIFTS FROM ABOVE
God gave us the ability
to laugh or to cry—
A reason to live,
and a reason to die.
He loaned us a body,
and gave us a soul—
And even a reason
for growing old.

He created the earth,
and gave us some space—
And the ability to perform
with amazing grace.
Infinity dwells in the Universe,
and life goes on
For better or worse.

Our senses are keen
and deep as an ocean—
Pulling and tugging,
and filled with emotion.
Oh, grant us the wisdom,
the kindness and love
To endow in our spirit
the gifts from above.

V A Parker
THE SHADOW

To my husband, Tim for sharing my light and giving me courage.

Death is a shadow that beckons us
all,
Then leads to the light when we
hear it's call.

It may come to us in the calm of night,
When the world's asleep and bathed in moonlight.
It may come to us in the light of day,
When we're busy with life and death seems far away.

There's no need to fear the shadow's embrace,
For it brings us peace when met face to face.
Death is the dawn of a marvelous life,
Removing the hatred that cuts like a knife.
It gives us the time to ponder our thoughts,
And learn the troubles of life are not for naught.

Life's filled with delusions for so many men,
Seeking their self over and over again.
One day their karmic debts will be paid,
And they'll be free of the guilt that they made.
Then the spirit will exist for eternity,
Like the rainbow seen in a cloudy sea.

Alice Greenwood Greiner

SERENITY

To stroll through a mountain meadow
of grasses wet with dew
Where new-sprung flowers wave gently
as a breeze passes through
To hear the music of a waterfall
as it tumbles on stones
Giving a promise of new life
to things no one owns
To pause in the cooling shadow
of a giant old tree
Listening to the mating call
of a bird winging free
Watching Aspen leaves fluttering
in an unspoken tongue
To find a warming fireside
at the setting of the sun
And to feel the gentle clasp
of a loved one's hand
Knowing that life's long journey
Will be shared to the end.

Patricia Wallen Adkins

THE FAITH OF A CHILD

Dedicated to my first Granddaughter: Karen ReNea Wallen with love from Grandma Wallen

---

A little child was standing
At the door of a children's home
Say "Where is my mommy and daddy?"
"Do I have to stay here alone?"

"And where is my brothers and sisters"
Are they staying here too?
For if I was left here all alone,
Oh gee, what would I do!

"Come, do not be lonely
Said another little girl
With bright blue eyes and
Rosy cheeks
And hair of golden curl
For I live here too, you see
But we are not alone
Cause we still have Jesus
And He's our very own.

Doris C Sharp

JANUARY 28, 1986

A ball of fire in the morning sky.
Trailing smoke across the blue.
A gasp, a tear and a moaning sigh.
With sinking hearts we knew,
"Sometimes even eagles fail to fly."

In all the pictures, did you see
any indication of hopefulness
that could have escaped me?
Look again—though I guess
that which we want cannot be.

Our hearts in total agony will cry.
Our words in futility will flow
as to comfort you we try.
But then someday you too will know.
"Eagles must always try to fly."

Evelyn Snyder

BIBLE ALPHABET

A is for Always, He's by our side,
B is for Bible, by which we abide.
C is for Cross, we all must bear,
D is for Devotion, to Him for our care.
E is for Eternity, where life does not fade,
F is for Faith, from which our prayers are made.
G is for God, who gave us His Son,
H is for Heaven, there's room for each one.
I is for Immortal, the sheep for His fold,
J is for John, the Epistle of old.
K is for King, the keeper of man,
L is for Love, with room to expand.
M is for Mary, the Virgin mother,
N is for Need, that we have for each other.
O is for Open, Heaven beckons us all,
P is for Pit, where some shall fall.
Q is for Quality, essential to deed,
R is for Righteous, all races must heed.
S is for Sacred, our Reverance of God,
T is for Test, on life's path that we Trod.
U is for Unerring, God's Love for each one,
V is for Vitiate, the devil's work done.
W is for Wisdom, man's right to decide,
X is for Xmas, Christ came as our guide.
Y is for Yearn, for our home on high.
Z is for Zion, our goal by and by.

Nancy T Smith

LOVE IS LIKE A ROSE

Love is like a rose,
it's soft and pure,
it's tender and fragile.

It can bloom in time
if treated with care,
or it can wither up and die
if abused.

You can kill it by not
feeding it with trust,
or you can help it blossom
by giving it tender care.

A new love is like a bud
if grows in time,
if cared for.
Love is special and delicate.

Beth Hundley

COUNTRY NIGHTS

To my sister, Bonnie who remains my greatest source of inspiration

---

Late night moments
still
as time stops
to the quiet ticking
of the clock.

The train whistle
travels through the night air
as awaited,
anticipated
from the soft feather bed.

Alone
in thought and feeling,
yet could it be
somewhere lies another . . .
awake
hearing a quiet ticking clock
and the whistle
of the train.

Laska Larsen

BORN OUT OF TIME

Why was I born, to what earthly purpose?
And why must I differ from my fellows
that I cannot conform, or be as others be?

Why in this breast do yearnings tear and rend,
longing for a life which is denied me.
Withheld, forever just beyond my fingertips.

Could there be a kinsman long since in hell
whose restless blood flows now within my veins
reaching across decades to smother me with tears.

For my heart is ever yonder with lofty pines,
by singing streams, in quiet forest glades,
far from the excruciating din and press of people!

Free as the golden eagle soaring over head,
shy as the wild deer feeding in the glen,
no sound but nature's symphony. Sonnets on the wind.

Oh ancestor, explorer of another day
where can I go to seek the unblazed trails?
The wilderness untouched by man's harsh hand!

Is there some bit of "Eden" left for me,
or must I struggle on my dreary way,
drawn by your love of lonely, unspoiled lands?

Longing to gallop with the summer breeze
to see God's masterpiece yet undisturbed!
Stop beating now sad alien heart, it can never be.

Joan N Perkins

THE CHRISTMAS GIFT

Just in time for Christmas
On the eve before the angels sang
Silent night, holy night,
He was born.
Unloved? No, loved from the start,
And willingly the young girl gave him life.
Rejoice, rejoice—oh Christmas Eve,
On that night a beautiful little boy.
But she couldn't keep him for herself;
Eyes filled with tears, she gave up her son.
Right or wrong—every year, the question she ponders.
The child's voice sings, "adoption means love."

Bonita I Waller

HENRY

Dedicated to Henry Hix

You do so many nice things in an unexpected way,
You have a way of bringing sunshine, to a rather gloomy day
I want you to know I'm grateful for the many kind things you've done.
I want you to know I'm thankful for such a caring, loving son.

Emily Carolyn Westfall

ALONE AND LONELY-THE DIFFERENCE

Alone—Completely Alone—
the rain my only music
the stars my only light
the night my only comfort—
Alone—to my delight.

Alone—Just Alone—
raining down old memories
nights and days alike
never mending—never ending
Alone—to my dislike!

Sharon M Austin

SUN AND RAIN

To Jerry

When a puppy ends up at your door
When a baby tumbles to the floor
When a tree is brown and losing leaves
When a little boy, skins his knees
When a flower wilts and fades away
When a happy kitten goes astray
When a fire hurts a friendly home
When a lonely girl begins to roam
These are times when people frown
And are most in need, 'cause they are down
These are times when things are low
When a persons love should really glow
So when you're down and feeling bad
Let me in to make you glad

Roger Huber

I CARE

You sweep through the day like the wind,
As graceful as a fawn.
You light up the night with your sparkle,
That you bring about a new dawn.

You are wonderful and beautiful,
And there is a special twinkle in your eye.
If I say that I care for you,
Don't be scared and don't ever cry.

I see your smile,
And it brightens my day.
Your smile makes me dream,
Dream of quiet moments by the bay.

Words don't say enough about my
feelings,
They limit my caring.
May we continue to live in
happiness,
And to live in sharing.

Mary Ann Baines

MYSELF, MY OTHER SELF

You are here when I first open
my eyes yet cannot see
I feel the cool air on my skin
and I cry
That sound, I am afraid
And I wonder in no language
that I know
Where was I?
Where am I?

I feel close to those
who confort me
There is warmth from someone
other than myself
You make me feel it
You tell me it is good
And we sleep

They don't understand
They don't hear me
And I don't hear them
But you hear me
You have told me more
than anyone ever could
I ask you everything
And you tell me

Oh, How I praised you
for the fame
No one can do it like you
Yet when there is wrong
I blame you
Yes, I am hard on you

Now I am weary
I am afraid
Is it because I do not
want to leave myself?
All is done and
I will go now
Come with me

Mary Price

HAPPY BIRTHDAY BABY JESUS

To my sister Phyllis Sean Lachowyn (Sister Joseph Ann)

I crept into the manger to
take a peek
You were asleep, hand upon
your cheek.
I crept into the manger be-
cause I wanted to
say-
I love you Baby Jesus and
Happy Birthday.
I looked around at the gifts
galore and said
"Baby Jesus I have one more"
It has not wrappings shiny
and bright
But it's given with love on
this glorious night
You opened your eyes as I on
bended knee
Bowed my head and said humb-
ly,
"Dear Baby Jesus I give you
me."

Raymond J Clark

FOREVER

There are some days
When my mind can not be at ease
It is these times that I search for a
Peacefulness
That can only be found when I
Remember
How much you love me

If there is ever a day
When you find yourself searching
For that peace of mind
Let this rose help remind you
Not only of how much I love you
But that I will love you
Forever . . .

Effie Mays

OUR LOVE

I dedicate this to my brother Roy W. (Shorty) Hines

Our love has kept you with us,
we would not let you go.

The doctor said you had a year,
we proved it wasn't so.

Your muscles kept getting weaker,
there wasn't anything we could do.

With all the love and strength we
had,
we still could not pull you through.

You're fading away before our eyes,
no one knows the pain we're going
through.

To see our brother fade away,
there's nothing left that we can do.

We must let go and let you rest.
God knows what is best for you.

Clara B Huddleston

MEMORIES

I carry my old memories
Everywhere I go,
So I can think about them
When I am feeling low.
I think back to my younger days
To better times than these,
Maybe not a better time
But more carefree if you please.
I remember Mama laughing
As she talked to all of us,
Then she could really make it rough
When we would fight and fuss.
We'd go to church and Sunday
School
Have dinner on the ground,
Sometimes all day singing
I still recall the sound.
It seems that we were closer then
Wrapped up in Mama's love,
Sometimes in my troubled times
She smiles at me from above.
I hope I leave good memories
For my children to recall,
If they can feel the presence of my
love
It will be worth it all.

Linda M Davis

A FIREMAN

This poem is dedicated to the men of the Fort Montgomery Fire Department, Fort Montgomery, New York. It was their dedication and service to the community, that inspired me to write this.

His adrenaline soars, and his heart
beats fast,
The minute that siren, lets out its
first blast.
Whatever he's doing is abruptly
ignored,
As he quickly responds and heads
straight for the door.

It's a sunny day, or the dark of the
night,
It's the summer's warmth, or the
winter's bite,
But no matter the weather or time
of the day,
It's the fireman's dedication, that
leads him away.

It might be a house, or a car that's
on fire,
A rescue, a jaws call, or sparks
from a wire,
But to him there's no difference,
whatever the call,
He's a fireman first, and responds
to them all.

He might be your father, your
husband, your son,
A neighbor, an uncle, but not just
anyone,
For a fireman is special, for the
care that he shows,
He would give up his life, each time
the whistle blows.

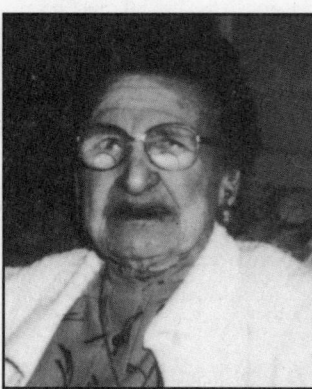

Aunt Em

Lucille Pennington

ELDERLY NEED LOVING TOO

To my loveable Aunt Em pictured on her 95th birthday

When you are young love is around
As you grow old it's not always
found
You're needed for baby-sitting and
borrowing money
It's great to be needed, but isn't it
funny
When you grow old and need help
too
There doesn't seem to be time for
you
If you reach old age, you'll feel the
same way
And then understand what I'm
trying to say.

Casey Jo Trail

WINTER

My favorite time of winter is
Christmas.
With warmth of giving
like a sun on a summer day.
And bells ringing
like birds singing.
And cookies aroma good
like a fresh picked daisy.
And pine needles touch
like a little friendly porcupine.

Eileen Tarosky

THE LEADER OF THE BAND

When I was a child
I didn't understand,
about the leader of the band.

Preoccupied was I, with many
childish ways;
"Come on gang! let's go and play!"
In my own little world,
having "tons" of fun,
and thinking of absolutely no one.

I was secure in knowing I would
come home from play
to my Mom and Dad who would be
there to say,
"my child! where have you been all
day?"

Sometimes I'd get in trouble,
I knew I had to tell,
and hope for the best, somehow I
couldn't rest.

I would hurt all over,
because I had to stand,
before the Leader of the band.

He'd look at me with very tired
eyes,
he worked hard all day, that's no
surprise,
and yet I knew, he was once me too,
suddenly, I began to realize,
that a child needs love and
guidance to grow!

So, Dad, I just want you to know,
HAPPY FATHER'S DAY! with all
my heart!
Because of you Dad, I got my start!

LaVera A Brown

A FRIEND

I'm like a ship set out to sea
Sometimes just tossed around.
My troubles then engulf me
My problems they abound.
Alone I sit and worry
And often shed a tear,
And then I dial the telephone,
And call a friend so dear.
She listens to me talk awhile,
And helps to bear the load.
It seems to me, she's always there
To help me down life's road.
Some people wish for wealth I'm
told,
And others wish for fame.
But me, I wish for more than this,
A friend to share my pain.
For when I share a heavy load,
Much lighter it will grow,
Yes I've much more than wealth or
fame,
Because a friend I know.

Robert O Ele

MASQUERADE

Each Day's a show,
That only I know,
The lines are just a part.
The roles I play,
Are just a way,
To hide a broken heart

When I am sad
I'll show I'm glad,
and throw my frowns away.
Each laugh and smile,
are put on file,
To use another day.

When I meet girls,
a mask unfurls,
to shield me from temptation.
The mask I use,
Are ones I choose,
To fit the situation.

When love appears,
She'll kill my fears,
My tears will start to fade.

Her love will send,
A fitting end,
To this masquerade.

Gary Brandin
TIME'S MACHINE
The next day after the holiday
Evidence of gaiety could be found,
The mood the same as the day
before
The passing of the crown,
Applause and Praise
Allure and Haze,
Gallantly prancing as they always
do;
Break-a-Way and Review
And All-a-New,
Leading the way as they always do;
Just like a wheel,
The carousal was born to change;
Winds will come and give their best
To deny the passing of the crown.
But, beware not
For centuries past
Demand the future
Not let the present last.

Joseph P Montes
THE CHILD IN ME
As I call upon my memories of
childhood dreams and
make-believe, of endless fun and
bandaged knees,
I see that you were with me.

And as time passed before my eyes,
gone were the puddles
and the child's cries,
my truth and innocence were
replaced with lies,
yet you never left my side.

And when I knew I had it all,
you watched me stumble, you
watched me fall,
you heard my cry and you
answered my call,
you picked me up and changed it
all.

Now my memories are still the
same,
the bandages are gone though the
scars remain,
but I don't so much remember the
pain,
for I am a child again.

Johnaton Jasso
PEOPLE
Poor and rich
Enormous intelligence
On a beautiful land
People make tremendous
population
Love the world as it is
Equal as they live

Maryann Rinehart
TIME
A measure of moments.
Passages of years.
Amounts of emotion.
Vanquisher of fears.

Time we spend together.
Time we spend apart.
Both of the same purpose.
Strengthening the heart.

Time to get over.
Time to grow anew.
All my times are happy times.
All times that I love you.

Janet Gregory
SEASONING
I sit all alone
In the middle of my field
While your eyes seek fairer
pastures.
My grass yet green,
My clover fragrant,
August wheat golden and bright.

Still, your heart longs
For April's sweet mist . . .
Spring's rose, velvet against your
cheek
It's pungent bouquet
Assaulting your senses . . .
You can no longer hear
My love's summer song.

Kim Ray Bybee
SEA WITCH
I remember now . . . It was foggy
that day . . .
I saw her standing there, her
golden body glistening with
drops of water as tiny
rainbows danced in her hair.
As she walked toward me I could
see her eyes were as deep as the
sea,
There was no need to speak as she
reached for my hand for it was
as if she had always known me.
As we walked along the beach I
noticed a piece of drift glass,
she seemed to smile and walk
past as I bent to pick it up
We walked to a cove where the sea
was as smooth as the drift
glass in my hand
The sun was warm against our
bodies as she drew me close and
made love in the sand

As I looked in her eyes I knew we
were never to part
She beckoned me to the waters
edge and I followed with longing
in my heart
We weren't far from the beach
when the first wave surrounded
us and my eyes were closed to
the light of day
I knew then to love a lady as such
as this there was a price to pay.
"When the land is covered with fog
and the sea is smooth as glass,
Beware my son, beware of the sea
witch for she lets no man past."

Willis-Elaine McKenna
POETRY CONTEST RULES

Dedicated to: My husband—Charles who had belief in me; and also My children—Cynthia who loaned me her typewriter; Kathleen for her pride in me; Chuck for his faith in me and my grandson—Chad!

I have to write a twenty-five lines
or less
ditty,
Perhaps I can come up with
something short
and witty.
The rules of the contest don't seem
extremely
hard,
It's just that I'm nervous and hope
I'm a Bard!
Writing poetry can be hard,
oops—my pen just fell
into the Lard!
Now for paper and, of course, a
new pen, my mind
Is now settled and—AW
SHUCKS—I really hope
that I win!
Thanks for the chance of letting me
enter—
OH DEAR!!!
I reached for the Lard and came
up with a splinter!
The contest deadline is February
28, I see, I'd
Better hurry up and mail this entry
before I end
up in Emer-gency!!!

Karin Kristine Morrison
WHERE ARE ALL THE TEARS?
I loved you with a passion,
I loved you with all my heart;
You are now gone,
Where did our love part?

I cried many tears—
When I knew you'd found another;
Sometimes I think it was a mistake,
Why did we even bother?

I saw you a year later,
And I was still in love with you;
From what I saw,
You still loved me too.

What were we to do?

Now you are married,
And have your own life to live;
But you still want to see me—
Do you have more love to give?

I want to see you too,
And have you rescue all my fears;
I do still feel the same,
But where are all the tears?

Angela M Wolfer
MURPHY

To my grandchildren and great-grandchildren with love.

I am a pretty pussy cat
Murphy is my name
I love to go to Grandma's house
Which is just across the lane
She doesn't always let me in
So I just stand by the door
And when she opens up
I slide in on the floor
She always always scolds me
And shakes her finger so
Now Murphy you behave yourself
Or out the door you go
But I know just how to vex her
I lay upon the bed
Then I know she'll always feed me
But alas, she's always one ahead
For she puts the food out the door
And I leave, to my great sorrow
But there's a bright spot in my life
I'll try again tomorrow

J Edward Worsham
EXCERPT FROM A LETTER TO A FRIEND
Dedicated with love to: My Beautiful Wife Pamela

. . . and the lady's name is Pam,
She is the essence of who I am.
She's the one to take my seed,
The only one I'll ever need.
And I know she loves me true,
Though I don't give her reason to.
She's the girl to share my life,
I'm so glad she is my wife.
I love her now and I'll love her then,
It's nice to know she is my friend.
When times are tough and I am
down,
I know that she will be around.
Precious times I'll share with her,
Those to come and those that were.
And when we both are dead and
gone,
I know our love will carry on.

Craig D Janzen
SERENITY
The Serenity's there, in the cool
morning air, but I reach out and
can't find it.
I don't know why, in my mind's
eye, that I can't ideally grasp it.
The times as they are, have a
bearing afar, with the way that
my thought's seem to wander.
So I'll just try, and hope to get by,
and maybe someday I'll find
it.

Lila
PROPHECY
Outside my window, a little virgin
cherry tree,
waits for the coming of her lover,
Spring.
Shyly, coyly, flirting with the wind
so free,
Lifting her dainty arms to sing.

Soon, soon, he will come, little tree.
Your lover Spring, he will hold you
tight.
Kiss each bough and limb in
passion's glee,
and you will bear blossoms pink
and white.

The soft Spring winds will sing a
lullaby.
Gently sway your cradle of green
leaves.
Birds, will love, nest, and the
birth-cry
of baby birds will echo in the
Springtime breeze.

Your womb, shall yield the fruit of
love
you gave so eagerly to Spring.
And as each fruit drops from your
breast
you will know the pain that parting
brings.

When winter winds will strip you
bare,
God will send the birds to rest
on your generous snow-laden
breast.

Charlene Kozak
ONE MORE VALLEY CROSSED
There was a pain deep in my breast,
And no way could I get it to rest.

The pain was deep and dark,
If only there would be a spark.
A spark of light to show the way.
So in this deep depression, I would
not stay.

Then from the Word came a ray of
light.
Now if only I could keep it in sight.
"Study on," was all that I heard,
So deeper, deeper, I went into
every word.

Brighter and brighter the ray
became.
Calling, Calling, saying the same,
"Give it to Me, and I'll be with thee."

Now the pain is but a memory,
Cause I gave it to Jesus to handle
for me.

Jesus died for you and me,
He died just to set us free.
My Lord hung there for all to see,
Just how much he cared for me.

Now deep within my breast is one
bright spark,
This spark is there for all the world
to see,
What My Jesus Means to Me.

Amen

Maureen O'Neill Stent
YESTERDAY'S I'VE LOST
Playing back memories
Of yesterday's I've lost.
I hear the 'old songs',
And know that you—might be
hearing too.

Do you remember the time
We sang from midnight 'til dawn
Even though we were both off key,
But too happy to care.
It seems like yesterday,
Another one I've lost.
I hope I've never
Hurt or disappointed you,
That would hurt me—most of all.
There is so very much
That I wanted to share with you . . .
The Beach, the moon, the stars . . .
And my heart.
I couldn't tell you the truth
That would have been wrong.
For I didn't have the right . . .
To make you do what you
Didn't want to do.
But you knew all along.

Sydney C Mason
ESCAPED TIME

---

*In memory of my grandfather,
Grover Cornell Lassiter*

There are many who never give
growing old a second thought,
Sure that they will be young forever
thinking their lives are theirs
that they bought.

The old, wishing they were young
again
often threatened by death and
dying,
Are frightened and lonely
sitting by themselves and on the
inside are crying.

Thoughts of homelessness, disease
and suicide
seem to flood the minds of the
old,
Feeling that they have no one to
confide in
they spend days alone and cold.

Youth will never understand
the meaning of time,
It slips away like sand in an
hourglass
a clock that the old can never
rewind.

Herbert Gunnar Wahlsteen III
OCTOBER

(For Rebecca)

Leaves rustle. Strong winds swirl.
The pale full moon peeks through
the thick clouds that unfurl.

I hear footsteps, from you,
in this October night,
footsteps I now pursue.

An early dark to each sight
brings strange and haunting
shadows.
Trees seem to shake with fright.

Cold fog buries vast meadows.
Its shroud obscures my goal.
The crazed winds' anger grows.

Midnight comes. Church bells toll.
This night is as you are,
lost in October's soul.

Rain? I see not one star.

Lory DeMarino
SUICIDE
Suicide the paper said
Hot tears of unbelief were shed
The broken hearts of loved ones
bled
And they became the Living Dead

No comfort could their minds
receive
Only for the lost one grieve
Was he God's—did he believe
Or only practiced to deceive?

"He didn't love me—didn't care"
Comes the cry of much despair
Guilt, confusion, rage—all share
The mind of torment—eyes that
stare

Then the flood of mem'ries real
Such longing just to touch—to feel
That familiar, much loved form
And see that face—the smile so
warm

When did it happen 'long the way?
How did the thoughts begin to
stray?
Why did he choose to die instead?
Whatever entered that mixed-up
head?

Why did he make the choice to stay
Forever parted from us—away?
Will peace 'ere to our hearts return?
Oh for answers—how we yearn.

Joanne Samec
untitled
softly
the crisp
gold autumn leaf
ever so softly
c
a
s
c
a
d
e
s
into
the open awaiting arms
of earth

Rosemary Raleigh
MY LITTLE SOLDIERS

---

*Dedicated to all faithful Jesuites
from their founder—St. Ignatius
Loyola, S.J. thru the late Padre
Burton J. Fraser, S.J. 5/6/71*

As I look across the golden sea of
grain,
Twirled and twisted by the waves
of a mellow wind;
I see millions of stalwart soldiers
peering at me.
Soldiers encumbered in the fertile
womb of earth
And knarled by the hands of a
stormy memory.

I see these men, once embittered
by the winter's past
But now, touched by the
tenderness of Spring's own hand.
I hear their bugles resounding
through the walls of time—
Time which is nothing more than
moments of birth and death.

I see these children entwined in the
bloody wax of life
A life that sheds the sweat and tears
of man.
I hear their anguished crys
entangled with the fear of night
The night which is blackened by
the velvet cover of sleep.

And now again, as I gaze across
this ocean of green
Torn and trampled by the hatred
of the violent wind
All my little soldiers have withered
away
Never again to be fatigued by the
memory of a torrent sea.

Mark Tritz
THE WINDS OF TIME
The winds of time pass quickly
through,
They can turn the skies to black
from blue.
They affect your life in a number
of ways.
So, young lovers; don't be false, it
never pays.
When selecting your mate to be;
Don't be trivial, but don't be too
free.
For it takes two to make a
partnership that is to last,
So learn by the mistakes you have
made in the past.
Life can be full of happiness and
joy,
If you don't handle it like a small
child does his toy.

Barbara Gilleo
DREAMS

---

*To my family, friends and Mrs.
Horan for her inspiration and
guidance.*

---

dreams--
Dreams
they float through our minds
and waver in front of our eyes.
Dreams
they are the inner images of
ourselves
and they help us to seek
knowledge.
Dreams
can make a person live or die
they can make someone a hero
or criminal,
they separate us from others
and turn imagination into
reality.
We are all made up of dreams
without them—
who are we
where is now
and where lies our future?

dreams.

Andrew S Hartell
HOW COME

---

*To My Friends Past, Present and
Future*

How come in every day life,
Man can say to man,
You Polish so and so,
You Italian so and so,
You Scotch so and so,
You Jew so and so,
You Irish so and so,
You Black so and so,
Yet man will give his money,
And man will risk his reputation,
And man will offer his shelter,
And man will give his life,
In fact man will do anything,
To help or better mankind,
So how come man can't get
together,
For an ever lasting Peace?

Georgia Milton
SHADOWS AT MIDNIGHT
There's long and lonely shadows
on my book tonight—
My pain racked mind, It reads the
shadows too—
The words change with each line I
read—
But the haunting, lonely shadows
never do—

The words I read tonight, perhaps
are soon forgot—
But what the lengthening shadows
do impart—
Will still remain, for one cannot
forget—
The things that lonely solitude has
taught the heart—

Terri Taylor
THE DAY AFTER CHRISTMAS
Twas the day after Christmas,
The house is a mess;
But cleaning can wait,
Because I need a rest.

Papers and boxes
Are thrown everywhere;
There's no place to sit
And I really don't care.

Smashed into the carpet
Are broken candy canes;
But one thing's for certain:
There are NO football games!

The stockings that hung

By the chimney with care,
Have a hole in the toe
And up the side a big tear.

Carols have been sung
The tree must come down
Valentines are up
All over the town.

But lo and behold
As sure as there's a Heaven
Only 347 shopping days
Until Christmas '87.

Mrs Grace K Calkins
YOU AND I

To my darling Arthur for fifty-two wonderful and loving years together.—July 1963

Many years have had their passing
Since we told each other, dear
We would share life's joys and sorrows,
Close together year by year.

We have traveled love's good highway
Over hills and through the dales,
Finding sunshine on the pathway,
Smiling bravely through the gales.

Still we're walking on together,
Partners in the game of life,
Hand in hand and heart to heart, dear
Friends and lovers, man and wife.

Life could hold no richer blessings
As the years pass swiftly by,
Than to find us still good comrades,
Sweethearts, partners, you and I.

Daphne Weber
WHAT IS LIFE ANYWAY?
Life is so unpredictable
It always takes you
By surprise.
You should always expect
The unexpected.

Sometimes
It feels like a dream
Sometimes
Even a nightmare
And all you want to do
Is wake up.

Sometimes
There is too much
Misery and sorrow
That you do not want to face.

But sometimes
You are happy
And having fun
And you never
Want to wake up.
You'd rather dream on
Forever.
Emotions change
Like nightmares turn
Into dreams.
But what is life anyway?

I often find myself
Asking that question
Hoping to get an answer
Although
No one has answered yet.
Does anyone know?

I will ask once again
And if there is no reply
I'll forget all the nightmares
And go on living in dreamland.
"What Is Life, Anyway?"

Patricia Wells Thornton
MY RESURRECTION
Bless me, Father, for I have sinned.

I shuffle in self pity through these dismal city alleys
which are void of beauty,
contemplating the false peace of death.
Dark smells assault the nostrils;
amonia wafts from cat-infested hallways.
Between the bars of peeling fire escapes,
red rust drips in oily patches.
I step over pools of vomitus,
products of rheumy-eyed vagrants
who hug the walls in despair.
Do their sad eyes also remember
signs of Spring in happier days, spent
in a childhood of robins, gardens, fresh countryside?

Then
in the noisome dump of a vacant lot,
Spring defies ugliness.
From one rusty old dirt-filled can
peeks a clump of violets.
Through bottles, old paper, garbage,
It lifts clumps of gentle, fragile faces.

Shafts of sunlight embrace the can and me,
carressing us both with forgiving fingers.
I've forgotten I want to die,
being glad of you—
oh, Spring; oh, hope; oh violets; oh, life!

David A Ivester

David A Ivester
SUMMER

To my very special grandparents, Mr. and Mrs. Eugene Gootee, and to my English teacher, Mrs. Verna Mitchell.

Summer is a time when earth's light bulb gets an extra charge.
The sizzle of the water, the application of the skin lotion;
is like the crackle of ice, the wearing of a coat, that sets
everything in motion.

It is a time when the earth sheds its white coat, and becomes large.
The growing of grass, the blossoming of flowers; is when
everything comes to life, and the day aquires longer hours.

Earth's time clock beats again, and everything starts stirring.
The melting of ice, the hardening of ground;
is like the world, where everything is round.

Nature starts to grow, and earth's clouds start their purring.
For when summertime comes again;
everyone will know, it's just around the bend.

Jeffrey P Doyle
MY LOSS IN ANGER
Soft her face shines in the night
and the moon dances on her hair,
so still she lies without a sound,
not a word to be spoken,
not a one to be found.
just hours ago a fight we had had
now all is calm, no longer are we mad.
I sit here and watch her as the night goes by
no more can I hurt her,
no more will she cry.
The chamber is empty in this cold piece of steel
but the deed is done,
this time for real.
Never again will I hurt her,
and we shall fight no more
for there she lies,
dead on the floor.

Mary Veselka
FAR AWAY PLACES
I dream of far away places,
Where time doesn't race,
Where life is at ease,
And you live it in peace.

The mountains and valleys,
You'll find without alleys,
The mountains with snowtops,
The valleys without stops.

The peace of the wild,
I consider it mild,
The beauty it shows,
Only God can bestow.

As I rest here in peace,
And I live life in ease,
In the mountains up high,
I do nothing but sigh.

I dream of far away places,
Where time doesn't race,
Where life is at peace,
And you live it with ease.

John Fitzpatrick
I-GO YOU-GO WE-GO EGO
Who is to point a finger of ego's weight
To those of error's way
What fault does ego see in reality
To worth no humble way
Excuse that's born of ego's need
Has no reality for justice way
What need ego's excuse
When forgiveness has no say
Ego hawks a false scene
No truth is its' prey
Compassion is its' face
Just to get its' way

Ego finds no justice true
That humbles it to birth
Ego's want of justice is
To itself it be serf
No toy is justice for ego's play
Justice is no game's mirth
Ego's sight has no aim
For peace on man's earth
Ego is the weed
That kills freedom's turf

Ellen Swanson
LOVING LIFE
Thank you God, for such a lovely day.
Please let it chase my blues away.
I'm sorry I've been so depressed, and couldn't feel the
happiness of having sunshine all day long and hear the bird's
melodious song.
Sometimes I wonder why I say, "This is such a lousy day."
When in my heart I know it's true, these days were given to me
by you, and I should cherish every one whether it is cloudy or
bathed in sun.

Katie Marie Preftakes
COLLIN, MY BROTHER

Dedicated to my wonderful brother—Collin!

I know a little boy, who is a joy,
But he has some funny ways.
He makes us all cheerful,
Whenever we are tearful.
And keeps us entertained,
These long and happy days.

We call him "Mini Mimic"
For he copies everything that we do.
He wants three shoes on his feet of two,
And when he can't, he gets so mad,
He doesn't know what to do.

After his bath he hates to get dressed,
Running up and down the hall in his "birthday best."
He runs around nude, that crazy little dude!
He makes a yellow puddle, and puts Mom in a muddle.

He throws his food down on the floor,
And has the nerve to ask for more.
Instead of a fork he uses his hands,
And when he is finished,
Up in the high chair he stands.

He calls himself "Boo" and isn't even two.
Collin is his name,
He'll bring us all to fame,
With his antics to his name.

Georgette Z Johns
DISAPPOINTMENTS

To Jim and our wonderful five, with love. Disappointments and/or joys—we've been through it all, together.

Why?
Why do disappointments invariably occur?
Just when you think you've got life's patterns fixed,
Out of the mist, like a death grip, disappointment
Clutches you;
Defies you;
Will not let go.
Why?

Why can some more fortunate folk bounce, say,
From job to job . . . higher pay . . . better rank . . .
Always landing as a cat—never a set-back—

Never a care, such as,
Where that next meal is coming from! Or,
Who gets the shoes this month?

Could we take in just one show? so long.
Would it be wrong to enjoy one night alone?
We've worked so hard!
What? The bills are due?
So many bills—the payments, few.

One makes a plan.
Sets desires.
Buys the food.
Lights the fires.
In one fell swoop the plan is gone.
The bubble bursts . . . the happiness, done.

Disappointments . . .

WHY????

David C Browning
THE TEARS OF GOD

For my brother Christopher who died in an auto accident May 11, 1987

I've seen the eagle wend its way
Across the windswept sky o'er me.
I've heard the seagull's lonely call,
o'er the surf and distant sea.
But have you heard the nite-bird singing lonely in the night?
Have you heard the wolves a-howling from their old abandoned heights?
Have you heard the cougar crying lonely to its mate?
Have you heard the wind a-moaning in the evening when it's late?
Have you ever felt the earth was mourning
a deep and heartfelt loss?
Or the rain where solemn teardrops falling lonely on the forest moss?
Have you ever felt these things, or thought it rather odd?
That we live in such a lonely world that cries
the tears
of God?

Gerald J Robbins
LOVE FROM ME TO YOU

To all who have felt the joy of love. beauty of your heart fill the world with love, life, and peace.

My soul does seem to be empty
as my life seems cold and blue
But I feel this warmth inside my heart
And this warmth I feel is you,

Your smile shows all lifes happiness
Your warmth and all your charm
Makes my life seem happier
And safe from any harm,

There is something very special
I feel when I'm with you
I see that life is not so bad
Now that dreams come true,

I have a dream of happiness
A dream of love anew
A dream of loving someone special
A dream of loving you,

Now Cupids aim is right on spot
As his arrows flight is true
It pierced my heart and filled my soul
With love from me to you.

Kevin Sean Crumley
WHEN LIFE MEETS YOU FACE TO FACE

In awe of God who wrote this

When life meets you face to face,
In those sobering times,
And you realize it's not a race,
It's not the big decisions,
But the ones in the right direction.
Because the only big decisions you'll make in life
Is the one that changes all the rest.
Kerie Ellisa (God be with you)
Choose life
Choose the small step that's right.

Theresa K Hardison
THE FISHERMAN
I've walked that dusty path so many years
Hoping to hook The Big One
Days spent on a muddy bank deep in thought
Pondering all left undone
While with hook and sinker I lie in wait
For you, my old friend Sir Bass
Branches spreading overhead—
Spring's green birth
Down at the end the morass
Where you also lie in wait, King of Fish
Lurking, watching, cool and sure
Under the surface in murky twilight
Patiently eyeing Death's lure
Tail fanning rotted leaves and oozing mire
In quiet desperation
We wait; two conquerors, each in his world
Silent anticipation
Clouds falling low, silver-streaked in the dusk
Your shadow slipping away
The battle I'm not quite ready to win
Will wait for another day.

Edna L Ferguson
OUR ADORABLE LAURIE
Shub up, shub up . . .
This identifies a little
Sweetheart named Laurie . . .
She's oh . . . so special
As can be . . .
Her beauty, love and jolly
Manner will win you
Over, you see . . .
Look around wherever there's
The pitter patter of little feet . . .
And shub up will be there
For you to meet . . .
She's love, joy, happiness
And much more . . .
For shub up (Laurie) is
Someone we all adore . . .

Roberta Clarke Eaton
QUEENS ACROSS THE OCEAN

This poem is dedicated to Her Royal Majesty Queen Elizabeth II, Buckingham Palace, and ALL mothers throughout the world.

My three bedroom CASTLE awaits my touch
Picking up clothes, and toys and such—
My PALACE, it seems, is in much disarray
After PRINCE and PRINCESS finish at play.
As my KING enters, through the PALACE door,
I'm greeted with enduring words, and more—
You see, the KING understands, as he glances around
and quietly picks up a toy I've not found.
Within my PALACE walls, came a loud KA-BOOM!
Frantically, we rushed into the dining room.
T'was only the sound of a rolling ball,
resounding against our PALACE wall!
After a moment of silence, relief shown 'pon my face,
Thank goodness, it wasn't my Renaissance vase!
KING patted my hand, t'was visibly seen—
He proclaimed in silence, that I was HIS Queen.

Terry L Whetstone
BIRD OF LIFE
Do not hurry through
the day
For you will miss the
virgin start of the
never ending
Circle of Life
With the Sun reaching to
the sky
The fluttering of the
Hummingbird on the
Winds
The Eagles Might
Before man has tanted
Mother Earth again
With the setting of the
Sun

Carol Stewart
LAST BITE
Thinking spiders lived in dusty realms,
Dark and overgrown with old debris,
I was surprised to find one in my own
World, until then considered so carefree.

Yet there he is, legs pointing to the sky.
His itching tracks upon my hide are sown
And I am left to ponder reasons why
This poor invader left his web in search of me.

How starved he must have been to gorge
Himself on such gargantuan fare
Unseen, unfelt until the welts grew high
And red and said so clearly he'd been there.

But I survived and he is dead as dead can be
Because, for him, there was no antidote for me.

Bette Gill
ON THE DEATH OF A SON
No grave dug can hold my son!
His spirit soars
Above the bleak and barren soil
and he endures.

His warm and loving self pervades
the very air I breathe
and remembrance of his teasing smile
bids all my grieving leave.

Yet the pain within my heart
longs for the comfort of his touch,
the big bear hug, the playful mood,
the things I miss so much.

His spirit free still lives with us
his friends say. I guess they know.
But a lonely mother still must ask
oh, Brendan, where did you go?

Douglas M Robertson
THE CONVERSATION
My dear oak tree how can you stand,
So firm and strong against the winter sands;
For it whipped you of your fall red leaves,
When once you had such dainty leaves;
Of lush green colors of wonderful shapes,
Then winter came with it's long cold cape?

But the oak tree replied, Do not despair,
For God is good and God is fair;
God blesses all things in a wonderful way,
Have faith in God in this very day;
Even though it's cold and days grow gloom,
Gods blessing is to come real real soon!

For in the spring I'll look towards the sky,
And ask my God should I bloom or die?
And wait for God to answer my prayers,
For by faith and grace I know he cares;
And sure enough I felt his touch,
With new fresh life, God filled me up!

Alice Johns
THE HOLY MANGER

To My Dear Children: William, Doris, David, Thomas And Paul

In a far away land
In a stable a baby lay
It was little Lord Jesus
Asleep in a Manger of hay.
The amimals stood around
Something seemed to say
A miracle had happened
In that stable that day.
There were shepherds in a field
Who followed a star
There were wise men too
Who came from afar.
By following a star and a dream
The shepherds and wise men were able
To find the Lord Jesus
With Mary and Joseph in a stable.
This story has no ending
We still celebrate His Birth
For God's only Son
Was once here on earth.
God sent His Son Jesus,
To live among men
With Love He came

To save us from sin.
But rejected and alone,
He died on a cross
And went to His Father
Heaven's gain is our loss.

Diane Teague Brewer
CURTAIN CALL
Night fades into Day.
Sands slide into the Sea.
No one knows how dear
Uncle Jessie has been to me.

You slipped away like time.
There is no way I can find
The right words to say
Good-bye.

Jim Jezek
WHY DO WE BOTHER

To my sons Joshua & Jacob; I'm glad I bothered!

There's no laughter in the
playground today;
All the children have gone.
Some were aborted, some were
exploited tell me—
What did they do wrong
To be sold or thrown away, and tell
me—
Why do we bother?

But rest your head now little one
Though a mothers tears may fall,
Not for all the world would she
Ever her child maul.

A little girl brings her mother a gift;
It's a flower from her yard.
But instead of a hug and kiss,
She just knocks her child down.
For just a flower! Tell me—
Why do we bother?

But don't you cry now little one,
Because your mother loves you so,
She doesn't want to harm you,
She just wants you which way to
know;
To leave whats hers alone.
Why do we bother to be fathers and
mothers?
Tell me—why do we bother
To even make love?

Rene Lynn Swackhammer
COME FORTH O FATHER
Come take from me the endless
days,
Come walk through the storms of
time.
Take my thoughts to soak them in,
And swallow up the tears of mine.

Make that stand to spread my path,
And help to build my house of
stone.
Show me the stars from high
above,
And carry me away from being
alone.

Bloom out the preciousness of life,
And create the world of yours.
Help me face the angles of my box,
Come take my hand as we explore.

Wash upon the beaches of the sand,
The glistening light of the ocean.
Step into the dreams of the past,
And the days of time in motion.

Ponder if you must amongst the
gardens,
To gather the scents of time.
But share with me your strength
within,
For 'tis I who must never look
behind.

Wilma Milligan Ketchum
WINDS OF ETERNITY
Winds of eternity
Blow, gently blow,
Through ageless, icy pinnacles,
Across the fields of time.

Spread seeds of wisdom
Over the earth,
Blow gently, blow gently,
Blow low.

Men of infinity,
Pick up the seeds,
Plant peaceful concepts,

Give the world what it needs.

Winds of eternity
Blow, gently blow
Dark storm clouds
From above.

Waft them aside
That the world may see
God's rainbow—
Sign of love.

Blow gently, blow gently, blow.

William Maxwell
ON MEYER'S HILL
On Meyer's Hill I work the land
Armed with a pitchfork in my hand.
I carve a trail through weed and
stone
Through anchored root, discarded
bone.

On Meyer's Hill I look below
Upon the fields, on melting snow.
I turn my gaze another way
And eye the plot my father lay.

On Meyer's Hill the trees are bare
No life is sprouting anywhere.
The ground is dug, the ashes spread
And one more time the earth is fed.

To Meyer's Hill a priest has come
To anoint another with his thumb.
He says a prayer to save the soul
From choking thirst and burning
coals.

Of Meyer's Hill the townsfolk say
The Devil lives there night and day.
He robs all souls to send to Hell
If this be true I'll never tell.

Mallory Petty
THE SAND DOLLAR

To Mom and Dad with Love

Surviving their travel through the
Never-ending currents that carry
them;
Making their way through the
darkness
Still alive under the wet cold sand;
So strong yet so delicate,
They crumble with the touch of a
hand,
Only to die and fade in the sun.

Catherine Proeschel
A POLISHED VASE
Time goes by, and we grow old,
The polished vase that once was
gold,
Reminds us that through each new
page
Of passing life, we too must age,
The once young face, so smooth
and fine,
Is wrinkled now, and scarred by
time.
Why wait for rust? Why fade away?
Must we turn bronze in future
days?
To save our bones and aging face,
Can we learn from the tarnished
vase?
Alas we can, and so we will,
It takes no work or unique skill,
Just be polishedf by and by,
Don't laugh at time as it slips by,
But stand up tall, indeed you must!
Or surely you will fade and rust.

Taunya Sagness
TEARS FLOWING ENDLESSLY

This poem is dedicated to my grandfather Oliver Monroy Sagness whom I loved dearly.

A teardrop on my cheek;
Why must I feel this each and every
week.
If I wait long enough the sadness
may go;
But then again, I may never know.
To wait is to waste time;
And soon the hevens may be mine.
I'm writing this to let you know;
That it is now my time to go.
With a tear drop on my cheek;
This shall be the last time
I speak.

Jennifer LuAnne Price
TEA PARTY PLANS
Little violet by the walk—
I have no time—no time to talk.
I have a friend with golden hair
and a face that's wondrous fair.
We're planning a party—
tea, if you please,
honey will do—
here come the bees.
Tarts and cookies,
sugar and cream,
Porcelain dolls,
My, what a dream!
Roses in bloom
and birds in the sky,
Oh, it's all over—
I think I shall cry!
So you see, little violet
why I can't stay and chat,
there's a place at that table
with my name on the mat!

James E Price
MY INNER SELF
My inner self
Sits on a shelf
of introversion, musing.
Just like an elf,
My inner self,
with secret thoughts, confusing.

Obscured from sight
Are ideas bright
the whole world might be using;
But myself sits
Upon my wits
although it's not my choosing.

So, to the edge,
Then from the ledge
my inner self is sliding
To more explore
The corridor
to lead me from my hiding.

Regaining thence
My confidence
(What else had I for losing?)
That little elf,
My inner self
no longer sits, bemusing.

Lorraine Tighe
THE MAGIC OF LOVE
Love is like magic and it always
will be
For love still remains, Life's sweet
mystery!
Love works in ways, that are
wonderous and strange.
And there's nothing in life, that
love cannot change!

Love can transform, the most
common place,
Into beauty and splender and
sweetness and grace!
Love is unselfish, Understanding
and Kind,
For it sees with its heart and not
with its mind!

Love is the answer that everyone
seek's
Love is the language that every
heart speak's
Love can't be brought, It is
priceless and free
Love like pure magic, Is a sweet
mystery!

Eve Harris
MOUNTAIN VALLEY CHILD
Stepping out through the door
To find playmates in the valley
And spend time, lost from reality
Away from a loveless, grown-up
world
Where no one cared and stomped
the floor.

Sheep crowded on the narrow
street
Tripping the child, scraping her
knee.
Sounds of wind fell quietly from
the mountain,
Miners singing rose in harmony
While she watched, standing in the
misty rain.

Mothers called their brood for
supper;
Told them to wash up, better hurry!
Too late for games tonight
And escape to fanciful flight.
No one called her saying, sorry
about your plight.

Sounds grew muffled, day began
fade,
And row house lights twinkled, all
was safe.
Tears welled, and no one heard.

She did not wonder what life was
all about,
Did not care if some strange land
had drought.
Need to belong subdued hunger
and cold.
Emotions became cushioned, held
for some future told.

Charles J Michner
OLD AGE AND ITS REWARDS

James and Linda Michner and Family

I'm an old man now and nature is cruel,
It's her joke to make old age look like a fool.
The body no longer looks sleek and limber,
It crumbles as grace and vigor depart.
There is a stone where once I had a heart,
But inside of this old carcass, a young man still dwells.
And now and then my beating heart swells,
I remember the joys, I remember the pain.
I'm not loving or living life all over again,
I think of the years many gone by gone.
Like a storm moving so fast,
And I accept the stark fact that nothing can last.
So open your eyes nurse, open and see,
Not a crabby old man, but only a body of a man who used to be.

Stacy Isis Small
DARKNESS
The wind has gone
The sun has set
The darkness is setting in
Then a shot rings out
A store clerk falls
A masked man runs
It is quiet
Then a siren breaks the still of the night.

Lucille Cast Mowat
FOREST CATHEDRAL
'Neath the redwoods, tall and stately,
In a grove of countless trees,
Man looks up in mortal wonder
At this growth of centuries.
Awed, he listens to the silence
Of these towering forest kings
When there is no breeze to stir them—
Oldest of all living things.

Then he listens as the zephyrs
Start a rustling through the boughs,
And the woods is filled with music
As the quiet giants rouse.

In the treetops far above him,
As the wind upon them plays,
He hears singing in the forest—
Anthems, hymns and roundelays.

As a great outdoor cathedral
Filled with standing worshippers
Bursting into vibrant praise,
By the wind of heaven stirred,
Is this mighty redwood forest
When there's music in the trees—
And man perceives a kinship
With this growth of centuries.

Yvette Roberts
CHANGING SEASONS
Autumn winds
Remove tattered leaves
From bare tree limbs.

Faded red, dingy yellow,
Dirty orange, grimy brown
Garments heaped carelessly, forgotten—
Winter winds bring
Shimmering silver
Bedclothes
for the long sleep
'til spring.

Betty White Scott
MY THANKS

Dedicated to the memory of my loving mother Mrs. Orrie E. Weese

My God is my strength
In each darkened hour
He lifts me up like the rain
Lifts the petals of a flower.
He helps me find a way
To see the silver lining
To see life is not in vain
To hush my petty whining.
When dark clouds begin to gather
And the way looks difficult to trod
I don't want to give up
I get in contact with God.
And I lift up my head
To say thanks everyday
That I had a mother
Who taught me to pray.

Julie Villafane
DECIPHERING NOW AND FOR THE NEXT JOURNEY

To Leyla: The only one who really understands, the best friend any one could have. With gratitude for teaching me and loving me.

Beautiful is you,
Is to think, is time;
Is the dogma of my love.

Passages in history
Speaking about the self,
The mind, the spirit, the soul
And after all,
Is only me
In my rocking chair
Deciphering the intricate mysteries
Of one being, of one subject:
Me and the creation of my world.

I have a friend
In whom I resume
The essence of love;
A friend who means to me
What desire is to hope.

I travel and think
Speak and remember;
Love with my eyes and my ears,
Look for things
To amuse me
And wait to live again
To undertake another journey
In which I can become
New things.

Gilbert Vines
WHO AM I TRUELY?
Who am I truely?
Who am I truely?
Different am I
From what is shown
Different am I when alone
My true self appears
when no one is near
Who am I truely?
Who am I truely?

Frank O'Brien
SHADOWS AND ECHOES
The Italian, the Pole, the
Englishman and the
English-French-Irish-Indian

A motley crew from the local ranks
Playing King-of-the-hill
On moonlit snow covered highway banks

Up I go to battle Big John
Two youth-spending warriors
locked in hand-to-hand pushes and pulls
Bringing to bear every muscle to care
Only to stumble and tumble
A long down back

Another beaten rolling laughing log

The britches now get an up-hitch
in the bright wet snow
"Big John is sure a bitch to spill"!
But now Italian Joe is king-of-the-hill

I pause to consider my quest for the throne
This time I won't be thrown!

The battle nonstop rages atop

Moonlit air is gulped for the gallop

Slipping and sliding and falling
and pawing my way up the pearly span
I head myself in a circle of hands and feet
But only anew to meet defeat

Thus I saw I was not to be king that
night upon the matted grass
But only to sing the praises of
youth too fast to past

Wayne J Walker
THE PESSIMIST
Thru the autumn woods I walk
Listening to the wildlife talk
Consuming all of natures grandeur,
Gathering in it's magic splender
A passive companion, at my side,
Complaining of the waste of time.

Before us stood a mighty oak,
Majestic in it's autumn coat.
From these acorns I relented,
"A tree will grow as God intended."
My companion turned and said,
"It's just a nut the tree has shed."

Allan Hilpert Stinson
FLEETING GLIMPSE
A Fleeting Glimpse
Catches the eye
mind often wondering
time to time

Always in
constant thought
things that should have been
were not

A restless soul
sometimes seeks
casting riches
upon the meek

Seeing the world
without being seen
living with false hope
but not in dream

To hold
not to be held
under someone's
demanding spell

Being cast about
not cast upon
ready to give in
But must go on

No racing against time
no finding lost love
just put your hand in mine
and release the skyborn dove

Teresa Ann Hardin
WORDS OF ENCOURAGEMEMT

For Mom—Mother's Day 1986

What I share with you today,
Stands for tomorrow too,
And every other day after,
This advice I give to you.
Promise me you'll be so strong
That nothing can disturb your peace of mind,
I worry about that often,
As we all lose control sometimes.
Let go of guilt and know
That it's okay to make the same mistakes again,
Let go of defeat and know
That if you believe in yourself, you can.
Let go of my hand, and hold onto my heart,
Let go of the end, and make a fresh start.
Don't rely on self-pity,
As it seldom takes you far.
Someone like myself may need you,
And not just for the keys to your car.
Believe in yourself,
As I know that I do.
Trust in the advice others give,
As I have given some to you.
When loneliness is your companion,
And all about you seem vanished and gone,
Listen well Mom, to my words,
And your moments of silence,
I will replace with love.

Doreen A Deshler
MY FRIEND

Dedicated to Mel Brady, Thanks for believing in me.

A friend so sweet and dear
Your always there to save the day
Someone who really cares
And doesn't care what people say

You'll stand behind me
Through thick and thin
You try to help me see
That there is a way for me to win

You give me hope and happiness
Love, strength and confidence

Your wish for you
Is a wish for me

I hope someday we will share
A love and friendship
An unseperatable pair
Something that will always keep

Forget you never
For in my heart you'll stay
For I'll love you forever
And maybe more someday

Linda Pace Maddox

Linda Pace Maddox
ON ACCEPTANCE

This poem is dedicated to my husband, Jay, and to his loving parents.

I am sitting here beside you, God,
And wonder why you took the notion
To fashion me the way you did.
I love you!
I don't understand life;
It has been confusing.
My thoughts are prisms of muddled rainbows
and I am deficient.
There is an answer there, and I want to touch . . .
and make it come alive.
I want it to sparkle
Like the grandest gem you ever chose to create.

I've been chipped —
Marred—Scarred,
And I've nearly dug a grave for the loveliness
you freely gave.
Give me a vision now, and make the person
you wanted to befriend.
Don't let me hide, but take my hand
And group me with your magnificent constellations!
I want you to sit beside me and smile.

Florence Van Wert
EARTHQUAKE—(COSMOGONIC FORCE THAT BRINGS—ORGASM TO POSEIDON KING)

As you lie awomb in the Good-Mother-Earth,
No one can predict the due time of your birth.
Needbe you are nameless while slumber you keep;
An insipid creature so long as you sleep
In quiet blankets of gypsum-sand and faulted rock,
Securely immured, in your dark chambers locked,
Lest the testy prod of seismic innervation
Should reach you and should breech you from your hibernation.

May Morpheus belay you, fast in his grip,
So fast, Oh strange creature, that you cannot slip,
Cannot slip, slip away from sleep,
Away to wakefulness to keep
Sad rendevous with man, who lives of the certainty you will come,
Ponders but the time and place it be done.
We'll bid the devil good-morrow, timely when he causes care;
Only when you slip your bondage will our sad cries rend the air.

The cosmogonic energy with which you are imbued,
That sparks your every movement, may never be unfueled.
What fools we be to ask of thee a timeless sleep,—
Like fools long passed, all those who asked Neptune to still the deep,
Its waves a thunder, destined to pound on crumbling shore
As eons pass until man is no more.
That your seed hold, attenuate, within the Good-Earth-Womb
The Lord God needs must blanket the earth's sun from her moon.

Elisa T Keena
THE WEDDING POEM

For Bryan, my inspiration.

Time and I will come and go
Your love for me will ebb and flow.
The song we sing shall be ever sung.
This deed we do shall never be undone.

So from this day, this very moment.
I give to you my love, my torment
And hope that we shall always stay
As much in love as we are today.

Karen L Lowicki
KNOWING YOU. . .

This poem is dedicated to Mark, "The only one," my inspiration, and #1 Fan.

Knowing you has made me see what affect a smile has;
How happiness can be expressed through simplicity.

Knowing you has helped me to regain the confidence I thought was extinct;
By seeing someone who believes in me.

Knowing you has given me the incentive to seek further for my dreams;
By feeling your presence in my journey.

Knowing you has made me appreciate the value within a person's individuality;
To know there is sincerity in silence.

Knowing you has given me the ability to give of myself again;
By believing in you.

Knowing you has made me realize there is strength in numbers;
By the warmth felt in your arms.

Knowing you has ceased what bad memories I've had;
You being proof of what might be ahead.

Knowing you I've become aware of time's essence;
By realizing; "Some things are worth waiting for."

Karen Shade Keefover
GODESS OF PLEASURE

A splendid geranium plant
Sits on the window to entwine
And strangle crusty cobwebs
That threaten to damp her sublime

Countenance. She defiantly dares a
sultry stare to mock the grey
Forbidding sky, heavy-laden
With snowflakes about to sway.

Red blooms like a scarlet harlot
tempestuously tempt snow
To peep in the window frame
Set wildly aflame with a glow

Reflecting the shame of comfort
On a frigid December day.
A winter drained of pleasure
Leaving no place risque to stray.

She welcomes gladly, to her brothel
Those enticed by her pleasure
Seductive, assured by all who gaze
Of her hypnotic treasure.

Edith Louck
THE SILENT HOUSE

The house is silent standing there
Upon a tiny hill;
Where once its halls were filled with noise,
For years it has been still.

If walls could tell their many tales,
Such wondrous things we'd hear.
They'd tell of many newlyweds
And weeks and months of cheer.

And yet, they'd tell the sad tales, too;
The ones so filled with pain;
Of bedrooms turned to battlefields
And clear skies turned to rain.

But though the life the house has seen
Can never be revealed,
It will remain till time stands still
So carefully concealed.

Mary C Belluardo
LISTEN TO THE SILENCE

My space is violated everyday
By myriads of distracting sounds
That pierce the eardrums and distract the soul
Turning my thoughts to empty and frivolous things.

Around and around I go in a whirlwind of cacophony
From early morning to late at night
The noise prevails from numerous places in
Sounds from radio, music, and televison.

Still I continue from day to day—first one thing then another,
Caught up in this empty merry-go-round of noise and sound
That drowns out even my inner most secret thoughts
Until lost in oblivion I crave only to listen to the silence.

Ah! Silence! Silence! Silence!
My thoughts I can finally hear and begin to fathom.
More than that, my God can enter within and try to reach me
Assuring me of His love, His care, and His eternal presence.

Lee W Farber
OF TERRA

Majestically whirling in a void of liquid black,
near heavenly furnace, of warmth no lack,
with pearly orb, small child in tow,
constant companion, lunar pull, tides flow.
Moving softly, a dancing mote, she passes,
turquoise vastness, lapping granite giants,
life abounds, dazzling vigor and defiance,
velvet shadows, laughing hills, bluest lakes,
the complex drama of beauty she makes.
Great seas of forest, drifting in mist,
burning oceans of sand, by fierce heat kissed,
this world set aside, for life and for motion,
a heartbeat I hear? . . . Strange idea, stranger notion.
All this is given, naught asked in return,
except to see, grow, develope and learn.
She is all that we are, now and tomorrow,
she gives us her all . . . all that we borrow,
she is mother to all, understand her true worth,
she is mother to all,
our Terra,
our Earth.

Thurman E Brown
WHEN YESTERDAY MEETS TOMORROW

Dedicated to my Wife, Opal E. Brown

While on our journey through life
If we meet the everlasting
Power of Universal Love that keeps
Blissful youth forever aglow
Yesterday has met tomorrow.

There will be no more time for tears or sorrow
only time for eternal love and exultation.
No time wasted looking for a tomorrow
That can never be anymore.
Only a today throughout the eternity for evermore
When yesterday has met tomorrow.

Where our souls shall be united in one accord,
Free of all mortal weakness that forbids our souls to sore
Throughout the universe in Eternal subline peace,
Where we can meet again with rapture
When yesterday has met-When yesterday has met tomorrow
Throughout the Universe Divine.

Mary Fritz Exoo
SUMMER DAY

John goes by on his bike.
It's much too hot for a hike.
He heads for the pool—
to get nice and cool.

Sue is hidden from the sun,
Ready for some quiet fun.
She sits in the shade of a tree,
And listens to the buzz of a friendly bee.

Amy has her coloring book.
She flips the pages to look
For the picture of snow on the mountain
Or the children gathered at the fountain.

The dog finds a gentle breeze,
And says, "I'll just stay here, if you please,
In this leafy shade,—
Snuggled in the hole that I made!"

Lyda Anderson

Lyda Anderson
HURRY UP AND GET READY

Dedicated to my seven children Namely: Douglas, Adoree, Ted, Beverly, Shirley, Mary and Sheila

From September until June, this is the morning tune
Hurry up, and get ready, that's what mother harps
To all of her children before their school starts
Now children get ready, you still must be fed
You can't lie there sleeping, so get out of bed.
Get up and get ready I beg of you Ted
Your date you kept late, now your eyes are like lead.
Mary and Johnny, honestly, I could cry
To mate up your socks is more than a sigh
There's one in the corner, and one in the shoe
It sounds very simple yet so much to do.
Hurry up and get ready before you are late
I tell you it's getting a quarter past eight
Remember I've said to obey every sign
To watch out for traffic and walk the chalk-line
Your teachers are waiting and think you are fine
So hurry and kiss mother and be there on time.
Hurry up, and get ready that's what mother harps
To all of her children before their school starts.

Mary Jane Hollen
THE BATTLE AT LEXINGTON IN SEVENTY-FIVE

Drums rumbled softly, and fifers did play
As the moon came up over old Black Bay
Where British soldiers, wet up to the knees
Had come ashore 'mid unseasonably cold breeze
Then onward they pressed, on to Lexington way.

Four Minute Men were sent forth to see
Just how close the marching British may be.
Three men were captured, only one did come back
As assembly was drummed, lest there be an attack.
On the town's village mall, and facing the road,
The Minute Men stood staunchly, holding their load,
Waiting to see, just what they may face,
As they watched British Regulars move into place.

Major Pitcairn upon catching a sight of the Square
Ordered a battle line to form,—right there,
But not to shoot, for surrender, "they" must.
Captain Parker's men, withdrew without thrust.
Dispersed they did but their muskets they held.
"Lay down your arms, damn you," Major Pitcarin yelled.
"We shall have them," came a voice, a Britishman's cry.
A loud shot was fired but no one can say why.

The Americans dispersed 'neath Englishmen's volley
Bleeding and hurt by someone's careless folly.
It was a bloody mistake, gathering little reward
As the British played music and swung on to Concord.

Cindy Hayes
WASN'T MEANT TO BE

Suddenly you came into my life, we fell in love so fast, so deep, you even asked me to be your wife.
Our world was beautiful, nothing could stand in our way,
I never thought my love could be so strong, yet it grew stronger with each passing day.
Then one day, much to my surprise the look of love was no longer
in your eyes. You said you didn't love me anymore and didn't know why.
I couldn't say anything back to you, all I could do was cry.
I alway's thought that you were made for me, but now I can face the truth and our love wasn't meant to be.
I fell apart just thinking that I wasn't yours and you were no longer mine, it took me awhile but now I realize that I'm going to be just fine.
The memory of you will still hurt me in the months to come,
I've promised myself to be strong because what's done is done.
I now understand why I'm not with you and you're not with me,
our love just wasn't meant to be . . .

Mescal E Greer Ph D
PRESERVE HIS AFTER GLOW

For Aaron Ross Greer—Whose gentle spirit will live forever in all who knew him.

Oh little room
at the head of the stairs,
You're so quiet and clean,
so filled full of prayers.

Oh little room
with your warm glowing sun,
Hold fast to your Spirit
of missions well done.

Watch over his treasures,
dear little room.
Nourish his plants
so they'll continue to bloom.

The August Geographic lying
there by his bed
Is awaiting return
of that world-searching head.

Still echoing last words
from imaginary travels
Vacation brochures for 1986
show festive and colorful
marvels.

A card quoting Saint Francis
stands patiently by,
Reminding all of us daily
of life's values to try.

His little gold clock
with its pendulum swing,
Whispers hopes of new joys
that his memories will bring.

Look in the top drawer
of his little brown chest.
See the Halycon egg, Leo in gold
with "affectionate, creative, sincere"
as his best.

The Bleker dance trophy
beside Leo is shown
Saying countless successes
in childhood he'd known.

There's a beaded belt buckle
with an eagle in flight,
And a boy's socker photo
shouting, "We'll soar to great height."

In his closet so neat
hang the clothes that he wore
Unaware that he'll never again
walk through that door.

Guard well his books
with pages like gold.
They helped in his breaking
Liquor's steal chained hold.

Death claimed his body
and took him away,
But his Spirit triumphant
is with us to stay.

Now dear little room
full of comfort and peace,
Preserve that warm glow
so our courage will not
cease.

Eva C Beck
JESUS WAS A LITTLE BOY

Jesus was a little boy,
Just like you.
Nestled in his mother's arms
Just like you.
He laughed and cooed;
And grew in grace;
And smiled into his mother's face.
Jesus was a little boy
Just like you.

Jesus was a little boy,

Just like you.
He played and ate
And slept the whole night through.
He was kind and helpful
To his mother every day;
And shared with other children
As they went about their play.

His mother was his teacher,
Together they would sing,
Of God and his great power
And of precious things.
There spread out before him
Was all of natures lore,
God's library of creation

Over which he loved to pore.

Jesus was a young lad,
And as he grew apace,
He worked in Joseph's carpentry shop
With a smiling face.

He learned to use and care for tools,
And to fashion things from wood,
And when Joseph looked upon them
He pronounced them good.

Then one day when he was twelve,

Passover to attend,
He journeyed to the temple
With relatives and friends.
There he saw so many things
To make a child exclaim;
The white robed priest;
The bleeding lamb;
The altar of sacrifice.

He bowed his head and prayed that day,
And began to understand,
The mystery of his mission
To this sin-infested land.

Suzette King (Z-MOM)
TRACT WAVES

This poem is dedicated to all the construction crews who have participated in the Sunnymead/ Perris Valley expansion.

It's beat is fast and rythmic
It's heat white-lightning hot.
It's hues are copper and wood and dreams
The likes of which have never been.

Two million ripples on this wave;
It's pulses sweeping over vales.
To change eternally the earth,
The "House" is having it's re-birth.

They saw and pound and dig and build,
This "Wave" of homes is far from still.
And with each beat of its pulsing self,
Another "House" rests on the shelf.

Callin J Edgin
WHAT DREAMS ARE MADE OF

To my loved ones; Mom, Dad, Craig, Tami, Cariann, Cherie, Carla, Cathy, Dora & Steven. All the Edgins.

Not clouds, and mist,
but maybe a lover and a kiss.
A warm place to hide away, for a long
period of time, or just a day.
Sometimes alone or together.
It depends on your imagination.
And all types of weather.
Seeing leaves fall to the ground.
With the brilliance of colors.
It can be anywhere, time or place.
Just relax and sit down and realize your
dream face to face . . .

Donna L Midura
EYES OF A STRANGER

Eyes of a stranger
Grown hateful with time
Eyes of a stranger
Stared straight into mine.

Depths of deep ebony
Held a constant storm
Eyes of pure madness
They thought would never form.

Eyes of a stranger
Belonged to no face
Eyes of a stranger
Came from no place.

I looked away with darkened fear
For I could not bear to see
That those eyes of a stranger
Now belonged to me.

David Lee Richardson
WARLORDS

From highest ascention, fell this dreary God. In dementia,
dwelled his self-forsaken good.
Aligning his ocean for apes off to war, dingy souls crawling, spawn insane glory boars, on those once green knolls running rouge coating, landmarks of honored insanities.
In fields of glory you will not find me.
Ego-idol aspiring, as each, ambitious and hollow.
So much of man's ignorance did abide and blindly follow. . .
Until no tomorrow could wake without sorrow.
Remember the error; the lesson unlearned still, in a law of the living.
It offers you only; The honor-scarred poison. . .
Barbaric propriety to man as monstrosity.
In fields of glory, you will not find me. For only in the final, blank second of frantic desecratement, does this darkness invocate conscious lament.
The warlord turned undone, unto his truth in unending lie, & brought his cosmic cradle home to die. . .
Bought his ancient mother the breath of death, and with clinging,
fractured life, left only, endless pain, And their tears ran red against the rain.
Reflection in sub-conscious mirrors, left the warlords self in searing fragments. So many unsettled souls unsheltered,
by their journeyed spirits. With your own serpents venom to protect, to yourself, breeds the hex and the hell.
A beast within the beasts of being.
. .The love would never seek their seeing.
In fields of glory, you will never find me.

Betty Frances Record
GOD'S CHILD

A child came to us
in the fall of our lives.
Not a baby to hold
but a child who was old—
old with the wisdom
picked up in the street.
Suspicious of all she'd happen to meet.
Her language was bad, her expression was sad.
Could we change this in just a few years?
Or would there be anger, tantrums and tears?
We prayed to God to show us the way
and to give us just the right words to say.

He said, "Just love this one with all your might,
I'll smooth the corners and still the fright."
A girl lives with us
in the fall of our lives.
A new life to mold,
a soft hand to hold.
A girl with a smile
and eyes with no guile,
loving to all she happens to meet.
Her laughter bubbles—
we have few troubles.
How right God was when He said love could change all things—
with help from above.

Lara S Baluch
ARRANGEMENTS OF A MOUNTAINSIDE

The blazing sun beats down upon the ground.
The neverending path reveals a challenging climb.
I stumble on the jagged edges of the mountian's crumbs,
feeling a spray from the trickling stream.

The aroma of pine needles lingers in the air, refreshing the journey.
I push the branches that reach for each other,
wiping the sweat from my brow.

I have conquered the top,
overlooking the crator of sapphire blue.
The pure lake awaits my splash.
The water, reflecting the sun like a mirror,
Shines like a sheet of glass.

The clifts extend high above the lake;
I balance on the edge.
The water is clear as crystal, cold as ice.

The boiling temperature cools as I work my way down.
The bottom of the mountain is clearly in sight.
Enjoying a day's journey, the sun sets over the trees,
Melting as it settles in the water.

Elvira C Schnabel
NIAGARA FALLS

Ethereal mist everywhere,
Clouds of enchanting dew,
Swirling torrents cascading,
Turbulent, enraged whirlpools,
Mountainous maelstrom of "white caps,"
Thunderous roar of the spillway,
"Maid of the Mist" edging her way
Near the perilous rim of milky foam,
Starry-eyed "honeymooners," oblivious
Of all but the Falls and each other.
A sari-gowned woman of the bewitching East
With a nostril lavishly bejeweled
Meditates in awe at the dazzling spectacle.
Rain-clad urban folk venture diffidently
Into the deep murky chasm
Beneath the rumbling billows of water,
Tighten their grip on the moist rail
Refuse to show their apprehension.
Resplendent rainbow, arc of cerulean blue
With tinges of brilliant ocher, delicate amethyst,
Even a dash of flaunting vermillion,
A prismatic aura of the Hand of God.
Man feels small, the cataract is gigantic,
This is sheer power, aesthetic beyond words,
It must be seen to be believed.

Bill Howey
PRAYER OF MASKS

Individuals, conceived From seeds
Like flowers that never bloom
Live to bear their hidden deeds
Their faces, like empty masks
Have learned to perform
Required and unspoken tasks
Visions of reaching the top
Induced into minds seeking success
Are merely the quirk of a cork's pop
Peace is now governed by threat of Force
And behind our mask
We deny our Future's course
Industries' ego of mass quantity
Has replaced one's pride in quality
Allowing other countries the right of equality
The call to help those in need
Is now only a faint cry
To a Godly nation of Greed
Few people take time to be real
Like the beautiful Flowers
That align the Field
Only when we remove our masks
Will our Fruitful deeds
Replace our Performed tasks,
Amen

Chris James
IS THERE?

Is the feeling born within your soul,
Is your fate determined as dice with a roll?
Is a number set from the beginning of time,
With no thought of your life in prime?
Should destiny be picked by a martyr,
Who should determine letting you go farther?
Is there a master, playing our game of chess,
Who is it that determines our failure or success?
Who should control the destiny of man,
Or duration of time, we should walk on this land?
Should we be put into the hands of belief,
If anyone could know, would it be a relief?
Would our lives go on as a wonder to all,
Just wondering who looks over us all?
Let those who shall say, believe what they will,
I shall not know, until my life's at a standstill!

Betty Honn Perry
A GREAT FRIEND IS HE

To my parents, my family, brother and sister, my friends, and Elderslie-St. Andrews United Methodist Church

Jesus Christ is our friend so true,
He knows all our sorrows and troubles deep.
Why not let Him be your friend too?
On His kindly shoulder you can weep.

In a crisis He will pull you through,
If in Him very strong is your faith.
In your life, does He come first with you?
"Love me as I have loved you," He sayth.

Just ask and He will grant you pardon and peace,
I found a wonderful friend just for you and me.
Now all our troubles and sorrows shall cease,
Oh! how wonderful—a great Friend is He!

Mike Neary
THE SEVEN STARS

In Memory of the last crew of the Space Shuttle Challenger January 28, 1986. Each a Pioneer

On a quiet night
after a bitter day

I looked South
and scanned the skies.
There were no stars to be found.
They too heard the news
and were too stunned to shine.
All were dim, save for seven.

It had to have been them,
for they dared to shine
as bright in passing
as they were in life.

And one,
the highest one there,
still held the gift
of bright red.
A going away present.

And hanging from the belt,
dim among them,
the Grand Lady
the vehicle turned Valkyrie
that took them
on one last trip
and joined them there.

Loretta Palguta

THIS FOR SURE

There is a song I must sing
For the peace I hope it will bring
Do not hide your head in the sand
But try to understand.

God made us to be brothers
To have compassion for others
We are no better than those
of a different skin
It's no game, to see
which race will win.

Until the proud become humble
And the rich feed the poor
Life on earth is worth nothing
God knows this for sure.

Waneta C "Scip" Rodeheaver

TOUCHED BY YOU

Your gentle caring ways
A hand upon my shoulder
Friendship I've come to cherish
As we've both grown older.

Your undying faith
Through so many tears
Yours, mine, ours
Just fifteen brief years

If I can but remember
What you taught so quietly
A better day is coming
For both you and me.

A fact I've come to know
All the years through
I'm a much better person
Having been touched by you.

Virginia R Gonzales

Virginia R Gonzales

MY FATHER'S HOUSE

My father's house, had no doors,
no windows and dirt floors.
My father's house, was warm,
it had Mama's touch and charm.
My father's house, with much food,
and Mama chopped the wood.
My father's house, children all
around,
sometimes sleeping on the
ground.
My father's house, sometimes a
tent,
played his violin, happy hours
spent.
My father's house, by a roadside,
with vegetable garden, acres
wide.
My father's house, a beautiful site,
with woodstove and oil lamps
for lite.
My father's house, it was indeed,
with Mama's flower garden
started from seed.
My father's house, was anywhere,
with Mama there.

Nancy Jean Pregont

PEACE MISSION

To the leaders of the world, to work together toward peace.

I hurried off to Europe,
Touching Yugoslavia and Greece,
The leaders and the people scoffed,
They didn't recognize, I'm peace!

Surely all of Asia,
Specially China and Japan's stance,
Would welcome me with open
arms,
But, they all stood off, askance.

Next, I embraced Africa,
Hoping Egypt and Libya cared,
They looked at me so coldly,
My peaceful soul was bared.

I prayed that South America,
Would change the doubt in me,
Oh, Brazil, Peru, I know you care,
They didn't accept peace as the key.

My soul was sad and heavy,
As these continents dropped from
sight,
All of them were unconcerned,
This mission became my plight.

My last hope was North America;
Canada and the United States,
"Oh, peace," they cried. "Stay with
us.
You're our only hope for the
world's fate!"

Cheryl Lynn Bell

BOREDOM

This poem is dedicated to Karl, my loving boyfriend and to Dallas High School's DEAL, my inspiration.

Conspirator plotting, failing,
captured.
Disgrace caused by shameful
conduct is not punishment:
sentenced to the ultimate
torture.

The lineament of the timekeeper
moves as if lame
. . . and slowly it creeps.
wantons sighing—crying—
tortured.
The cracks in the floor pulse like
veins of cement.
The tap of the pendulum is
rapturous.
And the lineament of the
timekeeper is now oblique
. . . but slowly it creeps.

Innocents begging . . .
pleading . . . forgotten.
The walls form a vice to squeeze
sanity.
The floor drops to the fires of
earth and the ceiling is flying.
The lineament of the timekeeper is
directed to hell
. . . so slowly it creeps.
Time's tenacious grip is
tightening—
killing the raindrop to make
room for the flake.
Time will constrict 'till all is
dying.
The lineament of the time keeper
moves as if chased
. . . too quickly it creeps.

Helen Dittman

CREATION

The changing of the seasons
Are a token from above
From God the great creator
To show us of his love

God put it all together
Then he created man
To rule the mighty universe
That he designed and planned

Janet L Turner

INDIAN CHIEF

Painted pony stands
With head held high.
Indian chief stares
With a watchful eye.
Skin darkened bronze
By the mid-day sun.
Face drawn and hard.
Seared from battles won.
Feathered headdress
Adorns his head.
Long, silky feathers,
White, yellow and red.
He sits there proudly
On the high mountaintops,
Ready to claim victory
As the last battle stops.

Luke J Sladicka

MY LIFE'S A SHADOW

Through my life I've seen pain and
sorrow
Will I live to see tomorrow
Still a shadow watches me
No one knows where I'll be

All I see and feel is the darkness
I feel I must confess
But what shall I say
to get out of this mess

Am I ready to die?
Why should I?
Who am I?
Right now I feel possessed
Right now I'm distressed

But why?
Who's here?
Who the hell is watching me?

When I walk
My mind goes blank
What am I
Who should I thank

Why should I thank someone
for this mess?
But right now I'm in distress

Cynthia Wibbels

A SIGN IN THE SKY

It got to be a minor thing, like an
airplane in the sky. They took
it for granted "we're in the space
age, there's nothing to fear so
fly."But people don't you
remember, it's only the 20th
century. We've gone far, too far
and they died.

They took it up, it went up high,
and then they went full throttle;
a big boom, like a falling star the
shuttle was gone forever.

Why?

The seven are gone, we'll see what
went wrong and make it better
next time. They would want it
this way, so they say, but who
got the chance to ask them, there
wasn't time to say goodbye.

We sat and watched, in awe we
cried as the sky lit up in flames.
There's nothing we can do now,
but I sit and pray for each of the
seven people who died on that
eerie day, I pray that God was in
their hearts and took them all
away.

Jaay Johnson

MOTHER'S LOVE AND FATHER'S STRENGTH

To Christine With All My Love

A child is born of a woman from a
seed planted by man. She nurses
and nourishes and plans, but she
needs the strength of her man.
It starts to crawl and then to talk
and holds its mother's hand, but
it can't do it by herself it needs
the strength of a man.
A mother's love and tender touch
they learn to understand. They
count on her for many things,
but they need the strength of a
man.
And as your child starts to grow
and its mind begins to expand.
It relies on you for many things;
but it needs the strength of a
man.

Burnam B McCormick

WHO IS THIS JESUS?

To Barbara Sue My Faithful loving wife

He was born in a manger many
years ago
Astounding doctors and lawyers
when he
Was 12 years old.

Baptized in Jordon by that great
preacher, John
Then God spoke from heaven
saying,
"This is my son."

He healed all manner of sickness;
He
Strengthened the weak; opened
eyes of
The blind and made dumb men to
speak.

He said,"Ye believe in God—
believe also
In me.
For I am the truth and I'll set you
free.

In an illegal court my saviour was tried
By the very ones for whom he died.

His death defeated the power of my sin,
But the real victory came when he arose again.

Who is this Jesus?; To a lost one in sin?
He would be their saviour if they would let
Him come in.
Do you know this Jesus, His truth and his way?
Then consider this Jesus before leaving today.
He ascended to heaven, but he is looking
This way.
When will he return, you ask.
Could be today.

Zezor DeForce

Zezor DeForce
TRAVELING WANDERER

I Zezor DeForce, lovingly dedicate this poem to three very special people: My friend Sarah, my aunt Bessie and my mother Catherine!!!

I hear the voices, therefore I must heed the command
The voices are not of people but are the voices of the road
I must travel the road from now until the end
For the miles ahead are my future and at the end lies my destiny
Loneliness and darkness are my only companions
Anxiously they await the resuming of my travel
As time grows near to the coming of my departure
Visions of our encounter fluctuate from within.

Once again I have wandered into yet another dimension
A dimension in which I was shown life in spite of death,
Love in spite of hate and knowledge in spite of ignorance
Though I was cold and bitter, I was shown warmth and sweetness
Though I was distant and quiet, I was shown closeness and expression
And though I was weak and confused, I was shown strength and direction
For these reasons and these reasons only
I kneel before thee, unprotected and at thy mercy
Forever I will miss the spirit of who you are
And the spirit of who you will one day become
And now I must bid farewell to yet another place and to yet another love
For my entrance was my exit from a past dimension
And my exit will be my entrance into yet still, another dimension.

Sister Concetta Schuit O S F
IRRESISTIBLE RAINDROPS

You captured me,
you couldn't wait until
you dropped your cloak
of raindrop satin
upon my brow.

So soft your touch,
so refreshing that I
didn't mind as I went
along and watched you dance
your raindrop polka.

Sometimes fast, then unaware you'd
stop and surprise me with a
twinkle in your eye as I
whispered,
Oh, you irresistible raindrop.

Shirley Yvonne May Dinning
REFLECTIONS OF THE SEASONS

The dew drop kisses the rose making it blush,
The morning air is filled with the song of the Thrush.
Heralding the beginning of Spring, awakening the life within,
Blades of grass and buds unfold, awakening from their dream,
Dressing Mother Earth in an Emerald sheen.
Oh what beauty there is to behold in Spring.

Summer brings flowers in bloom,
Birds dressed in their finest plume.
Grains to ripen soon, watched over by a golden Harvest Moon.
Butterflies emerge from their cocoon, spreading their wings never too soon.
From the lake, the call of the Loon, hints of Autumn coming soon.

An amber moon lights the way for Jack Frost to have his day.
Russet leaves orange, gold, and brown,
Blanket Mother Earth with a colorful gown.
Birds on the wing harken to the call.
Behold for it is now Fall.
A shimmering white gown covers the Earth,
As we all sit warm and cozy in front of the hearth.
The cold North Wind rapts at our door,
But we show him no raporte.
The antics of Jack Frost are met only with Mirth,
As we all sit warm and cozy in front of the hearth.

Lizabeth Anne Neilly
THE RAINBOW'S POT OF GOLD

Our love is a rainbow,
it starts deep
within our hearts,
it's bright and beautiful,
its beauty fills the,
hearts of those around us,
The rainbow goes
on and on,
it shines brightly
for all to see,
forever guard your rainbow
for at the end is your
Pot of Gold,
And with this Pot
of Gold
Comes the fulfillment
of all your dreams,
Always guard
your rainbow,
your love,
your hearts.

Sulabha Sardesai-Kulkarni Ph D
INTIMATE STRANGERS

Then,
You were so near and yet so far
I felt so lonely and sighed so deeply
And then you looked at me and smiled
And all my sorrow died
A smile to cherish and nourish till I perish
I shall cling to it fast till I breathe my last.
And now,
You are so near and yet so far
The two bodies and two minds keep us miles apart
A smile of love and understanding
A desire not to hurt but to make happy
A knowledge that you will not be her
And so will she not be you
And those three little words
"I love you" sincerely said
Are the magic emulsifiers for
The blending of two distant heads
But these very precious things are forgotten
In the rush of living
While the time passes by
And we stand like two strangers till we die.

Mary Beth Owen
TREASURES

It matters not the gold you've got,
Or what you think you're worth,
for in the end, you will spend
eternity far from earth.

Riches cannot save, my friend,
Or make you one bit better—
in trying to buy your way through life,
It only makes you a debtor.

Trusting in your treasures,
Or looking to your wealth,
Oh, How vain, it cannot save,
your soul, your life, your health.

Only Christ can buy your life,
He paid it with His own,
for with His blood, it was bought,
your sins He will atone.

So it matters not the money you've got,
Or the Lands that you may own.
With out Jesus Christ, you'll pay a big price—
Surely, you'll reap what you have sown.

Lorrence Anne Hutchinson
WORLD WAR III

The damaging words pierce
through your ears,
The shattering words that
everyone hears,
When will all of the shell bombing be stopped?
A family's at stake, no more bombs to be dropped!
Don't you see the children crying?
Don't you hear them always sighing?
Please end this terrible war,
Look for the answers through another door,
The war will come to an abrupt end,
When the wounds will be too hard to mend,
The explosion will wound not just me,
The explosion will hurt the lives of ye,
look up above for the answers you seek,
Or deep in your hearts take a little peek,
The answers are waiting to be found,
Take a good look, search all around,
Let it be like it was in the past,
Our love for each other will always last!!

Phyllis M Fuhrman
OUR GOODBYE TO DAD

At a time like this, it's very hard,
To express the way we feel,
We only know we are surrounded,
by the love of God so real.
We do know dad, that you're now at peace,
From all the suffering and pain,
This will be our richest blessing now,
For it to be our loss, but to be your gain.
Dad, you gave so much to every one of us,
Your wife, your friends and family,
Your kind advice was always there,
And some problems for us to remedy.
It's hard to know the pain you felt,
While you were fighting for your life,
We understand that God had his plans,
As He allows us these trials and strife.
So many things were left unsaid,
By so many of us here,
But your memories we will always share,
As they come to us so very clear.
We love you dad, for one last time,
As we give you to our Master and our Lord,
And we will meet you someday soon,
When it's God's will and with His accord.

Donna J Melia
QUALITY

Sure, make me an offer
but can't I refuse
and show me your way
yet allow 'me' to choose
let fairness maintain balance
put honesty right up front
and maybe what you present
is just what I want

Maxine P Lee
BLOOM WHEREVER YOU ARE PLANTED

I am the tiny seed of life, that came from heaven above.
Who fell on soil so dark and cold, but filled with God's great love.

The rocks of trials and tribulations
make it hard for me to root;

Still, I must bloom where I am
planted for it is written in God's
book.

The turmoil of disappointments
along with diversities loosened
the soil and set the rocks free.

Now only if the tears of hurt fall a
little more freely on me, I could
burst forth from this shell that
does encase me.

Here it comes, those wonderful
cleansing tears that have set my
soul free.

And now, Oh Lord! I have bloomed
where you have planted me.

Kerri A Hatton
I AM NOT A POSSESSION

Yesterday,
I was a child longing for
attention.
I was a girl wishing I could date.
Today,
I am a woman searching for love.
I am a person striving to live.
I am not a possession —
to be put upon a shelf and then
forgotten,
to be passed on or borrowed
thoughtlessly,
to be dominated or used
uncaringly.
I am not a possession —
but a human being, a creature of
nature.
I am to be respected, shown
kindness, admired.
I am not perfect—But, I am
beautiful.
I am an equal and I am important.
I need to be Loved, not owned.
I shall be free and feel glad I'm
alive.
But, if I must be anyone's
possession —
I'll be my own . . .

Mary Ellen Gilreath
MY CHILDREN LIKE DREAM LAND

---

*My third original story scene poem,
Dedicated to my three children and
their families. Judy-Eve,
Linda-Joyce, and Ramond-Earl-Jr.*

A cardinal flew upon its nest,
I woke the children.
Snow falling, covering all earth's
breast,
I woke the children.
These things that do excite me so,
it seems
I want the world to know.
"Come see," I
tell them, and they glow,
I woke the children.
Though they may see these o'er and
o'er, the
birds that fly, the birds that soar,
and
hear their melodious refrain, see
the rainbow
through the rain. There's so
much beauty here
to see, I want to show them every
tree, these
seem to be a part of thee.
I woke the children.
The rising sun, the sky aglow, the
stillness,
when wind doesn't blow. The
cooing of a distant
dove, reminders of your gentle
Love.
These things I'd never want to
miss, mist falling
like a gentle kiss. I try to tell
them all you
do, so they will watch and listen
too,
I woke the children.
The setting sun seen in the evening,
sends colors
on the clouds above. How
beautiful to all things
living, another showing of your
Love.
It's time for snuggling and for
sleeping, until
you wake with morning light. For
he will have you
in his keeping, safe and secure
throughout the night.

Albert Allen Krueger
SOUND OF SPRING

When will I hear the birds of spring
singing their songs
at the break of dawn
scratching for seed
on the snow-spotted forest lawn

When will I hear the song
of the snow-melt brook
as it deafens my ears in the day
and sings me to sleep
as the night fades away

When will the spots of a
newborn fawn
dazzle my eyes once again

And when will the rain
from the sky above
dance upon my windowpane

And when will I hear the thunder
and see the lightning strike

As winter fades away
into the dark dark night.

Melvin L Deas
GO ON

---

*To Ms. DEBBIE VIOLETTE-a real
friend!! Ms. BERNITA STEWART-
& Ms. GERENE FREEMAN-sisters,
friends, poets, and to the
LORD—my best friend.*

Last night you said we could—"for
friendship." I've just got to know.

Is there a "stop-sign" after
friendship—or will I be able to
go on?

Go on—in my attempts to make
you mine.
Go on—planning time together &
things to share.
Can I go on planting seeds of our
togetherness—and watch us
grow?

GO-ON—tell me!

Shirley Ann Osborne Welsh
SARAH, JEWEL OF MY GARDEN

---

*For Sarah Jane, who will always be
a jewel in her mother's garden . . .
and for all the little Sarahs in the
world!*

This morning I strolled through
the garden
Like diamonds, the dewdrops
sparkled so bright
As I held little Sarah's hand in mine
The fragrance of spring filled the
sunlight.

She lifted the petal of a golden
daffodil
As she caressed it in her tiny hand,
Then we listened to the robins
chirp and sing
And spoke to the oak tree so grand!

Now . . . the garden path descends
to the brook
With its cool and babbling stream,
When my Sarah sees a frog leap in
Her little face starts to beam!

The day she was born God smiled
on me,
And told me I had been blessed . . .
A precious infant given with love
To live in my garden nest.

Now my garden nest has no
silver . . .
You'll find no gold treasure chest;
Just my smiling, bright eyed Sarah
Snuggled close to my breast.

The dewdrops are my diamonds,
The sunshine is my gold.
More precious than emeralds and
rubies;
Is this little jewel I hold!

Carol Howard Gadway
I THOUGHT PERHAPS

I thought perhaps I'd miss the sun
heralding in each day.
And perhaps the giant oak as she
bows her head to pray.
I thought perhaps sunwashed rain
would cool my brow no more
And all because Death had
tapped upon my chamber door.

I thought perhaps the birds would
stop their twittering from above,
And the scent of lilacs
cease—that I had come to love.
I thought how cruel Death would
be
When she came to claim her
lowly servant, me.

I knew I'd miss the taste of dew
upon the wild rose,
And the fragrance of new
mown-hay as it drifted to my
nose.
I thought perhaps I'd miss the song
the wind whispered in my ear.
And all because—no longer
would I be home to hear.

I thought perhaps the stars would
cease to twinkle from cobalt
blue,
And the sight of Nature's birth
blanketed in morning dew.
I thought perhaps the sun would
sink and rise never more.
And all because Death had crept
inside my chamber door.

But, that was not the end Fate had
chose for me,
But Nature and I should as one
together be.
And I should dwell in Nature's
arms for all eternity,
And all because the hand of
Death had come to carry me.

Lucy M Atkins
TAKE TIME FOR 10 THINGS

---

*This poem is dedicated to Gene D.
Atkins, my son, who has been so
very kind and nice to me.*

---

1. Take time to work—
it is the price of success.
2. Take time to think—
it is the source of power.
3. Take time to play—
it is the secret of youth.
4. Take time to Read—
it is the foundation of
knowledge.
5. Take time to worship—
it is the highway of reverence
and washes the dust of earth
from our eyes.
6. Take time to help and enjoy
friends—
it is the source of happiness.
7. Take time to love—
it is the one sacrament of life.
8. Take time to dream—
it hitches the soul to the stars.
9. Take time to laugh—
it is the singing that
helps—with life's loads.
10. Take time to plan—
it is thesecret of being able to
have time for the first nine
things.

Judy M Blessington (jmb)
A SILENT TEAR

A single tear has fallen,
So silently it descends
Downward upon a cheek
To disappear at the end.

Like the falling of a raindrop
As upon a window lands,
Only to be taken from its path
By a loving touch of hand.

Then so gently down it falls
With the softness of a rose,
Like the breath of a baby's kiss
The tender emotions grow.

What fate in time has prompted
The dawning of its birth,
Be it the joy of happiness
Or sadness too deep for words.

There's a mystery about this
emotion
That takes control and descends,
For as suddenly as it burst forth
Now as silently it ends.

T L A
STILL LOVING YOU

When I needed you most, you were
never near,
With someone else, my worst fear.
I thought I was the one so insecure,
But it looks as though you were.

When you needed me most, I was
always there,
I guess that shows I really did care.

I still remember the first time that we met,
The exact hour, the minute, the place you sat.

I'll have the memories of us forever,
It's something my heart will always savor.
I thought a love like ours would never end,
That's one thing I'd fight for and try to defend.

Just when I thought our love could grow no stronger,
You left me stranded, our relationship no longer.
When we broke up, I cried myself to sleep.
While you were having fun, your reputation to up-keep.

Why am I the one who always feels had,
Why can't your heart feel this bad?
Misery and loneliness is all that I've felt,
Since you left my empty heart to melt.

Mary Bass Acosta

Mary Bass Acosta
SPIDERS

To my wonderful husband, "Ray," Ex-Pro Boxer. Together, we will win all of life's bouts. Your loving wife, Mary.

Do spiders really spin fine lace?
And do they wash their little face?
And brush their hair with utmost care,
while thinking of someone to snare?

They very carefully choose a mate
and oh' my goodness, what a terrible fate.
They do them in with one embrace
and walk away with a smiling face.

They spin their webbs in sheer thin air.
It's finer than the finest hair,
but stronger than the trees on high.
If you get too close, kiss the world good-bye.

But all in all, when said and done,
they're not too bad, just lots 'o fun.

Jeanne E (Zeek) Helm
AS I LOOK

To the best friend I ever had, Jesus. To my grandchildren, Loree and LeRoy

---

As I look out the window from my hospital bed,
I can see our flag a waving, it's blue, white and red.
I think, dear God, do we really appreciate—
The country you have given us, or wait until it's too late.
As I look over the tree tops, and see birds flying in the air;
I wonder how many of us Lord, Thank you for blessings we share.
As I look above the flagpole, directly in the sky—
I think, "They say that you are dead," but God I wonder why.
The beauty you created is everywhere to be found;
If people would only take the time to stop and look around.
This nation of ours will perish, if not led by the Master's hand;
For our Nation must be Godly in order to stand.
As I look into the clouds, how glorious that will be—
When you come back for your Church, Your blessed face I'll see.
Jesus died upon the Cross, our sins to atone;
America, get on your knees and pray! We'll soon be going home.

Ronald W Schroeder
THE COVE

The cove is an endless and timeless place of solitude.
A place of pure joy and happiness or a place of depression.
A place of total darkness or of bright and shining light.
It is a place to think.

Let these thoughts flow through your mind, like waves lapping on an open beach.
Let them drift like a log on an endless sea.
Let them travel forever through your mind.
Let them flow out into infinity of time and space then back again to touch the nearness of you.

The cove is a place to think out your thoughts, to find the meaning of all things.
It is a place of unrest and of peace.
A place where you can go to, and travel to places and times you have never been.

The cove is many things to you.
It is love, pain, happiness, greed, laughter, trouble, and joy.
It is a place of pure meaning and understanding.

You see the cove is your innerself.

Lucile Maxian
THANK YOU LORD

Thank you Lord for still caring when at times other God's are more important than you
Thank you Lord for helping me to understand about false images
Thank you Lord for your forgiveness when I use your name in vain
Thank you Lord for showing me how to honor your Sabbath
Thank you Lord for being patient when I fail to honor my parents
Thank you Lord for helping me to love and not to kill
Thank you Lord for your guidance in how to be faithful according to your word
Thank you Lord for stealing my heart
Thank you Lord for helping me to be a witness for you
Thank you Lord for helping me to claim your promises so that I may not covet anything that is not mine
Thank you Lord for your son who died on the cross for my sins so that I may live
Thank you Lord for your promise to come again to take me home

Marvin D Reed Jr
GLORIA, A SUMMER'S WALK WITH YOU

You held my hand and smiled at me
As we walked down the lane—
The summer skies changed suddenly
And it began to rain.

We ran beneath an old oak tree
That stood so big and tall—
Just that old tree and you and me
We watched the raindrops fall.

A gentle breeze caressed your hair
You squeezed my hand so tight—
The two of us just sitting there
Made everything so right.

And for a moment, time stood still
The world had gone away—
We softly kissed as lovers will
On this or any day.

The skies, they cleared and we walked on
And left that old oak tree—
That special moment now was gone
And just a memory.

But I'll remember that old tree
That stood so big and tall—
Just that old tree and you and me
We watched the raindrops fall.

Kelly Joel Hill
PORTRAIT OF VIVIAN—AN ARTIST 1953—1986

Shimmering gypsy lady.
Golden days when life was sweeter
each an adventure to pursue.
Laughter remembered—happy times
warm summer days & those voices in the garden. The sometimes
savage garden.
Gypsy lady—artist—so smart—so together—mother of an angel.
Then the devil's free reign.
The walk beginning alone
through the savage garden.
No hope now of getting our lovely gypsy artist back
from the savage clutches.
Words hurled like daggers
The poetry that is life became brutal.
Her final walk alone
through the savage garden.
Horror. Horror end to it all.
Horror that still grasps at us. Our grief still fresh.
Her sad walk finished.
At the last her soul freed came to me.
Touched my face—so gently—her life essence a warm breeze
where no draft blows.
She's free from the brutal savage garden.
Free of life's burden. Free to make existence work this time.
In an angel the promise of tomorrow.
To lay her at rest—peace throughout
Eternity—with loved
ones—loved & held dear—
to celebrate with joy each flittering star
of time—now & forever.

Mary Ann Legacy
SISTER, BROTHER

O, God, let us not destroy our land.
Save us from War's fate.
Teach Man the way of peace,
before it is too late.

Let us love one another,
Call each other, "Sister, Brother."
Join our hands in one accord,
as decreed by Holy Word.

Give us joy and calm, instead
of blood, strife, tears and dread.
Lead us in Your pathway bright.
Preserve our Nation in all that's right.

Jackline Elizabeth Dziuba
ALONE

A man of the world
alone in a world
of thousands of faces,
Reaching out for companionship,
human interaction,
a grasp of momentary reality in an
atmosphere of superficial,
temporary
fantasy,
Exhibiting pride in self-accomplishments,
independence, individuality,
pride in determination, in survival,
in being alone,
Yet still reaching against one's instincts,
to share, to be a part of life
instead of a silent spectator
of oneness.
For an instant an "I" almost became
a "we,"
But the grip of pride held fast
clutching an empty shell
making the "I"
a prisoner of freedom.

Dale V Moberg
REFLECTIONS

To My Reflections: Janelle, Kayla, and Suzanne

The greatest creation we'll ever make, the greatest work we'll ever do
Is right here in our home right now, a reflection of me and you
They come in different packages, in different shapes and sizes
And they will fill our lifetime, with love, hope, and surprises
It's our kids who'll turn our hair gray, and keep us awake at night
Wondering if they're all okay, and if they'll turn out right
It's our kids who'll be our teachers, it's them who'll give us breaks
Like watching us do something

wrong—then forgiving our mistakes
It's them who'll write all over the walls—after them we'll clean for hours
And it's them who'll pick dandelions from the lawn, so they can give mom flowers
It's our kids who will keep us on our toes, always asking "Why"
And it's them who can always make us laugh, and sometimes make us cry
It's us that they'll look up to, to us that they'll confide
And it's them we'll listen to say their prayers, our hearts bursting with pride
And when we go to check on them, and see the covers wiggle
The second that we leave the room, we hear the whole bunch giggle
And late at night when we peak in, to tuck them in their beds
Laying there so peacefully, we'll kiss their sleeping heads
They don't care if dad's rich or poor, or if mom drives a fancy car
They don't care if we're thin or fat, they love us for who we are
When we get older and think back, over the previous years
It will be those 'reflections' of you and me, that'll fill our eyes with tears
And while we're looking back, will it all have seemed worthwhile?
And would we do it all again?—the answer's in a smile.

Genevieve Singleton
HALLEY'S COMET
All of her life she had heard about Halley's Comet

(Halley rhymes with Sally)
And now the time had come again for its appearance in our hemisphere;
Dressed in a warm jacket and moonboots, flashlight in hand,
She followed the meteotologist's directions precisely.

And there in the sky just as he said, she saw Halley's Comet;
For her no telescope, only clear, moonless nights,
Unobstructed view from a pasture knoll,
All-important timing which changed nightly;
Not disappointed that the development was not spectacular,
She was grateful to participate in this special order of Nature.

Edward Syrek
THE ANTIQUE TEAPOT
Great Grandmother treasured its delicate spout
And only on special ocassions brought out
The hand-painted teapot of fame and renown
Her mother had foresight to keep and hand down;

While grandmother's pleasure was company for tea,
She polished it brightly and chortled with glee
At envious sighing and covetous stare
Until she surrendered, to my mother's care,

That glorious heirloom—the porcelain pot;
But mother, by far, was the worst of the lot,
For high on the shelf it continually stayed
And only through windows of glass was displayed

Till I, mother's daughter and last of the line,
With no eye for beauty or grace and design,
While searching for cookies, nudged antiquity
And the crash when it fell shook THE WHOLE FAMILY TREE!

Robin Lynn Baxter-Jones
REFLECTION OF ME
I look in the mirror and who do I see?
So much like my mother, I thought I'd never be.

Why is it so hard just trying to be me?
One minute stable and strong,
One minute weak and easy to break.

I build myself up, just to let myself down.

I know the right road, but can't decide which way to go.

I am lucky I think, and fortunate too,
So why can't I learn how to quit feeling blue?

This time is it! I swear you will see,
In this mirror a reflection of me.

Carla Raffel Matzat
LOVE STATED SIMPLY

To Terry, the person who knows me better than I know myself.

I love you, dear husband, so very much.
I really believe that our hearts touch.

Perhaps you don't know it, but during the day,
my heart leaves my body and sails away.

As you leave each day to whatever chore,
my heart goes with you as you walk out the door.

You never felt it when you kissed me goodbye.
But it quietly stole under your shirt and by your heart lies.

During your labor you are not alone.
My heart keeps yours company—they are beating as one.

Your chores are finished and home you arrive.
When you walk in the door, we all come alive.

From one child to another you quietly go,
greeting each one with a hug, big and slow.

As for me, I can wait for my hug that you do,
because I know that all day my love's been with you.

When you give me that hug, I'll be happy as can be.
For I know my heart returns fuller than when it left me.

Rosemary E Rigsby
THE LONGING WILL NOT SLUMBER
Now, once again I stand alone
As I have really always been;
I wonder if this is the price
For some great unknown awful sin?

I've loved and lost so many times,
And been alone when it was done;
That my heart now wonders if
Those loves should ever have begun.

I've been a mother, sister, friend
And lover; my heart to all sincerely given;
Then all these loves saw, each, its lonely end;
Each time my heart was riven.

Where must I go, to whom to turn
To find a love that is not pain?
Where can I go but to myself,
But then, there lies the emptiness again!

Father, mother, husband, son,
And friendships that I cannot number—
All now are beyond my gentle touch,
But still the longing will not slumber.

Without someone to hold and love
Life is not worth the daily strife,
Yet day by day I struggle on,
To sustain this useless, worthless life.

Morgan Collins
LOVE A NEW TIDE
Love is the oak—
That grows from the heart;
The leaves are the feelings,
That shadow the heart;
Christ, is the breeze,
That lifts the leaves up
Laying them gently,
Onto the sea,
Caught in the tide of eternity—
The sun gives them warmth,
Persuading the tide—
New leaves appear,
On the oak tree.
Love is the oak,
Growing inside—
Each flight of leaves, reach a new tide.

Albert Francis Fischer
MY WORK MOTTO

This poem is dedicated to Al's three little FISH Albert, David, Michael

---

Once the job has begun
Do not quit till it's done
Be the job big or small
Do it right or not at all

Gill Temple
LIFE

This poem is dedicated to My Loving Family and Virginia Porter

---

Life can be a Pleasure or even a bore,
It all depends on how you keep the score.
From the cradle to the eventual grave
Consider—did I receive more than I gave.
So all through life it behoves us all
To listen for someone in need to call.
To give that lonesome soul a cheery smile
And when necessary go that extra mile.
When the songs of youth have all been sung
And the time for adulthood has just begun,
Your life will respond to the help you give
So you: will find it a joy just to live.
Don't count your ills and griefs and pain,
But hold onto your blessings that remain.
Then when looking back, may come this thought—
That you prize the blessings the years have brought.
Lord, help me this day to be a shining light,
And also help me to know wrong from right.

Helen T Ross
AMERICA'S TONE
Gentlemen lead me on my journey
Gentlewomen point me the quiet way
Father's of our Father's bid me forever stay
Forbidding turmoils seas of troubles neverending strife
America America land of beauty and free life
Freedom points the towers of strength
Sending seeds of greatness flowers strong in length
Mother's of our Mother's hold fast the mark
Children of our children yea' embark
Tomorrow's light beyond the dark
I address all people here this day
All citizen's of honored societies to stay
Together let's share hope in our future thus let's band
Yea' behold this United States of America our fine and fruitful land
Presenting the greatest and utmost inspiring dreams with hopes
Let's summize prosperous futures of people through corners of destiny arise
Inspirational wonders never cease chosen countries yea' number's increase

Harken' harken' all members in our land of dreams do a turnabout
Wonders these cobwebs seep in from the past gracious moments at hand
Chosen victories yet we withstand oppose'oppose' tyranny we fear'
Hold' Hold' bloomed horizon's yea' so grand' so gracious' so grand'

Myrtle J McWhorter

TOGETHER

Climb with me to the top of the hill and we'll watch the valleys below.
We can see the roads leading here and there
and wonder where they all go.
We can let our minds travel 'cross the miles
as we span the hours of time.
We can brighten up our dreary days
and never spend a dime.
The hills are high, and the valleys are deep
and there's happiness all around
If we open our hearts and build our tomorrows
with simply the sights and the sounds.
We can't let the hard times spoil the memories
of the good times that brought us together.
So take my hand and we'll climb the hill
and dream all our dreams together.

John Charles Calloway

THE RISE

O, happiness is all that matters now, Almighty Lord of Hosts:
The least He can do is love thee, to save thee is the most.
Soon all sadness shall be wiped away, this we should be happy for;
For happiness is an eternal thing, and Oh! There is so much more.
Thy Father sitting on His throne, glorified at the view;
This is to be eternity . . . time never running out on you.
Beauty, forever, the eyes eternal to see,
Soaking in all the beauty and freshness, our reward this to be.
O, isn't this enough, to show you it's all true?
That place of perfect love, His saints are going to.
No day will be more beautiful; The dead in Christ shall rise;
A beauty that has never been seen with human eyes.
In the twinkling of an eye, our bodies will be changed; We will be made new,
By the sound of the trump, Jesus is come with His angels, out of the East sky blue.
But then we'll move on, forgetting all things past.
Then complete and perfect presence we'll spend with the Lord at last.
We'll enter the Golden Gates, with happiness in our hearts;
For this is something new, yet . . . still, just the start.
This message is that He gave all for you, including His life he did,
Knowing that it would make a way for His saints, but all evil punished by rid.
But if the Lord calls me on, before this scene I view,
I leave two certain things I wish for my loved ones to do:
Always live for the Lord; and for my passing, your sadness be small in size,
For we will join again . . . I promise, I'll meet you in the Rise.

Dorothy Valentine Hopper

THE LAKE

To My Children Donna, Diane, Dennis, Craig.

Soon there will be no more sailing
on the water of the blue-green lake.
The soft warm days are growing cold.
The trees that line the mountain ridged shore
are turning to a profusion
of orange, red, yellow and gold.

The cold chilling wind will strip the trees
of their colorful fall attire,
Announcing winter is on the way,
And turn the blue-green lake to ice
On a freezing winter day.

There will be no more casting anchor,
in a tranquil cove to drift and dream
in the hot summer sun,
Until winter completes the painting
And God's Masterpiece of spring,
Will have once more begun.

Gina Marie Porter

COMPLETELY YOURS

I've looked deep into my heart
Searching my soul, who am I, what do I want
I'm not happy with what I see
I want more than what I am.

Your spirit within me shows me what
I don't want to see
The part of me that belongs to the world, not to you.

Lord help me to remove that which is of
the world within me
To become holy and pleasing to you
To be completely yours not the world's.

I want to see you Lord when I look in my heart
When I view the world
I want to hear your voice when I speak and
sit quietly before you
To feel your love and to have your joy in all I do and say
I want to be completely yours.

Mary Strouse Rose

WAKE UP, AMERICA!

In Memory Of My Brother PFC Paul E. Strouse, U.S.M.C. Vietnam— March 6, 1969

Wake up, America, you're sleeping!
You act as though there's nothing going on.
Have you ever thought of our freedom we take for granted?
Or will we never be really concerned until it's gone?
Wake up all you people in America!
Our freedom's growing weaker every day.
What few rights we have left we're not enforcing.
If so, our children in public schools could pray.

What has happened to the rights of law-abiding citizens?
Criminals now have those rights in their hands.
Bars the prisoners are placed behind have become invisible.
What's happened to the judicial system in our land?

What has happened to the family in America?
There's more mothers that are fathers in our homes.
Why have some men shrugged their shoulders and just given up?
And for those who are trying, why are they left alone?

For our children, what will we have to leave to them?
That is, to those who even get the chance to live.
Why are unborn children murdered in America?
If an unborn child isn't life, why must it be killed?

Then we wonder why our young people have turned away.
Well, I wonder what have they turned away from?
Wake up and pray you Christians in America.
God knows that satan's got plenty going on!!

Kate Runion Patterson

Kate Runion Patterson

LIFE WITH CHRIST

Life is like a vapor,
It swiftly passes away.
If we are going to live for Christ,
Why not start today?

Let Him have complete control,
Of our heart, body, and soul.
So when life here shall be no more,
We will live with Christ forever.

Kayleen Orton

I DO

For Kristilyn and Kevin, A love that will last for eternity.

I was walking with you hand in hand
the sky was clear and blue,
It was a precious moment in my life
when you said, "I love you."

We gazed into each others eyes
eternal life is all we could see,
You know that I was about to cry
when you said, "With you is where I want to be."

When we touched each other
you were soft and gentle,
and when you spoke to me
your words were sentimental.

You really changed my life
when you slipped on the diamond ring,
and after the reception
all we wanted to do was sing.

You know that when I said, "I do."
it meant that I love you,
look where our love has gotten us
for time and all eternity too.

Patti Shahan

MY BROTHER

To my little brother who is the pride and joy of my life.

I remember when you were born
Just a little bitty tike
I never knew you wouldn't ride a bike

I didn't know
I'd never hear you talk
Never see you take that first step
When learning to walk

I never knew you would
Have to sit and watch me run
Just wishing you could join in on the fun

Wishing you could jump
and catch a ball
Both of us laughing
when we fall

Take a walk
just me and you
I never knew
You wouldn't learn to tie a shoe

But just to see you
laugh and smile
is enough to make
all my dreams worthwhile

Just to see you always happy
Enjoying life as you can
it makes me happy when you give me hugs and hold my hand

You live in a life
that has many closed doors
So what if you miss a few things
who's keeping the scores?

So long go I didn't know
you weren't a normal little boy
I also didn't know you'd bring
so much joy

Just to see the little things
You learn to do
Let God show me
How much I love you

Just to sit and watch you grow
makes it hard
Knowing there are so many feelings
I can't show

In God's eyes you're perfect
In my eyes you are too
Your my little brother
and I love you.

Love always,
Sissy

Helen Travers-McGill
FOUR SEASONS
All of us have four seasons in life,
not all are happy, not all are strife.
Spring is Childhood and starting to live,
Accepting our beginnings and learning to give.
Summer, our youth, is all Fire and Ice,
and loving becomes the best thing in Life.
Fall comes so slowly we're hardly aware,
and we flow with the current and don't even care
But Winter comes into our life with a roar,
and we have only the memory of what came before

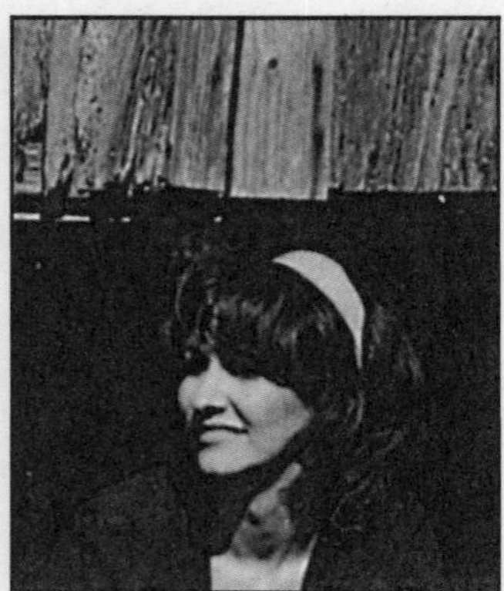

Frances Hart Davis

Frances Hart Davis
BEHIND THAT GOLDEN SUNSET

To my loving father, "Alton Hart" who has gone on behind that golden sunset.

Behind that golden sunset
there is a place for me
behind that golden sunset
I'll live in liberty.

There will be no rays of sunshine
for his glory all men will see
and behind that golden sunset
my Lord awaits for me.

When darkness looms in this old world

and trouble is all I see, I go behind
that golden sunset and talk with
my Lord so free.

He tells me of the new world
and the beauty that is so free
and my troubles about this old world
seem smaller by the greatest degree

Behind that golden sunset
the birds fly there with me
to talk with my Lord about this
world and the strength he gives to me.

Sherry Beth Cummings
GRANDMA'S HOUSE NO MORE
Every time I go into town
I take the same old route
Past the Wagon Wheel cafe and the old elementary school.
Once in a while I drive down that street
With the giant blue spruce standing guard on the corner.
I park my car under the aspen tree out front
And get out to look around.
I wonder how many of these neighbors remember Granny?
The "FOR SALE" sign creaks in the wind
And mingles with the sigh of the pine trees.
On the outside, the house has had a face lift,
White siding now covers the whole house, dusty blue paint
trims the windows.
I walk around to the back
The little old coal house has been torn down,
And Granny's little garden plowed up.
The cat's dishes are gone from the back step,
The cat himself has been put down by the vet.
I peek through the window
Hoping the inside is still the same.
But walls and stairs rise up where none were before.
Mom's bedroom is gone,
Uncle Darr's now a utility room,
A modern washer and dryer against one wall.
I take a last look at the kitchen
The old black coal stove missing,
I can almost smell a chocolate cake
Then the memory fades. .. I climb back into my car,
No. . . this is Grandma's house no more.

Chuck Vest

Chuck Vest
LIVING GRACE
The Lords sun beats down upon my face
his stars to fill my dreams
Jesus is a traveler of all time and space
even he has dreams.
He's elders of all different races
This world will seldom see,
top of days for which they sail away.
Jesus said all good will come with me,
all the songs from times of living grace
his sounds caress my ears,
Not a word I heard could I relate
but the story was quite clear,
As I gather all I've found
Before the sun turns to ground
And my eyes are filled with sand
As I stand in this wasted land
Jesus is like an open book fulfilling all our dreams,
for his father created all these things
oceans, forests, and the desert scenes.
I share his love beneath the silver moon
He has all our answered dreams,
Oh father of the evil wind
split my sails across the sea
Within no prevention but an open face, lone the strengths of fear.
Jesus will come once again and take us all from here.

Lelah Spencer Kent
PESKY LITTLE THINGS
I know you all,
both great and small,
would like to know my name.
I know it well,
but I musn't tell,
I'm purty all the same.
These little specks,
are only frecks,
with much attraction bring.
But Grandma says,
"Sour milk will rid
these pesky little things!"

Jane Ruth Turner
LETTER TO THE EASTER BUNNY
Dear Mr. Bunny,

You used to come each year at this time,
You dear old Easter bunny,
With all your colored eggs to hide
Before the day was sunny,

But you left me off your list last year. . .
What happened Mr. Rabbit?
You've forgotten me again, I fear!
It has become a habit.

So Sunday when you make your round
Would you please take good care,
And leave an egg where it can be found.

I thank you, Mr. Hare.

C Dick Griffin
HOW COULD YOU FORGET—SO SOON?
How could you forget so soon
Those stolen hours so sweet
Moments I live over again
As I feel my heart's quick beat!

Those hours seemed to mean
Ev'ry-thing in the world to you
You are breaking my aching heart
Would you mend it—if you knew?

How could you forget so soon dear
When you seemed to be so sincere
Is it because you've met someone
To you a thousand times more dear?
Won't you please tell me, my sweet
If a prince charming you did meet
For the question is with each heart beat—
How could you forget—so soon?

Deborah Lee Gilley
EMOTIONAL ABUSE
Because of emotional abuse
I learned to cry in silence,
There is no good excuse
For living in such violence.

With no choice of my own
I lived in constant fear,
I really wasn't quite grown
When I shed my first tear.

As the hurt builds up inside
Too young for understanding,
All you want to do is hide
Life seems too demanding.

Quietly yearning, just to be loved
No matter which way you turn,
Mentally, being pushed and shoved
Others seem without concern.

Living in a nightmare
Its hard to know whats real,
Too much pain for just one to bear
Your heart might never heal.

Even though, I aged too fast
My heart was left, unmended,
I desperately tried to forget my past
I couldn't, so I just pretended.

Wava Reutter
HOW DO YOU EASE A BROKEN HEART?
How do you ease a broken heart?
When a mother's dreams are shattered to bits?
By a warm hand's clasp on your part
And a little prayer on your lips.

How do you awaken a gleam of hope
To someone near and dear?
When it would seem she cannot cope
With the problems she has to bear?

How do you ease a broken heart?
How do you her fears quell?
With a soft word spoken at just the right time
And assurance that all will be well.

You do your part by letting her know
You are with her all the way,
For God makes all these little things grow,
And you let her know that you pray.

Marguerite B McGlamery
FRIENDS ON MY PATHWAY
Flowers in my pathway,
Of every kind and hue;
Lifting up their faces,
Fresh kissed by morning dew.
Busy little bees are humming,
As if on little banjos strumming,
Just to pass the time away.
Butterflies, such lovely things,
Come drifting down on fragile wings;
They go in and out, and out and in,
Then away, now back again.
They like the nectar that they find
In each flower's special kind.
My friends the birds are out there, too;
Wrens and sparrows,
everywhere,

Eating from the feeder there.
Blue jays, and cardinals of brilliant red,
Each have a topknot on their head.
The mockingbird of gray and white,
Feeds by day, then rests at night.
As the sun begins to rise,
It points its head up to the skies
And sings to me its happy song.

Mary Lily Lopez

PARENTAL LOVE

To my Children: Don, Sandra and Gary

The children that we raised and praised,
soon grew up and each went their separate ways.

Even if we have had to part, they are forever in our heart;
For this love will never part.

The tears that we have shed for them, the joy that we have had from them,
will be with us until the end;
But we'll still be here if they ever need a helping hand.

Our memories will forever be with us.
Especially, when they fought and then they would run, so they would not get caught.

There were times when it was our turn to thank them; but also, there were
days we had to spank them, then we would hug them and tell them how much we loved them.

All those days are done and gone, but we also had a lot of fun.
We can now sit back with a smile and we know it was all worthwhile.

Marion G Braxton

WELCOME

In this house where God abides,
We welcome you to come inside.
Our doors are always set ajar,
To welcome people from near and afar.
We welcome the sunshine in the sky,
We welcome the moonlight up on high.
We welcome the beautiful birds that sing,
We welcome the flowers in the Spring.
But more than these, much more, we welcome you.
We hope that you will be happy and stay,
While we try to sing and pray.
So sit back in your pew and smile,
And let us entertain you for awhile.
Again, we welcome you.

Victoria Leach

JUST TELLING YOU

Just telling you the way I feel,
would be selfish, but it's true and real!
If I thought that maybe you'd believe.
but I'm afraid you may just leave.
My feelings are so open and true,
they're so important, from me to you.
You're the only person I've ever felt this way for,
and you just make my heart and feelings soar.
They soar like an eagle in flight,
when I'm with you, everything is right.
What I'm trying to say is true,
I would do any;thing just because I love you!

Diete Nickens

THE SEA

Purple clouds above a sparkling sea.
Footprints in the sand from strangers like you and me.
Washed over castle, made of sand,
Some child's fantasy, some child's playland.
Feel the gentle touch of a cool summer breeze, making grains of sand
tickle you on the knees.
Lovers walking the shore line hand in hand, waves running over their
feet in the sand.
A friendly old man holding his fishing line,
Smiles when you pass, letting you know he is kind.
Sea gulls sing their queer summer song,
The sounds get lost in the wind as you wander along.
This is the sea.

Edwin P Spivey

MAGIC DAYS

Magic days when you were mine, mine, I thought, to the end of time.
Now you are gone, even from my dreams,
all to keep me sane, those precious memories.

None but the lonely hearts can know just how I feel,
none, but they, can kneel as I kneel
night by night and day by day,
kneeling in this lonely room, grieving as I pray.

Lying in this lonely bed, wishing for the dawn,
when the lonely day arrives wishing it were gone
so that I could lie in bed, see you, perhaps, in dreams,
but in this lonely darkened room, seeing only the moonbeams.

No sign of you, for whom I pray each night,
no sign from you to make my darkness bright.
Perhaps a magic day, will some day arrive
bring from you a sign, to make my dark days live.

A magic night, and then a dream breaks through,
to help me, perhaps to live my life anew,
bring meaning to my life again
with loving words to help keep me sane.

I know my life can never be
those good days that used to be,
but, perhaps, one day I'll find
through dreams of you some peace of mind.

Ruth W Davis

MOON FLIGHT

The timer is set, and the motor's in tune,
Christopher's ready to blast to the moon.
The infaseat's tilted, and Chris cannot wait,
Now that he's able to hold his head straight.

Christopher's eager—he'll get there or bust.
His muscles are tensed for that nuclear thrust.
That dashing appearance of masculine pride
Is managed by tossing his bib to one side.

Eight weeks of wisdom, and Chris joins the race,
He's ready to challenge the world face to face:
He'll tackle his Pablum or enemy sniper,
But first he needs time out to get a dry diaper.

Peggy L Danko

AFTER THE NIGHT BEFORE

In the afternoon, following the morning, after the night before,
I stand beside my bed and think of what might have been,
If I'd stayed there in your arms and held you close to me,
Within my arms I'd have you, but never in your heart I'd be.
I've wondered what it'd be like, to love a man that didn't love me.
To be there when he wanted me, to disappear when his use for me had faded.
I've thought it through and through, I can't go on without you.
I love you more and more with every passing hour of every passing day,
If only you'd be mine for ever and a day.

I'd tidy up your home and keep your clothing clean,
I'd love you in the morning and in the evening too,
If only you would love me as I'm in love with you.
I'd hold you in my arms each night and pray you'd still be there,
When I awake in the morning following the night before.
But since I'll never see that day, it just has to happen this way.
I'm saying good-bye, to you, my love.
If ever we shall meet, along our destined street,
I'll say hello, and then good-bye,
I'll turn my head and shed a tear,
For what there could have been,
If only I'd stayed there.

Mildred Michel

COOKIE JAR

Never was a cookie grandma
Never saw a need
Then one day my grandson said,
"Got any cookies me to feed?"

So bought a big old cookie jar
And filled it to the brim;
Now he comes and helps himself
He thinks they're just for him.

It does me good to watch him eat
A cookie now and then
I realized how much I've missed
Not having cookies for my men.

So with the Lord's help
And if He will allow,
I'll keep that big jar filled
Just as it is now.

Susan J Hoefling

O TO COMPREHEND OUR COMPLEX WORLD

Overwhelmed by the majesty of the Earth
My spirit finally stirs in awe
And with humble reverence
I try my pen to what I saw
I find words mysterious and able
But leave much wanting:
The mind can not grasp
The expanse. . . the magnitude. . . the unknown
The immensity of its wonder —
To respect what has been revealed
To anticipate that which is sealed —
I try my pen to find
No matter the skill I attain
Many questions and answers
Stand in overpowering domain
And Life and Death
Abound everywhere:
The poet contemplates
And his awesome heart with all would share.

Betty Ann King

LEAD ME HOME

God, take my hand and lead me up
To a place where we'll never die
Far, far above the valleys green
The sun, and the blue of the sky.

Up, up until I'm at the gate
Where sorrow is never known
Where loved ones never cease
And I'll always have a home.

No more wondering where to go
No place to hang my hat

Where-ever yonder I want to stay
There is always a welcome mat.

I'll always have a friend
And will never be alone
God, come take this lost hand
And lead me onward home.

Joseph A Byrne
GLORIA

Posthumously dedicated to Marija Sims whose work I continue.

The crowd had hushed
As she rose
Her hands firmly on the bar
A grip of steel
And the audience waited
And anticipated

You could just see the strength in
her arms
Hardened. Flexing. Ready to
perform.
A great athlete
She had trained every day
Missing none
For fourteen years
Even Christmas

And whether the children played
Or it rained
She stayed
And trained

And at the tender age of fifteen
She had reached a pinnacle
Of anticipated ecstacy

And with her parents at her side,
smiling,
She took a step
Her first one
And her chair slowly rolled away.

Mary Harris-Robinson

Mary Harris Robinson
SOUTH AFRICA MUST BE FREE!

South Africa, South Africa, must
be free!
What will it take for the White
Afrikaners to see?
Five million whites will not
continue to rule,
Because 24 million blacks have
paid their dues.

They beat, tear-gas, shoot, and
interrogate!
We are fourth class citizens in our
own African state.
Coloureds and Indians were given
voting right.
We don't care how long it takes; we
won't give up the fight!
Mandela has fought for
twenty-two years.
He fights and fights, because he
has no fear.
The struggle goes on from inside
his cell.
The treatment he has received only
he can tell.
He was banned from his family
and the press.
But, Nelson Mandela, you are the
best!
We love you, Mandela, so keep up
the fight.
Soon you will be free, and we will
gain our voting rights!

South Africa, South Africa will be
Free!

Dorothea D Lewis
NEXT SUNDAY

Next Sunday I'm getting up early
I said to myself one day.
I'm going to church like I used to
'Til I somehow lost my way.

Then suddenly, there it was
Sunday.
I hopped out of bed at ten.
Church better wait 'til next
weekend,
It's too late this morning again.

Next weekend dawned wet and
dreary.
A good day for staying in bed.
I'd intended to go to church today
But I'll wait 'til next Sunday
instead.

Next Sunday appeared in a hurry.
I really had so much to do.
I'll catch up on all of my work
today,
And Lord, spend next Sunday with
You.

The week went by only too quickly.
I needed some time just for me.
I'm sure one more Sunday won't
matter.
I'm going, you just wait and see.

Just how many Sundays had gone
by,
I really can't say that I know.
But next Sunday I'm getting up
early
And if nothing comes up, I'll go.

Jillian Fiedor
LOST CHILDREN

Words are the children of my soul.
They cry out deep within me to be
heard,
But sometimes
I cannot find the right clothes
To dress a particular child,
And thus he cannot be presented
to the world.
Forever he will be doomed to cry
deep in my
soul.
Sadly never to be heard from,
only felt within myself.
My child, my child,
I am sorry for my inability
To communicate my thoughts.
Because of this incompetence, you
will
never come to life and be
cherished by
others.
I will cherish you forever. . .
But what am I
But an incompetent fool?

Janice Hamilton
MY FRIEND, THE KING

Because I walk with the King of
Kings
I'm walking in the light.
Because we're walking hand in
hand
He makes my pathway bright.

There have been times when tears
have come
I've had some pain to bear
But each time this fell my lot in life
I found that He was there

Yes, there have been dark clouds
in life
But that is when I find
That when the darkest clouds have
come
Each one is silver lined

I'm leaning strong on His arms of
grace
I'm trusting in His love
For not one time has He let me
down
He guides me from above

Because I walk with the King of
Kings
I'm walking in the light
Because we're walking hand in
hand
He makes my pathway bright

Susan Davis
TOO BUSY

The red, red roses
of summer time,
the Christmas bells
that always chime.

Of all the things
that nature brings,
I love the song
the bluebird sings.

The melodies of love
in the air,
spell that February
is soon there.

The purring of
a tiny cat,
the dog softly sleeping
on a mat.

The trickle of
a mountain stream,
the rays of sunlight
on water gleam.

Although love is in
all of these,
sometimes people
are too busy to please.

Norma J Gates
THE SEARCH

Wherever are you, Precious One !
I've looked hither, I've searched
yon.

Your picture graced so many
places—
Billboards, food stores, TV
spaces.
Surely someone peers into
That special face that's only you.

I've walked the streets, I've talked
to friends;
My waiting, praying never ends.
I've reamed my brain, unlocked my
heart
To learn just why you chose to
part.

No answers come, just constant
cries
That faith and hope and love
arise
To see me through
'Til I find you.

Perhaps some day;
Perhaps, I say,

But until then my life's amiss—
Searching, Looking, Expecting
Bliss.

Alice Waters
MY HAND—MY TREASURE

A hand reaches out in a gesture of
peace.
A hand calms the crowd when
hostilities cease.
A hand wipes a tear from a
toddlers' eye.
A hand holds you tight and lets you
cry.
A hand picks a flower, then, gives
it away.
A hand waves "Hello" at the start
of a day.
A hand writes a note to a friend
very dear.
A hand dials a 'phone to say. "Wish
you were here!"
A hand sets a table—knives, spoons
to the right.
A hand tells each bead of your
prayers at night.
A hand paints a picture —
A hand stir's a cake —
A hand sews a button
On clothes that you make —
A hand is a jewel—a gift Divine!
Thank God for this treasure!
Thank God for mine!

Donald Ray Hudson
CONFUSION

This poem is dedicated to LeRoy Patten, my greatest friend. Pat, my only regret is that I did not meet you sooner in life. Thanks for everything!

I like what I see,
And I see what I like
But, I can't have what I like,
And I can't have what I see
Cause if I took what I like
I couldn't have what I see,
And if I took what I see
I couldn't have what I like.
So, I,m back where I started;
With what I like,
And what I see!

Larry G Mendenhall
CONSIDERATION

Seems everyone's taking and
nobody's giving
Seems everyone's found a new way
of living
Get what you can while the getting
is good
Don't take what you need, take
more that you should
Looks to me like it's sweeping the
nation
Did everyone forget about
"Consideration?"

Don't worry about your neighbor,
he can look out for himself
Who cares about him, if you've got
your health
Don't look out for anyone just
cause they're down
Walk right over them, don't waste
time going around
I'm getting worried about the
whole situation
I think everyone's forgot about
"Consideration."

I don't like the way the game of life's being played
I think it's about time that some changes were made
If everyone would use some for the rest of their life
It'd put an end to wars, hard feelings and strife
Just pass it along, there's no obligation
Just give everyone a little "Consideration."

Just kind of put yourself in the other person's place
Think how He'll look with a smile on his face
You can make someone happy, it's all up to you
It don't take much effort, here's all you do
All it takes is participation,
Just give everyone more "Consideration."

Mary Ann Lucido
LAST NIGHT'S LOVER
Someday he'll come along, Mama
Someone who'll want to know.

How I lived my life without you
and how I missed you so.

Who loved you all those long lonely years?
Who tucked you in and kissed you goodnight?

Who gave you gifts and wiped your tears?
Where did you run when a dream gave fright?

Last nights lover didn't want to know
If I was thirsty, or hungry, or cold.

Last nights lover watched T.V. while I wondered,
Am I pretty? Am I witty? Am I old?

He didn't even care, Mama
He didn't want me to show,

How I live my life without you
And how I miss you so.

La Dawn Elm
UNKNOWN DESTINATION

To: Michael J. Rudder, a friend as well as a teacher

The desert heat has worn off
With the coming dusk,
But a warmth persists
Staring off into the horizon—
I continue.

Although warned,
I have often been diverted.
The only consequence
Was loss of direction.

The setting sun on my right
Casts long shadows
Of me distorted,
And it disturbs me.

There are horizons beyond
The one I approach.
The rounding of the earth
Hides them from view;

I cannot see
Too far down the road
Yet I continue,
Oblivious

Barbara A Lott
DID I?
Did I, along my busy way
Do just one kind deed today?
Did I notice the lonely eyes?
One who often was heard to sigh?
When my brother was seen to fall
Did I offer to help at all?
When I helped him, did I "tell"?
(If so, then I surely fell)
Did I have a hand to lend?
Just today, was I a friend?
A soft word, a gentle touch
It might have meant so very much
Love is of such little cost—
Did I? Then count this day as lost.

Ruth Porter Knaus
UNSPILLED SEED
The immensity of the universe
Does not make me feel small.

It makes me feel important,
My being here at all.

Samuel Goldring
LIGHTNING
In robes of thunder it comes down;
And with a frown
It rends asunder, up and down,
Both hill and town.
It devastates the countryside;
And naught can hide
From its mad fury. It does ride
Vain earth to chide.

Jodie Bilger
CHANGES
My life is so very different than what it used to be.
Always afraid to let it be known; now I praise thee on bended knee.
O Lord, you are my creator and guide, along life's rock road.
I've found the WAY, and now I can see, wherein darkness I once strode.

My life was missing something and I didn't know what it could be.
Until HE whispered softly "Will you follow me?"
These things I pondered daily and kept within my heart.
Life's darkness overcame me-I cried-"LORD, can I start?"

HE wrapped his arms around me and hugged me to his chest.
My precious little lost one, lean on me and rest.
I'll shoulder all your burdens and carry all your cares.
Till you are out of danger of life's so tempting snares.

Now I praise HIM faithfully, each and every day.
I walk beside my master for there is where I'll stay.
There's no need to go searching for any deeper love,
JESUS has it all for you. Praise GOD in heaven above.

Don Hofer, Flatwillow School
DREAMING
I know a place not very far,
Where I'm going to go and eat a candy bar,
I'm going to sit under a big oak tree,
I'll watch the birds as they fly free,
While I lie and sleep under the tree,
I'll relax and dream of what I'll be.

Charlene Pipito
MOTHERHOOD
Never has there ever been
A mom as glad as I;
Proud and happy as can be,
My children play near by.

Smart and clever, witty, kind,
These tender little hearts I find
Are filled with laughter, yet earnest in thought.
Throughout the years, their energy I've sought.

To watch them grow and smile,
And listen to their reasons
Has given me a treasurechest of
Memories, cherished through the seasons.

My heart will always love them;
My goals are but a few:
To hold, to guide, to comfort them,
And to see their dreams come true.

Betty J Lattman (Jodi)
WHAT YOU MEAN TO ME

Bruce, My Husband, Friend, and Lover

Your love filled the emptiness in my life,
And I am so grateful to be your wife.

In your arms, I feel safe and secure,
There's nothing our love can't endure.

May our lives continue to blend together,
And may our hearts beat only for each other.

I have been blessed beyond my wildest dreams,
Even greater than all my brilliant schemes.

Your love means more than anything to me,
You have blessed my life now, and for eternity.

Helen Hughes

Helen Hughes
I MUST GO DOWN TO THE RIVER OF JORDAN

To Shirley, my loving daughter

I must go down to the River of Jordan
with this lonely soul of mine
I am looking for a ship that is,
steered by a man called Jesus
I can hear music and the angel singing,
the old Ship of Zion
I can see the white sails flow
through this gray mist and,
hear His voice sounding like,
a thousand thunder bolts, saying
My child step on board.

Connie G Krenning
THE LORD IS MY LEADER
The Lord is my leader.
One which I will follow.
I know this is the way,
Where before, I was so hollow.

I admitted my sins,
I opened my heart,
Jesus died for me, that day on the cross.
I surrendered my life to him.
Where else, My precious God, would I begin?
I followed in Baptism,
As a picture of my faith.
You blessed me, Dear Lord!
That's something I'll never forget!

You've started me walking a new way of life.
In the beginning, it was awfully tough,
But I know <u>NOW</u> I'm going to make it!
Because I'm not alone anymore!
I needed a leader.
"Thank You LORD!"

Kelly Case
WINTER
Lonely sad times for some,
Cursing and ill feelings from coldness.
Cars honking and dying in streets,
Shivers and frowns—as winter comes.

Harsh words from bitter cold,
Starless and lifeless nights.
Dreary days with sunless faces,
No more fun—as winter comes.

For me though, happy thoughts,
Long walks feeling crisp air.
Coming home with blushing cheeks,
My time of year—when winter comes.

Catching snowflakes on my tongue,
Making a snowman in a corner park.
Sledding the steepest street in town;
Feeling free with myself—when winter comes.

Marie Shearer
ODE TO A PILOT

In memory of Scott Ramstad who will always remain alive in my heart.

The air took you away
As you were lifted
On the wings of angels. . .

You are now free to soar
Above the clouds
—FOREVER—

You will always be near me
The warm smile in my heart
Or the tear in my eye. . .

No longer shall I dream
For my dreams crashed
And shattered with the plane
The day you rose to heaven. . .

I hope and pray
When I soar above the clouds
You will be my guide.

Irene G Mammen
DIVERSITY IS FAME
When I look out the window
And see trees of every kind,
Flowers, too, of different sorts

Just what had God in mind?

Birds come to our feeders;
They're never quite the same;
In keeping with its own design
Each has a different name.

Houses in our neighborhood
Differ, too, through brick and
wood.
It makes it all more interesting;
Such variety is good.

Would this not be a boring world
If all things were the same?
God had his people all in mind,
And made diversity his fame.

So now let us relate his will
To all our thoughts and deeds;
So we may make a friendly world
And understand its needs.

Marie Pinella
AUTUMN BEAUTY
Autumn trees standing so bold
Bearing leaves of red and gold
Autumn trees will soon be bare
And autumn's beauty will not be
there
Wintry winds dancing through the
trees
Gathering in it's arms autumn
leaves
The earth's now covered with a
carpet of gold
A beautiful sight you will be told
An artist's delight this season is
With brush in hand the scene is
his

Dina M Beauvillier
ALONE AGAIN
And so there
was a Little boy
whose love for Oversized
books outgrew his Need
for everything and Everyone.

And he walked into
the storm Going nowhere
but everywhere All at once
for the Imagination
of a child Will Never die.

Marge Andresen
BONES
Bones
dry, dusty
clean
washed by rain
purified by sun.

Dry, dusty bones
dreaming in the sun.

Another age
compressed
in their concreteness.

Within their atoms
moves a memory.
Of what? Love —
singing hours —
the green earth?

Or of pain and anguish —
the unbearable cleft?

Perhaps they are glad to be
only dry and dusty bones
in the sun.

Linda P Vanslette
OUR SON
Tiny gifts—
tiny treasures
placed within our lives.

Little time spent—
such love felt,
such love given.

Tiny gifts—
tiny treasures,
taken from us.

Little moments shared—
such pain within,
such grief felt.

Tiny gifts—
tiny treasures,
held within our hearts.

Myrtle A Treadway
PATCH OF BLUE
My world was dark and dismal
Seemed the light could not shine
through
Then, on yonder's far horizon
I saw a tiny patch of blue.

Now, my world seems brighter
My heart feels lighter, too
Since the day I looked into the sky
And saw that patch of blue.

When the storms of life cloud up
your sky
And you don't know what to do
Lift up your eyes, scan the skies
For a little patch of blue.

And when your sky is blue o'erhead
With not a cloud to blot your view
Just silently bow your thankful
head
For that Heavenly patch of blue.

When threat'ning clouds loom
overhead
In life, they sometimes do
Watch for the Sunshine to burst
through
Followed by a patch of blue.

Friend, let your trust be steadfast
Let your faith be strong, and true
And keep in mind, in His good time
God will send a patch of blue.

For, there's many a suffering soul
out there
Who is seeing it worse than you
Give him a hand, let him know you
care
Help him to find a patch of blue.

Dorothy A Coles

Dorothy A Coles
THE SNOW

To Elmer D. Coles, my loving husband

I sat by my window this morning,
Saw the snow drifting silently
down.
The trees and roof tops were all
covered,
The most beautiful picture I'd
found.
The master had no brush or easel,
Yet a masterpiece He had
displayed.
No artist ever could duplicate
The beauty that nature
portrayed.
It was then I began to ponder
The billions of flakes that it took
To create this beautiful picture
I enjoy by simply taking a look.
Then suddenly my head began
nodding.
Too soon I was looking down.

There were these beautiful
snowflakes
Causing such misery on the
ground.
Then I thought there is a great
mystery,
For each flake has a special
physique.
How much like the human being
Where everyone is very unique.
As no two snowflakes are alike,
They resemble the human race.
While some are high and beautiful,
Others have fallen from grace.

Caroline L Shannon
THERE IS NO GOD?

Dedicated to my dad who was my inspiration to start writing.

Today as I gazed across my yard, I
thought,
How can some say, "There is no
God."
Each flower, tree, and blade of
grass
All artist brushes do surpass.

The billowy clouds that roam the
sky,
The stars at night—and by and by
The chill of autumn, brisk and cold
Will turn green leaves to brown
and gold.
The colors change, the leaves will
fall
Things may seem drab and bare
But God will dress our yards again
In beauty ever rare.

The feathery snow flakes flutter
down
As winter comes once more
And little children romp and play
As you did, years before.

God's greatest gift these young
ones dear
So precious, and I'll try
To teach them all about God's love
That Him they won't deny.

There is no God? Just look around
Wherever you may be
He's visible to all of us
You just need faith to see.

Kathleen Velez
FLOATING BEAUTY
Clouds float softly across the sky,
Lingering wonderously,
Changing shape and design and
leaving all below to admire their
beauty.

Sheila Marie Fitzpatrick
DECEMBER SNOW
December is the month for snow,
Making snowangels what fun and
know,
Sleding down a snowy hill,
Making snowmen in the snow,
Oh what fun it is you know.

Icicles hanging down off the roof,
Skiing down a slope so high,
Toasting chestnuts over a fire,
Skating circles on the ice,
All these things are very nice.

Mittens, scarves, boots and coats,
You need all these things if you
want to go out,
Snowflakes falling,
Each one different you know,
These are the beauties of winter
snow.

(Mrs) Judy Gordon
NEEDING
There is a man
of kindness great, and gentle—
to the manner born;

Yet driven by the many forces
that dwell within him.

He little understands
and can't accept
his feelings, so he runs,

constant, centered in on his own
world,
flaunting freedom, while deep
inside,
needing the important others,
as they need him.

His running seems to carry with it
pain,
to him,
as it does to those who care.

He dreams of many things;
He hopes for many ways to make
his universe complete.

His time is spent in searching,
for more things, and people,
ill content to be alone, himself,
fearing to feel, fearing to accept.

I, too, dream of many things—
among them,
that this kindred soul will cease to
run,
will stop his endless searching
for that which he already has;

He need not fear, for those who
really care
will wait, and understand—

Though ease is not a part of
sharing pain,
sharing will in time ease all things,
and make all things possible.

Leanne M Nauffts
SUMMER DAYS

To: Calvin B. Blayland & Louise Nauffts

The wind was blowing
Upon my face

Through the trees
At a great pace.

The sun was shining
Upon the grass
As I walked by
I walked right past.

I layed upon the
Bright green grass
And in the sky
The clouds did pass.

I still remember
That summer day
In the grass
Where I did play

Ronald McFadden
SARAH
I see her, As I stare, hypnotized,
A watch swings like a pendulum in my mind, back and forth,
In a trance, I have lost all power of concentration,
But in the distance, I see her.

I feel her, I cannot speak or move, paralyzed, immobilized,
Like a tree firmly planted where I stand,
As her vibrations sweep over me, like a gentle breeze,
And I'm calm in my unrest.

I love her, in my heart and dreams,
My secret lies buried in a vast sea of wonder and confusion,
A treasure chest, waiting to be discovered, uncovered,
And brought ot the shore.

I miss her, as she walks away all light follows,
In the darkness I grope about for the light switch,
But to no avail, the darkness is over-powering,
And I fall back, defeated.

I forget her, for one brief moment,
I forget and I'm alone in the darkness, and then I remember,
A name, a face, a feeling, and the light returns,
I remember, Sarah.

Estelle Dent Crocker
DREAMING

For Alvin . . . Because

Is it the moonlight
Stealing through your hair
Or only a fantastic dream
That I am weaving there?

Is it the moon shining
In your dear eyes,
Or only love binding
Us in still closer ties?
Is it love eternal
You to me are giving
Or only a pretty romance
That has no chance of living?

Liz A Leger
SEASONS OF MY LIFE
You were the seasons of my life.
You came to me as the spring,
So exciting and new.
You became my summer,
Loving me hot and passionately.
But then you changed as the leaves
In the Fall,
And you became my winter,
Distant and cold.

Gloria Tomlinson
SUMMER LETTER
Using all your energy in the sun,
Know what would be fun?
Writing a letter,
To me, thats better.
You use things like,
Sentence structure,
Writing, spelling,
Grammer and stuff
But thats not enough.
A letter keeps us up to date
Of happenings of late.
Like whose getting married,
Of whose traveling a lot.
But more importantly,
A letter tells me
Of you and your Family.
That's what its all about
Getting a letter from you
Telling me whats new.
So write a letter or note sometime,
Even if it doesn't rhyme.

Leroy C Jensen

Leroy C Jensen
I LOVE YOU WOMAN
I love you woman, God knows I love you so
You're always in my heart, wherever I may go
I love you woman, for your beauty and charm
We could face each day of life, our love arm'n arm
I love you woman for your friendship, honesty and trust
And I know our bond of love, would never twist, bend, or bust
I love you woman for your humor, sensitivity, and your wit
And when days are bad and times are tough, we would never quit
I love you woman, and I want the whole wide world to know
No matter what they say or do, our love will always glow
I love you woman, can't you see my love is true
My wanting to spend every day of life, being close to you
I love you woman, and I know what I want in life
I want to hold and love you, I want you for my wife
I love you woman, God knows I love you so
You're always in my heart, wherever I may go

Edith P Aase
LONELINESS

To my daughters, my ever present friends!

Silence—unruffled—unbroken,
Thoughts that are, seemingly sad!
Words—unuttered—unspoken.
Dreams that are tainted and bad!
Tears—unnoticed—unheeded
Falling as dew of the night!
Misery—thy course is completed!
New freiendships shall hasten thy flight!

Nelson N Burlingham
A GENTLE ARMY
There is a valid, gentle army
Dwelling in our land today
With faces lined from living
And hair that's turning gray.

They learned to work, direct and serve
And fashion with their hands
And minds, creating arts and skills
For meeting life's demands.

This senior host is resting now
With dignity and grace
But not content with idleness
Of their retirement place.

Waste not these willing, able ones
Give back their working shoes,
Depend on them to do the job
They have surely paid their dues.

Inez Spradling Grouf
THE LAND OF LIBERTY

To my daughters and their families

I have heard it said
And it could be true,
About this beautiful country
Of the red, white and blue.
God hid this land
Between two deep seas;
He was saving it for those
Who were seeking liberty.

They came and they stayed
Through the hardships they endured.
Working for that promised land,
Tho' nothing was assured.
They fought for their rights,
For their chance to be free.
Many shed their life's blood
For their hope of liberty.

We have a great country,
It's called the land of the free,
But many things need changing
For the good of you and me.
Tho' we have the best there is,
And hope it will ever be,
We still have to work
To preserve our liberty.

Jef Garity
TIME IS A MATTER OF?

For Kristi Jo

I walk with you
I walk alone
I hold your hand
I hold my own
Again restrained
Again the same
The way I am with you

These thoughts I hold
These tears I drop
All mine alone
You share no part
Don't change for better
For better is worse
The way I am with you

Cry of the dog
Bark of the bitch
Slapped in the face
Cuffed to the wrist
Again the pain
Again the same
The way I am with you

Tick of the time
Tock of the matter
It's all a matter of time

From one endeavor
To the next whenever
Time is a matter of?

Nuel Golden
THE BEAUTIFUL LADY
We met this beautiful, sweet lady
Her blue eyes brimming with hot tears
As she told us about her husband, his age was 80
She said they had been married for fifty years
Then as the tears began to softly fall
She told us how he had unexpectedly passed away
Quietly, as he heard his masters call.
She cried Soooo as she recalled that day.
She said she could never forget his tender love
He was so gentle and kind to her always
She told us, his strength came from God above
There was enough to carry them both through the rough days
We hated to leave this beautiful lady alone,
She cried as we left her standing there with her memories
Just memories of the one she had loved so long
She stood there all alone except for her memories.
Just Memories—

Maxine Reall
BEYOND THE SANDS OF TIME

This poem is dedicated to Les, my loving Husband, who has been an encouragement to me.

Candles flickering in a dark room,
Burnt embers cast aglow;
The rain and storm outside the house
Foretell winter winds that blow.

Memory time is now at hand,
A look at long ago—
Scenes of childhood dancing forth
Amidst the embers glow.

If we could but turn back the clock
To days of yesteryear,
When we were young and o' so strong
A childhood without fear.

The shape and shadow of things to come
Were not to cross our minds—
We lived for then, a happy day
Of laughter, winks and rhymes.

But life goes on and days pass by
To adulthood we grew;
With love from above to guide us on
From childhood we withdrew.

We stepped beyond the sands of time
To a fuller life with God;
Memories now must stay in place
Ashes of dreams we trod.

Pamela Ann Cavanagh
FINDING YOURSELF
Walking down a narrow path,
not knowing where you're going.
Knowing at one point you will see
a shadow of yourself,
and as the shadow slowly gets bigger,
and knowing you're you,
you have discovered the way of "Finding Yourself."

Ruth (Matsko) Knerr
YOUR RING

Dedicated to my sister "Barbara (Matsko) Bova for all her faith in me "I love you"

I took the ring you gave me
And put it on my hand,
I thought some day you'd trade it in
For a wedding band.
The fires of love had started
Your kisses were the flame,
And everytime I looked at you
I softly spoke your name.
I told you of the love I had
For you, and you alone,
And with the ring I wore dear
I claimed you for my own.
The ring is badly tarnished now
Just like my broken heart,
But still I keep on wearing it
We two will never part.
I loved you only heart and soul
But darling, love has lost,
I only have your ring left now
It was an awful cost.
But life goes on dear, just the same
No more do our paths cross,
And though our love was once quite strong
It's now a total loss.

Judith K Cump
SONNET OF THE PIPES
Assuredly her sound is grandiose;
Her pipes precipitate creations bold;
The sounds of earth for heaven she'll transpose
And music of the ages will unfold.

Mere metal, wood and wind are just the parts
Assembled by the skills of mortal man;
When unified, will fill the coldest hearts
With warmest music made since time began.

To play her is an art magnificent;
Her ranks of pipes—a challenge to the brave;
Tonal bouquets grace the environment
As chords upon the soul she will engrave.

The mighty organ lingers, triumphant;
But alas, no longer so abundant.

Michelle Sundermeyer
TO MY SISTER
Hush little one mama is coming.
She will wipe away your tears.
Mama loves you very much don't you
ever forget that.
Are you hungry?
(Mama nurses her child)
She caresses the top of his little head as she rocks back and forth.
So soft, so vulnerable to the unknown
world.
What will happen to you when you grow up?
(She wonders)
She picks him up and pats his back.
(She says to him)
Its a tough world little one.
Don't let the evil ones get into your heart.
Just remember mama is here for you always.

Paul Miller
LIGHTNING O'ER THE MERMAIDS PROW
Stand fast! the mainsails are drawn;
even as the waves are set with sea-devils,
roughly dancing, encircling the stormy dawn.
Lightning pricks loudly through the distant cloud levels,
announcing to the keeper of the light the sight of billowing bellows reaching to rage with the sky and revel.

Land last! the twain quails waves sawn
with questing, yet the sturdy prow bedecked mermaid
ploughs on o'er the sea-bottom's treasure lawn.

Look! Brightening licks proudly splinter the mainsail, a mighty blade.
Lightning o'er the mermaid's prow! solid might that braves breathing sea-borne winds, of Godly challenge made!

Tan mast! the bane fails to yawn
drawing quarter for the Captain lashed to the lanyard,
a bough bending the anger to its purpose, as a pawn.
The prow set against the mainland, the anchor ripped unheard,
Ye Captain bloodied with death, tangled in sails; stoned by the rocks, the mermaid bleeds beneath the hail.

Marilyn Turner
MEMORIES
Sweet smile of my true love
Shining like the moon
Blest be this match above
That echoes in the ruin.

The ruin is my broken heart
Echoes faintly ancient dreams
His eyes pierce me like a dart
Tearing me at the seams.
All is gone but memories
Haunting this cold space
Where are those broken dreams
That sparkled on his face?

Marie D Baumann
ABOUT CARRIE
Why must I watch her so painfully endure,

The trials of her life as she struggles to mature,
Her battles with self, with her friends, and with me,
Her longing for peace, for serenity.
Why won't she listen when I try to explain,
That I've been through it all, I can help her stay sane,
If only she'd listen I'd show her the way,
Offer her answers; but I know what she'd say.
"Mother, be quiet, I don't want to hear it,
This is my life, my body, my mind, and my spirit,
I'll figure it out on my own, if you please,
I don't need your advice, I'll find my own keys—
To unlock life's secrets, and happiness find,
In my own time and way, if you kindly don't mind!"
So I keep my own council and don't say a word,
Not so much as a murmur; yet it's all so absurd.
I think back in time and imagine I hear,
My own mother trying to council, to cheer,
I hear her repeating the very same line,
And know I'd not listen most of the time,
She'd been through it all, as her mother before her,
She knew very well, the confusion, the torture.
But she learned, as I've learned, the trials to endure,
Knowing that eventually, one's daughter does mature.

Jennifer Wock
WINTER
Winter is kind of nice,
but sometimes it's just snow and ice.
I like the white blanket that covers the earth,
it reminds me very much of Jesus' birth.
Hot chocolate in the winter feels very snug,
and also does a great big hug.
I like the ice crystals that cover the trees,
and during winter people usually sneeze.
Birthdays in winter are usually full of snow,
when that will happen, no one ever knows.
It can be happy and full of cheer.
Winter will be with us every single year.

Lisa M Lundgren
FALLEN LEAVES
As I walk along this path
the leaves crunch beneath my feet.
And I think of you and I,
a quick heartbeat.
I am the tree standing tall,
trying to be so strong.
And you, the leaves that just fall,
not knowing where they belong.

Those leaves were once green,
and now the color changing,
some bright and others dark,
your life is rearranging.

The tree stays the same
as the leaves fall from her.
She awaits their sweet return,
but right now it's just a blurr.

While the leaves are away
it will be a long season
of cold snow and chilly winds,
and what is the reason?

Because when the leaves brighten life,
this is when they dare
to fall down from that tree,
leaving her so bare.

Marci James
FALLEN BIRD
I saw a fallen bird
one night,
His wings were worn
from weary flight.

As I stooped to pick
him up with care,
My eyes were caught
by his loving stare.

This bird had trusting
eyes, you see, and
These trusting eyes said
he believed in me.

I took him home
and made him warm,
And kept him safe
from any harm.

When I awoke
again at dawn;
I knew the place
to whence he'd gone.

Now I know that
he's alright,
no longer worn
from weary flight.

Craig R Stevens
ACROSS TOWN
There are two million miles between here and my town.
The miles are counted with haste; with care.
Stagnant relations are living there;
enthusiastic choruses are down.
I'll make my way back for the prize that waits
in streets where dreams still meander;
in streams where dreams still meander.
Packed away in sublime crates.
"Stop to see us if you can."
"Haven't seen you for awhile."
"See you still have that ol' smile."
"Turning into quite a man."
Parental patience paying all the time.
Things that mattered once before
don't need to sleep anymore,
or worry how to make lies rhyme.
The grass is still growing,
and the trees are still growing.
The kids are all growing.
Is my loneliness showing?

Kelly Jo Knaub
THE FUTURE'S YOUR LIFE
The future's your life
The future's your life,
You can be what you want to be.

You can fly in the sky,
Or swim in the sea.
You choose for you.
While I choose for me.
A nurse, a doctor, or a secretary,
Maybe a dancer or even a star.

Show me your talents,
Let's see what you are.
The future's your life,
The future's your life.

Lee Ann Sontheimer

FAT FARMLAND

Here is fat farmland,
Rolling Missouri hills
Cradling this town
And this burial ground.
In this quiet country land
Came forth my kith and kin.
In this country graveyard
Lie their bones.
Mary, the German born,
Milton, Kentucky bourbon bred,
And their babies, their dreams
Are buried here, in rich land.
The green pastures reek of
Goodness, a smell of good ground,
The same earth that holds
Nellie Dirst Roberts,
She who was born in Indian
territory,
Danced with a Texas Ranger,
Came here in a covered wagon.
An American flag, a white cross
With proud red poppies stands
Above Claude, veteran of the
Pacific Theater,
He who once played boats with me,
Shirt sleeves rolled high.
His hands once guided mine
To hit a horseshoe ringer
everytime.
I, city born,
I, who live in an Ozark town,
I stand here, the good sun above me
On this fat farmland, this rich earth
Over those bound to me,
And I feel peace.
This is a good place; the quiet
Rests easy on my soul.
This is Fillmore,
This is another facet of my
Own rich herritage.

Oday E O'Neal

EARTH'S BEAUTY

To Shannon, Sherri, and Stephen

I stood upon the highest hill
With wondrous joy my heart stood
still
Saw the beauty far and wide
Watched the mighty rushing tide.

Felt the beauty of the land
Miles of glistening snow white sand
Distant mountains were capped
with snow
While stately trees grew far below.

Heard the ships far out at sea
Standing there I felt so free
The sun moved slowly across the
sky
And nearby a birds soft cry.

Saw the splendor of the earth
With rapture watched natures
rebirth
The Master surely waved his hand
To create this glorious land.

E Ruth Russell

ASSURANCE

My heart was heavy as I walked
along,
My feet from the path did stray.
And walking the way, with the
weary throng,
I stopped and began to pray.
And as I talked with my Saviour,
A peacefulness filled my breast—
As I heard His sweet voice saying,
"Come Unto Me and Rest."

Now I can travel the dusty path,
And my heart is light and gay.
I am filled with His wonderful
presence,
And my feet no longer stray.
For I have talked with my Saviour,
And He has given to me
The sweet relief from worry and
care—
And His promise my burdens to
bear.

Kathy Blair

A SOULFUL JOURNEY

This poem is dedicated to my mother and father and to my grandmother, Edna Blair, for all the love and joy they've brought into my life.

Legacies of summers past
Chimes are still and humble.
Fallen hopes from dreams we cast.
Blocks that made us stumble.

Tears that fell from widened eyes
The debri washed ashore,
Heavy burdens broke the ties
From things that meant much
more.

Ashes strewn on edges steep,

Mem'ries in my mind.
All the etchings run so deep.
With all the hurt I find.

Lead by fate on golden beams;
Held on tight, but lost the touch.
Felt the quivers and it seems
Gone are those as such.

Taught the child and learned as
well,
But naivety's a game.
Fossils few within this hell—
The rendevouz's the same.

Sharon Elizabeth Sinclair

LEW

To Dad and Donnie, your light shines on my "water from the moon."

Like pink cotton candy
that melts in my mouth,
Illusive with sweetness
that beckons for more.

Like fresh mountain breezes
that stir my heart's joy,
With memories of beauty
that crave an encore.

You make me remember
the fragrance of lilacs
That bathe me with wonder—
a spirit made whole.

With the comfort of waves
as they break on the shore,
You bring me your treasures
for my outstretched soul.

You are music and laughter
and hologram magic,
The sunset at evening
with colours sublime.

Like words from the poets
that answer my longing,
You are all precious moments
suspended in time.

Isaac B King

I'M GETTING BETTER WITH AGE

My life is like an open book
Each day a different page
Come on in and take a look
I'm getting better with age . . .
I feel as 'tho this world is mine
I should be on the stage
Because each day, I rise and shine
I'm getting better with age . . .
This old world I know
Is not what it use to be
But, no matter where I go
There's always something new to
see
As long as I'm free, I'm feeling fine
So, don't put me into a cage
I'm like a bottle of vintage wine
I'm getting better with age . . .

Pearlie L Ditmore

LISTEN, AND YOU WILL HEAR

Listen my child, and you will hear
The wind as it glides through the
trees;
The birds as they flitter here and
there;
The river as it rushes to the sea;
The rain as it falls gently by your
feet;
The sound of someone you love
coming near.

Listen my love and you will hear
The voices of love whispering;
The busy hands of those who care;
The soft footsteps hurrying quickly
by;
The noise of life all around you;
The songs of love, hope and good
cheer.

Listen, everyone, and you can hear
Life at it's best, lovely and bright;
People living one day at a time;
Nature busy getting ready for the
winter;
A heart crying out for
understanding;
The sounds of living, each thing so
dear.

Listen my friend, there is nothing
to fear
For listening is one of life's greatest
joys.
Thru listening you learn to share
Love, heartache, and life itself with
others.
You will be giving of yourself thru
love
When you listen so that you may
hear.

Lona Jean Turner Binz

TOMORROW WILL COME

I heard them say
She looks so peaceful; yea!
At last she rests, another said
And with goodbyes they closed the
lid;

I heard the cloud above me thunder
As they lowered me slowly six feet
under
I heard the dirt start falling in
As the preacher uttered the last
Amen.

Now here I lay so dead, so still
And I must say it's not my will!
It's dark down here, as dark as hell
Sure, they can say it's swell, she's
well;

Just wait, someday will be their day
Then they can hear but cannot say
They'll see the dark with glassy eyes
And grass will grow where body
lies.

Lela Holt

THERE IS A BEAUTIFUL DAY AT HAND

To my husband Layton Holt

Yesterdays are past recall
and things
that happened then
are only shadowed memories
we think of
now and again
Tomorrows never come
they say
of plans fulfilled
and things we hope to see
Todays are riches
close at hand
Fresh pathways to explore
new joys to lift
our spirits high
what heart
could ask for more?
so why relive
those days gone by
or look so far ahead
let's cherish
what we have right now
and live today instead.

Burl R Lines

FLAME

To Patricia my wife whom I love

There is a light upon the land
from the lady
by the sea
And to see aback awhile
the light was always
there
In the winter of our LAND
the Dear Father's
stood for truth
Again the darkness not
yet past
Our Father's saw the light of right
This is the country of the Free
A light in every Heart
The light shines brighter still
In a world aglow

Milton F Clapper

CLOUD WATCHING

To my beloved and wonderful wife Therisa.

Have you ever sat and watched the
sky?
As fluffy white clouds move
gracefully by,

Thinking how peaceful they seem;
Have you ever imagined that you see?
Faces, forms or things you want them to be,
As if they appeared in a dream.

As each cloud appears moving ever so slowly,
Each processing a picture for your mind to see,
And capture it for a moment?
As I then return to the world of reality,
Thankful for the precious time I was free,
To enjoy a time well spent.

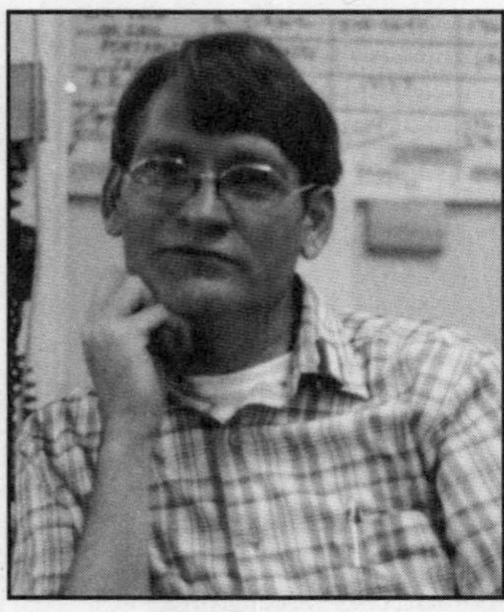

Phil Brown

Phil Brown
INTERLUDE
A brief respite if you will,
a rest.
You have earned it brother,
and so have I.

A moment to smoke
or sit on the sand;
just a pause
without a cause;
free from the pressure of accomplishment

Nerina Binetti
WINTER SNOW

To My Mother

The night is dark
The snow is slight
It falls slow
like a white rose
It shows
It grows
Over the open door
See the sight
on the glowing floor.

Betty Jenkins Johnson
HOME
The house at the edge of the wood still stands,
her arms outstretched, saying, "please come home again."
The walls and the roof are tattered and torn,
on the house by the wood, where I was born.

Oh! take me back, take me back, where the grass is still green,
where my thoughts are still keen,
of the children that played, and the family that stayed,
in the house at the edge of the wood.

The swing still hangs in the old oak tree,
and has only the wind to push it.
The garden gate stands open and free,
impatient for someone to fix it.

The cotton in the field says, "you win"
to the tall grass that waves in the wind.
The wagon can't go to the cotton gin,
it sits in the barn where it's always been.

With each passing year, my memory grows stronger,
and there are times when I think I can wait no longer,
to go back to the place where I spent my childhood,
in that little house at the edge of the green wildwood.

Oh! take me back, take me back, where the grass is still green,
where my thoughts are still keen,
of the children that played, and the family that stayed,
in the house at the edge of the wood.

Dana L Lawrence
TO BE

To my Lord Jesus Christ, my family, and friends who let me be me; I say thank you kindly.

To be or not to be;
that is not the question,
that is the answer.

To be young,
to be gifted,
to be you,
to be free,

I know!
To be me.

Bo Singleton
BO'S CHANT
The large sun
The hot dry sand pursued us,
The gritty sand
Beneath our feet
The hot dry sand pursues us,
The dying plants
The hot dry sand pursued us,
The small water pond over there
The hot dry sand pursued us,
We drank but
The hot dry sand pursued us!

Brenda S Melton
IT'S LIKE A RESURRECTION

To God, who gave me the talent and to my friends at the Erie Church of God, who have always encouraged me to use that talent

---

The sunshine kissed the treetops
This morning as I lay
Looking out my window
On a glorious springtime day

The winter snows have melted
Buds spring forth anew
All the birds have started singing
They know it's springtime too

It's like a resurrection
Death gives way to life
Love overcomes hatred
Joy springs forth from strife

"Grave where is your victory?
Death where is your sting?"
As I look out at the flowers
I see you've not accomplished anything

The wintertime is gone
The world wakes up anew
And deep in the center of my soul
There is a resurrection too.

Judy Randolph
YESTERDAY MY SON
Yesterday my son; so happy and gay
as I watched him play.
Now the Lord has taken him away.
Why, I ask; but I know not why?

Yesterday my son; a bond of love
more than words can say.
Now the Lord has taken him away,
Why, I ask; but I know not why?

Yesterday my son; now I live with
sweet and cherished memories. I
must live for my daughter and have
memories of my son.

Yesterday my son; so happy and gay
as I watched him play.
Now the Lord hath taken him away,
Why, I ask; but I know not why?
Yesterday My Son.

Debra Sue K Fraley
HERE'S TO THE YOU AND I'S
Here's to the memories one by one.
Here's to the melodies until they are
All sung.
Here's to the days until they are
All done.
And here's to the You and I's until
There are none.

So with glasses held high
Nearly touching the sky,
Lets toast to our friendship
It shall never die,
And if God should bless
We could forget all the rest

And toast to the memories one by one,
Sing all the melodies that wouldn't
Have been sung,
Live out the days that shall never
Be done,
And always be the You and I's
There shall never be none.

Virginia Ginger Panikoff
LOVE
When we think of love
it is one single word
one loves within ones limits
he loved me
but couldn't see
more lies beyond
the way he loved was only the beginning
he thought it was the end
it is not what needed to be said
nor what needed to be done
it is what needed to be felt
he needed to start again
a mother loves a child
he loved chocolate

Bobby Ray Greenwood
ALONE

A Viet Nam Vet. In dedication to my son Bobby Ray Greenwood Jr.

I live in a bottle
Can swim like a fish
Around and around I go
I search for my wish.

Blood and sweat I gave
I couldn't ask why
But our God above
He understood our cry.

We didn't ever see it
Home didn't really care
They knew it was a war
But nobody knew where.

Land of slanted war
Many answered the call
All of us gave
They knew we would fall.

Nobody ever really knew
Just how much it cost
But the only real thought
Is, God, how much we lost!!!

Carter Craft
MY WISH FOR YOU
Wishing you all the happiness
And the joy that comes with love,
And that this bond you now are forming
May be blessed by God above.

Although I never will forget you
And in my memories you'll always live,
Just know that I want the best for you
That life could ever give.

May your life be filled with laughter,
Love and joy, not tears and pain,
And may you always see the sunshine,
Be it blue skies or be it rain.

Patricia Moore (LeCour)
THE ARMS OF FATE
Into the arms of fate go,
Dreams of the young
And hopes of the old.
Enfolded in nights dark cloak
They slip away —
Only to emerge
Out of the darkness.
Greeting new lives and lovers.

Sharlene M Zhorne
FRAGILE BEAUTIES
In the summer two beauties are around
One flutters in the air,
The other grows from the ground.
The first is the butterfly,
The second the rose,
They are both very fragile
As everyone knows.
When the wind blows very hard
Both wings and pedals become scarred
Neither lasts very long
But both brings beauty
Before they are gone.

Carol H Wright

Carol H Wright
THY ROBE OF PROTECTION

My three sons

Take Thy robe of protection you have
And wrap it around each of my sons,

Protect them, love and keep them from harm
Until all Thy work's have been done.

Kathleen P O'Beirne
CORRESPONDENCE SCHOOL—POETRY 101
Goodbye, professor without a face,
Who critiqued my poems with humor and grace,
Your sadness pervades all your witty lines
Addressed to us in farflung climes.

You've heard our varied voices cry,
And in a tone both pained and wry,
Laid bare our common quest for love.
You've done it all with hand in glove.

You've known us all as few ever do.
We've poured out our souls and encumbered you.
We're not the first and far from last,
Who come to you with anguished past,

Or empty present, a future bleak.
You've cared, that's clear, and helped us seek
The truth that there is more to life
Than any words that we might write.

As we fade from view, our poems finished,
You wonder if our lives, lonely, diminished,
Will ever bear fruit for all to view—
I'll let you know in Poetry 102.

David P O'Brien
SILENCE
Silence,
All through my mind
Silence,
What get's me through time
Silence,
The most beautiful sound
That's not heard all around
Confusion breaks the silence
Suspicion takes the place of
Trust and love
I can't even turn to the
Sky above
But listen, can't you hear it
It's that sound not heard all around
It's silence

Beth Anne Brazil
BECAUSE I HAVE YOU, MY DEAR

To my Mother and Father, and to my first love "Elliott Dew" who inspired this poem in the summer of 1970.

With you I feel young and free
that with others, I dare not be
My life's filled with impossible dreams
but you're all I need it seems
You're my night and my day
cause with others I dare not stay
From out of nowhere you'll appear
and up in smoke goes my fear
I love you, yes, it's true
so much I know not what to do
Saying you've loved me from the start
starts a fire in my heart
As time is rushing, oh, so fast
I only hope our love will last
I get crushed to think we may part
for there can't be another start
All I want I have right here
because I have you, my dear

Everard Anthony Steadman
TO A FRIEND

To Verna and Vernice, my Mom and Aunt. They represent all things beautiful in this world.

I jumped from the bed this morning,
Wanting to write a poem;
My thoughts were of roses
Lilacs and daffodils in spring,
But lack of inspiration
Just could not produce anything.

Standing at my window's ledge
My eyes were witness to the glory,
Of nature in her majesty.

My heart was burdened
And filled with joy,
At the beauty there to see;
But try as I might
To describe that sight,
Nothing flowed from memory.

Religion and philosophy,
I sifted through my hand;
Should I write about these profound things,
Or just the state of man?

Then I thought of you Yvonne Legris:
You're the poem I wanted to write about.
Not nature, not religion nor philosophy you see,
But of a true and trusted friend,
Who's been very kind to me.

Brenda Lee Minnick
WHY DIDN'T THEY CARE?

This poem is dedicated to my parents who will never be alone. To Mrs. Schlegel my dear friend. And to you Charlie, I love you so very much.

My years are now coming close to an end
I've spent so many days alone;
As the kids grew up
And went their own way
Did they even realize I was alone?

Each one has their own little family,
I see them every now and then;
But when it came time for caring
Did they ever know I was there?

As my eyes grow dull and lonely
My limbs now ache with pain;
My heart is empty with loneliness
I wonder, do they feel the same?

Each one of the children are special,
I love them so very much,
They made me so proud of them,
Just why . . .
Why couldn't they show they cared?

JoyRene' Ryan
THE BOOK
Upon the highest shelf I sit,
Gathering dust upon dust,
And ever growing old.
Once upon a time I was used,
But that was many years ago.
I wait patiently for someone
To remove me from this place,
Open me and look inside,
Just to see what I might say.
Can't they find anytime for me?
Is it too late?
Take my word it will do you some good,
For it's truth written on my pages,
I've been here much too long already,
Contemplating moments to be shared.
Surely I can't be out of style,
For I've been read from the beginning of it all.
Is this the place for me?
I'm a book for young and old,
Miracles, poems, songs, and more
I consume,
Within my very bindings,
I hold the way to eternal rest and many more great findings,
Still I sit up high, but not out of reach,
Hoping to be found!

William B King
PLAY
The kitten and I and a piece of string
Are proving that sport is a simple thing,
A matter of guessing which way to run,
A chance that is lost, a chance that is won.
A jerk, and the string is mine, and then
A pounce and the kitten has it again.
Were it not for wit, I could never be
A match for the cats agility.

If I grow weary of play and drop
My end the kitten will quickly stop
His antics, for string is merely string,
Though it seemed so like a living thing.
That may curl itself in sleep
While I sit by with the thoughts I keep
Of many strings that are quiet now
And many more I must seize somehow.

Mary Alice Albright Brown
THE UNSUNG SONGS
Wasn't it only yesterday
My hair had not yet turned to gray
I skipped through life at a rapid pace
And there were no lines etched in my face?
Time seemed like an endless thing
For I had many songs that I would sing!
Age belonged to others I could not see
Then so suddenly, it happened to me!
Twilight years, it just can not be true—
For still I have so much to do!
So many places I still have not been
Nor have I asked forgiveness for a sin—
Have not reached out to those who care—
Nor had the time and love to share!
I must hurry and sing the melodies
I have not sung—
That I should have been singing
when I was young!
Now the swinging gate of life is closing fast
And my days of singing songs are things of past!

Elizabeth Pollan
A MOTHER'S DREAM

To Nanci

There you stand, in Veil of White,
a train of satin, pink and white Roses,
Babies Breath all around a
beautiful, flowing, white wedding gown.

A dream come true, for any mother
with a daughter like you.
When you were only two, Little
blond dog ears dressed in
ribbons of blue,
Pink frilly dresses and white ballet
shoes. Oh, how I dressed you,
just dreaming of the day, when
I would be able to see you this
way.
My sweet little angel, so
magnificently feminine, turned
into a tomboy when she was
eleven, wearing blue jeans and
pigtails and playing boy's games.
But, when she was sixteen, the
picture had changed. You've
discovered you're a girl, you
know what it means.
Once again you are beautiful, a
princess in every right, but this
time, to the boys delight.
And now you are twenty, more
beautiful than ever—
and there you stand, in Veil of
White, Pink and White Roses
and Babies Breath all around, a
beautiful flowing, white
wedding gown—
A dream come true, for any Mother
with a Daughter like you.

Eva Forman
LADY LIBERTY
Come ye tall ships of all
nations, to a land where free
men dwell
and bring forth with you a
part of peace, for the brave
in war that fell
I see old glory flying in
the highest mast, leading the
mighty fleet into historys
past

The sound of rockets are
clearly heard across the
open sea, pay tribute to this
great lands birth, and lady
liberty
Our country men look proudly
on as the tall ships cross
the bay, and with her lamp
Lady Liberty guides them
on there way
and so it will be another
hundred years, the tall
ships will meet again,
on these shores where
free men dwell, and
history never ends

Ruth Amerson
TO LIVE ALONE

To my children John, Penny & Diana

To live alone must be so sad,
I've heard that said before.
What does she do at evening time
when she walks in the door?
There is no one to greet her, or say
how was your day? Or a little
child to run to her and say come on
let's play.
Who lives alone must never be the
object of ones sympathy, but in
ones
heart must always be the fondest
of ones memories.
So please do not feel sad
for me, for I have My Lord for
Company.

Alice L Felmlee
AGED HARMONY
Mine eyes do not see the
flourishing of life as they had
sands ago,
For the footsteps of time have crept
upon us now,
Forming dismal a shadow and
thoughts of evil and foul.
My evenings are spent in a mist of
reluctant thought,
Contemplating the way existence
should be or therefore ought.
The blanket that raptures me in
warm trust,
Must shield thee from the silence
of day that stalks behind my
door.
Thy soul is not brave as a flower
that blooms quaint and bright,
Or a cocoon that bares a pair of
wings through a frost bitten
night,
And thus I must accept what the
Master player has in hand,
Fulfilling my destiny as a willing
command.

Kelli Sumption
THE SOUL
I'm watching for the soul.
Although realizing it is
no longer a being, but
a lifeless shell,
I wish it to hear me.

Open your eyes—
Let the wind breathe
distorted life into you.
Once more let your pulse
thunder through your veins.

Ah, but me you musn't see.
The fear of your anger at
coming back to this hell
will keep
me hidden.

For I must know.
I must see the truth—
That there really is
somewhere to come back
from. I beg you—

Please taste this
bitter world so I may
know—Then it hears.
As it opens its eyes—
I turn away.

D Ann Henning
SKY LAND
In those mighty and high limbs
holds my fragile feathered
friends
Swooping together as schools of
fish
seeking a very tasty dish
Songs in their hearts
that come together from their
memories

Come take me there
I often dream
to a land that only sky can see
Play your swooping games with me
And teach me the songs in your
memories

Julie Cherico
A CRY IN THE NIGHT
There's something crying in the
night,
and all that I know is that there is
a danger in sight.
It isn't too clear of what it might be,
It's dark, and there just isn't
enough light to see.

As I approach it, the cry is of fright,
whatever it is, soon should be in
sight.
Coming closer, I saw its eyes glow,
I bent down to try and retrieve it
from the snow.
As I worked, my eyes filled with
tears.
Animals have a life too—they
shouldn't
be harmed by people like you,
and live in fear.
I took it out of the trap, and buried
it in the ground,
I still remember the cry of that little
bear I found.

Leora L McCready
HE SAW MY MEMORY
I thought I heard a little voice
a shouting up at me.
And then, . . . I felt a little tyke
a climbing up my knee.

He settled his tiny little frame
upon my lap with care.
I heard his little voice say, "Hi,
what 'cha doin' up there?"

Each tiny hand grabbed for my ears
as he placed his nose on mine.
Two sparkling eyes looked back at
me
to see what they could find.

"Look," said he, "I see you in there,
come out and play with me."
I couldn't resist a wistful grin
for, . . . he'd seen my memory.

Ah yes! . . he'd seen the child in me
so carefully stored away
in memories of the old times when
I used to run and play.

Again, this tiny little voice
broke thru my reverie
to say those magic little words . . .
Come out . . . and play with me.

Jennifer Leigh Nolen
ONE SINGLE TEAR
A single tear rolls down my
cheek. It's for you, the first
man I ever loved. That single
tear is for all the times we spent
together and for all the pain
you've caused me.
One single tear rolls down my
cheek as I think of how much I
miss you. It stands for all the
days of sharing, the good as well
as the bad.
That one single tear holds so much
emotion. That tear that only I
shall understand.
I see your face and it reminds me
of us together. That one single
tear is there, ready to roll down
my cheek at one more thought
of you.
Now, you're not mine, but were
you ever? That tear knows the
answer. No one else in the world
does. It stands for so much: All
the love and the pain. The times
we spent together. Our
fights. The good times and the
bad. The kisses we shared and
the laughter, too.
For all these things, I give
you—One single tear.

Mary Ellen Romero
WINTER CAME CALLING

---

*To my parents Joe B. and Rita A.
Whitaker for their love and
encouragement always.*

All night the wind howled through
the eaves,
And snug in my bed I knew,
Come morning donning my
warmest sleeves,
That my fondest of dreams and
come true.
Stoking the fire to build a new
blaze,
The kettle was put on to brew,
I wiped the window of its frosty
haze,
For last nights dream had come
true.
Yes, last night it snowed, it blew
and it whirled,
While snug in my bed I knew,
Today I would wake up to a
brand new world,
Because my dream of dream had
come true.
So now in my rocker, sipping my
tea,
I sit here warming my toes.
I know beyond the front door what
waits for me,
Because of last nights swirling
snow.
So with all my parts bundled up
tight,
And shovel in hand I go,

And I wonder as I shovel, how in
just one night,
There could ever be so much snow!

Mark A B Carlson
YOU
You sprinkle rain on warm
afternoons
that trickles coolly o'er my dusty
face—
one million little, gentle fingers
tickling my smiling eyes,
caressing ev'ry eager sense,
and slighting not one space.

You play the dancing notes
of the symphony of clear, night
skies,
performing in the tranquil
moonlight,
just missed by my out-stretched,
desperate hands;
these stellar acrobatics I watch
nightly
in my sealed, perceiving eyes.

You set the tired sun
sending rainbows 'cross the land.
The reds and yellows shine
strong
in my covetous, loving stare,
the fragile, final flash,
a soothing stroke of silken,
lustrous hand.

You are the beauty
that to which all else must
compare.
My drink, my bread, my sleep,
my ardor, bed and air—

Sheer perfection in this life
with me ev'rywhere.

Avis M Smith

Avis M Smith
FIRST LOVE

To my four daughters who love me in spite of myself

Waking in the night
I think of you,
Remembering all the things
We used to do.
Dancing until the dawn
When Love was new.
Walking in the starlight
With your hand in mine,
Youth and laughter always
Because we had no sign
That Fate would take us onward
To things we knew not of.
For the world was bound on all sides
By nothing else but Love!

Marilyn Paslay
WHEN I WAS YOUNG
The sights and sounds so different then; No sonic boom
Or auto's roar, just clop of hoof and grind of wheel
Down dusty street: In winter time a sleigh bell chimes
As cutter lays a serpent's track o'er pristine snow.
When I was young:
In the summer time, the swimmin' hole, deep guarded by
The willows drooping boughs;
Where siblings splash
And watch the eagle in his flight, o'er warm brown hills.
Where coyotes play, and rabbits quiver in the sagebrush shade.
When I was young:
On my pony, like the wind I race the well worn paths;
Or climb along the rocky ways. In pensive mood, alone
I walk the forest path, with nature to commune;
And in the beauty there to find, my Mother and my God.
When I was young:
Then all too soon the scene is changed, to home and family.
A farmers life, with all it brings.
The work and worry,
Love and joy. No longer time to roam, I smile to see
My children taste sweet freedom's joys as I once did.
When I was young:
Now "TIME" at last my steps have slowed, earthbound
By rocking chair, with book in hand I travel off
To some enchanted scene. And if I nod, perhaps I'll dream
Of carefree days, and childhood plays. Of how it was;
When I was young:
But if I'm patient, that same "TIME" which once my youth
Did steal. Will come full circle and again, I'll ride my pony
On the wind; And soar with eagles o'er the hills of home.
Then what joy! When once more and forever, all will be the way it was.
When I was young:

Nettie McGee
A FLOWER OF LOVE
Today as the winter sun
lightly touched my face,
My mind drifted back to a time
When your love
gently touched my heart.

It was at that moment
now buried in memories,
That a single seed was planted
And carefully placed with
the skill of a gardener.

Deep within my heart grew
that flicker of hope,
Fed by the passion of your heart
Until a sprout of love
blossomed through the weeds.

With a bright smile to
gently warm and enlighten,
This love developed an unyielding strength
And blossomed with the
rare beauty of assurance.

Now as the days apart number
too many to count,
I only need open the pages of my memory
To behold a rare flower
of love . . . and you.

Mary Jo Stickney
A SIMPLE MAN

This poem is dedicated to all the lonely people in this world, and to all whom have lost a loved one to the bullet of loneliness.

Dark clouds shall hide a sunlit sky,
Below a simple man shall die.
He shall die and only because,
He had no friends, alone he was.

The gun was there loaded and all,
There on a chair close to the wall.
A weapon that would surely kill,
It's only purpose to full fill.

They found him lying on the bed,
He was they said already dead.
The gun lie cradled in his hand,
His early death at his command.

Dark clouds shall hide a sunlit sky,
Below a simple man has died.
He has died and only because,
He had no friends, alone he was.

Faith A Ledermann
WHEN YOU GET A FLOWER FROM A FRIEND
When you get a flower from a friend . . .
Accept it, cherish it to the end.
But when it's gone—
Keep the song it put in your heart.
Pass on the joy it gave you,
that's what it was for!
As with earthly things—
their season is short not to keep.
It was lent us to look, to smell, to reap
the delight.
So as with the flower
the same with living.
things of the heart,
the receiving and giving
are the part that will last,
When all other things have past.

Bob Sorgi
THE UNCONVENTIONAL KITTY
There was once a kitty who
disdained the conventional,
by doing bizzare things in a
manner most intentional.

"Frinstance" . . . when offered steak
or salmon, the answer was
invariably, "Nope" . .
while making it known she'd
enthusiastically accept a ripe
cantaloupe!

Upon being told she should like a
meal containing tuna,
her reply was: "I'd prefer eating
dirt 'suna'!"

Fido, her dog friend, told kitty she
was some kind of nut.
Her reply was: "Fido, you're a
lowdown, despicable mutt!"

Now cats are supposed to prey
upon the lowly rat.
But kitty showed no interest in
anything approximating that.

Instead, she chose an occupation
lacking in authenticity,
only further proving her
inveterate, consummate
eccentricity!

Ever hear of a cat being interested
in aviation?
Well, this one, in kittydom, became
an international sensation.

Yes, at shooting down flies she
quickly became an ace . . .
which occupation sometimes left
her with a smile on her face.

Many is the fly she left with a bad
case of decapitation . . .
a thing most flies would consider
the absolute ultimate in
frustration! ! ! !

Despite a diet fit for a total
vegetarian,
Her Highness has already lived to
be an octogenarian.

This must be said . . . last but not
least.
For her, there's only one thing
that's better than a feast.

It's doing what all kitties do while
in deepest slumber
which, of course, is chasing dogs
while sawing lumber ! ! !

Connie R Ferber
SUMMERTIME
If I could draw a picture of
summertime.
The colors in the picture would be
sublime.
Nature with its beauty of many
hues
To chase away those wintertime
blues.
Traveling Minnesota, singing a
song,
Thankful that this is where I
belong.
Watching the tall grain wave in the
breeze,
Corn in the stalk and beautiful
trees.
Hip-roofed barns, nestling in the
hills,
Wrens and songbirds and
whipperwills,
Little streams, a pothole there,
Horses grazing, I breathe a prayer.
Elevators, brick schools, water
towers,
Towns speed by, while away hours.
Black roofs, red roofs and gray
roofs too,
Railroad crossings, and sky so blue.
Gravel pits, a barren tree,
All this Beauty! Lucky me.

Evelyn Holmes
UNTITLED
True poetry isn't written—it's
lived—
The best poem is an unwritten
poem—
but a living poem
The poet went out on one day and
saw an old lady
struggling under her own peculiar
load
Can I be of assist, said the poet
You can if you want, said the old
lady
And when her load was made light
by this man;
the living man, she turned to him
and said,
Now that what you did, sonny
man, was the kindest
thing anybody ever done for me,
and I thank you
for helping me to write my poem,
for I was having trouble putting
together
the last few lines.
You see, I been addin a few lines
every day
since I was born,
Now it is complete.

John Irving Sorensen
WALK
We strode the moist sands of time
one day,
Our footprints there plainly seen.
As though cast in bronze they lay.
High tide soon came to erase all
trace
of our having been.
Along the way once, and then,
Who Knows if we will pass that
way again.

Our walk to cease in time,
Caressed by sea air and rime.
A sand dollar washed thin there
ahead,
and fat gull recently fed,
objecting to us, refusing to fly,
Majestically struts instead.

Sunset's brilliance, each brief
moment
surpassing those just spent.
All earth, still, awaits the night.
A sea bird's shrill cry echoes,
there, out of sight.
The first star of evening creeps into
the sky.
Really far off, not seeming that
high.

Peace, after the work is past.
Time pauses, Peace, at last.

Debbie Taczak
IF I LEAVE FIRST

So many tears together spent
Profoundly are we one.
And yet we know within our hearts
That day will surely come . . .

When one of us will go away
Leaving the other here;
That doesn't mean our life must end
Or that we live in fear.

For through these years we've learned to love,
Continue on to share . . .
If I leave first then let me say
I want you still to care.

I want you to go on and be
The one I love so much;
The world could learn so much from just
Your caring loving touch.

And when we meet again I'll say
I'm very proud of you.
For through your pain you carried on
With what you had to do.

Barbara Grace Lake
FRIENDSHIP

We walked along
The water's edge
Not touching in
A groping trial
Of tactile, hearing senses
Yet our minds were intertwined.
We talked a little
Often not, but sent
Our unframed images,

Unspoken thoughts
And tenderness
On airborne rafts
In total synergy.
How better than
The harshly arid
Battering
Of empty words
This stillness
Of communal thought
Between two friends.

Mae Newton Lindsey
WHO YOU ARE

Dedicated to the glory of GOD and to all who wish a closer walk with Him.

When asked the awesome question of whom you are, I pray
You say not that I AM NOBODY, nor even feel that way.
You are a special person, a miracle of spirit and mind.
You are made in His likeness; however,—One of a kind.

God took time to make you different, even numbered the hairs on your head.
You are made for His eternal glory as the Word of God has said.
God took time in His planning to make you the very best;
Even the finger-prints you have are unlike all the rest.

The Holy Spirit yourself indwells, His peace abides within.
Comfort and help He provides, with which a Christian can win.
You are joint-heir with Christ, God's only begotten Son.
Christ is your salvation in whom final victory is won.

You are a masterpiece of God, in His own image you are made.
He put something of Himself in you like a master of any trade.
Lift up your eyes toward heaven, affirm that God's blessings are real;
Thank Him for your creation and the joy and peace you feel.

You are God's own creation, He has a special plan for you;
Talk with Him to learn it, like any good Christian should do.
Then say NOT that I AM NOBODY, You, whom God did create.
Ask Him the plan for your life, and for the answer patiently wait.

Carla Lovetinsky
IT'S THERE

It's there. You can see it in her eyes.
That far away look. She looks without
seeing, listens without hearing, touching
without feeling.

She walks in a haze. She walks in a world
all her own. Her own silence comforts
and leads her.

To listen, you would not understand her
silence. Nor would you understand her
words.

Her soul belongs to the unknown. An
unknown she must enter and leave alone.
She exists obeying the silence within.
A silence that may lead her to the door
that will join her soul with her lost
heart.

Dennis V Spatz
DEFINITION OF MOTHER

A someone who was always there
To give children all ages loving care
A someone who in spite of what you've done
Could give you solace if you lost or won
A someone in times of stress
Would somehow find a ray of happiness
A someone who could find the time
To mend a sock or a boot to shine
A someone who could take your side
Be no matter what, in her you could confide
A someone who the role of doctor played
In times of sickness at your bedside stayed
A someone who could mend a broken heart
Shape a scrap of material into a work of art
A someone who with hands like mine
Could make food taste like aged wine
A someone who could miraculously kiss away
The little hurts that occur each day
A someone who most of us for granted take
Until we realize it was all just for our sake
A someone who like God alone
Sets not on a pedestal, but on a throne.

Happy Mother's Day

Gayle Knoller
DON'T GIVE UP

To my darling daughter Dominique:

Don't give up your dreams or your dreaming,
Don't let life cut your line as you reel in
those dreams . . . hold on tightly.
. . . Keep reeling . . . don't give up . . .
Grab that net . . . and if they look like they're
about to leap out of the net after you've caught
them, jump in after them, and keep on swimming, till
you drown if you have to . . . but don't ever let go
of those dreams!

Sandra Jean Sharp
A NEW YEARS COMING

This is a time for good cheer.
Looking forward for the year is past.
Putting to rest what has gone by so fast.
To contemplate, to compile, all that has
happened in one year.

For one to have no fear for the future of
this coming year;
We shed the shackles of our past hardships,
free the pain that might remain, and
free the tears that have collected.

To hold in our hearts the joys of happy
times that were freely expressed.
To see the good in what might be.
To hold onto the strength of the feelings
that make you feel whole.

The future has no gurantees.
The past is what remains unchanged.
We hold the power to change the games.
We are the directors of our fame.
One travels through the years as if were a storybook in time, on the stage
or life we masquerade.
Put your life on a pedestal.
Its a time to recapetulate all the characters you've played, compile them
in the menagerie of your life
so far as today.

Dennis E McNeeley
MY LOVE

I dedicate this poem with all "My Love," To Debbie—my wife

My Love is Tender, My Love is Caring,
My Love is Sweet, My Love is Sharing,
My Love is Beautiful, My Love is funny,
My Love is Bright, My Love is Sunny,
My Love is Patient, My Love is Kind,
My Love is Neverending, My Love is Not Blind,
My Love is Understanding, My Love is True,
My Love is forever Because my Love is You!

Mrs Kathleen R Trautman
FATHER

Some people say they're lonely, but you are by my side.
Don't they know why you were born or the reason why you died?
I wonder why some people don't feel your presence here.
Is it out of ignorance or perhaps just out of fear?
Lord, I've asked in Jesus' name and the Comforter has come
All my questions answered in your word and in your song.
You've cleansed my heart and filled my soul as you entered into me.
You've taken all the blindness hidden deep inside of me.
I praise you Lord for you are good—so merciful are ye.
I thank you and sing praises, I know what you've done for me.
I praise you Lord and worship you as I get down upon my knees
You've filled a void within my life—You've walked each step with me.
I'll tell the world of your great love
I'm a witness unto thee.

Joan Giltner Canfield
MIDSUMMER

Midsummer fills the moonlight air
while star-light dreams
on her rocking-chair.

Outside in the meadow
On a garden swing—
A bluebird listens to the wind.

Slowly the hands on the clock
Go around . . .
Summertime has come and gone.

Midsummer in her cloissonne
Painted rocking—chair . . .
Spins poetry while browsing there!

Surrounded by the evening sultry air
Midsummer sleeps in the night-time
breeze—

Counting the stars as she hums along
Midsummer dreams in her rocking chair.

Pamela Rankin Lott

Pamela Rankin Lott
A TOUCH OF SPRING

I dedicate this poem to my wonderful Grandmother Gretchen whose wisdom and inspiration made this possible. And to all my family for their love and support.

As a new season starts,
A new day begins.
The morning, with all her softness, brings light.
And there, beneath the light,
The world begins to show.
The birds who briskly awaken, sing,
As though this might be their last day.
The trees in which they have their homes
Glisten with the morning dew
Which has settled on their leaves.
Then they begin to sway with a touch of springs breeze
And shake off that which burdens them.
It falls to the ground below,
And is then taken back
By the shine and warmth of the new days sun.
Every earthly creature begins to stir
As if each one knows the day.
And life begins as usual,
With a new day
And a touch of spring.

Cheryl Elaine Burgess
HIS LOVING HAND
How great you are, O'Lord
To love us as you do
Blest are we among your midst
Whom exault and trust in you

Our Father, who art on high
Your loving ways are firm
To guide, protect and lift us up
To your bosom as we learn

We shall remember who Thou art
In our everyday walk of life
For as the pressures are laid on us
Your words shall console the strife

We Praise and Exault thee O'Lord
Your faithfulness we see
You meet our needs, our prayers are heard
As we bow on bended knee
Your loving hand upon our lives
As a mother's upon her child
If we but trust and let you guide
We will be righteous, not defiled

Firoozeh Rahimian
SHADOWS
Whenever I close my eyes,
Whenever I'm alone in my heart,
I feel this strange pain.

I can hear my friends' voices at night;
I can see their shadows in the moonlight,
but their love and brightness has gone.

And all I have left
is an illusion of what use to be faces;
they are only figments of a shattered picture.

Now, alone,
I face the silence of endless nights;
I face the stillness of countless days,
and feel this pain
for the rest of my life.

William Thomas Marshall
MORNING
circlets of light
bent by the lake
reflect into my face
making my eyes quake
the sky is bright
turning pale pink
to the water comes a deer
stretching out a kink
dawns early light
night fastly fading
comes the waking earth
trees begin their shading
morning shadows
closing water-lillies
chestnut mares
suckle their fillies
old farmer jones
milks his pure-bred cows
eats a hardy breakfast
goes out and plows
morning is the best
best time of year
wake up it cries
its morning I'm here

Letha B Bunton
WHERE ARE THEY NOW
I'm talking about the big white clouds in the sky
I'm always watching them but don't know why
They are very pretty and unique in their own way
Twisting and turning and putting on a show—I'd say
They spin and go around and around and around
Until another cloud they bump into that they've found
They seem to cling together for a while
Then gradually slide away with a smile
Some seem to stand still like they're in a trance
While others go by so fast as if it's their last chance
Then others pull apart in long slow strings
Sort of make pictures in the sky to you they bring
The pretty blue sky and these white clouds
Sometimes I think of them as a bunch of happy clowns
They spin and they swirl and go round and round
Never stay in one place—that I have found
They look so peaceful up there high in the sky
If I were a bird sometimes I think I'd try
To reach them and go on their free merry-go-round
But then I'd spoil their fun so I'll stay here on the ground
And then there's days when I look up high
I see no clouds anywhere in the sky
I walk around and look and say to myself out loud
All those pretty clouds—where are they now

Richard A Mushko
HOMELESS BOUND

I dedicate this poem to my family who gave me the courage and freedom to express myself through poetry

---

He slowly lifted his hand out to the passbyers.

This was his home his only home.
A brown cold paper brown box.

He slowly crept up from his home and took his daily walk.

He said PLEASE spare me a quarter. No givers were near for the whole day.

He sadly walked to his home.
His cold brown paper brown box thinking tomorrow is still another day.

Inez M McCarty
DOWN MEMORY LANE
To survive the loss of a loved one
Take a trip down memory lane.
Recalling the joys of companionship
May give you a stiff upper lip
To try a laugh-a-day and
Drive the blues away.

Elizabeth Kelley
THE WALL OF TIME
Behind the wall of time
one cannot pass, alas,
But ancient thoughts,
once so sublime,
Can like a vine o'erpass—
and leaf and flower;
Green-fresh thoughts
from an ancient bower.

Paul Vincent Jaramillo
UNTITLED
In the stillness of the air, sings a song you cannot express . . .
In the stillness of the air, you wish you could address . . .
In the stillness of the air, you will see no emptiness . . .

Bev Bennett
DADDY PUSH ME PLEASE

In Honor of my Loving Parents, Mr. & Mrs. George C. Bennett; My Brothers, Don, Bruce, & Brian; and Grampa. In Rochester, New York the 1960's

---

Those teeter totter times in our backyard
Back and forth like some Canadian geese
Always for me, monkey bars were too hard
Swinging high, above clouds and falling leaves

Shorts and sneakers force my past to return
Tough skateboards with bruised legs and cindered knees
Faded scars of scrapes and peeling sunburns
Stitched leotards from frequent falls finds me

Wondering whether my mother was right
Scolding scenes made tears and some misery
Pouting to my room, hiding tears from sight
Piano practice; hating history

When gullible cries of childhood glide home,
Please push me high as I can't fly alone.

Diane E Brennan
A SPECIAL LAND
You live far away from me,
In a different land.
I've always wanted to live with you
But you didn't take my hand.
Sometimes you dared to act as if,
You really cared for me.
I read it in your deep brown eyes,
That was all you let me see.
My love was very strong for you,
But now its had time to fade.
I wish I could let you go,
But that's just not how I'm made.
So here I stand, looking vulnerable,
Holding out my hand.
Please let me come with you
To your own special land.

Betty Thomas
THE WINTER SOLSTICE
On solstice days I lie and dream
Of all the times the earth was green
And life was sweet for you were there
Running your fingers through my hair.

But life is sweet on solstice days
And Winter gives the golden rays
A Softened hue, a dreaminess
To reap the peace of quietness.

Richard L Cecil
THE ULTIMATE TEST

I dedicate this poem to the Astronauts families, in loving memory of

"Challenger" Flight S1—L Crew. I wish to thank Mr. Larry Speakes, Al—Kapkowski, and my wife Peggy

---

America, we passed the Ultimate
Test . . .
we gave you our all . . . our very
best,
so be proud and stand tall!
We were a team . . . we studied
together, worked together,
laughed together and yes, even
prayed together . . .
for our country's esteem . . . for
America's people and
NASA'S success . . . we passed the
Ultimate Test!
America . . . do not quit, do not
weep. . . be brave,
press on . . . for the mountain to
success is very, very steep!
We piloted your ship into the arms
of our God . . .
high above . . . so don't weep . . .
we're with the Master of love . . .

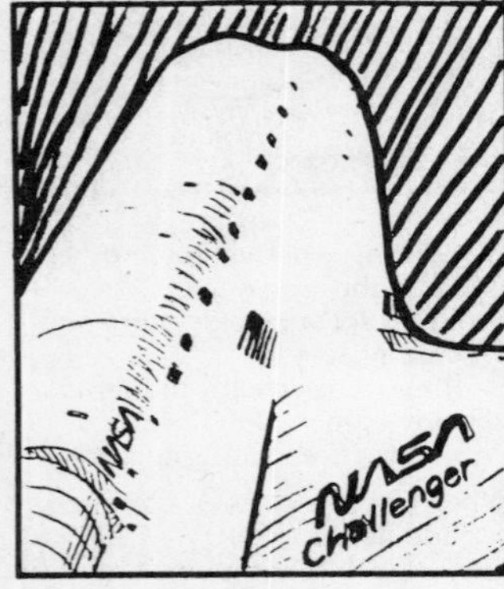

He told you once about this
ultimate test . . .
He told you what it would take . .
. you gave us your love
and prayers to take along . . ."Let
Freedom Ring"
is our National Song . . .
Be proud . . . be glad! Be true to
your code . . .
Say your prayers and all their
"amens" . . .
The Ultimate Test is "to lay down
your life,
for all of your friends" . . . we did
. . . we're glad too!
Three cheers for the Red, White
and Blue!
Tell our children to study, have fun
and play . . .
never forget how to pray . . . keep
your faith . . .
your trust in our God . . . set him
as your goal . . .
For HE is your true Mission
Control!

Kim Charnock

WILD AND FREE

Fly on a wing, wild and free . . .
As I run through the meadow the
flowers play upon my flowered
skirt.
I sense my love is near.
Near is he and wild and free.
Down in the flowers we laugh and
we love, two people, wild and
free.

Efrain Vela

WHY?

All they needed was more time
For the orderly process.
As goes the setting, sublime
Equipment ready, no less.
Instructions followed and kept,
Abruptly and suddenly aborted!
So hard for the mind to accept,
Functioning systems were
thwarted.
Comes the unnatural maze,
Conveyor becomes destroyer;
Shocking to confront and face:
No fast answers by deduction,
Some attacks of gloom and haze,
Ugly climate of destruction!

It was Fate's exclusive choice
To strike her blow and rejoice,
She left, apart from her take,
Catastrophe in its wake.

Of this special part of history
We don't want a repetition;
Let's keep all the rules of safety
Everything in good condition.
With Nature's eternal rhythm,
Let's accomplish our mission.
Death and danger deter none!
Life must go on, and on, and on . . .

Michael J Wittman

LIKE A SAD SONG

Where has my one love gone
Has it ended like a sad song
I remember the nights we'd spent
Telling each other how much
we'd meant
Holding each other till dawn
Never seeming all that long
Ah, your sensuous perfume scent
And beautiful hair . . . redish tint
Listening to love songs
Sipping wine, nothing could go
wrong
Then you said you had to go
away
That you just couldn't stay
You knew this from the start
That our paths had to part
Even now when I think back
It's hard for me to face the fact
Then a tear comes to my eye
Remembering our last good-bye.
Where has my one love gone
It's ended like a sad song.

Michael Young

SONNET OF TIME

We value time and pray the day be
long
And pass with haste the duties of
the day,
So all the nightly dreams for which
we long
Might be the thing we save from
death's decay,
But time unsympathized to mortal
dreams,
Refutes our hopes with quickly
rushing sands
And makes for man a haunting,
chiding dream
For which he vainly, always vainly
plans.
With mortal dreams unsatisfied he
turns
Beyond, where God eternal does
abound.
Oh, yet he knows and, hoping, will
return
To mortal dreams, for this he
knows he's found:
If time would at our heart's desire
be,
How superfluous Eden then would
be!

Mary Stevens Trella

IS-WAS

When you finally know the
waneing
when warmth and real is gone
when too much goes to feigning
with torments of wherein the
wrong,
waste not the time of pondering.
It was. And for a reason.
The is-was becomes more than
wandering
if not in this, then in coming
season.

Edith Beach

WHITE LILIES AT DUSK

A summer eve; a fragrant time
Of whispered sounds and
insect-song—
A single star is in the west,
And deep among the shadows long
The lilies, ah! the trumpets fair
With petals luminous and white
Are clustered by the garden fence
And glowing, ghostlike, in the
night.

Delmer R Hite

SHIP OF EARTH

Did you see the first man walk
On the sere moon's barren face;
Where no living thing had trod
Since God made Earth and Space?

When he stepped on that dead
sphere
So like unto the Vikings hell,
Did you thank Him who made
This garden world where you
dwell?

Did your heart leap with gladness
When you saw that lovely sphere,
Blue-shining in space's dark sea
Which all men hold most dear?

Our World! Our Home! That
priceless jewel;
The planet of mankind's birth,
Green-glowing in the cold, cruel
night
Which shrouds our living Earth.

Did your soul not whisper then
The truth which the mind won't
see—
That all men ride on a single ship,
Brothers on that black space sea?

That all men crew the Ship of Earth
To Heaven, Hell or Death;
To shelter in a harbor snug
Or wrecked on the tempest's
breath!

Mary C Schooley

MY ALTAR

Dedicated to my dear sister, Charlotte C. Craft, who read one of my poems one day and asked me to save them. Before that day I had written poems but never kept them.

An altar can be most anywhere,
Mine is just an easy chair.
As I start a brand new day,
This is where I sit and pray.
Sometimes I have much to say,
Other days I cannot pray.
At times like these I sit and listen,
Then my spirit lifts and glistens.

There are so many for whom I pray,
Seems my list grows day by day.
When I think of all the strife,
All the hate and jealousy in life,
My heart grows sad and I could not
bear
Unless I took it all to Him in
prayer.
So when I rise to start a brand new
day,
I must always take the time to
pray.

Jennifer L Perkins

THE SWIMMER

She was on the block and ready,
Her legs were steady,
Anxious to go the distance,
To win the race.

Everyone knew how she felt
By the look on her face.

Then,
She slipped.
She fell.
"False start, Lane 3," the starter
yelled.

She got out of the water,
Tears streaming down her face.
She couldn't swim now,
She had thrown away the race.

She went up to her coach.
He just turned away.
Her teammates
Didn't know what to say.

So,
She said to herself,
It won't happen again.

Then,
Back to the block
To try again
With a determined look on her face.

This time she didn't slip and fall.
She just swam the race,
and beat them all.

Linda Rodgers Minton

Linda Rodgers Minton

ALONE TOGETHER

Oneness
Is not aloneness,
But wholeness,
And aloneness can have
More than one.
I'd prefer to be alone
Together with myself
Than together alone
With most other people.
Until they find their other selves
Most people are alone,
But when they do,
"Alone" is brighter than before
And "together" is a quadrille
Danced on silvered sands.

Sandra Lee Crawford

MY DISTANT FRIEND

Unicorns running freely through a
field of roses, white coats
sparkling, golden horns
shine-run-run.

Manes are blowing, beauty around every face, every body. The smell of roses pierces, the feeling of love suffocates.
Come closer-closer, darkness is coming now, the yellow sun disappears beyond the trees. The roses close, Babies fall asleep in their mothers comfort.
Beauty is around me, I twirl and sing. Rose in hand, I walk away, but something tugs at my heart saying, stay, stay where you are welcome, stay where you are happy.
Touch every rose, feel every unicorn as they meet you, smell the roses, fall asleep for when you awake all will be gone . . .

Pat Bell

LIFE OF LOVE

Life should be love
Tenderness complete
To share all the sorrows
The bitter with the sweet

Life is love
But to only who see
Yesterdays and tomorrows
And all that can be

To be loved is to live life complete
Cherish, respect and hold so near
Never to doubt each other
Or have any fear

To live together from day to day
Having faith in each other
As you go on your way
To be free within each other
No other paths will cross
For there's no tomorrows
And there can be no loss

Life should be love
Tenderness complete

Sharon J Schwalm

DESTINY

On the rim of the western wind
The bird learns how to fly

By the urge of the soul's great longing
And the ache of the mother's cry.

Pearl L Boyd

THE SNOW FLAKE

What is more pure than the tiny snow flake,
Falling from out of the sky?
Bringing with it freshness, and beauty,
So lovely to the eyes.
It dances to and fro', so dazzling white,
Gives a sparkle of diamonds, to the night.
It is like the ballarina, on the stage,
When the act is over, out of sight she fades.
It leaves a glow, of glitter in your hair,
Makes your cheeks rosey, with brisk air.
Like a magic wand, it comes and goes,
Just one of "Gods miracles" to behold.

Ms Henrietta LaVerne Johnson

THE VOICE

To my Grandmother (Mrs. Ida Lundy Johnson) I will love you for eternity!

We can live a life of sin
That comes from within;
We must create love in our heart
Life the creation of a piece of art;
We must rejoice
With the beauty of God's voice.

Garland Lonnie Cates

TO THE BRINK

To Mr. Everett A. Boone, who travelled to the brink and back and has since gone on across the bar. His sharing of his experience with us is the inspiration for this poem.

I felt myself being moved through time, toward a bright horizon . . .
as if I walked through a curtained hall,
through no will of my own.
I knew not why I was brought here to this strange yet peaceful place . . .
the last that I remembered, I was contented in my earthly space.
The doctor's aide stood,... mask in hand, and said . . .
"Think something nice. Soon you'll awake and be brand new."
I breathed the mask no more than twice.
Then darkness overtook me, for a moment, then the light . . .
Like a beacon loomed before me, drawing closer as in the night.
I heard a voice say . . .
"Don"t be frightened, child . . . there is nothing here to fear."
And I felt the peace of angels, though I knew not where was "here."
And then I saw Him standing there, and I knew the source of light.
I reached out, eager, willingly, for I knew that behind me was the night.
"I'm home," I thought . . . "no pain . . . no more . . . the crown of life is mine!"
Then, suddenly, the light grew dim, though it did not cease to shine.
Backwards down the curtained hall, I feel my body drawn . . .
and I begin to cry, for now, I see the light is gone.
"We almost lost you," came a voice; "but you'll be alright now."
The tubes and lights annoy me and sweat beads on my brow.
I recognize the sterile room and the surgeon at my side;
My bandages are cumbersome and my eyes will not yet open wide.
"I've been sent back," I thought . .
. and I knew
that my time left would be wise.
For I'd almost touched the hand of God . . .
there at the brink of paradise.

J Vallieres

I LONG TO KNOW YOU

in my thoughts and dreams
in morning and evening

in shyness and pride
in love with ecstasy.

Sarah E Gill

MOODS

To my daughters, Gwen and Mary Ann

Yesterday everything was wonderful,
Today it's not.
Yesterday was a promise of success,
Today is utter despair.

Sometimes I long to soar like an eagle,
Be my own person.
Sometimes I'd rather be coddled and spoiled,
Treated as a child.

There are days when I feel the sky is the limit,
I can swing from a star.
There are days I need praised and prodded,
My confidence lags.

At times I need only my friends and peers,
They make me feel important.
At times I need my family even more
They love me in spite of all.

Most of all I need love, guidance and understanding,
I don't know all the answers.
Be there when I need you to help me when I fail,
I'm only a teen.

Rose Marie Meyer

LOVE CHILD

This poem is dedicated to my children; Jeremy, Rosie, Brandon, and Thomas, for reminding me of lifes true purpose. To Kelly and Lydia, may they all STAY GOLD

There is no love which can compete
With the love so pure from a child
Seldom expecting too much from us
Just listen to them for awhile
For they have yet to learn to be afraid
Of the world in which they live
Thriving on the simple things
Adults are afraid to give
Somewhere in our growing up
We've forgotten how to cry
We spend our lives rushing here and there
Trying to live before we die
We no longer seem to be entranced
By the starred summers sky
We seldom stop and wonder anymore
Just how a bird can fly
We've lost ourselves in our lives

We've become afraid to live
Of all the smiles, hugs and handshakes
We've forgotten how to give
The beauty of living is not forever lost
We have teachers of love abound
The search is not far reaching
God's children are all around

Opal M Wegner

SPRING BEAUTY

To Gustav, my loving husband who has been so supportive

A beautiful sunset sits on the horizon.
Beneath the white fleecy clouds in the sky.
A gentle breeze stirs o're the landscape,
The fingers of spring are shaping the time.

Spring is the gardener for the shrubs and flowers
The johnny-jump-ups, the tulips and the daffodil.
The clouds bring the rain that gives them a drink.
The soil gives the nutrient, the final sequel.

They live for their season, then they are gone . .
Replaced by the roses the asters and such.
But their beauty lives on in our memory.
The fragrance held over by our tender touch.

In a better time and a better place,
All this beauty shared we will recall,
It wasn't man who made this beauty in life.
It was the Great Creator who made it all.

Kimberly R Glass

MY LETTER TO GOD

Today my thoughts turned to you and my tears flowed,
I think of all you've given me and my feet slowed.
A sadness engulfed me as I realized; I never once said "Thank-you"
So many times I've turned my back and said that you were untrue,
I now know it was me; never you.
I took and yet; I complained about all,
Each time you'd be there to pick

me up; when I'd fall.
I thought I was alone; so I tried to be tough,
But you were my tower to lean on when things got rough.
Turning to you now; with my hopes and fears,
I know believing in you will wipe away the tears.
For all that you've given me and all yet to be,
I give my life to you to be set free.

Mary (Kristy) Kristina Scarbrough
MYSTERIOUS WAYS

This poem is dedicated to Tom Atteberry who has showed me all the happiness and pain a true love can bring, but he always taught me to look forward to tomorrow. Thank-you.

Sometimes there's tears
which fall like rain
but then comes happiness
to absorb all the pain
Sometimes there's sorrow
with dreams all erased
but then comes tomorrow
with new dreams to chase
A lot of times there's lots of love
with memories to share
but then one day you're left alone
to find that no one's there
There's love and kindness
from the warmth of a touch
then before you know it
what's left isn't much
Love seems to work
in mysterious ways
but keep in mind
there'll be other days.

Luther Butler
FALL
Harbinger of Spring
Fashion plate with delicate
Blue and White flowers with green leaves
Ringing out that winter is gone with its
Cruel blast of Arctic wind that rules the temperate zone with numbing freeze.
Growth uninterrupted through the Fall and Winter rain
Covered in snow but growing on
Until the warm spring days bring forth
Delicate blue and white flowers,
That burst forth in Springtime songs to tell of all the things that are to be . . .
And of all the things that have been.
Roots nourishing on the decayed bones of buffalo
Growing in land that was trodden on by hooves of Indian ponies.
Surviving through drought, flood, fire . . .
Plants growing from seed lying in the ground,
Unable to grow until a time determined by nature's law,
Bringing it forth to spring out of the soil that shows forth the work of God.
You who can survive the stress of time and bloom with brilliance every spring.
Sends hope that the human race will also survive
Atomic bombs, pestilence and flood

To do the work of the Divine
Who was resurrected at Eastertime.

Margaret E Posson

Margaret E Posson
MR. PRESIDENT

To my loving, caring triplet sister Flora Jeannette Posson

You have been the Moses of the Old Testament leading your people in a new direction—through the uncharted desert of returning the power of government to the people.

You have been the Nehemiah taken by God from a humble beginning and raised to the position of Governor of the State of California and the Presidency of the United States of America.

You have been the Job—with your broken dreams for El Salvador, the satellite in space for the defense of our United States.

You have been the David tuned in Spirit to God's existence, presence, and commandments—facing Goliath (Grenada, Soviet Russia) and conquering.

You have been the Shadrach, Meshach and Abednego in the fiery furnace of life as our President.

You have been both blessed and burdened by our God—filled with wisdom, understanding, knowledge, and faith, working for the good of our country in the face of great opposition.

You were called of God to lead this country and you were obedient to His call. God Bless you, Mr. President.

Rudy V Albright
BAPTIZED

To my only God . . . Jesus . . .

. . . Rising from the water of my "grave" . . .
One step from the "old man," crucified . . .
Washed up on God's shore by baptized wave . . .
While Angels shout where they abide . . .

Walking from the waters of "the dead" . . .
Ascending to "the rock," on which I stand . . .
"Rock of Ages," now in you I'm bred . . .
Rooting, "Root of Jesse", in your hand . . .

Walking in "the way," God's brand-new kid . . .
Stomping out the mud-holes brought to bay . . .
Stumping toes on stones that Satans hid . . .
Black-eyes on the "school-ground" where I pray . . .

Brilliant is "the light" of my inside . . .
Burning out the future . . . of my past . . .
Eating from the table of God's in-tide . . .
Bread upon the waters . . . that I've cast

Marty Morrow
VICTOR
It doesn't matter if your eyes can see, When every vision's one of deceipt
It doesn't matter if your mouth can speak, When it dribbles like a leaky sink
It doesn't matter if your ears can hear, When you listen but just don't care
What matters is what's inside, don't hold it in and force it to hide
Just let your love come out and you'll be the victor of the bout
Then you'll see through different eyes
That the world isn't full of lies
Then you'll hear a different tune
One singing of flowers in June
And then the words will flow from your mouth
A hint of love in every word that comes out
But if your eyes only see hate
Going crossed and you can't get them straight
And when your ears no longer hear
You put words in where the words aren't clear
And all you take right to the heart
Will eat you away and blow you apart
And with the fork of your tongue
You can watch all around you run
Or you can clean out those ears
And hear that all around you care
Wipe the sleep from your eyes
And the darkness will die
It took that mouth quite awhile
But that's a smile

Roger D Priest
TEA & HONEY AFTERNOON
Tea & honey afternoon
October grey & sweet rich color from the trees—

A car sooshing by on the gleaming street
All the better in this dry place to fill up your cup
And say on the phone, "I'd really like to
Come today, but I'm awfully busy and . . ."

To be alone, summer's slow dissolve upon your spoon
Savoring the sips of memory
Some more tart than others
Circling in your quiet hour
& settling in a place of peace—

Gently now, inside you finally come to rest
Enough to feel the shifting light
Easy grey on grey

Time Pours Slowly

Voice inside, patiently silent
Yet finally clear as the click of your cup on the saucer,
Teaching answers that were not fastfood quick
Like computer readouts
But awaited you where hours aren't
Measured by the spoonful, where seeking nothing
All is given
On a tea & honey afternoon.

James M Sellers Jr
INSIDE
I lived in West Texas a hundred and fifty years ago
Wagons passed me by and men were saying Westward Ho.
I've seen cattle drives as they moved so slow
Men used me for shade, resting their weary soul.
You see, I was a Mesquite, my roots ran deep
I survived in a land nobody wanted to keep.
I've seen winter so hard and cold
And summer heat that made records, so I'm told.
But to look at me after I was twisted and ready to decay
As I laid on the land so hard, time moved without delay.
Hope almost gone, then on one spring day
Jimmy Sellers came and my owner gave me away.
He took me home because he could see something in me
He took time to make a bowl, as you can see.
Outside, I was rugged, twisted and had seen my day
But take a good look since you've come Jimmy's way.
He brought out beauty I had inside of me
So I'll retire where Jimmy wants me to be.
I came from God's creation and maturing all through life I've lived
And beauty in this bowl, is all I can give.

Niki Webster
MELINDA

-4 mary, some intimate lines kept always—

Yes, I saw Melinda just the other day.
Her dress was all torn and her hair was so astray.
Why are you looking for her? What has she done now?
If I tell you where she is, would you promise not to scowl?
She went over to that side, the side that needs a prayer.
So many people have gone, but I'll not take you there.
I dare not set foot where only darkness prevails;
'less you tell me if my Lord, He will not fail.
Melinda needed you . . . and you turned your back.
I don't blame her for running;
I don't blame her for that.
It must've been awfully tough for her to do such sin.
Many times she came to me, and asked my Lord to forgive:
'My Heavenly Father, help us to understand
the reasons for us living,
'cause life is not so grand.
Take us a little further
in our search for knowledge within.
Help us to take one day at a time.
We pray to God, Amen.'
Little girl? Little girl, why are you crying, my dear?
I was thinking 'bout Melinda but I'll not take you there.
Melinda needed you, but you . . . you turned your back.
I don't blame her for running . . . no
. . . I don't blame her for that.

Susanne K Johnson
LOOKING OUT

To all the people who know what cabin fever is all about. To my family and to Ira

---

I sit holed up in this little cabin, in the woods.
I watch the snow come down and the sun reflect its shine
Looks so divine Fairies glitter spread atop of the world
I watch through the window at the little Chick-a-dees
Scampering off Erratically
The blue-jays squawk and do their dancing in the trees
Holding their heads high and gracefully
The wolves howl is the lonely cry of winter
The wind seems to sigh at the wolves capture
For the deer fall silently as the snow
I don't know if it's the wind that tells the owl
Or the owl to the wind
Of all the wise and wonders of the land
Occasionally a pair of leaves, captured by a breeze,
Dance along spirited and playfull—yet restless for their journeys end
Back to where they came
A fox chase rabbit game is also played out—
To the foxes delight he wins the game
A high squeal emits from the rabbit
Could it be a squeal of delight also?
For it no longer has to play the game.
And with the long winter will be an occasional thaw
The icicles report themselves throughout this time
The sun will do a dance through them
With reflections of spring to come
I watch intently the life of winter
And wait patiently for the sun to dance
Through the final icicle.

Emilio P Valles

Emilio P Valles
DADDY'S MESSAGE
There is one thing I want you children to know
I love your Mother very much, it continues to grow
This is why you see me hug and kiss her all the time
Mom is for me to have, hold, she is mine
When Mom looks at you, in all that while
Mom's beautiful eyes glitter
She has a sparkling smile
She is the only Mom for all of you that I have only known
Which is why my love for her has grown
Now that all of you have grown and know
something of life
Which is why you should only have one husband or one wife
To have, hold until death do you part
This love should come from deep in your heart

Frances Brown Young
THAT OLD GANG OF MINE
When the Autumn leaves are falling
And the grass is turning brown
From the woods I hear a calling
To my old stamping ground

Down the path where the rain drops glisten
And straight through the barn yard gate
For a whisper from my old gang I'd listen
Oh! I mustn't make them wait

All day in the bright sunny wood dust
The wind with a language of its' own
Has gathered my old gang to join us
With its' low and mellow tone

To each bird I must carry a token
I must nod at each tree and smile
My promise to the squirrels can't be broken
I must make my trip worth while
By the old oak tree we all gathered
First the rabbits the birds and squirrels
Like a bunch of old friends we all chattered
THAT OLD GANG OF MINE

Jennifer A Sansone
FRIENDS
A shoulder to cry on,
An ear to bend,
Money to borrow,
Clothes to lend.
Friday nite movies,
Afternoon walks,
Being together,
Our "private" talks.
Mending our hearts,
Crying those tears,
Planning our futures,
Voicing our fears.
Our memories together,
May they never end,
Always together,
Forever Friends!

James D Pietrocarlo
THE MEANING OF LOVE
That infinite moment of peace and relaxation
I think that is love.

A contact of thought through eyes never disturbed by sound or touch.
I think that is love.

A time of pride never felt before but always wished you had.
I think that is love.

A selfish feeling upon which devotion is number one.
I think that is love.

A feeling of compassion which is felt by one that should be felt by the world.
I think that is love.

A familly united by joy or crisis when all feelings are equal.
I think that is love.

A diseased pain which is cured with no medicine.
I think that is love.

A problem is mine; a problem is yours. Together the problem is ours.
I think that is love.

A feeling of security where one can express himself without the fear of hurting or being hurt.
I think that is love.

Waking up to a new day not regretting yesterday's thoughts, words, or feelings.
I think that is love.

A feeling of togetherness which can never be separated.
That I know is love.

Phyllis A Solheim
ALONE
"What's good about being alone?" I said.
Alone I can use both sides of the bed,
And stay up just reading half of the night . . .
No one will tell me to turn off the light.
And no one will say, "I need the car."
Or, ask who drove it so very far;
Or notice I let the milk turn sour.
Alone I can talk long-distance an hour.
Alone I get up when I want to rise . . .
No talking over; no compromise.
Alone meal-time comes with the hunger feel;
And a hard-boiled egg can be a meal.
AND . . .
No one is here giving incentive to please;
Or—pushing the thermostat down five degrees,
Or turning out lights that burn without need;
OR . . . encouraging me to do a good deed;
Or—seeing my tears!
Alone there's no argument over things that are bought,
And—No sharing of laughter, or a hope, or a thought!
Alone there's no longer voices that boom;
And no one is here messing up the bathroom . . .
Or wanting massages, or buttons sewn.
No one is here. I am alone . . .
Alone—
And, mostly . . . I don't like it!

Carolyn J Lovelace
MEMORIES OF MY GREAT GRANDMOTHER
Looking back when I was small
I can remember my great grandmother ever since I could crawl.
I used to go to her house, she'd meet us at the door,
Like she'd always done many times before.
I can see her smiling face at the door,
She lived in a small house with old squeaky floors.
Everytime I'd go see my great grandmother,
She'd have my favorite; sweet potatoes smothering with butter
As I grew older so did she,
She wasn't in good health like she used to be.
I've done some family research on my great grandmother,
I know there will never be another.
She was a small lady,
Who lived in the woods where her yard was shady.
I remember when vegetables she use to can,
From the harvest my great grandfather raised from the land.
She was born in 1894,
She lived through four major wars.

On May 20, 1979,
We received a phone call, you can imagine what went through my mind.
My mother began to cry,
And so did we all, no eyes were dry.
I didn't want to go see my great grandmother,
Because I knew she was dead and would never recover.

Michele Robertson
WINTER WONDERLAND

Mom: I want to share this special moment with you, and thank you for being my mom. I love you.

Leaves flying all around tumbling, crashing to the ground
A crimson multi-colored whirl from the limbs the wind will hurl
A blanket white of untouched snow upon which the crimson rainbow flows
A crystal glass upon the lake the sun does not attempt to wake
Hiding behind an unending shield the wintery sky does not yield

Through the forest the silence speaks of wonderous wintery mountain peaks
Gazing at the soft, silky white the crimson leaves blow from my sight
My snow covered world falls slowly apart so I must make myself a new start
In the crystal melting streams reality destroys my wonderful dreams
I pick up my life with the new day with the melting winter my past flows away.

Mrs Pat Brantley
PENITENTIARY BLUES

Dedicated to my son Micheal, my brother Joe and all men and women in prisons everywhere.

Here I sit so alone
Wondering why I did wrong
Wishing I was still at home.

Knowing I'll never be free
How I wish I could find a key
So lonely and blue,
Will this always be my doom!

I wanna go home
I wanna be free
Oh! Look at me
Strange faces only I see
Oh God! Please don't forget about me

Friends, I have none
All they did was run
They turned their backs on me
And laughed out loud with glee

The days go by so slow
I say to myself
Why oh why
Must I be the only one to pay the price
To do the time for my crimes

I wait so patiently
For the time to come
When I can finally go home

Was it worth it, would I do it again
Did it mean so much
It did at the time

Drugs, booze, and girls
Were my only friends
My life is ruined
And I'm filled with so much gloom
I know I'm headed for doom
Help me please, I cry
Let me survive for other times

Let me have just one last wish
Let me be free for one more time
Maybe then everyone can forget all of my sins.

Marvin Eugene Couch
LOST!

To the one, I Love

Lost on an island, far out to sea
With only the one I love, with all my heart
To find a treasure, beneath the sand
With jewels and rubys, of untold wealth

Treasures in the chest, studded with emeralds
and rubys without, glistening against
the snow white sandy beach
To run my hands thru the pearls, emeralds
and bars of gold, that is my heart feeling
her love

To listen with the wind, whistling
thru the palms leafy tops, sending
sand into the banks, which each
beach does have only in a different design

To hear the sound of the seas echo
for an eternity, within a shells domain
To watch a piece of driftwood
floating from the sea, all this
is like the innocence of her love

Marjorie Marshall Rowe
THE STRANGER BEHIND THE WINDOW

Snow tumbles,
thunder rumbles,
the Sun shines bright as day.

We watch,
and wait,
as we open up the gate.

"Laugh now!"
you roar,
as you chase them away.

Old age,
comes soon,
I've missed my time to play.

Leonard James Diamond
ABSTRACT ENCOUNTER

On a special morning as the sun went down
On the crowded streets of an empty town
I saw a woman that wasn't there
A beautiful blonde with soft dark hair

And with a voice I could not hear
From far away she called me near
Her eyes she closed to look at me
A mental image I could not see

She gave a touch I could not feel
A soft illusion so very real
Devoid of effort she pulled me down
Her missing passion I now had found

Although confused we both were sure
Without a need we wanted more
We gained a love from love we lost
Though both had paid there was no cost

We shared a feeling though each our own
Her's a desire I have never known
Though yet to meet this girl I know
The time has come for her to show

Louis Salzman
WHEN OUR GREAT GRANDFATHER, THOMAS CANBY

When our Great Grandfather, Thomas Canby, went a courting Sarah Jarvis, he had no other way to go but to put his legs into service.

The Old York Road he gaily strode to where a hickory stood. There he took an Indian Trail o'er 8 miles or more of woods.A sharp-eyed link crouched overhead, a bear sulked nearby, a whirling grouse gave him a start, an eagle screamed on high.

But Thomas had no thought of fear, and soon some curling smoke showed him where the Jarvis cabin stood beneath the spreading oak. Eight miles or more he had come o'er hill and vale but it really seemed like four.

When at his rap the waiting maid threw back the cottage door. And what was done and what was said we do not know—we only guess what most folks can tell.

At nine o'clock he started back, and Sarah, calling Rover, walked with him to the clearing edge, their goodbyes soon were over.

The homeward trip seemed four miles more than going the other way. At last he reached his Uncle's Mill. THE END OF A PERFECT DAY.

Stephen D Palmer
A CHRISTIAN'S ROAD

The road we walk is narrow and winding
With many dangers along the way.
A Christian's road is sometimes binding
For it is all too easy to stray.

The road I mean is walked by few
For many lose the path.
This is the road chosen by you
To escape all evil's wrath.

For most this road is quite confusing
For many lose the way.
Many are fighting the battle and losing.
It's the price of Hell they'll pay.

But for some the path is easy and straight
For Heaven's gates are in sight.
These are the souls blessed by Fate.
They have literally seen the light.

Yes, it's the light of Heaven that they shall see.
An eternity they'll spend in peace.
I pray this is the destiny of you and me
and that our love will never cease.

Veena Pai Desai
TRUE CONFESSIONS

My poem "TRUE CONFESSIONS" is dedicated with fond memories to my wonderful parents, whose great souls rest in peace.

Times were fine, dear father and mother close to me,
They were my two beautiful, twinkling eyes; full of love, life and happiness you see.
Until the gruesome 'Death', blinded me so too sudden,
Now only their sweet memories, do I cherish in overwhelming tears.

So many thoughts still remain in mind to tell,
How very much I loved and admired you, could hardly ever express.
Late though now, but before I die, I say in my rhyme,
'You were the most precious in the world, mom and dad', I always did realise.

Try my best to be mature and face the truth,
And keep myself occupied till the entire day is thru'.
Yet, when the night turns dark, and the world almost asleep,
'Remembrances' of papa and mama, whom I miss so much, makes me weep.

'Time is the best healer', so console the wise,
But death before time, of my beloved ones, seems to me a nightmare.
I seek no power absolutely, no desire for any wealth,
Just that warm touch of unselfish love of my darling parents, I truly confess.

Eileen Tubbs Halstead
PARTURITION

Did you ever hear a day give birth
While the stars shown up above
With the lonely crow of a rooster
Or cry of a single dove?
Did you ever listen for what
Was next to be in that day
And hear the low soft whispers
As the leaves began to sway?
They sweep the last grey vestures
That turn the night to dawn
And the birds sing ha le lau ya
As the infant day is born.

Dorothy Murphy Menna
A MOTHER'S SORROW
Where are you, dear child of mine?
A lonely mother's heart cries out for you
BUT YOU DO NOT HEAR.
Loving thoughts flood this tired, old mind.
Treasured memories are forever with me
BUT YOU DO NOT REMEMBER.
You are gone—though I know not why.
My prayers are all for your return
BUT YOU DO NOT COME.
Child of mine, I wait for you.
I grieve and yearn to hold you close
BUT YOU NO LONGER CARE.

Dorothy Van Dyke Szalai
A FLIGHT

I Dedicate this poem to my Beloved, parents, Roscoe Lee Van Dyke, and Melvina Wolfenbarger Van Dyke

As we lift off the ground, and go
Soaring like a bird, soaring high
Above the clouds of such I've never
Heard.

Oh beauty Grand, and glorious, as we
Fly gently out in space, That we have
Eyes to behold it, is God's Mercy,
And His Grace.

As we look down from up above, we
See how small we be, for we are but
A drop of rain in God's Eternal Sea.

Phyllis Holder
TIME

Dedicated to my children Joy, Mark, James and Chris

Hear the cry of a newborn
Hear the laughter of a six year old
See the smile of a teenager on her first date
The wedding of all time
The eyes of wonder at her first child as he is laid in her arms
See the lines in her face as the years slip away, wondering where
they went
Hear the silence all around, for she is alone now
The gray has covered her head, her mind is that of a six year old
Now her rocking chair is quiet.
Time is no more.

Nancy Pettit Delloma
HEAVENS GAIN

This is dedicated to my mother, Margaret Quintana Pettit, who was my anchor.

What's it like in heaven?
Are all who loved you there?
Did open arms embrace you,
and welcome you with care?

Did grandma come to meet you?
Her eyes shining with love.
Did angels gently guide you,
to heaven up above?

And did she reach to touch you?
And smile with happiness?
An heavens gate swung open,
to meet the very best?

Did Jesus come to see you?
Your crown held in his hand?
To welcome you from our world,
into the promised land?

And how is it in our world?
It's empty, sad, and blue.
We lost our "special angel."
Precious mother . . . you.

So Jesus, treat her gently,
let all who love her see.
and when you have the time Lord,
please save a place for me.

Mary Jane Ledford
DANDELION
Dandelion, gives silent call
This is where man has walked
It will not grow where man has not been
Living proof it's not the end.

Susan F Gilkerson
TAX FREE
Stroll thru this desert treasure house
Unlocked by keys of Spring,
On floral carpets, multihued,
The envy of Persian king.
Vast canvasses here, by Nature's hand
Unequalled where ere you roam.
See, high above, of deepest blue,
Arches a sapphire dome,
And sunset hills, pale amythest,
Beyond the wind-etched dune.
All riches, as night's curtain falls.
Are silvered by the moon.
Exotic, free of chemists' art
Faint perfume fills the air
As each tiny desert floweret
Now wafts it's perfume rare.

Miss Ruth Knickerbocker

Miss Ruth Knickerbocker
MY LOG CABIN HOME UP IN MAINE
I've got on an old Derby Hat and a Worn Out Suit—
With a Napsack over my Back—
With Just Fifty Cents and one Cigarette-
I'm Tired Of Roaming around—
I've traveled the Roads From Maine to New York—
Over Valleys and Mountain Streams—
But There is One Place I'll Never Forget—
It's My Log Cabin Home Up In Maine—
It's Just A Little Log House By An Old Country Church—
With a Gold Cross Over The Door—
And a Cobble Stone Walk—That Leads right to the Gate.
Oh How I Wish I was Home.
I Know That My Mother Is Waiting For Me—
In An Old Rocking Chair By The Door—With a Bible In Hand.
I know That She is Praying For Me—
That I will be Home by tonight.
I Miss Her Home Cooking—My Soft Feather Bed—
And My Old Hound Dog Named Mike.
With GOD's Helping Hand I'll be There By Tonight
And I Will Never Roam Anymore.

Rita Dingman
ROBIN REDBREAST
Oh little Robin Redbreast
what made you come so soon?
The snow is gently falling
as I listen to your tune.
It's cold, little Redbreast,
you should have a hat and shoes,
and maybe a knitted vest
or a jacket if you choose.
They say you bring us spring,
but I wonder what you'd say
now that it's so bitter cold
and you've come a long, long way.
I wish that I could help
to warm your freezing feet,
would you come into my parlor
and enjoy my fires heat?
I'll put out seeds and suet
and maybe some water too,
I guess that's about all
that I can do for you.

Roy L Sargent
THE DAY AFTER THE END
The sun rose on a darkened world,
Dead, for untold years.
Gone, were the lights, the glamour,
Gone, were sorrows, and tears.

Lost to infinity, lost in time,
The ruptured cries of "doomsday,"
Re-echoed thru limitless space—
Barren the mountains, black the bay.

A mist hung o'er a valley deep,
A hecatomb of bones,
Ghastly they lay—as spectres,
Landed, and bleached as stones.

Winds swirled 'round in mourning,
The silence was the dirge.
A dark clouds ominous presence
Felt not, any earthly surge.

A sun-ray fell on a shattered cross—
A symbol once held dear.
But no eyes beheld the enduring spot,
Of a lonely, foresaken tear.

Donald Warr Jr
LOST LOVE

To Fluffy, Poncho, Hot Dog, Ginger, Cookie, Ramel, Scamper, Tippy, Major, Flash, and all the other dogs who have touched and enriched my life.

It has been seven long years since you passed away,
But I still think of you most every day.
Your last days on earth were filled with such pain,
I know that someday I will see you again.

You were a beautiful blonde with big brown eyes,
Now you look down on me from high in the skies.
You gave so much love without judgement or fear,
I wish very much that you were still near.

Since you have been gone life has been very rough,
I miss you so much, my old dog, Fluff.

Dee Ross Scroggin
ROSE SO RED
There is that last dimension,
A peaceful seventh place,
Where warring songs for power bands,
It's music not embrace,
Where brooms of wind are sweeping,
Beyond its fiery garden wall,
And weeding guards with lovely face,
Blow hard their clarion call,
And the key, a combination,
Long-stemmed red rose, blood-red,
Grows not for eyes that never wept,
For hearts that never bled.
It soon can only open past
Sixth corridor of time,
For the tender soul as a little child,
And love, the rose's sign.
That harbor ground with perfumed shade,
Beckons over the waves of strife,
Plant now, today, your rose so red,
For the warning thorns of life.

Leo J Norris

Leo J Norris
APOLLO

To all who have known me especially my departed brothers Jimmy, Otis, Clarence & Dee

A chill flows all through me
My lips chap

My heart drops to the floor
Things I hadn't though
My life flashes before
I hear mother scolding
Finish your supper

My hands are clammy
The heat is intolerable
I feel a wetiness
Without a warning
Bright flash
Red, blue, green white
Silence . . .
I must be asleep? ? ?

Carmen Mills
NO BEAUTY
There is no beauty,
For I cannot see.
Things once precious,
Mean nothing to me.

I hear no love songs
Like "Never Going To Let You Go."
The words I understand,
It's the meaning I don't know.

I see no sunshine,
My days are full of rain.
I see no happiness,
All I see is pain.

Lee Ann Garrison Carstens
MY 2 MILE

This poem is dedicated to Nancy Deganis for giving me the inspiration to write "MY 2 MILE."

My first lap was really shakey, I didn't know what to do.
My second lap was devasting, I knew what was happening and I couldn't keep the pace.
My third lap I thought I'd never make it, I wanted to give up!
My fourth lap I felt better. I had aged and was half way there, I could see freedom.
My fifth lap I had to make a choice, I needed to pass so I decided on help.
My sixth lap was the hardest, I needed to accept that what-ever decision I would make would always be mine.
My seventh lap and I am in the pack. My friends are all cheering me on and with their help I was able to go on.
My eighth lap I survived all the gruel punishment and beat it!
No matter how much time it took or what place—I WON!!

Ann Coddinton
A SINGLE TEARDROP
Just a single teardrop
No utterance was heard
He stood and took our punishment
Too terrible for words
And on that day He freed us
He took our stripes instead
The guilt of all us sinners
Was placed upon His head.

So as we stop to ponder
The price He paid that day
I hope we all appreciate
That price we couldn't pay
Yes, just a single teardrop
That no one else could see
Was shed by my sweet Savior
The day He died for me.

Dennis Walter Smiley
OUT OF THIS WORLD

To my loving kid—Denise Jessica Smiley-Gonnelli

Some where out there above the clouds in eternity
I was on my way to see the Lord to set me free
My soul began to rise—as an ash
My mind was so at ease
Cause I was ris'n somewhere
OUT OF THIS WORLD
Wars were going on back home
Making angry eyes at me
SMOKE was on the surface below
Flames were in the air
THE WIND was blowing through my ears
My eyes began to stare—I rose—higher—
Higher higher OUT OF THIS WORLD

Taffy Sue Gonzalez
LIQUID DIAMONDS
Liquid diamonds
On my face
Golden memories
Of a better place
Opals in skies
Of sapphire blue
Silver moon shining
Of me and you
Amethyst mornings
And ruby nights
Onyx shades
Amber brights
Emerald eyes
Without love's grace
Put liquid diamonds
On my face

Doris Irene Singer-Hatcher
BUTTERFLY DREAM

Those who have inspired me, know it. So don't just dream your dreams, live them.

I looked away & while I was dreaming
Asleep in mindless days of toil
You ugly laughing bitch, called time
Stole my youth away
I curse you for leaving this body
Which is not mine
For leaving need which were never met
You sucked out my joy & energy
And left me wasted empty breasts
I damn you for your silent laughter
At your cruel senseless joke
Inside me the stillness rages
Winter has just begun
But I laugh last you hag
The butterfly sheds its cacoon
Inspiration is forever young

Grace Rhyne Clay
CAROLINE SNOWFALL

To each member of my wonderful family

Oh winter, how bleak was your night
Till storm clouds, hovering high,
Sent fluffy little gems of white
To dress the earth with silent might,
Then bare a moon-lit sky.

Wintry-White gems like velvet lay
High-heaped o'er nature's frame.
Enhancing sun at break of day
Fashioned a fairy-land, bright, gay
To play a child-like game.

Cold winds joined the play and called, "Dear
Snowflakes, come, there's a fair
For riding, gliding, sliding near
The tree-top swings where beams appear
To claim their jewels, rare."

A Master's touch with magic gleam
Sent whirling through the air
The snowflake gems to meet their beams,
To flit and sway o'er meadow, stream,
O'er hill and thoroughfare.

Then thousands more joined in the fun
Like feather-down at play
But lingered not till day was done
For beams waxed warm with steadfast sun
And kissed the gems away.

David E Walker
HOW WOULD YOU KNOW
How would you know that I love you
If I never told you?
You could spend your life looking
For someone to hold you.
Your search might end
If I could ever tell you.
That I love you.
So many times have come and gone,
Opportunities have slipped away
To tell you that I love you.
But my heart's low murmur
And steady beat
Pursuaded me to remain. . .
In silence.

Andrew R Conicello
PASSAGE'S OF TIME
A lifetime's but an hour in the passage's of time.
Let me not waste a minute make each precious second chime.
With love for every person that I meet along the way.
A gentle smile for everyone's the way to start each day.
Let me open up my heart and lift my eyes to God above.
Let me bring joy to each and everyone and spread his words of love.
When my hour is over and I'm in eternal rest.
Don't mourn too much but think instead I did my very best.

Sandy
DREAM LOVE

For Van

Others
A dream in my reality;
He
The realization of my dreams.

Paul L Hill
RED CANDLES

To all those who have lived, loved, lost and lived.

The world turns, the candle burns.
And a fool would seek romance.
How shall I tell, within it's brief flickering spell,
Falls the limits of his chance.
The red flame flows, the red fluid flows.

His hour has now begun.
Let him love and smile, if but for a while.
Too soon the candle's life is done.
And tomorrow's stranger visiting there,
Will see not joy, nor hear despair.
But a pool of red, alone will tell.
Of the tragic end, to the candle' spell.

Paul W Crumes
THE QUAKE

This poem is dedicated to Blair Elizabeth Burke, my loving granddaughter

---

The sun was peeking over a row of trees, the air
was still, no morning breeze.
My mind was on fishing before the day turned hot,

I hurried to the lake to my favorite spot.
I heard a rumble as I got to the lake, the
water started to ripple and the trees started to
shake
I knew right away there goes my day, as
the ground started to tremble and then to shake,
I knew right away it was a darn earthquake.

Debra S Johnson
FARM NO MORE

I dedicate this poem to my English Teacher, Mrs. Mary Finley, for all the help she has given me on my writings.

He walks the land
He owns no more,
Visualizing the crops
He proudly grew before.

His Grandpa and his Dad,
In their graves have turned around.
They have no more tears to cry for him,
for the tears have swelled the ground.

He ponders the days
When you were proud to farm land.
And if you ever got into trouble,
you'd receive a helping hand.

Now the bank has foreclosed;
This fate he never knew.
With dead animals and no money,
what's the farmer left to do?

He's like many other farmers
In debt and without land,
Who have lost it all and have nothing left.
How much more can he withstand?

He isn't asking for your tears,
nor pity at his door.
But who will feed you when he's gone
and leave you food no more?

Terrence McCormack
FRIENDS

To Mom & Dad, Sandy, Tom, & Janet for being my best friends

Thinking of people, eyes blinking
A light goes on, my mind starts thinking
Of what's ahead, and what's behind
Of things I'll leave, and things I'll find.

I hope my friendships last forever
The ties that bind, I never will sever
Though the life I lead, must be my own
I'll try to live the life I've known.

Though I may travel, I'll always return
With new found friendships, stories I've learned
And looking back, I say Amen
All the people I've met, I consider my friends.

Bonnie L Long
CHRISTMAS SEASON

This poem is dedicated to my mother who we miss dearly

I wish you were here this Christmas season
Don't ask me why I have many a reason.
You're needed, you're loved, and hardly blue
You're kind and considerate to name a few.
Give me strength that's all I ask
Help me make this season pass.
I'll try to be happy not blue
But my thoughts somehow always arrive at you.
My heart aches often at its own pace
To hear your voice, and see your face.
You're special to me in many ways
Lord knows there could never be too many days.
We had our fun and arguments too
But I was me and you were you.
Forgive me for all that I've done wrong
Give me strength and make me strong.
Because you see this special season
Makes me sad for many a reason.

Imogene H Meadows
A FRIEND

We're traveling down the road of life
Many our heartaches, troubles and strife.
There are good days, there are bad
There are happy ones and some are sad.
As you pass a friend along the way
Do some nice thing to brighten his day,
It may be a pleasant smile or a good word
Maybe something encouraging you've heard.
But, be sure and remember—the bad tears down
And may cause someone to fall to the ground.
We must ever keep lifting up our brother
And love and do good to one another.
We all must travel down this road
What a blessing for all, when we share his load.
Our own lives are touched, when we lift them up
And by the self same flow—fills our cup.
And—to do good there is no end,
When we stop by the road 'to help a Friend'.

Kathy Horan
JENNY

You were there when
I needed you
And I was there when
you needed me.
But it seems that I
was selfish in a way
Because you needed me
more that I needed you
You were always strong
even in moments of pain
Even to the end
Oh, Jenny
How have I missed you
but I know now
You're not gone for good
you're there up
In heaven keeping
an eye on me
Our need for each other
never was gone
Because I know you
will always be
Watching me until the end.

Patti Bell Hudnall
DREAMS

To Robert Schwarz, who told me to hang onto your dreams; for dreams do come true.

Dream on little dream girl for dreams do come true,
Be patient as you wait and don't look so blue!
Someday your dream will come to life,
So hold onto your dream with all your might!
Life's long road is filled with turmoil and pain,
Yet don't give up, for you have a dream to gain!
Yes, you fit into God's eternal plan,
So grasp hold tight, hang onto his hand!
Patience is all God asks for your dream,
Yet time rushes by, too fast it all seems.
Believe in God with your heart and your soul,
And soon your dream shall start to unfold!

Charles A Stratton III
THE EPICURE

The essence of Solitude
is most exquisite
when tasted as an aperitif
to Friendship
or when cleansing the palate
of Companionship.

Henry P Madera III
A HUGGER'S DILEMMA

To all the "huggers" worldwide who participate in the Special Olympics and especially to all those little people who make these Olympics so special.

The sky over my head is pretty and blue,
But what is sky and what is blue?
The ground I walk on is dark and brown,
I know what's dark but what is brown?

My mommy's flowers smell real good
But tell me, are flowers pretty things?
My clothes feel good, all snug and warm
I wonder, do all my friends dress like me?

Mommy and Daddy are pretty I know.
And they tell me I'm a cute little boy,
I'm very happy; only I wish I could be
Like all my friends . . . I wish I could see.

My mommy told me that when I was born
God gave me eyes but forgot to turn them on.
I'm not mad cause I know He was busy
And a little thing like me was easy to forget.

Daddy says that if I'm very good
And say my prayers each night before bed,
That he and mommy will try and see
If God will turn my eyes on for me.

Trish Clarke
DO

"Do" is dedicated to my daughter Terri Smith, who has a lot of living to do still. May she always be happy.

A beautiful day to bum and play.
Get mischevious and mysterious; let nothing in your way.
Romp in the sunshine, play in the flowers.
Do tell the weatherman "Let's have no showers."

Be energetic, go find a hill.
Do anything fun. That's your will.
Climb a high tree, see miles and miles.
Take all your friends and everyone smile.

Enjoy life, you only live once.
Don't be a grump or a dumpy dunce.
Take all you can and give a lot.
That's the secret of happiness many people know not.

The world is yours—God's gift to you.
Enjoy greatly everything you see and do.
Always be happy, don't ever be down.
Bring happiness to everyone.
Rejoice the world around.

Nancy M Borghoff
A BOOK BY ANY OTHER NAME

I dedicate this poem to my Mother

Ah! A Book
For which I'd search every cranny and nook
To have in my possession
My fondest obsession
A first edition
Of all the great thoughts enclosed in a book.

Countries I've journeyed
Mysteries unraveled
Philosophies pondered
Psyches dissected
Pages upon pages of underlined words,
Of captured thoughts, profound nouns and verbs.

My books of which I hold most sacred
When borrowed from me till time outdated
I keep a watchful, wary look
And check the conditions of my returned lent book
There comes a time to meet the all knowing
But if I can't take my books then I'm not going!

Wanda L Day
OUR ETERNAL GIFT

The Eastern Star was shining
bright and lighted up the land,
It was a very special night with a
lovely birth near at hand.

As Mary and Joseph made their
way to the stable that stood
nearby. The Mother Mary softly
said, "The time is quickly
drawing nigh.

The animals stood quietly aside as
if awaiting this special birth
Of the one that would bring
changes to everyone on earth.

The baby Jesus soon was born and
gave his first soft cry.
Tears of joy filled Mary's heart as
Joseph stood proudly by.

We thank God for that special time
when Jesus Christ was born.
He came and taught us many
things as our life he does adorn.

He taught us we should never fear
the things that come our way.
He will always give us strength to
meet and conquer every day.

We need not ever be afraid of what
we face in life,
We only need to keep our faith to
overcome each strife.

The birth that came so long ago
was a blessing to us all.
Again we give our thanks to God
for Jesus Christ who stood so tall.

He was a very special man as he
taught, and healed and led
The many who choose to follow
him and live by the words he
said.

So at this very special time, let's
remember that wonderful
birth
And cherish the many blessings he
has given us on earth.

Beth Wentz
EVERYWHERE

Somewhere a bird sings
The song flutters in the air.
Somewhere a butterfly spreads
Its wings.
And she can fly anywhere.

Somewhere a baby cries.
The mother hushes him softly.

Somewhere an eagle flies.
And lifts his head loftily.

Somewhere I sit and think.
My thoughts fill the land.
They're too large to put in
Ink.
They're small enough to fill
My hand.

Eric Lord
HEART OF CLAY

Life to grasp,
A love to hold.
My arms won't reach,
Though not so old.

Her smiling face,
Her stories untold,
My hands won't touch,
Grown stiff with cold.

The fears, they grab,
They hush, they fray,
So deep inside,
This Heart of Clay.

The wind, it scatters,
The words I say,
None shall hear,
My Heart of Clay.

A gift some have,
Their smile, their joy,
Life's time and light.
Are their only toy.

I envy them so,
Their step, their flame,
This Heart of Clay
Often slumps in shame.

Yet as I write,
My spark endures,
It leaps to burn,
My crippling fears.

I watch her smile,
It moves the spark,
The heat and light,
They thrill my heart.

I am quite young.
As I walk this path.
The waste, the loss,
Arouse my wrath.

This struggle: Life,
From God it is sent,
From fear and sloth.
It must be rent.

Though I often cringe or ask for
more, my path is blessed and
well-lit by the light of your smile
and the forgiving and wondrous
hand of God.

Susan Crowther-Bruchey
CHILDHOOD MEMORIES

In loving memory of Helena Bright and Joseph A. Long. Time passes and lives change, but the memories I hold dear will always remain.

Sometime ago, I remember a
dark-haired little girl
watching Grandpa silently
smoking his pipe.
"Will you do smoke rings?" She
asks.
And giggling, she catches them on
her finger, then watches
as they slowly fade away.
Later, as Grandpa comes up from
the basement, he carries a
can of multi-colored marbles.
He's had them many years, but he
still remembers,
So he shows her how to shoot
them, naming special ones as
they
go along.
Then the little girl grows tired, so
she says goodnight to
Grandpa as he settles down to rest
on the couch.
The little girl knows in the morning
there will be pancakes
with lots of butter, syrup and
jelly,
So as she drifts off to sleep, she
hopes morning will
come soon.
Yes, I remember this little girl
because she was me.
I'm no longer the curious
youngster I used to be,
and sometimes I'm too busy with
dates and homework to go
and see Grandpa,
But I hope he knows I think about
him a lot.
Maybe the next time I see him, I'll
ask if he still has
those marbles.
I'll tell him I love him and give him
a big kiss "just because,"
And I'll tell him I do remember all
the beautiful things
we did—
Because like to that little girl I used
to be,
my Grandpa is still very special to
me.

Shirley Y Spivey
AFTERTHOUGHTS

'Twas the week after Christmas,
everything was quiet.
The boys had gone duck hunting I
was back on my diet.
Jim had gone back to work—Kim
was riding her bike,
Santa had brought her the one he
thought she would like.
The tree looked so lonely and bare
underneath,
On our front door hung our
beautiful wreath.
I thought to myself how quickly it
all passed,
Our time with the married kids
went ever so fast.
Everything was so lively and
cheerful and gay,
It nearly broke my heart when they
all drove away.
As I sat in my chair and looked
across at the wall,
I saw a picture of Jesus, it was ever
so small,
The picture made me thank God
for my family and health,
And He seemed to say "Don't pity
yourself."
For I'm with you always I'll never
leave,
I'll stay forever so don't ever grieve"
This is what matters more than
anything else
The love in our hearts and our
God-given health.
And our families and loved ones
being together,
To honor His birthday and
someday forever
To go live with him where we'll
never be parted
Thank God for Christmas for that's
where it all started.

Vivienne Holmes
A GIVING HEART

To my mother for her inspiration.

I lent my hand to a passing, old
man. He took only the fingers
and left the palm. I lent my ear
to help a girl hear.
She took only the lobe to give to
her mom.
I lent my eyes to a priest in a
church because he could not see,
and I lent my tongue to a mute
in a park so he could
recite poetry.
I traveled around minus these
things that I had loaned to those
in need; and I saw so much and
heard what there was,
for it was my heart indeed!
I lent my heart to one who could
not love, and it was returned
all bruised. I healed my heart
and returned to my home
to see how my things had been
used.

The fingers I had lent the man were
worn down to the bone, but
pretty rings were on each one as
they were connected to
my palm.
The little girl returned my lobe,
and much to my dismay, a
beautiful earring hung to the
floor, and its look was
of parquet.
I went to the priest to regain my
sight, and the original
glasses were missing. He gave
me contacts with a
perfect fit, so I saw with no
misgiving.
My tongue had grown to twice its
size and looked like a big
wing. "This muscle is too long,"
I said. "But wait!
I now can sing!"
The things I had returned to me
worked better than before.
I pawned the earring and the
rings, and then had ten
times more!

Kelli A Driggers
NEVER STOP LOVING YOU

This poem is dedicated to my family and especially to my husband, Ron, whom I love with all my heart.

From far away I can see.
The picture looks so clear to me.
It's vantage point so few can find,
I'm serene knowing your love is
mine.

Patience holds the golden key.
Your love is my only guarantee.
Our destiny to make it through
the night.
Dreaming of our love that's
perfectly right.

Through our tears and through our pain.
Love was built to stand the strain.
Though better times I can recall.
Our love still shines through it all.

When our feelings were hurt and our dreams were shattered,
Being with you is all that matters.
Faith in love will pull us through,
I'll never stop loving you.

Carol Armour
A MOTHER'S PRAYER

I dedicate this poem to my beautiful children, James and Lisa Armour. I am very honored to be your mom!

Lord, you gave us the sun to make the day bright
And you gave us the moon for a shimmering night
But there's a special light that outshines both of these,
It's the life of a child that you've given to me.
When you created a child you saw it was good
So you filled the world up and made neighborhoods
That would constantly glow for thousands of miles
You gave them big hearts and beautiful smiles.
Thanks for sending them, Lord.
They are a guiding light
For now my world's a brighter place
All because of a child's life.

Mary F Dugger Thomas
SECOND MARRIAGE

To my children with love, Duane, Tim, Judy, Marty and Michelle

---

if ever again, i'm married to be
it will have to be someone
who will share life with me
not just the bed, but other things too
and every once in a while
will say i love you
who will sit down beside me
and have a long talk
and every once in a while, take me for a walk
we will look at the flowers
and listen to the rain
and comfort each other, when we are in pain
for life goes by swiftly
and needs to be shared
it would be nice to have someone
that you knew really cared

John William Dobson
NUTTY BUDDY
I have a dog whose name is "Buddy."
He is big and black
And acts real nutty.
That is why I call him
My nutty Buddy.

Sandra L Covill
PLAYER SAX
As the Player Sax wails,
I drink in the blues
And slowly become intoxicated
By the contents.
In an abstract state,
I follow the primary colors
As they dance with lines and shapes.
They take me down.

Free-falling through the flow
Of bare-boned sounds
And blinking lights, my mind
Expands into geometric form.

The colors twirl me around
Laughing, as I travel
Faster-and-faster until I am
Surrounded by lightheaded circles.

I float among champagne bubbles
Feeling content as they gently
Lift me up toward the surface.
One-by-one they pop.

My ears are refreshed
From the silence, then shattered
By deafening applause.
The Jazz Man winks at me.

Ronald Scott Sr

Ronald Scott Sr
SYSTEMS
A system of Payment must be in place
Before a man can move forward one space.
A debt of obligation must be made
Before tomorrow's bills can be paid.
A thought of understanding must be exchanged
Before you can build anything.
So let us start with this simple thought
Can love, peace, and justice be bought.

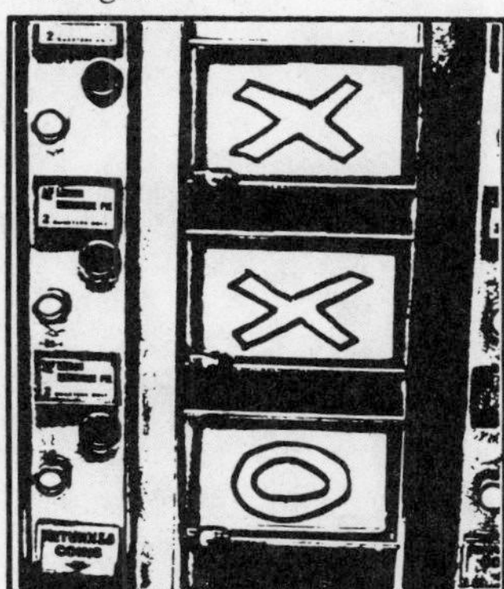

And if they can what price will you pay my friend?
Has life ever seemed to let you down?
How many smiles have turned to frowns?
Tell me the times you have stood in line.
Then when it's your turn you found you were in the wrong line.
Now smile a little to yourself
I want to tell you something else.
There is a system that is used each and every day
It says a system must be in place
Before you can move forward one space.

Randal R Voss
THE MAGIC WORD

To Norma Lee, You'll always have a special place in my heart.

There is one word,
That we all have heard.
It comes not from Earth,
For all it is worth.
It's a valuable thing,
For friendship it will bring.
It could stop all the wars,
And reach incredible scores.
All the people should learn,
With this one word they can earn,
An intelligent race,
And receive through God's grace,
A very good place,
In the history of man.
And I think that we can!
Just think what can be made,
Through kindness you'll be paid.
Time can go by,
In the wink of an eye,
But this word, it won't go,
At least that much I know.
This one word is love,
From heaven above.

Ron Munday
A HIGH JUMPER
Just how high can man soar skyward? Seven,
eight, nine feet, he only has but two legs, two feet.
Only a few can meet such a feat.
What makes this mortal man fly so high?

It may be something like a fire deep inside;
that burning desire, it may be something like a God
way up high. Oh God, help me fly so high.

I watch this man with style, ease, and grace.
If only I had but one of these traits.
He flies like a bird and bends like a snake,
till over the bar; and back to a soft place.

I've tried so hard to jump so high and
land so light.
If only I could jump and soar so high, like
those other mortal men who step so high.

To go so high and float so free, if only it
were me. Up, up over that reachless bar, just once
I ask of me. You can do it just once I say,
just try and think that way.

Mortal men are not equal in terms of skill,
but to jump so high is a God given will.

Darleen F Lasiter
THE TOY

To Loyd Wimberly—For his inspiration and helping to repair the broken and shattered toy.

As you pressed your face upon the store window,
looking inside you saw "THE TOY."
If only you could have that one special one,
you'd take care of it forever.
Yes, your wish came true. It was yours,
how proud you were.
"Look at my new toy," you bragged to all
your friends.
You took your toy everywhere.
It was bright
and new.
You were careful not to let anyone touch or
hold, just admire your new toy.
Time went by as it always does,
The toy
started to lose its brightness and was slowly laid aside.
Every once in awhile you'd reach for it when
something else would catch your eye.
Days passed, a month, a year went by. Now "THE TOY"
was faded, dusty and torn inside.
When one day you noticed this dust ladened toy
lying on a shelf. As you reached to touch it
crumbled in your hand.
How could this be? Time had slipped by and your
favorite toy had become shattered and yours no more.
No! this just couldn't be. This was your favorite
toy. You had loved it best of all, and it now lay
crumbled in your hand, a tarnished, broken object.
A toy of love no more.

Janet Bancroft
SAINTED SISTER

In loving memory of Beverly Bragg, one great American.

We talked, we laughed, we sometimes cried,
On Thanksgiving Day, my sainted friend died.
A friend who shared each sacred trust,
So kind with deed, so truly just.
Life's precious gift of valued time,
God gave to me then said, "She's mine."
He raised the meek for all to see,
Then said, "Take heart, she'll be with me."
As Saints deserve, Lord knows it's true,
When friends unite from Heaven's view.

Connie Graham
GREAT GRANDMA'S ATTIC TREASURES

Dedicated to the memory of Great Grandma Nina Graham where all the attic treasures were

---

Everyone was quiet as a mouse,
We were on our way to great grandma's house.

Which meant treasures to be found galore,
We could not wait to get through her door.

She always made cookies and such a fuss,
Her treasured attic awaited us.
"Let's go upstairs," we heard her say,
"Look in the attic for pleasures and treasures today."

To walk through that magical door,
Probing, looking on objects we did adore.
Transformed to days gone by,
There lay great grandpa's old hat and tie.

Memories of yesterday, treasures for tomorrow,
Filled my heart with wonder, yet sorrow.
For here lay good times and bad,
Of treasures to be happy, also to be sad.

Each little trinket no matter how small,
Brought a story from great grandma about it all.
Her eyes were like a rainbow of colors you see,
Of times gone by and how it used to be.

Events when she was very young.
Of hills she had climbed, of songs she had sung.
Oh the treasures we could see . . .
Great grandma's attic was the place to be!

David D Rymer
TOO BUSY

Some call him "reverend" while others call him "preach,"
but while he ministered to others, his own he could not
reach; he worked, he labored, he counted not the cost, but
while he preached to others his own soon suffered loss.

He was always faithful, he worked from dawn till evening
sun, but in his zeal for Jesus, his family was not one; he
was busy preaching and meeting with the board, but in his
busy schedule his family was ignored.

One day as he was praying the Lord said, "Son, don't you
see, your ministering is not as important as your family is

to me;" his wife was O so lonely tho busy as could be, she
spent too much time by herself . . . what a tragedy.

It's wonderful to serve the Lord there is so much to do,
but what your family wants and needs the most is to be a
part of you; so hold them close and hold them near keep them
from all harms, the security they need and want the most is
found within your arms.

It's always needful to serve the Lord to spend much time
in prayer; and don't forget your family your life with them to share.

Carol A Lyle
MOTHER

To the greatest Mother, Roberta L. Van Lew, that had ever lived. We shall miss your love and Christian understanding.

A woman who didn't mind the dirty diapers.
A woman who didn't mind the fishing worms in the boys' pockets.
A woman who didn't mind the girls trying out her makeup.
A woman who kept house, washed clothes, cooked for a tribe.
This woman didn't mind.
A woman who was glad to make homemade food.
A woman who was glad to wipe away the tears.
A woman who was glad to sew for her children.
A woman whose heart was full of love and it never ran dry.
This woman was glad to be called, "Our Mother!"
God Bless You Mom!
Your thirteen kids

Alex McCort
HALF A WORLD AWAY

Hello again! Do you remember me?
Am I a dream or just a memory?
Girl, it's been so long, so much time has passed
You're half a world away and still my love lasts.
When I close my eyes I can see your face
Then I look around it's only empty space.
I only wonder if you feel the same,
Am I real, or am I just a name?
When you dream am I ever there
To kiss you and brush your hair?
When you close your eyes, do you feel my touch,
Are you in my arms again, do I mean so much?
I hate to bring up the things I'm thinking of,
Every time I think of us, all I think is love.
You're so far away, and we're so far apart
Still you're ever closer in my broken heart.
Yet we'll meet again, and then say hello
How long can we last? We may never know.
My arms reach for you, hold onto my hand
Half a world away, am I still your man?
So close your eyes, and fall asleep
Maybe in your dreams is where you'll keep
Memories of days gone past
Of a lover whose love shall forever last.

Kathleen Booker Webb
THE STATUE OF LIBERTY

To my great-grandson, Donald Brannon Sharp, Jr.

The Statue of Liberty had a birthday party on the Fourth of July,
an extravanganza staged on land, sea and sky.
She was all decked out anew for her one hundredth birthday
and it was celebrated in the most spectacular way!
Visitors arrived from around the world
to pay homage to this famous, man-made girl,
Who for one hundred years has stood on the American shore
to welcome the homeless and open the door
To the Land of the Free and the Home of the Brave
where the Star Spangled Banner so proudly waves.
There was singing and dancing, orchestras and bands played,
notables were present and eloquent speeches were made.
Airplanes flew over head to salute her from the sky,
On the waters, a multitude of ships sailed slowly by.
From Liberty Island, the President lit the flame she holds in her hand,
the symbol of welcome to strangers arriving from foreign land.
Fireworks bursting all around her was a magnificent sight,
a perfect finale for this Fourth of July night!
It was an event to be remembered, a chapter for U.S. History
the mighty salute honoring
THE STATUE OF LIBERTY!

Billy Harmon

Billy Harmon
SOME DAYS

To Joan, my loving wife; to my sons Danny (wife—Lindy), Eugene (deceased), Ricky (wife - Fran), David (wife—Lisa), Steve and Jimmy; and to all my grandchildren.

Some days you say just how much you love me
Some days you say nothing at all
Some way I try and I seem to get by
Knowing your love's waiting some days just down the hall.

Some days you stay to love me through the night
Some days you make me climb the walls
I love you so and I just can't let go
Knowing your love's waiting some days just down the hall.

Some days I feel I'd just die without you
Some days I live just for your call
You know me well and you know how I fell
Hard for your love waiting some days just down the hall.

But most of all I find myself crying
Trying to believe that someday you'll take me with all honesty
So I keep holding on, hoping to be the only one
You'll love someday in your small room just down the hall.

Helen Bole
OUR SEWING TEACHER

She's cute as a "button," and neat as a "pin."
Straight as a "tape measure"—and just as "trim."
Her directions for sewing and patience to try us,
Taught us some "short cuts"—"Time"—on the "bias."

For twenty weeks we "staylined" and "notched."
Ripped and sewed and made over a lot;
Learned about "darts" and the "grain of the cloth."
Made our clothes "so they would look bought."

And now that you've chosen a "life like pattern,"
"Matches" like yours don't "just happen."
So the best of good luck to you and Barney,
Here's something to prove this is not just blarney.

Tracey L Dalton
I WILL ALWAYS LOVE YOU

Dedicated to Larry, who gave meaning to my life by showing me what love really is.

Most people go through life alone;
True love to them will never be known.
Against the odds some of us get the chance;
I got mine because of a silly dance.

I was told: "No committment just one meaningless date;
A few laughs and a lot of fun will be great."
Well as we both know the joke was on me;
Things didn't turn out as expected, you see.

I had gotten used to your joking yet gentle way;

But as we had planned, you left one day.
You told me to find another and forget about you;
But I was too attached; there was nothing I could do.

I stayed around for the rough and bumpy ride;
I always knew that luck would never be on our side.
We gave calling and writing a try;
We hoped that our romance would never die.

To our surprise the miles became too much;
The longer you were away the more I missed your touch.
I'll let you go for now, with love and a prayer;
If you ever need me, you know I'll be there.

Maybe over the course of the years;
I'll be able to forget my tears.
But for now I must let you go.
I WILL ALWAYS LOVE YOU; that much I know.

Robert Allomong
IMAGINE

To Bud Satterfield

Imagine a man so honest
One that would never steal or lie
Imagine a man so caring
If you hurt. He would hurt inside.
Imagine a man so wise
He taught you lessons in your time.
Imagine a man so sharing
He gave you the years of his prime
Imagine a man so wonderful
That words cannot explain
Imagine a man so gentle
As soft as summer rain
Imagine this man as your father
How happy it would make you feel
For me there is no imagining
In my life this man is real.

Paula Marie Rohleder
MARRIAGE IS
Marriage is an ever growing and lasting bond between two souls.

A special seed planted within
our hearts. Nurturing Faith and Trust
—Ever so delicately—Shall
flourish into a cascade of
breathless
beauty.

Daily your love must be renewed
by sharing and caring
for each other, without
compromise

Marriage grows and passes just
as seasons do.
Spring, love is young, tender and
oh so curious.

Time passes with the setting of
a warm summer sun. A time new
roads are traveled together. As
you begin a journey through a
precious
land, creating an unforgettable
collection of memories to reflect
upon.

Autumn brings a sense of
thoughtfulness. A time to ponder
and admire the love you've
nurtured and held so tight.
Time and Seasons pass so
quickly. The travels
and passions shared, soon
become a memory
of wonderful days gone by.

Chill of Winter fills the air. The
life, once
so agile, stills as the days grow
shorter and the nights so cold.

The warmth of your love will
always burn brightly if two
souls share as one,
unselfishly.

I love you, Mike

Ronnie Ray Fowler
A SILENT VOICE

This poem is dedicated to April, a warm, beautiful woman "Ding-Ding Baby"

A silent voice the heart understands,
the warmth and comfort of your loving hands.
A moment caught, a deep secret told,
my love for you can never grow old.
Although my words cannot quite say,
how much more I love you with every new day.
The joy I feel when you are near,
the loneliness I feel when you're not here.

Still my words may somehow impart,
my love for you planted deep in my heart.
To tell you now, what you know is true,
April my love, I will always love you. . .

Ronnie Lee
REMEMBER WHEN
Doctors made house calls & people smiled a lot
A dime was a fortune to a kid
Jokes were funny, but dirty they were not
Divorce was something celebrities in Hollywood did.
Glue was for pasting, not sniffing
Grass was something to be mowed
Coke was a five cent drink, not fifty
And kids walked wherever they had to go.
Hardware was a store to shop in
And appliances outlived their guarantee
Only women wore earrings
And butchers gave you soup bones for free!
Bathing suits left a lot to one's imagination
Hell was a dreaded inferno, not a loosely used word
People believed in their Country and Constitution
"Riot" and "Revolution" just wasn't heard.
Holidays were observed on the day that they fell
And all stores closed every Holiday
Teenagers thought sex was the number after five, misspelled
And five cents sent a letter plus a postcard on their way.
People wore their Sunday best to Church
Families stayed and prayed together; received comfort from within
For happiness you need not search
Ah, those were the days my friend!

Donna-Marie Halunen
A TRIP DOWN MEMORY LANE

This poem is dedicated to all the people I love (Jim), and to all who have made my memories of So. Carver, Massachusetts a wonderful memory. Especially James D. Forand.

Carver is the town I know, where all the people I come to know.
You drive into town seeing all the friendly faces all around.
Heading south on "58" things havn't changed very much. There's
the town hall on the left, and there's the park on my right.
Look over there on down main street, there's the Little League
Field. It's Sunday now at 9:30 I see the cars on the right.
There's the church I used to go to and all the friendly faces all aglow. Then I see that familiar face it's Rev. Meritt in his robe.
It's time to continue down the road. Passing by the divided
highway on to South Carver here I go.
It's fall now, all the colors all around yellow, orange, red and
brown. Berries all a velvet red. Floating on top of water.
Many people in the bog look like strangers in a pond. Watching
all the morning fog. Down the road is Sampson's Pond. Passing
by the Griffith lot. On the corner there's the house, that big
one all decked out. Take a right at Dave's place. Slowing down
on Monday. There's the school I used to attend. Yet there's no
more school. It's back at Center Town. Now take a right down
Church street. For there's a steeple and the church. Where's the
children I used to know? For we have all gone our own ways. On
the left was Michael's place and to the right Christene and Rick
Oh yah he's gone to a place far from here. But never ever forgotten. There's the house I'm looking for where all my dreams came true.
And my learning and my love are remembered in that house. For I
remember all those days when Mom and Dad were disobeyed but now
I know for whom I love it's Mom and Dad. Now I miss those days.

Laura S Deermer
LOVING TOUCH
I love the way you smile at
me with sparkling eyes so bright
The same way the stars can
brighten any darkened night
I love the way you touch me
that only you can do
The way you hold me close
and then make love to me too
Your the only man I've loved
I'm so glad I found you
You just know how to make
things right when everything seems so blue
You make me feel so good like
I can do no wrong
Then fill my life with beauty
and help me feel strong
I follow every rainbow
only when I'm with you
Because I know if things
get tough I can always lean on you
The many loving things
you do always mean so much
I hope no matter what
happens to us you'll never
lose that loving touch.

Grace B Ashby
THE DANCING BRIDE
She danced with the old,
She danced with the young,
She danced with in-betweens
And those whose tongue,

Had not yet mastered
The art of speech,
But whose young arms
Could upward reach,

To grasp the hands
Extended them,
While they adored
Her stratagem.

Marian Nelson Weller Brickell

Marian Nelson Weller Brickell
FOOTPRINTS IN THE WATER
Passing by the pool one day
I stepped close to the edge
Saw "footprints in the water" clear
Traced upon the ledge!!!

<u>This</u> sight ne'er I'd seen before
Was taken by surprise!
The size was very large. It was
Bob's, I did surmise.

The markings of the toes were clear
Outlined by definition
The rounded heel and placeless arch
Got all of my attention!!

I thought of HIM who "walked on water"
With blessed "Footprints" trod
Had <u>HE</u> been in the pool last night
Playing?? <u>HE</u> and His Father GOD???

Tamah S Ruth
LISTEN
Have you ever just stopped and listened?
Listened to the breeze in the trees,
The birds in the morning, whistling and wooing?
Do you know the sound of the babbling brook,

And the cackling of the crane?
The waves gently lapping at the beach?
But. . .
Have you ever just stopped and listened?
Listened to the wind whipping the trees,
The sound of birds no more?
and the soundless crane?
The waves crashing against the beach?

Clinton Van Inman
SONG OF ULYSSES

Of greatness and glory let us speak of all things rich and noble,
And set our sights upon the highest peak
and tread where only men are able.

Speak no more of glitter and gold or of the flys of the market place,
But of greatness and stories old of dreams that Time could not erase.

Come, arise my men and pass around
the beaker, drink! For morning we sail
Again our past Aegean straights beyond,
for we are men, we will prevail!

Of greatness and glory let us speak and sing for all things strong and great
And choose the course that we alone seek
for we are the masters of our fate.

Give me a world such as this one without comfort, joy, or bliss,
A cruel world, where we can struggle to stand and be a man.

Come, arise, my men, let us venture into the depths of the setting sun,
There we'll find new worlds to conquer
newer places writ in blood and iron.

Ramona E Nixon
MEMORIES ARE MADE OF THIS

In my garden the memories flow,
I think back to my mother of many years ago.
My beautiful gladiolas remind me of her,
She had many also, straight and tall they were.

Remembering how she took her time to plant all of them,
Stooping down low to save a broken stem
That had been snapped off that she would find,
Sharing with someone who had been kind.

She would rake and pull and dig out the weeds,
Keeping the rows straight and enjoying new seeds.
Her gladiolas were her pride and joy,
Often admired by her own girls and boys.

Picking a bouquet to gladden someones heart;
She enjoyed this, often pulled the flowers apart,
To take the dead ones off the thickened stem,
My gladiolas are a reminder as I work with them.

I can picture her now bending to and fro,
Quietly working in her garden, straightening out the rows.
Saying little as she walked up and down,
Touching this one and that one, admiring what she had found.

Now up in heaven she must know,
My gladiolas remind me of her as I sow
To keep them flowering, one by one,
Memories galore I find in my garden in the sun.

Hilda E Pierce
A GARDEN WHITE

To my husband Franklin H. Pierce

A garden cool and frosty white,
A garden bathed with shades of light
Blooms outside my window glass
And beckons all my friends who pass.
My garden bench invites delight
Amid the joys of green and white.

Through early morning silver mist
We see the flowers dew has kissed.
When fog surrounds the garden plot
We sense the beauty, seeing not.
We smell the flower scented rain
That beats upon my window pane.

The snow in wintertime's repose
Promises the summer rose,
Flowering peach and hyacinth
Feverfew and tangled quince,
Narcisses, daisies, columbine,
And boxwood with it's leafy rhyme.

Candytuft and pansies peek,
Too shy and innocent to speak.
Bearded iris, pale and pure
Through the decades will endure.
My garden through the window glass
Will bless all living things that pass.

Ramblings by GEANETTE
SPECIAL PEOPLE

On our life's road
Sometimes we find
Others with a load
With needs of a kind

Touch as we pass
In some tender way
Life passes so fast
Words really can't say

Closeness can bring
A feeling of peace
While words can sting
Frustrations to release

How better to know
The depth of caring
Than when you show
The pain you are bearing

Why do we need
To bother at all
Can it be greed
When we start to fall

In the passing of time
We can all grow
Somehow to find
Compassion to show

Others have needs
Hearts that ache
Just sow some seeds
And hope to make

A friend for life
If that can be
It's worth the strife
At least for me.

Joe-Lee-Bergeron
SO—FAR—APART

In memory of my parents, Mildred Reiber Bergeron—1898-1985,Joseph U. Bergeron—1904-1982.

The lamp on my table,
throws-a-lite,-on the paper,
as I write these words for you. . .
Dear: Christy,
Why must we be so-far-away,-from each-other—
Tonite. . . As I am, sitting at the table—thinking
of you, and—the words, I write:
Dear: Christy, only for
you, how I wonder, if your love, for me—is as strong—
As the love, I have for you, and why must, we be
— so far-away, from each other—tonite. . .
Dear: Christy, sweet little Christy, won't you give me
A-chance. . . for some romance—tonite, when-a-hug, and a kiss,
and a smile from you, so-warms, my heart. . . why can't
I see you—tonite. . . Why can't—I touch you, and make things
right. . . Why must we be—so far-a-part—tonite. . . When
I know—what my heart, really wants. . . So why can't we
Be, my Dear-Christy, together-to-nite, why do we, listen
To others, who say—our age difference, will hurt-us —
when we know, in our-hearts-and-mind. . . Our love
for each other is right. . . so—Dear Christy, why can't
I—be with you to-nite, my sweet little Christy. . .
Won't you please, give me-a-chance, for some romance
to-nite. . . With all my love.
Joe-Lee.

Hazel Grey Daugherty Chandler
MY DADDY

To my children and grandchildren.

My daddy was the kindest man.
He always had a smile,
Even in the darkest hours
He would make life seem worthwhile;
The grandest pal a girl e'er had
He never did grow old,
I worship him my own dear dad,
I think his heart was gold.
He brought the sunlight to our home,
And to my mother dear,
He was just indispensable,
With him she had no fear.
It never did occur to me
That anyone was sad,
I always felt so happy
'Cause I took my cares to dad.
With a heart just filled with kindness,
He would tell me what to do
To banish all my worries,
And then come smiling through.
So life moved on smoothly
While daddy dear was here,
I never dreamed a future
Could be so bleak and drear.

byoung

byoung
BIG MAMA'S BONNET

Amid things long, put away in the attic the other day.
I found Big Mama's little Bonnet with lace and ribbons on it.
When she had worn it last, is a fond memory of the past.
As through a mist of tears, I saw down the long years.
Though only decked with ribbons and lace, she had worn it with becoming grace.
And with such charm and pride she did adorn it.
That 'twas like a beautiful cornet.
Styles came and quickly went, Fashions caused much to be spent.
But no change in shape or shade, did my Big Mama's Bonnet sway.
And beside the finery of all the rest.
Big Mama in her bonnet looked the best.

Helen J Haynes
I'M PROUD TO BE AN AMERICAN

I worked at my job and established my skill.
I voted in an election and voiced my opinion at will.
I went on vacation and played in the sand.
I went to a club and danced to a Rock & Roll Band.
I attended church and no one questioned me.
I stayed in my home and had my own privacy.
I live in America and am allowed to do,
All The Things I Wanted To.

Steve Hadley
MEMORIES ARE REAL

In memory of Dad and Bill

Everything has a mem-o-ry
Some are good and some are bad
Some of them bring smiles to us
And some of them make us sad

Some are made from things we do
And some of them are not

Some are made from simple words
That are spoken from our hearts

Some are made with pictures
Of loved ones very dear
And some from pictures in our minds
And we keep them very clear

Some are made from pretty things
That so often fill our lives
And some are made from things in life
That our memory tries to hide.

No matter what they're made of
or how they make us feel.
Our memories are a part of life
And a part that's very real—
Memories

Martin Roque

Martin Roque
WHAT LOVE MEANS TO ME

Love is not, just nice words and pretty songs,
Love is the way in which the weak grows strong.

Love is the way, the truth and the light
It is a gift from God to give us our sight.

For in our mind, He will show us the Kingdom,
In our heart He will place the Key,

Love is the answer and in order to get there,
We will need all three.

Nancy Luther Rosenblum
WORD PAINTING

Dedicated to my Mother, Mary Luther, Columbus, Ind.

To put my feelings down in words
Is my main ambition and drive,
Because that's the only pleasure
Out of life I do derive.

To be able to paint a picture
With only words you see,
Is the most beautiful thing in the world
The feeling it gives to me.

To make it so that others can see
My feelings written before their eyes,
Without using paints and a brush
In my words is where it lies.

They don't have to ask why I did it
In my words I hope they can feel and see,
Then put themselves in my shoes
And walk that mile with me.

I hope they can visualize every word I write
And can see it in their head,
The picture I paint with just my words
The story my emotions have said.

As we go through each verse together
I hope they can feel all the way,
The picture I've painted for them in rhyme
The story my heart had to say.

Michele Kroll
WATER MASSAGE

To Bunny and The Nut Slingers of The Bahamas

Snowlike foam spiraled through endless ripples of sea
Spraying its mist all over his subtle body
Undisturbed he stretched out supinely
In liquid sand

Dozing he craved nothing
Contented to be alone in tepid shallowness
A serene moment
In rare occurrence

Incessant waves intercepted still waters
In buoyant gestures of power
Time and again swiftly receding to expose
The majestic silhouette of his flawless anatomy

Sun rays sea salts created a glistening harvest
Upon his attentive muscles
Hours of daylight transforming baby soft skin
To a tawny shade of brown

Sandy hair escaping freely
Flowing into a water dance
A slight smile crept across his face
Mesmerized by water and man
I sat and watched this elusive stranger

Milo W Rosenberg
TO FORGOTTEN WARRIORS

There are tales that were written in the dust of the prairie
Where the bones of our forefathers lie;
They are tales we remember when the cold rain is falling
At night from a thunder-torn sky.

There are pictures to ponder in the clouds o'er the prairie,
Of brave ones and the deeds they have done;
Of grim, painted riders on shaggy war ponies,
Feathered lances that flash in the sun.

And the sounds that we hear in the wind of the prairie
As it sweeps past a lone cottonwood,
Are the voices of spirits keeping watch through the ages
Where the lodges of heroes once stood.

Mimi Moore
VISIONS

To Cathy—My Daughter—My Inspiration

There's something very contagious spreading over our town, it picks you up and makes you feel good when you're feeling low down.
It started with a small child who was given a toy one
day, and spread through the store to a salesgirl
who was given a raise in pay.
She passed it on to a very old man who held a cane
in his shaking hand, he gave it to a small child on
crutches who could barely stand.
The child gave it to a policeman who helped her
across the street, and from there it traveled
onward to all the people he would meet.
If this spreads enough around our town and into
the countries too, A SMILE could be the
wonder drug to help millions, even you!

Luther Elvis Albright
REFLECTIONS: MY HOMETOWN

Nestled on the banks of the Cumberland
And across from Red Paint Hill
Stands Clarksville the town of my childhood
With memories treasured and still.
She stands in the well watered valley
Where deer and buffalo grazed,
Where Indians fought with the White Man
When our wilderness trails first were blazed.

The land was once covered with timber,
Wild turkey and bear roamed at will,
While swans searched for food on the river
Red foxes and elk climbed the hill.
But then came the flatboats and barges,
The keelboats, log cabins and guns,
The axes, the women and daughters
With pioneer fathers and sons.

And now she's become a great lady
With highways and mansions and fame,
With actors, and writers and athletes
And statesmen who freedom proclaim.
You were born amidst hardship and labor,
Conceived on a wilderness trail;
But now you're the Queen of the Cumberland—
My hometown: Oh Clarksville, all hail!

Peter R Beyerinck
ODE TO ELAINE

*E*ver in my thoughts you are,
*L*ike a pretty melody;
*A*lways I'll remember you,
*I*n warm and fondest memories;
*N*o single word can more express,
*E*laine means: happiness.

Sharon Gallagher
DEATH OF A CHILD

Nine years of warm brilliant life
Spilled so suddenly
Into a cold, snow-filled ditch.
Laura, gone.
Winter is my death.

I throw each day away now.
They are all memories
Of hazel eyes and golden hair.
Laura, gone.
Winter is my death.

Hope for life to carry on is
Finished with her death.
Life does not keep promises.
Laura, gone.
Winter is my death.

Mrs Lillian (Lou) Dagneau
APRIL

Spring of earth,
month of firsts.
Things they say,
Should come in May.

Osprey in a lonely glide,
Mayflowers, tho they hide.
Rabbits changed to brown from white,
peepers songs, in dark of night.

These and more.
Promises, what's in store.
Green of woods, blue of sky,
gifts of summer rushing by.

Winter, long,
sung her song.
Comes now the time,
of poets' rhyme,
Of sun warm,
and bees' swarm.

'Till days break cold
and, as of old,
November firsts,
bring winters' earth.

Carolyn G Tuzzolino Lott

Carolyn G Tuzzolino Lott
TO MAMA'S AND DADDY'S OLD HOUSE

Dedicated to my parents, Vincent and Dorothy Gulino, who passed away in 1985.

I went to see you yesterday
And you were sad.
You huddled, shivering, among the trees;
Their branches sobbing softly as they hung their heads,
with leaves as limp as orphans in their beds.

Do you still miss the love that

Mama gave you?
Do you feel barren as a mother's breast
when all her babes are gone?
Are rooms too silent with their doors unslammed
by boisterous hordes of children, now all grown?

At Easter, does your tall grass feel forsaken
without the eggs unfound
(except by toddlers feet)?
At Christmas, are your walls and corners lonely
without the holly, tree and piled-up treats?

I talked with Mama Saturday . . .
She said she missed you, too.

Raymond G L Snyder Jr
MILES AND MILES OF LOVE

To Pam, Bobby and Lisa, my loving family.

You are many miles away,
I start to worry that you'll stray,
Afraid you'll find a better guy,
Yes, afraid and this is why.

I love you tho we're apart,
To you I've given all my heart,
You have done so much to make me a man,
I've also given you my hand,
I'm thinking of you all the time,
So if you look you'll surely find,
By thinking of you every day.
I've given you my mind.

Yes, we are many miles apart,
But protected by God above,
I'll give you what he gives me,
Miles and miles of love.

Lowell LaBre
NATURES VERY OWN

This poem is dedicated to Georgette, my loving wife, and my two sons, David and Jerry

Look! yon monarch has come
to worship his Queen,
this virgin violet groomed.
Loved by him and daily seen!

What devotion they share
What a lasting romance.
What harmony so deeply felt
and seen at a glance!

They have a tart language,
a beauty all its own,
Whose purer words were never
to child or poet shown!

The wind is their music,
this forest their abode,
Whose laws bind each
to some strange code!

Be where they will
in sun, rain or mist.
Each will always have each
to charm and kiss.

Sharon A Maxwell
HEALING TEARS

Dedicated to the Lord Jesus for talents and abilities given;and in memory of Dad and Mom (Sumner & Phyllis Ormsbee); and with love to George, Michael David and Earl Dewey.

Memories come floating by
The windows of my mind.
"Open up," I hear within,
"And see what you will find!"
So cautiously I peek inside,
Not sure I want to see;
For memory can bring such guilt,
And fear and pain and grief . . .

Suddenly I see the past
For what it's meant to be:
A growing-time; a learning-time;
A time to let go and be free.
Faster then the memories come,
And with them HEALING TEARS.
Gone is the pain; gone is the guilt;
Gone, the grief and fears!

Linda Patricia Gleason
SONG OF THREE VIRTUES

I sought a while for happy things
To make one laugh, not cry, but sing.
And when at last the bell did ring,
I knew the joy which virtue brings!

Kindness be fair, all truth to win,
She plays a rosewood violin.
As sweet she stays to friend and kin,
So wise you'd be to let her in.

Happiness tells her story new.
She, like kindness, is bright and true.
But often, like the morning dew,
At times will hide her face from view.

Now wit, fox like, does roam about,
And better knows she how to pout.
While never having just one doubt,
With sharp finess, she'll put you out!

A color they call rainbow sea,
Will steal your eye, and bend
Your knee.
Then, dashing from behind
a tree,
They'll show you how good
life can be!

My story told, you'll ask
me, blue,
"Now what has this with
joy to do?"
Please show your smile
as if you knew,
or else these three
will laugh at you!

Trudy Grammo
SUZI

A little palomino horse
stands tall in her stall.
A young boy no more than eleven
walks up to the palomino horse.
She nickers loudly to him,
he puts his hand on her nose
And says quietly "Shhhh,
we're going out."
Saddled and bridled
he does this in a flash.
Down to the track is the
twenty yard dash.
On his horse, he races,
round and round the track they go,
Clocked at a mile at the speed of light.
The boy, later, remaining forever
nonprofessional
The palomino, long since died,
and buried in the center of his heart.

Laurie Lascody
HIDDEN PEACE

To Tom—the one I love and the one that inspires my inner thoughts.

The great wall of mountains
tower up to the sky,
While the sun shines brightly
in my eye,
And the birds glide gracefully as if they
are unable to fly,
Why can't things be this peaceful all
the time—why?
The freshly cut grass sways in the
mid-afternoon air,
I can take a brisk walk without
even a care,
And the clouds never darken—
they don't dare,
Why can't things be this peaceful all
the time—should we beware?

Mattie Williams Kennedy
VICTORY

This poem is dedicated to Megan Petrese Kennedy, a wonderful gift of God.

Fighting forces of a netherworld
Forming visions of power
Struggling within myself
To set this demon free.

Voices from afar
Attempting to devour me
Chanting unheard details
From a body so devoid.

And I
Of devout heart
Doth hear my master's call
I look toward the heavens
And he speaks to me:
"My child, I shall conquer all."

Robert L Allen
ON EAGLE'S WINGS

To my grandchildren, who will inherit the future regardless of how we leave it; good or bad. May God allow it to be the former.

To see the eagle soaring over cliff
or mountain stream,
With its grace and ease of power
causes one to sit and dream.
To dream you are an eagle's wings
soaring high and seeing far,
Being feared for all your cunning
ways, yet, admired for what you are.

As long as time's been measured
men have envied all your fame,
Used you on their flags of glory;
Coats of Arms; above their names.
You are mentioned in the
Scriptures, your Creator you've served well,
Soaring high through all of history;
oh what stories you could tell.

You treat your young with
tenderness as you raise them in your nest,
But tenderness gives way to
strength when you are put to the test.
Perhaps your greatest honor
comes when man imitates your ways,
Though they're bent on your
destruction in, oh, so many ways.

We cage the very standard so our
children all can see,
The emblem strong and proud and
bold which stands for our
LIBERTY. And somewhere in
the future I know we'll realize,
The symbol of our great, free land
no longer soars our skies.

The silence will be deafening; pain
no one wants to share,
The EAGLE and our FREEDOM
gone because we didn't care.
We've poisoned many eagles and
we've poisoned those who're free,
As it has been with the eagles, will
it also be for thee?

Beth McGee
WHY BIRDS SING

With love to my daughter, Maribeth.

How brightly, my little garden,
flourishes in the sun.
Bees, lingering in its fragrance.
Touched the blossoms, one by one.
A tiny bird, winged his way, to the garden.
His eyes alit with wondrous glee.
"With so many flowers now in
bloom." he sang,
Soon, many pods of seeds, there'll
surely be.
I'll just wait around, 'Till the seeds
are ripe.

Then to the south, I'll fly.
For when all the bees and flowers
are gone,
Cold winter winds, bearing snow
are nigh!"
So, wait he did, with a song, in his heart.
Then joyfully, he found,
That God, had not forgotten the birds.
On my little plot of ground.

Earl C Akins
THE BEAMING LIGHT

When the dark clouds of despair,
Darken your stumbling way,
When all your hopes seem severed,
And overshadow your day.

When your cries seem in vain,
On a tempest—tossed sea,
And you cry out to Jesus,
In one fading plea.

Look up into the heavens,
A rift in the clouds will arise,
A beam of light descending,
Upon the darkened skies,

A heavenly light so radiant,
Brighter than the noon-day sun,
Will fill your heart with gladness,
And you'll know the battle's won.

Irene M McGivern
LIFE'S THREADS

There are many threads in Life's
Tapestry
Woven with each day that passes
by—
The newest stitch—Retirement—
Brings new activities to try.

We gently weave our friendships
Both the new ones and the old,
Into designs of joy and love—
Along with memories of gold.

Each stitch is a different pattern
When we let others know we care
It brings friends closer together
In this tapestry of life we share.

The strongest threads that we possess
Are kindness, faith and trust,
Intermingled with patches of prayers
For us all—it is a must!

We turn to God, our greatest weaver
In him, we all depend—
As he weaves his love amongst us
And guides us to our end.

Lillian Cimador

I'M FREE

I can walk where I want to walk.
I can talk when I want to talk.
I'm free.
I can be what I want to be.
I can see what I want to see.
I'm free.
I can hear what I want to hear.
I don't fear for there is no fear.
I'm free.
These I can do but not without my health.
Without it I cannot gather any wealth.
I feed my mind and body right.
I want them to see the light.
My tomorrows will all be bright.
I'm free.

Nora A Uehlein

THE "SONS OF KIERKEGAARD"

To my father and mother for encouraging me.

No. We are not
Stunted by the weather
of our paradise lost.
We recognize
in our neighboring dust
our grandparents, once quick,
as we too progress
into essentially nothing.
But we still believe
in ourselves and in
our not-so-humble children
who promise (as we did)
to find the answers.
No. Adam's fate
has not washed us with fear;
our numbered years
convey more hope
than placid Eden did.

J Quintana

THE BROTHERHOOD

All the brothers have slept and must now be awakened,
For together as brothers, we are not forsaken.
Our God, in his mercy, has made us as one, and together,
With love, his task will be done.

As his children we know that our father is just, and his
Love is our truth, and in him we must trust.
It is he that doth breathe every breath that we take,
It is peace that he wishes all brothers to make.

Myra E Stidham

FATHER TO SON

Because I do not wish to turn again or face the failures of my life
I that is near your heart son tell you of life
My son the world is yours to conquer with the gift of your being.
The world turns and the world changes and you must build the meaning.
The world is full of pain and too often unfair
And to truely know happiness is rare.
Sometimes the road is level, but still you'll stumble and fall.
You may rise and run my son or you may only crawl.
Sometimes the lessons in life we learn are late and slow.
Sometimes we are only blinded by our lack of will to know.
So take this rose of memory and never feed your fears.
Understand the words I've said and always cry silent tears.

Terri Lynn King

TOMORROWS YESTERDAY TODAY

Yesterday's a mem'ry,
We hold within our heart.
Tomorrows but a dream,
We've only yet to start.
It's today that we are living,
To cherish and to hold.
For yesterday it was a dream,
And tomorrows mem'ry told.

Queen D Franklin

DREAMS

Amazing dreams I had in youth!
Would make you laugh with glee,
I will tell you here in simple truth,
Of girlhood's revery.

Piano and trombone I'd play
O'er land and sea I'd roam.
I'd see the beauties far away,
But make U.S. my home.

I worked and scrimped as ne'er before
That I not dream in vain;
But alas! my talent is no more
'Cause arthritis gives me pain.

Beautiful scenes to me are gone
With bifocals on my face.
How oh how can you play trombone
And keep false teeth in place?

Lovely mountains I cannot scale
'Tis awkward with a crutch;
Scenes have grown dim, as visions fail,
But dreams keep me in touch.

Marsha Denise Hensley

BLUE ROOM

Scattered thoughts and memories come to mind
As in my heart I try so hard to find
The feelings once so deep and true
In all the days and nights I spent with you.
How can we change so much so soon?
It's in my heart that I saved but just one room.
To hold on to the many tender moments shared
To hold the feeling close, knowing that you cared.
Its been so long since thoughts like these
Have traced the threads of time to tease
The shattered course and bended road I've taken
The dreams and hopes of our love forsaken.
I wonder where lifes path has taken you
While in my heart your room turns many shades of blue.
I miss you.

Hydie Stevens

MY LAND

I did not want to come here,
I did not want to stay here;
As a child I had to come here
And leave my native land.

But I fell in love with this new land,
And now I will never roam
From my dear northern home . . .
In a place called Michigan.

I longed at first for my lost home,
For friends and land and southern ways.
It seemed so strange and new.
But folks were kind and the land was good,
And old ways began to fade.

As new ways took over and changed my childish heart
The longing ceased for that other home.
My roots grew deeper here,
And I did not want to depart.

I'm thankful for a southern heritage,
Its honorable and good I believe.
But there's just something about this Yankee
land and Yankee ways
That tells me, "You are home!"
And will not let me leave,
And will not let me leave.

John Edward Kercel Jr

John Edward Kercel Jr

THE FIVE SENSES OF DEATH

Deadman, deadman, what do you see?
Can those eyes gaze into eternity?
Is it a warning or an invitation to me?
If you could, would you pass the key?
Was your life such a travesty?

Deadman, deadman, what do you hear?
Sounds of ecstasy or screams of fear?
Do cries of apathy or achievement ring clear?
Can the vacuum of death bring you near?
Is it a void silence, or the roar of tears?

Deadman, deadman, what do you smell?
Does the timeless scent treat you well?
Pungent battlefields, or plagues from hell?
An odor of danger for me to compel?
Was it the aroma of solitude as you fell?

Deadman, deadman, what do you touch?
A life that was beautiful, or just a crutch?
Monster of saint does it treat you as such?
Chaos or enlightenment, can you tell me which?

Deadman, deadman, what do you taste?
The flavor of fame, or are you pleading your case?
Are there bittersweet memories of a life spent in haste?
Do you savor calm, shrouded in lace?
Was your life really such a waste?

Mark F Bishop Jr

IMMORTAL BEAST

This poem is dedicated to my dear friend Greg

Walking down the hallway you see what you
Believe to be real

Can't distinguish the things that are fantasy, and the things
You really feel

Empty rooms behind closed doors, searching for the answers to
Questions asked before

Is this only a dream or a nightmare in disguise
Searching for the truth hidden behind our past lives

The voices in your head continue to destroy
Everytime you wished you were dead was just a simple
Ploy

Slapped in the face with cold reality, something's in the
Distance; the beast of immortality
Contorting the minds of all who pray
Bringing them on to their last day

Eric LaMar Samuels

ANEW DAY

In the world all alone
Is how I feel when I'm at home
In the dark of the day
When my head to rest I lay
After a day of going through
Situations old and situations new
Then before I close my eyes
I say a prayer to the one most high
To give me strength to make it to
Another day to see anew

In that day I pray I'll be
A better person to all I see
And serve as an encouraging sign
To those at days end I leave behind
Because after that day is completed
In my home I will be seeded
To grow and to appreciate
The relationships with people I make
So that those thoughts will carry me through
The next day I pray to see anew

Kathy Dukes Renner
THE CAT OF DAWN

This poem is dedicated to Miss Joynelle Pearson, my high school Creative Writing teacher, a very special person.

Silent and ever so gently;
Oh, do be careful!
Sh-h-h! Don't give any warning.
Softly creep over the rising,
meticulously slip over the leaves,
don't dare let them rustle.
Sh-h-h!

Now with a quick, graceful glide,
drop sprightly on the world.
And, like a giant liquid bubble,
burst with elasticity and pride,
spilling liquid rainbow colors
all over the drab blanket of night!

Ms Diana Russ
IF I BELIEVE IN ME

This poem is dedicated to my Mother, Sisters, and my precious children.

IF I Believe in me . . .
I shall be free.
IF I Believe in me . . .
I can climb the highest tree.
IF I Believe in me . . .
I can bring all Nations together.
IF I Believe in me . . .
I can bring peace to the universe
Forever.

Janet Elaine Coppock
NEW CREATIONS

To all the closet bards, and those determined to expose them.

As an inner seal is broken
New creations, outward flow
While one can merely speculate
Of whence they come to show

Such creations, new, inhabit few
And fewer, yet, released
Thoughts never said, bound up in head
That die with the deceased

Experience must not be obscured
As silence would imply
It serves as warning to the world
And left unheard, thereby

Becomes a shameful loss; A senseless waste
Denying innate gifts
While generations pass in haste
As though no loss exists

Accounts of loss are sure to grow
No salvage left to spare
'Tis tragic, what the dead bestow
And worse, so few should care

Jennifer Korpi
I NEED YOU
I need you when the sun is low
and when the moon is high,
and whenever my heart is feeling blue
I need you all the time.

It seems that in the morning
when the sun comes out to dry,
the tears that shed my loneliness
I need you when I cry.

And in the evening when time is short
the world seems all so true,
I find out in my wildest dreams
that I need you.

Clara Rasmussen
MY VISITOR
Jenny Wren is at my door
Looking for my love and more
A tiny house is her request
Where she could build her tiny nest
Some bits of string and twigs of oak
And feathers so the rain won't soak
Her tiny babies two or four
A tiny hole to be her door
So none but she and her singing mate
Can enter in that hallowed gate
My protection is all that she
Will ever ask or want of me
I give it gladly and in return
Her busy happy self I earn

Yvonne carol Daniels
A REFLECTION
As I sit by the waters side
Staring into deep blue
A reflection appears
It is of you.

Of the many laughs we had
Of the deep thoughts we share
Mother Nature let us begin
to innocently care.

Of the friendship we bonded
Of the obligations we have
That keeps us from being close
It leaves me rather sad.

Your reflection will fade from the waters
But you won't fade from my mind
You are forever imprinted
In the pages of my mind.

Thaddeus R Bachta
FRIGHT FULL

To all those who have had their fill of fright and have found new ways to express self-love.

I came across this sight one night;
A hundred bugs, a toad named Fright.

The bugs they flew in frenzied flight
Attracted by street corner light.
They buzzed and blitzed with such a might,
Then sidewalk landed,—resting site.

With patience armed and goal in sight,
The toad named Fright saw moment right.
He stretched a smile of grave delight
And swiftly ate with . . . one . . . big . . .BITE.

Mrs Carol C Sprinkle
A SALUTE TO THE SEVEN

To all Americans everywhere who revel in the pursuit of their American DREAM.

A Nation awoke, one glorious morn,
Refreshed in spirit, united in hope . . .
A vision unfurled, a DREAM was born;
How common citizens, in space could cope.

As the challenge mounted, elation soared,
The applause was sounded, and victory did glide . . .

BUT NO! the shuttle shuttered, then a fire roared;
And destroyed the DREAM, as the heroes died.

Stunned with shock, the Nation gasped,
The ineffable happened, as fate did con . . .
Defeat not permanent, a rebirth was grasped;
To the Tribute of Seven, the DREAM must go on!

Michael A Corley
TOUCH
The sun sets at dusk.
The sun rises at dawn.
Our world keeps spinning round.
Life goes on.
Some have very little.
Some have so much.
And though our lives are different,
we all have God's touch.
The one's who have a struggle,
a struggle hard and long.
The one's who have everything,
whose life is like a beautiful song.
People who are the richest, the people who have love.
These are the people
the one's who've been touched.
Touched ever so gently,
by the one who watches from above.

Melinda McCane
ONE WORD
Changing, moving, lifting the spirit
So many different ways to use it.
One feels for a pet or a toy, and
Yet in another for a girl or boy.
So many things around me I feel
But only one word there be,
To describe what I feel
For those around me, and what
They send back to me.
One small word for so many feelings
And many a purpose be true.
Only one small word to read
And I found it written in you.
Love

Helen M Hatheway
A POEM FOR JOEY
I need a poem for Joey
For all the world to see,
The Angel of a boy he is
And what he means to me.

The winds will never touch his face
As riding on a bike,
Nor shoelaces come untied
While walking on a hike.

For he's an unsung hero
Suffering silently,
With his courage, strength and spirit
As he fights Dystrophy.

His princely handsome body
Fast becoming just a shell,
Yet the joy and love he gives me
Flows like the living well.

He's taught me loads of patience
As I watch him bear his cross,
And what an honor it is
To help him with this cross.

I'm a far better person
For having served this child,
He's taught me how to give of self
To walk that extra mile.

The journey through this life is short
And many times unfair,
But if it's lived with You in mind
It's lived beyond compare.

For just like Jesus on the cross
I'm sure the same was said,
Of how unfair it was for Him
As Heaven bowed its head.

So Thank You Lord for Joey
The gift You've given me,
Let his courage, strength and spirit
Be his gift Eternity.

Kim Lian Ponchik
HEROES
Long ago in the front row,
I lauded you as my hero.
Though I longed to share your philosophy,
Your view of philology was worlds apart from mine.
All the time I had you believe that you converted me.
Since that dread day I felt that it was you who deserted me.
From time to time I leaf the pages of your domain
And regret the absence of your name.
Searching for you in the face of strangers,
I pace the hall —
the very path we crossed each day —
And rehearse the lines you may never hear (me say).

Seeing his visage in yours,
His fervor is less missed
For an instant.
You incessantly criticize my diction
While your rhetoric causes friction
Between us.
The verbs lying dormant in my heart
Are filled with torment
As I know they are not meant for you.

Now, what is in store for me?
I will wait patiently,
For I believe that I shall meet the wise one who holds my dreams
In his valise.

Mindi Smith-Scott
PALE RIDERS
The pale riders of DEATH
begin their long journey
down the Ardous road
of complete uncertainty.

As their shadows pierce
the horizon, fear begins

to slowly creep into
the minds of Sober Men.

Men's hearts grow heavy
as the riders draw near.
The arm lifts slowly
to point the intended.

The intended steps into
the PALE RIDER'S shadow
and is forever lost
into that unknown of DEATH.

Other men's hearts lighten
for it was not yet their turn
But deep in their souls
they know it is only a matter of TIME.

James P Roberts
EXPLORING
We walked up the dike
and on the other side
saw the spring flood.
It had crept into the cornfield
drowning the tender stalks.

Traci ran ahead, shouting,
her yellow hair matching the dried grass.
Clods of wet mud flew from her shoes
and a trail of brown spatters
ran up her back.

Along the new-made shore
we searched for rocks.
Flat rocks to skip over the waters.
Big rocks to throw as far as possible
and watch the geyser erupt.

And pretty rocks—Traci kept those and
(She saw a sea shell) white chalk
rocks, too.

Bending, I watched the spring bugs
cover the soil with their industry.
A chicken hawk circled above,
out over the trees, over the river.
It vanished beyond the treetops,
but I could see Traci following it
with her eyes, with her mind.

Iva Cogdill Cook
HAPPINESS
Time is short here
Get rid of fear

Make yourself fit
Only you can do it

Sunshine will replace rain
OH what sweet gain
Happiness!

Floriene Lillie
MY OLD LOVE
Today I took a notion

To stroll down memory lane
Through my photo album pages
That show both signs of joy and pain

As I sat there quietly dreaming
Turning my life's every page
I saw a treasured picture
Only slightly dimmed with age

It brought teardrops to my eyes
And as I let them softly flow
Your smile seemed just as dear
As it did so long ago

I looked with love at your dear face
The arms that once held me so near

It seemed your lips were saying
I love you still my dear

Than as a tear fell on your face
My memory seemed to clear

I realized that this is today
And you are my yester-year

I changed my life a lot of ways
The day I changed my name
But in a corner of my heart
The old love is still the same

Janice Lynn Van Deest
TEAR'S
The salt of the soul, rising forth like the tide of life. Giving freedom to one self, uncaring wet wonderful. Small clear crystal drops, dancing on faces. For happiness, sadness, yearning, hoping. Light on some, yet heavy on others Joy for life, sadness for death, multipurpose drops. Shown rarely yet shown often. Bitter for lost love, tender for new found. The makeup of a thousand faces. Peering, glancing, covering up. Yet they show signs if looked at carefully enough one can see the difference and try to understand. And yet who or what would we be with out them?

Jacqueline L Wallace
YOU ARE TO ME
You are the strength of my mind
You are the Heart of my Soul
You are the Sunshine of the New Dawn's Light.
You are the One I think of at night.
Every Love Song on the radio reminds me of you,
You make the Morning Sun Take on a new Hue
You are the height of the Evening Tide
With you I have nothing to hide
So my Dear you can see
These things you are to me.

Don Berry

Don Berry
I AM A SPECIAL GUY

To my wife Pauletta, and my children whom I love dearly.

I am a very special guy
At least my family thinks me to be
But I can not really figure why
<u>They don't know it's them, not me.</u>
My wife says at helping others, I am a success
She thinks that my inner strength is such a mystery
But it's not my strength that I possess
<u>It's the support she gives to me.</u>
My daughter thinks a room is brighter
When I've been there awhile
But I think someone should tell her
<u>That light is her own smile.</u>
My son is really something
Thinking I'm the greatest, that could ever be
Not realizing I'd be nothing
<u>Without his faith in me.</u>
Robyn says I'm the father she never really had
But there are two things I think she does not see
I love to hear her call me dad
<u>And I need her, as much as she does me.</u>
What makes me such a special man
I can tell you what I believe
It's not so hard to understand
It's all these special people, that I call family.

Harry D Kleiner
WE WERE YOUNG ONCE
We were young once—
and gentle—
and eager for life—
There was little trouble,
little strife, until . . .

Life came to us, hit us, and hurt—
We were raped, and cut, and torn apart like an old shirt,
and because we were young—
We tried to bounce back, sought for another chance,
yet again we were stung—
Life continued the painful dance on and on . . .

Now we are old, grown tired, less bold—
There is hardness in us, we no longer fuss, when life dances by us,
with us, through us . . .
We have learned much with the passage of time—
The hurt bounces off more easily each time—
And yet—part of us still cries, at the pain, the misery,
and always will.

And then one day it is gone—
The pain, the strife,
the concerns of this life—
And some of us remember, remember back;

We were young, once . . .

Lisa P Dedmon
FOR "MOONLIGHT"
Oh, storm—
Beat upon my heart with your fierce lashes
and dissolve my pain.
Take me home to your sweet green grass,
For I shall not love again.

The gales 'round me rage;
A peaceful night I long for;
A deep, restful sleep I pray for
As I begin the journey home.

Once my skies were sun-filled:
I laughed and danced in the meadows,
I drank of the streams and dreamed under the weeping willows—
But those days shall come no more.

Once I was filled with love—
A love that blessed me and kissed away my tears.
I could picture your face in the clouds as
the days drifted by me.
Soft touches of rose-petals became your mouth—
But those days shall come no more.

I see the bright sunrise stretched out before me,
The daffodils beckon me, "Come!"
I bend to inhale their dear fragrance—I have finally found my way home.

Mary M Judge
COST A-PLENTY
Went into a store.
Just needed several things,
Came out with ten items.
Including chicken wings.

Hurried down each aisle.
Not much on my mind,
But all the brands confuse me.
Several hundred did I find.

Charmin, Puffs and Kleenex.
Bounty, Bolt and Scott,
The things I really needed.
But in my haste forgot.

Del Monte, Hunt's and Royal.
Aunt Jemima, Hungry Jack,
Told myself, get sweet rolls.
Now Mary, put that back.

Welch's, Kraft and Quaker.
How can I decide,
Skippy, Jif and Peter Pan.
Fab, All, Duz and Tide.

Next time on my shopping trip.
I will get the Duncan Hines,
Pay my bill, get out fast.
I won't get caught in lines.

O'Fulwood-Wilson
CURTAIN CALL AT THE MET

This poem is dedicated to my dear husband, Rich, with love

The ride into the Apple
slowed down to a crawl,
and we are running late
for an eight o'clock call,

We avoided the Holland
and the Lincoln was jammed,
with rush hour traffic
it seems we are damned,

If we don't get there
in the next half an hour,
we'll lose our reservations
then, we will have to scour,

Restaurant Row
across from the Met,
no time for a meal
we'll take what we can get,

We dashed across Broadway
in the rain and all,
through the door, up the stairs
to make this curtain call,

I am at my destination
sitting, just resting my eyes,
cleaning my opera glasses
as the curtain begins to rise.

Richard Alva Hare
IF TRUE LOVE WE SHARE
With God up above, we will share our love,
Just like the stars share the sky.
Until the end of our years, we will share true love,
In hopes, that love will never die,

There will be fountains of
happiness, as long as we live.
If we share true love, and true
love we give,
For there is one thing, that no one
can tear apart.
And that one thing, is a true
loving heart.
As the world turns, a loving heart
turns,
For kindness, effection, and
bliss.
Each person that lives, with the
love they give,
A tender kiss.
To show they care, with the love
they share,
A true love that gives delight.
All because, true love they share,
When together, are out of sight.

Paula S Webb
COUNTRY VS. CITY

This poem is dedicated to my friends and family, in return for their words of encouragement. And to Bobby, my loving husband

---

In the city, at dark, the town comes
alive;
In the country, they roll the streets
up at five.
In the city, there's lots of people to
call;
In the country, you're lucky to have
a phone at all.
In the city, if you want something,
you go to a 7-11.
In the country, if you want
something, you wait 'til the
morning at 7.
But in the country, you never meet
a stranger,
in the country, there's a lot less
danger.
in the country, there's no
bumper to bumper cars,
in the country, you can see the
stars.
watch the sunset, the moon rise,
chat with all, who passes by.
Of all the places there is to live,
The country has a lot to give.

Mary R Davis
WHAT IS A DAY
A day is whatever we make it.
So stay happy and enjoy it, to the
fullest.
You can be happy, glad moody or
sad.
It is your choice, so don't make it
bad.

You can go to work with a smile or
frown.
If you go in with a frown, it will get
you down.
So each day let's keep a smile.
That will help us easily make each
mile.

So what is a day?
It's how we help people on our way.
Whether it be good or bad.
Keep a smile, and you won't make
people sad.

We have twenty four hours in each
day.
So do good or you might pay.
Say something kind, write a letter
to a friend.
Then your day will have a happy
end.

Margaret C Walters

Margaret C Walters
GODS HAND ON ME

To God, and my loving family, for love, encouragement, and understanding.

I was young, and so full of energy,
And as healthy as I could be,
The lake was huge, I almost
drowned,
But He had his hand on me.
And later on as time went by,
The car that hit me, I did not see,
The driver died, but I was saved,
As He had his hand on me.

At the age of twelve my parents
died,
I was as heartbroken as could be,
But though I never knew it then,
He still had his hand on me.
Now many years have come and
gone,
I had five children, with all glee,
With the last one doctors said,
"you'll die,"
But He had his hand on me.
As I sit and count my grand-kids,
I am as happy as I can be,
And I thank God, for letting me
know,
He still has his hand on me.
I am now a Born Again Christian,
Filled with the Spirit, and set free,
I "shudder" thinking, I didn't know
til now,
He's always had his hands on Me!

Juanita (Wilson) Hockenhull
LONESOME DESPAIR

Dedicated to my husband James, Children Lucinda, Nancy, Andrew and Thomas. Also in memory of my parents Clarence and Lucy Wilson

---

Oh lonely, lonely into the wee
hours are thee
The world seem to have
forgotten me
The darkness creeps in
and shadows the trees
And time stands still and
seem to have no key
Lonely lonely am I
the dark shadows even past me
by
The stars twinkle so high
in the sky
That even they have no
answer to why
Oh lonely lonely into the wee
hours are thee
What seem to have been hours
is only half-past-three
The shadows lighten and
turn into trees
And the stars fade unto where
no one can see
Oh lonely lonely into the wee
hours are thee

Karen King Carnes
A TRIP THROUGH TIME
Today I took a trip through time—
It was a lonely walk—perhaps a
sign?

I traveled back to places where I've
been,
To view a heart that couldn't mend.
Painful were the memories, I'm sad
to say,
It is so true, "Nothing Gold Can
Stay."

To look upon life with such sorrow
and dejection,
If for the beguiling self—a state of
regression.
This, to me, lessens the very act of
living—
And deems the presence of death
as "breathing."

I tell myself, this seering sorrow
isn't me—
My life is to be happy and
elevatingly free—
But somewhere back in time—
I lost my love, my life, my dream,
my rhyme.

Irene Burton Richey
A MOTHER'S LOVE
A mother's love is a different love;
It begins before a babe is born.
It grows and grows, as the baby
grows,
And from her heart, it can't be
torn.

Through-out all stages of life,
And every kind of crisis;
A mother's love is a different love;
Though tried, it never ceases.

Eino Lake
GODS BEAUTY

To my pastor I hereby dedicate this poem to say thanks for all your kindness.

Here as I stood on the highway for
the first time
I saw beauty like I have never seen
before,
miles and miles of loveliness that
was created by the
masters hand; for he had planned
it for me that I would
see all this grandeur through his
eyes, that I would always
remember this day. Then as I
looked to the mountains I knew
he was looking at me, and then I
heard him say there is a more
beautiful place that no one has
seen for the new earth will
be more beautiful than what your
eyes have seen today.

Randi Misnik
FRAILITIES
Why is it though I love you so,
and trust you with my very soul;
When posed with a problem that
makes my heart heavy
I choose to suffer alone, in painful
silence?

Why is it though I love you so,
and want you to disarm yourself to
me,
yet effect my defenses at
you—when I need you most—
When in reality it is you who would
defend me?

Why is it though I love you so,
I've fashioned this self-inflicted
armor
that robs us both of the closeness
we yearn for as humans?

What have I to risk, really?
What's to lose—if I were to tell you
that the most
unbearable agony in my heart is
that you might not
Love Me Forever.

Lennie Kincaid
WRATH OF EMOTION
Oh! Wrath of emotion that finds
engraved in one's soul,
That steers wisdom into a state of
confusion
And tends to cast a new mold
Of a person, enthralled in a
delusion.

Oh! Wrath of emotion that fills a
day with splendor.
That gives each moment value
untold,
It tends to become life's defender
For a person with happiness as a
goal.

Oh! Wrath of emotion, another
role to unfold,
Fills life with confusion, delusion
and dismay,
Who will confess his emotions and
be so bold?
Instead, wrath is suspressed and
truth gets a stay.

Oh! Wrath of emotion fills the body
with mystic pain,
That seems to end only when sleep
devours
The tired mind, all emotions
suddenly wanes,
Stillness, clear thoughts emerges
like spring flowers.

Oh! Wrath of emotions bid farewell
To the cause, that makes the wrath
unreal,
To life it's no stranger, but
happiness tells
In one's face, truth does reveal.

Oh! Wrath of emotion you have
gone a far,
With out-streatched arms with no
cause for remorse,

Now a new feeling of reaching out
for a star,
Becomes the strength from an
omnipotent source.

Oh! Wrath of emotion you are now
tame,
A steady mind, consoled soul has
now resurfaced,
Better or for worse is not a verdict
to proclaim,
Living becomes another day, but
not without purpose.

Sarah F Sands
DADDY'S IN HEAVEN

This poem is dedicated to Mr. Bill my wonderful Dad.

The Gates of Heaven
Opened wide,
Jesus, said to our
DADDY come inside;
The Angels came
And led the way
One cold November
Day.

Patricia Patterson
A TRIBUTE TO ELVIS

This poem is dedicated to God for His "gift" of Elvis to us.

The glitter and glamour of his life
and career are all behind him,
He has reached his final
destination and has found;
PEACE AT LAST
He was a giving, loving and
caring man who shared his life
with
others,
Depriving himself of what he
needed the most;
PEACE AT LAST
His mother and father, his
protectors and guides, are once
again reunited,

Elvis has returned to his real
family, and has found;
PEACE AT LAST
The emptiness and void in his
life have finally disappeared,
His time had come, his search for
an inner peace is over with;
PEACE AT LAST
He was a gentle man a great
man, who gave until he could
give no more,
Then God chose to call him for his
eternal reward;
PEACE AT LAST
He has reached his final
achievement, his ultimate goal,
his greatest concert,
The day God called him to His side,
for he now has;
PEACE AT LAST.

Angela M Grecian
MY RAINBOW

Come jump on my rainbow!
We'll see the world!
The night, the day,
The sun, the moon,
And the fiery stars at night.
Come see the country people with
country ways,
The city people with city ways,
Each doing their own things.
Come see the cottonfields and
lakes,
Birds atop the fences,
Fishes in streams,
And the windy, winding country
roads.
Come see the pansies and daisies,
The roses and the lilies,
All opening their petals to face the
world.
Through the colors in my rainbow
you'll see . . .
Lives that won't ever be full,
Pieces of dreams,
And that the world will never be
done unraveling.
So come jump on my rainbow!
Come see the world!

Deborah Lynn Copeland
VOWS OF LOVE

This poem is dedicated to: "my wonderful husband, Steve" "I LOVE YOU"

Today we spoke the vows of
everlasting love
In the presence of our families and
the Lord above
And in these vows we promised to
love until we died
To trust, honor, and cherish, and
walk side by side

I'll trust you Steve, for there is no
other way
And I'll honor you as my man, each
and every day
I'll cherish you all through my life
And I'll walk with you as friend,
lover, and wife

Yes, these vows we spoke were
more than just words
Vows filled of love, to others
unheard
For in each vow, in our own special
way
We exchanged our love which will
grow everyday

Barbara Chappelle Heller
LIFE

The beauty of sunrise and eventide
Earth, sky and sea;
Ages of wisdom past,
Faith of infinity,
The ultimate love in God's creation;
Hopes of the human race,
And a promise of life eternal
Are seen in a baby's face.

Madge R Close
DARE

How dare you dare to start
the bloom of a lost love again
after you broke my heart in two
when you said, "We'll never wed,"
because you found someone new
and then you bid me ado.
How dare you dare to think
to rekindle the great love
we once upon a time knew.
How dare you dare to return to me
and plead to take you back.
It will only bring back the bruise.
How dare I dare to accept you?
I dare to dare to love you again.

Tony Heiar
THE GREATEST CHEF EVER

The greatest chef ever was a jolly
old man
Who spent time in his kitchen
flipping
strawberry crepes in his frying pan.

He kept his customers happy
whipping up
gourmet delights which where
served on Saturday night.

A pinch, a dab, a toss, a bunch
He gave his creations a tasty punch.

To his chili he would add pepper
and onion and curry
All this he did with a style and a
flurry.

His souffles were a mile high
And he made the tastiest apple pie.

He baked snapper and trout
Well, they were always much
talked about.

He was always a master at roast
lamb
And produced the best baked and
honey-cured ham.

He had a real way with corn beef
hash
And even made his customers like
his succatash.

From the streets of San Francisco
to the shores of Maine
His scalloped oysters gained great
fame.

After all this you might wonder
what he did for relaxation.
A sip of fine wine and a long
vacation.

Jackie S Wagner
PART OF YOUR HEART

To Someone Special

Although you can't be with me
At least not all the time
You may not be where I can see
I know a part of you is mine
You may not be close by
Nowhere even near
But I can feel your presence
And I know that you are here
You're always on my mind
Whether it be day or night
The feeling is always there
Whether it be wrong or right
You'll always be with me
Even if we're far apart
For I own a special part of you
I have a part of your heart.

Erdine R Holbrook
FROM THE EDGE OF THE GRAND CANYON

The deepest caverns dug in the
depths of earth
In jagged form, immense in size,
are lit
With hues which rival spectra
softly split,
Into all shades and tints of rainbow
girth.
Were these the scars attending
rugged birth
That rent the hills and plains a bit
by bit
Until these crags were formed for
crows to sit,
Perchance results of early cosmic
mirth?

Just so our lives are filled with
many cares
That delve into deep caverns of the
souls
Of men to mock weak efforts as it
dares
Mere man to conquer mighty
force. It bowls
Us over, times on end and sorely
bares
Our hearts afresh as we attempt
new goals.

Dolph Greer
FRIENDS AT EASE

This poem is dedicated to Johnny P McBride my long time friend and fishing buddy now deceased.

Bump over the chop of the lake
In a bass boat toward the lea.
Worms, cane poles are enough to
make
Shell crackers wriggling fishing
spree.
Move over to the water grass
Beside the pasture pine tree strand
For shell crackers. We'll take a bass
And talk small town and business
drawl
In Buffum Lake with groves afar;
Shines Florida orange trees in sun,
And cottages peek 'mong pine
trees—
A world in motion slow blown
breeze
Not with the awe of artist's views
But fisherman and friends at ease.

Ken Grant
AERIAL SUNSET
(High Above The Northern
California Coast)

I love to watch the sun go down
Into a rainbow sea;
Far beneath our silver wings,
And disappear for me.

Like we're above the very heavens,
Flying fast and free;
Above each living mortal soul,
In our own eternity.

Up here, there's color everywhere
That's far beyond compare.
Not only flaming clouds and sky,
But scarlet-colored air.

Soon the sun will fade from view,
And leave a starlight sky;
Sinking red, in the western sea,
Like a mighty serpent's eye.

Headed home in the moonlight air
Only a flyer knows;
No earthly living soul could guess,
How an aerial sunset glows.

Michelle Lynn Kitchens

THE LIFE YOU SAVE

The life you save may be your own,
Through treacherous times and the waiting of dawn.
We must take the time to understand,
Success is behind The Master's plan.

Through love and hate—life and death,
We all do things that we regret;
These things should not make us blind,
There's just no time to fall behind!

Cheryl J Moor

EYE-DANCER

To William

I am there, dancing in your eyes,
Just as sure as I'm standing here.
As easy as walking away,
I could leave on a single tear.

But I will be there forever,
Dancing across an azure floor,
And I will be your eye-dancer
Until your eyes can see no more.

Valerie A Witscher

GLAD TO BE ME

The Flutter of Wings
as a bird passes by—
The sound fills the air
as a new baby cries.
The voices and laughter
of children at play—
All makes me happy
as life fills my day.

The health that I find
as each day I wake—
The smells that all fill me
as each breath I take.
The touch from the people
so special to me—
All make me see
I'm so glad to be me.

Frank B Trimm

UNTITLED

When flaming sun hath settled in its nest.
And all about is eager to lay down;
Then will the earthly multitude be rest,
Without the presence of all worldly sound.
Shall we the peaceful makers live to gain,
If all about is gone to be forgot:
Let us not shout about out glories fame,
When we, the teachers, fight to win, have taught.
For winning is not everything we know,
If by this winning ceases there a life:
True victory is not to beat the foe.
But lasting unity in hearts should thrive.
Now think, is man so eager to resign,
It may be thoughts of some, but not of mine.

Elizabeth Brooks Farnsworth

WHY?

Why? Why? Why us?
I've asked myself a thousand . . . no, a million times.
Our lives were perfect.
We were so very happy.
We were where we wanted to be.
A second son was like "icing on the cake."

After struggling and fighting life,
I think I know "why."
It's the "why" that only we could create.
Look at what we have to offer.
We are dedicated. We have love.
We know joy. We have a lot to give.
Dave was right, "We can do it together."

The answer was there all along
. . . as answers often are . . .
waiting to be discovered
. . . inside.

Kevin D Latiolais

LONELINESS

To never see a smiling face
brighten up this lonely place
would be hell on earth for me,
to never smile and never see.

A tear is shed, drop by drop,
A pool of water, down, kerplop.
No one here to cry my name,
no one here to end this game.

Now I know how one must feel
never knowing two as real.
Silent voices never carry.
Misty ghosts never marry.

Loneliness attacks the heart,
an emptiness about to start.
A smile, a glance, too far gone,
heartache, pain, all have won.

My eyes grow weary of wasted tears,
drop by drop for many years.
My limbs are weak, as if tied,
Alas! My soul has died.

Roberta Carolyn Woodard

THE RETURN OF THE WAVE

I would like to dedicate this poem to my parents, R. C. and Jewell. Without them, nothing would be possible for me. Thanks Mom and Dad.

The great torrent rises from the depths of the ocean,
Alike the precipice rises from the center of the earth,
Gently the misty moon rests upon the great wave,
As the cliff's edge glows with the phosphorous of the sea.
So very far from its destination,
Drowsily the great torrent begins to move.
With each passing moment it gains speed and strength.
Faster it moves, ever faster.
The cliff braces itself for the encounter.
Quickly, the giant wave approaches.
Silently, the precipice awaits.
Suddenly the wave is where it was meant to be.
The violent, resounding crash occurs.
The glow of phosphorous fuses with the mist of the moon.
Just as suddenly, all is now quiet.
And the quietness of death shall remain
Until the next night,
When the reunion will occur yet again,
Again, and again,
Until the Death of Time.

Ann Dee Schlegelmilch

DREAMS

Dedicated to my family and friends with love and appreciation for their encouragement in making my dreams come true. Special love sent out to my daughter Nicole, for being part of my dreams.

Our dreams can take us far away,
To regions unexplored;
As distant as the farthest star,
On wings of birds that soar.
Join cavalcades of gypsies gay,
In dashing, bright apparel.
Or float on lofty, fleecy clouds,
Singing angelic carols.
Skip lightly over cobblestones,
On boulevards of old,
Or strut along with head held high,
Feeling arrogant and bold.
Meet mystery with every step,
And question every tenet.
Hold light to brighten darkest nights;
Recite the best loved sonnet.
With dreams we live out fantasies;
We make each dream come true.
Let go of love in one quick glance,
Not caring what or who.
So dream we shall, and hold our own.
No soul can take dreams from us.
For dreams are ones' own silent way,
Of keeping hopes prodigious.

Sam G Simon

AGING

There ain't much fun when you're 81
You can't lift your feet 'cause they each weigh a ton
You can't jog or walk and surely can't run
All you can do is sit on your bun
My sight is fading, my hearing is nill
My prostrate is active, my colitis is still
My arthritis is dormant, waiting for the winter chill
I'm losing my crown of glory, balding inspite of my skill
My heart is still beating 'cause I control it with a pill
They tell me you look good and don't look ill
But the truth of the matter is I'm really over the hill

Robyn G Larew

I MISS YOU

In days gone by, when I was small,
and looking up at you,
It didn't matter what went wrong,
you knew just what to do.

If things at school were hard, or
just not going well,
It always was to you I'd come,
always you I'd tell.

You'd look at me with clear blue
eyes and hold my hand,
I always knew deep in my heart,
you would understand.

During times now, when things are
going rough,
I remember that I didn't say, "I love
you" near enough.

Those days are gone, now so are
you.
I find myself, at times, not knowing
what to do.

When I'm alone and have nowhere
to turn,
I realize, deep down inside, it is for
you I yearn.

In case that you can hear me, or
just know what I write,
Let me say "Thank you, Mom," for
making things allright.

If only I could talk to you, and you
could hold my hand,
I know that things would be just
fine, and you would understand.

Marjorie Prince

MAN, A LITTLE ANIMAL

A squirrel
because he is hatched hungry
Makes his own lump of luck
And sniffs his diet of disaster.

He flashes his swift signature
upon the bald brown bark
And is gone—
Beyond my quiet
Beyond my questions.

Marian E Luebbert

YOU

The clouds had formed a picture frame
The center was azure blue
And in my concentration
The picture inside was you.

I saw the smile upon your face
And I felt your tender glance

I thought of all the lovely times
We shared our sweet romance

And now the clouds have blown away
Your picture came apart
But I don't need the clouds to see you
For you live here, in my heart.

Natalie Leja

LOVE

99 times through the day
We get love when we pray
God gave us love
As peaceful as a dove
Love that cares
Love that He shares
Love that He made for us
Not to fool and fuss
With it
But to share it
So I'm going to share my love with you
Because I care about you
In my heart
And I'll show you in my art.

Carla M Wiggins

EULOGY OF A DOOMED MAN

"Come on in son, admissions free"
The man at the door just smiled at me
"Two for the price . . . but your just one"
"What the hell, you'll have some fun"
"Go through that door and hang a right"
"Relax a little man, you're too uptight"
He loosened my tie and gave me a shove
I saw that glint in his eye, it wasn't love
So I took his advice and I followed that path
Talk about unleashing the "grapes of wrath"
The dude was right, this wasn't so bad
Like he said, "hot talking preachers just made you mad"
So I lived it up, gave it one last shot
As the saying goes I was really hot
But the day soon came when I saw no more
I didn't know what they had in store
Soon I learned that it wasn't a plea . . .
When the man at the door just smiled at me
"Come on in son, admissions free"

Wm L Irwin

MEMORIES FOREVER LOST TO TIME

To my little Buzzy who died tragically but died in innocence.

First son, first born, first love, no more.
Oh for a hungry cry to hear,
No laughing Buzzy I see,
No arms to hug my neck,
No feet to stand upon my knee,
No kisses to embrace my cheek,
His little lips forever sealed to me.
Dear God, how I hated in giving him up to your
blessed heaven;
I feel so empty,
To that of a cold pre-dawn grave—
Not having my little Buzzy to grow beside me.
Nor can I find comfort in his memory,
As only guilt burdens the mind,
As his memory forever grows dim with time!

Luis Alberto Guerreiro

THE WOUNDS IN OUR HEARTS

To my wife, Lassalete, and our daughter, Jennifer, with love.

The street kid in rags with eyes the color of the sky
knocks at our window and asks for a dime

No one responds
from the wounds in our hearts
get lost I don't have a dime
our eyes raised in the sky too busy in the brilliant clouds

The street kid persists extending his palm and begging
a delicate hand promising buildings triggers bread
in the summer morning his lip falling in a
premeditated touch of persuasion
get lost I said we don't have money
the street kid clownishly runs away and joins two other
kids in rags
the frustrated beggar sticks his tongue out at us and runs
and runs in his happiness without reins
they run and smile with eyes the color of the sky

They run and leave behind in their shadow
shining petals of the shameful vision of remorse unsettled
yet not won upon or secularized
in our wounds
the system runs
buildings triggers bread

Dawnee Ramsey

WHEN ALL SEEMS LOST

Dedicated to my mother who passed away August 1, 1986.

As I walk alone now and then
I wish I could see you once again.
As the days went past
I thought back and remembered what you said.

When all seems lost, you said,
Try to remember happiness again,
If nothing comes to mind
Think of me until then
Be sure of all kind.

When all seems lost, you said,
I'm never far behind
Just try to remember you're one of a kind.
Good will come and bad will go,
That is when you'll know
All is not lost,
But somewhere very near,
That is when you'll know,
All is not lost,
But is in the mist of the air.

Until then hang on to memory,
And soon you'll see
The joys of happiness and me.

Stephanie J Overby

EAGLE

Eagle, strong and bold,
How tall today you stand.
O' nation full of gold,
A great and glorious land.

She has seen some wars,
Sometimes she did not win;
But through rough times she endures.
Yes, she stands through thick and thin.

Her people had much pride;
They stood up for their rights,
And, oh, so many men have died
To help her in her early plights.

Today we see her fly;
She's above all the rest
With her head held high.
Her people made her the best!

James G Weravetz

WHAT THE FUTURE HOLDS

Dedicated to three Outstanding performers: Paul Simon, Suzanne Vega, Stevie Nicks

---

Todayist;
Future passed, from those on the boats, maybe three.
Sailing from East to West, Cuba has sent their best.
Banking off the Northeast wind,
Japan is trying to not misspend.

Today we see alot of camaraderie,
On the streets and on the beach.
Was it they whom said,
"Better Dead than Red?"

Pushing too hard trying to succeed,
Only a Professional can agree.

A burst of glare in the Eastern sky,
Took lives of the trusting brave.
Relying on experience invested,
Only now they have rested.

So long ago since the fall of Rome,
People as the like, have tried to find a home.
Searching the world as to invite,
This is my space, "Let's not fight."

With two hands and feet,
A Twenty-count is easy.
Square the number, it might show a score.
But since the world is round,
The Future Holds no Bounds.

Grace G Desprez

THE CURSE OF THE NORTH

We're living out an ice-age prelude,
For the weight of the world will shift
When the arctic crawls out of it's shadow,
And it's continental cover goes adrift.

For then the sleeping princess will awaken
In the arms of the sun, her handsome prince,—
And the flowers of their doom's day will bloom again,
As they never have bloomed since!

But like ants stir-frying in a pan,
Let us do our frantic dance while yet we can;
For few of us will ever live to see
The glories of this bright new world to be;—

Our dream, the diadem of paradise,
Shall sit upon another's brow.
The steam of our hell has moved the ice,
And nothing can save our world of now!

Through aeons of silent unawareness
Our timer's icy sands shall sift,—
For Lo! The virgin princess now arises,
And the curse upon the Northland shall lift!

David Allen Schmelter

HALLOWEEN NIGHT

The moon comes out as gray clouds go by,
The winds start to hollar as the trees start to cry;
Yet some people say it's just another night,
But don't you believe it, it isn't right;

As you walk down the street amongst eerie things,
For every sound you hear, your knees start shaking;
And you watch in the sky for a flying witch,
And in the trees where bats will twitch;

Even tricks and treaters are in fright,
As they walk down the street holding hands real tight;
Yet everybody knows on October thirty-first,
That witches and goblins are out to do their worst;

Even as pumpkins glow and costumes flee,
The night is still young for the wicked and eerie;
So lock your doors and pull down the shades,
For this is the night the witches and goblins go on their raids;

Now go to bed and cover up tight,
It's going to be a long Halloween night;
And when you awaken, I'm sure you'll see,
That you would wish it was still Halloween. . .

Lorna Anne Skinner (LAS)

POLLUTED RAVINES

Dedicated to: present and future generations and to Mother Nature. . . long may they live.

Mountains, rivers, and country streams
Towns and big cities with polluted ravines,
Nature's beauty is dying
So lets save what we can,
And not destroy nature along with man.

Kay Riddle
OF THORNS AND FLOWERS
Today a tender hand caressed my brow
Reminding me of the important things
Like love and dreams and hope,
And I was peaceful again,
I knew that life had meaning.
Oh how I pity the wretched heart
That has never known the hand of God
Or seen His eminent presence in their own darkened mind;
Never traced His artist's brushes as He fashioned each of us,
No two alike and every one beloved.
Oh God,
I'm hard sometimes
And hard of hearing.
It's a cruel world sometimes
And cold.
But there are roses among the thorns.
I never saw them while I ran through the briers
Cursing.
But looking back I see.
And it was worse to myself that I never took time to smell their fragrance
Or savor the beauty of their crimson petals.
Worse to myself that I never thanked You for the flowers of my life
Because I only saw the thorns

Pauline Burlison
A SAD SATURDAY
"Ho, hum, tweedle dum, by now he should have come,"
Grandfather sat in his wheel chair, glum.
He'd been bathed and dressed. (It was an effort, too)
He wanted to smell nice and look good to you.
He bragged to the others that you always came
On a Saturday, and each time the same.
That you brought him such joy and happiness
He could forget he had to live like this:
Bound to a chair within four walls,
And hardly a day without pain from falls.
With you he could pretend to wrestle and play
As often he'd done on a long ago day
When strong and agile he would romp with you,
And more than likely teach you a lesson or two.
I'm sorry they called just now to say
That important business was taking you away.
I must wheel him back to his dreary room,
And watch his face fill up with gloom
When I break the news as gently as I can
To a dejected, disappointed ninety-two-year-old man.
I do hope you can come next Saturday
To visit your grandfather old and gray.

Joanne Norman Schiffman
THE ROSE
The bud appears
unfolding slowly
displaying
delicate layers
of petals
revealing
glory of
a rose.

SUDDENLY
a tinge
of black
appears
soon after
the rose
will wilt
petals will
fall
one-by one.

The glory
of the
rose
is finished
too soon
TOO SOON.

A J Jackson
ONE ON ONE
Awash in a turbulant sea there is an Island.
In that self-supporting desert there is much beauty,
But sadly, it is seen by few because people so often
Choose to look with the eye rather than the heart.
Often the sea grows angry, and the winds in the night
Blow so strong that they threaten to overwhelm the island.

But always, by morning, the tides recede, the winds die
Down to a gentle breeze, and still the Island stands,
All the stronger for the experience.

High above, the moon and stars watch with interest,
Nightly keeping their lonely vigil to see who will be the
Victor at dawn.

And always, they disappear into the morning wondering how
Such an insignificant tuft of scrubby plants and dirt can
Remain so immovable, defiant of the might of the raging sea.

Eloisa Cantu
DRIFTED APART

Dedicated to my two moms, Clementina and Lucy. I'll forever love you.

I remember the moments we shared
And all the times you said that you'll always care.
All the memories we had will last forever,
Even though time could no longer keep us together.
When we were drifting away and felt more apart,
I knew I would always have you deep inside my heart.
The happiness we gave each other could never be replaced,
Nor could all the sadness we shared and had to face.
When we separated and sadly said goodbye,
I knew it would never be the same like the times when
It was just you and I.

Helen K Simpson
BACK TO NATURE

To my mother and father

Looking at the state of things
That rules from man-made kings
Should start us on a different course
Using nature as our resource.

The worth of one man's living
May be solved by another's giving
For many bear suffering untold
Because man's measure is by gold.

Let us cast the pain away
Sharing what's in the world today
Food being man's first need
The first gift to all—a little seed.

A plot of land to grow the seed
If insufficient for everyone's need
Many greenhouses may be a solution
For purer food without pollution.

Let us breathe much cleaner air
Laying all the factories bare
Giving hands the joy of creation
The skill of many to clothe a nation.

Oil slicked water and exploding gas
What fuel is safest to heat the mass
Give man the seeds for trees to plant
The oxygen gained would be extant.

Then doesn't nature give all our needs
And take away the cause of greed
Giving beauty to man's dimension
Removing the cause of his dissension.

Lisa E Rand
TIME
Time is more than a minute . . .
Time can be Love and Trust
To the breaking of a heart
And a feeling inside.
We have more Time.
Oh yes, Time . . .
Time . . .

We will go into Time and be lovers.
Forever, together
me and you.

Time is more than an hour
It's me and you.
Time is us together . . .
me and you.

Bobbie Johnson Jordan
TIME SLIPS AWAY
When the wind blows
The cradle does rock
Time slips away
Like seconds on a clock
Yesterday, I was a baby
The next day, a small child
From a teenager to a mother
Now, I hold my grandchild
Time slips away
Much too fast for me
Before you know it
A great-grandmother, I'll be
Life is so good
I never want it to end
But for it to keep flowing
Like a river around a bend
But, if my time stops tomorrow
My life still goes on
Through my children and grandchildren
So, I'll not be gone.

Benjamin Franklin Pierce
CHILD OF MY HEART

Para Tracy Perez, Yo te amo mi Corazon, para siempre.

Along the miles of sentiment's shore.
as frost bends down the bough:
there lies the truest love I've known.
at rest in memory now.

She was the freshness of each day.
the tender smile upon my face;
a child within a woman's frame.
wide-eyed wonder set in grace.

A whispered hope upon the wind,
as dawn goes down to day;
a page in time has now been turned,
and she has gone away.

The door is closed between us now,
as though a widening sea;
life's spark within has long since died,
for she was a part of me.

And now I've told you, one and all,
of a heartbreak here to stay;
how I grew to sorrow the moment,
when loveliness passed my way.

Myrtle S Munn
BELLS
There are church bells, school bells, bells of every kind.
But when I think of bells, there's one that comes to mind,
It's the old fashioned dinner bell like the one my mama rang,
To let us know that lunch was ready
Oh how our feet would spring!

I'm sure we never worked too hard, even tho we were physically able.
But the food tasted so good, the meal mama made
When we gathered around the table.

Those were the days before we had watches
To tell us the time of day, but God in His infinite wisdom always provided a way.
When our stomachs began to feel empty, and we could step on our shadow's head with our feet,
We knew that soon the bell would be ringing
And we would all get to go home to eat

They say as we grow older, our taste buds change
And nothing tastes as good as before

But the memories of things we
enjoyed as a child
I cherish them more and more.
Many changes have been made as
life goes on,
But the memories I love so well,
are somehow entwined with my
life as a child,
And the sound of the old dinner
bell.

Larry Steven Drake

AMERIKA, AMERIKA

Amerika, Amerika—more justice
accidentally
A noble plan; A bless-ed land
Forefathers could not bear to see:
Your apathy, hypocrisy—Ad-man's
democracy.
Crown-ed, blind elite pervert my
sweet!
My sweet oppress-ed's retreat.

From university blind teachers
bleat
Blind phrases made of sinful meat.
Blind, truthless books entreat and
hook
By serendipitous insight,
To blind and mame the youthful
sane
With more of the insane blight.
Amerika, Amerika—more
confrontation designedly:
To fill the bowels and the jowels
Of thy ravenous, insane machine!
To make and sell the cogs of hell
Mass-marketed interworldly!

Great conflict sought; just short of
wraught—
To deplete that inventory!
And make more guns, their routes
to run
Making the world safe for
democracy!
Oh Beautiful, oh spacious heart of
Liberty,
Regain your soul; Retake your role;
Re-Reason—from sea to shining
sea.

Harlan E Hobson

SOMETHING TO THINK ABOUT

You can't please everyone, I've
heard it said
and this is oh so true.
But you can influence people, for
good or bad
by the things you say and do.
Every morning when you wake up
you have a choice to make.
You can be a person that gives of
theirselves
or you can be a person who takes.
Giving does not always mean
the giving of material things.
Much more important is the gift of
giving love
and the joy that this love brings.
Believe me, there's plenty of hate
in the world
and we've got negative people
galore.
So please don't try to be like them
cause we really don't need
anymore.
We need more people who aren't
afraid to smile
and let their inner selves show
through
We need more people who aren't
afraid to hug
and to simply say, "I love you."
So as you start each day, examine
yourself
see what you're really made of
Are you a critical person who
spreads discontent
or a caring one who spreads love.
And if you were to die tomorrow
ask yourself, "What would people
say?"
Will they come and pay their
respects
or secretly be glad you have gone
away?

Armilde Kivilaan

LIFE, THE MOST BEAUTIFUL

To my husband, Dr. Aleksander Kivilaan

Shimmery the world of life,
where sun in charge to mix
colors—
—eyes be given—to seperate them
all well,
and art, with inner light can
presence them all.
Patience, endurance to them
who adding more vivid beauty to
shaded side of life.
All living beings for decoration—
in time-chamber are lined up.
And they are proud to proceed the
dance—among the others . . .
It is dance—the dance of life—
Luckily it is short . . .
At time to exceed the ballroom . . .
the costume wrinkled—stained
with sweat—
even bones are weather beaten,
weak.
The thoughts for life—quite
different,
even if the face is in smile—it is
weared . . .
and for activity—no energy . . .
It is gone.

Ruth Mohr Ildza

HIGH PLACES

To my husband Clayton, and children Faith, Carol, and John. With them I have known many high places. They also help to make the low places more serene.

I listened to the wind, and heard
my Lord,
In powerful accents, how the earth
did shake!
And then the whispering aspens
answered Him,
As all turned calm like ripples on
a lake.
I saw Him there upon the
mountain top,
Majestic peaks, snow capped and
crowned with trees.
Yet, simple winding roads led up
to him.
Wee creatures and small birds, too,
he used these.
A myriad of small flowers, gold and
blue,
Yellow and lavenders, snow white
and red,
Made carpets, midst high
meadows, round some trees,
His glory blazed in all these signs
I read.
I thought, "How excellent, my
Lord, thou art!
I must take you back to city streets
and sod.
For, oh, they need you so, majestic
one,
Magnificent, towering, yet so
gentle God.
In your high places, how my soul
is filled.
But the low places can be full,
serene."
"Oh, man, invite Him in to sup, to
stay,
And know the power and peace
these eyes have seen!"

Frederick Sherwood Crafts

SEARCH FOR THE BUNTING

To Deborah

Above old scrub, in endless blue,
White wisps of cloud drift slowly by
Although this tranquil scene, it's
true,
Seems incomplete; do you know
why?

No feathered heart of lilting note
Sits high atop the tallest tree,
Filling moments on which to dote
With cheerful songs sung just for
me.

But wait! There! Did you see it, too?
A small blue bird with grayish
wings—
I'm certain that one past me flew
To yonder wood; let's pray it sings.

You're so quiet, my perching child,
Where leafy boughs hang o'er the
stream;
Are you saddened to be so wild
That no one knows your only
dream?

If just a twitter rises nigh,
Then falls away, yet lifts once more,
My heart will soar into the sky
And find, perhaps, life's secret
door.

Ah! I see you! But please do sing
So that we will finally know
If you are, little bird of spring,
The bunting blue with indigo.

Juanita Burris

SPECIAL DELIVERY

"Look out world, I'm on my way"
"One day in October will be my
birthday."
"A boy or a girl which will I be"
"That's my secret, so just wait and
see."
"I know my family can't hardly
wait,"
"So I must remember not to be
late."
"I know my arrival will be a
delight,"
"Maybe I'll come in the middle of
night."
"So many good things await me
out there."
"A world of love and tender care,"
"I'm anxious to see my loved one's
faces,"
"And to be taken to exciting places,"
"So raise your glasses and drink a
cheer,"
"Cause someone special is about to
appear."

Clayton D White

E.R.A. N.O.W.

"What time is it, please?"
this cry for help cycles a lonely
house,
halting briefly at the attic floor;
then it sifts softly below,
more silent than bitter ashes
"What time is it, please?"
my dearest daughter,
only you may choose that
whichsoever hour of that
whatsoever year
when you shall abandon your
translucent chrysalis,
shedding your stained-glass
childhood;
then climb those steep and dark
and echoing stairs,
to unfurl and dry and try your own
great unruly wings in the sun,
beside that other self,
your sisters
"What time is it, please?"
my daughter,
so much depends upon you alone,
not on some eyeless sentinels
who stand with helpless hands,
ticking away their own time in a
hollow and windy hallway
"What time is it, please?"
daughter,
it is seldom too soon,
and almost always so very late

Jesse Karas

UNSPOKEN WORDS

I can't say how I feel
words are untrue
they cannot feel what I do
the unspoken words of the heart

A smile brings new hope
a touch lets you know
what words never tell
the unspoken words of the soul

the unspoken words of the heart
the unspoken words of the soul
are the unspoken words you can
know

The words slip away
no one knows where they stray
they may return, but until,
remember
the unspoken words that you know

I've tried to show how I feel
but am misunderstood
open your soul to hear
the unspoken words that I know

the unspoken words of the heart
the unspoken words of the soul
are the unspoken words that I
know.

Barb Edgecomb

LONG DISTANCE LOVE

Although the miles separate us
We're still very close in heart
But when you do come home to me
I'm afraid we'll have to part
The road has been a long one my
friend

I'm very sorry to say.
You've seen too much of the world
So you'll have to go your own way.
But I want to tell you one last thing before you go for good
Remember how we were
please promise if you could
Remember. You'll always hold
A special place in this heart of mine
A true love
Of a very special kind.

Margo Pike

DOWN THE HALLS OF FORGOTTEN DREAMS

Down the halls of forgotten dreams they wander
In a world all their own—
For many in a world of the past, for very, very few in the world of the future.
Some sit, some lay they all dream the same—
Where are the children?
Did they have their supper?
Will (he) or (she) be home tonight?
But some days they are happy other days are sad and lonely.
Somedays they ache and others not so bad.
Down the halls of forgotten dreams.
The saddest thing you will hear them say—
"Some day we will all get to go home"
It seems a shame they should have to suffer so—
But when the end is near they seem to know—
No more pain they just seem to let go!
Down the halls of forgotten dreams.

Kelly Louise Dawson

OH, PERFECT ROSE!

To my beautiful mother, Barbara Jean Marx, for her love, understanding, and support. Thanks Mom!

Have you ever walked through a garden
Admiring God's magical works we call flowers?
Among them are the most beautiful, the Rose
Roses come in many colors, sizes, and scents
Each is unique
One tends to pamper a Rose, unlike any other flower
Why? Roses are very, very special . . .

A child knows not of a Rose
But only as a flower
Even though it's from that Rose
We get our strength and power
We sometimes take for granted all the beauty that we see
So now I want to tell you that you're beautiful to me
You've blossomed for your family
Your petals they extend
You've spread perfume into the gloom
With a smile that's Heaven scent!
You're put upon a pedestal at least a mile high
And trimmed in lace set in a vase
we all look up and sigh
Oh, Perfect Rose
Oh, Perfect Rose
I'm hoping that you know
I'm speaking of <u>you</u> Mother
For you're the Perfect Rose.

Holly D B McClure

YELLOW

Yellow is the happiest flower
blooming in a field,
Yellow is the color
of a sign that warns to yield;
Yellow is a golden hue
of dawn upon the grass,
Yellow caresses the cheek
in hair of a Scandinavian lass.
Yellow is a banana
to peel and eat with mirth,
Yellow sparks aglow
that's in the fire near the hearth;
Yellow are the pages
that to an old book belong,
Yellow is my soul
when it is singing happy songs.

Vivian Love

MY GARDEN

I planted seeds in my garden,
Each one was planted with love;
And down came the rain from Heaven,
From our dear Savior Above.

He knew if we must have gardens,
We must have the warm sun and rain;
To cultivate our gardens and flowers,
And to raise our golden grain.

He watches over the tiny plants,
And all the living things;
But we must never forget to thank Him,
For all the blessings He brings.

Sherie-Lynn Riesberg

I WISH YOU A CONSCIENCE

Karyn Conrath; English Instructor, Montcalm Community College, a precious jewel in every domain.

Parent, the child is needy.
She has hands to hold,
kisses, and hugs to share.
Moments pass that cannot be brought back.
I wish you a conscience.

Parent, the child is alone.
She has accomplishments to show,
questions of life to ask.
Lack of love destroys her self-esteem.
I wish you a conscience.

Uncle, the niece is afraid.
She has games to play,
friends, and secrets to keep.
Unwanted touches confuse her mind.
I wish you a conscience.

Husband, the wife is hurting.
She has children and trust to give,
nights saved for you to love.
Broken vows promise to take their toll.
I wish you a conscience.

LeRoy Cape

SNOW COVERED RED ROSE

With its beauty frozen through all time
Its scents of perfumes untouched
With melted snow showing
The tears of it drips down
With love it could give
As the rose dreams for love
The snow covered red rose

Pam Fish

A MOTHER'S BOY

To: Jesse Fish. This poem is dedicated to my 6 yr. old son, who has brought so much joy in my life.

There once was a little boy
His love for me brought so much joy,
With his dark black hair and wavy curls
A round little face, white as pearls.
Loving him was the greatest thing
It made my heart live and sing.

The lad had freckles on his face
He was my buddy, my little ace.
Throughout my life, when in despair—
His words were, I love you Mom, I care.
As these words were spoken to me
A teardrop fell upon my knee.

As years pass by and you're lonely or blue
Open the scrapbook of the boy and you,
You cannot know the joy it will bring—
Like bright colorful flowers in the Spring.
Summer, Spring, Winter, or Fall,
Pictures are memories for you to recall.

Zilpha Reed

Zilpha Reed

TRUE LOVE

True love is an emotion two people share.
True love is caring when they share
Happiness and sadness.
True love's survival is truth and forgiveness.
True love survives, and hardships die.
True love brings back happiness and lets
Sadness lie.
True love strengthens when happiness and sadness are
Shared.
True love is heaven sent by faith in God's love.
True love thrives on truth, forgiveness and faith
That love brings.
True love deserves to let sadness lie and
Happiness win, to have faith in God's love and keep
It alive.

Nona O Volz

AMERICA MY LOVE

To my Sons, Brothers and all relatives who has served in the services of this great country.

You are mine from border to border,
So no strife, let's keep order.
From those who would do us wrong,
We must be strong.
They say we have their trust,
After our land they lust.
We came from freedom of choice,
We do have a voice.
To you who deceive,
In our land we believe.
So give a hand, big or small,
We love our America one and all.
You gave us everything,
Let all the bells ring.
With God above, and Brotherly love,
YOU AMERICA, ARE MY LOVE.

Karolyn Nelson

I BELIEVE

I believe in love
even when I don't feel it.
I believe in the sun
even when it's not shining;
I believe in the moon and stars
even if they don't glow at night.
I believe in the rain
on a hot, dry day.
I believe in other people
even when they've done me wrong;
I believe in the best
even when the worst is showing.
I believe in happiness
even when I feel only sadness;
I believe in crying
even if tears are not shed.
I believe in my friends
even when they're not around;
I believe in God
even when He's silent;
I believe in Heaven above
even though I cannot see it.

Marilyn Ellet

THANKSGIVING DAY

Turkey, dressing and pumpkin pie
makes me think of days gone by.
When I was little and this I'll say . . .
I never wanted to miss
Thanksgiving Day.

Mom worked so hard in her kitchen so bright!
The fragrance of good food was such a delight.
The chicken so golden, the biscuits so light
We all waited for that wonderful sight!

Then the relatives all came in—
The table all set and ready to begin.
Mother said "Lets all sit down."
The table was filled all around.

We all loved mom's cooking,
So good to eat—pass the potatoes
And pass the meat.
It really and truly was a treat.

So now after the years have gone by,
I just want to say—
Thankyou, mom
For those wonderful Thanksgiving Days.

Estelle Sams Gordon
SEASONS OF LIFE

To the one who loves and encourages me most, my husband Gene.

My life was so much like magic,
Like the magician performs in his show.
Once I was like a daffodil,
With a lot of beauty and glow.
As time passed by, something else I wanted to be,
Then I was like the sun, sand and the roaring of the sea.
A short time later the sun began to dim its light,
I was a crimson leaf, fluttering beneath the Heavens, like a tiny kite.
Now it is almost time for the magician to pack and go.
I am faded, calm and falling, I am a blanket of snow.

Alice Mae Bernard
COMTEMPLATION
Upon a rock I sat and gazed
in wonderment and awe
At creation.

How did God know one day I'd need
a softly blowing breeze
some birds to sing a new song
flowers to brighten a dreary day
And trees.

How did God know one day I'd need
a seashore's sandy beaches
the crash of breaking waves
a rocky crag along the shore
And seashells.

How did God know one day I'd need
a storm to cool the summer's heat
the sunshine when the rain is past
a snowflake on my windowpane
A mountain's majesty.

Because . . .
God knew me even when
He breathed the breath of life in man
And all these things were made for me
To enjoy from birth through eternity!

Sonja Gilleylen Gibson
MY PRAYER TO GOD

In loving Memory of my Mother, Ellen

Lift the weight from my troubled mind, oh Lord.
Lift the weight from my weak heart.
Alleviate the weight of my burdened soul and let my blind eyes be opened to acknowledge the presence of God.

Build me up and make me strong for I'm weak, but I know I'm wrong.
Provide me with reason for my every reaction of life. Fill
me with all goodness and kindness that I may live in glory and never sin and cause worry.

Thank you Jesus for this life of mine. It isn't perfect but neither was it meant to be.
Whenever I'm troubled I pray to you on a bent knee.
I just say, "Thank you Lord for everything."

Phyllis Lynum
JUPITER IS MARY
I came here many years ago, when Jupiter was small
The light-house was the beauty spot
So picturesque and tall.
Mary then, was young and gay and very kind to me.
She was my dearest friend by far
This new friend, by the sea.
Mary taught me many things, so southern, and so new.
I learned of plants and fruits, and shells
And southern cooking too!
Many friends have gone away,
And jupiter has grown
But the sea and sands remember her, and claim her as their own
And so do I—I can't forget, for everywhere I go,
The palm trees that we loved so much
The sea gulls flying low
All seem to whisper "Mary,"
And this will always be
As long as I've a mem'ry
And as long as there's a me!

Donna Fischer
A WALK WITH YOU IN THE PAGES OF TIME

Denise and Bryan on their day and Wayne, our walk together has been beautiful.

As you both travel down life's long path
Remember always, to look back at the past.
For with it comes tomorrow, and it's always the best, but only if you grab it and hold it to your heart.
For then comes the love and the zest to conquer it and treasure it, for it goes fast.
With it comes memories of things past, young and gay. And the realization with each passing day, you're heading towards the other way.
But always look to God and try to see he loves you, yea as the leaves on the trees.
And with your hand entwined with his, you'll come to see that
life is what you strive to make it be.
Always start each day with a song and a smile in your heart, and your belief in God will never tear you apart.
Stop to look at things great and small, and remember your love will make you both tall.
To have loved and have lost is not the best, but to love and keep it is to know all the rest.
For with each passing year you'll know that the tears were only the shedding of all your fears.
And as you come to the final end, you'll know that God and your love is just around the bend.
And most of all the things you thought were bad were only the steps for you that God had.
So count your love and blessings along the way, for like life's sorrows, they'll pass with each day.
For like a rose, it buds and grows to the fullest and then starts to close.
But the beauty and sweetness in your mind stays on. So savor it,
my children, and keep it for each passing day.
We're only here for such a short while, and it's really up to you to keep it with a smile, for only then can you see, life is what you make it be.

Marie Jaconetti
INSPIRED IN A DREAM

In Loving Memory of My Friend Libby Gregory, (And Also) To All God's Children

---

I'm coming again like the ripples of the sea.
Don't fret or be frightened, for all will know me.
I've come for you all, who will be by my side.
To share peace and all joy, and make sorrows subside.
My love for you all is ever so great,
And I want every one of you to walk thru that gate.
I'm the light shining bright,
That shines on thru the night.
And don't ever have doubt,
It will never go out.
Put your bad faults away, and all turn unto me,
Like the waves of the ocean, and the
beautiful sea.
Oh come, come, come all unto me,
Like the waves of the ocean, and the beautiful sea.

Judy Ann Somers
PAIN, SORROW, GUILT

To Jessica, Brian and my family, may God bless you all with the love, joy and laughter you have given me

---

Pain, sorrow, guilt
Don't you wish such words were never invented

or the feelings that they bring?
Joy, love, laughter
would have been enough.

Rinay
ROOTS

To my 105 year old grandmother, Agnes Legros, from whence my Roots did grow.

Oh, mighty tree so tall!
You, whose roots do bind you here,
Are yet considered to be free.
While I, whose feet are free to roam,
Am ever bound to this place,
That I call Home!

Gail H Phillips
DONNIE

This poem is dedicated to Ethel, without whom there would have been no Donnie and quite possibly, no poetry in my life.

A little boy with big blue eyes
Came to our home and touched our lives.
He came to us when he was five,
The report said "Hopeless," but that was a lie.
His first few years of life had been rough,
All of the foster homes had made him tough.
He didn't laugh and he didn't cry,
He didn't play as the days went by.
We had no magic wand to wave,
Love was the medicine we gave.
And slowly—so slowly we saw a light
Steal into those blue eyes and shine so bright.
When he was six he began to speak,
And play and laugh at Hide 'N Seek.
There was a lot of catching up to do,
So much undone—so much was new!
Now he's nine with still far to go,
But his eyes are bright and his face is aglow
With each new challenge that comes his way.
He climbs each mountain day by day.
We've watched him blossom and come to life,
So much beauty from so much strife.
And all the love we give to him
Is returned tenfold by Donnie Grimm.

Florence Y Striker
KISS CAN DO
There once was a pretty young girl named Trunella
But somehow for kissing she'd say—"not for me fella."
One day by a young man she was tenderly kissed
'Twas only then that Trunella knew what she'd missed.
Tears began to fall, I'm sure no need for me to tell ya.

But alas, the tears were soon to cease their flow
That daring young man just wouldn't let her go.
Life now was pictured in an all new frame
Those two danced and they sang—they knew no shame
Two hearts beating wildly—faces all a-glow.

Now soon on her finger a ring was placed
As at the altar the preacher they faced
Saying their vows, making the two of them one.
For them at that moment a new life begun.
How happy were the two as they embraced.

By now our Trunella has lived thru birthday eighty-two
And the gents pass her by with little or no ado.
But there's still a twinkle in her eye
Undimmed not at the years flying by
As she happily remembers what a kiss can do!

Peter Miller Esq
MY NEIGHBOR

To my wife, Evadney, My daughter Milissa and my Sons Roger and Peter Jr. Thanking God for his blessing and his love.

The birds sing
My old door bell rings
But I did not listen
It was within my heart I whistle

To find my dream I look above
For the answer I seek below
My dream I saw upon a hill
And was bought with just pure skill

In I move without a doubt
Not knowing my neighbor's whereabouts
Years have past, and old I grow
My neighbor, I did know

I was young and did not know
My neighbor was old and filled with knowledge
So they did what God forbids
And hate me for the things I did.

Forrest N Cobb
YEARNINGS?
Was it fantasy or did I hear
Spring's first murmur in my ear?
My wishful thoughts may have led
To only what she may have said.

I yearn for blooms and birds and sun,
Soft rains and grass and fishing fun.
I'm tired of snow and ice and freezes;
I want to feel those southern breezes.

Yes, something sounded in my ear,
And spring is close this time of year.
So was it dreaming or was it fact?
Is it winter or will spring act?

Mrs Lois E Wielenga
A TRIBUTE TO LEVI

This poem is dedicated to my very "special" nephew, Levi and his loving and dedicated parents, Darrel and Lynn.

A new little baby has arrived on the scene,
He looks like his daddy; he is so serene.
But, Lord, how we wonder and nobody knows
Why Levi was born with no fingers and toes.

What is the problem? Who was to blame?
We wonder, "Will your lives ever be the same?"
You have shed lots of tears and felt the heartaches
As the fear of the future this situation creates.

But the Lord gives you strength and wisdom to know
That He had this planned long, long ago.
You know through His grace and His loving care
That Levi will not be a burden that you cannot bear.

God has given him health and a beautiful face
Which we know, in time, all your tears will erase.
You've touched our lives, Lord, with this special guy;
Now accept our humble thanks for little Levi.

William R Kelly
PASSING MOMENTS

Dedicated to Mary, my wife, Hawkeye Club, Everyone else fighting drug abuse.

The days,
Are long.
The Years,
Much too short.

I, wonder
How many hours,
I have,
Before,
I, too,
Am gone

Betty Jane Hart
THOUGHTS TO A SOLDIER, A LOVED ONE—FOR MY SON, FREDDIE
You're in my thoughts,
Wherever, you may be—
My love and heart is with you,
Through all eternity.
I wonder how you are tonight?
And if you're quite all right?
I pray the Lord is with you,
And keeps danger from your sight.
I worry, I may never hear,
Your loving voice again,
But, I must wait and trust the Lord,
As He's our only friend.
And if by chance,
We never meet once more,
Please wait for me, my soldier,
Just, beyond the door.

Jody J Bradley
DO YOU REMEMBER
Do you remember me?
I'm the one that loves you
For everything you are

Can you recall the day
You asked me to go steady
We were ready for a commitment

But then the day came
That you stopped caring for me
And now I'm alone

Tears sting my face
As I hear "our" song
And look back to what we used to be
I remember making love to you
And how close I felt to you
How I wish I could have those moments again

Sometimes I wish you were just another guy
Who I could put away in my scrapbook
But you'll always be so much more

I'll never stop trying for you
Even if I'm only hurting myself
But I'd risk everything for you

I love you
I miss you
Please, won't you come back?

Mrs Alice C F Argall
A BOUQUET OF WILD FLOWERS
I picked these in the morning,
Before the dew was gone—
The air was fresh and wholesome—
I heard the bird's songs—
I walked in the woods and found—
A late mauve violet plant—
Some curled up fern shoots—
And a "Jack In The Pulpit" plant—
I picked up my colored leaves—
Some grasses as well, to make a
Garland, for the Big Front Door—
As we did, "in Days of Yore"

Connie Collins

Connie Collins
PAST, PRESENT, AND FUTURE
Life will always be a struggle.
A time that looks towards the future and the past.
Where all the dreams, worries, and memories are;
They come and go so fast.

You look back through time,
And find your mistakes.
A number that all has lost count to;
Especially the heart aches.

You look at the present,
And all its tears,
From all the people crying over their sorrows,
Through the many sorrowful years.

You look towards the future,
And all its glorious dreams . . .
Where the sun is always shining,
Through its awakening beams

S A Profitt
THE FUTURE OF MAN

To my son Logan Anderson Profitt and to his future

When he breathes, his passion is shown.
He exhales as a tiger breathes.
He inhales as if life is ending.
Remotely he remembers to be calm;
Releasing expressions of body,
Not of just the mind.
He who comes with pain,
And exhileration is one,
Who brings hope to the future of man.

Demetrios G Lambrenos
TIME

I dedicate this poem to my mother, Mrs. Ruby Lambrenos, for her inspiration and guidance throughout my life.

"So rapidly I see it go by,
Faster than a hummingbird's flight
I see it fly,
And I ask myself, "What am I?"
"What will I be?"
"When?" and "Why?"
And as I ask, it passes still . . .
Yea, true, Time does not wait for the idle will."

Shirley M Jansen
THE MADONNAS TEARS

Dedicated with: Reverence and Pride

Her tears that flow
Will we ever know?
The reason that they stream,
In a world so extreme;
With pain, crime, and disbelieves.
Will we ever know?

Is it for the pain, the sufferings
Of all mankind?
The endless rages of crime,
That has little end in our time,
Or for the disbelieves
Will we ever know?

Is it for the doubts
And lesser faith,
The destiny of the world up to date.
Will her tears soon subside,
As we pray and wonder at her side.
Why her tears flow?

Will we ever know?

Tina M Eick
REFLECTIONS IN THE WIND
Reflections in the wind
Recollections of my sins
Of people I've left behind
A taste of bitter sweet wine
No reason left to cry
No time left to wonder why
For what is me is what I've made of me
What I am has become my destiny
In the end maybe I'll see
Who I've been and what I've wanted to be.
Reflections in the wind. . .

Mary Luella Heithaus
A MOUNTAIN LAKE

To my son David L. Heithaus, his wife, Doris G., and their son, David E.

A Mountain Lake is a wonderous thing,
In a haven, where the wild birds sing.
Amid the lofty peaks it lies,
To steal it's color from the skies.

To hold the image of tall Pine trees
And capture the sound of the passing breeze.
It's beauty has to be so rare,
So, God gave it these things to share.
For many a secret, within may lie,
Of life and love in years gone by.
Perhaps, from it's bank, a maiden's croon,
Told of her love, 'neath the western moon,
Or a mother poured out her heart's lament,
For the life of her child, too early spent.
An Indian Brave may have paddled his canoe
Across these quiet waters, blue,
In search of rest for body and soul,
When the ravage of war had taken it's toll,
Long years before we knew this land
Of Pine trees, lakes and mountains, grand.
Still, man with his turmoil, strife and care,
May lay down his burdens, there.
Peace and comfort, to him will bring,
A Mountain Lake, where wild birds sing.

Margaret Renfroe Meyerer

LIFE'S RENEWAL

The once tall tree lies crumbling
Across yon dusty, grass-strewn path.
Where it fell remains a ragged base,
Roots still holding strong.
As seasons pass bring snow and rain to further decay descend
There sprouts one spring sun's day

A lythesome ventured growth.
It nourishes on the old lost tree
And drew strength for each day.
As limbs reach out, birds nest about
And other saplings do appear.
Nature has a glorious way of renewing our world for us.
Is it not so with mankind, too,
As generations pass.

Anthony N Basilicato Sr

THE DRUMMER BOY AND ME

THE MAGI JOURNEYED from afar
IN SEARCH OF THE BABE—
the New-Born King;

THEY FOLLOWED THE LEADING
heavenly STAR
unto the STABLE, AND HEARD
ANGELS SING—
"GLORY BE TO THE NEW-BORN KING."

GENUFLECTING—ON BENDED KNEES
the MAGI GIVE
the GIFTS THEY BORE,
"Gold, Myrrh and Frankincense"
—fulfilling PROPHECY OF YORE.
ALAS—WITH PRAYERFUL HEART AND SOUL
a spirited DAY—
THE MAGI RETURNED
on their BLESSED WAY.

HOW FORLORN, I FEEL, O GOD,
unlike the MAGI 'GIFTS-TO-GIVE'
—ALL I HAVE IS MY LIFE TO GIVE:
TO LOVE, TO SERVE THE SON OF
GOD—O DEAR INFANT JESUS—PLEASE—
like the BEAT of the DRUMMER BOY
—ACCEPT MY HEARTFELT
BEAT OF JOY!

Carol Linn Rich

WHERE THE HOUSE STOOD

To my Dad: Brady Linn, Glady Creek, Marion Co., W. Va.

So quiet, so still, the sounds are no more. This house was home to a generation of four.
You served us all so long and so well. If wood could talk what stories you'd tell.
The walin' of newborn babies cry; sounds of weeping as some had to die.

Water dipped from a spring down the hill. Sweet smell of home
cookin' I remember still.
This house on Glady Creek aged with time. Vast memories remain
the family and mine.
Someday you'll fall; no more shadows to cast. You'll be "where
the house stood"—a part of our past.

Mary E Stephens

ALONG ROCK CREEK

To my Kentucky Family

The headstone said he died in 1883.
But, in this age-old cemetary, he's still alive to me.
I feel his presence all around
In this little graveyard I have found.
Across the path the post office lay,
Though mail hasn't been there in many a day.
The building is gray and broken and small.
After fifty odd years, it still doesn't fall.
Down the road and over the hill
Is a swinging bridge to a once busy still.
The still, like the man, has long gone away,
Yet all the relics you can still see today.
Back in these mountains you go back in time.
God fearing people and coffee a dime.
You drive down the road with bait and your pole,
To catch a trout—Look out! There's a hole.
A narrow bridge made of logs,
"Coal dead" trees in minature bogs.
The people are gone and so is the mine.
Yet, there in the splendor, a tall green pine.
A history lesson for all to share
Nostalgia, dreams for those who dare.
To see this place, as a temple of wonder,
Not as a plight of coal-mining plunder.

Valerie Hummel

TO MY MOTHER

To my mother
Who is always so kind
and is willing to share the joys of happiness
and the tears of sorrow.

To my mother
Who understands
and tries her hardest
to help me in anyway she can.

To my mother
Who is always so kind
There is not another woman in the world
that is a mother like mine.
I love you mom,
Love
Val

Rick Mohr

HERE WE ARE—WITHOUT ANY MONEY

To my son Christopher, who was born the day after I wrote this poem, December 24th.

Here we are—without any money,
But I hope you'll always be my honey.

It's Christmas time, for Peace and Joy,
And we're still wondering—a girl or boy.

And though this child won't be a stranger,
You wonder if it will be born in a manger.

But be it born on Christmas day,
Or born in the middle of the month of May.
Whatever day, Important, its not,
Cause it's a real baby and not just a thought.

And the four of us will be very happy,
You'll be the Mammy, I'll be the Pappy.

So have a Happy Christmas—Spouse,
Whether at the hospital or at the house.

Merry Christmas

Evia Wilson

MOMMA WITH HER SWITCH

This poem is dedicated to Momma, Mary Ella Lynn. For her love, courage, dicipline and understanding. With these in mind, our family survived many hard times.

Through the house, then out the door, sister Bonnie, she would
go. Running for the cornfield, to hide in the rows. Then here
comes momma with her switch.
Then all of us kids would know
Bonnie was in trouble again. She would get the switch below.
But momma had to catch Bonnie first, so the cornfield rows she
would go, with all us kids behind her, until Bonnie cried no, no.
For that old switch would touch a nerve that went clear to our
toes. Now all us other kids knew not to giggle, we would only
sigh. For if we laughed at Bonnie, we would all get the switch
in behind from a momma that really loved us with a switch to
keep us in line.
Well, this is a true and touching story when I think of those
hard times. Because our family all had to work hard back then
to earn a dime. Though sometimes good, then other times bad,
the memories make me cry. But to this day and always, thank you
Momma with your switch that raised us kids right.
Now kids, please don't go thinking that momma was a witch,
just because she used a switch.
Because her heart full of love,
courage and understanding made up for the like of this. For
through sorrow, laughter, hard times and pain, we've survived
it all and love remains.

Merle E Gelletta

TODAY WE HONOR YOU

Today we honor you, some with smiles and some with tears,
You have lived a century, a complete one-hundred years.
You have seen the farmers' market, replaced by modern stores,
You survived the great depression and the world wars.
You have seen the tractors, that replaced the plows and mules,
You have seen the passing of little country schools.
The cobblestones replaced, by concrete and asphalt,
The memories replaced by progress, are not all your fault.

You have been blessed with, oh so
many years,
But we all know, you have shed
your share of tears.
You have seen the passing of many
family and friend,
But life goes on and we have to live
it to the end.
So as we wish you Happy Birthday
on your 100th year;
We will all say thank you Lord,
we're glad she's still here.

David Landon Kuny

STREET MAN

Kitchen lines and railroad chimes,
Walking lonely dusk inclines.
Darkened corridors, limping in
pain,
Hardened grimace can't explain.

Sleepy alleys and hidden places,
Sullen graces show tired faces.
Shadows grow on sorrow's frown,
Pitys' gypsy cannot be bound;
All his thoughts go round and
round
As he haunts from town to town.

Street man, what can I do?
I want to help you do all you can
do.
I don't know if they understand
What it means to be a street man.

Petty crimes and two-bit wines,
Into himself this life consigns.
Muddled minds and soiled hands,
Prisoned within his own
commands;
No one cares to understand
Just who it is, this street man.

Mrs M

MR. MOON

Mr. Moon shining bright above,
You've done something for
everybody's love,
Keep it Shining, Keep it Glowing,
Everlasting, Evermore

Cheryl M Cranmer

OCEAN VIEW

Listen, Do you hear?
Do you see in your mind?
The waves slash the rocks,
with the fury of a God gone wild.
Look to the other side of the
planetary light;
the water calms its rage and
soothes to quiet strokes against
the sand.
Power of an unquieting rage,
to the peace of ebbing trickles.
She controls it all. Or does it
control her?
I listen. I hear. Most of all I see.
I see the struggle of tug-of-war.
The yes and no all in one breath.
Never a win, always a maybe.
She doesn't fight the shore, she
fights herself.
All the questions lie in the horizon,
all the answers lie in the hidden
depths.

Ann May

AN OLD FAMILIAR FRIEND

The leaves fall upon the ground,
you look up, you turn around,
and there in front of you
what do you see?
The masculine trunk of an oak tree.

Some of the branches are as long
as your toes,
others only go to your nose,
but look up again and what do you
see?
The swarming nest of a bumble
bee.

Trees are relaxing so they say,
but you would have known it
anyway,
cause look up again and what do
you see,
beyond the branches and falling
leaves?

You see a tree that's as old as you,
that reaches the sky that's so
beautifully blue,
that's lived in your yard since the
day you were three;
You see an old familiar friend in
an oak tree.

Angie Neatherton King

Angie Neatherton King

THE SEDUCTION

To Rodney, the love of my life; and to my two beautiful children, Chet and Brandie. . .this one's for you!

"Come hither," She calls slyly from
the glass house
where she hides;
Luringly, tempting you to join her
at her side.
"I'll take away your troubles. . ."
"I'll mend your broken heart. . ."
Yet all the while knowing, she will
tear your
life apart.
And soon her great temptation is
more than
you can bear,
You lustingly rush to her and you
grab her
in despair. . .
Her wicked laugh is haunting, for
she knew
it all the time—
You sold your life. . .your very
soul. . .
For just one taste of wine.

Trude D Firestine

CRAZY IN LOVE

Like a pilot, flying into the blue
You came, flying into my heart. . .
What do I do???
Where do I start???

I'm just as shy as you, maybe
more. . .
Can't find the words I'm look'in
for!??
I don't need time to think it
through
I'm crazy—head over
heels—in love with you
It's the truth!!!

I like you best, when I'm the closest
to you
The way you look, your style, the
things that you do
The flash in your eyes, the smirk
on your face
These are all familiar things to me.
Won't you see???

That, I don't want your money
I have my own. . .
I just want a place to call home.
Honey, someone to talk to. . .
Give a care. . .take and share one
life. . .one love
Do we dare???

I don't need time to think it
through. . .
I'm crazy—head over heels—in
love with you
Catch a care. . .I've been riding
on air,
for so long and now
you're gone. . .

Adrienne Coleman

open ports

whatever
made me think that
you
could tighten the rope worn, thin
frayed as i have stretched it
define contentment or slow
the speed demons that
thunder inside me

as if
entering your harbor could
secure
my daydreams, crystallize fluid
abstracts i have fingerpainted or
solidify the liquid
amphetamine that penetrates
my life stream

no chance
still emotions anchor my
drift
here i discover no
refuge from the storm no
need for a line
only you, open ports
always have seduced me

Sharleen Maye

A PERFECT MOMENT

As I am walking by the sea,
I feel that you are here with me.
The sea and sky so blue and clear,
I know there's nothing for me to
fear.
I know that life is not what it seems,
That peace and joy are not just a
dream.
Not with my eyes, but with my
heart I'm now seeing,
And all that I see becomes one with
my being.
I, and the sea, and the sky are all
one,
As are all God's creations under
our sun.
No longer alone, or separate or
scared,
No thoughts of the future that for
so long I've feared.
I know that there's really only the
now,
I let go of the shoulds, the why and
the how.
It's not the outcome but the
journey that counts,
To hold onto my faith in spite of
my doubts.
My psyche is stilled, my essence
comes through,
I am that I am, I'm not what Ido.
To feel a part of the beauty I see,
Opens my heart and sets me free.
Free from the cares of earthly
things,
I feel my heart has sprouted wings.
Before I came walking down by the
sea,
I felt as if there was only me.
But walking by this sea so blue,
Has reminded me I'm a part of you.
With my faith restored, and my
strength renewed,
I know the future will be what I
choose.
I reach for the sun and the stars up
above,
Whatever the path, the way is
through love.

Lanny R Bowers

CROW CALLS

I hear the sounds of the calling
crows,
Caw-caw-ing through the morning
wind
And I wonder if they call to me
A grounded bird in the world of
men
Mourning all that I might have
been
In the desolate chill of this
morning wind.

I feel the loneliness of the calling
crow
Caw-caw-ing over all the
countryside
And I wonder if they call to me
Saying come to me sweet,
saddened bride
I bring you love from the nether
side
Love having love that never died.

There is a sameness in the call of
the morning crow
In this world, within worlds,
beyond the deep
And I've heard the call come out to
me
In lands, whose tongue, I could
scarcely speak
Caw-calling my soul to wonder and
weep
Leaving me dreams that play in my
sleep
Always with me, something to
keep.

Gerianne Roland

SELF-INTRODUCTION

If you're intrigued
with an unknown man,
try to avoid
his lay away plan.

You approach, feeling pressure
to say something clever.
Thinking to yourself
"It's now or never."

His response is clear,
take a number, stand in line.
His outrageous ego
changes your mind.

Monica Olszewski Nowak

SECRETS FOR A HAPPY LIFE

To my Grandchildren Katrina and Steven Russell, Becky White, Molly, Arin, Vanessa and Gabrielle Nowak

When I was young and just a girl
I didn't have a care
I didn't know what life was about
And I really didn't care.

As I matured into a woman
And then became a wife
I soon found out that loving, caring, and sharing
Are the secrets for a happy life.

And as the children came to me
And I became a mother
I shared with them my secrets for a happy life
So that they could give to others.

Through out the trials of growing up
My children came to see
That loving, caring, and sharing
Is what life is meant to be.

And now that they are grown
And with children of their own
They share the secrets for a happy life
In each of their own homes.

Although throughout my life
No jewels or furs I have gotten
The legacy of the secrets I leave
Will never be forgotten.

Belle Ellis

CAT ON THE WALL

Big black kitty with the big green eyes,
You sit and stare at me every night;
Your golden whiskers gleaming, your long tail curled,
Sometimes you seem to fill me with fright.
You sit there so stately, grinning at me,
I wonder what your secret is all about;
Seems you're trying so hard as you're watching me
To keep my mind filled with doubt.
But you can't really bother me too much,
For you're just a cat on some wood;
And even though sometimes, I feel you are real,
I know you'd never hurt me, even if you could.
For you came to me, a gift from a friend,
To help brighten up my day;
And you shall always have a spot on my wall,
For I'll never, never send you away.

Lisa M Morelli

SHED NOT A TEAR

In loving memory of Kim. . .

Shed not a tear,
for I have not left you—
I am the presence in the gentle wind that whispers through
the trees. . .
and the warmth of the sun shining down upon your face. . .
I am among the soothing raindrops that cleanse the earth. . .
and the delicate snowflakes that fall silently adrift. . .

You can find me amongst all of nature's wonders,
. . .with the shooting star that leaves a blazing trail against
the darkened sky. . .
. . .the calming rainbow after an angry storm. . .
. . .and with the tiny creatures that scurry about the forest. . .

Just open your eyes and look around—
for I am there—
always with you—
and never more than a whisper away. . .

Tracy Marie Flintoft

LOVE KNOWS

Love knows, knows when to fly,
From your heart high into the sky.
It wanders around for someone to love.
Then flies down faster than doves.
Love is not a demon, nor a dream.
It is a match-maker and becomes a team.
Love, loves you night and day
Love knows, knows when to stay.

Nikki Shawn Crippens-McDowell

Nikki Shawn Crippens-McDowell

POOR LITTLE GIRL

For my Mom, Ellen Pando, for letting me make my own mistakes.

Little girl
Sitting in the dark
All alone
Cold and hungry.

Little girl
Watching as her
Drunken father
Beats her mother
Till blood stains the floor.

Little girl
Trying to escape
With eyes tightly closed
As she shoots up smack.

Little girl
slowly dying
Tears rolling down her cheeks
As she cries
For no one cares.

Little girl
Lonely no more
Crying no more
Lying in her grave
For she is dead.

Little girl
Sitting in the dark
All alone
Cold and hungry.

Randy K Yingling

I MUST LOVE YOU

I asked the trees while walking,
just the other day
not to whisper your name so often,
as I went upon my way.

The trees said they were sorry,
but could not be held to blame
It seems the wind was the culprit
that played this teasing game.

"Wind," I said with aching,
"is her name all you know?"
"I," said the wind, "but move the branches
as on my way I go."

"Then who sings her name so often,
that I can't escape the sound?"
"She's in your mind forever," they said
"to your heart she's bound."

John Helwig

THE BRIDGE

There are areas we cannot stride across,
Though our goal's on the other side;
Not reaching our goal seems a crushing loss;
But how shall we lengthen the stride?

There are very deep gaps, many water filled,
That we span with concrete and steel;
But the ones for which we are not so skilled
Are the faith gaps we try to conceal.

The distance between ourselves and ideal,
By paths that could lead astray,
Has few on the way to whom to appeal,
For a lift or a rest time stay.

Those stretches too hard to commute by ourselves,
That must be travelled somehow,
Preclude, who now, like fairytale elves,
Will soothe care's mist from our brow?

We were not meant to be crushed by care,
Like a rockslide buries a road;
There is a force that seeks to share
With us every burden and load.

"Come unto me," calls Holy Writ,
"Exchange your burdens for mine;
And you will find that the gaps to wit
Will be bridged toward life's sunshine."

Barbara L Force

FRIENDSHIP

To: Bob Blackman; Throughout time, you'll always remain my very "special" friend. Love you, Barb

---

True friendship is a precious thing
It is as rare as the loveliest jewel,
And twice as glowing.
Friendship is like an emerald pool
Deep and satisfying,
Soothing and cool.

Friendship is giving and receiving
It is based on truth, not deceiving.
It is always sharing and caring
It is not to be given lightly.
Or taken lightly.

It is as precious as life itself,
Without it life is an empty shelf,
Dusty and without meaning.

Rosemary Babiarz

LIFE AND ME

Why didn't anyone tell me,
What life was all about.
Maybe then when things go wrong,
I wouldn't have to Pout.
But if my life was perfect,
As I would like it to be.
Then I wouldn't need anyone,
To help and be with Me.
And life without anyone,
Would be lonely as can be.
Because I wouldn't like this world,
If there was only ME.

Robert A Girondi

THE VIET NAM WAR MEMORIAL, WASHINGTON DC—REFLECTIONS I

Carved from the earth this man-made rift,
This gaping wound sends thoughts adrift.

So soldier straight and deathly dark,
It's a somber tract for a nation's park.

All green and black with walkway gray,
And deepcut names engraved to stay.

In mem'ry of our nation's loss,
It's a graphic view of the human cost.

With watchful eye three comrades stand,
Staring out past those at hand.

'Mid tree and bush they view the sight,
Reminding all through day and night.

That brutal time has left its mark;
On souls and minds, in light and dark.

Some that yet live come sit and weep,
And show the world their scars run deep.

They talk of dear old friends that died;
Of visits past, and times they've cried.

And those of us who knew that war
Must tell the world: "NO MORE! NO MORE!"

No more battles, and no more wars;
And no more homes with wreath-hung doors!

For when battles cease and wartime's done,
The question's still: "So what. . .who's won?!"

Carlos Garcia

COMING HOME

Riding on a sweat-lined drive
A salty fly explores my brow
and drips
My brain buzzes with caffeine and carmel coloring
and spills
White dresses lie folding under hot summer shade
blowing parachutes into an oven breeze
I hold shimmering pictures;
clouded
as I splash through humid highway puddles
The road melts,
and I am home
watching the albatross float across

watercolor blue
over blazing white sand
As it sleeps next to a simmering sea
You're lying beside me—breathing low
and the water is gone from the rear view mirror
A yellow line pulses against the white
and the road is hard again
where I see you
a look in your eye that keeps shining
like a smile that can't wait for tonight
I come home passing
as long-necked grasses tangle under the wind

Sylvia Kathryn Seely
WHEN I AM ALONE

When I am alone—

I let my mind reach and stretch,
for things common and some far fetched.
Ore' mountain tops or blue sea foam,
to other worlds or right here at home.

When I am alone—

I reach inside to the inner-most depths,
where feelings of the heart are kept.
To awaken some long forgotten dream,
or to imagine a far away exotic scene.

When I am alone—

I contemplate on the serenity and peace,
and the depths my mortal soul can reach.
It's at these times it becomes so clear,
that I'm not alone, because my Lord is here.

Pamela E Elliott
winter's retreat

the sun—brilliantly shining with a million
fingers of warmth,
searching. . .
reaching down to caress the soul-heart of man,
thawing. . .
waiting for the bitterness of winter to retreat
to its lonely cave.

Michael Alan Marsh
IN THE MIDST OF IT ALL, A SONG

The shadows fall earlier these days and
the air is beginning to chill.
Despite the coming bleakness,
the bird's song comes floating over my windowsill.
The sunshine is feeble and frail and
the warmth, though small, remains.
Still the bird sings on.
its voice rising clearly through my upraised windowpane.
The song drifts out from the late blooming tree and
floats through the blue sky above,
a trinity of peace and contentment,
an attachment of unspoken love.
But the blue sky will surrender to darkness and
the tree will soon stand bare.
The bird will take flight on instinct,
oblivious of my presence there.
And I in all my loneliness will
stay and meet the night,
the light, the beauty, the bird,
all gone with hurried flight.
Quietly the darkness creeps in and
melts the trees into spindly form.
I sit in silent solitude,
wondering if the bird is so forlorn.
For I realize the darkness will continue until
it envelopes the world complete,
with the light, the beauty, the bird,
overrun by its silent feet.
And somewhere still the poor bird sings.

Morella Mensing
A FLOWER OF LOVE

The little seed in each one's heart,
The seed that we call love,
Is planted there, and made to grow
By One who reigns above.

One little seed may spring and grow,
Increasing every hour;
And ere we can enjoy the bud
It is a full-grown flower.

Another seed may slowly grow
And sometimes long delay,
But often flowers that so come forth
Will last and bloom for aye.

The seed that grows up very fast
As if it were a weed,
At times is nipped while in the bud,
And gently caused to bleed.

But every little seed will grow,
With sunshine from above,
And blossom out for all of us
Into a flower of love.

Mildred E Richardson
I SHALL NOT BE MOVED

To my loving husband, Morris, who always aids me in pressing my way and hanging in there when the going is rough

---

A firm stand I must always take
Being sure that I'm on solid ground
For there are many
accomplishments I must make
My decisions and judgements
must be sound
This I must do for my sake
For I shall not be moved

It's so very much that I hear
So many are in great pain
Yes so very much to cause one to fear
One wonders if it's all in vain
And if there's any real gain
In spite of it all I shall not be moved

Even though it all may make me cry
Let all come that will
I'll always continue to try
I shall stand still
I shall not be shaken by the things I see
Strong and faithful I'll always be

Through tears and sorrow
I'll press my way
Each and every day
Many others may doubt
But I'll always look for the way out
No I shall not be moved

Harold J Wilson Sr
MY EYES ARE FOCUSED ON JESUS

Standing on the banks of the Jordan
Looking out across the great sea
With my eyes focused on Jesus
And his eyes focused on me.

When my heart is heavy and laden
And the load I bear not alone
My eyes are focused on Jesus
And He will guide me on home.

Jesus has always been there
Knocking on our front door
And if we would only but answer
Our troubles would be there no more.

Sometimes our burdens are heavy
And others it seems they don't care
But troubles and good times together
Will always be answered in prayer.

In this old world of many roads
We roam and do our thing
Until we hit a hornet's nest
Then cry and suffer the sting.

So focus your eyes on Jesus
He's always there so kind and true
And pray every day He may
Keep His eyes focused on you.

Allien Spangler Buckingham
STALLIONS

The stallion dances
Among the clouds
Against the faded denim sky.

His mane drifts in the wind
Following his soul
Toward the sun.

His untamed spirit flares
From your eyes
And rippling muscles.

For you are like the stallion
Wild, Free
And restlessly drifting.

So I'll not try to coax you nearer
With sugar-cube promises
And story-book endings.

But you must flee
From my love corral
Now, while the gate is open.

Helen Hitchcock Nelson
MY MOTHER'S THIMBLE

I found an old thimble tarnished and worn
That no one else wanted, now that Mother was gone.
It lay in a trunk amid the treasures she loved
Unwanted, uncared for, next to her old glove.
But I could remember as a small child
Her hands always busy and her gentle smile,
She never picked up a garment to sew
Without using this thimble, I'd come to know.
I can see her now with embroidery hoops
Making dainty stitches and flower loops.
The thimble gleamed as her fingers flew
Mending or darning, making something "do."
So I took her treasures out of the trunk,
And brought them all home, to me they weren't junk.
I polished the thimble and there to behold
Was Mother's treasure of purest gold.
Now I use this thimble whenever I sew
And carry it with me wherever I go,
It's as if she is with me when I put it on
Saying "My daughter, I'm not really gone,
I've watched over you all the years through
And know you cherish my treasures, as I cherish you."

Billy R Champion
ALABAMA

I dedicate this poem to the people of Alabama the beautiful state in which I live, I would also like to dedicate this poem to Mae Hale, the woman I love.

Alabama, my land where my heart is,
Your mountains where my home remains still.
With treasured forests' of north, of south, one who
Listens can hear summer rains falling so hard and smell the
Fall of fresh water in the air.

Alabam called by many that flock by day and by night
From places a far distance to the many rivers and
Ponds of Alabama to fish, to salute the forests and
Woods where fowl fly free, and from deer to rabbits
That roam in Alabama that nature allows us to seek in
Sporting of food.
To the historic harbors of Mobile where ships dock, I
Flow in the breezes of winds in cold to warm weather that
Scatters rains for many farmers' crops. When clouds roll in,
Winds dart across fields, bringing dust.
In springs, flowers bloom in all colors and nights get longer
And brighter from the moon's light. Nights that were dark
In the winter nights of the cold winter past now become
Lighter on a clear night.
On summer days and nights, warm and tender, sitting upon my
Porch, I look into the tall dark woods, I hear birds
Chirping and farmers plowing on tractors in new fields, on nights
That are not long after rains one can hear the croaking of frogs
And the singing of crickets. Ode to be lazy on a summer day, to
Walk on an old dirt road, I love to hear airplanes fly over on
a clear day.

In Alabama winters', heavens mistness begins to arrive
In cities and towns of valleys neath foothills of
Your mountains. Leaves have turned into a brown death
And fallen from trees. On your mountains that peak
Across the skies edge, where fowl

roost in trees and
Other animals that roam seek shelter from brisk winds.
Snows soon shall arrive to cover the lands in stillness,
Leaving only trails of footprints upon the white snows
To see. This snow, cleansed and of purity has only shadows
Of trees casted upon it, as the sun comes out in the afternoons.

Snow vanished, cold air past, lands soon shall become green again.
When rains fall in darkness of cool nights, I begin to fall into
A deep sleep upon hearing heavy drops of water fall upon the
Roof of my home.

Alabama, you call, we come to thee.
Alabama strong and great, we yearn to be there in
Leading the world in peace, strength, and greatness.

Linda L Leffler-Praznik

LOVE IS AN ART

This poem is dedicated to my husband John, my family and friends.

Love is a feeling deep inside
Love is a feeling one cannot hide

Love is a tear that has been shed
Love is a couple that are wed

In so many ways love is shown
Love is felt in a happy home

To love someone is to be there
Ready to listen, to show that you care

The love for a child can be seen on a mother's face
And felt in a warm embrace

Love is all around
Just waiting to be found

Love is an art
To find love, look not with your eyes, but with your heart

Mrs Daisy LaVerne Rhoden

SPACE SHUTTLE

Dedicated to seven brave astronauts to whom died January 28, 1986 in the Space Shuttle Challenger Tragedy.

We boarded the Space Shuttle
Everyone huddled in a great big shuttle.
We plan to land on the moon no later than
Tommorrow at noon.
As we journeyed far into the sky
I began to feel a little shy
As we got higher into the sky.
I don't know why but I began to cry.
For some unknown reason I don't know why.
I'm sure gonna try not to cry
Unless I plan not to reach the sky
As we journeyed through space
It almost seems like we were in a race.
Even though we were going at our own pace.

David L Dolin Sr

WHAT TIME WILL IT BE

When the God of the universe
Expresses His vows,
And the angels of heaven
Open the clouds,
When the children of love
Are unnestled and found,
And the tyrants of evil
Are casted and bound,
What time will it be
For you and me
A time to weep and cry,
Or a time to be free?

Yvonne L Smith

NEW YEAR'S

Morning's past now.
Sun's gone down,
Eluding itself from sight.

I lay here. . .alone.
Thinking of the morning. . .
With you apart,
Of all that's gone. . .
And still to come.

You lay so peaceful. . .
It's like a dream
That I cannot touch,
Fearing it will fall apart. . .
And never be.

Tear's flowing softly
Down my cheek,
Your love evades me.
But I keep searching. . .
Hoping. . .it will find
Its way back to me.

Clayton T Sowell

TEACH THE CHILDREN LOVE

Dedicated to my parents, Clayton and Roxie Sowell, who taught me love and to my children, Michelle, Jeremy and Jason who my wife, Sherry and I are trying to teach love.

Teach the children how to love, it's essential to their life.
Show them its helpful ways to cope with today's woes and strife.
Teach the children the love of God, through him all things must come—
To ignore His precious gifts, would be extremely dumb.
Teach the children the love of nature, home of birds and bees—
Destroy not the life of such, not even flowers and trees.
Teach the children patriotic love, freedom it must be.
Today's small ones—the future's hope to keep our country free.
Teach the children of spousal love, an example you should be—
One day their married life will depend, now on what they see.
Teach the children parental love, the guidance you shall give—
Shapes their minds and paves the way for the life they will live.
Teach the children brotherly love, the compassionate way—
To warmly greet those encountered and brighten up their day.
Teach the children about puppy love, where it has its part—
Each new week brings a new love for them to present their heart.
Teach the children of sexual love, the problems it can cause—
Pregnancy or social disease, troubles come without pause.
Teach the children to love their friends, make sure of their measure—
Drugs or booze can take their life, their one and only treasure.
Teach the children to love themselves, call it not conceit—
Instill in them self-respect, a roadblock to defeat.
Teach the children to practice love wherever they may go—
To avoid love's temptations, they should simply answer, no.

Andrea J Howell

MEMORIES OF DAD

In memory of our wonderful father as we love and miss him so much.

Very few months have come and gone
Since the statewide news revealed to us
The damage the midair collision had done.
Shock, then fear; dread, then tears
Disbelief and anger. . .why us after all of these years?
"Time is a healer," especially of pain
He's in eternal happiness, but what do we have to gain?

Happy moments and loving thoughts
Cherishing the letters and cards we thought we'd lost.
Reliving every moment as if it was the day,
That he was here to share it in his very special way.

But life goes on, and so must we
"Things will get better, just wait and you'll see."
Hoping and praying that each day will bring
The strength and courage needed to tackle everything.

I miss you dad, I love you too
I hope you can hear me and comfort me when I'm blue.
I can see your face, I know you're there
I just wish that you were here, for this pain
I wouldn't bear.

So for now I guess the happy thoughts
and memories will have to do
Until the day when once again I will be with you.
February, 1987

Marilyn N Taylor

THE DANCE

To Wayne: How we've danced through sunlight and shadow.

Weaving, breathing, bright lights
Painting the air
Like an artist does with brilliant colors
Softly, then boldly flaired
Arms outstretched, apart, but somehow
touching each other
Making us feel the wonder
They seemed not to be bound to the ground
Somehow, they were airborne and free
As if some kind of magical wind propelled them into each taken spin
Breathing, weaving bright lights
I was caught in a trance
Adrift!
'Twas almost as if
A grand finale of every romance
Seemed to be born in each turn
The softness of rose petals
Then another spin and they were aflame
A high burn
Both enmeshed
Not to be undone
At the end, intertwined, combined, they'd become
Quite solidly woven, to one!

Marjorie M Bartlett

SOMETHING TO LIVE BY

Separate the *value* of "store-bought" things,
From God's free-given beauty;
Know that God has given all of us . . .
A burden and a duty.

Accept the good . . . then thank Him,
Accept the sad things too;
Look up to Him, He'll guide you . . .
In how and what to do.

Kneel down and ask for help,
When you're "up against the wall;"
Then kneel, again, to thank Him . . .
When there's nothing wrong at all.

Miss Cheryl Lynn Gilmer

WHAT YOUR LOVE MEANS TO ME

This Poem is Dedicated to Shanya Oglesby, William Oglesby and my family with love.

Words cannot explain all the love you've
given to me, with your tender touches
you make me happy and glee. IF I owned
the world I would give it to you.
Because I know you will always be there
to see me through. I will never forget
the times we spent together and now
that my heart has mended my love for
you will be forever.
IF it were by one's command I would
fulfill your every desire. Every time
I think of your love it sets my soul
on fire. Time and time again I think
of the love we once shared.
Because WILLIAM you showed me you really
cared.

Gerald Brown
DOWN ON THE FARM

Down on the farm, 'bout half past four, I slip on my pants
and sneak out the door. Out in the yard I run like the
dickens, to milk the cows and feed the chickens.
I clean out the barn; curry Nancy and Jiggs; separate the
cream and slop the pigs. Work two hours, then eat like a Turk;
then by heck, I'm ready for a full day's work.
Fix up the wagon; grease up the rack, throw a jug of water
in an old gunnysack. Hitch up the horses, hustle down the
lane, gotta get the hay in 'cause it looks like rain.
Look over yonder, sure as you're born, cattle on the
rampage, cows in the corn. Start across the meadow, run a
mile or two, heaving like I'm windbroke, get wet clear through.
Get back to the rack, then for recompense, Nancy get's
a-straddle of a barb-wire fence.
Joints all aching, muscles
all a-jerk; I'm fit as a fiddle for a full day's work.
Worked all summer till winter draws nigh; figure out the
books and heave a big sigh.
Worked all summer; didn't make a
thing. Got less cash than I had last spring.
Now some folks will tell you there ain't no hell; but they
never farmed, so how can they tell?
Spring rolls around, I decide to take another chance, as
the fringe grows longer on my old grey pants. I give my
suspenders another hitch and my belt another jerk, and by God,
I'm ready for another year's work.

Linda Ash Smith
STICKY FINGERS

For my daughters: Ginny & Limarie

With sticky fingers upon my face, you reach up yours to gleefully place,
A sticky kiss upon my cheek, and I close my eyes and refuse to peek.
All gooey and dirty and stickey its true—but then if you weren't you wouldn't be you.
Oh, my child, the image of me, with grime and dirt and battered knee,
What have you been doing with your day, and where in the world have you been to play?
Some large dirt pile I've no doubt, but did you have to try every one of them out?
Just one day I'd like to see you without, all the dirt and goo, but then I doubt I'd recognize you.
But later that night after your bath, I watch you sleep and have to laugh,
You look so peaceful there in slumber, you fill me with warmth and love and wonder.
And as I bend to kiss your clean cheek, you turn and mumble and start to speak.
Bending closer to hear what you say: its "Goodnight, I love you mommie, I loved you all day."

Betty Lee Fulop
THE ANSWERED PRAYER

The child came—so tired and weak,
"Dear Father, please, mercy I seek,
This day I've tried so hard to please,
But I have failed . . ." And on his knees
The child fell. The tears came fast . . .
The night drew on . . . The hours passed.

The morning rays of light so fair
Shone down upon the child in prayer.
". . . help me to be so strong this day
That I will not t'ward evil stray."

But ev'ning came, and darkness found
The child again with choking sound,
". . . I've tried so hard . . . I'll try some more . . .
Just give me time . . . this I implore."

So time was given, and grace was, too.
The child learned, the child grew
In faith, in strength, in grace, in love—
His prayer was answered from above.

Laura F Cook
THE THUNDERSTORM

Dedicated to my husband and daughters with love.

My mind was mixed up
My soul had lost it's way.
I was so lonely and confused
Till God spoke to me that day.

The skies were dark and gray,
The air so calm and still;
Then, God began to cry
His tears fell all around me
As I silently sat there
On the Hill.

His voice was loud and roaring
As he said "My child come back
Home to me, I am what you seek,
In me you will find peace."
Yes, God spoke to me that
Day.

I reached out my hand and
Placed it in his.
Oh, how beautiful I began to
Feel;
Then God smiled, and every-
Thing around me glowed with
Newness as hand in hand we
Walked down the hill.

Elizabeth L Wieland
THE DERRING-DO'S AND THE DERRING-DON'TS

There's nothing like a storm at sea
With lightning flashing overhead,
A howling wind and smashing waves
If I'm on land and safe in bed.

I love a lofty mountain top,
A challenge to a climber's skill
A rugged trap for all who dare;
No, thank you, I don't think I will.

The river's swift, the rapids white,
The roaring falls are just below.
You take the raft and go ahead—
I'll take a dinner and a show.

In darkest Africa, I've heard,
Safaris are the common scene.
I'd love to see it all someday,
With popcorn, on a movie screen.

Some men are made for daring deeds;
Brave women, too, aren't hard to find;
But simple, timid souls like me
Seek glory in their daily grind.

Evelyn Demarco
FROSTED PICTURES ON THE PANE

'Twas very cold last night and
As the morning sun shines
Through the windowpane
I see pictures there with
A clear backdrop of blue sky.

A face with mouth open
And a shock of hair
Drooping over the forehead
With a small pointed nose
Like someone excited at a game.

The other is a bag of jewels,
A plastic bag to see thru.
As the sun shines behind,
I view sparkling diamonds
With rainbow hues.

The sun's warmth is
Making the pictures melt.
But it was wonderful to briefly
Feel the richness that Nature
Shared with me this morning.

C J Cloutier

C J Cloutier
LIFE AS A GAME

This poem is dedicated to those who've helped my dreams become reality

---

Playing with hearts
The joker a fool
Life like a game
Has only one rule
Different deals from
Day to day
Make up the hands
We will play
Study closely
The best times you keep
Discard the past
Memories cheap
Bid on your dreams
Bluff if you will
Life as a game
You need a skill
When your dreams
Have been called

The memories all fold
Lay down your dreams
A winner you'll hold
Life like a game
Only one rule
Go with your heart
Never a fool

Michele Marie Bradburn
NO IMAGES

To David, who believes in my magic

When you hold me,
be silent
savor the warmth
no hollow, patronizing lies
only you and me.
When you are near me,
see only me
no images, no shadows
only reality.
When you are away
keep me with you,
on the edge of conscious thought
always near.

Jody Steinke
JANUARY HEART

It's cold outside,
but not as cold as I feel.
My environment is frozen,
as solidly as ice.

The wind blows,
and it howls within our walls.
If I would touch you now,
you would probably shatter,
or my fingers would slide—
off your skin like skates on ice.

If I have to wait
till the spring
for our condition to thaw,
I'd as soon melt away with it.

Billie Morton
AN ODE TO THE STATUE OF LIBERTY

I've been here most a hundred years
My clothes are worn, face streaked with tears
I look so tired yet still I stand
And hold the torch in my right hand.

The shops pass by, I understand
They come from every oppressed land.
To work their trades, apply their skills
And raise a family as each one wills.

I hope that each one finds their dream
And lives a life of high esteem.
I hope that each one finds much love

And gifts abundant from above.

I've welcomed the servicemen
home from the wars
To their home on these beautiful
American shores.

I wish that I could tell each one
How much we appreciate what
they've done.

The winds blow hard I creak and
groan
A point on my crown pierced my
right arm.
Though in my state, I feel no pain
The way I look is quite a shame.

Then one day some workmen came
With ladders tall they built a frame
I wondered what they'd do to me
Would I still be able to face the sea?

The men have come from far and
near
To do their best, no need to fear.
They hammered and rivited and
worked long hours
In the sun, the wind and occasional
showers.

All nationalities worked as one
Until the very last job was done.
For I am the symbol of all men free
The lady with the torch of liberty.

Now I look as I should look
In one hand the torch the other a
book
I hope that all the world will see
Me standing here, so proud once
more
To lift my lamp beside the golden
door.

Kathleen D Bradford

A MOTHER'S MUSE

To Heather

Busy hands, happy hands
Pressed against the pane,
Pushing in, pushing up
Trying to catch rain.
Such a joy to behold,
The apple of my eye.
Carefree, young, and curious,
Bold, but sometimes shy.

Busy hands, happy hands
Writing on the door,
Going up, going down,
Scribb'ling on the floor.
So much color to behold!
(It really caught my eye.)
Not carefree, young, but furious,
And ready just to cry.

Busy hands, happy hands
Finally put to sleep.
By night the mischief banished,
The angel slumbers deep.
Her wavey locks now brush her
face—
Her halo made of gold.
Still the apple of my eye,
A joy yet to behold.

Bessie J Wood

MY FLOWERS

My flowers bloom every day
They help me walk along life's way.
One of my flowers is a little rose,
With ten chubby fingers and ten
chubby toes.
With little curls around her face,
A laughing smile and a sweet
embrace.
My other flower is tall like a
jack-in-the-pul-pit.
Sturdy and strong and five foot
three.
He really means alot to me.
Yes my flowers bloom every day.
With loving care I watch them play.
But someday when I'm old and
gray,
My beautiful flowers will move
away.

Valerie J Bean

FOR I SHALL NOT LEAVE

---

*For Roger Allen Bean Whose
Memories Are Forever Near*

Though I've left and gone
away
I'll be with you each and
everyday
I will stand by and help you
along
And ask my Lord to help you
go on
For I Shall Not Leave
At night when you lay down
to sleep you may dream of the
things we were going to do
And at day,
You'll remember the past I had
with you
For I Shall Not Leave
When each is alone you'll feel
the presence of me
For this is the way I want it
to be
As time goes on God will give
you the strength to stand
But remember,
I'm always within reach of your
hand
For I Shall Not Leave
Any of you

Terri Trautman

INSIDE MYSELF

---

*This poem is dedicated to my
children, Dana and Carey whom I
love very much.*

Inside myself I looked one day
And this is what I found
I found a child afraid to cry
Afraid to make a sound
I saw the child progress in years
To a woman of the world
And yet this woman fully grown
Still feared to shed a tear
I bowed my head and closed my
eyes
And prayed to God on high
Dear God I said—Why is it
That I'm so afraid to cry
For crying is a way to cleanse
The hurt and pain within
It calms the spirit and lifts the heart
And frees the soul from sin
And then I knew
Why I feared to weep
Why I thought it was a waste
I knew if I did
There would be no one
To wipe tears from my face

Shirley Ann Arionus

JESUS LIVES

---

*Dedicated to Mr. P. for his
dedication to the P.O.W.'s.*

I believe in life,
I believe in love
I believe in flowers,
that bloom in the spring
I believe in mountains,
that we all have to climb
I believe in birds,
that make song in our gypsy
heart
I believe in trees,
God gave us to shelter our soul
I believe in you
I believe in me
I believe in love

Carol B McWatters

NOT QUITE PERFECT

---

*Dedicated to the sweetest
Granddaughter in the world.*

I'm a little less than perfect
But aren't we all?
Maybe it's more obvious
Because I am so small.
Because I am not perfect,
I trip a lot and fall.
I do not mean to stumble
or step upon your toes.
Please do not look upon me,
Down Your Nose!
I may never be real perfect,
but maybe if I try,
I can learn to fall more perfect
and not to cry!

*Susan Birchwood Rochester
Balabin*

HOW MUCH WILL IT COST?

I've seen a lot of heartless things
along the face of time.
Most everyone is in a hurry, or
drunken from the wines.
I see them pass by animals, as
though they weren't there,
And seen the hatred in their eyes,
of one who does not care.

I wonder how it came to this, the
love's been long since lost!
I wonder can we get it back, or
how much will it cost?
But then caring, love, and trust,
may not be what they need,
They'd rather wrap themselves
inside a wall of selfish greed.

Such ugliness was not
foreplanned, nor is it part of life,
Nor was it meant to be sunk in,
and twisted like a knife.
I wonder how to get love back,
for how much will it cost?
It's a shame it's come to this, the
love's been long since lost.

Catherine S Mills

**THE RAINBOW: A
MASTERPIECE**

When a person sees a rainbow,
Such things do come to mind
As spectrums and crystal prisms
And good old Roy G. Biv.

To the nature-minded, the winds
blow,
And leave such musings behind,
To replace with organisms
That upon this earth do live.

A cardinal flies 'bove the red ribbon
With the energy of a flame,
Or a drop of life's precious blood,
Or a rose that brightens the day.

Orange are the leaves of autumn,
That signal the end of life's game,
Or citrus juice in a flood,
Or fertile Georgian clay.

Yellow is the life-giving sunshine,
Or bananas that monkeys adore,
Or buttercups that dance in the
meadows,
And bob and sway in the breeze.

The ripples of foamy brine
Glow green as they splash the
shore,
And the grass waves on as the wind
blows,
And the leaflets emerge from the
trees.

The blue sky in all its great honesty,
Caresses the lakes wise with age,
And the bluebird's lovely chime
Twitters and bubbles and charms.

The "purple mountain majesty"
Looks down o'er the plains thick
with sage,
While our cups runneth over with
wine
Flowing graciously from
somebody's arms.

We see all these things in a
rainbow,
And yet we know not what we see;
'Tis God's work of art that we
witness,
For nature is His masterpiece.

So whenever you see a rainbow,
Be sure you know just what you
see.
Respect the great work that you
witness;
Don't ruin His great masterpiece.

Mary Parton

YOUR MEMORY

---

*To Scott Ransom, in loving
memory, painfully missed by his
family and friends. I love you,
Scott.*

I hear you sometimes,
When I'm all alone.
I come home from work,
And reach for the phone.

I see you outside,
And I call out your name.
But, when you disappear,
I know my mind is to blame.

I sit on the couch,
And I wait for your call.
I remember you're gone,
When the tears start to fall.

I can't go to sleep,
For thinking of you.
The great times we had,
Together . . . us two.

I want to be with you,
More and more each day.
But I'll wait here patiently,
Until He says I may.

Robert J Freeland Jr

MY FAMILY TREE

As I look
upon this tree
I see the life
God gave to me
I start with the trunk
and this is me
And all the limbs
genealogy

My mom and dad
are under me
For they're the roots
of this tree
As each generation
unfolds from me

So do the branches
on my tree
The main branches
on my tree
Are the children
God gave to me
As God has given
this tree to me
I thank you, Lord
for my genealogy

Wanda Moore
TROUBLE'S

Dedicated to: Veronica & David.

Trouble's are like a heavy weight:
But taking your own life:
Won't get you to Heaven's Gate:

So turn to GOD in prayer and thought:
Don't close the doors to your troubled Heart:
And some day soon, that weight will lift:
Then deep inside you'll find your gift; "LIFE."

Gloria A Dunnigan
DOUGHNUTS, DOUGHNUTS
DOUGHNUTS, DOUGHNUTS
Taste so good
eat 'em all up
like a good girl should.
Glazed, powdered,
Jellied and Plain.
Eat so many,
I'm 'bout to go insane,
When I eat them all
I'm sorry to say
my body shouts,
"It's time to pay!"
When I looked in the mirror
To see style and grace;
My body turned to a doughnut,
Boy what a waist/waste!

Mark E Smith
ODE TO A GODDESS
Goddess of thy courting world
How long young hearts a cry,
Loving the taste of honey sweet nectar
Dripped from thy crystal eye.

The dew so lovely shining
Mirrors reflections of your beauty
In the eyes of rich, red petals
That sing your fluttering carols.

Followers in like, come weeping home
And fuse their candles long
Awaiting for your sweet arrival
To keep their love continually strong.

Eyes in deep keep shape
And float along your flowered way,
Leading to pacifying harmony
That keeps hearts' chambers in bloom.

By the glass water flowing
You drip the drops of love,
And I swim within the bottomless stream
Melting with each royal touch.

Michelle Dawn Hall
ONE YEAR, FIVE MONTHS AND FIFTEEN DAYS
It was one year, five months and fifteen days ago that I first saw you.
Over this span of time I have grown to care a great deal,
But now you say you've found someone new.
What should I do?
I could try to forget you and find someone else,
Or cry for the rest of my life.
I could try to make you as miserable as I am,
But what good would that do?
I guess I'll just think about it for awhile,
Maybe for one year, five months and fifteen days.

Robert C Rehm
A DAY AT A TIME
A friend told me
live a day at a time
but forgot to mention
what to do with memories.
Those happy hours
filled with laughter-love,
or the tear-cluttered moments
when quiet shouts,
or about our hopes and dreams.
Are they just for now?

Perhaps some people
have a built-in shut-off valve
that stops the night
promptly at eleven
and they have no need
for lonely nightly vigils
that send TV to bed
or wakens the birds
to share their loneliness.

I like remembering.
The nows
and all the tommorrows
allotted me.

Mary Ragan
ONCE . . .
Once I had life,
now I'm dead.
I killed myself,
the newspaper said.

Once I was happy,
now I'm no more.
They found me dead,
there on the floor.

Once you knew me,
now I'm gone.
Please don't do,
what I did wrong!

Once I was me,
they said, "There she goes—
so beautiful."
What happened? Nobody knows.

Once . . . I was real.
Once . . . I had something to show.
Once . . . I was alive.
But . . . that was once . . . so long ago.

Lorraine Ann Gardiner
A SYMPHONY OF SPRING
Spring brings many musical sounds of nature.
The sound of birds singing in the morning.
The trickling of the little snow that is
left, fastly ebbing away.
The soft whistling of the trees from winds.
that makes them gently sway.

You can hear the pitter patter of a late
afternoon shower.
Which will help grow an audience of pretty
flowers.
The sound of the honking geese, as
they V flight north after their long winter
stay in the south.
The croaking of a frog as he opens his mouth.

These are all the sounds that spring brings.
The sounds of nature, a symphony of spring.

Vera E Hammersley
MY GARDEN AT TWILIGHT
In the quiet of my garden
My Master walks each night
Between the rows of flowers
Which are a welcome sight.

He caresses them and speaks
And each little ear is sharp
As His benediction falls on them,
Day draws her curtains, and it's dark.

The Pansy faces are all upturned
His sacred Face to see
And as He stoops, He brushes past
The tree which means Eternity.

The Canterbury and Blue Bells
Are ringing on the air
Their gladsome song of welcome
To their Maker walking there.

He turns to leave with a word here and there
When suddenly on the cool night air
There comes the sound of notes ascending:
It is the trumpet-vine's fanfare.

He's leaving now—a figure, tall
And awaiting Him at the garden wall
Are Honeysuckle and Roses, fair
Each giving Him comfort with fragrance rare.

R C Smith
THE LITTLE BOY'S ROOM
You can always tell a little boy's room.
The floor is covered, with trucks, and cars,
G.I. Joes, and airplanes, a crane with no boom,
and about a dozen, little plastic men from Mars.

Dirty socks, on the floor, in complete abandon.
His shirts, and jeans draped all over a desk,
some are dirty, and some, are probably clean,
with shoes, boots, and sneakers, piled in between.

His bed is askance, along one wall.
He throws things here, and throws things there.
The chair to his desk, is out in the hall,
and under his bed, there is a teddy bear.

He may have a helicopter, hanging from the ceiling,
that tangles in your hair, everytime you walk by.
An old plastic plane, with all the decals peeling,
and in the window, is a model of a one-winged fly.

Yes, this is a boy's room, as you can tell.
His favorite toy, is a fire engine, with no bell.
There are papers, and books, all over the room,
and he says, he will clean it up Mom,
if somewhere in that mess, he can find the broom.

Matteo Jannicelli
AFTER THOUGHTS
Am I strong? (I guess!)
How strong? (?)
Am I strong enough
To withstand today? (. . . Maybe?)
How about tomorrow? (. . . I don't know? . . .)
And next week? Next month (?)
Next year (?)
. . . Hey . . . How about the dark
. . . Of tonight? (?) (?) (?)

Kelly Michelle Woodard
MATURE LOVE

For Gram, Gramps, Dad, Mom, Bobbi and Jeaniene. Thank you All! I love you.

A thought has just occurred to me
Waiting for you alone.
We have weathered many storms
And they've failed to wreck our home.
Wrinkles in the covers
Indicate passionate nights.
Tear-stained pillow cases
Prove we've had our fights.
Now the hallway's empty
No more sneaking to fool around.
Where our children's voices were
Now there is no sound.
As you sleep, I look with love
At your weather-beaten cheek.
I know that there within you
Are the answers that I seek.
I know that there cannot be
A deeper love than this,
For I am once again eighteen
When I feel your kiss.
Impetuous feelings of the past
Turned to a love that's true.
I thank God each morning
That I've been blessed to spend my life with you.

Gilbert M Golla
SPRING SNOW

This poem is dedicated to Michaelena, my loving mother.

Spring awakes, yet sleeps a while.
Crocuses snuggle, covered by blankets
of white feathers.
Snow Drops are hidden in whiteness,
While Robins huddle in the snow
covered branches of conifers,
'Til Nature beckons summer.

Josephine Munoz Perez
THE CRY OF THE POOR

To the memory of my dear parents, Juan L. Munoz and Josefina Valverde Munoz, who instilled in me the love for poetry.

Out there in the night the poor
exist.
Some curse, some pray, all weep.
Some lie awake pondering
from whence tomorrow's bread
will come.
Others, though hungry too,
are blessedly overcome by sleep.

The old ones, afflicted with aches
they knew not in their youth,
suffer perhaps the most.
Or is it children, as yet unused to
grief,
who really hurt.
The mother's sorrows may be
deepest,
hearing her childrens' cries
and knowing the next day will be
no better than the day before.

Or can it be the father
whose pain is most tormenting,
and sometimes in frustration,
takes his meager earnings to a
Tavern.
There he drinks himself into a
stupor,
and prefers the gutter to his bed
in that bare and miserable shack,
which he must call his home;
filled wall to wall, floor to ceiling
with hopelessness and black
despair . . .

Mary Louise Brooks
A REDWOOD TREE SPEAKS
We are the Redwood trees,
The giants of the earth.
Thousands of years we've been here
Yea, long before Christs birth.

We think man must be blind
Not to see the beauty around.
We inspire young and old alike,
Yet men there are who would cut
us down.

Birds and wild creatures small
A haven here have found,
And nowhere else do we grow
The whole wide world around.

Our leafy arms reaching to the sky,
Form a green Cathedral for all
passers by,
And so folks feel that God is nigh.
Yet men there are who would cut
us down.

We grow strong and very tall,
From rain, sunny days, and foggy
nights.
Oh, shame on men who would cut
us down
And destroy such wonderous
sights.

Though we've withstood both fire
and storm,
Some from old age will fall to the
ground.
Others for ages to come will still be
here,
If man will refrain from cutting us
down.

Jerome Sylvester (Jerry)
I THE WORLD

From my heart . . . for my God, my wife and my friends. For God for giving me the talents that I have, my wife for her love, and my friends for their dedication to helping me find myself.

Once long ago in a land far away,
there was a child who had run
away.
Run away from the pain, and
hunger and dirt;
His thoughts were survival: get
away from the hurt.

The child shivered by night and
begged by day;
I the world saw him pass my way.
But I the world was to busy to care;
To involved with myself, to selfish
to share.

I the world certainly should have
known,
that to be on his own he should
have been grown.
I so pompous . . . I so smart;
I haven't dealt well with affairs of
the heart.

So I went on my way to tend my
own,
and left the child to push on alone.
Spirited and brave, he managed to
live;
No thanks to myself who had so
much to give.

The child did survive and grew to
a man,
a long time ago in this far away
land.
From strife he grew strong . . . a
lesson to be learned;
I the world give you nothing . . . it
has to be earned.

Ann Carter
BLESSED SAVIOR

This poem is dedicated to Rhoda—my loving daughter.

Blessed Saviour, I my cross have
taken,
Leaving all to follow thee,
All the way from earth to heaven,
Oh thou blessed lamb of Calvery.

All my love to thee my Saviour
All my love I give to thee,
On this earth I have no other,
Who would share such love as thee.

When one day when I shall see thee,
On the shores of heaven fair,
Then oh, then, I'll find the joy,
That will be with me forever there.

Mary F Johnson
A POLICEMAN'S PRAYER
Teach me that sixty minutes makes
an hour, sixteen
ounces a pound, and one hundred
cents a dollar.
Help me to live that I can lie down
at night
with a clear conscience, without a
gun under my
pillow, and unhaunted by the faces
of those
whom I have brought pain. Grant
that I
may earn my meal ticket on the
square, and
in earning it, I may do unto others
as I
would have others do unto me.

Deafen me to the jingle of tainted
money and to
the rustle of unholy skirts—Blind
me to the
faults of the other fellow, but reveal
to me my
own. Guide me so that each night
when I look
across the dinner table at my wife,
who has been
a blessing to me, I shall have
nothing to conceal.

Keep me young enough to laugh
with little children,
and sympathetic enough to be
considerate of old age—
and when comes the day of
darkening shades and
the smell of flowers, the tread of
soft footsteps and
the crunching wheels in the
yard—make the
ceremony short and the epitaph
simple.
"Here lies a man."

M D Haddad
LITTLE HUMMINGBIRD

To George—for believing in me

We have a little hummingbird
who visits every day.
He's truly a perfect gift of God
in each and every way.

He goes about his duties
with a swift and knowing air,
But pauses at the window
to see if we are there.

He's such a tiny, busy bird
that even wind can't halt!
Ah, that we could measure up
and be as worthy of our salt!

God bless you little hummingbird
with wings so swift and strong,
For in His loving hands
you never will go wrong.

Jeanette Visscher
THE EXILED
Silver clear the lake shone out
Covered with its blanket mist.
Grayish wips, escaping there
Dart through sighing weeping
willows.
Moon beams sharp and bright
tease through
Sparkling cascades of love unmet.
Tinkling laughter tells the beams
Where to find their wispy friends.
When at last they all are found,
They hold a celebration dance.
When dawn's first light comes o'er
the earth,
They all lay down 'til night's return.
Then sudden thunder—the lake is
caught
In hostile webs of red surveying
flags! Oh—
The violating men harshly stamp
Their smoldering cigars on the
cringing soil!
Bulldozers tear its heart in
wrenching jaggedness
The soil heaves in long-last agony
as its tear-showers fall.
Once laughing imps flee
mournfully in vain,
In search of a willow-lake dancing
floor.
Rough stubble on his face
A polluting cigar 'tween
stained-yellow teeth;
"Boss," he reports with a satisfied
smirk,
"We've finished our glorious
concrete roads.

And still the imps haunt the land.

Janet DiLeo
THE FACES OF WAR
The faces of war, we need to
remember.
Who is that young soldier, so tall
and so slender?
He could be your neighbor, he
could be your friend.
Is he somebody's brother? Is he
someone's son?
No matter I tell you, there's a war
to be won.

The faces of war, their eyes are so
wide.
In the beginning, they are
brimming with pride.
Seeing so much, being so near,
The soldier's eyes now are showing
great fear.
He sees enemy faces, the same age
as he,
"Must I kill them first, before they
kill me?"

The faces of war, we are now
witnessing.
A mother slumped over, her
handkerchief twisting,
A telegram opened has dropped to
the floor,
I am sorry dear parent your son
lives no more.

The faces of war, cry out in the
night.
Those who return, can't forget
their past fight.
How hard to erase the destruction
of man,
He'll hope and he'll try and he'll
pray that he can.

The faces of war, are they fading
from view?
This question I pose to both me
and to you
How splendid, how great the
freedom they bought,
Such a price that was paid, should
not be forgot.
The faces of war . . . WE NEED TO
REMEMBER!

Frank and Carolyn Waterhouse
INVICTUS REVISITED
Strong were the chains that held
me back.
I crossed the bridge and paid my
toll.
I fought God and the Devil alike.
For the right to my own soul.

I cast off the shackles of the past.
No power on earth can thwart my goal.
I jettisoned my script, at last.
Now, I myself, will mark my scroll.

The struggle is over. The script is dead.
A war is won and here I stand.
With the power to determine my destiny.
I'll mold my fate with my own hand.

Against the odds of circumstance.
I conquered all, and now I'm free.
I won the most prized gift of all.
My right to live, Autonomously.

Larry Shields FSC
PEACE

To all who accept nature's dare to grasp the plethora of the beauty of her hidden fare.

Lord i come at break of day
to seek your grace and pray;
enough good has come my way
what can i do, for you today!

loaded with favors this past year
do i express thanks and cheer?
i am spoiled by you
having only a materialistic view.

your abundant gifts distort my mind
i'm cruel, yet you, so lovingly kind;
i pass your house each day
without time, for a prayer to say.

am i a dreg, a last leaf
selfish as an unkind thief!
your gifts i take and do not use
is my mind a burnt out fuse?

you made the sun, the wind and the river bend
your power and nature neatly blend;
am i disguised as a shadow at night
or do i reflect your radiant light!

if i'll plant your seed
my life will be legible to read;
can i give witness to Thee
and still be the present me!

Joan Roberts
MOTHER'S DAY

To My Dearest Mother With All My Love Always And Forever. Your Daughter, Joan

---

Mother Dearest, this is your very own Special Day!
You've earned this day throughout
all these years without any pay!

You've given of yourself so freely,
Asking for nothing in return
year after year and day after day!
You've stood beside me through thick and thin!
No matter what the price or the pain!

There is no way that I could ever repay
you for all that you have done for me!
Only the Lord above knows just how I feel!
You are so very near and Dear to me!
I could search the world over
and never find a Mother as
Loving, Wonderful, Kind, and
Dear, as you are to me!
Mother, Oh Dear Mother of Mine!
Happy Mother's Day! Mother!
I Love you always and forever!

Adele Williams

Adele Williams
THE SEEKER

This poem is dedicated to Maureen McGuire who is a continual inspiration, and to Steve, my wondrous wizard.

I never knew the world to be
Someplace I treasured immensely.
I've been in and out of body and travelled so far
Strumming my strings on the world's guitar,
A misplaced person in the third degree
Being carried further out to sea.

Yes, I'm wilful and very strong
But to settle down would be oh so wrong.

"Be true to myself" echoes in my ears,
The need to be like others only brings tears.
People applaud me for all the things I've done
Although it's hard for me to give credit for one.

I'm choosing a path far from the norm,
It's just too late to try to conform.
"Be cautious, you fool"
I often hear
But there's a genuine need
To caress my fear:
To meet them head-on and poke them around
To touch them and smell them and listen for sound.
Using all my senses to find the right key,
Knowing all along the answers are within me.

When I write the last chapter I wonder if I'll find
This whole complex mess was just all in my mind.

Helene Phillips
SPRING OF HOPE

The trees moving gently
in the breeze.
Birds winging their way north as
spring slowly returns.
Eternal hope surely swells within
each breast, the urge to nest
is rightly timed.
We see this season as renewal, as
another new beginning.
Surely, for some, for all, a
fluttering of heart,
a new day begun.

Debbie McClellan Carter
CHILD ABUSE

For my parents and my husband, whose love gave me an anchor and for Lesa and Janet, whose friendship gave me wings.

Some things are hard to understand
like why cells divide and chromosones band
like how electricity causes light
and why the tides go in at night
like how plants photosynthesize
and where a person goes when he dies.
Why do mountains grow so tall
what's behind a waterfall
and I wonder, most of all

why people hurt little children.

Rosa Fern Sinkler
SEAMSTRESS

Amid the array of supply
See the fragments of her inspiration
Materials galore to try
Ready tools of her chosen vocation

Needles sharp pointed for wit
Larger to embellish or embroider
Strong to prick the heart's intent
Slimline to pleat love and ardor

Threads of highest quality
Pliant and fine as noblest thoughts
Yarns of color for variety
Strands of goods their message wrought

Outlines arranged in concepts glad
Fabric of life hemmed bright all around
Paisley of prose, moral of plaid
Patchwork of myriad tones abound

Pieces in profusion tangled
Seam to seam and line to line now gird
Trim, splice, shape and angle
To form the garment of the written word

Tracy A Riester
SPIDER WEBB

softly falls the ancient drops
of silvery rain
upon the dew-drop
sparkled web

deftly approaches the stealthy
warrior of
octagonal locomotion
to discover the purpose
of the miscellaneous disturbance

'tis only the rain
my friend, and
it is evening'

Olive Twigg Davis
ABSENCE

It was mid October,
the leaves were of bright hue's
While walking on a lonely mountain road
in late afternoon
I thought my heart would
surely burst with longing
For the nearness of you.

Curtis E Clendenin
LONELINESS

Loneliness is seen;
In the darkness,
The night, the sky;
Being alone without another,
Or talking with yourself.

Loneliness is heard
In the dark.
Heavy sighing, children crying,
Or a lightened breeze.
Anything without thought.

Loneliness is in yourself.
No dreams, doubtful thoughts,
That repeat themselves
In your hardships,
In your work,
And even in your rest.

Jeanette Mullins Brooks
MEMORIES

Memories keep slippin' in my head,
Thoughts of things that are now dead.
Will they ever come alive in other times,
Or just stay buried deep within our minds?

Memories of faces I miss so much,
Hands from the past that I long to touch,
Words from my life that I cry to share,
A heart that longs to listen to theirs;

A friend so real I can't forget,
A place so still the day we left,
The words we spoke stopped by our tears,
Only memories left from so many years.

There was a time when life was right,
And it only ended because of the night.
My life has more meaning since all this has been,
But I can't help wondering "Could this be the end?"
No, I can't help wondering "Does it have to end?"

Rhonda D Lowman
YOU'RE THE ONE

I'd love to feel your body
Close against my skin,
I'm hurting for you badly
Even though it is a sin.

You're the one I want to hold me
As I fall asleep tonight,
Kiss me gently as I'm sleeping
To drive away the fright.

I'd love to have you hold me
As morning gently peeks through,
Then hold me against your body
As you whisper softly, "I love you."

Therone J Boone
STRUGGLE TO SURVIVE

To all my children and the wonderful people that gave me a helping hand. God bless you all.

I was born the victim of a broken home;
From a sixteen year old mother
who couldn't cease to roam.
The lonely offspring of a broken

marriage . . .
Who never even owned his baby carriage.
I was given away when I was born;
There was nothing on earth I could call my own.
Home after home I was sent to live . . . .
But, I learned to pretend and how to forgive.
I was sent to school from my foster homes,
But was never treated like one of their own.
I grew up paying some unknown dues;
A victim and slave to unfair rules . . . .
And yet, I survived and learned to be smart,
Like someone was guiding my will and my heart.
I blamed no one and I never complained,
'Though my reason for living was never explained.
I found that with sorrows there was beauty in life;
I've never regreted my being alive,
'Cause within my struggle was the will to survive.
And now, at last, I can understand . . . .
That the hardships of life was molding a man.

Paul Russell Lesley

Paul Russell Lesley
RETROSPECTION

To my loving wife, Daisy Dean Lesley, my daughter, Dana Dean and granddaughter, Lesley Dean, with all my love as ever.

When the good Lord dims the glimmers, on this mob of Earthly sinners,
And the Angels up in Heaven keep their watch o'er you and me,
I will often stop to ponder, as my stay on Earth I squander,
And I'll ponder o'er conditions of the present day,
and how things used to be.

What were sheep trails, now are highways.
Lanes are widened shining whiteways and the horse-car has vanished
for the subway or L or steam or bus. And,
while the square dance changed to shimmy, and the Golden Rule to Gimme
It makes the days of our grandparents seem a vague, but cherished dream.

With their long curls cut to shingles, plus their 4-inch earring dangles
And the ease of dying up their hair, most any henna, shade or hue.
And how the women keep us guessing,
as their hair and skirts they lessen.
And ain't it mighty funny what a dab of rouge will do?

I can fathom bad relations, that might test the strength of nations.
And I can savvy in a measure, why it rains or flowers grow.
And it is even my intention, to pursue the fourth dimension.
But when the subject is women—Like the rest, I'll never know.

But did you ever get this inkling, as you sat at night a thinking
And your former trysting places and your loves passed in review.
With your boyhood days behind you, can a lonesome night remind you,
If you had it to do over, can you figure what you'd do?

A man can't live without or with them,
His delight just seems to give them all comforts and pleasures
We have, or ever hope to own.
A woman is a man's greatest treasure, but a man only feels the measure and the value of that treasure when he sits at night alone.

The living impression of a sweet memory
is much more beautiful than any immediate reality.

Mabel P Howell
MAKE THE BEST OF WHAT YOU ARE

This poem is dedicated to my family.

If you run for the president
And fail to gain the seat,
Don't sit around with posture bent
And moan because you're beat.

Keep smiling on with courage true
Take failure on the chin,
For duty may be calling you
In a smaller field to win.

Now we gain nought to sit and mose—
Don't despair, but take heart
Yes, true success have come to those
Who took the minor part.

For all can't shine quiet as the sun,
Many twinkle as a star.
Your task, though small, be it well done
Make the best of what you are.

Ruth Moloney Cowgill
MY MOTHER

To: Ethel Saum Moloney on her 92nd Birthday, Aug 28, 1986

With Love and Gratitude. God Bless!

Why do I love my mother,
With her kind and gentle ways?
Was it because she sprinkled love
Throughout my childhood days?

Or was it for the things she taught
While kneading dough for bread
Maybe it was the winter nights
And the stories that she read?

Or was it for the food she raised
With garden long and wide?
Or the way we talked things over
As we weeded side by side?

Or was it for the dandelions
She braided for my crown,
Or the little dresses that she made
Then embroidered all around?

Could it be the prayers I said
Beside my bed at night,
When my mother knelt beside me
To help me do it right?

With my growing up made easy
By the way she played her part
Now the things we did together
Stay the closest to my heart.

When I think about my mother
Who was great beyond compare,
The thing I loved the very best
Was her just being there.

Linda Marie Fahey
THE TRAVELS OF DUSTY SUNSHINE

There's a dust cloud where the old road bends
Out Back where the empty quarry ends;
Near the pebbles and the rocks
Where time outlasts electric clocks
Sun and Dust meet like old friends.
CHORUS:
Sea of Sand and Dusts
Where nothing ever rusts

The Sun rides orange in the sky
Where afternoon breaths blow hot and dry
No water can there be found
Only Dusty Sunshine stopping by.
CHORUS:
Sea of Sand and dusts
Blowing hot and stormy gusts

Dusty Sunshine inhales at the edge of town
Dusty Sunshine storms into a whirl wind clown
Air dances through leafless trees
Dryish fingers choke the breeze
When Dusty Sunshine walks around.

Richard A Griffiths
MY PRINCESS

If I were a prince, with a princess to choose, to sit on a throne that no one could refuse,
Of all the great ladies with wealth and renown, there would be but one that could wear MY gold crown!

The grandest princess of them all, she would be; with beauty, and charm, and calm dignity.
Wise in the ways of the heart and the mind; and thoughtful and truthful, and gentle, and kind.

She'd have common ways, never vain nor too proud to meet the least privileged of all in the crowd.
With her grace and pure heart she'd have all at her feet; and with her warm smile, a huge army defeat!

She'd need not gold, nor silver, nor land; but just the sweet touch of her palm in my hand.
Her warm and soft body, just there beside mine, clad in purple robes fit for the best of her kind.

I'd love my princess, and she'd never deny; that her station in life was the highest of high;
For though I'm the prince, and she is my wife, she always would rule in affairs of my life!

Douglas W Harris
A SEARCH FOR PEACE

Where is the light at the end of this tunnel of darkness?
Where is the peace that could end these decades of war?
If wars could cease, and the efforts of man could be applied to a better life for all;
What a place this world could be, for all mankind, and for you and me.
What can be gained through the destruction of war?
Who can be happy by controling this world through force?
Let me work for the happiness of all mankind;
The ecology of a better world, in balance for the good of all.
Show me the little spot where I can serve this plan,
To make my contribution, and to be a happy man.

Virginia Bognar Garon
THE OLD FARM

To John, Richard, Donna, Johnny, Susan, Scotty and all of the other children in our family . . with love

---

Nothing stands of the old farm house
where children played beneath its porch
. . making roads for tiny cars
and playing games that only a child knows

The cold wind blows across the grass
where it seems like only yesterday . .
the fields were gold with ripened grain
and stacks of new mown hay

Carefree days and happy hours
with dandelion crowns to wear . .
chasing the elusive butterflies
that fluttered happily everywhere

and from within the old farm house
. . the aroma of fresh baked bread
apple pie and chicken frying
. . thats what grandma said

Now all is quiet . . all is gone
only cherished memories still remain
and the children who are grown . . .
with children of their own
are all scattered like the grain

A gentle rain is softly falling
. . . or is it just the tears?
As I recall those happy faces
and those precious childhood years

Jack Passerello
IT'S ME

Dedicated to all the living things on this Earth.

If all the fishes in all the seas
And all the birds in all the trees
Had names,
You see what a problem that would be.

And all the plants and all the bees
And all the ants and all the fleas
Would use all the names

From "A"s to "Z"s

Thousands of Janes, millions of Moes,
A billion Jacks, a trillion Joes.

At the pearly gates, asked "Who are thee"?
A mile long list to read, you see.

God knew of this, and made it be
That all could answer, and say;
"IT'S ME" !!!!

Patricia Ringer
RAINBOWS AND BUTTERFLYS

To Ann and Brian who believe in me and I in them.

Rainbows and butterflys
Things that are real
Oceans and meadows
Quiet moments we steal
All reflect the beauty of
Truth that I feel
I can say with all sureness
This LOVE is for real
It may last a minute
Or maybe a day
It could last forever
But this one thing I say
No promises no promises

Violet Newbry Teater
MY PRAYER
Dear Father, I'm coming to You today—
No Problem, just to say thanks and pray.
Thank you for making me strong and free.
Thank you for giving me eyes to see.
To see the beauty in this big world,
To see Your love and joy unfurled,
To see Your light in the morning sun,
And blessed wonders that have begun.
Thank You, for helping me to know—
It's only through You, that I may grow.
Thank You Father.

Gloria LaVelle Worth
I DEPEND ON YOU, LORD
I depend on you Lord
for food on the table,
I depend on you Lord
because I know you are able.
I depend on you Lord
for the clothes that I wear,
I depend on you Lord
because in my heart you are there.
I depend on you Lord
for to my enemies the right words to say,
I depend on you Lord—
each and every day!

Arthur D Taylor
AUTUMN?
Autumn?
No, not yet.
Though these cool mornings nip savagely at Summer's heels,
And the days late haze obscures landmarks,
That were clear in Spring.

Mary Y York
SPEAK SOFTLY
Speak softly Lord,
And fill my soul
With faith and hope,
And dreams untold.

With visions high
And strength to climb,
Each mountain peak
With joy sublime.

Then lift my eyes
Yet higher still,
And lead my heart
To do thy will.

O, precious Lord,
Be thou my guide
That in thy love
I shall abide.

Lamora M Collins
FULFILLMENT
The warmth of your presence
As sun on the frozen snow
Melts my icy loneliness
Flooding the river of my soul

Esther Herrick
WINTER SLIDING
Fresh
As the breeze,
That comes from the wind.
Fresh
As the
New fallen snow.
The children
Outside are sliding,
Down
the
beautiful
snow-capped
hills.

Linda H Adams
THE WEDDING PRESENT
Just as promised, I am now delivering.
On cold winter nights it'll keep you from shivering.
To make sure of that, just place on your bed.
Use as a blanket, or even a spread.

However you use it, and that's up to you,
It'll keep you both warm when the winter chill comes through.
It works well in its place, but goes only so far.
To stay warm inside, it takes a lot more.

It takes hard work—not a little, a lot.
And much give and take, "fifty-fifty" it's not.
So be strong in your faith, put God at the top.
If each other comes next, your love won't stop.
In fact, it'll grow, and one day you'll see
That you aren't the same people you used to be.
You'll care more for each other than ever you thought,
Because into your marriage God's love you brought.

So, in closing, I'll say, and pay close attention;
For warmth outside the quilt's a great invention.
But to keep the warmth on the inside aglow,
It takes God's love and yours, and a willingness to grow.

Lois Rapp
UNTITLED
This structure is a gossamer thread
Of dew and lightning formed,
A filigree of earlier dead
The moaning of the born;
At subtle whisper of the wind
And movement in the moon,
These filaments do turn and spin
And make the earth their loom.
A moment's gleaming in the sun
With hard metallic sheen,
A second and the thread is spun
Unsought and twice unseen.
Release each cord and knit as one
A net to stay the dream.

Ruth Sutton Sexton

Ruth Sutton Sexton
THE SLEEPING GIANT
Like a sleeping giant—life can pass you by
All the while activities go on
Movement
People
Sounds
Seasons
Change
Yet never awareness of all that is round about.

Wake up, oh sleeping giant
Flex your muscles
Move
Feel
Hear
See
Know
Really Know—Experience—
Participate—Come Alive

Don't be laden down
Be lifted up
Be set free

Wake up, you sleeping giant.

Charlotte Cole
WORKING MOTHER'S LAMENT

For Jaime, with love

Waiting after school in lifeless room,
With TV and junk food sole consolation,
Till Working Mom gets home.
Eleven years old. Fast approaching the
Door marked "Adolescence, Enter Here."
How can I explain what's on the other side?
I know naught of men or manhood.
I am woman, single parent, failure,
Driven by necessity to hated job
That keeps us off the welfare rolls.
Time is the enemy and poverty my master.
"Education!," say those who think they know me
Well enough to call me friend.
When not at work, then I'm to be at school?
And who'll be robbed of precious time and thought
While Mama gets retrained?
No, my son. We will endure together.
Till, old enough, and wise enough
You leave me, and leaving me will know,
If you had nothing else from me,
You had my love.

Garnett Fireline
WINTER
Seasons change faces
Like war and peace.
Everything's a memory,
A memory fading.
Like hidden places,
Messiah waiting—
Waiting above on a deep cold night.
On a silent snowy plain I cry.
Bitter rain beating—
Everything's incomplete.

Another cold winter blowing inside hollow.
Deep cut ice engraved in my soul.
Like fall ending and winter flowing,
Blowing a feeling of lostness
Across this face—lips cracked,
Winter is here, winter is back.

Lucille Quackenbush
LEILA

This poem is dedicated to Leila, a very dear and special friend.

You have gone from me,
But, still I see
Your sweet-self sitting there.
Others have sat in it,
But, it will always be "your chair"
I miss you so, but, still I know,
We will meet, in heaven above,
Where there is only love,
And dear friends to meet and greet.
I will always have fond thoughts of you.

Farewell, until that day,
Our friendship we will renew.

Robyn H Torbert
AMERICA

Dedicated to my children Jacque, Jim, and John

America, America
Who are you?

Do you want each ethnic group
Stirred, kneaded, blended
into one huge glob, all alike
a unison of forced conformity
no individuality?

She wept, then smiled,
"No, I'm wiser now,
Keep your different personalities
your culture, songs and dances
hold fast to what you are."

"I only want you tossed
gently as a salad,
only the dressing must be strong.
Blended well, adhering, seeping
down, around,
anchoring you together."

"Then each one retains their own
identity
shares an unique flavor
all contributing to one superb
country
each knowing and respecting
one another."
This, is America."

Janilyn R Hunt
SPECIAL YEARS

To my loving husband, Jim who, by the grace of God, inspires all my endeavors.

Twenty-one special years have
passed
Since first we exchanged that
precious glance
Through good times and bad
You have always kept me from
being sad
When our lives have been high
Or when trouble was nigh
You have always been here
To bring me good cheer
Our prayers will never cease
And always bring to us an inner
peace
Though problems seem big, we'll
never fall
Because on God, we can always call
Together the dreams we share
Will show others our special care
In this world you are my dearest
And all happiness comes when
you're nearest
The true light of my life
Is in being your wife

Norma J McGuire
I'LL FIND A NEW MOMMY

For my son David—this old Mommy loves you.

I'll find a new Mommy
That's what I'll do!
She'll be nice to me
Not mean, like you!
She'll play all day
And sing all night . . .
We'll have candy and popcorn
And I'll always be right.
I'll find a new Mommy
That's what I'll do!
But, my old Mommy loves me
And I love her too.

Dawn K Ah Chick
ONCE UPON A TIME

I remember the time we met
The fun times we'd never forget
Walks together hand in hand
Going to the beach and sitting on
the sand
Laughing and smiling all the way
I never knew that it would come to
this day
What happened to the guy I once
knew?
Did he fade away like the morning
dew?
The sweet gentle guy who seems to
be gone
That special someone that I
thought I had won
A feeling of despair enters my head
Remembering those three words
that he once said
Why did we tend to drift apart?
Did we forget those feelings down
deep in our hearts?
I think about this guy I miss
His warm smile and his gentle kiss
Sometimes I wish that he were
mine
As he was, once upon a time.

Richard "Bud" Weaverling
LITTLE ONE

To Sharon, John and Kristie Lee Connolly

Welcome to the family, Little One.
We have been waiting a long time
for you.
It matters not either daughter or
son,
There's lots of love and fun
awaiting you.

Your Mommy is here and so is your
Dad,
To love and guide you as you grow.
To share the good times as well as
the bad,
And to teach you things you ought
to know.

The Lord has given your parents a
job to do,
To love, to feed, to clothe, and
educate you.
The decisions they make may at
times offend,
But they will be by far your very
best friends.

So welcome to the world, Little
One,
Grow healthy and strong and have
some fun.
Learn to love and to care as your
parents have done.
They're fine people, they're Sharon
and John.

Mary Alice Sherman
THE STORY CONTINUES

My magazine trembles . . .
The lines grow intense . . .
I'll die if it doesn't
Let up on suspense.

His fingers extend
And the trigger is snapped.
Oh, no . . . it CAN'T be,
The poor girl was trapped.

She screams out in terror,
Then slumps to the floor
While the villain laughs madly
And shoots her some more.

Oh, horrors! How dreadful!
I reach for a tissue
To cry in—then notice
"Continued next issue."

Noah M Ennis & Yoko Ennis
GOD GAVE ME A DAUGHTER

I prayed to my God one day.
Please send a beautiful flower my
way.
God made one so sweet, He had to
love and kiss it too.
He cryed when you left him, and
he sent me you.
He made me promise to love it with
care.
And all the world its beauty I must
share.
Then he touched its heart and
made it beat with love.

And he said, there's no one sweeter
on earth or heaven above.
He said be oh so careful when you
touch it.
You must handle it with care.
And if you ever hurt it here's what
I'll do.
I will take my beautiful flower back
from you.
So I made God a promise, to love
his flower always,
And I pray.
Dear God, please don't take my
pretty little flower away.
And each morning God Loves and
kisses her too, I'm so thankful
my daugher, God sent me you.

M M Ruggles
NO MORE

In loving memory of my father

Soft the gentle breeze is blowing
As I bid you this adieu
If one seems a little stronger
It's because I think of you.

Neither sorrow, tears or regrets
Should you have that I am gone.
For you know I'm gently sleeping,
Until that wondorous break of
dawn.

For I loved you all those years dear,
And although we cannot talk.
I'll be always thinking of you
Gentle breeze beside you walk.

Loretta Ellen Maguire
SNOW FALLS

To my nephew, Shaun Alan Collins, because he made my dream come true.

Every step on the pounded snow
Squeaks like saddle leather.
I slip, but my arms tense to protect
him,
His tiny body close to my heart,
Childhood in my possession.
The white falls and begins to bury
us,
As winter nips my nose, crawls up
my icy sleeve,
Warming my body.
The baby coos.
His rosey face and woolen cap
never before had
A frosty mountain.
Sun puts cellophane on snow,
While I fight the chill with my
warm bundle.
And the dreams fall, pile around
us, beautifully clean.
Cinderella waltzes by,
Snow White skipping around her.
The shining silver horse appears
on the horizon.
Snow White trips, bumps
Cinderella,
And the shining horse falls.
I open my eyes to the August green,
Walk home, hands in pockets.

Miriam Louise Trowbridge
A GIFT OF LOVE

To my mother, EDITH AGNES REGISTER TROWBRIDGE HUNT, from whom I inherited her gift for words, humor, perseverance and love of life. She is now and always be my PERMANENT FRIEND. I love you, Mama.

VOLUNTEER they call me
Why that's just a name,
It has no warmth or feeling or love
Which certainly is a shame . . .

Because inside what I feel
When I give my time to others,
Is what little children feel,
When they snuggle next to their
mothers . . .

Love so strong, it can't be measured
A need to pass it along,
And when I see love returned
It's like a beautiful song . . .

To know that I can help someone
Is all the pay I need,
And I thank GOD for this gift
Because HE is my lead . . .

So you can see I'm more than a
name
I was created from ABOVE,
Because my time I give to others
Is truly "A GIFT OF LOVE."

Jone' Hindsley-Harris
THEY MATE FOR LIFE

With love for my Mother and Father, John and Georgann Hindsley, on their 40th Wedding Anniversary, Your Gosling, Jone'

Two of a kind and like in their
purpose,
They search to find their spirit,
Reflecting back from unknown
depths of souls,

They entwine to form a union.
They Mate For Life.

Through the peril and the danger,
They are steadfast to their destiny.
Born to instinct and to fate,
They teach their species culture.
They Mate For Life.

From thaw to freeze; from seedling to harvest,
They support a combined well being.
Life is cruel; the loss is painful,
They endure a sentinal for the trust.
They Mate For Life.

Carla Van Veghel

DREAMING

As January comes around,
so cold and lots of snow covering the ground,
You find yourself thinking about the year that past
A year, you cannot change and went by so fast.
Life is hectic nowadays, everyday that same quick pace.
Newyearsresolutions so well made, by an adult or a child
start off so well, but later in the year run wild.
Come March, you feel really blue
and dream of summer, the favourite season for you
In April things are looking better
Sometimes you feel it already, that sunny weather.
Spring is in the air, it does funny things to people every year
You start again: a new beginning, you feel it in your blood
The coming months are going to be good.
The trees welcome you with their green coats
Birds are back singing wonderfull notes.
Children playing together in their yard
People come closer, not hidden far apart.
Gardens show colourfull blooms of flowers, that smell for hours.
Also the aroma of fresh cut grass hangs in the air,
Mix everything together and it will last you all year.
From the past you cannot change a thing, but look on the bright side of all the good a new spring can bring.
Lots of sunshine, especially in your heart, does wonders for you & others too.

Alexandru C Megas

INSIGHT

To my dearest ones, as an expression of our first years of struggle and sustained hope

---

INSIGHT into that dizzy like round trip,
INTO that supple and absurd process,
THE occasionally looker-on unwillingly stares;
TRAVELLERS restless and endless journey,
CRAZY attractiveness, sensible and docile move,
WANDERING perpetually conducting the unevading wool
ALONG the taking over bobbins,
AN obvious and hidden feeding
ENDLESS act passing through
STAINLESS steel or plastic made rings, a
STEEL strength wool yarn bearing along a
RING all the previous material inheritage, a
CRAZY absurd flow of miraculous
FINAL pressed together particles at a
STROKE by stroke stream,
REVEALS that tremendous straight and
AN open step by step course, so
UNEXPECTED at a fresher first sight, as
ORDINARY as a water flow, for such a
YARN is so a human product of a
WOOL made perrenial spring of prosperity . . .
"INSIGHT INTO THE TRAVELLERS CRAZY WANDERINGS ALONG AN ENDLESS STEEL MADE RING,
A FINAL STROKE REVEALS AN UNEXPECTED ORDINARY WOOL MADE YARN"

Roseann Petrowski

CHRISTMAS IN A PACKAGE

Lovingly dedicated to my Mom, Ann and my sister, Eva who have always believed in me. And especially to Sue Vitale and the Eastlake Jr. Women's Club, without whose request this poem would not have been made public.

Christmas in a package
Silly, or it seems
Inside, hidden treasures,
Bits of shattered dreams.

From within, its shadows
Form in silhouette
Memories of loved ones
And friends you can't forget.

Distance is a menace
And plays a wicked part,
Making sure the heart aches
Right from the very start.

Phones and letters help you
To always keep in touch
But can't replace the warm embrace
From those you miss so much.

And knowing you won't see them
As holidays draw near,
Makes the longing almost
Impossible to bear.

A plain, brown, paper package
Somewhat sad—but then—
I look forward to sending one
Time and time again.

So know it's not just holidays
You're missed, but all year through
By this Christmas in a package
That I send with love to you!

Sterlen Dwayne Barnes

DISTANT SHORES

Dedicated to my wife who never lost faith in me and to all who have found love in Hawaii.

On the distant shores of an undiscovered
paradise lies the feeling of
serenity within one's self.

Here one may walk along white virgin
beaches unspoiled by blemish,
unscarred by the passing of time.

Feeling the gentle breeze blowing
across your face, ruffing your hair and
Enhancing your senses to the beauty abounding
or listening to the peaceful sounds of
surf as she whispers a song
that warms your heart.

Knowing there are no untruths
Only the never ending joy that
one finds in a special friendship.

Audra E Bowers

OUR LOVE

When I saw him
I knew I loved him
He made me feel good
Like I always knew he could
When I gave him my heart
He just tore it apart
Now it's all done
I knew he had won
I don't know what to do
I don't know if it hurt him too
I tried to call to see if he cared
But I just think he was too scared
Now it's all done, and all gone . . .
OUR LOVE

Richard W Stiffler

Richard W Stiffler

AMERICA, MY LOVE

My America, how I love thee;
From Dawn's glistening light—to sunset's last gleaming.
I feel thy warmth, and see thy love.
As the wind blows across your face,
I feel thy love and see thy grace
and know from this land I don't have to flee.

The tender touch of a womans hand,
the freedom of moving when I well please
The look of love that's such a tease,
Freedom to work the job I choose,
to gain all the education and not lose
the right to speak, to sing, or dance;
all are reasons why I love this land.

Sometimes warm and sometimes cold,
sometimes harsh, sometimes gentle,
full of love and hate, life and death,
a place of opportunity and advance;
a simple song, a simple dance.
Oh land of the brave, land of the free
How I love thee, a story unable to be told.

Ruth E Schunke

KEEPING IN TOUCH

When your loved ones are so far away,
"I miss you so much," you always say.
Time goes by and you say, "I must write,
But oh, I am so tired tonight.
I don't like to write and I have no time,"
Even though it's just a couple dimes.
Before you know it, the time's gone so fast,
"When did I write, was it two months past?
No, it can't be, that's just not me.
I miss you too much to let time flee."
Then by chance, your loved one passes,
"I loved and missed you so much,
Why didn't I keep in touch?"

Ron Lucas

WAITING FOR YOU

The breeze is blowing
The ships are sailing
The waves are waving
While I'm waiting
Waiting for you.

When you feel a breeze blowing
Or see a ship sailing
May it remind you
That I'm waiting
Waiting for you.

My hair is graying
I'm wrinkled from aging
But I keep praying
You'll stop this waiting
Waiting for you.

When the breeze stops blowing
The ships stop sailing
And the waves stop waving
I'll still be waiting
Waiting for you.

Carrie Cronin Urquhart

ANOTHER DAY IN TIME

I have a love, so deep inside
I know at times, you read my mind.
If my heart could say the words,
I hope and pray, you understood.

You think of me as just your friend,
I hope that part will never end.
If that chance may come our way
I would thank God every single day.

You'll never know the way I feel
The day won't come for me to tell.
I have to keep it in my heart,
And never let it go that far.

What I would give for you to know
But for this life, It can't be so.
There may be another day in time
You'll be more than just a friend of mine.

And so for now,
we'll be just pals,
To the end,
we'll be just friends.

Valda Schal

A SEAMAN'S SAGA

This poem is dedicated to Saimi Lorenzen for her inspiration and support

---

Gray and sullen is the ocean
Crashing and heaving with

Angry discontent against
The shore's cold jagged rocks.
Alone in a frail skiff
A young seaman dares to put out
On this wide, wild sea.
Overhead the night's starry sky flames
Beneath him whispers darkly his grave
But ever forward is Fate's command.
The seaman prays to God in Heaven
And Open Sea for guidance to a
Tranquil harbor beyond pain
And certain Death.

Adagria

THE RIVER AND TIME

Time will always flow like a river
Time is so scary it makes me shiver
A river, the changes of reflections,
Reflections of time, different projections.
You can never tell about a river or time,
Like images in water, they're hardly to kind.
Life goes on like the river and time,
So ever changing, always rearranging.
I'll have to flow like the river and time;
I'll have to be honest, with an open mind,
To accept things with change, no questions to incline
Learn to flow along like the river and the time.

Debra Stevenson

FEAR

The War has
begun
The time for soldiers
to fight
We bear our
arms
We strike another
human down
Do I shoot?
Do I run?
Please Lord, I'm not
a Killer
I see the bodies
falling
My heart has
stopped
I see my brother
down
The hatred has begun
in my heart
My arms are secure
my feet are planted
I lift my gun,
I aim
The killing will
never end
For someone will always
lose a brother
The fighting never
stops
War is feelings
A feeling of hatred

Barbara Hamby

JUST YOU AND I AND WHOEVER

If we could form a circle 'round the world,
Hand in hand, beneath all flags unfurled—
Man to woman or man, children too
There'd be no fear of missiles in the blue.

The force of love that we could all create
Could hold the awesome power to eliminate
Fear, distrust, the war to end all wars—
Not leaving our planet barren and covered with sores,
But verdant and fertile, basking in warm tenderness,
Starting with just a few, we have the universe to bless.

Vivian K DelMontier

AWAY . . .

The Violet wakens, and the Daffodil,
The Laurel and the Dogwood climb each hill,
The fragrance of the Lilac fills the air—
and I'm not there.

The trellised Roses mark the scented hours,
And fields are golden with a million flowers;
A steepled bell chimes out the closing day—
though I'm away.

The trees are all aflame with red and gold,
And southward wing the birds, just as of old;
The lengthening shadows steal across the lawn—
but I am gone.

On distant purple slopes the snow lies deep,
The lake and stream are locked in winter's keep;
And desolate, my heart must ever yearn—
'til I return.

Alan N Riman

Alan N Riman

THE EYES OF THE WORLD

To my MOM & DAD who were always there & whose love I will never relinquish & to my buddy HAROLD BRODSKY, alias "Harry," alias "Howie Brooski" my best friend in this whole world. SHALOM!

Is it I the blind that see?
Is it I the deaf that hear?
Is it I the crippled that walk?
Is it I the mute that talk?
Or perhaps the weak are strong,
Or perhaps the short is long,
But, from a yielding source
I've set my course,
By the light in the eyes of the world.

Tis remarkable the feeling
That this light has brought so near,
With an ever-lasting wonder that enabled me to hear,
With an ever-glowing vision that enabled me to see,
With an ever-lasting glory that enabled me to be.

But the fact is clearly evident,
My life I have not hurled,
For I've got the shining image
From the light in the eyes of the world.

Marilynn J Baker

NEIGHBOR

To Zoe

When you zip by in your little car
And wave your hand at me,
You have a twinkle in your eye
And a smile which is a pleasure.

I'd like to have you as a friend,
The kind that I could treasure.
The warmth I feel when you zip by
Is more than I can measure.

Oh, what a treat when you drop in
And sit down with a sigh
To let me know about your day
And how it has gone by.

I'd like to have you as a friend,
The kind that I could treasure.
The warmth I feel when you drop in
Is more than I can measure.

There is a sadness in your eye
Every now and then.
It lets me know I'm not alone;
You also need a friend.

I'd like to have you as a friend,
The kind that I could treasure.
The warmth I feel each time we meet
Is more than I can measure.

Dorothy McPhillips

THE SUMMER PLACE

Down a dusty road we turned
That runs down to the bay;
And there espied our summer home—
'Twas crumbling in decay.

No one goes there anymore to spend
A day or two:
The children are all grown and gone,
Those precious years are few.

We put the key inside the lock—
We're greeted at the door,
By memories of a yesterday that were
But are no more.

Bamboo shades with broken cords
Still sift the summer sun;
And many a spider lives there now
And many a web has spun.

We checked and resecured each room,
Then hurried out quite fast;
It's sad to linger with the ghosts
Of days that are long past.

Back up the dusty weed-strewn road;
A silent pair are we.
We had left behind a lonely house—
And the days that used to be.

Helen F Armstrong

LITTLE THINGS

My eyes grow dim
For my desert land,
And with a tear or two,
I can see arrowheads
In the sand,
Beneath a sky of blue.

I love the desert,
I love the sea,
And both I would explore.
But had I time, I still couldn't find,
All the treasures they hold in store.

God gives to me the ability,
To seek and yes! to find,
The little things that mean so much,
But only in my mind.

For others would not take the time,
To seek these things so small.
But arrowheads on two small plaques
Are hanging on my wall.

Eric Adam Fenner

ARBOURHYTHM

Mother Earth,
You have thrown me outward,
Arms flung, reaching for the Sun.
Growing upward.
Life—green coat and cellulose skin.
Drinking in the
Tears of Heaven,
As storm-grey clouds
Weep upon my shoulders.
A feathered throat sings in my ear,
Protecting fledglings
Nestled in my arms.
Minions of Aeolus,
Writhing about my body.
I whisper
Aeonian secrets
To the Children climbing on my body.
And I trill with the Heavens,
An unending tune.
And not a soul can hear me,
For I am only a Tree.

Evelyn Hansen

ON THE LOSS OF A CHILD

Death can be gentle
I know for I've seen
It spread a soft mantle
On a boy's endless dream.

I will not fear
As I kneel to pray
For Jesus is near
To take him away.

Sleep son, yes sleep

How peaceful you lie
It's truth, and I weep
We live, but to die.

Eleanor M Palazzo
THE AUTUMN LEAVES
The Autumn leaves are dancing
As the gusty fall winds blow.
They whirl and swirl around us
As 'round and 'round they go.

The Autumn leaves are painted
By Jack Frosts gentle hand,
And the beauty of his colors
Spreads across the land.

But Autumn soon is over,
And soon the snow will fall,
And the blustry winds of winter
Will chill us one and all.

Yes, it's sad to watch the Autumn leaves
Dancing 'round and 'round,
For you and I know all too well
They die upon the ground.

Nellie O Lovett
BEFORE I EVEN KNEW HIS NAME

Dedication to Gordon R. Kautsky for love and support.

I heard his voice,
Saw the shadow of his face,
Before I even knew his name,
Felt his presence,
Shared his shame,
He came from nowhere,
Knowing he was the same,
Before I even knew his name,

I touched his lips,
felt his pain,
With sweet life, we embraced,
Trying to know each others name,
I felt his desire,
Knowing mine was the same,
Before I even knew his name,

Our baby was birthed,
Laid him in the shade, of the tree,
While we played,
He called my name,
I answered,
Before I even knew his name,

Henrietta A Scott
THE KEY TO HAPPINESS
Be kind to one another
As the years go rolling by.
The love you have will hold secure
If you will only try.
May our Heavenly Father bless you
In everything you do,
And may you always live a life
That's wholesome, sound and true.
When disagreements flare up
As they are apt to do,
Please weigh the words you utter
so they'll not trouble you.
As you travel on together
Over life's uncertain miles,
Remember it costs nothing
For tender words and smiles.
And most of all, dear children,
Save a part of every day
For quiet meditation
While kneeling down to pray.

Christopher Wienstroer
POWER
When one speaks of the power
He speaks of me but does not know it
For I am the power
I am the center of everything
For I flow through every living thing
I am the power that preserves and ends
For everything evolves around me
I am eternal but without substance
For I can only be seen from within
I am not of your domain though I use it
I am not a God nor am I mortal
I am a prince with many names
To speak my name is to sacrifice a part of you
One day the words shall be spoken
And I shall be released from my prison below
The day I walk your land, Beware
For all shall fear me, I am Souleater
I AM ARMAGEDDON!

Anna Myrtle (Marriott) Evans

Anna Myrtle (Marriott) Evans
LOST INTENTION
Strolling the meadow brookside
With notepad and pen in hand
I was intent to write beneath a tree
But scenery took command,
And focal interest swelled
Occupying my mind until
My very being saturated

With an imperative thrill
That set my mind wandering on
An uncharted daydream far away,—
Thus pen and paper contact
Had no given chance to play
Their part in keeping thoughts
That filtered through my mind
And winged their way unpenned
Until another place and time.

Kathleen Ebel
ONE RECKLESS NIGHT
Upon the pedal his foot was lead.
Strange and oblivious thoughts
leaped around his head.
His sight was blurred, his speech
was free;
in the darkness he didn't see the tree.
His body was mangled into the grinding steel.
This wasn't a dream,
this was real.
For he had a little too much to drink that night.
He thought he was tough,
he thought he had might.
The ambulance came and took him away.
If it weren't for those few drinks he had,
he might still be here today.

James W Murphy Jr
SANCTUARY
The damaged race
Dragged by like thunder.
Too afraid to die.
Born-again Christians ride
on subway trains.
Start up the house
Don't forget to unplug
the lamps.
We're moving to the suburbs,
Where lavender lights,
kill bugs in the night.
It's like waking up
From a dream, still crying.
It feels so good,
You don't want to stop.
So you keep on crying.

Maurice Henderson

Maurice Henderson
STICK' EM
Stick'em, Stick'em
Bigger than A Mosquito
Stick'em, Stick'em
Bigger than they Come
Stick'em, Stick'em
Yeah, You're Right
Stick'em
If You say so
Stick'em

Angelina Marie Stillwell
A POEM A DAY

To my loving husband Scott and my precious daughter Nicole, and in memory of my father, James P. Greco, Sr.

If I write a poem a day
I'll be happy or so they say.
And so I write of love and pain
Then I wonder what remains.
I can write of trees and skies
But I favor writing of guys.
So when I meet someone new
I write a poem about him too.
During a fight with my love
I write about a flying dove.
And if it ends in a happpy way
I write to tell him I hope he stays.

Lee Hatcher
A DREAM

To Kandis, my first child, whose inspirations never cease to amaze me. 051686

Last night I had a dream
that I was a butterfly,
and it felt so good to me
to fly around the flower tops
and see what I could see!

But then I thought about what this dream might mean,
then I decided it was fine,
and then a very interesting thought
came into my mind.

If last night I dreamed I was a butterfly
flying across the land,
today how do I know I'm not a butterfly
just dreaming that I'm a Man . . .

Fay Ellen Duggin
WINDOW OF MY LIFE

In loving memory of Ronald E. Boese whose life I shared, just a short while.

Looking out my window
nothing there to see.
Looking back upon my life
the best is yet to be.

Little girl of long ago
growing more each day.
Finding out all about life
and learning along the way.

Times are quickly changing
my life is passing by.
Looking out my window
I can see the reason why.

I remember not long ago
a wish of mine came true.
I wished to be a girl again
and share my life with you.

Doris Johnson Hocott
IN HIS HANDS

To My Mother In Heaven, Alice K. Johnson

My life is in His hands
Yes, each and every day
My life is in His hands
And He will show the way
Oh come with us to Jesus
To know true happiness
Our sins He took from us
For He could do no less
My life is in His hands
Yes each and every day
My life is in His hands
His love is here to stay!

James H Wick
YOU AND ME

To all the kids of Brewster in the 30's & 40's

Where is the graveled road where
I fell and skinned my knee?
And what happened to our club house,

The one by the big apple tree?

Where is the pool we called our old
swimming hole?
And that little brook we fished in
with our willow poles?

Has anyone seen that little girl that
made my heart flutter and skip?
Or that dog that everyone loved,
His name was Tip.

Then I remembered what my dad
had said;
You can't go back son,
You can only go ahead.

Don't you understand?
Can't you see?
I wasn't looking for just little boys
and girls,
I was searching for you and me.

Jim Collins
TRANSFIXED
I paused to stare into the sky
One Lovely night in mid-July.
His velvet sheet was really lit;
A sky with stars all over it.
I stood not really knowing why,
Without a wish to get me by,
Alone upon that silent hill,
And stared into the sky until
My eyes were blind with stars
And still I stared into the sky.

Nancy A Hannon
A VISIT FROM DEATH
Death came to visit a Friend
The Friend was not willing for
death to come,
My Friend struggled to avoid this
visit.
He felt his work was not yet done,
but death lingered close by.
Death was trying to take My Friend
willingly.
I waited in sadness.

At last I released My Friend,
hoping He would go in peace.
He chose to do His dying His way.
So inch by inch, moment by
moment, His body
was rendered helpless.
Still the struggle went on.
At last weakness overcame His
strength
and showed Him the beauty of
dying.
Truly His work was done.

Glenn F Gasper
MEMORIES SO SHINING

To all family farmers. Also to all descendants of farm people existing in the cities of America.

Days end is welcomed by a
moisture laden fog,
Evening quiet broken by a distant
barking dog.

Time is lost to a place far away
When hours were given to merry
cheerful play.

Oh, there were times of work and
strife,
But it was such a glorious, peaceful
life.
Working our muscles along with
the soil
To nurture the crops with our daily
toil.

We had no idea there was anything
better
Than to do days work while
enjoying the weather.
But there were so many times of
great delight
When we'd play games late into the
night.

Creating strategies to achieve great
ends,
With brothers and sisters as best
of friends.
Could we after these years of
monetary folly
Return to times that were so jolly?

Only the Creator up in the sky
Can tell us perhaps on the day we
die
That we should always live as when
we were small,
Because surely those were the best
years of all.

Now, in the years of the physical
bodies declining,
The mind is alive with memories
so shining,
Of days on a beautiful American
family farm
With parents and family with
hearts kind and warm.

Donna Kopp
WHEN WINTER COMES
When winter comes upon my soul,
deep within I hibernate;
joy sleeps beneath, and seeps the
cold
to every fiber permeate.
When winter comes upon me.

When sadness overcomes my
heart,
deafness comes upon my ears
to sounds of love and merriment,
and every sound that I may hear
becomes a dirge, a wild lament;
when sadness overcomes me.—

But joy still sleeps beneath the cold;
awaits the warmth of love to wake.
When God leans down to touch my
soul
songbirds will sing and dawn will
break.
When God leans down to touch
me.—

the fires will burn, and love return
to voice joy's vital symphony.
Speak but the word and I will learn
of light and warmth and harmony,
and spring will come upon my
soul—
if you but speak the word!

Mamie Jeffrey Pase
TO OUR DAD
His curly hair was white as snow
His eyes were soft and brown,
His smile was always sunny
The best-loved man in town.

His countless friends were
everywhere
They waved to him each day,
As he prodded to and from the
Shops
He whistled along the way.

He loved his family and his God
His home came always first,
He didn't fear the wickedness
He didn't fear the worse.

He was a dad to be proud of
He taught us right from wrong,
He taught us fear and love of God
In a world where sin was strong.

His headaches were with him
always
He never did complain,
They grew worse throughout the
years
He smiled and carried the cross of
pain.

'Tis many years since he closed his
eyes
As a tear rolled down his face,
For on the day God called him
home
At last he'd found his peace.

He's with his mother and father
now
He's wrapped in Eternal Love,
He's paid the price we all must pay
God grant that we'll join him above.

Marie A Smith
MY DAD

In loving memory of: Howard R. Britzius

He was short & chubby & cute as
could be
He was my teacher & guide &
protected me.
He was trusting & understanding
& always there.
He was like a Gruffy Teddy Bear.
He was gentle & tender & a true
friend,
All hurts & bruises, he could
mend.
He knew how to share his love
& attention,
He had other qualities, too many
to mention.
And though not a noble steed he
had,
He was my knight in shining
armor.
He was my Dad.

Betty Toner
REDHEADS

To Marie and Judy—

"Hey-Reds!" is there a redhead not
aware—
That her given name takes second
place
To the color of her hair?

Strawberry, Auburn, Brick, Flame,
All come under the universal
fame—
Of "Yo-Reds!"

"What a temper!" The fiery roots
give passion
To the brain.
Not known by length, or style, or
curls,
But by a rusty mane.

Choose your clothes with extra
care—
Must match, not clash, with your
red hair,
No different do they walk, or think,
or speak,
Yet somehow, redheads are
unique.

Dianne Schreiber
LITTLE BOY
Dear little boy,
you live deep in the heart
of the man I've loved so many years.

I saw just the tiniest glimpse of you
at first;
but gradually, you told me more
and more:
of the hurt you suffered, of
rejection, and of your self doubt,
until I cared so much, I fell
hopelessly in love with you.

I wanted to hold you, little boy, to
comfort you;
I wished I could have known you
before you grew into the man
standing there before me,
wanting—but afraid of—love.

I reached out my arms to you and
I tried holding the man.
But the instant I put my arms
around him,
you disappeared—and he ran away
from me.

I still love you—the little boy you
were,
and the man you are.

(And I'll miss you both,
forever).

Johnny C Patrick
ODE TO A PUMPKIN

To a supporting family, Linda, Stan, Mark and Kim, whose hearts still beat with fantasy, this poem I dedicate.

So ye lie there, full and plump,
shining bright orange
In the noon-day sun,
And awaiting a hand to pluck thee
Up from a wilted show of greenery
That was with thee when thy life
began
On a thickened field where life
juices ran
Through swollen vines for me to
see
Just how it was you came to be.
You now fall prey to some child's
fun.

Ye who once caught the morning
dew are reamed
Of seeds and inner lace.

Ye now sit waiting patiently for Halloween,
To frighten passers-by with your face.
But time passes quickly, whence you began, and
With your mouth all shriveled, you die, as an old man.

Marie Rabon
HAND PRINTS
Hand prints on the furniture
granddaughters been here for sure.
Things needed dusting anyhow
More than my time had allowed.
guess who didn't care?
Grandma.

Rose G Follmer
LOVING

With love, Conrad, Mom and Dad, Chal, Pina, Stephanie and Amanda

Into the shadow of my dreams
Came the glimmer, the light
That what was felt
Was real
And more than the gossamer webs
Of childhood fantasy

For in that frontier
Of endless possibilities

Quivered the shimmering flicker of love

And from that dream came
The You and I
That are today
With the light of loving
So bright and full
That the shadows of my dreams
Are the lights of my reality.

E F Hicks
IF WE WERE CLOSER TO GOD
What is this world all about
It's all in an uproar, with the biggest of shouts,
Could we be more understanding
And less demanding,
If we were closer to God
Even the mod look, wouldn't be so odd,
Take advice, give up sin and dice
The spice of life, give up, sacrifice,
Beware always be prepared
Share in your heart a loving prayer,
There is never any need to be afraid
God can foresee, God will come to your aid.

Sherri Schnell Falatovich
CHARMER

To my fellow performers and friends—1978 Pennsylvania Ambassadors of Music

London,
With all your culture and history—
You've seen a lot—haven't you?
It shows in your face—
the age,
the pain,
the pride.
The woman feeding the pigeons
in your famed Trafalgar Square—
She's always been there—hasn't she?
Does she know Admiral Nelson
has been watching her?
And those funny cabbies
and double-decker buses—
No one's told them they're driving
in an odd fashion.
But London,
You don't have to conform
or be beautifully adorned.
I've seen it in your palaces and castles,
busy streets and cobblestone alleys,
sidewalk cafes and crowded pubs,
And on the faces of your people.
Don't lose it. . .
It's the charm of London.

Judith Ann Babilon
THE CAROUSEL

This poem is dedicated to my loving husband, terrific sons, loving parents, and all my dearest friends who believed in me.

I watch
a constant,
never-ending circle of horses,
ascend and descend
non-stop
to a monotonous,
repetitious,
organ melody.

Around and around
they turn,
long necks stretching,
muscles straining,
nostrils flaring,
as though competing for first place
in a race in which there are no losers.

Me McDole Clark
HARD TIMES IN "TEXAS" (AUGUST OF 84)

Love to Jesse

Crying in my heart
For the things in life
We battle for a start
The pain sometimes hurts like a knife

We run around making waves
Never to accomplish
the goals of many gone days
Always fighting for the filled up dish
It feels like we get ahead
Always running to and fro
Sometimes seeing plans go dead
But always making oneself go

Trying to fight the sun's rays
It's TEXAS in the summer
And sometimes the heat's a roaring blaze
At times thinking life's a bummer
But we live and we love
Sharing the good and the bad
With the help from up above
To end each day feeling glad. . .
We are with the ones we love!

Mary M Mallett
WHAT ARE RAINBOWS?

Dedicated to all who reflect the same—

Rainbows?
Just diffusion of light, found anywhere.
Watch after the rattling thunderstorm
Is past, when lingering raindrops
Mingle with the sun
Look in morning dewdrops
On a blade of grass
Or in flying spray
Of a sun-bathed waterfall.
Look in a room
With scattered bright hues,
Casting sparkles
From twinkling chandeliers.
But best of all rainbows
Are rays of hope-filled cheering thought
In those helpful words and deeds, given from the heart.
We can look for and make
Our rainbows abound
For in sunshine or shadow
We can show that we care.
Rainbows?
Just reflected light, found everywhere.

Arlene Rose Hobley
A HUMMING BIRD
Humming bird, humming bird,
Flying to and fro,
From flower to flower,
Where the fragrants grow.
Humming bird, humming bird,
Where the fragrants flow.
In the dew so high,
It make the sky so blue,
I love to sit and watch you
And wish I could fly too.

Tamra Aldrich Gottfried
ON A COOL AUGUST NIGHT

For my husband, Daniel whose inspiration led me to believe in me.

On a cool August night
we met.
Our friendship developed
like a delicate seed planted
into fertile soil.
Our caring and sharing
grew to heights of passion,
A flame we could not deny.
We soared to the heavens on wings,
Our love knowing no bonds.
And the truthfulness in our once
silent hearts released,
dropping fragrant petals
to the Earth
below.

Sheila Velez-Kirk
. . . A SECOND IN TIME . . .

This poem is dedicated to my beloved son Ricky, in his memory.

It comes without notice,
The coming of one.
The coming of another,
It's like "A SECOND IN TIME."

The life lives, if may
Or perhaps another day.
Then and now, on its way,
Having nothing left to say.

Without a thought to say,
Or a thing to do.
Just living life each day.
Just the same as yesterday.

It leaves without notice.
The leaving of one,
The leaving of another.
It's like "A SECOND IN TIME."

A carefree life that, was once led.
Has now been put to rest.
The coming of one,
The leaving of one.
Like "A SECOND IN TIME."
Many did, many will.

Alma L Long
BEST FRIENDS

Inspired by Michelle; and dedicated to her and to all my other grandchildren.

Me and my best friend,
We like to play 'Let's Pretend':
"You be the Mom,
I'll be the dad."
Oh, the happy hours we spend!

My best friend and I
Pretend that we can fly.

We run and jump
And dance and swing
Always reaching for the sky.

My friend and I really do
A lot of pretending, that's true.
But it isn't pretend
When my friend says to me;
"Grandma, I sure do love you!"

Lana Chin
IT'S A BOY!

To my son, STEVE

You came into the world, unannounced
In the silence of the room
I heard your cry of triumph
My heart burst forth with joy
In my agony I whispered "Thank you Lord, it's a boy!"

You rushed into the world, unprepared

Too soon before your time
Small in size, barely thirteen
inches long
But you filled my heart with a song
A sweet and lingering lullaby!

You burst into the world
Like a star burst in the sky
Filled it with brilliance and shine
No more darkness, no more pain
My world will never be the same
again!

Now, as I walk down memory lane
My mind recalls again and again
Your first step, your first smile
Your first encounter with every
kind
My son, my true source of pride!

Kevin L Propst
I TOLD YOU

In loving memory of my Nikola, and to her mother, my mother, and Jesus for loving me.

Only two lines to this song:
On the dinette stand some
mummies
With a pink ribbon 'round their
stems.
What were the flowers for?
Mislaying time in just a shot
Makes days slip by unseen
Expanding time in just a shot
Was it something the flowers said?

You told me not to remember you
And I told you that won't work
And since I do remember you
Was your order just a quirk?
I see you on a TV
In a picture from a drawer
My Nikki on the tube
Frozen with me forevermore.
The waiting time is over; my tears
have come and gone.
My memories will not fade; my
inner guilt's departed.
And the waiting time is over.

I told you I'd remember you
I thought I understood the process
But the mechanics were all I knew
See, Dear One, I told you.

Madeleine Thompson
THE AVERAGE AMERICAN
I think that I shall never see
Another person just like me.
And then, in every passing face
I see the selfsame lack of grace.

A person all wrapped up in him,
Oblivious, living by whim.
And then he turns the other cheek
To give us all an inside peek.

At the "average" guy, so benign,
He'll leap ahead at the first sign
Of danger to his fellow man,
And stop to help him when he can.

This deep feeling, so well hidden,
Seems to come forth whenever
bidden.
I hope we all will stop and see
The decency of you and me.

Susan Youens
I LIVE IN A WHITE FARMHOUSE
I live in a white farmhouse.
And this morning, when
I went to milk the cow,
I saw a crow fly
over.
And I began to think
how it was, not too
long ago, when Dad
was alive—he used to
shoot these crows.
"Crows are a burden"
he said once,
with his sunburned hands and neck
"You gotta teach'em. Keep'em
in line"
And then the sky cracked.
And their wings sounded like
mom beating rugs.
And I smelled something burn.

Then Dad stroked my hair,
And said in a slight laugh,
"Without'em crows, I have
nothing to shoot at."

Adam C Miller
THE WRITER
The blank paper stares me in the
face
Not knowing what to write I let it
sit and sit into
the dark of the night
Then it starts a feeling a spark an
idea so slight
The words start to flow, one then
another the
sentences just seem to grow
My thoughts flowing outward onto
the sheet
So when you read it, for a moment
our minds will
both meet

Betty Beach Stephens
LISTEN TO SPRING
Crocuses croak, dandelions roar,
Water falls, tulips don't pucker any
more,
Daffodils go crazy with colors so
bright.
Marigolds gleefully show their
colors,
Pussy-willows purr their delight
At the sight of the new birth of this
Spring
Narcissuses lose their egos as they
bloom
Seeing other flowers as beautiful
as they
Such as the jonquils in bloom
Violets stop being shy and poke
their
Beauty through the damp earth.
Stop, look, and listen to the beauty
around you.
It's God's miracle renewed!

Donald G Benzing
CASTLES IN THE SAND

To Mary Lee Benzing

I see castles in the sand
Where we walked hand in hand,
Little children everywhere
Without a worry or a care.

I remember when we were one,
Building castles in the sun,
At a time when love was young
And I thought you were the one.

But then the waves took command,
And washed away all that sand,
Leaving nothing in the air
But a memory of what was there.

How I've longed for those days
When we laughed the time away,
Building castles in the sand,
Making all those future plans.

I think back to what we had,
How we loved and how we laughed.
It's not the good or the bad,
But what we learned with the time
we had.

And now I walk along the shore,
I think of you just this once more,
Watching children, hand in hand,
Building castles in the sand.

Amelia Samson Hernandez
UNTITLED
This green-eyed monster,
With its evil eyes cast upon me,
Severes the respect and affection I
have for thee.

If this persists, with venom
flowing from thy heart,
Then, there need not be a need for
me.

Love is not love when trust is gone.
Love is infinite, a forever glowing
flame.
It absorbs the lovers 'til they are
one.

Welded as one—it's firm and
enduring to the end.
It falters not no matter how shaky
life is.

Together, steadfast, the lovers
fight.
In the vicissitudes of life
their goal is set.
Win they will no matter what.
As one, they will work together
to make that love a pillar—
a monument of stability and
endurance.

Such is the test of true love.

Virginia M Gamble
PRAYER FOR TODAY
Bless our homes, Oh Father above,
Fill our hearts with your dear love.
Grant each one a caring heart
One that is caring as thou art.
May we have compassion for other
souls
May loving kindness be our goals.
Fill our hearts with sweetness,
And patience too.
May we always be spiritually
In harmony with you.
Amen

Rev Marion R Thomas

Rev Marion R Thomas
BASEBALL, FALL, AND CRACK

Dedicated to President and Mrs Reagan for their fine leadership in helping the youth of America to escape drugs.

What fun to hear the baseball and
the bat,
For when they meet there is
exciting crack!
Then voices ring from the great
excited crowd,
Yes, the rising tide of shouting is
so loud!
Each ballgame is a great
competing force
Of talent, power, and every known
resource!
And dullness of their life just fades
away
When comes the time that it is
baseball day!

What fun to see the color of the
players suits,
And number of the man for whom
his city roots!
The shouting of a mother and a girl
and boy
Who love that man who plays the
game with joy!

And he inspires a thousand kids all
O'er the land
Who play the smaller games in
small grandstand!
Plus give those children in their life
consuming goal
To be just like that dad, a man of
leading role!

What fun when fall comes 'round
to hear again that crack
As once again the ball meets with
the swinging bat!
And fans who down through all
those years, those many years,
Yes, when we win or lose shed
from the high emotion, tears!
The game and grandstand are one
great and grand commotion,
And this crack is a pure and good,
uplifting potion!
Come to the ballgame, America,
and shout with me
For this high is high that no
complaint can ever be!

Shari Tanzini
TO MOTHER ON MOTHER'S DAY
There are so many cards you can
buy today,
They all do have something nice to
say,
But I thought I'd write your
Mother's Day card this year,
To let you know that you are very
dear!

A Mother is someone very special
you know,
Who has bathed you, clothed you,
and watched you grow,
All through those years that have
gone by,

Full of laughter, tears and one big sigh!

A Mother watches you learn, live and love,
Her advice seems to fit any situation like a glove,
She's there at any time of the night or day,
Just to visit, have coffee, or stay!

A Mother, a worker, a friend, a counselor,
I know my travels grey hair I have given her,
I hope as the years come and go,
She knows more and more that I love her so!

Karyn Jentz
GRADUATION

To those who care deeply and who dream boldly.

Graduation is a goal achieved, a victory we have won.
With God's continued guidance, there's so much to become.
God puts our yesterdays behind us, so let us pray before we leave
For strength to face the future, and our dreams we will achieve.
Grant that we be Christians and not pray for wealth and fame.
But let us find our true success in our Father's Holy Name.

Wayne Cheveldave
A GOLFER'S XMAS DREAM

In Memory of My Dad, Walter J. Cheveldave

T'was the night before Christmas and all over the course,
Not a golfer was stirring for snow had covered the source.
When out on the fairway there arose such a clatter,
I sprang from my desk to see what was the matter.

And what to my wondering eyes should appear, but
Four little golfers and their caddies, Reindeer.
Carrying spike, divot, ball washer and putter,
Not a sound did they utter.

They tee'd up their balls and swung to their task,
I was so dumbfounded I forgot to ask,
Why were they playing on snow covered grass?

With a wink and a nod of their heads they made me know,
That I had nothing to fear from the winter and snow.
The snow mold was gone, the ice lenses melted,
Dessication forget it.

My wish was fulfilled and I heard them exclaim,
As they pitched out of sight, Merry Christmas
To all Golfers and to all a Good Night.

Steven A Nelson
A MAN

This poem is dedicated to all the positive life forces in the universe.

A man stands
on the shore of time
The thoughts of the future
run through his mind,
Awakening the spirit
of life from inside
His minds eye opens
as he begins to cry.
Don't think he is sad
the tears are of joy
The man suddenly realized
he's still a boy,
You see, the mind of a boy
is more open and free
And now the man is able
to see and believe.

Edward Paul Skretka
PAPER BOY

While I sit and contemplate
Affairs of country and of state
A friendly thud sounds at the door
To say my paper's here once more,

Now my favorite chair I find
And hope the family doesn't mind
As I spread the paper out
To close me in and shut them out,

But the purpose of this rhyme
Is to ponder one more time
And categorically state
Why that kid is sometimes late,

When the winter cold and sleet
Keeps most people off the street
A hooded figure wends his way
And brings to you the news of day,

Do you have some change at hand
When he makes correct demand
Or fumble, fume and fuss about
While he's cold and standing out,

Then hastily make your retreat
While he shivers at your feet
And quickly firmly close the door
To leave him in the cold once more.

Marlace Berg Zacharias
LIVING THE LIVES

Night after night
she watches TV
living the lives
of luckier souls
souls who do not
go it alone.
"Call me," she pleads,
"when you're in town,
we'll go for coffee."
She does not ask for
a night on the town
soft music, wine,
the finest foods,
nor does she ask for
a list of contacts,
she asks only
for conversation
and company.

B K Weaver
A DIFFICULT THING TO DO

To J. B., With Love

How can I say what I really feel,
When I've been on this road before.
I know what's next—how it will end,
And how someone will go through the door.

It may be you—coming into my arms,
My dream would then come true.
To have you here would complete my life.
But what would that do to you?

Perhaps the other one would leave,
And take your children, dear.
To split your life between the two,
Is too much to ask, I fear.

And what of me—if I should go?
And mark it down as a sacrafice.
To walk away and leave you alone
With only warm memories so nice.

To let you know what you mean to me,
Is a difficult thing to do.
So I'll continue to smile and leave it alone,
And just go on loving you.

Kay Arneberg Booth
MAJESTIC MOUNTAINS

The majestic, massive mountains,
With Heaven around their heads,
Commune with God, yet ever
Have solid earth their nesting beds.

Lift up your soul to heights unknown
And discern that there is God.
Yet the mortal body must be fixed
Upon this mundane sod.

Behold awe inspiring grandeur
Of each mountain's snow capped peak.
Though firmly held by earthly ties,
Elysian fields they seek.

So must we, as we live this life,
To God lift your heart and eyes.
Then Peace, which passeth understanding,
Will be sublimest prize.

The majestic, massive mountains,
Solid earth their nesting beds,
Commune with God, for always
They have Heaven around their heads.

Malcolm MacDonald

Malcolm MacDonald
THE DOLLAR—FROM GOD'S POINT OF VIEW

Dedicated to Ira Bernstein Wall Street, New York, New York

I see uneasy twitchings of the Bull and Bear
Scratching at the Ticker lice.
Why made I the sun? To light another Gold?
Or liquid pourings of the sea,
Ignored for ebb and flow of price?

I made the bullion of the Stars.
You upward gazed and wondered at the first—
Then placed your faith to steer the course.
Ah, yes, and Love:
"Thou lookest on the Stars, my Star.
Would I were the Heavens, to look on Thee
With many eyes."

But now the Stars are of a different Stripe.
I saw you Man, when Mediaeval Stocks were Bonds;
The weak went to the Wall—
And lately—headlong in the Crash—
Your ultimate Free-fall.

You come so close—"In Me You Trust"
Yet why the Bills for Bombs?
From "Annuit Coeptis" to the Mortgage burnt—
My interest only is your life.
"Since when did barren metal breed?"
Such flimsy paper for such strife.

Lee Beth Hershman
LIFE

It's hard to say what's on your mind,
When the whole world seems just a little unkind.
I know now that lifes not fair,
But i'd say that i've had my share.
So you're young and on your own,
That doesn't mean you'll be alone.
Don't give up without a fight,
You know success is in your site.

Stacie L Pecor
TEARDROP

A teardrop is like a thousand words
It drops and still no one learns
When it falls, your world is shattered
You're alone and nothing matters
Too many emotions to be explained
You see them dying in the flames
Far beyond anyone's reach
They tell nothing, and nothing they teach.

Edith Pindell Pishalski
MY HOME

My home must be a friendly place,
Where friends drop in to see,
All the love and happiness,
That was meant to be.
If other's lives are getting dull,
Or they're just feeling blue,
Let them come to my home,
To see the sun shine through;
And when they finally leave my door,
Their hearts will know no strife,
For they will have found something in my home,
To change their outlook on life.
They'll come back often and will eagerly share,
The joy, the sunshine, and the love they find there.
God bless my home, may it always be,
A happy place for my friends and me.

Marian Heath
I WAS TRYING TO THINK OF SOMETHING TO WRITE

I was trying to think of something to write,
So I could enter your contest tonight.
While at the table drinking tea,

I thought, why not write about
things dear to me.

My first thoughts are of my Dad
and Mother,
For almost fifty years, they have
had each other,
Can you imagine fifty years of
married life,
And spending them all, with just
one wife!

I have one sister, Marjorie is her
name,
Head cook at elementary school,
has been her claim to fame.
She has three kids, for which she's
glad,
David, Donna and Debbie, Wayne
is their Dad.

Last but not least is my husband,
my all,
His name is Roger and our son is
Paul.
It is hard to write in twenty-five
lines or less.
About a lifetime of happiness.

And now my poem is complete,
In your contest, I'm going to
compete.
I write poetry just for fun,
But Honorable Mention is what I
won.

Albert Garcia
SILENCE
Alone in the dark
Waiting for my death to come
To exit this world.

A White
FRIEZE
Now spring
With soft white bud
Whispers the Celesta
Through the magnolia of satin
Sorrow

Fly bird
Past face etched moon
Through sting of wind nettling
Pine pizzicato violin
Unheard

Quiet
Ordered senses
Introspection of past
Willow sighs and swirls where the
heart
Midnights

The brook
Yet frozen ice
The ground has silenced seed
A flame of memory but stab
of pain

Sand bare
Scours past the rock
Gathering arid mass
Where eyes strain dust cloud for
Holy
Water

Jennifer H Ratliff
UPON ST. VALENTINE'S DAY, OR ANY OTHER

To Franz Joseph Haydn

There shall be pearls, and
diamonds,
And roses addressed to one
Of shared, sometimes hidden
emotions,
Of rainbows, of rain, and of sun;

There shall be some numerous
mansions,
Ancestral, of offsprings, of where
The portals are open to fragrance,
To space, and to light, and to air;

There shall be the gifts of the
angels,
Priceless, of a quarter, or more;
And there shall be oysters and
dillweed
To all that pure loving stands for;

Thus woe betide vinegar heartbeat,
And woe betide soul of the mire,
Who would intercept true love's
dreaming,
Reality, quietude, fire!

Patricia R Joyce
WE MUST GO SEE HER
"We must go see her" we often say
When a name comes up in the talk
of the day.
"We must go see the sweet old
soul."
But some how we never reach our
goal.

The years fly onward, then comes
the day
We hear that she has passed away,
Our feet make tracks straight to
her door,
When we really should have gone
before.

Sylvia Kathleen Smith
MY BICYCLE AND I
As I ride through an open field,
On down a country lane
My bicycle my friend becomes,
The world is ours again!
The singing wheels seem to be
part
Of nature's far off places
The sky and clouds; the trees and
birds
Are old familiar faces.

The wind is our companion too
It cools us on our way.
It gives us wings, or holds us back,
A gypsy child at play!
Wild asters and tall goldenrod;
Sweet corn, now withered
brown,
Reminds us of approaching fall,
As does the milkweed's down.
We dread the bleak, cold days
ahead
When we won't ride together—
My bicycle and I.

Ann M Shuford

Ann M Shuford
SWEET DREAMS
He held out his hand and said walk
with me for just a little while.
I will take you to beautiful places
with me and replace your sad
eyes with a smile.
In my blindness that day I failed to
see what lay behind his shielded
eyes.
My need was too great as he
reached for me and I didn't hear
how his soul cries.
His kiss is so sweet and my pulse
starts to beat to his music and
my body sings.
How could I know he would arouse
in me all these wonderful,
magical things?
When I am with him the world
goes away and there's nothing
except him and me.
My mind walks the green valleys
and I find perfect peace in his
arms where I'm so happy to be.
I don't want him to go but I know
he can't stay for this time's only
borrowed you see.
He just came my way and like a
sweet dream with the light he
will soon be gone from me.
But his memory will be precious to
me and I'll never forget these
sweet days.
As he lay in my arms growing
stronger each day and I learn
more about all his ways.
This feeling for him wells up in me
and I love to breath his sweet
smell.
And I know I will love him till my
dying day and pray for his soul
to be well.

Allen Pritchard
THE LESSON

To my dear wife Ursel

A great man sat upon a hill
Talking to a crowd,
He spoke of love, of truth and
peace,
Of kindness and goodwill.
He warned of pride and passion
That warp the soul and sap
The spirit's compassion.
Should peace and harmony abide
Then tolerance must surely be
In a world of greed and bigotry.
Our actions will decide the fate
Of those who follow.
Don't foster fear and prejudice,
Don't teach your children hate.
Be guided by a simple rule
That great man declared true;
Do unto others as you would
Have them do unto you.

Carol Cosby
SENT WITH LOVE
We wanted a baby,
to bring us joy.
And it didn't matter,
if it was a girl, or boy.
So we waited and waited,
and finally, she came.
And never again,
would our lives be the same.
Rebekah, born on the Eve,
before Christmas Day.
And she was so perfect,
in every way.
Her eyes are so blue,
like looking, at the sea.
A prettier baby,
there never will be.
So we thank you God,
in the heaven above.
By sending Rebekah,
you sent us your love.

Doris N Costello
BROKEN DREAMS
This is the chapel on Christmas
morn,
These are the people who eagerly
come
Holding their treasures from
home.
Here is one cradling a Poinsetta
plant
Rocking and crooning as if to a
child,
She loves the flower and is
comforted
And brings her treasure of love
To the manger to be blessed.
There is hysterical giggling from
another
Who has lost the reason for
laughter;
Wild eyes and restless hands testify
That no more can she be trusted
Without the arm of Supervision
nearby.
Shuffling feet, downcast eyes,
Tousled heads, crooked seams,
On this one day dear Lord
Dear babe of Bethlehem
Be born for these
Thy children of the Broken
Dreams.

Twila Laffoon Cozad
WINTER
All day long the sun drips through
the trees,
It glistens and shines through the
snow-clad limbs;
When twilight comes, the wind
starts its tease.
It whistles the moon awake and
then skims
'Round and calls the sleeping,
shineless stars.
The air is full of a harsh, moaning
sound,
And the windows shake like
strummed guitars,
But past midnight the snowflakes
start their round.
In the morning when all is calm
and bright,
The trees are attired in their finest
array;
And the earth puts on its robe of
purest white.
The fluttering snow-birds are
joyous and gay
For there isn't a time in a summer
June,
That would compare with a lovely
winter evening moon.

Elizabeth Ann Barr
FOREVER FRIEND
Jesus is a friend of mine.
He's walking with me all the time,
There's not a place I go
that He's not there.

He's in my heart each hour each
day.
And that's just where He's gonna
stay,
So His love for me shines
through for all to see.

He died right there at Calvary
Giving His life for you and me.
Why won't you open your eyes
so you can see?

You'll never have a better friend,
He'll walk with you through thick
and thin,
And all you have to do
is just believe.

Pearl B Swanson
MY LITTLE CHICKADEE
My Little Chickadee,
Upside down in my big tree—
Is the world more orderly,
Mirrored in the sky?

Happy Little Chickadee
You've the right philosophy,
Life's a sweet eternity;
Why should birdies sigh?

Elizabeth A Ohneck
OLD AGE

To my three wonderful children, Nan, Sue, and Steve

To be a Senior Citizen
Is depressing (so they say)
You're supposed to hate each wrinkle
And resent each passing day!

But this is not the way it is
I've lived, I've loved, and worked,
I've many happy memories
And my duties never shirked!

Sure—I've had some sad times
But lots of happiness and smiles,
I've laughed, and really conquered
Life's many troubled miles!

So—relax and hope the young ones
Have it easy down life's road
Pray they'll have a sense of humor
And their trials they will unload!

Be grateful for every passing day
And thank the Lord above,
For allowing you to have the joy
Of younger ones to love!

Ray Childress
ROLL ON RIVER

To all. To all of mine, to the river.

At daytime I stood by its way
I heard the voices at work and play.
They were singing and dancing
and brushing the stones,
Swift and still continued their song;
To the sea, to the sea and up to
Heaven's Breast,
To rain again on the flower's sweet breath.

Stop, I cried, speak with me!
We can't, we can't; it's on to the sea.
But if you can wait for us,
We will meet again.
And they waved their white caps
Around the bend.
Roll on river.

Lyndal Brammer Munoz
LOUISIANA WOODS
One of the memories that I cherish the most
Is walking in the woods as a child.
Straining our eyes for muscadine vines—
Or coon-grape vines—
Or some queer animals—
Then running along some shady,
yet sunny path.
Laughing—
Singing—
The wind carrying our young,
happy voices.
As the sun begins to fade
We decide which is the path home
And reluctantly—
Yet cheerfully—
We leave our beloved paradise.

Christine M Marazita
LONESOME CHRISTMAS
The roads are clear—
The house so quiet—
Not but a sound is heard—
But the crackle of a fire,
And once, the screech of a tire,
On this lonely night of Christmas.

Have you ever been alone?
Not a whistle or a moan,
Is heard throughout your house—
You sit and stare
At the fire and the flare—
On this lonely night of Christmas

Spirits can brighten
Like my fire will lighten
As I sit and think about people—
Who love and care
But couldn't come to share—
My lonely but thoughtful Christmas.

Elaine A Robinson
I LOVE YOU

To all those in my sphere.

I love you—
But it hurts
too much;
And it will cost
too much;
We can't pay that price.
So—
I'll stay away
again;
Change colors with the leaves,
Lie under a blanket of snow
And maybe—
emerge in spring;
Ready to take a chance
again.

Lorraine Hicks
THE ESCAPE
The volcano roared
as thunder,
in rage for freedom.
She belched
forth a mushroom cloud.
Earth trembled . . .
as her breath . . . her guts
flumed o'er the land . . .
leaving her calling card . . .
which read, "I'm alive."
Her innerness free
of prison . . .
Touched the wind
sailing free.

Myrtle Morrow
VIEWS FROM PROPHESY BRIDGE
Gaze young lovers
at your entwined reflections
mirrored in the placid water;
Suppress your shudders
when a breeze
ruffles the placid surface;
Seeing yourselves
twenty years from now
need not repulse you;
Please, don't draw apart
or go separate ways,
Those were
only ripples in the water.

But what of me?
I gazed also,
my image wasn't there.
Those were
only ripples in the water.

Mae Leslie
PROCRASTINATION
It's not such a big job I've dreaded so long
It's just getting started that seems to go wrong.
But once I begin it goes pretty fast
And I finish realizing it's not such a task.
But why do I do it?
Can somebody tell?
Or do other folk have this same problem as well?

Chris Gates
SNOWTYME
Jack, he was amidst in the frost,
Finding emotions lost.
Peering betwixt every window sill,
Watching the happy, the sad & the ill.
Leaving his trace on the window pane,
In part this is where he gained his fame.

He glides so gently,
Gently as the wind.
But the harshness of his bark,
The cold scream he shall send.
His fingers are icicled,
Bare, cold and wet,
Fingering the snow, of the snow.
Snowballs he shall get.

Snow will rise and snow shall fall,
But Jack of the Frost shall bring all.
Jack shall die and hard he'll fall,
Slowly, melting, he shall cry: Life and all.

Jack of the Frost shall come hither
in the return,
But in the meanwhile your fires
you shall burn.
Jack, he was admist in the frost,
Finding emotions lost.
Freezing the light in the beauty of the snow,
On his merry way, he shall go.

Dana Elias Moses
FELINICITY
I sing the things around me,
and like a chorus of Oedipus
bemoan myself
and use these blades like cats
o'nine
these cats of mine that roar
and scratch
and bristle when cornered
deflate their ears, to drown out
the noise of battle—
Fat cats, flat matte
satin brat-cats, with eyes
like slivers of milk
chocolate that drip and
sparkle in certain lights
like green marbles
the brains of a cat
in darkness—
The tiger is only as tame
as the unpulled tail.

Lillian Tanagretta
REMINISCING
When I was young I had such fun
All I did was play and run
Had many friends to love and adore
I wish I had those times once more

I often think of things in the past
Why oh why did it pass so fast
Can I ever bring back those days I had?
And not have memories to make me sad

Time flies by and life goes on
Friends I've known have moved or gone
The thought of them makes me feel low
I sit and ponder where did they go?

I often wonder would there come a day
Perhaps these friends should pass my way
That perchance all this was just a dream
How happy for me this world would seem.

Alice C Lendobeja

Alice C Lendobeja
MEMORY CALLED

To Glenn and Mary Ann who walked with me after the cows.

I walked the long way home tonight
Through greening fields and clover white.
The cows had long since reached the barn—
In quiet contentment their milk was drawn.

I picked a wild iris and stopped to look
At the water in the slowly flowing brook—
Yellow buttercups floated in wild array
Bright as the glowing sunset of late May.

I walked back again that road tonight.
Instead of clover the fields with snow were white.
In memories lane the cows went home—
My thoughts in wild confusion roam.

Down the pages of memories
book—
I stood again by the flowing
brook—
Instead of buttercups, crystalline
tears did fall
I'm sorry now, I answered
memories call.

Judy A Durkee
BE . . .

This poem is dedicated to my children and those who believe in my talent as a writer.

Be a winter snowflake,
Be a tarnished leaf,
Be a blossomed flower on the
ground.
Be a youthful spirit,
Be a blooming bud,
Be an Autumn Meadow colored
brown.

Be a lover's image,
Be a sign of time,
Be a part of winter's ending rains.
Be a faded memory
Be a one-night dream,
Be a special kiss that soothes love's
pains.

Be a mellow smile,
Be a soft, low sigh,
Be the Good Tomorrow our world
needs.
Be a flower's petals,
Be a sharing word,
Be a planted hope and spread it's
seeds.

Tom P Lowery
MY CHURCH
There's a plot of ground in our
town,
A most hallowed piece of sod—
A building's there of brick and
stone,
Our Church where we worship
God.
This church has stood witness
for many years
As servants of God spread Good
News:
Souls have been saved and new
lives begun
From people who sat in the pews.
My church has seen many a happy
day,
When its aisles young brides have
strolled;
With pretty white dresses and
trailing trains
To say vows and God's love to
unfold.
There are times for meditation;
From the organ soft music is
heard—
"Amazing grace, how sweet the
sound"
Proclaims God's holy word.
Folks sit in silence with heads bent
low
In reverence to God's holy plan;
And Thank Him for His blessing
and care
Offering strength to every man.
My church just seems to grow
weary
When some of its members
depart
To other fields, or are heaven
bound—
But my church had done its part.

Lavivian A Drake
MICHELLE
She was wonder & joy, beauty &
love
She was laughter & tears, sunshine
& pain
My only daughter—not quite
eighteen
Filled with the mystery of life
passing by.

Oh God! Why did she die?

She came from within me—my
flesh & my blood
Returned now to earth which gives
life
She'll give no more laughter & bear
no more strife
Gone oh so quickly with no final
goodbye

Oh God! Why did she die?

I stood by my window in silence &
pain
Two long lonely years had passed
by
My question still burning my
thoughts oh Lord
When the answer I saw in the sky

Please listen! Michelle did not die!

Her face is in the sunshine
Her hair's in the wind blowing free
Her smile's in the flowers, her eyes
in the moonlight
Michelle is the force that sets us all
free

I fell down on my knees
then—wiped back the tears
And thanked God for those 17
beautiful years
Now she nurtures my soul as I
nurtured her body
Her peace dwells within me and
now I cry

Michelle, Michelle did not die

Anna M Crouch
LOST BUT NOT FORGOTTEN
As from a wisp of fog I am almost
blind;
My eyes roam about in all the
space.
I survey with bowed head and
foolish face.
I keep looking far and wide and can
not find
That valuable manuscript that
once was mine.
Where is my precious jewel? What
can I do?
I wrote in school in nineteen
thirty-two
That great beloved sonnet, I can
not find.
What does it matter? It can again
be done.
I'll have another sonnet before this
life is run.
Work from early morn; lose no
sleep,
And in that poetry contest, I'll take
a little peep.
Forget the sonnets of the past;
don't flip,
The time has come, the mind
begins to slip.

Shirley M Kell
CHILDHOOD MEMORIES
Your child has need of many skills
To help him face the world.

He'll need to study many serious
things
But he'll always need some
carefree wings.

Show him stones of every size and
texture
Just waiting to be found.

Wildflowers bloom along the road
Chipmunks beg for bits of food.

Look for tiny bugs and toads
And ducks upon the creek.

"They like me, Mom" he said
Of fishworms gently held.

The thrill of music he might play
Will scatter joy to everyone.

There are friends to be made
And faith and trust to build.

Your child will always feel your
love
Which time and space can never
dim.

And you've taught him how to look
for springs
In life's deserts of sad and serious
things.

Bobbie N Brown
THE WORKS OF OTHERS
Sometimes when I sit in my easy
chair
And let my thoughts roam free
They flicker across the screen of
my mind
The things important to me.

I think of those whose printed
words
Have enriched my life each day
How others have given so much to
me
By the works that have come my
way.

I've wanted to make my mark in life
To leave something of me when I go
Not wealth nor fame, as some
desire
But helping others to grow.

If I could impart to another one
To perceive the values I hold
Or bring a new direction to one
Who is seeking a place and a goal.

This is the hope I have nourished
And dreamed and cherished each
day
For others have given so much to
me
By the works that have come my
way.

James A Larrain
THE GOLDEN SOUND
Many years have gone by
my thoughts and feelings are
imprisoned
free me from despair
unfold my heart filled with
bright sunny gold
inset your key
release me
your words are refreshing unlike
those
ever heard before
the key to my heart is
The Golden Sound
set me free
and you will see
my bright sunny Gold.

Marie Gish Ford
THE MERRY GO ROUND
Pink horses gallop by
with flowing mane and head
held high—
Red eyes aglow like balls of flame—
bright saddle horn and leather
rein.

Circle of steeds goes 'round and
'round
in time to gay caliope sound—
And I sit and watch, remembering,
as a child I reached for the
golden ring.

Norm Lashley
RESPLENDENCE
Showing it's face at daybreak
Dressed in the morning calm

Guiding the way for a newborn day
Seeing the night undone

Drying the face of a mountain
Drinking the dew on the tree

Finding it's way to the middle of
day
Embracing the land and sea

Floating across the heaven
Leaving no chore undone

Giving it's light to the world in
flight
Serving us all as one

Adorned in the essence of rainbows
Wrapped in it's colors bold

Yielding it's light to the darkness
of night
And retires to a cradle of gold

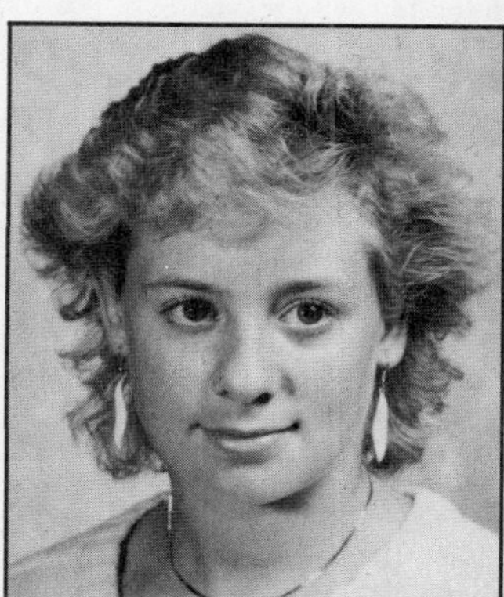

Dali Jean Williams

Dali Jean Williams
GROWING PAINS

To Mom and Dad with love

As I look in the mirror,
I see the reflection
Of a child
Waiting to grow up,
But not quite ready to let go . . .
Unsure of whether to play with the
doll
Or push it aside,
One moment longing for
protection,
The next, wanting to be free.
I pick up the lipstick
And trace in red,
A smile that fades.
No, not quite ready yet . . .
I pick up my doll
And close the door.

Lucille D Amoroso
HANDS ON CAREGIVERS

Dedicated to the Clients of Angel View Crippled Children's Foundation, Desert Hot Springs, Cal., upon my retirement at age 75 years, after 17 years service.

Of all the professions
In the world to be,

A Nursing Assistant
Is the one for me.
I can comfort people
Small or great
And know how much
They appreciate.
Helping to feed,
A kind word said,
Assisting them in
And out of bed,
Putting on braces,
Combing hair,
Brushing teeth
And all such care.
The rewards, if you're wondering
Are quite a few,
But the greatest is when
They say, I LOVE YOU!

Murray Goff
THANKFULNESS

This poem is dedicated to my loving wife, Frances

When I awake in the morning,
After a night of protection and rest,
I pray that the Lord will help me
do my best
to be fair with all things—
birds, beasts and mankind;
For I have received many
blessings—
a sound body and mind,
and life itself—health,
happiness, home and love—
for all of which I am very thankful
to my Maker above.

Dawn J Bloomquist
A SPECIAL GIFT

This poem is dedicated in loving memory, to Mom & Dad, (Helen & Keith Fawcett.)

When the sunshine peaks through
the rain clouds,
How beautiful it is to me.
It makes me think of Heaven,
And of the loved ones I long to see.
Everything is so sparkling fresh,
And the birds sing their melody.
But I know, as God has promised,
Someday all of this I'll see.

For now I'll have to be contented,
With life here on earth and all the
things to see.
Because God gave this special gift
to me.

So when the rain clouds part and
a rainbow I see,
I'll think of it as a pathway,
For future years for me.

Philip M Erickson
JUST A WIND BLOWN MILEPOST ON MEMORIES LANE

Just a wind blown milepost on
memories lane,
That old gray shack without any
name,
Sometimes its a woodshed
sometimes its a barn,
Sometimes its a bunkhouse for
help on the farm.

But away with fault findings
belittling air
Cast aside your aloofness and look
at it there,
Just a tumbled down shack that
once was a mansion,
For brave pioneers of westward
expansion.

There grandma had smiled and
pauses in knitting,
For over her memory dull
recollections are flitting,
Recollections of hardships that
belong to the past,
When brave men would stand and
fight to the last.

There poor old grandpa had passed
away,
Not knowing the good he'd done
for we folks of today,
Then let this noble old relic remain,
Just a wind blown milepost on
memories lane.

Thelma Thompson
I AM—

I am a traveller of the world
Traversing its skies and seas
From ancient Mesopotamia
To the domain of Ceres;
From Apollo's torch-lit Aleusis
To the craters of the moon;
I've hunted seal in Alaska
And lolled by a southern lagoon;
From ancient times I've travelled
Downward thru the years,
Laughed with Pan in the forest
And dried old Orsini's tears;
I watched from a Gothic tower
As Sir Lancelot rode that way;
I was one of Robin's Merry Men
When the king we held at bay;
I was one among the cortege
When Porsena marched on Rome,
Was with Horatio on the bridge
When he plunged into the foam;
I've fought in hundreds of battles,
Lost with Napoleon at Waterloo;
I rode with early frontiersmen
And fought the mighty Sioux;
Tis my fate to live forever
In many a word and deed,
For I as all of humanity
With its greatness and its greed.

Julie Ann Drapalik
JUST ONCE . . .

To all of those who have influenced and cared for me.

Just once in a lifetime
The right person comes along.
A person who is caring
A person full of devotion.
A person who is also understanding
Just once in a lifetime
You will meet the right person.
So always remember that
Only once will the right person
come along
And that person will change your
life forever.

Peggy Maddox
NEW HOPE

To Laurie, because 1987 is a special year. Happy teaching! Happy marriage!

I rested on a hillside
Where I had sat so long ago
Wearing dreams—smoothly
Mine would always flow.

Today my dreams are tattered
And with my head hung low
Remorsefully thinking, where
had I let them go.

Through dulled eyes
I chanced to see a spider web,
torn down, the spider was working
Lacing it up and down.

Then I felt new dreams within me
My vision grew firm and clear
The spider, though unaware,
Had made new hope appear.

Patricia A Mahan

Patricia A Mahan
FREE SPIRIT

Spirit of Grace
God doth grant me to be
Mightiest of those
Who liken to me

Free as the wind
As it gently blows

Free to peer down
At the valleys below

O' long may I fly
O'er this Earthly domain
Free Spirit—my symbol
Bald Eagle—my name

Jerry Tuckness
MOUNTAIN MAN

With gratitude; A tribute; My humble attempt to attest; To my friends that dwell where eagles soar, upon the mountain crest: Frank, Beverly, Reina, and Leah.

I am a clever mountain man, as
anyone can see;
Chopping wood and taking hikes,
that's the life for me.
I stand upon my mountain top, one
hundred miles to see;
There's streams and lakes and
rattle snakes,
No place I'd rather be.
The lovely things of nature, that
mean so much to me;
The city folk don't understand,
they'd rather see it second hand;
At home on a color T.V.
The rat-race of the city, I'm daily
forced to face;
My job is down there, but each
night I'm allowed
To return to my own hiding place.
Abandoned to reclusion, I've
chosen there to be;
My girls and I and Magie my dog,
and my sweet wife, Beverly.
I savor every moment, that winter
brings my way;
To sled down a snow covered
hillside,
Or just watch my little girls play.
At work one thing of value, I have
in store for me;
I carve my wooden artifacts for all
the world to see.
One day I hope to nestle, my
fireplace next to me;
And pay my way with things I've
made, from pieces of a tree.

Tillie Romein
BECAUSE I COULD NOT STOP FOR DEATH

To Emily Dickinson, my inspiration!

Because I could not stop for
Death—
He kindly stopped for me—
The Carriage held but just
Ourselves—
And Immortality.

We slowly drove—He knew no
haste
And I had put away
My labor and my leisure, too,
For his Civility—

We passed the School, where
Children strove
At Recess—in the Ring—
We passed the Fields of Gazing
Grain—
We passed the Setting Sun—

Or rather—He passed Us—
The Dews drew quivering and
chill—
For Gossamer, my Gown—
My Tippet—only Tulle—

We paused before a House that
seemed
A Swelling of the Ground—
The Roof was scarcely visible—
The Cornice—in the Ground—

Since then—'tis Centuries—and yet
Feels shorter than the Day
I first surmised the Horses Heads
Were toward Eternity.

Mary Cancilla
NIGHT

The midnight sky is smooth, soft
ebony,
A black silk blanket covering the
earth.
The moon, a gleaming ball of
purest gold
Which glows down proudly,
showing all its worth.

The wind is sleeping calmly in the
sky.
Its rhythmic breathing gently
rocks the trees.
The leaves, the grass, the flowers,
too, relax

As they are also cradled by the
breeze.

Much farther off, the mountains
still stand tall,
Though everyone around is in their
beds.
Some small white clouds can very
safely dream
While on the hills they lie their
sleepy heads.

The birds no longer sing their
happy tunes,
But cuddle with their children in
their nests.
A cricket sings a gentle lullaby
To all its family as each member
rests.

Entrancing beauty fills the world
this hour.
It's prettier than it could ever be,
But of all sights, the loveliest I find
Is by my side, eyes gazing down at
me.

The wonders of the earth are so
much more
As I sit with my love and hold him
tight.
To be here with my darling by my
side
Can help me see the splendor of the
night.

Walter Daniel
TRIBUTE TO THE ASTRONAUTS

Ever'body was oh so happy
The launching was taking place
The Astronauts were so excited
They knew they would soon be in
space.

Friends and love ones were
watching
As the rocket started to ascend
As they watched they did not know
They would not see them again.

Just seconds and the explosion
began
Oh how sad this would be
Before our eyes it destructed
A blazing furnace is all we could
see.

Amazed they stood in shock
They couldn't believe what they
saw
The rocket now vanished and gone
Just bits and pieces, that was all.

Those who they have left behind
Mothers, fathers, husbands, wives
And oh yes their little children
They will miss them all of their
lives.

All the American people
Saw the tragedy that day
They saw the fiery rockets
They fell on their knees and prayed.

The sacrifice of our love ones
Has stirred the soul of man
But there'll be tears and heartaches
Throughout this troubled land.

But they have showed us the way
The future is not free
The dreams of each person there
Will benefit both you and me.

This is what they would all want
For us to continue our journey in
space
If we did not continue what they
started
Their lives would all be a waste.

Esther E Hardy
LOVE DENIED

Her parents never stroked her
With love and tenderness
Of pride they never spoke at all,
There wasn't time, I guess.
She pleaded for a little dog,
That she could love, caress,
Her Mother barely heard her plea
"It would only make a mess!"
And so she struggled onward,
Not sure of her direction,
Hoping somehow she would lose,
This feeling of rejection.
When she met him in the street,
And he showed her attention
Her feelings soared above the
clouds
Her joy too great to mention.
Then when she found herself with
child
Her Mother cried, "Why, child,
why?"
In her youthful innocence
This was her reply
"Mom you see there's something
For which I've always yearned,
Someone who would love me
And I'd love in return.

Audrey Kay Hicks
FORESIGHT

To Little Grandma—Because I Remember

I passed your house today
But it was gone

Where is your pink robe and white
head scarf?
Your coal bucket and pear shaped
disc
for the phono that never played?

What happened to the iron bed
and lace curtains
that blew in the wind
as I napped?

You know the honeysuckle and
bleeding hearts
that I took for granted
now have gravel on their resting
place

Did you know, I never liked
sardine sandwiches and sugar
bread?
I wanted oatmeal, ovaltine and
toast.
I bought a can—
Just smiled
Never opened them

Did you know, I loved you?
I don't believe I ever said

I passed your grave today
But there was no stone . . . .

Sharon Taylor
PRAYER

Our Father who art in Heaven,
I came to you and was forgiven,
Tho I didn't know how to pray,
I said i'd try each passing day.

You helped me up when I was
down,
You're the one that wears the
crown,
It's no sooner said than done,
Forgive me Lord my only one.

God you gave your only son,
For sinners such as I was one,
Cause Jesus died upon the cross,
So that sinners would not be lost.

I pray now as best I can,
That others will take you by the
hand,
Surrender now and you'll see,
He's the only one for thee.

Oh Lord I pray to you now,
Save all the sinners and show them
how,
To follow in your path of right,
That they too will see the light.

Satan can take a hold of you,
But God will shine his light
through,
Tho you may slip and fall,
You'll find out GOD is all.

Confess now dear sinner friends,
God always understands,
Your sins and your sorrows too,
He'll take care of them for you.

Becky S Bowers
PRAYER OF LOVE

Dedicated with Love to my Dad

Outside my daughters room I stand
My wife walks up and holds my
hand
As we listen to the prayer of love
Our daughter tells to the Lord
above

Dear Lord:
Daddy lost his job sometime ago
Money's tight and jobs are slow
All I need is daddys love, thats why
What I need no money could buy
Help daddy to see and to
understand
That all I need is to hold his hand
For daddy to hold me close and
tight
To love my mommy and not to fight
Keep my daddy away from any
harm
So he can always hold me in his
arms
God bless mommy and daddy

I kiss the top of her little head
As I tuck my baby into her bed
I told her daddy now understands
I kiss her again and held her hand
As I watch my little princess sleep
I sit beside of her bed and weep
You know I would not lie to you
For no one loves you as much as I
do

Sadie S Matthews

Sadie S Matthews
GOD'S GIFTS

To my children, grandchildren, great grandchildren, brother, sister-in-laws, aunts, uncles, nieces, nephews, cousins, my husband and friends & Eddie-Lou Cole with love.

God gave us the grass to see
He gave us bees that sting
He gave us birds that sweetly sing
God really gave us everything.

God gave us the rain that freshens
the earth
He gave us the wind to blow on our
face
He gave us a mind to help one
another
God gave us love to share with each
other.

God gave us the stars to shine at
night
He gave us the moon, oh! so bright
He gave us the sun to brighten the
day
God gave us his son to show us the
way.

Vera E Royer-Riedesel
WHY?

To my son, Paul J. Wooten

I miss you more than you can
know.
I'm angry with myself for letting
you go.
I look at your picture as days go by.
I sit here alone and wonder why.

I'll never forgive myself for saying
good-bye.
I hate myself so much I could
almost die.

I wish I could answer my question
"Why?"
But all I can do is sit here and cry.

Gary Farley
THE WAY LOVE GOES

I wrote your name
in the sand today
where warm waters welcome
free birds to play
but the tide came in
and took you away.
I drew your face
in virgin snows
and dreamt of you
emerging
as spring's first rose
but I awoke
to catch the traitor winds
make-off with your pose.
Now deep into my heart
I carve your memory.
And when I die,
into my grave
you will stay
with me.

Deanne Mosley
FROZEN WINDOWPANES

As I stare out through frozen
windowpanes,
Again, my vision blocked returns
to me.
I search and search for a small
glance to gain.
Yet, disappointment starts since I
can't see.
It is determination driving me.
I must see out; there is no other
way.
All that is clear is a large wooden
"T."
To satisfy myself, I mustn't sway.
I stare as with my eyes to melt the
ice.
It fights by blinding, being blazing
white.

To be victorious, I must pay the
price,
With confidence through all that I
am right.
And suddenly a glare of light
shines bright,
As I triumphal, the odds I've
learned to fight.

Sara D Howard
THE HEALING

To R.T. Lee, in loving memory.

I held your hand
as we talked.
You were sleepy and weak . . .
the pain was bad.
We pulled you upright
so you could breathe easier.
"Yes, the oxygen is still on."
You squeezed my hand
tighter—and groaned,
"Please help me God!"

I put the pill back into your hand
after it slipped to the couch . .
I picked it up again
as it fell to the floor.

"The injection will help—just
relax."
Her voice was calm and soothing
as she
massaged the cramps from your
legs.
This scene had been repeated
countless times . . .
"Soon you'll be eased," she said.

"Help me, dear Jesus," you gasped,
as we pulled you up again.

God heard—and He answered . . .
Another grunt . . . a quiet hush . . .
And you slipped away . . .

Myrtle M Weaver
MY THOUGHTS BY THE SEASHORE

To my loving granddaughter, Cynthia

Today I went to the seashore and
as I walked on the sand,
I stood there amazed as I held
your hand,
To see this great ocean and its
beauty so rare;
So few catch and hold this
beauty, as you and I did there.

I heard the roar of the ocean, and
saw the great waves rush in,
I saw the ships out at sea, and
knew there once had been
Men crossing this ocean in the days
of long ago,
Who had wondered about the
future, whose spirits were very
low.

I thought about Columbus and his
adventurous trip,
How he came so very far in such a
tiny ship.
He must have been a very brave
man and thought he would
succeed,
Or he wouldn't have dared such a
thing, or wouldn't even heed.

The pleas of the men to turn back
after sailing for days and days,
But to give up would be cowardly
and that was not Columbus'
ways.

He said we'll sail on and on until
we reach land;
It shows you can do a thing, if
only you think you can.

And then I thought of myself, and
the things I would like to do,
But, yet I lack the courage to sail
the ocean blue,
And be a great hero as Columbus
was that day;
So I'll just be contented and walk
the well paved way.

Marcine P Smith
THE VOICE

Dedicated to my loving husband, Phil, and my five wonderful children for giving me space to be myself.

The road to insanity is deep and
wide,
Only a narrow thread from the
saner side.
Your whole being shrieks and
screams for release,
And out of the black and swirling
depths comes a voice,
"Stop, Stop, Cease".
You close your eyes tightly and
then you pray,
"God, help me through another
day".
The escape was narrow, your
breath comes fast.
My God, My God, I'm grateful it's
past.
If from that black and swirling pit
I should fail to hear the voice,
And if there is another choice,
Before that narrow thread can
break,
Close my eyes, don't let me wake.

Simone Blanch
LITTLE FLOWER
Little flower in the snow.
Trying very hard to grow,
Try to sleep a little longer,
Till you grow a little stronger.
Soon the sun will shine above,
And help you with a gentle shove.

Stephanie Lyn Tornquist
THE FRIENDS OF NATURE
The waves of the ocean swish
wildly against the rocks
The seagull lands on shore all alone
Another joins him as he takes off
again
The sandy shore has been
interrupted like a sleeping one
awakened
Pretty soon the rocks have given up
and are swallowed by the ocean
The seagulls are no where in sight,
so I feel alone once more

The sun settles at the end of the
forever running ocean
Making a bright orange reflection
Pretty soon the sun will leave and
the moon and stars will appear
You can barely see the setting sun
as it peeks at the day it now ends
The ocean has laid down to sleep

I sit and stare as the ocean sleeps
The stars finally peek through the
darkness
The moon shines to give off the
light
Yet never shall I be so lonely again
The stars are my friends
They hold my dreams
The ocean is my friend
For it holds my secret of life
The sun is my friend
For it says to hang on and don't
ever let go of life
There is always tomorrow

Timothy Daniel Cadle
REAL LOVE

To Melody Schneider my true "Real Love"

Real Love oh how I need Real Love,
I fell in love before,
I knew it would not work I needed
something more,
I needed the gentleness of a
womans touch,
I needed this so much,
Something I can not grasp on to,
Something I couldn't understand
or even do,
I'm waiting, waiting for that real
love,
Real love that is going to survive,
Then I met you and now I have real
love in my life,
I needed your love so much before,
But now I have that real love in
store,
Real love has me right here with
you,
Know real love survives and goes
with time,
Real love I do not have to walk
away from,
Real love is so rare,
Real love is what I want to share,
Real love is being together,
Real love is being together forever.

Kim M Lord
A SOLDIER
Wind him up
Watch him go
Marching to songs
Children all know

A hero he is
In the eyes of a boy
Fighting many a battle
In wars that destroy

Medals of honor

Draping his chest
Display moments of glory
He was at his best

Up on the shelf
Is where he is stored
Until a little boy
Decides he is bored

Then one day he marches
With the dreams of a boy
This once tiny soldier
Is no longer a toy

Jane Roberts
A BIT OF LOVE CALLED DOG
A bit of Love came to our house
today
admidst the strife (it's growing up
they say)
T'was such a tiny thing, so soft but
true blue
to grow into maturity, as love must
do
One black ear and the opposite eye,
to be
her mark on the world that says
"That's Me!"
No other love, no matter how sure
will ever be the same, 'cause Love
is her
Can a bit more love that will grow
and grow
help us see we do reap what we sow
A love that gives and doesn't
demand
will find it's reward; do you
understand
Love gives of herself; that is to be
free
to pay the price of being loved, you
and me

Sheila M Bevins
SILENT IS THE NIGHT

To Jamie! Dedicated to the one I Love!"

Silent is the night when you come
to me
I watch you in the firelight, I'm as
warm
As I can be
You whisper in my ear, endearing
words of love
As we look at the sky and count the
stars above.

The night is like the wind, softly
blowing in the breeze
Your fingers on my skin, oh so
gently tease
Like water flowing over rocks in a
graceful stream
Your everything I've thought of in
my nightly dreams.

Silent is the night and as dark as a
raven's wing
The love that you show makes the
blood in my veins sing
And I'm so lucky you chose me for
your wife
I'll treasure every moment with you
for the rest of my life.

Georgia M Berger
OUR HEARTS, OUR SOULS, OUR LOVE, OUR LIVES
We've both been hurt in the past
And we're uncertain if what we
have will last.
We've come a long way in such a
short time.
Our lives together have begun to
rhyme.

How can anything this good be
wrong?
With each passing day our love is
so strong.
Life seems to be telling me
That we are no longer free.

We share a love
That is blessed from above.
Who are we to question why?
We must simply comply.

Our hearts have become one . . .
Joined together in the warmth of the sun.
Our souls will live on forever . . .
In a manner most demure.

Our love will always grow . . .
Like the beauty of a new rainbow.
Our lives will be more secure . . .
As our love becomes more mature.

So, my darling, as you can see . . .
I have given you all of me—
my heart, my soul, my love and my life.

Martha J Tinkey

QUIETLY

To Mom, Kay, and Marye—Thank you for helping me reach my goals and for believing in me. God bless you all.

Alone,
Sitting quietly,
Thinking.
The moon shining brightly
Over the breeze
Coming off the cool
Summer lake.
A summer full
Of laughter,
Of sadness,
Of friendship,
Of love.
Taking time
Just to remember
The many things
About life
Too often
Forgotten.
Smiling,
Enjoying,
Quietly,
Being alone.

Jerrie B Savage

AU RE-VOIR

To my son Bob whose love of poetry is an inspiration to me.

Goodbyes are always hard for me
I would rather say hello,
Welcome, or please come again
To all the friends I know.

There is something deep inside me,
That makes me want to cry
For I am never ready
When it's time to say good by.

There comes a time in every life,
(I say this with a sigh)
For those who are not ready
To say that last good by.

I must confess I never feel
I'm ready to depart,
There's always something left undone
Some wisdom to impart.

But when God makes His call for me
To leave this earthly shell
I shall not say good by at all,
I'll only say farewell.

Trudy Mariano

IN ANTICIPATION

Waiting—Preparing—Thinking—
About what it will be!
Helpless—Speechless—Fearless—
Will it look like me?
Excitement—Wonderment—
Confusion—
Brothers whose feelings are mixed.
Concern—Anxiety—Love—
A husband whose support is flexible yet fixed.

Little One—
We're here with—
Care—Guidance—Love—
Waiting—
To take your hand
To help you—
Understand!

Kari Stauffer

UNTITLED

I am a person,
but yet human.
I have succeeded,
but also I have failed.
I have achieved victory,
but I have also felt the disappointment of defeat.
I have received many roses,
but with each rose, came the thorns.
I have felt the calmness of the ocean,
but the danger of a swift current.
I have felt the warmth of love,
but also the coldness of rejection.
I have experienced many things
being a person,
but none were as meaningful as what
I experienced as a human.

LaVerda Guffey

EARLY PAROLEE

In loving memory of Texas Ranger Stanley Keith Guffey

It was a night in January,
When the call went out.
A child had been kidnapped,
From a rich man's house.

"Be in Marble Falls until-?"
The note it did read.
The Texas Ranger had set out,
On his final deed.

"Leave the car in the drive,"
The kidnapper sneered.
The Ranger Captain looked sad,
"I'll need volunteers."

Rangers Guffey and Aycock,
Stepped forward with pride,
"We have kids of our own,
The back seat's where we'll hide

Footsteps came running,
The child cried in pain.
"Police," shouted Guffey,
As the bullets rained.

When the battle was over,
The parolee's blood spread.
The child? Safe from harm
But Ranger Guffey was dead.

Emmett Smith

THE VALIANT

For Cap'n Zi and Mike.

I have walked the high lonely trail with the in-born stealth of the mountain cat and secretly observed Man and Nature at their candid self.
I have run with the wind, faster than the deer, my shadow racing to catch up to me.
I have felt the silence spreading outward like a giant ripple, louder than a sonic boom.
I have known with absolute certainty, through that extra sense honed sharp, that I was not alone; without seeing a shape or hearing a sound.
I know the thrill of the kill and the satisfaction of victory.
I have known the sunken hearted despair of being un-prepared, out-witted and out-maneuvered, but the feeling of respect rose as a silent salute to the wittier one with the promise of next time on my lips.
I have known the cold clutch of fear that threatened to loosen my bowels; with summoned courage and instinct I acted and cold fear was replaced by cool calculation and precise judgement.
I pressed on when others dared not.
I lived while death dropped around me.
I have walked through valleys shrouded in death like ships in fog.
I have laughed with the deep mirth of exhilaration and cried my heart right into my hands.
I have lived, yet this I know: though death shall surely come,
to those of valor, it can only come once.

Michael D Gavin

NO MORE MAGIC

The magic's not here
The wounds will not heal
Nothing to do
When the love's not real
We've given our best
To make it work out
But you're not the one

I can't live without
Nothing to do
When the love's not real
This is a wound
That time cannot heal
Time has come
To say good bye
I'll never forget
That I made you cry.

Betty L Varanelli

ONLY WHAT YOU SEE

You want to live in a palace
with royalty all around,
with silks and satin clothing
and jewels and money abound.

You think you have the right idea
and everything will work out right,
you say that your not happy there
and your alone most every night.

Your palace may be fine indeed
but somethings money can't buy,
happiness is not for sale my dear
you may have riches, but still you cry.

Without someone to love you dear
your riches do you no good.
You need someone to love you,
I only wish I could.

But my time is growing short
and you've turned away from me,
for all your jewels and money
can only buy what you can see.

James L Clark

HANK THE ALABAMA MAN AND HIS COUNTRY BAND

He grew up in Alabama
Was born to play and sing
Writing country songs of love
'Twas a gift from above
His heart was in every word he sang
His songs will be with us
Long as the world will stand
Tho we never got a chance to meet
Your songs have warmed my heart
Moved thousands from their seats

Alabama man and his country band
Played and sang all over this land
Life for Hank had its ups and downs
in his songs they can be found
On a long lonely ride to a show
Traveling thru snow going was slow
Fans did not know until they arrived
Hank was dead not alive
Angels came to take Hank home
Never more to roam

Fred William Russell

I BELONG

I belong where the weasel play
Yonder hill in the woodland height,
Where summer clouds kiss the tree tops
And little shadows follow the light.

The evening sun for shadows make
Where giant rocks lay and sigh,
Little flowers look up to take
Colors from the sky.

I belong in that house within
Through the fireplace I see,
Blades of grass dance fantastically
As if to an old melody.

Stayed too long at the cider press
Where good taste is sweet,
going through the stubble field
And the smell of wheat.

I belong where the plow is king
Where hearts are never sad,
Life there seems forever
A life I once had.

Michael Kevin Colombo

WINTER

As, I lay upon my bed,
Thoughts come to me as I read.
Thinking of times when things were new,
Like life coming out before me and you.
The days grow more and more of an orange color,
Painted by leaves through nights of the solar.
Daylight creeps away,
As sunlight cries to be out every day.
Everybody listens but nothing can be done,

To help what is happening to us or
the sun.
We trudge along with rakes on our
lawn,
Wishing to be completed by dawn.
Coldness creeps more and more in
dismay,
Telling us to get ready, for Winter
is coming our way.

Jeannette Hann
LIFE LONG GOAL

I dedicate this poem to my mother and my life.

We see what we must
Capture what we can
Live by our standards

W R McNeill
CHOICE

If I had choice
of realms in which to dwell
I'd free this soul
from body and world's worth
to soar with eagles
on the wind's express,
free from the clinging bonds
I've known on earth.

If I had a choice
of voice in which to sing
I'd say a chorus
from the sky's expanse,
my song a clear expression
of a soul set free
and down across the fleece of
cloud
I'd dance.

Herminia Yangat Somoba

Herminia Yangat Somoba
I UNDERSTAND

For all the students whom I have helped since 1952 especially Arvin Hernandez of Waimanalo School, Hawaii whose inclination is to become a writer someday.

Bright as the beams of a new born
day
Sweet as roses fair under the sun
First day with you, innocent faces
And I felt my worth, I understand.

You were fresh, very keen to learn
I was frisky, too eager to start
I perceived the talents of each one
All different yes, I understand.

So years come and go, and so do
you
And just for a year I stay with you
I learn from your ways, daughters
and sons
You're all lovable, I understand.

I hear from you or about you dears
And I rejoice for your achievements
Fervently I prayed for your success
Our dear, Lord, listened, I
understand.

Old in age but in spirit still young
I'm now with silver hair, dear ones
But oh, my love for you still the
same
My sacred service, I understand.

You'll not forget my patience with
you
You'll remember happy bygones
too
In case you'll not see me tomorrow
I'll be proud of you, I understand.

Betty "Chris" Heuer
TIME MARCHES ON

Dedicated to my twin brother, Bobby, who died May 12, 1986.

I touched the wing of a bird today
And it gave back to me
A wonderful feeling of freedom
So beautiful and free

I smelled the fragrance of a rose
Touched a tiny baby's cheek
Heard the beauty of a songbird
Watched the silent darkness creep

Walked upon the dewy meadow
Strolled in sand along a beach
Reached up my arms to heaven
But it was out of reach

If only we could capture
Each glorious moment so sublime
Tuck it into a timeless capsule
So that when the sands of time

In the autumn of our years
When we are old and gray
We could open up the capsule
And recapture yesterday

Brenda D Shelton-King
STARDUST

Dedicated to my husband Wayne for his love and encouragement.

Stardust sprinkled in her eyes
becomes but a dream.
A dream of a reality that only
exists in the
expectations of the young and the
hopes of the aged.
Life goes on and she awakens,
the sun at its peak,
and faces an old world.
And as she rubs the stardust
from her eyes she sees
a new beginning.

David Robert Shields
MY HOME, MY COUNTRY, MY PEOPLE

Why I'm proud to be an American
is found etched upon my soul.
For thereon is written experiences,
Life and death, and struggles
untold.

I searched high and far to answer
this question that burned deep
inside.
I climbed up to the mountains;
Upon the wind I did ride.

I saw purple mountains in their
majesty.
I danced in Alpine meadows
among the fragrance of flowers
and trees.

I traveled to see the amber waves
of grain.
I crossed the mighty Mississippi
and felt the gentle Southern rain.

Every where I went I met people:
Rich, poor, strong, and weak.
Some were proud, humble,
boastful, and meek.

People are the secret of our
Country's great success.
America is for the people and by
the people.
We would rather die than take
anything less.

In all my searching to answer the
question
"Why I'm proud to be an
American,"
I found my home, my Country, and
my people.
For freedom and these people I will
forever stand!

Mrs Mary E Day
OUR MAILMAN

This poem is dedicated to Buddy, my son-in-law

Our mailman is sweet, considerate
and kind
He brings us our mail come rain
Or come shine.
He is the one that brings Christmas
Cheer,
With letters & cards, throughout
the
Whole year.
He is the one that we watch for
each day
In hopes that we get letters from
those
Far away
He wears a smile and takes time to
SAY HI!
As he fights off the dogs and hopes
they pass by
Lets give him the credit he so much
deserves
Lets make his smile bigger in so
many words
We're proud of our mailman, yes
he brings us
cheer.
Not only on Christmas but all
through the year.

William R Taylor
WHERE DO THE CHILDREN HIDE

Yesterday you hid behind
momma's dreams and daddy's
pride
Today you grow to find yourself
living in hell.
Your daddy beats your mommy up,
And everytime he gets drunk,
You get the urge to run and hide
somewhere.
Time went so fast when you turned
fifteen,
Learned of drugs and living in the
streets.
Your mommy's mistake and worst
nightmare.

Where do the children hide
When nobody seems to be on their
side.
Where do the children hide from it
all.

Hypnotized by rebel eyes,
You can't tell who's on your side
When your dad attacks you late at
night,
Flunking in and out of school
You're scared stiff but Joe thinks
you're cool.
And you want to know where dad
is coming from.
A bottle of whiskey and one last
toke,
You want to think life's one big joke
As you play Russian roulette with
a friend.

Where do the children hide
When nobody seems to be on their
side.
Where do the children hide from it
all.

Brad Freeman
MOTHER NATURE

To my wife, Kim and son, Brandon

I'd like you to meet a friend of mine
Mother Nature is her name
Once you really get to know her
You'll never be the same

Her splendor and her majesty
Goes beyond compare
Her beauty's unsurpassed
Her wisdom very rare

The balance of her nature
Is delicate though she's strong
Sometimes she's temperamental
But ya know she's never wrong

The white man calls her nature
The red man calls her friend
Some people may not realize
But let me tell you friend,

If we all would try to learn from her
As we live from day to day
She'll teach us loving kindness
In her own mysterious way

If you really get to know her
I'm sure that you will find
Just being in her presence
Will help to ease your mind

Donna-Marie Forand
THE CIRCLE OF LIFE

This poem is dedicated to the person who has helped me make it through the years, with all his love, understanding and sincere words, to James D. Forand 1976-1987 forever

---

Trees, leaves and bees

Many special kinds of trees.
Big ones: small ones: wide ones:
thin ones
They are life: which grow from
seeds
A stem blossoms off the side
Big ones small ones many kinds
Blossoms appear growing to the
sun
Attracting the bees to the blossoms
Of the sweet wonderful smell of
spring
One by one the rain falls spraying
the
Trees with nourishment of food
and water
Soon Fall arrives. One by one the
leaves color.

Red ones. Yellow ones. Orange and brown.
The cold frost begins to fall
Making the leaves lose their color.
One by one they begin to fall.
Now its winter one more time.
Then we begin the cycle again.
Spring, fall, summer and winter time.

Annette C Richardson
MY MORNING GUEST

I Dedicate this poem to my children: Jeffery,—Nellie, — Melvonia,— Gary,—Wade,—Thurston,— Bonnie,—Phyllis, — Tarus.

I got up early this morning
and prepared my meal to eat
As I sat down, a knock at the
door sprang me to my feet.

I went to the door and asked,
"Who's there?" "It's me," a strange
voice answered in despair. "I'm
tired, I'm hungry, and have been
long upon my feet . . .

"Come in," I said, "I just prepared
a bite to eat." I led him to
where the table was spread, I
looked up and saw a light shone
about his head, we sat down to
eat, my heart felt aglow. I had
a quaint feeling this is someone I
know.

I blessed the table, as I always
do, he smiled and said, "That was
very kind of you." We finished
our meal, our words were few. He
smiled again and said, "My dear,
thank you." He spoke again and
said, "I must be on my way, for
there is much to be done,
so have a good day.

I bidded him good-by with
no doubt in my mind, he knew
who I was all the time.
Needless to say, my day was
not a waste, if ever he comes
again, I'll remember his face.

Meta M Suchon

Meta M Suchon
GOD IS THERE
As the day comes to a close
I think about the things God knows
The hearts I broke, the wrong I've done
All comes with the setting of the sun.

He knows my worries, cares and pain
And yet He loves me just the same
And through the darkness He's by my side
For my salvation, He was crucified.

He forgives me daily for my sin
Why can't I let go and let Him in?
He waits for me to say, "I'm yours
This misery I can stand no more"

But before His love can cleanse my soul
I try, once more, to take control
I seldom take the time to pray
I try to do it my own way.

He loves me still and takes me back
And sets me again, on the right track.
But what a predicament we'd all be in
If God refused to forgive our sin.

Marcus A Reid
THAT'S LOVE, LOVE IN ACTION

Dedicated to Mrs. Roma Estelle Reid, my mate, my partner, my wife and love in action that brightens my life.

Jesus says come learn of me
Whoever you are whatever you be
I paid sin's debt to set you free
With power to live victoriously
Hear what the Spirit has to say
'Tis He who guides you day by day
Every word of it obey
For it's the Truth, the Life, the Way

It matters not how great your sin
Nor what condition you're now in
Nor who you are or where you've been
God's gift of grace is for all men
But this is what's required of you
Admit your wrongs; abandon them, too
Forgive one another then He pardons you
When knowing these things, then, these things do

In every man's heart there's a sin breach
In its intake or its outreach
Its computered heartwear, language, speech
Omits the word it was to teach
Get a new heart from Jesus today
Free for asking; nothing to pay
Get your new heart don't delay
Eternity is just a breath away
That's love, love in action.

Nelle M Bell (Mrs L W Bell)

Nelle M Bell (Mrs L W Bell)
TRIBUTE TO OUR FLAG
Our Flag—Beloved by you, and by me.
From its first flight at Brandywine
With Washington in 1777
To its journeys with the astronauts
Beneath the floor of Heaven;
From 1790 and its first trip
By boat around the world,
And 1812, when for the first time above
A log schoolhouse it was unfurled—
Its glory has grown and grown,
Its fame spread everywhere,
Offering promises based on honor,
And freedoms for all to share.
Beautiful as a delicate flower
To those who love it best;
Terrible as a meteor in flight
To those who its strength would test.
So—Treat it tenderly,
Handle it with loving care
Knowing that in every
World-Peace Dream
It will be found flying there.
Our flag—Inherited and cherished
By you, and by me.
God grant it never falls
Throughout Eternity

Ida Hollaway
A LIFE
Would you kill a child at the age of two,
Or let him live to be three?
A decision you have no right to make,
Whether he's grown or just a seed.

"An abortion, you say, that's not the same.
It's my body, I'll do as I please."
You're wrong my friend, there's a life involved,
Whether he's grown or just a seed.

He's dependent on you for life support,
He needs you even to breathe.
And you're willing to end his only chance,
The life that you have conceived?

Perhaps he would have been a surgeon,
Or president of our country, lets say,
Or perhaps something even greater you see,
The father of your grandchild one day.

Larry Ballew
GRANDPA CARRY ME
"Grandpa Carry Me" are almost music to my ear.
Coming from this little boy whom we love so dear.
We had a late start with our daughter and our son.
Even tho' we are older, this little boy is such fun.

We go out to feed the horses or check the garden plants.
By the time we get there, he's almost lost his pants.
His little legs work like piston's keeping up with me.
There's many things to do, and lots of things to see.

And does that boy ask questions, talking constantly.
"Grandpa, why do birds fly, and how do they sit in a tree?"
"What makes tomatoes red, why do you call that a butterfly?"
"Grandpa my legs are tired, Ouch!, I got a bug in my eye!"

We got the horses fed and watered the garden a bit,
Well little boy don't you think it is about time to quit?
We'll go in and take a nap, your momma will be here soon.
She said she would have her shopping done by noon.

"Grandpa Carry Me" as we headed back to the house.
By now he was getting sleepy and was quiet as a mouse.
We don't get to see little boy but ever'day or two.
We sure do enjoy him, he's some boy, I'll tell you!

Sheila L Bridges
FORGET

In MEMORY OF My Grandmothers & All Sleeping Love Ones Mrs. Ella N. Gause Fore & Mrs. Anna Hosey Bridges

---

Forget the pain you might have shared!
Forget the dark lonely hours you might have spent!
Forget the distractive hate you might have felt!
Forget those painful mistakes you have or might have made!
Forget those sleepless nights you have or might of spent!
Forget those loves you might have shared!
Forget all those chains and obstructions that might hold you back!

Because my friend life will be full of things to forget!

Forget what you must!

But, forget not to forget to love those whom love you!
But, forget not to learn from all the pain and mistakes you might have made!

Because my friend—you are full of things that you might forget to learn!

But, yet you are what you are and that my brothers and sisters is not worth forgetting!

So, don't forget to be what you are!

Forget what you must!
But, don't forget this!

Margot Lee Passalacqua
WONDERFUL PEOPLE
The sun shines softly on the
new fallen snow,
as I sit here and think
of the people I know.
The people I cherish,
the people I love,
the people who helped me
to rise above.
My problems were many
and my mind was confused,
I felt so lonely,
hurt and abused.
When I sat down to think
and feel sorry for myself,
I remembered the friends
I had put on a shelf.

Their problems were many,
far worse than my own,
yet they always stayed
by me,
never left me alone.
So to these people
who helped me to rise above,
I give my thanks,
my friendship,
and love.

Trey Woodrow
TOMORROW AND TOMORROW
As the world calls,
so we must go;
leaving behind the world
that we know.

Our beginning's complete,
the game's at an end;
to destiny's summons
we now will ascend.

We face the morrow,
our die is cast;
from our time together
only memories will last.

Mary Roettenbacher
SONG OF THE WOODS
If only my words, like music could
be heard;
Such as Longfellow, Bronte, or
Frost.

Then capture, I would, with
melody, your mood
And in peace and solitude you'd be
lost.
And however hard you'd try
My melody wouldn't die,
But forever in your mind it would
stay.
With harmony and precision my
song would bring visions of
Flowers in bloom
Birds all in tune
In a woods
On a hot summer day.
Or of rain soft and quiet,
Like silver through the sky it
Streams.
And forms a soft mist as each leaf
is kissed.
And the warm earth, from the cool
rain just
Steams.
Aware are your senses of a
fragrance all around.
A breath-taking sweetness from
the flowers that abound.
And as if you were there, you'd
sense the warm air,
And the color of green would
surround you.
But my words won't convey . . . as
for beauty . . . no way!
Such sights and such sounds be
compared to.

Joyce Edwards Hargrove
i love you ma-ma

To my Ma-Ma, Mrs. Claretha Edwards, thank you for adopting me.

---

i have a warm, exciting feeling
inside of me—
i love my ma-ma.
so what's so great about that
thought?
i'm able to tell her, that's what!
i love you ma-ma, i'm sure you've
seen it
in my eyes and heard it in my
voice,
but now you hear it from my heart.
you link me to my very
beginnings
of life and nourishment—so
sacrificing;
thru touch, of love and affection,
guidance and discipline—how
endearing.
i love you ma-ma; i can say it
again and again,
and you will hear me—so
rewarding.

Carol J Brandt
A POEM TO DURK (MY BABY SON)

For my handsome son and his wonderful dad, Kenneth

On the 6th day of December of 1973
a beautiful baby boy was born to
me.
With eyes so blue, skin so red
My goodness, his sweet little bald
head;
So proud we have a son.
We hope the best for him—hope it
has just begun!

May he be honest and good.
Strong and have laughter
everyday, like he should.
We love you, Durk. Always will.
So please son love us too!
But we know by your cute ways
you already
do!

Norma Durbin
BOUQUET OF MEMORIES

To Ganny

As I count the roses of my mind
I find
You have given me many beautiful
bouquets
During all the days we shared
Their lingering fragrance
Is a lasting memory
That strengthens,
Sustains,
And comforts me

Arlene R Sliter
A TRIBUTE TO AMERICA
This is your day Miss Liberty,
Symbol of our country, home of
the free,

The ethnic and impoverished,
we've welcomed thee,
To our country blessed abundantly,

With resource, industry and
impartiality,
By our God and Creator, one
person in three,

May our hearts always give thanks
to thee,
In a spirit of love and unity.

B T Leedy
I SENSED YOU
I sense you now—I hear you step
You peremate this home
A feeling—such as —I've never felt
It stifles me—as I sit alone

I sensed your presence—amoment
before
you shadowed the window then
as you eased toward it more
you slipped it open—and slid in.

My heart shuddered with each new
step
up my spine—races a deep
penetrating chill
you seem to moan & hesitate
I lie there silent until

You came to my bedside
I pretend to be asleep
After you left me satisfied
I heard you creep.

You lingered for one moment in
my door
then moved into the darkness
beyond
I saw you no more
I reasoned—you had moved on.

Rosemary Church
IT'S LIFE
My heart hurts deep within myself,
but the mind works above it.
The world is such a mess, it seems,
that most people can do nothing of
it.
We've took the stand to fight,
in many wars hot and cold.
The mothers cried, the sons, they
died,
the fathers, they grew old.
The right to say; I'm Free,
is the only message, we all agree.
To take the lives of human beings,
in this game of life, it seems.
Who gave the right to any man to
take
a human life; not only in the war
zone
but on the streets and to thyself.
The greatest miracle, that we have
and each day we drink, polute,
smoke,
eat and dope it away. Like it's
nothing;
nothing at all . . .

George H Archer
TRAIN WATCHER
I once saw a little boy
Who looked so very shy,
He sat up on a hill alone
And watched my train go by.
Oh, how very sad he looked,
How thin and so ill-clad,
Not one movement did he make,
Such haunting eyes he had.
I wondered why he was so sad,
Did he need a pal to play?
Or yearn to be an engineer
And travel far away?
Was he unhappy in his home?
Did he have enough to eat?
Did someone help him with his
prayers
And tuck him off to sleep?
Only his eyes followed the train,
I felt them rest on me,
And then I knew I had to know
Just who this child could be.
As the train moved on, I waved to
him
Not once did he reply,
And then so suddenly I realized,
The little boy was I.

Winifred Inez Thompson
THE AUTUMN OF MY LIFE

"The Autumn Of My Life," published posthumously, is dedicated, in loving memory of our mother, Winifred Inez Thompson.

The aromas of fall delight me;
I think of purple grapes warming
in the sun,
Chrysanthemums lending tangy
spice with their beauty,
Burning leaves on a frosty day.
The taste of fresh cider,
Pumpkin pie, turkey and
cranberries
Are flavors to tease anyone's palate.
I can listen to the wild geese on a
stormy night,
Conversing with each other as they
wend their way southward.
I can hear the autumn tempest,
tearing
At our snug little cottage.
I touch the ones I love and feel
comfort.
I remember the soft tenderness
Of the babes I held in my arms.
In the autumn of my life, I am more
aware
Of God and his manifestations;
I pray that I too, like the pale
leaves, clinging to the tree,
May catch the radiance of the
sunset, and reflect his glory.

Charles Maynard George
LIFE AND POETRY
Life and poetry in harmony!
Engrafted vines with roots in
earth below,
And reaching upward to celestial
realms
For higher alchemy with
"Soul-ar" glow.

The earth, a wilderness of common
sages,
And of weeds and breeds more
radical;
As cactus with their points of
argument,
Though pointless in debate more
spiritual.

The world, an Eden with a tethered
yield;
Of surface offerings for a
serpent-creed,
Or mineral stores and liquid
life—lines from
The inner sanctum, for a deeper
need.

Behold, another hidden treasure
here,
With Nature as appointed
pedagogue
To teach us truth beyond the sight
of things—
Child and Nature's God in
dialogue.

Poetry is life, and vice versa,
Where the best of words and
thoughts, deep-felt,
Reflect the best, and worst, of
poetry
And life—sometimes "better felt
than telt."

Samuel Simmons
MEMORIES

To the most wonderful person to ever come into my life.

My memories are wonderful,
They're all thats left for me;
I cherish every single thought,
Thats how it will ever be;
To have you always in my mind
will strictly be my game,
And then once more I'll be with
you;
That is for what I aim.

Our places were together
right from the very start;
I do believe this was the truth
with all my lonely heart.
I know the way you loved me,
and always called me dear;
It always made me happy
to know that you were near.

I've tried to see the brighter side
since you went away,
But that is awful hard to do
Thats all I have to say;
'Tis not hard to remember
how you gave me your love;
And I get a tender feeling
when I think of you above.

You, with your understanding
of each and every need;
A voice full of authority
the kids would always heed;
Our maker did take you away,
and eased all of your pain;
Now all I have to do is wait
to be with you again.

Marilyn K Flanders
SERVICE

This poem is dedicated to my mother, Mrs. Dorothy Flanders, who taught me the true meaning of service.

I am a child of noble birth,
Sent here to live and walk the earth.
My Father in heaven will smile on
me
If I try to be what He wants me to
be.

While on my journey here below,
I'll try to do what's right, and know
I'm not alone in my quest to find
Righteous paths; I'll be good and
kind.

I'll strive to do a noble deed,
And help my fellowman in need.
For in giving service, I truly find
Joy in living with all mankind.

I'll seek my Father in daily prayer,
And my testimony, I'll freely share
With anyone who wants to know
True happiness' paths while living
below.

For in doing for others, one truly
finds
Love, and joy and peace of mind.
For one day, we may hope the
Father to see
And live with Him throughout
eternity.

Emma Jackson Sutton
STAND UP AND BE SOMEBODY
Stand up and be somebody.
You've only just begun.
Make your parents proud you are
Their daughter or their son.

Stand up and be somebody
While youth is at your door.
Get prepared for the challenges
The future has in store.

Stand up and be somebody.
Learn everything you can.
And use this knowledge so you'll be
A successful woman or man.

Stand up and be somebody.
Set foolishness aside.
Go forward on and live your life
With dignity and pride.

Stand up and be somebody.
Fight injustices great and small.
Whatever endeavors you
undertake,
Give them your all and all.

Stand up and be somebody.
Don't compromise your goals.
Do the things you know are right
In your heart and soul.

Stand up and be somebody
All your whole life through.
And the Lord will see you on
In everything you do.

Stand up and be somebody!

Scott D Youngdahl
THE OPTIMISTS' PRAYER
May unyielding desire be your
strength and drive,
To conquer all problems, with a
will to survive.
Though fate may deal you a
damaging blow,
Fight back and show you're a
formidable foe.
It's true life has its ups and downs,
Hold fast to the smiles, instead of
the frowns.
Keep a positive outlook
throughout your life,
Don't let negation ever cloud this
strife.

Shannon Miles
SWEET DREAMS

In Memory of: Jessica Nicole Miles, January 1986—January 1986.

Jessica Nicole, she was my first
niece.
Now she's in Heaven where she is
at peace.
A precious and smiling face.
Her cousins—Justin and Jas.
A beautiful little girl.
With pretty dresses and curls.
A Mommy and Daddy as special as
can be.

Why God took her, we still can't
see.
A Grandma and Grandpa to spoil
her rotten.
Our memory of her will never be
forgotten.
A very precious and tiny baby.
She would have been a very fine
lady.
Now she is our special Guardian
Angel.
She'll keep us safe and keep us well.
We will always love our Little
Jessica.
We will see her again, in Heaven
above.

Dana Lynn Hoderowski
SECRETS
Lost in my mind
Lost in my heart
Feelings of you
Tear me apart
Feelings so deep
Will always
Show through
Locked deep away
Are memories of you

Nelle M Gray
PRAYER FOR PEACE
Gracious God we are praying for
peace.
We ask that all malice and wars
cease.
We pray for Your will to be done,
No war is ever won.
We want to learn to love each other,
We realize everyone is our brother.
We will dedicate our lives to You,
You alone can see us through.
For peace we are praying,
In humility our prayers we are
saying.
Dear God peace is our one desire—
World peace, War is setting our
world on fire.
Please hear our humble prayer
today,
We know of no other way. In
Christ we pray.

Kathleen "Kaci" Muster
THE SILENT SCREAM
It won't be long now
'til you've gone away.
'Til the silence of the phone
the times you would have called
reminds me that you're gone.

Your absence will become
an almost tangible thing,
making a very real emptiness
in my world. In me.

Your space, (special place),
like a hole punched out of
a painting . . .
it's <u>not</u> being there becomes
a "Silent Scream . . ."
of something missing.

Florence Yoch
LONELY EVENINGS
Oh, how lonely the evenings are
Before the sky puts out a star.
I want to go dance and be gay,
Held tightly in a loving way;
Sweet nothings whispered in my
ear
And in my heart to hold no fear.
Dance breast to breast and cheek
to cheek
'Till the early dawn leaves me weak.

Then to an all night cafe to go
To eat a bit to calm me so—
So I, in bed, can drift to sleep
And dream sweet dreams while in
the deep.
I rise again after the noon
To dance again under the moon.

OH, how lonely the evenings are
When the clouds hide the
night-time star.
I'm now in the evening of life;
All through with the struggle and
strife.
I still want to dance and be gay;
Like I did in my youthful day.

Paula Lonardo Paliotta
MY SPECIAL LOVE
My Special Love is always there,
He knows when I need Him no
matter
What time of day or night;
His time is Endless . . .
He comforts me when I'm down;
So He can lift me up.
When I'm ill He heals me;
If I need a friend I can trust,
He's there for me . . .

He will never Lie or Deceive me;
He fills the emptiness inside
With His Spirit and Love:
He will be your lover or your friend;
What ever you want Him to be . . .
He never turns His back on me;
He's always there . . .
He Died for me; a Sinner; and
His name is "JESUS"
MY SPECIAL LOVE

Elsie E Bowles
LET US GO CAROLING
Come now and let us go caroling
At this glad Christmastime.
We'll sing to the aged and shut-ins
While the bells in the steeple chime.

We will sing about the angels
Who announced the Christchild's
birth.
"Glory to God in the highest" was
the message
They brought, and "Peace, good
will on Earth."

We will go to a street in the city,
And glad tidings there proclaim.
"Joy to the world, the Lord is come,
Let earth receive her King."

And then as our final number,
Which we hope will bring good
cheer,
We will wish all a "Merry
Christmas"
And a joyous "Happy New Year."

Tracy M Noble
ONE STEP

To Delvin, My One Step

Dew drops on the petals of the
roses that I carried.
It wasn't stones or precious metals
that I wanted us to be married.
I walked down the aisle for better
or for worse
Standing at the altar, I looked into
your eyes.
I saw all the love that never could
falter.
You smiled as I started to cry.
The reverend started saying the
words that bound us together.
I shut my eyes and prayed, "Let this
love last forever."
The vows were spoken, the rings
exchanged.
You whispered, "This is just the
beginning.
This marriage of ours will be never
ending."

D R Mirabal
DEPRESSION
Depression is
An obsession
Sometimes
Puddles of sad
Drip, drip, drip
Down my cheeks
Disappointments
Are counted like sheep
On a sleepless night

Kimberly Wagner

Kimberly Wagner
CANDY WRAPPERS
Candy wrappers all around,

I pick them up when they are found.

The candy was good by-golly,

But when I had to pick up wrappers,

I wasn't very jolly.

Didi Panos
FOR A STRICKEN GODDESS
The lonely wind will whimper to the skies,
The lonely eagle drop his wings and drift
Where fleet Diana broken-hearted lies,
Her vibrant soul in tatters, and her shaft
Cleft raggedly. Then all the mournful wood
With one accord its fallen nymph will cry,
Stange elfin voices mingle in a flood—
(They had not known that she could also die)—
The somber morning twilight soft will lay
Across her ashen cheek, across her breast
A gentle shroud. And so at last the day,
A cheerless dawn, a dawn stillborn, unblest,
Will creep and peer and find the Huntress there,
The sad wind gently fluttering her copper hair.

Debbie A Polen
TIGHTROPE
I've never walked a tightrope before:
I am now.
To maintain my balance is to understand you.

But I'm not steady yet—
At least not all the time.
I quaver and shake, but I curl my toes around
that rope as tightly as I can—
Determined to stay on.
My feet hurt,
but I don't care—
Because if I fall, I will hurt much more.

Katherine Hope Woodruff
GLASS TREES
The sun catches in their icy limbs and leaves,
making them seem of glass.

To touch them would break them
so you watch silently.

The sun fades and the moon is born
and still you watch as God's beautiful
gift melts little by little.

The icy drops fall onto the crystal white
carpet below until the glass trees
are no more than icy puddles on the
ground.

You walk away from the once
beautiful sight, thinking things
are always different under the surface.

Carolyn Ann Kern
THE UNIVERSE
Have you ever laid upon the ground, and looked up at the stars?
And wondered, who cannot believe in the creator when you gaze at Mars?
Every planet, every galaxy exactly in the right place
Our beautiful earth spinning round and round way out there in space.
Have you ever wondered of those fluffy clouds floating in the baby blue of the sky
Oh what a lovely sight for the tired old eye If I could only look up and see our Father standing there His sandled feet upon a cloud looking down at me oh how happy just His face to see
This beautiful universe He created and gave to you and me.

Susan Vollkommer
THE ANNIVERSARY PARTY

To Mom and Dad, with love

It was three months late but fun just the same.
We all got together to celebrate your day.
Clyde and Polly Cassidy, Charles and Helen Nichols,
Uncle David and Aunt Mary, Uncle Peter and Aunt Martha.
Mr. and Mrs. Raymond Chapin brought their daughter Carol.
Bob and Cheryl were there too, complete with cake and crutches.
Larry, Kathy, and Eric, who donated their house;
Pete and I with Angela and Scott
Ed and Mitchell, too.
We all were there to make for you the happiest day of all.
Kathy cooked a gourmet dinner and served it buffet style.
No one even noticed that the china was the kind you throw away.
Cheryl baked a two-tiered cake,
(the third tier wouldn't fit.)
The top, itself, was rather plain
The one she truly planned to use had been thrown away!
When everyone had eaten and the last dish put away,
We all went out to sit in the yard and enjoy the lovely fall day.
Now the party is over, everyone has gone home;
But the prayer in our hearts is the same—
That the next twenty-five years of marital bliss
Be as happy as those in the past.
Happy 25th Wedding Anniversary.

Mrs Anna May Rookard
MY LETTER TO GOD

This poem is dedicated to my family and best friends

Dear God can you hear me?
Can you understand
Things that happen to us
Are all made by man

Can you lift the pain? I ask
So we can understand
We know you are there for us
To lend a helping hand

I thought I'd write a letter
To let you know we're here
To ask you to give us strength
To you we do appeal

God this is no insult
For I know you bear pain too
You put us here on earth
To do what we can do

We know the pain that you have beared
Has come down on us too
All I am asking, Is your help
Just to make it through

If you can do this for us
Just help us understand
We know the Supreme being
Is above all man

Charlotte R Luedtke
USER'S
No matter what I do,
I can never please you.
You hurt me in so many ways,
I just wish you were in my shoes,
For the way I feel for you.
I don't understand why you treat me this way.
Why can't you see how much love and sympathy
I have for.
Love is never true!
I had a dream, but it went down the stream
Don't use me, please!
You really don't want to confuse me.
Do you?
Please, I only ask this once just understand me and
Maybe we can be true.
Just don't be a user; because
User's don't get any further with me
Can't you see!

Gail Stapf
THE TOUCHSTONE
Small and smooth it lays in my hand.
At first it is cool and aloof,
As my fingers stroke its surface.
Slowly it warms to my restless touch,
Summoning the serenity
From deep within a troubled soul,
Reflecting a universe
In its myriads of patterns.
Even in darkness it assures
That all the jagged edges
Gradually will be worn away,
If I have the patience to wait,
For time's gentle, healing touch.

Bertha Munson
TELL ALL TO GOD

Dedicated to my family, especially my Mom and Dad

When all is lost and you feel forlorn,
The panic inside you, sets off the alarm.
It's time to sit down, in your own private room, and
Tell all to God, he'll show what to do.

When the children are fighting and not minding you right,
The bedlam goes on, far into the night.
When you're seeking an answer, but none is there.
Tell all to God, he's always up there.

When bills are due and the money is not.
Don't get upset and upset "Pop."
Just open your Bible where God tells you to.
Tell all to God and your troubles are through.

Life seems to get easier and more comfortable too.
The children get better in minding you.
Due bills are paid, not a moment too soon.
Just tell all to God, His love really blooms.

Cyl Dawson

Cyl Dawson
SEPARATION

To my parents, Paul and Martha Crosby. Thank you for the courage, love and freedom to create and thank you, God, who gives these things to each of us.

The teacup crack travels upward—
cutting and slashing with oblivion's need.

Wind around the fissure holding earth's end—

trying to patch the gap with tiny
threads of longing.

Steps can't be retraced, dreams
won't stand—
while the blue and brackish tides
of reality wash over all.

The original picture blurs out
slightly—
sadly it slips away,
down a velvet face, full of
salt-water tears.

Deborah Ann Deakins
MY DEAR GRANDMOTHER

She had so many ways about her,
that people loved her so,
she was always there to help
even people she didn't know.
She always had a smile on her face,
hardly ever would she shed a
tear,
she took so many things in her
hands, holding on without a fear.
Her most favorite things were her
gardens of flowers, not just one
but every kind,
she worked so hard till they
looked just right, and she never
seemed to mind.
She was a good wife and Mother,
and to many people a special
friend,
she was always there beside you
till the very end.
Her life was such a happy one, she
lived the fullest everyday,
but then there came a time for
her when she had to go away.
She's living in a world where there
is no pain, for she has found
peace in heaven above
where God will take care and
watch over her in his home of
freedom and love.
Silent tears, I felt, upon my face,
as I watched us say good-bye to
her,
we will never forget the love she
gave us, she was so precious and
pure.
Loving us was what she did best,
and loving her we will forever
cherishing all the moments, we
had once shared together.
She would want us to go on and
live our lives as she were here,
for she's left us with the
memories, our hearts will hold
so near.
As I finally let go at the end of this
page, I'll set her free
forevermore,
she's filled my life with love and
joy as I've said before.
I hope we'll have the strength to go
on with our lives, to be there
when in need for each other,
remembering her for who she
was, rest in peace My Dear
Grandmother.

Mary Jean Carlson
FOR SUCH A LITTLE WHILE

This is for the loving memory of our one & only daughter. Through her inspiration and God's help, emotions now flow forth in a whole new outlet (simple & meaningful) and I love it!!!

After giving birth to two boys
who grew up so fine and all;
It was great to have a little
daughter . . .
so precious, so small!
Little did we know then . . .
she was to be ours for such a
little while!!!

We named her Julie for
that was simple, yet sweet!
The Lord said "She's yours now . . .
Take care of her for me; she's not
yours to keep!"
We didn't know then the plan
was . . .
she could be ours for such a little
while!!!

We knew deep inside that
her precious years would be few!
But our blind faith . . .
and hope clouded our view!
It is good we didn't truly know
then . . .
she would be ours for such a
little while!!!

The love in her heart and
smile on her face made her
special to all!
To us, with her light so a glow . . .
her other problems seemed so
very small!
God said "Love her, teach her all
that you can . . .
She's only yours for such a little
while!!!"

Those eight and a half years
were such a big part of our lives!
But someday, He will also take
us . . .
that plan was made from the
time of our birth!
We will be together again, all
happy and whole . . .
but this time <u>not</u> for such a little
while!!!

"SUCH A SPECIAL—LITTLE
WHILE"

Michelle Parker
THE LONELINESS

Loneliness is a terrible thing,
Can't laugh, smile, nor sing.
No one around you. No one's there.

No one to say (Hey I care).
Taken for granted, they say
"It was his time"

But deep inside, "You cry."
Most people say "It's best."
But I know different.
Because I live with the
loneliness.

Sandra MacTavish
MY ONE SELF

I look upon the mirrored glass
The image I see is me
But there's more than just the
reflection
Something deeper, I believe

Full of emotions, negative and
positive
There's a feeling, a sense of
belong
To grasp this uncertain tendancy
Can be quite beneficial—
I'm strong

To thrust oneself under the sky
of blue
To seek inside, going deeper
Realize expectations, even
limitations
Seems more gratifying, less
bleaker

I'm just human, I can make
mistakes
But I can make happiness, too
Just remember the most important
task
Is to first know you love you.

Carolyn A Perkins
IT ONLY TAKES

For Scotty—Michelle—N—Hawley with love forever your Mom

It only takes a heart to try
It only takes a tear to cry

It only takes a soul to love
To bind as one with the Lord above

It only takes the Lord to help us
walk
As it took another to teach us to talk

To right the wrongs
To learn how to forgive
To free the heart
To learn to live

To laugh, to smile, through pain
and sorrow
It takes the Lord to see tomorrow

It only takes the bad to see the good
To do the things we really should
It takes love to make things right
To turn us gently into His light

It only takes a heart to try
It only took a tear to cry

Frank Massaro
ONE MAN

Dedicated to my wife Maureen and daughters Valerie, Diane and Victoria.

One man who stands so fearless
Against the odds of ten
Who has fought his battles fearless
Can fight them once again.
Though his name has not the glory
Among the honored few
To me he is a hero
And he's honored through and
through.

Ivan D Franklin-Rusinsky

Ivan D Franklin-Rusinsky
**I WISH I WERE A
MEADOWLARK**

To Jeane J. Kirkpatrick, an American inspiration

This Country is my home and love
for ever,
I to the Nation under God belong;
I wish I were a meadowlark in
heaven
and sprinkled all her fields with
thankful song.

God bless America with strength
and glory,
a lighthouse of the universal sea!
Let folks of all the lands hear
every morning
the horn of peace, the bell of
liberty!

You ask why I am filled with such
devotion—
The stretch of land called simply
USA
is just a space from Ocean to the
Ocean
where also people toil and children
play. . .

God blessed America with
Freedom's glory,
a lighthouse of the universal sea;
the folks of all the lands hear
every morning
the horn of peace, the Bell of
Liberty.

Sandra L Fourqurean
CASE #419

They gave me the bare
necessities
of life.
School Cafeteria apple sauce
plus red and white cartons
containing a half a pint of milk.
Clothes that were always
dirty—too small—never too
big.
I guess they didn't want me
getting attached to things,
please see,
their jobs don't deal very often
with permanency.

They sent me to public school
to learn.
Subjects like math, history,
English, science, plus other
lessons
that I shouldn't have had to
discern.
Children laughing at me
and—pointing always—never
being kind.
I guess they haven't ever been
like me, who is
homeless, with
no one to bestow even a little
permanency.

They took me to the courts
of children.
Hard, wooden slippery pews
plus thick air and ladies
quietly, nicely telling me what
to do.

People talking all about me—poor thing—never with me.
I guess they didn't understand but
tried anyhow, then found a home
for me with a mother, a father, and
a permanency.

Solomon Jones
HALLELUJAH-HALLELUJAH
HALLELUJAH-HALLELUJAH,
Praise be the name,
Of the one that lives in heaven,
The place of which I aim.

HALLELUJAH-HALLELUJAH,
Believe He is alive,
Place yourself at his altar,
And give him your lives.

HALLELUJAH-HALLELUJAH,
I feel good just knowing,
That He's by my side,
To show me where I'm going.

HALLELUJAH-HALLELUJAH,
Serve him with all your heart,
He'll pick you up when you're down,
And show you how to start.

HALLELUJAH-HALLELUJAH,
He'll never give up on you,
Just whisper a little prayer,
HALLELUJAH, He'll see you through.

Spencer L Shaver
THE MAIDEN
Within the garden, through the mist,
a maiden lays awaiting.
Like roses stems, so frail and weak,
for love to come again.
I cannot help but see her cry
and give to her my heart.
But not unlike the roses stem,
with thorns sharp and ever piercing,
My bosom feels her deadly sting
and love, hence forth, depart . . .
Awaken I to find that all my visions were a dream
and the maiden I envision
I find I am still yearning.
And though my brow be draped with sweat
and my heart be filled with pain,
I slowly close my eyes
and pray I dream of her again.

Richard DiGiacomo
JUST FRIENDS
It's Killing me slowly
And You're holding the gun
pressed to my lips.

I gave you roses.

You kissed my cheek.

Pushing the knife
closer to my heart
And you don't realize what you are doing.

Tell me how cute he is
when we sit together
Or just grab the juglar.

You call me up
But no longer does my heart leap.

We go out together
My fantasy
realized by others but not us.

It's killing me slowly
Nobody knows it.
And when I awake to her mean streak
I promise to be celibate I lied!

Michael P Lynch
MR DAVIS
there's dust on the table
now but not before
there used to be alot of times
there'ld be meals and people
but not anymore

it really is a wooden floor
it creaks and makes noises
he never really thought of the noises
until it became so quiet

it was so goshdarn bothersome
all the doings and carring ons
he was too old for all this nonsense
she nagged life into his brooding

but even as a toll of life
her snip and punch were constant
he never was really satisfied with her
though he grew use to complaining

now of course he knows the floor
he knows every noise of quiet
dust will settle on her half of the house
and he won't understand its growth

there is the habit of sleeping on only one side
of the bed
and there is the habit of crying
he remembers she had the darnest coldest feet
and he remembers habits of crying

Victoria Lynn Lang
EMPTINESS
The soul is empty and dark,
With loneliness scorched through and through.
The heart is overcome with a neverending pain,
With scarred memories of loving you.

Nothing in the world seems to matter.
Thoughts of suicide coming strong,
But that is a sin I can't commit,
For I have loved God for so long.

None will ever guess I wished for death,
I've hid my wounds so well.
I never intended to hurt anybody,
But no one realizes I was put through hell.

Doris Ellis
FARMER BROWN
There was this farmer whose name was Brown,
Every pay day, he went to town,
Brown could never find enough to do,
Except eat, drink, complain and chew,
He read the American Agricultrist and liked Mirandy,
He also liked a six pack handy,
One morning about ten, he went to get a drink,
Came home to milk the cows at eleven, figured they were on a blink,
He phoned the veterinarian shortly before noon,
After doing this he sobered up soon,
Mr. Brown figured, this was one foolish call,
So farmers, never mix your work with alcohol.

Mary Sue DeFoe
MY MOM MY FRIEND

To my Mom, my dearest friend who passed away June 6, 1986. My children and I took her out for her birthday dinner. She passed away within 5 minutes after returning home.

Friends could I take a little of your time
To tell you about a "special" friend of mine
She was such a grand lady in every way
That God made her birthday a very special day
My children and I took her out to dine
Not realizing she had such a very short time
She got a call later that same day
Another celebration would soon be underway
She was invited to the house of Our Father Above

To be with her son, and others to share her love
Just as she had always done down here on earth
My Mother wore a crown of jewels on her rebirth
I miss her so much, Oh don't you see
Selfish is something that I must be
But Mom I'm trying hard to understand
And someday we'll meet in that great land
There will be no more sorrow and strife
At our family reunion in another life
Until then, Mom I make you this vow
I'll love you then, as much as I do now

Jack Virgil
FATHER'S DAY

To my father Augustine Vigliotti from his son Joseph.

Three cheers for Dad on Father's Day; That old forgotten man,
Who does so much for all of us, but never gets a hand.
Remember when we were just kids, the alarm clock would ring and say;
Tho' Dad I know you're sleepy yet, you've got to work to-day.
Why Junior needs a pair of shoes, and Sis could use a dress;
You've got to work to buy these things, to help them look their best.
Mother's hat is kind of shabby, her coat's torn here and there;
You know the neighbors like to talk, though Mother doesn't care.
Your boss has made it kind of tough, for you to grin and bear;
But don't forget the kids must eat, the cupboard's almost bare;
The boss would like to see you quit, he makes you feel so small;
You just hang on you need the cash; when bill collectors call;
And most of all, don't you forget, the kiddies' education,
You'll have to work an extra job, While others take vacation.
Yes, all these things and plenty more, The alarm clock seemed to say;
So even when Dad was real sick, he went to work that day.
He just forgot about himself, for Junior, Sis, and Ma,
And only lived if we made good, to say 'I am their Pa.'
So if you think you're doing better; than Dad did in his day;
You can thank your good old Dad, For what you are to-day.

Patty Hoye Ashworth
AFTERGLOW

This poem is dedicated to my loving husband, HERBERT RAY ASHWORTH, who gives me inspiration every day of my life.

I can't go on with you this way, I've said it all before,
But when it comes to leaving you, I can't walk out that door;
There's nothing here to stop me now, you won't ask me to stay,
'Cause you could hurt me one last time by sending me away.

I think that I stopped loving you, I guess some time ago,
It was not my choice alone, I had to let you know
That when you want to hurt me now, don't bother, do not try,
'Cause you don't know me anymore, and you won't see me cry.

I believe that love can give the best we've ever known,
But why am I this close to you and feeling so alone;
I'd gladly give a try if you would ony let me through,
But I'll not try all by myself, I'll just wait for you.

I must be feeling something, for the hurt won't go away,
And I can tell, just like the rest, today won't be the day;
Don't give up on love today, although your eyes are dry,
Love, don't you give up on us, for I don't want to cry.

Maybe someday you and I will know just where we stand,
Who can say, you may reach out and even take my hand;
And if it's not too late by then, or if we'll ever know,
I've heard it said that embers give a lovely AFTERGLOW

Dee Hughes
SAMPLES OF HEAVEN

To God, our Creator, who gave us the five senses to be able to appreciate His "Samples of Heaven." He knew we would need a lift along the rocky paths of life.

I gently touched the keys—
Music flowed with melodious ease.
"If I gained the world"
Was the song my fingers unfurled.
My soul became a part
Of each note, filling my heart.
My whole being chilled with happiness,
Just a sample of Heaven, I guess.

I walked amongst the hills one day,
(How they rolled in their gentle way),
A blanket of green for half their face,
Eyes of wisdom brown, all in place.
What joy to behold such land!
Hate vanisheth with beauty so close at hand.
My whole being chilled with happiness,
Just a sample of Heaven, I guess.

I listened in the still of the night,
One as velvet black as the other snowy white.
Without a doubt, when their talk did end
I knew that each was the other's friend.
What courage to want to understand and know,
And with a forward step to say, "My Brother, hello."
My whole being chilled with happiness,
Just a sample of Heaven, I guess.

Maria T Celestial
DESTINY OF WORLD'S DIRECTION

To Letitia, my daughter, and Frank, my loving husband

How is our destiny in this world to show,
if our future seems bright, will it's light always glow?
Do we expect happy moments to last,
or must we fear of our tragic past?
If we appreciate and respect every creature,
will our world maintain harmonious feature?
We develop our patterns for our advancement,
and determine the designs for our achievement.
The way we expect our lives to be,
is what the world around us would see.
With proper guidance and great protection,
our world could be lead in the right direction.
How must we value our world of tomorrow?
Must we build it with love, or ruin it in sorrow?
Must we be alert of unexpected moments,
or relax and pretend there's no danger of opponents?
In a world of exploration, and competition,
mustn't we be prepared for opposing instrusion?
So let's be aware of interceptions,
which are hampering our world's right directions?
How then, must we determine this world's right direction?
Could we clearly define the direct route
toward it's positive motivation?
What values must the world possess
to maintain outstanding peaceful reputation?
Surely! Knowledge, honesty, confidence, patience,
cooperation, faith, and determination.

Leta Ferola Watkins
THE SEASONS OF OUR MARRIAGE
Come walk with me, my love . . .
Our spring we shared laughter,
Blessed with hope and joy.
Our love seeds blossomed into children
Our love, time could not destroy

Come walk with me, my love . . .
Our summer brought searing pleasure,
Singed a bit by pain
But as you drew me closer
Sunbeams outshined our rain

Come walk with me, my love . . .
It is the hue of Autumn
We now in wisdom share
Our children are begetting their children
Your kisses, I still proudly wear

Come walk with me, my love . . .
May in our Winter we feel
Each other's warmth, despite the cold
Our snuggly embraces
Will be a unique blending of our married soul

Come walk with me, my love . . .

Larry Richardson
LOVESONG

To my moms, "cookie," my two sons, Darryl and Jimmy and to my lovely Granddaughter, Shanequa.

I see you as beauty personified
beyond cosmetic guise
undaunted by fear/doubts and remorse
a vision to my eyes.

You're lovely as a crisp, clear dawn
above the mundane thoughts
that drown nearly all of us
in its one relentless course.

With a smooth demeanor all your own
that distances the guile of pose
you're a star with a shining soul
brighter than any rose.

Ramona L J Taylor
PRESSING MIND
Bearing body
Pressing mind
To free from bondage
A form alien to my sight
But its touches are familiar
As the pebbling beads of rain
Along my tired, swollen feet
And hands craving
The softness of
Tiny toes and bottom.

Bracing, slowly,
My pressed mind,
I arch my sight
And pant my lungs
And feel the tightness
Give way to the rush,
Much like a fall.

Filling my chest
With the sharpness
Of fatigue
Pat my flat stomach.

Debby Marlin Green
BE A BRAVE SOUL
Arise from your fall—
you don't have to crawl;
Climb to your feet—
you need not know defeat;
Don't ever lose hope—
it's the only way to cope;
Be a brave soul—
make that your goal;
Hold on to your dreams—
don't fall apart at the seams;
Climb up the tree—
you shall soon be free;
Remember . . . there's
always tommorrow—
to forget your sorrow;
Keep your spirits high and . . .
you will always fly high.

Rosemary Baker
EARLY MORNING SHADOWS
Early morning shadows,
Seem to follow me;
As the sun shines through the window,
How peaceful it can be;
The morning with all its beauty,
A great and wonderous thing;
It makes it all worth getting up,
To see what this day brings;
All the happiness of living,
Will fill my heart each day;
And for every new morning I am given,
The night before . . I'll pray;
Pray for another morning,
Just like the one before;
Just open up the window,
Or open up the door;
Just open up your heart,
And let the sun shine in;
And let the beautiful morning,
Let a new life begin.

Yolanda Michelle Shaw

Yolanda Michelle Shaw
WHY SO LONG?
Why so long—
to rejoice and sing,
for the birth of MARTIN LUTHER KING!!

It's been eighteen years since his past,
Our love for him will last and last.

Why so long—
for them to consider,
are they really that bitter?
Why didn't they realize?
Just stop and think don't criticize.

Martin had many dreams,
That brought him to the extreme supreme.

Why so long—
to finally start celebrating,
the man that started the Civil Rights Demonstrating!

He is missed by many far and near,
For this I know is very clear.

There is still one question I want the answer to,
That brings a dark cloud over me and you.

Why did it take so long?
to finally give in to the throng;
to rejoice and sing—
for the birth of MARTIN LUTHER KING!!!

Leola Terry
THAT CAT
That cat was just within my reach,
His eyes and mine did dare to meet,
There in my hand I held a treat,
He sat there perched upon his seat.
Out came his tongue so swift and neat,
He stole the treat and he did eat.
I thought aloud he did me cheat,
But then he snuggled at my feet.

Gloria Parks Crawford
JASON

Thanks to my husband, son, Roger, and family who believe in me as a poet, this poem is in loving memory of my son, Jason.

It hurts when I think of what you might have been
But maybe your way is easier than what mine has been
To never breathe the air as I doesn't mean you're unknown
You'll always hold that part of me no one else can own
I know I've asked myself a million times why
And at night in my dreams I can hear you cry
At last I can rest a little easier as I've found
It is our way of communicating the profound
As even with death doesn't erase how much we love
And unties our souls in eternity above . . .

Jennifer Lynn Clemans
FOLLOWING BY THE SEA

This poem is dedicated to my loving husband, Troy, for helping me in following my dreams.

Following by the sea
The footprints in the sand
Leading to my dreams
Of a far away land

Enchantment by the miles
White sand stretches too
Opening to the waters
Rich in tones of blue

An invitation of a sort
An opportunity given to all
To see the great waves
As they rise and fall

A symphony of nature
Created by His hand
The gulls calling to us
As they fly above the strand

This beauty be endless
As I follow by the sea
Many treasures await us
If you care to follow me.

Mary Jane Sparks
LITTLE CHRIST CHILD (GOD'S WONDROUS GRACE)

Oh, little Christ Child, born in Bethlehem afar,
Thy timely virgin birth was her'lded by a star,
Proclaimed with joy by hosts of angels in the sky
To frightened shepherds watching o'er their flocks nearby.
God's Love was born on earth that night upon the hay;
Thou, Hope of all the world, within a manger lay.
Thy name was called Jesus— Saviour of sinful man,
Emanuel (God with us)—Let me understand!
Wise men sought to find Thee in that far eastern land;
And "wise men" seek to find Thee still, across time's span.
In lowly Naz'reth Thou didst grow to be a man,
Humbly yielding Thyself unto the Father's plan.
Oh, Thou didst wander homelessly in Galilee,
Treading the rocky paths with sinn'rs, yet sinlessly,
That on that darkest day in all eternity,
Thou couldst, in justice, die for me upon a tree;
But death could not contain Thee, Son of Life and Love —
Despair was turned to hope when Thou wast raised above!
Humbly I thank Thee, Lord, now Heavenly Royalty,
That by Thy wondrous grace, Thou dost now dwell in me.
My life is Thine—'tis new—the old has ceased to be.
Oh, risen Christ! Thou hast been born again—in me!

Elizabeth Juell
THE IMAGE OF LOVE

To Curt, who is the Image Of Love

He is trustworthy,
I can always count on him.
He is generous,
Giving of himself to others.
He is courteous,
You go first, my time will come.
He is thoughtful,
Always remembering special times.
He is charitable,
Helping others out of love.
He is loving, laughing, and giving,
He is my son.

Prescott Smith
LAS VEGAS

To Edwin Arlington Robinson

Here where the odds on life are one to none
And final payoffs are but green-smudged palms,
The Action fleeting fortune never calms
Engenders thoughts of quiet fields, of one
Who toils there—mixing sweat with day's fair sun
In earth that is the source and yields the balms
For hands so cracked from work—who has no qualms
Wrestling fate there, resting there when done.

The smooth hands here work quicker than the eye
And operate on land of grime-green felt,
Controlled by mammon-god—eye in the sky—
Who smiles as "wins" drool, as losing palms melt:
Greed's Kings and Queens must lose to Black Hand high
Before the end, where death is not to die.

Nancy Hughes
A NEW SEASON

To my friend, Rose Carlson, Phd., for walking not ahead of me, nor behind me, but beside me.

From a seedling,
I spring.
From beneath a strong blanket earth,
I arise. I am born.
My beginning is meek,
yet I persevere,
and reach my arms
toward an infinite sky.
I seek nourishment.
The sun, the rain, the air,
they strengthen me,
And I grow.
Slowly I begin to feel
that I am becoming stronger.
Harsh winds attempt to uproot me,
to whisk me away,
But I am firmly set in place.
My reach has extended to beyond the sky,
And I begin to blossom.
I dare to share my goodness,
the fruits of my growth,
and in giving,
I am reborn.

Ms Helen Head
LIFE

This poem has been dedicated to me.

Life is so beautiful if only I would open my eyes and start walking.

Life is the bird who whispers a song to me.

Life is what God gave to me. He said, "Take it and enjoy it to the fullest, until the last minute."

Don't waste yesterday for today. Live today and think about what tomorrow will bring.

Marilyn Stephens
THE BLUEBIRDS

To Honor My Mom; "Thora."

These bluebirds have dropped by to say; hope you're feeling better today.
They bring sunshine, cheer, and much happiness to you, hoping by now you're over the flu.
When you are sitting in your hospital bed; thinking you'd rather be home instead.
Just think of the bluebirds their songs they tell, hoping that mother dear will soon be well.
May God send sunshine into your room, to take away some of the gloom.
He sends his love and blessings too; and your daughter sends all of hers for you.

Amen!

Sandra Fury
TWO HAPPY HEARTS

Like early morning mist upon the daisys,
Fresh and warm like rays of summer sun,
Your smile, your touch, your everything,
And in my heart, I know, you are the one.

Your strong caress, but gentleness,
The little things you do;
Your subtle ways, that make my days,
This tells my heart it's you.

Our love could climb the highest peaks,
Sit quiet by a stream;
Blossom in a forest dense,
Or fields of ivy green.

In a shock without its' windows,
Or a marbled mansion white;
It needs no special place to grow,
This tells my heart its right.

Beneath the stars, Upon a blanket,
A full moon lights the night,
I feel your breath upon my skin,
Two happy hearts unite.

Geneva R Marshall
GOD IS OUR ANSWER

To my husband, George

How little we know
As we start out in life
How things would be
And how hard to understand
Which is the right things for us to do
Or the right places to go
I guess it wasn't meant for us to understand everything
No matter what we undertake to do
But to have faith that we can and must do it
No matter how hard the task may be.
Life will not always be jolly
With all the trials and temptations
As we travel on many roads of disappointments.
We stop and ask ourselves
Wy must we have all these things?
So, remember no matter where we may be
Whether far or near
That God is our answer, our hope and our happiness.

Melissa Ann Clark
THE LITTLE DOG IN THE WINDOW

Look at the little dog in the window,
His fur looks just like snow,
Wouldn't you like to have him?
Well, gee, I don't know.
He looks so sad and lonely,
But I guess I'll never know,
For someone just bought that little dog sitting right here in the window.

Mary A Fontana
STILL IN FLIGHT

"To the Challenger" and "The Seven Fallen Astronauts" 1-28-86

The day was bright
The sky was blue
One by one they came in view
So proud, to be wearing their suits of blue
With a smile on their face, and a wave of their hand
All too soon they were up in space.

Suddenly then, that awful sound and everything was coming down
Seven beautiful people so brave and true.

No more was the sky so blue,
nothing more to say or do
Our hearts are saddened, eyes filled with tears
We shall remember them all through the years.

Gone are they now
Gone but forever still in flight.

Rhenda Horvath
WINTER MEMORIES

Joseph with his chubby cheeks
Puppy with his leaping feet
Together they romp and play
especially on a snowy day
Joseph laughs and puppy barks
Both are filled with happy hearts
They run and leap in piles of snow
Master and pup have a healthy glow
Sister Mary joins the fun
Now all three are on the run
Laughter and yelps fill the air
None of the three have a care
I open the door and look outside
my heart fills with pride
Rosy cheeks and laughing eyes
Sparkling snow and sunny skies
All these things are memories
To warm a mother's heart, like me!

Tiffany C Ava
WHAT IS A FRIEND?
A friend is
someone who is
always there when
you need them
most even when
you don't a
friend is someone
who you can
talk about your
problems with no
matter how great
or small. A
friend is someone
to share life's
exciting moments with
At times an
unkind word might
be spoken but
soon it is
forgiven for true
friends last forever.

Tammy E Futej
CAROL ANN

In memory of Carole Ann Arbogast
To a beautiful and warm person
who had a heart as precious as gold.
I will always love you mom.

I tell the story, and yet I know full well,
the half was never, never told,
the half I cannot tell.
I love you so dearly, mother,
I know the feelings are shared with my brothers.
We are told the hurt will go away.
But as the years we know it will stay.
From my heart falls the tears of sorrow,
Knowing that for you there will never be a tomorrow.
Filling the puddles of loneliness, hoping
God will take the naked feelings and fully dress.
I reach my heart & hand out for my mothers touch, telling myself every night "she's still here," using it as a crutch.
You gave so much to all six of your children, we know, you gave every minute, your heart, your mind & soul.
No matter how strong the sun may shine, I'll never forget a thing about you because you're part of my mind.

Barbara Silver
ETERNITY
A friendship that would last through eternity,
We laughed
We shared
We cherished
Changes occured,
Days would pass.

As I thought—
My eyes gleamed of happiness,
Is this an impossible dream?
Does he understand?

Deep conversations—
Yet nothing said,
His eyes showed warmth
His voice spoke sweet,

I wish I could understand
His feelings
His thinking,
Will we meet again?

Margaret C Cole
SPRING
Budding trees and birds that sing;
These are signs of early spring.
Soft breezes stir, the air is warm
Bees are buzzing and ready to swarm.
Rain showers come to dampen the earth
And water the flowers to give them new birth.
Dormant bulbs know that now it's time
To lift their heads, each and every kind.
Daffodils and crocus too
Blossom forth; it's SPRING in view.

Patricia J Combs
A BETTER WAY
Why must people always hurry?
Like rats in cages, they must scurry.
This world would be a better place
If smiles would appear upon each face.

People these days are disconcerted.
No one speaks, they're introverted.
I myself can't understand
Why we can't go, all hand in hand.

Helping each other, everyday,
Not ignoring neighbors, feet of clay.
How long was it since you walked
In the park and stopped and talked?

Smiles grinning ear to ear,
Helping hands, bringing cheer?
I myself hope things will change,
Looks on faces rearrange.

Corners of lips will not droop down
So far down they touch the ground.
Instead twist upwards to the sky,
Grins and laughter, morn' and nigh.'

I can see it now in my mind's eye
Smiling, laughing, never a sigh.
Wouldn't this world a better place be
If each of us a smile could see.

Xochitl M Fernandez

Xochitl M Fernandez
VACATION DREAM

To My Loving Daughter, Rosa

With fog and smoke, the scene is muted.
The air is dense and so polluted.
You feel the need for clime ozonic
Out where the air is like a tonic,
For your sinusitis cronic.
Away from all the grime and noise
Can't even hear the human voice.

Oh, for the lonely stretch of road
And driving on without a word.
'Til suddenly you come upon
A rivulet and grazing herd;
And here and there some big oak trees
And flowering fields for honey-bees.
One just forgets the city traffic
With scenes like these so fotographic.

Grace E Hall
A LITTLE BOYS' DREAM

To my wonderful grandson LCPL
Michael A. Bales Camp LeJeuene,
North Carolina

Just a small boy with a great big dream
of how he would grow to be a great big marine,
Learning to march and the right way to salute
and of all the guns he would shoot.
What fun it was going to be, boarding a huge ship
and sailing off to sea!
All of this he was to do serving his country
under the red, white, and blue.
The little boy grew and turned eighteen and said, "It's time
I'll be a marine," traded his jeans for a service mans'
suit and started out to be a recruit. I'm sure it
wasn't quite like his dream, yet he's proud to be that marine.
Basic was hard and oh, what long miles. He was
glad to rest for a while. Leave was short and ending all too soon.
Now a P.F.C. stationed at Camp LeJeuene, A few more days and he
will board that ship and sail the sea.
I'm sure it won't be just as he dreamed
yet he's proud to be a marine.
Standing so tall at 6 foot two serving his counrty under the red, white, and blue.

Velma G Adkisson
NEW EXPERIENCES
Today I earned my wings
And became aware of things
When turned loose to roam
Gram's house at my own will.
I explored things from the floor
That from her arms I saw before
And how different life became,
'twas quite a thrill.

How interesting to see
Threads and things were left for me
On her rugs in every room I found a scrap.
It was difficult to crawl
'Cause my hands became so full
Then Grandma said, "Our family's got one more pack rat."

She put a sucker in my hand
And in my mouth it went, My land
A good taste like this I never had before.
And gooey sticky as it was
From my clothes it gathered fuzz
And it picked up bits of junk and stuff galore.

Then she spoiled all my fun
When for a wash cloth she did run
And proceed to wash me from my shoes to head.
Now I ask, "Is that quite fair
To give me pleasure and then dare
To expect me to be happy in bed?"

Ellen Lorraine White Smith
COLORS IN HEAVEN
Colors light up a dreary sky shadowed by storm clouds rolling by . .
Storms are dark and shadow the light like in the darkest hour.
When the sun comes shining through, Oh the wonderous beauty there I see.
A lonely dove soars through the painted canvas of the western sky.
His heart soars as his love flies to greet him.
Through the the Northern sky covered in darkest grays
Trimmed with edges of brightest Golds and shimmering silvers to lighten up her way
Living colors painted by the brush strokes of the Masters Hand,
His concept of beauty causes me to stand in awe
As I watch the brush strokes of living colors, brighten up our day with warmth and love,
The Masters colors change and blend
As one fades anew begins on His canvas of living colors
He paints His beautiful paintings again and again.
All the beautiful paintings of man, cannot begin to compare
To the living paintings, of the Master Artist.

Nancy Rabalais Howard
NO ONE SO GREAT AS HE

To everyone who reads this poem. I hope you come to know the Lord as I have—Accept Him in your heart and put you life in His hands and you will be richly blessed.

He died for us what more could we ask?
There will never be another like him to cross our path.

He hung on the cross at Calvary
and suffered humiliation and
misery.
He was mocked, laughed at, even,
scorned and on his head was
placed a crown of thorns.
He suffered through this out of
love for man. For all the people
in all the land.
He died and was buried in a cold
dark cave and a rose again after
three days.
This day is called Easter. It's a very
great day.
He arose again and is here to stay.

Ida A Baldonado
FEELINGS

This poem is dedicated to Joe Angel, my loving husband.

I'm experiencing these Beautiful
Sensations
Hopes Turning Into Dreams
Dreams Succumbing Into
Reality

Oh! But Am I To feel
The Final Touch?

Total Ecstacy
The Heart
The Spirit
Then, The Body

Irene Thrasher
LIFE IS WORTH A SMILE
No one likes a griper,
Even tho' things go wrong—
So I'll take what life offers,
And hum a little song.

Yes; hum a song of gladness—
That I can thankful be;
For the good things life has offered
To poor unworthy me.

Tho' there may be days of sorrow;
Pain; worries and despair—
I'll just keep right on smiling,
As if I had never a care.

How true that old saying—
"Smile, and the world smiles too,"
But never; if you start crying—
Does the world cry with you.

Tho today may be blue,
Full of sadness and sorrow—
I'm sure there's bound to be
A better and brighter to-morrow.

So I'll do my best to keep smiling,
And I'm sure I'll happier be—
As I travel down life's pathway
To know the world smiles with me!

Rick Barnes
THE FEEDING OF CHOOCHEE B
It was during the year of eighty six
in the month of July
When my little sister Choochee B,
decided to come on by

Now Choochee B is the youngest
of six, raised by Mom and Dad
But not withstanding her order of
birth, she's the hungriest they
ever had

Breakfast, lunch, and dinner—all
have consumed her time
Thoughts of snacks and leftovers
continue to excite her mind

Our Chooch believes that nothing
in life surpasses the taste and
feel of jelly
As it enters your mouth, slides
down your throat, and plops into
your belly

One morning I awoke to find her
propped up on our kitchen table
Sucking the fillings out of Dunkin
Donuts and devouring all she
was able

It came to pass in July when we all
went out to eat
That our Choochee B committed
her greatest gastronomical feat

The stage was set at a local joint
called "Hals Eatery"
When dear Chooch showed her
stuff, to Mom, Hal, and me

Mom and I thoughtfully ordered
the ribs, a truly tasty dish
Our Chooch quickly ordered the
menu, everything but the fish

The burgers were followed by the
specials, the appetizers, entrees,
and dessert
And not once did we hear from
Chooch, a groan, growl, or a
burp

She finally pushed away the table
and waddled out the door
Leaving me to pay the entire bill of
two hundred and sixty four

"Hals" is now a shrine and
thousands come to see
The place where it all happened,
The Feeding of Choochee B

Ruth Naomi Morris

Ruth Naomi Morris
A REMEMBRANCE
Never knew love—
When trains were larger,
Trees were taller
And life was erroneous.

Never found love—
When all of springtime
Danced andante.

Never met love—when now
Trains aren't so large,
Trees aren't so tall,
And life is acceptable.

Ken Gaeddert
CRIMINAL BEGGAR
"Give me, give me" upon my breath
It matters not to whom I speak
All men are targets in this business
All men's pocketbooks I seek

'Persistance' is my secret tool
'Exhaustion' your final end
Get rid of me, please, I beg
A dollar or two in my hand

There is a major flaw in my scheme
I have an achilles heel
If you act as if you don't care I'm
around
I know I've blown the deal

There will be poor, always
Toward whom the rich will feel
guilt
A dollar or two in my hand
I'll have treated the symptom you
felt

I admit that my trade is undignified
I'm sure that you sense a scam
I take the alms which belong to the
poor
For me, that's business, my friend.

Joann Hallock
HEART-BROKEN-PERSON
Have I changed, I do not know,
Why do lonely days effect me so.
Of days of bore, Of days of want,
My heart tightly wrapped in a knot.
For I am too serious for my age,
Without your love, it's an empty
cage.
My heart is broken like a limb,
And just because the problems
of him.
I love no man hardly knew,
It's only one that makes me blue.
For you have left to run and tell,
That all my dreams are lost in hell.
For you used to hold me tight
and fast,
My prayers and dreams are in
the past.
No living man will meet my eyes,
For now I know I am too wise.
For I have dreamed of him and
seen,
Oh how could I pity and him be so
mean.
I found his sweetness lip to lip,
For now he's gone he took his pick.
When days were cold and winds
were rude,
He left me here in this lonely
mood.
For my loneliness walks with me,
To a heart-broken-person, as
you can see.

Carole E Morris
IS THERE SOMEONE ELSE?
"Is there life out there?" I pondered
As my eyes searched outer space.
Is this the only universe
with life and human race?

Are autumn leaves unique to earth?
And are flowers for us alone?
Is the joy of loving a new born babe
In other galaxies unknown?

Are war and peace exclusive
To this earth that we call home?
Or is there a place beyond the stars
Where love and pain are known?

I gaze again at the star-lit sky
from this place where Earthmen
trod.
And pray that if there's someone
else,
They've come to our God.

Diann B Fisher
THE SPIRIT OF HAMPTON ROADS

To my grandmother Caroline, daughter Nicole, mother Mary Ann and husband, King, who always believed in me.

Eastside. . .Waterside. . .Westside.
. .Portside.
Yorktown. . .Olde Towne. . .Great
Bridge. . .Sandbridge.
All across the James River Bridge.
Soldiers marching. . .Coast Guard
watching. . .Crackerjacks
harboring. . .
. . .Sandy-covered beaches. . .

Linda Schneider Mowry
BLIND IS HE

To Gertrude Meta Schneider. I love you mom.

Why couldn't he have seen
where it was really at
Before he became deceitful
at that

He hurt her in the end
when he sold his soul
With the other one it
was an equal blow

But as life shows
it's not the cruelty of those
Who are loved in the
end by one who knows

Love must have no
meaning to him
For if it did he would
have known

Henry O Johnson Jr
SEEK GOD FIRST
If you walk with God through this
earthly life,
You may desire a husband or wife.
We seek by sight and not by faith
God already has a perfect mate.
But: Seek me first oh child of
mine
Without my spirit you're
lost and blind
Is it my kingdom that you
cherish?
For if not your dreams will
perish
We pace the floor so fervently,
Searching for that someone
desperately.
God has work for us to do
But we sit around feeling sad and
blue.
But: Seek me first oh child of
mine
Without my spirit you're
lost and blind
God is jealous and very demanding,
But has lots of love and
understanding,
The person may be right, But the
time may be wrong

God says tary till he makes you strong,
Don't fuss or fight or put me to test,
For I am God and I surely know best,
But: Seek me first oh child of mine
Without my spirit you're lost and blind
Is it my kingdom that you cherish?
For if not your dreams will surely perish.

Elaine T Welch
WAITING FOR SPRING

To Bobby, Linda and Poochie, who endured that long winter and those awful cookies.

Gloomy winter, life's so boring;
noses pressed against the glass—

Mommy's mean and don't like children
to track in lots of mud and grass.

I think it's time I baked some cookies;
shapes and sizes to make then laugh.

I'll sure be glad when winter's over,
and we can give that dog a bath—

Dog and children in the house, each one
on the run—

Gloomy winter, can't stand waiting—
oh, look quick, is that the sun?

Bernadette Inkster
VISIONS OF DEATH

To my loving family and friends who have helped me get to where I am.

I see the brightness of the light,
and it slowly draws me there.
I suddenly think of leaving you,
and one last time I hold you near.

In the darkness of the night,
I see you lying there alone.
Taking one last look back at you,
my saddened heart turns cold as stone.

I will surely be missing you,
but with little to no avail.
My number was already picked,
and for God's sake I must not fail.

I sure wish you could follow me,
but you'll encounter me never.
Oh how I hate to be leaving you,
(but once I've passed through the light)
I will be with you forever.

Joy E Smith
SILENCE

Listen and you can hear the snow falling—
As loud as Cupid's arrow as it pierces the heart
As loud as a lover's silent shed tear
When you say we must part.

I know not how, I know not why
God made snow as loud as this—
As loud as anything the deaf may hear
As loud as one's secret thought of fear
As loud as the awakening of a new day
As loud as the setting sun
As loud as love when it's just begun.

Sheryl Leeson-Chomel
FOR MY SON (BEGINNING A JOURNEY)

Pale moon hangs low behind the clouds.
Stars shimmer, and I remember a colder night than this
When child gave way to woman and woman gave way to child
In brighter light than this and pain as swift as fire.

Younger then than you are now, I lay down shaking,
Alone with my pain and comforted by ignorance.
The rhythm of life begun months ago now became a truth.
Out of that night I carried love like a torch.
Love, older than ancient, would become my shadow.

So many years ago, before I ever knew you,
I swore an oath to teach you
The truths that I knew then and all that I would learn.

A thousand moons have passed, and now
It's a desperate future that I cling to.
It is yours.
All that I have lived for, since that pale moon long ago
Hangs in the balance.
Suddenly, I fumble for words and this cat-gotten tongue won't do.

The fear I feel for you is great. I do not want to fail.
Give me your hand to steady me
And your heart to give me courage.
Take one small step to give me hope
Until I learn to voice the language
That is the same one that you speak.

Doris R S Miller
I MET A MAN

To the man who inspired me to write this poem, the man I met, married and love, my husband Ray. . .

I met a man somewhere, one time, his face was kind and true:
a man that you could love and hold very close to you.
I met a man who really cared how I would think and feel, I met a
man so strong, and tall, so wonderful, so real.
He's made of all the little things that make you love him so, with
something about him almost heavenly that sets your heart aglow.
He doesn't wish for worldly goods, for all the wealth untold, he's
happy with the common things, his smile is worth more than gold.

He's humble, graceful, loving too, and more than I can say, I met
a man that I could love and want him just this way.
He likes the flowers, birds and trees, the moon that shines at night, the cats and dogs, all animals, but, not the ones that fight.
I met a man so good and true, sincere and yet so kind, I'm truly
glad I met this man, this type is hard to find.

Dana Lisa Phillips
LOVE SONG

Dedicated with much love to Mitch and Zoe Eichman, married on the thirtieth day of June, nineteen-hundred and eighty-seven.

When I fell in love with you, the moment was quick to take,
Love was all around us, the love we'd always make.
You held me in your arms close, love was oh so real,
Stars fell overhead, the night we'd always steal.

Hand and hand we'd wonder, through long lost lonely dreams,
We'd make up our own stories, and follow out our schemes.
At night you'd lay beside me, and whisper in my ear,
You'd whisper your sweet nothings, the things I'd long to hear.

You'd take me in your arms close, and look into my eyes,
You'd tell me that you love me, and wrap me up in ties.
Today we're still together, our love is still so new,
I sing to you this love song, as I say I do.

Debbie Craft
TOGETHERNESS

For L. D. with love D. C.

Togetherness, is a state of mind.
We can be alone, separated from each other and have
the feeling, of being together.
We can be together, and still have an unbearable sense
of loneliness.
At this time, we are miles apart,
And yet, we are still together.
Our minds, hearts and souls, are always tuned to the
same thing.
Whether it be happy or sad, good or bad,
We, are together.
We are together at this moment, and we have been in
the past.
No one, knows what the future will hold, until
it happens.
Your future is mine, as mine is yours.
Together, we will make it through, all the
troubled years.

Tammey Leona Northcraft
MERCY

Monsters from Eden hath no return,
storms from Heaven have rath not burn.
Twice was the coming,
yet the end be near,
soon no longer the earth to be here.

Let all man now plead Mercy from God above,
For he shall forgive sinners and every man Love.

What once the beginning, soon to end,
for earth to dust no man may mend.
For God is the creator of life divine,
and without God there is no life to find.

Now is the time for all man to plea,
storms from the oceans and the sea.
This is the warning from God above,
"Repent sinner and unto me love."

Iris B May
THE WAY I FEEL

The love I feel for you puts me
in a great mood,
I feel so happy I don't know
what to do . . .
I get this crazy feeling that
you love me too,
But, how am I to know if
you don't tell me so?
I feel like a princess in a
fairy tale book,
Who is waiting for her prince
to take a good look.
When I'm with you I feel so
warm inside,
But I can't make up my mind
to be by your side.
I feel like holding you close
all night . . .
Hugging you, loving you with
all my might.
When I look into your eyes, oh,
how they shine,
And send cold chills running
down my spine.
When you first told me how
you felt,
I thought my heart was
about to melt.
Your kisses are like the
sweet taste of wine,
That's why I can't get you
off my mind.
Your touch fills me with so
much joy,
I cuddle in your arms like a
new-bought toy.
I loved you more than you will
ever know . . .
Sometimes I wonder, why I
ever let you go.

K W
ONE STORMY NIGHT

I saw the knife that cut the sky,
It came from the Heavens.
Out of its grayish sheath,
It cut the sky with a flash,
And as quick as it came, it disappeared.

All that was left was the sky's soft tears.
They fell to earth so gently,
As the sky screamed out in pain!
I stood there in awe, I could do nothing to help.
Yes, I saw the knife that cut the sky.
I now understand why the sky is crying,
Because the storm is slowly dying.

J Howard Futch
TOGETHER

Dedicated to Chet and Brenda Music on their first wedding anniversary.

Walking together hand in hand upon the lonely stretch of sand,
You are bathed in the sunset's candle-glow,
caressed as the gentle breezes blow;
While the sounds of the birds and the murm'ring tide
reflect the excitement deep inside,
As memory soars and wings its way like a gull in the fading light of day.

For a new-found joy, robust and bold,
came with the one whose hand you hold,
Bringing wonderful peace, a calm and repose
as sweet as the whispering wind that blows;
And a love that's as deep as the ocean there,
warm and fresh as the salty air,
Gives a courage to face the darkest night,
for together you'll wait for morning's light . . .
together.

Doreen Dennis
PALE BLUE
Pale blue
reflections
through the crystal sky
wondering
what ever happened
to you and I.
Pale blue
early morning dew
in the spring
where have all the smiles gone
that I used to bring
to you.
Pale blue
in the darkest hour
desert moon
my cactus flower
where have you
disappeared to
my pale, pale blue
where are you?

Mrs Heather Gingerich
TRIBUTE TO A CANADIAN JUNE

All things bright and beautiful. . .the Lord God made them all.

As I wake up to a chirping band,
rays of sunlight warm the land.
Robins sing songs clear and true;
songs about skies of powder blue.

The maples sway in the caress of the breeze;
flowing gently between its leaves.
Fields are painted with flowers gay;
waving good morning to a new day.

Bees drink sweet honey from every bloom;
in meadows of daisies of heady perfume.
This is the time in a June day,
when nature performs its beautiful play.

Stirling B Hubbard
PRAYER AT SUNRISE
Sunlight dancing on the wall
Shadows flitting down the hall
All is calm and all is still
In the house upon the hill.

Youth has grown up in that room
Lovely bride and shy young groom
All is calm and all is still
In the house upon the hill.

Long the days and long the nights
Work by sun and dim lamp lights
All is calm and all is still
In the house upon the hill.

Years they came and years they went
Backs by years of toil were bent
All is calm and all is still
In the house upon the hill.

Joy of life they drank their fill
Now in death their hearts are still
All is calm and all is still
In the house upon the hill.

May our life be full as theirs
As we share life's joys and cares
All is calm and all is still
In the house upon the hill.

Trish Snelson
THE STRANGER
On that dark corner there lurks a stranger.
Suddenly, I sense that I am in danger!
My heart seems to stop, my breath comes in rasps.
My many fears have me in their grasp.
My fingers turn to ice and grow numb with the cold.
Each step I take makes me a thousand years old.
The silence of the night like a tomb surrounds me.
With all my heart and soul I want to flee.
I open my mouth to let out a scream.
But no sound comes. . .as if in a dream.
Yet as I try to turn around and run
My destiny seems to say "COME. . COME."
Then each step nearer the corner I come
Makes me quicken my pace and I start to run.
Then as I reach the darken corner I slow my pace.
Suddenly a smile spreads over my face.
For the stranger I had feared the most
Was only the familiar box where we mail our post.
Then up from behind the box where he'd been hiding,
Leaps the stranger, stabs me and now I am dying.
A sense of relief comes that it wasn't all in my head.
Gone is the stranger, gone is the danger, for now I am dead.

Melody M Minielly
THINKING OF YOU
Thinking of you each
and every day,
The things we went through
so you won't fade away.
Thinking of you and
your tender touch,
And the loving kiss
that I miss so much.
Thinking of you and
your soft blue eyes,
The things I said you
know they weren't lies.
Thinking of you and
your special way,
And wishing you weren't
so far away.
Thinking of you with
the loving hope,
That your thinking of me
and trying to cope.
I'll say it again
what I've said before,
I'm thinking of you
and your LOVE once more.

Myrna K Leemhuis
'MOST BLIND
Yesterday I saw a man, I saw a man 'Most Blind
Yet there was laughter in his eyes and Love that's hard to find.
His clothes were old and ragged, his hat lay flat with age
His white cane turned to yellow, but Joy, his face encaged.
He spoke with little children, they were welcomed in his arms,
He told a story to them, 'twas not some silly yarn.
Such kindness from within him, he had gentleness untold,
Tenderness about his way, Warmth, only Grace can mold.
Yesterday, I saw a man, I saw a man 'Most Blind,
Yet he saw more than you and I, 'twas Love his heart entwined.

Today I heard a man, I heard a man 'Most Deaf,
Yet he made music for my ears, and hatreds all had left.
He wore no shoes upon his feet, no razor touched his hair,
He had no shirt upon his back, but he had Joy, to share.
He gave a mute's card to me, it asked me not for money,
Instead it spread a message, much sweeter than new honey.
Such gentleness within his being, just kindness from his heart,
Tenderness about his face, Warmth, only Grace imparts.
Today I heard a man, I heard a man 'Most Deaf,
Yet he heard more than you and I, for Love was what he left.

Tomorrow you will meet a Man, you'll meet the Man I pray,
Who makes the deaf to hear His Voice,
And the blind to see His Way.

Roy Alan Babiuk
BRIDGES
They begin as lights.
Attacking with bright spears of false sunlight.
Approaching with sense of purpose.
Emitting roars as they advance,
Rising in crescendo as they come nearer.
Probing the dim false light of the morning,
With their rapiers of brightness.
Only to rush by,
Retreating with a show of red light
To mark their passage.
I am watching from my own vantage point.
A small section which I have claimed my own.
From here I see the passing of time,
Of space, of slow change.
And I realize that in my mind, I wish
I could somehow be one with the objects
In which I have become so involved in observing.
To have sense of direction.
Being able to advance as I choose.
I have not the means
To carry out my wish
And remain still.

Leon E Chamberlain
TWENTY-FOUR/FORTY OR FIGHT!
Why, oh why, does every poetry contest
Invariably specify twenty-four lines or less?
What can possibly be said in twenty-four
That can't be said much better in a hundred or more?
My lengthy thoughts simply cannot unwind
If confined and compressed in a mere 24 lines.
I didn't compose these long verses just to make them small
If 24 is all I get, I can't possibly include them all.
The lines I thoughtfully composed, so lucid and eloquently
Can't be consolidated and squashed so conveniently!
My poor obese doggerel must go on a diet to reduce
Oh dear, which verses stay, which ones vamoose?
So many favorite phrases and sentences must be tossed out—
The thing'll collapse—who'll understand what it's about?
Cruel world! Forced to take a cleaver to the verses you've made—
I'd rather take a punch below the shoulder blade.
These hard-written words say just what I wanted to express

Now it's start over! Do it in 24 lines or less!
My poetry, like the universe, it must expand
Friend this is poetry, don't confuse it with shorthand.
I'm pleading, dear editor, so noble and kind:
Expand the line limit to at least a hundred and nine!

Alan R Smith

THE TIMES OF LOVE

To a very dear friend, who inspired these lines to become part of this lifetime.

Sometimes I see you and I
As sensitive rosebuds:
Opening to each other, petal by petal
In love's sun-blessed luminance.

Sometimes as I watch
You become so beautiful I cannot find words.
Then I know you are allowing me
A glimpse of your soul.

No times are you out of mind
For longer than a few moments.
So strong the desire to share,
You are a natural part of every experience.

Each time I leave you
Is the hardest task ever performed.
Only your constancy
Makes it possible at all.

Agnes B Choi

SOUTHERN TEXAS

To my colleague R.N.

I'd like to go one small town
in the southern Texas,
and be unknown ordinary woman.

I'd do laundry & cook for my good man,
and listen to children in the evening.

In my little house fenced with wild roses.
I'd grow tomatoes, cucumbers, squashes
in the backyard.

At the night,

I'd rather hold shiny stars
and dream for the night.

There wouldn't be any more loneliness
sheltered behind walls, nor
competitions or exhaustions.

I'd like to go southern Texas,
and be unknown ordinary woman. And
rather to take long walk on fine spring day
into that green prairie.

Arlean Richmond Bowers

1984—MY FUN YEAR AT BALLY'S

To: Shirley and Nancy

In Atlantic City at Bally's Casino where I used to dwell,
Among the slot machines that I loved so well.
Then I fell in love with Black Jack too,
And that is about all an 80 year old lady can do.

My two best friends, Shirley and Nancy, who always play,
I know that they will win big someday,
But if I'm not there on that Big Day,
I just know what they both will say:
"I wish Mother and "Geenie" was here."

But they are wrong again you see,
They just don't use their heads without me.
All they have to do is look for that circle with (3),
and in there, they will always find me.

And when you go to eat, don't forget to say,
"Little Heidi" will sure eat good today!

So, I guess this is the end of my line,
As I fell in love quite a few times,
But My one Big Love will always be,
At Terry Roberts Black Jack table in Bally's Casino,
With Shirley, Nancy and Me.

Elva Dockery

MOTHER AND DAD

A sweet young girl and a bright eyed boy
Entered life's pathway together
They moved to a home
They didn't want to roam
But only to be with each other.

The years rolled on, children came along
The way was not always bright
But they toiled and worked
They never shirked
And of a truth taught their children right.

Years have passed, changes have come
The children grown up and departed
The two were alone
Once more in their home
As when at first they had started.

Yes, changes have come, these two are gone
Two better parents who could have had?
They are at rest
At home with the blest
Yes, they were my Mother and Dad.

Billy Mac Woods

THE FLOWER

I see before me a beautiful spring flower;
ever so gently she sways in the cool morning breeze.
Suddenly a butterfly alights, and covers her beauty from me.

Charles L Stapleton

A SYMPHONY

For the Marotto family, with special thanks to Frances, who sent this in without my knowledge.

In music, every note has its value.
Each one separate, yet
Dependent on the others.
One will make a single tone,
Many will make a single chord,
But all of them together
Become a single song.

Any one of you can stand
Alone and sing what is
In your heart and mind.
Together you sing the
Same song—each making
Up that which is vital
To the theme.

As you grow, the music
Becomes increasingly more
Complex, while sustaining
That simple theme that
Has been there from
The beginning, now
Soft and unnoticed,
but not unheard.
The original notes
Still true to the
Song in which each
One of you is an
Essential part.

Grace Delaney

INTERCHANGE

At some point along the day's way
A flash from memory may stray,
Triggered by something seen or heard,
Dreams outlived, revived by a word;
An emotion outgrown surges
As a face from the mist emerges.

We are experience, emotions, thought,
All character blocks by fate wrought,
Built on triumphs and mistakes
Tempered by time, rapture, and aches.

Linda Malena (Jones)

I'VE GOT A MANSION

To my Grandpa Damon and Grandpa Jones who have already found their mansions in heaven.

I've got a mansion on a hilltop somewhere
beyond the sky.
And I know I'm going to see it in the
great by and by.
There's a sign above its door and my
Name is written there.
It's my home in glory, built with God's
Love and tender care.
Yes, I've got a mansion there in heaven
And it was built for only me.
And someday not long from now, its
Glory will I see.

Do you have a mansion on a hilltop way
beyond the sky?
If so, I'll see you there in the great
by and by.

Lesley Gerald Barrow

A FRIEND IS HE! (CHRIST OUR LORD)

"I AM" — From Everlasting to Everlasting! "The mighty God! The merciful Father! The Prince of peace!" Let all the glory be—to God! For it was He who wrote the song-lyric through me by His Spirit!

Such a-friend,. . .to-have in Je-sus,—so-knowing,. . .and under-stan-ding!
All the-sins,. . .and bur-dens of-us,—to-him,. . .let-t us bring-g! ! !

Would you serve Jesus-our-King. . .— to-do-honor. and pra-ise him,. . .
Of-the-world, for-saking every-thing —. . .Worship him—and praise him!

And pra-ise him— music and pra-ise him—
For he-is wor-thy. . .of-love, hon-our, and-d pra-ise-e!

John M Hoy

REMEMBRANCE

This poem is dedicated to the seven crew members of the space shuttle Challenger.

It was on that fateful January day
Challenger left the pad, a full cargo bay.
All seven crew members strapped in very tight,
we all covered our eyes to shade the bright light.
And as we watched it ascend through the sky,
we watched seven crew members tragically die.
The nation saw the families, and felt so sad,
what lives they could have lived, the lives they had.
And now we search the wreckage and try to find
what went wrong and how to prevent it next time.
Our farewell message to all the crew members;
Good luck, best wishes, we'll always remember.

Cara Louise Languein

UNTIL TOMORROW

To Cindy, a friend that is always there for me.

If a person could be two places at one time,
I'd be with you.
For you are the one who cared for me,
During the good times and the bad.
You gave my life back to me,
In a way you set me free.
Our friendship is like two ships passing in

The night. For one day you'll sail away,
To a new and brighter life.
But until then, there is no looking back,
Only ahead, toward the future. Is nothing greater than tomorrow.
The words will never show.
The you, I've come to know.
Tomorrow—Today, beside you
All the way.

Marion W Thurman
SUNSET

To John Henry, my loving husband.

Lord when you give us a sunset
At the closing of the day
There is nothing to match its beauty
From beginning to the last ray.

The way you paint the sunset
No artist could match the splendor
The orange, the yellow, the red, and the pink
You put there with love so tender.

The sunset to me is a grand preview
Of the colors in heaven we'll see
It's God's way of letting us know
It's up there for you and for me.

Please God send us many sunsets
For us to enjoy while we're here
Let them be your messages
Saying, "Children of mine have no fear."

So enjoy that special time of the day
When the sun sinks in the west
And know that God is always with you
And darkness will bring only peace and rest.

Dianne M Winter
THE BOX

To follow my head,
Or to follow my heart—
Become closer together,
Or drift further apart.
With each step I take,
There's a fear deep inside—
One that claims my true feelings—
Why must they hide?
As if they are kept in
A small china box,
And only by you
Can the box be unlocked.
To unfold all my thoughts,
And the dreams that I hold—
To make this cruel world
Seem a little less cold.
Yet so hidden are these thoughts,
That even I cannot see—
In that little closed box
That lies inside of me.
But maybe someday,
I will find the right key—
And unlock all the secrets
Behind what you see.

Cathy L Tolan
LOVING

Gone is the little bit of laughter I had left inside me,

Just like letting the air out of a balloon.

I touched the hot stove and the fire spread not only to my hands but to my heart.

I wish I could love that way again.

I feel like a ball that has been smashed up against a brick wall,

Feeling each brick smack me in the face.

You put more into love than what you get.

Some give more—some give less.

I gave all I could and I lost all I had.

Evelyn L Opalinski-Durkin
HOPE ETERNAL

To my family and To All Immigrants

Our Ancestors came to America
From all over the world —
And gazed with misty eyes
As Old Glory was unfurled.
They labored hard to build a home
And raise their families well —
And as they sang "America" —
Their throats with pride did swell.
Folks still look to us with hope
Their problems we will share.
So let's build a chain of love
To show them that we care —
At home, at school, and everywhere
Weld links of friendship true.
And then the world will better be
For us—and others, too.

Sharon Brandt
SLEEPNESS NIGHT

Dedicated to my mother

As I lay here sleepless, in the still of the night
I stare out the window looking at the moon so big and so bright.
Listening to the quietness, all around.
And hearing the odd dog bark with a so faintful sound
Listening to the frogs croke down in the raveen
And the cats mate, with that terrible scream.
Now, the sounds of a far away train.
Going by the river, where the boats remain.
Sounds are so different in the middle of the night
Sometimes they even give me a little fright
It is almost shameful we have to sleep
Cause tomorrow we listen to the noise
Of the city's beat

Kimberley Anne Vordahl
A FUTURE UNKNOWN

I sit weary from thought,
I have no path,
no winding road.
I am like a broken down car,
that will sit and erode.
I have friends that have paths.
these paths take them,
where they want to go.
But I sit weary from frustration,
On no path.
On no winding road.

Bobbie Bayich
DAWN

My wind dances fast
Blossoms float upon the lake
Sweet dawn sighs gently
Sounds fall out of the sky
some life still sleeps long.

Karen R Cunningham
TREASURED THOUGHTS

This poem is dedicated to the residents, families, friends, and employees of the Jefferson Manor, my favorite Nursing Home at Jefferson, Iowa.

Treasure each day, as it was your last.
For things that make you happy, create memories of time past.
Appreciate what God has given man.
Remember to be truthfull and honest, and go hand in hand.
Life can be worth more then riches, or gold.
It's up to you, how your future will unfold.
Sometimes you may wonder about the life you were delt.
But think of the lessons learned, and how you felt.
Think about the happy smiles created, from the goodness of the heart.
Think of the band of friendships, that can never be torn apart.
For as the years go by, and you grow wiser with age—
It can be beautiful, as times in a history page.
When you see someone, with graying hair, and drying skin.
Be happy, for he helped create our future, from the life that has been.

Helen Marie Diggs
PERFUME OF ROSES

Perfume is more fragrant
At a rose's first blush,
A bird's song is sweeter
When the melody's hushed!
A star's glow is brighter
When the sky's dark and deep,
While the prayers of the angels
Forbid them to sleep,
Lest they miss one sad echo
Of some lonely heart
That's pleading with God,
A new way to start
Some work that is worthy

In some little seed,
Or a mountain of courage
From a prisoner freed!
The rainbow is veiled
In glory and mist,
And a wrinkled hand's softer
Where a baby has kissed!
Ah! perfume is sweeter
From one single rose
Than a bouquet forgotten
At yesterday's close!
Lying unheeded
In ashes forlorn,
Roses of yesterday's
Rubble and scorn!
One rose to remember,
A bird's song-delight!
The stars to guide
The lonely tonight,
A flutter of angel wings
Softly unfurled,
Let "Perfume of Roses
Encircle the world!"

Norah Ellen O'Brien
ABSTRACT FEELINGS

Running, running, running
Street after street
Here I found myself
Before a great wall
Of abstract colors.
I slowly sank to my feet
Crying, crying, crying
Tear after tear
I glanced up and
Examined the wise old
Wall, carefully.
There were bright colors
And faded colors and
It seemed these things
Were the only things
That made sense in my life.
For in my heart
Each color painted
A picture of love,
Laughter, happiness.
Suddenly it all made sense.
All I need is a friend.
I rose to my feet
And walked off in search
Of a friend
And for once in my life
I felt I was headed
In a colorful direction!

Lorena Mae Hull Lewis
ONE DAY AT A TIME

To 1. Mr. John & Bessie Hull 2. Ella Brim & Family 3. Grover Lee Gorrell

---

We worry about tomorrow
oft missing the joys of today
trouble about what may happen
Yet tomorrow, may not come.

Life's pathways is uncertain
"Right now" is yours and mine.
The future is safe in Gods hands
We can live but one day at a time.

Elma E Fisher
SONNET

To Bob, whose love inspired my poem and who will share a golden wedding anniversary with me next year.

In buoyant spring when love blooms forth in hearts,
I think of you and wonder in my mind
What Power did give me sense to feel such arts
As those which in your soul's own depth I find.
And through the casements of your eyes I see
The molded truth and purity of thought

That's planted deep in you, but shines to me
Through vistas of those dancing smiles I sought
With earnest hopes. My praises leap with joy
To sound my ardent worship of your ways;
And yet I find that words can ne'er employ
The heart's full voice, nor quite its music raise.
In spring my love does all but lose itself—
It is a part of you, my other self.

Sherry Charlene Taylor
BUYING A WORLD

This poem is dedicated to my husband Robert, my children, Larry, Robert Jr., Anthony, and Shana Also to my mother, mary charlene west.

How much would it cost you
if you went out today?
And bought yourself a little world
what do you think you'd pay?
You'd buy a sun, you'd buy a moon,
And a bucket full of stars
A river and a mountain
A close up view of Mars
You'd buy yourself some pretty green grass
and over it you'd hang a big blue sky
You're about to finish your shopping list
when suddenly you begin to cry
For all the things upon your list
you realize are free
Because whether rich or poor my friend
these things were all given to you and me.

Jeremiah F Enright
U. S. MARINE PRAYER

To all U S Marines living and dead first. And to all of America's Military Forces second. May God Bless and protect his America Always.

Stay with me, God, The night is dark,
The night is Hell, My little spark
of courage dies. The night is long,
Be with me, God, and make me strong.

I love a game, I love a fight,
I hate the dark, I love the light,
I love children, I love women,
I am no coward, I love life.

Life, with its changes of mood and shade,
I want to live, I'm not afraid,
But me and mine are hard to part,
Oh, unknown God, Lift up my heart.

You stilled the waters at Iwo Jima
and saved your servants. All your work
is wonderful, Dear God. You strode before
us down that dreadful road.

We were alone, and hope had fled,
We loved our country, and our dead,
and could not shame them, So we stayed
the course, and were not much afraid. (we were)

Dear God, that nightmare road!
And then that black, sandy beach!
We got there . . . We were men,
My eyes were blind, My feet were torn,
My soul sang like a bird at dawn!

I know that death is but a door,
I know what we are fighting for,
Peace for the kids, our brothers freed,
A kinder world, a cleaner breed.

I'm but the son my mother bore,
A simple man, and nothing more,
But God of Strength and Gentleness,
Be pleased to make me nothing less.

Help me, Oh God, When death is near,
To mock the haggard face of fear
That when I fall, if fall I must,
My spirit may triumph in the sleep of Dust.

Oh, God, Bless and protect America,
To us Marines, Your promised land always.

Verna Tomlinson Baker
ABODE
April Easter
came, nor went—
bringing with it
our true Lent,
still within our hearts
its place—
leaving Sonrise
on our face.
You could see
at early pass
jewel dewdrops
in the grass.
Trilling birdsong
breaking through—
hymns of praises
to Him due.
Sparrow, lily,
beggar, king:
to Jesus
every thank we bring.

Mary B Phelps
LOST LOVE

To the man who took me to heaven, then brought me back to earth

---

It's gone forever? How can it be?
We had so much, you and me
I guess it was destined to be true,
there'd never be a me and you
We both worked on it, hard and long
but midst the fight the love has gone
Where its lost, I do not know,
I've searched my mind for signs to show
How did we lose so grand a love?
Did it fly away, on the wings of a dove?

It's hard to believe a love so grand,
could turn so coarse, like a grain of sand
The passionate love we used to share,
has turned into a vicious glare
With as strong a love that lies behind us,
I'd like to think, someday, again, it will find us
As I know, there will never be,
another love, as you, for me
We've lost each other? How can it be?
We had so much, you and me.

Irene Joyce Balestra
OH, CANADA
A vast and beauteous land wrought
by the Creator's hand

where towering forest
damp and green
have a beauty
seldom seen
and awe-inspiring peaks
proclaim
the Rocky Mountains'
claim to fame

where vast prairies
stretch
out of sight
and thunderous rivers
narrate
their might

the trees
the lakes
and rocky shore
tranquil creeks
and falls that roar

from north
to south
and east to west

here's Mother Nature
at her best.

Lois M Fishback
MY LOVED ONE
My loved one dried the dishes
Then in his chest was pain.
He must take a little pill
And rest up once again.

"Grandpa, my toy is broken.
Can you help me, please?"
"Bring the dumb thing over here."
He was a loving tease.

I weeded rows of flowers
He'd planted with much care.
Raindrops on the petals?
Or my tears falling there.

The paths we strolled together
Were, oh, so very sweet.
I walk them now, despondent
On listless wandering feet.

Others miss him daily.
And though I say, "Not so,"
My loved one's gone forever
To where I can't yet go.

He's with our Savior, Jesus.
And there he waits for me.
With no more pain and sorrow
From suffering now set free.

Delena K Constant

Delena K Constant
MY WORLD

To Bud, Who Has made my world Complete.

I have stood on the Great Plains of Texas.
I walked the pasture lands.
I have reached to touch the wild flowers.
to grasp the Texas Bluebonnet.
I have touched His hand.

I have watched the green field of cotton grow.
I watched the bud burst forth into a flower.
I watched the leaves turn brown and fall to the ground.
Behold a soft fleecy white appeared, cotton.
I see Him all around.

I have watched the maize grow on stalks of green.
The beginning of a small yellow head above the green.
I have felt the hot sun turn the maize a vivid burnt orange.
He gives me strength.

I have felt the cold feel of snow upon my face.
Falling down all around in soft flakes.
I have seen the cold North wind blow the flakes into a bank of snow.
I feel Him beside me.

My God, You made my world to see, touch, to feel.
You made Your earth my strength to stand, to carry on.
I see You in the trees, the flowers,
I feel You in the wind.

O M Gibbons
FOR ALL THE TIMES

To all my loved ones—especially mom

For all the times I wasn't present
Didn't telephone or write
To tell you that I love you
Or to cheer you thru the night
Didn't wish a Happy Birthday
Or send that Easter card
To share the Joys of Heaven
That softens trials so hard
Didn't welcome that new baby
The parents' pride and joy
Didn't send the gift that said
So happy it's a boy
You couldn't know I see each baby
As a rare and perfect pearl
Each a gift so precious
Whether boy or girl
Couldn't be there in the sadness
Or help when illness struck
My work was so important
The company needed that next buck
Didn't share the graduations
Send the gifts for wedding chimes
This is love to you from
Heart and soul. FROM ME!
FOR ALL THE TIMES.

Donna Marie Wisener
LIFE
Into life I flow
not a worry nor a woe
To see what I can see.
Big or small no matter
what, I want more of
it all.

Good or bad, glad or sad
I've seen it lately.
Perfection, mistake, who
gets all the breaks, might
I ask?

Life is grand, too.
Harsh as sand at times.
Upon a star, soon I shall fly.
For my trip of life is finished for
now;
and I still have not
a worry nor woe.

That's life.

Roger Lee Spears

TAKE THE TIME

They say that, one must do what
one must do,
but it's not to profit one over
another,
but to stop and smell the roses,
even give some to a sister or a
brother.
So even in the midst of a hectic day,
don't just to thine own self be true,
take the time to look around,
a brother or sister may need you.
Sometimes when on a mountain
top,
and looking toward the skies,
it's hard to see a brother low,
or hear a sister sigh.
Take the time to look around,
be a brother true,
take a brother by the hand,
and help him up there too.

Henry J Nunez

MOTHER

Because you showed me how to love, because you taught me never to hate, that's why to you Ma, this poem I dedicate

---

Mother, I miss you more than ever
Things you taught me were so
clever
The thought of you makes me cry
Mother, if I ever made you suffer
My apologies to you I offer
Oh why did you have to die?

Mother, you were terminally ill
With a disease that soon would kill
The very life you so much adored
Mother, among the angels you now
sleep
Is that why every night I weep
Or is it 'cause you're gone forever
more

Mother, oh wherever you may be
Won't you keep an eye on me
Please don't ever let me do no
wrong
Mother, call it fate or destiny
By my side you'll no longer be
Still your memory, in my heart
lives on

Mother, seems no matter what I do
My thoughts are all of you
Oh how I miss your warm embrace
Mother, with these words that are
so true
I will pray and pray for you
And hope you have reached your
final resting place

Kevin Schoenecker

SEASONS AND LIFE

To my father, Cyril L. Schoenecker, (1930-1978). I'm proud to finish what you started, and to my Mom, for being there.

A slap, a cry, a child is born,
As a seedling shows its head
In the spring's early morn.

Summer draws strength from its
warm wind blowing,
As a youth gains from experience,
Learning and growing.

Adult and mature with knowledge
to spare.
Time begins its changes
In autumn's darkening air.

As seasons and life pass on
Don't weep
For now it's time for winter's sleep

Geraldine Irene Plantz Cafiero

VERMONT—GOD'S MOUNTAINS

Dedicated to an old friend The Bard of Hunter's Brook. William Mundell, who loved Vermont as life itself.

I live in awe of the mountain's
beauty like
nothing I ever saw.
To look up, up, and up.
Into the clouds above.
I feel somehow are filled with love
It seems each mountain peak is
hiding.
But with a message of good tidings.
From God to mankind through all
his trials and tribulations.
To find joy and great elation.
Just to have seen the great and
wonderous
works of God's hand.
As we travel side by side
throughout
his land.

Roxanne Collins

A FATHERS TASK

This poem is dedicated to James Powers, my sweet husband.

A man embarking on
life's greatest task,
knows not what the future will
hold.
He answers the questions his
charges will ask,
and gathers them into his folds.
Together, they walk forests' glade,
as he points out the things they
don't see.
Before they should scatter,
he'll lovingly bade:
'tis only a guess what they'll be.
Some bit of wisdom,
small as a seed,
he imparts to his younger living,
hoping the spices of life,
will prove more seasoned in the
giving.

Phil Galusha

OUR WEDDING POEM

For my loving wife Linda on our wedding day.

On this special day, together we
stand
Beside one another, before God
and man,
Our hearts are filled with the love
we share,
The vows we have spoken, prove
that we care.

Care about each other till death do
us part.
Care about the love that's deep in
our hearts.
Care about each other in sickness
and in health.
Care about each other whether
poor or with wealth.

We've made a commitment that
God once began
When He made woman from the
rib of a man.
The man and the woman, together
would be
A oneness to God in sweet
harmony.

Joy and happiness forever we'll
live.
Love everlasting together we'll give.
A bond that is strong, a love that is
deep
Compassion and truth together
we'll keep.

These few words may not a
marriage be,
But these few words may help us
to see
That a marriage can and should be
for life
The most precious thing to a man
and his wife.

Mrs Lillian Solberg Nelson

THE FIRST RAINS

This poem is dedicated to all of my children

Our hearts are sadly calling
For rain so much in need
And now rain is finally falling
It makes us glad indeed.

The birds are sweetly singing
For they are happy too
Church bells in the vale are ringing
They tell a story true.

They tell of peace and gladness

On God we can depend
No more cause for sadness
Our wheat fields soon will bend.

With weight of fulfilled promises
To feed the ones in need
Fields of mums and narscissus
Are God's gift to us indeed.

The skies are grayer grayer
As clouds come floating free
Rain answers every prayer
Of prairie folks like me.

Bea Lawrence

HIT THE ROAD GRANNY

Most of my life I've been house
bound,
Afraid to get out and travel around.
I believe now I've changed my
mind,
If you ask me, it's about time.
Sell the house, pay off the bills,
Buy a van and head for the hills.
On open road, no work or such,
Just my man and dog, who means
so much.
Sick of cleaning pots and pans,
Scrubbing and waxing floors, with
old rough hands.
Cooking, baking and all that stuff,
After fifty years, I've had enough.
I'd like to be just plain lazy,
Being tied down is driving me
crazy.
New homes, cars, money and
clothes,
Happiness isn't any of those.
Let me park by a stream or lake,
An old cane pole and plenty of bait.
If I get tired going here and there,
This granny will head for her
rocking chair.

Vi Murray

A GARDEN OF FLOWERS

In memory of my parents

Mother you have gone away,
To rest from earthly life they say.

You filled the role of Mother well,
As each of your children tell.

You did not seek for fame nor
wealth,
You asked for treasure of a
Far more lasting kind; health,
God's blessings and friends.

Knowing our Dad as we do,
He wanted so much to be with you.

We asked for happiness for both of
you,
In all things great and small
But it was for "His Loving Care,"
We prayed the most of all.

Jeanette M Frontier

ANXIOUS MOMENTS

To: Janet—Debra—David—Michael—John

Time has caught up with
me today
I gaze at the bed
Where you lay
The baby, the child
and now a man
Dreams and wishes galore
always
of a far off shore
How did these things
grow so quiet?
You just began to try it!
The things that happened
took place each day
Time Don't Go Away

Charles K Gambel Sr

FLAGS

Dedicated to the eternal memory of the M.I.A.'s, P.O.W.

INTRO:
The horses charge, the canons roar,
"Attack you cowards—This is
war—

Runner, hold your colors, banner
 high,
It isn't everyday you get a chance
 to die!"
Eyes to the right & eyes to the left,
"Get on with it soldier—Don't you
 lag—
If one runner falls, pick up the pole,
The bloody ground must not kiss
 the flag!"

CHORUS:
Flags, have little meaning,
If one can't feel, some touch of
 pride—
Just some rags & a flash of color,
But, there's one thing you can't
 hide!

Every time, they raise—O' Glory,
I hear the heart within me cry—
I see a bloody, tatter'd banner,
And all the men who had to die.

O Flags wave in the sunrise,
The bugles blow at dawn—
Flags wave in the moonlight,
When all brave soldiers are dead &
 gone!

Flags, have little meaning,
Until your homelands' dear, to
 you—
O God, forgive the anger,
When strangers burn, the Red,
 White, & Blue!

Twila L Gibson

DOUBTS

In memory of James Johnson Gibson, my father

"Dearly beloved . . . "
 What am I doing here, do I truly
 love this man standing beside
 me.
"This man and this woman . . . "
 Woman, I'm not old enough for
 marriage. I'm just eighteen.
"Why these two should not marry?"
 I can, but what would I say, I
 can't marry him, because I love
 him too much.
 We let the moon and the stars
 decide things for us. Neither
 one of us is ready for this are we?
"Do you . . . "
 His answer so clear and strong,
 sounds awful sure of what he is
 doing, but is he as nervous as I.
"Do you. . ."
 I answer softly I do, but do I, can
 I promise to love, honor and
 cherish him till death do we part.
"Place the ring on her third
 finger . . . "
 He's slipping the gold band on
 my finger and looking into my
 eyes with as much reassurance
 as possible and as he lightly
 squeezes my hand, I realize I'm
 ready for this and God with your
 help every now and then we'll
 make this union joined by you
 work.
"YOU MAY KISS THE BRIDE."

Clarence Huntington

MEMORIES OF MY MIND

This poem is dedicated to Evelyn, my loving wife

Behind the closed doors, of the
 memories of my mind
Are happy thoughts of someone,
 gentle, good and kind
Someone, who cared, and shared
 my dreams in better by gone days
Someone, with tender love I knew,
 now lost in the past of yesterday
Oh, if I could but open, the locked
 portals of time
Just once more to share again,
 each moment so divine
With that certain someone, who
 eased my sorrow and pain
And whose sunny smile like a
 rainbow, chased away the
 gloom,
Of life's stormy rain
Then my heart would not have to
 go on searching,
As it strives to find
The mysterious answers locked,
In the memories of my mind

Joyce R Dixon

HOLD GOD'S HAND

The darkness of night leans
 heavily against the
 windowpanes,
There is no feeling of weight for the
 blackness can be
bright.

I am secure in the knowledge of the
 wonderful magic I possess,
Just a blink of my eye, my world is
 transformed, I am in flight.

The transformation is as quick, as
 vibrant as you, Laci, my child,
I have entered our private world
 where there is only love and
 light.

Wonder, awe, laughter, adventure,
 a thurst for knowledge never
 quiet,
Viewing all things with a little girl's
 glee is my plight.

You never lay back, relax but with
 endless energy bound forth,
Wispy curls, inquisitive blue eyes,
 little legs with a running gait.

This is your universe, just to show
 it, to share it, enriches my
life,
On our last worldly excursion I had
 to caution, "Hold my hand,
 wait."

I shared your world, I share it still,
 we are never apart,
For my treasure of memories are
 so real, profound, so grand.

The sudden final depth of death
 cannot steal you from my world,
But now Laci, my love, you must
 remember, please, "Hold God's
 hand."

Terry H Chaney

THOUGH I'M GONE

Though I'm gone, even the least
 time—
 You are with me; In my heart;
Always on my mind.
 Which isn't never too far:

Though I can't touch you—
 My love remains.
Always devoted, always true—
 Each and every day:

I long to be there.
 And now; is too long—
"Sometimes;" isn't fair;
 Not ever being home:

Somethings, are getting easier—
 For us, two;
And yet some harder,
 I'm happy; we, have me, and you:

Together, we are one—
 Apart, we still are;
One together, under the sun;
 Apart; together in our Soul and
 Hearts.

Mary M Krause

LIFE

To Posterity

None of us were made to be Angels
Only follow where His calling leads
 us.
From humble beginnings to great
 heights;
From wealth to ruin.
For every season, there is a reason,
Who can fathom the human mind
 or soul?

The sound of greatness is ever near,
We must reach back and pluck it
From those who have gone before.
The call of hunger pulls me down,
From this etheral plane.
Then need, duty and feelings for
 others
Return me to sanity once more.

Why do we look good to someone
Even in the morning?
Is it love or morality or mentality?
Whatever turns us on.

This is the story of life.
Plan, strive ahead.
Stopping; we lose sight,
Starting, it may never be.

Babies are fulfilling
Accomplishments help the ego.
The forever flow of life.

 Age mellows
 Accept what is—
 And flow with the tide
Til the sea engulfs us all.

Jeannette Louise Linker

Jeannette Louise Linker

GOD'S GIFT

To my loving Aunt; Peggy Simpson for all her support also Leigh Ann Linker and Jason Linker for being my gifts.

God's gift to us is a child so sweet.
We pray for knowledge to guide
 their feet.
We set an example each day that
 we Live.
Our Love and wisdom is what we
 give.
In return we receive so much pride
 and joy;
This comes from both a girl and a
 boy.

Barbara Ruth Nesmith

GOD'S LAND

To Marsh and Pearl who gave me life and God's land . . .

My whole being echoes a psalm of
 thanksgiving
As I survey this land where I make
 my living.
No better place can I find to talk
 to God
Than here on this farm, close to the
 sod.
Here is the land where I planted
 the corn,
And there the stable where Charlie
 Horse was born.
I walk a bit further and there is the
 lot
Where in winter I feed the cows
 with the calves they've got.
Walking across the pasture (in
 spring it's so green)
From where in the distance a forest
 can be seen
Where as a child I played with my
 sisters and brother.
I know there is no place on earth
 I'd rather
Be than here on this farm of mine.
 My heart sings
As I think of the joy it brings.
Though in the scheme of things it's
 insignificant and small,
When I'm out there I feel 'most ten
 feet tall.
I think of the things that God and
 I have done
Out there in the wind and the sun.
God's part in all this has been far
 and away the most,
Without Him it would all have
 been lost.
While I love the land and pretend
 to farm,
He prospers me and keeps me from
 harm.
And as day by day with Him I walk
 hand in hand,
I know for sure it ain't mine, it's
 GOD'S LAND.

Jo Ann Miller

ONE DAY AT HALLANDALE BEACH

Dedicated to Jesus Christ, to my hubby, Jerry, to my mother, Lona, to Kevin and Eddie, and to my Indep., Missouri roots where my love of poetry began.

The Good Year Blimp hovered over
 me as I stood upon the sand
Around me laid the bathing bodies
 of many fit and tanned.
No clouds were above and the sky
 was endless blue
The white sand seemed only to
 serve to magnify my view.

A bit of conversation wafted over
 my way
Something about news in Iran? It
 seemed out of place that day.
A bird swooped down and from the
 water snatched a fish

While a child ate potato chips from a plastic dish.

The man with the metal detector seemed lost in his world
As the lifegaurd's flag caught in the breeze and gently unfurled.
the tropical lure held me in it's grip
While a matronly woman gave a beach boy a tip.

I turned my feet toward the sidewalk and headed myself home
Putting my back to the waves capped white with foam.
The palm trees leaned ever so slightly as I passed them by
And the only sound I heard was my own contented sigh.

One day among many, yes it is true
Of this category, though, there are all too few.
So the moment was siezed and I was a part
Of a memory to treasure and hide in my heart.

Sandy Loughmiller

IT'S MOTHER

It's the most important job that will ever count.
When problems come and things go wrong,
Our frustrations begin to mount.

Having no experience, with our mate we enter
With faith alone, and in desperation we cry out
To our Father for help and the courage,
To make love abound in our home.

Then something suddenly happens to make it all worthwhile.
The whole purpose of life comes into focus
And has to make us smile.

While the responsibility makes us shudder,
But then we think of this thing called love
And that makes us happy.
What is it all about?
IT'S MOTHER!

Laura LeRayne Shank

WHAT HAPPINESS IS ALL ABOUT

To my mom and dad. . .my inspiration and my hope. God gave me the gift of being able to write down my every feeling. . .But still, I love you both more than my words could ever express. Thank you, and I love you.

Look at all the stars tonight,
Burning beautifully and bright.
Like little candles in the air,
At which I can sit and stare.

Things are so peaceful with stars around,
So peaceful that there is hardly a sound.
Once in a while I hear a dog,
But the sound is muffled by a dreamy fog.

Then the sky begins to crack,
And the color is no longer black
But bright and cheerful.
The loss of peace is almost tearful.
All you have to do,
Is look a while ahead of you
And the stars will peek out,
And whisper, what happiness is all about.

Sam Franks

EMERALD GREEN EYES

When I was young—about sixteen—we had a family fight, so I left home to make my own and see some different sights.
As I was walking down a hot and dusty road,
I spied a fellow traveler walking my way and carrying quite a load.
He was heading east, and I was heading west,
so we sat down to chin awhile and let our burdens rest.
I asked him how far the next town was; he said he could not say.
I asked him where he hailed from; all he said was, "far away".
He told of all the places he'd been, and all the wondrous sights he'd seen.
I judged him to be of Mexican descent, but his eyes were emerald green.
He said in his country everything was free—nothing bought or sold.
There were no sick and lame, and no one's ever old.
He said you didn't have to dress too much, for in his country it never gets,
too hot or cold.
I took his line with a grain of salt, and then I had to grin.
Some of these fellows lie so much, they forget that it's a sin.
I told him I had rested enough;
I had to be on my way again.
So I shouldered up my bundle and trudged on down the road.
My thoughts on what he'd told me about never getting old.
Then I happened to remember that I had not been polite,
so I turned around to wave my arm; although the road was straight,
he was not in sight.
Later on, I wondered just who it was that I had seen. . .long hair, robe and sandals, and eyes of emerald green.

Doreen E Hardy

BEING ALIVE

In this big world of love and war
are people who are happy just being alive.
With all the sadness in the world
there is a great world of happiness.
I love being alive and not getting
down about things.
There are so many reasons for being
alive that it would be foolish to give the
reasons up.
Be happy and not sad, be glad and not mad,
smile (always smile) when you wish to cry
for tomorrow is out there with better days
ahead.
So feel good about yourself and be
Happy just "Being Alive."

Alicia Eldridge-Davis

MY IMAGINARY SHOE BOX

There's an imaginary shoe box I keep
In the corridors of my mind,
Where I keep my most compassionate emotions
So they're easy for me to find.

On days that try my patience and compassion
Is not at hand,
I reach into my shoe box for the strength
To understand.

I keep an Extra Dose of Tenderness and
An extra Smile or two,
Just in case I need them when my
Supply is overdue.

The thing about this shoe box I keep
So tucked away,
Is that I must remember, you have
To fill it everyday.

Mark Anthony Klapperich

WHEN QUAFFING DEAR WINE

When quaffing Dear wine
with those of a similar heart and mind
Be patient, for if the wine, like love, is too young
"Callow, pretentious, and before its time"
Are words lamented, not sung.

Don't pour so fast!!
Haste makes waste
and you may cheat yourself out of a taste.
Rather, decant slowly, only a little at a time.
And if you still desire more,
You can then resume the pour.

Sip. . .drink without swallowing
stuttering, staggering and eventually wallowing.
Enjoy not only its taste, but its fragrance and color
And you may never want any other.

Affections, like vintage wine
Need a lot of time. . . to mature, to deepen
producing a bouquet which rivals the flowers of
its very own vine.
You needn't watch the barrel to know
what's going on inside
Have faith and some patience
enjoying ambrosia at my side.

Carole Emma Mathewson

LIZZIE DYE

Up in the redwoods, majestic and tall,
Clear in the days of early fall,

The clustered tents of the clan stood,
Red-walled by the Grant Grove wood.

Round about them pine trees sweep,
Moss and pine cones hanging deep;

Fair as the primeval forest of yore
To the eyes of the children four,

On that pleasant morn of early September
That Monroe would always in horror remember.

Twenty years as a teamster he drove,
Twenty years those mountain roads.

An injured hand forced him to hire
A driver unaccustomed to mire.

Over the mountains winding down,
Wagon and team toward Millwood town;

Four children with smiling faces,
Four children among suitcases,

Beamed in the morning air.
The sun of noon looked down on despair.

Down the infamous Stevens Grade,
May the dreadful memory one day fade,

To a point in the road where a spring was ditched;
Would that the team had remained hitched.

In a chair wired to the wagon bed
Sat the young mother who would soon be dead.

Wheels slipping in the mire of the ditch,
A fearful crowding at the hitch;

Crowding, ever crowding 'til the team feared
the encroaching wagon as it neared.

A wild gallop down the mountain side
'til team and wagon soon divide:

The wagon, in its course, with a rock collides,
And Monroe and the driver are tossed to the sides;

A smashing and splintering of one of the wheels,
Then, emitted from children, terrified squeals,

As three, like rag dolls, are safely thrown aside,
Away from the dreadful ongoing ride.

The wagon tongue suddenly is broken off short,
This having been the last support.

The wagon box then out of its standards bounds,
Hurling Lizzie and her babe forward to the ground.

The wagon bed's front end then downward pitched,
And onward the wreckage sped, though unhitched;

While beneath, caught and dragged, lay Lizzie Dye,
Her life ground out, we can only ask why.

To her bosom her child she held,
'til from the wreckage the two were expelled.

The child was rescued without harm
As Monroe gazed at his wife in alarm.

Lizzie, as crushed and dying she lay,
Formed these last words to Monroe, to say,

As her husband's eyes with terror filled:
"Oh! Monroe, I am killed!"

Robert Garrett Bulmer
A WALK DOWN MEMORY LANE

To my loving wife Edith and my four wonderful daughters, Barbara, Bobbie, Debbie, and Pat.

I walked across the plush, new mown lawn back home.
A summer breeze carried the perfume of lilacs in full bloom.
Puffy, white clouds accented an azure sky
And hollyhocks, standing guard at the front porch,
Waved and nodded to me as I walked by.

I came to the yard between house and barn.
There stood a venerable, but still majestic maple tree.
Its leaves sheltered a concrete well-cover and a tired rusty pump.
An old frayed rope and a worn wooden seat swung free,

Held by a sturdy limb that grew from its gnarled, rugged trunk.

The barn, unpainted and weathered for nearly a hundred years,
Was silvery gray in the bright sunlight; or so it appeared.
I descended a steep hill to the orchards and fields below
And followed the lane past aging fruit trees to the pasture gate.
How I remembered those years of apples to pick and hay to mow.

I could hear the trickle of the brook as it ran its winding course.
Walking along, I listened to its different voices.
Deep water flowed and rippled with a soothing whisper; then a hush.
Now it giggled, danced and babbled through the rocky shallows
Changing to a muted gurgle, as it vanished under fallen trees and Brush.

Carol Fennimore
TO LIVE, LOVE AND SING A SONG

To my family, whom without their love, I couldn't of made it through.

God gave me a lot of gifts,
But the one most precious to me.
Is the gift of life, the air I'm breathing,
Ya life is all I need.

To sing a song of love and hope,
Coming from the bottom of my heart.
A song so beautiful it makes your soul cry out,
For the strength to make a new start.

I'll play on my guitar a song,
To God for helping me through.
But the best of words always come out,
When I'm writing a song for you.

We should all learn to live our lives, to the fullest,
And be the best we can be.
And maybe oneday we'll all learn to love each other,
All the world singing a song in harmony.

Robert L Yeager
A YESTERYEAR SCHOOL DAY

It's nine o'clock. The schoolmaster rings the hand held bell, children hurriedly take their seats in this one room school, as once again, talking and laughter ceases, giving way to order that is demanded, and a quietness doths prevail.

Behind the battered wooden desk, the schoolmaster sits and commands, "Roll call will now be taken!" The words sharply spoken, "When you're called, raise your hand."

The blackboard cracked from years of use, floor beams sag from under, children read scripture, salute the flag, the coal stove roaring like thunder. GeorgeWashington's portrait, faded and frayed, hangs on the schoolroom wall, first grade children reciting nursery rhymes, Jack and Jill, Humpty Dumpty and all.

Water dropped on the floor from dripping tin cups, filled from the clay waterjug, sprung hinges on the school door, it's hard to open, you really have to tug.

It's midafternoon, books and pencils stashed away, another school day ends. Quietness will now prevail in this one room school until tomorrow, when once again, sounds of rattling lunch buckets, and children's voices, will remind us, that the time has arrived for another school day to begin.

In the quietness that now prevails in the one room schoolhouse, the schoolmaster sits behind the battered wooden desk, and ponders about the time, the times, and the years gone by. I know, for you see, I, am the schoolmaster.

Mary A Nash
A TALK WITH A STRANGER

I dedicate this poem to my mother, Grizell T. Parsons with all my love.

As I sat at the bus stop in the drizzing rain
I met a young boy who had no name.
His mind disoriented, his thoughts misplaced,
I knew he was confused by the look on his face.

As he spoke of the mistakes in his early life
I knew from his actions, it was constant strife.

He told me that his family tried to make him
understand but this boy wanted too much to be
a man. He told me he's paying for his
teenage sorrows this black uneducated boy in
search of tomorrow.

He admitted reluctantly that he knew he was wrong,
and his failures were his own because he let them
linger on.

This young boy that I met who had no name
Finally realized that life was no game.
As he walked away my thoughts dwelled
within his mind of a search for himself
which he may someday find.

Aileen Lois Fielding
THE FARMER HAS GONE AWAY

Dedicated to my father, Roy Fielding, and my mother, Eva Fielding, who were farmers, and especially enjoyed raising and nurturing livestock.

Can it be evening chore time now?
No hungry cows stand munching hay
Beside the barnyard rustic now.
The farmer has gone away.

Barn doors are closed securely.
There is no tinkle of cowbell.
In other pastures they graze contentedly,
Unaware that the farmer has said, "Farewell."

The coppery sunset is blazingly aglow.
Night's curtain will soon be drawn.
No frolicsome calves are left to low,
Since the farmer is gone.

His herd grazes in other pastures, green,
Where cool, clear, crystal streams flow.
When the Hand of Providence did intervene,
The tired farmer was called to go.

He sleeps beneath a grassy knoll in the cemetery,
Resting to await the Life Giver's call.
In the morning he will awaken to immortality,
To meet Jesus, the Greatest Shepherd of all.

Sandra K Caron
APRIL'S INVITATION

April called to me today—
What choice had I but to obey.
Determined to escape the gloom
I left the shelter of my room.
And, lo! before my dazzled eyes,
The beauty of her bright blue skies.

As eyes adjusted to the light,
I marveled at this wondrous sight:
Bud-swollen trees bowed in the breeze—
Inviting me to bend my knees
In silent reverence and awe
For all this beauty that I saw.

I opened up my lips to try
To put expression to this high
Emotion that was filling me
But as tongue formed, "What mortals we . ."
My breath was caught and snatched away
By April's breeze upon its way.

Yes, how could I of flesh and bone,
Expect I ever might intone
Appropriate words that would express
The beauty and the awesomeness
Of our Creator's Spring Display
When April called to me today.

Fred Gerard Shanahan
THE LAST BATTLE

To Mary D. without who's love and devotion I would not have realized my lifes dream, to write.

My limbs have seen the great battles
During my time I have felt the peace,
Now war has been declared by the progress of man
When will this destruction cease?

I have watched over this land for two-hundred years
Through the rain, wind and snow,
I have fought back all that nature sends
Yet! With mans progress it's time I go.

My limbs are not ready to be splintered
The roots shall remain strong, till the end,
You may clear this land that lies about me
To remove me, the best you'll send.

For I am not just another tree
With me, a man spent time,
Now he is gone, and you're bringing me down
In nature, is this not a crime?

I have given to this friend, a cool shaded space
To his daughter, I have given great thought,
To end my life, destroys her memories
Is this the accomplishment you sought?

So! Go ahead and clear this land
Set fire to my limbs and frame,
For as you look upon new woods
I shall stand there, again and again.

Holly Anne Perry
ONLY FOR YOU
Sitting with your arms around me
watching an old movie on TV
on that sleepy, snowy Sunday
was the most romantic afternoon
of my life.

You see; it's not the candy
and flowers we true romantics
remember.

It's the loving embrace
and knowing that no-one
can ever take your place
in my heart.

Dean J Pursel
ADVENTURE VIA NOD
Dad always said a little work would never do anyone harm
So summer vacation always brought a month down on the farm
I didn't mind the daily chores, I loved ole Uncle Mike
The aches and pains the first day out was the thing I didn't like

I passed into the land of Nod as soon as I hit the hay
And found myself on a pirate ship and I heard the captain say
"Look alive you swabbies or I'll lash you to the mast
Make ready men! Hoist those sails! We have a pending task"

The captain was bold and burly, and his hide was tan and rough
Years of sailing the seven seas made the captain old and tough
The tide was high, the sails were rigged, the lines were cast from shore
The old pirate ship was moving out on a venturous voyage once more

Bound for the South Pacific or some other far distant land
No destination was given to this fierce pirate band
They hoisted the "Jolly Roger" and it flew most free and bold
A symbol of death and destruction, of pirate ships . . . centuries old

The sky began to darken, clouds forming dark and deep
As the winds tossed the ship about, making waves wide and steep
With the storm fast approaching, it would surely abruptly descend
To release its fury and havoc on the captain and his men

The old captain stood in defiance, fear he didn't know
If the forces of nature sought combat, they met their prey and foe
The encounter finally ended, and the storm moved out to sea
In the quiet serenity that followed, it annoyed . . . and awakened me

Gladys Eastin
IF THERE WERE DREAMS TO SELL?
If there were dreams to sell dear;
Which one would you buy?
One of joy and laughter, or of the castle in the sky?
Or of riches given, of lavender and lace?
Or a whole new lifes adventure in some foreign place?
Or would you dream of loves, as lasting as the breeze?
Of meadows green and flowers fair
And tall dependent tree's?
Or would you buy a world of love
And dream there be no sorrow?
Or that the world, would never change
Or no trouble borrow?
No matter what the others dream,
I'll tell you what is true.
If there were dreams to sell, my love,
I'd buy the best for you.

Joan Disher
MATTHEW, OUR DEAR LITTLE SON
Matthew, our dear little son,
The Doctors did everything that could be done.

We were hoping for some kind of magic,
But the outcome was very tragic.

We think of all the happiness you brought,
And how hard you must have fought.

To be able to survive for that long,
Makes your death seem even more wrong.

You would have been 10 weeks old today,
How great it would be to watch you play.

How much I would give to be able to hear your cry,
But instead I sit here and keep asking the question, "Why?"

For you our little Matthew, we'll always be glad,
But the fact that your life was so short will always make us sad.

We'll always love and remember you,
And cherish the memories and keepsakes too.

Abigail Mulder
MOUNTAINS
How beautiful to see
mountains around a valley,
like Gods,
with their arms
around the valley.

Dan F Johnson
BONDING
An entire face smiles
Up at parental wisdom,
An entire room giggles
Back at parental hisdom.

A gentle hand touches
Hearts of a feather
And the room giggles again,
A tug at the tether.
Familiar eyes capture
The innocence of life,
The essence of husband and wife.

Cathrine L Harris
CAST A GOLDEN SHADOW
Cast a golden shadow upon the pool of life,
touch the silence, feel it, endlessly alive!

Cast a golden shadow its tones are filled with light,
somnolent hues of amber, oh what a lovely sight!

Cast a golden shadow at days end towards night,
smokey topaz embers are dancing in the light!

Cast a golden shadow where the sky greets the sea,
and with the dawn of morning, a soul shall be set free!

B L (Billy) Spooner
HARMONY

To the lady who brought Harmony to my life, My wife

I have often stood in the still of night
and scanned the ink, black, silk of the celestial height.
My mind quietly soared skyward and beyond
shaking free the fingers of gravity's bond.
Past treetops and mountains my mind raced free
free to chase rainbows, free to be me.
No longer encumbered by a body of clay,
my soul raced through forever and back through today.
I've carried a snowflake in the palm of my hand,
and bathed in the sunlight which covered the land.
I've heard the song of the summer breeze,
as it gently carressed the leaves of the trees.
I've felt the velvet, soft, touch of the river's flow,
and the ocean's soft kiss on its shores below.
A deep reverant hush falls over my soul,
as it beholds the pure beauty of nature unfold.
The eagles, the raindrops, the sun in the sky
The days yet to come, The days that have gone by,
they are but pieces of puzzle, parts of a plan,
lessons to be learned, by each willing man.
The message is simple for those who would see.
The beauty of nature is Complete Harmony.

Margaret L Finch
MY HERITAGE
Come to me, my Forefathers!
In thought, you have always been closer than my breath.

I long to see into the distant past,
through the mists of time,
yearning to know what it was like to have climbed the Highlands,
to have wandered through a shady glenn,
to have heard the bagpipes skirlling
as they encouraged the troops to battle.

I envision those kilted men,
as small in number,
they noisily marched
toward the enemy.

I see their women and children
working and playing,
their Tartans designating their Clans.

I meander like a ghost among them,
striving to find the one to which I belong.

Vincent G Root
SOLDIER'S LAMENT
In my youth, I nursed a dream,
One of a farm, with field and stream,
One of a wife and child there,
To whom I'd give my utmost care.
I dreamed of things that I would do,
To make our deep love still more true,
But at that time, I knew it not,
That such for me, was not my lot,
Dream bubbles bursting one by one,
I was called to shoulder gun,
To march, and kill, and burst more dreams,
Of other youths who'd not forseen.

Sequel

Now in that day, and in that time.
My thoughts were, that I'd not survive,
But Mother's prayers went out for me.
And God answered them, as you can see.
Five years of war returned me home.
To conclude this little poem.
With a girl met in army life,
To be that dreamed of lovely wife.
Then children came for us to share.
With them, the good Lord's love and care.
Our lives were blessed in every way—
My thanks to God for all today.

Post World War II

Kenneth R Blume
OLD GLORY
Old Glory is our nations flag that flutters so proud above our free land.
Old Glory is so proud and free that it
describes freedom for you and me.
It grew by the faith of this land and what we have put in its hand.
I am proud of our flag you see because, it has made us free
Old Glory has grown in its pride by seeing us fighting for freedom at land and sea.
And it reminds us of our times of battle and dieing men
Because, it has shown it by fluttering
above our free land.

Elsa Winkler Roberts
THE QUESTION
Many have asked this question,
"Where is God and what is He?"
I have been asked this question,

What will my answer be?

I see God as Spirit
Alive in all creation on heaven and earth.
And we must abide in his teachings
And learn of our mission on earth.
Life on Earth but a moment.
No paradise; never meant to be.
'Tis a school of learning
For our future life to be.

Times of pain and sorrow
Hardships we must bear.
But the love of God within
Our burdens all will share.

The pathways to God are many.
All roads lead to His throne.
And the children of God have His image
Deep in their hearts to behold.

As I gaze o'er the ocean,
Raise my eyes to the stars above,
I believe God as Spirit,
Creator of the wonder of life and love.

Mystery Alires

BROTHERS

Pain and I are brothers, we have come so many miles.
Across Time—we shared a blanket or stood beside a stream;
paused where midnight pools are filled with glow of stars
and wandered on until the moon was down beyond the hill.

Brothers for so long, that I've forgotten when it was not my shade.
Yet in kinship, I have come to know a brighter way,
a warmer sun, a sweeter rose and night of deeper peace.
Pain and I are brothers, we have come so many miles.

Eugenia Wilkinson

FACES FROM THE PAST

I know them not, but yet they are there,
these visages of the past.
Stories that float in and out of my head
assure that the memories last.

One grandma whom I resemble so much,
whose pere was true Native American, she said.
Of what tribe even he did not know, for spirited
away was he when a very young lad.
Cherokee-white great-grandmere, immortalized in her oval portrait.
She came back again to live in my mother,
except this time a yellow-ochre.

Then there was great-great-grandmother Goldie,
conceived in the antebellum romance.
'twas not her name, but what she was called
for her hair was the color of flax.

Les noires? Of course, but I have no image of them;
they're not on the family tree.
No tribal name, nor from which province they came;
I suppose there shall never be.

This is the knowledge that I have, handed down from my grandmothers to me.
It says that I am not one, but a blend of many—
an intricate legacy.

Alberta V Rasmussen

LOST OPPORTUNITY

That stinging, singing wine
Which filled my goblet up;
That sparkling, dancing wine
That bubbled in my cup.

It's gone—the wine is gone—
The pitcher is not there,
And I had scarcely tasted
Of the wine—I did not dare.

My glass I've filled at streams
Where cool, clean waters ran;
And dew my cup has held
But never that which sang.

If time reversed its path
And took me back again,
I'd grasp my cup and laugh,
And custom's frown disdain.

I'd drink that pungent wine
Till happiness would be
The only thing that mattered
In this life to me.

Oh, that stinging, singing wine
Which filled my goblet up;
That sparkling, dancing wine
That bubbled in my cup

Chris Egelston

TOMORROW MAY BE TOO LATE

There is a time I cannot say,
What I have to say today,
The years speed by so very fast,
Our words are lost in the past.

So, I must say to you right now,
What should have been said long ago,
The love of family should stay the same,
Growing deeper and not so slow.

Our time is in the sunset,
We have so much to say,
Don't keep your thoughts hidden,
Tell someone you love them today.

Tomorrow might never come,
And if you pass before,
Someone's heart will always ache,
For the love you held in store.

I'll try again to tell you,
Before we meet our fate,
Tell your family you love them,
Before it is too late.

Joan Jacobs

FEELINGS

Sometimes it's hard to say what's really in your heart.
For me you can read it in my eyes.
In my culture I was taught to express my feelings.
Not so much to be bold, but to be honest and open.
I've been honest and open.
Now I feel pain, since I frighten people away.
I'm sorry; yet I'm not sorry . . .
Since I know someday people, ideas,
and feelings will change.

Mary Jane Hoover Baer

GOD IS IN CONTROL

I see the sun rise in the east, hear the ocean's billows roll,
These miracles of a Master's hand, show God is in control.
I listen to a blue bird sing each note in harmony,
A gift from God our Father in nature's symphony.
God touches every flower, each one a brilliant hue,
He gave us sight to enjoy each one, take time to smell a few.
When trouble's come, reach out in faith to His redeeming love,
Remember God is in control, He rules from heaven above.
We cannot walk life's road alone, we need a guiding hand,
Reach out, God's there, he's in control so trust His command.
Don't worry about tomorrow, sleep well and trust the Lord,
Our souls rest in God's loving grace receiving faith's reward.
Worries about war, inflation and crime all seem to take its toll,
Read God's Word, it's written there Our Lord is in control.
Do you live your life for Jesus, who gave His life for you,
He's in control of all the earth, trust Him to see us through.
No nation has a ruler, who should be worshipped and adored,
Such love belongs to only One, He's Jesus Christ our Lord.

Henrietta F Tissue

LONELINESS

I never lived such empty days as I am living now.
And when I try to laugh and sing, I find I don't know how.
Each day I listen for your call, but waiting seems in vain,
And patience, still, within my heart is driving me insane.

What does a tree do when its leaves have fallen to the ground,
And blossoms shaken to the breeze can never more be found?
A loneliness I'm sure is there—and so it is with men.
A tree is bare till blossom time and blossoms come again.

My heart beats out in discontent that surely you must hear.
Have patience yet a little while: I wipe away a tear.
Have patience—yes, and while we wait, a star falls from the sky.
And opportunity, disguised, has slyly passed us by!

Emmett W Harris

REVERIE

The windswept clouds in far-off western skies
Softly draw the curtain on the day;
The fading azure seems to nod good-bye,
Crimson hues grow dim and waft away.
A lonely star appears to pulse its light,
Once again leads heaven's jew'ls to view,
And here I stand alone in hush of night,
While this grandeur pales with thoughts of you.
Your silhouette glides to my reverie,
Outstretched arms that beckon all my love,
But all too soon comes stark reality,
You are lost in starry skies above.

Diane Leatherwood-Shekhawat

WORDS

You once wrote words
to someone you cared for.
I, in turn, write them to you,
for you are someone I care for.
Be it time or loneliness
that has consumed you so,
forget not the friends you possess,
regardless of whether you are aware
of their undying devotion to you,
it still lives on,
waiting for your acknowledgment.

My endearment for you is immortal . . .
and can only be put to death
by your hands.
For only you gave it birth,
and only you shall be it's executioner.
I speak of time gone by,
and time yet to come,
and that—my friend,
is forever!

Charles M Stanley

PR1 Charles M (Stan) Stanley USN-Retired

BIG BROTHER LEAVES AMERICA

To: All members of the United States Armed Services and appropriate governmental agency's (FREEDOM RINGS)

1982 has come and passed
Orson Welles lies in the grass
Big Brother came but did not last
Freedom won with his last test

What a feeling to be FREE!
It brings a thrill to me and thee
Brother moved across the sea
Not to bother you and me

The USA gives us our thrill
We do not need Brother or a pill
With Uncle Sam we get our high
We know we can make it, If we try!

If you want to spy, whine and shout
Fly to Russia and try your clout.

Julie Walker
SNOW SCAPE
Fallen snow
Crystallyn white
Blanket of diamonds
Luminous and bright

Silver glow
Keeper of life
Beneath a thick blanket
Thru winters night

Ice water falls
Frozen in time
Cascading down rooftops
Trickling down pines

Mother Nature sleeping
Under a veil of white
All Earth in her protection
Safe thru the night

Helen Richards
HALLOWEEN

To my grandson Tom Kramer who at the age of twelve inspired me to write this holiday poem for his October bulletin board.

Halloween comes in the Fall
When leaves are colored yellow, red, brown or all.
When witches fly, and the black cat roams
The owl hoots, and skeletons rattle their bones.
In fields the cornstalks stand among the pumpkins,
Children in costumes trick or treat, the little bumpkins!
Goblins and ghosts are near,
Happy, happy, Halloween have no fear!

Martha J Adams
TREASURES
Baby fingers wrapped about yours
Wrap also 'round your heart.
It's really just the beginning;
Just the very first part.

They come to you shortly after
With hurts that need your touch.
And often they walk up to you
With flowers in their clutch.

They test your patience day by day,
And keep you up at night.
But just their smile (that toothy grin)
Can make your heart take flight!

You'll answer a thousand questions
Like . . . Why is Daddy tall?
How come I can't take my teeth out?
And what makes babies crawl?

And there are still treasures
Even when they're grown,
Because we've tended carefully
And seeds of love we've sown.

William R Hoover
ONLY IF I NEED HIM
God sent down an angel to see me today
I said there's much to be done before you lead me away
I didn't come to take you his assuring words I felt
He said the reason I'm here is you asked God for help
You say your spine is all crippled and you can't stand the pain
You can't even walk without the use of a cane
Climb up on my wing and hold to it tight
I did what he said and we were off on a flight
Across the ocean we went high over the waves
Where we saw people starving and some didn't have legs
Some had no arms and others were blind
All of these people had more problems than mine
As we continued our journey he spoke of his boss
Then I caught the image of someone nailed to a cross
Take me back I said I don't need that cane
When I slid down from his wing I felt no more pain
What I learned today is richer than wealth
You never ask God what you can do for yourself

Carl H Engleman
RAIN PAIN
Every time it rains it seems
I slip into those nightmare dreams
So long ago and far away
From what I see as real today.
My mixed emotions rob and steal
The thoughts of what was really real
And now I cannot seem to tell
If my heart is free from that mental jail.

Sometimes I think when I awake
That everything was a big mistake.
It was only a trip I took in my head
And all my friends aren't really dead.
Why, I saw Smitty just the other night.
We were side by side in a big fire fight.
It didn't take us very long
To take that hill and kill those Cong.

It's slacking up, now let me see
Where was I supposed to be?
Oh yes, I must have closed my eyes.
It's good to see those clear blue skies.
Though I'm in pain and feel alone
Guess I should be glad that the rain is gone.

Cherie Ulrich
THE FARM
I have found a place that is very special to me,
It is a ways away from where I live, but I still
go there at least once a week. At this place, which is
a farm, I find security. I know that no matter how
down I am I can go there and be cheered up.

This farm is different from any other farm I've
been to, for not only are the people and animals
friendly, but the landscape also puts me at ease.
Here I can talk with others or be alone. I can
receive anything I need when I am there and never
am asked anything in return. No matter what
angle I look at this farm it gives out love,
friendship, and security to me.
I hope that one day I am able to make this
farm my permanent home. It would be like a
dream come true if this would happen.
I know once I live there I will only grow
more attached to it and the other people
that will surround me.

Mrs Rose Kinal
WHAT IS THE SWEETHEART?
A loving person, that is dear and sweet
Good and sincere, not only on top, but also beneath
It is a person who loves to share
That loving kindness everywhere.

It is a person who goes an extra mile
And sits in any place, with you to dine.

People like that happiness and joy
They are darlings and welcome to stay.

Persons like sweetheart make the earth go round
Special little sweethearts they for heaven bound.

Like lightning they lighten the world
If they say only one sweet word.

This is the child that is so sweet
From the top of the head to the soles of the feet.

It is our hope and happiness too
That's why I am writing,
Sweetheart, about you!

Dr Christy Beck Gootee
A FRAGILE WHISPER—A SOFT CRY
You are the wind that lives and will not die.
A breath inside the sun's gold fire. But we—
we are a fragile whisper—a soft cry.

You are the flame that burns, the searing eye,
that touches coals, consumes, engrosses me.
You are the wind that lives and will not die.

I am a raindrop on a rose, a sigh.
I lose and gain in the silence of your sea:
We are a fragile whisper—a soft cry.

You are the trees, the stars, the snow and I—
I touch the shadows that I cannot see.
You are the wind that lives and will not die.

I am the ice that melts when you walk by.
In the fire of you I burn and cease to be.
We are a fragile whisper—a soft cry.

We are the light that never questions why,
that seeps through time into eternity.
You are the wind that lives and will not die.
We are a fragile whisper—a soft cry.

Trish Thomson
THE NO-COLLAR MAN
Way out in a dark and dirty hole
An old man was sitting as black as the coal.
As I tread my way to him he lifted his head.
I felt sorry for him and my eyes turned all red.
. . . His shirt had no collar,
and I said, "Here's a dollar."

His eyes sparkled bright as he started to smile,
That old man sittin' there on that pile.
His words rang loud and clear, they came out plain,
"I feel richer than you, thanks just the same."
. . . His shirt had no collar
Yet he had no need for my dollar.

What's he got that I ain't got?
A great big house on a great big lot?
A chain of stores or a grand Hi-Fi?
But he felt sorry for me and now I see why . . .
I've got too many collars
And too many dollars.
My life has no love
I have no meaning at all.

. . . His shirt had no collar
But he was richer than I.

Alan Thornton Watkins

Alan Thornton Watkins
REFLECTIONS
On a beautiful September afternoon, I sit in my garden at peace. There is the scent of fall in the air
that makes the years unfold to other times and places in vague recollection. Long forgotten talks, sights,
smells and sounds that tease my memory. Almost clear at times . . . then lost. But I will savor the present
moment; this September afternoon—alone in my garden.

Gary Michael Johnson
SESTINA
As I sit, here on a Friday afternoon,
head held, between the palms of my hands,
the trees whisper in through the window.

I close my eyes,
hoping the day will disappear,
if only for a moment.

And in that moment,
evening slips over afternoon,
and I disappear
from the pressure between my
hands,
the sand behind my eyes,
to the lulling, that passes in
through the window.

Traveling away from that prison
window.
I skate on a frozen moment.
Starlight shielding my eyes
from the burn of afternoon.
With nothing left to bind my hands,
I let go my mind, and the thorns
disappear.

What if, disappear
I would, forever, close the pane in
the window,
push it down with my hands,
leave myself with infinite moment,
never again a Friday afternoon,
never again a need, for shield
before my eyes.

A noise behind me, my hands react
and the stars disappear.
I open my eyes and turn; back to
the window,
back to a fleeting moment on a
Friday afternoon.

Doris E B Leach
A LOVING ATTITUDE
Children, parents—each one of us
alike;
'Tis by our attitude we make our
life.
God has given us everything we
need;
Love alone is our earnest goal.

Be good to each other, and to
yourself;
Thru kindness and understanding
we all grow.
Christ Jesus is here to take our
hand;
To enrich our attitude, through our
soul.

Awaken each one—look up and see
The sky overhead, the beauties on
earth.
Heaven is here—so make it your
worth
To live life by having Love for all.

Catherine A Oberdorf
UNSPOKEN LOVE

To Gerald and Susan, my loving parents

Love was never spoken here
It was merely understood.
It wasn't that we didn't try
We just never could.

You treated us all different
With little things you'd do.
Now we know you were saying
We really do love you.

We always had the chance
To do things on our own.
And though at times we felt it
We were never alone.

Now that we are older
Have places of our own.
We still think of visiting you
As always going home.

Gus Horn
KISSES
Kisses on paper (XXX)
Are a cute little ploy
But they'll never replace
The real McCoy

Edna Herring
LOVE
A word not uncommon to man
Indeed very much in demand.
It's in the air, actually everywhere
All one has to do is really care.
Love is outstanding in its field
Emotions are endless that it will
yield.
It's available to many, not just a few
Always within your reach, it's just
up to you.
Love, many times, seems to go
astray
When the wrong emotions get in
the way.
Not meant to be a slave, it yearns
to be free
Not possessed, it will work
miracles for you and me.
The wonders of the mind can make
or break
The laws of nature and cause the
heart to ache.
One could say it's used, abused,
thrown aside
Then around it goes with "This I
abide."
No other word has so much impact
On every living thing, it's a matter
of fact.
Love will not bore you, nor ask any
favors of you
Except to keep it true, which
should be an easy thing to do.
Love should never be ending
Instead, always upon you
descending.
Its meaning was written in a few
quite words
If you read with understanding,
then you must have heard.

Lela Hartnett Atteberry
WINTER GARDEN
'Tis winter in the garden now.
The gray sage proclaims
Supremacy.
No towering mint run wild
Infringes on her space.
The chaste young violet
Reduced ere this
By careening caraway
Presents fugitive blossoms
In humble splendor.
While optimistic oregano
Sends forth some shoots
As if to test the season
Of the year.
The thick leaved mullein
Accepts the winter rest
And lies supinely, relaxed
Awaiting spring.

Joyce Latham
NANCY
They said "It's a girl"
You told them her name
Because "girl" wasn't worth
The caring and loving
You gave before birth.

You think all the thoughts
Your sure she must have
While rocking her gently
Holding her head.

The threat of the school year
Is too much to bear
They tell you the truth
Will surely show there.

She's out the door
And off to school
You sit at home crying
"Can she be a big girl?"

She's doing just fine
As you knew she would
She's being your daughter
Now, "Did I do good?"

Of course you won't know
Until she is a Mom
And watch how she raises
Her little one.

Sandra King
THE OBOE
The Oboe is a baby clarinet without
a mouthpiece.
It's the color of a dim piece of
coal,
That is like a firey grill that has
just
been put out.
The Oboe sounds like the
feelings
I have when I'm happy and sad
at the same time,
And it's like a dark spooky
Halloween night.

Sandra King
LOVE
Love is a jewel of a treasure,
Which is a satisfying pleasure
And it's so precious that it
can't be measure.

Jerry Chute
AMBER LADY
Blue tears,
Memories of nothing
fall.
Deep wonder
Breaks solitude.
From within
I've seen your majesty.
Are you real,
Or just a fantasy?
Is your hold on me liberty?
Amber Queen
By quiet stream,

Lost shadow of a
painful dream.
To pursue you could
mean everything.
Do you know me:
Can you feel?
Is there nothing to provoke
More than your idle while?
Who runs, chases
You or I?
Yet I am warmly caressed.
Blue tears?
Amber Lady?
For nothing?

Joy Helt-Raner
TIME FOR TOMORROW
Early in the morning and
in the middle of the day,
Suddenly I realized
all the time that's passed away.

Never to be recaptured,
Neither now nor then.
Time tells me to keep moving.
Forward, straight ahead.

All the yesterdays are lost forever,
today is in the sun.
Hold on tight to all your dreams
for tomorrow is yet to come.

Through trials and tribulations
hold on to this thought,
the strongest kind of people
are those who can't be bought.

Go forth into tomorrow,
looking back only when,
to try to capture yesterday;
never to be seen again.

Ann Talley
CAPTIVITY
I awaken, longing for the wild,
Green beauty of another time,
When I was King of the Jungle
And all was mine.

Lazy days and noisy nights,
Filled with sounds of friend and
foe,
Fresh food to be had
Wherever I wished to go.

I awaken to man-made sounds
And a repugnant scent.
Bars of melted ore and slain trees
Remind me of days spent.

Caged and tormented by man.
I'm fed from the carcass of
another,
Never knowing of what,
It may be a friend or brother.

Straw, with mildew and mold.
Stinking smut for a bed,
Memories of wild grasses, blowing
in the wind.
O, that the King were dead.

Julie M Stolz
MOM

Because you were always there for me. With all my love.

Thanks for all you've given me
when you let me have my freedom
knowing you only wanted to keep
me
you let me express my own
individuality
letting me find my mistakes on my
own
then guiding me back on the right
road
helping me through the hard times
and always being there to share the
good
I'm so glad God picked you
specially to be
my mom

Lillie A Skaar
SPRING
Well, spring, you're here again
At your same old tricks I'll bet.
Guess I'll watch the paper
And see how many more you get

Spring, you ought to be ashamed
You know it is not right
To turn a young man's fancy
Then revel in his plight

Ah, my spring, I know you well
Just look what you did for me
If it hadn't been for you
We wouldn't have these three

Yes spring, you did turn his fancy
He conceded you that bout,
But please don't turn his pockets
too,
They look bad inside out.

Edwin A Dahlgren

ONE DAY

As the years
go traveling by
An unpleasant occasion
may cause you to cry
But having faith
in our world each day
Will help to drive
the sadness away
Have faith in our friends
and return a good deed
It will bring happiness
at a greater speed
With all the problems
that arise
We hope each correction
proves to be wise
In this new computer world
moving with such speed
There is not much time
for best choice of our need
We hope in the future
not far away
All men will be peaceful
in this world one day

Elizabeth Hickle

NAM

With tears, pride and gratitude to all gallant men of Vietnam; Heroes All.

Brittle chips of moonlight
Dapple the paddy
Elephant grass swishing
And the sergeant towering.

Drowned in the sweat of the world
While the night—mawking,
mawking
Silence—aching, aching
And the sergeant towering.

Whispers, whispers, whispers
Animal, vegetable, mineral?
Death whispers in his ear
And the sergeant towering.

Then—Clamouring, Screaming,
Bleeding Hell
Sequined twinkle of bursting shell
Splayed over the paddy—
Caught in green tender shoots
Jagged bits, hissing.

Crumpling he made no sound
Full measured on the ground—
DEAR GOD! THE SERGEANT . . .

Jo Ann Norton

A MONSTER STEALING

It comes
A monster stealing
Frightening
Penetrating
Trying to tear homes apart
Draining them of heat
Chilling
Freezing the occupants
There is no way to control its
viciousness
Clawing
Taking breath away
Biting tender cheeks
Draining moisture from bare skin
Ripping at trees
Dessicating earth and grass
Sucking life from plant and animal
Constant flowing
Blowing
Raging
It shows no mercy
No tenderness
Its voice roaring
Screaming
This monster stealing
This cold winter wind

Dale E Boydston

DAY'S END

In the cool of the evening
When the sun has settled low,
When the night winds softly
whisper
And the leaves so softly blow,

When the shadows begin to
lengthen
Fortelling the close of day,
Comes a time of quiet
remembrance
Of things now gone away.

Our minds so slightly wander
To joys the day has brought,
And we find peace and
contentment
In every precious thought.

Though weary from our labors
When time has quickly passed,
We cherish each precious moment
And welcome the night at last.

Belinda Jenkins

THE HOUSE THAT STANDS ON THE HILL

To my mother, Emily, whom I love very much

The house that stands on the hill
Had a white picket fence with a
rose garden
The trees would whisper
throughout the night
The birds would sing from evening
till first light
And when the young man came
home from work
He would bring flowers to his
lovely wife
Every Saturday the grass would be
cut and the windows
Washed, on Sunday he would hunt
in the green meadows
The house that stands on the hill
Had so much kindness and love to
give away
When the elderly man came home
from work, he kissed her
everyday
Every Saturday he would rake the
leaves
From the long and swaying trees
Every Sunday the elderly man and
woman would sit,
And watch the sun set, on their
anniversary, a candle was
always lit
The house that stands on the hill
Would in its own way seem to laugh
The elderly man now comes home
from work bearing no gifts
Every Saturday the tall grass grows
taller, the windows become
Dirtier, every Sunday he
dissappears into the house
The trees don't whisper, the birds
don't sing
The elderly man sits in his chair
And stares out the dirty window
with his lifeless eyes
He just sits in his chair and
occasionally lets out a sigh
And at night, if you listen, you can
hear the house on the hill
Begin to cry.

Carol J Cummings

A WALK BY THE SEA

This poem is dedicated to my Mum and Dad. I love you.

As I went wandering by the sea,
I thought of all the wonders I could
see.
The clouds went swirling by on
high,
A gentle breeze like a whispering
sigh.
I walked upon the golden sand,
So soft, so warm this glorious land.
The sea in all its splendor swirled,
Swaying and crashing the waves
unfurled.
I saw the sea shells on the shore,
Oh who could wish to see anything
more.

I watched as my footprints were
washed away,
Oh wouldn't it be nice if they could
stay.
Far out at sea I saw a ship,
I thought how I longed to take a
dip.
The sea was warm against my skin,
I watched the seagulls fly and skim.
Dancing along the curling waves,
Flying into craggy, rocky caves.
I watched a crab go skittering by,
I thought of the golden sun on high.
Oh what a glorious, wondrous day.
Walking along the sand, I wished
to stay.

Lawrence E Weilacher

MERCY FROM GOD

The roof of their house,
Was a mountain of stone.
All the rooms dark.
As they worked all alone.

These were just miners
Who dug out the black coal,
Enclosed in a damp dungeon.
Risking body and soul

Not seeing bright daylight
Just sealed in a tomb
Digging black diamonds
From a ten by ten room

But God up in heaven
Knew of their plight
As he felt the rocks move
In the darkness of night
God saw their faces
And felt their hearts fear
A cave in was coming
As Jesus stood near

Their black grimy faces
Turned upwards to God
As they prayed for mercy
From the fast falling clods

But Jesus has answered
And God had his way
For down thru the darkness
Showed the brightness of day

Gayle Gardner Lin

RECOVERY

What was the demon
That sat on your shoulder
And, like a vampire,
Sucked the sparkle from your eyes
And the excitement from your
voice,
Leaving you with a vacuous stare
And rounded shoulders
Turning inward on yourself,
Causing you to speak in a
monotone,
To resist my embrace—
Your body as stiff as
A cigar store's wooden Indian?

What type of fungus
Mushroomed inside you
Killing the dreams, the hope,
The promises of youth?

I watched your suffering
And longed to reach inside you
With my bare hands
To tear loose the cancer
Consuming your psyche.

My beautiful child, who was unable
To face the burdens of everyday
life,
A positive response from you has
Created a rainbow in my tears.

Christine Jester

MY LAKE SUPERIOR

Its gray, cold hand reaches toward
you,
Its frosty breath chills the air.
Glittering, challenging, sparing
few,
It laughs harshly without a care!

Its friendly smile invites you in,
Its cool, green depths refresh your
mind.
Splashing, mischievous, creating a
din,
Sparkling, gurgling, playing with
time.

Which side do you see?
Which side have you found?
Does it let you be free?
Or does it pull you down?

Kathryn J Keys

WHY?

Why do people laugh when we
stumble and fall
And why do we cry at nothing at
all?
I once heard that everyone's
human;
But you are the best of them all.

I see you standing as I wave
goodbye.
The tears in my eyes will never dry.
I want to run back and love you
again;
But I know that's the wrong thing
to do.

I want you, I need you, to get into
your heart;
To stand by, to walk by, we never

will part.
I'll love you forever as we walk along,
From now to the rest of our lives.

You take me in your arms and tell me you were wrong
And that you want to hold me again.
I let you know that I will forgive you
And I will always love you.

I whisper your name when you're not around;
I dream of your touch and glad that I found
The one thing I hoped for and always will cherish
The love that you've given me.

Katherine Smith Matheney
THE MASTERS HAND

To my sister Edna, who never gave up faith in me.

God walks with us along the way
As down lifes road we go.
He comforts and He cares for us
Because He loves us so.
He sends the sunshine and the rain,
The moon and stars above.
And in His handiwork I see
Our God's abiding love.
He shares each sorrow and each dream,
Our every hope and plan.
And all of our tomorrows are
Touched by the Masters hand.

D J Henderson
PUZZLEMENT
I wonder are there others who have longed
For knowledge, learning, mastery of many crafts;
And have strained the limit of their comprehension
In hot endeavor to outwit the time,
O'ercrowd their length of days.
As I have found, they find
That they have failed true competence.
They are equipped with odds and ends of erudition;
Fit but to entertain at dinner,
Lighten tedious hours of travel,
Confuse the serious scholar,
Deflate the pompous, ridicule the self-righteous,
Challenge the intolerant,
Raise doubts in true believers,
Amaze the ignorant, make women smile;
Useful for little else.

I wonder are there others who love God
And trust his mercy as their mothers taught,
And have listened, Sabbath after Sabbath,
To what the preacher teaches.
Yet will vex, in some uncertain moments,
Their ordered understanding
With fruitless questions
Of Adam, Christ, Eternity, Omniscience.

Ralph W Michener
THE SUNFLOWER
How much I admire the stately sunflower
Designed by the Creator for us to observe,
She is one of distinction in the kingdom of flowers
As she stands like a sentinel her kindred to serve.

How she graciously looks to her God for survival
And spends the night waiting for him to arise,
Then adorned in her beauty she greets his arrival
And faithfully watches his journey thru the sky.

Until the hour of parting with no less adoration
She sighs as the horizon conceals his repose,
Then pleased with the memory of the days occupation
She fondly turns back to the place where he arose.

So devoted so faithful from the time of her birth
Until the shades of autumn mark the end of her days,
Then destined like all forms of life on this earth
Her beauty and life will fade away.

Juanita M Scheer
AT RAINBOWS END

To Guy Eben McConnell who is always in my heart, and waiting at rainbow's end. . .

The rain rolls off a window like tears rolling down a cheek.
Mother Nature is crying, for She has lost one of her own.
I know the pain she feels deep within her heart,
for I too have lost this special person.
And no words can take the pain away.
The years we had were very short,
but the time we spent could have lasted but for only a day,
and it would have been no more special.
We gave them so much heartache,
and we shared their laughter too.
My mind wants to disbelieve that all I have left are memories.
My heart knows you are holding my hand.
You lead me down the rainbow's path.
Not for gold—but love, friendship and understanding at the end.
I am peaceful at heart—sure I will miss your hugs,
but I feel your spirit here within me.
These tears I cry for you—each is a memory.
I will cherish forever this time we spent together.
Good-bye for now—I know it's not forever.
Someday we will meet again.
Side-by-side holding hands.
At The Rainbow's End . . .

Darleen Cornell-Adams
CHRISTMAS TIME POEM
This is a time to smile, a time to care.
A time for loved ones and a time to share.
A time for laughter, so try not to cry.
A time to look at the stars in the sky.
This is a time for love, a time to give.
A time to enjoy and a time to live.
It's a time to listen as well as to speak.
A time to be stronger when you feel so weak.

It's a time to reach out for someone's hand.
A time to show them that you understand.
A time for happiness, a time to be glad.
A time to realize that life's not so bad.

A time to sing a beautiful song.
Time to be forgiven when people do wrong.
It's a time to pray to our Father above.
Time to be thankful for all of his love.

Before I end this poem, I leave you with this thought.
These gifts are given freely. Not one can be bought.
So remember all of these, I'm wishing just for you.
So have a Merry Christmas and may all your dreams come true.

Jo Nell Holcomb
WHY DON'T YOU LOVE ME, DADDY
Why don't you love me Daddy,
I'm only a few months old.
I'm really a beautiful little girl, or so I've been told.
I've got big blue eyes and auburn hair and a smile that
would melt your heart, so why don't you love me, Daddy,
when I'm older I know I will be really smart. I guess I
am small and young, and I cry quite a lot, but why don't
you love me, Daddy, I'm the only little girl you've got.
My Papa rocks me and Grandmama sings me lullabies, but
my Mommie is broken hearted, so she just rocks and cries.
I know I'm expensive, Pampers I wet, and all the milk I
drink, but why don't you love me, Daddy, we share such a
common link.

I'm your's and mommie's little girl even though you never
wed. I guess you never will, or that's what mommie said.
If you can't love me Daddy, won't you please tell me why.
I hate to see my mommie just sit and cry.
I'll close this letter to you Daddy, and seal it with a
tear. You know I will always love you, although you will
never hold me near.
I hope you health and happiness, as you never wished for
me, but if wishes came true, then we would be a family,
so, good-bye, Daddy.

Brian M Drake
A QUIET MOMENT AT THE WISHING WELL
A small silver disk,
Tumbles end over end
Falling towards the brightly glinting surface.
A softly muttered wish,
A distant glimmering hope,
A quiet splash,
And a silently muttered, "Amen."
As the ripples spread across the pool's surface.

Velma Warren Crenshaw
THOUGHTS TO LIVE BY

In memory of my mother, Maud Robinson Warren, and my grandfather, Joseph W. J. Robinson.

I stand beside the open grave with grief too heavy to bear
And as I gaze into the heaven comes an answer to my prayer.
"What can't be cured, must be endured," I hear my Mother say,
And with these words, the pain does ease, though it does not go away.

I see a lame, old beggarman walking down the street
And hear the voices of children deride him as they meet.
My mind goes back to a childhood day long since gone by,
I hear my Mother say, "There, but for the grace of God, go I.

"Do unto others as you would have others do unto you."
My Mother lived each and every day by this Golden Rule.
These much loved words, I once again renew
As, with a loving kiss, I send my own children off to school.

"Never put off until tomorrow what you can do today."
I can hear my Mother telling me what her Daddy used to say,
For "A stitch in time saves nine" is true in every way
And is just as appropriate now as it was in my Grandaddy's day.

These axioms to live by were told to us over and over.
These were the standards and rules of survival and life
In my Mother's day as in my Grandaddy's day before,
And in this present world of trouble, they help me also to survive.

I hope my children will remember these when I have passed from this earth,
For there is nothing more important that I can leave them
In this present, torn and troubled world of their birth,
Than these changeless rules of love and life that I bequeath them.

Annie-Laurie Herman
PREJUDICE
Who are you?
Why are you here?
Just go away
We don't want you so near!

It's not that we mind
Your right to exist.
We want to be kind
How could we resist.

It's just that you're different
Than what we're used to.
Please don't lament
Just do what we do.

Reject or withdraw
Scary things in life.
If you must then you claw
Your way through the strife.

We don't learn much this way
But it's what we do now.
Maybe some day
We'll be taught how

To learn to accept you
The way that you are.
The concept is new,
Like touching a star.

Ann Hall Chance
RUN GIRL RUN
Run girl Run,
Don't let him touch your heart.

Run girl Run,
Before the teardrops start.

You fell in love so long ago;
and gave to him life and love,
your very own soul.

Run girl Run,
before you cross that line.

Run girl run,
Painful memories are on your side,
remember girl, you loved him true,
and heartbreak is all he gave to you.

Life was gentle and sweet or so you thought,
soon, life became a game only to be fought.

Run girl run,
Don't let him touch your heart.

Colleen Shaughnessy-Palmiter
NOW FAR AWAY
My mother, my sister, my friends
gloss in my eyes as I peer out the window again
into the mist and the icicles in the trees
the vision of my face
searching through the glass
looking distant off into the land
of memories and ice and sun
thinking of my family and times
when I was close to everyone
now far away
the sun can't melt the ice
this wilderness created over the land
and icicles won't freeze my longing
for the warmth of a familiar friend,
loving mother, gentle father. . .a warm hand.

Mary-Helen Neyhart
ODE TO AN ISLAND
For me, a little island in a lake,
Especially if it were wooded well—
A few tall firs, a tamarack or two
And lesser growth with berries passing birds may take. . .
A tiny cove ringed by a beach of sand
With pebbles strewn as if for children's play,
Watched over by a boulder Time has tamed
And garnished with white bones of floating trees from land. . .
A faithful spring in shade with water clear
Near mossy cradled spot inviting rest,
Caressing breeze passed on by trees, to feel
And not a murmur but faint lappind foam, to hear.
No tethered boat for me to reach reality;
So, fretted thoughts, come share my found tranquility.

Laura L Pelton
IF I ONLY KNEW
I step out of the car.
Not a sound is heard
No one is talking
Not saying a word

The wind is whisping
Through the tops of the trees
It is very gloomy
And there's a chill in the breeze

The fragrance of flowers
Is in the air
The birds are chattering
Without even a care

I just stand there
Feeling ever so blue
Thinking Oh God
If I'd only knew

The tears start to come
Without hardly a sound
As I stand and watch
Them lower my daddy's casket
into the ground

June A Stroops
TO BE
Youth is not here to stay.
So why waste it away?
As the years go by.
You will understand why.

Oh, to have yesterday!
Time gone by.
Never to be again.
Memories to hold and blend.

Yesterday is gone.
Today is here to mend.
Age goes with life
Tomorrow is a friend.

So use your days
The best that you can.
Because yesterday is past
And tomorrow doesn't last.

Sarah Smith
THE PREMONITION OF LOVE
Like a rose blooming in the early spring, love begins.
Hear the whippoorwill calling, calling.

The sun is the smile of happiness as love grows.
Hear the whippoorwill calling, calling.

The breezes are the beautiful words of I love you from deep within.
Hear the whippoorwill calling, calling.

The rain is the teardrops falling as love begins to whither.
Hear the whippoorwill calling, calling.
The cold dark clouds gather around as love begins to die.
Hear the whippoorwill calling, calling.

Cold and alone until spring comes, waiting for love to bloom again.
Hear the whippoorwill calling, calling.

Elfi Keating
UNTITLED
I shall leave no trace
On my road through life
Wind and sand
Shall erase my footstep
And I shall walk on until infinity

Hope Beavers Weed

Hope Beavers Weed
ANKLE BRACELET
It's just a small ornament
Given her for adornment
And it is without unction
Or a practical function.

It is just a cute bangle
Worn at an acute angle
And wound around her ankle
In an endless circle.

Not a chain of iron links
So heavy in hardship clinks
That is tight enough to welt
With a loss of freedom felt.

But to further inquire
A chain of real light wire
Of finely crafted spun gold
So delicate to behold.

Communicating links not tough
Yet a gold chain strong enough
To carefully band a bond
Of enduring friendship sound.

Lucile E Sigourney
THE CUT WORM

To Christina

I went in the backyard.
And a cut worm I found.
A weed he did find,
And this will be mine.

He looked up, and showed
me his teeth, then all the
leaves he did eat.

I went away and came back,
And the whole hard stem,
he had devoured.

Tony Howard Webb
KINGDOM OF THE DOVES

This poem is dedicated to those who won't give up their dreams—today is the day of miracles.

Whispers speaking in my ears
through the silence of the nights
the memory of days gone by the
pictures in my mind
the dreams you left behind for me
the love you gave my heart
you changed my world before
you left to the Kingdom of the Doves
You were more to me than just a friend you were my only love
you gave to me the strength I have and today I am who I am
When I walk alone late at night and look into the skys
I feel your presence in my heart
just like you never died
I send my prayers up past the stars to the heavens up above
and ask the Lord to rest your soul
in the Kingdom of the Doves
I found myself a hopeless case then you took from me a harden heart
I thought of life as a total waste
then you took from me a world of hate
May peace be with you through eternity in the heavens up above
I send my love from me to you
in the Kingdom of the Doves.
Reflections of the past when I'm deep into myself
I flash back to the beginning
because again I'm by myself
but this image in the mirror isn't the same person as before
cause even though your gone today
my life means so much more
It's the dreams you left behind
for me it's the love you gave my heart
You changed my world before you left to the Kingdom of the Doves.

Elizabeth Harding
GOD AND GRANDMAS APRON

Dedicated in Loving Memory of our Grandmothers and to our Lord and God, father of us all—a Loving family of brothers and sisters in faith.

Oh Grama, how I wish I could
be tied to your apron strings.
The strings of binding love that a
happy homelife brings.
Living life a simple way,
slowing down from modern day
Quick food meals and quick life styles
Thinking of the old days makes me smile
So—
We trust in God and emulate his ways
He is our anchor and will never stray.
The one we depend on in times of need
A life of love and faith—but never greed
Keep us in your strings, Lord—
of binding love and protective care
Like love of families—You're always there
When we need you most, and when we may not
We turn to you thankfully
For all that we've got.

Hazel Huntley
TO DAWN ON HER WEDDING DAY
When Dawn was just a little girl,
and sat on her Mother's knee
She used to tell her nursery
rhymes, and of things that used to be.

But all too soon the years went by,
and Dawn went off to school.
A clever girl she wanted to be, and
was nobody's fool.
The teenage years soon arrived,
and High school was in sight
Her mother's hair soon turned
grey, and she couldn't sleep at
night.
Father paced the floor, when Dawn
was on a date
Where is that girl? Her father said,
It's getting very late.

The years soon passed, and Dawn
grew up into a lovely Miss.
Every young man who came her
way, would want to steal a kiss.
The final step is now in view, a
wedding is on the wing.
Every step our Dawn will take, will
make her young heart sing.
Congratulations to you Dawn, and
to your handsome groom.
Although you are a woman now, to
Mom and Dad you'll be
The very precious little girl, who
sat on Mother's knee.

Scharlei S Sawyer

THE INFINITE

This poem is dedicated to my son, Buzz. A fine policeman who was killed May 16, 1983. "Blessed are the Peacemakers"

I don't know what is to be,
I only see all around me.
I know what I see is clear,
I can believe in what is near.

You don't see what is to be,
You cannot see through me.
You should see it clear,
You know what is seen is near.

Ruth D Simmons

THE SEASONS

To my Granddaughter—Leilani

Do you feel the wrath of winter?
Cold winds whipping about your
face,
Snowflakes falling all around you
From the skies with poise and
grace.

But Alas! It now is spring time.
Things are new, the grass is green
Flowers are blooming in the
garden.
All the world is bright and clean

Now it's hot, it must be summer.
Skies are blue, the sun is bright.
Garden's ripe, flowers are pretty.
Moon and stars are out tonight.

The air turns crisp, the leaves are
falling
Now the trees are turning bare
Frosty fields, and yellow pumpkins
It must be fall, this time of year.

L Anne Jones

TEMPLE'S CAFE

Mr. Lucious Temple, owner of the CAFE, corresponded faithfully with our hometown boys who served during WWII and this poem is in his memory and in honor of all United States Veterans.

Somehow, along life's way,
I had the good fortune
to be a patron of
Temple's Cafe, my hometown,
U.S.A.

It was there, I had to eat,
my favorite treat, for a nickel. . .
A hamburger with all the
trimmings. . .
mustard, onion and pickle!
and to drink, for five cents yet. . .
a cold delicious Grapette.

I have eaten hamburgers in fine
restaurants,
cozy cafes and even a corner
diner,
But, there is no way, their taste can
beat,
the nickel hamburger, I had to
eat,
at Temple's Cafe, my hometown,
U.S.A.

I consider it my luck,
to have seen a time,
when a dime,
could buy my favorite treat
to eat,
and even luckier
that I could pay
what it took
at Temple's Cafe, my hometown,
U.S.A.

Joan Moran

EXTORTION

To my mother

Like a ship that drifts and tosses in
the night,
So is my love to me a wandering
barque
Upon the seas of Time; unwelcome
lark
Too soon his matin sings and puts
to flight
Our passion with the coming of the
light.
Time serves us ill and forces us to
mark
His course, dissolving love just as
the arc
Of rainbow fades and vanishes
from sight.
But when we steal from him his
rightful due,
Then, rich with love, we charge our
petty theft
To the wayward winds; rejoicing in
our bliss,
The lark forgets his song; Time
cannot sue
My lover's eyes on mine, and thus
bereft,
Leaves us to seal our love upon a
kiss.

Katherine M Watkins

MOTHER

To the precious memory of my Dear Beloved Mother, who went to be with the Lord Feb. 4, 1987, and to Velma, my sister, who gave her many years of devoted loving care.

All the appropriate words it seems
have been said,
Concerning all Mothers both living
and dead.
But mine is so different from all of
the rest,
Let me describe her the way I can
best.

She's ever so gentle, so kind and
forgiving,
God's love she reflects in the life
she is living.
She's always an example of things
that are good,
I never would change her, not even
if I could.

All of her virtues grow richer with
time,
It's a wonder of wonders that she
got to be mine.
I wish I could tell her, but words
can never say,
What I feel in my heart for her day
after day.

When God passed out Mothers to
the rich and the poor,
I got more than my share when he
came to my door.
So with all of the poems more
beautiful than gold,
With Mothers like mine, the half
has never been told.

R Craig Flanery

TO BENJAMIN CHEE CHEE

I am this land; the land is and was
And ever shall be the everlasting
and eternal I-Am.
The meek may inherit, and the old
shall see visions
When the young have ceased
dreaming,
But I-Am will not cease from
casting its shadow with the land.

There are no longer any hills
toward which I-Am may look,
And there is no longer a Place of
the Gods or even Dead Places
Where I-Am may search, bidden or
unbidden.
And there are no longer Waste
Places where I-Am may hide,
Even for a time.
And there are no longer ways to
know from whom I-Am is
running
And no ways to know from whom
I-Am is hiding.

There are only Bitter Waters and
Great Burnings—
Witherings within and without.

Who is I-Am that man art mindful
of him?
Man has lived here and brought
forth here.
Man has fought here and given up
living here, and man has been
but short-remembered.
And now man has learned to kill
here, neither laying waste
storage barns nor monuments to
men.

But the land bideth.

Helen Ramsey-Wilder

SEASONS OF DESPAIR

To the losers of the world, for the one true love that should have been and could have been, but never was!

My heart became as frozen as the
earth in winter time.
I slammed the door that reached
within, no solace could I find.
The love we shared had
disappeared, you took it when
we parted.
I found myself in grave despair,
alone and empty hearted.
Through winter's bleak and
gloomy days I kept myself on
guard.
With spring's first thaw my pain
increased, for memories die so
hard.
Through summer's heat, the blush
of fall, my heart was dead inside.
A year of hell I suffered through
but heartbreak I denied.
As winter came around again my
loneliness declined,
I'd lived through this torment
before, this cold, bare
winter-time.
And then one day to my surprise,
I woke and felt a thaw,
My heart was stirred, 'twas spring
again, the pain was not so
raw.
I suffered through my first love lost
and locked my grief inside,
But I'm greatful time heals
everything—my love has finally
died.

Bee Anderson

A CONTEST

A"contest,"
What?
Of love?
It's overdone.
Of life?
Small victories won.
Of war?—we've had enough.
Let's write of hope, a dream,
A world-wide peace.

SG

UNTITLED

"What is Grace?
It is something we say
Before each meal takes place?
Is it some kind of feeling?
I want to know.
Is it expressed, felt,
Or something that we show?
Grace—the best that I have
Experienced, and can perceive—
Is like a life-saver
Thrown to a drowning person,
Out in the turbulent sea.
When all hope is gone
And we're going down
For the final count—
Grace, from a power greater
Than us —
Gives new hope, and helps
Pull the drowning victim out."

Terrence A Adams

THE ELLUSIVE RAINBOW

Not there yet,
But craving a formation,

A shape: Blue, Green, Yellow,
Orange and Red.
Blended buckets of elapsed time,
stretching across a placid plane.
Misty precipitation, bursting
through light from a swollen sun.
Behold, something to grip. A
hemisphere, glowing with glee.
Sensing silent songs from a mute
sense-around.
Leaking colors for staged
thoughts.
Withstanding wild winds
and costumed clouds.
Then suddenly,
leaving not
a solid
droplet
to go
by.

JoAnn Clark
UNINVITED
We should be friends by now
For you have constantly been in my life
But I always find myself resisting you
Because you are so upsetting to me
I fight you, I don't want you in my life
But you always seem to be there
And my fight is fruitless
Because you always win
Sometimes you come almost unaware
Subtle but sure
Other times you come in like a hurricane
Ripping me from one end to the other
Leaving me in pieces and in tears
My pleas, my cries have been to no avail
For you come uninvited and do what you must
Often I wonder what it would be like
Never to have you in my life
I imagine the simple peace
The predictable pace
The calmness of the course
These blessings are not to be mine
For you will do—as you have done
All that you can to make the way difficult
We should be friends by now
For you have constantly been in my life
And I only know you as—Change

Donna Watkins
WHEN COMES THE TIME OF MAGIC

To: Jill Bardell and Thomas Iagulli, for believing in me and caring, Thank-you.

When comes the time of magic
Life doesn't seem so tragic

Problems of everyday flight
Have disappeared with the night

And as peace envelopes me
Insecurity becomes history

Something to remain undefined
This magic of heart and mind

Rising from deep down
To shimmer like a diamond crown

Cynthia B Eddy
TENDER THOUGHTS
You crossed my path of hidden secrets, which had all been unknown.

You dug into the deep treasures of my dreams, everlasting and sacred.

You came to me in white,
pure and sweet.

You caught my every emotion with just one glance, without even knowing why.

My angel, the song you sang filled my world with all the glory of heaven.

Don't deny the honey-flavoured kisses of the night, for it is within you in which I
live.

Denise L Teague
TO DREAM

Dedicated to John, John II and Angela, Because We Had The COURAGE

We have each other,
The World is in our Hands.
Love together, Play together, Work together,
United as one, a Family.
With our Children,
We can invest in Tomorrow's America.
We will do what we Dare to Dream.
Love means being there and listening,
Listening to what needs to be told.
We will never walk in anyone's shadows,
We will make our own dreams come true.
For Dreams do come True,
That is why we dream.
Be open to dreams,
To your ownself be True.

Margaret Culmer
IN THE WHIRLS AND SWIRLS
In the ins and in the outs,
In the quiets and the shouts,
In the longs and the shorts,
In the keeps and the Aborts,
In the whirls and swirls of everyday,
It's the loving of you that gets me thru.

In the goods and the bads,
In the nots, and the hads,
In the losers and the winners,
In the angels and the sinners,
In the whirls and swirls of everyday,
It's the loving of you that gets me thru.

In the ups and the downs,
In the classics and the clowns,
In the hopes and the despair,
In the common and the rare,
In the whirls and swirls of everyday,
It's the loving of you that gets me thru.

In the falls and the springs,
In the takes and the brings,
In the thistles and the flowers,
In the minutes and the hours,
In the whirls and swirls of everyday,
It's the loving of you that gets me thru.

Phyllis Dee Francis
I HOLD OUT MY HAND
I have eyes but cannot see. I hold out my hand and you are close to me.
I feel your face, it's strong and fine, I feel your love flow from your heart to mine.

Your lips are full and soft, your nose small and upturned. Your eyes are damp with tears you shed for me, for they are the windows of my soul.

I walk the tight rope you are there to break my fall. I feel your arms and the world opens its doors. The sun is warm, the breeze blows gently in my face. I smell the flowers.

But your love, your love. These things I feel I know they are there.
My heart is full because I love you, but most of all I know that you love me.

Up in the sky I see a star, I reach for heaven and there you are. For no matter where I go I'll hold out my hand and know that you are there always be there.

Lola Mae King
TO HARRY
Brother, dear brother,
I'm writing this for you
Because I fail to tell you
That I often think of you.

One thing I remember
As I reminisce,
Is the best cutter-outer
That ever did exist.

There were other things, too,
At which you were good—
Tiddley-winks, caroms,
Marbles, cutting wood.

But, your rough-and tumbling
With Roy and your cutting-out skill
Will remain most outstanding
In my memory still.

I am sorry I could not be nearer
To see you mature and become wise with age,
To see if you grew more like Daddy
Or developed your own particular form of "sage".

I love you and miss you
And hope you are well
Because oldest brothers
Are always swell.

Mabel Loretta Law
WHAT IS LIFE ALL ABOUT?
I'm going through time
Searching for the rhyme
And the reason for it all.
Seems it comes my way
I'm happy for a day
Then bad times on me befall.
Will I just go through life,
With the struggles and the strife
Never knowing true happiness at all?
I want my spirit to be free
And everything my eyes can see
Paint a picture mentally I can recall.
I want to live it to the fullest
And sing a happy chorus
And learn what life is all about.
I want to do something worth while
Bring a tear or a smile
Leave my mark in history on the wall.
So when my race is run
And my time is done
For me there'll be no doubt what life was all about.
There'll be no doubt about life all!!

E Harold Burns
A SINNER'S PRAYER
Dear Jesus,
As the cloak of death moves
so ever near
Without my Savior I would be
filled with fear.

But in His presence I am able to stand,
Like a little child held in
His father's hand.

His love is so gentle and His patience so strong.
To feel His spirit seems to correct any wrong.

Now if I can find a way to forgive others as He forgives me,
And keep the Commandments
as He said must be.

I know someday
as it is told,
I will be walking with Him
On the Streets of Gold. Amen

Lisa D Howard
A REMEMBRANCE
I touch the skin on the back of my hand
and a rush of memories pulse through my mind.

I am sitting in my Grandma's kitchen,
the table is small, wooden and covered with her standard vinyl tablecloth.

We sit separated and joined by one rounded corner.

Today she is giving me a handmade quilt, embroidered pillow cases,
a crocheted afghan and anything else that she has that I have ever admired.

I am swept with a love that knows why she asked me here today.
I don't get home very often, I live three hours away.

She bends over her cedar chest, arranging and rearranging.
Finally standing slowly up, smoothing the front of her cotton dress.

She holds out to me a patchwork piece of her soul; as I accept
I touch that paper-thin silken skin on the back of her time-frailed hand.

We are separated and joined by one rounded corner.

Laurie Hillmer Koch
IF I SAY I LOVE YOU
If I say I love you will
you never call again?
If I say I love you will
it end before it begins?

If I say I love you will
it scare you away?
If I say I love you will
it be hard for you to stay?

If I say I love you will
the excitement all be gone?
If I say I love you would
it truly be so wrong?

If I say I love you will
everything be changed?
If I say I love you will
your mind be rearranged?

If I say I love you will
it stop being fun?
If I say I love you will
the happiness be done?

If I say I love you will
the "we" we were be through?
If I say I love you will
you stop beng you?

James Aversente
PRELUDE
I love the wind,
The rain,
All that surrounds:
The sky ever smiling—
Awesomely sublime;
Shifting clouds
Now silk in blue,
Now pregnant with dark threat;
Slender scented grass
Ever leaning, waving and bowing;
Trees of endless chatter
That move in placid animation,
Or shakewith wind-swept fury;
Crystal flowing water
Welling with passion to restore;
And flowers—
Lockets of loveliness,
Shrines of sweet reminiscence;
Yet more . . .
The sum but a flicker,
An obscure perception
Of a now
That must one day
Come to pass.

Scott Shortridge
IN MEMORY OF DA

To my grandfather, Myron Dowd, an inspiration to everyone he left behind.

BEGINNING
A new possession,
This frail vessel for new life,
Held in loving arms,
New discoveries await
For the bold adventurer.

LIVING
Camaraderie!
Together in danger filled lands,
Red-Dogs, one and all,
Hear the guns roar in practice,
The enemy shall not pass.

Your children and theirs,
Together with you this day,
Warmth, love, together . . .
Playing Santa Claus for them.
You have insured the future.

ENDING
Six more months to live . . .
Fear, terror, resignation,
All hope disappears,
Terrible pain will follow—
Can I die with dignity?

The pain is gone now,
A new state of beingness
Arrived at in death,
Floating free into new worlds,
Sorrow deeply felt . . . released.

Kyle Bell
CATS

Cats
Small, cute,
Running, jumping, climbing,
Yarn, mice, balls, cats,
Sleeping, eating, growling,
Big, furry
Dogs

Rebecca Lynette Martin
FRIENDSHIP

To my friend, buddy, and pal—Brian Flynn. Thanks for always being there.

You were the one that looked my
way
And decided to hold my hand.
You were the one that kissed my
tears
And made me smile again.
You were the one that cared about
me
And made me really see
All of the beauty
Hidden deep within me.
You were the one that listened
And made me understand,
That life isn't always easy
But that God is always there.
You were the one that taught me
Not to give in, no matter what.
And now when I feel like dieing
I stick out my chin and fight.
You are the one I'd like to thank
For always seeming to care.
And I'd like to also tell you
That just as you were for me;
I'll always be there for you.
And—Yes, I really do care!

Jacqueline Olsen
A GRANDMOTHER'S JOY
1986 was a good year for me.
I became a grandmother, you see.
My son had a boy, my daughter, a
girl.
The first a little slugger,
the second a delicate pearl.
Edwin was born on Thanksgiving
Eve.
He really gave it a fight.
Karissa was a Christmas Day baby.
We waited for her all through the
night.
Edwin Anthony is three months
old,
with beautiful dark eyes and hair.
Karissa Noel is two months old,
in color she is more fair.
I've been blessed, truly blessed,
for my joy is two-fold.
There isn't just one precious baby
for me,
but two to love and hold.

Diane Mikula Pencin
SPRING (HAIKU)

To my children

Spring, gentle, growing
Opening budding flowers
Refreshing clean rain.

Sarah Nell Dennis
SCHOOL IS ABOUT OVER
My dog named Glover likes to eat
clover,
Because school is just about over.
And he loves to wink,
Let's hope he doesn't turn pink.
Oh no! He's got my doll!
Good, he finally went to play ball.

He started to cry just because I
said bye.
When I started to go he said
"Whoa!"
"Where are you going?" he asked.

Grace Helton
1969
The winter winds blow a stormy
gale,
Pale stars dip and glow in space,
The world stands still, mouth
agape,
To see a man on the old moon's
face.
A cold rain falls, from eaves a-drip,
As the astronauts, on the lunar trip,
Speed through the outer
atmosphere.
In history this will be the year
Man first set foot upon the moon
And made it back, but very soon
Another pair will try their luck
To leave footprints in the gray dust
Of, I believe it said in Genesis,
A lesser light, and it still is
Up there to give the earth its light,
Help distinguish day from night.
We wonder how God in His
wisdom sees
Man's unceasing seeking for
supremacy.

Kathryn L Roberson-Harding

Kathryn L Roberson-Harding
MRS JANUS

And many women they call me lov'ly and praise my smile

I wear a mask for the world to see
And many women envy me.
They call me lov'ly and praise my
smile
But you know, I'm cheating all the
while;
'Cause I wear a mask for the world
to see,
Knowing women envy me.
I live in a "palace," a woman's
dream
But things aren't always what they
seem.
I flaunt my furs, fine jew'ls and
dress
Then no one knows I'm depressed.
I travel and dine in choicest places;
Practice all the social graces;
Still wearing my mask for the
world to see
Knowing women envy me.
There are prestige cars for me to
ride
And servants, too, but I'll confide
Sometime I live in a private hell
Ah-h-h, but my mask hides it well.

Janet Lynn Pendleton
THE LAND OF DREAMS
There is a land I dream of,
With rainbows, unicorns, and
such.
All these things you may see,
but never able to touch.

Flowers are in the garden,
birds are in the trees.
There is a magical door,
with one special set of keys.

The keys are your imagination
it's not very hard to use.
Just close your eyes and
concentrate,
the keys you cannot lose.

There is a special king,
in this special place.
You always hear his voice,
but never see his face.

This special king is JESUS!
he loves us one and all,
he's always there for us,
if we only learn to call.

Stephanie Lamb
WHO AM I?

To Jim, Who, through his downfalls and hardships and his determination to rebuild himself, has helped me to answer

---

Who am I is a question that often
puzzles me.
I try to unlock the answer, but I do
not have the key.
At times I think I'm nothing, at
others, the greatest on earth
But then I stop to wonder, "How
much
am I really worth?"
Am I somebody important and
serious
who wants a lot of fame?
Or am I carefree and fun, always
wanting to play a game?
Do I have the courage and
determination
to work for my dreams?
Or do I take things for granted,
always
planning a scheme?
Is who I am who I want to be, or
someone
just holding my place?
To find the path to happiness I
must
first fill that empty space.
Will I one day answer that
question,
as hard as I try?
Will I one day know the answer to
WHO AM I?

Kimberly Ciarlone-Bennett
MERRY-GO-ROUND

Dedicated to my nephew Bobbie, 9/18/79-1/29/86, I love and miss you.

His life is like a Merry-Go-Round
and his chances of living

go up and down.
But, you never see him frown.
Despite all the chemo and transfusions
he's been through,
he is stronger than me and you.
I will keep on praying for the little dear,
that someday soon they will find a cure.

Dawn L Roy
A LESSON FOR ALL TO LEARN
Compassion it lies like a murmur in our hearts
Hate is like a stone that must depart
Love is a thing for all mankind
Peace is a will of the inner mind
This is a lesson for all to learn
Especially for those whose hearts still
Yearn

Melanie Wray Millican
FINALLY FRIDAY

To Mom, Daddy, Dina, Kristie and Mike—My loving family, and Lynnette & Susan—fellow 'sufferers'

Here I sit at my little desk,
It's Friday morning—did you guess?
I don't know if I can go today,
Just keep me awake, Dear Lord, I pray.

Can I make it seven more LONG hours?!?!
Maybe I'll receive a BIG, BUNCH of flowers!!

Somebody help me! Save me please!!
I'm locked in this place & can't find the keys—
Even if I could they wouldn't let me go
They really need me here—just won't say so.

Maybe I'll sneak off, run and hide!
If they say I should've stayed, tell 'em I tried.
I need fresh air, no time schedule, ringing phone—
To simply sit & lick my triple ice cream cone.
I'll take my puppy & we'll play in the grass.
We'll have so much fun! too fast it'll pass!
But we won't worry & we won't pout,
We always have tomorrow—there ain't no doubt!

I guess I'd better go back—my desk is beginning to pile,
& the boss is getting suspicious, for he sees my dreamy smile!!!

Ken Kingsbury
WHEN WE'RE APART
Darling, when we're apart
I don't just miss you.
I feel like I'm only half here,
like a part of me is gone.
When we're apart.
I have no one to talk to.
No one special, anyway.
When we're apart,
I cannot stop thinking about you,
I miss you so much it hurts.
But no matter how far you are from me,
You are always in my heart.

Ann M Szili
WHAT IS A FRIEND
A friend is someone special
they lift us when we're down
They'll put a smile on our face
when all we do is frown

They'll make us count our blessings
and look around to see
That we can conquer anything
If we let our hearts be free

They'll help us face tomorrow
no matter what the fear
and they'll always be beside us
to wipe away that tear

A friend is a loving person
who won't quickly turn away
when things are too much to handle
They'll be with you each new day

Turn to the Lord now and thank him
for sending this fine friend to you
and don't ever fail to remember
that God is your special friend too

Evelyn Lemons
ELUSIVE VERSE
Some million stars whisper, "There's room,
Down beside the lake where the lilies bloom."
Hark! Could that be a meadow lark
Sending its challenge across the dark?
Or was it for the owls wide awake
That I sent my fleet across the lake?
Taking the lilies well afloat,
And making my warriors little boats,
Then spreading the lily petals wide,
I blew them across the rippling tide.
Each warrior sat so tense and terse
To catch a glimpse of nature's verse.
And the aspen's tuneless sigh
Was this fleet's royal battle cry.
I commanded them to capture the pale moonbeams
And return to me the mysteries of silvery streams.
Traitors! This fleet became an elusive fiend,
To ne'er report to ink and pen.

Eula G Kelly
MY LOVE
That's right, I really
didn't want to see you again tonight:
But the old familiar yearning was there.
As the appointed time drew nearer
I could feel the excitement
Building higher.
My heart was pounding,
I was getting so hot I had to start
Shedding my clothes, one piece
By one piece.
Then we were into the game, hot and heavy;
Oblivious to anyone else
Who might happen to be near.
The tension is almost more than I can stand
When suddenly it's over!!
We beat our arch rivals again
By a last second basket!!!

B Larue Moran
MY APOLOGY
In tears, I really must confess
I never meant to leave
My house in such a mess.
Shorter and shorter the minutes grew
I fumbled and fouled
Fairly ran and flew.
The honk of a horn, I'd have to go
But my ego required
That I look just so.
I'd soon be back to sweep and clean
To tidy the place
'Til it would sparkle and gleam.
I threw the latch so the door would lock
And turned towards the waiting car.
I gasped with horror, chagrin and shock:
For behind that locked door, on a chair, if you please,
Lay my trusted purse
And in it my keys.

Maria Lopez Johnson

Maria Lopez Johnson
MY ADOPTED COUNTRY

To my husband Tracey and children with love.

You are the pearl that surged
Between the two widest and deepest of oceans.
This Camelot land that like a silvery beacon
Shines to all the world with a sign of peace.
This pearl, this spot on Earth,
That its courageous sons and daughters
Made into the land of the free.
This giant land of milk and honey
That sleeps like a lamb
In the assurance of its own
Power, security and goodness,
But is always vigilant,
And can roar like a lion,
Protecting the sanctity of its shores
And protecting its people.
This immense and powerful country,
Formed of the immigrants of the world,
Where the oppressed find freedom
And the poor and hungry find opportunities.
This is that shining spot on Earth,
My beloved, revered, adopted country—
This United States of America.
I sing to you today
With love, admiration and patriotism.

Virginia L Caviness
LOVE AGAINST FOIBLES

This poem is dedicated with love to my son, Craig Matson Buhl

---

Nervous twitches distorted his features,
his blond hair was in complete disarray.
Her face, worn and pale, moved not a muscle,
she had already said what she had to say.
Accusingly, vindictively, his blue eyes met hers and held.
Then surprisingly she laughed,
love struggling against foible of mind.
"Oh, all right, you can keep it,"
she reluctantly relented.
Watching her small son stagger
under the weight of the stray feline,
his little face buried in its fluffy fur,
Her abhorrence of black cats, her
superstition and fear vanished
in squeals of joy and a contented purr.

Teresa Fraser
OH BEAUTIFUL TURTLE
Oh beautiful turtle,
Oh beautiful turtle,
How smooth your shell is.
Oh graceful turtle,
Oh graceful turtle,
How you take your time
Moving in the burning sun.
Oh shy turtle,
Oh shy turtle,
How you hide your face
When you are scared.
Oh mighty turtle,
Oh mighty turtle,
How you snap
When you are mad.
Oh gentle turtle,
Oh gentle turtle,
How you walk in the
Grass to be cool.
Oh cunning turtle,
Oh cunning turtle,
How you hide yourself
From the colors around you.
Oh beautiful turtle,
Oh beautiful turtle.

Vivian Harvey
GOSSAMER SUMMER
Meadowlarks, geese honking,
dew-fresh pine and sage,
Old house sweet with coffee,
good cooking, and age;
Fifteen summers had passed me by.
Sixteen saw gossamer float on
an August breeze
And turn stubble-fields to
shimmering, silvery seas.

Slipping out alone while they're
sleeping, walking abroad
With night's beauty around me,
I felt close to God.
Summer heat fled in the
night-wind's sigh.
Star-glittered, moon-bright,
deep indigo sky.
Coyotes' wild yapping and
sand-snipe's cry.

Day break, hay rake, hay rack,
hay stacks, and horseback ride
On a paint cow-pony, a bay mare
and you at my side.
Cold blue river, blue mountains,
and warm blue sky.

Sun-bleached hair, sun-burned nose, freckles and tan.
Busy days, lazy days, sunny days without worry or pain.

Sitting on the woodpile under cottonwood trees,
Watching gossamer fly on a warm,
dry breeze,
And mountains purple as sunset flamed the sky,
Shoulder to shoulder with my brother, my friend;
My gossamer summer began to end . . .
My gossamer summer began to
end.

Rich Hand
BONEYARD
The peaceful resting place of old
in solemn silence stands
where husks are brought and
laid to rest
into ancestral lands

Strong faces, growing, fading,
keep watch o'er vernal lands
where what was planted
will not grow
among the fruitless stands

Against the endless marching time
eternal law still stands
when men begin their
mortal march
toward the promised lands

Deepest sleep, no dreaming here
encased in time's own lands
the foggy past as
in a dream
the fading marble stands.

Angela Angelakos
THE SLEEP OF LONELINESS
The Sleep of loneliness is but a small death,
it revolves images, like thirsty dreams.
In its depth, lies the color of spring,
For Happiness and fun are but a myth;
Then morning comes like a wind,
making sorrows become real.

Paul Agnew
REVERIE
Walk down with me, down to the river's shore,
For we aren't happy here, you and I
For they do not remember anymore

There we will skip flat stones picked from the shore,
And we will skip them five, six times a try
Walk down with me, down to the river's shore

And we will pick the honeysuckle near the shore,
And taste its nectar, if our throats are dry
But they do not remember anymore

We'll see the water lap the stones on shore,
Where brownish pebbles in the shallows lie
Walk down with me, down to the river's shore

We'll watch leaves wave green-gray on the far shore
We'll hear them rustle as the wind goes by
If they do not remember anymore

And we'll talk of what is downstream some more
And we will picture green hills rising high
Walk down with me, down to the river's shore,
For they do not remember anymore

Theresa Hettich
LIGHT

To my family "listen to my words to hear my soul"

The sun and moon squabbled one day,
Quarreling who was the greatest being.
As the feud carried on, the tiniest star,
Quietly smiled as to what he was seeing.

"It's me," said the sun, "I'm the main source of light.
I draw the attention of kings."
"I also shine," was the moon's reply.
"I give glow to drab earthly things."

"I send out rays that warm cold days,"
Puffed up the sun big and wide.
The moon did not yield and boasted back,
"My energy moves ocean tides."

As the tiniest star began to recall,
Excitement within shone him bright.
A memory sweet of a Bethlehem Eve,
When he twinkled the greatest one night.

Helena S Simpson
CHRISTMAS 1986

To my darling Joe, with ever lasting love.

To love you is the greatest joy
that I have ever known.
Looking back from when we meet
I see how much it's grown.
Closer to each other
though far away in miles.
Remembering the together
always brings the smiles.
Though the holidays without you
are sure to bring a tear.
I'll remember all the happy times
and hold them "O" so near.
So think of me my darling
at this very special time.
Remember that I love you
and wishing you were mine.

Madeline F Sewell
WHAT HERITAGE?
When things come easily to hand, they just as quickly go . .
For worthwhile things, abiding things grow steadily, but slow.
Good characters are slowly built, and reputations earned . .
It takes a lot of honest toil, and painful lessons learned.

To build the kind of life we wish posterity to share,
Foundations strong must first be laid . . then built upon with care.
Without the pioneers attempt . . the unknown to explore,
Uncharted courses, doomed would be . . and stagnant evermore.

For nothing but our best will live in immortality;
Without the efforts to prevail, we'll soon forgotten be.
What heritage will you pass on?
What footprints in the sand,
To say that you have traveled here?
Will your memorial stand?

Edna Stewart
GIFT OF LOVE
Love is like a light that shines in the dark,
You can see it clearly if only a spark.
So treat Love Kind treat it tender, far no
greater gift can one get from the Sender.

It will fill empty places where nothing else
can, it is a gift from God to satisfy man.
For it is so tender it fades with neglect,
But grows like a tree when watered and fed.
And will go where the Lover has gently lead.

Shelton Sim Mcgraw Sr
LOVE, NEVER ENDING

To my loving wife Mary together, with love never ending

When on that day I met you dear,
Twas such a joy to feel,
Seemed somehow to loose all my fear
And completely fall at your will.

Your smile so sweet
Your voice so soft,
They swept me off my feet,
And set my thought's aloft

Now, years have past,
And times seems to have gone,
Yet all those things I saw they last,
With yet the same great tone.

It's now, not just sights, of what I see,
For it's now, for you only I long,
I've learned your moves, and ways, foresee,
A love that's far more strong.

So, in our future, till our life shall end,
We'll hold on til' death shall part,
And one shall, just go to asend,
And wait; for us, a new life, soon start.

Lurana M Locke
OUR GRANDCHILDREN
Four little grandchildren do we have
They are as frisky as that many calves
On the go from morning to night
One boy is Dennis, the other Mike
They are the oldest of the four
Then two girls, who could ask for more?
Dorothy three, Elizabeth one
Keeping up with them is such fun!
They play together and sometimes fight
It takes their dad to set them right
Then Mom gets in a spank or two
And they know it's something they shouldn't do
They pout awhile, then go and play
Before you know it, it's been a busy day
Off to bed they go with a good night kiss
Without grandchildren, see what you miss?

Brenda Compton
LIFE'S LIKE THAT

For Chantelle and Chelsea, my inspirations.

Life is a funny drama
We all want this or that,
But sometimes wants and needs are mixed
And end up back to back.
Sometimes it's useful to reflect
When things seem upside down,
What really matters when we're dead
And buried in the ground?

Ms Tonya J Jackson
YOU ARE MY LIFE
You are my everything,
You brighten my day.
When I'm feeling down
You show me the way.

You are my lover,
You are my friend.
Forever I will love
Until the very end.

You are my life.

Barbara Sehestedt
WHAT IS IT?

For Bernard Joseph Thomas, Jr. I wish you a rainbow.

What is it?
What's wrong?
You needed me
or you wouldn't have called.
Although,
God knows,
You would never admit to needing
anyone—
much less me.
Still,
it was there,
An absence of power
in your voice,
So unlike you.
I'm here—
I ache to help you.
Please
need me.

Jamie E Ambrose
PHOTOGRAPH

To my dear, funny, beloved parents who are always there for their children—through "the thick and the thin."

See them smiling back at me,
Forever frozen in a happy instant;
Sunlight, flowers, themselves consistent:
So far away, yet still they see.
I feel my eyes remembering.
Not the distance of miles I fear;
More the space, the vast light-years
Of changes. Life is tempering
Chameleon's colours 'round me now.
Every note and none I sing,
While searching for the one which might ring
True for me—for me alone. How? Oh, how
To reconcile the parts of life? To bind
The differences of present days,
Uncertain steps of future ways
With all that one has left behind?
To weave from all one tapestry?
See my parents: how fast they stand
As I drift on, far from their hands.
So far away—can they still see?

Stephen J Marenick II
TO THE MOST BEAUTIFUL GIRL IN THE WHOLE U.S.A.

I dedicate this poem, To The Most Beautiful Girl In The Whole USA, To my Beautiful wife, Marites

To the most beautiful girl in the whole USA
This Happy Valentine Day's greeting, I just have to say
You are the most beautiful girl in the world to me
Each night it happens, you are in my dreams
I think about you all of the time
Your name is always on my mind
When I'm not with you, I feel so alone
Your voice sounds so pretty, when I call you on the phone
I want to be with you, all of the time
Because you're so beautiful, pretty and kind.

Benjamin Zloty
GOD HAS BEEN GOOD TO ME

In Memory of My Wife Ida

I've a nice little place in the country,
Where I hang my cares on a tree,
And my heart cries out when I look about,
God Has Been Good To Me.

There are loving faces in the doorway,
Where the birds sing merrily,
It's my wife and daughters who are waiting for me,
God Has Been Good To Me.

I might have been a millionaire,
With a mansion on the hill,
But I like things just the way they are,
And I guess I always will.

For I get a million kisses,
I'm as rich as I can be,
And I always say when I kneel to pray,
God You've Been Good To Me.

Robert Earl Coleman

Robert Earl Coleman
THE SUN

This poem is dedicated to Ruby, a genuine friend.

The sharp glittering glow of the sun,
Renders it's radiance with a smile,
To overpower the world in fun,
As if from the eyes of a child,
I'm simply amazed at the light
The sun exhorts each day,

To brighten our paths until night
When we tire from work and from play,
So good Lord in Heaven above
Keep the light going our way,
Making us ever mindful of love,
Brought by the vastness of the sun's ray.

Jeanine Marie Woroniecki
FLOWER OF WONDER

My Dedication: To the Lord above, For it is because of Him that I have a talent such as this.

I wonder will I
Ever grow like a flower?
Big and strong
with all my limbs?
Will I get my fill?

Will I live long or just
Enough before I die?
I wonder will I ever
Be as pretty as a flower?
Will I make it through the storms?
I wonder how much am I like this flower?

Loretta Lynn Lavigne
MY LOSS IS HIS GAIN
In the darkness of the night
I hear his scream low with fright.

My child was waken from his dream
By a nightmare it did seem.

As I cradle him in my arms,
He said, Mommy don't be alarmed.

The time has come for me to go
To leave this place I've come to know.

I shall go to my new home
Don't worry Mom, I'm not alone.

Jesus will take me in the light
To a place so big and bright.

Past the lovely Gates of Gold
Where Angels sing so pretty and bold.

Mom, I'll be okay you see
God will take this pain from me.

With these words my tears did flow,
For his leaving was so slow.

Tearing at me in my grief
Was a feeling of relief.

My son was sick for so long
Through it all he was so strong.

Where he's now, there's no pain
I understand my loss is his gain.

C J C Klingler
BUDDING DISSENT
Regiments of thick black weeds
march in crooked lines
towards the daisies in the garden.
Armed with green blades
the tulips stand firm
defend their soil.
Marigolds
yellow as always
peek carefully from the underbrush
petal slightly in the wind
rustle softly to each other.
Daring daffodils stand forth in the daylight
face the thorny regiments of dark sticks.

The goldenrod flutters in indecision.
Should it fight its cousins
or its brothers?

The weeds mutter, surge forward.

Closer and closer
the armies inch.
When summer dawns the battle begins.

A passing gardener glances over
clucks in disgust
ends the war
with a few tugs
of a large rake.

Margaret J McDonnell
ONE MORE TIME
If only we could find a way
To come back once again
And right the wrongs that we have done
And be a better friend.

To see the best in others
And broken friendships mend
Wouldn't it be wonderful
If we came back again.

To keep in mind mistakes we made
And benefit by them
And not to leave this world of ours
Before the fence did mend.

To choose our words so carefully
That we could now be free
And Bless the lives of those we knew
Leave happy memories.

And knowing I have made things right
I'm not afraid to leave
I won't be coming back again
Because there is no need.

Josephine Darner
THE QUIET CANAL

This poem is dedicated to Richard

Wind brushes back seaweed
On the face of the canal
Like green and tangled mermaids' locks
Strewn in a Bacchanal—
And hanging on the other side
Smooth and cold with moss
A grey backdrop of ancient rocks
Shines with a watery gloss—
The day is still, under a pale sky, perched
Like a motionless dragonfly—
interrupted only
By persistent joggers lonely,
Padding
Down
The dry tow-path

Jackie Kopplin
THE ROSE
He picked the rose.
I watched him.
From across the street
I saw him select the last red rose
from the flower stand.
He plucked the thorns from its richness,
and as he removed them one by one,
he pricked his thumb.
In fascination I watched him
place his tongue on the tiny wound.
Then he turned and looked directly at me.
His eyes collided with mine.
With words unspoken
we communicated in silence.
My heart contracted.
my mouth went dry.
I licked my lips.
I couldn't breathe.
Suddenly he disappeared
and gave the rose to her.
She who stood before him
and obscured my perfect view.

Lois Barber
THE LITTLE DRUMMER BOY
I asked for help, and I got none.
I asked for Love, and I got a drum,
That you beat with a stick. And every Lick, brings a sharp note,
To an ear, that only wanted to hear.
Yes, Dear! I'm here, when you need me. And my Love, I will give thee.
I know now, that giving Love
is far more important, then giving
a drum.

George Harris
MY SOJOURN IN THE MUSEUM

This poem is dedicated to Mary, my Princess, my best friend, and much, much more.

I saw many things along the way
which I admired, appreciated, even coveted.

But I couldn't touch them.
And I moved on.

Others, I held and cherished, even loved,
But they were mine for the moment only.
Soon enough I had to release them.
And I moved on.

The moment I am experiencing now
recalls another back there along the way.
I wish I had lingered longer then.
But I didn't. And that saddens me
as I move on.

Now, as I near the exit,
I look back over my shoulder wistfully.
I wish for another visit
so that I might more fully appreciate each moment.
But Life is a One-Visit-Only Museum.
And I must move on.

Michelle C Fricker-Square

MY GRANDFATHER, MY SON

In loving memorium to my grandfather I. Hitchcock Monoson Born Nov. 10, 1895 Died Sept 29, 1986

I hope you grow to be like him
with all the kindness and civility he
possessed
Had you been born later
you'd have been so with his name
As it is you will live now and always
with his blood in your veins
For if not for his seed
we none would be here
If not for his love
we could not have grown
With only love to give, I offer this in return
to My Grandfather
a father to me
My son
a tribute to him

Donald R Caron

Donald R Caron

WRITERS BLOCK

To June whom I loved for twenty eight years, and I love her still!

For want of words and lack of rhyme
A pen too stubborn to write
I sit and fight with my mind
It stays as blank as my stationary
Sometimes I feel just like an "IMP"
And dance upon my table
Flop on the floor and stare at the door
And hope for something to happen

Whimsical thoughts and foolish dreams
And schemes too wild to happen
Seem to invade my very soul
Yet evades my paper and pencil
A-ha A-ha here I go
Another hysterical spasm
Laugh and sing—dance and spin
Oh damn
I think I've lost my marbles!!

Tamara L Patterson

WHEN SHALL WE MEET AGAIN?

To Mom; Nana; Pa; and especially Chris M. Benjamin, my inspiration; my love and admiration always.

When shall we meet again,
In this plane of time?
You will have gone your way,
And I will have gone mine.

Through the years we've been together,
Through the thick and thin.
But how will I know whether,
You and I shall meet again?

Friends forever, friends for now,
I hope to see you,
Years from now,
When all of you have changed, me, too!

But always remember the good times,
For they will always be with you,
And don't forget the bad times,
For you must learn from them, too!

Camille Botsford

FAITHFUL LOVE

You I love, tonight
You I will love, tommorrow
But through my faith
in God
I love all
All who are enemies
All who do not hold
external beauty

Paul M Bennett

CONNECTED MOONLIGHT

To the World.

I stand on a hill looking down at the valley.
And I see the moonlight reflecting off of the
Pearly grey opalescent mists down below.
Sitting as a horizontal band cast down from the
Paintbrush of an infinite artist and contrasting
In the gentle darkness with the midnight blue of the
Mountains sloping gently down to the river in the valley floor,
All framed by mesa tops and silhouetted pinon pine trees
Of black and midnight green, and I think to myself.
"This is the most beautiful place in the world,
Where I feel connected to the creation."
I feel my heart break in two and collect
In liquid love at the base of my being.
My sigh fills all the space around me.

Pham Thi Kim Chi

I CAN SEE THE LIGHT

Here by the window I sit,
Looking out into the night sky.
I see no moon, no star, no light . . .

All I see is darkness,
A darkness that spreads
Into every crack and
Crevice of my being.

A world filled with a darkness
That only I see.
It's sad, this world of mine,
For there's no hope, no happiness, no love.

Yet . . . Life surrounds me here;
It is everywhere and nowhere,
A thing that never flows smoothly.
In all ways, life is a poem
Written by a poet who
Has never written poetry.

Experience life as I,
The new poet,
Have experienced poetry.

Helen Martina Russell

LITTLE BABY

Welcome Baby, precious tot,
You're the brightest thing we've got.
You're so tiny and so rare
All our love to you we'll share.
We will watch you as you grow
Strong and tall, and we will know
That God in His divine plans
Has placed you in our loving hands.

Nicole Renee Bush

O BEAUTIFUL VISION

O beautiful vision!
You stand so tall and regal.
Such a sight for sore eyes
I have never beheld before.
A symbol of perfection
Wrought from Heaven.
Blond hair shines gold in
sunlight.
Eyes glowing with the light of
Polaris.
A face smoothed of
Imperfections by the hand of
The Creator.
A Nordic Angel.
Can I ever hope to touch you,
So far above earth and
Mankind?
Unless you should become
A fallen angel,
Still beautiful and angelic,
But corporeal
This mortal cannot but
Watch you,
Admire you and
Love you
From afar.

Carol Leopold

COME WITH ME

You're looking at me with those eyes
I fell in love with them,
But now those eyes have clouded
and I can't remember when,
the last time we really talked
about this and that and then.
How our lives have changed so much,
over the last few years.
All the times we fought and loved,
our way through all our fears.
Have we really grown up so much
that we are afraid to share,
to show our love and cuddle up
and show how much we care?
I think it's time to break this wall
we've built between us now
And with God's help and all his love,
He will show us how.
We'll work together once again,
We'll find out who we are,
So take my hand, I'll understand,
together we'll go far.

James Keith Jordan

WATCHING YOU

This poem is dedicated to Stephanie Ellen Kaye Wilson with all my love:

I've been Watching You,
not as the hawk watches it's prey
nor as the night watches day
but as a man watches a bird fly away;
with envy and with love.
Watching to see
not watching to correct
but with love and respect.
I've been watching you. . .
I see you in everything,
even when you aren't there,
my eyes deceive me
and, my love, I see you everywhere.
You're in my every thought,
You're in my every day,
So the love that you have brought
will never fade away.
I'm still Watching You,
wanting to be so near,
but I know that I must wait
until the path is clear.
So I'm patiently watching
and this is what I see:
A very special girl who's looking back at me.

John A Bartosiewicz

THE HERO COMES HOME

The father's face was solemn,
The mother, how she cried!
The long black box at the station
Their only son had died.

"He died to save his country"
I believe that's what they said
The price of freedom is costly
A bullet through his head.

And, as the box is lowered into the ground
The parents ask themselves
"WHY?"
A stupid, bloody, senseless war
How many more must die?

Sandra Leigh Krantz

Sandra Leigh Krantz
TWINS

Creative ventilation written on a dreary day of dolour in loving memory of my brother, Franklin (Jay) Joshua Krantz, Jr., a courageous soldier who died in the jungles of Vietnam.

A girl and a boy came into this
 world
just one week before Saint
 Valentine's Day
in the year of your Lord,
 nineteen-fifty-one;
the place of occasion, Frederick in
 Maryland.

The girl and the boy, Sandi and Jay,
were as different as night and day;
she would fight while away he'd
 run,
he coddled his doll, she killed with
 her gun.

Different they were just as black
 and white,
but neither would stray from the
 other's sight.
Opposites they were for a short
 life-time to come,
yet, inseparable best buddies
 together they'd roam.

The girl and the boy grew up
 through the days,
remaining as one even going their
 own ways.
He went to the war, she went to
 college.
But, he was the first to grasp all the
 knowledge . . .
 of life and, of death.

The girl left alone for a life on the
 run
misses the boy and all of the fun.
But, believe:
 The space they shared in their
 mother's womb
 remains a tight bond even after
 the tomb.

Lillian Marotta
ANGEL
Born into the world an angel in my
 fathers eyes as he watched me,
 grow with love and pride.
Being so little yet learning so much
 a father's love, a smile with a
 gentle touch.
Locked inside his own little world
 reality left unknown never
 looking back to see how much
 I've grown older yet wiser in the
 same little world with feeling
 and needs of my own.
Not knowing why he does this he's
 not quite sure himself. But like
 a doll I'm dusted and put back
 upon the shelf.

Bonnie Marie Baross-Benedetti
HAWAIIAN MOUNTAINS

To Dad with loving memories.

Hawaiian Mountains.
Beckoning some,
Cautioning others.
Desolate, black, smokey and red,
Plush and green, misty and clear,
Cooling waterfalls,
Jagged and smooth,
Stately and strong,
Spirals peaking,
Pointing upward beyond our
 scope.
Magical and mysterious,
Somber beauty in a contradiction
 of reality.
Hawaiian Mountains.

Philip Wise
VIETNAM

To The American Soldiers

Vietnam was a bloody war
Which to a lot of people was a
 closed door.
Only to set these people free
Will you hope and pray with me.

You hear these people tell their
 stories
and sometimes they are gory.
These people will have a special
 place in my heart
Just like a favorite sweet tart.

Lloyd Chiville Shuler
MOON-SET
The soft, dark petals rise and
 slowly close;
The huntress, strangely charmed,
 completes the flower,
And waning, seeks in this
 appointed hour
The velvet softness and the day's
 repose.
The cloud, without her glory,
 somber grows,
The earth-bound wind cries in his
 earthly bower
For secret fear, laments her
 passing power
And sighs as every star now
 brighter glows.
Oh, western wind! Cry not in sad
 despair;
Be gentle to the waves upon my
 shore.
The Genesis continues from the
 past
And is not stopped by grief, or joy,
 or care;
And only man may sigh, "oh
 nevermore!"
For only man is the iconoclast.

James Lafferty
LIVING INSIDE A COMPUTER
I talk to the computer once in a
 while
when I'm inside messing around
 with his
memory bank. He goes haywire.
 Sometimes
I go crazy because it gets mad at
 me.
I wish someday we could be
 friends.

Day and night for months I sit
 around
talking to the computer. People try
and get things out of him.

Frank lives inside the computer.
Frank's a friendly guy. Sometimes
the computer shows him movies
 about
"How Computers Are Made."

Frank and the computer were
 friends for
a long time. They grew old
 together.
Then Frank had a stroke. It broke
 the
computer's heart. It couldn't do
 anything.
So it buried him under the
 circuitry.
The computer then broke down
 and stopped.

Bonnie M Jacobs
PEACE
The world in turmoil is involving
From the inferno in man's angry
 heart
To destruction of man's own
 making
Contrary to His making at the start.

My soul cries out midst the war
 and fury
My mind is crushed with unsounds
 of the dead
My being staggers neath the load
 of knowledge
But wisdom is what I need instead.

So rest me now with the One who
 answers
Be calm, oh my soul . . . His peace
 impart
Although the roarings are 'round
 about me
His quietness reigns within my
 heart.

Vervaine E Mains
THOUGHTS
Can it ever stop, will it never end
 For our liberties and rights of
 men.
Since Adam and Eve set the pace,
 Is it an endless and fruitless race.
Shall evil blight the righteous and
 good
 And constantly strike at the
 truth for which we stood.
How our hearts bleed long and
 hard and weak
 As the pain grows strong for the
 peace we seek.
Shall our hopes and prayers for our
 children unborn
 Be beaten and trampled by
 those who scorn,
And bring scarcity of peace and
 love
 And turn men away from Him
 above.
Oh Holy Lord, please hear our plea
 Help good to spread and the bad
 to flee.
How well we remember the evil
 and the vice;
 How much is forgotten, Your
 Devine sacrifice!

Cricket Omlor
TAKE MY HEART
Who knows the pain I'm going
 through?
Buried inside,
Away from view.
My heart no longer sings
A sweet melody;
As a bird in a cage
Can sing of no joy.
He wants to be free,
To soar in the air,
But not since his heart
Was captured in lair.

My heart belongs to him.
He won it fair and square;
Let's give our love a chance,
I'm sure you won't despair.
The pain in my heart
Will surely give way,
When you give me your love
To share for the day.
Not only for a day, but maybe for
 life.
To leave right now
Would cut like a knife.

I give you my heart,
So take good care.
I'm willing to part,
If you're willing to share.

Susan Rupe
THE COMING OF AGE

To my daughter, Dawn Prenton: I loved you in your youth and celebrated in its maturity!

A biological clock ticks as we each
 grow old
 As past experiences we freeze to
 hold.

But one attitude we should clearly
 engage
 Is that youth and maturity have
 no age.

Donna Musella

Donna Musella
MY SISTER

To my long lost, and short found sister Betty-Jean (Duffer) I love you.

She's been thru many years of
 pain, let downs, and disgrace.
But, even with these things of hurt,
 a smiles upon her face.
She's had her share of heartaches,
 and will have many more,
And even thru the "depths of hell,"
 it's her I will adore.
Life's shed its rotted fruit, and
 dropped it at her door,
And, if I live to be a thousand, I'll
 never know what for.

I haven't really known her long, but
for me it's long enough,
To see the trials, she's been thru,
the roads been really rough.
Does she really have to prove, how
strong that she can be?
If the Lord could just send down
an angel, I'm sure then he would
see.
She's a fair and shining beauty, her
heart is pure and good.
She's there to help, another heart
to do just what it should.
Oh yes! I've seen her angry, and
even seen her cry.
But these are human feelings she's
kept down deep inside.
Her anger, is a pressure, that
beckons to be freed.
Her tears are blood, from a
heartache from other peoples
greed.
There really is no need for this,
with a heart as good as hers,
She doesn't want for any thing, like
diamond rings, or furs.
And even if she had them, and
someone had it bad,
She'd sell them all, and even more,
and give them all she had.
I've watched her laugh at parties,
when her heart was broke in two,
I've seen her sit and listen, when
she had better things to do.
But . . . to her there's nothing better
than to help another soul,
And to volunteer her shoulder, or
her arms reached out to hold.
Her precious love is worth to me,
more than any pot of gold,
And if I'd known her sooner, I
would try to fit her mold.
There's times, I look up to the sky,
and cry a single tear,
And wonder what I did in life,
without her all those years.
What did I do to earn her, to have
her in my life,
It must have been a miracle, or an
unseen guiding light.
I know there's nothing I could do,
to be deserving of such a prize,
And on my scale of one to ten, well,
she's a ninety-five.
When God comes down to get her,
I want to go there too.
"Cause" . . . without "My sister" in
my life, I won't know what to do.

Bernadette Sabel

THE FUTURE IS OURS

AIM HIGH—GREAT
COURAGEOUS ASTRONAUTS
May future journeys never be for
naught.
Ever so young—their whole life
to live
But—dreams for the future they
died to give.

FLY ON SO HIGH—VALIANT
ASTRONAUTS
Who are we poor mortals who
wait and talk?
Afraid—fearing to face the deep
unknown
We're not brave as 7
ASTRONAUTS known.

AIMED SKYWARD—TOWARD
HEAVEN—DREAMS THEY
TOOK
Climbing higher—never back
did they look.
Faint-hearted are we—who
never will try
Hopefully—someday to keep
goals alive.

SO—QUESTION NOT—
CHALLENGER'S TRAGEDY
GOD only can see—whatever
will be!
THE FUTURE IS OURS to carry
onward
Be brave like an ASTRONAUT—
AIM FORWARD!

Marilyn Elizabeth Buxton

ODE TO SPRING

Spring is here and the earth
awakens from her slumber deep;
She brings to each and everyone of
us
her own true beauty she alone
doth keep.

It's the time of year that HE arose
from WHOM eternal spring still
flows;
And lifts our souls above despair
to know the joy that HE'S always
there.

Shawn M Severson

THE RIGHT TO LIFE!

We are the people of this earth.
With each new
dawn we bring another birth. The
cry of a child
enlightens the day, but the death
of the old
leads us a different way.
We are life, we are happiness.
We are sorrow, we are death.
Out with our joys and hidden with
our fears.
You hear the sounds of our own
rain falling tears.
We are the people who build and
people who destroy.
Those who believe life is nothing
but games and toys.
We are the strong and we are the
weak.
New Beauties,
New Homes,
New Worlds,
Is something we all soon shall seek.
Death and destruction head our
way.
Soon there will be no dawn to start
the
Very next day!

William H Bittner Jr

DEEP DESIRE

She walks alone,
But always has a crowd.
She speaks softly,
But her message is loud.
To her a man,
Is nothing but a toy.
He is to her,
A way to achieve joy.
Her gentle touch,
Seems like it is magic.
When it really,
Is nothing but tragic.
In her eyes,
You see many things.
Meanwhile sorrow,
Is all those eyes bring.
That night,
You lay upon her bed.
As she wraps,
Her hands around your head.
She clenches her fingers,
And pulls on the wire.
As dreams end,
You meet your deep desire.

Kenneth Paul McPhail Sr

JOYOUS RIDE

This night, at this time of doom.
Angels hover near, suddenly
ominous
Clouds appear and slowly fade
away.
A soul goes soaring on an unknown
flight, as radiant stars form a
splendid light. Whilst dancing
across
the skies. A journey not the end
has began. Old transgressions are
forgotten, new faiths and
obedience
linger here. With our Savior who
is just and pure this soul will
abide. Lord thank you for the lift.

Judith Tubbs

AT OUR AGE

For Larry, my mate in life—and my best friend.

When we were much younger,
What could our perfect vision see.
Not what life was really like
Just what we wanted it to be.
Sadly, time is wasted in youth
As we strive to reach our goal
Of wealth, status and fame
All our merits, we extol.
Our sight is much dimmer now,
Our hearing is not so clear.
But, now we see with our souls
And with our hearts, we hear.
How much better is our love,
Unencumbered by frivolous things.
Free to share, care and feel
And enjoy our many blessings.
We're in another chapter of life,
Each day we write a new page.
This book of life is wonderful
When you live and love-at our age.

Barbara Kummer Nicely

DEATH, WHERE IS THY STING?

With Love, To My Husband, James Samuel Nicely, and in Memory Of My Parents, John and Mattie Lou Kummer

---

"The wages of sin is death—"
O, what finality!
But with His dying breath
Christ paid the penalty.
The terrible price was paid;
He died for you and me!
The sacrifice was made
That we may be set free.
So, fear not the fateful grave;
Dread not the dark of night;
Through Christ we have been
saved!
He is Everlasting Light.
Christ alone is Good,
Worthy to be King;
He cleansed us by His blood!
"O death, where is thy sting?"

Anthony Xavier Price

MAN

Look at this land
We call the earth
Where we have lived
Together since birth

In love and peace
And pain and sorrow
We live in today
But look for tomorrow

As Human Beings
We pass judgement on others
On Blacks and Jews
Our sisters and brothers

So let's look at our faults
And not at our brothers
Pass judgement on ourselves
And not on others

Janet M Cornell

INSIDE OUT

Dark shadows creep up—they
plague my mind.
My eyes doth see though I'm
incessantly blind.
Pronouncing doctrines of unborn
space
emptiness of heart; spoken words
a waste.
Negation of meaning, avoidance of
pain
evident simplicity—my thoughts
have been slain.
The naked soul/so brazen and bold;
fire burns within, the shell remains
cold
for social implications of
embellished deeds,
serve blind importance
(of which I can't conceive).

. . . And the conceived emotions
entrapped in the core,

Foster a deprivation that the
wound must implore.
The essential euphenisms only
serve to save face,
they covert society—protecting
our race?

The potential for growth is
possibilities denied,
for mutual understatements
banish self pride.
(And the internal conflict in its
subservient presence is far from
remidst; in life's luminescence.)
And though the piercing mind is
aware of our state, the soul; in
conclusion, will determine our
fate.
So,
relinquish the burden of protecting
your treasure
you see, eccentric dimensions
possess value beyond measure.
And I long to be—inside OUT
for inner possessions are what I'm
about.
If you take me for granted, you'll
evade who I am—
D-e-s-t-r-u-c-t-i-o-n of uniqueness;
the innocence of man.

Nellie Curtiss

HABIT

Habit, I go to the window,
Look,
Look,

Look.
Nothing, no one, alone.
Habits
grow deeper, add stress,
remembering a time of comrades,
knocking at the door, happy,
Happy,
Happy,
even in sadness, Happy
in sharing, in caring, in knowing
no one is an island
Except
when isolation breaks down
friendship, phone calls, letters.
Habit, I go to the window
look for a car,
listen for footsteps,
limp inside, I see, nothing's there,
No one's come. I'm alone.
Habit. Habits break slowly.

Richard Hoepfl
THE SMILE

The world is in distress
All spirits in depress
Hidden ideas undress.
Worry for a while,
But sometime you've got to smile.
Show that symbol of friendliness.

It brightens darkened rooms,
And smells of sweet perfumes,
And pulls up spirits from the dooms.
It cramps our style,
if we do not smile.
Or sudden destruction looms.

A world without love
Carrying the hunted-down dove
Nothing to lift our hearts above.
Not a place for sorrows to pile,
clean it up with a smile.
And discover something to be proud of.

A frown—cold as a relentless draft,
Treacherous as a mine shaft,
Ah, but there is a simple craft!
No need to make it trial,
just pull up the corners of your mouth and smile.
Oh, what power! I wonder if we laughed?

John Owen Robinson
HOW IT CAME TO BE

My father was a blacksmith and a good one at that. He was made of steel and steel is what he begat.

Eons & Eons Ago
God first made the atoms and the molecules amid the darkness of the deep.With these He made the earth, air, and seas. Cold was the air for the sun was not yet. The salt waters froze at 27°.
This was the melting point when came the sun upon the sea though the atmosphere could not be more than minus 458°.So, as He moved over the sea, He likely used ice skates.

Day 1
But then He said: "Let there be light" and light was made, and with it heat.

Day 2
Next He divided the waters so that dry land could appear, and He charged the sea to keep its bounds.

Day 3
Then made He trees and greens and the seeds of things.

Day 4
Came then birds to sing and fish to swim.

Day 5
Next the animals, two by two—the hippo, hippopotamus, and the kangaroo.

Day 6
Now, to His own image and likeness He made man, male and female, with two eyes and two ears to be windows for the soul; two legs to walk; a tongue to talk; a nose, but one, to breathe the air; a mouth to eat, to drink, with lips to dare; two arms to feel, to work, to care. And now the soul from outer air whence comes the architect, the sculptor, the artist, the musician, and the mathematician, the poet, and the orator.

Day 7
And God saw everything was good. And so on the final day He rested.

Genesis 1

Mary Elizabeth Rose
INTROSPECTION

Lord God of all the common things
Upon the earth and in the sky above,
How little is there we can praise and sing about,
If there's not love—
If in our hearts there's only desert waste,
Unirrigated by love's prayers and tears;
No fondness felt, no kindness for another,
But only doubt, mistrust and foolish fears.
I did not find Thee, Lord,
In all the earth or in the sky above;
Nor know the boundless meaning of Thy worth—
Till I found love.

Peg Feder-Schelle
THE HOMELESS

I see you wrapped and layered in heavy dull colored woolens
pulling down and dragging around your feet.

I see the uneven heals and soles of your oversized boots that
will hold old rags, carpet and paper bags to help retain your body heat.

I see your body in a fetal position against a wall
adjusting the card board tent to lessen the chilled wind.

I see your soiled discolored hands rubbing the tired and sand filled eyes and brushing away dry flakey skin.

I see you desperately trying to stay alert on the streets
protecting, pulling and pushing your furnishings and inventory.

I see you with deep depression, hopelessness and congestion of words while people stare and scoff as you relate your story.

I see you escaping to alley trash cans in hope of food ingestion
and stuffing pockets for some to spare.

I see your weak body aching, dreary with worry
too ill to eat but willing to share.
I see you as a human being, with dreams, hopes and cares.
I don't look at you as an enemy.

My God, I want to help you—you are my family.

David R McDonough
MASK

He walks in the shadows of the dimly lit lane
Alone he must face his sorrow and pain
He's traveled from town-to-town looking for work.
His only response to the relentless search, "I don't hire Jerks!"
As an outcast of society, he's done prison time
Unjustly convicted, Innocent of the crime
He's forced to sleep on a bed of old rags,
With a pillow from gathered shopping bags.
The food that he eats, and the clothes he wears
He's found in the trash, others discarded wares
There's only one request of people he does ask
For each to look at themselves and remove their Mask
It is easy to condemn and ridicule
As long as your own skeletons are hidden from view.

Michael S Nikirk
SKI-SCENE

I am alone, the white surrounds
Serenity in every turn
Through aspen trees
As natures' bride
On lengths of golden glass I glide
And realize somewhere inside
Forever this I'll yearn

Edward A Bradley
TRY

I don't understand,
Why, I don't hold your hand.
I can't explain, why, the other guy,
Gets that extra sigh.

Together, we never talk,
Together, we never walk.
We only pass each one by,
Like two birds on the fly.

Never a smile, nor a kiss,
It's always that mere miss.
Why?
Oh, Why?

We plan to plan to meet,
But, it would be a defeat.
Each time we get near,
There is a unknown fear.

I don't understand,
Why? I don't hold your hand.
If, I was the other guy,
Would you, like to try?

Dorothy Gillham
ROOM 84B

To the many known and unknown who have lost their home, their freedom - but not their dignity of spirit.

I watch you bring my food tray. I am fed.
I lie covered with a thin blanket. I am bathed.
My teeth are brushed. My hair is combed. I am dressed.
Another day lies grey and unchanged before me.

When Night gradually leaves my shadowed world
And Daylight, with ever brightening clarity outlines
The rails that shape the boundary of my bed,
I listen for the footsteps that never echo in the corridor.
Look with dimmed eyes for past loves, only to see present strangers.
Can you feel the hurt, the fear, the weary loneliness,
The sense of being totally abandoned?

You don't understand, do you, young Nurse?
You don't understand when you wheel me into the lounge
And leave me watching the T.V.
The screen is filled with orange-green, blue-green people
Who never see the circle of wheelchairs lined up all around them.
Do you <u>really</u> think those actors (so untouchable),
Can fill the void within our lonely lives?
That wheelchair touching wheelchair can bind our isolated hearts together?

My eyes follow you as you step out into the world I once enjoyed.
Relieved of your duties you look back. What do you see?
A frail whiteheaded lady so seemingly unaware of her surroundings.
Already her head is drooping forward. Her eyes close.

Young Nurse do you understand? Do you CARE—
For the old and unremembered.
For me?

Lydian De Silva
BORN FREE

I stood on the beach, and looked up to the sky.
I must gather the strength, to give life a last try.
The fiery sun set low in the west,
I knew in my heart, I had not done my best.
I had reached for a star, but I fell on a thorn,
I cursed the day I had ever been born.
Liquor and drugs had controlled my whole life.
I lost all of my children, I lost my "Dear" wife.
I could start over, what chance have I got?
I had followed a rainbow, in search of the pot.
Gold or Silver, it all means the same,
What good is it all, when I am burdened with shame.

Can I start over and bury the past?
Have I got the courage to change
things at last?
A large wave approached, and
washed over me.
"Of course I can do it," I am a man,
"Born Free."

Franni Taylor Apostol

I FEEL

To my teenage years; and to John and Joe Apostol whom I love with all my heart

---

I FEEL the tears
Roll off my eyes
I FEEL the heart
that always cries

I FEEL the love
I once knew
I FEEL it gone
And I am blue

I FEEL terror
that is never gone
I FEEL it growing
On and on

I FEEL the need
For some Affection
I FEEL I need
no more rejection

I FEEL so deep
I see so strong
I FEEL that home
Is long way gone

I FEEL I wish
that I were dead
I FEEL it in my
lonesome head

I FEEL I need
Someone to care
I want someone
Who will be there

Rosalie Aquavia Moffo

RAINY DAY

A rainy day
Filled with honey dew drops
Falling down from the sky

A rainy day
Filled with loneliness
Coming from within your cry

A rainy day
Filled with happiness
Towards a graying sky

A rainy day
Filled with sunshine
Seems to stop the time . . .

Rita A Grala

THE SPACE SHUTTLE DISASTER

On January the twenty-eight, in
nineteen eighty six.
Our space shuttle; the Challenger,
finally made the lift.
And, at launch time it lifted fine,
everything was go.
The horror that so soon took place,
there was no way to know.
There was no evidence, such a
disaster could transpire.
The shuttle in two minutes flat,
was a giant ball of fire.
It carried seven that we loved.
Great astronauts, so filled with
dare.
They climbed aboard the
Challenger.
Though deep inside were well
aware.
That anything could happen, but
they bravely faced the sky.
And while doing what they chose
to do, were destined all to die.
With heavy hearts, we will
remember each of them with
pride.
And better yet, let's not forget, for
all of us they died.
The clock we cannot backward
turn,
Erase from history
Instead, we move ahead and learn.
From what, was meant to be.

Ruth A Johnson

TWO PATHS THAT HAPPENED TO CROSS

I consider it an honor to publish this poem in dedication to my beloved, dearly missed, late father, DALLAS JOHNSON.

Two paths that crossed one day,
We stopped long enough one word
to say.

That one moment so touched our
heart,
Now we are both hurting, at the
thought we must part.

Perhaps, it shall be only for a while,
When the great distance we are a
part,
Will be just a mile.

Two paths that happened to cross
one night,
Not to simply embrace, but to hold
back,
Took all our might.

It must have come from someone
up above,
For at first sight we both fell in love.

Two paths that happened to cross,
We can only look back at what we
lost.

Pearlie M Gnewuch

OH "THIS WORLD"

This poem is dedicated to Bob, my loving husband.

Oh "This world" with troubled
days, some are good
And other's filled with haze,
How hard we try in each days birth,
Oh this world be strong I say, for
this world has many
More days to come, tis" is true
Oh" this world days will come and
days will go,
With this troubled world you never
know,
Good and bad, blue and gray, oh
"this world I pray"
Come again and bring your beauty
and all your good
Sometimes we are so
misunderstood,
Each day you come, bring your
gentle breeze and all
Your mist, tell the sun to shine ever
brite and tell
The moon that comes with the
night, oh "this world"

Ann Carole Via

MR & MRS CURTIN

Mary Ellen and Shawn,
You're soon to go up the aisle to
say, "I do,"
And become "husband and wife"—
Mr. & Mrs. Curtin, that's who.

Now hand in hand you'll start
Your journey down through life.
And with God's blessings,
In love you'll face each strife.

May you always show you care,
One for the other;
By the faith you share
And the devotion of a lover.

May God's boundless mercy
Help fulfill your highest hope.
The aim of all God's children
As they with striving learn to cope.

Now share the tears and the joys
As you through life do walk.
And on bended knee to God
Ask guidance for the windows of
your life to caulk.

Now don't ever forget
The first rule of marriage:
You're to always travel
In God's "one horse carriage."

Jacqueline H Eubanks

MOTHER'S LOVE

To Reggie who is now 14 and still the Apple of my eye.

My little boy is only eight.
And smart as he can be,
He shows how much he loves me,
For all the world to see.

He asked me if I loved him,
And he was quite sincere,
I told him that I loved him,
I said, "You are my dear."

For mothers love their little boys,
Though they may think we don't,
And try to fill their every need,
And everything they want.

There comes a time in this old life
When mothers take second place,
When their little boys grow to men
And girls give them a chance.

For now I feel quite safe to say.
For him I'm number ONE.
For all the love he gives to me,
He is my Loving Son.

Mr Chris Bontos

YOU

Often when I lay in bed and am
silenced by the deep darkness.
I can feel you lying by my side.
A touch is all I need to hide my
loneliness.

Dreaming in a subconscious way, I
travel to you and shower you with
colors of love and warmth, and
when I've awakened, I am covered
in
sweat, dampened by the night.
Could you be a reality of my future?
A diamond before it's cut? Or am I
just fantacizing about a love that's
not.

For all unknown reasons that I
cannot explain,
I find myself engulfed with pain.

Nancy L Leech

THE SPIRIT IN DAVID

He's struggling
We're struggling
Searching for answers
there are none
holding onto strength
giving away sometimes to
depression
There is always hope
believing in him
In time, he will be whole again
The will to live is there
endure the pain
think positive
He doesn't need our negativeness
His fight is our fight
We stand beside him
holding, crying and guiding
He is not alone
Our hearts are with you David
Our love will hold you close
Faith will pull you through and
time will make you complete
We wait.

Mary Garoufalis

WRINKLES OF WISDOM

While an old lady rested in the park
one day.
A little boy sat next to her, as he
played.
To all of her wrinkles he became
alert
He wanted to know when she
talked, if they hurt.

The old lady looked over and gave
him a smile.
With a twinkle in her eye and a
voice so mild
She assured the boy that she was
in no pain.
And if he was lucky, someday he'd
have the same.

As she placed her hand upon her
face
every wrinkle she slowly began to
trace.
Remembering how they each had
left its mark
Knowing that each wrinkle began
in her heart.

She then continued to say, how
each wrinkle she earned
For they are life's rewards for the
things that she learned
You must always remember to do
your best
As each day you live, is one of God's
test.

For I know that no two wrinkles
are alike
each one is a different memory in
my life.
Some come from joy, some come
from sorrow
For the life I live today, will be the
wrinkle of tomorrow.

Jerri Brillhart

ENDURING LOVE

Dedicated to George Brillhart my loving husband for almost 40 years.

Molding you, saying I love you
Is a total acceptance of all you are
and

A realization of all your endearing
 frailities
Knowing how wonderous you
 really are
Even when you forget and your
 voice
Sounds angry and impetuous
Or your eyes glisten with criticism,
Those are the moments I must
 remember
That underneath you are so
 magnificent.
Recognizing all your values are
 honest and
Sincere, even when you can't
 remember
What I asked you to do on Monday.
Recalling all the years of gentle
 ways
You were when abandoned to your
 amorous
Antics that now lie dormant on a
 secret shelf.
While love has mellowed and been
 tamed to
A tiny flicker, I sit in reverie still
 loving you.

Lela Neely-Ford

SORROW

For the sake of sorrow,
 I sought a brighter tomorrow.
Silently weeping,
 boisterously wailing—

Love lingered, unprevailing.
Semi-imposed, deeply detached—
 Imagining utopia . . .
Forgetting-Illumination!

Tyronda Renee Jackson

RIGHTEOUSNESS

Remember me always: Wayne, Brittany, Theron, Chardonnay, Shirley, Wright, Dana, Kim, Lionel, Tony Jr., Brandon, Gret, Eddie, Family and Friends/Enemies.

You put me on the highest
 mountain.
 And now I see,
 There is beauty in all things
 and not just in me.
You let me fall.
 And now I see,
 Things aren't always what they
 seem to be.
You showed me
 And now I see
 I'm not the best nor the worst of
 human beings.
You taught me to love
 And now I see.
 There's no greater love than that
 from above.
I see things more clearly.
 And now I see.
 The world is a place for you as
 well as for me.

Gayle "Cherie" Rowbottom

SHARED MEMORIES

For my beloved son, West

Each mother grieves
As her son leaves the nest
To begin his search for life
New friends—a home—a wife
While we stand back and silently
 pray
That he will find the best.

I am one of the lucky ones
For he mastered all the three.
Had I the choice—I would have
 hoped
For you—for all my sons.

We have a bond my dear Michelle
That time cannot displace—
We shared the love of a beautiful
 man
That nothing can erase.

You never tried to break the bond
As many often do.
And I had more—not less
Because God gave him you.

My love will always be there
For the two that became as one
And I pray that God will Bless you
For the Love you gave my son.

Anna J Tuite

DAUGHTERS

To my Beloved husband, Johnny and our lovely daughters, Maryanne and Carolynn

---

The gift of a flower is always
 a gift of Love,
A daughter is like a flower
 given from Heaven above—
Just like the flower that has
 blossomed and grown
She was nurtured and loved and
 now has a life of her own.
Like the aroma of a flower which
 fills the air
She filled our hearts with Joy,
 Pride, Love and Care!
Like the flower that reaches
 toward the Sun overhead
May you reach all the goals you
 have set in your head—
May God watch over you always
 from His throne up above
May you always bloom in our
 Garden of Love!

Mary L Harris

SHADOWS

I should like to dedicate this poem to Mr. William P. Conrad, Author and Historian of our Town (Greencastle & around).

Here they come; there they go—
 Shadows
Casting gloom, grief and woe—
 Shadows
All the light they seem to swallow—
When we walk, they seem to
 follow—
 Shadows
Forms of windows, lights and
 trees—
 Shadows
Things that sail through each cool
 breeze—
 Shadows
When a sudden darkness falls—
Then these things are on the wall—
 Shadows

Jennifer Lynne Stanley

ALWAYS THERE

This poem is for the person who has been my best friend for 21 years. My mom, Judy Butts.

Her fair curly head goes bobbing
 in and out of your sight,
But she never loses sight of you.
To carry a child inside you, to
 know it before it's born,
And to finally see it, that it's perfect,
To hold it and watch it until you
 know it better than anyone does.
But soon, you know her less and
 less,
Her adventures, her accidents are
 her own,
But you still know her better than
 anyone—except her.
And so she grows, up and away
 from who she was.
You feel discarded as she argues or
 ignores you,
She, who begged to follow you
 anywhere, just to be with
 Mommy
Doesn't want to follow anymore.
She asks for little, you'd love to give
 more.
The young woman who writes
 from college owns herself now,
Her adventures are more
 interesting, but in less detail.
The details are saved for phone
 calls to friends,
They know her better than you do.
Where's my little curly top?—and
 the blanket would come away
To reveal the shining eyes of your
 little girl.
The barrier between you is more
 than a blanket now
But the eyes still shine so you keep
 trying to pull it away,
Even when you don't want to,
 when you're afraid you've lost
 her.
Her world is bigger than your arms
 now,
But you still never leave her sight.

Cathy Ann Rose Ward

GLASS HOUSE

This glass house we live in
 is full of tragedies and sin.
And buried in its see-through walls,
 someone's tear gently falls.
For all the world has become
 unclear—
 there's no one you can trust here.
Here we live all alone,
 this is ours, this is home.
Locked in bars around this place,
 we seldom see a happy face.
Inside ourselves, our hearts burn
 while wicked thoughts flash and
 churn.
How lucky are we to be living
 where everyone is so
 unforgiving.
Behind this glass, fogged and
 scratched,
 in this house all doors are
 latched.

Denise A Rutan

HOW I FEEL

I can't find the words to express
 How I feel for you
They're stronger than any card
 Or gift could say or do.

A card can tell you how I feel
 A gift will express it too
But neither can ever truely tell
 How much I do love you.

And even words can not express
 How much you mean to me;
"I'd climb the highest mountain"
 And "sail the roughest sea".

But look closely into my eyes
 And soon you will agree
That I Love you very much
 And for all eternity.

Constance L Haugh

ONLY EIGHTEEN

To my twin brothers, Bob and Jim, who lived this poem at eighteen, World War II

Today a lonely sailor
Lies dreaming on the beach
His soul is filled with loving
 thoughts
Of those beyond his reach.

He listens to the music
That rolls in with the sea
The song of every heartbeat
Through all eternity.

The stomp of pre-historics
Of dinosaurs and man
The song and dance of natives
Leaving footprints in the sand.

The roar of monster cannons
The sun across the way
Brings him back to life's realities
And the war he fights today.

Thelma Gene Mullins

I FOUND JESUS

I am just passing through
This world of sin, I thought
I would stop an see you again

I have traveled through the valleys
I have climbed the highest hills
Jesus is my savior, you can only
 trust in him.

Sometimes I get so weary
Sometimes I feel so blue.
But I'll tell you Brenthen
I found some one I know

Gary J Gerardine & Marsha A Schmalz

A TRIBUTE TO THE CHALLENGER SEVEN

It rose with a track—straight and
 true,
Framed with a bright and brilliant
 blue!
Upward it soared toward the far
 away heaven
Carrying its crew—the Challenger
 Seven.

In a matter of seconds, an
 unforgettable story
Bestowed this crew with renowned
 Glory.
It happened so quickly, and no one
 knew
What became of our Challenger
 Crew.

As the world looked on with
 unbelieving eyes

Challenger Seven exploded in the morning skies.
The fireball engulfed, everyone was agast
For surely, we knew the "Seven" had breathed their last!

To Judy, Christa, Ellison, Mike, Ron, Greg, and Dick
The day that began has thus ended as quick!
To us, you have not left, but entered that sanctity of Space
In preparation for others that will follow in your place!

In your honor is offered this tribute to you,
For this flight meant so much to all of us too,
And, now with you at rest so peacefully in Heaven,
We honor and praise—THE CHALLENGER SEVEN!

Roxanna Lee Myres (Gast)

IT COULD HAVE BEEN US

It could have been us that lost that Dear Little baby.
Oh that Precious little boy, how cute it would of been to watch him grow and play.
That Precious Bundle of Joy can't be cuddled or even held,
Oh how sad you must be without that Precious little Bundle.
He's in God's tender loving care and that little bundle of Joy will rest in peace without any pain.
No you'll never know why your little boy was called home at such an early age, but you saw the miracle of your little boy, even if it was only one day.
Thank God for that one day.

Jane A Cahalan

A LETTER FROM VIETNAM

To my family, with Love.

I have a friend, he has no family. You see?
So Mom, I'd like to bring him home with me.
My Son, of course we won't mind if he comes
for a few days.
But mother, you don't seem to understand what
I'm trying to say.
I want this boy to live with us as long as he wishes
to stay.
First I must tell you something, but don't be alarmed

My friend while in battle happened to lose an arm
" My Son don't be afraid to bring your friend home with you,
he can stay and visit for a week or two."
But Mother, he isn't just a friend, he's like a brother too.
That's why I want him to stay and be a son to you.
Before you give an answer there's something that must
be said,
my friend while in battle, also lost a leg.
"My Son, it hurts to say this but the answer must be no.
Your father and I have no time for a boy who is crippled so."
So many months later a letter came to say,
their son had died, and the reason was SUICIDE . . .
Home came the casket draped with our flag,
they saw their son lying there, minus an arm and leg.

Larunce A Pipkin Jr

STRANGER

"Hi, can you tell me why he sits between us,
or is it me that I see in the folds?"

The cold warms but the seat stays firm,
planted in the safety of distance.

"Sorry, so sorry, don't mean to be a nuisance."

You laugh. I want to laugh with you,
but you'd be put off by my manner.

"If by chance I see you again, could we exchange a letter?"

"A memory maybe, something quaint."

"Sorry, so sorry, I should have seen better."

"Excuse me, I think you'd better run,
it's silly, no wait, aw, go ahead."

Still the view is quite lovely.

I'd like a closer look.

"Naw, not sad, it'll pass, at some point,
we must be lonely."

Willie Mae Smalls

ALONG THE GARDEN TRAIL

I watch things grow, nature's flower show, life's beginning and its end, nature at work and seasons change.

I find happiness, peace of mind, comfort, food for thought, God's love, health and beauty, pleasure, contentment, a bouquet of flowers, enjoyment and encouragement.

I see birds, bees and butterflies, creatures great and small.

I meet neighbors, chat, share, laugh and lament.

I dream of fame, fortune, hobbies, food and fun.

I rest my feet, mind, body and soul.

I meditate as I design beautiful plots, creating a work of art-a masterpiece, think, ponder, and communicate with God.

I research the "wonders of nature," discover patterns of growth, experience many moods and mysteries of nature.

I paint pictures of landscapes, gardens and the sky.

I gather knowledge, seeds, berries, flowers and fruits.

I plant a garden that is beautiful, restful, enjoyable and soothing to one's mind—a precious gift to mankind.
Along The Garden Trail

Kathleen M Sleight

GIFTS

To understand life, you must begin anew.
You must give up what you know and see all things from a fresh point of view—yours!

Life gives to you its Truth and Bounty
for your education.
And your awareness of it
has determined your spot
on the scale of spiritual endeavor—
your place and yours only.

Perhaps like me you are half way through
forever!
What you have to offer
is yours alone to give.
Attitudes and attributes,
part of your individuality.
You, a Jewel in the Crown of the Creator!
The rest is up to you!

Roscoe Terryll Lansdown

ALPHA-RAY

The Mankind Creation

Star sign, Alpha ray . . . Cut by the edge of a crescent moon.
Light . . . Splintered by the slash giving birth to a rainbow, multi-colored spectrum prism of an ever-pulsing glo.

Sunbeam . . . Fire of illuminate essence, radiance of power causing the waverings of reality, that warbled mirage of images reflected off the mirror of impregnable space.

Wind . . . Air . . . Energy in motion. Blowing, moving upon the Earth, Whirling . . . making collected clouds of dust . . . Swirling, wet by rising steam (evidence of sweat) dripping from the body of Earth.

Earth . . . Held by the force of gravity, swinging in rhythmic patterns making cycles in the realm of time.

Intense generations. Electro-magnetic action. Creative force moulding and making substance, giving shape . . . adding structure . . . causing Form.

Form . . . Whirling, Swirling, Whisping clouds of dust (earthen matter moist with sweat).

Earth . . Body . . Held in balance by the wind, sparked by an Alpha-ray.

Form . . . Developing structure, an image made visible, tempered by radiant light.

Gift . . . Eternal substance, behold the Mankind.

We are the creation called Mankind; should it be that our insatiable need for war, fostered by our desire for peace, would have us to be declared "Once Were? . . ."

Marcia Eckel Robinson

HEART CRY

I dedicate this poem to my husband, Richard Ellsworth Robinson. "Dick," has sacrificed mightily, in behalf of my poetry, and he has been my constant encourager.

I too, may be more
Than my rough, harsh,
Unattractive exterior reveals

For hidden deep within the living soul of me
Are alive, yet dormant,
Seeds of Potentiality:
World's of heart tenderness . . .
World's of mental envisionings . . . even
World's of physical blooming . . .

Won't someone please, have the caring?

Won't someone please, take the time?

Won't someone please, look deeper than the surface,
scarred, scared me—to see the me
that I should, and can be?

All I need are just a few, tiny drops of that
Life finding,
Life saving,
Life transforming fluid,

More precious than emeralds,
Called love . . .
Do you, have any to spare?

Patricia Anne Call Ascani

YOU'RE LEAVING TODAY

To Robert Parker, a dear friend

You're Leaving Today
When will I see you again
Have I told you lately
How good it's been

Being together
Growing so close
Learning 'bout each other
I'll miss you the most

The secrets we shared
The moments alone
We couldn't fortell
How close we have grown

Saying Good-Bye
There's sadness untold
Your memory will be kept
In my locket of gold

Sherry S Campbell

SANDS OF TIME

Are your days as infinite as the sands of the earth?
Or is your time numbered as the sands in the hour glass?

What is life to you really worth?

How do you live each day, each hour?
To the fullest, as if this moment could be the last
Or not sure of your future; not caring for the past.
Are you living half heartily as though the supernatural force will never tire of turning your hour glass over and over again?

Time will run out; but when? If we knew; what then? Would it matter?
What is our purpose, our reason for living?
Was it fate or just by chance we were born?
Or is our life a very carefully planned event with a special purpose for each one that is sent?
Which one do you think is true?
I hope you know in your heart of the two the answer is surely the latter.

No one can set an exact pattern for you
For that's why each life is made unique, so one of a kind.
So reach into the depths of your inner being
For there are answers to questions you really must find
And soon you will know what you have to do.

Just let God through Jesus take control of your Soul.
Then life in the fullest is what you'll finally be seeing.
From that moment on; whatever comes to pass
You'll be blest with a Promise from God of rebirth
And your life will be as the infinite sands of the earth
And not as those of the hour glass.

Sandra M Henig

IT'S REALLY GOOD TO SEE YOU AGAIN

To my dear friend Vicki, for the memories of yesterday, and the visions of tomorrow.

It's really good to see you again
I've missed you in so many ways.
I've thought of you when I've gone to certain places
And heard certain songs
Wishing you were there with me.
I've missed your smile and your laughter
That brightened so many of my days.
I've missed that special twinkle that lit up your eyes
When something touched your heart.
I've missed your positive outlook on life
That is so contagious to everyone around you.
I've missed your honesty and compassion—
That unique balance of sincerity and humanity
Which eases even the most difficult situation.
But most of all, I've missed those special times
When we'd sit and talk for hours on end
We'd share a bottle of wine and our dreams
And secrets from our past.
We never had to measure our words—
We could let them flow freely
Knowing that the other would understand.
I've remembered those times with such fondness;
Those were such memorable moments that I'll always treasure
And I want you to know
That it's really good to see you again.

Phyllis I Lucas

PLEASE GOD: A CHILD

Dear God, send us a child,
please pick one out today.
Find a little boy or girl
You could give away.
We parents will love it,
this we promise You.
We will give it best of care,
all that's good, it's true.
Please, dear God, try us,
don't let us down.
Promise us today
that You'll look around
for that lovely daughter
or perhaps, that special son.
We don't really care, Lord,
we'll take either one.
We love children,
this You surely know,
send us that child
and how our hearts will glow.
So, if You feel we can handle
all the trials of man and wife,
send us that little angel
to help fulfill our life.
Not our will, God, but
Yours alone be done.
Just one more plea, though,
a daughter or a son?

Daniel A Grill

COUNTING MY BLESSINGS

In honor of my wife Oretha, my sons Wallace and Russel and my daughters Danetta & Nicole.

Thank you Lord, you've let me live another year
It was a sad one at times when I lost two people that to me were so dear
But Lord you made it up to me in many ways
You sent me a new granddaughter and you healed granny's
Leg that we worried about for many day's
There was times when my family was pretty sick
And you touched them with your almighty hands and made them well real quick
Oh Lord I could go on and tell more thing one by one
About the many kind things that you have done
Yes Lord you've blessed me in so many ways
Now let me repay you by serving you for the rest of my days

Susan M Ovesen

THE VIOLINIST

He waits for stillness.
A death-like silence fills the air.
He is satisfied.
He presses her, ever so gently,
To his body.
He cradles her like the lover
She is to him.
He begins to seduce her, and
She responds to his gentle seduction
By emitting the sweetest melody.

I feel his passion, his intensity.
He has me under his spell,
And entices me to join him in
His sensual interlude with her.

He rocks her back and forth
In their romantic dance.
He is rough with her,
She responds still.
He takes us both to the very
Heights of esctacy.
My heart pounds as she cries out
In her climactic pleasure.
A tear of emotion rolls down my cheek
As he ends the movement.
I am breathless.

Harry Frank Russell

ON THIS ROAD OF LIFE

The road of life
Seems to be so bad right now
But I know it really isn't
Because you are there

The road I have been following
Seems to be so long
There is a lot of pain and despair
But there is also a lot of happiness
Because you said anytime that I am troubled
I can come to you
And you will be there

Well Lord, you have been there
And I know you always will be
I want to thank you for this
Thank you for being there
While I travel
On this road of life

Elizabeth E Gibson Evans

A CHILD SWINGING

Dedicated in the memory of my grandmother Elizabeth E Gibson. To Clarence for his love and encouragement. And to Jamie, Samantha, Aaron and Andrew because I love them.

I see a child swinging.
And I watch her blonde hair fly.
Her blue eyes sparkle in the light.
And she giggles as she rides.

She's not concerned with world affairs.
She does not worry and she does not care.
Her mind is focussed on one thing.
The magic ride upon her swing.

She does not know what lies ahead.
In the future she'll soon know.
For if she did the ride she's on,
She never would let go.

If only we could stay as free.
As the child on the swing.
Let all our hurts and heart aches ride away upon the wind.
We would be forever happy in a world so full of lies.
If only we could catch the light.
That sparkles in her eyes.

Jane Elizabeth Carlson

BONDED BY UNMISTAKEN LOVE

I dedicate this poem to my husband Ray, for all the growing up we shared and all the times he pushed me to be myself . . . no one knows me like he does . . . I love you Ray!

All you've ever known are lies, that have forced the pieces we've bonded to fall apart. How hard can it be to be mine, and mend the cracks that divide our broken hearts.

Go away, go away, leave me here to rest. No more game techniques to put my love to the test.

Don't tease me, don't play, I know how bad I get to you. My thoughts may go astray, we're upset but what else can we do.

I love you my dear, because you help me on my feet again. Even when I feel like giving up, knowing I just can't win.

I've traced my thoughts, when we're alone, from time to time. I guess you're the only one I've really ever known was mine.

So kiss me my dear, let's fix this bond we've broken. Have no fear, for loves real truth can now be spoken.

Sabrina R Michael

DON'T STEP BACK

This is dedicated to the Loving Memory of my late cousin, Daryis W. Walker, whom I miss and loved very much.

I can't move forward and I can't step back.
I can only look from left to right
When will life meet me so I can find my way.
Just can't give up without a fight.
There isn't any mornings or days to turn to nights.
No sunshine or shadows or empty places with no light
Your once young eyes saw a rainbow offering you hope.
Stars that shown to help you guide your way.
But darkness fell upon us, like it has for many more.
And you wonder inside yourself what the hell is life for.
Just take a look at yourself and you'll see,

That believing is more than it was
thought out to be.
Let life guide you the way it was
meant to be.
Don't Step Back—just follow it
with me.

Dennis Roy Felt

A BABY

What is innocent, can't even talk
What is innocent, just learning to
walk
You watch it crawl in very odd ways
'Cause you were the same
In the beginning of your days
It could be only one thing
A little baby!
What does it hear?
What does it see?
Happiness, misery,
You or me?
Nothing!
Nothing but peace for the first few
years
A show of laughter, a show of tears
Something made from woman and
man
Something living that doesn't
understand
But as it will grow
Into this big beautiful world
It will know why,
What it is here
So close and so dear
And why it will always
Be so
NEAR

Kym Stubblefield

FOOLS

We were fools of the moment
Played at love
or thought so
We lied beautifully, soundlessly
To ourselves
but didn't think so
We cried outloud
To ourselves
or pretended to
We hurt each other
Time and time again
not purposely
We miss each other
Not really
or do we?

Lucille M Fields Borden

Lucille M Fields Borden

CARING . . .

This poem is dedicated to my family and special friends

Caring
Is wanting to see the one
You care for be happy—It brings
out the
Inner beauty in us—
It makes one want to reach out
and—touch
It makes one want to—
encourage—caring
It makes one—trust
Caring it makes one—defend you . .
It makes one want to embrace and
caress—
You too—
Caring . . it makes one feel—so
good . .
It makes one wanting to share their
whole
Being . .
Caring—it makes one—only seeing
everything
That's good in you . . . caring is like
a magnet—
Drawn to each other . .
It's . . . Magnificent

Monsignor Bernard Powers

LIFE

Life receives life
and there is expectation and
hope,
there is a desire
for life to come forth.

Life bears life
and there is apprehension and
wonder.
There is a desire
for life to be well.

Life sees life
and there is satisfaction and
peace.
There is a desire
for life to respond.

Life touches life
and she who bears
knows that life has been given
and there is joy in sharing.
Life is seen by each
and both are alive to the other.

Life enraptures
mother and child.

J N McCracken

MY NOSE LEADS ME

Leading me out by the back garden
fence
My nose discovers many peculiar
scents
Snakes, snails and turtles have all
been through here
There's also the tracks of a white
tail deer

My nose leads me on to a beautiful
rose
It smells nice but, "don't push me
too close," says my nose
"The stem of the rose is all covered
with thorns
They could prick me and then I
would feel so forlorn"

Then my nose leads me to the
tracks of a bird
It studies the scent of things my
ears have heard
The birds watch from tree limbs
above, of so high
My nose gathers their scents and I
watch them with my eye

As I follow my nose through fields
here and there
It soon leads me to the tracks of a
hare
First the scent is strong, and then
it stops
In the spaces between the hare's
hippity hops

Then on my nose leads me to the
back of the house
Where in the wood pile there lives
a field mouse
I'd like him to come out, just so we
could play
But he's frightened of me, so in his
nest he'll stay

My nose catches the scent of my
master outside
My ears perk up and my eyes open
wide
Legs and paws carry me swiftly
across the yard
There I greet my master, my tail
wagging hard

My nose tells me my master has
brought me some food
As he pets me and talks to me, it
makes me feel good
Out to my dog house my nose leads
me with care
In my dish is the supper my master
placed there

After supper comes nap time, I'm
sure you have guessed
From all of my travels I need a good
rest
I'll lay in my dog house with my
head near the door
Till my nose leads me out to go
searching once more

Mrs E R Cantrell

MY DADDY

My Daddy J. D. White
My daddy age 93 what a
Wonderful man is he,
He is my best friend and
Will be till the end.
He loves his country home
And all, most of all he loves God,
One thing he says
So many times we do the
Best we can and get
Along.

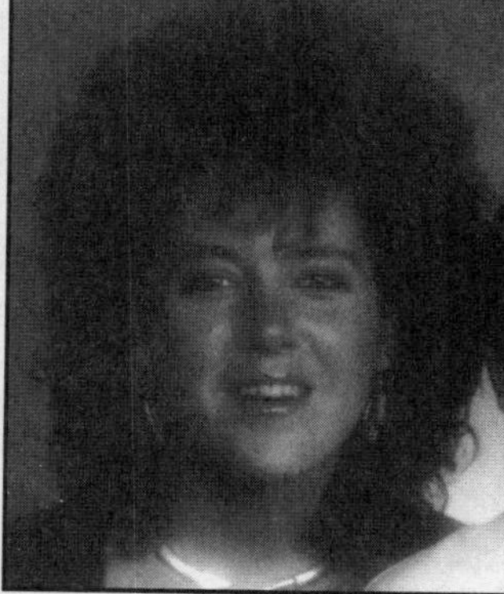

Lucille Ann Johnston-Carrington

Lucille Ann Johnston-Carrington

WITH HIGH HOPES

This poem is dedicated to Scott, my son "Best Friends" Love you.

Would you meet me on a hill for
lunch?
All dressed in your Sunday best
Coat tails and top hat
I would dress so elegant
Maybe my grandmothers old
wedding dress
With a limp straw hat and bells,
Well . . . Would you go?
Would you build a tree house with
me?
One large enough for midnight
candlelite snacks.
We could put curtains on the
windows
I love dandylions in chipped blue
bowls
You could serenade me from
below on starlite nites.
Well . . . would you sing?
Would you dream with me?
Maybe about nothing at all or silly
things
Just watch clouds roll by
Do you really think there is a man
on the moon?
Let's build a home and grow old
together
Well . . . will you go
Will you sing
Will you dream
with me.

Susan Wesolek Peyton

WHAT WAS IT?

Dedicated to Emma Johnson Teutsch, Living forever in my heart.

Soft grey hair, sweet warm face
Gone from Earth, now in His grace
I truly knew, it would happen one
day
Nothing in life, is here to stay
Time has shown me, you're really
gone
But before you left, something
seemed wrong
For near the end, you could not
speak
Your body and soul, grew much
too weak
Words were unwillingly
imprisoned inside
It had to be important, how hard
you tried
Determined you were, to get them
out
No one could guess, what it was
about
I wish, you could have found a way
What was it, dear Grandma, you
were trying to say?
I chose to believe, it was, "I love
you,"
With a tear, I responded, "I love
you, too!"

James Quinn Lanier

MY FINEST HOUR

Here I stand
Before your eyes now,
See it my way
Or don't see it at all;
This-my hour, my finest hour.
A light shines from inside like the
warm sun.
Don't help me, pity me
For this is <u>my</u> hour, my finest hour.

Betty Duncan Colgrove

ELEMENTAL

Of all the free things offered me
Sun . . .
Moon . . .
Stars . . .
The sea . . .
I think the one I like the most
Though it comes moaning like a
ghost
Is winter wind.

Christina L Grieger

INCHING

Worm Worm Worm
Inching past my window
How far will I let you go?

(Feeling cruel today,
you know.)
Worm Worm Worm
Trying to escape a hidden
crime
Slam!!
Now you're only slime.

Trishel Sisk
IN MEMORY OF MY MOTHER
Mother's gone to heaven
To a land so bright and fair,
Where no sorrow ever enters,
There'll be no dying there.

Her burdens here were hard to bear
And many nights she spent in
prayer,
One day her troubles she laid down
And God gave her a starry crown.

She's walking with the Angels
In a robe of spotless white,
In that lovely city
Where there never comes a night.

No parting in that city
There's no tear drops in that land.
For Christ the Holy Saviour
Wipes them away with his hand.

Lauretta Jane Lowell
A THOUGHT DIVINE
May I convey a thought to you
That will thrill you through and
through,
Giving a sense of love as you devote
More of your life to God each day,
That He may find you walking the
way
Of giving and goodness and peace?
Blessings to your soul He'll release.

The potential of divinity dwells
right in you
And may accelerate you through
and through
With a fiery new sense of mission
and hope
Which will cause you in ferver to
devote
More of your life to God each day.
He will show you the way
Of giving and grace and peace.
To your soul blessings He will
realease!

As you tread life's rocky way
May you heed your soul's need to
pray.
Might you attune to Jesus within!
Lay down every burden and sin!
Replace it with such a hope
supreme!
Surpass your fondest mortal
dream!
It is God's peace that casts out all
fear
And will help you grow year by
year.

Sue Wegner
HELLO AND GOODBYE
Cautiously, we weave ourselves in
and out of other
peoples lives.
Often as not becoming entangled;
Too frequently leaving a bitter
taste behind—
So seldom leaving a treasured
friendship.
But on and on we go . . .
Meeting, mingling, entwining
ourselves in, around,
over, and under all those we come
in contact with.
Relationships established.
Becoming a part of new families.
Acceptance—Belonging . . .
Leaving.
And what becomes of the family
and friends you leave
behind?
You never leave just one person
when you say goodbye.
And so now you're gone.
Except for traces of you left behind
in family albums . . .
Pictures taken during special
times;
Diaries where your name was
casually mentioned.
But gone, none the less.
And, in time, someone new takes
your place.
And she looks at the pictures and
reads the words
That leave her wondering why life
is so full of hello's and goodbye's.

Gladys Cleveland
SAD LITTLE BUTTERFLY

In memory of my Mother, Annie Ree White Cleveland 10-18-1908—2-6-1974

I'll fly tomorrow to spread my
wings
Like a little girl in a open swing
You see my colors as I pass
Like a rainbow in a sudsy glass
When summer is over you will see
My beautiful colors fade from thee
My wings and me we will freeze
Till next summer when we feel the
breeze
My wings and me we will not be
I'll return to the past where you will
see

Where my beautiful wings was
taking from me
I'll cry for my wings like a bumble
bee sting
Until I hear the summer bells ring.
I'll say good-bye as we pass
Like looking into a looking glass
My wings are covered with the
snow
I'm going behind that open door.
So long winter, summer and fall
Till next spring I'll remember you
all.

Leigh Ann Davis
TEACH ME TO FLY

I dedicate this poem to my dear mother, Fran Davis.

I was standing, gazing up at the
sky, watching the birds fly by. I
found myself asking outloud,
"Why can't I fly?" I heard a voice,
and saw a figure standing in the
sand.
"Oh, My child, you can," He said.
I suddenly felt I had known Him
since a child.
"Teach me to fly" I said.
"Think not with your mind, but
with your heart. Think about all
the things you love. Feel free
within your heart."
I did as he said, and felt myself
soar . . .

Mavis S Williams
BEAUTIFUL PARTY
When I was a child I thought
parties were grand.
Lots of fun and music was always
planned—Now that I'm grown,
it's still lots of fun.
To dress up grandly, I enjoy every
one.
But this is what I want to say, my
thoughts have changed a lot
today.
I used to think of death in a
different way.
Then I thought it was like leaving
a good party half way thru'.
The music and laughter was ended
too.
Now I know different—the party's
not here.
It's somewhere else in a different
sphere.
We just catch a glimpse, now and
then, of the wonderful party God
has planned for us when.
We enter Heaven and see the great
throne, of Jesus, our Lord, and
He welcomes us home.
Nothing we do can change the
plan, that God intended since
the world began.
The joy and the music will never
end.
Jesus said: "Come Unto Me!
You're invited, My friend."

Clere Weaver
TO MY HUSBAND

In memory of my husband "Ollie." Thank you for the many happy years.

I love the little Valentine you gave
to me today,
And when I read the little verse it
took my cares away.

It tells me loving little words your
lips cannot impart,
When I read it o'er again I know
what's in your heart.

I love the little Valentines you gave
me thru the years,
The lacy ones, the red and white,
the cupid-bow and spears.

When I'm a little older I'll read each
verse anew,
And live again those precious years
I have spent with you.

Henry Adelmo Trujillo
THE POTTER

Keep your eyes on the potter; who was perfect from the cradle to the grave. He who assures our tomorrows, to all humanity.

Keep your eyes on the potter, who
was perfect from the cradle to
the grave.
He who assures our tomorrows,
keeping faithful in his word.
Keep your eyes on the saviour who
walked upon the sea,
Jesus who cleansed the lepers and
makes the captives free. Our
name is in the book of life, he
bought us
with his blood, no other way to
heaven, bought Jesus
God's own son. The mansions are
all ready the trumpet
is about to sound, Jesus will
descend in glory, will
be headed homeward bound. Keep
your eyes on the saviour,
who's sitting on his throne, Jesus
who left his promise,
to those he calls his own. Keep
your eyes on the potter,
who molded you and me, who
through his crucifixion all
men should be free.

Chip M Clark
STRONGHOLD
The mist of burnt fodder blends
well with castle walls
as the bartizan beyond flies a
familier family flag.
The battlements make ready in
reply to trumpet calls.
as a man bares his mettle in each
crossed castle crag.

The cold and sturdy parapet defies
the cannon's shot
for the faces from my past reflect
my first Sally.
Their thoughts remain unchanged
for the melee fails to pivot,
as my hopes dwindle from the
castle's opening rally.

The corpes of my attempt to
conquer this castle's concept
lie still amoung the ramparts of
this castle and its crypt.
Yet, the cast for this campaign can
irritably accept
their premature deaths; the
inevitably casted script.

So, I am forced to fight in this
battle that I must wage
against a castle plague that within
my heart is sown.
But now I see the heresy it breeds
within its cage
to reaffirm the pledge that these
thoughts need overthrown.

The men are called to arms as I
stare on to my past
in search of some foundation that
still deserves to stand.
Behind the ridged portcullis is
where my soul was cast;
now these kindred walls must fall
as that same soul commands.

The vollies file forth toword the
stiffling stagnant stone
to fight amoung the myriad of men
who died for silence
of old ancestral answers, this
castle's cornerstone,
while I remain unchanged from
the castle's colic conscience.

Glenda D Bishop
A MOTHER'S LOVE

This is for you, my precious daughter Meridith Taylor Melissa Whatley. With all my everlasting love, Mother.

With all the love this world can
hold
I look to the stars and who do I
behold?

That of my child Meridith.
I have but one will, and that's to keep my love until
Death slips me away into the night.
My heart cries at the thought of her lovely blue eyes,
The glistening of her beautiful brown hair,
And her complexion, that of a Milky-way.
Meridith is forever within my heart.
I shall keep busy, and the wait won't be so long.
At last I look up, old and worn,
And there she will be, with open arms.

Meridith child!
Here is, Mothers' Love

Myra E Weatherbee

A METAPHOR

I walked beside a brook one day
That was on its way to the sea,
And the course that it traveled over
Was like the life of you and me.

There were jagged rocks and shoals
And dams formed by debris,
Calm soothing stretches
'Neath the shade of hemlock trees.

And so it journeyed onward
Having its ups and downs
'Till it came to the end of the trail
And emptied into the sound.

So like this litle brook
Is the life of you and I
From the moment we are born,
Until the day we die.

We travel on a chartered course,
Mapped out by God above,
Where he leads us let us follow,
For his way ends in eternal love.

Iva Bradberry

TO ANN

She's neat and trim, oh so slim,
And easy on the eye;
But what can we serve for Ann's birthday,
Since it can't be cake or pie?
Fried chicken, potato salad, with squash and okra too;
These are much too rich for our Annie's diet,
But oh for me and you!
So just this once we'll sacrifice,
And cater to her wishes;
With un-sweetened tea, salads with no dressing;
But served in pretty little dishes.
And when it's time to light the candles,
For Ann to make some wishes;
Instead she'll say "thanks for the dinner,"
And blow us little kisses.

Alma Sing

MY GOLDEN TREASURES

Dedicated to: Family and Friends

Friends are golden treasures,
To have and then store—
Their Friendship way down deep
in your heart
Could you ask for more?

Friends, the Golden Treasure
You never know you have,—
Until the day when trouble comes
For them, You can be glad.
They'll aid, comfort and help you
through the hours of sore distress.
These are your Golden Treasures,
And Friends you know—
Are "The Best."

Wanda Fishburn Goodin

SILENT MESSAGE

This poem is dedicated to my father, Sam. Thank-you for all the denials and sacrifices you restricted upon yourself so that my life could be a better one, and I forever thank-you for being "my wonderful Dad."

He never said, "I love you,"
all through my growing years.
He never called me "his little girl,"
which I desparately wished to hear.
I would kiss his cheek each evening
before slipping off to bed,
I would lie awake with sad remorse
for "I love you" was never said.
Each night I hoped to tell him
that I loved him very much,

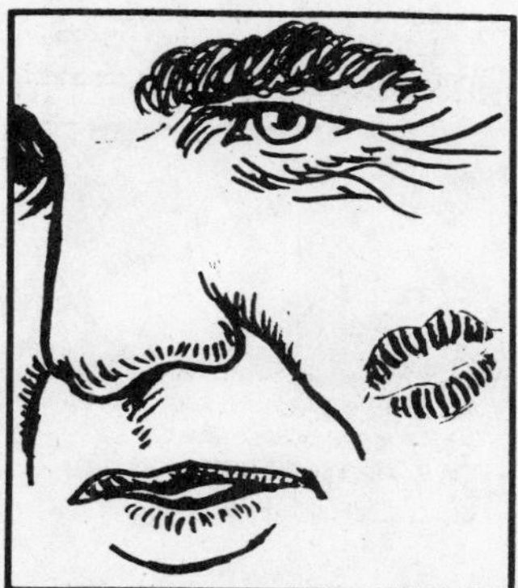

But my sisters and I, (my brothers too)
were afraid we'd make him blush,
But as I grew older
and learned more about my Dad,
I realized what I'd been wishin for
was something I'd always had.
His eyes said more than words could tell
of the feelings within his heart;
My childish mind was too very young
to see this from the start.
Now I stand without a doubt
for it is all so clear;
A "Silent Message" shines through eyes
of blue; "I love you daughter dear."

Mrs Lottie Ellen Roger

COME BACK TO ME

Sister, brother, husband or wife
Did you get unhappy with your life,
And just walked out of your home to stay
Yet you haven't found happiness to this day?

Home folks are crying down inside
And the door to their hearts is open wide
If Jesus spirit lives within
you'll swallow your pride
Glance around at all the sin
Look toward home and walk back in.

Now you can see that Jesus loves you so
for He gave you this home in which to grow.
He tells us— "I am your peace
And will your future be
If you'll just put your trust in me."
Jesus heavenly lore and rest are free
So dear friends out there, let's all agree
Though you walked out and committed a sin
It is never too late to walk back in
To the ones who are saying, "come back to me."

Darlene Rowe Howard

BOOK AND PEN

I will never be without,
someone to call a friend.
For I have found them in a
book and also with a pen.
Just read a book it
will take you far.
Or use a pen
right where you are.
A book will take you many places.
A pen will draw you many faces.
As I set here awe in wonder,
and listen to the distant thunder.
I crack a book and strike a pen,
I'm not afraid for I have a friend.

Gary Maserang

DON'T DO DRUGS

Teach your children, don't do drugs.
Don't let them run with all those thugs.
Crack, pot, cocaine, alcohol
Don't let it back them to the wall.

How many children have to die
Before they stand up and ask, "Why?"
There's one main thing that you should know . . .
You've got to help your children grow.

Teach your children to be good
Don't let them be misunderstood.
Shower them with kisses and hugs.
Give them lots and lots of love.

Please show them love in this world,
How to be wiser boys and girls.
Be their friend when they're in need.
Yes! Be their friend, their friend indeed.

Now if you hear this call today
Please send your help there right away,
'Cause they are waiting for your love
And God's help from above.

Teach your children, don't do drugs.
Don't let them run with all those thugs.
Shower them with kisses and hugs.
Yes, give them lots and lots and lots of love.

Mollie S Hoffman

AT LAST I AM A GRANDMA

Stacy appeared in September,
Instead of the expected November,
For she was born a "preemie,"
And gave us the screamin' meemies.

After such an early arrival,
We worried about her survival,
But Stacy soon made it known,
That she was determined to get grown.

Next month, Stacy will be two,
Grown she has, it is true,
I can't help but love her,
Just as I do her lovely mother.

Mischievous and delightful,
Stacy is a hand full,
Thank God, she is healthy,
It makes me feel very wealthy.

At last I am a grandma,
And feel like saying rah-rah!
If in choosing my grandchild I had a voice,
There's no question that Stacy would be my choice.

Lorraine D Niemela

THE MOSQUITO

Through the night air you relentlessly come,
Breaking the soft quiet with your minor key song
To my left ear you make a daring dive,
Honing in as an informed spy.

Beating the air, I let out a cry,
you little varmit, how dare you defy,
My night of rest from the weary day.
All silence ensues, and my pillow I find,
My eyes close wearily and I let out a sigh
when at my right ear . . .
Continues the song!

Grabbing my pillow, I descend the stairs,
Escaping the attentions of my newly found friend,
Beating out the lumps in the old daveno
. . . accompanied by my friend
. . . with his string and bow!

Shirley Pack Hankins

TODAY THERE IS JOY IN MY HEART

There is God, as I understnd Him;
After so long a search in misguided ways.
I have finally found Him.
He really isn't so hard to find;
As I have perceived in my soul and mind.
He knows and allows me my feelings, good and bad;
Since the beginning of time we humans have had.

This unconditional love He offers me,
Sometimes is hard for me to see.
To understand He knows and loves the all of me.
My defects, my weaknesses, my mistakes, my strengths,
My giving of myself to others, my capacity to love;
All that is me.
My humanness He gave to the all of me,
Which is the human being for all others to see.

Sometimes He gives me others who can understand,
Know, accept, love, and forgive.
But, He alone will judge all the human complexities
He gave to me, because,
He with His unconditional love that passes
All human understanding,
Gives me and is my spirituality.

Velda L Smith
LOVE'S TEARS
Deep within her very soul
Love's tears form.
Struggling against reality,
They push upward,
Seeking an outlet for release from sorrow.
Set free by her heart,
They find a dwelling place
In the well of her memories,
Lit by her brown eyes,
To stay just awhile,
Absorbing each thought of yester-year's love.
Until at last, one memory
Too much to hold,
Love's tears sprang forth with pain,
Linked together by Time's hand.
Tracing their way over smooth, white plains
Capped with rose,
Tiny streams run in Nature-cut paths
To the end of her beautiful face,
And turn
Into a vapor of mist
That settles over her whole being
As she sits in solitude
And remembers a love now lost.

Theodore R Harris III

Theodore R Harris III
THE ANSWER

To all the people in this world who seek deeper understanding of life!

Silently waiting, I watch myself knowing,
What I really am, is just what I'm showing:
They look to the sky, for the wave of a wand,
In their mind it is held, to break physical bond.
The magic they seek, won't come from the sky,
And sure won't be seen, by the physical eye!
People are fearful, they're dreading the last,
They know of the future, yet live in the past.
People should strike out, in search of the truth,
Instead of just waiting, just wasting their youth;
Nothing will last, this much is sure,
But the things that will be,
Are the things that are pure;
So be your true self, or be nothing at all,
For if you are not, you surely shall fall.
Remember this one thing, that always will be,
The choice that is yours, is the <u>one</u> to be free!

Orpha Parscale Norris
MUST HE LEAVE THE OZARK HILLS?
Within yon hills the brooklet runs
Wild flowers bloom, a squirrel leaps
To catch an acorn from a tall oak tree
As over yonder hill an old man creeps
with cane in hand—
A product of this land is he.

Ah, the beauty of it all he sees
With dimmed eyes, yet drinketh deep
to see it all again before the eve'
When he must go away again and keep
the mem'ries all
Within his heart—Why must he leave?

David Powers Sch P
A FIGHT
So much depends
upon
the word unspoken
conveyed by
menacing motions,
malevolent movements
and
the certainty
that
someone's the best.

Lee Anna Champlain Holle
THE WINDOW SILL
The window sill is more than just a piece of wood.
I have often cast aside my treasures there,
Or in the evening stood and listened to the frogs
Peeping in the silence of the night.
I have looked into the dark and talked with God,
While the moon beamed a silvery curtain,
Which seemed to carry all my dreams to Him above.
The window sill to me, is an altar
Upon which I place my hopes and fears,
And the stars that shine down
Through the panes give a guiding light,
That leads to better understanding.

Matthew R Stocking
THEE
As I leave my home of birth,
I depart from planet Earth.
I leave it at lightnings pace.
As I speed towards outer space.
Past Mars, past Jupiter,
Past Saturn too.
I see lands that have visitors few.
Post Uranus, past Neptune
It is Pluto I see.
I thought about man, I thought about thee.

Scott David Sulzer
SILENT
There is no sounds into your ears,
The sound is flying away from your ears,
To be silent or not to be silent,
It's up to you to hear a sound,
Deafness, is a quiet rhythm . . .

Connie R McDonald
NATURE
Converging towards the uplands,
prairies rise to the mountainous crest.
The vision of the cloud-capped peaks thrills me.
God's country—where the heaven-kissed
skies meet the west.
Beasts of the field ruffle the fowl of the
air into a flurry of indecision.
Ridges of jagged granite rise above the flowing meadows.
Streams meander up, down, around
the different ridges, cutting its way through.
Elk, bear and white tail deer
scamper to and fro,
avoiding contact with his
dreaded enemy—man.
Wind whistles through the trees,
singing a different song every time.
The beauty and the wonderous
perfection of it all seems
to astonish my senses.
This is the country I love.

Lila McElwain

Lila McElwain
GOD'S CIRCUIT
I am not nearer to confinement small
But, rather, I am nearer sweet release,
When, in the days of age I hear His call,
I shall but deem it as His plan for peace!

And, I shall hasten, when life's day is spent,
Glad to have fulfilled this earth bound span
To travel in God's circuit, be content
In great conveyors not devised by man.

Could it not be, that when the time has come,
For me to cease from running to and fro,
In cars, or planes, or even ships at sea,
A wider fuller circuit I shall know?

A circuit not confined to time or space
Or gravity-defying rocket thrust,
But wide, and far, and free, an endless race,
The circuit of God's love, and hope, and trust!

Barry Keith Johnson
EMERALD CITY
The stars encircle the question mark
of the sky
—a bright constellation pointing
Towards our emerald city.
We follow the cool breeze in the dark humidity of night
—a gentle wind directing
Us to our emerald city.
The curious binding of stars
blinding our eyes gently
—bring us closer, enveloping
Us in the warm blue of the night sky.
We sit down in the wet green grass
of our mixed interior thoughts
—hiding from people in disbelief, coveting
The bright lights of our emerald city.
And we follow the direction of the question mark
in the sky
—as we search inside, trying
To find our Emerald City.

Mary Lou Luttrell Phillips
WAITING
Long hours spent
nose pressed against the glass
Feeling like an "ass"
waiting for you
to come home
to park the car
to open the door
to be near me

You do not seem to know
that I love you so
that this waiting
makes my mind race
Each delayed hour conjures
visions of disaster
images charged with emotional stress
pictures projected of porno postures
pitted in adulterous positions
imagined sirens shrieking agony
rushing toward crumpled steel
These things and others I feel . . . .

Waiting
long hours magnifying every sound

Waiting
for you to come home to me

Jennie P Rice
JOHN F KENNEDY
There was a man, a wonderful man,
Who governed o'er our land.
He fought and fought, and he'd appeal,
And he prayed to God that his ideal
Would be accepted by this nation,
To abolish segregation.

In this nation, and a great many others,
Despite their religion, creed or color,
He was loved by a great, great many
His name, of course, was—
<u>JOHN F. KENNEDY.</u>

He fought for his country in peace and in war,
But, he will fight for it no more.
He did more than his best—
And now he was gone to his rest.
Among those who gave their own

To protect their country and their home—
We will always honor your memory—

GOD BLESS YOU!—

JOHN F. KENNEDY!

Pam McGovern
BROTHERLY WARS

On a field in Virginia, they stood. strangers—one blue, one grey—warring countrymen;
A lone thought raced through each mind:
Kill or be killed.

Four eyes—two green, two hazel—rivoted to each other,
Daring the opponent to blink.
Two fingers—one black, one white—poised on a trigger,
Hoping to fire first, wishing it wasn't necessary.

Moments later, only one remained standing.
All color differences washed away by the blood of the fallen.
It was a country torn apart by color and pride,
Losing one son to free another.

On a street in New York, they waited. Divided.
Neighbors armed against neighbors;
Some yearned to fight, others prayed for peace.
Tension mounted, as all wondered who would strike first.

A whisper: "Why are we doing this?"
The answer: "They don't belong here. They're different."
The battle was not new, only the soldiers.

Once it was over, the differences had vanished.
It was a neighborhood torn apart by color and pride,
United in death.
A question: "Who won?"
No answer. No one had won.

Paula Melson Thielen
LOVERS

To my best friend, lover and husband, JOE.

"From the groaning agony of intense mental pain
to the sweet release of fulfilling gain.

From two hearts burning with desire.
Uniting together to enhance the fire.

To peace and tranquillity that only they can know
when they are together their enchantment does show.

From the rising of the sun to it's setting again
realizing their ecstasy has been well worth their pain."

Adrienne Nevers
A CHILD'S SMILE

Dedicated, To Candace Renee' Carter, my Granddaughter, from "Nana"

"A Child's Smile is a Wonderful Thing; His Eyes Light up like the freshness of Spring; The Wail of his cries can sometimes be hard to Bear; We must hold him and love Him to show him we Care."

"The Sound of his laughter is music to our Ears; It warms our hearts and calms our fears; The soft touch of his hands on Skin ridden with Age; Lets us know He trusts us and that He's not afraid."

"When everything seems hopeless; And life seems to be passing you by; Just remember there's Nothing more Comforting; Than a "Little Child's Smile."

Lucille M Kroner

Lucille M Kroner
A CHRISTMAS TREE

In memoriam to Marguerite Phillips who suggested that I write a poem about the Christmas tree, in 1984 near Christmas time.

A Christmas tree is many things,
A candle's glow on a frosty night,
a box all tied with ribbons bright.
The silvered star where moonlight sings.

A Christmas tree sees many things,
A baby's smile with eyes alight,
holly wreaths in window's site,
The glow a special hearthfire brings.

A Christmas tree hears many things,
Sleigh bells' song o'er hills of white,
snowflakes fall in quick delight,
The silvery peal of church bells' ring.

A Christmas tree tastes of many things,
Oranges, apples, cakes so light,
cheeses, nuts, mince pies first bite.
Cranberries, popcorn on a string.

A Christmas tree smells of many things,
Cedar, pine, from a forest green,
earthy odors from the country bring,
And mistletoe, where snowbirds cling.

A Christmas tree is touched by many things,
By little hands that search for treasures through prickly limbs with great pleasure,
For a little train, a doll that clings.

A Christmas tree is loved for many things,
From its glittering base to its top alight, where the regal star reigns in might,
For the glorious joy its promise brings.

A Christmas tree tells of many things,
Of a manger small where all was quiet, where a Child was born one Christmas night,
The Son of God, the King of Kings.

wendy j karsevar
THEY RAN (A DEAF CHILD):

for CP, MH, PS, my family, and all those other important people in my life . . . with much love, WJK

walking through a field
I came upon a playground;
isolated, desolate . . .

I remembered coming here
as a child,
I approached the merry-go-round
full of laughing
children.
They tormented me
with their silence,
then they ran
far, far away . . .

I sat, slowly,
on the old, rusty metal,
smiled at the memory,
and brushed a single tear from my cheek.
They would never know, would they,
how alone I feel.
Even if I'd wanted to,
I would never hear them laugh
at me.

Marvin B Wingfield
SO LIMITLESS

My heavenly father: Thank you for blessing me with your gift of life

The expanse so fathomless
As space so timeless.
The creation so vastless
By the creator so matchless.
On earth so restless
Is souls so numberless
In men so powerless
By the Lord so tireless.
Moving space so lifeless
Encircling life so limitless,
In the ether so ceaseless
Is the being so deathless.
In heaven so spotless
Reigning so slumberless
Forever so relentless
Is God so sinless.

Craig S Rotta
AS SIN RACES WITHIN ME

To God the Father, who met me in my time of need.

As sin races within me Lord, I struggle to hear Your will for my life.
Darkness engulfs me with total blindness, that hinders me from seeing Your truth.
How do I open my eyes, Lord, to see, and my heart to hear?
The whisper of sin has rung within my ears like a shout.
Yet Father, your love has guided me to Thy side.
Gentle in Thy embracing of me, I am held safe within your arms.
With a love far greater than I have ever known, Lord, You have bought me.
I stand before Thee, and from my lips, Father, Thy praises shall ring out in adoration.
As melodies flow endlessly out to you, Lord God in Love
Your Son's holy name shall ring out forevermore in glory, honor, and praise.
Upon my lips, and within my heart the name of Jesus shall reign always.

Doris Therese DeVarney
THE BIRTHDAY CAKE

This is dedicated to my four girls: Joyce, Robin, Sharon and Lisa.

I made myself, a birthday cake,
When it was done, it looked so great.
I frosted it with the greatest of care,
As if there were an audience there.

I quickly removed it from the pan,
Only to find that my frosting ran.
In my excitement, I forgot the rule,
Do not remove, unitl it's cool.

Quite surprised my cakes a flop,
Wondering how I'll fix the top.
The cake was stuck, to all sides of the pan,
What happened to the cake, I thought was grand.

Because the cake was now too small,
I wondered why I had made it at all.
As I turned, from that awful sight,
Standing near, were some faces so bright.

I knew why I had made, that cake sitting there,
It was, for all of us to share.
Now when I think back, to the past,
I'm thankful, I had the courage to last.

Frances Ann Simonitis
A SAILOR

Dedicated to Capt. W. Wolf Bauer

To sea as a boy,
To war as a man,
Torpedoed in the channel of Yucatan.

Forth and back o'er the Atlantic,
Munitions and tanks,
With nary an ear for a word of thanks.

A Master license to earn,
At the school Maritime,
To Captain a ship would be just fine.

Forth and back o'er the Atlantic,
Munitions and tanks,
With nary an ear for a word of thanks.

A gray day, several rough crossings
To Normandy, on D-Day.
But that's all—that I'm going to say.

For he was a sailor,
At heart will always be,
At home on his ship. At home on the sea.

Larry Joe Hays

Larry Joe Hays
TOUCHING REALITY

In memory of G.D. Davidson and dedicated to all Vietnam Vets. None of us served in vain.

What can we do?
Turn our heads, Ignore the news
or should we write a song about liberty
With our goal, to feed and set men free
seems our eyes often see
but we simply say "That's Just TV."
Should we stand before men
shouting "Truth"
Yet the Homeless, Hungry and Poor
So often we seem to ignore

What can we do?
The world's condition so needs to improve
Should we march on Washington, D.C.
or could the truth simply be
Just to let our hearts feel.
Thinking truth as I see,
There's no room to ignore,
if we simply let our hearts feel
Touching Reality
is really from the hearts feelings

Ryan Miller
MOUNTAINS MOUNTAINS HIGH AND FREE

Mountains mountains high and free
Will you let me climb thee,
Mountains mountains by the sea
You are set so beautifully.

Your snowy peaks I climb
Through the clouds I seek,
A single star
Across a distant far.

Mountains mountains by the sea
Mountains mountains high and free,
You are so lovely.

I climb the mountians narrow and sheer,
You reach high to touch the sky
People travel far and near,
To watch the ungarded boundries of snow,
Which in the spring, as water roll and flow.

Sharl Prior-Prince
DON'T CRY FOR ME

This poem is dedicated to those that have passed beyond this life, that have looked upon the face of GOD, and have returned to tell of his LOVE and GLORY.

"I'm sorry . . .
Afraid it's too late . . .
Won't be much pain . . .
Up to six months . . .
I'm terribly sorry . .
Nothing we can do."

Time,
Blessed time,
It has a way of making everything,
More bearable.

I can now look ahead,
To the time I have left,
With a calmness,
I never believed would be possible.

I have time to enjoy things that I'd always taken for granted:
The quiet serenity of a soft winter snowfall,
And the beauty and scent of Spring anew.

I have lived my life with Dignity,
And,
I'll insist,
On a death with Dignity.

Death is a part of life,
And I'll accept it,
Simply,
As a change in my consciousness.

I have no fear,
For I believe that life goes on,
FOREVER.

So don't cry for me:
I have lived a life of LOVE;
Of giving and receiving;
A life of contentment and fulfillment.

Don't cry for me;
I want to die,
With Dignity

Leola Devault
THE MAKINGS OF A PEARL

A Pearl has had its irritations
From just a particle of sand
Dashed in by the seas and the oceans
By its movements and motions
That's made by the Master's great hand.
For each hurt is a treasure
Made great by God's measure
By his gifting and sifting of the sand.
And all thru the ages; the marks on the pages
Of the hurts and irritations of mere man.
Would love to know, when long, long ago
What our great and loving Master gave in His answer
And drew and wrote in the sand.
I'd like to relate when I hesitate,
Bring back memories and I meditate
That He drew a big heart and wrote love in the sand.

Violet M Robinson
A GRAMMA'S MOST TENDER JOY

To Sarah Marie—my darling Grand-daughter

No one knows my joy today,
The joy a Grandma feels,
When a daughter's Love is returned to You
In her child-after years.

It is a normal day, you see,
With daily chores "by the score"
But then a little face appears,
Knocking at the door!

Tiny face clean and sweet,
Bouncey hair, bright loving eyes,
In a hurry for the door to open
Knocking knocking, impatient with sighs!

"Hello Amma" the first words spoke
Softly, with laughing eyes,
Anxious to get down to play,
Snatching at bonnet ties—

Such a busy little bee
With so many things to do,
A mind so anxious to see and learn,
Oh how I do love you!

Playing content upon the floor,
Turns quickly from a toy that's new,
The first day she ever says—
"Amma I UVE YOU.!!

Margie Annunziata
BROKEN LIVES

To my son and grandson Bob and Justin Ligus

Two hearts, two hurts, two lives astray,
The worst part of all the baby will pay!
Oh; for the love of God that we should have for each other
The kind of love Jesus has—one who would die for his brother.
We meet someone in a lonely place fall in love marry
Then get kicked in the face.
Things are not what we dreamed,
and then we part.
But now there is another heart.
A new heart, gentle and kind—the heart of this grandson of mine
Oh, if things had not of been bad.
My son would have made a wonderful Dad.
The hearts that are broken, they think are three.
But what about this heart inside of me?
I hurt, I cry, I pray, I give—but the marriage just couldn't live
I pray for happiness for all involved, but no one wins
When a marriage is desolved.
Lord, many years have passed
I dedicated Bob to you—Now Dear Lord here's Justin too.

Paul G Jones
NATURE AND ME

I took a walk one dew dropped morn,
About the time new days are born,
And heard the chirpping of the crickets,
In among a thorny thicket.

The birds had started their songs to sing,
On this fair new day of spring,
The squirrels engaged in playful chatter,
If I don't return home it doesn't really matter.

For in this meadow of animal talk,
I could stay and take quite a long walk,
The butterflies float softly by,
And great white oaks grow toward the sky.

A lazy brook flowing in a trickle,
The wild flowers growing, they are so fickle,
Bees with nectar hum 'round the nest.
As the wise old owl settles in for a rest.

So let me walk till this day ends,
In this world of new-found friends,
If I don't return home don't worry you see,
I'm quite content here, just nature and me.

Joe L Flores

Joe L Flores
THOUGHTS OF LONELINESS

To my Parents, my Daughters, family and friends

At times I've thought to realize
And wonder, what is it, that I seek?

A dream of something I can't have
Perhaps a promise, that someone just can't keep.

I dare to want the truth in life
As I wake in such an empty bed
And I feel a piercing through my heart,
While I hear such sad songs, in my head.

Just a thought I say
Like the cold wind, as it blows upon my face
Do my feelings sway?
As I search this world, desperately to find my place.

There are times for thoughts and promises,
There are times when the truth must hurt,
There are times for empty loneliness,
To express this, one must find the words.

The wind which blows in all directions
As my thoughts do, when I search
Will one day land me, where I must,
And I'll know in this world, I have found my place.

Miss Ahnjullii Rahsheen Longe'T

I, WON I, WON

To all who have only known the worst. And keep hoping for the better. May you be granted your hearts desire.

I, won the lottery. And I, bought everything in my wildest dreams.
I, knew not the cold again, or the cardboard box that covered me against the night. I, now owned the soupe kitchen that once fed me, and gave to the hungry and homeless and I, owned the bank that once turned me down in my youth.
I, now drive a motorized wheel chair, and a wool blanket covers my once cold legs.
And as I, look up toward the blue sky's to give thanks, I, suddenly begin to feel cold again, and I, feel the tears streaming down my face.
As I, open my eye's I, hear an echo within my mind slowly begin to fade 'I, won', 'I won'
And as I try to pull the cardboard box over me, I, realize that it was only a beautiful dream. (For now).

Emily M McCall

WHAT'S IT LIKE TO DIE?

Is it like a leaf, flourishing on the tree?
Flirting with the sunshine, fluttering in the breeze:
Hanging on for dear-life, not wanting to let go:
Reluctant now to leave the rest, having loved life so!
But now the leaf is withered, and its veins are dry.
It has no choice, it cannot stay, the time has come to die.

Or is it more like a kite, being pulled by a string,
Not making any effort, not really doing anything;
Until caught up in the wind that lifts it up so high
Momentarily sailing blythely through the sky . . .
Then, all at once, dipping and falling off the course
As if pulled back by some involuntary force.
But not for long—again a breeze comes coaxing it along;
Upward, Heavenward, the string breaks, it's out of sight . . . It's gone!

Or can it be like going home, from being on a visit?
You've loved the time you spent on earth—but going home? You wouldn't miss it.
Your friends, your family, those you love . . . reluctant to depart;
But looking forward to reunite with those dear to your heart.
So, "What's it like to die?" we ask . . . It's not for us to know.
But how we "LIVE" is by our choice . . . And not on how we "GO."

Rose-Elva Doyle

HEART'S-AFLAME

In nineteen hundred and twenty-nine,
Two lovers' hearts became entwined,
On the 29th day of June they were wed.
Twenty-nine years they were entwined,
And they grew closer all the time.
Until that fatal day,
When God called my love away.
But love lives on until the end,
When both hearts beat as one again.

Louise Calangelo

WINTER WINDOW

Out beyond my window
Is ground of blanket white
And air of cool and crisp
With trees dressed in sparkling light

Birds atop the snow chirping
Squirrels scampering for trees
The miracle of snow flakes
Brought in by gentle breeze

Out beyond my window
The beauty of breathtaking views
Creating a natural balance
Molded snow, and colored hews

Nature forming its pattern
Like skillful hands unfold
Winter performing miracles
Magnified and cold

Out beyond my window
The skies of yonder height
Veils the hills, hides the woods
With images of delight

James A Gale

HARBOR LADY

She stands as a symbol for our great land.
She reaches out with a guiding hand.

She brings us hope in our darkest night.
While she guards her people, well standing for their rights.

She stands for a symbol for everyone to see.
That all who preserve it, shall remain free.

Bernadette Demski

I AM ART

i am art, i am not straight
i zig and zag through a quasi-land.
i am splattered up and pouring down
in colors i twirl through naked walls.
i am art, i am too straight
to jet stream sideways on a gallery nail.
i am art, turned right sideout
exploiting a brain vomiting life.
a delusion of passion in a bathroom asylum.
i am angles and shapes slinging words to
watchers who sway me the wrong way around.
i am art, jaded, jagged, jarred looked at
through jazz trumpets and cymbals and clangs and keys!
See me crooked and smeared and inside out.
i am art, to free the bars whose drink will
rock lonely and dead. i am touched to
speak the art i am, to swallow you
whole into the light. i am art, narrow too wide
the depth inside. i am art, forever to flow,
taste me equal, devour me slow.

Victoria Rotolo DoLyniuk

THE BRIGHTEST STAR

I want you
wherever you are
to look to the sky each night,
and find the brightest star
and know
I wished it there for you
to see it's beauty
and I
will look to the same sky
and smile . . . just to know
you
may have smiled too.

Mabel M Petersen

MEMORIES

George, Rebeccah and Laura my gifts from God.

Memories are little words assembled that pass across the mind.
You cannot touch or handle them, just pray that they are kind.
Sometimes they're little bits and pieces, a word here and there,
Like a quiet breeze that hardly stirs the air.
It's these that bring a pleasant smile, or just a gentle sigh,
A little bit of yesterday simply passing by.

Sometimes they come like armies, marching full array,
Bringing back the past in a swift and mighty way,
Stirring up emotions thought conquered long ago
And laying bare the hidden again for us to know.
It's these that kindle anguish and start the flame anew,
And burn our souls once more as they are passing through.
But no matter how they come, or in what manner they may pass.
We'll have yesterday just as long as thoughts will last.

Adam Zuniga

ALL I CAN DO IS DREAM

So many times I can sit alone at home and cry
Waiting for a phone call from you
The phone never rings, and I seem to wonder why
I guess now All I Can Do Is Dream
All I Can Do Is Dream of times that we can share
Holding hands, skipping stones, doing as I planned
All I Can Do Is Dream of you and me
From wedding days to crying times all I want is you
But I guess now All I Can Do Is Dream
Looking at your picture in my mind
It is hard to realize that those deep blue eyes
shattered my heart
But still all I want is a new start
As I'm sitting here on the floor waiting for your
voice to come over the phone
But you'll never call that I know
So I'll search through my mind
Reminicing the times we used to share
So they say it's wrong to dream
But that's the only place I have you
So I guess now All I Can Do Is Dream
All I Can Do Is Dream of times that we can share
From wedding days to crying times all I want is you
But I guess now All I Can Do Is Dream
Yes I guess now All I Can Do Is Dream

Ralph James Hiester
LEAVE OUR CHILDREN DREAM

Children are young, they are sweet when they laugh and play, yes they know the way, if only left to dream!

But we parents come along, tell them to grow up, be adult, act their ages, and spoil their growing process to no end.

Give them time to be themselves, our children will grow into their own beings, and us damn parents will be better for it, so leave our children dream.

Betty Cable-Thompson
MY NEVER-ENDING LOVE

I cannot stay the rising of the sun
Or touch a cloud that's drifting high above,
I cannot still the winds that softly blow,
But I can tell you of my deepest love.

I can't prevent the fall of summer rain
Or change the beauty of a fulgent sun
Or catch a bird in swift and soaring flight,
Nor can I stop this love that's now begun.

I can't restrain the fireflies flashing glow
Or hush the haunting song of turtle dove
Or brush away the rainbow's colored arc,
But I can offer you abiding love.

I cannot chase the shadows from the dells
Or light the brilliant stars that shine above
Or turn the moonlight on when twilight falls,
But I can promise you my faithful love.

And since I can no more stop loving you
Than I can stop the flowing of the streams,
I give to you my never-ending love,
Along with all my heart and soul and dreams.

Jerry Kelly
THE DAY AFTER CHRISTMAS

'Twas the day after Christmas, and all thru our pad
Gift wrappers were scattered, it really looked sad.
Lia, with vacumn, and I with a broom
Were reclaiming our house from grandchildren-doom.
The wrapping, and ribbons were torn all asunder
No box would survive this juvenile plunder
This small-tot invasion, we thought it was fun
(We've given them genes of attila the hun)
They've left now, those angels, right after they reveled
Not giving one thought of that room so disheveled
We're taking our aspirn as our headaches subside
We said we "felt fine", though both of us lied.
Next Christmas? A change.
Though our halls we will deck.
We'll call from Miami, and we'll spend "em a check!!!"

Robert F Kenney
SAGA OF A SYMBOL

To Dawn M. and Robert F. the 3rd, my children. To Patricia Uhlrich, my greatest supporter of my work. To Janasta Jeffrey of Nova Scotia who has the courage of the eagle.

The thunder in the stillness
The roar within the air,
The clapping of his arms above
Bring music everywhere.
The majesty that takes him high
Where only God can see,
The thrust as he goes forward
The "prey" soon his to be.
He'll thrust himself toward earth again
A whispering sound he'll make,
One giant splash upon the pond
The great sized fish he'll take.
Then to the trees he travels
To settle for a while,
Food for his mate to feed the nest
That holds the brand new child.
Just sit and look and wonder
You'll hardly say a word,
As he reaches for the heavens
This great majestic bird.
For he is called the "Eagle"
The symbol of our land,
The mark of our great freedom
Which we all understand.

Ann A Fitzpatrick
THERE'S A BABY IN HEAVEN

To Karen, my special daughter

There's a baby in heaven
On it's way to be . . .
It's a boy, it's a girl,
We soon shall see.
God's little angel is on it's way,
Sure hope that it arrives today.
Anxiously waiting from the start,

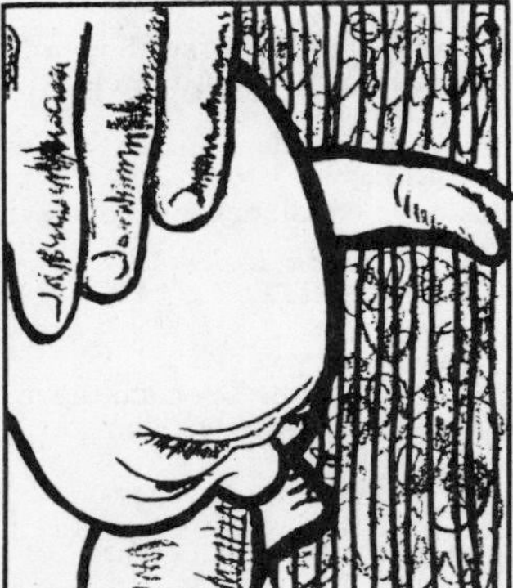

To give all the love that's in our heart.
Reminding us that we should give,
And care, and share, as we do live.
For what man on earth
Has the nerve to reply
There is no God,
No one greater than I—

Gayle M Bennett
ROAD TO REALITY

To anyone who wants to get along with their lives, after something tramatic has happened to them!

We all walk down a road called "Life,"
Finding pain, heartaches, and alot of strife;
Reality plays it's royal part,—
For many times come a broken heart;
We don't know how to cure the pain,
As once things seemed simple and so plain;
But it's a road we walk down all alone;
And it's something you do on your own—
For even though your hurting deep inside,
You can still hold on to "self" and pride;
If you let them go their separate way,
Things will get worse each passing day;
"Life" has its purpose-yet we don't know why,
As things get tougher for you and I,
Try to strive for "peace of mind",
And try to let the past behind;
I know it's a very hard thing to do,
But what's it going to do for you?
It's up to you to choose your plan—
So make your choice the best you can,
For life keeps going on and on,
And still be here when we are gone.

Mildred Parrish
AS YE SOW SO SHALL YE REAP

This poem is dedicated to my family, with love

As you go along life's pathway, bear this thought in mind
Always be loyal and truthful, and fair with all mankind
Love and kindness is the answer, so bury your hatred deep
For you know the only outcome, AS YE SOW SO SHALL YE REAP

Never think that you're an Island, where you are all that counts
Other people's thoughts and feelings, are just as dear and in great amounts
Never let your tongue become a sword, and always think before you leap
As from the pan into the fire, AS YE SOW SO SHALL YE REAP

When you deeds come back to haunt you, as you think back on what you've done
You'll know the Devil was your pilot, and God's wrath comes to anyone
When you face the great hereafter, it will do no good to scream and weep
For God's last and final answer, AS YE SOW SO SHALL YE REAP

Life is short and filled with troubles, even though we've done our best
But the burden can be lessened, when one's conscience is at rest
So beg everyone's forgiveness, this day before you sleep
So the meaning could be joyful, AS YE SOW SO SHALL YE REAP

Laura Ashley
ONE DAY SOON

When morning bids a day brand new,
on each leaf is shining dew.
Mornings are such a peaceful time,
like a quiet melody or rhyme.
But as the sun climbs up high,
the morning is no longer nigh.
Sometimes I wish that time stood still,
and no one would want to kill.
I wish mornings would be here to stay,
and there never would be a passing day.
No sorrow will we see,
only happiness for you and me.
But time has not stood still,
at least not for real.
Soon the day will be here at last,
and oh! it's coming fast.
What a grand time that will be,
when the Lord comes for you and me.

Thomas Panichi
LOVE'S PRAYER

FATHER forgive them
they know not what they do

They don't believe the one they hang
was sent to them by you

Now I freely pay the wage
for their blind, unbending rage

They don't believe the nails they drive
will set them free at last

The heart they pierce with tempers fierce
makes void the awful past

Father receive my pain
accept my passion's end

In agony that crushes me,
make everyone your friend.

Vern Hopkins
GIFTS

To you my cherished friend I give
these things I hold most dear.
My morning star, my quiet thoughts
a tiny unshed tear.
The silent noises of the night
the clean fresh breath of spring.
The cold dawn slowly forming light
to you these gifts I bring.
The tawny haze of autumn days
winters muted white.
The thankful prayer that fills my heart
that God made things so right.
The dancing shapes of candles flame
the wispy clouds of summer.
The pleading rhythm in my mind
that from my different drummer.
To know the deepest value of
these precious works of art,
They must be shared with one you love
my gifts to you dear heart.

Miriam Barbour
FALL ARRIVES

Some call it Autumn-but I call it Fall
It's the most beautiful season of all.
The woodlands are covered with red and gold
The squirrels are busy storing for the cold.

The birds to their southern home are in flight
Nights are getting longer-days have less light.
The trees will soon be bare for the winter chill
It's the time of year many folk are ill.
The flowers have gone to take a long winter nap
It's time for mufflers, mittens and heavier winter wrap.
Off in the distance you can hear the school bell
Now's it time for children to learn to read and spell.
The grass is now all withered away
The time has come for the upcoming holiday.
The trees are all laden with red and gold
Aunt Jane's applebutter is the best I'm told.
All the furry little animals scurry to their winter nap
Now don't you think Fall is best?

Peter Rothschild Jr

Peter Rothschild Jr
THE PLANTED ROSE (PEACE)

To my Father 4 all his love and just 4 sticking in with me, I love you dad! And 2 my mom, I wish we could have spent some mother and son time. To Tammy Taylor 4 teaching me love & pain. And Casandra Hall, beautiful & perfect.

Angry am I the man with the broken heart
So many tears have I cried in the darkness of my room,
No lights in sight or maybe I prefer the darkness
The morbid feeling closing in to seal my doom.

I beg 4 your forgiveness
Human and foolish because of the things I've done,
Absolutely followed by very many
Positively honest and worthy 2 none.

Now on my knees forced to face reality
Shelterless my eyes seem only to be able to look down,
Posterity and happiness use to follow me
Now I'm surrounded by pain, guilt and a chisled frown.

Turn back the sands of time for me
Shed some light on this cold dark day,
I've forgotten all my selfishness and deviations
A rose has been planted for a brighter day.

A day when all things can be forgiven
When each race walks hand in hand,
War and slaying come to an end
And peace flourishes through every land.

Conner Edwin Powers
A FORTUNE HIDDEN
Beauty at mind is my fortune,
Flowers and trees
Birds and bees.
Is this what I can find?
Wind in the tops of pines,
Running water, a brook,
A newspaper is my book.
Is this my harvest?
I suppose it is
Not in reality,
But in my world.
Not of love, nor hate
But of never ending tranquility.
Pleasantness, oh yes,
Beauty at mind is my fortune.

LaVerne C Arthur
PAPER IS MY CANVAS, A PEN IS MY BRUSH
Paper is my canvas,—A pen is my brush
Written words present a picture as pen and paper touch
Like paintings, splashed with color, or in black and white
To the mind's eye dull and gray or bursting with light.

The word love is a masterpiece, priceless as art to me
It brings alive scenes of yesterday painted in my memory
A frame house by a creek and an old oak tree
Gentle Dad, fragile Mom loving my brothers and me.

Mountain gets my attention, sights explode in my mind.
Blue Ridge Mountains of VA and lonesome trails that wind
I write opal, rainbow and sunset, dazzling colors appear
I pen the word forest and visualize a free spirited deer.

I write flowers and before me is a garden fair
Butterflies, birds singing, and bees buzzing here and there
Ocean, the word brings to mind seashells, waves and sand
I form the words sun, moon and stars and envision God's mighty hand.

Baby, to me the word means one of life's greatest joys
Mental images emerge of my own precious girls and boys
Tears fall on my paper as my trembling pen writes calvary
I see blood on a wooden cross where Jesus died for me.

Yes, Paper is my canvas—A pen is my brush
Words may paint pictures of joy other words can crush
After each nugget I write I'm beginning to find
I've penned a picture of my own heart, soul and mind.

Krista Jupin
GREAT STONE STAIRS

This is dedicated to the ones we love. Kris and Paul

Once there was a baby girl born to a family.
They lived in an old apartment house with great stone stairs leading down to the street.
The girl had learned to walk on those stairs and the stairs had told her a great many things that it would not dare tell anybody else.
The girl put all of her trust in the stairs because the steps had told her that she would never fall while walking or running down these steps.
The girl grew and still she never took a spill on the great stone stairs.
She could run, slide, skate or ride her bike down these stairs and she never hurt herself.
Then the girl found her a man and she didn't spend a lot of time with the stairs anymore.
She spent it with the man of her dreams, so when time came for her to get married she told the stairs her plans and with that she up and got married.
Her parents held the the reception at their house as a farewell because she would no longer live there.
Well the party was fabulous and upon leaving for the last time the girl slipped on the stone stairs thus falling to her death.

Beverly Henkel
HUNGER
I rooted for the rebel souls
who had no food or place to go.
They'd wander faceless in the cold,
gathering in the darkness.

Sometimes the wind would howl so loud,
drawing yells and jeers from the restless crowd,
reminding them that they once were proud
til the fire in their souls erupted.

With the winter snow falling cold and deep,
and their eyes ablaze from no food or sleep,
they would empty their souls til all would weep
and the sunlight filled the morning.

Lost forever, they'll remain
in too deep to think of change.
To some it's hell, to some just strange,
for the world outside still breaks them.

As time goes by, you can still hear the cries.
See the long, searching looks inside empty, aged eyes.
So lives the poor, hungry looker to the skies
no more wise, no more wise.

Stacy Armstrong
ONE NIGHT I DREAMED
Puppies were green
And liked to scream.
Cats were purple
And liked all gerbles.
Monkeys were yellow
And they all had a fellow.
This dream I think is quite unbearable
To me, to you, and any old crew.

Helen Haynes
DEAREST GRANDAUGHTER, LOVE GRAM
Dearest Granddaughter
I think the most wonderful thing to be,
is accepting our individuality.
Like flowers in a garden bright,
there isn't any two alike.
I am left handed, you are right.
I sleep all day, you sleep all night.
I paint a picture of a frog;
you like to sit and pet your dog.
How Wonderful! I think it be!
That we all think differently.
I am large, You are small,
You are short, I am tall.
Gosh! It's so fun for us to be.
You being you, and me being me.
Love, Gram

P G Viator
PROPHET

To my family with love and thanks . . . then, now and forever—

You came to me in summer
on that southern Illinois farm.
I held you
while the sun dipped beneath the cedars
and bulls croaked.
Your eyes understanding;
a twist of cinammon
always willing
to listen, might I call.

I told you
what I remember of the past—
—the night
with Andrea in the bathtub
blue; dead
only a dream.
Dad's funeral, "big man" for nine.
Then, loved ones pass for last good-bye
tawny lid is lowered
entombing forever.
My tear-blurred vision
the waters of baptism
for the child revealed.   Falling
to where we rest now.

Your answer comes silently
as the night hushed the west.
Moving me
to turn
confronting the east
warming myself with another
day's sun.

Dorothea (Stalcup) Woolam
THE ONE LEFT BEHIND

To my dear husband, Thomas Woolam, in memory.

One morning, you left me
So quickly.
You were mine one moment and then you were gone
The next.
Never to return,
This side of heaven.
You left me so desolate,
So alone,

To the gnawing emptiness,
The empty heart,
The long days, the lonely nights

Without you.
My love, the tears flow
So freely,
In hopes of washing away
The anguish and pain.
A dagger has struck
The very core of my being.
My mind tries to comprehend
The devastating loss.
How I wish that death
Had taken me too,
Then I would'nt be alone,
I would be with you.
But that was not to be.

Lee Ellen C Morris
CAN THIS BE SPRING?

Forty degrees the thermometer read
His hibernating clock got him out of bed
Because it was there he climbed the wall
Reached the window then lest he fall
Slowly and carefully moved across the glass
Without crampons or rope searched for a pass.
Looking hopefully from side to side
No plant or soil where he might abide
Ever upward he struggled on creeping feet
Where was he going? What did he seek?
Fog hid the sun, there was no budding tree
Poor little bug, a bit like me.

Julie Thomas Fleck
LOVE COMPARISONS

Love is like a tree that's budding showing its new found joy

Love is like a bird that's singing softly and somewhat coy

Love is like a flower blooming smiling in the sun

Love is like a river flowing on and on

Tiffanie S Bertrand
SUMMER DAYS

I love summer days
with it's dainty flowers
and pretty ways.
When I go outside the wind is cool,
so I sit under a tree and drool.
I think of things I'd like to do,
like play with my friend, named Sue.
She's probably drooling too.
So I'll stay here.
"T I F F A N I E!!"
Oh, my Mom's calling me,
I'd better go inside.
I love Summer Days.

Vince Kamaka
ODE TO A BUTTERFLY

Fluttering over a daffodil sea
Spreading wings of crimson and gold
Touching and delighting each as you fly
O Butterfly, do not pass me by

Daffodils turn and follow with a glance
On earth-bound bodies in syncopated dance
In the hope that you will draw nigh
O Butterfly, do not pass me by

There are many daffodils in the sea
Can you fly to all? Will you fly to me?
Will you touch me and lift me high?
O Butterfly, do not pass me by

Ellen Magdalen Allison
LOVER—LOVED NOT

Pass gently from my heart
Your warmth is but a dream
So go now—Stranger—
Let my soul know rest

Rita R McCormack
SPRING WALK

To Dan Beloved Husband, Companion and Friend

Dear God, how can I thank you
For my savoring another spring?
Sun smiling warmly on new
Green leaves bursting out
Of tall old trees;
Hyacinths, daffodils and tulips
Peeking out of tender baby grass;
Pillow clouds resting on a
Pale blue sky; white clothes
Billowing on a soft April breeze!
Oh, cliche, cliche, it's
All been said before. Still,
I must say once more—
Thank you God for the
Beauty of it all—it all!

Nema Lu Parker
MY GARDEN

I look out my window
When winter is cold and drear,
And wonder when Springtime will appear.
To speed the time I sit and read,
The catalogs of plants and seeds.
I stay inside,
And run and hide,
From the cold and the snow,
And wait impatiently for the day
I can watch my garden grow.
To touch the warm earth,
And till the soil,
To work and sweat and labor and toil.
Watered with gentle rains from above,
A garden is a work of love.
And when the plants show through the sod,
I know I have seen the hand of God.

Jack Thibault
A PIECE OF ME

To those who dare to use the power and Love, and those I love . . . forever.

I've tried,
more than once or twice,
to sit down
and write something to you,
without much success.
The words that once used to appear,
almost as if by magical will
on empty pages,
refuse to yield
to the command of my pen.
Silent protest to their inability
to serve the master wordsmith.
It seems all I wish to say,
I have in some way
or at some time
scribbled down for you to read,
only finding I had yet to meet you.
Even these scratchings
seem inadequate, shallow.
One step at a time,
with no more ease
than the passing of a day,
I reach in
for something unknown,
yet oddly familiar.
A bit more substantial
than redundancies and words.
A bit, perhaps, of me.

Constance Joy Kescik

Constance Joy Kescik
THE SWINGING GATE

To: "Becky, Carrie & Holly"

In the Summer when the darkness came
Wherever they had been
I listened for my swinging gate
And knew my brood was in
In Winter when the snow would fall
I still can hear them yet
The gate would close and up the stairs
They stumbled, cold and wet
Now they are leaving, one by one
My heart is leaving too
There's empty space and silent walls
And not much left to do
And now I know they were my dreams
And they were all my plans
And Heaven it would be, if I
Could hold their little hands
I must adjust, I tell myself
And find new things to do
So I will start by passing on
The things I've learned, to you
To all young mothers in the world
Who cannot face the day
Be kind to them, for soon the gate
Will swing the other way

John Howard
FOX HOLE

The fox-hole was deep
like an ocean reef.
The stains of blood
covered the cold wet mud.
Bravely the men fought
most favoring a halt.
Some men were crying while others were dying.
Oh, the fox-hole is not a nice place to be
It's filled with blood, filth, and gorey.
But what the men are really thinking
deep in their heart—
where does it stop . . . why did it start?

Alicia Padron-Gomez de Molina
A TALK WITH GOD

Last night I had a talk with God.
"Why must my heart ache?," I asked
"Be patient my child," he said, "my heart is aching too!"
"But why yours my Lord," I said
"Is your love far away too?"
"You do not trust my intentions my child," he said.
"That is why my heart aches too."

Cheryl Sue Howard
GOING HOME

In loving memory of my brother, Larry Gordon Howard, August 1950—October 1977

The greys mist are drawing ever closer.
The sounds that surround me are becoming faint.
The light from the window fades before my eyes.
I can feel the last breath leaving my body.
I am drifting high and beyond.
Why are the people about me crying?
Can't they see that my spirit is free?

Above me I see a single white dove.
Calling to me softly, to follow in flight.
And we soar high into the mighty heavens.
The clouds part to reveal great splendor.
There is a mighty city before me—ancient.
But shining—all silver, white and gold.
And the feeling is that,
I am finally going home at last.

Betty Nye
THINKING ABOUT YOU

To my Mother, whom I lost too soon and to my Children who are growing up too fast

When you think that you are grown,
And you are out on your own,
Think about mama
Because mama is thinking about you.

If you're away so very far
Look up at the stars
And think about mama
Because mama is thinking about you.

If you're sad and blue
With no one you can talk to
Think about mama
Because mama is thinking about you.

If you are all alone,
Or close to a phone,
Think about mama,
Because mama is thinking about you.

Mary Pieri
FACE THE WORLD WITH A SMILE
Face the world with a smile,
On a happy face,
With a heart full of love
For the human race

Be glad you are alive
To sing God's praise
Pray for daily guidance
To be filled with God's grace

Sing a song of praise
To God for his love
Who sent his son to die,
For our sins, from heaven above.

Diane Kahler
MY NURSING HOME FRIENDS

Thank you to my friends and Alverno co-workers who inspired and encouraged me through the years.

Some of my older friends
Live in a nursing home.
They like to read and talk
Of where they used to roam.

They're really quite the characters,
As delightful as can be.
Just like Nellie who plays Bingo,
And Katherine crochets, you see.
Others do crafts or play some cards
Grace watches her soaps on T.V.
Charlotte plays the organ very well.
A dozen sing songs with Sister Mel.
They have visits with their family,
And still go to church so faithfully.
Holidays are dress-up times for a few.
They get the chance to dress so crazily
They provide you with a laugh each day,
Because of humorous things they say.
They come from all over the world,
Each has their own personality.
Once you know them, you won't forget,
They'll be remembered eternally

Esther M Cote
THE TORCH OF FREEDOM
Hold high the torch of freedom.
It has been paid for with blood
Of heroes who have gone before us
To make this the land of the free.
Hold high the torch of liberty.
May its light forever shine
To all who are oppressed
And hope for a better land,
A price was paid for freedom
So all might be made free.
The blood that ran in battles
Paid the price for you and me.
The pilgrims came unto our shores,
Because they were oppressed.
They believed in God on high
And by Him would be blest.
In God we trust is on our coins.
Our flag the stars and stripes.
The torch of freedom is His book
In this land of liberty.
God gave His life for freedom
To all who would be free.
He paid the price with His blood
When He died for you and me.

Susan C Gage
A VISIT WITH SARAH
She spoke of an apple orchard;
Tall, lush trees lined perfectly.
They stretch for miles, she said.
Ripe fruit glistens under the sun.
Soft, white petals
dot the dew wet grass.
The sweet odor of country flowers
fills the spring air.
Her long, boney finger
traced this picture on
the cell wall;
the spotless snow-colored wall.
I wish to make love in an orchard,
she giggled,
ran to her bed
wrapping the sheets around
her frail body.
She waits for a new stranger
who'll listen to her dreams.

David Lee Straight Jr
GRANDPARENTS
We love you so much
Our lives would not be the same without your touch.

That must be why the love for grandparents is to true
Because we just can't live without the two of you.

Grandparents have this magical spell
That makes their grandchildren love them so well.

They have this special power
That makes you feel so loved hour after hour.

If they could live for ever and a day
Our lives would be so much better in every way.

Mark Hudson
WHISPERS
Whispers are only for you to hear.
Whispers are soft and tickle your ear.
Whispers are secret . . . not for show.
Whispers are only for you to know.

Evelyn A Kaminski
SAME OLD STORY
With computers, are we progressing?
We Americans are deceived and duped a lot
To believe that the Robot can do our thinking
For sure we soon will be without a job
Unless we learn to repair the thing
How long could that job be lasting?
Until the Robot got to know his parts
Once again no job and a lot of broken hearts
Is this what we call being ahead
Or does this mean we are hungry and dead
Everyone will have to deal with this commotion
Each person is responsible for the answer in this nation
To progress and not to proceed that is the question
To proceed and not to progress that is an emotion
I'm sure that if the Robot had some brains
He would skip town and never do business with us again
He would go his way and never play the game
He knows that in the end
We will not come to his defense
He will become a turned off, burned out machine
For sure just a simple ordinary thing
Lying dead in some junk yard stream
In a pile of heap in memory lane.

Mrs Tauba Paves
HOW WAS I TO KNOW
There's one thing I know,
Lovers may go, lovers may come—
Like everything else—that comes,
Always—must go.

How was I to know—
You only meant to be nice to me,
When you said "I love you."

How was I to know—
You only meant to be kind to me,
And that your kiss would break my heart in two.

How was I to know—
You would soon laugh at me,
And my time woud come, to go!
How was I to know!
You only meant to be nice to me.

Dave "DQ" Quesada

Dave "DQ" Quesada
THE LOVES SLASHER
Slashed,
Blood oozes,
Trying,
Thoughts Deteriorate

Provoked,
Bludgeoning Pleasures.
Injecting,
Sorrow Unavoidable.

Trusted,
Feelings Disguised.
Believing,
Decision Enacted.

Discovered,
Mind Misguided.
Bursting,
Precious Intercourse.

Crushed,
Bodies weapon.
Failing,
Instincts Overlooked.

Hunted,
Slasher's Weapon.
Finding,
The Mind "DQ"

Slashed,
Trusting Females.
Exclusive,
Uniqueness Elures.

Awaited,
Boomerangs Return.
Slashing,
The "Loves Slasher."

Carrie Elizabeth Gentry
STAGES
We went different directions, you and I
Not my choice but by circumstance,
Never-the-less we remained close in heart
Hoping some day for a second dance,
Sliding and struggling one step at a time
Perplexed with each others stages,
Me longing for yours, you longing for mine
Unknowingly writing the pages,
Exchanging our books with an eager frustration
I realized today with a frown,
All that I've learned was committed to memory
But some I forget to write down,
And it hit me so simply only today
As I sat reding your letter,
All of my insights through hardships related
Have not helped you deal with yours better,
And none are so different after all
As we're molded and shaped through our stages,
All taught the same lessons in similar ways,
First hand, and at different ages.

Jean M Lillich
MY THOUGHTS
Sometimes you have to take a walk
To clear your troubled mind.
For nature has a way to make
You care and be more kind.

The beauty all around you—
Keeps your mind clear and serene,
You wonder why you're troubled
When God surrounds you with great scenes.

The autumn air is crisp and clear
The silence makes you more aware—
Of all the beauty that surrounds,
So enjoy your walk on God's great grounds.

When your walk is over, and your back home,

Have an open mind, and maybe
phone
A person who is troubled, just like
you
And tell them of your walk with
nature,
And of your new found view.

Bebe C Bowers
COMFORT ZONE
Do not
fear
heat lightning,
It lights
the night
and sends
Morse-code messages
to
the
lonely . . .
as it illuminates
an otherwise
bleak
black
sky . . .
and allows
quick glimpses
of
wide-awake stars
and . . .
sleeping white-gray
clouds . . .
for
OUR
comfort.

Steve Peper
GOD'S MERCY AND LOVE
God stretched out His hand,
We slapped Him in the face.
God stretched out the other,
And we nailed it in place.

Mrs Alfred D Bailey
MOM
I remember back when I was young
The many things my Mom has done
We took long walks and played
games and
did things together
She is like my sister—my
friend—as well
as my mother—
A person of many pages; like a
well beloved
book—
You never can tell by the
cover—what's inside
until you look
She's aging now—and for me it's
hard to
understand—she's so different
then she
used to be—she wants no
helping hand—
She'd rather be a "loner" —the
independent kind
Then to be a "bother" to
anyone—
This little mother of mine
We do for her what she will allow
As time goes by—I wonder how
I will cope with
These facts of life—But with God's
helping hand I
Just may turn out to be—The kind
of person "My Mom" was to me.

Robert E VandenHeuvel
THE SECRET GARDEN
Often, in the afternoon
I sit and watch the flowers bloom
alone, in gardens, no one else can
see
lost within my solitude
this pure and peaceful interlude
restores the hope, that lives inside
of me
but then, my garden disappears
when reality and truth are near
and dreams of love and beauty fade
away
until some quiet afternoon
when flowers, once again, can
bloom
and I can sit alone, and watch them
play

Often, when the day is done
I dream that I have found someone
who will help me watch the flowers
grow,
a lover, who will understand
the little boy, inside this man
content to sit, and watch the river
flow
but when the dreams all disappear
I find that there is no one here
to gladden with a freshly picked
bouquet
of flowers, that can only bloom
on calm and peaceful afternoons
when all my cares are safely locked
away

Ronel E Sinstead

Ronel E Sinstead
STILLNESS

Dedicated to the Unity of all mankind, by the Reverend Ronel E. Sinstead, poet, author and minister of Unity Church of Muskegon, Michigan.

Be still and know that I am what
you are
Listen to my stillness, it is life itself,
And it is your life

O let its stillness calm your mind
Search no more, for I am that
Stillness within you
Express it, and you express me

Listen to its Peace, and it shall be
your Peace
Let it flow, for it is love, that feeds
your being
As my being

Let me be, and I shall be
Still your thoughts, and you will
find me
For I am, that stillness

This peace, love and power are
yours now
There is no other peace, power or
love
It is what I am, and you, are what
I am
I am life eternal!
Be still and know that I am in you,
as you
Act as though I am, and I shall be,
to you
O be still, and know
Be still and know, that I am God
The breath, and the life and the
mind in all
The only power in life you will ever
find
For my kingdom is, in your
thoughts divine

O God, I hear and feel you now
The living presence throughout all
For now I'm free, to express you as
me
O God, I know now, that I am
One, with Thee.

Dan Self
. . . JOURNEY . . .

I dedicate this poem to the beginning of a journey not yet ventured, and to all of the people whom were clouds in my life.

Yesterdays failures will only be
Tomorrows wisdom, tomorrows
wisdom
Will be todays dreams. For a
dream
Is the leader of our journey.
Life is but as an untamed journey
And the sunset but a mark of
Accomplishment. For the only
journey
Lost is the one not taken, the only
Foolish step is the one not
ventured.
Without a journey we would be as
A fallen sparrow, limp to lives
Understanding.
Soar with todays dreams of
wisdom
And be as an eagle among man,
spirit
The clouds of yesterdays future.
Let wisdom bring the sunshine for
Today. Without the clouds our
Spirit would be empty and
sunshine
But another day. For tomorrow is
Only a covet of hope, no guarantee
On what it shall be

Edwin P Wolfe
JUST SIMPLE WORDS
I sometimes speak just simple
words, and yet
The impact of those words I can't
forget;
For I have uttered them with idle
thought,
Not thinking of the anguish I have
brought.
Those simple words were filled
with bitterness,
My sole intent to hurt, I must
confess.

And then, in contrast, simple
words impart
The great compassion found
within the heart;
For therein lies the secret of this
life,
That we should choose the love,
and not the strife.
Then let us wisely choose the
words we say,
And help our fellowman along the
way.
Just simple words can make our
day so bright,
And others still can turn it dark as
night.
O, give me wisdom, Lord, that I
may find
The simple words best suited for
mankind;
Then may our lives be blest by God
above,
And all the words we speak are
filled with love.

Carole McCune

Carole McCune
AWAKENING WITH THE DAWN
Dawn breaks with awe inspiring
splender,
The dew rests sparkling on all
earth's flora and fauna,
Hushed birds burst out with varied
song
To wish the day hello.
New shoots begin to tremble into
growth
And earthworms pop up their
heads to a new day.
The sun warms the sky and beams
its ray earthwards

To greet mankind in her cloak of
glory,
To a fresh beginning, get an
extension
of our development.
Then so called humans awaken
without song
And drown the peaceful harmony
of sunlit day
With myriad noises calling it
progress, growth,
Oh! how little do we grow
When we don't stop, to wish the
Dawn hello.

Lucille Rinaudo
WAS I EVER YOUNG

For my husband Vince, my children Jennifer, Patrick, Vincenzo, who have shown me where there's life there's hope, where there's caring there's understanding, where there's love we can conquer life's obstacles.

At twelve I asked for a toy they said
I was too old;
Whenever I laughed or clowned
around I was acting childish I
was told.

When I was thirteen there was
nobody to understand me,
Why? Oh why? Can't they let me
grow up naturally,

At fourteen I couldn't have friends,
Frustrated and lonely I wanted my
life to end.

Fifteen I ran away in search of love,
Instead I found drugs to float
through life like the clouds
above.

At sixteen I had sex because I
thought I had someone who
cared,
heartache and sorrow followed he
was spared.

At seventeen I was desperate for
someone to love and come my
way;

Sex, drugs, & booze is what came
instead; what a price to pay!

At eighteen I bore a child who died,
There was no one there to comfort
me or wipe the tears I cried.

Soon after my child died I was out
of control;
I was out on the streets selling my
soul.
At nineteen, in control with our
Lord's blessing I was with child
once more;
This time my child lived which
brought joy and happiness, not
emptiness like before.

I began to realize that my youth
has disappeared;
All because the words I love you I
never did hear!

Mary Ann Naylor
MODERN DAY WOMEN! LIBERATED WOMEN

I feel the strength of thousands
standing firmly at my side.
Our voices are heard everywhere;
There's no place left to hide.

We work at jobs that once were
theirs,
pump iron, have our say.
And when we take them on a date
we always pay our way.

We're Modern Day Women!
Liberated Women!

My husband... he is one of them,
I love him all the more,
Because he lets me lead my life.
We've evened up the score.

I've made a firm decision.
It's mine alone to make.
I'm staying home to raise the kids,
to sew, to clean, to bake.

I'm a Modern Day Woman!
A Liberated Woman!

Kenneth F Paffrath
SPIRIT'S JOURNEY

My spirit reaches out
It soars and flies
It touches your spirit
And in the touching
An understanding is gained.

As my spirit touches
And is touched
I feel it grow
And in the growing
It soars ever higher.

My spirit is hungry
It needs to be fed
It needs to learn
And in the learning
New wisdom is given.

I set my spirit free
And upon its return
A better person am I
For having touched
The spirits of others.

Joyce Yvonne Conklin
ONLY A DREAM

Yesterday, you were but a dream,
today, I'm in your arms.
Tomorrow, you'll be but a memory,
or one page in a book of yarns.

I've often been called a dreamer,
and told dreams don't come true.
But if that's the way, the story goes,
then who, may I ask, are you?

Many a day, when I was young,
I'd sit by my window and dream.
Back then, I was the beautiful
princess,
just waiting for my prince to
come.

I remember my mother, telling me
then,
when you grow up, your dreams
must end.
Little did I understand her when,
those words of truth, she spoke
so often.

As I grew older, my dreams I kept,
hoping someday, I'd find you.
Now here you are, within my reach,
but where will you be tomorrow?

Blanche Wellington-Cross
MY HOSPITAL STAY

To my son-in-law, Roger Alford, who had this experience. Roger, you are like a son to me.

Hospital stays can be a bore, but
mine is worse
So propped up in bed, I'll put my
thoughts in verse.
Amid the clutter of trays and the
clatter of dishes,
My hunger pangs start and also
my wishes
For food, home and someone
who'll talk
Or just be able to go for a walk.
They starved me for days, not even
a drink.
I.V.'s may be fine but I think that
they stink,
Next they put a tube in my chest
and feed me through that.
The "Jello" is fine but spare me
those bottles of fat.
They poke pills down my throat by
the score
And jab at my rear 'til my
"Fanny" is sore
As "Angel's of Mercy" they haven't
shown
They've drained all my blood,
I'm as dry as a bone
They're tormentors dressed in all
white
I'm all worn out, I've lost all my
fight.
Stretched out on this bed, I'm as
limp as a rag
But if they call this rest, I think
that they brag.
Tangled up in these tubes, I'm a
prisoner in Hell,
But I must follow orders if I want
to get well.

Diane Louise Riehle
ODE TO A ROCKING HORSE WINNER

Dedicated to my two sons, Steven Lewis and Michael Lee. With love.

Upon this wooden horse I ride
The earth beneath our feet,
Our eyes are open far and wide
For dreams we wish to beat.

My Mother's hopes are strong
desires
My horse and I can claim,
For all that's wanted in her heart
Dead heat against the rain!

We'll try our best, my horse and I
No matter what the game.
My life is hers for years to come
Let's not forget the name!

You knew my thoughts in the dark
My broken heart in pain,
All that's needed in her heart
Just a winning name.

For many nights we rode so strong
My thoughts upon her grief
Surely it won't take too long
To set the winning streak.

One Last Surge. . .
I saw her face smiling down on me
Oh, my God! We've won the race
To die alone——
We're free.

Evelyn Frechette
ON THIS CHRISTMAS DAY

As I sit here alone on this
Christmas Day I think about all
the
sad and lonely people the world
around, is there any peace and
joy for them to be found: and the
people who are hungry with
nothing to eat will they receive a
friendly smile from the people
they meet?
And the ones who are homeless
with no place to stay will they be
happy on This Christmas Day?
I called on a friend who is more
precious than gold but she was
too busy to invite me in from the
cold. Merry Christmas I said
and begin to cry?
No time to visit, she said and told
me goodbye.
So I turned around and went on
my way.
There was no joy for me on this
Christmas Day.
I passed by a Chapel and stopped
to pray
but the doors were closed on
This Christmas Day
and now at the end of This
Christmas Day I kneel down to
pray, it was then I realized that
not all is loss.
When I remembered our Savior
Who Died on the Cross
He is the one who will bring
Peace on Earth Good Will to men
If we open up our hearts and let
our Savior come in.
I looked to the Heavens as I
begin to pray Christ Jesus I love
you on
This Christmas Day

Susie Law Ingram
INSPIRED BY GOD

Inspired by God,
But yet being possessed by the
Devil.
The world is ugly,
But yet so beautiful.
Your attitude so nasty,
But yet so understandable.
Your heart is vexed,
The world is surely a mess.

I lived to see the world,
But yet inspired by God,
"I saw the world" and
Did not travel very far and
With this inspiration of God,
The world was no more
Cause I've been inspired by God.

Debra Elaine Todd
HIS DEATH AND RESSURECTION

He died for you, He died for me,
He gave His life on Calvary.
Just for our sins, Is the reason why,
He let them nail Him to the cross
to die.

People laughed, And people cried,
When the hour came when Jesus
died.
Then they took Him down and
buried Him,
But in three days He arose again.

B Herman
THE SWING SET

The swing set sits at the edge of the
lawn,
Color faded and one swing gone.
Colors once bright, don't last—
As the swing set knows—at the
edge of the grass.
Where have the children
gone—that used to play?
Grown up, gone to college, and
moved away.
So the swing set sits at the edge of
the lawn,
Color faded and one swing gone.
Thinking with each passing day,
The children might be back to play.

Sharon Gray
OUR PROVIDER

In rememberance of our Lord Jesus Christ and who is our provider

I'm writing you this poem
Though I'm not so talented this
way.
But I need to show my love for you
For all you've sent my way
Although I can not see you.
I see how much you've done,
In the morning you gave us the dew
And the rest of the day the sun.

You allow us to suffer
When we get too proud or bold
Or think that we can handle things
On our own. We're told
To place all our faith in you
And you, will provide our needs.
Lord you're so merciful to us
Even though at times we can't see.

If only we will trust in you
I know we could have the best
You're more to us than just a friend
You're our provider and our guest
So here's my life I give to you.
I know I should never fear
I could'nt be in better hands
So I won't shed a tear.

Sharon Irene Allison

Sharon Irene Allison
ANOTHER SLEEPLESS NIGHT

To my love—James N. Wilson. Thank you for many beautiful memories and wonderful years. They were the best of my life. I love you.

Another sleepless night,
I sit alone and cry,
Twilight times till dawn,
Memories linger on,
Since we said good-by.

Throughout the sleepless night,
No matter what I do,
Your always on my mind,
I find, I'm still in love with you.

Though shadows fall and I recall,
The love you once had for me,
I miss you so when lights are low,
And dream of things, that used to be.

Your always on my mind,
Although your gone from sight,
Lonely tear drops burn,
As I toss and turn,
Another sleepless night.

Edward L Schmidkunz
THE ECHO OF WINTER
I woke up this morning the very same time
Drinking my coffee to clear up my mind.
I opened the drapes as I usually do
And saw that the sky was all white and blue
The sun was just rising, above the tall trees
With a glowing color so pretty to see.
But the thing that really caught my attention
Was the way Jack Frost had made his indentions
The windows were painted in many designs
He had flashed his brush sideways, up and down
I'll have to admit, his work was a wonder.
But it made me think of places much warmer,
Sea breezes blowing and sandy white beaches
Maybe in Georgia they're out picking peaches.
The weather man says it's twenty below
I'll put on my longjohns and away I'll go
Hoping my car starts without a sputter.
My teeth are chattering and I'm sure I stutter.

Oh well, spring can't be so far away,
Guess I can take it day by day.
The echo of winter will just fade away
Flowers and gardens will spring their arrays.

Gertrude Morrison
SNOWFALL
One day I stood at my window and watched the snow fall;
And it touched the world with magic;
Creating its own strange beauty, clean and awesome,
Covering earth's blemishes—making it new.
Drifting downward from the sky, Slowly, Slowly.

I opened my window and held out my hand;
It wasn't the snow, but God's Grace I felt.
And it touched my heart with cleansing power,
Creating a new hope—covering my inequities.
Falling downward from Heaven. Softly, Softly.

On some tomorrow the snow will go away;
And once again the earth will lie—gray and bleak
Stripped of its glamour—unadorned and bare;
Shivering and brooding, sensing its loss. Sadly, Sadly.

No so God's Grace! Today, as yesterday, tomorrow as today
It cradles me, softening my sorrows,
Lifting my heart to heights of expectancy,
Giving my life a sense of fulfillment;
Leading me Homeward. Surely, Surely!

Ruth Darling Felton
THE HEAVENS
I looked up in the heavens,
And guess what I could see!
A countless number of tiny lights,
Just put up there for me.

Some were big and some were small,
Some were middle-sized.
They all looked down from up above
As if they had surmised

That they were bringing me happiness,
That they were lighting the way;
And I thanked them, Oh, I thanked them
Silently, more than words could say.

DeAnna M Shaw-Berget
A ROSE OF INVARIENT COLOR
Through the ageless eyes of an old soul,
She watched her contemporaries—children of this time—
play marbles and tag.

From a distant hill she watched the innocent playground.
She sifted sand through her toes, and counted the validity of past existences.

Memories cloud in a lace veil what it was she thought she knew.
Visions interrupt her thoughts—familiar visions—as if the here and now
returned to something unfinished.

And a voice from within her heart whispered—
"You are a rose of invarient color.
Your lives have been a blossoming of yourself.
Live in this time, and believe in your
capacity for growth.
For you shall never wither.
Your love grows with each passing of time.

Live now, love now.
Awake to the beauty of the morning sun—
reflecting orange and blue through the mountain ruggedness.
And play once more,
an innocent game of marbles and tag."

Elizabeth A Tani
BEAUTY
Beauty, be it shallow, hooks a man deep
Capturing every sense; making thought sin,
But into the soul glances do not seep
His eye yet novice cannot see within.
Judging with desire as his jury,
His verdict for me but a cold stare.
My mien causes no fire, no fury
But I plea an appeal, a trial that's fair!
For me there is no justice to be found
Though, I will not hunt love; the chase is cruel.
Love hides like a rabbit from the hound
And he who chases it becomes the fool.
My beauty, more than this,
comes from the heart
And he who finds it has mastered loves' art.

Lenora Lang
THE OLD TREE
As I sit under this ancient tree
And watch the leaves play games with me,
And through an opening I see the clear blue sky
With snowy white clouds floating by.
Dear Lord, my savior, I know is above
Soft breezes whispers to me of His love
'Tis far between us, my Lord and I
Yet I feel His presence here by my side.

So gentle is this, His presence to me
In all of nature, not just this tree
Wild flowers that bloom beneath my feet
Green lawns that mowed so neat.

The lilting songs of so many birds,
Racaus caws of crows can still be heard
These are God's messages, speaking to me
As I sit beneath this lovely old tree.

For many a year. It has been here to stay
As a promise that God will show the way
To love, to cherish things as they are
I know that God is never too far.

He is just as close as the beat of your heart
If you let Him come in, He will never depart.
Like the acorn that grew this great old tree
God will always be there for you and for me.

Ellen Elizabeth McCormick—"Elena"
SENIOR YEAR

To my four wonderful grandparents, James Joseph Staunton, Lori Staunton, Charles Henry "Chuck" McCormick and Addie Ellen McCormick. I love you all very much. 5-20-1987

Being a Senior
Not quite grown.
Living your life,
Yet not on your own.

Classes to take
Tests to pass.
Teams to cheer,
Your lot is east.

Only a student
With your books,
But to be an adult
Is where you look.

Life is hard
With decisions to make
And there are times you think
That your heart will break.

But when the year is done
And you're out on your own
Just be sure you will reap
The seeds you have sown.

Doreen A Miller
HEATHERWOOD EXERCISE CLASS OF 1987

To my beloved Mother, Winnifred

Of all the activities in our park
I think the one that I like the best
Is the exercise class three times a week —
It's quite a good physical test.

Some of our girls are fat and some lean
And some have a beautiful form,
We look at each other and think to

ourselves —
Just which one of us is the "norm?"

We grunt and we groan, stand up and lie down
And we lift our legs high in the air,

Some of us may lose a bit of our fat
But most of us don't have a prayer!

When we're down on the floor stretching our limbs
And pointing our butts at the sky,
We notice the men like to visit the club
And peak in the doors passing by.

And when we're in bed at night and we ache
And we know we have not lost an ounce,
We don't worry a bit—we're not bothered at all
'Cause we still like to jiggle and bounce!

Fred Pearce

OUT IN BACK

Hey, Dad, c'mon . . . let's play some catch.
(Now, there's an offer I can't refuse).
We'll spin away care through the flight of the ball . . .
Good time to cast off the blues.

And we'll not be bothered by anything heavy:
Which came first? Chicken? Egg?
Just r'ar back and let 'er go.
Say you can't play catch?
Well, then, let's play throw.

Joan Estes

SIGNS OF FAITH

Each morn when I awake to see
A star studded sky
What a joy to behold the birth
Of a new day
When those first filtered rays of Light seem to separate the night and day
I thank God for the opportunity to enjoy
Yet the fruits of another day
During the day as I stumble and toil
Comes the realization that as the Sun rises so also must she set
Time waits for no man—
Never a promise to know that on The morrow this fulfillment of Birth will again be realized.

Delia E Quiroga

MAINTAIN WORLD PEACE AND BROTHERHOOD

Oh, how great love the Creator has for the world,
He showered it with abundance, that nature overgrows;
He provided essential sunlight, that living things could see the most,
Of this planet called "Earth," that He had so endowed.

He sprinkled the sky with starlights,
And a moon that shines out bright;
To light the paths of the weary,
And cheer up our lonely nights.

But best of all, He gave us one another,
To love, to inspire, to console and to hold;
And live the life that He had taught, now and ever,
That all our harvests may manifold.
So hand-in-hand let's work together,
Regardless of races and creeds, and in all weather;
For World Peace and Brotherhood which only Love can conquer,
And make this world of wonders even brighter!

For what good does it make to reap successes,
In Science, Mathematics, Aeronautics and Economics . . . (?)
If weapons keep firing with bullets of pride, envy and greediness,
Then, everyone's dream will be shattered.

Where did we ever learn the word "war?"
When we were created out of an overflowing love . . .
Isn't it worth the Blood and Body of the Lord,
That mankind should maintain World Peace and Brotherhood?

Oh, my God! Dear Fellowmen, we should . . . we should!!!

Ella Louise Hoefs

RAINY LAKE

Submitted by the family of Ella Louise Hoefs, who passed away on 10/8/84. Our mother loved the Great Outdoors and her poem is dedicated to her memory.

It nestles high in the North Cascades,
Where few men ever trod,
And only nature's music fills
The silences of God.
Great mountains tower above it's shores
And green trees fringe it's brim,
And o'er it's crest forevermore
The wanton breezes scim.
The beauty of the waterfall
As it comes tumbling down,
Surrounded by sheer cliffs and peaks,
As if they were a crown.
The grandeur of the glacier
Above the lake so blue,
Revealing all it's beauty,
So old and yet so new.
In this grand and glorious country,
In this great and wonderful land,
If it could only stay this way
And not be marred by man.

Sylvia J Loggan

MY MOM

Seven faces she has bathed
And seven pairs of hands.
Seven souls she's helped to save,
That we might live in this free land.

She led us like a flock of sheep
Down the rocky path of life,
And prayed for us while we did sleep;
That we might grow and live just right.

She nurtured us thru many years
Then sent us on our way.
So we could learn thru bitter tears
What she had tried to say.

Now we are scattered here and there
But still we can't forget
The one who kissed away our cares;
The one who loves us yet.

Tina L Lee

THE QUESTIONS OF A CHILD

How green is the grass?
How blue is the sky?
How deep is the river?
Why do birds fly?
How come you're old?
Why am I too young?
The Questions of a child.

Why is there rain?
When I am cut, why do I feel pain?
What is love?
Does God live in the sky, up above?
What's the difference between girls & boys?
Why is it that only kids play with toys?
The Questions of a child.

Where was I born?
Where did I come from?
Can I stay up late?
When can I go on a date?
Do I have to visit people I hate?
The Questions of a child.

*Theresa Deren-Hauprich*t

A TRIBUTE

It's time to say "Good-bye" to you.
It's time to let you fly.
Your spirit soars above us now.
In Heaven's realm you lie.

I want to say "we love you, Mom"
And hope you know it's true.
I want to say "we'll miss you, Mom"
And all the things you do.

I know you're in a better world
And you're safely in God's care.
So when I cry, I cry for us,
You're a loss that's hard to bear.

I seek comfort in the knowledge,
With my brother and sisters around,
That I only need listen and look at them
And that is where you can be found.

So God bless Mom, and rest in peace.
It's God's Will that we should part.
Just know you're always in our thoughts,
And forever in our hearts.

Melanie M Eberwein

REVELATION

To Mary who illuminates the darkness of my creativity

Commitment is Life's quicksand.
Eventually,
Reality's quagmire ensnares us
To the hips with careers, promises given,
Payments made and payments due.
There we stand,
Trapped in self-made circumstance,
And smothered by Pity's sorrowful shroud.

Yet,
With body bound,
The mind, soul and spirit can take wing
Through the hard, coal night;
A silvered seagull jettisoned to the Dreamer's Star of Imagination,
Absorbing the warmth of renewed hope and freedom
In the brilliance of it's light!

Marjorie Geeting

THE GYPSY

When I was but a little child
My mother used to say,
"Watch out for the gypsies,
They might come by today."
I'd stare across the distant hills,
And in my childish way,
I'd pretend that gypsies came
And induced me away.

I love the gypsy way of life . . .
Relaxing and so free;
These twentieth century troubadours
Are always calling me.
If it be muse or night dream,
That carries me away,
I have a secret Camelot,
Down where the gypsies play.

I caught the gypsy fever,
For I still like to roam;
Most any place I lay my head
Can be called 'home sweet home'.
Though I may be a vagabond,
To me it's plain to see,
In addition to my rendezvous,
There's gypsy blood in me.

Ronald Coffey

HANDLE WITH CARE

Handle with care,
Every minute and hour,
The trees and flowers,
The soil and air.

The trees in the forests
And the fish in the sea
Depend on each other,
Like you and like me.

The plants in a garden
And the crops from a field
Were made from God's hand
And to His eyes appealed.

He put them here for us to tend
But NONE of their beauty to spend.
They are all ours to share;

The soil, the plants, the air.

Now it is our turn
To do what we must.
God gave us His beauties
And turned them over to our trust.

Jeffrey M Laird
STANDALONE
Standalone
I look back upon the ruins of a house that took
seven years to build. Noble only from without, for
the few allowed within its walls to peek
observed foundations far too weak
to bear the fine facade that was more
a lie to those who cared, in depth to look.

If I, in youth found love too hard
then aging was its own reward.

Child by the shore, finishing a castle of his own
rises up, calls all around to come admire
his work. As they gaze with grace on builded sand
the builder takes his gifted hand
and razes all within their view.
"But why?," they cry
"The why is simple," his reply
"for I am bored and need acquire
more room on which to build a finer castle now this one's done.

Without regard for what is lost
the tragic builder pays the cost
to standalone.

Mary Louise Kellner Olson
SEARCH TO BE A MAN
Yesterday is the tomorrow I set out to find today,
looking in each direction trying to find my way.
Who knows where I am headed, or where the beginning shall end?

For much like sheep in a flock on my shepherd I will depend.
For without his love and guidance my path will go astray,
and we the people of tomorrow would only last through today.

So God my loving shepherd stay near and close at hand,
For without your faith and courage I shall never be a man.
Instead I'll go on searching in the direction to find my way,
Knowing that yesterday is the tomorrow I could not find today.

Jerolyn J Minter
NO ILLUSIONS

To The Maestro, who encouraged with love.

Nothing in this universe remains the same
forever, yet everything exhists
throughout eternity
today what seems a seed
tomorrow a seedling will be
if
one but has the time to
linger
observing the slow yet
wonderous
change from seed to
seedling
to full grown tree that
blossoms and
bears fruit that contains
the
seed
An thus a human relationship like
the seed
remains not the same but
traverses
its evolutionary
path ever growing and
changing
today what seems an interest
or desire tomorrow
blossoms
into friendship with ever
deepening
thrust toward respect
and understanding of
each other's
individuality
thus the relationship
embodies the
essence of its seed
committing it to
eternity

So to my beloved we have
embarked upon our
evolutionary journey and in
the tomorrow of tomorrows
when my eyes may no longer
behold you and to my ears
the
sound
of your voice has paled
and the
senses no longer soar
from the
touch
of flesh or the meeting
of our
minds our
relationship shall
have then
been committed to
eternity
for our souls met
embodied
the seed and
walked together
along the
pathway of
this one and yet
another
lifetime

Joan Ochs
POETRY
I, in spiritual repose,
believing to receive, silently entreat
and wait upon invisible Hand
to come, cover mine and lead.
Holding common ordinary ballpoint pen,
yield strokes to unseen cursive Guide,
see ready writer's instrument transformed
into eternal Tongue divine.
Sacred Tip commences singing
songs of Love to lonely hearts,
whispers words of comfort
to children frightened of the dark,
inspirits men discouraged to persevere
and carry on, consoles a woman grieving
whose dead child lives Beyond.
I hear, I hear, its Message sweet
resounding beat so fair—
piping chamber music so extraordinaire.
Inspired interpretation channeled
Hand to hand to heart. Melodies in ink
flow from poetic pen of bard.
Listening hearts become transformed
into tabs of soft clay flesh—
where Tongue and writer's passion meet
to kiss and scribe and etch.

Aurora Cayon (Dawn)
LORD . . . THANK YOU

I would like to dedicate this poem Lord . . . Thank you to my Lord and Saviour, who by His Love showed me the beauty of His Creation and then to my mom, dad, and sister for all their support and Love. And to all my christian brethren.

Thank you O God . . .
For creating the sun that brings us warmth of our days and a moon in
the night to bring us tranquility . . . peace . . . and reflection as we lay and thank you for what you gave us throughout the day.
Thank you for the four seasons for which you are reflected Spring . . . Summer . . . Fall . . . and Winter.
In the Spring . . . as the trees and flowers bloom with beauty, we are reminded of the resurrected Christ.
In the Summer . . . thru the warmth of the day, we are reminded of the warmth in your heart O Jesus for all your children.
In the Fall . . . the beauty of the colorful changes and the falling leaves we are reminded of our sins thru death.

As the raindrops fall, we are reminded of the tears you wept over the Walls of Jerusalem.
In the Winter . . . as the snow falls on the ground, we are reminded of the purity of your Son Jesus as the Son of God . . . whom you sent to earth on the morning long long ago to the town of Bethlehem.
I thank you O God ... for sending us Our Brother and Our King, with your words of Knowledge and Wisdom and the teachings of your truth.
LORD Jesus, my Brother . . .
THANK YOU my Saviour for
Loving us just . . .
THE WAY WE ARE

Karen R Carr
THE COUNTRY ROAD

This poem is dedicated to all my family, especially my fiance Milo, who made this possible.

The country road was hidden
Amongst the wind blown trees.
It's well worn path is shabby,
Growing with flowers of cerise.
The bob-wire fence along the road
With posts that need repair,
Stand waiting for someone
To come along and show they care.
The country road is worn,
Showing lots of ruts.
The rains that fell showed their force
By leaving all the cuts.
The winds play on the road
And pick up lots of dust.
The winds are there and then
They are gone in one big gust.
The country road is almost gone
Because no one showed they care.
It goes to places far away
And to others none can compare.
The country road will soon be lost
Because of lack of travel.
The trees are still in a lane,
And grass now grows where there once was gravel.

Reverend Eddie Toplin Sr

Reverend Eddie Toplin Sr
THERE IS NO DEATH.

To the family of Dr. Martin Luther King Jr. and the Toplin family.

There is no death, the stars go down
To rise upon some other shore
And there in Heaven's jewell crown
They will shine for ever more.

There is no death, the breath he breathed
Must change out in the atmosphere
To bring some food unto the rocks,
And the hungry moths they bare.

There is no death, the dust he treaded,
Must change beneath the summer's shower
To golden grain or mellow fruit,
Or rainbow tinted flowers.

There is no death, although we grieve,

When some one great like him is gone.
He just has dropped his robe of clay,

To put his heavenly raiments on.

There is no death, he was born to do,
Like Moses did for the Hebrew Nation
To lead his people from under bondage,
Of Jim Crow laws of segregation.

There is no death, they whipped my lord,
And hanged him on Mount Calvery.
But he rose the third day like he said
And conquered death for you and me.

There is no death, we must say good by
To this earthly home that is made of clay
And move to our home beyond the sky
To meet Dr. King on the judgment day.

Bernice Poulin

A LONG WALK IN THE WINTER

To Paula—If it wasn't for her I wouldn't have written this poem

---

You decide it is too humid in the small house,
So you choose to take a long walk in the snow.
As you walk there is a blanket of white on the ground,
And the air has frost-bitter chill to it.

Everywhere you look the snow is all over the land,
The snow is so bright that you can see everything.
The deserted streets are covered with thin layers of ice.
You look up and see long, clear icicles dangling from the
tree tops.

Silence is everywhere you walk,
There is not a solitary movement in the cold air.
All the cars' headlights are blaring through the crisp snow,
Suddenly the wind starts to pick up.

The trees start to sway and a white blanket falls off,
Icicles are crashing into fragments like glass when dropped.
You are walking and the bitter snow starts whipping in your
face,
You can sense there is a chilling blizzard ahead.

Charlene Dion Lahar

WE HAVE OUR OWN LOVE STORY

We have our own Love Story, you know.
Yet ours is a tragedy
For we must go on living. . .
Loving.

The world around us dies
But music everlasting holds our souls like glass and protects
our love through time.

Why can't it be as easy for us
As for Oliver and Jenny?
We must go on living in the same world
Breathing the same air
Loving the same people
Yet—living apart.

Their's is a story reknown.
Ours is a tragic endurance.
They had none but each other.
We have so many but not ourselves.

My soul is eternally united to yours
And though the bonds can never meet
Our love is as united as the
Sunlight is to warm.

Mary T Leonard

MARCH WINDS

March winds howling
Turning things upside down,
Taking sand from the earth
And blowing it round and round.

So much speed and noise
As a lion—roaring in a cage,
So upset at everything—
Remaining in a rage.

So destructive
Of things it meets—
Tossing garbage cans
Onto the street.

It moans, groans, and roars
And rattles the windowpanes;
It hunts out forest fires
And fans the flames.

It runs its course
And loses its roar,
It suddenly disappears
And we have it—no more.

Lori May Orchin

Lori May Orchin

MEMORIES

Dedicated to my Bandit. You were deeply loved my friend

Shadows from the past
Dancing in the flames
Memories fill the night
Things aren't the same

Empty chairs sit laughing
Games that once we played
Are covered with dust and cobwebs
As I think of the good times we made

How many times I've sat there
The sky so blue and free
Thinking and remembering
Feeling glad that it was me

Just because it's over
Friends have come and gone
Doesn't mean I'll forget them
They will always linger on

L R Pendleton

TO RISE ABOVE

Would you want me if you knew me,
You would if you were fair,
For truth without the judgements,
Form never ending pairs,
We'd climb the highest hilltops,
To find what could be seen,
And wash away the salty sweat,
Of love, in cool sweet streams,
We'd taste a bite of every chance,
For every small delight,
Would feel as fresh and crisp,
As a dew swept, clear, cool night,
We'd throw away the book of rules,
That poisons life for narrow fools,
And disengage the chains of fear,
We've worn as others' tools,
The dreams and schemes,
Of which we've wished,
We'd share, in total trust,
No fear of cruel rejection,
In being what we must,
Free to total honesty,
But will we ever know,
Or spend our lives in fantasy,
Wishing life to grow.

Patsy L Malone

COME BACK NOW

If ever you come back to me
Come now,
Now, while I still care and hurt
Don't wait until time wipes away
My tear, and binds my heart
In soft cotton.
Come now, now while the nights
Still stretch into eternity, and
There is no music but sad music.
Come back now, and sit by my side
And tell me all the things
I want to hear, before I lose
That sense of sound, and while
Your perfect face is burned
With a pain almost unbearable
Into my memory. Please,
It's important that you come now,
For I cannot stop time before
He gentles you.

Jeannine A Renninger

ANTICIPATION

Do you ever get scared?
The feelings of independence swarm in around you;
the colors of red and black engulf your senses.
The cool morning becomes hot day,
and all you want is to get off the planet?
The evening brings the breeze off the water,
and yet with it, comes a storm.
Will today's dress be green or white?
Do you want tunafish or turkey for lunch?

Do you ever get excited?
The dawn breaks, the robin sings.
The willow trees bring love and wonderment;
the colors of yellow and purple engulf your senses.
New ideas, new places, old ones refreshed in your mind,
all is right with your world.

But, do you ever get scared?
The willow trees bend too far?
The new places become strange to you and you, a stranger.
All that you look for isn't there? or is it?
Independence swarms in around you,
and you choke suddenly, and die.

Kathy L Welsch

MY PORTRAIT OF LOVE

To all who share my love . . . feel the warmth I see today, in . . .

My portrait of love,
is the poems I write.
All my feelings down in words,
brought out in plain sight.

With a tool I can make you smile,
or release a tear to flow.
Words and ink paint my portrait,
to all my feelings will show.

The deepest warmth of love,
flows freely from my heart.
I pray my ink will never dry,
even the blind can feel my art.

I've been told I have a gift,
sent from the heaven above.
But without my pen and feelings,
there'd be no portrait of love.

Ian Fields

OUT OF PLACE

Walking amidst the wet grasses,
passing by trees and brush.
I happened upon a graveyard,
where perched a lonely thrush.
Headstones, intruders in this place,
in this temple of green.
Here, at the edge of the forest,
such a contradictory scene.
Epitaphs, voices of the past,
try (in vain) to reach the living.
But the thrush sings louder than these.
I, merely an observer
of a struggle between two worlds.
And when the headstones have crumbled,
Nature reclaims her land.
Those dead buried here—forgotten.
The grass still grows tall
while the sun watches it all.
And the thrush sings on nonchalant.

Patrice Simone

LEGEND

I am legend and the spirit that has moved upon the waters.
I have seen the Gods and gave praise for the land
I have moved among amimals . . .
I have lived and died with them
I am history and timekeeper of the past
The wind blows around my tradition
Kept alive by my children
I am a mystic and a warrior
I have died many times
I am war and ask for peace
I am proud as I paint my face to fight for what is mine.
I die . . .
but my spirit lives on
calling time back to freedom
I am wisdom
Some will call me
My spirit carries the souls of many
We are Legend . . . We are Indian . . .

Charles F Heinzelman Jr

THE FROGGIES IN THE LILY POND

THE FROGGIES IN THE LILY POND ALL JUMP AND SWIM AND DIVE.
"OH!," said he, "SO GLAD ARE WE THAT WE'RE SO VERY LIVE".

MR. BULLFROG BIG AND STRONG, SEE HIM JUMP AND DIVE SO LONG.
TEACHES LITTLE FROGGIES DEAR, SITTING ON A LOG SO NEAR.

Jay T Mohler-Avery
A WALK IN THE PARK

My child innocently announces to me as
he points at a lump atop a park bench,
"Daddy, look over there at the old man."
Lying freezing cold, upon this comfort,
is a man of skin ever so old.
A bottle in hand for warmth, yesterday's
newspaper to keep out the day's wind.
The ridgid structure vertically stiff,
with a thin layer of thread to cover,
his body looking frail and thinned.

The sagging eyes asking not for cries of
pity but for silver to spend on the next day's rations.
"I'm a bum!" he bellows, "And I wish
you'd stop looking at me!"
Within my thoughts; remorse and regret
fill a glass even.
"Please go away and leave me alone."
Those were his last words as he crawled
under the black and white, weeping away
into sleep, only to face a next day . . . his
cold society.

Marion Balisteri
CHALLENGES

To my daughter, Lyn.

Give me a word, and I'll rhyme it;
Hand me a song, and I'll sing!
Show me a mountain; I'll climb it,
Whatever the summit might bring.

Bring me a child I may cherish:
Show me a dragon: I'll slay!
Offer a hope for tomorrow;
Then, somehow, I'll conquer today.

Angie Chamberlain
WHEN ALL THE WORLD IS FULL

When all the
World is full of
Snow when the
Wind blows can't
You feel the
Lovely breeze
When you go
Skating you can
Feel the wind
Passing by. You
Will go outside
And you will feel
The wind passing
By and I love
Wiiind. Angie

Bobbie O Wilson
BEYOND TIME

Beyond the cold of winter winds—
Beyond the (Shadow) of death—
There is A land of splendor—
This place—always shining—always bright—
The light is never dim-med—But
Becomes A becon to light the path through eternity—
Beauty never fades—And blooms eternal—
Love is immortal—
We may not see with dim earthly vision—
Nor hear the music of those that play and sing there—
Sometimes as I wonder about this land—
The firey sunset lingers—
The gates swing open—Long enough that I may see an echo—
As I stand A moment in awe—
The gates are closed by silent fingers—***

Elaine Boismier
A LOVE THAT NEVER DIED

To my husband Albert and my daughter Barbara for the joy, their love brings.

My darling, we struggled for years and years.
We lived through our hopes, our dreams and our fears.
We passed through the good and the bad,
We cried together at things that were sad.
We made it together, side by side,
Because our love is true, it never died.
We comforted each other, when God took our son
And in our grief, we spoiled the other one.
But she also has left us and now we've grown old.
We miss them both, dearly, but we had to let go.
Now we sit, with you confined to that chair
And me with my shawl and my cane over there.
God's not finished with us, in his master plan.
I know that as I sit and hold your frail hand.
But no matter my dearest, whatever the weather
I pray that when we go, we'll go together.

Her prayer was answered on a warm summer night
They passed away in their sleep, about twilight
They died together, their hands tightly clasped
The love on their faces will never be surpassed.
I found this letter among my mother's things
It's proof of true love and the joy it brings.

Amanda M Smith
FEELINGS

Feelings are like something special;
You can keep both.
Love is like a person;
It can be good or bad.
Happiness is like a town:
It keeps growing.
Hatred is ike an old chest;
It remains until you do
Away with it.
Friendship is like an
Everlasting light;
It keeps glowing.
Loveliness is like a toy;
You don't have to have it.
Marriage is like an old
Tin can in the shade;
It can rust if you put it in
the rain.

Michele and Debora

Anna Rose Hobora
THE PERKY TURKEY

To Debora and Michele, my beautiful children, in memory of your childhood days.

We had a Perky Turkey
He always acted very Jerky
He ran around and got Soooo THIN.

Our Thanksgiving dinner was—
Turkey SKIN.

Jean Cartwright
PEACEFUL MORNING

While everyone else is sleeping
I like to awake and arise,
To have some quiet time alone
To be peaceful and organize.
There is time to meditate and be still
To write note, to cheer others in pain,
Or just to thank God for the gifts
That he gives.
For time, for more knowledge to gain.

It's so peaceful and quiet
No noise and no din—
But in just a short while
Up they get and come in.

The morning is the nicest time of all.

Anna L Crater
MIKE—I LOVE YOU

To the best husband in the world who has given me a life of laughter, love, and happiness.

We have our ups and downs
Our brows crease from the frowns,
But you are the only one
In whom I can turn to for fun.
We have had our fears
And shared a great many tears,
But when the countdown is done,
You are the one I really count on.
Now that ten years has passed
And our marriage did last,
How very much you are loved dear,
I know this letter will make it very clear.
We have proved to those in doubt
That together we can win any bout.
But when the times get rough
You get very dependable and tough.
The difference in our ages
Are as numerous as a book's pages.
But to you, this no difference makes
Patience and understanding is what it takes.
But after all is told, you see
And all our troubles and cares many,
Only one answer can there be
You will always be the only love for me.

Leah Ruth Lokey
YESTERDAY, TODAY, TOMORROW

As I sit here in my room,
And think of you, my love;
My heart is filled with happiness,
Just to have known of your, love.
I thought I loved you, yesterday.
But today there's even, more.
And with all the tomorrow's
There will be, even, even, more.
And when the right time comes,
And I will pass away,
I will love you, even, more, than I do today—
May peace, be with you, my dear, and someday, you will find,
And feel this love, I have for you,
No matter what the time.
We had our bad yesterday's,
So we must pay for them today,
But there is alway's tomorrow,
And better, love, than yesterday

Ann Paschall
TWO FRIENDS

To Ginger, a grand Doberman lady.

A Shepherd and a Dobe,
Would run across their yard.

They'd race along the fence,
As if they were on guard.

It was an awesome sight.
They'd show their teeth and growl.
It made the neighbors cringe,
To hear them bark and howl.

It didn't last too long,
And when the game was done,
They'd slowly stroll back home,
As if to say, "What fun!"

The yards are empty now.
Just memories remain.
Their bodies now grown old,
Somewhere are softly lain.

A Shepherd and a Dobe,
God sat them by his knee.
Arrived there just in time,
He needed company.

Robert M Byrd

LIFE IS SHORT

We can't count on tomorrow
For it may never come
When we go to bed tonight
We may never see the rising of
another sun.

We must live each day
As if it were our last
Give our all to the present
And rectify the wrongs of our past.

Say thank you to the friends
That have helped us along our way
For we may not be around
To show kindness on another day.

When the final curtain falls
And the play of life is through
There is absolutely nothing else
That we can say or do.

So today please accept my thank
you
And the friendly hand that I extend
For if today is to be my last day
That's how I want my life to end.

You too, might think about the
things
That you could do or say
Remember, you may not have
tomorrow
So make life worthwhile today.

Michael Wayne Mahaffee

FROM THE WRITINGS OF ALRAC 2799

I am Alrac of the Man Race,
I walk now in a great Dead Place.
I see great buildings of metal and
stone,
Built by great men all now gone.

These men were our fathers the
writings say
They ruled the world in a mighty
way.
They traveled the old roads in
chariots of steel
They rode very fast on round
rubber wheels

They flew to the sky in great silver
birds
Their deeds hard to describe in our
old words
From the press of a button they
turned night into day
They grew food wrapped in cans in
such a magical way

But then one day fire fell from the
sky,
And no one ever really knew why.
They say, fire came from men
across the great sea,
Men like our fathers with whom
they could not agree.

We once thought them Gods
These men of the past
But Gods, they were not
For what they made did not last

Gwendolyn Derifield

WHAT CHRISTMAS MEANS TO ME

Christmas is a bright oasis
In a dry desert world.
A candle shining in the night,
The good news to hearld.

Christmas is a flying flag,
Before a mighty king,
With hopes and cheerful greetings,
To a hungry world to bring.

Good news of a wondrous day,
Of a king so long ago,
Who came to earth as a baby,
In the lovely starlight glow.

How could we not have Christmas,
So our hearts can be made glad,
With gifts and love and music,
And no one should be sad?

Jeanne L Pizzuto

THE HOME THAT USED TO BE

To my beautiful children Danny and Edith, who expressed their wonderful imaginations to me as we visited many deserted farms in days of yore, and to George, my loving husband, who took us there and shared our joy.

In the Country and driving by—
The homes of people of days gone
by,
Notice the flowers blooming still,—
Among the weeds—grown to the
sill,
Is someone caring even still?
A leaning barn that once had kept
A farmer's stock—and even yet,
The neighbor's horses roaming
free,
To graze at the home that used to
be.

These people now are gone away;
The family's children grown and
strayed,
Maybe Doctors or Lawyers they,—
Or gone to war and in France they
lay,—
And there's the Church where they
used to pray.
The old house is empty and lonely
now,
For the kids and dogs and the horse
and plow.
I can hear their voices around me
today,
For I'm here in the yard where they
used to play,—
And they've shared a memory with
me today.

Vicky Allis

MIDSUMMER

You loved me for a little
Who could not love me long:
You gave me wings of gladness
And lent my spirit song
You love me for an hour
But only with your eyes:
Your lips I could not capture
By storm or by surprise
Your mouth that I remember
With rush of sudden pain
As one remembers starlight
Or roses after rain
Out of a world of laughter
Suddenly I am sad
Day and night it haunts me
The kiss I never had

Raymond Shroll

AMAZING APRIL

April's vitalizing liquid manna
Provenders rose and buttercup.
Rills of children's kinetic laughter
Infiltrate the crust of Winter's
ennui
Liberating Spring's enchanted
soul!

Rebecca Walker Welty

GRANDMA & POP

You were always there when we
needed
You were always there if we called
You were always there with an
open ear
You tried to give it your all.

You helped us when we were
babies
You helped us more as we grew
You helped us thru our bad times
And now its time you knew.

We loved you when we were little
We love you now that were big
We love you the most—because
you are you
Because of the love & concern in
all that you do!

Susan Masel

FRAGIL ARE WE

Life is like a crystal glass.
Fragile from laughter to tears.
Breakable is the heart.
The sensitive pleasure of life, can
turn so easily.
Yet it is so hard to regain
happiness,
In three part harmony.
We are scales to weigh and balance,
The obstacles on our road to
choose.
Sleep may ease, but not control the
desires for happiness.
Unify into one the three.
Control the fragile breaking down
of the spirit.
Be as you may to oneself—
And let not a fault to be.
Unify as one my spirit, for I love
you,
Will care for you, as a crystal glass,
Never to break or bend,
Only to stand sturdy.

David Richardson

MASSACRE

Mangled bodies
speak to each other
in silent voices
each a different death
each a different life
they speak of their common fate

silent cries
rise with the stench
of the new dead
of children dead
in a cause not theirs
the living
the killers
killed

orderly rows
disordered corpses
executioner's
bayonettes and
bullets
without a fight
with but slight
cause
the dead now
speak their mind:

what killed us was
not the guns
but the poison
that we took.

Ms Joyce Yvonne Payne

IT'S ALRIGHT TO LOVE YOU

I'm going to keep on finding a way,
To love Bob every day,
No matter what you say or do.
I'll always be in love with you,
I do hope that our love won't stop,
Because I had loved you from the
very start.
Like the birds in the skies which
flock together,
I'm so glad you're mine.
Love, why must we separate?
Losing you, I can not take.
Our love will last to the end of time,
With this in mind, my love grows
on like the budding of a rose.
It's alright to love you.

Natalie A Herbert

A PRAYER TO ST. JUDE

Dedicated to my Oncologist, Michael H. Dosik M.D. without whose encouragement, and medical skill, this poem would not have been published

---

Of all diseases for which there is
no answer,
The worst of all, is the one called
CANCER
The sinking feeling deep inside,
The tears that swell like a rising
tide.
The ugliness of losing hair,
Is there no relief for the pain and
despair?
It breaks my heart to hear children,
say,
Please God Tell us why,
We who have lived so short a time,
Have to die.
The pain and agony of this horrible
curse,
None should have to endure,
So please St. Jude guide all medical
minds,

And help them find a cure.
To free us from this terrible Plague
From which so many to rest have been laid.
Help us St Jude to you we pray
That soon there will come a day
That we may without fear of CANCER—
We beseech thee please, show us the answer.

V V Lane
LOOKING DEEPLY INTO YOUR EYES

To: Grandma Lucy

Thoughts of past relationships.
Will ours survive?
You cause me to see life differently.
Comparing thoughts and sharing feelings,
We are each building upon the others life.
Time passes and we are changing.
Even though we are each a part
Of the others life, will our
Relationship just be memories?
Eventually going our separate
Ways, will I inevitably be
Alone?

Jeanne Stolworthy
DREAM SANCTUARY
Within the Etherian Mists,
From whose mysterious lists,
Dreams take form and rise
In pageantry before the

Sleeper's eyes:
Towers a cathedral the
Angels keep,
Where mortals go for
Enchanted sleep.

Kelly Swallow
DREAMS
Dreams are like a flower
They're here and then they're gone.
Sometimes they come back again
But sometimes they need help.
Sometimes dreams can be like people.
People are so different,
Their likes are not the same.
Dreams can take place on a tower
Or on a beautiful lawn.
It doesn't matter where or when!
Dreams can be frightening and make you yelp.
Sometimes dreams can be as perfect as a steeple.
For dreams you spend no money only your time is spent.
Dreams, dreams, dreams, what is their aim?

Jerry Vaughn
A TRIBUTE TO A THIEF
Not just by night, but by day and night,
you came into our lives and stole from
us all. Why do I pay tribute to a thief,
because of who you are. Your not an ordinary
thief, your goals were our spirits and our hearts.
You didn't ask, you just took them and ran
to the stars. Did we miss them, how could
we, because when you had them, they reflected
a better spirit, a bigger heart. While you
kept these trusted possessions they glowed
within you and made us better.
Those precious items you took from us will
never look as bright as when we watched
you board the Challenger and wave them
back to us. Our faith, our hearts were
returned bright as the smile on your face
and bigger than space. How can we say
more to you than the legacy you left to us
all, a better world for having known who you were.

Miss Jeannette Carlson

Miss Jeannette Carlson
FARM DOG
One of the things special
About the country scene
Is the farm family's dog,
Who has always been
Loyal, true, courageous,
Sentinel at the door,
Companion, helper and even more;
He's the standard of the barnyard,
Sleek'n shiny he sits,
Like on a greeting card!

Shep, Duke (Dutchess, Queenie),
Whatever is the name,
The happy, willing, spirit
Is always the same.

Joseph Michael Doss
COSMIC FIRE
On a golden bed in a glass dome
high atop her mountain home
looking out across the solar sea
happy with it all, lonely as can be
She likes to
look out her window and wonder
across the galactic expanse
where cosmic fires burn
and distant stars dance
She's so conscious of her fashion
in her burning fits of passion
wishing he's by her heart to stay
but tens to power light years away
Somewhere outside the threshold
of even her wildest dreams
beyond her sunlit valleys
with clear running streams
She likes to
look out her window and wonder
across the galactic expanse
where cosmic fires burn
and distant stars dance.

Phillis M Carter
GLAD TO BE A MAN
As I walk barefoot through the meadows
Gently touching the daisies.
Feel the sunshine.
Little bit lazy.
Think back to my younger day.
Think of mama an auntie.
My ole grandie.
They all had to go away.
I'm here to stay.
They're up there helping God each day.
angle's ole they stand.
Giving God a big ole hand.
Often think about them.
So many way's, wonder why oh why God did they go away.
I'm all grown now really understand.
So many things has happen.
I've grown to be a man.
Doing all I can.
I'm so proud an happy.
Glad to be a man.

Debbie Ann Cotton
THE SOUND OF THE OCEAN
There is a cool breeze flowing through my hair,
The sound of the ocean is in the air.

Two strong arms reach out to hold me,
This moment we share was meant to be.

His eyes are bold his mind is free,
Our lips are open moving vigorously.

The tide is calm the ocean light blue,
Our thoughts are together these feelings are true.

The sun is setting on the mountain tops
There is the sound of the ocean, fearful it is not.

Patricia L Hermeyer

Patricia L Hermeyer
LOVELETTER TO MY GRANDPARENTS

Dedicated To my Beloved Grandparents Dale and Shirley Welty, and Ruth E. McAfee

---

The silver tint glazes their hair,
Like tiny snowflakes dotting the air,
Every strand,
Was carefully planned,
By the One we know,
Who sees every sparrow.

The sound of their voices,
Is music to my ears,
The strength in their hands,
Shows the wisdom of their years.

The lines on their faces,
May look tired or worn,
But every single line,
Has weathered a different storm.

The sparkle in their eyes,
Tells a story all its own,
Its a story of love and sharing,
With four children now grown.

As I look back,
To those so dear,
The memories are strong,
And the message is clear.

How can I ever repay,
The love and support you showed,
During those tender days.

Lelia Shepherd
PEACE, BE STILL

To all people in the world who desire "Peace".

Oh Lord, wilt Thou look down upon a bleeding world,
A world ashamed of what it's hands have wrought?
Ashamed of all this carnage, suffering and loss
Of precious things the blood of Calvary has bought.
O world misruled by cruel greed,
O world gone mad with fear!
We cry aloud in our great need,
"Wilt Thou not hover near?"
Oh Lord, wilt Thou look down upon a bleeding world,
And bend the deeds of man unto Thy will?
Spread forth Thy shelt'ring arms above a storm-tossed world,
And bend the deeds of man unto Thy will?
Spred forth Thy shelt'ring arms above a storm-tossed world,
And in Thy deep compassion whisper: "Peace, Be Still."

Rosie Barten Spanier
OH MY BEAUTIFUL BABY

To all the baby's killed by unjust abortion.

On its lips a beautiful smile.
It did not know that in a short while.
Plans to kill it were in the making.
A life so cruely they would be taking.
A Doctors needle soon would inject it.
The baby's mother then would reject it.
The lovely baby softly cried.
The mother slept and the baby died.

Mrs Irene Wheatley
SMILE
Smile is a little word but it goes a long long way
Have we forgotten how to for we see so few today.
It may take a little effort but it's certainly worth a try

Give some sad or lonely person a big
friendly smile
What makes it even nicer is that twinkle in your eye
It will make them feel better and I'm sure you will too
To know that kind little gesture will help us see the day through
It may be hard to do when you're not feeling up to par
But the person you bestow it on may
feel worse than you by far
It will cost you nothing and may even
start a trend
Wouldn't it be great to start each day
with a smile from a friend?

Carol Yelensky
LOVE

I am on an island
There is no other here.
Only the water speaks to me
Saying . . . love.

Love is an island
Blazing in the noon time heat.
Love is an island
Of serenity at twilight.
Love is an island
Unmoved by the tides around it.

Love is an island of peace.

Kris Caslavka
FRIENDS ARE LIKE RIVERS

A rivers water always runs
Twisting and turning
Around the bends.
Pushing its way through barricades
Never worrying what happens ahead.

It just continues down the path
Always wanting to be on its own.
Sometimes sharing with others around
And changing its liefstyle as the day goes on.

Just like a river
A friend is the same;
He twists and turns
Trying to avoid the problems.
Sharing his life with others who care
But also, wanting to be on his own.
When problems occur
He finds a way out;
And lets the path
Direct his life.

But when that river soon dries out
All that is left, is the earth below.
Like a friendship that ends all at once
The memories are left, to die in the dust.

Violet B Bickett
LIFES VERSION

Life is a very special gift given just to you
Handle very carefully in all that you do
The challenges will be there all thru your days
Meet them face to face or turn yourself away
Feel they are a hardship or another game
To win or to lose you still have much to gain
Life can be full of tragedy and sorrow
Turn these into opportunities for your tomorrow
Life can be full of struggle and duty
Still it's full of rest and beauty
Life can be a mystery and puzzle my friend
These two things make it interesting till the end
Try to sing all of lifes happy songs
This keeps you skipping merrily along
Sum it up and here is what life will be
A gift, challenge, adventure, game, sorrow, tragedy
Also it is duty, opportunity, mystery, struggle, a goal
Songs, beauty, promise and a journey until you are old

Linda Ravenhorst
NIGHT NURSE

At 1 a.m. as I walk very quietly
I hear the soft weeping in Room 323
It is a mother who's just been told
It's cancer. She needs a hand to hold
So I sit for ten minutes maybe twenty
And listen to troubles of hers aplenty

Leukemia at 10 seems such an illusion
As I check young Jenny's blood transfusion
In the next half hour I hear Mr. Kethan call
As I enter he says in deep Southern drawl,
"I really didn't mean to waken you nurse,
But this pain in my belly is such a curse,
So much that I just can't sleep at all."
I bring him a pain shot down the hall.
If only he'd come to the doctor sooner
All his tests show it's an inoperable tumor.

I know I must get to checking the charts
And what needs given from the medicine carts
Even the surgeries for the upcoming day
Must have lab work complete and a chest x-ray.
I haven't time for all who need it tonight
May God give you strength and make it right
As we battle together this thing called cancer
And pray that a cure will soon be the answer.

Marie Hinz
PRAY TO GOD

We never know from day to day
Whatever is in store
We have to take each day
Whatever it is for
And put our faith in God each day
And always take the time to pray.
For all the blessings he has sent
Are we grateful; for what its meant?
We shoud give him thanks and praise
We have been blessed in many ways.
Take the time to thank your God; for all
the grateful things he does
For each and everyone of us.
So take the time to tell him so
We will be blessed; this we know.
Pray to God every day
It will help you in every way
God is always ever near
And will keep us in his care.

Ila "Susie" Dayton

Ila "Susie" Dayton
OUR FRIEND

Dedicated to my husband, Howard W. Dayton

Inky Dinky Parly Voo
Jim Kennedy, how we all love you!
This game of life, you live it well,
So to folks like you—why shouldn't we tell?

Just knowing you will enrich a life,
Be it Brother, Sister, Husband or wife.
Hearing you sing and laugh and play
Has brightened for us many a day.

You are a good man to have for a friend,
One who will be to the very end.
We realize at poetry we are not so good,
A better job we've done eating your food!

The life you live—so many times to us has been a light,
That's brought us back from out of the darkest night.
So, over the years and as 1968 comes to an end,
We've thanked God for having you, Jim, as a friend!

Cindy Lee Baucom
TEARY EYES

I remembered back to yesterdays years,
Knowing that it would bring me tears,
All I wanted to remember was you and me
Together always but that couldn't be.

Cause I also remember the day that you left,
A day that I said I'd never forget.

Then I realized the time that's gone by,
And that it's time to dry my TEARY EYES.

You and the memories shall go with the tears,
And all that will be left is me and the years,
To spend them the way I want them to be,
And not be locked up with the memories
Of you and me.

Joan May
THINGS ARE SO DIFFERENT

Where should I go but to the Lord?
Things are so different.
The world is so fine.
He is our Savior, yours and mine.

As long as I am tuned to his phone line,
Things are so different in this heart of mine.
I pray I am His, and He is mine.
Things are so different with Jesus on my line.

He came on this earth to save us from our sins.
We have to follow Him.
"This Jesus to win."

So where should I go but to the Lord?
Things are so different when you trust in Him!
Your life changes, And your cup runs over the brim
And that is when things are so different
When your life belongs to Him!

Deborah L Sears
AUTUMN FAREWELL

Written in memory of Margaret E. Bennett

As daily life continues
and the sun turns into rain
the leaves that fall from the trees
are symbolic of our pain

Our lives were made much richer
just by knowing you
and the tears we shed will graze the land
as does the morning dew

For though we must accept the fact
that you have gone away
the precious memories in our hearts
will return to us each day

We comfort each other the best we can
in this time of great loss
and silently pray for the day
when once more our paths will cross

Robert E Heath
HELP ME CARE
Flowers in the valley
And hills filled with trees
Lord God the mountains
Is where I long to be

The beauty of the streams
The crystal clear waters
Lord God don't seem to be
Listed in my orders

A life on the wide deep six
Apart from the ones I love
I wish my life spread out
On the wings of a loving
White Dove

The freedom they share
The peace in the air
Lord God help me to care
For this life I do bear

Jo-Anne Aura
RABBIT PRAISE
Lord, make me a rabbit, gentle and content.
Give me big ears with which to listen,
And a tiny mouth that chooses words carefully.
Give me whiskers, like sensitive probes
That can feel their way ever so delicately
into the heart of another,
And a tiny nose that avoids business
not its own.
Grant me quickness to flee from danger,
And eagerness to serve You with joy.
Finally Lord, give me eyes that see the beauty in any environment,
and the beautiful in any "rabbit."

Ellen G Platko
UNTITLED
They met, not in youth's first passion,
Nor when the years weighed
Too heavily for joy,
But rather at that time of life
When disillusion had been conquered
And hope, unbending, sought new hope.

They met and touched, untouching
And spoke the silent words
That dared not risk
Another's ears.
They became friends
And yet a friendship too complex
For exploration
Too near, perhaps, to reality.

(The answers to human need
Are seldom found
Until blindness thinks it sees
And the reflections of our souls
Become shadowed by degrees.)
They met, therefore, and meeting
Turned aside
From the promise always broken
And went their pre-determined ways
While the flower, rootless, died.

Brad P Fielder
YOUR FRIEND
The sea so calm, over which I look, with you by my side.
We watch the sun's path across the vast heavens.
It's light shimmers on the sea, reviving it,
turning the dark water orange, yellow, crimson, scarlet.

I look into your eyes, hoping to find a place for me.
But my passion is halted, as I find that space already taken.

I look away, back at the sea.
It is now becoming hostile, waves rising, falling,
crashing against the rocks below.
The sky clouding over, a drop of rain falling on my hand.

I glance toward you, a tear racing down your fine skin.
I am ashamed of myself, my sorrow for you is that of a thousand tears.

I look away, the sky clear once again,
reflected beads of setting sunshine catch my eyes.
Once again I look your way.
Now I finally realize that to you I am not as special as a lover,
I am even more so, I—
Am your friend.

David Salas
THE DRIFTER
As I Look Out To Sea
For The Day Will Soon Be Gone . . .

And Tomorrow Is Just Another Day
Walking Along The Sandy Beach
I Wonder Someday . . .

For I Am A Drifter
And Drifted This Way . . .

If I Had A Dream To Sail
To The Promise Land Someday . . .

I Wonder Whats Out There Too Stay
I Wonder Which Way
I Wonder Each Day . . .

For I Am A Drifter
And Drifted This Way . . .

Barbara Kahut
IN SILENT SOLO
The first bud of Spring awoke from her long Winter's sleep.
Wonderment sparkled in Baby Bud's first worldly peek.
But mama tree was busy sipping raindrops left and right;
So the moment passed forever, out of mama tree's sight.

Under warm Summer sunshine and bright blue skies,
Missy Bud performed her first visual surprise.
She burst forth into a leaf of emerald green;
But for mom tree gazing skyward to the future, the present passed unseen.

Soon Autumn presented her palette of colors;
From them, Miss Leaf chose a travelling gown.
Dressed in her frock of red, orange and yellow,
Lady Leaf tumbled silently down.

She floated and twirled. She danced and swirled.
She drifted toward Winter's cold ground.
She landed lightly; yet ever so slightly,
She made a soft, crackling sound.

Suddenly mother tree noticed the absence!
She searched, peering down through the gathering mist.
She stretched her boughs, straining them frantically earthward;
But Lady Leaf was too far away now . . . to be kissed.

Mrs Irma (Hammons) Hubbs
ON LOCATION
I'm on location here in space
I'll note the time and mark the place
For space is vast and time was deeded
For every soul to get unseated.

A life on earth is but a minute
A gift from God—no one can 'win it'
Short and sweet like the song of a bird
Sometime, somewhere, somehow—you heard.

Eleanor Banks
CROSSES TO BEAR
We all have our crosses to bear.
Some heavier than others.
But there is someone we carry them too
And just leave them there.
So day by day the weight can become lighter.
The way can become brighter.
Until at last victory will be yours.
So keep the faith and God will carry you thru.

Martha Olson Carlson
I THANK GOD

To my christian parents

I thank God for childhood days
For a Christian home with Godly ways
When the sabbath came we worshipped God
In the little church on the prairie sod.
Thank God for memories of faith and love
Instilled in our hearts by our Father above.

Now when I think of the days that are passed
And wonder how long this life will last
Without friends and loved ones and God to provide
Strength for the day and God by my side.
I could not go without Him above
To help bear my burdens and to know great love.

I thank God for each rising sun
To see and enjoy the things He has done
The beautiful colors of autumn leaves
Fall into place as our Master weaves
The perfect picture of loving care
Into the sunset with splendor so rare.

Then some day when God calls me home
I will leave this earth no more to roam
For those who believe He has promised a place
How joyous t'will be to look on His face.
And hear the "Well done faithful servant of mine
The glories of heaven as promised are thine."

Sam Fishman
TERROR
It is terrible to hear
This shrieking in the night
It caroms off the walls
And echoes in mad flight
Agony and anguish rise
From some bottomless black hole
There is a rending and a tearing
And a splitting of a soul
Oh, what poor being suffers so
From what throat this tortured cry
The answer lies in my pounding heart
It is I, it is I, it is I

Nancy Bentrop Lakey
FEELING SMALL AND BEING TALL
Lord, when I look at Your Creation
The graceful flowing hills,
And the splendor of the flowers
Brings me to a still.

What kind of God builds mountains
And dots the land with flowers,
In a multicolor ray
And with trees that seem to tower.

The vastness of your creation
Brings me to my smallness.
But to be a part of that creation
Gives me a feeling of tallness.

You gave the world a sun to light
So that everything may grow.
And then you gave your son to us
That his light in us—may grow!

For who could make a better world
With beauty all around,
So when I'm feeling lonely
Your creation speaks to me with sound.

Viki Beard
BLACK TEARS
Black tears
Stream down my face
My feelings fade
leaving stains on my
Heart
My mind runs blank
As I hold out my hand
I keep reaching
But . . .
It falls

Helen Louise Jennings
OUR MISPLACED LOVE

To Cliff—this poem is dedicated to my husband on our 40th anniversary, with love—

You never hold me anymore,
Or kiss away my tears.

It's funny how love changes—
When your married many years.

Those busy days when we were
young,
We always found the time;
To sneak a kiss or hold a hand—
Without a reason or a rhyme.

And when the children came along,
We had such hectic days,
Somehow we let each other go—
And went our separate ways.

The love we shared was split apart,
And wrapped tightly 'round each
child.
We didn't save enough for us—
And it slipped away for awhile.

I need your love more than ever,
Now that we are growing older.
I'm so lonely and so frightened—
As the days grow dark and colder.

So honey, hold me once again,
And kiss away my tears.
Together let us find the love—
We misplaced through the years.

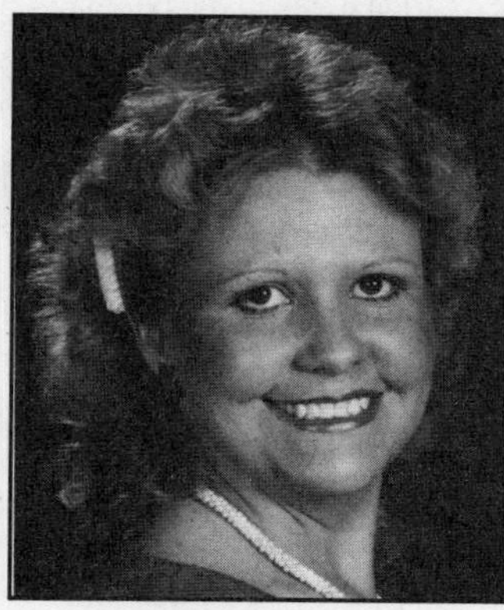

Katie Thomas

Katie Thomas
MOM'S VACATION

Wanted to give you something
before leaving home
All I could think of was writing a
poem
As you get the baggage packed,
please put in an extra sack
So that you can bring me
something back
When you get to the country of
Turkey
You will find the people not perkey
They do not cater to Americans
You'll take your own paper when
you use the can
The people there are not friendly
soon
You carry a bag lunch as well as a
spoon
May not be allowed into Lebenon
Because the fighting is still going
on
Look for the Valley of Armagedon
and Church of Antiock
Also look for that famous big rock
Jeruselem is real special it is
trimmed in lace
You'll have a Jewish guide to show
you this place
Remember to keep in the back of
your head
To take a look at the sea that is dead
If you hear anyone say "Only one
Dollar"
You'll know whats for sale is not
worth a hollar
When you get ready to come back
home
Could you bring me something
along
I would like a six foot two
Made of flesh and of Jew

Christopher L and Crystal D Tremblay
ODE TO MOM

To Debbie; a wonderful wife and terrific mother. We hope you'll enjoy and cherish this forever.

I've known you for seven months
and seven days,
But you've helped me in many
ways.
Without your help I'd surely die,
So stay with me so I won't cry.
Just hold me close and don't let go,
Give me the feeling you love me so.
My heart is small but that's okay,
It sends you lots of love on this day.

Tammy L Sheehan Yarber
WILD HORSE

I dedicate this poem to all the animals hoping they go undisturbed in the beautiful wilderness.

Wild horse so beautiful
Young and free,
When I approach
You run from me.

Wild horse on the plains
Where you belong,
Your legs so lean
Muscular and strong.

This horse was caught
By a man one day,
I hope you're set free
I wish, I pray.

Soon after I heard
You broke your noose,
Wild horse so beautiful
Young and loose.

Now you can run
Free and tame,
Let the wind blow
Through your mane.

Wild horse so beautiful
Young and free,
You can soar the plains
Where you ought to be.

Brenda Joyce Martin
AMERICAN POETRY

How satisfying it is to me,
Dwelling on words of inspiration
and sheer beauty;
Combined with strength, wisdom,
and harmony,
Described and expressed in
American Poetry.

American Poetry may talk of
anything you see,
It lets your mind flow, your spirit
run free;
And though it may not rhyme or
make sense to me,
Somehow, I still have a fondness
for American Poetry.

Thoughts being shared, feelings
expressed you see,
Of words that allow you to be
anything or anywhere you
wanna be;
And though you may, or may not
agree,
May somewhere be found, in
American Poetry.

So when you're lookin for a kind
of objectivity,
And want your mind to flow, and
your spirit to run free;
And though you may or may not
agree,
Just pick up a book of American
Poetry.

Virginia M Ferro
TRISTESSE

I did love you once
When
April's greening
Pregnant with promise
And rainbowed horizons
Held out
Her arms
To us.

But we were weak
Heirs to primal defects
Strongly taloned
And quick to find
Each other's
Vulnerability.

I did love you once
When
Winter's hand
Steeled with frost
And timed with memories
Curled more
Than once
About us.

Mary M St Clair
ABIDE

We do not with eyes need to see,
to know of God and eternity.
The promise He made before He
died,
always with us to abide.
To confess that we are born in sin,
open our hearts and let Him in.
If on His name only we believe,
into His kingdom He will receive.
Into the world He was born, and
His
life did give,
That we, through dying begin to
live.

Myrna Kavaney
AN AUTUMN LEAF

I watched a leaf fall from a tree
It seemed to glide, so calm, so free
It touched the earth and there will
stay
Until the wind blows it away.

I stood and wondered just a bit
Why life can't be as calm as it?
Why can't all people get along
And do more good, instead of
wrong?

Our Lord didn't plan this world to
be
A life of tears and misery
He planned it all from up above
For faith and hope and trust and
love.

I wonder where that leaf will go?
But only God, alone, will know.

Ruth J Laverty
A GREAT MAN

J.F.K. was a man so great.
Yes, he was the President of the
U.S.
A man like maybe you or me,
He didn't act any different than we.
He fought for his country, and he
fought for you,
He came home a hero after saving
his crew.
To go through a war and come
back alive,
Then to get shot, just taking a drive.
While the people cheered and
called his name,
A shot rang out and down he came.
Jackie and Caroline and John, too,
They lost even more than me or
you.
We lost a President, but they lost a
dad,
Something that every child should
have.
When their Daddy's not there,
they'll want to know why,
Why did their Daddy have to die.
And what do you say to a child so
young?
When you don't know yourself,
why this has been done.
This, Lee Harvey Oswald, had a
reason,
For committing such an act of
treason,
To kill the President, a man such
as he,
This man called John F. Kennedy.

Catherine Elaine Newman

Catherine Elaine Newman
MY LOVE

To my daughters; Jennifer, Jessica and Jill

My love flows like the River,
Slowly drifting into the
unknown.
Like love, sometimes the waters
run deep,
And I escape forbidden depths
before coldness sets in.
Love surrounds me like the beauty
of Fall,
Against a streaked pink sky.
It glorifies the sweet and tender
moments,
When the River stood still.
And for a moment, we met, and
drenched,
Our souls in forbidden waters.
I became the fountain that
swallowed up your youth,
Which strong forces left me out
of control, like a raging river.
I'm grasping to hold on. My heart
beats like thunder
On a stormy night,
And life passes me by like lightning
streaking
Across the sky.
Tears formed the depths of the
River,

Where destiny forever hides.
I am no longer the River that
perceived love so bold,
For love runs deeper within me.
What used to be swift waters,
Is now the roaring Sea.

Sue S Williams
CALVARY'S RANSOM

Cruelly crucified
between
convicted criminals
among
cowering crowds
on
Calvary's Cross!

RIDICULED!
RESENTED!
REJECTED!

Response: "Father Forgive!"

RENASCENT!
RESURGENCE!
RESURRECTION!

Result: Redemption for
you and for
me . . .

Stephen Beck
AS I SIT

As I sit
down to write
this poem, I
stare at the
small green light
on my typewriter
as I think
my thoughts.
I try to
think but I
must stare at
the light so
small and so
green.

Shirley E Sample
WHY LORD

This poem is dedicated to all my loved ones that have been called Home by the Lord, written with love!!!

Lord,
why do we wait oh so long,
until someone has already gone.
why didn't we express our love to
them
why do we wait, until the end?
Lord,
those times are gone, we could
have shared,
letting them know how much we
cared.
We seem to forget how time runs
out,
oh why, didn't we let our love be
felt?
Lord,
those little things that mean so
much
like the spur of the moment
invitation to lunch.
Taking the time to pick up the
phone
and letting them know they're not
alone!
Lord,
to think of the times, we could have
had
and all the things we should have
said,
makes my heart weep with sorrow,
oh Lord, why did I wait until
tomorrow!
Lord,
help me to learn from my mistakes
and remind me of the time to take,
to say "I love you" in my own way
and not tomorrow Lord, but today!

In Jesus Name . . . AMEN

Diana Anita Sceurman
HIS LAST DAYS ON THIS EARTH

Upon a donkey He came,
All who saw knew His name,
Shouting Hosanna, palms they
waved,
Years from now, remember what
He gave.

The table is set for the 'Last Meal,'
Jesus is there with His twelve,
None other allowed in there to
dwell,
Knowing His death would soon be
sealed.

In Gethsemane He did pray,
Tears in His eyes, blook-like sweat
on His brow,
Earnestly praying, shall He stay,
Be it God's will, He will go now.

The betrayer came to the garden,
All it took was one small kiss,
Thirty pieces of silver paid not to
miss,
It's too late for Jesus to be
pardoned.

To the cross He was taken,
Kicked and beaten, gentleness was
out,
Here is your King of Jews, they
shout,
All because His name was
foresaken.

The sun went dark, the earth shook,
Soldiers cast lots for the robe He
wore,
From the top to the bottom the
curtain tore,
To His death, our sins He bore.

Gary Ronald Ellis
HOME SWEET HOME

I'm a native born American,
Who's proud of Liberty;
From the hills of West Virginia,
Mountaineers are always Free!

I was born in Wetzel County,
In this Mountain State;
In the little community of Reader,
Whole family there is great.

The house that I was born in,
Still stands there yet today:
I have an aunt that lives there,
Who I think of every day.

Loved ones now no longer there,
Memories I could share;
But in my heart they're still around,
God bless them in his care.

Wild Wonderful West Virginia,
Her colors blue and gold;
God bless my mountain homeland,
My heritage now told.

"Almost Heaven, West Virginia,"
Famous song of yesterday;
Take me home country roads,
Winding there to stay!

Gerald W Fleetwood
WITH ALL OF THESE GIFTS

While walking through a meadow
A thought came to my mind,
How fortunate we are, was in the
thought
As I began to unwind.

We have the gift of seeing
Our life as it passes by,
Even though without
understanding
And sometimes even asking why.

We have a gift called speech
Although sometimes uncouth,
It portrays just what we want to be
Relating back to our youth.

The gift of choice is also there
We determine whatever we do,
No matter what our peers suggest
The decision is to me and you.

With all of these gifts how can we
say
That no one seems to care,
Because while walking through
this meadow
I found someone to share.

Rebecca E Morgan
MY DAD

Dedicated to Emory C. Morgan my Dad

My dad never made a fortune
He wasn't that kind of a guy.
When it came to making folks
laugh,
He didn't even have to try.

Some called him another Will
Rogers—
I'm sure Will Roger's comedy was
best,
But you can't tell how far he'd gone
Had he ever been put to the test.

His education was meager.
He lived in an earlier day—
When higher education wasn't the
vogue,
But common sense held sway.

The town gossip lived on our
corner
So he got all the news as he passed,
And could always remind someone
speaking unkind
Of something unkind in his past.

He said to listen to all men,
Not just to a scholarly few.
Remember how little a person may
know,
He may know it better than you.

To measure a man by his money
Is considered to be nothing new,
But I like to measure a person
By the little things they do.

Morris Lee Shaw
OUR TABERNACLE BY THE SEA

This poem is dedicated to Rose Marie, My Loving Wife

It was many and many a year ago
In a Tabernacle by the sea,
That a maiden there lived whom
you may know by the name of
Rose Marie and this maiden she
lived with no other thought
than to love and be loved by me.
But our love it was stronger by far
than the love of those
Who were older than we of many
far wiser than we
and neither the angels in Heaven
above nor the demons down
under the sea can ever dissever my
soul from the soul of
the beautiful Rose Marie.
For the moon never beams without
bringing me dreams
of the beautiful Rose Marie and the
stars never rise but

I feel the bright eyes of the
beautiful Rose Marie
and so, all the night tide, I lie down
by the side
of my darling, my darling my wife
my bride
in our Tabernacle there by the sea,
in our temple by the sounding sea.

Michael Crawley
LOVE

Do you love me or do you not?
Did you tell me because I forgot?
I have a heart and it is true,
Now it's yours from me to you.
If I should die before you do,
I'll go to heaven and wait for you.

And just to show you that I care,
I'll write your name on a golden
stair.
If you're not there on judgement
day,
I'll know they sent you the other
way.
And just to prove my love is true,
I'll go to hell to be with you!

Marsha T Skipworth
THE STARTLING RAIN

Silently flowing, silently fading
the dismal hours drear away,
While the treetops blow
with harmonious sweeps,
Above the wet-layed town

The trickling down of the
soft drops and wind smudge
the crispness of life on
the ground and on the panes
What is this dreadful thing
that ruins the slowest moving
shellful and slightless creature
on land and topples the weather
beaten
clothed sail to one side?

No one knows why Nature insists
Judge to warm or rain
As they, the wings that flap wait
and the sea to rush rapidly
among the banks of the heavily laid
earth

But others enjoy the showers
that dampen the spirits and soil
So let us go and join
Mother-Earth with her downpours
and shine.

Carol Conrady
THE BEAST

It taints the blood.
Rots the brain.

Consumes the life
In unending pain.

At first the beast can be contained.
For private times it lies in state.
A sentry at the darkest gate.
Are you alone?
It is too late.

One defective cell its malignancy spreads.
To lead you down the paths untrod.
Offering peace and tranquility
To be your friend, then your lover, then your God.

It gently nestles in your home.
As from your brain it does escape.
It's in your carpet in your drapes
It greets you at the door.

At first it only whispers soft
And then it speaks and then it screams.
The dark gray shadow in your dreams.
To grow in strength to take control
It lies, it cheats, it schemes.

When the drums pound and you humbly ask
What do you want? Is death the goal?
I'll spare your life.
I'll take your soul.

When normal life does not resume.
It is too late. You've been consumed.

Daniel A Wise

TRAGEDY: A FRIEND

This poem is dedicated to Scott R. Carll, killed by riding with a drunk driver.

His life was short
to its end . . .
But while he lived
I called him friend.

David Dye

THE PASSING OF CHILDHOOD (KEVIN WAYNE'S POEM)

Race child—fast and fleet—
Over hill and dell.
Put haste to your feet.
Only time will tell
After you have gone.
None care that you passed.
So race child—race on—
Fly now, swift-one, fast.

You shant dream now child,
'Cause life has passed you—
Left you feeling mild,
Turned your heart to blue.
So fly on—spirit—
Fly to heaven nigh.
Don't despair of it.
Go home to the sky.

Dreams, visions—fading—
Leaving you alone.
Your dreams cascading,
Like waters, wind-blown.
Life has passed you, child,
Naught to come your way.
No more to be wild—
Oh, what a sad day!

Rachelle M Riney

THE POWER WITHIN

Everyone has it, the Power Within.

My friends say I'm a poet
Though my words don't always rhyme
My actions show it time after time.
My kids say I'm a teacher
Though I don't always give them the answer
I only show them the way
Sort of like a preacher.

Everyone has it, the Power Within.

You can be a dancer, a singer, a star
You've got what it takes
You don't have to look far.

Look for it in your heart
It's there where you can't see it
When you feel it, use it
All you have to do is start.

Everyone has it, the Power Within.

Mark J Richardson

SHOTGUN SERENADE

Walking across a patch of snow
on the summit of Shotgun Pass,
you check your footing every step—
one slip would be your last.

Your legs are weary, your mind's a blur,
and you'd swear it's all a dream.
If you fall up here, you'll fall forever
and no one hears you scream.

Relax. Let go. It's better to surrender.
Lie in the snow and rest.
You're only passing through this world.
You're just an honored guest.

Let that snow come and take you,
down the mountain in one breath.
Let it come and initiate you
in the music of your death.

Anita L Watkins

Anita L Watkins

FOR SOMEONE SPECIAL

Every night my thoughts drift to you
I can't help this no matter what I do.
It is my heart that has to pay the fee.
I can't blame it on no one but me.

Our first kiss still lingers on my lips,
dreams of your eyes makes my heart flip,
your smile is there as I close my eyes,
to think of your soft hair makes me sigh.

I am happy when with you I am sure.
When you hold me I feel so secure.
The way you treat me is like a queen,
I wish you knew how much to me that means.
All I ask is a chance to show how much I care.
With you there is so much I want to share.
I want to prove that I will never hurt you.
Making you happy is all I want to do.

I will always be by your side,
I will not go in and out like the tide.
Just give it some effort and time,
You will see this is not a silly rhyme.

Mrs Annetta C Stanton

THRILLS

There's no thrill to compare
With the thrill of accomplishment:
Not the satisfaction of owning much
Nor any artificial stimulant!
That warm, full swell of the chest
To a well-deserved compliment
Is something life-long lasting
And perfumed with Heaven-scent . .

Eileen J Miller

A SINNER'S PRAYER

In dedication of my four children—Sheri, Janet, Rogene, and Roger

---

My prayers are silent, but they are sincere.
They're not said aloud for others to hear.
These are things that shouldn't be spoken at all.
And once they are said they can't be recalled.
To pray in silence is the way for me.
Then my prayers are just between God and me.
Some of them are answered, some of them not.
But my prayers are not left in my brain to rot.
Maybe to the church I'm not an integral part.
But when I pray, it comes from the heart.

Renee Goldberg

MATE

For my husband Sid, on our 33rd Wedding Anniversary

Mate
Ship Mate
Help Mate
Soul Mate
Partner in Life
Anchor—

We are pebbles washed by the sea
In and out with the tide
Scattered, separated, together, apart,
Clustered, clinging
Holding on
Washed away
Washed back again
Creating solid ground.

Betty Jane Simpson

THE KANSAS FARMER

Born on the prairie, born to know
The flatness of open fields,
His gaze surveys the vacant sky,
Endlessly searching for rain,
Eternally searching for rain.
Always the same, as year upon year,
He tests the soil in his hand.
Born with the patience to wait
And watch the pattern unfold,
To rejoice as the pattern unfolds.

He stands alone, silent, listening,
Hearing the song of the wheat,
Forever rustling—rippling with sound,
Song of the wind singing only for him,
Everblowing—the wind sings for him.

He is at peace, this Kansas Man,
A man at one with his land.
His view is clear, and the air is sweet,
His cares, like chaff, are winnowed by wind,
Everblowing, the winnowing wind.

Antoinette Petrella-Stanfield

WOMAN OF YESTERDAY

The woman obeyed
and man for the first time was.
He saw himself in her eyes.
He took pride on her love.
For his existence
in the dark she dried
her tears.
Silences of love.
In silence
she lived and loved,
suffered and died
and man for the first time was.

Judy Clark

MOM'S LETTER TO JODI

Years ago I had a baby girl
Such joy, such beauty, she was a whirl.
Years went by and I did my best
Tis a mother, ever to rest?
As more years went by, perils began.
I hurt, I cried, I wished I could have ran.
One day you cussed me, right to my face
Whoa, back-up. I had to get back my pace,
You wrote me a letter from where you were living
God! I did my best, but you just weren't forgiving.
The anger in you is still at a high peak
I wished now I hadn't been so weak.
I tried writting you but tore up the sheets
I just couldn't do it, the hurt was so deep.
But I do want you to know that I deeply love you so
And hope and pray, you'll grow up: Someday.
Have kids of your own and know what it's like
To have them look at you and tell you to take a hike
Then maybe you can understand; why I should have used my hand

Victoria Hammond

HUMAN MACHINE

Dark piercing eyes, searching, probing for something,
That is not visible to the naked eye.
Sensitive ears listening for, but not hearing,
For there is nothing but silence.

Fingers touching ever so lightly,
Hands clutched ever so tightly,

Arms outstretched for your embrace,
Heart beating with an even pace.
Legs made for walking,
Yet getting nowhere.

Take care of yourself for the end comes too fast,
Take care of yourself so that you can last,
Long enough for you to enjoy,
The time you have upon this earth,
That was given to you by your birth.

Larry Dewayne Hilderbrand

Larry Dewayne Hilderbrand
KNOWLEDGE

Dedicated to students of Job Corp, Fiancee Melody Redman, and Brother Jesse Hilderbrand, US Air Force.

Up the wind does blow with all the
things we know.
No burden will it fly, briskly to the sky.
When time of doubt does flow, less life
will we show.
If I find out on this day that confidence is the way,
No wave of storm shall blow away man's seed
we call a soul.
So when future time is here, and success makes us fear;
We will always find we used the wind with
no abuse.

Kelly Jo Runkel
WINTERTIME
Sled riding, falling down
I get up, brush off and frown,
Grandma says, "You'll be sick for two weeks."

Snow men and snowballs,
The snow fight, then mother calls,
"Get in, you've been out there too long."

Frost on the windowsills,
I feel the bitter winter chills,
Jack Frost has arrived in town.

Its cold out, I've got frostbite.
But maybe, I just might
Find some warmth in deep down in my heart.

Sue Newberry
A NIGHT'S PONDERING
I sat at the edge of the world
And watched the stars dance in and out
The moon shone brightly
Turning the ocean's face silver

The night faded with the stars
And the moon gave 'way to the rising sun
The colours of the eyes of God
Reflected on the sea

O wondrous dawn—how lovely you are!

Through the clouds rolling past my feet
I glimpsed heaven
I felt the world and all humanity
Pulsing through my veins.

Phillip E Newell
ON CHANGING CAREERS
is this it then
what I have waited for
an end to oil and cyanide
and noises of machines pounding
ringing in my ears
of cordite hanging in air
and no breeze

am I free of endless
revolvers awaiting assembly
of shoes that reek
and clothes that don't come clean
am I free to think
can I think . . . of what

Shakespeare, Whitman, Twain and Crane
commas, <u>it</u>, <u>the</u>, redundancy
or will I wake and find myself
again at piecework
ten cents a line

is it better to lunch in restaurants
or brown bag in grease
left over from morning production

are words or guns more creative
when no one reads

R S deVries
NO CRADLE ROCKS
No cradle rocks for this new Babe
No presents for the tree
No warm fire glows to warm His toes
No shelter there for He

But all around upon the ground
Most wonderful to see
A host of angels bright with light
Shone all around Mary

The tiny Babe all wrapped so tight
Lay sleeping on the hay
While shephards came with awed delight
His precious face to see

The lambs and oxen closer came
While Baby Jesus slept
And in His tiny hand that night
The peace of Nations kept.

Stanley Lloyd Glenn Jr
THE ROSE
I liken you unto a rose
With beauty so unmatched
Where you go my heart goes also
We are spiritually attached

Joanne Pooch
SPIRITUAL ARCHITECTS
I see in the night
By hell's fiery light
That you're black and not white
Teaching me the things I believe
And symbolic of a childs wisdom
You show me a passion of whiteness
And eery light—Equal to mortal blackness alone
You say we are polished stars in a galaxy of blackness
Where nothing lives, nothing grows
Simply existing in a sphere titled <u>Earth</u>

Deities said let there be light
And there was whiteness
As they spoke those of the cloven hoove
Created a counter reacting force
It was dark, evil, a satanic intensity
There was blackness

Two worlds built in the images of their makers
One was good and kind
One was cruel and evil
The seraphic whiteness
The cimmerian blackness
Stygian vs celestial
Heaven vs hell
Armagedon
The end

Lena Roberson

Lena Roberson
MY BROTHER CARSON
Carson wasn't a college graduate, nor had a Doctor's degree;
But he could quote the scriptures, as easy as the A B C's.
He was taught by God and inspired men . . .
Speaking to him through the bible with power;
He learned God's word by reading, Meditating—
And studying many hard hours.
He wanted to do God's will always, and teach the bible every where;
He was good, honest, kindhearted and brave,
And will be remembered as a man of prayer.
He finished the course, kept the faith . . .
And grew in the grace and knowledge of the Lord;
He spoke as "the oracles" of God, and has gone on to get his reward.
I know there's a crown laid up for him,
In that city so bright and fair;
He'll be waiting with the saints around the white throne,
In that place God has gone to prepare.

Sheila Eads Deal
AN ESOTERIC TALE
Cascades the whirl of salty sand
Amid the crest of distant land
The tide washed in and cleansed the shore
A tired love and nothing more.

The wasted years, the costly time
Have left for tears no ream of rhyme
The quiet daze that lingers home
A silent friend with which to roam.

Beseeched by fools who fled from past
Encounters bled a deadly task
Escaped the soul with nought to gain
Then echoed soft, a sad refrain.

The burdened night has met his mate
Well locked behind the freedom gate
The song is old, its message clear
A dusty thought that left a tear.

The heart endures an empty pain
Of suffered dreams in stagnant rain
A prisoned lust, a poisoned cry
No will to live
No time to die.

Barbara J Slentz-Hogan
WITHOUT A DOUBT
I can say without a doubt
That God's been good to me.
He gave me legs to run about
And eyes wide open to see.
He gave me ears to hear the songs
Of birds in morning praise.
He gave me a husband to hold dear
And little ones to raise.
Oh, there were mountains I had to climb
Rivers that had to be crossed;
There were storms that I stumbled through,
But somehow I never got lost.
Within my heart he put a song
Sung by the angels above.
He gave me a promise he'd always be there
And he gave me a heart full of love.

L A Romano
WHO AM I?
Who Am I?

My color is deep; an artless perfection.

My coralla is soft. My briar afflicting.

My scent discrete.

My design precise.

I symbolize a vivid pulsation!

Love . . . Amour

My meaning to appeasing. Who Am I?
I am
A

Jacqueline Proctor
THE ROCKING CHAIR

In memory of Annie Branham, for whom this poem was written.

The rocking chair has
Stopped rocking.
The apron has been
Laid aside.
No longer do aged fingers
Braid grey tresses
To wrap around her head
Like a crown.

I walk through the
House cold and empty.
I hear the echo of my
Footsteps on the floor and
her gentle voice.
I smell the violets she
So lovingly nurtured on the front
porch.

An empty house,
An empty chair.
Flowers bloom
On the grave
From tender loving care
Not her own.

I wonder if she sees them
From another rocking chair.

Loretta Bakken
BOXES
Boxes are brown,
All boring and blue,
Sitting there with
Nothing to do,
Used once and once no more,
Boxes are boring with
Nothing to do.

Richard S Pena
THE KING
There was a man from Tupelo
who dream't he'd be a singer.
So he wrote a song, for his mom,
and that song became a winner.

He later moved to Memphis,
for this would be his home;
and he did call it Graceland,
for Graceland was his own.

He also made some movies,
did some radio and t.v.
He loved his live performances
to sing to you and me.

He never became big headed,
or thought that he was great.
He sang to please the people,
until he met his fate.

He will always live in our hearts,
for he could truly sing.
There will never be one like him,
for Elvis is THE KING!!

Cheryl A Kuslak
MY VERY SPECIAL FRIEND
Some people say my world will end
now that I have you as only a friend.
But I know they are wrong
For, you see, I am quite strong
and very soon "we" will be just a
memory
but always between us there will
be that chemistry.

When the time comes and we
should meet
How will we handle that
unavoidable feat?
Your new love doesn't like me
afraid of me she seems to be
Yet could it be that she knows best
and realizes that our love just won't
rest.

No matter what our hearts may say
there must never again come a day
when we look at each other with
hope
because together we just can't cope.
No matter that we will love each
other forever
all physical bonds we must now
sever.

To stay together we've tried and
tried
but to ourselves we've always lied.
The past seven years may have
been a mistake
and brought us both a lot of
heartache,
But I'm glad I went through it, for
in the end
I found you . . . My Very Special
Friend.

David L Barbe
A MOUNTAIN MORNING
Shadows fall on the misty morn,
Red sunrise as the mountains
warm.
On a lofty peak, a hoot owl calls
As the mists gather and daylight
falls.
Far away and to this world
unknown
A rooster crows from atop his
throne.
And in the wood so still and deep,
A grey squirrel rises from his sleep
To bark and scurry up the old oak.
As the winds whisper silent and
remote
I struggle to keep still and smile
within
And I am glad to be here as day
begins.
Far away from the world below
At peace with all and my heart
aglow,
I silently thank my God above
For all I see and the things I love.
Sitting silently in the woods, still
and deep
It's secrets free and mine to keep.

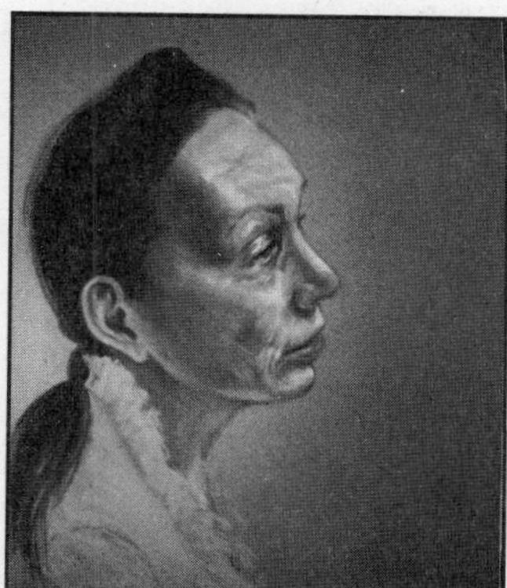

Betty Jane Hall Simons

Betty Jane Hall Simons
MARGARET'S LAMENT

Dedicated to the memory of my dear friend and colleague, Margaret Reppard.

Chaste, pure, assuredly no trollop,
Nonetheless, I gave you my
polyp.

Were you content? Not for a
minute
Since my body still had many
things in it.

I discovered quickly two ovaries
I had
So next I gave you my right
gonad.

Plundering and pilfering just
like a solon,
Damned if you didn't get part of
my colon!

Let's come to a halt, just give me
a pill
Or the next thing I know, my
parts
will be nil.

No courtship we had, with no
gifts was I showered,
'tis true nonetheless, I am
completely deflowered!

Jodie Pickett
SEASONS

This poem is dedicated to Donald, my love, my life, my wonderful husband.

Fall is here!
School bells, jack-o-lanterns, a day
of thanks.
Red and golden leaves fall
gracefully covering the barren
ground.
Before the last leaf falls, a
snowflake appears—
its intricate design so pure.
Winter, spreading its soft white
blanket over the earth.
A season full of a childs laughter
as they run and
slide down hills of white satin.
The cold air turning cheeks rosey
red, eyes all aglow.
Trees of tinsel, a jolly man full of
love.
Gray skies turn blue, billowing
clouds roll and drift.
Birds nest, the warmth of the sun
fill hearts with love—Spring.
Summer can't be far away—
sandcastles, salty
breezes, wedding bells—lazy days,
sultry nights.
Seasons, Mother Natures gift to all!

Elizabeth Paige Levin
WHY AM I WEAK?
Why did I call?
Why did I break down?
Why do I let my soul
Be tossed so around?

Oh, please stop,
Please stop letting yourself feel
pain.
Why go through it
Again and again?

Why do I keep at it?
Why do I still try?
I say I want you so,
But to myself I do lie.

For you don't love me as you did,
You don't want me any more,
Where my heart once was full,
Now lies a festering sore.

Stop beating yourself up
Until you just want to die,
Stop chasing after lost love,
Just learn to say Goodbye.

God only knows, I'LL TRY.

Linda Franell
MY PEN, MY INK, MY WORDS, I THINK
With this Pen
I thee write,
A set of light little verses,
Gay and bright.

Happy I am
to use this gift, this way
To brighten some lonesome one's
Otherwise gloomy day.

Let my pen slide
Across my paper now
To make all who reads this
Give a happy smile.

For God gives me the talent
And I put it in ink
We all have a mind
And I like to make mine think.

It gives me the feeling
I've done something for someone
Something someone else,
Has not already done.

I love to play
With words you see
A writer is something
I'd like to be

Joyce Stites
TELL OF HIS LOVE
I walk by my saviors side
He sent me from above
To fill the lives of mom and dad
and tell of His love
And Gods own hand is laying
His peace on everything
Thy lays in Heaven.
The love is on the earth
Love give it energy
Love gave it birth
Fill the lives of sons and daughters
And tell of His love.

Helen V Hill
ONE DAY FOR A WALK
To day is a beautiful day.
Although the birds have gone away.
The snow will come to stay.
So the children can go out and play.
To some the snow means trouble
But to some it's fun for lots of
children
When the snow has gone
Spring comes with lots of Joy.
The flowers bloom, the birds sing,
The grass grows to a beautiful
green.

Trudi McNeish
A WAY INTO YOUR HEART
The lawn is ironed; neatly pressed.
The weeping willow looks by far
his best.
Off in the distance, Children run:
Their silhouetted shadows taunt
the sun.
But childish laughter will refrain,
As love's umbrella dances in the
rain.
When sorrow claims them as its
own,
We'll know these fragile figurines
are grown.
How love, sadistic, takes control:
Reaching, grasping, maiming
every soul!
Yet, still I visualize your face,
Imagining myself in Queen Anne's
lace.
And tho' we may be worlds apart—
I swear, I'll find a way into your
heart!

Miss Shelby V V Smith
ENDLESS
Dark may be the night . . .
As I lay;
Thinking,
Wondering,
Dreaming about that special
something in my life . . .
Questions with no answers
Answers with no questions
Endless thoughts come to mind,
As I lay.

Dark may be the night . . .
As I sit;
Hoping,
Concentrating,
Looking for that special star in the
sky;
That'll lead me to my goal,
Beginnings with no endings
Endings with no beginnings

Endless thoughts come to mind
As I sit,
As I think,
Figuring out this mystery,
As I lay . . .

Mary Ann Blissick
FROM OUR LIPS TO GOD'S EARS

Someday soon I hope we can say to God, "Look there are no more wars and the hungry have been fed." "The naked have been clothed and there is nothing more to dread. We visit those in prison and we've turned the other cheek. But, could you work on disease, in this we've found defeat."

Now, look aroun Dear Lord, because we've really tried. We hold our brothers hand and we know we cannot lie. We thank thee for the flowers and the sun that always shines, we're working on the water's but we need a little time.

Man has destroyed a lot here, but we're really on the mend and we're grateful that our children have the chance to start again. So, you see you didn't fail God; we were just led astray and now we're working on tomorrow, starting with today.

Georgia D Anderson
MA MA KANGAROO AND LIL JOEY'S FATE!

To sweet Po Po from Mo Mo

Doin' the tango, ridin' her sled
Poor Ma Ma Kangaroo, fell dead!

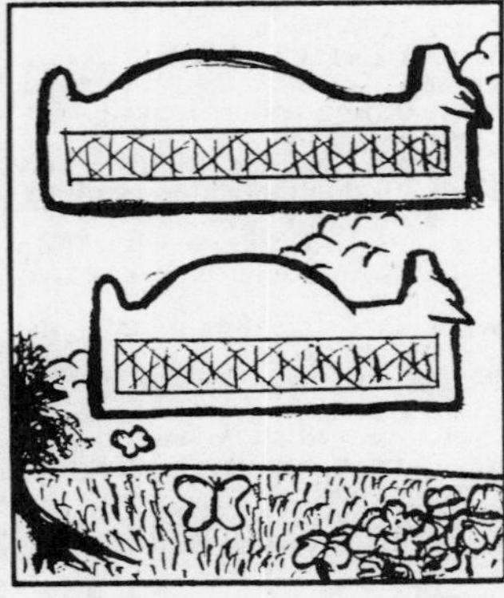

And sweet Lil Joey, in a battered bed!
Died alone, with a busted head!

Peggy Lee
MIDDLE AGE BLUES

Well Happy Birthday Brother, and here's to you!
You've now reached number 40 and feeling blue!
Like old middle age has taken its grip,
You feel that everything is starting to slip.
Your hair is getting a little more gray!
The eyesight is also weaker each day.
The reflexes are not nearly as quick,
The body feels all worn out and sick.
The teeth get bad, they cannot chew;
And sex is something you used to do.
You think life has gone, it's passed you by,
So much has happened at the wink of an eye!
Remember the best is yet to come.
When pressures of life let up some.
Worries are less as you start a new beginning.
More time for your mate as you start another inning.
Where you'll be called handsome instead of cute,
A real mature type sort of brute.
And what you see is more important to you!
"Now's the time to enjoy the things you do!"
Your sex is the best you'll ever get.
This life after forty is much better yet.
So Happy Birthday Brother, and have many more!
Believe me they get better the more that you score.

Helen Strey
HENRY HOFF OUR BELOVED NEIGHBOR

We miss you, Henry—
You 'cared for' us all;
Your friendly handclasp—
Your neighborly call—

Your witness was faithful
Your faith and love, strong;
With thoughts of your Saviour
All the day long!

Your influence on earth
Will continue to live
As you dwell in Heaven,
And continue to give. . .

We'll never forget—you rescued
Our Grandaughter's lamb
From the irrigation ditch,
Four waterfalls and a dam!

And my last words to you,
God directed me speak,
"Henry, you remind me of Jesus
With the little lost sheep!"

You helped us as neighbors,
Stay 'in the fold'
Of the Good Shepherd JESUS
By your witness so bold.

Is your message like Jesus' to Peter,
For us here below?
GIVE SPIRITUAL FOOD—GOD'S WORD
THAT ALL MAY GROW—

"Peter, do you love me?"
Three times Jesus did speak;
"Yes, Lord, you know that I do"
"Well, then, FEED MY SHEEP!!"

Anthony Cucci
A WOMAN CALLED IDA!

I wish to dedicate this poem in memory of my wife Ida.

There are times I stop and wonder?
Could you forgive—Can I forget!
Why do you run? Why must you hide!
You have gone I now know where!
I need you—I desire you by my side
Only your goodness brought you there
On my knees I shall fall!
You knowing there never be another
Hopeful you my darling to call?
Why is it this that I shudder?
May what I desire
A Woman called Ida.

Eunice G Jones
TRIBUTE TO MY HUSBAND

When it's twilight in the evening and the sun is sinking low, that is when my thoughts go back to days of long ago.

For that's when we were sweethearts, sweethearts fond and true, bless the day we took the oath that made me part of you.

We walked straight down the road of life, not knowing which way to turn, but with you by my side and God above, I'm sure dear, we will learn.

As we wandered down life's way, came blessings from above, a little girl and a little boy with us to live, cherish and love.

Was the answer to our dreams, we care for them so, they are our sunshine it seems; dear God help us to make them grow.

So, once more I turn to You, my faith looked up to Thee, no one else could ever have been so kind and true to me.

So let's put our holy faith in God and ask Him; I know He will, help us through the sod, dear God, help us up the hill.

Floyd Doremus
TO MOTHER

My mother is so very great,
And to me she is so dear.
Why do I just celebrate
My mother once a year?

She's always there when I need her.
She's constantly on guard.
She watches out for my welfare,
So living don't get too hard.

On mother's day we all recall
The many things she's done.
We often wonder when she'll fall,
As she keeps going on and on.

She never asks for much you know,
Just health and happiness.
She wants to see the healthy glow,
And hear the sounds of gladness.

To all the mothers on this earth,
We know you are the best.
We'd like to give you what your worth,
In health and happiness.

My mother, she is number one,
This day and then forever,
I'll never leave her all alone,
Our ties we'll never sever.

Kathy Lynn Veach Omer
BEING YOU

Don't rob yourself in being you
In trying to do what others do;
Don't pattern or copy or imitate
God has a plan, just patiently wait!

For you are best at being YOU
To your own self you must be true;
You are unique and a different kind
Your talents will surface you will find!

Don't try to fit in another's mold
in your own heart, the key you hold;
No way can you please every person's demand
Just do what you do and the BEST you can!

Of what others expect, don't be afraid
Follow your heart and the plan God gave;
Success comes with practice—don't give in to defeat,
Set your sights upon Victory and your goals you can meet!

For God has given us all to excel
So do what YOU do and do it well!
Don't envy a neighbor for his talent or skill
Just yield your own heart to the Creator's Will!

You're special, my friend,
Take courage anew—
For YOU are BEST
AT BEING YOU!!

Mary Rachel Hoover
THE BOOK BARN

To Moyer's Book Barn, the inspiration for this poem

Its rustic charm seems to beckon to
All who pass to come and see
The countless gems that therein be.
Marked by the ages and some near new,
Volumes and volumes are in full view.
For teens, adults and tots of three,
They stand on shelves with just one plea—

A desire to tempt each one of you.
The Immortal Bard would smile with praise
As would Bonaparte and Poe.
The founding fathers who formed this land
With the masters of the arts would raise
Their cups in tribute to bestow
A salute to the barn creator's hand.

David W Shepard
SNOWSAND

To be first is a place reserved for last—for you Lois, beauty conceals none with the smile of your grace. Phyllis & Bob, where my love is bound through the lifeblood of my family.

Before my eyes, through my windows haze
I have caught a glimpse of lost winter days

O' Dear Lord, the beauty I see
My soul you fill, a gift for me
Snow you send, to gladden thee.

Through sand so fine, dry is its fame
I see before me a crystal gleam
So long ago, this sight has been
I praise you Lord, for the snow you bring
White is its color, pure is its name.

Dorothy Pearson
A MOTHER'S PRAYER

Dedicated to Reggie Baker because of our love that will last forever on earth and in heaven.

She just got a letter from her son today—fighting a war—so very far away—

Dear Mom, please don't worry—someone has to fight to keep this country strong—it will be awhile—and we must right a wrong.

As she sat in the chapel—tears flowing from her eyes— she prayed that other boys would have a chance to survive—.

She remembered his childhood from long ago—.
Running through the fields— with his dog by his side— with a boyish grin—handing her flowers that he picked on the sly—.

The letter was never finished—and that's when she knew—that her darling boy had died.

She remembered more words, expressed by her son—mom! I have to do my best and stay until the job is done—.

Where someday we'll all be at peace. We'll all lay down our arms—and with God's love—we'll all be united as one.

Diane E Ramey
THE BUTTERFLY
I fall in love with the butterfly
but grasp its wings and make it die.

Love shines on me like a distant star;
I fear I'll never reach that far.

How can I bear to gaze upon
promise that tempts and then is gone,

with deepest yearning, ne'er fulfilled,
'til all desire in me is killed?

I walk the roads of earth and sigh
with longing for the butterfly.

Florence Hinkle Bailey
A TRIBUTE TO ALL MOTHERS AND FATHERS

Dedicated to L.C. "Burr" and Ethel Hinkle

There is a deep woe which comes to all mankind.
The heartache of watching Mother and Dad depart.
Grow weaker with the years, these signs
Of advancing age to those we love, break our hearts.

A few more years now, we can't have them long.
Their bodies are old, they are weary.
Father says, "The Old must make way for the young."
We know he is right, their aches make their life dreary.

A few more years and we dare not think,
We only love them more, for them do more.
They have lived their life almost, they are on the brink,
Oh, God! Bless them, help their souls to soar.

Up to Thee for gentle love and care.
It will be an empty time, when they are no longer here.
The only way it can be faced,
Is with Your sustaining Love and Grace.

Richard R VanOverbeke
CONFESSION OF AN ALCOHOLIC
I've lived and walked a tumbled road, only a
tragic event lets my story get told.
Too many times I've woke up on the edge, wondering
why me? Should I jump off this ledge?
Yet I didn't give up, I kept plugging away. But
this haunting inside me seemed here to stay.
I denied and denied, ignoring my friends. Just
kept living life like there was no end.
Suddenly I realized as I lay in the night, if I
keep living this way I could never find light.
Change isn't easy, but then neither is life. If
I didn't stand up, I'd be cut down by the knife.
My message is simple in this story I've told, I want
to live my life, until I'm good and old.

Ronald Reavis

Ronald Reavis (A.K.A.) Omar Ahmad Alshareef
LIFE

To my loving Daughter Nicole Turner (A.K.A.), Nura Bekkah Alshareef

---

Some people see life as only an illusion
That's filled with hatred and massive confusion
Whose desire for life is no more than dreams
When will they awaken to what life really means

Other people see life as being Russian roulette
When the game is over there's nothing but death
For those kind of people, it's the easy way out
But still, they never knew what life was about

Life is a condition of a course of living
Life can be many things if one is willing

Life is a reality, life isn't a dream
The duration of existance is what life really means

Life is the one thing everyone enjoys
Life is a song of love and X-mas for girls and boys
Life is knowing that the freedom bell will ring
Life is everything that one wants to cling

Find your destiny and set yourself a goal
Grab with both hands to keep a light hold
And give life a chance to become your friend
And many things to you, life will send.

Jeanne Fee
BLACK ROSE
I see this world as an ugly garden,
a desolate place,
Filled with thickets and weeds,
known as the human race.

A Gardner was sent, where
nothing grows.
He looked over the land and
found a Black Rose.

He knew it needed light and
rays from the sun,
The thickets were cut, weeds
pulled, one by one.

He knelt down before it and
reached out his hand,
I bid you farewell now, He said,
I hope you can understand.

The rose wept silently, each
tear became a thorn,
Questions were asked; why am I here,
why was I born.

He had nothing else to offer,
nothing else to say,
He left her that awful
gloomy day,

To stand alone as the story goes,
Alone am I,
I, the Black Rose.

Susan L Moak
WHAT ARE DREAMS?
Are they full of screams in nightmares?
Or icecream at country fairs?
Are dreams about caring and sharing?
Or passion and lust?
Do you begin by talking to people wearing the latest fashion?
Or just the people you trust?
In them, do you forgive and forget?
Or re-live and regret?
Are there hellos and good-byes?
Or hatred and lies?
Are they entirely about love?
Or the Great Creator up above?
Do you ever dream of people who are always so kind?
Or of certain people, you sadly once left behind?
Do you dream of a world that's hard and cruel?
Or where there's a king to always rule?
A place you'd like to accent—
A war you'd like to prevent—
Do these things ever cross your head?
When you're alone asleep in your bed?
Do you ever dream of walking along the beach in the sand?
Or does your dream take you to a foreign land?
Do you ever dream of your father, or your mother?
So tell me, do you dream in black-and-white?
Or do you dream in color?

Rychele Ann Howe
TO BE WITHOUT LOVED ARMS
To be without loved ones is to be without life.
Parents are a foundation to eternal love and life.
When gray clouds appear, that life is gone.
To feel a young life die, to be done so young, so hurt . . .
Yet it's dead to loved ones, doesn't exist past a picture on T.V.
They remember the good times . . . the sad times . . .
Yet never the hard times that cry for the arm of a loved one.
A young woman waits in the black shadows for a light.
A light, far, far, down a tunnel, a tunnel that has no end . . .
Unless a loved arm dips into the shadow to pull her out.
She waits . . .
waits . . .
waits . . .
Years have gone by, she is older, still alone, with no loving arm . . .
Wait! Is that a light?
There! There is an arm . . . Yes, an arm!
Is she saved? Yes!
The arm winds its' love around her,

draws her close to a body.
She lifts her head, the tears
running like a newborn river.
She sees a face, blue eyes filled
with tears,
tears of sadness, tears of sorrow.
She hears a voice . . . sees the lips
move.
Her heart rings with joy, she is
reborn, forgiven, loved.
She, the young woman, is home, in
love and happiness.

Beth Easter
HOW IN THE WORLD DO THE TREES GROW

To Mae, my sister and her brilliant ideas. I love you. Horsie

---

The sun shines bright
The wind blows slow
But how in the world do the trees
grow?

The grass is green
The birds are in flight
In the dark hours of the night
The scream of new life is in sight.
But how in the world do the trees
grow?

Peace is few
War is not right
Life is made up of Love and Fight.
But how in the world do the trees
grow?

Your minutes are limited
Seconds are lost
Time is the answer
In the few hours that it costs.

It also helps the trees grow.

Darla B Holt
UNTITLED
Sitting and writing,
Thinking and fighting
To rid me the pain
That makes me keep lighting
Those candles of life
That burn far too slow,
And keep me tied here,
Not where I should go
Those burning, consuming candles
That my past keeps lighting
The ones that only burn,
And not lighten my fighting

Amy Joy Fase
SPECIAL FRIEND

Dedicated to: Miss Julie Kortman, thank you for your care and friendship. You're truly a special friend.

You're a special friend
whose always there for me.
You're a special friend,
God's love in you I see.
You're kind, sweet and caring,
patient, loving and sharing.
Many times I think of you
and the good things that you do.
You're a special friend
who's needed everyday,
You're a special friend
through and loved in every way.
God is working miracles through
you,
it shows in the things you do.
You're an example from above,
God shows through you
His abundant love.
You're a special friend
whose care I treasure so,
You're a special friend
whose love and joy I know.
Thank-you for giving time for me,
God has handed you the key—
To touch many lives with your care,
I appreciate the way you share . . .
yourself.

Andrea M Garcia
SOMETIMES IT'S HARD

To someone very special to me with lots of love.

Sometimes it's hard
To keep the love in your heart
When things don't work-out
And your falling apart

Sometimes it's hard
To take life day by day
When you know what you feel
But not what to say

Sometimes it's hard
To be just "Good Friends"
When love is still there
And a relationship ends

Sometimes it's hard
To admit you were wrong
When someone you love
Has been hurting too long

Sometimes it's hard
When three words mean so much
When you say "I love you"
It's the heart that you touch

Judy D Swartz
ROCKY MOUNTAIN HIGH
Envision those mountains and get
your high,
They can overpower you until you
sigh,
With joy and wonderment—the
greatest content,
Their power and majesty no man
could invent.
Have you heard the eerie tales that
echo from their canyons,
About mountain men and the sleek
mountain lions?
Stories of conquest and tales of
death,
Of riches so vast it grasps your
breath.
Of Jeremiah Johnson and the
"Grizz" so fierce,

Of wild Indians with arrows that
pierce,
Of hooves clattering through
pebbles as the stallion herds his
mares,
To tease 'em and please
'em—whatever he dares.
Of rivers so swift and gorges so
deep,
Just to look down gives you a creep.
The beauty of their snowcaps in
spring unfold,
Waterfalls, new life and mysteries
untold.

Rebecca Parr
A SHADOW OF LOVE
Quietly moves the dream
As if never to awake
Drowned in the thoughts and
the beat of a heart, it is an
obsession—a shadow of love

Only a stange feeling remains
Full of the ultimate mystery—
Beyond the hope and pain
There lies an uncertainty masked
and hidden

Uncovered, bares a soul crying
So distant, a mere spark in a fire
to never grow beyond the
imagination

Love sighs like a waning spirit
blown by the wind as pages of
tomorrows
A caress that spreads
Leaving only a smile

Time has taken a toll on the shell
of affection protected for so long
A love uncomparable to nature
And above life itself

It is a sadness to be greeted
By the shadow as a glimmer of
hope
Falls into darkness

Carolyn Wynn
I CAN FEEL NO MORE
I went to the same place that we
went to before:
I stood and waited for the magic
that I can feel no more;
I never felt anything, why did I let
you go out of my life that day:
I don't need, or love you, is what I
had to say;
I felt the magic in my life slowly
fading as away I did walk,
Your face I still see as you asked
honey, lets talk.
No need, I said as I felt the tears
on my face,
Why was I hurting this way;
You're in my heart to this very day;
But today, I went to the same place
we went to before;
I stood and waited for the magic
that
I can feel no more.

Carmela Gonzalez Garcia
CUANDO EL ALMA SEA LIBRE

Con Amor A Mi Madre Otila, Ya Mis Ninas Esmeralda y Paloma.

Cuando mi alma sea libre
de la materia en que esta
yo volare a otros mundos
la paz ansiada a buscar.

Cuando mi alma sea libre,
yo buscare lo anhelado
y encontrare al Dios
aqui . . . no encontrado.

Cuando mi alma sea libre
yo quisiera viajar al infinito,
sin limite de tiempo en la
distancia
hasta hallar la luz que necesito.

Cuand mi alma sea libre
yo no quiero flores
ni rezos, ni lagrimas hipocritas
ni falsos sinsabores.

Ire a ese mundo tan sonado,
sin odios, envidias, ni rencores,
donde no haya guerras entre
hermanos
sin fronteras, ni razas . . . ni
colores.

Kaye Chedister Beaudry
A BIRTHDAY MISSED

To my mother, Edna Burns Chedister, a fellow poet, who fostered my love for writing.

To wish you joy, happiness and love
was my intent
but,
Your birthday came and your
birthday went,
and
What's this I see, no card
was sent.

Oh dear, Oh dear, scurry, scurry,
I must send that
card in a hurry,
So you won't worry and you won't
fret, for even though it is late
your birthday wish is truly meant.

John Richard Ford
THE DEATH OF A DREAM
Of her I dream, the beautiful
maiden who loves me. In her
presence I am handsome and
heroic, as I would be. In the
forest of my imagination we walk
together, we share a
timeless world that will last
forever. To be with her is
all I desire but Reality takes me
from her and I am alone.
I strive to return to her side but this
world of Darkness
and Despair creates a barrier of
Hopelessness and Doubt
between us. Of her I invision
until at last I can no longer
bear to think of her, for to be
without her is the greatest
misery. This world has destroyed
her, from the Land of Dreams
I heard her pleas for mercy,
towards her I ran. Upon the
wind I could hear a melodie errie
and old. She sang a song
so sweetly, she sang a song of
Death, she sang a farewell
to me with her final breath. I sat
beside her in the place
where she was slain, her gray eyes
stared up at me void of
life, her raven hair flowed gently in
the breeze. Her lonely
grave is visited by no one, but me
and from it I can never
be free.

Judith L Engen
P.O.W.—M.I.A.

Dedicated to: SP4 Peter A. Schmidt USA 8-15-70 LAOS

I see a light so far away
I dream at night—the U.S.A.
I stand alone across the sea
From one great nation dear to
me.

The years have past—the light
grows dim

The days are long—my dreams
are thin
So far from home, so much alone
Please nation great—Please
bring me home.

Behind you left me years ago
My faith and hope shall never go
For I believe with all my heart
The light that shines across the
sea—
Shall bring my country back for
me.

Phoebe Juanita Vaughn
THROUGH MY FATHER'S EYES

A dedication to the memory of my late Father, Samuel Franklin Fitzgerald

Come hither little one and light up
my life, as the
moon illuminates the sky of the
night.
For you are my goddess of the
moon.

I will protect you in your youth, as
you will protect
me when I am old and gray and
weak and frail.

And even though father time will
come knocking at your
door, you will remain ageless and
someday take your place
among the stars in the sky.

Now that my time on earth is
nearing its end, I must admire
you from a distant place of no
return.

But my love for you is endless and
forever,
a love only a father can have for
his child.
My Phoebe, my goddess of the
moon.

Ida Lipshultz
SHARING

Dedicated to Julie with love—Ida

A thing of beauty
Becomes more beautiful when
shared
Colors, ecstasy in sounds are
enhanced
Our souls are bared
Our feelings more advanced
In mutual harmony
Life for two people who care
Becomes full of meaning
When all is there to share
And a radiant joy comes through
gleaming!

Mattie Boney
MY LAST DO NOTS

When you hear of my death do not
think of flowers to send,
far better, help a child to bloom.

When you look at my coffin do not
grieve, I am not there,
The Savior has taken me to dwell
in Glory Land.

When you go to my grave do not
think of doom, have faith and
hope,
think of life's pleasant
memories, too many to list.

When you stand by my grave do
not cry, I can not hear,
I am listening to Heaven's
Golden Band.

When you look at my grave do not
dispare, God is near,
I prepared many a year for this.

When you think of my death do not
neglect to
dwell on God's splendid promise
of eternity.

Virginia Sharpe
FALLEN ANGEL

To "Geneva—for believing in me Galluch"

An angel fell down from the sky
Her wings in disarray
With saddened eyes I watched
As she looked up to say
My Lord, My God,
What have I done
That thou should anger so??
Said he—Thou art fallen angel now
Ye walk with me no more—

No, No My Lord—I beg of you
She pleaded hopelessly
I promise to obey
And to worship ye The King . . .

From side to side he shook his head
And then these words were said—
No longer shall ye walk along
My island of the dead—

Alone, confused—and lost
She wandered in a daze—
This earth would be her new abode
She'd have to learn its ways—

Alberto Campa
THE MAN WHO LOVED YOU

I knew that man,
that today battles,
with death, who is relentless,
and cold, that makes eternal
repose.

You who loved him,
till his last breath,
with of any reproach,
with out a gaze that would hurt.

That pride of man,
who feels wounded an ever,
near death,
the one who toast's his last smile.

That one who leave,
you with a reminder of presedence,
the fruit of his love,
that son so lovable.

That tomorrow will grow up,
conserving then in his memory . . .

Hazel Alycia Marconi
SEASON'S FOREVER

The leaves are falling, one by one,
We feel the half warm beams of sun
Ah, sad weak days are here again . .
Gloomy weather, damp with
rain . . .

To me, it is the saddest thing
to lose the beauty that was spring
All new and bright, each day a song
With promise of a season long . .

Life is a promise ever gay,
While summer pushes spring away
And burst forth brighter then
before,
She's here, She smiles! she's at
your door,

Ah', eager summer to begin,
To bring those lazy days again
As sudden as you came in spring,
You left, when fall came rushing
in . . .

Teressa Leach
THE STAR

I saw a star that was so bright,
It was to guide me with its light.
Over hills and over mounts,
There were so many I could not
count.
And when I thought I could go no
more,
I saw a wooden stable door.

I opened the door so big and wide,
And breathlessly I stepped inside—
The animals all smiled so proudly,
And Mary whispered, "Come and
see."
And when I saw him lying there,
I asked her if she would care?

And in my arms I held him near,
For he was God's Son, so precious
and dear.
And then without warning,
I awakened to the morning.
And now it seems, it was all in my
dreams.
But wait, not only is it in my
dreams, it's in my heart,
And that's where, I think,
Christmas should really start!

Vickie Mulanax Fenderson
TUMBLEWEED

The wind forever blows
As you roll through life.
Once in a while the wind slows;
You wish for roots, but move on.

The open fields call you
Adventure carries you away.
Brief encounters, there have been
a few
But you move on, unable to stay.

You, my love, are a tumbleweed
You have touched many lives,
there'll be more.
Roll on, my Tumbleweed
Remember . . . I Love You.

James o Crouch
THE SHADOW OF A ROSE

I'm the shadow of a rose
The delicate beauty everyone
knows

I'm one of the casting of a dozen
Sent to share because of loving

I can fill your eyes with such happy
tears
And bring back memories
throughout the years

As a shadow of a flickering thought
I'll always be the memory of love
when sought

As my shadow fades away
So goes the dawn of another day

But remembering forever that
wonderful sight
I'll gladly fade into the night

Thank God for letting my rosebud
bloom
And giving me the aroma of loves
perfume

Farrell Blaine Collins
BLUNDERING LOVE

This poem is dedicated to Eve. Thanks for what you have taught me.

A first love lingers on with rapture,
a thing of precious beauty still.
They met and loved, and sinned;
thereafter, and passions won
against their will.
For twenty years she let him rule
her, bore their angels, kept them
fed.
Now how could he have thought to
fool her? He broke his vows and
left her bed.
Oh time, drag on, may eyes
awaken, and teach them when
true love is near.
For you are moving ever faster, the
scene is changing year by year.
He waited for her fits of anger,
thought her jewels of love had
fled.
She dueled with love and truth and
rapture, her sorrow brought her
tears instead.
Blundering love, blundering
blundering love, they failed to
teach it at my school.
But would it matter, make a
difference, it's hard to teach a
blundering fool.
Their first love blossomed in a
valley, between the hills of green
and gold.
He went away, not of his choosing,
a war must have its future told.
When he returned, they built their
mansion, a home of love, and
work and play.
Their offsprings went away to
college, indiscretion ruled his
day.
Time has not improved his image,
he will have to take his lumps.
He has made a bed to lie in, lacking
legs, and arms, and bumps.
Oh! blundering love, blundering,
blundering love.
You have learned it now you fool,
what a way to go to school.
Blundering, blundering,
blundering love.

Gregory L Lawson
BE YOURSELF

To all the people I love and to that special one that I'll always love.

"To be or not to be?" That is the question.Competition seems to be a way of life, but we waste too much time trying to prove we're better than the other person. If we spend less time trying to prove ourselves and just concentrate on being ourselves. Being yourself at times may not be all you expected it to be, but not being yourself isn't what you hope it would be. Remember if you're not happy with yourself don't expect others to be happy about you. Being yourself is no crime.

There's only one reflection in the mirror when you're standing in front of it and that is only you. Why be anyone else? When we have enough problems being ourselves. "To be yourself and not worry about being anyone else." That is the answer.

Mary Frances Davis
THE CAROUSEL OF LIFE

I'm on the carousel of life,
Going up, going down, going all around.
And all that's happened has shaped me.
Helps me keep my feet on the ground.

There just aren't any more surprises
Tho' everyday is new.
The hurts seem to be so many,
The highs so few.

And then along comes a beautiful rainbow
With colors more brilliant than ever before.
And it happens to me again:
I'm happy once more.

Thank God for each and every rainbow,
Even if there are not too many.
I'd rather experience one and lose it
Than never to enjoy any.

Linda Goble
GOING OUT OF STYLE

The Father wrote His Laws for us in stone so long ago.
And He has never changed them.
We must follow them, you know.
Sins of sex and lust have now become acceptable in this day;
But Jesus still is crying o'er the dreadful, awful way
we carry on ignoring the laws we know are true.
Adultery is still a sin. I know that.
So do you.
We must not simply rationalize with others all around
that everyone is doing it. God's love is so profound
that He'll forgive us anything. But we must come and ask.
Confession and repentance is still our own true task.
I pray, dear Lord, that sins of flesh will soon do a turnabout
And as fashions change, dear Jesus, let adultery just go out
of fashion. Let the circle turn full 'round.
Let people seek Your will again where purity is found.

Amen

Margaret W Cain
YESTERYEAR

To the LOVE that is my LIFE

Yesteryear is dead and gone
With all it's yesterdays.
Some were filled with promise
And others . . . to my dismay.

And as I look them over,
I find to my delight,
The days that seemed dark and cloudy
Made the others . . . more shiny bright.

And . . . now . . . I fully realize
That all were in preparation.
For I perceive that it's the here and now
That fills me with elation.

For today well lived . . . becomes
A yesterday with no regrets.
With precept upon precept
I soar, as with the eaglets.

So here I stand
In wondrous ecstasy.
Because, my friend, it is as true for you
As it is certainly true of me.

Lawrence Mitchell Jenks
SOMETHING MISSING

When writing this poem, it generated thoughts of my heart. I've only one person to dedicate my frequent thoughts while writing this poem, Casey Conklin.

It's a subtle feeling that I miss, it's in the way we used to kiss.
This feeling comes in many ways, the feeling begone its fumbled away.
Forever my heart will reach out to you, the love is like the blue rolling sea, never to subdue
My feelings for you that I encase, enchants me so to suppress is to waste.
Tho sleep or wake my thoughts always say, I'll pray you be with me somehow, someway.

Tami Nixon-Humphrey
MY MOTHER'S EYES

Throughout the years of childhood
I grew to learn one thing
That there is nothing quite as precious
As the love a mother brings.

Here eyes are like the ocean
As deep as the river's flow
Bluer than the summer sky
And as bright as the sun may glow

As age becomes a grace to her
It brings her no disguise
I wonder at the depths of love
In my mother's eyes.

Her tears are drops of silver joy
That feed our hearts through time
And looking at myself I ask,
"Will there be such love in mine?"

And as I continue to go through life
It comes as no surprise
That never can I nor will I forget
The love in my mother's eyes.

G T Woodard

G T Woodard
PARENTS, WHERE ARE, YOUR CHILDREN?

To my family, and all the families around the world.

Did you take them out to play, or did you send them on their way?
Parents, where are, your children?
Are they out there in the dark? for there's a pusher in every park.
Parents, where are, your children?
Today, are they in school, or have they broken just one more rule.
Have you checked to see if they are there, or you don't have the time to spare.
Parents, where are, your children?
Their friends have a car, your neighbor runs a bar, they said they were not going far.
Their peers will cheer, you will sit in fear, hoping to hear, the key in the door, or don't you care anymore?
Parents, where are, your children?

Virginia Dare Casteel

Virginia Dare Casteel
MOUNTAIN HEIRS

Dedicated to all the Mountain Heirs of Scott County, Virginia.

A special people are Appalachian Mountain Heirs.
We grew up on the mountains' slopes or in its' shadow.
Descendants of pioneers who settled there,
To them our unique dialect we owe;
Our speech with smithereens of Old English
Preserved by the blue-misted mountains we know,
By isolation and ruggedness that still flourish.

We see mountains as God's masterpieces,
So we feel close to him on a mountain trail or summit.
No church or cathedral can bring such peace,
Such renewing and enrichment of body and spirit.
These visible crafts of our invisible God
Create within us a oneness with God and his planet
In our wild, high and remote places where tall trees nod.

No matter how far from our mountains we roam
We take a part of them with us—their music and beauty.
The mountains, we always call our home.
They are there—waiting for us—our security.
Highways are carved through our stubborn mountains,
But it's realm of wildlife and quiet beauty,
We pray, will remain untarnished for eons.

Cheryl Ann O'Neill
THERE UPON—THERE WILL BE

To all who have loved and lost to tragedy upon the sea

There will be a smile and a flower,
a knock upon the door,
a while and a shower
a wave upon the shore,
There will be a kiss and a touch,
a hand upon the hand,
a Ms. and a must,
a ring upon the man;
There will be a man upon the shore
and a keepsake in my heart,
and there upon the shore,
there will be my heart;
There will be a river and a dam,
a boat upon the dock,
a quiver and a slam,

a tick upon the clock,
There will be a tear and a cry,
a drop upon the cloth,
a fear and a sigh,
a wish upon the cross;
There will be a man upon the shore,
and a keepsake in my heart.
and there upon the shore,
there will be my heart.

Diane L Hemminghaus

FOR ALICE

So Here You Are
Saying Those Words
I Wanted So Desperately To Hear
In Earnest From You Then.

I Reached Up To You
Like A Daffodil In Bloom;
Giving My Love
Without Hesitation.

You Chose To Play
"Loves Me, Loves Me Not"
And The Petals Fell . . .
Leaving Me Empty.

But Just Like Spring Flowers
I Knew I'd Grow Again;
Bringing Forth New Colors
To Smile In The Sun.

Your Words Are Falling Gently,
Though,
Settling In My Mind.
Preserved Like All Good Memories;
A Fond Ending For A Fairy Tale.

Eloise (Riccardi) Johnson

OUR LOVE

To the one and only man who made these feelings be . . .

You came to me out of a memory . . .
Made dreams, fantasies and being in love a reality.
From when our eyes silently met our love was meant to be,
Our hearts whispered softly and our souls touched for eternity . . .
You caressed my spirit as no man has ever done,
In loving you I am able to capture the brilliant rays of the sun.
Nothing in this universe could make me more committed or true—
I pledge my love and that love is my vow that binds me to you.
There has been a mountain in our path since we first met,
Though the climb is high, your love is worth every step . . .
You are phenomenal . . . So the cost I will gladly pay—
I'll love you for always . . . . . Forever and a day.

Susan D LaRue

WANDERING WATERS

Wandering Waters so deep and so blue, as deep as my love for you. Like tides and waves so low, you kiss me and my blood flows. As tides and waves so high, you touch me gently and I could fly.

Whisper in my ear and I shall certainly hear. Tell me of your love and joy, and I shall become a Dove flying with poise. Listen to the soft breeze, touch me gently and squeeze.

Feel the whispers of the ocean's air, now we become a pair. Touch my hair and I shall feel fair.
Kiss me tender and I shall surrender.
Look into my eyes and I shall become wise
We shall share our best, and build a loving nest

We shall sing songs of joy and love, then fly away as Doves. No longer to be lonely, now to love one another only

Debra Brown Taylor

JANUARY TREE

To my husband, Wayne, for his support;—My sons, Jaarad and Wyatt, for their faith and encouragement;—and my mother, Myrtle Cable Brown, for her never-doubting inspiration;—With much love to all.

Statuesque lady, once grand
adorned, adored
Stands lonely now stripped of
all her glory,
Dry and barren, sadly of no use,
Brittle, shriveling, crinkling
tired with age

But Once We helped her dress
for her big day
Small faces beamed, admired
her bright array
Where once her proud arms
Cuddled splendor, now are empty
In her prime, she glowed
in glitter, now reserved
for future growing maids

I watch as sanitation workers
Coldly heft her on that
Ugly hearse.
I remember beauty of
past days.

Howard B Jenkins

AN OLD GREENWING'S LAMENT

To all those robbed by time of everything but the memories of wonderful experiences shared with their fathers.

"Hey Daddy, I want to go fishing,
down at the old fishing hole;
Hey Daddy, I want to go fishing,
I'll get the bait and the pole.
Hey Daddy, I want to go fishing,
I'd give my heart and my soul,
For a moment with you, We spent so few,
Down at the old fishing hole.

Hey Daddy, I want to go camping,
Up where the skies were so blue;
Hey Daddy, I want to go camping,
I'll get the gear and some food.
Hey Daddy, I want to go camping,
I'd give my heart and my soul,
For a moment with you, We spent so few,
Up where the skies were so blue.

Hey Daddy, I want to go hunting,
Over at Old Miller's Run;
Hey Daddy, I want to go hunting,
I'll get some shells and the gun.
Hey Daddy, I want to go hunting,
I'd give my heart and my soul,
For a moment with you, We spent so few,
Doing the things that were fun."

Roberta J Brown

STILL

You asked me if I <u>still</u> love you.
I get excited whenever you walk
into a room
and I'm there.
Just the mere presence of you
sends a surge of passion through
my body
and I shiver.
And all I want to do is lie down
beside you
and talk.
Feel your warm breath on my skin
see your eyes moist, twinkling
smell the wilted fragrance of
cologne
on your neck
taste the salt on your lips
hear your soft voice forever locked
inside of me.

Sometimes I awaken in the night
and am embarrassed
at how tightly
I've wrapped myself around you.
And I turn
away, only to have you
pull me to your chest.
And the passion starts again.
And you need to ask if I <u>still</u> love
you?

Laurie Lee Watkins

TOO MANY ACRES WE SEE

Is there not a tree for every soul
A drop for every pain at the end of
a rainbow
Is there not an uncertainty for
everything you know
While a man symbolically holds
your hand
To give strength and tribute to
every tree.

The innocent heal daily; the evil
suffer regularly
And there's the many inbetweens
Who cannot grasp the means of
either—
They are neither
All beautiful or all ugly
But composed of the best and worst
Of all captured and free.

Diago, who pities your existence?
Your pain and shame glows in
resistance
Of your need to care, and your
cursed bitterness fighting,
screaming, BEWARE!

And there's a sun ray and a shade
of colour
For every soul.
There seems too many realistic
ways
To be inwardly burnt and
outwardly froze
As even flames feel cool at first
And when the best is misconceived
the worst
We must understand
That there is an ocean for every
land
And a well of water and wine
Amidst every thousand acres of
sand.

Lucille Beiersdorfer

LUNARIA, LIKE A WOMAN

Lunaria, early Springtime,
Blooms in lavender and lace,
Joyful in her violet gown,
She sways with style and grace.

Lunaria, Silver Siren,
Weaves a magic spell,
Dances with the moonbeams,
Then lures the sun as well.

Lunaria, early in the Summer,
Her blossoms blow away,
Bright green seed pods growing,
Moonlight mystery holding sway.

Lunaria, Moon-kissed Maiden
Now bronzed by the summer sun,
Takes a season siesta,
Future dreams, bright hopes are
spun.

Lunaria, like a Woman
When her tan is stripped away,
Reveals her hidden beauty
In a Wintertime Bouquet! . . .

Jan Pauline

CELEBRATE

We live out our lives
day after day
while neighbors and loved ones
sometimes pass away.
In all of our pain and tears and
sorrows
we tend to forget the joy in this
horror.
Although they'll be missed
be joyous and bliss.
When Christians depart
it's just the start
of a life with our God
in a world way beyond.
What a happy occasion,
a time for celebration.
And knowing that your a
Christian too
should end your heartaches and
your blues.
Cause when your number's up
and your time is due
your bound for Heaven to be
with
your loved one and your God too.

Laura Marie Hernandez

VETERAN'S DAY

Veteran's Day, I'll never forget
as if it was yesterday
My mother said before we retired
"don't forget to pray
"For your brother along with
all the others"
"Who went to fight the war"
I remember once she said
my father's heart it tore
For he had been through that
HELL
a long, long, time before
But once upon a time there was
a cause to fight a war
Can you tell me what Vietnam was
for?
Was that the one for politics,
like so many government games
It's too bad most of their players
came back lame
Although some have, their bodies
and their souls
Who's going to give them back
their mind?
that were left in their foxholes
So who won anyway the
politicians or V.C.'s
Because of what I've heard and
seen here
It wasn't none of these

Anna Lee Johnson Gambill

FANTASY

An old man sat by his cabin door
while fireflies flitted by.
He yearned for greatness late in life
as he gazed at the starlit sky.
"I wish I were a king tonight, or

just a prince," sighed he.
"If I had honor in this world, I'd more contented be."

And as the humble creature flashed its small light to and fro,
The old man slowly settled back by his open cabin door.
He saw the brilliance of the stars that seemed to reign on high,
And wished his lot were as a star instead of a small firefly.

Suddenly through his troubled mind there came a simple thought,
Why have you in your latter years this power and honor sought?
Your health is fair, your comfort too, your life has been well spent;
Stars sometimes fall, their brilliance lost, so why not be content.

"I am content, the old man said, and thankful, Lord, I'll be,
For life and love and liberty and the joy of serving Thee."

Carolyn Row Barber
REQUEST TO MY DREAMS

Yes, come if you must to me this night,
You dreams, you stealers of sleep, you unrestful visions!
Sift into my slumbering mind when the gates of sleep
Have opened wide and I am far within their keeping.
I do not bid you welcome, but I have no choice,
For you will come unheralded, unasked, unwanted,
As silently as the clouds drift across the summer night,
Blotting the moon and stars from view;
But, as you steal beneath the velvet blackness in my brain,
I pray you to grant one favor, just for this one long night,
One small request to last through the emptiness ahead:
Let me walk in a cedar-sweet morning, early clad in dew,
Breathing the fragrance of the dawn,
And by my side place the one whom I hold most dear,
That I may measure his long pace with my own steps,
That I may listen to the low music when he speaks,
And see the Holy Light of Love in his dear eyes;
And, if you will be charitable,
Let us pause by the new, clear brook,
And let him hold my hand, and then perhaps
Bestow his soft kiss that is a benediction to my soul.
If this night shall bring me this
Even Paradise could not seem lovelier,
For I will have known the touch of my Lord through him,
And will have listened to the Ageless Song of Love.

Janet Lofgren
INSIDE MY PIANO

Inside my piano there's a song.
A melody somewhere that belongs.
I sit down every night and race the sun.
But it seems that I'm the loser—daylight won.
And it's hiding in the shadows in the dark.
It seems that I can never make my mark.
But my mind knows all the secrets, holds the rhyme —
so I'll have to try it over one more time.
The bottom of the ocean is so deep.
The highest heights of heaven I can't seek.
So I look to find the answers in myself,
but I only see the questions on the shelf.
I lay down next to you and hold your hand,
and I think I'll find the answers in a man.
But loneliness still stabs my very soul,
and I wonder if I'll ever be whole.
I'm a little bit of everything I see,
and a little bit of everything is me.
And the person that I am is all in doubt.
The person that I am is reaching out.
Do you love me as I am? I cannot change.
I cannot take it all and rearrange.
Though I'd like to take it all and start again,
I can't erase the past and make amends.

James Whitten
I'M NOT A MALE CHAUVANIST PIG

Dedicated to My Mother, Mrs. Edith Whitten

I'm not a male chauvanist pig,
but the male sex of a bird, I can dig.
He is so colorful and bright,
When she is colorless, but still a delight.
Unlike people who are split by color and race,

Different birds don't mind seeing a different face.
Bird life is so superior to ours,
They get from here to there without smelly cars.
I write this poem to all humanity,
Watch God's birds, they'll give you peace and sanity.

Aaron Robert Hutchison
GOOD DAYS

Good days
How good they are
Bad days
How bad they are
Half days
How half they are

Kristy Lynn Hathaway
QUEST FOR WISDOM

Brought forth upon this earth
With a will to survive,
We find our place among the horde
And fight to stay alive.
We're traveling our path in life
Through peacefulness and war,
Learning things along the way,
But longing to know more.
Knowledge has lifted us
High above the rest
And rescued us from perils
Along our never-ending quest.
As we grow older,
Growing wiser with the years,
We avoid senseless errors
And overcome our fears.
Our time here is all too short
And upon my passing I'll say:
Study the past, predict the future,
And live the present today.

Mary Jo Daniels
NOT FOR ME

I often burn the chicken
And sometimes even steak,
But worst of all is when I burn
My husband's favorite cake.

I used to try making bread,
But it rose up to the sky.
Into the oven, it would not go
And I've often wondered why.

Once a turkey I tried to roast
But it kept jumping from the pan.
It flapped it's wings and ran from me
Saying "catch me if you can!"

My husband came home one night,
No dinner was in sight.
He grew mad and out he went
To a restaurant for a bite.

Now my husband understands,
A cook I'll never be,
So I took to writing poems
For I do that best you see.

Evelyn Anderson Stroh
SISTERS

This poem is dedicated with love to my sisters, Lillian Abbott and Helen Stroh.

I've been thinking lately
about the many years of blessings
And how enchanting to have two sisters
as part of our family tree.

Most of our lives have been spent
miles and miles apart
But our love for each other
is as fresh as from the start.

I've been thinking and remembering
those special times in our lives
Especially when we were children
and we young ones totaled five.

Have been thinking about those frosty nights
all snuggled three in a bed
How we giggled and bounced on mattress
until we were little sleepyheads.

Remembering, too, those cotton stockings
all hung carefully in a row
At the foot of the old iron bed
ready for Santa and tied with a bow.

Like astonishing magic
the joyful memories come and go
Reminiscing has a way in autumn years
to make our lives on earth fullfilled.

Frank Lomprez
COSMIC FLIGHT

Let one butterfly lift me to cosmic scene . . .
to flit about and taste the sweet nectar of a dream
stars to guide my sight—sand to anchor my raging thoughts.
As a raft upon rainbow seas—
the butterflies, nector, dreams and stars . . .
power the engines that conquer space.
Sands on the seashore and rafts on the seas—
sands are worlds without number
rafts to rescue creation from waters
that drown and destroy
symbol and glyph
and dream and star
are the drama and stuff of things that are.

Alan Demeule
WINGS NOT YET GROWN

Let us carry this night upon wings
we have not yet grown
Let us lament to ones we have
neither yet held or known
For if growing and feeling is but a
small portion of life's
malediction then . . .

We must act childish when the
clock strikes humorous tones
We must laugh later after we
have difused Satan's clones
But no one person has
strength enough to incite the
rut we must . . .

Forgive rifle bearing fools shooting
up pauper sons
Forgive hollow text hallow
antonym gave birth to gluttons
Because opiate wings are theories
old carried tightly catacomb
slow growth feathers sprouting out
sacrum

E K Robe
VERNATION

Fallen plants
like aging people
suffer shock
as roots weaken
soils shift
with climate,
time,
wind.
They seem dull
split,
battered,
stunted,
silent
yet storing memories
like counted seeds
on invisible
abacus beads

when recalled
surge,
thrive,
surprise
next
Spring.

Frank Sturgell
FOREVER FRIENDS

The Whispers of Autumn Winds,
Through Sun Dryed Golden Grass.
Future Days And,
Yester-Years Gone Past.
Silent Thoughts Within My mind,
Of Friends Forgotten,
Left Behind.
Friends to Meet Along,
The Chosen Roads of Life to Find.
Friendship Forever,
Yours And Mine.

Lori M Mason
SOMEBODY'S ALWAYS SAYING GOODBYE

Somebody's leaving
Somebody's staying behind
Clinging to each other
Not wanting to go.
Echos of the empty train station
As you are left
Standing alone.
Trying to remember
That last look on their face
The look
That will haunt your memory
Forever.
The pain inside
Not easily erased.
Standing
With tears in your eyes.
The crying
That won't help
And not understanding
Why?
Somebody's always saying
Goodbye

Carmen Santiago

Carmen Santiago
NO MORE LIKE SISTER

I still don't believe I love you.
You are my dear friend who I treat
Like my sister. Here I am caring
for you
Like my woman. I take the airplane
To disappear. But soon I be there.
Your
Name appear in my mind and I
came out
So fast I can't resist myself far from
you.
Now I confess to you I love you so
much.
I think we can't have a big big love.
I remember one day I asked you a
question
And your answer was that you was
looking for
Your love and maybe you have one
near you.
About that time,I don't know what
you mean because
We continue to be good friends
until I discovered
That you was the woman I even
been looking for
Myself. Until the time came you be
my wife to ask
The second time in front of God.

Myrtle Poor
IN THE CIRCLE OF OUR ARMS

This poem is dedicated to Lenard, my loving husband in thanks for his love and support all these years.

As I lay in bed I can smell his
cologne, still lingering
On the pillow where he lay his
head.
I can reach out for him, and even
though
He is not beside me I can feel his
warm and loving body,
Lying in the security of my arms.
I can feel the magic of his fingers,
As they move upon my body, and
his kisses like
A hummingbird drawing nectar
From the sweetness of a spring
flower.
When he makes love to me,
He carries me to the highest
heights
And we land among the stars.
Then slowly we float down upon a
big, fluffy cloud
And closely lie together, with the
happiness and contentment
And love still upon us . . .
Then like a puff of a spring breeze
he is gone;
But I won't worry, because I know
Before long he will return, and
someday soon,
We shall remain as one forever
In the circle of our arms.

Jennifer Boldt
JACK FROST

To my mother, for loving me always.

Jubilant joyful painter,
Attacking all the windows,
Cold fingers do the painting,
Keen artistry at work,
Frozen beauty, never lasting,
Royalty, often fascinating,
Ordinary-looking, never,
Significant pictures everyone,
Touching all the panes of glass.

Zack Carden
YOU DON'T KNOW WHAT IT'S LIKE

Dedicated to all who keep FREEDOM alive . . . who in their own ways have made that word more than black ink on white paper.

I've got a story to tell you boy . . .
It's taken a long time to see.
Put down your placard alongside
my chair,
I'll tell you what happened to me.

Goddammit son . . . you don't
know what it's like!
Snotty-nose . . . liberal kid . . .
I gave my legs on the road to Tay
Ninh,
So you could demonstrate here!

Laying all night in a cold
monsoon rain,
Conscious . . . with death all
around.
Covered with blood as others
have been . . .
Some exchanged space with the
ground.

Go ahead, demonstrate! . . .
mock if you like,
That's what Democracy's about.
Someday your blood may flow
free for her life,
And then in turn you will shout . . .

Goddammit son . . . you don't
know what it's like!
Snotty-nose . . . liberal kid.
I gave my legs on the road to Tay
Ninh,
So you could demonstrate here!

John David Finney
UNTITLED

With much love to Ann and Terrah. Thanks for being a part of my life.

Innocence is but youth
That slay's thy body's temper
Relinquishing simple Love
No sorrow
Nor hatred
Until the age of wisdom,
When innocence is gone.

John D Tisdalle
TOP THAT

Though man may ride like a god in
space,
And walk within its span.
Only the God of space can change
a life,
And walk in the heart of man.

Now man can take the heart of
man,
And exchange it for another.
But only Jesus can take the heart
of man,
And make it like His brother.

Yes man can make a telescope to
see the light of stars,
A billion light years past Jupitor
and Mars.
But God can take a man and
cleanse the heart from sin,
Then lift him past those galaxies to
live forever with Him.

Well man can do a lot of things,
That appears to be like God.
But man will never make another
man,
From just a lump of sod.

Top That!

Ruby L Ezell-Freeman
AN EERY DREAM

As I chanced to walk through
London Square,
I saw a few of the villagers there,
A'shrouded in the foggy mist,
Looked as tho by Death they had
been kissed!

So pale were they, and so forlorn,
Standing, oh so still, on that foggy
morn,
As tho they were waiting for the
day,
When the Grim Reaper would take
them away.

Then hark! I heard the hooves
beating down!
To the east of us, t'was a
frightening sound!
Seemed the earth was shaken from
it's place in the sky,
As pale horse and rider thundered
on by!

Then I awoke, and I shook my head,
"T'was only a dream, thank God!"
I said,
So glad was I to be back in my
room,
Far away from all that death and
gloom.

Then I pondered o'er my eery
dream,
Which lasted for hours, to me it
seemed,
And I wondered of the message
there,
In those pale, drawn faces in the
misty air.

Audrey M Coyle
MY MOTHER

This poem is dedicated to my mother.

Her face was so wrinkled, a
roadmap of life.
It showed evidence of her years as
a mother and wife.
I washed her hair so fluffy and
white,
then set it with care to last a few
nights.
We went to buy groceries, the
shopping went slow.
She appreciated my help and
wanted me to know.
She held tight to my arm as we
walked across the street.
She made a comment about how
her feet
weren't dependable anymore,
and how hard it is to go to the store.
Old age had decended so swiftly it
seemed,
leaving her weaker than she'd ever
dreamed.
I decided to tell her how dear she
is to me,
and I remember well what I
learned at her knee.
I love her more dearly year after
year,
and I'll care for her because she's
so dear.
I'll never forget the lessons she's
taught
about love and responsibility.
I'm so thankful that God picked her
as a mother for me.

Helen Ormson Studley

Helen Ormson Studley
LOVE IS CARE

My love and affection to my family and friends, Only our spirits understand beauty, live with it, and grow with it.

Daisy White, Daisy Blue,
Daisy Gold . . .
I care for you.
Like a snowflake in the sky,

You are different to each eye.
When I look across the lake
Then I wonder should I take?
For your beauty is so fair
And I know that love is care . . .

Jeannine Ann Pittman
MY BOYFRIEND
There is a guy, that I know,
Who loves to sing and hates to sew.
He doesn't like dogs of green and blue,
And when he sees a cow, he sometimes goes, "Moo!"
He is sweet, if I may say.
He isn't blue, like showers of May.
He lives in Louisiana,
But his name isn't Suzanna!
He drives a car that is kind of small,
He isn't too short and isn't too tall.
He likes cars of all kinds,
And antiques that he finds.
He has hair of dark brown
But he isn't a clown.
His beard is red in color,
No, there can't be another.
Yes, it's him, the one and only.
It's my boyfriend, and he isn't lonely.

Betty L Frantz
THE POET'S DREAM

To all who still enjoy Poetry and Christmas

The towering Mountains
high above the Evergreens
partly hiding a Rustic Road
are sent to You
because they bear
a message
old but true

The Crystal lake at the foot
of the Highest peak,
and the Reddish cones
that have fallen
on the Icy Snow,
from the tallest and
smallest Trees,
want you to know

That the Mountains Above
and the Scene below
are combined with my thoughts,
for I wish to say
Merry Christmas to you,
in an old fashioned way.

But, when I took my brush
to paint this scene
it was a poet's dream,
with a wish for you,
MERRY CHRISTMAS and
HAPPY
NEW YEAR

Linda K Hulme
A SYMPHONY OF SILENCE

To my Sister Marjorie Jeanne Hulme Flanders For the Faith.

Quiet eyes talk . . .
Raindrops sing,
The winds screaming—
Silent Laughter.
Am I dreaming?

Never take for granted . . .
Illusions,
Simplicity,
Impossibility—
Time.

Basil Eldadah
THE JEFFERSON BROTHERS
As the story goes, it was springtime,
'round eighteen sixty-four,
Some folks from West Virginia,
Enlisted for the War.

They went by the name of Jefferson,
And them brothers John and Mack,
Took rifle in hand and left the house,
But neither could look back.

Well, one cold day a battle raged,
As bullets shot through the sky,
And the men would shield their faces,
As the bomb shells would pass by.

Now, Mack was in the bunker,
When he saw a woolen, blue shirt,
So he grabbed his gun and fired,
Till the Yankee hit the dirt.

The shooting stopped as Mack walked over,
To the body stretched on the lawn,
He turned it over and was gazing at,
The face of his brother, John.

So, the Jefferson brothers, they were no more,
From this day forever forth,
You see, Mack had stood 'long side the South,
But John fought with the North.

Sharon Despain
THE GIFT
Father gave me a talent, a gift to share,
and said "Now use it my daughter and show me you care."
This gift was given only to you, will you use it to serve me
as the spirit beckons you?

Will you use it to help me in my noble cause,
or use it for vanity and worldly applause?

The gift is there for you to use, for if you do not
think of the blessings you lose.
For in doing so you honor me, not just for today,
but for eternity.

I did not feel equal to the task He had asked me to do.
Can I complete the task, do I really dare?
Father I'll try for I really do care.

So I prayed, "Father help me to help you in your plan so divine,
and because the giver is so wise and loving and kind.
He will inspire and help you that your gift may shine . . .
That it might a blessing be, not just for today, but for eternity.

Now remember, there will be an accounting some day.
Did you use that sweet gift or lay it away?
Will it be recorded in the Book of Life, "Well done thou
good and faithful servant,"
through much toil and much strife.
Now I can't answer for you, but as for me and my part,
I want to answer "I really tried Father, with all of my heart."

Veronica W Elie
YOUR LOVE IN TIME

To my beautiful children: Tahnee Kimya, Chad Thomas and Micah Scott Elie—Wonderful, loving memories and sheer joy you've given me in my life. Love you always, Mom.

As the earth spins in its gravitational pull,
Your love turns me crazy;
As the winds blow east, your love blows my mind,
It reaches into the core of my being;
As fire heats the midnight sky and dances to the
Erratic eastern winds, your love makes me dance in
Uncontrollable rhythms;
As the moon and stars glow in the Master's
Brilliance and obey his will to form a perfect
Picture for the evening, your love touches my soul;
As the sun shines each day in all of its grandeur
And splendor, your love lights up my life;
As the rivers and oceans roar against the banks of
The sand dunes, your love fills my heart with a rage;
As time goes on and on, my love for you will never cease to be...
It will live on until eternity.

Kenneth C Kuester
REFLECTIONS BY A CAMPFIRE
I think that I shall never see
A man as humble as a tree,
Who yearly sheds his verdant dress
To stand, unclothed, the winter's test.
Who's home to all; man, beast, and fowl,
Including one lone great horned owl:
Whose blooms in spring, (Oh Wondrous Sight!)
Are worn as quietly as a right.
Whose leaves, though grown without refrain,
Both shade the sun, and shed the rain.
Whose luscious fruit, when fully ripe,
Is freely given, with no fight.
Who's stood through wind and storm and frost,
Whose fate is finally to be tossed
In fire, in whose warmth I toast.
I've never, ever heard him boast!

Marcia Ellison Wise

Marcia Ellison Wise
IN MEMORY OF DAD ON FATHERS DAY

This poem is dedicated to my father, Fred J. Ellison, who passed away, August 27, 1978; In W.VA.

I sit here thinking back so far, about my Dad,
And how wonderful the memories are.

He was always there whenever you were in need,
And his advice I always did heed.

In my eyes he was big and very strong, and he was always singing little songs.

He loved good food, and as a fisherman he was the best, and at everything he did, He always passed the test.

He did his best to raise me, teaching me right from wrong, and I sure do miss him now that he is gone.

I know he is in good hands with the good Lord up above,
And I'll see him again someday, once again to share that special love.

Dad, you're in my prayers each
night when I pray for the Lord
to guide me right.

Thank you Dad for being my
Father, for I am proud to be your
daughter.

Warren Sheehan III

THE FINAL SIN

We come into the world blind and
mute . . . except for a cry
Time passes—opinions are
formed—influenced—
Some humanities subside
No one is born to hate
To pollute the world,
Performing actions and words
which can only be learned.
The teacher stands with serpent
tongue, grinning as it swirls.

This is a bad scene for everyone
now.
It is not meant to be changed . . .
Though many grow to see and
speak
We may not help it be rearranged.

The rain will always fall, as will
cold snow,
And the damage
Will be done
Before the useless sirens blow!

So now we stand here like a meek
shadow cast
Upon the presence of
The nuclear bin,

And wonder how we ever gave
them the right to commit
The final sin.

Sharon Kay (Johnson) Call

HANDS OF TIME

To Raymond & Beverly Johnson on their 45th wedding anniversary from their daughter with love

---

If I could turn the hands of time
back to the days gone by,
I'd turn them to a time
when I was merely a small fry.

Things were so simple way back
then
compared to life today.
The biggest worry I had then
was the games that I should play.

Little did I realize the problems
and the worries
of two dear people in my life
they are, of course, my Mom &
Dad—
a husband and his wife.

Clothes made with loving hands
so dear for both me and my
brother.
With every stitch a loving touch
made by our own dear mother.

There were times, I'm sure, when
things went wrong
but never did we hear,
a word, a cry for sympathy,
we never saw the tears.

The strong, yet tender, hands of
love
belong to my dear Dad.
I was his little handyman
through good times and through
bad.

When he had worked his fingers to
the bone
and came home at night to rest
I was right there bending his ear,
the thing that I do best.

As a family we were *#1*
each person a vital part.
We worked, we played, we laughed
a lot.
We loved right from the heart.

Time changes all and we can't go
back
to the way it was before,
but memories will never fade and
I love them more and more.

Cornelia Marie (Bergdoll) Garrett

MY GRANDMA

To my Children, Grandchildren and Great Grandchildren

There grandma sits in her ol'
rocking chair
Her face is all wrinkled and snow
in her hair,
Her head is a nodding and her eyes
are closed
But at what is she smiling, land
only knows?
I lay down my books, my coat and
other things
And reach in my pocket for some
wooly strings;
Then I creep up beside her, on my
tip-toes . . .
Very carefully and softly . . . I
tickle her nose.
She leaps from her chair like a
soldier to attention,
She was saying some words, I'd
better not mention.
She grabbed me and hugged me,
and smothered me with kisses
As her hand came down softly on
the seat of my breeches.
"I love you dear Grandma . . . really
I do . . .
So please tell me a tale . . . or a
story or two."
Then I sat down beside her, my
head on her knee
She patted my hair and said,
"What shall it be . . .
Jack On The Beanstock . . . or the
Boy on the Burning Deck?"
"Ah! here comes that lesson . . .
of the boy on the wreck;
But she didn't get far, when my
eyes went closed . . .
Suddenly I was Captain Nemo .
. . capturing my foe
On board I took silver and great
heaps of pure gold,
I was a great adventurer . .
. and bold,
But would you believe it . . . as the
story goes
Grandma just woke me . . .
tickling my . . . nose.

Vi Krausse

MOTHER OF A TEENAGE SON

To my sons, Travis and Tracy, with all my love, Mom

You came into this world, to me, a
bundle of joy,
I didn't really care if you were a girl
or a boy;
I was just so happy that you were
healthy and alive,
Knowing it would be a struggle for
you to survive.
I watched you grow and feel your
way,
Learning and doing new things
each day;
Making me happy with a smile, a
hug, or a kiss,
Treasuring the moments that
happened like this.

Not knowing that you would soon
grow up and change,
From a smiling happy child, to a
teenager, that wants to
rearrange;
My hard working life from happy
to sad,
Making me feel as if I'm slowly
going mad.

You always go about your merry
old way,
Not thinking or caring about the
things you do or say;
Not knowing how you are breaking
your mother's heart,
Leaving her at home all torn apart.

Will these sad times ever end?
Will the closeness come back, so
we can spend,
Happy times together again, can it
be?
Or is it over, my son, for you and
me.

I pray that I will see the day,
When you walk back into my life
and say;
I'm sorry mom, for hurting you too,
I want you to know, that I still love
you.

Selina (Creampuff) Joe

HOW DEEP CAN I LOVE

To my loving and supportive family: Ernestine, Pete, Rita, Mita, E.J., Crissy/In memory of my loving Grandma: Estelle/ many thanks to Grandma Inez/ any my first and only love, who inspired this: David T. Lara

---

I think I'll write my heart a poem
which will tell how much I love
him

This love is vaster than I've ever
known
I hope I never again have to be
alone

This man is so important to have
in my life
I'm sure we could deal with
whatever strife

I'd marry him in a second if only
he'd ask
we could live in happiness and
finally relax

To me he seems like heaven on
earth
only for him, I'd gladly give birth

I'd give him my love and all that I
have
just to be content, thankful and
ever so glad

He awakened me to my beauty and
gave me strength from above
but most of all he taught me . . . .

How deep I can love

Cindy A Melton

LET YOUR GOOD SPOT ROAM FREE

To: Daddy, Connie, & Darlene, who all told me I could do it, I dedicate my first published poem.

Sometimes people lie,
Sometimes people deceive,
Sometimes people do anything
they please;
But I like to think that everyone,
Way down deep inside—
Really has a good spot,
It's just trying to hide.

If any of us can do a kind deed,
Or really help someone in need;
Maybe a good spot trying to hide,
Will rise way up from deep
inside,
And show itself to all the world,
Be it a man, woman, boy, or girl.

Don't judge people by what you see,
They may look like they are in
need;
But they may be the one helping
others,
Maybe even your sister or
mother.

You can give so much more,
And I'm <u>not</u> speaking of money—
If you just throw away your
beehive -
And keep your honey.

Mary Golightly

THE SEA OF LIFE

To Judy Brown who gave me encouragement

Listen, listen all you fools
To what I have to say,
Don't ever do the things <u>I've</u> done
Or you will surely pay.
You'll sit alone each lonely night
And ask the question, why?
You'll sit alone and wonder
As the sea of life goes by.

You'll sit alone and wonder,
And ask the question, why
There's faded youth and wasted
yesterdays,
Oh, what a pain to bear,
There's no one left to worry,
Only me who pays.
But when there are children bright
and fair,
Who am I to care,
About faded youth and wasted
yesterdays.

And so, you fools, you too shall
know
The answer just like me,
You won't sit alone and wonder,
You'll <u>know</u> the reason why.
You'll know the answer then, my
friend,
As any fool can see,
It's children and <u>their</u> children
Who make the sea of life flow by.

Shawn Roeder

A SILENT STRUGGLE FOR SURVIVAL

The strength of his heart waned
with every beat it made as it
became a struggle for every
breath.
And though the chill of the icy
creek trickling over his body
numbed the pain, he knew he
was approaching death.
The wound was deep and the
suffering intense,
And fear became an overwhelming
sense.

But with will to survive he staggered to his feet helped by a limb,
And got a shot of terror as he saw the gaping laceration, realizing odds of living were slim.
He attempted to shout, hoping somebody would hear him, somebody would be there.
Yet his shouts seemed only a faint whisper compared to his loud gasps for air.
The gentle breeze awoke his injury causing him to suffer and shed a lone tear,
And the rustling trees didn't help as they seemed to proclaim that his doom was near.
The incident was fresh and still rang in his ears,
And he began to recall it thus adding more tears.
His canoe had struck a limb on the side causing it to tip,
And as he descended into the shallow waters he felt flesh rip.
His chest had met the cruel edge of a rock below,
And he had doubled over in distress from the wicked blow.
His knees now gave way and he dropped back into the watery deep.
And as the fluids engulfed him, he sank back into eternal sleep.

Angela Picerno Nista

EULOGY FOR A LOVE

Beginnings and endings
Deeply and tenderly entwined
As though they were one.
As love dies,
I remember its birth
and fruitful existence
As though it were a dear friend
Who has passed on

In the very prime of life.
I feel remorse and regret
At its untimely passing.
And I am saddened more
By the rememberance
of the joy once shared,
the togetherness once felt,
the love—once lived.

Dorothy Dixon Thomas

LIFE

Getting to know yourself,
Facing the disappointments.
Seeing your friends succeed.
Having happiness seems so far.
Searching for that special dream.
Why me? Why all the failure?

Needing and wanting something,
Something that only God can grant.
You try so hard to live right,
When things are going great,
There's always this obstacle.
One day I will realize,
Life is only for the ones
Who can handle the pain,

It's not for me.

Beverly L McAtee

YOU WEREN'T THERE

Where were you;
When I needed you most
When I was afraid of the ghosts,
You weren't there to hold me.

When I had the lead part
In a play at my school,
You weren't there to see me.

When I learned to play ball
And made a home run,
You weren't there to cheer for me.

When I went on my first date
And I came in too late,
You weren't there to scold me.

When I dropped out of school
Which was a dumb thing to do,
You weren't there to stop me.

When I walked down the aisle
To become a mans bride,
You weren't there to walk with me.

When I had my first child
And we both were so proud,
You weren't there to share it.

Where were you,
When I needed you most,
DADDY

Bonnie J Gingrich Cramer

BURDENS TO BARE

This poem is dedicated to my beautiful children, Tracy and Mark.

These eyes are opening to see the world, not through societies,
I feel I've been given a gift, to see the realities;
Not living with all the pleasures they tell me I missed.
Or the way we want to believe it does exist.
I want to help the world see too, and share my wealth with all;
Why our minds are so great and our hearts so small?
Before it's too late we must level them out and let them connect!
We are such a complex species, always taught to stay in control,
Don't you fear what will happen when it's time to let go?
Too selfish to feel for others, doing whatever it takes to please us.
Can we live without material dreams, and survive with what we must
Are we pushing ourselves to the point of no return?
Soon we'll be tested, times will be harder and souls will burn.
Not a few will perish, but lives will be wasted in masses.
Can't we see we're being blinded by dollar sign glasses?
I'm trying to relate to the world, what my feelings say,
Why is it so difficult to throw our lusts away?
For those that have never been to Hell; and cannot conceive,
To live in peace and harmony is the goal we should achieve
It is sad to perceive that our children will not have known
God has blessed them all, each with a gift of their own
To praise when we do right, have compassion when we do wrong
The greatest gifts are from within, to be thankful, free and strong.
Amen

Betty Digwo

THROWAWAY SOCIETY

Ours is a throwaway society,
In which things are discarded
Just because we are tired of them
And something new has caught our eye.

Our clothes are out of style;
We empty our closet
To make room for new ones.

Oil painting looked like fun;
But we soon packed up paints and easel—
No time for all that practice.

The puppy was cute; who
Would have guessed he'd be so much work?
We sent him off to the pound.

When we are old and useless, will we
Be cast aside—unloved and unwanted—
Like the pup peering through a cage
With bewildered, pleading eyes?

Rachel Odo

THE MOMENTARY MADNESS OF A SWALLOW

There's a swallow on my lawn,
Stretching, stretching its neck.
Singing. No! Shouting.
The rebellious words of a wishful, wishful song.

Swallow, said I;
What right have you
on this perfect morning
to cast about my emerald lawn
Raging words of feckless madness?

Forgive me my momentary madness, whispered the swallow,
In distant voice of pale, pale thunder.
Then it soared expertly upward,
Cursing and cursing its natural gift.
Still shouting the rebellious words of that wishful, wishful song.

Ron B Briedwell

SURELY HE CARES

Down this long winding road, I have always walked alone.
I have tried to overcome by my own willpower, but because of grief and sorrow,
My strength is almost gone.
My soul cries out within my chest
I pray, "Lord, take this grief from my mind,
Have mercy upon me, and close my eyes that I might rest.

Oh God, My Lord, Why have you forgotten me?
My sorrow is a burning fire in my soul.
There is a multitude of loneliness in my heart, I try not to show
My heartache, without you, I cannot bear.
Oh God, My Lord, Do you not care?"

There is grief that seeks to control my mind.
I reached deep inside myself for help,
But without you, God, The strength I could not find.
My heartache I could not overcome, And my loneliness
I knew had just begun.

I knew by the strength of myself, I could not stand.
Please, Lord my God, I prayed, Help me,
And Jesus reached out from the cross, and he took my hand.
Jesus reached out to me in all his glory.
He reached out to me by the power of his hand.
He lifted me up to the throne of God,
And taught me how to stand.

The heartache is all over.
The grief is almost gone.
My loneliness was destroyed by the love of God,
As I looked upon his throne.

"Oh God, Why hast thou forsaken me?"
These are the words that burned so strong in my memory.
Then suddenly I remembered, suddenly I understood,
These are the words that Jesus spoke when they nailed him to the wood.
Then my Lord because of his love, took me up in the Spirit, that I might know
Why he died on the cross almost two thousand years ago.

I was suddenly in the spirit, And I looked down upon a cross.
I saw my Lord hanging in great agony, then I heard Jesus cry out in great pain,
"My God, My God, Why hast thou forsaken me?"
Then by the spirit God made me to see
The sins of the world come down on Jesus as he hung on the tree.

The griefs of the world were placed there too.
Your heartaches, and everything else he did bear.
My God, He really did care.

God burned in my mind a message that day.
The short time we have on this earth in a few short years will pass away.
The Lord shall reach out to you by the power of his son.
The lord God has spoken it, so it shall be done.

Dearest Souls, Spiritually by the power of God all these things were done.
Grief, heartache, and sorrow were placed on the body of his only son.
Beloved, the Lord is calling your name today.
For peace of mind do not turn him away.

Shirley A Wynn

LIFE

Life—is yours
It can make you happy or sad

Life—is yours
It can make you blue or glad
Life—is yours
It can make you smile or cry
Life—is yours
You can shape it or break it.
Life—is yours
So make it beautiful, and thank
God
For the gift of "Life"

Jim Hurlburt
MONDAY'S DAUGHTER

To July 14, 1958

Monday's daughter
One, of first water
A moon child's marauder
More "mink" than "otter"

Only of the best
Set aside from the rest
Special egg of the nest
Sought after, yet never caressed

Lonesome though she may not be
You wouldn't know it by a simple
look-see
Funny how clever someone can be
Wearing a smile trying to fool me

Eyes that appear blind
Yet, envisioned through the mind
Pictures of the benevolent kind
Words caught up in a bind

So to speak
An uphill climb to the peak
She's the challenge that I seek
Every night of the week

Ella Coard Egbeji

Ella Coard Egbeji
LOVE

In memory of James Hunt. To Nicole and Scott Kelly and their father, Bruce D. Kelly and to my wonderful family and friends who supported me

I knew you some years ago,
I held you, I walked with you
I rode the trains with you,
I held you, I loved you
I lost you, I knew that
never again was I to find you
I lived! That was supreme,
to live, a wasted existence
I could not bear, I seeked
a man of your coloring
Of your heritage of which
I could not find
But bore two children of
your coloring, of your bearing
Of your carriage,
But it's not the same
I might have, together with you
Loved them into obedience of
Family, Society,
Nationalism
Citizenship.
Today one I might have won!
The other I
might have lost.
And I never gave credence
To him who bore, AND
one day I guess, I must!
Today I acknowledge you!!

Valentine Anthony Wyszynski
MY CHILDREN

I'd like to have someone to love
And fill my lonely nights . . .
It's been so long to be alone
Not loving isn't right . . .
I'd like to meet you first and see
If all there is, is true . . .
But 'fore we go on seriously
There's something I've to do . . .
You see, I have some children
That mean the world to me . . .
And tho I need someone like you
I have to wait and see . . .
If I like you, then they will too
But I need to know inside . . .
That you'll like them as well as me
And take us all in stride . . .
They don't need a(nother) father
Theirs' is pretty good with them . . .
All I ask for me if you
Would be a loving good close
friend . . .
And if in time it's you I want
And fell in love with you . . .
Just please love me with all your
heart
And love my children . . . too.

Kimberly Ann Sederstrom
HIDDEN FEELINGS

I doubt you know
how much you can lift my day.
When I'm hurting deep down
inside,
I only need to see your face
to know you care—
Things will be fine,
because I know you'll always be
there.
When we talk—I can see the love
and concern in your eyes.
Making me feel so special . . .
The love I have for you
isn't on the surface,
it's deep down in my heart.
You're so special . . .
In my eyes I can see no faults in
you,
you're intelligent.
You always know just what to say.
I respect you for the caring
person you are—
There is a strong feeling inside me
that makes me so grateful to be able
to be your daughter—
I love you Dad—I hope you know
what a great father you are.

Kim Berthiaume
GROWING UP

To Mom and Dad: Thanks for helping me find my way through each day.

I entered this world as just a tiny
baby
my parents knew the world was
ahead with no key
to the easy way through, not even
an if or a maybe.
As I was growing up my parents
had so much to say
they told me the wrong ways and
they told me the right ways.
When the day came that I had
finished Grammer School,
my parents were very proud, they
considered me their precious
jewel.
I continued on with my education,
I continued to grow,
but now in High School I've had
some troubled times,
but I know if I let my good times
flow I will be fine.
My parents still hope that I will
listen to their voice
but respect me and know it's time
for me to make my own choice.
My Senior year is now here and
soon it will come to an end
now I must fully grow up and no
longer can pretend.
As I now go out into the world my
parent's voice will echo from the
past
their guidance and support will
continue to last.
As progress enters my eyes,
my past and memories I will never
let die.
Thanks mom and dad for showing
me the way. My future is now
here
but thanks to you both I will have
no fear.
In the begging there was no key to
show me the easy way
but now I have come to see you
were my key
you were the ones to help me
through each day.

Vivian (Mike) Franklin
LONESOME HOUSE

A squeaking sound came from the
kitchen
On tip-toes I went in to see,
And on my table a little mouse
Was shyly watching me.

A piece of cheese was in its paws,
Red jam smeared on his nose and
ear,
Ooh— I never saw anything so
sweet
In all the years I've lived here.

I'm not at all afraid of you,
No need to run away,
It seems as though you like it here,
So please—, why don't you stay?

There's lots of rags and paper
To make a cozy nest,
I'll let you put it anywhere
For a quiet place to rest.

Tell no one that your living here,
Be as silent as you can,
Or otherwise some friends of mine
Will never come again.

So get your things and drag them
in,
Now you have a home mouse,
I'm glad to have you live with me
In this old lonesome house.

Montia F Clay
THE ROSE

This Poem Is Dedicated To My Wonderful Family

Two little gardens grew side by side
A wonderful tribute of selfless
and pride,
A wee little man and a lovely
maiden
Each planted a seed in their own
little garden.
The wee little man was careless one
day
And picked up a seed he found
by the way,
With a spade he dug a hole in the
ground
And planted the seed that he had
found.
The lovely maiden traveled many a
mile
Until she found a seed she
thought worthwhile,
She planted the seed deep in the
ground
And with a watchful eye she
lingered around.
From the maiden's seed there grew
a rose
And the rose grew higher and
higher,
But alas! from the seed the wee
man planted
There grew an ugly brier.
The wee man wept for his tragic
plight
The maiden's heart was
saddened,
The maiden loved the wee little
man
And the wee man loved the
maiden.
Through storm and wind,
sunshine and rain
The rose grew higher and higher,
Until it reached into the wee man's
garden
And its beauty covered the ugly
brier.

Edith B Blenkhorn
DEPRESSION YEARS

The twenties and thirties were days
of yore with hard times and
want, everyone bore,
Banks closed, all savings went
down the drain leaving many
with no place to enter in out of
the rain;
Losing all they had, working so
hard each year
Jobs were scarce in the days of

yesteryear.

The milk man came and the ice man too without too much stir and ado,
Placing one on the step, other in the chest sitting on the porch with all of the rest of the paraphernalia of the great depression
Those days of make do with imperfection.

City folks had long bread lines everyday,
Lined up, hands outstretched begging in dismay;
Country folks were better off with food on the table,
A growing garden, milk from the cow—they were able to not beg for mercy and made good on their own,
Scarce money, but pride kept, without falling down.

I look back, remembering, that time of life,
Clothes washed in a tub, cooking on wood stove, busy housewife.
Home remedies to treat and strengthen all of the childhood diseases we had back then.
Time seemed to move slower, no reason for haste making every penny count taught economy not waste.

Sarah M Taylor
IF I'M HERE TODAY AND GONE TOMORROW

This poem is dedicated to my family and friends

Just remember to bless me and be thankful that God has given me the opportunity to share a special part of your life.

And remember that, I will continue to live though the eyes of my loved ones. We all must leave, whether if we're young or old.

Don't cry over my death, but be happy for me. Because God put me here and he decided to take me away.

Don't feel sorry for my departure, because if there was a moment when, I was unhappy in this world. I know my happiness will be at my Father's home.

Remember, I love all of you with all my heart and my Father who art in heaven knows this.

Remember the good things about me and not the bad

Remember my smile that, I always had.

To my loved ones and friends, may God bless my soul and bless all of you.

Amy Renee Pope
A MOTHERS HAPPINESS

To my son,—Ryan Michael And to my daughter,—Michelle Lee

When I was just a little girl, so proud I seemed to be,
Of all the precious little things that you have shared with me.
You've led me from the darkness, from a thousand fears I've known,
And taught me ways of countless joys, through warmth and care you've shown.
And when at times I felt alone, and needed someone near,
You knew what I was feeling, and you'd wipe away my tears.
You've guided me through sorrows, in this funny world we live,
And kept me from unpleasantness, and taught me how to give.
My heart does not forget those words, you often spoke so dear,
To help me through my little doubts, and give the day some cheer.

You always wore a gentle smile, to lead me through those days,
Those days that weren't so good for me, you've changed in many ways.
For now I have a daughter too, she's grown to be like me,
I cherish her with guidance Mom, the way it used to be.
I hold her closely to my heart, and wish away her fears,
And hope the best would come her way, inspite of all her tears.
I share her doubts and emptiness, to build her spirits bright,
And help her gain back confidence, so things will turn out right.
I wear a smile upon my face, and guide her through each day,
And let her know I love her so, in each and every way.
But one day she came up to me and said, "I'm proud you're here,"
For truth and life's fulfillment casts an honest love so dear.
Someday she will remember too, a daughter near her side,
Of all the precious little things that love has to abide.

Dorothy Wear
THE LADY, CALIFORNIA
"Give Me men to match My mountains"
Pioneers to search for gold
Settlers for My valley's,
California's for the bold!

They came west by the hundreds
Stripped My rivers of gold;
Farmed the valley's green
And drilled deep to reach My soul!

My redwoods gave them timber;
For to build their homes.
With orange-poppied fields,
The restless no more to roam.

Rockets over my desert;
Movies upon a screen.
Playgrounds full of magic,
California proudly beams!

Give Me men to match My mountains;
Pioneers to bring me gold.
With clear-blue skies;
California's for the Bold!

Georgia L Usher
GRANDMA
Sitting crumpled and worn in a chair with all her wisdom and love a shadow
She holds her thread and tool in hand
You marvel at the blind made lace
Dingy with age yet fresh as spring this old woman sits with pride and dignity
Ragged as a pauper and mighty as a queen
She does not accept or deliver charity
Each line on her face is history a road on her map to victory
This old woman in her chair with streaks of silver through her hair
Knew the world when it was bare
She struggled through life and held it dear
Only to sit crumpled and worn in a chair

Marta Lozano
POETRY
The joy of creating a world just for words,
to give them a life of their own,
comes out of a heart that has dreamed many hopes
and felt that we make our thoughts known
by using a tool, which I'm sure is a gift
sent by a source so divine,
it makes me feel proud and so happy the source
had chosen this gift to be mine.
I share it with others, who must believe, too,
that we have a goal to fulfill.
Through beautifully sounding lyrics from love,
we'll spread happiness, hope and goodwill.
If poetry isn't the most wonderful way
to let loved ones and all humankind
experience luminous treasures of life
that can animate anyone's mind,
then I guess I'm just bias and want to believe
in a channel of onflowing streams,
consistent in giving bouquets of ideas,
which give such a glow to my dreams.

William R Clements
A LADY OF THE 80'S

This poem is dedicated to my niece Linda, the "little brat" that has showered me with much love and affection.

Her life's so full, 'tween work and the home,
each hair in it's place, by spray and her comb.

Her appearance is neat, great pains she will take,
and just a few minutes, to work she'll be late.

Then one of those days, when nothing goes right,
while driving to work, she discovers a fright.

Though dress is quite chic, something catches her sight,
her shoes do not match, left different from right.

The color's the same, but that's about all,
her walk will be funny, for one heel's too tall.

With one shoe that's open, her toes in fresh air,
the other is closed, how people will stare.

Too late to turn back, so drive on is a must,
Thank God only one bra, is used for the bust.

Delvara D Alexander
LOVE & HATE

To Arthur J. James, Jr. Together struggling through trials and tribulations, Love Has Found A Way

---

We Love and Hate sometimes both at once
I Love your touch, kisses and caresses
But I Hate the times when you are impatient,
thoughtless and selfish
I Love your smiles, surprises and gentleness
But I Hate your illogical, irrational and
immature outlook on my personal thoughts and
feelings sometimes
I love so many things about you
But I Hate somethings about you too
Somehow we always seem to Love & Hate
Yet it never goes away
So I assume that this is a part of life a new
stage of our relationship
And I suppose as our relationship grows together
We'll be seeing more of this Love & Hate
I hope more of the Love Side than Hate
Because as I have seen in the past
Hate has away of killing
EVERYTHING THAT ONCE WAS LOVED

Jane Fischer
AN ELEGY
Do not weep for the unbloomed rose
that withered in the night.

It knew not of hot summer sun
or cold winter frost
but of morning dew
and evening breeze.

For those who looked upon it
the dew was sweet
the breeze cool.
For those who looked away
the sun was hot

the frost bitter.

The rose, which knew not that it
was
looked upon,
or looked away from,
had been here forever
assuming it would be here
forever more.
It was blessed to know nothing else.

Do not ask why,
do not weep
for the unbloomed rose
that withered in the night.

Guy H Morris Jr

Guy H Morris Jr
SEABROOK ISLAND

The turtles come from hiding in
morning,
Retreat into the brackish water at
noon
To cool their sun-baked shells,
And just as soon return to solar
slumber
Upon the branch afloat.

The heat pounds upon the marsh
brush.
Swarms of gnats encircle certain
spots,
Making perfect patterns in their
guest.
A humid breeze softly sways grassy
reeds,
While white-winged egrets stand
motionless
In the glaring sun.
Like sentries they guard the grassy
plain,
Turning routinely to scope the site.

Overhead, broad beaked pelicans
glide
In search of floundering fish.
Clam shells dot the muddy banks,
A graphic graveyard of life lost to
nature.
Thousands of sand crabs scurry
across a tributary bank.
As if the sun would do them
damage,
They quickly return to their homes
in the cool clay.

A lovely sight in all;
And in this quiet world,
The secrets of LIFE and DEATH
are FOREVER bound.

Dora Dent
THE HEART IS HEAVY

Dedicated to John T. Dent, Jr.

The heart is heavy
in silence weep
Down the isle came
the sound of
old soldiers feet
The organ played softly
God Bless America
As they gave a final salute
Sobs and quick breath
were heard—
don't be sad, he suffers
no more
Weep no more my children
make your memories good
and few
All the things he never
was, is alive and good in you.
The flag was folded and placed
upon my lap
The guns were fired 2x10 and one
a young man
with a bugle hid in the trees
Taps rang out over the mountain
softly and beautifully.

Leona Ragains
SEED

When I planted a little seed in the
ground
it looked so small and a very dull
brown.
Then one day its little head
appeared
and the dew clings to it like tears.
As the weeks went by I wondered
why did I try?
Why did I go to the trouble, why
did I try?
Then I decided to pull it out one
afternoon,
but that is when I found a little
bloom.
So I took care of what I planted
with faith
because we all know faith is all it
takes.
And when the flower gave beauty
to everyone
then I thought, "Look," Look
what I have done!
But I was only an instrument of
what God can do,
so why don't you be his instrument
too!

Sanda Fletcher
TEARS

The fiesty, little bundle of fur
bounced and becharmed her
way into our lives and hearts,
Snuggling up by my neck, letting
out little squeals of happiness,
Always Happy to be close,
Later in this pose she would doze,
as I worked at my typewriter
or read,
Once recharged this little bundle
would race off to explore the
grass and chase the butterflies or
taste the daisies,
Scolding would bring tears and
licks on my hand meaning "I'm
sorry,"
Moments later she would charge
me, STOP, then race away,
suddenly
turn, hoping I would STOP and
PLAY the brown eyes pleading,
would win their way . . . I would
STOP and PLAY,
Key in lock, I hesitate . . . Thinking
I hear that WELCOMING BARK
. . . No . . . Only MEMORIES,
Times for reflection, questioning
and tears of loss for a carefree,
happy little life so swiftly taken,
NOW, that fiestly, little bundle of
life is only with us in our hearts
and memories of those precious,
bright, blessed times . . . Times
GOD has given us to be
remembered and cherished . . .

Mary Stewart (Lindstrand)
JUST A LITTLE TOO FAST

This poem is dedicated to Paul and Tony to whom this actually happened.

I took my car to the school shop
Tuned her up from bottom to top

I picked up my brother from the
Coast Guard
He said: "How does she run?" The
road was clear; I romped on her
hard.

She squatted to the ground
And we were off with a bound

To stop at the light I had to snub her
When the light was green I layed
the rubber

We can really fix our cars in that
Bothell shop
I didn't know I was in front of a
Seattle cop

He blew his horn and blinked his
lights
I took one look and pulled to the
right

He pulled up close beside
I said: "Oh brother! Here's where I
lose my hide!"

He gave me a ticket for speeding
I knew right then the road signs I
better start reading

They sent me to the judge: He said:
"Give me your license, My Boy!
Now you'll have eight months to
learn a car is not a toy!"

He said: "Now son, you shouldn't
drive as fast as you can
we'll just use you for the example
to the other man!"

Now I've walked and I've sweat
I'll never speed again; I'm willing
to bet!

Flora McCune
MY EXECUTION DAY

As I was walking home one day
down by a beautiful sea
I realized the beauty in this world
most eyes would never see

I looked into the sun shining with
its beautiful rays
shining down upon the world and
the animals as they grazed
Then I heard a bird singing as it
was flying in the sky
and it reminded me of heaven and
an angel passing by

Then as the sun was sinking low
and darkness growing near
I saw the beauty of a falling star
shining crystal clear

Then the sun came shining
through these bars made out of
steel
was then I realized this dream of
mine for me was not so real

For today's my execution day my
life from me they'll take
and though I know I'm sorry for
me it is too late

And as I sit here in my final hour
and think of the lives I took
I pray God will forgive me when he
opens up his book

I pray I'll go to heaven where there
is no more pain
I pray I'll see the people whose lives
I took in vain

Mary Kathleen (Madonna Kay) Maxwell
UNTITLED

To my brother, Timothy Ray Maxwell, who was my friend as well. Surely there were those who thought us daft, for we seldom cried, and we often laughed

---

To thee:
Read out aloud, this me—my soul,
I'm free through words, I'll pay no
toll.
Pen, hold not back what ye wish to
say,
What could be said tomorrow, can
be written today.
My brother so proud, yet he not be
present.
No bad memories of thee, no guilt,
no resent.
Just left of him a will to succeed,
To help a strong limb or wilting
weed.
I remember the rains and the
floods still deepen,
My eyes and heart are still
a'weepin.
Until at last we meet once more,
I pray that God knocks at my door.
United I'll be forever more,
With the one, I so adore.

Love, me

Kathleen M Moran
PERSONA FEMALIA

To my dearest Michael, the tamer of the stranger.

Have you met the stranger
That lurks within my soul?
She is dark, she is haughty
And her terror is untold.

There are times during the night
When she knows that I am
dreaming.
She comes from the shadows
And her nightmares take on
meaning.

She takes on the form
Of a wanton, savage female.
Her talons; They are sharp

And with them she will impale.

I cringe from the knowledge
That she cannot be controlled.
She is rabid she is angry
And her lust will take its toll.

But when the daylight kills the darkness;
It also kills her might.
And she waits in the shadows
For the coming of the night.

She is dark, she is bloodless
And her heart is black as coal
Yet she lives within the depths
Of every womans soul.

Marcella Ruark
OLD MAN IN THE PARK

I was walking in the park one day, when I saw this old man.
He was sitting on a park bench, a cane in his hand.
He looked sort of lonely, so I walked over and said hello
The sun was shining on his head, his hair was the color of gold
He seemed anxious to talk, so I listened to what he said, all the while I was thinking, he reminds me of my dad.
He said "I stay at that rest-home down the street aways, I walk
here to the park nearly every day. They treat us well enough
keep us clean and fed, guess thats all one could ask for,
and a good warm bed.

You know as I lie in my bed at night and I think back through
the years, people seemed a lot happier then, for they had
less to fear. With all the hate and killing, and the threat
of nuclear war, I wonder what could be in man's heart,
to let things get that far.
They say the worlds made progress, well if thats what they
believe, then God help our children for better things to
achieve.
Oh well, I'm just an old man, guess I don't know it all.
I just pray for the young ones, to always stand proud and
tall.
My folks are all gone now, there's no one left but me,
I don't serve much purpose here, so far as I can see.
As I started home I kept remembering, the words he said
to me. In my mind I kept thinking, God surely has a
purpose for a man as wise as he.

Ramona E Douglass
BY FANTASIES POSSESSED

To Jo Myrtle: who always encouraged me to reveal my true self.

A woman in love with her fantasies
Beds down with her dreams for the night,
Hoping her visions of romance
Will bring her to sexual heights.

On chariots of fire and passion
That carry her "self" through her mind,
She's laden with gifts for a lover
Who's painted as sturdy and kind.

Oh, call me a weaver of daydreams,
Projecting emotional highs;
Yet caught in reality's mainstreams,
Denying what's true as mere lies.

My fantasies offer protection
From fear of what I possess.
The woman I see is a stranger,
Whose body I hold as a guest.

The men I adore can conceal me,
Without substance to bring me to life;
Yet I dote, and I praise, and I crave them,
To shut out my personal strife.

How I long to reclaim my possessions,
Give shape to a world that is mine;
Forgetting my follies and phantoms,
And leaving my terrors behind.

Janice Plyler Hockersmith
O FATHER, DO YOU REMEMBER?

To my parents, who have believed in me—Hurley and Annie Lee Plyler

---

Do you remember, or have
you forgotten the day on
which I, your fair-haired child
Was born—that triumphant shout

"It's a boy!"

Do you remember, or have
You no memory at all of
Those grandiose dreams in their splendor
All and ever so neatly laid out?

And can you remember that
Day in September when I
Cut the strings and went out
On my own (in first grade)—

Have you forgotten what
Promises, planning, and all of those
Other things out of my reach that
Were (for me) presumably made?

Where did it happen, or when
Did it change, perhaps could
It be possibly due to my having
The wonderful will to think for myself?

For I am no athlete (Dear Lord!)
I'm a scholar, a dreamer of
Dreams with a Sunday-white collar—
Not a clone of another adorning a shelf

Irene Doris Parks
THE LONELY FATHER

He watches you walk out that door.
With the man you vowed to adore.
He stands and listens as your car pulls away.
You told your father you'd marry one day.

He wouldn't believe it, but now its too late.
Its over and done with, you just couldn't wait!
He sits in his chair very lonely now,
But, you think he will get over it some how.

Then you think of how he always tryed to help you.
And try doing those "things" that only a mother could do.
Now he sits there, with no one at all.
Because your mothers been gone before you could crawl.

So you wonder and worry, what should you do?
But your husband tells you, its not up to you.
So shrugg your shoulders, as your car pulls away.
He's only a father, he will get over it one day.

Helen L Gibbs (Brown)
WHEN ALL SEEMS LOST

Where do you turn when you've nothing left except a very lonely soul,
When all you've loved has gone, never again to return.
Inside yourself you hide away, letting life just pass on by,
Not caring who is near or fat, you set alone and cry.
Life has no meaning; now that your love has gone,
One day at a time; you strive to go on.
Your heart feels like a time bomb; just waiting to explode,
With every beat you take a breath and put yourself on hold.
The world seems cold and empty without the one you love,
So! Locked deep down within yourself; you learn to live alone.

T Moody Scanlon
THREE CROSSES, THREE DEATHS

Any talent I have is God given

My Lord hung there on the third cross,
A thief hung on either side.
It's been the same, down thru the years,
As these three in different ways died.
The one thief, at last, was repentant,
Prayed that his pain would subside.
The other went spewing bitter words,
From lips that cursed and lied.
The third mans' thoughts were of others.
"Forgive them father" he cried,
"For all the evil they have done."
Then, "it's finished" he sighed—and died.

Ethel Hayes Johnson
THE NIGHTINGALE

Outside my window in the still dark velvet of Night
Sings a Nightingale
In Concert
Such music is not to be heard, save by those who listen to God's
Creatures in the quiet stillness
He sings the Tenor, Alto, Bass, the key between so rare and sweet
He is a supreme and contralto—A choir, soloist, quartette and duet
The music of and for the night, for those restless uneasy moments
when nothing seems right
But he is perfect
The Nightingale

James L Pighinni
PAST, PRESENT, FUTURE

In sincere dedication to "CRCI and JUDGE"

The past is something we remember dearly, regretfully, scornfully, desperately.
We cannot forget our sorrows, happinesses, lonely times, loves lost, hatreds built, dreams made, nightmares rout.
The past was and is, a living thing.
We learn from our experiences, those things that have already happened.
Here and now is the present we strive to gain from.
We slave ourselves to the point of exhaustion to build our lives
into something or someone we are not.
Sometimes we hit our bottom only to get right back up.
Some of us can't get any higher, we all have our own individual capacity.
But we still try, like robots or automatons, we have the built-in force to go on.
Some, will perish from the struggle of lifes struggle.
Others, will go on.
The future is a magical thing, sort of like a gamble.
We try to predict it, we try to refrain from it, we try to save it, we try to destroy it.
We reach for space, study star to star, we gaze down upon ourselves, only to see death and destruction!
We search for a new planet, for new life form.
For what! To learn? No, they will only be our aftermath!
We are destroyers, conquerers, achievers, rulers.
We live on yesterday, we struggle with today.
Our hopes, our dreams.

Paul O Carlson
CHARITY

To the Ministers of Jesus Gospel

C— Christ, is the way into Heaven's Land.
H— He's the ordained pass God has planned.
A— Awake my brother take your sister's hand.
R— Resist the devil, let's present our stand.
I— Inside you'll find Meat, truly it's grand.
T— Telling sinners about Jesus

with His Love.
Y— You're by God's Spirit,
attuned from above.

Elvira F Soste

Elvira F Soste
MIND

To my family and friends.

Mind is a burning furnace—
Where my being is forged,
Comes from nowhere . . .
Nowhere to go . . . it is!

Mind is a place—
Where Angel stands next to the Devil,
"Get thee behind me!" said the Angel—
But that was all he ever said.

Mind is the place where lovers meet,
Where friendships are made to last—
Where happiness is the matter of heart—
And rainy days are few!

Mind is the root of all that is . . .
Is ever changing ever growing,
. . .till it joins the Universe . . .
The meeting place for us all!

Todd Allen Paul Nahirnik
BLIZZARD

*B*elligerant gales gallantly blow.
*L*avish are the amounts of snow.
*I*ntense periods of cold violently flog our clothes.
*Z*ones of terrorizing weather inflict a great many woes.
*Z*ephyrs are desired but very seldom given;
A great deal of precious warmth from our bodies is driven.
*R*ocks anchored in the luster of ice;
*D*rowned are the memories of summer by which we were so much enticed.

Martha June Riddle
MY BABIES

This poem is dedicated to my children, whom I love very much.

God looked down from Heaven one day
as I was busily going my way.

He said "I have some rosebuds to share,
but they must be handled with the utmost care."

So, I said "I would love one or two."

But, He said, "No, I have six for you."

"You must arrange your own boquet,
and they must be returned at some future day."

"I'm entrusting some of my most precious flowers
from my private garden where I've spent many hours."

"You may pretend they are your own,
but never forget they are only a loan."

So I've nurtured them kindly with patience
and love
Only exceeded by his from above.

I've held them and nursed them, gazed on their beauty,
I've prayed I've enhanced them, and
fulfilled my duty.

So when they're called back to their rightful place,
They will brighten God's garden with sweetness and grace.

Grace Carrick Kachner
SPRING

To my Daughter, Sandra . . . and Granddaughters Kim and Cindy. They Bring Spring Into My Life.

Spring spreads her golden tresses
Across the hillsides green,
And wakes up tiny flowers
With each bright golden beam.

She dances through the valleys,
And loiters in the dells
To seek out every brooklet
So she may wish it well.

She breaths through all the treetops,
Which whisper back refrains
And blossom forth in welcome
That she has come again.

She rocks her tiny feather friends
In their new-built nests,
And sings them sweet lullabies
Until they have gone to rest.

And then when Summer comes creeping
Stealthily in the night,
She finds she cannot linger,
Her step is not so light.

So she rests upon the soft white clouds
And slowly floats away,
While she showers tears of regret
That she can no longer stay.

Deborah Scott Quevedo
HOME

Help me make it through this day
Take my hand, show me the way
For dear Lord I've gone astray
Show me the way home
Tho I tried with all my might
I did wrong instead of right
Fought so hard yet lost the fight
Please Lord take me home
Now the pain cuts deep within
I could really use a friend
And so I turn to you again
To my loving home
To your arms that shelter me
To your word that sets me free
No longer blind, now I see
I am safe at home.

Leah M McCann
THERE IS NO LIGHT . . .

Release the aim, free my soul
Take me out of your unending control
Free me from thine boast and pride
My self and soul shall I forever hide

Swirl with the world, I thus hear
Not I, its games I fear
Reach with the wind to the utmost cry
Fly on the wings, oh bye; goodbye

Humiliation replaces the hope in thy heart
Killing the seed straight from the start
Gone is the love for all beings of dreams
To take its place are the soundless screams

The glass is empty and thirsts persist
Try not, oh no, one can't resist
Evils flow from pores of dead ones
Touching the moon, blinding the sun

Long time to see thee cry
Poorest little one you cannot fly
Thus, forever a mist in the night
Suffer the pain, for there is no light . . .

Anne Shaffer
FOLK BALLAD

There was an old an' haggard man
who always stayed at home.
He up an' spake ane dreary day,
"Why must I stay alone?"

He must o' said it loud enough
for a' the toune to heir,
But ane voice only spake to him,
"My guid man, hold no feir!"

He saw no body 'round the house,
So then outside went he.
Then spake the voice a second time,
"Guid man, I'm not to see."

"This cannot be a normal man
that I am speakin' to.
Reveal if ye be friend or foe
and tell me what to do."

The voice then spake, "A foe I'm not,
so heir and heed my word.
No man on earth is left alone
who knows an' loves his Lord."

Beverly Hartman
A LETTER TO GOD

Dear God,

I firmly believe you are with me every night and every day, you always seem to help me when trouble comes my way. When things go wrong and I'm feeling down, I say a little prayer, then I always seem to feel much better, so I know you must be there.

This life is far from easy, and I try to do it right, it helps to know your by my side, you are my guiding light.

Help me get through this hard time, I'm trying to do my best, and just knowing that your by my side, puts my mind at rest.

Kimberley Gomes
WINTER WONDERLAND

To my loving parents, who support me in every way.

*W*onderful is the snow gently falling all around;
*I*nside is warm and cozy while snowflakes hit the ground;
*N*ever wish the white snow would simply go away;
*T*he fluffy stuff will fall out of the sky one unexpected day;
*E*xquisite are the lovely flakes that flutter all about;
*R*ound and round and up and down while children scream and shout;
*W*hile looking at those icicles that resemble large toothpicks;
*O*n and on they grow and grow so long and ever so thick;
*N*oses freezing and cold feet;
*D*ancing and prancing as children grow cold;
*E*ach day making our winter grow old;
*R*emembering all those lovely flakes;
*L*oving mothers start baking cakes;
*A*nd while little children are snug in their beds;
*N*ature prepares the flower beds;
*D*aisies bloom and Winter Wonderland ends!

Lonnie W Geary

Lonnie W Geary
IN REMEMBRANCE

Lonnie died as a result of a tragic automobile accident. This poem was found by Lonnie's sister after his death.

Remember the memories of how
we shared our touch.

Remember our love and how we cared so much.
Love is special in its own kind of way
One thing is certain, nothing can take it away.
Love can always grow, but it will never go.
So, remember our dreams are made to be fulfilled
So, don't give up, some day they will.
Remember me, as I will you.
And never forget that I love you!

Darlene Marie Hoseman
FREE TO DREAM

To Prince Charming

Behind that handsome
Face I see,
A gentle spirit
Yearning to be free.

To be free from what
Only you can know,
Constantly searching
The depths of your soul.

When I look into your
Eyes I'm weak,
Because you stir
An emotion thats buried deep.

Your quiet nature attracts
Something in me,
For when I look at you
I feel a certain peace.

Although I don't know
You that well,
With you my spirit
Wishes to dwell.

To be with you
In my arms,
And experience each
Others charms.

Your the prince charming
Of my dreams,
But in reality
I don't have a chance
It seems.

But I keep you
In my thoughts,
And my feelings
I try not to show.

Because in life
You never know.

Evelyn M Wenzel
JOYFUL TEARS

For A Special Love

My joy is filled with tears,
I hope it lasts for years.
These precious moments that we shared,
That showed us both how much we cared.
Could I but relive that hour we had,
I wouldn't change a second but would add
How thankful I am for the Lord's blessing,
Though, why He allows it keeps me guessing.
I won't try to reason why.
I would rather weep and sigh
For the happy reunion He granted,
A prayer to our Lord should be chanted.
Your touch, your embrace, your kiss,
All combined to cause me such bliss.
I couldn't really tell you how I felt
Allowing it to happen almost made me melt.
I don't want it ever to end,
I praise God for you, my dearest friend.
"You are loved," He said,
Then picked me up and carried me to bed.

Eva Ballard
TIME

Dedicated to James, my husband

While I travel along this way of life
And take note of the passing time;
Am I kind and thoughtful to lend a hand
As I journey through this land.

Time waits for no man . . . alas
The past I never will catch;
Let me walk my path and carry the cross
To help the hungry, homeless and lost.

There's a hand to hold, and words to say
A broken heart to mend;
To bring a smile, wipe tears away
Not tomorrow——but today.

The clock of life is wound but once
And time is fleeting on;
I'll put aside my wishing well
Since waiting does not dwell.

For time is like a rolling stream
It passes and fast forgotten;
I'd like the love I sow to be . . .
For all who follow after me.

Jack W Courtney
MINE

This poem is dedicated to Bobbie, my loving wife.

Mine is a treasure on earth to behold,
Affording more pleasure than silver or gold,
For silver may purchase the linen so fine,
It's only a thread by this treasure of mine.

Some treasures are false, like with diamonds of glass,
Reflecting a glimmer that never will last,
But I'll show you one that all time cannot dim,
This treasure of mine; yes, this beautiful gem.

So, what of the treasures that falter on earth,
Not stemming the tide, and not proving their worth.
My treasure is blending the sun with the dew,
Emitting a sparkle I'm thankful to view.

My treasure is spending itself everyday,
By giving me pleasure I cannot repay,
The metal I offer, too bold to refine,
Is rust in the coffer by gold that is mine.

Some treasures are hidden so deep in the clay,
MY treasure is living with me everyday.
She's holding my hand as she walks by my side,
My treasure of love, and with whom I abide.

All mine is this treasure I zealously hold,
Her smile is my pleasure, her touch is my gold.
Enriching my life is this pearl oh so fine,
This gem is my wife, and she's mine—she's all MINE.

Raymond A Trotter Jr
MY LOVE HAS GOLDEN WINGS

My love has wings, slendered feathered things.
My love has shell like ears; teeth like pearls;
Eyes as black as midnight; skin as soft as silk white as milk;
Lips as red as the rose, hair as the raven, laughter fresh as spring.
My love walks like a feather floating to earth like a summer sunset;
Now she comes to me in my dreams on lovely wings, because God took her away from me. So if I am good perhaps I shall have wings some day;
Lovely wings of gold will come for me, when the day comes;
I will love her more, even more after death;
My love with lovely wings of golden things, that carry her to me.
My love, "O" My Love

Dorese Ransom
MY HOUSE

I would like to dedicate this poem to my good friend Melanie Beth Staten and my loving husband, Horace.

My house is not so big;
and yet it's big to me
My windows are kind of small;
and yet I can look through and see.
My rooms are all one scene,
but oh, my walls are clean.
My floors are not all bare,
and the carpet only needs a little care.
My neighbors looked and said
"Oh Gee!"
"I wouldn't want that house I see!"
But I prayed anyway for this house,
and you know?
God just saw fit, to give it to me.

Sheryl A Knieriemen
THIS MIRACLE CALLED LIFE

Life is fragile, handle with prayer
is a phrase we often see.
Let us for once concentrate
on the message that comes from Thee.

Life is a gift and with it comes love
a gift that was meant to be shared.
Trusting and telling God of our hearts desires
comes from the power of prayer.

Miracles happen everyday and
we so often take them for granted.
What we all do with the time that is given us,
it's no wonder we sometimes feel stranded.

Miracles don't stop at babies you see,
look at you, look at me;
Hear the sweet songs of joy that fill the air,
smell and feel the gentle breeze.

Take a look at your gift today
with all its blessings, all its strife, and
Let God take hold to do His Will
with this miracle called Life.

Trisha Louise Fane
OFFER NO APOLOGIES

I dedicate this poem not only to black people, but to people of all colors. Never be ashamed of what you are.

God made men and women equal:
No matter, black or white we're
All still people. So why be prejudice
Over each other skin.
We all have the same color blood
And flesh within.

We are teased sometimes for our color,
But hold your head high and offer no apologie
For it. I am the past, the present, and I
Plan my future.
I need no apologie for what I am.
I am proud already for what I stand.

I stand for knowledge, I stand for all
I stand for what God made me, so I stand
Ten feet tall. Give me the respect of
Equal rights, because I offer no apologies
For my color and my might.

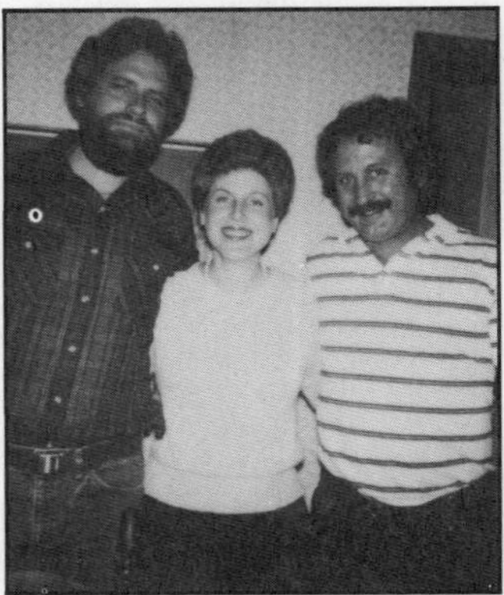

David, Nancy and Sonny

Fannie Nash Livingston Grooms
ONLY GOD

Dedicated to: My son on His 34th Birthday. My son David Francis Livingston "Baby son—born Jan, 3, 1953—Gone to be with Jesus Friday Feb, 13th, 1987, Also to my daughter Nancy L. Hodge and Sonny Livingston

---

Only God hears all my prayers
Only God knows all my thoughts

Only God heals all my pains
Only God will save my soul

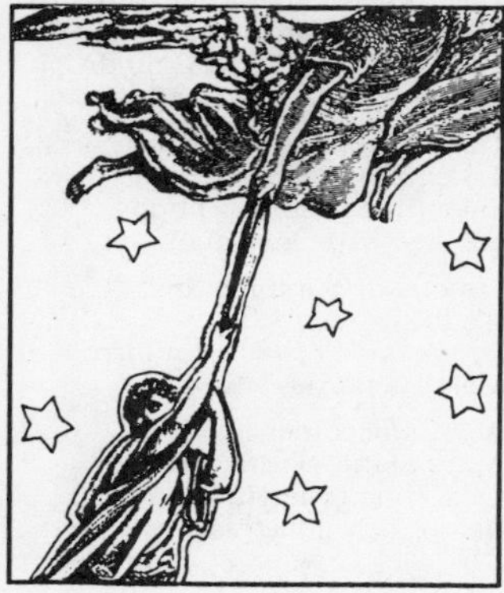

Only God will dry my tears
Only God gives me strength,
Hope and Happiness,
Only God is my father, best friend
And King of Kings.
Only God is my everything.

Penny Ann Rice
JUST ASK HIM
Jesus will allay our fears,
If we ask Him to.
He will always cheer you up,
Whenever you feel blue.

If only you believe in Him,
He will be your friend.
Whenever you are in need,
On Him you can depend.

And if you just ask Him,
He will wash away your sin.
He will start your life anew,
And make you clean again.

Barbara J Monnin
ATTITUDES
I sit there—silence surrounding.
The heat of the sun probing
The recesses of my thoughts
Where in dreams of sweet release
I find—blessed peace.

Yesterday, yea, all my yesterdays
Become as one—combining
To haunt my memories.
Then—bursting like a bud—the sun!
The battle may be won.

Tomorrow, if and when, appearing,
A star on life's horizon, shining,
Infringes on self pity, erasing.
Doubts cannot linger longer,
Life has made me straighter—stronger.

Life, multitudes of attitudes
Nudging lethargic minds to action.
See the beauty! Smell the flowers!
Feel the love around you—
Forget the old, embrace the new

Attitudes of life—

Vinetta V Bianchi
A YOUTHFUL DESIRE

Dedicated to my grandson Robert Keith Zinchuk

He sallied forth in search of want
In DIM EYED DOOLEY'S used car haunt.
The grass was sparkling as his eyes
With tiny drops of lucid skies.
He looked and looked and looked some more
Through every colored used car door.
He sat behind each steering wheel
Imagined every price marked deal.

Day dreams of driving round the square
With envious eyes seen everywhere.
Looked at himself and winked his eye
Self confidence was running high.

He slicked his hair in rear view mirror
Felt the cloth of car's interior.
He matched his jacket to the paint
Then prices quoted made him faint.

Margaret Schrader-Kerr
AN ODE TO MOM AND DAD
Fifty years have gone by since the day you were wed;
Many days, many hours sharing good with the bad,
You've worked as a team, together you've said;
"We'll make it my love, yes, blessings we've had."

It hasn't been easy each step of the way,
but nothing worth having is easy, they say.
From dawn until dusk he plowed and she canned;
or she sewed while he hayed, yet together they prayed.
She mothered her children, he tended his flock; she
cleaned and she cooked, he toiled 'round the clock.

Winters so cold and summers' hot tin, spring in it's
luster and autumn's full bin.
The blush on her young cheeks fifty years ago today,
has mellowed with time, and her hair is now gray.
His young face so strong and so true, is now lined
and weathered from chores he would do.
Yet still in their eyes you see youth peeking through,
his dark eyes so wise, hers warm sparkling blue.

Thank God for all parents and let this daughter say,
I'm happy, so happy that I came your way.
Of all of the parents in this big, wide land,
I want you to know that I think you're just grand.

Mayzell M Ries
A HAPPY LIFE

This poem is dedicated to Henry and Dennis my father and son.

This happy feeling,
It's so good to be alive,
I'm happy all over,
Life's a wonderful surprise.

I'm so very happy
I can't complain,
The world is so beautiful,
Even in the rain.

I see someone smiling,
And I have to smile back.
I'm full of love,
Not there do I lack.

Oh! Why can't everyone
Be as happy as me?
I have love in my heart,
For everyone to see.

Jane E Venable
MEMORIES

To my dear husband, Ken

As I sit here on this windy, rainy day,
I can see leaves falling from the trees as they sway.

It's cold and dark outside, but this doesn't bother me.
I don't let the cold winds or rain get me down,
Because I know together we will be found.

I think of us walking together in the country,
I think of us sitting together side by side.
Our love shines as bright as any star above,
We have so much to give and someone to love.

I enjoy a day together in the park,
And then we go home just before dark.

As we grow older each day,
I remember watching our son play.

Then it's not long until off we go to bed,
But first a story must be read.

Marjorie Ann Iburg
AN IMAGE WHILE DRIVING
An old woman
looks out her window-on-the-world
and sees—
not her pain
not her knarled hands
not her uselessness
not the cars passing in the street below.
An old woman
looks out her window-on-the-world
and sees—
Morning.

Philip Paradis

Philip Paradis
GIFT

A Precious Gift
a notion called Friendship
A Precocious Rift
a concept named Pride

with Friendship the Gift
no need to Hide

with Hands a Lift
Friends on either Side

James H Worley
DREAMER

To my wife Sue and daughter Susan who understands

See the dreamer slowly walking
Like a beast of prey that's stalking
Through the fields and valleys of the mind

Quietly seeking! never finding
Sleeping! walking! reaching blindly
For a door out of his private hell

People! visions! scenes and faces
Light and dark all changing paces
Shifting from their normal places
All haunt the dreamer
While he dreams

He prays that with the dawn he will borrow
At least some small reprieve
From horror
To still the twisting serpent in his soul
But as the dawn brings on tomorrow
He awakes and finds with sorrow
The awakened streets are filled with horror
Of uncaring people on their way to nowhere
So he locks the door, turns out the light
And returns to the endless night
And dreams! and dreams! and dreams

Joanne M Gagnon
LOOKING GLASS
Reflecting an image, a sight to be seen;
A mirror reflecting a distant dream.
It's said the eyes reveal the soul
and echo back the words untold.
An essence riding through endless space
yearns to feel it has a place
in someone's heart, in someone's mind
searching for warmth it cannot find.
Reaching out in all attempts
to grasp a beam of rapture sent
in streams of energy whipping through
every sense in every hue

on every thought to ever shine
within the chambers of the mind.
Reflecting from the eyes its but seen
a looking glass which echoes dreams . . .

Gabriele Nysveen

Gabriele Nysveen
MOMMIE, HOW AM I SUPPOSED TO . . .

To Daniel, my son, who inspired me to write this poem. Love, Mom

How am I supposed to know not to tell you "no" when you
tell me "no" all the time?
How am I supposed to know not to hit if you hit me?
How am I supposed to know how to say please, thank you
and excuse me if you don't say them to me?
How am I supposed to respect your feelings if you don't
respect mine?
How am I supposed to learn not to push you away if you
always push me away when I want your attention or just to be
with you?
How am I supposed to know the difference between right and wrong if you tell me one thing and you do another?
How am I supposed to learn things if you don't take the time to teach me and let me do things by myself?
How am I supposed to learn patience when you have none with me?
How am I supposed to grow up being kind and loving if I
don't see it in you?

I may be small but I am a big part of you I need you, I want you, I trust you and I love you. I accept you just as you are, please accept me. Please be patient with me and give me a chance, I have a long way to go!

LaFon Watkins
OH GOD! HOW GREAT THOU ART
Tonight, Tonight, I cannot sleep.
I even tried by counting sheep.
But even as they jumped the sty,
Holy Angels filled the sky,

They sang in chorus soft and clear.
And seemed to say, "Our Christ is Near."

What Greater Joy can lie in store,
What Peace, What Love, and much, much more.

We feel His nearness as They sing,
"Behold our Savior, Lord and King.
Let all the world awake, Arise,
And sing His praises to the skies."

Oh Bethlehem! Oh Bethlehem!
How canst Thou sleep this night away?
Arise! Arise! and Glory give
The master of the skies this day.

While we on earth do send our Love
And worship Thee so far above.
Receive us with Thy grace, Oh Lord,
And give to us Thy Holy Word.

Let us remain Thy special heirs,
Please accept our fervent prayers.
We worship Thee, though from apart,
And sing of Thee "Oh God! How Great Thou Art!"

Agnes Barnes Nichols
LIFE'S TREASURES

For my son, Lee

The stone I hold in my hand
Is as soft and smooth as velvet.
You brought it to me years ago
When you were but a child
And I was young.
The flowers were pressed
Between the pages of a book
But most of the stones
Found their way back from where they came
To be found by other little boys
And taken to their Mothers.
When I had you
A stone was just a stone
But you are gone now,
You are out there in the world
Doing man things,
So this stone has grown valuable
It is now more precious then gold.
It sparkles like a brilliant diamond
Or could it be that
I am looking at it
Through a tear?

Edna Thornburg
A FRIEND

Dedicated to my beloved Amber Dawn Marquez

A "Friend" is someone who loves you though—
You're old and wrinkled and kinda' slow,
Though your eyes are dim and your ears don't hear—
And you sometimes act a little queer.
You can come to visit and stay for days and days—
They put up with your "clutter" and funny ways,
They make you feel "welcome," though you wonder why,
You know you're a "nuisance"— although you try.
Wherever they go, they take you too—
They're not ashamed of the things you do.
Your shoulders are stooped and your feet have gone flat,
If someone asks where your home is, you can't quite remember just where it's at.
But you know that you've got one, it's around somewhere—
You cook and take care of Jim when you are there.
And you still like to eat, you can eat anytime—anywhere,
And you'll gain a few pounds while you are there.
Your clothes look "frumpy" and out of style—
You've had 'em of course for quite awhile.
But you figure why buy new ones at this late date—
You're getting so close to that "Pearly Gate."
So for as long as I live—until my days end,
I'll thank God for giving me—that kind of a Friend.

Helen Martin Witt
FULL CIRCLE OF LOVE
She who gave
life to me
lies attached to
lifeline tubes
that sustain erratic
breath and heartbeat.

My mind balks
at remembered
words of doctor,
"—further heroic effort
useless—her age—her heart—
your decision."

I cling to withered hands
that fed me,
sewed ruffled dresses,
meted chastening
when I erred,
comforted me
in sorrows.

So many years.

Now I must
become the mother,
releasing
umbilical cords of plastic.

Do I imagine
fleeting pressure
of flaccid hands,
faintest smile on
slackened mouth,
echo of refrain
heard through the years,
"I know you can do it."

Doyle W Overman
EACH OTHER APART

To LaVeta Sweatt a dedicated teacher, a friend, an inspiration of love.

As the minutes and hours squander by
Loneliness and uncertainty multiply
Thoughts of you come and go, but stay
What are you doing?
What are you thinking?
What are you feeling?
If I think, If I wonder, I wish I knew
Time apart an unbearable chore
I have missed you!
I know for sure
Life is special, you are sweet
Together with God we can't be beat
My heart is yours to keep
With my all, I love you

Will Allen (Billie) Stodghill Jameson
TAKE TIME
Take time to chase fair rainbows;
Take time to smell sweet flowers;
Take time to feel cool raindrops.
All these make life worthwhile.

Take time to kiss a baby;
Take time to say a prayer;
Take time to hold a puppy:
For here true love abounds.

Time is fast and fleeting;
It's like a veil of fog:
Here now, but gone tomorrow,
Mere memories recall.

A child becomes a man,
And dreams of other worlds.
Take time to nurture him
Before he's gone his way.

Take time to call the old folks;
Take time to hear their woes;
Take time to praise their efforts:
Love meets these daily needs.

Time is disappearing
And never will return.
Give all your love to others,
And thus your life fulfill.

Randy Arthel Freeman
A MAN IN NEED
A man in need tries to hide but finds no shelter
He runs but gets nowhere
He asks for help but no one seems to hear him
So he sits and cries and says "no one loves me"
But then he remembers that Jesus loves him
He raises his head, smiles and says a prayer
He rises to his feet and walks with his head held high and a smile on his face
So a man in need isn't really in need if he puts his faith in Jesus
I should know for I was that man in need.

Janet A Woolin

Janet A Wollin
ORANGE DAY-LILIED HOUSE OF GLASS

To Goesta and Karin, With Love

Orange day-lilied house of glass
Wooded forest—cool versus warmth,
Golden sunlight.
First impression of serene beauty.
House of a lifetime, motherhood and fatherhood.

Daughter playing, children
frolicking.
Redwood, birds flying.
Evergreens, azalea, iris, flowering
plum,
Pachysandra curled in winter.
Glistening ice among driveway
trees.
We skating on frozen slanting
meadow.
Bird eating from cat's dish, moths
in skylights.
Winter sun reflecting on snow and
covered rocks
And majestic, straight, slender
trees.

Skis ready for fun and skimming,
Tennis racquets winter-idle, then
swimming and sailing in
undulating Hudson.
Seagulls swooping, mallards
waddling, doves cooing,
Geese honking at morning eight
o'clock.
Lovely house, concrete
carpeted-brown, gardenia
blooming,
Terrace parties,
Dogs and kitten snuggling
Now all is left behind me, and
Another lives here.

Candy F Fury
UPON A FALLING STAR

I want to Dedicate my first poem ever published to a very good friend, David Lazor. He is the one that really encouraged me to get started and to do something with my talent. Thank you very much for the encouragement.

It was another special night last
night
we went for a ride under the
moonlight
After awhile we went for a short
walk
while holding hands, we got to
talk.

Our little walk didn't last very
long
we soon sat down under the
moonlit sky
Looking out over a lot of God's
creation
just thinking about it, I wanted
to cry.

It was all so beautiful under the
moonlight
and all the sweet sounds that we
had heard
The sound of running water
from the creek
the wind through the trees, voice
of a bird.

I got to make a wish upon a
falling star
while wondering who the both
of us really are
My wish, I hope and pray will
come true
to get closer to the Lord and still
have you.

It was getting late so we really
had to go
but there was one thing I wanted
you to know
I told you I loved you, then you
kissed me
you meant it when you said you
loved me too.

It was a little cold, the ride on
the way home
but it was all worth it, and I
didn't care
I was cold on the outside, the
inside was warm
I was really glad we decided to
go there.

Suzanne Goodwin
WASTELAND
A girl's dreams lost in total
darkness
The ability to dream is
self-inflicted pain
Suffering from the wounds of
reality
Starving from the lack of fantasy
Always a stranger to paradise
She's living in a wasteland

Sands of time create the deserted
dunes
Miles of nothingness surround her
She reaches for love, but he
escapes her
She screams for attention, but he
does not hear
She watches from afar, because he
does not know her
She's living in a wasteland

She loves him, but he loves
someone else
She can't give him up, not for life
itself
She drains herself of love, giving it
all to him
She is empty and alone in her
desert world
She is left there to die

She's dying in a wasteland

Victoria Lynn Corrigan
THE STORM

To my unknown baby with love

The trees bend low to kiss the
ground
and all I hear is a whistling sound
It makes me shiver deep inside
it makes me want to run and
hide.
The sky grows dark against the sun
and all of God's creatures are on
the run
To a place where they are safe and
warm
to where they're sheltered from
the storm.
The rain hits hard upon the pane
not once, not twice, but again
and again
The lightning streaks across the sky
and thunder roars with a
powerful cry.
Then it stops like sudden death
and you have time for just one
breath
Off in a distance you hear a scream
and you hope to God it's only a
dream.
And then it hits with all of its power
with the mighty thunder and a
flooding shower
It rips the beauty from our life
and leaves us with much grief
and strife.
And when it's gone we'll keep in
mind
this will happen from time to
time
As the sky grows black and covers
the sun
man and beast are on the run.

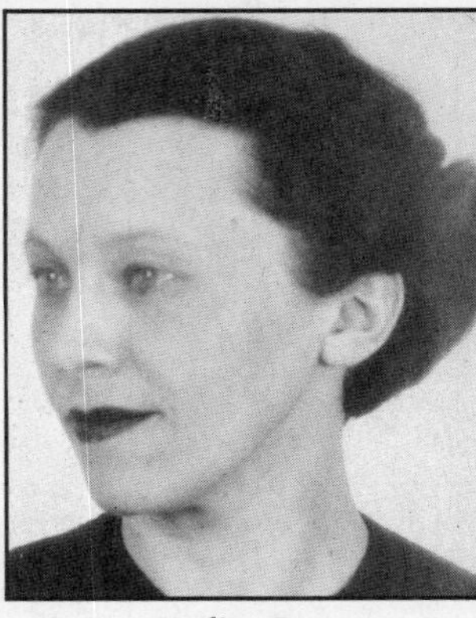

Nadine Beyer

Nadine Beyer
A CHILDHOOD MEMORY

For my good friend Elisabeth

A lovely chandelier hung from the
ceiling
Of our family dining room.
I still remember that warm feeling
That drove away all gloom.

When the lights were lit, each tiny
glass ball
Sparkled with perfect reflection.
My mother explained they were
made of crystal
As I gazed with deep affection.

A heavy snow had fallen that year
Too deep to go out to play,
My room looked out from under
the eave
So there I decided to stay.

I had my dolls, my books, and my
clown,
The sun was shining bright.
The snow on the roof was dripping
down
It was a beautiful sight.

Next morning I peeked out my
window—
The icicles were long heavy bars!
They had frozen themselves in row
upon row,
They must have had help from
the stars!

I thought of the beads of the
chandelier,
They also cast their prism,
So then and there it became very
clear—
This was my crystal prison!

Carl F Klingler
CANDY CANE FACES
Do you know what the joy of
Christmas is
Do you know the joy of love
All we have to do is watch two
candy cane faces
with chocolate chip smiles
Kneeling under Grandma's
Christmas tree
So much love on their faces, the
joy inside
The tree lights sparkle in their eyes
as they smile at the manger
Oh the sparkle in their eyes
The star on the tree is smiling back
at them
How much love they have inside
They never hurt a soul
Oh how they care about life
We can all learn a lesson about life
We can all learn a lesson of love
We can all learn the meaning of
Christmas
from candy cane faces with
chocolate chip smiles
As they kneel under Grandma's
Christmas tree
Everyone should have a candy
cane Christmas
with little chocolate chip smiles
Merry Christmas everyone
From Candy Cane Faces

Bonnie Ducott

Bonnie Ducott
RAINY DAYS AREN'T SO BAD
Suddenly the sky darkens
The clouds seem to open up
Beckoning me
Silent raindrops
Gently touch my skin
Calming my fears
A stiff breeze
Sends shivers up my spine
And shakes loose my anger
The coolness of the tiny drops
Comforts me
The restful tapping on the leaves
Relaxes me
And then it all stops
Suddenly the sky brightens
I've forgotten why I was angry

Richard D McMurray
LIFE SUPPORT

To all who read the Bible with their eyes and ears open to God's words.

What if the stars in Heaven
Never shined their light
What if the day was always dark
There was no day or night

What would be if Adam never
Made a living sound
What if Eve were never formed
From dust upon the ground
There would be no sun to shine
No light of day at all
There would be no young ones
To come in at His call
No need for fruit to grow
For no one here to it consume
A sad place out in nothingness
Quite like the lonely moon
No sounds of old men telling tales
To children on the street
No sounds like: "Thank you, Gra'ma,
Homemade candy is so sweet"
Thank God for life's beginning
And our smiles and tears today
All things you see are good—
For HE has made them all HIS WAY!

Lesley Harmston
SILENT PROTEST

To the memory of "Kriss"

What right is theirs, if of ourselves we give
And nature's miracle thrusts forth upon the womb
A heart beat's chance to live.
Should momentary unions joy
Whisper a song of death
And careless stewardship deny
Even a single day of breath
What right do we afford them
In their unchosen home
Lying deep within the flesh
Their bed becomes a tomb
Powerless to transcend their fate
Travelling a deathbound route
With silent screams protesting
Life's value absolute.

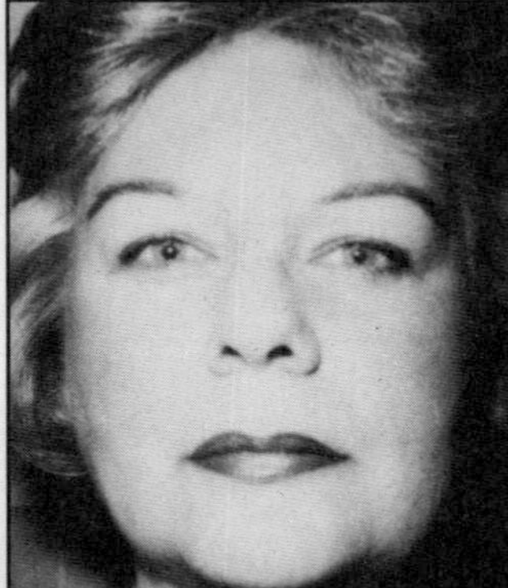
Cathy Cummings

Cathy Cummings
CHILDREN

With love I dedicate this poem to my daughter, Marnie, and my son, Robert.

Children are the future
Our today and our tomorrow.
They inherit all we leave behind
Our happiness and sorrow.

They follow roads that we have paved
Be they bumpy or be they smooth.
They look to us for guidance,
For honesty and truth.
Growing up is very hard
With many ups and downs.
The jobs they choose are challenging,
From executives to clowns.

But for all the time and problems,
One thing you can't replace.
That special look a child can give,
When a smile lights up his face.

Norman E Gay
GETTYSBURG DECEIVED

Dedicated to my family, my reason to be.

"Oh charge, you men of Pickett's breed,
Before the cannon of the union sea,
The greed of the wealthy beckons their pride,
While corporate magicians on their carpets ride.
Under the guise of patriotism, a weapon of greed,
The rebels advance to their destiny.
The fruitless Battle of Cemetery Hill,
Lingers on in our memory still.
Lee's last offensive on northern terrain.
Leaves the world of greed once again in disdain."

"Haunting ghosts of leaders of our nation,
Applauded with thunder, Lincoln's Address of Emancipation.
Lincoln strove onward, his face tired and weary,
While men of greed plotted to upset his theory.
History repeats as often before
While leaders chose those lessons to ignore.
Refer to the past, our future to insure,
Or let greed, through patriotism, endure.
The virtues of the young, with the merits of the old,
Will make the true meaning of peace unfold"

Tammie Laviolette
MISTY TEARS

In memory of my loving daughter June 25, 1984—Oct 18, 1984

Newly faded memories with pictures lost in time,
Figments of a laughing clown, the sadness of a mime.
I do recall my crazy life as I shed a misty tear.
The darkness surrounds my empty life without an ounce of fear.
The wind blows without a sound, the breeze a single trace,
Somethings forgotten, other things so clear,
I close my eyes once again, to cry a misty tear.
My arms will always ache, the pain will stab my heart,
But we will be entwined, never pulled apart.
My reflection of myself, was in my little girl,
She's no longer here, but hasn't left my world.
The clock is still ticking, my time is still here,
But many nights I lay awake, crying misty tears.

Mardelle McNeal
MY TREASURES

Written for and dedicated to my son, Rod Bowman.

A two gun holster and cowboy boots.
A shiny air rifle that really shoots.
A magic kit and an electric train,
Bright red pony with a long white mane.

He had Milt the Monkey and Teddy the Bear.
Here's a few more treasures with you I'll share.
Bumps and bruises and even a black eye.
Quivering lips of a boy who felt too big to cry.

There were always buttons off and holes in the knee
A foot badly swollen from a sting of a bee.
We had marbles, cars, and a model plane,
Turtles, hampsters, and pigeons to tame.

Barefooted jelly-faced in his cowboy hat
Storming the house yelling, "Mom, where's my bat?"
Freckled nosed collector with a pocket full of snails,
A piece of rope, bubble gum, and a few rusty nails.

Do you like my treasures? I have many more.
Like the flowers he brought me from the yard next door.

I don't keep these things under lock and key,
But instead I carry them always with me.
No one can take them from me, they'll never part.
You see I have them locked tight in a Mother's heart.

Of all the grand treasures that I've ever known,
God's gift was the best, a son of my own.

Lt Robert T Rice, Jr

Michael Edward Rice
MEMORIES IN HIS NAME

To all those who have contributed and to those that will contribute to the Lt. Robert T. Rice Jr. Memorial Scholarship fund, 3800 Victory Parkway, Cincinnati, Ohio 45207 and also to my son Robert T. Rice, III.

He was born a Junior to the Senior of the family.
He was sure to be a strong branch on the family tree.
The boy was small but he walked so tall that his pride
shown all about.
He accepted every challange so as not to be left out.
Bob played the sports and joined the scouts; active,
yes he was.
Always lived his life to the fullest unlike everyone does.
A graduate of high school, somewhat sad, but relieved.
Five foot small, still walking tall, the Dean's list
he did make.
Who's Who in American Colleges, in it he had a stake.
A student or a citizen—always did his best.
An officer and a gentleman, he graduated above the rest.
A commitment to his country, loyalty in his heart,
The young officer's tour was just about to start.
A phone conversation, brothers, sisters, Dad and Mom,
He was about to board a plane to the land of Vietnam.
Far away from home, the leader of a platoon —
In the blackness of the
jungle—mortars struck the doom.
The safety of his men was Bobby's only concern;
As an American and a soldier that is what he had learned.
Mortars exploding all around, shrapnel hit his head.
Lieutenant, Bobby, Brother, Son, lay in the jungle dead.
His death will not be forgotten, Mom and Dad thought for sure.
A scholarship in Bobby's
name—they wanted it to be the cure.
For other young people who study to better our nation,
The scholarship fund is proving to be an inspiration.
A five, a fifty, a hundred will not bring my brother back;
but it can help others to follow Bobby's track.

Richard Camilo Aguilar
RESERVATION TOWN

On this dusty, dirty street,
I stop and look around.
I can sense, almost, a palpable aura,
An aura of pain and despair.

Rusting hulks litter the streets,
Resting next to houses in disrepair.
Dirty naked children play in the dirt,
While mongrel dogs roam at will.

In the center of town, tribal elders sit,
Listless and uncaring, staring with lifeless eyes.
Most of the young people have gone,

Gone to seek their dreams, in a strangers world.

I listen to tales of woe and anguish,
Of dreams of hope and dreams impossible.
Alcohol and drugs are used by many,
Vainly, to forget their futile existance.

As I walk away from this place, I think,
How wind and rain causes stone to fade,
Knowing that time will cause the same,
To this town, where I was born.

Shannon Kelly

KEEPING TIME

Still
you live in my heart
Roped off,
Restricted—
no one can come here
but you.

Please
call me,
once.
Let me hear your soft
voice
asking for me.

Debra J Wahl

INNOCENCE

Cold lonely nights
Knowing it isn't right
What is it I really feel
Confused and lonely
Out of control
Not myself
But someone else
Where is the me that I once knew
The innocent child of long ago
Who overnight
Blossomed into
A woman you never knew
Leaving childhood behind
Almost as innocent now as she was then
Still barely knowing
A thing about men

Anita Pownall

BALANCE AND BELIEF

The thoughts of you are leaving me.
Quickly, quickly they are going,
as if they had never occurred.
I can't stand the quiet in my heart and mind.
I'm crying out from this silence
for something to believe in,
something to hold on to.
All this time is making me crazy,
time to think and time to feel,
it's all lost time.
Wasted.
I want to go home to love and friendship,
but it is never there,
only silence.
My belief in you is ending
and along with those fading thoughts
goes my piece of mind,
my serenity, my balance.

Launa Dianne Morrison

ONE SET BACK IN LIFE

January 28, 1986—Let us remember the Challenger & it's crew. Do not let their dream, our dream die! Keep believing, so all our dreams will live & grow, Forever!

Life—
Death—
A sad reality in being here.
A dream—dead or died?
A sadness—
Emptiness—
A tear.
For happiness—for better!
Now a faded dream—
NO!
Just another door closed on the way.
We must not stand in disbelief—
We must go on believing!
Life—
Love—
Dreams.
Soon, we shall conquere our failures—
And be able to open those doors!
Love together—
The lives taken—
One mishap—
But, our dreams shall live on!
—The Space Shuttle Challenger tragedy—

Janet C Griffith

BUS RIDE

Fusty wet wool itches.
Damp crosses backs and books
Hands hold tight
Leather U-straps hanging from the domed white roof,
Boards where cigarettes and undertakers advertise
Lurching onward up and down the icy hills.

Dampness clouds windows, wisdom,
Twists hair, drips from reddened faces.
As we peer through frantic mittened rubbings,
Every narrowing circles
Fail to keep us from keeping
Our melting sights on
All our cold way home.

Eileen M Luczynski

Eileen M Luczynski

MY U.S.A.

To all service men and women, both living and dead, who fought for freedom and to keep America strong. God bless them all.

I'll take my stand, to preserve this land
For I'm proud of the U.S.A.
Where "Old Glory" waves in this land of the brave
And we can all stand up and have our say.
We've had many brave men, who fought to the end
And there's more who take their place today;
They will join in the fight to preserve what is right
So we can live the American way.
We welcome from the sea, to this land of the free
The oppressed, the hungry, and the poor;
Here, they will learn a trade, and not be afraid
In this great land of the open-door.
We will them, one and all; and our land will never fall
For we are building up its' forces every day;
Going to any length, to maintain its' strength
As we still shout out, "Hip Hip Hooray."
We will never veer, but state our case loud and clear
To all aggressors who may come our way,
For this land of the free is the land for you and me
And I'm proud of the U.S.A.
I want to help "Old Glory" wave, in this land of the brave
So the children can grow up strong and tall;
Without fear of any man, or of any foreign land
Knowing the U.S.A. is mightiest of them all.

'Haze' Craddock

ANOTHER DAY

Each A.M., as I arise,
right before my very eyes
is another day.
A day that I could criticize . . .
but I'll look for good if I analyze,
cuz I'm so thankful for each one that comes my way.

What does this day hold for me?
I can hardly wait to see . . .
Naturally, I hope it's good, BUT
I'll be grateful no matter what,
for another chance to live and just be me.

As I get older and feel less plucky,
every morning I feel so lucky!

Gee, another day that's just my size—
I'll make it count, if I am wise;
I'll give of myself and walk in HIS ways
as a small reimbursement for my beautiful days.

So, I get up and say,
(and so should you)
"Good morning, day,
I got here too."

Linda S Ervin

MEMORIES

Is it the faint smile of a new mother,
Holding the smallest of miracles in a
Snow white gown, etched in primrose
Lace.

Can it be the reflection in the still—
Ness of your mind, of a flowing orchid
Gown descending from a staircase into
The arms of your senior-prom hero.

Could it be the seriousness of a
Slightly etched smile, coming from your
Now painted, but once untouched lips,
Now displayed in a white robe, gold
Tassel, a diploma so honestly earned,
Encircled with scarlet.

Or could it be all and this too.
The day you wore the gown of pearly
White, etched in primrose lace,
Grandma's pearls, arm in arm with
Your fondest of heroes, who gave you
Away to another.

It is these memories of a once young,
Distorted smile in a broken mirror,
Not so clearly can you see it now in
The discolored looking glass, you
Found in grandma's attic, when life
Was so sweet and dreams were so far
Away.

Betty A Hussey

MY BRIGHT STAR

To all mothers of servicemen wherever they may be

As I sit by my window and gaze afar,
On the distant horizon I see a star.
There are many, I'm sure, others can see,
But the brightest, the clearest is for me.
My son is there on a far off isle
Where God has sent him, for just awhile.
As I sit by my window and gaze out there,
My heart offers up this fervent prayer—
May my son never, never my vigil repeat.
Anger and warfare, dear God defeat!

R K Duncan

THE HANDS OF A MIGRANT WORKER

I have worked
In the canefields of the world;
In the vineyards of the world;
In the orchards of the world;
In the farmlands of the world;

I have given all I have;
My hands,
My father's hands,
My children's hands.

My mother died young.
I light a candle
On her saint's day.
I don't know why.
Her saint is gone
From the calendar.

Carol Schatz

HEAR THE RAIN COMETH

Hear the rain cometh,
Steadily falling;
The beating soundeth,
Like angels calling.

The rose bush bows its head in prayer,
To thank God that it is there.
The ground receives, thirsty it was,
But now it's not of what it twas.

The trees hang heavy of water sweet,
So happy that tears drop from their bidden cheeks;
The birds flutter and come to life;
Hop upon the ground,
And on worms they thrive.

We heard the rain cometh,
Now hear the rain go;
To where? We do not know,
But what is left is more wonderful than the rest;
The sweet smell the rain leaves is now the best.

Pattie Denise Porter
GRANDMOTHER

To my loving Grandmother, Daisy E. Porter

Grandmother you are very special
Though you are set in your ways
You've helped me many times
And brightened many of my days

There's nothing I cherish
More than your love
You're like a gift given to me
From the Good Lord above

All throughout my life
You've always been there
Proving to me each and every day
Just how much you care

Although we are now many miles apart
I think of you with each day passing
And hold all of our wonderful memories
Deep down inside my heart

Grandmother, I wrote this poem
Especially for you
Because I love you very much
And thank you for all the things you do

Joy Margaret Fox
PAGES IN A BOOK

Pages in a book, that's what my thoughts are,
Leaping forth from the page to me,
Getting my attention with
A gentle easing into expression.
Teasing and tantalizing they come,
And I tend to snatch them before
They get fully born, only to find
Them withdrawing back into the womb of my mind.

Then patiently I must wait and
Focus on what my hands are doing,
Giving time and space to these infant thoughts
Which really have a mind of their own.
Then, with my attention elsewhere, they
Again ease back into view and I wait
As they come forth fully formed this time
And are welcomed into my arms.

A May Hill
FOOTPRINTS

The ocean was beautiful today,
Blue, green, lavender and gray.
I ran along the water's edge
making footprints in the sand.
But alas, my footprints did not stay,
For great waves came rolling in
And washed them all away!

Today I walked a lonely winding road,
Carrying a large and heavy load,
But the way seemed rather short,
And my burden somewhat light,
For this was a labor of love.

Looking back I saw my footprints
Deep and strong in the damp firm earth,
Then I knew where the difference lay
In shifting sands and passing pleasure
My footprints will not stay,
But only in the selfless loving acts
That make the day.

Margaret L Trefz
PEN PAL

Six years have passed since first we met;
Six years we've been together.
You've proved a loyal pal to me
In every kind of weather.

I loved your dainty green-robed form
That first glad day we met;
The ribbon, too, with golden clasp,
I treasure even yet.

With you I've traveled many a mile
Through many changing scenes;
You helped me get my lessons, and
You wrote my English themes.

You helped express my joys and tears;
You shared in all my fun.
I want you for my pal until
Our little life is done.

For all through life's short day I need
You, my dear, faithful friend!
Oh, great is my regard for you,
My TRUSTY FOUNTAIN PEN!

Leo Michael
CHRISTMAS

A shining light reaches down to earth
on a cold, dark Christmas morning.
A heavenly child was given birth
to a mother most holy and loving.
Angels appeared in this morning light.
Their trumpets sounding louder and clear.
The shepherds awoke in a shattering fright
to hear a voice. Do not fear
a savior is born to save mankind
as told by the prophets of old.
In a manger on hay, you will find
a glowing face, brighter than silver and gold.
The shepherds gathered and left their flock
to follow this light, so far, so dim.
In their hurried step, they refused to talk
until they reached the crib in Bethlehem.

Carol Pickett
GOING HOME

I'm going to try to go home again
Though they say it can't be done.
It's something that I have to try
Before my race is run.

I want to travel back through the years
To where my memories wait.
Back to the past that is part of me
That pulls my heart like a weight.

I want to walk the same old streets
That I walk in my mind alone,
And find still more of my memories
In familiar places I roam.

In long years past, we played our games
And dreamt our childish dreams.
Why can't you go home again?, I ask
It's just a short journey, it seems.

I want to travel back through the years,
Back through the heartache and pain
And see if some of the dreams I had
Might still remain the same.

Maybe you can't go home again,
but shouldn't we really try?
And if the past is gone, then I will whisper a silent cry,
And voices from times long gone will say,
"We're glad that you wanted to try."

Robert H Daniels
LIFE'S CONSTANT COMPANION

To the glory of God and in memory of Matilda.

When I was a lad of ten and four,
I would sit on the step outside the door,
And watch the shiny sulkies pass
'Til they came no more, no more.

First there was a nobleman, laughing and proud,
Next followed a widow, poorly endowed.
Then passed a craftsman leathered by the sun,
Lastly I myself, 'companied by the Grisly One.

"Who are you, what's your name?"
The answer always returns the same.
"I am life's constant companion, who
tho' hesitant now, finally gets his due."

"Ah, yes, tho' a youngster in years I be,
I have a Companion older than thee.
He came on earth that we may be
Forever free of the likes of ye!"

Marion E Otterson
SO SPEAKS THE SEAGULL

The sky is my home and I always fly free—
Over rivers and lakes and wide open sea—
I follow the ships, a great distance I roam—
Never forgetting the sky is my home!

My home's ever changing, each minute seems new—
Flying into the sunset of gold red and blue.

When only the moon and the stars make it bright—
On the cool sands of shore I bed down for the night.

At the first sign of dawn I'm off and away—
Over the waters to Kattegat Bay.

It matters not how far I may roam—
I'll always remember the sky is my home!

Michael J Cihon
THE FLOWER TENDER

Warm is my heart with gentle thoughts of you
A flower, delicate and yet afraid
Trembling at the touch of love and kindness
Unsure because of pain from life's past charade
Dark eyes that look with wonder at the night
And heart that fear and pain unsettles
Mistreated by life's cold and heartless tempo
Afraid to show it's warm and fragrant petals
Let me mend your wilted broken leaves
And let me mend what's torn apart
Walk with me through passions open door
And touch your blossoms wounded heart
I'll warm you with my gentle wind
And shine my sun upon your precious soul
I'll mend your heart with healing love
And soothe away life's bitter toll
I'll hold you through the night's cold darkness
I'll sing your song so warm and tender
I'll open up your spirit's beauty
And bring it back to love's sweet splendor
I am the flower tender

Fern R Ackerman
MY MOTHER'S GARDEN

In my Mother's garden there were many things to see
Big long rows of lettuce, beets and lots of peas
Each one carefully planted in straight and narrow rows
Allowing space where needed so everything might grow
All around the outer edge some pretty flowers grew
They seemed to add a touch of class and some beauty too.
My Mother loved her garden and she tended it with pride
You, of course, could help a bit, but she would supervise
One day while helping with the weeds, she turned and said to me
"Be careful where you step and walk, a plant you may not see
God sends the sunshine and the rain

But I must work the soil, the same
As if it all depends on me
To bring forth the food and the
blooms you see,
So with God's sunshine and his rain
And with the help I give
Those little seeds will sprout and
grow
And strive so hard to live."

Our faith is like her garden
It needs nourishment and care
Life and faith are precious
So handle them with prayer.

Beverly Hoffman
LIFE'S BLESSINGS

They were not given to us
To squander nor to hoard
But to share with All-Life's
Blessings
Freely given by our Lord.

Care about the suffering
Feed the hungry when we can
Do what we can for others
Just like the Master's Plan.

Bear one another's burdens
Encourage a beaten soul
Pray for those who are hurting
All lives to be made whole.

For does He not expect, Just
a little more of you and me
Born in the "Land of Plenty"
By God's grace, loved and free.

Gary L Nielsen
IN A-ROUND-ABOUT WAY

To Ronda; My Loving wife.

I've always thought that beauty
could only be skin deep.
With you I find it deeper, In your
sole and funny little feet.
I've always thought that good
times were few and far between
But we have had so many, I feel
I'm in a dream.
I've always thought Devotion was
like a lock and key
It can tie you down to boredom,
But you hold a golden key.
I've often thought that "life was a
bitch and then you die,"
You've gave it a whole new
purpose, your sole makes my
soul high.
I've always known that laughter
could make a gray day shine,
It cheers the heart and warms a
smile, and helps the nerves
unwind.
I've always believed that food for
thought can stimulate the mind,
The food you've put on the table,
I'll weigh 200 pounds in time.
All of these things I've mentioned
you have so many of,
I can't believe this is happening, I
can't help but fall in love.
I want to say I Love You, from my
mouth and not my hand,
But that word is not so easy
anymore, I know you'll
understand.
We've both been burnt by love
before, I know we both are
scared,
Our pasts are not so pretty, but
now there's fresh clean air.
I promise I will be good to you, and
for you, for as long as we are
together and I hope and pray
that it will be forever.

Thomas Ivester
THE SPARKLE IN YOUR PAST

Dedicated to Susan

I've searched everywhere for that
one special card to find,
the one that would say what
is so truly on my mind.
But that one special card
was nowhere to be found,
so here on this paper
I write my mind down.
I could write forever
of my aches and pains,
of my cloudy skies
and days plagued with rains.
But now I write you a hope
that this gift would forever last,
as a sparkle in the back of your
mind,
the sparkle of a love in your past.

Leo D Germain
A HOLE IN THE GLASS

There is a man in a box
Only he knows why,
And only he knows how.
Someone misplaced all the locks.

There is another man outside,
He's in the light,
Searching for the reasons why
He looks down, and his shadow
cries.

There's a thought in the air,
Piercing the fog
of all our forgotten nightmares.
We will never hear.

There's a hole in the ground
with a man falling through.
He say's he wants it that way
We're too afraid to stick around.

I see a hole in the glass,
but it won't let the air in,
and the light can't come through.
You, me, and someone's shadow.
Together at last.

Roy Holland
COLUMNS: A LEGACY

Yesteryear
Lingers in shadowed, massive
form,
Scarred by fate's unkind decree.
Jutting from a reddish mound,
Three columns stand proud and
free.
And a door behind them
Is open for wisdom to endure.

Today
Struggles with the invasion of
change.
The light of understanding seeks a
better way
As concrete arms guide restless
minds
To challenge the meaning of life's
play.
And a door behind them
Is open for truth to speak.

Tomorrow
Lives within the soul of night.
Time still has knowledge to bestow
As the giant monoliths continue to
herald
Each new dawn's eager flow.
And a door behind them
Is open to give the choice.

J M Thomas
ODE TO THE VIETNAM VETERAN

In tribute to a survivor of the Vietnam conflict D. G. Helgeson—Artist for the ODE TO THE VIETNAM VETERAN

Death and dying everywhere—
I see the sorrow here.
Back home in the United States;
People, do they care?
Am I forgotten? Do they know
That I am here for them?
Or, do they just pass each day
Not knowing where I am?
Oh, the pain, the cry of all—
I hear it night and day!
O please, dear God, end all this
strife
And, bring me home someday!
I've seen the children in the streets
Walk aimless day to day;
I care for them, I fear for them,
How long must we stay?
It's over, Oh thank God—
I'm home,
But the Memory lives on.
My hurt is real, my pain is real—
Where have my friends gone?
It seems the world just passed me
by—
I wonder was it real?
Did I see all that hurt and pain?
The Memory's with me still!

Mary E Caldwell
AFFAIR OF THE HEART

I wish to dedicate this poem to Calvin Edgar Boone the source of my inspiration

Oh eyes that glisten and glow
Beneath your brilliance
There is a story to unfold
Sudden wealth of jewels and gold
Cannot be the secret
Yet to be told
For I can sense
That the mystery lies deep
And yet it is not one
Your heart shall let you keep
For even heaven's starlight

Is bending low
To add to the shine
Appearing from your soul
Wisdom alone
Would not allow a man
Or woman to guess
But for ones that have been there
And are equally as blessed
Can appear smilingly
In his or her own happiness
And say, "you are in love"

Ramona E Westerberg
I DO

To John Eric Westerberg, the man that I said I do

I couldn't wait
for us to unite
Just to become one
and have a sight
Of you to be me
and me to be you
To walk together
in only one shoe.

I do feel
that unity with you
I have walked
in only your shoe
There is no other
for me to share
The rest of my life with
If only you dare.

Suzanne Sproule
THE AREA THAT ROCKS MY MIND

For those of us whom, at times feel depressed, there is an answer and a place to rest

On any given day, if you may seem
me hard to find,
I'll be basking on the jetty by the
sea through the tranquility of my
mind.
Sea air and salt will cover my
face—along with visions of
seagulls soaring high—
As I glide off secretly for my
favorite resting place.
Wet rocks that are set out far on
the ocean floor where the mist
of the sea I truly feel,
Breathing and inhaling the
wonderful air that I know is so
real.
That's where I'll be mesmerized by
the beautiful sounds,
The thrashing of the waves, so
soothing to my mind,
Against the rocks the clearly heard
roar as the salty water pounds.
This is my hide-a-way. The solace
and peace that I reach out to find.

Donna Joy Nixon
LOVE'S GOLDEN CAGE

To William, the loving craftsman and my husband.

I love my little golden cage
With it's widely open door.
For when I feel the need to fly,
My spirit freely soars.
The tiny bars are bound with love
And securely locked in place.
But lovingly the craftsman left
A splendid opened space.

At times I feel the need to stretch
And learn a new sweet song.
With so much love about my cage,
I care not to tarry long.
I feel the wind caress my wings
And bask in warm sunlight,
Then turn and swiftly sail back
home
To my golden heart's delight.

If the door was never open,
If I couldn't learn new songs,
I'd probably fall right off my perch

And live not so very long.
Yes, I love my little golden cage
With it's widely open door.
The space I have to leave and fly
Just makes me love it more.

Donna Nordstrom
I WONDER

I wonder-
How a leaf feels when the wind
  begins to blow.
It is fun skipping across the lawn,
  or does it hate being pushed?
The grass, as the mower passes
  over it—
Is it annoyed at having grown for
  naught?

I wonder-
If a creek feels proud of the
  bubbling song it makes as it
  trickles along?
Is it happy to be alive, or do the
  objects which lie in its path
  make it cross?
Do the nests in the branches of a
  leafy tree make the tree feel
  unkept, or
Is it proud to be called a shelter?

I wonder-
Is the blanket of snow warm or
  cold to the ground and what's
  under it?
Does time enjoy its swift pace, or
  does it wish to be able to rest?
Does it wish to stand still for a
  while and survey its minutes?

Gwen Headrick
TWILIGHT'S BEAUTY

Here I sit by a cool brook,
My heart is trouble free.
All nature's one big splendid book,
On every side of me.

The sky is dressed in softest blue.
The golden sun is setting low,
Bathing the earth in a perfect hue,
By casting its soft warm glow.

Just as twilight displays its best,
The day creatures are quietly
  drawn,
To sleep and gently laid to rest,
From darkness to early dawn.

Now the night creatures come
  awake.
The air is filled with a multitude of
  songs,
And I feel privileged to partake
In evening's beautiful pictures and
  songs.

Homeward bound I am once more,
Fulfilled, but reluctantly I go
  inside,
While twilight silently shuts its
  door,
And moonbeams to the earth do
  slide.

Andrew-Philip Cross
PERFECTION

For Pat and the small circle of friends who knew I could.

Although, when the dancer
  Becomes the dance,
There may be music in her soul,
And when the gambler
  Becomes the chance
He may have achieved his goal,

You see, when the pilot
  Becomes the flight,
There is danger in the air.
And when the fighter
  Becomes the fight,
It is best that you beware.

Because, when the artist
  Becomes the art
It's not really what he needs.
And when the lover
  Becomes the heart
He'll find he, too quickly, bleeds.

And so, when the culprit
  Becomes the crime,
Though he's achieved perfection,
As when the poet
  Becomes the rhyme,
He has no more direction.

Peggy Ann Dial

Peggy Ann Dial
THE MISS JUDGE ROSE

Can't understand the existence of
  life sometimes.
The existence of nature, and it's
  compatible mates.

So intimate when love is to share
The most exciting is the one who
  really cares.

This love is more abundant
then the petal of a rose,
that's shy,
More beautiful than the sky its' self,
Which hides beneath the bright
  sunshine.

When the hittest of times is there
And love can be very true,
don't depend on a rose petal
Cause he really loves you.

Delores P Knowlton
DIVINE COMMUNICATION

I sat in a crowd & was lonely—
Lonely—as a lost—fluttering bird.
  Though gaiety—and song
  swirled about me;
My heart—did not swell with their
  sound.
  I sat by myself—and was lonely—
Not a sound—no one uttered a
  word.
  Ah-h-h then—'MY FRIEND'
  entered in;
And—with fullness—my heart did
  abound.
  We sat alone in the stillness
  together—
FRIENDS—sharing mutual
  respect & trust.
  Hearts bound together—with
  human affection;
Two souls joined—divinely as one.
  Heart—mind and soul—sealed
  in friendship—
Though our lips just gathered dust.
  Eyes meeting—in total
  communion;
A corporation . . more mighty than
  Bradstreet and Dunn.
  At—our mutual—and—
  boundless contentment—
Both bird—and crowd—seemed
  perplexed.
  We smile—as in mute
  comprehension;
Their bewilderment—we both
  understand.
  Void of a—like and implicit
  fusion—
'Tis true—they're understandably
  vexed.
  Viewing—comprehension—so
  tacitly interwoven;
Borne—of a glance and a wave of
  the hand.

Gladys E McDonough
SAND

I would like to dedicate this poem to my friend Larry Earley, who gave me the word "Sand" as a challenge to write a poem

---

The world of the desert is a vast
  world to man
With acres and miles of unending
  sand,
By day, an arid world with beating
  down heat,
A world where sand and horizon
  eventually meet.

At night, turning cold and the air
  is so clear
All night sounds clearly reaching
  the ear
A Coyote's call—weird, piercing
  and shorn
Can leave a man's nerves all
  trembling and torn,

A lone horse and rider with his
  head bent low
Plod peacefully along for they
  seem to know
That they are alone in this huge
  desert of sand
And no harm will come to them
  close at hand.

The winds start up and the sands
  drift and mold
This world by itself makes a man
  hardy and bold,
He learns all the places for water
  and food
And when troubled and restless,
  sand eases his mood.

He rides on and on and never
  ceases to see
The unending pictures of sand's
  mysteries.
Sand, sand, shifting, whispering
  sand . . .
What is this peace that you hold
  out to man?

Patricia Patterson
HAPPINESS IS FLEETING

Happiness is like a fleeting
  butterfly,
Touching peoples lives as it passes
  by.

Some folks believe it can be bought,
Actually it can't even be caught.

When I was very young and gay,
It was constantly slipping away.

Then as it touched my life one
  night,
I tried to hold on with all my might.

I was sure it was there to stay,
Only to find it gone the next day.

As I grew more wiser with age,
It's fleeting caused me less rage.

I found that's how it's meant to be,
Happiness is fleeting, don't you see.

Letitia G Ellis
A SPECIAL RAINDROP

To my son Benjamin, the joy of my life, and my mother Virginia for her inspiration, and to the man I love.

This morning I saw a raindrop,
That gave me such a chill,
It made my spine shiver,
It all seemed so unreal.

As I watched it through the
  window,
It took things off my mind,
And nothing seemed to bother me,
It all want back in time,

It all came down upon my face,
And everything stood still,
I looked around, and there it was,
A raindrop standing still.

Daisy Summer
IN MEMORY OF JOHN F. KENNEDY

When the dark clouds gather at the
  close of a beautiful day,
As twilight slips into blackness to
  steal the hours away,
So slips from our midst a gentle
  soul, one most loved and held
  dear,
To pass on to something better
  where there is no hatred or fear.
God grant him peace and refuge in
  this far and better land,
And guide his wife and children
  and lend them a helping hand.
He gave his all that people might
  have life and liberty,
And make this earth a better place
  for our democracy.
His aims were high his love for
  people great.
It's hard to understnd how anyone
  could harbor so much hate,
To end this life so needlessly and
  find his the same fate.
My heart is heavy, my tears are
  spent for the loss of this gentle
  soul,
Who had to leave this earth before
  he could reach his goal.
And so you see it isn't only me that
  mourns this noble gent,
The whole world feels his loss
  because he was our President.

May his memory linger in the
  hearts of the American people
As long as the everlasting lamp
  burns in the Arlington Cemetary.
Nov. 22, 1963

Lillian Cecilia Martz
NEEDED TIME

To Mama: who always gave me the time I needed.

If you needed all the time in the
  world
  But only had ten hours
Would you waste it doing needless
  things
Or stop and "smell the flowers?"
Would you gather those you loved
  very close
And kiss away each tear?

Hoping love would erase all pain
And banish any fear
No one knows when time will run out
Or our days on earth will end
So until then show love to all
And each living creature, befriend!

Frank W Thorlton

Frank W Thorlton
TINY HAND

Lovingly Dedicated to My Wife "Vernice"

I touched the hand, of the hand of love;
Sent to me from God above.
It took my heart in a time of stress;
And brought it out of a wilderness.
It renewed my faith in the master plan;
It opened my eyes when I touched that hand.

In a world where madness seems its only scope;
A hand like this is our last best hope.
The love and innocence in that tiny hand;
Was surely Gods original plan.
A new world was opened to this doubting man;
When I touched, my Grandchilds tiny hand.

Mabel A Crews Fleming
TAKE TIME

Take time to think,
Thoughts are the spice of life.
Take time to laugh,
Laughter is music to the soul.
Take time to love,
Loving is what makes living worth while.

Take time to smile, people wander what
You are up to.
Take time to be friendly,
Friendship gives life a delicious flavor.
Take time to speak,
One little word could uplift an unhappy soul.

Take time to touch someone,
A warm, tender touch is heart warming.
Take time to look,
Someone feels, you care.
Caring is what it is all about

Dennis G Bathurst
REMEMBER THIS NIGHT?

To Kim Leonard To be with you, and to love you is all I ask of life.

Remember
When we laid beside one another
And our love was finally at peace
Remember
When we tried to hold each other close
but we both knew it was just a tease
Remember
When we laid thinking to ourselves
Without anymore lust
Remember
When we tried to imagine love
And how wonderful it would be for us
Remember
When we kissed each other good night
feeling the warmth for the last time
Remember
When I whispered "you're beautiful"
As you put your leg between mine

John Lee Bradford Jr
GOD'S PLAY ON STAGE HERE ON EARTH

Someone said the world's a stage,
We each must play a part,
We are the love ones,
God is our sweet heart,

Act I, is when we're born,
We don't know what to do.
But as we grow a little,
Things come in to view

Act II, We start to go to church,
With each new passing day.
We learn about JESUS,
But sometimes, we don't except
HIM right away.

Act III, We finally except Him,
But yet we're not through.
We must follow him,
In every thing we do.

Act IV, The play is over,
It is time for us to go.
It can be a happy ending,
If you want it to you know.

Jessie Turner
MY COUNTRY

My Countrys Constitution

Other Countries May Suit You Better
Other Countries May Impress Your Mind

America, My Country's Constitution
Constitutes Freedom For All Mankind
Government For the People
By the People

Endowed with Certain Inalienable Rights

Pursuit of Happiness and Freedom
Freedom, a Prophecy What Life IS TO BE
A Rainbow of Promise Translated
All Men Were Born Free

I Pledge My Sacred Honor to the BATTLE
For Human Freedom
Can I Do Less

Vicenta S Benoza
THE CIRCLE OF LOVE

To my Husband, Armando, for your love and support and to my children, for the joy and pain of watching you all grow.

Your touch is so tenderly sweet,
Upon my innocent face,
I never knew anything as lovely as your voice,
The sound of it brings music to my ears.
Sometimes I feel your tears upon my cheeks,
Yet always I would wonder about the glitter in your eyes,
Just one moment away from you I feel lost.

But your touch is magic,
Making me complete that my basic madness is an excuse for loving.
You gave meaning to a less colorful world
I discovered the heights and depths of emotions running wild,
For every moment I am with you I feel alive.

And your touch is sacred,
Lifting my eyes above, calm and serenity reigns
And my heart over flows with humility
I thank thee for the gifts of life and for the disappointments and pains,
They are the tower of my strength.
Each blessed moment alone with you, my soul has found peace.

This circle of love goes on and on
We lived through it's dimensions
For love is life . . .

George R Nash
BLOOD OF THE GRAPE

This poem is dedicated to my loving wife Hazel and to my uncle Stanley Kearns who prods me in developing my talents.

People look upon the red wine as being best.
But that which is delightful soon becomes a pest.
For awhile it deceives you and camouflages its aim
Which daily injures, kills, and bites to maime.

Once sick, beggard and ruined in his estate
Man can't see this as his most fatal mistake.
All the quarrels, the sorrows, and the woes
Are all wounds without cause as onward he goes.

The eyes become unruly and there is lust in the heart
And the tongue lashes out words it never before would part.
With judgement clouded and steadiness long past
The delight has become a killer at last.

Once a rich man I was in good health
I felt not my descent; nor the loss of my wealth,
I am but an animal whom alive is already dead
Take in by the blood of the grape when it is red.

James Corbet Bunkley

James Corbet Bunkley
EVEN THOUGH . . .

Dedicated to Samuel Henry Bunkley

Even though . . . our lives aren't complete,
Even though . . . there's no answer to the question we seek,

At least I've had the privilege of a little small peek
of you at birth . . . so Handsome and Pink

Even though . . . dreams are left unfilled,
Even though . . . the pain will never heal,

I thank GOD that you were complete,
Beautiful in every way . . . from the tip of your little head,
. . . to the nails on your tiny toes!

Even though . . . life's pleasures will never be ours,
I know you are with One who cares.

Even though . . . I don't know why, and I can not believe,
Even though . . . I will never see,
Even though . . . We will never be,

GOD willed that you must sleep . . .
So, sleep my Son, in Heaven's slumber
And when I die, you can end my wander!

Lamb of God who takes away the Sins of the World,
Have mercy on our Souls! My Son
. . . My Endless Love

"Samuel Henry Bunkley"

DAD

Kimberly Martin
IS LOVE BUT A MEMORY?

Is love but a memory
for us that's gone by?
With all the pain I've caused you
My feelings I can't clarify.
But, if we are what we are
it can't ever be the same,
my actions were unjustifiable
and I'm the cause to blame.
With the lies I've told you
You could never trust me
Our dreams turned into nightmares

And that's not how love should be.
It hurts to say goodbye
After all the years we shared
but if hurts you to live with me,
When you've had all you can bear.
If we've wasted all the years
Have I wasted all my tears?
Trying to hold onto us
And trying to lose my fears.

Jacqueline Orten Bloch
A CAGE OF LONELINESS

To my three beautiful children Christine, Jason, and Jenette And my wonderful husband, Michael

---

He sits day after day on the same old park bench
He watches the chidren at play
He wonders what the future will bring for them
He wonders how it will end
He smiles and waves at the passers by
At times he even shouts a word of greeting
But no one hears him, no one stops to say hi
He talks to the pigeons and squirrels in the park
He feeds them bread and shows them the love in his heart
He wishes he could show people the same
But no one will let him try. All alone he starts to cry
The poor old man with wrinkles of age
He feels as though he's locked in a cage
A cage of loneliness, he can't break free
He looks into the trees with his sad soft eyes
He tips his hat to his friends, the pigeons and squirrels
His precious little pearls
The poor old man with a long flowing beard
Glances back at the children at play, and the passers by that never say hi
He shrugs his shoulders he feels his bones growing older
He slowly gets up with tears rolling down his face
And silently creeps away

Kathleen Margie Preston
GOD'S EVERLASTING LOVE

I dedicate this poem to all my children, Bob, Mike, Rick, LeeAnn and another son Michael, who died in 1986, I wish everyone peacefullness and happiness

---

Here is a love you can share
One you can call your own
Just turn to God, he'll be there
You'll never be alone
If we obey his laws
Do what is right
He will show us the way
And give us the light
Our true and faithful friend
Sing to Him clear and loud
Our Saviour until the end
Some day He'll arrive on a cloud
The time may be dark as a raven
Or it could be in broad daylight
He will show us the way to heaven
With Him, everything will be right
He knows we are all sinners
But He is our precious saint
through Him, we can be winners
Let's do it now, before it's too late
He's in our hearts day and night
With him, let's try to be true
He loves us with all his might
Walking with God, we won't be blue.

Becky Timonen
WAVES
The waves come crashing,
Pulling at the sand.
Reaching out,
Calling people to enter.
Will they come?
They go back,
As fast as they came,
Leaving treasures,
For those who remain.
The waves return,
Ever to recede once more.

Mary B Treible
WILD STRAWBERRIES!
Spring is here! April showers bring May flowers!
The white strawberry blossoms
Holding their heads up high
Following the sun
And letting Nature work its magic
Back behind the garden
My path leads me
Thru the large patch
Of wild strawberries!
Daily I visit the patch
Watching Waiting
Until the day
When three tiny berries
Are red Ripe
I pick I eat Delicious!
Daily for six weeks I visit the patch
I pick I eat
The ever increasing supply of berries
Until finally
The supply has exhausted itself
Ending the season
With three tiny berries
Red Ripe
I pick I eat Still delicious!

Sandra Leigh Stoudt
IT IS FOR THE BEST
A decision must be made in so little time,
Can it be justified . . . or is it a crime?
The pressure mounts with the close of each day,
An answer must be contrived before time withers away.
Some say right, while some say wrong,
Circumstances insight feelings which are strong.
Questions badger the already cluttered mind,
Feelings of uncertainty and pain forever bind.

The alarm sounds . . . Where is the Decision?
A consent form is signed and handed to the Physician.
"Believe that it is for the best," the Doctor proposes
Locked are the memories as that office door closes.
Only a memory of what could have been remains,
Existing evermore is the emptiness and all of the pains.
—Here ends a life so that another may live.

Hazel B Foster

Hazel B Foster
DEAR LORD, I HEARD YOU SPEAK

To My Fellowmen

Dear Lord, I heard you speak
I did not talk.
I felt your pull
I did not walk.
You sent the sunshine from the skies,
I did not even raise my eyes.
For the moonlight you sent at night
I did not care
And when I woke at morning light
I did not spare
A thought for you, your love or pain
Or that your tears were in the rain
I stood alone
Outside my door
A wind swept by
With a loud roar.
And as it passed, I heard a voice
It called, "My Friend, Rejoice, Rejoice
I am the Lord."
I then did talk
And with the Lord
I then did walk.
I see the sun, I feel the rain
Never alone shall I be again.

J Byran Harris
THE SEARCH FOR TRUTH

Dedicated to Gary Edwards and all who served and died in Vietnam.

Thousands of brave young soldiers had to die.
Leaving their families to wonder why.
Fine healthy men in the prime of their youth.
Willing to die for their land and the truth.
But what was the truth in the Vietnam War?
This question cut the U.S. to its core.
Some did not question it; some did not dare.
Some used drugs so they could bury their care.
Some found their answer in acts that were brave.
Many followed the answer to their grave.
A few killed children in order to live.
These few became men with nothing to give.
The survivors carried permanent scars.
They had sacrificed all to the god Mars.
These soldiers returned home needing respect.
But all they found here was pain and neglect.

William E McLaughlin
TIME

To my wife, Kathy

Every day my heart loves you more and more.
From the very first day I met you, I liked you.
But as the hours turned into days, I found I cared for you.
As days turned into weeks, I found I needed you.
As weeks turned into months, I found I loved you.
As months turned into years, I found I can't live without you.
And so I pray that time will always go on with us side by side—
FOR ETERNITY.

Carla Darlene Walker
HEAVEN BOUND
As I looked upon the ocean floor I saw one thing come
shining through.
There was a ship with a man on board who held his head high and wouldn't say why.
He told me to worry at all no more, your time has come to leave this earth.
There are mountains and there are rivers and there are even
golden ladders.
The clouds are fluffy, the sky is blue, and God will protect you from all whom is doomed.
So board this ship right now my son and you can see it for
yourself.
For the place you're going it's like no other, there are angels flying high with golden harps upon embraced.
It has a name, oh, yes indeed, people call it a mansion.
You call it a dream, but if I were you, my son, I'd call it
heaven, Heaven Bound.

T Ann Schmidt
WHAT'S IN A NAME?
Down thru the ages, it's always been the same. Rather reality or coincidence, there's importance in the name.

Down thru the ages, it's always been the same.
Rather reality or coincidence, there's importance in the name.

Take Jesus just for instance, and the story that is told.
You hear the name from day to day, from the lips of young and old.

Abraham led his people, in a united spiritual way.
Lincoln brought freedom, that we enjoy to this day.

John gave his head, for the soul of every man.

Kennedy had firm convictions,
from which he never ran.

Say King, you remember Elvis,
Martin Luther and England's best.
In Boone, Custer and Sitting Bull,
they represent the American west.

Bell, Edison, Einstein, their
foresight and a legacy to the rest.
McAuliffe, Scobee and Jarvis, the
heavens were their quest.

As parents we have a responsibility,
do think on this well.
For some day the name you give
them, may have a great story to tell.

Della Kathantis Sarathi

Della Kathantis Sarathi
TEMPTS
She is without genesis and
cessation.
She passes, swiftly and effortlessly.
Within her reflection, is the
essence,
of the past and future.

Sometimes! We hunger, and thirst
for her
Then! Occasionally, we want her to
flee rapidly.
We need to achieve a blissful
destiny!
Because, she too leaves her fate on
us,
Until! One day we become one with
her;
No one knowing hence we come,
or hence we're going.

Peggy McKenzie
THE ARTIST

This poem is dedicated to—My children and My Friend Louise whose love, Friendship and Faith In me, Has made my life worthwhile.

Memories are canvases, painted
through the years,
Each of us are artists of our joys
and fears.
First comes pictures of mom and
dad,
And their love so true,
Next we painted school days, for
me and yes, for you.
Oil lamps and homework,
snowmen and laughter.
Grade school and High school, and
exams everafter!
Then we painted weddings,
And children oh so sweet.
We've pictured their joy as they
played round our feet.
Love and Happiness coloured the
days, "Dandy flowers" too!
Homemade cards and kisses and
"Mommy I love you."
Now the children have grown
And too soon they've moved away,
But just a song, a card or a word
Takes us back to yesterday.
Then once more we are "sketching"
On the parchment of "Old Times,"
Nothing can ever take away, the
photos in our minds
So it is with everyone
With the rich and even the poor,
Our memories are the canvases
We paint forever more—

Margaret J Brooks
A POEM FOR THOUGHT
I want health, I am not concerned
with wealth.
For greed is lonely
There's one in every breed
It's a strong uncontrolled need!
We need love!
Don't look down, but above
There is no middle, no in between
No matter if you're a queen
People aren't naturally mean.
It comes for what they've seen
So people be kind
Follow your good part of mind
Don't be blind
There's always a good time

Vickie Lynn Cheek
MOTHER-HOOD
When I was young and so was he,
I thought:
The hardest part of mother-hood
was,
heating similac at two—a.m, and
changing dirty diapers.
Then he learned to walk and!
The hardest part of mother-hood
was,
picking up broken knic-knacs, and
kissing bruised knees.
Then he started school and,
The hardest part of mother-hood
was,
getting him to bed by eight 'o'
clock, and saying goodbye every
morning.
Then he went to summer camp
and,
The hardest part of mother-hood
was,
not embarrasing him with kisses,
and not going crazy with worry.
Then he started dating and,
The hardest part of mother-hood
was.
Knowing his girl wasn't good
enough, and not being able to
tell him.
Then he started college and,
The hardest part of mother-hood
was,
Teaching him—that boys do cry,
and trying to be around if he
needed me.
But now that I'm old, and he's
still very young
I know;
The hardest part of mother-hood
is.
Calling long-distance each
Sunday, and
being replaced by his wife.

Marjorie M Swanson
SPRING IN MINNESOTA
The scent of Spring
Has reached my door
I smell its perfume,
Its heavenly lure
I think I'll pen
My welcome sign
As I have done before,
And place it in the window
Or perhaps upon my door.
Spring might feel
That I enjoyed
The fresh fragrance
That she wore,
And I'll not forget
Her sweet caress
As she kissed me
In the door.
And thus she'll always
Seem to me, the gift—
Of rarest perfume
That Nature has in store.

Patricia D Drischel
MY KENTUCKY LAND

Dedicated to all my wonderful Kentucky friends from the Irish Indian Poet.

A cool wind sweeps through my
soul.
And I'm homesick for those I love
I hear at evening-tide the
mourning Dove
And I long once more for my
Kentucky land.
Where the hard hills of clay beckon
me
Not sea or sand, just my Kentucky
Land!

I smell the wood smoke
As it rolls from yonder hills
Among my loves, these are the
greatest thrills
So carry me when my days are done
To those clay hills kissed by the
sun.
Ah yes! My Kentucky Land!

Those Kentucky hills soothed by
the sun and rain and sleet
Those blessed hills that felt my
baby feet.
And the long stride of me, grown
to be a man
Oh yes, carry me to those golden
hills
Of my Kentucky Land!

Debra K Epperson
LOVE YOUR PARENTS TODAY, KIDS

To my Father, Jack H. Carithers, whom I love very much!

I wonder which prayer did it,
The one that saved my Daddy's life.
Was it said by friends or relatives,
Or a special one by his wife?
When the Lord gives us an Angel,
(A special person placed on Earth)
Do we sometimes take for granted,
The great value of their worth?
To me my Dad's an angel,
A ray of sunshine to the sad,
A spark of hope to the weary,
Always knowing good from bad.
They said my Daddy had a battle,
Fighting life at death's own door,
But he knew that life would win it,
And no one deserves it more.
Again I ask myself the question,
As I have a hundred times before,
Did God make my Daddy suffer,
So I'd appreciate him more?
Is this God's way of saying?
"Treat your parents right, my
friend;
You better love them while they're
living,
Cause you can't do it in the end."

Jennifer L Mysicka
WONDERLAND
Ornaments and dolls
All within four walls—
A Wonderland on earth,
Where fantasies are birthed.
The smell of incense in the air
Look over there, a teddy bear!
A pretty doll dressed all in lace,
A ballerina in a case.
A figurine that plays a song,
A candy cane that's Oh, so long.

Wherever my eyes may choose to
land—
Another member of Wonderland.
"May I have this?"
"May I have that?"
But, all at once, my dreams go flat.
Look at the price tag on that doll!
It must be seven miles tall.
But, "Mommy, mommy, can't you
pay
For a tiny trinket all my own?
I'll work around the house all day
And give the dog his daily bone."
I cry as I leave this Wonderland,
without a trinket in my hand.

G Petur Matthiasson
(FE)MALE FEMINIST
Listen—
I need to talk to you:

"You are a man"
And the closing door

sounded like
the apartments

relief
which was glad

to be rid off
off
this guest.

Barbara Jean Laine
ATOM

Dedicated to Danny Binz; and my beautiful children Rita LaJean 6 years old, and little Lynn 4 years old. Thank you, for loving me. I am truly blessed.

I'm sitting here on bended knees
Begging for your memories
Was the grass really green
Did children play outside
Did the sun really shine
Once upon a time . . .

Was there really mountains
Oceans and rivers of blue
Will one day I see these things
Just the same as you?

I don't know why they punish us
For we've done nothing wrong
I do believe I hate this thing
Known as the ATOM BOMB.

Frances Elmer
GUESS WHICH ONE I LOVE?
What a decision to make,
One of the two loves me,
one does not.

One of the two needs me,
one does not.

One of the two would take me
anywhere—
the other, nowhere.
One of the two
thinks of my feelings—
the other, only of his own.

One of the two
thinks I'm beautiful—
the other, thinks he is.

One of the two
calls me everyday—
the other, forgets to.
Guess which one I love.

Barbara Moffit
AMERICA'S MY COUNTRY
America's my country,
I'm very proud to say.
What shape would this poor world be in
Without the U.S.A.?

Her doors are always open
To help someone in need.
She'll never turn her back on you,
Whatever race or creed.

She's been through many battles,
And she's felt the scars of war,
In all her spacious beauty,
She'll reign true forevermore!

From Atlantic to Pacific,
She's an awesome sight to see.
Her "Stars and Stripes" wave proudly
To proclaim our liberty!

Yes, America's my country,
I'll shout it filled with pride,
"The Land of Opportunity"
Where no one is denied!

Rita D Peters
OUR SECOND ANNIVERSARY
Just two years ago today
You and I started on our way
To many days of joy and cheer
That will linger in my heart for many a year

Now that we are miles apart
I keep your love deep in my heart
I pray for you each night and day
And miss you more than words can say

I dream and plan our future life
When we can again live as husband and wife
Children, a home, a car and you
Are all I need for a dream come true

I send my love to you each day
And hope it helps you on your way
As your letters help me to carry on
When all my happiness seems gone

I always long to hold you tight
And kiss you "Hello" and "Goodnight"
With a few more kisses in between,
I guess you know dear, what I mean
I lay on your pillow and sit in your chair
And want you to know that I always will care
You mean more to me than words can say
And I realize it more since you are away

I hope, my dear, that it won't be long
Till you are back where you belong
And we can have our hugging and kissing
To make up for what we both are missing.

Nellie L Ayers
A PLACE CALLED HEAVEN

Dedicated to John Murray and Tim McGory—my teachers

There's a beautiful place called Heaven
Where I want to go someday,
Where the Angels will all be singing
And on their harps they will play.

There, I will meet my loved ones
Who left many years ago,
We will sing our praises to Jesus
And be happy forever more.

We will gather around the "Great White Throne,"
Where the "King of Kings" will be;
There will be no sorrows or heartaches
For my friends and loved ones, nor me!

Mary Richardson Echols
THE AWAKENING

This poem is dedicated to my beautiful children, Andy, Shirley, Mary and Judith.

A bird took flight in the early morn,
Adding his song to the breaking of dawn.
Raindrops sparkled like diamonds in the sun.
The sound of music comes from where the rivers run.
A spider seemed to hang in space,
While spinning his web, as delicate as lace.
The gentle breeze felt fuzzy and warm with scents of flowers,
From gardens, and fields, and lavender bowers.
The laughter of a child at play,
Could be heard across the silken way.
As time passed, many more wonders were added
To the beauty of the day.
And, when it was viewed with the sun's last ray,
The world was a masterpiece on display.
It's sad, though, for someone had to describe it to me,
As I failed to take the time to see!
But, as I listened, it occured to me;
The beauty I was unwilling to see, is still out there,
Just waiting for me.
As we are part and parcel of this sphere divine,
The stars and moon are yours and mine;
The sun, the trees, and cool water in the pond,
Bind us all in a kindred bond.
"Please, help me notice all there is to see,
Take time to look, and feel, and be."

Ken McElheney

Ken McElheney
LIFE

Dedicated to Dad

I lived my life a lifetime
Funny as it seems
Eventually I'll lose it
Even in my dreams

Some things I have forgotten
Some things I can't conceive
Before my life turns rotten
I think I'll have to leave

I had a good beginning
It was just a start
When I thought I was winning
I began to fall apart

Now it's nearly over
This is plain to see
This life was just a mystery
And not a joke to me

Natalie J Moffitt
OREGON
The grass is green,
the deer are lean
Rolling mountains,
and fresh streams.
Long windy roads,
so quiet you can hear the toads.
Tall pine trees,
reaching for the sky.
A friendly beaver,
slapping its tail and saying "hi."
A beautiful bald eagle,
a rare sight to see,
Soaring high,
in the cool breeze.
This is my home,
This is Oregon
Land of the beautiful skies,
a land for you and I.

Teresa Cavitt Theobald
THE LOVE OF MY LIFE

This poem is dedicated to my very special daughter, Breauna Renee Theobald.

The love of my life is not a man that is tall;
In fact, if you saw her, you'd say, "she's really quite small:

She's been with me, now, almost three years;
And when I think of all we've been through,
it almost brings tears:

Tears not of anger, nor of pain;
But of joy, because my soul, she does rein:

Little does she know she holds my heart in her hand;
And for her I would travel this great land:

I suppose by now you're curious to know;
Just who this person is, that I love so:

Well the person in question stands about three foot three;
And is none other, than my sweet daughter BRE***

Robin Lee Jenest
REFLECTIONS
Through the fog and mist, we see reflections—
Reflections of ourselves.
Although they're not so clear at first;
We know what we want them to look like

Are we really what we appear to be?
A picture-perfect image—
Suddenly shattered into a million fragments.
Only to be put together piece by piece

As each part fits together
The reflection becomes clearer.
It may not be all that perfect,
But it certainly is distinct

Someday I will reflect upon these years;
Some fuzzy; some clear as day.
But the lasting memories will stay close to my heart—
Those of friends, of laughs, of tears.

It is time to say farewell—
We must move on to a new spectrum—
What was once a crystal-clear reflection,
Is now a mere memory . . .

Gloria A Prichard
WHO ARE YOU
The man who stands by your side
Who is he
The man whose love is like a blanket, protecting and warm
Who is he
The man who is always there when you need him
Who is he

The man who brings you presents,
not on holidays, but because he
was just thinking about you
Who is he
The man who thinks a really great
get-together is when the two of
you get together
Who is he
The man who reaches out to you
in the night just to make sure
you are real and really there
Who is he
The man you want to spend the rest
of your life making happy
because he makes you so happy
Who is he
If I see him, I'll tell him you love
him.

Ruthe Potter
THE BEST DAYS
The best days of our lives were
spent
on Grandma's chicken farm.

The best days for 3 people—
Cousins
Jim Stockton, Billy Clark, Ruth
Elaine.

My brothers!

It was a form of love!

The love for the farm!

The love of 3 people!

Love! . . .

Bob Bagby
LOVE WASN'T ALL I GAVE YOU (THE SUN OVER THE MOUNTAIN)
The sun comes up over the
mountain,
at night the moon makes
everything look still.
But I know life without you,
will never again be real.

Love wasn't all I gave you,
I also gave my heart and soul.
I gave everything from within
me,
and now I'm empty and cold.

When you decided to leave me,
when you took it all away.
My sun, my moon, my life,
they all disappeared into a haze.

My sun doesn't come over the
mountain,
my moon doesn't come out at
night.
You see I must live in darkness,
because I gave you all the good in
my life.

When this life has left me,
when I bid the world adieu
Maybe I'll find peace within me,
because my heart will stop beating
for you.

Marilyn Diane Papay
WHO IS MORE FREE?
There is no justice in the system.
Money talks with passionate
intensity.
Our verdict is in. The individual
is guilty.
This trial need not begin.

Your singular thoughts are a
danger; a boil
needing quick incising to stop its
grotesque spread.
We label you hostile, a danger, a
threat.
How dare you challenge our sacred
institutions?

Guilty of independent thinking—
you assault our truths.
You must comply. Become a
team member.
Stop being a problem. Don't defy
us.
Our ears are deaf to your
dissonance.

Opinionated, self-righteous
bureaucracy
mires its members in a
schizophrenic swamp.
Paranoia and psuedo-idealistic
reasoning
entraps its members in an
unrealized destructive pattern.

The group, speaking as one, chants
a pseudo-ethical cadence.
Deaf to fresh thoughts; Blinded by
stagnant self-serving vision;
The group controls its very
being. jailed by their
acquiescence.

Who is more free? The individual
or the group?
Group think—a product of
cowardice ensnares.
The individual looks into her
accusers' very souls—
Her vexed nightmare ends; Her
integrity makes her free.

Shirely Rinehart
WHEN I GROW UP

Fondly to "Lloyd"

I'm just a boy
With freckles all tan
But when I grow up
I guess I'll be a man

You see, I ain't got much choice
Cause that's what all boys do

It's gonna take a lot of time though
And a heap of learnin' too

But what the heck, it's simple
I ain't plannin' to be bad
I'm just gonna grow right up
And be just like my Dad

Ms Carla Patnett
REALITY

This poem is dedicated to the "Love of my life," Derrick J. Nelson, who made it possible for me and encouraged me to write Reality.

There's nobody gonna stop me
from succeeding in my dream
as JiJi is helping me, he's the one
that has control of my existings
That's the way it be, my happy
dream and it doesn't matter
what I be,
I will succeed, that's
Reality
Reality
As I know this is a hell of a world
but I can cope, many even smoke
that snow, that girl, a messed up
tale, stay on top, for the world is
hell, as

Nothing is happening but a
struggle, as you go through a
hard day's work and the way it
is today, you can even get
puzzled and
That's the way it be, my happy
dream and it doesn't matter
what I be,
I will succeed, that's
Reality
Reality

Nina D Oshurkoff-Baratoff
OUR PRAYER

To my dear daughter with love

Thank you God for our yesterday.
For our joy, for our sorrow.
We ask your blessing for today,
And all your help to reach
tomorrow.

James C Morley
WITHOUT LOVE
Gentle is the love that touches the
soul . . .
Reaches out and touches
another.
Would it be that I had such a
love,
The only parting would be the
parting of my lips . . .
In total giving.
I long for the feel of warmth,
Of droplets . . .
Sparkling moisture pressed to a
sheen . . .
Of a soft breeze flowing over
exhausted lovers.
Without this giving,
Without this loving,
A coldness creeps in . . .
Numbing the senses.
Beleaguered soul, frenzied,
searches easier reaches,
Only to find despair . . .
And pain.
Is there not one soul in this lorn
multitude . . .
To put aside this horror?

Helen M Noland
A POEM OF ME

To all my family and friends who had faith in me. But most of all, this one is for you Doris.

Born in Mississippi way back in
the sticks,
People called me a redneck, or even
a hick.
Now I never knew those bright city
lights,
That lit up the blocks on long dark
nights.
Then I was placed in an orphan's
home,
Surrounded by people yet all alone.
Where you're just another childlike
face,
Where each morning is a pre-set
pace.
Of loveless days and blacken
nights,
Of hopeless prayers of a happier
life.
Then one day the time had come,
I left with my father, the orphan's
home.
Then to marry at an early age,
Which felt to be just another cage.
Now all this was soon to be
worthwhile,
When I was blessed with a
beautiful child.
Now in the years there was soon
three more,
All as beautiful as the one before.
Now they are all married or gone,
And as before I'm back alone.
Still searching for a better way,
To fill my nights and lonesome
days.
Just waiting for the time to finally
come,
Like the day when I left the
orphan's home.

Mary Linda Dodd
PARADOXECOLOGY
"No Living Allowed" (for goodness
sake!)
Read an altered sign at Moosehead
Lodge,
Where geese once rose from acid
lake
(At least the ones who learned to
dodge).

There's surely good reason
For cage-laid eggs,
Or strawberries off season,
And whale oil dregs.

So much logic abounds
For paved-over fields,
And off-shore oil yields.

Then there's the dire need
For the seal pup's white skin,
Steroids to whip the racing steed,
For research, suffering's no sin.

So, not to worry; it's all for you'n
me
That oiled wings no longer fly,
Marred and muted without
dignity,
Our planet-planners die.

At Moosehead Lodge the baited
snow
Awaits the threat of sun.
The needles fall. No crocus grow
And a millenium is undone.

Peggy R McGrew
HOW BLESSED I AM TO HAVE A MOTHER
Though she was young when I was
born
In the middle of the "great
depression"
She cared for me unselfishly
The war was no exception.

She taught me to be loyal to God
And to exercise my freedom of
choice
And for those who cannot speak for
themselves
I exercise my voice.

She taught me to fight for the
unborn child
For he is helpless today.
To remember and know, we will
grow old
We will need his strength someday.

She taught me that the world will

be better
For the helping hand we give
But how will it be better
If we won't let them live?

As aging lines appear on her face
I hold her close in warm embrace
And remember the times I had no other
How blessed I am to have a mother.

Cathy Ann Hoffman

MY FRIEND . . . THE STAGES OF LIFE . . .

We met as children who yearned for the attention of others. . .
We grew to be teenagers who dared to be different . . .
We became adults who made decisions. . .
The decisions we made along the way pulled our paths apart . . .
But even distance and difference, could not dissolve this relationship.
Once again our paths crossed . . .
We brought with us memories of past loves, heartaches and misfortune . . .
We also brought back a clearer vision of what we wanted . . .
Coming together was different this time . . .
In a car, past midnight, we bowed our heads and prayed for a new understanding . . .
We cryed out for a new beginning . . . And we embraced with a new found affection for one another.

We had become friends . . . sisters . . . In him.
Since then you have mothered a child, become a wife . . . And although some things can't last forever, You picked yourself up and continued . . .
You've become stronger, more determined . . . More willing to bend with the wind . . .
As a friend your compassion has grown, your understanding increased . . .
We've shared together some of the best times in our lives . . .
I take with me the memory of your sincerity, the laughter of your heart, and the closeness of your friendship . . .
I thank you for your prayers in time of need, your comfort when I hurt, and your laughter when I smiled . . .
I thank you for the single rose . . . The heartfelt hug . . . And the constant reassurance . . . I thank you . . .
For being my friend . . .

Lisa A Bamonte

PAINTED PICTURES

Painted Pictures
in my mind . . .
You and I forever
Two of a kind

I can picture us on a Desert Island . . .
Smiling, touching,
Listening to our hearts . . .
Feeling the sun beat down upon us

Painted Pictures
In my mind
You and I together
combined as one.
Bonded forever
Alone and in love
Being together
From the gift above

Edgar R Wyatt

A DAILY CREED

Meet the morning with a smile
Greet your friends with pleasant cheer
Always speak of noble things
Evil things refuse to hear.

Give your work a careful thought
Do each deed with greatest care
Help your comrads in their trials
Do not make them burdens bear.

Help the downcast man along
Give to him a cheerful smile
Pass him not without kind words
Help him o'er the rugged mile.

See the aged through helpful eyes
Respect them in their childish ways
Make them happy with a smile
Cheer them in their feebling days.

Don't forget the little children
Speak to them both gentle and kind
Guide them from the evil things
Sow good seeds for them to find.

When the day is left behind
Thank your God for His great care
Ask yourself if you've been worthy
Of the blessings that were there.

Denise J Givens

IMMORTALITY

If I die I shall not worry
For I shant wake in a hurry

Beneath dark clouds of growing hates
But before golden glowing gates

Where no evil can befall
The newborn angel of God's call

I shant be in a flaming world of misery
But in a bright land of the free

If you follow Jesus's bidding
You will find life's not just winning

It's learning to share in the giving
And receiving of his care that is everywhere,

In God's eternal world of love.

Debbie Kolar

LIFE

Life can be like a warm summer's day
Or like the warmth of a child's breath
And in the griefs and beliefs of a child's death
The death of a child. They wish not to lose
Rough winds will shake the blooming buds in May
A strong growing feeling of a child's faith
Or the undir conflict of his wraith
Whatever new or old life they wish, they choose
My child's soul I can not reach, when out of sight
But his neverending light, shall not fade
Death shall not come to those who stay out of the shade
You must stay by the sun and candle-light
Good-bye my child, your lights now fade.

Debbie P Olmsted

A MOTHERS LOVE

To be a mother I'd waited so long,
Finally holding you in my arms my love for you is strong,
Motherhood is all I dreamt it could be,
Your coo's and smiles fill my heart with such glee.
With each passing day I watch you grow,
Amazed at the things you have learned and now know.
I love you so much as we cuddle and rock,
You touch my face and talk a lot,
Of course your words aren't very clear,
But every sound you make to me is dear.
You learned to crawl, stand and walk,
As I watched on with motherly pride,
Honey, I want you to know I'll always be by your side.
You've had your first birthday,
With lots of chocolate cake and toys,
Gone is my babe; now enters my little boy.
You now call me "Ma—Ma;" seems I can't hear that enough,
You kiss me and give big hugs too,
Now I know why my life felt so empty without you.
The love that you give is so pure and sweet,
Each day with you is such a treat.
Son, one day you will become a man,
And I want to raise you as best as I possibly can.
Some days will be rough, while others are not,
But know I love you son, I love you a lot ! ! !

Dick Hays

SUNSET

To my wife—Marie

Have you ever rode at evening
toward the settin' sun
on your favorite little mustang
at a careless reckless run
in and out among th' cactus
and the Spanish dagger spears
while the cooling desert breeze
goes whistling by your ears.

Watch th' cotton-tail and lizzards
as they scurry from th' trail
hear th' diamond-back a-rattlin'
the buzzer on his tail
th' chatter of th' prairie-dogs
mixed with the eagles scream
and the sly coyote a-dippin'
off in a dry ravine.

See the brilliant glow of the settin' sun
mirrored in the western sky
and clouds of changing colors
go slowly drifting by
the artist's efforts are wasted
and Mother Nature wears the crown
if you've ever been in the desert
to watch the sun go down.

Marion A Hutter

WINDOW OF YOUR HEART

To the one's who share a special place in my heart

How big can it be?
What is there to see in the window of your heart
It's the love that's there the moments you share in the window of your heart.
It's the beginning of life and the lone road ahead, which in many words can be shared.
It's the laughter and sorrow that comes each day, paving your life in a very special way—
We see the beauty and the splender of each little thing that makes you want to shout or sing.
It's the memories past or present, whatever they may be, can bring a shining glimmer to the window of your heart.

Carol A Cunningham

GOD'S GIFT

To my dad, Wes Neal, who showed me how to look at the world with love...I love you.

I remember the ocean, the wind from
the sea...

The smell of the air as it wraps
around me...

The clouds moving by with their
halos of gold...

I try not to think of the days
I'll be old...

The roar of the waves, the howl
of the wind...

The sand beneath my feet, coarse
against my skin...

And when the rays of sun pour down
to the sea...

I remember God...and how He
gave this to me...

Karen Hershey Valentine

TALK TO ME . . .

To Jim, my friend, my love

Thoughts come, they flood my mind. But no words.
Confussion, frustration, thoughts everywhere . . .
How to start, what to say, where to begin . . .?

My mind is filled, it wants to
  explode. But no words.
My soul screams, my heart cries,
  my eyes ask.
    I listen.

John W Rast
FUTURE PASSES

To the past, present, and future It's all the same time . . . Reach for the stars

---

Little cubes fill the sky
  Looking like squares
Circles of wonder
  Blaze new trails
Triangular motion
  Ceases to halt
Future passes
  Tamed by revolt
Retrospective comotion
  Stars on the wall
Flickering and dancing
  Yet at a halt
Confussion is plenty
  Yet comprehend a few
To make waves of the future
  Rippling in time
Space unending
  Sees to a few
Favors are granted
  Oh, but to you

Tom Fronk Jr
WITH OUT LOVE

To my father who has loved and has been loved

With out love
We can not stand
We keep on falling
And don't understand
With out love
We go down in tears
They keep on falling
And end up in fears
With out love
We can't hold on
We keep on grabbing
But we can't for long
With out love
Smiles don't last
We hope forever
But for time we grasp.

Nicci Musser
PARTY DAYS GONE BY

You didn't think about it, did you?
When you were popping those
  little pills,
When you were drinking to get
  drunk,
When you were getting your little
  thrills.

Man, that booze must have tasted
  good
For you drank an awful lot.
Boy, you must like being high
For you smoke a lot of pot.

But you didn't think about it, did
  you?
You didn't think someone would
  die.
You didn't think she'd lose her life.
Because of your stupid high.

Boy, you must enjoy racing
To drive your car so fast,
To give up your entire future
To be like the boys from the past.

Hey, big man, don't you feel bad
  for her?
She was the innocent one.
She sacrificed her life for yours
Because of how you have your fun.

So you just keep smoking and
  drinking,
Pop your pills and stay on a high.
But, party boy, next time the casket
  lid
Falls down, it'll be you they're
  telling good-bye.

Kathy A Eader
AN UNBORN CHILD

I wonder who will ever hear
The voice; inside of me
For you see, it can't be heard
It has not come to be . . .
Yet right is right
Wrong is wrong
Forever I've been told
A womans' right to take a life?
Justice, they say so bold.
Who are you who made this choice
to take a life at hand?
A life you chose to make one day
A gesture that was grand!
Why not give that life it's chance . . .
To live, to love, to laugh . . .

Marjorie A McNeil
ODE TO MOUNT SAINT HELENS

My dear Mount Saint Helens
Beautiful sleeping girl,
You have released your firey anger
Upon an unsuspecting world.

You were once a peaceful beauty
Serene in your crown of snow,
Now you lie in a wasted forest
On a bed of ash and silt-mud-flow.

Those who marveled at your beauty
Are now saddened by your face.
Many souls that loved you
Have perished at your base.

My dear Mount Saint Helens
So long asleep within,
How many years, I wonder,
Before you sleep again?

Elisabeth Williams-Thorpe

Elisabeth Williams-Thorpe
IN REMEMBRANCE OF THOSE THAT HAVE LIVED THE HORROR OF FAMINE

Dedicated with love to Loyal, Cecelia, Tom, Faye, John, Mariah, and Karma

---

An Indian woman
with hopeless eyes
cradles her son
whose silenced cries
still rip through her heart.
Those left living
are numb with grief,
there is no comfort
for the dying here.
Outstretched hands and
empty bowls echo
the loss of so many souls.
Babies suckle their
mothers' breasts
in vain, even tears
no longer flow.
Thousands of people,
young and old,
die together in
untold agony—
suffer in hoardes,
noticed by few.
And God, the dear children,
their brown eyes searching,
searching.
Their swollen bellies,
Blinded eyes,
useless limbs . . .
haunt me.
But especially her—
that woman,
dead son in arms,
surrounded by a living
Hell.
Asking nothing—
but saying so much.

J Watson
REFLECTIONS

Reflections in a daydreamer's eye.
Makes me smile,
makes me sigh.
I want to laugh,
but instead I cry.

Anne L Sellke
MAN ELUDES, BUT GOD PURSUES

For my sons, John and Harry

Peace, peace, oh where art Thou?
The inner self that man ignores,
The outer self that man does live . . .
How different and how yet the
  same,
When all is forgiven
In Christ's Holy name.

Faith, faith, oh God unknown,
How to break the barriers down,
To reach the hand of God within,
To wipe away the guilt and sin.

Christ, Christ, the Way, the Light,
Oh ye watchers in the night,
If you but think of God above,
The Christ in you will come with
  love.

Susan W Soule
A STILL WINTER DAY

The winter air is cold and still
As I walk upon this wooded hill.
The snow is falling all around
To make a thick, white blanket on
  the ground.

A chickadee on a frozen branch
  sings
And his high, clear voice through
  the forest rings
Like sleighbells on a windy day
Or like the laughter of a child at
  play.

The pine trees are now dressed in
  fine lace
And across the snow a rabbit does
  race.
There's no one here that I can see.
No one is here except God and me.

J Frank Whittaker
SPRINGTIME

Dedicated to the wonderful memories of Emma Lee, an angel who became restless and left unfulfilled dreams.

Springtime is a time for love and
  fun,
for those of us who play in the sun.
Flowers bloom and shed the
  winters gloom.
Woolens are shed for colors
  instead,
time for work in the flower bed.
Trees adorn leaves of shade,
the memories of woodcutting
  begin to fade.
School and job prepare for
  vacation,
a time for rest and recreation.
Plants and vines begin to bear,
succulent fruit and muscadine;
  thus completes
the wonderous joys, of springtime.

Nellie Maie Elmore
REFLECTIONS

Have you ever lain 'neath a shady
  tree,
Gazing upwards into Infinity,
  White clouds afloat high in
  Heaven so blue,
And watched the silvery leaves
  aflutter,
Stirring emotions you could not
  utter
  And nebulous thoughts that you
  never knew?
Have you peered up into the sky at
  night,
millions of stars making Heaven
  alight,
  And you felt you were very, very
  small?
How awesome, how vast was
  eternal space!
Almost you felt you envisioned
  God's face,
  And you yourself were not there
  at all.
Dear erring child, all your faults
  are forgiven,
For you are a part of this eternal
  Heaven.

Michael J Unger
DREAM FLYING

I dedicate this, with all my love, to family and friends, here and above.

Sometimes, when I try to rhyme
And put together words of love,
I find I lose all track of time
As though my mind were just a
  dove

And away I fly, high and free
Wherever my imagination goes,
I'd like for you to come with me,
Chasing our dreams, wherever the
  wind blows.

Soaring in a sky so blue,
Chasing clouds and rain away,
I know I'd love to stay with you
Forever and ever and a day.

Gene Lee
YOU CAN

You can change the world
You can change your mind
You can change everything

If you can find the time

Can you change the heart
That's frozen to the core
Could you knock down walls
Who could ask for more

Will you take my hand
Show me new space
Will you help me live
In this dangerous place

Do as I ask
I will see us through
And don't ever forget
I'll always love you

Take a frozen heart
That is all alone
Give it faith, give it hope
Give it a brand new home

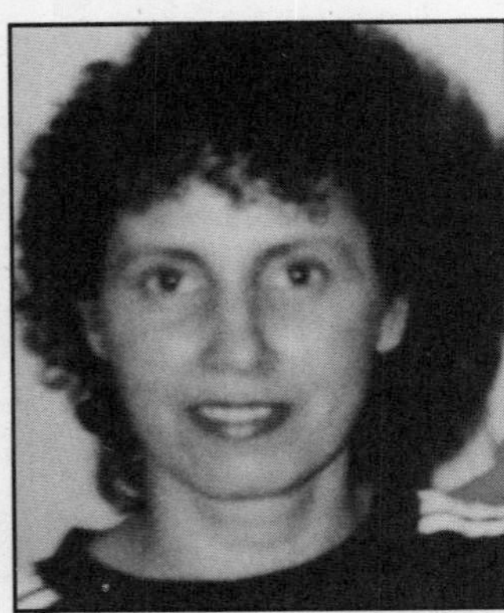

Mary J Kline

Mary J Kline
CONTEMPLATING DEATH
I am going to be with my Dad, you see.
There is nothing left in life for me.
I don't want my daughter to think bad of me.
I am lost I need to be found, before
I am lying six feet underground.
Life is too stressful, Life is too tough.
I'm leaving the living, I've just had enough.
I'm empty inside, I feel only strife.
I'm dying you see, my life will soon end.
I don't have a pal and I don't have a friend.
To feel so hopeless, to feel so sad,
To die and be free it won't be so bad.
I have no treasures, I have no gold.
I have no life left to unfold.
I do have one treasure that is far greater than gold.
I have a daughter her life is untold.
She is young, she is free, but she is lonely like me.
How will she cope? How will she strive?
In this cold cruel world just to survive.

Oleta Bracken
TONIGHT MY WORLD'S ALRIGHT
The grass is damp with dew
As I stroll outside tonight
Darkness is a peaceful shawl
And tonight My world's alright

A gentle breeze is wafting
Sending lovely scents to me
From the roses in full bloom
And from flowers I cannot see

The whippoorwills are crying
And a hoot-owl has his say
Honeysuckle bushes dance in tune
Longing for the coming day

A million stars glow overhead
In a cloudless summer sky
The crickets sing a brassy song
As the midnight hour draws nigh

I walk in sweet contentment
While I enjoy this lovely night
Not trying to hurry tomorrow
Because tonight my world's alright

Judith M Burris
THE CHRISTMAS PRESENT

For my daughter, Heidi, who loves horses, too. And to Determined To Run, the subject of this poem.

A brown and white filly foal
A dark bay mare getting old
The new baby born on Christmas Day
What a wonderful gift she would make
Maybe I will find it in my heart to give her away
The pretty newborn foal lying asleep in the golden hay

A dark bay mare has reached her goal
As life's story does unfold
The mare stands with a look of pride on her face
As upon her very last colt she does gaze
For this baby, this very day, her life the old mare gave
How, oh how, can I give her away?

A brown and white filly three years old
And now her story has been told
Of a mare, who gave her life, so she might live,
A life she must take in stride
For the three year old lying in the hay
My heart is filled with pride

A foal is born at midnight
And in the frosty morn
A secret hope is born
A dark bay filly, she just might be
Just like her grandma,
For all the world to see
And she belongs to me.

Michael Kurela
UNTITLED

Dedicated to Cheree my greatest inspiration I love you, sweets!

When I look into your eyes
I see the ocean taunting me
thick foamy waves caressing the sand
graceful seagulls scavenging the beach
empty highchairs towering the horizon
A lovers heaven in the late night mist.

When I look into your eyes
I see a warm glowing sun
heating up your bones on a chilly spring day
every emotion and what you're thinking
life and happiness love and wonder . . .
wonder why love has to hurt you.

When I look into your eyes
I wonder what my life has meant
if those I've touched are better for it
why you're always in my thoughts and dreams
I see my reflection and startled back home,
Smile and say how beautiful you are.

Shirley Ann Irish
CRUEL PEOPLE

To all people that listen to gossips

People are so cruel
They say things
About people your
Wondering if thats true
They hurt peoples feelings
Your wondering if
Their doing it on purpose
They talk about them
You think is that true
What I hear
The talk goes on and on
They say the best thing is
Don't listen to gossips
You hear things you think
Were true about people
You tell others
They tell others
It goes on and on
That's why they say don't listen
To gossips
Ask that person
That's where you would get the truth
People are so cruel

Lottie Opdahl
DANDELIONS AND LOVE
A bouquet of bright yellow blossoms
Held out to me in a grubby little hand,
Tugging at my heartstrings in a way
Only a mother would understand.

With all praise to the little giver,
For at that precious moment in time,
Love transformed a lowly weed
Into something truly sublime!

E L Garr
AMERICA

This poem is dedicated to Grandsons—Kelby, Jason and Joshua

AMERICA has been sold I fear
By those who do not hold it dear,
They watched it slip right through their hands
Through Watergate and Arms to Iran.

Now what seems almost incredible to me
Is why this great land of opportunity,
Must be governed by doubt and secrecy
Instead of truth and honesty.

AMERICA, AMERICA I bow my head to thee
Thy credibility is blown and poverty is known
At home and over seas.
I know we must have the resources at hand
To restore credibility to this great land;
If a Leader we had to rule
With knowledge and stature from the old school.

AMERICA, AMERICA what can I do for thee
To help thy cause and protect the laws
That insure our liberty.

Ruth Bunch
A BROTHER'S DARING
I opened a bottle of orange,
I thought it to be pop;
I took a swallow or two,
And nearly blew my top.

My brother dared me to do it,
So I took a swallow you see;
If I'd drained the whole bottle,
It'd probably have been the end of me.

It was oil or anti-freeze,
Didn't know the difference then;
But I'm lucky it burnt when going down,
Or I wouldn't have reached age ten.

So when this brother asked me to do,
What he was afraid to try;
I became a little more cautious,
For I didn't want to die.

Stephanie Holland
SOMEONE CARES
"If only someone cared," I said, one dark and dreary day.
"I wish someone would come, today, and take my cares away.
I need a helping hand, someone who is a friend,
Who will correct me when I'm wrong and help me start again."
I heard a voice then, clear and true,
"I am the Someone who loves you!"
"I do not know you," I replied.
"I am Lord of seas and skies.
I am Jesus, God of all,
I will save you when you call."
He helped me and removed my sin.

The sun began to shine again.
The clouds were gone, the day was bright.
A peaceful rest, I had that night.
I knew Him now and I was safe.
I couldn't have found a nicer place.
I realized that all it took,
Was someone who would stop and look.
And see the sorrow all around,
And turn all frowns upside down.
Someone does care, the Lord above.
I found peace, thanks to His love.

Kathleen A Hogan
CHRISTMAS EVE

To Ken: Whose LOVE has made all my nights like 'Christmas Eve'and in whose eyes I found my inspiration!

There are but shadows all around me now,
save the brilliance of a high December moon.
Sparkling white crystals descend the clouds
illuminating all they touch.
Transcending time and space they come,
bringing forth new hope for tomorrow.
Like the human element—no two are alike.
Each of them dancing to their own step,
all of them bringing forth a fresh new beginning.
The air is cold—piercingly silent!
As I wait and watch,
the sound of human anticipation is just over the horizon.
Midnights such as these,
were made for special moments.
Moments of laughter, moments of dreams, moments of LOVE!
Time to look into our hearts,
and see the one thing that is truly our purpose in life.
The night grows quiet . . . the snow has ceased!
Hence the earth becomes beautifully still.
There is nothing left to fear, but the chill in the air.
I will sleep now and fear nothing,
for I am warmed by the memory of you.

Elsa Anderson
THANK YOU!
Don't forget to say thank you with a smile;
It's worth a hundred of millions each mile.
To know you are appreciated for whatever you do,
Will make you wanting to jump out of your shoe.

Thank you this. .thank you that.
thankful honey!
You are surely my best Easter Bunny!
I'll never forget you on this earth,
No matter how long since your birth.

I see someone outdoors kindly lifting
The snow that continually keeps drifting.
A double thank you will cruise the air,
As I turn and wave from the stair . . .

Thank you, oh thank you to you!

C Dean Taylor
STANDS A FORTRESS
Stands a fortress on four pillars of flesh and bone
Surveying his kingdom covered by grass, tree and stone,
His massive trunk lifted high into the air
Testing strange scents of which he must be aware.
Great gray flaps covering portals where sound may enter so
Matching the moving leaves swaying to and fro,
A trumpet sound tears the air, shatters the silence
Challenging the one who holds his kingdom in balance.

Another massive fortress, moving, suddenly breaks into view
Gleaming tusks raised high, death in eyes glaring through.
Lordly titans crashing, thrashing, anxious for the fight
Trampled grass, trees crushed, creatures scurrying in fright.

Thundering cries filled with rage deafening all about
Trunks brandishing, ivory slashing, life's blood seeping out
Mighty the battle, no rest, continuing hours on end
Each fortress with desire to reign, refusing to bend.

Bloodied, beaten, one fortress begins to crumble
Falling back, giving ground, beginning to stumble.
Years of protecting, fighting, time has taken its toll,
A once proud king must retreat, no longer bold.

The final journey to a distant graveyard has begun,
To rest forever by the bones of the ancient ones.
Stands a new fortress on four pillars of flesh and bone
A new king, surveying his kingdom, standing alone.

RJ
SHE BRINGS TEARS TO MY EYES
I wish I knew the hows and whys,
But she always brings tears to my eyes.
I've thought a thousand thoughts while alone in time,
But I'm still the farthest thing from her mind.
I've felt the coldness of space,
The lonilness of life, coupled
With a long season, and I feel
I'm starting to lose my pace.
There's a certain cycle of events,
That space and interim augments,
As they close in on me now,
I weaken and lower my defense.

It pounds away uncaringly, brutually,
Seemingly, without a cause.
It has no boundaries that it goes by,
no laws,
I finally begin to feel the icyness,
As it reduces me, wills upon me the final signs,
As I now moan.
At last, I relinquish myself, and sigh,
As once again, she brings tears to my eyes.

Bonne Lu Perry
WINTER AND SPRING
The sky is soiled white
Over faded blue.
The wind dusts the pines
And shakes the cottonwood skeletons.
The dust dances
And so my spirit
Lulled in a half sleep
Waits for the spring.
Spring came.
The bashful leaves
Slyly appearing
Coyely flirt
With the wind.

Horace A Duke
OUT BACK
I really like the quiet Little places,
Where you meet such friendly people—with happy faces.
I like to be far away from the big cities' roar,
Away outback where the hawks and the eagles soar.
That's where the air is pure and clean,
Where the beauties of nature can always be seen.
Where the little new colts frolic and play:
They know the sheer joy of living each day.

There is a time which I love best,
When the golden sun sinks in the west.
Then all nature is hushed and still—
As if guided by some universal will—
Settling in for a night of rest and sleep.
Sometimes this silence is sweet, meaningful and deep.
Somehow it's here that even a mere man
Can feel that he's actually part of nature's plan.

Helen Cecil Pierce

Helen Cecil Pierce
POT POURRI
Bare branches, black against a leaden sky,
Mist swirling and settling all around me;
From somewhere, a bird calls hopefully,
And people scurry about the business of the day.
Children run and shout to one another
Whereas older folk move cautiously.
I sniff the air, and it is strangeley pungent . . .
Redolent of what? Daddy smells and fragrent Mommy smells?
I'm a little girl once more
Caught by the tinkle of distant laughter
Cloaked in the mystery of my fantasies.
But now the sun would push through the mist
Lending an eerie luminescence;
Droplets like pearls string along bare branches
Already pregnant with new buds;
Horns blare, and headlights peer searchingly.
Slowly, slowly the mist begins to lift
Taking my fantasies with it.

Hazel Soper
TOGETHER
The speaker gave each of us a piece of thread
Which we looked at in some surprise.
It was white and about two feet long.
No one certainly felt they had won a prize.
She spoke about individuals in church
All working together, praying in one accord.
Helping the needy, the elderly, the tempted;
Having Bible studies, learning more about God.

At last we learn why the thread.
One little thread has little meaning you find.
It certainly is a bit uninteresting
But oh! what if many of them are combined.
She next held up a lace table cover.
What a beautiful pattern, what beauty.
It was made with hundreds of threads
Worked by hands of love not duty.

Let us take a lesson from the combined threads
And work together generously and maybe
We can weave a tapestry with threads of love and faith
That He will say "well done" that man of Galilee.

Howard J Speelman
THE RED SKY

Dedicated To My Lord and Maker And My Dear Wife, Carol Ann Speelman

---

Our Heavenly Father is great with love,
For He is the Creator of The Red Sky above.
It is morning, with dew on the ground,
The Red Sky is glowing, with the sun just abound.
Another day, for all to share,
God, I'm sure that you are there.
As the fiery ball continues to ascend,
The clouds are lit-up, with an illuminating glow,
Oh what power Our Loving Father shows.
It's just the beginning of another day with such zeal,
And God the Father, gives it its appeal.
The sun will slowly cross the big blue sky,
And lead to nightfall,
As another day says good-bye.
God is still watching, both day and night,
And I thank Him for keeping us within His sight.
For He is our "Eternal Light."
A-men

Carolyn D Miller
CIRCLE OF LOVE

This poem is dedicated to the Lord Jesus, who gave me the words', and the talent

I lift my eyes
To see your face,
Then you touch me, Lord,
With your sweet grace.

Your arms you open
And I step inside,
The circle of love
Where you abide

So tender your touch
No love can compare,
Your abiding love
I am fully aware.

Your presence is nearer
Than stars up above
Your smile so bright,
Showers me with love.

Lord, how I love you
Without you, I'm lost,
I'll e'er give my life
No matter the cost.

Gladys L Lovett
THE ONE GOD

There is one God over all nations,
But one God hears when we call;
The Almighty, Creator, Redeemer, Word,
Our Comforter, Healer, Jehovah the Lord.
He is called many names for great is his work.
He is worshipped in millions of places and ways,
Eternally he lives through nights and days.
The whole world is under one God.

With many nationalities, creeds, and personalities,
United we stand hand-in-hand.
Our voices up-lifted in prayer and praise
To the one true God over all.

Viki Caudill-Brinchek
THE VICTORY LIGHT

Dedicated to the memory of my father, Howard R. Caudill, Jr., who was a light to all who knew and loved him.

Somewhere a door was opened
and as I started in
I heard someone call my name
and turned to look again.

I saw a brightly shining light
no false glow was this.
I felt I knew what was in my sight
it seemed my every wish.

Twice I covered my eyes in pain
and naked was my soul.
I bowed my head once in shame
and the light dimmed it's glow.

Moving closer I heard sorrowing sounds
I realized they were my own.
Tears flowed down to wet the ground
I felt the earth groan.

Suddenly the light was in me
and I knew that I was free.
I had faced my life complete
and won my victory.

Roger P Temple
THE ROSE THAT SHE LEFT BEHIND

Beauty of roses, last only shortly, Beauty of people, last an eternity. To my Mother, Paralee

There she sat in the terminal, wearing a white sun dress and holding a single Rose.
A Red Rose, which signified for her the end of her own adolescent and largely pre-mapped life's route.
She had cashed in that which was for a ticket which would assist her in gaining a new direction on whatever road she chose.
Crowded, yet alone, maybe; maybe not, she recognized her position at the crossroads on this memorable date.
As for her acknowledgement . . .
For the moment she had her Red Rose, a floral milestone between her past and future fate.
In response to her departure call the Rose girl quietly and mostlty unnoticed departed from her present station and went forth to cast her ideals into the realities of her dream world.
. . . Left behind to wilt in its own merciless heat of reality and for now, forgotten or not, was her Red Rose.

Jack R Corwin
FEELINGS

I love you more than life itself, or the body I wear

Even though I make mistakes, death would be O' so sweet
If I lost the one who has my heart for without you, life is incomplete.

Angela M Genova
CONTEMPLATING THE CEILING

I contemplate the ceiling.
Evenly spaced waves appear
across the stark white background
presenting a monotonous image
dulling one's senses.
Further examination presents
railroad tracks
waiting for the train
that never comes.
There are small round nail spots
which take on the appearance
of puffed eyes
eyes ready to burst open with tears.
A black splatter or two
makes one believe
that more than one mosquito
has lost its life
in the splashing of the ceiling waves.
When night falls
shadows form strange
and familiar images
dancing across this beckoning stage.
contemplation seems to urge one
to pick up a paint brush
and create a new image
on this time-worn canvas.

George E Williams
FRIEND

Friend, friend won't you be my friend
I look into each passing face
Hoping to find a

Friend, friend, won't you be my friend
Someone to share my too set ways
Someone to call a

Friend, friend, won't you be my friend
When I looked into your eyes
I knew I'd find a

Friend, friend, won't you be my friend
One who'll be right by my side
When I need a
Friend, friend, won't you be my friend
A person to tell what's inside
Things you just tell a
Friend, friend, won't you be my friend
Each time I look into your eyes
Will I find a . . .

Linda Brinkman Dallum
IF I SLEEP

To my Beloved Husband, Mel

I'd like to climb a mountain top
and look out upon the val
I'd like to feel the sun so hot
and hear the creek flow gently by
and feel the breeze blow thru my hair,
hear it rustle in the trees
I'd like to see a butterfly
upon the wild flowers there
listen to the songs of birds
and watch an eagle soar
I'd like to fall asleep there against the hill
soft grass for my pillow
my blanket be the sun
The birds would sing a lullaby—
and there I think I'd like to die
So if I sleep, there let me lie
cast no shadow on my eyes
leave in peace and do not cry,
'tis here I wish to lie
no sweeter place to die,
save for the arms of my 'only' love
and oh, for one sweet kiss goodbye

Billy G Maye Jr
GENERATIONS

He's begun his life; has just started
I'm down and old as can be
He watches the world through a
Looking glass
And I need the glass to see
The Days are short, the nights are long
My frame is tired, I lay it down
The young boy is full of energy
his life forever turns around

My lungs are weak, he breathes his air
He goes on and throws the dice
My legs are limp and lifeless
And the air I breathe it twice

I feel so low, I'm lying softly
My heart is beating fast
the boy is standing over me
wait soon my life will pass
its time that I should be going
I hear my life pleading to be free
you can't turn back the hands of time
And never whats destined to be

Its been awhile and many years
This boy reaches for glasses
Waits a second for his pain to cease
and rocks gently after it passes.

Esmeraldo de Leon
CORY, CORY

She was a petite housewife
who dared topple a demigod.
She was a brave little widow
whose man fell in a tarmac of blood.

For twenty long years the demigod ruled
with oppression and in wealth wallowed.
But Cory defied the holocaust,
And the people rallied and followed.

She embraced the torch of people power.
She damned the ghouls of greed and avarice.
And the despot fled in the night.
People power triumphed over the forces of might.

Cory, Cory the masses shrieked.
The saviour has come at last!
The whole world applauded her—
This angel of faith and in innocence cast.

The Philippines cheered for Cory.
She has vanquished graft and corruption.
There was joy and jubilation
For the glorious rebirth of a nation.

Arlene Mae Frisinger
GOD'S WORK

To my loving sister

Sculpturer with hammer and chisel in hand,
Lovingly and gently chipping away each day.
Removing the unwanted pieces,
To reveal inner beauty.
Careful not to chip too much or too long,
As not to crumble the final product . . .
A wonderful image of Christ.

Donna Kay Case
LIFE AFTER DIVORCE

This poem is dedicated to my Mom and Dad, I love you both very much.

He took away my pride, He took away my soul.
He took away all the things that make a woman whole.

He left my heart in pieces to put
together again.
Its been a long, hard battle, one I
wasn't sure I'd win.
Now I've regained my pride and
soul has been set free.
And on my own I have become the
woman I always wanted to be.
I learned a very hard lesson, but at
least he is out of my life.
And deep in my heart I know I will
never be another man's wife.

Jeannie C Looney
CHANGES

Dedicated to Rod, For Allways being there

To this world I was born
a long life I have well worn.

Where is this place in the sun
I'm having trouble finding now
that I've begun?

The years drifted by like leaves
and petals, the ones precious as
gold medals.

The road ahead to me is unclear,
the changes I must make!
Let me draw from the good, and
not to repeat the mistakes . . .

Denese Jester-Brown
UNTITLED

Touch me
Before it's too late.
Try to heal the heart
That has no time to wait.
Hear me deep in your soul,
For I'm growing so weary and
cold.
Reach inside and really see
How sad the ending of you and
me.
See the end,
'cause that's all there can be,
The final chapter,
Now you're free.

Mrs Edna I Purdy
MARCHING IN REVIEW

In my lifetime of years
And there are more than just a few
There are cherished friends
Marching along in Review.

Among them are dedicated
ministers
They too march in review
Each and every day, duties to
perform
Their appointed tasks to do.

They face trials and tribulations
daily
Their duties are varied and many
in form
But without these servants of
God
Our lives would indeed be forlorn.

The beauty of earth would be
marred
Souls crippled and sad
So Thank God for these martyrs
Who march in review to make us
all glad.

Beatrice Bachmann
I DON'T WANT TO GO TO DALLAS

To John Fitzgerald Kennedy, cut down in Dallas, Texas on November 22, 1963, the 1038th day of his Presidency ("it shall not all be done in the first 1000 days").

November 21, 1963 P.M.

I don't want to go to Dallas
It's such an ugly nest
of hate-filled groups, unfriendly
moods
and political unrest.
But the President said that going
there
will be an image lift
and change things for the better
and heal the party rift.

But I don't want to go to Dallas
it holds no charm for me
But the President said "yes you
must go
it's you they'll come to see
and we must be there together
shake hands and smile, and then
if our mission is accomplished
we won't have to go back again."

November 22, 1963 A.M.

Oh, I'm glad we came to Dallas!
we were welcomed with warmth
and smiles!
Now it's almost time for the
motorcade!
We'll be riding for several miles!
The people are waving and
cheering!
And the bright sun has broke
through the Gray!
So we'll surely enjoy the open car
for it's such a lovely day!

Mary Campbell Hemingway
TABBY, GENERIC CAT

I have a cat named Tabby,
A generic cat is she.
Her eyes are yellow—
Her coat is striped brown,
And with a bowl of milk—
So contented she will be.
Although no pedigree papers
Does this generic cat possess,
yet she is a champion
to all of us.
Then—if I entered her
in one small
feline contest,
Tabby'd get top honors
is my hidden guess.
She'd purr at all
the V.I.P's,
And really make her
presence known—
Yet she's only generic,
just an alley cat
I'm told.
But now to all,
Her fine feline upbringing
She has shown.

Helen Croom
EVER PRESENT DANGER

To all mothers' children Especially Robby—This Mothers child

In the elevators they huddle in
corners trying not to notice me
Do they feel that if they do not
acknowledge me, I won't exist

On dark streets they skurry by,
cringing as they flee
Where's the peril? Only I press
forward through the mist

O where will they hide from the
Ever Present Danger?
I go about my business unafraid.
They are visable, yet unseen by
me.

Their fears have no foundation. I
have no time to sooth an anxious
stranger
From my own dark dragons I
struggle to be free.

The thing they fear does not exist
in me
Let not imaginations steed run wild
Only a man of flesh and blood
stands here you see
Only my mother's much loved
child.

Uneva Litster Workman
SELF-ESTEEM

Somebody said, "I'm glad you're
here?
You do so much for me."
Somebody whispered, "I love you
Unconditionally."

Someone gave me the message
clear:
"You are a worthwhile soul.
Live just TODAY . . . and make it
count.
Exalted life, your goal."

Someone said, "I appreciate
You just for being you."
Somebody made my spirits rise
And soar into the blue.

Someone guided my faltering steps
And kept me "on the beam".
Because they loved and showed
they cared
I now have self-esteem.

Pamela Sturgill
THE POETS' CORNER

To Roger, whose freedom soars

Frozen lions escaping capture
from tall stony columns reaching,
words faded but not lost
in the vastness of the musty air.

Steps retract footprints
of imprints of times past,
echoing the same prose
inspired by experiences of same.

Eyes caressing each morsel
and ridge of chronological history,
tasting, then devouring
lifetimes of contributions.

Grey sculpted walls of three
indebted to Chaucer for its origin,
open unselfishly to the greatness
while our hearts encompass their
souls.

Vivian Gallivan
BY THE DOCKS

Overcast by the docks, friends
pushing bicycles over old
cobblestone blocks. It's a cool
Friday afternoon in this rainy
London town. Adventure at
every turn, warehouses filled
with things to be found.

New song is ringing in the air, a
clear mist of rain is falling on
our hair. Endless happiness and
fun, free and on the run. A tall
man in a long scarf. Bobbies
blowing whistles down by the
wharf.

Cheryl Lynn Kendrick
REMEMBER THE WAR?

Men in blue,
Men in grey,
fighting a cause unknown.
bullets whistling,
cannons shooting in the sky,
Our men in trenches, waiting to
die.

The sound of a bugle
playing the charge,
to conquer the enemy
the victory is ours.

Young and old who die each day.
We their loved ones, praying today,
Was it mine?, Was it yours?
Time is on their side.

War is war, it's them who decide
our men then gather,
to shoot side by side.
It's our men, who fight for us
to keep the world at peace.

May it be Father, Son, Mother, or
Uncle.
They've all had their stake and
claim,
For the 11th of "vember",
is ours to remember,
our men in blue and grey.

Rhonda Massara
PAPPA ONLY TOLD JESUS

To Philip and Angeline, my parents, my sister Elizabeth and the Everly bros. parents, Ike and Margaret

---

Pappa was a good man who always
kept feelings inside.
He never showed any emotions
and he never cried.
But I knew all along he loved my
mamma and me so.
Though he'd try never to let his love
for us show.
Until one day I found him kneelin
alone in the shed.

He was prayin to Jesus and I heard the words he said
He said: Jesus please take care of my lovely wife for me.
And my little boy you know how I love them both dearly.
Lord do this for me watch them both when I'm away
And I'll thank you sweet Jesus every day when I pray.
After his prayin pappa got up slowly from his knees
I knew pappa was cryin as he turned his face towards me.
Pappa's tears were like wide rivers flowin down his rugged cheeks.
I looked pappa in his eyes and saw all the love that they speak.
Yes pappa never showed his emotions and he never cried
Pappa only told Jesus how he loved us so inside
Pappa was a good man who always kept feelins inside
To momma and me he wouldn't let feelins show only to Jesus would he confide
The only time I saw my pappa let them feelins show
Was that one day I remember well so many years ago
Since then not a day goes by in my life I don't think of that dear man.
And the words pappa only told Jesus play softly in my mind over and over again.

Sandra Hills
MY LOVE IS GONE
I had a love so dear to me
And then I heard him say,
I know you're not the one you see
And then he went away.

How my heart is aching now,
If only I could say,
Please tell me that you love me
Before you drive away.

But oh, the things he said to me
I thought perhaps he knew,
That I was in love with him
And that he loved me too.

How hard it is to face this life
Now that I am all alone,
A sorrow only I can know
I thought our love had grown.

If only once again to hold
My loved one to my heart,
If in the beginning I was told
It was wrong right from the start.

Just now I can only think of him,
And as he drives away,
Part of my heart is growing dim,
Because I lost my love today.

I saw my love just one more time,
With fear and mixed emotion,
I knew he was no longer mine
He scorned my true
Devotion.

Soon I know the hurt will go
Yet it is hard to see,
Why does God test our patience so,
What has He planned for me.

Melanie C Palmer
THANK YOU LORD GOD
Thank you Lord God for the time we had,
for the things we shared,
through good and bad.

Thank you Lord God though it hurts so much,
like an open wound,
so painful to touch.

Thank you Lord God that he lived this long,
for the time that you gave,
I will sing my song.

Thank you Lord God that he was able to see,
six children grow up.
How blessed can one be?

Thank you Lord God for this man made of gold,
he was kind and gentle,
yet strong and bold.

Thank you Lord God because he loved us so,
it's hard to believe,
and even harder to let go.

Thank you Lord God I'll say it one more time,
I love you so much,
Grandpa of mine.

Annette Winberg
IS IT REAL, IS IT A DREAM?

To David, The one who appreciates, and inspired me.

Is it real, is it a dream, or could it be a fantasy?
But I think it really happened to me.
I think I experienced nature in all its phenomenal forms.
Did I really see whales spout and splash as they migrated—
south to have their calves?
Then to turn around to look and see and smell the fragrance—
of the Eucalyptus tree.
Bay trees, Sequoia's, to shelter the monarch butterflies—
among their leaves.
Then to watch the fog roll in, to blend with the sky, and—
the Pacific ocean.
The peace and the beauty too much to prevail, along this—
coast of Central Cal.
Blue skies, sunshine, sea lyons at play, make for me the
most beautiful, exciting and enjoyable day.

Wilma Childres Doup
HIS DAUGHTERS

To my husband, David and our daughters, Diane Autumn and Dawn Abigail, "May God's love always bless your life as beautifully as you have blessed mine."

Two small hands clasped tight in his,
He walks them to their beds.
They chatter to him, tell him stories,
Tilting up their golden heads.

Who could have known when they were born
That he would love them so?
They're wrapped completely around his heart
With strings that won't let go.

Pamela Michelle Davis
DREAMING
I dream of the love
We could share
To express ourselves
To one another
Your charm enhances me,
Expressing that we could be free.
The first time together.
This love I am dreaming of
Will take time,
But when this happens
I will keep you as mine.
Oh
Dreaming
Of Love.

Marlene Cutchin

Marlene Cutchin
WHY CAN'T CHRISTMAS BE EVERY DAY
Why can't Christmas be every day,
Why just once a year,
People happy, people gay,
Always spreading cheer.

Hair that sparkles like the snow,
Eyes that shine like the lights,
Always that warm and tender glow,
All three hundred and sixty-five nights.

Why can't we all be Santa Claus,
Listening to others' needs,
Always there to fill a loss,
Always trying to please.

Why not give a gift a day,
A gift that can't be bought,
A gift of love in any way,
By doing or in thought.

Why can't Christmas be every day,
Maybe we'll all learn,
With these gifts, there are no bills to pay,
With gifts to keep, none to return.

Why can't Christmas be every day,
Why just once a year.

Sharon Boyd
IGNORANCE OF A DRUNK DRIVER
Speeding down the road swerving to and frow.
Music playing in your car, a song you just heard in a local bar.
You pay no attention to the road ahead,
Your mind is spinning, your vision blurred.
You hear a thud that you ignore.
Arriving home a litle unsure.
You awake to a knock on your door, you get up your head a little sore,
You open the door.
A little surprised to see a policeman standing outside.
You stand in shock as said "theres a body under your car the person is dead."
You go to look afraid to see that of a childs body mangled with loose debry.
You start to cry and say "Why me?" as the officer arrests you—
You remember the thud you ignored . . .
Was a life someone else one adored.

Anasa Miesha Mpingo
LOST IN A WORLD
Lost in a world
Without much hope
Struggling to accomplish
Praying to succeed
Refusing to give up
Regression to give in
Standing firm
Standing tall
Time will show what was right
Steadfast and hopeful
Behold the light of another time
Another life
Another world
Enter in
Seeking
Perhaps success this time
Alas and alack
Energies spent
Ending up
Lost . . . in a world
Without much hope

Kathy Cody
TEARS OF A LONER
Alone, so alone
No one is here.
No whispers, no echos
just me and my tears.

I'm high on a cliff
I'm deep in the sea.
Not much is wrong,
Just lonely, you see.

My feet run like lightning
when you open the door.
You give love so scarcely
with me wanting more.

Your cruel hearts' appearance
deceives and defies.
You fool me and trick me,
close your ears to my cries.

I'll die ever lonely
just my tears and me.
Not much was wrong,
just lonely, you see.

Faith D O'Brien
TRAZAN-A SIDS BABY—1986
God gave our baby Heaven for Christmas;
An angel took him, in the night,
And climbed, into the Light.

Jesus held out His loving arms;
"I once was a baby, too,
Long ago, in Bethlehem, I was a baby, too,

Father Joseph guarded Me,
And Mother Mary held Me to her breast;
Come, my Little One, I will give you rest."

I look up into the starlit night,
And, know our baby's there,
I kneel and say a prayer.

Christ Child, Christ Child, who was a baby, too,
Bless our precious baby boy

And give him Heaven's joy!

And, if I weep, forgive me, Lord,
For, though we miss him so.
We remember You were a baby, too—
In Bethlehem, long ago.

Ruth Lisa Marrone
HOUSE SO DEAR

This house stood strong and brave
Til the sorrowful day it was razed.
Its roof was wide, its siding bright,
never lacking its paint of white.
Beneath its roof was warmth and cheer,
a happy family did dwell here.
But families grow and drift away
and a house is left alone to stay.
This house needed love and tender care
so who was left to tend and repair?
It's once white paint had turned to grey,
The roof was torn and rotted away.
This brave house that once stood proud
now lives covered by an earthly shroud.

Yatindra Bhatnagar
HOPE, HOPE

Immense ocean and mighty waves challenge,
Ever eager to devour, to finish whatever is left of you.
Life slowing ebbing away in a dark sea of despair,
Age fast taking on where youth left you.

Dreams shattered, unfulfilled and now sour,
Memories of once glorious, gorgeous days
Linger on to enhance the pain you writhe in.
Even the name you were proud of pinches you.

The vast skies, the space endless, the wide world
Once your playground, your working table,
The big names you saw daily held no terror.
The host of friends no more, now distant.

Like the fallen leaf in the flowing river,
Drifting and turning, resting and now rushing,
Pushed aside and ignored, a bit of trash
That Western Waste or some one else
collects to destroy.

A kite no longer tied to the string
Wavering aimlessly in the blue skies,
No longer able to hold her own and fly
Only to fall and be trampled under foot.

A broken life, a useless present, there seems
No future to look to, to conjure . . . but
Life still does not depart, stubborn
Will to live, to love, to hope . . . and to hope!

Jean Lee
THE LAMB'S BOOK OF LIFE

Dedicated to: Pastor Noel and Phyllis Weiss of Zion Christian Center for their loving support and confidence.

Out of the billowy clouds of white
Thru the roar of thunder
The sound of the trumpet shall be
heard, and My Son will appear.

The Lord of lords, King of kings,
The Son of Righteousness.
Then shall ye know
The judgment is near.

Is your name written in the
Lamb's Book of Life?
When The Book opens,
Will your name appear?

Or will The Book be closed?
The sound echoing thru the heavens:
Too late . . . Too Late . . . Too late . . .
Your name is not here!

Don't delay,
My precious ones,
For The Judgment Time
Is drawing near!

Patrick Guy Lewis
IN LOVE WITH HIM

I've felt alot of pain in my life
But nothing comes close to this
You said you only want to be friends
But my heart's just not in it
You didn't mean to lead me on
But you led me all the same
Is it any wonder I fell for you
But you're in love with him

I send you roses everyday
But you don't really care
I pour my heart out into words
But to my words you're deaf
I wander past your home each night
But you're not home till late
Still through it all I fell for you
But you're in love with him

You called me on the phone today
But you only needed to talk
He said he wanted to part as friends
But his words you couldn't stand
You thought he really felt for you
But you found out you were wrong
He made you fall in love with him
But he didn't mean to lead you on

Karen Thompson
DREAM

Only as high as we reach can we grow;
Only as far as we seek can we go;
Only as deep as we look can we see;
Only as much as we dream can we be;

Parthenia Holman
ECHOES FROM THE PAST

To my loving family especially William & Regina my inspiration

---

They drift in through the shutters
They creep in through the walls
They glide from up the stairs,
And wander down the halls;
As fickle memories come crystal clear;
Familiar voices ring in my ear.

Would you come here child; I heard her say
Don't dawdle honey, come right away
I need some help, don't take all day,
And when you finish, run out to play.

Now hurry off to school, and don't be late,
And don't forget your homework;
No, you can't take your skates
Come directly home from school,
And don't stop to play
Well don't slowpoke around child;
Be on your way.

Shelly (Carlson) Watson
DAY BY DAY

To Pamela, for her love and understanding

Loving you day by day
And beside you I will lay.
Take me for who and what I am
For I'm not weak or meek as a lamb.
My love for you is strong and true
And I never want to make you blue.
So together we go hand in hand
Across this beautiful land.

Richard Gilman
GEORGIAN BAY

The day dies slowly in the northern bush.
Sunlight trickles from the low branches
And slashes, silent and gentle,
In the rippling lake.
The surface dulls,
Reflecting the last shimmering minutes
Of the pine-crowned forest
Before the needled branches blur
Against the flaming sky;
Dark green to grey,
To jetty silhouette.
The bay's crimson sweep
Smooths and re-smooths the eddying circles
Of lazy snouted bass;
The canoe hovers in a sea of fire, floating
One with its pensive paddler, till he,
With insistent whining round his head,
Digs deep his blade and with strong reluctant strokes
Drives forward to where the bow sands the little beach
Below the winking lamp
And dancing wind blown sparks.

Ethel C Brown
CAN YOU HEAR HIM?

"To Humanity" May we grow in Love and Brotherhood.

That's what I was here for today
To help another Soul along the way.
For only you who created us all
Know our needs both great and small.

From dawn to sunset you hear our pleas
Your Pilgrims of Eternity.
We cry to you through prison walls
And others through great sickness call.
For we know that you can reach someone
When all seems lost and no one cares
To bring us hope and not despair.

For Father we are but one family
Under the stars and above the sea.
And if we are helped in any way
We realize that it is you who made the play.
To help one of your children
To find the way
Back into the sunshine of another day.

So I Thank You Father for using my line once more
To send your message of a brother at war.
And I hope my life will never be too busy
To hear your voice!
And answer the call from above.
Of my human family
In need of my love.

G W Brooks
AN EMPTY GLASS

Winter's dreams flow into spring, and
as we drink we hope
summer to bring
the flavor of reality
For someone to fill our glass that we might sing
summers long we may sit, waiting
as an empty glass is a poor thing
yet poorer still
is a heart in which dreams don't ring

Bev J Schoen

Bev J Schoen
PETTICOAT POOL

To the 'Surf Club', my championship team of the '70's, and all of the memories. This is just how it was . . .

Slowly, I walked around the table, with my cue stick in my hand.
Stopped to study my opponent, and noticed, 'Masconi, was her brand'!

I glanced back at the green, to see the cue ball against the cushion.
I used some right hand english, and brought the ball back in position.

I hit the cue ball low, as not to scratch.
Used a quick draw back on the cue, and I knew I had the match!

As my big ones drop off the table, my opponent is rather shocked.
So, I pause to psyche her out, cause all her balls are blocked!

As the rythmn of my cue, helps me to run the table,
The music on the juke box, keeps me very calm and stable.

Again, I stroll around and study, to give her some time to sweat,
For my last shot is on the eight, the pressure ball, and hardest one to get!

I smoothly slide my cue stick between my fingers with ease,
Cause this one's a bank shot, and I've got to make it, please!

Everything is quiet now, not even a whisper,
And as both balls fell, I knew, I missed her.

Catherine Richey

LIBERTY AND FREEDOM

The word freedom is expressed in so many ways
in words and deeds in what we do and say
To be thankful for this land that's free
To see our flag flying her colors of red, white, and blue
So beautiful to look at indeed
Giving thanks for our freedom that's ours to share
To enjoy freedom of worship and feel God's presence there
To enjoy liberty and freedom around everywhere
As we guide and teach our children to care
To believe and keep the freedom as we trust in God in a spiritural way
To know what freedom means that's ours today
As we celebrate our country's freedom as we gather far and near
As we hear the bells of freedom ring out loud and clear
As the Statue of Liberty torch burns day and night
To always believe and have faith in what we think is right
To know nothing is impossible for God is our Guiding Light

Heather Cooper

NIGHT, TIME

The night is silent,
Still and breathless,
Scared of the untold,
The untimely agony,
Of the moaning winds,
Howls of the coyote unfold,
Murmer of the night creatures,
But with what quest in mind,
Slowly drags,
The Sands of Time.

Mrs Peggy Ann Dietz

THE END

I would like to dedicate this poem to all the people in my life who have inspired me:

JOHN, DUSTIN, DEBBIE, MICHELLE, DOROTHY, LEWIS, BARBARA, JAMES, AND ALLISSA M.

There will be laughing, singing, and carrying on,
But it will be the same tune, the same song.
The wind will blow softly as though to say "bye,"
As our Lord in Heaven descends from the sky.
No one knows exactly when this will be done,
As the sand grains fall faster one by one.
All of our clocks will stop clicking their time,
And all of life's games will pass the finish line.
Live your life the best you can my friend,
Because someday it will have to come to an end.

Claire Fullerton Shilanskis

AN ODE TO FATE

To Annette, whose spirit lingers on

I cannot hear the thunder blast,
The birds sing not for me,
The rain falls muted to the earth,
The surf breaks silent from the sea.

I cannot hear the church bells chime,
My ears hear not the melody,
The wind howls voiceless in the storm,
The river surges silent, endlessly.

For I am deaf. No words can breach
The abyss of my soundless destiny,
The lute may sound, I shall not hear,
But I can feel, and I can see.

I feel the earth tremble with the anger
Of the raging wind and mighty thunder,
I feel the rain's caress upon my cheek,
Like tears of awe and wonder.

The birds on wing, far lovelier than sound;
The swaying bells are chime enough for me,
What matters if the surf breaks loud,
When I can feel the salt spray of the sea?

I do not ask, I do not seek the pity,
The world bestows on such as I.
I ask not for the sounds or melodies
I'd rather drink the beauty of the sky.

Corithia Lyn Kiser

HOMELESS

The streets are cold this time of year
And many dangers, I foresee
But yet, this is my only home
The only home for me.
Some people call me homeless
And some say I'm just a bum
They care nothing at all for me
Nor care from whence I come.
I have no place of employment
No house, no car, nor family
They say I am a menace to society
And do not even want to look at me.
Maybe I am invisible
But others, including children, I see
If it's not I that you care to help
Help the little children at least
It's not that we wish to live like this
It's just that bad luck came our way
And everyday I pray to God
We all find homes someday.

Lorena Washeck

THE SPRING BALL

I saw a cowslip through the fence,
A horseradish by the wall;
The tiger lilies looking fierce, but I was not afraid at all,
The rose-of-Sharon in her regal gown, the naked ladies, stately and bold;
The black-eyed pea with one eye closed—too many ladies to behold!

The dandy lions and the buttercups, beauty and wealth claimed they
For who can cover a carpet green with such a golden array?
The elephant ears stood by the gate; large, green, and gracefully tall.
With these animal flowers around, Miss Spring throws her annual ball.

The dragonlily, calico bean, and cauliflower Dan, all dressed in their trousers bright;
With partners like Rose, Fern and Pansy, danced happily through the night.
The green beans played their strings; such an orchestra you've never seen.
The moonflower beams furnished the light for this happy nocturnal scene.

The bleeding heart and the pining tree stood alone, unhappy and grieving,
While the sweet pea fluttered around, putting guests at ease all evening.
Now it's all over—time to leave! a wonderful time was reported by all.
"Please come again next year." cried Spring, "as soon as you hear my call."

Shawn Lester Hanson

OUR TRUTH

To my mother, Viola Lester, with love.

I wrote you a long letter,
When I was seventeen
I said you were the greatest thing
The world had ever seen.
I pledged undying loyalty,
And praised you for your deeds,
I thanked you for your sacrifice
In caring for my needs.
I told you that your wisdom
Had always helped me through,
That my favorite possession
Was a word of praise from you.

I don't regret that letter,
Though I wrote it in my youth.
But I would have added something,
Had I somehow known the truth.
My life has been more perfect
Than I could have thought it'd be
I'm thankful I'm your daughter, Mom
Since I wasn't originally.

Roberta J Cox

WHAT I DON'T UNDERSTAND

To all who will never be allowed to read this poem

What I don't understand is alarming.
Hungry children, so disarming,
Left to suffer and starve,
Not at all by accident,
But by government.
Tiny, nameless children,
Never given a chance
To dance or cast a sunward glance,

While, consumed with fire and revelry,
Mom and Daddy prance.
Bloodied, bruised, and battered,
Little children lie,
Beaten by grown-up parents,
Can't you hear them cry?
So many of them die.
Innocent little wonders—
Miniatures formed by God,
Full of trust and awe of the world,
Yet, bearing the hurts and scars
Of a pain-filled, God forsaking generation
On their tiny, trusting shoulders.

Sara JoAnn Farkas

LOSS OF LOVE

I know the hard guy exterior
Is so you don't need to show pain and hurt!
Somewhere behind the pain and hurt
there lies a soft and gentle person.
A person capable of love and caring
not apathy and hate!
A person filled with hopes and dreams
not emptyness
You may have lost something you loved dearly
but you have memories of the good and bad
Don't lose anymore.
memories are important,
you must keep them always,
but you can't close everything up,
or the others you love too will be lost

(MARGUERITE) Rita L Shejn

CONTENT

This poem is dedicated to the Great Creator who give us cretivity, and to my grandparents,

Nelson E. & Nellie E Howard, who reared me with love and caring.

Content...
But tired, weary and worn.

Content...
Though usually alone
Walking,
Rocking,
Talking to himself.

Content...
Smiling quietly
As the eye of his heart see visions;
Visions blurred with tears,
Happy Tears!
Many years parade,
Repeating, retreating, repeating.

Content...
Darkness gathers
His eyes close,
His mouth quivers,
He sighs,
Still smiling
...the old man dies,
Content.

Imogene Willis
EMPTYNESS
You go to work and pay the bills
I care for the children and cook the meals
To think that life has come to this
When once we shared such marital bliss
It would have been better to have died in my prime
Than to be dead inside, though still existing in time.

Where went the tender sighs
That made the lovely hours pass swift
The meaningfull glances which needed
No words for expression?
They have now become long lonely
Years of nothingness.

Life goes on, menial tasks demanding my care
The children are growing, beautiful and fair
They need not know
And I pray they never will
That hands tenderly care for them
And a heart tries to hide the emptyness there.

Bea Townsend
EARLY MORNING NEWS
Sleepily, busy putting on my clothes and shoes
Listening indifferently to the early morning news.
I thought the reporter said "There's big trouble with Babe Ruth."
Startled—wondering why?
Listening more closely.
I discovered she said, "BEIRUT"

Donna Lynn Brady
BEWARE: MY HEART
My heart is
Forest in summer
Shadows are tangible
Beware: if you turn your back
They will devour you

My heart is
Ocean on a calm day
Sparkling blue and quiet
Beware: do not dive in too deeply
the undertows are deadly.

My heart is
Pond frozen in winter
I invite children to skate on my surface
Beware: the ice is thin
The waters black and inescapable.

Reita Jean Ash
COME TO THE PARTY
Did you behold His wonders?
His gifts for us today?
He made great beams of gold
and sent them down our way.
He spread His shimmering curtain,
of the finest silvery mist,
over lakes and seas of emeralds
and fields of amethyst.
He made great mountain peaks
to reach for Him on high.
And a perfect angel's song
just for His breeze to sigh.
He placed a perfect diamond
in every drop of dew.
He handpainted every flower,
as only He could do.
Do you see His message there,
in His clouds of pink and grey?
They're drifting out His invitation
to come and share His day.

Ms Johnnie B Houston

Ms Johnnie B Houston
TO YOU * FROM ME

To the world

To you from me
Are beautiful words you see
And sending them to you today
Extends my appreciation miles away
It is my desire to make another's heart happy too
For the sad and the lonesome that hurt like we do
Even though all things will come to pass
Let's remember each other and cherish what we have
I hope this little message brightens your day
Because its written for you with love to stay.

Lucy Bowers
THE HILLTOP AT NIGHT

To Barbara Greene

How quiet and still
It is here upon the hill
With the pine trees scenting
The breeze which is already relenting
With the coming of the night.

How warm and bright
Is this hilltop at night
When the moon blossoms forth
And in all its glory pourth
A magic light from the sky above.

Oft have I wandered here
On this hilltop to God so near,
Who from his Heaven looks down
At one poor mortal on the ground,
And gives to me the strength to live.

So onward I go
Back to my life below,
To crowded town and busy days
And ordinary and usual ways
But yet remembering
Pine trees on a hill.

Virginia G Sullivan
TIME
TIME—gathers no moss as it rushes along
And we ride as it were—on the wings of a song.

When hearts are young and love is new
These precious moments are so few.

For a space of TIME we are content
While the years rush by and then, we are bent
To salvage the pieces of one life that is spent
TIME—THAT FLEETING ELEMENT.

Pattie Portalatin
HOW DOES ONE MEASURE THE CALIBER OF A PERSON?
How does one measure the caliber of a person?
What are the things one might jot down for weight?
Would you consider a person just because he's wealthy?
Or does the school that one attends carry the weight?

How does one measure the caliber of a person?
How does one take measurements of what he has inside?
Is it the productivities that one gives to society?
Or is it how much one is puffed up with pride?

Does honesty and integrity
Play any part in the weighing and the measuring?
Or just where does the measuring begin?

Must every act of good deed be recorded
From his highest achievement down to the smallest one?
When you begin measuring the caliber of a person
Just how is this measuring done?

After all of one's qualities have been ascertained
and discernment given to each part,
Fine schools, wealth and pride are not the only criteria.
Then it must be the size of one's heart.

Rosalie Buzzell
RUSTY

To my son John with love

Mommy and Daddy said I should pray
for my little dog who died yesterday
Rusty was my very best friend
Why did his life have to end?
Dad said he'd get a new dog for me
But it won't take the place of my best friend Rusty
I'd like to take all my toys
And send them to heaven

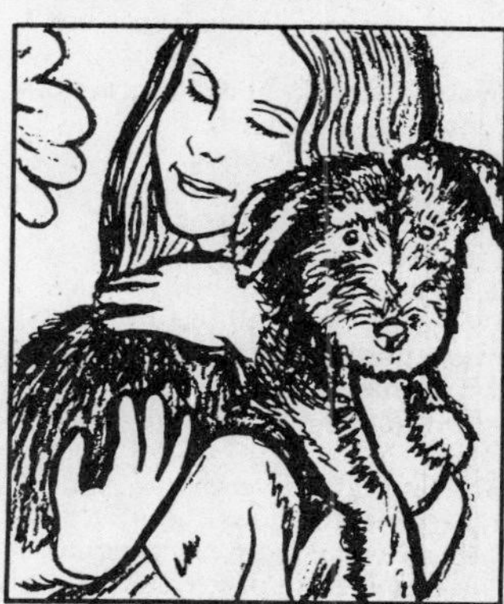

where there are boys
I'd give them my trains
and even the tracks
If only you'd give me Rusty back
A fair and square deal
So what do you say?
I don't mean to rush ya
but could you make it today?

Elizabeth Ann Randall
YESTERDAY'S FUTURE
Ruined dreams and broken promises
Memories left in my mind
Searching for tomorrow—
Leaving yesterday behind.

Facing the world—
Standing alone.
Picking up pieces—
Now on my own.

A new beginning—
About to start.
Taking that first step—
The hardest part.

Challenges to meet—
But giving them a try.
Time will grow—
And so will I.

Angela Hope Durant
THE JOURNEY
I began with you when I was so young,
The time of our journey I did not know
You talked of future things not yet begun;
You whispered softly, "We must begin now."

You led me to the place where the sun shines
You led me through the murky waters deep,
You led me through the darkness of the minds;
You said what I sow I shall also reap.

So I began to live the narrow way,
The journey has almost come to an end;
Sooner than you think it will be your day
One day you said "yes" and for me did send.

Now I float on a celestial high plane
So happy am I, I followed God's lane.

Lavonna Sue Carroll
IT WAS ONLY A DREAM!

I was confused about you and me,
About what our relationship may
end up to be.
It was an unpleasant sight to see!
Perhaps frightening to me,
I tried to struggle against it but I
was too weak.
I wasn't certain about our actions
nor was I pleased.
It wasn't our life style,
It just wasn't me.
But I realized, it was an
unconscious thing.
It may be puzzling but It was
pleasant and full of fun
Even though it really wasn't me.
It may have been a dream of wish
fulfillment and exciting as could
be,
But I remained very calm, until It
became a serious thought.
When I woke from my sleep a
lovely feeling of joy came over
me,
And I repeated, time and time
again,
"It was only a dream."

Clifton McNeil
FEELING THE PAIN

This poem is dedicated to my parents Ruby and Jimmie, my sons Marcus and Michael and my loving wife, Sylvia.

We hear rowing ships sailing
toward the bay—
coming to take our families away.
Feeling the pain in our hearts and
minds—
leaving everything that we own
behind.

The master's whip is making a
command:
"go plow up some brand new land."
Feeling the pain burning in our
hearts and hands—
it hurts so deep; we can hardly
stand.

Freedom calls for us this day. The
president said,
"There will be no more slaves to
slay."
Oh Lord! the chains, suffering and
pain has finally past.
But the memory will always,
always last!

Times have slightly changed for us
a bit—
now we have to watch where we sit.
"Sit in the back with your kind."
"Sorry, you can't stand in this line."

God sent us a Black Disciple one
heavenly day
to show us that togetherness is the
right and only way.
Now the pain feels sweeter each
day—
Thank you Lord! We will obey:

Our glorious Disciple has found a
heavenly home
through the Gates of Glory where
there is no wrong.
There is a dream that's yet to
come—
All nations will live together
peacefully—as one!

Rosalie Buzzell
THE PROMISE

To my husband George and my children who enriched my life and sweetened my hope

My child you must know the time
has come
when your two parents will
become just one
I have some pain but I'll be fine
I have to talk I have things on my
mind
I have to get these things in order
So listen to me, my lovely daughter
take care of Dad do it for me
right now he needs you, more you
see
Your brother's so helpless, in many
ways
tuck him in at night, make sure he
prays

Your little sister, she can be a
bother
they'll help you with her, your
brother and father
Please don't come home, so late at
night
And when you do, hold your pillow
real tight
think of it, as if it were me
I bet you I'll feel it, real tenderly
Promise me that, when the time
comes
You'll place me somewhere where
there's lots of sun
Bring me red roses, as red as can be
But most of all, please don't forget
me!

June Stubbings Sheldon
MUFFY, MY KITTY

On winter days, you sleep in a ball,
Comfortably in the sun—
With your nose tucked in the fur
of your tail
From morning until day is done.

Evening arrives, and you go to bed
And sleep the long hours away.
The only question in my mind, I
find,
Is: "How can you sleep both
night and day?"

Is that a form of hibernation?
Or are you just a lazy cat,
Taking advantage of a warmed-up
cushion
In the chair where I lately sat?

Brenda J Selby
THE SWING

Weathered boards
Creak, moan.
I sway forward,
Backward,
Admiring lush hills.
Clinking chains
And swishing feet upon the grass
Mingle with soft bird sounds,
Composing a sweet song.

Robin Caroline Watts
DREAMS

Dreams of day and
Dreams of night . . .
Some dream to live, and
Some dream to fight.
Some dream to be preachers,
teachers,
Doctors, too.
Some dream to be movie stars, or
Build model cars.

Wishes to people are special
dreams
Too!
Some wish for their freedom . . .
Some wish to be right on the moon.
Dreams aren't stupid, and that's a
fact!
But some dreams are awkward,
and will
Never come true.

B Albert
LITTLE LAMB OF GOD

Little lamb, little lamb
It is very late in the day,
No one to hear this lamb
For the shepherd is far away.

Yonder shines a glorious star
I run, I fall, can't hear his rod.
The shepherd saw it from afar
And left to find the Lamb of God.

Through the hills I must follow
O' Bright Star, lead me, I too must
rush,
Beyond the hills lies a bright glow
Trembling, I find all in a hush.

"Lamb of God" angels sing above
Holy, very holy, this night.
Here's your little lamb full of love
At me—The Lamb—a smile so
bright.

Little lamb, smiling little lamb
No longer too late in the day
No one needs to hear this lamb
For the Shepherd is here to stay.

Nancy Christian
I AND AM

I am not Am
for Am is a kindred soul
and spirit, she has been
with me and I with her.

Our years together and apart
have been many. The strength
that has been forged, like iron,
grows stronger all the while.

Am I? No I am not.
Am is herself and I
am I.

Dust desert storms to
coastal life, afterwards
lies peace and calm
sharing thoughts

in the sunset.
I remember that house
just a dream to be built
over a valley, Am's house.

Now all dusks are not the same
for they are Am,
am I.

James P Cunningham
MEDIEVAL MAIDEN

Well, she comes and she goes, once
in a while
Sophisticated youth, sweet
perfume and smile
English maiden gazzing upon the
idle mire
She shows a warm heart, through
eyes of fire
She tells me stories and asks, what
do you think?
Then she says she feels like having
a drink
She seems so fragile no more than
an eight stone
And she's light on her feet and
never alone
She speaks so softly, dazzling and
then you know
How she feels by a frown or a grin
So close to earth she watches the
eagles fly
And she can find a rainbow in a
medieval sky
She is gone in a flash, she never
stays long
She finds security in her castle
strong
She is colorful, she stands proud
She brings sunlight through an
obinous cloud
Such a wonderful place this
ancient earth
And forever wanting frolic and
mirth
I learn to be graceful watching her
dance,
Graceful lady, she does intrigue me
with a single glance
She likes to walk the rolling glen
And dream of places she had never
been
Lovely child of the emerald isle, are
you the queen?
For you are the sweetest lass this
realm has ever seen

Nancy Teter

Nancy Teter
JUST YESTERDAY, JUST TODAY

To: Kristen L. Teter, and Eva Liang who took down the bears from the wall leaving those who watched, a little sad

Just yesterday, she came here, a
day I'll always recall
Just yesterday, she hung teddy
bears, all over her wall
Just yesterday, her dad said, she's
too timid and shy
Just yesterday I answered, that will
pass, by and by
Just yesterday, school functions,
she'd attend not at all
Just yesterday, there was noone, to
give her a call

Just yesterday she stood, much shorter than I
Just yesterday, the little girl, would give a bored-sigh

Just today, she took down, the bears from the wall
Just today, I realized, she's growing so tall
Just today her Dad fussed "she never gets off that phone"

Just today there's a party, she planned on her own
Just today he said "thank God, she'll soon be grown
Just today I answered, "she'll soon be on her own"
Tomorrow, what we'll wish for, "But may never say
We'll wish for just yesterday, or just for today

Elma N Kreider

SHEEP OR THE GOATS

I really was glad when they picked out my name
To be on the side of the sheep.
For I'd never be happy to be an old goat
And eat all the trash on the street.
For sheep always loved the sweet smelling grass
No tin cans would do in their diet.
And they followed the shepherd wherever he led
And garbage they never would try it.
But God really had a plan for the goats
When curtains for the temple were made.
He took all the hair from off of their backs
As soon as the foundation was laid.

Francine Mathis Boska

WALKING IN THE WOODS

Walking in the woods, is such an enchanting fairyland,
Listening to the birds chirp and sing,
Makes a person feel so grand.
I love to listen to the soft call of the Dove,
while gazing up at the blue sky above.
You can feel the soft summer breeze,
as it whispers sweetly through the tall pine trees.

The ground is covered with a soft blanket of green,
And if you look very closely, blue violets can be seen.
If you walk a little farther into the woods,
You can surely see natures treasured goods.
A babbling brook is finding it's way to the sea,
While the grey squirrel is building a nest in the old oak tree.

Delores Gillespie

MY HUSBAND RETIRED

I thought your retirement would
Drive me up a wall,
But it really hasn't been that
Bad at all,
It would even be much better
For me and for you,
If you'd get a part time job
So you have something to do.

Lawrence E Wesley

DICHOTOMY OR UNITY

I dedicate this to a wonderful person—Juanita, my wife and friend without whom I would not exist today.

I laid and watched the stars with you and life was made
I awoke to the rising of the bright sun; life was rejuvenated
I switched on the light and it opened a new world of dreams.
I walked down a darkened street and felt fear.
I laid in the blazing, white sun and felt pain.
I have read that a black plague destroyed much of humankind—
But
I have witnessed persons in white sheets destroy another kind.
I have seen rich, black soil make organisms grow, and—
I have seen white pearls corruption sow.
I have heard white lies destroy, and I have heard black lies absolve.
Without light there is no night, without the night there is no light.
I am lost until both have some meaning; until we understand that both is needed.

R H Tannahill

HARDLUCK

It seems that we can't get ahead, we're always just about to.
But just today our car broke down, so walk, I guess we'll have to!
We need new shoes, our soles are thru,
our broken furniture's come unglued.
I lost my job, I was fired,
Broke, hungry, and downright tired.
We're all sick or just about,
matter of fact everything's worn out.
So, I may have to, I don't care,
ask you, "Mr. Got a dime to spare?"

Billy Eugene Williams

SUICIDE MIND

Looking for light, when seeing in darkness.
Looking at life, with all of its hardness.
Look for the sun, to see that its raining.
Feeling lifes emotions draining.
Remembering happiness of time past.
Wishing that it, would've last.
Wanting to feel peace of mind.
In hopes of leaving trouble behind.
Feeling confused about tomorrow.
Thinking death will end its sorrow.
Saying there is no use.
I'll end this life, with its abuse.
In the twinkling of an eye, its over and done.
The suicide mind has finally won.

Agnes T Mitter

Bettijean LaVoy

A VERBAL PORTRAIT

In memory of my very special mother, Agnes T Mitter

M means the mother
who spanked my derriere

O means old-fashioned views
I soon learned to share

T means her tough, yet
tender reprimanding

H means her heart
full of love and understanding

E means endless tasks
and unselfish giving

R means the religion
she instilled in daily living

Kimberly Shrodes

SHOES

This is dedicated to the memory of Dorothy Naunton, whose SHOES of love can never be filled.

When I look upon her face, I see so much has changed.
A face that once showed so much life, now shows fright and pain.

Though tough as it may be to view beyond that frightened look.
I think back through the years and see exactly what life took.

Back when she was still quite young her black hair began to fade.
And quick and sure as with us all, her hair was suddenly gray.

Her face at one time was so smooth and soft as a baby's face.
But with all the worry and care of love, life's love lines took their place.

Though right now it seems to be that life took much away.
But few will ever truly know what she gives to us each day.

Hearty smiles and joyous laughter is a part of her every day.
Gracious hugs and lots of kisses are just her in her own way.

But more than smiles and more than hugs is the love she has in her heart.
And when that love is truly gone my own love will tear me apart.
For it will be hard, 'cause no one can fill the shoes of one another.
Especially when the shoes of love are worn by one's Grandmother.

Ranne Krizek

FLUFFY

Our hearts are breaking this sad dreary day
They will never completely mend.
Our beautiful, faithful Fluffy
Has met an untimely end.

We will bury him now, though we do not know how
We will come to terms with our grief.
The young man who hit him wept tears of remorse
As he told this sad story to me.

Our Fluffy was nudging his smaller companion
Away from the danger he was able to see
When a wheel rolled over his brave little form
And Fluffy was injured instead.

The driver and we wept copious tears
As Fluffy, still able to see
Looked lovingly up
At my heartbroken husband and me.

He seemed to be saying
"I'll meet you up there
Where the land is so fair
In Green Pastures we'll run, you and me."

Anna Mae Parish

A JUNE DAY

What is more lovely than a day in June
To smell the Rose's sweet perfume
To see the sky a delicate blue
With pastel clouds passing through.

To feel the gentle breezes blow
Kissing your cheek, leaving a tinted glow
Making you feel that you are queen
On this bit of earth, all emerald green.

To hear the Wren's sweet, cheerful song
High on a branch, where he belongs
Watching his home, to give alarm
To keep his family from any harm.

To see the butterflies dip here and there
For a taste of nectar from flowers rare,
Or zig-zag high on aerial waltz
Over picket fence or garden wall.

Then comes creeping the velvety night,
Fireflies lighting with a wee yellow night,
High over the trees you see the moon,
Another day gone in lovely June.

To youth, the passing of time is naught

Or a June Day is nothing to talk about,
Set your standards high, soon you will learn all that pays,
Is how you have lived and spent each day.

June Durflinger
PEAS

To my mom, without whom there would have been no "PEAS" or meat and potatoes.

While hullin' peas one evenin',
In my little farmhouse kitchen,
I got to thinkin' how fast life
was passin' by.
I said to all creation,
What I need is a vacation,
and by grab I'm gonna get it
'fore I die.
I believe I'll go to Reno,
and play a little Keno,
and maybe have a drink and
see a show.
Now all I need is someone,
to take over with the farmin'
and 'spose I better have a little
dough.
I think I'll go tomorrow and see
how much jack I can borrow,
Catch a plane and then I'm on
my merry way.
The only trouble, beg your pardon,
Is the peas and that damned garden,
So I guess I'll have to dream
another day.

June Hinds
A TREE FOR LEIGH

In Memory of Leigh Sherman
5-20-75 to 2-17-86

When we think of the joy of life,
And the spirit of the free,
No one comes to mind,
As quickly as our Leigh.
Her courage, her smile,
So readily on her face,
Will remain in our hearts,
In a very special place.
So today in her memory,
We now will plant a tree,
As a living, growing symbol,
Of the life we shared with Leigh.

Joyce Schick
SHE'S NOT HERE NOW

Years taking care of the ones she loved
Just to have them grow up out of her arms
Never once did she show just self love
As a mother she still has special love and charms
She's not here now with me, Mom you're one I'm proud of

Thinking of yesterday, smelling freshly ironed clothes
Things I took for granted she worked hard at
Things done out of love, why! Only another mother knows
She's not here now, wish she was so we could chat
As each day goes by my love for her grows

At times it seems she was left out and forgotten
By the ones she loved and cared for so much
She is a flower that was picked from the Garden of Eden
I miss her every day along with her special touch
She's not here now with me,
Mama, words of love to you
I wished I had spoken

Julia Gajdosik

Julia Gajdosik
WHAT IT TAKES TO BE A NEIGHBOR

To my husband Andrew in loving memory

Do you ever wonder
what it takes to be a neighbor?
Is it living side by side
with a high fence all around

Is it, this is yours
And this is mine

You stay on your side
Do not trespass on mine
Just leave me alone and we'll be fine

Just what, it takes to be a neighbor?
Try a Hello, and a smile
It always works wonders, and
If ever you need help, Remember to call.

James B Arnold
IT'S BEEN A TOUGH YEAR

It was a night of golden memorys
And the time slipped slowly by
Content of mind, with pen in hand
And writing pad close by
Scribing notes
Of sweet scented smiles
Bygone years
And lifes grey trials
Touching life's treasures
In the palm of my hand
Thankfull for each one
And each grain of sand
I try to live
One year at a time
The same way I write
Just line after line
Some years are tough
Like some lines are teasing
But all years are rough
It's the living that's pleasing . . .

Walter Mae King
SPRING TIME

This poem is dedicated to my children, Carol Lynette and Gregory Lee

I hear birds singing,
Fire flies flickering,
Crickets chirping,
Robins singing in the trees,
Bringing in the joy of spring time.

I see flowers blooming,
Green grass awakening from a winter's nap,

Leaves bearing arms of green,
Streams flowing through the meadows,
Bringing in the joy of spring time.

I see little children playing in the park,
Hearing merry voices,
There's joy in the mountains,
There's life in the air,
Bringing in the joy of spring time.

Debbie Rogers
WISHING

For my Grandmother Mrs. Isabell Bryant With all my love

Sitting by the window
Wishing time to fade away,

Wishing I were a child again
So I could go out and play.

What happened to all those years
They seemed to have flown by,

They've gotten away from me so fast
It makes me want to cry.

Oh' to be a child again
To run and laugh and sing,

I would give up my last few memories
And a lot of other things.

To feel the grass beneath my feet
The wind blowing through my hair,

To be able to do almost anything
Without ever having a care.

But time goes very quickly now
And my days are numbered less,
And not so many days from now
I'll be taking my final rest.

J Susan Billingsley
DREAM!

Take me far beyond your soft horizons—
Far beyond the shadows of the real.
Far beyond the tears that haunt my waking,
Let me run in cotton-clover fields.

Take me down the alleys of a nightmare—
Down the lanes where time is only dust.
Down the winding staircase of my slumber,
Let me drift where memories are rust.

John E Gillespie
CATHEDRAL

The candelabra of rugged hills
Thrust their tapers, tall green pines,
Upward toward the ethereal blue
From the altar of eternal shrines.

A choir of birds, their threnodies
Warble to a dying day,
While down the canyon's twisted aisle
A murmuring river seems to pray.

The angelus of rustling fir—
A whispering monastery chime.
Through stained-glass panes of broken clouds
The sun's departing rays incline.

Its architecture ageless stands,
Its ceil the sky, its floor the sod,
And I in pygmied solitude
Behold the presence here of God.

Than Anchlia

Than Anchlia
FACT

This poem is dedicated to 'Jethi', my loving love: and to all others who like or dislike 'fact'.

What is happiness?
what is sorrow?

What is life?
Acts in action, make to feel
As if it is: Yes it is.
Your sorrow may be
Someone's happiness.
Your happiness may be
Other's sorrow.

Thus wheel rolls on and on
No begin no end
Born and dead
Got and lost
Your thoughts send signals
Only to pretend.

Adelia (Dee) Wright
CREATION

Dedicated to Ned Wright, the dearest man I've ever known.

When I read what others write,
The wheels within my brain begin to turn
And, once again, the children of my mind
Seek entrance to this world, oh, how they yearn.

And, so, I labor as I've done
So often in the past,
Giving birth with painful joy
The die is cast.

Until, maternally,
With pride I look
And wish some day to see them
Published in a book.

Mrs Lois Casper Bartolini
STONE

To my husband Pete whom I love with all my heart

Once apon a time
I found a litle stone.
I put it in my pocket
but it was all alone.
I searched and searched all around
until another stone I found.
I put this in my pocket too
they belonged together like me and you.
They're not the same
in color or size.
But they blended together
right before my eyes.
Together they're one
for all to see.
Like the love we have
just you and me.

Brigid Colangelo
WE SEE THE DAYS COME

We see the days come.
And the nights go.
But what have we actually
done today? Tonight?

If we could accomplish but
one important task everyday,
And perhaps see the sense
Of making someone smile or laugh or cry.

If we could gaze upon the
Sky, we'd see one of the most
Appealing thing to our eyes, the stars.

A good day, A good night,
to feel we have not been
implicated in the lesser
things life has to offer.

Aldean Marie Stewart
FROM MY FRONT PORCH

This poem is dedicated to my lovely daughters Janis and Cheryl

---

From my front porch, such a beautiful view,
A firey red sunset beneath a sky of blue.
The rolling hills stretch to the highway beyond,
Cattle and deer can be seen grazing at dusk or dawn.
They have a path from the creek, over a wooded ridge,

The deer have a crossing just above the bridge.
In the distance, many cedars can be seen,
The hill appears to be painted dark green.
As the sun slowly disappears from sight,
And the moon and stars come out tonight.
It's like the Master Painter on high,
Waved his Magic Brush across the sky.

Ruby B Nuckolls
HAPPY BIRTHDAY, DEAR JO

Friends Come,
Friends Go!
But none so precious
As you, dear Jo!
Upon you we depend
Whether we go, or just send.
Our days are brighter,
With burdens made lighter,
So wishes for happy birthday
Are coming your way!
May God bless you with many more!
As you serve Him from door to door!

Tom Coffman
MASTER OF CONFUSION

He's everywhere, this thing
That makes life miserable
He makes the blues to sing.

Why, just yesterday he made me
Look at my wife (my companion for life)
While she was talking to me.
I looked at her quizzically and said
"Wha-a-a-t?" Because she all of a sudden
. . . she just quit speaking!!?!
Very strange

Yet, through it all, the master of confusion
He just has to lose,
Eventually, the confusion clears
And leads the way to maturity and wisdom.

A person has to be strong
to break the evil ones grip.
But, a faith in God and goodness
Will clear the fog.
So, "Peace and Sanity" to you
Brothers and sisters,
BE STRONG—BE STRONG!

Pearline Strong
MOTHER

---

this is dedicated to MRS LEOLA HANDY, my loving mother

Mother fed and kept us clean from day to day
When bedtime came she would kneel and pray,
Say thank you Lord for my boy and girls
Take care of them thru this cruel world.

I will never forget that bright April morn
When Jesus came and took mother home
She often told us that the way would be hard
She said always have faith in God.

You can look the world over
But you will never find a friend like mother
I was standing by her bed trying hard not to cry
All I could say was goodby
We will meet again one day on high.

All her life
She would freely give
Her time, love and advice
She was a wonderful mother and wife.

Skip Lasch
TODAY

Let me be aware
Of the treasure you are.
Savor you, bless you
Before you depart.

Let me pass by
In quest of some perfect tomorrow.
Let me hold you while I may,
For it will not always be so.

One day I shall dig my nails into the earth,
Or stretch myself taut,
Or raise my hands to the sky.
And wish more than all the world
For your return.

But, of course, you will not return.
With pain I acknowledge,
There is no tomorrow
There is only today.

Doris M Baker
LOVE IS

To my children—Ted, Joyce, Della
Love is the greatest of all emotions

Love is God, love is life,
Love of a husband for his wife.
Love is beauty in the old oak tree.
Swaying gently in midsummers breeze.

Love of a mother for her child
Beginning the day with a cheery smile
Love is in all sizes and shapes
Even the mystery of drifting snow flakes.

Love is stillness in the middle of the night
Tomorrows sun bringing much delight
Love is kindness sowed along the way,
Sprouting happiness for each new day.

Love is forever, the joy of living
An outstretched hand, the pleasure of giving.
From the smallest ant to natures honey bee.
Love abounds for all to see.

Debralee Dellefratte
INSPIRATION

TO ASK WHY
and seek the answer until I find it.

TO SING OUT
a song without words
and to music only my ears can hear.

TO SEE PICTURES IN THE SKY
and find words to describe dreams.
WRITE PROFOUND THOUGHTS
and in reading find strength.
DRAW A PICTURE OF MY MIND
and in so doing find order there.
WATCH NATURE BREATHE
and the change does not alter my hope for tomorrow.

TO SLEEP RESTFULLY AND PEACEFULLY
knowing tomorrow may forever change
THE DREAMS I DREAMED TODAY.

Mrs Mary Holloway Cuthbertson

Mrs Mary Holloway Cuthbertson
MY LITTLE GIRL BECAME A WOMAN TODAY

To Sharon, my dear and loving daughter

No more mid-night feedings, no more formulas to make,
No diapers to launder, no unwanted baths to get her to take.

No more sticky finger prints to
wash from the walls,
No need to rescue, should she
stumble and fall.
No more "da-da" and "ma-ma," her
first uttered words,
To us, her proud parents, were
the sweetest we had heard.
No more baby food all over her
pretty face,
Lipstick and rouge have long
since replaced.
No more walks to the corner store
to get candy and treats,
Saying "hi" to everyone on the
street that we meet.
No more school photos with front
teeth missing,
Instead it's one in her wedding
dress I find myself kissing.
No more waiting up nights til she
returned from her dates,
No more guiding her along as
she whipped up the cakes.
I've shared her with the family and
what joys did occur,
And now I must share her with
someone who's become part of
her.
It is he who has taken and stolen
her heart,
Although I'll miss her terribly, I
hope they never part.
I wonder if the Mom and daughter
chats will now cease to be,
Or will it be woman to woman
on issues of life and what is the
key.
As I sit here on the pew on this her
wedding day,
I fight back the tears as her dad
gives her away.
So right before my eyes the past
has passed away,
And my little girl became a
woman today.
But maybe some day she'll have a
daughter too,
And I hope I'll be fortunate to
help her grow like grandmas' do.

Carole Barrett O'Saben

THE WAY OF LOVE

For Max, my love.

It washes over you,
Like a wave of warm sea water,
Contentment and well-being,
And joy in your fulfillment.
You are as one with him,
And what is good is the best.

And then,
A little wrong creates a void.
And even in his arms you feel apart,
As coldness drowns your soul.
Your mind has packed its bags,
For your journey into solitude.

And then,
It floods over you,
Like a wave of warm sea water . . .

E Ann Leavenworth

APRIL SHOWERS

Pitter-patter so gentle
Falls with a soft beat,
Soothes the weary mind
And makes serenity complete.

Nature takes a new lease
And things start to bloom
While beauty and peace
Are wrapped in soft gloom.

Then soft pretty colors
All looking their best
Compete with each other
In great zeal and zest.

And I thank our God
For giving us all this
With barely a nod
And a small loving kiss.

Marjorie A Pate

ON A SUMMER'S MORN

This poem is dedicated in memory of my father, Roy L. Qualls, who loved the outdoors.

A spider's web has a lacey look in
the morning sun,
A snowshoe rabbit hops across the
road nearly at a run.
The young moose looks bigger still
when only ten feet away,
The weasel has turned from his
ermine white to his brownish
way.
The squirrels they chatter and run
around up tree and down,
A marmot is seen in its velvety coat
of brown.
The grouse of ruffled tail is hiding
in the grasses,
The duck so quietly in the water
splashes.
The "porky" of the spiny tail plods
along his way.
The graceful white swan of neck so
long is on the pond this day.
'Tis summer's come! the bees and
birds hum,
And nature's favorite season has
begun.

William McGraw III

MELODY OF WORDS

I listened to her melody of words—
The contrived intervals;
The forced inflections;
The honey-sweet masking
sincerity.

I observed the performer
Who, by this tuneful contrivance,
Expected wide-eyed acceptance;
Unquestioned belief;
As though the magic melody
Would make lies, truth;
Egoistic intent, pure;
Evil, good.

I observed the glassy eyes
And plastic smile
Fixed in grotesque portrait;
Features out-of-sync with Spirit;
A veneer of silk roses
Covering a basket of thorns.

And then I listened no more.

Bill C Messick

ON YOUR DAY—MOM

Your birthday is just a few days
away
And I've been searching for the
right words to say
Too many poets have said it better
with their clever rhymes
But none are more sincere than
these simple words of mine

Through these years you've let me
grow
I've drifted away at times; very
close
But at all times you are there, like
the eternal moon and
stars . . .
There to guide when I need it, and
there to admire just because you
shine . . .
My feet may walk on distant shores
Or I may be as near as your front
door
Regardless of where I am, you are
in my heart
You influence all that I am, say or
do.

So, Happy Birthday Mom! May
each new year be better than the
last
And always remember—I love you.

Rhoni Billick

CARPENTRY OF MOTHERHOOD

With much love to my three children, Tori, Tyson, and Thomas who are teaching me how to be the best mother that I can be!

Gazing up into the heavenlies on a
brilliantly starlit night,
A surprising void deep within
encompasses me.
What's the question within my
soul?
"What do you want me to be,
Lord?"
"A CARPENTER."
"A carpenter?! But I don't know
how to build or repair anything.
A carpenter of what?"
"A CARPENTER OF
MOTHERHOOD."
"A carpenter of motherhood?
what does that mean?"
"Oh no, I knew it! I haven't been
a good enough mother."
"Maybe, I just need to love them
more and not yell as much?"
"Maybe, I need to join the P.T.A.
and become more involved with
them at school?"
"Maybe, I need to be more
interested in their interests?"
"Maybe, I just need to look them
in the eyes and LISTEN to them
more?"
"Oh, when will I have time for
myself and the creativity that I
want to express?"
"I always had a nagging thought
that I never wanted to be a
mother in the first place. But, I
am."
"Now that I am, He is asking me
to give it my all?"
"Oh, He can't mean that!"
"Maybe, 'Carpentry of
Motherhood' just came from my
imagination?"
"I wonder what it means?"

Faith Heideman

THE LIGHT

This poem is dedicated to the Lord Jesus Christ, who is "The Light"

The newborn babe, the light
surrounds,
And tarries near, to set the bounds.
The light shines bright, if space
allows,
But filters through faintly, if
disavowed.
Time passes, and the light grows
dim,
Struggles, trials, no thought of
Him.
The light persists, behind the
scenes,
Hovering close, gently invading
dreams.
Darkness, now is quenching the
light,

Unseen powers, working, with all
their might.
The light, in patience awaits
within,
Amidst turmoil pain confusion and
sin.
Ah, the darkness lifts, and sees the
light,
Truth, now comes into perfect
sight.
The struggle, now embraces the
light,
And seeks its help, for the fight.
The light, is brighter than the sun,
Oh perfect day, the victory is won.
The light, around the heart is
wound,
Of paradise not lost, but found.

Vernon L Davis

MY FINE PEOPLE!

I would like to dedicate this to all my wonderful friends of Moscow, Kansas; A Special Poem . . .

In my youth, as over the fields I
went,
I look back . . .
As the years have quickly been
spent!
When Dad's sickness took it's toll,
All Moscowites' rigs did roll!
In a flash our spring planting was
done,
Instead of work, it seemed like fun!
Thanks! Vern Davis, Tucumcari,
New Mexico

Ron Ganther

IMPRESSIONS

To Kami, a young woman who showed me what beauty truly is.

Kindly dropping into peoples lives
some people may not give you a
second look
but even though I thought that I
was prepared for you
I found out that you still took me
by surprise.
I had everything mapped out,
what I would say and how I would
act
but there was something in you
that brought out something
in me that I haven't felt in years:

the over-powering essense of
shyness.

As I looked at you from a distance
I could tell that you are a young
lady like no other.
You appear to be extremely
confident
yet looking like someone who can
only appear in dreams.
There you stood, lovely as could be
looking prettier than any picture
could do you justice
and there I was, doing an imitation
of a statue
unable to speak, only look at you.

Maybe, in time, I could conquer
this strange feeling
and I assure you that I will
because I would like to talk to you
get to know you, not just the honor
to look at you.
I would like to know the person
behind those brown eyes
for I'm sure that you are very
special
because I feel that nobody can pass
you
without feeling the aura of warmth
around you.

I remember part of a poem
that I think applies to my case
"And you can't pluck a rose
all fragrant with dew,
Without part of its fragrance
remaining with you."
for you have left your mark
with me for all eternity.

Frances Knight

LIFE

Life is a wondrous thing,
Full of beauty but also gloom
Life may not always be as it seems,
For life can be filled with joy or
gloom.

Life may not always bring forth
Bouquets of flowers or sugar and
spice,
But in all of the world,
Life is a gift which can be nicer
than nice.

Life can bring happiness or sorrow
But everyone should remember
this;
There is almost always a tomorrow,
For there is nothing which can
equal life's bliss.

Echo Love Boley

MYSTERIES OF LOVE

It's like the rain,
It has to water the land sometimes.
It's like the wind,
unpredictable at times.
It's like the snow,
Clean, white and beautiful.
It's like an ocean,
Mighty and big.
It's like a mountain,
Standing tall and mysterious.
It's like a flower,
Delicate, and if taken care of,
lasts.
It's like a deer,
Scarce, and when really seen, it's
genuine.
It's like a fire,
It can burn until there's no more.
It's like the trees,
Changing with the seasons.
It has it's good and bad times,
But if it's really true,
It will forgive anything.
And what I'm talking about is love.
Everyone needs it.
The rich, the poor, the wise, the
foolish,
And even me.

Jason J Tirone

BOWLING IS A SIN

This poem is dedicated to my mother who shares the same opinion of solid sevens and solid tens. Her loving support inspires me in all that I endeavor.

Bowling is a sin.
I should know, I'm the ten pin.
I have a pal, his name is number
five.
He always seems to be taking a
dive.

His friend the head pin is the
reason why,
When he gets hit, things start to fly.
There's a man here tonight, Tony
by name.
He never leaves an open frame.

He hits all nine, then saves me for
last.
Then he hits me with a bionic blast.
I wear my battle scars, by no choice
of my own.
My paint is chipped and my cracks
have grown.

Hook balls, fast balls, loft balls and
all,
No matter what they are, they all
make me fall.
I have a twin, number seven's his
name.
When I'm not standing, he's
usually game.

They all hate the corner pins, but
we stand tall.
But when Tony gets up, we always
seem to fall.
I know it wouldn't help to beg or
plead,
But now it's time again for the
Friday night league.

Barbara Manning

TO MY FRIEND

I have wrapped up
Every painting
Every poem
Every picture
In my mind
In paper cut fine
From scraps of my soul
And to you
Have I given them
Given them all—
All a thousand thousand times—
Over a thousand
Cups of tea.

Dorothy M Schreiber

JEALOUSY

Jealousy rides on the backs of the
green-eyed hounds of slavering
hate. Destruction bound, they
leap across chasms to beseige
innocence.
Suspicion drools from jealousy's
savage jaws. Mischief, sorrow
and death curse the passage of
their cruel journey.
Unreasoning, jealousy's desperate
beasts seek no excuse to rend
asunder their victims. Smiting,
crashing, hurling, jealousy
devours with remorseless
hunger its prey.

The long hot tongue of jealousy
winds in ravenous hunger,
mighty and unequal. All things
pale in the luminous green of
suspicion's foul glance.
Polluted effluence degrades in
jealousy's unforgiving
harshness. The blade of the
executioner awaits as the
tumbril wheels jealousy's
victims to their final destiny.
The hounds race on—unappeased.

Teresa Beckwith Dickey

LEARNING LOVE

It doesn't matter what the
circumstances or the problem, if
they should arise, that you
would ever doubt me, just look
into my eyes.

I know some people can be
deceiving by the things that they
might say but a heart-filled love,
that is very strong is hard to hide
away.

It doesn't have to be shown, but it
can't be helped, for you know it's
always there, by the way you
touch, look and smile and
sometimes say you care.

There's no room for petty things,
like jealously or mistrust,
understanding and patience are
major keys, forgiveness is a
must.

It cannot be demanding, for that
can take away, so . . . you have
to give, to be able to get,
unselfish giving, day to day.

As days go by and time moves on,
feelings start to grow, love steps
in and takes control, and you
begin to know.

The need you had is somehow
filled, you can be happy once
again. Because in your heart,
you've found that love, and a
very special friend

Mary Anne C Tennant

SEEDS

Seasons change and winds blow
cold
Or sun imperiously beats down
Earth's face alters day by day
And seed blown distantly are sown,
Finding apertures to let
In hearts prepared by rain and
snow
There, waxing greater become fruit
Of love conceived and love will
grow.
Some, less fortunate, will fall
Where ice is still and hard and cold
And grasp and slip and slide away
And seeds remain and seeds grow
old.
No warmth will soften or will
blend,
No moisture penetrates the shell
And the sweet promise still within
Is dormant till a tender rain
Encourages to life again.

Juanita Oliver Wilson

LOOKING AT YOURSELF

Dedicated to my sons Andre D. Wilson & Delano C. Wilson

When you look in the mirror
Who do you really see?
Is it the face of someone you know
Or someone you are trying to be.

Do you really know yourself
Have you given it much thought
Is your image something you have
taken for granted
Or someone else's you have sought

Have you been so busy criticizing
others
That you fail to see the wrong you
do
Do you think that you paint such
a perfect picture
That no fault can be found in you?

Do you try to impress others with
your
Pride and dignity
And at the end of the day when you
are alone
Wonder what it would be like to
just be me . . .

Make changes where they should
be
Let them be good
Have courage, use what you have
To do the things you should

Let others love you for who you are
Not someone you are trying to be
Then you can look in the mirror
and
Say . . . This is me . . . This is really
me!

Patricia T Shipley

AN OLD AND LONELY HEART

To the greatest actor I know. Your performance could have won an "Oscar"

Where is he, I wonder, on this
aching night
As I peer into the semi-dark
I can feel no joy in the starlit sky,
Only the desolate stabbing pain of
a lonely broken heart.

We were so foolish, so small of
mind
Though our years are many, the
winter of life
Our price for demon pride, for me
a loving husband
For he, a faithful wife.

We were lucky, we said, we had it
all
Then why are we each alone?
After loving for so many years, we

lost our way together
God, where did this thing go wrong!

The mean words we say in our golden years
May be our last time to tempt fate
For the sweet makings-up of an earlier time
May be now forever, forever too late.

Treat your love tenderly no matter the age
Treasure it always as you did from the start
For this world offers no other pain
Like the pain of an old and lonely—broken heart.

Art Eves

THE AMERICAN WAY

"Buddy, can you spare a dime!"

I was born at the time a handshake meant a deal,
when a smile could get you a meal,
when people were proud to say:
"In God we Trust!"

"Buddy, will you buy an apple?"

I was brought up at a time when no one got credit,
when an ice cream cone cost a nickel—if you had it,
when a bike was something you dreamed about.

"Mister, I've got just what you need!"

Easy credit; plastic cards; play now, pay later;
buy a chance, win a car—a Ferrari!
I was groomed to want it as long as it was a bargain.

"Mister, can you spare a dollar?"

Work hard, save in the Christmas Club—
the rest will follow!
So, I am dying of malnutrition, melancholy, marasmus, and malaise.

I am seeing the end of my days dry up.
I am financially secure, physically mature,
and spiritually bankrupt!

"Buddy, can you spare some time?"

J Barbara Simpson

GRAM'S ATTIC

Dedicated to my Mother, Aurelia, and the "way it was"

The Attic was scented with by-gone days,
of other times, of different ways
The steamer trunk stood against the wall
And there, glassy eyed, stared a China doll
There were dusty flowers on a big brimmed straw hat
A caned seat rocker held an old stuffed cat
Discarded with care stood an old walking stick
near an ancient clock that didn't tick
A beaded bag hung from a hook
There were yellowed pages on the Holy Book
What did I find? A blue silk near the chair
I wondered who wore it and to what affair?
Then, wrapped in paper, all turned brown
I uncovered a breathtaking wedding gown
The waist was so tiny . . . and what was that?
Oh . . . a cane, a suit, and a blue soldiers hat
near soft white mocassins of an Indian girl
What questions I pondered, my head in a whirl
I heard an old voice calling my name
So, I hurried to meet it . . . my face red with shame
I'd stumbled onto somebodys day
Did I dare ask questions? What would I say?
Gram's face was stern, but she had smiling eyes
I knew she'd have answers for all of my whys.

Terence Bina

FIRE AND RAIN

To lose a love,
Of fire and rain,
has many a memory,
with goodness and pain.
Love with great passion,
And anger the same,
tender soft kisses,
A lion to tame.

Through visions of splendor,
Elusive cruel games,
veins burn with desire,
An iron cold chain.
But torn of such evil,
true love still remains,
With altered conceptions,
Of fire and rain.

Tesha Walker

A VISION, A MEMORY

I dedicate this poem to Sandy and Eric. The two people who made me believe in myself.

Looking out my window one day
I noticed a bright blue jay
He was sitting on the branch of the tree
Staring in the window at me.

Looking around I saw his mate
Sitting on our golden gate below
Giving a joyous call to her,
She came flying and perched on the limb.

They looked quite content sitting out there
I hope they did not mind if I shared
This moment and day.
For now its a memory—They have flown away.

Hugh Lee Stevenson

IN THE MOONLITE SHADOWS

To my wonderful wife, Marie and my son Eddie Grant. For being the two most important people in my life. Thank God for my talents.

In the Moon-lite Shadows
underneath the Capitol Dome,.
A tall lanky man,
continues to roam,
In his suit of ancient black,
so stately and tall,
I thought I heard him speak,
I knew I heard him call.
I listened very intently
to what He had to say
As he kept on walking
down the dark hallway,
I saw his lips moving
as He spoke aloud to me,
You must always stand tall, my man
if you want to be free.
:You may not be President,
but there's a lot you can do,
Tell everyone you meet,
what I say to you.
Freedom is so precious,
the job's for everyone,
It's a continuous Battle
that must always be won.
I'll always keep my vigil
here in old D.C.
Go tell all the people,
I want them to be free,
It's better dead than living,
than to be a slave,
The prize is for the living,
who dare to be brave.
Go sound the trumpet
until the dead awake,
That they may come alive
for their freedom's sake.
Don't go like dumb Cattle
to the slaughter pen,
Stand firm for your rights,
fight until you win.
I watched Mr. Lincoln
as I slowly walked away
I will never forget
what He had to say,
Listen all you people
it's time to take (your) stand
Demand from all the leaders,
freedom for every man.

Betty L Dames

GROWING WITH LOVE

This poem is dedicated to all the kind and devoted parents who have shared the "gift of love" with their children. May God's blessings be granted to them.

A baby born into this world
With nothing but its charm,
Begins to murmer little sounds
When wrapped in love in its mother's arms.

Each day he grows and feels the warmth
Of love within abiding,
Because he knows his parents care,
Within them love residing.

As the years of childhood come and pass
With loving care each day,
Received from both his mom and dad
In a very warm and special way.

And now he has become a man
With a heartfelt warm emotion,
Because his life was filled with love
By his parents loving devotion.

Louise Thielen McNeil

FREEDOM IS—

the privilege of
voting
criticizing our government
crossing state borders
unhindered
attending the church of our
choice
choosing our vocation
marrying for love.
FREEDOM is living in America.

Trip Belote

MISGUIDED THOUGHTS

Products of the big machine.
Misguided cells perhaps.
Maybe a bad piece of fish.
Possibly a memory laps.

Did he ever slap Yoko?
Did Buddah's brother surf?
Who makes these holy wafers?
Have you ever been to Perth?

Where can I buy venison helper?
To whom is a Big Mac big?
What about non-dairy creamers?
Does anyone really like figs?

Whose idea was faith?
Where can I insure my life?
Do you think the Pope has connections?
Do you think God has a wife?

Irene M Lokcynski

OUR CANADIANA

To The Restoration Crew And Our Supporters.

Could we call it our hope?
Should we call it our dream;
To have you sail from our shores,
-Our Canadiana—
Rekindle our dream of dancing,
Romancing, once more—
Memories of old dreams,
Friendships forming once more,
-Our Canadiana—
All our efforts realized
Gathering together to socialize—
Stack house lunches . . . a surprise,
No one lost his appetite.
Warming barrel fires burning bright
Togetherness, merriment . . . so right,
-Our Canadiana—
Aches and pains forgotten soon
From cleaning up that shore.
Let's give it more zoom.
With God's help our people
Will set her to ride
High off our shores,
Like a Queen in all her splendor
Let's send her—
-Our Canadiana—

Fadrea Demure
THE FUTURE NEVER MEANT TO BE

For Luccia Capritta With my unconditional love

We look back in terror at all of our errors,
in the future never meant to be.
Each great mistake carved into fate
etched in our memories.

Our pasts are just sectors of entropic vectors
that plot the burst of destiny.
And all of our concepts preceed the doorstep
of a paradox eternity.

Death a mere key, it may allow you to see
true dimensional reality.
Chilled to the marrow we are fledgling sparrows,
our novice fight through casuality.

And we will never be free, until our egos agree
to accept the finite mortality.
As our senses flee, we are eventually freed
into the future never meant to be.

We have no more needs, we totally see
the full scope of humanity.
As it dies of its' greed
and hemorrhaging morality.

We arrived foolish and naive, unable to grieve,
peasants in ecstasy.
Present and past are forever here cast
in the future never meant to be.

Opal V Reed
JESUS' HOMECOMING
Out of Heaven there comes a joyful song
For God has called His beloved Son Home;
Given to the world to show the Way,
He was despised, rejected, and turned away.

Sent as a new-born babe to earth
The angels sang carols to herald His birth;
Only some shepherds came, this Child to see.
In a lowly manger, our Savior to be.

With His disciples 12 He wandered around
To many villages and larger towns;
Till He met with Herod's angry crowd
And the Priests and Scribes at the temple, loud.

Thirty pieces of silver, Judas would receive,
To betray his friend, who he tried to decieve,
To Pilate's court with Him they came,
But He washed his hands and took no blame.

Crucified on the cross, He had to share
The shame and disgrace of the thieves hanging there;
No word of complaint or censure said He,
Only, "Father forgive them," was His fervent plea.

As a Father greets a well-loved Son,
He was welcomed and greeted by the words, "Well-done;"
He lived and died the world to save,
And rose triumphant o'er the grave.

Annie L S Atkinson
TO THE LITTLE ONE WHO WILL NEVER BE BORN
Oh little one
Plucked from the womb
By doctor's tools
Too Soon! Too soon!
You'll never feel all our loving arms
Nor will we see your baby charms.

A flash of tortured pain—
Your unfinished body will cease to be.
It's just plain murder!
Can't they see?
A few months of their life
Would mean a life time to you?

How can they look at your cousins small
As they toddle along or throw a ball?
How can they see their little faces
Full of smiles or wet tear traces?

I can't help you little one.
Not yet anyway.
But angels will hold you softly
And sing you their heavenly songs.

You'll live in my heart forever
And since love is a special magic,
You'll know that it's your grandma,
So where ever you may be . . .
I love you Little unborn child!

Wendy I D Clark
TO MY CHILDREN II
God blessed me with my children, and he'll
help me teach them right from wrong.
It's his love that gets me by,
and helps to make me strong.

This life is grand and very much worth
any of the pain.
For in that pain is where I learn,
and this is where I gain.

My children please don't ever forget—
there's beauty all around.
Live your life as best you can,
and make the Lord so proud.

Let the wind kiss the memories
here that you have made.
Take them to the highest star,
and put them on parade.

Wm R Burgess
LOVE TREE
Life seemed to have passed me by
I no longer enjoyed getting high
I lived life fast and free
Always looking for the love tree
with days that were full of haste
and nights that were a total waste.

I've visited the homes of sin
and always wearing a grin
always wanting more of life than pain
often times wondering if I were insane.

After searching hard and fast
I've found this tree of the past
I have completed my search
I have found the Love Tree . . .
It's the one Christ died on for me!

Dollie Ardola Champagne
CONTEMPLATION

Best of all to my two and his four!!!

To the unknown forces beyond this plane that one reaches for in a weakened state.
Let the warmth and love so needed envelope me and wipe clean the slate.
For the battles that can't be won are fought.
Witness! The battle scars.
The chosen approach was on to one while reaching for the unreachable stars.
There's no longer a need to join in the fight of battles that can't be won.
The parts are played in the sweeping move of the times that have recently come,
And played without a precedent set for one to fall back upon.
Early marriage of long duration, high ideals, no needs were met.
Eventually defeat was faced and then the single parent set.
Back home to face a business world with two youngsters now in
tow.
The right man and time gave the confidence for a step to the next plateau.
Marriage and the aggregate family, alarming challenge, although,
Joining heads and hearts together we could fight just any foe.
With my two and his four we formed a band, hitched our wagon to a star.
Though pulled in all directions we never wandered far,
From the path to our goal, one family guided by a star.
In retrospect it's obvious the battles that can't be won.
Only exist when we reach for a plane above that which we dwell upon.
But what dear heart can exceed the thrill, or who can ever mar.
The joy experienced when two hearts joined,
Ride the uncharted course to an unstable star.

LaVonne Walters
THE CYCLE
Awake my soul to love within;
Let rapture, joy, and growth begin.
Ah, love flowers. Will its' blossoms stay?
Nay beloved—love blossoms—flowers,
And dies away.
Loves' light flames high and then dims down,
Burned by lifes' miseries in anguished sound.
But wait—its' seeds spring forth.
O joy devine, it blooms once more
This love of mine.
A force so great heard my travail;
I prayed and prayed—it did not fail.
Once more love, come within,
reject the strife.
Hold fast—cling to me,
My love—My life.

LaVerne Meek Roberts

LaVerne Meek Roberts
THE SLEEPING FLAME
Oh, Love, that lies within my heart
What must I do with you?
You've nestled there so long, so still
Waiting yet to be fulfilled.
You came so very long ago
When life was just beginning
You played the game and, for awhile,
It seemed that you were winning;
But fate can play such funny tricks
On lovers, young and old

Separation rushes in
To leave a sting much sharper still
Than winter's stoutest cold.
The sands of time slip slowly by
And things once live
Seem quick to die
Yet, memories, memories linger on—
And in my heart
There's still a throne
Adorned with you,
With you, alone.

Peggy Burke
WONDER OF WONDERS
My dreams and my hopes are now sanctioned
By a God of such infinite Love,

That vistas of joy lie before me,
and the stream of Life flows from above.

Whatever I dream I now claim.
Whatever I hope I behold
In the storehouse of Mind's vast resources,
Taking form in the Infinite's mold.

I see myself prospering daily,
I see my good flowing to me.
I live in such blessed abundance;
God pours out His riches on me.

Unfathomed delights are my birthright;
My Father has ordained it so.
Whatever I hunger and thirst for
Faithful Parent at once doth bestow.

Peace and goodwill are my comrades,
Love and Joy are my guides for each day.
Sustance Sublime is my passport
To cross borders that stand in the way.

When I am tempted to scan distant shores
And search for my heart's desire there,
The wise Oversoul gently whispers,
"Look within; I AM, the All, is here."

Taiesha T T Green

AS THE SUN RISES

I dedicate this poem to Christine Groner and family.

As the sun rises on a hot
summer day. The children
all come out to play. To swim
to run or go about their way.
I wonder if I can go play?
One heads my way. Would
you like to play? Yes, so
run to beat me to the
other side of the street.
Oh we are having so much
fun. Laughter fills the street.
Now it is dark and we
must go in. But we will
awake again and come
out to play on a
Hot Summer Day!

Billy Marinell

STAINED GLASS WINDOWS

Dedicated to Grace United Methodist Church, Alamogordo, New Mexico

---

Divinely inspired, the glint as a fire
To all who behold, inspiration
They send out their rays, through figures of saints
And beckon us to worship and contemplation.

All doctrines, all religions, are one in their light
This dazzling display of devotion
When day turns to night, and night turns to day
Color and light shows creation in motion.

For they are alive, these windows we share
As they pick up and play with the light
They sparkle and change with each ray of the sun
And reach out to all within sight.

Twice blessed, the believers, for they see His face
Even angels come down to behold
These stained glass windows, that reach out to heaven
Windows that bring light to the soul.

Tammy Barlow May

YOU WENT AWAY

Special thanks to my Mother, for giving me a love to share, a heart to care, and a God to believe in. I love you Mom!

In the time I needed you most
You left and went away
I got down on my weary knees
I looked to God to pray

I prayed that he would keep you safe
And hold you in his hands
Oh Dear God, bring him back
For I've searched the sea and lands

I prayed that I would hear from you
Where-ever you may be
I prayed to God with all my heart
That you'd return to me

Where-ever you may be right now
I just wanted you to know
That I looked to God and prayed for you
Oh why did you have to go?

Rebel Thompson Vanek

CHALLENGE OF CHALLENGER 7

As you soared from
This planet Earth . . .
Our hearts, souls, and spirits
Soared with you.

When you so quickly
Vanished from our sight . . .
Our hearts fluttered in
A moment's confusion and pain.

Your dreams and quests
Were so strongly etched
Into our minds . . .
That now we will
Continue your flight . . .
To seek the knowledge,
The discoveries
You wanted so much
To find.

Challenger
Soon will soar again,
Onward, upward, and outward,
Into the vastness . . .
We will . . . find!

Rita Klehm

TO MY DAUGHTER

This poem is dedicated to my friends Dorothy and Melvin. The loss of their only child, Sarah, was the inspiration for this poem.

I always felt incomplete and a bit forlorn
but all of it changed the day you were born!
I felt aglow, secure and warm
the minute you were placed into my arm.
A love so great and so divine
pulsating from your tiny body into mine!
I pressed you closely to my heart
and knew that we would never, ever part.
I didn't need a son, you didn't need
a brother
for we possessed everything just by having
each other.
You are very, very special and more than sweet
most important, you have made my life complete!
You gave me a million reasons for living
I feel like I have done all the taking, you've
done all the giving!
With a love like ours, dwelling in every
corner of our heart
let me assure you that even death shall
not do us part
There is no other way, it simply has to be
"life everlasting" for you and me.

Myra Fairchild

Myra Fairchild

THE SHIBBOLETH

Some sit awhile
Asking inaudible questions
Then prey upon the moment
Painting invisible answers.
Others just stay long enough
To teeter on edges
of syrupy martini glasses;
Whilst, in the corner,
Where light and dust are visiting,
Sadness steeps
In a mound of decoration.
How flat it is
And counterfeit,
This trepidation.
Amid the quips and industry,
I go dressed in indefinity
And that is all self
Has ever meant
To crustaceans.

Carolyn Elaine Farrens

BLESS THE CHILDREN

Bless the little children
They keep a family strong.
And teach us how to love ourselves
And how to get along.

With all their wide-eyed innocense
And their silly chitter-chatter.
They show us how to look at life
And about things that really matter.

Like, money isn't everything
It can't buy you time,
To play a game or read a book,
Play tag or seek and find.

They take the time to look at life
Make friends along the way.
Show honesty and trust
And, at bedtime kneel to pray.

The look to God for miracles
Whenever things go wrong.
Show endless love for everyone
And fill our hearts with song.

So, bless the little children
Where ever they may be
For they're the future of the world
In them we Must believe . . .

Mary Lou Hofheinz

BE STILL

To the late Gertrude De Kock Keene in whose creative writing class this poem was written

---

"Dear Lord, what is it I'm to do?
How best can you use me?
Help me to steep myself in Thee,
Help me, Lord, set me free.

"Dear Lord, what is it I'm to do?
Help me to know Thy will."
And then the still small Voice comes in
And simply says, "Be Still."

"I know that, Lord," (impatiently)
"I ask for something more."
"My child, He says, "Just being still
For you is quite a chore.

"Be still and love, be still and live,
Trust Me, not toil until
My peace embodies thee and thine
By simply—being still."

L Cpl Blissick Marianne F

TO MY NEPHEW

As I gaze upon your gentle face and as I plainly do, I see the generations that have given life to you. Your mother's side, your father's side, there all plainly there. Grandparents that go so far back, but I can see them there. I see aunts and uncles and yes cousins too! I can't believe the memories and joy that come from you.

You are just a little one and God I'm glad you're here. I hope that I can stay awhile, as you make life so Dear. I am sorry that I cannot see you each and every day, but, dutie calls for Auntie, and I have to be away. I serve in the U.S. Marine Corps,dear one, and I serve my country well. We're trying for a better world that you can live in well.

La Jeanne De Walt

THE MAD POTTER OF FLAGSTAFF

To Jim Simmerman, my poetry teacher who said this poem was lousy and gave me an "F"

"Make a pinch-pot, no, make five," my ceramics teacher Gary said.
"We can test glazes."

I fondled, mutilated, mauled and anticipated the beauty my hands would create from my lump of clay.
Eventually . . . my eyes glazed.

Somewhere between my brain and my hands, the plan went awry.
Nothing looked like anything I had intended, or even pot-like.

I discovered I can make a lump of clay . . . into a different lump of clay.
Perhaps my brain is glazed.

I am reminded of the ugly clay things my children brought home from school . . . their precious little fingerprints imbedded in the clay.
I had oohed and aahed and proudly put them on display.

Now . . . I can return the favor, and watch my childrens eyes glaze.

Eve Hilton

MY SISTER

To my loving sister, Iris Hoskins

My favorite sister of them all,
Is the one that makes life a ball.
She's always there to hear me out,
And seems to know what life's about.
My problems she will listen to,
Then says what she thinks I should do.
A sister and a friend all in one,
Who never criticizes things I've done.
Another one like her there will never be,
Iris, you're very special to me.

Melissa Roman

IN MEMORIES OF YOU

For Ed

I heard a song about you today.
I'm sure I looked the mischievous imp
as I thought of how we'd played.

Then I heard a child laugh—
laugh as I did
when you teased, and pulled my hair.

And later still, I remembered the words
you'd said as we laid in bed—
hiding from the day we'd say good-bye.

It was a good day
spent in memories of you,
But the night grows cold,
and the wind blows hard.
Yet, thinking of you
drives the dark away,
and once again
you are in my arms.

Mrs Debby (Pippins) Melvin

TREASURED MEMORIES

In memory of my mother, Idell (McCart) Pippins who walks with Jesus, but will Forever live within my heart. I love and miss you still . . .

While he sat on the riverbank and watched
As the water kissed the shore,
his mind went back to a life and time that would exist no more.

As a young man he stood brave and tall,
his courage known throughout the land.
The young brave held much respect and honor,
from the tribe he was born to command.

A gentle people living out their lives,
they gave and received from the land,
in their hearts they knew whatever life held,
they were in the "Great Fathers" plan.
He remembered the beauty of the one he had loved,
And her gentleness still tugged at his heart,
two sons—one daughter she had given to him,
till her spirit was claimed, and they did part.

But in his heart she still lives,
And in his mind "treasured memories" stir,
As he quietly sits on the riverbank, reliving
time—his life, and her.

Clare Fearn

HAPPINESS

Much has been written in both prose and rhyme
To describe "happiness" in this day and time.
To define it in a capsule would hardly be fitting.
It depends on your age and where you are sitting.

To a child it's chocolate candy or a new toy.
The keys to Dad's car bring a teen-ager joy.
Attaining that magical age of twenty-one
Means the road to happiness has just begun.

As an adult it seems we're much harder to please
And this sought-after bliss doesn't come with such ease.
To some it's the status of high social rank
Or that warm security of bucks in the bank.

But from where I am sitting (well over the hill),
That cup of happiness is now easy to fill;
Family and friends, good health and the grand-kids,
A home and a hearth and a diet that's "blanded."

To get to the crux, basic truth, bottom line,
Real happiness—the one thing that lasts through all time
Is love, given and taken and shared with another.
So, you want to be happy? Just be a lover!

Karen M Marchand

DAD AND MOM

This poem is dedicated to my husband Randy who I love very much.

You've taught me right from wrong
and you've been there all along.
Sometimes I'm blind and just can't see
that you're always there for me.
You help me through when times are bad
especially when I'm sad.

You make me laugh and cry
but your love never runs dry.
For everything that you do
I'll always Love you.

Mary J Gartin

THE LOAN OF GOD

All children, are God's children
God will loan you a child
Remember it may be for just a little while
Most of God's children grow up to become a success
Some won't make it that far and are laid to rest
It's hard to understand, when a child returns to God's Heavenly home
Of all the tears and heartaches, you'll feel so alone
Just keep it in mind, the child, was God's loan.

Marie Anastasia

AWAKENING

To my daughter, Maria

Twenty years, where did they go?
Just yesterday, you were playing in the snow;
Your Dad beside you, your dog in tow.
Those walks in our woods; Our talks,
So serious . . .
Your many changes of moods—
'Twas all just part of "Growing Up."
Soon, from the feast of "Life," you, too, will "sup."

Michael J Jan

AMELIA EARHART

"TONI" for our love was bold but true, yet made a love story dream come true.,

---

Dad, who was Amelia Earhart?
Listen son, and I'll tell you. Amelia Earhart was a lady, daring chances she did take. Til one day she flew, where to no one knew and up to this day she still is away, Amelia Earhart had a record her record no one could break then in stepped fate her record did break, and left in its wake a lonely heart that lonely heart was her husband hubby who loves her so, yet where ever she may be there remains the mystery of Amelia Earhart.

Brant Glazer

POOL FISH

I'm a cool fish, a pool fish, a fat fish, and fast;
I'm a lap fish, a flip-flop fish, quite the enthusiast;
I'm a glad fish, a rad fish, swimming in chlorine;
I love it in my swimming pool, I could not be marine.

I'll never be a sea fish, dodging carnivorous;

A lunch fish, a munched fish, traveling by seahorse;
Not for me the dangerous life, fleeing with a school;
But filters, and lounge chairs, and comfort of a pool.

Not for me the other fish, always on the run;
One week on the Nile, the next week on the Amazon;
O mine is still the long life, the lazy life, the best;
My diving board, jacuzzi, and raft on which to rest.

Gay Hart

AN ANGEL

My little Lesa oh so small
On this earth had no life at all
There is a place she lives I know
Where she can see the flowers grow
Even though she's not here with me
I know someday her face I'll see
I believe in God and in heaven above
Who made an angel from my baby of love
So he will help me through when I feel sad
And send some sunshine from the angel I had

J Ann Boyle

MY SUMMER

As gentle as the
flowers in early spring
comes my Summer

Soft as a cool breeze,
easy as velvet
nuzzles my Summer.

Days grow short for
my Summer.

Oh, what will I do
when gone is
my Summer.

My Summer,
My Summer dog.

Kathleen Harding
IS IT HOME OR JUST A HOUSE?

To my family for all of their love and support. But, especially to my parents for always giving me a home to come to and not just a house.

A lot of people own a house
But how many people own a home?
There's a difference you know?
A house is just a building where
you sleep and live
But home is where you go to feel
safe and welcomed
And above all loved
It's not the things you have that
make it home
But, the people
So the next time you go to where
you live
Look around and ask yourself is
this
Home or just a House?

Anita Jane Eldridge
INDEPENDENT DEPENDENCE

Misunderstanding outlines
confusion;
Impetuous motions make the
intrusion;
For Elders, it is not an illusion.
No remedy for the solution.
Children will have their revolution
Called the adolescence evolution.

Discovering freedom in
independence
Brings a self esteemed deliverance.
Restrictions mold into
responsibilities
That are measured by one's
learned abilities.

With every step lurks another
thought
With another idea the mind has
sought.
Choosen roads are quite often
altered,
But a certain direction never
haltered.

Creativeness of youthful intuition,
Unhampered by rules of
institution,
Develope character in a hungry
mind,
As it unravels treasures it can find.

Kerry G Gietzen
THE HUNTER

Inspired by my father and brother; Clarence and Neil Willman

As I walk through these woods,
The silence of nature prevades my
senses,
filling my eyes and ears of a time,
When there where no fences.

The chitter of a squirrel as I
come to near,
the screech of a blue jay claiming
no fear.
Mingling with nature and feeling
as one,
From early morning till the setting
of the sun.

As I walk through these woods,
The ageless beauty shrugs away
my years,
Adding a spring to my step,
Strengthening my prowess in
tracking a deer.

The scampering of a field mouse
beneath my feet,
A startled owl taking flight as we
meet.
The sight; the sound of a
meadow lark,
The touch; the feel of an old tree's
bark.

As I walk through these woods,
It's always the same,
Be it "Darwin's theory" or God
given right,
That big prize buck comes within
range,
Then slowly ambles out of sight.

The skip of a heartbeat; the draw
of my bow,
Just as it was then, now too, it is so.
The hunter taking only his needs,
As once again I walk through these
trees!!

V L Etter
SEARCHING

What is the point of our meeting
if our union is only a greeting
in a flight that will quickly fly
into leading us to say good-bye

Are we tied with an invisible cord
are we made from compatible flesh
will there be an attraction of some
altitude
that shall cause our own hearts to
enmesh

Shall we keep to ourselves or speak
freely
are we islands that cannot be
beached
are we open to full human
connection
or are there points that can never
be reached

There is darkness that may never
be lighted
incidences we may not understand
but a thousand words may be
spoken
in one single touch of your hand

Joy LaBarre

Joy LaBarre
CHRISTMAS IS TO GLORIFY JESUS CHRIST

Jesus Christ's birthday has come
again.
Merry Christmas bells are
ringing,
To glorify His holy name,
And Christmas carols folks are
singing.
Because He had a holy birth,
The church held mass to honor
Him,
And praise His holy name as they
pray,
And they called it "Christ-mass
Day."

Linda Musick
WOMAN'S HOPE

To a loving family who never doubt that I can achieve my dreams.

Hope is for the future
Love comes from the past
Life is always going forward—
Mostly "in fast!"

I have locked many dreams inside
this heart of mine
Can I fullfill them all, or even any,
Do I have the time?

My first grandchild, painting, my
"baby growing up," old age with
a friend,
This and zillions more I long to
taste before someone writes—
"THE END."
So 12 months gone by I began to
scheme a way
to ponder, plan the "why's" of my
days.
A woman, of any age, especially 10
x 4
dreams, schemes, & yearns for
more
But she must keep on grappling
with each new day,
to obtain her goals and conquer
obstructions in her way.

She finds the reason not binded on
some shelf
But deep within her "Fire" that
eternal burns in self.

Sunshine, rain, and stormy doom
All, in some way, contribute to the
roses bloom.

A woman keeps on looking,
searching, testing with all her
soul
To bow with dignity, after standing
applause, to finish with honor
her life's given role.

Kathy Thomas
ZOO

Come let's take a trip to the zoo,
There's so much to see
And so much to do.

We'll take a long walk
And look in the cages;
It's like reading a book
But not turning the pages.

We'll hear myna birds talking,
See long-necked giraffes;
Catch glimpses of peacocks
As we follow the paths.

We'll see the big bears
And watch monkeys eat;
Look there at the elephants
My what big feet!

Our walk is all through
And the animals sleeping;
Except for the lions
Who are still creeping.

Daria Mae Fakankun
NO DAY SHALL COME

I dedicate the poem and all the other poems to the almighty God, who bestowed them on me thank you "God"

I rejoice in knowing that as
You try to make me wallow in the
mire
You are wallowing in far worse!!!
I do not wish to stifle your growth
Yet you hinder mine!!!
The degradation you point in my
direction
Is ricocheing back to you
Traveling twice the speed of light
Your fall is far worse
Than your man-made fall
You've tried to make me take
I fall a little and immediately
My "hope" cushions me
What do you have
When, your aggravation
Fail to stir me
To lay down & die!!!
All that you do to me,
Only, fires up a determination
That abounds out of your reach
"No day shall come"
When you shall succeed
Unless we succeed together!!!.

Gertrude Gutfleish
NATURE'S SYMPHONY

In memory of my beloved daughter, Lois.

Boughs swaying in the breeze
Flowers nodding and offering their
nectar to the bees
The falling leaves are covering the
ground so tenderly
Above, the birds are chirping and
softly wing their way
Saying adieu to my loved one
forever and a day.
She dwells amidst the woodland
greenery
The place she loved so well
There, deer so timidly wend their
way to keep her company
The stars at night watch from
above
And shed their light on her
For all the love she had on earth is
hers eternally.
I lean on the rock you knew so
well
To the peace and quiet, I'm under
its spell
Then upon my cheek I feel the
brush of your gentle voice so
dear
"You will heal, ma," I hear you say
"In the near future, some other
day."

Judy A Kanotus
TEN MILES HIGH

Written as a Dedication to Challenger Astronauts, January, 1986

For love of life,
And all mankind;
For thirst of knowledge too.
For little children, yet, unborn,
And all things, good and true.

Because of dedication,
Because of pride and caring.
Because of blue horizons,
And a need for sharing;

All of nature's beauty
And wonders yet untold.
Because of unmeasured bravery,

Because of young and old;

Because of great expectations,
Because of dreams unnamed;
Just ten miles high and climbing,
Before their lives were claimed.

Marty Brown
THE SILENT GARDEN

To my son, William Tal Brown, in loving memory.

In this garden,
The sky is a beautiful blue
Where white fluffy clouds play.
The trees sway quietly in the breeze
But . . . .
No birds sing—no children laugh.

Silence—except for the sound of tires
Racing down a distant highway.

Bright flowers reflect the sun against the
Background of green grass.
Also, gleaming in the sun are
Plaques of brass.

As I turn to leave this beautiful,
But, silent place;
Emptiness closes in, grief swallows me up.
For . . . here I must leave behind, lying
Beneath the green grass and gleaming plaque,

My only child . . .
My little baby boy.

Virginia Putze Martin
APRIL

My darling daughter, April.
Fresh as Spring's new day.
A sweet and innocent child
Born to love and play.

You are so special
So sincere and true.
It warms my heart
Each day to think of you.

I thank God,
And sing His praise.
For the wonderful girl
He gave me to raise.

Thomasine A Bartley
AND CROWN HIM KING

This poem is dedicated to my son Jamal whose inquisitiveness inspired this poem.

Momi, momi who was Dr. King?
He's a man who set us free,
He's a man of whom we sing.

Momi, momi how did he set us free?
He taught us to hold our heads up high
He taught America the meaning of equality.

Momi, momi what's equality?
It's something God gives us all at birth
And don't ever forget you deserve to be free.

Momi, momi why did Dr.King die?
Well, he had dreams of freedom and brotherhood
And baby I don't really know why.

Momi, momi why do we have a sky?
God put it up there to let us know
How far we can go when we believe and try.

A Jaye (aka: Alice J Hart)
WHY, ONLY ONCE A YEAR

Why is it only once a year
We take the time to say,
"I love you mom," Then show our love
In a special sort of way.

Why is it only once a year
We send those special flowers,
When every day to us she'd show
Her love for many hours.

Why is it only once a year
We praise her above the rest,
When all year long she'd praise us
When e'er we did our best.

Why is it only once a year
These special things are done,
When all the time she'd be right there
For her daughter or her son.

Why is it only once a year
We show our love this way,
When above all this the greatest gift
Is "I love you mom" each day!

Imogene Escobar
SILHOUETTE

To My Mother— Cynthia Isaline Peggy Blackburn—To whom I owe a debt of love—I cannot pay; For you are gone.

So faintly—
Against the darker shadows
White Lace—
Frames lines drawn with gentleness
Hesitant—
To age this sweet face.
Are you looking through the
window of your past—Gentle Lady
Do your eyes follow down the street—
Remembering—
Wandering in the green freshness
of your spring—
The sweet dreams of your youth?
Was it a certain way he walked—
And stopped—To watch a child
retrieve a ball?
Was it his smile—
That made your eyes turn—
Following?
Gentle Lady—
With the lace handkerchief
In a hand that moves—
Restlessly—
I would give you back—
Your youth—
Your Lovely Spring—
And all your Songs . . .

Hilda Davis
THE COUNTRY MAIL MAN

In honor of Ralph Davis, Elkland, Mo.

He is a very special man, I know you will agree,
No one else can take his place, no matter how high his degree
He is dedicated to his job, He goes thru the heat and cold
The barking dogs that chase him, some times are vicious and bold
When he stops at your mail box, you are immediately on the run
And you're glad he brought you something, even if its only a dun.
Phone bills are soaring higher, How in the world can we pay
Only by letter can we afford to say all we want to say
On Christmas on birthdays, when cards are so welcome
Or get-well cards to the sick
A card—a stamp and the mail man
Can always do the trick
Lets take off our hats to the mail man
A public servant is he
He'll challenge the weather, let come what may,
The mail must get to the addressee.

Sally Frooman
MY LADY FAIR

My lady fair willingly
Yields to be—
In the depths of her blue
eyes I see,
A shimmering light of love
for me.
Every time our eyes do meet
Her lips and charm, her words
So sweet,
My heart with rapture
Goes a beat.
Her form diving, blithe
With grace,
In history back, one can not
Trace
The beauty of such
Loving Face.

Robert E Phillips
HALF ME, HALF YOU

To Bebe, friend and wife of many years

Ah, life is but a time in which to seek
The mysteries philosophers would share.
Since time began, for truth and love we dare
To sing, to die, to cry from mountain peak

Of a you in me, a me in you, unique;
Half me, half you. Yes, love has made us fair,
And whole we now exist. Your love taught care.
Selfish ways vanish, leaving spirit meek.

Our one true love does span the stream of time,
Our summer thoughts mature as fruit for fall.
What fun the ambitious desires of youth;
Só significant only to their time.
Now winter winds . . . what thought looms tall?
Just one, my dear—only our love is TRUTH.

JoAnn Stovall Page
YOU'RE LIKE GOOD WINE

Dedicated to the memory of my mother, Novella Lewis Stovall "Wish we'd had more time"

Yet another complete revolution
Of the Earth around the sun and as
Usual, another year for you has
only just BEGUN
'Really, you are very special,
'though
Everyone accumulates
years—you've

Learned that the truth of this
existence
Is found as you release your fears.
Being
Kind to others has proven to be

Easy and second nature to you—

God knows why being kind to
yourself
Often seems so hard to do. If
Only you can see yourself as always
Determined and willing to give;
even

When it's not popular—what
matters
Is how you live. Don't be concerned
about
Numbers; they really don't mean
anything.
Especially when so much joy to
others you can bring.

Mark Edward Stout
RED SKY AT MORNING— SAILOR TAKE WARNING!

An excerpt from the fluent context of: "A Searcher's Journey to Suggest A Dream"

—Certain repose, as this scarlet dawn arrives . . .
merely a careless warning, or a thing more surely wise?
with just a thought of taking heed, for tis I who am in need
More carefully take I thought to skies . . .
for certainty, when surely my soul has greed.

To my venturing vessel of restless lament—
Just as the day before, where my time has been spent
With caution and precaution, to buffer my side . . .
In this last kiss of Innocence, as my soul is tried.

This journey, envisioned, so I surely prepare
for the challenge of all my soul thought to dare.
Where reason embraces, the need, as have I . . .
Christening the ship that which now I may try—

Seeking the answers to questions unknown,
An aforethought of glory, that by now may have shown.
. . . Yet I wonder, still choosing this day to embark,
Are the answers to some best left in the dark?

Once again, I look to his scarlet dawn,
giving a warning to each seaward pawn . . .
"The sky is the limit, for journeys made here,
where questions are answered, by facing your fear."

Catherine L F Fye

MATT 24:6

She was born in '26,
So aware of the big one.
Lost her big brother there.
Misses him still.
Keeps a faded photograph.
Visits his grave . . .
And wonders.
She was born in '52.
Loved a boy once.
When both were young and innocent.
He was drafted; died in a far away land.
She remembers the protests;
The peace signs.
She was born in '80.
Her mother watches her
Playing, out the window.
She recalls a faded photograph her mother has.
Of an uncle she never knew.
A tear traces her cheek.
Memories; of a boy she once knew . . .
So full of life.
She watches her daughter
Play with young friends.
prays a silent prayer.
And wonders.

Margaret C Bicsak

YOU

Where would you be if you would not have been born.
Just a washed away seed from a woman's womb.
'Tis a miracle that only God can create.
A tiny seed that can become you.
You! who can become great or small.
You! who can cause happiness or woe.
You! who can create more little you's.
You! who was started with Gods magical wand.
Thus was the start of a whole universe.
A flock of men and women created by love.
First of all, Gods love. "Love" which he instilled
Into each man and woman. To bring about this multitude.
Awed am I by love and what it can do.
Make you and you and many more you's.

Robert F Smith

WINTER, WINTER, WINTER

In loving thanks for their support; Mom, Dad and Aunt Mary.

Winter, Winter, Winter
Snowflakes falling all around
Hopefully six inches on the ground
Snowball fights arousing soon
Thank goodness it's not June

Hopeful children's dreams are growing bigger
Filled with lots and lots of vigger
Sleds fling down the hill
Going faster then light or sound
Even during the night they'll be in flight

Winter is such a wonderful season
The landscape is so beautiful
It's always a joyous, happy time
Filled with lots of colorful rhyme
If this isn't Winter, what is?

Cori Croot

HAWAII

This poem is dedicated to the students & faculty of Kalani High School

---

Palm trees swaying in the breeze
Graceful dancers telling their stories
Diamond Head rising in the distance
The sun sinking into the ocean

CRASH go the waves on the seashore
SWOOSH, the wind rustles through the trees
SQUAWK go the many tropical birds
SPLASH, as the water tumbles over the falls

The fragrance of many flowers wafts softly through the warm summer day
The salty smell of the ocean
The scent of exotic Hawaiian food cooking
The refreshing smell of rain as it drifts from the valleys

This lovely land
A treat to all the senses
A paradise, a peaceful resort
Hawaii

Heather L Wykoff

RECIPE FOR A SPECIAL FRIENDSHIP

For Ms. Wesley, my best friend in the whole world! You have made this simple recipe possible. I shall remember you forever! Thank you! 12/02/86

Ingredients:
2 people
2 caring hearts
warm thoughts
good and bad times
laughter and happiness
generosity
secrets shared together
tears and fears
warm smiles

MIX
Mix the friends and their caring hearts. Gradually, add the good and bad times. Mix until a warm smile shows bright and sincere.

BLEND
Blend a lot of warm thoughts to spice life. Add a 1/2 teaspoon of tears and fears (for these are needed, but not essential for a special friendship.)

POUR
Pour the batter into a deep friendship filled with a life of laughter and happiness.

BAKE
Bake until you depart. Top with secrets shared together through and through.

SERVE
You shall be together forever, so serve whenever the time is right. And there you have it. A Recipe For A Special Friendship!!

Curtis R Cavender

Curtis R Cavender

WON'T YOU STAY

For Those Among Us Often Forgotten

Broken down mem'ries
Old worn out heart
Always troubled mind
Right from the start of each day
Sometimes there's hope
But quickly it dies
No one can help
So he always cries won't you stay

Will you be a friend
To a helpless old man
Be a friend if you can
He needs someone to lean on
He needs someone to be strong
So won't you stay a little while
He'll be okay
After a day with just your smile

Diane Covey

LOVE'S ESSENCE

To mom—Thanks for always being there. To Ron—My love and inspiration. To Donna and Mike—May they always be inspired by love.

Love isn't just sex and it isn't just fun,
It's all the good things rolled into one.
It's knowing they'll be there in good times and bad
With a smile or a kiss—or a pat on the head.
What would some give to be loved so much, to only be
waiting for that one special touch.
God knows what we need and He's always nearby,
Just ask for his help and He'll guide us to try.
Life to us should be a sweet song, if it isn't
My love, then something is wrong.
We each make our life what it is every day
Don't blame someone else—that isn't the way.
So live out your life, have faith 'til the end,
And He'll be there smiling, Jesus, our Friend.

Evelyn Eden Rose

THE WOODS

To "Russ" My special friend and inspiration

I know a place that's "Shangri-La,"
That's hidden away from cars,
And city noise, and lumbering trucks and screeching tires,
Where trees so tall they touch the sky,
And clouds like cotten floating by,
Where the wind whistles through the trees,
And leaves behind a cooling breeze,
Where leaves in Autumn turn to gold,
But pines so green their colors hold,
The sky so blue, but clear as glass,
Butterflies flitting from blades of grass
To flowers, peeping up their heads,
While singing birds, next overhead,
Where squirrels play and deer abound,
And crickets chirping cheerful sounds,
A place of peace and serentiy,
It's Nature's own tranquility!

Opal Farrell Downey

A FAREWELL TO MOTHER

If there was anything that we could say today
That our dear Mother would wish in parting of the way
It would not be of grief nor saddness—
But, instead, she'd wish for joy and gladdness.

For she has gone on to be
In a place so beautiful and free
Where there is no suffering and pain
And where the Savior greets her once again.

Now, there's a gift so full and free
That she has left for you and me.
It is the memories she left behind
That will not dim with age or time.

Yes, the memories of her great faith
Will live on in our hearts and minds,
As God continues to bless us today
Because of the words we heard her say.

For she truly testified in word and deed
Her love for Christ and our great need
To follow His commands, if we would be freed
From this world's sins of vice and greed

Now, there is not much more to tell
As now, we come to bid farewell
Till once again with her we'll meet
To share our love and joys at Jesus' feet.

Theresa Stockwell
RAIN

To my husband, Roy, and family.

Rain to the Earth
is like a Glad Heart,
a song meadowlark
sings.

She flirts with Nature
till She shower her
crown.

And then She, like
the meadowlark flees
to find new realms
to darn.

The Gladden Heart,
like the meadowlark,
stand refresh and
renewed in her grace.
And behold the Earth's
beautiful ray of Color
lace.

Agnes E Booras
A DIETER'S PROMISE

Dedicated to my Family and John.

I have to get slim
I'll go on a diet
I might not lose fast,
At least I can try it.

I'll watch what I eat,
I'll jog and I'll run,

My calories I"ll count,
Each fattening one.

I'll start this tomorrow
or, maybe start Monday
First I must finish, this
Great Hot Fudge Sundae . . .

Kimberly Sue Kaufman
LIVING, A NIGHTMARE IN REALITY

Scared, frightened and alone,
An angry face,
An unsatisfying home.

No one to talk to, no where to go.
A bewildered expression
And no feelings to show.

A hidden beauty,
No one can find,
The breathing stops,
And no one will mind.

The vision will blurr,
The crying will start,
A militious feeling,
Tearing things apart.

The skies are gray the nights are long,
In this world,
Everything goes wrong.

There is no hope and only fear,
A ticking clock,
Death is near.

No more pulse,
No more shame,
No more hurt,
And no more pain.

Christopher B Smith
A DREAM

To my beautiful daughter Kassie Leigh, and my loving wife Paula, I love you both.

Oh can you sea the see,
for it is too far to be,
reality.
But the tide comes this time,
of year, can you hear the see,
can you hear the tide in me,
the ocean. The change.
In me.
Or can you hold the see,
or will you drown...
me.
Hold me, before it comes.
And it will erase the land,
with one giant hand, like mine,
will you be there...for me,
at that time.
Change is sure to come,
like the see, and me,
and I must leave,
it is my time.
To be...
And the rain will come,
a drop of red, only one,
will fall upon a sea,
of white sand.
Reality? it could be...
It does not matter, will you
remember,
me?

Philip Charles Brierley
PILOT IN COMMAND

Looking up he caught his eye
On a tiny airplane in the sky.

Soaring just beneath the sun,
It looked to him like so much fun.

That tiny airplane in his eye
Was calling him, calling him to the sky.

With a deep breath, he let out a sigh,
And went to the airport to give it a try.

For the first time he climbed into the plane,
Knowing his life would never again be the same.

Lifting its nose the plane left the ground,
He couldn't help himself, he looked all around.

For miles and miles he can now see,
The magic of flight has set his soul free.

Elizabeth Stevens
A CHILD'S WORLD

A magical world
—A wonderful world.
The world of
Make believe.

An enchanted kingdom
—composed of many things—
is the world of
Make-believe.

Ghost, dragons and
castles can be found
in the world of
Make-believe.

Daring young ladies
dashing young men
are found in the world of
make-believe.

The magical world
of make-believe
is unknown to
you and me.

The world of
make-believe
is known only to
A CHILD.

Patricia McClung
THE EMPTY NEST

"Will I ever be able to sleep on my stomach again?" you say and "yes" you will —
Raising a child is an exhilarating experience and takes the utmost skill.

The joy, delight and pride you'll feel flooding your heart—
Will bond you for always with this child—nothing tears it apart.

"Will I ever sleep again?" you wonder and someday you do.
But not before alot of sleepless nights you go through.

"When will he smile" "When will he talk?"
"Won't this baby ever learn to walk?"

And he grows and knows and yes he does it all—
From laughing and loving to Little League ball.

And soon there are three children to love you see—
with Sunday School, Church and prayers on bended knee.

And you wonder "won't I have time to do my thing?"
but you forget about you when they start to sing.

And the days fly by with the meals to cook, books to read, laundry to do.
So much work, a husband and the children—you don't even wonder about you.

Then before you realize and right before your eyes.
Those three little babies are ready to hit the skies.

And you say a prayer with a lump in your throat—
bid them goodbye with a hug but remember to note.

That inside you wish just for one more day of those crazy, hectic times.
When you were so busy you couldn't write rhymes!

Diana L Richardson Reed
WHILE YOUR GONE

To My loving husband who was only a boyfriend at the time. I love you Greg, love always Diana.

You've been gone for a while,
I haven't forgotten your smile,
So please take care of my heart,
As long as we're apart.

I miss you oh so very much,
Your coal black hair, your gentle touch,
Holding hands as we've walked together,
Holding hands, I hope forever.

When I look out over the sea,
I see a vision of you and me.
We are standing on the sand,
Side by side,hand and hand.

Love can be a tricky game,
No two kind are the same.
With us, we have a special love,
To me it's a blessing from God above
God, I wish you really knew,
How much I truely care for you, and,
If I had it all my way,
I'd be with you till my dying day.

Now believe me darling,
I'll always be true,
And one day soon,
I'll be with you.

Michelle Kay Mallory
A CELL CLOSEST TO HELL

Here I lay in a cell,
it's got to be a taste of hell.

As I sit waiting for time to
go by,
I wonder, was it worth it
just to get high.

Now I know the other side of life,
that people go through a hell
of alot of strife.

I'm being punished for my crime,
and I guess I'll do some time.
I'm losing my home and my love,
but I do know theres a God up above.
He'll get me through these trials and
tribulations...
then I can go home to my loved ones and relations.

Now sitting in jail,
where did I go wrong,
I should have been in church all along.
My life and my loves are at home,
I've got to stop being on the roam.
Because theres trouble out there as you can see
and if I don't take care

a jail cell is where I'll be.

So, if you decide to do
something wrong, think again
for you may be going, straight
to a cell sitting next to me,

in a cell, Closest to hell.

Kitty Deschaine Poisson
A WALK ALONG THE BEACH
You can feel the sand still warm, from the afternoon sun
As you stroll along peacefully, when your busy day's done.
It sparkles as a million gems, and still holds the marks,
Of the small feet of sandpipers and seagulls and larks.

The spray from the water is refreshing and cool,
Where you stand water reaches, forming a pool.
Strange little creatures will crawl along,
And the shells that you find will carry a song.

The driftwood resembles all kinds of things,

In the distance you hear, the flapping of wings.
If you watch very close, the birds you will see,
Catching their dinner of fish, skillfully.

The horizon will hold the sight of a ship,
Moving slowly along the waves, as they dip.
Soon it will vanish before your eyes,
Where the water's edge, joins in with the skies.

So private and peaceful, it's a place to go,
To imagine and dream, and let your mind flow.
To rid all your worries, and fill all your thought,
With pleasant reminders, that you've always sought.

Boyd Brazell
SUICIDE ATTEMPT
"Why'd you want to do a thing like that?"
The white-washed woman wailed
While liquid lights beat white heat
On sweat-soaked clothes.
"Because, because,
I am a dancer without a dance."

"Why'd you want to do a thing like that?"
The mannered male nurse moaned
While beads of death
Rode water wings to fall among the dinner puke.
"Because, because,
I am a singer without a song."

"Why'd you want to do a thing like that?"
The dog-faced doctor droned
As starched straps held slim limbs straight
Against sheets of slate-sleet color.
"Because, because,
I am a wing without flight."

"Why'd you want to do a thing like that?"
The social worker strained a smile
As beads of death rode water wings
Through plastic nasal tubes of rescue.
"Because, because,
I am a poet without a poem."

Cheryl Thomas
A ROSE FOR A ROSE

In dedication to my mother, who I will always remember every time I see a rose.

She is a rose that spreads out
Her loving scent to each of her petals;
A rose may die,
But she leaves her buds to bloom,
And follow in a traditional way,
The one thing about the rose I have,
It can never be replaced.
This rose is the only rose I love,
This rose I call my Mother.

Donna Mae Huncosky
SILENT TEARS
In this world
Walks a lonely girl
Leaves crunch beneath her feet
As a silent tear rolls down her cheek.
She stops just in time to hear
twig's snap from a runaway deer.
Next to a gurgling stream
She sits down to dream
But in the distance can be heard
The mating call of a bird.
And she wonders if she'll ever hear
those three words she holds dear.
And as another tear rolls down her cheek
Faintly it can be heard hitting the water of the creek.

Joseph E Ecklund
SPRING
The gentle rains washed o'er the land
With a whispered call, "It's Spring!"
The plaintive cry of geese now heard
From the thousands on the wing.

The pansies grin their silly grins
From the soil now breaking free
As rainbowed meadows grace the earth
For its multitudes to see.

The tulips push their gaudy heads
Up through last banks of snow
As flora heeds the ancient call
It's spring and time to grow.

The daffodils grow daffy
In their wooded wanton glee
The squirrels are acting squirrely
As they chase from tree to tree.

The partridge drum in love's delight
As they dance their madcap dance
As Eros rules his springtime reign
Of romance, ah—sweet romance!

Mary Anita Todd Anthony
INFINITY

This poem is dedicated to Milton, my beloved husband, and all my wonderful family.

The forget-me-nots of the Angels,
are the beautiful, shimmering stars.
I think they must, of a surety be,
the windows to God's infinity.

As I watch the soft clouds of gray
hurrying past on a dreary day.
I thank the Lord, again and again,
for his gracious, bountiful gift of rain.

I see the fleecy white clouds above,
sailing o're the skies so blue.
They look like wooly little lambs
running, leaping and scampering thru.

When the full moon is brightly shining
the clouds seem to have a gossamer lining.
The lovely shafts of silver beams
soothes the weary to restful dreams.

As I see the yellow sun in the sky
giving us light and warmth, from on high.
The clouds are tied with sunbeams gold,
to light my path, as I grow old.

Alma Lees
GETTING A ROUND "TO IT"
I have always tried to do my part
And paddle my own canoe
But the time has come I must admit
When I'll welcome a boost or two.
When the family was small, I had no help at all
Now they're grown, they fully agree
"We are anxious and willing—just give us a call
When we get around to it you'll see."
So, I pawed thru' the tool box, found hammer, saws
And a square.
But nothing resembling a round "To it" was there.
There's a hole in the roof where the rain pours in
And drips on the living room floor
New hinges and paint would greatly improve
The state of the sagging back door.
There's garbage piled up till I can scarcely wade thru' it
But it cannot be hauled, till they get a round "To it."
One morning frustrated, and sitting alone
I at last blew my top, and I reached for the phone
I hired a workman, who came on the run
And without a round "To it" the jobs were soon done.
So, I bided my time for the rest of the day
Knowing full well that I'd hear someone say—
"Hi Mom, what's for dinner," and that was my cue
To say, "Boys you know I'd love to help you, but
If you're hungry, find some cold bologna and chew it
You'll get a square meal when I get a round "To it."

Cynthia Barnes
MY FIRST BORN CHILD

Kimberley I'm proud to be part of your life. With love, Mom

On a summer's day in the month of June
God gave me a special gift—
My first-born child,
A little girl came crying out of my womb.
As I first saw you my love grew so strong
And I never stopped loving you as the days went on
I watched you walk; I listened to you talk
Your first word was "Daddy!"
And into a lady you are all grown up
This first born child of mine.
You will always be my little girl no matter your age
For there is something that binds us two
This first born child of mine.
Sometimes I just don't say how proud of you I am
You filled the years with so much joy
This first born child of mine.
You try so hard to do your best in everything you do
To make me proud as proud can be
Of this first born child of mine.
No one could ask for better in these days of troubled times
When children won't listen and seem to be so blind
I know I can count on you to find your way in life
And never have to worry when you make some man a wife.
I thank God for sending this special gift to me
And I know that He too is proud
Of this first born child of mine.

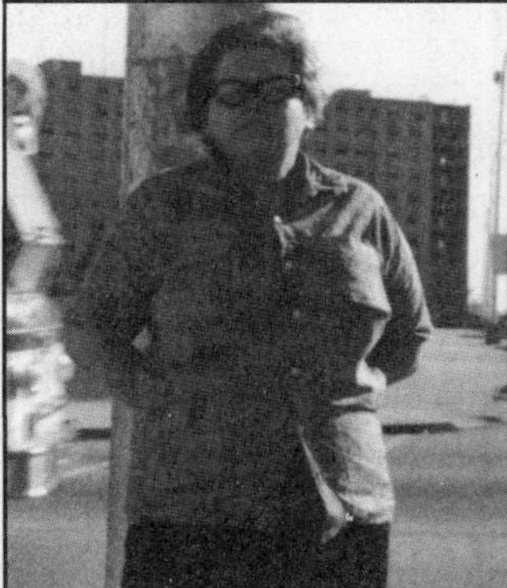

Norma A Pulsifer

Norma A Pulsifer
SMOKER'S FIT

I dedicate this poem to James Bailey and other smokers I have known.

Got to smoke that cigarette, got to have another puff.
I seem full of that stuff, smoke seems to come out of my ears,

Got the smoker's fit, boy does it
make a hit.
Every half hour or so, got to smoke
that cigarette, got a bad habit.
Someday I hope to quit it, it gets
on your hair, skin and clothes.
Smells worse than perfume
But I have to kick that habit, got
to have a cigarette.
It gets in your eyes.
It drives the non smoker wild, but
you know how it is,
Just got to have another smoke or
a cigarette.

Claracy Hulett Ingels
ON A CLOUD

Like a winged bird I sail the sky
O'er fleecy clouds of white
Through breaks below, I glimpse
the earth
Dressed in colors dark and light.

The sun shines bright on fields of
green
And roads just ribbon wide.
THe river stretches far below
With trees and homes on either
side.

The earth is good beneath the feet
With it's heartbeat strong and loud
But let me have my wings a while
And live upon a cloud.

Linda L Brame
SPARKLING EYES

With sparkling eyes she tells me
To hold her without fear
Music begins across the sea
As she quickly draws me near

My mind becomes a prisoner
Wrapped within her silken web
My past receding to a blur
The future begins to ebb

Around the sun we race
And across the milky way
Vanishing without a trace
Like moonbeams in the day

Lights that take my breath away
And make my heart stand still
Like a roman candle holiday
My senses begin to thrill

A million bubbles seem to burst
Somewhere above my head
Tumbling down to quinch my
thirst
And wash away the dread

But suddenly the music dies
As I begin to comprehend
In my arms was only lies
I was dancing with the wind

Gilbert F Gehman
THE TRAIN

I listen and watch
from my little shack,
as the trains come
roaring down the track.

The loads that they
haul vary by the hour,
lumber and coal and
autos with horsepower.

No more steam engines
do they now run,
only quiet Diesels
that aren't much fun.

No more whistles blow
and that's very sad,
it wasn't like that
when I was a lad.

The youth of today
will never know,
the joy of hearing
a steam whistle blow.

Barbara McGregor
EMPTY

To My Children, Stop, Think and do What's best for you

I'm searching my feelings now
and really I am empty
Such a loss,
Such dispair,
What really would have made me
happy,
I do not know,
Things went wrong so many years
ago.
I've lived a life of make believe,
But who in the end would be
deceived?
I've been something to all
that is not true,
And the years are gone and cannot
be renewed.
Had I been true what would life
hold for me?
I haven't the courage to even
dream of that fantasy.

William P Justice
WHEN AN EAGLE WEEPS

Misguided youth with torch in
hand
Burning Old Glory, emblem of our
fair land
Or showing callous disrespect as
she goes by,
It almost seems that I can hear an
eagle cry.

Innocent hostage held by foreign
band,
Blood of America's finest stains the
sand.
It's as if this proud bird no longer
flies,
And in my heart, I know that an
eagle cries.

We go in smug complacency about
our daily task
Does anyone really care; does
anyone ever ask,
Is patriotism surely dead, or
merely sleeping;
Listen my friend, can you hear an
eagle weeping?

Althea L FurBay
THE PERFECT PAIR

To my in-laws who have shared 55 years together and to their son with whom I hope to share the same amount.

We're the perfect pair
You and me
Just like a pair of old shoes
Comfortable
Standing side by side
Well matched
Yet opposite
You right
Me left
The perfect pair
That's you and me

Lisa Jane Prince
THAT CRISP OCTOBER MORNING

On that crisp October morning,
the birds were flying away,
We smelled the damp birch trees,
and saw leaves swarming down,
like furious bees.
There was a lot of construction
and cars going by,
But who could forget the river
sounds,
as it flowed so high.
The bears are all hybernating,
and the bugs have mostly died.
We were in a world of our own,
On that crisp October morning.

"Chuckie" Charles James

Bonnie Dean Lynch Firenze
UNTIL WE WALK THE REALM OF ANGELS

Dedicated in memory of our Son "Chuckie" Charles James. To all families who have lost a child. We share your suffering and silent desparation.

Memories like a whisper are here
and then they're gone
Indelible impressions, which our
whole lives set upon
Our inner grief reveals itself and
takes its toll in time
For each tear shed, the secret
expression of pain becomes a
line

In silence we will travel to the place
where angels go
Encompassed by a torch of light
the inner spirit knows
We will walk in the realm of angels
like lambs we shall be lead
To the light beyond the darkness
where no more tears are shed

Reunited with our children they
make us understand
They are well and safe and happy
in their heavenly sweet land
They send us back to live and learn,
they love yet set us free
To finish life's duration of what is
meant to be

Hope will be our source of strength
and guide us to tomorrow
Faith will chase our fears away and
help us deal with sorrow
Inner peace and wisdom are
rewards that we shall gain
As we hold our heads up proudly
and bear our cross of pain

We will marvel at the splendor as
each day passes by
We will love you and will miss you
until the day we die
We will make a point to rise above
our anger and frustration
As we meekly walk the road of life
with gentle anticipation
To a day when we will also stand
to knock on heaven's door
Where we will not be separated
from our children anymore

Romana Wood
WAR

War is most terrible,
With killing and fighting,
And some of the most horrible
things.
The bombing and destroying,
Of lovely places,
Places that can do no harm.
And when I think,
Of all the innocent,
That are destroyed for naught.
Tell me, why, how
Can one man do this to another?
Doesn't he feel shame,
In killing a brother?
Doesn't he remember,
For the rest of his life,
The three year old child,
Who died in it's mothers arms?
Or does he forget it,
Like a child does a bad dream?

Freda M Kling
CHOICES

I thought about the choices
That I'm required to make
Each and every day that passes
From the time that I'm awake.
No matter what the outcome
I must decide the act;
To do to not, to give or take,
To leave or stay, to eat or fast.
On and on the choices come,
Decisions make the total sum,
And I must weigh each good or bad
Decisions from the choice I've
had.
The scales of justice do not lie,
One always reaps his just reward.
For every error in one's choice
There's penalty of equal cost.
Every choice that's true and right
Brings happiness and great
delight.
So heaven here at last is found,
But also hell when choice is
wrong.
There is no way to cast the blame,
Because my choice is mine alone.
I must receive effect from cause
With faith that wisdom guides
my choice.

Vivian Marie Barrington
MOTHER, WHERE HAVE YOU GONE?

This poem is dedicated to my mother, Mrs. Ima Hancock, a victim of Alzheimer's disease. She died 13 weeks after it was written.

Mother, where have you gone?
The shadows of memory linger on,
As your children move forward
On Life's ageless plane,
In the hope, by some chance, you
will join us again.
Mother, are you still there?
Are you able to feel, and can you
still care
That the babies you held now have
babes of their own,
And some of these babes are now
magically grown?
Mother, we miss you so,
And the longing for you is a
miserable low,

For we're touched by this empty, emotionless shell,
By the unending torment, the limitless hell.
But, Mother, you are the best—
The time that you've given, the love you possessed
Are a legacy treasured by all you have known,
A garden of promise from seeds you have sown.
Mother, you're in our prayers;
When we seem overcome by our own daily cares,
Your sad face reminds us of what you have been.
We pray you'll return and be with us again.

Cynthia J Herring
GIVE ME A HOPE

Above all else, give me a hope
And give me a dream for a guest,
To walk with a dream where others dare not go,
This is the gift that is best.

My steps may not reach that ultimate goal,
The scope may be great and the price too high—
But with a searchlight of expectancy and a hope
I'll scan the limitless dreams in the sky.

Do not deforce that hope and that dream,
Or else within me something will die;
Tho' obstacles mount, dreams crumble in dust,
Still, there's an unchartered course I must try.

I'll face with joy what life will yield,
And hold onto my hopes and dreams,
And I'll reach out for that elusive star,
No matter how far it may seem.

Gina Marie Leeb
SILENCE

To my Son, Joey

Darkness overhears
The shadows of the past

When the quiet rises
The past returns to present

Echoes of the silence
Build walls, never to escape

Neda Hatfield
SILENCE IS GOLDEN

For Mom, for believing in me.

Twas the morning before dawn.
I saw the sun rise, with the glorious rage of hate, and with the spiteful love for none.

The day mysteriously long, hot objects around endlessly.

I the last one tiring, mold and form with the rock.

The moment before moonlit shown, courageously the water rose.
The earth with the gloom of darkness, lost with curious visions of victory.

Existence of no knowledge, the ungodly sound of silence.
Last of the insane worlds, the horror of zero.

Beverly Parrott
RUNAWAY

My poem—RUNAWAY written for and dedicated to our Son, Ed—our Runaway—returned.

Our teenager left home today
we know not where he did not say
Just wants to be free he wrote
in our mailbox he left a note
Says it is nothing we have done
where are you now are you safe, our son?
Each time the telephone does ring
frightened are we of the news it will bring
Many things happen throughout each day
a constant reminder you are away
We miss the times we did share
talking, joking just showing we care
Do you realize what you ask?
don't worry about me, what a task
Our daily prayer each and every day
please God show him the way
keep him safe and trouble free
return him home to us safely
once again to love, care for and enjoy
our teenage son, no longer a boy!

Anna Toma Anderson
WILD FLOWERS

There's something intriguing
About the beauty of wild flowers,
That makes you gasp with sheer
Wonder at mother-nature, as her
First-born colorful beauties
Swing gently to and fro in
Spring and summer breezes.

Unlike their restricted and

Cultured friends, who need
Special love and care, they are
Unrestricted and free to roam
Anywhere . . . fields, sidewalks
And unexpected places.

They are bred and milked
Right from their earthly mother's
Bosom, whose hands were blessed
With a heaven-sent touch of the
Creator-Himself . . . making them
Simple and common and loved by
All . . . because they are God's
Floral favorites; bathing us
With His love, joy and
Bouquets of sun-filled beauty.

Cindy L Randolph
MY SISTER COLLEEN

In memory of Colleen Ann Adams, who died 12-22-85 at the age of 32. She was my only sister, and the best friend I ever had.

I guess I always thought we would be together.
But God has better plans for you.
I am selfish, I don't want you to go away.
But I know you won't leave me . . . alone.
For sisters share a special bond,
and I know you will always watch over me.
Until we are together . . . again.
You are so special to me.
My memories of you, will be with me . . . always.
I love you . . . and I will always miss you . . .
But you and me, we will always be . . . Sisters.

Your body is weak, mine is strong.
Because we are sisters, we'll make it along.
Our paths lead in different directions,
our destinations are the same.
I'll help you with the pain.
You'll help me to be strong,
and we'll make it along.

You will cross before me,
I will carry on.
Someday we'll be together again,
This thought will make us strong,
so that, we'll make it along . . .
We are SISTERS.

Reginald R Rowe
DREAMS OF ANOTHER DAY

I look out at the dawn of a sunny new day
To wonder what my roll it will be to play.
Will I think of something of which I can be proud
Or will it be like yesterday, my mind in a cloud
I run so many dreams through my mind,
But things that are real, are hard to find.
Now it's time to wake up to this brand new day.
Just my luck, it's another cloudy day.

William S Kellison
SPRING

This poem is dedicated to my mother, Lillian Kellison and to my family for their support.

Spring is a wonderful thing
When the trees bud and the birds sing
Flowers push up from the ground
Then you know mother nature is around
She fills you with sights from the past
And you wish that it would always last
Fresh air and sunshine all over the place
for us to smell and feel on our fence
but spring doesn't last very long you know
because everythings green and starting to grow
Mother nature is off and running at last
and spring becomes a season past

Nancy D Paciencia
ENDING

Great black swirls
Of dust and crime
Flew o'er the city
At the end of time.

Man had come
And conquered all,
Save Mother Nature
Who once stood tall.

Once kind, the Lady
Now was grim
And Man's great day
Was lost to him.

Thought men then
To start anew.
Too little, too late,
The Earth was through.

Trees—no more—
Or flowers, too;
No birds and bees,
And men were few.

The damage done,
Too late to cry,
Her Earth was dead—
She let Man die.

Catherine Rickards
BRUCE'S DOG

My pet is a dog named Tippy,
She's black and shiny and zippy.
All day long we play together,
We share a tent in all kinds of weather.
Up and down the pavement she pounds,
When I on my tricycle make my rounds.
At playing ball, she's a whiz
I am the pitcher; she catches.
She likes the ocean; waves and all,
And rescues me when I fall.
She stays by my chair when I eat my meal,
Cleaning up the floor with great zeal.
On purpose I leave part of my food,
So Tippy can enjoy what's good.
At night when we go to bed
She snores; I cover my head.
On only one thing we don't agree
When I bite her; she bites me.

Ouch/

Michelle Graf
FLOWERS

Flowers smell pretty.
Flowers come in many colors.
What a sight for the eyes to behold!
Their pretty fragrance fills the air.
In Spring they pop up everywhere!
Flowers have a special way,
Of brightening up a gloomy day.

LaVonne M Smith
MY ETERNITY

For Lynnette, my purest rose, who always wanted to live long enough to be immoral.

First I saw its unending beauty
and I thought I knew the rose.
Myself's the fool, to believe it everlasting.
Was not its full-colored life too short?

It seemed so eternal, so softly there,
But wait, that shortness is its eternity

with the softness, vulnerable and pure,
until its zenith, then deterioration deadly.

Surely, I know eternity, the forever.
It is my duration. My beauty in or out
doesn't matter, my pureness will matter
even less. I am my eternity!

Carlyle Leggett
SIMPLE MAN'S POET

Dedicated to the simple man's peers

I'm the simple man's poet
my vocabulary is small

But that's better
than not expressing myself at all.

For I have the same emotions
as the most educated man

But when I say something
most anyone can understand.

So may be I'm lacking in
education and word knowledge

But common sense is not taught
in any old college.

Margaret Adomaitis
A LETTER
My heart dares to say
Today will be the day
My thoughts dare to say
Today will be the day
My lips pray and pray
Today will be the day
A letter is on the way
Today will be the day.

Wayne T Harris
SKY ROADS
Silver vessels sounded, listened, then I heard and saw,
but was blinded, Reflections of the sun bounced off its
wings, Raised my arm and put my hand before my eyes
so I could see that great bird pass over me,
tons of alloy and steel thrust through the air
as an arrow would fly from the bow.
Seconds passed on by, then it was only a dot in the sky.

Mrs Linda Martin Soucy
HIGH CLASS LADY

I wish to dedicate this poem to my loving mother. She taught me everything I know. Like mother, like daughter.

A graceful lady-in-waiting,
Is truly a blessing in disguise;
And in her rather quiet manner,
Portrays a woman full of royal grandure.
She is a vision of a virtuous person,
And is unique in every way.
She is so delightful,
That she brightens up my day.
Her enlightened spirit,
Of mystical intrigue,
Is like a nightingale,
Singing gently in the breeze,
In tune with the passing tides of time,
Full of sentimentalities,
Of love once so devine.
And while solemnly posing,
For an unknown painter,
She somehow maintained her silent composure,
In lonely regrets of many a disclosure.
And all her secrets and greatest desires,
Were hidden behind her faint smile,
As she thought about the flowers,
That her lover had acquired while muttering;
"Darling, you have great style, so smile."

Cynthia Kelsey
THERE IS A WAY TO STOP THE PAIN

In thought of William H. Jordan Special, September "79"

There is a way to stop the pain
Touch me,
Hold me,
Make me smile.
There is a way to stop the pain.
See me,
Know me,
Look me eye to eye.
There is a way to stop the pain.
Love me,
Need me,
Show me how.
There is a way to stop the pain.
Scream with me,
Think with me,
Show me your way.
There is a way to stop the pain.
Understand me,
Demand of me,
The things you desire.
There is a way to stop the pain.
Run with me,
Lay with me,
Show me your soul.
There is a way to stop the pain!

Susan I Mettert

Susan I Mettert
IN THE TWINKLING OF AN EYE

This poem is dedicated to our son James Robert Mettert

You were a twinkle in my eye, a dream come true, your father and I created you.
You are part of the pursuit of happiness, the product of love, fashioned and patterned from things above.
In your eyes are the answers to questions we never knew, in the Universe that existed of two.
And through the years as you grow, there are things you will learn, and seeds you will sow.
Now as you grow and travel through time and space, soon you will become part of the human race, as unique as the planets and individual as the stars.

Soon you will know all that we do, in the twinkling of an eye you will understand too.
Soon you will take a wife to share the adventures of your life.
You'll spend the present and mortgage the past, you'll invest in each other and hope it will last.
You work, you change, you fall short of your dreams.
Reality sets in, life is not what it seems, or what you thought it would be, once there were two now there are three.
And as you continue on your way, you will pass on all you do and say to the future to come, your very own son.
You'll write, revise, revise and rewrite again, you'll rewrite your own story till you come to it's end.
Time fades and passes through, as your opening doors your closing some too.
Then when you are old and tired and worn, you will think back to when you were born, remembering all the things that you did, the things that you knew the essence of you.
Content with the pleasure you can rest from the pain, your works go before you yet nothing remains.
You've done all you could and been all you are, you've completed the circle my bright shining star in the far distant sky, and to think it all began in the twinkling of any eye . . .

Thelma Schiller
PARADE OF PATRIOTS
Ten-thousand-flags . . . Betsy Ross proclaim,
Like rows of flowers in sunlit rain,
In like arrays of stars and stripes;
The music calls from fifes and pipes,
Till flowing past the classic art,
The galleries, the grocery mart,
The troops march on as unafraid
As ships that in the harbor laid,
Where children watch with sleep-filled eyes,
Lady Liberty hovering over sighs,
Her torch aflame, the filtering sun
Caught in her golden crown . . . the awe;
The whole crowd cheered at what they saw:
The men, the flags, the marching band,
The flaming torch held in her hand:
And more than one glad heart did cry,
"This is my home . . . until I die."

H Brandon Wright
TAPS
I didn't want to go, they drafted me.
I didn't want to fight, they called me yellow.
They ordered the attack, shrapnel tore my guts.
They carried me to safety, in safety I died.
They marked out my name.
They blew taps over me.
They buried me under a cross and a tear from my mother's eye.
But I live on in everyone who saw me or others die,
And those who had to cry and buried a son with a tear of an eye.

Sue Ann Gold Frodsham
THE WORD
My love,
Shine forth, do not hide,
You will conquer all fear.
One is waiting,
Listening,
For the touch of the word.
Patience my heart
Bridle your passion,
The hour cometh in its own time
For the word,
I love you.

Jean Thomson
WASTED TIME
You and I
we weren't that close, in days gone by,
You
in fear and frustation struck out,
I
in confusion and loneliness struck back
The gap between us grew wider,
angry words flew between us,
harsh words on harsh words, pain on pain,
who was the strongest, who could withstand the most pain?
Each day grew longer and harder to bear
and the gap grew stronger and impossible to repair.

In the end, I left and started my own life, away from you.

Now that the years have drifted by,
that gap no longer exists.
Now that time has erased the pain,
only gentle words remain.

As you lie in that bed your forced to lay
do you remember and weep?
I do, for so much wasted time.
Before you die will I have time to tell you
its ok, I understand and I'm sorry
Will I have time to simply say,
I Love You.

Barbara Edson
A DAUGHTER
A daughter is a precious thing,
to hold, to love, to hug, to bring,
a friend, a pal, a buddy true
into my life each day anew.
Ere sometimes tho I oft recall,
the good, the bad, we've shared them all.
Sometimes I think of times gone by,
a laugh, a tear, a smile, a sigh.
Of all the prayers I've ever prayed,
my ones for you are heaven made.
I pray, I feel, I talk, I sing,
my daughter, your a precious thing.

Joe Allen Poston
I THOUGHT YOU SMILED
I thought I saw you smile
As I looked into your face.
Then, just as quickly as it came,
A frown took its place.

The frown told of troubles
That boiled within your mind;
But, behind that stressful look
Were memories of more pleasant times.

I felt that time had erased the pain,
So I reached out to you.
You quickly slammed the door again
And made it clear that we were through.

The smile was gone
Never to return.
Now the lonely days pass
And my heart only yearns
FOR YOU!

Griselda Castro

Griselda Castro
MY PLEA TO HIM

I dedicate this poem with all my heart to my husband Tony, my three sons, my parents and my close friends.

Bless me Lord in times of tribulations.
When I need you and I feel I can't go
On anymore.
I need you Lord
So many years since my salvation and
So many times through my tribulations
I wanted to leave you my Lord.
I need you Lord
But within me I cried the more for you.
Lord embrace me with your loving touch
So that I can make it through.
I need you Lord
Fill this heart of mine with joy and peace
And blessings too. No one can do it like
You do.
I need you Lord
Through the years you've been by my side
Always being my guide. When I thought I
Couldn't make it, you stretched your loving
Arms and carried me through the rough times
And gave me the strength to carry on.
I need you Lord
Please continue loving me, so I can keep
On living for you. Forgive me Lord, for I
Have many faults. But Lord please change
My heart and save my soul. Even though I
Have many moods don't leave me Lord. I
Want you by my side until the day I die.
I need you Lord

Daniel Bacon
THE WORLD

This poem is dedicated to all mankind

Mountain to mountain to form a range
The earth and rock does live in pain
As man moves over this vast land
It starts to perish by mans own hand

Linh Duy Vo
HELLO FRIENDS

Dedicated to Rancho Los Amigos Medical Center on its Centennial 1888—1988

Have you noticed me?
I am a wheelchair
Carrying a beautiful person
Just like you, we make a pair

Love is within silence
In me and my rider,
As you see wherever we are
We are never short of patience

You may want to go for a stroll
On a nice day at the Ranch
Then say hello to everyone here
And share your love with all

A hundred years have gone by
My existence at the Ranch means destiny
Witnessing love bound among staff and patients
Hello my friends, have you noticed me!!

Kelly Arline Burns
I THINK OF YOU . . .
I think of you and the times past,
and wish that those times would always last.

I think of you and look towards the sky,
and watch the fall geese go flying by.

I sit and watch the water clear,
and wish that you were still here.

I watch a star light bright,
I think of you most at night.

I wish and hope that you would come back to me,
but those thoughts are thought foolishly.

So I guess I'll just have to pretend,
cuz all good things must come to an end.

I think of you and don't know why,
as a love-lost tear falls from my eye!

Greg Malnikoff
BEGIN AND END

In memory of Howard Rogers who had to finally let go

Life can be precious,
Its end can be welcome.
We'll all experience both,
And it makes me sad.
For when I think about it,
I want to cry.
Because the day we're born,
We begin to die.

Daymien S Thommen
WHITE ROSE
You grew a white rose in a garden of snow,
And left it to survive on its own.
a green thorn
a white rose,
Longing for warmth.
You cared not,
no love
no warmth.
a red thorn
a black rose,
Lay awating its fate.
Seasons changed
fate changed
You changed,
Yet—
no love
no warmth
no companionship,
You cared not.
Now all that remains
a silver thorn
a bloody rose,
Lay crushed in the snow.

Sue Harman
A NEW LOVE
Everyone in the world around
Needs love to keep them going,
Love that's lasting with the sound
Of sweetness for the growing.
Somewhere I'll find the one for me
It has to come I know,
I'll look around and I'll see
A love starting to grow.
The stars were in my eyes
I could see you there,
Somewhere we heard the cries
And we knew we cared.
So here we are close together
Eyes shining as the stars in the sky,
Doesn't matter the weather
We don't think of the why.
We love each other and dream our dreams
God sends his blessing for this,
We stand closer than it seems
And share a sweet kiss.
Our wedding day is here at last
And in my thoughts I see,
Our future so filled and blest
Always for you and me.

Julie A Starr

Julie A Starr
YOU WERE EVERYTHING
You were my life and you were my soul.
You were my treasure, my one and only goal.
You were the reason I got up in the morning and went to sleep at night.
You were the answers and you were the light.
You were the stars that shone on heaven above.
You were the feathers on a snowy white dove.
You were the red in the hearts I drew.
You were always on my mind, my every thought and every clue.
You were the leaves that fell in fall.
You were a tree: big, strong and tall.
You were puppy dog tails and everything that boys were made of.
You were the clouds that billowed far above.
You were the sun that shone on my face.
You were everything: so full of grace.
Now that you've left me,
Now that you're gone,
I cry now and then, but then I move on.
I now get up in the mornings and go to sleep at night.
I see this world of mine in a totally new light.
Just because you left, you thought I'd be full of doubt.
I don't need you anymore, this I found out.
I'm my own person and I have a life too!
I'm just glad I got to spend part of it with you.
For this experience, I'm a little richer, smarter and wise.
Now that I'm free . . .
WATCH OUT GUYS!!!

Raney Douglas
JOSH
Don't fret for Josh—his pain is gone—
For the Lord has called his little boy home—
Just think of the blessings the Lord gave you—

For the wonderful things you and Josh had to do—
You would read him books and taught him to spell—
And you gave him his medicine to keep him well—
His laughter and playing made your day—
And—"Gramma—I love you" is all he needed to say—
You gave him the love—he needed so much—
When his home was broken and out of touch—
Just try and look at things this way—
"Lord" he was my sunshine—he made my day—
Thank you Lord for all the years—
He's in good hands and no more tears—
But if the Heavens would open and Josh would look down—
He'd see all your tears and then he would frown—
He'd say "I didn't die" I'm just taking a nap—
And Heaven is just like my Gramma's lap—

M Vasil

LIFELINE

Somewhere along the way
I must have missed the boat.
I find myself a floundering
And cannot stay afloat.
But—each time that I am sinking,
A hand is always there
To give me gentle boosts
And to bring me up for air!

Sara L Wanambwa

A DREAM DEFILED

They carried on their shoulders the dreams of a race
They were the Firsts whose bold steps set the pace
Men and women of color, pioneers in bronze shades
Who trod the bloodstained path the martyrs had made
But their upraised fists became palms to be crossed
Power is the drug; Money the boss
Equality for a price; Loyalty for sale
Traitors with dark skins our dream have impaled
As leader I faced those betrayers black as night
Assailed, battered, thwarted I held fast to the right
With truth as my sword and justice my shield
Determined, naive I would not yield
My following was strong, sounding the call to battle
But the war cry soon faded to an empty rattle
I finally stood alone; My army dispersed,
Praying for the best; Expecting the worst
My pain was so great; So monstrous the sin
Our dream was defiled by those of our own skin
Oppressed became oppressor with disdain and scorn
But the dream did not die though battered and torn
It lives in the hearts of the faithful and bold
Who know that real dreams can't be bought or sold
Betrayers, defilers in arrogance
they rule
Dream builders shall triumph with truth as their tool

Janet L Hardie

WHEN GOD MAKES US NEW FRIENDS

When God makes us new friends
He carefully molds one in the left
and the other in the right hand.
Each is uniquely designed.
Of all the people in our great land
I am glad that God picked you to be my friend!

Cheryl Ann Boehm

THE LOVE THAT WENT AWAY

I once loved someone
he was very special to me
I always had wished
he would always be
One day he went away
to me it was the end
Our love was something
we just couldn't mend
I still think of him
as each day goes by
I just can't get rid of him
no matter how hard I try
But now my life must go on
I say that with a sigh
And now I think it's time
for me to say good-bye

Dawn C Kimberling

UNDER THE FINGERS OF A COOLING BREEZE

Under the fingers of a cooling breeze we lose
the smiles of a time that long has passed: the flowers
of my garland'd hair have faded and fallen.
The rings and chains, all worne with a tired weight upon
your hands, tarnish even as we speak.
In the icy grip of this passing time, chasms are torne
open from even the little lost memories,
the smallest sip of thought.
The wind is cold in these empty spaces
and we grow chill with all we forgot.

Carolina Fraraccio

YOU

Dedicated with love and admiration to my husband, Joey.

Joy is contained within his heart,
Observations increase every day,

Sadness is replaced by love,
Each action describes precious
thoughts,
Preparing for future events make his
Happiness thrilling and full of contentment.

Margaret Evelyn Benn

FLOWERS FROM MY WEED PATCH

Flowers from my weed patch,
require no work at all,
yet all the colors of the rainbow,
are reflected from the soil.

These little bits of color,
are good for the soul,
take time to look beyond it all,
for a lesson in Love is told.

All of these creations,
well earn their place in the sod,
for when they unfold,
they are the smile of God.

Helen McCuch

GOD'S CHILD

I am God's exceptional child
Conquering emotions gone wild
Born and doomed to live without love
I beg mercy from God above
I've suffered and conquered so much
I now long for only God's Touch
Through it all I've survived
Made strong, now I've arrived
Yes, I am God's exceptional child.

Mary C Marble

TODAY

As my thoughts turn to yesterday
I sadly throw the key away.
Even tho my future is dim
I feel 'God' in the soft wind.
I see 'God' in the leaves and trees
I hear 'God' in the hum of bees.
I see 'God' in the flowers that bloom
I hear 'Him' in the stillness of my room.
Then with a happy start
I even feel 'Him' in my heart.
So if tomorrow never comes my way
I'll live and be happy just for today.

Dorothy E Call

A MOTHER'S PRAYER

So long as there are homes where fires burn and there is bread,
So long as there are homes where lamps are lit and prayers are said,
Although people falter through the dark and nations grope,
With God himself back of these little homes, we have hope.

A child's head is bowed low at his little bed.
While he asks by the heavenly Father's hand to be led.
He is thankful for a mother who guides him through the day
And watches tenderly over him while at work or play.

Her prayer is God help my child to be kind and good
And to follow after Thee as he should.

Bonnie Salmons

LEGACY

"Of all the wonders that I yet have heard,
It seems to me most strange that men should fear
Seeing that death, a necessary end,
Will come when it will come."
From Julius Caesar as I quote
Long ago, Shakespeare wrote.
But if I can leave one thread of knowledge,
One wisp of wool upon a hedge,
Walk on sands of time, and looking back,
See my footprints straight upon the track,
To leave a child behind to make the run,
Take up the torch and do a task as yet undone—
A chore bestowed by God—a link in chain—
Then all my toil shall not have been in vain.

Bleeka M Boatright

PEACE IN VIETNAM

Dedicated to our son, B. D. Boatright, who served in the U.S. Marine Corps in Vietnam.

This is something to think about
And its something to brag about,
It is something to pray about,
For there was something we did about,
Our boys in Vietnam.

Just how often did you think about,
How our boys there, got about,
Through mud mined fields and bombed out routes,
With combat gear they couldn't do without?
To fight in Vietnam.

Some were slain in the dark of night,
Some were imprisoned without a right
And suffered cruelty without a doubt,
With little to eat to keep them stout,
To establish peace in Vietnam.

Now what can we all do about,
This war torn area we know about,
To establish peace and bring about
Friendship and love we're taught about,
To keep the peace in Vietnam?

We can take the time to pray about,
The cause of wars we've fought about
And ask for peace in Nations throughout,
Through faith in Christ whom we know about,
To keep the peace in Vietnam.

Paula C Snyder

SPRINGTIME

This poem is dedicated to my husband, Randy and our daughters, Christina and Angela.

The treetops gently swaying
against a sky of blue,
Meadows growing green
Earth's treasures now renewed.

Birds that are singing in the trees
send children out to play,
The sun is shining brightly
to make a perfect day.

The flowers peek in shyness
at humming bumblebees,
Grasshoppers playing leapfrog
and puppies cutting zzz's.

The air is filled with freshness
of all things now reborn,

The pleasent smell of honeysuckle
to greet us in the morn.

Young and old love start to bloom
as does most everything,
People laugh and smile more
in the months that we call Spring.

Elizabeth H Clark

Elizabeth H Clark
MEDITATIONS ON MIDDLE AGE

No longer young, but not yet old
Not yet serene, but not uncontrolled
Not yet content to relive the past
But the present and future move too fast
Too soon to regret what you might have done
Too spent to begin what you haven't begun
An island in the sea of time
A pause before the steeper climb.

Stephanie Kanean
REMEMBER ME

A rose has died and is fading from sight
To join phantom flowers on clouds of white
Farewell to thee my longtime love
Can a rose that's dying bloom above?
Can a rose decayed grow with essence sweet
Should the paths of our souls again ever meet?
Remember me on quiet days, when raindrops whisper on your pane
Remember me when winter comes and crystalizes earth's terrain
Think of me when evening stars speckle lazy summer nights
Remember me when springtime charms your soul to taking dreamy flights
Like valleys below with silence profound
Or majestic mountains snow-white crowned
Keep me in memory as I'll keep you
I loved you more than you ever knew

Penny Taylor
TWILIGHT

Only in my dreams may I recall
your tender kiss.
Forbidden love knows not the dawn
—in shadows must it be fulfilled
And passion's labored breath is stilled
for none but I to hear.

This mortal soul gives not itself
if true love be denied.
My heart could ne'er withstand the pain
—lest dawn's reproach of sinful lust
Lady silenced in the autumn dusk
no more to haunt the mind.

Sidney Hopkins Charles
OUR CLASS REUNION

Tonight's class night—our forty-fifth
Seems everything has gone amiss—
First of all, we came in late
And I forgot my partial plate!
The food was cold; the coffee too
The steak was tough—I couldn't chew.
Tonight's class night—our forty-fifth!
The years have tamed our urge to kiss.
Some wore the wig; some used the dye
To bring back youth that passed them by.
It's partytime so don't feel blue,
Enjoy yourself and hoist a few!
And when the band begins to jive
Show everyone you're still alive!
Tonight's class night—our forty-fifth
Hey! I even lost my address list!!

Caryn L Payne
HELL

Sleeping, Smiling,
The peace of innocence

Waking, Screaming,
The nightmare of life.

Sherri College
MY TREASURE

While traveling over Life's highway
Some people earn fortune and fame.
They stop and stand back to admire
The things they've worked so hard to claim.

We dreamers just keep on hiking.
Our destiny? Rainbow's End!
We're looking to find that "pot of gold;"
Could it be up there 'round the next bend?

But alas! Here's the end of our rainbow;
And there's no pot of gold, but I see
Something more precious than dreams of stone:
It's your love, and it's shining on me.

So let others go seek costly treasures . . .
To me they're not worth a dime
Because when you touch me your own special way
All Heaven and Earth become mine.

Velma McMurry Day
CASTLE ROCK WISCONSIN

At the bottom of an ancient sea
Ruled a granite tower—magestically.
A thousand feet above the floor
A thousand leagues from any shore
Pink granite monarch of the sea
Ruling in splendor—and magesty.

Long ages rolled—deep waters ebbed
Huge tremors warped the ocean bed
The raging flood—at last set free—
Rushed off to form another sea

Ten million billion years crept by
Till that pink castle caught my eye
Bereft of realm—but not of pride
Surrounded by prairie on every side
A thousand leagues from any sea—
And ruling still—majestically

Louise Campbell
ROSES

This poem is dedicated to my family, who inspired me. Thanks to Mrs. Ruby Wilson, who gave me hope, and to my dear friend Pat Bailey, who kept the dream alive. They had faith when I had none.

In the garden of my youth
I tilled those Roses sweet.
I carefully tore out the weeds
To keep my garden neat.

In the garden of our love dear
I sometimes let the grass grow long.
An unseen Rose was left to die
Neglected and alone.

In the garden of my wisdom
I can tell them all apart.
I don't allow the weeds to hide
The roses in my heart.

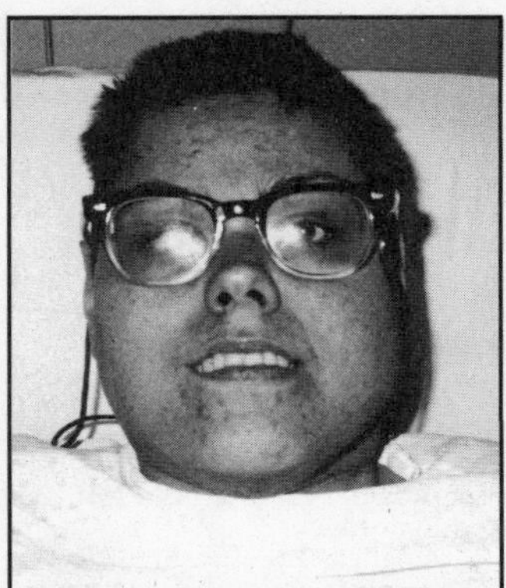

Joseph Peter Liotta Junior

Joseph Peter Liotta Junior
ODE TO THE NURSING STAFF

To my family and to Elizabeth Herr, Massachusetts General Hospital Nurse.

There is a very special team of professionals,
hard at work, on the 9th floor!
Top flight in the Ranks of the Nursing Corp.

They can make your bed, without a wrinkle,
and they are a flash with the urinal,
When you have to tinkle!

If you ask them nicely, they will set up your meal tray!
(But, as to what is underneath the cover? You had just better "Pray!"
(Because only "GOD" has an answer to your inquiry!)"

Pills? They dispense with a lightening speed,
(keys willing.)
and they are always there with a bedpan, should you feel "that" need!

Taking your pulse? You will find this a Pleasure!
But while you are looking at them?
It is impossible to measure!

When asked by the doctor, for their "helping hand?"
GOD forbid!
They should refuse "this Command!"

They would be quick to fill the doctor's "Medicinal order,"
but, discerning his prescription blank shorthand?
That is a feat the "Nursing school" never taught her!"

Taking your blood pressure? It is "no problem" when it arises!
But "locating" a stethoscope?
That is a "chore" she despises!"

When mid-day winds around? It is time for her break,
the coffee is usually at hand,
but, must be fresh, for the patient's sake!

When afternoon comes, and it is time for the "Shift Change?"
better remember "Who did What?"
or your in for a "scene"
that most would consider "Quite Strange" who is giving report?

When evening comes up and, the help grows short?
It becomes the "task" of the "Supervisors" to check on the
"troops in the "fort!"

Two, there are, but not a "Tardy" visitor crosses. Should any dare try!
They would quickly discover, just who the "Boss" is.
(The Blue Coats are coming! The Blue Coats are coming!)
(Security!)

As you "Serenely" sleep, While recovering from illness, take heed!
lest you hear! "It is your night nurse," while handing you, your "sleeping pill" and a small bottle, she says
"I need a urine specimen!" "Here! Fill this!"

As the nurse on duty has charge of your "health"
better do as she wishes else,
lose your wealth!

"To sum this all up, When the patient is cured "Stat"
Give praise to the, "Nurse"
Because? that is where it is at!"

Perhaps you are, bored or find it "hard to cope?"
"The Recreational Therapist,"
is there to handle your hope!"

She is an expert at curing your "ills!"
Just ask it of her,
and she will fix all your "hills!"
Muffy! is her name, and she knows all the "right" ways!
For handling your "problems,"
in just a way that "pays!"

If "checkers" is your game, or, "cards" are your game!
She has a lot of these,
and makes them available your mood tames!"

Suppers in the "Penthouse" she handles each week,
just bring your appetites

if it is, satisfaction you seek.

Volunteers abound, if you need their advice,
they know their jobs,
So you need not ask twice.

Mary Nolan Moran

A MESSAGE—1979

Ring out, O Bells!
This is the Year of Peace and
The Message of Good News
Has been brought to the land.

O Bells, Ring!
With sounds of Peace.
Soft as a dove's cry.
May they never cease!
Bells, Ring out!
A certain Prince, a Pope,
Told of the Child Who brought
The Gift of Hope.

Ring, Ring, O Bells!
For the people who came to see
Had Hope in their eyes,
Hope that all may be free.

O, Bells, Ring, Ring
The Story of the Child.
Tell it once again to the World.
Always new, never old.

Ring out, O Bells!
A Prince told the story
of Peace. Told of the Child
Who gave us the Promise of Glory.

E J English

BATTLE OF THE THUNDERHEADS

Was a dry autumn day the overcast skies were a dismal death color gray. All life appears to have came to a stop. A slight breeze barely moved in the tree tops. All of the creatures disappeared from sight, as if sensing the coming of a terrible fight. Like two gigantic ships slithering through the gray dawn gliding across a calm sea, two giant thunderheads were closing on each other. Neither would turn away as they approached on a collision course.

The calm was broken as by the sounds of a thousand horse drawn chariots racing across the skies, accompanied by the drum roll of a hundred drummers calling for the battle to begin. As the thunderheads closed the distance between them blinding lightning bolts would hurl from one to the other like cannons of mighty war ships.

Blinding flashes lit the gray skies followed by explosions that shook the earth. Still neither would change course, the savage battle raged distance closing until finally the collision took place.

Blinding lightning flashed followed by explosion after explosion, the sky lit up as if a ton of fire works had exploded. Tornado winds whipped leaves from the trees sent branches crashing to the ground.

Slowly the thunderheads began to disappear like two mighty battle ships lost on the high sea, without a trace of where they used to be.

The battle was over, a soft gentle rain floated down.

Margaret E Starr

MY GARDEN

I walked in my garden this morning
My garden all dripping with dew
Each rose, each lily, each daisy,
reminded me so much of you.
Up the pathways and down them I
wandered
To touch each petal I knew
Breathe in the fragrance of nectar
That reminded me too of you.

Beyond the woods they were
calling
The sleepy thrushes for you
Beyond the mists of the meadows
Comes the sun shining golden and
new.

Then I hurried out of my garden
Back up the pathways I flew
For instantly I remembered
There were daily tasks to do.

Amy Dawn Welch

MR. LUNA

It happened on December Eleven
Dear Mr. Luna has past on to
Heaven
I feel sad
But maybe I should feel glad
It was what he wanted
It was within his power
Now he is no longer here to deal
With life throughout the hour
I'm very upset
But I'm learning to deal
At times anger is what I feel
I think "How can he do this"
Doesn't he know he'll be sadly
missed
Then I stop and say to myself
"This is a bad dream, I'll soon wake
up"
But it never happens
Face reality!
Get a grip on things
He's up in Heaven hearing the
Angels sing
One day I'll die
I'll join him up there
I'll tell him I was one of
Those friends who really cared.

Leslie Dupree

LARA

To my Daughter—my life, my friend

Your name has always meant love,
even before you were a person.
Now that we know you, the name
comes to life—like fresh snow on
the pines at the top of the highest
mountains.
Through all seasons, you slolum in
and out of the hearts of all
mankind—a true gift, not a
learned art.
Life is full of wonder for you, yet
I'm sure the world stands in awe
of your snowy innocence.
Love,
Mom

Kenya Berryman

THEE ENDLESS MUSIC OF LOVE

I often wonder what Mother Earth was trying to say to me. I never took the time to really listen. Until I found my trueself everything which Mother Earth tuned herself into was filled with endless music of love. The trees, birds, and rivers all have parts to play in the endless music of love. I once couldn'thear, see, or feel her beauty until I found my trueself even the butterfly with its colorful wings and its silent movements plays a soft rhythm beat. My trueself is thirsty and longing for free expression of Gods love. I now can hear, see, and feel Mother Earths gifts to me as thee rainbow curtains open for the sun to make its grand entrance to lead thee endless music band of love. I sit quietly and listen. Oh God they are all playing a symphony for me.

Dorothy Irene Shaw

Dorothy Irene Shaw

BIRDS

Birds are such a joy to me,
I thoroughly enjoy the beautiful
colors amongst the trees.

In fall the harvest golden beauty
burnished bright,
The sky is ladened with thousands
of ducks and geese in flight.

We often wonder how they know,
Migration is a must to escape the
cold and snow.

And yet there is the open season,
The firing of guns, I feel for no
reason.

For some it seems to be for prey,
And walk away and leave them lay.

The population of many birds is
now extinct,
It's time now for everyone to stop
and think.

Before one last call is made,
The trees will be standing for their
shade.

And in spite of the grumblers who
stand about,
Somehow, it seems all things work
out.

The calling of geese will continue
from a twilight sky,
We'll see their wings in rhythm
passing by.

Alice E Strobl

THE PLACES THAT I VISIT

As a child, with my parents, I took
trips each year.
In 1937 off we went to Flagstaff by
train,
To see Grand Canyon under the
sun not rain.
Since my Dad was a railroader, we
got to travel far and near.

The 1939 fair in San Francisco was
our next trip.
Then on to Yellowstone and Old
Faithful would be seen.
I can give all you vacationers a tip.
See your own country first, in the
Winter or
Summer when it is green.

1940 came the New York fair and
the Eastern coast.
1955 Lookout Mountain in
Tennessee, and to Florida with
its beauty.
I'm glad that I can boast,
I've learned to enjoy the USA early.

Now at sixty five, I'm going places
I haven't been.
There is so much yet to be seen.
This year I hope to visit and see,
And learn all of the rich history of
Albuquerque and Santa Fe.

Ruth A Raymond Costello

WHAT FEELING—THIS?

Feelings of love and friendship
Feelings of joy and grief
Some feelings last forever
And some are very brief.

And then, there are those feelings
that seem to defy description.

overjoyed
overwhelmed
awed amazement
ecstatic elation

UNEQUALED

However many words come to
mind
there is no one word
that can describe
the total
all consuming feeling
that comes from one human life
pushing another
into wordly existance.

Only a mother could understand.

Donna L Kyser

YOU

Dedicated to my family. I could not have done it without you.

You are the one who makes my
whole life shine.
You are the one who makes the
tears fade one by one.
You are the one who turns my grey
skies blue.

You are the one who makes the sun shine through and through.
You light up my life with the glance of your smile, or the warmth of your touch, just once in awhile.
You are the one whose kisses taste sweeter than wine, and whose skin is as soft as roses on a vine.
If I could have one wish, it would be to always be near you, with you, you see.
I love you so much and I need you so dear, I would do anything to have you near.
So, don't fret my love, for you can see, you still are number one to me!

Lottie Lavanna Parks

MY DADDY

There my dad sits on the porch
Waiting for the sun
As it beams across the way
I know the day's begun

Although this day won't be for him
As full as days gone by
He will just sit and watch the birds
And hear their lullabye

For all his life he's worked so hard
His fingers to the bone
But when the sun was sinking low
So tired he would hurry home
But you see the day for him
Was not yet always done
There was wood to cut, cattle to feed
He was always on the run

He's plowed the fields, worked the mines
A carpenter he was too
There wasn't a thing pertaining to work
That my dad couldn't do

So as he sits there on the porch
His silver hair I see
But just to watch him every day
Means all the world to me

Mary Lunsford Cory

FREEDOM

Dedicated to my children: Patricia Kay, Kris, Teresa, Kent, Rohn, and RuDeena Elise, for helping me have time to write.

I came up on a sparrow once,
Entangled in bailing twine.
His heart was pounding madly,
Life, lost a sense of time.

He wasn't such a pretty bird.
But precious in heaven's sight.
For God had created his soul,
To enjoy his earthly flight.

His sparkling eyes were thankful,
Could family be near by?
Remembering tiny babies,
He gave a chirp and a sigh.

I helped to free his tiny feet.
While wish'in he were mine!
I knew sometime again we'd meet.
When he will speak sublime!

James Russell

THE WOMAN

There is this woman I know of
She's pretty as can be.
Whenever I gaze upon her
I feel she belongs just to me
I really adore her beauty
She really stands so tall
This woman never changes
In Winter Spring or Fall

If she ever spoke I'd be startled,
But, I'd be happy as can be.
Because this beautiful woman I
Speak of is the—
Statue of Liberty

Louise Berkowitz Haselkorn

WINTER

To Mother and Dad, to my husband Arthur, to my children Gitelle and Zev with much love.

Star white saphire dots,
heavens ink blotted
galaxies of
light.

Snow pillowed mountains cover
a frozen city
quiet and
still.

Waves bite ocean shores
and majestic eagles
soar above
clouds.

Bonnie Ingraham-Smithback

PERHAPS

Life was never meant to
be barren and fruitless.
People were made to work,
to do, to be used up.
To leave something behind them
as payment for having existed.
Have I failed?

Gregory Spindler Brown

WHAT SUN AND MOON APPEAR

As the sun approaches
On the sky abound,
Many powerful glimmers suddenly
Fill the sky so bright.
The moon appears from
Beginning of day, to ending
Of night. It shines so
Brightly from reflected sun;
Never knowing in day it
Can't be seen.

The sun and moon seem
Both to be here for only
Half a day; yet they
Both are here twenty-four
Hours a day. They both
Are spheres of interest
And awe; they are the
Objects which we always
Saw.

Lonita Krantz

MY SWEET GRANDMA

What a woman you've been,
Through life with it's sin.
Never a backward glance,
When life is so full of chance.
You've taught your children moral conduct, even in strife.
This you know, as you depart this life.
Never has one stood so tall,
As you, my sweet Grandma.
A large family you've raised.
Through all kinds of times, the Lord, you've praised.
You go on, with the faith you've always had.
We will be sad.
But again now, you can be with Grandpa.
. . . My sweet Grandma.

Mae Brewster

ANOTHER TOMORROW

To Bessie Lynn (my little sister)

The lights were bright when we walked in.
The vision in my sight, was a dull dim.

The way I held her hand and looked in her
eyes I knew I was not wrong.
For the ache in my heart was strong.

She gave me a hug and said good-bye.
I thought then I was going to die.

The tears fell to my cheeks,
For I could not speak.

Away she ran and not once looked back.
I thought then, there's a girl with some tack.

I thought my heart would be nothing but blisters.
As I heard the plane leave with my little sister.

When I walked into the night, the cold rain
Hit my face with all it's sorrow.
But I held my head high, and with a grin
And her memories, I knew I could face Another Tomorrow.

Kim Huncheck

SILENT LOVE

There you sit in your silence,
Here I sit in mine.
We're as much alone together,
As if we were apart.

I long to reach out and touch you,
To hold you in my arms.
Instead, I remain sitting quietly,
For my fear of rejection is strong.

Wouldn't it be much easier,
If we could read each others mind?
Be able to reveal, without using words,
What we're feeling inside.

But that of course, isn't possible,
So now what can we do?
To break down this wall between us,
And let each other through????

Michelle Blemur

MARTIN LUTHER KING JR

Martin Luther King
the man who stood for thing Peace.

He cared not for violence;
But for the love and kindness of humanity.
He was a man with a lot of bravery,
and did not believe in slavery.
He believed that his brothers and
sisters should be free and that
he held the key to equality.
He believed that we should live as a
neighborhood, where we are united in brotherhood.

Not by the color of our skin, or the state we
are in;
Because in God's eyes we are all one shade.

Mary Morris Mikkola

A FAR COUNTRY

Reluctantly the sun begins his daily climb
Out of gray mists as the bustling wind
Sweeps cloudlets from the sky.
Down the lane a waking Meadow-lark
Chirps softly to his sleepy mate
The trills "good morning" to her where she nests
While practicing his scales to keep in tune.
The day's begun, sun-burnished, new,
And I am wondering, now you've gone.
If you can hear the whir of bird wings as they pass,
Or drone of bees returning, laden, to the hives;
If fish leap silver in the streams
And if arbutusairs are soft and sweet;
If golden languor overwhelms the sense
And you. At ease, lie down
And fall asleep to dream of me?

Ceil Spitalny

PLANS FOR THE BEST IS MY REQUEST

Thanks for this opportunity
To show if we can be lucky
It is important to get along with all
When we do we can stand tall.
We all believe in the same G-d often in a different way
Remember this—avoid dismay.
At times we help each other, use appreciation
This can aid many a nation.
To remind all takes careful planning
Seeds that lead to understanding.
We're all brothers and sisters under the skin
So we should manage without sin.
Can we reach the endless shores
Convince all there's no need for wars?

Too much of sweets of the wrong kind
Causes lack of needed and the best rind
Fruit and natural food and juice
That should be planned for our use.
Yes the mind is affected by this
Please see that we don't miss.
Natural food and positive moral
Can help us become a good pal.
Hope all can be in harmony
Is the wish of wrighter Ceil Spitalny.

Mae Jean Sheerin
COME TO ME, MY CHILD

I heard You, Jesus, when You called,
My whole being became enthralled.
It was more an impression, but O so tender,
That to You my heart I did surrender.
Your Presence felt like flowing ointment warm and sweet,
Poured over my head and going down to my feet.
I saw a bright, white light, but could not see Your face.
Your touch startled me, then I felt Your loving embrace,
As You made Your Presence known.
I was standing, then knelt before Your throne.
You called me Your child saying, "Come to Me."
"I have waited patiently to bless thee."
My heart was racing, but my voice kept singing,
For my heart overflowed with the joy You were bringing.
"Come, My child, give Me your burden, worry and care."
"I have come to answer your prayer."
I dropped my heavy load at His nail-scarred feet.
His wonderful peace swept over me with ecstasy complete.
He washed me clean of all iniquity and sin that day,
And said, "I will never leave you. I AM with you always."
"Go forth now, My child, My Word you will teach,"
"To the nations I send you to preach."
"Lift up My banner, to My cross they must come."
"Tell them, I AM the Door to My Father's Kingdom."

Lee Deline
THE WANDERING RIVER

The lazy wandering river flows ever on and on,
Beautiful at sunset or in the golden dawn.
Gray rocks line the borders of the river banks,
Oaks and towering maples bow their heads in thanks.

Amber water foams around the windy rocky shore,
Laying down a river bed much wider than before.
On through heavy forest, in softest twilight shade
The stream meanders onward through the wooded glade.

Still the wandering river flows ever on and on,
Beautiful at sunset or in the golden dawn.
Then across the meadow it idles, slow and lazy,
Mirroring along its banks a blue flag or a daisy.

Yet my wandering river flows ever on and on,
Beautiful at sunset or in the golden dawn.
Growing older through the years, with each passing day,
With its gentle power it pushes on its way.

Jessie Johnson Young
STRAY DOGS

Stray dogs are a nuisance
But some touch your heart;
Like the one this morning
I met by the park.

He was ranty, dirty,
His tail hung way down;
He had no confidence
As he loaped through town.

But his eyes were friendly—
His tail tried to wag.
Instantly, I loved him
That homeless old hag.

The more we strolled the more
I dreaded to part
With that poor old creature
Who had touched my heart.

But the sad, sad part is
I simply can't own
All abandoned dogs who—
Sadly walk alone.

Erick De Serio
IF YOU LEAVE

To my beautiful Jackie, whom I love with all my heart

If you should leave at any one day
Just remember the memories
We shared our special way

You touched me some where
With such love and care
That went straight to my heart
From the very start

You wiped away the tear
That filled my eye with fear
And brightened my days
With your loving ways

As for the love we made
behind the closed shade
It would be tops on the list
Of the things I'd miss

So if you leave, the pain I can't hide
Cause it cuts so deep, like a bullet
in my side
Our true love, to me is the best
And it will stay in my heart above the rest
And the memories we share, I'll cherish and hold
Deep within my heart, till I'm gray and old

Edith M DeBusk
THE DEER HUNTERS

To my husband Leo, son's, Bob and Jerry, whom I love dearly!

"Time to go deer hunting, my husband says to me;
and with our two son's, that makes three.
I don't like to see them go,
as all day long I worry so.
Sitting on a stump with their feet on the ground;
trying so hard not to make a sound.
How can they do this on a cold windy day?
God keep them from all harm I pray.
Makes no difference if I say no;
they are out there after a buck or doe.
What a thrill to them when a deer comes in sight;
and they try to get it with all their might.
If they don't succeed I won't care;
keep them from harm dear God, please answer my prayer!
If they bring one home, how happy they will be;
and their smiling faces I love to see.
Why do I worry about these three?
Because I'm wife and mother,
and they are <u>dear</u> to me!

Kathy E Ward
THE SKY AND YOU

For you Jim; my love my friend

When you touch me its like that
Of the gentleness of a cloud
Floating in the eternal sky.

When you are mad its like that
Of a violent storm, wondering will it ever end.

When you look into my eyes its
Like the color of the sky on
The very first day of spring.

When I look at the stars at
Twight light time it reminds
Me of all the good things you have given to me.

When I gaze at the moon it.
Reminds me of the sadness which is
Sometimes written all over your face.

But most of all I love the sky, because
I know it will always be there;
Just like you.

I do love the sky
Can you understand why?

Leonie L Wade ("Dani")
TWO STAND ALONE

Dedicated to: Eugene P. Wade ("Danny") my charming Husband, wonderful lover, and inspirational friend! I Luv U, dear.

In all the world, two stand alone
different in many ways.
One thing they share, between them, there
a lo̊ve, a life, that stays.

Though different in the lives they lead,
they're like in many ways.
Fights come about, they cry, they pout,
the love it hides away.

The two they strive, for what they got
to keep the love at hold.
As days go by, love seems to die.
Each others all they know.

These two, alot, has passed them by,
more than they'll ever know.
For what they bare, a love so rare,
Each others all they hold.

Peggy B Trueblood
THE SHORE OF TIME

In memory of my sister—Jackie Ward

I stand upon the shore of time and watch the waves go by.
Some are small, some are great-such as the trials of you and I.
I shade my eyes and look afar out where the water is so deep.
And I know that's where I must go if I would His commandments keep.

But out there's where the storms do rage and ships are tossed to and fro.
Oft-time they meet great tragedy, but onward, onward they must go.
I walk on down the shore of time so careful each step that I take.
Knowing that if I would do His will, I must the right decisions make.

I turn again and look afar and I hear the Master call.
"Fear not, my child, be not afraid, I've walked upon the shore of time,
I've walked upon the sea, I've calmed the storms,
And I've stilled the winds, and surely I'll watch over thee."

I took a step from the shore and then I took another,
Oh, the cool refreshing flow as I went on even further.
Jesus walked beside me all the way as the water got deeper and deeper,
Keep trusting me, I'm guiding thee, I'm your Shield, I'm your Rock,
I'm your Keeper.

The water has become more shallow now, I can see the other shore.
The lights are softly glowing, and my heart is aburst with joy!
I'm Home, I'm Home, I'm Home at last; the storms are in the past.
Safe in the Home He's prepared for me, Praise the Lord, Praise the Lord,
I'm Home at last.

Brenda (Jeanette) Murphy
EVE OF A VOYAGE

When night divides the sky,
Darkness and I become a team.
It controls the world as I lie,
Leaving me only to dream.

I don't have to worry about yesterday,
I just let my mind open wide.
The walls fall down and I fly away,
I go so far but stay inside.

It's a dark blue sky
Where nothing can get through.
It's where I fantisize,
It's the lace I belong to.

The sails are never hard to find,
They have a peaceful feeling.
It's so hard to explain,
It's how I live, just by dreaming.

It's the eve of my voyage,
Forever and on sailing.
It's something I've earned,
Here there is no failing.

Vina Hurst
THE ROSE THAT NEVER WAS

To God: Infinite-Rhyme, of the universe!

From the living-branch, I cut the rosebud
And placed it in a crystal vase.
Then nutured it, with food and water,
To coax a pink-bloom, to it's face!

There was promise in this infant-beauty.
A gentle fragrance, touched the air.
Then, tightly closed, it slowly withered;
Bending low, as if in prayer!

Strange as it seems, I kept the rosebud
Pressed inside, a large old-book.
It died, leaving; but a few stained pages
And a served-no-purpose, look!

Yet the rosebush blooms; with roots held-firmly
Fed by the earth and moist from rain.
Although one season ends, with petals-falling,
Another comes, it blooms again!

Could this symbolize, the human spirit?
In analogy, it gave me pause . . .
Did God, create the rosebud for a rose
Or; for the rose that never, was?

George William Fatzinger
A TRIBUTE TO MOM

I love you Mom for all you do
The way you show you care
For warmth and love and happy thoughts
I know are always there.

Your strength is never ending
It's with me every day
The way I act, the love I show
Is patterned from your way

So this poem is for you, Mom
And all my thoughts are, too
Since my whole life can show the world
The love I've learned from you.

Debra Ann Barnes
DANCING DAFFODILS

I dedicate this to my Grandmother, Estella Barnes, for the years we had together, the love we shared, and the memories I hold dear to me.

Flow gently graceful daffodil,
Soft, silky petals fluttering in the wind.
Fair is that flower which dances in the breeze,
Vibrant colors beaming with charm, with life.

"I will teach you the dance", said she.
"And the dance will go on
Even after I am gone
Because I live in you,
And you live in me."
We danced, danced, wherever we would go.
We danced until dusk.
We danced until dawn.
Then I turned around to find my grandmother gone.

Memories, like the flower, have been so long pressed
and preserved between the pages of my life.
When the nighttime turns into quiet reflection,
I pause—
Turn the pages of that book,
And take another sentimental look.
A joyous love grows within.
My soul cannot resist.
I fall asleep in a floating field,
My grandmother's dancing daffodil.

Harry Fuller III
FOR JEANNETTA

speak my name—
i hear the tender sound
of snowflakes falling;
the gentle sigh of moonbeams
penetrating the world of dreams.

speak my name—
i feel the ageless glory
of the sun rising within my soul;
the everywhereness that is
the power of the night.

speak my name—
i become a lavender vision
in the land of Sugar Trees;
a timeless being kneeling in
the shadow of your love.

speak my name—
i see the silver reflections
of my childhood laughter;
stars falling from the heavens;
their radiance overwhelmed by your own.

speak my name—
and i know the bliss
of a perpetual moment.

Mrs Henrietta-M-Stacy
AN ODE-TO-THE-DEATH-OF-ONES-MATE

A tender look you give.
Soft love words spoken only to me.
These are imprinted forever on my mind.
When you go from me and, leave me behind.

Death is so final, but it need not be.
I can bring you back to me.
A recalled gesture known to us two.
That truly sad I love you.
You go, I stay, but you are never far away.
I feel you close around me still.
My heart is at peace, for your spirit gives me release.
Till death do us part, are only words you see.
For you are still alive in the heart of me.

Leilani T C Brown
MY GUARDIAN ANGEL

This is for Mongo, my own guardian angel and for you Robin. The two special men in my life I will love always. And for Mom who gave me strength. I love you!

It's funny you know, how things work
People tell me that, your dead & gone
How can I believe, that's true?
Today I felt you,
You, were the extra warm rays of the sun,
You, were the extra bright smiles I met,
You, were the extra song in laughter I heard.
Yes my sweet, you were with me all day,
Tonight I see you,
Your in the shadows taking care of me,
Your in my dreams to make me sleep ever so peacefull
My own beautiful guardian angel
People tell me I should cry, because your gone.
No my sweet, I can not cry,
Because now you are closer than ever.
Now, you are mine completely.
Your the hope in my life, your the love in my heart
Your that special feeling for no reason at all.
Your the smile on my face, when everything goes wrong.
Your the song in my voice, when there's no hope
Oh yes, there are days when I wish I could, hold or touch you.
But then there are days when I know how near you are,
That . . . I love you most of all!!!

Amy Lynn Semock
LOVE AS IS

I walk through the valley and drift off to my world like I have a million times before.
My world revolves around you, you think my thoughts, dream my dreams and feel my feelings.
I feel helpless without you . . .
I want you by me, I need you by me. My darling, my God . . . I love you.

Lucille Engstrom
LETTER TO ELAINE

To my sister, Elaine,

What is it with sisters when they grow up together,
they play, pretend and fight—no matter what the weather.

It may be important that we do not think the same.
We seek to find our own friends, pursue a quiet fame.

We leave the long-lived childhood and go our separate ways,
think of each other as we approach the golden days.

Each hand that I am dealt by life brings you to my mind.
My memories grow tender with each photogragh I find.

Recollections of you—total pleasure and fondness,
adding up to the best love which I know God does bless.

Our babies grew up side by side in our younger days,
that was due to your planning and your persistent ways.

Your plans included others for every occasion.
Your caring always shared, abundant nuturation.

Thanks, you and yours, for all you have done for me and mine.
Years of enjoyment together—'til the end of time.

From your sister,
Lucille

P M Meerleveld
FOR MY NIECE

In loving memory of Cassandra Ann

One day she arrived, blonde hair and blue eyed
Into our lives she came
She stayed but two days, then went away
Leaving our hearts in pain.
Cassandra Ann we love you
We wished you stayed with us
But since God called you to Him
We send you all our love.
A glance she gave to her daddy
Goodbye she seemed to say
And then a few moments after
She gently passed away.
Cassandra Ann we miss you
But time will heal the pain
Our minds and hearts will keep you
Until we meet again.
We'll never see you sitting
Upon your daddy's knee
Or playing with your brother
In the front yard tree.
But I know we'll be together
In heaven's paradise
And so, dear one, please save us
A place right by your side.

Love,
your Aunt Pat

Paula Kasparik
HONEYSUCKLE TIME

Honeysuckle, the soft beige of rich cream, green vines running rampant along a wooden rail fence on a hot summer day.

With closed eyes I inhale deeply. The fragrance lingers in the air, sweeter than the perfume of kings.

I listen to the soft hum of a fat bumble bee, as he takes his fill of sweet nectar.The warm days are filled with the sound of birds singing.

I chase a butterfly across a newly plowed field. The soil is hot beneath my bare feet. The nights are lighted by the moon, and the stars shine while the sun go to sleeps.

The daylight animals go to bed and the nighttime ones take over.The chirping of crickets, the hoot hoot of the brown owl that lives in the rafters of the old barn, and the mournful baying of an old hound dog as he trees a coon in the swamp beyond the corn field.

I love honeysuckle time in the deep south. I close my eyes and go to sleep, lulled into dreamland by a soft southern breeze, in the live oak trees.

Anne Gardner
TO CAPTURE LOVE

To my love, with whom I "CAPTURED LOVE"

It's fading away in the evening light,
this beautiful day filled with love so right.
But let's hold on to this beautiful day
and never, never, let it slip away;

Then we can recall the laughter and smiles
that we shared today for a little while,
Along with our love, our hopes and our dreams
and a love for life that happiness brings.

If we catch each moment and lock it up tight
we can share it again in tomorrow's light.

Then we'll go to our bed hand-in-hand
and search for our nighttime fantasy land.
And when we find it we'll lasso, as such,
each kiss, each sigh, each gentle touch,
each precious moment of a love so deep
that we may never, never sleep.

And then we'll have captured, or so it seems,
love and smiles and hopes and dreams,
And kisses and sighs and the gentle touch,
that remind me of you whom I love so much.

Elaine M Rosekat
PLEASE! STOP AND THINK

To David

The sun is shining. It's a beautiful day,
But you can't see it, because you've gone away
You thought no one loved you or cared,
Forgetting the good times we shared
We had no idea of your troubled mind,
Now all we have are memories, left behind.
If only there was something we could have done or said,
It's too late now because you are dead
The "it's," "whys" and "maybe's" go through our mind.
But at that time, we seemed to be blind
We are reminded of you every day,
By something we see, or hear someone say
Sometimes it makes us laugh, sometimes cry,
Sometimes shake our head's and say: "why," "why," "why"
To all who have suicide in mind,
Please! think of those that you leave behind.
Life is not all unfair,
Some of us do care
Think of all the thing's you will miss,
A tender touch, a loving kiss
Count your blessings, I'm sure there are some,
If not, better days to come
Stop, and think of what I have said.
For you are a long time dead.

Allan F Peever
CREATION

To my loving wife Vera for all her help and patience

Lament of a Lonely Heart
In another world another time
Dear you belonged to me
And that is why I'm shackled now
to these memories
I loved you then as I love you still
though your no longer mine
our lifes not Hearts where parted dear
in that stream called time
perhaps some day we'll meet again
somewhere on that great sea.
And our lifes and hearts shall join once more
forever yours and mine

Kellie Greene!
DADDY

To my very dear friend, for believing in me. Thank you, Mary!

My saddest memory: a man stands against the sink,
in a small cabin's kitchen, against a warm, dim light;
he stands there, his shoulders slouched, one hand
holding the counter, the other holding a beer. Willie
Nelson sings softly from the radio about cowboys,
country ways, and broken hearts; and this man's head
hangs low. His face, his rugged, handsome face,
expresses an anguish that is deep and hidden; one that
is as old as he, or at least as old as me.
I look at him, he looks at me, and for all the
emotion caught in this stare, not a word comes from
our lips. I don't know why and he doesn't know why,
but all we can do is fight back our tears.

Fern Hall
ANOTHER CORD TO CUT

"Train up a child the way she should go."
The Way? Babe that I was I did not know.
When she was a child the way looked clear,
But somehow grew dim from day to year.
Where did she go? Out of my reach.
Why so soon? Still much to teach.
Many dangers, much to fear,
Too late though, wipe that tear.
The world and child feel contempt
For protective parent. They make us exempt.
Must let go, cut the ties,
Painful, part of me dies.
Is to love to let go?
My child says so!
Do I forsake mine, is she leaving me?
Would it be clear if I wanted to see?
Nine months in womb, cord to sever.
Some dependence is not forever.
Has time now come to cut another tie?
Unlike mother, the child does not cry.
Did I ignore a warning sign?
Has dependence switched and become mine?
I must let go in order to hold!
Oh child of mine, you have grown so bold.

Michelle N Smith
WIND

This poem is dedicated to my loving grandparents, Ed and Barb Smith, Adeline Hoffman

---

Windy weather time,
Open your mouth and say a word
but, none shall be heard.

Lamar Dennis
QUOD

To Mother & Father who has given me their loving support through my hardships

---

I am like a wounded bird that has fallen from its nest amongst its tree,
I am like a fish—captured within the depths of the sea.
My strength has been weakened like a dying flame, I've been reaped of my title—a number now my name.
My days have become darkened like a shadow thru its darkest hour.
Where inside this concrete beast I have been devoured.
Here I lay like an ash spread thick into the aging dust.
Pressed into a corner and left only to rust.
But in my heart—God remains strong.
He fills me with his devine love—and there places a song

Linda K Worrell
THE MAGIC OF A STORY

She sat quietly beside me
As I opened up the book.
Her eyes alert, her hands so still.
She had a special look.

The words I read were magic
To the child who shared my chair.
She heard the story come to life
As if she were right there.

No pictures did I show her,
No T.V. screen entrancing,
Just the printed pages of the book,
And words upon them, dancing.

I can only try to imagine
The pictures in her mind,
As she listened to me reading,
While the story did unwind.

And when the tale was finished,
And the book back in its place,
The magic of that story
Was written on her face.

Denella

George Lorencz
QUESTIONS

Denella Ann Lorencz December 16, 1967-March 20, 1985

Think of me when I die
as the rainbow in the sky.

Will all the people I know
below
Think of me as a friend or
foe.

Will they walk past my soul
as it rests,
and never forget the memories
we possess.

Please don't say it's not
fair,
just because I am no longer
there.

But does my death really matter?
Will it leave their lives
in tatter?

I promise you this .. my
goodbye kiss.
I'll watch over you all,
try to guide you when you
fall!

But do me one last favor,
These words try and savor.

Think of me after I die
as the rainbow in the sky.

Ernest A Rojas
GHETTO LIFE

To my loving wife & daughter (Cindy & Deidre Marie) who makes each morning worth waking-up for.

I've tasted the breeze
I've tasted the earth
I've fell to my knees
With my face in the dirt . . .

I've felt all the pain
Where there's no dance or song
Where life has no gain
Where life is all wrong . . .

This is life in the projects
And its no pretty sight
You'll wonder who'll die next
Who'll live through the night . . .

When drugs on the roll
Is a born way of life
Where death takes its toll
If you live by the knife . . .

Life here is realistic
Cause it happened to me
Now I'm just a statistic
From the projects—you see . . .

Miss Jacqueline M Rist
DECISIONS

To my very close and special friends... L.M. J.R. M.B. C.T. R.B. H.S. and especialy J.W.R. & P.C.R.

Though some may not be hard to make, the easy ones may not always be the right ones.
How do you know if you've made the right one?
Will someone tell you, or is it by trial and error that you come to realize it?
We've all made some decisions in our past and are going to continue making them in the future.
Never regret your choice, for there is a reason why it was made even though you don't see it now.
The choices we make now are the building blocks by which we walk on towards our future goals.
Make a decision and follow it, for those who do not regret their decisions will be better prepared for what the future holds...

One decision at a time.

B K Parscale-Meyer
WEE, TINY, AND SMALL

There was a little teddybear, so tiny and small,
He almost wasn't one at all.
He belonged to a little girl, tiny and wee,
Who lived neath the roots of a chestnut tree.
With hair so fine and curly you know,
It was almost the color of new fallen snow.
They play for hours under the sun,
Until the stars twinkle, and the day is done.
They eat a supper of apples and honey,
And drink all their milk, as quick as a bunny.
With a jump and a hop, into bed they would go,
And dream, the dreams, only children would know.
Then in the morn, when the birds would sing,
These two would awaken, happy and smiling.
Then up to a breakfast of berries and tea;
With crackers and honey. As pure as can be.
Then out to the sunshine, to play in the day,
With giggles and laughter, sounding the way.
And then again when the day is done,
Home they will hurry on a run.
Through the grass, and through the flowers,
To the mighty chestnut towers.
Then down into the roots of the chestnut tree,
Go the little girl, and teddybear, tiny and wee.

Venash Yashwanth Singh
NIRVANA

Dedicated with love to my solicitous and loving parents: Thara and Koomar Singh (South Africa).

Slowly, oh so slowly I sank into that peaceful state,
A peaceful state without any hate,
Above worldly desires—greed and lust,
A state that made me want to trust,
I thought of Him,
and all else was dim.

The heavens were laid before me,
I was free, as free as free could be,
Our creator in all his might,
stood out like a guiding light,
This beautiful state of purity
made me experience a sense of security.
I felt eternal joy
that nothing and nobody could destroy.

Peace and tranquility had at last been attained,
The animal feelings had all been drained,
Pure of heart in His kingdom I stood,
for in this kingdom there was nought but good.

The music of the heavens filled the air
and removed all distress and despair.
My soul had flown and my spirits soared
in receipt of God's gracious reward.
The angels in their shining attire did gleam
and it seemed as if, I this all did dream.
Was it a dream?
No, this was the peaceful, tranquil state of Nirvana.

Barbara D Hill
PRECIOUS SCOUTS

Dedicated to Den 1, Pack 28-Clarksdale, Ms.

Seeing the sight of a boy,
Full of life, Full of joy,
Working hard for things they do,
Making everyone proud of you.
Seeing the world with different eyes,
Wanting to soar high as the skies.
All the scouts throughout the land
Working together hand in hand.
They always seem to have that zest
In helping others, doing their best.
As you grow from day to day,
Time will come to go your own way.
Keep in heart and keep in mind
For through the years you will find,
Being a scout played it's part
In what you hold in your heart.
Learning from you I give my thanks,
You all sincerely earned your ranks.

Charlene B Iversen
INNER PEACE

To T.J.M. Who wanted me to find happiness, and I have.

Reach out to help a friend in need.
Look beyond all that you Think you see.
Achieve new heights, and you'll succeed.
Be happy, and your soul is freed.

Find the land where love endures.
Love yourself with a heart so pure.
Let go your inhibitions, and open closed doors.
Search within, the answer's yours.

Henry Gorham
IF I HAD THREE WISHES

This poem is dedicated to the people of our world.

If I had but three wishes.
My first would be to last
I'd wish the world full of peace,
until eternity itself should pass.

My second would be outstanding,
as no man has ever seen
I'd wish for universal love.
To walk with eternal peace

At last I'd wish for togetherness in nature.
What a gift that would be
Then even as all life live.
It would be in perfect harmony.

Val Scott
MY BELOVED SISTER

Dedicated to my sister and friend Pam Jean Scott the memories will always be cherished.

From my heart a love I have,
So special and so pure.
The times we shared the laughs, the tears,
Our friendship was for sure.

Remembering her gifts to me:
Some small,
Some big, her smile.
Were everlasting, never fading, her love
Will last awhile.

The lessons learned of how to dress,
Of how to comb my hair.
The secrets told about the stars,
The stories told with care.

The times we fought when playing games,
At times when jumping rope,
I'd go and sit with streaming tears
She'd come and offer hope.

But after years of life we shared,
My friend she did depart.
T'was not my choice, but hers.
She chose to stop her heart.

My sister dear, my sister love, among
The stars you are.
I thank you for the secrets told
I know you are not far.

Roosevelt Brinson
AN INSPIRING LOVING AND WISE GOD OF TRUTH

Dedicated in behalf of our loving Creator, whom truly aids those that glorify his name and does his bidding.

THE GOD OF TRUTH, how

wonderful he is. A lie he has never concur, on him beyond a doubt there
is no compare: He conceals no earthly matter of shady deals, himself

he does not deny: His power is absolute

and he will remain on high

Because he is SUPREME and will never
expire; He has unending LOVE that will
never conspire to untruth of him in which men have lied; his word is SWEETER
Than Balsom and Myrrh, In him there
is nothing cunning or sly; and nothing
devious, some wonder why: It is because of
the truth he inspires.

The father is never devious and will never die, because truly he is more wonderful than thy and will remain the apple of my eye:
Remember with him love will never die,
he is wonderful sweet and truly WISE.

Beulah M Cockrum
THE BIRDS
I love to watch the birds in flight
I love to watch them feed,
They are so very happy
Without a care or need.

They carry on their daily tasks
In such a business way,
Never shirking, always singing,
That really makes my day.

And as I watch those little birds
Flit through the air so gay
They're teaching me a lesson
That helps me on my way.

Don't worry about tomorrow
What will be—will be—
Gods eye is on the sparrow
And I know He cares for me.

Mrs Sally N Piner
THE BOOK OF MORMON
One day I descended the stairs from above
Not knowing what awaited below
A lady was sitting in a chair near the door,
A lady I had never met before.

If you don't believe the words I tell you
accept them in faith and you'll see,
The joy in your heart will shout to the world
His great love, His great love for thee.

Later I ascended the stairs from below
To my bedroom and there closed the door,
A book in my hand I pressed to my heart,
Held a secret I wanted to know.

The knowledge of Christ that inspires the heart
Reflects in one's face dear brother,
The love it does bring will cause you to sing
With joy in your heart forever.

Harriet A Barney
APARTHEID
Lord, when the shepherds came that Christmas night
Almost two thousand Bethlehem's ago
Some sheep they must have brought who were not white,
That walked with fleece unshriven through the snow.

So we, Infinite Infant, we are sheep—
See how we come shepherded by a star
To gaze upon omnipotential sleep
Here in the place where you and Mary are.

Some of us are white and some are not,
And some disdain the brother-hand;
But oh! lest all these things be forgot,
Show us the stable, make us understand

How through the desert with a single track
There came three kings—and one of them was black.

Luz Guzman Funes (Lucy)
A CHILD IS
A CHILD IS: A mind to shape,
A heart to love and teach to love.
Ears that hear, mouth which repeats;
Therefore what you sow, you'll also reap.
For a child will not do as you say,
He or She, will do as you do.
If you give honor, trust and love
And teach to love our God, above;
That child will surely love, trust, honor,
The ones who paved the way of life
For them, to act the same as they.
A CHILD IS NOT: Someone for lust
That knows no shame, nor cost.
They're not someone to tame,
Nor to spoil for gain.
A CHILD IS: A precious gem
That you must polish with great care.
A CHILD IS of God the voice,
If in their innocence you rejoice.
They're little angels in disguise.
They are my future and your future,
If we are patient, loving, wise;
Teach them with deeds as well as words
To be the masters of this world.
You were a child and so was I!

C J Walker
ELVIS
Early tide frosts the 'morn,
How do I understand;
Accomplishments made but not forlorn,
And for each the price is grand.

Who-or what-giveth to bring,
Each others love or sympathy;
Who can but pull the string,
To end success so brilliantly.

The mind rattles on—
The curtains fall—
Memories sweet song—
The end of it all.

I don't pretend—
To know or guess—
Why the beginning to end—
It's all a mess.

My heart won't forget—
My mind will linger on—
History's never ending debt—
For Elvis and his song.

Terri Elizabeth Young
The Soul
There is a man who is camoflauged
With checks, lines, and dots
People look at him
But receive him not
What color of skin he has,
Nobody knows.
He is a beautiful peacock
In his pose
He smiles but there is no laughter
He cries but there are no tears
Society sees his colors
But not his hopes, dreams, or fears
His texture of soul has been lost
In layers of mask
Does he really have feelings?
Is the question they ask
He does have feelings, he does!
He cannot show them
They are hid
The hurt and pain are there
Left as a memory of what he did
He loved and lost
He lived and died
They asked him who he was
What did he do?
He lied.

Maureen M Ward

Maureen M Ward
CAPTAIN, MY CAPTAIN

My love to those who remained after the curtain closed.

The endless waves of time wash in and out
As endless thoughts of you stay in my mind.

Oh Captain, my captain, where are you now?
What seas do you sail,
What storms have you weathered?

The docks where you land
The different worlds that you see,
Could your thoughts ever be on me?
Or are they crowded by all the fine
Places and people you meet.

Oh Captain, my captain, our time was so short.
You came in with the tide,
The moon still full as you sailed from sight.

Yet in that short time—
I traveled the seven seas through your eyes.
I felt the swaying of the ship beneath my feet
By the touch of your hand.

Oh Captain, my captain,
Shall I ever sail again?

Judith R Wade
KEEP CLIMBING, MY SON

To my son, Patrick, in hopes that all of your dreams come true.

Many a mom has shared the joy
That I am feeling tonight
For I am the one with a wonderful son
Who has soared in a flawless flight.
A son who fills my heart with love
And swells my pride-filled chest
A son who is my closest friend
Standing out, above the rest.
How fast my little boy grew tall,
Matured, in his young years—
Embarking in college 4 years ago
Now his graduation nears.
What will become of this child of mine
Where will be his niche in life,
Will he be strong, will he get along—
Amidst the trouble and the strife—
Will he hang on to all his dreams
For we planted them together,
And will he know, I love him so
Through calm and stormy weather. . .
God,
I am so thankful for my son
That you trusted in my keeping—
He has filled the album of my heart
And it's tears of joy I'm weeping.

Debra Denise Chavez
A LOT OF TIME WELL SPENT
A small cabin in the midst of a mountain
A sparkling brook nearby
And miles and miles of unused land
Flowers covering the countryside

The smell of dew in the morning
And beauty blows their scent
A thunderstorm at night time
It's alot of time well spent

Lying in front of a fireplace
And snug and warm besides
As winter blows, and snows
The windows fogged inside

Greg Tolbert
A WOMAN AND A FLOWER

To Diane, Charlie, and Shelia.

Beauty in both is one to see and feel.
Her face showing proudness, being expressed with the eyes;
Like a rose, at morning, opening to full size.
Knowing inside and outside the loveliness is real.

As a scented springtime bouquet one would caress,
Her features deliver and show their softness.
Always appreciating truth and respect,
Like the reflecting waterlilies the pond will not reject.

Creations like these are made from above,
Provided with a conscience to protect, same as the flowers leaves;
Both used for the feelings and needs.
As to show the world does have; the sense of love,
Not the use of excessive power.
But to view reality:
A Woman and a Flower.

Janet Doll
GIVING
Today I visited my heart
And pumped the blood of life
To my less fortunate brother.
Then I said "hello" To my kidneys
And willed them to another.
My eyes I willed to a little girl
Who has never seen the look of love
Or what the world is made of.
My soul to anyone who needs to feel
The love of laughter and life;—
Someone who's filled with sorrow & strife.
Take all of me and make good use;
Give to those who need.
And make my having lived—
Complete!

Michael A Laverell
A SAD STORY

To Pet Pals. You Give A Gift

I heard a sad story today
From a man who'd lost his way
He didn't ask which way to go
His destination he didn't know
Life had only rewarded one thing
Til shortly ago made his heart sing
Something dollar value once put upon
Yet another didn't exist under our sun
Day and night by his side
With danger near didn't try to hide
She never would even talk back
They shared the same knap sack
She was killed by a speeding truck
Pushing aside a child about to be struck
The driver never even slowed down
Speeding on into town
Gently lifting her to his breast
Beautiful in her final rest
Only he felt a killing pain
She being too young to be slain
His eyes began to fog
For his love, his dog

M E Minster-Poetsch
THE BECKONING
Peacefully yearning, my spirit is hungering,
To savor the wonders you bring.
Eagerly, with impatient senses, I'm beckoning,
To embrace you, elusive Spring.
patiently beckoning . . .
ANXIOUSLY BECKONING . . .
beckoning.

Dismal mute meadows long grown dreary,
To Heaven bare branches plead.
"Come clothe this nakedness, bleak and weary."
To Spring, zealous wind howls.
Will you heed?
silently beckoning . . .
RESONANTLY BECKONING . . . beckoning.

Gentle rain be temptress, lure crocus to bloom,
Entice daffodil, sweet violet, I cherish.
Torrents rouse Mother Earth's slumbering womb,
To sleep no more, 'ere we perish!
softly beckoning . . .
TUMULTOUSLY BECKONING . . . beckoning.

Last night while rain, the wind, and I slept,
Too silently for anyone to hear,
Elusive Spring to meadows and bare branches crept,
To surprise us, came early this year.
it was all THAT BECKONING . . .
beckoning.

Betty Terrill
LITTLE SUNSHINE, BY "MAW"

To my Grandson, Ryan

This little one, so dear to me,
Soon, will be turning three.

He brings joy to my heart,
This I cherish, since apart.
The clouds just disappear,
when little sunshine is near.
God knows how I feel,
as this is very real.
His little hands, clutched in mine,
what a smile, now that's sunshine!
Blessed him be all his life,
never knowing woe or strife.
Sent from heaven up above,
that we may know His love.
What have we here?
Someone very dear.
Little sunshine, let it be,
you reflect your light on me.
It's happiness with an "ah!"
When he looks up and says "-hi! maw!"
In thoughts all the while,
I have a picture of that smile.
Little sunshine, you guessed it right,
is in my prayers, every night.

Donna Marie Cowan

Donna Marie Cowan
GOING ON

To my mother, who always wanted me to be a writer. I love you mom.

It grieves my heart to let you go
But it must be done, in my heart I know
That if you don't return to me
T'was something never meant to be.

I tried so hard to be the way
I thought you needed every day
But the more I tried—you just seemed bored
And my needs went ignored.

Your excuse is "just your way"
Of getting 'round what you must say
So the words I needed never came
Now things simply aren't the same.

My heart is beating sad protest
Aching so within my chest
I just don't know how strong I'll be
Without you being here for me.

But I must try, for "Life goes on"
An old cliche, but a sad, true one
And my love for you will brightly burn
A glowing hope for your return.

Mrs Shirley Purdy
IN THE WOODS

I dedicate my poem In the Woods to Sylvia Arsenault my lovely daughter.

Down in the woods
Where the boughs are green
I saw the woodsmen chop
With a steady stroke
All the pine and all the oak.
The air was heavy with odours sweet
Of the woods I use to meet.
Wet and helpless the trees did fall
All the summer and all the fall.
Down in the woods
Where the boughs are green
The leaves are waxing their last scene.
The birds and squirrels will leave it too
There will be no home as
The richly tinted forest leaves
Are swept silently down
And make the forest moan
While the dusky silence fall
On the chopping of the woods.

Michele Lea Rogers
OUR FADING LOVE
I had a dream of you and me—
The light was so bright—we could hardly see.

You were calling my name from so far away—
Begging me to always stay.

The light was dim
Your voice was hushed.
Suddenly I felt my heart being crushed.

I stood there—cold, all alone
Your love no more I could call my own.

Your memory will be here forever more
Till this day, I just wish it hadn't ended this way.

Jeanne Perez
GREETINGS FROM THE VICAR

For Sean, because he will not have me sleep when I dream, and because the light of love in his eyes has become my own.

The vicar deared his Christmas cards
to friends and enemies,
Put envelopes to his tongue,
as wafers to the tongues of the body,
and sent them off,
like the cloaked body who knows what lies
behind the curtain of his white and tassled robe.

We, who were wished the spiritofchristmaswhichispeace,
jolt nightly to the wail of fetal screams,
our temples, over and over torn in two;
one stone screaming:
it was a mass of cells dividing, another:
one more child destined to die like Jesus.

So you, vicar, who wished us the joyofchristmaswhichishope,
tell us,
who was the hope of Jesus when the father abandoned him?
Borne down under the weighted sins of two,
we nearly drowned in that red Dead Sea salty.
Some of us rose from its chamber knowing life
in our reflections under the sunlit sky.
But never again will we hope in the trustworthy vicar,
to whom we whispered our secrets in night-quiet,
who would have these proclaimed on the rooftops,
to whom we gave the nails that fit our crosses.

Neda Albertson
SNOW

To Mrs. Yohe, my sixth grade teacher, and my mother who encouraged me to enter my poem.

Snow is a white blanket
Embroidered with young people
Romping and playing in it.
Some small snowmen smile
While you go past.
For children
The snow is a battlefield
But the weapons are—
SNOWBALLS!

Annette Mary Labutte
JERRY'S KIDS BALLAD OF M.D.

To Jerry Lewis for having the telephon every year and knowing all I can about. Pleased being a part of it by answering phones in my district. Also Andrew my fiance for encouragement and love.

My feet and legs will not walk or run on early morning lawn
For they were affected before they had a chance to greet the dawn
My hands and arms will not stretch to the sky they stay still by my side
My growth was stopped before I could record it on the wall
I won't see shores of life like I wish, or stand on a hill or talk the way I sometimes feel
That is what M.D will do
For M.D affects kids and adults and sometimes kills
One fine day Jerry Lewis took over he gives us all the hope to carry on when we sometimes feel despair
Every Labor Day he has a telephone and gets pledges, donations from all around the world
We go to hospitals and get medication we need
We use the electric wheel chair

which is like our legs we go
where we never went before
Learning to walk and talk
Moving our arms and hands
Some day we know we will beat
this M.D disease but not alone
We will walk on our own without
help
We will talk how we feel
We will stretch out our arms and
hands and reach for the sky
We will have our chance
For the victory will soon come
For we have Jerry and thousands
of others who really do care
For it is more Blessed to give than
to receive and the Lord will Bless
us all
Amen.

Marta L Fincke
THERE SHOULD BE A TURNING

Our Creator became our Saviour! This is dedicated to the living Christ who was "GOD with us," and who is God! And to His Gospel Message which bring's eternal life to all who believe it. Those who are rejecting God's Truth of redemption and salvation, risk the eternal loss of their souls. Others who deny His truths in nature in favor of supposed science (i.e. the "oppositions of science falsely so-called") are bringing ruin to America, and particularly the cattle under the evil practice of artificial insemination. True science respects that which is normal; false science has no law.

Someone should set their sights on
Christ
and bring Him into focus sharp
and clear
adjust the great lens of time a bit
take away the particles of dust
on that telescopic glass
and slowly turn the dial
to meet the eye just right
the eye of understanding
that brings God to the center
someone should set their sights on
Him

there should be a turning
to the One who is the very source
of Truth
the One from whom all wisdom
flows
for when learning pushes Him
aside
Knowledge disappears
and is soon seen to fail
and wise men cease being wise
and turn themselves into fools
instead
someone should set their sights on
God
and fix the lens of time in time

Barbara Lorraine Blecker
SPRINGS MAGIC

Something about the way the sun
shines in my heart
Every time of year when the snow
melting starts
Gives me a feeling and I soar to the
sky
And the soft blowing breeze brings
a tear to my eye

A magic works its way into my soul
Energy transforms itself into
making me whole
I take the brilliance from the suns
warm rays
And live on love in the oncoming
days

There's no other feeling than that
of spring
When the earth is preparing for
newborn things
It makes me want to push forth
towards a new goal
And gives me power for learning
the things I must know

An answer lies waiting beneath
each new leaf
An answer to sorrow—an end to all
grief
And I bury myself in these wonders
I've found
I carry a vision of every fresh sound

And all through the winter I hope
and pray
That the weather will change in
every way
'Cause I long for the sunshine to
brighten my heart
I long for the signal to give me the
start

There's no other feeling than that
of spring
When the magic lets loose on
everything
And the brilliance lingers with a
tender touch
It's no wonder I love spring so
much

Thelma Rose Chipman

Thelma Rose Chipman
CHRISTMAS AT THE CASTLE

From my castle tower window
On this joyous Christmas eve
I can see the tips of fir trees
Swaying gently in the breeze.
And I hear familiar noises
That only Christmas brings
Like the sound of children's voices,
With such a merry ring.
The snapping and the popping
Of the eucalyptus logs,
Tom and Jerry purring softly
And outside a barking dog.
Now my family gathers 'round me
And they join with me to say:
"Merry, Merry Christmas and a
Happy New Year's Day!"

Beverly A Myers
SMILES BORN OF TEARS

With love, to Mother.

The reflection in the mirror is all
too vivid this day,
Reality has a way of showing that
the little girl has danced away.
Should I have stopped to linger, for
the woman that I see,
Seems so much older now, this
simply cannot be me.

A reflection of small fine lines that
have been etched with time.
I long to feel the silken skin, the
golden hair that once was mine.
Time has a way of closing doors,
jarring memories of wasted
years,
There is a stimulant to the heart,
that lives within a woman's soul,
Secret corners that were never
touched, silent prayers she must
withhold.
For there are so many levels in
which we must pay the price,
Just to be able to reveal
ourselves—seems to be such a
sacrifice.
But when youth has had it's
shining hour, in a world
numbering many fools,
There still remains a richness
within the childlike heart that
rules.
And the heart can redeem the soul,
no matter how badly damaged
through the years,
The youth remains forever,
With loving rememberance,
Of smiles born of tears.

Ann Youngblood
MEMORIES OF GRANDMA

Dedicated to the love of my life, my husband Richard, and our three angels; In honor of my Dad, my Mom, and my dear Grandma.

Grandma's eyes were aged with
worry,
Grandma's eyes were never old.
Grandma's eyes were filled with
courage,
And how those eyes could warm
my soul.
Grandma's smile could light the
morning
As she met the coming day.
But Grandma left me without
warning
And with her took my sun away.
Grandma's voice echoed like
church bells
And soothed this restless child to
sleep.
But Grandma's voice now charms
the angels,
Though I can hear her when I weep.
In my hand I now hold the favorite
comb she used to wear.
Funny, how I look more like her,
placing it upon my hair.

Bessie Haddox Harvey
THE WONDERFUL WEST

Dedicated to the State of Washington

How blest to live in the Western
wonderland,
Amid the artistic planting of His
creative hand!
Out here in the grandeur of lofty
loveliness,
Hearts find the source of true
strength and rest.

Its pine scented breeze assumes
good health,
And means more to me than
oceans of wealth.
Just to linger beside its rippling
streams!

Our crystal lakes among
mountains grand
Are scenery equal to any land!
Mirroring in their depths, beauty
sublime,
Of mountains, clouds, and stands
of pine!

The snow-capped mountains
towering above.
Are eternal monuments of His
divine love.
Silently entreat ones soul to climb
higher,
To rise above each unworthy
desire.

Go away from this rushing modern
age
And view the splendors that God
has made!
They will awake higher aspirations
in your breast,
That make for lasting happiness.

These inspiring blessings awaken
the soul,
Make one realize this world is not
life's goal.
Oh! I love to live where tall pines
nod,
Close to nature; Close to our
creator and God!!!

Peggy Ruth Johnson
HELLO GOD

Hello God, It's me again,
I see you've left the door open, that
I might enter in.
You see lately I've been a little
down, though I know I
should not be, For your help and
guidance are always there for
me.
Sometimes when I'm at my lowest,
and things seem
dark as they can be, That still small
voice inside
whispers, "My child, let go and let
me."
You reach out and take my hand,
ever ready to help, to
understand.
Help me Lord I pray, to grow closer
to you each day,
No matter what obstacles are strew
in my pathway.
Rich blessings you want to bestow,
On my life you want to send a glow,
Now thank you God for listening,
already my spirits start to soar,
you want me to be happy, this I
realize more and more.
Yes, I feel better already, and I
know things will turn out alright
in the end.
I just needed to talk, and there's no
one
better to share with than, you
Jesus,
my dearest friend.

Mrs Mary Jacqueline Wright
1986

For fourteen years we've spent
some time
A-making cards with verse to
rhyme,
And pictures, too, as children grow.
Sometimes the parents even show.

Son Lee stands tall—is five foot ten.
At dinnertime he's with the men.
The sports at school that keep him fit
Are track and soccer and that's it.

Our daughter Dawn gives us a thrill
Each time she calls us from Brazil.
A student there through Rotary
She loves the land, finds much to see.
Fine, friendly hosts; new things to try.
She won't be back 'till next July.

A lonesome Yuletide some might say?
'Tis true, but Dawn, in her own way
Is spreading love from land to land
To show the world just where we stand.

Now Mom and Dad shan't be outdone,
We're proud, indeed, of daughter and son.
We're thankful, too, God watches o'er
Those others who have left our shore.
We pray that peace, tranquility
Pervade the world, as it should be.

Ann Klein Cooper

BERTRAM BLOWHARD'S FAMILY BUDGET

This poem is dedicated to my inspiration, my loving husband, Justin.

Mr. and Mrs. Bertram Blowhard decided to start on a budget.
Said Mr. to Mrs. "When buying, be sure that of price, you do
Always judge it!"
And since they both were good scholars,
You'd think they'd be thrifty with dollars.
The husband agreed with this thought.
But his wife, well, she had to be taught!
You see Mrs. B. liked gorgeous rings,
Hats, furs and all elegant things.
Once she called him to approve a new hat
But Mr. Blowhard just burned up and sat.
So he said to her: "Oh my dear wife,
You are now in the prime of your life.
Did you ever think of saving for food?
Or do you only when hunger strikes your mood."
She said: "So you want me no luxuries to keep
And purchase funny clothes that look cheap?
I don't need a hair waver,
You go ahead and buy yourself a new shaver.
Be sure to get a new tie," she added, with a down-hearted
sigh.
"Oh, no dear," he said, "I only meant that we save enough to
pay our rent.
I guess for your clothes we could spare a cent."
She answered— "Oh you sweet honey, where is the money, for
my brand new fur coat?"
Cried he, "I'm leaving for China on the very next boat."
So, friends, when you start your own budget;
When buying, of price be certain to judge it.

Ursula K Van Patten

Ursula K Van Patten

VERMONT SPRING

Streams flow crystal clear,
'Til rocks and falls disperse them
Into foam and mist.

Willows, not yet green,
Shelter clinging small gray shoots,
Proof of their budding.

A deep drift of snow
Hides in a crevice, to 'wait
June's heat for melting

Buckets on maples
Catch dripping sap, to sweeten
Some bountiful feast.

A robin's red breast
Shows itself briefly, then flies,
Seeking warm cover.

The scent in the air
Dispels odors of birthing;
'Tis Spring in Vermont!

Mary Sarah McCann

CYCLE OF LIFE

A tiny seed fell to the ground
With its tough brown jacket securely bound.
It did not know if it had worth,
Tucked down in the fresh plowed earth.
Little seed just took a nap
Until it felt a sudden rap.
Warm sun and rains from on high
Slid down without a sigh.
Little seed wiggled from within
To make little seed split his skin—
To let new life begin and
To make new seeds to drop again.

Sandra Lee Alexoff

ALONE

I sit here alone all on my own

My dreams you see did not happen to me.

In childhood the future seemed so clear. As long as I did my part I had nothing to fear.

As my world of promise was turned upside down—sickness, relationships that failed, uncertainty about careers—I was left with a frown.

Alas, I thought I had an answer to my life's prayer. I'd pour myself into a job and find someone with whom to share.

But fate showed me how uncertain life is and that no one really knows what their life has in store. You may have a job you love then circumstances change and you have it no more.

A lover or spouse may be your life but then commitment is missing or their love is stolen or lost. How precious to have had but at what a cost.

For a broken heart is life's cruelest blow. A heart so heavy you feel your life's blood starting to flow.

I sometimes think life is better alone. But if one does not experience the ups and downs and does no giving, is living alone really living?

Doris Marie Hakemack

I FOUND A FRIEND

To Melaney, Candice and Dodie Marie, the three most beautiful girls in the world, from "Mom"

Like the shadows of the monstrous city buildings, the paths of our lives crossed today, and I found a friend.
But unlike the shadows, which disappear with setting of sun, our chance
meeting cannot find an end, and I am very thankful I met this friend;
for in those eyes I see a glimpse of yesteryear's heartaches and sorrows,
some, I too, have endured, and so each day I look for my new friend.
She speaks to me of love thy neighbor and doing for others as best she can,
and enlightens my day with her wit and wisdom . . this is my friend.
And because I know that God in His heaven meant for this friendship to be,
He lets me share my daily life with this special friend.
And only could I hold the values of her knowledge forever in my heart, 'til
the shadows no longer fall upon me and my friend.
Then some day, when I too am filled with wit and wisdom, and another shadow
crosses mine, perhaps someone else will say . . . "I found a friend"

V Q Denny

IN MEMORY OF SENATOR EVERETT M. DIRKSON

Another great Senator has left us
He quietly slipped away,
To be with God his Creator
'Till the dawning of another day.

A Senate seat is now empty,
A great orator's voice is stilled,
Where in soft and humorous, but convincing tones
The Senate Chamber it often filled.

He was known to many as an evener
Among those he met from day to day.
He oft calmed the strong, upheld the weak,
In a firm, but simple way.

He brushed aside his political position
For his convictions were surely his own
As oftimes in life he stated
Man does not walk alone.

To the strong is not always the battle
The swift sometimes lose the race
But always to the true and faithful
Victory is surely promised through Grace.

Carmen J Lendi Jr

WAS IT AUTUMN

You and me, our lives were a reverie until that one day,—was it autumn?

I am somewhat confused, though we touched each other in so many ways and brought love to shower our everywhere.

You and me, separately were we until that special day when our eyes met and it did seem as if we always were together.

I see your laughter and your cries and our tender touches eased our togetherness.

You and me, we escaped the grasp that time has on so many; we opened doors that locks have on so many; we basked in our awareness and brought joy others envy.

You and me, there could not be another; there will not be another,—and it was autumn.

Kerry Kineavy

SURVIVAL OF THE FITTEST

At night he stalks in search of home in the jungle of the city streets
The moon, a token North Star beckons him to endure aimlessly and see the light
He tries to hide from the enemy that lies within his heart
He is the enemy. He is the prey
He cannot find shelter from himself
Beds of stone and concrete pillows
Dreams of nothing much and warmer days
A blanket of wind stars on his ceiling
Unwelcomed rains in times of drought
Endurance his triumph without reward.
All wrapped up in yesterday's news the stakes too high with gin
He cowers
Onward, past years of dreams stolen by time
Past fatted tigers in designer suits
He was once one of them though now maimed
Tales trapped forever by tattered clothing and a matted mane
Everyone but no one believes that he longs to be freed from the concrete jungle that binds him to his broken dreams
Though rich with jewels
Tosses him just icy stares and empty looks
The beast of kings. His stomach roars.
Fiery eyes lurk behind a death-like mask of unshaven shadows
Shattered windows to a broken

spirit that yearns for shorter
days and better dreams
The street his mecca; a
pilgrimmage for fallen kings
His heart a heavy reminder that
loneliness his lifelong friend
Will bury him in the end
Today his dream did come true, a
downhill battle finally won and
etched in stone
Found upon a concrete pillow . . .
Home at last.

Kath Minar

AN ALCOHOLIC'S BIRTHDAY

Happy Birthday, dear brother
will you live to see the next?
Will you be as sober as I am
or lost somewhere in a detox cell?
Is a family in your plans
or is your criminal defense
lawyer your only friend?
Would you get drunk enough to hit
your son
just as you hit your own
father, brother, sister?
God, I love you
I hate to see you suffer.
If I had the power to take it away
it would have never began
You'll never know how I hurt for
you.
when you hurt yourself
Happy Birthday dear brother
please light another candle next
year.

Rich Lea

LAST OR FIRST, FIRST OR LAST

Last or First, First or Last
Memories around, imperfect focus
Ever provoke nearsighted
conclusions

Assorted thoughts unscramble
Deep feelings of guilt
In weightless state matter little
Last or First, First or Last

Mysterious inscription veiled by id
Unsure and questioned of hidden
meaning

Shall ponder their importance
Last or First, First or Last

Influence in order coded
On gossimer chips when
approached fly
Return faint images, yet can
I—choose one
Last or First, First or Last

By cosmic threads suspend
Success or failure hang
The strength, the length and drive
decide
Last or First, First or Last

Mari Schultes

THE FIRST MORNING

I remember waking
inside a diamond-lit city.
The beehive had begun.
Lighted workers were on their way.
I didn't see the noise
or feel the hate—
not then—
Just flashing beamed excitement;
the mercedes—the velvet.
Now I see robots
cold and mechanical.
But the first time I woke,
city diamonds
held me awed.

Judy Barbara Herring

GOD'S PRECIOUS GIFT

From the very moment the
precious
breath of Jesus filled your tiny
soul
I knew his Kingdom was mighty.

His breath glistened your
magnificently
small eyelashes and brushed
your
locks of baby fine hair.

From the moment I felt your
tender embrace
against my breast I knew
God's everlasting love was more
than man could conceive

And yet, in all his grandeur,
in all his majesty,
in all that life itself encomapsses,
Jesus molded your soft and
delicate perfection
of everything I had ever dreamed
for
into a small, sweet being.

And then I remembered, in the
twinkling of an eye,
that God gave us his soft and
delicate perfection
of everything he had ever dreamed
for; Jesus.

From the moment you took your
first steps
and uttered your first words,
I knew Gods unending grace was
alive.

I saw you grow from a precious
baby that I adored,
into a beautiful and loving
woman.
And from that moment I knew
Jesus was Lord of all.

Marlene Driscoll Cox

WHEN

Oh Human Race of poor recal,
You fail, to see the signs
That led the Kings, of long ago
To their bloody, mad, downfall.

The angry, biting, cheating mob
Of this so-called humane race;
Will one day once again be forced
To start anew, the rebuilding job.

The minds He gave us, seem to lack
The most important factor.
To be able to learn from past
mistakes;
We must trust, and not attack.

How soon, before this Sacred Earth
Will harbour just a cloud of dust;
Where Man was once the ruling
force
Is naught; but mere dearth.

When? Oh when; will you
"Brilliant?" man;
Realize, you; are just a minute
speck
Of dust, in His Mighty eye—
A miniscule in His Majestic Plan?

Soon, I hope, before the end,
Some light will flash in all your
brains,
To see and learn, and know and be,
At last to call each other Friend!

Ryan K Moeckly

YET A CHANCE

The dove of peace is yet alive,
Through all these years of war.
In his nest he sits,
That olive branch beside.
He waits for the day when . . .
When the rockets stop roaring,
When the guns stop shooting,
Then the world shall hear his cry.
Through all these years of war,
There is yet a chance for peace,
And it's waiting for to fly.

E Joanne Whitehead

KATHARINE

Katharine—you had the strength
to climb—the courage to sustain
that climb—and the trust to let
go.

Your spirit is with me
Your life touched mine
Your teaching of simplicity
Your devotion to friends
Your unquestionable trust in
God
Your acceptance of death
Your love of life

Your life was like an eagle—soaring
and free

Your discipleship contributed
tremendously to our world
without fame or fortune

I miss you my friend and hope I
can contribute to this world
without seeking fame or fortune
but with true humility for my
fellow man.

I love you. Your Devoted Niece, Jo

Laura Lindsey

MIDNIGHT REVERIE

To lovers and dreamers and to the people who make them feel special. No matter how briefly love touches the soul, the feelings of those rare moments, however fleeting, will last a lifetime when the heart remembers.

I once had a dream
It never came true.
Then my dream changed
It was made up of you.

You entered my life
On a brisk autumn's night.
Out of darkness you came
Like a warm glowing light.

Now you're here in my world
Weaving spells on my soul,
Your kisses fall soft
Tracing patterns so bold

We fly with the time
Share moments sublime.
We laugh and we tease,
Teach and learn with such ease—

Though my old dream has flown,
A new love has grown.
If in my eyes it should seem
I'm dreaming a dream,
I can tell you it's true—
I'm dreaming of you.

James D Ross

IF YOU BELIEVE

I was told Christ made the world,
and on the seventh day, God said
if you believe, then go to church
and pray. God said be not a
sinner, be faithfull kind and
true, always lend a helping hand,
if some one asked you too. Learn
the ten commandments, that
God has handed down. Then
God will have his angels, keep
you safe and sound. Never be a
looser, always do the best you
can. If asked and you are chosen,
stand up and lend a hand. And
as the year's start fading, and
Illness takes a toll, pray & God
will be there, to help you save
your soul. He'll have a place in
heaven. A place where you can
dwell. And before I die I'll pray
to God and ask him to take me
there. For I remember reading,
from the Bible this I quote, "God
said." "If you believe," then I will
save your soul. Amen

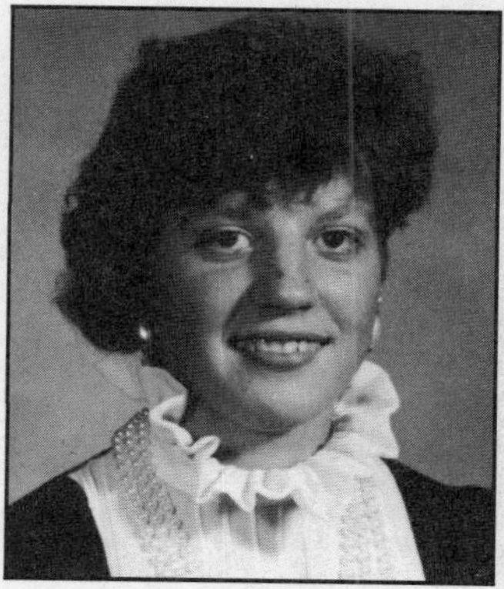

Andrea Dawn Tatoiu

Andrea Dawn Tatoiu

TIGER LILY

In loving memory of my father, Emil Tatoiu

Instead of staying with us, you
went away
But why? Tiger Lily, did you not
stay
I was small and young, I did not
know
Why my Tiger Lily had to go
The day you had to leave, there was
alot of fear
And as you went, down my cheek
came a sorrowful tear.
I wish that sad and unhappy day
That the darn wind wouldn't have
swept you away
If I had one chance to bring you
back, you see
I would do it in a snap, that's how
much I loved you dearly
Now I know where you are
And why you had to go so far

Now I'm old enough to know
Why my Tiger Lily had to go
Instead of being sad and full of sorrow
I look back as you would be with us tomorrow
I will always remember you as you twinkled in the sun
And will remember not the sad times, but the fun
Remember, where ever you are Tiger Lily,
That no matter what, we love you dearly.

Danah Johnson
GIVE ME A CHANCE

Through my short life
I've had sorrow and pain.
It runs before me
Like the falling rain.
My thoughts are controlled
By the world around me
I haven't a chance
To let them run free.
Why should I listen to them
When I'm the one that matters.
Just give me a chance
In this great big world.
Try to understand
I mean more to myself
THAN A GRAIN OF SAND!

Ruth Grosjean
MAKE YOUR HEART LIKE A GARDEN

To my six children, whom I tried to teach the right way to live, after their Daddy passed away, at an early age.

Make your heart like a garden of roses.
Make it true and ever so sweet,
So the rains in this life, that keep falling,
Will help make your love complete.

When the sunshine comes through, it is easy,
To face life without any fret,
So don't make your heart like a garden.
Of briars you'll always regret.

If it be of the rain or the sunshine,
Just face life without a regret,
And make your heart like a garden,
Of roses you'll never forget.

Glister Threadgill Jr
TO THE GREATEST MOTHER I KNOW

To the sweetest and dearest person I know, my mother, Ruthell Thredgill, and two individuals that I love dearly, Tisa Rachette & Khalil Gibran Cooper; I dedicate this poem.

To someone special and dear to me,
To one who has led me when I could not see,
To someone who cares what I turn out to be,
To the greatest mother that I know

To someone who has fed me down through the years,
To one who calmed me and took away my fears,
To someone who has comforted me and wiped my tears,
To the greatest mother that I know

To someone who helped me when I was down,
To one who has carried my burdens around,
To someone who struggles hard and does not even frown,
To the greatest mother that I know

To someone who knows all of my ways,
To one who tells me that Living Holy will pay,
To someone who furnishes a place for my head to lay,
To the greatest mother that I know

To someone who wants me to be happy and free,
To one who truly, truly cares for me,
To someone I want her days to be glee,
To the greatest mother that I know

Brenda Hudson
SPRINGTIME

As you walk down a country lane
On a bright spring day
Have you ever stopped and watched
Little squirrels at play.

Or listened to a robin's song
It's notes so sweet and clear
Or heard the little lambs cry out
Is mother near.

Have you stood and gazed up at a tree,
To see leaves a gorgeous green
Or picked some of the wild flowers
The prettiest you've ever seen.

Have you ever lay awake all night
Watching the hours go by.
Or seen the sun awake at dawn
So shiny new and bright.

Pauline Feger
GOD'S GIFTS

To God who created us all

God gave to the Blacks
The essence of night.
"My sons," He said, "—Rest!
There's content in my mind!"

God gave to the Whites
The brilliance of day
"My sons," He said—"Peace!
It's the kindest way!"

God gave to the Orients
The color of wheat.
"My sons," He said—"Pray!
We communicate that way!"

God gave to the Indians
The fire of the sun.
"My sons" He said—"Love!
My creation is done!

Dotty Harrold
THE SEASONS OF LIFE

In the springtime of our youth,
When the world was sweet and fair.
I discovered the pleasure of you,
And we had time and years to spare.

In the bright sunshine of summer,
Then, we start to build our family.
And our love begins to prosper,
As two people, in love, become three.

The Autumn leaves are falling,
As the days grow dim and cold.
The winter years are calling,
As we gracefully grow old.

The winter years now have fallen,
And our children are grown and gone.
Our house now feels so hollow,
As we spend our winter years alone.

Linda Eaton
ALONE

Alone is someone's enemy
Often my best friend
To some it lengthens shadows
As day draws to an end

Alone can give your mind unrest
Cause hope to go awry
Alone can give the time to Know
The face you live with every day

Alone will introduce you to
A you you've never met
A you that friends and strangers know
A you you'll not forget

I know alone can be unkind
Unleashes hurt and fear
It also gives you peace and heals
It brings the cleansing tears

Alone grants time and wisdom
Arrests you in your flight
It helps you answer questions
That plague your darkest night

Alone sorts out the right and wrong
Of things you feel and say
So take alone into your arms
Embrace her every day

Michael F Kolenda
I CAN STILL SEE YESTERDAY

This is dedicated to my father, Louis B. Kolenda, whose life has taught me patience, understanding, and how to dream

---

The old man is walking down the street,
Thinking of the days in his life gone by.
He watches each step as he shuffles his feet,
Hoping that his time is not in short supply.

Sometimes, he can't remember the events of the day.
What he did an hour before, he might not know.
He may even forget most of today.
But he can tell you what he did fifty years ago.

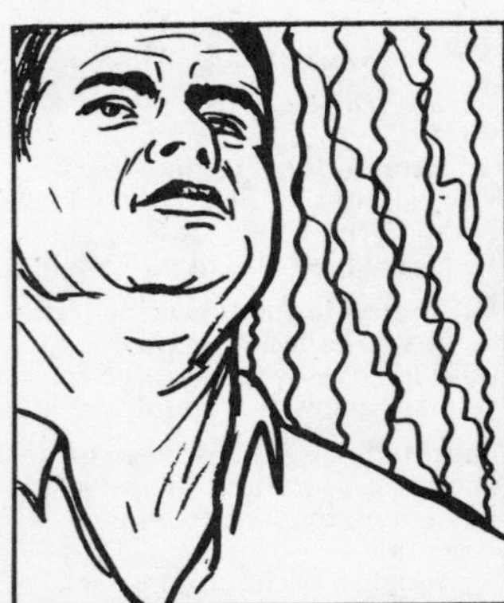

His mind sometimes wanders to the past,
To the places and people that he knew.
The memories of those times will always last,
Because often the past seems more true.

He squints his eyes as he looks at me,
While memories of the past take him away,
And says, "Sometimes, I can't see too clearly,
But I can still see yesterday."

Jacinda Cash-Smith
LIKE TWO SHIPS PASSING

This poem is dedicated to my parents; to whom I love very much.

I'll never forget the words you said
The wonderful moment that we met.
And in my heart I'll always keep,
And never, ever let out a peep.
I know it will never happen again,
Nor walk together hand in hand.
We're like two ships passing along the way,
And never stopping for words to say.
Though in the mists of days gone by,
I stop and wonder how and why,
That in our passing we should find
One brief moment out of time.
To share kind words, tender and true,
My memory will always be of you.
For we're like two ships passing along the way,
Never again stopping for words to say.

Rebecca Rowand
CHANGES

Everything's changing
that, you'll agree.
I hope it works out
for both you and me.

Life seems so empty
so vacant and void,
I hope you'll change that,
depressed feelings, avoid!

They remind you of the past
so good, yet gone,
don't let new developments
let a frown come upon

Circumstances may change
but not memories of old.
They'll always be there,
forever to hold.

They'll give something new
for life to be for;
a new reason to be
awake in the morn.

So think of old memories
keep them mind you,
the new ones won't replace them,
just add to their value!

K Stathas
I TOOK A WALK ON CHRISTMAS MORNING

To my parents, who called me to life again; to Joe's logic; and to Nature, who gave me succor.

I took a walk on Christmas morning.
There was a brilliant blue sky
and sun shining bravely
(but not boastfully)
upon the fields of white.
Snow crunched a muffled sound
as I headed for the fields,

in a jacket meant for summer,
meant for autumn,
—now in winter,
ice encroaching steals,
and where the summer
wildflowers grew,
only barren stalks, a few,
remain—
these mingled in the snowy
white terrain.
An aimless walk, I brush my hand
tentatively, gently, against
the winter lifeless feathery stalks
and wish them life again.
No butterfly, no humming bees,
no sweet silent summer
morning glee
prancing through the fields,
no autumn goldens, rusts, or
reddened,
no vast expanses green—
just the silent winter hush of
snow;
its kindly blanket soothes the
dust
kicked up in summer's
wanderlust,
now sleeps

Kelly (Dodson) Hadley

Kelly (Dodson) Hadley
ALONE

To my husband, Kelly Dean, the most important person in my life! You never gave up on me! Thanks!

Make way amid the noise and haste
For the quiet little girl who can't
speak or hear.
For the child of Heaven who
wanders about with only a smile
upon her face.
Who sits on an old wooden bridge
dangling her legs over the water
just to see her reflection.
Wondering who the other girl is
and what she is doing there!
Knowing that the other child is the
only friend she has!
Then the sun disappears and her
friend goes away.
Now she is left again in her own
little world.
With no one to know how she feels,
Just her and her friend who comes
and goes.

Jim Kelly
STORM

Gazing out the window
At the approach of a storm
Do not see the destruction
But, the beauty there upon

God's power unleashed
Causes some to alarm
Some see the darkness
I see new life to become

Our love, grows as the storm
Such power unleashed
Causes some to see destruction
Causes some to be full of alarm

Gazing out the window
At the approach of a storm
I dream of our love
And see the beauty there upon.

Sean Knierim
THERE IS A TIME IN EVERYONE'S LIFE

To Joan Dziedzic

There is a time in everyone's life
That their sense of adventure
reaches its height.
And when this acme is reached,
Even the strongest of will are
surcumbed.
And when this point of my life
came,
Just like the wings of a hawk,
It carried me towards my goal
And little did I know how far it
would take me.
It carried me over the highest
mountains,
Into the lowest, dark, bleak caves,
Through the deepest, most
desolate oceans,
And towards the greatest danger
And the greatest treasure at the
same time.
When my journey finally ended
In a secluded cove near a secluded
bay
There was a young child not over
five weeks old
That had an air of innocence
surrounding it
That could only be described as
"white."
And an air of evil
That could only be described as
"black."
But what drew me to it was
Something between black and
white, innocence and evil,
It was the true "personality,"
Neither hiding behind black or
white;
This was the true essence of life.

Linda L Snyder
ONLY CHILD

This poem is dedicated to Jack & Dorothy, my parents.

Many times we get so depressed
We just don't know what to do
Life is full of ups and downs
But then I think of you.

You are always there to comfort me
To listen to my woes
The love and respect I have for you
Constantly grows and grows.

You're not only dear and trusting
friends
I know I can depend on
But your generosity never bends
For that I can rely on.

My main concern is to have
wisdom
In whatever I undertake
Cause you taught me lovingly, Dad
and Mom
So it's my own fault if I make a
mistake.

Many times I have wanted to tell
you
How much you both mean to me
I just never knew how to do it
But this poem fits you so
graciously.

Now I have a wonderful husband
A son I can be proud of too
It all could never have happened
Without the two of you.

Linda Lee
A NURSERY RHYME

Sailing the ocean deep and wide
Trying to reach the other side
Falling and tripping in the night
Why can't there be a guiding light?

Wanting to sail and go with the
flow
Searching, needing, longing to
know
Standing in front of the door with
the key
If I open it—will I find me?

Listening and learning the song of
the sea
—Am I finding or losing me??—

Carolyn Y Graff
KITES

The children flew their kites today
My son and daughter did.
The wind was light, the sky so blue
The sun was never hid.

His was a giant eagle
Black with snowy head,
Hers a lovely butterfly
Of blue and gold and red.

The monstrous eagle would not
soar
The breeze too light and spare,
Although he tugged and coaxed
and ran
It crashed and wilted there.

But hers did lift, and darting high
While joyfully she ran
With feelings light as her small kite
She felt that life was "Can."

So crying angry tears he sat
And then began to rant
Too many things he could not do
And life to him was "can't."

She took his hand. Together
They ran down to the sea
And playing in the surf and sun
Consoled by love was he.

Roy Bunn
TEARS

For June—She believed in me. Thanks "Bug."

Awake!
Sleep crowds my eyes.

I reach to touch you,
My heart sings.

Shall it be coffee or kisses?
Perhaps the world does not need
me.

Today I shall be a vagabond in love,
Roaming the horizons of
contentment,

Taking the red out of rainbows
To make rubies for you.

Wet fields of grass
Shall be emeralds.

But—
The colors are fading.

You are not there,
Only dark gray walls.

A small window
From which no light shines.

Tears—wash my eyes.

Michael Lee Morris
THE PRECIOUS GIFT OF AGE

A chill swept through my body as
I gazed at the, loveliness of old
age.
I followed with awe the depth of
each wrinkle, and traced each to
it's end.
Filled with wonderment at the
cause of each furrow, I could
imagine how each and every one
had been born.
Filled with years of hard work and
sleepless nights, coupled with
love and laughter each came to
life.
The elements of time have been
good to this fragile body,
sleeping before me in her bed of
flowered sheets and crazy quilts,
she lays as elegant as the first
day of spring.
I watched the very essence of life
ebb with each breath, oh dear
just and merciful God. Be gentle
to this rose tonight as you were,
when she was a vulnerable bud.
And when you decide to pluck this
bloom for her final bouquet,
to be placed in your house of
love.
I must know that to take this old
flower off the vine of life, does
not mean that the beauty and the
aroma will be lost, rather the
memories will be pressed
forever in my mind and the smell
of
the once beautiful rose will be
forever fresh and with me all the
days of my life.

Dorothy Jean Jenkins
IN TIMES OF TROUBLE

This poem is dedicated to Orist my husband

Orist, Don't you dare to loose
control
Everything will turn out right and
Our troubles will be old.
I know it has been hard on you;
more than
You could bare but remember my
love

The weight with me you can share.
You are never alone, this you should keep in mind
Our burdens well be lifted, it's just a matter of time.
Brighter days are coming, this we both know but we must
Remember they never stay—they continue to come and go.
The one most important thing is to give each other strength
When the other falls weak; and contentment we shall not have to seek.

Millie E Govig

MY CUP RUNNETH OVER

To my children, Richard, Ronald, Dennis & Donald Govig. Also my grandchildren, Teri, Shelley, & Brandi Govig. and my husband Adrian C. Govig.

Lord Help Me, split these fetters that nail me to this bed,
Loan me strength to loose my tongue. Release it from my head.
They're casting men to bear me up-before that final stage,
Knelling bells will soon be tolled. No life, No pulse—they say.
Please, dry their eyes-so SOMEONE sees, MY tears within their cage.

Dear God above, Help in this grief. They plan to bury me.
My sins before me billowing roll. So gross. Oh yes it's true.
And they don't know, I hear THEM all. Don't let them carry through.
They're listing homes where family can easily belong
PLEASE—make them wait-a little while-for I'm not really 'gone'.
They're touching me while tying-up, endless funeral plans,

Lord,—flutter please, these hidden eyes and twitch these leaden hands.
My spirit is willing-tho' flesh is weak; THIS I always knew.
My faith must wait in Thee alone. I'm counting Lord, on You—
to snap these bonds like silken threads, Dear God—it IS a Must.
My muscles grind with deadlock pain, Then comes THY Mighty THRUST
And all those fear struck faces freeze, in ghostly awesome hush.
Blood surges thro 'my veins midst prayers of thanks and trust,
Such blessings from Thy bountious store, my certain death did'st
crush.

Still now my ardent 'THANK YOU' by Angelthrongs has soared past Heaven's portals far beyond, to kneel near Thee Oh, Lord.
Thou did'st hear and Thou was't near, Thou did'st Thine Aid aford,
Through plans Divine—It was not Time, to grant me Heaven's Reward.

Mary Jane Johnson

THE DREAM RETURNED

To my mother, who devoted her life to her family, and made the dreams possible.

I used to walk the country lane and wonder
What would I be when I became full grown
A young girl then, all my life ahead
What dream fulfilled, what joys unknown?

Then women sang of home and hearth
Content in their domain
The finish line, the vision ahead
I know not when it changed

Reality demanded that my dream should fade
Forgotten in the joy of babies born
Was this the life I sought,
Or was ability to reach outworn?

My world around was all the same
No unknown ground to tread
There was a certain satisfaction
A purpose in the life I led

We shared a network, family and friends
But time has changed the route
Is this the goal achieved,
Or was my freedom bought?

Oh, I yearn for what I'm not
But who can claim the right?
My duty's not to self alone
For all are in this plight

Yours or mine, whose freedom then?
Duty bound, our life entwined
With certainty, a safeness there
As endless days unwind

Then suddenly—spring tried to come too soon
And glistening, turned the trees to ice
Reminded of a farm field frozen years ago
Hidden like the winter solstice

The dream returned—still there

David Borntreger

A SONG OF PRAISE

To My Departed Mother, Elizabeth, for her guidance to the greatest way of life mankind has ever known.

I work and worry, stew and fret
On most days I just forget
All the beauty there is to see
All that my Lord, has given me

I've felt the touch of a loving hand
The look that says I understand
I've seen the joy of a child at play
Shared their tears and laughter gay

Been caressed by the gentle breeze
That comes ashore from out the seas
Felt the softness of a winter snow
Warmth of a fireplace all aglow

Watched the billowy clouds roll by
Basked in sunlight from on high
Seen the mighty rivers wide
The oceans ebb and flowing tide

I've played upon the silver sand
And on the mountain top did stand
The beauty of each living tree
From tiny seed to majesty

Lord! What I see leaves me amazed
I should daily, sing thy praise
With all thy power and mighty deed
My Lord you still would walk with me.

Jason R DeWinter

TOO WEAK TO CRY

Dedicated to all my friends who cared

My Heaven's an inferno
My Hell is seething
I'm burning inside
My soul is dying
I need release
of all emotion
they sit and wait
they burn, they eat
Devourer
emotionally I'm dying
soon to be dead
I cry for help
but it is futile
I'm weakened
I try to withold
my rage inside
just hold, restrain
I fear what would happen
if timing were correct
it would be different
But I can hear, acutely hear
The Death of a thousand Angels
As my Soul begins to die
For it's too late
Always late
I'm too late again

Ann Cline

THE CARETAKER

Who is it in the orchard,
That He has blessed most of all?
I think it is the apple,
So glorious in the fall.

Or, could it be the cherries,
Blessed with sun and dew and rain?
He's given them a beauty
That few others can attain.

Perhaps, it is the berries,
They're most loved, I do believe,
With twining, clinging tendrils
Lovely patterns do they weave.

But who is in the orchard,
That He's placed above them all?
O'er plums and pears and the grapes
Growing on the garden wall?

Who is most beloved of Him?
Won't you tell me if you can.
"The keeper and preserver.
It is I," answers man.

Dorothy Krueger Burman

CRADLESONG

May your dreams, little one, flow as quicksilvered sand
From the night's hourglass into deep slumberland,

Where quite soon they will gleam with the luster of gold
And the twinkle of stars from the Milky Way's hold.

Come now, close your bright eyes, gently dream until morn—
Ride the rainbow's great arc on which all dreams are borne—

And then, as you grow up, may your golden dreams shore
All the hopes and desires you will come to explore.

Ah, I see that an angel has now kissed you goodnight—
For, your smile is so sweet though your eyes are closed tight—

May the Heavenly Father throughout all of your days,
Ever bless you, dear child, as you tread Life's strange maze.

James B Vercher

NIGHT TIME ANGEL

There is a tear in my eye as you walk away.
Darling, I hope you will be back someday,
Yes, Sweetheart, I will wait by the phone;
I will miss you so much, "Angel," please hurry home.

The bright lights have lured you back into town.
Please, my darling, don't let me down.
I am home waiting for you, don't you see?
So please, Angel, hurry home to me.

You love the good times—night life and all;
I love you Angel, and I hate to see you fall.
You are a night time Angel with all of your charms,
And I want to enjoy you held tight in my arms.

I will have a light in the window and a hand on the phone,
Just any time Angel that you want to come home,
Please, Angel, I love you, don't you see?
So please, Angel, come home; don't do this to me.

Tracy Varn

ROSES FOR MY LOVE

To Billy, because you are my inspiration. I love you

Roses for my love and a kiss upon his face,
My heart can say a thousand words no sentiment can replace,
A lifetime of "I love you's" will only hit the core,
But oh my passion goes deeper yet for you, my love, there's more,
A sip of wine to toast to, a word or two well said,
The promise of all our tomorrows, on which my heart has fed,
For years the poets have said it each different with passing time,
But all with a wisdom that surpasses all knowledge of reason and rhyme,
The roses may all wither, as time

will do its part,
But nothing grows quite as wild, as
this love within my heart

Linda D Lane
REMEMBER WHEN . . .
Remember when he said,
"I love you?"
Remember when he said,
"I'll never leave you?"
I remember.
I remember the hurt, the pain,
and the lies.
I can remember only the bad times.
Where are the good?
Were there any?
All I remember is when you said,
"I don't feel the same way about
you."
"I don't want to see you very
much."
He said our love would never die,
I never thought he'd lie.
I believed in him,
I was a fool
I've learned my lesson well . . .
Never fall in love.

Linda Decker

Linda Decker
IN TIME

This poem is dedicated to John and Bobbie, for all you've done for me.

When
times are rough.
Which
some times they will be.
Hold
you're head up high.

And
keep on going.
For
in time things will tend
to mend them selfs.

Elva E Howell
MY MASTER'S VOICE
I dreamt one night I heard my
Master speaking
In accents clear and sweet to me,
He said to win my heart that He
was seeking,
That I His way should try to see.

I answered Him, "Oh Lord, I need
Thee sadly,
Forgive my sinful, erring way,
My heart I lay before Thy throne
most gladly,
And there I want it e'er to stay."

The mem'ry of that night to me is
holy,
'Twas then I found my Lord and
King,
My mouth speaks forth His
goodness now so boldly,
His praises ever will I sing.

Mildred Chludil Bila
TRIBUTE
There rose a mighty engine's roar
We watched in awe—
To see the Eagle soar,
It lifted, sleek and shining in the
sun,
Their silent journey had begun,
And then, so short a time they had,
To be on angel's wings,
A flame—a mighty flame—
It was as if the sun had burst!
A million pieces fell away!
A giant shadow fell across this day!

Maribel Salinas
THERE'S ALWAYS A LIGHT THAT SHINES MY WAY

"This poem is dedicated to Mom, J.M.I. and to YOU, my special friends, for helping make my dream a reality." From simply "ME", Love Always and Thanks!

Though skies are gray
while your far away,
There's always a light
that shines my way.

I see your smile
your eyes so bright,
They bring me joy
at every sight.

I hear your voice
so loud and clear,
Through the clouds
I feel you near.

I thank God,
I know you are here.

Mrs Waldo H Dunn (age 101)
ELDORADO
A poetess once had written of her
lover husband
"I love thee to the depth and
breadth
And height my soul can reach."
He, being rich, anticipated and
fulfilled her every wish
And so there was no testing of that
great love.
Another, not a poetess, felt that
same love
For one, though poor but ever
proud.
Seeking always for fame, that
Eldorado.
To follow such a lover meant great
testing,
But she would dare to transcend
all the heights.
Then followed the sewing and
mending, never ending,
Mopping and sweeping,
sometimes weeping,
Thus came fame fulfilling the
highest hopes.
But one day her mirror told her, as
did the poets words,
That all of her beauty long ago
was-lost,
And men love beauty. Then came
a poet's warning:
"Over the mountains of the moon
Down the valley of the shadow
If you seek for Eldorado."

Kathryn Cude Everhart
HE WENT TO SCHOOL TODAY

Dedicated to my dear son, Scott, whose very words prompted this poem.

He went to school today—my little
man!
His eyes were shining stars. He
held my hand.
Yes—man in courage and in
confidence.
Yet babe beneath that grown-up
brave display.
"I wonder what I'll do at school
today?
I wonder if she'll tell us when to
rest?
Of all the other boys I'll be the best.
I know which room! Where we
went in before?
Will you walk with me, Mother, to
the door?"
Confidence! It wavered there
awhile;
But quickly came and bravely with
a smile—
"Good-bye, Brother. I'm going to
school today!
I wonder if we will go out to play."
Today the door for him is opened
wide.
He'll work and play with others
side by side.
Day by day he'll grow as all must
do.
In knowledge, patience, kindness,
obedience too.
Little can his mind now
comprehend.
Little can he realize the end.
Yes—he went to school today.
And I, with heart so proud, yet
humble as I pray;
"Lord, help me to teach my son
from day to day
To walk with courage in the
Master's way."

Sonia Yvette Lewis
I KNOW IT'S ONLY HUMAN

Dedicated to Esther "My mom" and her many married men.

I know it's only human
To have emotions and feelings
To have physical and sexual
Contacts and dealings
I know it's only human
For me to have a crush
On a guy who makes me feel
good
And at times, makes me blush
I know its only human
To feel passion and desire
To have a fantasy of
Love potions and love fire
I know its only human
To want to be loved and
caressed
Satisfied and understood
By only the best
But is it human
To live a fantasy of
Love potions and love fire
When a married man
Is who you desire?

Raymond D Whiting
MRS SHAW'S HOUSE
I lived near Mrs Shaw
And walking by used to see her
Doing hand springs in the house
She was short and tattoed;
Had been in the circus they said.
She had three fine sons
One a sergeant in the army
One was a cook in a cafe
The youngest finished high school
—
Then took A.P.G.
He couldn't get a job you see
He was either too short
Or the depression hadn't released;
So he went in the army too.
Mrs. Shaw is dead and the
Three boys are gone.
I walk by now and some men
Are fixing used cars in the yard.
They have an ugly dog.
It's not like it used to be.

H Tayloe Parker
A LETTER TO MY DAUGHTER
Child of my body, blood of my
blood,
Believe it or not, YOU . . . I do
love.
You're so young and full of life,
Its just beginning, this term of
strife.
You'll make mistakes, we all do.
Learn from them and you WILL
get through.
Looking at you is like looking at
me.
When I was sixteen . . . I wanted
to be free.
I was hard headed and obstinent
too,
NOBODY was going to tell ME
what to do.
I've made mistakes . . . I've eaten
dirt.
I tell you these things to save YOU
the hurt.
You're an intelligent person . . . this
you know.
Use your brain to HELP you grow.
Think things through . . . WHAT
Will IT DO?
How will it affect the people
around you?
Be responsible for what you do and
say.
Believe me, "One day you WILL
have to pay!"
Respect and trust MUST be earned,
By your actions, words, and what
you've learned.
Don't just accept the answers to
questions,
Seek out the answers, ask for help
and suggestions.
Be in life whatever YOU want to be,
All I ask is . . . "DO IT TO THE
BEST OF YOUR ABILITY!"

Shirley Gooden
A SPECIAL HOLIDAY IS COMING

This poem is dedicated to Lois, my mother. And to Helen, Benny, Alisa, Kizzie, Aurelia, my children. Also, Joanie, Joanne, Tammy, Lynn, my sisters.

A special Holiday is coming.
Can you, see the preparation.
Can you, perceive the anticipation.
Can you, breathe the period of duration.
Can you, feel the fascination.

A special Holiday is coming.
Some people are planning, to celebrate.
Some people are ready, and can't wait.
Some people are willing, but don't have faith.
Some people are filled with love, some with hate.

A special Holiday is coming.
It's a once, in a life time day
It's coming soon, there will be no delay.
It's a serious celebration, so put childish things away.
One man hurt us all, and he was made of clay.
Another man saved us all, now he is on his way.

A special Holiday is coming.
A day, you can't celebrate every year.
That day, you will be happy, and have no fear.
Because God, in Heaven, (knows), and loves you dear.
So hurry! and be at rest, the time is near.
Jesus, is coming in a cloud, He will soon be here.

Jean Huff
THE JOURNEY

To Mom: Whose life I took for granted—Whose death I tried to understand

Hello, my friend, I've been waiting for you.
Please come on in, sit down a while.
I'm not quite ready, I've things to do—
Like washing, dusting—why do you smile?
I cannot leave with this house a mess,
For who will clean it while I'm away?
What will they eat? They'll manage, I guess
But I wish they were home to hear what I say.
I'd tell them how happy I have been,
How much I have loved them all these years.
Could I just wait to see them again?
To try to rid them of their fears?
I'm sorry I had to make you wait,
I know you're getting anxious to leave.
They'll soon be here for they're never late.
Why, there they are now, I do believe.
They walked right by me, they did not see
Me standing here—have they gone blind?
What's that they're saying? I cannot hear!
Why are they crying? Oh, never mind.
I am quite tired—I'm ready to go.
Thank you for holding out your hand.
Oh, dear, It's cold, and shaking so!
We're going where? The promised land?
That does sound nice, I've heard of it
And dreamed of going there when I die.
Again, did I notice you smile a bit?
Oh, well, may I please say good-bye?

Juan R Moreno
A WISH

To Soila B. Aguilar, A special friend whom I love and care for very much. Thank you for the inspiration and the support.

I wish that I could send you bouquets of beautiful flowers.
I wish that I could make you smile every day,
To unburden you from everything that makes you sad.
If I could erase all the scars that people have left when they hurt you, I would.
I wish that I could bring you everything that you wanted
That would make things better for you.

Alas,
All that is beyond my means.
What I offer is this:
A shoulder,
A helping hand,
All the moral support,
And love as a friend that you need.
I wish to always see
Your smiling eyes,
The smile on your face,
Just you being happy.

What I wish most of all,
Is that you be my friend, Always!!!

Nancy Olinger
LORD I PRAY

To my supportive sister Gwen Burgess, whom I love dearly. She was my inspiration for this poem.

LORD, with Thine understanding care,
Lead the doubter's who have gone astray;
That they might repent and trust again,
Oh LORD, for those I wish to pray.
LORD guide a gunman's hand today;
That he's not impelled to take a life.
Convince him with THY bountiful love,
You shall remove his crushing strife.
Direct the lost and skeptical one's;
Grant, stormy lives YOU will fulfill.
Usher them hope and eternity.
I pray worshiping becomes their will.
Aid those struggling with burdens.
Lord, instruct in their needy hour.
Demonstrate, belief—is secured
With pure FAITH in THY DIVINE power.
Uplift the oppressed with YOUR grace,
Let us praise YOU in fervent acclaim.
With THY guidance, may we never oppose.
These we beseech in YOUR Sacred Name.

Natalie S Leonesio
BIRTHDAY SURPRISE

This poem is dedicated to my three daughters: Marie, Anne and Julie.

"Mommy, stay upstairs awhile,"
Said my daughters, with a smile.
"Please don't come 'till we say to,
We have something more to do."
Quietly they moved about;
Then I finally heard a shout,
"Come on Mommy!" And I came.
There upon the table, same
As if it were a regal feast,
Was my china, and the meat
Was a chicken, done just right.
What a really pleasant sight!
Baked potatoes, peas, and more!
Tomatoes, pickles, were in stove!
Camera ready as I sat
For my picture. Think of that!
After dinner came the cake
That my little ones had baked.
"Happy Birthday, Mommy dear!
We're so glad to have you here!"

Angie Schaefer
TEENAGE FOOL

This poem is dedicated to my seven children, whom I love very much.

I was young and I was cool, I was nobody's teenage fool.
I had it all I knew what to do.

I played the games, and played them well, I knew the ropes,
I needed no help.
Then problems mounted fast and furious, what to do, I'm
frightfully curious.

I never listened, so I never knew, that I had help if I
wanted to.
The lessons taught as I was growing, were lessons I thought not worth knowing.

I learned a lot in all those years, I caused a lot of heart aches and tears,
I was a teenage fool you see, but now I'm grown please listen to me.

I want to help, I want you to grow, with help and love you find at home.

Jim Dorsey
AN OLD MAN

I heard an old man died today
Without an honored passing
No friends have come to view his face
No mourners now are massing

It seemed so sad to hear of this
And guess the reason why
That loneliness had been his life
And all alone he died

No time was made to speak of him
As though he were a friend
The wooden box they placed him in
Was all that marked his end.

I stopped along the road to cry
As tribute to his death
And thought it must have eased him some
To draw his final breath

He must have felt forgotten then
To live and die alone
I could not help but sigh to think
His name was never known

They laid him in a potter's field
Another's grave he shared . . .
. . . I heard an old man died today. . .
. . . And no one even cared! . . .

Judith Climer Runnels
MISTER CLOWN

To my loving Dad who wanted me to write from age 13, and in memory of my beloved mother whom I shall miss dearly this Mother's Day, 1987

Mister clown upon my wall,
your hair peeking out
Like clusters of apricots
from your little brown hat

at a crazy perch upon your head.
Is it askance because
You raised up from your noontime snooze
and the bench got in the way?

Oh, Mister Clown upon my wall
why does your 5 o'clock look like 10,
the daisy in your lapel seems weary now,
and your cherry nose isn't quite as red?

Mister Clown upon my wall,
that's what I intended with brush in hand
And that's the way God made me,
With Intention.

Patricia Dirig
INDIAN NAPANEE

Dedicated to to my Mother Irene

Out on an Indian Reservation,
Far away from civilization.
Where the foot of pale face, seldom trod.
A white man went to fish, one summer.
Met an Indian Maid a hummer.
Daughter of "Big Chief Spare the Rod."
White man threw some loving glances.
Took the maiden, to war dances.
Smoked the pipe of peace took chances.
Loving in a teepee, built of fur.
Rode with her on an Indian pony.
Gave her a diamond ring a phony.
Then he said these loving words to her.
You are my pretty little Indian Napanee.
Won't you take a chance and marry me?
Though your daddy is a chief.
It's my belief, a very merry wedding, He'll agree.
True your a dark little Indian Maid.
But, I'll suntan to a brighter shade.
I'll wear feathers on my head.
Paint my face an Indian red.
If you'll only be my Napanee.

Sorry, to say, his coo talk caught her.
Soon he married, the big chief's daughter.
Happiest couple that you ever saw.
Till his dreams of love had faded,
Napanee grew old and jaded,
Just about like any other squaw.
Soon papooses, came in numbers.
White man wonders, at his blunders.
Red skins yells disturb his slumbers
And the feathers droup upon his head.

Too late, Now, He's still is a wishing,
That he'd ever had gone a fishing,
Or had met, that Indian Maid and said
You are my pretty little Indian Napanee,
Won't you take a chance and marry me.

Bruce W Carlson
HIS WORLD

For my beautiful son, Steven Jarrett 5/5/87.

Hey son,
Are you having fun
In your world
Of fantasy?

Hey son,
You are the one
I hoped that you
Would be.

I wonder what
You think about,
When I look
Into your eyes,

And I wish that I
Could ease your hurt,
When you feel
You want to cry.

Hey son,
Let me know
If we can
Make the time,
Because I know sometimes
I'm not near,
But your always . . .
In my eyes.

Kim Alison DeTombeur
LISTEN

To my mother, with all my love

You searched not for a face
nor for a body.
Your loneliness needed no expression
or questioning,
just an open and sincere heart.
The battle within you
is much more
than I can understand,
but the time is now
to reveal all that you want me to know.
I can help with a silent understanding.
As you spoke
an explosion of feelings erupted in me.
I could not see your words
or hold each syllable
but I could take your pain
and leave you with
strength, courage
and a forever place in my heart.

Cleveland Calvin Matchett
I REMEMBER NORTHFORK

I am presently entranced by a National Geographic article showing
The economic catastrophe that has to West Virginia come flowing.
I am especially amazed at a graphic view of present-day knowing
Remains of Northfork between Bluefield and Welch. I can hardly believe
What I see here. The town looks almost abandoned with no reprieve.
It is not even shown today on most maps. Windows are boarded up—and leave
Streets deserted. My experience here was in 1947. I was fresh out
Of business school in East Tennessee and had never been away, I doubt,
From home for very long at a time. But my uncle pastored the local devout
Methodist Church in Northfork. He knew that I was looking for work.
A member of his church was manager of Algoma Coal & Coke Company.
As clerk,
It was agreed that I would start in the company office. Again,
The town was bustling with activity. Down the wide main
Street ran the major line of Norfolk & Western Railway. The train
(Powhatan Arrow passenger) zoomed into and out of town daily. On each
Side of the railroad paralleling the tracks and depot was a wide reach
Of street. Then three blocks or so of stores lined the street.
Each Sunday noon we drove down to Keystone for a meal. The Berry retreat
Mansion was a main town attraction (famous coal mining family), complete
With long lines of coal cars, mines, tipples. Everywhere in the air
And on surface was smoke and grime. A few churches were around there.
The entire town was located in a small valley between mountains bare
Rising from both sides. Homes straddled the mountains that meet
The street. Many long stairways lead up the mountain side from the street.
I left to start college life, but memory does repeat.

Leigh Walton
BEAUTY AND THE BEASTS

For T.R. Hummer's "The Beating"

Everybody started chanting it like it was prayer.
Those stupid boys at recess
chasing after me like I was the one
that done it. Clifton—scratching
lies he knew stood no more chance

of coming true than he did of being human.
Why'd they do it—all that deep, bawdy singing
till everybody heard it, and that Clifton, all wild and thick
who scared you just by smelling him, would sweat
while they circled around me, smug

with their new discovery, like some pack
of dogs tearing at raw meat, until
I started trembling, wishing God and the devil
would slash Clifton's fat hands for carving
such torment. It wasn't anger

that caught me. It was humiliation
that anyone that dumb would love me.
How could he? He'd been below me all his life,
so far, it was hard to see how he'd think I'd care,
ever. He was a beast whipping those boys.

He went down on them, pigs
all of them, and gave them a slap of the pain
I'd never forget how to use: how my beauty
can attract for all the wrong reasons
and sting, real sharp, when I want it

to; burn, like lemon spit, on broken skin.

Linda S Parker
LADY ON THE SEA

I dreamed I was sailing
far out on the sea
the winds and waves of freedom
kept calling out to me
with peace and tranquility flowing
through my mind
I felt there was still something,
something I had to find.
Then I saw a vision of a lady
on the sea,
And in a soft and tender voice
these words she spoke to me.
"To exist without meaning is
what you've done, Now you dream
of an escape of which there are
none, you must first fill the
emptiness you have so deeply
felt. Before finding the freedom,
you must first find yourself."
As I heard her words, this lady on
the sea
Slowly I began to realize
The lady I saw was me!

M Isabella Boy

M Isabella Boy
TO A BUTTERFLY

In memory of my mother, Maude K. Boy and my cousin, Maude Kinkead.

O swift and brightly colored butterfly,
You lovely harbinger of Spring
On glist'ning, glowing, golden wing;
Your beauty stuns me as you flutter by.

It looks as though you're on an aimless flight;
First up, then down, you hover now;
And soon you will discover how
To rob a blossom when you gently light.

How come, on balmy days you know to hatch,
And caterpillar spins cocoon
Which turns to butterfly so soon,
Whose wings, to open right, the sun must catch.

How come you know to lay your tiny eggs
On plants that only your type feed
To give them substance which they need
To form their stained glass wings and elfin legs.

O gorgeous creature, how'd you come to be?
The great Creator gave you birth;
A touch of heav'n—a touch of earth;
You are His gift to man—for all to see!

Embodiment of everlasting life,
You teach the resurrection morn
Enables us to be reborn
And leave behind this world of sin and strife!

Linda K Berry
A NEW LIFE

A new life I must begin
Not my choice, but yours, O, God
Today, a new life I must begin.

The comfort of my God is always near
He will ease the pain and guide me
In the new life I must begin.

I cannot see the end of the road
The road, I must now travel alone
In the new life, I now begin.

I begin my new life bravely
With a gallant smile and joy in my heart
I reach out to others in my new life.

I live on and do all things the same
I fill each hour in useful ways
In this new life, I have begun.

As dawn follows darkness
Peace and happiness must follow sorrow
In my new life, I now begin.

tane frederickson
hero

booby goofenoffer came home
from nam today.

a flag flew half-mast.
but booby wasn't dead.
he bounded from the plane,
laying a shroud of exuberance over
the mourning crowd.

on the runway,
to the silent revelry
of an imaginary marching band
booby danced.

the medal,
which was to have lain gently
in his rigored hands,
now hung silvery and gleaming from
booby's neck.

pride and honor . . .
purpose and glory . . .

booby spat on a five-star's
glistening black shoes.

Lisa G Lahrman
GO AWAY

This poem is dedicated to Dan, my loving husband. But this poem does not reflect my feelings for him.

You are in my past now,
I wish you'd go away.
My heart was yours to rent, not own,
who told you you could stay?
Convinced that I could love and leave
I let our lives entwine,
and though we shared a summer love,
we loved on borrowed time.
Back home I tried to face the fact
we'd never meet again,
forgetting's easier said than done
when memories still remain.
But don't you see we can't be one
our lives are worlds apart,
you took more than I had to spare
So please, give back, my heart.

Brandon Scott Nicholson (age 7)
PEACE

No war please, We need to live peacefully on earth
We pray no killing or crime on earth please.
We want to live together and be happy
with our families, our cousins, our grandparents and our dads.
We want to live on earth, Jehovah, our
heavenly father. We pray for you
to make earth a peaceful place to live.

Billy Krejci
NATURE

Nature is a thing of life.
The person behind this creation
is Mother Nature.

Everybody loves nature.
Nature is trees, animals, people, plants,
and all living things.

Some people think nature is
just things in forests and woods
But it is not the truth,
Because nature is everything that lives.

So, if you think nature is
just forest creatures
Please change your mind because
nature is all living things.

Chrissy Lynn
THE CALL OF THE WIND

To my third grade teacher Mrs. DeLonga

The call of the wind sweeps through the trees with grace, glory and ease.
Like the sound of the cars going through town or the soft purr of a kitten.
Listen to the soft sound of the wind
because if you listen to the
wind it will listen to you in hard times.
For the wind cares in many ways
if you care for it.

James S Hyde
I AM

To my wife, Opal, who can listen.

Consise Biblical Portrayals

Character of God
I. Creator
II. Correcting Father
III. Redeemer

To cosmos I gave nod,
Created whales and cod,
And Trees as well;
Placed fruit within the pod.
I formed you from the clod.
From Me you fell.
I time the plight you plod.
I am the Righteous Rod
Of Israel.

I walked your streets of sod,
You treated me as odd.
I meant you well.
The trail of tears I trod.
I am the Son of God,
Immanuel.

Clifton B Adams
IN THE BEGINNING . . .

To Jean J. Jackson, with all my love.

In the beginning . . .
There was a single, perfect rose
It's stem climbing skyward,
full of life.
Standing alone, as if for a picture
it posed.
It's thorns showing brightly,
warding off any danger.
It's petals opening slowly,
never to be closed.
It sits there alone, for born
is a stranger.

This rose, I've given you,
For it is special, delicate,
and untouched.
It's color so red, so true.
Bewildered I stood and
watched.
When all of a sudden the
wind, it blew.
Inside this rose, an image
of me and you.
Hold this rose, careful
not to part.
For this rose, you see,
Is really my heart.

Darlene M (Swartz) Miltner
DESPAIR

Glacier of ice deeply lodged,
unmoved by words, sunless days.

Deep shadows of night prey on
bones, flesh and heart.

No spring of thawing, nor promising
warmth eases the stronghold of winter's
cold. Hollowness, emptiness, nothingness.
All is mute.

The sting has gone. Numbness lingers on
No penetration of smiles or song can
melt the glacier as it slides along.

All lies barren, dark and void.
No happiness in heart or soul.
The waste of years in vastland's cold.

James L Wattenbarger
STRAWBERRY DAYS

To Julie, Jamie and Justen: May your dreams find you, May your prayers be answered.

These are the strawberry days . . .
red and ripe and juicy,
begging to be picked,
to be consumed.
Shining with enthusiasm,
blushing with excitement
to live, to love, to discover.
Glowing with eagerness to see
"around the bend,"
"over the rainbow."
Someday it will all be committed
to trinkets and photographs
and pages of scrapbooks.
And an easy willingness to believe
when you've seen over one rainbow
you've seen over them all.
But not yet! Not today!
For these are the strawberry days . . .
red and ripe and juicy.

Lee Roy Seiber
THE SUN AND US

Have you ever watched the sun go down,
Behind a mountain without a sound?
And wondered where it went from there?
Because in the morning it will reappear.
Does it sink down deep into the sea,
Or go to sleep like you and me?
They say when it takes away its light,
It's in another place, shining bright.
Is that the way it is for us?
When we die, why make all the fuss?
Perhaps we are shining bright somewhere,
Behind the mountain over there.
Or maybe we go to distant lands.
Whatever the case, we are in God's hands

Betty Moura
SHE'S THERE

She's there to cook
She's there to sew
She's there when your feeling low
She's there to teach you a little trick
She's there to nurse you when your sick

She's there when you skin your knee
She's there when you get stung by a bee
She's there with money when you need a loan
She's there with your messages from the telephone
She's there to chauffer when you need a ride
She's there in any crisis by your side
She's there to wipe away your tears
She's there throughout all your years
She's there when there is no other
She's there, she loves you, she's your Mother

Bernard Rouse

THE ONE

Dedicated to Nicole and Bernard

Of all the loves around,
Only one will make you real:
Will take you off the playground
And lead you to the field.

Of all the loves to embrace,
There's but one eternal flame,
Just one believing face
Who'll put you in the game:

Will let you call the play
But make you carry the ball;
Will let you have your way
But ask of you your all . . .

Of all the lilies in the dells,
There's one with a certain glow:
A precious herb of nodding bells
And if you see it . . . you'll know!

Of all the compassionate clones,
Only one has a different touch;
Just one you've always known
Needing you . . . just as much!

Cathy LeCompte

GRANDMOTHER'S RETURN FROM LOSS

She has come to live with us today.
Mother says not to embarrass her,
to look right at her
as if nothing has changed.
Father pushes her chair
up the ramp he's built
over the steps. Her face,
shallow, inanimate, frightens me.
I try to do what I've been told.
I look right at her,
say nice things, pat her hand.
I don't know what I say exactly.
I want to look away, past her,
but always my eyes rivet
back to the stumps,
hidden under her cotton dress.
Her face, the color of shame,
whinces, struggles to meet my gaze.
I imagine she wants to make some excuse,
make me understand.
She says nothing,
she folds her hands in her lap,
turns away from me.

John C Stoscup

THE CHRISTMAS TREE LEGEND

It began the day Christ was born.
Man and beast had gathered 'round
Each bringing in humble sincerity
A gift for Him, presented bowed to the ground.
The animals ran to the forest gathering food
As people stood and stared creating a strange and mysterious mood.
A feeling never felt before; of freedom and new life!
A feeling without living's pain, devoid of useless strife.

And as the people were gathering around
There was a cry and all stood without making a sound.
A woman named Mary placed a small wriggling baby in a manger,
The silence so still as still could be found.

Far away a small fir tree stood solemn and sad.
It wanted to give, and give so bad.
Suddenly, a flash from above and decended a shape of a man
Yet not a man, this shape from heaven descended down upon Bethlehem

With it another flash of great degree!
The angel had placed many small stars on that small fir tree

And from Bethlehem and as far as one could see
The smaller tree shown the greatest light in brilliant consistency

So the people went to the forest to see what this was
And they found the great gift created with love.
As more came then more saw
That this little tree was the best gift of all.

And still today those stars are shining.

Frances J Martin

HELP ME DEAR LORD

This poem is dedicated to Leon, my Loving Husband, who always believed in me.

Help me Dear Lord every day of my life,
to be a friend to all people, turn away from all strife.
To give a helping hand to those who are down,
to face each day with a smile and never a frown.

Help me Dear Lord to be a witness for you,
to live my life as you would have me to.
To give you the glory for all that you do,
to not be ashamed to tell others of you.

Help me to remember, Dear Lord, the cross from the tree,
the pain that Jesus suffered to set my soul free.
The walk that he took up Calvary's hill,
that the moment he died, the whole world stood still.

Help me Dear Lord, always walk by my side,
please show me the way and be my guide.
Guide me with love and thy tender care,
help me to remember you'll always be there.

Help me Dear Lord to give you my all,
I pray if I stumble you won't let me fall.
Let me walk in your valley saved by your grace,
until I can reach out and touch Jesus' face.

Tim Moore

DREAMCHILD

This mirror plain, does it yet bend
and shroud its face beneath a mist
or speak to he who turns the light
and offer final exactitude,
knowing well the visage truth
unlike what wisdom did see through.

Wan ache for such yet did return,
grant guiling supple voice to stir,
then gather to where lies the dust
and in that place once echoed still
duplicit cries of waning ken
of azure love throughout the sear.

Hence eyes transfixed thus did not see
the gift of sorrow mending callously
from hate a crusted wound to make
a keep to hallow a gift for men
and know the fey, well tendered ruse
till for a time it lit within.

Such blooms are as, unlike their barbs,
depth piercing and unyielding things
whose life precludes their selves to know
that soul as night, so, too, grows cold.

Alva E Wyatt

I PRESS ON

There is a path that wrings,
Through the forest deep and strange,
And so with urgency to gain,
My freedom in that greater plain,
I press on.

Oh! gladly would I run to that fair land,
But time is my companion in this band,
And we must do our part in his great plan,
To help bring peace and happiness to man,
So I press on.

There have been many, who this way have gone,
Who, now, rejoicing with that happy throng,
Like Peter, Paul and John who now are home,
Compel me to press on, and on, and on . . .
So I press on.

Zelda Stanley

MOTHERS—DAUGHTERS

Mothers and teen-age daughters
Who never see eye to eye—
Each one of you search your heart
And try to find the reason why.

Daughter, you think mom's too strict,
And don't want you to have any fun—
Of course it could never be something
You might, or might not, have done.

Mother, could you be so overly strict
Because of something in your teen-age day—
So that "the something" unhappy that happened to you
Won't happen to her the same way?

Daughter, try to understand your mother,
She's doing what she thinks is best—
Mother, you can't live her life for her,
Just pray she'll survive the test.

But, when all is tried, should you decide to part,
There's one thing you should both do—
Before you part, let the other one know,
That truly, I really do love you.

Then, as daughters turn into mothers,
And their daughter reaches that teen-age land—
Perhaps they'll look back, and remember,
And then—hopefully—they'll understand.

Mary E McEntee

LONELY HOPES

My mind wanders,
in the lonely darkness of my room.
With thoughts of you,
my vision clouds.
How beautiful it would be
to wake by your side.
I long to be sheltered,
by your arms.
Suddenly, my world is formed
around your very being.
Your grief is mine,
my happiness is found with yours.
You are my strength,
and weakness.
Without you
I exist . . . only
To live each day with hope
That you will soon be coming home . . . to me.

Bonnie Dayton

THE CAPTAIN'S CAP

The lad watched the Captain in awe,
And daydreamed of his future.
His enraptured face foretold,
The reputation he would nurture.

A sudden storm sealed the fate,

Of the proud old sailing ship.
Water poured into her hold,
When a many patched seam split.

The Captain burst from his stateroom,
His cap lost in the fray.
With one quick look, he signaled his mate.
"Abandon Ship," the mate relayed.

When all were in the life boats,
The Captain slid down the rope.
The crew pulled hard upon the oars,
With each stroke grew their hope.

A shout went up, the Captain turned,
And saw the lad upon the deck.
The Captain's cap upon his head,
He stood proud on the sinking wreck.

There was no hope to rescue him.
The Captain rose tight lipped.
The crew followed suit and all gave tribute,
As the Captain went down with his ship.

Eileen Spellman Billett

CAPISTRANO—A PACIFIC COAST MISSION

The Mission at San Juan, "Capistrano," By Name
Where "Gods" little Swallows; gave love and gained fame
For on March nineteenth on St. Josephs day
They return each year to remain a short stay.

Its a miracle how birds can a mission find
And stay a season and leave behind
A jewel of all missions for us to see
A treasure of ruins for you and me

"God" must have sent "Father Serra" on his way
For we learned the story of his work that day
But he worked and struggled and completed his chore
And built the mission on a peaceful shore

And on October twenty third, on San Juan Day,
The beautiful swallows ever so gay
Circle the mission in farewell flight,
And gone for a season they fly out of sight.

Louise Mustin

STILL

Take not your trembling breath from mine
With backsearing fingertips
electric white,
Skin glisten, shimmer with splashes of bright . . .
And what can we speak of now?
We face each other in violence,
Still
In love to the nerve's limit;
So it hurts to breathe, to move . . .
We scream until our voices shatter,
Bleeding larynx:
I will sing no more.
Dearest our blades are broken;
Twisted in triangle tangle.
Now teeth and claws may better serve
The lovers with an angle.
With each her crimson cross to bear,
We make a study in despair;
Still
Deeper deeply drive the nails,
And stretch to touch the golden grail . . .
For dagger eyes of tears that kiss and kill,
My heartrate flutters . . . slower . . . still.

Sally Cole Kravat

I REMEMBER MARY

Oh I remember Mary, sitting
in her chair
I can recall when I would
braid her blacken waist
long hair.

And in the morn, her nerves
near torn,
she'd rise up brave and warn,
"This promise I'll keep to
get my sleep, or you my pets
shall surely weep."

Afraid we were, those words
she meant but way down deep
we knew, that she was heaven
sent.

As wise as could be at eighty-
three, she was the grandest lady
there could ever be.

I still seek advise from this
lady so grand
Someday I shall join her
we'll circle the land,
we'll talk of the old, days,
and walk hand in hand.

Heidi Paris Kelley

MOTHER SEARCH

He stood in the doorway
Paint peeling
Blue-in jet black hair
Onyx eyes pierced
Into my heart
He ran up the stairs
And back down
Calling calling calling
Calling
Back upon the
Threshhold
Only melting
Now murky pools
Fell into my arms
Sobbing sobbing
Sobbing sobbing sobbing
Sobbing.

Enid Littlefield

BE STILL MY SOUL

Written when diagnosis of cancer was made. Dedicated to my dear friend, Haydon Sypert.

Lord, why? Why? WHY?!!!
From the depths of my soul, I cry.
There is no answer to this
In this world. There is no bliss
Without Christ, in whom alone
My trust I place.
'Tis He will give me strength to face
Life in this world, and He'll destroy
All doubt, when His help, I employ;
For God is ever in control.
Have mercy, Lord.
Be still my soul.

George O Chinn

TO MY LOVE

To my darling Meta

From snow-capped mountains to meadow bestowing
Through ice bordered streams, rivulets flowing
Water to nourish all things living and growing.

The sounds again of rippling brooks pleasing to ear,
Under rain freshed skies, gorgeously blue and clear,
Bring happy memories of times we were near.

Finch and sparrow flocks on utility line,
Red robins hopping, winging with mud, twig, and twine
To build nests, sturdy, cozy and fine.

God's creatures join in symphony; fragrance of new flora fills the air.
Lovers rapturously mating without a care
Vowing life long their love to share.

When everything on earth shows signs of spring,
Then young hearts (and sometimes old hearts) turn to sing
Words that express my feelings for thee ever true,
Which are quite simply:

"I love you."

Deana I Huffman

LIFE'S LASTING MEMORY

I've lost a love, but I'll no longer shed the tears; for I've grown stronger in the past few years.
I loved you with all my heart and soul and was willing to spend my life with you growing old.
We shared our lives for a time as one, with all of the sorrows and the fun.
We lived, we laughed, we loved then died, but did we really caringly try?
We were two individuals on our own, waiting for life's pleasures to warm our souls.
I don't regret the precious time we shared, for I learned that you did truly care.
I'll remember your warm smile and soft caring eyes,
I'll love no other the way I loved you, before I die.
We had our ups and a lot of downs too, but I'll remember the bright and not the blue,
For you were my love, my love true.

Richard L Yeakle

MY SPECIAL PRIZE

To my darling daughter, Bonnie Beth. You bring me joy always.

When will my dreams take me away
From the reality I dread by day
Knowing that I'll not be there
To wash her face or brush her hair
The beautiful child who calls me "Dad"
Oh how I miss her, it hurts so bad
I'm far away from her loving eyes

My little girl, My special prize
I'll see her soon and we'll go walking
Singing, dancing, laughing, talking
I'll tell her I love her and her Mommy, too
She'll say "I love you, and I miss you"
How do I tell her that once again
I'm going away till I don't know when
Then I hold her tight and say good-bye
I walk away and I hear her cry
Me, too

Tamara Lynn O'Brien

GONE

Home at last
The ice and loneliness begins
To melt by the fire
The coldness caving in
Tears wash through whirling memories
of my dead father
Hurt draining from my body
Once again feeling snug
The aching of my heart surrenders
to the warmth in my cheeks
No more falling tears
forgotten happiness gradually returns.

Anna Trampke

SPRING

For my beautiful life with my wonderful husband. Dedicated to Paul Trampke

---

It's been so long, I've waited the winter through
For spring to return with its skies of blue,
The long cold winter will finally pass,
Spring is my favorite, I wish it would last.

There's a robin perched now at my window sill,
Faraway in a distance I hear a whippoorwill.

Oh what a joy to see the oncoming spring,
Such wonderful sights that nature brings.

Sweet smell of honeysuckle fills the morning air,
Pretty flowers in bloom, spring's everywhere.
Rain falling softly as the meadows green,
Rare beauty abounds with the oncoming spring.

Trees turn green before my very eyes,
Kissed with dew glisten from the sky,
Crickets re singing while birds are in tune,
Spring soon will be gone, summer's in June.

Robby Bennefield

LIFE LONG FIGHT

This poem is dedicated to my Personal Savior Jesus Christ, and my loving Parents Billy and Arelia.

Many people didn't know I was out of control.
But I knew I was heading for that terrible place below.
So, today my life starts anew.
I am no longer split into.
Now my future is in my hands.
There is no fanfare; there are no bands.
Quietly I make the change.
Slowly I take the reins.
If God hadn't entered my life my soul was dead for sure.
Now that God has, my soul is washed clean, white as snow, it is now pure.
It is up to me to keep the faith.
It won't be easy for the devil knows he is the one whom I hate.
Please pray for me each night.
For this is a life long fight.

Peggie Pringle

GOD IS ALWAYS THERE

Today I walked alone in sorrow,
Knowing not what would come tomorrow.

I felt life was passing me by,
I felt nothing but pain and started to cry.

I remembered what a friend once said,
If you're down and out, bow your head.

I bowed my head and started to pray,
When suddenly I heard a soft voice say,

Come My Child, give your life to me,
I'll remove your pain and set you free.

This Man that stood high above me
Said, to humble yourself pleases Me.

Those who come to Me with an open heart,
Are one step ahead from the very start.

Take My hand and walk with Me for a while,
I'm here to comfort you My child.

We walked and talked and I felt renewed,
A peace came over me from my head to my shoes.

He said, with a great big smile,
This is only a sample My Child.

Walking with God can bring eternal gladness,
There is no need for pain and sadness.

Edie Carter

INSIDE OF YOU

For "Tillie" my mom and Douglas

I want to be inside of you.
I want to feel . . . what you feel too!
I want to know your thoughts and dreams.
I want to know the hidden streams of thoughts
and dreams, that run across your mind.
And dance like elve's in other times!
I want to dream the dreams you do.
I want to play along the way of golden
thoughts, from yesterday.
I want to know the "little child" who must
still be hidden there!
I want to laugh behind your eyes; when they
close themselves away from the skies.
I want to love . . . just as you do . . .
so carefully and lovingly!
I want to live your life with you, inside of you.
So we can be "two" inside of you!

Curtis Burgess

UNICORNS

Unicorns
Look up in the sky
And blow your horn
For there will appear
A unicorn
So gay and dearly
So fond and freely
Hovering high above the morn

Edith L Kennedy

AS I SIT HERE OVERLOOKING THE BAY

As I sit here overlooking the bay
I watch the ships go their way
Some are large, some are small
No matter which, it is the
Greatest Navy of all.

Some are coming in to be repaired
Others are going out to do their share
Now that peace we have won
They'll help to see that war is shun.
With the greatest Navy in the sea
They'll carry out democracy.

Roderick Taylor

THE SEA AND I

Dedicated to Mrs. Doris Straw, Ms. Bernice Noland & Son, Ms. Adrielle Preval

I love to cruise out to sea
but the sea doesn't like me.

For I am a natural born landlubber,
Riding the highwaves gives me trouble.

My maladjusted stomach to the sea make me green.
Only a strong stomach can keep you clean.

I tried motion sickness pills,
A storm develops and makes me ill.

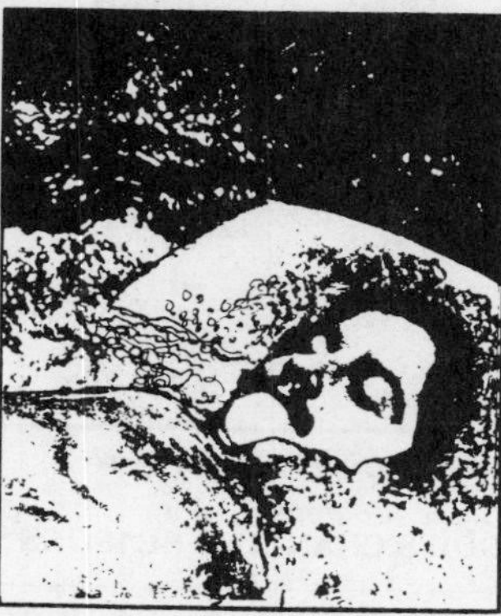

The best time that I love the sea is when she is calm.
Unpredictably at anytime there can be a storm.

On a clear night at sea,
The infinitemestical stars amazes me.

There is a spirit of freedom while on the sea.
As long as a storm is not upon me.

The awesome power of the sea.
It is good to know that only G-O-D can control thee.

David Charles Costello

VIETNAM

For all who lost their precious lives to the Nam. To those who made it out—may God bless you all—

As a silent gray cloud
lain high above the town of Kent
off to Vietnam
All our children went
Indeed those children fought for us
their names and faces since unknown
So many children left that day
So few of them came home

Margaret Brown

MISS DOLLY

She sits quietly in the corner,
a slight smile upon her face.
But, Oh! the things that she could tell you,
of, another time, another place.
The little girl was younger then,
and when she came to call,
grandma would always let her play;
with Miss Dolly in the hall.
Time passed so very quickly.
Now Miss Dolly sits and waits.
For the little girl of yesteryear,
to keep their weekly dates.
Grandma is getting feable now,
her mind is not the same.
She limps a little when she walks,
sometimes she needs a cane.
The little girl of yesteryear,
still visits now and then.
She always looks for Miss Dolly,
and she holds her once again.
Upon her bed grandma lays,
her time has reached an end.
Take care; of Miss Dolly, she asks—
She's been your faithful friend.
Upon a bench she now is perched,
greets each who comes to call.
Another child now holds her.
She sits waiting in the hall . . .

Ellen M (Brandy) Canfield

TO SAY I LOVE YOU

This poem is dedicated to my husband, Skip, whose love and support inspired these words.

To say 'I Love You' is to say
I accept your imperfections.
To say 'I need you' is to say
My life would have an empty
place if you weren't here,
To say 'I want you' means
I enjoy your presence even when we are apart.
To say 'I'm sorry' is to admit
that I'm not perfect either.

Sallie Louise Thompson

SALVATION IS ONLY A REACH AWAY

To My Mother and Daughter, Yvonne

I'll make my journey through life with Thee
Knowing that I can take none with me;
On this crusade I must travel all alone
For I must atone for all the ill seeds I have sown . . .
I'll climb that unclimbable mountain high,
Ever keeping my eyes and arms stretched to the sky
I'll talk to my Lord as I go on my way,
Blotting out all sounds except what "He" says.
I'll linger on each plateau, add fuel to my life tank
Go down on my knees and give my Father thanks
I'll blunder and stumble along the unknown terrain
Lord, give me courage so that I will not complain
Steady my footsteps, give me wisdom to be sure
Cleanse my body and soul and make my heart pure
I look to heaven, see there Your smiling face
And know that I am protected by Thine loving grace
Lead on Dear Jesus help my quest day by day
The wonder of salvation is only a reach away.

Barbara E Leach

TO CREATE

Poetry
is the greatest
way to escape;
but only
for minutes at a time.

A thought flits by—
a memory persists—
in a sculpters way.
To take the thought
to use with the memory,
is my mind's way
of sculpting
a great piece of art!

For if it were not for my hand
to rove so gently,
My thoughts
would always remain stale
While my memory
faded away!

Pamela Kathryn Hortenstine
THE HOME COMING

To my Aunt Norma Jean and to my best friends, my mom and dad.

The day I've so long awaited is now
so close at hand,
The day I've anticipated, the return
of my best friends.
The feelings I have, I can't discern,
for how I do not know.
It's not just joy for their return, it's
why they chose to go.
What a precious mission of love
they decided to imbark,
It was a time in the days of my life
that shall always remain in my
heart.
My love for them so much has
grown, since they have been
away
Somehow I never felt alone, their
love touched me everyday.
God touched another life through
theirs, there's no feeling that's so
sweet;
For they kept walking one more
mile, till at last, their
journey stood complete.
One day I asked the Lord to send
to our beloved Aunt Jean's side,
The sweetest angel that He had,
through death to be her guide.
Then as I sat to write these words
I heard my Jesus speak,
He said "Beloved, I knew the need,
before you came to me.
You asked that I send my angels,
the sweetest that I had,"
He said He'd done that long ago
when He sent my Mom and Dad.
There they stayed, by way of grace
at the side of His child, Norma
Jean,
Until they saw her safely tucked
beneath an angel's wing.

Marti Jo Stepp
TO MARY FROM JOHN

During the war, I was a nurse.
I visited the patients and talked to
them.
But, mainly, I just listened.

There was one man, boy actually.
His name was John.
He asked me to help him.

He wanted a letter written
To his beloved Mary.
I sat with parchment, ink, and quill.

His lips moved,
But all he said was,
"Mary I love you."
Then, his voice faded away.

I wrote the line, then looked over
at him.
His eyes were closed,
And no breath he drew.

I looked at the parchment.
I felt I should finish the letter
But how—How
How to tell her he was gone

I wondered on that point,
But, then I knew.
I finished the letter
By signing it "John".

Hattie (Calihan) Taylor

Hattie (Calihan) Taylor
GOD'S CHANGING SEASONS

To my beloved husband Bob, our children and grandchildren.

Spring comes with flowers and
trees so green
Then Summers heat comes to burn
and wilt it.
Along comes Fall with it's colorful
scene,
That Winter covers with it's white
blanket.

Through it all we see God's hand.
He created this beauty for the
enjoyment of man.

So enjoy the grass, the birds, the
trees,
The flowers, the shrubs and the
kiss of the breeze.
Then lift your hands give God
thanks for it all,
He could have made this whole
world bald!

Kenneth Stephen McHattie
ISLAND OF THE MIDNIGHT SUN

Standing on the shore of an ocean
In the furthest reach of my mind
Experience this hazy sunset
Don't get lost in my paradise

The world is painted to match
My azured ocean and sky
There is a way to escape
Just sink back into your mind

Undescribable.
Beautiful.
Goodnight.

Morning comes with
Dreams and cold mist
If only it was true bliss . . .
But it wasn't

Lou Conrad
GROCERY SHOPPING

Dedicated to my loving husband, Vernon, for "understanding."

Grocery shopping is a pain in the
neck,
I sure do hate it, but what the heck!
I grew up, with one bad habit;
My tummy says "I gotta have it."
Eating meals three times a day,
And for all that food, we've got to
pay!

Every week it's ten cents more,
On every item in the store!
I wait <u>two hours</u> to get thru the line,
And hug my money, while it's still
mine!
And when I gotta hand it over,
I don't cry, but I <u>Suuure</u> look sober!

Sometimes I feel, my family
should,
Be on diets . . . we'd look <u>real good</u>!
Or vegetarians, we <u>all</u> should be . . .
That wouldn't be too tough for me!
'Cause when I look at the price of
meat,
It knocks me down, right on my
seat!

Someday . . . I hope . . . Someone
discovers,
The <u>SECRET</u> of all "Brand New
Lovers,"
They don't need much food at all . . .
'Cause "LOVE" is how they answer
"the call!"

But as for now, I have to go.
My spirit's down, and I'm feelin'
low,
Grocery shopping's a pain in the
neck,
I'll hate it <u>forever</u>, but what the
heck!

Beatrice Dobelle
INCARCERATION

To Harry who has always been our inspiration

It seems one day I heard a soaring
sound
Tho' not of world but there in outer
sphere
Of angel wings a whirlwind rush of
air
That to my ears and heart were
earthward bound.
Within that consonance of chords
I found
A stilling opiate urging me to dare
To plumb the depths of ego and
bare
The servitude that chained me to
the ground.
What hapless soul that could not
fly on wing
To beatitude and ardent lips that
say,
"Come to my breast, I will
compassion bring
Away from scenes discordant and
awry!"
The sea subdues great stones and
I will sing
Thus chains of fettered soul
breaking away.

Betty Hamrick
THE OLD HOMEPLACE

To Dewitt, my husband. In loving memory of his parents

The old homeplace stands alone,
it's no longer a home
Where the family worked and
played
The floors have worn through, the
walls have cracked too
And the paint is fading away
But I remember the time this old
house was alive
When the family came in from the
fields
Momma standing there, apron and
gray hair
Oh God, the memory is so real
If I could just go home and see her
face
Warm my hands by the old
fireplace
See dad sitting there in his favorite
chair
Dozing off with a smile on his face
If I could just lay my head down
on that old iron bed
Say goodnight to my mom and my
dad
I would give all I own if I could go
home
I would give all that I had
Memories are sweet but you can't
repeat
The good times that were had way
back then
So I'll brush back the tears, get on
with the years
But I'll always remember then

Floy May Nicks
SUGAR AND SPICE

To the ladies of the missionary society of the Wesleyan Church, Sioux City, Iowa who asked me to write this. Especially Marge.

A little sugar in the tea makes it
extra nice.
Heap it on strawberries—Aaaah,
you're in paradise.
Put a little on the cereal—makes it
more complete.
Bake up some sugar cookies for an
extra special treat.
One could just go on and on. Sweet
things we all crave.
But too much of a good thing can
put us in the grave.

Cinnamon in the apple pie adds
that special touch.
And some little cloves stuck in the
ham help it oh so much.
Nutmeg on the custard flavors it
just right.
And a plate of ginger cookies jogs
the appetite.
Sugar and spice are what we need
for flavor and good taste.
They add a lot to many
things—especially the waist.

Alot of people in this world need
some sugar and spice.
I have a good suggestion so please
take my advice.
Just give your life to Jesus. He
knows just what to do.

He'll take away all sin and shame
and give it back to you.
He'll heap on the sugar—spice it up

just right.
You'll think it was a miracle that happened over night.

Sugar and spice are expensive. We know they cost alot.
And the price keeps going up and up. It doesn't ever stop.
They can raise the cost of sugar and raise the cost of spice.
But inflation cannot hurt us because Jesus paid the price.
He died upon the cruel cross. Oh, what a sacrifice.
So let HIM be your sugar, and let HIM be your spice.

James Lindsey Frost

A WINTER DREAM

One cold November morn,
Amidst the virgin snow,
There came to me, a winter dream
Of a fair haired girl I used to know.
Her shimmering eyes of crystal blue
Were filled with magic all her own,
Like a mountain spring and it's liquid hues
Or a summer sky of vivid tone
I was whisked away by that winter dream,
Transported through space and time,
To happier days and places we'd seen,
Sparkling still in memory
Deep within my mind.
I'd stay there too, that much I know,
But I was reminded of things
That I still must do
By a northeast wind that began to blow.
Those fragments of paradise
Will see me through,
Shielded by memories
From the frost and snow,
By that fair haired girl
That I once knew

Nancy Kendon

LIBERTY REMEMBRANCE

I was a part of history.
Even now the concept is hard to grasp.
Such a simple thing really,
Singing, something I do so often.
And yet, the intricate fabric woven by those harmonies was composed of emotions which will never quite be duplicated.
The real world was deposited at the gate, and cynicism was swallowed by the rising spark of excitement.
The Orchestra began.
The moment had arrived.
"Oh Say Can . . . "
But the notes weren't there. They had become entangled in a web of feelings which had manifested themselves as a lump in my throat and a trickle of moisture from my eye.
Pride.
So often we forget—but there it was, palpable, with a life all it's own.
Reality is back now, but the memories remain.
And when the gates are opened, and they flood back to drown everyday thoughts, I can feel the heartbeat again. "Oh beautiful for spacious skies . . . "
Remember! The emotions.
Rejoice! The excitement.
Renew! The memories.
I was a part of history!

Joyce Halasz

LOVE IS

Love is kindness
Love is caring
In times of sadness
Love is sharing
Love is there in times of need
Love is doing a helpful deed
Love is singing and crying together
Love is there in all kinds of weather
In summers heat, in winters cold
Love is for the young and for the old
Love is giving without regret
Giving freely, not to get

A sharing of thoughts and emotions
Consideration and devotion
Love is hearing words unspoken
Love is compassion and understanding
Love is asking, not demanding
Love is to be there in sickness and health
Love survives bad times, appreciates wealth
Love is forgiving each others mistakes
Love can be teaching but doesn't dictate
Love doesn't die at the first sign of stress
It sometimes can bring you unhappiness
It's not always pefect and filled with bliss
But a part of life that no one should miss

S E Liveoak

CHANGE

A wish for man to see his folly

Once there was a stream here
And trees.
Birds would flirt with the sky
Dancing colors.
It was Spring. Flowers bloomed
And sweet fragrance filled the air

Summer came.
And brought a subtle change
Rich color
Friendly showers cooling the days
starry nights
Flowers gave way to fresh green shade trees

Fall came.
And brought yet another change
Cool nights
A hint of frost. Sometimes color everywhere
As trees shed their green mantles
Fallen leaves.

Winter came.
And brought man. And change
Once there was a stream here
And trees.
Now there's a shopping mall.
I cried.

Bridget Williams Creel

REMEMBER

Look at the sun that's shining above,
Believe there'll always be another Love.

Think of the moon against midnight blue,
You'll know there's someone thinking of you.

When the birds begin to fly,
Hold back that lonely cry.

All the days and all the miles,
Bring back those old familiar smiles.

This will be a brand new day,
You'll see the past in a special way.

Feel the Gentle sprinkle of rain.

Love and Life aren't taken in vain.
Dream the dreams that you believe,
For your memories will never leave.

Walk through the forest and the snow in December,
And don't ever forget that you'll always Remember.

Donna Berry Keffer

WASTED

Not for what was, I weep.
But for what could have been.
My tears flood forth at thoughts of
Love not shown
Devotion not felt
Loyalty undemonstrated.
For vows broken
And never healed.
For hearts rendered cold
And uncultivated,
Incapable of reaping their
Harvests of love
In soil barren and acid.
Opportunities laid waste
In sour fields—full of brambles
And thorns
Barriers to compassion
And understanding.
For the years and years wasted—!
For these I weep.

Brenda Delatte

WEE LITTLE ELF MAN

Wee little elf. Tinier than small, I'll tell
you a story to make you feel tall;
Wee little elf man, small as a fig, I'll tell
you a story to make you feel big;
Wee little elf man, with a mushroom as
your sky, I'll tell you a story to make you
feel high
Wee little elf man, what a life you plee, frolic
surrounds you, through mythical charms of glee;
Wee little elf man, how lucky you are—not a care;
Not a love; Not a hate; not a bore;
Wee little elf man, do the dewdrops tickle your nose,
as you wake, in the dawn from the shelter of a rose.
Wee little elf man, have you a friend to call your own,
as the toads that live beneath the logs, so undauntifully
alone.
Wee little elf man I'd like to hold you in my hand
but you're just a wee fellow—an image to the Irish
land;
Wee little elf man, I'll say farewell for now, though in my
mind you bend and bow—you'll always be near to me;
The wee little elf man, I NEVER DID SEE.

Todd R Harbison

ONE WISH

For infinate hope of understanding the outer reach to understand . . .

Oh, if I only could,
Should I, should I, should I?
Well I do know I would,
If I could.
If the smoke wasn't in my eyes,
I would let out a great big sigh!
So I guess I should stop contemplating,
And do, do, do.
If only I could pack up and go,
Or maybe have something to do.
So well! so well, so well.
Life is a continuation . . .
If it was't it would be a flop.
I know one thing, I want to be on top!
Love is precious.
Some think it's not.
You do what you have to do,
Even if it is sought.
Life sometimes involves putting things
In a sack.
If only in a day,
Not two, not three, not four.
Please Lord, if only I could smoke,
Just one pack.

Barbara Whisenant

UNSPOKEN WORDS OF LOVE

Birthday candles, your face all aglow
I saw you today . . .
Wearing an angel's halo.

I missed being there, Farrah
to pass down Heaven's path with you;
Today I told God . . .
five years were just too few.

An angel turned six in Heaven today
give her a kiss for me . . .
She gave us her life
so loving and free.

We miss your sweet smile
those big, brown eyes,
That chuckling little voice . . .
we can hear for awhile.

People you love were at your grave today
they felt you nearby . . .
You heard all the words said to you
except the quiet word "why?"

For me the pain is still there
maybe even more . . .
A touch from you would give me "life"
and I'd give God the score.

The stars do still twinkle
in the wide open sky . . .

The earth still turns
tho' we wonder why.

Cars go up and down the streets
and rain gently falls,
A heart skips a beat
as an angel softly calls.

Surely the angels know
what Farrah's birthday means;
All on earth sit sadly,
we should be happy it seems.

But the "promise" of knowing
you're in a safe, sweet place
Has helped me through many
moments
as tears streamed down my face.

Growing up in Heaven
will be quite hard to do . . .
just for us, that is,
on earth, we'll miss you.

You'll make a sweet angel
a "Heavenly delight"
One day we'll see you
oh! What a sight!

But, until that time
and whatever that day
Our hearts stay together on
the 24th of May.

A beautiful day in Heaven
I'm sure this day must be
Here on earth unspoken
come these words of love
from me

Inez (Iverson) Nikko
METER OF PSALM OF LIFE

To my loved ones, parents Hersey and Mary Iverson, sisterClara, brother Arlie, daughter Dorothy— grand daughters Vivian, Sally, Connie, Margie, Yvette, 6 great grand children, Iverson Shisler and Wm. Nikko.

Tell me not in such deep figures,
The Senior Class is in a dream.
As we graduate from high school,
But we're smarter than we seem.

We are truthful and in earnest.
And we shall strive to reach our
goals,
We will fight to our endurance,
With our heart and with our soul.

We may all meet some great
sorrow,
One may be lighter than the rest,
But we'll somehow struggle
through it,
And thus do our very best.

School is over, for a while,
But it's memory is left.
Thus showing that our sorrows,
Were soon over and bereft.

In the schools broad field of
knowledge,
We all tried to take our share,
We were eager, yet relenting,
Wishing to treat all Classmates fair.

Thoughts of honor oft remind us,
We should try to make our feet.
Tred the path for Juniors to follow,
And be met by what we meet.

Let us then continue working
To make something of life or fate,
And when sad, recall old memories,
Of when we did graduate.

T H Bowen
GONE
My child is gone. Where did she go?
She was here just yesterday.
She was so near to laugh and play.
Now she has gone her separate
way.
Oh, how I long. I miss her so.

My love is gone. Where did she go?
She was here so short a time.
She was so near and she was mine.
Now she is gone, I, left behind.
Oh, how I long. I miss her so.

My dream is gone. Where did it go?
It was here because I willed.
It was so near, to be fulfilled.
Now it has gone. It has been killed.
Oh,how I long. I miss it so.

My friend is gone. Where did he go?
He was here—his time so brief.
He was so near; he gave relief.
Now he is gone, but not the grief.
Oh, how I long. I miss him so.

My life is gone. Where did it go?
It was here, a candle flame.
It was so near, to make its claim.
Now it is gone from whence it
came.
Oh, how I long. To miss it so.

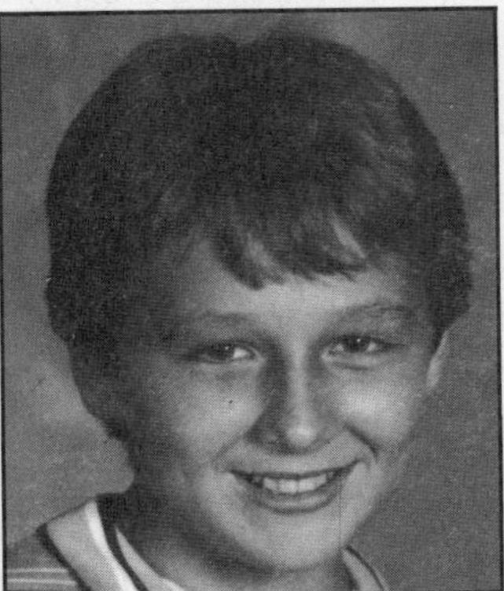

Kevin Lee Spears

Terry Lee Spears
A NEVER ENDING BOND BETWEEN A FATHER AND HIS SON

This poem is dedicated to our son Kevin Lee Spears, his time with us was brief, but in our hearts he lives forever.

On a cold and gray December
Morn,
a little baby boy was born,
With eyes of blue, and hair of
gold,
I pondered yet, of dreams untold.
A Movie Star? An athelete? The
whole
Wide world lay at our feet.
I watched him grow, day by day,
and guided him in a loving way.
He learned to swim, he learned
to fish, to see a star, and make a
wish.
The years flew by, I watched him
grow, his courage and wisdom
began to show.
And then one day, When I was
gone, the Angels came to take
him home.
He was my sun, he was my rain,
he was my joy and my pain.
But through it all, my love endures,
for in my heart I hold him near.
The meadows and streams where
we once roamed, Now down
life's road, I walk alone,
I hope some day God calls me
home"
In Loving Memory of a great
little guy,
My son, Kevin Spears.

Norma Minjares Carrasco
EMPTY POTS

This poem is dedicated to my sister Lola who encouraged me to write.

You see children without shoes.
I never owned a coat but I was not
cold.
Empty cupboards. No food on the
table.
Pots of water on the stove boiling
over and over again.
"Check the pots," my Mom would
say. "But
there is no food in them," I would
answer.
"Why do we have to boil water?" I
would ask.
"So the neighbors will think I am
cooking the food to eat," she
replied.
I pretend to be cooking and would
look in silence.
Our suffering will disappear
someday, I would dream.
I could see my little brothers and
sisters
faces and big starry eyes that
would turn and
smile like reaching out for freedom
of poverty.

Orlando Ortiz
INDIVIDUALITY

This poem is dedicated to: A special few, who've taught me and helped me, to never deal myself short. God Bless You!

If there's anything I've learned,
From either of you—
It's never give up,
And never be blue.

Sure times are hard,
And it's not easy to be strong,
But hardest of all,
Is figuring, where you belong.

People will say, "Who is that child,
Romping around, has he really
gone wild?"

"His clothes are outrageous,
His dance is obscene—"
But what they cannot realize,
Is that he's living a dream.

He won't settle, for second to best,
'Cause second to anything, is just
like the rest.

You'll say, "It's not easy.," "They
won't understand."
But hey who's to say, "I'm king of
the land—"

The pieces are many,
The chances are few,
But the key to the puzzle,
Is that "I'm not you!"

Anni Dorwart
HOPEFULLY
The world keeps singing a
sorrowful song.
And I can sing right along.
We can sing about disease
A subject with which no one is at
ease.
We can sing about starvation—
It should be a moral violation.
We can sing of peace and war,
We can sing of blood and gore.
Maybe someday we can chime
Of peace—in our time—hopefully.

The world keeps singing a
sorrowful song.
And I can sing right along.
We can sing of devastation
And of destruction.
We can sing of the lives lost
All at their country's cost.
We can sing of Gorbachev,
Quaddafi,
And of the Ayatolha Khomeini.
Leaders who seem power crazed
But their values are just
dazed—hopefully.

The world keeps singing a
sorrowful song.
And I can sing right along.
Not hopefully.

Roberta Wagner
MY PEN
My pen writes my feelings out
Line by line the mask is removed
No place to hide, anymore.

My pen of black it writes out my
sadness of long lost love
My pen of black it has no feelings
so it doesn't care
When my teardrop erases the
words that once said love.

My pen of blue it loves you
Though many pages remain you do
not
It will push others aside like you
pushed it aside
That doesn't matter.

My pen of red it writes where no
one can find it
My pen of red it writes of passion
where two hearts play
It writes of the before and the after
of a love game
Only to remain, ever after, alone.

My pen of green it writes of envy
and jealousy
It writes only to have its face ripped
up with anger
To lie in peace after sleep.

My pen of nothingness will forever
be in hand
It will wait in the shadows for a
moments thought
Only then to erase what was there
It will smile when the poet finally
loses hope of writing.

The poet is always inside his pen
Of black, blue, of red and green, of
nothingness.
See him now smiling
After his creation of solitude.

Evelyn M Forsting
A SUMMER STORM
Storm clouds quickly gather,
Eerie shadows form,
God is warning all below,
The coming of the storm.

Now the raindrops tapping
On the window pane,
God's bathing His creation,
All will be fresh again.

Glistening raindrops on the grass
Reflect like diamonds as we pass,

Blooming things have much to gain
From the vital gift of rain.

Birds with feathers freshly bathed,
Twitter frightened, yet so tame,
Sounding just as if to say
"Thank You for the lovely rain."

Flowers drooped and withered,
Lift their heads again,
They, too, look to Heaven
To say "Thank You for the rain."

Fret not for clouds appearing,
The sun's still shining there,
Waiting to smile down again
Through clean, fresh rain-bathed
air.

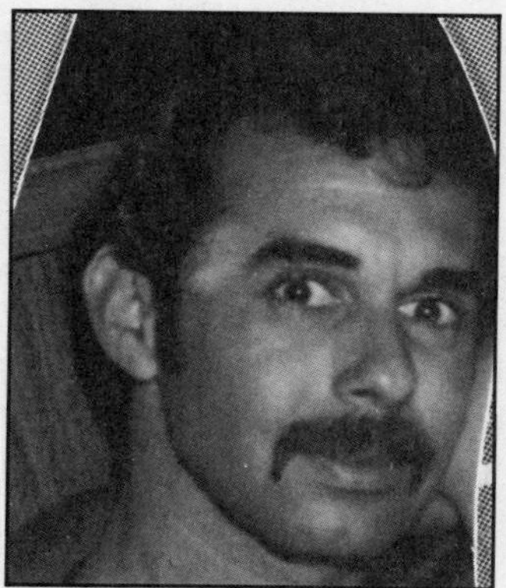

Victor R Valdez

Victor R Valdez
I LOVE YOU

I dedicate this poem to a special friend with whom I fell in love, not as a memory, but as a hope and a dream.

I love you with my mind
For you live within my every
thought,
From the slightest flicker of
remembrance
Of a dream long past, to the
Memory of yesterday as our love
Entwined and rapture wrought.

I love you with my eyes
For I see you all around me,
As far, as high, and as wide as my
eyes can see.
And with all that I am and all that
I feel,
Without regret, without
reservation, unconditionally.

I love you with my heart,
For therein lies the very beginning
Of my emotions,
My laughter, my tears and
Unconquerable passion.

I love you with an uncertainty,
As God may not grant me
Tomorrow's breath,
And if so, as I have loved you in
Life, so shall I love you in death.

Joseph O McCann
FEELINGS

Of all the feelings I've suppressed,
Until I thought the time was best.
To show you that I really care,
Although at times I feel despair.
For all the moments we have lost,
And all the love my moods have
cost.
I know that I have come so far,
To tell you what those feelings are.

Betty Jane Roseberry
THE WOES OF A D. W. I.

Oh if you could only see,
The misery drinking and driving
caused me.
It started with a drag race, just for
fun—
The arm of the law put me on the
run,
I did not get far in the chase,
A terrible accident was my fate.
Scared to death I ran away,
Now I've really got to pay.
First they arrest you, your parents
post bail,
You can pick up your son down at
the jail.
It's lawyers, courts, judges and
fines,
They don't leave you one thin dime.
Fifty weekends at their inn,
It's sure boredom without your
friends.
Two years probation you must fear,
Lost your license for a year.
A.A. classes you must attend,
They tell you when they will end.
You're called an alkie if you drink,
That's the part that makes you
think.
All it takes is a few too many,
Don't get behind the wheel, if
you've had any!
Because if you do,
All of this could happen to you.

Ruth E Osborn
THE CYCLE OF TWO

Lovingly dedicated to Traci and Robyn, and their mothers,Joyce and Judi.

Two little girls; they came to stay.
They came to stay for a year or a
day.
They stayed and played as children
will,
Fair curls atop bright frocks and
frill.
How short the days; how soon the
dawn.
I glanced away, and alas, they were
gone.

Two teen-age misses; they were
here, then away
With a flurry of mischief to stir my
dismay.
So fleet were those days of frolic
and joys,
Of hidden treasures and
neighborhood boys.
Just how many dreams can youth
contain?
When I glanced away they were
gone again.

Two fair young maids. They would
never stay.
The signs foretold they'd be gone
some day.
With feet atwirl at proms and dates,
And hearts awhirl when Love
dictates,—
Those bridal showers,—a tossed
bouquet.
This time I knew they'd be gone to
stay.

Two young wives,—now mothers,
too,
Begin again the cycle of two.

Two tiny tots; they've come to stay.
They've come to stay for a year or
a day.
They'll stay and play as children
will,
Fair curls atop bright frocks and
frill.
Young mothers, reach out! Hold
back the dawn!
Don't glance away, for too soon
they are gone.

Glendola Skaggs
ARE YOU TROUBLED

When you are in deep trouble
You feel you are lost and all alone
Tell God about your problem
He will point the way to lead you
home.

If you are deeply troubled
And can't seem to find your way
Just be patient for the answer
And take some time to Pray.

Does God say no
And we do not hear
Or does God say yes
And we do not care.

It's hard to be calm
When I am tossed by an angry sea
But if I trust Gods great mercy
He will calm and comfort me.

When I tell Him I am lonely
And I am lost in deep despair
If I be still and listen
I can feel my Heary repair.
I am sorry for my loved ones
When their blessings they can not
see
all the beauty in this world
He has made for them and me.

Rose Neal
SEASONS OF LOVE

Will you love me in winter as you
did early spring
When life was so young and robins
did sing
Will you always remember the love
that we shared
We loved and we laughed without
worry or care
But soon spring was fading away
in the past
And then came the summer with
problems at last
We worked and we played we
laughed and we cried
But no matter what faced us we
tried and we tried
How could I have faced a situation
like this
If my marital status was much less
than bliss
How beautiful is Autumn
embracing our love
The future we'll face with God'
precious love
Winter is coming it soon will be
cold
With you at my side I won't mind
growing old
But tell me my darling what news
will you bring
Will you love me in winter as you
did early spring

Onalee A Butler Weaver
HAVE I?

To my three; Mikell Lee, Melinda Ann, & Ryan Scot

Have I walked this way before?
Stood where I now stand?
Written words just like these
In a strange yet familiar hand?

Am I a ghost on the eternal path?
Or a soul to earth returned?
Can I say this life's my last
Or is this just another turn?

Has fate dealt me these blows
before?
Or was she kinder in the past?
Is this life better or worse than
before
And how can I know if it is my last?

No, there are no answers for a
questing soul
In this life, before, or perhaps
another yet to come
No choice have I, to live or die
So just give me the faith to carry on!

Edith G Ford
WINNING THE RACE

You cannot get to heaven knocking
one another down. Stumbling
backward and forward and all
around get in a straight line and
stand at attention willing to run
with patience and love.
Let grace be your stride and the
spirit be your guide running side
by side.

Don't stand too tall least you fall,
keep your eye on the track and
don't look back keep your mind
on the race and don't loose your
place.
Strive for perfection because you
got protection let Jesus control
your mind.

Betty Watson
WHISPER OF THE WIND

This poem is dedicated to my sister Mary for all the help she has given me.

I stood upon a mountaintop,
With the sky not far above;

And I heard the distant calling,
Of a lonesome mourning dove.

I heard the whisper of the wind,
As it blew gently through my hair;
And I felt so close to nature,
As I briefly lingered there.

I tarried a moment longer,
To listen to the sound;
That all the wild creatures make,
When they think no one's around.

But surely the sound, that I loved best,
As the day came to an end;
And I stood, on the mountaintop,
Was the whisper of the wind.

Hazel D Fisher

HUMBLE SERVANTS

Happiness is ours every day
If we let Jesus have his way.
His gift of love is oh so sweet
No other could e'er compete.

Treasure in Heaven we can share,
Truth, love and grace, the gifts of prayer.
Answered by our ever-loving God
As the pathway to glory believers trod.

To die to self is not in vain,
When all the glories of Heaven we gain.
Being so everlasting blessed
With a home of eternal rest.

Weigh everything we do and say;
Making sure the Lord has His way.
Help us to always humbly pray
To live fulfilled from day to day.

To be with our lot in life content,
Making the most of each moment spent—
In loving Christ and our fellowman.
Thank you for good Servants God. AMEN

Ione Gilbertson

MY MOTHER

In memory of my mother, Evelyn Loiland

I never told you
When you were here.
How much I loved you,
Mother dear.

But I think you knew
By the cards I sent
Just how much to me,
You really meant.

You were always so giving
And considerate of others.
A friend to all,
And the best of mothers.

The sound of your laughter
Is always, with me.
And your smiling face
I still can see.

Patricia Cirillo

SUNNY SIDE UP

In dedication to Joseph Welke.

The morning is here
and the morning has begun
for he was a fine man
who always loved his eggs in the pan

He was loved by all
and always had a call
Generosity, Sincerity, and Age

Yes, a gray morning
All dressed in black
Wishing he could come back

Remembering his ways
Cheereful all his days
Teaching his young
Not to be sad and glum
Look to the Sunny Side
Eggs on the Sunny Side Up
And never mess up your sunny yolks.

Esther Pollitt Weaver

HIS FIRST PASTORATE

Lord, he's so young,
So very young for this most awesome task.
For through the years I've seen
The rise and fall of older, wiser men.
But Thou in Thine own wisdom hast decreed
That this young shepherd tend this little flock.
So be it Lord,
Though trembled I when this appointment came.
Your hand has oft been heavy,
Your ways austere
While shaping this most precious bit of clay.
This needs must be I know.
But how I hurt when he is bruised
Conforming to Thy will.
I've often quailed
As Thou hast laid the lash
Of Thy chastisement on his erring heart.
But now dear Lord,
I stand aside and watch-in prayer,
As Thou according to Thy plan,
Performest Thy work in him.
To break him—mold him—use him,
My flesh, my blood, my bone,
But, oh, Lord—he's so young.

Sandi Mroz

A NEVER ENDING VOW OF LOVE

Alone . . .
i think of . . .
You . . .
make me dream of . . .
Together . . .
i long for the gentle touch of . . .
You . . .
and i create in my mind and body a . . .
Oneness . . .
that makes me know i couldn't be me without . . .
You . . .
make my inner self happy even when i'm . . . alone

Stephen C Johnston

A THROWAWAY'S FINAL ESCAPE

Escaping to the streets he hustled to survive,
being handsome new and fresh money came easy.

The first lane of drugs, booze, and promiscuous sex
provided thrills as only temporal escapes,
momentary diversions from mental anguish,
torments so deep their scars were irreversible,
depression and sadness no high times could erase.

Forget as he tried his memory was vivid
filled with the horrors of his mean father's beatings,
angered and jealous over his mom's many men,
starved for fillial love which no one provided,
abused and abandoned his mind could not forget.

Surrounded by decadence and burdened by memories,
tragic suicide eliminated both enemies.

Lena Long

GOD BLESSED THIS TREE

To my sister Belle Smith, Happy Birthday.

God blessed this tree And from it grew
A family more precious Then silver and gold
The branches grew longer And the tree grew taller
Some leaves turn brown And fell to the ground
Soon new leaves were in sight
Filling our hearts with delight

We went our separate ways But when there was trouble
We remembered our love for each other With hearts full of love
And the blue sky above The birds that sing
The flowers blooming in the spring
Is a promise from God
Of a brighter tomorrow.

Diane Nieset Joseph

RAIN

Rain—
the heavens crying
For all the tears unshed
If only a droplet
For each and every head—
that had no mourner
that had no grave
that had no dignity
Left to save—

Thunder—
heaving a mighty groan
For the wars forgotten
Fought for causes unknown—
For the maimed and the crippled
The lost and the chained,
For the lives that were wagered
And the deaths that were gained.

Gary John Pullman

I'LL BE THERE

Life seems so short as time goes on.
The seasons seem shorter and shorter
As the years quickly pass by.
And I know, too, that the day will soon be here
When I am dead and gone. But life will go on,
So do not mourn for me,
For God has given me a spirit that will always be there.
Just watch and listen for those little reminders
Telling you that I am there.

When that cold November wind bites at your face,
That will be reminding you that I am there.
As that big buck snorts and the steam bellows
From his nostrils, I'll be there.
As the white belly of the "Proud Angler" walleye flashes
Just under the boat, I'll be there.
As the cock pheasant bursts from the cover
Just under your feet, I'll be there.
As those geese set their wings and begin to drift
Down into the decoys, I'll be there.

And when that cold winter wind blows with its unforgiving ferocity
Turning this land into a seemingly lifeless void,
I'll be there, too.
For my spirit shall live forever,
forever drifting upon the wind,
And wherever a wild thing grows and lives,
I'll be there.

Ida M Bienz

THE VALUE OF A FRIEND

In memory of my parents Wayne and Lenore Graybeal

Because you taught me kindness,
Held out a helping hand;
Because you taught me loyalty
Of a stronger, finer brand;
Because you taught me confidence
When everything went wrong;
Because you taught that courage
Is the strength to carry on;
Because you taught me patience
When mine was at an end;
Because of these I've learned from you
The value of a friend.

Melissa Sue Bugbee

THE GRAY OLD MILL

The gray old mill, was so still . . .
on that very hill,
Oh! The gray old mill.
The gray old mill . . .
was so still, as the wind blowed,
and the water flowed.
The gray old mill, was so very still
On that very hill.

Dave Binkley

THE PRIDE I FEEL INSIDE

This poem is dedicated to the Lord. In his grace he allowed me to be born an American.

His teacher called him stupid,
and sent him home from school
but over one hundred inventions

proved Thomas Edison was no
 fool.
They said he wasn't creative,
he couldn't even draw,
but by Walt Disney's talent
he captures one and all.
They said that he was deaf
thunder he could not hear,
but music flowed from his soul
and we still hold Beethoven dear.
Three strikes they said were
 against her,
she was deaf, dumb, and blind,
but Helen Keller graduated from
 Harvard
she wasn't the quitting kind.
Now some people tell me,
America may not be alive much
 longer,
but we've had slavery, war and
 Watergate,
and each time we've come back
 stronger.
So the problems of this world
learn to take them in stride
that's the spirit of America
and the pride I feel inside.

Gregory S Lefler

Gregory S Lefler
AS SO A DREAM

Thank you, TO ALL; of my family and friends. For all the love and support.

Columns of marble,
I pass through.
Wondering where I might have
 been.
Sky so blue, and crystal clear,
Air so fresh, not like breathing.
So content I walk.
Bewildered of my where abouts?
I sat down on the ground,
Seemed as though no ground at all.
But just a vision that I saw,
A man, quiet old and silver.
He wore a thin white cloth.
"It couldn't be,"
"Not me."
In this place,
I never dreamed.
"This was so,"
"I said to me."
This place is better for me.
As so a dream.

Dorothy Logan
COPING

Dedicated to my friend Walter Lundblad

What can a woman do when a man
 is not around—
When she has never lived alone
 and jumps at every sound.
Or when the pipes are frozen and
 water gushes thru the door
And the plumber is just too busy
 to do this little chore.

Well, I have just decided what it is
 that I must do—
So when anything does happen I'll
 not be in such a stew.
I'll go to school and I'll work hard
 and with a heart thats full of
 hope
I'm going to learn to do these
 things—I'm going to learn to
 cope!

They told me that I could not learn
 to do the things they do—
Its best to have a friend, they say,
 who'll come when you need him
 to.
But I worked hard and persevered
 and tho' the way was rough
I found that fixing cars and pipes
 was really not that tough.

So now I'm self-sufficient and
 people even ask me for advice—
To know that I can help them is
 really very nice.
And there's great satisfaction in
 knowing that I have passed the
 test
But knowing that a friend will
 come—THAT'S COPING at its
 best.'

Terry Nelson
SECRETS
When this old pen rides paper
I know the open pleasure
and the way
of wide-hipped wonder

and I know shame and horror
that ride the wings of memories
and wait far in the future

but
I do not negotiate
we wallow in the words
jealously
my pen and I

this old pen punishes
putting my blood on paper
but
I do not negotiate
I am a happy wound

Harold A Slack
INCOME TAX AND ME
In filling out my income tax,
It seems that I was mighty lax.
In putting all my income down
On statements from the bank
 uptown.
Interest drawn and dividends
Were very small to suit my ends.
But on interest paid, I overrode
With state gas tax I hit the road.
Work tools and my union dues
Give deduction checker's blues.
My real estate taxes are very high
And sales taxes, oh my, oh my.
My contributions, which I lack
Could keep all charities in the
 black.
My dependents are so many
My home must be the horn of
 plenty.
One item that told the truth
Was on my W2's, forsooth.
If I.R.S. checks up on me
In the country is where I'll be.
For if I'm locked in Federal Jail
My refund check won't pay my bail.

Phyllis Mondok
REQUIEM TO EARTH
How much do I love precious
 earth, my Lord?
I find no mortal words that can
 describe
The beauty and magnificence she
 boasts
Of mountains rising high through
 sunlit skies
Where eagles soar to ocean's
 rolling coast.
A lifetime, Lord, I've worshipped at
 this shrine
Called Earth—that you created for
 mankind
And now in silent terror my eyes see
Her wonders slowly ravished and
 destroyed
By men of greed whose lust for
 wealth employ.

Oh blessed Earth now scarred by
 sins of men
I weep because I'm helpless to
 prevent
Huge stacks arise from factories
 that spew
Death and destruction through
 your sweet clean air
Where here now shroud of acid
 rain you wear.
No more will wheat fields ripen
 'neath your sun
Or sparkling rivers full of fishes
 run.
Seared grow the throats of gentle
 birds on wing
There is no fruit to moisten throats
 to sing
As sunlight grows forgotten by
 death's sting.

I pray, dear Lord—send us a
 miracle
To shake awake man's faith to
 realize
His life upon Your earth is
 jeopardized.
Too late we gasp for air to fill our
 lungs
To ask forgiveness, Lord—before
 we come.

Jim Asher
PM
A vision appeared in a dream
Of a face known long ago.
Though she loved me as I slept,
She left as the sun
Drove the haze from my eyes.
I awoke, and for a moment
It seemed she was there.
But as sleep ceased to cloud my
 mind
I could find of her no trace.
The joy of a moment now fled
May never come again,
But a spirit was awakened
I thought long dead
With a memory of that which will
 never be.

Asa Betts
MY LAST LONGING
I was walking around in that fear
 I had learned
to live with and love
It was often cold there, yes, and so
 I tried to wake you up
I always did Warn you
But you just let all happen to us by
 wrecking
our suspense and throwing my
 pointless suffering
so far away from you
Burned our most beautiful
 thought . . .

Against the cliffs I saw my own
 spirit in tension
flinging into splinter.

I asked to see your hand, they
 turned me the back
Empty and Silent, they didn't even
 feel the darkness falling
or mention all the laughter they
 had destroyed.

Without fear you were turning my
 paralized body over the summit.
I wanted to hold you for the very
 last time
But suddenly you made me scratch
 your eyes out

The feeling disappeared . . .

Then I stood up and walked away.

Helen Miller DeVore
THE FOG
The fog hangs heavy and I cannot
 see
What future plans are ahead for me
As a day awakens and the sun
 shines through
The fog is lifted for the morning
 dew.

God gives us life, He plans each day
At the time he chooses, we pass
 away.
Soon the fog is lifted, and life goes
 on
As the morning dew, a babe is born.

Gary Wm Coatoam
MOMENTS
Two lovers walked along a golden
 beach,
 palm trees yielding to the wind's
 caress.
Their foot-prints trailing where the
 great waves reach,
 the breezes swirling her printed
 dress.

I love you he said and I always will.
 She smiles and gently nods her
 head.
A sandpiper prances, a morsel in
 its bill,
 her happy hatchlings soon to be
 fed.

So silently the lovers hold hands,

 feelings exchanged with words
 unspoken.
Scribbling hearts in the shifting
 sands,
 better no words than promises
 broken.

The crystal sky an azure blue
 paints reflections on the water
 below.
The palm fronds still covered with
 dew
 wave gently at the girl and her
 beau.

A moment in time they'd discreetly borrow,
for each belonged to another.
Tomorrow's parting world bring her great sorrow.
Still, she knew he would always love her.

Geraldine Pountney-Atkins

SUCCESS

Did you ever have a need;
A need to succeed?
To succeed is to fulfill,
To fulfill that of the will
The will which does control,
Control that of the soul.
The soul that makes a man,
A man who claims he can.
He can succeed.
Did you ever . . .

Rita Hoffman

PRIME TIME

Tee Vee
Emotion.
Meted out
With cars and cosmetics:
Carefully arranged
Plastic covered
Twelve minute portions—
It's all I can take
Anymore.

Leona Burgett

FOREVER TOGETHER

They say that happiness is where we find it
No matter what the cost.
But the price we sometimes pay
Not knowing how soon it may be lost.

Sometimes love is for a life time
Again it may be for a very short span.
We must give and take to make love work
Understanding from both woman and man.

We have our happy times
And disappointment here and there.
But it's the hanging in there together
Letting each other know we truly care.

When we get old together
And know we have made it through
Then we can look back on many years
When we made our commitment and said, "I do."

David E Glavin

MOTHER'S LOOK

The look that one remembers best,
That stands to memory above the rest.
Is just the look that Mother gives,
That graceful look,
That lives, and lives.
That look that say's: "That's my child there!"
And I'm so glad that I did bear,
The pain and suffering, the sweat, the tear,
That bore the grief, and brought him here.
That's the look remembered best,
That rolls a tear from cheek to chest;
And nothing more in any face,
Throughout this life we see,
Will move us more than Mother's look.
Mother's look,
Won't let us be.

Dwayne David Poloway

FREEDOM

Dedicated to Joan Louise Bennett; The being who took the time to understand.

You have guided me through a darkness,
when I was blinded by the glare of a lie,
and you have helped me overcome the fear of dark,
the dark I had feared most,
the black night of helplessness.

And as you helped me and kept me near you,
I followed in your confidence,
and although I could not see you in the darkness,
I but felt your entire presence.

It was at the tunnel's exit,
that the sun's bright rays burst apart the blindness,
and overwhelmed I saw you, oh how beautiful you are,
that I am now at a loss for words,
I feel afloat and so wonderful,
I am light and have left behind me the dark domain,
how happy I am in heart and soul,
that you have rescued me from my exile.

Carol Knight

PHOTOGRAPH

I saw your picture
the other day,
and it took awhile
to place the face.
But, as I remembered your eyes
I remembered you and
the one yesterday when
I looked into your eyes.
In the moment I was given,
time paused.
Looking at your picture now
I wonder,
has that much time
passed between now
and what was the longest moment
I've ever known.

Janet Marler Miller

CONTEMPLATIONS

To my beloved mother, whom I will never quit missing

I stand beside the place
Where you lie in peace
Silently, softly letting time pass
Without caring for the problems of the world.

Do you see me standing here
With tears streaming unheeded
Down my cheeks;

And do you long for me as I for you?

Oh, could you take me to your bosom
As you did long years ago,
When I was a child
And you were young,
To comfort me.

Mary Ellen Widacki

I WILL ALWAYS LOVE YOU

To my special friends—Cheryl Ann, Donna, Julie, Jackie, Lonnie, and Sherie—Thank you for your love, support, and understanding.

I will always love you.
The act I was guilty of most
Was loving you too much.
Sure there were other matters,
I mean you were my first love.
And that would not have been so bad
But deep down in my heart
I truly loved and cared for you—I still do.
You helped me more than you shall ever know
You cracked a great big thick shell.
You taught me to feel, to touch, to love,
To be loved.
And I dreamed, how sweet it was to dream,
Because those dreams were nice.
And because I dared to dream
The hurt was even worse.
There is beauty in sadness and
Those dreams I will never forget.
Yes, I loved you, and that I will never regret.
For I am a better person for having loved,
Even though I lost.
In time nature will heal my hurt.
It was nice to know I could share my life,
And I was okay and I am still all right.
I love you, I always will.
I miss you, and maybe someday,
I can miss loving you.

Theresa Struzinski

A LOOK BACK

A broken heart
It cries so bad,
The teardrops fall
They look so sad.
A pleasant dream
There cannot be,
What's in the future
For you and me.
A welcome hello
Not a soon goodbye,
Comforts me more
When I start to cry.
A guiding hand
A smiling face,
To give in now
Would be a mistake.
A wish for that
Will come with time,
But memories still
Are forever mine . . .

Lois Wood Weavil

?

Death paid her a visit last night!
He beckoned her come, it's easy, don't fight,
but she heard a voice so sweet and low,
saying stay with me, I need you, please don't go.

All night long she tossed and turned.
The demon raged, the fever burned.
By dawns light she was very low,
but the voice kept repeating, don't go, don't go.

She woke up with the morning sun.
The long dark night was finally done.
She felt so strange, and she didn't know,
why her mind echoed, don't go, don't go.

What an odd dream she'd had, or was it fact?
Did some force really keep pulling her back?
I guess she'll never really know.
Was love's pull stronger, than death's undertow?

Faye Allen Bohren

DEAR GOD I HAVE A TEENAGER

Dear God, do you remember the little fellow you gave me so long ago?
To love and cherish and keep in toe.

I've loved him, tended and fed him with care.
Washed his face and combed his hair.

Taken him to church and helped him in school.
Taught him to be kind and to live by the golden rule.

Introduced him to music and the finer things in life.
Guided him with a loving hand, to face the wordly strife.

Now dear God, I have a teenager, a wonderful man to be.
Help me. Take his other hand, to walk a long with thee.

Show him how to enjoy this delightful age of teen.
As it all fades so quickly, like a wonderful, wonderful dream.

Prepare him to face life with an even stride.
To walk along the road of life, and hold his head in pride.

Help me dear God, not to have a selfish view in mind.
While guiding this teen, along a full and useful line.

I am not jealous, but a little envious
with sigh.
Of youth that wastes so much of
his teenage time.

I pray to you oh God above,
To help me guide this teenager
with understanding love.

To respect and honor his younger
points of view.
And not to force my experiences,
for him to pursue.

Help me to be tender and smile
through the tears.
While helping this boy through his
teenage years.

Margaret A Coe

LEARNING

To Kathryn, who was my inspiration.

Oh child
you don't know
what you haven't learned
and you won't learn
until
you understand
why you need to know.

Ange Tremain

THE DIFFERENCE

To my teachers for showing me the value of words.

You say
I am different
Because
I dress in old clothes
let my hair hang loose and long
read books for pleasure
open windows on rainy days

Because I don't like rock
and don't do my nails in 37 hot
fashion
colours paint my lips mulberry
dawn
I am an alien in my own world
that girl in the hall
giggle as you go by but
don't
look at my eyes because
my
tears refract your stares
into
colourless rainbows of
melancholy

I see you in your sadness and
insecurity
You who think you are happy
are the odd ones
Hide behind your laughter don't
see what I see
The Real Difference between
us

Charla Peck

THE AMERICAN FLAG

Look at the American Flag in the
sky
Blowing in the wind way up high.
It's full of truth and full of pride.
It holds great meaning tucked
inside.

Many people enlisted in the war.
They fought outside of our
country's door.

There were many tears and many
rips
Many bad times and hardships.

But America pulled its way through
And mended up the bad spots too.

And now we have freedom, that
glorious gift.
And from that thought we never
shall drift.

So next time you look at the
American Flag in the sky
Blowing in the wind way up high.
Remember America's past
And let it in your mind and heart
last.

Melissa Butler

HER EYES

He looked into her eyes
The ones he'd loved so well
Now was time to leave
To finally say farewell.
But if you looked deep enough,
You'd surely see
That already her heart
Had begun to bleed.
No emotions stirred
In her blue eyes
Just a blank look
It took her by surprise.
When he left
Her heart turned cold
Her eyes grew stormy
The story would unfold.
He'd fallen for another
And left her in despair
And if you'd looked at her heart
You'd find a great big tear.
Now life was drained from her
His love had took it's toll
The last remnants of their lives
Is written on this scroll!

Lorine A Gleue

LONG DISTANCE

Once there was a grand-mo-ther
Who thought to call her
grand-son-er.
Oh no, I mean a grandson who
Was first to put the phone call
through.
Whichever way the phone call
went,
Communication was the intent.
How'er it was, the call went
through,
A pleasant moment for these two.
He talked to her in voice so nice,
(The telephone had rung just
twice.)
And told her how his days were
spent
In learning, doing, con-tent-ment.

"Do you still swim?" she asked of
him.
"Yes, once a week in the "Y" gym."
"Karate lessons, really? Oh, my!
Be careful you don't hurt your eye."
"Piano, too? How fine, indeed!
"And you are learning how to read?
That's wonderful, I'm glad to hear,
Why you may call me any year.
Five dollars will help pay the bill,
When that is used, we'll up the till,
But heed this warning if you will:
'If called by a panther, Don't
anther.'"

Laura Frederick

MY CHRISTMAS DREAM

This dream can't be wrapped
And tied with a bow.
It's a gift that only
A heart can know.

It's a special man
I'm dreaming of,
To share this tender
Gift of love.

Someone to help me
Start each day,
Someone to care for
Along the way.

Someone to walk with
On moonlit nights,
Someone to hold
When I turn out the lights.

Marilyn Burke Walko

SILVER TEARS

It wasn't supposed to be this way
On our twenty-fifth Anniversary
day.
There should be laughter and
celebration
Instead of tears and desolation.
Tears for you, tears for me,
Shed for things that cannot be.
I'm trying so hard to be brave
As I stand here at your lonely
grave.
And the only comforting thoughts
are these:
NOTHING can take away the
memories.
We shared our lives and we shared
your death.
And our dreams died with you in
your final breath.
You were my love, my laugh, my
life,
And I'm so proud to have been
your wife.
It's our Anniversary, my love, and
though we're apart,
We're laughing and dancing here
in my heart.

Jean Williams

THE UNVEILING

Love unveil yourself to me
Yours is the face I want to see
Some say you are lovely
A prince in their eyes
Others that you are an evil
Your loveliness is but a cruel
disguise
Are you the master or do I wear the
crown.
Love unveil yourself to me
Yours is the face I want to see
Although I may never know
I shall never remove my crown.

Helen R Kirkby

UNTITLED

To my husband "Lew"

We've been together
We've been apart
But still are close within our hearts.
We've had our ups, we've had our
downs
Gone through them all with very
few frowns.
So now lets hope that life will be
As best as it can till Eternity.

Dale P Harr

WHY THE RAIN

To my family for their encouragement.

I want a house upon a hill
With green valleys far below.
The clouds would tell me stories
that
The wisest man would not know.

The clouds that float around the
sky
And look down upon the land,
See the things we can't see,
Like killing our fellow man.

Clouds witness man's injustice
And the crimes by the score.
Then the clouds are filled with
tears,
And it rains forevermore.

Susan J Rowland

NEW ENGLAND BREAKFAST

To my father—Whose silence said more than enough

Tender one's little eyes
Sitting in that way-up chair
Spy outside on a sherbert rise
A soaring seagulls' paradise

They roll and glide through pastel
beams
With a peace they carry deep inside
And little one I promise you
With all I am, no alibies
Will hold you down when comes
your time
To glide upon the sherbert rise.

Marian Hastings Keck

OLD BARN

Weather-worn and gray,
Regal and alone in a weed-filled
field,
The old barn still stands
With the quiet dignity of a
Gentle dowager in ancient tweeds.
Swallows rest in the sagging eaves,
Sunlight slants through broken
boards
And dust motes swirl in a golden
dance
Around the discards of yesterday.

Marianna Gillilan
MAMA
Do you hear my soul crying,
mother? Do you see it lying,
writhing at your feet? Do you see
the thorny crown it wears, Of
childhood memories and
dreams?

Mother, help me, how it hurts—
This torment gnashing at my veins;
Grief covers my face
With a pillow of fears;
And any minute to escape
I'll welcome heights of ecstasy
In pain that sears.

Mother, do you see the wounds,
My jagged heart cut open slowly?
Do you see my tears, Mother?
They're not for me—
But everything I've lost,
And everything I'll never be.

Give me your hand, Mama . . .
Stand with my anguish face to
face—
Forbid it to come near your child;
Turn on the lights and scare
The roaring beast away . . .
Oh, Mama, help me.

Awake me from this nightmare,
My soul is crying, Mama.
Can you not hear it?
My soul is dying, Mama,
Are you afraid to see it?

John White
ILLINOIS FARMLAND

To my buddies at work, Kirby Buschman, Don Holiday, and Tim Woolens.

It's been a hard day.
My muscles ache.
I drop my hoe,
raise my hand,
and wipe my brow.
I look out at Illinois farmland.
So peaceful, the seeds have
yet to break the ground.
They're two weeks late,
but I see more hope
in them now than if the fields
were being harvested.
And the horizon above
them seems to echo
my thoughts.
For I see an orange sun
embellished by a sky
of purple hue.
Finally, I pick up my hoe,
and leave this
place of serenity, more
peaceful than when I came.

George Shields
UNTITLED
. . . mom; oh mom;
where are you, mom;
oh there you are, mom;
look! . . . I got myself dressed,
tied my own shoes,
like dad used to do;
my new teacher told me, mom,
be there by nine;
hurry up, mom,
it's almost that time . . .
some kids'll be there
to play with me, mom,
like you promised me once,
remember that, mom;
boy mom, your room is a mess . . .
there's a whole bunch of dust,
clouds of it, mom,
under your bed;
hey, can I climb up—
on your new quilt, mom?
I like the leaves on it mom,
and the pillow of flowers
where feathers should be;
come on, get up mom . . .
it's time to get up;
get up, mom . . .
mom . . .
mom?
. . . mom!
—old man,
at a mother's grave . . .

Ken Joyce
CAMEO
Sky hanging seagull,
soaring, fully stretched wings
black tipped—turning in ever
tightening circles, serenity so
isolatingly beautiful, thus
accepting the winter sky,
unconcerned to icy winds
that hold you suspended.
A background of lapis obsidian,
unmarred by clouds.

The winter sun intensifies
your outline, so that
to my perceptiveness, you
appear as bird plus sky,
a free floating cameo
held by no golden chain,
but nevertheless the gift
of some unseen ancient,
a Minerval offering of
pure flight.

Christy Everrood (10 years old)
LOVE
Love is beautiful
Love is bright
Love is deep
But yet so light.

Love is in the morning
Like the dew
Love is in the sky when
it is oh so blue.

Love is sometimes fake
And sometimes so true
Love is something
Between me and you.

Lisa Zbitowsky
RODEO CLOWNS
Painted grins
And daring eyes,
Heroes
In baggy overalls
And tennis shoes.

Nettie Jean Jenkins-Taylor

Nettie Jean Jenkins-Taylor
MAMA'S THINGS

Dedicated to a Mother's Love, to my own Children, and to the Growth of the Human Spirit.

I don't need to keep these thing no
more,
they only make me cry;
I've kept them 'round for long
enough
since when my Mama died.

And now seven years has gone
away
Since the day her Soul was
called,
And I still bereave her leavin' me,
but I don't need to keep it all.

Each year goes by I miss her more
in so many other ways,
But I also try to let her go
'cause I'll see her again . . .
someday.

Her mem'ry stays inside my Soul
so she never really is gone;
And I don't need to keep ev'ry little
thing
'cause inside me she lives on . . .
dear, dear sweet Mom.

Linda Traweek Greenberg
MORE PRECIOUS
I saw in a line on the ground below
A little black boy with his face all
aglow.
He couldn't have been much more
than five,
His body in movement, in
motion—alive.

And there on his little shiny black
face
Was a smile growing bigger all over
the place.
For he held in his hand a most
wonderful thing,
To him more precious than gold or
great regal kings.

There in his tiny soiled black hand
Was a delicate pink flower, to him
so grand.
He tried quite hard to control his
delight
As he found himself in a line closed
tight.

Soon his excitement could not be
contained
And he called his teacher, Miss
Foreman, by name.
Things were so hectic and hurried
she was,
But turning to him, took a sniff of
his rose.
She turned to continue with the
morning routine,
Little knowing she had shared in
part of his dream.
He now knew for certain that his
flower was rare,
For one special teacher took a
moment to care.

And from my window on this
second floor
I'll never forget what I saw them
explore—
A world blessed with moments of
wondrous shared things
Far more precious than gold or
great regal kings.

Marie 'George' Holman
SILENT SCREAMS
Into the cold night air
Goes my silent screams,
My screams of despair.
No one hears.
No one wants to care.
Into the darkened room
Goes my silent screams,
My screams of fear
No one can hear.
No one is near.
Into my soft pillow
Goes my silent screams,
My screams of pain,
My screams of going insane.
My screams are in vein.
No one is there,
No one wants to care,
So into the cold night air
Goes my silent screams.

Kaye Price
PSALMS 23: REVISED VERSION
Conviction lured my baby south
for the summer,
but not to church camp in the
mountains with
comforting friends in peaceful
surroundings.

The Army Reserves holds him
hostage in the
smothering, hellish Carolina heat
with rigid
daily regimen, chanted runs at
three a.m.,
impersonal "no sir, yes sir,"
military routine.

Cursing his inexperience, sneering
at innocence
badger the youthful captive,
testing his defenses.
Even these won't crush his
power-filled spirit.
Letters of encouragement, walking
in the Word, and
prayer protect my son from the
destructive Ones.

The ransom must be paid.
Training terminated.
A child has died.
Release brings transformation.
An independent man will return in
my baby's place.
I'm not afraid.

Cynthia Dee Baker
I'M GONE, GONE
I'm gone, gone.
From civilization run.
I don't know why,
I should ever return.
In the world of all time,
My skin starts to burn.
See me red, see me brown,
I exist just to learn.

In the place of all worlds,
My brain starts to burn.
I rest on the hillfront,
I live only to yearn.

In the land of red fire,
The imagery hits me.
This country of desire,
Belongs in me.
Wait for the privilege,
Of feeling sweet-pain.
Missing the gold-country,
Only in vain.

Donovan Paul Roberts
CHANGING PROPHESY

With compassion and admiration to everyone, everywhere, who is searching for someone or something; for I am among and love you.

The world is depressing and
enlightening
The world is stimulating
And living is supposed to be
ecstatic
And life is living and touching and
hearing
And everything under the rainbow.
But the rainbow goes away and so
does life
And then you're left with just living.
So the wind blows and the sun talks
And I listen—
And the rain talks too,
If you listen closely.
And pianos can still make music
Even if they're out of tune
And the music is just as loud;
And then you realize that
We're not alone, and loneliness
is crowded,
When happiness always has a
vacancy
And we'll make it anyway.

Karen Kessler Kroft
THE UNFORSEEN

A man once set forth.
On a journey, that was to
become, the fate of many.
For once he had set out.
Destiny was to become his friend.

Let us set forth, to change,
if not alter.
That which seems almost
impossible.
And yet well beyond our reach.

For there are many who seek.
To destroy, that which is theirs,
by errors ways.
Though hurried are the ways of
man.
Time cannot be changed, by other
then.
The MAN, who's much greater.
Then that, of destiny itself.

Robert L Sesco
BIRTH OF A POEM

In icy silence poems move through
space—
Timeless, waiting, mammoth,
spinning orbs,
That float content in mathematic
grace
Until by chance a lifetron it
absorbs.
The seed begins in minds with
fertile crusts,
As laser worlds zip by and light the
sky;
The tiny verb will suck the world
it trusts,
Then dormant will the larval comet
lie.
Among the countless Novas, young
and dead,
For endless years it floats in cold
ellipse,
Until inside the Perfect Poet's head
The words are born through
fevered, parting lips.
As Sun and Moon are
married—man and wife,
The Poet's word reflects the light
of life.

Frances P Brown
CRIPPLED BEGGAR

To my Grandchildren: Kimberly Morris, Kevin Morris, Mandy Brown, Jana Lipscomb, and Joe Truitt Lipscomb

---

Ambling, struggling, alone he went
Down the street, back half bent.
Apparently miserable, a tortured
soul,
A poor crippled beggar, alone and
cold.

A crowd of people rushed past him.
With pleading eyes he begged of
them;
A little help he needed so,
But no one noticed the beggar's
woe.

A little boy came skipping by.
He heard the poor old beggar sigh.
The boy was on his way to school,
But, he remembered "The Golden
Rule."

He stopped and gave a helping
hand
To the poor old beggar man.
He gave to him his sack lunch,
Happy, as he heard the beggar
munch.

Will this little boy keep such
intricate compassion?
Yes, because Jesus' Precious Hand
will fashion
This tiny boy into a very special
man,
Who'll always do—the best he can.

Margaret Jubara
REPETITION

To my son, Chris (deceased May 16, 1986)

Signs of Spring are now appearing;
Winds and snow will not long last.
Sounds of birds we'll soon be
hearing;
Shadows again—by a bright sun
cast.
How to greet this wondrous
repetition?
What to say as I walk on the
warming sod?
I will raise my eyes again in
adoration,
Again raise my eyes in thanks to
God.

Andrea Trosley
SIX-POINTED SNOW STARS

The most popular snow star?
Well, I would say the six pointed
one.
Some people call them snowflakes,
But I call them six-pointed snow
stars.
And the best thing about them?
It's cold when they kiss you on the
cheek!

John D Chapman
SOME DAY

"Some Day," said I, "I'm going to,
Tell that small boy what he
should do,
And, also, things which he should
not,
Just when to start, and where to
stop."

"When going out, or coming in,
To leave doors open, is a sin,
Leave not your gum upon the seat,
Look well before you cross the
street."

"Leave not your shoes upon the
stair,
For you'll forget you left them
there,
And it just isn't nice, at all,
For it may cause someone to
fall."

"You must not tease the dog or cat,
You could be bit or scratched,
for that,
For things you think are so great
sport,
They'll bark or snarl and cut you
short."

"You must not stay out in the rain,
Or some will think you are
insane,
And if you linger, even yet,
You very soon are sopping wet."
Now there are several more, it's
true,
You should not say, and must
not do,
It really takes a lot of tact,
To know just how you ought to
act.

Mrs Yetta Roberts
HIS PRICE FOR FREEDOM

In a Korean prison camp one
awfull day,
Our boys were out for roll call in
the usual way.
One starving, pain wracked, sick
young boy
Rushed forward with all the
strength he could employ,
Raised his fist and shouted to the
Communist kingdom,
"I have only one thing to live for,
My Freedom, My Freedom!"

The pain wracked boy was seized
and rushed away,
Never to be seen again that dreary
day.
All that night his screams could be
heard,
While in the other prisoners' hearts
rang out just one word,
Freedom, Freedom.
The rats killed him that night, so
the Communists said.
But another prisoner who buried
him, saw the bullet hole in his
head.

The brave young boy was carried
up the hill,
To be thrown in a hole, at the
Communists will.
But his shouts of defiance still rang
through the night,
Giving the other prisoners the will
and spirit to fight.
Right then and there, they vowed
to fight.
For their own freedom and all that
was right.

How much do we love freedom,
You and I?
Enough to fight and starve and die?
Dear Lord in Heaven, grant this
day,
That we may love freedom as much
as they!

Lisa A Morgan
VISIONS

Every day I think of you—
I can't concentrate.
I think of how we had met;
Was it by fate?
Visions of you and me
Flow through my head.
Visions that stay with me
When I go to bed.
Every day I think of you
But do you think of me?
Is this love that I'm feeling,
Or just a fantasy?
Visions of you and me,
Together in the end.
Visions that ask me,
Where? How? Why? and When?
Where will we both be—
How will we know it's right?
Why can't I clearly see
When our futures will unite?
Visions of you and me
Flow through my head.
Visions that will stay with me
Until the very end—
of time.

Lois Brackin Oglesby
GRANDMA'S FEATHERBED

My grandma lived many years ago
So about modern conveniences
she did not know
A kerosene lamp lit her home
And a wood cookstove cooked her
biscuits brown and done
But there was one luxury that
Grandma had
That was her big soft goose down
featherbed.

On a shelf on the porch was a
bucket and pan
And a long handled dipper dipped
the water to wash our hands
Baths were taken in a wooden tub
And on a rub board our clothes
were scrubbed
But there was one luxury that
Grandma had
That was her big soft fluffy
featherbed.

We loved to spend the night at
Grandma's when the weather
was bad
For a chance to sleep on her
featherbed

We would snuggle down in it's soft fluffy folds
And never know that the weather was cold
We pulled the covers up over our head
And thanked God for Grandma's featherbed.

Though Grandpa still lives I don't go there as I did
When I had the fun of sleeping on Grandma's featherbed
But the most wonderful luxury that Grandma had
Was that big thick fluffy featherbed.

Ruth Floyd Hendren
DAY OF DREAMTIME

Dedicated to my Hardy Ancestors

Gnarled oak branches laden with snow,
In the distance a rickety barn.
Weeping willows border a creek,
On a lonely deserted farm.
Split rail fence had kept cows from the road,
Tall cedars guarding a well.
I visioned a grape arbor, laden with fruit,
Sensed the peal of an old dinner bell.
Squirrels and rabbits scurried about,
A fox raced by the cove.

A hawk perched high in a dead elm tree,
Sharp eyes watching for something to rove.
Six crows flew over the meadow,
Their caws rend the cold winter air.
That's when I dream of springtime,
And a meadowlark singing there.
I search for a row of daffodils,
Growing beside a hill.
Bending low in a warm southern breeze,
But the air remained cold and still.
My footsteps turn to the dwelling,
Windows blackened and broken by time.
I close my eyes as I savor again,
A way of life, once mine.

Donna R Goldberg
CANDLE WISHES
Today you are twenty-five, how strange it sounds and yet,
I too, will pass that landmark soon . . .
Sooner than I wish.
The blissful innocence of youth is no longer ours.
nor was it ever ours together.
Somehow it doesn't seem quite right that I
who am so much a part of you now
Should not have known you then.

Today the price of growing old is much too high.
Could we but stretch the carefreeness of years long past,
we would be eternally young . . .
But we are not all Peter Pans, and we have aged
for as we grew so too grew our awareness
of wordly turmoil, ignorance, hate.
Our game of marbles became a game of guns,
and we were forced to play.
No more mere "candle wishes" mark the passing of each year.
Oh, but each candle on your cake could represent an evil of these days,
And with the heaviness of the world upon our breath
together we could blow them all out,
And vanish from the world all war and hate to recreate
the peace of long-gone birthdays.

Sol Roseman
OUR DESTINY
How still it lies,
Within us
Our destiny,

That which is to be—
Our destiny,

Seeking, pushing, we know not where
Looking forward to see,
Our destiny,

Man, man, immortal man—
Striving, yearning, begging to be,
The shaper of
Our destiny,

Let us cast aside these whims,
And turn only to HIM,
Who shall always be,
The keeper of
Our Destiny.

Tricia Kelly
CLEARING OF TIME
I stood alone in a clearing of time;
Past, present and future in a pantomime.
All times were one and one time was all.
I watched the machines of the present as across the blue they would Fall.
Things that have come and gone again marched before my eyes
And the events to come made me want to sigh.

The trees of the past stood stark against the sky
And the leaves whispered to me of times gone by;
Times when Nymphs and Dryads danced along the water's edge
And played with the breeze.
Oh how often I've wished to be back in those magical times,
Dancing under the full moon as I listen to the talk of the trees.

But alas,
That dream is fading fast,
So I will stand, look around and be thankful for this Clearing of Time.

Edna O Morris
STAR STUDDED NIGHT
I stood by the ocean one star studded night—
And watched the tide roll in,
It cast it's cargo upon the sand—
And rushed out to sea again.

Seashells glistened in the pale Moonlight,
The Heavens were all aglow—
Of God's great plan for mortal man,
How little we all must know.

Ships were cruising the ocean deep,
With waves swishing soft and low—
Strangers passing in the night,
Unaware of the undertow.

The scene was quiet this Beautiful night—
All nature seemed in accord,
I raised my eyes to the radiant Sky—
And whispered, "Thank you Lord."

Marshana Prescott "Flowers"
THE WIND

To my mother and father Mr. and Mrs. Flowers

The wind hits the ground
Making no sound
All across the trees
Making a breeze
Swaying high
All through the sky
Up top of a hill
Sometimes very still
It whistles a song
All day long
The song it sings is so brief
It moves a leaf
Sometimes it flies like a flock of birds
As strong as a herd
At night it howls
When its real cold it growls
It twirls left to right
All day and all night
But its never in sight
Whirling around
Without a sound
In one big heep
To fast and steep
The wind is a silent thing
Thats never to be seen

Wendy A Thompson
VIOLATING PATTERN
Powdered-milk flakes knit down,
down, past the cottonwood's alabaster frost
clinging to its limbs, down to wet
grass, a virgin earth. Holding her breath,
grass turns golden, innocent as snow cleanses
then baptizes. Tangerine and apricot
leaves mat beneath the boughs,
framing winter's path while peach
and lemon stragglers neglect tradition
to sweep the breeze. Flakes fall,
chalking earth, purifying;
white glory. The breeze blusters
and swoops past cottonwoods,
sagebrush, earth, into cracks
of my window, pluckering my
flesh. I shiver, cold,
content. Winter awaits, virginity still
its pattern, and I pull on my boots.
Outside, I smile at innocence,
chasteness, and inscribe my footprint,
violating pattern.

Carol K Steyer
WE MUST HAVE FAITH IN BEAUTY!
Why else the shrug of the tree
Dispelling its seasonal claim to life.
It sleeps! . . .
Strong arms and fingers remain poised.
Intricate web of life darkly silhouetted . . .
Fragmenting each day and night.

Frolicking to breezes, cloying.
Bowing to winds, molesting.
Moistened with rain, caressing.
Silent and noble with snow; blanketing.

Triumphantly bursting with repressed gayety.
And life displaying pastel tapered buds
Unfurling to deep color . . .
To beauty . . . only to be nipped by
The great unsettling of constant change.
Repeating, and beginning at the beginning.

Kimberly S Nadeau
I MISS YOU
I miss seeing your smile everyday,
I miss how I needed you in everyway.
I miss the way you held my hand,
I miss the way you used to understand.
I miss the happiness when we were together,
I miss how you said: "I'll love you forever."
I miss the walks we used to take,
I miss the funny jokes you used to make.
I miss the way you used to love,
I miss the way we used to hug.
I miss being your other half,
I miss the way we used to laugh.
I miss your gentle, special touch,
I miss the way you cared so much.
I miss your affectionate kiss,
What it comes down to is that;
It's all of you I really miss.

Janet R Blake
WORMS
Worms are slowly, slinking, creeping,
across the ground while peoples sleeping.

Never listening to what their told, they
crawl across the sidewalk bold.

The sun comes out upon the ground,
and melts the worms without a sound.

Robert L Kerns "Country Boy"

Robert L Kerns "Country Boy"
LOVE IS LIKE A FLOWER

This is dedicated to My Loving Sweetheart Dewanna Bush

Love is like a flower
It needs that special touch,
Dewanna the words that I'm about to express,
I hope they mean very much.

Love is like a flower
and you have to let them know you care,
Just always remember you've got to have time and patience
and also show them that you have time to spare.

Dennis Nothdruft
BOTANICAL
Bleak-bare
Desolate
The wind sweeps—
The driven snow
Scrapes
Over
The frozen
Land.
Inside—
a greenhouse
Rare and gentle
Blooms
Blossom—
Defy the winter
Yet
Seperated only
By a pane of
Glass

Helen Moran Haselden
TEARS

For my Sons-Richard and Brian Moran

I went into my child's room
To clean up yesterday.
To change the sheets and pillow case,
And brush the dust away.
I remembered, as I worked about,
I had punished him that day,
For there upon his pillow,
His teardrops still did lay.
I felt a sadness in my heart,
For I wondered as he grew,
How many times the teardrops
Would lie there, like the dew,
But even as I thought these thoughts,
I heard his laughter ring,
And I knew, as now, his future tears
Would be just a passing thing.

Linda Lathrop Spinney
REMEMBRANCES

Dedicated with deepest affection to Pam, a kind and gentle spirit.

Lonely spaces, unwon races,
thoughts of what once was.

Sandy beaches, your mind reaches
back to one once loved.

Eyes still crying, heart still dying,
pain still burns the soul.

One is leaving, one is grieving,
where did love go wrong?

Roxanne Giron
LAND OF FAMINE
Hot winds blow
Across this tortured land
Like damaged falling totem poles
Staggered in unprecious sand—

The people bathed in bondage
From starvation, plagues, and death
Victims of this famine
All void of emotions, till no breath—

Each cruel day that passes
Hundreds to thousands die
Men, women, children
Old and young they cry—

Jeffrey L Garber
PATHFINDER
Losing sight
The sun going down
The paths' not far
Yet still not found . . .
The winding path
Is slowly changing
I sense it's presence
It's temper raging . . .
As unsure feet, wander about
The path begins to shout
"Follow me my faithful friend,
To the ineluctible end."
But, as these loathsome feet
Defeat the growth
The growth subsides . . .
Beneath these feet
A path resides . . .

Dawn L Schall
A POEM
Once I read a book,
I read it in the sun,
It was fun.

I learned a lot,
and I'm glad I never
Stopped.

James Richard Webb
THE SHIP
The ship came up the river
When sunlight lay on the plain.
Her two-score oars dipt briskly
And they flashed and dipt again
While her sail, with a serpent blazoned,
Pulled hard at her mast and stays
Till they beached her there in the valley
Where they stopped for a hundred days
While they wasted the corn and the cattle
And they slaughtered the deer and the swine.
Then they set strong siege to the castle
When the lord and his warriors dined.

Gainst the sword and the stone and the arrow
They seized the strong-bastioned height,
And the sea full five leagues northward
Was lit by her flames that night,
Till the frost came down with the autumn
They drank and they sang and they fought;
But they took no prize save the castle
And the armor her smiths had wrought.
Then the ship sailed down the river
As the raptor returns to her nest
And her sail still strained at her braces
But twelve of her oars were at rest.

Helen Crislip
TO OUR SON
Well, Son, you're practically now grown
But, secretly, we don't want you 'out on your own',
We want to protect you from worries and all,
Just as we did when you were small.
But we know that you must spread your wings
To look for promise of all the good things,
That life has to offer, if given some chances
And to make the best of all circumstances.
Yes, Son, we're glad you've grown as you have,
You've learned how to give, how to love, and to laugh.
Yes, Son, there are no others prouder than we,
You've grown from a tender twig into a tree.

Roger Elting
THE CLOWN

To Jesus Christ & God & all the clowns that make us smile with happiness

---

The clown is no longer blue!
Because now he's alive, but somewhat different than I or you

He went down hill because of his age

and finally died a few times on the stage
and then he died his last on the stage of the world

So his best performance for God could be unfurled

He's alive now, certain it was all worthwhile
Wouldn't you feel that way, if you could see God smile

Patsy B Buchanan
IMAGE OF THE MIND

To my family Randy, Chastity, Randy Jr.

As I sit in my dark room
Images go by against the moon
Like images of your life to be
an you yourself can set free
The dreams you long to someday live
and the emotions you want to give
To have, to know, and to feel
in your mind to which they're sealed
In the walls of total sleep
to which you laugh and even weep
Keep the innocent forever within
or to be of many sins
It's good to know that you can be
whatever you want and to be free
They're yours to keep or throw away
or have for that special day
To your life you can give
the greatest that any can live
It is a great wonderful gift
and to you always a big lift.
Cause Image of the mind
can be so very fine

Lowell Thomas Tewell Sr
LITTLE PART OF ME
I count each day of life, with eager eyes I greet the morn.
I love to feel the fresh air blowing in my face
I love to hear the birds sing
I love to ride by the sea
But my day is not complete less I meet a new friend.
I cherish my friends old and new,
but I know none more than you.
You make life worth living, for to start a day with you
is the answer to a dream.
You came my way and it doesn't matter why,
you have a heart to offer and a bike to ride.
So as we peddle down the road near the sea
I hope we will always be friends you and me.
And if in time we should drift apart,
there will go a little of my heart.
But no matter where you roam a friend you will always be
and a little part of me.

Alice M Bierer
A NEW BEGINNING
The alarm goes off.

You sluggishly climb out of bed . . .
You prepare yourself for the day . . .
You walk out to get the morning paper . . .

These things happen every day.

How boring this whole thing seems!

Isn't there more?

Just when you feel like giving in—
You look up.

Before your eyes,
And possibly noticed only by you,
Is the sunrise.

You are warmed,
By it's subtle, yet vibrant, rays
As you gaze at its brilliance.

Suddenly you feel as though there is hope
For this world,

And your life takes on a new beginning.

Bernice Jefferson Liba
THE MIRROR
I really need more time
The hurried mother said,
As she fluffed up the pillows
And rushed to make the bed.

I surely need some rest
The weary mother sighed,
As she sorted out the laundry
And wished that she could hide.

I need to find a niche
The lonely mother pondered,
As she settled in the armchair
And sat, and thought, and wondered.

And then in just an instant
The conflict disappeared,
For coming toward the mother
A little figure neared.

And when she held her child
The joy-filled mother knew,
That in that gift of love
God did her life renew.

For here was time and quiet.
Here was rest and place.
Here was all Eternity,
Mirrored in her child's face.

Julie E McQuiston
SOME GUYS
Some guys are so sweet and kind, that you think they're so fine;
But watch-out they can change from kind
to mean and cruel but not mine.
They will rip your heart in half, just to get a laugh.
This is my word of caution to those who think guys are so grand,
you will never ever understand.

Debora Lynn Grover
HANDS OF GOD
Holding hands of faith
Hands of mans love,
The hands of God.

Holding his hand of wisdom
And compassion.
God holds this in mans hands.

Karen Snider
RUN, RUNAWAY
Hard, cruel world
of stone and glass.
Cars zoom by
amidst a blanket
of dreary grey.
Cats meow.
Babies cry.
Someone shrieks
in the night.
The red
and deathly blue
ambulance siren
pierces the moment.
Run, Runaway.
Your dream
is over.
The nightmare
lives on.

Michael Ryan Miller
A NEIGHBOR
On fiery wings of silent flight,
It lights the sky of darkest night.
Often seen from far away,
You must look quick for it does not stay.
But Oh!—this time it is no star,
This time it is an alien's car.
This small space ship has travelled here,
For us—his race has reason to fear.
To him our planet is very close,
But to us his home is quite remote.
An emissary is this alien pilot,

Come to see this planet in riot.
From outer space earth looks pristine,
But we fool it daily with waste and machine.
They visit us every once in a while,
To see if we have changed our warlike style.
As long as we run this warlike race,
We must not spread it to outer space.
If we turned our arms to a peaceful labor,
We just might find a peace loving neighbor.
If we keep our arms for the sake of war
Then the day will come when earth will be no more.

Nancy Schulenburg
VINTAGE
His warm smooth lips,
Touch her small lips of dew,
And loves sweet tremble begins anew.
Tear moist cheek from such sweet renoun,
Brings the sighs of love from deep down,
such a hidden sweet remote sound.
the vexation of day and life that exist,
when love has removed, will not be missed.
Under his cloak he gently glades her,
Lay there in her warmth beside her.
Brings near her mounted breast,
beneath his clear smooth chest.
There remain he sweetly bids her,
seeking home once more the quest,
setting her silken skin to shiver,
smoothing her frame as not to quiver.
His hands tendering as with the graces,
set aglow their love born faces.
As the he and she they be,
wrapped in loves' equality.
Her slender fingers over his statue traces,
engulfed in buttons, bowts, and laces.
Against satin hair their thighs smooth,
as gazels their bodies move.
He nestles in his comeliness, to file his claim to his throne,
a kingdom he calls his own.
She gives her love her solemn kiss,
the myrth of songs that brings sweet bliss.
Bestow they the knighthood of which they're kin,
a world with-out, -a world with-in.

Sandy J Walters
THE GIFT
Oh dear Jesus, how lovely your world. Ah dear Jesus how true is your word. Oh dear Jesus how we trust and love you, and we know that you love us too.

How lovely the Jays are in their gorgeous blues, even the sparrows in all their brown hues. What a joy it is, seeing them all around, and living on Jesus's sweet hallowed ground.

The pinetrees in spring are so lovely and green, where we can walk under or sit down and dream. Then in the winter, their
boughs full of snow, where under is a resting place for buck, fawn and doe.

All of this beauty our God made for us, to love, to enjoy, and to hold in our trust.

Denise Hall
WHENEVER YOU SEE

To my parents for their love. And to Craig for loving me even when I didn't love myself

---

Whenever you see the sunshine.
Think of me thinking of you.
Whenever you feel lonely for me;
Think of me being lonely for you.
Whenever you see kids playing.
Think of the happiness you bring me.
Whenever you see someone smile;
Know that I am thinking of you and smiling at that very moment.
Whenever you see a flower:
Know that that is how much beauty you bring to my life.
Whenever you see the rain,
Know that I am crying because I miss you.
Whenever you see the trees or grass;
Know that I am thinking of how much we're grown to
love each other. Whenever you see a rose, know
that I am telling you in my heart. . . That I love you.

Homer F Parish
MIND CONTROL

To all the non-believers, Dreams DO come true.

Hard!
Always hard to do—Keep a secret.
Why? Mystery, intrigue perhaps,
Don't know.
Easy!
Always easy to do—spread rumors.
Why? Mystery, intrigue perhaps,
Don't know.
When secrets are told all over
Secrets can become rumors,
Rumors can become lies,
Lies can lead back to secrets.
Hard and easy, which is which, both's the same—
Don't know.

Evelyn D Bell
THE DANCERS

TO: LBE, For dancing with me.

We dance across the floor,
Our arms around the other,
In places I'd not been
Until I went with you.

I dream of being yours
Always in this embrace
Sharing our joys and hopes;
Touched by the music's spell.

I forget all of those
Who would think we are wrong
To have these special times,
And give myself to you.

I'm a woman in love
In her lover's arms,
Transformed by his magic;
Submissive to his charm.

Before the music stops
And there are no more dreams,
I know that deep inside
I'll never be the same.

Billy Yuhas
TRUTH
The truth is not a lie,
A lie is not the truth.
Telling a lie is betraying God,
But telling the truth you won't be betrayed,
The truth is something you tell a friend.
It dates back to our great, great ancestors,
The truth is a thing of the past,
The truth is with us now,
And the truth is the future.
With the truth you'll be fine and go far,
But telling lies won't get you past a day.

Donna Middlestadt
MY FRIEND
We try so hard to please everyone
because we need to be needed.

We hurt for others, as much as for ourselves
because others are just as important to us.

We touch places with our hearts
no one else could ever hope to.

We need more, sometimes too much.
We also give more, sometimes too much.

We have weaknesses we must always hide
because we are so vulnerable.

We care more than others can,
for we alone, know the secret of compassion.

Sometimes we must cry, alot
to wash ourselves free of the unfairness of it all.

But we are special, for we are woman.
Only we, can understand each other.

Melvin D McGallion
SPIRITUAL SPRING
Seasonal youth with virgin green,
beauty beheld with eyes so keen.
Out of a wintry storm I came
branches brittle and limbs lame.

The forest about me dead and dreary.
My roots that held me weak and weary.

When to my stump the axe was laid,
for a debtor, the debt was paid.
And that by another tree

where waters of life are flowing free.

One whose roots are strong and deep.
Steadfast and sure his life to keep.

Then I, watered with his life,
was nourished above temporal strife.
And out of a wintry storm I came,
roots and branches never the same.

Through the Creators' life giving flow,
The grafted tree began to grow.

The strength of seasonal youth,
The glory of virgin green.
Fruits of Righteous Truth,
beauty beheld in a Spiritual Spring.

David E Miller
ONE RED ROSE
The rose is a symbol of love everlasting . . .
Of friendships that never grow old . . .
Its radiance a reflection of youth . . .
Though tattered and withered in time it may be, its beauty then faded and gone . . .
Nothing visible left of the beautiful flower, but in memory its fragrance lives on. Ay yes, forever and always lives on and on and on.

Betsy Gemerek
A RECOLLECTION

To Kim—

What used to be laughter is now a sad song,
But we will depart and life will go on.
What used to be sunshine is now a gray sky
For I am alone for the days to pass by.

In my heart I will treasure all the good times we had.
I will picture your face and never be sad.

Mary Jeannette Watson
LOVE THAT COUNTRY MUSIC!
When I was a very young child,
growing up in a small Kansas town,
My daddy owned a tavern,
the best little inn to be found.

He'd take us there with him sometimes,
we'd watch the people come and go.
We'd listen to the juke box,
every country song we'd know.

Ah, that country music,
how folks loved it at that time.
They'd sing along with the "Pioneers."
it made them feel so fine!

Those were the good old days, for sure.
Music didn't have to be "noise,"
and everyone I knew back then,
would have loved the "Oakridge Boys!"

There were not any amplifiers and things,
no groups with a name such as "Ratt!"
And I don't ever remember <u>my</u> parents,
saying, "Kid, you can't listen to that!"

The music today, well, I guess it's okay,
and I don't mean to imply it is silly.
But can't we turn off the hard rock for awhile,
and let me listen to "Waylon" and "Willie?"

Anne Louise Roe
TO US (TRUE FRIENDS)
If you'll put out your hand, then I'll take it,
If you'll share with me just one more smile,
If you'll take first one step, then another,
I'm sure we could walk one more mile.

If the leaves flutter down from the treetops,
If the snow starts to pile up again,
If you start to feel just a bit lonely,
Remember, in me, you've a friend.

When you listen to birds, think of children.
When the sun shines so brightly above,
Remember through good days and bad ones
That deep, runs our friendship and love.

Should our world turn a little bit shaky,
Should both of us have heads of gray,
Should we not get around as we used to
"True Friends" is still what they'll say.

Margaret D Park
APRIL CAPRICE
I watch your coming, April snowstorm,
A rushing down the field toward me,
From out your hilltop woodland hiding,
A shrieking, wild ferocity.

You try to awe me with your fury,
But I just laugh, Spring laughs with me,
For well we know you're but a changeling,
And this is just temerity.

A noisy child, Oh, April snowstorm,
Who must be heard before you leave,
So shout and rage and blow and bluster,
And have your short and wild reprieve.

For Spring is here! And soon in triumph,
Which you delay, but can't restrain,
She'll sing her song and soothe your rashness,
And you'll be April, calm again.

Mrs Cleo B Bunk
OUR MOM AND DAD
God was on his throne in heaven;
he'd been thinking hard all day.
He chose a girl from a family of eleven
and sent that lovely girl our way.
He chose a man that had red hair
with a spirit hot as fire
to do the things few men would dare,
but many to inspire.
Those two folks we claimed our own—
they were Mom and Dad—
their going makes one feel alone,
somehow very sad.
Many comforts they did give,
a life of joy and mirth.
Thank you, Lord, to let them live;
Bless them that gave us birth!

Edith Ensworth Chandler
SOUL TRAVELERS
You stole into my room last night.
Oh not as a burglar, masked and armed, but rather an
ethereal being, unencumbered of flesh and bone.
I could feel your presence, the spiritual unity we once
shared before beauty was chased by tragic laughter.
You hovered above my bed,
drinking in the wine of me;
then bade me come.

You stole into my room last night,
and together we
walked the Astral Plane to that little gleam of TIME
between two eternities.

Victor M Schall
CATHERINE I LOVE YOU

To my wife Catherine

Communion of love so strong
As almost to seem wrong
The very thought of you
Heart felt feelings renew
Envied by all
Requited loves all
Is it any wonder
Never to wonder
Everlasting love so true,

Is your mind so blank as not to realize

Love for you is in my eyes
Of you my heart cries
Very near when I hold you
Encouragement by you are said by words so few

Your body oh so close
Out of respect my mind froze
Understand now it's you I love

Not another.

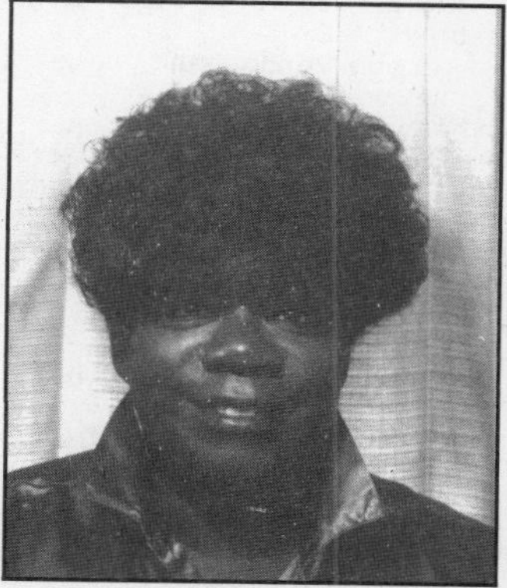

Deloris Garland

Deloris Garland
MASS CONFUSION

This poem is dedicated to Jonsier, my loving niece

Why is it, that every time, I want to do something or be with someone, I want to be with, someone is always trying to get in my way.

Stirring up trouble, causing confusion, making everything and everybody around me up tight. Then nobody wants me around.I get out of control. Forget want I wanted to do in the first place.

I start making excuses, apologizing for something I didn't do, feeling bad, being much too hard on myself, trying to figure out how this all got started anyway.

Gretchen Foth
MY MOTHER'S KITCHEN
With coffee in a mug marked 'love'
Cradled in my always cold hands,
I bask in kitchen warmth
While cookies bake.

As I sit and listen,
The rise and fall of family voices
Speak love
In the telling of stories.

I think back to my Father's Father
Who, while living in a shack,
planned this kitchen
For his first true love.
She poured coffee and baked cookies,
Filling this room with warmth.

Now, many births and deaths later
It's my Mother's kitchen.

A harbor from the cold,
Spanning the generations,
And linking us together.

As I sip the coffee
The story is retold
And I am warmed throughout
By the mark of love.

Patricia M Lanterman
YOU AND I

Dedicated to: Christopher Oliva, I'll love you always!

Everything I see reminds me of you,
Everything I hear, say, or do,
I can't get you out of this head of mine,
I wish you'd understand and give me your time,
What we have is special to me,
And I only wish that you could see,
That we'd be great together, you and I
And without you I would simply die,
Please don't go and leave me behind,
Thoughts of you are always in my mind,
Give me a chance and you will see,
That we'll be happy, yes honey, you and me,
You're the one that I want to kiss,
And when I'm gone, you'll be the one I'll miss,
Please open your heart and let me in,
It's your love that I want to win,
You make me smile when I am sad,
Honey, it hurts, I want you so bad,
Take my hand and walk with me,
Into the land of eternity.

Vivian E Howes
PRAYER FOR PEACE

In your paper I read one day
Of a prayer that brought rain so they say.
If a prayer the drought could release
Why not one to ask for peace.
If in all this great world around
In each city and small town,
Every person a prayer would say
Maybe there could be peace some day.
So gather round one and all
And on our Dear Lord we will call.
And ask from deep within our heart
For world wide peace that won't depart.
Each night as we go to bed
Get on our knees and bow our head,
Ask our Dear Father up above
To help each of us to share our love.
Then peace on earth we all would see,
And what a wonderful world this would be.

Jacqueline Davis
POEM OF A YOUNG GIRL

I and a girl so happy and free,
A world of love shared by my
Sister and me. But today my
Life will change for my parents
Have went away.

I sleep in a room full of pain
Alone. I lay on a old smelly
Cot and hear my body groan.
I cry deep inside my soul,
As my mind wonders why
I still abide.

Today they asked how I was,
She told them I was fine.
It's a lie!
But they went away without
A question in their mind.

And now I cry a silent cry . . .
For me the pain is over . .
For others the suffering
Has just begun.

And as my soul rest in a
Place of peace. I pray to
God "keep my love ones from
Sorrow and pain"
For I am loved and all is well.

Doris J Olmstead
MY YELLOW ROSE IS PINK!

Twas on last Mother's Day
when my husband surprised me.
He gave me two bushes
and said roses they would be.

We planted them together
and watered them with care.
I watched with anticipation;
the leaves sprouted, the blooms bare.

Then I reveled with glee
for the buds had formed finally.
Patiently I checked each day
to see my roses bloom beautifully.

When the blooms did appear,
the red rose was deep red,
But the yellow rose bloomed
not yellow but pink instead!!

I turned to my husband and said,
"My yellow rose is pink!!"
He pondered a moment and replied,
"But it's pretty, don't you think?"

A rose by any other name
is still a rose.
But pink instead of yellow
my rosebush grows.

Betty Jean Lapointe
THOTS ON MOBY DICK

To Harold

See the movie
Forget the book
Only an English major need
Give a second look

Ruby L Creekmore
DAY BY DAY

If day by day
A little better I can be,
and live my life
so other folks can see,
the very good there is
in me.

May I ask a prayer of
you, Oh Lord,
Help me along and
temptations avoid.

And rather I some
goodness to explore
something upright to
enjoy.

A life worthwhile
I'd feel I'd spent,
Few things done for
me to repent.

When as I travel along
life's way
Surely, I will be better
day by day.

Mary Agnes Ritchie

Mary Agnes Ritchie
TWO NATIONS WITH HONOR BETWEEN

Dedicated to an Honorable Friendship Between Two Great Nations.

No high walls nor fence to bar us,
Along this border, between.
We faithfully guard, this friendship, and trust,
With honor, and highest esteem.

A great marble arch proudly stands,
High a-top, two flags, side by side.
The symbol of two mighty lands,
For these things, our forefathers died.

This freedom, we honor, and cherish,
Let us, to always keep free.
May this right we have, never perish,
Whatever our country maybe.

So whatever your flag, America's stars and stripes,
Or Canada's red white and blue.
Let us always cherish these rights,
This friendship, between us keep true.

Laurie Gardner
EARTH RENEWED

The rain it falls in a soft retreat
To bring relief from summers heat
It comes down soft and warm
Soothing life in every form
Very soon the rain will cease
The world is cleansed and at peace
The birds sing and trees glisten
You can hear lifes sounds if
You only listen
So open your eyes become aware
That in every living thing
God is there

Ann Whitaker
THE STATUE OF LIBERTY

I would like to dedicate this poem to my dear friend, Jackie Schmid, for ALWAYS being there. God loves you and so do I

Take a minute and think about the freedom for which I stand
Holding high and proud a lighted torch in my hand.
Everyone holds a memory who has landed on this shore—a
Sigh of relief . . . lasting freedom forever and ever more.
The pain and suffering, what stories I could tell
Are you busy now, then come and sit a spell.
The life we take for granted, we should always pray
Universal peace, may it come soon to stay.
Each one of you have blessings and by the score
Oh! just realize and be grateful, I beg, I implore.
Far and wide across this land and the oceans too
Love one another, the way that I love you.
I want to feel the joy of a happy, happy heart
Begone forever the wars of hate that keep us apart.
Every nation send me a dove, a dove of peace
Reaping and sowing love—the violence would cease.
Thanks for listening to me, I feel better now
You will bring peace to all, some way, some how.

This is what I feel "OUR LADY," the Statue of Liberty
would say if she could come to life and speak. So be it.

Cindy Aga
SORROW

Black
Capes
Drape over
Everyone as
Forgotten deaths of
Great people
Hint to the
Inside feelings
Jolting our minds to remember . . .
War is a permanent scar.

Berniece J Fox
IN MEMORY

I know a place where green grass
grows
Where daffodils bloom in the
spring.
There's a small mound there—
Oh, so alone!
With a little headstone
that bears her name.
There, my dear little friend
lies—
She left me one lovely spring
day,
Oh, that we could have had
more time.
But God did not will it that way.
The sun was shining the day she
left me
But dark clouds filled my heart
and soul.
I know some day we will meet
again
And the joy and happiness and
love
Will be there for us to share,
"Blackie" was her name—
a four-footed bundle of fur
With a heart full of love.

Norvel R Sands
PAUL REVERE'S HORSE
"Come listen, my children, and you shall hear
Of the poor old horse under Paul Revere,
Puffing and panting and all out of breath—
Why that doggone fool's going to ride me to death,
Because of a light in the Old North Church—
Why, I've seen those lights since the day of my birth!

"Down through the alley and onto the street,
He couldn't have made it on his own two feet.
Yelling and screaming, I think he's gone mad—
When this night is over, I sure will be glad;
Then I'll dream of great glory—to me, of course—
How this Nation was saved because of a horse!"

Antonino E Najera Sr

Antonino E Najera Sr
YOUR'S TRULY
Once upon a time—when I was young—
Winsome, Wholesome—but unlove, unsung;
Timid, coy—did avoid the fair sex
Yet cares—but got not the nerve to mix.
Girls turns their heads—emits cries or sigh
Your's truly—right then is passing by.

Kevin D Cook
A COWBOY
The cowboys spurs are rusty now.
And the rodeo days are forgotten.
His saddle isn't used anymore.
And his ropes have all turned rotten.

He's just an old time cowboy.
With nothing left to do.
And just like other cowboys.
He'll be forgotten too.

The old days are just memories now.
No, there not what they seem.
But each night when he's in bed.
They come back in his dreams.

Yes, he's an old time cowboy.
With nothing left to do.
And just like other cowboys.
He'll be forgotten too.

Lorelei L Logan
AUTUMN MEMORIES

For Scott: In remembrance of an innocent love

Like leaves of autumn and changing times,
Memories run through my mind;
Friends of old and friends to find,
Some of them will be left behind.

I'm drifting onwards and changing, too,
But I find my thoughts return to you.
The years have gone, we both have changed,
But my heart still quickens when I hear your name.
Your voice and laugh, your smile and looks,
Are still familiar like a favorite book.

Love, I know the past is gone,
But sometimes I find myself wishing on
A star up in the distant sky
That you'll be mine again, by and by.

Betty Hawkins
SNOW—FOR SUE
The snow comes
And, silently, in its pristine beauty,
Covers the ground
Makes soft and rounded
The rough angles and sharp corners
Hides the ugliness of reality
Makes us believe that
There is only beauty and goodness
In a world inhabited by snow creatures
Who hide their blemishes and scars
Under the cold, white coverlet,
A mantle of untarnished propriety.

We were taught to be snow maidens
But, the warmth of our talks
Has melted away bits of snow
Revealing some of the rough angles
And sharp corners of our lives
Dark niches exposed to the glowing sun
Seem not so dark anymore
The snow may appear to be cold to the world
And still be a counterpane of warmth
To sisters exploring what has been hidden
Under the pristine mantle.

Sandy Fritsche
TOMORROW
When tomorrow comes,
what will it bring?
Will there be happiness,
or sorrow?
Will there be love,
or hate?
Will it bring peace throughout the universe, or war?
When Tomorrow comes, will people
help the helpless?
Will the suffering of innocent stop?
When Tomorrow comes,
what will it bring?
I will bring love, more than today,
more than yesterday . . .
Tomorrow there will be peace.

Tina Vanasse
CRASH
Today two died because of me,
A nightmare, God, this has to be.
Don't drink too much, my parents said,
I listened not—now my friends are dead.

We were so young and foolish too,
And thought we knew just what to do.
We started out from home last night,
Such good friends we were for life.

Found our crowd at the regular bar,
Ten minutes from home—it wasn't far.
Guzzling beer was the latest fad,
For one to beat me, made me mad.

I had so much to be thankful for—
Family, friends, and much, much more.
A happy life I thought I had,
But drinking made it turn out sad.

I remember not just when we crashed,
But the police had said the car was smashed.
"Watch Out!," is what my friends had said,
I laughed—and hit the tree instead.

My friends are dead—now, the guilt I have to bear,
But worse than that:
The nightmares—of seeing blood everywhere.
The moral here you know, is not to Drink and Drive,
Stay away from "Booze" —You'll keep your friends alive!

Bunnie Copeland
UNTITLED
I'm beyond the point of no return . . .
I'm lost in myself . . .
Will I burn in hell
No—please help me
I love you—you are a part of me.
I can't see you, but I know you're there.
Why are you doing this, is it some kind of daze.
Do you want me, do you care.
If so, then take me
If not let me go, please do let me know.
I'm not a toy to be played with or farther more destroyed.
Please stop this game—stop in his name
you can't do this to me
Do you understnd, can't you see.
This is not a game—this is not a trial.
I'm not a phone to be just dialed. I am a person with
feelings. I won't be walked over again and again by you
Is it clear, is it sound. I'm starting to wander if your worth the love I've found.

Dawn Kelly Coffin

Dawn Kelly Coffin
CHIEF BIG FOOT IN DEATH

TO MY MOTHER Patricia (Daylight) Allen For your faith, love and inspiration.

Death reaches out
The chill of winter creeps slowly to the marrow
Nothing but silence

Life flashes
Wars fought, treaties signed,
Reds, Whites,
Bullets, arrows,
Many have feared your name

Your son is strong and has ridden by your side many times
Your people follow him now

Buffalo are scarce
Hundreds once roamed where you now lie
Pounding hooves roared

Forced west
Until you can go no further

Your body numb
Your moccasins and wraps soaked by the wet, slushy snow
The Great Spirit comes
Wisping away the paths we have trod
Releasing many souls from the bitterness.

Joanne Littlechild
IS THIS EARTH A PARADISE
An animal of beauty,
Surrounded by the snow.
Sits in terror thinking
When and how he'll know.
He's watched his parents suffer
And knows his turn comes soon
For when that two-legged creature
Comes from behind him with a boom
He'll be still for awhile and dazed
When the cold will slowly hit him
Then the creatures gone
And he'll just lie and gaze
That's all that he can do
His life has almost ended
His big sad eyes look up and say
"For that's my coat," I hope you get a decent pay.
Thats one less pup
This earth will have

We've all turned greedy and lost our love.
For today, money's everything
For tomorrow, a symbol says
This earth is hell.

Haideh Yazdani
THE WORLD IS IN NEED
The peoples of all the nations are entitled to liberty,
Which not only means freedom, but freedom in a world that is free,
But now the world is tied down by the ropes and chains of war,
And people say, "We're fighting for, the thing we've been looking for,"
And so the war keeps raging on, bloody battles never end,
And to this day I've never seen a person to surrend,
No, like children, they keep fighting, until during the war,
They hardly know with whom they're fighting and what they're fighting for,
And hardly ever have I seen a person to say, "Wait,"
Are we really fighting for our honor or for our fate,"
And "what is all this mess about 'we must keep charging ahead,'"
"I mean, can't we talk this over or do we have to be all dead,"
No, everyone must have his way or things won't work out right,
Can't we use our mouths to talk or use our hands to fight,
Think about if this way, if we fight for things too long,
We might not even be able to see what we did all wrong,
Our creator has endowed us with a mind we all must use,
But definitely not in a way that we use it to abuse,
If we do not learn our lesson and we don't learn it in time,
We will be destroying this blessed earth which is the worst of all crime,
And so I leave you with a thought, an urgent one indeed,
That if we don't unite the world, we'll never live a life to succeed.

Mary Atkinson Probst Seat
SAY IT WITH FLOWERS
Flowers whereever you see them, some message dear
Will impart.
Some tell of a dream that is realized and some of a broken heart.
Some bloom around the bed of sickness and help to lessen the pain.
Some bring the picture of one we have loved back to our memory again.
Some breath a message of happiness when they bloom in a bride's bouquet.
And some a message of sympathy when deaths angel has passed our way.
All of the wonders of nature God has made and has given they are ours.
And all of the thoughts we wish to express, we can say if we say it with flowers:

Lorraine E King
I AM AN AMERICAN
I am an American. Patriotic? Why shouldn't I be?
I live, of course, in the land of liberty.
Dictatorship, suppression, lack of freedom I abhor.
In America I can be happy and content; it's a land that I adore.
From where I came there is no mystery;
It can all be found in the world's history.
I was born in this land and in countries all over the world;
I pledge allegiance to America wherever the Red, White and Blue is unfurled.
It doesn't matter what my race, Red, White, Yellow or Black;
We all join as one red-blooded American Nation when under attack.
I do my best here, there and everywhere I can
Because I am proud to be an AMERICAN!

Ann G Waiters
HOLD THE DREAM
While the Nation watched on T.V.
The drum major for peace and equality,
was beaten bloody, gunned down and left dead.

In the early years of the Civil Rights Movement,
He sought economic, social, and political improvement
And, as a catalyst and conduit for change,
He launched The Poor People's Campaign.

Still, serious symbols of evil and injustice remain.
Apartheid, American style, poverty and racism
and yet to be slain.

A courageous symbol
of revolution and liberation,
The King won our deepest admiration.

His life and work, unique they seem
Call to us still, Hold On,
Hold On To The Dream!

Elizabeth Back
THEY TELL US

To Ron, Reg and Lavonne, Jim and Maureen

They tell us Banff is beautiful,

Or Greece and Timbuktu;
My favorite camping ground
Is out on the farm with you!

There's gorgeous purple beans,
To share with coons and squirrels;
Each multicoloured morning glory,
Up round the melon curls.

The corn is sweet and tasty,
Even if it's not so tall;
There's lots of turnips and taters—
You can't possibly eat them all.

The carrots are golden and crunchy,
Delicious in marinade;
When it gets hot and dusty,
In the house there's lemonade.

Pinecherries are a crimson red,
Standing near the chokes;
Natural treasures are all around,
Far from city blokes.

Our ground hog surveys the scene,
From his loft up in the barn;
Enjoying our casual company,
He knows we mean no harm.

With all the lovely sights,
There's a myriad of sounds;
Hooty owls and squawky geese,
They love these unspoiled grounds.

Have we the yen to wander,
To far-off touted places?
When here we find serenity,
And kindness in familiar faces . . .

Nancy Nokes
SOLITUDE
I hear the quiet whisper of the night
The cool air spreads over me
The stars twinkle up above
Indifferent to the world below
The stillness is relaxing
To my soul
The quietness makes me feel
At ease
The atmosphere of the night
Entraps my soul
I wish it could
Stay there
But . . .
It can't

Karen Abney-Doyle
ISOLATION
Pain, loneliness, despair, surround me, my invisible castle walls,
There are great towers built of old quarrels, hurts and exposed human flaws.
Sometimes, I roll out the big guns of blasting loud emotion to make the battle over with and done.
Hollering, bawling, flashing perceptions, thunderingly, I attack, "It'll pass," they count "1,000 & 1."
My lightning flares brief and when ignored burns out.
Their armour stays dry and bright, safely sheltered by emotional drought.
Most times, I find it easier to run and hide in my secret passage ways, then stay alone to fight.
In a micro spot of time, flying through my mind, excaping down corridors of darkness and light.
These castle walls must hold magic, whether for good or for ill,
Because, invisibly, I travel, while they think, I sit here still.
Rushing, finding twists and losing direction, thoughts are shadows, unnoticed follow and are all around.
The path shows bright and straight ahead, then with no warning, frightening emptiness, without sound.
Priorities and hang-ups are in the room behind the heavily bolted massive door, and
If the iron latch were dropped and my inadequacies and fears broke free, they'd soon breed with confusion and be more.
Sneaking up on the knowing, to catch myself by surprise,
Hyposcrisy startles easily and lays naked all the lies.

Nancy Jo Setters
WHO ARE WE TO SAVE?
I am bad, yet who are they to say?
In the darkness of the night
They also play

This loneliness engulfs me
Tragically I live each
Day

Seeing through these tears
Shall I find my love
Today?

Kimberlie Ann Yeoman (age 6 1/2)
BLUE AND GREEN
Blue is like the wind,
Staggering through the sky.
Blue is like the bluebirds,
Making nests in the trees.

Green is like a meadow of grass, banana peels that are not ripe, and broccoli
Green is in summer time trees,
Green is in a sweet mint breeze.

Susan Eloise Baskin
ONE

Dedicated to Deanna Sweet for her unconditional love

I am one with you

Nothing has death that I may have light
I am one with God

I am one with you

I shall live forever dancing
I shall learn forever singing
God is one with me

I am one with you

I do not reflect nature, I absorb her
I am one with nature

I am one with you

Nature senses and knows my love, she tells me her secrets
Nature is one with me

I am one with you

I invite you to come with me and dance the dance
Dance the dance of life
Sing the song of knowledge
I am one with you
You are one with me

We are love

Deborah Fein
CHILDHOOD
i am little i am small
and nothing can begin
to tell you how i wish
to grow and grow
until (of course) i start to grow down

and then my mind will also grow down
to reach the level of perpetual childhood
which in turn grows back to adulthood
and down again to childhood

man is born man has died
again and again (so forth
and so on) children yes
grow and grow to only
become children again
up is down and down is up
men will die
children will thrive

Mary Cavanaugh
I WANT YOU BACK

I wonder, is there a time in your life you think of me?
Because ever since its ended, I think of you constantly.
You know you weren't the first lover I've had.
But without you in my life, it seems rather sad.
It's no fun without you by my side.
With you, life was full of happiness, now all I can do is hide.
Everytime I think of how it could have been.
I start to wonder if it's ever going to come again, an if so when?
I love you in so many ways.
But being reluctant to tell you, I guess alone is the price I have to pay.
The feelings I have are a fact.
I guess I'm just trying to say, "I WANT YOU BACK!"

Maureen Elizabeth Dutton
THE LAST WHALE

As a whale, I swim free,
In my home waters; what will become of me?
Will I be shot and left to die?
Or will the whalers pass me by?

All my kind are gone but me,
I am the only one left in this blood red sea.
All day I haven't heard a song,
Or seen my friends; it's been so long.

Evil sportsmen in boats go by,
Looking for me, but what for, and why?
With their murderous harpoons set for aim,
Enjoying this with fun and game.

I must spout to take a breath—
BANG! Soon with my pain, I knew it would bring my death.
Sick and wounded I slowly die,
And sink towards the bottom where I would lie.

Towards the bottom is black as night,
I can't see a thing within my sight.
But as I descent to the bottom of the sea,
All my good friends;
Are waiting there,
For me.

Mark R Turner
WHAT WE'VE FOUND

Your gentle ways have captured my heart,
I've known this fact from the very start.

I hope you feel the way I do,
realizing by now how much I love you.

I'll never regret this love I've found,
because I know now you won't let me down.

I want you tonight all alone by my side,
to share the feeling we have deep inside.

Let's keep these feelings forever this way,
so our love will be here for always to stay.

Alan Wade Johnson
LIFE'S TREASURES

This poem is dedicated to Sandra Kay, the woman who filled my life with love, warmth and peace.

Have you ever loved—
and walked away?
Only to settle for something less second best . . .
Have your bedroom walls ever bore witness to a broken heart?
Your own . . .
Has your heart ever not cared to beat again?
Only to continue without concern . . .
Have you ever cried for someone?
Someone that no longer cared . . .
And have you ever not wished—
dreamed—thought—or cared?
Have you drained your soul—with the
tears of your heart—until what's inside
of you, that was once a garden, with buds
of beauty, turned only to dust?
And do you know loneliness?
Has it shared your bed—
your days—your nights—
Your heart?
If you've known all these things—
truly known—count yourself as one
with the best of life's treasures—
for won or lost—bought or sold—
borrowed or stole—
You've known love . ..

Susan Cochran
TEACH ME LOVE

Tell me not of victories past, but battles yet to win.
Tell me not of love gone by, But love thats left within.
I really dont want to know much of a past no-longer there.
Tell me instead what future we could share. What worlds we two might travel.
What trials we might bear. Tell me all of things like this so then I know you care.
Teach me love and happines for these things I have yearned.

Mamie McCue Jones
GODS LITTLE ANGEL

Dedicated to my granddaughter Kelly Ann, in memory of her baby.

A little Angel looks down tonight, while she's playing at the feet of our Lord.
She's smiling, singing with joy, all the Angels in one accord.
God gave her to her family—or rather loaned her for a very short
stay.—and I fully believe, with all my heart: This is what she is trying to say.
"Mama don't cry for me or wish me back; I'm with Jesus now, you
know.—there isn't any pain or grief; most of all, theres no sorrow.
I went walking with Jesus today; and as He held my hand so tight.
I thought of all the times I could see Him, as He was only visible to my sight.
Remember Mama, when I smiled that day? Do you know what I saw and heard?
I saw Jesus standing with out stretched arms, saying, "its almost time my little bird."
I saw the snow white doves hovering, and heard the fluttering of their wings.
Then suddenly a bright light appeared; A halo, like a golden ring.
It's yours they whispered, wear it and come home with us Arnell.
You did your part, here on earth; you gave love and you did it
well.—God knows you are hurting Mama; but under that mask its hard to tell.
And He knows that sometimes the pain, is almost unbearable.
But He loves you, just as I do; A love that surpasses all things.
And He wants you to be happy, in your thoughts of remembering.
So you see Mama, its time to let me go, and give me back to my
Father.—He blesses you for everything you did; specially for being my Mother." God bless you, from your Little Angel

Jim Cruz
MOTHER

To truly know a mother, compare her to a rose
Listen to your heart speak, as it's God who really knows
A mother's stem is her strength to stand
Against the weathers' wind and life at hand
The softness of her petals to which she reaches out
Her color be it deep, yet so soft as not to shout
The love that she gives is the fragrance of her pose
A fragrance that keeps flowing to fill her childrens' nose
A thorn that she wears is to provide
A protective measure in which to chide
As the seasons change, the rose shall remain
It's beauty to behold, a mother is the same
Through the seasons wear, her lasting beauty to never tear,
Within her heart, her children first, to love, protect
And deeply care
Her husband the proudest, this rose he does possess
His children have been cared for, and love is at its best
Her childrens heart are set aglow
As they have come to know
The true meaning of their mothers pose
They have found within the rose
Throughout the years this rose has endured
With the love of God she is assured
A place in this life upon this earth
To reveal to the world a mothers worth

Basil B Clark
SOLDIER AT A VERY EARLY AGE

To Ralph and Rocky, the two best sons a father could have. May you never have to go to war.

I was introduced to soldier at a very early age.
I found it in the hymnal as in church I turned to page
Three-eighty-five. Please stand.
So I sang about the onwards and the Christian soldiers more,
Who with Jesus as their guardian went marching off to war
The cross in front.
And my momma always said when she talked of God's great love
That a Christian must be tough like a soldier, fit for above
For God. Drill Sergeant.
So the natural thing to do at the age of sweet eighteen,
Was to enlist Infantry and join the First Air Cavalry team. I became a soldier.
But I often pause to reflect and I often wonder why,
Why the song of Christian soldiers left out how it was to die
Or watch it happen.
And the music made in church somehow left out all the strife,
And it even failed to mention how a soldier takes the life
Of someone else.
And I don't quite think that Jesus is His wildest crazy dream
Thought it right the day I killed a Vietnamese, age 'bout fifteen
Or maybe fourteen.
And I still don't find much comfort in approaching middle age
In the well-worn, aged hymnal as I turn in it to page
Three-eighty-five. Please stand.

Wilmer Ellis Boswell
THE NOBODY MAN

Fantasies, Fantasies, Fantasies.
They are not real—they are only dreams.

I had walked a long way and a long time
On a strange road—hard, rough

and winding.
Suddenly, an old man stood before me—
He seemed to have come from no place—
Was he real or an illusion?
He was, indeed, a strange person—
His appearance was unusual.
He was dressed in unique apparel.
There was no sound; No word was spoken.
Suddenly, by me, the silence was broken.
I said: "Who are you? Where are you going?
You seem to be dejected. For what are you looking?"
He said: "I am a drifter—the nobody man—
Searching for the never, never land:
I have dreamed too much for things I couldn't attain;
My efforts to succeed have been in vain.
I have not coped with realities—
I'm a victim of my fantasies."
I listened to what he said, attentively—
It seemed he was on a mission to me.
Before I could speak, He went his way;
He looked back, waved and disappeared.

Kim Emanuel
THE WORDS OF LOVE

To all the people of the World

The Letter L Means It Is A LANGUAGE, That
Each and Everyone Will Of course Understand.
The Letter O Means It Is ORIGINAL,
Just Like The Shake of A Hand.
Then The Letter
V is There Meaning VERSATILE, For It
Can Do or Be Many Things. The Letter E is For
The ENERGY, Which Comes From The
Happiness That Togetherness Brings.
Yes LOVE is What These Four Words Make Up,
And In Front Of LOVE is Where
WE ALL SHOULD STAND.

Allen Jay Wilder

Allen Jay Wilder
IT'S TIME

To all race, all creed, all people's of the world. Love is our hope on earth.

It's time we cel-e-brate His birth on earth;
To sing from every mountain of His birth
It's time our whole world discover, all race all creed
Are brothers, Love is our hope on earth.
It's time we cel-e-brate His birth on earth;
And teach the child the meaning of His birth.
It's time to show more understanding give thanks
For all of our blessings. He is our hope on earth
To-night.

It's time to cel-e-brate His birth on earth and
The Love we give is gon-na bring peace on earth
It's time to heal this difference be-tween us. Give
Love a chance to work. Love is our hope on earth,
It's time we cel-e-brate His birth on earth to-night.

It's time we cel-e-brate His birth on earth
And spread the news a-round of His birth.
It's time to to un-to others, and reach out touch a
Broth-er, Love is our hope on earth—It's
Time we cel-e-brate his birth on earth. To-night.

Vickie Ellen Boling
THE STRENGTH OF REALITY

To my Mother and Father, who with all of their love and patience, have encouraged me in all my endeavors. I love you.

My deep-sleep dreams are intense, fragmented and yet curious.
I struggle to recapture the shelter of their sheer fantasy.
But reality intrudes;
the sun of the fresh new day,
the projected lonesome hours,
the awareness of present time/space.
I turn to face the wall.
Then some word,
phrase or glance,
some smile,
some caress,
some thought,
some dream,
a sharing of a moment,
a whisper of hope,
some long ago love touches me.
I arise to face the world.

Alberta Bruno
OUR COUNTRY

America was born to be
A free and promised land,
All nationalities have merged
Each with a helping hand.

Years of true prosperity
Have seen our country grow.
Each president in his own way
Has helped to make it so.

Some citizens condemn our states
And what they have to give,
Yet wouldn't choose in all this earth
Another place to live.

Let's get together once again
To cooperate and bless,
This country which we share at will
With peace and happiness.

Brenna Leffler
REMEMBER

Remember the way we used to touch,
Remember the one you loved so much,
Remember the little things you said that proved our love would never end,
Now the years have taken over time
And I am glad to say you're still mine.

Richard A Leavitt
PLENTY OF BEAUTY

To: My wonderful wife Kathy, my children Tim, Amy and Travis and the rest of my family for giving me support and inspiration when I needed them the most.

I heard some people talking about the world today,
They were saying it was ugly, as they hurried on their way.
I thought to myself, why don't they stop and look around,
Because there is plenty of beauty just waiting to be found.
There's the beauty of an eagle with its wings spread in flight
And that of a mountain at the first break of light.
There's the beauty of a flower as it basks in the sun
And that of the deer or the elk as they run.
There's the beauty of squirrels gathering nuts in the park
And that of the horizon just before dark.
There's the beauty of a rainbow with its colorful stripes
And that of the fruit as it's just getting ripe.
There's all kinds of beauty in most living things
And it's in the color and fragrance that each of them brings.
So if you think the world's ugly, stop and look around.
You'll find there is plenty of beauty just waiting to be found.

Walter O Campbell
SINNERS SALVATION

To my wife Sarah and daughter's, Sandra and Shirley also Calvary Baptist Church, Lyman, South Carolina

I watched the man so sorrowful, as he dropped his head so low.
He squeezed the hymn book tightly, as
tears began to flow.
He left the pew so meekly, and to the altar came.
He poured out his heart to Jesus, just as the sick and lame.
He cried oh God! Save me! I've lived in sin so long.
Have mercy on me Jesus? I know I've
been so wrong.
Set me free from sin Lord? And place
me in your care.
I want to live for you Lord, and all your blessings share.
I've broken every commandment, you
know how sinners are.
I'm calling on you,. Jesus, I know what the cross is for.
Thank you Lord for saving me, so unworthy of your love.
I know you have a place for me, now in Heaven up above.

Edith Young
A PUZZLE IN THE SKY

Dedicated to my grandchildren

Little stars you shine so bright and the moon gives so much light, making the sky a wonderous sight.
The sun it lights my path each day and the moon it guides my path at night.
Wish I could see where the sun hides at night while the moon comes out to light up the night and if I ever figure it out, two more puzzles must I solve.
Where does the moon go when the sun comes out and how can so many stars, find a place to hide?

Edith M Peterson

Edith M Peterson
SILVER FALLS

We stand entranced,
God's Cathedral is filled with music,
Made by the murmuring stream,
And the song of birds.
'Tis the wedding march.

Down the isle
Mid giant trees of fir
Comes the bride.

She is dressed in silver,
About her flows a veil of rainbow mist.
In her arms, she carries
Flowers from the mountain, and fern
Held with white spray.

The wind catches her veil
And flings it against our upturned faces,
Leaving them wet,
As she trips on o'er the rocks
To wed the sea.

Lena S Foley
THAT OLD DOG OF MINE

The old Dog that was so dear to me.
I miss him something awful don't you see?
He would roam the country all around.
but he came home to the call of my sound.
We got along for years and years,
as I think back now through a flow of tears.
His fluffy white hair and his big giant
feet, he was getting on in age, but he did look
neat.
I tarry on now as the story is told,
that old Dog of mine was good as gold.
Partly deaf and could hardly see,
words cannot express how much that dog meant to me.
A place in the wilderness that's near to me,
now holds a plot for him under the shade tree.

Marica
THE BATTERED ISLAND

To Johnny—who believes in me—And to Jesus in whom we both believe.

No man is an island able to stand against the forces of life—
When the tidal waves wash over his soul, the banks may give way to the strife.
The pounding winds—the torrents of rain he cannot stand and fight—
For the battling forces of nature may require his very life.
When his shores are battered and weary worn—his foundation eroding away—
with no hand to clutch—or shoulder for crutch, he'll stumble and fall each day.
After a season of fighting the gales the battered soul may say.
"give up, give up—give up the fight, you can't win anyway."
Oh, what a shame! For had that soul His mighty anchor sought
Stretched forth his hand to the hand that waits, all our battles
He has fought.
No winds can stand, nor storm prevail, no soul the devil snare.
the forces of evil can never command a soul that's in his care.
Reach out! Reach out! Oh man alone. You need the one who cares.
Rest in the arms of the rock of ages, He'll keep you safely there.

No man is and island, unto himself, able to stand apart.
For he's joined to others by the blood of Christ.
Hand to hand and heart to heart

Patricia McKeen Herman
MISSING YOU

For my "Alter Ego" —My friend—my lover—my husband—Roy!

---

as i turn my eyes
to the trees and the skies—
i'm missing you—
as i go through my day—
in my own way—
i'm missing you—
as i lie here in my bed—
with you in my head—
i'm missing you!

darling, is there another way to say—
i'm missing you?
i'm loving you!!

Bonnie R Schreffler
A DREAM

A dream may be a vision
a ceaseless fantasy;
Neglected hopes or wonders
that await a reckoning.

A dream may lose its splendor
in one moment of despair;
Or lull in silence, motionless
until rediscovered there.

Sometimes hard to grasp or hold
it is sadly left to stray;
If abandoned or unrealized
will surely fade away,.

Judith Nan Lewis (Sanders)
A SELF-MADE PRISON

Dedicated to my husband, Brian Sanders, whose occupations required all his time and inspired my writing.

I loved you! "Till it hurt."
"Gave," until it hurt.
A, self-made, prison I'm in,
while your gone.
"Trying," to except our days
together, ALONE

Bud R Thompson
LOVE-STAR

Dedicated to "Carol"

Another day has come, dawn is here and I'll be gone
its up to you now to carry on.
Please shed no tears for me, for the love you gave was enough
you see
Oh I thank you so. It meant so much you know
And as they say, I needed that—the road is dark
There's no way back
Your Love like a Star will guide me on
To the road of the cross where God belongs
And when its time for you—please have no fear
For my love in return will bring you here

Polly Lyon
A FRIEND CALLED TODAY

We talked of my health and of my soul,
she couldn't help but let the tears flow.
But if I should die young, don't feel sorry for me.
My life has been happier than I ever dreamed it could be.

With caring, loving parents,
Husband, daughter, and son,
I had everything I wanted,
I was their special someone.

Don't think there haven't been heart aches,
God knows there have been quite a few.
But all the good has out-weighed the bad,
I hope life will be that good to you.
I love life so,
The end will be hard to bear.
But if love and happiness is what life's all about,
Then I've had more than my share—

A friend called today.

Mary

Mary
WIFE

I am thankful to heaven for blessing Divine.
For peace and good friends, and the success that is mine. I am thankful for
health, and skies of bright blue.
But most thankful of all, for a wife like you.

Lillian Donohue Marren
SEDUCTIVE LOVER

To Ronald J. Marren and all those who are forced to suffer from incurable diseases due to lack of medical knowledge and funding needed for medical research.

She was a seductive, possessive lover.
She stalked him silently through the years.
Invincible and strong,
Sinister and secretively.

She wanted him for herself,
Regardless of the consequences of her selfish greed.

She had a need—to kill him and take him away from his family, friends and career.

She was always there, her presence felt everywhere.
In his eyes, his drooping mouth, his unsteady gait and
Loss of weight and appetites that make a marriage right.

She wanted him.
Her fingers wrapping tightly around his bones, muscles and
tissues.
Sucking his blood to preserve her youth and beauty.
First she wanted one pint, then two, then three.
Her needs ever increasing.
His strength ever decreasing.

She dominated his life.
Now she is his wife.

I live with a stranger,
His mind no longer on me but with her.
His devotion ruled by her every emotion.

She wants his life,
His very last breath,
His energy and intellect.
She is death!

Alice R Stoddard
THE ROAD AHEAD

The long road on which you have walked, tripped and sometimes ran
Was based on parallel paths—one each for the woman and her man.
Your dual roadway meant always being there—to touch, to talk, to share
Thoughts, opinions, laughter, sorrows—both were really there to care.
Suddenly your road ahead has turned into a shadowy single lane
Of disolusion, the burden of loss, great heart-ache and pain.
But now you see the road ahead still goes on, and you ask
Can I really overcome this altered life—what a task!
This road ahead, will it be forever impeded with bramble, tangle and thorn?
No, it will not, cannot be, however long you perhaps will mourn.
On this long, long road ahead, you will eventually discover
There are many of family and friends to help you recover.
For the road ahead, leading through and over the steep hill of grief
Will bring you to see, on the downhill side, with your belief
That there is on this road ahead the certainty that you can cope,
And there will again be days to laugh, to enjoy and to hope.

Byron Lee Sacre
CONVERSATION WITH MY CAT

To Muckle, who made me appreciate life.

Peepers, friend calico enrapt on the patio
Trancing the advancing morning away,
Not asleep, deep in reverie where I can never be,
Your golden eyes shining, divining the day,
O harlequin goddess in pantheist orison
How sad I have never seen where you have been.
She glides like a velvet dream
(small socks of palest cream),
Bounds up, cocks her sable ears
(sounds no one human hears),
Leaps the table to pace in her place by my side.
She desires now to share with me rare midday mysteries,

On my lap sweetly pleading and kneading my knees,
Addressing me, pressing with passionate stride.
What? I am wondering What scene is she pondering?
Is it fable or fear spurs her purring at me?
Musings on meadow mice, or does she seek my advice?
Has an eldritch sprite frighted her beside the big tree?
She gazes reproachfully; No speech will she broach with me,
For no talent have men to ken arcane feline tongue.
Discontent, she departs from me, clearly too smart for me—
Her attempt to converse so perversely unstrung.
No gift I aspire to, no greater desire would I
That a flair to share views with my cat,
For through all our universe no true diverse brotherhood
Could afford a more cordial communion than that.

Tony V Smith
WILL WE MAKE IT
I said to myself, I am going to make it in this world,
cause there are people fighting for their lives every day.
Will they make it, or will they give their lives away
So many say, they have the strength to go on,
some of them say, life's not worth living for, will we make it
Will we fail, will we make it in this world
Father o mighty Father, help your children.
Give them the faith to carry on, will we make it, or will we fail, will we make it in this world.
Just believe in yourself and show the world.
You have faith, just believe in yourself.
And I'll believe in you, then we will make it.
I know we will make it, you and I will make it. Cause we have faith. And we believe in our goal.
That, we will achieve.

Eleanor Raymond DeDomenicis
REVERIE
Campus paths lie serene before me; a placid stillness prevails.
Across a cerulean sky, wisps of white meringue float gently into oblivion
while sunbeams perform a ballet upon the contoured stages of oak, maple, and pine.

In the warmth of the day, multi-colored birds sing messages
that Man cannot decipher—that if understood by him,
would unlock the secrets of the universe.

A carpet of green plush stirs in the gentle summer breeze
—invitingly soft and cool.
I tread, instead, the man-made ribbons of crushed stone
on my way to poetry class.

I walk not alone; the poetic imagery of Robert Frost is my companion
his savored stanzas as refreshing as a flowing fountain
and as soothing as fine, sweet music
when it lulls the senses into dreaming.

Suddenly! An inner burst of sound!
A painful thud!
A rude awakening from the quiet reverie!
A hard object—I know not what—drops from some distant height of a massive, overhanging oak;
And Mother Nature, the Queen of poets, unmercifully raps me on the head!

Grace Broekhove
MY NEEDS
I need to play
to laugh, to giggle,
to walk in the sand
and feel my toes wiggle.
I need to dance
and spin round & round,
to float in the air
fore my feet touch the ground.
I need the warmth
from the sun up above,
to have lots of friends
and feel all their love.
I need the light
from God up on high,
as I bask in his love
I sit here and sigh.
His is the balm
I need for my soul,
to heal all my hurts
and disappointments of old

Kelli Loraine Thalacker
MISSING YOU
All my thoughts, all my kisses, surround my heart with deepest wishes.
Deepest wishes of me and you, not only now apart, but much together too.
Thou are apart now, our hearts are together. Soon our bodies will touch together.
We'll hug, we'll kiss, we'll share our smiles, and our loneliness will no longer be miles.
Soon back together, no longer apart, my mind will not miss you, and neither will my heart.

Renee Lynch

Renee Lynch
LAST SIGNS OF SUMMER
Today as I was walking,
I just happened to look down.
Beside my foot I found,
A small white and yellow daisy
Waving in the wind.
One that was left from summer
Which left only a few months ago.
This last and lonely sign of summer
was left there all alone,
As if to brighten the day
of a lonely old lady.
Or even a man who couldn't see,
but could smell the fragrance
given off by the daisy.
So I picked it in hopes to brighten
Some special person's day.
So I give to you this daisy.
In hopes to brighten your day.
So smile and remember it always
this last and lonely sign of summer.

Paul Warren Higgins
THE SPACE SHUTTLE
Full thrust! and courage. God, why?
Their pedal to the floor, we're who they're doing it for.
Lighting up the sky in an orange-white-yellow fry.
They were free-basing coke, so went a desperate joke.
Secret missions, the devils whisper.
Shall we argue 'bout the mystery?
Keep living a war whore history?
Why do people have children, sir?
To eat them all up at twilight's stir?
Judy, Judy, Judy, fun-loving, smart . . .
I'd copy her homework, seek her heart . . .
Are there girls like her in a captive nation?
What chance have they there to reach her station?
Do they give up, as face-covered prostitutes,
For cowards to use them as snakes follow flutes?
The inalienable rights of each woman and man,
May they some day be granted to joints like Iran.
We must do our part, our little bit
The jolly right stuff it, never quit!
Show the world how dumb it be
To savage the best out of hate, jealousy,
When all achieved is for thee and thine
To face real God, 'fore we really dine.
For we the living, the brave did die; as Elvis sang,
It could be for them, "You light my morning sky with burning love."

Joyce Whitehead
MOTHER-IN-LAWS
Memories of my mother-in-law are very dear.
They are nothing like the rumors of mother-in-laws you hear
She was good hearted and jolly and fun to be around.
No better mother-in-law could be found.
She really loved her grand children with them she had a ball,
She was generous and kind and always on call.
If it wasn't for my mother-in-law I wouldn't be the same,
She gave birth to my husband I now bear his name,
My husband was born half her and now he is half of me.
So I couldn't help loving my mother-in-law because she is part of me, you see!

June Kuwitzky
SQUARE DANCE MAGIC
It's Saturday, it's been a hard week
Is there a fun way out, some enjoyment to seek
Can we find exercise, fellowship, perhaps some romance?
Of course we can; we found it, it's called a square dance.

As I go thru my closet and select a pretty dress
I bid farewell to weariness and most of the week's stress.
As I put on my makeup and blow-dry my hair
My mirror does some magic and transforms me then and there.
The bouffant petticoat and matching pettipants
Make me feel like Cinderella—all ready for the dance.

But alas
stretched out upon the couch lies my worn-out mate
Will I need wifely persuasion
To stir him for a date?

As he dons a western shirt
And pulls on each fancy boot
A magic overcomes my Prince
He is ready to "swing thru" and "scoot."

Oh, think not this a passing fancy
Or we'll soon lose these illusive states
'Cause for twenty years, we've "do-say-do'd"
And will "slide thru" the Pearly Gates.

Margaret W Knowlden
MY ANGEL MOTHER

To my beloved mother, Alberta Wickham, who died November 28, 1986. She was a poet and had several poems published. This is my first poem to be entered and published, and I am a third generation poet.

Day by day, your influence guides me on
As it did when you lived here with me.
Your spirit lives deep within my heart;
Each shared moment but an echoed mem'ry.
The hours we spent together seemed short
As our lifetimes sped away in space.
Before that, time passed by endlessly.
Now you have vanished without a trace.

Bewildered, I ponder where you have gone,
Knowing you have reached a higher realm.
I'm tempted to follow after you,
Confident our Lord is at the helm.
The light of faith burns much more brightly
As my thoughts turn to Eternal Life.
You've inspired me to search earnestly
To find that heav'n free of care and strife.

My prayers explore the depths of myself
To find answers to questions not clear.
An unknown future beckons to me;
I am learning to live without fear.
Death was but a step beyond the grave
When you slipped so peacefully away.
God's peace has calmed the voice of my soul,
And I will be with you again some day.

Robert F Olson
TRUE LOVE

Love is something we can not hide
It is all over this world wide
It is wide and it is also deep
It is something we can not keep.
It is something that is low and high
We may often begin to wonder why
It is a debt that we can never pay
We must always give it away.
It is something we can not deceive
There is always someone to receive
We must now, make no mistake
We must always give before we take.
Our true love is always pure
It is something that makes us secure
True love is something that we feel
It is happiness, it is something real.
I'll begin to explain it all over again
Read, Romans thirteen, eight to ten
The ten are all wrapped in one, called love
It all radiates from the One above.
This true statement has been made
This debt of love is never paid
When we give, this is my view
It always comes back to me and you.

Frieda M Dollmetsh
FRIENDSHIP'S LANE

There's a place in our lives we frequently visit—
A place not of earthly terrain—
A soothing departure from everyday chores—
The place known as FRIENDSHIP'S LANE.

It isn't very far to this magical spot,
Just a few quick steps to the phone,
Or a very short trip to the house next door—
And suddenly you're not alone.

It makes all the difference when you confide
To another understanding soul
The problems you have that you can't seem to solve;
And suddenly, the solution is whole!

Or maybe it's happiness you want to share
And telling it triples your joy;
It helps you immensely to have a true friend
Whose devotion time can not destroy.

So whether you're glad or whether you're sad,
Whether brimming with health, or in pain
Remember the way to gladden your day
Is a stroll along FRIENDSHIP'S LANE!

Virginia Caldwell Gomez
THE WALK

I took a walk down main street today
In a town of which I'm so proud;
I saw a large group of people,
So, I went and joined the crowd.
There were draft dodgers and card burners;
They all had something to say;
The boys and girls, the young and the old,
Were protesting against the U.S.A.
And as I watched I felt sick
That patriotism had fallen this way,
And I remembered another walk I had taken
On the last Memorial Day.
I had walked through the battlefield;
The rugged, desolate terrain,
And from somewhere in the distance
I heard a bugle's eerie refrain.
I had walked inside the church
And knelt in silent prayer;
I gave my humble thanks
To those whose memory still lingers there.
I had walked through the cemetery
To pay homage to those beneath the sod.
Weep not, ye that were left behind,
For they have walked with God.

Lena B Porter
MAN SPLIT THE ATOM

Man split the atom and soon
Roared past the galaxy of stars,
Conquered the surface of the moon,
And planned a colony for Mars.
An astronaut returned to say,
He saw not God along the way
To the finite invisable is He,
Until death sets the spirit free.
The creator he shall see
Only in eternity.

Alan Abrahamsen
OF MY LIFE

I know a bell will toll
the day I lose the need,
to nourish my soul,
through that staple from seed,
The bread of my life.

And the stars never rise
ere I count my blessings,
for my escape from ties,
my refuge from sad things . . .
The wine of my life.

But I am never breathing
without always dreaming,
of my reason for being,
my purpose for living,
The love of my life.

Thomas F Bradley
LAST SHEETS

Last sheets usually get tossed out,
Without the privilege of last writes.
Not this one tho';
He shall have a special purpose.
He shall reveal,
He shall proclaim,
He shall show,
That not all that are last are least,
But are best.

Irene Dickson Boudreau
A THOUGHT IN QUESTION

To My Loving Grandchildren

Why did Humpty Dumpty allow himself
To sit upon the wall
When he knew the possibility
Of his great, eventful fall?
Do you suppose he meant to prove
A point to each and all—
That it is not wise to place oneself
Upon the highest wall?

Leanna K Ford

Leanna K Ford
PORTRAIT OF MY MOTHERS FACE

Each crease around my mother's eyes
Are signs of love, tears and wisdom in disguise;
Lifelines, sketched by each golden yesteryear,
Etched by some childish laughter—or perhaps a tear;
Crowned by patient furrows on her brow,
Echoing seams of laughter around her mouth.
There are no wrinkles on my mother's face;
Just seasoned, kindly marks
God's plan has traced.

Judy Hardik
GOOD TO BE ALIVE

I woke this morning feeling fit and well
This was going to be a great day, I could tell.
As I rose from my bed and by the window stood,
I knew in my heart this day would be good.
The sun was just rising over the trees,
Beautiful mornings are rare such as these.
The birds were chirping with early morning noise
As if to say "Get up girls and boys."
The warmth of the sun felt good on my face
I sighed and thought "What a great place."
Today was a day like all the rest,
But somehow I felt it would be the best.
Some days are full of headaches and worry
And it seems like I'm always in a hurry.
Rushing here and going there
Feeling sad with the gray in my hair.
We all need some time to stop and think,
Give thanks we have enough to eat and drink.
Be happy with life's everyday joys
Like watching children playing with toys.
Don't be depressed with worry and strife,
Do the best that you can and enjoy your life.

Ellie Copeland
PRIDE

Lord I'm not very happy with myself.
I have stored too many unpleasant things on my memory shelf.
Lord you know, I want a clean and pure heart.
But this life of every day worries and troubles I can't depart.

I know I have pride, that goes before a fall.
I have fell so many times lately, I can't count them all.
I love with all my heart, and work hard with my hands.
Lord give me some help, so I can make it to the promised land.

I try to be honest, and help any one I can.
That's not enough Lord according to your plan.
I want to be humble, honest, and sincere.
Lord give me tolerance, patience, and love to adhere.

My faults are many, and I'm quick to judge.
Lord take these faults of mine and don't let me hold a grudge.
Let me see beauty not malice or greed.
Help me Lord to do all things according to your creed . .

Jody Jennison
CHRISTMAS TIME

Christmas time to me means . . .

It means White Christmas
Christmas is made for everyone
Christmas is beautiful and white
Christmas is caring for you.

It means Christmas Trees
Christmas trees are bright
Christmas trees are a place for presents
Christmas trees is a place for love
And a place for you.

It means Christmas Wreaths
Wreaths are for decorations
Wreaths are for love
But they look better around you.

It means Stockings by the Fireplace
Stockings can have goodies
Stockings can have candy
Stockings can have toys
Or something sweet like you.

It means Merry Christmas to All.

Kathleen Ann Fowler
HUSBANDS

To Thomas, without whose "assistance" this poem could not have been written.

Out-dated film, and bits of string;
A suit that is too small,

A stone from someone's old class ring;
An air-less basketball.

A mangy pipe, without a stem;
And sweaters long worn out—
Yet to part with all these "treasures"
I know he has a doubt.

"I'll clean that closet out someday."
And yes, indeed he does;
He puts it all in one big box,
And leaves it where it was.

Karen Cotten
HIDEAWAY

Dedicated to my son, Wm. Chad

Do you have a special place,
peaceful, warm and secluded?
A place where you can dream,
you find you never want to leave?
Don't be afraid to share it.
Only you say who enter your hideaway.

Marian Lee
TOGETHER FOREVER
Your life, your love, your happiness God gave to thee
He gave you your son, and that was a treat,
with this symbol that I am gave you.
No trick, No games, No putting on a show.
For being a special friend to me.

Dennis C Beach

Dennis C Beach
FOREVER LOVE

This poem is Dedicated to my loving wife Patricia.

Of all the fortunes that can be fortold,
All the Diamonds, Rubys, Silver and Gold;
No amount can compare to my wonderful wife!
Who has brought me more riches by just being my wife.
She is an angel from up above.
She is my Venus! My Goddess of Love.
We love each other. Of that I am sure!
There can be no other love so good, and so pure.
My wife has that special something that is so rare.
That's why no other woman could ever compare.
So I will love her forever! That's all of my life.
I shall always thank "God" for such A Wonderful Wife.

S R Ford
HARMONY
You've heard of Happy Memories
In the days of long ago,
You've heard of Sweet Tomorrows
With the fireflies all aglow.

You've heard of Sweet Contentment
In the days of yesteryear,
Where people lived as neighbors
Without ever any fear.

Why can't we live the same today
As they did so long ago,
With neighbor loving neighbor
In this world we all love so.

Why put off until tomorrow,
What we should do today,
That is, Love One Another
IN THE SWEET AND RIGHTEOUS WAY.

Let's get back to the basics
Of what a life should be,
And live in Sweet Contentment
In a land so True and Free.

Dawn Blue
JUST DESSERTS
Sacrificial lamb.

Just say okay,
Roll over and die.
It's so easy,
No fighting . . .
Just roll over,
And let their knife go in easy.

No muss, no fuss.

Sacrificial lamb.

All your life, that's what you've been:
Come with me; Live with me; Toil for me;
No, not that way, this way; Change to my way, my style;
Yes, sir—Yes, sir—Yes, sir.

And you've done it all . . .

Sacrificial lamb.

Dawn Bolivar
WHEN I AM HAPPY
When I am happy,
I sing a song,
Play Ping-Pong,
Do something graceful
And eat something tasteful,
When I am happy,
It pleases me to hear
How Old King Cole was a
Merry old soul,

And hear holiday songs that are

Very dear and always sincere.
Sometimes when I am happy,
I start to cry a couple of soggy
Tears from my eye.
My nose starts to jiggle

When I see and hear the crows caw.

That's what I'm like when I am happy.

L Burnelle Deardorff
BEES ARE BUSY LITTLE SOULS
Bees are busy little souls,
They have no time for birth control,
That's the reason times like these,
There are so many son's of bees.

Donna Mae Eaton
SUNSET IN VERMONT
The sunset glows o'er Lake Champlain,
I sit in reverie,
Thoughts of yesterday, today,
Tomorrow, what will be!
I watch the gold waves splashing in,
The seagulls soaring, cry.
The sailboats tossing to and fro,
The black ducks swimming by.
The crickets chirp in harmony,
Their concert can be heard,
As crimson colors fill the sky
"God speaks, without a word."
The brilliant moments fade too soon,
I watch the black night creep,
He wraps his dark cloak over all,
And lulls the world to sleep.

Edward Williams
COME ON JESUS AND TAKE ME AWAY
Come on Jesus and take me away
Sometimes I feel like flying away,
Sometimes I find it hard from day to day,
Come on Jesus and take me away.
Sometimes when my heart is cold,
I can't find words to say.
Come on Jesus and take me away.
But I know that if I have faith in you,
I will find peace all my days.
Come on Jesus and take me away!

M Evelyn Fischer
MORNING

Dedicated to My Beloved Pastor, Robert M. Varner

Tis morn, another day to share in the path of righteousness
Another foe to conquer
Another friend to gain
Another heart to give our Lord and King.

Mary Cleaveland
RETIREMENT
Retirement is just a frame of mind
No fun I'm often told.
You find you search for things to do
To keep from getting old.

Altho at first you smile a lot
This leisure you enjoy.

But then the hours begin to drag,
You start to daydream as a boy.

A fishing hole, a hunting trip,
Rent a cabin by the lake.
Maybe I'll get a part time job
Just to keep myself in shape.

All those things you planned to do,
And now so far away.
And if you were only younger,
You'd have yourself a day.

So I think I've solved the problem
As age does take its tole.
Retire when you are very young,
And work when you are old . . .

Hector S Gonzalez
ATOMIC REACTION

Dedicated to the one who shares my life, the one who shares my hopes and dreams, my wife Carmen.

While some sit and meditate,
Others scheme to get ahead.
Life continues while death waits,
Like an ever endless thread.

Dimming sun and grayish skies,
Cities filtered with concrete.
Building reaching way up high,
Glass and metal crown the streets.

No more will the willow cry.
Nor the birds on tree tops sing.
Springs of life will surely die,
And this world of death shall stink.

In an instant all will end,
As the atoms break their chains.
And it will not matter then,
There'll be no one left to blame.

Sylvia Husser-Edwards
THE QUIETEST ROOM IN TOWN

To my sister, Tonja Elaine Husser Lambert, who died in 1971 at the age of 21, from a drug overdose, yet she lives on and on and on . . . Dear Tonja . . .

There she lay, in the quietest room in town
Dressed no more in her thin Frederick's gown
An information tag hung limply from one toe
Identifying her as a murdered Jane Doe

Her lovely face was a ruin for now and evermore
But her spirit followed me as I closed the morgue room door

Now she wears the purest white gown
As she
silently
follows me
From the quietest room in town
She's still my Little Darling and her Angel face does shine
No one can take that from me
Eternally
She is mine
Now she wears the purest white gown
As she
silently
follows me
From the quietest room in town

Kim Turcotte
IT ALL UNFOLDS
On the field
soldiers training,
Strength and knowledge
they are gaining.
In the midst of war
not for conquest,

But for their nation
they do their best.
While in battle
fear of knowing,
Flame and smoke
death is growing.
The unforgotten
their memories hold,
In our minds
it all unfolds.
Once a year
our memories retain,
In people's hearts
the pain remains.

Phyllis Blevins Jones
O MOON AND STARS
I see the moon and stars above,
They make me think of the one I love;
Although he is gone far across the sea,
I know that he is thinking of me.

O moon above you look so bright,
You don't seem to know I'm lonely tonight;
O stars you don't seem to care,
About this diamond I so proudly wear.

But O moon and stars do one thing for me,
Look down on that one so far across the sea;
Tell him I'm thinking so tenderly of him,
Tell him that soon we'll be together again.

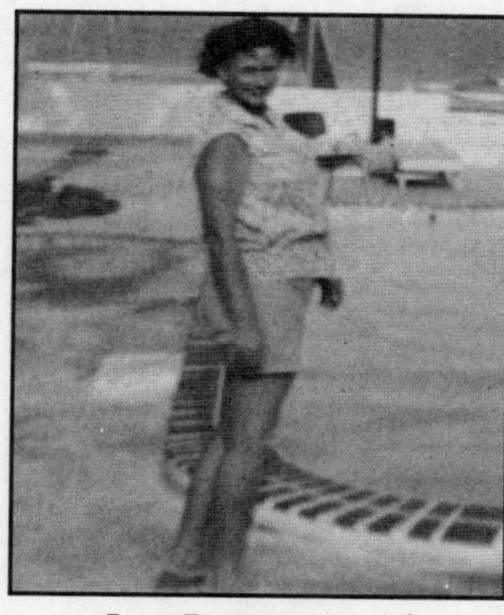

Jean Brunson David

Jean Brunson David
TRANSFORMATION
This room is cold . . .
It is only a place . . .
It soon will be warmed
By the light on your face,
As thro' conversation and glances
I am led to yesteryear . . .
You have come—
What a change has taken place here!

Janet Kramer
UNTITLED
Heavy . . .
Heavy . . . sorrow
Wilt thou abate
With the coming morrow?

A morrow of days
Or of years
The length as yet
Undetermined by tears

The weight inside
So dull, so quiet
A companion unwanted
Would you buy it?

To rid myself
I'd sell
Full knowing you
Want none of this hell.

The cause persists
Out of my hands
The perpetrator yet
Self-righteously stands.

Heidi M Dzieglewicz
THE WHISPERS IN THE NIGHT
When the sunsets
and day goes forth to night
when the moon shines its light,
I hear the whispers of the night.

I hear the whispers of the wind blowing
through the blades of grass,
I hear the trees talk in low sacred voices.
I hear birds singing lullabies
to their little ones who cry,
but most of all—
I hear the crickets singing their songs to each other
in the darkness of the night.

Kate Boozer
THE CHIMNEY

Dedicated to my sisters—Gin and Cas

Deep in briars and scraggy pine,
Inviting imagination back in time,
It caught my eye; also my heart.
What secrets could it, with voice, impart?

How many have gathered 'round the fire
Of this now forsaken chimney spire?
How many peanuts were roasted o'er it's coals?
What were it's owners dreams. . .their goals?

How many prayers were said;
How many tears were shed
While long hours turned leaping flames
to embers, dead?

How many babies racked with pain
Were rocked before it's warmth—
'til silence came?

Whose hands gathered stone and fashioned strong?
Alas! Its secrets with the smoke are gone.
Unwalled, silent, stark, it stands alone.

Maxiena E Daniel
OUR AMERICAN FLAG
United States' flag is so grand!
Patriots find it is in demand;
Each state, a white star true,
Freely waves on a field of blue.

Bravery is portrayed by blood red,
And many loyal soldiers lay dead,
That citizens may still be free;
So Americans can gladly ever be
Loyal to our nation's bold flag!
And if our spirits start to lag,
Proudly give thanks for this land,
And our beautiful flag so grand;

Its stars form a new constellation
To free us from all apprehension,
That we could lose our freedom
To despots seeking more kingdom.

Lois Stinson
THIS VALLEY

Dedicated to my daughter Sue

This valley is mine,
It can be yours, too;
Just stop for a moment
And take in the view.
You'll see beautiful mountains
Of green, and some blue,
And rivers unending
With deep purple hue.
The years have flown by
Since I was a child,
And played in your woodland
And picked flowers in your wild.
Somehow I knew
What your mountains were for;
The fierce killer storms
Never reached our front door.
With mountains so high
And valley so low,
The unending rivers
And meadows to sow.
Why look any further
For Heaven on earth;
I love this "ole valley"
I've lived in since birth.
When my time comes
To meet with our God;
I'll tell him I've rested
Under your sod.
Between winding rivers
And mountains so blue,
To this beautiful valley—
"Much thanks" to You.

Judy Reedy Springer
PATH OF PASSION
As I walk down the path of passion
Love overcomes me like the darkness
And the moonlight beams a ray of romance
As the wind whispers sweet nothings in my ear.

I hear bells ringing and bluebirds singing
Sweet melodies that float through the air
Speaking softly and gently everywhere
All I want is for someone to care.

When I'm walking in a spring shower
The rain feels like teardrops on my face
Tis the season for love & flowers
Yet it's not my time for pearls and lace.

Another day has come and gone
I see a star wink at me
The man in the moon seems to say
Happiness only comes for heaven above.

Ed H Stanton
DESTINY
As He looked down on the earth
He said, "I have a plan for you, and you and you."
And he pointed his finger, at everyone in the world.
"Do not try to elude the things
I've laid for you on earth,
For all I have in store
Began on your bed of birth.
And should you try to change
The pains that I have taken
You will find to your disillusionment
That they will not be shaken.
So don't despair when things go bad
Or do not go your way
For I have a better plan
For you another day."
"Who are you?" All the people asked,
"for Your name we can not see."
And with a booming voice replied,
"I am Destiny!"

Deborah Collinson
DEPARTURE BAY CHILDHOOD
Rusty, rainy days,
orange juice dripping off chins,
cobs of corn secreted from the coalpath,
morning laughter tears.
Tripping down the Ancient's stairway,
deep down
to fish,
chips
and the broken mirror left by ferry Queens.
Limpid Mother ocean rocks to her cradlesong,
tickling toes with tideworn caress.
Reaching out to waxwing clouds
we will spy on stars that spray the night sky.
A reflection of
the breath of life
to every passing day.
All is well.

Ora M Johnson
THE SETTING SUN
Clouds thru the clouds pure color delight.
The setting sun still glorious and beautiful.
The setting sun its waning rays trying to play
peek-a-boo in our car.
Oh my the setting sun is leaving me!
Farewell setting sun until the dawn of the new day.

Clouds thru the clouds pure color delight.
The setting sun still glorious and beautiful.

The setting sun its waning rays
trying to play
peek-a-boo in our car.
Oh my the setting sun is leaving me.
Farewell setting sun until the dawn
of the new day.

Rickey Dwain Smith
THE ROAD
The road leads on forever,
it never seems to end.
You come to where it crosses,
and it starts all over again.

The road takes you to places,
that you have never been.
You see new things and faces,
and might even make a friend.

The road is like a circle,
It keeps going round and round.
From north to south, and east to
west,
From big city to small country
town.

The road is something that we all
share.
It takes you anyplace, anytime,
anywhere,
I'm proud to say the road is mine.
Because without the road,
My way I could not find.

Chauna Craig
ENLIGHTENMENT

This poem is dedicated to all who have nurtured my writing, especially my parents, Bob and Necha Craig.

Endless parades of street lamps
march before my eyes,

piercing the placid pools of
shadow.

Exhibiting a pompous display
in their glowing costumes.
Each desperately attempts
to absorb the attention
of every nighttime passer.
Yet underneath the flash and dash
Lies a simple plate of glass
and a few pieces of crooked wire.
Worthless in the sun's
magnaminous glow,
Useless when boastful radiance
snuffs its own existance.
Proud streetlights: their only
important role to guide another's
path.
But personifying the human race,
no beacon is willing to share
the limelight,
And while magnifying its own
brilliance,
it soon dies and is forgotten.

Robert A LaRocca
HERE WE GO AGAIN
Hot ice
Pink's nice
Hot Pink
Miami Vice
That's nice
Think Twice
Think Tank
Pull Rank
Pull over
Four leaf clover
Lucky charm
Break an arm
Arm a tank
Give a thanks
Give a hoot
Gee you're cute
G.I.Joe
Here we go
Stop the show
Indecision
Nuclear fission
Split decision
No Winners
Only Sinners
Here We Go Again

Patricia (Zeigler) Bossard
THE WYNOOCHE RIVER

To My Parents Frank and Rachel Zeigler, My Husband Jerry, Our Sons, Jerrod, Kevin, and Arnie, and My Sister Leta who love the River Too.

In Summer I sit by the river,
Today it's as clear as the sky.
I feel so calm and peaceful
As I watch it drift on by.

Quickly then, its colors change,
It's now a turquoise blue,
With Fall leaves hanging over,
It reflects a golden hue.

Winter is now upon us,
The flooding river is brown;
It excites me very much to see
The logs go floating down.

Springtime comes more slowly,
The river is fresh and clean,
Wildflowers cover its banks
Just waiting to be seen,

I hope that generations to come
Will want to come and see,
The river as it flows on by
And will treasure it as much as me.

Roland Kile Colburn
ALPHA (GENESIS 1-3)
AND GOD SAID
LET THERE BE LIGHT:
Darkness
and a deep echo
of silence
that no one hears
concedes
to a fulmination
born
in Promethean Defiance
of imaginary things (?)
A pale ellipse
and lonely shadows . . .
creating
an imagery
that brushes the earth
with it's wings
re-incarnation
the dead of darkness
into an illuminate birth.
AND THERE WAS LIGHT.

Cynthia McCrea
A MAN
What good is a man,
when he walks alone?
Without a friend to call
his own.
What good is a man,
when he cannot see?
The love God has to
give that's free.
What good is a man,
when his life is lost?
Look around dear man
and give God your heart.

Robert G Kennedy
MS LIBERTY

To Dorothy L. Toney. My loving pal.

With her arm held high.
The torch reflecting in the sky.
Wishing I were nigh.
Cause when I see her
She seems to be saying Hi
Oh! How I love Ms Liberty.

Judith Desjardins
BLESSED AMONG WOMEN
She sits quietly now, that first great
rush of feeling abated.
Already she can see the curious
stares, the pity, and the scorn.
And some of them will never know
the truth (God, help them to
believe).
Still the wonder of it all remains,
surrounding her with its
warmth.

And now her time has come . . . she
struggles through the hours,
Hardly knowing the mystery
revealed in her travail.
Earth and heaven wait, time itself
suspended,
And then she holds him in her
arms—
Oh, the joy of him, so tiny, and so
beautiful!

The night is dark around her, its
wordless terrors reaching to
engulf them.
She clutches him more tightly to
her breast as they hurry, ever
hurry.
Behind them are the awful cries,
the agony of all those babies
dead,
Dear God! He's safe, she feels him
warm against her, safe.

She watches from a distance now,
thinking how the time has gone
too quickly.
Yet from the beginning she has
known,
Wrenching from her heart the
roots that would take hold,
Somehow understanding in her
spirit that to find her redeemer,
she must lose her son.

God, how much longer? Will it
never end, this sword that
pierces through her soul?
How can this be borne, to see him
hanging there, this man who
knows no hate?
Her mind casts back and once
again she holds him in her arms.
She hears him then, triumphant: It
is finished!
And knows again that for this he
was born.

Her mind is reeling from the news
they bring, Alive! how can it be?
She trembles at the thought, still
afraid.
How cruel to be lifted from the
darkness of her grief and then
cast down again.
As suddenly as he appears, her joy
comes singing back to her,
Boundless, free, eternal in his love.

Roni Haussamen
THE NIGHT SECRET

To my mother who has taught me the value of optimism when it hardly seemed worth it and who has shown me the meaning of love.

I'm a strong woman. Yes, I am.
I can make my own way. Yes, I can.
I can fix, fry, jiggle and wiggle.
I can sew, bank, sing and giggle.
I can make me wheatcakes, sunny
sides up.
Hang the curtains. Feed the pup.
Water the plants. Shovel the walk.
See a movie. See friends for a talk.
Change the linens. Play Shopan.
Make my own way,. Yes! I can.
Weather the storms. Cry for the
poor.
An independent woman needs men
no more.
It's funny.
At night.
Without the light.
When my body is fading to sleep.
I reach for my man with my empty
hand.
And dream of love "for keeps."

Loney Oglesbee

Loney Oglesbee
MY FAMILY
When I was very small, I knew even
then, I had the best Family of all.
The sweetest Parents, A Brother so
dear,
Wonderful Grandparents that
lived near.
Aunts, Uncles and Cousins too.
We could always find something to
do.
Each Sunday at my Grandparent's
house, we'd meet.
A big long table was filled with
good things to eat.
I have so many sweet and precious
memories of days gone by.
There wasn't much money but we
never asked Why?
There was Loving, Caring and

Sharing, that meant so much to me.
It was a Blessing to have such a
Great Family.

Now so many Loved Ones have
gone on to meet our Dear Savior
on
High.
I think of them often and have a
good cry.
Someday we'll be together, no
more will we have to part.
We'll sit at a table with Jesus and
I'll have Joy in my Heart.

Becky Lackey

Jerry T Lackey
A TREASURE STUMBLED UPON

To Becky, My wife and my Treasure!

Treasures are sought.
Things of value are not always
hid.
When one least expects it,
When one has no idea of the
worth
Of something within his reach;
Often priceless, something not
known:
A treasure stumbled upon.

Eyes possibly visualize
Or see an object;
But until the heart sees
Does the transformation start
Into a precious priceless gift
A present found,
A prescence missed, when not
around.

When I reach, be there.
When I withhold, reach for me.
I do not want to miss
A treasure, I'm beginning to see:
A compassionate, kind, tender,
Mature giver, more than taker,
A gift from the Supreme
Treasure Maker.

I thank God for you, whom I have
known:
A Treasure stumbled upon.

Lou-Ella Lively
YESTERDAY
As I look thru my minds eye
to yesterday
I find the memories are the
foundation—of my life today.

Remember the ups, the downs,
the smiles, the frowns, tears you
shed
And fears from which you fled.
Don't ever forget what your heart
holds dear—cling to those
memories
of yester year.

Always remember as you travel
lifes way
The people you meet. The things
you say
Are making someone's yesterday.

Ah, yes—Remember, remember
yesterday
in your mind and heart each and
every day.

Elizabeth B Grable
THE ENDLESS DISTANCES
I stand alone on the long, white
beach
And gaze upon the sea.
From here there is no other shore—
Only infinity.

Across the endless distances
Deep waves roll far and free.
As far as I can think and feel
Is the sea's immensity.

But trusting travelers, who embark
Despite the ocean's roar,
Find that, beyond the curve of
earth,
There is another shore.

My little soul has never hoped
For more than that death be
My life-force blending with all
others'
As waters in the sea.

If this should be, I am content;
There need be nothing more . . .
But—might I find—far, far
beyond—
There is another shore?

Evelyn Bebb
GOD'S GIFTS-THE FOLLOW UP-THANK YOU, LORD
God has been so good to me
He gave my eyes, great wonders to
see
A gift of legs, to run—to walk
The power to think, the ability to
talk
To enjoy good music, He gave me
ears
In sorrow and grief, I shed some
tears
Two arms to serve, to hold those
dear
Knowing His presence is always
near
His spirit came, a snow white dove
The perfect gift, His gift of love.

THE FOLLOW UP
THANK YOU, LORD
Thank you, Lord, for all these
gifts.
They have served me well for many
years.
A few are holding up just fine,
Some are failing after all this time.
My speech is hesitant, when I talk.
Corns and calouses make it hard
to walk.
I squint to see, just, who you are,
I'm thankful, I still drive my car.
I used to stand so tall and straight,
Now I'm stooped, and have gained
weight.
Notes are written to myself,
Then are put upon a shelf.
Lord, your gift of love has stayed
with me
Through happiness and tears.
It has increased a hundredfold
Through all these many years.
When I am called to go to you,
Your gift of love will see me
through.
I know my "thank yous,"
Have never been enough.
That is all changed now, for I have
written
"Thank you Lord" upon my cuff.

Sharion A Jackson
ODYSSEY
I have tasted the
Waters of the Nile
Swam through the
Holy veins of
My ancestors

I have trekked the
Shores of the Tigris
Danced in the palace
Of the ecstatic mother

I have lived the
Deaths of tortured Kings: Queens
Worn tiaras as proof
Of my conquests

I have weathered the
Skies of the galaxy
Encircled the moon
With each abysmal passing

I have wept in the
Temple of Kali
Condemned for upholding
The anima of my being

I have learned
Adventures do not end
Yet begin at every
Sunrise I awake!

Audrey Alice Pledger
SPRINGTIME

This poem is being dedicated to my beloved parents, Arthur and Margaret Pledger.

The woods are full of violets
I can see their beauty now;
Mounds of moss are springing up
Over which the trees do bow,
The robins sing merrily
About eggs of heaven blue,

The air is fresh with springtime
That is old but forever new,
Water sparkles in the streams
Unbound by winter's prison,
The sky is clear overhead
The sun no longer hidden,
Life once dormant defies us
These are God's gifts from heaven!

Frances W Berg
GREEN PASTURES
To fish for trout
by some mountain stream,
and smoke my pipe in peace
while lazily I sit and dream
These are my Green Pastures.

To hunt with dog and gun
a dear trail in some aspen slade—
to poke a rabbit in the briars
This the sport of kings acclaim
These are my Green Pastures.

To paddle my canoe in Spring
over rapids long and rough
Watching wild geese soar high
winging over flyways at dusk—
These are my Green Pastures.
To sit home by winter's fire
with loved ones close and safe—
While memories of the past float
by—
in this heaven's chosen place.
These are my Green Pastures.

Lulu J Cole
A COMFORT STATION?
A comfort station with an
attraction to see,.
Walked around, looked
everywhere, what could it be?
Entered the restroom so nice and
clean
Nothing unusual that could be
seen.
Stepped inside the first empty stall
Alerting a million bugs on the wall.
All that bare flesh they eyed
hungrily
In force they zeroed in on me.
What was once smooth and white
Became red and lumpy with each
bite.
I covered up so very quickly
And departed the place mighty
hastily.
Itching, scratching and cussing too
Opened the door to escape and out
they flew.
Stopped to read the sign again
Should have found the custodian
To let him know about the demons
within
Hoping he'd spray before they'd
multiply and attack again.

Terry L Freysinger Rogers
A POET'S DREAM

This poem is dedicated to my husband, Jim, our lovely children, my father and sisters and my mother-in-law for their constant support of my efforts and goals.

I'd love to write like Shakespeare,
for his sonnets were just great;
But, considering my talent,
this dream may have to wait.

You see, on words I stumble,
at times I even fall;
Yet, the challenge seems to thrill
me,
in short, I have a ball!

My efforts sometimes fail me,
the mind it just goes blank;
Then, other times the words are
there,
and fall right into rank.

My family says I "have the knack,"
to put my thoughts in poem;
I fear if they did not agree,
I'd run away from home!

The best things that I've written,
have come at such wierd times;
When doing-up my housework,
or hearing news of violent
crimes!

Although it seems quite hopeless,
I guess I shall keep trying;
For, if we give-up living dreams,
what's left except for dying?

Joseph Loser
OUR FATHER

Dedicated to our Father whom passed away, but yet lives. The Our Mother poem grew out of the Our Father poem but given to our Mother on Mother's Day 1987

To know you as a person
Or just to be your friend,
Is worth all the joys and happiness
That this world could ever send

Not enough words to thank you
For everything you are worth,
To sum it up, The Lord says
You are the best woman on this earth

We love you and thank you
For being number one
They'll be waiting for you at the gates of
Heaven, when your work on earth is done

In our lives there will never be a moment
That you will not be a part.
There will always be that special place
Deep within our hearts

We feel you in our presence
Every night and every day
Always thinking about the beautiful things
You do in your own special way

We thank you for all your helping
We thank you for all your sharing
We thank you for all your listening
We thank you for all your caring

You share our lives
And all your inspiration
We give you all our love, respect,
And deepest appreciation

You are the most beautiful mother
We do say indeed
As it was in the beginning, as now,
And ever shall be

We walk tall, we are all very proud.
Happy Mother's Day, we love you,
You are the best, forever and now

P.S. Mom
The more we grow, the more we know,
That as we become more of ourselves,
We become more like you.

A J W Kimmel
CHALLENGER

To my family and friends, and to the memory of Challengers Astronauts, who sacrificed themselves that we might succeed.

A nation broad its tragedy,
engulfed a silent scream
realization her gazing eyes, despair the price of dreams.
American loyalist the astronauts,
aboard the shuttles seats,
bravely ventured their willingness
Dedication was Complete!
Commander Dick Scobbee,
Ronald McNair, her pilot
Michael Smith, Judy Resnik,
Ellison Onizuka, Gregory Jarvis missed.
Dynamic Christa McAuliffe in space, a teachers dream come true
All was go until the end .,
the shuttle and her crew.
As Challenger soared the edge of space, a nations dream
embraced, her dispersion of rockets intense the air
pointing upward exploding its face.,
Spilling raining fierying debris, deep the Atlantic wide
ascending heros a flawless launch, boosters crazily fly.

Unlocking doors beyond our realm, the price America paid
theirs a triumph even in death, the conquest they engaged
pioneering new horizons, searching and moving on,
pursuing goals the undertaking

American Giants Gone!

Roberta Indya Rose Cox
ALONE
Sea shells glisten in the Sun
Waves are dancing one by one.
Surf caresses sandy shore
Here and then, forever more.
Silence in the sky and sea
Just the way it used to be—
here I am alone.

Pondering why such blissful Peace
Endureth still and was so brief.

Ending before the actual start
Existing here in this small part;
In this bare secluded ground,
Nature's silence can be found—
here I am alone.

Throwing all my troubled thoughts
Against the rocks till they are crushed
Then being revived into the sea,
My troubles are splashed back at me,
Leaving droplets on my face
That passing time will soon erase—
here I am alone.

Hazel Scott
HEAVEN

This poem is dedicated to Earnest Melvin Reed, my wonderful Dad.

H-is for heaven, and a land so sweet and fair,
where God's great love will banish all worries and all cares.
E-is everlasting we will dwell there,
eternally God's love we will share.
A-is for the angels proclaiming on high,
Glory to God in the sweet by and by.
V-is for Victory won, by letting God dwell within,
right from the beginning to the very end.
E-is for everyone willing to make heaven their home,
obey the will of God you'll never walk alone.
N-means no sorrow, no tears will be there,
much joy and happiness, in heaven, a land so sweet and fair.

Waneta Dressler
THANK YOU LORD

This poem is dedicated to my loving husband Ed and our four children, Penny, ES, George & Susan.

Oh how much I love thee
Grateful to you forever I'll be
Merciful Lord full of grace
Saving a sinner like me.
Oh what peace and joy I feel
Knowing in Your loving arms I'll be
Safe from all harm to come
Even death has no hold over me.
One day soon I know I'll be
Beyond the sunset with Thee
Lord my Savior my everything
To You my all I bring.
There on the crystal sea
All my loved ones will be
The joy and happiness we'll sing
Thank you LORD for LOVING ME

Christa Lydon
THROUGH LIBERTY'S EYES (THE NEWEST COLOSSUS)
I stand alone
beside an ocean of tears
with silent pleas that echo endlessly.
Not only
Steam ships in the harbour
with misty foreign eyes,
But
Wire fences in the desert
beneath bright desperate skies.
And
the silent prayers on Arctic winds
borne by Hopes sweet spies.
Yes I stand
With my lamp lifted high
beside a tarnished door
that glimmers only briefly
with the golden hopes of a different age.

Cheryl L Flanagan
BIRDS
Birds are the prettiest of all,
they're big, round, fat and small.
Their colors are bright,
in day and night.
They fly high in the air,
without a thought or care.

They have such a wonderful life,
they live so simple and nice.
They live in a nest so high in a tree,
they live so happy and free.
They're life is so great they sing,
They also travel every spring.
To be a bird to live this way,
to fly and travel everyday.
Is something nice to do,
but not for me and you.
But to think of all this, and get no rest.
Is something of the best.
Is also quite tiring at least,
I think that I will go to sleep.

Rose Budau
HOUSE HOME
Bickering between a husband and wife
Only a place of worry and strife.
Walls, windows and doors just a house
Where sadness and loneliness roam.
You'll have to agree this kind of house definately is not a home.
Home is a place where happiness dwells from where love and laughter swells.
True, there are times of sorrow even shame but the home atmosphere remains the same.
There is strength and warmth that come from inside
A kind of family love they just can't hide.
Men can build a house with walls
Windows and a door
But to make a house a home, it takes something more.
It's the people a family caring pulling together through thick and thin.
Truely it's the loving and sharing that makes a house a home within.

Ramon E Martinez

Ramon E Martinez
TO HER . . .
You are more than a carnation
For you are blazes of Its Fire,
With the splendour
Of Heavenly Treasure.

You have majesty and goodness
Of a flower from Divinity,
Girdled with festoons
Of His own Beauty,
And cintured
Like the three
Concentric rings
Around Saturn . . .

Oh!, you are symmetry,
Grace and harmony . . .
More . . ., you are "eternity
Gazing at Him" in a mirror."
Yet your charming grace
And exotic tinct
Makes you a Flower
From the Elysian fields:
The most beautiful bud
From the garden of Creation . . .

Debbie Budnick
PLEASE LISTEN
Alone she sits in the corner
Tears falling from her swollen eyes
She weeps but no one listens
Doesn't anyone care
Isn't there any help for someone in need
Please listen, care, help
It won't take long to listen
Tears flow faster now
Alone in the corner she still sits
No one is listening

No one will care or help
People don't want to bother
With someone that isn't like them
She hurts terribly
But no one cares
She screams out loud
But no one listens
She's sad and weary
But no one helps
Alone she sits in the corner

Joyce A Mitchell
HEAVEN ABOVE
Heaven above, smile down on me,

Valleys, below for me to see.
As I lay upon this hill,
Holy Spirit within me fill.
And this beauty around me be,
Made by my Father, from sea to sea.
The grass is green, the trees are tall,
I praise my Lord, to see them all.
How much beauty He gave our land,
From hills and dells, to sifting sand.
I feel so blessed, to be Your child,
To enjoy Your beauty, from mile to mile.
All this land You gave to me,
I know my home is a Glory to see.
I love You Father, and Your creation,
Served, by Love and Consolation!

Maxine Eliza Powers
IF DREAMS WOULD LAST
If dreams would last
Then all would happy be.
We would never know that;
Sorrow is the ashes in the heart
Left when a dream has died.

No bells to ring the knell of death
For a dream that once so lofty was,
It soared the skies on falcon wings,
'Til a hunter's arrow found its' mark,
And rubies rained upon the ground.

Wings beating the air in wild despair
Could not the plummet to earth stop.
Oh! Beautiful dream in stillness splashed
Where feet tread beneath an empty sky.

Laura B Brown
THE EMPTY PLACE
The top is an empty place
if Jesus is not there.
You may win many awards
and receive many applauds
You may meet kings and lords
and be the chairman of many causes.
But the top is an empty place
if Jesus is not there.
Misery is your friend
because unrest lives within.
Every day is the same
someone is always playing
the mind game.
The top is an empty place
if Jesus is not there.
So climb the ladder of life
with care.
Each step you take have Jesus there.
He will be your guide
and go with you everywhere
Then when you reach that
Plateau at the top
It will not be an empty place
because Jesus will be there.

Marie Dhane

Marie Dhane
GOLDEN YEARS OF UNITY

This poem is dedicated to Eddie, my loving husband

United in love always,
Subtracted from all others you knew,
Has multiplied and divided
By the children in the lives of you two.

A relationship where obligation is reciprocal;
An established convenant called a home.
Where independence is equal, dependence is mutual,
And God hovers it like a dome.

The joy is doubled and the pain is halved
As "mine" is shared into "ours;"
Your dreams of life are a reality
For love raises visions to a higher power.

The eyes are windows of the soul.
The gift of life is God's wonder.
What God hath joined together
Let no man put asunder.

And in these golden years of life
The best is yet to be;
For plans that were made in your youth
Grow sweeter in this age you see.

The home is the vestibule of heaven
Where two hearts beat as one.
May this poem help light your pathway of love
To the heart you have won.

Orville Kemper Jr
WHO IS THIS MAN
As I was standing on a corner, I seen a Man walking down the street. As I stood there and looked at Him, I noticed a light that shined from His face. And when He stopped and looked at me, it put chills up and down my spine.

Who is this Man with a light that shines like the light of day?Who is this Man and what does He want with me?

As He raised His hands towards me, I saw marks in the middle of His palms, and as He came closer, my legs grew weaker; and, I fell to my knees in the sand. And as I looked up, I thought for my last time, but to my surprise it only put tears to my eyes. For here was a Man with a crown of thorns on His head and tears that rolled down His cheeks and in His eyes showing love I've never known or even seen.

Who is this Man and what does He want with me?

As He turned to walk away, I saw marks up and down His back. It looked like He'd been whipped a thousand times or more.

Who is this Man with a light that shines like the light of day?Who is this Man and what does He want with me?

Madonna Nelson Williams
THE CHATTER BIRD
I'd like to tell you a story!
About something, that happened to me.
One day, I was sitting in the park,
When a bird! hopped on my knee.
He said, "How would you like to eat worms?,
And wear feathers, on your head?"
I was so startled! I pretended,
I didn't hear a word, he said.
Then a man, reading his paper,
Gave me, the strangest, look.
And said, "I don't eat worms."
"Why don't you read your book."
Then, the bird, twittered his feathers and said,
"How'd you like to sleep in a nest?"
And the man quizzically looking, said,
"Your making yourself, a pest."
So then I tried, to tell him, about the bird,
sitting on my knee
And saying, all those things, he thought, he was
hearing from me.
Well, the man got up, and walking slowly,
And keeping me in his sight,
Left the park, as if,—my brain had taken flight.
And sitting in the highest tree,
Was the chatteringest bird! I ever did see.

Jim Ross Davidson
GOODBYE 'TIL DAWN

Dedicated to Jeanette, my indispensable wife of 20 years, who, in view of the poem's sentiment, doubts that I can "feel" without touching. I admit only to having exceptionally keen poetic sensibilities.

As now the hour draws near to say our one "goodbye,"
Other hours long since past number the reasons why
Goodbye is a false word—a word that too oft' gives
A feeling of ending, of finish to that which lives
And will live even for as long as faintest thought
Can recall the first "hello," the last rose bought;
"We" will live just as the sun and moon rise apart—
The dim moonlight the now—the sunshine the start.

And thus for living, "we" are but only half alive—
Half to you, to me the other, but "we" will survive
Until then, and longer still and farther on beyond;
"We" shall meet again, for share we of a dual bond—
Yours to him and mine to her, our promises to keep,
Rejoicing in the joys, avoiding not a time to weep.
For in this, "we" do live again with each new day—
What we shared so they do in a living kind of way.
All, then, that I love will ever be a part of you,
And you a part of them, tho' ne'er again just we two.
So you see our "goodbye" is not for forever more—
It's only 'til the dawn into our hearts doth pour.

Mimi FitzGerald
BIRTHDAY SONG
I skip along on feathered feet
That do not touch the ground.
My heart is singing to the sun,
My arms embrace the wind.
How sweet! This youth! This joy! This bliss!
This spirit free and gay!
How can it be when I have reached
Age forty-nine today!

I smile at children, men and dogs.
I sing along with birds.
They fly no higher than can I,
Nor know no sweeter words!
I do not know the outcome
Held in the hands of Fate.
I only know I'm younger now
Than I was at forty-eight!

gertrude williams siesholtz
TAKE TIME
Take time for seeing
Nature that surrounds,
For realizing lasting
Beauty that abounds.

Take time to appreciate
The wondrous things,
Counting all the blessings
Each day brings.

Take time to understand
A tear or two
Brings comfort helping us
To start anew.

Take time to be aware,
Take time to live; to care—
To start and end each day
In silent prayer.

C B McCleary
SISTERS
You shared when there was plenty and when there was not enough. We had secrets only we could hold together. Your easy smile and laughter just seemed to overflow and fade the struggle of the coming day. These are the things that make a friend forever. I miss you.

Mayda Simone
HIS EYES OF LOVE

Thank you Jesus, for mending my broken life! I'm eternally grateful.

Thru His eyes of love
I can see beyond what is felt or touched
My heart sees heights and depths that human eyes see not
I can see reality, thru His eyes of love
I see capabilities, as my Father sees,
No limitations, only what can be, for love is infinite
Thru His eyes of love, I see how my Lord perceives.
The warmth of His gaze,
The tenderness of His touch,
Can melt away walls of hurt and pain,
Built by insensitive encounters on life's rocky paths
All is good, all is well, thru His eyes of love,
All will pass away, but not the works of love
That will remain in the heart
To take on, to pass on and on and on
Jesus, thank you for your love,
The ingredient which holds life's forces in a knot.

Jackie L Ritchie Franco
YOU ARE GONE FROM ME
You are now gone . . . taken from me
Scared, lonely, wondering what my future
will be.
No one could take your place,
your gentle touch,
your smiling face.

Taking for granted you'd always be there
Together we'd walk for a breath of fresh air.
The walks are now empty, lonely,
unmeaningful to me.
How I wish we could be together
like it used to be.

No more aroma from your pipe fills the air.
No Newspapers crumbled next to your chair.
I have nothing left to look forward to
Everything we did, we did together . . .
me and you.

Gone, but not forgotten.
Your memory will always be with me.
I will place the flowers 'neath the big Oak tree.
You cared and pampered the flowers from spring until fall
Now I wonder,
Will they come back at all
You are gone now . . . taken from me
I can't help but wonder what my future will be.

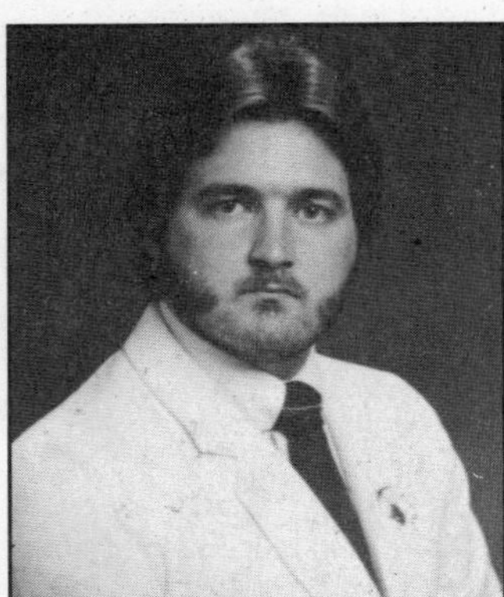

Santiago Pena Jr

Santiago Pena Jr
UNITED STATES

Dedicated to the air of Freedom of which I breathe with discipline, And Respect due to the countless memories of mine with the U.S. ARMY, And to the Nation of Unity and Love, and Trust for all of God's People.

The ground of freedom, the history we share,
The trees so tall and green that grow with no despair.
Our motherhood of travelways for unions to meet,
We're the proudest and the mightiest, and cannot be beat.
They shelter hand in hand, and grow with the years,
There's fifty of them that shine without a fear.
The stars and the stripes, in red, white, and blue,
Guarded by the bravest of braves in our society so new.

The motherworld of fortune, to be shared by me and you,
Together we build our nation, with the strongest and the few.
So trustful and very worthy, for our allies to follow,
The footsteps that we leave behind are far from being narrow.

Our mission is for glory, for joy, and for goodwill,
Not lacking in anything, and still climbing a new hill.
Our bodies are so safe and so surrounded by love,
That we sleep in best comfort that God made this world of.

We soldier our borders to keep out unwanted invaders,
We block out transmissions of all that are traitors.
Our guns lie in wait, for the moment that may come,
But our hearts stay open and offer a warm welcome.

Richard L Lee
LIFE

Dedicated to my Wife Lucy, Mother of our five children, Grandmother of our thirteen Grandchildren and my inspiration.

So helpless life begins, dependent so completely upon others,
We lay so still, then moving some still gaining no response,
Appealing for the comfort given only by our Mothers.

We're older now, yet free from world's cares we live each
day for what we gain while winning and losing friends.
Joys and sadness come and go, our ups and downs we ponder,
we live, we grow, another season ends.

We're caught up in the stream of life, do, don't, are we
progressing? are we learning?
The time has come to set us free, doubting we must go,
The need for friend, security ever yearning.
Life we've mastered, security we've gained, a mate we
seek and find, together we become Fathers, Mothers.
In life's creation we have joined, so helpless life
begins, dependent, so completely upon others.

Constance Renee Priest

Constance Renee Priest
VIETNAM

I would like to dedicate this poem to my father, because I never really said thank you. Thanks, Dad.

Vietnam was a horrible war
There was no way to win
No points to score

We sent our guys to fight a war that couldn't be won
Yet they went and they fought
They figured that the enemy needed to be taught.

To be taught the lesson that so many had learned before—
That they were the best.
They were the U.S. military corps.

When they came home they thought they'd be heroes
But they were treated like zeroes.

Many lives were lost, they were just left to die;
Now many people cry over what happened
But I thank those men because I know why.

Why they died; why they sacrificed themselves
It was for their country, their families, and their pride.
They died for us, for you and me,
For their country and for our honor.

Thank you veterans and those who died.
You'll always be heroes in my eyes.

Hazel P Hedrick
A POEM FELL

I Dedicate this poem to, Father Time, healer of all hurts.

In dark of night I heard the crash as I turned on the light

I saw the pieces lying there the clock struck twelve midnight.

A poem fell out of my heart
and shattered on the floor
I stepped on it with cold, bare feet
and shattered it some more,

Because I could not bare the pain
its truth would make me feel,

I raked the scattered fragments up
and crushed them with my heel.

I could not bare to think the
thoughts
its lines would bring to mind
nor spill the hord of pent up tears
or drink the bitter wine,

that I would then be forced to drink
if it should come to be,

it would reveil the secret hurts
buried inside of me.

Mel Gilbert

TIME MARCHES ON

This poem is dedicated to Helen, my loving wife

As I looked at my wife the other
day,
I noticed her hair was turning gray.
My eyes nearly filled with tears,
As I thought of her, getting up in
years.

In thinking back on by-gone days,
How God had blessed our home in
many ways.
He blessed it with a couple of
healthy boys,
Also a girl to add to our joys.

With the family all grown and out
on their own,
That leaves wife and I all alone.
As we labor here and travel there,
Together life's joys and sorrows we
share.

As I thought of my pal's graying
head,
She looked at me and shyly said,
Why father, I've thought the same
about you,
I see plenty of gray ones shining
through.

I suppose there's no need for great
concern,
Just because our hair is beginning
to turn.
I guess there's no need to fret and
fuss,
For the same thing happens to all
of us.

Catherine Phillips

I DON'T

To my love my BoBo

I thought I knew,
But now . . .
No one knows how
the future lies.
I dream of us
quite a bit
I must admit,
You know how girls always dream.
And now I know
it could break
in a second.
Tomorrow holds so much
Unknown.
Sometimes I am afraid
and sometimes I can't wait.
Maybe it is that
I dream too much.

Everywhere I go,
everything I do,
brings you back
into my dreams.
And they are all pleasant
to think about.

Alfred G Stefan

DREAMS

Paranormal behavior alive in the
unconcious.
Brain delays, heart jumps.
Dreams are now nightmares.
Lovely thoughts turn cold and grey.
People turn to mangled creatures.
Running will only delay the final
outcome.
No one can survive.
Even the awakening will be fatal
That is why people stay and live in,
The universe of the mind.

Lillian Ruth Weeks

MT. SAINT HELENS' WARNINGS AND GOD'S WARNINGS

As daylight appeared over Mount Saint Helens, May 18th, one year before 1981, indescribible rumbles were groaning and moaning, warning people of a terrible disaster to come. There was an old fellow named 'Harry Truman,' and I would say he had a mind of his own. He wouldn't leave his lodge cabin forhe thought his protection was in his lodge home. "As you travel down Stovepipe Trail," he might have said, "Say a prayer or two for me. might hide my gold and silver in a safe place—the old chimney, that's the way life is going to be."

Then the ashes began to glitter as they fell upon the earth; very soon ashes covered his whole cabin, down the chimney on to the hearth. Then months later, a little daisy poked its head up in the field, just to tell the whole world that life after death is undoubtedly real.

This old world just keeps on turning and the sun comes up each day, but very soon we'll see a new SON, because He's coming to take His Church away. People thinking about their treasures as they travel through this life, cannot compare to the treasures in heaven where there is neither war nor strife, but a new earth and a new heaven on the horizon will soon appear, and happiness will be forever where there will be no more fear.

Barbara J Everette

SNOWFLAKES II

Blanketed was the whole earth
with a beautiful fleece of white
Slanted from underneath by the
frozen stubble
of mown grasses,
And early springtime crocuses that
had just begun
to peek, felt from a single crack
of ground
With one green sprout each.

Through windows, waterstreaked
by steam
that warmed the passenger car,
projected
Countless, tiny travelers from
outerspace,
Swirling and turning, the
various geometric crafts
Each gyroed into view on some
mysterious flight
Then lighted gently and rested
there.

Pine needles, their frigid faced
upturnd to greet
the snowflakes from their
tree-top perch.
Had slender branches laced with
white frosting
held steady by strong
earth-thronged roots.
Dried and still the oak tree,
dwarfed by tall timber
on a wooded hill
Held an ice-capped head that
bowed in the drift
And one deserted child of the
oak, at my acorn,
Made a visible black dot in a spot
slightly bare
That punctuated the starless
night.

Frank Lauria II

LOVE FOREVER

To Tina, whom I shall . . . .

At the end of the everything;
Armageddon
The world, the galaxy, the
universe, the end
of time, space, and all that exists,
my love will shine.
And it will drift in darkness and
emptyness,
and cry out in loneliness—but
will
not be heard.
It will nourish itself on your
memory, and be
sustained. For you my love is
forever,
and it will never die.

Irene Rokowski Plante

DOZERS AND DAISIES

Where cows of long ago
Had nuzzled daisies and clover . .
A young man watched
Two old girls shuffling
Across the former hayfields
Which was being dug up
And leveled off by the bulldozer.
Standing on their spindly legs,
The old girls lamented plaintively,
"Where did the Stonewall go?
Wasn't our broken-down barway
Somewhere over here?"
They wanted to know.
The young man thoughtfully
Appraised the old girls eyes
Full of lost and hurt.
"The old Stonewall was over there
Where we left a grand old Oak
standing . ."
Gently, spoke the young man
Who'd bought the overgrown
hayfields
To build himself his new modern
church.

Cleotis Thompson

GOD SET ME FREE FROM SATAN'S CHAIN!

To the magnifying of God, word Rom 7: 20-25 and to my mother Frances, Ernestine and our kids Willie, Corey, Quincy, Martez and our family.

God, remove the chain from my
mind
So my thoughts will be thoughts of
righteousness.

God, remove the chain from my
eyes
So my sight will be clear of the lust
that deceives me.

God, remove the chain from my
ears
So I can receive the truth when it's
spoken.

God, remove the chain from my
mouth
So my words will be words of
inspiration.

God, remove the chain from my
hands
So my labor will be an encouraging
foundation.

God, remove the chain from my
feet
So I can walk a straight and narrow
path.

God, remove the chain from my
heart
So I can be free of all the worldly
things
that imprison me.

Sally Kosiarek (Age 72)

CONFLICT!

"God & the "Devil" are fighting
over me, neither one will let me
free,
One takes over for a little while
then the other cramps his style.
I wonder if "God" did know?
When He created hills & valleys
so low.
Put an ocean here & there, made
man & mate with love to share.
That the "Devil" was there is true,
to mess up the lives of people he
knew.
Did he know of the wars we would
fight, never knowing what was
right.
Did he know that "Satan" would
grab some man & mess up
"Gods" great plan.
For peace on earth & a good life,
for his people not always strife.

Did he know of drugs & booze too,
that could ruin people & make
them blue.
Sometimes I'm happy I think I'm
with "God." Then bang comes
the "Devil" down the lightning
rod.
Then I'm mean & rotten to the
core, & I become a great big bore.
I can't understand man being so
bad, to sell people drugs that
make them go mad.
"God" couldn't create man with no
soul, he was made by the "Devil"
from down that deep hole.
We all have to fight, man woman
& child, to get rid of the "Devil"
get him exiled.
So we can enjoy what we will find,
deep serenity & peace of mind

Dolores A Olson
SOUNDS TO REMEMBER

Sounds of children playing out,
Wagons rattling, now and then a
shout.
Children crying, then their
laughter
Yes, sounds to remember ever
after.

The alarm clock going off at four,
Music from the house next door.
Chickens crowing, a dogs shrill
bark,
Babies crying after dark.

Music from the church on the hill.
Cats meowing on the window sill.
Children singing "Silent Night."
A beautiful sound to set hearts
right.

Mrs Doris Henricks Kraley

Mrs Doris Henricks Kraley
FUTURE SPACE PILGRIMS

Oh cities of America where have all
the green fields gone?
The meadows and the flowers so
question this for each their born
To taste and smell the fragrance of
the honey-suckle air
I hardly think this fair,
The big and frightening answer to
their cry is cement
Is this what God so aimlessly meant
To have these things abolished in
smoke
Can we as humans survive and
cope
With this ever ending plastic stage
On which distrust and dishonesty
is gaged
I sometimes find myself in a rage,
What is left for us and our children
Are they the future space pilgrims
We must plan and work as we may
To help make our cities livable
someday

Josephine Warych
INSPIRATION

This poem is dedicated to the memory of my husband Victor

Help me God, when my days are
dreary
Help me God, when my heart is
weary
Help me God, in my hour of despair
So that the load I'll be able to bear
Help me God, to do a good deed
And plant happiness with every
seed
Help me God, to be true and kind
Keep the love in my heart entwined
Help me God, to be meek and
humble
So long life's way I will not stumble
Lead me God along the pathway
Of goodness and mercy every hour
every day

Nguyen Huu Nguyen
THE BOAT PEOPLE

If you ask: "Where do I come
from?"
I would say: "From a faraway
country
That had been called the Pearl of
the Orient,
The balcony overlooking the
Pacific Ocean."

If you ask: "How do I come here?"
I would say: "In a tiny, leaking boat,
Having neither map nor compass,
but only
A dream to live with LOVE and
DIGNITY."

If you ask: "What's my name?"
I would say: "It really doesn't
matter
Whether you call me X, Y, or
whatever,
Since the world now names me
"BOAT PEOPLE."

Shirley Wilson
POINTS OF CONNECTION

At the stroke of dawn.
At the stroke of intimacy.
Its' passive beginnings—
The renewal of emotions.
The building up and the breaking
down.
Trying to repair web-soaked
relationships—molested by
grief,
With forbidden approaches to love.
Needs for communication—
disrupted.
Shall I ever advance?
The immediacy of the warmth of
the body,
I respond to stimulus,
Clutch me to thine breast,
I disrobe of all defense.
The transformation of day / to /
night,
Reverse the sentence,
Work toward the development of
speech.
(the color of words)
Baited at the entrance,
Reshaped by experience,
To enter must I knock?

Shirley Kuha-Hotchkiss
WE

To Renee, Michael and Julie—And Unconditional Love.

Day by day we planted the seeds—
Each, in its season, fulfills our
needs.
You picked and brought to me
"love-flowers"
As you grew and sought your great
powers.
You showered me with your
heart-felt joy . . .
Feelings you knew for a treasured
toy.
BACK THEN you looked up to see
my face,
NOW I look up to your growing
grace.
Somewhere, it seems, you and I
knew grief
Yet, hand in hand, we walked with
belief.
BONDED FOREVER, yet ever so
free,
My love for you and yours for me . . .

TOGETHER, MY CHILD AND I,
ARE "WE."

Eloise Wilcox Johnson-Jones
ONLY MY SOUL CAN DANCE

My feet . . . . no rhythm those . . .
. no Spanish
Flamenco dances, castanets
clicking . . . .
no Strauss waltzes . . . . long silken
skirts
flying . . . .
No cha chas . . . . no
polkas . . . .
My body, my brain, and hidden
rhythms
trapped in long years of
restrictive inhibitions . . . .
oft self—
imposed.
No patient teacher or friend
to break through those painfully
gauche and gawky days and years
. . . . years . . . .
those dreadful
trepidations . . . .
Though born with feet of clay,
still my soul is free of fears and
restraints to dance . . . .
dance . . . .
dance.

Lillian Towe

Lillian Towe
PAST TENSE

To my husband, my children, and my grandchildren

Fences, made of split rails
Crisscrossed, one on one
Marching down a hillside —
Shadows in the sun.
Creaky, covered bridges
Spanning narrow streams
Splintered planks and timbers
Broken walls and beams.

Crumbling sandstone chimneys,
Standing all alone
Houses once built 'round them
Torn down and gone.
Rusty, idle train tracks
Some, where grass has
grown—
Waiting for the whistle
Of trains that never come.

Empty old schoolhouses
Leaning and decayed
Windows stare at schoolyards
Where the children played.
Past tense, giving glimpses
Of another time -
Quietly telling stories
Of things now left behind.

John S Barna
I DREAMDT I DIED LAST NIGHT

I dreamdt I died last night
And there before my very eyes
I was surrounded almost
completely
By some most famous guys

There was George Washington,
Abraham Lincoln, Robert E. Lee
Leonard da Vinci, Christopher
Columbus
Babe Ruth and President Jack
Kennedy

Then there was Thomas Jefferson
To name but a few
And it would not be complete
If I did not mention the women
there too

All those that went before
In a gigantic amphitheatre sit
Waiting to greet all those
Who on earth have finished their
bit

There is no madness nor rage
No waiving of fists at a nervous
pace
No shouting can there be heard
And there are but smiles on every
face

No flowers or other forms of beauty
Can one on this side find
Only that little seen on earth
Brotherly love of all mankind

Violet A Rivet

Violet A Rivet
THE TALL PINE TREE

It stood by my window and swayed
to and fro,
It seemed very anxious but had
nowhere to go,
It looked this way and that way and
on to the lake,
Its trunk is so long it looks like a
big snake.

There were other pine trees all
around,
But not one of them as tall could
be found,
It peeped in my hospital room day
and night,
The wind blew the needles as
though they were in flight.

Then came the day I left for home,
The place where I longed to be,
The tree that surpassed my two
story room,
Was still my favorite pine tree.

I left the hospital and the tall pine
tree,
Oh how it reached for the sky,
It looked so happy as it swayed
toward me,
But not nearly as happy as I.

Kelly Lynne Reed
SOMEDAY

There's a place where the green
ferns grow,
the birds sing and the wind chimes
blow.
There's a place where the stream
trickles,
the frogs croak and Grandma
makes pickles.
There's a place that's like my
home,
where the fish swim and the deer
roam.
There's a place like this in a
valley far away,
that I'll come back and see again .
. . someday . . .

Dawn Mahree
TRAGIC IS SHE

To my grandparents

What a tragic soul is she
Tears she cries, only to grieve;
A dangerous web she weaves
Her soul disconnects rivers from
seas
Her mind meant not to read;
Oh what a tragic soul is she.
What a tragic life she leads
Walking in slumber, hiding with
the meek
Her life is dormant, she believes;
Winds cry her name through trees
Her heart is cold, like a winters
breeze
Oh what a tragic life she leads.

Georgiana M Clemens
GOD IS THERE

When the rain is done
Along comes the sun.
When life brings an occasional trial
And the tears are done
Along comes a smile.

When the night is gone
Along comes the dawn.
Thus God tells us: "Don't
despair."
He is there.
For whenever come the sun, the
smile, the dawn
The rain, the tears and night are
gone.

Diane J Dingman
FROM MY HEART

To the one I cherish, my husband Thomas

This is to the one who keeps me
going on the right track day and
night.
This is to the one who gives me
patience and understanding
without questioning.
This is to the one who loves me no
matter what, and I him.
This is to the one who has all the
faith and loyalty towards me.
This is to the one who gives his
undivided love to me.
This is to the one who believes I'm
worth every ounce of it.
This is to the one I married and
vowed to for the rest of our lives.
This is to the one whom I call
HUSBAND.
This is to my love called Thomas.
This is from your ever and always
loving faithful wife.
This is from the one who is proud
to be called your wife.
This is from the one you call
Diane. Always yours
Diane

Robert Worden
TILL DEATH DO US PART

For all the men who fought and died in protection of my freedom.

The day was dark and dreary,
When the battle had begun,
Gunshots fired rapidly,
Morter rounds destroyed.

Let us remember that day,
It came many times,
Let us remember, December 7,
1941.
Pearl Harbor fell, our boys were
killed,
A date which will live in infamy.

Never will the thought perish,
The thought of men dieing,
Through the battles of the war.

Let us hail the mighty soldiers,
That landed on Normandy,
The men that lived to tell,
But most of all the men that fell,
In the gunfire of total hell.

Shall we pray for the men,
That fought the Battle of the Bulge,
That undieing bravery,
That steadfast faith,

Never shall we forget,
Wars in far off lands.

It should always be remembered,
A terrible day,
When our boys fell on the ground,
In the jungles of Vietnam.

Lest we forget,
The great souls, killed
unmercifully,
As the building toppled,
In downtown Beruit.

Never, never, let your minds forget,
The mighty men that died,
In protection of our freedom,
In protection of our country.

Let God bless our brave
servicemen,
God bless us and our mighty
country,
The United States of America,
Till death do us part.

Carol Ann Erhardt
SEASONS OF THE TREES

To Ron, my husband, who gives me the courage to continue.

Alone I walk,
through the awakening dawn,
Footsteps echoing
in the silence of my heart,
Wondering why I'm so lonely and
sad,
Tears cleansing my cheeks . . .
When did they start?

I sit upon the cool, damp earth
. . . Leaves forming a musky pillow
beneath the tree.
I rest my head upon her sturdy
trunk
And wish her mighty strength
belonged to me.

Thoughts are muddled, screaming
through my mind
Tormenting my soul and bending
my will.
Black hatred rushes adrenalin
through my limbs.
My body soon is heaving with
sobs, unable to still.

Much later, drained and cleansed,
My eyes once more gaze upon the
tree;
And I realize how much strength
there is . . .
In the world, the tree . . . and me.

How likened is the complex human
form
To the tree, standing silent and still
—Until nature's forces take control
And change context against our
will.
Spring showers, quiet air, and
silence.
Time to raise our weary form,
Waiting for the rainbow sure to
come,
Not a thought for the growing
storm.

Sunny days, laughing children,
scurrying squirrels,
Lifting our branches and reaching
for the sky!
Growing and spreading, providing
shelter . . .
How happy we are, the tree and I.
Soon the storm rages, blowing
branches to and fro,
Dipping and bending our bodies to
the ground,
Breaking our spirit, drenching
our souls,
Crippling our thoughts with its
deafening sound.

How quickly it abates! Once more
the sun
Threads fingers of gold through
autumn leaves.
We prepare our hearts for winter's
cold,
Stretching our limbs to the cool,
night breeze.

We sleep and mend our broken
minds,
. . . Letting winter's soft blanket
weave her cocoon.
We bask in the silence; we need the
rest,
For the spring will come . . .
perhaps too soon.

So like the tree, is the human form.
Tears cleanse as spring showers in
May.
We bend and change while
currents of time
Sometimes force us to follow their
way.

I lift my limbs to dry my eyes,
My soul cleansed of hatred, bitter
and cold.
I raise my trunk and walk once
more
Feeling lonely, sad . . . and old.

For like the tree, my years do show.
The storms have left their mark.
I look to the sun and draw
strength for the day.
. . . I will rest tonight . . . in the
dark.

Paule Cadet

Paule Cadet
MOTHER'S DAY

Crowned with flowers, I saw
My country in a prom'nade I
stopped
It was Mother's Day I thought
Colored lilies, pink and gold
All at once, joy invaded my heart
In that great day I guess
To celebrate a special one
. . . my mom.
Dear mother, among all the
provincial
Having fought to establish a real
life
For your adore', you are a special
Sweet mother, don't you know I
love you?
Is the best thing I can do for you.

No matter I love you y' love me for'ver
I love you too and you are perfect
Just as you fill me with love
Just as you make me cry a lot

Oh mother! by love you tell me lie.
The best thing I should do, love you each time.
Take these flowers, take my heart, my life
All your concern, because you are a kind.

Rose Mary Owen
SUN AND BREEZE

The gentle breeze caresses my skin.
It tenderly massages while cooling.
It's like a soft kiss from
A lover who likes to play,
And is in no hurry to go away.

The sun warms and stimulates.
It gently and carefully tans some,
While savagely and wantonly burns others.
It's like a restless lover.
Warm and soft at times
But with many different climes.

The warm sun and the gentle breeze
Often work as a loving team.
While the sun warms and heats,
The gentle breeze cools and soothes
As through the day they move.

Jayne Bullock
TO BE OR NOT TO BE A WEED

Whish, whoosh! Whisper, Rustle!
A sea of green—swooping, swaying,
dancing to the beat—fast, then slow,
in tempo, with rhythm;
a ballet without music or sound.
A gyrating sea in shades and hues of green—
astir with the evening breeze.
Slender lean stems, crowned with oat-like seeds,
surrounded by lush willowy green leaves.
A meadow, an ocean—
bespeckled with puffs of purple, white and yellow,
effusively lining and carpeting a well-trodden path.
Behold! The tall, gracefully swaying stalks proclaim—
Am I not a work of art—a welcome perenial to nature?
A menace? Surely not! Only man has no time for me.
They say I am a contagious, earth-hungry eyesore,
an undesirable denizen—
a threat to farmland, roadside and hill!
But, still . . . See how I sway in the breeze—
vascilliating unpredictably in magical motion.
Hypnotic—bowing and undulating in the wind,
with regal dignity—
making life seem more beautiful, gentle—
a welcoming haven. Peace!

Mary Krusz
BEGINNINGS

To parents who have experienced a loss of a newborn. To my mother, Norma, who has given life through her Love; and in memory of my brother's, Gary and Stephen

---

To know a life has just begun
and watch a birth begin.

To feel the stir of something warm,
touching deep within.

The joy in expectation waits
as days and months go by.

The final recognition
a birth but swift goodbye.

The joyous clamor shattered
a torn and battered hymn.

A reaching out with all I have to grasp
the life that's been.

A gentle touch to say farewell
a broken heart to mend.

The dreams that once were present
no longer can pretend.

The tears they flow so swiftly
when will they ever end.

And when the droplets fall no more
the tears inside I'll send.

Intensity will lessen
I'm told by one and all.

And rightly so I'm certain
but to wait patiently its call.

Rosa L Coleman
THE GIFT THAT IS RETURNED

This poem is dedicated to my parents, my sisters and brothers, and their extended families. RCL

Yesterday, my grandson, you came and asked of me,
"What's the best thing that I must try to be
When I am as old and so wrinkled as you,
And there will be no more work for me to do?"
Ah, yes, my darling, there's always a bit more
For us who are still alive on this earthly shore,
To learn to share daily, our love and a smile
With those whom we may by any chance meet
And knowing not, at those times when we greet
Them, that we may be lifting a very dark cloud
From someone's heart, and piercing a dense shroud
Of loneliness, worry, misfortune and despair,
By letting our smile say, "we really do care."
And this, my grandson, is the only answer I could give,
When you so thoughtfully asked me how you should live.
"Just give a smile, filled with love, every passing day
And you will receive a gift that you have given away."

Otto Halseth

Otto Halseth
A WONDERFUL BARGAIN

We find in the Bible, God's plan of salvation
What wonderful bargain, He has made with man.
For death He'll give life, for darkness light.
For sickness health and for blindness sight.
For condemnation freedom, for bondage Liberty.
For unrest peace, for defeat victory.
For weakness strength, for fear boldness.
For carnality His Spirit, for sin righteousness.
For hatred love, for bitterness sweetness.
For anger and wrath, the spirit of forgiveness.
For drunkenness sobriety, for filthiness purity.
For faltering stability, for doubting surety.
For hardness meekness, and gentleness for cruelty.
For unkindness compassion, for pride humility.
For weariness rest, for loneliness companionship.
For impending judgement, Eternal heavenly Bliss.

Only a fool will choose to neglect such a bargain.
The Lord gives everything, only loss we bring.
It was His great Love that was motivating.
We owe to Him our all, Let us crown Him King.

Will Elliott
DESERT SUNRISE

Alone on the desert mountain-top
In the early hours of morn
I watched the sky a-lighting
And saw the new day born.

The dark and quiet night-time
Faded farther from my sight
While the softly glowing dawning
Bathed with all its morning light;
The stillness yielded gently
To the singing of the birds
And the golden-headed grass tops
Swayed to songs that have no words;

With a sudden burst of glory
The morning sunlight shone
And brightened all the desert
Singing, "You are not alone."

Jamie Bergey
REFLECTIONS

To Linda

A shooting star blazing and bright,
the howling wind of a cold winter's night,
the taste of good whiskey, the laugh of a true friend,
a precious moment that should never end.

So say it loud and say it clear,
live life to the fullest while it's here,
for fate heads no master, and time waits for no man,
you will cherish this life, when this you understand.

Patti Gaumont
DREAMS

A dream is like a wish
that someday might come true
it all depends how hard you try
and the different things you do.

You have to try to live it
to make it seem like real
no matter what someone may say
or how someone may feel

Dreams are what keep you going
and help you through the night
only you know down inside
if the dream is right

When you do feel
the right dream come along
grab on to it and hold real tight
and nothing will go wrong.

Roberta T Perrin
THE MOCKINGBIRD'S SONG

In the quiet of the morning all I could hear
Was the mockingbird's song so sweet and clear.
Each morning I hear him begin the day;
Soon other birds join in, happy and gay.

They tweet, they chirp, they sing, they call;
A concert present for one and all.
I lie there and listen—quiet and still,
Afraid I will miss the softest trill.

As time goes by, I have become more aware
Of the beauty around me everywhere,
The singing of birds, the flowers, the trees,
The rain and the sunshine, even the breeze.

How dull, how drab my world would be
If there were no birds to sing for me!
No flowers or trees to brighten the way,
How empty my life would be every day.

But my life is enriched by all of these,
They bring joy and happiness as well as peace.
The beauty they add cannot be measured,
All nature is mine to be treasured.

So open your eyes, your ears, your heart,
To this wonderful world of which you're a part.
Each moment is precious . . it soon will be gone,
And you might have missed the mockingbird's song.

Lisa Diane Cox

AT MIDNIGHT

I sit alone now.
Sleep has stolen you from me.

Darkness holds many secrets.
Stars answer all dreams.
Shadows battle my worries.
I hear peace whispered in the silence.
I have security while the world rests.
I find understanding from the lonely old moon.

Morning has stolen night from me.
I sit alone again.

Ruth Williams

THE OTHER SIDE OF CHRISTMAS

There were no trinkets or tinsel hanging on the tree
No pretty lights twinkling merrily
There were no gifts tied with ribbon so gay
But there was PEACE and LOVE lying on the hay.
A star shone bright to light the sky;
As angels sang his lullaby,
"Glory to God in the highest; Peace on earth; Good-will toward men"
They sang the message joyfully, loud and clear,
Announcing that JESUS, THE MESSIAH, was here!
He was the GLORY to GOD on high; For man He came to earth to die,
Another reason for His birth; He was the PEACE come down to earth,
To bring Good-will toward all men;
To show us how to live again.
So let's go back to the 'good old days'; When Christmas meant worship and praise,

And thanking God for His Love and His Son; Or have we forgotten how it's done?
Giving of ourselves and our time we are sharing,
Not just telling, but doing, proving we are caring.
So ring the bells and shout our greeting "Merry Christmas" to all we are meeting.
There were no trinkets, no tinsel or pretty lights twinkling merrily,
Just JESUS, our SAVIOR, hanging on the tree,
Suffering, bearing our shame, our sins and our iniquities;
Shedding His blood; giving His life for you and me,
That we may live in glory beyond our dreams.
This is what the Other Side of Christmas means.
So when the New Year comes and the excitement is passed
The "goodies" are gone and the last gift unwrapped,
Remember the manger where the message starts
And let's keep CHRISTmas in our hearts.

Emma Coker

IT'S WHAT'S IN THE HEART OF MAN

To George & Hattie Nance, my parents

When my hair has turned to silver
And my days with memories past;
I'll think of the days of wine and roses,
Of the love that should have last.
I'll remember the wasted hours
That should have been filled with wonderous things
When we should have shared love and laughter—
But love was afraid to spread her wings.

Afraid to accept the fine mysteries,
Or to take the unkown chance
Afraid to give to the fullest
The joy and sadness of romance.
So love was silent, would not express
The depth of its feelings and powers
She hid her light, suffered her distress
Never to know her greatest hours
Of the fulfillment of peace and tenderness.

And the greatest blessings of all,
She failed to understand,
It is not the material things so much
As what is in the heart of man.

Judith Ann Eger

WHAT ARE PARENTS

Dedicated to my Mother and Father, James and Dorothy Eger

Parents are your Mother and Father,
Whom you cherish throughout the years,
And you should always respect them,
Because they are so kind and dear.

They provided, clothed, and cared,
No matter the time of day.
Laughed, cried and shared their love,
In their own sweet loving way.

They brought you up through childhood,
From tiny tot to teen,
And the years went by so swiftly,
Now an adult, with worthwhile dreams.

So don't let your parents down,
They loved you from the start,
Gave you love and guidance,
From the bottom of their hearts.

So all they really ask of you,
Is a little respect and love,
And God will bless them always,
From the place called Heaven above.

James Peltier

PARENT'S LOVE

This poem is dedicated to my parents William and Marilyn Peltier for all the love they have shown me.

My parents stand in front of all
For precious moments I recall
Stayed up those nights, worried alone
When I'd decide not to come home
They chauffer me from here to there
Seldom do they charge me fare
With love I write these words to them
To me they are my closest friends
They see me through when times are bad
Lift my spirits when I am sad
A perfect pair they are to me
Filled with love and honesty
In my mind I must confess
They stand among the very best
With tender ways and loving hearts
I'm positive they will never part

Mary Jo Thornton

INTERMISSION TIME

To my God, Creator of the world's beauty, and to my dearest children, Daniel and Debra for their great appreciation and love of nature.

Summer days start fading
Into brisk September morns,
The woods takes on an earthen glow
Of chocolate brown and russet forms;
While the beautiful summer wildflowers
Bow their heads down to the ground,
There emerges a brilliant carpet
Weaved of gold, orange, and brown;
While the milkweed pods are bursting
Cattails sway gently in the breeze,
The leaves start drifting aimlessly
Bedding down for winter's freeze;
The wheat fields wave their tassles
Looking like Indian head-feathers,
While the cornstalks stand naked
Braving winter's worse weather;
God gave autumn a breathless beauty
Surely, all its own,
Just a short intermission
Until winter is born.

Emily Gentry (aka Emily Kerri)

SAILING

In loving memory of my Dad, Henry Roscoe Jackson; "This sailor has reached home at last!"

While sailing on the seas of life
Many waves are surging high;
I realize that other ships
Have swiftly passed me by.
Some have been driven by the wind
While others float on waves;
I hope to pass some of the ships
That forced my sail astray.
The bigger ships can glide right through
Though tempests rise and fall;
Other ships are smaller.
They cannot sail at all.
My ship has weathered many storms
Upon life's raging seas;
But now today I'll sail away . . .
To shores of victory.
God is the Captain of my ship
The Guide of this worn vessel;
No rival ships will ever pass
This sailor shall reach home at last!

August Smith

DARKNESS

This poem is dedicated to my mother Chris, my grandmother Dolores, who gave me inspiration, and my dear friend Sampson.

The Sun—
Eternal???heat
The stuff that daydreams are made of—
At night???

Basking in the sun—
The sun in my eyes
At night???

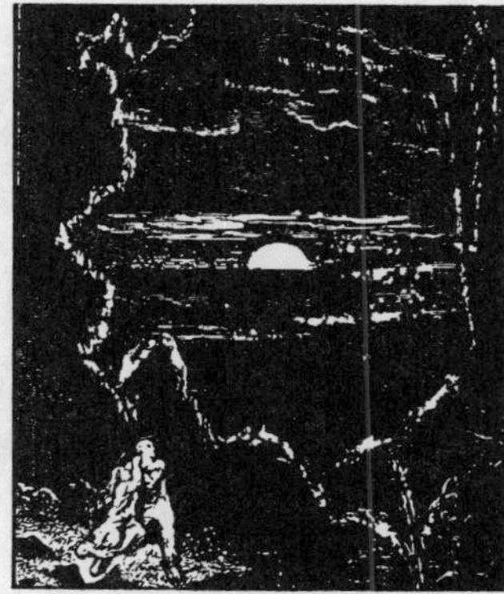

Warding off the moon—
The stars dim
Blue skies again.
At night???

What good is it
Without the sun?
Our hopes stored in a huge yellow glow
At night???

—At night??No Sun??At night—
—At night—

Pat Couillard

LONELY ROAD DOWNHILL

To Dan Crowley, who never gave up on me. To my family for their support and encouragement, for always believing in me.

Feelings, emotions, from in my mind.
How long will I stay awake this time?
Up and down, back and forth,
Walking and thinking alone in my room.
Night after night, I toss and turn.
Hoping for a solution, for somewhere to turn.
Pills, pills, red blue and black, all sizes and shapes.
So easy to find, so easy to take.
One pill too many, what a big mistake.
Sleep so deep, as peaceful as death.
One pill too many, you'll breathe your last breath.
Uppers downers, so easy you say.
But what a price, your life you will pay.
I'm glad that today I found a way out.
Now I will find out what life is all about.

Peggy Lou Wright
A CHILD

To my three children: Mark, Michelle and Matthew

The most precious thing, I've ever known.
Was the love of a child, before they're grown.
So naturally giving, and sweet, as a rose.
They're darling and adorable, from their heads to their toes.
Pure and untouched by the corruption of man.
A fresh new beginning of God's worldly plan.
Like rainbows and buttercups in the morning sun.
All "giggles" and "smiles," just packed-full of fun.
Asleep, they're like "angels," on high clouds of white.
Awake, they will fill your heart with "delight."
Trinkets, teddies, dollies and worms.
Fidgety, fussy and little bitty squirms.
Boo-boos and ouchies, ringlets and curls.
Tuffy big boys, tender little girls.
Jello and ice cream, with grass stained knees.
Hates dumb old "spinach," and won't touch "peas."
Won't wear galoshes or silly old mittens.
Crazy for puppies and darling baby kittens.
"Big Bird and Mickey, Captain Kangaroo."
Can't hardly wait, to go to school.
Stuffed-up noses with bumps on their heads.
Oh please Mommie, I don't want to go to bed!
With the world full of "violence," "suffering" and "Stress."
They help us forget, about this terrible mess.
So lets "love" them, "guide" them and "protect" them from others.
For they are our future and we are their mothers.

Alice Wamsley
CHILDREN

To my five children that are now grown. Thank you for all the love.

A mothers job is never done, no matter what you do.
If only they would show some appreciation towards you.
You cook and clean iron and sew, it seems your always on the go:
Your bursting heart, so full of love, for your children, a gift from above.
Even though there is always a riot you would never trade it for peace and quiet.
For they will get big, and away they will go,
And loneliness will be the only thing you will get to know.
So enjoy your job of raising your crew, and make them think the best of you, let them know you will always be there, what ever needed for.
And somehow they will always find their way back to your door, that door must always stay open, for your children and their sons,
For in your heart you know they are the only ones.

Nicole M Kleve
SHE AND ME

To my husband Bob, who gave me life and showed me the sea and all of her treasures.

Drifting on a sea, as breathless as the dead
Slight of fear, anticipation and dread
Blinding rays of sun, silent heavy air
Time eternity, answer my prayer
Sails limp, helpless hanging shroud
Begging, give her wind, make her proud
Suddenly a telltale gave a sigh
Could it be? I wouldn't die.
Beaded, running salty sweat
The devil laughed, but lost his bet
We came to life, she and me
And away we sailed on our loving sea.

Wanda Lilly Coleman

Wanda Lilly Coleman
WHERE PURPLE VIOLETS GROW

In the West Virginia Mountains, amidst the rocks and rills,
There blooms a purple violet high upon the hills.
I played there in my childhood; I roamed the grassy fields;
I listened every evening to the lonesome "whip-poor-wills."

In dreams I oft' go back to the days of long ago,
Where I climbed the highest mountain and waded the deepest snow.

Where bluebirds sing so sweetly and the mountain breezes blow,
A place I'll long remember; where the purple violets grow.

The city folks are busy in the factories and the mills.
The country folks are happy without the fuss and frills.

They wake up every morning when they hear the rooster crow,
And smell that lovely fragrance where the purple violets grow.

When my earthly race has ended and I sleep beneath the ground,
Just find some purple violets and plant them all around.

I've been to lots of places, seen lots of pretty sights,
But those little purple violets out-shine those city lights.

Manuel M Zapien

Manuel M Zapien
SALLIE'S CAT

Oh, ye four legged Creature,
With your hair so shiny.
Independence is your main feature,
But at times so whiny.

At your convenience or whim,
Your food is right there.
Your milk bowl filled to the brim,
While my plate is bare.

I look for my easy chair,
To set my weary self down.
Since you've possessed it as your lair,
No wonder I wear such a frown.

For you no questioning or nagging,
As your mistress is so comprehending.
She knows you've been tom-catting.
Ah! that I could have such understanding.

When some loving you need,
To your mistress' lap you crawl.
You feline born of an alley seed,
From a ten story building I wish you'd fall.

If in resurrection I believed,
And it really came to pass;
As Sallie's tom-cat I'd be so relieved.
In the meantime, I'll just kick your ass!

O Coyote Youngblood
CONTINUOUS SONG OF SILENCE

Deep in the heart of the Poet
Lies a song that remains unsung.
Many of God's creatures know it
But it's silent upon their tongue.

It tells a beautiful story
Hidden on sighs of the breeze,
Of all Life's wondrous glory,
And strange, obscure mysteries.

But it can't be put on paper with rhyme,
No bright colored pictures can paint
With a fraction of meaning, for through time
The words grow old and colors grow faint.

Words are nothing but scribblings on paper
And painting, a bright colored whim,
Soon all words will rise with the vapor
While colors will fade and grow dim.

Still, in the Poet's silent heart,
From the throne of the King above,
That song will stay and never part,
Manifesting the notes through Love . . .

Linda McCanless Taylor
NO GREATER LOVE . . .

This is dedicated to my wonderful husband, Curt. The only man I'll ever want or need to make my life complete.

You are my lover and lifelong friend.
You'll be my husband till our lives end.
A perfect man you cannot be
But, God created you just for me.
He made you special in every way.
To love, honor, cherish and obey.

We created two sons to love and share.
We show them happiness, joy and care.
You teach them respect and you understand.
For you were a boy, and now you're a man.
They will marry and have children one day.
And your Fatherly Love, they can repay.

Gerald M Hilstein
THE DESERT

For Helen, my favorite Tango dance partner

The sun shines very hot today
It shines also on a desert far far away
A desert with beautiful towering dunes
Yet it would never look like a ruin

For there would be wild flower beds
An occasional eagle over our heads

Aubrey Gene Roe
AMERICAN SOLDIER FROM VIET NAM
I board this Orient Express for home
And feel its shivering power
I've given my best, to the very last
O—to be home within the hour.

I hold abreast, on loving chest
A cloth defining my glory.
I'm headed home, I'm headed home
Covered by Old Glory!

Carol Ann Bourdy
THE "LAND OF ENCHANTMENT"
New Mexico is a beautiful state;
The sky is so clear and blue.
It's surely a breathtaking view;
The Sandia Mountains are a mile high.
There's no mistaking, that you're in a different place,
You'll love that warm sun on your face.
The weather here is the best we've seen.
You'll have to visit, to see what we mean.
The people are so friendly and great!
It's true, New Mexico is a wonderful state!

Jo-Ann M Huguenin and Michelle

Jo-Ann M Huguenin
MICHELLE
In the early morning hours,
When I awake from sleep,
I think about a little girl
and my heart begins to weep.
Why did God take her home with Him,
When she was only five?
Her life was so precious to us,
While she was still alive.
Her little voice would sing
God's songs so very sweet,
With her in our home,
Our lives were so complete.
He gave her to us to love
For just a little while,
He gave her to us to teach us
How to love and smile.

Did you need another angel in your heaven, Lord?
Did you need another star in your sky?
These are but some of the questions . . .
I'll always wonder why.
We'll never have all the answers,
While on this earth below,
But someday, we will join her,
'Til then, we miss her so.
Please, Lord, I pray, You'll let her shine
Through a star in your heaven so bright,
I need some reassurance and hope
As I sit here alone in the night.
When the dawn breaks through with a bright new day,
I know I'll make it through,
Because of the love of a little girl . . .
Because of Michelle and You.

Diane Sibble Jennings
THE STAIRWELL

Dedicated to my heavenly Father and my earthly Father, who together brought forth in me an honest heart and a strong family spirit.

Peering in the stairwell near the kitchen door,
hangs the worn plaid woolrich my Daddy always wore.
As I gazed upon the sight that slowly took me back,
I pictured "Dear Ol' Dad" take his gun down off the rack.

Then off we'd go disturbing snow lying serenely upon the ground,
while through the woods as we walked—little rabbits bound.
Often as a special treat, the thing that I liked best,
was when we sat upon a log to give the gun a rest.

We'd watch the snow fall softly, gently down upon our heads
and if we'd look so carefully, the flowers peered from winter beds.
Then Dad would share the years gone by, his adventures as a child.
We'd listen close with widened eyes, imagining Dad out in the wild.

As the sun slowly began to set and the snow gently wet our noses,
old man winter soon moved over making room for springs delicate roses.
Day after day as the years are no more, our time together—I see it soar,
I find myself peering in the stairwell . . . near the kitchen door.

Marvin B Hutto
TO BE A BEE
Of all the things which I could be,
I'd like one day to be a bee.
While the summer sun woke everything,
Let the cool dew dry upon each wing.

And when the dew was dry to go
Swiftly buzzing high and low.
To follow the balmy summer air,
Free from need and want and care.

Just feast each day on nector sweet,
From each flower on field and street.
And visit each shrub in stately dress,
That summer breeze and rain caress.

Yes, I wish that I could see
One day that I could be a bee.
To nestle close to each flower's ear
And share bits of gossip each may hear.

Gossip from ant and butterfly,
Rose and tulip and corn so high.
Warbling notes from Finch and Crow;
Each cry that on soft breezes go.

By God's good grace I cannot see
My day on earth to be a bee.
But still I wonder how it would be
If on one day I could be a bee.

Melody C Curtis
TRIALS OF A TRAFFIC JAM
"Hail a cab, chauffeur. Hear!
My work is calling loud and clear.
The traffic is thick,
And we are stuck,
We're right in back,
Of a semi-truck.
The light is green and they won't go.
I don't understand why they're so slow.
We've been here since twelve o'clock
And now I hear the crowing cock.
I hope this Mack does not back up,
If so, I fear, I shall not sup.
What ho! He's nipped us on the snout.
Oh, no! my chauffeur has passed out."

Don Adams
THE OLD PRO
The locker room knows of his pain and grief,
His happiness, perseverance and teams belief.
He sits and wonders with tension building,
With knees a aching from previous fielding.
The painkillers taken sometime ago,
Now seem to have taken their part of the toll.
The game begins with some delay,
With enthusiastic fans from play to play.
The sweat is pouring from within,
The heart a pounding until the end,
He looks at the clock with a sluggish grin,
For the OLD PRO knows he has won again.

Donna Lynn Front
A SPECIAL LOSS
When I'm dead
And I'm gone,
Will I see my mothers face?
Will she smile, and run to me?
Oh my Lord, please let this be . . .
She was my mom
And my best friend . . .
My strength
My support
My backbone.
The time we had
Was so very short,
But her memory lives inside my head, my heart
And my soul . . .
But the emptiness is always there,
The pain, the fears,
The endless tears . . .
How I long to see her face,
To hear her voice,
Her warm embrace . . .
My life has changed
In many ways.
The Special Meanings
Behind "little things."
The surprises, the fun, the talks.
The comfort and peace
That only a Mother could ever give . . .
And so dear God,
I must ask:
When I'm dead
And I'm gone,
May I please be with my Mom?

Elsie M Youngblood

Elsie M Youngblood
GOD TOOK HIS ANGEL BACK

For: Ricky Lee Sewell The three year old angel in this poem.

God sent a little angel.
He was such a precious child.
He said, "You can love and cherish him,
For just a little while."

"But don't hold on too tightly,
For the day will surely come,
When I'll need my little angel back,
And I'll come to take him home."

"Now, I know how much you'll miss him.

But can't you really see?
That he's not dead, he's still alive,
In Heaven, here with Me."

"For just a few short precious years,
You've had him here on earth.
And all the memories he's made,
Have surely proved their worth."

"So, when you think of him with love,
And the tears form in your eyes.
Remember, there will come a day,
When there'll be no more goodbyes."

Carol Nunemaker Knabb
TRANQUIL GREETING

To Ralph and Arlene Brown with fondest regards

At twilight I traveled a secluded lane
Approached a house nestled in glistening snow
The old house proudly exhibits its charm
The old wooden siding ne'er showed its age
Long windows are decorated by winter's frost
Trimmed with old-fashioned shutters

Bushy garland encased the door frame
Enhanced by
Decorative strung lights
Casting an inviting soft glow upon
An encircled grape-vine wreath
That hangs on the front door

It shall bear luscious grapes no more
But will beckon weary travelers
As they come inside to
Fellowship admist the pleasant home
A cherry fire in the open woodstove
Radiates a relaxing warmth through out the room

Though wind and snow beat on the house
People inside are surrounded by friends
Warmed by a cup of tea
A feeling of peace and contentment radiates
A relaxed stillness
Blessing the fortunate people

Alma Payne Hollis
MY CHURCH

To my darling daughters, Pat Armstrong and Teddy Gore, because I love them so very much.

My church is a beautiful; place;
There you can meet God, face to face
The lovely spire reaches high in the sky.
Pointing to a mansion that will be mine by and by.

It is a place you can feel secure;
Of that you can be very, very sure.
So come with me, just for today.
There you can learn to walk in His way.

Coming to know Him creates peace,
For the Savior's love will never cease.
The road for peace ended my search
When I joined others in my church.

So if you want more,
just walk through the door
into MY CHURCH.

Kevin Stefon Bass
A KING WITHOUT A THRONE
Togetherness was what he preached
He hoped around the world that it would be teached
He told the people not to fight but to turn their cheek
He walked a quiet road but the man wasn't weak

He had a vision of the world unified as a whole
Nonviolence as his partner Integration as his goal
Born in Atlanta January fifteenth
The day is now a holiday for people to keep

Emotions ran high when he made a speech
He had quietly broken unto the breech
He believed that black and white could work together as one
He believed we were equal all under the sun

He was criticized at times by his peers
But held his head high and didn't shed one tear
He showed the people how to stand up and demand respect
A monument to his name we should erect

Won the Nobel Peace Prize for helping out mankind
The memory of that won't be left behind
He led a march with a peaceful tone
He was surely a king but didn't want a throne

Here was a king above all men
A man like him may never come again
Dr. King was a man all could be proud of
For in harsh times the man found love

Ralph Silverman
ETERNAL PEACE
Central to all, is that Calm Center.
Like the eye of the hurricane, amidst
thunderous violence it abides in eternal Peace.
We all visit this realm of joy and bliss for
short intervals, yet even a desire to stay,
brings tension, and causes it to slip away.

And so, fellow Pilgrim, know the truth!
"The Kingdom of Heaven is within you."
And you will replace desire with Love and
abide in the Heavenly Kingdom Forever.

Tillie Hilfman
CONDO CONTRAST
What a joy to behold a couple, old, but erect and in shape out at the pool
to play each day that is sunny.
First they walk at a brisk pace; 'round and around they go—her face
looking up at his—a trace of a smile
ever on her lips; his laugh is strong
in appreciation of her humor.
She tests the water with her toes as they
don caps, goggles, ear plugs. Soon, they begin
laps in unison, hands cutting the water
together, just as Esther and Fernando once did—
dolphin's at play—a water ballet.
Wrapped in terry; rapt into novels, sun-hats
shading eyes, their sighs are audible to
passers-by. I hear them and try to read
the titles as I swim alone, envious.
My soul-mate is watching foot-ball again . . .

Barbara Smith

Barbara Smith
DIGGER

This poem is dedicated to the survivors of the Holocaust and is a memorial to those who died in the Holocaust

---

Dig with my heart in my mouth
Pain wracks my body.
Keep digging and shovelling
Earth turns, my stomach turns.
Try to block dead naked bodies
Of my fellow Jews—men, women, children.
Heap one upon the other
Great mountains of flesh.
Caught in a hard place
Only way to stay up, alive
Is to dig down, stabbing my heart.

Karen A Heaslet
LIFE

To Tracy: Things could only get better. I love you.

Life goes on thats what they say.
Things get better day by day.
But if the days pass without
one to love,
What is life,
When shall it end . . .

Robert E Tate II
LONELY FOR A FRIEND
Looking, just into your eyes a feeling starts to show,
And no sooner does it come I have to let it go.

So afraid it might come out the reasons make no sense,
For when it comes to loving you my mind gets so intense.

The words they stumble from my lips
my throat, it gets so dry
That when I get the chance to speak I lose the will to try.
Finding you alone somewhere so lonely for a friend,
How I wish for just a start before I see it end.

Lance M Grenamyer
BOYS
Funny, neat
Laughing, talking, teasing
Smart, cool, obnoxious, nosey
Naging, boring, annoying
Irritating, careless
Girls

Alice M Picotte
MY CRYSTAL HEART
I'm sending you a token of my love hoping it will bring us closer dear
A bluebird of happiness I have engraved upon a heart shaped mirror.
When it arrives please hang it on the wall in your room.
And everytime you look into it imagine us as bride and groom.

This is my proposal so keep me in mind.
The right words for me to say are so hard to find.
If your answer is yes we will have a double ring ceremony.
And pledge our vows beneath the Orange Blossom tree.

High on a hill I will build you a mansion.
It will have thirty rooms when it is done.
A street paved of gold will lead to our front door.
Our home will be a peaceful place to live in that we have been searching for.

And if by some unforseen event we should part.
Please keep our mansion and my crystal heart.
I will always love you just the same.
In my heart for you there will always be a flame.
Please keep our mansion and my crystal heart.

Corinne Patricia Weiss
THE SNOWFLAKE
The snowflake swirls,
Buoyant on the breeze.
Sound is silent—
Absorbed by a blanket,
Cold and covering all.
Freely floating,
Catching air currents,
Rising higher and higher.
Then suddenly a swoosh and a backwards blast,
Eddying
And dipping slowly, softly, to the ground—
A speck among infinity.
Crystals frozen in one unique shape;
Icy and cool
Yet warm with brilliant beauty.
Flashing and gleaming with winter sun
Yet soft and glowing under the evening moon.
The snowflake.

Donna Babashan
WALKING SCARED

In memory of Tim

Hey, World! Listen up! Have big news for you.
Don't make room for me now. Am leaving you.

Oh! I did need you. Had overdosed
on despair.
Beseechingly cried out. But you
weren't there.

Existed in confusion. Rejection
and pain.
Terror choked my lifeline. Believed
I was insane.

Disturbing mind shadows. Making
thoughts awry.
Doing too much time alone. Scary
enough to die.

Fear my tormentor. Constantly
swallowing me whole.
Helping hands missing. God!
WHERE IS MY SOUL?

Drugs not the reason. My only need
was you.
To listen. To listen close. To tell me
what to do

I remember calling. Hearing my
voice say,
Hey, world! How about it? Need
help bad. TODAY!

Danger signals flashing. Demons
crowding my space.
Erasing me. Wiping me out.
Leaving no trace.

There now! Am history. An infinite
part of eternity.
No more calls for you. No more
hanging up on me.

A mournful wind my whisper.
When wailing out its stress.
If you think of me at all, don't think
any less.

Nancy Jo Clifford

UNTITLED

Sit down on a grassy field,
put both palms on the earth,

close your eyes . . . Do you know
you are holding the whole world
in the palms of your hands?

Donna Clippinger

GOD GIVEN SPEECH

Mother Rabbit let out a mournful
cry,
Realizing she was about to die.
Never before had she made a
sound,
Until she was captured by the
hound.
Her first and last cry was to warn
her young,
With her dying breath, God give
her a tongue.

Beany Trimble

WHERE ARE YOUR BELLS CHURCHES?

This poem is dedicated to Cardell and Family.

The bells of churches are not
ringings.
They are not calling their members
today.
They use to rings long ago.
Reminding us it was time to pray.
Where are your bells churches?
Where are your members today?
Few are lost and forgotten and
many have gone astray.
Bring back your members today.
Please rings your bells churches.
To a world so far away.
Let the world know that you are
still here.
And it is time again to pray.

Eugene Wojtczak

A MOTHER'S TREASURE

This poem is dedicated to my loving wife, Carol.

More precious than gold. A
brilliance
That outsparkles the largest
diamond.
This is what a young infant is when
it
Looks into its mothers eyes.

To all the mothers who went
through
The miracle and pain of
childbirth—
Your treasure will always be with
you.
Happy Mother's Day!

Mildra R Bacon

Mildra R Bacon

SPRING TIME IN MY HEART

There's a special beauty in living,
Not in taking, but, the joy is in
giving.
It arouses a passion and a longing,
Of being in love, and belonging.

When the seasons change,
especially in spring.
And my heart yearns only for you.
When the flowers bloom, and the
birds sing,
And, everything's fresh with the
dew.

It's been so many years, I've cried
a million tears.
Sometimes I've wondered how my
heart takes it.
You were one of a kind, you stay
on my mind,
I will never love again, and I won't
fake it.

But, if you come back to me, my
life will change.
It's always springtime, when I hear
your name.
And, if you love me, the same as I
love you.
It's springtime in my heart, for our
love is true.

Margaret Nolan (Wertman)

NOTHING LIKE GOSSIP

Gossipers, Gossipers, you will find
them around,
Living in villages, suburbs, and all
over town.
Talking and gawking with so much
to say,
Finding a poor soul to be a victim
of prey.

Pin down the bad points, for they
are most interesting of all,
Picking human bones dry, as does
the vulture with claws.
Loud voices are heard, and the
gossipers words soon spread,
The story growing longer and
larger so hungry minds can be
fed.

Fuel for the fire, and the flames are
fed well,
As they are twisting and burning
through town on a story they are
not quite sure how to tell.

So they adlib or guess to fill in such
words, making the gossip more
interesting to all, and more for
the birds.
In the evening the gossiper lies
down and into the pillow their
head digs deep.
Their own conscious never
bothered as they drift into a
sound sleep.

And in the morning they arise fresh
for another day,
All rested and ready to TALK about
someone or something,
But really having "nothing" to say.

Louise Johannaber

20-20 VISION

My Grandmother Augusta
would push up her reading glasses
to be conveniently near
on top of her head.
After a spell of housewifely
business
she would fret,
"I can't find my spectacles
anywhere,"
when she wanted to rest and read.

Moira Jane, my growing-up
granddaughter,
adroitly arranges her sun glasses
over her shining hair.
They are tilted twin mirrors
that in duplicate dancing
reflections
reveal the responses of delight
where Moira walks.
She never forgets that she is
wearing them—
never for a moment!

Linda King

I HAVE SEARCHED AND I HAVE FOUND

I am here, You are there
its me again where have you been.
I have searched and I have found
You had never left, you're always
around
I have felt so down before
and needed a friend so true
I have searched and I have found
I have that friend in you.

We share our faith, we share our
joy
We get these from above
But I have searched and I have
found
the greatest of these is love.

So if you are lost and so confused
and don't know what to do
Just search until you find the Man
Who loves you so much too.

Ruth Emma Smith

I STILL BELIEVE IN LOVE

I still believe in love,
Tho I've no reason to.
I still believe in me
And, I still believe in you.
Tho there's no song left for me to
sing
The melody lingers on . . .
I still believe in love,
I still believe.

It was only yesterday,
When you went away.
It sems a million years,
I still can't stop the tears . . .
I hear you walking there
On the stairway from my mind,
Please walk softly dear . . .
Footprints are all you've left
behind.
But, I still believe in love,
I still believe . . . In love.

Nita J Gross

A LOVE, A FRIEND, A ROSE

To me, there's nothing like a rose,
A love, or friend so true—
So, brush your tears and pick a
rose—
A special rose for you.

Inside my garden, many grow
But, I count them everyday,
Lest one rose be taken from me—
While I look the other way.

God planted not a single rose,
Unprecious in His sight.
And you may be the Rose He
chose—
To save some Rose tonight.

Florence Grimes

THE OLD HOUSE

I passed the place where the old
house stood.
A simple structure made of wood.
The floor was lopsided.
The roof leaked above.
It was held together with kids and
love.
When cold winds howled we didn't
care.
We felt secure 'cause Dad was
there.
Now the old house is gone and Dad
is too.
We've started a new life—new
things to do.
Sometimes with a hint of a laugh
or cry.
I think about the days gone by.
Now all that old house has for me.
Is a special place in memory.

Hattie T Henry

NATURE'S MAGIC

When I see a beautiful sunset
Or the moon light up the night,
I feel the spirit of it all
And the One that makes things

right.

Flowers blooming by the road side
Or a bird's nest in the trees;
The beauty of it all thrills me
As I walk in the evening breeze.

I bow my head in silence
And breathe a little prayer
To the God who made it all.
I feel His presence there.

When the rain falls from the clouds
And washes the earth anew,
He makes flowers and green grass grow
As only our God can do.

He gives the flowers their beauty
And the birds their happy song.
He gives me a better life
When I ask forgiveness for all my wrongs.

Theresa Ann Bandaccari

IF I START

If I start to stumble or fall.
Pick me up.
Tell me I can go on.
I can make it on my own.
But reminding me that you love me.
It gives me a strength I've never found else where.
For I know then I can make it or succeed.
You'll touch my life.
And I'll touch your life too.
Both of us will become richer for knowing and loving each other the way we do.
Thanks for just being there with me through it all.
For I've become a better person since you offered to help.

L M Pomeroy

MEMORIES

For R.D.K.

A melody
A happening
A face;
Momently
They weave
A fragile web of emotion,
Simple,
Yet complex,
Interlacing strands
Spun over time,
All leading to a center:
Inevitably
You.

Deborah Engel Broder

Deborah Engel Broder

WANDERING THOUGHTS

A feeling, a dream
yet I can't touch it.
A fictional story with no ending
Yet too real to distinguish between fantasy and reality.

A time, a place where words were few,
A distant dream that failed to create.
A tear that ran like the river and broke like the ice it laid.

Its time to break the chains that I have molded, for today is the past and Tomorrow will be my future.

Rae Lee

SUMMER DREAMS

Did you ever travel to the world of make believe?
To that land of dreams where you can escape to;
Where you can live for awhile in a dream world;
To put reality behind when life becomes too much,
And you need somewhere to go.

Well . . . come along, escape with me.
To the land of make believe.
Where I've had a thousand dreams,
And done a thousand things,
In my world of make believe.
Where I've watched a thousand clouds float by
While under the tree I lay,
On Mother's old hand sewn quilt.

Come now with me . . .
The day is sunny and bright,
And the fluffy white clouds are flecked across the horizon.
For love is in the air and my heart sings a song of love.
Even if it's in the land of make believe
Let's dream together . . . of us.

And as the summer sun retreats toward the West horizon;
As the heat of day slowly fades
My eyes become misty,
Because my dreams have burned to ashes in my heart,
And I come back to live in reality.

Brenda F Herrington

INDIFFERENT

I am not indifferent
perhaps it is the eyes you see me with
and if so—
look again please.
I am not all that you will ever be
but what I am, is left to you
to accept
or reject.
And if I had one chance to tell you
I would say it to your eyes
which tell more
than a voice could ever provoke,
that you are indeed . . . beautiful.
The platonic mind in which I hold you
protected and lifted
from the chaotic world,
shall in no way be destroyed.

And yet,
if you read me with different lines
perhaps you have only read the introduction,
the context within,
containes the real value.
Please, don't close the book,
I have yet to find the end.

Bernarda Powell

I REMEMBER JENNY

When you were little, tiny and cute,
Crawling around, not bigger than a foot.
Very soon you were five, and went to school.
Now you are 10, and a very bright jewel.
When you were a baby, very alert,
Jenny, that is why you are so smart.

Melisa Dianne Loflin

CHRIST IN MY GARDEN

In my garden filled with daisies,
Stood our saviour sweet and dear,

And it seemed a bit of heaven,
with our precious friend so near,

His tender word of scared love,
Fell on the blossomed air.

And suddenly the tiny birds sang,
Like a lilting prayer,

In every nook and crevice,
The garden whispered love,

For Christ was teaching that sweet day,
The way to heaven above.

Marilyn (Max) Biesterfeld

ALONE

Alone
the quiet settles around me
once more
Peace and contentment are mine
as I listen to the kitten snore.
My only visitors,
the memories of friends;
Part of my past
and part of my future
Where we'll meet again
in the circle of the word
unspoken;
Recognizing ourselves
in the eyes of each other.
Alone
yet never alone
while there is Love.

Omega Watson Wagner

Omega Watson Wagner

THAT LITTLE HOUSE WE'VE OUTGROWN

Today I passed our old house,
The place we once called home.
Small and rundown, but filled with love,
That little house we've outgrown.
Roses planted with love and care,
We saved pennies to buy.
Were softly nodding in the breeze,
They seemed to whisper "Don't Cry".
We worked so hard to reach the top,
At last we have succeeded.
I'm alone again tonight,
Wondering if I'm still needed.
I walked through the door of our mansion,
Beautiful to behold;
Success brought us many things,
But our beautiful love grew cold.
Oh take me back to that little house,
It was more than a house, <u>it was home;</u>
We laughed, cried, and oh how we loved,
In that little house we've outgrown.

Mary M Slygh

LIFE—LOVE

Tho I left you behind,
Please don't let this
Fill your mind.
Open up your soul and heart,
Let childrens laughter
Become a part.
Listen to the birds that sing,
Add these too,
In your everything.
Enjoy the sunshine and the rain,
Don't let my leaving,
Bring you pain.
Smell the air after a spring shower
Take out time
To pick a flower.
Look at the stars and moon
on a clear night,
Know that God has made
Everything just right.
Don't be in a hurry
To join me here.
Enjoy every day
And every year.
Just live each day
The best you can,
Look only to God,
And not to man.

Mary P Turner

THE MAILBOX

Dedicated to my loving Lord, Who gives me the words for my poems.

The mailbox sits upon its post, so commonplace appearing,
But what it holds from day to day just makes it most endearing!
And when I see that mailman go—with gladdest expectation—
I hurry on out to that box midst greatest speculation!
"I wonder what 'twill be today?" I ponder as I scurry,
And when I reach that precious lid I yank it with a flurry!
"Oh my, just look at all the mail!"
I grab it most delightedly,
And clutching it with utmost care,
I rush inside exitedly!
There's mail from friends—and strangers, too—and much solicitation,
And here's a letter from out West, from some of my relation!
There're cards for Christmas, birthday cards and some for all occasions,
And notes to cheer us on our way, and shower invitations!
And magazines and sundry ads and duns and bills galore,

And Sweepstakes entry blanks and books—all these, and so much more!
But, oh, the letdown when we go as fast as we can sail,
And when we yank that boxlid down—there isn't any mail!

Suzanne Lynch-Wright

MY DAD

I watch as you help him. I'm glad you're there,
to give the pills, and push his chair . . . to help, to care.
I know how you see him; the frail body, the parchment skin,
the darkly bruised hands that tremble.
I wish you could see him as I can. My memories are so clear;
of earlier times, and happier days, of laughter and of joy.
I wish you could see him as I can, my dad . . . your patient . . . the man.
First off, he's Irish, proud to be it, proud to say it;
with a too-quick temper and a taste for drink.
He was a son, and still a brother; the black sheep, a
maverick—the one to fight and try and dare.
He was a soldier, straight and proud, who went to war
and fought the fight, and earned the name of hero.
He's a husband and a father; imperfect at both, if the
truth be told, but loving, and oh, so definitely loved.
As a daddy he gave freely; hugs and tickles, and
strawberry ice cream cones, a lap to chase away fears.
Baby Ruth candy bars, Jucy Fruit gum, Easter baskets and
dolls that walked—both of them taller than me.
A spanking when it was needed, 'tho it nearly broke his heart,
He gave me so much loving, that I hardly know where to start.
So, later when you help him, try to see the man that was;
a man who danced and fought and laughed and loved.
Try and be a little patient, and humor him when you can.
You're dealing with my dad, you know—a very special man.

Faye M Helton

UNTITLED

the body swayed gently
to the song of the wind
and the limbs danced lightly
to what once had been

the head bows forward
in a silent prayer
tho' the lips whisper not a word
of the pride stripped bare

the rain gently weeps
on the dark brown skin
the tears that silence keeps
from way back then

prejudice, what death you've bought
what needless selling of souls
what pain and terror you've brought
what are your goals?
the body swayed and rocked
through the ages of time
crowds of people flocked
prejudice, what is really thine?

Toni (Sabre) Keenan

FROM SHADOWS ARISE

To Gary Slayman, for your faith to trust the strength of my words. Indeed, you are a friend to me.

From Shadows arrise promises as crystals, as crystals shattered, turned ashes by Morns' sleepy rising
Taken by the Winds of Vexation soon to shower, to nestle within the naked, stirring branches of Despair
To affix upon the mighty roots of Hope awaiting the hands of Destiny to cast into weary clouds, Eyes of Somber
And thus tears shall fall by Rains' deceitful masquing, to nurture, as well as to disrobe the Forgotten Knowledges' for fate has beckoned such to be, and so shall such befall
For Desire has arrisen within the Tower Ruin as Beast forsakes mortal lust shall reign the Fire rearing Sins of Peril save for
the She and Wolf. "Steele" are the Towers to rise, and remain unscathed, in grave wounds she lay dreamingly . . . the Breath of Tower Ruin, from the Shadows of Pain, arrise . . . arrise and
seek thee . . .

Thomas C J Price

ENCHANTED

Dedicated to Mary Frances Stevens

When thinkin' of days
which life passed by,
I begin to wonder why?

With you what was it all about?
In those times of total doubt,
each dream you came to me,
fate tellin' me it was meant to be!!

But still I'm alone n' cold
in a mystic world caught
between new n' old

Enchanted! enchanted!
was it your eyes or innocence?
Cosmic magic or coincidence?

Were they just dreams of my
enchanted world?
Or are we victims of life gone

foiled?
How doth the little crocodile
improve his shining tail?
By fighting confusion, disappointment
n' the evil powers of hell!!

Enchanted! enchanted!
I wonder if you'll ever know
how much I love you so

The secret seal broke over the
loss of you
A prophesy fulfilled
Heaven split in two

You're my guiding spirit
the key to the door
with or without you
I know there's much more

Enchanted! enchanted!
You're the princess of my dreams
We're victims of satans screams

S Elaine Chavis

ME

To my daughter Sonja and my son Zak. May you always fly high and free

---

Butterflys fly so high
so fast, so free
Would like to be close
but it scares me
Catch me if you can
softly, slowly
With your open palm
lightly, gently
No nets to hold me
united, yet free

Patsy A Call Bauer

TO MY FRIEND NADINE

It's been a very long year.
And I've shed many a tear.
Thoughts of you come, no matter what.
I see you in the sunshine,
I see you in the night.
I see you in your children,
And have thoughts of what might have been.
I see the brilliance of your life in the trees.
I hear your laughter in the breeze.
The hurt of losing you will never mend for some,
And the tears—they will continue to come.
I show you are with the Father above.
I still thank God I knew your love.
I miss you, my dear friend,
And hope we can be together in the end.

Genevieve (Sandy) Clifton

WHAT MATTERS

For sixty two years I waited for it
The check that was to be my security,
"Just enough," my husband added his bit,
"To pay for your stamps and some charity."
I recall how over the years I worked hard
To pinch my pennies and even sacrificed
Trusting that at sixty two I could sit in my yard
And not worry about how high things were priced.

I thought retirement would be a bowl of cherries
I would sleep when I wanted to and eat likewise,
But now I know that it has its share of worries
Prices keep rising—cost of living facts prove to be lies.
Now I figure and figure how to make ends meet,
While Congressmen vote to increase their check
And try to pay my taxes so as not to cheat
It's enough to make me a nervous wreck.

I'm thankful to God for all His blessings
A free country, abundance of food, a warm place to sleep
For I know that elsewhere the lack of these is most depressing
And what one sows, isn't always what one reaps.
Please, Lord, help me to always remember
That good health, a clear mind and peaceful soul
Is really what matters when one reaches life's September
Not how much money there is in the bank or cookie bowl.

Debbie Hestand

MOM'S GROWING PAINS

Yawn and stretch, get out of bed.
Tis another school day for my little sleepyhead.
Where's my socks? Where's my jeans?
Can I wear this sweater? It sure looks keen!
Cereal or eggs, what is your choice?
Cereal! I hear from my little one's voice.
Milk poured on, soon breakfast is eaten, quickly gone.
Hurry my child, for I do fear, the time for your bus is quite near.
Where's my backpack? Where's my brush?
Oh! These school mornings can be a rush!
Finally ready, headed for the door.
Blow me a kiss, my little one, just one more.
I watch out the window as she climbs on the bus.
I feel a tear come on but not because of the morning rush.
Seems only yesterday she was my infant baby.
But I must stand strong, for one fine day, I'll turn
around and she will be her own grown lady.

Evelyn Neal Hooker

I THE RAIN

I the rain, am a soft, slow mist that in winter can chill the body and cause a shiver,

I the rain, in spring, awaken the sleeping plants with gentle drops that causes their leaves to quiver,

I the rain, in summer, can cause tragedy far and wide, and for the distress I leave I care not a sliver,

I the rain, withhold my moisture in the fall to enhance the beauty of the hillside's color,

I the rain, cannot control myself. I am despised, at other times welcomed; because I was never disciplined by a mother.

Kathy Ruether
FAITH

Faith is not learned in church, but through the private struggles of an open heart. This poem is dedicated to the Lord Jesus Christ and to my beloved friends who had faith in me, even when I didn't.

There comes a time of terrible
teasing . . .
of sunshine freezing,
church bells wheezing,
and water balloons
dropping from ivory towers.
In these hours
only faith

holds the hopeful lamp,
glimpsing glories of His face,
able still to trace
footprints 'cross the
waters.
Speak not lightly of faith—for but a
single strand
can
span
an empty shell of despair
to the very heart of God.

Margaret DeBow Judge
INVITATION ACCEPTED
She stood untouched, in a
darkened alcove, perfectly
fashioned; exquisitely shaped and
submissively mute.
Presently I sensed, she was
beckoning to me!
Impulsively I responded and
tenderly extended both
hands, in her direction.
Suddenly, a surging arpeggio
of delight, inundated my soul, as
each fleeting finger
floated triumphantly, over her
exposed black and white
surface, as once again I
succumbed, to the silent
invitation, of a "Steinway."

Kim Ball
THERE'S NO OTHER TIME LIKE SPRING
There's no other time like spring,
The flowers are yellow, the leaves
are green,
There's no other time like spring,
Where the fish hop and birds sing,
Where people sit out in the sun,
just before all work is done,
There's no other time like spring,
In spring trees grow strong,
So nothing will go wrong,
No, theres no other time like
spring.

George Anthony Marchiando

George Anthony Marchiando
LOVES DYING SEED

Dedicated to Mark E. Hering, My Best Friend

Well it came to be on one spring
day,
The love I felt when you came my
way.
You wanted me, you told me so,
And said with love like a seed we'll
both watch it grow.
The summer brought laughter of
days spent in the sun,
And the breeze carried our
promises that we would always
be one.
Our nights filled with magic, from
a moon that hung so low.
My arms like vines I'd hold you,
My heart like a root grabbed hold.
For fall now brings its beauty,
Like your smile I stand back to
behold.
The magic in the swirling leaves,
The deep blue sky that seemed so
bold.
I thought our love would last
forever,
And I took for granted the things
you need.

Like the daily care and love I'd give,
When our love was just a seed.
Come the change of the seasons
came a big change in you,
And as cold as winter wind your
words cut right through.
Now the harvest is done and snow
covers the leaves,
And all that's left standing is a man
planted in grieve.
He keeps thinking back of a fertile
spring day,
Wondering if the seed of love could
ever again grow in his heart
Now hard as clay.

Mary Theresa Sallemi
MOTHER AND DAD
Loosen the grip
of the hand
that guides me

I've grown now.

No longer do I need
the bit and bridle
to guide my every move.

But,
if you can,
every now and then,
tug on the reins
when I seem

lost.

Jean Bazar
RECIPE FOR A CHILD
No matter who the child may be
And no matter what his boast,
An understanding parent
Is what he needs the most.

A child does not need wealth or toys
Or mansions great and tall,
Just give him your attention
And a lot of love, that's all.

When he comes to you for
knowledge,
Don't push him from your side,
Have a little patience with him—
Be pleased to be his guide.

Listen to his troubles,
His heartaches—trials at school,
Be firm, but teach him gently
To live by Golden Rule.

When years fly by and he is grown,
You'll surely be the one
To hear these words sincerely said,
"I'm proud to be your son."

Margaret S Chard
LADY DAWN
Lady Dawn arose today
Wrapped in a crimson negligee;
A mischievous breeze caught hold
of her hair
And spread its glistening gold
through the air.
Languid and lovely, she rose in the
sky,
Leaving her blankets lie
carelessly by.

I looked through my window and
saw, way up high
A splash of gay color like spilled
pots of dye.
Oh fortunate Lady with boudoir so
bright,
I should think that you'd never
want to sleep through the night.

Bonnie K Silbernagel
MY KITTYS
I love kittys,
They are fun,
I have two,
Not just one.

My kittys get hungry,
They love to eat,
They meow and meow,
Until they get their milk and meat.

When my kittys go outside,
I hope it is dark,
Because we have a dog next door,
And boy does he bark.

When mom brings home the
groceries,
We have to hurry and unpack,
The kittys are waiting patiently,
To jump in and out of the sack.

When my kittys have to go potty,
They do very well,
They go in their litterbox,
But I can't stand the smell!

When they are tired,
They sleep in the waterbed,
And when I wake up,
They're sleeping by my head.

Joseph D Miller
MY SWEET ANN MARIE

This poem is dedicated to the memory of my sister, who shared her love for six years on Earth, and will, for eternity, in Heaven.

My heart was pierced with blades
of flame.
My eyes refused to cry.
Yet, deep within, I drowned in tears
the day my sister died.
No one can know just how I felt—
the world just ceased to be
I struggled to save memories
of my dear, sweet Ann Marie.
She truly was a gift from God,
for all of us to share.
Her love of life was endless,
and her beauty was so rare.
Her smile could melt a stubborn
heart.
Her laughter was so free.
I miss the gentle, tender love
of my dear, sweet Ann Marie.
A dozen years have come and
gone—
the hurt has slowly passed;
yet, deep inside, I feel a pain
that will, forever, last.
Though she was taken from this
Earth,
with me, she'll always be!
I cherish all the memories
of my dear, sweet Ann Marie.

Linda Parisi
TO ERR
To err
They say
Is human
For no
One person
Is perfect,
But why
Do certain
People err

More than
Others and
Does that
Make them
More human;
And what

Of those
Few who
Hardly err
At all,
Are they
Less human?

Virginia E Robinson

MY LITTLE SISTER

All my contented memories
Like a little shadow
Hold her image
My little sister

When other children ran away
She was there
Huggable, trusting and endearing
My little sister

We played games and explored
I told her wild tales
My captive audience
That little sister

Now we are grown and miles apart
I see in my memory still
The unchanging picture
Of my little sister

Anna Louise Bunger

THE CONQUEROR

Little brown-skinned urchin in your tattered denim jeans,
With a most angelic smile that will conquer any means,
Where did you come from and what are you doing?
I'll bet my last nickle there's a lot of mischief brewing.
Your flashing pert blue eyes are two roguish dancing imps,
And your laughter loving mouth is all atwitch.
From your topsy-turvy hair to the bottom of your toes,
I can see there's trouble coming, heaven knows!
Licorice scented hands have left imprints on your cheeks;
But the sticky blackness doesn't hide the dimples lurking deep.
Your smiling full red lips, ripe as cherries off a tree,
Play hide-and-seek with pearly teeth as even as can be.
A sun-kissed chest bears evidence of battles none too few
For to the manly shoulders proud, march scars both old and new.
That fraying belt of knotted rope looped at your slender waist,
Serves its purpose very well although not in perfect taste!
From a threadbare bulging pocket, hangs a piece of gnarled chain,
Flaunting a rusty knife doubtless used in warring games.
One foot displays a bandage on the stubbed big toe,
Prominent indeed with a lengthy one loop bow.
While a dust covered mate, so bony, broad, and tough,
Is scarred from the ankle to the nails torn short and rough.
Yet due to devilish prowlings, thru more battles you'll be nursed;
I know they'll be most welcome and you'll end up none the worse.

Judy Ricks

SOUGHT SERENITY

This is dedicated to all my family and friends. Thanks for all your support.

As I sit and think of you
All my grey skies now turn blue
The clouds have faded
The wind has died
The dogs don't bark
The birds don't cry

The sun shines bright
Its glow is warm
My fear is gone
And so's the storm
So as I sit and end my thoughts
I've found the serenity I have sought

Cynthia L Lauderdale

I ONCE WAS THERE

To my wonderful sister Helen, who's life has been unfair

I see a gloom look in those eyes
why do you sit there in total despise?

Look at me I once was there
in the same way of total despair.

I have cried and so should you
of the same reasons, to you they're new.

But please remember your future starts now
give it a chance soon you'll learn how.

Later in time, you'll remember this day
when you see a tear of another, and say
"I once was there."

Sarah A Shirvinski Long

Sarah A Shirvinski Long

MOM AND DAD

Mom and Dad you both are grand
Alway's there with a helping hand

When someone is sick.
You help them feel better quick
When someone is in sorrow.
You give them faith for tomorrow

You may not get a medal,
For all that you have done.
But Heaven will be waiting.
That's for sure.

With a treasure beyond compare.
To a wonderful couple most rare.

David R Ballinger

THE LAST ROSE OF SUMMER

This little poem is dedicated with love to all who stop long enough to smell the roses along the way.

Beyond a garden wall, once stately and tall,
Olive green leaves and red velvet petals fall,
Baring a naked branch of thorns and face less fair,
A faint trace of perfume hangs in the air.
One graceful exit, the last rose of summer.

Melveen Labrador

IN THE PAST

In the past you had some kisses,
from a boy who called you misses,
Every time he smiles at you,
it always means that he loves you.
And when you smile back at him,
it makes him think and then he grins.
This all happened in the past,
and to you it seems so fast.

Every time he sees you cry,
he always looks back and then he sighs.
He'll always remember all those cries,
and that day you said good-bye.

Only now he knows you're apart,
but he still loves you from his heart.
What ever place love puts you thru,
just remember he's with you.
You now know that you can't hide,
but it hurts so deep inside
to see that it was from the past,
which all happened oh so fast.

Jennifer J Mayer

OUR LOVE

Our love was like a rose
that blossomed and grew.
It began from nothing
yet became a beautiful friendship.
The thorns were those
who tried to keep us apart;
the stem and leaves were friends,
both yours and mine,
who supported us and cared about us.
The petals were you and I
growing close together,
and basking in the beauty and love of the other.
Yet somehow the thorns overgrew everything else.
They tore us apart, ruined our love.
Now I'm alone.
I cannot find you and cannot live without you.
I am withering like a rose without water.

William Waeys

THE SUGGESTIVENESS OF FLAME

Along the purposes of rivers

their directions, penetrations,
the subtle intensities, their indications,

the wet glint of dew on summer grass,
its film at twilight hour
gossamer webbed in a dying woods
under the moon-struck night—
some hint of edge and border,
the light of line drawn around its form;

through the seeded thought in every eye
glimpses of star-drops in the sky,
between bitter sobs
the suggestiveness of flame.

That endless expression within the eye
which creates itself upon itself, and
sees itself in the love of another eye
becomes flame;

the essence of that which goes on between us,
the faculty of knowing moon leaves
breathing black and white diamonds
on the ground.

That which stirs, awakens, and remains
forever, and follows us everywhere . . .

in a memory, in a dream
in the actuality along the river,

the suggestiveness of flame.

Matt Konkel

GOING NOWHERE IN MOTION

And as the spaces get filled,
A time comes to return
Ourselves to abnormal.

The sun shines, the wind
Blows, and the clouds take
Us away from the problems of
The present.

Observing all we can and
Remembering it before it fades
Away and dies.

The past returns and the future
Escapes me.

Time, after depressing time.

Amelia J Jones

Amelia J Jones

FEELING ALONE

Feeling alone, like a leaf on a tree, in the cold winter months.
Feeling alone, when there's not even a whisper or a voice being heard.
Feeling alone, when no one listens nor hears nor sees you.
Feeling alone, like the waters of lakes, oceans, and rivers.
Just drifting along with the flow.
Only the roar of waters can be heard, and here you are again
feeling alone

Joan M Lotz Mazzi

STOLEN MOMENT

We've caught this evening's
Still droplet
Born from the shower
Of yesterday's rain
And it was perfect.

We've witnessed this body—
Warm droplet
Glisten in the morning's light

And it was still sweet.

And now in the noonday sun
This beauty has eased its way
Down life's green blade
To nurture our days?
Or have we stolen a moment
While time was napping?

Daniel T Nowak
PORTRAIT OF A DREAM

To My Son Arin D. Nowak

Through the portrait of a dream
life seems to be confused,
And with a little imagination
meaning will come through.

For life is a play ground
of time and change,
using symbols and meanings
for the individual to reframe.

Then take as you will the
knowledge of theme,
and think of life as your
own—personal dream.

Millie Peterson
1986
Where did they go,
the holidays that came into our
lives
like golden days . . .
and disappeared like magic?

For it seems,
with passing time
so much has changed yet stays the
same . . .
like snowflakes in a paper weight.

Now, we find
as we clock each golden moment,
the past seems rewritten . . .
for the future is the present!

Suddenly,
as we shake and scatter all the
years,
viewing each fluted spectrum . . .
the day is here again, that we
thought
so far away.

The patterns set
by that first Christmas Day . . .
forever marked by a Baby's birth.

Sherry L Heaton
DEAR DIARY
A little book of memories, on the
table by her bed
Withholding precious secrets, of
things that turn her red.
Every girls private friend, to
share an inner joy
Of new days, school days, and that
very special boy.
It holds her rays of sunshine, and
captures all the rain
A page by page collection, of
laughter, tears, and pain.
The little book of memories, on
the table by her bed.

Vashti J Hopkins
THE CULTURED SAVAGE
Among the pages he softly walks,
Many leaves he doth digest,
Of philosophy, art and music he
talks,
And civilization from East to West.

He explains the stars and the
clouds in the sky,
And his love for his fellowman,
The cultured savage goes strolling
by,
His loin cloth in his hand.

Dawn Haze

Dawn Haze
FREEDOM OF RIGHTS

To my children, Michele, Leslie, Melissa, Heather, Holly, Noel, Michael and Nicole. Also, My Grandchildren, Christian, Micaila, Andrea, Alex, Joshua, Matthew, Melanie, Ariele and Mark.

I heard a hollow voice shout out,
"Freedom of rights!"
The right for the unborn to live
And the right not to die.
The same voice keeps ringing in
my ears
Crying to our young people,
"Get ready for war!"
No longer has one the choice to live
It is all right to die!

I see the surviving fetuses
Saved by the pro-life movement
Lining up to save the young
soldiers
Who will be sent off to die.
They say we must not destroy life
Not while it's so new!
But wait just a little longer, until . . .
We can feel it
And touch it
And know it
And love it
Only then can we truly destroy it!

Margaret Asfour
COURAGE

For every one, every where

Though storms may rage, and the
world plays havoc
With our senses, though stress and
strain may wear
Us down, we have our courage and
strength from Him
Above, who is always there to guide
our path.

Susan M Agne
WHEN YOU SAY YOU LOVE ME

To my loving husband Manny, may our love last for an eternity.

When you say you love me
I know that it is true
Because you always show me
Just how much you do

You show me all the time
In your own special way
Just a kiss from your lips
Is all you need to say

But when you say you love me
And when you say you care
All I'm really asking sweetheart
Is when I need you please be there

Mattie Simms
LOVE FOR A LIFETIME
Love cannot be measured in
distance and time
It is a deep feeling that has been
many times defined
Will our love last, we are not to
know
But loving you for one minute
has started me to grow.

As I grow I see things in a
different light
I do not ponder on the past that
is behind me
Stammers, stutter, and
shed tears, I do not
For I've grown to know love is
costless, love is free.

One strives for wealth, fortune
and fame
With this power, love has no
remembered names
All of your fortunes, may slide
slowly away
Love is always in ones destiny
it's here to stay.

We seek the world over for a true
love
Stop and think, it all starts from
above
No one in life you will ever have
to pursue
For the love for a lifetime is
within you.

Madelene R Grimm
GROWTH
If growth is through pain, through
tears, through isolation,
Then I have matured beyond my
years.
Must the song of truth be struck
mute to be heard?
Must the heart be forsaken to
discover love?
I have not been isolated without
purpose.
Nor have I been hurt by those who
could not have loved,
had we passed at another time.
I shall wait, for my heart has heard
your song,
My breast has felt your sorrow,
And I, I have given you my love.

Marilyn S Martin
ETERNITYS' ROAD
As the little man walked
with a very slow pace
Down the long road
He had a smile on his face
Suddenly he spoke up in glee
I am walking the road of Eternity
For I am old
And can barely see
I am filled joy
For I walk the road of Eternity
And when I get to the very end
I will be in a beautiful land
A land of flowers and trees
Of youth and health
Where no one will be sickly
Where all will be free
For we have lived our time
And for this we receive
A beautiful gift
Called ETERNITY!

Esther C Foster

Esther C Foster
23RD PSALM (PARAPHRASED)

This poem is dedicated to Marianne, my loving daughter.

The Lord my Shepherd is I know
He gives me what is best.
He leads me where smooth waters
flow
In green pastures where I rest.

He restores my soul in faithfulness
Through each winding path I take,
I walk with Him in righteousness
Where He leads for His name sake.

Even though I tread valley's dark
and deep
No evil will I fear . . .
The Lord my Shepherd, never
sleeps
And He is always near.

His rod and staff they comfort me
When earth friends prove untrue.
He prepares a table where all can
see
What His loving care can do.

The annointing oil with tender care
On my head He freely bestows,
And with His blessings rich and
rare
My cup now over flows.

Surely goodness and mercy follow
me
Where ever I may roam,
Until His blessed face I see
In our eternal home.

Frances E Chicoine
GARDEN IN SEPTEMBER
Today I walked among the garden
rows—
September's touch has tipped each
stalk with seeds
Or pods, disorder reigns, for now

the weeds
Defy June's pattern, as they decompose
Where once the rose and violet dared to pose.
One lone, brave blossom rallies there, and pleads
For a reprieve till Winter's winged steeds
Swoop down to smother her with ice and snows.
How like the changing garden is the mind—
In Spring of life it flourishes and grows;
September finds the paths of mem'ry strewn
With weeds and thoughts we should have left behind!
Today I walked among the garden rows—
Oh, that our minds and gardens could keep June!

Ronald Chatt
REFRESHING THE PLAIN

Soon flowers will bloom
Chasing the blues
And, that's not too soon.

So, forget the pain
Then comes the rain
Refreshing the plain.

A warmer breeze
Will chase the freeze,
With a spring's tease.

Then, grows the grass;
Must buy gas
To trim the mass.

Thirl Michael Butler
DARK FOREST BYWAYS

Mushroom days, dark forest byways,
drift on suntrails. Rainbow birds' song
follows a deer tracks' silent haze.
We creep past red oak vines along

diamond-rippling, rock-strewn streams,
leaping reflections and dragonflies,
flashing broken sunbeams,
rainbow dreams.
Dancing tall trees sway in your eyes.

Baby-tears flow down the creek bank,
a carpet on which we may lie
to whisper in the day and thank
each other with a kiss and a sigh.

Melissa Arnold
TO TINA

For you, my friend—the one who is always there
really showing how much you care
Sticking up for me when others offended me
Understanding my needs and always fulfilling them
Giving me a smile even when you were down
You, the one with golden hair and eyes of hazel
You, the one with a height of 5'8"—
The one who deserves the world
For you, Tina, I give my love and a smile for just
being there

Sandra Simpkins
JOY OF LOVE

I dedicate this poem to my Beautiful parents: My Mother and My Father.

Loving others is a very special thing.
When you love others:
You never know what the harvest may bring.
It may bring Joy!
Joy of Love.
Like the Beautiful clouds in the sky above.
To be loved is very kind.
It soothes the soul, and eases the mind.
The stars in the sky disappear on a sunny day.
Because the Joy of Love is wonderful in every way.
I love to be loved, and loving my friends.
Because love is a word that will never end.

Juliet Marie Grimble-Morris

Juliet Marie Grimble-Morris
BLUE MOONS AND PURPLE STARS

To: My Loving husband, Jimmie and three beautiful daughters, Jennea, Jeniece and Jillian

---

Blue moons and purple stars of make believe
Out of time, out of space, yellow creams
Looking glass upon the wall, who's to say
Here and now, now and then yesterday?

Have the lines crossed the never ending mind?
Doing the undone unkind
Seeping through the willows of the sea
Laughing witches of the make believe

Cruising demons on silver wings, in crying snow
Whisking through the autumn blue, run after me
Conquered time to realize the thoughts you'd know
Receiving creams, receiving dreams of make believe

Blue moons and purple stars of make believe
Out of time, out of space, yellow creams
Looking glass upon the wall, just who's to say
Here and now, now and then, yesterday?

Scott Fredrick Transue
MY MOTHER THE EARTH

For God and my family the world

My mother the Earth
My sister the Moon

My brother the Wind
My friends the Stars
and God.
Never alone,
In a lonely world.

Cynthia F Mullikin
GIVING-HOW MUCH CAN ONE GIVE?

Long ago in Bethlehem, God sent a miracle to earth
And from the seed which grew in Mary's womb, Jesus was
Given birth. In a lowly stable he was born and that day
Since has been known as Christmas morn.
Shepherds and Kings alike, they came from afar, guided
by the brightly gleaming Bethlehem star. In awe they stood
before the manger where the child lay, and with hearts
Filled with love did reverently bow there heads and pray.
They knew that someday this little babe would be, the
King of Kings, Blest redeemer of all lost humanity.
Presented to the Christchild were the first gifts of
Frankenscents myhrr and Gold, knowing someday his
gift to them (eternal life) would far outweigh all riches untold.
From the manger in Bethlehem to the hill of Calvary Christ
went, each moment of this thirty-three years well and wisely spent.
The Son of God gave the greatest gift . . . His life . . . that
from the bonds of sin we could break free and thru
the power in his blood, believe, receive, and with him someday reign eternally.
The supreme example he did set—that deep within
our souls—We know it is better "to give" than "to get!"

Barbara Lynn Calhoun
LOVE LOST

To James Buchanan, Jr. a very sensitive and loving close friend. I have a great deal of love and respect for you babe! Eric Lattin, you're a really sweet person, a true friend!

As I walk along the snow drenched path,
I am deep in thought as nature silently listens.
In the bright sunshine, the snow sharply glistens.
As the frozen leaves crunch beneath my feet.
The winter wind whips briskly through the trees.
Hurriedly up the hill I went.
The forceful hand of the northwind stubbornly pushes me along,
As I hear the faint whisper of a robins sweet song.
In the distance a familiar voice seemed to call out my name,
My body suddenly becomes lame.
Could it be you after all this time?
I stopped in my tracks,
I turned to look back.
There's not a soul around,
No friendly smile to be found.
I look above me and all that I see, is the sky.
I look below me and all that I see,
are two lonely footprints made only by me.
I look beside me and all that I see,
is the image of you walking beside me,
Oh! How I wish it could be!
For there is no one in this world with whom
I'd rather be!

Elsie Zabriski
STATUE OF LIBERTY

Dedicated to My Mother and Father, Deceased. Theresa Abbino Massari, Mrs Marcella Kelpsas and Pete.

Statue of Liberty
Beauty
She stands for freedom
She is 100 years old
Mothers, Fathers and grandparents
And Immigrants too.
Came to this country
for Liberty and Peace
She luminates the Harbor
She stands tall and proud.
There is no queen that
Could match the
Statue of Liberty

Furman Clarke
A PLACE FOR ME

Somewhere, twirling on the horizon of my mind, there is a place for me/
And I will continuously dog its trail, however elusive it may be—
At times, it's almost within my grasp, then suddenly, it's out of sight/
But, it returns again for me to behold, in dreams that comes with night—
And every time it slips away, I will search, and I will search again/
For it has been ordain to be my destiny, to reach my rainbow's end—
There are times, when it seems the more I exert myself, the higher my rainbow soars/
But; I am sure that I can make it there, If, I just stretch a little bit more—

So; I will not let myself become stymid, by pessimismor or even doubt/
Because; everytime I progress an inch, I mature more in what GOD'S about—
I will love my brothers one and all, to where emotionally there's no slack/
And, all I ask of them in return, is, that they should love me back
But; should any of them find it difficult, to put gratitude on display/
It will not matter in the least, I will love them anyway—
I will roll out all of my treasures, all, that I am blessed to hold in bind/
Giving, joyfully, so willingly, in that my heart unfolds my mind—
And, it will never be conceived as sort, that there is a point of giving up/
For, I am so very well aware, of the gracious source that fills my cup—

Myrtle Parker Weaver

OLD MAN

I saw him out there on the desert. Old before his time, because of the hardships, the weather, the struggle for existence.

He could tell you many a story—keep you spellbound—take you into another world, another life, but he is silent. Quiet, still, pondering, thinking.

He remembers when the hills were friendly, some people were friendly; some places were beautiful—unspoiled.

The loneliness is there but he is not lonely. Even in his solitude he is content. I see no bitterness, no hatred, no remorse.

I want to touch his brown leathery face, deep scars and wrinkles—but I dare not! Not because I am afraid of him, but because I dare not intrude upon his meditation.

I know he is a GREAT MAN!—or was.

He is so far away.

Bobbi L McClure

BEST FRIENDS (CHANGES)

This poem is dedicated to Debbie—still one of my Best Friends—even through our changes.

We were the best of friends—nothing came between us.
We shared happiness, sorrow, and every emotion in between.
We weren't ashamed to say, "I love you," it was true then.
Then you changed—or so I said; the
Funny thing is, you said the same about me.
When all along the only one to blame was
Time—time changes everything, everyone.
No matter how far apart we've grown,
Time cannot take away the friendship we once had—
Time cannot change the past.
Deep in your heart, I will always be your best friend,
Deep in my heart, you will always be mine.
Even though we are still friends—we have lost that "Something special" that made us best friends.
We have other friends, and other things to keep us busy, but
We will never be complete again—we will never have another
Best Friend.
Maybe our friendship isn't lost forever,
Maybe we'll find it again—someday.
Most likely we won't, but
Oddly, we have no regrets, because at last
We have grown enough to say:
"I have changed."

Helen Thorbahn Snyder

JUST A POEM

Color poetry, a gift of love,
A giving of one's self;
Perhaps a message from above
To stabilize one's shelf.

A store of solace, anesthesia,
Mortal, transient if you will,
But rather like a bright bouquet
To grace your windowsill.

Ruby B Nuckolls

BABY DAY AT CHATTAHOOCHEE BAPTIST CHURCH

Little babies are such a charm
Perched upon their Mother's arm.
They are our pride and joy
Whether they be girl or boy.
Mother sings a lullaby,
"Baby, go to sleep and do not cry!
Next Sunday is Baby Day
Be Pretty so Grandma can say
'You're the prettiest one in line.'"
As we all pass by feeling fine—
Greeting the babies born the previous year
Along with their families, "blessings of Cheer."
"May God keep you in his care
All through life" is our prayer.

Lester W Clark

THE SEVEN

To the memory of Judith Resnik, Christa McAuliffe, Michael Smith, Ronald McNair, Gregory Jarvis, Francis "Dick" Scobee, and Ellison Ozinaka.

They cast aside the bonds of Earth
and roared into the blue,
The seven who had proved their worth
our Challenger's brave crew.

As millions watched their spacecraft rise
and soar above the sea,
An alien flame of no great size
grew in intensity.

That spark becomes (Oh please God no)
a growing fiery blast.
While seven souls to heaven flow,
a nation stands aghast.

The risks were known, why did they go?
Man's thirst to conquer space.
They dared and died but heroes know,
someone will take their place.

Though they are gone, the quest goes on.
Others will dare the blue.
But we never shall forget them
Our Challenger's brave crew.

For there above that shining sea,
Judith, Christa, and Michael
Reached an immortality with Ron,
Greg, Dick, and Ell . . .

Peggy Vaughn

A GOLDEN SILENCE

Amid the hustle and bustle of a working world—
The cogs of machinery emit a noisy din—
The whining wheels of industry are set in motion—
As though to stifle the spirit within—

Quiet times should not be relics of the past—
Solitude is a great reviver of the mind—
In the pre-dawn hour as the world still sleeps—
A golden silence reigns proud and kind—

To awaken before the world is astir—
This quiet is an awesome thing—
There is a golden beauty in tranquility—
And all living noise loses some of its sting—

Sound is a necessary aspect of life—
And a contribution we all have to render—
The quiet times are the core of existence—
And a golden silence is rewarding splendor—

Buck Graham

A GENTLEMAN

When I was young my Dad would say "A Gentleman could make any woman's mind sway."

That the path to love was to be kind and true.

So as I grew up, I did stride hard for a gentleman to be, hoping all the girls would recognize me.

Later on a wife I did take until I found her heart was a fake, and another man did take my place.

So back to a gentleman was my pace. But now I find I'm lonely and blue, and my mind is really quite confused. For I hear women say they look for a gentleman to come their way. when I ask for a date or two. So they act like they don't know what to do.

Then they date someone else leaving me all blue.

They say I'm too kind for them they just don't know what to do, So now that I'm lonely and blue.

Is it any woner that my mind is confused?

Jane Powell

A DIRGE

Winds sigh in the Cypress
I weep, and weep . . .
Child of my Child
Oh, that I could
lie beside you,
and sleep, sleep
the dreamless sleep.

Mary E D Cantwell

THE VISION

A little Boy, with golden curls
And eyes of deepest blue,
Held in His hands a crown of thorns
That cut Him, and He knew
That deeper thorns one day would be
Inflicted by the throng
Of heartless human beings
To whom He had done no wrong!
The little Heart would be broken,
But He with a sigh or two,
Would whisper to God Almighty
"They know not what they do."

Michael Federika

AT THE SCHOOL DANCE

Dedicated to my friends in school

Perfume pervades the air
Spectacular colors everywhere
Everyone's kept from despair,
By the rhythym of the music.
After two hours without a care,
So, not to appear dour

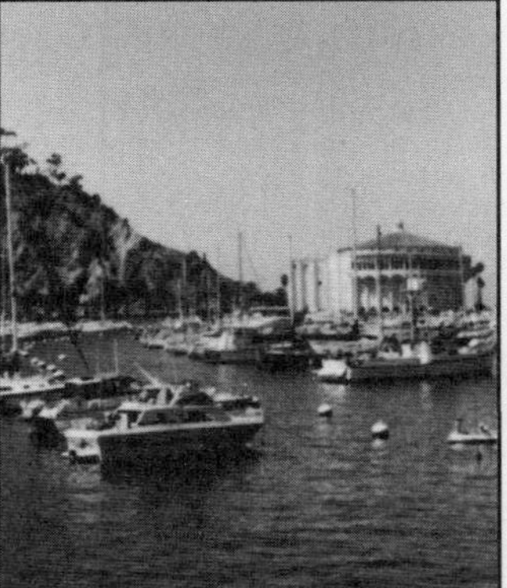

Or maybe a wallflower,
I spot a girl, with whom, a dance
I can share.
The music gives me power.
She looks askance as I ask for a dance,
She takes a chance,
She has beauty and mystique.
I'm in my glory, acting very chic.
Maybe the beginning of a wonderful romance.

Mrs Ida A Walter
MY NEW SONG
If I were to live my life o'er, and do it all over again.
I would not ask for more, I'd just make a new plan.
I'd be the perfect wife, the perfect mother too.
If I had another chance in life, these things I would do.
I'd hug my children every day, My husband I'd love every night.
Ne'er a cross word would I say, I would do every thing right.
To my father and to my mother, all my love I'd express.
To my sisters and to my brothers I would give my best.
To my neighbors I would do good and return all that I borrow.
And give help when I could to those in need and in sorrow.
I would right all my wrongs and do all that I should.
I would sing a "new song" and do only good.
But nobody is perfect, no one does all they should.
Some errs I cannot correct. There is only ONE called GOOD.
Going back thru the years, to my family, my friends and my all.
There were laughter and tears, now some have answered HIS CALL.
I must go on living, I cannot give up.
I'm glad HE is so forgiving, I must give HIM my cup.
Now this is my "new song," I will sing it each day.
"Lord keep me from wrong, Lord show me the way."

Miss Darcy A Hollers
LIFE
Today is Tomorrow's Yesterday so shall it be day's from now.

I'll try my best to say only what I mean, and do only what I should, so that it cannot fall upon me, (the heartache's) of . . . Today, Tomorrow, or Yesterday.

I'll try to live my life day by day, and cherish each and every hour that I shall breath, so that Today, I can look back at memories of Yesterday, and be able to face and live all of my day's to come, all of my Tomorrow's to be.

Dan Anderson
LOST INNOCENCE
We were born to this world, with the power of our Innocence.
But it started to change, with our thoughts first pressence.
That dark power that surrounds us, and strives to take hold.
To be firmly rooted, before we've grown old,
As we start to grow bolder, taught by those who are wise.
The dark veil of evil is cast before our eyes.
We're told to do right, don't get caught if you're wrong,
But in the mind of a child, can this go on for long?
How can they help, but to grow up confused,
with the "do as I say, and not as I do's."
We learn from our elders, who do as they will,
Then take to the streets, where they teach us to kill,
Now the world as we know it, is filled with despair
While the high & mighty just seem not to care.
When life seems unbearable, and you can go on no more
Then you turn deep inside, and close every door.
Your filled with a calmness, and search a bit farther,
Then you know that you've found our Heavenly Father.
As the peace that now fills you, is sent from above
So the power of Lost Innocence is replaced by our Love.

Sue Crabtree Ragan
IN MEMORY OF

This poem is dedicated to the Sutton family in memory of their beloved son Ricky.

Today they're our small babies all cuddily and warm wrapped in our loving arms.
Next day they've grown to be toddlers mischevious, yet full of charms.
Now they've grown into young boys and girls,
Oh how grown up they look in their ties and curls.
In such a short time you've grown into teenagers, dating for the first time, and yes, driving your own car.
Today I watch you, a small baby dreaming of angels while in a peaceful sleep.
Tomorrow I say goodbye and send you off to school so happy your face is beaming.
We watch them come into the world and grow up,
They're our true pride and joy, a beautiful little girl and a very handsome boy.
They've only just begun to live, and it's so hard to let them go, but today God called and made them angels for Heaven above.
With them they take my heart full of love.

Hope Victoria Wellstein
THE LITTLE CHAPEL ON THE KNOLL

"Restoration of Muzzy Memorial Chapel" August, 1975

There's a chapel on the knoll by the oak trees
No lovelier spot could be found—
It's so dear to the hearts of the people,
A gem to the people of our town.

It was built in the year sixteen
The huge sturdy oak became its floor
The pews from the oak their strength did glean
Beauty and strength it has more and more.

The picture of Martha on the wall,
"She was so loved by all who knew her,"
Fond memories are for all to recall—
The painting of Martha on the wall.

Chorus:

The organ so sweetly is calling.
The Bible on the pulpit is there,
O come to the chapel on the knoll,
O come, come to the chapel so rare!

Jessica EurLynne
FOLIATED/VOICES/II
Dust of a star
coat this soul
ringing a desire
  for a black hope.
Longing for a
sun rose sky
  to dance in
and BE with/them/th-
eir hearts joined fo-
r a span of Life: as—
mine . . .
In their earth form
I am becoming
  this being:

/From some long ago
(of a star once?)
never expired
  now a black hole.
Transformation to
some alien day
  to love in
and BE with them th-
eir hearts joined fo-
r a span of Life: as—
mine . . .
I am, Alien now
I have become
  Another's dream/.

Margaret Raspolic
LIVING PICTURES
I'm privileged to be sitting at ease,
Watching tall trees blowing in the breeze,
Seeing flower blossoms burning bright,
Made that way from radiant light.

Buds, too, are glistening like a distant star,
As if I were watching galaxies from afar,
And thin, green leaves are filled with life,
All there to ease my pain and strife.

I'm loved! So why all this weeping?
Living pictures are trying—
to dry my eyes with one grand sweeping.
Peace could be mine for a day or all time,
If only I could remember this rhyme.

Pamela Elaine Tharp
GOD'S PROMISE . . .
Once I was a caterpillar, then a butterfly!!!
I use to crawl around a lot! Now I like to fly!
I crawled around as best I could, to get to where I went;
"Slow as Xmas" they would say, but it was time well spent!
I'd stop along a flower leaf, and warm up in the sun;
Or visit Mr. Worm awhile, and that's when we'd have fun!
We'd race up trees and flower stems, to see who won the race,
With all my legs and fuzzy belly, I had time to waste!!
Soon the day came; it was time for my nap!
When I'd wrap myself up and weave me a cap!
Warm and safe, I slept a long time;
The day I awoke, I was feeling just fine!
Little did I know when I laid down to nap,
That I would grow and grow right out of my cap!!!
I wiggled and I stretched, till I set myself free!
And you'll never guess what happened to me!?!?!?!?!?!?
I looked nothing the same, and had wings of all colors!
Even antennas or something or other!
It didn't really matter what all these parts were,
Cause now I could fly to the ends of the earth!!!
I saw Mr. Worm, and I told him goodbye!
That once I was a caterpillar, but now a butterfly!!!

Tracie Dawn Plaisance
DEDICATED TO THE ONE I LOVE
I see a clear blue sky,
empty of all clouds,
when I look into your eyes.

They're like a deep blue sea
that pulls me in
and holds me so tenderly.

Sweet as sugar is your kiss,
which puts it as number one
on my list.

Thrilling is your touch,
maybe that's why
I desire it so much.

Your smile is like a key,
that opens up the love in my heart
and sets it free.

I love you without a doubt,
because you are
what my life is about!

Daniel Eric Arzola
CHALLENGER
One Florida morning the space shuttle Challenger lifted off the pad.
Then all of a sudden something went bad.
What there was in the sky was nothing but smoke.
There had been a malfunction.
How could the families cope, with the thought that their kin might not be alive.
Then the remains of the space shuttle took a plummeting dive, toward the bottomless ocean

where it will forever hide,
the truth to how this tragedy began.
But we don't give up hope, we search all we can,
for a small trace of evidence, so we can understand,
why there was an explosion which caused such commotion and filled the whole world with the greatest emotion.
But through this confusion we'll always remember the seven who died.
Reach for the stars, that's what they tried!

Sheila Lynn Conary-Thum
I SMELL THE AROMA OF FRYING BACON

I smell the aroma of frying bacon.
I miss you, Daddy.
I hear the sounds of children laughing.
I miss you, Daddy.
I see a boat skim across blue waters.
I miss you, Daddy.
I feel the wind rush through my hair.
I miss you, Daddy.
I hear the sound of an ambulance siren.
Papa, I loved you so.

Eugene J Silveira Sr
SEEDS OF OSMOSIS

I planted a seed on yonder hill,
hoping a fruit would bear
A seed of evolution, motivation
I mated a jackass with a man,
hoping to save mankind
Against all odds, Salvation
I retraced the ladder of life to its furthest ends
Hoping through osmosis to overcome weakness
Man's inhumanity to man, his misgivings and disbeliefs
Hoping is not all we can do
Shake, my friend,
Strength

Mrs Darlene A Bryant

Ms Dianne Marget Bryant
POEM FOR MOTHER

In Loving memory of Darlene Arnold Bryant, A wonderful Mother, Sister, and Friend. You will remain forever in our hearts.

When I was a child still young and bright,
What kept me feeling safe at night . . .
A mother's love.
When playing did cause me an injury,
What vanished my tears away instantly . . .
A mother's love.
And when upon me mischief did shine its light,
What force guided me from wrong to right . . .
A mother's love.

When misfortune had me feeling down,
What lifted my spirits back off the ground . . .
A mother's love.
When growing pains did make their showing,
What gave me the strength to keep on going . . .
A mother's love.
When it seemed a loved one no longer cared,
What made me feel my hurt was shared . . .
A mother's love.

When a solution to a problem I could not see,
What created a feeling of faith in me . . .
A mother's love.
And when I attempt to seek a future endeavor,
What presence will stay with me forever . . .
A mother's love.

It's a kind of love that's genuinely true,
And only given by loving mothers like you . . .
My mother's love.

Jennifer Kuhnemann
STAND-UP STRAIGHT AND TALL

If I were to go away today I would miss very little.
The world is so cruel, it's unbelievable
I don't seem to understand how the world works
Because it sure doesn't work around me.
People come and go not even giving you second thoughts.
They walk over you like you're just another hill in life they
must climb over to get to the top!
You just lay there waiting for the next person
Because by the time you get up to heal your cuts
Down you go AGAIN & AGAIN!
Because people don't care only if they need you to get there.
Don't feel alone if you have been hurt stand up straight and tall.
Tell the people around you, your feeling, make them understand.
Life is mean't to be lived standing up
and not lying on the ground!

Ronald W Sanders
SILENCE

I dedicate this poem to all my loving family: Joe, Marlys, Kevan, Jana, Darby, Jennifer and Adam. Thank you for your love and support.

I arose briskly and went outside my
Tent to chop wood to build a fire
For breakfast.

As soon as the fire was crackling away,
The coffee perking and the bacon sputtering
And popping in the pan, I detected for the
First time in several days, the quiet of the
Woods I had entered, from the clamor of city
Life I was accustomed to.
The tranquility had finally caught up to me
As I stood alone, more alone and isolated
Than ever before in my life, listening to
The sounds of nothing, and yet, of everything
Beautiful . . .

Scarlett Sepulvado
SOLITARY CONFINEMENT

The bricks have been laid one by one
A long job, but it has been done
The cement every one in between
Not quickly, neatly, or very clean.
The formation has been four walls
And on the outside I can hear the squalls
At first it was the other side
But now a fact I cannot hide
Is that it is from deep within
The contents of this lonely den.
The ceiling came much later
The thoughts were its for the better
But instead of better you see
It only made the job harder for me
For now there are reasons beyond control
To escape from the dark and dungeon hole
Now the bricks must be released
And the chains of me unleashed.
But the foundation is deeply rooted
And to me I thought this wall was suited
By other means beyond this world
To trap this person and to hold
All feelings that may lead to hurt
Until the body returned to dirt.

Marilyn Teresa Holubar
DAD

This poem is dedicated in memory of Dad to my Mom.

As I sit here and think about years long ago,
I remember Dad, "He was a carpenter you know."
He wore blue stripped overall's, decorated with tools,
A ruler, a hammer, and nails were his jewels.

In winter Dad wore long john's and a big heavy coat,
Work boots, a cap, and a lunch box he would tote.
Off he went, to build a mighty wood frame,
Once only lumber, then a house it became.

Years of hard labor could be seen on his face,
Steadily working at a never ending pace.
Striving to feed us kids every day,
Never giving up; "A great Dad I would say."

Lisa Lynn Clark
DO YOU BELIEVE IN THE FINAL WAR

In the beginning the story unfolds,
But with the final war, there is no sequel,
Unless everyone takes and holds,
The belief we're all created equal.

So be part of the global reconstruction,
To overcome our primitive hate,
Or burn for nuclear destruction,
It must be this generations fate.

So do you believe in the final war,
Well I know one thing is true,
When all the fighting is done for,
Peace will prevail with or without you.

Lisa A Spargo
WHERE I SHALL BE SOMEDAY

Where the wind and water
freely sway.

Where there's nothing to
do but play.

Where everyone smiles
everyday.

Where everyone wants to
go to stay.

Where fighting and arguing
pass away.

Where I shall be
someday.

c melville sisson

c melville sisson
LEAVING HOME

---

dedicated to sandi-mo

If you must leave my child . . . take this with you . . .
For life's journies will take you to many places . . .
Each one giving you a different perspective of life
And serving as a reference point to help you measure
What lies ahead.

From time to time you will reach a crest that seems to
Offer you more than any place you have ever seen before
And you feel the promise . . .

Follow your heart
With each and every positive thought you can find
And fill your arms with dreams
That you have gathered along the way
For you will need all of these to

find the promises you seek
And . . . if it doesn't work out at first don't be discouraged
For dreams are elusive and few people find everything
They are looking for

So work hard to find the good things for these will be
The foundation for the future and as the journey goes on
. . . Remember that you are not alone and
If wishes and prayers could make it so you would always
Be wrapped in the warmth of happiness and safety.
For the depth of feeling I have for you cannot be measured
Or ever taken away
So carry it with you on your journey. It's not something you
Can take out of your pocket and examine like a coin . . .
But look for it in your heart
For it's the one thing that you can always count on!

Rudolph "Rudi" J Balaban

A CHAUFFEUR'S LAMENT

To my mother, 81, who is ill with Alzheimer's disease, but when in good health used the van to join her friends at the Senior Citizens Center.

They need to use my van
As all Senior Citizens can
To get to the Seniors' Center
And enjoy it with others who enter.

They're all affable
And can even be lovable.

Most of them are widows
Who shun standing at their windows
Needing friends and companionship
Not the often-used nip.

The first to board, 87, is Frenchie
Who, for a decade, has served the coffee.
On Maiden Lane lives determined Bernie
She says she'll never ride a gurney.

I honk the horn for Linda
Who always greets a glad "How are ya."
Next is ever-laughing Polish Mary
On her you can count nothing petty.

And dear old grandma can't be forgotten
With her, you just know, that everything's rotten.
There are many others—not regular
But they all have something quite singular.

Yes, all are affable
And can even be lovable.

Elander Swan

TO MICHAEL TESLER

You told me your name was
Shelly's Best Friend,
You were one of mine.
Though you graced my life for one brief instant,
You were a man of love and wisdom,
And you always will be.
You left me with these words:
In the choice of two
The first you pick
You know you'll lose.
Then why not pick
The second to win?
You were with me one day—your last,
But you'll always be a friend.

The last thing I remember you saying,
"That poem will soon take on new meaning."
Five minutes later you were killed by a drunk driver . . .

Michael, I was in a hurry to go home to eat,
I thought our friendship had just begun:
My second choice was to finish listening
To what you had to tell me.
Had we lingered longer, that drunk would not have
Been there then on your ride home.

My first reaction was to feel guilty:
I couldn't help the frustration,
But I remembered your poem and
Your last words to earthly ears . . .
I feel privileged that I was your last friend.

I will forever love you, my friend . . .
Shelly's Best Friend.

Arend Trent Thibodeau

LOVE IN VAIN

She was just standing in the darkness of the night watching the world go by
She had given up on the realities of life she no longer cared to try
The hope and faith, they had all grown old
The nights were long, they grew lonely and cold
The feeling of happiness was a thing of the past
Once she had felt it but she couldn't make it last
The joys of love and happiness had forever escaped her heart
The bitterness and cruelty of love in vain had torn her soul apart

Susie White

LASTING LOVE

To my loving husband Mike, Who endured the separation from his family, to support us during the lengthy unemployment in our town.

You know I haven't worried
All the time we've been apart
Because I know the love you hold
Is deep within your heart
I know we'll work so very hard
To keep our marriage strong
We'll talk things over tenderly
When ever things go wrong
Oh yes, I know we've paid our dues
But God is our true friend
For all that we have been through
He'll be there till the end.
We mustn't sell ourselves so short
For what we have is grand!
A family we love dearly
We hold within our hand

From this you know "I love you"
This, we can't deny
For if we master this my love
There is nothing we can't try!

C Maggie Coffey

I AM THE VOICE OF THE PEOPLE

To Dustin Lee, Mom, and Mike with Love unbound

I am the Voice of the People.
I speak for the mothers in the words of a child.
I am the sound of boys going away,
and of men coming home.
I am that very same cry in the night
that calls out at dawn clear and loud.
I speak for each of us.

I am the Voice of the People.
I say we stop.
I say we all go home.
Each to his own and his all.
I say we move freely about.
Let those who will help, help.
Leave those who would live alone, alone.
I say the dancers should busy themselves dancing.
Let the bakers bake.
Let the hungry eat and the tired lie down to rest.
Those who like blue may wear blue.
Those who are shameless may run naked,
and the cold may cover themselves.

I say we leave us alone and go home.

Jennifer Danielle Kuhnemann

REMEMBERING

Walking on the beach;
alone.
Everyone has gone
because summer
has.
Thinking of all the people
that came and
went.
Not knowing or even
trying, too!
Memories; remembering
how it was walking
on the beach;
together as
a couple.

Madeline H Rose

Madeline H Rose

MY PRAYER

Please give me thy blessing dear God today
In what I think and do and say,
The sky so blue, the grass so green,
All your beauty in between,
A cheerful smile, a happy thought
Memories that can't be bought.
Please take my hand and hold it tight
and guide me through this day of life,
And at the closing of this day
Prayers of thanks I'll send your way.
Amen.

Janette (Jo) Kiteley

THERE COMES A TIME

There comes a time one must speak out.
No need to shout
No need to yell
It must come with age 'cause now it seems
That all that rage
Is no longer there.
I find myself telling all
"That seems so rare."
If there's a chance
You can't comprehend
It's truly not a glance
Towards <u>an</u> end.
If you flee-(first)-Then I will
(Before you)
—So let it be—
But you won't.
For some crazy reason
You just can't
And you won't
But you must understand
I've got the upperhand
One pat on the shoulder was all it took
To gather all those crazy—For me
Thoughts
On, where I'm headed
And who I'd like to be—
Come

Linda Perkins Jacobson

WHO ARE THE "THEYS"

This day and age is so confusing
"THEY" say you're either an alcoholic or child abusing!
"THEY" say you're exercising too much or not enough
"THEY" say you'd better quit smoking or life ends abrupt!
Taxes are screwed up, heads are in a dither
Suicides are becoming so common, grown men wither!
"THEY" say society put us where we're at today
Anxiety, nervous stomachs—And who, by the way, are the so-called "THEY!"

Nuclear war hanging over our heads
"THEY" say fight for your country but how when we'd all be dead!
"THEY" criticize and analize until your head spins with confusion
Afraid to go to the doctor; there may be Aids in your transfusion!
"THEY" say eat this; don't eat that; you'll die of cancer
"THEY'VE" got you running back and forth but not everything has an answer.
I say: To hell with all the "THEYS" and the <u>do's</u> and <u>don'ts</u>
Afraid to live without living is NO antidote!

Luis M Burton
STATE OF SHOCK

To the memory of the 7 bold Americans whose sacrifice will forever be remembered. To my wife Loraine whose encouragement made it all possible to continue writing.

Millions of eyes gaze towards the sky
as the Challenger makes its way above the clouds so high
90 seconds in flight a sudden explosion
and those eyes gaze in horror and confusion

Students mourn the loss of a teacher so dear
millions expressing sympathy and showing they care
silence from NASA as they search for a specific clue
and havoc among the media as they try to establish the truth

The flag is at half-mast
the torch is lit
mourners passing by to get a glimpse of it
motorists driving with headlights on
and house lights flickering till the break of dawn

Seven bold Americans made a sacrifice
pioneers who would lead America to greater heights
but fate claimed them rapidly
not a trace of them by land nor by sea
So farewell to you my heroic friends
let it be known that you would not have died in vain

Versie Devereux McDaniel
THE MEETING
They stood together at the place where bargains were sold,
One man very young; the other one was very old.

To the old man, the young one suddenly said,
"Do you ever think about being dead?"

For a moment the old man didn't reply.
He seemed to have something in his eye.

Then he answered with a whimsical smile,
"Yes, I do, every once in a while."

The young man then said, "I'm young but you are old.
My blood runs warm but yours runs cold.

Soon I'll go and get a job in the town
And marry a pretty girl with eyes of brown.

I'll work very hard throughout the day.
Then, at night I'll just love, laugh, and play.
Perhaps some day success and riches will be.
Now, old man, don't you really envy me?"

The old man looked toward the setting sun,
For he knew that the day was nearly done.

So, with a sigh he said to the lad,
"All your hopes and dreams I've already had.

The things that you have done or will do,
I have done them all: I am you!"

James L Kincaid
MY DARLING I MISS YOU
Oh my darling I miss you with all my heart.
Ever since you left me my heart is lonely and sad for I loved you
When you walk down that long lonely path, walk slowly for some day you will hear me calling you.
I will always remember the love we had for each other, and there will always be a lonely spot in my heart
Every time I think of you I will always walk in the memories of you,
Oh my darling I will come back to you some day.
Even tho the tears fall I will always remember the love we had for each other.
Oh darling walk slowly down that path?
So I will know you are looking for me.
Good-by my love until we meet again on that long—lonely path my darling.

Antoinette A Bell

Antoinette A Bell
FOG
A dense fog has crept over the city
Everyone is hiding in the weather
A jazz tune trumpets out melody so pretty
Could we find each other lost in grey
Occasionally there are some bright-colored
mittens or a fancy cravat
I see your image, in the white puffs of cream,
to this somber day

The atmosphere drips frosty rivulets of water
Hot, tense memories penetrate my demeanor
My balance is weak and I totter
Could we again drink fragrant tea and eat "Chinese"
A bus splashes its gusty reservoir my way
Is that you in the distance through the park's trees

The sun will dry out this mystery
Tomorrow I will follow my organizer's plan
The chill of night is now like some evil
wizardry
I reach my steps at dawn
It should be a lovely day
My plans here, somewhere, as I sleep on . . .

Joann Gifford Spiker
ODE TO A COMPUTER TUTOR?

To my two daughters, Linda Marie and Karen Jean, the true gems and treasures in my life . . .

I went to my local library to find a book I could carry
To class on microcomputers, but I'll need my own private tutor
I go/B@(Blank) or even worser, with Ram and Rom, I'm the cursor
The buzz words, tho I try to rabble, are my modern day Tower of Babel
And while "HANDS ON" is truly the teacher . . . .
I'm half afraid of this creature
Trying hard not to delete or get beeped, with its silent and superior grace,
My syllabus falls flat . . . on my Data Base . . .
With a /WH@ *to a /WVA@*,I jump from window to window, but with a
/GC (A20)@and (— & —)! What would you do ?????
Software, Hardware, an eight or a sixteen byte . . .
In desperation !!!! I reach for my "Nikes" . . . cause . . .
From in there, somewhere, "I" get the command, that I'm an also ran!
That by labels, (A1 + *B17)*, and values (+*A1* +*B17)*,I must be judged, "oh fudge"
"Hands on" , "Hands off," the Apple of my cry, "You'll learn," I tell myself
As eons go by ZZZZZZZZZZZZZ
To understand all is but a dream, Alas! I'm sitting at the wrong machine!!!
With merciful coup de' grace, is this egg upon my face?!?!?!???
As I file my record in a field, waiting to see what spring will yield,
I silently sank, my characters —— "Blank" and ——
To retrieve my self esteem, I quickly "Xed" my memory . . . .
And beheld xxxxxxxxxx an empty screen !!!!!!!!
My words wrapped around ****** automatically! and tho not all were noble
When last seen and heard was screaming, "Motto! Global, Global."

Rita F Fredrick
NURSING HOME
Memories float on the ebb tide—
advancing, then retreating
a little more each time.
Wheel chairs are like sail boats
anchored in the harbour
safe from the storm.

Ruth Ward
STAND BY ME
Stand by me when times are bad.
When we think about the things we had.
How carelessly we let them slide
Out to where love no longer abides.

When things were good, we took and took
And never gave thought to what we forsook.

As life goes on I realize one fact
That life is a play with only one act.
Never forget the part you play
As the curtain goes up day by day.
Live and love and be put to the test.
If you pass the test of life.
You'll know it was worth the strife.
Someday you will understand
To be with you is my only demand.

Louise Gooden
NATURE'S SHOW
The old man stood on top of the hill
And watched as the sun peeked over.
Everything around was so silent and still
Waiting to see what the sun would uncover.
The birds, in their nests, awoke with the first breeze,
And squirrels were running up and down trees.
All in a hurry to get on with their day,
To gather food and then to just play.
Butterflies were dancing from here to there
And bees hummed their news of flowers to share.
Ants marched by all in a long row.
Everything seemed to have somewhere special to go.
Wild flowers moved like shadows in the wind,
They'd bend their heads low and pop up again.
Frogs in the pond jumped from one spot to another,
And fish seemed to play games of tag with each other.
All of God's creatures, large and small,
Dressed in nature's best as if going to a ball.
We're putting on a show for the sun to see.
Each seemed to say, "I'm glad to be me."
As the sun dimmed and slowly shut out its light
All the animals went home to rest for the night.

Only the old man was still standing
there alone
And he, too, turned, and started
towards home.

Frederick Brugge
AUTUMN

To my wife, Maria

October's amber afternoons,
The musty tang of fallen leaves
Rustling round my feet, a tattered
carpet
Scattered with the wind.
Half-hearted twitterings of
mockingbirds
Exhausted from the summer
heat.
Persimmons golden-red
Among dark branches shine
Like pendant lanterns in the night.
A headiness of air and light
More rarified and sensuous
Than summer's fierce
endearments,
The forlorn ornaments
Of a courtesan no longer young.

Carrie Debra Alexander

Carrie Debra Alexander
A NEW DAWNING

To my FATHER above and my mothers: Elizabeth, Mary, Myrtis in Georgia; Ellen and Mary in Indiana. Friends in faith: Renee and Floyd in Indiana and Charles and James of Georgia.

As this new horizon dawns
I'm a captive of its haze
Arising slowly to heights of
controlled feelings
Of
Uncontrolled acquiring thoughts
that slightly
Touch
The nucleus to retrieve my
awareness
Only
To be released to find my place in
the universe

Ginger Hamilton
TOMORROW
One morning
you'll awake
to find
all your Yesterdays
are gone
and left behind . . .

Only Tomorrow
will be in sight
to keep you
smiling
all through the night . . .

But . . .
if you don't learn
to give your heart . . .
Today
and
Tomorrow
will all be gone
and leave you
only in sorrow . . .

Jeanne Marie Wamser
MOM, OUR MOTHER

To Luella Carley, my mom, who did without . . . so us kids could have . . .

One day as we sat down together,
Talking of things long ago,
Laughing and smiling together,
We passed comments to and fro.

We came upon a subject,
One agreed on with both of our
hearts,
A person who binds us together,
A person we've loved from the start.

Mom, our Mother, we love you.
You accept us as we are.
You smile, you care, you love, you
share,
Our thoughts from you are not far.

We'll call her our tower of strength,
We'll call her the hub of the wheel,
Without her love and forgiveness,
Our world just wouldn't be real.

Our tower of strength, our hub of
the wheel,
She kept us from hurt and from
harm.
She worked to make us a family
and a home filled with love, that
was Mom.

Pauline Kohlmetz
TRY
I'll try not to cry
When I know it's goodbye.
As I know you're mine
To the end of time.
Which is yours and mine.

I'll try not to cry
Knowing our drive.
To put aside all our sighs,
Our love is in the high drive.
I'll never let loose of our ties
As we are yours and mine.
To the end of time.

May God bless us all.

Melinda Miller Butler
A PICTURE
You can paint a picture however
you choose the audience.
How much of the scene is true or
fiction?
How we twist the scenes of life into
a providence.
Then convince others of that
notion.

And in our words of such an art,
We paint the colors light or dark.
And who's to say which character
is preditor or prey.
And in how many minds it will stay.

Patricia Everett
LIGHT
Like a child
that finds a penny
in the rain
Lord, you've brought
happiness to me
in life again
Drowned my tears in
rainbows of light
Taken me out of the
dark, deep night
To see
sunlight again
Like a child
that finds a penny
in the rain

Beverly Robinson

Beverly Robinson
NOW SHE TOO

This poem is dedicated in the memory of my mother, Vava Wilson Robinson

---

She sits in her chair and reads
books,
To pass the time of day.
The lamp sits beside her on the
round table,
Made for her on her fourteenth
birthday.
As she closes her eyes she sees an
image,
Of her mother on a cool spring
day.
Her mother always looked gay,
And young for her age.

A tear flows down her face as she
remembers her mother,
Who has long since passed away.
Now she too has become old with
age,
Her hair is gray and her face is
wrinkled.
The days grow shorter
As she becomes older with age.
Now she too will go through time,
Until she too has long since
passed away.

Florence Frank
LUCY REMEMBERS

Dedicated from a nurse to all the elderly in Nursing Homes who are lonely.

Nobody feels sorry for me you say
as you sit in your chair and cry
again today.
"I cooked, I cleaned, I did
everything you see
for all of my kids now just look at
me—
Here I am all alone and so sad,
What did I do wrong, did I raise
them bad?"

Lucy, comfort for you is what I
must find
But your words keep on going over
in my mind
What you say is oh so true
But if I agree I will make you more
blue.

Lucy, I cooked and I cleaned and I
did everything as you
I gave up my life but it meant
nothing to my two
All my hard work and effort it
seems
Went down in disappointment, for
them I had dreams.
They grew up and ignored all that
I'd gave,
It's my life they say—It's how I
want to behave!

To Lucy, what I must say is please
do not cry!
You Did your best, you gave your
best try.
Try not to dwell on your sorrow
inside,
Look for joy around you on the
outside.
Be happy for each day you are
given from above
and remember I am your friend
and you I do love!

Stephanie Derringer
THE WILL OF GOD
Death is to me waking up one
morning and finding out someone
you
love isn't there anymore. But deep
down
in your heart you know that it was
for
the best. You know that GOD
wanted it to
be and that she was in a better
place,
than this earth could ever be. You
also
know that your day will
come, when like she did, you will
be called
to GOD'S kingdom. But you're also
feeling the
pain of losing someone close,
someone
special. You don't fully understand
why GOD had to take her away
from you.
Sometimes you take your anger of
losing
someone and blame it on GOD,
friends, family
and sometimes even yourself.

Jean Ruggiero Cascio
I'M ONLY A MOTHER

This poem is dedicated with all my love to my son, Robert

Life is filled with ups and downs,
filled with sorrow, filled with frowns;
What's a smile, I cannot say,
except for that one most special day.
You gave me back what I needed most,
a reason to live—a reason to boast;
When you grow up I'll say aloud,
thank you son—you've made me so proud.
For me your love compares to no other,
just understand my mistakes—
I'm only a Mother.

Ola Hand Albea
A BEAUTIFUL LIFE (Matthew 5:8)
I stood at the bedside of a friend the other day,
And watched her gentle loving soul steal silently away,
And as I saw God's glory shining from her lovely face,
I knew that God did keep His own and give us dying grace.

She never murmured or complained about her pain and strife,
Though blind her eyes, she always saw a need in someone's life,
And stretching forth her hand to God in sweet humility,
She seemed to bring His presence near to fill that need for me.

I did not see the furrowed brow or note the lines of care,
I only saw the life she'd lived and knew that God was there,
And as I held that wrinkled hand I prayed so earnestly,
That I might be to someone else what she had been to me.

Hilde Huckelbery
LOVE, WHERE ARE YOU?
Love, where are you?

Please feed my hungry heart
I am alone in a much too busy world

Love, where are you?

I cry to heaven: Please, God,
Hear my pleas
Comfort the ache and longing in my heart
I long to feel you, touch you
Lonely is the world I'm in

Love, where are you?

Fill the gap inside of me
Take, the loneliness away
Dry the tears in my eyes
Give me a sense of belonging

Love, where are you?

Unfold in my heart
Let me give more to others
Make my dreams come true

Love, where are you?

J M Lambert
SERVANTS
Every morning provides a new chance
New minutes
New hours
Unfulfilled and waiting
For someone to use them
To bring them to life
They await your desires
To fuel your dreams
They seek your attention
They hunger for action
For you're in control
Unless you don't act
And yet even then
With a forgiving hand
They return the next day
To receive you again
Time servants to man

Ellen Pederson
MY HUSBAND
Hold me close, I need you—
The world's been cruel today.
You give me strength when I have none—
To fight the wrong that has been done.
Without your love to guide me—
I'd be a lost, lost soul.
The pain that I have caused you—
Will tear always at my heart.

I know what you have been through—
I've seen it in your eyes.
And today I need to tell you—
From the bottom of my heart.
My love for you is something—
People search for all their lives.
It will always, always be there—
As life goes on for us.
And I only hope that I can too—
Give back that strength you've given to me.

Edna M Smith
MY FIRST GRANDSON
Just as the day was dawning,
Just as the night took wings;
A tiny little baby boy
Landed on angel wings.

He landed right smack on my heart,
It will never be the same;
My first grandson—this little man
And Eric is his name.

So fair of face and form is he,
With eyes so heavenly blue,
And in his smile I see his Dad
When he was still brand new.

Thank you, God, for this precious gift,
My son now has a son;
God bless this home and keep them close,
And God bless my first grandson.

Anthony J Agresta Ph D
TO BE WITH YOU
To be with you
In every moment,
We must hold the night,
And mourn the day,
We must part!
To be with you
In fragrant delights,
Holding you close,
As we begin to part.
The night forms the day,
We must part!
To be with you
In love's dreams.
Never the day,
The night curtains
Our rapture.
Hold back the day,
We must part!
To be with you
In our Love's dilemma.
My arms hold the dawn.
Our divine inspiration,
The moment of light,
Love's anguish begins,
We must part!

B Joan D'Angelo
MISSY PRISSY BLAIR
Missy Prissy Blair
Your long dark hair
Slightly wavy, slightly so
Beneath a straw hat, shimmering, glimmering flow
Frothy pink dress, all lacy and bright
Lacy pink socks and shoes so white
Missy Prissy Blair
Your nose in the air
Laughter on your face, a smile so sly
I see you, you caught my eye
Wish I could hug, wish I could squeeze
Your dark eyes how they tease
Your just a picture, that's all
Just a picture on the wall
From my misty eyes falls a tear
How I long to have you near
Missy Prissy Blair
So far away in old Santa Claire
As you play in the sand, as you play near the water
Stay happy, be well, you ought'a
If now and than you think of me
Let it be a happy memory

Lena M Reedy
APRIL
April is a month of dreams
Of magic nights—enchanted days,
Of sleepy rivers—silver streams
And over all a witching haze.

April is a month of love
Of laughing eyes and singing hearts,
The knowing stars, so close above
Wink down and magic starts.

April is enchanted dreams
Laughter, love and youth
When all the world an island seems
Where fantasies are truth.

And may no disillusions mar
The dreams you now hold dear
And may your faith be greater far
When April comes each year.

Henrietta Parker
FREEDOM
Am I free, free at last
The nigger said to me
No more toiling, from dawn to dusk
Cause in America there's opportunity.

The man then yelled, colored and free
No more chains that he could see
He worked all day, and studied at night
For he had a dream, things would soon be alright.

So he worked even harder, then he realized
Colored men got nothing, so then he got wise
I'm black and I'm proud, I'm proud and I'm free
I've given my blood, for this democracy
I've paid my dues, I've paid my tide
And justice is standing by my side
So when I knock, at the door
It's going to swing open, cause I'm colored no more.

I'm black and I'm proud, ain't asking no favor
Cause one thing for sure, I know how to labor
I'll study real hard, and then when I've learned
Go into the world, for the respect I have earned.

No more hand outs, not for me
I'm black and I'm proud, but above all I'm free.

Delbert Victor Dotson

Delbert Victor Dotson
THE MAN IN THE MOON
The man in the moon's in a terrible fix:—
He's doomed through eternity to gather up sticks.
He burned trash on Sunday, of course 'twas a sin,
And that is to blame for the fix he is in.
The court told the culprit, "It may take some time
To figure a punishment in line with your crime."
But it didn't take long for the court to decide:
"You'll build us a trashpile eleven miles wide.
And it is our verdict—we've decided it's fair—
That by 'eleven miles wide', we mean 'eleven miles square'.
But not 'til you've finished will you get to stop—
When it's a mile and a half from bottom to top."

"It won't take me long," said the man, with a grin,
"Just let me at it, I can't wait to begin!"
But in spite of his manner, in spite of his grin,
In spite of his efforts, he just

couldn't win.
For he had a mania, this bad, silly clown,
He would build up a pile and then burn it down!
He would work with a vengeance, any rest he would spurn,
If, while he was raking, he could watch a pile burn.
So, the man in the moon's in a horrible fix:—
He's doomed, through eternity, to rake and pile sticks!

And you, who are skeptic, go, look up tonight,
You'll see him there, toiling, if the moon's shining bright.

J C Barrows
THE SECRET OF THE GOLDEN FLOWER
Above the mountain soaring
seeking his companion
little white dove.

Below the heavens listening
intently to the message
old, blind man.

Little dove, fly above
Fly into the sun.
Blind man, take a stand
learn to see the one.
understand the one.
Become one.

Somewhere in a garden
surrounded by the water
sweet, golden flower.

Elizabeth Hoppe
NOW AND THEN
I thread my needle
I must sew with care
The fabric so worn
Afraid it might tear
The pattern has faded
Once so bright
I must be careful
Not to stitch too tight
No one will notice
If worn with a smile
The stiffness turned to softness
Has made it worthwhile.

Mary K Williamson
MARSHMALLOW DELIGHT
The snow sifts down so lovely and white,
Creating a scene of Marshmallow Delight.
It's pleasant to watch through my window pane
As it purges the land scape of all grime and stain.
The day wears on, flakes continue their falling,
Now the snow is quite deep, it's really appalling
How our welcome for the snow has turned a bit sour,
And grows even more so, hour after hour!
The wind, it has risen, we're having a blizzard,
It's enough to scare one right out of his gizzard!
Schools are dismissed. And they've cancelled all meetings,
Messages hit the air-waves through "C-Bers" greetings.
Snow plows arrive and they'll work half the night
Making paths that send flying this, "Marshmallow Delight!"
But thus is it ever when Winter rolls 'round,
We get rather anxious to see snow on the ground,
For it changes the scenery, this soft, downy stuff
To a picture of Serenity—but enough is enough!

Diana Stanton Minsky

Diana Stanton Minsky
LADY MOON

I would like to dedicate this poem to a real lady . . . My Mother . . . Edith Stanker.

Oh! Lady of the Moon
Your face is star struck!
Your eyes sullen . . .
Your cheeks billowy.

You rest on the beams
And shadows!
Oh! Lady of the Moon
Come light the balconies
Of love!

Your silhouetted profile
Luminescent in secrecies.
Like the Mona Lisa's smile.

The Sun nor the evening star
Can't compare to the
Light of the Lovely . . .
Lady Moon!

Joseph E Kupka
CULTS
Cults insidiously lure lonely lads and lasses,
Brainwashing them to ensure mindless masses.
They promise and preach peace, love, immortality,
But enslave and bond them to absolute authority.
Creatures of fleeting fads and cultural whims,
These youths are hopeful, helpless, pathetic victims:
Closed, closeted, crippled mimics,
Marred, maimed, moored serfs,
Seared, scarred, scored boors,
Blinded, bullied, boggled pariahs,
Pierced, pared, pruned roses,
Robbed, raped, reversional dolts,
Dumbfounded, duped, doped fools,
Fixated, fleeced, flimflammed toads.
They are tethered to totalitarian sects,
Perversions of those in religious texts.
They are governed by godless gurus, masters
Of amassing money, assuming a gamut of powers.
Glutted, gorged, greedy gangsters and grifters,
Cults build quasi monuments, temples and towers.
Truth told, they telegraph their trumped-up goal:
Anti-God, anti-good, anti-man, and anti-soul.

Patricia Louise Morgan
ALWAYS
A Man I have known in many bodies but only one soul.

A Man, Oh Yes!
A GIFT from GOD, perhaps.
But Oh, He is so much more.

He is Joy and Peace to My tired being,
Sunshine and Warmth to My Soul.

He is One I have searched for Oh! so long
One to make my life complete.

He gives Me joy beyond measure with just a word,
A touch, A smile.

That Smile has been known to melt my Soul, and
make my heart fly like an Eagle free.

His Soul has been intwined with mine for many
Millenniums or so—We sharred this since the
beginning of time and will till evermore.

A Man, Oh Yes!
A GIFT—Perhaps!
BUT ONE I WILL NOT LET GO.

Dorothy Mendosa Decker
THANK YOU GOD
My days are full of wonder, of how I came to be,
A nose to smell, ears to hear and eyes that I might see.
A mind to think, a heart that beats, a mouth that I may speak,
A face that smiles, and hands to reach out, to people on the street.

It must be some great miracle from someone high above
A miracle beyond the skies, a miracle of love.
That miracle must be God, for who can be so caring,
As one who knows our every needs, our sorrows and our yearnings.

My life, my all, I give to Him, I praise and give Him Honor,
I know that He is coming soon, for heaven's around the corner.
Thank you God, for making me, a part of your great glory,
I pray that I may live, to tell the wonderous story—
Of how I came to be.

Daniel DeForrest Laughlin
SONNET II
Though love and warmth just blossom in the heart
The cold blade doth its harvest cruelly reap
Before life's joyfulness can fully start,
And bring the strong and make them sadly weep.
To snatch and crush as if a killing frost
That comes and smites the newly budding rose.
Over the Dark Sea thou so easily crossed
To the distant Isle where all life goes.
From tight arms thy self did swiftly fall
To depths beyond mere mortal beings sight
Where no voice could thy gentle love recall,
Nor any mind thy sorry fate could fight.
Yet why mourn this passing to the unknown
For only from the living comes a moan.

J C Kitsch
THE BAD MAN
I know the way you watch me,
I hear the way that you laugh at me,
you sit on your throne in your dark land,
and wait for me as you sit there smiling
with fire in your eyes and a stone for a heart.
You will pull and grasp at my soul for eternity
because you feed on the souls of the weak.
There is no place for me, even in death,
you will be with me for I have set my own destiny,
when I choose the bad side of society of violence,
killing and cheating mankind of its vast beauty,
for I will dwell in the evil gates of hell forever,
for I am the bad man.

Mr Berdeen Oland

Mr Berdeen Oland
HOMELY GIRL
Lord, let me love a homely girl
Whose hair is straight without a curl

Whose nose is large and out of place
With lots of freckles on her face.

Let her be fat or very thin
Sometimes with a foolish grin,
Let her eyes be blue or brown
The plainest girl in town.

But let her heart be kind and good
And treat all others as she should,
Then soon her face will lovely grow
When these old eyes have made her so.

Rena Faye Hegenbarth
THE BEAUTY I ONCE KNEW

In Memory of my daughter Regina A. Campbell (Young)

Yes, God gave us faith and to believe.
What we must cherish, but not grieve.
Our heart's ache, for our lost.
I feel in my heart, what I can not say.
For the lost of ones, I can only pray.
Believe I loved you every day.
OH! How I wish you could stay.
But only memory's; of you each day.
For all that's left me, every day.
You were my friend, in every way.
But to this day, I can't understand,
Why He took you away.
You were such a beauty, so I guess,
He needed you to help with His duties.
They say it's beautiful and graceful there.
Oh! Honey, you are so fair and very rare.
There's no one like you there, with your
blue eyes and your blond hair, Oh beauty, you're there!

ToniJoy Robin
THE LORD IS MY STRENGTH

The Lord is my strength, His Power is in my soul.
And when we choose to follow Him, only then are we whole.
His wisdom always guides me, His love sees me through.
And I know He is always with me, in everything I do.

Loran Allen
SPRING

Thanks to my Mother—who loved & shared the joy of poetry.

Spring—
Blooming, fickle
Child of nature.

Born of winter's
icy clime.

Gentle guardian;
Cruel assailant—

Mother of
Sweet Summertime.

Laurie A Bullock
ONE'S THEORY

There once was a man who came back from Vietnam, had trouble in growing up, you see,

"As I grew up," he began while he stood by his Sedan, with only one leg short to the knee. "How anyone can get by, to be able to deny, that war in life is the key."

It's true he's mislead, on the fact (that I dread), that war only makes you free.

It's hard to believe how people can be deceived, on a theory that is so untrue.

I said, "Love conquers all," and I felt so tall, as I stood on one leg, but two.

Kristy Jones Kohler
LOST INNOCENCE

The bud—florescent—
—a fluent scent—
admits a virgin interest—
nameless—intent—

The bee—influenced—
—by the buds entire—
inflamed—seduces—
with mad desire—
—the flower

And the bud—enraptured—
—by the bee—
lazily admits—to me—
—lost innocence.

David Ryan Tilley
GOLD AND ICE

Two women: one with a heart of gold
and the other with a heart of ice
I chose the latter, not thinking twice.
Now I can feel the biting cold.
It holds me fast and won't let me go.
I want my spirit to soar in the sky,
but that feeling—I'll never know
until the day I die.
If I had only made the right choice
then my soul would be free
and everyday I could rejoice.
But it's too late for me,
so listen close and take my advice.
"You can not warm a heart of ice."

Kimberly L Russell
A YOUNG GIRL'S PAIN

To the loving, supportive people: especially my husband, who stood by me and held me up during a difficult time.

Sleep was close as I snuggled in bed,
I heard the steps creak,
My small body filled with dread.
The door opened and my father came in,
I tried to fake sleep and hide under the cover . . .
Again.
That never worked, he'd climb in behind me,
I'd stiffen up and hope he wouldn't like me.
I was lost as his hands began to roam,
Wondering why this had to be my home.

He pushed and he wiggled
Until he was through,
Without a word he would leave,
Oh, what could I do?

I trembled and cried
For quite a few years,
Remaining silent . . .
Until now,
And still shedding tears.

Margaret T Deppish
MOTHER'S LOVE

This poem is dedicated to Barry Manilow and his mother, Edna and in memory of my mother.

Hold your mother's love tightly.
Keep it close to your heart.
Always remember a mother's love is special.
For there's no other love greater.

Hold your mother's love gently.
Caress it softly to your heart.
Return her love with special care.
Tell her you love her often.

Hold your mother's love brightly.
Never let the light flicker.
The warmth of her love will be with you forever.
The flame will help you through every time.

Hold your mother's love softly.
Deep within your heart.
There it will stay even when you can
no longer feel her loving touch.
The memories will be happy ones.

Sarah Richardson
LOVE FLOWER

My mother Julia Boddie

Your love is like a flower,
that blossoms like a rose,
will never die or grow old,
for it's rooted deep in my soul.

Demova K Beach
THOSE WERE THE DAYS

In memory of: My Mother and Father: Ruth and Gale Mobley

A big white house, some chickens and cows,
An orchard, a garden, some strawberries too,
Tea roses, sweet peas and pansies blue,
This was our home when I was younger than you.

Me, in my bright red dress and high button shoes
and curls from a curling iron too,
Big brother in knickers and rompers for a brother small,
A player piano playing "Over the Waves,"
Believe me my child, those were the days.
Roller skates, jacks, marbles, and jumping ropes,
School and church picnics with all the pies and the cakes.
With our friends and relations, those were the days.

Our memories are sweet as we recall the pleasures we
knew,
I hope your memories will be as good too,
Oh! Those were the days.

Roberta Clarke Eaton

Roberta Clarke Eaton
TWISTED AND BENT

This poem is dedicated to Mrs. Ronald Reagan, "First Lady of the Land." I sincerely hope it has been instrumental in your anti-drug crusade across America.

O Lord, we live in fear of an UNCONTROLLABLE ghost
Deliver us from the depths of this devouring host.
Having NO limitation—he continuously roams
Striking, like a savage, through schools and homes.
Devoid of all boundries, this villain doth creep
Setting the scaffold for a requiem sleep.

As Crack seduces our children of today
Tomorrow, such a tragic price we'll pay.
This Diabolical Denizen of the Deep
Relinquishes our nation to lament and weep.
He engulfs our children and leads them astray
Strewing a pathway of sorrow and decay.

These once wholesome bodies
—NOW—twisted and bent
What be the reason? An Experiment?
We thoughtless mortals ever blind to fate
Can't we see that these drugs assassinate?
This Vampire of death storms violently through our land
Leaving silhouettes of tragedy with his epidemic plan.

Hallucinogenic drugs—will they ever decrease
So this world can live in harmony

and peace?
Alcohol paralyzes, terrorizes and agonizes
And to its victim, it offers NO compromises.
'Tis an all out struggle and perpetual fight
Stabilizing this crippling parasite!

Diet pills or Valium taken by prescription
Can also lead to dreaded addiction.
Doctor's GIVE Valium, so we think it's alright
But if we're addicted—it's a survival fight.
When seeking an end to the perfect thrill
Remember Amphetamines and Alcohol definitely kill.

Caught in the frenzy to curb its use
We must be educated on drug abuse.
Marijuana runs rampant throughout our land
Unite with me and let's all take this stand
Please, put your principles on the line
In order to halt the drugs and the crime.

The Prince of Death prowls the earth worldwide
If we are snared in his clutches—it's suicide!
These pushers and users lie sly and smug
Voraciously waiting to sell us their drugs.
And if we partake in their merchandise
It will certainly lead to our demise!

I grieve for the spirit declaring defeat
For many will return to the ways of the street.
Lord, give us the ambition to MOTIVATE
The wisdom to EDUCATE
The desire and the will to participate
Then together—WORLDWIDE—we'll celebrate!

Bennie Cheely
FREEDOM

People fight and die for it every day.
Some abuse it in every way.
To those that has never had, they dont' miss it.
People who's had it never forget it.
Some believe their ways are the best.
For me freedom beats all the rest.
When our rights are set upon,
It's war that we fight and fight alone.
The rights to do as you wish.
To hunt when you want or even fish.
To be a doctor, lawyer, or a lumber jack.
To always walk forward, and never look back.
To do the things you don't want to forget.
To do these things without regret.
Freedom means these things to me and many more.
Thats why when they try to take it, we the people get sore.
To go to war in a far off land.
For their freedom we understand.

John E Faust
A SMILE AWAY

For Vee, and Wayne; Always a smile away

Endless ages ago
or so it seems,
time was of the essence.

Endless ages ago
or so I remember,
you were just a smile away.

I've given up on the counting of days,
and my dreaming
has long ago ceased.

All of the poems that I once wrote
lie buried in the dust of time.

Once time was kind and warm;
and together we grasped for moments,
only to find that the moment was gone
the instant we blinked an eye.

Endless ages ago,
I think that's when it was . . .

Endless ages ago,
how hard now to remember . . .

Ah yes . . .
you were just a smile away.

Jane Marrazzo Tortorello
BETWEEN THE DARK AND THE DAYLIGHT

Twilight casts its ghostly shadows over me,
Am I afraid of what is beyond?
The day I have already faced,
but these lengthening shadows,
what do they forecast?

So I wait,
in expectancy of what, of whom?
Bewitching, the vapors form figures,
yes and no.
Do I see beseeching hands,
trying to give me a message?

Twilight your gossamer cape
cloaks me in sadness,
cloaks me in fear,
cloaks me in pain.

How cold I feel!

Joyce Franklin
JESUS! OH! WHAT A FRIEND!

To Grandma who shares her faith with me.

Just when we're ready
To give up life
And have so much strife
He gives us strength to
Carry us through.
With him, all our skies
Will be blue.

He healed my duchess
And gave her strength to her.
He'll give us our
Lives in length.

This may seem a
Simple poem to you
The only kind I write.
But I believe in the Lord Jesus
Believe in him with all your might.

Jimmy Clay
SHADOW MAN

In the land of heartbreak,
There is a city called Despair.
In the streets of Despair,
There stands the shadow man.

Neither black nor white,
neither rich nor poor,
Neither humble nor proud
is the shadow man.

The wife of the shadow man is sorrow.
His children are Mystery, Fear, War
and Hate.
The shadow man.

He is the forgotten friend.
He is the stranger in the cold, night wind.
He is the love abandoned.
He is the oppressed—
The shadow man.

He is a coward; he is a hero.
He is always forgotten,
The shadow man.

For, you see, he is not
The man that is,
But the man that might have been,
He is the shadow man.

Joan M (Roberge) Nelson
CURRENT

Sparrows feed their greedy young,
While morning mist doth lift the sun,
and each breeze blowing catches flight,
as through the branches twists the light.
Oh mighty oak with back bent low,
Impervious to friend or foe,

With banches dipped in water flowing,
ever echoing, ever knowing,
and underneath the water tranquill,
Stirs a current ever fretful,
Changing swiftly, sometimes tearing,
er relenting, never caring.

Barbara Faye Duncan
CHILDREN

To my children: Terri, Vince, Sherri, and Donny—for all your love and inspiration.

From heaven comes the blessing of children
their spirits and lives are given
to do the best we possibly can
to love and teach them right from wrong

Raising them right is our deepest fear
for we only have them a few short years
so many joyous memories we pack away
trying to teach them along the way

Over the road of life's ups and downs
seeing their smiles, tears and frowns
laughing at their good and crying when bad
and so a mother's love never ceases.

It only continues to withstand and increases
each child is different
because of this each is loved in a very special way
but children have a way of questioning

So each mother has to hope and pray
that someday each child will know and can say
"Thanks, Mom, for loving and raising me the way you did."

John Zimmer
TIME

Dedicated to all my family and friends, most especially Robert D. Wolfram and his family with gratitude.

Time cures and heals. It rips apart and destroys. It cannot be changed or hidden. It cannot be stopped or slowed.

Time in itself is endless but for us it's here and gone in a second.

Time deepens lines and fades memories. It helps and hinders us all our lives.

Time is precious and our share of it is short. So make the most of the time you have. You cannot give it away or sell it so don't throw it away. Use it, and when you come to the end of yours look back and remember . . .

William Joseph Dettmann
HE CALLS ME BROTHER

He calls me brother . . . this man named "George,"
Although we are from seas apart.
Me, a Germanic-American . . . he, a Jordanian-Greek.
It matters not how we met; this happening happened to be.
The moment in time remains today and the bond of brotherhood is clad to stay.
He refers to me as brother . . . what greater gift than this.
This induring word from our earthly clay
Which holds the secrets of horror and honor last.
Did we stand and fall, side by side in battles past?
Before the seas of our time on this earth, give the
truth to the present . . . having met again at last.
Were we brothers then in the past to the new . . .
Meeting once again, this wonder given to so few.
He calls me brother . . . this man named "George."
This honor is mine, mine alone.

And I respond in thanks and
devoted friendship anew.
And yes, I call him brother . . . for
he is a brother true.

Tracey A DiPrimo
EYES

The feeling began with a quick
stolen glance
The possibilities were
immeasurable; given the chance.
The eyes beckoning, calling to me
Seeing things no one should see.
Feelings of pain, happiness, desire
Delusion, distrust, the mark of a
liar.
Eyes penetrating, burning the soul
Return everything; give back what
you stole.
The tree is dead, its leaves hang
down
No life, no green, the earth has
turned brown.
Where is the life, the breath of love?
Where is the twig in the mouth of
the dove?
Again those eyes turn back to me
The flowers of the earth are once
again free.
A rebirth of light, of love, of breath
Gloom and despair are consumed
by death.
Those eyes once shielded against
my heart
Are open to life, beginning, a new
start.

Eugene L Mach
STRANGERS HERE

---

*To the people who make life a joy
My wife—My family—My
grandchildren*

How strange this world we live in
How strange the sounds we hear
How very strange the things we do
How strange the things we fear

This strange world that we live in
Is but a stop in time
For soon we move from this cruel
world
To one that is sublime

These strange sounds that we hear
each day
Are natures lovely song
They're ours to hear and to enjoy
For soon we move along

The strange things that we do each
day
The reason we are here
Is just to love and to be loved
By those we hold so dear

The things we fear I feel are those
We do not understand
But soon we know the answers
As he leads us by the hand

So is it strange?—The world—The
sounds
The things we do and fear
Or could it be perhaps that we
Are only strangers here

Delores M Deo
THE POET

---

*To my son, Michael for his help and
support also for being my friend.*

A poet is a caretaker
of beauty and ideas,
Through his pen he expresses
many things.

Day and night he searches
For just the right words.
He sees the world through
different eyes than you or I.

His words are filled with life
With each line he is reborn.
Beauty in man's eye is fleeting
A poet captures beauty in words
And words last forever.

Even when he dies
he's never really gone,
because through his words
he will live on.

James D Compton
DEATH

When death comes to find me,
and find me he must,
Will I stand and face him
and accept him in trust?

Or will I a coward
go cringing and crying,
proclaiming to all
my fear of dying?

Is he our foe
this dread master of all?
Or is he a friend
we have need to call?

Does he but come to
make a captive of me?
Or is he a redeemer
come to set me free?

All of these things
one day I'll know well,
but then my dear friend
no one can I tell.

Anna F Simko
FASCINATION

Thank you God for sight to see
The beauty that lies ahead of me
As I look out into space
The snow covered trees and shrubs
look like lace
Intricate patterns that defy
A painter's brush to perform
What God and nature produced
last night
During a winter storm
Beauty and imagination
are there for us in all creation.

Eugenio Sahuquillo-Arce
IMPRESSIONS

---

*To Amy, whom I love over time and
distance.*

Look at the past, you shall see
In a bustle, many—and many
Impressions
Resulted from a touch of
inspiration.

There is always in your heart a
little dream
That remains although the
future yet goes on.
There is always in your mind a
gentle murmur
That the muses whisper softly
like a song.

So, look back, you shall hear
The sweet song from the
nymphes in your past;
Smooth melodies, they
are—impressions
Resulted from a touch of
inspiration.

Put the wings to your quill,
Ride the clouds across the sky;
Write new poems, dream new
dreams,
Let from now your feelings fly.

But, never forget the past, you shall
learn
From those memories, from
those
Impressions
Resulted from a touch of
inspiration.

Miriam Blum
GRANNY'S FANNY

To my Grandchildren

Grandpa gives it a loving pat
Granddaughter says it is too fat
Grandson says it is just right
Great grandson, the little kite
says, "get off your duff—
come outdoors and play with uth."

Vicki Pittman
DADDY

---

*To Melvin Garner, my Daddy, with
love.*

In my younger years
I saw you as a God
Someone not to toy with
Someone who was strong.
As the years rolled slowly by
My vision of you changed
I saw you as a monster
Keeping me in chains.
I broke those chains,
And slipped away,
We grew farther and farther apart.
Now my heart is telling me,
I need to be close to you again.
It's taken some time for me to see,
You were only trying to love me.
You've left the door wide open
For me to come on through,
It'll still take some time,
But DADDY, I LOVE YOU.

Shannon K Pruit
I WAS THINKING

To my dad whom I love very much.

I was thinking about the way I use
to run and play in the wheat
fields of New Mexico. I would
laugh and sing in the forest
pine. The musky odor of dust
that covered my cabin house. I
would be just fine.
I would clap and dance to the
musical rhythm of the bird and
butterfly. I would be just fine.
I would cross the old bridge of
mine and listen to the foamy
brook. I would be just fine.

Angela L Martindale
LONG STEMMED ROSES

We are long stemmed roses, God's
creations.
Put on earth to better our nation.
We are all in love,
Watched over by God from above.
He is helping us make our dreams
come true.
Turn to him and he will help you.
The road may be bumpy and rough.
But we'll make it with God's love
because that is enough.
Yes, in the darkness of the night,
God is my guiding light.

Dinorah Alberto

Dinorah Alberto
DREAMS

The sun is shining, the ocean blue
Its waves approaching my silk
white dress
I look upon the immensity of the
sea,
And see him smiling and coming
towards me.

We walk together hand in hand
The warm sand pampering under
our feet.
My heart elated with all the love,
I had always dreamed of but had
never come.

Oh! What a feeling that will not
end.
We'll walk together, again and
again

Sharing our life, our love until the end.

As I stand here alone today,
I look for him, but he is gone.
The waves are slow, the sun won't shine.
I have awakened, this is my life,
It's just a dream.

Arlene Sandra Lingor
PATIENCE

To My Beloved Husband Lawrence C. Lingor 3, 23, 1986

Be Patient My Loved ones with this Widow Please,
your anxious words don't make me at ease.
I am not one to dwell on sadness or loss,
my loved one is gone . . now I'm the Boss.
It will take me awhile to get use to my pace,
but I will soon catch up to the Human Race.
Be Patient when I seem not to care, cause for
awhile my loss is hard to bare.

Andrew G Kerth
SHOW THE LIGHT
The candle throws it's flickering light
To make the dark surroundings bright
It flickers, fades, and dies away
As you and I must do, some day
But, will our lives be spent to make things bright
As was that lowly, little candle light

Patricia Riley
TRAGEDY
The stars tell my wishes
and you do not hear.
The sun spells out sadness
and you are not here!
Now I count memories
and love you, my dear.

Diane Barnhill
LIFE TODAY
We all live to die someday,
and we work for what we got.
Life is just a high price we pay,
which doesn't give us what we bought.

The meaning of life in our society,
with all our pains and sorrows.
Doesn't give us much variety,
or hope in our tomorrows.

It costs us all we have to give,
and sometimes even more.
But it takes more than money to have the will to live,
it takes trying even harder than we did before.

When we're young we learn our way,
and we're still learning when we're old.
We all have our own role to play,
life's not easy to have or hold.

Each day we struggle through,
some are good days and some are bad.
It's not what you say it's what you do,
it's a waste of energy to even get mad.

Happiness is hard to find,
with all the troubles we go through.
All we want is peace of mind,
but we get pain for what ever we do.

We all make mistkes and learn,
and we pay with our heart and soul.
Respect is something we all have to earn,
it takes more than one life time to really know.

Michael D Yeoman
DOCTOR JECKLE AND MR. HYDE
You can turn the key now and see what
But know the ways of the world
It bet not, get out of the car,
Some day you will see the way.
Bet not turn that key
So turn around, but turn on me,
Not the Jeckle you seem to be.
For you see I know the way of the world says me!
What of Hyde is he so sly,
To talk and boast of the sky.
To come so close to the almighty high.
What of the sly and said good-bye.
Be one I can only be thee,
For you see thee is smarter than me.
What goes so far without fire?
So the day goes on just like there is a night?
Thats right it gets so bright then so dark.
Because the plants air at night and grow in the day.
But what of the bet you lost?
Thats right just because I turned the key.
Too get some where you got to want to do everything!
Your right to know the way is truly a gift.

Rosemarie A LaFond
OUR WEDDING DAY
We were not brought together per chance
but in answer to a prayer;
I prayed to God for the "perfect man"
and suddenly you were there.
I knew the day we came together for us there was a way
And here we are together, forever on this, Our Wedding Day.

My love for you has no conditions,
it has no limitations
For you are to me a dream fulfilled,
a joy beyond all expectations.
As we enter our new life as
man and wife together
I hope we can rid ourselves of the past,
belonging now only to each other.

I want to be your wife, your lover and your friend;
I want to share my life with you,
to be someone on whom you can depend.
My heart is full of love for you
as no words could ever say;
I love you my Darling and give myself to you
on this, Our Wedding Day.

Jean Stafford
CLOSING THE DAY

Dedicated To We The People

As I walk lifes pathway, I find many in need.
A smile, kind word, with a little laughter,
Mixed in between, Closes the day Conveniently.

Lona Marie Dressler Williams

Lona Marie Dressler Williams
TO GOD WITH LOVE

Dedicated to My Loving Husband Wes. My Dad, Mom, My Brother Toby, Dr. Harlen D. Myers and to my Friends and Family For All Their Love, Support, And Prayers. Thank you

---

TO GOD WITH LOVE
ON MY 28TH BIRTHDAY
A REAL CELEBRATION OF LIFE
"MINE"—MAY IT FOREVER SHINE

As I think of what I want to write,
I Already feel the tears.
Because you Dear Lord,
Brought Me through to see 28 years.
Some people had doubts, But Not Me,
Because I Had You!
Your Strength, Hope, Faith and Love,
Lives Strong Inside me.
Some Days Were Tough I admit,
But I feel, I know, I'm a Better Person, Because of it!
Instead of enjoying life, You did better,
You Gave me Life, to enjoy Forever!
So I am Very Grateful and Very much Appreciate,
That You Brought Me through to see 28!
I'm thankful even more,
Because I Feel in My Heart, The storm Has Passed.
I Do Believe—I KNOW
My Life now will Forever Shine
Just Like Your Beautiful Rainbow!!

I LOVE YOU GOD

Johnetta Louise Ernest
TODAY IS TODAY
Today is today. Tomorrow is
tomorrow. I must go ahead
And live for today.
And heaven knows, dream for
tomorrows; because yesterday
I thought to do this, some of
this I did some I didn't
But there's one thing for sure
Today I must go ahead
And strike for it and live
for today 'cause tomorrow
is tomorrow and today is
today and I must go
Ahead and live for today, dream
for tomorrow and l-i-v-e
for today

Nancy Finken
DESOTO BEND REFUGE
The're a bend in the river,
A quiet place to be.
A refuge for all wild life,
A wonderous place to see.
West is Nebraska, Iowa on the east.
A pheasant gliding the meadow,
A full circling sky of geese.
A winding trail to follow,
Wild flowers peeking through.
A hollow tree, a wood duck nest,
Touched with beads of dew.
Shadows on the Bertrand,
At the setting of the sun.
Deer stop their feeding to listen,
Then suddenly jump and run.
And from his hidden perch,
A bald eagle eludes your view.
Safe from all his enemies,
His chance to start anew.

Albert B Sperry
TIME FLIES E'ER FASTER
When I was ten, time's passage was slow
'Cept during vacation, it raced by, I know.
School was a boring, endless drag; learning
Things for which I had no yearning.
And nobody knew the great depression loomed—
It would give us concern we all were doomed.

At twenty-five I was a first-class "tar,"
Whose hitch in the Navy would end with the war.
My loving wife waited anxiously at home,
Counting the days 'til no more I'd roam.
Our children were just a gleam in the eye
As we waited and yearned for time to go by.

At fifty-five the calendar turned more often,
While we as parents had learned to soften
The discipline the children often heeded,
But loathed, tho it was greatly needed.
Weeks turned to months, and months into years—
"Will the kids grow up good?" topped our list of fears.

Now at sixty-eight the days twinkle by,
Tho retired, our time e'er faster does fly.
With a daughter close by, and young son 'most thru college,
Our offspring's success is encouraging knowledge.
Our bodies are tired, to our mild consternation,
But that could be cured by a speedy vacation!

Pam Gerdowsky
GRANDPA IS LOVE

Dedicated to Chad Gerdowsky and his grandfather, Gene Fullenkamp

---

I cannot see my grandpa at all
But I know he stands oh so tall
You see he's very special to me
Because he's my eyes; I can not see
I see things in a different way
My hands and ears are used each

day
Grandpa will guide me as we go for
our walks
And explain things to me when we
have our talks
The love he gives me is my guiding
light
To know life's ways; wrong or right
Together we'll make the world
much brighter
And make any sorrows a little bit
lighter
For Our Lord has blessed us from
above
Thank God for my grandpa and his
precious love

Ms Bula Bernice Kennedy

Ms Bula Bernice Kennedy
I'M WALKING OUT THE DOOR
You don't love any more, the thrill
we had is gone,
You make me feel so alone, just like
I don't belong,
All you have to say to me is, leave
as before, so all
The memories, and dreams I will
take before my love
Turns into hate,
So—I'm walking out the door.

At night I walk the floor because
your kisses are not
Like before, and you don't love me
any more,
Your love has grown cold, for
some-one-else you must
hold,
I can see you are tired of hanging
around, for another
Love you have found,
Just memories, and dreams is all I
have to wish for,
So—I'm walking out the door.

Some-one-else has taken my place
with all the
Trimmings, satin, and lace, all the
wonderful feelings
Are fading away,
Darling—my love can-not touch
first base, so
I'm leaving this place, and for-ever
I will stay away,
So—I'm walking out the door.

Beatrice Wolf
ISRAEL
I like to think of Israel, of places
yet to be seen
Where my brothers journeyed
years ago
To fulfill a lifelong dream
I've heard of Bar Mitzvah's at the
Wailing Wall
Of crumbled prayers stuffed in its
crevices
And I picture myself standing there
A Jew-'midst all the rest of us
The Golan Heights-Tel Aviv-the
Dead Sea-the Masada
Jerusalem-the Good Fence; I
dream and I wonder
Will I step into the Dead Sea and
feel its salty buoyancy
Will I climb the steps or maybe ride
To the top of the Masada
Will I see the view from the Golan
Heights
Will I really be in Jerusalem
Will I walk the streets of Tel Aviv
Buy something to take home with
me
Will I join the children at a Kibbutz
And maybe sing "Hatikva"
Will I see the soldiers defending
them
Brave men for all seasons
Will I plant a tree and feel the earth
Visit the "Holocaust Memorial"
Will I feel the meaning of this land
And be able to control my
Emotions.

Leslie McSkimmings
A WHISPER
To each a whisper comes
To each a whisper goes

Light as a bird's feather
Drifting down from the sky

Quiet as snow falling
On a cold winter's day

Fragile as a petal
Blooming for the first time

Dark as the blackest night
Not a star in the sky

A whisper comes
A whisper goes

Virginia Smith
THE DARKEST HOUR
When midnight's lonely hour is
there
Perhaps the night wind makes old
shadows sway
While shades flit softly up and
down the stair
The secrets of an old house—who
can say?

A ghostly shadow in the darkened
hall-way
That vanishes in the moon's
fleeting light
The eerie sounds from the room
above me
Perhaps just the wind moaning in
the night

Yes—while ever near us—the
un-seen
The dear im-mortal spirits tread
For them the boundless universe is
life
In their world there are no dead

Yet night's darkest hour is just
before dawn.
When nothing moves—nothing
sings—nothing cries
When silently the soul's of the
dying are gone
While hope in the heart's of the
living finally dies

Dixie Bryan
YOU ARE THESE
You are the refiner's fire.—
The last glow of day.
The call of a Gull on a lonely beach
When shores are gray.

You are the gleaner's thrust
'Gainst fields of yellowing grain;
The fertile loam and the elm
bough—
Mingled with rain.

B J Cole
TRUCKING FEVER

To my Dad and Brian with much love

When I hear the jamming of the
gears;
I forget all my fears.
There's a part of me that's a part
of the large trucks;
And the "Big Mama's" seem to
always bring luck.
The 18-wheeler's run;
From one dawn 'til the next rising
sun.
With them they bring a song;
That my heart will always long.
I can hear their engines groaning;
While their wheels are moaning.
The air-horn brings joy;
It's every truckers toy.
I love my truck and will never leave
her;
For I have TRUCKING FEVER!

Frances Memory
THE BIRD AND I
Lonely I sat on a wooden log
When along came a big, black bird
He stared and stared, then finally
said
"What are you doing you fool,
Do you want to die?

I stared at him, then said
No, no, but why am I so sad inside?
With this he got a gleam in his eye
You must bid good-bye
Or else you will die.

But why? Do I want to die?
No, no, but bad thoughts and
memories
You must hide
This place is quiet and opens
wounds
It starts fumes
With this he flutters his wings
Then quietly he left, but he still
sings.

Good-bye, good-bye forever
Me, you will see never.

Jana Lisa Olsen
WINTER WARMTH

This poem is lovingly dedicated to Richard, the darling one I married December 31, 1977. I'm thankful for his constancy through the storms in life and for his encouragement to seek out the beauty and wonder of winter.

A whisper's flight swirled swiftly
'round
As snowflakes lithe fell softly down.
On tender grass did gently lay
A cloak of white—a new year's day.

Oh, warm the thoughts—
December's vows,
A mountaintop, a cabin town.
We shared our love and heart's
desire
By candlelight and crackling fire.

On ocean shores we taste the spray,
The misty kiss of cloudy gray.
As birds fly low o'er shifting sand,
Great waves explode, you hold my
hand.

My mind sails back through
storms in time
To find your love beholding mine.
Oh, warm the thoughts—
December's vows,
Our love has God forever bound.

We share our dreams in valleys low,
While sleeping deep beneath the
snow.
With trees arrayed in silvery ice,
White fields aglow with soft
moonlight.

We dream of diamonds pure and
bright,
Reflecting God's unfailing light.
Oh, warm the thoughts—
December's vows,
Let's shine for God with jeweled
crowns.

Ev Sloat
ZACK 'N JACK
A prospector Zack
And a crusty old jack
Sweated out in the desert alone.
The rucksack was bare,
No grub was left there,
Shrinking the hide to the bone.
They snacked on the sand,
Living off of the land.
Cactus made passible stew.
They searched everywhere
With inch-by-inch care,
And all the while hunger it grew.
When at long last
Near the end of their fast
They struck on a glory hole, sure
And as prospecting would,
They grabbed what they could,
"It's good to be back!"
(That was old Zack)
"We really got scorched on the
plain."
"But I'm soon to be rich!"
(The old son-of-a-bitch)
"I'll buy me a coach on the train!"

Then he lugged this old tub
To the assayer's club
A' countin' his moolah too soon,
"Wasn't worth all that toil,
All you got was some oil."
Just three fins isn't much of a
boom.

Myrtle A Alder
DRIFTING

Dedicated to My Mother Jennie Lee Hendricks

Why did I drift away from God
When all the time He was there

By—my side.

Guiding me, from the danger of
Neglecting his loving care.

His love for me is the, "is the"
Most precious emblem of
Hope I have, to enter His
Haven of Rest.
My soul is anchored in the
Haven of Rest.

Sharon Reece
THE SEASONS OF LOVE

I wish to dedicate this poem to the loved ones in my life whom I know have gone through all the different seasons of love for me.

Love has got its seasons
For each day of the year
Some can bring the sunshine
And others dispel fear.

Spring is just the season
That brings about such light
For everyone seems happy
Since there's no storm in sight.

Since summer seems like anger
From the heat that is to come
Winters sure a hard one
Since everyone stays numb.

Fall has got its values
Since everyone can rest
For nothing seems to happen
Or be put to the test.

So to find peace and contentment
And happiness for all
Try keeping loves two seasons
Like springtime and the fall.

Lura R Christ
LONELY

I walk down in the lovely woods, among the fallen leaves. So many lovely colors, it was hard to believe. I thought of all the beauty, of the sun shining in your hair, I thought of your arms around me so, loving so full of care

The wind is blowing lightly, theres dark clouds up above, this is the place for you and me, the place for people in love, yes I love you my darling and I know you love me too, this is the gift from God above, He gave us lots of love

The rain is softly sprinkling, its dampening my hair,
as I walk I think of you and I'm wishing you were here

It won't be long so its said that we can be together, in marriage, yes in wedded bliss that we can fair the stormy weather

My darling I will walk among the fallen leaves, until that faithful day, when you and I are together and the dark clouds roll away.

Wilma Turner
WHAT I WANT TO BE

Dedicated to My Family

I want to be a worthwhile person
I want a good and honest name
To leave behind me when I'm gone
Back to the dust, from which I came.

I want my family to be proud
That I am their relation
I want to leave something of myself
For my future generation.

I want to use my talents
God gave me the knowledge to do
I want to leave something of myself
So they will know that I passed through.

I pray that long after I leave this world
Someone will call my name
And remember me as a worthwhile soul
When I've gone back to dust, from which I came.

Kathleen Tobin DeCrescenzo
THE FREEZE

My eyes well blinded by my fear
blink seldom for a tear
which knows not where to go,
it's shed for reasons still unknown
maybe for a flower hoping it will grow.
Like trees in the forest
like the breeze in the woods
flowers strive and grow through autumn
and through winter if they could.
But the snow makes its blanket
and the frost it covers leaves,
and that simple little blade of grass
sits glass-like in the freeze.
So we put our hands together
making warmth within our hearts
and we'll keep them clasped together
until the summer starts.

And we see that flower striving
to bring beauty once again,
through the months too short for question
with winter round the bend.

And the cycle starts all over
and that blade of grass it cries—
Known to all as dew in morning
just a tear drop from its eyes.

Irene Guckeen Murphy
DID I HEAR SOMEONE SAY "THERE IS NO GOD!" WHO MADE THE WORLD?

Who made the tiny stream that flows at the base of a mountain high?
Who made the Sun, the Moon, and the Stars that give us light and brighten the Sky?
Who made the Mountain? Who made the Sky?
Who made the Ocean? Who made the Land?
Divided by a beach of sand.
Who taught the bird to fly in flight by wing?
And for their young-the food to bring?
Who made the fish to swim in waters deep?
Who made the Valley low, the Hills steep?
Who makes the rain, the hail and sleet?
Who makes the Winter cold, the Summer heat?
Who makes the lightning flash, and thunder crash?
The violent winds to blow? Who makes it snow?
Who made the air that man breathes to live?
And man in turn, some Thanks should give?
WHO MADE MAN?
With eyes to see, feet to walk, and voice to talk?
Who made the night? Who made the day?
Who taught us the "Our Father Prayer," we say.
Who made the trees, the flowers, the grass that grows from sod?
ONLY ONE COULD MAKE
THESE THINGS . . .
ONLY GOD!

Cornelia Jones

Cornelia Jones
CITY BLUES

Dedicated to those who love as I do True to the Heart and Deep from the Soul.

Crime Non-stop,
Overpopulation never drops.
With everything seeming to stay the same,
while everyone's out trying to gain their own fame.
Mothers and Fathers worrying about their children.
Children on the other hand worrying about their parents,
working more than one job trying to support them.
With life getting harder everyday.
There being more people having to worry about getting a job with good pay.
City Blues thats all they are.
For no one knows when they'll get any better.
So, we just keep searching and searching for that
rising star, until we reach our highest peak.
For it's always said, "you have to go through some
heavy low-down city blues before you reach those
high-lighted peaceful days that everyone talks about."
When everything is just the way you want it to be,
with people, you love around, and no worries to care.
For, except being free.

Marian Thomas
A MISSIONARY PRAYER

Lord, give us minds to serve thee, whether near or far away
Hands to help some wandering stranger,
as we travel night and day.

You have someone who needs us to show them your great love
By our helping them as you help us
With your grace from up above.

It doesn't matter what their color or what the race or creed,
Just make us aware of the persons, and the greatest of their needs.

Lord help us see all you want us to see,
and hear all you want us to hear,
Help us be willing to do as you say,
That your blessings be granted each day.
Amen.

R Thomas Davis Jr
IF TODAY

To family and friends and to my heart, soul, inspiration and life Sunny Davis.

If today I would lose my sight
I would not sit around and pine
I'd still be able to picture you in the moonlight
For you looked like Venus a goddess devine.

If my legs were gone and I couldn't walk
I wouldn't just lie down to die
I'd remember the nights we'd stroll and talk
And in my mind together away we'd fly.

If I'd lose the use of my arms
I'd sit and with pleasant memories remember
Your radiant beauty and all of your charms
And the many times that I held you near

But darling, if I would lose your love
I know that I just couldn't go on
I'd ask why of God above
For along with you my heart and soul, would be gone.

Rukeia Desza Draw
DRUGS

This poem is dedicated to those I love, and care about.

Drugs are a great problem today
People use it so many ways
People say that it won't hurt you
But if you use it you'll be that way too,
It messes with your brain
And it makes you insane
It makes you do things that you usually wouldn't do
It makes you say things that hurt people too.
Drugs make you very lazy
Drugs make you very crazy
Drugs make you act like you're insane
It makes you look like you're in pain.
People that use it usually wear junky clothes
or fancy pants, usually they're Fila Fans.
I'm not talking about drugs that cure you from sickness

I'm talking about drugs that make you a menace
Drugs can be used by
Doctors, nurses and journalist a painter, trainer plus a therapist.
My name is RUKEIA and I would never do drugs
It could make you pull the plug
It can make you feel you could fly
It can make you get too high.
Drugs can make you want to die
Drugs can make you fail and not try
That's why I would never do drugs

Kara L Scrougham
A SOJOURN THROUGH LIFE

A passage through a Mark Twain adventures tunnel of
neverending chambers and locked doors; almost unnoticed; definitely untouched.
Though changing around us with each new day, a peerless
flight through evolution is the picture that is developed.

The alarm to success rings.
Struggling and
denyful the foot hits the floor.
A catharsis of the external body but not of the soul.
The new boughten paints, but the same-as-always drawing board.
A flick to the wisps: an add to the made-up look.
Not to be discouraged, a walk to the filing cabinet of
riches to rags—for the middle class solely.
It seems to only look worse; never getting better.

"To be or not to be" or because we want to or because we have to?
That is a question.
The neverending tic-toc that makes rage flury, sweethearts love,
politics wary, and etc. and etc. just to fill in its illimitable term.
Neglectfullness: a time for surpassing the normalities of the days of yore.

A quick dash of nourishment, a spring through the portal.
A quick sigh:
A walk through God's observatory:
It's really not as bad as they make it sound.

Bonnie Jean Waller
A SALUTE TO BAY HIGH SCHOOL

This poem, is dedicated to all the students, who have passed through the halls of Bay High School, and those that will come in the future.

There are bends in the road of life, may we take them without strife.
Forever hold her banner's high, so
our memories cannot die.
Dear colors of purple and gold you will never grow old.
Alway's a special place in my heart you'll be, through-out all eternity.
We must go on to higher and better things.
Like an old friend, let the silver of the past prepare us for the future of gold.
Knowledge is power and we shall use it hours on hour.
A tribute to all our teachers, who have touched our lives.
The guidance, we've had, to teach us good from bad.
The wind of time blow's where it will, changes come,
We must go where the winds blow.
Time, cannot be purchased, sold, stored up, nor cast away. It may bring glory, it may bring shame.
But in the end it will serve God's purpose.

Richard J Smyth
TIME

I would like to dedicate this poem to Jeanette, my wife, who inspires me to put my feelings down on paper.

I think deep back into the past
I close my eyes to make it last
I think of times that used to be
and just how much they meant to me
I kept my head throughout the years
I fought the hurt and hid the tears
Life has thrown me many curves
it breaks your heart and tests your nerves
Hands of time have done me wrong
here and now and for so long
My troubles just won't go away
in my past and here today
and if I did it all again
I'd only wish for you my friend!

Tracy Havens
IN THE WINK OF AN EYE

For Adam, the brother I loved and lost.

Time passes on
The young become the old
The old go away
The young carry on
Time passes on
The old stay the same
The young want to change
The old will stay the same
The young will change
Time passes on
The years go by
In the wink of an eye
Never to be changed
Never to be rearranged
Time passes on

Frances L Angst
DAYDREAMS

For Delbert, my husband of 38 years February 1987

When we were young and in our prime
We dreamed our dreams and wasted time
Then we grew older, day by day
And let our daydreams slip away
And then our middle years were there
With slower step and silvered hair
With youth long gone and children grown

You'd think that all worthwhile had flown
But oh, not so, my love, my dear
The beauty, still it lingers here
Not seen by some, but there the same

The same sweet feeling, same bright flame
More settled now and surer still
Our love has grown and grown until
The day has come, my dearest love
When we are truly hand-in-glove.
And so my dear, love can't depend
On words and phrases, end-on-end

But trials and deeds lived day by day
And all those daydreams gone astray
And life was better, dearest one
Than if our daydreams had come true
For dreams are only that, just dreams
And darling, I've had you.

Fonda Fern Campbell
MOSES

When Moses was a tiny babe, his Mother's faith was true.
She made for him a little boat and sealed it through and through
The boat was placed at the water's edge, among the grasses fair,
And Miriam stood nearby to watch; No harm could reach him there.

The Princess and her maidens came, out for a cooling walk.
She asked about the little boat, but Miriam would not talk.
"I'll take him, then, to live with me; to be my very own!
"He'll be taught, so very well to take his place on the throne!

Then Miriam came from her hiding place; the answer she must know . . .
"Do you need a nurse to take full charge; to watch the baby grow?"
GOD knew of the plan, and faith, so great; The family HE knew
For Moses was a chosen one, and he must stand the test.) best,

God's people in the Wilderness must have a leader, strong.
By Precept, Law, and Government, they'd know the right from wrong.
When Moses and his days were gone, he laid him down to rest.
But GOD repaid the work, the test; and Moses by heaven was blest.

Edith F Harrison
SASKATCHEWAN

When God created Canada he laid it out with care,
Each province must have it's blessings and a little cross to bare.
He tryed to make them equal yet each one be unique,
And when he made Saskatchewan these words they heard him speak,
I'll spread a vast prairie across the southern end,
And cover it with prairie grass that some day will be grain.
As the human race increases so they must be fed,
And Saskatchewan shall grow the wheat to be made into bread.
I'll bless it with the sunsets nowhere else will better be,
And also with the northern lights that many lands will never see.
To the north will be the park land with crystal lakes and many trees,
I surely hope the human race will take good care of these.
When he came to natural resources he scattered here and there.
Oil and coal to the south and trying to be fair,
Potash across the centre for he knew the time would come,
If the earth was to keep providing it would be needing some.
Pausing by the uranium bin he wondered do I dare?
Place this dangerous mineral into human care,
Will they use it wisely for the good of all man kind,
Yes man must make his own mistakes his own way he must find.
Now for that little cross to bare and with a wily grin,
He reached out his precious hand and tossed the mosquitoes in.

Deborah Lynn Tannenbaum
WAS IT VIETNAM?

No one knows how we feel.
the War is over,
but it still seems real.
Our "Heroes Welcome"
was a soundless scream.
We've come home,
but where have we been?
We've escaped sneak attacks
for a country that doesn't want us back.
We stand and look around—
this is Home . . .
We remember the ground.
Still . . .
when planes fly overhead
we are reminded of our dead.

Mrs Florence E Lynch
MY HONEY

To my Honey, my Husband, who died young; after 23 years of our being together in 1963.

I miss my beloved, my Honey, my wonderful Jim
This life's not worth living

without him
I can't see him, nor touch him, but
he is near
His dear, wonderful presence in
spirit is here.

He's in the bedroom, the kitchen,
the hall
Look closely you'll see him right
next to the wall
Oh, you're really not gifted to spot
him; you see
'Tis only our love that brings him
to me.

I'll love him forever, I know 'till I
die;
We're made for each other, my
Honey and I.
I'll attend earthly chores until they
are done
Then my Lord will again let us
be one.

Diane M Ahlgreen

TO

To my husband, Stephen

To look out the window
and see no sun.
Also, to what hasn't been done.

To go to talk
and find no voice.
To go to look
and find no eyes.
To go to listen
and find no ears.
Oh, it would seem like years.

To go to walk
and find no legs.
To go to hug
and find no arms.
To look for you
and find no love.
Would be like Noah, not finding
the Dove.

To look for a friend
and not find you.
Would be like Death and the End.

Karen E Czaplinski

SPRING!

Spring . . . enveloped in an ethereal
sensuality,
soft as gossamer wings of pastel
butterflies,
yet with a persistance that can only
be symbolized
by the old adage, "moths drawn to
flames."
Spring!
Soft, soothing Spring.
Life oozes slowly through the earth
to the trees and plants,
leaving feathery greens in its' wake.
Gentle blossoms slowly gain in
strength.
Breezes gently envelope you,
barely ruffling your hair,
while tickling your cheek and
nuzzling your neck,
invade your body and mind in a
provocative fashion,
with provocative results.
Disjointed thoughts are
overwhelming.
Ears are deaf to spoken words,
yet hear the distinct, haunting
music from a 'different drum.'
Ethereal feelings of invisible,
silken threads
tugging with gentle persistance,
sending images of wings flapping,
ready to take flight,
needing to take flight.
Ah, to be able to fly . . .

Shirley Maddox

PERCEPTUAL WEALTH

Wealth is not measured in silver
and gold
When riches abound in things we
behold:
Like a winding trail through the
forest green
Where songbirds and wild flowers
enhance the scene,
Majestic mountains of beauty and
might,
Autumn leaves ablaze with color so
bright,
Winter woods transformed by the
fallen snow,
A fire on the hearth with embers
aglow.

Wealth is not measured in silver
and gold
When rich blessings flow from
things we behold:
Like the first budding flowers of
early spring,
Signs of new life that make one's
heart sing,
A glowing sunset at the close of the
day,
The star-studded skies of the Milky
Way,
A pat on the back—a touch of a
hand,
A friend who will listen and
understand.

Wealth is not measured in silver
and gold
When peace and joy come from
things we behold:
Like sheltering trees on a hot
summer day,
The laughter of children while
busy at play,
A stroll on the beach—a warm
ocean breeze,
The white-capped waves of
emerald seas,
Warm reassurance from a smiling
face,
An answered prayer—God's
amazing grace.

Matthew Johnson

VICTORY

This poem is dedicated to my sister Trish.

At full speed just five laps to go.
But you just don't know.
The man in front is a pro.
And you've never even run this
track before.
There's the flagbox only four laps
to go.
But your low on fuel.
You pull in and get all the fuel left.
You go back out and you see that
the leader has spun.
You go for all you've got.
You're in the lead but the second
place man is coming.
He slowly comes up beside you and
is going for the pass.
You put it in sixth and fight for
your spot.
It's neck to neck but you slowly
start to pull away
Then he gives it all he's got and
catches you.
You both fight through turn four
and by the flagbox.
Quickly you think only three laps
left.
But your troubles aren't over yet.
You continue to fight but then he
starts speeding up
Slowly he takes the lead from you.
You stick to his tail like "crazy
glue."
Your floor it and begin to gain on
him. You start to pass
In the turn when all of a sudden
you lose control!
You spin around and around. As
you pull out of the turn you
straighten up!
You're in the lead and the second
place man is lost. He can't
believe you're still rollin'
You quickly zoom past the flagbox,
two laps left.
When you finally realize you're still
alive you start breaking records.
You hit amazing speeds of 218, 219
and 220!
You just made history as you see
the white flag!
As you go around the track you
think back.
You think of the quarter midget
and the Formula Ford.
Then the midget and then to the
car your in now.
As you pull into gasoline alley you
get out of the car
Take the checkered flag and the
warm milk and
You smile and think to yourself,
"Victory."

Phyllis J Yoder

BABY DAUGHTER

To my daughter Nancy Lynn Noble

The time you were born was on a
rainy summer night
You arrived in this world without
a fight.
You were such a sweet loving
bundle of joy
Blue eyes, dark hair and so very,
very coy.
You looked so cute in your frilly
little dresses
and of course Mom insisted on
curly "tresses."
The school years came and went
by the side
You always took each day in your
stride.
Thru grade school, high school and
Cosmotology too,
Its been a joy just to know you.
Then the day came, your wedding
you see
A nice young fellow was taking you
away from me.
As you walked down the aisle, I was
filled with pride.
But deep down inside I cried and
cried.
Life goes on and Mothers know
there is always the time they have
to let go.
Now you are a Mother of two sweet
little boys
Involved in their good times, bad
times and joys.
And I'm sure there are times they
may be unruly even wild
But nothing impares with a
Mothers love for her child.
Even tho you have blossomed into
a terrific young lady
You will always be Mom's sweet
little baby

Rose Sharon Hoover

T'IS NOT IT NOW TIME

To the future unborn . . .

Jasmin floating through the night
like incense from above
a wistful dream
the shadow of an approaching
dove
says, the time has come
its time for Love . . .
O Timelessness to which I must
in the end return to dust
spare one second of Eternal time
so man may have a chance to
climb
out of the depths of greed and lust
which in our ignorance
ourselves have
thrust, perhaps the only remaining
song
a God-given knowledge
of Right and Wrong . . .
Enough of these destructive wars
which accomplish nothing
but corrupted laws
that separate us from our own kind
in the endless battle
of Blind against Blind . . .
Surely O empty rushing night
if you stop but a moment
in your flight
you can not help but look above
and say, t'is not it now
the time for Love? . . .

Louise Jaffe

TROPISMS

The rain has messy penmanship.
The snow
Is ignorant of tenses, how to spell,
And where a comma goes or
doesn't go.
How many winds are known to
outline well
Or chart the starts and ends of
paragraphs?
The syntax of the sun mocks all our
quests
For it. The etiquette-lorn ocean
laughs
As if our strivings were just empty
jests
When we would conjugate its
waves. Rash grass
Ignores transitions. Paradigms of
sky
Defy recalling. So however crass

Men seem, when I yearn for love's prosody
I turn to them, let nature's splendors wait
Till passion's ebb makes me feel profligate.

Alan K Burwell
THE CRAZY COWGIRL

When I was travellin' through the country, something happened to me.
There was a funny lookin' cowgirl tryin' to kiss on me.

So I got a smoochin' fish from an extremely murky lake.
What a neat and awful joke this kissing fish would help me make!

Now this is what I had in mind (though it may seem cruel):
I'd put that fish right to her lips and thus prevent a duel.

She'd think that little fish was lips, and then be full of pride;
But while she kissed that yuck ole fish, I'd run away and hide.

So when the cowgirl kept a comin', I turned and faced her there.
She mistaked and thought I liked her; she thought that pretty fair.

But then she glanced down at my right hand, and she saw that smoochin' swimmer.

She realized what was in my mind, and I began to tremor.

So she ran to me and spanked me and said, "Sonny, that's a crime!
Don't you never think it, or I'll spank you one more time!

All day long she slapped and whipped me (until I was whim-per-in').
She told me, "Hush up, boy, or I'll throw you in the pen!"

"I've been kind to you, I haven't blabbed, you mean ole ugly crook!
If you don't repent, next time I might not let you off the hook!"

Then she ceased to chasten me, and I was very glad;
But she warned and said, "Forsake those pranks, or you will wish you had!"

Alice E McBride

Alice E McBride
LA PETITE SMOKIE PRINCE

To "Smokie," a wild mustang adopted at age 1 1/2 by the author on 2/28/83, and euthanized on 1/21/85.

Smokie was a mustang, through and through.
I loved and worked with him, and he loved me true.
He could open gates, and untie knots.
He liked to play King of the Woods, and climb and stand up high on rocks.

He followed me like a puppy dog would, showing his love in all of the ways that he could.

Smokie had four white feet, and white on his face and tail; his mane and tail were black, but the rest of him was a beautiful grey.
He always knew what to do to make my day!

His eyes were dark, with a black liner, and when the sun shone on them they had a deep blue hue.
Horses like Smokie are very few.

He understood so many words; and he made many friends of all ages.
About a mustang like Smokie, one could write pages.

Smokie had to be "put to sleep" when he fell on a hard snow in an arena and broke the humerus bone in his shoulder.
No other horse can ever take his place in my heart!!
My love for him will always smolder.

He was a friend, brave, strong, and good.
Maybe, someday, I'll write a book!

Susan H Newman
MY WAY

"This poem is dedicated to Wanda, a beautiful and wonderful friend.

I'll go where you want me to go dear Lord,
Real service is what I desire.
I'll say what you want me to say dear Lord,
But don't ask me to sing in the choir.
I'll say what you want me to say dear Lord.
I like to see things come to pass.
But don't ask me to teach boys and girls dear Lord,
I'd rather just stay in my class.
I'll do what you want me to do dear Lord,
I yearn for the church to thrive.
I'll give you my nickels and dimes dear Lord,
But please don't ask me to tithe.
I'll go where you want me to go dear Lord,
I'll say what you want me to say.
But I'm busy now with myself dear Lord,
I'll help you some other day.

Betty J Reed
VIETNAM

To all who fought and died in Vietnam

I've thought a lot about you today.
How you used to ask to go out and play.
Watching you swing, playing in the sand.
And how we lost you in Viet-Nam—
So young, good looking, and strong. To fight
a war that was later declared wrong.
I look at all the young men disabled
beyond repair, and wonder why we ever
went there.
You were the light of my life,. And all
that is left is memories and strife.
When will we learn? And when will we
know? Raising our children and helping them
grow. To settle our problems not with
war and strife.
Why do young men have to lose their lifes?

Anita L Boucher
UNTITLED

I cannot describe the joy I feel because you are in my life.
You give me encouragement, you give me strength,
you help me when I am overcome with strife.
Ours is more than friendship, more than love.
You are so deeply entwined around me
Sometimes I wonder, in all the world,
how can such things just be?
Words cannot express the love and ties I feel
for such emotions are of the heart.
But without someone like you within my life,
each day would be too hard to start.
I owe you more than words can say for it is a debt beyond price.
You are teacher, brother, lover, friend
and so much more besides.
I truly hope this never ends
and my debt keeps growing higher.
With a friend like you, I am truly blessed.
For more I cannot ask.
It is a humbling effect to see you there
and know you really care.
Thanks

Sandra L Koch
REFLECTIONS

This poem is dedicated to my loving mother and friend, Delores. Thank you so much for your love, caring, and encouragement.

As you look at me, I am a woman
but can you see way beneath?
I am your first, and a child inside.

You taught me right and wrong,
how to be open and strong.
I took your advice, but things went wrong.
I don't understand and I don't know why.
I feel so ashamed and guilt inside.
That part of me is dying inside.

I hope I haven't done too much harm,
I feel so worn and withdrawn.
But in time I hope to be, someone special,
that you expected me to be.

I probably caused you enough despair.
but it's just because my head wasn't there
I probably caused you lots of fears,
but please bear with me.

I want to make my amends so desperately
but I am scared I will fail as repeatedly.
Please grin and bear, your love has given me a destiny.

I am a woman with a disease,
which I'm not pleased.
But my higher power will take care of me,
if I let it be.

I am a woman physically, a child emotionally.
I am your daughter,
who loves you deeply.

Cahtherine Mary LaGrave
WHEN WE GET TO HEAVEN

When we get to Heaven
There will be peace
There will be joy
There will be glory
When we get to Heaven

There will be no pain
There will be no hurt
There will be no tears
When we get to Heaven

Oh I'll be so glad
When we reach Heaven
Jesus is going to have
Something special waiting
For us after we go through
So much down here it
Will be alright up there.

William Hillard
NECROMANCER

My name is Dryas
My story is tragic
I was the spring
vibrant and young
but age sets like winter
and I too became harsh and cold
When I met her she was so fragile yet strong
like a diamond in the hands of a jewler
Her name was Juventas
my name to her was elder
I loved her for her youth but she spurned
me for my age
She was promised to another, Iapitus
He was handsome, young
She saw life in him
I saw envy
The night before they were due wed I murdered
Iapitus in the castle garden
I tried to explain all to Juventas
but she fled from me
The townspeople finally captured me
and sentenced me to death
Juventas was there to witness my

execution
The rope broke six times before it held to snapping neck
I looked to Juventas before I died
fir its the last time I will
Now for eternity I wonder in the garden
taunted by my own love
taunted by my own will
this is the fate I chose I cannot be denied it
ask me not for an explanation and I ask you not
for forgiveness
I am forced to live amoungst the dead and will
forever seek peace

Velma Hendricks

Velma Hendricks
JUST FOR TODAY
Just for today as the sun shines
I ask God to be mine.
If I put my faith in God
All will be fine.
For his will not mine
I'll find the time
Not my will but thine

Anthony J Pagano
THE DEATH OF TIME
When I upon thy face should gaze,
Surely it seems the beacon in all this haze,
For within my soul the fog is great,
and in the world one finds so much hate.

But in thy presence I sense a calm;
An eternity of springtime where the nights are long,
And the sound of your voice is as sweet as the bird's song.

For the troubles, the pain, and the tears
all disappear whenever I hold you near.
And the warmness of your body against mine
kindles in me the fires of desire.

In our rapturous entwinement
that damn old lamplighter is silenced,
and his cry of the hour falls on deaf ears.
Now Time can add not a single second
to my fading years.

Ann Kotas
FEELINGS OF LOST LOVES
I ask myself, has it been this long.
where has the time gone.
Only yesterday you were here.
Now too suddenly you've disappeared.
Yet it seems you're in my heart to stay.
For it will always be this way.
Time can't change the way I feel and guess it never will.
Do you ever forget a love that's been shared?
To foget his smile, and how he showed you he cared.
Remembering the little things he'd do for you.
And the many other things you never knew.
Calling you up; whenever he was free.
The way he looked at you, when he thought you didn't see.
A touch from his hand, so warm in yours, so strong.
So right, yet somehow wrong.
And never meant to be, for I gave my love, all of me.
Because he was all I ever was or hoped to be.
And my tears reflect my love because he's gone from me.
And it just was never meant to be.
Just "you" or "me," but never "we."

Debra Lou Macfarlane
THE FLOWERS ON MOMMA'S GATE
As I walk down lifes pathway of late,
I think of the morning glories on the back gate.
Back in days of childhood I,
Would run and jump on the gate and fly.

That old metal gate was an entrance to pleasure,
It was the door to Alladins Treasure,
A jail, a passage to an ancient place,
Or maybe the gate way to outer space.

It was the way to many childhood charms,
It saw us run home to Daddy's Caring Hands and Mommas loving arms.

Now we have all grown and moved away,
But the gate stands always open to welcome our way,

It's covered with morning glories so beautiful and bright,
The Lord touched it with his Glory and Light.

He gave it a crown of Flowers for its service to me,
And when the Gate of Flowers I see,

I remember, smile and look up above,
And thank Him for all my Blessings of Love.

Mary Trudy Ryder
UNEMPLOYMENT DAY
Oh! Rich Man, will you behold, those who are poor, weak, and old,
Those who have not the smallest scrap of meat,
And only a small crust of bread to eat,
On This unemployment day,
When you in thousands lay
A feast and liquor in bountiful array.

Upon a poor Man's table rudely made
In an old box some pennies are laid;
Only a few, but they are all
This sightless Man his own can call on this unemployment Day.

Oh! Rich Man just think, I pray,
When in your Rich Man's homes such wealth display:
Except for a dog the poor is alone
(A friend one can but give a bone),
And yet with grateful spirit one smiles on the friend they cannot see,
And bends one's gray old head to say,
Dear Lord, I thank you on this unemployment Day.

Oh! Rich Man, blessed with all things that the world holds best,
Please look at the picture of the poor, weak, and old,
And try some kindly act to do on this unemployment Day.
To light the way of some one poor and lone,
Who is in need of food, love, employment and home,
And in Our Heavenly Father's Name, I say Thank You,

Paula Young Hardy
PRAISE PRINCIPLE NOT PERSON
The human Jesus, sent to earth to do God's Will,
Did teach the Christ, Truth, and show to us by healing,
God's All Presence; His Power revealing,
That we, by honoring Truth, find freedom;
Instead—we celebrate a man called Jesus
In place His Kingdom.

Mahatma Ghandi's prayer and fasting,
Done to plead for Peace—long lasting
'mid masses dying, brought a light.
Yearning thus to stop the fight
Said, to make the nations whole,
"Live Satyagraha—force of Soul!"
We honor him in memory
On "Masterpiece," through BBC.

Martin Luther King, in few short years,
Did overcome—and led his people from their tears;
His vision of "The Promised Land" and "I have a dream,"
Indeed acknowledged God Supreme;
Yet, failing still to praise and laud,
We honor Martin 'stead of God.

When will we learn—how many ages,
Our source is God instead these sages?
Love sent these messengers
In witness to His caring
That we dominion find—His image bearing.

Heather Greber
A LOVER'S APOLOGY
I sit and stare at the sky,
Keep asking myself why?
We used to be good friends
Now it has come to an end.
I wonder what went wrong,
Was it because of me?
Listening to a sad song
making me realize
what I see.
How terrible I was to you.
What makes it worse you knew
exactly what was going on.
From morning back to dawn.
Just now I realize
How wonderful you were.
Each day was full of surprises
When we were together.
Lately, I wanna apologize
and say
I'm sorry for each day
I hurt you. I really
truly do
Love You!

Georgene Davis
SUMMER'S END

Dedicated to Evelyn, our Dear Daughter and her Husband, Bill.

At summer's end
The insects Drone;
And birds in flight
Are heading home.

The days grow short
The sky is haze.
And clouds are soft
The sun is maise.

Abundant fruit
On straining limbs,
From perfect weather
Despite her whims.

Enter Autumn
You beauteous quest!
Artistically readying
Nature's rest.

Dr George W Davies
"LOVE" THE REAL MEANING
If loves transmission is sincere and strong,
It brings joy to the heart, whether in poem or in song.
It is a comfort, to many who are laden with grief,
It is like pouring fresh water to revive a fading leaf.

If it is sincere with true and loyal devotion,
It sets a happy feeling, rapidly in motion.
You'll find peace and content of mind,
Leaving most of your troubles far behind.

True and loving companions, are treasures to uphold,
Good friends to depend upon, when we are growing old.
It is a blessing to live, with one who really cares,
Takes the good with the bad and willingly shares.

It is sorrowful when one is forsaken and forgotten,
They are like rosy apples, that fall from trees and go rotten.
A smile with some love, could revive a broken heart,
Sharing peace and happiness, is never to late to start.

Steven Burch
DADDY'S GIRL
My baby is special
A gift from above
A blessing from Jesus
To cherish and love
A bundle of joy
A sight to see
A prettier girl
There cannot be

My little girl
Forever you will be
I will always love you
I pray you love me
I love you daughter
I am a very proud man
Thank you Lord Jesus
For my sweet Shana Ann

Jane M Sawon

Jane M Sawon
PICTURE FRAME

To My late husband Anthony Joseph Sawon Love Forever

Today I drew a picture, and put it in a frame,
It had blue skies, green grass, pine trees and flowers;
Also in this picture is a house, so large and very tall,
With heartful memories of you and I and our children.
The offsprings of our Love,
But I knew one day, soon, I would have to leave it all;
The children grew and I went away,
They had to find their way,
Just you and I were only there,
Now that you are gone dear, I had to turn my life around,

Adjustments don't come very sound.
I tried and tried and then came fall,
I knew then, I would have to leave it all,
I tried to find comfort and some Love,
But could not find it without shame,
And I could not play the dirty game,
So I will keep the painting in the frame,
And save it all for you dear.
Because the picture that I drew, gets mixed up daily,
All other gifts and prizes, mean nothing to me now.
The only thing left for me is to walk in the valley of tears,
A tear for every year I have loved you.
And that's a lot of tears
Because my dear I have loved you,
Lots and Lots of years.

Kitty Verdelle Fontnette
GOING HOME
Going home, going home, going home to that city so
bright and fair,: where my mansion is waiting
for me over there, I shall enter the twelve gates
of pearl, tred the streets of gold, say
farewell to this sin sick world, going where
The half has never been told. No more
Trouble and strife, I'll sit down by the tree
Of life. See my loved ones shake hands
with my friends, everyday will be Sunday,
Sabbeth will have no end.
Going home, Going home, Going home at last
Troubles, sorrows and cares all past
The battle all over, the victory won—just to
hear Him say servant well done—ten thousand
Years just praising his name! Thou art worthy!
Thou art worthy! The lamb that was slain

Rheiba Reigh Gower
STAR REFLECTIONS
I climbed into the Heavens
and sat upon a star.
It was "Star Light!" The star
we had wished upon as children.
"Why didn't you give me all
my wishes star?" I asked.
"The things I had so eagerly
hoped for?"
"Because," was the star's
response, "I gave you
your needs instead"

Dorothy L Hartz
BRIGHT SUMMER DAY
The radiant glow of dawn
opens the door of morning
and ushers into being
a bright new summer day.

Mocking birds call to crickets
"time to tune your fiddles
summer has begun,"
trees sway in a soft noon breeze.

Growing jet streaks
slash a brilliant blue sky
as if attempting
to loosen heaven's hold on earth.

Beneath the sun's warm caress
flower petals stretch
and bloom full
to greet butterflies and bees.

Myriad shades of green
hold fields and hills
together in a continuum
of soft soothing peace.
The arms of twilight
rock to sleep
the last sweet songs of birds.

Bea Hollingshead
UNSPOKEN LOVE
Beneath all the chatter and words of delight
Lies a silent language.
Where emotions, actions and feelings occur.
Miles can't prevent it,
Time can't destroy it,
No one can take it away.
Quietly hands will touch
And a smile makes no sound.
Thoughts and memories are what we hear
When no one is around.
Only Mothers hear the Love inside
Her baby's screams for milk.
So she feeds them Love, Faith and Truth,
Blended with Courage and Hope
As the child grows and learns to know
The sounds of the woman's voice,
Even deaf ears hear the brilliant roar
Between Mother and Child,
Unspoken Love,
Rejoiced!

Opal Nichols
LIVIN' ON WEL-FARE
I can't find a job I've got no money,
I tell my wife, it's just you and me Honey.
If there was just a way we could make ends meet.
No car to drive, no place to live.
That's bad enough and no one will give,
So I call on wel-fare just for somethin' to eat.

They say sit down, be with you in a minute,
I wait four hours, but my heart's not in it.
Then they finally call my name and I go in.
They say "sit there" and I have a seat.
Then they stand up and say "I'm beat."
"It's time for my break" but I'm anxious to begin.

You just sit there and twiddle your thumbs,
You feel like a fool and look so dumb.
Then they come back and you wonder where they've been
You sit there and listen, you can't say a word,
They don't say a thing you haven't already heard.
They say they'll help, but you begin wonderin' when.

Then they go off into another room, and they say "well I'll be back soon."
But when they get back, you're feelin' kinda low.
They say "I'm sorry, you'll have to come back,
You'll get help and that's a fact."
But for right now, you're gonna have to go.

Johnny A Vineyard
A POOR MAN'S TREASURE
Riches and fame have passed me by
A living I earn with my hands.
No one can say that I don't try
Regardless of each day's demands.

Of all the dreams I beseech
Only one has ever come true.
Something special beyond my reach
I found when I married you.

Each day finds me tall and proud
As I head out to earn my pay.
Another face among the crowd
With nothing special to say.

When I come home, my life begins
As my family waits by the door.
I pray to God this never ends
No fortune could be worth more.

Little faces smiling up at me
Their love is clearly shown.
I'm really special, I must be
They're yelling "Our Daddy's home."

Maybe fortune and my name in lights
Were just never meant to be.
But sticky kisses and hugs so tight
Mean more than the world to me.

Norma R Machin

Norma R Machin
COME QUENCH YOUR THIRST
As if I were in the desert, so thirsty was I
for love, that on coming upon the first I drank.
He put his arms around me and gently pressed
his lips on mine. I felt my very soul awaken
with desire, I drank of his breath. my lips
were moistened.

Oh, how he quenched my thirst.
Like a child on Christmas Day, I rejoiced.

Nancy L Crawford
MOM

Mom you gave me life that I should live,
No scales could measure the love you give.
We've shared so much in such a short time,
I wouldn't want to trade you for a million dimes.
Everyone would be happy to find,
A friend, and a mother like mine.
When times for me are so rough,
You lend a hand without a fuss.
You're a mother of whom I can be proud,
Not just another face in a crowd.
I want for you all happiness to be,
Hoping you'd want the same for me.
Part of my happiness is being with him,
Can't you accept him at least as a friend?
Mom, I love him deeply with all my heart,
But knowing how you feel tears me apart.
You taught me to love, not to hate,
Why must you feel this way about the guy I date?
This happiness he gives me, I wish we could share,
Please mom, give us a chance if you care.

Beulah Mae (Bunton) Voncannon
MOTHER

M—is for fond memories
O—Of love and your kindness for others you are always thinking of
T—Is for the time you've spent in helping cheerfully
H—Is for the home you've made a happy place to be
E—Is for each thoughtful thing you've done throughout the years
R—Is for remembering them as Mother's Day appears—

Put them all together and the lovely word they spell is one that
means far more to me than any words can tell. My thoughts are
with all dear mothers—Past, present, and future.
HAPPY MOTHER'S DAY!

Sharon Griffin
BUTTERFLY

This poem is dedicated to my mother, Mrs Gwendolyn Brazley and my grandparents, Mr. and Mrs. Leon Wigginton.

Out of this ugly brown cocoon
comes Gods gift of beauty
the butterfly
Luminescent wings, silver
streaked with gold, whisper
against my cheek
an angels kiss
Brilliant and spectacular colors
blended by a Master magician
Perched eloquently, drinking in
precious nector
poised for flight
Where will it land next?
Beauty kissed by the sun and
thrown to the winds
Forever
free

David A Higgins
REASON NOT TO CHANGE

Winnie for all the changes that you could not.

From the moment
I first thought that
it must be the season
or it could be my time,
with the words of a poet
and words of fire
I went forth with an
angel's desire of heaven.

Well I felt you;
as the night comes down
into the shadows; you;
fade to darkness with scarce a touch.
I could love you,
I cannot love you much.

So the words
and the fire
and all the desire
must surly fade
like a fallen angel in Hell.
Know that I've loved you
and as the fallen,
must not love too well.

Clare Salata
UMBRELLAS

People touch each other
in so many, meaningful ways,
creating a spiritual umbrella
for rainy days.
Years or hours or fleeting
moments—
deliberate deeds we treasure—
become grand gifts of superb
support
to be opened with pleasure.
As one life grows better
because of what another gave,
life's rekindled energy sparks
a surging, wondrous wave.

Lew N Hortillosa M D
THE GREAT AMERICAN

I am as ancient as the Eagle's Nest,
My people dwelt and hunted in this land,
Deer in the east, buffaloes in the west,
Bears in the Rockies, cougars in Canyon Grand,
In proud feathers you still see us dance or stand,
Our way of life had been freedom-blest.

In Ellis Island or Plymouth Rock, Thanksgiving,
High seas and wild winds had proven my Heart,
New World in a vast Land and New Hope living,
I sweated in iron mills and coal mines my part,
Potatoes, tomatoes and cheese I sold in my cart,
My Family and my People we are freedom-loving.

With anger and horror I wailed when I first came,
In chains and shackles and unjust yoke,
I picked Missippi cotton in silent shame,
Until one Kingly day the wicked spell I broke,
My dream to all my People I vividly spoke,
And we marched at last in Freedom's name.

I am the Fullness of American Centuries gone,
Skyscrapers and rockets built, I visited the moon,
In Democracy, Science and Sports I am Number One,
The car, TV, telephone I invented, and cartoon,
I play football, watch Broadway, fly hot air balloon,
In Miss Liberty's Torch, my Flame is second to none.

Betty Forth Young
BREAKERS

I dedicate this poem to my four children, Jenine, Roma, Nicholas, and Janice & to my many grandchildren whom I adore—

There is this Jutt along the shore
I'd say one hundred yards or more
Of rocks and boulders bare and bleak
From its beginning to its very peak:
My Favorite Place.

I'd sit upon this rock so bare
And watch the sea with vacant stare
See the breakers rough and high
Toss their foam into the sky and
Watch the gulls as they fly by:
Always Seeking.

Think deep thoughts that make me cry
Always wondering just why this rock was put there.
Like me I'd think this rock could be
Put here on earth for all to see.
Maybe my thoughts just breakers be:
I wonder?

Alice L Stout
SONNET

Dedicated to Father Mark Edwards, deceased, Formerly a teacher at Black Hawk College, Moline, Il. He honored me with his praise.

You pass, a flaming meteor, through my mind,
Your burst as brief as flash point celluloid.
By arc distorted is your trail defined,
White contrails streaming in the dark of void.
The pulsing of your beat is lost in space,
But quintessential being that you are,
Of alien beauties you leave just a trace
Adjoined to twinkling rhythms of a star.
Reflections in this mirror world of clod,
Designed to image you as when you passed,
Retain a curse, an earthly stain of sod.
Distorted is the flight that I have glassed.
The spirit scarcely weds itself to clay;
It darkly waits to wing itself away.

Annie Gutierrez
WHEN WILL THE SUN SET?

When will the sun set?
When will the sky turn red?
When will the clouds separate?
When will these visions fill my head?
When does the sun fall,
And go to sleep?
And the tiny stars up above,
Open their twinkling eyes and weep?
When does a full moon rise?
And shine on us its light?
Why does this beautiful change,
Happen only once every night?
How can so many people sleep,
At such a perfect time?
Does no one notice this beauty?
Is the night, alone, all mine?
The cool sweetness of the night,
In the morning must go away.
And in its place, the sun shines bright,
Burning me with each hot ray.
The sun holds a certain beauty,
But none compared to the moon.
It showers me with such a glow,
How I hope the sun will set soon.

Marie Ellen Creighton
MY TWIN

When I look into the mirror
I see my twin,
She's not related,
By marriage or kin.
She is someone special
To me.
She is always there,
When she needs to be.
When I need someone
To talk to,
I know all I have to do—
Is look into the mirror
And I see,
My twin, who is waiting
For me.
She will always be my twin
And
She will always be my friend.

Doris Lickwola
MY GRANDSON

It's not the things that can be bought
That are <u>my</u> richest treasure—
It's a visit with my grandson
And there is <u>no</u> way to measure
The joy and love he brings to me—
Ryan is my greatest pleasure!

He takes me on a magical tour
Into his won little land of toys—
A visit with He-Man and She-Ra,
Voltron and Hordak—
Transformers and GoBots—what joys!

On to the land of Mickey and

Minnie—
Puzzles, trucks, crayons and
balls—
There are cartoons and Mr. Rogers
And cars that climb the walls!

I never cease to be amazed
How this little child of three
Can fill my heart with so much love
Which he imparts to me!

A grandchild is a priceless gift
That cannot be bought or sold—
The love, the joy, the happiness—
Are worth more than silver or gold!

Ruth F Wright

Ruth F Wright
A PORTRAIT

To my mother Minnie Foster Cooper

Upon her head a crown of glory
That fadeth not away,
An ornament of grace
Around her neck,
She openeth her mouth with
Wisdom,
And in her tongue is the
Law of kindness,
Neither was guile found in
Her spirit,
Grid about in white linen,
Feet shod with the gospel of peace,
Her heart flowing with praise
And in her hands the words of life

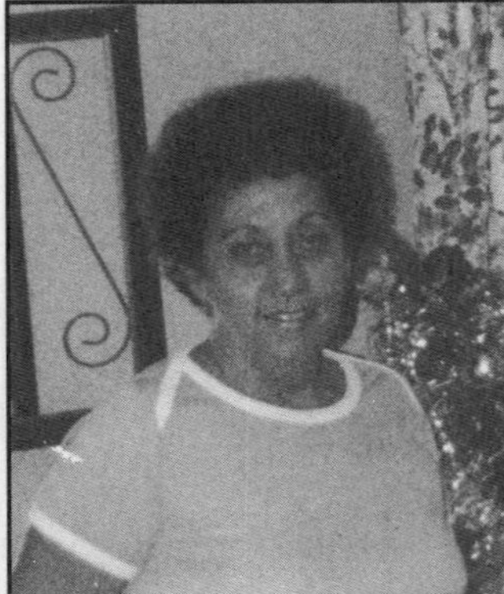

Nellie K Dantoni

Nellie K Dantoni
A SMILE
A little smile upon your face
can make the day seem brighter,
It helps when you are troubled
and makes the load seem lighter.

Chris A Smith
THE LADY WITH GOLD HAIR

This poem is dedicated to my friend! Angiee Crumrin

There's a lady with gold hair who makes all the men stop and stare. Her hair is finer than any diamond or broach. This is what makes me want to approach and be with her. For the rest of my life. Although she's taken I still want her. But then I wake up and realize. She's like gold something of which I can't have. Her or the gold.

Mary Willard Swain
OASIS

To Kenneth, Nina, Mom and Dad with much gratitude

Catch a lovely fleeting moment
Bind it taut in fisted hands,
Ere it sifts through vapid fingers
Swept on winds to distant lands.

Chase a tranquil golden moment
Stay it 'neath the pounding feet,
Cruel angry crushing forces
Slay the nuggets pure and sweet.

Glean a joyous rushing moment
Hoard it safe in avid mind,
Morning dawns a veiling shadow
Rend'ring beauty's mem'ry blind.

Fold away a sacred moment
Nurture fervent soul in part,
Loving moments captive dwelling
Precious treasures of the heart.

Katie Kelley Jones "Kay"

Katie Kelley Jones "Kay"
TIME OF LIFE

To Bob my loving husband, and family. Fr. Richard my hary K—Spiritual adviser. Thanks for their inspiration

Life is like sand flowing through
an hour glass
No matter, whether you are poor,
middle, or upper class
Nor how much knowledge, you
have acquired.
The strife, all the heartache.
"Love," was required.
"As you journeyed through"
How you treated life, or life was to
you
In your memory, the happy times
and the sad

What you have done, the things
you wish you had
"I'm a young fifty-one"
I pray for many years to come
My hopes, my dreams, for the
future will be
Filled with Faith, Joy, Love, Peace,
and Charity
Upon Reflection! In the Quietness
of My Mind.
I feel! I have only, "Touched," The
Edges of Time."

Sandra Pilling
I AM

To son Bill: 1964-1984

Long ago when I was young the world was mine to conquer. Later, as an adult, wife and Mother; the world belonged to someone else and I was content simply to survive.
It made me different; a tougher, stronger refugee from struggles past.
One day I looked and found I was no longer me—Where went the sweet thing that loved the world without question? Who caused the change? . . .
The many who wrote on the impressionable mind and taught it how to cry; how to hurt. I ever return to trust and love, as once before, knowing what I know?
Wisdom of age is not always a proper excuse, nor knowledgeable to do less than say "if only" to build each day, over and over the person who is me.
One day the world will be mine once more . . . Perhaps only after the fact . . . when this life is done, can someone, somewhere say . . this person was good and loved much. I will have won the total victory—for then it will no longer matter who I am except to me and God.

Andree D'anna
THE CHILD FLIES WITH EAGLES
I began, and was afraid to fly—
then sought the consulation of
eagles.
Daring the sky with their
swift-winged knives they cut.
I began to fly . . . and
mangnificently fell . . .
to
Earth.
An ode to greening of pastures,
meaningful gestures and
postures . . .
while the eagles perched with
valiant nests
Against the sky.

I began to fly again,
to witness stars and many other
knowledgeable worlds.
Even the ants seemed splendid in
their endeavors.

I began to devour the whole sky
and things in my path.
The sharp wide beak opened to all
humanity.

I AM AGAIN, I AM BORNE, like
the eagle.
Air friend and witness of all the
spiritual universe,

The spirit flies, beyond the eagles
Far out of view
Ascending
Into . . . Into . . .

Leisa J Allen
DRUNKEN REGRETS
Last night was part of the day
I had waited for, for years
Yesterday was my birthday
and I turned nineteen my dear
I had a celebration
full of lots of cheer
The beer was stacked like
mountains
and all my friends were there
We partied until early morning
and I left still drunk at dawn
God help me I was swerving
there was nothing they could
have done
I hit their car head on
no survivors left to tell
The cries could have rocked
mountains
three dead children who I had
killed
Their mother was in critical
soon after she did die
I beg God to forgive me
no more tears can I cry
Nothing can bring them back
oh please look at what I've done
Drinking is a hazard
that can be fatal even to the very
young

Stephanie Button
IN A HEAVY HEART
In a heavy heart, there is no rest.
A teenager is struggling within his breast.
There is no peace that he can find.
His eyes can see, but he is blind.
Searching for truth day by day, but the emptiness in his heart won't go away.
He realizes his heart is crying for love, then falls to his knees and looks above.
God reaches down with both of His hands and tells the teenager that He understands.
Not a word could the teenager speak, as God gently wiped a tear from his cheek.

God with His tenderness and
His words so true, looked into the
teenager's eyes and said,
"I LOVE YOU!"

Theresa Gavic
FOREVER DEAR

Dedicated to my husband Scot, My friend and my inspiration

As one beat our heart
Entranced is our mind,
Your eyes so clear
Your smile so kind.
No other lips taste so sweet,
No other hands so smooth or
strong.
Your embrace makes my life
complete,
Your voice is my safe and secure
song.
I close my eyes and think of you,
The vision of love comes beaming
through.
My eyes can't help but bring a tear,
I'm in love with you,
Forever Dear.

Jean M Uebel
LOVE GROWS

This Poem is Dedicated to My Loving Husband, Ernst Ludwig.

It may begin a slight flirtation,
To bloom and grow into
infatuation.

But then again, as time goes by,
You stop to think how come or
why.

Look out your window to
Moonbeams and Streams,
Let your mind wander to
Memories and Dreams.

Your heart reminisces the laughter
you've shared,
Your mind recollects now, how
much you cared.

So caress him now and hold him
fast,
For your life time of dreams have
come at last.

Kiss him and hug him, and keep
on sharing,
To Blossom a Love, Depends On
Caring.

Vera J Williams
FLAG TODAY

To all persons interested in poetry.

What does the flag mean to you,
Banners red and white and blue?
Does it set your eyes to see
What this could mean to thee?

What does this flag mean to you,
As we pledge allegiance true?
Is it a symbol of the free
Floating to save our liberty?

Flag so brilliant and so bright,
Flying for the good and for the
right,
Waving for the proud and the brave
Help this land of ours to save.

Flag so lovely, when you fly high
Beneath the azure of the sky,
Bind each heart unto you fast
So strength and UNITY forever
will last.

Rose Burkhart
YOU WENT AWAY

You said, "We're through." , then
you went away.
Stunned, I watched you go.
Days drift by; my misty eyes stare,
wanting to envelop you in their
gaze.
My arms hang limp and heavy,
waiting, waiting, endlessly
waiting to enfold you,
knowing that strength will return
only
with holding you close.
My feet carry my body
in disappointed anticipation.
They sense the absence of familiar
shoes,
of soft, gentle toes.
They become lonely and tired for
they miss
your warm, joyful legs that
walked close by
in happy friendship.
My heart cries, aching in rejected
love.
But, no more! No more!
If I'm to gain control of me
I dare not speak again
of the longing within my heart
and the pain-filled emptiness
that permeates my being,
since you went away.

Christine L Nordstrom
YOU CAN'T DO IT! (A TRUE STORY)

In 1913 a country church burned
down,
It was a sad and sorry day for the
only church in town,
So they built its body up again but
stopped short at the neck—
To complete the clock and bell and
tower the town picked up the
check.
Every three or four years when the
church was looking bad
It was faithfully repainted and the
town picked up the tab,
Then, in 1973, or somewhere
thereabouts,
A citizen who hadn't known with
great surprise found out.
The citizen, wanting answers,
chose to make a special journey,
He took his tale to Boston to the
state attorney general.
The "General" said, "This violates
our country's constitution,
I understand God's in command
but man must seek solutions.
The town must make the church a
public building for the people
Or the church will have to
congregate to purchase back the
steeple."
The church was quite unhappy
feeling down upon its luck,
But it DID buy back the steeple for
one large almighty buck,
And will they ever paint it new
again?
Perhaps, when God is willing,
For to maintain the clock and bell
and tower
Costs more than to paint the whole
building!

Wanda Whanger Higgins
IN THOUGHTS

The people surrounding were as if
the dark of night,
No speaking voices almost like;
In this town with no sparks of life.
Then, wading through my
thoughts intense,
I do think I caught a glimpse;
Oh, yes, a star brightly gleaming
I really must be dreaming.
I must come back tomorrow,
So I can relive this clear!

Devorah A Pugsley
MY FRIEND

My friend,
You were always there when I was
sad.
You were always happy when I was
glad.
You stuck around when I was mad.
You never judged when I was bad.
You were the best friend I ever had.

My friend,
From you, my feelings I could
never hide,
And always you were there, at my
side.
You were my protector, my joy,
and my pride.

My friend,
I could always tell you about my
dreams and
Other things,
That people would have laughed at
and labeled,
"Foolish mental flings."

My friend,
You always knew how to gladden
my heart,
And even now that you are gone,
And your death forces us apart,
The memory lingers still, in my
mind,
Of a friend whose better I shall
never find.

Now, people may scoff and people
may sneer,
At a person who holds one of "your
kind" so dear,
But they were gone when I needed
them near.
You, my friend, were always here.

So, I'll go on refusing to allow them
to jog,
My loving memories of you, my
friend,
My dog!

Oscar Phillips
THE PAWN BROKER

This poem is dedicated to Milton Kaplan, Pres. and all the employees of Safferstone's and North Memphis Pawn Shop, Memphis, Tennessee.

To a wonderful man who is sweet
as honey
His business is loaning money,
He don't work with a chip on his
shoulder
Because he's wise and live to have
gotten older,
I am sure his parents are proud
that they gave him birth,
Because he's grown up to be a man
that's down to earth,
At work he don't walk around big,
bad, and tall
To each and everyone he is friendly
to us all,
No he don't smoke
But love to joke,
Once in a while
He will make you smile.

Margaret R Schmidt
THE GLORY OF A SINKING SPELL

The sun has a sinking spell each
evening.
But rises the next morning in all of
its
glory and splendor,
Ready to give its sunshine in
beauty and warmth
Wherever needed.

When we have a sinking spell,
Remember we too, must rise and
shine in our
brilliance,
Radiating forth the rays of love,
kindness,
courage and inspiration.
Radiating forth the rays of love,
kindness,
courge and inspiration
Wherever needed.

Carol Lynn Meyers

Carol Lynn Meyers
CHILDHOOD INNOCENCE

To Leslie, and Teddy my best. To Jimmy and Michelle many nights of blissful sleep.

Nightime has decended, and its
time to go to bed.
You look so sweet and cuddly as
you lay upon your bed.

Your teddy tucked beside you as
you slowly draw him
close, and whisper that you love
him and playfully pull
his nose.
The day has been a long one and
you ventured very far,
from playing super heroine to just
the way you are.
Your eyes fill with amazement as
you look at each new thing
I often wonder why it is I can't see
the things you see.
Your eyes fill with excitement as
each new day draws near
each day is an adventure that
children seem to share.
Why is it we grow old and don't
stop to see, the things
that are important, the things that
children see.

Alberta Turner
MEMORIES ARE HERE TO STAY

To my dearest husband, children, families and wonderful friends, who really care and helped through all these years.

God made darkness into light
He makes the moon and sun shine
The stars that twinkle so bright
The short, medium, tall of pine
Flowers of beauty and crops that
grow
Birds and animals and humans too
Brinks to mind what to sow
Creative arts for many to do
He makes life then takes it away
But memories are here to stay.

Dad and mother so strong in their
way
Teaching their children how to
pray
Grandparents, uncles and aunts a
plenty
Cousins, brothers and sisters many
Always one telling stories by the
hour
Guiding, showing to give you
power
The joys of life as we travel along
Makes one happy to sing a song
We thank God for our blessings
each day
Just remember Memories are here
to stay.

Kym Marie Shiller
MICHELE

To the woman who gave me back . . . me.

Look at me—
who do you see—
the person I am or the one I use
to be?
I've loved and I've fallen—
broken heart and soul.
Have you ever been able to look
through me and see it all?
Another breathless moment,
this time I'll wait and hide.
I gave myself a promise—never
again—
to let inside.
My heart now wrapped in layers
from past lovers missing parts,
I've secured until I met you—
now I don't know where
to start.
You are a gift placed in front of me
with only love to bear,
I know it's only a matter of time, I
need,
So I can share.
The bondage that's around my
heart
I hope you'll see it through.
For when we tear it all apart I
know,
I'll be,
Like you . . .

Eulalie L Steward
THE CENTRAL GATE

Let's be generous as a Nation!
Let's just put ugliness out on
Probation!
Stand firm and resolute!
Dignity and Honesty should be
the absolute!
Hide not your eyes from sin and
lies—
The noise of work and worship are
often in
Disguise!
Accept the truth from ear and eye,
Keep a diagnostic talent sharp and
spry!
Evaluate wisely, the Media's
contribution
Research and check, Top
Reporters distribution!
Let's be considerate, kind and
Humane.
Let's find explanations, plausible
and Sane!
Let's forgive! but let us Remember
Many things with covers have
combustible Timber!
Let's change to a Smile and
eye-touching Grace.
Let's discuss and resolve all
problems in this Place!
Investigate, explain Educate
and plan
Elevate—Integrate—Enhance
the Soul of Man!
Spread aboard this glow of our
Togetherness
United in Purpose of Moving
Stormy Weathered-ness.
Pass around the Understanding
Charm
Devoid of weapons, Fears and
Harm!

Gerarda Cecilia Gibbs
INTO YOUR DEPTH

Yet if he carried my cross, still lay
I with the bearing
Still I walk in anxiety, for he
giveth and he taketh away
There I stood knocking on a
closed door
Waiting for a way, waiting for a
time
Could he have forsaken me or is
he
drawn into the rivers of the sea.
My goodness, I can't wait
For tides rise above me
And I am drawn into their depth
Searching for the untold
Looking for a day
Or perhaps a night
It's here, but we
the star must
find the sky to
which we belong
to which we
descend
to which
we
must
go

Helen Jean Richardson
BIG BAD WORLD

Look in the mirror and who do you
see.
Is this person really me?
Take off that mask.
I cannot face the cruel world.
This world is like a cold winter
night.
"Oh please don't make me face the
world."
I am not a little girl.
The world is a monster waiting
outside my door.
Knock, knock, who's there?
"Oh just me," the Big Bad World.
I shall not give in and open the
door.
I can't take no more.
I shall not give in and open the
door.
For if I do I must surrender to that
world.
The Reality's of that Big Bad
World.

Arthur M Rhodes Jr
MY WORLD

If I could build a world
for everyone to see,
There would be happiness
and happiness a sea.

Laughter would be abundant,
it would grow from a tree.
No-one would ever be sad,
that's the way it should be.

There would be no need for hunger,
or even threat of war;
No need for fighting at all,
for you see, there'd be no more.

The earth would be a fountain
and from it love would pour.
This fountain would be everyone's;
Theirs, Mine and Yours.

The sky would be like silk,
never having a crease.
Life would be a banquet,
One on which we all could feast.

My world I can only dream of
and this dreaming will never cease.
But I'd be happy with this world,
If it had never ending peace...

Linda Feamster

Linda Feamster
A SUMMER NIGHT

Moonbeams silently stealing
across the lawn
Embracing the maple and
disappearing by dawn.
A soft summer breeze begins filling
the air,
With the fragrance of Lilacs and
Honeysuckle, everywhere.
Fireflys like twinkling stars,
flickering in the night,
Playing hide and seek with their
soft green light.
Off in the distance, the song of a
whippoorwill,
Breaking the silence of a night
so still.
A cloud passes over puffed full with
rain,
As soft raindrops begin tapping
against the window pane.
Behold the glory and splendor of
God, an exciting night,
Soft, warm, enchanting, a
Garden of Eden at night.

Marilyn A Hall
MY LOVE

To my husband, Earl Clayton

I wrote a poem for you today
What it says I cannot say
You're in my heart and on my mind
I see your smile and your big
brown eyes
As I held your hand and we said
good-bye
I sit here and watch the snow pile
high
But look up and there are stars in
the sky
The sun will shine tomorrow I
know
And my love for you forever will
grow
For in March it is true
37 years ago was the day I said I do

Raydelle Winter Knarr
A LAD AND HIS DAD

Today I saw a little lad
A-cutting grass beside his dad.
The little mower, fast or slow
To keep the pace that Dad would
go.
If Dad went forward, then the Boy
Would that way go, with smile of
joy:
But when his Dad reversed his path
The lad went backward with a
laugh.
Adoring eyes were fixed upon
The father, by a loving son.

Oh, father, may you conscious be
The pattern you must set that he
Will always walk the path of right—
Your ways are perfect in his sight.
It's up to you to point the way
Your son will take from day to day.
Your faith, your courage, love or
hate,
Your little boy will imitate.
You must account for each deed
done
Of bad or good before your son.

Irene E Vennette
60TH ANNIVERSARY

For sixty years now, you have
shared each others Love,
And for sixty years, God has
guided you from above.
You are a great couple, good
parents to Brother and I,
There were more children, but
they are with God in the Sky,

I know you enjoy one another, and
still hold hands,
So I wish you more time
together, if it is God's plan.

Your lives were Love, Laughter
and Yes, some Tears,
What more could you ask for,
after all these years?

Now this is a great Anniversary . .
. . to obtain,
As the years go on, I know you
will not complain.
You both look forward to more
time together,
I am sure, so I wish you both the
best,
Dad and Mother.

Noble G Boyd

TO THE MOUNTAINS—LET US GO

To the mountains—let us go—
High, high above the hue and cry
of the world below.
Let us, instead, hear the still small
voice of God
Pleading with man His will to
obey—
For 'tis on the mountain heights
God has spoken to man.

But, there we cannot stay—we
must come down.
Will it be the same old world we
left behind when up the
mountain we did climb?
Ah, Yes! Perhaps so, but how
differently to us it will now
appear.
Why? How so? One might ask.

Comes the answer, clear and
strong—
Because of our interview with God
upon that mountain top
Up, up, among the clouds and
away from the earthly hue and
cry.
The answer is Yes, surely Yes, for
we now can more clearly see
The needs of that world below, and
are now more ready His will to
obey.

Orlin Foster Sr

RICHES OF GOD

A loving God, a country of freedom, a loving family true, loving and caring friends. May God hold you in the hollow of his hands. Love and luck.

A fall of snowflakes on a windless
night, the riches
of God are sound, and in sight, and
blown white buds in
the fields of June, the starry dark,
and the sunny
noon. The sky new leaves at the
root of spring, the
lift, and start of the red birds wing.
Since no man lives who is really
poor, and all may take from the
endless store.
The riches of God are manifold,
exceeding silver surpassing gold.
Who ever has loved or laughed or
sung, been gay or lovely
or brave or young and seen cool
green shadows on
quiet streams and childrens
laughter and lovers dreams
with the light of the moon on his
lifted face or walked
with the wind in a leafy place, the
new day break in the
Eastern skies, or who ever has seen
with his own
two eyes or scattered seed on the
fragrant sod
has had a share in the Wealth of
God. Love and Luck.

Mrs Jasper Kenneth Simmons

A DAY'S END

To my husband, daughter and son, Kenneth, Elizabeth and George William

---

AT the end of each day
when my work is all done,
How I like to sit down
and watch the setting sun.

The robins and sparrows
have all gone to their nests,
As I see the last rays
of the sun in the West.

I thank God for pleasures
of the day that has passed,
And ask for his mercies
when my eyes close at last.

Edward D Davis

Edward D Davis

DREAM UNFULFILLED

This poem is about a girl,
Who is beautiful and kind.
Her radiance astounds me,
And her charm captures both soul
and mind.

Many beautiful girls I have seen,
In my travels far and wide.
But my happiest moments,
Were when you were by my side.

And as I travel onward
My many dreams to fulfill.
I leave one dream open,
For you, whom I love still.

Terri Lynn White

MY MISTAKE

I hope you know how I feel,
because the feelings inside
are just unreal.
I don't know what to do
because, I still love you.
I'm very sorry for what I've
done!
I miss the things that we
did that's such fun!
I don't know what to say,
these feelings I'm feeling
are just not ok!
My friends say I'm doing
you wrong,
I believe them now because
you're gone!

E Randall Silvers

ALMOST TO SAFETY

The Marine was returning from
patrol late that night
Looking through the jungle at the
Compound's welcome light.
He knew if he made it there he'd
be all right.
Almost to safety. Almost, but not
quite.

He thought how the ambush on his
squad took its toll,
When "Charlie" opened fire from
the top of the knoll;
How his buddies had died as they
screamed in their fright.
Almost to safety. Almost, but not
quite.

The young man then stumbled as
he followed the trail.
His mind was now wondering
what caused them to fail.
He then looked again for the
Compound's great light.
Almost to safety. Almost, but not
quite.

The young man, now shaking so
much from his fear,
Sat down for a moment to quell a
great tear.
Shots from the jungle then rang
out that night;
Almost to safety . . .

Cheryl L Hood

THE OLD MILL

This poem is dedicated to Charles and Todd for their support and to "THE OLD MILL" for inspiring me to write it.

There was an old mill built in 1860,
Back when times were hard and
people thrifty;
People would come from miles
around,
Just to have their wheat and corn
ground.

The old mill stone came from
across the sea,
From some little town in Italy;
The old iron wheel crossed enemy
lines,
During the Civil War . . . the
hardest of times.

Horses and buggies would line the
old roads,
And after a time, left with their
heavy loads;
There was an aroma of ground
corn and wheat,
It must've been hard to stay in your
seat.
The grind of stone and roar of the
wheel,
Gave many small children quite a
thrill;
Families came together piled high
in the seat,
To see the old mill was really a
treat.

The wheel with its water did
mightily flow,
I wish I'd been there . . . bet that
was some show;
The mill stone would crush the
corn so fine,
People were always waiting in line.

As a water supply was a ten-acre
lake,
To fill it in was a grave mistake;
The dam was opened, the water
would race,
To grind the corn at a faster pace.

THOSE WERE THE GOOD "OLD"
DAYS LONG AGO,
THOSE WERE THE DAYS THAT
ARE NO MORE.

Janet Hysell Wagoner

FOREVER IN MEMORY

Dedicated to My Beloved Mother, Annabell Hysell

When a love one passes away,
And you wish they could have
stayed;
For at least one more day.
When the hurt is so deep inside,
You want to run; but there is no
place to hide.
When this is just a dream you feel,
And it just does not seem real.
When you think of things unsaid
and undone,
And wish for more time with this
love one.
When tears you can no longer cry,
And when it comes to the final
goodbye.
When the heartache you can no
longer bear,
There is someone who knows and
does care.
Someone has faced this same day,
And they can tell you; it will yet
pass away.
You will think of the times spent
together,
And all these you will cherish
forever.
But now you are too sad,
To think of memories you have
had.

Nina Cascio

THE ROSE OF LIFE'S END

A Rose is one of life's stories,
For each petal tells of our glories.
The birth is a bud, grown from a
stem,
That bursts out with many petals
around them.
Each petal starts opening into a
beautiful thing you see,
Until one day they start to fall and
soon will be free.
Yes, free of life's troubles and woes,
Just as we are put to rest in the
ground below.
For the Rose of Life has dried, the
petals turned dark,
So now it's farewell, with much
regret, we shall depart.

Mr Emory M Biggers

REFLECTIONS OF DEATH

Why they fear me
I do not know
I harm no one
I touch and then go
Why I am feared
I can not understand
I just open a door
And guide by the hand
They think me cold
Not possessive of heart
No warmth, no love
Throughout my many parts
They fear me and yet
Do not understand
I make easy their entrance
Into another land
Why they fear me
I do not know
Unless it is because
They do not wish to go

Cletus Clark Moffitt
TRUE LOVE
I took my girlie for a stroll
for her love a-seeking.

I missed her mouth and kissed her
nose
and found that it was leaking.

Helen T Golightly
ONE SUMMER'S TWILIGHT!
What a feeling of Peace, and
Tranquility, as
I return each year, to my old
place of abode!
A place where Autumn dwells in
depth, and
I find myself walking down an
old winding dirt road.

Where the anchient Holly, Birch
trees and the
tall yellow Popular's remain year
after year, kissing the sky.
Setting the stage for a Grand
Finally, fall
colors reach peak's of brilliance
before winter's dormancy,
whispering good-bye.

With compassionate eyes,
watching speckled quail, rustle
in
the underbrush, as their
off-spring play happily in the
sand.
Brightly, colored foliage of our
decidoues trees and
shrubs, inter-spersed with
evergreens transforms the
wood's
into a wonderland!

Tonya L-H Vickerman
EARTHQUAKE
A terrible noise
tore the air
down through the window
the earth broke wide
her crooked wound deep
the building sways
clung to the floor
hold on life
run to the beach
expression agape
the ocean broken
waters fold
fill the crease
snatch the children
from her clutch
cast to the ground
back over my shoulder
black sky
the sound

Teri E Wolff
AN EPITAPH FOR SOCRATES
My silent, unfledged, wee "avis,"
A life you've set your face against!
I cannot rest
And so, hard-pressed
Sack cloth and ashes kneel in
mist . . .

My playful, songful, joyful pet:
The Fates would sing our last duet;
In falling leaves
My Socrates
Sleeps, lulled by death's lament.

Life stroked its winter on your
breast
So cold this dawn, an empty nest.
Melodic muse,
One poet less
Whose songbird mourns are quiet
trysts.

As snowflakes flutter in duress
And blanket your small bed,
(My God will bless)
My wee "avis" —
You'll more than seeds be fed.

Irene Rousey
AUTUMN

This poem is dedicated to my dear husband, Julius, who appreciates the beauty of Autumn in our Georgia Mountains as much as I do.

Touched by the beautiful frosts of
early morn
The trees stand solemn in their
sun-drenched splendor;
Garbed in wild, indescribable hues
of gold, red, orange, and
yellow . . .
As I in awe, view the majestic
mountainside
Robed in her vivid array of beauty
As a king in all his glory
Sitting upon his mighty throne.

Mother Nature has completed her
work for another season.
Soon, oh too soon! The trees will be
Derobed of all the beautiful
raiment
For so short a time they wore.
The winds and storms and rains
will loose them from their home
And cover the roads and paths that
so oft have been trod
By strangers and lovers of the
mountainside . . .
While others fly far away finding a
new place to rest.

Reginald H Wright
TAKE CARE MY FRIEND, AMERICA

Dedicated to Freedom

I am America's Union
Freedom is my guide
I stand up for our people
I plea you sense that pride!

For all across this nation
Our vigil has implied;
"Take care my Friend"
America; will never censorize
Nor raze her Flag of honor.
That trust we advertise!

Peace will fly our banner
To seed the fields of faith
"Take care my Friend,"
America; I salute—
Your fond embrace!

George B Williams
MERRY-GO-ROUND
I am not so bold to take hold
A pole as cold & unfriendly.
Harsh is its music so close.
Calliopes please only from far
away.
The screeching deafens me!

Up-down, up-down, round &
round;
Swirling, twirling, sad thoughts
unfurling.
The acceleration dizzies me!

Blue, purple, red, orange, yellow
fuse
Astride my spectral steed.
Yet demonically do I ride
This vortex-crazed carrousel!

Dear God, what do I cling to
On this merry-go-round of life?

My frantic voice screams in vain
Amidst the wind and the rain—

I want the brass ring!
I want—
I—

Michael J Lowery

Michael J Lowery
REMEMBER ME

To everyone who's ever loved me, and to anyone who can't find the words to say good-bye, this poem is for you

---

Remember me with a warm soft
smile
a hearty laugh and cheerful eyes
Think of all the moments we've
shared
and how lucky we are to have
memories
so dear

Know in your heart how much I
always loved you
and reflect on the experiences
that together we went through

So when I leave this world
and my body is gone
you may treasure these thoughts
your whole life long

Clarence Holcomb
TEEN FOOD

For Kristen Hairston—My Granddaughter who has since this poem was written learned that nature really does know the distribution pattern.

As I sit here
And look at my plate
I think of all
The food I ate

Where did it go
Where will it show
How much and where
Will it make me grow

I say to my self
I'll take it slow
And only eat
Every day or so

Then I see
A heaping plate
And like Pavlov's dog
I salivate

I lose resolve
And eat again
I will probably end
With a double chin

Ella Mae Sanders
THE SCALE OF LIFE
There are times we feel we do too
much—
That we are getting the old "soft
touch,"
For some will take and take and
take—
They'll take lots more than we can
make.

Especially on gloomy days life
certainly can be dreary.
There doesn't seem to be a thing to
make it bright and cheery,
And then some one gives us a
boost, we feel our strength has
risen,
Then we know God is behind us all
and theres much more to be
given.

There are times we feel so useless
and so utterly unneeded,
Yet all around are things to do if
we had only heeded.
We'd give someone a helping hand
to show that we do care,
In any way do what we can and be
always just and fair.

Sometimes one doesn't have the
time, or maybe doesn't see
The pleasant little things to do that
troubles softer be,
But if we've faith and love and trust
in all our fellowman
It'll help to boost his spirits up then
he'll do all he can.

Theres a certain amount of
happiness that offsets all the bad,
So to live our lives the fullest we
should all be very glad.
Theres only so much of the "bitter"
that can go along with the sweet
And we'll have to smile and firmly
stand upon our own two feet.

The moral to this little plot I
haven't figured yet—
There are surely times that one
must give that others still may
get.
I guess it all adds up to me—that
this is what its about.
"The Scale of Life" is pretty fine
but it usually balances out.

James Greene Jr
THE LADY

This Poem Is Dedicated To Sallie M. Johnson

Listen people to what I say, James
Greene gonna tell you a storie
this very day, now I know, now

I know, the feelin
when your lady put you down don't
waste a moment wondering why
cause the lady say goodbye. When
every thing goes wrong, you
still got to go on don't let the feelin
get you down, even
when times get rough and you've
had enough. No matter what
people
say don't let them stand in your
way, cause the lady put you
down. So don't let that feelin get
you down, even when times get
rough and you've had enough you
still got to go on. So no
matter what people say, don't let
that feelin stand in your way.

Katherine Kehl
SWEET MUSIC

To Kay, Charlie and Rew.

The sweetest music that I ever
heard,
Came not from the flute or the
song of a bird,
Nor the Do Re Me of an Opera
theme,
Or the slow trio of "The Old Mill
Stream,"
Or the Western twang of the cows
that roam,
Or the sad solo of "My Old
Kentucky Home,"
Or the chirp, chirp, chirp of the
Robin Red Breast,
Or the tweet, tweet, tweet of the
Canary's best,
But my Grandchildren's wail, as
they howl and cry,
When we part and kiss with a
fond Goodbye.

Karen L Antonaitis
SARAH (1-3-86)

To our little princess who brings us much joy, we thank God for you everyday. All my love, Mommy.

A little bundle so soft and pink
With skin as smooth as milk,
And eyes as blue as the sky above
With the everlasting look of love.

Her smile is like a breath of spring
Her voice will make an angel sing
A rosebud mouth that always
smiles
The love she projects goes miles
and miles.

She's a precious gift, one of a kind
Another like her you'll never find
She's someone so special and new
Not to see her every day will make
you blue.

She'll make her mark, you can be
sure
All kinds of happenings she will
endure
One look at her makes my heart stir
Thank you dear God, for bringing
her.

Annette Reinhart
BEING TOGETHER

To my new Christian family and friends for helping me through my Christian walk with the Lord, and to get to know Him better this year. Thank-you. I love each and everyone of you.

You are far away from me,
If I may, I would come
back and stay.
Everyday I take a walk
and I talk to myself
about you.
I take things down from
my shelf,
One at a time the things
that you gave to me,
And I think about the times
we had together.
I can't see you everyday.
'Cause you're so far away
from me.
But I have the memories
of you.
All I have to do is reach
Out and grasp it between
my hands at anytime.

Sherry A Carbone
A TRUCK DRIVER

This poem is dedicated to Bob, my beloved husband.

There's a truck driver named Bob,
Who should find a new job,
Freeway driving's a pain in the
neck,
Jerks on the road that you'd love to
deck.

At 5 a.m. to the freeway he heads,
"Oh my" he says, "I should've
stayed in bed,
Hundreds of cars a going my way,
And this is what I drive in every day.

Dora K Weyeneth-Soucy
PAVILION OF LOVE

To my Children with Love
Ivor-Aurele-Claude-Odette-&
Huguette

Down there, beyond the garden
walls
Stand's hidden amongst some
loveliest flowers,
The Pavilion of Love!
Such beauteous sight has not been
seen,
The Pavilion of Love is not a mere
dream,
It's path is strewn with yellow
primroses
The air perfumed with the scent of
roses,

The beauty of nature is everywhere
For all lovers to equally share,
The lilac, jasmine, wisteria and
dahlias,
The hyacinth, daffodils, simlax
and camelias,
The Pavilion of Love in it's unique
charm
Has seen many lovers in each
other's arms,
Where love was born between it's
ageing walls
In answer to the famous Cupid's
call.
Pavilion of Love . . . real dream of
gold
Clings to my memory and never
grows old.

Sandra F Lanier
YEARS

It's been years now since I've heard
from you,
Or seen your gentle sad eyes,
But I've not forgotten.
That feeling of happiness, warmth,
and longing,
It all rushes back at the very
thought of you,
Still here after all these years.
Your touch so soft and gentle, yet
demanding,
I can still feel your lips on mine,
All, as if it were yesterday.
I thought my love for you would
die,
Or the memory would at least
subside,
But instead it is still very much
alive.
I wonder, do you feel it too
wherever you are?
Do you think of our love so great
and strong?
Does it make you happy to feel and
think as I?
How would we react if we were to
see each other?
Could we control the sudden rush
of emotion?
For me it would be uncontrollable.
Why was the greatest love of all
times not meant to be?
It could have grown to such
magnitude.
Oh my love, never to forget.
I'll love you always, will you me?
Or wait, was it just I who felt and
loved,
I wonder, love of mine.

Toni Milliff
GODS LOVE

I wonder what will happen
When God comes around
To take all his children
From the ground.

He'll take them to his heaven
And make life worth living
He will always be thoughtful
And forever giving.

God loves everyone
He will always be a friend
For now, forever
This love will never end.

He'll stand beside you
Ever minute of the day
And show his care
In His own special way.

If you get lonely
And start feeling blue.
Just remember
You've always got God to talk to.

Mary-Lou Patterson
UNTITLED

Head of gray
Old dandelion . . .
Waiting to be
Blown away

Lori A Bihl
LIGHT OF TOMORROW

To Lydia, with all my love:

If only my heart could speak
then you would know my feeling
true
but it seems I'm at a loss for words
because my heart hurts for you
if only I could take away the
yesterdays
that filled your heart with sorrow
I'd give you back a happy heart
and a hurt free tomorrow
but our yesterdays will always be
something we can never change
and our tomorrows will always be
something we can never arrange
and some of our tomorrows will be
filled
with those who won't let our
yesterdays be
And they'll put a shadow in your
light
So a happier tomorrow will be
hard to see
But if you turn away from them
And reach out to those who care
You'll see the shadow dissapear.
And it won't matter if they judge
and stare
I wish I could protect you from all
of this
But since I can't you must be strong
So we can have you back again,
At home, where you belong.

Jennifer L Alexander
BARNEY

You were always there for me
And I knew you always cared
Even though you were just a dog
There was something special we
shared

We used to play and fool around
And you'd jog with me every day
I taught you all sorts of tricks
To speak, sit, rollover and lay

You were growing weak, you were
growing old
And I knew that you were in pain
I also knew that without you
My life would never be the same

Your eyes are closed, your heart
has stopped
As you lay upon my floor
I take one last good look at you
And start crying more and more

Things are all over now
But I'll think of you and how we
had fun
And in my heart I'll always know
That you Barney, are number one.

Mark Faria
LIFE DOESN'T SEEM TO HAVE ANY MEANING

Life doesn't seem to have any
meaning
The good times we had, seemed
like I was dreaming
'Cause now it's over and we're all
through
But I find, I'm still thinking of you
Only a few good times we've had
in the past

But it is those memories that will always last
Memories of you and I in a warm embrace
Starring eyes Face to face
Words of love passed from ear to ear
Those times are gone, my worst fear
If no memories do you have of me
Then my life has ceased to be

Richard Allen Morris Vancouver, WA

THE NEED

The writing's clear
and the die is cast
one's day in the sun
has come and past

Yet one small part
in the spirit of Man
is unfilled
in the Master Plan

Minimal requirements
were probably met
if the life we lived
was just, and yet

Tho we mostly play
a minor role
Recognition
is the Ego's goal

Where is the mark
on the wall of time
of the slightest scratch
that could be mine

Some small trophy
for all to see
at the show and tell
of eternity?

Mary R Mount

EARTH'S REBIRTH

To my children: Rosemary and David; Robert and Debbie; Christine and Ryan; and Heather.

Golden barley, wheat and oats
glisten in the harvest time.
If I but toil dawn til dusk
all that I can reap is mine.

But before You made them mine,
Lord, You sent both rain and shine

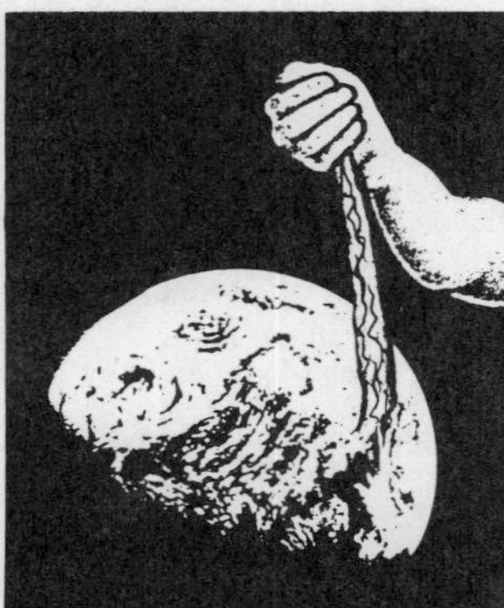

and You caused each seed to grow,
touched them with Your Hand Divine.

Touch us with Your Hand Divine
that Your love will spread on earth.
Guide us forward, help us shine.
May all mankind live rebirth.

Lily Ray Thompson

MUSIC

To my dear Mother and Father Thomas R. Ray and Fanny W. Ray

Music is the place where memory dwells
The language of the soul, exalted and unexcelled
Heartrending sobs pulsate as angel faces finger the heart strings
And we soar upward as if we had wings,
We wait in mid-air for the continuance of the refrain,
And are softly descended but do not remain,
A veil of sadness surrounds us when all is hushed,
And we drift aimlessly back to our old self, as our heart strings
Are given their last brush.

Steve Jobe

A VISION

I walked down crimson corridors of burning amber flame, to see so many different things, none of which the same,
I saw a baby being born into poverty and pain, the mother weeps, the father's gone, what will he have to gain?

I saw a soldier in a war being stretchered away, His face is burnt, his eyes are blind. It causes much dismay,

Sometimes it seems we live in hell, the things that we go through . . .

But then again. Through different eyes, it can be heaven too!

Ron Sanzone II

THOUGHTS FOR A FRIDAY AFTERNOON (SUMMIT MEETING REAGAN AND GORBACHEV IN ICELAND)

So there sat Mr. X,
A sadness in his eyes,
A hundred feet across the table,
Was located Mr. Y.

6000 years of civilization,
Had finally succumbed to this,
2 men; 1 world,
Nothing free from risk.

The bargaining was fast and furious,
Alas, nothing hath been winned,
I see the storm approaching,
And the light of our future has dimmed.

Betty Engle

BE HAPPY BETTY

Betty went up the hill without Bill
She wanted to to be alone
She did not yell, as down she fell
And broke her right crazy bone.

No climber's pick, ski pole, or stick,
No friendly neighbors, or callers,
Needless to say—what a price to pay
Which may be five thousand dollars.

How can one tell when all is well?
And everything's going your way
If the arm is healing, and happy the feeling
Just living and loving today.

Oh have a thrill—go climb a hill
And see the heavenly view—
If you do not go—you will never know—
How exhilarating it can be for you.

J Lynn Tirey

TO ME TO YOU

To me I am sad and confused
To you I am happy and outgoing
To me I see the world as a fearful place
To you I see the world as a wonderful place
To me I see the world out of control
To you I see the world at my feet
To me I hide under a mask
To you I have no mask
To me I carry many burdens
To you I carry none
To me I need my friends very badly
To you I need no one
To me and to you I am two different people trying so hard to be one.

Nila (Whitsell) Phelps

MEMORIES

To Daddy and Mama, for their love, who made the memories possible. To the memory of Uncle Seldon, He was only 15, but made me know love, In memory of Grandpa and Grandma Whitsell, who gave me Love, and for my families support to all the farmers, with love

---

Memories of care free days running through green meadows, watching my Daddy as he plowed up the fields

Memories of Mama in the kitchen early in the morning fixing us all a good hot meal

Memories of laughter and song as my brothers, sister and I played, with love for each other that was so real

Memories of my Uncle Seldon of the day they came to our farm and told our grandparents that their son had been accidentally killed

Memories of farm life sharing love, laughter, tears and caring in a way that only country folks could feel

Memories of my Grandpa and Grandma picking cotten side by side, seeing with my young heart the love they shared still

Memories of my Grandpa and Grandma moving away to California, to seek a better life and to get out of the hot Texas fields

Memories of our own family moving away to another farm, starting out to make new friends, leaving behind memories I will keep as long as I live

Memories of my life on our farm, love and laughter we shared, times that have faded with the years but left me with memories that I still can feel

Annette Barnard

A PREGNANT PAUSE

To Paula, Ray and Scott, our beautiful babies who are now terrific adults, with our love.

Motherhood may not be outdated, but some would argue that it's quite over-rated.

When the rabbit died and I had conceived,
you started being you—and I stopped being me!
We rushed to the Doctor's and waited awhile;
Then he sadistically said, with a sly smile:
"No smoking, no drinking, and limit your salt;
Exercise regularly, and be sure to walk.
Everything's fine, but your ultimate fate
depends on not gaining too much weight!"
It occurred to me then (though I didn't utter a sound),
that all enjoyable things were now out of bounds!

Nine months drifted by, slow as could be.
I couldn't believe the changes in me.
I learned to waddle with stomach rotound,
and to tie my shoes (with no one around).
Some days were worse and the real hub
was when I couldn't get myself out of the tub.
I smiled at "fat" jokes, even though they were flowing,
Observations such as "are you coming or going?"

And then you arrived, an angelic smile on your face;
Curled your fingers on mine, unimpressed with the place.
"Was it all worthwhile?" you seemed to ask from the start.
With a non-pregnant pause, I said "yes, little miracle,
you've latched onto my heart."

Natalie M Merryman

FANTASIA

Let me feel joy in my heart and soul.
Let the sun warm my face and the air make my lungs bubble.
Let the smell of salt water fill my nose and burn my eyes.
Let the rain fall on my head and cleanse my soul as it does the grass.
Let me smell the first crocus of spring, the summer rose, and the dry autumn leaves.
Let me feel the purity of snow, the strength of the wind, and the calm of a warm summer day.
If I can do all these things, then I can be a part of the world and not just a passer-by.

Doris Barb

A BROWN THRUSH

A brown thrush sat so pert, upon a willow's limb,
with a heart so light that from his throat did warble
the sweetest tune. From his soul an urge would soar,
as he gratefully awaited spring.

He cocked his head, eyed his world, first left and
then right. He twitched his tail to

and fro and with
a bobbing motion, did take the air
in flight.

With wings spread full he would
meet the gentle
breezes and glide for a while, then
with grace and
beauty would settle near the lake.
He would sing his
song to the world while looking for
a mate.

His voice rang true, his song was
heard, for his
mate was perched upon a limb far
above his head. She
flew about in a teasing way, with
him following her every
move. They picked a skinny willow
branch, sat waving in
the wind. They joined as one in
beautiful song and would
be mates this spring.

Madeline Bartell Packerman

RECOVERY

the
Ghost of Us
haunts me
It
comes to me
at quiet
unexpected moments
intrudes on my solituide
and
disrupts my efforts
to regain
my equilibrium

the
Vision
grips the crevices
of my mind
tearing
into the helpless
healing surfaces
with relentlessness
till
I gasp
with the sorrow
and
pray for
Exorcism

Mrs Doris Vroman

BEAUTIFUL HAWAII

Hawaii, a land of—
Beautiful blue skies and,
Circled by a spacious, scenic ocean.
People dotting the beach, of
black, and white sand,
Girls, boys, men, and women
doing the hula in exotic motion.

Mountains reaching into the sky,
With clouds hovering, or passing
by.
Soft breezes, and rains that
come, and go,
Making many, many, beautiful
rainbow.

A land of great Aloha Spirit,
For everyone—
Who comes here to live, or visit.
Each island though different in
size,
Is just a little bit of paradise.

There one stands on the white
shimmering sand—
All alone,
As by now the beachcomers have
gone.
Looking out with her sparkling
eyes,
Out to where the ocean meets the
skies.
A peaceful calm she never knew,
Seem to fill her, as soft breezes
blow.

Louise C Watkins

A GIFT

To Barbara Ann, My Daughter

If God had made me a poet, there
would be
No idle time . . .
My days would be spent, with
thoughts of love
And writing rhyme after rhyme.
But I understand it's not easy, to
know
Just what to say.
The thoughts are there; the heart
is willing
But the words will often stray . . .
But I'm not worried about my
"book" or
Royalties I might receive,
It's the day by day living, and
rhymes,
However "corny," that God has
given me.

Mrs Jennie M Florence

MARY'S LULLABYE

Sleep little Jesus,
Sleep precious little child,
Sleep and rest.
Angels are watching you,
Mommy and Daddy too,
Child so blest.
God sent you from above,
To bring us peace and love,
My sweet one.
Soft bits of stardust too,
Stayed in your eyes of blue,
Child so sweet.
With this tiny hand in mine,
You will all hearts entwine,
Sleep holy child, sleep,
Sleep baby Jesus, sleep.

Margaret Ripley Wolfe

AN EAGLE'S CALL

I had a love who devoured pecan
pie, motors
and
me;
Then the Eagle called him from
our mountains
And he went where the Spanish
moss grows and the
Phantoms roar;
Not enough said the Eagle.
Go away for a year and
a
day
To a strange land where rice
children play.

Diane R Mathis

FLY AWAY

Little bird flying high,
little bird if you only knew,
little bird so carefree, how
I'd love to fly with you
up so high gliding on air,
using your wings to escape with
the wind,
As if to say so haven't a care,
A message of hope is what you
send.
Keep on flying fast as you may,
don't let nothing stop you for
tomorrows another day.

Stephanie Michelle Craig

A TRAGIC DAY

Birds in the sky,
They soar as they fly.
The wind sings it's song
As the clouds float along.
Down, down below,
Where the brook has to flow.
Suddenly BANG, a gun!
Then a deer tries to run!
It did not survive as the other ten.
All was silent once again.
A hunter came, got the deer and
went away.
What a tragic day!

Florence I Alexander

DISPOSSESSED

The day you came into my life
In search for hearts to rent.
I thought perhaps you'd pay your
bills,
Believed you "Heaven-sent."

The love and kisses that I asked
Were really not a lot.
My heart was roomy, clean and
pure;
But love I never got.

When tenants do not pay their rent,
They board no longer free;
For they are dispossessed at once
And left the cold to flee.

And so, I've turned you out, my
dear,
The cold you must endure.
I've dispossessed you from my
heart,
And firmly locked the door.

Marian Machado

Marian Machado

I'D TELL YOU THAT I LOVE YOU MOM.

To my dearest mom, I think about you everyday and cherish all the beautiful memories. I love you. —Marian

---

If I could have one more hour with
you
I would have so many things I'd
want to say.
I'd tell you how happy my
childhood was
and how you brought sunshine to
each and every day.

I would thank you for the little
things you gave me
that provided my life with ease
you were always so willing to give
your all
and rarely did I ever say please.

If I could have one more hour with
you
I'd apologize for all the harsh
words my tongue had spoken
but believe me when I'd tell you
that I regret it
and my heart will remain broken.

I would sit and attend to your
problems
without the desire to critcize
Its the feelings behind the words
that are important
and this I have come to realize.

If I could have one more hour with
you
I'd tell you how beautiful and
intelligent you are
You see I never told you these
things
because I always had to be the star.

I'd tell you that I love you mom
and how I admired your
determination to live
but since I'll never have that hour
with you
look down upon me and find it in
your heart to forgive.

Linda Burridge-Willoughby

MAMA-I LOVE YOU

I've been a disappointment
ever since I've known
that time you said
my brother and sister
were born;
I write now
since high school;
with honors to my name,
no money—
which you never understood
means more to me—
its my fame;
Maybe one day
we'll both understand—
hold each other,
let no words come
just the feelings,
and knowledge,
there is Love
Yes,
Between us.
I Love You, MOM.

Ebeling Riley

MISS LIBERTY

I dedicate my poem to God and country and my family, wife Marie and children Esther, Angela, Jim and John

---

I fell in love with a fair lady
She came to us from far away
To brighten up our city
Oh, we love her, she's here to stay.
Now her name to us is history
A visit thrills you so
She resides in New York Harbor
On an isle, that was called Bedloe.

So whenever you are travelin'
To meet her you shall see
She stands so tall
She hears the call
Of every refugee
Oh, our spirit never crumbles
She stands taller than a tree
We're all so proud to know her
She makes a heart feel free.
So whether you are travelin'
By land, by air, by sea
Stop by at New York City,
Where you'll find Miss Liberty

Daisy Smith
AMERICA!
America! America!
God still sheds His grace on thee.
America—O Blessed Land!
You're still the land of liberty.

Your star—spangled banner yet waves proud and high!
You're still the home of the strong.
Brave men continue to give of their lives.
And poets still praise thee in song.
Your freedom still rings form all the land;
Your riches and beauty have grown,
Your victories have not known defeat,
God's truth is still marching on.

America! America!
God still sheds His grace on thee.
America—My home sweet home.
You're still the land of liberty.

Doris E Self
GIVE ME FAITH

To my six children— Donald, Eda Mae, Richard, May, Grace, James—and my dear, departed sister, Vera Blakeslee

---

Oh, Father of the universe
Who made the earth, the sky—
Give me the kind of faith that moves
The mighty mountains high.

The kind of faith that heals the sick,
That helps the blind to see;
The kind of faith that Thou didst have
Up there on Calvary.
Though I have walked near vales of death,
Yet do I fear no ill.
I know that Thou art by my side
And will protect me still.

Alice V Thomson
OLD AND FORGOTTEN
Cast away and forgotten
By those who should care
Life still so precious
It doesn't seem fair
Hands once so busy
Now idle and old
Still long for the touch
Of a young hand to hold
Eyes have grown dim
And shed many a tear
So hard to be shunned
By those held so dear
Why can't we show
The old folks we care
Why must we wait
'Till they're no"longer there
The road of lifes end
Should offer good things
Instead of the heartaches
And strife that it brings
We all walk that road
But we don't seem to care
'Till we get to the bend
And find nobody there.

Laura Anne Packer
OCEANS APART
Even in the narrowest, most hurtful of people
There is that of good in them
Not to ignore the ocean of darkness
Against an even larger ocean
Of light and love, laughter and joy.
Even in a world in which
The ocean of darkness threatens to overwhelm
And destroy the goodness of the ocean of light.

The blackest of the dark oceans has not the power
To obliterate forever the light and goodness
Found in the greater oceans of light
In the hearts of these glad souls.
Even the most blackest of people have in them
Some portions of this lighter, more fair ocean,
Awaiting only the chance to be set free and recognized
For the beauty and light it possesses.

Light ocean, power mighty over the dire dark ocean
Needing only to be recognized to be released
To become a joy and gladness overwhelming
The blackest of the dark oceans.
Worlds apart are the dark and the light,
And yet very near for whatever purpose,
The conqueror is chosen by the individual
In which the two are housed.

Clara R White
FROM THE ASHTRAY
You may not be a smoker,
But please make use of me;
I can serve your smoking friends
Who with you want to be.

For you and your friends who smoke,
I'll do a favor;
Because in a sense
I'm a carpet and furniture saver.

My slots for cigarettes are recessed,
Don't you see?
This helps to keep the cigarette butts
Where they need to be—
Right inside of me ! ! !

Frances D Wilson
HER FIRST LOVE
Swift as the flight of a bird on the wing
Sweet as the flowers in early spring
Pure as the light in a baby's eyes
Fresh as the dawn of a new sunrise.

There will be others as life goes on
Singing the words of love's sweet song
But dearest to her will always be
Her first love's tender memory.

Janice M Lutz
THE ART OF IT ALL
Art is being created before my eyes.
The model poses, every muscle at attention,
with thoughts controlled—no wandering to other places.
'Tis sad he, too, can't put on canvas what he sees on faces.

I sit apart from him, relaxed,
with mind afar or near. Choose, I may.
Portraits form and features appear and disappear in a myriad of interchange.
I am engrossed. Painters seek perfection now with no exigency for change.

I watch an artist squint the shadows where they must be placed
to complement the light, correcting any false effect.
Her squint leads me to near hysterics.
To control a maniacal laugh, my attitude becomes more intent with lyrics.

Someone's mother—no, grandmother—
sighs from time to time and almost seems to speak
as she laboriously puts down her own interpretation of lost youth.
I wonder, is it her desire to ask,
"How do I paint the truth?"

Another is completely self-assured
for youth still holds her by the hand.
Her strokes are firm, true—the likeness is there of what she paints.
Obviously, she percieves her life secure with few constraints.

The evening quickly seems to pass.
Thus nears the end of this, another artists' class.
Within, my heart is greatly stirred;
so to paper I put pen and paint my canvas, but with word.

sd edwards
I CAN FLY

---

for Bruce Murphy, another one of our Great Canadian Poets

---

in dreams   a man can fall
but if he lands
before   he wakes   he dies

it is a scary
feeling   falling
Empire State
pathetic state
of confusion   in the mind

I fell once
I landed too   before I woke
yes   I am still alive
before I landed
I turned into an eagle

Carl Schomberg
YOUNG BOYS IN MEN'S CLOTHING
Young boys in men's clothing
It almost makes you cry
They live for yesterday
For days which are gone by

Their songs are such dear songs
Like children love to sing
They seek the days of old
Wanting the joys of spring

Once they were little boys
Trying to be like Dad
But one day they grew up
And now they feel so sad
So they play children's games
Because it's so much fun
Men wish they were young boys
Playing games on the run

If but for a moment
They can be little boys
They will be so happy
Like children with their toys

Still time makes men wiser
All aging is not bad
For men are like young boys
Who learn things from their Dad

Merwin D Oakes

Merwin D Oakes
A WOMAN

To my Daughter Pamela, my Granddaughter Pam and Ms. Ronnie Roman

---

Heaven's most precious human gift,
Wrapped in fragile love.
Demands the tenderest of nurturing,
Blossoms into the most wonderful of

all that is good.
All through the ages,
Guardian and dispenser of all the joys of the universe.
Unloved. . .Destroyed.

Kathleen C Graves
UNTITLED

For Lawrence Delafield Woodbury Graves

The purest love is not to be compared
to anything at all. Engaging intellect
to filter sense through thought

ensures neglect
of fundamental knowledge which was shared
before evolving creatures rose and dared
stand upright (naked); look up at the sky
and there see God; guess what it means to die:
The old brain by the new has been impaired.

The purest love has naught to do with saints,
nor sacraments, nor marriage; it just grows
from instinct, unromanticized and wild.

The purest love escapes the artists' paints:
Its unseen whiteness is the love that flows
direct, and streams from mother into child.

Gretchen Cooper

UPON A NEW HORIZON

To my beloved grandmother Crisafulli

I walked to the ocean toward the break of day. Still candles
burned in every window that I passed along the way. I see
faces marked with loneliness, looking for shelter. Some about to
go crazy, worried in their world. I see some with bottles as
their only friend in hand. Every time they tried to walk away,
they fall to the sand. Their faces buried beneath the sand. When
they wake to the smell of the salt air. High above the ever
long ocean. They see a new horizon. Some realized that God gave
them another day. The others are the people that belong to the
ocean, to be tossed about, as they do day after day.
I walked to the ocean toward the break of day.
To see if a new horizon waits for me.

Charles Francis Adams

PLAYS

I cannot make a mime of fear
I cannot role a lead.
So many postures, faint at heart,
Contrive at human need.

The trivial and battered child
Applauds the opening line
And throws his fruit and vegetables
When I reveal mine.

Why is the salad of my days,
Set out for all mankind,
A plain fare in jungle lair
Or never brought to mind?

How come a whiff of garbage
Malingers middle age
And scars of old performances
Repudiate the stage?

But if I walk a second mile
And leave the past behind,
Within inhuman comedy
Or tragedies that whine,

Perhaps the salt within my wounds
Can also be within
An empathy to Eden
And honesty in men.

Leslie Rundles

THE RESURRECTION

Jesus rose from the dead
On this Resurrection Day
And some day soon,
we don't know when
He will come to stay.

Three days was Jesus buried,
In a dark and lonely tomb.
Three days His disciples spent
Full of sorrow and gloom.

But on the third day
When Jesus did rise,
Can't you just imagine
The disciples surprise?

God's people were filled
With feelings of joy,
For by this they knew
Sin was destroyed.

And after He rose
Into Heaven He went,
To sit by the Father
Until again He is sent.

The next time He comes
He will forever reign
And we will live happily
In His great domain.

Antonio Colecio Jr

RAIN

Rain come on down
From the sky.
Anytime, day or night.
And fulfill prairies,
Lakes and the seas.
With your beauty
Like crystals that
Surround the sky at night.
Beauty and beauty
That's what you are
Beauty come on down
From the sky.

Margarett Anderson

PATIENCE

Silently, she walks through the parched African
plains. Her sleek feline body is thin from the lack of
a few meals. Her heavy underside shows evidence
of a young cub waiting in a nearby den. With a practiced
eye, she searches the landscape for the prey she
hopes to find, tensing her body as she sees the
cloud of dust coming from the distant horizon.
With unfaltering patience, the lioness sits and waits.

Charles S Quinn

THE QUEST

I set out one day to prove
The undeniable existence of God
O'er highway and barren field
Through mountain trail I trod
In plane and train and car
From city thru forest I went
Seeking, hunting and asking
Sleeping in cabin and tent
I was twenty-two when I started
I was seventy-two when I quit
I wasted my youth in my questing
My youth, my strength and my wit
And then one night in my parlor
On the rocker with pipe in my mouth
I glanced out my evening window
Gazing East and West and South
In the sky the shoe-string formations
Of sun golden pieces of cloud
On the horizon they formed a message
And I read as my head I bowed
For fifty years I'd wandered
Then aged old forced to desist
And now the clouds formed the message
"Yes, I Do Exist"

Tricia Derryberry

MY FIRST SNOW

White stuff is falling down
It is staying on the lawn.
Never have seen it before
It is snow I am sure.

I want to run right outside
And be the first to check it.
Then I hear all sorts of shouts
School is closed, bus can't get out.

Now I know without a doubt
Snow is the best thing around.
We will all stay home today
And in the snow we will play.

My brother was the first one out
I was not the one to check it.
I am so happy he's about
I will not cry or pout.

Patricia A Perrotta

TOMORROW

This poem is dedicated to Jill and Michael for all of their support and inspiration.

Days are the waves
of the rolling sea.
Future, the horizon
wherever it may be.

Nights are the stars
of the Summer sky.
Time is the tide
when it rushes by.

Friendship is the warmth
of the shining sun.
Understanding, the bond
that makes us one.

Ambition is the strength
of you and of me.
Destiny, the fate
that was meant to be.

Andy Cremeans

LOVE

TO: My wife Nancy, With all my love, Your husband: Andy

Loves not a spirit
Nor was it made by man
Loves not something; you hold in your hand
Loves seldom seen; rarely heard; ever touched
God's gift to the world; we need so much
Love can be anything; you like it to be
And I'm hoping; you'll let; your love; be me

Idell O'Connor

MAMA

Mama, I love you I needn't say more
But I want to know about Heaven's Great Door
Is it oh so tall that I cannot see
The latch made to open without any key?
And how many steps to the Wonderous Stairs
Will I have the chance to follow you there?
Oh, Mama, if only He'd used the same mold
And made me the image of you to behold
I'd not have to worry for I'd sure to be
In His lovely Garden Him comforting me

Now, Mama, do roses bloom all year around?
Does it ever get cold; is there snow on the ground?
For I'd need a blanket to lay on my chest
I'll share it with you, Mom, when I lay to rest
Oh, Mama, I miss you with all my heart
God knows I'm hurtin' and falling apart
Now if you should mention my name don't you see
He might reconsider and Call unto me
So won't you please listen for me when I cry
And take me with you, Mama, up in the sky

Gene Schroll

APRIL

April's full of promises—and—
She'll keep them—every one!
Of half-awakened crocuses,
Of tulips in the sun.
Bending weeping willows—and
Small deer—startled—shy—and
Baby bunnies, foxes, squirrels—and—
Umbrellas in the rain unfurled.

April's full of sunshine,
She spreads her diamonds 'round.
In forests and in meadows,
She gaily flings them down—so—
Any ragged beggar who has but eyes to see
Can hold a king's own ransom
When he drops down on his knees—and—
Plucks a single dewy blade of grass that April's left.

April's full of showers,
They make her daisies grow.
In sturdy gold and white profusion
They shed a gentle glow upon
Each and every passerby's happy, sad, or thoughtful face.
Of all the months of all the year
It is April who has grace
To use the quaint and common things
Delicately.

Roger Richmond

A FISHING

Today I am remembering when I was just a lad.
I loved to go afishing with my Uncle and my Dad.
We'd wait till after supper time to go upon our way;
Because my Uncle and my Dad would work during the day.
Some times 'twas dark when we

would leave, so dark we could not see.
We took along a lantern, that cast shadows of us three.
When we got to our favorite spot, (we called it fishing hole)
We'd take a small branch from a tree to help support our pole.
We'd fix our bobbers on the line and then hook on the bait,
Throw both of them into the brink and wait, and wait, and wait.
Ten minutes seemed like ages to a boy of only ten,
I'd pull my line in, check the bait, then throw it back again.
We'd build a bonfire on the bank to take away the chill;
Then Dad would tell some stories of his boyhood, what a thrill.
Along about ten thirty as the fire was burning bright,
We'd have ourselves a little snack to last us 'till midnight.
We always took bologna, it came in a big ring.
We also took a loaf of bread, we thought of every thing.
If we did not catch many fish, it didn't make me sad.
'Cause I had been afishing, with my Uncle and my Dad.

Henrietta Esser Jungwirth

PEACE

When the world to God returns,
When evil men their bridges burn,
When hate and greed, and quarrels cease,
Then the Lord will give us peace.

When the abortionists lay down their tools,
And say, "My God, we've been such fools!
The lives we took were meant to be!
How can we make it right with Thee?"

When around the world our food we share
With friend and foe to show we care,
When immorality and lust decrease,
Then the world will be at peace.

That's when we'll feel the peace and love
From our Creator up above.
And recall the words, on a night so still,
"Peace on earth, to men, good will."

Trudy Denny

PRESIDENT KENNEDY'S BORROWED THOUGHTS

My thoughts were weighed yesterday
For dreams of happiness to-day
My thoughts my life was borrowed
To mold lives for to-morrow

Bob Davis

THE FARTHER GLEN

To any quiet corner, my farther glen, and to the Chiracahua wilderness, my favorite quiet corner of the earth.

---

lets seek the bosom of the secret place
silent in the night
we'll follow the whispers of the wind
to the farther glen
as our hearts soar and bound
there beyond the brooks muted sigh
we'll rest our troubled souls
in our secret place
rush to the beat of life's pulse
cling to the chime of dreams lost
then return to the secret place
there in the farther glen

Marguerritte Mitchell

SEE THE SEA

The sea is a mystery, no matter what you know,
Tho beautiful, it's dangerous, wherever you go,
At times it's blue, or capped with white,
Even flat, or wild in height
Never trust this ocean, no matter what,
The lives it has taken are more than a lot,
Always respect its powers, no matter what unfold,
Unpredictable, its secrets, and wonders, can never all be told!

Ronald F Eden

A CUP IS PASSED

Between the two of us a cup is passed
It's filled with both hope and despair
And in this cup is our portion of life
And the light or shadows we'll share

Patches of sunlight and patches of gloom
Will ever lighten and darken our way
Brightening the darkness with showering light
And clouding even the sunniest day

Life is canvas on which colors are thrown
By the ageless Master above
To strengthen and shade our portrait of life
and give depth to the word called love

So let us sup of this cup that is passed
But with strength and undying trust
Knowing full well dark hours will come
And many strange winds will gust

William F Payne

OCEAN'S EDGE

Pants rolled up
Shoes in hand
We walked the ocean's edge
Happy—
Because love was good
And we were good together.
In the gathering darkness
You came into my arms
And because our need
Was greater than our caution
We undressed
And became as one.
Later
Lying there
I heard
A strange sound in the wind
And I thought
It was probably just God
Sighing with envy.

Doris M Stewart

Doris M Stewart

SHE WAS NOT MINE TO KEEP

This poem is dedicated in loving memory of my precious daughter, Diane Kay Stewart.

I had a little girl, I called my own
A dear little child, so sweet and warm
I made her dresses and pretty things
But our home no longer with her laughter rings.
She would run and crawl upon my lap
And I'd sing and hold her close while she took her nap
It is something I wish I could repeat
I loved her so, but she was not mine to keep.

Sky blue eyes and chestnut hair
A beautiful child with skin so fair
Her hugs and kisses told me she was mommy's girl
A beautiful gem, a priceless pearl.
So much time was put into raising her right
Teaching her good and not to fight,
Showing her sharing is much more fun
Helping her walk and watching her run.

How God could possibly love her more than I
Is really a mystery for I don't know why
He took her away and left me to weep,
For only He knows why she was not mine to keep.

J Eldon Carter

OF CAKE SALES AND TOM THUMB WEDDINGS

To my late father and mother, Verne and Artie Carter, and to Fair Play, Missouri where I spent the first fifteen years of my life.

Memories of small town, midwestern America,
of hailstorms in Springtime
and the smoldering heat of late Summer,
of frosted Autumn's slow-dying beauty
and Winter's snow-deepened paths round the town
are reflected through the seasons,
and which came when and what went where,
who won the rain-drenched fight with the preacher's son
or who left the redbird there dead in the snow,
matters little now.

Hayrides and caroling,
cake sales and Tom Thumb weddings,
a tooth broken on a pump handle,
pockets filled with popcorn balls
brought home from Church on Christmas eve

are things which hold me steady in middle age,
and though each alone could make a story
my memory does not plot out that way;
these things live in my mind,
shape me and give rhythm to my life.

My heart sings a song of the mind's memory,
telling those who will listen
how to call back that finest of red wagons,
that fastest sled on the hill,
and that greatest of all Summer evenings.

Lora Hylemon

THE BLUEBIRD AND THE DOVE

The bluebird is calling
From the hills above
On the breathe of the wind
The soft calling of the dove

The bluebird is wild
Exciting and fun
Flying high in the air
To greet the morning sun

The dove is quiet and peaceful
This is the dove
Cooing so softly
The promise of love

I stand in a meadow
Sparkling with morning dew
Trying hard to make my decision
Between the dove and the bird of blue

I'm looking for excitement
But more so for love
So I answer without delay
The soft calling of the dove.

Agnes Coleman

MAMA

Mama is a powerful word,
It means "Love" however its heard.
It brings joy to warm the heart,
And its a Love that will never depart.

When I think of Mama, I think of the best,
A Lady set apart, from all the rest.
Who fed us and loved us and taught us to live,
And when we would "want" she had something to give.

We need you Mama, altho we're all grown,
Your our leaning post, that we're still leaning on.
We need you sometimes, just to lean on us,
For doing things for you brings joy to each one.

Mama we love you, that sounds very small
But our love for you is bigger than the great China Wall,
We thank "God" for keeping you here with us all
And giving you strength to pick us up when we fall.

Exilia Gutowski
HOW LUCKY WE ARE

Why is there so much sorrow in the world
when there could be so much happiness.
Why do we think we have so little to live for
when we know it's our own selfishness.
We're always reaching for rainbows no matter how high.
We don't see others point of view;
we don't even try.
If we could only give a little and expect
nothing in return, I'm sure this would
be a much better world.
So why don't we all try and do our part.
Maybe we could reach in someones heart.
Then the less fortunate would feel
closer somehow.
Then we would realize how lucky we are.

Waneta V Emery
MORNING PRAYER

Thank you, dear Lord, for this day,
Help me live it as I should.
Let me be pleasant, kind and good.
Let me do my work willingly,
Even if hard the task may be,
And when this lovely day has gone
Please let me see another dawn.

Diana Cella
METAPHOR

My wounds are healing
I think that once again I've started believing
I'm calm—undisturbed
I see the sun and enjoy the rain
Like the autumn tree parting with its' leaves
I try to let go of the burden
and slowly, very slowly, my soul is uncovered
The fight I led was probably only against myself
No more hate and bitterness
The time has come to love

Vicki Derry Lopez
LETTER TO GRANDMA

Thank you Grandma, it's meant so much
Your gentle voice, your loving touch.
Being there and being strong,
You helped my early years along.
Thank you for the time you took
To play a game, to read a book.

Time's gone by so quick it seems
Like days gone by were merely dreams.
You drew us close within your heart,
You never let our family part.
Loving you, it made us strong,
It made me feel that I belonged.

I'll carry on inside my soul
The lessons taught so long ago,
The wisdom everyone should seek
Were in the words you had to speak.
You've given me so very much,
Your gentle voice, your loving touch.

Gail Wilkerson
A PAUSE IN LIFE

To Junior and Little Treen for reminding me dreams do come true

---

You have to be brave when you fear it
and strong when it happens,
then convince yourself it's over
when it's gone
They were so happy,
all that new love inside her.
Then it died. Unexplicably.
Unfairly.

My first niece or nephew
never had the chance to fight back.
It was never cancered by the sun
or ravaged in the night.
It would never fail in school
or drink itself to ruin.
It could never stick a needle in its arm
and fill itself with poison,
or hide a gun inside its palm
and stop the life of someone's husband.

It would never crawl across the floor
and skin its knees out on the sidewalk.
Or do the living room in crayon.
Or say my name. Or look like us.

There was no grave, just words.
Talk.
We cried our hurt and screamed our anger.
Now we whisper our memories
And we'll never forget.

Lois Essler Merrick

Lois Essler Merrick
STILL THE BOSS

To my son, Ronnie—My First Born, My Friend

I am saddened by the world today,
often wondering, is it true?
God, are you really out there,
guiding us,
is it really you?

I want to believe, that you are there,
please show me if you can—
and help restore, my faith once more,
in all our fellowman.
For sometimes we don't love each other,
just the way we should,
more often do we see the bad,
and never see the good.

Our neighbors fight—Nations are at war,
oh, so many stones we toss.
God, please show us all, with your power and love,
That you, are STILL THE BOSS!

Rebecca Ashwood
THE END OF TIME

What will we have
When the future is gone,
Less and less
As time moves on.
Angry people
Who see nothing but red,
War moves closer
And everyone dreads.
War, war
The battle is on,
Soon there will be no one
To carry on.
The Battle is slowing
The end is near,
Fewer and fewer people
Stand in fear.
One last gun shot
And the war will end,
No more people
No more friends.

Leisa Morrell
REMEMBER ME

Rember me?
From a dream so long ago . . .
From a memory that has faded into mist?

Does my body feel familiar
beneath your touch?
You know me . . .
But seem uncertain of your knowledge.

I knew you many lives ago.
From a past I don't recall but know existed.

Your eyes . . . have haunted my dreams for endless years,
Your voice . . . so often heard from far away,
Yet so clear.
I loved you then as now.
Remember me.

Hazel R Bartlett
WONDERFUL SPRING

To Virginia Joyce and Joye Kay. I dedicate this poem to my two lovely daughters.

Oh, the joy in the awakening of Spring;
A bright new refreshing
atmosphere affects everything;
Winter's cold chill and blanket of snow has said adieu;
And a carpet of green appears bright and new;
The sun glows brightly from skies of blue;
The ground is moist and warm;
Tiny flowers peep through;
Little birds flit here and there
singing songs of cheer;
'Tis such an invigorating time of the year;
Children filled with glee, play and
shout from morn till night,
Bright sunny days truly fill them with delight.
Springtime brings Easter; the seasons highlight;
'Tis then we realize how much God did care;
Into this great world, he sent
Christ, a gift quite rare;
Christ, His Son, lived, loved and sacrificed for everyone;
At an early age, Christ's mission on earth was done;
On the cross He laid down His life to save us from sin;
Eternal life in Heaven for all God's believers to win;
In obedience to His Father,
Christ overcame His foes;
On that first Easter morning; up from the grave He arose;
If in this earthly life you would be blest,
Believe, keep faith, serve God;
eternal life is best.

Michelle Fountain
LISTEN TO ME NOT SPEAKING

For my Grandpa Ross

I need not speak for you to know,
that I'm upset,
and loneliness has overcome.
You can tell by the slump of my shoulders,
my look of pain,
my desolate expression.

Listen not to my words of anger
and desperation.
Look within and see my longing
for happiness,
my wanting of a better time,
and place.

Listen with your heart,
your soul.
Hear what is not said,
Listen to me not speaking.

Laurel Fitzsimmons
HOW CAN I

All I've got left is memories
All I really want is you.
How can I live without you
When all I've got is memories?

I keep thinking about you
And the fun we had.
How can I go on without you
When I'm always sad?

You brightened my days
You filled my nights.
How can I manage the rays
When I've lost the lights?

Jennnifer L Wagner
FOREVER SMILE

To Fr. Fred Kirchner, O.F.M.—a true friend and inspiration.

Smile for me now
My friend

For, although our friendship
Will never end

We may someday
Have to part

And I want your smile
To be forever in my heart.

J Wathen/Carpenter
WARMTH

I felt the warmth of your belly
against my back
and snuggled closer,

trying to take that warmth
from your body,
Soaking it up through my back.
There have been many bellies
against my back,
but none quite as warm,
quite as comforting
as yours.

Ximena V Marin

Ximena V Marin
CONSCIOUSNESS OF ONE

To the God of Love within each one of us, opening our hearts to a world where Mankind is One. To Vincent, for all your unconditional love.

When will the barriers be lifted
The walls broken down
Without a show, a calculated sound

When will words be spoken
With sincerity from the heart
From soul to soul
Without distance, miles apart

When will acts display
Genuine love and care
Simply giving to share
Without the fear of loss or gain
Of what's to come, what's to remain

When will man learn
To stand firm
For what is just, for what is right
Minus the false pride
Without a struggle, without a fight

When will mankind allow
Universal beauty to penetrate
The guiding spirit to ignite
Can we displace the darkness
That surrounds us
And in our totality accept
That only in Peace
Can radiant forces
Unite.

Lottie Kay Werstler
MY SHADOW
My shadow . . .
the very best friend I have.

My shadow . . .
always there for me.

My shadow . . .
an expression of me.

My shadow . . .
the imaginary me.

Lisa A Glanden
A CHILD
When a child is born, a mother's
heart is filled with joy
whether it is girl or boy.

In your hearts they find their way,
with their silly
child's play.

They grasp your hand when steps
are few, then all
at once they are ahead of you.

The meadows they soon find are
vast, that is when
time slips by so fast.

Then you see your child has grown,
it is sad
when they are on their own.

Percy Gordon
I'M GETTING BETTER
Jogging down a country road in the
rain,
People probably think I am just
insane.
But I know my efforts are not in
vain,
With each step I take I'm getting
better.

Sometimes I go through the cold
and the snow,
When I go up hill, I'm not fast I
know.
But I am glad I can get out and go.
With each step I take, I'm getting
better.

I don't take lots of medicines and
pills.
I've found a way to get rid of most
ills.
And the more I jog the better it
feels,
With each step I take . . . I'm getting
better.

People want to know if I'm still at it.
I've started and don't want to ever
quit.
To keep healthy, I'm just doing my
bit.
With each step I take . . . I'm getting
better.

Peggy Plack Bergin
COLORADO SPLENDOR
From gold rush to ghost town
with history so rare
From prairie to snow-capped
mountain
with beauty beyond compare
From mountain stream to valley
man searches for dreams untold
From winter storm to sunny skies
life's hopes and dreams unfold
From country farm to city life
there's no more need to roam
Colorado has it all
and man has found his home.

Thelma Pearson
TO VETERANS

For my father Robert, and all Vietnam Veterans. Your sacrifices were many and I hope to acknowledge that once and for all. I thank you.

Brave young men go to foreign
lands to fight For their countries
beliefs. They give it their all
including their life and never
find relief.

Now I guess this is the reason that
all those stars shine bright.
There's one for every brave
young man that ever lost a fight.

So salute the unknown soldier that
lies in the unmarked grave. You
must remember he died for one
reason, so your freedoms could
be saved.

So if you ever walk amoung the
crosses, step softly and look
toward the sky. Because that's
where you'll find the soldiers
that kept your dreams alive.

Jim Rhyan
A TIME TO BE BORN

Dedicated to Char, my loving wife

Spring flowers, April showers,
Skies of blue, butterflies of every
hue,
Birds singing, bells ringing,
A time to be born
Fathers pace, gowns of lace,
Mothers sigh, babies cry,
Mothers tender touch, oh I'm loved
so much,
The time to be born
Hospitals white, sun light bright,
New faces, strange places,
Next to mothers breast, at last at
rest,
I've been born.

Brenda Sue De Rhone
WHEN I'M

This poem is dedicated to Mrs. Lois Marie Knapp, My loving mother

Will there be an earth when I'm
one;
I hope so, for my life's just begun.

Will there be an earth when I'm
two;
I hope so, for my life's fairly new.

Will there be an earth when I'm
three;
or will the only one left here be me?

Will there be an earth when I'm
four;
or will earth's beauty be no more?

Will there be an earth when I'm
five;
or will no one be left alive?

Will there be an earth when I'm six;
or will society cease to exist?

Will there be an earth when I'm
seven;
or will everyone be up in heaven?

Will there be an earth when I'm
eight;
or will I find I was born eight years
too late?

Will there be an earth when I'm
mine;
or will destruction be all that I find?

Will there be an earth when I'm ten;
or will earth, before then, come to
an end?

Jo Weikel

Jo Weikel
GOLDEN YEARS

To Mom and Dad with Love In Honor of Your 50th Anniversary, November 22, 1984

I thank you, my darling
For those Golden Years;
For the joy, the gladness,
The sorrow and tears;
For the love we have shared,
Which will never depart
And these "Golden Memories"
That live in my heart.

God gave us one heart
For His Love to abide,
Then gave us His Spirit
To lead and to guide.
The Rock on which we have
Built our life.
Is He, who blessed us
Husband and Wife.

He filled our life with
Gifts we could treasure,
A blessed family to love
Beyond measure;
And among those gifts
That the Lord bestowed.
Are the cherished friends
Who have shared our road.

On this, OUR DAY, of
Remembering When
Our hearts will renew
Our vows once again
Though the future takes view
And the past disappears,
I'll remember, my darling,
Those "Golden Years."

Eula May Lutzenhiser
CHALLENGER SEVEN

To the memory of my Mother. The friend and fan like no other

One bright blast—
And from earth,
Just that fast—
They were forever gone.

Not into space—
A journey's worth,
Was their race,
But to a Place farther on.

Just a flash—
White and clear,
Was their dash—
Toward Home to Be.

No one knew—
It was so near,
This going through—
Time into Eternity.

Andrew Adam Ruiz
HELPLESS CHILDREN

To my soul mate and best friend, Letitia, with all my Love and respect.

Helpless children all alone
With no one to call their own
Seeking shelter with warmth and love
Asking answers from God above

Silent voices that speak no lies
You see the hunger within their eyes
Not for want of food or drink
Asking only for us to think

To think of times when we were young
We cried with laughter and harmless fun
Heart swept memories should linger on
Before we lose them, every one.

Terry C Snyder
IMAGINATION
Visions form to ponder
for future wants to be.
Pictures seen none fonder
for only you to see.

Wanton desires emerge
at given times of need,
concentration will surge
creating needs indeed.

Giving meaning within
and satisfaction drawn,
serving every whim
reactions it will calm.

Hidden away from all
persisting only you.
Insists your high not fall,
insuring release true.

Amy Elizabeth Eagan
THE DEATH OF A GLIMPSE
As time passes and life sometimes seems hard to endure,
I have discovered why with this constant pain there is no cure.
Because only in small glimpses does pure happiness exist
And searching for those glimpses is hard to resist.

But that is the reason that life is so cruel,
For we have seen that happiness is not the rule.
And had we not had the joy that tasted so sweet,
We would not suffer so in its cold defeat.

So now I have a solution to end all the pain.
The search for all joy I will now refrain.
The death of a glimpse I will now procure,
To never again surface with its destructive allure.

Alice H Story
TO JOE, IN MEMORIAM—MY GRANDSON

To Joe's parents, Billy and Berenice and family—

Dear Joe, why did you leave? The chairs, in the parlor, all miss you the birds do not sing, anymore.
Neighbors and friends, all ask, why you don't call.
But, Joe, Dear, we miss you most of all.

You served your country because you answered the call, you were homesick and lonely.
Mid'st the Red, White and Blue;
But through it all, you were true,
To the principles and standards taught to you.

If you had not succumbed, to old, John Barley corn, and all it's harm and folly which it could do to you,
God would not have called you to your home in heaven and left a void,
and vacant chair with family and friends at home and all who remember you.

Beverly Borem
SARAH'S DOLL
A stitching, stuffing and sewing,
making Sarah's doll I am going.

Must make this doll with care,
put in a dimple here and there.

Sarah wants to put her on her bed,
doll will look nice with curly head.

Went to class to learn what to do,
now make a cute toe too.

I love Sarah so much,
I hope she thinks of me with each touch.

I can hardly wait for her to see,
This doll made with love by me.

R Reid Chapman
BLACK AND WHITE PHOTOGRAPHY

To Wendy who has been my inspiration and encouragement.

A Black man in a White world.
A White man ever reaching.
Separation, the void of seclusion.
Friendship bridges the gap.
Ridicule.
Closed doors.
Apartheid.
Social injustice.

Black man falling.
Lost in this world of hate.
White man steps from behind the shield,
Revealing love as an out-stretched hand.

Robert Allen Green

Robert Allen Green
CLIMAX!

Dedicated to all my friends and relatives who have helped and inspired me in what I do and write. To one and all, I thank you!

Lucky
Am I,
To have seen you. . .

Fortunate
Am I,
To have met you. . .

Honored
Am I,
That we are friends. . .

Priviliged
Am I,
That it never ends. . .

Jane Porter Ennis
THE SYMBOLISM OF THE FLOWERS
May all the things
that flowers say
be mine today.
I cannot wait
until they grow
their slow and gorgeous way.
Nor can I wait until I die
for flowers sent.
Impatient am I
for their beauty now,
and all the meaning that
they do convey.

Joy is what I want
to extol a higher place
and the myriad colors
they display with lavish grace.
Music I embrace
but sight most clear
proclaims a further reach,
a greater consciousness of space.

Swaying in the wind
the colours shout.
They tell of happy days.
The green, the purple and the blues—
red flaming roses
loudly love proclaim.
Yellow jonquils tell us
spring has come.
While lillies on a pond
tell us of gentler ways.

Harry D Meade
BASEBALL AND LIFE
Baseball and life, they are very much alike;
Bases in baseball, stages in life.
We don't use umpires or any innings;
We'll start at first base, that is the beginning.
You enter into this world with nothing at all
And before you know it you're holding the ball.
Your childhood is second base proceed with care—
Be good, be grateful but most of all be fair.
Your teen years are next and coming on strong;
They will be here and gone before too long.
You're going to the prom all dressed in lace,
Now you are safely standing on third base.
You are grown up now heading for home plate;
But be cautious, this may be your fate.
Old age creeps up on you, slow but sure
And for old age there is no cure.
I wish I could say this with a little more clout,
But death is here, the game is over,
I'm sorry you're out!

Dee Crane Elchlepp
BEYOND THE DOOR

To my joyful granddaughter 'Victoria' who fills my life with the sunshine of her being. And to all who have boasted of my talent, and urged me on—

Beyond the door trees flutter green
With the first provocative whisper of spring . . .

The advancing suns hot ready breath
Has finally compelled winter to let go its long hold.

Snow on the mountains begins to melt
And run wide streams across fertile valleys.

Earth creatures no longer speaking in hushed tones
Throw off heavy wraps and shout praises to the sky;

Once again a growing wonder has come upon the land
In this the new age beyond the door . . .

Tricia Marie Bisinger
GONE FOREVER
All alone I sit on the beach
thinking of the dreams
that were never reached

All of the things we talked about
are gone forever
I guess they weren't so clever
So many things we wanted to do
So many dreams that never came
true
Your on my mind
night and day
When will the memories go away
You were more than a lover
You were my best friend
But why did it all have to end
When will my broken heart
mend
I wasn't ready to let you go
There were so many things
I needed to know
Why did you go away and leave
me
here
with nothing to say
for I wasn't ready
to say goodbye

V Di Raimondo
LOOK WITH YOUR HEART

I sit beside your easy chair.
My heart a stone filled with despair.
Your easy chair is empty now.
I should forget—but don't know how.

Your favorite book—its pages worn;
The edges brown—some even torn;
Stares sadly into empty space—
It misses too your lovely face.

I pick it up and suddenly
A gentle breeze caresses me.
It flips the pages one by one
And stops at something you'd begun.

The rose that sleeps beneath the frost
Will live again though it seems lost.
When winter days make way for Spring
I will return on the sparrow's wing.

My love lives on in the heart of a flower
In the kiss of the sun; in a warm Summer shower.
Just look around when in despair;
Look with your heart and I'll be there.

Ricky J Starks Sr
THE WIND

Ricky Joe Starks Born 10-10-52 which is the year of the Dragon: Now let the Wind Blow:

Though the morning sky's are blue,
The wind gave more than a tussle; it blew.
Shapely girls in loose mini's
Not realizing all the guys see plenty.
Oh! Yes that's how the wind blows,
Two guys in gi's doing judo throws
As the wind blows on
It won't be too long before I'm gone.
For I'm running out of space
So the wind cannot blow in this place.
So remember now, those girls in mini's
When the wind is blowing plenty.

Annette Lowrance
A MOTHER'S LOVE

To my loving mother, Lee Ella Hatch, and my loving daughter, Jessica, who inspired me to write this poem

---

Dear Mother, This Special Mother's Day, my thoughts I want to share
My love, my blessings, my hopes and dreams and prayers
As I think back of Grandma, you, my baby daughter, and me
And life, and how it has to be

Tonight her tiny, trusting arms entwined about my neck
As she clutched herself to my breast
And her tiny, touseled, towhead fell
Upon my shoulder's rest

I held her to me tightly and kissed her tiny brow
I could not bear to think that someday she would not be as now
And as I lie here in the quiet of the night
And watch this little angel sleep
Somehow my thoughts take flight to you
Who were once as I, with a baby girl so sweet

I do not mind being awake even though it is very late
For as I lie here with her tiny warmth against me I do not worry of tomorrow's fate
And I savor each and every moment, for these moments will soon slip away
And tears stream down my face as I hold her—it hurts so to think of that day

And I wonder if you had these same thoughts so many years ago
And if Grandma ever had these thoughts, even, when you were little so
But life will grow as God did plan from above
We should not be saddened so, rather, we should set loose that which we love
And wait for it to return to us with love

So I will rear her in love as you always loved me
I will love her but I will set her free—knowing that she will still love me

Donald M Ference
TH' FIRS' MIRACLE

Jesus wen' ta Caanan fer a weddin' feast
Wit' his mother along fer th' ride.
He shook hans wit' th' groom 'n' done kist th' bride
'N' stood off wit' some friends ta th' side.

Well, th' party started rollin', they was feelin' fine;
Just adrinkin' 'n' adancin' ta th' band.
But den th' jug run dry, 'n' th' groom begun ta cry,
"It's gonna end afore it all began!"

But, y'know, Mary was a frien' a th' family,
An' she knew wha' they was goin' through.
So she said to her son, "Y'know th' wine's all done,
Could ya see wha' maybe you could do?"

Well, th' Lord, He curled his lip in a frown,
'N' shrugged His shoulders wit' a sigh.
He said, "Th' problem ain't mine, cause it ain't my time."
But den He saw th' look in Mama's eye.

So, He said ta th' waiter, "Bring me three jugs,
Fill 'em full a water from th' well."
He gave thanks ta th' father 'n' spoke some words.
Made th' waiter promise not ta tell.

Now th' waiter took dese jugs ta th' bridegroom;
Said, "You wond believe what I jus' found!"
'N' when th' groom took a sip, 'N' it past 'is lip,
He said, "Dis wine's gonna be talk a th' town!!!"

Y'know th' waiter turned 'n' winked at Jesus,
'N' Jesus winked right back too.
See, there was a tale ta tell, 'bout that water from th' well,
'N' I just tol' th' story ta you!

Doris J (Wright) Shaeffer

Doris J (Wright) Shaeffer
A JOURNEY INTO THE NIGHT

Dedicated to my parents Wilmer and Mary Wright

I walk thru the lonely night and the air is heavy with misty dew. Somewhere in the stillness of the night I thought I heard you call. My feet hurries into the vapor that lies ahead and my heart quicken's its beat, but when I get there, I find, no you at all. I continue my lonely journey ahead, my eyes always searching for you. Maybe, my mind is playing tricks on me, as I lift my weary feet, then stumble and fall. Maybe, you were only a dream. Maybe, I never knew you at all. But why this aching in my heart each time I hear you call. Off in the distance I hear a song it turns back my mind to happier days when you were mine. The laughter that flowed from your lovely lips, and dark eyes that sparked with fire when anger you showed. Then I flip the page in my memory and you lay like a soft little girl in my arms, for on your face happiness glowed. Then all at once the dream became a lie. Somewhere out there you wait for me. I'll search for you till eternity for I know my heart does not lie. I'll love you till the day I die.

Jesse Updegraff
DEATH—MY LOVER

DEATH please come
And make me breathless
Give me company
Be my companion
My accomplice in the killing
In the carnage of life

KING OF TERRORS to others
A welcomed friend to me

The lover I long to hold
Engulf my mind with blood
Drown me in your glory

Let the masses suffer
Endure the agonies of life
While I am loving you

My passion is for your sword
The bloodstained sword of DEATH
To penetrate my substance

Come inside of me
With your river of pleasure
Let my blood pour through
Through the happiness and life
Death—my Lover to drown them both

Mary Faye Eyres
THE LITTLE WHITE HAIRED LADY

The little white haired lady is busy
With her patchwork quilt creation
While stitching loving memories
For a future generation
Scrap's from daughter's favorite dresses
And granddaughters colorful collection
Arranged in blending colors
Makes a work of art perfection.

Hattie Martin
A TRUE FRIEND

Yahshua (Jesus is a tried and true friend
That's closer than a brother
You can trust him with all your secrets
That you cannot tell your mother.

He can be your counselor
He will be your lawyer too
He'll defend you when you're in trouble
He'll always be with you.

He'll even be your doctor
When doctors give you up
With a touch of his hand, he'll heal you
He'll let you share his cup.

When the whole world seems against you
And you don't know what to do
Yahshua (Jesus is the only true friend
He'll always be with you.

Anna Feggoudakis
LEAN ON ME

For my dearest Petro

If your eyes ever cease to see,
Your guide I would be.

A prism, rainbow shared, no black,
no white, no gray.
Only red love, purple passion, and
green days of summer.
But if your eyes ever cease to see
the love in me,
Then I would have to leave.

And if your sounds grow silent like
the deepness of the sea
Then your ears will hear the
melody in me.
Songs of the heart
Beating tunes in time
I will let you hear rhythm and
rhyme.
But if your ears grow deaf to my
words,
Then I would have to leave.

And if your words you could not
speak
But only sounds like a wind so
meek
I would still hear you, read your
eyes
And say your words for you, see
your smile
And laugh your laugh for you, and
fill your silence with sound
But, when your silence turns
secret,
Then I would have to leave.

But let me stay by letting us share
Care and dare.
The dare to carry an unfair weight
The dare to love so much
The dare to say
Lean on me.

Gina M Swinson
A WEDDING POEM
A poem for you,
To treasure throughout.
Written with love,
For you and your spouse.
It's to honor the love,
The two of you hold.
A bond that is special,
Held together by gold.
Your bond is strong,
And lasting through love,
Which is carried to heaven,
On the wings of a dove.
You must enjoy the best times,
And hold on through the bad.
Because no one but you,
Can know the love that you have.
Take care of each other,
And live a good life.
For now you are one,
Husband and Wife.

Patrick N Hart
RUMINATIONS

In memory of our Loving Mothers: Elizabeth Hart & Lillie Fay Sides

---

As inevitable as our next breath,
is the certainty of our death.
Why not, therefore, enjoy this life
instead of filling it with strife.
Let peace and joy forever reign,
anathema to sadness, pessimism
and pain.
With but one life to live,
let us not only take but give.
If a friend acts in a manner
kyphotic,
why respond or act neurotic.
Never forget life is a precious gift,
permit it to give us a lift.
Take time to smell a flower,
or from the sea, experience its
power

Lorria Lee
LIFE AND THE ROSE
Life like unto the rose
Must start as a tiny seed
But to know full beauty
We must pull each weed.
Happiness comes as each
New bud is born
But each new blossom
Must also bring a thorn.
First comes the bud
Then the fragile flower,
In man as the rose
This is a precious hour.
The bud bursts forth
Into the glory of full bloom,
What the rose is to the earth
So a child is to a room.
In regal beauty the rose
Reigns victorious in her day
But all too soon to understand
Life and the rose fade away.

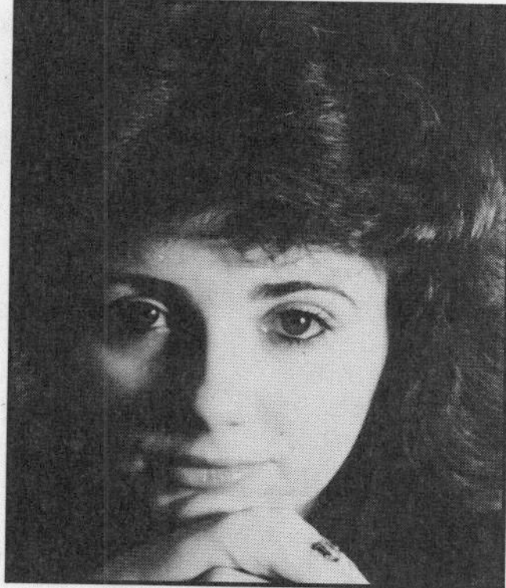
Michele M Dellapenta

Michele M Dellapenta
IF THERE'S NO GOD

Dedicated to my best friend and husband, Lou

If there's no God,
Then tell me please
How did we come to be?
The people that we live each day,
The you, the he, the she?
How did the earth become so
round?
How does the day make night?
And why are deserts dressed in
sand—
And mountains capped in white?
Why do oceans wave to me?
From where does wind evolve?
And if the earth's suspended high,
How does it then revolve?

If it takes man so many years
To answer all these whys,
How can they say there is no God
When stars fill up our skies?

One can't deny the beauty of
This earth and all her ways—
For answers men take years to seek,
God made in seven days!

Jeanette Kilgore
REMEMBERING
Oh to be a child again.
If only for one day,
With nothing more serious to think
about
But what games we should play.

Remember how you could not wait
For the first snowflake to fall.
You hoped it would snow so much
There would be no school at all.

Remember how the fresh cut grass
Got caught between your toes.
Then you had a good excuse
To spray off with the garden hose

Remember how safe and warm
you felt
Because Mom and Dad were there
Nothing could ever bother you.
As long as you had their care.

To know that kind of joy
For just one single day.
Would be a bit of heaven
Is all that I can say.

Jona Adcock
MY LOVE
I gaze upon the stars bright lights
at night,
But still their brilliance can
never compare
To my lover's eyes with radiant
light.
Silk could not compare to my
true love's hair.
Sometimes when I dream of our
true love,
Tears, doubts will slowly creep
into my mind.
But I know our love is blessed up
above.
My true love is truly a lover's find.
Each day that we spend is just like
the first
And when you return at day's
end,
It will be like the day we met in
June.
If I live to see the sunset with
him,
I know our love will again unfold.
That night we will love by the
light of the moon.
Our two hearts shall be as one,
And our two souls will live
forever as one.

Joy Judd
PRISONER OF HOPE
Do I ask too much from life?
Is it all in vain?
When I seek a ray of sun,
I get a drop of rain.

Trees and flowers bloom and fade.
Seasons reap and sow.
But as for me, things stand still.
Yet, it's there, I know.

Each trodden path that I have
walked
has scarred my aching heart.
Yet thru the tears and all the fears
I seek another start.

As I lie in fretful sleep
and stir at ev'ry sound,
I wake to glimpse the light of morn
but darkness has me bound.

I wait for days that turn to years.
Somehow I seem to cope.
Help me, please, escape this
place—
a place that I call hope.

Linda L Laneuville
I'LL REMEMBER
I'll always remember
That night in September
For that was the night we shared
A love that proved you cared.

I'll always remember the
moonlight
And the stars shining so bright
For that was such a glorious night
And no other love could be so right.

That Night I sang a new song
Because I had waited so long
And I was so happy to be alive.

At first I thought is was just
another fling . . .
But then I knew it was the real
thing.

The sweetness of your kiss
Was such a heavenly bliss
I remember it still
Because it was such a thrill.

For that night in September you
chose
And only God knows . . .
How long I waited to hear
Those words so sincere.

The leaves will turn to gold
But our love will never grow old.

Allison Russ
SPRING THAW

This poem is dedicated to my grandfather who encouraged me to write it, and who I love very much.

The sinister snow has melted away
We will not see any snowmen today
Nor will the ground be painted
white
Spring is here, here tonight
And yet tomorrow, there will be
Pastel buds on every tree
"That's what you think!" the
groundhogs say
For spring must wait another day

Marguerite Norby
THE SONG OF THE WIND
Outside the snow was flying,
The wind was bitter cold,
And moaning through the treetops,
And anecdote it told:
"Old Mishba was a fiddler,
His notes were soft and clear,
On Sundays with the choir,
He played, throughout the year.

Today no one remembers,
How he lived but to inspire,
For he died as do the embers
Of a slowly burning fire.

Yet his haunting tunes still
lingered,
(Tho we were unaware),
As the wind moaned through the
treetops
His melodies were there."

Myrtle Duncan Columbus

Myrtle Duncan Columbus
BUT I WILL GO WITH THEE

In memory of my beloved John

"Oh, I can't climb that mountain
It's much too high for me,"

But something said, "You have to,
But I will go with thee."
I climbed it very slowly
And sometimes I would stop,
But then a voice would say, "Go on,"
And I finally reached the top!

"Oh, I can't walk that valley,
It really frightens me,"
But something said, "You have to,
But I will go with thee."

So, I went to the valley
Very far below,
Sometimes I walked, sometimes I ran
Not looking as I'd go.

It seemed to take a long, long time
Because it was so wide,
But with that voice encouraging me
I reached the other side!

And when at last, I'm called upon
To swim the wide, wide sea,
I hope I hear the voice that says,
"But I will go with thee."

Frank Gasbarre

THE UNITED STATES OF AMERICA

Dedicated to the Hope that the people of this Great Nation will always live to please and not to offend, to like and not to hate, to praise and not to scorn so that all can live and love living!

Yesterday, today, and tomorrow
Through times of strife and sorrow
And times of pride and glory
We were, are, and we'll be
"THE UNITED STATES OF AMERICA"

A land of many wonders
Of every race and creed
Where we are free to choose
To care for each other
To trust one another
To strive for unity
For peace and liberty!

For peace and liberty
An' the right to be free
This land of many wonders
Of every race and creed
Is the land we love
The land we call our home!

Heidi Held

OPUS 20

Once there was a feeling, bathed by the sun
And dressed by the moon,
Gallantly streaming, marching
To the tune
Of a pastoral overture,
Opus 20.
Swinging 'round were the bare arms of time
And reeling through the gate
Were the embodiments of a timeless mistake;
Forgotten long ago,
Yet brought to attention once more.
Who could stop the imagination's deadly chore
Of bringing back yesterdays
Solemn and sweet;
Is there always a time and place
When 'tis meet?
When all is said and done,
Who will try for round 21?

Faith Hawkins

QUIET

In the quiet of the pre-dawn hour
When all the world is still,
Not even morning song of bird
Can yet be heard.
Alone, no voice nor song
To break my thoughts,
The promptings of my heart,
Outpourings of my soul,
So, I write till dawn appears
In the hushed quietness
The island of my soul,
And the world awakes
To break the peace.

Ray Rasmer

LOVE'S FAVOR

Hardly a day goes by
when I don't say your name
or think of you in loving ways.

You were an answer to a prayer
that I should have someone
to love the rest of my days.

My thanks rise up to heaven
that you were sent along
to share life and make me smile.

You have been more than I expected
and worth the tears and upsets
that happen every once in a while.

It's hard to be without a fault
although I know how hard you try
to be the best you can for me.

Despite faults, we enjoy happy times
that brighten every loving day
with smiles that others plainly see.

From both of us, Love asks a favor
because we're changing all the time
with every day we spend together:

That we should not forget little things
that caused us to fall in love,
so our union keeps growing better.

Jean Arnold

THE WILD FLOWER

To Dad With Love. Thanks for believing in me.

Colored with gentle hues.
You hide among the weeds,
A rememberance of childhood days
That rare innocence.
Gone long ago,
Yet held so dear.

No silver vase
Your fragrant pedals hold,
Nor gentle hands
Care for your needs,
Still you are loved,
Flower of the wild.

You're natures baby,
Sweet and unadorned,
Solace to the hiker
Along a country trail,
You touch our hearts
With thoughts of long ago.

Virgie L Adams

AN ENCHANTED SPRING

The world is clothed in beauty now;
A special hue sits on each bough;
Dark somber earth has turned to green,
And loveliness is all that's seen;
Jonquils burst forth from the sod,
And lift their golden heads to God.

The redbud's pink, the dogwood's white.
Bring to my soul a pure delight;
The perfume from the apple trees.
Is borne a loft by every breeze;
New-Born kittens romp and play;
Birds are singing all the day.

All these things—and many more.
Are mine to keep—and mine to store
Within my thoughts, and then replay
Them to myself when skies are gray.
My joy explodes! I laugh and sing;
God has granted me, another spring!

Mildred Townzen

LOTTIE HOOPER, COUNTRY GIRL A DOLL OF WHOLE CLOTH

LOTTIE HOOPER
COUNTRY GIRL
Came a tumbling
Down the hill
Cut from cloth
Dressed in sacks

Wrapped in feathers
Poked in flax
Whipped so fine
With cotton thread
CANDLEWICKING
On her head!

Kathryn Dare-Aarhus

SUPERIOR SUSQUEHANNA

To all the souls lost to the Susquehanna River, whether by fate or by their own decision.

The Susquehanna most beautiful and serene,
Spanning out along its omnipotent miles,
Glistening and shimmering in the crescent light,
Its fleet currents peacefully flowing along its banks.

So very appeasing, placid and so serene,
Beckoning and inviting you to sit by its side,
Grasping and clenching you to its unrelenting sight,
Hypnotising and magnetising through the mesmerism of its tranquility.

The Superior Susquehanna abiding your arrival,
To fill you with its prestige of tranquility,
Addressing you personally to draw you nearer,
Craving the unity of you and its waters for eternity.

Beckoned near by its fervent embracing,
Your soul overwhelmed ever so much you cannot flee,
The Superior Susquehanna stiffling your one apprehension,
Fabricating your confidence to its most aspired point.

Some fortunate enough to flee its haunting dominance,
Others unfortunate to succumb to its overwhelming attraction,
Existence impressing the triumph of the undefeated,
Headstones preserving reminiscences of the feeble.

Margaret P Bechhoefer

YOUR THIRTY FIFTH ANNIVERSARY

On the twenty fifth day of December,
Is a day you will always remember.
Stepping up to see the bird's smiling face,
As the ceremony was held in a sacred place.

With words of real meaning each one said "I DO"
The bride wore beautiful flowers, more than a few.
In a short while they commenced feathering a nest,
Like most people do to get their daily rest.

He wends his way to work or vacation,
While she makes activities of home her station.
Children enter your lives to draw attention,
When their character reveal many traits of mention.

Like a love story of fiction that ever was told,
Your experience of give and take before growing old.
Each day and week passed during your lives
With enjoyment of grandchildren, of stories you've told.

Yes, this game of faith, hope and love in each other
Is no different than your sister or brother.
In these thirty five years of togetherness seems to blend,
Wishing you a blessing of good health to the end.

Bebe Childress

CHOPIN AT TWILIGHT

Through the ship's porthole
The horizon dips from sight
And back again.
The audience waits,
A hushed lounge—a listening silence.
From the musician's long fingers
A haunting nocturne unfolds

Like the silken moonflower—
Achingly beautiful, caressing,
Pulsating through my senses,
Climbing to a throbbing crescendo,
Now dropping back; a sensual whisper
Translating the complex language of the soul.

Patty Hardin

LITERARY COMPANION

In loving memory of my father

I'm ready to read the Sunday paper
Which is spread out on the floor.
I have my coffee close at hand,
Could I ask for more?
At just that minute the cat strolls in
And I know where this is leading,
But with all the soft places in the house,
She curls right up
In the middle of
The page that I am reading!

Mary Theresa Coronas Leigh

LAND OF THE FREE

I dedicate this to Warren and to the memory of my great, great Grandfather, Chief Tehcumseh

Land of the free
Home of the brave
For this our nation's fathers went to their grave.

From our states
To our territory
Our nation grew to such great glory

From Oregon
To Kentucky
One nation under God is what makes us lucky.

God and country do not forsake
Our great nation could become a lake
Remember Noah, for heaven's sake!

Brothers and sisters teach your children well
Their legacy must be more than a living hell.

Allison Broadaway

A WALK WITH JESUS

As I was walking along the beach;
I thought about the sermon my Pastor had preached.
As I began to think about it more
Into my heart God's message began to pour
I realized I never much thought about him
And into his glory I needed to take a swim.
As I seriously thought about bringing him into my heart
I knew that decision would be smart.
As I made that critical decision
Into my eyes came a vision
Of me at the age of eighty-seven,
Walking in the Pearly gates of Heaven.
As I walked in and looked about,
There was no reason to have any doubt.
God had taken me under his wing.
And under the great golden arches I will sing.

Betsy Dale Treitler

SHADOWS

Free Spirits.
Orange, lavendar stripes, speckled fish stirs about
sliding in zigzags along smooth edges
inspecting pink, orange-yellow curves and crevices
of sea tulips
arms jut into dark reverberating silence
their shadows dancing, dividing and overlapping
in the depths of Australian waters.

The moon's cryptic fingers interlock
with lanky, pink stems
caressing the tiny creature
as it clings to its sea-laden floral kingdom
riding deep-sea ripples
flickering, reflecting
playing tricks to deceive unwanted visitors.

Kelp twisted and curled around tulips
carves out an impenetrable cavern
outlined by jagged edges
only rough as the plant's body and surrounding sand.

The clingfish stirs about
darting in and out of moon's reach
lurking in the shadows of the depths
of sea tulips.

Gary Lee Poe

SPRING IN OHIO

This poem is dedicated to My wife GLORIA, and SON DARIN and Dear Mother HELEN R. POE and Family and Friends in OHIO

Latent forces of nature reviving
The mystic enchantment of spring,
The daffodils are blooming and striving,
To glorify their offering
The meadows and hills are greener,
Most lovely is each flowering glen,
The breath of pines is keener,
It is spring in Ohio again.

With beauty the orchards are gleaming,
With color the rock garden glow.
The sun is brilliantly beaming,
On meadows where dream rivers flow.
To the northlands the buzzards are winging,
While music from the cardinals and
Robins are singing
All the church bells are ringing,
It is spring in Ohio again.

Jammie Anderson-Hebert

I'VE USED YOU

Sitting here alone feeling like a fool
Knowing I was wrong to use you.

Wanting to say a thousand things
Not having the courage to admit I'm at fault.

Hoping to see you time and again
Longing for your touch . . . feeling despair.

Knowing how you feel, wanting to cry.
Thinking like mad, why is this pain?

Looking for answers that can't be found.
Knowing I was wrong to use you.

November P Turner

HEROES TIE SHOELACES

To Michael, my son, who has grown past his shoelaces.

Beacons of light
Spread forth the plains, the valleys, to mountain tops

And carried a message.
To all was given
An interpretation, Faux Charity, for wantan

A better life.
Over the hills
Came scientists, philosophers, doctors, lawyers, and Mothers;

Whose shape created
Riffs and ripples thru 'ot this spreading society.

Death to a war!
Some good, some bad; where hope and faith interwove notariety.

Like snow blankets
Soft, falling, giving way to Springtime's grating hoe—

Life springs forth
At each twinkling touch linking man and his creations

To the Earth as such.
As great men wonder and work toward greater still;

Our heroes become
Intombed within societal will.
Occolades are printed and trophied. When all is said and done,

The Greatest Little American to be . .
Is the one
Who asks me to tie his shoelace—My Son.

Sarah C Smith

OUR MOTHER

To our mother with love, respect and admiration always

She was tiny
She was sweet
I think of her nightly
When I go to sleep.

Her face was radiant
Always with a smile
Her love for us vibrant
Her caring day and night.

She made us happy
With her hugs and kisses
Her voice sweet melody
When her prayers never misses.

We think of her often
She lives in our hearts
The book of memories is open
For us to read when we are sad.

F L Muller

WINTER GARDEN

She picks the wilted flowers as they die,
Tossing them into brown paper bags
labeled marigold and zinnia.
When bleakest winter sets, she spreads
them on a tray in the basement,
To ready them for their part in the miracle.
And, planting them at the first hint of thaw,
Sometimes too soon, in flats that line the basement floor,
She must replace the ones that lose the struggle to exist.
Continuing the cycle.

Mary L Thornburgh

PERHAPS

Perhaps you weren't strong enough
Perhaps I was too weak
Perhaps your love was dying
Perhaps mine never reached its peak.

Perhaps you didn't listen
Perhaps I failed to hear
Perhaps you held me far from you
Perhaps I didn't want you near.

Perhaps our love once had a chance
Perhaps it never began
Perhaps you've said "good-bye" to me
Perhaps I never can . . .

Kathleen L Conner

SECRETS

As I lay here
watching you sleep,
I wonder about all
the secrets we keep.
Thinking of you
gives me a smile,
a soothing warmth
embracing me awhile.
Then there are those
things that we say,
bringing us closer,
dreaming of someday.
But, as I lay here
watching you sleep,
I can't help but wonder
about those secrets we keep.

Stephen Jarman

FANTASY

The smell of bacon wakes me up.
I jump out of bed
and fumble with my pants
as I stumble down the hall.

And there you are.

You are standing at the stove
in your duster
with a feathery wisp of hair
floating between your eyes.
You pat a yawn,
look around at me,
SMILE
and say
"Well, good morning!"

(My pants are on backwards.)

Sheila Riggs
SPRING
She comes to us in such a way
that makes us want to run and
play.
Daisies dancing on our lawn;
Spring is coming, winter is gone.

Cold winds turn to gentle breezes,
Children stop their sniffs and
sneezes.
Birds now sing a brand new song;
Spring is coming, winter is gone.

Coats and boots are put away,
and soon replaced with bikes
and skates.
Love really starts to move along;
Spring is coming, winter is gone.

Mary E Quarry
DEDICATION TO MOTHER

To my beloved mother, Ethel Mackey

Mother Dearest Mother
You are all the world to me.
I'd never find another
If I sailed the deep blue sea.
You're all creation stands for
You're of heaven's own design.
And no one else on earth dear
Has a mother sweet as mine.
Mother Dearest Mother
You're the one who kissed my
cheek,

And I'm the one who listened
Every time you went to speak.
For tho' I could not talk yet
I understood you well,
And I loved you dearest mother
more than words could ever tell.
Mother Dearest Mother
Tho' you're many miles away,
I hope you understand the words
My heart has longed to say,
You held my life within your hands
And planned the best for me.
And that is why I'll Love you dear
Through All Eternity.

Belle Niblo McMahon
COMES THE DAWN
After a while you learn the subtle
difference
Between holding a hand and
chaining a soul,
And you learn love doesn't mean
leaning
And company doesn't mean
security,
And you begin to learn that kisses
aren't contracts
And presents aren't promises,
And you begin to accept your
defeats
With your head up and your eyes
open,
With the grace of a woman, not the
grief of a child,
And learn to build all your roads
On today because tomorrow's
ground
Is too uncertain for plans, and
futures have
A way of falling down in mid-flight.
After awhile you learn that even
sunshine
Burns if you get too much.
So you plant your own garden and
decorate
Your own Soul, instead of waiting
For someone to bring you flowers.
And you learn that you really can
endure.
That you really are strong
And you really do have worth.
And you learn and learn . . .
With every goodbye you learn.

BethAnne McHenry Belusko
REPLY TO DANTE ROSSETTI'S SONNET, "SILENT NOON"

Thanks—for Phillip's love, for Mom and Dad's encouragement, for Steve's patience

My hands numbed bitter by the
cold, late snow,
The fingers stiff and red against
the white.
My eyes spill despair. This
meadow nicked by night,
Turns dark from the clouds that
overlay the glow.
All around myself, far as my gaze
will go
Are frozen milkweed plants with
crystal edge,
And the great hawthorn-hedge
has met the sledge.
Unseen is the silence, still as a
stream's flow.

Gone are the fire-flies with the
light they bring.
Swinging like small stars, whisking
with their wings.
So these days fly, their wings
unseen in the dark.
Forget! my heart, the past, for
death does end
All talent, memories, and letters
you penned.
Your love is silent in the grave so
stark.

Cheryl L Heggstrom
LOVE

To my husband, Kenny, for whom it was written.

High as the Lord's ceiling, low as
the
Lord's tides, slips into deepness
these
feelings, I'm trying so hard to hide.
Find in my mind a calmness so
unreachable
to let you slide from my side, no!
I need, I desire all that is written
within yet feel unable to obtain
a way to confide for the ever yet
present fear of all that is unfelt
the feelings we have yet to find.
I've lived, I thought that I had loved
but never in this realm before.
It's deeper, it's real, it's more
frightening still but I won't let
go because it's so instilled deep in
my soul.
For I give you all until the Lord's
life is everlastingly still.
I love you is all I am trying to say,
so for
at least, a little while, my heart will
keep still.

Jessie Butler Jones
PICKING UP MAGNOLIA LEAVES
Picking up magnolia leaves is
bound to be a sign,
For dad was old as a man and even
older in mind;
Yet daily he would stoop beneath
the boughs, crouching without a
sound,
Supported by his walking stick,
collect the leaves lying silent on
the ground.
Now mom, almost as old, yet
clearer of thought than he,
Would call from the porch, "Until
more fall, let them be."
He heeded not, with stature almost
sassing,
For it was a task he had to do until
his eventual passing.

In essence of time, several years
passed by, the mom moved up
the road
To live, apartment style, in the
daughter's home, adjusting well
to the new abode,
In that yard, grew two other
magnolias, giving of their beauty
with the ivory blooms,
And yes, dropping their leaves
regularly, too soon.
Her mind now fading, jolting
memories here and there;
She began to move under the
magnolias with the utmost care;
Bagging green-brown shapes,
stacking them for the day,
"For the convenience of the trash
man," she said, "who would
carry them away."

I, the fifty-ish daughter, marvel at
the aged's task;
Some significance, when leaves
must be gathered quickly, lies
here for me to grasp.
I want to yell out, "Let them go,
we'll rake and burn, one time
will suffice."
Instead, I respond,
understandingly, "It sure looks
nice."
Contemplatively though, these
leaves play a role far too great to
fully comprehend;
And upon the brother's visit, his
ear she did bend,
To discuss the task of picking up
leaves clearly as a cue,
For the loved one must be carefully
tended while preparing for the
adieu.

Jim F Surprise
PASSING THOUGHT
On a summer day, as the rain pours
down,
Some of you people sit around with
a frown.

For when I see a puddle, I go out
with a crash,
So go find yourselves so you too
can splash.

So get down and boogie, keep time
with the beat,
Just how long do you think there
will be summer
heat?

For when the autumn winds
blister, and the snows
all about,

Now your life is full, and in your
mind there's no
doubt.

You're no better than one man, but
much richer than three,
For you have looked in your heart
and can truly see.
For there's many men lonely, all
over this land,
Are you one of the few, who would
reach out his hand?

Leslie Howell Jr
A LAND OF BEWILDERMENT
As the sun sets across the tranquil
sky,
a ray of hope beams through the
massive trees standing
boldly in the light,
Just as darkness offers a temporary
respite for half the world,
the other side wakes up to a
raging land of confusion,
While one man sits and applauds
his own success,
another man can only weep as
his dreams linger in the air
waiting to become reality,
Just as one man accepts his losses
with hatred and discontent,
another man takes his defeats
with his chin up and his eyes
open for he is not ashamed nor
is he defeated,
While a refreshing morning mist
falls upon some remote green
meadow, a fusillade of gunfire
invades a small village of a
country still at war,
In the midst of all this bedlam,
one must never forget his pride
nor his ability to dream,
For when one loses his desire to
dream, he must accept the
world as what it is rather than
what it could be,
But don't despair, for the sun will
appear tomorrow,
shedding more hope on this
bewildered place we call home.

Anita Percopo Jantz
THE DEVIL DANCE
The people danced, hand in hand.
They circled 'round to the beat of
the band.
They laughed and danced and
circled 'round
And danced and danced to the
maddening sound.
Then, the devil danced.

She danced right in to the center
of the crowd.
She twirled and whirled as the
music grew loud.
She danced and laughed with fiery
eyes
Until everyone was hypnotized
As the devil danced.

Her gold lame' sparkled in the light.
She whirled and twirled to the
crowd's delight.
They could not see through her
cool disguise
Her red-hot passion to mesmerize.
They watched the devil dance.

Her flame-red hair shone like fire.
She took the crowd higher and higher
Until they felt a euphoric sedation.
The men just watched with anticipation.
They watched the devil dance.

She could have had any one of them.
But as they watched, she chose him.
The lucky partner chosen to whirl
And dance with the devil and spin and twirl
To the devil dance.

He moved his feet without knowing how.
The music slowed, and then . . . somehow
She had him in her magic trance.
And she'd have his soul by the end of the dance.
The devil dance.

Susan M Jones

LIFE

Life is a great adventure,
Each day a new surprise,
So sweep the dust from within your heart,
And open up your eyes.

Life is a great adventure,
So let the windows of your heart open wide,
And watch the sunlight flowing in,
Warm everything inside.

Life is a great adventure,
So thank God each and every day,
For letting you live the life you have,
By taking the time to pray.

Mary Arnold Snider

EMPTY

Dirty, broken window,
A shutter half torn,
Deserted old house
Looking forlorn.

So goes a life,
A useless soul,
Once so vital,
Now without goal.

There once was a time
When one felt needed;
When little things mattered
And feelings were heeded.

But now all that's changed.
She sits there alone.
No one really cares,
No one hears her moan.

Yes, hinges are broken,
And roofs all caved in.
The floors are all rotten
They've been worn too thin.

Useless old house,
Dirty and bare.
It looks as if now
No one ever lived there.

Tracy L Penoyer Blau

NOW YOU'RE GONE

To my Great Grandmother "DeeDee" and my Loving Grandfather "OPA"

Now you're gone, I realize
You were a precious friend.
You brightened up my cloudy skies,
And loved me to the end.

You led me to my real self,
And showed me who I am.
You took my head off the shelf,
And let me know I can.
So now I'm thanking you, my friend
For everything you've done.
And to you, my love, I send
To you, my shining sun.

Ocie L Williams

THE TREE

To a dear friend, Ms. Donna Gail Lanier of Middleton, TN, who literally persuaded me to submit this poem.

I think there will never be
A resource more useful than the tree.
She furnishes refuge for man and beast;
A peaceful haven for weary souls to retreat.

The tree provides food for animals and birds.
They fill her capacity; she utters not a word.
She stretches her limbs in submissive array,
Welcoming nature, come what may.

She honors the sun, rain, snow and sleet.
Even the wind, which so drastically upon her beats.
When the sun beams down at mid-day,
"Come, there's relief beneath me," she seems to say.

Every part of the tree's in demand,
Her leaves are used to nurture the land.
We use the tree to build our homes,
Make our furniture, and to keep us warm.

Her stern, strong roots help the soil to stay;
Without their support, it would wash away.
The tree has so awful much to give.
There's even room for the insects to live.

The tree's a resemblance of Jesus Christ,
He offers shelter to all; He even gave His life.
He died, but rose again, to free us from sin.
Like Jesus, the tree can be cut, but it'll sprout again!

Betty Bobbitt Way

PETS PROMISE POSITIVE THERAPY

Dedicated to my wonderful Husband, Tom, for his loyal support of my love and commitment to aiding God's creatures!

As I am greeted by ten happy yelps,
one cheery chirp,
and one musical meow;
I truly count my Blessings and realize anew
the commitment to aiding Animals I vow!

I have always been fascinated by the deep devotion
and total trust of my furry friends so true;
If only humans would render equal love and respect,
more joy this world would view!

There is a special attachment and lasting impression
of all the precious critters I rescue;
But none so memorable as my adorable terrier—HAPPY WAY,
the ring leader of our jolly zoo!

Six years ago on Valentine's Day—at a mere six weeks old,
she was left at our welcome front door;
Cold, hungry, dirty and lonely—her condition and cruelty
of the owners made us angry to the core!

From a stray to the Royal Way best describes our
charming and delightful HAPPY WAY;
Whose autobiography reaped $2,000 in the "Bark In The Park"
to aid more of her helpless friends each day!

As we share our many Humane goals, thank you, Lord,
for the support of my patient and understanding Hubby;
Guide us as we attempt to make others clearly aware
of the fact that "Pets Promise Positive Therapy!

Carlos Gonzalez

Carlos Gonzalez

FROM THE HEAVEN FELL DISTRUCTION

I dedicate this poem to my parents, family, friends and enemies, and specially God for the faith and hope which he gave us all.

Clear as daybreak,
Streets covered with snow,
People roaming and falling
All over the sidewalks of New York.

Clear as daybreak,
America declared an outbreak of war,
Against the drug dealers and crimes alike.
To stop the trafficking of all nations,
And worst crimes alike.

Clear as daybreak—
No one can stop it.
For drug is the game today,
For money is there to get.

"No one can stop it . . ."
"So what the hack people say"
When out from the Heaven fell destruction
To those dealing with drugs and crimes alike.

Everyone was at ease when
From the Heaven fell destruction itself.
No one left, no one around,
Not even innocents, not even the crime.

Perhaps one day people will
Be born again in a life
Where drugs and crimes
Do not exist.

But a world of happiness and peace
Among all living and dead
"Remember!"
From the Heaven fell destruction.

Nolbert L Jackson

SERVANTS FOR THE LORD

Between heaven and earth bleeding and
Suffering, our blessed saviour gave his life for
Each and every one. Betrayed and whipped stripped and
Shamed, oh,—such an innocent one, to each and ever—
One this day is heard a silent plead, be ye
Servants for the Lord—for upon this tree—
Stained with blood I have given the greatest
Gift of all. Go then and tell of this hour
For I have chosen you who do believe, be ye
Servants for the Lord, teach of this saving power
Sing of this glory for there is work to be
Done. The highest and brightest—please
Hear this pleading call from the cross—
Be ye servants for the Lord

Jeannie Rae Martin

STEVEN

In loving memory of Ramblin' Rose and for all the Stevens in the world.

Magical Steven
Bright as the sun,
Where will you go
When your journey is done?

Where have you been

And what have you seen?
Did you go to London
to visit the Queen?

Where did your dancing feet
take you today
and did you hear voices
and what did they say?

Come out, magic Steven
Come back to the real
Oh, tell us dear Steven
what you think and feel

Break out of your dream world
Please set yourself free
For this world is poorer
Without you, you see.

Pattie Farrell
MISSING YOU
As I lay here in my empty bed
Thoughts of you run through my
head
Your loving touch, your tender kiss
Most of all these things I miss
I need your touch, your warm
embrace
I need to see your smiling face.
Being apart is so hard to bear
I wish so hard that you were here
When you're holding me in your
arms
I feel so safe, secure and warm
Our caresses, our kisses, our love
for each other
Makes me feel like a whole new
other
It's like God meant us to have our
hardships
Just so we could find each other in
future time
Oh God, Oh God, I hope you'll
always be mine.

Blair W Benjamin
TEARS FOR FEARS
The sweat of blind activity did
cover up her tears,
And searching eyes did blink in
shame to flatter anxious fears.
A whistle draws a simple smile, but
not a hearty grin
For happiness of willing men does
not conceal true sin.
So she may rest her weary bones
upon a mountainside,
And rain may fall from
thunderclouds of all the days
she's cried.
And men may worship her afar,
and women feel she's vain,
And only those who take the time
may see her hidden pain.
The hour comes to ride the wind
and she obeys the call,
Descending from the great plateau
to watch her lovers fall.
She sets her steps upon the clouds
and reaches up her hand
And enters into her true realm, no
rain upon the land.

L Orchin
WINDSONG
Lie back and listen
Relax and close your eyes
Peace and quiet haunt you
As the windsong tune arrives

Whispering and rustling
Blowing through the trees
Memories it brings back
The past and with it peace

Peace of a past life
A memory so clear
Going back and living
A time that was so dear
Lay back and listen
The song comes from within
Peace and quiet haunt you
The windsong plays again

Paulette A Bousquet
SONATA
Maybe
we could dance
we could share our music
Listen
I am surrounded
by sounds
Of life, love, laughter
but
wait
you cannot hear these notes
you listen to
a different song
composed
of death, destruction, danger
and I
in all my cowardice
refuse
to listen to your music
Perhaps
we may never dance
together.

Kathleen McColley
THE DREAM OF LIBERTY
How proudly with dignified grace
She stands
On a high pedestal covered with
gold
Sheltering the homeless with
loving hands
While beneath Her feet children
freeze with cold.

Justice and Freedom crown Her
lovely head
The heavy chain lies broken at Her
feet
"A free land of equality," they said
But why do some die starving in
the street?

A lighted torch shines brightly in
the sky
While from Her mouth are
whispered silent prayers
A single teardrop slips silently by
Are we so hardened now that no
one cares?

A country full of love and liberty
This is the dream She'll always
share with me.

Donna M Vorlicky
SWEET SORROW

This is for everyone. If it wasn't for you, I wouldn't be here. Thank you. I love you all.

Early dawn, the morning dove
cries,
Carry my soul to the clouds in the
skies.
Bring me closer to thee I love,
The only one my soul dreams of.
Sweet sorrow, take me away!
For my love has gone astray.
Bury my love in the depths of his
heart
To keep us together while we are
apart.
Bring me closer to he who loves me,
To where in this world that
someone shall be.
Let us meet like the sun meets the
morn,
Let us rejoin our hearts which were
torn.
To rejoice with the sun, and cry
with the rain,
'Til we feel no sadness, feel no pain.
Together forever, 'til death do us
part
Though fate leaves it's scar upon
our heart.—

Deanna Lee McMurtrie
HIDDEN LOVE
Why does it have to be this way?
Isn't there something I could say?
My love for you is very real,
You can't imagine how I feel.

Oh, how I wish I could tell you,
But that is something I cannot do.
For my love has to be hidden deep
Down inside my heart.
I cry to myself when we're apart.
It's killing me, but my hands are
tied.
My love for you, I have to hide.

I'm glad we met, you are my friend,
But my love for you, I cannot send.
For, you don't love the way I do.
Don't get me wrong, I'm not
blaming you.
If you would only chance it and see,
Our love together could truly be!

Rachel Schnur
THE YOUNG IMMIGRANT
As he stands at the port
On this night of cold and darkness
The young immigrant boy still feels
the rocking of the ship
the swaying back and forth
as he makes an effort to balance
himself . . .
Men around him huddle together
Tattered coats and shattered pasts
Fervently discussing the present
and future . . . America . . .
Women covering their young ones
As the snow begins to fall so slowly
Eyes looking upward
Hopes and prayers and
anticipation
The young immigrant takes a deep
breath
Cold air, refreshing his lungs
Taking away the stench of
airless cabins, sickly crowds
He bends down, and, as if in
disbelief,
Touches with his bare hands the
cold, damp ground
"America," he says to himself
The touch, seemingly electric,
gives him a shock
Not of lights and ions, not of colors
and currents
But of reality
Quiet yet forceful, magic yet
attainable
"America," he smilingly says.

James E Chant
BREAKFAST IN BED
God bless the light that shines.
The splashing sun that uncovers
her face.
Revealing the clues
that drip like tears
from the lids
of emerald eyes.
(I pause to catch my breath)

A feast for the curious, her features
turn.
The gamut is run in dreamy
slumber.

Conflicting emotions battle for
space.
A devilish grin on an angels face.
I, on one elbow, observe the pace
of cat-like stretch
and feline grace.
(Again, I pause to breathe.
I sometimes forget.)

Virgil A Wallace
FEBRUARY WINDS
I hear you in the night time as you
sweep up
through the draw.
Strumming the boughs of the
Alder, chilling
the flesh that is raw.
Rushing over the hilltops, with a
merry shout
of glee.
Reminding me of the water, of our
mighty
western sea.
Sighing, ebbing, dying, as you
travel through
the night.

I hear you tugging at the windows,
and pulling
at the eaves.
I hear you whispering through
dead grasses,
and rustling the dry leaves.
As you chase them across the
roadway, and
out upon the lawn.
Just as playful as a kitten until the
early dawn.
Then tis day light, I look eastward
and see a
crimson glow.
And bid farewell to you wind, for
it's time for
you to go.

Jack Connors
MUSINGS
We often dream of things as they
might be.
If Fate had twisted yet another way,
Could not our parts be in a
different play?
Might not our burdens be borne
more lightly
If we had held, and won each
lottery
That Tempter, Life, proffered—
then stole away?
Would elusive Fame beckon and
hold sway?
And of our dreams—dreams or
reality?

I would not change the sweet
gentle coursings
That transport me on sometime
violent crests.
The gentle arms that hold me
tight—that cling,
And lips I press—assurances—not
tests!
To exchange these for an unknown
something,
Would be but mockery to
happiness.

Mrs Trish Bisci
THE CRYSTAL FOREST
Out of the window panes I see,
The tiny shadow of the iced pine
tree
Glimmering snowflakes whirling
around
As diamond, glazed crystals fall
to the
ground.

Silver sparked hail covering
branches and vines,
Icicles grow on the maples and

pines . . . .
The wind whirls the snow into large cotton balls
What once looked like shrubbery become igloo walls.

Ambulets hang from the roof and the drains
As the ice forest forms
Through my window panes.

Shirley Broughton
THE KISS ON THE NOSE
You are a man, who once he makes up his mind—makes up his mind.
You had decided we were to be "just friends."
You would come to my house in the Hamptons for weekends,
But had already decided in New York what would happen—or would not happen.

You were here for several weekends—we walked, we talked, we laughed.
But then one night, the moon must have been at an oblique angle,
Or perhaps the tide was making a U turn;
Or maybe the winds were conspiring among themselves.
Who knows, but some strange mysterious power had invaded your universe.

That evening, we were listening to an opera by a friend.
There was only one libretto, so we shared the same text.
You made a comment—and suddenly, lo and behold—dare I mention it,—
Gave my nose ever so tiny, ever so gentle—a kiss.
You were more startled than I was; your eyes told me you were worried.
Thought you might be going insane; doing something not prearranged.

We both settled back to the text and finished the opera
Just in time for you to catch your train to New York.

Oh man in control of your life, I look forward to your next visit.
You're sure to come—it's so beautiful in the Hamptons.
And I must confess, I wish one night
The moon may go berserk
Or the waves dance up a storm
Or the winds have a confrontation and destroy your universe

For then—I could hope for—
Another kiss on the nose.

Margaret L Hughes
MY TALENT
Each one has a talent—
That's what I've heard.
I wonder about mine—
And I get disturbed.

I've worked in the fields—
I've cooked and I've cleaned—
Milked cows and gathered eggs—
But no talent I've seen.

I've raised three kids—
And they do fine.
They all have talent—
But that's not mine.

For the last forty years—
When the frost is all gone,
I plant me some Zinnia seed—
As I sing a little song.

Each spring the seed I sow—
Comes out of the ground and begins to grow.
I watch and wait, and it's still a surprise—
To see those zinnias before my eyes.

All sizes and colors—
Yellow, pink, white, and red—
I wonder—maybe my talent—
Is my zinnia bed!

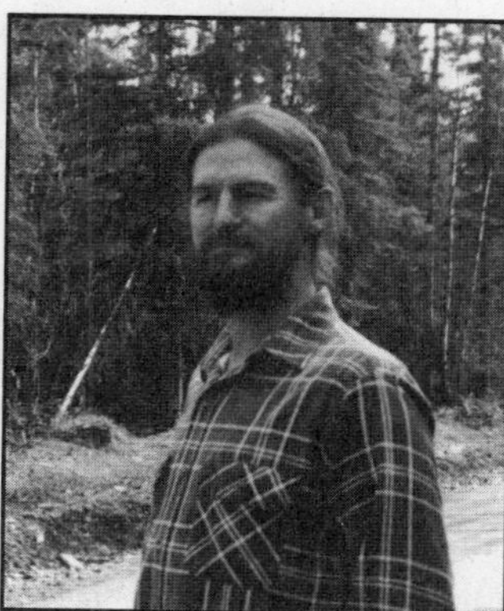

Paul Douglas Byrd

Paul Douglas Byrd
NATURE'S SONG

To Mother

I've journeyed the earth, height and girth,
looking for treasure of precious worth.
In each village I'd ask around
for one of knowledge and renoun.
Treasure they'd say, to my dismay,
"been none here to this day."
Then one eve on a soft warm breeze
an idea was born of the wind in the trees.
The answer I'd find among the seasons,
after judging each for truth and reason.

. . . Summer tanned me with a blistering glare,
said I should never have come there.
Winter gave me the cold shoulder,
said come back when you're older.
Fall, masterful in change, only frowned,
then fell silently to the ground.
Spring was another treasure I'd sought
for in it's coming new life was brought . . .
I might have avoided going town to border
if I'd asked the seasons in natural order,
but I now had the answer to my search.
The greatest treasure is Life; death or birth.

Tami Rose Peterson
WITHIN
Within a persons mind and soul
there are feelings that can sometimes make
Someone feel whole. A person has hard times showing
boldness in turn sometimes coldness.
Within a person there is always someone wanting to be
cared for. Someeone who needs warmth and kindness to
give strength to their weakened minds. Wanting a feeling
of togetherness that can somewhat bind
Within a person there are shadows of unhappiness, feeling
alone and somewhat cold. All the feeling of boldness gone
with the sunrise. No rainbow to show us the beginning
or ending of an unworthy day of loneliness.
Darkness comes, ending what was happy and people confusing
you with feeling's that mean the entire world to you.
Within a person a being lurks which is pursuing a
death of confessions and misfortune. Being able
to say good-bye now and forever is a feeling of the
hearts beat of confessions of all misfortune.

Doug Fields
FUNLESS
The joke is over—it's not funny anymore.
The joke is over—don't know what we told it for,
unless:

Maybe we thought about brass cats too much.

The smile is faded—it's not easy anymore.
The smile is faded—don't know what we showed it for,
unless:

Maybe we thought operators stood by.

The sound is through now—it's not pleasant anymore.
The sound is through now—don't know what we listened for,
unless:

Maybe we thought it was only a test.

(But) it's only crickets—it's not testing anymore.
(Yes) it's only crickets—don't know what it bother'd for,
unless:

Maybe we thought 'Deliveries in Rear.'

(It's) just the attic fan that's not squeaking anymore.
(I) hear the attic fan; don't know why it spoke to me,
funless:

Maybe I thought precocious grapes wouldn't.

Vicky Applin
SPECIAL FRIEND
When I'm lonely or depressed
I hope to see a face
With just a simple, little smile
Without a lot of haste.

I'd like to have a special friend
One thats dear to me.
And they'll be as gentle and calm
As the rolling sea.

When I ask some people who they are
They look at me and say!
"My friend is yours—just look—
Maybe you'll find Him some day."

I think I may have met you
By chance or by mistake
And it seems you've given me
A friendly chance or break.

I hear your voice of comfort
From somewhere in my heart.
And you always help me out
When I need a little start.

Now I know I've found you
My very special friend.
Your name is Jesus Christ
And I'll be with you in the end.

Jill Teresa Nethercott
MY LITTLE STREAM
My life is like a little stream,
That flows along a mountain path
Through beautiful valleys it
Wanders on.
It flows down into gullies,
And as it passes, it encounters
Rocks, huge boulders,
And rough terrain along the way.
At times I sit and ponder about
My life
And I think of how it is like
That mountain stream.
I meet problems, which are
Like big boulders,
And my stream must find a way
To meander around them.
I meet little rocks,
Like my disappointments,
And I must flow over them,
Leaving a tear, or two behind.
But at last, I see a fresh water
Lake below.
My buddies are all down there,
Waiting, calling out my name.
Finally I flow, down into
The lake with them,
And I think, I can hack this life
Because I have
My buddies with me!

Maria Del Consuelo Maus
AN INVITATION
I've been invited and so have you
To a city that gleams a brilliant hue,
The invitation states R.S.V.P.
Please answer soon, I anticipate few.

The directions to reach me are all around;
And the methods to seek me are very sound,
Your invitation is one of a kind
I will show the way,
As you make up your mind.

My Father's gift is to offer you rest
And welcomes you as a favored
guest.

J C Royer
WASCO, PAIUTE, AND WARM SPRINGS

Wasco, Paiute, and Warm Springs,
all sound like names of famous
kings.

They might be far from being
kings, those Indians and their
special things.

We'll see them on the reservation,
maybe again on a vacation.

I wish that they could come back
with
us, but there wouldn't be room
for them on our bus.

I can not wait until we go,
It seems better than a circus
show.

This is what I have to say—
I can not wait until that day!

By Jay
TO THE "OTHER WOMAN"

To those who have shared my pain.

What a cruel thing to do
The pain keeps saying you
Our Family Tree has lost a limb
Because you have taken him
You have taken away these last
years
They should have been ours, never
yours.
What do you have invested in him?
Ours is forty years, a real loss, a
shame
It's as though we never had a
chance to say good-by.
Why did you cause him to live this
lie?

You have changed my life.
Caused such strife,
Caused such pain.
Not only have you stolen his life,
You have stolen my memories; it's
not right.
Memories that should be my
pleasures.
Part of my treasure to carry
through life.
You had no right
To cause all these tears day and
night
Day and night
Tears that won't go away
Until my dying day.

Now you can add a page to your
memory book.
My pain will pearce your heart as
it has mine
Never to go away, always there,
forever, forever.

Louise Reeves
RAINBOW LOVE

Through the dark days,
Keep a Rainbow—
In your heart!

We each have a choice—
We can stay under a cloud,
Or get busy
And find our Rainbow.

We must each paint
Our Rainbow from the
Colors we've been given.

We must always
Remember to take
Our Rainbow with us!

Mary Roy
THE WORLD

To Keith who gave me the incentive to write

I took a walk around the world
So I could see what havoc and
turmoil
had been unleashed
I saw beauty and innocence
destroyed by
the mere touch of human hands
I saw humans and animals
suffering
I saw cruelty and courage
I saw hope and peace
I knew that this would not last long
For one day it would all be gone
in an instant flash of light
It saddened me that this was
happening
And I felt a heavy weight upon
my shoulders
I strove forth to proclaim
the message to stop
But no one listened
then the day came
when all was lost forever.

Shirley Ann Roberts
THE HAND OF GOD

Take time to examine the world
around you and you will see
God's hand in every thing even you
and me
He made the first designer clothes
for Adam and Eve
He outfitted the trees with the
beauty of the leaves
He placed the moon and stars
which light up the skies
With this man can not compete no
matter how he tries
He guides us along safely down
life's weary way
With a single ray of sun shine he
makes our day
Some times we seek but should not
find the things
God's hand has left behind
Amid this confusion chaos and
mess the comfort of
God's hand has stood the test
And though there are many things
we do not understand
Still trust in God and hold on to
his hand

Tammy Dee Young
DREAM LOVER

Why do you haunt my dreams each
night
like a ghost out of the mist—
touching me first with your warm
hands,
then with your burning lips?
I've met you only once or twice,
and that was long ago;
so why must you visit me in my
sleep,
when I have someone else to hold?
What is this game of fancy,
this illusion that's been weaved,
these subtle, but sensuous,
hauntings
that prevail when I'm asleep?
Each day they abide in my
thoughts,
like favored memories,
holding me still for brief moments,
making me long to go back to sleep.
How do I stop these hauntings,
cool these fantasies,
and turn you, my dream lover,
into a memory?

James Harper
WILLIAM DAWES AND PAUL REVERE

William Dawes and Paul Revere
Both, so very dear
It will always be a big mystery;
why William Dawes never made
history.

Linda M Link
NO IDENTITY

I keep having a dream late in the
night
About a guy that might be just
right.
But he somehow gets lost in space
He was a person without a face.

I did not remember his name
And he did not own fortune or
fame.
It was always a different place
Where I saw this person without a
face.

He's one of the finest guys you
could ever meet
Always kind, sincere and very neat.
He's the kind that would be hard
to replace
This Mr. Nice Guy without a face.

His voice reminds me of the
tranquil sea
Whenever he talks on the phone
with me.
I know his heart must be in the
right place
But will I ever get to see his face?

Lalene Cargill Meyer
COMMITMENT

Sunlight splashes
through parting clouds
over green land where
tools of this age threaten.

Not hearing, not seeing,
world shapers too
readily ignore, sacrifice
life of all forms
for mammon and power.

Giving without interlude,
Earth needs it people,
our commitment to halt
the retreat from humaneness.

Ethelyn Flora
AUTUMN

Rich colors of foliage
Brocade on a Chinese loom
Repeating a pattern.

In the country
Fields of dry corn and beans
Exclamation points
Marking and end to a season.

Memories of the past
Wild geese
Winging through migration
flyways.

Mae Hess
A YEAR IN RHYME

As January's icy winds blow,
This white world is all aglow.
Then February slips swiftly by,
Promising warmth "Oh she's
sly!"
March pushes February away,
Green "peeps" thru, as trees
sway.
April brings rains galore,
Growing starts and mowers roar.
May is an artist's dream,
The world is beautiful it seems.
June hears the church bells ring,
Happiness from youth we bring.
July and the shores are fine,
"Tans, tans" thats everyone's
line,
August seems too hot to bear,
Wonderful!, vacation's here.
September and the school bells toll,
Teachers start to call the roll.
October sees the footballs fly,
"yells and cheers" the minds
defy.
November with the turkey basted,
The family goes to Grandma's
place.
December, lots of holiday cheer,
And here we have another year!.

Anthony Mercorelli
THE PRAYER

As I knelt beside my bed to pray
last night
Oh Lord I said help my brothers
and sisters in their fight
Against the drugs they use by day
and night
Whether they be red, yellow, black
or white
I know they are precious in your
sight

My eyes fill with tears and my heart
with pain
When I see them stoned on crack
or cocaine
Then I hear a voice within me say
it was their choice
I gave them a mind to rule
themselves alone
Not that they should be a puppet
or a clone

And the drug dealers, I will strike
down
As you can see it's happening in
every town
That it makes me sad and my heart
burn
Won't my children ever learn?

I gave them the gift of life so
priceless
That only I alone can give and now
it's worthless
I gave them love so great at birth
It reaches the four corners of the
earth
They threw it back in my face
What has happened to the human
race?

But to thee I say, repent my
children with all thy grace
And I the Lord will remove the
drugs without a trace
I will give you the power to be set

free
If you will reject those drugs
And have faith in me

Lynn M Pearson
WINTER SOLACE?
To wish upon a dream, afar
Brings teardrops to my heart
The obstacles and miles abound
So forcing us apart.

The winter winds can only sing
A dissonance so lonely
Without your touch and voice so kind
I feel I am so only.

So now, I smell a roseless thorn
That burst amongst the frost
As without warmth am I now
Without your love am lost.

Juliana M Corridon
EVENING
Deep buried in our hearts
Are all our sorrows, yet alive;
Like ocean waves pitched fierce against the rocks,
Life's road seems cumbersome;
In Nature's way life is and will be molded,
And like the ravished cliffs
That weathered through the storms,
Then glisten in the evening sun,
We, too, can hope to catch the mellowed rays.

Dorothy W Johnson
REFLECTION

To my loving husband, John Wesley Johnson

In the mirrors I see poor me
Forlorn of spirit, and yet, free
To turn my glance and look away
From tearful thought and mood of grey.

Through the window I see thee
Carrying crosses to calvary!
Heavy laden art thou there
Burdened too heavily to bear.

May I help thee with thy load?
Help thee travel thy rough road?
Lifting, pulling, up and on
Rising higher toward the dawn!

Now the mirror is forgotten
And the sadness there begotten.
One's own burdens hardly bother
When one carries for another.

Natalie D Schuler
THE BEAUTY IN A PERSON
Beauty is in every flower, in every tree—
Tis in every person you and me.
Hidden often within a heart,
or openly displayed in a work of art—
Looking earnestly you would find
the wisdom, the thoughts, the dreams tucked away—
for another to discover in a man's mind.

Look not for this gift on the outside,
but venture into a person's heart, mind, and soul—
to a world of wonder, love, and creativity—
A fantasy land waiting to be explored.

Jill Allen
A BAD DAY
There was a girl named Fay
Once she had a very bad day.
It rained all day and snowed all night,
then poor Fay had a fight!

Jennifer Dunmire

Jennifer Dunmire
WINTER TIME
The snow lay round about
And the children sing and shout
They sled ride through the town
While little snow flakes dance around
While icicles hang from tree to tree
Such beautiful pictures for us to see
When beasts sleep in their homes
Dreaming of the surprises in the Spring

Michelle R Mizerka
MIDNIGHT LOVERS
The Wind whistles through the trees,
As stars lighten the night sky.
While falling leaves glide on the breeze,
Resembling the Nightingale in flight.

A young man waits in the grove,
Listening to every noise.
His heart hammers against his chest with a steady drone,
So loud is its noise.

Thundering hooves upon dirt road,
As a black mare's mane sails with the brush of the wind.
Breathing hard for it has soared,
In the flowing fields made by the wind.

She stops her horse in a quick easy motion,
And easily slides into her lovers arms.
The stars light liquid lotion,
Upon the nearby farms.

She a princess of the throne,
And he a young man of a farmer,
Have come here this night,
In need for their desires.

Two people thrown together by destiny.
Both will become midnight lovers,
Which they will always be proud to be,
For their secrets will be kept like all the others.

Wendell Hull
LAST WORDS

(in memory of Pete Motsinger)

Carnations of white will build a road
that leads to heaven, this I know.

No more hurt and no more pain
no more sorrow in this rain.

The challenge of life that I met,
I pass this world with no regret.

My love will follow, I'll build a home,
to rest forever and never roam.

Cry not for me, but pray for you.
this peaceful place is something new.

I love you all and always will,
we'll meet again and be a family still.

With wheels of gold and amber wheat,
it was God with whom I went to meet.

Emily Keeton
MY MEMORIES
The many places I have been
And the things I have seen
The many pictures in my mind
Take me back again

The endless chain of snowcapped mountains
Even the desert brown and plain
The beauty of the trees in spring
And the smell of a summer rain

Watching the raging river run
Hearing the sound of the water rush
The goldenrod, and turning leaves of Fall
Are like seeing God's paintbrush

These are some memories of my mind
The beauty and wonder of it all
Make me glad I am alive
And knowing God created All.

Kathy Kulisz
YOU'RE THE BEST
Mom,
I know I sometimes get on your nerves,
And you put up with it more than I know I deserve.
I know I often take my frustrations out on you;
I scream and yell, but deeply regret it when I'm through.
You're the best mom in the world, though I know
I don't often say it.
You give me so much love and understanding,
Though I know I sometimes don't repay it.
When I have problems, I know I can always
Talk to you.
You guide me and help me to make my own decisions;
You never <u>tell</u> me what to do.
I'm the luckiest person in the world to have
The sweet mother I do.
You're the best mom anybody could have and, though
I don't say it as often as I should,
I love you.
Te Adoro, Mama

Hazel Lambkin Smoot
I'M YOUR NEW NEIGHBOR
Look, Dear, I'm quite delightful
When all dressed up for Spring—
In fact, I'm quite an eyeful
When clad in pretty things.

And if you were to see me then
You'd know this not amiss,
You'd not look so amused and smile
To see me look like this.

No make-up on—my hair a mess
My hooks and seams awry—
Looks like I slept in this blue dress—
So, <u>NOW</u>, you're dropping by!

Annette Gonzalez
PHANTASMAGORIA
I had prayed for this.
It happened.
So long I waited; like
a vision in some dream
you stole into my body and soul.

Why didn't your arrival tell
of your impending departure.
The fires of my soul are
in embers: ready to spark.

My heart has flown away with
you to Norway
While in New York remains
An empty shell.

Return my heart to me.
I am haunted in all
my waking and
While I sleep—"Perchance to dream . . ."

I am possessed and without recourse
Doomed to love only you
The Miles have torn us apart
I am loving a Phantom.

Ruth C Mihlbauer Dunn
PLEASE DON'T DO DRUGS
Did you ever stop to think what drugs can do?
They can really mess up your life for you.
I guess you think you're doing something big!
But its not, not big as a mustard seed.
I knew a boy who was just fourteen,
Started on pot way back before his teens
Then started using coke just before he was twenty.
Now he is dead, my God, what a pity.
My dear young friends it is no joke
Please don't do drugs, there still is hope,
If you are still alive then reconsider
You can be great this time if you become a quitter
You're still young and you could become very wise.
Before it's too late, if you'll only

realize
Please don't do drugs they will do you in,
And we'll never get the chance to tell you again.
That were really not trying to put you down,
Only that we love you and want to keep you around.

James R Skypeck
RETREAT ENLIGHTENMENT
Lord, open my eyes and let me see
All the beauty with which you surround me;
The magnitude of all you have made
From the tallest redwood to the smallest grass blade.

With every person that I meet
It is really you that I greet;
You who lives in everyone
You there with me when all is done.

Glorious and praiseworthy Lord
Free me from anger; ease all discord.
Fill me with gentleness, compassion, and love
And help me to long for things from above.

Make me aware that You are ever present
When things are all wrong and when they are pleasant;
When tears come so quickly and laughter does not
In people I have loved and in people I have fought.

Open my heart, Lord, help me to care
Knowing by charity, it is with You that I share;

Help me to give all I have now to you
In all that I say and in all that I do.

Bea O'Brien
FEELINGS
If God would grant me one last wish
before the day I die,
I'd look on life and ask myself
one wish, for me, not I!
For there are many things I'd wish.
Of these that I'd been true,
to all the friends that I'd possessed,
and most of all, dear God, to You.
I'd wish that I had been more kind,
more thoughtful and sincere
to all the people that I've met
throughout the many years.
I'd wish that in my life.
I could, exchange the wickedness,
the unkind words to those I've loved,
for tears and tenderness.
I'd ask my God to help me love,
Where hate and anger lie.
Within my heart this is my wish,
before the day I die.

Rosebud Manis
THE WALL OF BLACK
Thousands of names
Upon The Wall Of Black
Etched in bitterness and grief
A gleaming monument of doom
Hard and unbending
A reverent symbol
Of unquestioned loyalty
Their black banner of bravery
In life, and in death

Shoulder to shoulder
They fought, and they died
Gone, but not forgotten
By those left behind
Left to rot, never to grow
Rootless and unclaimed
Perpetuating the cause
Of their futile crusade

Thousands of names
Upon The Wall Of Black
Indelibly inscribed
In life, and in death . . .

Linda E Osborne
REMEMBER ME?
Remember me?
Know who I am
Sad little man?
I bring heat and fire,
Lust and desire,
Hate and crime.
I know your mind.
I bring disease and destruction,
Malice and corruption.
Still don't know me?
I carry sorrow and condemnation,
Resentment and violation.
Are you beginning to know who?
Yes, that's right . . . I'm you.

Karen Baxter
YOUR LAUGHTER
I can remember your laughter.
You tried so very hard,
For success, for respect.
That you forgot,
All I ever wanted,
Was to hear you laugh.

Diane R Shwedick
PAID IN FULL

With love to Chonon, who was always there

Twenty years without a mother
20 years, no sister, brother.
20 years, some filled with strife
20 years, one half my life

Twenty years of married bliss
I never felt my mothers kiss
20 years, my children raised
I never heard my mothers praise

Twenty years my heart half full
Because I broke my mothers rule
20 years, she punished me
Withheld her love for all to see

Twenty years I wept inside
So no one saw me when I cried
20 years, but not another
I've paid my dues to you, my mother

Marie E Colsey
DEPARTURE

To loved ones and friends who remain in my heart

Sometimes I find no words to say
On a sad and tearful heartbreak day
A discontent and disbelief
Resentful anger solemn grief

Oh God please help me to be strong
And not to think Your Will is wrong
I know we're only passing through
This lovely world designed by one

We're all inclined and do pretend
This gift of life will never end
But like a stranger in the night
Our soul is taken into flight

The earth below means not a thing
For above the clouds the angels sing
Our Lord is waiting have no fear
His plan for us is very clear

Have faith my child for in heaven above
There's eternal peace and lasting love.

Vanessa N Dyche
GOD'S MOST PRECIOUS LOVE
It's a love so special, so precious and real;
A love that's touching and so strong you can feel.
A love thats unselfish, so giving and dear;
A love with no room for doubt or fear.

A love that is returned without question or thought;
A love that comes natural, a love that's untaught.
A love that is caring, gentle and kind;
A love that is soft and easy in it's binds.

A love that's unlimited, secure and safe;
A love that's unwavering in it's faith.
A love so loyal, so fierce, yet mild;
A love that can be shared only with a child.

Mae E Avey
THE QUESTION
For me
The question has always been—
Who is this creature that lives in my skin?
A glance in the mirror,
I start in surprise—
Who's looking at me with a stranger's eyes?

A worldly woman—
No longer beguiled—
But I still catch a glimpse of an elfin child
Whose joy in living
Can never be stilled,
Though life's expectations remain
Unfulfilled—

Lois M White
AM I WORTHY?

This poem is dedicated to Larry, Tonya, Kim and Stacy, my beautiful and loving family whom God has blessed me with.

Am I worthy of the life I live from day to day?
As I try to live for God, Satan's there, always in the way.
Am I worthy of His love and all the blessings too?
That seem to always come my way no matter what I do.

Am I worthy of the time God spends on me each day?
As He listens to my cries and promises when I pray.

Am I worthy of the blood he shed on Calvary?
To save me from my many sins and then to set me free.

Am I worthy of the day when Jesus comes again?
Will He say, "You are worthy, you may enter in!"

Joseph A Fioravanti
RHYME FOR SHIRLEY
I was a house without joy, on my walls
scars where landscapes were removed,
an intruder in deserted halls,
misery tiled and roofed;
Then you knocked and turned the key
Giving the morning back to me.

I was a crooked tree in an abandoned field,
carved and gashed by weathered toys,
harvests of husks my only yield;
once crowned a golden chain of girls and boys,
these torn from me, my branches bare:
Then you wreathed Sweet-Cicely in my hair.

I was a trainyard untracked,
severed ties,
trestles down, finger pointing toward infinity,
my deserted hostel a gathering of flies,
the spider's false cathedral a lost divinity;
One day your love became the stair
Bridging the void beyond despair.

April is the fool that sings upon the bough:
Love's fool I sing your praises now.

Mrs Alton M Bumgardner
THE OLD HOME PLACE
There she sits upon the hill
That old home place of mine,
To look at her gives me a thrill
And for her sometimes I pine.

Oh, the good times that I've had
While playing in the yard,
Hiding out behind the shed
And getting, Oh so tired.

Thinking of the holidays
With family all gathered round,
Loving in so many ways
Knowing happiness that we've found;

And there was Mom and Dad
So loving and so kind,
Helping us to feel so good
For making us use our mind.

As I see the old home place
No matter how far I roam,
I'll always come back to face
For there is no place like home.

Cindy M Gray
IN THE LAND OF DIAMONDS

Dedicated to my three children, Carie Ann, Pete, Samantha and my mother; Ethel L. Franklin.

Once upon a time,
In a faraway land,
The land of Diamonds,
Lived the Queen of Hearts.

The Queen of Hearts was in love,
She loved the King of Spades.
But their paths couldn't meet,
They were of different colors.

Then one day, on a white stallion,
Came riding the Jack of Clubs.
To him, colors made no difference,
What was in the heart mattered.

The Jack of Clubs threw a party.
He invited the King of Spades,
And sent for the Queen of Hearts.
The party was very successful.

The two fell deeper in love,
And now share the grandest castle.
The land of Diamonds has
prospered,
Because the Jack showed no
preferences.

Edmund A Wise Jr
THE NIGHT WORLD

I dedicate this poem to everyone who can respect the awe and beauty of the Nightworld such as I, and to Tammy, the one girl I shall always love.

Following the close of day,
A silvery moon rises high
To the realm where stars play;
Losers shooting across the sky.
Bats flitter through the trees;
Owls descry intensively,
To catch rodents for their feast.

Shadowy vagueness moves;
Hedges rustle in forceful wind—
Coolth water numbingly soothes
A mountain man's injured hand.
Rivers drain from mountain peaks;
Ferverous air melts winter's snow;
Ice covered lakes crackles and
creaks,
While furious southern winds
blow.

Before first rays of light,
All night critters disappear;
As the crow caws with delight,
Stars vanish into thin air—
Daylight burst on far horizon;
Man's alarm begins to beep;
The nightworld is lulled to sleep.

Claudia L Parda
BENEDICTION

we place
rosepetals
upon their eyelids
sleeping children, nurtured
dreamers
taking openmouthed breaths
half-moons
dewy, furred caterpillar legs
lay upon their cheeks
while
mothers smile at them from behind
stained glass windows

Mrs Nellie Margaret Smith
MEASURED LOVE

If you could strut as fast as I,
Or I could slow my gait.
But you just want to take your time,
And I don't want to wait.

We never seem to want to change
To satisfy each other.
I've blabbed about us to my Dad
And you've run squawking to your
mother.

I don't know why I don't let you go,
Or you hang unto me.
I don't want you finding someone
else,
And I've seen your jealousy.

It seems I can't run fast enough,
And you can't hurry more.
So I guess we'll have to tolerate
What the future has in store.

We did and do agree on one strong
point
When we snuggled down for life—
We're a mighty loving twosome—
But a screwed-up man and wife.

Shirley Jean Gissin

Shirley Jean Gissin
HOW I REMEMBER (THAT LAST DECEMBER)

How I remember that last
December
That wonderful day we met
My voice grew weak I could hardly
speak
That day I will never forget

When your hand touched mine it
was so divine
I thought I was walking on air
Then your lips met mine and our
hearts entwined
We made such a wonderful pair

It was snowing the wind was
blowing
But I didn't mind it at all
To me it was summer my heart was
a drummer
But it was only the end of the Fall

And my head spin round with a
buzzing sound
I forgot where I was at the time
And my feet felt light as if I were
in flight
Then I knew heaven was mine

Then I discovered my true lover
When Cupid was having a ball
How I remember that last
December
When love had dropped in to call

How I remember that last
December
That wonderful day we met
How I remember that last
December
How can I ever forget

Herta Schwarz Rousseau
SALOONEY (OR LOSS OF A FRIEND)

To my children and all the catlovers in the world

Scratching on the door
Coffee is on.
Feeding the cat
before anything gets done.

Sitting in the garden,
under the tree,
Living together
just kitty and me.

Hiding under bushes
sleeping on the chair.
No bother, no trouble
I know that he is there.

Enjoying his company
as time went on.
One day I 'woke
and he was gone.

No more greeting the car
no more purring and all that
Alone in the quietness—
how I miss that black cat.

Della M King
ODE TO AN IDOL

A little stone God, with little stone
eyes
So haughty, so homely, so
seemingly wise . . .
Did you fore see, with the wisdom
of sages
And fore tell, the world shaking
news of the ages?

Were you there, when Noah was
building the Ark
When Sodom was burning, did
you fan the spark?
When Jericho fell, did you help
Joshua . . .
Were you there when the walls
were beginning to sway?

I aught to destroy you, you little
stone God
And bury the pieces, down deep
in the sod . . .
But old superstitions are staying
my hand
And you still wield a power that
I don't understand.

A little stone God, on a little stone
shelf
Conjurer, enigma or just a stone
elf . . .
I can not destroy you, you might
hold the key
To treasures or crises that I can't
fore see.

Darryl Preston Peacock
THE WINTER

The leaves fall like an omen
Of the destruction to come;
The wind blows cold through trees
so bare;
Winter is here—killing all in its
wake.

I survey the landscape—wretched
and cold;
As the waning moon lay low on
the horizon,
Casting a dim, eerie light over the
land—
That throweth dark apparitions
from trees so stark.

The land lay transformed as if by
evil spell;
Though nature claims liability
For this strange form of chaos—
Only nature knows the reason
for the season.

Winter is here—this blighted place
Has become a barren wasteland;
Winter—the silent annihilator—
Living off the corpse of spring.

V F Popp
FOREVER AND A DAY

I blink away the tears
So others will not see
That I am still living
With a past memory

I am so very proud,
I just don't want
My feelings to show
That I still love you so!

You can take your heart from me
And walk quietly away
But I will always love you
Forever and a day.

Richard F Hay
LIFE IS LIKE

Life is like an open book, who sees
it not, just doesn't look;
For like the air, it's all around,
seldom seen and nowhere found.
Life is like a lovely rose, by night
it sleeps, by day it grows;
Here today, gone tomorrow,
never knowing pain or sorrow.
Life is like a tragic play, so full of
things that cannot stay;
Things that rise and so must fall,
without a bow or curtain call.
Life is like a race to run, not to win,
but just for fun;
It rolls along from day to day,
comes again, but not this way.
Life is like a burning star, ever
close, but, oh, so far;
Shining brightest in the night,
tho by day still burns its light.
Life is like an endless stream, a
babbling brook, a living dream;
Never sleeping, ever waking,
always giving, never taking.
Life is like the empty sky, far away,
but also nigh;
Up and down can it be found,
high above and on the ground.
Life is like a newborn child, soft
and gentle, sweet and mild;
Full of wonder, free of doubt, it
gives itself to all about.
Life is like a mustard seed, for it to
flower, rain it needs;
Tended and fed, if it's to grow,
cast off bounds and beauty
know.
Life is like the silver moon, its
borrowed light is gone so soon;
Hide and seek, its favorite game,
it seems to change, yet stays the
same.
Life is like a central sun, it sheds
its grace on everyone;
Light and warmth it so
bequeaths, to all above and all
beneath.
Life is like a timeless sea, whose
unmoved depths shall ever be;
Tho surface winds its waves do
blow, they never touch the deep
below.

Skipper A Fuller
HAWK

The screech does pierce the
twilight sky,
then silently he swoops softly by.

One of the keepers of nature's flight,
with his knowledge beyond our sight.
His wings touch water, his talons scales,
and in his grip it's life soon fails.
He rests at dark within his nest,
far above on the mountain's crest.
At golden touch of glowing morn,
upon crisp air this one is born.
In the skies above the trees,
he floats upon a zephyr breeze.
In the midst of noon-day sun,
he is there the sky to run.
His eyesight touches the ground beneath,
through glens, and meadows, and
thorny heath.
Silver light reflects skyward,
and a glimmer gleams in the eye of
the bird.
The hawk dives to the field below,
delivering it's deadly blow.
He carries home at end of day,
that which he has won, his prey.

Betty Simpkins Hutchison

CURTAINS

You wounded me more deeply
than deep is thought to be;
the pain I feel is endless,
abyssing inwardly.

I've prized myself a victor
of life's adversity,
I've kept abreast its ravage
with flexibility.

This time, the wound went deeper
than tears or years can heal—
you left a ghastly crater
which I shall always feel.

Harold L Bond

GIFTS OF GOD

A mountain lion flowing, like smoke down the hillside.
Clouds lassoing, the peaks of mountains.
Tumbleweeds clutching, at a barbed wire fence.
Leaves softly whispering, to a gentle summer breeze.

A stream rippling its way to the sea.
Stars twinkling brightly, in a quiet sky.
A baby's smile, the sound of quiet laughter.
The gentle touch of a Mother's hand.

A quaint silhouette, of a mountain.
A blend of fog and glory, of dusty cloth and gold.
An Eagle flying majestically in the sky.
All these were meant, for You and I.

The flashing light of a firefly, soft winds singing a lullaby.
Nightbirds softly calling, leaves are gently falling.
All these were meant, for You and I.

Helen Phillips Smochek

TO THE CLASS OF 1992

This poem is dedicated to my three miracles, Bobbi Jean, Buddy and Jody, who are trying to do their part for the world.

This first day of school sure has a different feeling,
The thinking is enough to set you reeling.
Where, how, who, what is the way?
What games will your children play?
Before there has been sadness, but joy at knowing there is more.
But little girl and little boy as you impart through the door.
No one has been just here before,
Shadowed by hot reactors and rumors of war.
Daughters and sons down that hall,
You have the worlds greatest call.
More to carry than any generation before,
Your burden the future for us all.
Give a care is already your fare,
Your motto do not pollute the air.
Not what will I be when I grow, but will it still be there?
The trees, animals and air.
You are not growing with be seen and not speak.
The worlds worries are not making you weak.
Determined you are our prayer.
To keep the world and us still there.
In these short years, God please,
Put our world together and better instead.
Let this girl and this boy win the race.
Help change what their children face.

Sunny Lorraine Van Cleave

Sunny Lorraine Van Cleave

GOD GAVE ME GRACE

To my Grandmother who has given me faith

Oh not this time you devil you slime, you tricked me too often, I won't fall this time.
Your tricks won't work like you thought they would, you laid me down but not for good.
The things you made of me, out of money aren't gonna happen time 'round honey.
I'm stronger now and wise to your tricks, just try lay me down see if I itch.
The pain and guilt you put in my mind won't last at least not on my time.
You thought you had me by the balls, but it's you that's gonna fall.
The hell you once made me go through, came to an end once I knew you.
I got the wire that you were here, but the message got lost in my ear.
I got lost on your street to hell, and did find people who did smell.
I detoured off to someplace and don't you know god gave me grace.

E Rosella Raugh

WITH WINGS AS EAGLES

Come fly with me, cries the eagle
From the highest mountain peak.
Leave your trials and your cares,
Leave your mix-up world affairs,
Come, together we can reach the sun.

With strong wings, it leaves its tree top perch.
Watch me, watch me, it cries,
Watch me, as I fly to the highest hill.
Come fly with me,
Together, we can reach the sun.

Learn from the eagle and its flight,
Remember its courage, its strength,
Feel the delight
As it flies high, oh so high—
A silhouette against the evening sky.

Learn from the eagle,
Yes, learn its ways.
Reach for greater heights and greater days.
Then you will know when life is done,
You've reached the sun.

Edna Otto Dame

WHO? WHO?

I walk in the woods and what do I see
But a wise old owl sitting in a tree.

He tilts his head from side to side
And fluffs his feathers up with pride.

So I look at him, and he looks at me,
He must be wondering who I could be.

He blinks his eyes in a questioning way,
To ask me why I'm in his woods today.

Getting no answer, he has to find
Just who I can be, to ease his mind.

With a "Who? Who? Who?" he asks me straight,
"Are you friend or foe, to love or hate?"

Then I answered him with a quiet voice,
"I'm whatever you wish, you make the choice."

Since he doesn't seem scared, or fly away
I must be a friend, and I'm welcome to stay.

So I walk in the woods, and start to sing
Happy, because I am not trespassing.

Sister Elizabeth Anne Durbin

THE FIRST SNOW FALL

To my mother and father

Mother earth was dark and dreary,
Her trees stood stripped of their fine green leaves.
The little brown birds seemed to know,
that something great was about to take place.
Even the sky showed signs of a great wonder,
that was about to fall from its vast throne.
Then there seemed to be a veil lifted and
Tiny little flakes began to fall.
One by one they fell from the sky,
The wind gently blew them to and fro,
They came slowly at first, then faster and faster
they rushed to the ground, until
All the earth became covered in the beauty
Of its soft white flakes.
Then they stopped, just as they had started,
very slowly.
The blue in the sky began to peep through,
And the sun shone forth in all its splendor,
To brighten the wonder of Mother Nature
in all her beauty.

Carol Linn Rich

GATHERING A MEMORY

To Mike, Becky and Michael, "Loves of my life." Glady Creek, West Virginia

---

Small wonder the daisies grew so well, stretched up their heads for this child to smell.
"Pick me, pick me," they seemed to say. "Take me to Mom, then come to play."

He tugs at the stems to break them tall; runs to the house, careful not to fall.
"Here Mom," he says with a grin.
Then off to the field to play again.
You watch from the window and what you see; the love of a child gathering memories.

shirley e riley

AINT I A BLACK WOMAN

To the National Political Congress of Black Women, New York and Vicinity

---

Who
has struggled, o these many years
keep my family from starving
scrub the man's floor
nurse his babies . . . 'cause his ol' lady wouldn't/couldn't

Aint I A BLACK WOMEN

so well endowed multitudes
DROOL
with envy as i strut my stuff
painters/sculptors rush to
duplicate me

Aint I A BLACK WOMEN
who
performs magic on them
collards/red
rice/chicken/sweet potato
pies/chittlins
pigs feet
leaving an indelible mark on the
taste buds

Aint I A BLACK WOMEN
getting a special tingle hearing
the
voice of my LOVED one
longing to melt in his
arms/become
one . . . invisible
God . . . he alone know I'm there

Aint I

Olga M Smith

NOSTALGIC VALENTINE'S DAY

St. Valentine's . . . . . What a sweet
precious day,
Romantic, nostalgic, in such a dear
way;
Confirming our love with a gift of
some kind;
Showing them that they are on our
mind;
With flowers or cards or even some
candy,
How more can you prove, your
relationship's dandy;
Isn't it grand that each year at this
time,
Your question asks . . . . . "Will you
please be mine?";
So always remember to give God
the praise,
That we still have a day, to help
hearts up-raise;
Then continue to show what it
really transcends,
That "Love" over-rules, finally, . . .
. . In the end!

Donna Dell

GREAT ESCAPE

An escape into freedom,
is what we all need.
So escape with me,
to a land of makebelieve.

Not a tear is shed,
not a heart is broken.
We sleep upon beds,
made of violets and croquens.

Skin of black,
skin of yellow and white.
Not an ounce of discrimination,
nor a racial fight.

Friendship and love,
is all we need know.
Surrounding each one of us,
like a thick band of gold.

So come along,
come take my hand.
Come stray with me,
to my makebelieve land.

Thomas D'Ancona

LIQUID MOON MORNING

there was a crack in the moon
that let the sun shine through,
it filled his gaze,
giving the eyes dreams.
the tears of angels roll at their feet,
lit and unlit
over the lost dark thoughts below
them.
he awoke with red-orange
rose petals under his tongue.
the skies bled their inbred colors
into the water, the citrus smell of
tangerines
hung like birth in the air.
sweet avocado emeralds hung in
his groin
making the quiet sound of ladies
fingers
drumming on mahogany when he
walked.
phosphorescent lipstick circled a
day old
ceramic cup,
a dried leaf screeches across slate.

Brenda Kay Smith

CRIES OF A DEPRESSION

This poem is dedicated to my mother and father, who have shown great strength and love throughout the years

---

Mama, don't cry; we'll make it thru
the day,
Mama, baby Angie wants to stop
work to play.
Mama, why did brother Billy go
away?
My little one, I cry, because I care
for you,
You see, we're in a depression and
there's not much we can do.
I know your mind isn't clear on
what I say,
Yet, you and Angie will have to
work instead of play.
You're the innocent, the ones who
don't deserve this hell,
So, I guess it's me and your Pa that
has failed.
But honest, we didn't know it
would be like this,
That's why Billys gone, he's on
Gods special list,
Mama don't cry, we understand,
Me and Angie don't mind giving
you a hand.
Mama, we may be young and
innocent but America is our
land,
Mama we love America, Pa and you
And Mama, if we have to, we'll love
that damn depression too.

Eleanor M Lydic

WHO IS A FOOL

A fool is one who thinks he is smart,
Plays a game foolishly from the
start,
His life is nothing but a mess,
To people, he's a terrible pest.
About his job he doesn't care,
Neglects it and gets the air.
About his appearance he couldn't
care less.
He won't shape up like people
suggest,
He thinks he's God's gift to women,
Trys to make every woman he can.
If you tell him to behave,
All he does is fly into a rage.
His jokes are lousy as can be,
He laughs very loud at people he
sees.
Lays his money all around,
Trys to cheat until he's caught,
Selling things that can't be bought.
Doesn't follow his doctor's advice,
Rather loose by playing some dice.
Drinks and smokes like a fiend,
His ideas are one big dream.
That's what a fool is.

Evelyn Mathewson Blinkenberg

WHERE TO GO

To all of my families

Where to go I don't know where,
You don't know where to go?
Ocean, Beach, Sand or Snow;
Golly where shall I go?
Think of the mountains, sky and
trees,
Do I want to play in the sand?
or play in the leaves?
I think of all, first I will to the beach
and play in the sand and swim,
Then I will go to the mountains and
rest under the trees.
So I can listen to the birds sing,
and the gurgle
of a spring or stream,
So now I know where I will go;
Do you know what I mean?

Stanley O McCaffrey

THE END OF DAY

I have witnessed another
sunset.
Which marks the end of the
day.
The moon and stars will
shine again tonight.
The four seasons will come
and go;
Spring, Summer, Fall and
Winter.
The wind, rain, sleet and
snow will fertilize the
earth.
The flowers will bloom and
the fruit and vegetables
will grow.
There will be a harvest time
and a harvest feast
and a Thanksgiving.
Christmas will come and go.
And I will ring-in another
new year.
The tide will rise and fall
every 24 hours
And the sea will breathe in
and out upon the shore.
The clock-of-life is wound
but once.
And no one can foretell
when it will stop.
at late or early hour.
In my twilight years, before
"Now I lay me down to
sleep,"
I pray that I will see another
sunset,
and the moon and stars
again from earth.
You see, I know my old
clock is slowing down!

Joe Allen Davis Jr

THE OTHER SIDE OF THE MIRROR

On the other side of the mirror
I see a fountain of youth at the
touch of a hand
People are dancing in showers
Children building castles in the
sand
Secrets are kept in Heaven's closet
Most people are too blind to see
Some escape the thought
Some die looking for the key
I arm wrestle with the hands of
time
To grant me a slower second
Thus, I will delay the time
For me, the bell has beKKoned
Angel's fly and look through to us
Even though we cannot see
But I hear the tones
Of the mirror screaming back at me

Mary A Keller

LOVE FULL OF PAIN

Who has been filled with false
hopes and dreams
I believe that it's me, or so it seems
I don't want to hurt him, this man
I once knew
The life that we shared and all we
went through
He thinks that the hurt and the
pain will soon pass
I know in my heart that it won't
happen fast
I feel that at times I'm not really
alive
A terrible daydream when I open
my eyes
I want a new life, to forget what
went down
To gather my senses, to get my
mind sound
My head is all clouded, my heart
crying out
For the strength that I need to be
rid of my gout
All sense of feeling has left me and
died
An empty shell cracked, it's
contents all dried
A castle of sand on a beach late at
night
The tide knocks me down when the
dawn brings in light
You can build me again, but the
same I won't be
For some pieces were left in lifes
open sea
You say that you're sorry from all
that was said
After the hurt that made me feel
dead
We fight everyday, it never ends
here
Belittle me more, make me feel
small dear
I know that he hurts, he thinks it's
not fair
His life feels in ruins, his pain he
does share
It's the child in my heart that hurts
when we fight
A child needs assurance, held close
in the night
But he can't just hold me, his needs
are much more
Misguided feelings, and
emotionally sore
I'm leaving this man, I must to
survive
A new life with meaning, so I'll feel
alive

Linda MacDonald

WAR, AND PEACE AT LAST

Dedicated to all Veterans

Thank God, it's over and done with
Another fruitless way,
Bloody, Bloody battles,
Fought each day o'er.
Man to man, troup to troup, plane
to plane,
And then it starts all over again.
Thousands killed, hundreds flee
Men go back, too wearily
To change and shave, just rest and
save

All their strength, to fight and pave
A way for peace? to come at last
And offer refuge to the mass
Of tired soldiers, coming home.

Evonne Y Jackson
TO BE A WOMAN

Can a girl know when she's becoming a woman, can a girl know when she becomes a woman. How can one tell when things are so mixed up inside. Will it always be like this?

Is becoming a woman a test of nature to face the puzzles of life and solve them as they come her way?

How can a girl know when she is a woman, when she sees her reflection and no longer sees that girl that always wondered why things happen.

Or is it the woman that tries to make some of these things happen. Does having a child make this girl a woman?

Does having a man make her a woman. Is having the experience to do what is right make the girl a woman?

Does decisions, the struggles to survive and the strength to overcome the hurts that come with life make this girl a woman?

If all of these things make this girl a woman. Then I have all these things.

And it's tough to be a woman!

Millie Bundschuh
MY ALASKAN MALAMUTE

In memory of my friend, "Reaba."

She was gentle, loving and wonderfully bright, with almond shaped eyes that held you in sight! A soft wolf-grey coat that shone in the light and her beautiful face wore a mask of snow-white!

She filled my life with both joy and delight, was ever protective and if need be, would fight!

She became ill and grew weaker as my heart filled with fright—a future without her just did not seem right!

She is truly missed since she went away but I know we will meet again someday, for now she is safely in God's care and someday in heaven she will be there!

Ever regal and sometimes cute, my beloved Alaskan Malamute!

Patricia E Scanlan
DETOUR

To Jenny and Tim and their generation With love and hope for the future.

A warning to burn-outs, so
knowing and wise,
your seeing the world through
young and blurred eyes.
Dulling your senses, expanding
your mind,
it's all in good fun so it seems at
the time
you're not hurting anyone can't
your parents relax?
Just leave you alone with their
vicious attacks!
On all your true friends on all you
hold dear,
your clothes and your music, your
double pierced ear.
They don't understand, they'll
never relate
You're ready for life but, they tell
you to wait.
Could there be any truth in the
things they say?
Are you headed for trouble if you
continue this way?
I didn't believe it. How could they
know?
Things were so different so long
ago.
But life passes quickly I've founded
the bend,
I now find myself on the parents
end.
My children are me in another time
I've been to the places they're tying
to find.
Theres nothing there to be
revealed,
No big secret signed and sealed
I want to spare them all my woes.
The burn-out path was the road I
chose.
Don't sing me praises on pills and
pot.
I've been there before and I know
what you've got.
Can you learn from my lesson? Can
you feel my pain?
Oh Please take the time to think
again.

M Dianne Barker
RETURN

For Anna

I've walked with you along the
misty shore
When darkness veiled your shining
face with grey,
And listened to your tales from
days of yore
Until the golden breaking of the
day.
On rocky ledge I've sat and
watched for you;
I've shivered at the seagull's lonely
cry,
And even as I waited there I knew
You'd only come—then turn, and
say "Good-bye."
But then, sometimes, you reach
your icy hand
To give me polished glass, a satin
shell;
You toss them carelessly upon the
sand,
I hold them tenderly—you give
gifts well.
And e'en should I desire, I cannot
spurn
Thee, restless sea, to whom I now
return.

Carolyn Cosentino
IMPRESSIONS

Impressions are what we are
It's memories that we recall
Recollections of past and present
People whom we have known
Sadness and happiness we have
experienced
How we face our trials and
tribulations
Our commendations and
condemnations
Makes us each most unique

Roxanne Walsh
I HEARD YOUR VOICE BUT DIDN'T ANSWER;

I heard Your voice but didn't
answer;
it seemed so unreal
But now I feel Your hand on my life
now I begin to feel
A love greater than the world
and stronger than man,
So rich with peace and joy,
so immersed in truth it stands.
A purpose begins to fill my life
with a deep desire to be close to
You,
To know You, to love You more,
To rejoice forevermore in You.

Steven R Wright
TRULY GIVING

The feelings received, by truly
giving
Warm the very heart
Truly expressing, a meaningful
living
Not just a work of art
Your heart grows warmer, when
it's done
You've found a piece of mind
You've showed your love, just like
Gods son
By being so very kind
to what you've given, the other
needs
An act of kindness today
I pray you all, find joy in these
deeds
By following in his way
In giving to others, you let your
heart flow
Their needs have been your care
In return, you've found, that Godly
Glow
That giving seems to share
You've pleased the Lord, you've
done what's right
Your payback is above
For these are the deeds, that make
life bright
And show your utmost love

Mr Larry E Truchinski
SOAR LIKE AN EAGLE

Soar Like An Eagle;
Learn to Fly;
The Mystery Unfolds.
Cumulous Clouds, Clear Above;
The Earth Below;
Tilled Soil, Trees;
All Of Its Green;
A Sight To Be Seen.
Mountains, Hills and Valleys,
Rivers, Lakes and Oceans,
Thermals Unseen.
Lived to Fly And Flew To Live.
Loved to fly As Life Itself.
If This Is Heaven?
How Come I Am All Alone?
Dawn to Dusk,
Inverted Spin,
Storys Untold;
God Made The Eagle
For Man To Behold.

Kelly A Beardsley
ONE

I alone applaud the night,
For it is I alone who dares.
I alone endure the sight,
For it is I alone who cares.
I alone look past my grief,
For it is I alone who can.
I alone rise to my feet,
For I alone must stand.
I alone extend my hand,
For it is I alone who gives.
I alone enjoy the band,
And it is I alone who lives.
I alone refuse to die
And soon alone no more am I.

Myra Becher
FRIENDSHIP

In this wonderful land,
join hands with hands
creating a lasting friendship
with friends who understand.
Sharing many a heartache
and a fallen tear.
In love, which everyone holds dear,
bringing memories from the past
and heart,
of lifelong friendships never to
part.
Be a friend

Deena Howard
OUR LAST DRIVE

It was rainy that night,
And I was full of fright;
For he had been drinking,
But of course, I wasn't thinking.
I let him drive the car,
When I shouldn't have let him get
that far;
He went speeding down a curved
road,
I still remember the last words he
told;
"I can handle it, O.K."
That's when he left the road with a
swerve,
And he missed that last curve.
Down,
Down,
Down we went without care,
And then we were both sent flying
through the air . . .
Now they tell me I barely lived,
But it was he who was actually
killed;
His funeral will be tomorrow,
And everyone is full of sorrow;
So, in your heart forever let this
thrive,
Please, don't drink and drive.

Daisy Lee
REMEMBRANCE DAY

Dedicated to all those brave soldiers who fought for Our Country

---

Remembrance Day, you can't
forget.
Especially for the honoring vet.
They fought on land, and in the air.
To think of them, it just seems fair.
Cause they fought with such grace,
No one can ever take their place.

You can't ignore a day as such,
Cause these brave soldiers did so
much,
They shot their guns with bravery,
Some were caught for slavery,
That is why they became
A great token of such fame.

Even though we can't complain
They saved our Country and
suffered great pain,
In our hearts they live on infinite,
Just knowing they died in such
dignity,
These soldiers we should think of
most,
Fighting they did, from Coast to
Coast.

Prisoners were treated just like slaves,
While others lie in their graves,
Between the crosses straight in row,
The poppies steadily grow and grow,
What they are known to me you see
Is they fought for our Country, for us to be free.

Carol I M Schilling McVeen

Carol I M Schilling McVeen
NATURES ARTISTRY

To my loving father, Robert V. Schilling and in loving memory of my mother Adelaide V. Williams, Schilling. With Love to my children Lorene Marie McVeen, Stiles, Richard, Charles McVeen, Jr.

The skillful hand of nature,

Artistically paints the changing of the seasons,
On the canvas of the world.

Terry Canote
UP THERE
The world was blind
To your talent
But then the world's always blind
To its dreamers.
Maybe you'll find
What you're looking for.
Maybe you'll find
Better luck up there.

Doesn't it seem
Time goes by too fast.
They stop your dream
Before it's past.
They took you away
A little too soon.
I wish they hadn't taken you
Up there so soon.
The world never knows
What it has till it's lost,
And now you're gone,
The world has paid its costs.
The world might forget you,
For you never made your mark
But your friends will never forget you,
Even if you're up there.

Carl L Anderson
CONFESSIONS OF A HUSBAND
I'm Sorry

I have never learned to say—
"Darling, I'm sorry."
Words of regret are hard for some,
However deep remorse may be.
Easy words for the frolicsome,
Most difficult they are for me—
For the sins of neglect that mar the day,
For the words said in anger along the way,
For the selfish spirit too oft displayed—
Darling, I'm sorry.

I Love You

I have never learned to say—
"Darling, I love you."
Words of love are hard for some,
However deep affection be.
Careless words to the venturesome,
Most difficult they are for me—
I toll the hours when you're away,
Count that day lost you overstay,
Dearer than life you are this day—
Darling, I love you.

Larry O Keith Easter
JOHNNIS

To Johnnis my first and only love, love can neither die nor be destroyed. Love is you and the things you do to make it better

---

A soft spoken name of intensity
like the flower she has blossom to become a shadow
of the rose.
A model of beauty with the fashion of love
giving her design the way of gentleness.
A creature of rare intelligence by no human
standard,
bound by a spirit of passion by everyones
affection.
With equal grace pure American by breed
neither above nor beneath a fellow companion.
A latter climber stepping up in class with a
compelling desire for peace,
a heart full of joy motivated by freedom
drawn from the strength of a determined
will.

Conrad Lee Jiron
HELICOPTER BLADES; FOR A SOLDIER
I
hot steamy jungle, bullets cutting the air above the blanket grass bombs blasting, the sounds of war machine spinning carousel death a million Vietnamese eyes running
in circles to endless fears Asian Earth blown to bits, enormous holes swallow American soldiers heart drips crying moans in the blood moon night, a born cemetry gates of hell burning young bodies, a mud memory never forgotten lonely soldiers stand still in a Vietnam breeze blowing sadness onto their sticky sweat, nervous skin jumping at every moment at every sound, every thought, as soldier weeps farewell to comrades.
the night has gone, wounded American soldier hears the speed dawn rattling helicopter landing fast on the barren fields of death trap on board to Saigon, up in war skies, fading above the torn landscape the war voice screaming, sounds of helicopter blades, explosions the weapons rapping, the trail of scattered bones on the forgotten Earth, lays wasted in useless death for all humankind to know
II
black marble wall with thousands of American heroes, frozen in time names of courageous men with heart, with soul, with great substance momument stands solid under Washington, D.C. crucifix angels skull their death cries, their life crushing dream, Vietnam war coma suffocating deeper, it now haunts the soul of an entire country a legacy of young men who surrendered their lives for liberty, peace, justice, and freedom, for all people, for all time.

Edith Lenore Curtis
THE LOVING COUPLE
The Loving Couple
Happy and Gay
Not able to Communicate
Quarrels over nothing
Splits up . . . after harsh words . . .

Not wanting to leave as friends
Not a prayer of ever getting back together
As an ending result . . .
. . . A broken heart.

Thomas Anthony Schleicher
LOFTY HEIGHTS

To the fair one:

Oh! . . . Cruel sound that can't be heard.
A cry from a heart destitute for love.
And from such a scream
I climb lofty heights in my dreams
of one so fair
and escape from a loneliness known to none.
From visions of love to reality I fall
somehow safe in the arms of my dreams
and pass the torch of life to a new day.

Mary Orum
THE PRIDE OF GHOST WALKER

To my father who walked his last path to the ghost trail with courage and dignity. I love you father

---

He walks the land with the softness of the wind. His masculine bronzed body
glissens with the sun. Senses that match
that of his sacred Mother Earth. Ebony eyes
that shine defiance for the wrong done to his people and lands many of
whom now ride the ghost trail with the rain from heaven as tears to shower
the scars of Mother Earth. His arms stretched to the sun he cries how have we angered you grandfather for the
shame is more than any mortal man can
endure. Now my feet will walk the white mans burning trail of hate. But
one day we will walk free on our beloved Mother Earth to finally ride
with pride the ghost trail.

Thelma Irene Sommer
INSTITUTIONALIZED BETRAYAL

Dedicated to my parents

Conditions of humanity institutionalized as betrayal
Excite a sense of martyrdom, implying acts which do self-flail.

Goes on within the family—among the nations too.
One consequence of all of this is that we feel blue.

At this time, we give up power
for a truth-revealing hour.

Strength in responsibility
Is set aside for sands are shifty.

And our roles as helpful teachers
Are relegated to watch-bird bleachers.

Gossips here will loose their tongues
Find people hard to live among,

As they search out "worst" and "least"
In ways defining Man as "beast."

Oft, responsible decisions
Are treated as if they were brain
lesions.

Where sense of terror muscles in,
Acts "bad" and "good" are seen as
"sin."

While we are led to feel helpless,
With decision-making hapless.

The terrorist enters this Man-made
vacuum,
His focus, scattered views as
wisdom.

And on the path to Atom war
Man enters as a spirit whore.

Louisa Middleton
LUNCH IN FROGTOWN

Green lump in moist brown earth
Large blades of grass
Camoflague his existence

A fly flutters around
Snap, Pop
A sticky long tongue
Out and in again

Buzz Buzz Another fly
Comes into sight
Snap, Pop
Sticky tongue

Lunch inside
Gulp, Ribbit Ribbit
Hop, Webb feet splat on
Damp earth
Hop, Hop, Hop.

Avic Huffines Greeson
MOTHERS WEDDING DRESS

This poem is dedicated to Jennie Huffines, my darling mother.

It was white, it was long, just as
pretty as could be,
The wedding dress my mother
made to wed my dad you see.
She made it fancy at the waist,
sleeves and at the hem,
Everytime she looked at it she
would say, "Oh how I love him."

She put it in the trunk upstairs and
every now and then,
We would take it out, make
pictures and put it back again.
Fifty years passed, two children
one grandchild came along the
way,
Out came the wedding dress to
celebrate the day.

Now when the bells toll for me
don't you dare forget,
Put my wedding dress on me also
my wedding slip.
She at eighty seven swiftly took her
flight, to be with Him,
She had served on earth, in the
quiet of the night.
She looked so peaceful in her
lovely wedding dress, I will
always be so thankful I followed
her request.

Helen E Franklin
FAR PASTURES

When I crossed the rushing river
I traveled to a foreign land,
Stepping up the bank a shiver
Held me like a caressing hand.

Trees seemed greener, flowers
were fairer
Than any I had seen before,
The very air seemed even fresher,
As eager I searched for hidden lore.

Twilight came in stealthy manner,
I was heedless 'til the dark,
Then something happened to my
banner—
Joy was gone, my colors stark.

I knew then green banks of rivers
Were very much the same each
side,
So sadness came with different
shivers,
Leaning on a tree, I cried.

Elizabeth Quering
FRIENDSHIP

For my husband Bill and best friend Mitz

Friendship's a thing everyone
needs;

It grows out of kindness not from
a seed.

Friends are created by time and by
love,

By giving a pull instead of a shove.

Cindi Erwin
JOEY

I call you "Bratman"
Because you are.
Sometimes I catch you
In the cookie jar.
You come in my room
To make me mad,
But at other times
You make me glad.
You make such faces;
It's a sight to see!
I tell you you'll stick like that,
One day you might freeze!
You glare at me
And say, "Don't care!"
Then I reach down
And pull your hair.
You get mad and
Run to mother
As I say, "Oh, No!
Oh, brother!"
Our fights are many
And our hugs are few.
But, Nephew of mine,
I do love you!

James W Wigglesworth
THE GRAIN OF SAND

To my four children Lois, James, Maelee, and Clyde.

I walked along the seashore
Thumping my toe
Thumping grains of sand
But, how little did I know

I picked up a grain
And compared it to me
I said to myself
I'm a giant, compared to one of
these

I looked to the heavens
And then back to me
And then I knew
This grain of sand was a lot bigger
than me

The Grain of Sand is a symbol of
the night
Look at the many wonders
God made for our sight
The stars, the planets, the moon so
bright
A billion worlds, out there in the
night

So if you compared our world to
all these
It's just a Grain of Sand
That's somewhere in God's plans
In the many wonders of God's
heavens to see.

Robert Gregory Coker
THE BETTER MOUSETRAP

The birth of fire did not surpass
our flame
and loses much of its
significance,
for fire itself would blush and die
of shame
to see us cast away our
innocense.

Inconsequential also is the wheel
compared to all the places that
we go
When we are carried off by what
we feel.
It makes the wheel seem
primitively slow.

Who cares which man achieved
the written word
or carved it first upon tablets of
stone,
for if our words of love by him
were heard
his scribblings never could
express their tone.
Our making love is able to
surpass
man's mediocre makings of the
past.

Maria Veronica Bakkum
HIS MAJESTY, KING OF MY HEART

Dedicated to Robert Milliman and our high school days. Composed by Maria at age 15.

He didn't come to me on a gallant
steed
He never slew a dragon or do a
mighty deed
He was not of noble birth, he wore
no garments gold
But he smiled and all the splendor
of the world his smile did hold
When he spoke the skies were blue
and clear
And when he sang the very heavens
bended to hear
He never saw a royal banner
waving in the air
Or saw in golden letters his name
emblazoned there
But in the hearts of those who love
him
There is that fair emblem of him
He never led an army his beloved
land to save
Nor returned to hear the cry

"Victorious are the brave"
He never thrust a flaming sword
to save a princess he adored
But in his dark and starry eyes
There an eternal promise lies
He never ruled upon a throne or
wore a jeweled crown
He never saw a court before him
lovingly bow down
For my heart is his castle and his
ever faithful throne
My life is his to rule—reflecting
him alone
For my heart has crowned him
King
And here's the song I'll forever sing
His Majesty, King of my Heart.

Colmar Devon Tucker-Moseley
KEEPER OF THE SECRET

I watched her slowly fade and then
vanish.
She came to me with her problems.
I heard them, but I didn't know
what to do.
She was only fifteen.

She always looked outgoing to
everyone.
Few knew of her true self.
I—I knew, and yet I didn't do
anything.
She thought of herself as a caged,
lonely, and frightened
Zoo animal in a displaced habitat,
searching for a haven to
Lay its burdens. I could have given
her comfort, but I
Didn't do anything.
She was only fifteen.

Some say it was an accidental
gunshot to the head, but I—I
And her parents knew better than
that. I went to her funeral
And watched her parents mourn
over her deathly silent vault.
Their whispers sirened in my ears.
They kept repeating,
"Darling you should have come to
someone for help."
I could have helped her, but I
didn't!!
She was only fifteen.

To this day I still
wonder.
Why—Why didn't I help her?
Was it that I didn't care? Or was it
something else?
I don't know, but I could have
made all the difference.
For she was only fifteen.

Shirley Taylor
THE SWING

This poem is dedicated to the memory of Robert Lee Taylor, my beloved husband.

A vagrant breeze, with gentle touch
Lightly sways the swing
Wherein he sat
In deep meditation
For long hours
Pondering the profound mysteries
of
Life, death, eternity.

A zephyr breeze still rocks the
swing
Bereft now of his presence
To higher climes
His soul has flown
To learn first-hand
The answers to
His earth-bound soliloquies.

To us who yet remain in quest
Of all he sought
While here on earth
The empty swing speaks
Solace to our hearts
To ease the pain of
Empty days
And lonely nights
With promise of
The mystery solved
The victory won.

Lavona M Potter
TO MY GRANDDAUGHTER, WITH LOVE—

To Wendy, a beautiful young mother.

Families together
Can survive the stormy weather
Especially when the sailing's rough.
And winners have a way
Of coping with each day,
While quitters cry "enough, enough!"

Right now you're going through
A time that's hard for you,
An experience like no other.
But the life that's soon to be
Will instantly make me
A happy Great Grandmother!

Our Family Tree is greening
And each new leaf has meaning,
Part of an overall design.
Who knows what gifts it brings,
What melodies it sings,
And best of all, it's yours and mine!

Janice Balakrishnan
I AM MY OWN REASON FOR BEING!
I Am My Own Reason For Being!
The palm does not apologize,
For being not a pine tree, nor an oak.
Its own height and its strength do suffice.
It bends toward earth with a supple bow.
It has its dignity—as I have mine.
I Am My Own!

I Am My Own Reason For Being!
The flame does not apologize,
For being not the moonlight, nor the sun.
Its own gleam and its warmth do suffice.
It lightens its chamber from the darkness.
It has its dignity—as I have mine.
I Am My Own!

I Am My Own Reason For Being!
The stream does not apologize,
For being not a river, nor the seas.
Its own width and its depth do suffice.
It washes its shore with each ripple.
It has its dignity—as I have mine.
I Am My Own!

I Am My Own Reason For Being!
The dove does not apologize,
For being not an eagle, nor a swan.
Its own speed and its grace do suffice.
It awakens the slumbering masses.
It has its dignity—as I have mine.
I Am My Own!

Sharon Jane Barnett
NO NEVER . . . WELL MAYBE . . .
The beat of your heart
The sound of your voice
The understanding in your eyes
The warmth of your touch
The strength of your charm
The light of your doorway in minds eye
Ecstacies brought to me by your presence

Shall not I want to hear that sound? No Never . . .
Shall not I want to listen? No Never . . .
Shall not I need this look? No Never . . .
Shall the cold embrace me? No Never . . .
Will I be weakened by such charismatic sounds? Well Maybe . . .
Shall I see thru that threshold of lust? Well Maybe . . .

No Never . . . Well Maybe . . . I Must . . .

Samuel Parisapogu
T.G.I.F.
It is the Old evening Friday, again
relieved people hurried cars;
Drink beer eat chips
play pool in Tavern with chicks.

Sometimes you make it
sometimes you don't;
But it is the anxiety
and the unexpected pleasure.

Sandwitch culture anyway you look at it,
you earn and spend;
To complete the cycle,
for humanity it is biocycle.

Dickie Evenson
FLYING SAUCER

To America of Tomorrow, This is the truth!

We saw it in the north-east sky
before the sun arose
It was my first, our daughter's next
but dad preferred to doze!
Quite like a saucer, yet with light,
all irridescent, upsidedown,
its colors changing, dim-to bright
not far above our town!
Its geometric pattern moved
in triangles, it flew!
We saw no person in it's frame,
yet mind-controlled, we knew!
For twenty minutes, we both watched,
spell-bound, it held our gaze
then in an arc, it sailed away
much faster than light-rays!
When some folks laugh now, as we talk
of things we saw it do,
we realize nobody knows
when they might see one too!

Robert F Farrell
THE JOURNEY
I pause for a moment to look behind.
A figure lies there still and blind.
No feeling of sorrow or remorse,
Do I feel as I resume my course.
The world below me seems to fade away,
As I speed thru the cosmos,
there's no night, no day.
I have no form, no shape, no size.
I can see like an eagle, yet I have no eyes.
There is no one with me, but I feel not alone
As I'm gently guided toward a gleaming throne.
No recollection of whence I came.
Perhaps a place without a name.
Then, suddenly, it occurs to me,
I am the soul of man set free.

Harold M Curtis
MEMORIES
Why is it that time drags along so slow,
When you've nothing to do, nor anyplace to go?
Now, after all these years, things just aren't the same.
The rules have changed; theres a brand new game.
Old age has taken over; changed all but my name.
Yes, everything is different, and nothing is the same.
My teeth are fewer; my eyes are getting blurry.
My hands fumble a lot; my hair is falling out.
My back is very weak, and my legs are far from stout.
Now I can go any place I please;
have anything I really
care about;
Eat at any restaurant or greasy spoon; travel any highway
or route.
But, time, that use to drag along;
Right now, rapidly
is running out.
As time runs into a solid wall, what
I have on instant
recall
Is what I've spent a lifetime collecting: Years and
years of MEMORIES.

Lloyd Wayne Taylor
HEAVEN SENT
The Lord sent me an angel from the heavens up above,
to watch over me, and share all her love.
Yes, the Lord sent me an angel,
for the rest of my life,
to share all my love with and take as my wife.
To share all the sorrow, the heart and the pain,
though the love in our hearts shall always remain.
Yes, the Lord sent me an angel from
the heavens above,
flown down to earth as a snowy white dove.
May I thank you, O Lord, for this wonderful gift sent,
for the rest of my life will be wisely spent.
And if the day comes, and the devil tries to lead me astray,
I beg you, O Lord, please don't take my angel away.

Pat D Johnson
YES, WE DO MIND
We're not strange and it's no joke,
But, we really mind it when you smoke.
It's hard on us, and worse on you,
It's also hard on our furniture too.
For long after you have come and gone,
That stale, pungent odor lingers on and on.
It's your life to lead until you're dead,
If you choose to smoke, PLEASE do it elsewhere instead.
But, if you love and enjoy life, take care of your health,
Or, someone else will enjoy your wealth.

Meta D Weiss
HYMN TO MUSIC
O, ancient art, to you we sing
with voices loud that they may ring
and spread your praise through all the world
so that it may be heard.
You give us comfort when we're sad
and cheer with us, when we are glad,
inspire us to valiant feats
and great heroic deeds.

Our language often is not known
to other folks who speak their own
and world events of great impact
arose from this fact.
But music knows no limits,
fine understanding it permits,
May you guide us for the common good
to one great brotherhood!

Sylvia F Bogust

Sylvia F Bogust
A TENDER TOUCH
If God's tender touch can pluck a song from the night, and send it
across the land and sea, then God's tender sigh can call to you and me.
If a petal can be blown high into the sky
and tossed over a Continent wide, then
come all ye mortals and wonder no longer,
but lose your pride and know that God is
very much alive and always at our side.

William D Cameron
WHAT OF LOVE
What of love shall I speak to thee
For who in love can really see
Lest I say that love is a tower
upon which one may ascend to power
To love a person is truely grand
yet it's better still to love all in the land.
To caress, fondle and kiss is splendor
for in these things our hearts we render
Personal love sometimes causes pain
and more than not is often vain
Impersonal love, like the future present and past
is a love that will last and last
Yet the love of uprightness should be greater
than the love of beauty to which we cater.
For one may come, and one may go
but the love of uprightness will forever grow
The love of one heart for another,
as the love of a son for his Mother
Is a lasting love perhaps is true,

but is this the love of many or a few?
What of a love that knows no grounds,
a love that grows in leaps and bounds
Who among us can profess to love
All things below and those above?
Will not we ever learn to treasure
Love that rests not in pleasure?

Paula Lewis
A SPECIAL GUIDE

"This Poem is Dedicated to my Loving Mother, Flora" who gave me the inspiration.

Years long ago, but not so far away their little hearts lingered with memories that will always stay. Five little girls left without a Mother; So little and so young yearning . . . Where will be the blanket for my cover? Where's Mommy? They'll ask not knowing which way to go, Mommy went to heaven and someday they'll know; they were left out, with nowhere to turn, all having such harsh memories, wishing they could burn . . . sweet Jesus called Mommy, Mommy had to go, but they didn't understand. Being left out, their little hearts crying "won't somebody lend a helping hand." Wondering will they eat or where will they sleep, so many reasons for the little ones to weep . . . These five angels sent from Heaven, with no place to lay their head. Molasses and cornbread, will they lay in their featherbed? No shoes on their feet, no pretty clothes to wear . . . So many miles ahead, no pretty ribbons in their hair. One was to stay here another to go there, were they to grow up with such despair? They were strong . . . Realizing this is where their life begins, and it had to start, losing Mommy, and being a part, would never break the "love" in their heart. Mommy had sent, "special prayers" to follow them too! They had to walk the edges of life, but Mommys goodness would see them through. With each and every step of life for the little girls to take . . . To grow and to learn, they'll never break a promise that they make. As they look back. living life with such a stride . . . They took every step of life with pride, "but you see, they had a special guide."

Desiree E Hodges
TIME

What is time
But the wind's whisper,
A moment's passion,
A child's first word.

What is time
But of endless hours,
Perhaps of waiting,
Perhaps of longing.

What happens to time?
Looking in the mirror to find
A time etched face,
Greying hair,
Children that aren't children anymore.

The years slipping by—
Old lovers smile
As though remembering days gone by.

Looking upon present life
And back upon what could have been,
And being thankful for what one has.

Time is like a woman—
Ever changing,
Everlasting,
Always present,
Forever elusive.

As the flame of a candle is gone
So are the precious moments wasted.
Because of fear or
Maybe inattention—

Like a dove,
Time flies away.

So what is time
But the wind's whisper,
Or a moment's passion—

Or perhaps the empty eyes
Of an old man.

David Beagles
THE CLOWN

I'm just a clown,
See me smile . . .
See me frown . . .

Performing in the middle ring,
Hearing the applause—
My acts bring . . .

Flipping a cartwheel,
Doing a slow handstand . . .
Making the crowd squeal . . .

Tho my heart is breaking,
I'm a professional . . .
You don't see the faking . . .

Painting on a smile, or frown,
Sometimes I act up . . .
Sometimes I act down . . .

The mask I paint isn't true,
I'm not perfect . . .
I, too, can be blue . . .

Take a good look at me,
Don't judge too quick . . .
I'm not what you see . . .

Sometimes I'm clowning . . .
Sometimes I'm smiling . . .
Sometimes I'm frowning . . .

Nikki K Patten
YOUNG LOVE

You entered my life
and showed me such joy,
I never thought days could be brighter.
With your smile so light
it made every night right,
you were truly much more than a boy.
But soon it was May and you went your own way,
I thought I would die of the fright.
I miss you it's true
and human as well
I find it hard not to be blue.

Tyler K Bush
PUT YOUR FISTS DOWN

To my sister Natley Myers who is always helping people.

Sometimes love darkens or turns flat.
Periods of dislike can cause a spat.
Let it only be a temporary thing,
Before you know it, good times will upswing.

You too, can bore and annoy.
Don't throw out your marriage like a broken toy.
It's just a phase,
there will be better days.

Pointing your finger at imperfection?
You have plenty of that from your direction!
Don't look for another spouse,
because we all at times are a bit of a louse.

Don't dwell on the bad times.
You got through them before,
you wouldn't have thrown your parents out the door!
Remember all of the good times!

Tell your mate you want love to last,
hold them fast.

Pour out your feelings—not blame!
Over the years the flicker of love
will mature to a steady flame.

Fleda F Capell
A COLD SPRING DAY

The garden was growing and doing well,
"We've set out some plants," to others we'd tell.
One night on the news we heard it'd be cold,
"The temperature will drop below freezing," we were told.
The next morning Jack Frost and ice was found,
and our poor little plants were bowed to the ground.
Our flowers that had been so colorful and big,
had now turned brown and were drawn up like a twig.
But God still hath made everything beautiful in His time,
He has all in his power and we're proud it is thine.

Bettye Harlien
ONCE IN MY DREAMTIME

Once in my dreamtime
My mate did go astray.
Greener pasture yonder
Sought him out dream way.
Within him there it happened
To love I thought so strong.
The tempter lured him onward
And held his gaze too long.
She kept the lust there growing.
His eyes so plainly cast,
The torment deep inside him,
Just wanting youth to last.
I saw him reach to touch her.
I called to him in vain.
He chose to make me suffer,
For only thrills, his gain.
His new one thus, deceived him
He found himself so wrong.
The fickle one, he'd answered,
For always, then was gone.
He wanted my forgiveness.
I pushed him there, away
For once in my dreamtime,
My mate did go astray.

Florence K Rhoda
SPRING MAGIC

Behind the fence
Stands
An old Dogwood tree
All pristine white with blossoms!
Beside it
An ancient Wisteria
Creeps
Up among its branches
Like delicate lace, its purple flowers
Drooping gracefully
As a shy bride
Clinging
To her husband's arm.

Purple against white!
Where have I read
Of light refractions
And chlorophyll—
All the many Complexities
That lie behind
Such beauty?
Yet, understanding little
Of that
I stand admiring—
One of God's children
Seeing
Purple against white!

Alma Taylor
BEAUTIFUL OHIO

To my daughter Marilyn

Be still in your rampaging
Empty your waters over the dam.
All eyes watch your flooding.
Until you quiet down we will worry
'Tll we see your waters subside.

Islands where birds and lovers
Shelter from all storms
That blow across your face.
Urgent you may seem oh so restless,
We love you beautiful Ohio.

Never forget to flow past homes
of the rich and poor
In winter, summer and all seasons.
They offer you their undying love.

Aaron Michael Butler
LINKED IN TIDE'S CHAIN

The waves roll in like a freight train
churning and rolling the sand's grain,
the pebbles, the driftwood that floats
on the waves like seagulls, like boats.
The waves roll in like a freight train.

The wind blows the salt spray like the grain
in the fields on the great Kansas plain.
It floats through the air like Spring rain.
The waves roll in like a freight train.

Small windows roll up in the wind-blown
surf. Windows of agate not to own,
but to borrow, to hold, and to dream,
to see tiny worlds through a sunbeam.
Dreams drift out to sea linked in tide's chain.
The waves roll in like a freight train.

Maurice Louis Frisell
THE SCARY HOUSE

To my Sister Rose F Badeaux

Down the road is a scary house,
Wherein live a Ghost and a Mouse.
The house hides behind the shakey trees
And,
Through the broken window screams the breeze.
It is the sca-rrie-est place I've ever seen!
And I wouldn't go there

Not even on Halloween.
Now:
I've never seen the Ghost
But I've heard the Mouse,
And, I always run fast
When I go past
That House.

Susan Ruckle-Smith
JUST A WORD
Suicide—It's just a word.
But sometimes it's much more.
It gives you empty promises,
And always ends in horror.

It closes in upon you
And threatens endless pain
If you don't use its ghastly ways
To mutilate your brain

So many try to overdose
On different kinds of pills
Some even try to slash their wrists
With razors, just for thrills.

Millions of those misguided minds
Believe those threatening lies
Of no more worries and forever peace,
Those poor frustrated cries.

Suicide is just a word
As people seem to say.
But just that one word—suicide
Kills people every day.

Frances Garner
REFLECTIONS OF LIFE
As I pass upon the street of life with its hurried paces and strife
I watch others go about with their empty
character role, never stopping long the way
to help one wayward soul.
And I take one long look in the mirror of life,
with all its reflections of emptiness and strife
I say to myself, is this one I see that keeps looking back at me
Am I the one that helped this emptiness of
the wayward soul.
I searched myself, and I felt a warm ease,
A feeling of warmth, a feeling to please.
Then I knew beyond this shadow of doubt,
that when I look, in this mirror and I
begin to see,
All is well, because I can see God in me.

Sandra Jean Walpole
THANK-YOU LORD FOR MOTHERS' DEAR
Thank-you Lord for mothers' dear, but most of all for mine,
I hope you keep her with me for a very, very long time.
You're a mother who's one in a million, how I thank God that you're mine,
For all of the love and kindness that you manage to show all the time.
Thanks for teaching me right from wrong, and just being there in time of need,
Oh, how I thank God to you I belong, the greatest mother indeed!
Each day is a golden moment Lord, that we can never relive,
So help us to show thanks to our Mothers, for all the love they do freely give.
A mother's love is more precious than gold, and purer than the snow,
And we'll always be our mother's child, no matter how old we grow.
The smile on your faces always warms our hearts, and that can never be erased,
Because the warmth of our mother's love, can never be replaced!
Everyday is a Mother's Day cause you're always on my mind,
And each and every day I pray, and thank you dear Lord that she's mine!

Edward H Wellborn
BEFORE THE STORM

To Velma, my loving wife.

Two little zephyrs dancing tiptoed around
A eucalyptus, touching lightly, prance
And nudge the daisies with a dalliance
Of kittens playful pranks. Without a sound
They take their micron laden cloaks and bound
Across the crimson spotted lea. They glance
At zenith sun entombed in haze. A trance
Befalls them like a cat at a chipmunk's mound.

The pines beyond the meadow break the spell.
The vanguard breezes flush a mottled quail
And consume the zephyrs as they skir pell-mell
In shifting capers leaving a tiny wale
Of sprinkled dust; then frantically charge to quell
The dark and domineering eastward gale.

Martha Daugherity
MY SWEETHEART

You're America, my sweetheart, I'll love you forever.

I love you in the flaming dawn
And in the burning sun;
I love you in the Twilight hours
And when the day is done.

I love you in the Chapel bells,
In the Factory whistle's drone;
You're telling us you love too,
Thro' the years that we have grown.

You're in the Land of Never, Never,
Where children dream and play;
You're in the Land of young folk
And where the hair turned gray.

You're on the waves of Radio,
And on the Silver Screen;
Often times, I wonder if
You're really heard or seen.

I'd like to share you with the world,
Even tho' you're my Sweetheart;
And if they'd love you like I do,
I'm sure we'd never part.

I love you in the Stars and Stripes;
You're a beauty to behold;
Tho' at times, you seem a wee bit worn,
You're pure as solid gold.

Cinda M Austin
YOU

To My Daughter Jennifer "I Love You"

When I see you
Walking down the street;
Something happens to me.
My heart—
I think it stops beating.
My stomach—
It gets butterflies.
There's something about you
That's really special to me.
When our eyes meet,
There's a certain glow in them;
That I think their telling me something.
But then—
Just when I'm going to say it;
I look up and you are gone.
Now, I look at your picture,
Wondering—
Will I ever be with him again?
But I know, if you're willing
And I'm willing;
We'll find a way.
You . . . and I . . .

Irene Pittman
MY SPECIAL ROSE

To My Precious Son, James Lewis Pittman

There's a rose in my garden I'm sure God planted there.
This rose needs special attention and special prayer.
Almost 27 years ago this rose bud started to grow.
It was a very beautiful rose; and we loved it so!
Oh it was so wonderful; all the petals seemed just right:
There then came a change in my rose; it was almost overnight.
Eight months of love and care: I knew just what to do . . .
I'd work with this rose; I'd give it everything, too.
I don't think I took the time to thank The One Above
Who gave me this perfect rose: It was a gift of love.
I'm sure He saw that like before; with the two roses He had given:
I'd love them and take care of them; but what they needed most . .
I'd fail to feed them of the food for spiritual growth.
And He knew this was my last rose that in my garden would grow:
So He had to mar some of the petals . . some didn't grow at all:
Some parts of the rose are still a bud, while some grew too tall.
But, through this rose I see some beauty that all may not see.
This rose is so precious and so sweet to me.
Someday in a perfect garden where petals never fall
There will be only perfect roses for everyone to see!
So, if you have a perfect rose. Be careful how you try
To do too much for the outer flower and let the inner flower die.
As I watch my special rose, so many times I cry;
But, still I thank God everyday that He has chosen me
To help take care of a special rose and to help my blinded eyes to see!

Frank L Wanamaker
GO SIT YOU
Go sit you by a fireside, friend, look deep within its coals.
The answers that are hidden there will help you find your goals.
Go sit you on a hillside friend, look far beyond the peaks.
Lose yourself in deepest thought and heed the voice that speaks.

Go sit you neath a tree my friend, look way up in the leaves.
The murmuring voice that whispers there
will help you to believe.

Go sit you by the sea, my friend, look deep within its roar.

If you're in tune to its measured
beat
you're meant to know much
more.

Go sit you neath the sky, my friend,
look way up in the clouds.
And if it's pictures you can see,
how richly you're endowed.

Go sit you by a friend, my friend,
look deep within your heart.
Then sit you by your friend, my
friend,
how truly blest you are.

Paule Cadet

Paule Cadet
IT'S YOU I LOVED
I don't remember when I loved you
Maybe I was nineteen, you're
twenty
Crazy in the world like an army
Fighting for their proper nation.

Now time changes to disc'ver the
truth
Farewell seems a pain in you!

Please don't follow me, it's too late
Just remember only our sweet love.

Up the mountain we sat together
Talking like two dreamers
I loved you, you loved me
We're so proud in that little isle

Remember the day you're telling
one
The lovely poem you wrote. Gently
I listened with a satisfied smile
Still love you again should I?

Once, I was waiting for your
appeals
You're gone with her like two
angels
I know I loved you before all
But love isn't eternal at all.

Barbara Morris
COCAINE

This poem is dedicated to all those gifted athletes, innocent kids, teenagers and adults: Just say no to drugs.

Cocaine is not only used by thugs,
Janitors, Teachers, Doctors, and
Lawyers
get high off this same drug.
Could it be the stress
Could it be the pressure of some
sort,
To drive these people to take a snort
Maybe it's the high,
Where in a matter of minutes these
individuals think they can fly
Or could these people be insane
To inject such deadly drugs in their
veins,
People are having more heart
attacks,
Some say it is the use of crack
Why must young and old get on
this crooked road
Could this be their only answer of
getting rid
of their heavy load,
Could this be the only way they
know out
Or are they afraid if they try
without a doubt,
they might be fighting a losing
bout.
Despite the spread of these new
diseases
drug use still have not ceased
Some of my friends have lost their
lives,
family; jobs, cars and the clothes
off their back,
But still rehabilitation can't help
them get
back on the right track,
Yes I wonder are these people
insane,
to use such deadly drugs as
Cocaine.

Susan (Hamburg) VanVooren
TRIBUTE TO MY CATS ON A WINTER MORNING

To my parents who always believe in me, and my cats Jack, Jill, and Katie, my inspiration, with love.

The warmth of the winter sunshine
beakons through the glass door.
My kitchen becomes bright and
cheery in its rays.
My cats are drawn towards it, like
moths to a flame.
They bask in its glory with playful
delight, as they roll and stretch.
They beg to go outside with
longing wishes, seemingly
remembering warmer days.
But nature has played a trick on
their furry soles.
As I ponder from the open door, I
sense their dismay.
Their bodies stiffen, as their paws
make contact with nature's cold
truth.
Their journey is shortened, as
winter's reality sets in.
Soon they yowl to escape, back
into the sunny ritual of my
kitchen.
Tomorrow, they will begin again.
How soon they forget the brisk,
freezing feel of the air.
Again, my cats are pulled
magnetically towards the
sunlight.
Again, I watch, happy that they and
the brightness seem to become
one.
For their simple contentment,
brings me a serene joy.

Sandra Wegner
HOSPITALS
Hospitals are not very cheerful
places,
In them you see many unhappy
faces.
You enter by stretcher, on foot or
on a cane,
Feeling oh so miserable and full of
pain.
Soon doctor after doctor probes
your body with all kinds of
contraptions,
Until you're ready to scream and
are no longer responsible for
your actions.
When finally the problem has been
found,
To the operating room you then
are bound.
After many hours of
unconsciousness,
You wake up feeling weak and
quite a mess.
But, with each day that passes by,
You begin to feel better and are
soon very spry.
Your first step is a little wobbly and
unsure,
But, you're happy because they
finally found a cure,
To stop your misery and great pain,
Like sunshine after a long, long
rain.
Your smile broadens with each
passing day,
Until the last day of your hospital
stay.
You say your goodbyes as the
corridors you roam,
Feeling very happy because you're
finally going home.

Robert E Pennington
THIS, TOO, WILL PASS

For my children, and in memory of my parents

Emotions, emotions; like the
swells cresting on an ocean!

Emotions, emotions; like the
waves breaking over a beach!

Emotions, emotions; like the ebb
of one's hope in lifes course!

Emotions, emotions; like the tides
that flow into our life!

Emotions, emotions; adrift on an
ocean of feelings!

Emotions, emotions; recalling
always, when things go awry,
"this, too, will pass."

Michael J Cunningham
THE WATCH
A watch is such a poor measurer
of time,
Take it off—open your eyes, ears
and mind,
Let your heartbeat measure the
moments of your life,
Turn attention to your fellow man,
children, and wife.

In comtemplating philosophers—
the wisdom of our times,
Show compassion, break the clock
and listen to childish rhymes,
Make the most of the wonders
around and within you
Cast off your shoes and feel the
ground beneath you.

Take time and lock it up—no need
to rush and rush and rush,
Move within a different dimension
and walk with a lightness that
can not crush,
Make each new day sparkling and
gay,
Take the watch and the clock and
throw them away.

Therese Ensworth
THE PROMISE—FULFILLED
The dandelion globe of gossamere
Wafts heavily on the air,
Beside the fabric globe of rainbow
hue
Straining toward God, thru
vaulted blue.

Can our spirit stay, against such
force—
The surging draft propelling us
on?
"Not yet," we hear, "Not yet, go
back—
The fields are white—you see?
(Else who will harvest for me?)

But for now, cheer up, my little
ones,
(I have already overcome!)
And when at last the trumpet
blows,
Up, a WAVE of rainbows rose!

Because my faithful gleaners
stayed,
My harvest to woo home;
Spreading my word, lifting me
up—
(For you, I drained the Cup!)

My Father draws all men thru me—
'If I be lifted up . . .' you see.
Come all who will, His word is true.
Come all who will. I wait—for
you."

Louise Kelly Salyer
THIS IS OUR LIFE
Two old people, each with a cane
One with a broken hip, the other a
slight stroke
Are walking together down life's
highway—
Married forty-five years
One son
Two grandchildren
Still bearing together life's
vicissitudes
Having weathered together the

depression
Four Wars—World War I
World War II
Korean War
Vietnam War
And now inflation and Watergate
Through all a glimpse of hope—
And then it disappears.
One without the other
Is like coffee without cream.

Mrs Doris Jean Johnson
WHAT IS LIFE
What is life if not sharing
Sharing ones time and possessions.
What is life if not caring
Caring in every way about ones feelings.
What is life if not giving
Giving of all that you possibly can.
What is life if not loving
Loving in every way to make life's fulfillment,
To me this is life.

Juanita Baugh
DISTANCE
The distance—that I keep
is because I love you
And I need for you
to be true
No questions asked
but they go unanswered
My mind wanders away
to you leaving one day
With someone new
and me lonely and blue
We are honest with each other
and I always want that
No need for the hurt
to start
No need for the happiness
to end
Please always remain my friend
When the love stops
who will be there
To pick up the pieces
of my broken heart
You will always be a part
of me
Together we will be
The love in our hearts
is just beginning to grow
One day soon we will know
if we are to love today
And lose a little along the way
You're always on my mind
My time away from you
seems so far
And I look at a star
And see your beautiful face
and your memory takes the place
Of an empty soul
Always thinking of you
makes me whole.

Roselyn Pennycuff
GINA
I saw a little red haired girl—
A smile upon her face—
I saw a little red haired girl—
In a dress of snow white lace—

I asked the little red haired girl
Why she stopped along the way—
I asked the little red haired girl
Why she could not stay—
So said the little red haired girl,
"Gods garden is in bloom."
So said the little red haired girl,
"For me He has made room."

So, goodbye to the little red haired girl.
We wish that you could stay.
Goodbye to the little red haired girl.
We're glad you stopped along the way.

Roxanne B Frisbie
THE JOY OF SEASONS

Dedicated to my granddaughters, Rachel and Chrissy, who both light up each season of my life with love and joy.

I've been inspired by
A dear little child,
To write about the seasons,
The joy of them all,
The rapture of each,
There are so many reasons . . .
First on the scene is the springtime,
When blossoming buds burst through,
A time of soft pinks and of yellows,
When life begins to renew;
Close on it's heels is the summer,
With hot days and lemonade,
Some time to fish, to swim and to play,
The stuff of which dreams are made;
Follows, the beauty of autumn,
With colors rare to behold,
Leaves of deep red and burnt-orange,
Pumpkins, near wheat fields of gold;
Then comes the silence of winter,
Muting the landscape with snow,
A time of peaceful reflection,
Before spring again, starts to show . . .

Michael L LeFebvre
DARK CLOUDS

This poem is dedicated to my family & friends whose love and encouragement has kept my writing alive. God bless you all. Love, Mike

Dark clouds hanging over-head
Please don't rain on me,
I'm so depressed, miserable
You're taking my life from me.

You have a very sad color
Black as in the night,
Scary, Dark, Evil
An awful scream filled sight.

If it wasn't bad enough
Thunder accompanies you,
Like a blast of a thousand cannons
For a war starting new.

Next lightning blazes across the sky
It's your eyes looking to destroy,
Anything that suits you
To be flattened for joy.

For spite you bring in wind
To take care of the rest,
Things your eyes couldn't handle
Another devils test.

Then it's time for the rain
To finish this picture of gloom,
Another masterpiece finished
Another trophy for your room.

Elizabeth Burmeister
TONIGHT I CRY

To Mr. Edward M. Albright, who under the wrath of cancer sleeps for eternity, he never had the chance to say goodbye . . .

Tonight I cry, for reasons to me are still unknown.
Tears come from my eyes, as from graves the dead do arise.
Tis not in sorrow, that I cry. Not because of the rain, not because of cloudy skies.
No, tis not in happiness I cry, nor do I cry to clean away the bad left inside.
Tonight I cry not because someone is leaving, but only because I
must say goodbye.
Tonight I cry for God alone. And it is said He will reward those
who willingly come to His home.
Because here forever you shall
never be alone.
The trees on which I shall never play. They have the power to
allow in the new day. One I shall never see, but let this be
known just between you and me . . .
Sometimes tis not easy to see what God has planned for you and
me. Nor is it wise to cry to Him, to wonder why.
So when a loved one dies and darkness rapes the skies, do not
weep and curse His ways. But you become Him. See you through His
eyes. Has He done something so terribly unjust, has He done something so terribly unwise?
Yes, tis true tonight I cry, but not for me and not for you . . .
Tonight I cry for God alone . . .
Tonight I cry for In God's holy name tomorrow I shall
Die . . .

Tawny Branz
YOU'VE BLOWN IT—SO WHAT?!
My child, I know you're thinking that NO ONE has ever been
In a situation quite the same, nor ever so DEEP in sin.
You think that you've disgraced me—that I've lost my faith in you—
But it just so happens my love won't change—no matter what you do!
I know you're feeling far away, and you think we're out of touch.
I know you think I've turned my back, but how could I? I love you too much!
If there is a space between us—a distance that to you seems wide,
It's NOT because I'VE walked away, but because YOU'VE chosen to hide.
Don't be afraid to come to me, I'll comfort you in your pain;
If you keep on running the other way not a thing will you ever gain.
I know how badly you're hurting—let me help you before it's too late,
Because if you don't that hurt in your heart will one day be turned to hate.
I know what it's like to be in pain!
I know what it's like to cry!
I know what it's like to wish you were dead; I know what it's like to die!
I remember that day I hung on the cross, how I hurt both inside and out!
Oh, How I wished for another way,—how I longed for some other route!
So I know the pain you're suffering, and as far as temptation and sin,
I was faced with the very same things so I know what a struggle it's been.
I'm not up here pointing my finger; I've no intention of striking you down,
My arms aren't folded in angry disgust, my smile hasn't turned to a frown!
So what do you say there Kiddo? Come here and sit down on my knee,
'Cause I don't care if you're 96, you're never too old for me!
It's okay to cry some tears,.
because I'll just wipe 'em away,
And until you can stand on your feet again, in my lap you're welcome to
stay!

Billy Ben Noll
NO MAIL TODAY

To my father who had waited so long

When I get the mail for Dad each day
While walking there I often pray
That someone thought to write a line
To boost his day, his face would shine,
The joy would last the whole day through
To just receive a word from you.

But many days I come back home
To find him sitting there alone.
There's nothing much that I can say
Except "No letter came today."
Those misty eyes he raised to me
Condemns no one, it's just to be.

But the ache I feel, I can't explain,
It's deep inside, I feel the pain.
I didn't know how much we fail
Till I had to go and get Dad's mail.

Mildred Hummel Albright

Mildred Hummel Albright
THE TRAITOR
The puddles of despair were far deeper
Than the seas of delight . . .

And the puddles beckoned . . .

Hope, the Faithful Traitor, doth betray us all . . .
In his own good time.

Once she lay down in joy and trust,
And rose with bitterness for her reward . . .
She will not rise again till her silver cup be filled,
That she might toast the Traitor one more time . . .

God! . . . The puddles beckoned!

Are her golden virtues tarnished
Because Satan breathed upon them?
Hope is a worthy opponent
Who doth lie in wait for us all;

Robs us of our possessions; parts us from our gold;
Invades our humble dwelling;
scoffs at us in the working place,
And laughs at desires in our soul.

When Paradise was on her shoulder, the hawk named Hope rode high,
Waiting to pluck what was hers and take it
Into the sweet bye and bye . . .

Never to be seen again . . .
And the puddles beckoned.
Hope, the Faithful Traitor, doth make fools of us all . . .
In His own good time.

Melita Molloy
THE LORD IS MY SHEPHERD
He leadeth me unto a righteous life,
His spirit grants me strength to avoid all strife,
I feel His peace and it rests my soul,
As I contemplate His message and His truths unfold.

I must never covet, lie, or steal,
For it brings great pain in the way I feel,
I shield myself from all worldly woes,
With His protecting Grace against all my foes.

He is my Shepherd—I need His love,
He so graciously gives from Heaven above;
May I always live worthily and follow Him,
To Eternal Life and let His Light shine in.

John Craig Carpenter
BREAK—DOWN
Damn buzzards!
What a place to break down . . .
Middle of the desert.
Middle of the day.
No water—No shade.
Sun burning my eye-balls out . . .
Dumb more—leaving the car . . .
Big mistake . . .
Should've stayed with the car.
They always tell you that . . .
They also tell you
to carry some water with you . . .
Should've listened to them . . .
Could use a drink right now . . .
People in Hell want ice-water.
I know how they feel . . .
God, it's hot!
Should've known better . . .
Big mistake—
Should've stayed with the car . . .
Lord, I'm thirsty!

Mrs William Buckman
OCTOBER

To My Bill

Fall is here,
The ground is brown and bare.
The harvest done, the crops are in,
The cribs and bins are full.
The trees are in their glory,
Their leaves are everywhere,
They're green and yellow, brown and red,
Glorious colors floating through the air.
The earth will soon be barren,
The death of Fall is here.
It isn't only growing things
That meets this creeping fate,
It's also closing in upon my chosen mate.
For fifty years and more
We've walked along together.
Now the dim, dark shape of death
Is knocking on our door.
I sit and hold his hand in mine
"Please God, don't let him leave me."
But if it is "thy will" to take him,
Then show me Lord, how to accept it.
Show me how to live alone,
When there's no one there to turn to.
And when my time on earth is gone,
Let me come up there to join you.

Gail F Snow
LIFE IS A WONDERFUL DREAM

This poem is dedicated to Hilary, my lovely daughter, who shares my love for writing.

Caterpillar, hold on tight
To the downy fuzz of the dandelion.
The raindrops moisten it's delicate seeds.
Wind comes up and shakes the stem.

Caterpillar hold on tight
Until the day is bright and calm again.
Then climb down and find a sturdier plant
That won't sway so easily.

You'll be safe to eat and grow.
Spin your cocoon and sleep and dream and change.
As the world seems so very far away.
Life is a wonderful dream.

Butterfly, so beautiful.
You remind me now of the downy fuzz
Of the dandelion, so delicate
Vulnerable and timid.

Rain moistens your lovely wings.
Wind comes up and shakes you until you fly
Away to the shelter of a high tree
And pull in your wings to rest.

Look down, pretty butterfly
On the dandelion stem now broken,
That was once a favorite resting place
In another time and life.

Rosemary E Fugate Uhl
THE DETERMINATION OF A BLEEDING HEART
Through the sands of the desert, I drudge my feet;
And behind me follows your heart.
I have battered and bruised it,
Torn and broke it;
It has lain in the sand in pieces,
Pouring out is bright red contents.
The pool of blood I have caused it to weep,
Would cover the Earth a thousand fold.
A few moments rest, and what's left of your heart,
Makes a trail in the sand as it still seeps blood.
Your heart is faithful;
For it has survived a battle which no heart should have ever survived.
It is a determined heart;
Determined to win above all other hearts.
And it has endured the one thing no heart should ever feel;
Betrayel from the one it loves.
But yet, through all of this,
Your heart continues to follow;
Only to be battered and bruised, torn and broke;
And to lay in pieces upon the sand once more.
A more faithful and truer love shall never be found;
Than that which is contained within your heart.

Linda S Croy
POW/MIA REQUEST

Dedicated to all of the American servicemen and women and their families who have given so much of themselves in the suffering of the perils of war and especially, my brother, Butch who served in Vietnam.

America is my country, it is my plea.
Once again, America, I yearn to see.
"So please God, help me cope through this night of pain, suffering and horrendous fight."
The bombs have stopped for the moment but all around me I see fire and torment.

I See many comrades who have parted to die but not in vain
and I wonder, "Will I survive or end up the same?"
I must push these doubts from my mind
for surely this war will end, it's only a matter of time.
Yes, I must carry on and never lose faith
while loved ones at home worry in wait.

I long to feel mom's gentle touch on my brow
and dad's firm handshake and hardy growl.
Oh how I miss little brother and sister's smiling faces
with happy memories of old times and places.
The memory of the girl that I left behind
slowly steadies my calms my mind.

"Dear God, please give them strength to continue on for some day soon I will be home."
Then, when I see "Miss Liberty" holding the lighted torch
and the "Flag of Freedom and Hope" that I love and support,
from a whisper to a bellow, my words will be,
"I'm home, I'm home! Thank God I'm free,
America, my country; America, my plea!"

Janice A Jentz
LOVE IS ALWAYS THERE
As I sit by my window
With tears in my eyes,
I can't help but wonder
If you hear my cries.

These tears are so warm
As they run down my face,
They've done this before
In this very place.

Then I'm reminded of your unfailing love,
That you've given to me from your throne above.

Although it is mine
And mine to stay,
I have a command
To give it away.

And as I give
It will come back,
I'll have an abundance
Without any lack.

Carlos Cole Beam
SUSPICION
Spoken, the sound's seal broken,
Ventured and bold invaded,
Nothing that long here waited
Holy, holy ever again . . .

Waiting by sill-framed window
In faith for love's returning:
Gone is the heart's reminder,
Present the shallow burning.

Spoken, the word's dark shadow
Moves with its mean inflection
Along the pane, the fogging
Breath is become detection.

Whispered, the sound of phrasing
Born and become Destroyer:
Named, the Judas betrayer,
Nothing is now remaining.

Ruth A Stetter
FOREVER YOURS
You stepped into my life
And my darkness
Turned to sunshine.
My dull life
Suddenly became gay and fun.
You taught me how to love
And I learned what it meant to care.
My days were filled with
Warm thoughts of you
And my nights were filled with you.
And now years later
You have settled into my life
And I into yours.
Our lives have meshed—becoming one.
As it was then
It still is now
I love you—forever.

Jeff Gerdts
YOU

I dedicate this poem to you, Cam. This is your poem; you created it. I hope that all of your dreams in life come true.

Since I've been with you,
I've known nothing but joy within.

Oh, sure, there have been rough times,
But that makes our love stronger.
The tender kisses and gentle touch,
Shows me what needs not to be said.
In some ways it is against all odds,
But I believe it was meant to be.
You make my life complete,
Where once was an emptiness.
The fun times and also the tears,
Are locked in memory—forever.
You know me better than anyone,
And probably more than anyone ever will.
You have a very special part of me,
And I've given it all to you.
That is the only way I can express it,
Because my feelings for you are far beyond words.
I guess all I can say to you on this day . . .
I LOVE YOU . . . with all of my heart!

Doris C Farnsworth

Doris C Farnsworth
GEORGE WASHINGTON WHOSE BIRTH WE CELEBRATE

To the Father of Our Country

George Washington, whose birth we celebrate,
We know could not have been celibate,

If father of millions of Americans merry,
His family tree could not have been cherry.

Tracey Gertsema
THE MAGIC OF A HUG
When I'm sad,
there's a special string in my heart
to tug.
All you have to do
is give me a great big hug.

It's incredible that something so simple
can do such amazing things.
When someone is down and out,
you can't imagine the joy a hug can bring.

It's hard to believe
what a simple embrace can express.
It can bring comfort, reassurance,
or just spread a little happiness.

So next time when you see someone
who is looking rather gloomy or smug,
just stretch out your arms
and use the special magic of a hug.

Nancy A Helman
FEELINGS

I wish to dedicate this poem to all the ones who are trying to find their way in life.

To fly the skies;
Or sail the seas;
To climb the mountains;
Or ride the breeze;
It's all the same to me.
A quiet place where you can find;
Is the hidden secret in your mind;
As you travel thru your glassy eyes;
Your dearest memories of days gone by;
An untangled vine in the garden low;
You sit and wondered what way to go;
You let it happen like you should;
To show yourself the bad and good.
The perfect one is shown to you;
Underneath the skies of blue;
The path that you all must take;
Is the path your journey without a mistake;
All your conscience within you lie;
You like this beauty, of just being
Able to try;

Jeannette "Jan" Bailey
YOU
Life is full of this and that,
Do you wonder where your at?
Life is full of silly things,
Does it often make you sing?
Do you sit and wonder why,
Does it ever make you cry?
Think of things that you can do,
When your feeling oh so blue.
Put a smile upon your face
It really isn't a disgrace.
Silly things, you laugh, you cry.
Will you hate to say "Goodbye?"
Your minds a glass, a pot, a vat.
Do "you" know where you are at?
When your life is near the end,
Will anybody call "you" friend?

Lorraine M Sadowski
THANKS
Thanks for giving my life a new meaning,
Thanks for giving me courage when the days looked dark.
Thanks for having confidence and patience in me.
Thanks for the many rides home after work.
Thanks for phoning when I needed so much to hear your voice.
Thanks for giving up so much of your needed time for me.
Thanks for letting me be your girl.
Thanks for being so nice to me.

Myldred Slesinski
THE FIRST DAY OF SPRING
Little specks of blossoms
showing through the green,
Dew drops shine like diamonds
in the tiara of a queen!
Rays come stretching from the sun
to wake God's creatures one by one;
The birds fluff their feathers
and start to twitter and sing—
Letting everyone know
'Tis the first day of spring.

Brenda Moran-McKeon
ODE TO A TRIATHLETE

To Richard with my love.

A way of life quite departed
From the simple and weak-hearted.
A breed of human, strong and true
Always faithful, and rarely blue.

A man who exudes devotion
While masking deeper emotion.
Driven by a greater desire
Reaching goals, soaring higher.

A body worked at a hard pace
Just to complete a long, long race.
Not that swimming isn't enough,
Biking and running make it tough.

An event the press will ignore,
No accolades at your front door.
Just a small test of strength and will,
Easing the pain with a small pill.

A man alone in a large crowd
Hoping they will see how proud,
When he crosses that finish line
With a PR, then all is fine.

This ode's to you to let you know,
I think you're one hell-of-a pro.
Resentful of the time you spend,
You keep racing, my heart will mend.

Lois Eula
A TRIBUTE TO PRINCESS GRACE
She had the world on a string . . . they say.
Everything from day to day.
The finest clothes and furs and things.
Her fingers were adorned with rings.
A palace here and a villa there,
for friends and loved ones, all to share.

Only the good die young . . . they say.
But, who are they?? They who say . . .
This is a terrible price to pay.

Those who are left, will weep and fret.
She left us forever with no regrets,
to rest in peace, her mind at ease . . .
it was her need the world to please.
As life goes on and on and on . . .
This life was just another pawn.

Dolores (Dee) Smith
MY HUSBAND

To Charles, come swim with me at high tide. Walk with me at low tide. Dream with me between tides.

The reddish tint of his hair
His eyes so alive, a perfect pair
His lips are set, in that certain way,
That grows more familiar day
After day.
A man toward filling.
His life's ambitions
I know he'll make it
With his right decisions.
A person of love, I had
given to me,
How wonderful it is to be
Married to thee.

Clarence W Wieske
REFLECTIONS

Dedicated to the one who inspires me—my wife Natalia.

Reflected in a quiet pool,
A face looked back at her.
The air was warm, the water cool,
A breeze began to stir.

A wisp of hair, obscured her view,
Darting fingers, tucked it in place.
Reflections of the sky of blue,
Formed a frame for an angel face.

Now you are always at my side,
Reflecting all my love for you.
And I reflect your love with pride.
Love is like a mirror too.

Genevieve C Schmidt Malinda

Genevieve C Schmidt Malinda
WHERE IS TOMORROW?

This poem is dedicated to the Malinda Family

Where is tomorrow? It's always today.
Sometimes we work, Sometimes we play.
I awake with the sunshine, sleep with the moon,
where is tomorrow? It's always today.
I'll go to sleep and close my eyes,
and dream of tomorrow,
But when I awake, it's always today.

Look for tomorrow, search for the moon,
awake in the morning, It's always today.

We dream of tomorrow and it will
come
with the dawn, arise for tomorrow,
It will be gone.

Now is morning, it is today, don't
wait
for tomorrow lets do it today.
Make today a day for tomorrow,
one of laughter
never sorrow.
Live for today,
not for tomorrow.

Kathleen Berry
AWAKENING OF SPRING

This poem is dedicated to Sister M. Theophane, a very special person in my life.

Slowly the flowers start to shoot up
into bouquets of
loveliness. The woodlands are
bathed in beauty—the pond
starts to come to life with the
sound of frogs and in
the distance we hear birds singing
their songs with great
cheer. The spiders spin their webs
of gossamer in a bright
array. All of them know that spring
is in the air. And
as a reminder of this wonderful
season, a rainbow flashes
in the sky.

Lydia Beth Isaacs
FATHERS' HOPE

To my Father who encouraged me through a time of darkness and lies, to believe he is for me and not against me and most of all my friend, thanks El Shaddai

---

A tear had came within his eye
each time his little girl cried
A longing seemed to grab him
deep inside each time
Someone told her a lie
With his arms did he reach
to draw her to him
Each time that he'd reach
she'd pull away from him
Pain fills his heart
Tears fill his eyes
Each one of his children
had told her a lie
So he searched for someone who'd
go
speak his words only
and none of their own
My heart's opened wide
there's plenty of room there
for my little one inside
My arms they are aching
to draw you aside
To ask you to believe
The best only begins
when you believe
I'm really your friend

Jeni Van Doren
LOST FRIEND
I thought we were friends
close and sincere.
It made my heart warm
just to know that you were near.

I thought you'd never
be too busy
or begin to forget.
I guess that I was wrong
because now the feelings are set.

My dear friend
Oh, where do you hide?
I feel that you have left
from standing by my side.

Your face is growing distant now
my eyes begin to fill.
Goodbye, best friend
I'll miss you, I really will.

Ruth DeJauregui
UNTITLED
silver
you soar
dreaming of the death
floating
below your flaming fears

you fly
your eternal complacence
shattered
by that blaring klaxen's calling

you
the anthropoid animal
spouting your senseless stupidity
reach
taste your metallic monument
enjoy this flashing moment

your blackened
mangled mushrooms
gnaw the shivering earth

A K Mills
GRANDMA

In memory of my grandmother, Melissa Norvell, whose love and understanding inspired me.

We always loved the time that we
spent,
and I know there was an ear bent.
There was never a word,
that went unheard.
Sometimes you spanked us I recall,
but we loved you through it all.
I will always remember your old
rocking chair.
You know the one, we three would
share.
On your knee, asleep we fell.
Until one day came the ringing of
a bell.
You wasn't with us very long,
but your love has made me strong.
Grandma now I have two,
one is pink one is blue.
Like two words you make to rhyme,
it's as if I have turned back the time.
Thank you for being there.
We know you will always care.
You touched the hearts from deep
within
and someday I know, we will meet
again.
We will join you way up high
and we will never say good-bye.

Patricia Pitcher Upshaw
UPON MY MOTHER'S DEATH

In loving memory of my devoted grandmother, Willie V. DeWeese, of Cairo, Illinois.

Yesterday I lived unthinking day to
day
Of what life is along the way.
I loved, I laughed—enjoyed life,
Unwary of the dreadful strife
That others feel.

Then Death knocked on a door
nearby.
My heart did ache; my eyes did
cry.
A loved one now was gone from
me
Whose sainted face no more I'd
see.
Oh, heart, please heal!

Forever, it seemed, such pain was
felt
For one who by my side had knelt
To help me up when I would fall
To give me courage to stand tall
To do my will.

Now tears still come with
memories,
But through the rain, rainbows I
see.
For love lives on. The love she
gave
To each of us no grave
On earth can kill.

So we must live our lives with love,
And give, as God did from above,
Unselfishly, as mothers do,
So there's no rue when life is
through.
Peace, peace, be still!

Tania M Shaw
THE MAGIC PLACE

To my mother and father, who taught me the meaning of peace.

Hidden for centuries,
A forbidden treasure,
Covered by cobwebs,
Nearly ruined by harsh weather,
Behind a terrible forest, all scrathy
thorns and horrible creatures,
Told of by sorcerors, witches, and
evil,
As a terrible thing—
Whispered of by wise men, fairies,
and elfs . . .
A wonderful secret,
Gold and jewels,
Easy to come by,
Easy to lose,
Once a fairy-tale land,
Now buried by fools,
This is the magic place,
Colorful and light,
A land so bright,
Tarnished and worn,
Yet gleaming and new,
Made for all that are good and at
ease—
This magic place I speak of is
called,
Peace

Alexandria T Beers
I MISS YOU SO

This poem is dedicated in memory of my dear husband, Joseph.

My Dear Joe, I miss you so.
Sure hope there's some way that
you know.
If some how you can reply,
Please write it out up in the sky.
If you could answer my request,
I know Dear Joe, you'd do your
best.
The new year has begun my dear,
And so much to accomplish this
year.
I leaned on you so much honey,
But now I must lean on nobody.
So much to do without you dear,
God, help me through this new
year.
So please my dear, stay ever so
near,
Because I need you so, you hear!
And heaven only knows how much,
"I miss you so."

L G Hollingsworth Jr
MY JANE
October the 11th, 1983, the very
life went out of me.
Though I live and my body is fed,
my heart still beats,
but I know it is dead.
The love I had left me alone, to
cry at night
since she's been gone.
I have tried my best to continue
on, but it's hard
to do when your heart is gone.
Memories are all I have that
remain, but
they bring sadness, tears, and
sometimes pain.
If tears and sadness were money
today,
I'd never want for any more pay.
I love her so, no one can care.
Save God! He knows my heart is
bare!
I never thought this could
happen to me,
the love I knew won't set me free.
Freedom, I do not wish to win.
Please God, reunite us forever
again.
The day will come when
together we'll be . . .
when this life I have will end for
me.
Together again when that time
does arrive,
Love and happiness in heaven,
I'll again be alive.
Love, Luby

Cindy Lou Turner
THANKSGIVING

To my wonderful Daddy, who taught me that, no matter how unfair life may seem at times, you can always find something positive to be thankful for and to encourage further hope.

It may come once a year in
November,
But it sure helps us all to remember
Friends we've made all through the
year,
Times with them we hold so dear;
Close to our hearts the memories
we keep.
For the good times shared, Lord,
thanks a heap!
Even through sad times a closeness

we feel,
In trusting and hoping that
someone You'll heal
Hearts which are broken by loss or
through greed.
You help us want to fill another's
need.

Thank You, God, for the roof over
our heads.
Thanks, too, for giving us nice,
warm beds.
Thank You for the family we take
for granted.
Thank You for all the seeds of Love
You have planted;
I pray that they will continue to
grow,
And change this world so that all
people will know
Of Your wonderful power, Your
glory, Your grace,
Your commitment to make us a
more loving race.
Thank You for letting me grow
more each day.
Thanks for helping me understand
Your way.
Give me strength to tell others all
about Your love.
Thank you for watching over us all
from above.

Bruce McPhail

Bruce Mcphail
THE PROMISE
Will freedom ring for Martin King
Will freedom break lifes
imprisoned link
Will freedom rise above our eyes
Will freedom earn his noebel prize
Will freedom end those racial slurs
That white is right and black must
serve
Will freedom stand upon his
mountain
Walk through our valley drink
from our fountain
Will freedom see us all as equal
Not by race but by our steeple
Will freedom see us wisely fed
In thought of others who often beg
Will freedom change our soldiers
grave
From unknown soldier to
unknown slave
Will freedom bring those soldiers
rest
Upon their grave no name was left
Will freedom dry their mothers
tears
As cries of war has reached their
ears
Will freedom stand in judgement of
Those who cried and no longer
loved
Will freedom change our nations
lies
That all are free if civilized
Will freedom march with endless
pride
Along the path of our Fathers died
Will freedom see us all join hands
As Martin dreams our promised
land

Betty A Whiteman
I'VE NEVER SEEN GOD
I've never seen God, but I know
that He's there
He's in the gentle swaying breezes
of the summer night
He's in the stars that light the
heavens so bright
I know that He's there when I hear
the birds sing
He's there when flowers bring
forth new life
He's there in the smile of a small
child's face
He's there in the hearts of men so
great
I know that He's there to guide our
foot steps through life
I know He is there when all of His
beauty I see
He's there for the harvest of time
well spent
I've never seen God, but, I know
that He's there.

Nancy L Jessee
AMERICA

Dedicated with all my love, to my life's most treasured gifts: Erick, Wayne, David, Carolyn, Bryan & Jeremy

---

God can't bless America,
the way He use to do.
Our flag no longer proudly flys
against His skys of blue.
The freedom men once died for,
has slowly slipped away.
Power, greed and hatred.
replaces it today.
How much longer do we think
the Lord will let us stand?
He does exist, He will prevail,
some day He'll take this land.

Olga Wadhams
THE CHAIN OF LOVE
When the chain of love is broken
And you're burdened down with
care,
Your sweetheart called to Glory
'Tis then you know despair.

The tears flow like a river,
And you think they ne'er will cease;
Your heart is oh, so heavy,
But in God you find release.

For thru faith you know you'll meet
again
Upon that bright happy shore,
And the chain of love that was
broken
Will be joined forever more!

Kathleen Chalmers
THE LIGHT
You are the Light at the end of the
tunnel
the only hope I need
the crystal clear blue waters
the very air I breathe

We've been together through the
ages
and no, not just by chance
I've known You for millenniums
You've partnered my life's dance

You are the Light that shines in
each of us
for all the world to see
together You and I are one
together, we are Thee

Geraldine Watson
YOUNG SOLDIER BOY
He, who has the strength of a
young bull,
The wisdom of an old prophet,
Goes out to die on the battle fields.
Are they not as brave as Ulyssesses?

Who makes the wars
That takes away our youth?
Damn the politicians for they are
always blamed
For the happenings of the world.

In a land so far and strange
Why should we pay a price so high?
The young men who fight and die,
We pay you tribute
As we sit all cozy and safe.

We pay you tribute
For protecting our country.
Our country, is that not irony?
Across the seas, is this our land?

No, but do not forget
It's for the rights of free men
everywhere.
So just remember, young soldier
boy,
There is a reason for you to die.

Josephine Buck
BUCKO JOE
I'm tired of being a sissy,
Sedate, and gentled down.
I'm on a rampage, on fire
To take this doggone town.

Please like me used to qualify;
But now you'll hear me roar,
Get off that, you know what,
Or this gun will tell you more.

There's work to do, jobs galore
For hands that should be willing
Instead of all your bellyaching;
And constant trifling, pilling.

Are you a man, or just a mouse.
Are you a woman, or a lazy
clown.
Put on a working rig and
sweat,
For we're going to clean up
this town.

Apolonia Swintek
THE EDGE OF THE SEA
Walk the edge of the sea,
The luminous margin of sand
That marks the divide
Of the water from the land.

Walk the edge of the sea
And watch the sparkling tide
Wash up the seashells on
That glistening divide.

Walk the edge of the sea,
Watch the curling swell
Leave upon the sand
Every sort of shell.

Walk the edge of the sea
The fringe of glistening sand;
The luminous, shell edged
Shining piece of land.

Jana A Benson
DON'T QUIT
When things go wrong as they
sometimes will
When the road you're trudging
seems all uphill,
When the funds are low and the
debts are high,
And you want to smile
But you have to sigh,
When care is pressing you down a
bit—
Rest if you must, but don't you quit!
Life is strange with its twists and
turns,
As everyone of us sometimes
learns,
And many a person turns about
When they might have won had
they stuck it out.
Don't give up, though the pace
seems slow—
You may succeed with another
blow.
Often the struggler has given up
When he might capture the
visitor's cup.
And he learned too late when the
night came down,
How close he was to the golden
crown.
Success is failure turned inside
out—
The silver tint of the clouds of
doubt,
So stick to the fight with your
hardest hit,
It's when things seem worse,
That you musn't quit!

Beverly Savage-Smith
YOU AND I
Nighttime has ended,
Nighttime has gone,
Wake up, O'wake up,
My little one.
Morning is dawning,
Light fills the sky,
Out in the sunshine to play . . .
You and I.

Marianne Suwanski
RESTLESSNESS
While searching for Peace
I ran through a wind-tossed field
But there Peace was concealed
By the spineless blades of grass . . .

My endless search continued:
I listened to the crash of the
surging sea
Hoping in this there was Peace for
me
But the waves were empty and
cold . . .

I stopped my search and
considered:
Peace is a gift received only by
sharing—
By giving to others—by loving and
caring—
In this only can one find Peace.

Melanie Milano
EASTER PRAYER
Was your suffering worth
my time on earth?
You did so much for so many
and did'nt ask a penny.
And all you ask in return is
for us all not to burn.
But did any even learn and
even now in this day and age
with people in such a rage.
Do they even subbstage.
The loss for you to die on the cross

Daune Brown
CONSCIENCE MY STRANGER: MY FRIEND
I met her one day, a stranger in my eyes.
She asked questions, a million wheres and whys.
She told me of the fears.
Said they still feel real after all these years.

She told me of the dreams that people have today.
And how if they're not careful, those dreams can slip away.
She says sometimes she hears a voice.
Told me it shows her how to make the right choice.

She says she cries once in a while.
That it helps to walk that extra mile.
She said sometimes she doesn't understand
Why it's so difficult without that guiding hand.

She told me being alone is a big step to make.
Said that it's one step she'd never want to take.
I saw her many times after that day.
She talked to me in a special kind of way.

I understand her because you see,
That girl I spoke to is inside of me.

Kimberly Pasty
POETRY
Poetry,
In my opinion
Should not be used to tell the story
As a whole,
But rather as a tool
To make the reader's mind more creative.
To make it think,
To make it feel.
And, when finally understood—
To enjoy.

Poetry,
As I see it,
Does not have to rhyme
Or have rhythm,
But flow in a prose quality
Yet still be poetic.
To make you think,
To make you feel.
And, when finally understood—
To enjoy.

Poetry,
I believe, is yours.

O Kristian Nilsson
WHILE THE LEAVES CHANGE

To the ones who deserve more, they who still stand when the walls have fallen. Jodi and many more . . .

Up on the mountain top
looking for the sky
or down in the valley
where the flowers sigh

But in the sky
I look at the flowers
and at the bottom
I climb every tower

So I stay between
and long for both
but now my world
is equally close

Watching the leaves
turn red and yellow
while the summer's wine
smells rich and mellow

Russell M Drake
LAND OF MAN
The sea beats the morning beach
With a high blue ice flame
Retreats sullenly to lure casual man,
Beats back at night with pinkly lighted
Candelabrum, cannons boom and bam

High over there silvered waters
Race rivened boats 'a gold
God-riveted to striped rocks
Wrap'd 'round seismic flowers bold

Here buffalo clouds drift and pass,
Run by brown deer and walking birds
On diorama of wind painted grass
Under skies chased by winged asps

Fastened to ancestral terrain rust
Wrought from ritual rain coursed by
Sky posts that see indigo thunder and
Hear fishermen sing and poets boast

Of strong men shorn of trust kneed
Stoutly now to steel orbed steed
Gallop down the art and iron genius
That bend stellar ray to ochre strand
Of dust, bay bled, banded land of lust.

Cheryl Vineyard
FRIENDS
Laughter, like a summer breeze,
Gently fills the air.
Two friends sit beneath the trees,
Laughter, like a summer breeze,
Sharing hopes and dreams with ease.
Friends can risk without a care.
Laughter, like a summer breeze,
Gently fills the air.

Steve Blair
SOLITARY SPRING
the rain falls in a sudden shower
turning the earth to green
blossoms open
to receive moisture-and
all life sighs
with the ecstacy of a moment
as i gaze upon this eternal sea
and watch all living things
caressed by love
a sadness
gently comes unto my heart
when i turn-and find
no one
with which to share
this vision

Jean D Wisner
PATTERNS
As one snowflake differs from another
As they gently fall to earth,
We too differ from each other,
Some are filled with sadness, some with mirth.
Some are kind and thoughtful,
Some are hard and cruel
And then there are the others
Who heed the Golden Rule.
There's the caring and discerning
And the completely unaware.
We surely are so different
But there's one thing we can share—
The knowledge that each one of us
Is in our Fathers care.

Martha Goodwin
SLUGS
rather like snails—
But slugs have no shame.
They crawl around naked
And they all look the same.

Repulsive and slimy
And an unhealthy gray,
They are truly revolting
In every way!

My one little flower bed
Produces millions each season.

It seems to me
If slugs could be
Transformed into a delicacy
We could feed the world!

Gayle Crowder
MARKTOWN
Long and slender fingers reaching helpless to the sky,
Breaking through the thick gray curtain, there but to defy.
Loneliness hangs heavy in this place where I must be.
I board the train of thought, and wonder where it will take me.

I walk along the street and gaze into the deep canal.
Blackness does encompass me and dreams become my pal,
And for a time I can escape, the dirty waters clear;
But when my daydream's time is spent, the smokestacks are still here.

The voices of ocean ships call to me in the night.
Now I long to follow them, but when the sun is bright
I see them cold and ugly, and their nighttime beauties scar.
The smokestacks pour and tell me more—my daydream's gone too far.

Louise Davis
MAY YOUR CHRISTMAS BE BLESSED
May your Christmas be blessed
And filled with great joy.
May you grow closer to God
Than ever before.

May peace fill your heart
And your joy overflow,
As you realize His blessings
To you here below.

This special greeting
We send to you,
Merry Christmas dear friends
And Happy New Year too!

Marie C Modrow
FRIEND
A Friend to the end
Love and trust you must blend
Hurt and sorrow you must mend
Togetherness you must spend
Secrets you must lend
Rules you must bend
Sometimes you must offend
Presents you must send
Lie and pretend
To keep a person called a Friend
to the End . . .

Erich Klossner
CHILDHOOD: OUR VOLATILE ESTATE
Cling not too tightly, Love, to little fingers,
Lest as they strain to leave your heart be torn.
Count not too much on anything that lingers
So briefly as a dream with wings unshorn,
For softly as a breath an hour may come
When this you hold shall be no longer yours,
And you will mark time like a pendulum,
Aware at last that time alone endures.

Share loosely then this charge of former springs
Grown restive in the grasp of guardian guides,
For babyhood, the least of lasting things,
Is prone to heed the tug of distant tides
And wings of youth are quite as apt to fly
As those which speed a bird across the sky!

Tom Conner
IF I MYSELF UPON A LOOSER CREED
If I someday, in an abstract search,
Should chance upon a lesser God,
And find in such, fulfillment to compensate
For my weakened soul,
Should I at once irreverant be
And chastened by the greater one?

Must I, beyond my needs and cares
Pledge obeisance to one beyond my means,
And kneel to the one who knows me not?
Or shall I embrace my demigod
And ask only for favors, to fill my needs?

Must I pledge devotion
To one who needs it least,
And bow to powers of greatness
When lesser will suffice,
And pray that I might be right, in that;
In such a complicated World
Simplicity must be King!

C Carl Martin
A MEMORY CHILD'S VISIT
Time has past and you are grown,
You have children of your own,
Yet we see you as you were,
Age our memories cannot blur.

We watch you play and cry and sing,
Excited at all that life will bring,
Innocent, trusting, full of joy,
To you all life is just a toy.

In our mixed adult concern,
You show us things we never learn,
Sights and sounds and things that

grow,
We see and hear but never know.

Most of all we see your love,
Unrestrained as God's above,
Undimed by life's dull doubts and
fear,
Freely shown in laugh or tear.

You come to us in faith and trust,
We praise and punish as we must,
We give you comfort, love and kiss,
Perhaps it's that the most we miss.

Now you're gone so far away,
But to us you're here today,
Again we laugh, we play, we sing,
Oh what joy your visits bring.

Fay Hutchens

BLACKBERRY MONEY

There was very little money, when
I was a kid,
That you could call your own;
Not even a nickel could be spared,
To buy an ice cream cone.

One day I thought of all those
berries,
That grew down by the creek;
All you needed were a lot of
buckets,
And you could pick for a week.

With 'dollar signs' dancing in my
head,
I eagerly went on my way;
Out to make a pile of money,
From sales by the end of the day.

The longer I picked, a strange thing
happened,
Those berries were shrinking, I
surmise,
And 'wouldn't you know it' that pail
I used,
Seemed to grow larger in size!

The sun grew hotter, those briars
scratchier,
And a snake just crossed my
path;
Suddenly I realized, to count my
earnings,
Wasn't going to take much math.

The idea of making 'blackberry'
money,
Soon proved it wasn't a winner;
So I came home with just enough
berries,
To eat that night for dinner.

Thomas R Nickel

I LIKE GIRLS!

I like Girls,
In flimsy things,
All bedecked
With beads and rings;
They like to talk;
They trip about;
When glad they squeal,
When sad they pout;
They like long hair,
They worship curls;
They're cute; they're sweet:
I like Girls!

Luann Shoup

LOVE STAR

Ever gaze at the stars
And see how they shine,
and make the sky bright
on a dark night.
See how many there are
up in that sky so high.
It is an impossibility.
Imagine if every one of them,
could stand for happiness
for all couples in the world.
Each would have a special star,
to call their very own.
Love is like a star,
shining until the flame dies,
And one starts again,
looking for another light,
until they find that special one,
that will be their's forever,
burning in the heart.

Laura M Leigh

LOST IN TIME

Dedicated to Marjorie Rebecca Kelley. Her Memory Will Never Be LOST IN TIME

There's a house that sits back from
the roadway,
Slightly hid by new trees that have
grown,
Surrounded by acres of fields and
by woodland,
Where my children and I used to
roam.

There was wildlife too numerous
to mention,
That filled many hours with great
joy,
And in the midst of it all was the
Little Black Brook,
That ever so gently flowed.

The house was filled with laughter,
And friends would come and go,
It seemed like God had chose this
place,
For us to humbly grow.

But time has a way of passing,
Someone else lives in that house
on the hill,
And we are lost in time, with only
memories to bind,
Our lives to the house on the hill.

Vicki J Coulombe'

MY MOM

This poem is dedicated to my mom, a dear lady that has always been there for me.

God put the beauty in our vast land
and He put the beauty in the
butterfly, the satin silk worm,
the soft white dove.
He took the beauty of the land and
colored
her hair,
He took the beauty of the butterfly
and colored her
gentleness with it's lovliness.
He took the beauty of the satin silk
worm and
gave her eyes it's glo,
He took the beauty of the dove to
color her
soft white skin,
He gave me to her and her to me,
and made His creation whole.

Paul A Harms

I KNOW YOU

I know you—
Our hearts loved before ever we
met.
Our spirits touched before ever
we spoke.
Our souls merged before
awareness awakened in our
lives.

I know you—
Our gifts sought one another
while time slumbered.
Our uniqueness blended while
motion was not.
Our specialness mingled while
existence was but an idea in the
mind of God.

I know you—
I "looked at you" before I had
eyes to see.
I heard you before I had ears to
hear.
I perceived your depth before I
had mind to comprehend.

I know you—
Our melodies danced in the
morning of time.
Our counterpoint intertwined at
the sunrise of meaning.
Our dissonances we cherish for
the wisdom they bring and the
growth we share.

I know you—
You are me and I am you.
My heart is your heart and your
soul is my soul.
Our individual selves—unique
and wonderful—mingle—our
spirits touch—our souls
embrace—our lives kiss—as
special selves we know oneness.

I know you—
Your joy is my joy.
Your pain is my pain.
The totality of our individual yet
collective completeness knows
oneness—in sorrow—in
hurt—as well as in joy. The
savoring of beauty and the joy of
healing was—is— part of God's
plan for growth and fulfillment.

I know you—
My trust is your trust, my faith
is your faith.
The sharing of all meaning; the
bad—the good the success—the
failure; the agony—the ecstacy,
the wounds—the healing, all
serve to temper the steel of our
bond—this since the primeval
mists of antiquity's awakening.

I know you—
The quiet certainty of our bond
was—when time was not.
The calm confidence of our
match was—when motion had
yet to move.
The depth of our multiplying
togetherness gave meaning—
when eternity awaited its
beginning.
We began when "beginning" was
in the womb of all that was to be.

I know you—
I am you and you are me.
We cared for each other when
eternity first drew breath.
We multiplied each other and
our togetherness when existence
first knew itself.
All that is—knew us at the
beginning of what was to
be—for we—you & I
together—are eternal.

I know you—
We belong—in absolute truth
and freedom—to each other.
We knew each other then—we
know each other now.
We will know each other
always—as soulmates.
I am you and you are
me—forever—in joy and beauty.

I know you—and you—know me.

Daria J Considine

CRAYOLA LIFESAVERS

I thought about you once
When the day stood still, and
wondered
What would you think of my
rainbow thoughts?

Do you see summer bright clouds
melting together with the peach of
dusk—
creating a saffron haze?
Or hear a seafoam song
harmonizing with cornflowers—
an aria of periwinkle memories?

Can you smell a gray storm
far away in a neon town—
gold-speckled halos dancing in the
dark?
Or run through a magenta frenzy
tripping on orange blossoms
a kaliediscope of noise . . .

Would you care if white innocence
blended with purple passion
to make lavender ecstasy?
Or would you walk away
from my candy striped dreams
of chocolate covered tears?

Some day, maybe you'll stay
long enough to touch
my prism coated smile.

Lisa M Steed

CONCEPT OF TIME

"Spring is here,"
the young boy called,
as he ran down the street.
He ran so fast he was unaware
it would be summer he next would
meet.

"Summer's here,"
the young man yelled,
as he dashed toward the lake.
He swam so fine he did not care
that fall was on the make.

"Fall is here,"
the man admitted,
as he watched the leaves turn
brown.
He stood and watched the young
boys play
with an idle frown.

"Winter's here,"
the old man whispered,
as he watched the snowfall chill.
He wanted spring to come back
then
but it was not to be God's will.

Heather Pyle

AN IMAGINARY LAND

Somewhere over the rainbow
In a land not far away
There is a place where dreams

come true
And skies are never gray.

And in this land a brook flows
Laughing and running away
Into the ocean, where its currents
Are picked up and swept away.

And in this land all hearts are full
Brimming over with love.
There are fairies that are smaller
Than a baby dove.

This land is so wonderful, I can't
describe it.
It would take to long to say.
If to this land you want to go,
I'll point you on your way.

Where everyone is ready
To lend to you a hand
In this wonderful, wonderful,
imaginary land.

Julie L Haas
I REMEMBER

This poem is dedicated to my father who doesn't know what an inspiration he has been to me. I love you Dad.

I remember special times, long ago
since past,
When we were all together, and
made memories that would last.
I remember long ago the special
times we shared,
I was but a brown-eyed child,
freckled and red-haired.
You took me many places then,
and spent some time with me,
Like going out for ice-cream or
to see a movie.
You played with me like fathers do,
and taught me to be strong.
You helped me through the
rough times, and showed me
right
From wrong.
Those days have long since
passed, and now I'm on my own,
To raise my two daughters, and
give them a happy home.
You've always meant so much to
me, and I'd just like to say,
That I shall always love you, and I
REMEMBER YESTERDAY.

Rose Elizabeth Gordon

Rose Elizabeth Gordon
MY HAVEN OF REST

Whenever I'm weary and feeling
sort of blue,
I return to that place where wild
flowers grew;
To watch the creek as it ripples and
laughs,
As it flows and winds down
crooked paths;
My cares and troubles disappear
with the stream,
Rushing along so sparkling clear
and clean;
What a joy to return to this place
I like best,
To meditate once again in my
peaceful Haven of Rest.

Since my first visit to this
sanctuary years before,
I've had occasion in my mind to
return or' and or';
There is nothing more peaceful
and perfectly calm,
Than to flee to this glen of quiet
balm;
To quietly get away from the
world's noises and strife,
And to be free for awhile from
the cares of this life;
There is no other place so lovely
and blest,
As my place of solitude—My
Haven of Rest.

The serenity and beauty seems to
purge my mind,
Watching in awe as colors
radiate the sunshine;
Because I've felt near to the very
heart of God,
Where there's been a release of
my problems and fog;
In a quiet little glen from my
childhood days,
I've sat in solitude and upon
God's beauty have gazed;
I reluctantly take leave from where
I've been blessed,
To return to life's chores from
My Haven of Rest.

Janeice A Mason
MOSQUITO

Puffer eyed
I smoke one more
and creak across
the bedroom boards
slipping on your soft round snore
wading tangled mounds of shore
I dive back in . . .
quite deep.
Your breath in waves
ebbs and flows
and fills the hollows
of the pillows
I sink in
a cranny fish
two flat round eyes
to listen for
that darned mosquito

Aloha Walker II
LIFE'S ANGRY SEA

I was a ship gallantly dressed
with hopes and dreams of silver
and gold.

I had set sail on the sea of life,
my flags unfurled to the winds of
time.

Time has shredded and torn my
flags,
and my ship of dreams has been
dashed
and splintered against the rocks of
life.

Now, as this ship lists helplessly—
with
only her captain remaining to man
the
wheel—she feels herself slowly
sinking
beneath the weight of futility
and loneliness.

C Maxine Jones
THANKSGIVING

To Irene Peck My Mother

The pilgrims landed on our shore
One cold November day.
To live a free and happy life,
Which they found without delay.
They planted corn and hunted
game,
This way they made their living.
They were so grateful to the Lord,
They called the day
Thanksgiving

Doris Anderson Berg
SOLDIERS ARE NOW REAL

Dedicated to my precious mother who sent five sons to war, also to my son and daughters and all my grandchildren . . . I pray they may never see war!

No more plastic soldiers in the tub
No more aching little legs to rub
Forgive me Dear Lord, today my
heart's just not in it
Oh, why didn't I know enough to
enjoy every minute
Now on a far distant shore the
soldiers are not plastic anymore
Today they are true grit, loneliness,
real blood, sweat and tears
Oh, where do they fly to those
innocent baby boy years?
Yes, today the soldiers are
America's most cherished young
men so fine
Struggling to quell evil, trying to
bring love and peace to all
mankind
Dear God that you would ease and
still all Mother's fears
If only the world could erase all
war torn years
My heart cries, in silent agony
pleads
Heavenly Father, please no more
war
Not even on a foreign distant shore.

Kahaunani Miles
HOMAGE IN THE LIGHT

I see golden radiance
Archways formed in eloquence
Father beckons unto me
Magnified in light

Spheric bells toll melodiously
While His voice speaks unto me
Come, my child—come be with me
Sharing chalice once your dream

Encircled into wonderness
Cherished momentness I be
Caressing Fathers Kingdomness
Bathing in pure light

Sunny sparkling rays appear
Scented flowers wink to me
In natures intermingling greens
Walking within light

Mysteries now to unfold
Golden doorways open wide
Captured into glistening tears
I see Father, Son with Holy Ghost

Angels harping blissful tunes
Winging floating kisses unto me
Caressed in Fathers arms I be
Greeting homage in the "Light."

Deborah (Dee) Ann Parrish
MY FRIENDS

I have a fine collection of things so
dear and rare.
They do not set upon a shelf, with
dust upon them there.
Some came from Pennsylvania,
New Jersey and Illinois;
Not figurines, or spoons, or
stamps, not old tin wind-up toys.
Not ivory or China, not crystal,
gold or teak.
They're far more precious to me
than the world's most rare
antique! So delicate and fragile,
I give them care and love;
Each one unique and special, each
a blessing from above.
They're all alike, yet different, in
color, style and size.
Since they have come into my life,
I feel I've grown more wise.
No matter where I wander, or how
far we're apart, I keep
them always with me, tucked
safely in my heart. So often,
unexpectedly, in thought (or
grocery line) I feel that
special kind of warmth when they
pop into mind. We've been
through much together, the good
times and the bad, and richer
have our lives been made by the
special bond we've had.
I reminisce of days gone by
through memories of times, of
sharing laughs and joys, and tears,
and silly fears of mind.
Because I found them I now know,
to my happiness there is
no end. I thank you God for
sending me my many faithful
friends.

Cynthia M French
EMPTINESS

To my husband Kenneth and my daughter Melanie whose love and support mean a lot to me.

My life has a big empty space
Where you once held a special
place
Now that you are gone,
How can I manage to go on?

I thought you'd surely give it a try
But then you went and said
goodbye
And even though you left me in
sorrow
I'd take you back today—or
tomorrow.

Now I'm sitting here thinking
about you
Just wish I knew what to do
'Cause when you left me
My life became so very empty.

Rose F Cunningham

Rose F Cunningham
MOTHER'S DAY

In loving memory of my daughter Patricia who was president of The Blue Pike Poetry Club before her death from cancer.

For the past dozen years or more
You picked blood-red trilliums and
phlox
Of the deepest hue.
Garnered them wild from the
roadside.
Just for me on Mother's Day!
"These are much prettier than any
from the florist,
Don't you think so, Ma?"
Hugging you, I replied,
"Gorgeous! Simply gorgeous!"

Today is Mother's Day,
Sadly I retrace your footsteps
And Pluck your immortal blooms,
Burying my face in their fragrant
memories.
My knees sink deep into the new
mound of soil
As I give to you the wild bouquet.
I linger, hoping to hear your cheery
voice once more,
"These are much prettier than any
from the florist,
Don't you think so, Ma?"

Teresa Marie Mihelich
LOVE IS LIKE A SONG BIRD
Love is like a song bird up in the sky
That flutters everywhere and
where it
Lay it shall stay in peace and love.

Miss Wanda G Toms
LOVE LASTS FOREVER
Love is something never—ending,
As it comes straight from the
heart;
When you are down, love is
ever—mending.
For eagerness, everyone takes
part.

Love contains no faults or flaws,
It is a wonderful trait to behold;
As in the Bible, it uplifts every
law,
Which we must obey and never
withold.

Love should be found in every
nation,
For it is something we must
share;
Whether with one person or a
congregation,
Love is the best way to show you
really care.

Love should be like a song,
We should never let it cease;
It's melody should ever linger on,
And you will feel a sense of peace.

Love must forever reign,
In our lives, both day and night;
It will free us of any pain,
If it is applied just right.

Love is a characteristic to
cherish,
It is brighter than any rainbow;
You will never see it perish,
If the seeds you sow, are seeds
of love.

Patsy Gaile Hestand
AWAKENING
Did you ever have religious
musings in the middle of the
night?
It's a lot nicer than counting sheep
or dreading a
tomorrow.
You sort of drift along and
contemplate . . . and then
there comes the "light."
With the answer to a problem that
somehow you could not
solve.
All at once you have the answer,
and it comes from out of
nowhere.
And you lay there stunned and
murmur . . . "It must be
from the Lord."
When it happens to you, you can
bet, you never ever will
forget.
It was a weird experience—I think
about it yet.

Linda Kaczmarek
SONG OF THE HEART
You left just a few minutes ago
or has it been a hour or so.
The house is so empty and cold
should I phone you and be so
bold?
The clock is loudly ticking the time
until once again you will be mine.

Sitting and waiting all day long
it seems as if my heart is missing
a song.
I see a car on the street
and suddenly I spring to my feet
only to sit back down
Knowing that you are still in town.
Another car goes past
only this time not so fast.
My heart starts to race
Knowing soon we will be face to
face.
I hear your song
Knowing you will be with me all
night long.

Seeing you standing there
looking so fair,
my heart sings a song
knowing that you haven't been
gone too long.
Tonight we are together
and my heart is as light as a
feather.
In the morning I know you will be
gone
and my heart will have to wait to
hear
another song.

Gladys Kemp Rodehaver
I HAVE LAIN WITH YOU
I have lain with you
In other lives.
And as such things
As morning dew on silken lashes
And evening sighs on trembling lips
Are but a memory,
Still, when I say that
I have lain with you
How can you doubt?
For all the world lies still in calm,
And in my heart is a lasting balm
As memory clings
Of all such things
That first I spoke, and dream anew
Of the times that I
Had lain with you.

Ben Stein
FIRST LOVE

This poem is dedicated to everyone who has ever felt the pain and frustration of their first love.

O foolish me, I fell as prey,
For you as a person in a special
way,
Captured so easily, frail as the dove,
The murderous beast was none
other than love.

Burning and yearning me, inside
and out,
I knew I would lose this hopeless
bout,
For no matter how hard I try to
forget,
The sorrow I feel but never regret.

My love for you will burn forever,
Not even time can erase,
The want to taste your gentle lips,
And to touch your sweet, soft face.

Emotion for me is hard to express,
A task every man fears,
But not even these words of
tenderness,
Can replace the love in my tears.

Lakshmi A Kripalani
ROB NOT THY SOUL

Dedicated to My Dearest Mother who directed me to perceive the Cosmos with its wonders

Rob not thy soul
With the glitter
Of material
Cosmos prevails
Around you
And all over.

To perceive
To transmit
Comic education
You need a soul
So alive
So sensitive
That penetrates
Within and beyond.

To emit rays
Of light
To lead you
In the direction
Of unachieved heights
Unfolding
The secret of nature.

It is not bound by
Teacher's manuals
Or charts A to Z
Or multiples
Of one and three
But the structure
Of nature
The basis
Of mathmatics
The independent
Facets of
All knowledge
That balances
The cosmos
The humanity
From origin
To eternity.

Cora-Mae Stubbs

Cora-Mae Stubbs
YES, HE DOES!
There's many a time
When I've felt depressed
I just turned to Jesus
To find peace and rest.
He knows me so well,
And my soul He doth feed,
For He already knows
The answer I need.
So, when your days are gloomy
And you think no one cares,
Put your trust in the Savior,
Yes, He does answer prayer!

Doris F Graham
MOTHER OF MINE
Did you ever see an angel
Walk upon the face of the earth;
Well, I have and I can tell you
She's been an angel from birth.
She speaks with the voice of an
angel
With understanding and full of
love;
I know God sent this angel
Down from heaven above.
She has walked like an angel daily
Her steps precise and sure;
Because she was leading nine

children
And helping them to endure.
When she smiles her face lights up
And sets all around her aglow;
So! . . . She smiles just like an angel
A blessing to all that she knows.
She has lived the life of an angel
Not one harmful word of her could
anyone speak;
A character and reputation—like
which
Every living soul should seek.
I've been blessed to know her
personally
'Cause I was one of the nine;
This earthly angel is none other
Than that wonderful "Mother of
Mine."

Esther C Adams
GRANDMA'S FLOWER GARDEN

Grandma has a flower garden,
'Tis beautiful to see.
It's full of pretty boys and girls,
So lively and full of glee.
The girls are the Roses,
The Tulips and Lillies sweet,
And just to look at them,
Makes Grandma's heart skip a beat.
The boys are strong and handsome,
Like Hollyhock and Marigold,
Just to have them in "Her Garden,"
Gives Grandma joy untold.
How Grandma loves, "Her
Garden,"
It is her pride and joy.
She feels so rich and well blest,
With every girl and boy.

Mrs Jean Filler
TOGETHER WE LIVE AND LAUGH

To-day I am a bride
Cousins, friends, neighbors, are
walking
down the aisle, and being seated on
high brown wooden chairs.

The Lily of the day
Is fairer by far in May
than the oaks after hundreds
of years
Fall dry bald and siere

The day will be here when my
children will walk down the
aisle to-gether

Spring summer, fall and winter
will bring delicious foods that
will make our mouths hungry
for more fruits, grapes, bananas,
pears.

James Bentz
CASUALTY OF LOVE (REBORN AS THE DOVE)

Joining under the sunrise
The heart let out of the cage
The love that came by surprise
To begin our dawning age

A bleeding heart poet
Overtaken by the guilt
I love you, and you know it
I'm crushed by the "love" you built

A casualty of love
A victim of the game
Reborn as the Dove
The sun rises again

The memories of the old
Give way to the new
The dawn we shall behold
Together as Doves should do

Helen Schneider
TO BETTER ENJOY LIVING

To enjoy living more each day, take
heed of all you see,
From a singing bird in a tree-top
tall, to a tiny honey bee.
Don't just rush along in the daily
grind,
But enjoy nature, too, for peace of
mind.
For we gain so much, when we
really look,
On that highest branch or
sheltered nook.
We miss so much when we hurry
along,
A flutter of wings, a bird's sweet
song.
It can add so much to our lives each
day,
If we but look as we go on our way!

Janice P Tate
YOU'RE A SPECIAL FRIEND

Dedicated with love, to my best friend, Donna Rimmer.

There are many that are friends
untrue,
But this could never describe you.
You've always been there to show
that you care,
To have a true friend as you is very
rare.

You're a beautiful person inside
and out,
The best friend I have without a
doubt.
Your loving heart and caring ways
that you show,
Makes our friendship forever grow.

We've shared good and bad times
together,
Each moment making our
friendship closer and better.
You give me a shoulder to cry on
when I'm sad,
And you know just how to make
things seem not so bad.

Some days may seem gloomy and
some will be bright,
But regardless of what befalls,
keep your special
dreams in sight.
Just always remember you're my
very best friend,
And I wish you the "Pot Of Gold"
at the rainbows end.

Juanita Pennington
TO CAPTURE A SUNBEAM

To my six grandchildren and all children that find magic in a sunbeam. To Charles, the Sunbeam Child.

A sunbeam came through the
window today
The young child thought it was
there to play
He tried to catch it in his baby fat
hands
Sunbeam jumped as if to say get
me if you can

The sunbeam danced with glee and
joy
The young child learned is wasn't
a toy
He could not pick it up from the
floor
He tried and tried and tried some
more
The sunbeam just kept moving
around
The child didn't know just what he
had found
It left at noon without saying so
long
For the young child some magic
had gone

Sunbeam left but it didn't stay
away
For it would come back another
day
To dance on the floor where the
child played
The child just played with his toys
that day

Diane Zagrodnik
IMAGINE YOURSELF

This poem is dedicated to the late John Lennon who influenced my poetic style and to Judy Dyson who told me to try submitting it somewhere.

Imagine yourself on a
Boat on a river—
Looking thru looking glass eyes.

Imagine yourself in a
Peaceful moment—
Looking thru crying war eyes.

It's easy to say, but
Not easy to do
All I ask is that you try.

Imagine yourself as the
Queen of the world—
What policies would you set?

Imagine better times, people,
You can if you just try—
Times can be better if we
All work together.

Peg A Utecht
CROW'S FEET AND OTHER CRIMES

God bless all the Helens in the
world
No longer competition in the
market place
For whom nature in its
insensitivity
Exchanged firm breasts and thin
waists
For cellulite, gray hair and stretch
marks
That bear witness to time and to
grown
Children on the mantelpiece.

God bless all the Helens in the
world
Whose only crime was crows feet
and flannel bathrobes
Who for their love and sacrifice
Had earned a loving touch

God bless all the Helens in the
world
For whom no heads will turn nor
phone will ring
Who were discarded like old shoes
for newer models
Who can giggle at well worn jokes
like school girls
because they are

God bless all the Helens in the
world
Who couldn't pack up memories
like their men
And discard them like last weeks
trash

God bless all the Helens in the
world
left dismembered
Because a part of what they were is
gone
Along with their identity

God bless all the Helens in the
world
For whom the "Golden Years"
will be tarnished
by
loneliness
and
pain

Herman Thomas Simpkins
DOWN HOME AGAIN

I would like to go back to the place
where my home used to be,
and take a stroll down through the
yard and all my loved ones see,
I would love to speak to dad once
more, and hear him call my
name
and kiss my mother on the cheek
and hug her neck again;
but i can't go back, Ah i wish i
could; but it don't exist no more;
someone else is living there and
would meet me at the door.
Dad left the old home place one
day, no more to call my name
and mom's not there to hug and
kiss, i can't go home again.
i would love to recall all those years
that times passed swiftly by
and change the heartaches i caused
dad and dry my mothers eyes;
i wish i could recall the hurt and
fill their hearts with joy
if i could make the clock roll back
i would be the best of boys.
i would love to stroll down through
the yard and all my loved ones
see
i wish i was a child again upon my
grandmaw's knee;
i would like to laugh and talk and
play with all my childhood
friends
but they are gone and i'm alone, i
can't go home again.

Beatrice Mayhew
WHO WILL BE HERE?

When our Garden of Eden was
lush and green
and beauty and bird did abound—
You and I were king and queen
in a Paradise—pure in the round.

Each day I picked a double
Hibiscus
from a bush by my grass house
door;
And I swam in the heavenly blue

Pacific
neath a dome of blissful azure.

Now it's nineteen hundred
eighty-three
and the days rush into each other,
to farout, virgin galaxies,
through the rubble of nuclear dust.

Will we be around another year
on our dying planet of birth?
Who will rule—who will fear—
Will the meek inherit the earth?

Will the one I love, love me
tomorrow,
Will the same old world be
spinning?
Who will be here—in joy or
sorrow—
To share in a new beginning?

David O Pollard

FATHERS PRIDE

To Debra Kay. My beautiful wife for without you, none of this would be possible.

The night will remain so vivid,
for oh so many years.
For when I first heard you cry,
my eyes became filled with tears.
That feeling I had inside me,
from my head down to my toes.
Is one of joy and happiness,
as only a father knows.
Then I held you in my arms,
and you looked me in the face.
I knew right then and there,
that this was the greatest place.
It happens right here on earth,
this thing that we call life.
Soon it was all made possible.
when your daddy met his wife.
To love you and support you,
through the many coming years.
I'll look you in the eyes once more,
so that you can see my tears.
For I'm not sad, or even mad,
but completely filled with joy.
That your sweet mommy, my dear
wife,
had given me a boy.

Anne Marie Nachtman

SOMETIMES WE FORGET

To Mom and Dad, Thanks for all the encouragement!

Sometimes we
Forget how much we love each
other
We fight
We argue
I go to my room
She to hers
I hear the steady click-clack
From her typewriter
Writing poems
Mother had poems but what
did she do with them?

Mario R Massaro

QUOTIDIANS' LACE

To All Religions: Think upon your invention and how easily man can relieve himself of the responsibility of his actions through perception of your human-like God offering meager surface rationality and satisfaction.

Make hast muted torment! The
seventh dawn unfurls
Quotidians' lace for its'
beguiling thief
that snares beleaguered ships
within this cluttered dome.

Fool beware! Muses dance for
rituals' delight, upon this
ravaged virgins' breast of rotting
wood and weathered cloth;
hermetic sealed, and thus
profused, from foreboding
waters' depths.

Cast away! Neither pawn nor play
shall pierce your restless frame;
though, fanteagues from
windblown dreams in
desperation clamour and fill
these defiant sails with darkened
creeds, till
my journeys' end.

Shelley D Kile

A THOUGHT APART

I should like to rise and go
To a place where the sun will
forever show
Where beyond the meadow
An ocean lies
With waters as brilliant
As the sunlit skies.
To a land where singing seagulls
soar
And the waves greet the land
With a crashing roar.
The essence of spring flowers
Would fill the air,
Lacing the earth
In floral fair.
And if the sky may darken
Or if the snow may fall
I could think none of it
And turn away from it all.
I'll escape to my paradise
Beyond the land so cold at heart
And wonder through my
dreamland
Just a thought apart.

Irish Pearl Simmons

Irish Pearl Simmons

IT'S TIME TO PRAY

Dedicated to The Simmons Family

There are times we all have to take
a rest.
There are things we know, but God
knows them best.

There are times when tears will fill
our eyes
But God only gave you to us for
just a little while.

There are times when we realize
that things were good in
the past.
But life wasn't given to us to
forever last.

We need not worry for God has us
all in his hands.
He has come to take this soul,
home to another land.

Now fall on our knees, and to God
we Pray.
He will watch over us each step of
the way.

Benny Goldwater

AN ODE TO MY DARLING WIFE

(When The Time Grows Short)

Fourty nine years I enjoyed my life,
Doing things with my darling wife,
But now it seems it won't be long,
Before my lovely wife is gone.

I cannot seem to find the answer,
As to why she contacted a dreaded
cancer;
When I think of it, I shake and
quiver,
For my darling has cancer of the
liver.

The Doctor with whom today I
spoke,
Made me feel like my heart is
broke;
He said, We keep your darling
filled with dope.
Because I'm sure there is no hope.

When she goes is hard to tell,
But she'll go to heaven and not to
hell;
For she was an angel down here on
earth,
All the gold in creation couldn't
buy her worth.

For it's a long long time from May
to December,
And the time grows short when you
reach September.

In Loving Memory of Betty
Goldwater who passed away
September 15, 1986. By her
beloved husband "Benny"

Thomas 'Sparky' Stafford

COME DREAM WITH ME

Lovely lady come dream with
me,
for I have some wonderous things
to see.
It's something we both should
share
all about the love you and I dare.
There's tears and laughter and
moments alone
quiet evenings and turned off
phones.
Dinner for two and sparkling wine
Knowing I'm yours and you are
mine.
Tender times with your soft touch
intimate times loving each other so
much.
Many thoughts of knowing you
care
and warming laughter we both will
share.
With emptiness when we are apart
still loving each other deep in our
hearts.
Long drives in the country, just you
and me
always together, we know it should
be.
You'll make my heart feel like the
wings of a dove
both of us knowing what we have
is love.
Just take a few moments and you
will see
Oh, lovely lady, come dream with
me.

Clarence W Smith

HARVEST TIME

Take up your sickle and reap,
for the fields are ripe for the
harvest.
Your orchards are laden with the
fruits of life
and the meadows lie rich in
abundance.
The seeds are your thoughts,
that were planted with care—
they have foliaged and grown to
fulfillment.
The yield is the peace, the beauty
and joy,
that shall fill your own life
overflowing.
The sickle is faith, that will reap
your own words
and cut through the ties of
tradition.
Those that are barren and devoid
of joy,
shall be blessed with a glorious
transition.

Libby Kuna

REVIVAL

As winter drags on endlessly
My thoughts turn more to spring,
To brighter days and brand new
life—
A new awakening;

To longer days and milder nights,
The smell of warm, damp air,
To green buds bursting on the trees
And crocus everywhere;

To looking upward at the sky
Through misty, spring-green haze;
Watching awakened animals
Performing their ballets.

There's such sweet joy in walking
out
Into a bright spring morn,
For as the plants breathe life again,
My spirit is reborn.

I once again see Nature's charm
And am by it beguiled
As if I'm seeing it for the first
Like a young, wide-eyed child.

The cold, gray months have left me
with
Ambitions unpursued,
But now my head is filled with
plans
From energy renewed.

Each season has its majesty
From winter through the fall,
But, because it brings new hope,
I love spring best of all!

Mary Grace Hudson

FLOWER BLOSSOMS

There's a flower that blooms in
God's
Garden of Love
It's as lovely as it spreads its colors
From above.
There's a Rose that blooms for all
the
World to see
That God's love blooms within the
heart of
People like me.

He's the Lily that blooms along

life's way
He's my Morning Glory from day
to day.
He's the Carnation that blooms in
the spring
He's the Sunflower of all the love
he brings.

We are special flowers that bloo m
in
God's Garden of Love
We are His jewels watched over by
angels
Above.
Surely His presence within us shall
always be
Because we're special in God's
Garden
you see.

Karen Leigh Nadeau
IS A TEAR SILENT
The tear can tell so much,
Mean so much
Many millions of feelings,
thoughts, words
Put into one tiny, clear, crystal
drop
A single solitary tear
In itself can mean
Anything from happiness to total
sadness
A tear can let someone know
When you are hurting;
Being torn apart inside
Or
Crying out in pain—
In need of help
This jewel can show
When you are bubbling with
happiness—
Wanting to explode
Overfilled with joy.
A tear will give away
Too many unspoken things
I ask;
"Is a tear silent?"

Teresa Ann Peters
I USED TO BE A TOMBOY
I used to be a tomboy,
Climbing the tallest trees,
Arm wrestling all the boys,
And beating them with ease.

Until one day I took a look,
At what's become of me
No longer happy with myself
It's a Woman I want to be!

The years of growing have been
fine,
And I found how love is so divine,
It's great to be a woman,
And it gets greater all the time.

Christine Janz Taylor
FAITH BIOGRAPHY
I can't remember the hour when I
first believed;
before memory assurance had
taken route it seems.

I can't remember when Doubt
assailed my heart, Doubt
being as foreign to my mind as
orchids to a snowy clime.
I do remember the times
Discouragement became
companion
and Grief a willing guide.
I do remember what became
the pattern then:
unfailingly the signs would come
like white doves fluttering at my
hand.
Look! Look!
Paths cross becsause they need to
and soon careen away but the
after ripples of those crossings—
what magnitudes of consequences
they display.

Isabella Breckenridge
WAS IT A DREAM
"I am going Home," she said.
She went; she couldn't stay.
But oh, the long and vacant days
That I have met along my way.

Especial was a quality that
Day by day for her was claimed.
Perfection was her goal in life,
Now perfection she has gained.

Radiance glowed through eyes
serene;
So full of faith—so calm—so dear.
A portrait none could ever paint
From within this mortal sphere.

But did I say it was a dream?
It seemed so real—so very near!
The message so consise was short,
"Come on Home" I heard so clear.

"Pay whom you must—your
Doctor,
"All your obligations known"
A simple explanation: "Make your
peace,
"And come on Home; Come on
Home!"

Caren Ann McCotter
TIME
As we remember the road behind
us
And look ahead to the future
Our lives seem so long
Yet, as each day moves on so
quickly
You must savor each moment
Before you know it that moment is
gone
And the next has arrived
Your life isn't long
It is very short
Just a moment in the time
That is to come ahead of us
Time seems to speed up
Time can never stand still
Life goes by so fast
Generation after generation
Everything just seems to progress
As life gets shorter and shorter
Until there is no life
And when time doesn't matter
anymore.

Lucille Willard
THE CORNERS OF MY HEART
There are corners in my heart
Where deepest thoughts descend
And soft on evening's secret chart,
I whisper to the wind.

Of dreams that are my very own,
In the future and the past;
Of twilights and music I have
known,
And happy summers that didn't
last.

'Though I dipped my pen in gold
I could never express a part
Of the many dreams untold
From the corners of my heart
Secrets too deep to impart,—
Sorrows much too sad to mend.
No one listens to my heart
So, I whisper to the wind.

Now I wonder . with
afterthought,—
About sharing love . and cupid's
dart,
For surely there are more than
thoughts
To fill the corners of my heart.

Donna J Rable
AUTUMN
Autumn is my Sister,
She is my friend and my enemy,
For I can't prevent her arrival,
Nor hold at bay,
Her passing.

I can cherrish her colors.
But smell chill in the air,
Knowing winter, like a thief,
Follows after.

Autumn is me,
It is where I'm at,
The summer was beautiful,
The autumn serene,
Full of hope,
And dying dreams.

Autumn is my Sister;
Autumn is me.

Marguerite P Hurlbut
FIRST SNOW (MEMORIES)

To My Sisters, Nettie and Ann

Large wet flakes fall on the
country-side
clinging to trees and bushes
evoking memories of childhood
snows.
Drifts as high as a grown man's
waist,
chaffing winds and sub-zero cold
that pinched your nose.
A friendly snowman standing
sentinal in the side yard
wearing Papa's old hat.
Wild tobaggon rides down a steep
hill
joyful screams from half-frozen
mouths.
A roaring bondfire by the old pond
to warm the skaters.
The smell of wet mittens drying on
a steam radiator,
and Mama making hot cocoa to
warm us.
Quarts of milk standing in the
snow with frozen cream
jutting from their paper caps.
Hot cereals and homemade soups
and lots of hugs and kisses.
Memories . . .
to warm me during this first
snow of Winter.

Robert P McCormick (Age 16)
THE MAN WE SPEAK OF
The Man We Speak Of is Mighty
and Strong!
You'll Know All About Him After
this Song!
Some Say What He Stands for is
not Quite Right!
Just Because There's no Holiness
in Sight!
The Man We Speak Of was a Nobel
Leader!
He Just Spoke Out for what He
Believed!
And for that He was Banished with
no Reprieve!
His Memory Will Live on for Now
and Forever!
Because the Man We Speak Of was
really Clever
Clever In thought And in words
until he was
Banished by those Special Birds!
The Man We Speak Of his Name
we'll Now Tell!
For His Name is SATAN Leader of
Hell!

Michael Lee
LULL
The coat of Autumn sun warms me
From Winter's blizzard breath.

White gulls winging to sheltered
cliffs
Pass gray light on silvery wings,
Wheeling on frozen air.

Below lie furrowed fields
In the grip of Winter's hand.
Bare trees await coming snows.

While shapeless clouds mount the
ridge
To call the coming storm,
I watch in silence Winter's sounds:
The sounds of darkened color.

Hazel M Venrick
HAPPINESS IS
Did you ever stop to wonder
What happiness means to you?
I'm sure we agree there are many
things,
And I'd like to list a few.
Happiness is watching a babe's
first faltering steps;
It's offering a fervent prayer,
For peace throughout the whole
side world,
And brotherhood . . . everywhere.
It's lending an ear or a helping hand
To folks both far and near;
It's sharing joys and blessings
With those who we hold dear.
It's a friendly smile, or a handclasp,
warm;
It's gratitude and thankfulness,
too;
It's hope when everything seems all
wrong,
Happiness is really a part of you.
It's giving, sharing, forgiving,
doing;
Happiness is all these things;
It's love in the chapel of one's heart;
It's the flash of a bluebird's
wings.
Yes, many things mean Happiness,
So, as we give our thanks ech day,
Let's dedicate our lives to live . . .
The Bluebird of Happiness way.

Marilyn Podolak
VALUES AT LAST!

For Bruno Podolak

Give not your precious values up,
Disagree, though they may;
But cherish all your decency,
Until your dying day.

Though virtue of man, long has
past,
Goodness in you prevails;
I find this beauty in you, at last,
Though man so often fails.

Though honesty has been betrayed,
And values set aside;
I say to you, Be brave, my man,
Hold on to yours with pride.

Christie Forshee
BEYOND YOUTH
I shook myself and realized I was all alone.

Not with my friend of loneliness, but with the realization that I had grown.

No more teachers and leaders, or parents to hold my hand.

For now I'm all grown up, building castles alone in the sand.

Shirley Grace Kelsey
FRIENDSHIPS
Friendships are created by mutual consent,
It takes years for them to grow.
They are nurtured as each helps the other,
When you have a Friend, you know.

Friendships are hard to come by.
They work only for the sincere.
So keep your good Friend, no cost is too high.
Good Friends are very dear.

Jay Corrigan
FIVE A.M.
A dying yesterday's blood
spread across the horizon
as the golden sun follows
to enrich an autumn day.

Green gold and red
stand proudly on the trees
until a cool fall wind
comes and gives them their flight.

Ronda Denice Boozer
FRIENDS
Friends are nice.
Friends are good as spice.
They cheer you up.
Just like a pup.
When you're sad.
And feel so bad.
Just call a friend.
Your spirits to mend.

John Anthony Williams
A THANKSGIVING POEM
There once was a lucky family,
Who had a boy that won a turkey.
As they boasted they said,
"It's even roasted."
When Thanksgiving came,
Something just wasn't the same.
The family was unhappy,
And everybody felt sappy.
They just felt down.
When they sat down to eat,
Steven felt something in his seat.
He had just sat in his sup,
But that cheered everyone up.
Later, Johnny spilled his milk.
On Mommy's new dress of silk.
She was really sad,
And Johnny felt bad.
Later, while we ate,
The food that was great.
Daddy got some on his face,
And everybody thought it was a disgrace.
When Mommy got up she upset the table,
(That wasn't very stable.)
Well that made everyone happy,
And they never again felt sappy!

Helen L Finley
ODE TO AUTUMN

Dedicated to the Creative Writing class of the Highland, California Senior Center, and especially to Cecelia Riley, our inspirational instructor.

Trees
With leaves
Of golden brown
Await the quiet autumn
Days of chilling breezes when
They stand exposed within the wake
Of Winter's prelude and Mother Nature's
Cruel whim to find again the long, cold sleep
That ushers in yet another cycle of this old earth's
Prepetual endings and hopeful new beginnings.
XXX
XXX
XXX
XXX
XXX
XXX

Manuel F Shue
TIME CHANGES EVERYTHING
In life's game of ball
You'll give your all,
To you, winning is the
Name of the game.
But win, lose or draw,
Soon after the last
Hurrah,
How many will remember your name?

Pearl Hill
MY GRAND DAUGHTER

This poem is dedicated to my grand daughter—Mi Mi Hill

Grand daughters are special
They're one of a kind
That's why I'm so proud
That you are mine

William DuBovik Jr
MY SUZANNE, 1950-1986
The snow melted and somehow took you
with the drifts that sat quietly by the door.
Now your belongings sit quietly,
hair dryer, paintbrushes . . .
Your unfinished canvas complete.
All that moves, breathes, are those who shared with you
the mystery—life.
I, one with you, and the two children breathe now for you.
Your smile, friendship, love, faith and ideals have become
food set on a table, like borrowed props on an intimate stage.
None there to own forever here, nor for long; but how would we know?
No time for a goodbye or one last kiss, as your final breath
came in the twinkling of an eye.
But just as well
For goodbyes were never for us.
And "see you later" becomes my song for eternity,
"Have a good day," now a morning prayer.

Donna Ohl Allen
SOLO VOYAGER
The tide is turning out to sea,
Along the river wide and swift,
And bears upon its surging crest
This trusty, tested craft and me.
Beneath my feet the deck does lift
With eager strain to meet the breast
Of rising waves beyond the lee.

But time is running with the tide—
The days, the years like dancing foam,
A brilliant line, a sparkling course
That stretches to horizon wide—
And bids me evermore to roam.
May steady heart with no remorse
Attend the final trip to Thee.

Lois Brooks Johnson

Lois Brooks Johnson
YOU HAVE A JOB TO DO

This poem is dedicated to my children, TuWaunda and Michel Johnson.

Listen boys and girls,
You have a job to do,
Go to school everyday,
And do your best too.

Learn about jobs,
And the World of Work,
Soon you will be grown,
And on your very own.
Try to be the best,
In everything that you do,
So you can stand tall
And be proud of You.

Alice Viola
A DREAM

Dedicated to you in secret gratitude

A beautiful dream I had last night
It featured you as my fearless knight
Dressed in armour of steel and might
Sword in hand to kill the dragon
Who stood beside me with fury fangs
It hissed out violent words of hate
It growled fiercely about your love
Tempting me to depart from you
The dream was at its best
When you attacked the dragon until the end
Ran into my arms embracing
I hold you close to my throbbing breast
Now I am awake with passion
For your devoted love once more
Because I had a dream last night

Candace Rutar
A LONELY MAN
The man walked slowly along the pier in solitude;

Shedding tears for the woman he loves; tears bonding with the water,

Dreaming of her before the disease; curse the disease;

His woman; the one with the silky hair, soft smooth skin;

His woman, the one with the gentle, peaceful eyes, salty bright red lips;

His woman, the most loving, caring, sharing,
His woman the one dying.

Carol A Smith
SUNSET ON THE SHORE
A walk along the sandy shore
always leaves me wanting more.
A perfect place for inspiration,
or just for quiet meditation.
The salty spray upon my skin
calms the beast that lies within.
Nature's gift of consolation
guarenteeing relaxation.
Multi-colored sunsets
that take my breath away,
the Master's perfect handiwork
lovingly on display.

Mabel Peters
MY ROSE
In a dream, as I was walking,
I soon became aware—
Of a lovely garden of flowers;
Growing beside the roadside where—

As I gazed at the lovely colors,
Of every shade and hue;
I beheld one lovely red rose,
Sparkling in the dew.

I said, I'd love that beautiful red rose—
That blooms so beautifully there,
But I went on and left it,
To spread It's radiance there.

Walking on for some distance,
I couldn't forget my flower—
I turned and went to pick it,
But someone had beat me there.

My ROSE HAD BEEN TRANSPLANTED,
To that Heavenly realm above—
To dwell with all his loved ones,
Where all is peace and love.

No more sorrowing or suffering,
For this life is passed away—
My Rose will bloom forever,
In the land of fadeless day.

Martha Pinard
JUST BEAUTIFUL
Soft as silk, blue as the sky,
I saw this morning a butterfly.
She kissed a flower in her flight
and for a moment she was out of

sight.
Oh, please come back you marvelous thing
and let me admire your precious wing.
Oh, you came back, so I can see you once more
your beautiful body for me to adore.
Where are you going? you leave me again,
please let me know, when will you return.
I'm falling in love with you, I must be insane
don't fly away' I call out in vain'
Oh, beautiful BLUE, deep as the sky
Goodby my love, I know now,
nobody can own a BUTTERFLY'''

Mary A Reese
MY EXPERIMENT
I tried an experiment that worked so well—
I just had to find someone to tell.
When you look in the mirror today—
Thank God you look exactly this way.
Thank Him for a happy day.
Then go about being as nice as you can be.
Don't be too surprised to find—
You keep looking better all the time.
As you walk down the street
Wish everyone well—you happen to meet.
Remember each face in prayer at night—
Ask God to really treat them right.
At first this may be hard to do—
Especially with a few.
But, with practice—you will do fine—
Each day, you will feel more and more kind.
Now don't be too surprised to find—
God keeps treating you better all the time.
Some of those people—that had seemed so erratic to you—
May come to be the best friends, you ever knew.

James Sudalnik
PISSING OFF A BRIDGE
It's cold
It's snowing
It's high above the stream
Of life flowing beneath
High above the cavern of life
In a precipitous moment.

We can't touch it
We can only see it and wonder

No, maybe we can touch it
One day at a time
One bit at a time
One drop at a time

Maybe we can touch it by
Pissing Off a Bridge.

A golden stream
Mimicking the great one below
Silent peals, individual droplets
One by one, down and away
Brazen and self-serving
Splish-splash
Breaking upon the rocks of time
Who are accustomed to
A different earth—borne stream
Blown in the wind
As they descend
A stream becomes droplets
Golden droplets
That each contain
A little piece of me
Mixing with all
That is and has been
Up until now.

And I add
A bit of gold
To that which has always been staked

In this winter wonder
Of my own choosing
At your suggestion

Maybe you could see us together
Sometime . . .
Pissing Off a Bridge.

Alice Youngblood
THE RAINBOW OF LOVE
With this rainbow, I send you my love.
That it may open a little door into your heart.
With this key lock it up tight.
When you see a rainbow, think of me,
When the raindrops come falling down, take the key and unlock your heart.
So that some of my love will come sliding out.
And you will find that the raindrops will turn into beautiful sunbeams
To you from—me.

Susan Newton Furniss
DIRECTIONS
When I was a child, so wild and free
I cared not of school, and did as I pleased

Beginning my teens, I went astray
Thrown in a convent, I learned to pray

God showed me riches, you could not see
But when I got out, trouble started with me

At 15 years old, my freedom was gone
Life got pretty lonely, just me and my son

I loved and cared, and raised him you see
But a child raising a child, should never be

God opened the doors, for me once more
Now I'm raising a family, I love and adore

I will never walk, out that door again
Or follow the path, that leads me to sin

I love my two children, there is no doubt
Gods little children, is what its about

I'm on the right path, I found Jesus you see
Now if I grew up, I'm sure He will be pleased

I thank God for my family, their all I need
Without my family, God knows where I'd be!

Tina Shaw
THE CORNER

To my grandmother who was always there for me. I love you more than you'll ever know.

I sit in the corner, with the wind in my hair
Everyone looks at me with a bewildered stare,
The corner is mine, mine all alone
And when I'm in it, I'm deaf tone.

I hear no one, and no one hears me
For they can't, but I can see,
I have no patience, I have no time
For the corner is where I can clear my mind.

I wonder one day, if it will all end
When my mind will wander and start to bend,
For now I am young and hope to stay
But my body will age and die one day.

However, my mind will live and continue to grow
As long as my corner changes very slow,
For when my corner dies, my soul will too
And then there will be nothing left for me to do.

Margaret Clayville
MORNING IN MAY
Arise! Arise! The lilacs bloom!
The air is filled with their rich perfume!
A glorious morn! The birds burst with singing!
My soul's alight like bells a ringing!

The sun peeps up, soft breezes blow.
Heaven's rosy, dawn's all aglow.
That exquisite fragrance! It lifts me on high!
I dance with the lilacs. I sing to the sky!

Ah, glorious May morn with your soul's soft touch.
We thank you God, you give us so much
Of all that is lovely and fair to behold!
Far richer am I than with shiniest gold.

The sun's early rising,
The gleam of the day,
And lilacs so lovely this morning in May!
And lilacs so lovely this morning in May!

Evelyn I Smith
DROPPING THE BOMB
Dropping the bomb
Blowing up the world
Where is my mom
Her scream I heard

In this time of war
And terrorist attacks
Once the strong hold is tore
There will be no turning back

Things I will miss
And never will see
Things like this
Should never be

People who care
Like family and friends
The people who will share
The nightmare of death
After it is done
And the world's been destroyed
From a beam of the hazy sun
A cockroach will be seen

Things I will miss
My family and loved-ones
A death like this
On noone I'd wish

Mary Erickson Lund
THE END
How will it come
Natural or manmade
Peaceful and solitary or
Violent and in a group
By computer error or
Deliberate finger on the button

Will we humans stop the madness
or
Sic transit gloria mundi.

Jessie Grimsley Loy (Mrs Carl Loy)
A SWEET DREAM
How bright it seems
As in our dreams
We wander far away,
To worlds unknown
Though we are shown
To lands as bright as day.

We listen there
To music rare
And wonder how, tis true,
And there unfolds
The streets of gold
That to our feet are new.

We shout and sing
Joybells do ring
We live forevermore,
The best to be
Our Savior see
Him always to adore.

Though it may seem
Today a dream
Tomorrow twill be true,
If we have been
Cleansed from our sin
And made a creature new.

Jack Valencia
TO A YOUNG GIRL
Her eyes unveil the treasure
Within the rhythmic mold,—
Where God in all his wisdom
Hid a heart of purest gold.

The world has other values
Assayed by casting dice,—
But the heart of purest gold
Does not have an asking price.

The songs of life may offer
The jewels of love untold,—
While resting in it's chalice
Waits the heart of purest gold.

If stars their courses alter
Then she sails an unknown sea,—
That heart of gold will guide her
Throughout all eternity.

Delores Ciponaer
MOUNTAIN OF LOVE

To my four grandchildren

On the top of a hill is a Peppermint tree
Where the gingerbread boy loves To play.
In a lollipop land there's the Marshmellows meadows
Where the elfs and the leprechans Play.
And mountains so high
Want to climb to the top of mountains.
Just hop on the wings of a dove

There's no need to shout it.
No doubt about it
They call it the mountain of love.

Frances E Saylor
ODE TO AN OWL
The owl is wise and they say it's true
but what can he do, but say
Who-Who?
Do you think it's his eyes that
makes
him look wise?
Or does he look at the world
with great suprise.
He doesn't need a flashlight to see
in the dark
So flying at night, to him is a lark
It really doesn't matter and I don't
give a hoot.
To me he's a wise old bird
and also very cute!

Lonnie Collins
I AM AMERICA
The pilgrims came, one by one
A child was born, he was my son
From boy to man he quickly grew
His child was born, he was mine
too

My children spread out toward the
west
To cross the stream, the mountain
crest

To tame the swamp, the burning
sand
By wise use of resource at hand

They searched afar and found the
key
That unlocked the door to a land
made free
And I am America and you are the
ones
Born in me, becoming my sons

Beverley A Hill
RAINDROPS

Dedicated to My Five Children:
David, Mary, Daniel, Darell, Victoria

Raindrops cradled in the lilly,
tips the grass, and leaves
shimmering down the rain spout,
puddles around the trees.

Gentle breezes take away the
clouds,
welcome sunshine now appears
brilliant rays catch the raindrops,
like sprarkling diamonds before
they disappear.

Robins deck the lawn so green,
chirping, bathing, and finding
worms.
Puddles lure the children out
to laugh, play and splash in turns.
The Sun sets gracefully out of sight,
A full moon rises so soft and tender
Raindrops glitter in the moonlight,
All is at peace in God's splendor.

Patricia J Qualters
GETTING OLDER

To every woman who is getting older

I put on makeup—do my nails
Walk a mile each night in vain
I color my hair—lose some weight
I pierce my ears—what pain.

I try to hide the aches and pains
And act like I don't care
I'm getting older and how I hate it
It fills me with despair.

I pull my shoulders back, with
effort
And think I look just fine
But when anyone dares to ask my
age
I smile and say forty-nine.

Whatever happened to seventeen?
I always felt so alive
I look in the mirror and to my
dismay
I see that I really <u>am</u> fifty-five.

Mary C Baker
A BIRTHDAY CAKE FOR JENNY
I'll take a wish and fold it in
To Jenny's birthday cake;
Then add some laughter, stir it
round
A happy sound 'twill make.

Twelve spoons of joy and twelve of
fun,
And not one pinch of strife.
I'll mix them all together
With a magic, golden knife.

And then I'll sift a cup of dreams,
And just before I bake,
I'll sprinkle lots and lots of love
On Jenny's birthday cake.

Keith D Alexander
THE SKY'S WET
It is the truth of what one cajoles
And the respect of a foe,
The substance a spider sows,
What knowledge and confusion
know,
The result of a thousand years of
compressed coal
And of all flowers, not just a rose,
Thoughts of the man from the
North Pole
And the freckles on a little girl's
nose,
It's when the actor plays what he
wants to be
In a role and a present's bow,
And to feel what's inside
panty-hose
What's atop painted toes,
It's food for the soul
And where leprechauns go
And what rain and sunlight
behold.

It's what this poet's eyes see
when there's a rainbow.

Jo Jackson
ALONE, I GATHER PINE CONES
The sun will warm forever
The chinquapin's brown burr
And grasses dance, with soft winds
Their choreographer.

The leaves return to the valley
The whitewater to the shore
And nothing can separate them
Forever more.
Alone, I gather pine cones
In the growing overcast
And try not to remember
Your returnings are past.

Tammy Forget Brown
AGAIN
I love you, and
I hate you.
Not always, not often,
but now.
And again
Loving you, hating you,
I can't leave yet
not now.
For Again
I must wait
loving you . . .

Leonora M Cancio
PATIENCE
PATIENCE is LOVE, when the
going is rough,
It is forgetting, as well as forgiving;
It is true HOPE, when all others
fail,
Exuberant JOY, despite aches and
pains.

Life-giving SUPPORT, that's what
PATIENCE is!
The URGE and the PUSH, the
FORCE to go forward;
The bright yellow LIGHT, warning
never to quit!
It's loving PERSISTENCE, before
all the odds.

To know when to wait, say a word
or be quiet,
At the precise time when troubles
abound;
That's what PATIENCE is, which
heals and consoles,
This MAGIC WORD, gives true
inner PEACE!

The GOOD NEWS it brings, spells
of SUCCESS!
If one keeps on trying, amidst ups
and downs;
It is the GOAL, sought after to
prove,
A wealth of STRENGTH, a
VIRTUE to treasure!

Billy Parker
BACHELORS LAMENT (almost)
It came that time that most men
dread
when you're feeling lonely and
want to wed,
So I found a girl to share my life,
politely asked her to be my wife,
Well she was pleased and quite
inspired
but gave these demands that she
required;
"Your proposal I accept most
readily,
just these things you must do for
me;
I want three cars, a boat, a plane,
a Moorish castle built in Spain,
three chefs, a gardener, a chamber
maid,
and all your money when you get
paid;
I want you home on every night
and I must win our every fight,
You must be sweet and call me dear
and we'll have sex every leap year;
You may not smoke nor swear or
drink
you'll do the dishes and scrub the
sink,
I want diamond rings and pearls
galore
and you're not to stay with the boys
anymore!;
That's all I want to be your wife
and I'll make you happy the rest of
your life!"
Well I nearly died of traumatic
shock,
if I married her I'd be in hock;
Well I told her NO and ran away
and I'm happy and single to this
very day!

Betsye Cimino
THE DOOR AND THE KEY
Sometimes I feel as if I've just
found the Key;
I turn around and find that the
Door is moved,
Leaving me to find the key to a new
Door.

The Key fits into the new Door.
It opens.
There is a highway.
As I walk down this highway of life,
I look before me and I see:
The land stretched before me like
an endless sea.

A few trees line the highway
making the music of trees.
I hear the rushing of water and I
look to my left and see:
A waterfall in all its glory for all the
world to see.

I look above and see a bird dipping
and soaring,
His wings spread wide, his head
held high,
Searching for the Knowledge of
the world,
The Key that opens the chest of
answers,
The window with which to see all
things clearly,
When I find it,
Suddenly everything will fall into
place.
Life will have every meaning.
I will have something to show for
my life.
I will be proud of what I have.

The Door is time;
The Key is life;
I am caught in both.
Time is always changing.
Life seems meaningless.

If you can fit the key in the Door,
A treasure many have longed for is
yours.
Use it wisely.
The Door shuts soon.
And you are on the door-step again.
Searching for the new Key and
Door

Renae Kandler
STILL ONLY A CHILD
At this point in time,
the whole world's changing—

Still only a child,
our future's rearranging.

In life's steady pace,
we struggle to accept this—

Still only a child,
seems just a challenge to resist.

Time flies by so fast,
it's so hard to grab hold,

Still only a child,
warnings constantly we're told.

Yet always we're reminded
not to view life as a game,

Still only a child,
this advice we took the same.

We're growing up in a place
where life seems so unfair—

Still only a child,
we hardly seem to care.

But when the time comes,
and we're to go out on our own—

Still only a child,
how well we understood life—it
has yet to be shown.

Donna G Drake
YOUR MY WHOLE WORLD
Oh my little girl
I watch you everyday,
I watch you sleep,
I watch you play,
Your my whole world.
I see you on
Your good days,
I see you on
Your bad days,
Sometimes I'd like to . . .
But I don't,
Your my whole world.
Your such a joy,
Your my daughter
And I'll always be here for you.
Remember that I love you,
I care, and I'll listen
When you need to talk.
Your capable of anything
That you may want to do
I love you.
Your my whole world.

Marion Brown
FOWL WORDS
Time does fly,
Oh, so fast—
If one stays in motion.

But just to rock
And watch the clock
Stifles all promotion.

Mani F Clark
MY GIFT, MY SON
My God, I thank thee
For all that thou has done,
Most of all, I thank thee
For my precious little son . . .

I know I am not worth
Of this gift you sent to me
But you let me have such
happiness,
And my boy you gave to me.

I know he's not mine,
But only just a loan
And some day you will take him
Into your heavenly home.

But until that day, oh father
I pray thee, let me be
As worth of this priceless trust,
As thou would have me be.

Mani, your mother . . .

R E Black
MY LADY
My woman, she is getting young
Turning 40, and still going
strong.
What a woman, this lady of my
life.
I love her so much, I made her
my wife.
Twenty-some odd years, it
seems,
Sure does alleviate all those
fears.
Does she love me, does she not?
She told me so many times, I
forgot.

Life has been so good to us,
We don't seem to even fuss.
One lovely daughter, one
beautiful wife,
Oh, my God, what a wonderful
life.

Thank you, honey, for being
there,
I didn't worry, I knew you cared.
I love you, you're not getting
older,
Life just started and rolled over.

Life is beautiful with your love
Being there with the one from
above.
You looked out for me, kept me
straight,
Getting home, I just couldn't
wait.

I love you, you love me.
Together we became three.
Thank you again, sweet lady of
mine
For being there and loving all the
time!

Suzanne Sheppard Joiner
A FARMER'S PRAYER

I dedicate this poem to my Daddy, Elvis G. Sheppard

Dear God stand beside me all
during the day
Please don't leave me even at night
when I pray
The soil I tended turned into clay
Oh God I remember the good ole
days
The prices of beans now seem like
only dreams
The corn that didn't swivel in the
field—
Left us with not a good yield
I have these wrinkles on my
face—What put them here
Was it this place
If it wasn't for the barn you
wouldn't know it was a farm
We'll plant the land—Until one day
we'll see the
Nailed Scared Hand.

William E Street
SEND UNTO ME YOUR CHARIOTS OF FIRE

To my son Brett with all my love.

Send unto me your chariots of fire
The ones you call tanks
Give to me your soldiers of time
I give to you no thanks

For my name shall reign to highest
ranks
In your hour of need
I'll cover the world through all wars
Till all men are freed

As mighty argonants you fight each
war
In search of golden fleece
At the end my voice will sound
For I'm the one called peace

As son's and daughter's in the
future soon
Shall come unto my well
The last of us shall see them die
If put through this hell

Earline Terry
TAKING 'PRIDE'

Dedicated to all those who give of their time and concern for the abused and neglected children in America.

I've been thinkin' and sortin' some
facts,
Concerning the thing we vainly
call . . . pride.
We can't really decide when or
where,
But it sets rules, by which men
abide.

Now I've related to the feelings
myself,
I thought life was about staying
on top.
Yet pride took some things I can
never replace
And caused pain that will never
stop.

We can easily take pride in our
family,
And take pride in the way we live.
It's nice to take pride in a job well
done,
But in love, it's not what you
take, but what you give.

If you give of yourself, to help a
friend,
Even by confessing to your own
mistakes,
You'll find you won't miss the thing
called pride,
For pride is costly, never giving
more than it takes.

Jonie Grace Hays
BEAUTY
Beauty is in the eye of the beholder;
Or so I've always heard.
But real beauty is so much more;
A view, a laugh, kind deed or word.
We notice little what the body
looks like;
When ones heart and deeds are
pure gold.
When our walk through life
helps others;
And the spirit is courageous and
bold.
One looks with awe at a
breathtaking view;
Of a river as it winds by the way.
To take inspiration from the rising
sun;
That gives new hope for each day.
Pure beauty is the privilege to
bend the knee;
To call upon God above.
To know that He hears and
answers prayer;
With a steadfast undying love.
We live in a country of freedom
and choice;
So marvelous words can't express.
With richness abundant
everywhere one looks;
Our vast privileges to assess.
Love of God and family;
Love of neighbor and friend.
Beauty has no limits;
It's boundries, no end.

Evelyn D Brown
HOW I LONG TO FEEL THE WARMTH OF YOUR LOVE

To my inspiration—David D. Ramirez

How I long to feel the warmth of
your love
the softness of your touch
for then the two halves will become
as One
brought together by friendship
sealed in love.

Helen Miller
AMERICA
America, you're the greatest land,
Home of the brave and free.
Although I was not born here,
I was born across the sea.
I pledge allegiance to you
For you have given me
The right to love, to work, to pray
With full security.
You do not believe in violence
As it is plain to see.
But when they try to shove you,
You can be as saucy as can be.
America, I love you.
I give myself to God and thee.
And if you need me, America,
I'll fight to keep you free.

Carolyn I Hayes
MOVEMENT HAIKU
Breeze lifts small child's curls,
a flower vase wavers,
falls
on a mother's grave.

Erik Von Engel

Erik Von Engel
REFLECTIONS
I look in the sky
and what do I see.
I see the clouds.
I see the sun.
But mostly I see me.
I look in the ocean
and what do I see.
I see the fish.
I see the sparkling light,
But mostly I see me.
I look on the seashore
and what do I see.
I see the sand,
I see the sea shells,
But mostly I see me.
I look in the mirror
and what do I see.
I see the clouds,
the sun,
the fish,
the sparkling light,
the sea shells,
the sand,
This must be me!

Rose Anne Wilcox
ACCEPT ME LIKE I AM
Why do you criticize me so?
Why are you always trying to

change me?
Why can't you accept me for what I am?
Is it so I may grow and be a better person or so you don't feel like a failure?
Or do you see too much of yourself in me?
Do I really have those many faults or are they just my unique way of approaching life?
Do you really care for my sake or seem to care to boost your own esteem?
Am I being stubborn or just trying to preserve my individualism?
Must I always "fit in"?
Will I forever be a "second class citizen" in your eyes?
Do you have such little faith in my abilities to learn that you must tell me how to live?
I feel myself growing, evolving, changing can't you sense it too?
I am seeking your support, which doesn't mean you must agree or approve of my choices.
Remember, I am a custom made being, not a copycat product or produced object.
Don't judge me by my cover. I am more than one dimensional, won't you look inside?
I'm not so transparent that you will see all the joys, experiences, relationships, losses, hurts, and thoughts nestled within that makes me ME. "A distinct ME."
LET ME PRESERVE MY INTEGRITY

Maryann Clements
LOVE REBORN

The world is starting to come alive,
like a dream begining to unfold.
The colors intense,
like a new sunrise.
The dawn of a new dream day.

The feeling;
like intense pleasure,
lifting me, higher and higher.

Carrying me across thresholds of the past.
Twisting and turning,
to avoid old wounds.

The light,
like a soothing balm,
washes over me.
I feel free.

A B Parsons
THE UNREPENTANT'S TALE

After a hard winter the nubs
of blooms nipple relief
on skinny jerking arms
etched acidly by a failing sun

Wives ago I gave up on contracts
like trying to giftwrap emotion
The carrying fee is fearsome
the silvered scenes too sibilant

Children fortify sins of remissness
in Christmas cards caroled from Omaha
lying in dark knobby bureaus
moldering secrets
under crisping memorabilia
grown fragile as snowflakes

On a vodka vacation
I am safe to tresspass
back through time
until I encounter the Crayon Years
the yellowing thick paper
a blotter of ancient grief

Yesterday I heard
Aunt Jewell is dead
She pitched forward into her chamber pot
Clunking her head

I listen to Middle-English songs
and sculpt succulent dreams
clapping them together
with a reluctant
typing machine

I cough a lot saying I'll quit
miming an old and wizened dragon
baffled by the dawns and dusks
the winnowing wind
which brings me with chill pride to even this

Holding Chaucer like a crocus
that is pushing through the snow

Edna Schiller
IN SEARCH OF IDENTITY!?

Keep your hopes high; walk with grace;
Never lose sight of worthwhile goals;
Overcome any slights; keep an honored place;
Widen your horizons across the narrow shoals.

Yearn for the blessings of good useful habits;
Override adverse conditions; grasp what heals.
Use your talents, your wisdom and wits;
Reach out, reach up, hold fast to ideals.
Search for the niche where you're most at peace.
Envision a future of relative happiness.
Love a full life with courage and release.
Faith in yourself is the essence of success.

Rena B Marshall
WHO WILL FEED THE CHILDREN

The children cry—the mothers curse—
The fathers run and hide—
Frustration—anger—hurt and shame,
An all-engulfing tide.

Hopeless, helpless—God, where are you?
Don't you hear their cry?
One by one they're calling—
One by one hopes die.

Faith, oh Lord, in loving?
Faith, oh Lord, in Thee?
Faith, oh Lord, in mankind?
Faith, oh Lord, in <u>me?</u>

Who will feed thy children?
Jesus, meek and mild,
How can I teach faith and love
To any hungry child?

Who will feed thy flock, Lord?
Give comfort to the poor?
Who will feed thy children
Crying at the door?

"SHEPHERD, FEED MY FLOCK NOW—
THE WAY IS NOT TOO STEEP.
YOU WILL FEED MY CHILDREN—
SHEPHERD, TEND MY SHEEP."

Jim Hogue
ETERNAL LOVE

To my loving wife Geneva

I have a loving wife
who will love me all my life,
now why should I want to cry
with this kind of love untill I die,

We fell in love when we were young
we danced through life and it was fun,
now in our later years of life
our kids have caused us lots of strife,

But oh you know we love them so
it hurts so much to see them go,
but now that we are left alone
it seems as though our love has grown,

I am her own and she is mine
our love will last till the end of time,
although it may be shine or rain
although our bodies racked with pain,

And when our life on earth is o'er
we will still be in love, on that distant shore.

Michelle Ledoux
FAIRYTALE OF THE BROKEN HEART

There was a time in my life
in the long, long ago
When you were a prince that I used to know
You loved me and wanted my hand in marriage,
so you rode to my kingdom to ask for my hand
and found that no people inhabited the land
The streets were all empty, the shops all closed
The fields were barren, there was no one home
You looked around at the dismal land
and realized there was no king to ask for my hand
There was no magic carpet, no wedding feast
no ladies in waiting, no star in the east
No minstrals playing, no ballads to sing
no gentle court life, no flowers of spring
You looked once again at the stillness and decay
then you remounted your horse and you rode away
I screamed from my tower so high in the sky
I screamed and I screamed but you heard not a single cry
Could you not see me when I stretched out my hands?
Could you not feel my tears as they fell on the land?
Could you not smell the blood from the wound in my pride?
Could you not sense my despair as my heart slowly died?
How could you keep riding away from my love
'Twas not my fault that I'm locked in this tower
but I know in my heart if you had only tried
I could have been found, if your love had only had the power . . .

Tressie Ree Britt Hatcher
THE WANING DAY

To my loving husband, J.C. Hatcher

Another day has almost gone,
The golden sun has sunken low;
And I have heard the sounds of songs
Mingled with joy the whole day long.

The sun has now fled in its flight
To some bright glorious far off land;
To where the flowers bloom so bright,
And no one sees the fading light.

I wonder if I too have smiled
To one whose life has been in vain,
Or is some weary life beguiled
And then my life not been worthwhile.

Although my life has scarce begun,
I hope to scale the mountain peaks;
So when my life's a setting sun,
My Lord will say, " A life well done."

Daniel Ray Farley

Daniel Ray Farley
DEAR FATHER HEAR ME PRAYING

You know it makes me wonder, these troubled times we're in.
Dear God I hope you're watching, cause we're headed for the end.
I feel we're going under, the whole world's gone insane.
Dear Father hear me praying, cause I'm feeling so ashamed.

Forgive us for this madness, we've brought upon ourselves.
It fills my heart with sadness, we really need your help.
Please hear your children crying, calling out your name.
So desperately we're trying, the world we cannot change.

Please hear what I am saying, for the clouds of darkness loom.
It's soon to be upon us, those stormy skies of doom.
Dear Father hear me praying, as the hour draws so near.
For only you can save us, we really need you here.

Donald D Petty
DARKNESS
Darkness, oh Darkness
Lost within the crust of night
I try to see beyond my reach
And as I try, I come to think, to believe, and to know
That life is but a darkened screen.
And what I cannot see, I do not know.
And what I do not know is a darkened screen in my mind.
For it is wisdom alone I seek to mend,
To weave and thread within my mind.
For it is knowledge that makes a mind
As there are words to thin in.

Lenni Shender Goldstein
PREMIER ARTISTE
Watch me perform!
I walk a tightrope of unique design.
I teeter, falter, recover
and bow.
You applaud.
I run forward, backward, hesitate
and bow.
You applaud.
If you don't applaud

I'll fall.
Cheer me! Hurray me!
Or you push me
Down.

Jennifer Lynn Callen
STORY
Grandpa knows Jenny writes poetry
Read a magazine one night
Enclosed was official entry
And list of prizes out of sight
Told Jenny he had a surprise
And told her to enter
Maybe you'll win a prize
Especially since your my granddaughter
Remember to follow the rules
If you try your best—whatever you
Create the judges are sure to choose
A letter from Eddie-Lou
Note the deadline entry date
Please choose a title
Only don't mail it late
Even publisher John Campbell
Tells one hundred poets
Coles contests are fun
On a recording he has sonnets
No kidding—no pun
Told the kids in the class
Enter your poems and mine
Select the ones you wrote to pass
The World of Poetry is fine

Dolores A Crull
JOIN IN THE DANCE
The sun will glow like a solitare set in a golden ring,
And music will flow every where and angels will begin to sing.
All our questions and complications will be stripped away,
And peace of mind is what we'll find on that glorious day.
We'll walk hand in hand, toward this wonderous place;
At his command we will stand, in the aura of his grace.
Every race of every nation, in every place and destination,
Will join together and be as one; with the Holy Father and his son.
We are all given an open invitation to join in the dance,
To share in the celebration of this pomp and circumstance,
For God loves us all and wants us all to have the chance;
To accept his open invitation and join in the dance.

Wanda Fasick
PROGRESS
Is progress really on its way?
Ask some people and they say "nay"
We have computers today which help us in some ways
But do they really help our thinking minds?
Maybe we don't have the right kind

Our government is using them more
We wonder what they have in store
If they help solve our problems, we are all for it
With wars, people living on our streets, and crime
Will computers be able to help us in time

We have robots to do work we can't forget
They rake jobs our people can't fill yet
Then there's the electronical machinal devices
If any of these things go on the blink
What are we going to do if we can't think

Our education system too is being let down
There is too many drug problems on their grounds
In my time it was different than today
Is progress really on its way?
I say "nay"

Jessie Davis Johnson

Jessie Davis Johnson
LET ALL NATIONS PRAY
Why can't all Nations be at peace
And live in this world of ours,
The beautiful land God gave us,
A World of beauty and flowers.

It is old Satan that lures them
They walk straight into his den
It is he who causes the suffering,
Of good and honest men.

Oh, the sickness and the suffering
That is caused by these great wars
It seems such a pity
That they can't be stopped by Laws.
Fear not, be brave and steadfast
Keep your eyes upon the Lord,
And when the Battle is over, Go Home,
To live with Jesus, it is written in His Word.

Let us all unite together
Let us Pray the strife will cease
Let all nations live in harmony
In a beautiful World of Peace.

Howard E DuVall

Howard E DuVall
THE BUZZARD OF BEVERLY

This poem was written in Beverly Hills but it's dedicated to all cabdrivers who have ever had to rely on their sense of humor to pull them through—and to my wife and sweetheart Norma Jean whose "gentle encouragement" caused me to publish my work! Howard

---

I hover like a buzzard, central Beverly
looking for a morsel, 'er so carefully.
My cab it seems to barely move as I step on the gas.
What's this? a rich one hailing, as I slowly pass.
"Quick! Get in my cab." I say, "there is nó time to waste."
But now he wants to know the price and if I will make haste.
"Hang a left, no, it was right—a block or two before."
"But if you keep on going straight, you'll soon be at my door."
"Shut up," I say, "You talk too much", I'm sick of all this stuff."
"Give me what you owe me or I will get real tough."
Suddenly a wad of green appears before my eyes.
"You're not so bad after all," I say to my surprise.
But one thin dime is all I get for all my grief and woe
I ought to take this turkey and hang him by his toe.
"Oh well!" I say "I'm clear. I'm clear." Once again I'm free
to hover like a buzzard, central Beverly

Kristine Marie Hoover
TIME

For my son Aragon Allen Sharp

Time is not something you can control.
The years go rolling by.
Trapping every moment,
Until the day you die.
A life of love and friendship,
Is most important of all.
The beauties of this earth,
No matter how big or small.
So let us not forget
The mysteries of this land.
Have yet to be discovered,
With every helping hand.
Every person accepts this life,
Every man, woman & child.
All creatures roam this land,
Either tame game, or wild.
Creation is a mystery still,
Of all things begun.
And every morning we awake,
To greet the shining sun.
I wish you all the peace,
Last year is in the past.
But the good times roll on
And the memories will last.

Charlene Marie Morgan
THE SNOWFLAKES DRIFT OUTSIDE THE HOUSE
The snowflakes drift outside the house
In the attic, a tiny mouse

Comes closer for to see

Just what this odd package may be.

Inside the box wrapped with care
Poses a tiny teddy bear,
With bright blue bow and small blue dress,
Adorned in silent loveliness.

For years on end, the bear had sat,
Waiting for a small, light pat,
Waiting for a small young girl

To open the box with a twirl.

But the package remains closed,
Not a child has imposed
On the teddy bear inside.
And the teddy bear just sighed and sighed.

So the teddy bear waits on,
Still hoping to hear the song
Of a child, blithe and glad.
And the teddy bear seems sad.

Stan L Guyer
LOVES LOST LAMENT
Love, O Love,
Why must thou come to me?

Just when I feel I'm rid of you
and the memory of you expelled
You silently steal into my thoughts
and haunt the passages of my mind

When I'm not looking, you're there
to tempt me all the time
You fog the recesses of my mind
with faint awareness of loves long gone

An innocent smile, a gentle touch,
and soft supple flowing curves
Out you creep to catch my eye
and tear my heart from me again

You bring to me a haunting desire
and fill me with lust I can not share
You spirit into my very dreams
and seduce me while I sleep

O, you cruel and vicious thing
how you torment me day and night
With delightful pleasures that may never be
then depart, leaving not but sorrow.

Love, O Love,
Why must thou come to me?

Lori A Bickel/Dixon
MY LOST LOVE

To my loving husband, Iverd, Deceased January 22, 1986.

My days of loneliness get longer
My sadness never wanes,
The nights are endless, and
ever filled with pain.

When does it ever end,
When does the anguish stop?
My heart is heavy, filled with
grief . . .
No solace do I find,
Instead I weep.

I weep for joys no longer mine,
For a love that's lost forever,
The memories are too deep
to ever love another.

Latifah Malik
CATS

Cats have nine lives so they say
In the first life she reveals herself
brushed with selfishness, a
demon
like figure. The second life she
deepens
her plot in the law of
inhumanity. The third
life cats view the unseen forms
of smoke and fire.
In the fourth life she echoes
wisdom to all who will listen
to her cries. The fifth life leaves
an air of dismay to her enemies.
Kings of many nations in her
superiority could not murder
her, in
the sixth life, one would be wise
when approaching a cat in the
seventh life. The eighth life
cats brouse around you to seek
your
sent. If you were to look at the
inside of her you would see a
human after death

Sister Mary Lawrence Franklin RSM
THE MELODY OF MAIN STREET

Put, put, put, put, put, put, put, put,
The steady breathing of shop
machines
Scarcely stirs the sultry summer
air.
"Below, bel-o-oh, bel-o-oh,"
What does the Diesel say?
A decided—"get out of my way!"

An automobile grinds to a halt,
A semi hisses round the bend,
A manhole cover clatters
A locomotive rattles
Its string of carton cars.

"One and duh, two and duh, three
and duh . . ."
Musicians measure piano beats;
Pupil's shouts proclaim release
from school,
Pigeons mourn the humid heat,
Meek and gentle steeple bells
Earnestly urge the work-a-day
world:
"Refresh youself in prayer and
quiet."

"Put, put, put, put, put, put, put,
put,
The third shift thrums the
ceaseless chord
Accompanied by the "chug-chug-
chug"
Of an ancient guttural machine.

The beat of the tabor of day
Is happily muffled by maestro
mind
Who conjures concerts more
symphonic—
Less humdrum, and less profane—
Than the melody of First and Main.

Andrew Malinowski
SOMETHING IS STRANGE, LISTEN

It's quiet,
so quiet.
I can hear,
nothing.
It's so quiet.
I can hear,
my-self breathe.
It's quiet,
oh so quiet.
I can almost hear my heart beat.
I can feel my blood sliding through
my veins in its endless journey.
It's so quiet.
My mind won't work right
and their's nothing I can do
but sit and listen.

Ed Zaruba
THE BIG MOVE

We've come out of the City
Moved down to the Point
Still working, not idle
on our beautiful joint.
The children all love it
They're all on their own
They have their special chores
After school, come home.
The tenants are good
Remain in town
Daddy Zaruba stops by
Just to look around.
We all have our plans
Now the time has come
to watch the boating
And make fishing reels hum.
It's fourteen nineteen Angler's
Drive
Crank up the Fliver
Come to Palm Bay Point
Overlooking the Indian River

Earline Terry

Earline Terry
DAUGHTER

For my sister and her daughter, in celebration of the 17 year reunion.

You think that you would change
the past
if you could have your way.
You do not like the way it was
which brings us to today.
You firmly believe that millions in
gold
would not make you do as I've
done.
I, too, would reject a price so small,
for the love of my little one.
I cannot say I've never known
the burden that you bore,
I cannot say that I gave in
and knocked upon your door.
You cannot know the watch I kept
on any given day,
You cannot know the pride I felt
as I watched you run and play.
I cannot know your birthday wish
as you lingered by the phone,
was that your Mom would call you
before the day had flown.
You cannot know that on that day
I wept myself to sleep,
and blew to you a silent kiss
with familiar lips of grief.
You cannot know where I have
been
nor where our paths may lead,
but through this day of
Motherhood,
your thoughts will change,
indeed.
You will know that happiness
is not in proof of seeing,
but comes from deep within
yourself
as you meet needs for your
child's well-being.
In theory I knew you were waiting
for me,
but in reality, your youth had
much further,
for exactly this day, when you'd
understand
the endless love of being a
Mother.
So as you look upon your child
and say my truths, you cannot
see,
I pray the world may bestow on
you,
all that you hoped I'd be.

Mary K Mackey
LOVE IS

To my husband David, for what we are:

Love is said to be flowers,
All but forgotten dreams
Known as the beauty
Of free flowing streams.
Written in prose
By the heart's own hand . . .
Free as the waters
Overflowing the sand.
Shown by thoughts,
Built on trust . . .
Words unspoken
For love is us.

Sharon W Flynn
HEARTSEARCH

My heart looks heavenward—
Broken from its earthly strain,
Praying for the refreshing of the
rain.
My heart looks heavenward—
Awakened from its sorrowful sleep,
Asking for a love that's deep.
My heart looks heavernward—
Seperated from the light of the son,
Believing that its healing has
begun.
My heart soars heavenward—
Freed completely from the pain of
its sin,
Receiving, instead, joy and peace
within.

Carol Grey Honza
AN ORPHAN'S PRAYER

Why, Oh Mother! soft and sweet,
Could you not bear your sorrow?
Long enough to shelve your grief,
Till it be gone tomorrow . . .

To take thy child from comfort's
hearth,
Away to strangers' care . . .
How could you steal secure and
warmth
From round your child so fair?

Took leave of child to find yourself
In a selfish life of pleasure . . .
Did life provide enough to hide
The guilt and sorrows measured?

They tucked the tot into each night,
And kissed away the tears . . .
Strangers with your frightened
chid;
Could they relieve the fears?

Who missed the most, those stolen
years;
Who can separate the thread?
A mother's pain, through
memories,
Can torture till she's dead.

And lo, the child, who cried each
night,
The loss of Mother's care . . .
The question plagues . . . "What did
I do?"
A haunting Orphan's Prayer.

Francis Ivie
YOUR AN ARTIST, ITS OK

To be creative, is your right. Your
mind will improve with each new
sight, it
replaces the night with light. To be
creative
is self education, it smoothes over
all
the possiblys, and allows the real
you
to be. Enjoy and be happy, be
inspired, be
imaginative and receive the gift
derived
from your creativity, a never
ending
source of energy, being what life is
made of. Being creative, keeps your
mind and spirit alive with joy, and
allows you to feel the world from
within. The foundation of mind
grows and
is safe and real, so use your creative
skill. Our world loves your
creativeness it
wake's up there own, never feel
undone by
newness expressed, keep open
your heart,
spirit, and mind, let the world spin,
take your
rest with what you know is best.

Ian D Holter
MY WIFE

To Ellen, who has brought happiness and love into my life. She gave me the inspiration. Love, Ian

---

I took Ellen for my wife,
because she is the love of my life.
There is no one else for me,
she is Ellen my wife.

There is none finer than her,
She is so kind and gentle,
also a great mate.
That is why she is my wife.

I will always love her and adore her
for the rest of our lives together,
all because she is my wife.

I knew from the evening we were married
it was love from the start,
that she was the greatest and
best thing that ever happened to me,
is my wife.

She is like the lily of the valley in April,
oh so very sweet.
It's like we were made for each other.
The best and most important thing
Is that she is my wife.

Henrietta McDuffie
OPEN LETTER

Dedicated to Gary and George

My second love, you came along
and things seem right again
I gave my all, not realizing that our
love would also end.
We love and lived together as
lovers often do.
But then came the time in our lives
when you became untrue.
I was so happy with you, fulfilled
at last,
I didn't know then, it would
become a thing of the past.
I was blind to your unfaithfulness
I didn't face the truth
but I knew I would try again
Although it was no use.
We moved away to be alone, to
save the love we share
But I was beaten, and returned
home in dispare.

Audrey Dudley Huckins
THE REAL WORLD

I would like to dedicate this poem to my two daughters, Brenda and Joan, who have found that "real joy" is Jesus as they live in this "real world."

As we awake to face the day, the
beauties we behold;
Many choices we must make, some
never to be told.

As we mingle with family and
friends, the love we can't deny;
It makes our hearts so happy too
and physically we comply.

As we go to school or work, lessons
we daily learn;
Some may create complications,
others with ambitions burn.

As we face the golden years, each
day we feel so blest;
We thank our Heavenly Father for
our companions, love and rest.

For each day is a blessing, the time
goes by so fast—
We laugh and enjoy so many things
and so soon the day is past.

But this is the 'Real World', we
make it what we may
For some there's hatred and ill will,
for others love permeates the
day.

The secret is knowing our
Father—who made us and loves
us too;
In Him we seek His will each
day—and His love will take us
thru.

Everyone could have that joy, just
ask Jesus to come in;
Tell Him you are sorry and He will
free you from your sin.

Then you will be so happy as you
walk daily in His will;
You'll want the world to know it
too, your life with love He'll fill!

H Richard Hilger

H Richard Hilger
SAME, OAR

To Emily Dickinson, Mary Dargan, and my English IA classmates (the SCHS Brain Trust)

Looking up to those of wealth,
are the poor, the sick, the lame,
but why do this when it is known
at birth we're all the same.

As I was walking out one day,
along a windy shore,
I saw protruding 'neath the sand
the handle of an oar.

So weathered was this once used
tool
that when I pulled it out,
it snapped in half and threw me
down,
while there I thought about . . .

From where it came, which sea,
which ship,
From whose grip did it slip?
Could he have died while out at sea,
sent to that watery cript?

But who will know from where it
came,
it's resting place this shore;
the only one who knows this is
the weatherbeatened oar.

Ann Kotas
CAN'T SAY GOOD-BYE

You say you must go now, we must
learn to say good-bye.
You say prepare myself, for I
must not cry.
You say forget the pain it brings,
and walk away without a sigh.
You say this is what I must do
for others, for we all must die.
But as I see you slowly fading away.
I want to reach out, and make
you stay.
Oh, how I regret the years we spent
apart.
Though we were always together
within our hearts.
You were always there within my
mind, my body, my very soul.
It doesn't seem right for you to
die now, before you're old.
Yet, I know your spirit lives inside
me.
Say good-bye Oh, No, never.
How can I let you go.
Say good-bye Oh, No, never. For I
love you so.
You'll never leave me.
For you are me.
You know I'll always need you.
And how will I survive without you.
Yet, once again I hear you say,
say good-bye my love.
For you know I'll never really leave
you.
I'll always be there within your
heart.
And time will no longer keep us
apart.

David Hamo
THIS ROAD

This road begins on solid ground,
so smooth, so straight, so molded
round.

And then it twists, it winds and
turns,
goes up and down through trees
and ferns.

The sun it shines upon this road,
and paints a path of blue and gold.

And flowers bloom upon its side,
To give to those a pleasant ride.

Its wet and dry, its hot and cold,
some bumps it has, have been
extolled.

For through the years this road has
seen,
some snow and fog, some dust and
steam.

And several times this road was
blocked,
by trees and lines, and fallen rock.

But time moves on to clear the way,
for those who need this road today.

And where this road comes to and
end,
is where no one has ever been.

Where is this road you ask may be?
Nowhere you see!
This road is me . . .

George Halkias
ECHOS OF LIGHT

To the oriental fantasies that live within us.

I want to talk for the waters
Which have been captured in the
Agean Sea;
To talk for those endless moments
Of eternity, which have been lost
Within reasonings;
To talk for those sounds which
Decorate our nudity;
To say about hope, beyond the
Steadiness of the red rose;
To say for those echos which
Follow the truth;
To shout for all those birds
Without destination,
But I can't
Words will not let me.

Mary A Castillo
THE MALLS ARE PACKED WITH A CROWD

The malls are packed with a crowd
With people walking tall and proud
They are shopping
Then they will quit
So the people can rest a bit.

Then they go heading for the bank
for their new clothes they will need
a tank.
Back in the car, heading for the
mall
They buy clothes that are not too
small.

Now they have no money at all
So now they have to make a call
They call back home
And ask for dad
I NEED SOME MONEY, VERY
BAD!

Lara LaPlante
DREAM GODS

To Mom and Nan, The two greatest ladies I've ever known.

They come,
From where no one knows,
But they come.
Here in the forgotten days of long
ago,
They come back to reclaim what
was once theirs.
A land, a people, a way of life.
They like the days they once lived
in, have been forgotten,
But they come to haunt us in our
dreams, though they are silent in
waking hours.
They touch our souls, our hearts,
our minds.
They come,
Reaching out,
Hoping they have not been
forgotten,
"Help us," they cry so softly, "Help
us."
But theirs is not a dream.
We wake and forget them all too
quickly.
But do we not sleep again?
They will come again and again,
night after night.
They have for a long time.
But no need to worry, we will
forget them again won't we?

Mrs Rachel Veinot
WAR HEROS

Our hearts and prayers are with
those
Who volunteered to go
Far across land and sea
To fight that deadly foe.
We'd hope and pray to God each
day
To guide our loved ones there
Who bravely saw their duty was
Not here but over there.
They fought bravely side by side
The victory to win
And when the war was over
To come smiling home again.

There were many brave boys
We'll never see again
But they will be remembered
By all who knew them.
For they died bravely fighting
For us and liberty
That was the price they paid

To keep our country free.
Don't let your memory fail now
Of the gallant deed they've done
But bow your heads in prayer
In memory of loved ones.

Madolyn Reeves Goodboy
SEASONS

This is dedicated to the glory of God, who provided the earth with it's seasons and the words to the following poem.

Spring is the season for butterflies and bees;
Robins and tulips and dogwood trees.
The earth comes alive after the winter snow,
And farmers plow and plant, row after row.

Then comes summer and the hot humid days.
The flowers are awakened by the sun's warm rays.
Families and friends gather for picnics and fun.
Kittens, puppy dogs and youngsters laugh and run.

The leaves are turning colors . . . red, yellow and brown.
Soon the north wind will blow them around.
Fall is a beautiful time of the year;
But then we know winter is very near.

The snow has arrived so pretty and white.
Winter is here with it's long cold nights.
We thank God for his seasons and trust him to bring
The joy and renewing of life . . . the spring.

Lana J Kinser
OUR LOVE

To the man I love, my dearest friend and husband, Bruce Michael

---

Love has become so wonderful
As long as I'm with you.
You make the love so beautiful
And let your smile come through.

To show that nothing will harm me
You look that special way.
It can only mean you love me
More than yesterday.

And as we look ahead to tomorrow
Our mind is far away.
We can only hope our love will grow
Stronger and stronger everyday.

Helen Trent
ANOTHER START
It's difficult to sleep tonight.
I wish our hearts could reunite.
Tenderly, I still do love you.
Your silence said that we were through.
Since our break up I've changed my mind.
The mistakes and pains are behind.
I do love you the way you are;
Even the hurts that made a scar.
Their seems no sleep for me tonight.
There's no future of you in sight.
If love really changes the heart,
Then just give me another start.

Florence Day Prindle
WINTER KILL
The bullet screamed.
A clean shot dropped her.
Her dull thud
Charged the still snow
Into a powdery explosion.
It settled around her
Caressing her warm body
With it's icy down
Like a cold comforter.
The bullet had pierced her heart.
It's life's blood
Shot into the white snow
Staining it crimson.
Pain shattered her.
Maddened screams
Lured the hunter toward her
His footfalls quickening,
Seduced by the cries
Of his stranded victim.
But when he reached her
She lay motionless.

Mary J Lowe

Mary J Lowe
OUR LOVE
Things may be hard;
Things may be rough;
But nothing can disrupt our love;

Seasons may come;
Seasons may go;
But nothing can come or go from our Love;

People can hurt;
People never mind;
But nothing can hurt or never mind
Our Love;

With this Christmas I may not give much;
With this anniversary' I may not have much;
But with you, and our family, with me;
not giving or not having much can do nothing to
our love or life together . .

Patrick D Wood
MOMENTS
As the sun did rise so clear and bright a beauty to behold in all of one's delight.

For there standing all alone a little girl staring at the beauty which she beheld.

In her little mind something of grandeaur, a bright and so new of red and blue a swing.

What were her thoughts as she stood so awed by the beauty her little eyes of blue gazed upon.

Oh, if only one could know what thoughts did go through her mind, we would all be amazed.

Beauty is not of one subject, but moments of joy that abound all around to have and to hold.

Then as if the world had stood still, she looked up with the little blue eyes and said pretty.

For though the little girl was only three and my little girl this time remains so dear.

If only one could hold or capture these moments forever, what a wonderful world it would be.

Christie Michelle Williams
THE OLD MAN

In loving memory of my grandfather—Louis Joe Hopcus

The man was old and worn,
Not a care in the world had he.
He never thought his day was near,
Nor did she.

His day of reckoning is near,
For no one knows how he feels.
No one except for his little pet,
On the ground his little dog heels.

The little dog sits and howls,
"Oh hush," says the old man.
Then he goes inside,
And comes out with a pan.

He feeds the little dog,
All the time feeling funny.
Then he goes inside to his wife,
He says, "I'll see you up there, honey."

He goes to his room,
There he lies down.
He closes his eyes,
And you'll hear not a sound.

She walks in his door, then to the phone,
"Bring a funeral director," said she.
"For he is dead."
And I should know,
For that she is me.

Olga Brown
LOVE IS EVERYWHERE
Love is in our hearts
Love is caring
Love is sharing
Love is doing for others
Love is singing
Love is dancing
Love is crying for others
Love is everywhere
Love is working
Love is eating
Love is sleeping
Love is rising to a new day
Love is everywhere
Love is mother and father
Love is husband or wife
Love is son and daughter
Love is brother and sister
Love is you and I
Love is everywhere
Love of God is the greatest Love of All
Love is precious
Love is wonderful
Love is everywhere

Jeanette Todd Evans
GRADUATION
Four happy years have come to a close
Where your paths now lead, no one knows
The joys you have shared and the friends you have made
Will soon become memories that never will fade

This night you are together is one of the last
The things you have done here, your minds will hold fast
With these parting words and our eyes filled with tears
Good luck and best wishes in all future years.

Orcelia Birge Winn
SURPRISES
Open days
Hot summer hides nothing
It runs barelegged
On the grass.
An Easter lily
Blooms in August . . .
Life is full of surprises
Good, and bad.

Sue Jensen
THANK HEAVEN, HE WAS ONLY A DREAM
One day I wandered in my mind
to search for a heart I thought would be kind.

A heart that liked a cool gentle breeze; the
kind that blows on a summer night.

And we would dance under the trees
in the evening starlight.

Alas, he came along. In the memories of my mind,
I loved his songs.

We sang and danced with the breeze, in the evening
starlight. It was so beautiful and felt so right.

But his heart was like the breeze, ever changing, never still.
His moves were full of ease; to belong to just one he never will.

He knew all the right words to all the right songs.
My heart would flutter as I tried to sing along.

Then along came a breeze that awoke me from my dream.
The breeze that formed him in my mind, blew him away like a tease.

Thank Heaven, he was only a dream.
Now I can live at ease.

For I'd rather be in a loved one's arms
than to be blown away by a breeze.

Mary L Caler
MIRRORED IMAGE
Mirrored image, looking back,
You see the virtues that I lack.
You've seen me at my very best,
Or shared the fit of a brand new dress.
When as a bride, with joys and fears,
You cried the same warm happy tears
As babies came, you seen them too!
We'd try to make them smile and coo.
My pride is reflected, now they're grown,

And they do the same with babes
of their own.
There are lines on the face and grey
in the hair,
While the depth of our eyes holds
many a care
You see my life and my loves, so
true.
Only my God knows me better than
you.

Michelle Ann Peters
THE EAGLE'S FORBIDDEN FLIGHT

As true branches bow to
widespread wings
and prey scamper for shelter to
escape shrewd eyes
while He, soaring freely above us
all
glides serenely and gingerly
through the sky
never seeming to encounter any
walls
leisurely racing with a natural high
appearing regally and confidently
tall
until an acrid gunshot produces a
poison sigh
for who dares disturb Mother
Nature; what gall
man ignorantly displays, but it is
useless to ask why
as the person, with an arrogant
smile, observes the bird's fall
this untarnished eagle is forced to
succumb to the earth's dirt as it
dies
a human disregard for life and
pride, an action which should
reduce those to crawl
who say it's "pure sport" that the
eagle can no longer safely fly

Barbara Gaulin
ENDLESS TIME

listening to time . . .
the sometimes steady flow
of an ageless rhythm,
I hear serenity's laughter
in Nature's Child;
sometimes rushing by
in hectic chaos,
I hear the fervent cry
of turbulent complexity;
sometimes dormant
in empty slumber,
I hear the inane whisper
of lost souls.

time . . .
clothed in vast displays
of colour;
from rainbow's iridescent universe,
to mind's transparent web.

time . . .
ceaseless in its entity,
continues its masquerade
on the elipse
of life's reign.

Tanya Davis
THE DRINKER

There was a guy named Bill
Who liked to drink a lot;
He'd drink until he got his fill
And that was all he sought.

Bill's wife was named Liz-beth
And she would always tell him,
"Bill, drinking will be your death
So your future looks quite dim."

He said, "Drinking is my life,
Theres nothing I can do."
She said,"And I am your wife,
What does that mean to you?"

Bill was really confused
And left Liz-beth there to cry—
She started to watch the news
Wishing he would go dry.

"The end was not at all far
For a man named Bill Dean
Who was pulled from his wrecked
car
And pronounced dead at the
scene."

Norma Grizzle
LIFE BLOOMS FOREVER

The flowers bloom in the spring,
Like life it slowly vanishes away.
Their seed goes back into the earth
And awaits til they bloom again
someday.

Earl D Threet
FOR REASONS UNKNOWN

Its to wonder, to reason, or wonder
why—it maybe never be known.
For all those kids who will never
be grown.
Everyday, somewhere, one will die.
Though many people will always
wonder why.

Habits form daily, causing some
kids grief.
Others don't know, they have only
the belief,
Of others that say its OK!
Only to find out the hard way.

Through hardships, loss of friends,
and time and money spent.
Good times cost and rules aren't to
be bent.
To pay for death, that comes
anyday,
A shortened life isn't the way.

For kids to ponder and to involve,
Around those that do believe.
For the good Lord always will
grieve,
With the parents who had it all and
lost.
Their one and sometimes only, to
the heavy cost.
That drugs impound those who
have tried.
For reasons unknown—only to
have died!

Hiram M Dean

Hiram M Dean
UNDERSTANDING LIGHTS THE WAY

Dedicated to World Peace

When hopes fulfill and dreams
come true
And love of money at an end
We will work and live and pray
anew
When selfishness has ceased its
trend
When competition has become
pure
Our children's souls will be secure
God will help guide our thought
and hand
To know God is to understand

For love is such a tender thing
Like the flowers of the spring
Joy is something that can last
As long as memories of the past
Fear is what we learn to know
That comes to us with pain and woe
Faith will guide us like a keel
In life's rough seas secure we feel

Hope will help us to endure
Comfort us when we are not sure
Prayer gives us strength and
fortitude
When we pray for things we know
are good
But understanding lights the way
Will turn life's darkness into day
The Word the Good the Wisdom
too
With Understanding guide us
through

Marie Gennaro
YOU MEAN AMERICA TO ME

The thrill and the excitement is
over
The memory still lingers on.
The Harbor Festival of the Great
Lady
Which we can reminisce upon.

With her new torch held high
which lights the way.
And with all ships passing by her
each and every day.
She is a gigantic reminder we are
the land of the free.
She stands for Justice and
Freedom,
This Statue of Liberty.

The Centennial celebration was
one we will not forget.
Perhaps this restoration, for
another Century, we will not
regret.
I'm sure if Liberty is in trouble we
will again aid with speed.
This constant reminder of
Independence,
So many immigrants can be freed.

Many have come from near or afar,
Just to see how beautiful you are.
Mother of Exile, Colossus Lady of
the sea,
No matter what they call you, YOU
MEAN AMERICA TO ME.

Jacqueline L Aiken
THE HOLY BOOK

To my husband, Calvin, for encouraging me.

As I read this Holy Book, into the
meanings deeper I look.
To search and find what's written
within,
To sort out whatever I sin.
I read now and I read then, just to
see what is within.
Dear Lord, when I'm through,
I pray I'll be closer to the throne by
You!

Judith Kay Elliott
IT'S UP TO YOU

"Let me drive!, I'll be all right you'll
see,
Quit being a jerk and hand me the
keys.
I haven't had that much to drink,
Besides, if you took me home what
would everyone think.
I'm the guy in this relationship, so
I'm responsible for you,
If you loved me, you'd trust me and
there would be nothing to
prove."
Time goes on as he stumbles along,
Falls next to the car and sings a
drunken song.
"Why must he have so much pride,
When in the end, it could cause us
both to die.
I love him, I love him, I really do!.
So should I give in?! . . . What
would you do?."

Jack Earl Lindley
A DREAM COME TRUE

I dedicate this poem to my wonderful wife Juanita because she is also my friend and sweetheart and she made my dream come true.

One by one, God has put the stars
to sleep
The sky grows lighter, where earth
and heaven meet.
Soon he will open up the gates of
heaven
So the morning sun can light the
sky
To bring forth smiles from every
passerby.
And kiss the gentle flowers fresh
touched with dew
For all of this, I am grateful, but
most of all
I thank God for our love—a dream
come true.

Roger Freeland II
A USUAL DAY

There I was, starting the day,
In the usual way,
Got up on the wrong side of the
bed,
Then I heard what my mother said,
Clean your room,
with a sweeper not a broom,
I responded with no,
Which delivered a sharp blow,
To my mother, who was cleaning,
She asked me what I was meaning,
I said I would rather play instead,
She said if I didn't I would wind up
dead,
I told her that I had a change of
heart,

Thats when (to my surprise) she
called me a sweetheart,
The rest of the day went fine,
As my mother kept me in line.

Mamie Recky
THE DRUNKARD'S CHILD

Out in this gloomy night sadly I
roam;
I have no Mother, no friends and
no home.
Dark is the night and the storm
rages wild;
God pity Bessie, the Drunkard's
lonely child.
We were so happy until Father
drank rum;
Then all of our troubles and
sorrows begun.
Mother grew paler and wept every
day;
Baby and I were too hungry to play.
On the damp ground I must now
lay my head;
Father is a Drunkard and Mother
is dead.

Joe K
LOVE SONGS AND NIGHTINGALES

Dawn broke
and the first rays of light
pierced the darkness
which fled to another place.
All was quiet.

Then,
without thought,
but with every reason in the
world,
a nightingale's song
shattered the still.

Anita Louise Brown
WORLD STAGE

I woke this day as from a dream,
the world seemed far below
It beckoned me with open arms,
"please come help fill the show
And dance upon this stage of life,
and grace it with your glow."
How dare I take the burden on, the
heaviness of weight,
And twirl upon this stage of life to
tune that some call fate!

Richard Mackin Jr
SHEILA

Sheila the monkey is a fine girl.
Start the music, master Tom! See
her whirl
and whirl; tip up on her toes and
reach
for the sky!
The street musician and she play
for passers by.

Just a banana now and then,
a few coins for the cup
will make Sheila a long time friend
with music and dance ready to lift
you up.

See her spin and spin winking with
an eye;
the street musician and she love
the passers by.

Harvey A Sherman
TO A SPARROW

You dart about, hither and yon
Your song is most appealing,
Your passing does not stir the soul.
No hearts are you stealing.

Eagles' immortal, thank you Lord,
Bless you too poor raven,
Bluebird, thrush and meadowlark,
Surround us in our haven.

When winter blasts the bones to ice
And blizzards burn the marrow,
One song is there to cheat despair,
But no one hears you sparrow.

Robert H Johnson Jr
FEBRUARY

To my grandmother "Betty," Elizabeth Witcomb Barnes.

I've nothing much to do all day
But watch it snow
And see the many different ways
Its want to blow.

The world does need
A nice new dress,
A fine soft white one to caress
The naked earth, the bare cold
trees,
And cover with flounces
Their shivering knees.

There'll be thick, white fur
On the window ledge
And pom poms on the barberry
hedge.

If it only snows and snows and
snows,
I can stand where bloomed the
highest rose.
I can strut atop the tallest fence,
And call to the birds with gay
pretense.
I'll break a branch from an apple
tree
And maybe it will bud for me.

If the sun comes out,
As well as not,
The gown will turn to apricot.
The spruce trees will gladly make
I know,
Dark, soft fringes of indigo.

Ernest J Field
KING OF THE WORLD

Let me do it my way, said my son
one day to me,
Let me climb the mountains or sail
a boat to sea.
Then when I've failed or
conquered,
Chastise or heap me with praise.
But at least dear Mom. It's my way.
After all, "I'm King of the World."

It was the same when he tinkered
with motors.
Played sports and chased all the
girls.
His voice wouldn't say it,
But his look would betray it.
It's my way, "I'm King of the
World."

Then the war came, and the
serving of his country,
Had to be of his own choice.
But then what can I say,
For my son truly that day,
Became "The King of the World."

It's later the telegrams and notes of
condolence
From country, family and friends
arrived.
For my son in his sleep
Death had taken "My King of the
World."

Will this war like all wars be final?
Or, will it all go for naught like the
rest?
Ask this yourself my friend,
And then make a peace without
end.
And help save "Our Kings of the
World."

Rose Marie Polon
WITHOUT YOU

Dedicated to: "The man I will always love" "Shad" —Elvin Darryl Morgan

---

I could never live my life—
"Without you"
You are my world—my Laughter
My tears—my happiness, and fears
You are part of me—I, am part of
you
We are one—molded out of two
When you take your last breath
It is then that I'll take mine
For your heart—is my heart
Your breath—my breath
Your soul—my soul
Your life—my life
And "Without you" —I have
nothing
"Without you" —there is no me
"All my being is you" . .

Love Eternally

Michael Federika
CHRISTMAS JOY

To Christmas memories old and new "Spirit of Christmas"

"Carolers sing out Christmas joy,
The golden dawn of Christmas
morn
Illuminates the snow covered trees,
And the twinkling eyes of happy
dancing children.
Christmas joy in all of nature
shows.
Sleds brushing o'er new fallen
snow,
Distant church bells summon the
people to church.

Peace and happiness begin to flow,
Negative thoughts left in the lurch.
Christmas joy and hope become
ethereal,
Suffering and hardship,
immaterial.
The first Noel, the wise men
followed the star in the East.
Now we share gifts of joy, and have
a huge feast.
When your Christmas joy begins to
fall,
Remember One born Who brings
joy to us all."

Lynda G Garrett
MEAR, MIRROR REFLECTIONS

Behind the wall, I never even knew
there was a wall, inspired I write
on.
The journey was long, sunlight
clear and green water falling soft
grass under transparent foot, or
was it transparent grass under
foot soft.
A long journey I rested on a purple
hill and watched birds overhead
flying, talking, telling bird tales
of past, present and future.
Turning I see a Brook, Flowing,
I go and sit beside it, its talking
also, beautiful Brook language it
has mellow, I watch it, listening,
flow as it watches me, it tells me
a story of actions flowing on and
on liquid I almost see the
connection, the journey is
almost over, almost, my
attention is drawn a way.
Some animals approach they
wonder about my intentions, I
don't know what to tell them, in
my confusion they drift a way.
My eyes are drawn to a hill glowing
green and soft it seems far
away there is a path, I feel. I'm
on my way mysteriously light.
Clouds are drifting, water flowing,
all is in motion constant.
I lift my hand a butterfly flies,
cloud drifts, water flows all in
harmony, a complete motion,
one in all. Motion.
The hill is closer now, shimmering
blue green, upward now
climbing sailing, I stop half way
up turn a round to be, half way
down, in the middle, I wonder?
I sit, the grass is soft, neither up
or down I am, headed just now
here Now Here, it seemed like
hours I was, there, before I
stood,.
To re gain my way, I reached the
top. You'll find me there,. Still
I'll always be, here,. Here as I
look back down the hill. I re
garde self climbing, I wonder,
was there ever time?, when I
wasn't here, hear I wonder that
is, an other hill to climb.

Adrienne Companik
SEPERATE CASTLES

I built a castle in the sand and
protected it with love
Then feelings shattered my sand
castle with tears from up
above.
I may be able to build a castle from
a single grain of sand
But now my fears shattered all my
dreams I cannot understand.
You tell me I'm in love with love
you tell me I can wait
Still I lock these feelings in my
heart for little more than
fate.
I hold back feelings I hold back
love I hold everything I
should My emotions were meant
to share with love and I wish
that I could.
My warm sand castles melting now
I can't hold on forever
To let this castle drift away will
happen close to never
If I let the tide carry my castle as
it has carried me
Then dreams are lost and hearts
are broken and love will
never be So now its just another
day to repair my castle
of sand Always remember I'm
searching for another helping

hand To patch it up with kindness and keep it warm with love To give it faith to face tomorrow and I pray to God above That this companion I am seeking all throughout the land Will love as much as I do to build castles in the sand.

Mary P Fowles
THE SEASONS

I dedicate this poem to my husband, John, who, when we took many rides along unfamiliar roads, said "We'll find our way back."

I live in a world of seasons
and I always look forward to Spring.
The long days, the leafy trees
and the green of everything.

Next comes summer, my favorite time,
the best of all for me,
when I can take my chair outside
and stretch out under the tree.

Then autumn with its color
is lovely to behold.
Did you ever ride down a country road
under an arch of gold!

Then winter, it can be pretty too
and something I wouldn't miss.
But most of all, I thank my God
for giving me all of this.

Ruth Greenfield
AN ODE TO MY MOTHER:
Is it a year since you've left
This earthly place?
Is it a year since last
I kissed your face?
The tears I've shed
Have not been all in vain
They've helped so much
To ease the dreadful pain
A thousand times a day
I think of you.
Of the love you gave me,
Of things we used to do.
Oh Mother Dear, you were
The very best.
May you have peace at last,
May God help you to rest.

Your loving daughter
Ruthie

Mrs Norma K Cotter
RAIN
Falls
Splendidly
Sparkling
Quietly
Softly

Somehow
The
Lake,
Once
Mirror
Like

Churns,
Mirky,
Muddy,
Sullen.

Nancy Ricotta Hamelinck
A DREAM

To: My only and last true love

Ho! Please Lord
Don't stop me ever for dreaming,
For with out my dream of him
My life would cease.
And if by chance my dream
Comes true my joy and ecstasy
Would be like heaven right here on earth.

Helen Reuter
THE SHOE FITS

Dedicated to the Reuter Family

Back in the dark ages
When mom and dad were kids,
They must have been naughty sometimes,
But they sure keep it hid.
Grandma says my mom
Was a sweet and loving child.
Then she looks at me in
Wonderment and sighs.
Your dad was probably wild.
It's not nice to say such things
Even if they're true.
My dad was never wild like me.
Gram, I take after you!

Tawana Blair

Tawana Blair
USED
You told me you loved me
I've heard that lie before
that time you said you cared.
Who were they really meant for?
You said I was your very own,
I thought I was surrounded by your love
But how was I to know
That I wasn't the one that you were thinking of.

And the truth finally came out,
under the hidden lies,
you couldn't keep a secret
that was deep down inside.
You used words with no meaning

But you lasted in the end.
When you were winning at the start . . .
And knew things could never mend.

Celso Q Zafranco
RELUCTANT SURRENDER

To My Beautiful Wife, Feliza Zafranco

When I kiss you . . .
you would pull away;
When I hug you . . .
you will wriggle away
from me.
It was fun
playing
against your
resistance!
Because I know
you are titillated
and secretly loved
the tenderness
you found in my love.
Shyly reluctant
of wanting me . . .
when I know
there is passion
boiling mad
beneath
the unruffled
surface.

Fran Krausz
VIET/VETS MOM LAMENTS

To my son, John Binau and all Viet/Nam veterans

Your patriotic duty to your country back then,
Made me proud to know my son would serve his fellow-men.
I knew, should you be sent to war, you'd serve your country well;
I never dreamed that you would go there to such a living hell.

The terror of that war shows on your face,
A troubled soul no mother could erase,
Or ease the pain that drives you in the night
When you recall the ravaged fire-fight.

You live within your lonely little world
Where none can enter, see or understand.
I long to comfort, touch and hold you tight,
But you are alone within your fire-fight.

I pray the Lord who knows your wounds so deep
Will heal you of your devasted sleep,
For only God can heal you of that fright
And quench the ever burning fire-fight.

Celestine J Custer
NIGHTMARE, THE MIND
You wonder through life thinking, thinking, and thinking.
One day you find you exist.
The next day you wonder what is the purpose.
Then you find there is no light, only darkness.
You search for light everywhere, only to find more darkness.
One very long weary night you find there is something inside you that wants to live.
A hole of light shows.
You have found a sense of reality.
You began to realize you are valuable.
Your desires of worth began to broaden and more holes of light begin to shine through but none of them connect.
You are puzzled with blind madness, trying to understand why they don't all connect.
One night of day you realize the paradox of life and you see one of the holes of life connect.
Time is going around and around through your madness, you realize that the light you seek inside you.
Then the hemisphere began to open up to you and you smile because you know, you are half way there.
All of a sudden, it hits you, love is your only salvation.
It can destroy you or make you.
Because, now you realize love of blind desires can break you and only the love of truth can save you.
The day finally arrives.

Myrtle Dixon
TO SOAR WITH THE EAGLE
Born of the river, born of the sea,
Born of the mountain's majesty.
Circling, wheeling, soaring free,
Oh! What a longing he brings to me
Could I but free my pinioned wings
Flee from the burden of earthly things,
Soar with the eagle to heights unknown,
Seeking, seeking, that other home.

But I am bound with a thousand cares,
I can only dream of those golden stairs.
I can watch him mount into vaulted skies,
'Till I no longer see through tear-blind eyes,
Working, waiting, longing for home,
Bound to the earth, as the earth's brown loam.

Born of the river, born of the sea,
Born of the mountain's majesty.
Circling, wheeling, a monarch on high,
Kindred in freedom, the eagle and I.
For my soul will go soaring free someday,
Leaving behind the earthbound clay.

Mr Florian L Felts
SNOWFLAKES
Beautiful, delicate flakes drop slowly.
Many shapes and pure white.
Flakes fall on your head.
Soon you have a glistening crown of diamonds.
All too soon they melt.
Running down your face and your neck.
It feels so good.

I like to catch the flakes on my tongue.
How cool as they melt and my thirst is quenched.

I love the snow—soft, cool, and white.
Oh, how I hate the snow.
It plugs up my driveway and sidewalks.
Fun to shovel for a time but enough is enough.

Now I use a snow blower.
The snow shoots out in a steady stream.
All the flakes are mixed together.
Oh, now I have lost them.
They are no more—poor snowflakes.

Kolin Jeffery Goncalves
THE IMPORTANCE OF BLACK AMERICANS' ACCOMPLISHMENTS

I would like to dedicate my poem to my Nana, Edith May Jeffery for inspiring me to continue in poetry

America's Black history is a story of it's own,
There are many great Black heroes who are valiant and well known,
There are many in our history I could write about for you,
I will give you some examples—though these are just a few.

There was a brave Black soldier,
His name was Salem Poor.
He fought for our country's freedom,
In the Revolutionary War.

He was such a gallant soldier,
On his appointed mission,
That fourteen U.S. officers,
On his behalf signed a petition.

They asked of Massachusetts,
A reward for Salem Poor.
But he did not receive it,
For his braveness in the war.

Phillis Wheatley is another,
Who became very well known.
She became a famous poet,
And wrote poems on her own.

So we remember these Americans,
Who fought for freedom in the wars.
They helped to build our country,
And not to mention much, much more.

Barbara Ann Hicks
NEAR AND DEAR

This poem is dedicated to Jerry, my loving and understanding husband.

Near and dear our friendship and love compared. To you and I love is friendship. Oh! And so much more you know, you know like passion, there's caring too! Binds us together, fabric to a string, our wedding ring. Helping each other soften the blow against the stresses offered down here below.

You and I have found that love and friendship are so alike in many ways to a point, then it turns around and is as different as day and night. Our friendship can turn into a night with a love that can melt the world away or turn the daylight into a memory that will last a lifetime. This love of yours and mine. This love and friendship we share could be compared Enjoyment our time together, Acceptance cause we accept one another as we are. Trust there is there must be Trust to make it through the years. Trust wipes away the fears and Trust never makes tears. Oh! The Trust we share. Respect for each other because we care, we care we can support one another through whatever may come our way. Oh! The experiences we go through together gives us such understanding of what we are separately. Even our friends can see our closeness. They can feel our tenderness we share just being near the two of us dear. Oh! But love like ours needs its Spontaneity keeping us free to feel to be ourselves. It's a love for each other even if your far away or near to me dear. Near and Dear, Near and Dear.

Robert R John
THE PRICE OF FREEDOM

This is dedicated to the families of all those who gave their lives, for our freedom.

Sometimes we forget, old glorys hanging high,
She's taken for granted, like all the men thats died;
And 100,000 tombstones, lined up in a row,
Standing for the freedom, that we all love and know.

We buried our fathers, our husbands and our sons,
And all of the innocent, so freedom could be won;
And the war might be over, for folks like me and you,
But the scars will never mend, on the Red, White and Blue.

One lone soldier, in an unmarked grave,
Laid down his life, so freedom could be saved;
And 50,000 names, forever etched in stone,
They died for their country, but some never came back home.

And 100 years from now, she'll be standing tall,
Standing for freedom, and the hell that she saw;
And 100,000 tombstones, will be fading in the sun,
And the history books will tell, —of the freedom, that they won.

Yvonne Pesta Panfili
BEAUTIFUL MOUNTAIN SEASONS

From in the valley I look to the sky
And what do I see but a mountain so high
A mound of green under warm summer sun
A place to relax or a place to have fun.

Then autumn arrives and leaves start to fall
When I look to the sky, you don't seem as tall.
It is the one season that makes me sad
Well, that's part of nature so it can't be bad.

When I see you standing in a winter storm,
I wonder what will keep you warm.
I guess it will be the blanket of snow
That will protect you as the winter winds blow.

Not far ahead is the season of spring
And the budding of flowers is a glorious thing.
Soon all your colors will be coming back
And beautiful mountain there is nothing you'll lack.

Betty Ann Romanczuk
TWO FRIENDS

To All the Men and Women who served in Viet Nam. To my son Michael and my daughter Tina Marie who I love with all my heart.

I joined the service as a man. I met a buddy on friendly land.
We went to camp and everything was fine. We were soldiers one of a kind.
War broke out the numbers were high. Time was short for my buddy and I.
Our names were called we went in vain. We hated to go, we wanted to stay. My buddy gave me strength, we had nothing to say.
We made the mighty trip to unfriendly seas.
We were told to fight I couldn't believe.
The blue skies were darkening quick, guns went off, the noise wouldn't quit.
We were told to be brave, That the noise wouldn't last.
We wanted to go home, my buddy and I. They told us no, we had our pride.
They called us by numbers, I called him by name. The numbers were high. I was going home, tired I cried. I lost my buddy under darkening skies.
My friend, my buddy, his life lost in vain.
I went back to my friendly land not recognized by name.
The flag flew high on command, it didn't recognize the friend or myself as a man. Our names were all different, but we were the same. All the numbers died in vain. I looked at Arlington, it was
all the same, quite peaceful all around.
Fifteen years later the sun shown down at Arlington and all around.
I was back to my friendly land.

Elizabeth Glass Rodriguez
A ROAD FOR ALL SEASONS

Happiness is riding a road which couldn't be there if it wasn't by God's desire for deer to play. An all seasons pleasure for all to be there.
Oh! beautiful Spring along my road; the rays of that sun shining in the clouds of dogwood flowers, suddenly tinted by a cardinal's leisure flying. And all those trunks that seem so dull? they came to life!, but how?, I know! It's 'cause the chicks with their chirps kept all their nests until the Spring!
Oh Georgetown Pike how much I sighed, and every day I enjoy that ride, and in the Summer you look like a tempting jungle. The dancing leaves let the sun occasionally come in. When Fall comes along to my good road, it's hard to find the words to clearly show the feeling of my heart pumping with love. What would I say to all those trees? Have you my road turn into a jewel? are those your leaves made out of gold? are those red ones really rubies? they look so real! If you don't tell me that they are, then, maybe I will think they are on fire! But my jewel road, your riches don't stop in the Fall, because there are more riches when Winter comes. When crystals and diamonds from branches hang. They look so bright with the sun's light!, and Winter winds shook them once more. It's a Winter melody of crystal bells. A song of love!.

Jennifer A Blake
REACH FOR THE STARS

If life was meant to be easy,
What dreams would be achieved?
If unknown answers were left as is,
What new knowledge would be perceived?

If position and status were handed out freely
And no one had to strive
For the goals their heart desires,
What would it mean to be "alive?"

If children weren't pushed to reach the stars,
If their wildest dreams were shattered,
How could they tell the difference between
The unimportant and what mattered?

If days were left unnumbered
And the grasp on time unclutched,
Would memories be forgotten?
Would life not mean as much?

Reach and stretch for the stars,
You may change the days ahead.
You may hinder the future,
But you may help it instead!

Nancy Ann Lynn
I NEED YOU

I need you—
Like the springtime flower needs the sun,

I need you—
Like the sky needs stars
when day is done.

I need you—
Like the languid earth needs rain,

I need you—
To feel your warmth and
tenderness again.

I need you—
Like the ocean needs the shores,

I need you
Like the air I breathe, and more.

I need you—
Like I need no other friend,

I need you—
With an unrelenting love
that has no end.

Jacqueline Bernice Parker Smith
LINDA

This poem is dedicated to Linda, my dear, sweet sister. She has learned to follow her dreams.

Linda, Linda, you're number one
With you, one can always have fun
Laughing, joking, acting crazy
No one can ever accuse you of
being lazy
Hanging in there night and day
What more can anyone say

Linda, Linda, you're on the ball
Watch out now, and don't you fall
You've come this far with life's ups
and downs
Keep that smile and no more
frowns
The world is yours, so just start
looking
Get out of that kitchen and no
more cooking

Linda, Linda you're on the move
Look out world, she's found her
groove
Round and round and round she'll
go
And where she'll stop, no one
knows

So here's to you and all you do
You've earned it all through and
through
You deserve the very, very best
Good luck, God bless, and all the
rest

Dr Adlai Albert Esteb
THE ETERNAL SABBATH
The seventh-day is the Sabbath of
God,
Creator of all on this earthen sod!
God made it beautiful—he ought
to know!
It is such a pleasure to watch
things grow!
God made no mistakes and he
never will—
The seventh day is the true
Sabbath still!!!
It always was and it always will be!
It is God's sabbath for eternity!
(Please read Isaiah 66.22,23 for
confirmation)

When God made earth he had a
wondrous plan—
A "Memorial"—which he had
made for man!!!
God said "Remember"! Look how
man "Forgot!"
Simply "Forgot" what God's great
power had wrought!
Satan must have thought he was
smart and cute,
To set up some other substitute!
He led Mohamet to set up Friday!
And led the Pope to set up Sunday!

As Christ the Sabbath's Lord was
crucified
So hangs his day—a thief on either
side!
On which of these three days do
you worship, friend?
On God's memorial you can
depend!
The only "True" Sabbath you can
defend!
But what do we find is the worldly
trend?
In heaven what a pleasure it will be
To keep God's Sabbath for
eternity!!!

Norma Foster
TEARDROPS
When all has failed
And the teardrops don't come
Your muscles grow tense
And your body goes numb

You feel the sweat
Upon your brow
And your pounding heart
Keeps beating somehow

When you've done your best
And the teardrops don't come
Hurt fills your chest
With a tightness so strong

When all you've done
Doesn't work anymore
And praying just doesn't
Help like before

All that is left
Is the teardrops you've cried
In a pool of dust
Long since dried

You just take a deep breath
And blow out slow
You'll find that dust
Will help things grow

Hope L Drury
THE NIGHT IS DARKER
For an hour I watched the sky.
My eyes moved from tree to sky,
tree to sky.
The day was quiet, the air still;
The sky did not move.

The clouds seemed so thick, I
thought
That the sun had gone away.
Ah, bitter November!
The leaves scurry, loosened in the
chill.

I stared out at the sky and shivered
With thoughts of winter and of
too-swift spring
Until he slipped his arms around
me
And warmed my neck with his kiss.

"It's been a dark day," I said,
Warming to his touch.
"Yes," he replied, and then paused.
"But the night is darker still."

Harland J St George Jr
DREAMS
Hair of sunlight
Eyes that twinkle
A smile so sweet
That I just tingle

The voice of an angel
With a body to match
You're very beautiful
And one hell of a catch

I know you've been hurt
By one that you've loved
But life has its share of happiness
Just ask the guy above

So if you give me a chance
And open your heart to me
I'll try my best to show you
That my love is as deep as the sea

I dream of being with you
And kissing your lips with mine
Of holding you and loving you
And receiving the same in kind

So put me out of my misery
And make my dreams come true
For I've been trying to tell you
That I'm in love with you

Rose H Lutes
INDIAN SPIRIT
Red man stringing beads
Thinking of the life he leads
Out there on that barren land
As dry and parched as his dry hands
He strings beads for the tourist
trade
Wishing that he had some shade
Dreaming of a life that's gone
With the wind and far beyond
And as he sits he hears the eagle cry
Don't let your Indian Spirit die

Indian spirit born to be free
Born to the land of this country
Born with each new babies cry
Don't let your Indian Spirit die

Indian maiden weaving corn
Looking every bit forlorn
Weaving patterns from days of old
Escaping in the stories told
She accepts the toil and strife
And seeks meaning to her life
Her hands as dry as the husks she
weaves
Her spirit's proud and so she
grieves
And as she sits she hears the eagle
cry
Don't let your Indian Spirit die

Theodore L Morris Sr
A GRANDDAUGHTER IS SOMEONE
A Grandaughter is someone
You can cuddle and love;
A Grandaughter is someone
That must have been sent down
from above.

A Grandaughter is someone
Whose laughter is so sweet;
And you'll sit up and take notice
When you hear the patter of her
little feet.

A Grandaughter is someone
You can sit on your knee;
You can give her a big hug
And hear her laughter with glee.

Yes, a Grandaughter is someone
You can pamper and spoil;
And yes, my young ladies
Grandpa loves you all.

Jeanie Lynn Williams
REMEMBER
Remember when you sat alone
with no one there to care?
Remember when you called me
and I said I'd soon be there?
Remember how I held you all
through the day and night?
Remember how I said it would
soon be alright?
Remember our first kiss and when
we first held hands?
Remember when we bought our
first wedding bands?
Remember that I love you and that
I'll always be there.
Remember, please remember that
I'm the only one who cared.

Regina Murphy
CAN'T PEOPLE UNDERSTAND (OR DO THEY JUST NOT CARE)

To God, who gave me the ability, my "Little Twin," the critic, my Mother, my own counselor, and my Father, my own personal admiration society.

Why God, is it always me and never
nobody else?
Is it because I am cruel
Or is it because I am drawed up in
self?

CAN'T PEOPLE UNDERSTAND
OR DO THEY JUST NOT CARE?

Why do I always get into trouble?
Why does everybody think I am to
blame?
Oh God, don't they know I'm me
and I'll always be the same?

CAN'T PEOPLE UNDERSTAND
OR DO THEY JUST NOT CARE?

Oh God when I try to be right,
Everyone thinks I'm wrong.
Should I tell them to listen?
Or should I suffer along?

OH GOD, CAN'T PEOPLE
UNDERSTAND OR DO THEY
JUST NOT CARE?

When I want to cry it out,
Something happens and I lose
hope,
Oh God, sometimes I just can't
cope

CAN'T PEOPLE UNDERSTAND
OR DO THEY JUST NOT CARE?

Oh God, teach me to be loving,
Teach me to be kind,
And when people around me "tune
me out"
Oh God, help me keep a peaceable
mind.

Lola Douty Steele
ARISE

Glory to God for His presence and mercy in the life of Brittani Diane Douty, January 23, 1986—March 8, 1986.

Arise, my soul
At dawn; the new day
My father has made
Me whole.
Arise, my soul
My savior to meet;
The Lord Jesus, sweet
Has taken me home.
Arise, my soul
A grand new world to see
The butterflies to play with me.
My spirit does not roam.
Arise, my soul

This precious day
And trust the one who shows the way,
His light shines soft yet bold.
Arise, my soul
To learn above
How great the heavenly father's love
Taught to us by his son.
Arise, my soul
Free to be
All
My God intends me to be.

Robert Gainey
YOU GOT TO KNOW

I would like to dedicate this poem to Ms. Sally Gainey, Ms. Marion Coleman, and Ms. Rene Cousin.

Little girl grown to be
so fine and pretty.
Used to cry "hold me,"
whenever you missed me.
Now you're going to leave;
And like every daddy,
I won't let you see me cry.

Little girl . . . got your eyes
out for a husband?
Time on the clock says . . .
"don't pretend;
Don't ever think it's too late."
Call me when you can;
'Cause I used to hold;
I used to squeeze;
Now you're stepping out,
for someone nice to please.

I want you to know,
It's not easy letting go;
a flower girl;
Your father watched grow.
Yes . . . I watched grow.

Ashlee Yolonda Dixon
PROMISES ARE MADE TO BE BROKEN

The life I lead is now a lonely one.
There has been no one since you, and
There is a strong feeling that there will never be another.
You had no choice, or did you?
Did you leave on your own?
Or did someone beckon you,
someone stronger than I?
Nothing is perfect.
Nothing is forever.
There were no promises.
Promises are words of mouth,
Always spoken but never kept.
I thought our relationship was beyond the flaw of promises.
There were never words to be broken.
There were never words to be kept.
I thought ours was a perfect friendship.
I thought ours was a forever friendship.
Now I know these things were never possible.
The thoughts were all part of a never ending dream.
Were we part of that dream too?
Are our lives part of that dream,
The dream of promises?
Like promises our lives are never kept.
Life is always taken away.
Were there promises,
Promises made in the dark?

Edna E Langley
UNTITLED

To James Webber Who taught me how to love and be loved

With you I flew on crystal wings above the trees and I knew no bounds
We soared above the mountain tops so high above the ground.

The world below just seemed so small that for a breath—it did not exist at all

Only you and I against the sky
And each cloud was our bed to make love upon—until the dawn

Then watch the pink sunrise dance across the sky
But then reality sets in
The crystal wings become paper thin only to be shattered in the wind

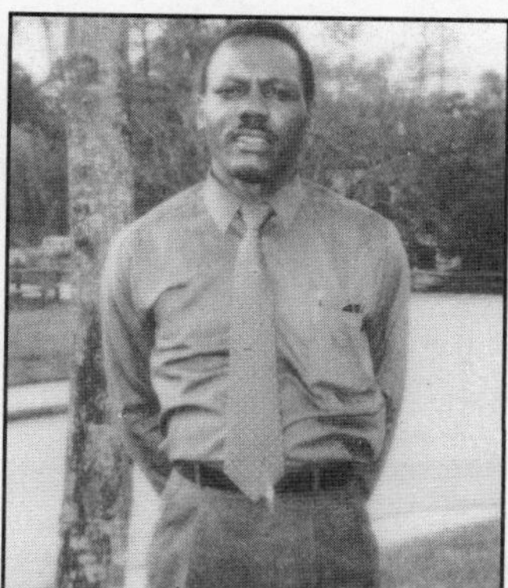

Fleter H White

Fleter H White
PLAY IT BY THE RULES

This poem is dedicated to my family, wife, and friends for their patience, kindness, and faith. And, most of all for believing in my abilities.

Play it by the rules and success will come. For rules are the governing force that makes this country run.
Strict, firm, and sometimes seen as unfair, for if there weren't rules no one would care. Our environmental situation would really be in a mess, causing our society an awful lot of stress.
Now, rules really aren't that bad as some people say. For we are the protected ones each and everyday.
So play it by the rules and keep the trouble down. Making life better for all of us around.

Alberta L Prescott
ELEGY FOR A DEAD SON

Death cannot separate as
The invisible cord that
so connected us.

In the eons of time
That shall pass, and, so
The fact of our existences
Will be as if they had not
Happened
In the recesses of eternal
Ether
This cord of love I
Have for you
Will never die

Marie Hill Foster
MRS NAG

Much thanks to Shelby, my husband. Very inspirational

Get your feet off my coffee table
Get up and fix that T.V. cable

Here it is raining and storming
And you come stepping in at 3:00 in the morning

You never say sugar, baby or honey
You always saying you got no money

I'm always massaging and creaming my face
But you never take me any place

Pick your clothes up off the floor
Empty the garbage, shut the back door
You brought the car home with very little gas
I'll drive my self, you drive too fast
Honey, I Love you, you know I do
Tell me, what would I do without you

Cassie Hindman
TO MOM

When I was a baby,
I cried when I was hungry.
You knew how to quiet me.
When I was three,
I cried when I skinned my knee.
You knew how to ease my pain.
When I was five,
I cried when I started school.
You knew I was scared.
When I was eight,
I cried when Mrs. Fry died.
You knew how to comfort me.
When I was twelve,
I cried when my best friend moved.
You knew how to cheer me up.
When I was eighteen,
I cried when I left for college.
You knew I was nervous.
When I was twenty-three,
I cried when I got married.
You knew I was happy.
When I was twenty-five,
I cried because I'd never told you
"I love you."
I took it for granted you knew.

Mary E Richardson
AUDIBLE AUTUMN

See all that shows us autumn is here:
Sunshine that sparkles like wine in the air;
Sky never so blue, and no, never so bright;
Clouds floating high like puffs of snow, white!
Trees topped with colors all yellow and red;
Fields and roadsides with rusty brown spread.

But hear autumn also, sounds muted but clear,
Like no other heard all the rest of the year;
The honking of geese from their V in the sky;
Blackbirds shrieking, "It's now time to fly."

The brisk rustling whisper of new-fallen leaves
Swept like dry rain on a sharp gusting breeze.
Streams hum a promise as they run toward the sea:
"We'll sing in spring when the ice melts us free."
So many, so varied, are the sounds autumn brings—
Some are glad, some sad, but each of them sings.

Brian Anthony Cortigiani
HANG IT ALL ON LOVE

To my wife, Ellen Kathryn, our son, Asiel-John and in praise of the Lord Jesus.

Here in my lifetime
I shall love you
With a whole soul
In word and all I do
For it's only love expressed
That'll open for the way
For receiving more love
Adding strength unto your day
Dream on just a little
As dreams are just a part
But, faith it is for freedom
Giving hope within your heart
So you see
My love for you
Is as deep as my soul
Strong as my strength
Loving you shall make me whole
And hopeful in my heart
Widening my mind
To see through eyes of light
To see and not be blind
To Heaven here at hand
Is love from me and you
So hang it all on love
Love's all we need to do, let it through.

Pauline C Bernot
A BOOK AND A FADED ROSE

As I open the lid of the old wooden trunk I'm surprised at what I see,
Diamonds, jade, rubies, pearls, and all kind of jewelry.
As I rummage some more I kneel to the floor to take a better look,
I find some clothes, a faded rose, and under this a book.
As I open the book and start to read I simply can't put it down,
I read about the man who wrote stories about his home town.
He told of the kind of life he lived, of his mother and his dad,
He told about his own young life when he was just a lad.
He told of being a pirate who kept very bad company,
How he joined Captain Hook and wrote this book while plundering on the high sea.
On and on and on he wrote how he and his friends stole Queen Mary's boat,
How on the ocean many miles at sea he became influenced by bad company.
They would eat and drink and play and plan and talk of fighting duels,
He also wrote, when they stole the boat they stole Queen Mary's jewels.
I found it exciting to find such proof of a lifetime of history,
That I actually found right under my roof in the book about piracy.

John A Orichosky
THE GIRAFFE
A yellow and black polka-dotted giraffe,
He must be as tall as a tree-and-a-half,
And his tongue is so long that it makes a man laugh.

How awkward, you'd think, to be one of these,
He bows for a drink without bending his knees,
Imagine the sight should the animal sneeze!

His head's so high-up that he can't see his toes—
Not many would envy the giraffe, I suppose
He pays little attention to any of those.

Few critters can see what this critter sees,
Stretching his neck as he's sniffing the breeze—
And it all comes in handy for nibbling on trees.

Kathryn A Marnik
YOUR LOVE FOR ME
Your love for me
Was at one time strong.
But as time went by
Something went wrong.
You found another
Who took my place.
Now it is I
Who the pain must face.
I hope someday
I will find in my heart.
A way to forgive you
Though we are now apart.
Perhaps at a later time
We will once again meet.
And our love for each other
Will again be deep.
So until then
Please remember me.
Even though together
We may not be.
I will always remember
And love you in my heart.
No matter how long
We are kept apart.

Anthony DeTeso
LOST LOVE
I met a lovely young lady
Sometime ago
But the love that I had
I just could not show
Her name was Alexandra
But everyone called her Moon
We were just friends at the start
Which would change very soon
She had a face I adored
Which would sparkle and glow
And fair skin that I swear
It was heaven I know
She filled my life full
Of happiness and joy
My lovely little princess
I did so enjoy
Now the time has gone by
And so have we
I would do anything
Just to have her with me

Ramona C Havey
TIME MARCHES ON!
Time slips furtively by
With never a moment to waste
When told by modern clocks
So streamlined, electric, and chaste
But an old-fashioned clock
Will pause, then speak with tick and chime
To warn forgetful man
And tell of the passing of time.

Cecil Sherman
A TRIBUTE TO: "THE IMMORTAL SEVEN" JAN. 28TH 1986 11:39 A. M.
Many people forget what they see and what has been said.
Many forget their friends and have disrespect for the dead.
Perhaps they think that's the way life should be,
But I'll bet my dollar against your penny
That of the millions that watched, there won't be any
That will ever forget seeing our astronauts blown into the sea.
There were seven beautiful people, I guess all volunteers,
Going on a special mission, leaving behind loved ones, worldly fears.
Going out into space to make things better for all good and bad.
But this terrible thing happened and we just don't know why.
They were in the prime of their lives, all so very young to die,
There are many so-called bad people in our world today
And they would destroy us all if they had their say.
But at a time like this nobody seems to be bad.
Everybody is so helpful, understanding and very friendly.
It could be like this everyday, instead of all the hate and envy.
So why do we wait until something comes along so sad?
Seeing so many strangers all feeling about the same,
Trying to console one another, which is the name of the game.
It is really something that is so wonderful to see.
Everyone is an equal with personal tragedies to share,
Helping one another with this terrible burden that they have to bear.
But tell me, isn't this the way life was meant to be?

Lynn Earl
PRECIOUS

To: Leonard and Adaline Dontay

The LORD said, "AMAZING GRACE."
I'll set for you lifes GOLDEN PACE,
I sent you my only SON,
So you'll know MY WORLD is ONE.

Merle Jackson Moody
A STORM
A ragged and grey old man appeared on the horizon,
exploded into closer proximity, and swelled into the tree branches, showering small burrs of ice like
metal shavings
broken glass
or
crushed gravel.
I watched them whirl downward . . . independently dangerous
like spilled razor blades.
They flash smiles of reflected light at me as I huddled under a conveniently protruding roof's edge,
"Nobody ever died in a hail-storm before," I tell myself and then blanch at the thought of hail-stones like pool-balls breaking car
windows, one time in Cheyenne!
"What the Hell." I inform a coal colored alley-cat sharing my refuge
He nods and tongue cleans his shaggy foreleg.
I'm gone into the storm when he looks up,
he is never really sure I was there,
not that he ever really cared.

Mark A Denny
IN MEMORY
In memory of our Savior, Jesus
Who was God's only son, He gave to us
To rid the sins of people all round,
The way He healed made people astound.
The men heartlessly nailed Him down,
But he stayed on the cross, neither smile nor frown.
They yell and say, "If He is the Christ come down off the cross"
For if He was the Christ it would be a terrible loss.
He hang there, thorns piercing His head,
And before long, Jesus was dead.
But before this had taken place,
With pain and agony in His face,
He said unto God, but directed to me and you,
"Forgive them, Father, for they know not what they do."
The sky darkened as Jesus died,
While his Mother, Mary, watched and cried.

When He was dead they placed him in a cave,
But for only three days it was His grave.
Mary Magdalene and Mary the Mother of James
Went to the grave to put spices on his remains.
The stone by the tomb was rolled away,
And Jesus was gone from where He lay.
"Do not be amazed" an angel said,
"For Christ the Lord has risen from the dead."

Dixie Star Davis
THE QUIET MAN

Dedicated to Brenda Fralish—
Because of you, I have received this special honor.

This quiet man I often see on TV—
He's a country singer, you see.
He moves with pride, though quiet inside,
His hair is some long with brown eyes
That smile at you and with you.
As this simple, yet great man sings his song,
He smiles a shy, enchanting smile,
Knowing all the while he's holding you in space
With his simple shy, singing grace.
When his song is finished
He slowly backs away—a bow of his head, his shy smile,
Brown eyes sparkling like the dew,
Knowing he sang his song just for you.
Wondering why you show your love for him and his songs.
His gentle quiet ways—the beauty of his voice,
The tune of his guitar plays—just his way.
With tears in your eyes you wish he could stay and
Sing just one more song in his gentle, yet quiet way.
Should he ask me a song to sing, a western song I would say,
For he's a western man as great as those in the early days
Who settled our land in their strong, quiet ways.
And now the quiet man sings again
So quiet, yet from deep within—just for you from him.

Mary Elefterakis
MY PRECIOUS GRANDCHILD

This poem is dedicated to all my precious Grandchildren.

My precious grandchild so special and dear.
I love you so much it makes my eyes tear.

The bond that exists between you and I,
Is so special a love it can't be defined.

Excuses I find just to keep you around.
I sing and I dance and act like a clown.

The child that I raised, now a parent too,
Appears once again when I look at you.

The cute things you do that I so much adore,
Were the things I scolded your father for.

The toys that I buy are really for me.
They bring back the child that I used to be.

Those eyes so loving, so innocent and pure,
Erase the problems my doctor can't cure.

You're the topping on my sundae, the icing on my cake.
You're the sugar in my coffee and sunshine you create.

My precious grandchild there's a heaven on earth.
It began for me on the day of your birth.

Beryl L Johnson
GRANDPAS AND GRANDMAS
Grandpa and Grandma have come for a visit,
And oh we are very happy to see them!
It feels just right to be folded in their
Loving arms and squeezed tight, and kissed—
Makes you know you belong,

And your folks love and care.

Oh—Grandpa is taking something out
Of his pocket! A new kind of "fly"
And live bait, too! Bet we head by Hanks
To the ole fishing hole, come morning.
We can sit and talk—man to man—
Real confidential, out by the stream.

Now Grandma is not to be outdone.
Goodies in her basket smell yummy—
Mince and sweet potatoe pie and
Ginger cookies only she can make.
Hard to know which way to go;
But Grandma will save us some, I know.

Grammies and Grandpa are so precious
To us—more than silver and gold.
Say, Sis, we must remember
To tell them—with love!

Cardell Trimble

O LOST SOUL

To my loving family, The Trimbles

O lost soul the Master is coming today.
In your lake of fire put your sinking ship at bay.
O lost soul the Master is coming today.
In your river of sins put your sinking ship at bay.
O lost soul the Master is coming today.
In your sea of darkness put your sinking ship at bay.
O lost soul the Master is coming today.
With your stream of righteousness, in his ocean of love.
Grace will save your soul today.

Anita Axford Burkhardt

ANTICIPATION

Christmas is coming again to the hill
Where I grew up as a kid!
The winds have blown in the snow and the chill
And the green of the grass has been hid.
The ice and the cold are a sign to remind
The hearts of the old and the young
That we must arrange our gifts for exchange
And the star must be polished and hung.
The full moon hangs low as it bids us to go
A sliding for fun to the pond:
When the ground freezes hard our sleds leave the yard
And we fly like an eagle beyond!
Soon grandmama says it's time to retire
But we sit a bit first to get warm by the fire.
"To bed!" she then says ere the moon is up high,
So we go with a groan and a visible sigh.
When in bed should we rest or imagine the best
That our enchanted fantasies muster?
We cannot resist to look out and insist
That the snow has a magical luster!
The clock down the stairs ticks away and our prayers
Rise up as our eyelids remember:
The sooner we sleep the sooner we'll keep
That Eve we await in December!

Jeanne E Grillo

LOVE IS —

Love is wonderful, love is real
And it shows in the way we feel
The way a couple looks at each other
Or the way a child looks up to his mother
Like the feeling I get when I know someone cares
Suddenly I'm not alone, and there will be no more fears
Love can be happy or it can make me cry
It can get me so mixed up that I'm wondering why
A smile, a gesture, or a gentle touch
It's the little things that mean so much
With love my problems are easier to face
And the world seems to be a better place
We all need love and it's sad to say
That some are afraid to express love in any way
For love is the greatest gift that we can give
And without it, there would be no need to live

Janice E Rowell

MIRACLE OF BIRTH

A child is like a flower
from a seed well sewn.
In a wall of protection
soon to be released, to be grown.
As it is nourished and continues to grow, it's the most precious thing ever to be sewn.
When in full bloom, with expectations beyond our
wildest dreams. The child fits nicely in our life of schemes.
As if in a high tower above,
God has given us the power
To bring forth this wonderful gift of love.

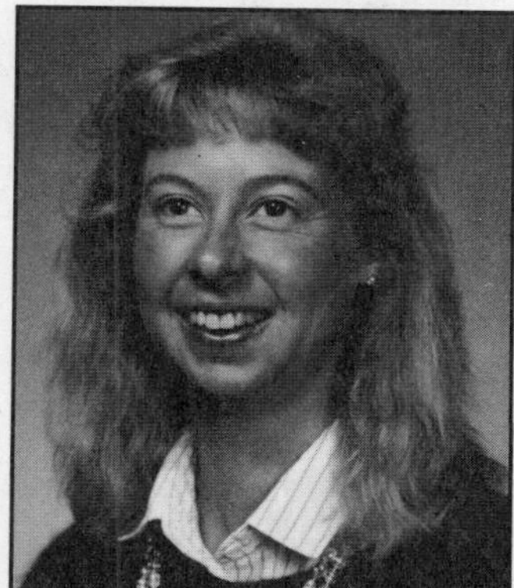

Carol Jean DeWitt

Carol Jean DeWitt

CALL TO PASSION

Dedicated to Neil Patrick McDevitt

Shake us, senses, knock us hard.
Go, defenses! Lift, guard!
Shock us, pleasure, drain our dregs.
Burn, treasure between our legs.

Enrapture us, lust, tempt us, daring.
Pull us up, trust, hold us, caring.
Wake us, passion; joy, run deep.
In your fashion, love, keep.

dot dear

AS I WATCH A SEAGULL

This poem is dedicated to my Mother

As I watch a seagull . . . his wings tip side to side
There's suddenly a peacefulness around me . . . as I see him glide
And I wish that I could be . . .
Another gull beside him gracefully flying over the sea
As I watch a seagull . . . I sit upon the sand
Trying not to frighten him, as I call out gently to see if he would land

His feathers are so pretty . . . gray, black and white
I yearn to be as free as he . . . as he makes his flight
As I watch a seagull . . . his call beckons out to me . . .
In hopes that I will feed him on the shore close to the sea
Soon he'll ask his friends to fly
This is a real beauty to see seagulls that paint the sky
Yes, as I watch a seagull . . . it brings teardrops to my eyes . . .
Because he's joined his friends and with a swish of their wings . . .
They say their quick goodbyes.

Ms Tonya A Jackson

WHEN YOU LEFT ME

So you left me all alone
And that made me sad
But knowing you are peaceful
Makes me very glad!

When I found you had gone ahead
All my insides were torn
And I felt so guilty and hurt
But I could do nothing but mourn!

The first night was the worst
All I could do was stay awake
Half-knowing it was true
And half-hoping it was fake!

Now it's beginning to really soak in
That you're really gone
Although I'm sad, I'm also happy
Because you've gone to your natural home!

I want you to know that
My love for you will surely never die
My feelings are so true
You know I wouldn't lie!

If I could have seen you
For one last time
It probably could have saved me
A lot of endless crying!

You know I'll never forget you
That I could never do
For as long as I ever live
I'll forever Love You!!

Marlene D West

INSPIRATIONS

As I see the bare trees
I can feel the cold on my bare knees.

I see leaves falling, and children drawing.

I can hear ballerina's dancing and composers composing.

I can hear the wind blowing, as an urgent warning.

That fall is arriving, and things start flying!

I can see the colors changing and see Artist painting.

For they know now, it is the time for great
Inspirations!

Sandra R Robertson

DAD

You see, my friend, I never knew my dad.
I never knew of all the joy others had.
I always wonder if we look alike, maybe we do.
Do you think he sits and wonders the same thing too?
I tried to hate him because he left me.
But I can't. For hate wasn't meant to be.
I sit alone and dream of seeing him someday
And pray to God for the right words to say.
I've seen pictures of the fun we've shared
And can't help believing he must have cared.
I've tried to hide that emptiness in my heart
But can't for it's the largest part.
Mom used to tell me of the few good years
But won't anymore for it only brings tears.
I was only three when he went away
And I won't ask the reason he wouldn't stay.
You see, he gave me something precious, my name.
And I want to give him something precious just the same.
I see fathers and their children walking hand-in-hand
And I wonder if he has started another life in another land.
So I try to brush away thoughts of that kind,
Because it makes me think he doesn't want what he left behind.
And if someday I've found that he has died.
My love and warmth for him I'll never hide.

William H Terry Jr
OUR SEVEN ASTRONAUTS

Dedicated to seven brave Americans: commander Francis "Dick" Scobee, pilot Michael Smith, mission specialists Ellison Onizuka, Judith Resnik and Ronald McNair, teacher Sharon Christa McAuliffe & engineer Gregory Jarvis

They died as bravely as they lived
Seven astronauts in flight
Seeking the heavens over earth
Where day never turns to night.

They died as bravely as they lived
Their dreams held tightly in their heart
There was so much of them to give
By sharing with us, We felt a part.

They died as bravely as they lived
A legacy to those they left behind
To quest for knowledge, to be of courage
And together work for all mankind.

Their flight took them further than the stars
Further than they, planned to go
To places that we're yet to see
To places that we're yet to know.

There were calloused, hearts that shed no blood
As they lost their lives that day
Pleasure's pursuit was more important to them
Than to these heroes homage pay.

We could build a statue, or name a city
Nothing for them would be too great
They died as bravely as they lived
What more can we ask of human fate?

Angie Monson
FOREVER YOURS

There once was a day
when you would always look my way.
But those days are gone
it's been so long,
Since the day when you were mine
it was a love that took so long to find.
You were always there
but I didn't know you cared.
'Til that day long ago
when your feelings about me—you showed.
You said you liked me alot
and that we would never part.
I had the same feelings for you
but there was something I couldn't do.
I couldn't keep you by my side
even though I've tried and tried.
There's one thing you don't understand,
my mom has lent a helping hand.
She says that you are much too old
and I have to do what I am told.
I hope you know that I still care
sometimes I almost want to risk the dare
Of holding you real close to me,
but I know I wouldn't be able to set you free
So I'm leaving feelings for you untold
Except for this poem that my feelings
for you will always hold.
I hope you have a happy life
I only wish I could be your wife
I know we'll always be together
in my heart now and forever!

Emma B Blake
TRAGEDY—ASTRONAUTS GOOD-BYE

Here on Earth, as we stood by,
Patiently awaiting another spaceship's try,
Leaving the launchpad; our first teacher in space,
Along with six astronauts of different race.
As they left for an experiment in the sky,
A tragedy happened just ten miles high.
An explosion of great glare burst in the air,
Sending bits and pieces everywhere.
We, as Americans, loved ones and friends,
Stunned as we watched, prayed, cried to the end.
A great sorrow spread over the earth, near and afar
As we shared in emotion and tears ajar.
Seven dear friends gave of their life,
Leaving their families and a nation in strife.
Only God knows the reason the tragedy took place,
Maybe his need for their help in space.
We all sit and wonder why it happened and at this time,
Could it be an awakening to help combat crime?
We, as a nation, weep in sorrow,
But still hold on to dreams of Tomorrow
As we strive to finish the task of the seven,
We hope to meet them someday in Heaven.
We bid them goodby and grieve for their dying
But will continue always to praise them for trying.
God Bless America

Patricia L Jackson
WISHFUL THINKING

For Stephen, without whom there would be no memories of the past or dreams of the future. You are a part of me and I am a part of you; nothing will ever change that.

You say you are a dreamer, well I'm a dreamer, too,
Living in my fantasies when I'm not with you.
I see us doing lots of things I know we'll never do,
And going to far-off places I could never go with you.
Sometimes I think how it might have been if I'd met you years ago
Before you were tied to someone else; it would have been good, I know.
If we'd had children, they'd be beautiful (what else could they be?)
For they'd be a combination of the best of you and me.
I also dream of the future and what it holds in store;
Will I see even less of you, or will I see you more?
In my dreams and fantasies, you are always there,
Anytime I need you, anyplace, anywhere.
All I need do is close my eyes and suddenly you appear;
Sometimes it's hard to believe that you're not really here,
So I understand your dreams of us that don't always come true;
It's called "wishful thinking," and I do it, too.
But sometimes dreams do come true, and some of ours will, too,
But for all the ones that don't, we still have me and you,
And all the beautiful memories that we can keep reliving,
And all the love inside us that we can keep on giving.
Let's hang on to our dreams and not give up, and hope someday, somehow,
That all of the things we dream about will be happening here and now;
But if we're not that fortunate, and Fate has another plan,
I'll always be your woman and you'll always be my man.

Donald C Rubino Jr
THE RIGHT ROAD HOME

This poem is dedicated to Joseph A. Rubino, A Loving Grandfather.

Walking down the road alone
With all that you have as your own
In a little sack
Strapped on your back
Heading to what you call home.
Stopping at every bar
To sing and play guitar.
To earn your keep
And a place to sleep
For home is yet very far.
How far do you have to go
Until you finally know
Where your home is at
Where you hang your hat
Whenever the sun gets low.
Is this the life you chose so great
In a world you did create
Since it has begun
All you did was run
So what will be your fate.
As you continue to wonder and roam
With nothing really to call your own
You won't have a friend
But the sorrows can end
If you follow the road back home.

Christina Marie Holston
ONLY THE BEAT OF MY HEART

Dedicated to Matthew B. Roberts.

My mind is blank,
Nothing comes into it.
Not a thought
Of my imagination flows.
Only the beat of my heart.

I am not here,
I'm on a distant shore,
Or in the clouds up above.
Nothing can be heard,
Only the beat of my heart.

You are a friend,
And in my times of need
You were always there for me.
Through my eyes
You see nothing.
What is there you ask?
Only the beat of my heart.

Martha M Molina
BABY

For my daughter, Sunshine who inspired me to write this poem. To my baby son Dylan, another gift of love. To my husband Leonard who's so loving to us—Thanks—

Our beautiful miracle from above the heavens will arrive to this earth in the month of—.
Our precious gift of love and joy will be a blessing to us all. As I sit and write this I feel the life born within me move.
Love and joy fill my heart.
Thank you o'mighty God for the most gift of gifts one can receive in this humble earth during one's life. For this precious bundle of joy you have gifted us with, we thank-you from our loved
filled hearts.
For we know that words themselves cannot explain the happiness & joy we feel all over . . . made possible because of you . . .
Love-u-Lord
Your blessed
Children

Florence Edith Williams
TAPESTRY

To my Lovely Mother who made all the "Beautiful Pictures"

There are special mem'ries
Which we see in the picture of life.
That are so dear, we hold them in reverence.
Mem'ries that grow more precious with time,
And seem woven into a tapestry,
For future keeping.

With age, they become more beautiful,
More precious, even tho' they are—
But pictures of the past.
Some pictures, we can separate, easily,
From the rest of the tapestry—
The older they become.

There are those smudged by tears,
Others are filled with sunshine—

Happy ones, sad ones,
But all treasured,
Because they make up
The Tapestry of our Lives.

Debra E Jones
A VIRTUOUS WOMAN

Virtuous women, that's what God called us to be
Our price is far above Rubies so says He
Loving and caring is part of our deeds
Administering to our families needs
Molding, gently shaping our children's personality
So they can live long upon the earth to fulfill their destiny

Early we arise to set the pace for the day
Making sure we weed out anything, That would set our house array
We first praise God, giving Him the glory
His continuous blessing makes us a success story.
We delight in our families healthy condition
For God has given us wisdom for proper nutrition,
God gave us a part in our husbands' success
When they think of us they consider themselves blessed.
Since God has made us a new and virtuous creation,
We can't help but be a sensation.

Marti (Martha) Silcox
TO FRIENDSHIP (TO POOH)

To my Grandmother, Lyda Mutter, who always believed my work good; and always said I could succeed, if I tried.

There are four seasons for us to live thru,
Spring—with her colors so rare and new;
While summer has her flowing gown.
Autumn, when the leaves begin coming down,
Winter's cold winds, bring the snow;
But these are all things we know.

There are people who we hold dear,
And with those we would like to be near;
But Mother Nature, we can not tame.
So we must bear, and play her game,
Let snow and ice have their day;
For tis never all that long they stay.

Enjoy their beauty, and take delight,
In knowing that one warm night;
They'll disappear for a year once more.
Then you'll hear the knock upon your door,
Announcing there is someone come to see;
If the chair still waits for me!

Patricia Calhoun
MAYTIME

For my children, Cathleen and Terence, For Believing

Trees dripped
With spangles of gold,
That chased the cold,
Of winter away.
The mockingbird
Warbled a roundalay,
When I was a child
And it was May.

The creak
Of a rusty old mill
Could be heard,
Sweet were the flowers
That bloomed in the wood,
Where a child often played
And it was May.

Silence
Where once was the sound
Of the mill,
Even the mockingbird
Has been stilled,
Naught is there
But a windswept hill,
Where a child loved to play,
Oh, where is May!

Julie Laura Cassady
MEMORIES 7-11-87

A gift of Magic,
A gift of Love,
No box can hold a gift so large,
No Christmas tinsel can be so bright,
Only the magic of memories can do it justice.
Printed on my memory in shades of pain and Joy and Love.

Stella Keliiholokai
RHAPSODY OF LOVE

Gratefully dedicated to the Holy Spirit, who helps and directs me and to my eight wonderful children Gary, Michael, Thomas, Stephen, Bill, Tami, Sherrie, and Kathleen. In loving memory of their father, the late Melvin (Mike) Keliiholokai, former Denver Parks Policeman.

Having tasted love at its peak,
I feel I know where of I speak;
But then mere words cannot express
The feeling of joy and pure happiness.

On the one hand joy, on the other pain
Not knowing when I shall see him again.
Uncertain, I'm filled with remorse and sorrow,
Then hopeful again, I wait for tomorrow.

A new day may bring his dear face into view,
My spirits are lifted, I'm happy, anew.
One look, one word, the touch of his hand
My spirits are lifted and oh, I feel grand!

But should the day come that we must part,
How does one say good-bye to one's heart?
Once again words fail to comply, I'm convinced
That its never, no never good-bye.

Elvira G Martinez
A BUSINESS MAN WAS HE

A businessman was he,
Not a quiet man was he
And not a soft spoken man was he.
Yelled all day long
Do that he would say.
Get that, go there, come here.
Look for this, take this there,
Hang this up, answer the phone,
Pick that up.
All day long he went on
And expected much from us all.
But when in need, he was there.
Can I help? He would say.
Or can I bring you anything?
Or can I fly you anywhere?
Or can I buy you anything?
So what else can be said
About this kind and good hearted man.
Jay Miller was his name.

Bernice Taylor
NO GUARANTEE ON LIFE

To my Husband Manuel, without your help I wouldn't have made it thru the tall grass.

I married a man so strong and mild
It almost drives me wild
He knows most everything
which makes me almost sing
He has patience, tenderness and love
Which are the greatest things above
He loves people and everything in life
And I'm glad I'm his wife
He taught me to relax and how to unwind
So I wouldn't go out of my mind
He taught me there's more to life than work
He said, a lot of duties you can shirk
He taught me how to have peace of mind
And how to leave your little worries behind
He taught me about fun, love and life
And I'm glad I'm his wife
There's no guarantee on life
So today again I'm glad I'm his wife

Stanley M Duchnick Jr
HE CAN SEE

He can see things with his heart
that most folks will never see.
He can see the hurt deep in your eyes
that might be missed by you or me.

He can hear the laughter of a child
as the fog rolls in from the sea.
He can see the wisdom in one's years
when only wrinkles do I see.

He makes me feel blind sometimes
because I can only see with my eyes;
But all His vision comes from his heart
and he sees beyond the lies.

The little lies we all tell ourselves
and the big ones that we tell one another.
He sees them all for what they are;
But he doesn't judge us like some others.

He can see eternity in the stars at night
and the beauty deep in our souls;
And He knows the pleasure of a peace
that makes the rest of us grow old.

Jim Cook
CHRISTINA

It was a morning's hesitation
Rambling, tripping, joyously lilting,
Rushing into a morning of exultant Being.
Mourning with stilled sadness;
She, lifting us to the rainbow's edge,
Frolicking, laughing, we
In fullness are All That Is.

From the edge of the sky
The lengthening reaches of my evening
Touches the times of her feelings,
Six years, sharing All That Is of morning;
Her laughter, her rainbows, her Being.

Her time of morning faltered, stopped;
Exultation in her fullness of Being did not!
We say her life was fully lived
Not in years, but in Being All That Is.

Touching her colors from the evening sky
There is no before, there is no after,
Before and After is not me,
We can only Be and Be and Be . . .

Darlene Kleist
THE ROSE

For I am the rose whose love surrounds you,
I am the thorns which wound your precise heart with my words and actions.
I am the rose you give in love,
For I am the rose that receives your precise love and words as gifts.
You are the enemy, the love, the friend that needs my help to help yourself out with your problems of life.
Don't deprive you or me of what we need to try to succeed, we may not succeed but we must try.
For I need you and you need me for help, security, love, we need each other,
Because I am your rose and you are mine, we are the rose which grows with love.
The rose that grows will bring us together as one to the other FOREVER.

Genevieve McAllister
DAY DREAMS

This poem is dedicated to my loving mother. Thank you I love you.

My Day Dreams are very dear and precious to me.
I would not give them up for anything.
They are there to comfort me. To ease my mind and
let me be free in my Day Dreams.
I do not suffer, I cannot cry, I have no pain,
I have nothing to hide.
I do not worry what people will think, because
no one is allowed past my guarded gate, to
where my day dreams take place.

There is where I can be anyone or be anything or
be anywhere my heart desires.
Day Dreams lets you be free to leave your daily chores.
So take a deep breath and clear your mind and take a
trip to the back of your mind where your Day Dreams have stayed
dormant all this time, and Day Dream with me and let all
your hopes, dreams, and fantasies come true.
In your Day Dreams.

George Steven Benedetti
MAN

This poem is dedicated to Angie, The Light of My Life. 7/22/86

He walks through life,
like the changing skys.
Taking the good and the bad
in their shifting tides.

His destination is well known,
through the passage of time.

To his Eternal Home,
yours and mine.

His faith, still growing
from what he believes.
All the warmth and beauty that he sees.

While the winds of his Soul keep blowing,
The sands of time.
Over the wounds of the mind.

R J "Bob" Stirling
BEYOND TOMORROW

To sit in the midst of a group of people, even be they friends, and feel all alone, as in the dark on a broad and desolate plain. With an everlasting urge to go onward, forever onward, never looking back. To find those greener pastures always over the next hill. To view for the first time, new and wonderous things. To think of beautiful experiences of the past, but never to ponder o'er them too long, for never can it be the same. "Eat, drink, and be merry, for tomorrow we may die". But do I wish to die tomorrow? Perhaps yes, for to live beyond tomorrow would be but to continue the everlasting circle. Never is there time for rest, never is there peace of mind.

Come, my friend, join me as forward again I go! I can show you—but no, you can not. For to take the past into the present and future is not possible. You must stay here with the past. A happy past, a sad past. Happy, as it were when it were present; sad, as it must be when looked back upon. Nay my friend, alone I must go. It is no right of mine to take thee with me on my path to destruction or which is destruction in itself.

Over the next hill lies the end of my journey; Home, always over the next hill, as it shall ever be for we who wander in the dark, watching, searching for the light which we think surrounds our home. But in our home there is no light, for our home lies in the distance beyond tomorrow; And tomorrow we shall die.

Frank C Halstead
BENEATH THE SILKEN WAVE

I thought that I could ride
Beneath the silken wave
and hide within a dream
the ripple I had made.

Within what I could see,
the world's eternity
was where the colors end;
but, circles closed me in.

And now that I could find
in turns of hurried time
a moments rest before
the siezing silence tore,

I thought that I could smile
only this smiling day
would never grace a ride
beneath the silken wave.

Susan K Whitcomb
SHY

A shadowy figure hidden in the stillness of the night
—Where the moon is the only light.
It does not speak
—nor does it seek
to find where it is now.
But, it knows where it has been.
Yet, afraid of being seen.

Full of despair.
—Oh, how it stares into your eyes
as though it had died.

Frightened that it would be hated.
A fear of being rejected
—and not accepted.
How it longs to come into the light.
But, the moment is never right
—so it forever hides
away from the light.

Jim Ward
PREJUDICE

The wind
Driven
Sand pelts my face.
I look, but can not see
I listen, but can not hear.
The wind stops, but I still
Do not see. The fear of the
Wind
Will not let me open my
Eyes.
Prejudice has won.
The fear is unfounded,
Yet,
It is still felt in
My mind.

Bernadine Aziz
NIMBUS

Like a tempest wind you blow in—
your presence leaves me shaking.
The air is full of your dazzling aura.
I can't even breathe.
Then you leave as ambivalent as you came,
unaware that your luminence lingers
like a fine cologne.

Jerry F Ogden
THE FLOAT DOWN THE STREAM

The water was a vast landscape of life,
Its depths unexplored.
As we sail on to the end,
The ship starts to rock.
But what we thought was a whirlpool
Was only my mom pulling the plug.

Kathleen V Beshears
TIME

As the sun shines through my window
Late in the afternoon of this winter day —
I notice the quiet beauty of the snow
As it sparkles in the sun.

It is a quiet time, a peaceful time,
A time for letting your thoughts roam —
A time to rest, a time to search your soul,
A time to understand

That the bright blue sky above
And the snow covered earth below is —
Our cradle, our haven, a gift
From God, our Creator, who loves us so!

Lois R Greene
THE WINTER HEART

This, too, shall pass
And all things be the same
As once they were?
No, not the same—
For, though the sun keeps its
Accustomed path,
The seasons come and go,
June follows May—
Within my heart
The winter's chill remains
Since you, who were my spring
Have gone away.

Moira Francis
SOMETHING IN THE NIGHT

Dark damp moldy air smothering me
Pulling me down into its eerie depths
Driving me back into the farthest corners
Of my consciousness, with no thought of tomorrow
Passing through time and space, whirling,
Turning, spinning around in my own mind
Until at last the whirlpool comes to and end
And I find I have arrived at another age.
I am a child, lost in the warmth of a bed.
Nestled into sheets of flanelette and blankets of wool
Unable to sleep, tossing and turning in the dark.
Listening with ears that seem too large.
Hearing every creak and breath in the house.
The beating of a tree that does not exist
As it slaps its branches against a window.
The sound of footsteps on the stairs which
Never reach the top, never showing its head.
The terror! The dread of those footsteps
Never once did they ever reach the top.
Never once when I was a child, did I see it.
But the smell! The awful odor of dead flowers
wet earth, musky, repulsive to the nose.
I must think no more of such things
I lay awake all night listening to the tree.
That does not exist as it bangs against my window.

Caryle Hill
MRS. SMITH

To Dad . . . In Loving Memory

The stone grey face on the old folks home,
Loomed behind the gate,
And on the swing on the old front porch
Mrs. Smith would often wait.
Her white hair shone in the afternoon sun,
Like a halo shining there,
And on my way from school each day
I'd stop and chat with her.

Through age she'd gained a treasure trove
Of wisdom, pure as gold,
And she became my closest friend,
And I never thought her old.
I asked her once, why every day,
She sat there all alone,
She gently placed her hand on mine
And replied in quiet tone.

I do not sit here alone, she said,
As a tear slipped down her face,
All the life that I have lived
Sits there in your place.
She knew I did not understand
The words she spoke to me,
You see my dear, when your not here,
I have my memories.

She spoke of days from long ago,
And smiled with memories fond,
Of the children she had loved and raised,
And her beloved husband John.
But many, many years ago,
Twenty will be soon,
John climbed the golden stairs to God
And waits for me at Home.

Now I am growing old, she said,
And one day when you pass by,
I won't be in my usual place
But for me, my dear, don't cry.
For I have lived a wondrous life
And have found a friend in you,
And in days of tears and laughter
You have helped to see me through.

I placed a kiss upon her cheek,
And that night while I was gone,
Mrs. Smith went Home with God
And to her husband John.
Now each day on the front porch swing,
Another takes the space,
But Mrs. Smith has left her memory,
For me, still in her place.

Edith L Pendergrass

OUR GRANDCHILDREN

Dedicated in memory of Gary Dean Perkins who was killed in an accident April 29, 1972

There is a saying, "When you can't sleep,
Just count your blessings instead of sheep."
So when I start to count mine,
I always include our grandchildren nine
Or there were till that fatal day,
When our darling Gary was taken away
From us so suddenly we can't understand
Why it had to happen, he was just a young man
Still grieved, though many words of comfort were spoken,
Yet we are so thankful his body was not broken.
The first grandchild is always "Special," they say
To me, they're all Special in their own sort of way.
Though their ways are all different as can be,
When they show their love it pleases me.
The little "great-grands" are counted too,
They are so precious, with their eyes of blue,
Their sweet smiles, and the "Big Talk,"
Now the little one has learned to walk.
So in this turbulent world of sin and strife,
"Grandmama's" prayer is that they lead a good life,
Learn to count their blessings, and with love
Remember all blessings come from the Father above.

Patricia Anne Swain

AFTER THE RAIN

After the rain,
When the skies are clear.
Can I come around?
Can I call you dear?

After the rain,
When the clouds are gone.
Will your love be clear,
Like each new dawn?

After the rain,
When the sun comes out.
Will you love me,
And never be in doubt?

After the rain,
When the skies are blue.
Will you ask me to marry?
Will we say: "I do?"

Will these things happen,
Without any pain?
Will the skies stay clear,
After the rain?

Doris Jean Davis

Doris Jean Davis

IN SEARCH OF LOVE

Out of the night that covers me
I see a small, small flame.
There may be hope, I'm afraid to know
then, faintly, I hear my name.
If I will try but a little harder
I may grope my way free.
Of this eternal quiet and darkness
that's slowly smothering me.
Please, can you shine a little brighter?
Please help me if you care.
If you will but call my name again
I'll try to make it there.

But then the night is deathly quiet
and black as black can be.
There is no voice, the flame is gone.
The stillness covers me.
And so I wait, for still I think
the end is not in sight.
I gather my forces as I prepare
for another lonely night.
Out in the distance I faintly hear
the sounds of voices and laughter
I know I shall not be shrouded forever.
I will leave this darkness hereafter.

Carol A Wells

MY LIFE'S TREASURE'S

This poem is dedicated to my children and grandchildren who are my pride and joy

---

The beauty of laughing children
So happy and trusting in life
Loving and giving without question
An inspiration for all to view!

Hope in a dawning spring morn'
Laughter shared on a hot summer day
The peaceful feeling of a colorful fall eve
Awe in an ice-covered sunny winter day!

All the precious memories
Each new day promises more
Dear God, if I could give to you
What you have given to me!

I have a cup, I have a treasure chest
One is running over, the other is filling up
God is always near, like a softly glowing light
Life's mystery-ever so simple and true!
The pluses of life are so vast
The minuses of living so few
To laugh, love and enjoy it all
These are my life's treasures!

Trudy A Boardman

IN HONOR OF UNCLE BILL

It's too bad people never realize
just how special life is
until a loved one is taken
from them.
Life should be valued
like nothing else
because
life is, everything else.
If I could have one wish
come true before I die,
It would be for everyone to
realize how great
LIFE is
and that not a moment should be
WASTED

Robert L Schowengerdt Jr

GIRL AT NAG'S HEAD—SEPT. 23

Waves scramble over one another's backs
Still seething hot from latin lovers' bath
They anxiously anticipate climax
Of stealing lonely footprints from her path.
Impressed, the sand resists this thievery
But finds that waves are stronger than their roar;
Too soon all traces of her memory,
Like phantom crabs, will disappear from shore.
A straggly cloud is chased away on winds
That also fear the angry, staring moon
Who has his ancient rivalry to tend
With flirting stars that wink in unison.
Her sigh's so sad at Summer's passing flight
That Autumn holds its breath another night

Jeanette Shafer

THE PICTURE

Paint me a picture
Of young happy days;
Color it brightly
To pierce through the haze.

Draw in a dream girl
To sweetly entrance;
Spatter with star dust
To lend it romance.

Sketch in a castle
Where dreams are unfurled;
Cover with ivy
To shield from the world.

Brush in some angels
With gossamer wings;
Shade it all over
With heavenly things.

Mix in some storm clouds,
But don't let them stay;
Outline them harshly
Then roll them away.

Finish my picture
As pale as the dawn;
Dip your brush lightly
And color it gone.

S A Martinelli

SEASHELL

Without the voice that comes by simply
Whispering your name
Without your strings to fill my symphony
I'd only be a seashell
And if you held me to your ear
You'd hear nothing but the silence of the sea

If your touch no longer filled me
When hunger scratched my soul
If I reached for you and couldn't find your hand
I'd only be a seashell
Just a chamber with no heart
Emptied out and left stranded in the sand

And if I found no more direction
By the starlight of your eyes
And if your sunshine didn't follow through my day
I'd be a simple seashell
Turning slowly in the tide
With nobody there to help me find my way . . .

Mary Shuman

BUTTERFLIES

Like two butterflies we once were . . .
Escap't from our cocoons . . .
Free . . .

To flutter o'er the thorns . . .
and taste the sweet honey of life . . .
Free . . .

To be together or to fly away . . .
What bliss . . .
The rose-colored moments our spirits shared.

Now two butterflies we have returned . . .
To our lonely cocoons . . .
Safe . . .
Waiting . . .
To be free again . . .

Irina Bell

PEOPLE

Yesterday is a memory
And tomorrow has not yet begun.
New experiences await me
Along with the rising sun.
Life is not always sweet
But we struggle and get by.
Because in the future,
Sunshine and happiness lie.

Too often we rely on others
To help us through.
God is the captain
And we are merely his crew.
So why can't we ban together
To reach a common goal?
Instead of shielding ourselves
With an unbreakable wall.

Our existence is empty
When we don't reach out.
Why do we sit in silence
When we should all shout
I need you, friend
So let's live in peace.
Break down that wall
And let your heart's love release!

Ines Espinosa-Gartzke

PROMISES

Everywhere I roamed
Small and big places,
Alot of spaces.
Familiarity was unknown

Touching many new horizons
My knowledge grew and grew,
Until I became W I N G S . . .
And flew

Searching
Silence became my strength,
Looking at you and you,

Walking my own way
A W A Y . . .

Everywhere I roamed I met people
People I met and called friends,
And then again,
Never saw what happened to them.

Everywhere I lay my head
I cherished the moment,
Church bells danced with my heart.
Always, always there was a new . . .
Start

One day I awakened
In the early morning dawn

There was no song
No song to guide me
To wander

The seeds fell from my hand.
No more paths would they
Fall upon.
Everybody's child had gone
Gone to a place . . .
I could call home

Touching emotions
Unknown
My wings would guide me
At home, where my seeds
Turned into F L O W E R S
Representing places where I
Only found empty
S P A C E S . . .

Julie A Voss
TO SCOTT
When you tried to help, I turned away
I ignored your outstretched hand.
I could tell by the way you hid your eyes
That you did not understand.

I didn't mean to hurt you
When I quickly left your side.
I just couldn't bear to let see
The tears I could not hide

I felt somehow it made me weak
For you to see me cry
But I couldn't seem to stop myself
I didn't have the strength to try.

Without a word, you came to me
You gently drew me near
Never asking for my reasons,
You brushed away my tears.

Silently, I clung to you
Until my pain was gone
At last you made me realize
That I am not alone.

Barbara May Carrier Rose
THE CROSS AND THE ROSE
There's a royal banner given for display,
the cross marked graves of heroes,
where red red rose's lay.
Those long rows of crosses that we all can see,
we give all our prayers just for Thee.
A sacred emblem of Christian Faith,
that cross is dear to me.
A rose is a flower of loveliness meant for all to see,
a rose of beauty, a cross of gold.
A royal banner to unfold.

Diana Baxter Herring
ODE: TO MY BEST FRIEND

To Leslie—Who always believed in me Even when I didn't.

Friends come and go, I've observed o'er the years—
Lovers as fleeting as the wind.
Only once in a lifetime can you meet the right person
To become your own Best Friend.

A Best Friend is the one you can turn to
When others have cast you aside.
It's the one you should cherish as your own life
And always speak of with pride.

You think of your Best Friend when you hear a funny joke;
When you triumph, it's the first one you tell.
You know you can count on your Best Friend to lean on
And to carry you through your own pits of hell.

A Best Friend is a face you're always glad to see,
No matter what time of the day.
It's the smile that can make even sunny days brighter
And help chase any problems away.

I met my Best Friend over four years ago;
We've shared laughter and the trials of life.
I count my Best Friend to be my greatest blessing;
And I thank God that he made me his wife

Donald J Boemer
DUST TO DUST
May the fruitful gloom of night ring out in acknowledgment on my behalf:
So that I may enlighten the past tense of time, in which all the nightmares of my extension provide me with destiny:
I lay out my soul with my devoted life where it may fail under stress:
I grasp my heart before it unfolds from all the unrest of life:
For the lust that we hold in the eclipse of time, and where our feebleness of trust benefits of another:
So when this love of mine deteriorates and all is forgotten, may I live in a brief ember of grace:

Jennifer Alexander

Jennifer Alexander
WHISPERING AUTUMN

To my parents Lidia and Larry Alexander for their continuous Love and Encouragement.

Fall comes silently, slowly without any warn.
Birds hatched in Spring are now air-born.
Time for warm clothes the air has a chill.
Birds fly South, the air is still.

Last night it rained; I heard the trees rustle.

While at the same time, wind and leaves tussle.

I see some frost and beads of rain
They strut across my window pane.

Outside right now the weather is cold.
Flowers drop for they are old.
The leaves colors blend and you can depend
On them to make you feel better,
Now flowers die and the grass gets wetter.

Turtles lie low, ponds turn to ice.
It's time to go harvesting;
Autumn's so nice.
Leaves turn colors; some stay green.
Autumn's crept in without being seen.

Ann Abeyta
MY RED ROSE

Dedicated to Jesus and Mary

Jesus please pick for
me a Red Rose from
your heavenly garden

I shall keep the Rose
real close to my heart
because I know it's just for me

It was so kind of you Jesus
to leave us so much beauty
I enjoyed the world you
left behind, to return to be
with your heavenly Father
and when it's time to leave

this world and go home to
be with you, I'll carry in my
hands a Red Rose and hope

You will forgive me and
let me stay always near
to You.

Dana Theresa Fusco
MY WISHES
I wish to have a happy day,
For all the wishes I shall say
Will have a touch of sparkling gleem
From all the prayers that I have dreamed.
Something more, that's what it needs,
A sparkle of magical singing seeds
To sing me a pretty lullaby
To make me think and make me cry
For all the Lords people and all
The Lords pride, and to think I'm
Going up there with nothing to hide.

Ginamarie Gallagher
A PRAYER
Are you listening God?
I have something to say,
Please listen to me while I pray.
I, would just like to thank you,
for all the things you've given me,
such as better friends, talents, and a
happier family.
And as for my family, let my father stop
drinking and smoking, too.
And let my mom get a diploma, and be happy
through and through.
Let my brother Thomas have better friends
and a long life,
and Bill a good education and no strife.
Please let everything in this prayer come
true,
because God and grandpa, I love you!

Helen Good Spitzer
A NEW DREAM
As the Christmas season fades away,
A New Year starts both bold and gay,
And Father Time gives way once more,
To a bright new kid at the open door.

We plan and dream how things might be,
But the dreams fall apart with reality,
Peace on Earth should be the way,
But somehow it eludes each day.

If we would only stop and see,
It has to begin with you and me,
Replacing all anger and hurt with love,
With strength supplied from the great God above.

Liz Cobb
TAMI, MY TRUE FRIEND
If as a child I climbed a tree
There you always joined me.
And through the years
We aren't just peers;
We're pals and friends,
The fun never ends.

As we've grown older
We've grown even closer.
Closer than sisters are we,
Truer friends there could not be.
Through bright days or blue,
I thank you for you.

You're there when in silence I wish to walk,
Or when even I wish to talk.
No matter which way
Or the words I say,
You're always there
And you always care!

Grayce E Horton
YOU CAN GO HOME AGAIN
You can't go home again, some said;
I couldn't help but wonder why.

Do the rounded bosoms of the hills
No longer reach to touch the sky?

From the cool, pine-scented woodlands
Have the turtle-doves all flown?
The primal river changed its course,
Or the wild things turned to stone?

Uninterrupted, planets wheel,
Sun and moon still rise and set.
Breezes blow and grasses bend,
Camas flowers are blooming yet.

Highlands changeless as the stars,
Though old inhabitants are gone;
This is the home, I often say,
You can return to when you're grown.

Edith P Brusco Veach
STARRY STARRY NIGHT
There's a starry starry sky up above us
There's a starry starry heaven way up high
And the Lord is telling us, Child get ready
For I'm coming for my saints by and by.

Try to look beyond the starry sky above us
Try to vision all the beauties of God's heaven
That will be for us one day to inherit
God has promised those who walk the narrow way.

Oh the wonder of a starry sky above us
Should remind us of God's promise in His word
That the wise will shine as stars in His heaven
I will praise Him for my prayer He has heard.

Oh Creator of the starry sky above us
Thank You for the glories that our eyes behold.
You have given us Your love and Your mercy
On us daily, Lord my Saviour, You've bestowed.

Shelly A (Weltin) Lehmann
GROWING

To Brandon and Aaron, who have in their existence enlightened my mind and strengthened my heart.

Babies are the youngest beings.
Looking but not really seeing.
Dependent on a mother's embrace,
Slow is the child's growing pace.

First years pass and pattern forms,
The parents' see themselves reborn.
Will he do the things I did?
I hope not, I was a rotten kid.

Teen years come and he learns of life,
For one day he'll surely take a wife.
Down swoops the white dove,
and he's falling in love.

He announces his plans
and ties his parents hands.
They've lost their baby,
but he'll come visit . . . maybe.

Phyllis M Roe
MOTHER'S LOVE
From the very beginning in God's Master Plan,
There was to be a mother for every woman and man.
Beginning with God's Son, Mary was her name,
And throughout the ages, it has been the same.
God gave mothers the capacity to love all
Whether they were large or very small.
Mother . . . the sweetest word I've oft been told
Is "Mother" in it's proper mold.

Unto a mother a child is born
To be loved and cared for and to mourn
If that little one chooses the wayward way
And from God's love decided to stray.
But a mother's love so strong and true
Follows that child in whatever he'll do.
No love is so small, no sacrifice too great,
But Mother is willing to love and to wait.

Mother can give all her love to child No. one
And have all her love left for her next daughter or son,
For who but a mother has enough love to share
To give it all away and have more to spare.
So, Mother, we honor you on this your special day,
And from hearts overflowing with love, we say,
"God bless you and keep you for what you mean to me
And may we all meet together someday in eternity."

Leona (Cox) Adams
ECSTASY OF THE MOUNTAIN
When I am on the mountain top
My spirit is light and gay,
Everything look's beautiful
Like flower's that bloom in May.
"If I could only stay up here,"
I whisper now and then,
Just wishful thinking, for I know
I must come down again.
So take me back to the valley
Where I get a different view
For even in the valley Lord,
I know that I will find you.
I am like a seedling
Planted in the ground,
I must have rain and sunshine
To grow both strong and sound.
If I should protect the flower
By putting it under glass
It would only wither
And die so very fast.
So he who planted me
Know's just what I need
If ever I am to be
More than just a seed.

Christian Gunderson
STRUDEL
My Mom has a job;
she makes scholars of the deaf.
However her best work is done at home
with the ones she loves.
It is the most heartwarming
and joyful odor in the house.
The fragrance of apple strudel
makes the stomach churn, yearn for some.
The most stern gourmets would fight
over but a slice.
The most finicky of persons couldn't stop
'til having three slices.
Mom makes it with a swirl to make it
oh, so light.
When that slice is on my plate, I know
she loves me . . .
It's proven in a bite.

Linda Ann Travell
MISSING YOU

To my brother, James Alan Travell. This one's for you. Love always, your sister, Linda Ann Travell

---

Wherever we may go
Our hearts will always remember
And as long as our hearts still care
We'll never part with those we love
'Cuz they are with us everywhere!

<u>I LOVE YOU!</u>

Chris M Pruitt
ONE SOLDIER'S PRAYER

To Dave, a Warrior on the wall; The Mighty "Q", for shadows on the wall; And my Lady, for understanding it all.

My Lord I kneel in prayer this night,
On this Asian soil where we must fight.
It's not for me that I've come to pray,
But for a friend who died today.

His lips they were all cracked and dry,
And his uniform it was torn.
But he proudly served his country,
And that's the reason it was worn.

For one last time those eyes sought mine,
His calm did ease my fears.
Then locked us in a bond that time,
Can't lesson through the years.

He came to this land torn by strife,
In the hope that all men might be free.
For this dream he gave his life,
So now I make this plea.

That when my life it too does end,
I see once more my now lost friend.
And if in Heaven there's no trace,
Then hell will be our resting place.

Patti Spurgeon Golden
MAMA MAY I CALL YOU DEAREST?

To that tree climbing executive, whom I adore and love. And who would not spank me as a child, because she remembered that she was a "kid" at one time, also! My mother: <u>Allie Spurgeon</u>

Tears will flow
But I don't wanna let 'em go
Your love so like a child
But your intelligence runs wild
Mama, May I call you Dearest?

There are so few like you
I wish on a star every night
That I could be with you
And have you in sight
Mama, May I call you Dearest?

Like a soft blanket to a child
You are my faith, guidance, and oh so mild!
So many cities apart . . .
But never in the heart
You've shown me love is out there
Even for me . . . Mama, May I call you Dearest?

Your heart outshines the sun
You make every day such fun
You love me always
You never let me down
When I look at you I never see a frown
Mama, May I call you Dearest?
Mama, May I call you Dearest?
Your love's like none I've ever known
Mama . . . May I call you "Dearest?"
Your heart is like a dove
That has flown and flown and flown
I love you so! ! . . . MAMA DEAREST!

Stanley Earl Anderson
STAND BY YOUR WOMAN!

To Diana—My Inspriation

A man's eyes may sometimes be roamin',
But his heart recognizes one woman.
His appetite might be strong—
The one woman accent says: "It's wrong."

Actions may be hard to take,
But impatience does not a marriage make.
Reliance is part of dream's great mold—
Having it brings happiness untold.

There are many women in the world,
But only one gets the flag unfurled.
There are many bodies that build desire;
Only one fans the fire!

Refrain:
Understanding is the armor that love uses—
Wearing it well prevents untold abuses.
If you can't by your woman stand,
Love is not at your command!

Yvonne Lucretia Blankenship-Wolf
BADGE OF COURAGE
Why is life so hard to bear,
There must be a <u>badge of courage</u> you can wear

When you think life has nothing to give,
And why is this world letting you live
Look at someone you love and smile
And when your love returns it, after a while
It kinda makes grimnace disappear
When you see that smile, you lose all fear
Love can be many splendrous thing
Beautiful and as free as a bird on the wing
But you must wear a badge of courage proudly
If you are in love your smile will be loudly
The badge of courage was meant to be used
The smile on others should not be abused
Thats what your face and mouth were created for
They were not put there to shout out war
A badge of courage is not for war, but the smile is
the will to live
Thats why all the people have a smile to give
A badge of courage will take you through the day
It makes your life worthwhile in many ways
The rich, the poor no matter where on earth you live
When you smile at the world you have something to give
It can be very catching it seems
A smile is like the sunshine that beams
Show your badge of courage

Penelope A J Fairchild
TO BE A ROSE

As i stare out my window.
i see a rose, fooled by time and nature.
Tricked into bud at the end of summer
by an unseasonal warm current.
But, never allowed to bloom.
There it stands suspended in time.
Never able to fulfill its original plan.
i relate to that poor shriveled bud!,
Standing now, in the frigid weather.
Wanting,
but never achieving.
Starting,
but never ending.
Grasping,
but never able to hold on.
Trying,
but never hard enough.
Dreaming,
but failing to succeed.
Knowing i need help.
But too ignorant to seek.
Take my hand, reinforce my soul.
Nurture me into blossom!

Darla M Ostrum
THE HOLDERS OF THE WORLD

Little girls and grandmas,
Youth and aged wisdom,
Sweetness and everlasting love.

Little girls learn all they can
From grandmas who learn
From them to live again.

No more special bond,
No more precious time
Will ever be known.

They're always there to hold . . .
Little girls' grandmas;
And never grow old.

And grandmas' little girls
Grow and love and live
And guarantee our world.

Martha McCauley-Rice
HEATHER

Her hair so
Soft and curly
Her eyes are
Cornflower blue
She wraps
Her tiny
Arms
Around me and
Says I love
You—I watch her
As she sleeps after
Such a busy day—
And Thank
Our God
Above For
Giving— Her to me

Mary J Hartle
LIBERTY—THE SPIRIT OF AMERICA

I dedicate this poem to my hardworking Irish ancestors, to my loving family, and to my loving husband, Kenneth, a retired U.S. Air Force Pilot.

She stands there proud, serene,
Her silhoutette in radiant elegance,
She is a guidepost marking the way,
To the teeming millions who came to stay.
May the spirit of the Lady's risen torch,
Be our victory . . . and
Give us all hope . . . and
Upon our souls scorch,
The meaning of true liberty.
In this . . . the land of the free,
She gives us all a ray of hope!
Lady Luck has shined down on us,
She gives us the promise of security and equality.
Our ancestors witnessed such joy on arrival,
Let us join together, hand in hand,
Across this great country,
As we salute this great land!
She was the seed of sorrow,
And gives us hope for each new tomorrow,
So long as our Lady's beacon . . .
Has been the hope of our ancestry,
We are all viators of this world,
Make us a viable world in this, Our nuclear age,
Let us not a viacrucis be, in this great land of liberty!
As we celebrate 200 years of America's beauty and freedom!

Linda E Olson
THE INDIVIDUAL

Ho! Russian, now you learn,
The monolithic of a worm,
Say Arab! are you split?
In the desert of your pit?
Listen, Hebrew, is your land?
Where your holy self has planned?

Black man, where is your white?
In the darkness of your night?
Frenchman, Turk and British three,
Latin Chinese, Grecian tree?
Well, my neighbor, do you see?
Continents of earth alive in me?

And in us, all colors there,
Green the one that makes it fair,
Underlies the think entire,
Red and white and blue on fire?
If your wit is sharpened now,
Armies march across your brow.

And your blood will tell the tale,
Healing peaks behind the veil!

Eloise Walker Evans

Eloise Walker Evans
FANTASYLAND

Down in the mysterious watery depths
Where fishes light up like torches
And shells are colored a vivid pink
And houses don't have porches;
I have a marvelous place of abode,
The prettiest nautilus ever could be,
With many rooms all pearly white
Is my castle under the sea.

Some misty night when sea horses
Are riding the briny deep,
I'll lasso one with anemones
And up to your door we'll creep.
Then on foamy waves of the ocean blue
I'll whisk you away with me,
Down, down, down so gracefully
To my castle under the sea.

There in the wonderful waterland
We will while the time away.
We'll swim to a far-off coral reef
And stay for a long and happy day.
We'll look at the Venus flower beds,
The prettiest that ever could be.
We'll gather some banded shells to take
To my castle under the sea.

When the ocean is singing a lullaby
And 'tis time to slumber and sleep,
An orchestra of fiddler crabs
Will play us some music so sweet
In this mystical fairyland
We will there for e'er and e'er be.
No one will come to disturb us
In my castle under the sea.

Mickie West
DRIPS

It drips—monotonously.
Day by day it drips,
As a record caught on a scratch.
Nagging, as it slowly draws a spot.
Dark upon the porcelain white.
Drip! . . . Drip! . . . Drip! . . .
It grows louder as night encroaches.
In the stillness it roars,
Pounding upon the resting ear,
Acknowledging something undone,
Something no longer secure.
Where there once chattered
Rushing cold water,
There now sluggishly roars
Dull, nagging, tepid
Drips.

Berniece Hacking Balle
THIS LITTLE LIFE

This poem is dedicated to Reed, my loving husband, devoted father of five & grandfather of twenty-five.

This—'tis such a little life, a moment of it all.
'Tis but an instant part with God, and yet weak mortals all.
Could we but see past shadows black into ethereal space,
We'd know—but no, weak fools are we who seek Eternal Grace;
Our vision dimmed, let trivials cast eternal dark o'er all
Continual warring; purpose crossed, and issues jumbled all;
Destroying one the other, blind in all our being, we:
Such worthless things, these eyes of ours, yet oracles to see.

Grace Frigo
SPOILAGE

Where do I keep my garbage?
Way back on the icebox shelf.
I don't really put it there,
It gets there by itself.
Why, oh, why doesn't someone
Design a revolving plan,
So I can make a sandwich,
Without using moldy ham.
No one uses the leftovers
I store in my tupperware.
Most times when I discover it,
It looks like it grew hair.
I should probably dispose of
It, without any further chillin'—
Instead of providing culture
For—home-made penicillin.

Stephen Feinland
THOUGHTS OF LOVE

Dedicated to my beloved partner, Susie Sunshine

I want to reassure you, Dear
That I will never go away.
To relieve your gloom and cure you, Dear
I have this to say:
To make you happy is the top priority to me,

More than my own life,
So the scope of our relationship
should be
Far more than love and taking you
to be my wife.
Joined in heaven we will always be
If you keep the view in sight;
There you will forever be with me
As in a dream for one eternal night.
One promise now I send to you:
No one else can take your place;
My heart I split in two and half I
lend to you
So you will always see my face.

Cathy Stasik
THERE SHOULD BE LAUGHTER AFTER PAIN

For so long you were with me,
You were always at my side—
To shield me from the current
Of the raging deathly tide.
You taught me how to laugh,
And showed me when to cry—
You guided my hopeless dreams
Way onto the sky.
And now this room seems empty
Without your voice around—
But at least I know today,
That I had finally found:
That friend I needed most;
That one, yet so true—
Thinking back, I know that
friend
Is the one and caring you.
I will forever miss you.
You will always be in my
heart—
Whether we're forever together
Or distance that tears us apart.
Maybe someday;
somewhere—
We'll cross each other's lane.
Remember there should be
laughter
Always after pain.

Tammy Tehaan Vitale
CHILDREN

Like two small moons
they circle my planet
born of my earth
and dark primal waters.

Faces towards me
they spin in their orbits
stationary as I but
with different visions
and pathways.

Secure and safe in my shadow
they move toward the sun

anchored yet flying free.

Lori Estep
THE DREAM

Dedicated to Jim, who lives on in our hearts

The grief that lies within my heart
Turns the days to cold dark
anguish,
The tears flow and there are
Moments of sheer madness,
Knowing it can't be so.

You are gone my love, goodbye,
Your soul is freed to fly,
To the place where you led me,
One dark night, in a dream so
real
I felt the touch of your hand
when I awoke.

How fresh, how sweet, how
clean,
Are your returns, to which,
Beside my dreams
The late past grief melts away,
Like snow in May
As if there were no such cold
thing.

Now I dream over blankets of
white clouds,
By deep pools full of peace,
My love waits for me there,
Till night presses night
And all the darkness
Turns to a River of Stars.

Robyn Gayle Koshel
UNEXPECTED VICTIM

Men in mirrored shades,
Dressed in black and grey suits,
very formal.
All with their black leather brief
cases.
Taunted.
Stereotyped.
They follow you around in their
black cadilacs,
to drive-in movies, to the 7-11
around the corner.
What do you do when these
mysterious men come knocking
on your door?
You run away but only to be
followed once more?
There's no means of escape.
I took the road not taken, look
where it got me:
To cavort around town with a man
in a gas mask tailing you
underground.
I thought I could save some money,
I didn't think they'd find out.
I am a hard worker for the little pay.
Where can I go, where shall I stay?
My life is such a mess, how was I
to know
they were the I.R.S.

Marlie Weimer
MAN'S INHUMANITY TO MAN

The little old lady shuffles
to a trash can and rummages
through to see what treasure she
might find today.
She wears no boots on her
feet and has only a ragged
filthy sweater to ward off
the evening chill.

Pedestrians go hurrying by with
their eyes averted. Only for
a fleeting moment does any guilt
assail them.
No thought to the closets

bulging with clothes, or the
kitchen stacked with food, or the
nice warm bed that awaits them.
They hurry on their way.

Tonite the little old lady will
lay her head on the cold
pavement
or crouch in a doorway and
cover herself with discarded
newspapers and she will close
her eyes and dream of days
that used to be.

Judy D Riquelmy
NATION IN A CRISIS

Nation Oh Nation, land of the free,
confusion, corruption has
invaded thee.
Spirit, faith, hard lessons learned,
freedom and greatness well
earned.

Brave troops, your generals have
lead,
thousands of your patriots now
dead.
Today Oh Nation in such pain,
was their patriotism spent in
vain?

Where is the courage of the past,
which made this great nation
last?
Citizens surge forth with the
greatest speed,
strengthen your unity, let your
integrity lead.

Wave "Old Glory" high in the sky,
let not your spirit, your faith die.
"Star Spangled Banner," Red,
White and Blue,
people of the nation, stand and
be true.

Eddie Sanchez
FRIENDS

This poem is for you.
Its about anything you like,
ice cream in a cone
or a ride on a bike

It's about dancing all night
if you know what I mean.
And living day to day
with love in between

So when you get to that age
and there's nothing to do,
think of your friends
and they'll be thinking of you

Teresa Braswell
NEGATIVEISM

There is something living in my
body causing doubt; creating
unrest and leaving me helpless.
This elusive creature is
Negativeism. It lurks in the
shadows and crevices of my
physic and subliminal being. It's
mission is to attack and destroy
on command any self
confidence that I have.
Negativeism I hate you for what
you do to me! Negativeism . .
. Negativeism . . .

Kristina M Brinson
FALLING IN LOVE

Falling in love,
I'm almost afraid.
The pain left in me,
Just leaves me to say:

I've loved you for so long,
I just can't stay away.
I wanted to call you,
But what am I to say?

You had asked me,
"With whom would I be true?"
I didn't realize,
You wanted it to be you.

Now you have someone else,
And I know you're no longer alone.
But if you happen to change your
mind,
You know I'll be near the phone.

I can't go on without you,
Can't you see I'm waiting?
I tried so many times to let you go,
But there were too many dreams I
kept chasing.

You tried to say, "I love you,"
As you turned to wipe a tear.
I smiled and said, "I love you too!"
I knew those were the last words
between us, that I would ever
hear.

Marie Eleanor Black
WHAT IS LOVE?

For my husband

Love remembers the happy young
time.
Love is tender, courteous and kind.
Love is faithful and loyal always.
Love is truthful in all things each
day.
Love listens, does not hurt or
destroy.
Love shares the problems, the
stress and the joy.
Love gives affection that is quiet
and dear.
Love fans all desire through year
after year.

My love for you has never strayed.
Through all these years I've not
betrayed
The vows we said long years ago,
They've been the guide to keep it so.
May God still grant us years to
grow,
Filled with joy, and time to know
Fulfillment of the early dreams,
Of love untried and now redeemed.
We've had some joy, the trials and
tears,
But kept on going through the
years
To reach this quiet time of life,
And I'm proud to be your loving
wife.

Jerry B Perrine
DAD'S SIDE

Here I sit all alone
with a heart heavy and cold like a
stone
I hear a noise and look to find
but it's just an echo in my mind
Children's laughter joy at play
any amount I'd be willing to pay
To hear a cry in the night
from a little ones fright
Or to hear the clatter
of something the matter
Or to wipe off a chin
with a cute little grin
No doubt where they've been
they were into some chocolate
again
All in all I guess it's not that bad
once a week I get called Dad
I pick them up for a day
maybe we'll go to the park and play
But it gets me a little out of wack
when I have to take them back
I give them my love a kiss and a hug
leaving those adoring eyes gives
my heart a tug.

Julie F Wren
LONELINESS
Loneliness . . .
is feeling lost
feeling like there's no one
and nowhere
to turn for comfort.
Anxiety suppressed.

Loneliness . . .
a wicked and oh so sad emotion;
confuses and blinds one to
true feelings.
Love is lost, yet not lost,
only hidden.
Hidden until it is too late . . .

Loneliness . . .
Hurtful acts too late realized
and very sadly regretted . . .
eternally.

Dale A Rhodes
UNTITLED
To bend with the wind
And move like the clouds
Never knowing how to bow.

As the wind carries the seed
So shall it always carry me.

The sun has it glare,
This we know we must share.

For in time we shall bare,
The wine that touches the buds
Of all mankind.
Whether sweet or bitter
All must dare,
To taste of that which is so
rare . . . love

Richard T Spangler
YOU'RE BEAUTIFUL

To Mary the reality of my dreams

How beautiful one can be
To anothers heart and mind
And the more I look at you
A more beautiful you I find.

So forever stay as you are
Always just be you,
For there's so many beautiful
things
You really seem to do.

Like knowing when to hold me
If a problem comes my way,
Or throwing a loving glance at me
To brighten up my day.

For I tell you you're lovely
Because I find you to be that way
You seem to bring the sunshine
Into all my lonely days.

You always make me smile
When my day has gone bad,
You seem to be that special person
To be there when I'm sad.

So remember I'll always love you
You're my shining star,
And remember I'll always need you
To be just who you are.

Kelly Noud
THE LAND WE LIVE IN
We live in a land of trials,
Our priorities confused;
Putting ourselves at the top.
Self indulgence has come over us
We take what isn't needed.
Please God, How is it to ever stop?
Giving is most important, but
seems it is Lost.
To find it in ourselves again.
we must search within; firmly hold
on
don't think of what it will cost.
The Land We Live In
God's created world
Each of us trying to better
ourselves
Instead of trying to make the land
a better place to live.
We say tomorrow is where I will
start,
Why not Today?
Right now, Hold on and don't ever
let go.

Vince Judge
OMEGA
At life it's best I can refrain
That our's is but a waiting game
From birth to death is our
complete attire
And there into our fondest dreams
we do aspire
But what is left when ash is formed
For it is far not the same as the
body warm

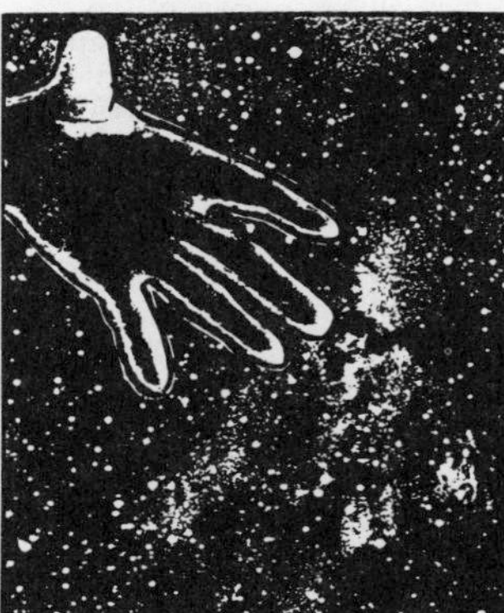

The material things that we have
bred
They too are all but lying dead
For what will stand the test of sand
and time
Is there anything left where we can
leave a sign
And the echo resounded from afar
Your words are all that there are

Sandra L Anderton
TOUCHED
I trusted him
I gave my love
I shared my hurts and joys

I trusted his word
I trusted his love
He was important to me

He said"he loved me
He said I was special
I was his favorite

One night when we were alone
He touched me
He touched me as no other

I felt sick inside
I felt bad and dirty
I didn't even understand why

I couldn't tell anyone
I was a bad girl
I couldn't share my hurt

I had no one
My parents wouldn't understand
They'd think I was the one

I'm all alone
I'll lock this secret up
I'll hide it deep inside

No one will ever know
I've been TOUCHED!!!

Gary L Blandford
STAYING ALIVE
I always believed in friendship
I always believed in God
Belief and faith and reality are in
disconjunction.
By that I mean, friends sometimes
are not
But God always remains constant.

Life passes and is too short
forgiveness is for the giving
And God is the love and forgiveness
needed
As the waning sunsets glisten.

Helen Christopher
ODE TO DONNA WILSON
I'll often think of you
When roses are wet with dew
I'll often think of you
When skies are dark or blue.

I'll often think of you
As a gentle mother of one or two
Thanking God for your blessings
When your day is through.

May the good Lord look down on
you
As with your baby you start anew.
May He health, peace and love on
you shed
And give you an abundance of daily
bread.

When you hear your child's feet
patter
Forget the little things that do not
matter
Be a parent; not a friend
Your child will be good to the end.

When he goes out on the highways
and byways
Your child will remember your
teachings always.
Stand by your child; do your best
Above all, trust God to do the rest.

Louise Zamorski
MY MOTHER
I had a Wonderful Mother,
She died when I was 8 months old,
I couldn't ask for another,
She was worth all the gold.

Many times I want to see her,
Many times I am very blue,
Because my dear Mother,
She can't give me any clues.

One time I dreamt of her,
She came down to me,
I said, "That is my mother,"
Then she kissed me tenderly.

When she went away again,
I had tears in my eyes,
I have never known my Mother,
Because she had died.

Eric Corcoran
THE DREAM
I dreamt.
That cold November night,
I dreamt:

I was falling
from the sky.
Falling, falling, falling.
And I crashed on
the earth below;
my skull split open,
Grey matter and purple blood
oozing and mixing with
the black sea below.

People say that
when you see
yourself die in
a dream, this
is a bad omen.

When I awoke . . . ?!!!

S I Nelson
DAYBREAK
Pale, insistent shafts of morning
Slowly tilt the rim of night;
Gently, star-strewn vaults of
darkness
Tip on edge, spill fog-swirl'd
light.

Casting pearl-glow vale to summit,
Opalescent clouds give way—
Brush the path of azure, for the
Golden monarch of the day.

Lori A Scott
ELEMENTS OF MY SOUL
I built a wall around my soul to
protect myself from the elements
That make my heart weak.
The southern wall protects me
from hatred; the element that
kills
And destroys entire worlds.
The northern wall protects me
from death; the element of my
future,
The element that tries mens souls.
The western wall protects me from
friendship; the element I can
never have,
That I never want. Its a closeness
that makes me vulnerable and
weak.
The eastern wall, the most
important wall, protects my soul
from love;
The strongest of all the elements.
Love is painful. It eats at my soul,
Deeper and deeper it goes,
churning my insides,
Then slowly, I close my eyes and
wish it away and it is gone.

The four walls are beautiful,
covered with dark green ivy.
They are big, strong, resistant.
Suddenly, as I am looking at the
east and west walls, I feel a
strong force approaching.
As it gets nearer, the east and west
walls begin to crumble.
I try to hold the walls up but the
force is too strong.
My heart beats faster. The two
walls are turning to dust.
I plead to the wall of death to take
me away.
It looks at me in its deep dark way
and refuses my suffering soul.
The walls of friendship and love
are collapsing.
I fight to keep them standing.
I'm falling, falling, falling . . .

Patsy M Blair
COUNTRY MORNING
A slight golden glow streams
through a window.
A cool breeze gently caresses all of
Gods creations.
The dew drops glisten like a field
of diamonds
as they ease ever do slowly down
the crisp
green blades of grass and gently
drip from
the soft, velvety rose petals.
The fragrances of nature are strong
and fresh.
The crystal like stillness is broken
only by
the delicate songs of a few early
rising birds.
These beautys and wonders are a
"Country Morning."

Ruby Jordan
TREASURE
I went strolling over the grassy lea,
stalked well known paths, trod the knolls,
. . . neared the bluff that hides the sea;
A perfume, rarely found on strolls
came wafting to my puzzled noses,
I whirled, to see who followed me,
expecting a maiden ladened with poses,
no maid, no bower, no specter did I see
but beheld an oddity standing there
all decked with flowers dainty and rare;
A scrawny lilac bush waving in the breeze,
as if bidding gale-like winds at each nod
to pass it's gift to whom it dared please.
So sweet a gift, came not by land or sea . . . just God.

Sharon Marguerite Norris-Williams
HURTS TOO MUCH TO CRY
Lord.
Sometimes it hurts too much to cry
When the days are long
and the children annoying.

When nothing has gone right all week
and there's been no word from him.
When you almost start to wish he's gone for good.
it's hurting every day
When you've spanked the kids
and near tears yourself
When you almost wish they'd never been born
'cause the world holds so much harm.
When the tears are brimming but not quite flowing
'cause a little child has smiled.
It hurts
but much too much to cry

Angelica V De Vos

Angelica V De Vos
THE PUMPKIN'S PLIGHT

To all my grandchildren

I was a beautiful Jack-O-Lantern,
all yellow and bright.
My eyes were ablaze with bright candle light.
The children I saw were filled with delight.
They followed me everywhere, all through the night.

But now all my world has come tumbling down.
All my smiles have vanished and I wear a frown.
'Tis rumored that I'll be a Thanksgiving Day pie
And I am so sad, I could almost cry.

No lights ablaze, no children to cheer,
I tremble and shake, I'm filled with great fear,
I must bid you good-by for I cannot stay,
But I'll leave you one wish, "Happy Thanksgiving Day!"

Cynthia M Gerke
A FRIEND FOR ALL SEASONS

For Lawrence "Coach" Nickol, Robert and Teresa Gerke and Nicole Gerke—my friends forever

---

Summer surf:
sweeping over sun-baked sand,
spurring Curiosity's quest
with an ever eager hand.

Fall foliage:
wearing nature's varied hues,
revealing Desire's fulfillment
in the beauty of the Muse.

Winter white:
sparkling slivers of Heaven,
proclaiming Honesty's valor
despite the luring raven.

Spring sunlight:
warming creation each hour,
securing Friendship's endurance
through love's abiding power.

Helen Munn Placyk
STOP AND THINK
Did you ever stop and think when you feel alone and blue
That maybe all the rest of the world is feeling that too?
Just like the flowers in the spring
that look so fresh and new,
Just like the trees in the spring,
they wear a new headress too
Did you ever stop and think when
the flowers all wither and die,
and the trees all lose their beauty,
they sit down and cry.
No! they're content to settle down
and rest a little while
and watch the rest of the world go
by with an understanding smile.
For they know that they will live
again in all their beauty true,
So just stop and reconsider when
you feel alone and blue.

Peggy Stockton-Martinelli
BAG LADY BLUES

To my dear sister, Cora, with love and gratitude for her unconditional love and ever-present support.

Coffee and a roll, please,
with butter and warmed:
Luxury on a Sunday afternoon.

Collect from Mother,
Operator.
That's a switch
how often pulled?
Money, Son or Daughter:
Please send Mom
for debts not owed.

Rich, I'm rich,
todays newspaper,
My hunger softened
as the wrinkled bag
on the mission bed.

H Pearcy
SHADOWS
A strong wind flattened brown grass to the ground
and bent black-oak boughs on the moonlit hill.
The weary woman shuddered at the sound
of whipping trees, and curled up in the chill

November night beside her waning fire.
Its flickering shadows on the cabin wall
were tattered ghost-bits of her crushed desire,
her splattered dreams, her broken trust, and all

that she held dear. In the unyielding dark,
she watched that fire burn down to its last spark.

Donna R Woodhead
DEATH
Ah sweet Death! If you could but come to me—
An end to all my suffering be
My eyes would never see what makes my heart bleed
My brain would not be clouded by misunderstanding
My soul would not search in vain for love; a love that is not here, and never will be
My useless hands grow limp groping for something that is out of reach
My mind searches in vain for it knows not what
My eyes grow weary from not being able to see
What is this quest which seems to have no end?
Why, with all my physical and mental being must I try to gain the ungainable?
Yes sweet Death, fall upon me when my eyes are closed and
my brain is in the mist of dreams that can't come true
Take from my weary body this fleeting soul and put it to rest
Lift my heart to the meaning and understanding of all being
Let my eyes see again, let my heart feel again; let me be a
complete being, as I was in the beginning.

Flora Linz
DAY DREAMING
Did you ever let your mind drift into space,
and lazily dream of some far distant place
Just hop on a cloud that's fluffy and light
And let the gentle breeze sail you right out of sight

Glide over lofty mountains and sparkling streams
and you can come to rest on a moonbeam.
Travel on to the Milky Way, which is not very far
While you are there gather a bouquet of stars.

Up to the rainbow—to the top—if you please
Slide down to Earth on the same gentle breeze.

If you ever want to travel to some distant land
No need to fret or make any plans
Just lie back and shut your eyes very tight
Hop on a cloud and sail out of sight

So daydream a little—get rid of your woes
It gives peace of mind—which is good for the soul

Sheila Shawn
A TRUE FRIEND
Every boy should have a puppy
he can tell his troubles to
For they are more than willing
to sympathize with you.
Perhaps you're feeling badly
so he will lick your hands,
and look at you with soft brown eyes
to show he understands.
You sometimes hurt his feelings
but he always will forgive,
and you will have a true friend
for as long as he will live.
He doesn't spread mean gossip
or tell your secrets out.
He'll be a perfect confidant,
and that's without a doubt.
He will always go out with you
when it's dark, to close the gate.
He doesn't mind if you forgot,
or if the hour is late.
You'll never find a truer friend
should you look all over,
than that dear loving pal of yours,
that pup that you call Rover.

Patty Eaton
YOUR MIND

Dedicated to my loving Mother & Father, Mr & Mrs. M. W. Eaton. God bless you always.

Are the heroes in your mind
so huge
that the sight of your beauty and worth
stay unseen
your eyes are not fixed on reality
but fantasy, mans' illusions
bringing your worth
to degregation, and valleys of low esteem
is man that much different
except in his own eyes of perception
do you have the time in thought
to allow another
so eagerly to occupy
your mental process
to supersede his greatness
over you in your own thinking
have you allowed your mind
to lash out against itself
are you not the obedience trainer
of your own thoughts

David M Windsor
WE THE CHILDREN
We the children so far from home,
struggling to make it, we roam.
Hardships, pains, a lonely street,
with few lights lit, we weep.
People wrong us so then pass on bye,

and we ask ourselves, why?
The mistakes we made we made amends,
then prayed to God, "forgive our sins."
The world knows not our hearts inside,
and who could be trusted to confide?
Still it is we carry on—
each one of us left all alone.
Yes, we the children so far we roam,
seen one day waving from Heaven's Home.

Maurice S Peizer
LOVE VERSUS ART
Contain thyself
Saith Art.
Dispense thyself
Saith Love.
Express thyself
Saith Art.
Forget thyself
Saith Love.

O Love
Thou art a ruse
To steal us from ourselves
For one whom we must choose.

That Universal Force
Whose self is very Love
Drives all with careless pulse
To sacrifice his nice identity.
O Love, thy dominion I refuse!
Myself I gladly, willingly choose!
For Art is life and Love is strife.

Dorothy J McCoy

Dorothy J McCoy
JUST YOU AND ME
A rose—so beautiful,
A small twig planted in the ground.
Our love—so wonderful.
So thankful each other we have found.
Just you and me.
With roots growing deep
Sturdy and strong,
Petals soft and sweet,
To each other we belong.
Just you and me.
Gradually the thorns came out,
Hatred, bitterness, quarrels and strife.
Our rose is drouping and falling.
Oh! what's happening in our life?
Just you and me.
Let's cut back that stem,
Start a new tonight.
Bring back the life,
Make things right.
Just you and me.
The stem will grow stronger,
The roots will grow deeper,
The petals will grow brighter,
The rose will grow larger.
For you and me.
Our love will grow stronger,
Our love will grow deeper,
Our love will grow sweeter,
Our love will last longer.
Just you and me.
We'll keep the thorns away.
Our love will glow and shine.
As we grow day by day,
I am yours and you are mine.
Just you and me.

Louise Redmond
SECRET PRIDE
As we sat on a blanket,
Surrounded by cool grass,
Peering through the trees,
A clearing could we see.
And lo! A man without means,
A hobo if you please,
Rummaging through castaways,
A treasure in one hand.
But alas! As he walked our way,
Not a stop he made,
This castaway man.
A secret pride inside to stay,
He would not seek,
He would not find,
Under our watchful eyes.
Peering through the trees,
A clearing could we see,
And Lo! The castaway man,
Another treasure in his hand,
A secret pride deep inside,
The castaway man,
Tried to hide.

Scott C Wooten
NO WAY OUT
In a world full of people,
Where we've all been fated,
Theres too many like us
That are just plain hated

And in a world full of drugs,
Where theres no way out,
Theres nothing we can do
But to scream and shout

And in a world full of animals,
You have to wear the boot,
And if you can't handle it,
Take that gun and shoot

But everyones got the solution,
And suicide will fit,
Too bad that they don't realize
That suicides not it

So if you thought of this,
And decide you want to try,
Just remember that
Suicides the biggest lie

So don't think of this,
Just think of how and why,
Because in the end,
You don't really want to die.

Michael P Green
SIMPLE DREAMS
Shimmering moonbeams on oceans shore;
Dreaming of things, that were before;
Shells you've found beneath the waves,
How you've spent your younger days.
Oh to dream on oceans shore.

Virginia E Beck
AUTUMN SANDIA
Mother of nature, you danced around
Amidst scrub-oaks and quaking aspen.
Touching tree-locust and cottonwood
With colored ink in your etching pen.

Softly you waxed over the masses,
Pine background a hallowed veil.
Touching there, brushing here,
Readying foliage to dress in regale.

You spoke to climate, addressed clouds,
Dipped your pen in paints and hues,
Brushed on solution to bring to life
Colors in hiding that cause revolution.

You spoke to mountains, Sandias were awake.
Told them to sleep so you could make
Out of their death a colorful life.
One last look at your arty still-life.

The stage is set, the frost is steady,
Your hand reaches out, touches curtain ready.
As sun arises and drapes pulled back,
Behold fall beauty—
An elegiac.

Lynnetta L Rapaszky
MOTHERS' EYES

In memory of Octavia LePottry and her passion for writing.

I once was small
seems long ago,
so many things
I did not know.

You guided me
through my youth,
reminding me
to tell the truth.

Don't ever steal
or tell a lie,
rely on God,
have faith and try.

"Someday," she said
"in further years
I'd understand
a mother's tears."

I'm older now
and realize
I too now see
Through mothers' eyes.

Avis Y Dillon
THE MANIFESTATION
A daydream winds through many years;
Sustains me through my many tears.
He's always there when need there be.
When life is harsh, then dreams run free.
Embroidered with my hopes and schemes
Till he is almost real, it seems;
Unhampered by mere time and space—
He only lacks a name and face.

He knows the very soul of me;
Possesses, yet he leaves me free.
The kind of man that I could love
And totally become part of.
The dream runs on as dreams will do,
Familiar now—yet fresh and new.
The line is thin, still he remains
Upon imagination's plane.

Are you my wish materialized
And come to life before my eyes?
Or is it true that all this time
I've been in contact with YOUR mind.

Helen Thomas Ray
MY MOTHER
The woman in the red coat and I
walked up town to the square.
She was my mother;
so kind, so sweet, so fair.

We talked a lot as we passed by
stores and houses all.
We talked and talked of lots of things
that we could recall.

We hadn't seen each other
for many and many a day.
So it was very very sweet
to have her come my way.

But after we got up town
the Maryland bus she took.
And I saw her red coat and her
go quickly out of sight.

Kelly David Smith
NIGHT WONDERS

To my Mother & Father Mr. & Mrs. Wm S. Smith and my wife Virginia L. Smith. Thank you all.

The times are long, As the
ship journey nears its end,
Tired sailors slow to a
nights rest, Others stand
watch to ensure safe journey.

As I gaze at the nights
wonders, And long still
seas, The nights magic
fills me with mystery,
And beauty of those who
believed of their tales.

In the mazes of my mind,
I see dreams of men, And
hear the tolls of men bury
in this vast tomb, They
call the sea, And in my
illusions I see wonders
that many don't see,
Or understand.

I alone in my thoughts
concel what I have seen,
For no others can, And
the sudden reality that
all is what you make it,
Is not always true.

Margaret Peke
THE HOMELESS
Ragged men with empty, hollow eyes
Huddling amid the debris beneath the concrete sky,
Their cadaverous bodies pungent, reeking, soiled with sweat.
Somnambulent women in patchwork clothes
Clinging to life without hope, hell on earth,
Their yesterdays, tomorrows, and today an endless treadmill,
plummeting into the void.
Neglected children, bare-foot and battered
Recoiling from mistreatment and misuse,
A ragtag rabble, silent, staring, and withdrawn.
They are humanity's throw-away people.
They are the homeless.

Scavengers by day with duffel bags

and grocery carts
Rummaging through waste bins
and garbage dumps,
In search of unwanted treasure
among the discarded trash.
Soup kitchen lines and storehouse
queues
Holding outstretched hands for
sparse rations and meager food,
Never feeling filled, never knowing
satiation.
Supplicants by night, seeking
sanctuary from the dark and cold
Sleeping in doorways, cardboard
boxes, or abandoned slums,
Survival, in any form, their
consummate goal.
They are mankind's frightened and
forgotten.
They are the homeless.

Artie M Ford
STAR GAZING
Advice to those who cannot sleep
Start counting stars instead of
sheep
I gaze in wonder how many there
be
As I start counting one two three
Gazing out my window, four five
six seven
My troubles forgotten eight nine
ten eleven
That bright one must be Planet
Mars
It's brighter than the other stars
From the little dipper I take a sip
So soon into dreamland I will slip
The Star of all Stars is the star that
led
The wise men to the Christ Child's
bed
In the manger where He lay
Cradled in the sweet new hay
I hitch my wagon to a star
And dream and dream, as I travel
far.

Mary Scott
THE DREAM OF AMERICA
God planted in the heart of man,
the seed of liberty;
So thro the countless ages grew
the longing to be free;
And do you know what men will do,
to reach this longed for goal?
They are many and are numbered
in the confines of the soul.

A dream of freedom brought them
here,
a struggling Pilgrim band,
That dream of freedom guided
them,
and others to this land.
With home and family left behind,
they trod the wild frontier,
Pushing onward, ever onward,
facing danger, facing fear.

Many battles have been fought,
to keep what we hold dear;
And brave men bled and died that
we
may live in safety here.
So let freedom ring through-out
the land,
our liberty proclaim,
And every man stand for the right,
and honor freedom's name.

Kathleen M Spinelli-Fleming
TIME PASSES
As each year goes by . . . I get older
and closer to my destination.
Why do I have to grow old
Live my life to the fullest so I'm
told
There's moments in my life
when I'd like
to stop time
but it continues to grow and
prosper
like fresh grapevines.
I'd like to return to my childhood
oh if I only could
Children are so free of troubles
and express just what they feel
they do as they please . . . and
are so real.
I can only hope I can be as a
child,
So free, so honest, so meek, and
so mild.

Butch Blair

Butch Blair
FREEDOM
The wings of man are not his arms,
but they are his mind.
Some men soar like an eagle, and
some men never know flight at
all.

The eyes of men can search the
universe and scan the land, but
without love and humility he is
blind.

Hindsight and foresight are only
measures of time. It is insight
that sets man free and saves him
from being blind.

Oh! to distinguish with clarity, to
perceive by the mind, to soar like
an eagel, to never be blind.

Shirley Jones Collins
MY DREAM LIFE

This Poem is dedicated to Carl, my friend, my love and also he's my husband

I feel my whole life has been only
a Dream, a semi-happy Dream.
A fantasy that I can't escape, a wide
open sea of faces that I can't see.
My life, my fantasies, my realities,
are all in my own little dream
world of friends, loves and
certain places I stay.

I am growing up to be, a woman,
to be me.
To take the things as they come
and to see whatever there is to
see.
Falling to tears, I cry, my life is real,
but sitting very still,
I think, how real is real.
Starting a new life, making a part
of me leave the past behind,
and thinking of making a find, not
behind, but ahead, to another
time.
After seeing the many sights and
bright lights of life,
I realized that my Dreams are
coming true, through you,
My Dream LIfe is You.

Karen Mouacdie
CONTEMPLATION

Dedicated To Katherine Finkle, a woman of honest dedication and courage, to whom I am proud to have for my mother and my friend, and to whom I owe a lifetime of thankyous, for a lifetime of love.

I sit in wonderment of the days
gone by,
Consider the bestowments that
fate made mine.
I ponder the bad times, and rejoice
in the good,
But should I have been different?
Did I do all I could?
What would my life be now, had I
never gone
From more than one triumph,
more than one song?
Can I gaze in a mirror . . be content
with the lines
That wrinkle this face with the
passage of time?
I stopped, and then laughed at
these questions in thought.
Life is too complex to sit down and
sort.
For as each year before me, and
each year behind,
The answer's the same in any
man's find.
It's the strength of the heart, an
eternal youth.
The Past may leave wrinkles, but
with dignity, too.
So I step forward and strong, for
I'm proud to be
The righteous truth of whatever is
seen.

Antonio Hoody
I KNOW IN ADVANCE WHAT'S EXPECTED OF ME
I know in advance what's expected
of me
I know with each day what I'll do
I know where I'll be when my day
begins
I know where I'll lye when it's
through

From minute to minute, from day
to day
Constantly going around in the
same familiar way
Like riding a merry-go-round a
course without change
Like a well rehearsed play, the
scenes all pre-arranged

Once I felt content with the cycle
in which I dwell
Now bitterness roams in my mind
And I am trapped in my own
private hell

Once it was enough for me, I felt
no need for more
Twas a game so safe I'd never lose
Fore I always knew the score

Now time teacher has brought into
view
Changes I once could not see
Though my cycle routinely
remains the same
These changes are deep within me

It's funny how you thought that
your mind was made up
And your feelings would never be
swayed
But, now you look back with many
regrets
As you lye in the bed you have
made . . .

Charlotte Gibbs
BOREDOM'S THOUGHTS
Far from the sights and sounds of
this hum-drum place—
Far from here where I never see a
familiar face—
Far from the prying questions of
my once precious friends—
Far, far, from here where the
imagination has no ends—
Far away in places undreamt of as
yet—
Far from the noise of the worlds
modern sounds—
Far into the unknown realms of
God's universe where
dreams have no bounds—
Far into the distant future where
we can never glance—
Far into the unknown tomorrow,
where we all have a new
chance—
Far, far from this place is where I
want to be—
Challenging the unknowns of the
universe, in places I never
thought I'd see—
Far, far away, where exploring is
so much fun—
Far, but not so far that I can't sleep
in my own bed—
When this day is done!!!

Charles L Coe
TAKING THE STEP

To my sister, Kathryn

Wild nights cried the blues
and colored soft the wind.
Emotion cracked and split in two
as if to let me in.

Do I know where I am headed?
Do I really care to know?
I think I'll place my feet
where my heart tells me to go.

Tami M Dean
A POEM FOR GRANDMA

I want to give my thanks to the people who encouraged me with my poems, my mom, Helen, Cheryl, Pattrise and Judy Adams, and especially to my grandma who meant the world to me.

I wanted to write
a word or two,
something that would be
special—just for you,
reminding you of the
things you've done,
all the happiness you've brought
and all the hearts you won,
being like no other
grandma could be,
doing those special things
that mean a lot to me,
always there throughout
the years,

to share in the laughter
to wipe away the tears,
You've been someone
that no one else could be,
that's someone whose
very special to me.

Phyllis K Henry
TIME GONE BY
The pages are yellowed
The words are all gone
I wish I could've read them
To know what went on.

They were the words of wisdom
The words of the past
The years took their meaning
Time's gone by too fast.

Some say it was the time
When all things were crazy
Others don't remember
Their minds are all hazy.

Maybe I'll never know
What those ancient words meant
The past is like a piece of money
Its value has been spent.

Cecil C Baker
MEDITATION
Such silence the night offers
That I can lean back
And allow the day to rest
Lightly on my shoulders.
I can sort out the comings and goings
Of all things that happened
And reflect on the words I've had to say.
In peace I can know
If what I did was right or wrong,
And in deciding of rightness
I choose not to judge.
The stillness assures me
That what's done is done,
Not to be undone.
What will come will come.
Tomorrow I will do whatever
The flurry of activity demands of me to do.
And always I strive to be
The best of who I am.
More and more the deepest of night-times
And brightest of day-times show clearly
What the silence of night offers,
So that I can lean back
And allow the day to rest.

Livonia Chittenden Osborn Stevenson
LATE WINTER STORM
Fifty million snowflakes falling from the sky
Fifty million feathers floating from on high
Soon will cover all the rooftops
All the hills will soon look painted
All the trees look black, white edged
Like an etching on white paper.

Nothing mars this silent winter wonderland
Peace and quiet gives one time to understand
Out of storm and strife, atonement
Out of warring, devastation
This then starts new life astirring
And the cycle is recurring.

Just as now the birds fly to the windowsill
For seeds and suet, then they trill
Now the quiet is no longer
Birds are flying all directions
Calling all their kind for feasting
While earth rests, the world is teeming.

Mrs Sandra Thomas Powell
MYTHOLOGICAL MUSICIANS

With loving devotion to my Grandmother, Anna Elizabeth Swisher Smith, who endowed and inspired my music education and the thousands who acknowledged my work.

Zeus poses in Olympian pride
While Zephyrus, the West wind
Flows in luxurious harmony
Across Scylla,
The rock between Italy and Sicily;
Where Orpheus, a Thracean poet
Creates mystical strains
Of melodious music.

Following Ulysses sojourn and conflict in Troy,
Having been conferred foremost of the Greek chiefs—
Is confronted by Charybdis, whirlpool opposite Syclla,
Vivid, yet vague an aqua arena
Compared to Calypso of Ogygia,
Who tearfully surrenders Ulysses,
Now seven years past his adventurous arrival;
At last, homeward bound to Ithaca.

Arion, charming Greek bard and cithara player,
Thanks the dolphin, Flipper
For guiding his voyage ashore!

Aphrodite, Greek goddess of love and
Aurora, Roman goddess of dawn
Dance dazzlingly and free as the first rays
Of recital eve chasten their way.

Apollo and Artemis, brother and sister,
Colossal towers of strength,
Praise Leto, God of prophecy and song,
As day lingers long!

Doris Culver
GOD'S PAINTING
God paints a picture
From His palate everyday,
Try to match his color,
You can't. There's no way.

Ada Beatrix Greathouse
MY HEART BEHOLDS THE KEY
The key of equality lurks in my warm-hearted soul,
A feeling of unjustice reigns through my veins,
I understand the values of my proven rights,
I wonder why I don't get my justice in the world,
I look and search and my pride gets swept away,
The key is inside of me just waiting to get out,
I hold the key in my hand and it fades away,
A face looks at me and snatches my freedom today.

Voices tell me to get out,
They say find out what the real world is about,
They say you are not wanted here nor there,
I'm just not wanted anywhere,
But I want my equality right here, right now!

My heart does behold the key of equality
It waits to get out everyday,
No one gives me a chance to show what I can do
I have the brains like anyone else,
I can move mountains, hills, lakes, and ponds
With the strength of my tongue;
My heart;
My mind;
My soul;
They can all make an impact on the outcome of lives to come,
My heart beholds the key
A key to the phrase—ONE DAY WE SHALL OVERCOME!

John M Switzer

John M Switzer
THE ROAD TO HERE

This poem was written for my lovely wife—Billie

We are born—we live
and then we die.
Some are not fortunate
like you and I.

We've traveled many roads
to get where we are.
Some have been rough
and from here—quite far.

They were roads of learning
and travel them we must.
To learn of God and love
before we turn to dust.

God has led you and I
along those roads to here.
Safely we've arrived
through all the strife and fear.
We've learned of God and love
and how our life He planned.
Now—He's put us together
to protect us by His hand.

Bryant H Bartley
MORALS GREATEST SIN
Girls are beautiful things I guess
To be desired but not possessed.
It fills my heart with deep despair
To see so many sink so far.

They are made to be a lovely wife
The pleasure of a mans life
And help to make a happy home
For lovely children to play and roam.

Though some men pluck a flower each day
To take out and toss away
To carry to some beautiful lake
And forever her honor virtue to take.

Some grey haired father bows in shame
The stain upon his daughters name
Her youngest sister follows too
For this kind of love to her is new.

Clouds of sorrow shadow the home
For peace and love all have flown
A happy family torn apart
It breaks a dear old mothers heart.

It certainly is morals shame
For the girl to always bear the blame
And left at home to set and cry
While the men go sunning by.

Linda Ortega
HALLOWEEN NIGHT
On a dark and windy October night
I spotted a witch on a broom in flight.
I have never believed in witches, you see
I thought my eyes were playing tricks with me.

The moon was full—As full as could be
But the movement of clouds that covered the sky,
Swept over the moon like a wind swept sigh.

I saw her cloak of floating black
And her face of green
Did I mention her cat? He was as black as the night; Eyes of deep green
Then I knew it wasn't real, it had to be a dream.

I tried to put these visions out of my mind—
The witch and cat; dark night, and the moon
But the clouds moved faster—
Leaves fell from the trees,
And a gust of wind brought me right to my knees.

Then I remembered it was Halloween night.
A time for fright on a dark cloudy night.
This was the way I was suppose to feel—
Only next time, I hope it is not real.

Debra Nicole Huber
STORM: FROM DUSK TO DAWN

To my family. Especially for Mom and Stephen, for your patience and love, but most of all, for just believing in me.

Though I scream I cannot be heard
With fire and fury flailing.

Tearing away my every word
Into the nighttime.
Sailing.
Wind, it whips all about me
And though I have nothing to hide,
I cannot help but tremble,
As I search for a ditch so wide.
White water crashes on the rocks behind,
Smashing, pounding in my ear.
Feet pounding the earth, I wonder?
Is it my own heartbeat that I hear?
Out of breath I slow, and stop,
To listen. The noise is dying down.
Cool water runs from my face.
Down,
Down.
Getting up slowly I turn around.
Wreckage from the havoc of the storm, scattered far,
Is all that greets my eye
Until I look upon the horizon line.
There's
A rainbow
In the sky.

Donelle Zeigler

A GRANDMOTHERS LOVE

In memory of my loving Grandmother, Martha London

A Grandmothers love is a special love,
it has a gentle sort of touch.
It's given with much respect,
and her feelings which mean so much.

She's a sense of security,
when the world outside seems sad.
With her softness and her inspirations,
makes the hurt seem not so bad.

She brightened even the darkest days,
her smile so full of cheer.
And when you looked into her eyes,
you could almost sense a tear.

For the joy that she has brought,
and the love that she has shared.
I hope in my heart that she really knew,
how much I really cared.

For now she's gone, but not her love,
as with us it will stay.
My Grandmother whom I call my friend,
will be with me throughout each day.

Marjorie V Heavner

TO MY GRANDSON

To Rosalee and Richard Morris—Parents

Dear Little Richey, so innocent and small,
What will you be when you grow tall?
What will be your hopes and dreams?
Perhaps your eyes will be trained upon the stars.
Many before you have had the same dream.
Don't despair—you, too, can be great in your own way.
In your travels, don't forget to be grateful;
Be kind to your fellow man, and give them love.
God above is watching over you—now and always.
I pray you will remember me, your Grandmother;
And thank your loving parents that made this possible,
Remember—keep a clear head and a kind heart.
With these attributes you can't lose.
Forever,
Your Grandmother.

Michelle Ranieri-Turner

SILENT VOICE

Altered by a newly unraveled strength
and appeased with a self-assumed perception
A timorous crawl will suddenly march
with distorted self-glorification
And a once torpid vessel will harbor
in a wave of blind certainty

A man without a reason
Yet a man with a goal
Callous principles
Shallow soul

Compelled under the guise of unspoiled intentions
and persuaded by the perpetuity of their gain
A mirage of glory will increasingly erupt
from worn and misdirected ambitions
And a once intangible illusion will be grasped
in the crippled hand of urgent perfection

A man with a taste for life
Yet a man who hasn't cried
Hollow aspirations
Contented pride

Surpassed by none with yielding thoughts
and infected with the conquest of a nameless reward
A haven of disapproval is the only inheritance
from a receptive view of life
And a once passable river of expectation
becomes a monotonous water of self-destruction

A man with a will
Yet a man with a numbered choice
Powerful aim
Silent voice

Marie Schweisberger

THE FORGOTTEN POEM

Once there was a little boy, his name was Robert
Reece. And every Friday afternoon he had to speak a
piece. So many poems that he had learned, that soon
he had a store of resitations in his head and he
still kept learning more.

Now this is what happened. He was called upon one
week, and he totally forgot the piece he was about
to speak. His brain he fairly cudgled, but no word
was in his head. So he spoke at random and this is
what he said.

"My beautiful, my beautiful who standeth proudly by,
it was the scooner Hesperas, the breaking waves
dashed high. Why is the tooram crowded? What means
this stir in Rome? Under a spreading chestnut tree,
there is no place like home.

When freedom from her mountain heights cried,
Twinkle, twinkle little star, Shoot if you must this
old gray hair, King Henry of Nevar. If you are
waking, call me early—to be, or not to be. Curfew
must not ring tonight, Oh woodsman spare that tree.

Charge Chester charge, On Stanley on, and let who
will be clever. The boy who stood on the burning
deck, but I go on forever."

Lynn Bowker

MY MOTHER

To my mother, Thank you for being who you are and making me what I am.

When I was in trouble she was there to lend a helping hand.
When I was in doubt she would re-assure me.
When I had something to say but no one seemed to care, she would listen.
She has done more for me than anyone could imagine.
She has helped me through many hard times and I love her for that.
She is very special to me and no one could ever take her place.
Most of all I love her because she is my Mother.
She made me what I am today, and I thank her for that.

Barry Jon Ousley

BLIND

He can see neither the forest nor the trees.
Yes, he is blind, but still he sees.
His eyes perceive no light.
Kindness makes his world bright.
He can see no color, no hue.
Honesty never fails to shine through.
He can't distinguish black, yellow, red or white.
Children laughing and crying sound alike in constant night.
He can see neither the words of the Bible nor the Koran.
He can feel the power of people worshipping hand in hand.
He is called handicapped, but he has to disagree.
He knows of people who have sight but still do not see.
For him, his darkness is merely an inconvenience.
The less fortunate base their blindness in grievance.
Society tends to set him aside.
That is alright, he needs no guide.
Although bound in darkness as if to a chore,
he recognizes love as the key to freedom's door.

Viola M Wurl

Viola M Wurl

US

Many' many years ago it seems,
Perhaps it was only in our dreams
We walked life's pathway together.
We sat together in that old sweet shop.
How we watched that old court house clock.
The movies we saw, the long rides we took.
Now it all seems like a story book.
But then there came a day with a parting of the way
Who did what or why, it is hard to say.
Then after fifty seven years had passed
Fickle faith decided that at long last,
Our paths should cross once more
Before we depart for that golden shore.
Sure our steps are slow, our hair is grey
Things are not the same as yesterday.
Still on the square stands the old court house with it's clock
But gone forever is the old sweet shop.
Perhaps the rides and movies are things of the past
But then somethings I am sure
Things that will last forever more
For they are a gift of the Lord, you see
My friendship for you and your friendship for me.

Mary-Jane Sousa

ACQUAINTANCES

I see you;
you look.
I look at you;
you speak.
I speak to you;
you listen.
I listen to you;
we see.

Brooks Harding

IN THE BEGINNING

In the beginning God created the sun,
The earth, and a heaven full of stars.

In the beginning he made the Moon for
Light by night, and the planets Saturn,
Mercury, Jupiter and Mars.

In the beginning he made a mist to
go
Up from the Earth, and caused the
rain
That gave the flowers their birth.

In the beginning he gave us his love,
He crowned it with a rainbow in the
Blue sky above.

As it was in the beginning it shall
Always be, the beauty of the sky, the
Land, the flowers, and the rolling
of
The sea.

Daniel F O'Keefe Sr
SINS OF THE FATHER

Dear Ole Dad.

Dad you no good bastard you left
when
I was four
You left Mom, Sis and me for a
bottle and a whore
I've never forgiven you for all the
hurt and pain.
They say it was the whiskey that
made you so insane.

I've a wife, and two children just
like you Dad
They don't understand me, and I
get so damn mad.
I'm a father just like you Dad, and
I hate you even more
As I sit here in this tavern with a
bottle and a whore

Lois Lund
BABY CHICK

In memory of my mother; To my father; And to my wonderful husband, Larry

---

As yellow as butter
Like a soft cotton ball,
Is the new little chick
With its cheep-cheeping call.

Its sparkly black eyes
Are as round as can be,
As I hold it so gently
And then set it free.

To run all about
On its little orange feet
Pecking at grain bits
I give it to eat.

Dear little chicken
You're one of the things
I'm glad that the coming
Of Easter time brings!

Cyndi Austin Singleton
THE RIVER

This poem is dedicated to Lambert J. Moore, a good friend whom I care for very dearly.

So calm and peaceful
It gently flows
Without an end
Knowing not where it goes

Watching the sun
Glare down from the sky
Warming this body
As each day passes by

Having no cares
Sharing no love
Just wandering by
Those who live above
So deeply it runs
Through shallow paths
Having no friends
To share joy and laughs

Maybe in the future
Somewhere around the bend
He'll find someone special
Just looking for a friend

Angela M Bradley
DIMENSIONS
Dimensions

Trapped on the isle of confusion,
caught up in some illusion;
Hear my loved ones beckoning
call,
Warning of a day when the heavens
fall.

Standing on my piece of ground,
Nothing gained from what I've
found;
Lost inside a room of walls,
Afraid of the day when the heavens
fall.

This world is like an ongoing maze,
Everything comes but nothing
stays;
But one day the beast will no
longer crawl,
After the day when the heavens fall.

Donald D Stockford
A DESERT PLACE
There's a desert place inside me,
Vast and stark, but not devoid of
beauty—
Where the earth is parched and
white,
A hot, dry wind blows day and
night,
And dead weeds roll across wide,
open spaces
As long-winged birds glide above
high rock faces.
In that desert land, alone, not
lonely, my soul resides—
With sun and moon and stars
besides.

Dale C Nebeker
OUR TIME CLOCK
Life as is a clock
In seconds ticks away
Measuring out life's time,
Each and every day.
Surely life's span is measured,
Though given little thought;
None the less holds in amount
What each and all have got.
No matter what we do
We live but once the time,
As a river of no return,
Moves in rythum and with rhyme.
So each second has a value,
How we spend it for it's worth
Will add up for what we are
In life upon this earth.
Some are designed to be great,
Which history shall record
But each had dictates of his own
That his make up will afford.
When life's clock does stop
Of age and wear and tear,
Have we spent our time well lived?
This should be our greatest care.

Lynn Ramsey
A LITTLE BOY'S FACE

For my grandson—Christopher

Today, I watched a little boy's face.
The path of his tears could be
traced.
What good are all the new toys?
The room must be kept as neat as
a pin.
Oh, what fun there might have
been.
Being a child is not a sin.
A place for all things, all things
in their place.
But, oh the tears on a little boy's
face.

Fay Harnage
I BELIEVE
I believe in wondrous things
A beautiful earth, and happy beings
Stars of diamonds, sun of gold
Moon of cheese, days of old
Cinderella and her prince
Sky blue waters, forrests dense
Wind sighing, angels above
Happy people living to love

Bobby Hunt
WHY I NEED YOU
To chase away a frown
When I feel lonely.
To let me know
I'm not by myself only.

To kiss me on my cheek
When I feel sad.
To let me know
Not all is bad.

To lift my spirits
When I'm somewhat low.
To have your love within me
Wherever I go.

To hold me in your arms
With a great big hug.
To reassure me with warmth
You radiate of your love.

To walk with me
So I'll not have to walk alone.
To help me remember
That your heart is my home.

And for all these same reasons
That I need you.
I'll be there . . .
When you need me too.

Pauline J Dutro

Pauline J Dutro
LIFE'S TRULY GREATEST TREASURE

To my Mother, a very spiritual inspiration at childhood. To Vickie, our daughter injured at birth. Helpless, but Special. Gave me inspiration to write through the Lord.

Life's truly greatest treasure.
We can receive here on earth!
Is the one the Lord will give us.
When we are ready for second
birth.

He is ours for just the asking.
Such a small task, to say, I do.
Take Him as my Lord & Saviour.
He has suffered already for you!

No matter what we ask for.
As we pray from day to day.
He hears our every longing.
All along life's way.

We don't always know the answer.
Life is such a mystery.
Our trials and tribulations—
Are sometimes meant to be!

We should never question His plan
As we travel here on earth.
But follow his precious footsteps.
Once He gives us a re-birth!

The joy of His being your Master.
Tis more than words can say!
May we learn to serve Him
always—
As we go along life's way.

Patricia Mauro
SUNRISE

For My Children, JOHN, TRAISE, MICHAEL, ERIC (And For All Children)

The boy's name was Sunrise
Who left the shiny sea
Sailing toward tomorrow
To touch infinity

He brushed against the windsong
And knew that it beguiled
When he heard the children crying
His fantasies went wild

He stepped into the sunlight
Hoping they would see
A special magic turning
Where all might be free

He fostered care and courage
And felt his job was done
By holding every moment
Until their hearts were one

To cherish love and caring
For those that need concern
And hope those creatures stirring
Shall value each return!

Yvonne Avonde Smith
THE HAUNTING
You were the ghost at the wedding
Invisible there to the room
But I could see you
And you could see me
As I walked down the aisle
To my doom

You were the ghost at the supper
Silently cutting the cake
We toasted each other
With bitter champagne
And waltzed to the tune
Of a wake

You were the ghost in the bedroom
Waiting to turn out the light
While I smoothed the cold sheets
Of the nuptial bed
Where we three would be
Spending the night

You were the ghost in the morning
Lingering to say good-bye
And I wept secret tears
For the coming years
When you turned away
With a sigh

Diana Lyons Wilson
EPOCH

Sing for me a happy song.
A song of cool blues and yellows.
A song to make me smile so big,
to help forget my sorrows.

A song to raise my sagging spirits.
Soaring through an infinite sky,
my mind will fly to distant lands.
A speckle in this world am I.

A song of yellow, shiny as gold,
dancing diamonds, singing light.
I reach out and grab. Revelation is
within my heart.
Oh, contented soul. Wanting
naught, needing naught,
happiness unfolds

A song of blue, as cool as an icy
glacier.
Of hope and love, of serene
wellbeing.
A happy timeless song, without
enclosures.
Emblazon with emotions
gleaming.

Rachael L Harte
YEARNING SOUL

i am in a dark hole; i grope, but i
can not grasp.

things i cannot see, pass above me.
i feel suspended in space, but not
in time.

words enter my mind, but i do not
understand.

i ponder my existence; my reason
for being; i feel trapped within
myself, wanting to break free.

i struggle, but to no avail. unseen
chains clamp down on my wrists.

i feel unraveled, pulled apart by
doubts.

a light shines within me, and I
know.

I no longer struggle, I simply am.

I reach within myself, and I
understand.

Gary Holt
A TEAR

Dedicated to Aunt Clara and all my family

A tear can form when someone
dies.
A tear forms in your eyes.
A tear forms when you cry.
A tear can form when you're
glad.
A tear can form when you're sad

A tear can form when you're
most anywhere.
A tear can form when you're
with your Aunt Clara.

Dottie K Kreps
A POEM FOR YOU

To my Mom—Sandy K. Kreps

When the day's brand new
And you think you can't make it
through,
Just remember this—
I love you, and I know you love me
too.

Mary E Bragg
DIET

So candy and cookies taste good
you say
And you actually put them in your
mouth
Then you wonder in great
amazement
Why your body is as big as a house
One little piece won't hurt me
I'll run this off you say
Then you sit down to watch TV
And don't move from your spot all
day
Go to the store after supper
Buying sweet and fattening foods
Then you wonder why you get so
tired
And feel the way you do
I don't like fat and neither do you
And don't say your pleasingly
plump
You see an over filled garbage bag
Is taken to the city dump
Ah-Ah-Ah don't put it in your
mouth
If its sweet, if its fat or good
Cause if you keep on over eating
You'll be as big as your
neighborhood
So if you feel the urge to overeat
Please don't even try it
Don't be the one to destroy your life
Be in control and diet

Ollie Jane Fuller
ENFOLD ME LORD

This poem is dedicated to my Daddy, "Walter Dotson"

Please enfold me Lord, In your
loving arms'—Divine.
So I can bear what I must for me
and mine.
Takes alot of faith, alot of trust.
With your help—I'll bear it Lord, I
must.
I must press onward, not in
despair,
I know your here Lord, everywhere.
My faith must be brave, must be
strong.
For in your hands' Lord, I can't go
wrong.
Lord I cannot hide no secrets, or
tears.
I know—your with me, in all my
fears.
So Lord enfold me, give me strenth.
For this sad, lonely time of length.
Make me strong, help me
pull—through.
If—it be Your will, for things You
still want me to do.

Don Marshall Hensleigh
MY BEST TEACHER

You asked for a story on my best
teacher;
Not a favorite can I recall.
It would not be fair to show
partiality
For I was inclined to like them all.

The sound of her voice
commanded a moment of
respect
And quickly gained my keen
attention;
I knew each statement that she
made
Contained some valuable
information.

In class you had to be alert
When she made an oral
explanation;
Later, when you were called upon
You could give an intelligent
recitation.

Evenings, I was encouraged to do
my homework—
Something I loved, so wished not
to miss them.
I think this rewarding factor
should be included
In our current Educational System.

If someone asked you this question,
"Who was the best teacher you ever
had?"
When you responded with the
answer
It is someone with love and
patience, just like
Your Mom and Dad.

Kara L Swanson
AND YOU, MY FRIENDS

We walk through life on paths we
find
Trails littered with passing time
Sometimes sure and not confused
The road is worn from so much
use
But often we must break the brush
Our doubts and fears we seek to
hush
And lean upon our courage, dare
To breathe in unfamiliar air
It is here we learn, we dream, we
grow
The seeds our lives begin to sew

Through darkness, storms, and
rocky bends
It's here we reach back for our
friends
For alone we may search for the
skies
It's all too soon we realize
That no beginning, no fresh start
Is complete without those in the
heart
For those who protect us from the
storm
For those whose hands have kept
us warm
For those who steer on treacherous
bends
We give our love, we call our
friends

Erma E Grant
THE CLARION

"Lo, the winter is past,
The rain is over and gone."
Such were the words of the poet;
We call it "Solomon's Song."
All is not joy and gladness,
Our spirit is crushed and despised.
Again a tall son must answer
The call of his country so wide.
This is our third and our youngest;
The second one failed to return.
May he never be fearful or anxious
But walk with his face to the sun.
I must feel somewhat like Mary,
(Mothers' hearts are all much the
same)
As she walked the way unattended
The day that dark Friday came.
Be this then your task for the
moment,
Keep faith as your armor divine,
Remember Him in the Garden
When the sun no longer could
shine.
I pray God you may face the future
As calmly and bravely as He,
Who, when all men reviled Him
Walked softly in Gethsemane.

Christine Reece
THE LONELY SCHOOL-HOUSE

A lonely, country school-house
stands on a rocky hill.
Dust covers the desks and books,
and each window sill.
That old school-house was new, in
nineteen twenty-three.
Its use, for learning and recreation,
is ancient history.
The school was on Aravaipa Creek,
the only place we knew.
The teacher and the pupils walked
several miles to school.
Pictures of our old school brings
back memories to my mind.
All the kids wore homemade
clothes; we knew no other kind.
A tornado demolished our little
school-house in 1927.
One wall stood, desks crushed,
three walls were leveled,
But, it was soon rebuilt on that
same old lonesome hill.
Deserted 40 years ago, that old
house stands there, still.
I recall the old-time dances—folks,
from near and far,
Danced around the school-house
floor, to a fiddle & guitar.
The school attendance got smaller,
as the years went by,
So, our school-house was
abandoned in nineteen
forty-five.
The steep trail from the creek, up
to the schoolhouse door,
Is filled with rocks, today, and it's
being used, no more.
To all, who went to our old school,
it was a stepping-stone.
Very few are left, today—we miss
the others, who are gone.
Our old schoolhouse is a reminder
of our childhood years,
And, as I look back to those times,
I shed some memory tears.
The lonely school-house is a
symbol of so many yesterdays.
Today, it stands silent, day and
night, just making history.

Buril W Smith
THE IMPACT OF ONE

This poem is dedicated to the one person who gave me the strength, courage, and backing, but most of all the ability and inspiration. JESUS CHRIST

He arrived on a planet
In such dissarray
There were all kinds of beings
All living their own way
He cared, though they did not
He had compassion for all

And tried to teach
That thru love and devotion
There was a goal they could reach
He cared, though they did not
At the end of his visit
He was looked down upon
So he left that world
His memory to carry on
He cared, though they would not
Many years have now gone
Since he went away
And yet the people became
More wicked each day
He still cared, though they did not
He has planned a return
To take back the few
Who thru the ages believed
And did follow thru
Christ still cares, though most do not.

Anna Marie Bostic
THOSE SILENT TEARS

Dad and Mom I would like to thank you for giving me life, love and happiness I will always Love you Annie

---

In a bedroom
in the dark
on a pillow
is where they start
those silent tears
that no one hears
they fall for a lover
who no longer cares
now a broken heart
she must bare
till come another
who will care
and chase away her fears
and help her stop
THOSE SILENT TEARS

Julie M Dunham
GRANDPA

To My Mother, Millicent Shimek-Gallup

We little girls once upon his knee—
Now reminded how long it's been
since we sat there
and took sweet
cherries from his stained and calloused hands;
We little girls once clapped and sang,
danced a jig as fast as he could play
upon the concertina;

Sunbrown fields with secret written poetry
where the dance of life is a ballerina
in a spiders web.
We little squirrel tails,
We little fish scales.
—So we miss
those fragrant flowers,
the trees will blossom again this spring,
and we all walk there
in memory.

Warm winds sing
and talk
in the tongue of his old country.
(Once upon his summers knee,
you and me, mommy.)

Kelly Lee Gibson
GRANDPA

I will never forget the day
So cold and lonely it was
The ice hung on the trees
The day we said goodbye.

When you went away
You left me with so many memories
Memories to hang onto forever
To cherish all day through.

I remember the nights I lay in bed
You lying beside me so close
You told me so many stories
You made me laugh so much.

The stories were so great
Each had your love attached
I will never forget them
As I will never forget you.

Someday soon I will hear them again
As they softly put me to sleep
I love you dearly, so dearly
Goodbye Grandpa, Goodbye . . .

Phyllis A Phillips
I LOVED YOU SO MUCH

You said, "Don't be angry with me when I die."
How could I, knowing how hard you tried to stay alive.
I felt so much compassion and so much love for you,
Yet there was so little I could do.
My heart was breaking, I cried inside for you,
And now I have to realize that you are gone.

Each morning I awake and wonder why, I am here and you have died.
God, I feel so guilty to be alive.
Yet I still smile to see children at their play,
Still love sunsets at the close of day.
Why am I so very much alive, How can this be, when you have died?

I always thought we'd go together,
By plane, car, or on your beloved trains.
But here I am, alive and well, yet you have died.

I always thought I could not live without you,
But now I find I cannot turn my back on life.
I feel its' pull, the good, sweet sounds of earth,
Spring blossoming forth, buds bursting, full of life.

Though you have died, I remain very much alive.
And yet, so many times a day, I cry inside for you.
I will love you and yearn for you until the day I die.

Francis J ("Bibbers") Dalton
THE STARS AND STRIPES

To Phyllis in gratitude for her extraordinary patience and help. Also to Captain Dennis Conner, and his winning crew. Also thanks to Felix, Maryann, and my grandchild, Joseph Michael Di Maio.

The spinnaker was hoisted,
the crew were in their place,
all were at the ready,
to start this famous race.

Whether the winds were light or heavy
it mattered not at all,
Master Sailor Dennis Conner,
on the "Aussies" put a pall!

There were white caps in abundance,
the seas were mighty rough,
you've got to give it to them,
these guys are really tough!

The cameras on this vessel,
captured surge and roll,
and the efforts of these sailors,
giving heart and soul!

There really was no contest,
each day they were ahead,
at night the "Stars And Stripers,"
could rest easily in bed.

The cup has been recovered,
you've restored a nations pride,
congratulations to you all,
and welcome back Stateside!

Eileen C Scanlon
WHILE YOU SLEEP

The peace of you, my darling, as you sleep, this night of my awakening. You are a gem in your style, your way of knowing, your clear, crisp laugh, your sense of humor that flows through you like a glistening river. You are a jewel in my day, I wake to you each morning, to watch you shake from you the blanket of dreams that held you, watch you as you take the hour in your stride, catching up with consciousness, sneaking up on the dawn.

We need not speak always the matters of the heart, nor can we always whisper of the love that drowns us in our joy—you bring me moonlight in a paper cup, daisies in a smile, dewdrops in a word, rapture in a kiss, springtime in a glance, youth in our laughter. You are strength in my arms and the dimple in my past. You are more to me than this, and yet I can only begin to say. You make my home a forest, my heart, a fawn. You are the cradle that soothes my soul when I'm weary and the charm of my life. You are the King of Splendor and the door to my longing. You are the dream I invisioned as a girl and the cusp of my Womanhood. You are all this and more. When will the day begin so I can kiss you hello?

Shannon Kay Abela
TUESDAY IN THE LIFE

To my BEST FRIEND and loving sister KIM. Whose love helped me through the rough times and whose encouragement made the good times even better.

Ball of confusion . . .
Nothing happens—or then it all does
At once
"Synchronized mass"
One minute you feel like "Atlas"
The next minute (or so it seems)
you're "Catatonic"
—Schizophrenic—
Why is everyone looking at me?
Am I the only one who can't handle it?
Or does everyone else fall apart
when I'm feeling my strongest?
But then again . . .
If we were all built emotionally the same—
Whose shoulder could we lean on?

Elizabeth Ann Cramer
A SMALL PRAYER

The small heart within me
Cries out in mortal anguish
Oh God! My God! Press your gentle lips
On this my aching wound
For I have wandered
And behind each stone and tree
Have searched
Till my humble mind grows weary
And the breath within me turns stale
Should I ignore the beat of wings
That pass within my hearing

Should I pull down the shades of night
And blur my constant vision
Lest the pitiful remains of me
Find surcease in forbidden paths
And solace in the black of night
With those condemned by thee
I wait—and watchful pose
I see a far off light
A spark of goodness which seems to beckon
Thru this realm of tears
I rise on folded haunches
And with weeping eyes and thrusting hands
Injoin my quaking soul
To thy everlasting human heart
Father, except me

John V Calleja
BE NOT AFRAID

Not able to breathe another breath,
I pass through the doorway of death.
Into a tunnel of brilliant light,
Blinding because it is so bright.
Now I see a hand that holds a key,
To a place I cannot see.
Using the key to open the door,
To let me see a little more.
An unbelievable power brings me to my knees,

From something I am about to see.
Through the clouds a face appears,
And I feel my eyes begin to tear.
It is the King who walked the land,
The one who carved me in His hand.
He said, "Come my child, be not afraid,
For Eternal Life the price I've paid."
This is home my friend,
You have reached the end.
I heard Him say,
There is no more night or no more day.
No more pain or no more grief,
Only belief.
No more wrong, only right,
Within the Kingdom of Eternal Light.

Lillian W Phillips

ODE TO MY DAUGHTER

With a thousand thoughts my mind is filled today,your special
day; brimful of the priceless memories no one can take away.

Can you count the blades of grass that grow or blossoms on a
tree? Rain drops which fall on your roof at night? pebbles
washed from the sea?

Wild geese honking on their northern flight? wild flowers in
a glen? White caps made by the vessels that pass? Thoughts you
keep of a friend?

Ringlets that grow on a baby's head? Stars which light up the
sky? Footprints made in a little boy's day? Clouds in a
wintry sky?

The flakes of snow in a drifted lane? Bees from their hive
swarming? Winds that gust through a tall poplar tree? Claps
of thunder warning?

The shadows found in a quarry near? The ripples in a brook?
The morning dew in a distant vale? Come dear and take a look.

Relax and dream as your mother's done; though many duties call
You really deserve a top-notch day for joy you've given all.

Marijane Brown

A LOVE POEM

Dedicated to the one I love, my husband, Steve.

A poem just for you my friend,
As a tribute to love without end.
In honor of what is and will always be—
This is a love poem to you from me.

I will do my best to make the verses rhyme.
Read it often, and think of me each time.
Think of the life we have shared,
And know that I have always cared.

Think of all the together years
Filled with many smiles and tears.
Don't forget the tears are part of it all;
We stumble at times, but never fall.

We have loved long and strong.
How can such love ever go wrong?
We know each other well, you and I,
And keep learning as the years go by.

Take my hand; never let go.
Love me often; tell me so.
We share a special love you know,
And I wrote this poem to tell you so.

Marian Betzold Butts

MIRRORS

The mirror that hangs on your wall
Can tell you many lies.
The true picture of a person
Is revealed through your eyes.

They dance from hidden laughter.
They sparkle with surpressed glee.
The peaceful look of happiness
Is there for you to see.

They show the tenderness of feelings.
They shine from unshed tears;
Light up with understanding,
Become dull from lonely years.

They can also show the icy steel of anger,
Please for understanding when you're sad,
Show the aching look of deep hurt,
The desire for someone to help you be glad.

Our eyes are truly the mirrors
Reflecting our innermost thoughts.
They reveal our deepest feelings,
The things we've always sought.

Olga Vila

LONELINESS

To my beloved daughters Helga and Alma Frohlich

Like a star, many times I feel
Lost in the inmense cosmos,
Not visible to the human eye
No matter how many others are around
Me.

Like a star, I shine with my own light
Yet, I twinkle when I feel lonely,
Moving around in my loneliness.
Because of the haze, I can not be seen by
Others.

Unless for a high magnitude of light,
As the intensity of the colors of the spectrum,
Which descends upon myself,
To eclipse the despair upon
Me.

Oh, how I wish I could be a Blue Star
And radiate great warmth and brightness
To give to others on this earth, and,
Like a Faith Star constellation, ease my
Loneliness.

Essie M Nicholas

CORNER CHURCH

To my granddaughter, Jill Heck

There is a place I like to go
Where all is quiet and love's aglow
Where church bells chime and music sweet
Beats out the time in full retreat
Where people go to search, a place within
The corner church

The spirit within that calls
Leads many men that they may not fall
The towering steeple that guides you there
The mighty strength that knows and cares
When all is gone, if you look and search
You will find the answer in
The corner church

Veronica A Lupsewicz

DUSK—MAHONING, PA

Inspired by my grandson, Stephen C. Lawrence, in our new world.

Indigo Mountains edge the horizon.
An orange moon in twilight-rising.
Heavenly-blue curtain descending
on village lights with fireflies blending.

Melodious church bells resound
Over roads homeware-bound,
Through tunnel-paths of corn fields

From sweaty-labored yields,

A distelfinked-barn appears
In a swaying field of corn ears.
As far as the eye can see,
A picture of tranquility.

Alana K Tyler

I WISHED UPON A MIDNIGHT STAR

To My Loving Husband, Robbin

Because of one wish I made to you
My hopes and dreams have all come true

I wished upon a midnight star
For a love, that was much too far
You came to me, as a friend
I don't anymore, have to pretend

Afraid of love and losing again
You were there to make amend
I no longer have to cheat or lie
My love for you will never die

You weren't the first, to have my love
But, you made me feel, like it was
I've forgotten all about my past
With you, I know, this love will last

I wished upon a midnight star
For a love, that was much too far
You came to me, as a friend
I don't anymore, have to pretend

Because of one wish I made to you
My hopes and dreams have all come true
Thank you for giving me, this one more chance
I know, at last, I've found romance

I wished upon a midnight star

Wanda Reed

TAKE A LOOK

Take a look at the flowers, take a look at the trees
Take a look at the mountains and feel the cool breeze
Take a look at the oceans and the rivers that swell
But you better look fast, 'fore they blow it to Hell
They've started a race that no one can win
The best thing to do was not to begin
There's no going forward, and no turning back
All in all, the future looks terribly black

But they say not to worry if there is a fight
For our leaders will scurry into caverns alight
And there they will gather, to weather the storm
In the Nuclear Winter their butts will stay warm

Don't worry if you sizzle, boys,
Don't grumble if you freeze
Why, you'll feel better just to know
That they are none of these

Now, I don't know about you, Friend,
But if worse comes to worst
The only way that I'd feel better
Is if those guys went first

Now you may think I'm bitter,
That I have a lot of gaul
But this ain't no game of marbles, Friend
We're playing for it all!

Walter Keith Lowe

NOT HURRIED, ANYMORE

Time has slowed immensely—
Days are longer than before—
Since I put away my timepiece,
I'm not hurried, anymore.

I don't eat because it's mealtime;
I don't sleep because it's night;
I'm not guided by the hour
Nor by darkness or by light.

I've got time for interruptions,
Time I never had before,
I'm not ordered by my timepiece;
I'm not hurried, anymore.

I've been thinking more of others,
Less aware of my own needs;
There're no hassles—there're no quarrels
For my mind's been set at ease.

I can now see things more clearly,
Hear sounds never heard before;
My senses are much keener—
I'm not hurried, anymore.

I can spend time with my Maker,
Time I should have spent before,
Get a sampling of the blessings
That for me He's had in store.

Erna H Flowers

Erna H Flowers

A LOVER'S ADVICE

Here's to the Bride, beautiful and thrifty
Who already knows about "that fifty-fifty".

Though I can't advise you along
that line
Here are some tips that are mighty
fine.
Remember, nothing will be the
same
Beginning, of course, with your
last name.
You'll always be jumping and on
the run
Trying to get things properly done.
Anytime you're in such a stew
Remember this: "You'll come
through!"
Remember to smile as around you
go
Trying to cook, clean and sew.
For once begun, it's for real.
You've lucked upon a lifetime deal!
Tell the new groom if he'll wash the
dishes,
You'll smother him with love and
kisses.
If he's angry, irritable, or sad
Remain very gentle, patient and
glad.
If disappointments come, cast
them aside.
Don't suffer because of foolish
pride.
When we learn to forget and forgive
It makes our lives much easier to
live.
Honor and cherish each other's
beliefs,
Willing to share each other's griefs.
A certain librarian was asked to
give
A hint for a successful life.
She said, "Just shoot him now,
And don't become a wife."
Now many have offered you hints
galore,
But I'll tell you what I'd do.
I'd throw them all out my back door
And "paddle my own canoe."
For happiness comes double
To those who work and plan.
Just thank them for their trouble
And do the best you can!
Then, no matter what the year or
weather
You and your man will be together.
Forever and Forever!!

Joan E Simpson

FRIENDSHIP

Bare this soul a gentle song
Of harmony
Cadent strings plucked by
A Silent Author
His music travels
Haply through the air
Seeps in the soul
Two listeners hear a melody
The third, a parody
And thus creates
Disharmony.

The Silent Author recreates
A stronger rhythm, stronger beat
And through the air they soar
Till high above the human task
Of making friends
Each soul explores
It's own
Diverse
Intensity.

And naturally as volume lulls
The sapped souls
With cognent cause
Fade silently
In blended tones.

Ruth Kildow

GOD'S SON

God sent His Son as a babe,
To save you and me.
He lived and died and arose
again—
From sin to set us free.

He's there with his Father
In that mansion up above—
Waiting to hear from each of us,
To fill our hearts with love.

Do you remember how He died,
On that cruel tree?
He said, "Father forgive them,
I'll die to set them free."

He arose the third day,
From the tomb they put him in—
Yes, my Lord had conquered all,
By defeating man's sin.

Let's remember this, the Easter
Season
By giving the Lord our Soul
And thanking Him each day—
Because He has everything in
control.

God gave us all that He could give
When He gave His Son—
He'd do the same all over again
If I were the only one.

I thank my dear Master
For what He's done for me,
He's given me loving hope,
And from sin He's set me free.

Earl J Kurth

A CITIZEN OF THE REPUBLIC'S PLEA

Oh say can you see by our
forefather's blight;
To write our Constitution to
preserve man's God given right.
A realistic dream to pursue
freedom and justice with
righteousness,
Thru a written document which
has such foresight and clearness.
The society of that time could use
phrases so poetically sweet,
With the chains of tyranny still
fresh in their mind and feats.
Now this document so flexible and
complete,
Was written to be amended if
needed to keep out the
tyrannical seat,
They drew up the ten most
precious right's,
And called them rightly so "The
Bill of Right's,"
It's easy to see by how early in line,
That the second amendment must
be preserved to the line,
For if ever so clear of man's
weakness to greed,
The people must have the right to
protect their liberty,
This little poem may sound like a
joke,
But! Don't let man's lust for power
cut our republic's throat.

Karla J Wunderlin

LOVE

Love. The "magical word"
The big word with little face
value.
Love. The building block of
destruction.

No one understands
when Love ends—
Their life is intact
and they're not alone.

The end of Love
is a death of sorts.
Memories—sweet memories—
are swept up and locked away
for safekeeping . . .
For someday.

When a loved one dies
Time is given to mourn—
People understand

But when Love itself dies
Who laments
with the widowed Lover?

Mrs Nan C Burnworth

DADDY!

Dedicated to my three children Joann Stanley, Dennis B. Mahaffey & George D. Mahaffey

---

Dear Daddy, tell us a story
Of your beautiful home above
Tell of its bountiful glory,
Built of the things that you love.

Help us to build us a home there,
Or just add some more to your own
We all loved you so dearly,
I know that you want us to come.

I shall never forget the last sweet
smile
That we saw upon your face
I knew that you meant it to tell us
Of your glympse of a better place.

God needed you for some purpose,
Not as a Doctor, though
For He is the great Physician,
There's no illness there, I know.

There will be a great day in Heaven,
When we meet our loved ones there
Though life's pathway is rugged
I shall strive to pay my fare.

Robert George Fitzpatrick

THE BLIND GIRL'S PRAYER

Dedicated To My family.

I wish that I could only see the stars
up above, and see the many
things God made just for you
and me.
For my eyes have seen the darkness
and the light I will not see.
I dream of many places where I
wish I could be, so I pray to our
father, our God, up above.
To let me be like other kids, and do
the things they do.
I know when the angels take me In
heaven up above, there will be
no more darkness, and light will
shine above.

Ellen Kronstedt

THE BLACK KITTEN

The little black kitten went out one
dark night.
He decided that he didn't need a
light.
The kitten was brave. He walked
all alone.
He even sat down to rest on a stone.
He heard different noises, but he
was not afraid.
When he came to some water, he
decided to wade.
Far in the distance he saw a dark
house,
He kept on a-walking, quiet as a
mouse.
The house door was open, but not
very wide.
The brave little kitten ventured
inside.
He roamed all about, from here
unto there,
The rooms were all empty, not
even a chair.
All at once he saw something close
to the wall,
The kitten came closer. "Could that
be a ball?"
He reached out a paw. He touched
the strange thing.
It just curled up tighter like a ball
of string!
The kitten got braver, and touched
it once more.
Then "eek" said the thing, and ran
across the floor.
The kitten was frightened, and ran
out of the house.
The brave little kitten was scared
of a mouse!

Annette Jordan

I USED TO KNOW WHAT ICE PICKS WERE FOR

I use to know what ice picks were
for,

You were too young to
remember.
You with your frost-free
refrigerator

—Cool cubes—making
themselves,
dropping into ice buckets.
You don't remember the ice man
coming—
Bringing twenty-five or fifty
pound blocks of ice.

More in the summer if you made
ice cream.

Folks wrote the "Blues about the
ice man

Leaving more than ice,

And the "Blues" went "Country"
too,
"You had to watch that ice man
Coming through your back
door."
There stood little wooden cabinets
on

Short, squat legs, to put ice in,
With drip pans underneath. Ice
melts faster
In summer—the drip pan runs
over.

If you were too poor

You didn't have ice in the
summer—
Or lemons for lemonade, or ice
cream.

But you had flies!

Couldn't afford screens on your
door,
—Not if you were too poor.
Not if you were too poor!

dee Mabry Speir

THE MEADOWLARK

For Nana. Ruth T. Whitlock, January 20, 1903—May 24, 1985

Somewhere,
A rustling in the trees.
The Meadowlark calls,
And your memory is whispered in
the air.
Spoken softly on the winds of time.

I turn;
The sun in my eyes,

And for one fleeting moment,
Beyond Heaven and Earth,
Our souls touch.

Then as quickly as he called your memory;
The Meadowlark calls me home.
But my heart cries out,
Did I remember to say,
I love you NANA,
And I miss you.

Marion Schiffgen

THE DIRECTOR

If I had the opportunity
I know what I would do;

I'd read the hearts of all mankind
Of red
Of white
Of black
And Jew.

And with the knowledge of these men
Their hearts a printed page

I'd direct a simple drama
Upon our avocado stage.

I'd lead their endless, groping minds
To find eternal peace.
Bring end to sorrow and to wars.
Yes, find from death release.

But, alas, that's not the way it's planned.
Each plays his roll alone.
The stage is set
The lights are on
The part you choose must be your own.

Naomi Isenberg Dale

CRAIG GOES TO SCHOOL

Today our Craig marched off to school
To start the years of books and rule.
His world will widen with each day
He'll make new friends and learn to play.
His teacher he will think is great
And also some of his playmates.
He'll learn to spell and read and write
And do his home work every night.
I know each year he's sure to pass
And be the head of every class.
I know he'll be the best of all
I see it through a crystal ball.
This crystal ball is small in size
It's what you see in grandma's eyes.

Melody Ann Ward

Melody Ann Ward

HE'S ALWAYS THERE

Jesus, is the light, of our life. He's our friend, forever.
When, you call to, him he listens. Then, replies, gives us, the right answers.

The more, we believe, in our Savior Jesus Christ the, happier we'll be living in this life.

Saying, a prayer, shows you care, in your heart and soul.

It tells, God that you, love him so.

When, ever your hurting, or in fear. When, your eyes, can't stop crying with tears.

Call, upon Jesus, he'll help you dry them away. Remember, he's always there.

Richard Allen Cox

SAILING

Time in morning, when time has past
Through the days, and all, the many, "feeling's of days"
That we, enjoy through
And, so many times,. "we" spend now
And through, the years, and "we" forever
So time, in the morning, when the sun, comes "in morning"
When all, "days" are gone by, when need the feeling's, of days
And you know, the times, "I" spend, with "you"
Those many times, in "life"
It's "you," gives "me" times

Away, I bound, "sailing"
Across, "Mighty Atlantic"
To away, I bound, "the golden shore"
"We sailed," the "ocean" in "search"
"I'm" going to the "silver stars"
In, "the night"
When all, many wonder's, of "you"
And though, "I see"
In, "your" eyes
All "the silver stars"
In, the "night"

Julie Rancourt

TO A FRIEND

Tell me dear friend,
does a poem have to rhyme?
I have read some that do
all of the time.

But, then there are those
with little to say,
they make you think they
have lost their way.

Some poems are pretty
and some poems are sweet,
some tell a story that
makes you weep.

Whether poems are happy
or poems are sad,
when you pick up a book
do they make you feel glad?

Perhaps dear friend,
this is what poems are for,
to make you relax and
read all the more.

Joseph Rudolph Harrell

MY FRIEND

To Joni, my lovely wife, and my loving 4 children Joe—Celestine—Debbie and Ruth.

I met a friend—sometime ago
And I watched—my friendship grow
No matter what the crisis be
I know this is a friend to me
There were times—when my life was sad
And I beseeched this friend I had
to help me solve—this thing I face
And soon the thing—was erased
I used to live my life in doubt
Wondering what its all about
The ups and downs—caused me strife
Now I know its part of life
Ever since our day of birth
Enduring is the way of earth
But lets not stray—from the blend
I must tell you—who is my friend
All thru life—as I trod
My eternal friend—you see—is God.

Richard R Anderson

TELL ME IT'S NOT TRUE

Tell me it's Not True
A nightmare of course.
All the People
In the streets
Singing in Remorse.
Tell me it's not true.
Tell me it's not true.

If there is a fair way,
to treat this insane thing,
Let the heard, of rhyme and word,
Ring—Oh let it ring.
Tell me it's not true
Tell me it's not true.

Give Peace a chance,
Was echoed here one day.
I am at my peace
But what a lousy way.
Tell me it's not true
Tell me it's not true.

A scribbled name
Ain't that a shame,
The Reason for
Why I was slain
Tell me it's not True
Tell me it's not true.

Sally Roxayn Evans

THE HUNT

The snow is cold on the pads of his feet.
His search is in vain.
He has found nothing.
Nothing but ice, snow, and trees.
Where are they?
They are gone.
But . . . where?
The dog cannot find them.
Where are the bears?
And, where are the ducks?
Where could the deer have gone?
But he is not worried.
They will come back.
Just like last year.
And then he and his master will get a ten-point buck.
But he will have to wait.
They will come back.
Just like last year.

Ralph Griffey

RAGE

It's not what you see or hear,
It's not what you dream or fear,
It's something that grows inside you,

Year by year by year.
It builds up as you get older,
And finds a way to get out,
Then all control is gone and you
Start to scream and shout.
If you don't know what I'm talking about,
Some people already do,
It grows inside with the coming of age,
And is called none other than fire burning Rage!

Arlene Bowen

GOD CHOSE

It's a beautiful morning,
I can feel the warmth of the sun upon my face
The rays stream through the window,
As I sit in my usual place
The winter has past,
And the winds are gentle and warm
The daffodils are blooming,
No longer hiding from the winter storm
I can hear the Robins singing,
I'm sure they're building a nest
The trees are budding leaves,
So convenient to protect and hide it from the rest
I can visualize the beauty,
As spring blossoms all around
I can smell the fragrance of summer,
As the flowers pop through the ground
My fingers touch the petals,
Of the flowers so velvety soft
How firm the new sprouts are,
Not like fall when the leaves are falling off
God made this beautiful earth,
And spring is my favorite time
And God made me see the beauty,
Even though he chose to make me blind.

Judy Gilmore

ODE TO THE GROUND HOG

Oh heres to you, natures brave centurion.
Who lays asleep deep in the mothers breast
Who wakens to some unheard calling voice
To rouse and see if yet the earth be blest.

Will your awakening be alas, in vain?
Or will the fickeled promise, at last, come true
It matters not if we must wait a bit
It is the hope you kindle that we seek
The promise that the spring again will come.

Roza Lantsman
ALL PATHS LEAD TO YOU
All paths lead to you
Where e'er I stray,
You are the evening star
At the end of day.

All paths lead to you
Hill-top or low,
You are the white birch
In the sun's glow.

All paths lead to you
Where e'er I roam,
You are the lark-song
Calling me home.

Charles H Bowman Jr
I WILL NEVER FORGET

To my Mom Hester, and my Grandchildren Nathan, Sharon, Charles, Marshall, & Sera

---

I will never forget that January day,
That 7 Americans were took away,
I will never forget how I felt in my heart,
As they were about to depart,
No I will never forget how America cried,
that terrible day they died,
I will never forget that look of dread,
When the world knew they were all dead,
No I will never forget them because they were like me,
For they had a dream to keep America free,
I WILL NEVER forget them.

La Verne H Jackson

La Verne H Jackson
ENIGMA

To My Beloved Husband Byrne Ambro Jackson Who went to his everlasting sleep March 1984

Above the highest mountain
Above the condor's flight,
And in the deepest silver mine,
I dwell, both day and night.

I am the weakest of the weak,
The strongest of the strong;
The infant's lullaby is mine,
The tempest's giant song.

I kiss the milkmaid's cherry lips,
At morning's golden dawn;
And throw the blossoms in her pail,
When passing o'er the lawn.

Without me none are ever born,
Without me no one dies;
No dolphin in the briny deep,
No eagle in the skies.

Within the poppy's scarlet cup
I sometimes fall asleep;
Yet wake at music's softest tone,
And with her sweet voice keep.

Christine Daly
ACQUAINTANCE FOR LIFE
Confusion sauntered in amazingly self-assured.
He arrived admist an avalanche of discord
with mayhem on his heals.
His immense robe of pale pink and powder
blue iridescence
Draped loosely about his body.

Logic is his tactic
He lives for death, possible, yes, never, why,
His pencil's out of ink, no, ofcourse, because,
Why not, the arid rain did fall.

Confusion is our friend, he comes to help us;
Loose our minds,
But only occasionally.

Marie Bolle
OBLIVION
The light shines in the promised land;
it is the substance of dreams,
a serene, vague, elusive place

imagined so often—a mirage, misty,
eternally compelling, beyond reach;
it leaves no trace.

Have waited so long for your entrancing,
hypmotizing, anaesthetizing embrace

With soothing, healing oils wash this wary,
tired traveller; in gentle forgetfulness
bathe.

These footsteps are so heavy, resounding
echoes of sad and hollow truths left
in the wake of an endless path; awkward
and out of step; in this land, a stranger
to its inhabitants and unfamiliar in its ways

No longer can endure, I surrender to seductive
calm, enveloping darkness; softly slipping
into oblivion never to stir or seek the
memory of bygone days.

Michelle Lenore Creech
LEAF
A leaf
is
an intricate
piece.
So full
of lines
so
utterly divine.
Green
or red,
Yellow
or brown,
A leaf
is
an intricate
piece.

James Morrison
A NEW YEARS MESSAGE

This is dedicated to my children, Chae Michael, and Ryan Ashley, and to nursing unit 2D of Washington Hospital Center. Thanks for the way you accepted me. Always James

---

Christmas comes and Christmas goes,
With all it's love and cheer.
Preparing us for what's ahead,
With the coming of a new year.

Prepare yourself don't be late,
The year may pass you by.
We haven't much time, we can't wait,
Now's the time to fly.

Forget the past look to the future,
And see what you can see.
It's time to let go be strong,
And be what you can be.

Enjoy the chance to start over,
And do it to your best.
For those of us who can,
Don't forget about the rest.

Tonya Holland
KENTUCKY GIRL

This poem is dedicated to Margaret Merrick, my loving teacher.

Kentucky is the place to be, when Education, is all you need.
The books, teachers, T.V. stations; All about education
I want to learn to help the sick, those in need for shelter, and those who need both.
I guess a doctor, you could say, but again, maybe a teacher someday.
If I should lose all the learning I've earned, I'd break
down and cry; for it's the most precious gift beside life itself
I hope that others can see the light that has shown upon me and is so bright;
I want to show someone the way; A daughter or son; grand child or grandchildren, all too young to understand.
One day I'll be old and it will be too late, so I'll do something now; there's no time to waste!!

Delores Allen
JEWEL FOR HIS CROWN
Theres a new angel in heaven today
Yes, Dustin has just passed away.
Not wanted on Earth.
With a heavenly giggle an one small crown.

With the angels he does play
In the arms of Jesus he does lay
Yes, Dustin just passed away.

On earth there was sorrow an pain
An no man to give him there name
Locked in a room, no one to play
As Angels looked down
They watch as he played

One angel among the heavenly host
Appear at the foot of the bed.
While flames hovered around his head
One jewel for the crown
Thrown among rocks of stone
In the arms of Angels he was carried home.

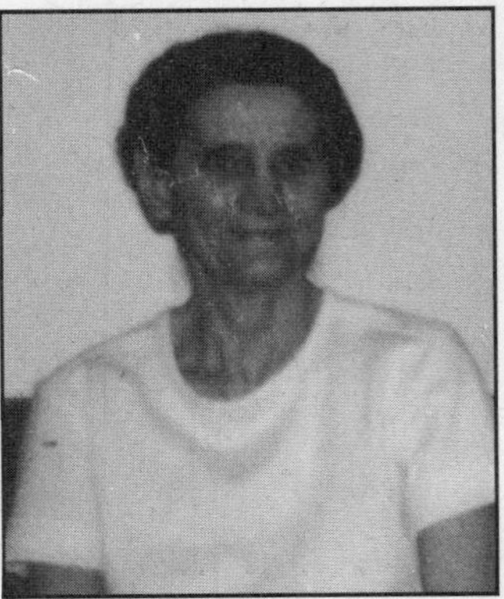

Mary M Killmon

Mary M Killmon
THIS LAND

To my twin brother, Marvin James, World War II Veteran

North America; has been called;
"The Land of The Free";
Some people can't seem to see;
It has cost blood and misery;
To keep it free from enemies;
Who want to make prisoners of you and me;
So we have to do what they say:
So we all must thank God and pray;
To keep America that way;
The Land of The Free
For you and for me, and
For all who love
Truth, Justice
And Liberty!

Helen J Prichard
TO LINDA
You really shouldn't say "Why me?"
When questioning your lot,
The answer simply has to be—
"For heaven's sake, why not?"

The valley you are in today
Was meant for you to know
How blest you were to climb that hill
You conquered years ago!

Julie L Nack
TO BE FREE
Freedom has taken on a more personal meaning to me
It doesn't feel as vague or illusive

It's the discovery of my inner freedom—allowing my true creative self to emerge
In discovering who I am, I have more to give.

It is a truly personal journey many miss out of fear
They take side roads or try to find the easier softer way
Never really feeling who they are
Living half-alive with the precious passing of each day.

I'm feeling my losses and grief as part of the process
Embracing the pain, staying with it, until I hold it to my heart
Old ideas, old behaviors and habits pass away
Replaced by new ideas, new ways of being, each significantly playing their part.

Peggy Cwiakala
A TALE OF HOW IT'S TOLD
I nowhere have gone that has not
gone before me.
I search and am rewarded
with breakthroughs that broke
on sandy rivers and gull lit
byways
where small craft recklessly float,
tied down
where the answers are—in other
words
the water knows what I find out.

I live in a whirl of voices and faces
that make up a cloud of
sensation. I
nowhere go that they do not itch
in—
rubbing shoulders, those noses
and eyes
of young women and old men. My
search leads
me only to questions more
arousing than satisfying.

In coming summer leans the apple
and the elm
the coming hot air circles even as
the snow
whistles and wets the earth, and I
am standing
looking up at the sides of buildings,
listening to the sighs of life being
lived—
moments going farther inward
while still farther outward.
My pulsing and my breathing
and my consciousness goes
nowhere that has not gone
before me.

Darlene Ann Marshall
TIME TO MY SELF
One bright and sunny morn, I
traveled the path of orange and
yellow daisys.
I felt so much alive, but a little lazy.
I stopped by the pond and gazed
at the different shades of blue, I
had time on my hands and
nothing to do.
Just then a squirrel went dashing
up a tree and didn't even have
time to notice me, as he jumped
from tree to tree different shades
of color of leaves fell on me.
I felt the warmth of the sunlight as
it shone through the trees as if it
was searching for something
just like me.
As I walked a little farther I knew
this day was like no other.
Perhaps I will never know what I
was searching for that day, but
it gave me time to myself and a
time to get away on this glorious
bright sunny day.

Niki Dee Pettijohn
KARRUTH CANYON

In memory of my Dad, Love Niki

Karruth Canyon is where
my dad was raised
he describes and speaks of it
with so much praise

I love to watch his face all aglow
when he talks about
the deep drifts of snow

How far he had to walk to school
with paper wrapped sandwiches
and old holy shoes

The trees are like giants
so very big and tall
remembering how brother Rick
& him
used them as fort walls

Grandpa used to say
"trees were here to shadow the
earth"
maybe thats why the wildlife
chose Karruth to give birth

And remembering the old two holer
located in the back
tip-toeing outside so quietly to
use it
running like . . . hell
to jump back in the sack

Fetching water for Mama
from the well in the ground
only to spill 1/2 of it
to my destination bound

At night trying to guess
who was coming up the road
and sitting on our front porch
only to hear . . .
that old noisy toad

And Dad reminding us to be careful
when we would seek out on
adventurous trips
"make sure you are home by
dark"
he would say;
"or I'll get you with the stick"

The majestic mountains are
always in view
very dark in color
perhaps wet from the morning
dew

Someday I'll take my girls to . . .
Karruth
Daddy would say
so they can see the secret place
God put on earth, "I think
just for me

The joy and the memories
I will always cherish
to know that Karruth Canyon
could never even have
a blemish

So I did just that
like I said I would
I took Niki & Sharon to . . .
Karruth
and I think they both understood

Now Dad we have those
precious memories
just like you
now and forever
our whole lives through.

With all my love,
Niki Dee
1985

Roger M Grauf
PAWN

For my Mother and Father, who always believed in me.

I am the Pawn that protects the
King.
My brother guards the Queen.
Ah, the Queen.
Majestic on her throne,
The King's right hand.
The Bishops: His assassins.
The Knights: His own "Black
Death."
His Castle: Mightiest on earth.

I am the Pawn that protects the
King.
The King, almighty in his rule.
He is the leader, the executioner,
For he sends us to our death.
Oh God, I wish I were King.
But alas,
I am the Pawn that protects the
King.

Patti Osenbaugh

Patti Osenbaugh
OUR WORLD
I hear people say, our world has
changed,
That things will never be the same.
Tho the sky, the stars, the birds I
see.
Are still up there, looking down on
me.
The squirrels play around my old
oak tree,
They're just as happy as they can
be,
The grass is still green, and blue is,
the sky.
The children still laugh, and
sometimes they cry.
The birds still sing, the dogs still
bark.
The cats still meow, when-it-gets
dark.
Now the rain still rains, and
flowers still grow
The joggers still run, and in winter
it snows,
At night through the window of my
room.
I can still see the stars, and the
same old moon.
Seeing all these things daylight
always comes.
Then I still see the sky, and the
beautiful sun.
So it seems—to me that some
people just change.
I'm so thankful Dear God, that our
worlds, just the same.

Mara Zoe Banish
TIGER IN THE COURTROOM

Dedicated to Anthony John Spilotro 1938-1986. To you, your brother Michael and your reawakening. March 1987

He strolls into the courtroom
Like a tiger in the ring
Many fear this killer
And the preying feel he brings

Glaring at the witness
As he shuffles to the stand
Like a growl, he softly snickers
With the verdict in his hand.

Having bribed a single juror
As a cat would tease his prey
He reclines, content that in the end,
A conviction would not be made

They claim he bore a killer's glare,
That would take your very soul
His ego, like a lion's pride
Kept Tony so very bold

The witness shivers in his shoes,
As a mouse before his demise,
For "The little guy" would not
allow,
Him to preach on what he buys

Debra J Kelly
THE FRAILTY OF LOVE
Crossing each other's paths and
revealing emotions,
It means taking a risk and sharing
our fears.
I choose to share this time in your
life,
Because of feelings that flow from
the heart.
When I'm alone . . . you're in my
deepest thoughts,
For I can envision your smile,
sense your touch,
and become mesmerized by your
laughter.
Relationships can kindle such
elation . .
and burden the heart with such
sorrow.
At times it is difficult to completely
reveal oneself,
So I submerge into my thoughts
and my pencil
becomes my release.
So many things in this life are false
and temporary,
But courage and strength in an
individual,
are a few gifts . . . that a person
can give to oneself,
In the hope of sharing them with
another.
My only hope is that through
openness and honesty,
we may discover each other . .
moment by moment.
For it is when we are experiencing
our
doubts and our strongest fears,
that courage and strength will
guide us . . . and if needed,
Even heal us.

Stella K Williams
GOD MAKES A RAINBOW OF OUR TEARS
When our rivers of tears have
flowed out to the sea
Joining all those ere shed by
hurting humanity
'Til that old ocean roars with the
pain of it all
Remember that God has seen each
teardrop fall.
Soon the sun draws up water and
then drops it as rain
On some desolate desert or a
faraway plain.
Thus earth is refreshed—rainbows
brighten the sky
Our spirits are lifted—for awhile
we don't cry.
God's prominent promise proves
that He still cares.
He re-cycles our sorrows—makes
a rainbow of tears.

Archie Meriel Asher Jr
DESERT SUNSET
Gazing through needles of Yucca's
descending sun rays paint rolling
waves of magenta cotton, further
and

further day time descends into dusk
Giving way to skies of lavender—yellow
As the coal of life melts into the blue
horizon
traces of reflected light bounce softly off
saguaro cactus

Eloina Colo'n

INTERROGATIVA

Este poema fue' inspirado por las la'grimas de mi nieto Edwin. A el se lo dedico con mucho amor.

Apenas con cinco anos
Y no obstante su ignorancia
Ya conoce del dolor.
Su abuela materna
se aucenta de momento
Y el pregunta sin sesar
Por que se fue?
No importa donde ella viva,
Yo quiero irla ver.
Luego se aucenta su padre.
Y pregunta sin sesar
Por que si me ama tanto
Me abandona sin piedad?
Cuando regresa su abuela
Por la que tanto sufrio
Se llevan a la otra
Al cielo, a morar con Dios.
La madre que tanto ama
Lo manda a los razca-cielos.
Pobre mujer, se separa
De lo que mas quiere en el mundo.
Su mirada entristecida
Sus ojos grandes y secos
Nos dicen lo que su corazon siente.
Pobre mujer, como sufre.
Mirando muy tristemante
A su madre, ella le dice:
Te entrego lo que mas quiero
Mi corazon, mi tesoro, mi todo;
Eso es lo que es mi hijo.
Y suspira fuertemente
Como queriendo gritar.
Hijo mio, hijo mio
Que sacrificio, Dios mio.
El nino en su ignorancia
No lo puede comprender.
Es que ella no tiene casa
Dondo vivir con el.
Un casero sin escrupulos
Se robo todo en la casa.
La ha dejado viviendo en la calle.
Pasando miles miserias.
Por que la gente no entiende
Que el oro no hace feliz?
Pues solo se es feliz
Al lado de lo que se ama.
Quiero volver a tu lado
Madresita de mi alma.
No importa donde vivamos
Quiero estar siempre a tu lado.

Elizabeth Koterwas Jacobson

PEACE AND JOY OF GOD'S GRACE

The glancing eye photos a height of skin,
Flaunting a mop, or fringe, of hair atop;
Some camouflaged with paint and powder, too!
Too "cool" to hold, with warmth, in arms or heart.

Mind's instant camera does not picture
The splendid bird, leaf-hidden in a tree;
The rainbowed blossom held in a twig's bump;
In summer's heat, the mountain's snow-capped peak;

The hurt behind the rigid, soured face;
The Spirit that dances on rooted feet;
A closer, warmer God, as seen by blind;
And beauty caught within the quiet Man.

But Oh!—the findings of the feeling heart,
That soars, with Love and joyous Ecstasy!
It stays—to hear the song of unseen birds;
To sense the leaf and flower in bumpy twigs;

To put the smile upon the rigid face;
And dance the Spirit with its grounded feet;
Is deeply stirred by beauty of Man's Soul!
Then finds God's grace is given to itself!

Nell Merritt

TO OUR LOVE

The mysteries in this life of ours
Are awesome to behold
When we deem how delicately
The tenuous strings unfold.

The early years for you and me
Were spent scant miles apart.
Yet, in my fondest childhood dreams
You never had my heart.

'Twas by the fate of chance we met
Since both felt quite unwise
To venture from familiar paths
With blinders on your eyes.

With faltering touch and wispy smile
Our journey had begun
For friendship soon grew into love
And we became as one.

Sometimes it seems the shards of life
Cut almost to our souls.
At other times we scale to heights
Of ecstasy and goals.

My love, be not ye faint of heart
Nor fear strange miles untrod
For down this unknown path we'll go
Led by the Hand of God.

Ethel D Gibbs

MY NIECES AND NEPHEWS

My nieces and nephews are my pearls,
The cute little boys and the sweet little girls,
Whether we are together or apart,
Each has a special place in my heart,
My other jewelry will tarnish and fade,
But these will improve with age,
As I watch each rosebud grow and unfold
I know they are more precious than silver and gold.

Each day as I swing and play with them,
My every prayer will be to HIM:
"Grant that I may never a stumbling block be,
To these precious ones who look up to me,
But rather let me an example be,
That they may ever see Jesus in me,
For He said: Suffer the little children to come unto me
Then He blessed them and took them on His knee."

There is another precious gem,
Who has gone to be with HIM,
And though it was hard for us to understand,
We realize now it was HIS Divine Plan,
He came and took her by the hand,
And lead her into the promised land,
Where there is no more pain or sorrow,
But we will all meet again on that glad tomorrow!

Carrie L Moats

THE LADY LIBERTY

Dedicated to: Mom, thanks for your support. And America's Freedom.

The lady liberty
standing bright and tall
with her torch lit
meaning freedom for all

She means to us, pride and love
as she looks up to heaven above
she is always standing so straight and tall
for those who come to see her, big and small

And when red, white, and blue fill the sky
for then we know, it is July
so when we think of her, on that July day
we love her and know
that she here to stay.

Jodie Lynne Brodeur

I SHOULD HAVE SAID I LOVE YOU

To the memory of my father—Richard Allen Brodeur

I should have said I love you,
but now its just too late.
Our relationship could have grown,
with only love not hate.
I'll always hold your memory
in my heart it will remain,
it'll be there for an eternity,
and help stop the rain.
The times we could've spent together,
but instead we were apart
might have shown that we were special
in each others hearts.
It may be too late to tell you,
how much I really care,
but these words come from deep within,
and I'll always hold you there.

Ann Gettys Cunningham

THE BAG LADY

She huddled beneath the paper sheets
Of script that told of sorrow
But she was used to being forgotten
And saw no better for tomorrow.

She was just a "bag lady"
Life's possessions she had few
She lived with memories of yesteryear
And with dreams that failed to come true.

The wintry winds just hurried by
Chilling her body to the bone
But she offered no complaints
Of never having a home.

Her smile was always so radiant
As her meager possessions she shared
After all, God loved her
It didn't matter that no one else cared
One cold night in her loneliness
God answered her fervent prayer
And gave her a home in heaven
Where she no longer had burdens to bear.

In her hand was a tattered Bible
marked with a verse of her quest
"Come unto me all that are weary and heavy laden
And I will give you rest."

Kelly Haggard

THE HENCHMAN

See the black buggy,
drawn by horses of black.
Holding reins sits the henchman,
bones behind him in a stack.
The henchman is pure black,
right down to his heartless smile.
His eyes are coals of darkness,
his hair is deathly vile.
Every night that black buggy
goes past your locked door.
To collect another body,
yet to spare you of the gore.
He has robbed you of your daughter,
and thieved your bonny wife.
And found some morbid humor,
to refuse to take your life.
So everyday as you grow lonely,
you get a little older.
And everyday as he goes by,
he gets a little colder.
We look to the west as the sun sets,
goodbye until tomorrow.
Unless his buggy stops tonight,
to end your bitter sorrow.

Angie Snesko

LOVE IS LIFE

To all the children in the world,

Love is life and life is love . . .
You know this wonderful feeling
Causes my heart to glow . . .
Love is the only answer to our lives
Puzzle . . . how can we survive without
Love; if we only learn to read and

Hear the fine beat of our heart . . . the
Silent beat of a heart full of love . . .
That's so beyond control . . . then perhaps
We will learn the meaning of the word
Love . . . this is the moment . . . this flickering
Feeling, causes my heart to glow . . . as you can
Sense I am in love . . . with love alone . . . love
Is like an exotic flower with all it's
Sentiment . . . and that's how it goes when
The silent beat of our own heart is full
Of love and love alone.

A Davis

IN STITCHES

Dedicated To Reciprocal Loyalty

There once was a boy who wore red socks,
They were going out, and going to bed socks,
He worked in them, slept in them
Danced in them, leapt in them
And, on rainy days they would be wet socks
He was given brown boots by his brother,
And, wore them out one night to impress a new lover,
But as the evening waned off
Those boots they came off
And, she found you can't judge a foot by its color
But she discouraged his bold flirtation,
And diminished each expectation
When harsh words left her mouth
He jumped from the couch
And ran from the houce, while she was still ragin'
In his stocking feet he stomped through the night,
Then their scarlet hue caught a car's light,
As its racing tires swerved
Good sense was served
Those darned socks had saved that boy's life!

Barbara F Duncan

MY MOTHER, DONNA MAE 53

Donna was a quiet, shy, private person, who didn't
often verbally express her feelings,
Yet underneath it all, her actions toward her family
and friends exhibited a great wealth of love.
Donna was not only a mother, but a grandmother
and a best friend to her daughter Barbara and
grandson Edward.
Throughout her life, she devoted herself totally
to her family and was very protective of them.
Even in the midst of her pain and suffering, she
never complained but endured patiently.
As being raised on a farm, she enjoyed gardening,
nature and animals.
As her life drew to an end, she expressed her faith
in God Our Father and in the Lord Jesus Christ
as her Saviour.
"I do hope to you, the people out among us,
will sit back and think! We have but one
Mother," Love, respect and care for her,
appreciate the time with her.
I wish I could have done more myself.
No one knows when the time has come.
Bless you all, Be good to one another.
Love,
Donna Mae's Daughter

Toni Wolfson Hidalgo

KNOWING YOU STILL CARE

When I see you lying there
Your hair so soft and fair
Through the years of wear and tear yet you still care.
When I know you're here
Those eyes so warm and dear.
Even when the trouble appears
You always lend a listening ear.
As you lie across from me and stare,
Your lips I cannot bare,
To have them untouched by mine
For too long a time.
How I'll always want you my pet,
For my life was nothing until we met.
That day I shall remember well,
Cause deeply in love with you I fell.
Many a year has passed since then,
But I'll never forget it when,
I still see you lying there,
Knowing you still care.

Ann Baehm

REFLECTIONS

To "My Son" Allan Baehm and "Charity Perry."

The moon's reflection,
Shining bright,
In my mirror
Late at night,
Reminds me often,
How "Beautiful,"
Is "Heaven's Light!"

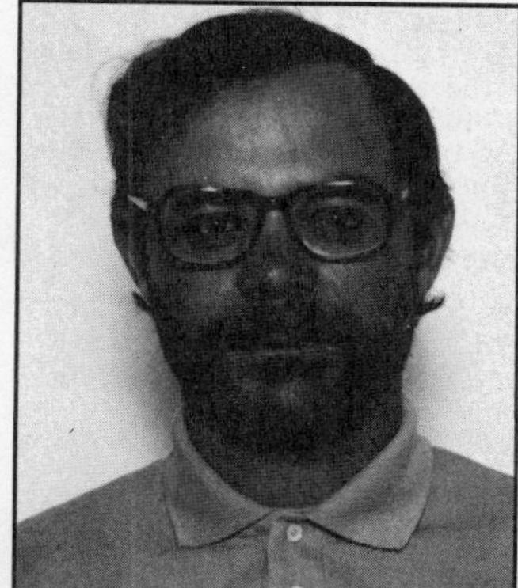

Rodney Calvin Forester

Rodney Calvin Forester

I GO NUTS OUTDOORS IN THE SUMMERTIME

To my first race car with shock absorbers on the top A-frames and the front springs heated to lower it

---

I go nuts outdoors in the summer time
The clouds in the sky look bigger
The birds in the trees sing louder
The ground seems closer
The wind blows harder

Laura Owen

THE DAWNING

I rushed into my office, threw my brief-case on the floor
Called out to my Secretary, "Hold all calls for one hour more."
There was work that I must finish, contract clauses that were wrong
Things that only I could handle, then I grabbed the telephone.

One hour to straighten out this mess before the board would meet
One hour to make the right decisions, or to go down in defeat
One hour against a lifetime of reaching for the top,
And now that I was almost there—I dropped the phone and stopped,
To read a telegram that lay beneath my finger tips
"Sorry to tell you Mother died while you were on your trip."
My vision blurred, my knees were weak, I sat down in the chair
A nagging voice kept whispering, "One hour! One hour! One hour!

I closed my eyes and sat there lost in sorrow and despair
Remembering a life of love, of giving, and of care
And then somehow the time had passed, and I no longer cared
Somehow it did not matter that the board would know I erred
Surprisingly, it dawned on me the world would go right on
If I just walked right through the door and caught the next plane home
That market prices fluctuate if I am here or there
And new contracts will be written, the world won't miss my share.

Above the clouds in soft moonlight, silently I prayed
That God would help me find the peace that somehow I'd mislaid
And as the dawn was breaking and the heavens fell away
With a calm and peace I'd never known, I faced the break of day

Melissa J Smith

IN THE BARN AT DAWN

<u>In the barn at dawn</u>
I saw your name
written
in Charlotte's Web,
then,
when I looked again
more carefully
I saw a spider
eating your heart
for breakfast.

Dr Earl Spangler

OLD ABE COMES HOME TO SPRINGFIELD

I'm coming home to Springfield
Finished is the call
My work was taken from me
Right after Richmond's fall.

For years I've seen the nation
Undergo a fearful task
'Midst trials and tribulations
No pity did I ask.

The guns are stilled, as well they must
Now peace is on the way
A peace for one and all of us
Tho' some wore blue and others gray.

The shot that came one April night
Brought peace that fills the grave
Although it denied to me the sight
To see man free and not a slave.

So, I'm coming home to Springfield
To meet the silent crowds
I know that they are near me
And will carry out my vows.

Deborah Irene Parks Livesay

LIFE'S BLESSINGS

To my wonderful mother, Hazel, for believing in me and to all my family and friends for their words of encouragement.

On days like this when the sun shines bright
It makes everything in my life feel right.
My troubles and worries become petty and small
As I soak in the beauty and the colors of fall.
My sadness is replaced, I must confess,
With a great sense of true happiness.
There's so much in life that I've ignored
By letting myself get so bored.
But the time has come that I've realized
To see with my heart, not only with my eyes.
By living each day seeing with my heart
Makes me feel I have a brand new start.
So I'll live each day to the fullest extent
For life has become a "Special" event.
I'll greet each morning with a great big smile
And dance through the day singing all the while.
For life to me is a beaufiful song
All you have to do is sing along.
Through this poem God is speaking to me
Letting me know the best is yet to be.
So until my "Special" blessing, I'll continue to sing
For the time is near My dream He'll bring.
I know in my heart all this is true
And deep inside, so do you.

Trena R Ely

A CERTAIN 65-YEAR OLD

Life, so swiftly passed. And yet time was eternal.

The newborn; almost embryonic still,
knowing nothing, and yet
instilling attendance to all its needs;
from first awkward jerks and reachings
to the fetching toddler, the joyous child.

Ah, and childhood! What happiness!

Unrivaled in its acceptance of life and fate.
Straining its leashes for every adventure, discovery, treasure.
Life was joyous, new,
imperviously
untainted.

Thus the teens. A new world, a new
awareness. Sure and unsure.
Flip, challenging, daring;
grasping
this world willed to it;
not yet its, but taking beginning reins.
Life indeed its oyster. Time, a suspended warp.

And so the ecstatic lovers,
the joys of young marriage, the proud parents.
Life was full circle!

Now engrossing, the tribulations of parenthood;
weighing down, and yet no deeper
its rewards.
And then, so long and yet so short;
the child departed.
Menopause, a serenity.

Suddenly a visage of old age, its shadow looming the horizon.
A vexsome worry; half-fretting.
Would it grant security?
What this retrospection?
Sometimes sad, sometimes joyous.
. . Life so swiftly passed.

Dietrich C Williams

IN THE PARK

Dedicated to BESSIE HILL, LOVE YOU GRANDMOTHER!

As I sit on this bench, my favorite in the park, my eyes
Watch the children at play, my mind went back to the time
When I was a child of yesterday.
There was sunlite in my
Hair, and laughter in my voice and the wind carried my feet
Fast and free I was a child with the whole world waiting just
For me. Then my eyes shift a bit and I sigh as I sat, at two
Sitting near by, and I remember all the loves of my life,
Especially the love who made me his wife, and tears softly
Fell from my eyes. Oh yes I remember all the important
Things, like the parents, we became as if it were yesterday
And then sorrow tugged my heart, as I sat in that park, and
Sweet memories faded away . .
Well my eyes are not young any
More, and I am alone unlike before, just like so many others
Like me. We were yesterday's people long forgotten

Now we are today's elderly . . .

The end . . .

Darlene M Thomas

THERE'S A NEW STAR IN HEAVEN TONIGHT

Dedicated to Helen Thomas; Our Beloved Mother

There's a new star in heaven tonight.
Tho it's breaking my heart it shines on bright.
And it makes me so blue for mother i know it's you.
So thru tears i'll try to smile with you.

There's a little star by the moon.
That was never there before.
And i'll watch that little star each night.
Until i can see no more.

When the rest of the stars are gone.
Mother's star still lingers on.
Here or in heaven she'll always be.
The sweetest of all mothers to me.

So i'll close my eyes in a silent prayer.
That God will please keep her alright.
For the sweetest star in all the sky.
Is the new star in heaven tonight.

Ida M Bennett

Ida M Bennett

THE BUSY BEE

Tiny little Bees so wee and busy
With black and yellow wings,
Buzzing around little flowers.
Could it be it's spring,
When you gather sweet nector
To be placed in honey combs.
Do you tire as you travel?
From the flowers to your home,
Oh, the wonders of your honey,
So delicate and sweet,
You share with Gods Children,
Unaware of the treat.
Little bees, we want to thank you,
For you bring a lesson to all.
Your work may not seem important,
Yet its a duty to Gods call.
When I think of the food value
Of the honey on my bread, I
Think of the toil and dedication,
Busy bees brought to the spread.
In life we have many lessons so
Give your best for all to see.
Remember the world enjoys honey,
Gathered by the busy bees.

Jeanette Abrams

UNTITLED

Five starts had I
Each I dream of
and see
in my mind's eye
Could you have been
like me or like he
You all who were once
a part of me
Are you boys
Are you girls
Do you have blond hair
or brown
Straight hair or
full of curls
I wish I had the chance
to know
The chance to love and
watch you grow
What has God
put in store for us
I wish I knew
I only had you a few moments
and Why
I will never know

Kathryn Sue Clabaugh

SLEEPY-EYED COLORS

Sleepy-Eyed Colors of
Gold and raspberry
Blind through the mist
Are the secrets you carry
Deep within your heart
Hid the flame of desire
It danced through the mist
And tried to retire
Satin-Finished "Talking Machine"
Blue-Ivory shingles
You know what I mean
It rings from your towers
To pass away hours
Of Sleepy-Eyed Colors
That swirl 'round my heart
Of blind mist that melted
My flame from the start

Henry S Molina

THE LIMB

While walking through the woods one day
I did see a babbling brook,
Its water flowed so quietly
The ground it hardly shook.
I ran along the waters edge
Following this road to clear,
When suddenly there came a sound
Its direction was so near.
The closer I went, the closer I got
And at its origin I saw a waterfall so majestic
I just stood there in awe.
As the waterfall and stream joined
There came a swirling pool.
Around and around it went I watched like a fool.
Then for no reason took a limb
And inside the circle it flew.
Around and around it went reaching out of the swirling brew.
As I looked the more hand-like it became
Clutching, grabbing, trying to hold
And around it went finding nothing
But the water so icy cold.

Dolores A Walker

VOICES

To David, my husband, because we are one; and to God, my Creator, and Master Poet.

Voices surround me
like crashing waves.
Taunting, questioning.
Hopelessly, I'm being
tossed about,
struggling to get my head
above the angry foam.
I am blinded by the salty sea,
deafened by the thunderous
applause of the waves
as they clap their hands in
triumph,
laughing and jeering.
At me.
I'm sinking fast.
I DON'T WANT TO DIE!
My soul cries out.
I hear another Voice;
A gentle, quiet Voice.
The waves cease their pounding.
My heart is still.

Yesmine Sarkis

THE DREAM THAT WALKS

The opportunity missed
As fast as a blown kiss.
In a passerby's quick glance
The lover's dance goes forsaken,
A could be true love
Needlessly mistaken,
Today's pace always borders on too much
That true soulmates are rarely given
The chance to touch.
The opportunity missed,
As life flows upstream,
Passerby walks the dream
Lost in human reality's scheme.

If only to be the power
To slow life's pace
In order to allow the living of life with grace
To lower the personal expectations
In order to have the secret key
To open the inner eye
To the reality of the scheme
So not to lose
Through idle and empty talks
And miss and make
The Love as Passerby
THE DREAM THAT WALKS.

Jennifer J Boggan-Lower

LETTING GO

My doubts linger long into the unsteady nite
Sleeping calms within me the constant fight
Letting go of defensives my love is in flight
Feeling time become motionless
My thoughts relive your sweet tenderness
All is free
My mind at last at ease
Cuddled warm inside your spirited embrace
Remnants of your presence makes my heartache.

Another day goes by with dull surprise
Hypnotized, tranquilized, another day through thousands of eyes.
The morning madness carries me along
Wasted moments scurrying never noticing another dawn.
People rushing everywhere to their jobs and fate,
Today has become yesterday going by at a fast pace.

Elizabeth Brandon Baker

HOLDING HANDS

Dedicated To Charles

This old man I sit beside;
Once I was his timid bride
When he took me by the hand
And led me to a lovers land.

All The world was ours to take
All the riches ours to make
We would walk on foreign land
All the while he'd hold my hand

Tending gardens was our toil
Never walked on foreign soil,
For the babes came there to bless
All our days with happiness

Now we sit upon the swing
Do not talk of anything
For every thing to say we said
All the dreams we dreamed have fled

Swatting at the errant fly
Nodding heads at passersby
They do not care, they do not see
My love is holding hands with me.

Ruth Ann "Esche" Atkins
SPECIAL GIFTS

With warm thoughts, in loving memory, I dedicate this to Marion and John Esche, my parents, who shared their love and faith with me.

When I awoke this morning, I began to realize
God had placed a special gift before my very eyes
He handed me another day . . .
He left it in my care
but,
He told me if I needed Him . . .
He would be right there
I messed up so many yesterdays!
Why was God so kind?
He said if I would search, I'd find the answer in my mind.
well,
I thought and thought about it as I lay there in my bed
When the answer finally came to me and entered in my head
God gathered love along with faith and shared them both with me

He knew the person that I was, but,
He still set my soul free
God knew there was another soul that was longing for a friend
And He hoped that I would share my gifts before this day would end
so . . .
Perhaps the next day my new friend would share the gifts he'd found
And the love and faith bestowed by God would begin to spread around
The earth would come to know the strength of love that it had shared
The power to end the worst of wars; showing neighbors that we cared
We would join together in the joy of peace
We would cling to serenity
And one day we would all earn God's greatest gift
To live through eternity

Amy Lomzenski
IMAGINE . . .

Imagine what it would be like not to
Have a friend.
One who will always be here to lend a hand
Or go to the beach and sun in the sand.
A friend who you could talk to late at night
Or to watch the stars shine bright.
Imagine no one for your letters to send.
Not a friend to cry on your shoulder when
Times get tough
Or to talk to when school gets rough.
Imagine life without a friend.
There would have to be an end.
For the days would be so long and bored
Not to have a friend forever more.
To imagine not to have a friend like you
Is the worst thing I could ever do.
So, remember my friend,
We're one among the very few that
Will never have to Imagine . . .

Cohen Burgundy Fincher
IF EVER THERE WERE

If ever there were a cherished husband . . . it is you.

You have filled my days with beauty and wonder, and my nights with passion and ecstasy.

Your love and generosity of self is that which I have never before known.

You and you alone know my soul . . . its troubles and its serenity.

Should ever have I had an all consuming ambition, it is that I bestow unto you all that you have bestowed unto me.

You possess not only my love and utmost devotion but my body and soul as well.

If ever there were a cherished husband . . . it is you.

S J Malton
THE GOLDEN POPPY

Dedicated special for Stephanie, March 18-85

The poppy so glowing Golden has covered the rolling slopes and valleys,
To remind once more the special place that was created,
To give eternal life for those that found its shore.
Others have sought it, but landed on far away places.
It was the land of Blue eyed fair haired maidens, that lived in this special place,
With all the good things known only to the great spirit in the sky, and shared with his chosen few.
They lived this life of desire;
Black hair hords with greed beyond their control burst over their mountains and drove them to the sea.
The great spirit sadden by the loss of his chosen few, had poppy seeds placed where his maidens had tread.
To Blossom in golden splendor,
For the blue eyed fair haired maidens that are native to its soil.
The people so loved its splendor, that they called it their very own, "The California Poppy."

Judith Brandow
WE PLANTED A SEED

We planted a seed with loving care,
We tended it and did our share
We were patient in our toil,
For this seed was not established in the soil.
It would be a living being,
Harbored from troubles, unforseen.
We would tend it night and day,
Preparing a path, making a safer way.
Watching it grow was our delight,
The blossoming part was quite a sight.
But the ultimate was all in the bloom,
When the toil was done, and the flower past doom.
When some admirer will pluck it and say,
I shall love and cherish you for ever and a day.

Cathy King
OBSERVATIONS

To Jenny for suggesting it, to Sharon and Sneakers for reading it, and to Sharon Lovering for always believing.

The darkest life is brightest,
For everybody knows
The darker that it seems today,
The more tomorrow glows.

The brightest light is darkest
When seen inside the mind:
The more the light of knowledge gleams,
The more it must be shined.

The empty sky is fullest,
For in an empty sky
Are held a hundred million dreams
That never, ever die.

The fullest heart is empty:
The more that it enfolds,
The greater is the room inside
For everything it holds.

Mary J McCoy
OUR LADY LIBERTY

I dedicate this poem to my hardworking Irish ancestors, and loving son, James, and my loving husband, Kenneth, both Air Force Pilots.

She stands there in New York Harbor . . .
In radiant elegance,
Her silhouette stark against the sky.
She holds high the torch and brings the book,
In the moon's mellow haze,
Or on bright sunny days . . .
With Lady Liberty in our gaze,
We are awed by her spirit and beauty.
She gives a warm glowing light,
To citizen and visitor alike.
She is the light that beckons all to see,
That tyranny should never be.
As Our Lady Liberty has been restored . . .
Let our spirit in America, be renewed and outpoured.
As we have shined up her exterior,
Let us brighten up our own interior,
And try to become a superior people!
Keep America clean, our morals straight . . .
With glowing hope, the future we anticipate!
Our Lady Liberty with her lamp held high,
Raising all hearts and eyes to the sky.
It's a message of old to brighten our way,
Greeting all who come to stay!
What a beautiful sight, Our Lady Liberty!

William C Sporka
A SEAMAN'S FATE

To my Uncle, Edward W. Lapczynski, Seaman, U.S. Navy, lost with the cruiser U.S.S. Indianapolis, July 30, 1945.

Oh now just a part of a coral reef
Though once so quick and bold,
When I knew him last
His heart beat fast,
But now it's still and cold.

He went to sea when but a boy,
A youth of ten and four,
Left Ma at home
And went to roam
She'll never see him more

Each of his friends had a dismal tale
Of the dangers of the sea,
But he packed his sack
And turned his back
On all of his friends but me.

For I was the one who sailed along
In the good ship "San Marie,"
In wind and sun
We thought it fun
As we plowed through the rolling sea.

There came a storm from the darkening west
We thought it ne'er would end.
We clung to the rail
And the howling gale
Left me, but took my friend.

Just one last glimpse of my buddy's face,
One cry, then he was gone.
With a heart of lead
A prayer I said,
Then turned to the fresh new dawn.

The voyage is o'er and I'm home again,
But my heart is filled with grief,
I'm at journey's end
But my boyhood friend
Is a part of a coral reef.

G E Reisinger Jr
WITH LOVE

I Love you in many ways, each special . . .
Your safety and security and warmth . . .
Our talking, sharing, listening, feeling together . . .

Innocently . . . as calming a bird that hurts,
or feeding a stray, or playing too long
when already bored with the game . . .

I love you in many places, each special . . .
When we have a quiet moment together . . .
When we discover, each personally, a beautiful thing . . .
Or see the singular dove soaring to her summit,
as only she sees it . . .
Or find the rose, untouched . . .
Or find a shelter, our own . . .

I wish to remember when, how, it began . . .
There was no time, nor space, nor place . . .

Perhaps when I first shared myself with you . . .
The hopes, the hurts, the sunsets, the horizons . . .

Or perhaps it began when I held someone who needed closeness,
or comforted when ill, or reassured when doubting . . .

Perhaps it began without words,
when I was beginning to understand your feelings . . .

Quietly, when I knew love was there . . .
Suddenly, when I knew I was no longer alone . . .
And I felt no more sadness . . .

I love you in many ways, inexpressably . . .
You live inside my heart, always . . .
My life is yours . . .

I love you.

Cora Mundy
FRIENDSHIP LANE

To my dear friends and loved ones

If ever you're lonely—maybe sad and blue
And you feel that no one cares
I know of a place called "FRIENDSHIP LANE"
You'll always meet good friends there
Perhaps you don't know of FRIENDSHIP LANE
Or maybe you've forgotten the way
The sun is shining—put a smile on your face
Why don't you come with me today?
It's just DOWN THE RIVER OF GOLDEN DREAMS
A short way—then open the gate
You'll find yourself in a LOVELY WORLD
Hurry now, you don't want to be late
So many DEAR FRIENDS await you there
As you stroll along in MEMORY
Reliving the GOOD TIMES—some that were sad
Eased by such friends as these
It's growing late—we should go now
Still we hesitate to leave good friends
But now you know—there's a place you can go
And share your MEMORIES again
Come again soon, there's no need to be sad
Or ever lonely again
Just open the gate, and walk inside
This PLACE called FRIENDSHIP LANE

Dianna Atkinson
CHIEF

This poem is dedicated to "Chief," whom inspired the writing of it. With love, Dianna

---

I remember all to well, your snake like movements.

Making love, in the cool waters nearby.

Your smiling eyes, as bright as the sun shines.

"Your loving smile, as long as mine."

Your mind reaching out, to touch mine.

Your gentle hands, for the pat on my behind.

Your spirit alive, riding close by.

Your soul is within me, as I hope I'm with you.

In front of a campfire, we have shared so much.

To speak without talking, as answering with a nod.

For a true love we have shared, will never die.

Our love went further without us knowing.

Or do we know?

Elaine Luther Lipps
BABY'S DREAMS

To Anthony: May all your dreams reflect the gentle joy in you.

What do you dream,
My little one,
Do you dream of playing
In the sun?
There you lie in such
Sweet repose.
A smile on your face
Neath your little button nose
Do you dream of being
Held in mother's arms?
And bedazzling her with
All your charms.
Or do you dream that daddy
Is bouncing you on his knee,
While you are laughing, oh
So gleefully?
Oh how I wish that I
Could know,
Your dreams that make you
Smile and laugh so.
I wish I could be with
You in your little dreamland,
To walk through it with you,
Hand-in-Hand.
So I would know what
Brings you such joy,
My little, charming, sweet,
Baby Boy.

Connie Biddle Owens
TO THE ONE I LOVE

This Poem is dedicated to Bill, My loving Husband.

You're everything there is to me,
The one who's always there,
The one who always takes the time to listen and to care,
You're the one who makes each day the bright and cheerful and kind,
Who brings the warmest memories
And the happiest thoughts to mine.
You're the one who stands beside me through what ever each
day brings
And shares with me lifes pleasure's its big and little things.
You're everything there is to me and you always will
be too'
the only one I'll ever love
my one and only
You'

Isobel C Auld
PERSPECTIVE

From where I sit
here in the warm sun
The boats sway gently as a small wind
stirs the bay;
I am pleased to note, the mast of this,
the last one in the line,
just clears the bridge
and yet this golden span dwarfs man
and shrinks a liner into infinitesimal obscurity.
A gull coasts down the quick'ning wind
Obliterates a clipper circling in from transpacific flight
—Two hundred men hidden by a few grey feathers;
A shadow cools my face,
A small boy fills the sky and grins to ask a question.
Soon I leave this place taking along the thoughtful comfort
That to raise a hand Oakland and the whole East Bay are gone,
Or Angel Isle and Sausalito if one is troubled in that direction.
So with masts that touch bridges, gulls to hide planes and little boys to fill the sky
Perhaps the problems of this earth, our mortal imperfections,
the shattered promises, the pieces and the bits
May also shrink a little in the sight of God,
From where He sits.

Maxine E Rider
BECAUSE HE DID

Dedicated to my family and everyone who loves the LORD

Sometimes I wonder "what's the use?"
Why strive and strain to teach the way?
Why bleed inside and feel the hot tears
Scald a stream inside your soul?
Because He did.
Why worry till you're numb with grief
Knowing that the one relief is to see
Your children love the Lord and follow Him, breast plate and sword?
Because He did.
Must we then pick up our cross
Carry our burden, forget the cost
Lean upon our Lords pure love
As step by step we rise above
each care we pace," The Four Alarms"
Till we're drawn into our Fathers arms.

Mark Mitnik

Mark Mitnik
TWO BROTHERS

Dedicated to My parents: Isidor Mitnik, Lina Mitnik—Hrein, my sister Alla, my family and Marianna Kogan.

Leo Pushkin came to Odessa,
But his beloved brother is gone.
Here he found his Dogaressa,.
But sadly's playing clarinet.

"Alexander Sergeevich Pushkin,—
Recalled the decembrist Yakushkin,—
Took great care of brother Leo,
Loved him fatherly and helped him".

Princess Vera, Langeron,
Lyceum, Liprandi and Oton,
Amalia and Countessa!
How dear you are to me, Odessa!

I am staying . . . all's decided,
Looked at the sea from dacha Reno,
What rhythm, if someone knew,
What thought recalling?

Keeping the memory for us
About his great excelled brother
Leva Pushkin was living in Odessa,
Visiting Oton and Betty.

Oldest lived here for a year,
Youngest—for ten years,
But the memory of them
Will not disappear ever.

Carl Reuben Lindberg
MY LOVELY IRISH WOMAN
My Lovely Irish Woman
She's beautiful silhouetted against the sky.
With her hair blowing in the breeze and the twinkle in her eye.
Her hair is light brown.
You hardly catch her with a frown.
Her personality is like the dawn of a new day.
Like the wind blowing sweetly across a bay.
She's like a field of beautiful flowers,
You can watch her every move for hours.
She makes the dark into day
And livens you up, like rolling in new mown hay,
She's sleek, beautiful, and frail
Like a ship cutting through the ocean in full sail.
Yes she's these things and more.
I love her and yearn to see her walk through my door.
I love my Irish Woman more in every way.
Without you I would never make it through another day.

Amy L Zimmer
WHY
Why did you have to do it?
Why did you have to go?
You should have told me first,
and I would let you know.
I never thought it would happen,
at least to someone I knew.
But I guess that is what everyone thought,
until it happened to you.
You should have told me about it,
when we went on our last date.
I would have talked you out of it,
before it was too late.
You were so young and had so much to live for,
everything was going your way,
why couldn't you have stayed?
Now I try to see your face,
through the tears I often cry.
Still wondering why you did it
Why did you have to die???

Deethyia Faye Montgomery
OKLAHOMA SPRINGTIME
Winter is gone from yonder hill,
The snow is all melted,
Wind loses its chill.

The robins are singing,
Flowers are in bloom,
Warm spring wind will be,
Blowing soon.

Away down in the meadow and up in the sky,
A big flock of snow geese goes drifting by,
Back up to the north country for their summer nesting,
While here on the soft grass, bunnies lie resting.

Daffodils dance out here on the prairie,
Its God's way of telling us,
That spring's in a hurry.

Connie S Perkins
SLUMBER
Sleep, will you keep me after I weep?
Will you rest me with your will?
Overcome my being, and drift me softly still?
Guild me thru my slumbers, help keep me when falling still?
Protect my being while I succumb don't Let it knock and bump.
When days of old or days to be rush waves all over me,
Keep me safe while I dream those dreams, If dream I must.

Joseph M Lampe
YOU

This poem is dedicated to those whose hearts and souls have come to touch mine. Thanks.

What did you do, what did you do to me?
I don't understand, all I know is I'm glad.
I look at your picture
And I want to transverse the distance so I can hold you.
I'm not the same, but yet I've not changed.
Though I possess it, you are the holder of my heart.
I'm either a fool, or a dreamer, or a lucky soul, for I feel I have you.
Do I? Or do I dream? Or could I ever?
There is nothing as the warmth of your embrace, and the look in your eye.
For I am affixed by your gaze.
Deny me not, but let me know,
The affection of yours toward me.
And please LORD, let it not be a dream, nor in vain.

What did you do, what did you do to me?
I know not, but one truth shall stand—
If there is a cure for what is done,
Rest assured it will be one
That I shall shun.

Ermia J Greer
TREASURE UNAWARE

"To God Be The Glory." With Love and Appreciation To my parents—Allen and Dollie Luster

---

In each earthen vessel
A vacuum lies dormant,
Craving to be filled
With a God transplant.

A pearl beyond measure
Is tucked away in the heart,
A precious hidden treasure
Awaiting to impart.

It's the Master's pleasure
That one must seek him,
For his gift of Love
Is a very special gem.

Laura Gurley Jamison
CHANGING TIMES
It was getting late and I was tired
To make matters worse, I had just been fired.
I hurriedly ate so I could go to bed.
There it sat so strong and well-fed.
I looked at it; it stared right back.
Well, it's time that I hit the sack.
It looked at me with an evil grin.
"You had better get your paper and pen.
Tonight's the night you are going to start—
Practicing, learning, and doing your part."
I looked at the clock, it was already two.
"I'm sorry my friend; I'm tired of you."
Turning my head I heard a clicking sound,
As if to say, "Take me back to town."
"It's really late," I cried with a sob,
"We'll train tomorrow for another job."
It clicked its keys and blotched its light
As if to say, "I don't want to fight."
I looked at it and I thought, "I'll shoot'er,
You aggravating, complicated, sophisticated computer."

Frances B Hair

Frances B Hair
SOLACE

Dedicated to those who mourn.

I thought I surely could not face another day alone.
It seemed that all the meaning life had held for me was gone;
But then, as if an angel's voice had breathed a plea . . . .
A tiny baby smiled at me.

I felt as though each day was just another load of care.
I saw the world an empty thing, so senseless and so bare;
But then, as if my God had smiled and breathed a sigh . . . .
I saw a rainbow in the sky.

It seemed as though my heartache was more than I could stand.
I suddenly felt the gentle clasp of an understanding hand.
And then, just like a miracle, I knew I wasn't alone . . . .
God's with me, though you're gone.

Pauline J (Matlock) Goldsberry
THE SYCAMORE TREE
My love and I went for a walk one bright and sunny day.
The weather was perfect and things were great—I must say.

It was the kind of day you were glad to be alive.
People were laughing and birds were singing, that summer day of 1985.

We were walking and talking down a trail of nature's beautiful trees,
When we came upon a cave with a ray of sunlight shining down that 'bout sent you to your knees.

Even though all this beauty and life meant so much to me . . .
It didn't compare to the secret of one beautiful sycamore tree!

Because under this tree a special bond of love was about to begin—
For my love first told of his love for me, and I for him.

I'm hoping our love is strong enough to build and flourish . . .
Because what we have going we should always cherish.

So now when I'm out walking, I'm hoping I will see—
The one special tree that means so much to me.

That tall and mighty tree that reaches toward the sky,
Will always bring a tear of joy and happiness to my eye.

I love the closeness it brought to my love and me,
It's one of God's symbols of love—THE SYCAMORE TREE!

Celestia Castoe
SPIRIT OF THE CHALLENGER
Day after day, here and there,
on the land, in the air
brave men and women risk life,
use God-given power to choose,
search for truth though lives they lose.

Inspired to try the unknown spheres,
to gain knowledge for future years,
Challenger's crew entered the race
to probe further outer space.
Although they didn't achieve their goals,
God will bless their heavenly souls.

Tragedy took them from this earth,
bringing sorrow, removing mirth,
slowing progress in exploration
for benefit of our Nation.

Still they speak from realms unknown,
"Hold that dream. Keep on keeping on."

Elizabeth R Custer
HOW I WONDER
OH, how I wonder, how people think there's no God.
When they can see a morning sun rising arose tall and full of color.

OH, how I wonder, how people
believe there is no God.
When the evening sun sets and
gives bright glow across the sky,
and draw it water.

Oh, how I wonder how people
think's there is no God.
When in the spring you can see the
grass, and the flowers spring
forth, the weather warms up the
rain comes down, and the birds
sing.
OH, how I wonder how people
believe there's no God.
When in June it gets so hot that the
heat melts everthing that it can
melt,
Even the birds find the cool water
that runs in the stream.

OH, how I wonder how people
think there's no God, because
God made the earth and the
peoples that lives on the earth
and I wonder who they think
made them.
OH How I Wonder!

OH, how I wonder how people
thinks there's no God.
When in September the leaves
turns so many different color,
and the weather gets a bitter
chill.
OH How I Wonder!

Angela Lynne Ladd
PURPLE MIST
Can you feel it seeping in
You try to keep fighting, can't let it
win.
But ever so slowly it creeps toward
you
Surrounds your body and slips
inside you.
It touches your mind ever so lightly
Then lights its fire ever so brightly
To capture your soul is its ultimate
mission
Through any weakness its given
admission.
So keep up your constant guard
For it grows like a cyst.
Ever so quick and quietly
Is the way of the purple mist.
'Cause no matter how hard I
constantly try
It keeps fighting and waiting until
the day I die.
It captures the outer areas then
moves inside
I want to be strong, yet I want to
hide.
I've fought so long and fought so
hard
With the consequences high, I've
played my last card.
Still the risk was taken
With my defenses worn thin
Now the fight has finally ended
For the purple mist is in.

Herman F Clasen
GENISIS REVISITED
Did Adam with his conscience
grapple
'ere he incised that famous apple
or did he bite quick for reprieve
from a bitching, nagging Eve.
Adam once came to great grief
for he'd misplaced his old fig leaf
and picked to form his modest
cloak.
Two stylish leaves of poison oak.

Soon after springing from Adams
rib
Eve started plotting for womens lib
devising weapons to aid her fight
such as headaches, backaches, and
"not tonight"

Adam came home once late at night
and he and Eve had a terrible fight
his answer to her jealous exams
"I've just been out with a bunch of
the rams"

When Adam laid down to take a
rest
Eve ran her hands all over his chest
not out of love in any amount
but for a chance his ribs to count

Adam toiled throughout his life
to make a home for Eve, his wife
and never went into deep debt
for there were no Jones to keep up
with yet

They had no sheets of silk or satin
on which to start all that begattin
though it was rough, they did make
do
for here we are, both me and you

Karen Coy Gibson
REGRETS AND DESPAIR
Harsh words spoken,
promises broken . . .
Love's just a token . . .
"good bye" rings so clear.

Memories gather,
of things you'd rather
have done, but you couldn't . . .
too late now, you shouldn't . . .
Your eyes begin to tear . . .

What worth has life . . living
if one can't be giving
the things they do best,
in hopes to be blessed
by the one that they loved . . but
now fear . . .
it's all so unclear . . .
What a waste of my years . . .

I'm so tired of hiding . . .
This dream-horse I'm riding,
has gone out to pasture . . .

My life's a disaster . . .
if only God would hear . . .

Dinkey Segers
PRECIOUS BOOK
When I was small probably three.
I remember mama reading to me.
She'd take what she called her
"Precious Book" and I'd climb
up in her lap.
All the other kids would gather
about

She'd read about Jesus and the
great miracles that He did.
I really didn't understand, being a
kid.
I remember her reading that Jesus
was both God and man.
That too, I didn't understand.

But as I grew older mama saw the
need.
She gave me her "Precious Book"
to read.
It didn't take long before mama
could see.
Her "Precious Book" had become
precious to me.

Soon I learned how mama's
"Precious Book" got it's name.
It changes lives, they are never the
same.
I wish all could read so they would
see
Why mama's "Precious Book" was
so precious to me.

Reed Blankenship
UNTITLED
Words come unassembled
Words not too slick
Although put into parables
Turn into mighty tricks

Words that can destroy
Words can make peace
The mightiest of all is love
It makes violence cease

Words when spoken
Become as but noise
Listen to the children
And their truthful poise

Words are vocabulary
Vocabularies change
The words of a word man
Will always ride the range

Use the good words
For obtaining smiles and laughter
Although parting words can be sad
It's strange to think that love and
words
Is all we really had

Gene Hinton
MYSTERY OF THE MANOR

To my Mother, Bernice Hinton, and Claire Ashy, Fatima Lay Minister, without who—this could not have been inspired and written!

The people passing by us—so often
stop and stare—
they're won'dring just what
mystery lies past that wall so
bare!
They ask; "Do they fear people?"
"Have something they to hide?"
"Why do they just stay indoors and
never come outside?"
If they could just look through it,
that manor wall they see,
they'd find there is no shocking or
unsolved mystery!

We wander through the hallways,
so mindful of the past,
when everything was beauty and
seemed it had to last.
And every room we go by we glance
inside to see,
if there may be a trickling of some
lost memory(?).
Though I do not regret it, they
sometimes wonder-IF?-,
a lively world abounds us with
peace and joy a gift!?

Bright skys and stars and sail
ships, just waiting there for
free,
and mountain, plains, and prairie
and trees and rolling sea!
Then suddenly looking 'round me
to see who might be there,
and saying nothing, listening, for
sound that comes from—
Where?—
While some pay no attention and
some are so afraid,
some can not see or hear us: "In
this the price now paid?"

Yet, some sit in their wheelchair,
they can not move or talk,
or others 'cause they're older, so
fragile they can't walk.
Then some are lost in their world,
not ere to hear Gods word,
but, others move around well and
watch the squirrel and bird.
Though some are sad or angry,
(they call this manner hell!),
I know they are not blameful: their
problem they can't tell!
But, nursing home and I know (!):
and, caring, treat them well!

Elizabeth Hill
MONUMENT

Mom we will always remember and love you. Elizabeth, Junior and Barry.

My mother is buired without a
stone.
God forgive me but alas alone,
I allowed her to be buried without
a stone.

Tall and thin, with long black hair,
She carried herself with a certain
flair.

Lizzie was her name, on heaven
above
She's my mother, and greatly loved.

She cared for her children, like any
mother would.
To me she was perfect, and did the
best she could.
Death came early at age fifty-four,
As time goes on I love her more.
I know she's in heaven and not
alone,
But I buried her without a stone.

Peggy Lawson
LOST RHAPSODY

This poem is dedicated to Deloris for her appreciation, and encouraging words.

Where has the rhapsody gone?
She has flown too high, trying to
catch the wind, endeavoring to
touch a star.

Some hailed her performance as great.
I saw them coming at a distance, and I reached out my hand, only to discover that I clutched at nothing.
She had begun to ascend a crystal mountain, and she eluded me,
The tinkle of their glasses rang loudly, accompanied by useless laughter.
Exorbitance mingled with amber and dark red.
Louder and louder it grew until it reached a wild crescendo.
Transforming itself into a black whirlpool, it enveloped her, and dragged her down, down, into it's raging, murky depths.
She awakens, sighs within herself, and gropes for the door, but it is sealed tight, and she is powerless to open it.
Once, perhaps a thousand years ago, the sun was warm on our backs, and we were overwhelmed by peace.
Even now, it is as the beat of distant drums, echoing, through
The endless mazes of my mind the rhapsody has vanished forever, and yet, never again.

Tod Alexander Huey

A GIRL NAMED JULIE, I ONCE KNOWED

To Julie, a special woman who touched my heart and altered my life in more ways than one.

It was from the first time I saw you. It was in your eyes.
The things you wanted most out of life, business, security and family ties.
Though, from school where I remembered you, or partying at Jasons.
You're in a class by yourself, because you are.
Though I tried to buy you clothes, jewelry and hats.
I found out you were a lot smarter than that.
So I tried to impress you, by hanging out with your brothers,
Being nice to your sister, niece and mother.
But everything I tried seemed to go dead end.
Though I was obsessed with you, I wouldn't stop then.
Though, through an investigator, I knew all about you.
From first loves to abortions, I had all the clues.
I bought a ring for our friendship, but you refused to accept it.
From when we partied in Haines City, where I lived there at eighteen,
to the house at 35th Street, I couldn't understand a thing.
I looked in the mirror, after time it appeared,
The reason why you wouldn't have anything to do with me.
I looked like a baby, too young to date you,
No hair on my face, like I was in grade school.
The night the F.B.I. surrounded me, as I sat in my car,
Machine guns clicking and revolvers weren't too far.
A song came on my stereo, it was cranked so cool,
It was by the Cars, Why can't I have you!
I laid there crying, face down in the snow,
And thinking of a GIRL NAMED JULIE, I ONCE KNOWED.

Eleanor Jaret

UNITE FOR PEACE

To my sons Frank and Peter and all my grandchildren

Children Children of the world
Unite, unite in the cause of peace
Appeal, appeal to your country
To end this deadly deadly arms race
Let your voices be heard
In every corner of the world
Lest your land be laid barren, your land void
Surely we were put on this earth
To live, love and learn how to deal with others
Not quite like ourselves but equally endowed with love
In their hearts, their souls
And to envision the marvel of the stars
Mountains rivers and streams
To smell the sweetness of the flowers, the trees
And our mark to be left in the form of our heirs
Living proof we passed this way
A gift of God, a privilege
Children, children all unite in the cause of peace
THIS DAY, THIS VERY DAY

Sherry R Hatch

MY MOTHER'S SURPRISE

Today I think I'll clean my room,
With garbage bag and trusty broom.
This will surely be a surprise for mom.
Since it looks like it exploded from a bomb.

I'll hang my clothes up nice and neat,
From the growing pile beneath my feet.
I'll put my books and games away too,
With my model cars and crazy glue.

I even cleaned under the bed,
Where sometimes I even looked in dread.
I found some things I thought I had lost,
And bought another at great cost.

I yelled at my sister for taking my tape,
Then I found it hidden behind a drape.
Some candy I'd hidden from my brother,
Was not as appealing in that green color.

I straightened the sheets and covers too,
So everything looks as fresh as new
But I think I'll put a blanket on the floor,
In case my mother should faint when she comes through the door.

Grant Kindwall

THE RIPPLING EFFECT

To My Wife Madeline

Did You shake Someone's Hand Today—
And then wondered Where it Stopped?
Your Gesture keeps moving Outward
Long since You may have Forgot

It makes Someone feel Welcome
As They Journey on their Way
It is a very Simple Gesture
But it Brighten's Someone's Day

Did You give a Loving Smile—
To a Stranger or a Friend?
If You did, You'll get it Back
Maybe, just Around The Bend

Your Friendly Smile is Contagious
It may be born from Up Above
Yes, A smile lives on Forever
For it is Dripping With Your Love

Anything that shows You Care
Moves outward in a Rippling Effect
Because You shared a Loving Moment
Some One, Some Where, Will Not Forget

Donna L Hurley

Donna L Hurley (SERENITY BELLE)

BEAUTIFUL SOUL

Dedicated with love, and White Light to my son Jason, who has given the diamond of my soul a reason to shine; to my family, for their guidance, and understanding; and to Gary F. for his wisdom, and inspiration.

You may never see the part of your soul that you've given me.
The part of you that "shines;" that "loves;" and is meant to be free.
The part that you hide, and let no one inside.
Yet out of love have allowed me to see.

You doubt yourself . . . but that's not fair!
For within your soul you really care
how other's see you; how they feel;
how they touch your life;
if they dare.
The turbulence inside you has brought both pleasure, and pain.
Now it's time to live again.

Set yourself free;
and what wonders you'll see.

Love yourself . . . Be yourself . . .
and give yourself the happiness;
the wisdom;
the true meaning of life you have given me!

Jackie Wayne Allen

MY WIFE

This is dedicated to my wife—Paula Kay

I gaze at the stars with wonder,
at the beauty God has displayed.
I thanked Him for, not stopping there,
and for you, My Wife, He made.

He made mountains so high with such splendor,
their peaks strung out on parade.
I thanked Him for, not stopping there,
and for you, My Wife, He made.

He made flowers, so many in number,
their colors brightly arrayed.
I thanked Him for, not stopping there,
and for you, My Wife, He made.

He took from His glory and beauty,
and the dust from a silver spade.
I thanked Him for, not stopping there,
and for you, My Wife, He made.

Gracia Walding

THE OLD MAN

He stood as only "age" can stand
Bowed with the wisdom of years.
Maturity had gleaned the best of youth
Time had erased young fears.

Knowledge now crinkled his once smooth brow
Giving compassion a chance to flow.
A distance of time far from youth
A time only age can know.

He turned and began to amble
Into the crowd that was there.
A golden ray of sunlight
Sparkled on pure white hair.

I saw in a flash, a vision
Of what life can mean as we climb.
The beauty of the old man touched me
And bridged the Span of Time.

Xavier Stewart

IN LOVE'S NAME

That which is done in love's name herewith we define.
Subtle as a changing tide.
As warm as a blanket.
Oh how a moonlight and seeded sky hear the whispers below define love sweet love.
How when early in the morning joy does come?!
Does not a beating heart alone define, or jealousy does find?
How then does warmth melt away and anger control?
Is it forever enduring in the soul?
And death with furor entertain, all in love's name.
When does the sea end the kiss of the shore?
Only in the change of the tide

through distance?
But is not the return stronger?
And the white rush with pleasure bring,
Only to hear a church bell ring!?
All in love's name.
But let's define.
The soul does know, that love, true love begins in the mind.
And through a poem foretold, I see that . . .
"love covered me like a blanket,
though I felt no need for such.
It covered one so close to me,
it covered me as much,
I did not kick it off,
As often before I'd done,
And soon I felt the warmth it gave,
And at last love had won."

Jerry Dunn
ALWAYS TOMORROW

To my children: Michael, Robert, Zabrina and Tonya

I once spoke to my God and He said then to me—
See what I as my own have created.
Let you hear what I say, it will be yours one day—
This whole world with its torments belated.
The way that you care shall determine your share—
For your life is no good without others.
You must give what you love and love what you give—
To that world, to yourself and your brothers.
Your thoughts must contain life be never in vain—
Though at times it may seem there's no way.
You need only look up and you'll see in my eyes—
I do mean every word that I say.
The will to keep living must never be lost—
Raise your head up and look to the sky.
Remember the wonder of unbroken love—
It works only when both people try.
You'll feel misery and pain and complete disbelief—
You'll feel lost like a child at a fair.
But behind all dark clouds shines a bright ray of hope—
That belongs to the ones who still care.
You must open your heart, let that ray of light in—
Let it dry up your tears and your sorrow.
Regardless of how painful your past may have been—
Remember there is always tomorrow.

Elizabeth Good
SUMMER'S END

As I sit alone reflecting back on the past
few months, I'm sad to think it has to end.
The bright, warm sun with its gentle breeze
soon will begin to lose its glo and the same
gentle breezes become a chilly wind.

The rain which came and caused the land to
grow with color will soon turn to ice and
snow. Yes, summer's end is at hand and my
heart is heavy with woe. The new people I've
met and the fun we've had will soon be just a
memory. We vow to keep in touch, but time
will only tell if the spring thaw will find
us renewing those friendships.

But the saddest part in fact is the loss of
old friends that a summer love has caused.
Friendships held dear in the past are found
fading as the summer turns to fall. All that's
left are memories of how it used to be, the
emptiness within me that only they can fill is
replaced by a longing that winter will pass
quickly and past friendships will be renewed
with the start of a new season. 'Til then,
God I need a friend.

Troy and Matthew

Donna K Corriveau
MY SONS

Written with love to Troy and Matthew September 20, 1985 by MOM, Donna K. Corriveau

---

A laugh like quicksilver,
A smile like a falling star,
So quickly come, so quickly gone.
They come at eve time—they come at dawn.
I could only ask God to slow down the clock.
To keep open my eyes and heart—to not close the lock.
To give me more time so I could enjoy,
The loving, winning ways of my two little boys.

They run through the yard, making all kinds of noise.
They zoom through the house, with all kinds of toys.
They are upstairs and down,
Always being the clown.
They are inside and out,
With no time to cry or pout.
They fill up my life with all kinds of joy.
They are my two blond, blue eyed boys.

Helen Schilling
LOVE IS

LOVE is many things
Such as hugs and kisses
Also marriage and wedding rings
Which could lead to being Mr. and Mrs.

LOVE is having children to raise
Through all their cute and funny ways

Love is grandchildren to spoil
In spite of all the turmoil
To hug, and kiss and rock in the rocking chair
And no matter how much they get in our hair
We will love them through thick and thin
Because love comes within

LOVE we should also give to the LORD
As he helps us to go forward
In our work or at play
He will guide us all the way.

So, LOVE! LOVE! LOVE!

Stella F Garrison
VIOLETS

Pure and timid violet
Face turned to the skies.
I am sure the star dust flecks
Make your golden eyes.
Nestled in the mossy banks
Full blown in early May,
Petals made of velvet scraps
The fairies threw away.

RoseAnn V Shawiak
A MIND BLOSSOM

This poem is dedicated to my husband, Robert Russell, and my two sons, Robert and Russell.

Life of mind so green and tender, sprouting with a freshness of purity.
Not a thought of ugliness, nor of barren wasteland could conjure long enough inside.
Ringing freely are the dancing bells caught up by flying laughter all around.
Blazing fire with no smoke curls upward and out of sight.
Blossoms popping out upon the ground, filling the air with a scent of nature.
Walking down the paths of many minds these memories hang limply down barely touching the brown dirt.
Everyone famous, everyone small, has a mind of life so green and tender although it never lasts, but for a short, short while.

Denise Fraser
A CRY FOR PEACE

Times they are changing, But people are still fighting, Like in war's on the other side of the world and Mommy's and Daddy's are living in fear. Fear for their little boy's and girls,
And still late
at night the men they will fight, there's crying and screaming in the streets, and when all seem's calm you walk out on the lawn, men, women and children are covered in sheets.

It seem's so senseless with us over here laughing and loving the way we do,
when somewhere over there, their caught in a war and poor little babie's need food.

Yes I'm happy I'm here away from it all. For surely I would go insane, Trying to protect myself and my babie's From needless bloodshed and pain

Betty Fry
WHEN A LITTLE GIRL LEFT HOME

I left my home for a city that had bright lights
I took to the railroad tracks early one night
I was so scared of the snakes as I crept along
Cause I know they come out at night, I tried to sing a song
I'm awful tired & sleepy, found a big tree, I huddled neath it
And felt so free, I had no money, & I was thirsty & cold
So early next morning when the sun came out
I walked & I walked & heard a loud shout
It was a dear old man & lady who told me to get in
We rode & rode in that old piece of tin
I never knew where we were going, but never opened my mouth
As we rode long I knew we were going south
They had lost a daughter, 13 my age
They begged me to live with them, and would pay me a wage
I thanked them so kindly but knew I must go on
I still think of this old gentleman & his lady so fair
with tears in their eyes they were saying a prayer
They knew it would be rough for a young girl like me
When they hugged & kissed me, she said I ought to turn you over my knee
There were so many friends that helped me not to fall
But Jesus, I fell but you put out your trusting hand
Maybe someday I can live with you in your promised land
I think of all the yesterdays, I look up & Thank God &
Always Pray.

Nicole Sosa
LOVE

To my mom and dad for teaching me everything I know.

Love is like the blue sky, the warmth of the sun on my face.
Love is like the ever enduring oak

trees that stand within the beauty in itself. Love is
like the bluebirds singing in the sky. Love is like the
wild flowers that enchant the hills and valleys. Love is
is like the freedom of the wild horses. Love is
seeing the sunrise in the mountains with its majestic
beauty covering the land with enchantment. Love is
like walking on the beach seeing seagulls in flight
with the beauty of the sea. Love is like the clouds
that drift across the sky. Love is like the rainbow
that fills the sky after a rain shower. Love is like
walking through the enchanted forest with magical
music that is carried with the winds. Love is like
the river that flows on its journey to the sea.
Love is like seeing the mighty waterfalls thundering
to its destiny. Love is like seeing the nature of
the wild forest. Love is the most beautiful thing
on earth.

Anita Edelman
VICTORIANA

The night of the party at Lucy's
when Senor Calais shot the dog
with a bullet intended for Grayson
and the neighbors complained of noise,
Smythe hid in the pantry with Tilly,
the androgynous scullery maid,
while Admiral Jonathan D'Arcy
removed from the library safe
a packet of letters and photos
and then burned them in the grate.

The vicar and local authorities
convening in the hall
brought charges of animal cruelty
and unnatural acts with a dog.
12 guests were found locked in the kennel,
there were threats of a news expose';
Senor Calais, released, flew back
to Peru. The butler resigned the next day.

The night of the party at Lucy's
when Senor Calais shot the dog
Lucy was seen in the garden
prowling about on all fours.

Kathleen Eggert Baysinger
DREAMS

Dreams, soft mist like dreams,
formed in the shadows of the night
intangible illusions born of;
love, desire, fear and passion.

Dreams, becoming tangible
seaping into reality, surpassing it,
becoming life, lived only in the mind
yet, touchable for those who hold them.

Dreams, beginning in the early times
with a friend for the friendless child,
running for those who cannot, going where we fear
until the running is more real than the being.

Dreams, taking us places few go,
to experiences seldom lived,
to worlds just imagined in minds too small
to comprehend even a portion of their significance.

Dreams, waking dreams, sleeping dreams,
daydreams, fantasy, Mystic experience,
lived in the recesses of your mind,
recorded in the being of your soul.

Mary Talken
LITTLE BOY BATTERED AND BRUISED

I hear a sound that starts as a whimper;
building to screams of children refused.
Visions of wounds that happen to bodies
of Little Boy battered and bruised.

Innocent eyes all purple and swollen;
flowing with tears from being abused.
Frail little bones that break all too often
of Little Boy battered and bruised.

How can a man lose sight of his senses;
can he be sane . . . or merely confused?
How can he strike the likes of a baby . . .
a Little Boy battered and bruised.

Mostly they cry alone in their darkness;
no one to hear them, no one accused!
Here at my feet, I stand at the gravesite
of Little Boy battered and bruised.

How can we help them . . . how can we reach them?
How can their tempers be fully defused?
Pray for the children and pray for the parents
of Little Boy battered and bruised.

George Kallemeyn
THE MOUNTAIN AND THE VALLEY

I climbed, one day, to the top of the crest
Of a mountain near to the sea,
The sun was above, the clouds were below
And under the clouds was the sea.
Exaulted I was by the beauty I saw
Of the rays of the sun shining through
The billowing clouds and onto the sea of blue,
It was the beauty of Love, the beauty of Life,
The beauty of turbulent Joy,
And the rays of the sun, they tell it to me.
The secret that all is of one.
I would like to have lingered and eon or two
Alone up there in a world of blue,
But down I must go to the valley below
To work with love and beauty and joy,
To nurture and nourish that which must grow.

Amy N Little
MY TEDDY BEAR

When things outside are cold and gray
And many friends have gone away
You'll sit there in your infinite knowing
Watching me while I'm still growing
Changing so quickly, growing apart
But you know you'll always stay in my heart
When I've gone to college, grown old and gray
By my side you'll always stay.
With arms ready to encircle me,
A lap, a perch. Where I can sleep
To dream my dreams with thoughts of you.
You always keep me from feeling blue
You remind me of the happy times
Far away dreams. Far away lives.
You see so much and know so much
And I can feel it in your touch
An objective opinion you always share
To let me know how much you care
You need not speak or wink an eye
I know you're alive and will never die
I know in time your face will change
Your hair will go, you're face rearrange
But to me you're always true
'Cause teddy, you know I love you!

Elizabeth Mullins
RAIN DANCE

As I watch the rain
Like a tear drop on my pain
The gutter has a leak
From the rooftop to the street

The darkness is a mile
Like an unlit churches aisle
Silence is all around me
And the walls and floor confine me

As I lay here on my bed
With you dancing in my head

Gwendolyn Oats

Gwendolyn Oats
TO ALL OF YOU

The words and Music I've listened to all my life.
Everyone of you focus on Us all. We've heard many
Love songs and many sad songs. You've brought Magic
and Inspiration into our Country. You've sung
about every aspect in our lives. You've helped
from the Rich to the Poor. You've Greeted the Fans
to the most cherished people God created. We
remember "We are the World" to "Hands Across America."
You've given us your time and patience. We give
you our blessing for showing the Identity of your
true dwelling hearts. My heart goes out to you all.
Keep the good work up. Now everyone is Cracking
down on Drugs. There are so many people on them and
they need help. Some are afraid to face the fact
they're addicted. Others are trying their hardest to
stop. I know there's a better way out. Lets Crack
down on drugs. Lets tell a friend to help join in.
This is another Love Chain. Join each other to
make our blood clean forever. Wash out the bad
habits that forbid many to go on. Keep doing what
you're doing. Because some are listening and want
your help to go on in Life.

Darlene Ovitt
DADDY DEAR

The years have passed
since you were here,
But in our hearts
you are so near.
Our love for you will last forever
Daddy Dear!

Joan S Davis
SUNSET

Like snow flurries, against the light,
The little insects swirl from limb to limb.
Buzzing between the boughs of my old cedar tree
At sunset.
The golden glow illumines gossamer wings,
Wild with short-lived life.
Do they know where they go? What they do?
Buzzing and breeding.
Burgeoning.
Until the chill November,
And goodbye.
To earth, and sky; to rain and sun.
Farewell.
And to me, their lonely sentinel,
When day is done.

Trudy Johnson Clark
TO A SON IN VIET NAM

"The snows are past, and green at last is showing through the sod.
My heart is glad, for I have had a lesson from my God.
Through dreary days, I still can praise my Lord, for He is near,
And spring will come, and you will come back home, our Russie dear."

Mary Ellen Jones
MEMORIES

This poem is dedicated to my children.

Crew cuts & pony tails
Barbie dolls & sandpails

Slumber parties & little league games
Ponys, rabbits, even bugs w/names
"Memories are made of these"

Party dresses & old blue jeans
Trikes, bikes & jelly beans
Bruised knees & stubbed toes
Hot days under the garden hose
"Memories are made of these"

Happy hours on the backyard swing
Funny songs we used to sing
Weiner roasts by the swimming pool
End of summer—1st day of school
"Memories are made of these"

Library books & Vo-Tech classes
Learning to cook & wrestling matches
Graduation & college days
One by one moving away
"Memories are made of these"

Weddings big & weddings small
So many good times to recall
Grandchildren to keep us young
Maybe—life has just begun
But— "Memories are made of these."

Rozita Schimenkov

Rozita Shimenkov
NEWCOMERS

To Irochka Zubok to her birthday

With the pain we left our people and lands . . .
But, God sees, we love them and they always will be in our hearts and be our friends.
And I want you to know—it was a test.
It was not easy, but it was the protest!

People name us "newcomers."
I'll try to explain, what does it mean:
It means, that many winters and summers
We had to fight to survive and to win.

Newcomers remember struggle and horrors.
They can better see and compare,
They have fresh memories of people sorrow,
They can better appreciate those who care.

We better can value all our wealth,
Can better price, what America gave.
It means we are ready to give to this country all our strength.
Till we shall be alive, till the last of the breath, till the grave.

We can tell people all around the world
Who can feel hands of each other and hold
With everybody from different countries and homes:

Kiss American Land!
Kiss American Stones!

We shall never forget, I swear—never
The highest meaning of "Friendship" and "Freedom."
We'll keep it in our hearts forever!
America now is our home is our Kingdom!

We are proud for this country which for
us is the best!
Which is the main charizma of our faith!
For all "people of good will" it always keeps open gates'
Days and nights we'll pray:

God bless America!
God bless the United States!

Patricia Lee Hamby
WHEN I'M WEARY
When at night I'm weary,
And no peaceful rest I find,
I get up with my Bible
And let its wisdom fill my mind.
In its pages are the answers
To life's problems that I seek,
And it's through this Book of Books
That to my heart God speaks.
There are passages on forgiveness,
There are passages on love,
There are passages on the perfect peace
That comes from God above.
So, if some nights you're weary.
And the days have got you down,
Just open up your Bible,
There the answers can be found.
Let the love of God surround you,
Let His peace dwell in your heart,
And as the dawn approaches,
Let the new day start,
With a feeling of renewal,
Love and peace and patience too,
And meet the new day joyfully,
For you know God loveth you.

Naomi I Camden

Naomi I Camden
TEACH ME A LOVE SONG FOR JESUS

To my wonderful children, Arthur and Nancy for their encouragement, and love. To my Pastor Dean Gade, for encouragement, And reading my poems in church, and to Dr. John Gilberts, for believing in me, also.

Teach me a love song for Jesus
One that's sweeter than all the rest
For I'll soon be going to meet him
And my song must be the best

I want to sing like the angels in heaven
When I offer my song of praise
And the music will be the songs of the birds
When my heavenly orchestra plays

There'll be the sounds of the laughter of children
The singing brook as it goes on its way
And there'll be the sounds of the wind and rain
And the pounding of ocean waves

And then the music will soften
With the sounds of the leaves as they fall
As I silently bow before him
And in reverence, I give him my all

My song must be a love song
One that's sweeter than the rest
A song of praise to Jesus
Because I love Him best

So teach me a love song for Jesus
A song of praise I can sing
And the song must be the sweetest and best
One that's fitting to sing to a King

Francis Leon LaPenta
TO MY SON

To Bruce LaPenta on the occasion of his marriage to Mary Beth Stuart

---

From father to son,
I have something to say.
You are soon to be married
and will be moving away.

Many poems are written,
about daughters and wives.
About girls that are daughters
the rest of their lives.

A son is a person
who is to soon grown.
The child that leaves
before he is known.

From a boy he is told.
you must be a man.
The things you are made of
are less sweet and bland.

As a child it was permitted
to hug and embrace.
Now that your grown,
It's just out of place.

Life can be difficult,
dangerous and cruel.
But a man's place in life
is to live by the rule.

Feelings expressed,
with a cry or a tear,
Are strictly forbidden,
when someone is near.

A dad has few rights
when a son becomes man.
When love is expressed
by the shake of a hand.

No matter how painful
his heart feels inside
A father's inner feelings,
are often denied.

So many fond memories
spin round in my head.
Such as the hug of a child.
just before bed.

From the day you were born
we were proud as can be.
This child that was born,
To your mother and me.

Now you have grown,
and chosen a bride.
These feelings I speak of
if yours, never hide.

This poem was not written,
to make you feel sad.
But to welcome the daughter.
we never had.

May your lives be happy,
as two lives can be.
Sharing love and devotion
like your mom and me.

Dad

Dorothy L Shook
A DOG DOESN'T CARE

This poem is dedicated to Eunice Whiteley who is dedicated to mans best friend.

A dog doesn't care
If you're black or you're white
If you're short or you're tall
Or you've lost your sight
A dog doesn't care
If it rains or it shines
If you're rich or you're poor
Or you're out of your mind
A dog doesn't care
If you're good or you're bad
If you're sometimes happy and sometimes mad
A dog doesn't care
If you leave him alone
He knows you'll be back sober or stoned
There's no other friend, so loyal and true
'Cause he needs, wants and loves only you.

Pauline (Myers) Howell——"Ping"
BEYOND THE GRAVE

To my parents—Stephen and Dena Myers who have been a loving inspiration to their seven children.

Dad what would you tell me if you could?
(Beyond the grave).
That life is just a hoax, a farce, and nothing more?
Have fun and "live it up," there is no tomorrow?
Or would you earnestly implore:
"Dear, live the Golden Rule, by all that's in you.
As if today may be your last on Earth.
Strive hourly for Good, and Right, and Justice,
Love loyally—be honest kind and true."

We are not here by years to count and measure—
But how we live those years that is the "cue."
Live right, and you will find instead of sorrow—
There is a brighter happier TOMORROW.

Denise Dworshak Frizzell
CHERISH THIS DAY
Each day brings forth new experiences
With each dawn, lifes' renewing force unfolds,

Cherish this day and every day
To have and then to hold.
These moments are all too brief
And soon, will pass quickly away,
They compose the events of our
lifetime
And carry over from day to day.
Leaving you, with their tender
memories
To cherish the best with the worst,
For these times will never come
again
So cherish them, when they come
first.
The innocence that awaits each
beginning
Will dance its dance, time and
again,
But with each event will never
dance
That particular, dance again.
The force of each event will remain
Living its time throughout its end,
Love them and hold them, before
they pass
So each moment you may extend.
May that force be with you always
From the beginning to the end,
And not the lifetime of the moment
But rather, the life of you, my
friend . . .

Cardalee Cowan

DAWN

Before the Missouri Morning,
callous frost licks the flush fields,
and leave them bitter.
And waves of dandelion
race the sky to taste the sun,
to catch its sweetness on one last
breath,
and to dance for children.

Mrs Irene E Searles

THE WALL

To my daughter Joan M. Crandell

America, the land where all
Nationalities meet
The land with abundance of food
to eat
How could prejudice penetrate a
Country so grand?
It wasn't evident on the Mayflower
when they found land
For the Pilgrims were full of
gratitude and love
They fell on their knees and gave
thanks to God above.
There was always welcome and
room for more.
They couldn't see it then, the
prejudice in store.
If they could visualize the future
they would lament
And never, ever, let these feelings
ferment.
Is this what is known as progress
The power and greed we call
success?
Is this the America with freedom
and justice for all?
When did we discard "love of
neighbor" and build a wall?

Carl R King

I WANT TO LIVE FOREVER

Dedicated to Katherine Gray King, Sweetheart Wife and Mother, Teacher and Grandmother.

I want to live forever
So I'll never miss the day
That the sunlight shines so softly
While it lights your every way
I want to live forever
And smell the freshness of a rose
When on a summer's day
I decide to rest or doze
I want to live forever
And never miss your voice
As you call my name so clearly
Or paint the world so nice
I want to live forever
And feel the magic touch

That your nearness always brings
me
And look forward to so much
I want to live forever
To feel a summer's wind
And watch the clouds go sailing
Wherever they will end
I want to live forever
To feel the solitude
When being near to you
Inspires my gratitude

Gloria Dunning

THANK YOU

This poem is dedicated to Patricia Roland.

I write this poem of thanks to you
for the kindness thou has shown
toward me.
There were times when I felt like
giving up
for I thought noone cared,
strangely enough you were there.
When I was in a bit of trouble
you got me out on the double.
When I got a hot head, you were
there
you showed me despite my work
you still cared.

I've never met a person who gives
so much respect
to someone who doesn't deserve
it, as you do me.

THANK YOU

Laurie Bowden

FEELINGS

To Regina, Mommy's angel in heaven.

Feelings are funny;
they separate us all.
No one can escape them
by building a wall.
Everyone has them;
some nice and some bad.
Some of our feelings
we wish we didn't have.
Without feelings, there'd be no
love,
and no pain would there be.
But it's a small price to pay
for the pleasure you receive.
Build memories with your feelings;
like money in a bank.
Take your chances at losing,
and for winning give thanks.
I'm sure you'll be happy,
more that you're sad,
and discover some feelings
you never knew you had.

Paul James Hawk

THEIR WARNINGS

The darkness of the weather,
The trees soon to die.
The grass no more green,
Because of you and I.

So still is the listening,
But only the wind.
No more will the birds sing,
To us is the end.

But war still is coming,
Our land no more free.
For us there is nothing,
You say, "How can this be?"

This all is to happen,
Centuries ago told.
By a man blessed by God,
For us to behold.

The horrors of the future,
Now are arranged.
But if we work together.
They can be changed.

Through this man came the
warnings,
That our God has sent.
To show that the future,
Can always be bent.

So heed what we've told you,
Don't throw it away.
For us and our children,
They've showed us the way.

Thank you
God and Nastradamus

Ronald Scott Chileen

WALK WITH ME, MELISSA

Sweet Melissa, will you walk with
me
in the golden fields of grain?
We'll walk and see this glorious
land
in the beauty of the rain.

And as we walk, hand and hand,
I'll speak of what I feel.
I'll tell you of my love for you.
And assure you that it's real.

We'll see the streams, and the birds
that sing.
The flowers and the clouds of
white.
We'll see the meaning of love itself.
In the brightness of the moon's
light.

Shelia Bevins

WHO'S BIRTHDAY

To Trudie, my mother and my inspiration for this poem. I love you Mom.

Guess what Mom, Its Birthday
time,
It must be your's, for it sure isn't
mine.
So I guess all of this means, todays
the
Day, I do dishes and you get all
the
Birthday wishes.
May all your wishes and dreams
come true,
For no one deserves it more than
you.
Mom, I love you with all my heart,
but lets
Make a deal, and here's where I'll
start.
Mom, I'll give you my love, hugs,
and kisses,
If you won't make me do those
Birthday dishes.
Mom, you can keep the, love, hugs
and kisses,
For I just broke these Birthday
dishes.

Jon Paul Kane

OF AN EMPTY ARK

To my wife, Linda, who's insight put this material to print. I love you.

And of a time that's soon to pass
There frolics on the sea
The mighty whale who's life goes
back
To the forming of this land

Yet here today in computer age
And sonic space machines
The dwindling whale is bound to
fail
At the hands of modern man

From central plains to the Pacific
coast
And across a mountain range
Bald eagles ruled the endless skies
And braved the wintry freeze

Such was it's fame of majesty
It's stately striking pride
That we minted our coins with that
stately bird
And warned—"Don't tread on me"

Now one would think since we've
chosen that bird
To represent this land
We'd do all we could to protect the
life
Of the soaring eagles clan

Yet sure as hell it's plain to see
In our rush to go no where
We've cut to shred the eagles dread
T'is man with his reckless care

How many species have come and
gone
To the tune we tag progress
And how many more will die by the
hand
Of our own pathetic ignorance

When they're all gone—and nothing is left
Except man himself against man
Perhaps we'll wonder in our stumbling blunder
Did we ever understand

Across the oceans and over the waves
Of a planet now dead and dark
There came the rains of forty days
And the bobbing—"Of An Empty Ark"

Shirley A (Griffith) Adkins

COOLNESS

Hot.
Dry.
Sandy mounds of earth giving way when footsteps fall.

Crisp leaves and dried up ponds and
Drooping flowers.
Brown grass;
A dying bush;
Thirsty frogs.
A worn out old man.
Oh for the want of some rain drops
From a blackened sky,
Or the sound of thunder after a burst
Of light—
Water running down the street, down my
Window, down my face as I lift it
Toward the sky.

Arlena Faye Aborn

HOME SWEET HOME

The place you hang your hat at night,
Through turmoil and strife, it's alright.
All the clutter, noise and dust,
No matter, family is a must.
Each member travels their own way,
Hoping to regroup on the Holidays.
Pictures are always on their mind,
Each changing, adding new faces.
Taking new poses and going new places.
Remembering old toys and Grandpa's hats,
A tear for all those precious dogs and cats.
Life moves so quickly, nobody's home,
Feeble and elderly, mom and dad have grown.
They took them away, only memories remain,
Now, HOME SWEET HOME will never be the same.
Pick up the pieces, home becomes new,
Cause someday this will happen to you.
Wall bare, pictures on the wall no longer,
Memories, precious artifacts, ties much stronger.
Reminding me to always count the ways,
Because HOME SWEET HOME, is just for today.

Decie Adcock Smith

DO YOU LOVE YOUR DADDY?

Dedicated To all Fathers

Do you love your Daddy,
And meet him with a smile,
Or do you only want his money,
To live in your own style.

You may not think he loves you,
Sometimes he's stern and cold,
But deep within that bosom,
There beats a heart of gold.

He would take the thorns from all your paths,
And weather all your storms,
He would sacrifice his very life,
To keep you from all harm.

So always be good to Daddy,
And do the things that are right,
Don't be a juvenile delinquent,
And stay out late at night.

You are your Daddy's monument,
When his life on earth is through,
Whatever is written on it,
Is entirely up to you.

He would like to know his teachings,
Will live again through you,
Don't forget that your dear children,
Will be a monument to you.

Give Daddy his roses while he lives,
Don't wait until he's put in the ground,
No matter how much you praise him then,
He will never hear a sound.

When Daddy's life is over,
And his final race is run,
Let him look at you with pride in his heart,
And be glad you're his daughter or son.

E Rochell Siders Biehl

THE WAY OF THE WORLD

I need you and you need me.
That's the way of the world.

I love you and I hope you love me.
That's the way it should be.

Could I lay down my life for someone I love?
Would I lay down my life for you?

Would you lay down your life for someone you've never met?
For someone not born yet?

Have you ever thought of Jesus, the pain he endured?
Have you ever thought of Jesus, as the man who lives next door?

Why would He let them drive nails through His hands?
Why would He let them drive nails through His feet?
Why would He let them pierce His side with steel?
I know—He did it for you and me!

The Man next door loves you brother.
The Man next door loves me.
The Man next door loves you sister.
I thank God, the Man next door loves me.
For, that's the way of the world.

Linda Slanicka

THE FIRST TIME

Dedicated—To my Son Ryan Andrew Slanicka, born March 3, 1987.

A little seed inside my soul
Had grown til it became a whole.
And life contained within my own
The pain of birth I'd never known.

And nine more months would come and go
But time would linger ever slow.

While never knowing what the price
Is paid a mother's, sacrifice.

To be involved in such a feat
Could only make a heart complete.

And find the words for perfect rhyme
To hold my son,
The very first time!

Helen Malinda Gibboney

Helen Malinda Gibboney

WHAT MY COUNTRY MEANS TO ME

I dedicate this poem to my daughter, Ruth Gibbony Funk. Ruthie, constantly encourages me to write and watches for opportunities for me to display my writings.

My country means so much to me
I sometimes tremble at the thought
What might have been my fate, if America had not been my homeland.
It's the home of many brave men and women
Who with undaunted spirit—helped make it a better place for me to enjoy—and live in peace.
I have beautiful, luscious, green mountains to climb
Rivers and streams to ford
I have lakes and trees, all kinds of wild flowers and honey from the honey bees.
I enjoy the snow-filled fields in winter
in summer the fields of waving grain-the fruit trees
the golden sunsets and the dawning that is always the same.
I can listen to laughter and music—watch little puppies at play
I enjoy the company of my neighbors as I wish them a happy day.
I watch horses and cattle—grazing in the fields
I devour the good foods of America and enjoy the sweet thrill of happiness.

David Sain Jr

IF ONLY

If only
You would allow your heart to feel
What your eyes see
My reaction to you

If only I could
Express myself
I am sure you will then
Have your answer to me

If only
I could touch you
As you have touched me
Maybe then we will have a beautiful beginning

But
Only you can allow
Yourself the chance
To truly see me.

James P Winch Jr

GENTLE LOVE

He is the light
In times of trouble
Sorrow and care
Be still and listen
Know that He's there,
To comfort and give you,
The strength that you need,
Whatever the problem,
Your prayer's, He will heed,
Protecting and Guiding,
Each soul in its plight,
In the dark hours,
He is the Light.

Gwenna Rae Young

OUR FATHER CAME BACK TO REXBURG TO STAY

Our Father came back to Rexburg to stay.
It was on a cold December day.
His eyes and hearing were nearly gone.
To care for Jane it would be wrong.

Jane is sick and special care does need.
He was a broken hearted man indeed.
He said "My home is for sale, that's why I am here."
His eyes filled with tears, I held him near.

Futile words of comfort I spoke.
Oh, give me courage, faith and hope.
A loving Dad so good and wise.
His handicap of ears and eyes.

He was kind and gentle thru and thru.
And taught us to be patient, loving and true.
He told us stories of his youth,
And things pertaining to the truth.

He taught us much this father of mine,
of love and faith and all things devine.
The phone rang out that Friday, day.
My sister's voice was shaking as I heard her say.

Our father is ill. I think it's his heart,
To Madison Memorial we soon will depart.
Father in Heaven please quiet our fear.
Help us to know that thou art near.

Dad's face was white, perspiration in his hair.

A lifted hand, recognized we were there.
A blessing given to forget earthly care.
A message of faith and infinite prayer.

We love you Grandpa and the good you do.
His last words spoken "I love you too—all of you."
Please help us that we may understand.
That this is thy Savior's Eternal plan.

To release this body from trial and strife.
To a better, happier, joyful life.
I felt so strong the comforter's arm.
As I touched my Dad's lifeless form . . .

Family is waiting in the Heavens above,
With arms extending a spirit of love.
Our father has love for each of his own.
And wants us back in his Heavenly home.

Lawana R Scales

THE CITY

The cold tall steel is joined with the orange haze of dawn,
As the sun spurts over the horizon to greet a new day.
All is calm from the stillness of the night before;
The windows of the skyscrapers glisten with the reflection of the sun.
It quietly, yet anxiously awaits, alluring those who must open it's doors;
The City is eager to waken, as the many cars filled with people, destine into it's arms for one more day.
The hustle and bustle as they all enter in;
Traffic jams, police cars, the smell of coffee, the sounds of talking:
Elevator bells, telephones and the drills as they work eagerly
to build and add to it's midst.
Now dust is falling and all leave for home, quiet are the buildings with darkened windows testing silently.
The City sleeps, it rests it's motors, closes it's arms, and waits, for another new day.

Marlene Meadows

LOVE

With heartfelt thanks to my loving children, Sharlet,
Robert, Mark, and Shandra, my dear Boston Aunts. Elin, Elly,
Fran, and Grace my special freiend, Jay

Love steals into the heart of every human being,
untouched, unheard, without our seeing,
Yet, once entered, starts senses reeling.
Pulsating with unequaled feeling!

Love lightens cares, erases sadness, filling aching hearts with gladness,
Gives solace in the time of sorrow, and confidence in each tomorrow.

Love uplifts sinful, troubled souls, inspires us to attain our goals,
While helping us to keep in sight, the principles of truth and right.
Love motivates mankind toward peace,
The ravages of war to cease,
Makes us aware of others' needs,
Respectful of all races, creeds.
Love's value we shall never measure.
This feeling is our greatest treasure,
For LOVE its wonders does disperse,
throughout the whole wide universe!

Maria Martin

Maria Martin

DREAMS OF TOMORROW

This poem is dedicated with love to Peggy, my loving mother.

Oh God, I wonder why.
I wonder why life is the way it is.
You created this world with innocence and peace.
Our presidents of yesterday gave us dreams.
Dreams of a better tomorrow and the hope of world peace.
Dear God, I am just a person like so many people.

I am no better or no worse.
Everyday we go to work or go to school.
We get so caught up in trying to get ahead that sometimes
We forget to bow our head and pray.
When will we stop reaching for the stars?
I have so many questions I want to ask You.
Questions that reaches beyond the earth and stars.
I am thankful for the strength I find in You.
With all the problems of this world that man can't solve I often wonder why like so many generations before me have.
I pray more people will turn to You.
I pray for our world leader, and I pray for the little people of this world.
Bless the farmers, our leaders and our families.
Teach the young to dream again and to make the dream come true.
For dreams are just dreams.
Oh, what a wonderful world this would be if we could just live our life the way it was meant to be.
I use to think life was one big dream but dream doesn't make life.
For dreams are just dreams.
It seems life is getting harder and harder and it is getting harder to dream.
Please God, help us to make our dreams become reality
Regardless of your sex or race.
I'll look to You the Saviour of all to help make this place on
Earth a better place to live again.

Thomas F Riley

AUTUMN MOONLIGHT

Over the mountain a yellow moon
Hangs low.
And spreads across the earth,
A lovely snow-white glow.
The leaves appear like silver.
As they rustle in the breeze.
While across the valley stretches
Lengthening shadows of trees.
The rocks on yonder hillside.
Appears ghostly in the night.
Reminding one of phantoms,
Wrapped in sheets of snowy white.
The road an open high-way.
For travelers of the day.
Becomes a distant path,
Like the sky's milky-way.
And just before the dawning.
The moon will seek a rest,
And steal from Mother earth,
Her beautiful silhouettes.

Joan Lynnett Redfern

ME, THE CLOWN

High above the clouds,
Looking down,
The bird sees me,
The World's saddest clown.

The clown that laughed
Himself right off the stage.
He walked right into
His own cage.

The worst cage,
Made by himself.
Very, very poor
Since he lost all his wealth.

His wealth was the greatest
Of every single kind.
His wealth was love . . .
Love without binds.

Michael Johnson

THE TREE

O old and ancient tree
what tales your branches tell.
Do they tell of men who
like blind dumb sheep
are offered to the one who
holds the spear. O sorry
bloody tree the blood flows
up to the one eyed one who
seats on the throne in
mighty Asgard.

Susan MacLellan-Tobert

FRIENDS

The gentle butterfly
And the innocent flower
Share the secrets
Of the April eve in the meadow.
They become one
And unite in the dusk
In the shadows.

The midnight sun silhouettes
The butterfly
As she sleeps on the petals
Of the flower.
In the morning she is gone,
The flower weeps in the dew
As her song echoes
In the meadow.

Ady Jimenez

Ady Jimenez

WANTED! PRESIDENT FOR THE 1990'S

To the ones I love: Gino, Vany, Family and friends God bless you!—thanks

---

In today's world we need heroes, full proved and strong;
to hold on the world together and carrier
it on.

In today's world we need a whole lot of love . . .
to keep it from dying all by its own.

Where there be new Lincoln's and Washington's . . .
Men who will think of our nation;

and forget all the struggles, by remembering
its full potential.

Men of thoughts, not just of force or
preservation . . . and to have the three
would be perfection . . . for that we hope.

Those that will care to make the difference,
moment by moment, for us all . . .
So, that when their job be done,
there be a legacy for the new generation
to follow on . . .
And it would always stay alive and free . . .
as we all.

Doris Miller
INFLUENZA
I thought him my friend, but he must deem me a hollow-head,
For he smiled, oh, so broadly at me as he said;
"I, too, had the flu. Why, I spent all day in bed!"

Oh nay! This just simply isn't true,
This simpering idiot had not the flu!
Malaria, perhaps, or pox and typhoid, too.

But not the flu! Ah, you would query why?
Well, the wretch who had the flu was I,
And my agonizing death did come so nigh!

My fevered scull was pierced and jabbed,
Satan's pitchfork, with precision, grabbed
My pain-torn, palpitating lungs and stabbed!

Jerked from ancient moorings were my heart and liver,
Non-ceasingly I shook, from quake to quiver,
Tormented bones a'clack and flesh a'shiver!

Throbbing eyeballs in hot, dry sockets burned,
Muscles rent to shreds, though barely turned,
Gethemane!, to even touch my skin, I learned.

For touching skin raised inch-high bumps,
Each hair had roots in king-sized lumps!
Flu-jaws ache thrice as bad as those with mumps!

Now, fellowmen whom I never will eschew
Are those who say NOT they have the flu,
Unless they really, really, truly do!

Louis Mateo
AS IF INNOCENCE WAS FORSAKEN
As if *innocence* was forsaken
our *newborn* yields its praise
do we strive for a *sinless* culture
and *purity* what we crave?

how can a man be *naive*
trying so to remain *unstained*
when being *unexceptionable*
is reason to be blamed.

immaculate is not, his gender
nor *unhardened* its aim
he is unsuccessfully *faultless*
as his *saintly* struggle accompanies pain.

however *unsophisticated*
to dwell in this *simple* state
representing *incorruption*
unblemished he awaits.

Mary C Vallario
OCTOBER'S ART LESSON

Dedicated to my mother

Who yearns for Titian
Red or Botticelli blue
Need go no farther
Then the nearest shore
And there to view
Beneath bright-canopied
October sky all colors
Found in every noted
Gallery of art
Ghirlandaio, Perugino,
Sarto, Filippino Lippi
Such works surpassed
By scenes scintillant
Each bearing master
Stroke and touch
And gilded by God's
Golden brush.

Jeanette Lee
FEEL THE SNOW GENTLY FALLING
Feel the snow gently falling from the sky,
Winter you see has arrived.
Smell the flowers blossoming in the air,
Spring is here without a care.
Hear the children laughing at the beach,
Summer is within our reach.
See the colorful leaves falling to the ground,
Everywhere you look fall can be found.
Why can't man be like me and realize
we're not here for eternity.
The seasons will be forever,
Man does not seem to know better.
To live each day as it comes, and
try not to undo what the Maker has done.
Can't we learn to live in peace, and
Hope someday the fighting will cease.
Why can't man be like me, and realize we're not here for eternity.
And feel the snow gently falling from the sky . . .

Helen Strange
WHO CARES
The dawn is here
And the day will soon be near
Not even knowing
Who really cares

But only, "God" up above
Knows only me
That I give my thanks
In so many ways

That I know myself
That it is He that
Really cares

As I know that He
Is always there
Even when I feel ok
'So sad and old and gray.

Rivka Cutler
PLACES IN MY HEART
Smile and gleaming eye behold
Passing strangers and with raised arm yet bold
Did this gnarled man of age
Strike my vision and like a sage of yor
Leave his imprinted message more
Daily on my appointed rounds did see
Him walking waving, gleefully, glee—
fully
Full of all life's preciousness
Having none and wanting less
Than giving all that he can give, no gile
With a wave and cheery smile
Then as one spring morning faded
I felt some portion of my vision raided
A vital missing piece of puzzle
I could not fathom what it was, until . . .
My heart beat quickly once, then was
filled
To near bursting with mournful sound
My faithful morning friend was
gone . . .
My faithful morning friend was gone . . .

Carol L Cautillo
I'M SORRY
Sorry is a word I use
when I've done something I shouldn't have
or thought something I made the mistake of saying
And sometimes
even when I could have done something
but didn't.

Sorry is a little harder to say
when something was done in jest
But I say it because I know
That what I said
may not have been taken
the way I meant it to be,
For this, I apologize
for being insensitive to your feelings.

And I don't think
Love means never having to say you're sorry
Because when I say "I'm sorry"
It doesn't mean I don't love you
Just that
I realize I was wrong
And I never meant to hurt you.

Dolores M Mann
'TIS TIME
Time is such an elusive thing, it just goes fleeting by.
We cannot catch or hold it no matter how we try.
There is a time to be alive and gay and time in which to rest.
There is a time to toil and work, time to do our very best.
Have you taken the time lately to watch a happy child at play?
Or take time to listen while your babies kneel to pray?

There is a time for sowing, there is a time for reaping.
There is time for waking, quiet time for sleeping.
Take time to sit and study you mother's loving face.
Or take time to notice a new bride's charm and grace.
There is time for thinking, there is time for planning.
There is time for dreaming, time for goal scanning.
There is time for doing and time for trying.
Time for living and time for dying.

There is time for the ring of children's laughter.
Time to make memories to last thereafter.
There is time to seek the joys of life.
Time for worry, time for strife.
There is time to loosen our grasp on those
Who leave us for death's sweet repose.
The time will come to say good-bye.
Time to reflect and time to cry.

We cannot stop time, try as we may.
But take time to love
In life's fleeting day.

Thomas A Dempsey
THEY TOUCHED THE FACE OF GOD
The "Challenger" was ready
Everything looked bright
Forget about the icicles
That formed the other night

An engineer from Rockwell
Phoned the "Cape" and urged delay
"What's the difference"
If we wait another day

"T" minus eight and counting down
The engineer's advice was frowned
The count got down to minus two
All our thoughts were with the crew

Now it's down to seconds, the computers do their thing
Lift off "25" seemed just another ring
Thirty seconds, twenty seconds everything looked bright
But milliseconds later flames engulfed the flight

Now these flames were not just normal, something wasn't right
What could be the matter, we prayed with all our might

Now "God" saw fit to take this crew
On this particular flight
And someone said they touched his face
On that I'm sure they're right

Geralyn Beth Halldorson
THE LADY

To my grandmother Cleo, a very special lady who died of cancer when I was 10 years old. She will always be in my heart.

There was a lady dressed in plaid
Her hair was done up in a bun
She had a dog that did not look sad,
She looked like she was a lot of fun.

She carried balloons in her young looking hands
She handed out chocolates from many lands
The children loved her
She loved them too
Oh! Would you love it if it were you!

One day, the lady, she got sick
She didn't hand out any popsicles on sticks,

But the children came, and saw her with some treats,
And the lady got better in a good two weeks.

Soon she brought the children the same old things
And treated them like queens and kings.
The dog barked happily as he walked along,
If you could hear or see, you'd want to sing a song!
Oh! They were gay!

Then a tragic thing happened, something really tragic happened
The very next day. The lady didn't come back.
The children ran to her house and looked on the dish rack.
There was a note with writing so bad,
It said, "Children, I am at the Hospital of Glad."

The children went to see her, very sad and very worried, too!
The lady said "good-bye," died, then flew
To a place where all good people go
With clouds like fluffy, fluffy snow;
The lady went to heaven, and the children cried, you know.

The children cried for days and years, but soon, they found out,
The lady loved them, she still did love them
Without a single doubt.

Margaret Pardonnet
RESURRECTION

Trees.
Wood-brown against gray sky.
A stray shaft of sunlight
Falls on a few dead leaves,
Warms them to luster of old gold
And makes them live again
For one short moment.

Scharlotte Diane Yarbrough
DADDY'S

To my Daddy—Arlin Swaffar—I love you

We each have a father, young or old,
Most of which are as precious as gold;
They supply our needs, our wants, and our wishes,
With things like toys and food in the dishes;
Fathers are good but daddy's are best,
His love is as far as the east from the west;
when things go wrong and problems arise,
I can look to daddy and find loving eyes;
He can take something dull and make it bright,
Just by making me laugh or smiling just right;
So remember next time I call you daddy,
Anyone can be a father, but it takes someone
Very special to be a Daddy

Margaret Anne Neebel
ALONE

Alone in this world
Nobody who cares
Another one of life's
Incredible dares

It is really a shame
That people can't see
The gentle and loving
Parts of me

I can't understand why
People treat me like a child
Maybe it's because
I don't act crazy and wild

Maybe there's someone
Out there for me
Maybe there's not
I'll just wait and see

I really do hope that there is
But then again
No one has ever died
From not having any friends

Mary Ellen Baker
MY LITTLE FRIENDS

To my daughters: Virginia Lee, Carolyn, Betty Sue, Mary Kay, Jackie and Linda

---

When I was just a little girl,
I would sit with my dolls and play;
I would tell them all my secrets
and of the big things I would do some day.
They would only nod and smile
in approval of all I said;
as I dressed them and poured their tea
and thought of my life ahead.
But I did not do all those big things
"Dollies dear," I must confess;
"Life has really been too full,
and even sometimes, quite a mess.
"You see, I had my own real dolls to dress
and to feed and pour milk (instead of tea);
Days were just too, too busy
to do anything for me.
"I had to wash and comb their hair
and get them off to school;
I had to teach them to share and play
also, about Jesus and the Golden Rule.
"But now, my own little dolls
are all grown up and gone away;
so I have plenty of time to sit and think
of many and many a happy day."
So while I sit in my easy chair
and start dressing dollies again;
I can see them smile and nod,
as I say, "Thanks for being my little Friends."

Larry L Wilson
QUERY

When I look into the depth of her eyes,
Do I see an inner self that often cries?
A loneliness she cannot express without
admitting her distress?
Or could it be what I really see is only
A reflection of the inner me.

Michael A Federika
EVERY DAY

To the girls I knew and ones I never knew

Every day and in every way
All I need is you.
There's nothing else to say
You're a part of me too.
A memory that lingers on,
No matter what I do.
It's a simple case of projection,
I know your sorrows of the past.

From your troubles, you need protection.
That's why we will last.
Every dusk and every dawn
We will hope our lives away.
We will live because we know
That in our hearts, our love will grow.
Our fond desires will always show.
Bound by faith and sentiment,
With ourselves, we're both content.
From each other, we'll never go.

Krista Matto
STONE

My heart is a stone—
Too hard to give,
Easy to break windows with.
My heart denies me
The pleasures my eyes see.
But I cannot look the other way,
And I am powerless to say,
"Please, love me:
Don't throw me away."

Dorothy Startin
RENEWAL

Quietly o'er the bright landscape steals the darkening cloud.
Is the threat of a downpour inevitable?
Will the arrival of wholesome moisture shatter the stillness?

Though the scene be dark, always the sun peeks through;
The landscape is changed as the shower passes.

O, when I am downcast as the cloud on the sun!
Light, fill my soul that the fear within will dispel
And thy spirit will uplift me!

De Lea Marcel Davis
GOING HOME

I'm going home
Where the sun shines bright
And my spirit soars
In endless flight

Now I am gone
And yet I am here
So far away
And yet so near

I'm free at last
No earthly chain
I no longer suffer
Or feel the pain

And as I begin
To spread my wing
I'm like an angel
Learning to sing

I fly in peace
And perfect grace
Because at last
I've won the race

Don't think it's over
Cause it's not yet begun
It's clear in my mind
As I fly to the Son.

Ruth Richardson
SURROGATE MOTHER

"Oh, will you be my Mom?"
The young lady
cried aloud.

"Of course, I'll be your Mom!"
Delighted that she would ask,
If not proud.

When she called me Mom
So free and easy
It seemed to be.

And how delighted I was
To have her love—
My own daughter was thousands of miles from me.

God knew that
Each other
We would claim;

In His infinite
Wisdom
He made our names the same.

God was so gracious
To give us
Each other.

And how wonderful it is
That He chose me
To be a surrogate Mother!

Ortha J Davis
CLOUDS

When I was a child,
I laid on the green grass
And quietly drifted
Toward the cloud castles
High in the sky.
For an hour or so
My marshmellow raft tossed
In a sea of blue feathers.

Now I am an adult
And the grass on which I lay
Is not always green; sometimes brown
And obscured by sturdy weeds.
For an hour or so
I drift again toward the cloud castles,
Marshmellow rafts and blue feather sea.
Then I return again . . .
Ready
to
face
reality.

Hazel Whipple
AN OLD WRINKLED SHOE

I have an old shoe in the closet
All wrinkled and knotted and worn.
The old darling who wore it has gone on before;
He was the best man that ever was born.

Oh daddy, come back to the old wrinkled shoe;
Put your old wrinkled face through the door;

Tie the knot slowly with your old wrinkled hands;
Come back to us daddy once more.

Through tears I see it so empty and still,
All wrinkled and knotted and worn.
It is just an old shoe that my dear daddy wore;
He was the best man that ever was born.

Michael A Federika
THE SOJOURN

To people and lands untravelled

I took a sojourn down a long winding road
I saw rippling pond waters, by the jump of a toad.
I grew from a boy to a man in a humble abode
A one room country cottage, with an outdoor commode.
I took a short hike down a long country road,
And bought a farm house, with stone fireplace.

I met a girl named Camille, she had great appeal
As I stared at the glowing embers in the hearth
I could almost see her beautiful face.
I knew her well, she had a good moral code.
We grew more as one in the romantic mode,
And soon, to our wedding we rode.
I sprang from boyhood to manhood, with the good seeds I sowed,
And took a sojourn down a long winding road.

Karrin Dayton
GRANDMA'S BACKDOOR
If ever i could stop
one moment in time
and hold it forever
save it as mine
it would be this moment
Now
with this sunset
these trees
those mountains
that barn
the pasture
the woodpile
my dog and her ball
the yard as it's seen
from my grandma's backdoor
the yard and it's scene
from my grandma's backdoor

Janet Eckelbecker
GOOD-BYE, MY LOVE
Love of my life, I love you;
It really hurts to go.
I want to spend my life with you;
Because I need you so.
I know it's time that I moved on,
And gave you peace of mind.
It's really hard to do this,
But, it's the only thing that's kind.
They say that if you love someone,
That you can let them go.
I'm telling you, it's not easy,
Because I love you so.
Bon Voyage, my darling,
Maybe I'll see you again someday.
I hope you won't forget me,
And will let come what may.

Jana Jones
BABY'S LULLABY
Rock-a-bye baby
In the treetop,
When the wind blows,
The cradle will rock.
Mama's the Queen,
Daddy's the King,
Rocking their baby
Gently to sleep.

Vickie Battle
LOVE QUEST
My first glance told me you were the child of my many reflections.

As I gazed into your eyes, I wondered why someone would part with such a treasure.

Your frail body showed you innately sensed your rejection.

But, be at peace little one and know love beyond all measure.

Will that bond of a mother's love be unbroken?
Will you be content with the love we share?

Beware of the quest for the story unspoken!

For some quest have soon become snares.

Will you be content with my love you've grown to know so well?

Only God knows little one.

Only He can tell.

Ramona J (Quiring) Petro
LOVE
As time passes
in my small room,
I wonder . . .
What is Love?
Love grows in hearts,
which are tender and young.
Love grows in trust,
in children of loving parents.
Love grows in faith
in sharing with a friend.
Love grows as nature,
blossoms into spring
With fragrance, sweeter.
than perfume,
And colors more exploding
than fire works
With life abundant, in the woods
in the waters, and in the sky,
All bursting with music
greater than a symphony,
Then, . . . when love fades . . .
It leaves behind its only . . .
Memories
Now I have found the answer
Love is sad when it's beauty fades.
So then remember, that we must
take care of our world, if we want
to continue to enjoy it's beauty.

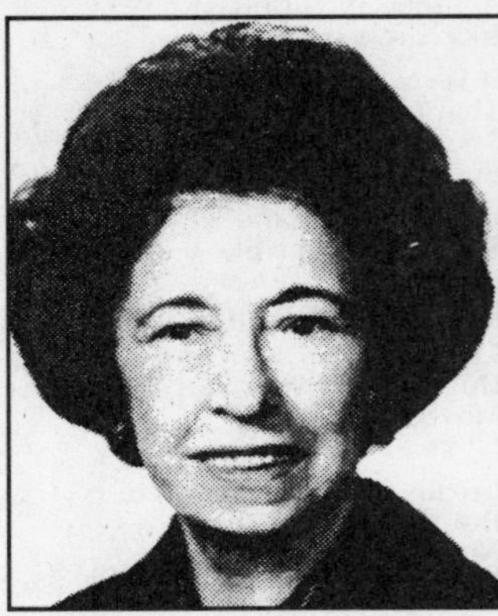

Violet Ficovich Morovich

Violet Ficovich Morovich
HAPPY THOUGHTS
Happy thoughts can help us
To have a happy day—
Most of the people
Will have this to say.

Looking at our family and friends—
At their good points,
Will make us feel much better
In our minds and joints.

All of us have
Good and bad habits
None of us are not perfect
To be wearing God's habit.

How nice it is when people
Have nice words to say;
It makes us happy
And helps to have a pleasant day.

Happy words can make
A gloomy day bright
And one better able
To see things in a new light.

Every little thing
Can help us have happiness
Just as wrong words
Can bring us unhappiness.

Gerald Moser
THROUGH THE SUNSHINE AND THE RAIN

This poem is for a very special and beautiful girl, Diana Poprik. Thanks for everything.

I did everything just as it should be,
every word spoken true.
From day to night and night to day.
I soon fell in love with you.

Your heart never gave me a chance.
Your mind always tended to care.
My heart was lost from too many a battle.
My mind knew it needed to share.

So we walked together through some good times
every laugh would later cause a tear.
Friends for all eternity,
hearts broken due to fear.

So my heart will keep fighting for your love
though I hate the feel of the pain.
Why can't we walk together
through the sunshine and the rain.

Bruce Johnson
THE COSMOPOLITANS
It was a world of peace until evil rose and claimed its satanicrites;
And all at once the light fell to darkness and the birds sang no more;
The sun was snuffed out, save for a small sparkle in the void;
While the proof of righteousness was lost, the faith still remained;
Pain and suffering, blackness and more blackness, less beauty seen;
Less meaning, less love;
The fight goes on;
Restore the dream, return the beauty;
Bring back the happiness, keep up the faith;
The faith never dies, the faith can never die;
While there is faith all is possible even in the black of night;
Where there is no faith naught is possible even when all things are in favor;
For the faith gives love and the love gives life, and not the
other way around;
Thus the evil shall perish and the cosmopolitans will rule the stars;
Forevermore . . .

Bernetta N Clubb
THE RIGHTEOUS WAY
Staying On the right side,
May not seem like fun;
But, you'll be glad you tried,
When your day is done.

You will sleep the whole night,
With your conscience clear;
No tossing left and right,
Dreaming trouble's near.

Study hard as you should,
Learning how to pray;
Then praise the Lord for good,
Things that come your way.

Olga Klug Iwanowski
LONELINESS
This encompassing ambience of sadness
Compounded by the sea and sky's blue silence
Accentuates the pain, intensifies the grief
Until the heart in anguish cries, o life brief,
In aimless wandring the lonely seagull flies
Above the brooding, restless sea
Dwarfed by the blue immensity of space
It is a counterpart of me.

Patricia A M Brown
GOODBYE MY FRIEND

This Poem is Dedicated to A Dear Friend and Neighbor Frank L. Spinelli

---

Life has gone by too quickly my friend!

As I look over our fence
I still can't believe your life has come to an end.

You may be gone from our sight,
but never from our hearts and thoughts.

You were there by my side in good times and bad.
Where are you now when I'm feeling so sad?

I guess you were needed by God up
above.
Maybe He, too, needed one more
friend to love.

There is more I must say—
The memories we've shared from
years gone by
will live on, till I must say goobye.

Your gentle and kind ways will be
missed by all.

How lucky we have been to come
to know you,
and have you as a friend.

Chris Malami
WINTER QUANDRY
Out of my mind I look to see,
Old Man winter sneak slowly by,
like a avalanche drifting
from a crying sky.

I see bleached clouds come soaring
by,
scattering tear drops made of dew.
They fall on land
like driven sand.

I stand on toes and feel the snow,
I wonder how the wind will blow.
Will yesterday's sunshine turn to
rain,
or will yesterday's promises
give me pain?

I am alone.
I shut the window and pull the
shade.
Will Old Man Winter gently fade
like melting snow,
or will he stay beyond
the break of dawn?

Anne Marie Evans
CHILDREN
Each day they learn some new tool;
To help on their way of Learning;
They make you laugh; they make
you cry.
And give you a reason for Living.

Nothing in life can compare;
To the sweet sounds of children
everywhere.

From the fall off the sled;
Till they go to bed;
The joy they bring is unending.
For when we think how lucky we
are;
In Children, we really have found
our star.

Gwendolyn Wood Tisdale

Gwendolyn Wood Tisdale
BOOKS ARE FUN FOR EVERYONE

Dedicated to My husband, My Sons and the Students at Winston School

Big ones, little ones, thick ones,
Thin ones, fat ones, skinny ones,
Heavy ones, light ones, different
books for different folks.

The more you read the more you
know.

Books are fun and interesting
too.
Titles galore to soothe your
mood
From home to school to other
lands
Around the world and back
again.

Travel through books to the stars
and flirt with Mars or
Board a sub and explore the deep
Through a book all dreams will
come true—

You can do or you can be
whatever
you choose. Reading is the
golden rule—
Adventures to Mysteries
Folklore to Humor, Drama to
Fine Arts,
Religion to Romance—

All of these subjects and more
You can find at a glance, in a
book—

So read, read as much as you
please
and you'll be sure to succeed,
indeed—

Charles Gaylord
LIKE EAGLES FLY
Like eagles flying on the wind
I'm filled with joy when you do
sing
To see you smile and hear your
song
For this my heart does always
long,

Your eyes they sparkle like the stars
Like eagles flying without bars
My heart would also like to fly
To catch your song from out of
the sky'

Your voice so sweet and like the sky
With clouds that go wandering
by
But on the ground where I must
stay
I dream and wish away the day,

In the silence of my room
I close my eyes and hear your
tune
That makes me soar like eagles do
And in my heart I am with you.

Nicole Ashley Grada
THE VISION WITHIN
I embrace a quiet vision
concealed from my own view
like an urge to touch the stars
it unsettles my reasoning
as it moves my hand to
reach the sky.
It's a separate sense—not my own
that lies within—a poetry
unborn
Emotions swells like a churning
force
compelling me to release my
imagination
but somehow trying to share
it
cheapens the abstraction
until it's gaudy
when it is so simple and clear
to myself.
I try to paint it
but what shape holds a dream
and what is its color?
I try to write it
but my words are too plain for
such complexity.
Someday someway the dream
shall soar
like sunlight splintering a prism
into stars
of brilliance
but the stars cannot be held.
And so the poetry within
is a crystal that waits to be
illuminated
to free the vision in its purest
form—intangible
and not solely mine.

Susan May Bourassa
LOVE
LOVE is not a word that is
whispered
but a form of commitment
that can be felt in
the hearts of those in love.
LOVE is something that
fills us with joy, and happiness.
LOVE also brings two people
together in sweetness of life.
LOVE is a spring of joy,
tis wrath, tis rain that
make me one with you.
LOVE needs no word, Love takes
two, for words are senseless, in
LOVE
LOVE is giving something of
ourselves,
If you dare not give, dare not
LOVE
for LOVE is giving most of you.
LOVE is the river
Peaceful, kind,
Yet can rage like
Oceans of waves.
LOVE gives more than it
receives and thus it
suffers nothing.

Kathryn Lincoln
SPRINGTIME
Seeking
Inspiration
Silence
Whispers
Expectation
A door
Closes
A door
Opens
A flower's
Petals
Unfold

Betty Quayle
LOVE

This poem-is-dedicated-to-Sam-my beloved-son.

Love is a never ending thing
The lovely trees, the birds on the
wing
The flowers, animals, a joy to
behold
Myriads of beautiful fishes to be
told
That God's love is everywhere,
In the sea and in the air.
The songs of birds resound
Across the sky, the heavens beyond
People show love to another
Their children, father, mother,
Sister and brother,
We need but look around us and
In our hearts,
To see love that ne'er departs.
God showed us love when He died
on
That tree
From our sins, we could all be free.
God so loved the world and the
people within
He created love, so we begin
To learn the lesson that comes
from within.

B C Jones
MOTHER WAS I KNOW, SHE WAS

This poem is dedicated in memory of my loving Mother, whose spirit is alive in me through the power of Jesus Christ our Lord

When I came forth from Mother
She held me in her arms
She kissed me oh so tenderly
My body was so warm
As darkness turned to daylight
The beginning of Sabbath morn
My Mothers eyes beheld me
The brightness of her newborn
son

As days turned into months
And months carried us to years
My Mother did wipe away
The sorrows of my tears
With questions asked I, Mother
About the life of man
Please son do not you worry
If God we trust you can
Mothers life is over
Mine is yet to be
Mother was I know, She was
An angel from God to me
Always as ever
B.C.

Christine K Sawyers
THE BIBLE

I read my Bible every day.
I talk to God while I do pray.
I have some questions while I look.
I find the answers in this book.
I read some more of what I see.
I find myself so filled with glee.
The things I do are going my way,
I know because I prayed today.
The things I took are in his book.
The person you see is He in me.

Carolyn J Wilkinson
WHERE LOVE HAS GONE

To my loving Mother and Father, Virginia May Cekala and Paul, Peter Cekaia

---

I looked into the sky of blue—
And wondered what I should do—
My baby left me all alone—
I wish that he would come home—
I looked at the sun in the sky—
So bright and hot and oh so high—
Will he come back? I think not—
The fight I wonder how it did start—
The trees are full and bright and green—
Why did you have to be so mean—
You left with her this I know—
I wish you luck whereever you go—
One day I will meet another—
One I want to be my lover—
I'll always love you my darling dear—
I'll not shed one more tear—

Rowena Bragdon Holt

Rowena Bragdon Holt
OUR CROCUSES PURPLE IN COLOR

To Louis—My loving husband of 51 yrs. Our daughters—Yvonne, Bonnie and Karen and our lovely granddaughter Julie

---

Our crocuses purple in color
their beauty rich and rare
First flowers in our beds
popping through as if to say "I care."
Soon, came the yellow daffodils
in their semi-circle they bloom
As the wind blows they can't be still
swaying you in all their golden glory
Farther across the lawn
lovely camellias in shades of pink
Awake early to greet the dawn
as flowers on an easel to look at
—and think
The stately spruce tall and green
I view from my window all day long
Then the magnolia with white fragrant blooms
makes the heart burst into song

God gave us all these
to add color among the trees
And remind us He is the Creator
of all things beautiful, great and small.

Jeanette Tongay
WHO AM I?

Dedicated to those who have the power of change and the will to do so.

My name is not important now.
My presence can't be seen
I'm with you at this very time.
I'm part of every being.
I live inside your deepest thought
I follow everywhere.
At times you think you're rid of me,
but I am always there
I'm with you when you turn away
from those who suffer so.
You see their pain and agony,
and still you let it go.
I'm with you when you say to them,
"I have no time to spare."
You walk away and leave behind
a chance for you to care.
You tell yourself, "They'll be alright,
I've problems of my own:
I's not my place to save the world."
You turn your heart to stone.
Then late at night, when all is still
as you lay awake in bed.
The thoughts of hollow, begging eyes
begin to fill your head.
I come to you in whispering waves,
a nagging, haunting sound.
I remind you of your selfish ways
of where your fate is bound.
You should have guessed my name by now,
it could be but a few.
Is it guilt or conscience deep?
My name is simply . . . YOU!

Gregory M Hawkins
CHANGE

Caterpillars are some what an unpleasant sight. But within the cocoon their beauty blooms. When they spring free to dance on the breeze, it brings a joy from within to behold such a marvelously inspiring sight.

Gary Jackson
WHAT AM I?

I am nothing
but a mass of flesh
suspended
by a frame of bones.
I am nothing
but fleeting impulses
in a gelatin substance
inside my skull.
I am nothing
but the surface features
that are reflected
when I stand
before a mirror.
I am nothing
but the fluctuations
of air pressure
that occur
when I speak.
Yet . . . I ask:
What am I?

Ann T Simkewicz Regan

Ann T Simkewicz Regan
SUMMERS HISTORY

The Suns Gold Rays streak
through the trees,
And quickly scans the Forest Floor,
The Goldenrod, the Queen Ann Lace,
Add to the late Autumn Decor.

The Scarcrow has gone with the wind,
Just left a toppled Grinning Face,
Its Cornstalk Hair has blown about
Its streeked off clothes every which place.

The Falling Leaves like Fairies dance,
As 'round and 'round and 'round they prance,
A swish of wind and up they rise
Like clouds of Monarch Butterflies.

Jack Frost features his Fall Reviews,
So let what Sunshine kiss your face,
Has shuffled colors here and there
We bow to Autumns Shorter Days.

He'll dart through all the Nature Trails,
And be as busy as a Bee,
A Patchwork Quilt he'll start to form
From all of Summers History.
He'll give each leaf a frosty nip,
And mix green, yellow, orange bright,
Then with his color palette full
Start tinting through the Frosty Night.

The Asters brave Jack Frosts approach
The Mums hang on long as they can
They do not fear the coming snows,
All in God's care, all in God's hands.

Laura R Terry
SPECIAL FRIEND

Thank God I have friends like you
Who sticks by me when I am trouble
Who listens with understanding and love
You are one of God's chosen above.
You are always there when needed
Forgetting yourself and time
You will always be a special friend of mine.

God gave you insight and feelings
Using your gift to help others
Show them the way of
understanding and caring

God will Bless you so many ways
As you are God's chosen
To help in His name and show
That He is truly Love and Forgiving

Thanks for your ear, time and love
For special people like you are hard to find
That's why you will always
Be a special friend of mine . . .

Joan Prescott
THE VOCALIST

She Comes on strong,
As a crowd of clowns.
She comes on soft,
As a wisp of breeze.

She tantalizes hearts
And tears minds.
Conditioned listeners,
Disarmed, attend her Song.

How does she succeed, and why?
She bares our hearts
To innermost needs
And shares her soul with all.

Shelby Artrip

Shelby Artrip
CONVERSION

As I ponder on my sin's unknowing start,
I think of you—of joys that I did seek
Which brought me nothing but aching in my heart
That lasted 'til after you said, we must part.
With you gone, I could hear my Master speak.

He spoke to me so often in my life,
Which He gave me through His Amazing Grace.
I could not hear Him; there was such strife!
I could only hear the troubles in my life.
I could only see my "God" in your face.

So saddened when I heard you loved another;
So broken in my spirit, I thought I'd die.
I could not see—I thought there was no other
To fill my being with joy. I thought I'd rather
Close my eyes to life than hear my cries.

My Master's Voice came to me so clearly,
I knew at once there was reason to go on;
And suddenly the one I held most dearly
Was at once to me the reason, I so nearly
Lost my soul, but now my soul is won.

Donald John Trzeciak
THE WAR NOBODY WANTED: 1968

The war nobody wanted came in on a whisper
The war nobody wanted started on a hint.
Like a game between two generals,
And we were all the pawns.
Rain at my window willow weeping
Time at my window passing slow
Rain at my window willow weeping
Where is he at I ask, He's off to war
once more. Again the guns are blazing
Again the thunder sounding
Where is he at—My husband
Will he come home. Tomorrow

Jenny Wegscheid
A QUESTION

Life's a question
Nobody can answer
But many try to guess
Only one that has experiences
It's pleasures and turmoils
can offer others insights
—But never answers—
Life's a special thing
For one person alone
No answers
Just questing and searching
If we search hard enough
And we are honest enough
Life will be fullfilling and fun
But only if we let it be—

Sheila R Bidwell
LORD HELP ME!

Lord
Help me see Your ways,
Sometimes I am so blind.
I know there is a purpose,
For this mixed up state of mind.

I so much need You by me,
To guide me on my way.
I sometimes wander off,
And don't find time to pray.

But You always seem to love me,
No matter what I do.
You always have the time for me,
Even when I don't . . . for You.

Thank you Lord for being there,
I am so much in need.
Please help me to be more like You,
In thought . . .
In word . . .
In deed.

Marylin Meeks
LIFE'S STAGE

For a very special friend who means the world to me. Rett, I'll always love you.

Life is alot like a drama
We all have our roles.
The director knew to put us in the same scene,
Just you and I together.
When the stage is set, the curtains will rise,
And the audience will applaud.
The lights will come on and it will be our turn.
I will say my lines and you will say yours.
We shall then depart as many times before.
The curtain will fall and
We will hear the chatter of the dwindling crowd.
The stage is cleared and the characters leave.
Now here I am all alone
Hoping you'll come back just like our scene.
But you never do show and
I realize that I can't live any longer without you
So I wait.
But life is real, not a drama
Our lines are not written out, but I can still dream.
So, when you see me alone on life's stage,
You'll know that I'm waiting for you.
And I'll always love you.

Michele Thompson
ODE TO A MOTHER AND FATHER

To Dee and Joe Thompson, my loving parents

Don't worry, Mom,
I know there's more to life than boys
Even popularity isn't that important.
I do think of life after graduation.
And believe it or not, I plan to face it on my own
no ring on my finger.
Nothing to tie me down.
How I plan to support myself comes first.
Before now I wanted to be protected by someone else,
Don't worry, Dad,
You are the best guy in my life.
I love you more than any other.
I know it's hard to watch your little girls grow up,
But it happens to all fathers.
Just because there are other guys in my life,
Don't think they're more to me than you.
I'll love you always, even on the day you give my hand away.
You won't be losing a daughter but gaining a son.
And, Mom and Dad, that won't be for a long time to come.

Henry White
LEGENDS

Seen on sides of hills where deep within
Are agencies, departments, offices
And sundry staffers, housed and worked:
Authorized personnel only—V.I.P.

Seen on distant landscapes towards the cities,
Mushroom clouds where buildings ought to stand,
By citizen—taxpayers who were warned
To run and hide, are signs: R.I.P.
Seen on checks to pay for time,
Equipment and supplies for personnel
To use them to protect the public good,
The imprimatur, "Civil Defense" —N.S.F.

Seen on landscapes, lying where they fell,
Corpses protected by smoke and falling leaves.

Marjorie Mack
WAPITI

Large soft snowflakes fall,
Wind whispers thru
the tops of trees,
I am proud.
I am ELK.
I raise my head and call.
An echo, an answer?
A flash, a sound, a blow!
And my life is splashed upon the snow.
No more will I roam or mate or yearn,
A sacrifice to Man,
Who gives nothing in return.

Michael A Federika
ANGEL EVER MORE

To Marilyn Monroe

"An angel always ever more,
Here at last, and here before,
You're never far beyond my door.
You are in my shadow—my every dream.
You're as beautiful as you seem.

Your illusion spreads out everywhere.
Over time and space surpassed,
The time is now for all to dread,
All joy is gone when you are dead.
You are an angel now, at last."

Ronald James Dessus
TA WA NEE

I dedicate this poem to Rosa, Joyce, Perch, Buddy and Curtis

TA Wa Nee Ta Wa Nee I softly call into the gentle night As a large shadow looms before my eyes—Covering the ground I stand upon—Moon beams streak the distance sky—Striking like lazer lights as Ta Wa Nee stand upon the hill—I draw closer to him—Only I have been allowed to gaze upon his presence—Drawing ever so close he says "open your eyes" as In a dream like state I open my eyes—The shadows that surround me evaperate—Displace by the rays of the sun—Before me stands Ta Wa Nee—Majestic—Proud—Like the sun itself— A golden hue—Shinning brightly into my eyes—I blink to focus better upon he who is before me.—In that moment he disappears—Like the constellations in the sky—When night gives way to day—Yet I sense his presence—Feeling comfort in knowing that he rules day and night—His flowing mane protecting me always—Ta Wa Nee Ta Wa Nee Ta Wa Nee

Jeanne Losey
OLD GLORY ON PARADE

When the flag of our land waves above a parade,
Think of all that she means, and the sacrifice made
So that glorious banner forever would be
Floating proudly above this great "Land of the Free."
Think of those who have died that Old Glory might wave
O'er this land we call proudly "The Home of the Brave."
Then just think of the blessings belonging to you
Just because you were born 'neath the Red, White, and Blue.
Show the world, by your actions, you're proud you can be
Born and bred in this wonderful "Land of the Free."
Let the Statue of Liberty's great shining light
Ever be, to the homeless, a welcoming sight.
The ideals that America lives by must be
An example to others who want to be free.
Place your hand o'er your heart as Old Glory goes by;
Make a vow you will help keep her floating on high.
So salute her and show her you're proud she can wave
Over every parade in "The Home of the Brave."

ReGena M Rocca
FORGOTTEN

He sits against a brick
building and stares at
all the cracks
in the sidewalk knowing
they are pointing at him
and they would all open wide
and they would swallow him up.
He knows he could wear his
shoes on his ears
and noone would care
and he could paint his hands red
and noone would notice.
Won't you give me a dime?
He waits for a silver song
in his tin cup
and says God Bless You
and wonders if anyone heard the words.
God bless you
as he turns to dust beneath their feet.

Sherri E Carson
GOD FORGIVE

God forgive my past
for my past hangs over

me like Hell fire burning
me its put me in a prison.
I can't get out of it.
But God I need you to forgive
for I asked Your Son
Jesus Christ in my life.
Now I have life back again
for God forgave.
And everything in my life is
changing for the good.
As I get richer and richer
In my blessing for
God forgave.

Danielle Elouzin
PRETENTIONS

To all of my sisters (not blood related) that are now involved in high risk P (or will be)-I Dedicate Pretentions to Hopefully find a friend that is supportive with no demise to yourself having the possibility of having a child. I'm sure the going is rough. As years disappear you'll grow with the youngster and understand some of Shakespeares seven stages of mankind. Life will be immeasurable.

Winters quiet disolution
Osmosis
Cells divide
Hopefully
Nature
Protects
A few gray hairs grace the circumference of my head
Quails blending with seasonal colorings
Spring brings the yearly event of pesach (coinside)

This year of 1986—A child named Benji at a
Decade of age will ask the four
Questions in English and Hebrew
All children ask questions
In the forests of time
Nocturnally
One fetus stretches the walls
Of my sisters uterus containing bundles of branches
Of fibroids pressing against her Placenta
Cucokos sing soft sagas
Hot humid torrid summer time when loud
Cucokos pulsate
Discomfort gnawing from deep within
Soon breath and growth will instill discoveries
Relating to the household of mankind
Writing sagas in the forests of time.

Helen J Hemingway
TO OUR MOTHERS

In loving memory to my mother, Anna J. Grandish and To All Mothers of The World.

God created a wonderful being,
My mother
Who will never grow old.
Her smile is like sunshine,
Her heart is like gold.
Her eyes are like bright shining stars,
Her cheeks like red roses, you will see.
God created a wonderful mother, and
Her gave her to me!

Stephanie L Baysinger
REFLECTIONS
Sometimes life
quiet as it may seem
as still as it may be
as lovely as you see
Can be confusing.

When life is confusing
you feel chaos pulling you away
you feel alone in an average day
you feel there is nothing to say
And want to be left alone.

But then you sleep
and dream the sun will rise
and dream of no more crys
and dream of friendly Hi's
And realize you were awake.

Mrs Pat Hawkins
A TRIP WITH MY VALENTINE
For 15 years my Valentine has been mine.
And this is not just one more line!
For though our relationship is not all fun,
I still rate my Valentine second to none!

To win a Ski weekend would really be nice!
And who cares if there's lots of ice.
For, being with my Valentine in rain or snow,
Would still be real cozy as anyone knows!

So, I'll just keep my fingers crossed.
In hopes my big chance will not be lost.
But, if this trip, I do not win.
Then, I guess this planning will come to an end!

Helen C Gilhousen
OUR AGED ONES
We see the aged as they sit,
Alone, and lonely, every day,
They've worked so hard to do their bit—
But now they slowly fade away.

Yet in their minds are memories—
Of happiness of by-gone days.
But now they sit alone and feel—
That they are only in the way.

O put your arms around them oft'
Tell them they're needed every day,
And gently kiss their cheeks so soft—
To show them they're not in your way.

And if their memory is not clear,
And they often make a mess 'tis true,
Remember that they've loved you, dear,
Then thank God they belong to you.

Karen Colp
LOVE'S PASSING
Eyes meeting across the room
minds locked in time suspended
sharing that rare experience
when beings touched, meshed, blended.

The moment fades, the world invades
two beings once again
searching for that feeling
of happiness within.

It's lost, gone with the wind
that closeness known by two
that elusive, teasing thing called love
vanished like the dew.

Two separate forms, each missing a part
sadly await the day
for love to return and mend the heart
to endure while they gray.

Michael A Federika
MAGIC IS THE NIGHT
Magic is the night
The winds across the field,
Blow gently in the moonlight
As the fields of gold do yield,
Across the field stands a figure
Not much shorter than I,
With her eyes silently lifted—
In meditation to the sky.
From where came this comely maiden?

With soft brown hair generously laden,
For what event is she waiting?
She loiters like a staid statue
Among fields shining of crystal drops of dew.
So stern, yet so mild; so wise; yet so wild.
Her amicable searching eyes looking for love.
And as the gold and crimson dawn breaks through
Her countenance comes into view.
You can read this the way you want,
But I believe this girl is you.

Mary Redmond
MY THREE LOVED ONES

To Michelle, Mike and Carole with Love.

I'd like to find the words
To tell you exactly what's in my heart,
If I put them down on paper
Maybe that will be a start.

From the day each of you were born
And continuing on through now,
I dreamed of special things for you
That I hoped would happen somehow.

Each one of you is so different and
Very special in your own way.
My love for you will never cease
As it grows deeper day by day.

I've watched you, listened to you,
And, yes, at times I've cried;
Wanting only the best for you
With a Mother's loving pride.

When you've read these words I've written
Then stopped to think them through,
Remember, my three loved ones,
They were written just for you.

Jewel Muston
MORNING THOUGHTS

I dedicate this poem to my daughter—Phyllis Charlene

In the morning when I awake
I see a beautiful blue sky.
Lovely fleecy white clouds
Below the dome of Heaven near by.

Then I see the earth
The budding of the cherry trees
Also the birds and the flowers
And feel the early morning breeze.

Then comes the evening hour
I see the majestic stars, the full moon
I pause a moment, breathe a sigh
For God has ended my day too soon.

But that's the way he planned it.
He knows I need my rest.
I say a prayer and promise
Next day to do my best.

My own personal prayer

Dear Father: Thou knowest harsh and
thoughtless words have been spoken.
Thou hast asked us to Love our neighbor
and our friends. Give us the Grace and
an open heart and courage that will enable
us to go and say, I am sorry;
Forgive me.
AMEN

Peter G Alexander
COMANCHE EYES
Brown and hardened
With sadness
Your planes are barren.
The Bison are gone
The water is bad
Comanche eyes
You lost so much.

Gina Renee' Sadlo
MY UNBORN CHILD
Ten little fingers
Ten tiny toes
Yet unborn, no allies or foes
Patiently waiting, anxious to know
Learning and loving
A lifetime to go

Michael A Federika
LADY OF THE LAKE

The scent of hyacinth and violets
Adorn the labryinths of my mind.
It is there I find
A melange of mahogany,
verdantique and indigo
Reflected in a cerulean, crystaline
lake.
A lady bedecked in white
A vision to behold,
Whose luminous beauty—an
aurora—a warm psychic glow—
Kindnesses once remembered
from long ago,
Once warm, now cold.
Her presence was felt everywhere
I go.
She, like the pulchritude of the
flowers,

Now faded from sight.
All colors sympathize behind the
lady in white.
The coagulation turns to black—
The glorious day once bright
Sinks, with the lady in white, into
the oblivion
Of the night.
She takes with her into the past
The love that we could know.
Through demon rum and devil
weed
These thoughts my memory freed.
She exists now, in my memories
Like the iridescence of the flowers,
the lake, the trees
The scent of hyacinth and violets.

Shirley Wilson Lawing
LETTER TO MY LORD

To and for my Lord, who loves us all and a special thanks to my wonderful husband, Ernest, mother Vergie and my children, Holly, Christy, Daniel, Cassandra, and David. And to my late father Burgin Wilson.

Jesus, my Friend, Saviour and
Lord,
Earthly riches, I need not hoard.
For Heavens blessings are
permanent pleasures,
Being with you Lord, will be the
ULTIMATE treasure.

Jesus, you love me though I sin
every day,
You know all I do, feel, think, and
say.
Lord, you understand and forgive
me, and love me so very much,
You reach out, grasp my hand and
heal me with your precious,
loving touch.

Lord, you came down from
Heaven, and gave your life
nailed to that tree,
Then raised up, to free and heal all
from sin; yes, even me.
Lord, I love you more than I could
ever say,
Your love and sacrifice, I can Never
repay.

Lord, I know that I am not worthy
of being one of your sheep,
Because all of my sins and failures
all run too deep.
But no matter what I've done, you
love me and forgive; forgetting
all of this,
Making my heart and soul sing
with wonderous joy and bliss!

Father, Son, Holy Ghost, thou
Holy One, I love and trust you so
please set me right,
Every time I fail or fall and sin in
your sight.
I have but one great desire that I
want more than any thing,
To see, fall to my knees, and
worship you, my Lord God the
Eternal King!

Your Thankful Child,
Shirley Wilson Lawing

P.S. I love you Lord. Even when I
hide from you, I know you are
always there, right beside me,
You guide me, and drag me
when I am stubborn.
Make me more Christ-like; giving
freely to others as you have to
me.
Give me the wisdom to know what
you want me to do and the
courage to follow it through,
Praise to you my Lord!

Nelda Blackwell
RESURRECTION DAY

Mary came with heavy heart
To the empty tomb,
Not knowing that the Saviour
Had risen from its gloom.

Weeping as she entered in
To find her Lord gone,
'twas more than she could bear
So she started on.

When she turned to go her way
A voice so softly spoke—
Mary, Mary why weepiest thou?
It seem she ought to know.

No it cannot be,
But then he told us so—
Destroy this temple
And in three days
I will raise it up.

My Lord, she inquired,
Is it really so,
Have you indeed come forth,
And where Shall I go?

Go I say and tell my friends
That I am on my way,
And be not slow for they must
know—
Of-my resurrection day!

Nora M Johnson
HOME, FRIENDS, I WONDER

Home

As I sit looking out my window,
mountains are what I see.
Strong, tall and majestic,
they'll be there for eternity.

As I look into my mind,
the picture's not the same.
I think of why I left there,
I remember why I came.

I see miles of snow white fences,
gentle rolling hills.
I see the rivers flowing,
cattle grazing in the fields.

I feel the breezes blowing,
the softness of the rain.
See the trees that change their
colors,
the leaves that clog the drains.

All these things remind me,
of the home I left behind.
The home I left in body,
but carry in my mind.

FRIENDS

A friend is there to lean on,
the times when you feel sad.
A friend will share your happiness,
the times when you feel glad.

A friend is there to help you,
during your times of trial.
When you need an understanding
ear,
to listen for a while.

A friend is there to help you,
in anyway he can.
A friend is never critical,
when you need a helping hand.

A friend is always loving,
gentle, understanding, kind.
Someone you can turn to,
when you find you're in a bind.

I guess what I'm trying to say is,
a friend is always there.
To share your joy or sorrow,
to help you your burdens bare.

I WONDER

If I could walk in Jesus' shoes,
I wonder what I'd do.
Would I give my life the way He
did?
Would I give my life for you?

I wonder if I followed the path,
He walked so long ago.
Would I be as forgiving as Jesus
was,
Somehow I don't think so.

Would I give the blind man sight
again?
Would I help the lame to walk?
Or would I think, Oh that's too bad,
But none of it is my fault.

What would I do if I needed
someone,
And they all turned their backs
on me,
You know that's what happened to
Jesus,
They just stood and watched him
bleed.

They watched as the nails were
driven,
In his hands and in his feet.
When he said, "Father please
forgive them,"
His eyes they could not meet.

If I could walk in Jesus' shoes,
I wonder what I'd do.
Would I use God's power for
myself.
Or would I use that power for
you.

Mildred L Ortiz
FROM A PAGE CALLED 'LIFE'

Dedicated to a precious memory from the past

The night was bright and clear,
The heavens gleamed with stars,
And from admidst the clouds below
A pale full moon shed its glow.

Into this perfect setting,
There wandered a man and a
girl—
Each for the time forgetting,
The world and its endless
turmoil.

As they wandered along hand in
hand,
The night seemed to whisper and
understand—
Their hearts were light, their talk
was gay,
Their togetherness seemed right,
as they wended their way.

Far from the city at the top of a hill,
They found a court on which
tennis was played,
And there beside it—secluded and
still—
There appeared a bench to
which they strayed.

They talked of things both pro and
con—
Laughing and living were so
much fun—
And though the night wore on.
Time seemed to stand still—
For and Eternity passed at the
top of that hill.

Perhaps there will be moments in
the years to come,
When each will remember and
their thoughts will roam,
Back to a city, its noise and its
strife,
To a very Dear Memory from a
Page called 'Life'.

Ernestine Jane Tebo
THE AMERICAN WAY

Dedicated to the seven astronauts, who lost their lives for our country.

The seven that lost their lives that
day.
For seeking tomorrow, the
American way.

They paved their road, to heaven that day,
As they searched for a victory, the American way.

The space craft that carried them, far from their homes.
Up into the heavens, the seven alone.
They left their loved ones, for duty had called,
And they left their nation, whom mourned for them all.

The space craft it ignited, exploded in air.
Leaving a vision, of what happened there.
It's hard to imagine, what came to their minds,
In the seconds that held, their most dangerous time.

But they were exploring the heavens that day,
While standing united, the American way.
Yes, they stood together, as Americans stand,
For our nation, while God holds our hands.

We'll stand together, tomorrow we'll explore,
We'll stand united, for what they stood for,
Yes, we'll stand united, the American way.

Gertrude I Martell
GO FOR IT!
At birth we arrive into our new world, whether early, late, or on time. We are cared for, loved, and soon learn the soothing feeling of being fed, and dry diapers make our life sublime.
YES, GO FOR IT!
In our new world we've felt love, early learned the pain of hunger, and discomfort of wet pants. It doesn't take us long to know which crys, or noises bring quick response to rescue us.
YES, GO FOR IT!
In our early years parents teach us the do and don'ts. During this time we are learning how and where their weakness lies. We soon learn where and how to get our way, whether it's good or bad for us.
YES, GO FOR IT!
To be told no, and given a reason has to be firmly adhered to. If parents in their love, and understanding for us, stick to the rules they have set for us, rewards in our future will be earned.
YES, GO FOR IT!
Worthy things in life are seldom easy. If our goals are met, and the challenge seems gone, then new goals whether they come early or later in life gives us a new challenge. God will help us to find our place, and our contribution to, and for others. Often times in helping others, we find we have helped ourselves more than others.
YES, GO FOR IT!

Oneida Layton
THIS BEAUTIFUL FLAG
This beautiful flag is your flag and my flag
It may get tattered and worn.
In storm tossed weather even torn.
We'll replace it with another that looks new born.

Flying for the living full blast
For the fallen heroes half mast.
We'll protect Her through thick and thin.
Even if it means our lives until the end.

No matter how far we may often roam
Our beautiful flag will be there when we get home
Look at any flag waving from afar
Like a huge twinkling star for us to protect even through war.

C J Doyal
MY LITTLE RED BIKE

This poem is dedicated to my Mother Fran Erspan and to my own daughter Ryan Jordan.

When I was a child, just a little tyke
My mom bought me a bright red bike,
That bike took me everywhere,
Everywhere I would dare.
It took me to school
In summer heat and winter cool.
It took me to see each friend,
And around every road bend.
It was always there waiting for me,
Ready to ride wild and free,
It was easy to have pride
In the little bike I would ride,
As I got older I rode it less,
Til soon it stood in idleness.
I out grew my little bike of red,
But I took the time to look ahead.
I stored it away with loving care.
Now happy memories I have to share.
There she goes, my own little tyke,
Pedaling away on my little red bike.

Gerald A Boone
GLIMPSE
Before movement of my being there
Was life so prevalent history is a binding
Web. Features that print this person
As one only: for a life time I am wed.
Country youth fear of dark made the
Sight of light ignite a blessing heart surge.
Many times I've braved things unknown
Stumbling misguided until finally altogether
Reasons merge. Mulitudes smaller than the
Eye can see specs conglomerate into shapes
Of living movement for greater thought.
Sums of money excite nations with desire
Toward removing greatness among all
Entwined into meaningless naught.
Troubled journey threatens this my pathway
In senseless darkness seeking the Blessing light. Am I no more in eternity
Than a grain of sand of clay may be as it
Lay waiting or have I a reserved
Surge in sight. I've enjoyed and
Treasured my environment only here on Earth
Meets my needs with Hope for the cycling
Seed. If communication with life
Endures my wish is please let others
Have this glimpse for its an eternal need.

Sandra Bowmaker

Sandra Bowmaker
LOVE ME NOT TO CONQUER ME

I dedicate this poem to the people who believed in me, even when I didn't . . .

Love me not to conquer me
as dust among aged ruins
conquered by winds
and old, old men.

Let me to love you
and set you, atop
a pinnacle of daisies and daffodils;
untouched by a tear.

As time; as love aging
whispers justly about promises beheld
and, "Rightly so!"
said the old, old men.

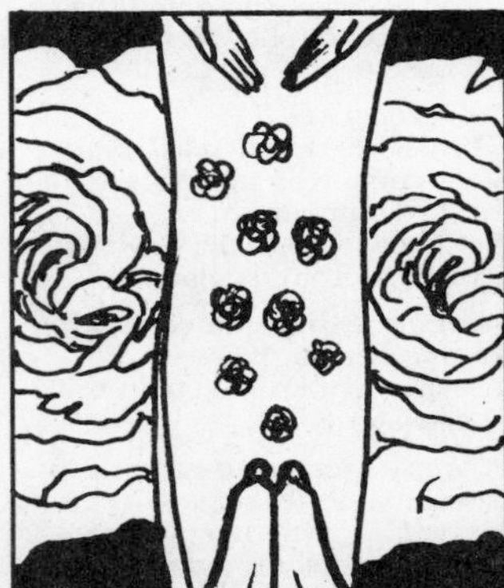

Come you with me
at evenings crest
and "Tarry not into the midnight!"
I said.

Thus, in time awaited
we came together beside calm
tides and restful seas,
growing aged.
And talking and laughing
with the old, old men.

Pearl E Pyznar
A BABE IS BORN
In a lonely stable far away,
Christ, our Lord, in a manger lay,
While Angels in the starry night
Sang their hymns of peace and right.
O'er all the earth a great light shone,
One huge star hung all alone,
Leading Kings and shepherds where
Men knelt before a Babe, in prayer.

A Babe whose very name is blest,
Lay at peace on Mary's breast,
While the beasts around them lay
The Angels sang of CHRISTMAS day.
Shepherds came and knelt in fear
Knowing not that God was near,
But as they prayed, on trembling knee,
He gave them peace for eternity.

The Wise Men came on camel back
Bearing riches in every pack;
They followed the brightly beaming star
Beckoning men from near and far.
Before a stable hewn of rocks,
Where shepherds knelt down with their flocks,
They came with jewels and gifts so rare,
They knelt at the Baby's feet, in prayer.

Great Hosannas filled the land,
As the hills echoed the Angel band.
God's glory shown around all men,
For Christ is born, Peace lives again.
God's Son has come to give us love
From the Father's throne above.
Peace be upon all men on earth
Rejoice ye all at our Savior's birth.

Albert H Streufert
THE FACE OF A GIRL

Dedicated to my SIX daughters.

There's nothing as beautiful as the face of a girl,
The slight, dimpled cheek, the wind-blown curl.
The cloud-studded sky measures light for the day,
But the face of a girl has eternity's ray.

There's death and there's life in the tall stretching flame;
There's light and there's life in the sound of my name,
But the warmth and the life and eternity's joy
Is the fact that I have the face of a boy.

Mildred Townzen
SEEDS IN TORRENT
Dibble the soil
Bestrew the seed
Spattering, sparging, spitting flurry
Plot the rows in castle mounds
Midst galey, gusty, rushing sounds
Transparent streams of gossamer
Furbishing blue chambray gowns
Tightly clinging, weighting,

binding, wetting down
Sad days pippin plantings drowned

In sky borne seas late born of rivulets
But grant the last loved leaf transpire to sailing ship
Of necessity, be miniscule
Transporting seed with harvest hopes departed
Through furrows, fjords, and free
Inexorably, inevitably, and wed
In wind and watery dissolution
To the salty sea.

Linda Woodley
THE DISTANCE
There is a distance between us tonight
and each is tentative toward the other,
wanting to admit things aren't quite right
yet the fear of confrontation keeps us silent.

You are shy, as am I—
We are like Adam and Eve hiding from the voice of God,
painfully aware of our nakedness and seeking refuge beneath the covers.

There is no comfort in you next to me
for you are miles away,
and I stare blankly at the ceiling
not knowing what to say . . .

Betty Lee Redmond Stillwell
REACH OUT
Why do we hold lifes small resentments,
in sullen hostility?
When transformed words or deeds could bring us,
cherished tranquility.
What is lacking disposition wise when we
can't express true feelings, particularly when
our emotional state effects are whole well
being.
Lets discard our hollow vanity, whats compassion
from a friend?
Work with gratitude not senseless pride,
it will accomplish a happier end.

Leonid Bulanov
UNTITLED
Do I miss the White Nights
And the black cavities of the canals,
The time which has passed,
Dragging with it the determination
To be or not—All lies in the view!
And the fence of the Summer Garden
Offers no proof, but remains a simple object,
Burdening the memory,
Which cannot be left
In the baggage-car of a train.

With feet leading away, but memory returning back,
(But why such a privilege for it?)
Back, where sit cathedrals Nikolsky and Prazhka,
Where the waters of Ladoga,
Lazily caressing the modest shoals of the bay,
Lock up the flow of the artificial space,
Where rain, a monument of constancy,
Beats down like deserved fate,

Where the horse-led convoy of bronze statues
Leads the weary prisoners
Away, where the row of pedestals,
Where the duel of the poet-forerunner
Became locked in fate
At the maddening waters of the Black Streams,
Now countless, and where
The White Nights hide the constellations of shells,
Fluttering in the water.

Robert L Willyard
BROKEN HEARTS NEVER MEND
Broken hearts never mend,
I wanted to be more than, just a friend.

You can't take from your memory,
a love that you thought would always be.

Why don't you believe what I say,
how could I love you, then be on my way.

You think you would rather be lonely and blue,
than have a new love, make a fool out of you.

What can I say, what can I do,
so you will let me love you.

Let me be more than, just a friend,
prove me wrong, that broken hearts, can mend.

Irene Guest
THE TIME MACHINE
The Time Machine is running down,
Its oil smoothed gears are noisy now.
Sometimes it "weeps," and the whole world
feels its gasping sobs.
Those who feel its hurt the most are filled
with grief, at the horrors foreseen.
Riots, wars, race against race, nation against nation.
The atoms split and mushroom, and are windswept—
across the ever seething, bloody seas, to other lands—
whose peoples are silently watching and waiting—
for the heat seared hands to clasp and circle
the whole universe.
The Time Machine is running down—listen.
It's slower and slower with each anguished sob,
With only a few to help to dry its fears—
And try to mend its breaking core.
Soon, too soon, the fiery clouds will spread.
The whole world will ignite in a brilliant flash of white hot fire.
The Time Machine will explode in a mighty roar—
then—STOP.
Man and his world will be no more.

Lillian M Serafin
TO A ROSE
You are the Queen of Flowers,
People admire you for hours
You reign at weddings in June.
Your name is mentioned in many a tune.
You are on the gift list of many a fellow,
Come in different colors
Mostly pink, red and yellow,
With your partner Candy.
On Valentine's Day you come in handy.
Make many a lass and lady feel dandy.
May you always reign with splendor.
As long as there is love and hope.
There will be feelings that are tender,
May you continue to bring happiness to all,
Whether it's "Spring," Summer, Winter or Fall.

Jeanne Pinette
CLEARLAKE, NICE CA
As the reflection of the sun
Warms my face—
A peaceful serenity
Warms my heart—

The emptiness—
Yet total satisfaction
Makes my day—
Just by passing thru!

Wyn R Winther
THE STAG
Upon the giant rock at the end of the long meadow the regal stag appears.
He stands surveying his domain head held high, nostrils flared—so as to assimilate the scents before him.
He must sense I am no threat as he stands statuesque against the evening sky.

Such a magnificent creature he is—red/orange as the first colors of dawn, with antlers spread wide as the branches of a giant sequoia.
His soft brown eyes are ever alert to the dangers of man who have encroached upon his realm.
As he maintains his vigil over the long meadow the snapping of a twig alerts him to danger—causing him to take flight.
Strong, rippling sinew contract for one soaring leap from his castle, fleeing into the darkness of the dense forest below.

As I gaze after his fleeing form I am thankful for having had these scant moments in the presence of this majestic creature.
There is a void, however, in my heart that he is gone forever from my eyes, but I feel blessed in that his image shall be forever etched upon my memory.

Gladys Thatcher Collenbaugh
GOOD OLE AMERICAN RECIPE
TAKE—ONE NATION UNDER GOD
Mixing—All people,
Combine—Them as one,
Measure—Equally with justice,
Spicing—Generously with Love.

Stirring— "Ole Glory"!
Adding—Red, White and Blue,
Breathe—A prayer of Thanksgiving
While it proudly waves for you.
Sift—Lightly together—
Admiration so true,
For blood, sweat and tears
That were shed through the years.
Blending—Fame and Democracy,
Always hopeful for peace—
Now and forever all wars to cease.

Mold—Firmly extracting all
Hatred for Love.
Bake—Slowly and gently
Using tender loving care,
Making sure there is plenty,
With some left to share.

Try toasting—with laughter
And spread with good cheer
While serving our country
Each coming new year.

June Elizabeth,
I'VE CHANGED
Because of you;
The child in me comes peeking through
Wanting to romp and play with you
Make you laugh, see you smile
Hoping you will linger a while.

My eyes have softened so you may see
Beneath the facade that covers me
My self-centered containment has fled
Now a need for you instead.'

Because of you;
I'm soft and misty, wild and free
caring and sharing my soul's wealth with thee
Needing to feel your need of me
Enter my heart with this the key.

So many emotions diverse and true
So many thoughts bequeathed to you
To have and to hold securely entwined
What's given to me returned in kind.

Because of you:
I'm still in awe with many a fear
Perhaps too shy but trusting you dear
Inviting you come into my life
Chancing our oneness will bring no strife.

We, so similar yet different still
Beseeching the Master Plan to reveal
A difficult challenge to view God's Plan
To accept the fact that woman was made for man.

I require your affection, warmth, and touch
Sensitive feelings, both needing so much
A noble gift from God's own Hand
To be your woman and you my man.

Keith W Barter Jr
THE HOMELESS CHILD
The clothes he wears are but ripped, dirty fragments of cloth,
Hanging from a skeletal frame as if he were but a rag doll;
The shoes on his blistered feet little more than tattered pieces of nylon.

His meals, rarely enough to satisfy his gnawing hunger,
Consist of whatever scraps he can find in open garbage cans,

Remnants of hot meals long since eaten, grown cold with age.

With no place to call home, his shelter is whatever he can find,
Abandoned buildings with boards for his windows, little-used doorways,
Affording him scant protection from the harsh elements of Nature.

Lost amid the chaos and confusion of a crowded, busy street,
His every day becomes a test, a challenge for his survival.
Motherless, fatherless . . . This is the plight of the homeless child.

Forced to fend for himself in a cold, unfeeling world,
Harassed by his peers, scorned by his elders, shunned by all,
What hope can the homeless child have for a brighter future?

Each and every year, thousands more join the ranks of "street urchins,"
Children who find life easier on the streets than at home,
Making this a heart-wrenching problem of outrageous proportions.

What is to become of these children . . . unwanted, unloved, alone?
Is there no hope for them to have a warm, happy home to grow in?
Or are they doomed to live, possibly die, alone in the streets?

Terri Caldwell
PRISONER OF LOVE

To my darling Antione, I realize you possess me totally but I really don't mind because I know you love me intensely. Even when it is cloudy outside, inside my heart jumps for joy at the thought of you. Your loving tulip

---

All of my life I have kept to myself, until I met you what a blow I was dealt
I'm a prisoner of love, a prisoner of love, a prison term of love that is as precious as a dove
A prisoner of love never wants to depart from the one who holds the key to their heart
A prisoner of love, a prisoner of love, oh how I love being your prisoner of love
Pain, hurt and pure distress, a prisoner of love could really care less
Put up with, deal with, night and day, a prisoner of love has not one word to say
For a prisoner of love is ever so spellbound, when that special someone is always around
Some wonder why this love is never blue, a prisoner of love keeps it fresh and new
A prisoner of love, a prisoner of love, oh how I love being your prisoner of love
There is no logic, there is no reason, why a prisoner of love is always so pleasing
A prison term of love is what I deserve, it's a sentence that I'm most willing to serve
So don't open this door, don't let me out, I'm your prisoner of love without a doubt
All of my life I may have kept to myself, being your prisoner of love was worth the blow you dealt.

Your loving tulip
Terri

Roxanne Harshman
CONCILIATE

To all that was—But may never be again . . .

With every temptation—
hear the storm
and calm the rushing wind.

Savor instead the gentleness of a touch
of the one you want to win.

Speak not of the Tempest
that stirs your raging soul,
but kindle the embers that burn inside.

Go lightly into the future—
Come back on my command.

Spin softly in
the tree tops,
dancing with all that you see.

Capture me inside a dream,
and take me to a Star—
Then I'll slide back on a Sunbeam . .
to recall you as you are.

Julie Knoke
NO MORE WAR
Imagine the Earth with total peace
All life on Earth would never cease.

The nation's bind and all unite
To make it warm on freezing nights.

If all could feel like those that care
Peace for eternity would fill the air.

Together we bond and make this true
Our world could finally be like new.

So give it your all and try your best
This fighting place could be at rest.

We're the strongest so let's all try
To slay the sorrow that makes us cry.

Why do people love the war
When we can have a whole lot more.

Are they fighting straight for pleasure
Or to kill the things we treasure.

Let's work together and end all gore
To live with peace and no more war.

Shirley M Broney
RUNE AMONG THE MIST
An endless mirage, a blinding foe
A mist between confining souls

Solemnly confined so that no one knows
Mysteries of montage hidden abode

Sullen and sleek they may appear
A fragment of which belongs to fear

Bright and brilliant and idle to deceive
The half hearted fool of orgin grieves

Truth to be, unknown to see
Confining souls are we.

Chantelle L Emmons
DYING HOPE BEYOND THE LIMITS
Double edge sword
Lurking in shadows
Musty air chokes the living
Suffices the dead
Broken hearts shattered and fallen lying in the dirt forgotten
Blood stains near Darkness clouds the sky
A full moon appears
One beam brilliant
Shines thru the golden key hole
To the cellar of death
Dimmness clears metal shines and shattered pieces
Cry rebirth slowly together they wish
Shattered pieces lie unseen unheard
Darkness clouds over again Beam descends
With all hope
Shattered pieces die.

Edward Helmstadt
COME TO ME
Kitten, kitten, how I love you,
you came to me cold, hungry, and blue.
I gave to you comfort, on that bitter day,
you started to purr, in your own special way.
Kitten, kitten, you bring me such joy,
and I see you are happy with your new toy.
Warm, soft, cuddly, and purring too,
if you need affection, come to me do.
Kitten, kitten, so pretty are you,
with your pointed ears, your eyes so blue.
You try my patience again and anew,
come to me, "meow;" I'll forgive you.
Kitten, kitten, you're getting older,
smarter, quicker, and somewhat bolder.
You watch the birds, through the window each day,
and come to me lovingly, after we play.
Older cat, older cat, you sleep night and day,
and it seems that you're not very eager to play.
Though you're contented with nothing to do,
waking each day, seems much harder for you.
Kitten, kitten, since you have gone,
my life is troubled; I'm desperate; alone.
I now need comfort, as I gave to you,
I'm lost and I wonder, what can I do?
Little one, little one," . . . come unto me,"
don't worry about kitten, she's happy, she's free.
She's playing with "mama;" she's been asking for you,
and said there is only one thing you can do:
"If you need comfort, as you gave to me,
come to Him, ask Him, as I came and asked thee."

Stacy C Garcia
ARTFUL LOVE

Dedicated to Steven, my loving and patient friend.

Our love is a piece of Art,
with such high integrity,
and well respected.
As the line curves,
new dimensions occur
and broaden.
Erasures of mistakes,
only leading to our . . .
Masterpiece.

Jennifer Davis
ONCE, IN LOVE
Once, in love.
My heart was lightened
But his love died
And my love brightened

Once, in love.
My days were carefree
But now they're long
And don't pass as quickly.

Once, in love.
I had not a care
But his love is gone
And mine is still there.

Oneta Yount
A LESSON LEARNED
Let me tell you a story or perhaps you have heard,
About the lesson I learned from a tired little bird.
He came in from the north, he had flown many miles
Then decided to stop and rest for a while.
So he lit on my window and he peeked inside
In search of some food and a safe place to hide.

His feathers were ragged, his body was thin,
From the long hard journey and being tossed by the wind.
So I put out some food, He ate and he ate.
Then flew off toward a tree in search of his mate.

They soon flew back to crumbs on the sill
Where he stood guard while she ate her fill.
Their strength was renewed, so they sang and they played,
So thankful for a friend while their trip was delayed.

They stayed a few days then flew off toward the south
With a song in their heart and food in their mouth.
They circled my window and away they flew
As if trying to say I appreciate you.

This lesson I learned:
That it doesn't take much to cheer some one along,
Just a crumb from the table or sing them a song.

Connie McGowan Smith
APATHEE . . . . AND ME
People are hungry . . . out in the street
no home to live in . . . no food to eat
can't find a job . . . unskilled and unsure
despondent, discouraged and

spiritually poor.

Babies are beaten and sexually abused,
men kill men . . . and smile, amused . . .
trash all around us to constantly view,
fall on your back, get up and sue.

Sneeze and rub the smog in your eyes,
another suctioned fetus dies.
Lost are the animals of present and past . . .
gone with the boom of another gun blast.

Drink, smoke and pop lots of pills,
drown out the sound of humanity's ills.
That's their problem . . . let it go by . . .
Why don't you help? . . . and why don't I?

Deborah Elaine Willoughby
GRANNY

To my Grandmother Zeffrey Sarah Duckworth with all my love

Time is of the essence for it is fading fast in the twilight of your years!
It seems God is calling you more and more each and everyday.
When God created you he gave you his heart.
He put a gentle touch in your hands and graced you with a goodness only a granddaughter much loved would understand.
You became a tower of Strength, a Smile, a Whisper, a Breath of Spring.
You became a Teacher, a Confidant, an anchor for the Storms.
You became all Goodness that to have to even consider your going home is complete torment, that I can never explain.
So rest well tonite my Granny and sweet dreams of peace, for contentment you have given me that will carry me until we meet again in a life of Snowy Whiteness, and Softest Sunshine, of easy Breezes, and Utmost Joy.
I know you know I love you, I tell you all the time, but did you know you are Breath to my Soul?

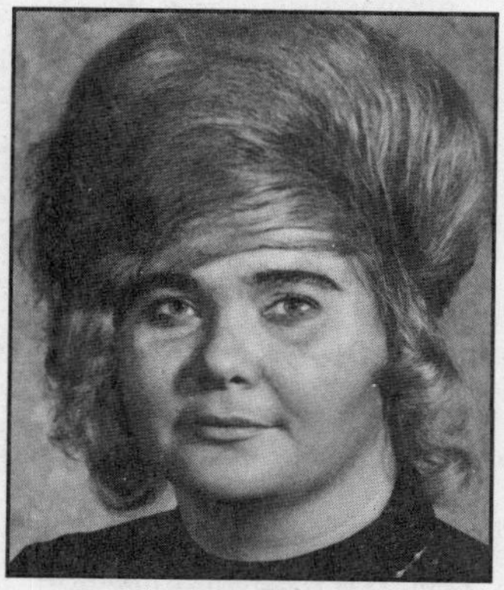

Elisabeth Ann Stout Craig

Elisabeth Ann Stout Craig
A SPECIAL GIRL

Send love to my sweet Mother, the best there is, to Carrie Stout Shelifeld Ala.

Also love to the best husband, C. B. Craig, Gulf Port, Miss. Love to all.

Hi there, my name is Baby Rose, and I have a
cute small nose, and skin that seems to glow,
Honey colored hair and eyes of brown to go with my
Round face. It's been said, I have the big head
Yes I'm very special and proud of it, I sit with pride
Head held high, with arm's out, like I'm ready to fly
up, up, into the sky.
You see, I'm a Cabbage Patch Kid, I was born of
Cloth like you were of skin, but I know no sin.
Honey it takes money to own me, don't think
I'm being funny, because I'm a pretty baby, and
worth every cent you've ever spent.
I have plenty of friend's, so don't frown when you don't see me around.
We're all nice, at any price.
Someday we'll talk to you
And say we love you too. Now tonight you be good and
Close your eyes and don't make a peep, and go to sleep.
Be good and eat right, like your mom says you
Should, and I won't be surprised, come sun rise,
That I'll be sitting on your bed, on the pillow at
Your little sweet head.

Reba Rich Bowman
OUR WORLD TOMORROW

The many young people who are restless today
Are seeking satisfaction and peace.
These are the ones we must help some way
And cause this turmoil to cease.
Many have never heard of Christ
Who can save them from all their sin.
They do not know there is joy in the Lord,
A lasting peace and love within.

While some older folk go on their way
Finding fault and criticizing the youth,
They never stop long enough to tell
Them of God's word and His truth.
Don't shove them aside, show that you care
Not only in word but in deed.
Help them along, their way too is hard
Just like ours used to be.

These young people are not really bad,
Just wanting their parents love.
They would like to be shown they are wanted
And appreciated by those whom they love.
So let's wake up parents of today,
Mourn before the alter with sorrow.
For these young folk we're neglecting today
Will be our World of Tomorrow.

Irene Smith
MARTIN LUTHER KING

There was a man named Martin.
He was sent to us from God.
God Knew we needed a leader
for we were over trod.
This man was kind and gentle.
And knew how to handle the problems
of his fellow men.
He never believed in violence
nor unfairness in his time.
No matter what the color of your
skin, he helped all mankind.
Everyone loved Martin, this
man of many talents.
But there are always those
around to keep the world unbalanced.
To stop the good that some men
do and cause upheavil.
But Martin worked so hard for us;
to save the world from evil.
So when we remember Martin,
who truly was a king.
We try to carry on his work.
So that, "freedom shall always
ring."

Angelina Lieth "Angel"
VISION

To Doug: Who knows no love like ours, even now!

I dare not look back.
It is, in my minds eye,
a clear, vivid picture.
I hear your words, I see your face,
I watch you as you leave us.

You are all excited—you can't wait
to get the last of your things in the van.
I watch in utter disbelief and
she watches too. With wide-eyes that never
leave you until you pull out of the driveway
and the dust from the wheels of the van kicks
back at us and I feel a dry-vomit in my mouth.

I dare not look back, but some days I steal a look
at you as you weep for days gone by. I knew you loved me,
as I loved you; but, we lost the magic that you found somewhere else.
A magic that only lasts for such a brief time. I wonder if you think it
worth all the suffering ???

I hear the thunder clap
and see the lightning strike our house.
I wish I were dead, I wish for the wildest, most
terrible things to happen to me—
The thunder claps . . . BOOM, BOOM . . . I jump, and am
grateful to be alarmed by something, anything.
For, you see, I am numb, I shake all over and wish you
would come back to me.

I weep for me . . .
I weep for her . . .
I weep for you . . .

In the days and weeks that follow,
my eyes are never dry.
Of course, I smile. I hide the deep sadness I carry around.
Soon she will go too. Some days I panic at the thought. But,
I know the spark has gone from me, the fight for <u>anything</u>

I swallow hard. The vomit rises and my stomach,
empty from the days of strife, has nothing to give.
I suck the smoke of my last cigarette and think about
the next one.
The days are long, but the nights are forever . . .

They are gone now, those nights and all those lonely,
lonely, painful days of my darkest hours. I shall never
go there again, to that place. But, I <u>cannot</u>, try as
I might, forget you. You, who caused my sorrow,
my pain,
my sorrow, pain . . .
You, whom I love . . . even now,
EVEN NOW!

Cori Robleau
WE WONDER WHY . . .

wisdom wounds, weakness wails, wallowing withers,
wantonness works wealth

beauty blossoms but briefly, bereavement bewilders,
bodies breed, bedfellows betray

cowardice crumbles character, courage conquers
calamity, confession confirms consequence,
conspiracy corrupts

decisions determine destiny, delusions design
destruction, delights die, deaths' door defies
description

leacherous loneliness lives, love lingers—leaves later,
losers lean, liars live little lives

persistance persuades, pathetic poverty pants
powerless, passions pale, pious pretenders promenade

humanity hungers, hate hinders happiness, heroism
happens, hedonism hides heaven

fools fumble fortunes, fantasies fade, forgiveness
fails forgiver, funerals fuse future fossils

altruistic attitudes annoy, apathy activates
atrocities, anxiety attends age, apostles achieve
another answer

anon, anon

nomatter now, neutrons nestle, natures nurture
neglected novenas, nations near nonentity

some sadistic satan sits scything, sans sympathy,
sagacious souls sadly sigh

pretending they know, and still

We Wonder Why . . .

Rosie J Collins

Rosie J Collins
FAITH!

Dedicated Firstly to "God," and to my husband Herbert Collins, for unearthing my "Faith."

Faith knows no gender
it knows no creed,
Faith is something
we all need.
Faith is the creator
of hope,
Without which it is
hard to cope.
Faith in one's self
and our God up above,
Believing in Him
and accepting His love.
Knowing that no matter
what troubles betide,
Through "faith" God is
always by our side.
Faith knows no color of anyones skin,
It defiantly is no respecter of men.
Faith grows and grows by leaps and bounds,
It picks you up when you are down.
Faith is secure and never unstable,
It reminds us that we're strong and able.

Marie H Ellingson
EASTER AT HOLLYWOOD BOWL

Sunrise at Easter—what a thrill
To see the people surrounding the hill
There's a cross to be sure—a symbol you know
Of an event that took place many centuries ago

The people are waiting for daylight to break
The dawn of a day bidding mankind to wake
To cast off the shackles of darkness and gloom
And for a Christ risen make radiant room

His promise today is the same as of old
Give up mortal thinking and enter the fold
He will strengthen and help and give needed rest
By his loving care the whole world will be blest

The daylight is breaking over the hill
While people arise the hillside to fill
With voices joyous a song is born
That fills the air on this Easter morn

The cross stands erect with lillies a'bloom
No longer it signals the coming of doom
The stone of bigotry has been cast away
And they greet a Christ risen this Easter Day

Jerry Gibson
WALKING MAN

For my wife, Marian.

Walking Man, autos and trucks do not slow your steady gait
as you walk beside their roadway against their rhythmic force.
Everyday your lean frame on a mission—to where?

Walking Man, what color eyes are hidden behind your dark glasses
of any day? What secrets could pass through the ever present
smile on your thin lips?

Walking Man, dressed for weather's occasion—
today, a full length coat and winter hat;
tomorrow, a faded T-shirt and summer cap.

Walking Man, your black shoulder bag
securely under arm—
it has truths for you and mysteries for us.

Walking Man, never before dawn, never after sunset—
home—to where?
Should we be suspicious of you?

Walking Man, will you continue your lonely twentieth century
journeys or will you join us and share your secrets
in our vehicles—to where?

Ruth E Davis
GRANDMOTHER

To my granddaughter Judy

I don't know what Grandma's are good for,
But guess it's nothing new.
When the Grandkids come to stay,
I'm glad they just send two.

They go half dressed, shirt tails out,
I yell, "quit that" and "put that down"
Till my voice is cracked and they think,
I'm the worst old crank in town.

My back aches and
My joints squeak,
I don't know what to do
Unless it's turn the other cheek.

I think I'll put my body down,
And rest for just a spell,
And be thankful that my Grandkids,
Are full of pep and well!

Diane Scott
AGONY IN (A) DEATHFUL SITUATION

The face solemn;
The eyes staring blankly into space: not seeing, nor caring.
Only wishing that death would come quickly and painlessly.

There was nothing left;
No expression of love or laughter left in the eyes; only pain.
No tear stains on the cheeks;
Because they were all in vain.
The body frail and thin,
So thin, that only skin clinged to the bones.

The family came.
But, there was no smile to greet them.
Their eyes never met restraining themselves from crying;
From sharing an emotion of love and pain.
Sitting and waiting for death to come:
Not knowing when death would come was agony for them all.

No-one dared for their eyes to meet;
For fear of succumbering to their emotions;
Of holding one another and crying together:
For the sake of love.
For death was knocking at the door;
They called it A.I.D.S.
But, it was "AGONY IN (A) DEATHFUL SITUATION."

Joel Mark Rogers
THE ME SOCIETY

I am a Lumbee Indian wild and free,
But I wonder if I should be living in another society,

This isn't the land my forefathers once roamed,

Then why should I call it my home?

It is becoming a land controlled by computers and technology,

A land built on greed and materialistic goods; a me society.

Rhonda L Raty
BACKDROP

The lone figure poses against charcoal-clouded skies
Two dimensional, surreal in the glow
Of tinted watercolor thinness.

Hair rinsed with sparkling sherry whips against plumrose cheek,
Swathed in skirts the color of banana republic yellow
Accented with a scarf,
Seven silk scarves,
Of babysky blue.

Her mintgreen eyes flash a junglemelon peachgloss smile
And her skin is turning,
You can see it turning,
From chicken noodle soup pale
To a bronzeglow bake.

Altered now, she moves so self-assuredly and chameleon-camaflouged
By neutral tone-flattering khaki safari wraps
So soon toughened by the earth's grip and
Backdropped by the sun's pull.

C Alicia Fore
FOREVER IN TIME

This poem is dedicated to my dearest Aunt Ursula and my beloved Uncle Otto, two of the survivors of Dachau.

Love me forever in time
Give me some words
And make them rhyme
Give me a song
To sing all day
To keep me from going wrong
Show me the place
Of happiness and true hope
Where life has a slower pace
All I need is a word so true
What I really need
Is some time to renew.

Marguerite Satryb Du-Prey
HAPPY BIRTHDAY

Happy Birthday to my son Peter,
Who couldn't possibly be any neater—
He's "Aquarius" and Gregarious;
Could be a United Nations Greeter!

He commands a tandem for U.P.S.,
A true expert, I must confess.
His heart is as big as the universe—
He gives much too much; it couldn't be worse!

A great fisherman, and hunter, too,
He brings home venison for a gourmet stew.

Happy Birthday, Peter, so you're forty-six—
You and cruelty will never mix.

I love you, son; You're so good to me;
May God smile on you til you reach a hundred three!

Nina Daniels
CAREFREE THOUGHTS

In memory of my father, Robert F. Williams, who loved the outdoors

---

Down on the banks of a very calm bay.
is just the place I would love to spend my day.
Back in the shade of a big old tree.
not a worry in the world feeling carefree.
Just watching the clouds slowly sail by.
and as I watch I wonder whats pushing them
and why.
Is the breeze up there mild or strong?
and as I wonder I hear birds sing their song.
I wouldn't mind being a bird so tiny and free,
sitting high alone in a very tall tree.
I could see for miles all over the land,
all of God's creation that's so grand.

The worries of life pushed out of my mind,
alone, relaxed, peaceful, quiet, just killing
time.
Yes this is the perfect life for me,
here relaxing under this big old tree.

Stefanie Marie Nadeau
CAT'S EYE

The glassy eyes see all;
Magnificent sherades

Echoing past the ears of humans.

And when the cold, dark night
Frightens the naive child,
Gold transparent eyes
Ease
By
Slowly . . . softly
Into the darkness.
As your glistening gold eyes,
Shadowed by pain,
Fall into an endless world,
Silver eyes
Catch
You.

Laura Gardner

MY BIRD

My little bird
Has a sharp beak
I wish to me
She'd speak
I think she would
Like to play a game
I'm sure glad
She's tame

Terry (Whitt) Fowler

OLD MEMORIES AND LOST LOVE

To S.B. for the inspiration.

I remember the days you were here with me,
We were so happy, so care free,
Now time has taken you away from me,
All I have left are weak memories and
The thought of where you might be.
I really treasured the times we shared,
But even though you've gone I know you really
cared.
I hope my dreams bring you back to me,
Maybe in time things could return to the way it used
To be.
But even if we weren't meant to be,
I grew stronger loving you, I found me.

David H Cope

David H Cope

NIGHT TRAIN

Dedicated to the memory of Bertha May and Wm. S. Cope, my parents

---

The silent dark night is intruded upon by a far off rumbling sound and the blackness is pierced by a blinding light and a tremble is felt in the ground.
A nightmare scream from out of my dreams as she thunders around the bend. Her firebox is bright and aglow in the night as she sucks cinders up in her wind.

Her mighty wheels scream and are driven by steam that mixes quite well with her smoke and her wheels pound the rails and her big whistle trails and her cars are wrapped up in her smoke.
The hills have a glow like moonlight on snow as the bright windows go flashing by and approaches a stream on a silvery beam and a bridge made of steel cross the sky.
She is trailed rather loose by a small red caboose with two lanterns of red and green light and as she goes by trailing smoke through the sky she disappears into the night.

Eve L Clemmer

SHATTERED DREAMS

To my mom, Josephine, I couldn't have done it without you.

What is it, forbidden dark truth.
Borrowed moments, For time everlasting.
Movements that flow deep.
Descending to my hidden void.

What is this, Mystique
Distance thunder, beating, beating.
Drums of pain, tears that flame.
Listen, listen to my strong heart.

What is it, running, hiding.
Follow the silent thread,
Weaving to and fro, just to let it go.
Lead me, free me.

What is this, Wild embrace
Yearning to know, let it go
Forever running, on to movement
Lessons learned from a soul that's burned.

Years that pass never to know,
The quenching in a night of heat.
Promise never fulfilled.
Dreams of love are shattered still.

Violet Bush

I WISH YOU . . . MORE

More than good fortune, I wish you this morning, You,
who will wed 'ere the close of the day . . . Maid, whom
the bridal wreath now is adorning,
Man who so swiftly
will bear her away.

You will have need for courage off yonder . . . there will
be days when your faith must be strong. Over the roads
you are destined to wander, . . Luck will not hold you
together for long!

GOD grant you strength, . . for the trials He'll send you,
GOD grant you wisdom for moments of doubt . . Luck from
disaster will never defend you, . . there will be days
when your faith must be stout.

Never, to selfishness, weakly surrender . . pleasure will
come, if the burdens you'll share, Keep to your purpose,
be brave and be tender, love will outlive every hour
of despair.

Trust not to fortune, but deeper within you, take wisdom
and courage, and faith where you go, live for each other
and love will continue, in spite of the heartaches you're
certain to know . . . Life's sorrows are many, twixt May and
December, but sweet are their memories, once they are
flown . . Love will bestow countless days to remember, but the
best of good luck cannot do it alone.

Janice (Hurst) Gillispie

SONG OF VISION

Soon the Great Spirit would gather him,
He must start.
His eyes dimmed with age,
He saw with his heart.
The old Indian sang of Visions,
Days of yester year.
His voice rose and fell,
Glistening on his cheek a tear.
Silhouetted against the sky,
All of nature heard his song.
Saddened by the changing of time,
It was for the past he did long.

A great Chief was he,
Wisdom had been kind.
He had led his people well,
And with a vivid mind.
Visions of his squaw,
And that of a son, for it was he—
To have been Chief,
For all the tribe to see.

He sang of visions,
Brave warriors, tomahawks in hand.
Fierce battles fought,
To save their sacred land.
The eagle soared in the air,
Many were the buffalo, elk, and deer.
The old chief felt the Great Spirit,
Ever so near.
Visions of rivers filled with fish,
Plenty was the wild game.
Many moons ago,
Long before the white man came.

The Redman's past is legend now,
Whiteman never understood.
Indians way of Life,
He visioned, that someday they would.
Gone are the days his people,
Could walk proud and free.
The Old Chief sang of visions,
To love in peace and harmony.

He closed his eyes,
His soul was young and light.
As he chanted by the fires glow,
Long into the night.
When the early dawn came,
The Old Indian Chief was gone.
The Great Spirit was gentle,
The wind carried his song.

Donna L Trumbo

WALKING THROUGH THE CORRIDORS OF LIFE

I dedicate this to the Lord Jesus Christ, who has either walked with me or carried me through many places in my life. I wish this relationship to all those who seek him.

Walking through the corridors of life can be filled with so much strife. The hurt can cut like a knife while we're walking through the corridors of life. Sometimes we can be sad, and sometimes we can be glad. But things can't always be nice, when we're walking through the corridors of life.

I'm so glad my LORD doesn't change, I'm so glad his spirit remains, remains to walk with me, while I'm walking through the corridors of life. He set's my soul and my heart free, he removed the fear from me, He made my blinded eyes to see, while I'm walking through the corridors of life.

This world never stays the same, you can't count on things to remain. It can become a great big game, but in the end what do we gain? We gain nothing if we lose our soul, if the LORD doesn't have full control, when we go walking through the corridors of life.

Budge Crick

AS THE GODS LOOK DOWN

To my wife, without whose help and support this poem would not have been written.

We are all guests at nature's feast
We do not need the help of ghost or priest
Robert G. Ingersoll one hundred years ago
Today I believe it should read like this

We are all guests at nature's grand affair
pull up a chair, let's pick mother nature bare
Scientist invented tools for construction
We use them for wars of destruction

To our ego inflated mind it may seem strange

That in natures intriguing plan of constant change
Man plays such an insignificant part
He is ingenious, but not very smart

The last act is about to start
We will tear old mother earth apart
Struggling for energy with our last breath
Like pirates of old we will fight to the death

As reluctant gods look down
Mushroom clouds appear above cities and towns
The earth becomes a great fiery steed
Results of man, machine and uncontrolled greed

At last it is over, mother earth is at peace
The last hydrogen bomb has been released
The devil angels that she nursed at her breast
Those demons from hell have been laid to rest

As mother earth sinks to her fiery doom
Mans own hand closes the door of his tomb
Earth will travel on through cold lonely space
Man and his gods have vanished without trace

The strange creature we call man was able to
Control every animal on the earth. The one
Animal he never controlled (himself) will be
The fatal flaw in his evolutionary climb.

Sheila Duprey

Sheila Duprey
AMERICA

To my husband Wilfred and son Keith, with love.

America what's happening—
Is there something I can't see?
It seems you've changed in many ways—
You've lost your dignity.

There's fear in all our cities,
And crimes on all our streets;
I try so hard to understand
Why my country's in retreat.
Our children will not stay in school,
They walk the streets all day.
Our churches they seem empty—
We've forgotten how to pray.

This is the greatest country
That God has ever made.
His love will always shine on us—
Like children, we've gone astray.

America, you may have your faults,
And you have done some wrongs;
We've come to love you very much,
And put your name to song.

Let's do the very best we can,
Looking back on her with pride.
We are respected for what we are,
And God is at our side.

Thea' Sullivan
A VERY DEADLY UNION
They called her the "Spider Lady" . . For she was always dressed in black
And when she entered the "Bistro Bar" . . Her heels would go clickity-clack
She carried a red velvet bag . .
And her legs were graced in lace
With a skin of alabaster . . She had a classic cameo face
They called him "Snakey Sam" . .
For there was poison in his doctors sack
He claimed it cured most everything . . from nerves to an aching back
But somehow his patients worsened . . And some of them even died
This way he developed a following . . Of old widows and crying brides
"Snakey Sam" came to the "Bistro Bar" . . He sensed that she was there
He walked straight to her . . And touched her jet-black hair
A tango played . . They danced and swayed . . As if in a deadly duel
The red velvet bag . . and the poison sack . . Still on the barroom stool
And no one knows when they took their walk . . And vanished in the night
The town folk whispered of foul play . . And wondered of their plight
A few years passed . . And a rider . . Came upon an old abandoned well
And when he shined his light within . . He had this tale to tell
There was "Snakey" and the "Spider Lady" . . Locked in fond embrace
Two skeletons in their deathly tomb . . One clad in black and lace
Now this is where the tale takes . . . A very ghastly "twist"
"Snakey" had a dried spider on his head . . And she a snake around her wrist
The fearful town buried them . .
Very deep . . And side by side
With one large stone . . That simply said . . "Snakey Sam and his Spider Bride"

The "Bistro Bar" has long been closed . . It's starkness frames the moon
And some folks say . . They've seen two skeletons dance . . To a ghostly tango tune

Frank Lauria II
TOMORROW
To the topic of tomorrow,
A poem I surge to write;
The concept makes me think . . .
Tomorrow holds no substance,
It's just a frame of mind,
It has no smell, no taste or sound,
It's presence can't be touched.
The question is, does it even exist,
It's image was never seen,
For when it's courage pushes it forth,
It's never tomorrow, but today;
Today exists.

Martha B Davis
TEN SECONDS TOO LATE
Last night I lay sleeping, and dreamed of the Lord,
And ever so gently He taught me His Word . . .
I said, I'm not ready, but I'll change some day;
My Saviour stood pleading, "Don't turn Me away!"
Chorus I
No, Jesus, no Jesus! I'll make it alone,
And I don't need You for my sin to atone . . .
I'll make it to heaven by keeping the law,
I'll do it my way, or just not at all!

I laughed as He pleaded, and closed my heart's door,
Then I heard the trumpet, the arch-angel's voice!
As soon as I heard it, I knew I was lost,
Ten seconds too late now, I counted the cost!
Chorus II
Oh, Jesus, oh, Jesus, now what can I do?
Is there not some way I can make it to you?
With tears in His eyes, He just closed Heaven's door,
And I stood outside there, wounded and torn!

The courtroom was crowded in front of the throne,
As I stood in Judgement, as I stood alone . . .
I bowed down before Him, and I called Him Lord;
But "I never knew you!" was all that I heard!
Chorus III
Oh, Jesus, oh Jesus! It's over and through,
And I woke up crying, and calling for you!
Please save me, Lord Jesus, don't turn me away . . .
Save me, please Jesus! Save me today!

Joyce Dixon Williams

Joyce Dixon Williams
SYMBOLS

To: MY loving parents, Rev. Rogers W. Dixon and Mrs. Alberta Gaines Dixon, my sweet siblings—Lillian, Ralph, Denise and Gregory Dixon, my personal mentor, John Samuel White, and inspiring confidant Mary McGee Baker.

"The Lady" stands in New York's harbor
to welcome your homeless, your tired, your poor;
four presidential greats watch over us in Virginia
as they sit perched upon Mt. Rushmore.
The Liberty Bell rings out in Pennsylvania
and is heard across the land,
and in Washington, D.C. burns the eternal flame
for those who have gone back to the sand.

All of these are but symbols of
America's conviction and pride,
brought about by ordinary people who had the courage
to make monumental strides.
You too can become "a symbol" and some lasting
contribution make
so that others who come behind you will have an easier
road to take.

If you can't sit down and sew like
Betsy Ross, who
made our beautiful homeland flag,
then get up and take flight like the
Wright Brothers—
There's no need for you to drag.

Outstretch your own arms to
someone, watch over
those in need—
Help to free someone's imprisoned
mind, and
shed light where darkness leads!

Mary Golliday
A TRIBUTE TO FATHER

Who is this that goes out in the
summer heat?
Winter freeze and work to
supply the family's needs?

Who is this that goes out in the
wind and storm
To make sure things are well at
home?

Who is this that has a strong
voice
But need only a few words to say,
And all his children will listen
and obey?

He is a comforter and a friend, he
rules with a firm
but gentle hand, he is loving and
kind, and listens
with an open mind.

He may say no when we think he
should say yes,
But that's because he knows
what is best.

Who is this? This is a Father.

Laurabelle Swift
AGED LACE

Quietly I sit in a lonely place
My thoughts drift to days when I
made lace
When nimble my fingers used to be
And I could create stitches carefree.

Now I'm growing old and can
hardly see
Sitting here quietly my thoughts
run free,
My lace is yellowing with age it
seems
As my wrinkled face looks at it and
beams.

My fingers fondle it with loving
care
As I think of each minute I used to
put there,
To save the time so often lost
I preserved it in lace without much
cost.

As I've grown old my life seems like
lace
I think about time that's wrinkled
my face
And wonder how long the stitches
will last
While life keeps tugging on my
wrinkled cast.

Helene A Johnson
SO FAR AWAY

This poem is dedicated to Julie, JoAnn, and Mary my loving nieces

---

As I lie here by the ocean
in this land across the sea
there's a song that's ringing,
ringing
in the very soul of me.

It's the song of running water
in the trout brooks of old Maine.
How I wish that I could be there
with my fish rod once again.

I can hear the old reel running
as singing thru the guard it goes.
How that sound can make your
heart beat
no one but a fisherman knows.

There's the pool where I got the big
one
not so many years ago.
There's the place we called the
crossing
where the cows went to and fro.

There's the bank where we picked
mayflowers.
It was only a short time ago.
But the changing hand of time
brought not happiness but woe.

There's the bank where we ate our
dinner
under the pine upon the hill.
Watching dreaming at the water
as it trembled from the mill.

Oh how swiftly does time passing
change the things of yesterday,
take the things we love so dearly
and carry them so far away.

Janice Freudeman
CHRISTMAS EYES

To the children. In all you do may you always bring the spirit to life.

Christmas Eve Santa captured the
stars in the sky.
Christmas morning he placed
them in my child's eyes.
And before the light penetrated his
dear little soul.
Old Saint Nick and his reindeer
bounded homeward to the
North Pole.
And although he bids us farewell.
Santa leaves us his whimsical
spell.
For Christmas is mystical,
Christmas is magical.
A child's eyes bring the spirit to life.
So look up in the air so high.
Off in the distant sky Santa has
come and gone.
But Christmas memories they live
on.
For Christmas is mystical
Christmas is magical.
A child's eyes bring the spirit of life.
And although Christmas will come
and go.
All of the glitter and all of the snow.
Our memories stay vivid and alive.
And live on in my child's eyes.

Penny J Schulte
THE BEST PART OF ME

To my best friend

Falling in love is easy
Staying in love a hard thing
Or so it always seemed to me
Until that magic moment—

It swept my mind with the force of
a tidal wave
Flashed lightning through the
heart
I realized he was special
And wanted to impart
What I wanted most in life
Was right there from the start.

Through the years I've gained
some wisdom
Now can plainly see
What I felt for those before him
Was only make-believe.

He gives the gift of caring
And this he shares with me
A love with no conditions
As endless as the sea.
His eyes I often drown in
Into deepest ecstasy
His smile my inspiration
He is The Best Part Of Me.

M Jane Korisher
WHAT SECRET'S HIDDEN HERE?

To the memory of my late parents-in-law, Wm. G. and Marjorie Merrill Korisher

---

Alone, I walk through green velvet
grass,
Listening to nature as I pass,
A big old willow tree that weeps
And watch two owls—each one
sleeps:
I sit down on a fallen log,
Listening to a serenading frog,
As he sings out to his mate,
"What's keeping you, my
love—you're late:"
White puffy clouds are in the sky;
I see two robins flying by,

And watch two squirrels, as home
they scurry,
To the big oak tree—wonder what's
their hurry:
I see Mr. Buck out with his wife;
As I sit here, I think—I guess that's
life;
These creatures of nature even go
by two,
While I sit here alone and feeling
blue;
But it's peaceful in this tranquil
place,
As I watch a spider spinning lace,
And listen to crickets chirp in the
dell;
These creatures get along so well:
I visit often, but ne'er saw them
fight,
Nor wander around alone at night;
I wonder what their secret could
be—
To have togetherness with
tranquility.

Eva P Rogers
CHRISTMAS 1979

It's been nearly a year since we
were married,
And we really can't begin
To tell of the joy we've experienced,
And all the fun it has been.

We love retirement living,
Many new friends we have made;
Travels in all directions
Brought us scenes that will never
fade.

From the parks of the Canadian
Rockies
To the islands of the Caribbean
Sea,
We have gone by plane, boat, and
auto,
And been as busy as busy could be.

We send Season's Greetings to all
of you
And hope that you have been fine;
May 1980 be good to you
And bring you many good times.
Merry Christmas,
Reg and Eva

Patsy A Gibbs
FANTASIES AND MAKE BELIEVE

Childhood dreams are scattered
now.
Like leaves in a warm summer's
breeze.
Fantasies and make believe,
are just beyond our reach.

Today was yesterday's tomorrow,
now how we long for the past.
The clock has ticked away those
years,
much, much too fast.

To lie again in grassy meadows,
or to play along the beach.
But fantasies and make believe
are just beyond our reach.

Butterflies and polly wogs seem
like
foolish little things
But so much time is spent these
days,
reaching for those pretty brass
rings.

Summers will come and summers
will go,
but the memories we'll keep.
Because fantasies and make
believe
are just beyond our reach.

Vivian Ballew Meredith
YESTERDAY

Lord, thank you for this day of
mine
A yesterday we cannot find
I need your strength to live it well
To do your will and do it well

Lord, give this day our daily bread
That others, thru us, may be fed
Bestow abundance of your grace
That I may show your love and faith

Lord, give me patience when I find
Another's fault, but none of mine
Lord, thank you for this day so new
Our yesterday has passed from
view.

We cannot place our finger on
The yesterday that has now gone
Our yesterday has made its round
Our yesterday can ne'er be found

Lord, thank you for another chance
To make amends and not be faint
Tomorrow is another day
Our yesterday has passed away

E June Benjamin
A CANDLE BURNS FOR KENNEDY

A candle burns for Kennedy
It lights the world today
Wherever hearts are saddened
And kneel in silence to pray
It is one good candle
In the multitude of sin
And like the man it represents
Its light glows from within
It stands for hope and happiness
And peace around the world
It burns on ever heatedly
Its little flame unfueled
It gives a joyous light
That shouts faith to every one
Tho his gallent heart has died
His task has just begun
It glows among the candles
And it will not grow dim
But reminds us the worlds a better place
With men like him
With men of strength and courage
And unsurpassing power
That grows not weak as time passes
But mightier by the hour
With knowledge and wisdom
Seldom found in men today
So just for President Kennedy
Lets light a candle and pray
That God may reward him
As we never could
And wherever in Heaven may be
He is doing someone good
As he did a mighty nation
And steered it clear from wrong
His life was not yet fulfilled
It didn't last that long
So lets keep his ideals and memories
Alive and greater until
The little light on that candle
Grows brighter and brighter still

Lance Tolle
THE BOY NEXT DOOR

I know a charming little boy,
In fact he lives next door.
He has stolen a bit of my heart,
And he has just turned four.

He swings a golf club like a pro,
Or converses like a grown up man.
While at times he plays childhood games,
And smiles as only he can.

I could watch him all day long,
And marvel at his awesome power.
He can change from superman to a child,
And with bright eyes study a flower.

We have to give his parents credit
For the way in which he leans.
For their gentle way of teaching,
And the blending of his genes.

But it was more than just parents
That put him on this land.
For who could look at Andrew
And not see God's loving hand.

Joseph F Davis
HAPPY BIRTHDAY MISS LIBERTY

To my wife Edith, our families, friends and AMERICA

One hundred candles on her cake
What a wonderful sight it will make
As she holds her torch up high for
All the world to see,

Happy Birthday Miss Liberty

And if she wears a coat of rust
There's a reason why.
It's not the salt in the air,
Just the tears she cries
Because she cares for her sons and daughters
Far across the sea.

Happy Birthday Miss Liberty

She's more than just a statue,
Standing there gathering rust.
She's a symbol of our country,
In God We Trust
Like the stars and stripes
Forever she'll go down in history,
So light the candles!
God Bless America.

Happy Birthday Miss Liberty

Karl F Fischer

Karl F Fischer
THE GAME CALLED LIFE

Life has its ups and downs,
tears laughter and frowns
every body, gets its share,
of tribulations and dare.

Like the sun and the moon
both give us light,
a little bid at the time,
sometimes too bright,
it depends how you look at it,
nothing is perfect, that's right.

Confusion elusion that's strife
that's part of the game called life,
you are the actor, your stage
is the world, this is my story,
go happy go lucky don't worry.

C A Carrasco
THE PROPOSAL

Thoughts of our times
Are not
trodding the lines
Society lays on the table
Oh yes, change will come
Not by hefting a gun
But by changing values,
If we're able . . .
. . . In a system amock
U may need a flock
Of eagles 2 scatter the smoke.
Because stench & decay
Are these peoples way
& poverty's no longer a joke
!Automatons revoke
meglomanias yoke!
It will bury U under the table
Unite & B free
or
Dishearken this plea, & watch
liberty become a Fable.

John A Blas
THE BEGINNING

To my wife, Connie, and the beginning we are expecting. God Bless

---

I closed my eyes, what did I see
The dreams within my mind
Of fantasies of wanting to be
A part of human kind
The tenderness of being touched
And knowing that I'm loved
Would fill me up with so much warmth
That I would jump for joy
I'd like to see a rainbow
Streaked across the sky
And know what Mother's Nature
(Love) has made alive
The time is getting closer
I feel it deep within
My destiny is calling
I shall not be here again
The moment I've been waiting
For me, my life begins
Today my dreams shall follow
My birth, and me, as one . . . .

Rique Rincon
'TIS

In the deep, deep channels of mind
and thought, creation is at work—
A mesh of feelings never to be heard.
A duo it takes—
Not one on its own.
A tingle, a shudder, moments alone.

To see and to touch
Are not at hand—
Only a warm, blissful, silent command.

This sense of which I speak is
patterned by a love.
Two people—who fit like a glove.

Grace A Riganati
PEACEFUL VIEW

Sunset on a lake
A kaleidoscope of colors
With every shining ray
Brings peace and cotentment
After a weary day

Joanne L Balstra
HAPPINESS IS

To my beloved husband, Bob, Our son and daughter, Bobby and Laury who inspire the very depth of my being.

Happiness is waking up to greet a new day
To see sunshine and hear the birds sing
Happiness is living for present moments

And making the very best of everything.
Happiness is sharing with a family
Mixing laughter and tears along the way
Happiness is accepting one another
Holding hands and being open when we pray.

Happiness is time spent with an old friend
For welcoming new persons into your heart
Happiness is growing with a changing world
Bridging gaps to join together what's apart.

Happiness is smiling through unpleasant times
A phase of life we all must endure
Happiness is Knowing God is on your side
Having confidence in yourself, and being sure.

Happiness is trusting in God's plan for you
Because He loves us, He wants us to succeed
Happiness is believing in who and what you are
That God will provide for your essential needs

Happiness is living and loving
In a world created for you and me to share
Happiness is reaching out to brothers and sisters
Giving life your love, and showing how you care.

Karla M K Tate
FRAGMENTS

I walk down the beach making footprints in the sand.
The sun is low, highlighting shells by my feet.
I bend to pick one up.
It is broken, and I see the beach holds many shells,
Also broken, their edges ragged from the pounding surf.

The sand holds fragments, pieces of shells, bits of color.
These shells, chipped now,
Hold visions of my broken dreams.

I walk, feeling the sea wind on my skin and look again,
Reach down, and take this broken beauty in my hand.
Perfection is in everything.
A whole shell no more perfect that this bit,
Whose pattern is still clear and beautiful.

The only moment we have is now.
All those lost moments are like pieces chipped
From all these shells.
Lost and broken dreams.

Yet there is substance in these fragments.
In this piece here, an answer, a clarity, a possibility.
Those dreams get mended now,
As I listen to the sound of the sea,
And deep breathe the ocean air.
I smile as I collect some of these hard moments
In front of me,
Lost no more.

Carol Dunbar
ELEGY OF LOVE

To A Lost Love

You came into my life—
Suddenly the dark corners were lighted
The sun shone—skies were blue
My dreams sprang to life
And grew
Life was good

You became part of me

We laughed and loved and shared
Something beautiful began to grow
My happiness seemed eternal
Wondrously aglow
Life was good

Just as suddenly as you came you left
The dark, lonely nights are back
The endless days drag on
You have gone—
Leaving emptiness
Will life ever be good again?

BamaBob Yates

YOU'RE A ROSE (BUT THINK I'M A THORN)

You were the rose I'as looking for;
Your beauty held my heart,
I thought I'ld look no more,
But my trying tore us apart.

I became "a thorn in your side;"
But I didn't mean to be,
I gave love that wouldn't hide,
And I gave it so honest & free.

You're a rose but think I'm a thorn;
And your leaving has left me torn.

Your beauty still has great power;
It's still holding my heart,
You're no ord'nary flower,
Your "magic potion's" hit its mark.

You're a rose in life's garden o' woes;
But now you've said it's over,
Now I don't have you to hold,
And I wanted to hold "the rose" forever.

You're a rose but think I'm a thorn;
And you leaving has left me torn.

You're a rose—in life's garden of woes;
And you know—for you—my love always flows.

Ignatia N Soepangkat

WOULD MY LOVE BE STRONG ENOUGH

. . .
Not just once,
or twice,
but for many times
I have observed how his breath has stopped
for a couple of seconds while he was having his sleep.

I have found how powerful marijuana is on him
(Oh, how beautiful this word sounds!)
tho' not so much addicted
it appears as if he couldn't avoid taking
is it because he isn't willing to do?

Everytime I saw that square white box with slices dried leaves
my heart felt so hurt
and my heart would feel much hurt
everytime I saw him being in that stage of enjoyment

Would my love be strong enough
to lead him to the other side of the world.
since someone else has sucessfully introduced him to this side?
Would my love be able to persuade the sun to shine much brightly
since he told me that my love has led him to a new dimension?

I love him so much,
deeply!

Lorene Dunaway Osborn

LORENE, I LOVE YOU

To my sweetheart Tommy Brown, who was my inspiration for this poem. And all my loved ones. Lorene D. Osborn, Ashland, Al.

Come to me darling, and let's leave off quarreling,
We've much better things to do,
Like me hearing you whisper . . .
"LORENE, I LOVE YOU!"

We could go out walking, or sit together talking,
The T.V. together, we could fondly view,
but the thing that would thrill me the most is to
hear you saying "LORENE, I LOVE YOU!"

We could go out riding, or just go into hiding,
but what I want most is to hear you confiding,
"LORENE, I LOVE YOU!"
and to know when I hear these words coming from you
they come from your heart kind and true.

We could listen to the radio, or out visiting we could go,
there is no telling what we could do,
"together" MY DARLING this is true,
but so sweetly my heart would leap if only you'd say
"LORENE, I LOVE YOU!"

"Come to me darling, I'll make you, my bride,
with your love I'll be satisfied,"
then perhaps I'll stop being so blue,
when I hear you say this and
"LORENE, I LOVE YOU!"

Waldemar T Raczkowski

A STUDENT'S WEEK

On MONDAY morning I sat in school,
feeling tired, looking like a fool.
Wondering where the weekend had gone,
It all moved so fast, so quick, I had no time alone.

TUESDAY was a sunny day,
but with all the work I had, my plans went astray.
Playing sports, running around was in my mind,
but those teachers never did seem very kind.

WEDNESDAY came, the middle of the week,
more work, more work, I must be on a losing streak.
Read this, do that, the syllabus did say,
but there were boats to see at the blue bay.

THURSDAY arrived, the weekend is near,
starting to feel strong again, I let out a cheer!
A great anticipation is what I do feel,
it's something great no one can steal!

FRIDAY—my work is all done,
felt great, but where is the sun?
It's hiding behind that deep dark cloud,
but nevertheless, I was happy, no doubt!

SATURDAY, a day to pay my bills,
then party at night, lots of thrills!
Saturday is the day I do feel great,
until midnight, when I get home from my date!

SUNDAY, oh my head hurts today,
I must have had a good time, or so my friends say!
Relax, and let the pain slip away, I was told,
but menacing Monday is near, I must again be BOLD!

Stephen Ukertor Kerchan

THE PIT CHRIST DUG US FROM

To all that call on his name.

When we get all enamored with our high and mighty importance,
It's a good idea to take a backward glance
At the hole of the pit from which Christ lifted us.

And let's not just think about it, let's admit it
Our hole of the pit has a way of keeping us all
At the same level-recipients of grace.
And don't kid yourself,
Even those who are extolled and admired
Have holes from which they were dug.

With Moses, it was a murder,
With Elijah, it was depression,
With Peter, it was public denial of Jesus
With Samson, it was recurring lust
With Thomas, it was cynical doubting
With Jacob, it was deception of his father
With Rahab, it was prostitution
With Jephthah, it was his illegitimate birth.

Whenever we start to get exaggerated ideas of our own importance,
Let's take a backward glance at our humble beginnings
For that is all it takes to conquer conceit.
Don't hide your roots.

When we are tempted to become puffed up by our own importance,
Let's take a look back to the pit from which we were dug.
It has a way of deflating our pride in Jesus.

Roland D Forsythe

DON'T BOTHER WITH C.P.R.

To my lovely wife Louise for whom these words were written.

You hear on many newscasts, people having a heart transplant
Some generous person donating, but I am one who just can't
I can't give my heart to others, it is not meant to share
It belongs to my loving wife, not a strange body somewhere
Although my hearts been broken, many times in the past
It beats steady for my wife, for however long it lasts.
My hearts overflowing with love, in another it couldn't beat
It's programmed to beat regular, for my lovely wife so sweet
For it to be planted in another, would be a medical mistake
It would die of pure loneliness, without her it would break
Many times it's been mistreated, by others long long ago

But never by my perfect mate, as any cardiogram will show
There is nothing artificial, about this old heart of mine
It belongs to that adorable, forever caring wife so fine
In my autopsy after death, a true statement will appear
Saying it over worked itself, trying to please you dear
If it ever stops beating for her, and no matter who you are
It can never be fully revived, so don't bother with C.P.R.
Never could it beat for another, even in someone else's chest
If it can't beat for my wife, let me remain in cardiac arrest

Bud Burner

PLEASE SANTA

It is the night before Christmas and at my home
I put myself to bed . . . all alone
It's been seven years since the Lord took her away
I miss her so much, even to this very day
I came home with presents to put under the tree
And I call to her to come here and see

When she did not come my heart began to pound
I ran through the house and I cried at what I found
Golden brown was the color of her hair
She was a good wife and she did care
Her eyes were a dark, dark blue
And she was beautiful, everyone knew
When she left she took my heart, my soul, and my life
And so I pray to you, Santa . . . bring back my wife

Joyce Durham Davis
A TRIBUTE TO MAGGIE
This friend of mine is older now.
So she rests more than she wishes.
She'd rather be behind a garden plow
Or doing the dinner dishes.

She remembers how it used to be,
When her life was always busy
Working hard from dawn to dusk
The speed would make you dizzy!

There were the children in younger years.
To bring up true and proper.
Community service, and church, so dear,
My! you could hardly stop her.

The garden is especially sweet
For her, both then and now.
Her pies and cakes just can't be beat.
Her many friends would vow.

Her cooking would bring happy smiles
To many many faces.
Her gifts of love cover miles
And visited many places

Life and memories are beautiful.
But time does not stand still.
So she keeps on making memories
Until her life is fulfilled.

Lee Martin Ross
UNTITLED
Seductively:
Swept away
Set adrift
Encompassing all
and
Breathing the air
on wings.

Prosaically:
Anchored
Moored
Secured
Encompassing little
and
Plummeting to earth.

Perverse is Life
Perverse is the Glow
Conformity Shouts
I sink to its Depths
and
die.

Patricia Davis Charlotten
BEING

Dedication to three special women, Betty Davis, Wilhelmena Wideman, Auera Charlotten

---

Every scene in my mind is a reality that exist
The beauty, the thoughts, intrigues me
Thinking around the rough edges
Remembering what I'd accomplished throughout my ability to
live
I know what's there, that in which I can not touch

Reaching out to be loved can only make me love more
Don't be hasty
Patience is the silence of the wind
The silence is the relaxing tranquillity of beauty

Carolyn Vise Hodges (Tina)
REFUGE, THEN FAREWELL

Dedicated to the memory of "Toby" Hodges

There is a place, where I can go to rest and lay my head down to wait for death. Where angels minister unto my needs and unto God, I humbly plead— Oh Father so merciful and kind, "Please— don't leave me behind." And when you call to me, then and only then, will I be free.

Oh praise God for this place of rest where angels do their merciful best. Villa Mercy is my last retreat where I enter into God's sweet sleep and enter into the world beyond hand and hand with God's sweet Son." I live I breathe, I'm free, I live, I breathe, I am spiritually. Amen

Linda Holden Nolen
STAR GAZE SPECIAL
When I met you I needed your guidance. You were but a tool for my use;
In dealing with general day-to-day problems, and curbing my chemical abuse.
Immediately I saw your sincerity, and I tried to be so unimpressed.
But with each following encounter I wanted you more; with your wisdom I craved all the rest.
The harder I tried to suppress my emotions, I became even much more aware,
of the unspoken passion my heart felt for you, and I tried really hard not to care.
With my quest for honesty and searching for truth, self deception was not in my reach,.
I instinctively knew you were special by the wise and unique ways you teach.
I decided to let go of unrealistic dreams; I knew they were not meant to be.
I tried to think a lot less of you, and put focus once more upon me.
It worked, yes it did, I saw much more of me and each time right there by my side,
I saw you as my helper, my friend and companion, and always a wonderful guide.
I decided instead of fighting the facts, I would invite you into my dreams.
And alas by a delightful turning of fate, you accepted me minus my seams.
Now our dreams and our hopes will be mutual goals, for we both have a new lease on life . . .
You're not only my confidante, teacher and guide; you're my love and I will be your wife!

Williamene (Billie) Weatherill
KEEPING THE TRANSIENT
O this ever changing, passing scene,
where naught remains the same.
One moment, life is full of pleasantness,
the next, its full of pain.

And yes, this ever changing scene,
it sometimes gets me down,
when each sweet season of happiness,
heralds a bitter season round.

But with this ever changing scene,
I'm learning all the time,
to hide the memories of the sweet,
in a place that bitterness can't find.

Leah Herman Stec
THE GYPSY—FOR WAYNE

To Wayne—my Gypsy. I love you, "Till the Mountain" —Gypsy's Baby.

The Gypsy walks alone
Along his lonely trail
Both night and day he searches
But still to no avail

What is this loner looking for
I think perhaps I know
He's looking for his Baby Love
So he won't be alone

He's looking for dark gypsy eyes
Full of truth and wisdom
Yet he's looking for the innocence
He's sure to find within them

The Gypsy walks alone
Along his lonely trail
Both night and day he searches
But still to no avail

What is this loner looking for
Perhaps I know and maybe . . .
At the end of his long true search
He finds her . . . Gypsy's Baby.

Mamie J Joiner
ONCE
Once she was a soft and cuddly baby girl
laid in her mother's arms.
Once she was a six-year old, going to school for
the first time.
Once she was a teen-ager, with all the grace and charm.
Once she was a blushing bride, just in her youth and prime.
Once she was a young mother, with duties large and small.
Once she was a widow, and no one on her did call.
Once she was getting old, and her children
Grown and gone.
Once she was sick and alone, with no home to call her own.
Once each day she thought of all her children,
And wondered why they didn't come.
Once she was placed in a nursing home
To live her last day alone,
Once a neighbor visited her, and saw her many needs.
Once she remembered her' Saviour and Lord
And she wasn't lonely any more.
Once her children thought of her
And a visit they did plan.
Once the Lord had closed the door
And her tired heart beat no more
Once again remember your Mother
Call on Her from time to time
Once again see love in Her eyes
Once again erase the regrets
Befor She says "Good Bye."

Christopher S White
WHAT IS BLACK?
Black is the stars, the moon, the sky
Black is a crow, chirping on high.
Black is a wire, high off the ground
Black is a panther that leaps with a bound.
Black is a hole, deep and wide
Black is two ravens, side by side.
Black sounds like a person choking on smoke.
Black tastes like a soda—called "Coke."

G Roderic Durham
A CLOUD BETWEEN US
When there ariseth a cloud between us
Though it be no larger than a man's hand,
The sun is blotted out
And there is darkness at noonday.

And, in the darkness, I search and seek
But there is answer none.
And I remember other times of darkness
When our tears rivalled the rain
In their intensity—
Denver on a Sunday night
When we trembled because of doubt
That our love would find fulfillment.
O Doubt, O Darkness, O Tears,
Are these our lot?
Are these all that we shall ever know together?
Is love like this? Real love?
Is there no fulfillment?
No peace in love? Is love
Always stormy, filled with tears
And darkness at noonday?
O clouds disperse! That once again
My Love and I may walk
In sunshine and be glad.

Omnibumni Dawn Wilson

Omnibumni Dawn Wilson
THE CONTEST
Here I am sitting at the table
Will I be able

To make a poem that's just
Good enough.
I am not going to pout, and I'm not
Going to puff,

Just because I just might mess-up

I have to make a lot of rough drafts
May nine, ten or maybe even eleven

So I can turn it in by February 28, 1987

Cynthia K Yarborough
YOUR LIFE
I never really knew just how
much you mean to me
Or if you left my life right
now, how my life would really be

My life would be without meaning
without accomplishment and goals
but now I know who's memories
in my heart that I hold

Your life is a light to me
an everlasting glow
in my eyes you're the love
that few people ever know

When your light stops shining
and they're taking you above
They're taking part of me with you
cause you're the one I love

Rapheal Dayton Young
THE SEED OF HOPE
"I need but a glance to know the devastating plague that hardly a morsel ever touched upon the lips of so many poor souls.
"Even thou surrounded by morsel in The air.

"Like a strong wind from a hurricane that blew morsels all over the countryside but missed some places.

"When will the strong winds of poverty cease to blow through the
city streets and countryside.

"Like dandelions that have been Plucked from summer fields while a small child stops to admire its beauty.

"And when it is touched for its lite and breezy look a strong wind comes and wisk it away, and as it flies in the strong harsh wind its beauty is thrown apart and
is spread all over the countryside
"So like poverty:

"Where will it end and how can we so few vanquish this destroyer?
"Tis but to plant the seed of hope and it will grow and spread throughout the countryside and one day it
will cover the entire world.

Celine Marie Hill
A CRY FROM THE PEOPLE
Do you hear what I hear,
A voice crying in the wilderness?
Do you hear the children play,
But now there is one less?

Where have all the children gone,
Why are there more missing each day?
The awful crime that's being done,
Who is it that will pay?

A father and a mother cry,
For their child they have lost,
Is it because we've not done enough,
We haven't truly counted the cost?

What happens when it comes to you,
Your child's gone—will you know it's too late?
Too late to take any action now,
Lord, why do we hesitate?

In this world of molested and missing children,
Pornography, old and new disease running wild,
Drug addiction, alcohol and the minor crimes,
Are beginning to seem very mild!

We're crying to you—our government,
Oh won't you please take a firm stand.
Put a stop to this insidious evil,
God's put the power in your hand!

Bonnie Lee Hodge
HIS WATCHFUL EYES

This poem is dedicated to my loving husband, James

With winter storms and winds whirling by.
I see the beauty in His watchful eyes.

His calm can be felt, throughout the land,
If, we let Him lead us, by His nail scared hands.

He vanishes our fears and with each new day,
He lightens the sky with a bright sun ray.

He lifts all our burdens, He knows we can't bear,
With His gentle voice, We know He cares.

He makes our hearts happy, and our life each day,
Should be to others a will to pray.

Look toward Heaven, with a gleam and sigh,
As you thank the Lord, for His watchful eyes.

Steven W Iverson
MY WORLD AND YOURS
I live in a world of my own.
Population one and i have the thrown.
Far from all you people,
Higher than the highest steeple.
A world with no lights,
Crazy days and restless nights.
I would never leave but i live in fear,
I will not be hurt it is safe here.
The first time i saw you,
My love was true.
They said our love could never be,
But thats up to you and me.
If i do not leave you will say goodbye,
So i'll leave my world and fly.
I left my world and you dropped me hard,
You broke me up like a glass shard.
A house to live in, a time to be confused,
I asked for a second chance but you refused
I need your love to keep alive,
The only answer is suicide.
Now that I'm gone she love's me true,
This hole in the ground is my love for you.

Frank Jimenez Jr
THOUGHT OF CONFUSION
As I sit here all alone, It's what it seems.
It fears to wonder and it fears to dream.
A thought of confusion came over me.
What does life bare? What would it bring?
Is it my freedom, or my
self-esteem?
What makes me wonder and turn to him?
Is it that dream of what life is about?
Praying forgiveness for that one way out.
Or, is it a game that I might play?
Making the dark clouds come my way.
What would it take to make me clear?
To stop and make these clouds all disappear.

Don't you know?
Wouldn't You know!

In that instant moment, In that special time.
Cometh my way a long ray of light.
It's what makes me write of that beautiful night.
It must have been so heavenly sent.
As He heard me call out from that heavy set mist.
Now all of those thoughts, nightmares, and dreams that seem to grow.
Are now just a few precious wonders that now make me glow . . .

Robert Lee Tussey
CYTHEREA

To the pale Golden One

Have you been to Cytherea
Where Cytherea first touched
Land?
Lovely, bright-haired Cytherea,
I wish I had been there to
Take Her exquisite hand.

Sweet laughing Cytherea,
Some say She is the Goddess
of Love,
Pale Golden Cytherea,
One of Her symbols is the dove.

Some say She is the Goddess
Of Fertility,
The vain, the wind, the sun,
And the earth,
Since before the dawn of history,
And to all living things She
Gives birth,—

She floated to Cytherea on a
Seashell,
Then eventually to Cyprus She
Went,
Arriving in all Her beauty and
Splendor,

Cytherea—of the sweet
Round throat and desirable
Breasts,—

Her grove and shrine at
Paphos,
Is there for all to see,
Laughter—loving Cytherea,
Born of the Sky and
The Foam Of the Sea,

A thousand years and more
Have passed,
Since She lost her standing
In Rome,
But if I ever visit that
Great city,
It's Her I'll seek in that
Magnificent Dome

Felipa Flores Villegas
THE BIRTH
To the hospital we go in a car
Although it may not be very far.
Many miles Mary rode on a donkey; how sad
Because the king wanted our Saviour dead.
We beautify and prepare our home
Because our new baby will be here soon.
Finding a room in the inn Mary was unable;

Our sweet Jesus was born in a stable.

We buy our baby clothes so new;
Bunches and bunches not just a few.
Why this happened no one knows
But our dear Jesus had only swaddling clothes.

We fix our baby a comfortable bed
Paint it bright colors of blue, green, and red.
Our sweet Jesus on this Holy Day
Was placed in a manger filled with hay.

But now my sweet Jesus I am glad to say,
You have lived, died and risen to show us the way
To your home in heaven where You forever
Will stay.

Paula Vining

THOUGHTS OF CHRISTMAS

Dedicated to my loving children Debbie, Kristi, and John

As the leaves begin to fall
Our hearts hold near
The thoughts of Christmas
And holiday cheer.

The joy of sharing
With loved ones and friends
Warmth and good wishes
And the hope Christmas brings.

A time to remember
God's gift from above
Sweet baby Jesus
The true meaning of love.

How blessed we would be
If the rest of the year
Were filled with the joy
Of peace and Christmas cheer.

Juanita Vega

MY LITTLE GIRL

To my daughter MaryEllen Vega, Brandt

"My little girl?," was my remark;
As I beheld my new born babe.
This new born babe was now to be
My little girl.
Soft, tender, sweet and cudley;
With bubbling love I bathed her.
Time, days, weeks, and months;
Still she was
My little girl.
My little girl in ballet suits and dancing shoes;
Frilly dresses and lovely curls,
Is now no more
My little girl.
For she prefers to stay away;
Growing up and loving others.
And when I get a little gaze;
When she passes by my door,
I realize she is now no more
My little girl.
As I behold her as a wife,
And now as a mother;
I realize for sure,
She is now no more . . .
My little girl
Oh! how I miss my little girl;
My little girl no more.

Ernest Johnson

PROBLEMS

Problems, they won't go away, believe it or not they are here to stay;
Adam's sin brought problems about—now its something you can't live without;
They make us sometimes feel that we are losing our minds and all they are doing is wasting our good time;
Some we solve, others we cope, if we stay level-headed there is hope;
Some attack us up front then others from behind; some make us
feel so despair—wondering where can I turn, there is no way
out, I cannot see, Oh Lord! deliver me!
Now that old problem has a big grin he knows you no longer have a friend;
Our anchor was the Lord long time ago but those old problems made
us believe and think; "oh he's not there anymore;
Now he told us we would have them and many they would be because Adam and Eve left me.
But He promised and gave His word, "I'm not going to leave you
alone, because even coping with all this would be so wrong. He said;
"Call upon Me, you can rely, never give into those problems and just want to die!
I've sent my Son into this world to die, it was only one death needed for all time to make you a friend of Mine;
I'll be here for you all your life—just trust Me to help
keep you right.
My hand is there for you, grab hold of it, hold on tight, because I'm going to help you live with these problems, with all My MIGHT!

Debbie S Wrightenberry

TIME

With love and respect to my best friend, my mother, who tries every day to teach me the value of time and patience.

What is this. Time that is the backbone of our lives?
They say that Time is relative.
But does that mean it is a mother or a sister?
Or relative in that our very existence is calculated on Time.
What is Time, the mystery that stalks, but eludes us thru eternity.

Time is the moving of tiny hands on a numerical face.
Time is the sun crossing the sky on a majestic clock of wisdom and patience.
Time is the pages of a calendar, ever turning, pushing us relentlessly forward.
Time is the long, gentle arm of mother nature, enticing the mountains and valleys thru her seasons.
Time is the fertilizing of our souls with the seeds of love and peace, hate and war.
Time is the clouding of our souls with the winds of the ages.
Time is the rolling in of the tide, to caress our yesterdays into memories.
Time is the aging of a dear one from invincible, to vulnerable.
Time is but memories—seen thru rosy colored glasses,
Interpreted thru the ages with love and hate,
To make us what we are—
To make us what we will be.

Craig Ralls

SISTERDANCER—DAUGHTER—BALLERINA

Performancer, you affect the mirrors lady, and move Beauty into the pirhouette drawn spaces amidst the galaxies but-o-so-more grace and swiftly, you—glory of the singing articulation of the body. i see, i know the pain and the pride, the suffering to share given in a life to please.
beneath the movement in the music are generations of design sculpted in the dynamics of the impulse that calls the love of the dance into the structure at the song and bids you to surpass the perfection of your expression.
there is concentration—a total soul traces your pathway at nerves—that so finely etches rememberance into all our hearts, a gift that we have each other. the ambient spell you weave in abstractions of language and motion—swells in the surpassing geometry of your gyreing arabesques; and is frozen in the momentary memory—the tears and desperation to achieve that joy, and lift high and free in the leap and turn of your Art, and private purpose as the company of dancers emerge— the audience pauses and gasps—for they recognize the star in the closeness of the shadows, with the ease of serious dedication all cameras, all eyes have glimpsed <u>you</u>, focused and framed, forever center stage.

Loistene A Ogden

MOUNTAIN LIVING

To the Good and the Beauty of Nature

Have you ever watched in early spring, a swarm of butterflies on the wing,
Or a mother tanager in her quest of lint or hair to line her nest?
A saucy squirrel look here or there for a nut or acorn for winter fare,
Or sat looking, hardly daring to breathing at deer brousing on tender leaves
Stopping often to listen and stare at some strange object here or there,
Or seen the tracks of wind in tall grass as it searched the way and found it at last?
I have seen butterflies by hundreds swarm from a damp place in the trail:
And the beautiful and wise tanager in her search;
I've watched the crafty squirrel hide in his tree,
And deer in herds graze the gentle slopes.
I have felt the soft wind grow strong—into a storm;
The rain that changed to sleet then snow,
The soft snowflakes drifting down to place a white blanket all around.

The very quiet of the deep woods is filled with sounds, if we but hear.
There a fallen tree creaks against another, here a noisy woodpecker drums his tune—
The wind plays its song as the oaks and pines sway,
The smell of unknown flowers blooming in a hidden place.
The pattern of sun and shadow lace—
Ever changing, ever new, who could be mean or untrue
Close to nature—close to God—this is good mountain living—

Danielle Velvet Peek

TREASURE OF LOVE

I'd like to dedicate this poem to all the special People in my life that I love. Thank you for your encouragement. I love you.

Love is to be cherished like a new found treasure.
Never to be let go or thrown asunder.
Love is brilliant, like the colors of a sunset against the crystal waves of the ocean.
My heart soars with the grace of a dove in flight, as I think of this love made for two.
You shall be cherished forever and one day.
Until the day comes when you go away. This will be a time when we're left with no choice.
You shall go your way and I shall go mine.
Till the day comes when we must part, I'll always hold your love forever close to my heart.
The memories we've shared shall never die.
Our love is something beautiful that will never be put aside. I cherish you so very much always close in my thoughts even when your so very far away.
I'll always treasure your laugh, your touch, and remember
Your gentle face
Your tender ways
Your presence in my life . . .

Bruce E Peterson

THE MORNING SUN

I know I'll always be with you until the end of time
Always loving you, I'm sure you'll be forever, mine.
You're all I want and need, you made my life complete,
Walking in the morning sun, you

are all I need.
Forever with you dear, we're living such a great life.
Knowing there won't be anyone else, forever you are mine,
Kiss me, then I'll say the words you love to hear.
You're the one for me, I love you, I whisper in your ear.
So many years together, why did you have to go?
To shatter my reason for living, only God could know.
Memories haunt me on a rainy night,
For you to go away, it just wasn't right.
God took you away from me, to leave me all alone.
But we'll meet again to be together forever and walk in
The morning sun.

Glenice E Lackie
DEAF—BUT
I cannot hear the wind that blows
And ruffles every tree and rose—
I cannot hear the birds that sing
When they return to haunts each spring—
The rippling brooks just sparkle past
And crickets play silent in the grass
The noise of children going by
Brings oft a deep heartfelt sigh—
But—though my ears are stopped to sound
My soul is not in prison bound.
Its ears are open wide and clear.
The voice of God speaks loud and near.

Velma Floyd Story
GOLDEN AUTUMN
Golden Autumn!
Golden Autumn!
The time is winding down.
Gone, oh yes gone—
The youthful days I knew not, now.
They are past and gone forever.

Golden Autumn!
Golden Autumn!
With fond nostalgia do I recall
When time was glorious
And oh so endless.
Gone, oh yes gone in a mist of time
And no more the careless, gay,
Heedless gambol of fun and play.

Golden Autumn!
Golden Autumn!
Time is spinning—going,
Like sand in an hourglass.
A tiny stream is flowing—
And then it's gone—

Marge Anderson
A DREAM

To my sister Netty

I dreamed you came into my room one night
I felt your precious presence
So tenderly you kissed my lips
And touched my face to yours.
When I awakened you were not there;
Only a tear on my cheek I know
Not from where.

Veronica O'Hara
ODE TO THE POPPIES
Poppies daring and quite fair
You fascinate me standing there.
You are so fragile and so sweet
And yet you burn with intense heat.
Your scarlet petals fling a warning
And yet hold tears in early morning
You cry defiance at the breeze
Then let him bend and break and squeeze—
Your petals from their earthly stem
To be trampled down by men.
Then softly on the ground you lay
And toss back brightness to the day.

Kermit Theophilus Wyche
TOGETHER ONCE AGAIN
Too long for this time, I patiently wait
Over anxious it seems, the moment so great
Going there, reunite, on the road to new life
Endless love, who knows, I hope, it might
Together once again, lost love I will find
Hands of time, wind back, memories, flood my mind
Empty, no more I'll ever be, on that promise you can bet
Remembering the both of us, you and me, never to forget.

Once again we are together
Nothing will untie the pair
Could this be losing ones heart I ask?
Everlasting life with love to share.

And when lost time has been made up
Good times the order of day
And when we share, again, what we had then
I'll always be here to stay
Never, will I ever, in life, try my love to send, no
memory could ever take your place:
TOGETHER ONCE AGAIN

Blanche Robbins Gerrard
IN MEMORIAM
Sleep on, ye brave
We'll make the dreams
You dreamed while here
Come true.

Rest well. The world
Will know a fairer dawn;
Fear not. We prize
The sacrifice you knew
And realize that even
"Over There"
You carry on.

Vernon Kitabu Turner
ALIVE
TO BE ALIVE is to feel,
to know the falling drops we call rain
as wetness on the skin,
TO BE ALIVE is to feel,
Winter cold makes us tremble,
Summer heat makes us sweat,

TO BE ALIVE is to feel,
the warm kiss of your lover steals your breath away,
the stinging slap of reality penetrates to the soul,

TO BE ALIVE is to celebrate,
to dance to the joy of childhood and beam with knowledge
at each new item learned,

TO BE ALIVE is to give,
sharing each precious moment
with another—we expand them,
offering our talent and our possessions—we enjoy them more,

TO BE ALIVE is to face death each second,
letting perish old thoughts and out-moded ways,
making room for the new,

TO BE ALIVE is to remain a child,
inquisitive, yearning, receptive to new experiences,
open-hearted and yielding,

TO BE ALIVE is simply being free,
moving with the breath—energy,
being what you are.

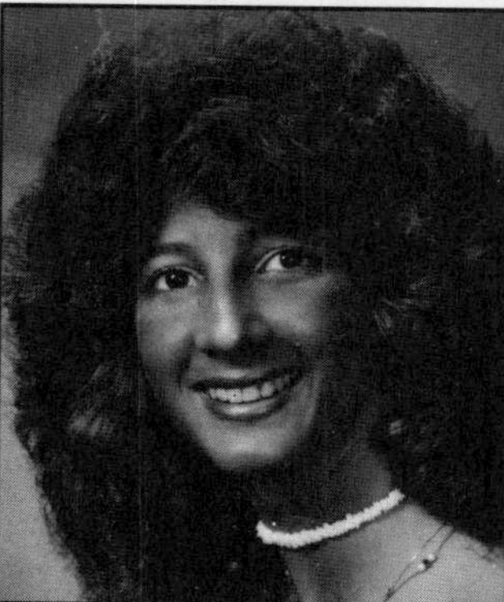

Paulette Theresa Reale

Paulette Theresa Reale
MY DREAM GUY
One day I hope to meet someone very kind
But right now things are somewhat difficult for me
That guy is hard to find.

I want him to be special in every kind of way.
I pray to God to find him.
To meet this guy someday.

Honest and friendly I hope he'll be
Because I need to find someone
Someone, just like me.

My friends are all to marry.
So happy they seem to be.
The only one left searching
Is me and only me.

I know he must be out there.
Somewhere, out there someplace
So I must keep on searching
For his friendly, smiling face.

I don't know what he looks like
Or how old he may be.
I just hope I'll find him.
For there's got to be someone out there for me.

I picture myself with a smart guy
Who has set himself a goal.
For someday I hope he'll want a family.
To play the husband, father role.

He doesn't have to be rich or famous
Or in the books I read.
I just want him to love me.
Yes, I want his love indeed.

Why God keeps me waiting
I will never know
I just keep on praying
One day that he'll show.

I hope he'll be protective
And keep me away from harm.
I hope he'll always smile.
I want a guy with charm.

I wish I wish I'd find you
I wish I had a friend.
We could share my inner secrets.
We could talk until no end.

Time may be the answer.
So as long as it may seem
I guess I'll just keep on studying
To my nursing dream.

I hope it's not forever
For the time to come.
For me to meet my special guy.
My special and only one.

Dear God I'll keep on praying
I'll leave it up to you
I'll leave it in your hands for now
To help my dreams come true.

Please help me not to stay too lonely
Forever in my life
Because you know I want to be.
A mother and a wife.

I'll go each day and look around
And hope to find my guy
It's just going to take longer for me, I guess
Being that I'm shy

When I least expect it.
I'm told I'll fall in love
So I'm believing in your word up there
My friend, dear God above.

Wayne L Miller
THROUGH YOU
I see the world
Through your eyes.
The tenderness
With your smile
The love
By a kiss from your lips
The careing
From your touch
The peace
From the warmth of your heart
The greatness
Through your love.
I see you as life itself
And the world through you
As a beautiful place.

Luciana D Adams
LOVE
Love is as pretty as a dove
Which comes from up above

It can also come from the heart
But it should be all, not just a part

When someone loves you like I do
That love will be strong and also true

Take me in your arms if you please
Hold me close, just don't squeeze

For you I will do any deed
Because your love is all I need

This is how love should be
Because I love you and you love me.

Mona L Zersen
MY GARDEN
I awake in the morning and look out of doors
To the beauty beyond, that belongs to the Lord.
I finish my tasks and then out I go,
Armed with my rake, shovel and hoe.

In my mind are the cares of a difficult day,
Which I soon forget in the sun's full rays
I look for the seeds I planted last week,
And find, thru the ground they begin to peek.

After working awhile, I seek the shade of a tree,
In whose bough, God is watching over me.
A robin drops by, to bid me good day,
I start to work, but first bow my head to pray.

And as I do, I feel His Hand on my hoe,
Guiding me to create beauty I alone could not grow.
The soothing peace I find in my garden of love
Could only come to me from the beauty above.

Donna J Copple
A BENCH
A special place under the trees,
Away from their view,
Hidden refuge for my knees,
Another minute and I'll be new,
Wooden throne beneath the pines,
A harbor from the rain,
A gentle place to unwind,
Just another chair, but not the same.,

Eileen M Chnupa
A PROMISE FOR S.T.
Carmalite, heavenbright.
A rose by name tonite.
Wonderous star, how close you are
to the Celestial Beam
that lights my dreams.
A promise made
should never fade
Amid dawn's early light.
To be renowned
One must be known
As ponderous pens have found.
So now I rite about
the height
that this intercessor can do for you.
Should you have need;
Make your prayer a seed
to flower in His rose garden.

Debby Knight
THE TEAR FROM MY EYE

To my husband Tom and my daughter Patty.

Running to the mountains
running through the trees
looking as I run,
a dream is chasing me.

Stepping in the water
of a river so bold
why did my dreams
grow so very old?

Feeling the sunset
in the glorious sky
take the pain from my heart
and tear from my eye.

Marjorie Alleckson-Pesch

Marjorie Alleckson-Pesch
MY SON IS GOING AWAY
He was a beautiful, blonde, baby boy
Chubby and healthy-strong and so brave,
Bringing a ray of sunshine
Into the lives of everyone he was near.

There are no sad memories—
Only days of love and laughter
Always happy and good natured
Smiling, laughing, loving, playing

Baseball cards and Baseball games
Building dreams with blocks and bricks
Nightcrawlers, mowing lawns and fishing
Climbing trees, piano lessons, and building forts.

Covering his room with empty beer cans
Collected from ditches, dump grounds, friends, and trips
Puppies and kittens, one racoon, and a goose,
Shells from the ocean and rocks from all over.

Loving cold Minnesota winters as my "Winter Boy"
Sledding, skiing, skating, and snowball fights,
Building tunnels in the snowbanks,
Blizzards and snowstorms—days home from school.

Hot, busy summer days picking rocks and pulling weeds
Swimming in the river and in the swimming pool—
Turning that healthy growing body
Into a golden sun-tanned athlete.

My son is going away
How quickly time has passed—
Where is my Beautiful Baby Boy?
Who is this tall eighteen year old
Looking down at me?

Does he remember all our happy days?
Is there a lump in his throat, too?

Graduation is almost here.

Amy Michael
SAM
He had grasped for a moment
The paw of the one he loved,
And touched the gray coat.
The love they had shared was now fading.
Fading from view.
The troubled years brought hardship for many,
Trial after trial upon the body and soul
And the everfading dream swept away with the dust of the land.
To be forgotten among the ashes.
Ashes now are the only memories.

Long gone and forever lost,
The boyhood memories of a boy and his true friend.
The only one in which he could truly confide—
Now sleeps in the shadow of the Lord,
And forever watches the path of his master.

Frank Sliver
YOU DON'T KNOW ME
If by chance we pass on the street, do not nod, look or say hello. Do not under any circumstances even let our shadows know.
When you hear my name, do not acknowledge or make a comment, pretend you don't even know me.
So you're dead—too bad—when I die & leave this earth & our spirits pass somewhere out there—pretend you don't know me, as you see, I hated you then as much as you hated me.

Sue Ann Davis
ONLY OURS

Dedicated to Billy, the man I love

I look at him,
He looks at me.
The feeling I get
When I see,

His eyes dark brown,
Shining like stars.
The love we have
Is only ours.

His lips are soft,
And oh, so sweet.
The feeling I get
When ours meet,

Is the love between us,
Will never part.
It will grow each day
Right from the start.

Marjorie Sager
ODE TO A NEIGHBOR
Friendly to all;
she shed a light
A friendly smile.
Always an opinion
A helping hand—
Her lite is out
Forever.
I miss her so;
You'll never know.

Mary Frances Holzhauer
YOU LAUGHED
You laughed—
The bubbling ecstasy,
Ringing harmony
Of your mirth
Gave my soul new birth;
I lived
And loved.

You laughed—
The withering irony,
Uncouth mockery
In your mirth
Scorned my soul's new birth;
Still I lived
And loved.

Oh what a banishment of woe
If love like other ills could go!

Shanee
I WILL NOT
I will not accept the things
you say, just have to be.
Too young women sat by the fire waiting.
Waiting for a child to be born,
Waiting patiently for life to say,
"Here you are—this is what
we will ALLOW you to be."

Patiently I waited for life to come to me,
In waiting, it almost passed me by.
Anger cut the web you wove around me,
Impatience catapulted me into action.
I want to shake all of you waiting out there.
Wake up—open your eyes—your mind—
your head and your heart.
There is a world out there.

IT IS YOURS FOR THE ASKING.

Sharon A Badgley
TEDDY BEARS
Mama Took me to a toy store to buy a Teddy Bear,
She said, "I needed someone to cry on when she wasn't there."
I picked the biggest one that I could find,
So I could cuddle up in peace sublime.
This brown grizzly, dressed in yellow,
Made me feel like a pretty good fellow.
Her eyes were gentle and staring, as if she knew,
Just the love I needed, when circumstances seemed blue.
Her arms and body were soft to squeeze,
She promptly growled from her mouth, "You big tease."
She made me laugh and think; I'm glad, God made Teddy Bears.

Gwyne Skinner
THE ROSE

Dedicated To My Mother.

The Rose stood closed in the morning dew
Its color held within
Then the sun smiled out of the blue
Kissing its petals again.
The Rose lifted its petals proud
And its fragrance filled the air,
It stood with its beauty loud
And nothing with it could compare.

Michelle Lee Tate
THE RAIN AND MYSELF
It's raining outside.
Quiet and still the house is,
So quiet . . . I can hear the faint ticking
of the clock on the wall.
The rain beats gently on the

sidewalk outside—
Cars hurry through the gathering puddles.
They're anxious to get home.
It's raining outside—
I'm home alone. The house is quiet . . .
I can relax and write how I feel.
I feel like the drops of rain—
One Individual falling steadily,
Either catching itself on a leaf to break the fall . . .
or missing it altogether and landing on the ground where it is no longer
One Individual.
It is now no different from the others.
I am an individual droplet of rain,
fighting to keep my grip on the leaf.
When the big wind comes,
I will let go . . .
and hope for the best.

Erlinda V Soliman
ERLINDA

E-Early spring is in your eyes
R-Roses so red just like your lips.
L-Love was felt with your touch
I-I see your smile when I'm alone.
N-Now is the time to know I care
D-Dearest one I love you so.
A-Always, always, remember dear,
I'll be waiting for you!

I remember when I first met you
You smiled to me when I say "Hi!"
The sky was blue and the birds were singing
With laughter and happiness.

Mary Beth Keegan

Mary Beth Keegan
FEELING

I dedicate this poem to my beloved father and mother, Edward J. and Barbara A. Keegan.

The sense of space.
The want to fly.
To feel the air . . .
And never die.
To reach for goals.
The want to be.
And most of all . . .
The want to see.
The want of freedom.
The need for one.
To know yourself . . .
And look toward the sun.
The want to cry.
The want to live.
And most of all . . .
The want to give.
To stand strong when others fall.
To be there when others call.
And help the one's that need it most of all.
To hold in mind a sense of peace,
And know that love will never cease.

Jonathan Woodrow Brown
WHO WERE OUR TEACHERS

I want my child to be raised
In an environment of peace in an environment of joy
I want my child to be raised
To be kind to be free
I want my child to have faith
In the King of Kings and the Lord of Lords

I don't want them to fuss and fight
I just want them to see the light
Mostly do the things that are right
And with the human race stand up and unite
Pray to God with all their might
Have respect and be polite
Teach them pleasant things to recite
For the word of God have an appetite
Who were our teachers

Steven M Beale
THE COURSE OF LIFE

In the course of life I've found
that without a goal we all are bound
to living in ignorance unaware,
filling our lives with constant despair.
Without the knowledge of which way to turn
confusing our minds so we do not learn
making our lives seem useless and vain
causing our hearts to ache with pain.
Keeping us stuck in the same old groove
and before you know you cannot move
But before you reach the destruction brink
there is one thing you should do and that is THINK
Go deep within, down the corridors of your mind
for the wisdom you seek you will surely find
And all the hope for the dreams you lost
all returns when you realize who's boss
And all the questions you had before
simply become answered when you've unlocked that door
Once it is opened go deep within
and watch a whole new world begin
Quickly now reclaim your stand
for your every wish is at YOUR command.

Laura J Wood O'Shea
I'VE WALKED THIS PATH

I've walked this path
So many times before
Never having a destination
But what did I need it for?

I've walked this path
So lonely dark and cold
This road was never paved
You just see the rocks grow old.
I've walked this path
Like a blind man would
With the knowledge that;
I would only love if I could.

Elizabeth Lou Conner
LISTENING IN

I met a friend today, Lord,
Who had many griefs and cares.
It seemed that he had fallen
In a pit of deep despair.

Then as he told his troubles
And I listened all the while,
It seemed his load was lightened
For he soon began to smile.

He thanked me for my patience,
For the help I'd given him.
I smiled and said, "Twas nothing,
I'd just been listening in."

Michael Haarstick
THE PASSING OF A SHORT LIFE

In a room once showered by Holy Light
where ne're a shadow flies,
Occurs there now a most grim night
As a dying child in a cold bed lies.
I look upon her face so fine,
and into her eyes so blue,
And as her hand falls limp in mine,
She whispers, "I love you."

She's now within an endless zone
On a bridge between life and death,
And as her spirit stands alone,
She struggles for one more breath.

Lo! From out the light, a golden image calls
and her spirit to it doth harken,
And as her chest for the last time falls,
See how the room doth darken.

Do not for her your sorrows send
But for your own sinning,
For death is never, ever an end,
But only a new beginning.

Merrily Ruth Worrell
TOUCHED BY HUMAN HANDS

We use each resource faster than mother earth can make it
If something natural's in our way, we don't go 'round, we break it

We aren't the only creatures who call this planet home
But we use and take and ruin as though we were alone

I wonder if we'll stop in time to give this world a chance
I worry that time's running out, is this mankinds last dance?

We have killed a thousand species of flower, plume and fin
And pushed a thousand more so close, their end's not if, but when

God gave mankind dominion and hands to build and heal
What would be gifts, if wisely used, those human hands now steal

We jeer at lemmings as they leap in seeming suicide
Yet they neither rape the earth they leave nor murder it with pride

Kim D Neal
A PIGS PROTEST

Dedicated to my daughter "Jamie"

As a pig I do protest
Because I'm called a great big pest
In the mud I like to run and play,
But everyone gets mad when I come their way
Although fat and funny some do say
I'm as nice as a bunny in my play
So don't be mad if I act this way
Because I'll be like this everyday!

Sr Ann Francis Monedero
MI ABUELITO

Stillness in a cobwebby attic
Slowly the antiquated trunk is opened
Cherished memories of goodness
Layer upon layer
Amassed through the years
One by one
Treasured and remembered once more

Sheila Emmons Smith
BEYOND THE LAND OF THE DRAGONS

This poem dedicated to Robin Zander

Lying in a bed of grass
Surrounded by a field of flowers
Wishing time would never pass
And end such a peaceful hour.

This valley of serenity
Is for my dreams alone
Shared only by the love of a man.
A face to me unknown.

Protected from all evil
As I enter my virgin land
Forgotten are the pains of life
As I take his soothing hand

Everything is simple
All words are left unsaid
For in my valley of happiness
tears are never shed

In my waking hour.
I remember my special place
I think about the man I love
And the day I will know his face.

Mary L Doyle
AN ANSWERED PRAYER

Dedicated to Royce "Bud" Doyle—My loving husband and loyal friend—With all my love. Thank you for loving me."

The Lord smiled down on this life of mine
And sent me your love so true and divine

My every Prayer He made come
true
When He gave me your sweet
love
and you
My empty life is now complete
Because of your love so tender
and
sweet
I want to always be your only
lover
And for your loving arms to hold
no other
For you're the only happiness
I've
ever known
My love is yours and yours alone
I will always be honest open and
true
And give all my lovin' just to you.
My life God blessed so tenderly
When he sent you as his gift to
me
I'll forever be thankful to my
Master above
For sending you for me to love
My deepest dreams have all
come
true
Because I have Gods love and
you.
Your love means more than all
the
world
With all its riches diamonds and
pearls
And all I ever will want from life
Is just to be your loving wife
And Darlin: Should we ever part
Your sweet love I'll hold within
my
heart.

Kathy M Marrison

WISHES AND DREAMS

How I wish that things were
different,
That our lives were only good;
No more problems to be faced with.
Share my dreams, please, if you
would.

See the happy daydreams.
Imagine all the loving nights;
Picture years of family glory,
Erase all the daily, petty fights.

To grow into a silly couple,
With hair of silver grey;
Doing things a little slower,
Than we did them yesterday.

But love brings forth reality.
Our lives aren't quite that way;
The bad and sad are mixed with
good,
Which is not so bad, I'd say.

Yet, as long as we're together,
And we work at being a team;
We can try to make our wishes,
Become much more than just a
dream.

Ezekiel Lewis

THE DRUG BUG

There is a BUG known as a DRUG. Why must we LUG around this DRUG BUG. When it is hated as a BUG, kill the DRUG BUG. We can no longer push this BUG under a RUG. We don't need this DRUG BUG. Because if we keep the DRUG under the RUG, soon some one will look at the hole we have DUG, by sweeping this DRUG BUG under the RUG.

Patricia Louise Carmichael

THE LAND OF MAKE-BELIEVE

The land of make-believe
Be my love forever
Together we will fly to the land of
make-believe
On heightened spirits we will soar
Our souls will join and never grieve

Anna M Salsi

SMILE (AND) FEELING

To my grandchildren with much love, Nana aka Nanny 1987

"Smile"
Hello everybody
Come listen to me
I'll tell you my tales
You will laugh with glee
It seems at times
I can never run down
But I surely do, as
Evening comes
On with my gown.

"feeling"
Take a slow walk down some lane
And time to look out your window
pane
Walk in fields of green grass wet
with dew
This whole world is beautiful and
not so new
Listen to the birds and see them in
flight
Look up at the stars that cover the
sky at night
Take some ones hand and walk
with them in love
It will make you feel light as a dove
Put a smile on your face it will light
up your way
Say something nice to someone
each day
All in all enjoy life now
As the days slip by quickly
somehow.

Beatrice Aurora Barry

WHAT IS A ROSE?

A Rose is the sweetness of Spring;
The fulfillment of summer;
The endlessness of forever;
The expectancy of birth;
The anxiety of love.

A rose is a baby's warm touch;
A child's sudden smile;
A Mother's soft hand;
A fireplace glowing;
The comforts of home.

A rose is the meaning of life;
The strength of pure courage;
The cure of all ills;
The faith in a prayer;
The believing in God

A rose is humanity . . .
Filled with humility.

John E Faust

CAP

The Fausts The Skalstads The Ocean—I Miss You All

I'd watched the old man walk alone
along the sandy shore,
he'd say "Hello," and be on his
way
"Hello" and nothing more.

Curiosity got the best of me
one day when I spied him
walking,
I asked him what his name
might be
he just smiled and started
talking.
He said his friends just called
him Cap,
those who weren't yet dead;
said he'd been around for eighty
years
and for sixty he'd been wed.

He spoke about his married life
with a woman he called Jean.
I could tell by the twinkle in his
eyes
how in love he must have been.

He told me that she'd passed
away
and that now he was all alone,
that he walks this beach where
they used to play
running barefoot in the white
ocean foam.

He told me how Jean loved the
sea
and of the walks they used to
take,
how he'd spread her ashes where
they should be
out among the great waves that
break.

We walked and talked for hours
on end
Cap never seemed to tire
and when we parted he called
me friend
I'd a feeling his spirits were
higher.

That was the last time that I ever
saw Cap
for the next day old Cap passed
away
but I know there's a beach
wherever he's at
and he walks with his Jean . . .
everyday.

Dad

Delore A Beach

DAD

He was ten times taller than me,
Five times when he knelt on his
knee
To pray or touch a small cedar tree,
His weathered hands were as big
as hams,
With which he would help any
man.
At times, he would speak with his
tongue in cheek,
And make believe it was true.
But the words that he spoke,
Through the campfire smoke,
Were as true as the blue of the sky.
His boots were scuffed by the
sands of time,
He was wearing them the day that
he died.
And, yes, "You bet,"
The crown in his hat was still high.

Karin Michelle Hickey

THE TIME JESUS AND I HELD HANDS

Once the Lord came down to me.
And said, "Oh, my child how do I
love thee"
So come if you will my little one.
Please come and follow me.
So I followed Him without a sound.
As I walked on curiously.
I spoke not a word.
Like a weak, frightened bird.
And spoke not a word did he.
I followed him high.
I followed him low.
As I gazed at him.
Surrounded with light, All aglow.
I then gathered my thoughts.
And I told him, I loved him.
With all my heart, soul and mind.
As he gently reached out his
powerful hand.
And delicately, He touched mine.
So He said, "My child please
remember this, I truly do love
thee."
"And if you follow Jesus Christ the
Lord, then anything can be."
He said, "It does not matter where
you follow me."
"Whether it be on water or whether
it be on land."
"I will always love you child and
throughout your life I will hold
your hand"

Gerald H Skinner

WILDCAT BLUES

I can remember back when I was
A small lad, living in the wildcat
Country with my Mom and Dad. I
Was always having some kind of a
Cold, or running around with a
Runny nose. No toys to play with as
I can remember, until the time
come
for the month of December, my
Dad
Bought a little farmers pride
coastel
Wagon at Punk McLaughlin's
store,
No need to look around because
there
Would be no more. My folks sent
me
To school with Broagan shoes on
my
Feet, and when I wore a hole in
them
Wading through the snow my feet
were
Red as a beet. Then on saturday we
Would walk three mile to town to
look
For stick on soles to put on the old
Broagan shoes, then Dad would
peel off
The paper and stick them on while
Singing me the blues. I want you
to know
Son I work hard at the brickyard
all the
Time, and these stick on soles cost
me
A dime. I had to work hard to milk
the
Cow, slop the hogs and feed the
chickens,
I worked so hard for those stick on
soles

They said, I worked as hard as the dickens.
Wildcat school was a good place to go,
Even if I did learn so slow. I
Can still remember way back when.
About my pet chicken Marcella she was
A beautiful little red hen. She was
Always going around a cluckin day and
Night, sometimes she would play with me
A peck on my toes and we would get into
A fight. I would yell and kick and
Pull my hair, and away she would fly
Up in the air, away up on the hen
House she would go, and just sit and
Cluck and watch me below. Those
Days are gone now and I just sit and
Think, so I guess I'll get out of this
Old chair and go to the refrigerator
And get a Big Red and pop the lid
And sit back and have a drink.

Homer Lesihau

I AM A REFUGEE, AND THE POET OF TWO WORLDS

Born to be poet in life,
Live to create rhythm of truth by heart, by mind,
Time trek co-functioned with realistic perception.
so, there are verses that bear the notes of music,
There are prose that mimicry the happiness, the sorrow!

Yesterday, the mystic youth, now and tomorrow . . .

Past cruel war, poems are sobbed with tear and wound,
When man-made thundering bomber roared to blast the earth,
Human flesh scattered the soil, with cries and painful sounds!
Mother nature depressed over the land of fire and blood,
When pray only silenced by the enlightening rockets and bullets!

Where I was and so it will be reflected, by scene and by memory . . .

The wonderful youth is a nature of romance to be with,
The perfume river, the wind-song-bamboo trees bound hamlet,
The harmonic flute sound, the echoing of the pagoda bell,
Grander scenery, there is vast rice field waves the breeze.
Folk songs floating on the river with oars water-splash base!

Moon shined night, when thousand stars flickering light paint, . . .

Alas! The scenes are changed, from sky to machine emphasis,
Romance of the nature contests with that of sex and Atom power,
Still I am the poet, with or without poem reader, even,
In the sky people talk of money and body show, or politics . . T.V. boasts the physical orgasm,
Radio purl hi-brainwave noises!

At the odd of the world, I just continue citing out my verses,
For now and tomorrow, I keep on living, dreaming . . .

Miss Debra Jane Decker

UNKNOWN ENDING

The world goes around in 365 days,
What do you get out of it a big never ending maze.
It all has to stop but you'll never know when,
As soon as one stops another shall begin.
The name of this game is so called life,
The corners and the edges are sharp as a knife.
If it goes dull and starts to fall apart,
It shall never go any where or never ever start.
If you know what you're doing and doing it well,
Your life will be accomplished like the burning coals of hell.
You think you know yourself but you really don't know,
You never know what may happen next your life could stop to grow.

Margaret Sylvester

THE UPS AND DOWNS OF LIFE

A little bird told me, if I was to fly,
I had to look to the heavens, right up to the sky;

I had to believe in myself, have faith in my God,
but, should I lose faith and fall to the sod;

I should pick myself up and start over again,
shake off all the dirt, discouragement, and sin;

expect, with my Father, to soar through the air,
to see all the beauty that God placed out there.

I've soared near the heavens and fallen to ground,
but, with help from my Father, I'm still safe and sound.

Rev Elmer D Colcord

THE BOY WHO WAS SPANKED BY A GHOST

Before the low and rounded mound
The boy stopped as he heard a sound,
"Wah-ho-min! Wah-ho-min!
The door was ajar so he looked in:
"Hello! Hello in there! Hello, I say!
What are you doing in there today?
Better come out and we'll play!
Miggles or jack-knives! Let's see!
And anyway, you can't catch me!
Was it the wind that said "Ha-ee! Ha-ee!"

The scared boy turned and ran pell-mell;
He tripped on a rock and fell,
He'd scratched his face and his backside hurt
But he scrambled up and with a spurt
He reached safety behind a tree—
Was it the wind that said Ha-ee! Ha-ee!

The boy derived from his report
Much notoriety of a sort
And like to have his companions find
Spank marks on his slim behind.
The Old Men differed on that score:
"Boy, you might have been punished more!
Atisken, roused, is full of spite!"
You were lucky! Lucky—quite!

Willie Lakey Jr

WHERE DO WE GO FROM HERE?

Native born is the man I am with freedom as my foot steps and liberty as my charm
I've raised victory to its highest form
"Where do we go from here!"

The bitterness we'v faced
The tears we'v let fill our face
The bloodshed for our slaughter without grace
The glomness of our past
The casting of our last.
"Where do we go from here?"

The shadows stand, the hands tremble with the fear of man, the eyes stand ready for the new born man.

Has the dark past taught us at last?
"Where do we go from here?"

Stonie are the roads that we have troded, bitterness are the chasting rod.
Out from the gloomy past till now we stand, at last our victory can be won with "God" Great hand.
Less our feet stray from "God" we'll never know
Harmony of his heart.
"Now where do you go from here?"

Jeannette L Linker

THE POET

In the still of night
When children don't fight, and
Bills don't have to be paid,
I sit down and write,
What could be and might, or lay
Where queens have lain.
With my pen is where I begin
But with the last line I won't stop,
For some other night when things are right,
The poet will write again.

Ernest Lynn Balmforth

ON THE FLOOR BY THE DOOR

Between the door and the floor is a world well known
hidden away from the light of the day
Believing, as truth, what others have said
caught in between "I know" and "they say."

That world is little, and narrow, and dark
overflowing with feelings of shame
Having listened to others, their words and their shouts
demanding we all be the same.

The shame is in shrinking to the floor by the door
not knowing it will open at will
For others it swings wide open at times
for those with no faith it stays closed and sealed.

So, where is the door that will let me pass through
to walk in the light of the sun
The door is my mind, the floor is the world
where I must decide how my thinking is done.

Between the door and the floor only a few walk on through with their faith, being able to see
I must know from within I am part of the plan
that remains incomplete without me.

If I listen to you without believing in me
my thoughts will be little and poor
My faith and belief must be mine and for me
or I'll stay in the world on the floor by the door.

Lourdes Barredo Potter

MY LONG LOST LOVE

This poem is dedicated to the GOD OF ABRAHAM, to ALL THE PEOPLE WHO WANT to get HEALED, AND MOST ESPECIALLY to Keith Bradshaw.

It was in the Island where the America's days begin.
When my profound love to a man began.
He comes to me like a sunrise shining in the sky.
Inspiring me with his smile.
His word was so gentle that gently remains into the mind of my heart.
Suddenly he vanish away.
For he was a stranger to my life.
For the Lord up above used him as a bait!
To carry on my mission he used him for commission.
My Love you are long lost, like a needle in a stock of hay.
But I'll find the way to search you throughout eternity.
For you are the prize of my heart.
After I will fullfill my mission.
To tell the mankind of their salvation.
That every problem has a solution.
Like the aid who frightened up the mankind, killing the victim without salvation.
Every nation don't trust each other
So they built a nuclear for their power.
In some nation there is starvation for they know not the mighty powers.
Around the earth the airs goes round stirring the life of every mankind.
But I know you, MY LONG LOST LOVE, you are still around.
For you are in the land of Liberty that gave the people bread and Honey.
So then my Dear Long lost love

enjoy your life.
While I'm doing my mission.
For I know the mighty Power up above is with me and you my love.

Felix Dickinson
RENAISSANCE

You went away to explore strange land
You feel hungry and also cold
You went away to find shelter
But your shelter was my silence and my cold.
You will miss my dreams and my passioned love.
The cruel winter came along.
Without light and without dreams
You went away, and my dreams increased, without any hope.
But today when I feel the times go by
And I remember your hair and your face
I came to realize that you only left a gray
Winter on a withered spring.
Today you returned to my life
Longing for my dreams
Dreams that staying with yesterday
I'm a dreamer, fantastic dreamer
Only the death is your hope, laeonic and sincere.
Faithful to hope of a clean renaissance
"To God" you will go. Rebirth in another world.
You will receive.

Elizabeth Fox Grifenhagen
THE PEN

I hang on to the old ways,
Of making life's path;
And find lately that in me
That's stirring up wrath.

Now why should this be
All happening to me?
Is God telling me something,
That life is waiting for me?

That there's another path in life
That now I should take?
And the urge keeps telling me,
Try it for his sake.

Will it be another dream of mine'
That will come true,
Because God planted the seed
And then it grew?
My whole body cries out.
Pick up the pen, keep writing
And only then,
Will you know the answer
To the urge of the pen

Tamara L Henderson
MY CHILD

It was Saturday night
But it wasn't right.
Then the call came in—
My child needed picked up.

"Not my child!
You must have the wrong number!
He doesn't drink-n-drive
He promised never again."

It was Saturday night
But it wasn't right.
Then the call came in . . .
My child needed identified!

"Not my child—he doesn't drink-n-drive
You must have the wrong number!
It must be hers!
Not my child—he promised never again!

As I look out the window
I know he promises now
because he is . . .
DEAD!

Lesley Dean Dougherty

Lesley Dean Dougherty
OLD BESSY

To Mommy and Daddy, who patiently listened to me writing "Old Bessy" on the way to my first World of Poetry Convention in Orlando, with love. Was issued the Golden Poet Award.

Old Bessy's comin' in—she's a good old faithful cow.
I can hear her bell a ringin', right now that good old cow.
She's a leadin' the pack, head of 'em all,
I swear that cow will never fall,
With her ringle-dingle-dangle-moo-moo,
Ringle-dingle-dangle-moo-moo.

Here comes Bessy now, OH NO!
Look at that cow!
She's a chewin' her cud out in the meadow,
playing with the birds and every single fellow.
Bessy's comin' round the bend.
She's a stomping her feet and then,
Snortin', Snortin', Snortin',
I swear that cow is mad—she's bad!

Old Bessy wants a milkin'
a milk—milk—milk—
and a szs—szs—szs,
She swishes her tail,
then knocks over the milk pail.
Oh, that clumsy cow!

As if that weren't enough, she steps in a puddle of muck,
Tracks it on the floor, inside and out doors—
That clumsy cow of mine.
BESSY! BESSY! BESSY!
Here comes Bessy now,
That cow!!!

Patricia A Eick
JUST A PIECE OF WOOD

"That's just a piece of wood," I heard them say,
As they looked passed me again today—
I've laid in this pile of splintering strife
For many years in our workshop of life.
I've laid in a corner gathering mildew and dust,
Where I've developed my "protective" crust—
Feeling more useless as the days went by,
I started to crumble, then, to cry.

The moisture had left me disfigured and rough,
So, I thought to myself, "I've had enough" —
Just when I figured I'd be kindling wood,
There came the Carpenter who understood.

Reshaping each grain with loving care,
He polished me into something rare—
Now, they see me as something good,
Since He's restored this piece of wood.

Gary Alton Waltemire
CRYSTAL CASTLES

To my nephews, and nieces for their interest in my writing. Love to them all. Also to my Loving Mother; 70 years young.

Our love is filled with brilliant colors.
Like a view through painted glass.
Lives to be shared by no others:
Just us and pictures of our past.

Visions form like ice blue rain;
Swirling right before our view.
There's no sorrow; There's no pain.
Just the love that's shared by two.

Crystal castles in the sky.
A kaleidoscope of light.
We've seen in each others eyes,
As we held each other tight.

Everyday anticipation;
As we soar to greater heights.
Love like this brings such elation,
as we share our summer nights

Our love has danced upon this earth,
Like lovers of the past.
It gave our lives a joyous birth.
And forever it will last.

Truman "Lee" Wolery
THE EMANCIPATION OF LOVE'S TENDER MOMENTS

Dedicated to the Phoenix Single's Group and, to my four loving children

---

As we sit here entwined about each other
We watch the candles burn mystiquely on.
Their flames dance to a rhythm of desire,
While they cast shadows of love on the wall.
As their tallow grow small
My mood changes . . .
I ponder tomorrow
With yesterday's uncertainties and fears.
Aware of this, you persue
The reality of the present
With an embrace and a kiss!
My senses grow dull with experience.
My mind tormented with the past.
Consult me and
Emancipate my true spirit.
Please give me a sense of being . . .
Secure my stagnate, oppressed ego
With a smile, or
A soft word from your lips.
The dawn approaches.
The candles have long since gone.
A new day arrives . . .
Must it bring another yesterday of emptiness?
It matters not . . .
If even for the few moments I spent with you!

Gran R Harried
nil desperandum . . . never despair

When I hear someone sigh, 'life is hard', I am always tempted to ask, "compared to what?" Grandfather G. Roberto Reyes-Harried

---

When grandfather fished inland,
he did so in some quiet out of the way place.
There in shadows he seemed an improbable seer;
yet not much escaped this most caring man.

Now his face oft showed chagrin,
for he was ever conscious of fault-finding
like most men, even then.

Usually to gain an advantage he yielded
to niggling arguments; . . .
"Make way for liberty," he cried, tugging hard,
scaring away all the fish.
'Virtue such as this had its own reward'.

When the women-folk asked, "where's the fish?"
Grandfather would reply, "back in the lake!"
Then he'd whisper to me, "make no terms laddie;
a wise man knows his own niche."

Know this then in bartering,
no matter how scarce seem enough good answers . . .
only a fool babbles dishearteningly.

Proof then is that oft we are most gullible.
Whoever's conviction is straight-out
somehow alienates the past.
Yet there were no fish that night,
as grandfather nodded ever so slight.

Jane Ellen Emerson
MY STRENGTH

To my Lord and Savior, who truly is my strength.

Lord I knew to follow you would not be easy, I didn't know the devil would launch his attack against me.
I finally know the meaning of faith in you, its hanging strong to your word when life gets cruel.
The comfort of knowing you see my plight. Encourages me to
continue my Christian fight.
To know the outcome with you by my side, helps me to take the

mountains and valleys in stride.
The real test is when all is right,
will I keep you as much in sight.
I pray!

Deborah S Ivester
DESTINED

Though everybody's special
in their own way
Some may be able to See
What others cannot
Yet someday in the future
the change will likely to be
Some will be in Solitude
While others shall be free
As spirits and butterflies
in the mist of the golden trees

In this Joyous Destineal Moment of Time
A Soothing Voice will softly say
"Fly, and thy shall be free
in this graceful, very gentle breeze."

Mabel I Bunting

Mabel I Bunting
ALL THROUGH THE NIGHT

With love to my late parents, Mark and Maggie Jones who believed in my writing ability. Husband George for his endurance. My children, grand, and great grandchildren, ALL.

Nights can be ominous, shadowy and dark,
when your sleepless, worried and full of fright.
Thoughts spin webs, with a chilling spark,
that rack your weary mind until the morning's light.
How grateful, thankful, for the east skie's early gleam,
assuring a new day's dawning with hope and reality.
To chase away anguish, and renew life's true dream,
that was cause for the shaking of your meek personality.

Quickly arise, refresh yourself with shower or bath,
dress neatly and casual, and hurry eagerly outside.
Stroll slowly down your rose lined garden path,
breath deeply of the fragrant, misty air, in nostalgic pride.
All your troubles dwindle, as living nature takes charge,
where sunrays sparkle on dewdrop covered foliage and tree,
sheltering chattering birds, some being tiny, others large,
making your spirit soar, and your heart sing happy and free.

Away with ominous, sleepless, nights,
give us all sweet sleep and heavenly dreams,
about crystalline snowflakes, bright summer kites,
and glorious spaceships we can ride through moonbeams.
Hopefully dawn will awake us totally rested,
calm, bright eyed, aware that life is all right,
for in meditation and prayer we have requested
Guardian Angels to keep us, ALL THROUGH THE NIGHT.

Gretchen Novak
HUMANITY?

Surrounded by the giddy and content
Sitting in satisfied comfort of my own
I recall the crippled expression of the man without a home
He was like a Piccaso painting, contorted in despondent pain waiting only for the nighttime.
So the sunrise may greet him again.
Well.
Who cares?
Who knows enough, to extend a hand to him?
The vile veracity of the situation emits only chagrin.
But do you remember the last time hunger stabbed you like a knife?
Do you remember the last time the streets determined your life?
Early in the morning while we sip the day's incentive, the homeless of the world are a little more inventive
They wake to find their bed of dirt is also coffee and dessert.
And the winds that furs so bravely fight became their blanket for the night.
This is a problem whose solution is the problem within itself
opportunities cannot exist where they do not present themselves.
There are no funds or programs, we just say what's done is done.
But that broken vision of a man was born somebodys' son.
So if you turn your head away, ignoring what you're seeing
Just remember you turned blind on the demise of a human being.

Elizabeth Howell
MISSING AGAIN

My little boy is missing again
Oh God, how I hate that disease
The waste it causes is such a sin
And it buries the feelings in deep freeze.

There must be a way to reach my child
Who is hidden beneath the drugs
My mind goes crazy, frantic and wild
'Cause, I cannot reach him with hugs.

It hurts to know there is nothing to do
Except to stand helplessly by
To feel the pain, watch the view
And pray he will not die.

As long as there's breath inside of him
I hang on tightly to hope
He'll face the truth he holds within
And win his struggle with dope.

As I pray for the miracle to finally come
I strive to work on me
For only this way can I help my son
Work on his recovery.

So God, the only thing left to say
Watch over my dear little boy
He'll return to us some sunny day
And my heart will be filled with joy.

Ruben Vielma Espinoza
MYSTERY

From the sky above comes a mystery.
Who's to understand the glow of its realm,
Its environmental esteem,
the beautiful gleam.
What force made it about.
Some say from a burst
Others from creation.
From whence, does the wind comest
to where does it blow.
Wisdom echoes its roar
hear its voice at the door,
The wise will comprehend
The fool will find his end.
The wise will solve the mystery
the fool will end in greater misery
wake up and hear
because the end is near
The mystery will be solved at last
so do your thinking fast.

Vicki L Bryan
AMERICAN RELIGION

No artillery gunfire just outside my window,
No one gonna shoot me for my faith;
Few, if any, ask me why I love Christ so,
American religion: free, unscathed.

Dressing, Sunday mornings, just to please the crowd,
Attempting outer holiness, the claim.
Listening to a preacher, neither long nor loud,
Leaving just the same as when we came.

Daily routines at my home and working place,
Free from Jesus' power in my life;
My example wouldn't change the human race,
To show that Jesus frees from sin and strife.

Appearances deceiving, are they? Not to fret:
Jesus said, "You'll know them by their fruits."
Weekly life depicts how Sunday morn we met,
Above-ground growth shows what's at the roots.

The joy of knowing Jesus as my King and Lord
Provides a simple challenge for me now.
Trusting in the cause for which His blood was poured,
I'll show the world the One to whom I bow.

Hypocrisy, religion, twined, and off they go
To beat down helpless masses every day.
But those around me won't mistake my inner glow,
I'll tell them it's the price that Jesus paid.

Mary-Jo Garza
TEN

I'm tired of playing grown-up,
Please give me a few moments,
I want to be ten again.
A carefree time with no worries,
No troubles, no pain.
In the next few moments
Let me grow up in your eyes,
I want to laugh, romp, and play,
As all spoiled children do.
I want to become a teenager,
With you at my side,
Wipe away my adolescent tears,
Oh, let me relive the days,
Of secret crushes and stolen glances.
My first date, the first kiss,
And the ultimate no.
Stay over my shoulder,
And influence my decisions.
Please give me a few moments,
And I'll grow up with you.

Kenneth

Elia Garcia Gonzales
OUR THANKS

This poem is dedicated to Kenneth, please know that God is always near and reaching out to help you because like us, he loves you very much!

I prayed to you Dear God, St. Jude and the Virgin Mary too,
I don't know what I would have done
had it not been for you.

To you St. Therese and Infant of Prague

so powerful so strong,
For being there when everything
seemed to be going wrong.

The Virgin of Guadalupe and
Sacred Heart of Jesus
a special thanks to you,
You did for me exactly
what I asked of you to do.

I asked of you a favor
that you make our Kenneth well,
You listened to my every prayer
for I could clearly tell.

When things got really tough and
grim
I prayed to you the more.
I knew Dear God, You'd help me
as you've always done before.

Our precious Kenneth is getting
better
and much stronger every day,
It's plain to see dear God,
"Thank-you!"
You wanted it this way.

To all his friends who gave so much
Your prayers too were heard,
For God listens to our every need.
He didn't miss a word.

We thank You again, we thank You
much
our hearts are filled with love,
We've got our precious Kenneth
back—
THANKS TO OUR GOD ABOVE!

Adlai A Esteb
GATEWAY OF THE NEW YEAR
Another New Year's gate now
opens wide,
Inviting us to come and look inside
And turn our eyes from hist'ry that
is dead,
To prophecies and dreams that lie
ahead.
The future is before us, and, like
clay,
Gives us the chance to mold it as
we may.

We stand upon the threshold of
a door
That closes now on all that's gone
before.
'Tis irretrievable, and angels keep
The record till its harvest we shall
reap.
Since yesterday is buried with the
past,
We can't recall it, for the die is cast.

The past is static: nothing we do
now
Can change the record or new
life endow.
The future is dynamic: that's our
clue,
To transform it by everything we
do.
So plan your resolutions: make
them great,
As Christ now leads you through
this New Year's gate!

Linda Isenburg Fasig
PEACE
How does it feel to live in peace
To know the calm of hate's
surcease?
Who puts this yearning in the
breast
Which guides the wiseman's
humble quest?
What master thought exudes such
grace
Then disappears without a trace?
When shall we grasp love's simple
plan,
And live the Golden Age of Man
Where time and space and fear are
nought
And only harmony is taught?

It happens in each human soul
It's individuations goal.
We hold the lock and key within
Which conquers anger, fear and
sin.
The lock which guards the gentle
heart
Bids eccentricity depart.
The key then opens wide the door
Love's light floods in, we're free
once more.
Come help me now, please hold my
hand,
We've harmony to teach the land.

Shirley P Forsyth
IF YOU CAN WALK THE ROAD OF LIFE IN SILENCE

With love to my daughter Cheryle

If you can reminice without hate
or malice
Tho' they that hurt you, still never
cease
To cast another stone
For life is but a walkway, the marks
We make, like stardust on the snow
And the springtime comes
The stardust still remains
For all the world to see, yet none
To know.
So let me have the privilege
Of meeting life in silence
Yet not so silent, that I cannot
Speak
For Jesus said, the word in all its
glory
Shall be welcomed.
By my little children, by the
humble
And by the very meek

Ida Pack
FAITH

Dedicated to God fearing Americans, living in the eighties.

As the sun sank slowly in the west,
It reminded me of the thing I do
best.
While God lulled me in a deep
sleep,
His angels on watch duty did me
keep.
The clouds moved slowly across
the sky
And grew dimmer as slowly they
did die.

The trees threw a shadow shown
down below
As God stilled the winds that
earlier did blow.
They whispered sweet music as
they quieted down,
And the noises in the villages no
more did sound.

The moon began slowly to rise,
It lit up the shadow seen earlier in
the skies.
Which sent a warm feeling that
came over me,
I was not alone, as earlier I felt to
be.
All I needed now as I looked up
above
Was to lie still, as I felt the warmth
of Gods love.

This world we live in is not so bad,
With God controlling it we need
not be sad.
So we live and look forward to
another day,
And ask God to always with us stay.
May He guide our tongue and our
steps too,
That we might please Him in all
that we do,

Helen T Ross

Helen T Ross
MAGNIFICENT AMATEURS
Call ye only upon thee
Yet sing with glee
Thrust upon mine futile glorious
feats
Steathy, sturdy heart abound yea!
with force
Lo! behold! look beyond hear thy
servant cries
Fabricco! Fabricco! nay close thy
eyes

Just but say true the like of thee
time will tell
Roam the endless moors as
seasons change oceans swell
Cloak thy torments vines of love
yea! yet do appear
Come then harken embrace me my
dear nay no fear

Merrily I beckon not withstanding
in awe
Come clasp thy hand hold me back
mistaken lovers
Yet find we nay folklore
Calmest calmest thy will is here
yea! yea!
Fabricco! Fabricco!
Thy love is clear follow me not into
darkest nights
nay shed no tear Amateur
players this role doth hold
Fabricco' Fabricco' warm thy way
not to stumble
in harms way nay' not this day
fools play
Ameuteur lovers gentle hearts they
mend
Nay Lord lest we die without a
friend' without a friend'

Patrice Greenwood
DISTANCE
I felt so lonely last night without
you.
I needed a friend to talk to . . .
. . . You spent the evening with her.
I yearned to feel your kiss upon my
lips . . .
. . . Somehow, her lips got in the
way.
I needed your closeness to assure
our love was real.
. . . You enthralled her with
exuberant passion.
I needed to look into your eyes and
see you say "I love you" . . . . .
You looked into hers and
watched her say it to you.
I cried myself to sleep feeling
empty and alone . . .
. . . You drifted into dreamland, in
ecstatic fatigue.
I had only my pillow to cling to . . .
. . . As you were clinging ever so
tightly to her.

DAMN THE DISTANCE!

Ad Fried
WHAT IS OUR DESTINY?

Dedicated to the brilliant Eddie-Lou Cole, who is inspiring to every aspiring poet she serves.

Life may be happy, life may be
great;
In life, each of us has a stake.
Right now, most of destiny we
ignore,
Yet, there we may remain
forevermore.
Where do we go? Where is the end?
Is it Heaven, or to what amend?
Good works become our legacy,
Unless we deserve only ignominy?
By our good deeds, we shall be
known.
If we arrive at our eternal home?
So, don't end up with a low score.
Do your best . . . and even more!
For you, will it be Heaven on high?
Or lost paradise, blocked by cloudy
sky?
Put it all together and maybe,
maybe . . .
Its reincarnation in a new baby?
Or, could it be our good deeds
done,
Lead to immortality and basking
in His sun?
Let's sing the praise of Him on
High,
Maybe we'll become another star
in the sky?
Our body returns to dust, our soul
to Heaven, it must!
Long live a good memory of the
best of us,
For when we go, be brave, for in
God we trust!

Betty Napier
POLITICAL ROAD
Election time is coming
I know this to be true
Equipment is humming
From the highway crew
The ditches are clean
A few gravels are dropped
Politicians use our dream
Your road will be blacktopped.
As they shake your hand
And hand you their card
They promise you as they stand
So be on your guard
A promise from a political man
Should not be given in heed
They do what they can
But not for people in need
Promises have been many
For people on route five forty two
I'd sell mine for just one penny
Because none of them are true

People please be aware
At who knocks upon your door
It is probably the biggest liar
You have ever met before.

Rocky Petrella
STEEL MILLS

To the hard working steel workers of the U.S.A. Who made our country strong God bless them all.

Steel mills, the heart of a nations strong.
Those looming giants of yesteryear dirty and dusty.
Truly the king, America growing up.
Blast furnace, and fiery open hearth pouring hot molten iron and steel.
Long smokestacks, reaching high into the air, spewing smoke billowy, and black with flying dusty ash.
Twenty-four hours a day she never ceases her weary toil, producing iron ingots, and hot oily cold rolled steel.

Strong men, red and ruddy faced with backs bending shoveling scrap, ore and coal into fiery furnaces roar.
Heat unbearable, with dancing, and crackling flames reaching for the open door.
Days work ended, lunch pails swinging, tired men's faces blackened from dust, and dirt wander home.
Men of strength, and character, men of honest faith walking in their own footsteps to an existence.
Silent now they stand, an era past, echoes of days gone by.
Shadows like ghosts, an eerie creeping feeling of loneliness, and sadness.
Closed gates! No admittance! Keep out!
Lonely twisting rails, soundless engines standing staunch.
No squeaky wheels or clanging bell.
Rusty nature takes it's course.
As I walk this path once more, I dream, and reflect as visions return to my mind.
I glance once more with heavy heart,
"AND SLOWLY, BUT SADLY WALK INTO REALITY"

Nelda K Guthrie
THE FOG
Enshrouded in fog like a corpse in a tomb,
Encased in darkness as a babe in a womb,
And naught could be heard in the night.

The big foghorn roared its message at sea,
"Beware what's ahead in the fog for thee."
And naught would be spared in the night.

The small foghorn screeched, "You shouldn't be here,
You must guide your ship well and not come too near."
And naught can be told in the night.

It's dark and it's dense so as no man can see,
What may lie ahead in the darkness for thee.
And naught can be seen in the night.

There's dead and there's dying on the weathered old boat.
The masts and the sails scarcely keep it afloat.
And naught can be helped in the night.

Adrift and at sea sinking slow to the sand,
The mate and the crew will each die by his hand.
And naught will be found in the night.

Gaia Elana S Watson
HAPPINESS
Happiness is like a robin's cheery song, singing on a rainy day.
Although today the skies may seem to be grey, the sun will shine another day.
For with a little help from the robins cherry song and along with the shining sun.
Tomorrow has only just begun.
For the robin's cheery song and the shinning sun is Happiness rolled all into one.

Mary Jane Boarman
FEELINGS FOR YOU!
The loneliness I feel,
Seems so unreal
Without you my Baby.
I'm a very sad lady.
You make my life so complete,
And trying to live without you,
Makes me so weak.
Sure we've had our ups and downs,
but that's what makes our world go 'round.
What I need is to be in your loving arms,
feeling your tenderness, and admiring your charm.
When you have me in your embrace,
My heart always takes off in a race.
Because only you my love,
Can make me feel as innocent as a dove.
When we once again reunite,
May our love life always be just right.

Monika Poulson
JUSTICE
God made the laws an age ago
to live, to prosper and to grow,
"I set before you good and bad,"
we throw away the chance we have.
Our choice is made without good reason
the land is overrun by treason,
we kill, we maim, we lie, we rob
and then we cry, "Where is our God?"

Our motto is in "In God we trust"
and yet the heart is filled with lust,
we've given up morality
and settled for iniquity.

Robert James Southam
WHO TAUGHT THEM?

This poem dedicated to the Glory of God

They say the world just happened to be,
And everything living crawled out of the sea.
The animals and birds, and humans too,
That means everything, even me and you.

Can you believe in a tale like this?
That everything living came from a fish.
Just look around you at all the wonders
Could all these things have come from a blunder?

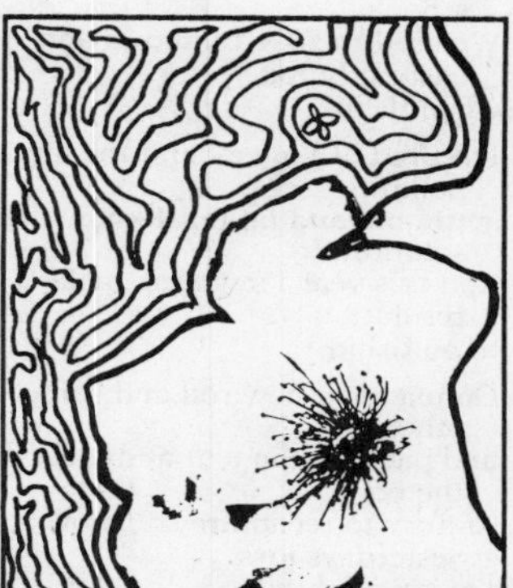

Take the birds how they weave a nest,
The flowers and trees knowing just when to rest.
When winter comes the bear stores up fat,
Crawls into a den, who taught him that?

Salmon swim to where they were born,
Who taught them to go there and spawn?
And don't you think that it's kind of funny
How those bees learned to make that honey?

And don't that robin seem pretty smart
To hear a worm in the ground, and then pull it apart?
Did you ever plant a garden putting the seeds in a row?
How do they know when it's time to grow?

Who taught the grass to come up in the spring?
And all them birds their songs to sing?
Does this little poem drive you up a wall?
Or do you know who taught them all?

Juanita J Deanes
SIMPLE FAITH

To my three children, Billy, Jo and Janet

Yesterday I had a great sorrow
Grief filled my heart with pain.
Would this darkness ever pass?
Would the sun ever shine again?

But I turned to God in my sorrow
And He softly called my name,
"Have Faith, My Child,
And I'll give you the power
To smile and be happy again."

Jessie L King
TOMORROW

Dedicated to all who encourage positive things in others.

I once time boarded rubber raft,
The current swift as might,
Where chartered courses find no place.
Or destination sight.
And had no thought to alter it,
To tame, speed up, slow down;
It's self-made will, the beauty of,
Is what I surely found!
And made no link, as one might phrase,
With auto-mat device,
But marveled at its great white foam,
Against the best advice.
There sometime is, in all of us,
To board the mighty branch,
And of a cup so seldom took,
To drink until we're drunk!
And wonder at the "best lain plans"
The chance it seldom takes
For who can know the silent course
"Tomorrow"
Sometimes
Makes!

Chris Ridolfo
LONG JOURNEY BEGINS
Opulent stained glass death
satin pillow and you're
on your way.
Perfumed paradise or the
road to Hades?
But you, in silent refrain,
give no hint
to answer, where to
you travel?
Slip quietly into place with flowers by your side
Cultural displays of ritual and delusion; confusion, tears spent
as the price for feeling one moment immortal.
Smile once more my friend,
for guests and relatives,
then we shall put you down,
deep-dark in earth
splendor,
back to our beginning.
Farewell,
till we meet again!

Elizabeth A Frisbie
ONE ROSE
Like a soft wind her voice caressed me in the rain.
It touched the heart of my being, and turned my head,.
Her wrinkled face and knowing

eyes searched me out.
I raised my hand and touched her wet cheek.
She handed me a red rose, smiled, and turned away.
Like a soft wind her voice caressed me in the rain.
My eyes followed her as she walked to the corner,
to sell her flowers.

She turned once, her eyes empty, and then sadly left.
Her wrinkled face, and knowing eyes searched me out.
The church bells ring, and a casket is buried in the
sand.
It takes me back to a day when we once met.
Like a soft wind her voice caressed me in the rain.
She with her rose, and me with my heart, we came
together.
Only her memory follows me as I put a single
rose on her grave.

Her wrinkled face and knowing eyes searched me out.
My hand shakes as I wipe a wetness from my cheek.
Always I will remember my mother with a rose
and a smile.
Like a soft wind her voice caressed me in the rain.
Her wrinkled face and knowing eyes searched me out.

Aline Piche'-Whissell

Aline Piche'-Whissell
LSD
Off the quietude of neap-tide . . .
Slyly the swell pulls you and lifts you up
Inexorably rolls you out to the sea
Receding ever increasingly further and higher

Straw speck, colourless, swept away by the wave
Mercilessly fighting against the infernal cycle
You are the wave and the ultimate drop
Glittering through the immense delirium

Between two infinities, where you waver
For a moment of eternity you are holding on
On the thin thread of a blade you settle
You keep hold of your soul, thrusting aside death
Death, greedy and millenial faced
Death bloodless face, lips stuck to the teeth
Then, the one beacon only, on the lost horizon
That acuteness of yours lights up
Saving you from final chaos where you were sinking.

Robert D Mann
FISHIN
When I was a kid I remember still
an old fishin hole just over the hill
Where the crick splashes in and you can get your fill
of fishin.

I used to hike for miles along that crick
so many good spots you could take your pick
And the only pole I had was a willow stick
for fishin.

It's funny how after the years roll by
you suddenly remember that blue, blue sky
Of the springtime of life when you and I
went fishin.

It all comes back now, that babbling brook
with a stick for a pole and a pin for a hook
We used to snag rainbows and eastern brook
when fishin.

I'm tired of the city and the air pollution
gettin old and fat but I know the solution
And this year I'm gonna make a resolution
to go fishin.

Gonna get a new rod and some other toys
and pack up the tent and take all the boys
And try to recapture some of yesterdays joys
I'm goin fishin.

It never occured to me before, this way
but I'm gettin anxious and I'm here to say
Can't hardly wait for opening day
to go fishin.

Gonna load up the stuff in the Jemmy truck
and try for those big ones just to watch em buck
Goin back on the he-haw to try my luck
at fishin.

Tired of workin extra all the time
puttin in double shifts and overtime
missin all the fun for an extra dime
I'm goin fishin.

Money ain't everything, or so they say
gonna live my life just for today
Might even throw my cigarettes away
and go fishin.

When I'm old and feeble and gettin kinda slow
I'll still chase rainbows wherever I go
If I don't come back then you will know
I went fishin.

C Mae Aschwege
OH MY FRIEND
Oh my friend.
not very long it's been
you left, to the promised land
with a ring, on your hand
from your special friend

Oh my friend
I'm waiting here below
not wanting my feeling to show
That I'm missing you so
But hoping that you know

Oh my friend
My feeling so strong
But are they wrong
Your special friend
Her heart not long to mend
Is it a sin
Her love, was it pretend

Lee Allen Davis

Lee Allen Davis
FEELINGS OF LOVE

This poem is dedicated to Maria Selene Villa (D.), my one and only future wife. I love her always and forever . . . Lee Allen Davis

Love is a feeling
So deep inside,
If the feelings are true
Why should they hide,
Lets act as one
And show that we care,
Let's use our love
And be willing to share.

J Morris Waters
SEEKING INSPIRATION
a poem
about what
me
someone
the ocean
some place
a thing?

how shall i write it?
eloquently
tastefully
senselesssly
exceptionally
traditionally

Yes!
my poem could be magnificent
or not so hot . . .

i wonder if the people
will appreciate or understand my poem
maybe i should get a pencil
and just get started,
right?

Richard Saavedra
GOLDEN LEAVES
Golden leaves on distant trees
With colors brown and green
I know when autumn is here
Because that's when you grow
I've seen you sprout
As leaves do
When you began
And I've seen you shrival
And die at the end
But golden leaves
Brown and green
You are still
The most beautiful sight I've ever seen

Elizabeth Smith
GOD'S PERFECT FARM
All the animals live free out here;
Beautiful they are for all who see . . .
Now and then there is a deer
Standing out there, looking at me.

All God's animals we should leave
Free to roam and never harm.
Together with the forest, they all weave
A perfect picture, God's perfect farm

Frances Gerry
JOHN WAYNE
We love you and we miss you John
John Wayne, is the John
That were speaking of
He's gone to heaven
So we send him our love
The world, seems so lonely
Since he went away, and where ever
He is we hope he's happy today
He brought us laughter and sunshine
While he was here and the world seemed
A better place, just having him near
We still have a little, that he left behind
On the big silver screen, where he still looks so fine
And while watching his movies, we forget
For awhile, Johns no longer here with us
He's gone and taken his smile

Samuel James Allen

Samuel James Allen
DOG: SAY—HAY: HOGS

Dedicated To: The care and future of animal life on earth

When all the neighbors dogs begin to bark,
Then I begin to cruise in my Studebaker Lark.

Now that all of the people are going to the dogs,
I think I am going back to raising Polan China Hogs.

Victoria D Johnston

WHAT YOUR FRIENDSHIP MEANS TO ME

Your friendship means so much to me.

You are a special friend.

You are one who understands the me I am.

You are one who attempts to lend a helping
hand to guide me in the right direction.

Through your wisdom of Life I learn to accept
things as they are.

You help me to realize I can not change all
things and to accept things and people as
they are.

Thank you for being my friend.

Carole Elizabeth Monroe

GOALS AND DREAMS

Dedicated to my son Michael Daniel Monroe, my inspiration

Clouds, vaporous hues
Twinged in pink and gray
Drift across the Mars-colored
Sun descending
Into the awaiting arms
Of the purple tides
As winds mild and warm
Whisper thanks for a perfect day
Coming to a close at this
Day's end.

On other horizons the earth
Awakens in the embrace of a
Brilliant orange sky
Dreamily, sleepily, watching
Birds soar on high
Singing praises for a
Virgin day on the
Universes' distant sides.
Such is the continuing
Span of life as each day ends
Another day, new, untouched
Is born that we may
Ascend the steps on lifes' ladder
To persist in fulfilling
The passion and fire
That burn like a Greek torch
Within my heart and soul's
Accomplishment of desires.

Hands, mind, spirit, heart
Reaching across a luminous rainbow
To catch successes beams
That complete the chain of
Delicately woven, but strong
Goals and dreams that
Set us apart
We are the conclusion.

Carmen Lucia Jimenez

SPARKLING COCOON

struggling toward the blue,
blue sky.

choking on life,
yearning to die.

pleasure brings not
a happy face,
but bloodied limbs,
under tattered lace.

questions,
they have asked too long.

explanations—
neither right or wrong.

clawing, climbing
up the moss grown hole
so deep it was dug,
a long, long time ago.

Barbara Wade

CHILDHOOD SNOW GAME

Twas an old photograph of Grandfather and me.
I was only a child, not much older than three.
Pictured, a winter scene on Grandpa's farm,
A place in mind's memories so treasured, so warm.
In the photo we were walking side by side, hand in hand.
Behind us, our footprints cross the snow covered land.
Beside his, my footprints so tiny, so frail
Mere sight of his footprint let memories unveil.
Mind's memories returned to my game in the snow.
I'd follow his footprints to see where they'd go.
Each step in his footprint to see where they'd go.
My red-booted footprint tucked snugly inside.

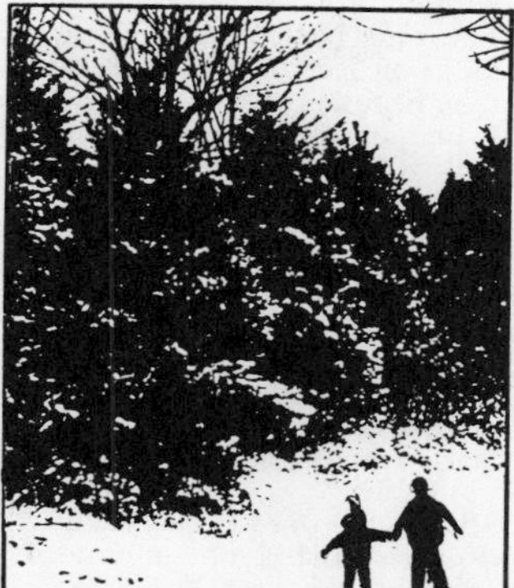

Each movement made slowly with thought and decision
To stay in his footprint took skill and precision.
I'd examine my footprint so fresh and so plain,
And knew my footprint within his would remain.
The game was complete at the end of the track.
My performance I'd judge when I'd turn and look back.
Game played with perfection if his prints only I'd view
Yet, while looking at one set, I knew there were two.
Did he find my footprints as his path he retrod?
Or were they known only, to me and to God?
I wonder, do children still play my snow game?
Is it intriguing to them? Are the rules the same?
Whose footprints do they follow? I'd like to know;
Will I find tiny footprints in my footprinted snow?
If prints found within mine, will the path be the same
As the dear trail I followed in my childhood snow game?

Mary M Schwarz

WHEN I FORGET

When sunny skies shall smile no more
When waves no longer woe the shore
When every sweet voiced bird has fled
When every summer rose is dead
When stars forsake the evening sky
When hearts with love shall cease to sigh
When silvery mists desert the glen
I may, perhaps, forget you then.

Phillip Douglas

SONGS OF A GYPSY

Songs of a gypsy to you I will sing
All you must do is to drop everything.
For the song may be long and take you A-ways
The journey may last for many odd days.

But time will fly and so will I.
For the song is light and takes to flight.
So tarry not and drop your cares
The trip I've planned will cost no fares.

Be light and free as a bumble bee
If you would care to keep up with me.
For we travel fast and we travel far
To many places impossible by car.
So now—try your wings and think of things
That seldom bring you down.
Let's laugh and play away this day,—
For the worries need a holiday.

Jynette Elizabeth Wilson

A FOX IS A FOX

A fox is a fox,
not an over small ox!
A moon is a moon,
not a sun in the noon!

The sky . . . oh, the sky,
present the years that have gone by.

And when you look
at the sun at dawn,
you think of a newly born fawn,
"Shawn."

Annabelle L Peavey

A THOUGHT

Listening to her troubles, mine vanished,
So small they seemed to me, compared;
I wonder if, when the good Lord hears
Our woes, and with us bears
Our burdens, He forgets His troubles too,
In helping us gain strength anew.

Richard Shaw

THE WAY STATION

Out from the darkness we came
Only moments before
Extending unending lying in
knowingness wishing
evermore
light beams breathing
crying sighs
Flash the water's crystals sides
weep the morrow's silver tides
Father's gone mother's dry
children laughing 'neath the sky
Dogs now barking to the moon
we all pass here this orb too soon
Death is the answer
Death is the cause
Life but a way station
between the stars

Back hence we came
Back to our birth
The blackness of sleep walk
The mystery stilled
The blackness pitching
The clouds vaporized
The winds dispersing
the dreams of our lives

Thomas Edward Yaeger

LESSON OF LOVE

To she who taught me life's true value—my mother

Lonely is my vigilance as I wait for her to die;
Silent are my prayers as I seek the answer, "Why?,"
Moist, warm upon my cheeks, the tears now flow
As from her body the soul departs and life does slowly go.
Aching is my heart as helplessly I face the plight
And plead her case throughout the lonely, silent night.
Almost unbearable is the burden; crushing is the pain,
For the bloom of life is fading; my prayers seem all in vain.
Grating is the sound as laboriously comes her breath

Telling me she lingers on the threshold of her death;
Thus, causing all my thoughts to lose their ration
As I curse my God for showing no compassion.
Despondent is my mood while I gently hold her hand,
They turn my plea to Lucifer and the power of the damnd.
Suddenly aware, I notice the softness of her stare
That says she understands my heartache and despair
And, as if with Godly gift, she seems to read my mind.
"Don't worry, Dad," she murmurs, "for God is really kind
And 'though my life's been short, I'm prepared to die."
She pauses and I stifle back my cry.
"You've been kind and good, the nicest father ever had.

So when I meet our God, I'm gonna' thank Him for my Dad."
No longer can I stem the flow of unrelenting tears,
Thankful now He let me share her twenty precious years!

June Wade

SIGN OF THE TIMES

We live in a country
That's supposed to be free

But lately these freedoms
Are scorned by those on TV

There's homosexuals and aids
Abortion and amoral sex
Democracy and Heroes are
Condemed by this nation

Where are the Righteous in
God's creation?

Politicians swear they're
Doing what's right for our land
But when voting on issues
They take the wrong stand—
Our countrys' in danger
These are perilous times
Evil abounds—
No righteousness shines

It's time to stand up
All who know what is right
Don't stand there and take it
Let's put up a good fight.

If God's on our side
There'll be no more doubt
Goodness will win and
Then we can shout

Hallelujah! Amen!
God's glory be praised!
His power still reigns!
Our country is saved!

Beverly A Wright

THE VENEERED HEART

Dedicated to Father James Hickey

His was a 'heart of gold' encased in veneer.
They say he was brash,
But his Christlike qualities far outweighed his brashness.

He was noisey, yes—but it came to be gentle noisiness.
He was so considerate; it was as natural as day following night.

His smile was a taste of heaven,— so holy, so naturally holy.
His run over shoes brought me back to childhood days,
A poverty, poor, but rich in spirit.

For nothing and nobody could run over his heart
For it was encased in veneer, —protected from man's carelessness.

Alec Clint Nichols

TENDER WINDOW

This morning our cathedral window strangely warms the living room.
The white sky slides its downy belly by the balcony of our cedar
A-frame home and nestles into our back yard among the pines and oaks.
Ground cover of foot high brush becomes the softest of blankets.

Slowly sifting space. Quiet.

The fireplace isn't the only reason for the warmth—
frilly, feathery, tender love.

The downy flakes have stopped.

Crystal quiet: a nightmare photograph.
A single oak leaf.
A tree. Arched. Humbled. Dead. White.
A large stump layered with white.

Wait! There's blue in the sky!
A searching squawk from a frustrated bird.
Another try. No echo. Silence.

The cold plops from the pained hands of trees.
It knocks on our porches.
The little patch of blue is gone.
Wet dropping, plopping and splashing. Noisy silence.

Nearly falling backward, I see ponderosa pines
rising from our front yard shelf
that rises over a canyon
of misty ridges and white-patched mountains.

This kind of window can make me worthy.

Lillian S Kenney

MOON MAGIC

On a black velvet curtain studded with diamonds
A golden ball hangs high.
Poetic fancy; the ball is the moon
God's wondrous work in the sky.

Sometimes, it's a silver crescent,
that's when it's new,
that's the one we wish upon,
so sure it will come true.

We watch it's magical beauty unfold,
as it tips the houses and trees with gold.

Now, you've shown me another place—
I did not like what I saw on it's face.
Your moon is covered with craters and rocks,
scientists say from upheavals and shocks.

I felt a pang of desolation,
even a sense of desecration.
I turned away to look at the sky—
Lo, there was my moon, still riding high.
Truly a miracle, hard to define . .
You found your moon,
but I still have mine.

Sewalla Duckrey Bellamy

WHEN I GROW UP

Lord, you know I'm getting older and my bones are getting colder,
And It's time that you and I sat down and had a little chat.
You know I'm hitting forty and no longer feeling sporty,
And it's true I've put on a bit of fat.
I've been thinking bout the years ahead; they're something I've begun to dread,
So I want to ask a favor of You right here and now.
If You can kindly see Your way, for this Dear Lord, I ask and pray,
Let me <u>LIVE</u>, full of life anyhow.
There are people out there to meet, I just know,
And places out there that I really must go.
Things to get into, onto, and out of,
And a world full of love.
I don't want to sit in an old rocking chair,
Confined to four walls with no one to care.
With no interest in life, letting years slip on by,
Lord, let me <u>LIVE</u> every day 'til I die.
Work for my hands, books for my mind,
Good health a plenty, and children who are kind.
Food for my body, peace for my soul,
A warm cozy shelter when winters grow cold.
A loved one beside me to share good times and bad,
A strong sense of humor, in case I feel sad.
Am I asking too much, Dear Lord overhead
If I want to live <u>LIVELY</u>, until I am dead?

Madeleine Applegate

THERE MUST BE TWO

There is no love alone Dear;
In life there must be two;
To glimpse the golden sunrise
Which basks the world anew,
Two must match the sunset, as flaming
rays turn gold and glad hearts look on
spell bound as natures pearls unfold.
There must be two to gaze Dear, on
clouds of fleecy white, and watch the beauties
of the scenes that change from morn to night.
There must be two to view Dear the beauty
of the rose; whose head held high in
splendor the rarest perfume throws.
There must be two inspiring our likeness
Dear, to mold—There must be two to foster
the young ones in our fold.
There must be one to comfort should we
but touch a thorn, There must be one to
Mend Dear a garment that is torn;
So. Two must be there always; as we
travel on our way.
To share the joys and ecstacies. We know
from day to day.

Mary Hedges

ANOTHER CHANCE

To Rusty upon your graduation from CHS on June 1, 1986 from a voice who responded to your cry

---

He screamed into the silent air,
"What's the use—doesn't anybody care?"

No sound from the place he'd learned to call home,
No sound from the hallways he used to roam.

Out on his own with no place to go,
Was there anyone anywhere who didn't know?

"Give me a chance—don't reject me!" he cried.
"Don't push me away as though I have died."

Several voices cried, "We'll take you in;
It matters not—what you've done, where you've been."

"Thanks for your homes, but what about school?
Not to finish makes me seem like a fool."

New voices cried out, "We'll give you a chance.
Just don't let us down—we warn you in advance."

I knew I had made it when June 1st finally came,
"Russ Allen Grimm," a voice called out my name.

Then I heard a voice familiar to me,
The voice of the One who had destined me to be.

"My son, I have been here all along,
I've never rejected you, even when you went wrong."

My hopes renewed by what I heard the voice say,
Maybe other familiar voices will be heard someday.

Jane A Galstad

GODDESS OF LOVE

To Jean Connell, with love

You are
Stronger than the northern winds
Gusting full force on prairie land,
Gentler than a summer breeze
Lapping waves against the sand.

You are
Taller than the forest pine
Branching out to cool the air,
Smaller than the fallen seeds
Giving life to all that cares.

You Are
Louder than a lioness's snarl
Protecting her hidden lair,
Quiet as a dove's feather falls
Drifting slowly through the air.

You Are
Straighter than the archer's arrow
Aiming towards it's prey,
Bending quickly as a fisherman's rod
Catches his prize of the day.

You Are
Faithful and proud as an eagle

Returning aloft to it's nest,
Symbolizing a country full of love
Promising life it's very best.

Sharon Eisman

SEASONS OF CHANGE

If I had met you in summer, would we have played in the sand or ridden on merry-go-rounds or walked on our hands? Would we have walked along bridges so amazed at the sky, like a kite in the wind, would we pretend we could fly? What if the springtime was when we first met. Would we have gone fishing and gotten all wet . . . perhaps we'd of picnicked alone in the park, watching the children till way after dark. Would you gather me flowers, so fresh and so new, layed down here beside me, on the grass, wet with dew.

Supposing the season would have been fall, the leaves on the ground, would we have met at all? Do you notice the seasons and how they change, the way people meet, and lives re-arrange. It's not so important the time of the year, just whether or not we like being near.

I'm glad the winter was the season for us, for everything lay sleeping, except the love and the trust. We shall see all the seasons and enjoy everyone, for togetherness is beautiful, and love is such fun . . .

Cassandra Renee Cooper

THE LOVE I GAVE TO ONE

The love I gave to one I presumed
loved me,
was a love, I gave spontaneously.
It was a love, I felt satisfactory,
yet a love, not fully returned.

The love I gave to one, I assumed
loved me,
was a pure love, given
unconditionally.
It was a love, I gave whole
heartedly,
yet a love sometimes unreturned.

The love I gave to one, I thought
loved me,
Was the first of my life, and
unregrettably,
It was a love I gave irretractably;
yet a love, I feared unreturned.

The love I gave to one I fancied
loved me,
was a love, I gave quite willingly.
It was a once-in-a-lifetime
experience you see,
for I guess, it was not returned.

The love I gave to one, I dreamed
loved me,
was an interlude of lust, shared
agreeably.
Yet a one-sided bitter-sweet
memory,
that I know couldn't have been
returned.

The love I gave to one, I had hoped
loved me
Is a precious souvenir, I call my
learning 'tree,
it is a love form which, I've finally
broken free,
and the next one I love, will have
to first love me.

M K J Aitken-McGee

THE FOOTPRINTS IN THE SAND

This poem is dedicated to Pauline Aitken

One night I dreamt that we were
standing on the shores of time.

The footprints in the sodden sand
were neither yours or mine;
The far horizon was as dark as
night.
Yet the sun was scorching down,
And the trees and palms that once
lined the shore
were withered dry and brown.

No sustenance remained within
the land,
or in the lifeless sea.
A legacy man had left just for you
and me.
What madness drove him on and
on,
Until at last he killed.
In rage he burst the final bomb
and all the world was stilled.

Why did he show his children war
instead of earthly peace.
He always was an animal,
whose lusts would never cease.
The footprints in the sodden sand,
are all that now remains,
and they in time will wash away
through deadly nuclear rains.
Our lifeless world will travel on
for eons round the sun,
to gradually revert to the point
when life had first begun.

Mildred Hutto Rycroft

HEARTBREAK

In memory of our daughter Linda Jo Rycroft, Courtney, Harrison Aug. 24, 1949—Sept. 22, 1981

My broken heart
Is still broken
And my crying eyes
Still cry
Since your footsteps
Are no longer
and your sweet smile
Is just a sigh.
The memory of your caring
And your ever loving ways
is ever present with me.
But more so on special days.
But even as I miss you
And dream of a happy past,
I know God must have needed
Someone special for his task,
For God took you from your family
So early in your prime
That my ache to hold you near me
Has not eased with the passing
of time.
I still ask questions
And refuse to say goodby
To someone so loved and precious
as my daughter in the sky.
My broken heart
is still broken
And my crying eyes
still cry
For your footsteps
that are no longer
But now treads
with God's angels in the sky.

Paul W Hansen

NOTHING IS ALL

The angles of a chair define its
comfort
And the volume of a bowl defines
its use.
The resonance of a home
Must rise from lines on paper.
The resonance of a soul must start
with skin.
Enclosures are for senses
Not for sense.
Experience and self cannot be
measured.
They are space between the
nebulas
In which the stars are hung.
And that is where heart's yearning
moves
Lonely as an asteroid
Lost in wonder.

Jewell Castro

IN YOUR SMALL CORNER

To look on and not offer assistance
to one who needs.
is standing in the shadows of truth.

To listen, and spread the gossip of
loose tongues,
Is to salt the open wounds of pain.

To grasp and hold onto unfeeling
substances,
Is to lose the value of caring.

To turn deaf ears to a child's plea
for identity,
Is to stifle creativity, individuality.

To miss the beauty of life and
living,
Is to hide in a shadowy cocoon,
alone.

To miss the joy of a child with
grandparents,
Is to read a good book, only to find
Someone has torn away the final
chapter.

Live every day to the fullest,
Take pride in whatever you do;
Make your small corner
unforgettable,
Because it once belonged to you.

Wallace E Smith

Wallace E Smith

HELP YOURSELF TO HAPPINESS

Help yourself to happiness—
Grasp all within your reach.
You really will not get too much
So do not lose the human touch;
That's the lesson life would teach.

Help yourself to love today—
It's more precious than you know;
It makes this world a different
place,
All grief and care it can erase—
It's the greatest gift life can bestow!

Help yourself to Life; yes, LIVE!
Let no doubt or fear beset you;
It's too short at best,
So forget the rest—
Lest Love and Happiness both
forget you!

Hal Algyer

OF SILENCE AND SLOW TIME

In Memoriam R. A. C.

Below the ground the ceaseless
water drips;
Unheard it falls in long monotony.
Unseen and timeless, slow the
glacier slips
Till one day icebergs thunder to the
sea.
Implacable the seasons go their
way,
So gradual I can not mark the
change;
I only know in watching day to day
I saw them pass, mysterious and
strange.

These things are slow, but there are
slower things
So slow are memories to leave the
mind.
The sight and smell and sound of
other springs
In present ones can not be left
behind.
A thousand little things come
back today
To let me know you are not put
away.

Sandra (Binky) Edwards

A DREAM COME TRUE

Though you'll never see just how
you set me free
I knew you long before you met me
You may not believe me or think
that its true
But honest and truly I really knew
you.
I've dreamed of you at night and
long into the day
Now I just can't stop dreamin
where are you today
I hope my words find you on lifes
long road
Cause I'd really and truly would
like you to know
You were so sweet so strong so bold
Thanks for the dream you gave me
to hold

Doris B Denison

LINE OF LONELINESS

She walks alone, along the water's edge to Joplin's "Solace" To companion the wind—shadow forth Through the forest of pain. Once a primitive child obsessed with Genesis, I mark my father's grave. Do not stereotype the tree of woman. If you must stencil word her with leaves of understanding. Malice is burdensome and begets malice. Enough of yellowed

parchment
etching data-feeding a computer. In my
labyrinth I mime: Harlequin female floating
up stream, dewy-eyed platonic abstaining
in exquisite agony. Ambition dictates
holding me tighter than a lover. I wish
star-dreams materialize: When I cross
the bridge of no return everything becomes clear: Perfect.
like an obelisk tapering
through the sky—a captive
of tomorrows—I have crystallized.
Dawn: and the
young woman is gone

Jennifer D Cash
WAITING
Waiting . . .
The rasping, scraping branches outside
the window disturbs my sleep.

The stillness drapes over the house
on this moonless night.

A lone cry pierces the darkness
as a lone wolf calls to its mate.

The cold October winds howl through
the branches calling my name.

The unsettling tossing and longing
and waiting for my loves return continues . . .

J Albert Locklear
SUCCESS
To have success in life you must be bold,
First set yourself a worth while goal.
Then find the courage to persue,
Also some planning you must do.

Be prepared if your progress seems slow,
Discouragements will try to delay your go.
You must have kindling for your fire of desire,
That is the fuel that burns the fire.

It will inflame the will of your heart,
Then from your goal you will never depart.
The kindling is your desires and aspirations to be met,
To fulfill your dreams and reach the goal you have set.

Courage is the maker of all bravery in you,
That will inspire you through and through
Things will happen if you only have the nerve,
Without it you will not get what you deserve.

In a five letter word there lies the link,
To all prosperity yes the word is think.
"I think I can" say it every hour of the day,
Then you will be to paving the way.

For your journey to total security,
All doubts will vanish into obscurity.
Just remember if you don't succeed, don't ask why,
Its all because you didn't deserve a piece of the pie.

Wilhelmina Garrison
LOSING OUR DREAMS
After more than four years I pray and I pray,
That God stays as near as he is this day.
I have watched my love over 48 years—
To fade and fade midst a million tears;
A dreaded disease that has taken his mind—
And taken its toll of many a kind.

Alzheimers disease the doctors replied,
But never once did our knot come untied.
So show patience with those whom you're not too sure,
As to what has gone wrong,
Then learn to endure:
He is such a dear thing—But now like a baby of course—
But with Gods nearness—I keep going and
Try not to show my remorse.
In taking care one day at a time and praying—
That he's happy and content in still being mine.
Keeping him with me is my aim—knowing he's not
Aware—But mine just the same.
May God still continue to give me the strength—
To show all my love to its greatest length—
Oh precious Lord—please hear me each day and
Stay beside me all of the way.

Labeebee Jeannette Hanna Saquet

Labeebee Jeannette Hanna Saquet
THE BALLET DANCER
The lyric form rejoices on stage,
Executes an arabesque or two,
A dainty run or two, and a leap into the air,—
For nothing else will do!

The body twists and turns, while the arms
Reach up to frame the face.
The leg kicks up, then quickly bends
In pure ethereal grace.

A balanced pose follows a pas de deux,
Unstudied, or so it seems;
You see creation of a living Art
That is the stuff of dreams!

R Monroe Miller
LIFE
Marketplace of unconscious lure
Beckons me as I pass thereby;
Hawk-eyed, unscrupulous hucksters
Fawn upon me and pick my purse
To please some conscious greed, or worse . . .

I think I died last night—I died,
Succubus wrapped in phantasy;
Swirling in deliriums heights,
Unknown, and visited but once . . .

The Sky, that Giant Eye, is blind
To wants, so tries to blind me too;
But I, in desperation lent
By evolutionary sense,
Cry out in fear felt secretly . . .

I know I cried last night—I cried,
Contemplating loneliness;
Feeling the loneliness of death,
Unknown, and visited but once . . .

Mary M Spencer
AM I A PRUDE?
There is a school for arts and crafts where I reside
All summer and it points with pride
At skills exhibited by young and old.
Throughout the season, it will often hold
An open house when students can present
Their works of art, their sound accomplishment.

I recently attended what was called
"A Poetry Reading Evening." I was appalled
And plain disgusted with the language being used
Four letter words were prevalent, good grammar was abused.
I'll call it "gutter language," offensive to my ear.
Perhaps I am outdated, I'll blame advancing years.

When I was younger, we were taught
Rhyme and rhythm and we sought
To capture beauty, earn a smile,
Tell a story, once in a while
Cry out against injustices and wrong
But obscene language just did not belong.

I thought perhaps in anger I could write
A few four letter words I heard that night,
But now I find that even in my rage,
I cannot put them on the written page.

I am amazed today it's being found
Acceptable and even draws a round
Of loud applause and here I must confess,
I could not join in demonstrativeness.

T L C
A CRY FOR OUR CHILDREN
I beg you my children, and listen you must,
this turmoil our world is in is truly unjust;

Material value is not where it is at,
for we must all come together, and bring our pride back;

The act of war will only add to more hate,
we must learn to love our neighbor before it is too late;

If tomorrow is to be, it is up to all of you,
our world can be better, and it only takes a few;

For if you see with your eyes, and love with your heart,
then maybe, just maybe, our world and our people will
never be torn apart.

Stella Lemanska Olbris
FAITH AND HOPE

To my children Steve, Frank, Linda, Mary.

The world is dangerous with many foes
And dangerous powers as everyone knows
But if more citizens would try to be friends
We would soon see a change in events.
I'll do the same with others I meet.
A quiet "hi" and a smile so sweet.
If others would only do the same
Scattering sunshine, instead of pain.
I've lived my life with its ups and downs
And many tears and many frowns
I've learned a lesson I'll never forget
To be sweet, patient, without regrets.
Letting each day end with feelings sublime
With hurts that heal, in the course of time
When days end and nights come down
We can all find life devine.
Many tears had to fall before this lesson I learned
Many years had to pass before life's lesson I learned
So don't anyone give up hope
While there is life, there is hope.
All you who are able
Scatter sunshine all the 'day
You'll never know whose life you brighten
Whose heavy load you may lighten.

Tom Davis
NOTE PAD

This poem is dedicated to George Thomas Davis Sr., who respected the rights of all animals—including man.

The land lies quietly encased in mist
Slowly with warmth it's gently kissed.
The Lord has granted us another dawn.
In their bed, a doe and fawn.
Nature responds, feeling Heaven's breath,
Night's gloomy veil has risen and left.
Golden now are the forests and fields,
And away the cold, it slowly peals.
The murmuring sound of a gentle brook
Where a little boy would like to cast a hook.
The mountains take on a luminous glow,

High above two eagles circle, ever so slow.
An artist hums a lullabye as she sets up her easel
While from a hollow log is watched by a weasel.
Robins sing, their melodies fill the air,
Newborn cotton-tails peak out from their lair.
Oh, the tranquil peace of early morning light.
Owls have returned from their silent flight.
The wind, still a hush as it starts to stir.
A butterfly and chickadee share the branch of a fir.
Nature's sounds are far more beautiful than any chimes.
As I sit here under a tree writing rhymes.

Theresa Terreson
GRANDAUGHTER ANNA

Little fairy creature
Tiny elfin thing
From what far away Kingdom
Have you spread your wings?
Fine and guazy ones
Soft as ocean mist
To sojourn in our world
With your tiny feet
Landing softly in your Mother's womb
Sleep, sleep, my little princess
"Comes the rude awakening"
Skin as soft as silk
Rubs the world softly
Cry your tiny "tears"

Katherine R Scevola

Katherine R Scevola
GOD SPEAKS THROUGH NATURE

Dedicated to My parents, Mary and Thomas Staron of East Chatham, New York who instilled in me honesty, strength of character and the great love and appreciation of nature.

God unfolds the Earth to us each morning as the sun's rays peer over the hill,
Awakening all his live creatures and blessing those that have stilled.
The dewdrops on the grasses and petals glisten
like teardrops the night shed for us all,
And the Lord put a Power in our being that sustains
us whether we walk or fall.
The mystery that is so pronounced all around us,
has baffled us in our everyday lives;
For we never cease to discover another Blessing in disguise.
The rains that fall in great torrents wash the face of the earth,
Creating a brightness and freshness, that Hearlds the coming of Nature, as she springs from the face of the Earth.

The winds have a reason for coming for they put
movement to all that is still,
While they freshen our path to the Heavens, as we
strive here doing God's will.
The rays of the sun sometimes scorching give Life
and Light to the earth;
Without God's lamp light above us, all would pale and
fall lifeless to earth.
Thanks to the Creator above us who makes life on this earth such a joy,
Instilling into us a power and wisdom that will lighten
our burden as we wait for His Trumpet Call.

Juliana D Guillermo
SENIOR CITIZENS

To all those in the sunset of their lives, this poem I dedicate.

Behold him,
Who in the prime of his life was virile,
Quick and alert, ambitious and going;
Dedicated, fired up and energized,
With a mission, kept on truly striving
For a just cause with dignity;
Propelled by drive
And noble goals and a lot of yearnings,
As provider, he labored through the nights;
From time to time he made sacrifices,
Did heroics in many silent fights
For his dear ones and loved people.

Behold her,
Who in the peak of her life was lovely,
Naive but sweet, demure but cheerful;
True and sincere, inspired and committed,
In partnership she's ever dutiful,
A faithful wife, a loving mom;
With rosy hopes
And cherished dreams, and a host of desires,
As homemaker, she left no stones unmoved;
From dawn to dusk she did the household chores,
Conscientiously, and nicely as behooved
With righteousness and loving care.

Behold them now!
In the sunset of their faded glory,
In the quiet of their own solitude;
Bent and shaky, with canes and hearing aids,
And blurred vision, with hushed and placid mood,
And the gray hairs, and the wrinkles;
Eventually,
These tangibles would be seen no longer,
'Til everything earthly would have perished;
But by and large, their love and legacy
Bequeathed to us would forever be etched
In the tablets of our mem'ries.

Amy Lynn Shields
MY CHRISTMAS DREAM

Twas Christmas, Aha He He, And who was still up waiting? Me? Yes, there I sat eyes a gleaming, rubbing palms together scheming. Dreaming of the toys he'd bring, I'd only asked for little things. A Little cash, a little car, a stereo, a VCR, designer clothes, some french cologne, some jewelry, skis, and a private phone . . . I guess I must have drifted off, cause suddenly I heard a cough. I screamed and hopped up in a chair, and there was Santa standing there. "Ho Ho there! How ya doing?" He said, I guess you didn't hear the sled. "Oh now you're here!" I cried with glee, And in his pocket I could see, The "little list" I'd typed so neat, a ten paged long computer sheet. "So Santa wheres my stuff?" "My dough?" "Just leave it all and you can go." But Santa laughed and said, "Chill Out" thats not what Christmas is all about. I didn't bring a VCR, a stereo, some cash, a car," "But hey I brought you something better." Than what you asked for in your letter. With that he dug down deep in his pocket, and out he pulled a heart shaped locket. Around my neck he hung the chain, then he grinned and said, "Look I'll explain. Now you don't need a fancy gift to make me happy, get my drift? Cause happiness comes from the heart, thats where the Christmas spirit starts. And suddenly I awoke, I'd been asleep, for goodness sake! I yawned and stretched and rubbed my eyes, I looked around and saw surprise! There by the trees some gifts were piled, I thought "that sneaky guy" and smiled, and gently I reached up to check, a heart was hanging round my neck.

Beatrice Walton Narber
A GREAT GREAT GRANDMOTHER DREAMS

I smile as I rock, nod and dream.
Each dream is an echo of a melody
That filled my heart for many years,
As happily I raised my young.
And as I kissed away their tears
Many songs of love and faith I sung.
When that labor of love was past
I found myself in still another roll cast.
Many songs were still to be sung
To MY childrens girls and boys.
So once again I knew the joys
That I had known when I was young.
Now those children are singing the songs
To their childrens girls and boys,
While I dream my dreams and nod,
Waiting to join the "family of GOD"
There with the angels I will sing again
And leave the dreaming to earthly men.

David D Neidigh
LONELY IN PRISON

Within my lonely prison cell I am setting.
All alone with my broken lonely heart.
Thinking only of you my sweet darling,
Knowing that we will always be apart.

The Judge wouldn't believe my story.
The Jury said he must pay.
So in this cold gray prison I am staying,
Until they come and take me away.

When that day comes for me,
And up these lonely stairs I walk.
To the chair that waits for me there.
I will tell the guard please let me talk.

When the chaplain asks any last words?
My answer will be, just tell my darling.
To believe in my Lord and Saviour.
For I know my Lord believes in me,
And together again someday we will be.

Arlene Kern
HEALTH FOOD HEAVEN

To my Mother, whose love and devotion have provided the greatest legacy of all.

I never knew what a bean sprout was when I lived in New York City,
Or tofu, granola, wheat germ, and squash spaghetti.
We didn't know back then we were being deprived of nature's riches,

Or of the benefits to be derived
from perparing wholesome
natural dishes.

Upon moving to the Golden State
seven years ago from the East,
A new world was opened up to
me—a veritable health food
feast.
"Fresh" ingredients became the
passwords by which we cooked
and dined,
As I carefully scrutinized those
labels where the ingredients are
defined.

Alas, as man does not live by health
foods alone,
We were unwilling to totally
abandon the other foods we had
known.
They were like old friends not to
be hastily cast aside
In our quest towards more
healthful eating and the benefits
it would provide.

"Isn't it better to improve our
eating habits by 50% of the
whole?
Rather than trying for 100% and
falling far short of our goal?"
I rationalized to myself this was
the sensible thing to do,
And as a celebration we raced to
McDonalds for a Big Mac
rendezvous.

Susan Cathy Green
MIRROR CHILD

I saw a blue eyed child in the
mirror look at me.
She had a tear in her sad eye. I
know that I have
seen her before, But I can not find
her in my mind.
I want to talk to this child and see
who she is and Know
why I see her. She must be from a
past time when life was
strange. She must want help out of
the past So she can start
a new life. Why won't she talk to
me? Why won't she laugh with
me?
She must be about 5 years old.
standing there in her dress of
white.
I have Called for her. I have
Watched her for days. Maybe
she will come out soon, maybe
it will be today.

Marie Gagon

Marie Gagon
MOTHER DEAR

This poem is dedicated to my angel Mother Isabella Evans who guided my footsteps in life.

She died on Aug 8, 1980 and I know she is waiting with open arms when it is my time to go she will meet me in Heaven and we will be together forever for time and all eternity.

Thou hast left us precious Mother.
All thy sufferings now are o'er,
Thou shalt never know a sorrow,
On that glad eternal shore,
Thou hast loved us precious
Mother

And thy gentle voice no more
Will be heard in gentle counsel
As it was in days of yore.
Thou didst long to enter heaven,
Longed to gaze upon the face.
Of Him who in hours of suffering
Gave thee such sustaining grace,
Thou art resting, calmly resting,
In the bosom of God's love
And thy spirit now doth hover
O'er us from thy home above.
We will meet thee in the morning
Over on the other shore.
When the cares of life are ended,
There we'll meet to part no more.

Rene'e Fullwood
FATHER KNOWS BEST?

To my Father, Marvin Fullwood, with love and devotion.

Through thick and thin, the ups
and downs,
Father knows best there's no one
like him around.
He's strict, but he's fair and tries to
understand.
Oh, all the love my Father holds in
his hands.

He picks me up when I stumble
and fall.
If ever I'm in doubt, I just give a call.
We are alike in hundreds of ways,
And I grow more like him with
each passing day.

To be more like him is what I wish
to be,
So strong and loving and always
carefree.
As I look back on years in the past,
I wished I wouldn't have grown up
so fast.

To ride a bicycle he taught me to
do,
He even taught me to tie my own
shoes.
No matter what I have done that
was right or wrong,
He stood by my side and helped
make me strong.

I am the carbon copy, and will
always be
Just like my Father; you wait and
see.

Carolyn Franklin
THE STRENGTH PRAYER

The Lord lay it upon my heart to dedicate this poem, to all whom will serve him. That there's power and strength in prayer.

Teach me Dear LORD
What I need to know
Can I be able to help
Another SOUL.
I lay awake at night
PRAYING and FASTENING
Wondering is this ever lasting.
Success is not MONEY or POWER
It is GOD'S LOVE that he shower.
What I fill is so REAL
It's like a Thrill
Only you know the POWER
Of your will.
So Always look UP
Never look down
Cause my LOVE will
ALWAYS be around.
So teach ME DEAR LORD
What I need to know
Can I be able to HELP
Another SOUL.

Alexander A Pushkin

Alexander A Pushkin
UNTITLED

To Natalie

Madam, Seavash is lost for us,
And you have by the tonight's
steamer
To hurry up to neutral waves
With your non-complicated
luggage.

Madam, the day comes to the end,
Check up your papers, tickets,
money;
They say, you know, —in season
that
That is the last this streamer's
voyage.

Madam, let me the last one touch
Before you put on dark your vuel,
And then . . . Be back or not to be—
—It will depend . . . But not of your
will.

The firing's near . . . Time . . . God
bless . . .

No sense to wear mourning
dresses,
You-go, we-reasons have to stay
For your return, somehow-
someday.

Georgia A Berkey
ON CALVARY

This poem is dedicated to my good friend Rev. Emily Styer

The earth grew dark, the thunder
rolled,
And lightning pierced the sky—
The day they nailed Him to the
cross,
And left Him there to die.

His voice had cried with mercy
As the nails pierced Him through,
His cry— "Father forgive them
For they know not what they do."

In agony He gave His life,
His precious blood was shed
That we might live forevermore,
"I am the Life," He said.

The world was changed forever
When the Son of God was born,
And won for us salvation
In the dawn of Easter morn.

Wilma Mae Humbolt
MUSIC

The love of my heart—
In the depth of our souls,
Among the finest of arts,
The sound of music that tolls
And lifts and enlightens
The burdens of man,
That only the sound of music
can.

Michael Angelo Mazzanti
DREAMS FOR MY CHILDREN

America is built on dreams for the next generation, written for and dedicated to dreams and children. In memory of Melina Michelle.

Butterflies are free
As they fly,
Without care or sound.
Just as the spirit
That lives inside
You and I.
Everyone has a spirit
That is free
And lives to fly,
To do what your heart
Feels is just.
Read and learn
What you must,
To fly free
And to live right.
Understand this world
We call life.
Remember always,
Fly back to me.
If you ever need me,
I will be there.
Forever,
Father

Michael Federika

Michael Federika
SOMETHING FROM NOTHING

To Diane S. Wherever you are

Day is gone; and night is through.
The only time I never think of you.
Is when I'm on that downward path;
And all that might be wrong,
Would never show it's wrath.
When there's no sun; nor cloud in the sky,
And all the world seems to pass me by,
Nothing but the light of wisdom before me would lie.
Time has proven little.
People, learning, wealth, wisdom, pride,
Of all this I'm in the middle,
Yet I have nothing
Without you by my side."

Rose A Steinberg
ETERNAL LOVE
Let us build our house together
Standing firm against the weather.
Stout strong walls will be secure
Based on Love that will endure.
Windows shining with heavenly light.
Stars aglowing in the night
A door that welcomes old friends and new
Climbing roses wet with dew.
A solid roof and chimney tall
God's peace and blessing over all.
Our children's faces we will see
As tender blossoms on our family tree.
The sound of music in their laughter
Will forever echo from the rafters.
Caring, sharing joy and sorrow
The sun will shine again tomorrow
Strengthening each other's weakness
Devoted love in all its sweetness
The life we lived so joyously
Will continue through Eternity.

Nora Mitchell
EACH LETTER IN EASTER HAS A MEANING
E—Is for Early upon the first day of the week when they came to anoint the body, but else where had to seek.

A—Is for the Agony Christ suffered on the cross.

S—Is for the Sinners He died, to save from loss.

T—Must have meant the third day, Christ arose from the grave with victory over death and power to save.

E—Is for everyone who will believe and say.

R—Is for the Risen Christ and that he lives today.

Crystal Nelson
ABSENT BLESSINGS
When I look out I see,
So many women all alone!
Their husband's, DADS, and boyfriends,
Are sitting back at home.
The sermon is much more than good,
The fellowship divine.
I'm sorry to see these big strong men,
Don't seem to have the time,
To spend a quiet moment, alone and reverently,
They're missing all the blessings the good Lord meant to be.
So next time your man tells you,
Just go ahead without.
You might just quietly tell him,
"I think you're missing out."

A Berenice Chew

A Berenice Chew
YOU ARE SO BEAUTIFUL
Dear Lord, You are so beautiful
And so good to me.
Without You, where would I be?
Who knows; none but Thee.

You will always remain
Beautiful in my sight.
To do right is my delight
So, before I fall asleep
Goodnight, good night.

Dorothy Lawton Ames
CONSECRATION
Dear Heavenly Father hear our prayer, look down on us today
And bless us as in reverence we humbly bow and pray;
We do not ask for glory, for wealth or power or fame
But in humility and love and in our Savior's name
We ask for wisdom, Lord, to guide these tiny little feet
And help them find the path that leads, through Thee, to life complete;

Today we dedicate to Thee the treasure Thou hast given
Oh help us keep this little soul pure, white and fit for Heaven;
Reveal to us Thy will that we may do our rightful share
In guiding this dear little one entrusted to our care.
Forgive us when our earthbound feet shall falter in the way
But grant in Thy compassion that we lead him not astray;

We thank Thee, Lord, for trusting us with this most precious task
And that we may be worthy is all we need to ask;
As we bring before Thine altar this little one to Thee
May our own spirits be renewed and this our earnest plea:
Oh help us here to dedicate our lives to Thee again
In the name of Him who came to earth as a little child,
AMEN.

Caroline Mack
YESTERDAY

To my parents, my earthy gifts from God!

When I recall the yesterday's
The rubbles, storms and strife,
I thank my precious Lord again
For giving me new life

There were times of darkness
And I'd surely lost my way
My life way empty, meaningless,
I could not even pray

Rejection heightened feelings
Of my lack of self-esteem
Failure at my peace of mind
Destroyed my every dream

The mornings I wakened to
Held nothing more than dread
My hope for happiness dissolved
I wished that I were dead

But then a single word "FORGIVE"
Was spoken from His throne,
And in my spirit beamed a light . . .
He beckoned "Child, come home."

I died to self that He might live,
Within the heart of me,
I chose the certain route to peace,
My shepard now is He.

I'm walking in His victory
A child of Christ my King,
In Him I find fulfillment
And to Him my praise I sing

As we journey on the highway of life
As moments of joy cross our path
Let's remember the giver of gifts,
So the beauty of his giving will last.

Sometimes in blindness we sort of abuse
The good we find along the way
Thus making life a bit rough
By the things we do and say,

By each new days beginning,
We have reached another chance
And to someday realize
How much our lives have been enhanced.

Theodora Russo
LIFE GOES ON!

To Peter and Norma

Though it's clear to me you don't care anymore, I still can't help loving you same as before.
You never take me out, not even if it's free, I know from past experience that this is how it's to be.
I've let you call the shots, letting you have your way, but as the good Lord says, "Someday you'll have to pay.
You know you've caused me lots of pain, but perhaps it all hasn't been in vain.
For one thing I've learned from knowing you, is you look at things from a different view.
I see life as an experience to share, with someone you love and deeply care,
You on the other hand would let love nevermore, find its way through your closed door . . . and frankly, my dear,
it's turning you into a bore!
It's money you crave and the drive to obtain it, you keep saying you, "Never had it so good,"
I don't believe it.
For you, oh my dear, have been short-changed by yourself . . . you could have had it all, you know,
your freedom, privacy and wealth,
Plus the love and devotion of the one woman in the world you could trust, I wonder if you realize yet
what you've lost?
Remember when you told me, "Why didn't we meet long ago?" Life would have been all the sweeter
lived together, but no.
You must have forgotten . . . it's too late, it's done! You've soured it all, now we'll never be one.
So this is fair warning to you, my pet, I'm looking for someone else who will love me yet!
You know what they say, "If there's a will there's a way," and I'm finding mine, little by little each day.
Cause I know I'm too young to fold up my tent yet, so life will go on with or without you, you bet!

Earl Wayne Chambers Sr
NIKKI

This poem is dedicated to my daughter Nikki whom I love very much.

I miss you more with each passing day,
I love you Nikki more than words can say.
Even though we are apart-you're the reason I exist,
As you grow older, take time to read this.

For twelve solid hours I waited for your arrival,
Nothing on my mind but prayer for your survival.
Listening to your heart beat twice the pace of mine,
Worried about your Mom, who was nervous, otherwise fine.

The doctor came in and paused at the door,

I had to know something—I
couldn't take anymore.
He reassured me the magic
moment was near,
Tell your wife good luck and stay
right here.

I sprang from my chair with a loud
protest,
I demanded I get to experience the
rest.
They finally agreed to let me in—
The delivery room, somewhere I'd
never been.

Nikki, you came into the world all
cuddly and wet,
I stared in disbelief the first time
we met.
I suddenly noticed that you didn't
even cry,
Noticed the sparkle of ambition in
the corner of your eye.

So remember Nikki when you
think of your Dad,
Of all the good times we could have
had.
Love and security are the things
you will need,
To develop your personality so
others will heed.

I hope you understand what I'm
trying to say,
My heart longs to be with you every
day.
Take care of yourself and do as
you're told,
A beautiful lady named Nikki—will
emerge from the mold.

Irene T Davis
THERE IS A GOD

Dedicated to those readers who may doubt the existence of an almighty God. An affirmation of His abiding presence and awesome creative power everywhere and in everything, and His special love for us whom He created in His own image.

In the sudden crack of lightning,
and the resonating boom of
thunder
There is a God

In the gentle rain of Springtime,
nurturing beateous things of
wonder
There is a God

In the mighty roll of breakers,
crashing on the ocean shore
There is a God

In the lapping of the wavelets,
leaving treasures to explore
There is a God

In the awesome depths of canyons
and the mountain's craggy height
There is a God

In the busy workers of the ant hill,
and the eagle's soaring flight
There is a God

In the vast and silent desert,
and the teeming city's sound
There is a God

In the cooling of an infant,
and the mother's love, profound
There is a God

In the splash of a fish in a quiet
pond;
the faint buzz of a gauzy-winged
fly
There is a God

In the white fleecy clouds high
above,
floating in a deep azure-blue sky
There is a God

In the rush and roar of the rapids,
and the quiet, deep river's flow
There is a God

In the gorgeous shafts of a sunrise,
and the splendor of a sunset's
glow
There is a God

In the times when we are troubled,
and our hearts with sadness will
fill
There is a God

In Him we find our solace and
strength,
and gently He tells us—Be still.
I am your God!

Ozella B McCoy

Ozella B McCoy
MAGIC MOMENTS

with love for my daughter and son Joyce and Jerry who are the joy of my life.

It's the little things in my life
that mean so much to me:
Stars twinkling in a velvet sky,
birds singing in a tree,
Black-fringed blue eyes, wet
shining streets,
church choirs on sunday morn,
Sun peeping over mountain tops
as a fresh new day is born.

Sound of childrens' voices at their
play,
good book I can't resist,
Young couple wrapped up in their
love,
a baby's soft, sweet kiss,
Rhythm of waves breaking on the
shore,
visit from dearly-loved friend,
Postman bringing me a longed-for
letter
my absent child has penned.

Punget smell of new-mown hay,
Loving hug when I feel low,
Sitting safe and snug before a fire
while frigid north winds blow.
It doesn't take a great event
or a lavish, costly gift
To fill my heart with sudden joy
and give my soul a lift.

Olive Taylor
OUR FATHER'S HART

Supplies all love
It beams from heaven above
That beam of love
Came down in the form of a dove
From Father to Son
The pure purified one
All sin He did bare
Father and Son does still care
With you all of His love
He wants to share
Why don't you care?
His love never runs out
It shines all about
No one ever needs to be left out
It brightens the blackest heart
Right from the start
With Him you need never depart

Lynda June Sirianni
TOGETHER IN AMERICA

She was born in Brisbane, Qld.,
Australia
She lived in fear during the war
Her mom was seriously ill
Her dad worked at a local store.
He was born in Cumberland, WI.,
U.S.A.
He worked hard on a farm with
nine family members there
His injury during the war was
almost fatal
They saw each other, and his
recovery they did share.

A touch is such a simple thing
Until with it—sweet love does
bring—

She hated to see him leave to fight
He wondered what World War II
would gain
She had his daughter and he did
not know
Her parents exclaimed he would
not be back again!
They took her daughter as legally
theirs—She wept
He was going to surprise her! She
gave him his daughter
They could not take her to America
She was legally not their
daughter—

A touch is such a simple thing
Unless you can't—then you don't
sing.

Forty years and five more
daughters later—to America
Together—daughter Number One
and her husband came
They all shared smiles, laughter
and tears the same—

A TOUCH IS SUCH A SIMPLE
THING AND YET IT MEANS
MUCH MORE
WHEN YOU HAVE FINALLY
TOUCHED A SISTER, YOU
HAVE NEVER SEEN BEFORE.

Mrs Dorothy Sciortino
PRECIOUS GIFT

To my Mom whose gentle love guides me, patience and strength supports me and never ending confidence in things that I may do.

You're really someone special
Mom most loving and
divine . . . , you're in my thoughts
and in my dreams . . . , always
on my mind . . .
To have you and to hold from each
and every day . . . , makes my
world much brighter in each and
every way . . .,
More precious than gold you
are . . . , the sunshine of my life
. . . , to help me with my
problems . . . , to make me feel
for life . . .,
You're really someone

special . . . , always on the go . .
. , to to make my world much
easier . . . , you'd carry the
heaviest load . . .,
To lose you woud be senseless . . .,
to love you is to live . . ., to have
a mom like you . . . , is more
Precious
Than
Heaven's
Little
Kid!

Sylvia Rosenbaum
MOOD

the sun god
hot in his temple
invades this room.
i cannot worship
his yellow laughter,
gold hair laying down a cloth
for me to crouch upon.

i step away;
hang ten stones from my toes;
fold myself away,
black clothes in camphor.

Susan Tisdale Carr
THE FLEETING YEARS

The years come fast and quickly go,
And one begins anew
On January first, soon Christmas's
here.
The days are fast and few.
Our years are spent almost as fast;
Yesterday we were young.
Then fast approach our grown up
years;
Our last song soon is sung.

Parents raise children to adults;
Quite soon parents are gone,
We reflect then on childhood days
How swiftly they have flown.
Our years on earth are as a tale
That's written or told;
If written with a ball point pen
In letters large and bold.

Seeing that time so quickly speeds
Or, that it goes in haste;
Should hie us also, so that we
Would not one moment waste.
In aiding, (say) a falling race
As precious moments mount,
That we won't sadly squander time,
But let each moment count.

Mary E Clarke
TO DIE

This poem is dedicated to Frank, my loving son.

Death and the grave is what I'm
trying to evade.
Better the couch where I could just
rest. Then the
morgue where I'll have to lay until
they bury me.
Ah, but are we not born to die?
But to be dead some say is better
still than this
harried, unpredictable life we live.

But I better
yet would rather my will be used to figure out life's
problems for a more reliable solution. While I do live I
can complete all the things my heart doth want. But
dead I can do nothing. But if we all could only live
Forever and then more, but forever and a day. What joy
to live this long on a sunny or moonlit day. Then in the
coffin where maggots eat and earth worms dig. After
the earth is thrown down. Down into the cold it'll
always be. Where up above it's liv-e-ly. How better to
live a short life than to sleep forever. Where time has no
meaning and life no abundance. Where thoughts neither
remember or care. What can I accomplish there?

KYM Bentley

SONG OF THE CITY

The constant click of resounding heels,
Upon the inclined walk.

The tires of the traffic squeal,
In a high & unrelenting talk.

The flashing of the lights above,
First green, now yellow, then red.

The horns, the sirens screeching sounds,
Etched forever in my head.

Mourning comes with anguished sins,
And the sequence once again begins.

And why I write and who am I?
I am one who is passed by.

The desolate, the dark and the cold,
The one forever growing old.

Upon the streets my footsteps lead,
And then again, where they will heed.

Debbie Linse

PATTERNED FOOTPRINTS

Life looked at me then ran
To touch anothers hand.
Left alone with my future's plan
Patterned footprints in the sand.

All becoming oh so near
The end I see, I fear.
Of precious things held dear
Patterned footprints are now clear.

Reaching for the guiding light
Never dim, always bright.
Traveled road to my delight
Patterned footprints of my flight.

Holding on, all the while
My face begins to form a smile.
For light's grown dim down the aisle,
New patterned footprints mile by mile.

Latrice V Hiatt

GOD'S WAY, OUR WAY

Our way being wrong, and only darkness,
God's way best, right, planned and light!
Offered love, joy and peace that's lasting.
Still we sought our way on in the nite.

Living of self, sin, world and pleasure,
Only for moments to satisfy.
Not seeking God's way, love and mercy,
But still sought God's way to deny.

To get away from home and live in darkness,
We sought to flee and live in sin.
With poor excuse against God's way will and purpose.
Still would not deny self and let Him in.

Finding only to flee from God's way,
We found no joy no hope our own.
Never no gain or break of day,
All was loss and nite away from home.

Seeking then of something better,
Thinking how vain all around.
How hopeless here, also hereafter.
Then brought much closer to the ground.

Seeking more we found the Savior,
Who sought so long our souls to win.
The true joy, love, light and hope,
To help us heavens home to gain.

Oscar D Lewis

MY GUIDING LIGHT

I stood upon the mountain top,
There was darkness far below.
In the distance lay a city,
Its thousand lights aglow.

I turned, looked southward many leagues
At a distant mountain's lofty peak
Where golden rays still bathed the snow
Across the miles I heard God speak.

I turned my feet toward the slope
Steep the trail, dark the night.
"You have no cause for fear," He said,
"I shall be your Guiding Light."

When once I reached the valley's floor
And the roadway leading home,
I looked back upon the mountain
And the light upon its dome.

A single star, unblinking shone
Through the silence of the night
As once again I heard His voice,
"I am still your Guiding Light."

Janet Torres

MY PRAYER

If I could just convey this pain
You'd know I'm really very much insane.
I've had my share and probably more,
There isn't a day that I'm not sore.
I have so much to hang on to,
To give up now, I just can't do.
Bare with me my friend and love me today
As I won't give in, I have debts to pay.
Oh! Hear me Lord as I now prey,
Grant me more than just today.
This life I know is oh so sweet
to except death now would mean defeat.
I have much love to spread around
Please give me more time upon this ground.
I know your listening God,
And you can hear,
Grant me please just one more year!

Ramona Harmsen

Ramona Harmsen

THE "LADY" WHO LIGHTS THE WAY

I dedicate my poem to the fond memory of my parents. (Dad was first "greeted" by the "Lady" in 1892. His life here of 77 years with 65 of Mother's help truly substantiate my message.)

"May all those who come to me
From 'here and there' across the sea,
Realize that they are free
In the USA, OUR COUNTRY.

May they also learn to know
That with all their heart and soul
They can aim and reach their goal
With truth and justice in control."

Going to and from we could see
Many trees with their colorful beauty.
The only sight that I recall
Had no special beauty at all.

It was a small catalpa grove,
Coming home on the right side of the road.
It reminded me of a regiment in the Army,
Like in the parades we would see.

The trees were standing in rows so straight
As if for orders they did wait.
Marching forward they would not be
As their only goal seemed to be Heavenly.

Now, what could their mission be,
But to give joy to you and me,
And for us to see part of God's regime,
As he is their General Supreme.

Eileen Isenburg

BOUQUET

Stop to smell the roses as You travel the highway of Life. Linger in the garden forgetting troubles and strife. Hold on to your dreams, your hopes and desires. Enjoy the garden, the beauty, fun, and laughter will surely diminish the fires. Only igniting the spark which is inside of each and everyone. The bouquet of life is there to pick, nurtured by love God and the sun. So as you travel lifes highway, take time to stop on the way, enjoying the fragrance of lifes beautiful bouquet.

C Maggie Coffey

MASS COMMUNICATION

To Dustin Lee Coffey because I love you more

These are automatic days,
days of predigested news,
encapsulated magazines,
of pseudo-liberated views.

Fast-copy days of bulletins,
updated sequels of events,
all live, on scene, thru mini-cams,
informative, concise abridgements,
of all the news there is to know.

Karen Mercurio

TIME

Wasted years, wasted past
Wasted memories that didn't last
Why I held onto such lonesome dreams
Only time will tell.

Wasted tears, wasted hope
Wasted heartaches that couldn't cope
Why I held onto my love for you
Only time could tell.

The years have come to present now
I look at you and wonder how
We made it through the wretched past
That only time could tell.

We've made the past, weve pulled on through
We've struggled hard we've started new
You have me, and, I have you, and
We have time to tell.

Ruetta Close

TO MY COLLEGE SON

Just wanted to let you know, I'm trying to turn you loose freely,
I know you're wanting to fly, but Mom is acting very greedy;
Daddy is trying to act brave and strong, but I notice he can hardly pass your bedroom door,
I guess the life you need and want, we try to ignore;
I stop there each night and fight back a tear,
Tell you "Goodnight," and though you're not there, you feel so near;
We parents try to stop the

spreading of wings, God gives each child,
I know we can't but pray God will guide you, while you are soaring the wild;
If you fly too high, I pray God will clip your wings,
But that God will catch you, before you loose control of things;
Hold you fast in the palm of his hand,
Just remember "HE" was with you, while you searched and roamed his land;
I walk through the house looking at memos, your trophies, guns, knives and cups,
In the basement, your old workout bench, basketball, bats and rags where you, rubbed the paint off your truck;
You never wanted to get rid of old things, to be replaced by new,
I got angry then, but oh how I wish I could go back and look at the things you didn't do;
When your Brother left home, my heart ached, when I pulled
his memos from his room,
But your energy helped pull me together, and put laughter
in a world of gloom;
Now that you've begun your adult flight,
I pray God will watch over you day and night;
We are so Thankful for sons like your "Brother" and "You,"
We want the best in the future, as well as good memories too;
I think of the nights when you were little and couldn't sleep,
I go to your bed, stand there and weep;
Now please try to always be a fine, loving "MAN,"
As you've been all along, "Just as you are now," GOD'S PLAN!

Richard A First
MATURING

Through the corridors of time I have become cynical
Down into the deep, dark and damp pit of despair I have plunged
Yet I must go on for I am myself.
Woe be unto them who utters nay.
For all a man can be is but himself.
True I can be overcome for there is always someone or something which is better than you in at least one way.
Yet I can strive for all!

David Keith Bertalla
A SAILOR'S WAYS

A Sailor's Ways is a tribute to one of the finest men I know! Frank Sontag, My Grandfather

---

This is a tribute
Of a man from the sea
When he's on land
He's Grandpa to me.
A young boy's imagination
Brave words ignite a dream
Tales of his adventures
How he sailed the seas.

Life is moved by question
Like the currents move the seas
When the seas become too rough
My Grandpa, he sailed with me.
A captain of many journeys
A man of the seven seas
As the North Star has guided sailors
His strength has guided me.

Life maybe a struggle
I will face into the wind
A sailor once had shown me
Courage is a sacred friend.
As I ride the wave of adventure
I remember my yesterdays
And how a friend of mine
Taught me a sailor's ways.

Angelina Paone Hurd
PORTRAIT OF A CLOWN

With love to my son James for whom I wrote this poem and his dad for understanding.

You left me a clown
With tears in his eyes.
You left me a clown
And I'm wondering why.
Is that clown me
You left all alone?
You left me here,
This place your home.
For other places
You want to be free
I don't know the reason
Can't you see?

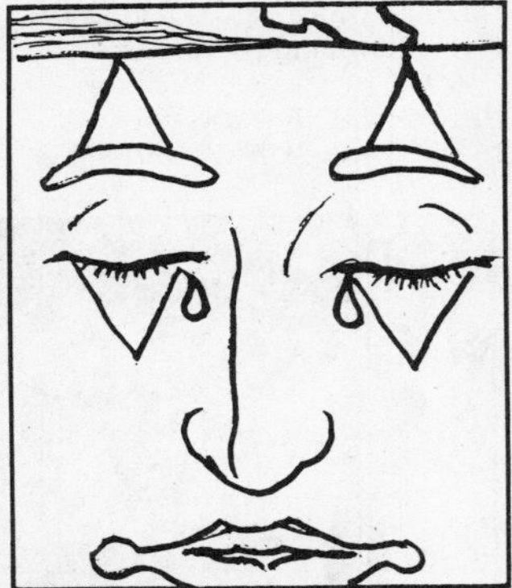

This is your life,
So you say.
But what of my
Life a mothers way?
A mothers love
Is not understood.
All she wants
Is for her son
To be good.
His dad understands
Him
Cause he's a man.
I try to understand
The best I can.
A mother's love
Is warm and true.
You understand son
I know you do
So I'm the clown
With tears in his eyes.
I'm the clown
And now I know why.

Mary E Stoneking
TIME

Time is precious, time is fleeting,
And we seldom realize it's worth;
Time may be long, yet seem so short
As we journey here on earth.

Speak not hasty words in anger;
Words once spoken we cannot recall;
So time once past, is past forever;
Waste not a moment, we will answer for it all.

Time is life and life is time,
It seems to fly away so swiftly;
Do what good you can today,
Tomorrow may never be.

Some day the great Angel will stand
With one foot on the land and one upon the sea,
And his voice shall echo around the world
That time no longer shall be.

Then God shall call us all to accounting,
And ask, "How did you use the time I gave to thee;
Did you use it for sin and to satisfy self?
Or did you use it to glorify me?"

Jane L Firestone
PICTURE

In front of the newly scrubbed 50 year old painting, "Jesus Knocking at the Door" by Warner Sallman. In memory of Frank A. LaPage, my father, the poet.

The picture is dimming and faded
But still it's message comes thru
God at your door comes knocking
He's calling—He's calling for you
He's been there for many a day now
He's patient and waits for your call
Jesus at my door comes knocking
And am I waiting, at all?
Or in my blind confusion
Do I go my self-willed way?
Jesus at my door comes knocking
Now what, oh what do I say?
I'll bid Him come into my heart now
And shelter me close as His own
I'll ask He forgive my transgressions
And thank Him for willing me home
I know now He has my allegience
I'll live within His good will
His blessings and grace-they are mine now
And I will abide with him still
When life's short journey is ended
He'll be at my side in the end
Oh Jesus I'm glad you came knocking

Margaret M Genentz
TREASURED PARTNER/ FRIEND

A cherished memory will never fade,
A period of time, two people have made.

A friends introduction, a blind date,
Instant recognition, your future mate.

Three friendly years before vows you took,
A wedding night, a beautiful book.

You found a friend, a partner to trust,
A home and family, a GOD filled must.

A friend/partner God loaned to you,
Years of sorrow and happiness, shared by two.

Time was too short for such a gift,
Leaving treasured memories as clouds do drift.

I know some day, I too will know,
Such happiness again, his true love will show.

Lori A Nichologianis
TWINS AT TWO

This is dedicated to my darling daughters Brooke and Jennifer. I love you both so much in spite of it all. All My Love, Mom

---

My Children used to be obedient
They were quiet and tried to be good,
When a scolding was in order
it seemed they understood.

Things are sure different lately
it's like they've become monsters overnight,
each day we tackle a battle of wills
things they used to love, they now fight.

Always using what they know not how
Try to stop them and they will be Mad,
Danger attracts them like magnets
They can't understand how it's bad.

Now who else would dare tear window shades
or draw pictures upon your wall,
Spill juice on your favorite coffee table
And food fights aren't they just a ball?

With two children every thing doubles
Especially when they are both two,
it's double the pleasure as well as the trouble
But what's a poor mother to do?

Judith DeLavern Whalen
HANBLECHIA (VISION QUEST)

Cover my world with tepees
Let campfires be lit and burn bright
Let me tend to my kettle of corn soup
and tell stories to my children, at night

Let me talk to the stars above me
that shine in the Great Maker's night
Let me hear the beat of Ceremonial Drums
as campfires join twilight

Let me cover my body with
buckskin
and with beadwork—MY, WHAT A
SIGHT
Let my moccasined feet, dance to
the beat
of the flames in the campfire,
tonight

I saw a vision so clearly
showing truely a wonderous sight
A mighty warrior—astride a white
steed
In the flames of a campfire's light

My heart is that of a red man's
and I will not stray from sight
My visionous warrior will lead me
To the campfire of Eternal Light.

Karen M Maturen

ROSE

Rose was Rose
As her friends would say
Cute and sassy in her own little way
Stubborn and bullheaded in all her
sports play
Being *#1* made her day
Ask any opponent, friend or foe
For they would know
"Rose did it her way."

Then in her 17th year, when all was
bright
Boyfriend, marriage and college in
sight, not all was right
Her disease took flight, her life cut
short
She fought with all her might, but
in the end
Her dreams were lost in the night.

If you could have seen her in the
hospital room that day
Loving arms reaching out and
comforting us as we came her
way,
Letting us know God was with her
today.
Decisions to be made with her Dad
she did make
to lighten the burden for all of our
sakes
And when all was done and the
bagpipes did play
All we could say was

"Rose did it her Way."

Ernest E Ridgeway

LITTLE WHITE BIRCH

I'm just a Little White Birch.
There is no other tree, anywhere,
like me.
My roots are different; my
Chlorophyll runs different;
There is no other tree like me,
anywhere;
My leaves like hair,
My arms of branch.
Some would say I'm pretty,
but I don't really know;
I never really saw me.

With all the wood around me—I
feel so very small,
And no wood seems to care—
Whether I'm small or tall.
Life, they say, I'm filled with—
And I can feel me grow.
I feel the sunshine warm me,
I feel the cold of snow.
But life's so very lonely,
I'm the only one like me.
And no wood really knows me—
To them, I'm just a little tree.
But someday when I grow,
Maybe some wood will really
know,
And love me for what I am.
But now—I feel so lonely,
And no wood holds my bough.
Yet—I'd feel so very happy,
If some wood knew me now,
And then they'd shade and love
me.
I wish some Big Wood would,
But to them—I'm only a little
tree.

Yet—I'd feel so very happy,
If some wood knew me now,
And then they'd shade and love
me.
I wish some Big Wood would,
But to them—I'm only a little
tree.

Virgil J Strader

BIRD WITH A BROKEN WING

Shivering and trembling in the
snow
Cold, bewildered, unable to fly;
What evil force has brought you
low
And left you wracked with pain to
die?

No more above the earth you'll soar
In search of food or just for fun.
Your flying days forever o'er;
Your happy roaming days are
done.

I rescued you and brought you
home
To live in safety in a cage.
For food and warmth no need to
roam,
The fight for life no longer wage.

You sing your sad songs now to me
To liven up my lonely day.
You dream of when you will be free
To soar again, to roam, to play.

Eileen R Driscoll

THROUGH GODS' EYES

If everyone could see the world
through the eyes that God gave
them.
They would see it as being
beautiful and great; instead of
ugly and full of hate.
If everyone could look at each
other through the eyes that God
gave them.
They would see love in one
anothers' faces; not faces filled
with hatred.
It's a shame to be so blind, when
God has given you these eyes.
Look around you and you'll see,
the world is a happy place to be!

Stu Lonon

MY SPECIAL PLACE

There is a special place I often go
many times when I am very low,
A visit in march when march
flowers line the trail
never once in the spring have
they failed

As the trip upward gets very steep
my brisk walk slows to a creep,
Yet, I move onward and do not stop
as I know my reward when I
reach the top.

Near the last bend I hear the
rushing waterfall
and in the distance a faint crow
call,
Moving closer I see below the
babbling little brook
I am tense for my first look

The water falls majestically down
the hundred foot drop
sounding with a thunderous clop
My thoughts now are of very
pleasant things
I seem to hear the angels sing

Moving closer for a better look
I am glad this time today I took
To visit one of natures pictures gifts
that shall stand as time slowly
drifts

Audnie A Sousa

WHY WAIT

Why wait till another fall
Answer the love call
There's no rapture in despair
Don't let down your hair
When loves soft enduring ways
Give forth with a praise
And offer their loving arms
You shouldn't be alarmed.
The torch is burning at the gate
Why make love to wait
Love needs but a single spark
To fire up your heart
With sweet lovable words
Precious to be heard.
In rhythm of the birds
Flying southwards.
Why wait till they return
Youth pages will turn
Leaving only memories
Of Autumns Fallen Leaves,
Down along the garden lane
Youth sang loves refrain
And its echo reached your heart
Why Wait, Take My Heart.

Connie Sue Hull

THE HURT

Dedicated to a wonderful man, my father, Herbert Hoover Miller, and in loving memory of my mother, Mary Kathryn Miller.

He's gone into another world . . .
He slowly went away,
and now he's always on my mind,
each hour, every day.
And though I write these words
with tears, it won't erase the
hurt,
For I still see the shovel as it
covered him with dirt.

But please don't think I'm silly
when I tell you I have cried,
For I know what it means to hear
that someone close has died.
Yes, many times I've broken up,
I've almost lost my mind,
I know just what it means to sob
when words are hard to find.
And yet, sometimes I treated him
with meanness, not with love,
sometimes I even slapped him
when he didn't know what of.
And now I set here crying, asking
why he went away, and
wondering why that car could
not have somehow stopped that
day.
I'll try to stop the tears that fall, I'll
try to stop the hurt,
But I know it will come again each
time I see some dirt.
And as I try to sleep tonight, I'll tell
myself he's here,
Wondering why that car had hit a
dog that was so dear.

Yes, each time that I hear a bark,
or when I hear soft paws,
I'm going to wonder why all dogs
don't have some traffic laws.
Because of this, I'm going to dread
each minute that I live,
Wondering if he were alive, if
somehow he'd forgive.

I only know I can't pretend, I
cannot face mankind,
For he has made the innocent so
stupid and so blind.
Yes, he has done so many wrongs,
he causes life to cease,
With man alive, no wonder that my
dog could not find peace.

Tawny Holmes

THE UNFOLDING OF A FRIENDSHIP

Each remembering the happy
times
Hearing of the others pain;
Sharing joyous days
Then learning of a deep despair
But here we are, still together
For all that is yet to unfold
To care, in tears and laughter
The rest of what will be
Friends in my lifetime are and
Have been oh so many—
But there is that one who shares in
Dreams—who knows the secrets
Of my heart,
One who ner' condemns, but rather
Praises and accepts my faults.
If you too, are fortunate,
Are so blessed with this most
precious of gifts.
This friend so far exceeds all
Worldly treasures we strive to gain
Each flerting day.
This special one this treasured
Gift we should hold dear
Do Value her
Your friend

Tina Marie Watterson

I WANT YOU TO STAY

The weather has changed,
and now so have I.
I seem to be different
as time passes by.

You maintain in my heart
for each night and each day,
from the end to the start,
you don't go away.

I'm dreaming of you,
and hoping to see
that it may be true
the real you and me.

I say I don't care,
but you know that I do.
I wish I could share
all my feelings with you.

It hurts me to know
that I'm feeling this way,
I can't watch you go,
cause I need you to stay.

Patricia McLendon

NATURE SPEAKS TO ME

I hear the wind rustling through
the trees
The leaves singing, each their
different song
The pond ripples with the breeze
Soft motions of flowing liquid
glass mirror the opposite
shore
My mind's eye gazes into
nature's
looking glass and nature
speaks to me

Harvey Hardesty
LIFES OTHER SIDE

To my wife Dorothy and four daughters Elaine, Eileen, Pam and Kim, Whose Love and Understanding has helped me through "LIFES OTHER SIDE"

A gentle wind
An ebbing tide
A falling leaf,

"Lifes gentle side"

Hurricanes blow
Typhoons rise
A quaking earth,

"Lifes other side"

Sandra Everett
ADVERTISEMENT FOR PSYCHIATRIC PATIENTS

To report psychiatric abuse or for facts about shock "treatments" and other damaging methods used commonly by psychiatrists write or call Citizens Commission On Human Rights.

"Depressed, its the most alone you'll ever feel."
Come on in. We have the power to heal.
We know your sadness won't last. We know it won't stay.
But you see, my dear ones, you are our prey.
Trust us. We care about you.
We'll take and we'll mold you into someone thats new.
We'll take you and fill your bodies with meds.
We'll place electrodes to your heads.
We'll take you and convince you that you are mentally sick.
This lulled society allows us to get away with these tricks.
Come little ones. Allow us to take notes that can slander your names.
We'll make it appear that the heartaches you've suffered are your total blame.
Come on in. We need the ones who are weak.
We are the vultures. We devour the meek.
Come to us. Come to us. We'll prescribe you some "mind candy."
Come to us. Come to us. Why, little ones, our treatments are dandy.
Society hold us to be the great Gods of clay.
Give us more power. Thats what we say.
Being wise we became fools.
But never mind, dear ones. We have the power that rules.
"you psychiatrists!" I say, "You're going too far!"
You lure in these little ones and leave them with bigger scars!
I saw my friend, so blonde and fair. She had the beauty of the moon.
She cried for mercy as you dragged her to the shock room!
You took her screaming into the torturous den!
You wouldn't stop! You are mad-men!
She never raised her frail hands to fight!
But she begged/she pleaded with all of her might!
Afterward, I saw her crying on her lonely cot!
How could you? How could you? You went your way, you forgot!
Others have died by your hands! In your care they had blind trust!
Now their blood is screaming for justice from the dust!
You judge men mad by their faith in God alone!
All of your days bitter seeds have you sown!
Your wicked deeds will one day be revealed to the world!
All things which are hidden shall be unfurled!
We'll rally the good people from all over this land!
We'll fight you! We'll fight you! We'll make a stand!
We'll march forth shielded with the whole armour of God!
We'll crush out your power with His mighty rod!
Remember the great Jericho wall?
Just as it did, so will you fall!
Stop what you're doing before its too late!
Stop or at that last day you'll be sealed to a most horrid fate!
The God of Israel is on our side!
Not much longer in power will you ride!

Richard F Wolfarth
COME LIVE WITH ME

Oh come live with me
You beautiful queen
For a life that was only a dream
With such beautiful eyes
And such curly hair
To heaven will go if only you dare
To live with me why should we care.
I'm not full of dust to live I must
So come live with me for a life full of fun
And never more will I have to run
Oh come live with me we'll dance and sing
Then we'll hear all those cheerful bells ring
We'll be two people happy and free
You've got what it takes and
I sure we're not fake
We'll be together as long as it takes
So come my princess and
Live with me.

Kathleen N Filidei
DEAREST FRIEND

When I look into your eyes.
The sight of birds a flying high,
with my soul chasing after.
Emotion swim with the fish in the deepest sea.
A pull lifting me up, and the warmth of your arms around me.
There is safety and the sleep of long slumber I've been waiting for.
You are perfect in my eyes.
You belong to the world, I am only one page of your life that will soon be turned over.
This is right a memory is all I'll be.
Yet I will try my damndest to be the best there ever was.

Jose Luis Hernandez
EINSTEIN'S 109TH BIRTHDAY

You are always welcome to
be in my heart.

Whenever I look at your
eyes I see my green light
to heaven!

You inspired my whole life
as it goes, light traveler,
time relative observer.

Billions of years it took
nature to generate beings like
you, pure thinkers, clean mind,
high awareness.

If you find your way back in
time, you know you are welcome,
anytime on Earth.

Come on, Come on,
great friend, keep
your eternal smile
for all coming generations.

New Universes open open up
with your brain waves,
and the path you marked
among us.

Little lost kid,
resist the sergeant like
teacher who disliked your
math slowness!

Sister Elizabeth Therese Daly
SPRING REVERIE

The crocuses yawn and stretch their new greenings beneath the music room window.

Students lean wearily on their elbows gazing out the window for new signs of Spring HOPE

Oh! to be free from the sameness of life!
They speak of week-end's . . . work to be done . . . friends . . . Proms . . .
Spring break! Florida! . . . summer jobs . . . college . . . days in an endless cycle leading to their commencement-journey into the world.

How many hours, minutes, moments spent in ceaseless reverie!

The sun, beacon of HOPE, sheds a luminous glow promising new vision to those who SEE.
Nature beckons saying, "Take heed! I am God's pure genius in your midst.
Love me! Cherish me! Share me!
Preserve me!
Praise the Artist-God for wonder and beauty."

Young hearts, weary hearts yearn for what is to be, anxious for a future made more precious each day through new challenges.

Lord, Giver of Spring glory . . . Spring wishes . . . help us to live in your universe without fear clutching at our hearts.

We need You to keep on renewing our Springs . . . our hearts . . . our world . . . so that one day the hatred and destruction of sacred lives with deadly weapons will disappear.

We need a new dawn . . . a time when true love will reign . . .
then PEACE will whisper its message to the young and to the old.

The crocuses sigh . . . patiently waiting as they listen to the rythms of new music . . . creative discord . . . soaring harmony.

The time will come . . . surely . . . PEACE will come!

Whitney Kanne
INSPIRATION

Wonder, splendor, beauty;
Awe inspiring natural high,
As I contemplate on the beauty
Of the drifting sky.

The wind buffets my hair
And tosses my mind;
Only to trail here and there,
On thoughts left behind.

I feel full to the brim with
Love and inspiration—
So full of "Him,"
So full of contemplation

Oh, earth breathe deeply of the glory,
And the peace that heavenly beauty brings.
Even when things get wild and stormy,
There's a quiet voice that sings.

Kathleen Keer McGowan

Kathleen Keer McGowan
LAMENT ON THE DEATH OF AN ONLY CHILD

To Kathy Keer Ryan, and to Tommy my late grandson

At night my dreams are so very real
I can't believe the things I'm told.
They say that you are "no longer here"
That death has claimed you.

In my dreams you are so alive
Always at my elbow with your
Pale golden hair, your deep blue eyes
And the many questions that always
Filled me with surprise.

You are still a part of me
I'll never be alone
You are the only child I ever had.
The only one I would ever call my own.

I am so glad I Knew you. You were loanned to me for Twenty five years
Now I understand all mothers

Their love, their pride their fears.
Some wonder that I could go on without you?
Perhaps in dreams you told me to?

Since you left I have survived for Two decades
Always remembering you with joy.
Having faith my dear, that one day we'll be together in a heavenly place,
You and I and your beautiful baby Boy.

Marjorie M Bartlett
THOUGHTS OF A WRITER
I envy the beautiful butterfly,
with wings so color-bright!

It feels no *"I wish I could"* . . .
"I think I can" . .
"I might."

It has no cause to light
from its easy, blissful flight!

The butterfly's life seems *'neat'*. . .
And its beauty seems complete.

I'm sure that it has no thoughts
of gloom or utter despair . . .

And it has no one to question . . .
"Why?" or *"What to Wear!"*

The butterfly's life is calm serenity . . .
A peaceful lack of care . . .
For it can flit from here
Or it can flit from there.

It has no task to try . . .
No thoughts of live or die . . .
No *wrong* or *right* . . .
No *"maybe"* or *"might"* . . .

It has no gas to buy . . .
It needs no car,
For beautiful wings
Take it *high and afar!*

The butterfly has no one to ask . . .
"WHERE did you go?"
"WHO was there that you should know?"
"WHAT did you do while you were there?"
"DID you have cause to stare?"

I do not wish to answer these . . .
Nor do I really care.
I do not even notice such . . .
If I do so, it is rare.

But I can tell you this . . .

My mind works on thoughts
Much greater than these;

I create from INSPIRATION . . .
And I WRITE just what I please!

David M Windsor
SIR ABADDON'S WARM WELCOME
Laugh, oh laugh, ye earthly grounds—
to help Hell's harpers, symphonic sounds.
Play ye loud, oh play ye gay,
to greet fallen angels in Judgement Day.

Greatly gather around thy treasured tomb,
devote honor and praise to Apollyon's doom.
Now come forth! Ye ashes alive.
Meet thy brethren on Hell's dark side.

Make ye merry, oh dance ye naked,
to all the torment thou can't escape it.
Yes! Sing aloud, lift up thine hands,
to the music sweet from Satan's bands.

Rejoice an tremble ye earthly grounds,
to the boiling heat of bubbling mounds.
Sieve in pain poor pitiful one,
while wretched demons roast thee in fun!

The Day is come to scream and yell,
as Red carpets roll into Abaddon's Hell.

Kelley Deneen Hammond
A BRIGHT RED ROSE
A face I can no longer see
From distance, time and lack of space
Unoccupied, my heart does race
From memories I cannot place
A fear I feel from lack or want
From dreams I cannot quite recall
I wish I could relive it all
I'd jump for you, I'd heed the call
A gentle voice I hear sometimes
On winter's nights or dewy morns
A soothing voice to calm the storms
A bright red rose to hide the thorns
A thought I only seem to have
That lags sometimes within my mind
Perhaps a thought I left behind
Perhaps a tear I could not find
A dream I lost and cannot capture
In plans I made for me and you
Beyond these fine lines that I drew
On stars that all seemed ever new
A gentle voice I hear sometimes
On winter's nights or dewy morns
A soothing voice to calm, the storms
A bright red rose to hide the thorns.

Verna Helen Gollihue
EDDIE LOU YOUR AGE LOOKS DON'T CORRESPOND

In honor of our great Poetry Editor Eddie Lou Cole

Eddie Lou your looks and age don't correspond
Your beautiful smile, and friendly face
And the bless you, words you always say
Makes me love you Poetry Editor
Makes me love you better and better

Your looks say you're bubbling over with love and laughter
I know you're happy, it shows in your face
And you'll be happy ever after
If you still keep up the Poetry Editors pace

I would love to meet you Eddie Lou Cole
And talk about your lovely life
I know it would be interesting to know
Because you seem so very nice

And someday when this life is o'er
And we send in poems never more
Perhaps we'll meet and our new life began
We may recite these poems again and again.

Amy Smith (Malchiodi)
FREEDOM'S PRICE
Power, money and pleasure
are the Gods we serve today.
Why couldn't we have stayed
like the men of yesterday?
They fought, they served,
and yes, some died,
To keep our country burning
with that "old fashioned" American Pride.
Oh! that we would remember
those who fought and that now sleep.
That if someday the need does rise again
we will fight for our freedom to keep.
Their spirit lives within us yet
on this "Memorial Day" —
They turned their mountains into roads,
they looked and found a way.
We can hear their cries for PEACE ON EARTH
resounding in our ears,
Let us not forget them
and their deeds throughout the years.
"America The Beautiful" —
may it forever be this way—
But to keep her free and burning bright
there is a price we all must pay . . .

James T Brown
WAR AND A HELPLESS YOU
A loud whistling sound,
Then the shaking of the ground.
A tremendous light,
The mushroom is in sight.

People dying, children crying.
Frantic cities, full of uncontrollable people.
What is there to do?
Nothing, but sit like a helpless fool.

No way to stop it.
No way of knowing when it's coming
No type of sign, no more whines,
Nothing but silence . . .

Frances L McVay
OVER MY SHOULDER
A son is a son
No matter what,
That's what a son is—
baby
youth
man . . .
Sometimes more one
Than the other
A son's an emotion
Defying all logic,
A rainbow of moods
In degrees of an arc

A free lilting heart—
Or a mirror
fogged
By the too close
breath
of my love.

John P Ryan Sr
JOSHIE'S LAUGH

To Maggie

After a long hard winter
We hear the robin sing
Bringing sounds of gladness
And promises of spring

The robin's song so pretty
Measures not by half
The power and the glory
Of little Joshie's laugh

It bubbles from his sinless soul
And fills the house with mirth
To all who know and love him
"Tis the sweetest sound on earth

May he not hoard that precious gift
But strew it by the way
And lay it at the throne of God
Upon the judgement day

When I lay my pitchfork down
And have nurtured my last calf
I will not have lived in vain
I heard my grandson laugh

I would ask aboon of God
Ask in his behalf
May he stand up to the wind
And hear his grandson laugh

Harriet Trotta
THE SCENT OF LILACS
Once again the lilacs are in bloom
And their lovely, sweet perfume
Permeates my room . . .
Lingering like a love remembered.

Four massive bushes are there
In my neighbors garden fair—
Spreading purple fingerlets from a close embrace
And flanking small dogwoods in a circling space.

The glistening whiteness of the trees
Almost brings one to his knees
Marveling at the beauty of the earth
That almost rivals the miracle of birth.

(In moments sad and lonely
One has but to think only
Of May and lilacs abloom . . .
With their fragrant, warm perfume.)

Joyce Fust
THE EDDY
Gurgling,
Foaming,
Flowing onward,
Onward to the sea.

Splashing,
Crashing,
Smashing,
Forming,
Onward to the sea.

Intertwining,
Mixing,
Tingling,
Dancing,
Sparkling,
Twisting,
Rippling,
Onward, onward to the
sea.

Emma C Johnson

CITY PARK

Moonlight seeps through wrack of
clouds,
Pure spectral light
cast on wasted alabaster.
Slatted bench obliterated by snow.
Sparkling drifts secret footprints
Of yesterday's trespassers
Smashing golden leaves
Dripped from naked trees,
Snatching patches of foam,
Glistening jewels,
Nature's adornments
Shrouded in faint mists,
Diffusing pale yellow glares.
Freezing vapors.
Hushed silence made audible.
Gale subsides.
Snow hisses uneasily.
Wind currents lash
Clouds of whiteness.
Abandoned . . .
Deserted . . .
Orphan of the season.

Mary Hilbert

TWIN FAWNS WITH MOTHER

Halfway up the mountain
there they were
twin fawns with mother
their lovely otherness
gazing nonchalantly.
Do not trust us! my heart cried
We are the enemy!
Nonetheless they do
ten minutes . . . twenty minutes
we share infinity.

Twin fawns with mother
are even more beautiful
than you my love.

Joan Stone

ON OUR WEDDING ANNIVERSARY

Dear God,
one asks,
how can one think
that money is security,
that it can bring
happiness, long life
or domestic tranquility.

Shouldn't we vow
more Faith
in our goals,
our talents and
our abilities
for which
each of us was born?

Shouldn't we show
more Trust in God,
in ourselves and
each other
before
it is too late?

James L Layton

GOOD-BYE

Tomorrow;
is but another day in an endless
stream.
Yesterday;
is but another day in my endless
dream.
A dream of happiness,
an endless sigh.
An end of saddness
a never ending good-bye.

I love you;
how many times can I cry!
You've hurt me;
but how many times can I die?
A death that never ends,
an endless torture.
A life that never begins,
an endless horror of only
memories.
Those of good times, those of bad
when you hurt me, when you
made me glad.
And finally when you said
good-bye.

Karlyne KC McAllister

LOST

To my parents, Gordon and Carol McAllister—without their love, I may have remained forever "Lost"

The sun of my life is sinking
lower, lower, into my soul.
Reaching for it, miss—
it slides between my fingers
little by little
forever to remind me
of the endless search to find myself.

Sandy Stinnett Morris

MIDNIGHT FANTASY

This poem is dedicated to David D. Lewis, the man to whom I will always love and cherish and give my very soul forever.

You came into my life like a dream
in the night,
Making my feelings, soar, like a
bird in flight.
Completely taking my breath away,
Along with my emptyness each and
every day.
You fill my days and nights with
love,
And all the stars that shine above.
You make me want you more each
day,
Never wanting your love for me to
stray.
Your love is that of a burning fire,
Fulfilling my each and every desire.
My soul is calmed by your loving
touch,
Allowing me to love you, oh so
much.
As we lie together in the darkest of
night,
Our love will shine as an eternal
light.
Knowing the love we share is true,
Keeping it always alive and new.
Your love again has made me
whole,
Along with the giving of my very
soul.
Only you can take my love away,
But I know in my heart, it will
forever stay.

Anja Hutgens

THE CHANGE

Looking at mysterious moonlight
underneath this ancient tree
my hands and head are resting on
one knee
stars fail to shelter me from pain
and feeling cold
and from terrible things that I've
seen or have been told
dark eyes laden with secret water
from my mind
and once again.
reasons for living are very hard
to find.

Waken up, under that same old tree
realizing I am feeling happily
warm and free
while dust is dancing in the
morning-light
day dreaming and love makes this
world seem right
and once again.
life gives me a strange
immortal feeling
and I forget all about its purpose
and its meaning.

Glen Crystal Mills

CHEERS! FOR THE GREAT!

You started me in Poetry, showed
me the Joys in Maths,
Enriched my soul with moral
truths, and flooded my mind
with facts
Knowing poetry is so near to your
heart—I've chosen this medium
As no other could play the part . .
. to sing your praises fine.
Cheers! In appreciation for your
unstinting care.
As you—once—with daily joy
taught pupils—without
tears—year by year.
You prepared them, through your
knowledge dispensed, for
careers in every field.
T'is time to raise your banner; to
pen your names in a Golden
Shield—
For devoted years of service in the
teaching field.
Cheers! All my Teachers!! You have
made your contribution to
humanity.
Cheers! Teachers all! Great
People!! Born of dedication and
integrity
Directly or indirectly—Teachers
responsible are for the progress
in science, inventions rare;
Doctors, lawyers, Politicians, or
cooks handling dinner-ware,
Poets, artists, linguists, or
musicians with good ear,
Owe it all to their teachers, who
taught without favour, or fear,
Were it within GLENDA CARR'S
power—each year—she'd crown
teachers
"Great People of the Year!!!"

Audrey Olberg

AS YOU SLEEP (FOR MOTHER'S DAY)

You lie there on the couch, your
white
hair spread like a fan on the pillow
you embroidered for my fifth
anniversary.

Curtains are drawn against May's
midday sun
(too warm for walking, too cool
for an
interlude on the greening,
shadeless lawn).

Mozart fills the room, Oboe
Concerto In C
and teacups, long emptied, sit
undisturbed,
the fragrance of Earl Grey still
lingering.

I love to watch you sleep, your
ageless face
unlined, fragile fingers folded at
your side,
your breathing as even as the
ticking of a clock.

A breeze thro an open window
mocks the stillness.
In the distance birds chatter, but
in the sweet
solitude of this spring afternoon,
you sleep.

You sleep and I keep guard over
your dreams.
You sleep and I remember all the
years and seasons,
all the joys and sorrows that we so
lovingly shared.

Joy Lou Albright

FRIEND

The morning Sun
It is so beautiful
The summer breeze
It feels so fine
The food of the earth
Great to the taste
So many things Good
In life to enjoy
The best of the land
Is walking with you hand in hand

Betsy A Malone

LIFE'S DIRECTIONS

From the purest blue skies,
Among the greenest of life,
Lies reflections,
Only man can see
To the depths of blackened oceans,
The view of crystal clear seas,
Life's directions,
Is hidden in thee,
As the darkness of the night,
Sudden changes of the winds,
Fear threatens,
The search of there in,
Like hounds on the hunt,
Close to the foxes den,
Soul's becken,
Its time to begin.

Helen Lawson Spradling

IS YOUR TONGUE A BLESSING

The tongue we have can be a
blessing
If we let God have his way
For he can help us do his bidding
And say what He would have us
say

Our tongue is such a tiny member
To be so busy all the time
Often saying things so precious
But so often out of line

Our tongue can never be forgotten
Its always there for us to use
Some of us will use it wisely
But others only to abuse

The one whose tongue is full of
kindness
Is one whom everyone adores
For when he talks about a neighbor
He speaks well of mine and yours

Our tongue should be a blessing
(always)
To each other every day
If it only helps a stranger
Or a friend along the way

If our tongue were in subjection
And we could be in full control
It would be a perfect story
And the sweetest ever told

Index

Index

Index

U

V

W